Presented to

Matthew Combs

By

Ronda Combs

On

Christmas 2004

COMPARATIVE STUDY BIBLE

COMPARATIVE STUDY BIBLE

NEW INTERNATIONAL VERSION
AMPLIFIED VERSION
KING JAMES VERSION
UPDATED NEW AMERICAN STANDARD BIBLE

ZONDERVAN™
GRAND RAPIDS, MICHIGAN 49530

Contents

PUBLISHERS' PREFACE, ix

King James Version

The Epistle Dedicatory, xi

Amplified Bible

Preface, xiii

New American Standard

Preface, xv

New International Version

Preface, xvii

THE OLD TESTAMENT

Genesis, 2	2 Chronicles, 1100	Daniel, 2222
Exodus, 144	Ezra, 1190	Hosea, 2268
Leviticus, 258	Nehemiah, 1220	Joel, 2296
Numbers, 342	Esther, 1260	Amos, 2308
Deuteronomy, 458	Job, 1282	Obadiah, 2330
Joshua, 556	Psalms, 1366	Jonah, 2334
Judges, 622	Proverbs, 1590	Micah, 2340
Ruth, 688	Ecclesiastes, 1668	Nahum, 2356
1 Samuel, 698	Song of Songs, 1694	Habakkuk, 2364
2 Samuel, 782	Isaiah, 1710	Zephaniah, 2372
1 Kings, 854	Jeremiah, 1884	Haggai, 2382
2 Kings, 938	Lamentations, 2056	Zechariah, 2388
1 Chronicles, 1018	Ezekiel, 2076	Malachi, 2414

THE NEW TESTAMENT

Matthew, 2424	Ephesians, 2998	Hebrews, 3086
Mark, 2522	Philippians, 3014	James, 3120
Luke, 2584	Colossians, 3026	1 Peter, 3132
John, 2688	1 Thessalonians, 3038	2 Peter, 3146
Acts, 2766	2 Thessalonians, 3048	1 John, 3154
Romans, 2862	1 Timothy, 3054	2 John, 3168
1 Corinthians, 2906	2 Timothy, 3066	3 John, 3170
2 Corinthians, 2952	Titus, 3076	Jude, 3172
Galatians, 2980	Philemon, 3082	Revelation, 3176

Contents

PUBLISHER'S PREFACE ix

King James Version

The Epistle Dedicatory, xi

Amplified Bible

Preface, xiii

New American Standard

Preface, xv

New International Version

Preface, xvii

THE OLD TESTAMENT

Genesis, 2	2 Chronicles, 1100	Daniel, 2172
Exodus, 144	Ezra, 1150	Hosea, 2265
Leviticus, 253	Nehemiah, 1220	Joel, 2290
Numbers, 3??	Esther, 260?	Amos, 230?
Deuteronomy, 438	Job, 1292	Obadiah, 2330
Joshua, 556	Psalms, 1300	Jonah, 234?
Judges, 622	Proverbs, 1590	Micah, 2340
Ruth, 698	Ecclesiastes, 1668	Nahum, 235?
1 Samuel, 698	Song of Songs, 1691	Habakkuk, 2364
2 Samuel, 782	Isaiah, 1710	Zephaniah, 237?
1 Kings, 85?	Jeremiah, 1881	Haggai, 238?
2 Kings, 938	Lamentations, 2050	Zechariah, 2388
1 Chronicles, 1018	Ezekiel, 2076	Malachi, 241?

THE NEW TESTAMENT

Matthew, 2424	Ephesians, 2998	Hebrews, 3086
Mark, 2522	Philippians, 3016	James, 3120
Luke, 2584	Colossians, 3026	1 Peter, 3132
John, 2688	1 Thessalonians, 3038	2 Peter, 31?6
Acts, 2766	2 Thessalonians, ??	1 John, 315?
Romans, 2862	1 Timothy, 3054	2 John, 3168
1 Corinthians, 2908	2 Timothy, 3066	3 John, 3170
2 Corinthians, 2972	Titus, 307?	Jude, 3172
Galatians, 2990	Philemon, 3082	Revelation, ??

Publishers' Preface

Today, as never before, Christians of every age, background and denomination are turning to Bible study to dig into the truths of God's Word and to find God's will for their everyday lives. A parallel Bible such as this one offers the Bible student the opportunity to compare translations and gain new appreciation for the richness, beauty and meaning of Scripture.

The *Comparative Study Bible* offers four of today's most widely read English translations in one volume.

Grounded in the best scholarship of its day and combined with its impressive, eloquent style, *The King James Version* has been a beloved translation for centuries.

The *New American Standard Bible* is the most widely accepted contemporary word-for-word translation. Recently updated to be even more readable, it is highly regarded for its scholarship and accuracy.

The *New International Version* is the best-selling modern English Bible translation. It is a scholarly translation that accurately expresses the original Bible text in clear and contemporary English while remaining faithful to the thoughts and meaning of the Biblical writers. Its readability, accuracy and beauty of style make it the most popular modern translation available.

The *Amplified Bible* uses a system of synonyms, punctuation, typographical features, and clarifying words or phrases to reveal shades of meaning of the key words in the original text. The first edition of *The Amplified New Testament* was released in 1958, followed by the complete text in 1965. Twenty-two years later, Zondervan Publishing House and The Lockman Foundation presented *The Amplified Bible, Expanded Edition,* the present standard text of this unique Bible version.

Of course, few things worth doing are ever simple. By its very nature, the *Amplified* text is longer than an average translation. Adding even a few references per chapter increases a Bible's length considerably; but amplification to the extent of the *Amplified* adds thousands of words. This complicates using this version in a parallel Bible because the format requires both translations to line up chapter for chapter on the page. In the Old Testament, the amplification tends to fit cleanly into the format of paragraph verses, and the other translations remain long enough to balance the pages with a minimum of white space at the bottom of the column. The New Testament is a different situation, however, as the amplification and footnotes cause the *Amplified* to greatly exceed the length of the other three translations. If left in a normal two-column format, this discrepancy would cause the *Amplified* to fill its column on every page, while the other three columns would always be far shorter, leaving wasted space for as much as half the column. In order to avoid that, we have used a moderately different layout in the New Testament. Selecting a slightly different column width for the *Amplified* text decreased wasted paper while improving the readability of the New Testament pages. The result is a less bulky and better designed Bible.

We hope and pray that this *Comparative Study Bible* will be a reliable, invaluable resource for you in your Christian walk.

THE PUBLISHERS

Publishers' Preface

Today, as never before, Christians of every age, background and denomination are turning to Bible study to dig into the truths of God's Word and to find God's will for their everyday lives. Any self-study Bible such as this one offers the Bible student the opportunity to compare translations and gain new appreciation for the richness, beauty and meaning of Scripture.

The Comparative Study Bible offers four of today's most widely read English translations in one volume.

Grounded in the best scholarship of its day and combined with its impressive, eloquent style, The King James Version has been a beloved translation for centuries.

The New American Standard Bible is the most widely accepted, contemporary, word-for-word translation. Recently updated for its scholarship and accuracy, and regarded for its scholarship and accuracy.

The New International Version is the best-selling modern English Bible translation. It is a scholarly translation that accurately expresses the original Bible text in clear and contemporary English, while remaining faithful to the thoughts and meaning of the biblical writers. Its readability, accuracy and beauty of style make it the most popular modern translation available.

The Amplified Bible uses a system of synonyms, punctuation, typographical features, and clarifying words or phrases to reveal the shades of meaning of the key words in the original text. The first edition of The Amplified New Testament was released in 1958, followed by the complete text in 1965. Twenty-two years later, Zondervan Publishing House and The Lockman Foundation presented The Amplified Bible, Expanded Edition, the present standard text of this unique Bible version.

Of course, few things worth doing are ever simple. By its very nature, the Amplified text is longer than an average translation. Adding even a few references per chapter increases a Bible's length considerably, but amplification to the extent of the Amplified adds thousands of words. This complicates using this version in a parallel Bible because the former requires both translations to line up chapter for chapter on the page. In the Old Testament, the amplification tends to fit cleanly into the format of paragraph verses, and the other translations remain long enough to balance the pages, with a minimum of white space at the bottom of the column. The New Testament is a different situation, however, as the amplification and footnotes cause the Amplified to greatly exceed the length of the other three translations. If left in a normal two-column format, this discrepancy would cause the Amplified to fill its column on every page, while the other three columns would always be far shorter, leaving wasted space—or as much as half the column. In order to avoid that, we have used a moderately different layout in the New Testament. Selecting a slightly different column width for the Amplified text decreased wasted paper while improving the readability of the New Testament pages. The result is a less bulky, and better designed Bible.

We hope and pray that this Comparative Study Bible will be a reliable, invaluable resource for you in your Christian walk.

THE PUBLISHERS

King James Version

TO THE MOST HIGH AND MIGHTY PRINCE

JAMES

BY THE GRACE OF GOD
KING OF GREAT BRITAIN, FRANCE, AND IRELAND
DEFENDER OF THE FAITH, &c.
The Translators of the Bible wish Grace, Mercy, and Peace
through JESUS CHRIST our Lord

Great and manifold were the blessings, most dread Sovereign, which Almighty God, the Father of all mercies, bestowed upon us the people of *England,* when first he sent Your Majesty's Royal Person to rule and reign over us. For whereas it was the expectation of many, who wished not well unto our *Sion,* that upon the setting of that bright *Occidental Star,* Queen *Elizabeth* of most happy memory, some thick and palpable clouds of darkness would so have overshadowed this Land, that men should have been in doubt which way they were to walk; and that it should hardly be known, who was to direct the unsettled State; the appearance of Your Majesty, as of the *Sun* in his strength, instantly dispelled those supposed and surmised mists, and gave unto all that were well affected exceeding cause of comfort; especially when we beheld the Government established in Your Highness, and Your hopeful Seed, by an undoubted Title, and this also accompanied with peace and tranquility at home and abroad.

But among all our joys, than was no one that more filled our hearts, than the blessed continuance of the preaching of God's sacred Word among us; which is that inestimable treasure, which excelleth all the riches of the earth; because the fruit thereof extendeth itself, not only to the time spent in this transitory world, but directeth and disposeth men unto that eternal happiness which is above in heaven.

Then not to suffer this to fall to the ground, but rather to take it up, and to continue it in that state, wherein the famous Predecessor of Your Highness did leave it: nay, to go forward with the confidence and resolution of a Man in maintaining the truth of Christ, and propagating it far and near, is that which hath so bound and firmly knit the hearts of all Your Majesty's loyal and religious people unto You, that Your very name is precious among them: their eye doth behold You with comfort, and they bless You in their hearts, as that sanctified Person who, under God, is the immediate Author of their true happiness. And this their contentment doth not diminish or decay, but every day increaseth and taketh strength, when they observe, that the zeal of Your Majesty toward the house of God doth not slack or go backward, but is more and more kindled, manifesting itself abroad in the farthest parts of *Christendom,* by writing in defence of the Truth, (which hath given such a blow unto that man of sin, as will not be healed,) and every day at home, by religious and learned discourse, by frequenting the house of God, by hearing the Word preached, by cherishing the Teachers thereof, by caring for the Church, as a most tender and loving nursing Father.

There are infinite arguments of this right Christian and religious affection in Your Majesty; but none is more forcible to declare it to others than the vehement and perpetuated desire of accomplishing and publishing of this work, which now with all humility we present unto Your Majesty. For when Your Highness had once out of deep judgment apprehended how convenient it was, that out of the Original Sacred Tongues, together with comparing of the labours, both in our own, and other foreign Languages, of many worthy men who went before us, there should be one more exact Translation of the holy Scriptures into the *English Tongue;* Your Majesty did never desist to urge and to excite those to whom it was commended, that the work might be hastened, and that the business might be expedited in so decent a manner, as a matter of such importance might justly require.

And now at last, by the mercy of God, and the continuance of our labours, it being brought unto such a conclusion, as that we have great hopes that the Church of *England* shall reap good fruit thereby; we hold it our duty to offer it to Your Majesty, not only as to our King and Sovereign, but as to the principal Mover and Author of the work: humbly craving of Your most Sacred Majesty, that since things of this quality have ever been subject to the censures of illmeaning and discontented persons, it may receive approbation and patronage from so learned and judicious a Prince as Your Highness is, whose allowance and acceptance of our labours shall more honour and encourage us, than all the calumniations and hard interpretations of other men shall dismay us. So that if, on the one side, we shall be traduced by Popish Persons at home or abroad, who therefore will malign us, because we are poor instruments to make God's holy Truth to be yet more and more known unto the people, whom they desire still to keep in ignorance and darkness; or if, on the other side, we shall be maligned by self-conceited Brethren, who run their own ways, and give liking unto nothing, but what is framed by themselves, and hammered on their anvil; we may rest secure, supported within by the truth and innocency of a good conscience, having walked the ways of simplicity and integrity, as before the Lord; and sustained without by the powerful protection of Your Majesty's grace and favour, which will ever give countenance to honest and Christian endeavours against bitter censures and uncharitable imputations.

The Lord of heaven and earth bless Your Majesty with many and happy days, that, as his heavenly hand hath enriched Your Highness with many singular and extraordinary graces, so You may be the wonder of the world in this latter age for happiness and true felicity, to the honour of that great GOD, and the good of his Church, through Jesus Christ our Lord and only Saviour.

Amplified Bible

About The Amplified Bible

The story of *The Amplified Bible* is a remarkable story of faith, hope, and love. It's the story of a woman, a foundation, a committee, and a publisher. Commitment, energy, enthusiasm, giftedness—these are the words that paint the picture, the picture of the making of a translation.

Frances Siewert (Litt. B., B.D., M.A., Litt. D.) was a woman with an intense dedication to the study of the Bible. It was Mrs. Siewert (1881–1967) who laid the foundation of *The Amplified Bible,* devoting her life to a familiarity with the Bible, with the Hebrew and Greek languages, and with the cultural and archaeological background of Biblical times, which would result in the publication of this unique translation.

Every vision needs visionaries willing to follow the cause. The story of this dream is no different. Mrs. Siewert's vision was seen by a California non-profit foundation called The Lockman Foundation, made up of Christian men and women who through their commitment, their expertise, and their financial support undergirded Mrs. Siewert's monumental translation project. The Lockman Foundation's purpose remains today what it was then: to promote Bible translation, Christian evangelism, education, and benevolence.

Commitment, energy, enthusiasm, giftedness—the things visions are made of—describes the efforts of the committee appointed by The Lockman Foundation to carefully review the impressive work of Mrs. Siewert. This Editorial Board, made up of dedicated people, lent credibility and organization to this unprecedented attempt to bring out the richness of the Hebrew and Greek languages within the English text itself.

One chapter yet remained to bring the vision into reality. A publishing house in Grand Rapids, Michigan, on its way to becoming a major religious publishing firm, seized the opportunity to participate in a project which all visionaries involved strongly believed would be used by God to change lives. The Zondervan Publishing House joined the team, and the dream became reality with the publication of *The Amplified New Testament* in 1958, followed by the two-volume *Amplified Old Testament* in 1962 and 1964, and the one-volume *Amplified Bible* in 1965.

Features of The Amplified Bible

The Amplified portion of the *Comparative Study Bible* features the text of *The Amplified Bible* with explanatory and devotional footnotes, and a reference system contained within the text.

The Text of the Amplified Bible

The text of *The Amplified Bible* is easy to understand, and is made even easier to understand by the inclusion of informative footnotes which give historical background, archaeological information, and solid traditional scholarship, both academic and devotional in character. Numerous Bible translations are among the sources cited in the footnotes, as well as some of the greatest lexicographers of all time and some of the best of Bible commentators.

To help readers achieve the greatest possible clarity and understanding in their reading of the text of *The Amplified Bible,* some explanation of the various markings within the text is necessary:

Parentheses ( ) signify additional phases of meaning included in the original word, phrase, or clause of the original language.

Brackets [ ] contain justified clarifying words or comments not actually expressed in the immediate original text, as well as definitions of Hebrew and Greek names.

Italics point out:
1. certain familiar passages now recognized as not adequately supported by the original manuscripts. This is the primary use of italics in the New Testament, so that, upon encountering italics, the reader is alerted to a matter of textual readings. Often these will be accompanied by a footnote. See as an example Matthew 16:2–3.
2. conjunctions such as "and," "or," and the like, not in the original text, but used to connect additional English words indicated in the same original word. In this use, the reader, upon encountering a conjunction in italics, is alerted to the addition of an amplified word or phrase. See as an example Acts 24:3.

Capitals are used:
1. in names and personal pronouns referring to the Deity. See as an example Psalm 94.
2. in proper names of persons, places, specific feasts, topographical names, personifications, and the like. See as an example Proverbs 1:2; John 7:2.

Abbreviations may on occasion be encountered in either the text or in the footnotes:
cf. compare, confer
ch., chs. chapter, chapters
e.g. for example
etc. and so on
i.e. that is
v., vv. verse, verses
ff. following
ft. foot
c. about
KJV King James Version
RV Revised Version
ASV American Standard Version

The Reference System

The reference system of *The Amplified Bible* is contained within the text. The Scripture references are placed within brackets at the end of a verse, and are intended to cover any part of the preceding verse to which they apply. If a verse contains more than one Scripture reference, the list of references is in Biblical order. A sensitivity to the prophecy-fulfillment motif is indicated by such references as [Fulfilled in . . .]; [Foretold in . . .].

About The Amplified Bible

The story of The Amplified Bible is a remarkable story of faith, hope, and love. It is the story of a woman, a foundation, a committee, and a publisher. Commitment, energy, enthusiasm, efficiency — these are the words that paint the picture, the picture of the making of a translation.

Frances Siewert (Litt. B., B.D., M.A., Litt. D.) was a woman with an intense dedication to the study of the Bible. It was Mrs. Siewert (1881 – 1967) who laid the foundation of The Amplified Bible, devoting her life to a familiarity with the Bible, with the Hebrew and Greek languages, and with the cultural and archaeological background of Biblical times, which would result in the publication of this unique translation.

Every vision needs visionaries willing to follow the cause. The story of this dream is no different. Mrs. Siewert's vision was seen by a California non-profit foundation called The Lockman Foundation, made up of Christian men and women who through their commitment, their expertise, and their financial support undergirded Mrs. Siewert's monumental translation project. The Lockman Foundation's purpose remains today what it was then: to promote Bible translation, Christian evangelism, education, and benevolence.

Commitment, energy, enthusiasm, efficiency — these things, again, are made to describe the efforts of the committee appointed by The Lockman Foundation to carefully review the impressive work of Mrs. Siewert. This Editorial Board, made up of dedicated people, lent credibility and organization to this unprecedented attempt to bring out the richness of the Hebrew and Greek languages within the English text itself.

One chapter yet remained to bring the vision into reality. A publishing house in Grand Rapids, Michigan, on its way to becoming a major religious publishing firm, seized the opportunity to participate in a project which all visionaries involved strongly believed would be used by God to change lives. The Zondervan Publishing House joined the team, and the dream became reality with the publication of the Amplified New Testament in 1958, followed by the two-volume Amplified Old Testament in 1962 and 1964, and the one-volume Amplified Bible in 1965.

Features of The Amplified Bible

The Amplified portion of the Comparative Study Bible features the text of The Amplified Bible with explanatory and devotional footnotes, and a reference system contained within the text.

The Text of the Amplified Bible

The text of The Amplified Bible is easy to understand, and is made even easier to understand by the inclusion of informative resources which give historical background, archaeological information, and solid traditional scholarship, both academic and devotional in character. Numerous Bible translations are among the sources cited in the footnotes, as well as some of the greatest lexicographers of all time, and some of the best of Bible commentators.

To help readers achieve the greatest possible clarity and understanding in their reading of the text of The Amplified

---

Bible, some explanation of the various markings within the text is necessary:

ft. foot.

New American Standard

Scriptural Promise

"The grass withers, the flower fades, but the word of our God stands forever."

Isaiah 40:8

Foreword

The New American Standard Bible has been produced with the conviction that the words of Scripture as originally penned in the Hebrew, Aramaic, and Greek were inspired by God. Since they are the eternal Word of God, the Holy Scriptures speak with fresh power to each generation, to give wisdom that leads to salvation, that men may serve Christ to the glory of God.

The Fourfold Aim
of
The Lockman Foundation

1. These publications shall be true to the original Hebrew, Aramaic, and Greek.
2. They shall be grammatically correct.
3. They shall be understandable.
4. They shall give the Lord Jesus Christ His proper place, the place which the Word gives Him; therefore, no work will ever be personalized.

Preface to the
NEW AMERICAN STANDARD BIBLE

In the history of English Bible translations, the King James Version is the most prestigious. This time-honored version of 1611, itself a revision of the Bishops' Bible of 1568, became the basis for the English Revised Version appearing in 1881 (New Testament) and 1885 (Old Testament). The American counterpart of this last work was published in 1901 as the American Standard Version. The ASV, a product of both British and American scholarship, has been highly regarded for its scholarship and accuracy. Recognizing the values of the American Standard Version, The Lockman Foundation felt an urgency to preserve these and other lasting values of the ASV by incorporating recent discoveries of Hebrew and Greek textual sources and by rendering it into more current English. Therefore, in 1959 a new translation project was launched, based on the time-honored principles of translation of the ASV and KJV. The result is the New American Standard Bible.

Translation work for the NASB was begun in 1959. In the preparation of this work numerous other translations have been consulted along with the linguistic tools and literature of biblical scholarship. Decisions about English renderings were made by consensus of a team composed of educators and pastors. Subsequently, review and evaluation by other Hebrew and Greek scholars outside the Editorial Board were sought and carefully considered.

The Editorial Board has continued to function since publication of the complete Bible in 1971. This edition of the NASB represents revisions and refinements recommended over the last several years as well as thorough research based on modern English usage.

Principles of Translation

MODERN ENGLISH USAGE: The attempt has been made to render the grammar and terminology in contemporary English. When it was felt that the word-for-word literalness was unacceptable to the modern reader, a change was made in the direction of a more current English idiom. In the instances where this has been done, the more literal rendering has been indicated in the notes. There are a few exceptions to this procedure. In particular, frequently "And" is not translated at the beginning of sentences because of differences in style between ancient and modern writing. Punctuation is a relatively modern invention, and ancient writers often linked most of their sentences with "and" or other connectives. Also, the Hebrew idiom "answered and said" is sometimes reduced to "answered" or "said" as demanded by the context. For current English the idiom "it came about that" has not been translated in the New Testament except when a major transition is needed.

ALTERNATIVE READINGS: In addition to the more literal renderings, notations have been made to include alternate translations, reading of variant manuscripts and explanatory equivalents of the text. Only such notations have been used as have been felt justified in assisting the reader's comprehension of the terms used by the original author.

HEBREW TEXT: In the present translation the latest edition of Rudolf Kittel's *BIBLIA HEBRAICA* has been employed together with the most recent light from lexicography, cognate languages, and the Dead Sea Scrolls.

HEBREW TENSES: Consecution of tenses in Hebrew remains a puzzling factor in translation. The translators have been guided by the requirements of a literal translation, the sequence of tenses, and the immediate and broad contexts.

THE PROPER NAME OF GOD IN THE OLD TESTAMENT: In the Scriptures, the name of God is most significant and understandably so. It is inconceivable to think of spiritual matters without a proper designation for the Supreme Deity. Thus the most common name for the Deity is God, a translation of the original *Elohim*. One of the titles for God is Lord, a translation of *Adonai*. There is yet another name which is particularly assigned to God as His special or proper name, that is, the four letters YHWH (Exodus 3:14 and Isaiah 42:8). This name has not been pronounced by the Jews because of reverence for the great sacredness of the divine name. Therefore, it has been consistently translated LORD. The only exception to this translation of YHWH is when it occurs in immediate proximity to the word *Lord,* that is, *Adonai*. In that case it is regularly translated GOD in order to avoid confusion.

It is known that for many years YHWH has been transliterated as Yahweh, however no complete certainty attaches to this pronunciation.

GREEK TEXT: Consideration was given to the latest available manuscripts with a view to determining the best Greek text. In most instances the 26th edition of Eberhard Nestle's *NOVUM TESTAMENTUM GRAECE* was followed.

GREEK TENSES: A careful distinction has been made in the treatment of the Greek aorist tense (usually translated as the English past, "He did") and the Greek imperfect tense (normally rendered either as English past progressive, "He was doing"; or, if inceptive, as "He began to do" or "He started to do"; or else if customary past, as "He used to do"). "Began" is italicized if it renders an imperfect tense, in order to distinguish it from the Greek verb for "begin." In some contexts the difference between the Greek imperfect and the English past is conveyed better by the

choice of vocabulary or by other words in the context, and in such cases the Greek imperfect may be rendered as a simple past tense (e.g. "had an illness for many years" would be preferable to "was having an illness for many years" and would be understood in the same way).

On the other hand, not all aorists have been rendered as English pasts ("He did"), for some of them are clearly to be rendered as English perfects ("He has done"), or even as past perfects ("He had done"), judging from the context in which they occur. Such aorists have been rendered as perfects or past perfects in this translation.

As for the distinction between aorist and present imperatives, the translators have usually rendered these imperatives in the customary manner, rather than attempting any such fine distinction as "Begin to do!" (for the aorist imperative), or, "Continually do!" (for the present imperative).

As for sequence of tenses, the translators took care to follow English rules rather than Greek in translating Greek presents, imperfects and aorists. Thus, where English says, "We knew that he was doing," Greek puts it, "We knew that he does"; similarly, "We knew that he had done" is the Greek, "We knew that he did." Likewise, the English, "When he had come, they met him," is represented in Greek by, "When he came, they met him." In all cases a consistent transfer has been made from the Greek tense in the subordinate clause to the appropriate tense in English.

In the rendering of negative questions introduced by the particle *mē* (which always expects the answer "No") the wording has been altered from a mere, "Will he not do this?" to a more accurate, "He will not do this, will he?"

THE LOCKMAN FOUNDATION

Explanation of General Format

FOOTNOTES are used only where the text especially requires them for clarification. Marginal notes and cross references have been deleted from this edition.

PARAGRAPHS are designated by a paragraph symbol and bold face verse numbers or letters.

QUOTATION MARKS are used in the text in accordance with modern English usage.

"THOU," "THEE" AND "THY" are not used in this edition and have been rendered as "You" and "Your."

PERSONAL PRONOUNS are capitalized when pertaining to Deity.

ITALICS are used in the text to indicate words which are not found in the original Hebrew, Aramaic, or Greek but

implied by it. Italics are used in the footnotes to signify alternate readings for the text. Roman text in the footnote alternate readings is the same as italics in the Bible text.

SMALL CAPS in the New Testament are used in the text to indicate Old Testament quotations or obvious references to Old Testament texts. Variations of Old Testament wording are found in New Testament citations depending on whether the New Testament writer translated from a Hebrew text, used existing Greek or Aramaic translations, or paraphrased the material. It should be noted that modern rules for the indication of direct quotation were not used in biblical times; thus, the ancient writer would use exact quotations or references to quotation without specific indication of such.

ASTERISKS are used to mark verbs that are historical presents in the Greek which have been translated with an English past tense in order to conform to modern usage. The translators recognized that in some contexts the present tense seems more unexpected and unjustified to the English reader than a past tense would have been. But Greek authors frequently used the present tense for the sake of heightened vividness, thereby transporting their readers in imagination to the actual scene at the time of occurrence. However, the translators felt that it would be wise to change these historical presents to English past tenses.

Abbreviations and Special Markings

Aram	=	Aramaic
DSS	=	Dead Sea Scrolls
Gr	=	Greek translation of O.T. (Septuagint or LXX) or Greek text of N.T.
Heb	=	Hebrew text, usually Masoretic
Lat	=	Latin
M.T.	=	Masoretic text
Syr	=	Syriac
Lit	=	A literal translation
Or	=	An alternate translation justified by the Hebrew, Aramaic, or Greek
[ ]	=	In text, brackets indicate words probably not in the original writings
cf	=	compare
f, ff	=	following verse or verses
ms, mss	=	manuscript, manuscripts
v, vv	=	verse, verses

New International Version

Translators' Preface

The New International Version is a completely new translation of the Holy Bible made by over a hundred scholars working directly from the best available Hebrew, Aramaic and Greek texts. It had its beginning in 1965 when, after several years of exploratory study by committees from the Christian Reformed Church and the National Association of Evangelicals, a group of scholars met at Palos Heights, Illinois, and concurred in the need for a new translation of the Bible in contemporary English. This group, though not made up of official church representatives, was transdenominational. Its conclusion was endorsed by a large number of leaders from many denominations who met in Chicago in 1966.

Responsibility for the new version was delegated by the Palos Heights group to a self-governing body of fifteen, the Committee on Bible Translation, composed for the most part of biblical scholars from colleges, universities and seminaries. In 1967 the New York Bible Society (now the International Bible Society) generously undertook the financial sponsorship of the project—a sponsorship that made it possible to enlist the help of many distinguished scholars. The fact that participants from the United States, Great Britain, Canada, Australia and New Zealand worked together gave the project its international scope. That they were from many denominations—including Anglican, Assemblies of God, Baptist, Brethren, Christian Reformed, Church of Christ, Evangelical Free, Lutheran, Mennonite, Methodist, Nazarene, Presbyterian, Wesleyan and other churches—helped to safeguard the translation from sectarian bias.

How it was made helps to give the New International Version its distinctiveness. The translation of each book was assigned to a team of scholars. Next, one of the Intermediate Editorial Committees revised the initial translation, with constant reference to the Hebrew, Aramaic or Greek. Their work then went to one of the General Editorial Committees, which checked it in detail and made another thorough revision. This revision in turn was carefully reviewed by the Committee on Bible Translation, which made further changes and then released the final version for publication. In this way the entire Bible underwent three revisions, during each of which the translation was examined for its faithfulness to the original languages and for its English style.

All this involved many thousands of hours of research and discussion regarding the meaning of the texts and the precise way of putting them into English. It may well be that no other translation has been made by a more thorough process of review and revision from committee to committee than this one.

From the beginning of the project, the Committee on Bible Translation held to certain goals for the New International Version: that it would be an accurate translation and one that would have clarity and literary quality and so prove suitable for public and private reading, teaching, preaching, memorizing and liturgical use. The Committee also sought to preserve some measure of continuity with the long tradition of translating the Scriptures into English.

In working toward these goals, the translators were united in their commitment to the authority and infallibility of the Bible as God's Word in written form. They believe that it contains the divine answer to the deepest needs of humanity, that it sheds unique light on our path in a dark world, and that it sets forth the way to our eternal well-being.

The first concern of the translators has been the accuracy of the translation and its fidelity to the thought of the biblical writers. They have weighed the significance of the lexical and grammatical details of the Hebrew, Aramaic and Greek texts. At the same time, they have striven for more than a word-for-word translation. Because thought patterns and syntax differ from language to language, faithful communication of the meaning of the writers of the Bible demands frequent modifications in sentence structure and constant regard for the contextual meanings of words.

A sensitive feeling for style does not always accompany scholarship. Accordingly the Committee on Bible Translation submitted the developing version to a number of stylistic consultants. Two of them read every book of both Old and New Testaments twice—once before and once after the last major revision—and made invaluable suggestions. Samples of the translation were tested for clarity and ease of reading by various kinds of people—young and old, highly educated and less well educated, ministers and laymen.

Concern for clear and natural English—that the New International Version should be idiomatic but not idiosyncratic, contemporary but not dated—motivated the translators and consultants. At the same time, they tried to reflect the differing styles of the biblical writers. In view of the international use of English, the translators sought to avoid obvious Americanisms on the one hand and obvious Anglicisms on the other. A British edition reflects the comparatively few differences of significant idiom and of spelling.

As for the traditional pronouns "thou," "thee" and "thine" in reference to the Deity, the translators judged that to use these archaisms (along with the old verb forms such as "doest," "wouldest" and "hadst") would violate accuracy in translation. Neither Hebrew, Aramaic nor Greek uses special pronouns for the persons of the Godhead. A present-day translation is not enhanced by forms that in the time of the King James Version were used in everyday speech, whether referring to God or man.

For the Old Testament the standard Hebrew text, the Masoretic Text as published in the latest editions of *Biblia Hebraica*, was used throughout. The Dead Sea Scrolls contain material bearing on an earlier stage of the Hebrew text. They were consulted, as were the Samaritan Pentateuch and the ancient scribal traditions relating to textual changes. Sometimes a variant Hebrew reading in the margin of the Masoretic Text was followed instead of the text itself. Such instances, being variants within the Masoretic tradition, are not specified by footnotes. In rare cases, words in the consonantal text were divided differently from the way they appear in the Masoretic Text. Footnotes indicate this. The translators also consulted the more important early versions—the Septuagint; Aquila, Symmachus and Theodotion; the Vulgate; the Syriac Peshitta; the Targums; and for the Psalms the *Juxta Hebraica* of Jerome. Readings from these versions were occasionally followed where the Masoretic Text seemed doubtful and where accepted prin-

ciples of textual criticism showed that one or more of these textual witnesses appeared to provide the correct reading. Such instances are footnoted. Sometimes vowel letters and vowel signs did not, in the judgment of the translators, represent the correct vowels for the original consonantal text. Accordingly some words were read with a different set of vowels. These instances are usually not indicated by footnotes.

The Greek text used in translating the New Testament was an eclectic one. No other piece of ancient literature has such an abundance of manuscript witnesses as does the New Testament. Where existing manuscripts differ, the translators made their choice of readings according to accepted principles of New Testament textual criticism. Footnotes call attention to places where there was uncertainty about what the original text was. The best current printed texts of the Greek New Testament were used.

There is a sense in which the work of translation is never wholly finished. This applies to all great literature and uniquely so to the Bible. In 1973 the New Testament in the New International Version was published. Since then, suggestions for corrections and revisions have been received from various sources. The Committee on Bible Translation carefully considered the suggestions and adopted a number of them. These were incorporated in the first printing of the entire Bible in 1978. Additional revisions were made by the Committee on Bible Translation in 1983 and appear in printings after that date.

As in other ancient documents, the precise meaning of the biblical texts is sometimes uncertain. This is more often the case with the Hebrew and Aramaic texts than with the Greek text. Although archaeological and linguistic discoveries in this century aid in understanding difficult passages, some uncertainties remain. The more significant of these have been called to the reader's attention in the footnotes.

In regard to the divine name *YHWH*, commonly referred to as the *Tetragrammaton*, the translators adopted the device used in most English versions of rendering that name as "LORD" in capital letters to distinguish it from *Adonai*, another Hebrew word rendered "Lord," for which small letters are used. Wherever the two names stand together in the Old Testament as a compound name of God, they are rendered "Sovereign LORD."

Because for most readers today the phrases "the LORD of hosts" and "God of hosts" have little meaning, this version renders them "the LORD Almighty" and "God Almighty." These renderings convey the sense of the Hebrew, namely, "he who is sovereign over all the 'hosts' (powers) in heaven and on earth, especially over the 'hosts' (armies) of Israel." For readers unacquainted with Hebrew this does not make clear the distinction between *Sabaoth* ("hosts" or "Almighty") and *Shaddai* (which can also be translated "Almighty"), but the latter occurs infrequently and is always footnoted. When *Adonai* and *YHWH Sabaoth* occur together, they are rendered "the Lord, the LORD Almighty."

As for other proper nouns, the familiar spellings of the King James Version are generally retained. Names traditionally spelled with "ch," except where it is final, are usually spelled in this translation with "k" or "c," since the biblical languages do not have the sound that "ch" frequently indicates in English—for example, in *chant*. For well-known names such as Zechariah, however, the traditional spelling has been retained. Variation in the spelling of names in the original languages has usually not been indicated. Where a person or place has two or more different names in the Hebrew, Aramaic or Greek texts, the more familiar one has generally been used, with footnotes where needed.

To achieve clarity the translators sometimes supplied words not in the original texts but required by the context.

If there was uncertainty about such material, it is enclosed in brackets. Also for the sake of clarity or style, nouns, including some proper nouns, are sometimes substituted for pronouns, and vice versa. And though the Hebrew writers often shifted back and forth between first, second and third personal pronouns without change of antecedent, this translation often makes them uniform, in accordance with English style and without the use of footnotes.

Poetical passages are printed as poetry, that is, with indentation of lines and with separate stanzas. These are generally designed to reflect the structure of Hebrew poetry. This poetry is normally characterized by parallelism in balanced lines. Most of the poetry in the Bible is in the Old Testament, and scholars differ regarding the scansion of Hebrew lines. The translators determined the stanza divisions for the most part by analysis of the subject matter. The stanzas therefore serve as poetic paragraphs.

As an aid to the reader, italicized sectional headings are inserted in most of the books. They are not to be regarded as part of the NIV text, are not for oral reading, and are not intended to dictate the interpretation of the sections they head.

The footnotes in this version are of several kinds, most of which need no explanation. Those giving alternative translations begin with "Or" and generally introduce the alternative with the last word preceding it in the text, except when it is a single-word alternative; in poetry quoted in a footnote a slant mark indicates a line division. Footnotes introduced by "Or" do not have uniform significance. In some cases two possible translations were considered to have about equal validity. In other cases, though the translators were convinced that the translation in the text was correct, they judged that another interpretation was possible and of sufficient importance to be represented in a footnote.

In the New Testament, footnotes that refer to uncertainty regarding the original text are introduced by "Some manuscripts" or similar expressions. In the Old Testament, evidence for the reading chosen is given first and evidence for the alternative is added after a semicolon (for example: Septuagint; Hebrew *father*). In such notes the term "Hebrew" refers to the Masoretic Text.

It should be noted that minerals, flora and fauna, architectural details, articles of clothing and jewelry, musical instruments and other articles cannot always be identified with precision. Also measures of capacity in the biblical period are particularly uncertain (see the table of weights and measures following the text).

Like all translations of the Bible, made as they are by imperfect man, this one undoubtedly falls short of its goals. Yet we are grateful to God for the extent to which he has enabled us to realize these goals and for the strength he has given us and our colleagues to complete our task. We offer this version of the Bible to him in whose name and for whose glory it has been made. We pray that it will lead many into a better understanding of the Holy Scriptures and a fuller knowledge of Jesus Christ the incarnate Word, of whom the Scriptures so faithfully testify.

The Committee on Bible Translation

June 1978
(Revised August 1983)

Names of the translators and editors may be secured from the International Bible Society, translation sponsors of the New International Version, 1820 Jet Stream Drive, Colorado Springs, Colorado 80921-3696 U.S.A.

The
Old Testament

THE FIRST BOOK OF MOSES, CALLED

Genesis

THE FIRST BOOK OF MOSES, COMMONLY CALLED

Genesis

King James

The creation

1 IN THE beginning God created the heaven and the earth.

2And the earth was without form, and void; and darkness *was* upon the face of the deep. And the spirit of God moved upon the face of the waters.

3And God said, Let there be light: and there was light.

4And God saw the light, that *it was* good: and God divided *a*the light from the darkness.

5And God called the light Day, and the darkness he called Night. *b*And the evening and the morning were the first day.

6 ¶ And God said, Let there be a *c*firmament in the midst of the waters, and let it divide the waters from the waters.

7And God made the firmament, and divided the waters which *were* under the firmament from the waters which *were* above the firmament: and it was so.

8And God called the firmament Heaven. And the evening and the morning were the second day.

9 ¶ And God said, Let the waters under the heaven be gathered together unto one place, and let the dry *land* appear: and it was so.

10And God called the dry *land* Earth; and the gathering together of the waters called he Seas: and God saw that *it was* good.

11And God said, Let the earth bring forth *d*grass, the herb yielding seed, *and* the fruit tree yielding fruit after his kind, whose seed *is* in itself, upon the earth: and it was so.

12And the earth brought forth grass, *and* herb yielding seed after his kind, and the tree yielding fruit, whose seed *was* in itself, after his kind: and God saw that *it was* good.

13And the evening and the morning were the third day.

14 ¶ And God said, Let there be lights in the firmament of the heaven to divide *e*the day from the night; and let them be for signs, and for seasons, and for days, and years:

15And let them be for lights in the firmament of the heaven to give light upon the earth: and it was so.

16And God made two great lights; the greater light *f*to rule the day, and the lesser light to rule the night: *he made* the stars also.

17And God set them in the firmament of the heaven to give light upon the earth,

18And to rule over the day and over the night, and to divide the light from the darkness: and God saw that *it was* good.

19And the evening and the morning were the fourth day.

20And God said, Let the waters bring forth abundantly the *g*moving creature that hath *h*life, and *i*fowl *that* may fly above the earth in the *j*open firmament of heaven.

21And God created great whales, and every living creature that moveth, which the waters brought forth abundantly, after their kind, and every winged fowl after his kind: and God saw that *it was* good.

Amplified

1 IN THE beginning God (prepared, formed, fashioned, and) created the heavens and the earth. [Heb. 11:3.]

2The earth was without form and an empty waste, and darkness was upon the face of the very great deep. The Spirit of God was moving (hovering, brooding) over the face of the waters.

3And God said, Let there be light; and there was light.

4And God saw that the light was good (suitable, pleasant) *and* He approved it; and God separated the light from the darkness. [II Cor. 4:6.]

5And God called the light Day, and the darkness He called Night. And there was evening and there was morning, one day.

6And God said, Let there be a firmament [the expanse of the sky] in the midst of the waters, and let it separate the waters [below] from the waters [above].

7And God made the firmament [the expanse] and separated the waters which were under the expanse from the waters which were above the expanse. And it was so.

8And God called the firmament Heavens. And there was evening and there was morning, a second day.

9And God said, Let the waters under the heavens be collected into one place [of standing], and let the dry land appear. And it was so.

10God called the dry land Earth, and the accumulated waters He called Seas. And God saw that this was good (fitting, admirable) *and* He approved it.

11And God said, Let the earth put forth [tender] vegetation: plants yielding seed and fruit trees yielding fruit whose seed is in itself, each according to its kind, upon the earth. And it was so.

12The earth brought forth vegetation: plants yielding seed according to their own kinds and trees bearing fruit in which was their seed, each according to its kind. And God saw that it was good (suitable, admirable) *and* He approved it.

13And there was evening and there was morning, a third day.

14And God said, Let there be lights in the expanse of the heavens to separate the day from the night, and let them be for signs *and* tokens [of God's provident care], and [to mark] seasons, days, and years, [Gen. 8:22.]

15And let them be lights in the expanse of the sky to give light upon the earth. And it was so.

16And God made the two great lights—the greater light (the sun) to rule the day and the lesser light (the moon) to rule the night. He also made the stars.

17And God set them in the expanse of the heavens to give light upon the earth,

18To rule over the day and over the night, and to separate the light from the darkness. And God saw that it was good (fitting, pleasant) *and* He approved it.

19And there was evening and there was morning, a fourth day.

20And God said, Let the waters bring forth abundantly *and* swarm with living creatures, and let birds fly over the earth in the open expanse of the heavens.

21God created the great sea monsters and every living creature that moves, which the waters brought forth abundantly, according to their kinds, and every winged bird according to its kind. And God saw that it was good (suitable, admirable) *and* He approved it.

---

a Heb. *between the light and between the darkness*   *b* Heb. *And the evening was, and the morning was*   *c* Heb. *expansion*
d Heb. *tender grass*   *e* Heb. *between the day and between the night*   *f* Heb. *for the rule of the day*   *g* Or, *creeping*
h Heb. *soul*   *i* Heb. *let fowl fly*   *j* Heb. *face of the firmament of heaven*

New American Standard

Genesis

The Creation

1 IN THE beginning God created the heavens and the earth. 2 The earth was *a*formless and void, and darkness was over the surface of the deep, and the Spirit of God was *b*moving over the surface of the waters. 3 Then God said, "Let there be light"; and there was light. 4 God saw that the light was good; and God separated the light from the darkness. 5 God called the light day, and the darkness He called night. And there was evening and there was morning, one day.

6 ¶ Then God said, "Let there be an expanse in the midst of the waters, and let it separate the waters from the waters." 7 God made the *c*expanse, and separated the waters which were below the expanse from the waters which were above the expanse; and it was so. 8 God called the expanse heaven. And there was evening and there was morning, a second day.

9 ¶ Then God said, "Let the waters below the heavens be gathered into one place, and let the dry land appear"; and it was so. 10 God called the dry land earth, and the gathering of the waters He called seas; and God saw that it was good. 11 Then God said, "Let the earth sprout vegetation: plants yielding seed, *and* fruit trees on the earth bearing fruit after their kind with seed in them"; and it was so. 12 The earth brought forth vegetation, plants yielding seed after their kind, and trees bearing fruit with seed in them, after their kind; and God saw that it was good. 13 There was evening and there was morning, a third day.

14 ¶ Then God said, "Let there be lights in the expanse of the heavens to separate the day from the night, and let them be for signs and for seasons and for days and years; 15 and let them be for lights in the expanse of the heavens to give light on the earth"; and it was so. 16 God made the two great lights, the greater light to govern the day, and the lesser light to govern the night; *He made* the stars also. 17 God placed them in the expanse of the heavens to give light on the earth, 18 and to govern the day and the night, and to separate the light from the darkness; and God saw that it was good. 19 There was evening and there was morning, a fourth day.

20 ¶ Then God said, "Let the waters teem with swarms of living creatures, and let birds fly above the earth in the open expanse of the heavens." 21 God created the great sea monsters and every living creature that moves, with which the waters swarmed after their kind, and every winged bird after its kind; and God saw that it was good.

New International

Genesis

The Beginning

1 IN THE beginning God created the heavens and the earth. 2 Now the earth was*a* formless and empty, darkness was over the surface of the deep, and the Spirit of God was hovering over the waters.

3 And God said, "Let there be light," and there was light. 4 God saw that the light was good, and he separated the light from the darkness. 5 God called the light "day," and the darkness he called "night." And there was evening, and there was morning—the first day.

6 And God said, "Let there be an expanse between the waters to separate water from water." 7 So God made the expanse and separated the water under the expanse from the water above it. And it was so. 8 God called the expanse "sky." And there was evening, and there was morning—the second day.

9 And God said, "Let the water under the sky be gathered to one place, and let dry ground appear." And it was so. 10 God called the dry ground "land," and the gathered waters he called "seas." And God saw that it was good.

11 Then God said, "Let the land produce vegetation: seed-bearing plants and trees on the land that bear fruit with seed in it, according to their various kinds." And it was so. 12 The land produced vegetation: plants bearing seed according to their kinds and trees bearing fruit with seed in it according to their kinds. And God saw that it was good. 13 And there was evening, and there was morning—the third day.

14 And God said, "Let there be lights in the expanse of the sky to separate the day from the night, and let them serve as signs to mark seasons and days and years, 15 and let them be lights in the expanse of the sky to give light on the earth." And it was so. 16 God made two great lights—the greater light to govern the day and the lesser light to govern the night. He also made the stars. 17 God set them in the expanse of the sky to give light on the earth, 18 to govern the day and the night, and to separate light from darkness. And God saw that it was good. 19 And there was evening, and there was morning—the fourth day.

20 And God said, "Let the water teem with living creatures, and let birds fly above the earth across the expanse of the sky." 21 So God created the great creatures of the sea and every living and moving thing with which the water teems, according to their kinds, and every winged bird according to its kind. And God saw that

---

a Or *a waste and emptiness*   *b* Or *hovering*   *c* Or *firmament*   *a* 2 Or possibly *became*

King James

Amplified

King James

22And God blessed them, saying, Be fruitful, and multiply, and fill the waters in the seas, and let fowl multiply in the earth.

23And the evening and the morning were the fifth day.

24 ¶ And God said, Let the earth bring forth the living creature after his kind, cattle, and creeping thing, and beast of the earth after his kind: and it was so.

25And God made the beast of the earth after his kind, and cattle after their kind, and every thing that creepeth upon the earth after his kind: and God saw that *it was* good.

26 ¶ And God said, Let us make man in our image, after our likeness: and let them have dominion over the fish of the sea, and over the fowl of the air, and over the cattle, and over all the earth, and over every creeping thing that creepeth upon the earth.

27So God created man in his *own* image, in the image of God created he him; male and female created he them.

28And God blessed them, and God said unto them, Be fruitful, and multiply, and replenish the earth, and subdue it: and have dominion over the fish of the sea, and over the fowl of the air, and over every living thing that *k*moveth upon the earth.

29 ¶ And God said, Behold, I have given you every herb *l*bearing seed, which *is* upon the face of all the earth, and every tree, in the which *is* the fruit of a tree yielding seed; to you it shall be for meat.

30And to every beast of the earth, and to every fowl of the air, and to every thing that creepeth upon the earth, wherein *there is* *m*life, *I have given* every green herb for meat: and it was so.

31And God saw every thing that he had made, and, behold, *it was* very good. And the evening and the morning were the sixth day.

2 THUS THE heavens and the earth were finished, and all the host of them.

2And on the seventh day God ended his work which he had made; and he rested on the seventh day from all his work which he had made.

3And God blessed the seventh day, and sanctified it: because that in it he had rested from all his work which God *n*created and made.

Adam and Eve

4 ¶ These *are* the generations of the heavens and of the earth when they were created, in the day that the LORD God made the earth and the heavens,

5And every plant of the field before it was in the earth, and every herb of the field before it grew: for the LORD God had not caused it to rain upon the earth, and *there was* not a man to till the ground.

6But *o*there went up a mist from the earth, and watered the whole face of the ground.

7And the LORD God formed man *p*of the dust of the ground, and breathed into his nostrils the breath of life; and man became a living soul.

8 ¶ And the LORD God planted a garden eastward in Eden; and there he put the man whom he had formed.

Amplified

22And God blessed them, saying, Be fruitful, multiply, and fill the waters in the seas, and let the fowl multiply in the earth.

23And there was evening and there was morning, a fifth day.

24And God said, Let the earth bring forth living creatures according to their kinds: livestock, creeping things, and [wild] beasts of the earth according to their kinds. And it was so.

25And God made the [wild] beasts of the earth according to their kinds, and domestic animals according to their kinds, and everything that creeps upon the earth according to its kind. And God saw that it was good (fitting, pleasant) *and* He approved it.

26God said, Let Us [Father, Son, and Holy Spirit] make mankind in Our image, after Our likeness, and let them have complete authority over the fish of the sea, the birds of the air, the [tame] beasts, and over all of the earth, and over everything that creeps upon the earth. [Ps. 104:30; Heb. 1:2; 11:3.]

27So God created man in His own image, in the image *and* likeness of God He created him; male and female He created them. [Col. 3:9, 10; James 3:8, 9.]

28And God blessed them and said to them, Be fruitful, multiply, and fill the earth, and subdue it [using all its vast resources in the service of God and man]; and have dominion over the fish of the sea, the birds of the air, and over every living creature that moves upon the earth.

29And God said, See, I have given you every plant yielding seed that is on the face of all the land and every tree with seed in its fruit; you shall have them for food.

30And to all the animals on the earth and to every bird of the air and to everything that creeps on the ground—to everything in which there is the breath of life—I have given every green plant for food. And it was so.

31And God saw everything that He had made, and behold, it was very good (suitable, pleasant) *and* He approved it completely. And there was evening and there was morning, a sixth day.

2 THUS THE heavens and the earth were finished, and all the host of them.

2And on the seventh day God ended His work which He had done; and He rested on the seventh day from all His work which He had done. [Heb. 4:9, 10.]

3And God blessed (spoke good of) the seventh day, set it apart as His own, and hallowed it, because on it God rested from all His work which He had created and done. [Exod. 20:11.]

4This is the history of the heavens and of the earth when they were created. In the day that the Lord God made the earth and the heavens—

5When no plant of the field was yet in the earth and no herb of the field had yet sprung up, for the Lord God had not [yet] caused it to rain upon the earth and there was no man to till the ground,

6But there went up a mist (fog, vapor) from the land and watered the whole surface of the ground—

7Then the Lord God formed man from the *a*dust of the ground and breathed into his nostrils the breath *or* spirit of life, and man became a living being. [I Cor. 15:45–49.]

8And the Lord God planted a garden toward the east, in Eden [delight]; and there He put the man whom He had formed (framed, constituted).

---

*k*Heb. *creepeth* *l*Heb. *seeding seed* *m*Heb. *a living soul*
*n*Heb. *created to make* *o*Or, *a mist which went up from*
*p*Heb. *dust of the ground*

*a*The same essential chemical elements are found in man and animal life that are in the soil. This scientific fact was not known to man until recent times, but God was displaying it here.

New American Standard

22 God blessed them, saying, "Be fruitful and multiply, and fill the waters in the seas, and let birds multiply on the earth."

23 There was evening and there was morning, a fifth day.

24 ¶ Then God said, "Let the earth bring forth living creatures after their kind: cattle and creeping things and beasts of the earth after their kind"; and it was so.

25 God made the beasts of the earth after their kind, and the cattle after their kind, and everything that creeps on the ground after its kind; and God saw that it was good.

26 ¶ Then God said, "Let Us make man in Our image, according to Our likeness; and let them rule over the fish of the sea and over the birds of the sky and over the cattle and over all the earth, and over every creeping thing that creeps on the earth."

27 God created man in His own image, in the image of God He created him; male and female He created them.

28 God blessed them; and God said to them, "Be fruitful and multiply, and fill the earth, and subdue it; and rule over the fish of the sea and over the birds of the sky and over every living thing that moves on the earth."

29 Then God said, "Behold, I have given you every plant yielding seed that is on the surface of all the earth, and every tree which has fruit yielding seed; it shall be food for you;

30 and to every beast of the earth and to every bird of the sky and to every thing that moves on the earth which has life, *I have given* every green plant for food"; and it was so.

31 God saw all that He had made, and behold, it was very good. And there was evening and there was morning, the sixth day.

The Creation of Man and Woman

2 THUS THE heavens and the earth were completed, and all their hosts.

2 By the seventh day God completed His work which He had done, and He rested on the seventh day from all His work which He had done.

3 Then God blessed the seventh day and sanctified it, because in it He rested from all His work which God had created and made.

4 ¶ This is the account of the heavens and the earth when they were created, in the day that the LORD God made earth and heaven.

5 Now no shrub of the field was yet in the earth, and no plant of the field had yet sprouted, for the LORD God had not sent rain upon the earth, and there was no man to cultivate the ground.

6 But a mist used to rise from the earth and water the whole surface of the ground.

7 Then the LORD God formed man of dust from the ground, and breathed into his nostrils the breath of life; and man became a living being.

8 The LORD God planted a garden toward the east, in Eden; and there He placed the man whom He had formed.

New International

it was good. 22God blessed them and said, "Be fruitful and increase in number and fill the water in the seas, and let the birds increase on the earth." 23And there was evening, and there was morning—the fifth day.

24And God said, "Let the land produce living creatures according to their kinds: livestock, creatures that move along the ground, and wild animals, each according to its kind." And it was so. 25God made the wild animals according to their kinds, the livestock according to their kinds, and all the creatures that move along the ground according to their kinds. And God saw that it was good.

26Then God said, "Let us make man in our image, in our likeness, and let them rule over the fish of the sea and the birds of the air, over the livestock, over all the earth,[b] and over all the creatures that move along the ground."

27So God created man in his own image,
    in the image of God he created him;
    male and female he created them.

28God blessed them and said to them, "Be fruitful and increase in number; fill the earth and subdue it. Rule over the fish of the sea and the birds of the air and over every living creature that moves on the ground."

29Then God said, "I give you every seed-bearing plant on the face of the whole earth and every tree that has fruit with seed in it. They will be yours for food. 30And to all the beasts of the earth and all the birds of the air and all the creatures that move on the ground—everything that has the breath of life in it—I give every green plant for food." And it was so.

31God saw all that he had made, and it was very good. And there was evening, and there was morning—the sixth day.

2 THUS THE heavens and the earth were completed in all their vast array.

2By the seventh day God had finished the work he had been doing; so on the seventh day he rested[c] from all his work. 3And God blessed the seventh day and made it holy, because on it he rested from all the work of creating that he had done.

Adam and Eve

4This is the account of the heavens and the earth when they were created.

When the LORD God made the earth and the heavens—5and no shrub of the field had yet appeared on the earth[d] and no plant of the field had yet sprung up, for the LORD God had not sent rain on the earth[d] and there was no man to work the ground, 6but streams[e] came up from the earth and watered the whole surface of the ground— 7the LORD God formed the man[f] from the dust of the ground and breathed into his nostrils the breath of life, and the man became a living being.

8Now the LORD God had planted a garden in the east, in

b 26 Hebrew; Syriac *all the wild animals*　　*c* 2 Or *ceased*; also in verse 3　　*d* 5 Or *land*; also in verse 6　　*e* 6 Or *mist*
f 7 The Hebrew for *man (adam)* sounds like and may be related to the Hebrew for *ground (adamah)*; it is also the name *Adam* (see Gen. 2:20).

King James

Amplified

⁹And out of the ground made the LORD God to grow every tree that is pleasant to the sight, and good for food; the tree of life also in the midst of the garden, and the tree of knowledge of good and evil.

¹⁰And a river went out of Eden to water the garden; and from thence it was parted, and became into four heads.

¹¹The name of the first is Pison: that is it which compasseth the whole land of Havilah, where there is gold;

¹²And the gold of that land is good: there is bdellium and the onyx stone.

¹³And the name of the second river is Gihon: the same is it that compasseth the whole land of ^qEthiopia.

¹⁴And the name of the third river is Hiddekel: that is it which goeth ^rtoward the east of Assyria. And the fourth river is Euphrates.

¹⁵And the LORD God took ^sthe man, and put him into the garden of Eden to dress it and to keep it.

¹⁶And the LORD God commanded the man, saying, Of every tree of the garden ^tthou mayest freely eat:

¹⁷But of the tree of the knowledge of good and evil, thou shalt not eat of it: for in the day that thou eatest thereof ^uthou shalt surely die.

¹⁸ ¶ And the LORD God said, It is not good that the man should be alone; I will make him an help ^vmeet for him.

¹⁹And out of the ground the LORD God formed every beast of the field, and every fowl of the air; and brought them unto ^wAdam to see what he would call them: and whatsoever Adam called every living creature, that was the name thereof.

²⁰And Adam ^xgave names to all cattle, and to the fowl of the air, and to every beast of the field; but for Adam there was not found an help meet for him.

²¹And the LORD God caused a deep sleep to fall upon Adam, and he slept: and he took one of his ribs, and closed up the flesh instead thereof;

²²And the rib, which the LORD God had taken from man, ^ymade he a woman, and brought her unto the man.

²³And Adam said, This is now bone of my bones, and flesh of my flesh: she shall be called ^zWoman, because she was taken out of ^aMan.

²⁴Therefore shall a man leave his father and his mother, and shall cleave unto his wife: and they shall be one flesh.

²⁵And they were both naked, the man and his wife, and were not ashamed.

The fall of man

3 NOW THE serpent was more subtle than any beast of the field which the LORD God had made. And he said unto the woman, ^bYea, hath God said, Ye shall not eat of every tree of the garden?

²And the woman said unto the serpent, We may eat of the fruit of the trees of the garden:

³But of the fruit of the tree which is in the midst of the garden, God hath said, Ye shall not eat of it, neither shall ye touch it, lest ye die.

⁴And the serpent said unto the woman, Ye shall not surely die:

⁵For God doth know that in the day ye eat thereof, then your eyes shall be opened, and ye shall be as gods, knowing good and evil.

⁹And out of the ground the Lord God made to grow every tree that is pleasant to the sight or to be desired—good (suitable, pleasant) for food; the tree of life also in the center of the garden, and the tree of the knowledge of [the difference between] good and evil and blessing and calamity. [Rev. 2:7; 22:14, 19.]

¹⁰Now a river went out of Eden to water the garden; and from there it divided and became four [river] heads.

¹¹The first is named Pishon; it is the one flowing around the whole land of Havilah, where there is gold.

¹²The gold of that land is of high quality; bdellium (pearl?) and onyx stone are there.

¹³The second river is named Gihon; it is the one flowing around the whole land of Cush.

¹⁴The third river is named Hiddekel [the Tigris]; it is the one flowing east of Assyria. And the fourth river is the Euphrates.

¹⁵And the Lord God took the man and put him in the Garden of Eden to tend and guard and keep it.

¹⁶And the Lord God commanded the man, saying, You may freely eat of every tree of the garden;

¹⁷But of the tree of the knowledge of good and evil and blessing and calamity you shall not eat, for in the day that you eat of it you shall surely die.

¹⁸Now the Lord God said, It is not good (sufficient, satisfactory) that the man should be alone; I will make him a helper meet (suitable, adapted, complementary) for him.

¹⁹And out of the ground the Lord God formed every [wild] beast and living creature of the field and every bird of the air and brought them to Adam to see what he would call them; and whatever Adam called every living creature, that was its name.

²⁰And Adam gave names to all the livestock and to the birds of the air and to every [wild] beast of the field; but for Adam there was not found a helper meet (suitable, adapted, complementary) for him.

²¹And the Lord God caused a deep sleep to fall upon Adam; and while he slept, He took one of his ribs or a part of his side and closed up the [place with] flesh.

²²And the rib or part of his side which the Lord God had taken from the man He built up and made into a woman, and He brought her to the man.

²³Then Adam said, This [creature] is now bone of my bones and flesh of my flesh; she shall be called Woman, because she was taken out of a man.

²⁴Therefore a man shall leave his father and his mother and shall become united and cleave to his wife, and they shall become one flesh. [Matt. 19:5; I Cor. 6:16; Eph. 5:31–33.]

²⁵And the man and his wife were both naked and were not embarrassed or ashamed in each other's presence.

3 NOW THE serpent was more subtle and crafty than any living creature of the field which the Lord God had made. And he [Satan] said to the woman, Can it really be that God has said, You shall not eat from every tree of the garden? [Rev. 12:9–11.]

²And the woman said to the serpent, We may eat the fruit from the trees of the garden,

³Except the fruit from the tree which is in the middle of the garden. God has said, You shall not eat of it, neither shall you touch it, lest you die.

⁴But the serpent said to the woman, You shall not surely die, [II Cor. 11:3.]

⁵For God knows that in the day you eat of it your eyes will be opened, and you will be like God, knowing the difference between good and evil and blessing and calamity.

^qHeb. Cush   ^rOr, eastward to Assyria   ^sOr, Adam
^tHeb. eating thou shalt eat   ^uHeb. dying thou shalt die
^vHeb. as before him   ^wOr, the man   ^xHeb. called   ^yHeb.
builded   ^zHeb. Isha   ^aHeb. Ish   ^bHeb. Yea, because

New American Standard

9 Out of the ground the LORD God caused to grow every tree that is pleasing to the sight and good for food; the tree of life also in the midst of the garden, and the tree of the knowledge of good and evil.

10 ¶ Now a river flowed out of Eden to water the garden; and from there it divided and became four rivers.

11 The name of the first is Pishon; it flows around the whole land of Havilah, where there is gold.

12 The gold of that land is good; the bdellium and the onyx stone are there.

13 The name of the second river is Gihon; it flows around the whole land of Cush.

14 The name of the third river is Tigris; it flows east of Assyria. And the fourth river is the Euphrates.

15 ¶ Then the LORD God took the man and put him into the garden of Eden to cultivate it and keep it.

16 The LORD God commanded the man, saying, "From any tree of the garden you may eat freely;

17 but from the tree of the knowledge of good and evil you shall not eat, for in the day that you eat from it you will surely die."

18 ¶ Then the LORD God said, "It is not good for the man to be alone; I will make him a helper *d*suitable for him."

19 Out of the ground the LORD God formed every beast of the field and every bird of the sky, and brought *them* to the man to see what he would call them; and whatever the man called a living creature, that was its name.

20 The man gave names to all the cattle, and to the birds of the sky, and to every beast of the field, but for *e*Adam there was not found a helper suitable for him.

21 So the LORD God caused a deep sleep to fall upon the man, and he slept; then He took one of his ribs and closed up the flesh at that place.

22 The LORD God *f*fashioned into a woman the rib which He had taken from the man, and brought her to the man.

23 The man said,
"This is now bone of my bones,
And flesh of my flesh;
She shall be called Woman,
Because she was taken out of Man."

24 For this reason a man shall leave his father and his mother, and be joined to his wife; and they shall become one flesh.

25 And the man and his wife were both naked and were not ashamed.

The Fall of Man

3 NOW THE serpent was more crafty than any beast of the field which the LORD God had made. And he said to the woman, "Indeed, has God said, 'You shall not eat from any tree of the garden'?"

2 The woman said to the serpent, "From the fruit of the trees of the garden we may eat;

3 but from the fruit of the tree which is in the middle of the garden, God has said, 'You shall not eat from it or touch it, or you will die.' "

4 The serpent said to the woman, "You surely will not die!

5 "For God knows that in the day you eat from it your eyes will be opened, and you will be like God, knowing good and evil."

New International

Eden; and there he put the man he had formed. 9And the LORD God made all kinds of trees grow out of the ground—trees that were pleasing to the eye and good for food. In the middle of the garden were the tree of life and the tree of the knowledge of good and evil.

10A river watering the garden flowed from Eden; from there it was separated into four headwaters. 11The name of the first is the Pishon; it winds through the entire land of Havilah, where there is gold. 12(The gold of that land is good; aromatic resin*g* and onyx are also there.) 13The name of the second river is the Gihon; it winds through the entire land of Cush.*h* 14The name of the third river is the Tigris; it runs along the east side of Asshur. And the fourth river is the Euphrates.

15The LORD God took the man and put him in the Garden of Eden to work it and take care of it. 16And the LORD God commanded the man, "You are free to eat from any tree in the garden; 17but you must not eat from the tree of the knowledge of good and evil, for when you eat of it you will surely die."

18The LORD God said, "It is not good for the man to be alone. I will make a helper suitable for him." 19Now the LORD God had formed out of the ground all the beasts of the field and all the birds of the air. He brought them to the man to see what he would name them; and whatever the man called each living creature, that was its name. 20So the man gave names to all the livestock, the birds of the air and all the beasts of the field.

But for Adam*i* no suitable helper was found. 21So the LORD God caused the man to fall into a deep sleep; and while he was sleeping, he took one of the man's ribs*j* and closed up the place with flesh. 22Then the LORD God made a woman from the rib*k* he had taken out of the man, and he brought her to the man.

23The man said,

"This is now bone of my bones
     and flesh of my flesh;
she shall be called 'woman,'*l*
     for she was taken out of man."

24For this reason a man will leave his father and mother and be united to his wife, and they will become one flesh. 25The man and his wife were both naked, and they felt no shame.

The Fall of Man

3 NOW THE serpent was more crafty than any of the wild animals the LORD God had made. He said to the woman, "Did God really say, 'You must not eat from any tree in the garden'?"

2The woman said to the serpent, "We may eat fruit from the trees in the garden, 3but God did say, 'You must not eat fruit from the tree that is in the middle of the garden, and you must not touch it, or you will die.' "

4"You will not surely die," the serpent said to the woman. 5"For God knows that when you eat of it your eyes will be opened, and you will be like God, knowing good and evil."

---

*d*Lit *corresponding to*   *e*Or *man*   *f*Lit *built*

*g*12 Or *good; pearls*   *h*13 Possibly southeast Mesopotamia   *i*20 Or *the man*   *j*21 Or *took part of the man's side*   *k*22 Or *part*   *l*23 The Hebrew for *woman* sounds like the Hebrew for *man.*

King James

Amplified

⁶And when the woman saw that the tree *was* good for food, and that it *was* ^cpleasant to the eyes, and a tree to be desired to make *one* wise, she took of the fruit thereof, and did eat, and gave also unto her husband with her; and he did eat.

⁷And the eyes of them both were opened, and they knew that they *were* naked; and they sewed fig leaves together, and made themselves ^daprons.

⁸And they heard the voice of the LORD God walking in the garden in the ^ecool of the day: and Adam and his wife hid themselves from the presence of the LORD God amongst the trees of the garden.

⁹And the LORD God called unto Adam, and said unto him, Where *art* thou?

¹⁰And he said, I heard thy voice in the garden, and I was afraid, because I *was* naked; and I hid myself.

¹¹And he said, Who told thee that thou *wast* naked? Hast thou eaten of the tree, whereof I commanded thee that thou shouldest not eat?

¹²And the man said, The woman whom thou gavest *to be* with me, she gave me of the tree, and I did eat.

¹³And the LORD God said unto the woman, What *is* this *that* thou hast done? And the woman said, The serpent beguiled me, and I did eat.

¹⁴And the LORD God said unto the serpent, Because thou hast done this, thou *art* cursed above all cattle, and above every beast of the field; upon thy belly shalt thou go, and dust shalt thou eat all the days of thy life:

¹⁵And I will put enmity between thee and the woman, and between thy seed and her seed; it shall bruise thy head, and thou shalt bruise his heel.

¹⁶Unto the woman he said, I will greatly multiply thy sorrow and thy conception; in sorrow thou shalt bring forth children; and thy desire *shall be* ^fto thy husband, and he shall rule over thee.

¹⁷And unto Adam he said, Because thou hast hearkened unto the voice of thy wife, and hast eaten of the tree, of which I commanded thee, saying, Thou shalt not eat of it: cursed *is* the ground for thy sake; in sorrow shalt thou eat *of* it all the days of thy life;

¹⁸Thorns also and thistles shall it ^gbring forth to thee; and thou shalt eat the herb of the field;

¹⁹In the sweat of thy face shalt thou eat bread, till thou return unto the ground; for out of it wast thou taken: for dust thou *art,* and unto dust shalt thou return.

²⁰And Adam called his wife's name ^hEve; because she was the mother of all living.

²¹Unto Adam also and to his wife did the LORD God make coats of skins, and clothed them.

²² ¶ And the LORD God said, Behold, the man is become as one of us, to know good and evil: and now, lest he put forth his hand, and take also of the tree of life, and eat, and live for ever:

²³Therefore the LORD God sent him forth from the garden of Eden, to till the ground from whence he was taken.

²⁴So he drove out the man; and he placed at the east of the garden of Eden Cherubims, and a flaming sword which turned every way, to keep the way of the tree of life.

⁶And when the woman saw that the tree was good (suitable, pleasant) for food and that it was delightful to look at, and a tree to be desired in order to make one wise, she took of its fruit and ate; and she gave some also to her husband, and he ate.

⁷Then the eyes of them both were opened, and they knew that they were naked; and they sewed fig leaves together and made themselves apronlike girdles.

⁸And they heard the sound of the Lord God walking in the garden in the cool of the day, and Adam and his wife hid themselves from the presence of the Lord God among the trees of the garden.

⁹But the Lord God called to Adam and said to him, Where are you?

¹⁰He said, I heard the sound of You [walking] in the garden, and I was afraid because I was naked; and I hid myself.

¹¹And He said, Who told you that you were naked? Have you eaten of the tree of which I commanded you that you should not eat?

¹²And the man said, The woman whom You gave to be with me—she gave me [fruit] from the tree, and I ate.

¹³And the Lord God said to the woman, What is this you have done? And the woman said, The serpent beguiled (cheated, outwitted, and deceived) me, and I ate.

¹⁴And the Lord God said to the serpent, Because you have done this, you are cursed above all [domestic] animals and above every [wild] living thing of the field; upon your belly you shall go, and you shall eat dust [and what it contains] all the days of your life.

¹⁵And I will put enmity between you and the woman, and between your offspring and her ^bOffspring; He will bruise *and* tread your head underfoot, and you will lie in wait *and* bruise His heel. [Gal. 4:4.]

¹⁶To the woman He said, I will greatly multiply your grief *and* your suffering in pregnancy *and* the pangs of childbearing; with spasms of distress you will bring forth children. Yet your desire *and* craving will be for your husband, and he will rule over you.

¹⁷And to Adam He said, Because you have listened *and* given heed to the voice of your wife and have eaten of the tree of which I commanded you, saying, You shall not eat of it, the ground is under a curse because of you; in sorrow *and* toil shall you eat [of the fruits] of it all the days of your life.

¹⁸Thorns also and thistles shall it bring forth for you, and you shall eat the plants of the field.

¹⁹In the sweat of your face shall you eat bread until you return to the ground, for out of it you were taken; for dust you are and to dust you shall return.

²⁰The man called his wife's name Eve [life spring], because she was the mother of all the living.

²¹For Adam also and for his wife the Lord God made long coats (tunics) of skins and clothed them.

²²And the Lord God said, Behold, the man has become like one of Us [the Father, Son, and Holy Spirit], to know [how to distinguish between] good and evil *and* blessing and calamity; and now, lest he put forth his hand and take also from the tree of life and eat, and live ^cforever—

²³Therefore the Lord God sent him forth from the Garden of Eden to till the ground from which he was taken.

²⁴So [God] drove out the man; and He placed at the east of the Garden of Eden the ^dcherubim and a flaming sword which turned every way, to keep *and* guard the way to the tree of life. [Rev. 2:7; 22:2, 14, 19.]

^bChrist fulfills through his victory over Satan the wonderful promise here spoken. See also Isa. 9:6; Matt. 1:23; Luke 1:31; Rom. 16:20; Gal. 4:4; Rev. 12:17. ^cThis sentence is left unfinished, as if to hasten to avert the tragedy suggested of men living on forever in their now fallen state. ^dCherubim are ministering spirits manifesting God's invisible presence and symbolizing His action (E.F. Harrison et al., eds., *Baker's Dictionary of Theology*).

^cHeb. *a desire*   ^dOr, *things to gird about*   ^eHeb. *wind*
^fOr, *subject to thy husband*   ^gHeb. *cause to bud*   ^hHeb.
Chavah i.e. *Living*

New American Standard

6 When the woman saw that the tree was good for food, and that it was a delight to the eyes, and that the tree was desirable to make *one* wise, she took from its fruit and ate; and she gave also to her husband with her, and he ate.

7 Then the eyes of both of them were opened, and they knew that they were naked; and they sewed fig leaves together and made themselves loin coverings.

8 ¶ They heard the sound of the LORD God walking in the garden in the cool of the day, and the man and his wife hid themselves from the presence of the LORD God among the trees of the garden.

9 Then the LORD God called to the man, and said to him, "Where are you?"

10 He said, "I heard the sound of You in the garden, and I was afraid because I was naked; so I hid myself."

11 And He said, "Who told you that you were naked? Have you eaten from the tree of which I commanded you not to eat?"

12 The man said, "The woman whom You gave *to be* with me, she gave me from the tree, and I ate."

13 Then the LORD God said to the woman, "What is this you have done?" And the woman said, "The serpent deceived me, and I ate."

14 The LORD God said to the serpent,
"Because you have done this,
    Cursed are you more than all cattle,
    And more than every beast of the field;
    On your belly you will go,
    And dust you will eat
    All the days of your life;
15 And I will put enmity
    Between you and the woman,
    And between your seed and her seed;
    He shall bruise you on the head,
    And you shall bruise him on the heel."

16 To the woman He said,
"I will greatly multiply
    Your pain in childbirth,
    In pain you will bring forth children;
    Yet your desire will be for your husband,
    And he will rule over you."

17 Then to Adam He said, "Because you have listened to the voice of your wife, and have eaten from the tree about which I commanded you, saying, 'You shall not eat from it';
    Cursed is the ground because of you;
    In toil you will eat of it
    All the days of your life.
18 "Both thorns and thistles it shall grow for you;
    And you will eat the plants of the field;
19 By the sweat of your face
    You will eat bread,
    Till you return to the ground,
    Because from it you were taken;
    For you are dust,
    And to dust you shall return."

20 ¶ Now the man called his wife's name gEve, because she was the mother of all *the* living.

21 The LORD God made garments of skin for Adam and his wife, and clothed them.

22 ¶ Then the LORD God said, "Behold, the man has become like one of Us, knowing good and evil; and now, he might stretch out his hand, and take also from the tree of life, and eat, and live forever"—

23 therefore the LORD God sent him out from the garden of Eden, to cultivate the ground from which he was taken.

24 So He drove the man out; and at the east of the garden of Eden He stationed the cherubim and the flaming sword which turned every direction to guard the way to the tree of life.

gI.e. living; or life

New International

6 When the woman saw that the fruit of the tree was good for food and pleasing to the eye, and also desirable for gaining wisdom, she took some and ate it. She also gave some to her husband, who was with her, and he ate it. 7Then the eyes of both of them were opened, and they realized they were naked; so they sewed fig leaves together and made coverings for themselves.

8Then the man and his wife heard the sound of the LORD God as he was walking in the garden in the cool of the day, and they hid from the LORD God among the trees of the garden. 9But the LORD God called to the man, "Where are you?"

10He answered, "I heard you in the garden, and I was afraid because I was naked; so I hid."

11And he said, "Who told you that you were naked? Have you eaten from the tree that I commanded you not to eat from?"

12The man said, "The woman you put here with me—she gave me some fruit from the tree, and I ate it."

13Then the LORD God said to the woman, "What is this you have done?"

The woman said, "The serpent deceived me, and I ate."

14So the LORD God said to the serpent, "Because you have done this,

"Cursed are you above all the livestock
    and all the wild animals!
You will crawl on your belly
    and you will eat dust
    all the days of your life.
15And I will put enmity
    between you and the woman,
    and between your offspringm and hers;
he will crushn your head,
    and you will strike his heel."

16To the woman he said,

"I will greatly increase your pains in
        childbearing;
    with pain you will give birth to children.
Your desire will be for your husband,
    and he will rule over you."

17To Adam he said, "Because you listened to your wife and ate from the tree about which I commanded you, 'You must not eat of it,'

"Cursed is the ground because of you;
    through painful toil you will eat of it
        all the days of your life.
18It will produce thorns and thistles for you,
    and you will eat the plants of the field.
19By the sweat of your brow
    you will eat your food
until you return to the ground,
    since from it you were taken;
for dust you are
    and to dust you will return."

20Adamo named his wife Eve,p because she would become the mother of all the living.

21The LORD God made garments of skin for Adam and his wife and clothed them. 22And the LORD God said, "The man has now become like one of us, knowing good and evil. He must not be allowed to reach out his hand and take also from the tree of life and eat, and live forever." 23So the LORD God banished him from the Garden of Eden to work the ground from which he had been taken. 24After he drove the man out, he placed on the east sideq of the Garden of Eden cherubim and a flaming sword flashing back and forth to guard the way to the tree of life.

m 15 Or seed   n 15 Or strike   o 20 Or The man probably means living.   q 24 Or placed in front   p 20 Eve

King James

Cain and Abel

4 AND ADAM knew Eve his wife; and she conceived, and bare *i*Cain, and said, I have gotten a man from the LORD.

[2] And she again bare his brother *j*Abel. And Abel was *k*a keeper of sheep, but Cain was a tiller of the ground.

[3] And *l*in process of time it came to pass, that Cain brought of the fruit of the ground an offering unto the LORD.

[4] And Abel, he also brought of the firstlings of his *m*flock and of the fat thereof. And the LORD had respect unto Abel and to his offering:

[5] But unto Cain and to his offering he had not respect. And Cain was very wroth, and his countenance fell.

[6] And the LORD said unto Cain, Why art thou wroth? and why is thy countenance fallen?

[7] If thou doest well, shalt thou not *n*be accepted? and if thou doest not well, sin lieth at the door. And *o*unto thee *shall be* his desire, and thou shalt rule over him.

[8] And Cain talked with Abel his brother: and it came to pass, when they were in the field, that Cain rose up against Abel his brother, and slew him.

[9] ¶ And the LORD said unto Cain, Where *is* Abel thy brother? And he said, I know not: *Am* I my brother's keeper?

[10] And he said, What hast thou done? the voice of thy brother's *p*blood crieth unto me from the ground.

[11] And now *art* thou cursed from the earth, which hath opened her mouth to receive thy brother's blood from thy hand;

[12] When thou tillest the ground, it shall not henceforth yield unto thee her strength; a fugitive and a vagabond shalt thou be in the earth.

[13] And Cain said unto the LORD, *q*My punishment *is* greater than I can bear.

[14] Behold, thou hast driven me out this day from the face of the earth; and from thy face shall I be hid; and I shall be a fugitive and a vagabond in the earth; and it shall come to pass, *that* every one that findeth me shall slay me.

[15] And the LORD said unto him, Therefore whosoever slayeth Cain, vengeance shall be taken on him sevenfold. And the LORD set a mark upon Cain, lest any finding him should kill him.

[16] ¶ And Cain went out from the presence of the LORD, and dwelt in the land of Nod, on the east of Eden.

[17] And Cain knew his wife; and she conceived, and bare *r*Enoch: and he builded a city, and called the name of the city, after the name of his son, Enoch.

[18] And unto Enoch was born Irad: and Irad begat Mehujael: and Mehujael begat Methusael: and Methusael begat *s*Lamech.

[19] ¶ And Lamech took unto him two wives: the name of the one *was* Adah, and the name of the other Zillah.

[20] And Adah bare Jabal: he was the father of such as dwell in tents, and *of such as have* cattle.

[21] And his brother's name *was* Jubal: he was the father of all such as handle the harp and organ.

Amplified

4 AND ADAM knew Eve as his wife; and she became pregnant and bore Cain; and she said, I have gotten *and* gained a man with the help of the Lord.

[2] And [next] she gave birth to his brother Abel. Now Abel was a keeper of sheep, but Cain was a tiller of the ground.

[3] And in the course of time Cain brought to the Lord an offering of the fruit of the ground.

[4] And Abel brought of the firstborn of his flock and of the fat portions. And the Lord had respect *and* regard for Abel and for his offering, [Heb. 11:4.]

[5] But for *e*Cain and his offering He had no respect *or* regard. So Cain was exceedingly angry *and* indignant, and he looked sad *and* depressed.

[6] And the Lord said to Cain, Why are you angry? And why do you look sad *and* depressed *and* dejected?

[7] If you do well, will you not be accepted? And if you do not do well, sin crouches at your door; its desire is for you, but you must master it.

[8] And Cain said to his brother, *f*Let us go out to the field. And when they were in the field, Cain rose up against Abel his brother and killed him. [I John 3:12.]

[9] And the Lord said to Cain, Where is Abel your brother? And he said, I do not know. Am I my brother's keeper?

[10] And [the Lord] said, What have you done? The voice of your brother's blood is crying to Me from the ground.

[11] And now you are cursed by reason of the earth, which has opened its mouth to receive your brother's [shed] blood from your hand.

[12] When you till the ground, it shall no longer yield to you its strength; you shall be a fugitive and a vagabond on the earth [in perpetual exile, a degraded outcast].

[13] Then Cain said to the Lord, My punishment is *g*greater than I can bear.

[14] Behold, You have driven me out this day from the face of the land; and from Your face I will be hidden; and I will be a fugitive and a vagabond *and* a wanderer on the earth, and whoever finds me will kill me.

[15] And the Lord said to him, *h*Therefore, if anyone kills Cain, vengeance shall be taken on him sevenfold. And the Lord set a *i*mark or sign upon Cain, lest anyone finding him should kill him.

[16] So Cain went away from the presence of the Lord and dwelt in the land of Nod [wandering], east of Eden.

[17] And Cain's wife [one of Adam's offspring] became pregnant and bore Enoch; and Cain built a *j*city and named it after his son Enoch.

[18] To Enoch was born Irad, and Irad the father of Mehujael, and Mehujael the father of Methusael, and Methusael the father of Lamech.

[19] And Lamech took two wives; the name of the one was Adah and of the other was Zillah.

[20] Adah bore Jabal; he was the father of those who dwell in tents and have cattle *and* purchase possessions.

[21] His brother's name was Jubal; he was the father of all those who play the lyre and pipe.

---

*e*In bringing the offering he did, Cain denied that he was a sinful creature under the sentence of divine condemnation. He insisted on approaching God on the ground of personal worthiness. Instead of accepting God's way, he offered to God the fruits of the ground **which God had cursed.** He presented the product of his own toil, the work of his own hands, and God refused to receive it (Arthur W. Pink, *Gleanings in Genesis*).   *f*The Hebrew omits this clause, but various other texts show that it was originally included.
*g*Some ancient versions read, "too great to be forgiven!"
*h*Some versions read, "Not so!"   *i*Many commentators believe this sign not to have been like a brand on the forehead, but something awesome about Cain's appearance that made people dread and avoid him.   *j*C.H. Dodd (cited by Adam Clarke, *The Holy Bible with A Commentary*) shows that it would have been possible for Adam and Eve, in the more than 100 years he estimates may have elapsed since their union, to have had over 32,000 descendants at the time Cain went to Nod, all of them having sprung from Cain and Abel, who married their sisters.

---

*i*i.e.*Gotten at the end of days*   *j*Heb. *Hebel*   *k*Heb. *a feeder*   *l*Heb. *at the end of days*   *m*Heb. *sheep,* or, *goats*   *n*Or, *have the excellency*   *o*Or, *subject unto thee,*   *p*Heb. *bloods*   *q*Or, *Mine iniquity is greater than that it may be forgiven*   *r*Heb. *Chanoch*   *s*Heb. *Lemech.*

New American Standard

Cain and Abel

4 NOW THE man had relations with his wife Eve, and she conceived and gave birth to Cain, and she said, "I have gotten a manchild with *the help of* the LORD."

² Again, she gave birth to his brother Abel. And Abel was a keeper of flocks, but Cain was a tiller of the ground.

³ So it came about in the course of time that Cain brought an offering to the LORD of the fruit of the ground.

⁴ Abel, on his part also brought of the firstlings of his flock and of their fat portions. And the LORD had regard for Abel and for his offering;

⁵ but for Cain and for his offering He had no regard. So Cain became very angry and his countenance fell.

⁶ Then the LORD said to Cain, "Why are you angry? And why has your countenance fallen?

⁷"If you do well, will not *your countenance* be lifted up? And if you do not do well, sin is crouching at the door; and its desire is for you, but you must master it."

⁸ Cain told Abel his brother. And it came about when they were in the field, that Cain rose up against Abel his brother and killed him.

⁹ ¶ Then the LORD said to Cain, "Where is Abel your brother?" And he said, "I do not know. Am I my brother's keeper?"

¹⁰ He said, "What have you done? The voice of your brother's blood is crying to Me from the ground.

¹¹"Now you are cursed from the ground, which has opened its mouth to receive your brother's blood from your hand.

¹²"When you cultivate the ground, it will no longer yield its strength to you; you will be a vagrant and a wanderer on the earth."

¹³ Cain said to the LORD, "My punishment is too great to bear!

¹⁴"Behold, You have driven me this day from the face of the ground; and from Your face I will be hidden, and I will be a vagrant and a wanderer on the earth, and whoever finds me will kill me."

¹⁵ So the LORD said to him, "Therefore whoever kills Cain, vengeance will be taken on him sevenfold." And the LORD appointed a sign for Cain, so that no one finding him would slay him.

¹⁶ ¶ Then Cain went out from the presence of the LORD, and settled in the land of Nod, east of Eden.

¹⁷ ¶ Cain had relations with his wife and she conceived, and gave birth to Enoch; and he built a city, and called the name of the city Enoch, after the name of his son.

¹⁸ Now to Enoch was born Irad, and Irad became the father of Mehujael, and Mehujael became the father of Methushael, and Methushael became the father of Lamech.

¹⁹ Lamech took to himself two wives: the name of the one was Adah, and the name of the other, Zillah.

²⁰ Adah gave birth to Jabal; he was the father of those who dwell in tents and *have* livestock.

²¹ His brother's name was Jubal; he was the father of all those who play the lyre and pipe.

New International

Cain and Abel

4 ADAM[r] LAY with his wife Eve, and she became pregnant and gave birth to Cain.[s] She said, "With the help of the LORD I have brought forth[t] a man." ²Later she gave birth to his brother Abel.

Now Abel kept flocks, and Cain worked the soil. ³In the course of time Cain brought some of the fruits of the soil as an offering to the LORD. ⁴But Abel brought fat portions from some of the firstborn of his flock. The LORD looked with favor on Abel and his offering, ⁵but on Cain and his offering he did not look with favor. So Cain was very angry, and his face was downcast.

⁶Then the LORD said to Cain, "Why are you angry? Why is your face downcast? ⁷If you do what is right, will you not be accepted? But if you do not do what is right, sin is crouching at your door; it desires to have you, but you must master it."

⁸Now Cain said to his brother Abel, "Let's go out to the field."[u] And while they were in the field, Cain attacked his brother Abel and killed him.

⁹Then the LORD said to Cain, "Where is your brother Abel?"

"I don't know," he replied. "Am I my brother's keeper?"

¹⁰The LORD said, "What have you done? Listen! Your brother's blood cries out to me from the ground. ¹¹Now you are under a curse and driven from the ground, which opened its mouth to receive your brother's blood from your hand. ¹²When you work the ground, it will no longer yield its crops for you. You will be a restless wanderer on the earth."

¹³Cain said to the LORD, "My punishment is more than I can bear. ¹⁴Today you are driving me from the land, and I will be hidden from your presence; I will be a restless wanderer on the earth, and whoever finds me will kill me."

¹⁵But the LORD said to him, "Not so[v]; if anyone kills Cain, he will suffer vengeance seven times over." Then the LORD put a mark on Cain so that no one who found him would kill him. ¹⁶So Cain went out from the LORD's presence and lived in the land of Nod,[w] east of Eden.

¹⁷Cain lay with his wife, and she became pregnant and gave birth to Enoch. Cain was then building a city, and he named it after his son Enoch. ¹⁸To Enoch was born Irad, and Irad was the father of Mehujael, and Mehujael was the father of Methushael, and Methushael was the father of Lamech.

¹⁹Lamech married two women, one named Adah and the other Zillah. ²⁰Adah gave birth to Jabal; he was the father of those who live in tents and raise livestock. ²¹His brother's name was Jubal; he was the father of all who play the

r 1 Or *The man*   *s 1* *Cain* sounds like the Hebrew for *brought forth* or *acquired*.   *t 1* Or *have acquired*   *u 8* Samaritan Pentateuch, Septuagint, Vulgate and Syriac; Masoretic Text does not have *"Let's go out to the field."*   *v 15* Septuagint, Vulgate and Syriac; Hebrew *Very well*   *w 16 Nod* means *wandering* (see verses 12 and 14).

King James

22And Zillah, she also bare Tubal-cain, an [t]instructor of every artificer in brass and iron: and the sister of Tubal-cain *was* Naamah.

23And Lamech said unto his wives, Adah and Zillah, Hear my voice; ye wives of Lamech, hearken unto my speech: for [u]I have slain a man to my wounding, and a young man [v]to my hurt.

24If Cain shall be avenged sevenfold, truly Lamech seventy and sevenfold.

25 ¶ And Adam knew his wife again; and she bare a son, and called his name [w][x]Seth: For God, *said she,* hath appointed me another seed instead of Abel, whom Cain slew.

26And to Seth, to him also there was born a son; and he called his name [y]Enos: then began men [z]to call upon the name of the LORD.

The descendants of Adam

5 THIS *IS* the book of the generations of Adam. In the day that God created man, in the likeness of God made he him;

2Male and female created he them; and blessed them, and called their name Adam, in the day when they were created.

3 ¶ And Adam lived an hundred and thirty years, and begat *a son* in his own likeness, after his image; and called his name Seth:

4And the days of Adam after he had begotten Seth were eight hundred years: and he begat sons and daughters:

5And all the days that Adam lived were nine hundred and thirty years: and he died.

6And Seth lived an hundred and five years, and begat Enos:

7And Seth lived after he begat Enos eight hundred and seven years, and begat sons and daughters:

8And all the days of Seth were nine hundred and twelve years: and he died.

9 ¶ And Enos lived ninety years, and begat [a]Cainan:

10And Enos lived after he begat Cainan eight hundred and fifteen years, and begat sons and daughters:

11And all the days of Enos were nine hundred and five years: and he died.

12 ¶ And Cainan lived seventy years, and begat [b]Mahalaleel:

13And Cainan lived after he begat Mahalaleel eight hundred and forty years, and begat sons and daughters:

14And all the days of Cainan were nine hundred and ten years: and he died.

15 ¶ And Mahalaleel lived sixty and five years, and begat [c]Jared:

16And Mahalaleel lived after he begat Jared eight hundred and thirty years, and begat sons and daughters:

17And all the days of Mahalaleel were eight hundred ninety and five years: and he died.

18 ¶ And Jared lived an hundred sixty and two years, and he begat Enoch:

19And Jared lived after he begat Enoch eight hundred years, and begat sons and daughters:

20And all the days of Jared were nine hundred sixty and two years: and he died.

21 ¶ And Enoch lived sixty and five years, and begat [d]Methuselah:

Amplified

22Zillah bore Tubal-cain; he was the forger of all [cutting] instruments of bronze and iron. The sister of Tubal-cain was Naamah.

23Lamech said to his wives, Adah and Zillah, Hear my voice; you wives of Lamech, listen to what I say; for I have slain a man [merely] for wounding me, and a young man [only] for striking *and* bruising me.

24If Cain is avenged sevenfold, truly Lamech [will be avenged] seventy-sevenfold.

25And Adam's wife again became pregnant, and she bore a son and called his name Seth. For God, she said, has appointed for me another child instead of Abel, for Cain slew him.

26And to Seth also a son was born, whom he named Enosh. At that time men began to call [upon God] by the name of the Lord.

5 THIS IS the book (the written record, the history) of the generations of the offspring of Adam. When God created man, He made him in the likeness of God.

2He created them male and female and blessed them and named them [both] Adam [Man] at the time they were created.

3When Adam had lived 130 years, he had a son in his own likeness, after his image; and he named him Seth.

4After he had Seth, Adam lived 800 years and had other sons and daughters.

5So altogether Adam lived 930 years, and he died.

6When Seth was 105 years old, Enosh was born.

7Seth lived after the birth of Enosh 807 years and had other sons and daughters.

8So Seth lived 912 years, and he died.

9When Enosh was 90 years old, Kenan was born to him.

10Enosh lived after the birth of Kenan 815 years and had other sons and daughters.

11So Enosh lived 905 years, and he died.

12When Kenan was 70 years old, Mahalalel was born.

13Kenan lived after the birth of Mahalalel 840 years and had other sons and daughters.

14So Kenan lived 910 years, and he died.

15When Mahalalel was 65 years old, Jared was born.

16Mahalalel lived after the birth of Jared 830 years and had other sons and daughters.

17So Mahalalel lived 895 years, and he died.

18When Jared was 162 years old, Enoch was born.

19Jared lived after the birth of Enoch 800 years and had other sons and daughters.

20So Jared lived 962 years, and he died.

21When Enoch was 65 years old, Methuselah was born.

New American Standard

²² As for Zillah, she also gave birth to Tubal-cain, the forger of all implements of bronze and iron; and the sister of Tubal-cain was Naamah.

²³ ¶ Lamech said to his wives,

"Adah and Zillah,
Listen to my voice,
You wives of Lamech,
Give heed to my speech,
For I have killed a man for wounding me;
And a boy for striking me;

²⁴ If Cain is avenged sevenfold,
Then Lamech seventy-sevenfold."

²⁵ ¶ Adam had relations with his wife again; and she gave birth to a son, and named him Seth, for, *she said,* "God has appointed me another offspring in place of Abel, for Cain killed him."

²⁶ To Seth, to him also a son was born; and he called his name Enosh. Then *men* began to call upon the name of the LORD.

Descendants of Adam

5 THIS IS the book of the generations of Adam. In the day when God created man, He made him in the likeness of God.

² He created them male and female, and He blessed them and named them ^hMan in the day when they were created.

³ ¶ When Adam had lived one hundred and thirty years, he ⁱbecame the father of *a son* in his own likeness, according to his image, and named him Seth.

⁴ Then the days of Adam after he became the father of Seth were eight hundred years, and he had *other* sons and daughters.

⁵ So all the days that Adam lived were nine hundred and thirty years, and he died.

⁶ ¶ Seth lived one hundred and five years, and became the father of Enosh.

⁷ Then Seth lived eight hundred and seven years after he became the father of Enosh, and he had *other* sons and daughters.

⁸ So all the days of Seth were nine hundred and twelve years, and he died.

⁹ ¶ Enosh lived ninety years, and became the father of Kenan.

¹⁰ Then Enosh lived eight hundred and fifteen years after he became the father of Kenan, and he had *other* sons and daughters.

¹¹ So all the days of Enosh were nine hundred and five years, and he died.

¹² ¶ Kenan lived seventy years, and became the father of Mahalalel.

¹³ Then Kenan lived eight hundred and forty years after he became the father of Mahalalel, and he had *other* sons and daughters.

¹⁴ So all the days of Kenan were nine hundred and ten years, and he died.

¹⁵ ¶ Mahalalel lived sixty-five years, and became the father of Jared.

¹⁶ Then Mahalalel lived eight hundred and thirty years after he became the father of Jared, and he had *other* sons and daughters.

¹⁷ So all the days of Mahalalel were eight hundred and ninety-five years, and he died.

¹⁸ ¶ Jared lived one hundred and sixty-two years, and became the father of Enoch.

¹⁹ Then Jared lived eight hundred years after he became the father of Enoch, and he had *other* sons and daughters.

²⁰ So all the days of Jared were nine hundred and sixty-two years, and he died.

²¹ ¶ Enoch lived sixty-five years, and became the father of Methuselah.

New International

harp and flute. ²²Zillah also had a son, Tubal-Cain, who forged all kinds of tools out of^x bronze and iron. Tubal-Cain's sister was Naamah.

²³Lamech said to his wives,

"Adah and Zillah, listen to me;
wives of Lamech, hear my words.
I have killed^y a man for wounding me,
a young man for injuring me.
²⁴If Cain is avenged seven times,
then Lamech seventy-seven times."

²⁵Adam lay with his wife again, and she gave birth to a son and named him Seth,^z saying, "God has granted me another child in place of Abel, since Cain killed him." ²⁶Seth also had a son, and he named him Enosh.

At that time men began to call on^a the name of the LORD.

From Adam to Noah

5 THIS IS the written account of Adam's line.

When God created man, he made him in the likeness of God. ²He created them male and female and blessed them. And when they were created, he called them "man.^b"

³When Adam had lived 130 years, he had a son in his own likeness, in his own image; and he named him Seth. ⁴After Seth was born, Adam lived 800 years and had other sons and daughters. ⁵Altogether, Adam lived 930 years, and then he died.

⁶When Seth had lived 105 years, he became the father^c of Enosh. ⁷And after he became the father of Enosh, Seth lived 807 years and had other sons and daughters. ⁸Altogether, Seth lived 912 years, and then he died.

⁹When Enosh had lived 90 years, he became the father of Kenan. ¹⁰And after he became the father of Kenan, Enosh lived 815 years and had other sons and daughters. ¹¹Altogether, Enosh lived 905 years, and then he died.

¹²When Kenan had lived 70 years, he became the father of Mahalalel. ¹³And after he became the father of Mahalalel, Kenan lived 840 years and had other sons and daughters. ¹⁴Altogether, Kenan lived 910 years, and then he died.

¹⁵When Mahalalel had lived 65 years, he became the father of Jared. ¹⁶And after he became the father of Jared, Mahalalel lived 830 years and had other sons and daughters. ¹⁷Altogether, Mahalalel lived 895 years, and then he died.

¹⁸When Jared had lived 162 years, he became the father of Enoch. ¹⁹And after he became the father of Enoch, Jared lived 800 years and had other sons and daughters. ²⁰Altogether, Jared lived 962 years, and then he died.

²¹When Enoch had lived 65 years, he became the father

---

^x22 Or *who instructed all who work in*   ^y23 Or *I will kill*
^z25 *Seth* probably means *granted.*   ^a26 Or *to proclaim*
^b2 Hebrew *adam*   ^c6 *Father* may mean *ancestor*; also in verses 7-26.

^hLit *Adam*   ⁱLit *begot,* and so throughout the ch

King James

Amplified

[22]And Enoch walked with God after he begat Methuselah three hundred years, and begat sons and daughters:

[23]And all the days of Enoch were three hundred sixty and five years:

[24]And Enoch walked with God: and he *was* not; for God took him.

[25]And Methuselah lived an hundred eighty and seven years, and begat *e*Lamech:

[26]And Methuselah lived after he begat Lamech seven hundred eighty and two years, and begat sons and daughters:

[27]And all the days of Methuselah were nine hundred sixty and nine years: and he died.

[28] ¶ And Lamech lived an hundred eighty and two years, and begat a son:

[29]And he called his name *f g*Noah, saying, This *same* shall comfort us concerning our work and toil of our hands, because of the ground which the LORD hath cursed.

[30]And Lamech lived after he begat Noah five hundred ninety and five years, and begat sons and daughters:

[31]And all the days of Lamech were seven hundred seventy and seven years: and he died.

[32]And Noah was five hundred years old: and Noah begat Shem, Ham, and Japheth.

The flood

6 AND IT came to pass, when men began to multiply on the face of the earth, and daughters were born unto them,

[2]That the sons of God saw the daughters of men that they *were* fair; and they took them wives of all which they chose.

[3]And the LORD said, My spirit shall not always strive with man, for that he also *is* flesh: yet his days shall be an hundred and twenty years.

[4]There were giants in the earth in those days; and also after that, when the sons of God came in unto the daughters of men, and they bare *children* to them, the same *became* mighty men which *were* of old, men of renown.

[5] ¶ And GOD saw that the wickedness of man *was* great in the earth, and *that h*every imagination of the thoughts of his heart *was* only evil *i*continually.

[6]And it repented the LORD that he had made man on the earth, and it grieved him at his heart.

[7]And the LORD said, I will destroy man whom I have created from the face of the earth; *j*both man, and beast, and the creeping thing, and the fowls of the air; for it repenteth me that I have made them.

[8]But Noah found grace in the eyes of the LORD.

[9] ¶ These *are* the generations of Noah: Noah was a just man *and k*perfect in his generations, *and* Noah walked with God.

[10]And Noah begat three sons, Shem, Ham, and Japheth.

[11]The earth also was corrupt before God, and the earth was filled with violence.

[12]And God looked upon the earth, and, behold, it was corrupt; for all flesh had corrupted his way upon the earth.

[22]Enoch walked [in habitual fellowship] with God after the birth of Methuselah 300 years and had other sons and daughters.

[23]So all the days of Enoch were 365 years.

[24]And Enoch walked [in habitual fellowship] with God; and he was not, for God took him [home with Him]. [Heb. 11:5.]

[25]When Methuselah was 187 years old, Lamech was born to him.

[26]Methuselah lived after the birth of Lamech 782 years and had other sons and daughters.

[27]So Methuselah lived 969 years, and he died.

[28]When Lamech was 182 years old, a son was born.

[29]He named him Noah, saying, This one shall bring us relief *and* comfort from our work and the [grievous] toil of our hands due to the ground being cursed by the Lord.

[30]Lamech lived after the birth of Noah 595 years and had other sons and daughters.

[31]So all the days of *k*Lamech were 777 years, and he died.

[32]After Noah was 500 years old, he became the father of Shem, Ham, and Japheth.

6 WHEN MEN began to multiply on the face of the land and daughters were born to them,

[2]The sons of God saw that the daughters of men were fair, and they took wives of all they desired *and* chose.

[3]Then the Lord said, My Spirit shall not forever dwell *and* strive with man, for he also is flesh; but his days shall yet be 120 years.

[4]There were giants on the earth in those days—and also afterward—when the sons of God lived with the daughters of men, and they bore children to them. These were the mighty men who were of old, men of renown.

[5]The Lord saw that the wickedness of man was great in the earth, and that every imagination *and* intention of all human thinking was only evil continually.

[6]And the Lord regretted that He had made man on the earth, and He was grieved at heart.

[7]So the Lord said, I will destroy, blot out, *and* wipe away mankind, whom I have created from the face of the ground—not only man, [but] the beasts and the creeping things and the birds of the air—for it grieves Me *and* makes Me regretful that I have made them.

[8]But Noah found grace (favor) in the eyes of the Lord.

[9]This is the history of the generations of Noah. Noah was a just *and* righteous man, blameless *in* his [evil] generation; Noah walked [in habitual fellowship] with God.

[10]And Noah became the father of three sons: Shem, Ham, and Japheth.

[11]The earth was depraved *and* putrid in God's sight, and the land was filled with violence (desecration, infringement, outrage, assault, and lust for power).

[12]And God looked upon the world and saw how degenerate, debased, *and* vicious it was, for all humanity had corrupted their way upon the earth *and* lost their true direction.

---

*e*Heb. *Lemech*   *f*Gk. *Noe;* see Luke 3:36; Heb. 11:7; 1 Pet. 3:20
*g*i.e. *Rest,* or, *Comfort*   *h*Or, *the whole imagination:* the Hebrew word signifieth not only *the imagination,* but also *the purposes and desires*   *i*Heb. *every day*   *j*Heb. *from man unto beast*
*k*Or, *upright*

*k*It is now well known that the age of mankind cannot be reckoned in years from the facts listed in genealogies, for there are numerous known intentional gaps in them. For example, as B. B. Warfield (*Studies in Theology*) points out, the genealogy in Matt. 1:1-17 omits the three kings, Ahaziah, Jehoash, and Amaziah, and indicates that Joram (Matt. 1:8) begat Uzziah, who was his great-great-grandson. The mistaking of compressed genealogies as bases for chronology has been very misleading. So far, the dates in years of very early Old Testament events are altogether speculative and relative, and the tendency is to put them farther and farther back into antiquity.

New American Standard

22 Then Enoch walked with God three hundred years after he became the father of Methuselah, and he had *other* sons and daughters.
23 So all the days of Enoch were three hundred and sixty-five years.
24 Enoch walked with God; and he was not, for God took him.
25 ¶ Methuselah lived one hundred and eighty-seven years, and became the father of Lamech.
26 Then Methuselah lived seven hundred and eighty-two years after he became the father of Lamech, and he had *other* sons and daughters.
27 So all the days of Methuselah were nine hundred and sixty-nine years, and he died.
28 ¶ Lamech lived one hundred and eighty-two years, and became the father of a son.
29 Now he called his name Noah, saying, "This one will give us rest from our work and from the toil of our hands *arising* from the ground which the LORD has cursed."
30 Then Lamech lived five hundred and ninety-five years after he became the father of Noah, and he had *other* sons and daughters.
31 So all the days of Lamech were seven hundred and seventy-seven years, and he died.
32 ¶ Noah was five hundred years old, and Noah became the father of Shem, Ham, and Japheth.

The Corruption of Mankind

6 NOW IT came about, when men began to multiply on the face of the land, and daughters were born to them,
2 that the sons of God saw that the daughters of men were beautiful; and they took wives for themselves, whomever they chose.
3 Then the LORD said, "My Spirit shall not strive with man forever, because he also is flesh; nevertheless his days shall be one hundred and twenty years."
4 The Nephilim were on the earth in those days, and also afterward, when the sons of God came in to the daughters of men, and they bore *children* to them. Those were the mighty men who *were* of old, men of renown.
5 ¶ Then the LORD saw that the wickedness of man was great on the earth, and that every intent of the thoughts of his heart was only evil continually.
6 The LORD was sorry that He had made man on the earth, and He was grieved in His heart.
7 The LORD said, "I will blot out man whom I have created from the face of the land, from man to animals to creeping things and to birds of the sky; for I am sorry that I have made them."
8 But Noah found favor in the eyes of the LORD.
9 ¶ These are *the records of* the generations of Noah. Noah was a righteous man, blameless in his time; Noah walked with God.
10 Noah became the father of three sons: Shem, Ham, and Japheth.
11 ¶ Now the earth was corrupt in the sight of God, and the earth was filled with violence.
12 God looked on the earth, and behold, it was corrupt; for all flesh had corrupted their way upon the earth.

New International

of Methuselah. 22 And after he became the father of Methuselah, Enoch walked with God 300 years and had other sons and daughters. 23 Altogether, Enoch lived 365 years. 24 Enoch walked with God; then he was no more, because God took him away.
25 When Methuselah had lived 187 years, he became the father of Lamech. 26 And after he became the father of Lamech, Methuselah lived 782 years and had other sons and daughters. 27 Altogether, Methuselah lived 969 years, and then he died.
28 When Lamech had lived 182 years, he had a son. 29 He named him Noah[d] and said, "He will comfort us in the labor and painful toil of our hands caused by the ground the LORD has cursed." 30 After Noah was born, Lamech lived 595 years and had other sons and daughters. 31 Altogether, Lamech lived 777 years, and then he died.
32 After Noah was 500 years old, he became the father of Shem, Ham and Japheth.

The Flood

6 WHEN MEN began to increase in number on the earth and daughters were born to them, 2 the sons of God saw that the daughters of men were beautiful, and they married any of them they chose. 3 Then the LORD said, "My Spirit will not contend with[e] man forever, for he is mortal[f]; his days will be a hundred and twenty years."
4 The Nephilim were on the earth in those days—and also afterward—when the sons of God went to the daughters of men and had children by them. They were the heroes of old, men of renown.
5 The LORD saw how great man's wickedness on the earth had become, and that every inclination of the thoughts of his heart was only evil all the time. 6 The LORD was grieved that he had made man on the earth, and his heart was filled with pain. 7 So the LORD said, "I will wipe mankind, whom I have created, from the face of the earth—men and animals, and creatures that move along the ground, and birds of the air—for I am grieved that I have made them." 8 But Noah found favor in the eyes of the LORD.

9 This is the account of Noah.

Noah was a righteous man, blameless among the people of his time, and he walked with God. 10 Noah had three sons: Shem, Ham and Japheth.
11 Now the earth was corrupt in God's sight and was full of violence. 12 God saw how corrupt the earth had become,

---

King James

¹³And God said unto Noah, The end of all flesh is come before me; for the earth is filled with violence through them; and, behold, I will destroy them *l*with the earth.

¹⁴ ¶ Make thee an ark of gopher wood; *m*rooms shalt thou make in the ark, and shalt pitch it within and without with pitch.

¹⁵And this *is the fashion* which thou shalt make it *of:* The length of the ark *shall be* three hundred cubits, the breadth of it fifty cubits, and the height of it thirty cubits.

¹⁶A window shalt thou make to the ark, and in a cubit shalt thou finish it above; and the door of the ark shalt thou set in the side thereof; *with* lower, second, and third *stories* shalt thou make it.

¹⁷And, behold, I, even I, do bring a flood of waters upon the earth, to destroy all flesh, wherein *is* the breath of life, from under heaven; *and* every thing that *is* in the earth shall die.

¹⁸But with thee will I establish my covenant; and thou shalt come into the ark, thou, and thy sons, and thy wife, and thy sons' wives with thee.

¹⁹And of every living thing of all flesh, two of every *sort* shalt thou bring into the ark, to keep *them* alive with thee; they shall be male and female.

²⁰Of fowls after their kind, and of cattle after their kind, of every creeping thing of the earth after his kind, two of every *sort* shall come unto thee, to keep *them* alive.

²¹And take thou unto thee of all food that is eaten, and thou shalt gather *it* to thee; and it shall be for food for thee, and for them.

²²Thus did Noah; according to all that God commanded him, so did he.

7 AND THE LORD said unto Noah, Come thou and all thy house into the ark; for thee have I seen righteous before me in this generation.

²Of every clean beast thou shalt take to thee by *n*sevens, the male and his female: and of beasts that *are* not clean by two, the male and his female.

³Of fowls also of the air by sevens, the male and the female; to keep seed alive upon the face of all the earth.

⁴For yet seven days, and I will cause it to rain upon the earth forty days and forty nights; and every living substance that I have made will I *o*destroy from off the face of the earth.

⁵And Noah did according unto all that the LORD commanded him.

⁶And Noah *was* six hundred years old when the flood of waters was upon the earth.

⁷ ¶ And Noah went in, and his sons, and his wife, and his sons' wives with him, into the ark, because of the waters of the flood.

⁸Of clean beasts, and of beasts that *are* not clean, and of fowls, and of every thing that creepeth upon the earth,

Amplified

¹³God said to Noah, I intend to make an end of all flesh, for through men the land is filled with violence; and behold, I will *l*destroy them and the land.

¹⁴Make yourself an ark of gopher *or* cypress wood; make in *it* rooms (stalls, pens, coops, nests, cages, and compartments) and cover it inside and out with pitch (bitumen).

¹⁵And this is the way you are to make it: the length of the ark shall be 300 cubits, its breadth 50 cubits, and its height 30 cubits [that is, 450 ft. x 75 ft. x 45 ft.].

¹⁶You shall make a roof or *m*window [a place for light] for the ark and finish it to a cubit [at least 18 inches] above—and the *n*door of the ark you shall put in the side of it; and you shall make it with lower, second, and third stories.

¹⁷For behold, I, even I, will bring a flood of waters upon the earth to destroy *and* make putrid all flesh under the heavens in which are the breath *and* spirit of life; everything that is on the land shall die.

¹⁸But I will establish My covenant (promise, pledge) with you, and you shall come into the ark—you and your sons and your wife and your sons' wives with you.

¹⁹And of every living thing of all flesh [found on land], you shall bring two of every sort into the ark, to keep them alive with you; they shall be male and female.

²⁰Of fowls *and* birds according to their kinds, of beasts according to their kinds, of every creeping thing of the ground according to its kind—two of every sort shall come in with you, that they may be kept alive.

²¹Also take with you every sort of food that is eaten, and you shall collect *and* store it up, and it shall serve as food for you and for them.

²²Noah did this; he did all that God commanded him.

7 AND THE Lord said to Noah, Come with all your household into the ark, for I have seen you to be righteous (upright and in right standing) before Me in this generation. [Ps. 27:5; 33:18, 19; II Pet. 2:9.]

²Of every clean beast you shall receive *and* take with you seven pairs, the male and his mate, and of beasts that are not clean a pair of each kind, the male and his mate, [Lev. 11.]

³Also of the birds of the air seven pairs, the male and the female, to keep seed [their kind] alive over all the earth *or* land.

⁴For in seven days I will cause it to rain upon the earth forty days and forty nights, and every living substance *and* thing that I have made I will destroy, blot out, *and* wipe away from the face of the earth.

⁵And Noah did all that the Lord commanded him. [Heb. 11:7.]

⁶Noah was 600 years old when the flood of waters came upon the earth *or* land.

⁷And Noah and his sons and his wife and his sons' wives with him went into the ark because of the waters of the flood. [Matt. 24:38; Luke 17:27.]

⁸Of *o*clean animals and of animals that are not clean, and of birds *and* fowls, and of everything that creeps on the ground,

---

*l*Enoch had warned these people (Jude 14, 15); Noah had preached righteousness to them (II Pet. 2:5); God's Spirit had been striving with them (Gen. 6:3). Yet they had rejected God and were without excuse.   *m*Noah's ark possibly had a window area large enough to admit light and provide ventilation.   *n*"Here can only be meant an entrance which was afterward closed, and only opened again at the end of the flood. And since there were three stories of the ark, the word is to be understood, perhaps, of three entrances capable of being closed, and to which there would have been constructed a way of access from the outside" (J.P. Lange, *A Commentary on the Holy Scriptures*).   *o*Noah had many years in which to interest travelers in securing these animals for him. The five extra pairs of clean animals were for food, and for sacrifice later.

---

*l*Or, *from the earth*   *m*Heb. *nests*   *n*Heb. *seven seven*
*o*Heb. *blot out*

New American Standard

13 ¶ Then God said to Noah, "The end of all flesh has come before Me; for the earth is filled with violence because of them; and behold, I am about to destroy them with the earth.

14"Make for yourself an ark of gopher wood; you shall make the ark with rooms, and shall cover it inside and out with pitch.

15"This is how you shall make it: the length of the ark three hundred *j*cubits, its breadth fifty cubits, and its height thirty cubits.

16"You shall make a window for the ark, and finish it to a cubit from the top; and set the door of the ark in the side of it; you shall make it with lower, second, and third decks.

17"Behold, I, even I am bringing the flood of water upon the earth, to destroy all flesh in which is the breath of life, from under heaven; everything that is on the earth shall perish.

18"But I will establish My covenant with you; and you shall enter the ark—you and your sons and your wife, and your sons' wives with you.

19"And of every living thing of all flesh, you shall bring two of every *kind* into the ark, to keep *them* alive with you; they shall be male and female.

20"Of the birds after their kind, and of the animals after their kind, of every creeping thing of the ground after its kind, two of every *kind* will come to you to keep *them* alive.

21"As for you, take for yourself some of all food which is edible, and gather *it* to yourself; and it shall be for food for you and for them."

22 Thus Noah did; according to all that God had commanded him, so he did.

The Flood

7 THEN THE LORD said to Noah, "Enter the ark, you and all your household, for you *alone* I have seen *to be* righteous before Me in this time.

2"You shall take with you of every clean animal by sevens, a male and his female; and of the animals that are not clean two, a male and his female;

3 also of the birds of the sky, by sevens, male and female, to keep offspring alive on the face of all the earth.

4"For after seven more days, I will send rain on the earth forty days and forty nights; and I will blot out from the face of the land every living thing that I have made."

5 Noah did according to all that the LORD had commanded him.

6 ¶ Now Noah was six hundred years old when the flood of water came upon the earth.

7 Then Noah and his sons and his wife and his sons' wives with him entered the ark because of the water of the flood.

8 Of clean animals and animals that are not clean and birds and everything that creeps on the ground,

New International

for all the people on earth had corrupted their ways. 13So God said to Noah, "I am going to put an end to all people, for the earth is filled with violence because of them. I am surely going to destroy both them and the earth. 14So make yourself an ark of cypress*g* wood; make rooms in it and coat it with pitch inside and out. 15This is how you are to build it: The ark is to be 450 feet long, 75 feet wide and 45 feet high.*h* 16Make a roof for it and finish*i* the ark to within 18 inches*j* of the top. Put a door in the side of the ark and make lower, middle and upper decks. 17I am going to bring floodwaters on the earth to destroy all life under the heavens, every creature that has the breath of life in it. Everything on earth will perish. 18But I will establish my covenant with you, and you will enter the ark—you and your sons and your wife and your sons' wives with you. 19You are to bring into the ark two of all living creatures, male and female, to keep them alive with you. 20Two of every kind of bird, of every kind of animal and of every kind of creature that moves along the ground will come to you to be kept alive. 21You are to take every kind of food that is to be eaten and store it away as food for you and for them."

22Noah did everything just as God commanded him.

7 THE LORD then said to Noah, "Go into the ark, you and your whole family, because I have found you righteous in this generation. 2Take with you seven*k* of every kind of clean animal, a male and its mate, and two of every kind of unclean animal, a male and its mate, 3and also seven of every kind of bird, male and female, to keep their various kinds alive throughout the earth. 4Seven days from now I will send rain on the earth for forty days and forty nights, and I will wipe from the face of the earth every living creature I have made."

5And Noah did all that the LORD commanded him.

6Noah was six hundred years old when the floodwaters came on the earth. 7And Noah and his sons and his wife and his sons' wives entered the ark to escape the waters of the flood. 8Pairs of clean and unclean animals, of birds and

---

g 14 The meaning of the Hebrew for this word is uncertain.
h 15 Hebrew *300 cubits long, 50 cubits wide and 30 cubits high* (about 140 meters long, 23 meters wide and 13.5 meters high) *i 16* Or *Make an opening for light by finishing*   *j 16* Hebrew *a cubit* (about 0.5 meter)   *k 2* Or *seven pairs;* also in verse 3

---

*j*I.e. One cubit equals approx 18 in.

King James

⁹There went in two and two unto Noah into the ark, the male and the female, as God had commanded Noah.

¹⁰And it came to pass *ᵖafter seven days, that the waters of the flood were upon the earth.

¹¹ ¶ In the six hundredth year of Noah's life, in the second month, the seventeenth day of the month, the same day were all the fountains of the great deep broken up, and the ᵟwindows of heaven were opened.

¹²And the rain was upon the earth forty days and forty nights.

¹³In the selfsame day entered Noah, and Shem, and Ham, and Japheth, the sons of Noah, and Noah's wife, and the three wives of his sons with them, into the ark;

¹⁴They, and every beast after his kind, and all the cattle after their kind, and every creeping thing that creepeth upon the earth after his kind, and every fowl after his kind, every bird of every ʳsort.

¹⁵And they went in unto Noah into the ark, two and two of all flesh, wherein *is* the breath of life.

¹⁶And they that went in, went in male and female of all flesh, as God had commanded him: and the LORD shut him in.

¹⁷And the flood was forty days upon the earth; and the waters increased, and bare up the ark, and it was lift up above the earth.

¹⁸And the waters prevailed, and were increased greatly upon the earth; and the ark went upon the face of the waters.

¹⁹And the waters prevailed exceedingly upon the earth; and all the high hills, that *were* under the whole heaven, were covered.

²⁰Fifteen cubits upward did the waters prevail; and the mountains were covered.

²¹And all flesh died that moved upon the earth, both of fowl, and of cattle, and of beast, and of every creeping thing that creepeth upon the earth, and every man:

²²All in whose nostrils *was* ˢthe breath of life, of all that *was* in the dry *land,* died.

²³And every living substance was destroyed which was upon the face of the ground, both man, and cattle, and the creeping things, and the fowl of the heaven; and they were destroyed from the earth: and Noah only remained *alive,* and they that *were* with him in the ark.

²⁴And the waters prevailed upon the earth an hundred and fifty days.

8 AND GOD remembered Noah, and every living thing, and all the cattle that *was* with him in the ark: and God made a wind to pass over the earth, and the waters assuaged;

²The fountains also of the deep and the windows of heaven were stopped, and the rain from heaven was restrained;

³And the waters returned from off the earth *ᵗcontinually:* and after the end of the hundred and fifty days the waters were abated.

⁴And the ark rested in the seventh month, on the seventeenth day of the month, upon the mountains of Ararat.

⁵And the waters ᵘdecreased continually until the tenth month: in the tenth *month,* on the first *day* of the month, were the tops of the mountains seen.

⁶ ¶ And it came to pass at the end of forty days, that Noah opened the window of the ark which he had made:

⁷And he sent forth a raven, which went forth ᵛto and fro, until the waters were dried up from off the earth.

Amplified

⁹There went in two and two with Noah into the ark, the male and the female, as God had commanded Noah.

¹⁰And after the seven days the floodwaters came upon the earth *or* land.

¹¹In the year 600 of Noah's life, in the seventeenth day of the second month, that same day all the fountains of the great deep were broken up *and* burst forth, and the windows *and* floodgates of the heavens were opened.

¹²And it rained upon the earth forty days and forty nights.

¹³On the very same day Noah and Shem, Ham, and Japheth, the sons of Noah, and Noah's wife and the three wives of his sons with them, went into the ark,

¹⁴They and every [wild] beast according to its kind, all the livestock according to their kinds, every moving thing that creeps on the land according to its kind, and every fowl according to its kind, every winged thing of every sort.

¹⁵And they went into the ark with Noah, two and two of all flesh in which there were the breath *and* spirit of life.

¹⁶And they that entered, male and female of all flesh, went in as God had commanded [Noah]; and the Lord shut him in *and* closed [the door] round about him.

¹⁷The flood [that is, the downpour of rain] was forty days upon the earth; and the waters increased and bore up the ark, and it was lifted [high] above the land.

¹⁸And the waters became mighty and increased greatly upon the land, and the ark went [gently floating] upon the surface of the waters.

¹⁹And the waters prevailed so exceedingly *and* were so mighty upon the earth that all the high hills under the whole sky were covered.

²⁰[In fact] the waters became fifteen cubits higher, as the high hills were covered.

²¹And all flesh ceased to breathe that moved upon the earth—fowls *and* birds, [tame] animals, [wild] beasts, all swarming *and* creeping things that swarm *and* creep upon the land, and all mankind.

²²Everything on the dry land in whose nostrils were the breath *and* spirit of life died.

²³God destroyed (blotted out) every living thing that was upon the face of the earth; man and animals and the creeping things and the birds of the heavens were destroyed (blotted out) from the land. Only Noah remained alive, and those who were with him in the ark. [Matt. 24:37–44.]

²⁴And the waters prevailed [mightily] upon the earth *or* land 150 days (five months).

8 AND GOD [earnestly] remembered Noah and every living thing and all the animals that were with him in the ark; and God made a wind blow over the land, and the waters sank down *and* abated.

²Also the fountains of the deep and the windows of the heavens were closed, the gushing rain from the sky was checked,

³And the waters receded from the land continually. At the end of 150 days the waters had diminished.

⁴On the seventeenth day of the seventh month the ark came to rest on the mountains of Ararat [in Armenia].

⁵And the waters continued to diminish until the tenth month; on the first day of the tenth month the tops of the high hills were seen.

⁶At the end of [another] forty days Noah opened a window of the ark which he had made

⁷And sent forth a raven, which kept going to and fro until the waters were dried up from the land.

ᵖ Or, *on the seventh day*   ᵟOr, *floodgates*   ʳHeb. *wing*
ˢHeb. *the breath of the spirit of life*   ᵗHeb. *in going and returning*   ᵘHeb. *were in going and decreasing*   ᵛHeb. *in going forth and returning*

New American Standard

9 there went into the ark to Noah by twos, male and female, as God had commanded Noah.

10 It came about after the seven days, that the water of the flood came upon the earth.

11 In the six hundredth year of Noah's life, in the second month, on the seventeenth day of the month, on the same day all the fountains of the great deep burst open, and the floodgates of the sky were opened.

12 The rain fell upon the earth for forty days and forty nights.

13 ¶ On the very same day Noah and Shem and Ham and Japheth, the sons of Noah, and Noah's wife and the three wives of his sons with them, entered the ark,

14 they and every beast after its kind, and all the cattle after their kind, and every creeping thing that creeps on the earth after its kind, and every bird after its kind, all sorts of birds.

15 So they went into the ark to Noah, by twos of all flesh in which was the breath of life.

16 Those that entered, male and female of all flesh, entered as God had commanded him; and the LORD closed it behind him.

17 ¶ Then the flood came upon the earth for forty days, and the water increased and lifted up the ark, so that it rose above the earth.

18 The water prevailed and increased greatly upon the earth, and the ark floated on the surface of the water.

19 The water prevailed more and more upon the earth, so that all the high mountains everywhere under the heavens were covered.

20 The water prevailed fifteen cubits higher, and the mountains were covered.

21 All flesh that moved on the earth perished, birds and cattle and beasts and every swarming thing that swarms upon the earth, and all mankind;

22 of all that was on the dry land, all in whose nostrils was the breath of the spirit of life, died.

23 Thus He blotted out every living thing that was upon the face of the land, from man to animals to creeping things and to birds of the sky, and they were blotted out from the earth; and only Noah was left, together with those that were with him in the ark.

24 The water prevailed upon the earth one hundred and fifty days.

The Flood Subsides

8 BUT GOD remembered Noah and all the beasts and all the cattle that were with him in the ark; and God caused a wind to pass over the earth, and the water subsided.

2 Also the fountains of the deep and the floodgates of the sky were closed, and the rain from the sky was restrained;

3 and the water receded steadily from the earth, and at the end of one hundred and fifty days the water decreased.

4 In the seventh month, on the seventeenth day of the month, the ark rested upon the mountains of Ararat.

5 The water decreased steadily until the tenth month; in the tenth month, on the first day of the month, the tops of the mountains became visible.

6 ¶ Then it came about at the end of forty days, that Noah opened the window of the ark which he had made;

7 and he sent out a raven, and it flew here and there until the water was dried up from the earth.

New International

of all creatures that move along the ground, 9male and female, came to Noah and entered the ark, as God had commanded Noah. 10And after the seven days the floodwaters came on the earth.

11 In the six hundredth year of Noah's life, on the seventeenth day of the second month—on that day all the springs of the great deep burst forth, and the floodgates of the heavens were opened. 12And rain fell on the earth forty days and forty nights.

13On that very day Noah and his sons, Shem, Ham and Japheth, together with his wife and the wives of his three sons, entered the ark. 14They had with them every wild animal according to its kind, all livestock according to their kinds, every creature that moves along the ground according to its kind and every bird according to its kind, everything with wings. 15Pairs of all creatures that have the breath of life in them came to Noah and entered the ark. 16The animals going in were male and female of every living thing, as God had commanded Noah. Then the LORD shut him in.

17For forty days the flood kept coming on the earth, and as the waters increased they lifted the ark high above the earth. 18The waters rose and increased greatly on the earth, and the ark floated on the surface of the water. 19They rose greatly on the earth, and all the high mountains under the entire heavens were covered. 20The waters rose and covered the mountains to a depth of more than twenty feet.l,m 21Every living thing that moved on the earth perished—birds, livestock, wild animals, all the creatures that swarm over the earth, and all mankind. 22Everything on dry land that had the breath of life in its nostrils died. 23Every living thing on the face of the earth was wiped out; men and animals and the creatures that move along the ground and the birds of the air were wiped from the earth. Only Noah was left, and those with him in the ark.

24The waters flooded the earth for a hundred and fifty days.

8 BUT GOD remembered Noah and all the wild animals and the livestock that were with him in the ark, and he sent a wind over the earth, and the waters receded. 2Now the springs of the deep and the floodgates of the heavens had been closed, and the rain had stopped falling from the sky. 3The water receded steadily from the earth. At the end of the hundred and fifty days the water had gone down, 4and on the seventeenth day of the seventh month the ark came to rest on the mountains of Ararat. 5The waters continued to recede until the tenth month, and on the first day of the tenth month the tops of the mountains became visible.

6After forty days Noah opened the window he had made in the ark 7and sent out a raven, and it kept flying back and

---

l20 Hebrew *fifteen cubits* (about 6.9 meters)   *m 20* Or *rose more than twenty feet, and the mountains were covered*

King James

⁸Also he sent forth a dove from him, to see if the waters were abated from off the face of the ground;

⁹But the dove found no rest for the sole of her foot, and she returned unto him into the ark, for the waters *were* on the face of the whole earth: then he put forth his hand, and took her, and ʷpulled her in unto him into the ark.

¹⁰And he stayed yet other seven days; and again he sent forth the dove out of the ark;

¹¹And the dove came in to him in the evening; and, lo, in her mouth *was* an olive leaf plucked off: so Noah knew that the waters were abated from off the earth.

¹²And he stayed yet other seven days; and sent forth the dove; which returned not again unto him any more.

¹³ ¶ And it came to pass in the six hundredth and first year, in the first *month,* the first *day* of the month, the waters were dried up from off the earth: and Noah removed the covering of the ark, and looked, and, behold, the face of the ground was dry.

¹⁴And in the second month, on the seven and twentieth day of the month, was the earth dried.

¹⁵ ¶ And God spake unto Noah, saying,

¹⁶Go forth of the ark, thou, and thy wife, and thy sons, and thy sons' wives with thee.

¹⁷Bring forth with thee every living thing that *is* with thee, of all flesh, *both* of fowl, and of cattle, and of every creeping thing that creepeth upon the earth; that they may breed abundantly in the earth, and be fruitful, and multiply upon the earth.

¹⁸And Noah went forth, and his sons, and his wife, and his sons' wives with him:

¹⁹Every beast, every creeping thing, and every fowl, *and* whatsoever creepeth upon the earth, after their ˣkinds, went forth out of the ark.

²⁰ ¶ And Noah builded an altar unto the Lᴏʀᴅ; and took of every clean beast, and of every clean fowl, and offered burnt offerings on the altar.

²¹And the Lᴏʀᴅ smelled ʸa sweet savour; and the Lᴏʀᴅ said in his heart, I will not again curse the ground any more for man's sake; ᶻfor the imagination of man's heart *is* evil from his youth; neither will I again smite any more every thing living, as I have done.

²²ᵃWhile the earth remaineth, seedtime and harvest, and cold and heat, and summer and winter, and day and night shall not cease.

The covenant with Noah

9 AND GOD blessed Noah and his sons, and said unto them, Be fruitful, and multiply, and replenish the earth.

²And the fear of you and the dread of you shall be upon every beast of the earth, and upon every fowl of the air, upon all that moveth *upon* the earth, and upon all the fishes of the sea; into your hand are they delivered.

Amplified

⁸Then he sent forth a dove to see if the waters had decreased from the surface of the ground.

⁹But the dove found no resting-place on which to roost, and she returned to him to the ark, for the waters were [yet] on the face of the whole land. So he put forth his hand and drew her to him into the ark.

¹⁰He waited another seven days and again sent forth the dove out of the ark.

¹¹And the dove came back to him in the evening, and behold, in her mouth was a newly sprouted *and* freshly plucked olive leaf! So Noah knew that the waters had subsided from the land.

¹²Then he waited another seven days and sent forth the dove, but she did not return to him any more.

¹³In the year 601 [of Noah's life], on the first day of the first month, the waters were drying up from the land. And Noah ᵖremoved the covering of the ark and looked, and behold, the surface of the ground was drying.

¹⁴And on the twenty-seventh day of the second month the land was entirely dry.

¹⁵And God spoke to Noah, saying,

¹⁶Go forth from the ark, you and your wife and your sons and their wives with you.

¹⁷Bring forth every living thing that is with you of all flesh—birds and beasts and every creeping thing that creeps on the ground—that they may breed abundantly on the land and be fruitful and multiply upon the earth.

¹⁸And Noah went forth, and his wife and his sons and their wives with him [after being in the ark one year and ten days].

¹⁹Every beast, every creeping thing, every bird—and whatever moves on the land—went forth by families out of the ark.

²⁰And Noah built an altar to the Lord and took of every clean [four-footed] animal and of every clean fowl *or* bird and offered burnt offerings on the altar.

²¹When the Lord smelled the pleasing odor [a scent of satisfaction to His heart], the Lord said to Himself, I will never again curse the ground because of man, for the imagination (the strong desire) of man's heart is evil *and* wicked from his youth; neither will I ever again smite *and* destroy every living thing, as I have done.

²²While the earth remains, seedtime and harvest, cold and heat, summer and winter, and day and night shall not cease.

9 AND GOD pronounced a blessing upon Noah and his sons and said to them, Be fruitful and multiply and fill the earth.

²And the fear of you and the dread *and* terror of you shall be upon every beast of the land, every bird of the air, all that creeps upon the ground, and upon all the fish of the sea; they are delivered into your hand.

ᵖPossibly overhanging eaves which prevented the rain from coming through the perforated window space had also prevented Noah from seeing the mountaintops. It is well to remember that the Architect of Noah's ark was the omniscient Scientist Whose "ways are past finding out," though men have learned much from them through the centuries. Nothing was lacking in Noah's ark to keep it from being suited for all that was required of it. The comfortable, light, well-ventilated, watertight, perfectly planned boat, large enough to accommodate all the original land animals intelligently and to permit the four human couples to live separately and in peace, needs no apology today. "In 1609 at Hoorn, in Holland, the Netherlandish Mennonite, P. Jansen, produced a vessel after the pattern of the ark, only smaller, whereby he proved it was well adapted for floating, and would carry a cargo greater by one-third than any other form of like cubical content" (J.P. Lange, *A Commentary*). It revolutionized shipbuilding. By 1900 every large vessel on the high seas was definitely inclined toward the proportions of Noah's ark (as verified by "Lloyd's Register of Shipping," *The World Almanac*). Later, ships were built longer for speed, a matter of no concern to Noah.

ʷHeb. *caused her to come of rest*   ˣHeb. *families*   ʸHeb. *a saviour*   ᶻOr, *though*   ᵃHeb. *As yet all the days of the earth*

New American Standard

8 Then he sent out a dove from him, to see if the water was abated from the face of the land;

9 but the dove found no resting place for the sole of her foot, so she returned to him into the ark, for the water was on the surface of all the earth. Then he put out his hand and took her, and brought her into the ark to himself.

10 So he waited yet another seven days; and again he sent out the dove from the ark.

11 The dove came to him toward evening, and behold, in her beak was a freshly picked olive leaf. So Noah knew that the water was abated from the earth.

12 Then he waited yet another seven days, and sent out the dove; but she did not return to him again.

13 ¶ Now it came about in the six hundred and first year, in the first *month*, on the first of the month, the water was dried up from the earth. Then Noah removed the covering of the ark, and looked, and behold, the surface of the ground was dried up.

14 In the second month, on the twenty-seventh day of the month, the earth was dry.

15 Then God spoke to Noah, saying,

16"Go out of the ark, you and your wife and your sons and your sons' wives with you.

17"Bring out with you every living thing of all flesh that is with you, birds and animals and every creeping thing that creeps on the earth, that they may breed abundantly on the earth, and be fruitful and multiply on the earth."

18 So Noah went out, and his sons and his wife and his sons' wives with him.

19 Every beast, every creeping thing, and every bird, everything that moves on the earth, went out by their families from the ark.

20 ¶ Then Noah built an altar to the LORD, and took of every clean animal and of every clean bird and offered burnt offerings on the altar.

21 The LORD smelled the soothing aroma; and the LORD said to Himself, "I will never again curse the ground on account of man, for the intent of man's heart is evil from his youth; and I will never again destroy every living thing, as I have done.

22"While the earth remains,
Seedtime and harvest,
And cold and heat,
And summer and winter,
And day and night
Shall not cease."

Covenant of the Rainbow

9 AND GOD blessed Noah and his sons and said to them, "Be fruitful and multiply, and fill the earth.

2"The fear of you and the terror of you will be on every beast of the earth and on every bird of the sky; with everything that creeps on the ground, and all the fish of the sea, into your hand they are given.

New International

forth until the water had dried up from the earth. 8Then he sent out a dove to see if the water had receded from the surface of the ground. 9But the dove could find no place to set its feet because there was water over all the surface of the earth; so it returned to Noah in the ark. He reached out his hand and took the dove and brought it back to himself in the ark. 10He waited seven more days and again sent out the dove from the ark. 11When the dove returned to him in the evening, there in its beak was a freshly plucked olive leaf! Then Noah knew that the water had receded from the earth. 12He waited seven more days and sent the dove out again, but this time it did not return to him.

13By the first day of the first month of Noah's six hundred and first year, the water had dried up from the earth. Noah then removed the covering from the ark and saw that the surface of the ground was dry. 14By the twenty-seventh day of the second month the earth was completely dry.

15Then God said to Noah, 16"Come out of the ark, you and your wife and your sons and their wives. 17Bring out every kind of living creature that is with you—the birds, the animals, and all the creatures that move along the ground—so they can multiply on the earth and be fruitful and increase in number upon it."

18So Noah came out, together with his sons and his wife and his sons' wives. 19All the animals and all the creatures that move along the ground and all the birds—everything that moves on the earth—came out of the ark, one kind after another.

20Then Noah built an altar to the LORD and, taking some of all the clean animals and clean birds, he sacrificed burnt offerings on it. 21The LORD smelled the pleasing aroma and said in his heart: "Never again will I curse the ground because of man, even though[n] every inclination of his heart is evil from childhood. And never again will I destroy all living creatures, as I have done.

22"As long as the earth endures,
seedtime and harvest,
cold and heat,
summer and winter,
day and night
will never cease."

God's Covenant With Noah

9 THEN GOD blessed Noah and his sons, saying to them, "Be fruitful and increase in number and fill the earth. 2The fear and dread of you will fall upon all the beasts of the earth and all the birds of the air, upon every creature that moves along the ground, and upon all the fish of the sea; they are given into your hands. 3Everything that

King James

³Every moving thing that liveth shall be meat for you; even as the green herb have I given you all things.

⁴But flesh with the life thereof, *which is* the blood thereof, shall ye not eat.

⁵And surely your blood of your lives will I require; at the hand of every beast will I require it, and at the hand of man; at the hand of every man's brother will I require the life of man.

⁶Whoso sheddeth man's blood, by man shall his blood be shed: for in the image of God made he man.

⁷And you, be ye fruitful, and multiply; bring forth abundantly in the earth, and multiply therein.

⁸ ¶ And God spake unto Noah, and to his sons with him, saying,

⁹And I, behold, I establish my covenant with you, and with your seed after you;

¹⁰And with every living creature that *is* with you, of the fowl, of the cattle, and of every beast of the earth with you; from all that go out of the ark, to every beast of the earth.

¹¹And I will establish my covenant with you; neither shall all flesh be cut off any more by the waters of a flood; neither shall there any more be a flood to destroy the earth.

¹²And God said, This *is* the token of the covenant which I make between me and you and every living creature that *is* with you, for perpetual generations:

¹³I do set my bow in the cloud, and it shall be for a token of a covenant between me and the earth.

¹⁴And it shall come to pass, when I bring a cloud over the earth, that the bow shall be seen in the cloud:

¹⁵And I will remember my covenant, which *is* between me and you and every living creature of all flesh; and the waters shall no more become a flood to destroy all flesh.

¹⁶And the bow shall be in the cloud; and I will look upon it, that I may remember the everlasting covenant between God and every living creature of all flesh that *is* upon the earth.

¹⁷And God said unto Noah, This *is* the token of the covenant, which I have established between me and all flesh that *is* upon the earth.

¹⁸ ¶ And the sons of Noah, that went forth of the ark, were Shem, and Ham, and Japheth: and Ham *is* the father of ᵇCanaan.

¹⁹These *are* the three sons of Noah: and of them was the whole earth overspread.

Canaan cursed; Shem blessed

²⁰And Noah began *to be* an husbandman, and he planted a vineyard:

²¹And he drank of the wine, and was drunken; and he was uncovered within his tent.

²²And Ham, the father of Canaan, saw the nakedness of his father, and told his two brethren without.

²³And Shem and Japheth took a garment, and laid *it* upon both their shoulders, and went backward, and covered the nakedness of their father; and their faces *were* backward, and they saw not their father's nakedness.

²⁴And Noah awoke from his wine, and knew what his younger son had done unto him.

Amplified

³Every moving thing that lives shall be food for you; and as I gave you the green vegetables *and* plants, I give you everything.

⁴But you shall not eat flesh with the life of it, which is its blood.

⁵And surely for your lifeblood I will require an accounting; from every beast I will require it; and from man, from every man [who spills another's lifeblood] I will require a reckoning.

⁶Whoever sheds man's blood, by man shall his blood be shed; for in the image of God He made man.

⁷And you, be fruitful and multiply; bring forth abundantly on the earth and multiply on it.

⁸Then God spoke to Noah and to his sons with him, saying,

⁹Behold, I establish My covenant *or* pledge with you and with your descendants after you

¹⁰And with every living creature that is with you—whether the birds, the livestock, or the wild beasts of the earth along with you, as many as came out of the ark—every animal of the earth.

¹¹I will establish My covenant *or* pledge with you: Never again shall all flesh be cut off by the waters of a flood; neither shall there ever again be a flood to destroy the earth *and* make it corrupt.

¹²And God said, This is the token of the covenant (solemn pledge) which I am making between Me and you and every living creature that is with you, for all future generations:

¹³I set My bow [rainbow] in the cloud, and it shall be a token *or* sign of a covenant *or* solemn pledge between Me and the earth.

¹⁴And it shall be that when I bring clouds over the earth and the bow [rainbow] is seen in the clouds,

¹⁵I will [earnestly] remember My covenant *or* solemn pledge which is between Me and you and every living creature of all flesh; and the waters will no more become a flood to destroy *and* make all flesh corrupt.

¹⁶When the bow [rainbow] is in the clouds and I look upon it, I will [earnestly] remember the everlasting covenant *or* pledge between God and every living creature of all flesh that is upon the earth.

¹⁷And God said to Noah, This [rainbow] is the token *or* sign of the covenant *or* solemn pledge which I have established between Me and all flesh upon the earth.

¹⁸The sons of Noah who went forth from the ark were Shem, Ham, and Japheth. Ham was the father of Canaan [born later].

¹⁹These are the three sons of Noah, and from them the whole earth was overspread *and* stocked with inhabitants.

²⁰And Noah began to cultivate the ground, and he planted a vineyard.

²¹And he drank of the wine and became drunk, and he was uncovered *and* lay naked in his tent.

²²And Ham, the father of Canaan, glanced at *and* saw the nakedness of his father and told his two brothers outside.

²³So Shem and Japheth took a garment, laid it upon the shoulders of both, and went backward and covered the nakedness of their father; and their faces were backward, and they did not see their father's nakedness.

²⁴When Noah awoke from his wine, and knew the thing which his youngest son had done to him,

---

ᵇHeb. *Chenaan*

New American Standard

3"Every moving thing that is alive shall be food for you; I give all to you, as *I gave* the green plant.

4"Only you shall not eat flesh with its life, *that is,* its blood.

5"Surely I will require your lifeblood; from every beast I will require it. And from *every* man, from every man's brother I will require the life of man.

6"Whoever sheds man's blood,
  By man his blood shall be shed,
  For in the image of God
  He made man.

7"As for you, be fruitful and multiply;
  Populate the earth abundantly and multiply in it."

8 ¶ Then God spoke to Noah and to his sons with him, saying,

9"Now behold, I Myself do establish My covenant with you, and with your descendants after you;

10 and with every living creature that is with you, the birds, the cattle, and every beast of the earth with you; of all that comes out of the ark, even every beast of the earth.

11"I establish My covenant with you; and all flesh shall never again be cut off by the water of the flood, neither shall there again be a flood to destroy the earth."

12 God said, "This is the sign of the covenant which I am making between Me and you and every living creature that is with you, for all successive generations;

13 I set My bow in the cloud, and it shall be for a sign of a covenant between Me and the earth.

14"It shall come about, when I bring a cloud over the earth, that the bow will be seen in the cloud,

15 and I will remember My covenant, which is between Me and you and every living creature of all flesh; and never again shall the water become a flood to destroy all flesh.

16"When the bow is in the cloud, then I will look upon it, to remember the everlasting covenant between God and every living creature of all flesh that is on the earth."

17 And God said to Noah, "This is the sign of the covenant which I have established between Me and all flesh that is on the earth."

18 ¶ Now the sons of Noah who came out of the ark were Shem and Ham and Japheth; and Ham was the father of Canaan.

19 These three *were* the sons of Noah, and from these the whole earth was populated.

20 ¶ Then Noah began farming and planted a vineyard.

21 He drank of the wine and became drunk, and uncovered himself inside his tent.

22 Ham, the father of Canaan, saw the nakedness of his father, and told his two brothers outside.

23 But Shem and Japheth took a garment and laid it upon both their shoulders and walked backward and covered the nakedness of their father; and their faces were turned away, so that they did not see their father's nakedness.

24 When Noah awoke from his wine, he knew what his youngest son had done to him,

New International

lives and moves will be food for you. Just as I gave you the green plants, I now give you everything.

4"But you must not eat meat that has its lifeblood still in it. 5And for your lifeblood I will surely demand an accounting. I will demand an accounting from every animal. And from each man, too, I will demand an accounting for the life of his fellow man.

6"Whoever sheds the blood of man,
  by man shall his blood be shed;
  for in the image of God
  has God made man.

7As for you, be fruitful and increase in number; multiply on the earth and increase upon it."

8Then God said to Noah and to his sons with him: 9"I now establish my covenant with you and with your descendants after you 10and with every living creature that was with you—the birds, the livestock and all the wild animals, all those that came out of the ark with you—every living creature on earth. 11I establish my covenant with you: Never again will all life be cut off by the waters of a flood; never again will there be a flood to destroy the earth."

12And God said, "This is the sign of the covenant I am making between me and you and every living creature with you, a covenant for all generations to come: 13I have set my rainbow in the clouds, and it will be the sign of the covenant between me and the earth. 14Whenever I bring clouds over the earth and the rainbow appears in the clouds, 15I will remember my covenant between me and you and all living creatures of every kind. Never again will the waters become a flood to destroy all life. 16Whenever the rainbow appears in the clouds, I will see it and remember the everlasting covenant between God and all living creatures of every kind on the earth."

17So God said to Noah, "This is the sign of the covenant I have established between me and all life on the earth."

The Sons of Noah

18The sons of Noah who came out of the ark were Shem, Ham and Japheth. (Ham was the father of Canaan.) 19These were the three sons of Noah, and from them came the people who were scattered over the earth.

20Noah, a man of the soil, proceeded*o* to plant a vineyard. 21When he drank some of its wine, he became drunk and lay uncovered inside his tent. 22Ham, the father of Canaan, saw his father's nakedness and told his two brothers outside. 23But Shem and Japheth took a garment and laid it across their shoulders; then they walked in backward and covered their father's nakedness. Their faces were turned the other way so that they would not see their father's nakedness.

24When Noah awoke from his wine and found out what

---

o 20 Or soil, was the first

King James

25And he said, Cursed *be* Canaan; a servant of servants shall he be unto his brethren.

26And he said, Blessed *be* the LORD God of Shem; and Canaan shall be chis servant.

27God shall denlarge Japheth, and he shall dwell in the tents of Shem; and Canaan shall be his servant.

28 ¶ And Noah lived after the flood three hundred and fifty years.

29And all the days of Noah were nine hundred and fifty years: and he died.

Descendants of Noah's sons

10 NOW THESE *are* the generations of the sons of Noah, Shem, Ham, and Japheth: and unto them were sons born after the flood.

2The sons of Japheth; Gomer, and Magog, and Madai, and Javan, and Tubal, and Meshech, and Tiras.

3And the sons of Gomer; Ashkenaz, and Riphath, and Togarmah.

4And the sons of Javan; Elishah, and Tarshish, Kittim, and eDodanim.

5By these were the isles of the Gentiles divided in their lands; every one after his tongue, after their families, in their nations.

6 ¶ And the sons of Ham; Cush, and Mizraim, and Phut, and Canaan.

7And the sons of Cush; Seba, and Havilah, and Sabtah, and Raamah, and Sabtecha: and the sons of Raamah; Sheba, and Dedan.

8And Cush begat Nimrod: he began to be a mighty one in the earth.

9He was a mighty hunter before the LORD: wherefore it is said, Even as Nimrod the mighty hunter before the LORD.

10And the beginning of his kingdom was fBabel, and Erech, and Accad, and Calneh, in the land of Shinar.

11Out of that land gwent forth Asshur, and builded Nineveh, and hthe city Rehoboth, and Calah,

12And Resen between Nineveh and Calah: the same *is* a great city.

13And Mizraim begat Ludim, and Anamim, and Lehabim, and Naphtuhim,

14And Pathrusim, and Casluhim, (out of whom came Philistim,) and Caphtorim.

15 ¶ And Canaan begat iSidon his firstborn, and Heth,

16And the Jebusite, and the Amorite, and the Girgasite,

17And the Hivite, and the Arkite, and the Sinite,

18And the Arvadite, and the Zemarite, and the Hamathite: and afterward were the families of the Canaanites spread abroad.

19And the border of the Canaanites was from Sidon, as thou comest to Gerar, unto jGaza; as thou goest, unto Sodom, and Gomorrah, and Admah, and Zeboim, even unto Lasha.

20These *are* the sons of Ham, after their families, after their tongues, in their countries, *and* in their nations.

Amplified

25He exclaimed, Cursed be Canaan! He shall be the qservant of servants to his brethren! [Deut. 27:16.]

26He also said, Blessed be the Lord, the God of Shem! *And* blessed by the Lord my God be Shem! And let Canaan be his servant.

27May God enlarge Japheth; and let him dwell in the tents of Shem, and let Canaan be his servant.

28And Noah lived after the flood 350 years.

29All the days of Noah were 950 years, and he died.

10 THIS IS the history of the generations (descendants) of the sons of Noah, Shem, Ham, and Japheth. The sons born to them after the flood *were:*

2The sons of Japheth: Gomer, Magog, Madai, Javan, Tubal, Meshech, and Tiras.

3The sons of Gomer: Ashkenaz, Riphath, and Togarmah.

4The sons of Javan: Elishah, Tarshish, Kittim, and Dodanim.

5From these the coastland peoples spread. [These are the sons of Japheth] in their lands, each with his own language, by their families within their nations.

6The sons of Ham: Cush, Egypt [Mizraim], Put, and Canaan.

7The sons of Cush: Seba, Havilah, Sabtah, Raamah, and Sabteca; and the sons of Raamah: Sheba and Dedan.

8Cush became the father of Nimrod; he was the first to be a mighty man on the earth.

9He was a mighty hunter before the Lord; therefore it is said, Like Nimrod, a mighty hunter before the Lord.

10The beginning of his kingdom was Babel, Erech, Accad, and Calneh, in the land of Shinar [in Babylonia].

11Out of the land he [Nimrod] went forth into Assyria and built Nineveh, Rehoboth-Ir, Calah,

12And Resen, which is between Nineveh and Calah; all these [suburbs combined to form] the great city.

13And Egypt [Mizraim] became the father of Ludim, Anamim, Lehabim, Naphtuhim,

14Pathrusim, Casluhim (from whom came the Philistines), and Caphtorim.

15Canaan became the father of Sidon his firstborn, Heth [the Hittites],

16The Jebusites, the Amorites, the Girgashites,

17The Hivites, the Arkites, the Sinites,

18The Arvadites, the Zemarites and the Hamathites. Afterward the families of the Canaanites spread abroad

19And the territory of the Canaanites extended from Sidon as one goes to Gerar as far as Gaza, and as one goes to rSodom, Gomorrah, Admah, and Zeboiim, as far as Lasha.

20These are the sons of Ham by their families, their languages, their lands, and their nations.

q The language of Noah here is an actual prophecy and not merely an expression of personal feeling. That Noah placed a curse on his youngest grandchild, Canaan, who would naturally be his favorite, can only be explained on the ground that in the prophetic spirit he saw into the future of the Canaanites. God Himself found the delinquency of the Canaanites insufferable and ultimately drove them out or subdued them and put the descendants of Shem in their place. But Noah's foresight did not yet include the extermination of the Canaanite peoples, for then he would have expressed it differently. He would not merely have called them "the servant of servants" if he had foreseen their destruction. The form of the expression, therefore, testifies to the great age of the prophecy (J.P. Lange, *A Commentary*). r Surely no greater proof is needed of the great antiquity of this portion of Genesis than the fact that it mentions as still standing these four cities of the plain, which were utterly destroyed in Abraham's time (Gen. 19:27-29; Deut. 29:23).

cOr, *servant to them*   dOr, *persuade*   eOr, *Rodanim*   fGk. *Babylon*   gOr, *he went out* into *Assyria*   hOr, *the streets of the city*   iHeb. *Tzidon*   jHeb. *Azzah*

New American Standard

²⁵ So he said,
  "Cursed be Canaan;
    ^kA servant of servants
    He shall be to his brothers."
²⁶ He also said,
  "Blessed be the LORD,
    The God of Shem;
    And let Canaan be his servant.
²⁷"May God enlarge Japheth,
    And let him dwell in the tents of Shem;
    And let Canaan be his servant."
²⁸ ¶ Noah lived three hundred and fifty years after the
flood.
²⁹ So all the days of Noah were nine hundred and fifty
years, and he died.

Descendants of Noah

10 NOW THESE are *the records of* the generations
of Shem, Ham, and Japheth, the sons of Noah; and
sons were born to them after the flood.
² ¶ The sons of Japheth *were* Gomer and Magog and
Madai and Javan and Tubal and Meshech and Tiras.
³ The sons of Gomer *were* Ashkenaz and Riphath and
Togarmah.
⁴ The sons of Javan *were* Elishah and Tarshish, Kittim
and Dodanim.
⁵ From these the coastlands of the nations were sepa-
rated into their lands, every one according to his language,
according to their families, into their nations.
⁶ ¶ The sons of Ham *were* Cush and Mizraim and Put
and Canaan.
⁷ The sons of Cush *were* Seba and Havilah and Sabtah
and Raamah and Sabteca; and the sons of Raamah *were*
Sheba and Dedan.
⁸ Now Cush became the father of Nimrod; he became
a mighty one on the earth.
⁹ He was a mighty hunter before the LORD; therefore it
is said, "Like Nimrod a mighty hunter before the LORD."
¹⁰ The beginning of his kingdom was *l*Babel and
Erech and Accad and Calneh, in the land of Shinar.
¹¹ From that land he went forth into Assyria, and built
Nineveh and Rehoboth-Ir and Calah,
¹² and Resen between Nineveh and Calah; that is the
great city.
¹³ Mizraim became the father of Ludim and Anamim
and Lehabim and Naphtuhim
¹⁴ and Pathrusim and Casluhim (from which came the
Philistines) and Caphtorim.
¹⁵ ¶ Canaan became the father of Sidon, his firstborn,
and Heth
¹⁶ and the Jebusite and the Amorite and the Girgashite
¹⁷ and the Hivite and the Arkite and the Sinite
¹⁸ and the Arvadite and the Zemarite and the Hamathite;
and afterward the families of the Canaanite were spread
abroad.
¹⁹ The territory of the Canaanite extended from Sidon
as you toward Gerar, as far as Gaza; as you go toward
Sodom and Gomorrah and Admah and Zeboiim, as far as
Lasha.
²⁰ These are the sons of Ham, according to their fami-
lies, according to their languages, by their lands, by their
nations.

New International

his youngest son had done to him, ²⁵he said,

  "Cursed be Canaan!
    The lowest of slaves
    will he be to his brothers."

²⁶He also said,

  "Blessed be the LORD, the God of Shem!
    May Canaan be the slave of Shem.^p
²⁷May God extend the territory of Japheth^q;
    may Japheth live in the tents of Shem,
    and may Canaan be his^r slave."

²⁸After the flood Noah lived 350 years. ²⁹Altogether,
Noah lived 950 years, and then he died.

The Table of Nations

10 THIS IS the account of Shem, Ham and Japheth,
Noah's sons, who themselves had sons after the
flood.

The Japhethites

²The sons^s of Japheth:
  Gomer, Magog, Madai, Javan, Tubal, Meshech
  and Tiras.
³The sons of Gomer:
  Ashkenaz, Riphath and Togarmah.
⁴The sons of Javan:
  Elishah, Tarshish, the Kittim and the Rodanim.^t
⁵(From these the maritime peoples spread out into
  their territories by their clans within their nations,
  each with its own language.)

The Hamites

⁶The sons of Ham:
  Cush, Mizraim,^u Put and Canaan.
⁷The sons of Cush:
  Seba, Havilah, Sabtah, Raamah and Sabteca.
  The sons of Raamah:
  Sheba and Dedan.

⁸Cush was the father^v of Nimrod, who grew to be a
mighty warrior on the earth. ⁹He was a mighty hunter
before the LORD; that is why it is said, "Like Nimrod, a
mighty hunter before the LORD." ¹⁰The first centers of his
kingdom were Babylon, Erech, Akkad and Calneh, in^w
Shinar.^x ¹¹From that land he went to Assyria, where he
built Nineveh, Rehoboth Ir,^y Calah ¹²and Resen, which is
between Nineveh and Calah; that is the great city.

¹³Mizraim was the father of
  the Ludites, Anamites, Lehabites, Naphtuhites,
  ¹⁴Pathrusites, Casluhites (from whom the Philistines came) and Caphtorites.
¹⁵Canaan was the father of
  Sidon his firstborn,^z and of the Hittites, ¹⁶Jebu-
  sites, Amorites, Girgashites, ¹⁷Hivites, Arkites, Sinites, ¹⁸Arvadites, Zemarites and Hamathites.

Later the Canaanite clans scattered ¹⁹and the borders of
Canaan reached from Sidon toward Gerar as far as Gaza,
and then toward Sodom, Gomorrah, Admah and Zeboiim,
as far as Lasha.
²⁰These are the sons of Ham by their clans and lan-
guages, in their territories and nations.

---

^p26 Or *be his slave*   ^q27 *Japheth* sounds like the Hebrew for
extend.   ^r27 Or *their*   ^s2 *Sons* may mean *descendants* or
successors or *nations*; also in verses 3, 4, 6, 7, 20-23, 29 and 31.
^t4 Some manuscripts of the Masoretic Text and Samaritan
Pentateuch (see also Septuagint and 1 Chron. 1:7); most manuscripts
of the Masoretic Text *Dodanim*   ^u6 That is, Egypt; also in
verse 13   ^v8 *Father* may mean *ancestor* or *predecessor* or
founder; also in verses 13, 15, 24 and 26.   ^w10 Or *Erech and
Akkad—all of them in*   ^x10 That is, Babylonia
^y11 Or *Nineveh with its city squares*   ^z15 Or *of the Sidonians,
the foremost*

---

^kI.e. The lowest of servants   ^lOr *Babylon*

King James

21 ¶ Unto Shem also, the father of all the children of Eber, the brother of Japheth the elder, even to him were *children* born.

22The children of Shem; Elam, and Asshur, and *k*Arphaxad, and Lud, and Aram.

23And the children of Aram; Uz, and Hul, and Gether, and Mash.

24And Arphaxad begat *l*Salah; and Salah begat Eber.

25And unto Eber were born two sons: the name of one *was* *m*Peleg; for in his days was the earth divided; and his brother's name *was* Joktan.

26And Joktan begat Almodad, and Sheleph, and Hazarmaveth, and Jerah,

27And Hadoram, and Uzal, and Diklah,

28And Obal, and Abimael, and Sheba,

29And Ophir, and Havilah, and Jobab: all these *were* the sons of Joktan.

30And their dwelling was from Mesha, as thou goest unto Sephar a mount of the east.

31These *are* the sons of Shem, after their families, after their tongues, in their lands, after their nations.

32These *are* the families of the sons of Noah, after their generations, in their nations: and by these were the nations divided in the earth after the flood.

The tower of Babel

11 AND THE whole earth was of one *n*language, and of one *o*speech.

2And it came to pass, as they journeyed *p*from the east, that they found a plain in the land of Shinar; and they dwelt there.

3And *q*they said one to another, Go to, let us make brick, and *r*burn them thoroughly. And they had brick for stone, and slime had they for mortar.

4And they said, Go to, let us build us a city and a tower, whose top *may reach* unto heaven; and let us make us a name, lest we be scattered abroad upon the face of the whole earth.

5And the LORD came down to see the city and the tower, which the children of men builded.

6And the LORD said, Behold, the people *is* one, and they have all one language; and this they begin to do: and now nothing will be restrained from them, which they have imagined to do.

7Go to, let us go down, and there confound their language, that they may not understand one another's speech.

8So the LORD scattered them abroad from thence upon the face of all the earth: and they left off to build the city.

9Therefore is the name of it called *s*Babel; because the LORD did there confound the language of all the earth: and from thence did the LORD scatter them abroad upon the face of all the earth.

The descendants of Shem

10 ¶ These *are* the generations of Shem: Shem *was* an hundred years old, and begat Arphaxad two years after the flood:

11And Shem lived after he begat Arphaxad five hundred years, and begat sons and daughters.

12And Arphaxad lived five and thirty years, and begat Salah:

13And Arphaxad lived after he begat Salah four hundred and three years, and begat sons and daughters.

Amplified

21To Shem also, the younger brother of Japheth and the ancestor of all the children of Eber [including the Hebrews], children were born.

22The sons of Shem: Elam, Asshur, Arpachshad, Lud, and Aram.

23The sons of Aram: Uz, Hul, Gether, and Mash.

24Arpachshad became the father of Shelah; and Shelah became the father of Eber.

25To Eber were born two sons: the name of one was Peleg [division], because [the inhabitants of] the earth were divided up in his days; and his brother's name was Joktan.

26Joktan became the father of Almodad, Sheleph, Hazarmaveth, Jerah,

27Hadoram, Uzal, Diklah,

28Obal, Abimael, Sheba,

29Ophir, Havilah, and Jobab; all these were the sons of Joktan.

30The territory in which they lived extended from Mesha as one goes toward Sephar to the hill country of the east.

31These are Shem's descendants by their families, their languages, their lands, and their nations.

32These are the families of the sons of Noah, according to their generations, within their nations; and from these the nations spread abroad on the earth after the flood. [Acts 17:26.]

11 AND THE whole earth was of one language and of one accent *and* mode of expression.

2And as they journeyed eastward, they found a plain (valley) in the land of Shinar, and they settled *and* dwelt there.

3And they said one to another, Come, let us make bricks and burn them thoroughly. So they had brick for stone, and slime (bitumen) for mortar.

4And they said, Come, let us build us a city and a tower whose top reaches into the sky, and let us make a name for ourselves, lest we be scattered over the whole earth.

5And the Lord came down to see the city and the tower which the sons of men had built.

6And the Lord said, Behold, they are one people and they have *s*all one language; and this is only the beginning of what they will do, and now nothing they have imagined they can do will be impossible for them.

7Come, let Us go down and there confound (mix up, confuse) their language, that they may not understand one another's speech.

8So the Lord scattered them abroad from that place upon the face of the whole earth, and they gave up building the city.

9Therefore the name of it was called Babel—because there the Lord confounded the language of all the earth; and from that place the Lord scattered them abroad upon the face of the whole earth.

10This is the history of the generations of Shem. Shem was 100 years old when he became the father of Arpachshad, two years after the flood.

11And Shem lived after Arpachshad was born 500 years and had other sons and daughters.

12When Arpachshad had lived 35 years, he became the father of Shelah.

13Arpachshad lived after Shelah was born 403 years and had other sons and daughters.

---

*s*Some noted philologists have declared that a common origin of all languages cannot be denied. One, Max Mueller (*The Science of Language*), said "We have examined all possible forms which language can assume, and now we ask, can we reconcile with these three distinct forms, the radical, the terminational, the inflectional, the admission of one common origin of human speech? I answer decidedly, 'Yes'." *The New Bible Commentary* says, "The original unity of human language, though still far from demonstrable, becomes increasingly probable."

---

*k*Heb. *Arpachshad*   *l*Heb. *Shelah*   *m*i.e. *Division*   *n*Heb. *lip*   *o*Heb. *words*   *p*Or, *eastward*   *q*Heb. *a man said to his neighbour*   *r*Heb. *burn them to a burning*   *s*i.e. *Confusion*

New American Standard

21 ¶ Also to Shem, the father of all the children of Eber, *and* the older brother of Japheth, children were born.
22 The sons of Shem *were* Elam and Asshur and Arpachshad and Lud and Aram.
23 The sons of Aram *were* Uz and Hul and Gether and Mash.
24 Arpachshad became the father of Shelah; and Shelah became the father of Eber.
25 Two sons were born to Eber; the name of the one *was* Peleg, for in his days the earth was divided; and his brother's name *was* Joktan.
26 Joktan became the father of Almodad and Sheleph and Hazarmaveth and Jerah
27 and Hadoram and Uzal and Diklah
28 and Obal and Abimael and Sheba
29 and Ophir and Havilah and Jobab; all these were the sons of Joktan.
30 Now their settlement extended from Mesha as you go toward Sephar, the hill country of the east.
31 These are the sons of Shem, according to their families, according to their languages, by their lands, according to their nations.
32 ¶ These are the families of the sons of Noah, according to their genealogies, by their nations; and out of these the nations were separated on the earth after the flood.

Universal Language, Babel, Confusion

11 NOW THE whole earth used the same language and the same words.
2 It came about as they journeyed east, that they found a plain in the land of Shinar and settled there.
3 They said to one another, "Come, let us make bricks and burn *them* thoroughly." And they used brick for stone, and they used tar for mortar.
4 They said, "Come, let us build for ourselves a city, and a tower whose top *will reach* into heaven, and let us make for ourselves a name, otherwise we will be scattered abroad over the face of the whole earth."
5 The LORD came down to see the city and the tower which the sons of men had built.
6 The LORD said, "Behold, they are one people, and they all have the same language. And this is what they began to do, and now nothing which they purpose to do will be impossible for them.
7 "Come, let Us go down and there confuse their language, so that they will not understand one another's speech."
8 So the LORD scattered them abroad from there over the face of the whole earth; and they stopped building the city.
9 Therefore its name was called *m*Babel, because there the LORD confused the language of the whole earth; and from there the LORD scattered them abroad over the face of the whole earth.

Descendants of Shem

10 ¶ These are *the records of* the generations of Shem. Shem was one hundred years old, and became the father of Arpachshad two years after the flood;
11 and Shem lived five hundred years after he became the father of Arpachshad, and he had *other* sons and daughters.
12 ¶ Arpachshad lived thirty-five years, and became the father of Shelah;
13 and Arpachshad lived four hundred and three years after he became the father of Shelah, and he had *other* sons and daughters.

m Or *Babylon;* cf Heb *balal,* confuse

New International

The Semites

21 Sons were also born to Shem, whose older brother was[a] Japheth; Shem was the ancestor of all the sons of Eber.
22 The sons of Shem:
Elam, Asshur, Arphaxad, Lud and Aram.
23 The sons of Aram:
Uz, Hul, Gether and Meshech.[b]
24 Arphaxad was the father of[c] Shelah,
and Shelah the father of Eber.
25 Two sons were born to Eber:
One was named Peleg,[d] because in his time the earth was divided; his brother was named Joktan.
26 Joktan was the father of
Almodad, Sheleph, Hazarmaveth, Jerah, 27 Hadoram, Uzal, Diklah, 28 Obal, Abimael, Sheba, 29 Ophir, Havilah and Jobab. All these were sons of Joktan.
30 The region where they lived stretched from Mesha toward Sephar, in the eastern hill country.
31 These are the sons of Shem by their clans and languages, in their territories and nations.
32 These are the clans of Noah's sons, according to their lines of descent, within their nations. From these the nations spread out over the earth after the flood.

The Tower of Babel

11 NOW THE whole world had one language and a common speech. 2 As men moved eastward,[e] they found a plain in Shinar[f] and settled there.
3 They said to each other, "Come, let's make bricks and bake them thoroughly." They used brick instead of stone, and tar for mortar. 4 Then they said, "Come, let us build ourselves a city, with a tower that reaches to the heavens, so that we may make a name for ourselves and not be scattered over the face of the whole earth."
5 But the LORD came down to see the city and the tower that the men were building. 6 The LORD said, "If as one people speaking the same language they have begun to do this, then nothing they plan to do will be impossible for them. 7 Come, let us go down and confuse their language so they will not understand each other."
8 So the LORD scattered them from there over all the earth, and they stopped building the city. 9 That is why it was called Babel[g]—because there the LORD confused the language of the whole world. From there the LORD scattered them over the face of the whole earth.

From Shem to Abram

10 This is the account of Shem.

Two years after the flood, when Shem was 100 years old, he became the father[h] of Arphaxad. 11 And after he became the father of Arphaxad, Shem lived 500 years and had other sons and daughters.
12 When Arphaxad had lived 35 years, he became the father of Shelah. 13 And after he became the father of Shelah, Arphaxad lived 403 years and had other sons and daughters.[i]

---

a 21 Or *Shem, the older brother of* *b* 23 See Septuagint and 1 Chron. 1:17; Hebrew *Mash* *c* 24 Hebrew; Septuagint *father of Cainan, and Cainan was the father of* *d* 25 *Peleg* means *division.* *e* 2 Or *from the east*; or *in the east* *f* 2 That is, Babylonia *g* 9 That is, Babylon; *Babel* sounds like the Hebrew for *confused.* *h* 10 *Father* may mean *ancestor*; also in verses 11-25. *i* 12,13 Hebrew; Septuagint (see also Luke 3:35, 36 and note at Gen. 10:24) *35 years, he became the father of Cainan.* 13 *And after he became the father of Cainan, Arphaxad lived 430 years and had other sons and daughters, and then he died. When Cainan had lived 130 years, he became the father of Shelah. And after he became the father of Shelah, Cainan lived 330 years and had other sons and daughters*

King James

14And Salah lived thirty years, and begat Eber:

15And Salah lived after he begat Eber four hundred and three years, and begat sons and daughters.

16And Eber lived four and thirty years, and begat Peleg:

17And Eber lived after he begat Peleg four hundred and thirty years, and begat sons and daughters.

18And Peleg lived thirty years, and begat Reu:

19And Peleg lived after he begat Reu two hundred and nine years, and begat sons and daughters.

20And Reu lived two and thirty years, and begat Serug:

21And Reu lived after he begat Serug two hundred and seven years, and begat sons and daughters.

22And Serug lived thirty years, and begat Nahor:

23And Serug lived after he begat Nahor two hundred years, and begat sons and daughters.

24And Nahor lived nine and twenty years, and begat Terah:

25And Nahor lived after he begat Terah an hundred and nineteen years, and begat sons and daughters.

26And Terah lived seventy years, and begat Abram, Nahor, and Haran.

27 ¶ Now these *are* the generations of Terah: Terah begat Abram, Nahor, and Haran; and Haran begat Lot.

28And Haran died before his father Terah in the land of his nativity, in Ur of the Chaldees.

29And Abram and Nahor took them wives: the name of Abram's wife *was* Sarai; and the name of Nahor's wife, Milcah, the daughter of Haran, the father of Milcah, and the father of Iscah.

30But Sarai was barren; she *had* no child.

31And Terah took Abram his son, and Lot the son of Haran his son's son, and Sarai his daughter-in-law, his son Abram's wife; and they went forth with them from Ur of the Chaldees, to go into the land of Canaan; and they came unto Haran, and dwelt there.

32And the days of Terah were two hundred and five years: and Terah died in Haran.

The call of Abram

12 NOW THE Lord had said unto Abram, Get thee out of thy country, and from thy kindred, and from thy father's house, unto a land that I will show thee:

Amplified

14When Shelah had lived 30 years, he became the father of Eber.

15Shelah lived after Eber was born 403 years and had other sons and daughters.

16When Eber had lived 34 years, he became the father of Peleg.

17And Eber lived after Peleg was born 430 years and had other sons and daughters.

18When Peleg had lived 30 years, he became the father of Reu.

19And Peleg lived after Reu was born 209 years and had other sons and daughters.

20When Reu had lived 32 years, he became the father of Serug.

21And Reu lived after Serug was born 207 years and had other sons and daughters.

22When Serug had lived 30 years, he became the father of Nahor.

23And Serug lived after Nahor was born 200 years and had other sons and daughters.

24When Nahor had lived 29 years, he became the father of Terah.

25And Nahor lived after Terah was born 119 years and had other sons and daughters.

26After Terah had lived 70 years, he became the father of [at different times], ʳAbram and Nahor and Haran, [his firstborn].

27Now this is the history of the descendants of Terah. Terah was the father of Abram, Nahor, and Haran; and Haran was the father of Lot.

28Haran died before his father Terah [died] in the land of his birth, in ᵘUr of the Chaldees.

29And Abram and Nahor took wives. The name of Abram's wife was Sarai, and the name of Nahor's wife was Milcah, the daughter of Haran the father of Milcah and Iscah.

30But Sarai was barren; she had no child.

31And Terah took Abram his son, Lot the son of Haran, his grandson, and Sarai his daughter-in-law, his son Abram's wife, and they went forth together to go from Ur of the Chaldees into the land of Canaan; but when they came to Haran, they settled there.

32And Terah lived 205 years; and Terah died in Haran.

12 NOW [IN Haran] the Lord said to Abram, Go for yourself [for your own advantage] away from your country, from your relatives and your father's house, to the land that I will show you. [Heb. 11:8–10.]

ʳAbram is only mentioned first by way of dignity. Noah's sons also are given as "Shem, Ham, and Japheth" in Gen. 5:32, although Shem was not the oldest, but for dignity is named first, as is Abram here (Adam Clarke, *The Holy Bible with A Commentary*).
ᵘAbram's home town was Ur of the Chaldees. As the result of extensive archaeological excavations there by C. Leonard Woolley in 1922-34, a great deal is known about Abram's background. Space will not permit more than a glimpse at excavated Ur, but a few items will show the high state of civilization. The entire house of the average middle-class person had from ten to twenty rooms and measured forty to fifty-two feet; the lower floor was for servants, the upper floor for the family, with five rooms for their use; additionally, there was a guest chamber and a lavatory reserved for visitors, and a private chapel. A school was found and what the students studied was shown by the clay tablets discovered there. In the days of Abram the pupils had reading, writing, and arithmetic as today. They learned the multiplication and division tables and even worked at square and cube root. A bill of lading of about 2040 B.C. (about the era in which Abram is believed to have lived) showed that the commerce of that time was far-reaching. Even the name "Abraham" has been found on the excavated clay tablets (J.P. Free, *Archaeology and Bible History*).

New American Standard

14 ¶ Shelah lived thirty years, and became the father of Eber;

15 and Shelah lived four hundred and three years after he became the father of Eber, and he had *other* sons and daughters.

16 ¶ Eber lived thirty-four years, and became the father of Peleg;

17 and Eber lived four hundred and thirty years after he became the father of Peleg, and he had *other* sons and daughters.

18 ¶ Peleg lived thirty years, and became the father of Reu;

19 and Peleg lived two hundred and nine years after he became the father of Reu, and he had *other* sons and daughters.

20 ¶ Reu lived thirty-two years, and became the father of Serug;

21 and Reu lived two hundred and seven years after he became the father of Serug, and he had *other* sons and daughters.

22 ¶ Serug lived thirty years, and became the father of Nahor;

23 and Serug lived two hundred years after he became the father of Nahor, and he had *other* sons and daughters.

24 ¶ Nahor lived twenty-nine years, and became the father of Terah;

25 and Nahor lived one hundred and nineteen years after he became the father of Terah, and he had *other* sons and daughters.

26 ¶ Terah lived seventy years, and became the father of Abram, Nahor and Haran.

27 ¶ Now these are *the records of* the generations of Terah. Terah became the father of Abram, Nahor and Haran; and Haran became the father of Lot.

28 Haran died in the presence of his father Terah in the land of his birth, in Ur of the Chaldeans.

29 Abram and Nahor took wives for themselves. The name of Abram's wife was Sarai; and the name of Nahor's wife was Milcah, the daughter of Haran, the father of Milcah and Iscah.

30 Sarai was barren; she had no child.

31 ¶ Terah took Abram his son, and Lot the son of Haran, his grandson, and Sarai his daughter-in-law, his son Abram's wife; and they went out together from Ur of the Chaldeans in order to enter the land of Canaan; and they went as far as Haran, and settled there.

32 The days of Terah were two hundred and five years; and Terah died in Haran.

Abram Journeys to Egypt

12 NOW THE LORD said to Abram,
　　　"Go forth from your country,
And from your relatives
And from your father's house,
To the land which I will show you;

New International

14When Shelah had lived 30 years, he became the father of Eber. 15And after he became the father of Eber, Shelah lived 403 years and had other sons and daughters.

16When Eber had lived 34 years, he became the father of Peleg. 17And after he became the father of Peleg, Eber lived 430 years and had other sons and daughters.

18When Peleg had lived 30 years, he became the father of Reu. 19And after he became the father of Reu, Peleg lived 209 years and had other sons and daughters.

20When Reu had lived 32 years, he became the father of Serug. 21And after he became the father of Serug, Reu lived 207 years and had other sons and daughters.

22When Serug had lived 30 years, he became the father of Nahor. 23And after he became the father of Nahor, Serug lived 200 years and had other sons and daughters.

24When Nahor had lived 29 years, he became the father of Terah. 25And after he became the father of Terah, Nahor lived 119 years and had other sons and daughters.

26After Terah had lived 70 years, he became the father of Abram, Nahor and Haran.

27This is the account of Terah.

Terah became the father of Abram, Nahor and Haran. And Haran became the father of Lot. 28While his father Terah was still alive, Haran died in Ur of the Chaldeans, in the land of his birth. 29Abram and Nahor both married. The name of Abram's wife was Sarai, and the name of Nahor's wife was Milcah; she was the daughter of Haran, the father of both Milcah and Iscah. 30Now Sarai was barren; she had no children.

31Terah took his son Abram, his grandson Lot son of Haran, and his daughter-in-law Sarai, the wife of his son Abram, and together they set out from Ur of the Chaldeans to go to Canaan. But when they came to Haran, they settled there.

32Terah lived 205 years, and he died in Haran.

The Call of Abram

12 THE LORD had said to Abram, "Leave your country, your people and your father's household and go to the land I will show you.

King James

Amplified

²And I will make of thee a great nation, and I will bless thee, and make thy name great; and thou shalt be a blessing:

³And I will bless them that bless thee, and curse him that curseth thee: and in thee shall all families of the earth be blessed.

⁴So Abram departed, as the LORD had spoken unto him; and Lot went with him: and Abram *was* seventy and five years old when he departed out of Haran.

⁵And Abram took Sarai his wife, and Lot his brother's son, and all their substance that they had gathered, and the souls that they had gotten in Haran; and they went forth to go into the land of Canaan; and into the land of Canaan they came.

⁶ ¶ And Abram passed through the land unto the place of Sichem, unto the plain of Moreh. And the Canaanite *was* then in the land.

⁷And the LORD appeared unto Abram, and said, Unto thy seed will I give this land: and there builded he an altar unto the LORD, who appeared unto him.

⁸And he removed from thence unto a mountain on the east of Beth-el, and pitched his tent, *having* Beth-el on the west, and Hai on the east: and there he builded an altar unto the LORD, and called upon the name of the LORD.

⁹And Abram journeyed, *ᵗ*going on still toward the south.

Abram goes to Egypt

¹⁰ ¶ And there was a famine in the land: and Abram went down into Egypt to sojourn there; for the famine *was* grievous in the land.

¹¹And it came to pass, when he was come near to enter into Egypt, that he said unto Sarai his wife, Behold now, I know that thou *art* a fair woman to look upon:

¹²Therefore it shall come to pass, when the Egyptians shall see thee, that they shall say, This *is* his wife: and they will kill me, but they will save thee alive.

¹³Say, I pray thee, thou *art* my sister: that it may be well with me for thy sake; and my soul shall live because of thee.

¹⁴ ¶ And it came to pass, that, when Abram was come into Egypt, the Egyptians beheld the woman that she *was* very fair.

¹⁵The princes also of Pharaoh saw her, and commended her before Pharaoh: and the woman was taken into Pharaoh's house.

¹⁶And he entreated Abram well for her sake: and he had sheep, and oxen, and he asses, and menservants, and maidservants, and she asses, and camels.

¹⁷And the LORD plagued Pharaoh and his house with great plagues because of Sarai Abram's wife.

¹⁸And Pharaoh called Abram, and said, What *is* this *that* thou hast done unto me? why didst thou not tell me that she *was* thy wife?

²And I will make of you a great nation, and I will bless you [with abundant increase of favors] and make your name famous *and* distinguished, and you will be a blessing [dispensing good to others].

³And I will bless those who bless you [who confer prosperity or happiness upon you] and ᵛcurse him who curses *or* uses insolent language toward you; in you will all the families *and* kindred of the earth be blessed [and by you they will bless themselves]. [Gal. 3:8.]

⁴So Abram departed, as the Lord had directed him; and Lot [his nephew] went with him. Abram was seventy-five years old when he left Haran.

⁵Abram took Sarai his wife, and Lot his brother's son, and all their possessions that they had gathered, and the persons [servants] that they had acquired in Haran, and they went forth to go to the land of Canaan. When they came to the land of Canaan,

⁶Abram passed through the land to the locality of Shechem, to the oak *or* terebinth tree of Moreh. And the Canaanite was then in the land.

⁷Then the Lord appeared to Abram and said, I will give this land to your posterity. So Abram built an altar there to the Lord, Who had appeared to him.

⁸From there he pulled up [his tent pegs] *and* departed to the mountain on the east of Bethel and pitched his tent, with Bethel on the west and Ai on the east; and there he built an altar to the Lord and called upon the name of the Lord.

⁹Abram journeyed on, still going toward the South (the Negeb).

¹⁰Now there was a famine in the land, and Abram ʷwent down into Egypt to live temporarily, for the famine in the land was oppressive (intense and grievous).

¹¹And when he was about to enter into Egypt, he said to Sarai his wife, I know that you are beautiful to behold.

¹²So when the Egyptians see you, they will say, This is his wife; and they will kill me, but they will let you live.

¹³Say, I beg of you, that you are ˣmy sister, so that it may go well with me for your sake and my life will be spared because of you.

¹⁴And when Abram came into Egypt, the Egyptians saw that the woman was very beautiful.

¹⁵The princes of Pharaoh also saw her and commended her to Pharaoh, and she was taken into Pharaoh's house [harem].

¹⁶And he treated Abram well for her sake; he acquired sheep, oxen, he-donkeys, menservants, maidservants, she-donkeys, and ʸcamels.

¹⁷But the Lord scourged Pharaoh and his household with serious plagues because of Sarai, Abram's wife.

¹⁸And Pharaoh called Abram and said, What is this that you have done to me? Why did you not tell me that she was your wife?

ᵛTo look with disfavor on the Jews was to invite God's displeasure; to treat the Jews offensively was to incur His wrath. But to befriend the Jews was to bring down upon one's head the rewards of a promise that could not be broken.   ʷSome books on archaeology frequently allude to the critical view that strangers could not have come into Egypt in earlier times, quoting Strabo and Diodorus to that effect; but later archaeological discoveries show that people from the region of Palestine and Syria were coming to Egypt in the period of Abraham. This is clearly indicated by a tomb painting at Beni Hassan, dating a little after 2000 B.C. It shows Asiatic Semites who had come to Egypt. Furthermore, the archaeological and historical indications of the coming of the Hyksos into Egypt around 1900 B.C. provided another piece of evidence that strangers could come into that land (J. P. Free, *Abraham in Egypt*).   ˣSarai was Abraham's half sister. They had the same father, but different mothers (Gen. 20:12).   ʸCritics have set aside the statement that Abraham had camels in Egypt as an error. But archaeological evidence, including some twenty objects ranging from the seventh century B.C. to the period before 3000 B.C., proves the authenticity of the Bible record concerning Abraham. It includes not only statuettes, plaques, rock carvings, and drawings representing camels, but also "camel bones, a camel skull, and a camel hair rope" (J. P. Free, *Archaeology and Bible History*).

ᵗHeb. *in going and journeying*

New American Standard

2 And I will make you a great nation,
And I will bless you,
And make your name great;
And so you shall be a blessing;
3 And I will bless those who bless you,
And the one who curses you I will curse.
And in you all the families of the earth will be
blessed."

4 ¶ So Abram went forth as the LORD had spoken to
him; and Lot went with him. Now Abram was seventy-
five years old when he departed from Haran.

5 Abram took Sarai his wife and Lot his nephew, and
all their possessions which they had accumulated, and the
persons which they had acquired in Haran, and they set out
for the land of Canaan; thus they came to the land of
Canaan.

6 Abram passed through the land as far as the site of
Shechem, to the oak of Moreh. Now the Canaanite *was*
then in the land.

7 The LORD appeared to Abram and said, "To your
descendants I will give this land." So he built an altar there
to the LORD who had appeared to him.

8 Then he proceeded from there to the mountain on the
east of Bethel, and pitched his tent, with Bethel on the
west and Ai on the east; and there he built an altar to the
LORD and called upon the name of the LORD.

9 Abram journeyed on, continuing toward the
nNegev.

10 ¶ Now there was a famine in the land; so Abram went
down to Egypt to sojourn there, for the famine was severe
in the land.

11 It came about when he came near to Egypt, that he
said to Sarai his wife, "See now, I know that you are a
beautiful woman;

12 and when the Egyptians see you, they will say, 'This
is his wife'; and they will kill me, but they will let you
live.

13"Please say that you are my sister so that it may go
well with me because of you, and that I may live on
account of you."

14 It came about when Abram came into Egypt, the
Egyptians saw that the woman was very beautiful.

15 Pharaoh's officials saw her and praised her to Pharaoh; and the woman was taken into Pharaoh's house.

16 Therefore he treated Abram well for her sake; and
gave him sheep and oxen and donkeys and male and female servants and female donkeys and camels.

17 ¶ But the LORD struck Pharaoh and his house with
great plagues because of Sarai, Abram's wife,

18 Then Pharaoh called Abram and said, "What is this
you have done to me? Why did you not tell me that she
was your wife?

New International

2"I will make you into a great nation
and I will bless you;
I will make your name great,
and you will be a blessing.
3I will bless those who bless you,
and whoever curses you I will curse;
and all peoples on earth
will be blessed through you."

4So Abram left, as the LORD had told him; and Lot went
with him. Abram was seventy-five years old when he set
out from Haran. 5He took his wife Sarai, his nephew Lot,
all the possessions they had accumulated and the people
they had acquired in Haran, and they set out for the land
of Canaan, and they arrived there.

6Abram traveled through the land as far as the site of the
great tree of Moreh at Shechem. At that time the Canaanites were in the land. 7The LORD appeared to Abram and
said, "To your offspringj I will give this land." So he
built an altar there to the LORD, who had appeared to him.

8From there he went on toward the hills east of Bethel
and pitched his tent, with Bethel on the west and Ai on the
east. There he built an altar to the LORD and called on the
name of the LORD. 9Then Abram set out and continued
toward the Negev.

Abram in Egypt

10Now there was a famine in the land, and Abram went
down to Egypt to live there for a while because the famine
was severe. 11As he was about to enter Egypt, he said to
his wife Sarai, "I know what a beautiful woman you are.
12When the Egyptians see you, they will say, 'This is his
wife.' Then they will kill me but will let you live. 13Say
you are my sister, so that I will be treated well for your
sake and my life will be spared because of you."

14When Abram came to Egypt, the Egyptians saw that
she was a very beautiful woman. 15And when Pharaoh's
officials saw her, they praised her to Pharaoh, and she was
taken into his palace. 16He treated Abram well for her
sake, and Abram acquired sheep and cattle, male and female donkeys, menservants and maidservants, and camels.

17But the LORD inflicted serious diseases on Pharaoh
and his household because of Abram's wife Sarai. 18So
Pharaoh summoned Abram. "What have you done to me?"
he said. "Why didn't you tell me she was your wife?

---

n I.e. South country   j 7 Or seed

King James

¹⁹Why saidst thou, She *is* my sister? so I might have taken her to me to wife: now therefore behold thy wife, take *her*, and go thy way.

²⁰And Pharaoh commanded *his* men concerning him: and they sent him away, and his wife, and all that he had.

Abram and Lot part

13 AND ABRAM went up out of Egypt, he, and his wife, and all that he had, and Lot with him, into the south.

²And Abram *was* very rich in cattle, in silver, and in gold.

³And he went on his journeys from the south even to Beth-el, unto the place where his tent had been at the beginning, between Beth-el and Hai;

⁴Unto the place of the altar, which he had made there at the first: and there Abram called on the name of the LORD.

⁵ ¶ And Lot also, which went with Abram, had flocks, and herds, and tents.

⁶And the land was not able to bear them, that they might dwell together: for their substance was great, so that they could not dwell together.

⁷And there was a strife between the herdmen of Abram's cattle and the herdmen of Lot's cattle: and the Canaanite and the Perizzite dwelled then in the land.

⁸And Abram said unto Lot, Let there be no strife, I pray thee, between me and thee, and between my herdmen and thy herdmen; for we *be* ^ubrethren.

⁹*Is* not the whole land before thee? separate thyself, I pray thee, from me: if *thou wilt take* the left hand, then I will go to the right; or if *thou depart* to the right hand, then I will go to the left.

¹⁰And Lot lifted up his eyes, and beheld all the plain of Jordan, that it *was* well watered every where, before the LORD destroyed Sodom and Gomorrah, *even* as the garden of the LORD, like the land of Egypt, as thou comest unto Zoar.

¹¹Then Lot chose him all the plain of Jordan; and Lot journeyed east: and they separated themselves the one from the other.

¹²Abram dwelled in the land of Canaan, and Lot dwelled in the cities of the plain, and pitched *his* tent toward Sodom.

¹³But the men of Sodom *were* wicked and sinners before the LORD exceedingly.

¹⁴ ¶ And the LORD said unto Abram, after that Lot was separated from him, Lift up now thine eyes, and look from the place where thou art northward, and southward, and eastward, and westward:

¹⁵For all the land which thou seest, to thee will I give it, and to thy seed for ever.

¹⁶And I will make thy seed as the dust of the earth: so that if a man can number the dust of the earth, *then* shall thy seed also be numbered.

¹⁷Arise, walk through the land in the length of it and in the breadth of it; for I will give it unto thee.

¹⁸Then Abram removed *his* tent, and came and dwelt in the ^vplain of Mamre, which *is* in Hebron, and built there an altar unto the LORD.

The wars of the kings

14 AND IT came to pass in the days of Amraphel king of Shinar, Arioch king of Ellasar, Chedorlaomer king of Elam, and Tidal king of nations;

Amplified

¹⁹Why did you say, She is my sister, so that I took her to be my wife? Now then, here is your wife; take her and get away [from here]!

²⁰And Pharaoh commanded his men concerning him, and they brought him on his way with his wife and all that he had.

13 SO ABRAM went up out of Egypt, he and his wife and all that he had, and Lot with him, into the South [country of Judah, the Negeb].

²Now Abram was extremely rich in livestock and in silver and in gold.

³And he journeyed on from the South [country of Judah, the Negeb] as far as Bethel, to the place where his tent had been at the beginning, between Bethel and Ai,

⁴Where he had built an altar at first; and there Abram called on the name of the Lord. [Gal. 3:6–9.]

⁵But Lot, who went with Abram, also had flocks and herds and tents.

⁶Now the land was not able to nourish *and* support them so they could dwell together, for their possessions were too great for them to live together.

⁷And there was strife between the herdsmen of Abram's cattle and the herdsmen of Lot's cattle. And the Canaanite and the Perizzite were dwelling then in the land [making fodder more difficult to obtain].

⁸So Abram said to Lot, Let there be no strife, I beg of you, between you and me, or between your herdsmen and my herdsmen, for we are relatives.

⁹Is not the whole land before you? Separate yourself, I beg of you, from me. If you take the left hand, then I will go to the right; or if you choose the right hand, then I will go to the left.

¹⁰And Lot looked and saw that everywhere the Jordan Valley was well watered. Before the Lord destroyed Sodom and Gomorrah, [it was all] like the garden of the Lord, like the land of Egypt, as you go to Zoar.

¹¹Then Lot chose for himself all the Jordan Valley and [he] traveled east. So they separated.

¹²Abram dwelt in the land of Canaan, and Lot dwelt in the cities of the [Jordan] Valley and moved his tent as far as Sodom *and* dwelt there.

¹³But the men of Sodom were wicked and exceedingly great sinners against the Lord.

¹⁴The Lord said to Abram after Lot had left him, Lift up now your eyes and look from the place where you are, northward and southward and eastward and westward;

¹⁵For all the land which you see I will give to you and to your posterity forever. [Acts 7:5.]

¹⁶And I will make your descendants like the dust of the earth, so that if a man could count the dust of the earth, then could your descendants also be counted. [Gen. 28:14.]

¹⁷Arise, walk through the land, the length of it and the breadth of it, for I will give it to you.

¹⁸Then Abram moved his tent and came and dwelt among the oaks *or* terebinths of Mamre, which are at Hebron, and built there an altar to the Lord.

14 IN THE days of the kings Amraphel of Shinar, Arioch of Ellasar, Chedorlaomer of Elam, and Tidal of Goiim,

---

^uHeb. *men brethren*   ^vHeb. *plains*

New American Standard

19"Why did you say, 'She is my sister,' so that I took her for my wife? Now then, here is your wife, take her and go."

20 Pharaoh commanded *his* men concerning him; and they escorted him away, with his wife and all that belonged to him.

Abram and Lot

13 SO ABRAM went up from Egypt to the *o*Negev, he and his wife and all that belonged to him, and Lot with him.

2 ¶ Now Abram was very rich in livestock, in silver and in gold.

3 He went on his journeys from the *o*Negev as far as Bethel, to the place where his tent had been at the beginning, between Bethel and Ai,

4 to the place of the altar which he had made there formerly; and there Abram called on the name of the LORD.

5 Now Lot, who went with Abram, also had flocks and herds and tents.

6 And the land could not sustain them while dwelling together, for their possessions were so great that they were not able to remain together.

7 And there was strife between the herdsmen of Abram's livestock and the herdsmen of Lot's livestock. Now the Canaanite and the Perizzite were dwelling then in the land.

8 ¶ So Abram said to Lot, "Please let there be no strife between you and me, nor between my herdsmen and your herdsmen, for we are brothers.

9"Is not the whole land before you? Please separate from me; if *to* the left, then I will go to the right; or if *to* the right, then I will go to the left."

10 Lot lifted up his eyes and saw all the valley of the Jordan, that it was well watered everywhere—*this was* before the LORD destroyed Sodom and Gomorrah—like the garden of the LORD, like the land of Egypt as you go to Zoar.

11 So Lot chose for himself all the valley of the Jordan, and Lot journeyed eastward. Thus they separated from each other.

12 Abram settled in the land of Canaan, while Lot settled in the cities of the valley, and moved his tents as far as Sodom.

13 Now the men of Sodom were wicked exceedingly and sinners against the LORD.

14 ¶ The LORD said to Abram, after Lot had separated from him, "Now lift up your eyes and look from the place where you are, northward and southward and eastward and westward;

15 for all the land which you see, I will give it to you and to your descendants forever.

16"I will make your descendants as the dust of the earth, so that if anyone can number the dust of the earth, then your descendants can also be numbered.

17"Arise, walk about the land through its length and breadth; for I will give it to you."

18 Then Abram moved his tent and came and dwelt by the oaks of Mamre, which are in Hebron, and there he built an altar to the LORD.

War of the Kings

14 AND IT came about in the days of Amraphel king of Shinar, Arioch king of Ellasar, Chedorlaomer king of Elam, and Tidal king of Goiim,

New International

19Why did you say, 'She is my sister,' so that I took her to be my wife? Now then, here is your wife. Take her and go!" 20Then Pharaoh gave orders about Abram to his men, and they sent him on his way, with his wife and everything he had.

Abram and Lot Separate

13 SO ABRAM went up from Egypt to the Negev, with his wife and everything he had, and Lot went with him. 2Abram had become very wealthy in livestock and in silver and gold.

3From the Negev he went from place to place until he came to Bethel, to the place between Bethel and Ai where his tent had been earlier 4and where he had first built an altar. There Abram called on the name of the LORD.

5Now Lot, who was moving about with Abram, also had flocks and herds and tents. 6But the land could not support them while they stayed together, for their possessions were so great that they were not able to stay together. 7And quarreling arose between Abram's herdsmen and the herdsmen of Lot. The Canaanites and Perizzites were also living in the land at that time.

8So Abram said to Lot, "Let's not have any quarreling between you and me, or between your herdsmen and mine, for we are brothers. 9Is not the whole land before you? Let's part company. If you go to the left, I'll go to the right; if you go to the right, I'll go to the left."

10Lot looked up and saw that the whole plain of the Jordan was well watered, like the garden of the LORD, like the land of Egypt, toward Zoar. (This was before the LORD destroyed Sodom and Gomorrah.) 11So Lot chose for himself the whole plain of the Jordan and set out toward the east. The two men parted company: 12Abram lived in the land of Canaan, while Lot lived among the cities of the plain and pitched his tents near Sodom. 13Now the men of Sodom were wicked and were sinning greatly against the LORD.

14The LORD said to Abram after Lot had parted from him, "Lift up your eyes from where you are and look north and south, east and west. 15All the land that you see I will give to you and your offspring*k* forever. 16I will make your offspring like the dust of the earth, so that if anyone could count the dust, then your offspring could be counted. 17Go, walk through the length and breadth of the land, for I am giving it to you."

18So Abram moved his tents and went to live near the great trees of Mamre at Hebron, where he built an altar to the LORD.

Abram Rescues Lot

14 AT THIS time Amraphel king of Shinar,*l* Arioch king of Ellasar, Kedorlaomer king of Elam and Tidal king of Goiim 2went to war against Bera king of

---

o I.e. South country

k 15 Or *seed*; also in verse 16   *l* 1 That is, Babylonia; also in verse 9

King James

2*That these* made war with Bera king of Sodom, and with Birsha king of Gomorrah, Shinab king of Admah, and Shemeber king of Zeboiim, and the king of Bela, which is Zoar.

3All these were joined together in the vale of Siddim, which is the salt sea.

4Twelve years they served Chedorlaomer, and in the thirteenth year they rebelled.

5And in the fourteenth year came Chedorlaomer, and the kings that *were* with him, and smote the Rephaims in Ashteroth Karnaim, and the Zuzims in Ham, and the Emims in ʷShaveh Kiriathaim,

6And the Horites in their mount Seir, unto ˣEl-paran, which *is* by the wilderness.

7And they returned, and came to En-mishpat, which *is* Kadesh, and smote all the country of the Amalekites, and also the Amorites, that dwelt in Hazezon-tamar.

8And there went out the king of Sodom, and the king of Gomorrah, and the king of Admah, and the king of Zeboiim, and the king of Bela (the same *is* Zoar;) and they joined battle with them in the vale of Siddim;

9With Chedorlaomer the king of Elam, and with Tidal king of nations, and Amraphel king of Shinar, and Arioch king of Ellasar; four kings with five.

10And the vale of Siddim *was full of* slimepits; and the kings of Sodom and Gomorrah fled, and fell there; and they that remained fled to the mountain.

11And they took all the goods of Sodom and Gomorrah, and all their victuals, and went their way.

12And they took Lot, Abram's brother's son, who dwelt in Sodom, and his goods, and departed.

13 ¶ And there came one that had escaped, and told Abram the Hebrew; for he dwelt in the plain of Mamre the Amorite, brother of Eshcol, and brother of Aner: and these *were* confederate with Abram.

14And when Abram heard that his brother was taken captive, he ʸarmed his ᶻtrained *servants,* born in his own house, three hundred and eighteen, and pursued *them* unto Dan.

15And he divided himself against them, he and his servants, by night, and smote them, and pursued them unto Hobah, which *is* on the left hand of Damascus.

16And he brought back all the goods, and also brought again his brother Lot, and his goods, and the women also, and the people.

Melchizedek blesses Abram

17 ¶ And the king of Sodom went out to meet him after his return from the slaughter of Chedorlaomer, and of the kings that *were* with him, at the valley of Shaveh, which *is* the king's dale.

18And Melchizedek king of Salem brought forth bread and wine: and he *was* the priest of the most high God.

19And he blessed him, and said, Blessed *be* Abram of the most high God, possessor of heaven and earth:

20And blessed be the most high God, which hath delivered thine enemies into thy hand. And he gave him tithes of all.

21And the king of Sodom said unto Abram, Give me the ᵃpersons, and take the goods to thyself.

22And Abram said to the king of Sodom, I have lift up mine hand unto the LORD, the most high God, the possessor of heaven and earth,

23That I will not *take* from a thread even to a shoe-latchet, and that I will not take any thing that *is* thine, lest thou shouldest say, I have made Abram rich:

24Save only that which the young men have eaten, and the portion of the men which went with me, Aner, Eshcol, and Mamre; let them take their portion.

Amplified

2They made war on the kings Bera of Sodom, Birsha of Gomorrah, Shinab of Admah, Shemeber of Zeboiim, and the king of Bela, ᶻthat is, Zoar.

3The latter kings joined together [as allies] in the Valley of Siddim, which is [now] the [Dead] Sea of Salt.

4Twelve years they had served Chedorlaomer, but in the thirteenth year they rebelled.

5And in the fourteenth year, Chedorlaomer and the kings who were with him attacked *and* subdued the Rephaim in Ashteroth-karnaim, the Zuzim in Ham, and the Emim in Shaveh-kiriathaim,

6And the Horites in their Mount Seir as far as El-paran, which is on the border of the wilderness.

7Then they turned back and came to En-mishpat, which [now] is Kadesh, and subdued all the country of the Amalekites, and also the Amorites who dwelt in Hazazon-tamar.

8Then the kings of Sodom, Gomorrah, Admah, Zeboiim, and Bela, that is, Zoar, went out and [together] they joined battle [with those kings] in the Valley of Siddim,

9With the kings Chedorlaomer of Elam, Tidal of Goiim, Amraphel of Shinar, and Arioch of Ellasar—four kings against five.

10Now the Valley of Siddim was full of slime *or* bitumen pits, and as the kings of Sodom and Gomorrah fled, they fell (were overthrown) there and the remainder [of the kings] fled to the mountain.

11[The victors] took all the wealth of Sodom and Gomorrah and all the supply of provisions and departed.

12And they also took Lot, Abram's brother's son, who dwelt in Sodom, and his goods away with them.

13Then one who had escaped came and told Abram the Hebrew [one from the other side], who was living by the oaks *or* terebinths of Mamre the Amorite, a brother of Eshcol and of Aner—these were allies of Abram.

14When Abram heard that [his nephew] had been captured, he armed (led forth) the 318 trained servants born in his own house and pursued the enemy as far as Dan.

15He divided his forces against them by night, he and his servants, and attacked *and* routed them, and pursued them as far as Hobah, which is north of Damascus.

16And he brought back all the goods and also brought back his kinsman Lot and his possessions, the women also and the people.

17After his [Abram's] return from the defeat *and* slaying of Chedorlaomer and the kings who were with him, the king of Sodom went out to meet him at the Valley of Shaveh, that is, the King's Valley.

18Melchizedek king of Salem [later called Jerusalem] brought out bread and wine [for their nourishment]; he was the priest of God Most High,

19And he blessed him and said, Blessed (favored with blessings, made blissful, joyful) be Abram by God Most High, Possessor *and* Maker of heaven and earth,

20And blessed, praised, *and* glorified be God Most High, Who has given your foes into your hand! And [Abram] gave him a tenth of all [he had taken]. [Heb. 7:1–10.]

21And the king of Sodom said to Abram, Give me the persons and keep the goods for yourself.

22But Abram said to the king of Sodom, I have lifted up my hand *and* sworn to the Lord, God Most High, the Possessor *and* Maker of heaven and earth,

23That I would not take a thread or a shoelace or anything that is yours, lest you should say, I have made Abram rich.

24[Take all] except only what my young men have eaten and the share of the men [allies] who went with me— Aner, Eshcol, and Mamre; let them take their portion.

ᶻOne of the notable proofs of the antiquity of the early sections of Genesis is that many of the original names of places about which they speak were so old that Moses, the writer, had to add an explanation in order to identify these ancient names so that the Israelites returning from Egypt might recognize them. Chapter 14 alone contains six such explanatory notes (Gen. 14:2, 3, 7, 8, 15, and 17).

ʷOr, *The plain of Kiriathaim*   ˣOr, *The plain of Paran*   ʸOr, *led forth*   ᶻOr, *instructed*   ᵃHeb. *souls*

New American Standard

2 *that* they made war with Bera king of Sodom, and with Birsha king of Gomorrah, Shinab king of Admah, and Shemeber king of Zeboiim, and the king of Bela (that is, Zoar).

3 All these came as allies to the valley of Siddim (that is, the Salt Sea).

4 Twelve years they had served Chedorlaomer, but the thirteenth year they rebelled.

5 In the fourteenth year Chedorlaomer and the kings that were with him, came and defeated the Rephaim in Ashteroth-karnaim and the Zuzim in Ham and the Emim in Shaveh-kiriathaim,

6 and the Horites in their Mount Seir, as far as El-paran, which is by the wilderness.

7 Then they turned back and came to En-mishpat (that is, Kadesh), and conquered all the country of the Amalekites, and also the Amorites, who lived in Hazazon-tamar.

8 And the king of Sodom and the king of Gomorrah and the king of Admah and the king of Zeboiim and the king of Bela (that is, Zoar) came out; and they arrayed for battle against them in the valley of Siddim,

9 against Chedorlaomer king of Elam and Tidal king of Goiim and Amraphel king of Shinar and Arioch king of Ellasar—four kings against five.

10 Now the valley of Siddim was full of tar pits; and the kings of Sodom and Gomorrah fled, and they fell into them. But those who survived fled to the hill country.

11 Then they took all the goods of Sodom and Gomorrah and all their food supply, and departed.

12 They also took Lot, Abram's nephew, and his possessions and departed, for he was living in Sodom.

13 ¶ Then a fugitive came and told Abram the Hebrew. Now he was living by the oaks of Mamre the Amorite, brother of Eshcol and brother of Aner, and these were allies with Abram.

14 When Abram heard that his relative had been taken captive, he led out his trained men, born in his house, three hundred and eighteen, and went in pursuit as far as Dan.

15 He divided his forces against them by night, he and his servants, and defeated them, and pursued them as far as Hobah, which is north of Damascus.

16 He brought back all the goods, and also brought back his relative Lot with his possessions, and also the women, and the people.

God's Promise to Abram

17 ¶ Then after his return from the defeat of Chedorlaomer and the kings who were with him, the king of Sodom went out to meet him at the valley of Shaveh (that is, the King's Valley).

18 And Melchizedek king of Salem brought out bread and wine; now he was a priest of God Most High.

19 He blessed him and said,
"Blessed be Abram of God Most High,
    Possessor of heaven and earth;

20 And blessed be God Most High,
    Who has delivered your enemies into your hand."
He gave him a tenth of all.

21 The king of Sodom said to Abram, "Give the people to me and take the goods for yourself."

22 Abram said to the king of Sodom, "I have sworn to the LORD God Most High, possessor of heaven and earth,

23 that I will not take a thread or a sandal thong or anything that is yours, for fear you would say, 'I have made Abram rich.'

24 "I will take nothing except what the young men have eaten, and the share of the men who went with me, Aner, Eshcol, and Mamre; let them take their share."

New International

Sodom, Birsha king of Gomorrah, Shinab king of Admah, Shemeber king of Zeboiim, and the king of Bela (that is, Zoar). 3All these latter kings joined forces in the Valley of Siddim (the Salt Sea[m]). 4For twelve years they had been subject to Kedorlaomer, but in the thirteenth year they rebelled.

5In the fourteenth year, Kedorlaomer and the kings allied with him went out and defeated the Rephaites in Ashteroth Karnaim, the Zuzites in Ham, the Emites in Shaveh Kiriathaim 6and the Horites in the hill country of Seir, as far as El Paran near the desert. 7Then they turned back and went to En Mishpat (that is, Kadesh), and they conquered the whole territory of the Amalekites, as well as the Amorites who were living in Hazazon Tamar.

8Then the king of Sodom, the king of Gomorrah, the king of Admah, the king of Zeboiim and the king of Bela (that is, Zoar) marched out and drew up their battle lines in the Valley of Siddim 9against Kedorlaomer king of Elam, Tidal king of Goiim, Amraphel king of Shinar and Arioch king of Ellasar—four kings against five. 10Now the Valley of Siddim was full of tar pits, and when the kings of Sodom and Gomorrah fled, some of the men fell into them and the rest fled to the hills. 11The four kings seized all the goods of Sodom and Gomorrah and all their food; then they went away. 12They also carried off Abram's nephew Lot and his possessions, since he was living in Sodom.

13One who had escaped came and reported this to Abram the Hebrew. Now Abram was living near the great trees of Mamre the Amorite, a brother[n] of Eshcol and Aner, all of whom were allied with Abram. 14When Abram heard that his relative had been taken captive, he called out the 318 trained men born in his household and went in pursuit as far as Dan. 15During the night Abram divided his men to attack them and he routed them, pursuing them as far as Hobah, north of Damascus. 16He recovered all the goods and brought back his relative Lot and his possessions, together with the women and the other people.

17After Abram returned from defeating Kedorlaomer and the kings allied with him, the king of Sodom came out to meet him in the Valley of Shaveh (that is, the King's Valley).

18Then Melchizedek king of Salem[o] brought out bread and wine. He was priest of God Most High, 19and he blessed Abram, saying,

"Blessed be Abram by God Most High,
    Creator[p] of heaven and earth.
20And blessed be[q] God Most High,
    who delivered your enemies into your hand."

Then Abram gave him a tenth of everything.

21The king of Sodom said to Abram, "Give me the people and keep the goods for yourself."

22But Abram said to the king of Sodom, "I have raised my hand to the LORD, God Most High, Creator of heaven and earth, and have taken an oath 23that I will accept nothing belonging to you, not even a thread or the thong of a sandal, so that you will never be able to say, 'I made Abram rich.' 24I will accept nothing but what my men have eaten and the share that belongs to the men who went with me—to Aner, Eshcol and Mamre. Let them have their share."

---

m 3 That is, the Dead Sea
o 18 That is, Jerusalem
q 20 Or *And praise be to*
n 13 Or *a relative*; or *an ally*
p 19 Or *Possessor*; also in verse 22

King James

Amplified

The covenant with Abram

15 AFTER THESE things the word of the LORD came unto Abram in a vision, saying, Fear not, Abram: I *am* thy shield, *and* thy exceeding great reward.

²And Abram said, Lord GOD, what wilt thou give me, seeing I go childless, and the steward of my house *is* this Eliezer of Damascus?

³And Abram said, Behold, to me thou hast given no seed: and, lo, one born in my house is mine heir.

⁴And, behold, the word of the LORD *came* unto him, saying, This shall not be thine heir; but he that shall come forth out of thine own bowels shall be thine heir.

⁵And he brought him forth abroad, and said, Look now toward heaven, and tell the stars, if thou be able to number them: and he said unto him, So shall thy seed be.

⁶And he believed in the LORD; and he counted it to him for righteousness.

⁷And he said unto him, I *am* the LORD that brought thee out of Ur of the Chaldees, to give thee this land to inherit it.

⁸And he said, Lord GOD, whereby shall I know that I shall inherit it?

⁹And he said unto him, Take me an heifer of three years old, and a she goat of three years old, and a ram of three years old, and a turtledove, and a young pigeon.

¹⁰And he took unto him all these, and divided them in the midst, and laid each piece one against another: but the birds divided he not.

¹¹And when the fowls came down upon the carcases, Abram drove them away.

¹²And when the sun was going down, a deep sleep fell upon Abram; and, lo, an horror of great darkness fell upon him.

¹³And he said unto Abram, Know of a surety that thy seed shall be a stranger in a land *that is* not theirs, and shall serve them; and they shall afflict them four hundred years;

¹⁴And also that nation, whom they shall serve, will I judge: and afterward shall they come out with great substance.

¹⁵And thou shalt go to thy fathers in peace; thou shalt be buried in a good old age.

¹⁶But in the fourth generation they shall come hither again: for the iniquity of the Amorites *is* not yet full.

¹⁷And it came to pass, that, when the sun went down, and it was dark, behold a smoking furnace, and *b*a burning lamp that passed between those pieces.

¹⁸In the same day the LORD made a covenant with Abram, saying, Unto thy seed have I given this land, from the river of Egypt unto the great river, the river Euphrates:

¹⁹The Kenites, and the Kenizzites, and the Kadmonites,

²⁰And the Hittites, and the Perizzites, and the Rephaims,

²¹And the Amorites, and the Canaanites, and the Girgashites, and the Jebusites.

15 AFTER THESE things, the word of the Lord came to Abram in a vision, saying, Fear not, Abram, I am your *a*Shield, your abundant compensation, *and* your reward shall be exceedingly great.

²And Abram said, Lord God, what can You give me, since I am going on [from this world] childless and he who shall be the owner *and* heir of my house is this [steward] Eliezer of Damascus?

³And Abram continued, Look, You have given me no child; and [a servant] born in my house is my heir.

⁴And behold, the word of the Lord came to him, saying, This man shall not be your heir, but he who shall come from your own body shall be your heir.

⁵And He brought him outside [his tent into the starlight] and said, Look now toward the heavens and count the stars—if you are able to number them. Then He said to him, So shall your descendants be. [Heb. 11:12.]

⁶And he [Abram] believed in (trusted in, relied on, remained steadfast to) the Lord, and He counted it to him as righteousness (right standing with God). [Rom. 4:3, 18–22; Gal. 3:6; James 2:23.]

⁷And He said to him, I am the [same] Lord, Who brought you out of Ur of the Chaldees to give you this land as an inheritance.

⁸But he [Abram] said, Lord God, by what shall I know that I shall inherit it?

⁹And He said to him, Bring to Me a heifer three years old, a she-goat three years old, a ram three years old, a turtledove, and a young pigeon.

¹⁰And he brought Him all these and cut them down the middle [into halves] and laid each half opposite the other; but the birds he did not divide.

¹¹And when the birds of prey swooped down upon the carcasses, Abram drove them away.

¹²When the sun was setting, a deep sleep overcame Abram, and a horror (a terror, a shuddering fear) of great darkness assailed *and* oppressed him.

¹³And [God] said to Abram, Know positively that your descendants will be strangers dwelling as temporary residents in a land that is not theirs [Egypt], and they will be slaves there and will be afflicted *and* oppressed for 400 years. [Fulfilled in Exod. 12:40.]

¹⁴But I will bring judgment on that nation whom they will serve, and afterward they will come out with great possessions. [Acts 7:6, 7.]

¹⁵And you shall go to your fathers in peace; you shall be buried at a good old (hoary) age.

¹⁶And in the *b*fourth generation they [your descendants] shall come back here [to Canaan] again, for the iniquity of the *c*Amorites is not yet full *and* complete. [Josh. 24:15.]

¹⁷When the sun had gone down and a [thick] darkness had come on, behold, a smoking oven and a flaming torch passed between those pieces.

¹⁸On the same day the Lord made a covenant (promise, pledge) with Abram, saying, To your descendants I have given this land, from the river of Egypt to the great river Euphrates—the land of

¹⁹The Kenites, the Kenizzites, the Kadmonites,

²⁰The Hittites, the Perizzites, the Rephaim,

²¹The Amorites, the Canaanites, the Girgashites, and the Jebusites.

---

*a*The reference is to the Lord as Abram's King. *b*This prophecy was literally fulfilled. Moses, for example, who led the Israelites back to Canaan after their 400 years in Egypt, was "in the fourth generation" from Jacob—Levi, Kohath, Amram, Moses. *c*The most important and powerful group of that region. The name "Amorite" later became virtually synonymous with that of the inhabitants of Canaan generally.

*b*Heb. *a lamp of fire*

New American Standard

Abram Promised a Son

15 AFTER THESE things the word of the LORD came to Abram in a vision, saying,
"Do not fear, Abram,
　I am a shield to you;
　Your reward shall be very great."
2 Abram said, "O Lord GOD, what will You give me, since I am childless, and the heir of my house is Eliezer of Damascus?"
3 And Abram said, "Since You have given no offspring to me, one born in my house is my heir."
4 Then behold, the word of the LORD came to him, saying, "This man will not be your heir; but one who will come forth from your own body, he shall be your heir."
5 And He took him outside and said, "Now look toward the heavens, and count the stars, if you are able to count them." And He said to him, "So shall your descendants be."
6 Then he believed in the LORD; and He reckoned it to him as righteousness.
7 And He said to him, "I am the LORD who brought you out of Ur of the Chaldeans, to give you this land to possess it."
8 He said, "O Lord GOD, how may I know that I will possess it?"
9 So He said to him, "Bring Me a three year old heifer, and a three year old female goat, and a three year old ram, and a turtledove, and a young pigeon."
10 Then he brought all these to Him and cut them in two, and laid each half opposite the other; but he did not cut the birds.
11 The birds of prey came down upon the carcasses, and Abram drove them away.
12 ¶ Now when the sun was going down, a deep sleep fell upon Abram; and behold, terror *and* great darkness fell upon him.
13 *God* said to Abram, "Know for certain that your descendants will be strangers in a land that is not theirs, where they will be enslaved and oppressed four hundred years.
14"But I will also judge the nation whom they will serve, and afterward they will come out with many possessions.
15"As for you, you shall go to your fathers in peace; you will be buried at a good old age.
16"Then in the fourth generation they will return here, for the iniquity of the Amorite is not yet complete."
17 ¶ It came about when the sun had set, that it was very dark, and behold, *there appeared* a smoking oven and a flaming torch which passed between these pieces.
18 On that day the LORD made a covenant with Abram, saying,
"To your descendants I have given this land,
　From the river of Egypt as far as the great river,
　　the river Euphrates:
19 the Kenite and the Kenizzite and the Kadmonite
20 and the Hittite and the Perizzite and the Rephaim
21 and the Amorite and the Canaanite and the Girgashite and the Jebusite."

New International

God's Covenant With Abram

15 AFTER THIS, the word of the LORD came to Abram in a vision:
"Do not be afraid, Abram.
　I am your shield,[r]
　your very great reward.[s]"
2But Abram said, "O Sovereign LORD, what can you give me since I remain childless and the one who will inherit[t] my estate is Eliezer of Damascus?" 3And Abram said, "You have given me no children; so a servant in my household will be my heir."
4Then the word of the LORD came to him: "This man will not be your heir, but a son coming from your own body will be your heir." 5He took him outside and said, "Look up at the heavens and count the stars—if indeed you can count them." Then he said to him, "So shall your offspring be."
6Abram believed the LORD, and he credited it to him as righteousness.
7He also said to him, "I am the LORD, who brought you out of Ur of the Chaldeans to give you this land to take possession of it."
8But Abram said, "O Sovereign LORD, how can I know that I will gain possession of it?"
9So the LORD said to him, "Bring me a heifer, a goat and a ram, each three years old, along with a dove and a young pigeon."
10Abram brought all these to him, cut them in two and arranged the halves opposite each other; the birds, however, he did not cut in half. 11Then birds of prey came down on the carcasses, but Abram drove them away.
12As the sun was setting, Abram fell into a deep sleep, and a thick and dreadful darkness came over him. 13Then the LORD said to him, "Know for certain that your descendants will be strangers in a country not their own, and they will be enslaved and mistreated four hundred years. 14But I will punish the nation they serve as slaves, and afterward they will come out with great possessions. 15You, however, will go to your fathers in peace and be buried at a good old age. 16In the fourth generation your descendants will come back here, for the sin of the Amorites has not yet reached its full measure."
17When the sun had set and darkness had fallen, a smoking firepot with a blazing torch appeared and passed between the pieces. 18On that day the LORD made a covenant with Abram and said, "To your descendants I give this land, from the river[u] of Egypt to the great river, the Euphrates— 19the land of the Kenites, Kenizzites, Kadmonites, 20Hittites, Perizzites, Rephaites, 21Amorites, Canaanites, Girgashites and Jebusites."

---

r 1 Or *sovereign*　　*s* 1 Or *shield; I your reward will be very great*
t 2 The meaning of the Hebrew for this phrase is uncertain.
u 18 Or *Wadi*

King James	Amplified

Hagar and Ishmael

16 NOW SARAI Abram's wife bare him no children: and she had an handmaid, an Egyptian, whose name *was* Hagar.

2And Sarai said unto Abram, Behold now, the LORD hath restrained me from bearing: I pray thee, go in unto my maid; it may be that I may ᶜobtain children by her. And Abram hearkened to the voice of Sarai.

3And Sarai Abram's wife took Hagar her maid the Egyptian, after Abram had dwelt ten years in the land of Canaan, and gave her to her husband Abram to be his wife.

4 ¶ And he went in unto Hagar, and she conceived: and when she saw that she had conceived, her mistress was despised in her eyes.

5And Sarai said unto Abram, My wrong *be* upon thee: I have given my maid into thy bosom; and when she saw that she had conceived, I was despised in her eyes: the LORD judge between me and thee.

6But Abram said unto Sarai, Behold, thy maid *is* in thy hand; do to her ᵈas it pleaseth thee. And when Sarai ᵉdealt hardly with her, she fled from her face.

7 ¶ And the angel of the LORD found her by a fountain of water in the wilderness, by the fountain in the way to Shur.

8And he said, Hagar, Sarai's maid, whence camest thou? and whither wilt thou go? And she said, I flee from the face of my mistress Sarai.

9And the angel of the LORD said unto her, Return to thy mistress, and submit thyself under her hands.

10And the angel of the LORD said unto her, I will multiply thy seed exceedingly, that it shall not be numbered for multitude.

11And the angel of the LORD said unto her, Behold, thou *art* with child, and shalt bear a son, and shalt call his name ᶠIshmael; because the LORD hath heard thy affliction.

12And he will be a wild man; his hand *will be* against every man, and every man's hand against him; and he shall dwell in the presence of all his brethren.

13And she called the name of the LORD that spake unto her, Thou God seest me: for she said, Have I also here looked after him that seeth me?

14Wherefore the well was called ᵍBeer-lahai-roi; behold, *it is* between Kadesh and Bered.

16 NOW SARAI, Abram's wife, had borne him no children. She had an Egyptian maid whose name was Hagar.

2And Sarai said to Abram, See here, the Lord has restrained me from bearing [children]. I am asking you to have intercourse with my maid; it may be that I can obtain children by her. And Abram listened to *and* heeded what Sarai said.

3So Sarai, Abram's wife, took Hagar her Egyptian maid, after Abram had dwelt ten years in the land of Canaan, and gave her to her husband Abram to be his [secondary] wife.

4And he had intercourse with Hagar, and she became pregnant; and when she saw that she was with child, she looked with contempt upon her mistress *and* despised her.

5Then Sarai said to Abram, May [the responsibility for] my wrong *and* deprivation of rights be upon you! I gave my maid into your bosom, and when she saw that she was with child, I was contemptible *and* despised in her eyes. May the Lord be the judge between you and me.

6But Abram said to Sarai, See here, your maid is in your hands *and* power; do as you please with her. And when Sarai dealt severely with her, humbling *and* afflicting her, she [Hagar] fled from her.

7But ᵈthe Angel of the Lord found her by a spring of water in the wilderness on the road to Shur.

8And He said, Hagar, Sarai's maid, where did you come from, and where are you intending to go? And she said, I am running away from my mistress Sarai.

9The Angel of the Lord said to her, Go back to your mistress and [humbly] submit to her control.

10Also the Angel of the Lord said to her, I will multiply your descendants exceedingly, so that they shall not be numbered for multitude.

11And the Angel of the Lord continued, See now, you are with child and shall bear a son, and shall call his name Ishmael [God hears], because the Lord has heard *and* paid attention to your affliction.

12And he [Ishmael] will be as a ᵉwild ass among men; his hand will be against every man and every man's hand against him, and he will live to the east *and* on the borders of all his kinsmen.

13So she called the name of the Lord Who spoke to her, You are a God of seeing, for she said, Have I [not] even here [in the wilderness] looked upon Him Who sees me [and lived]? *Or* have I here also seen [the future purposes or designs of] Him Who sees me?

14Therefore the well was called Beer-lahai-roi [A well to the Living One Who sees me]; it is ᶠbetween Kadesh and Bered.

ᵈ"The Angel of the Lord" or "of God," or "of His presence" is readily identified with the Lord God (Gen. 16:11, 13; 22:11, 12; 31:11, 13; Exod. 3:1-6 and other passages). But it is obvious that the "Angel of the Lord" is a distinct person in Himself from God the Father (Gen. 24:7; Exod. 23:20; Zech. 1:12, 13 and other passages). Nor does the "Angel of the Lord" appear again after Christ came in human form. He must of necessity be One of the "three-in-one" Godhead. The "Angel of the Lord" is the visible Lord God of the Old Testament, as Jesus Christ is of the New Testament. Thus His deity is clearly portrayed in the Old Testament. *The Cambridge Bible* observes, "There is a fascinating forecast of the coming Messiah, breaking through the dimness with amazing consistency, at intervals from Genesis to Malachi. Abraham, Moses, the slave girl Hagar, the impoverished farmer Gideon, even the humble parents of Samson, had seen and talked with Him centuries before the herald angels proclaimed His birth in Bethlehem." ᵉ"Nothing can be more descriptive of the wandering, lawless, freebooting life of the Arabs than this. From the beginning to the present they have kept their independence, and God preserves them as a lasting monument of His providential care and an incontestable argument of the truth of divine revelation. Had the books of Moses no other proof of their divine origin, the account of Ishmael and the prophecy concerning his descendants during a period of nearly 4,000 years would be sufficient. To attempt to refute it would be a most ridiculous presumption and folly" (Adam Clarke, *The Holy Bible with A Commentary*). ᶠThis, "it is between Kadesh and Bered," is further proof of the antiquity of the original names, since the place had to be identified to the reader in the time of Moses.

ᶜHeb. *be builded by her*   ᵈHeb. *that which is good in thine eyes*   ᵉHeb. *afflicted her*   ᶠi.e. *God shall hear*   ᵍi.e. *The well of him that liveth and seeth me*

New American Standard

Sarai and Hagar

16 NOW SARAI, Abram's wife had borne him no *children,* and she had an Egyptian maid whose name was Hagar.

2 So Sarai said to Abram, "Now behold, the LORD has prevented me from bearing *children.* Please go in to my maid; perhaps I will obtain children through her." And Abram listened to the voice of Sarai.

3 After Abram had lived ten years in the land of Canaan, Abram's wife Sarai took Hagar the Egyptian, her maid, and gave her to her husband Abram as his wife.

4 He went in to Hagar, and she conceived; and when she saw that she had conceived, her mistress was despised in her sight.

5 And Sarai said to Abram, "May the wrong done me be upon you. I gave my maid into your arms, but when she saw that she had conceived, I was despised in her sight. May the LORD judge between you and me."

6 But Abram said to Sarai, "Behold, your maid is in your power; do to her what is good in your sight." So Sarai treated her harshly, and she fled from her presence.

7 ¶ Now the angel of the LORD found her by a spring of water in the wilderness, by the spring on the way to Shur.

8 He said, "Hagar, Sarai's maid, where have you come from and where are you going?" And she said, "I am fleeing from the presence of my mistress Sarai."

9 Then the angel of the LORD said to her, "Return to your mistress, and submit yourself to her authority."

10 Moreover, the angel of the LORD said to her, "I will greatly multiply your descendants so that they will be too many to count."

11 The angel of the LORD said to her further,
"Behold, you are with child,
And you will bear a son;
And you shall call his name *p*Ishmael,
Because the LORD has given heed to your affliction.

12 "He will be a wild donkey of a man,
His hand *will be* against everyone,
And everyone's hand *will be* against him;
And he will live to the east of all his brothers."

13 Then she called the name of the LORD who spoke to her, "You are a God who sees"; for she said, "Have I even remained alive here after seeing Him?"

14 Therefore the well was called *q*Beer-lahai-roi; behold, it is between Kadesh and Bered.

New International

Hagar and Ishmael

16 NOW SARAI, Abram's wife, had borne him no children. But she had an Egyptian maidservant named Hagar; 2so she said to Abram, "The LORD has kept me from having children. Go, sleep with my maidservant; perhaps I can build a family through her."

Abram agreed to what Sarai said. 3So after Abram had been living in Canaan ten years, Sarai his wife took her Egyptian maidservant Hagar and gave her to her husband to be his wife. 4He slept with Hagar, and she conceived.

When she knew she was pregnant, she began to despise her mistress. 5Then Sarai said to Abram, "You are responsible for the wrong I am suffering. I put my servant in your arms, and now that she knows she is pregnant, she despises me. May the LORD judge between you and me."

6"Your servant is in your hands," Abram said. "Do with her whatever you think best." Then Sarai mistreated Hagar; so she fled from her.

7The angel of the LORD found Hagar near a spring in the desert; it was the spring that is beside the road to Shur. 8And he said, "Hagar, servant of Sarai, where have you come from, and where are you going?"

"I'm running away from my mistress Sarai," she answered.

9Then the angel of the LORD told her, "Go back to your mistress and submit to her." 10The angel added, "I will so increase your descendants that they will be too numerous to count."

11The angel of the LORD also said to her:

"You are now with child
and you will have a son.
You shall name him Ishmael,*v*
for the LORD has heard of your misery.
12He will be a wild donkey of a man;
his hand will be against everyone
and everyone's hand against him,
and he will live in hostility
toward*w* all his brothers."

13She gave this name to the LORD who spoke to her: "You are the God who sees me," for she said, "I have now seen*x* the One who sees me." 14That is why the well was called Beer Lahai Roi*y*; it is still there, between Kadesh and Bered.

---

p I.e. God hears   *q* I.e. the well of the living one who sees me

v 11 Ishmael means *God hears.*   *w 12 Or live to the east / of*
x 13 Or seen the back of   *y 14 Beer Lahai Roi* means *well of the Living One who sees me.*

King James

¹⁵ ¶ And Hagar bare Abram a son: and Abram called his son's name, which Hagar bare, Ishmael.

¹⁶And Abram *was* fourscore and six years old, when Hagar bare Ishmael to Abram.

The covenant of circumcision

17 AND WHEN Abram was ninety years old and nine, the LORD appeared to Abram, and said unto him, I *am* the Almighty God; walk before me, and be thou ^hperfect.

²And I will make my covenant between me and thee, and will multiply thee exceedingly.

³And Abram fell on his face: and God talked with him, saying,

⁴As for me, behold, my covenant *is* with thee, and thou shalt be a father of ⁱmany nations.

⁵Neither shall thy name any more be called Abram, but thy name shall be ^jAbraham; for a father of many nations have I made thee.

⁶And I will make thee exceeding fruitful, and I will make nations of thee, and kings shall come out of thee.

⁷And I will establish my covenant between me and thee and thy seed after thee in their generations for an everlasting covenant, to be a God unto thee, and to thy seed after thee.

⁸And I will give unto thee, and to thy seed after thee, the land ^kwherein thou art a stranger, all the land of Canaan, for an everlasting possession; and I will be their God.

⁹ ¶ And God said unto Abraham, Thou shalt keep my covenant therefore, thou, and thy seed after thee in their generations.

¹⁰This *is* my covenant, which ye shall keep, between me and you and thy seed after thee; Every man child among you shall be circumcised.

¹¹And ye shall circumcise the flesh of your foreskin; and it shall be a token of the covenant betwixt me and you.

¹²And ^lhe that is eight days old shall be circumcised among you, every man child in your generations, he that is born in the house, or bought with money of any stranger, which *is* not of thy seed.

¹³He that is born in thy house, and he that is bought with thy money, must needs be circumcised: and my covenant shall be in your flesh for an everlasting covenant.

¹⁴And the uncircumcised man child whose flesh of his foreskin is not circumcised, that soul shall be cut off from his people; he hath broken my covenant.

¹⁵ ¶ And God said unto Abraham, As for Sarai thy wife, thou shalt not call her name Sarai, but ^mSarah *shall* her name *be*.

¹⁶And I will bless her, and give thee a son also of her: yea, I will bless her, and ⁿshe shall be *a mother* of nations; kings of people shall be of her.

¹⁷Then Abraham fell upon his face, and laughed, and said in his heart, Shall *a child* be born unto him that is an hundred years old? and shall Sarah, that is ninety years old, bear?

¹⁸And Abraham said unto God, O that Ishmael might live before thee!

¹⁹And God said, Sarah thy wife shall bear thee a son indeed; and thou shalt call his name Isaac: and I will establish my covenant with him for an everlasting covenant, *and* with his seed after him.

Amplified

¹⁵And Hagar bore Abram a son, and Abram called the name of his son whom Hagar bore ^gIshmael.

¹⁶Abram was eighty-six years old when Hagar bore Ishmael.

17 WHEN ABRAM was ninety-nine years old, the Lord appeared to him and said, I am the Almighty God; walk *and* live habitually before Me and be perfect (blameless, wholehearted, complete).

²And I will make My covenant (solemn pledge) between Me and you and will multiply you exceedingly.

³Then Abram fell on his face, and God said to him,

⁴As for Me, behold, My covenant (solemn pledge) is with you, and you shall be the father of many nations.

⁵Nor shall your name any longer be Abram [high, exalted father]; but your name shall be Abraham [father of a multitude], for I have made you the father of many nations.

⁶And I will make you exceedingly fruitful and I will make nations of you, and ^hkings will come from you.

⁷And I will establish My covenant between Me and you and your descendants after you throughout their generations for an everlasting, solemn pledge, to be a God to you and to your posterity after you. [Gal. 3:16.]

⁸And I will give to you and to your posterity after you the land in which you are a stranger [going from place to place], all the land of Canaan, for an everlasting possession; and I will be their God. [Acts 7:5.]

⁹And God said to Abraham, As for you, you shall therefore keep My covenant, you and your descendants after you throughout their generations.

¹⁰This is My covenant, which you shall keep, between Me and you and your posterity after you: Every male among you shall be circumcised.

¹¹And you shall circumcise the flesh of your foreskin, and it shall be a token *or* sign of the covenant (the promise or pledge) between Me and you.

¹²He who is eight days old among you shall be circumcised, every male throughout your generations, whether born in [your] house or bought with [your] money from any foreigner not of your offspring.

¹³He that is born in your house and he that is bought with your money must be circumcised; and My covenant shall be in your flesh for an everlasting covenant.

¹⁴And the male who is not circumcised, that soul shall be cut off from his people; he has broken My covenant.

¹⁵And God said to Abraham, As for Sarai your wife, you shall not call her name Sarai; but Sarah [Princess] her name shall be.

¹⁶And I will bless her and give you a son also by her. Yes, I will bless her, and she shall be a mother of nations; kings of peoples shall come from her.

¹⁷Then Abraham fell on his face and laughed and said in his heart, Shall a child be born to a man who is a hundred years old? And shall Sarah, who is ninety years old, bear a son?

¹⁸And [he] said to God, Oh, that Ishmael might live before You!

¹⁹But God said, Sarah your wife shall bear you a son indeed, and you shall call his name Isaac [laughter]; and I will establish My covenant *or* solemn pledge with him for an everlasting covenant and with his posterity after him.

---

^g Ishmael was the first person whom God named before his birth (Gen. 16:11). Others were: Isaac (Gen. 17:19); Josiah (I Kings 13:2); Solomon (I Chron. 22:9); Jesus (Matt. 1:21); and John the Baptist (Luke 1:13).   ^h This prophecy and promise has been literally fulfilled countless times—for example, by all of the kings of Israel and Judah.

^hOr, *upright, or, sincere*   ⁱHeb. *multitude of nations*   ^ji.e. *Father of a great multitude*   ^kHeb. *of thy sojournings*   ^lHeb. *a son of eight days*   ^mi.e. *Princess*   ⁿHeb. *she shall become nations*

New American Standard

15 ¶ So Hagar bore Abram a son; and Abram called the name of his son, whom Hagar bore, Ishmael.
16 Abram was eighty-six years old when Hagar bore Ishmael to him.

Abraham and the Covenant of Circumcision

17 NOW WHEN Abram was ninety-nine years old, the LORD appeared to Abram and said to him, "I am God Almighty;
  Walk before Me, and be blameless.
2"I will establish My covenant between Me and you,
  And I will multiply you exceedingly."
3 Abram fell on his face, and God talked with him, saying,
4"As for Me, behold, My covenant is with you,
  And you will be the father of a multitude of nations.
5"No longer shall your name be called *r*Abram,
  But your name shall be *s*Abraham;
  For I will make you the father of a multitude of nations.
6"I will make you exceedingly fruitful, and I will make nations of you, and kings will come forth from you.
7"I will establish My covenant between Me and you and your descendants after you throughout their generations for an everlasting covenant, to be God to you and to your descendants after you.
8"I will give to you and to your descendants after you, the land of your sojournings, all the land of Canaan, for an everlasting possession; and I will be their God."
9 ¶ God said further to Abraham, "Now as for you, you shall keep My covenant, you and your descendants after you throughout their generations.
10"This is My covenant, which you shall keep, between Me and you and your descendants after you: every male among you shall be circumcised.
11"And you shall be circumcised in the flesh of your foreskin, and it shall be the sign of the covenant between Me and you.
12"And every male among you who is eight days old shall be circumcised throughout your generations, a *servant* who is born in the house or who is bought with money from any foreigner, who is not of your descendants.
13"A *servant* who is born in your house or who is bought with your money shall surely be circumcised; thus shall My covenant be in your flesh for an everlasting covenant.
14"But an uncircumcised male who is not circumcised in the flesh of his foreskin, that person shall be cut off from his people; he has broken My covenant."
15 ¶ Then God said to Abraham, "As for Sarai your wife, you shall not call her name Sarai, but *t*Sarah *shall be* her name.
16"I will bless her, and indeed I will give you a son by her. Then I will bless her, and she shall be *a mother of* nations; kings of peoples will come from her."
17 Then Abraham fell on his face and laughed, and said in his heart, "Will a child be born to a man one hundred years old? And will Sarah, who is ninety years old, bear *a child?*"
18 And Abraham said to God, "Oh that Ishmael might live before You!"
19 But God said, "No, but Sarah your wife will bear you a son, and you shall call his name *u*Isaac; and I will establish My covenant with him for an everlasting covenant for his descendants after him.

New International

15So Hagar bore Abram a son, and Abram gave the name Ishmael to the son she had borne. 16Abram was eighty-six years old when Hagar bore him Ishmael.

The Covenant of Circumcision

17 WHEN ABRAM was ninety-nine years old, the LORD appeared to him and said, "I am God Almighty*z*; walk before me and be blameless. 2I will confirm my covenant between me and you and will greatly increase your numbers."

3Abram fell facedown, and God said to him, 4"As for me, this is my covenant with you: You will be the father of many nations. 5No longer will you be called Abram*a*; your name will be Abraham,*b* for I have made you a father of many nations. 6I will make you very fruitful; I will make nations of you, and kings will come from you. 7I will establish my covenant as an everlasting covenant between me and you and your descendants after you for the generations to come, to be your God and the God of your descendants after you. 8The whole land of Canaan, where you are now an alien, I will give as an everlasting possession to you and your descendants after you; and I will be their God."

9Then God said to Abraham, "As for you, you must keep my covenant, you and your descendants after you for the generations to come. 10This is my covenant with you and your descendants after you, the covenant you are to keep: Every male among you shall be circumcised. 11You are to undergo circumcision, and it will be the sign of the covenant between me and you. 12For the generations to come every male among you who is eight days old must be circumcised, including those born in your household or bought with money from a foreigner—those who are not your offspring. 13Whether born in your household or bought with your money, they must be circumcised. My covenant in your flesh is to be an everlasting covenant. 14Any uncircumcised male, who has not been circumcised in the flesh, will be cut off from his people; he has broken my covenant."

15God also said to Abraham, "As for Sarai your wife, you are no longer to call her Sarai; her name will be Sarah. 16I will bless her and will surely give you a son by her. I will bless her so that she will be the mother of nations; kings of peoples will come from her."

17Abraham fell facedown; he laughed and said to himself, "Will a son be born to a man a hundred years old? Will Sarah bear a child at the age of ninety?" 18And Abraham said to God, "If only Ishmael might live under your blessing!"

19Then God said, "Yes, but your wife Sarah will bear you a son, and you will call him Isaac.*c* I will establish my covenant with him as an everlasting covenant for his

---

r I.e. exalted father   *s* I.e. father of a multitude   *t* I.e. princess
u I.e. he laughs

z 1 Hebrew *El-Shaddai*   *a 5* *Abram* means *exalted father.*
b 5 *Abraham* means *father of many.*   *c 19* *Isaac* means *he laughs.*

King James

²⁰And as for Ishmael, I have heard thee: Behold, I have blessed him, and will make him fruitful, and will multiply him exceedingly; twelve princes shall he beget, and I will make him a great nation.

²¹But my covenant will I establish with Isaac, which Sarah shall bear unto thee at this set time in the next year.

²²And he left off talking with him, and God went up from Abraham.

²³¶ And Abraham took Ishmael his son, and all that were born in his house, and all that were bought with his money, every male among the men of Abraham's house; and circumcised the flesh of their foreskin in the selfsame day, as God had said unto him.

²⁴And Abraham *was* ninety years old and nine, when he was circumcised in the flesh of his foreskin.

²⁵And Ishmael his son *was* thirteen years old, when he was circumcised in the flesh of his foreskin.

²⁶In the selfsame day was Abraham circumcised, and Ishmael his son.

²⁷And all the men of his house, born in the house, and bought with money of the stranger, were circumcised with him.

The three visitors

18 AND THE LORD appeared unto him in the plains of Mamre: and he sat in the tent door in the heat of the day;

²And he lift up his eyes and looked, and, lo, three men stood by him: and when he saw *them,* he ran to meet them from the tent door, and bowed himself toward the ground,

³And said, My Lord, if now I have found favour in thy sight, pass not away, I pray thee, from thy servant:

⁴Let a little water, I pray you, be fetched, and wash your feet, and rest yourselves under the tree:

⁵And I will fetch a morsel of bread, and ^ocomfort ye your hearts; after that ye shall pass on: for therefore ^pare ye come to your servant. And they said, So do, as thou hast said.

⁶And Abraham hastened into the tent unto Sarah, and said, ^qMake ready quickly three measures of fine meal, knead *it,* and make cakes upon the hearth.

⁷And Abraham ran unto the herd, and fetched a calf tender and good, and gave *it* unto a young man; and he hasted to dress it.

⁸And he took butter, and milk, and the calf which he had dressed, and set *it* before them; and he stood by them under the tree, and they did eat.

⁹¶ And they said unto him, Where *is* Sarah thy wife? And he said, Behold, in the tent.

¹⁰And he said, I will certainly return unto thee according to the time of life; and, lo, Sarah thy wife shall have a son. And Sarah heard *it* in the tent door, which *was* behind him.

¹¹Now Abraham and Sarah *were* old *and* well stricken in age; *and* it ceased to be with Sarah after the manner of women.

¹²Therefore Sarah laughed within herself, saying, After I am waxed old shall I have pleasure, my lord being old also?

¹³And the LORD said unto Abraham, Wherefore did Sarah laugh, saying, Shall I of a surety bear a child, which am old?

Amplified

²⁰And as for Ishmael, I have heard *and* heeded you: behold, I will bless him and will make him fruitful and will multiply him exceedingly; He will be the father of twelve princes, and I will make him a great nation. [Fulfilled in Gen. 25:12–18.]

²¹But My covenant, My promise and pledge, I will establish with Isaac, whom Sarah will bear to you at this season next year.

²²And God stopped talking with him and went up from Abraham.

²³And Abraham took Ishmael his son and all who were born in his house and all who were bought with his money, every male among [those] of Abraham's house, and circumcised [them] the very same day, as God had said to him.

²⁴And Abraham was ninety-nine years old when he was circumcised.

²⁵And Ishmael his son was thirteen years old when he was circumcised.

²⁶On the very same day Abraham was circumcised, and Ishmael his son as well.

²⁷And all the men of his house, both those born in the house and those bought with money from a foreigner, were circumcised along with him.

18 NOW THE Lord appeared to Abraham by the oaks *or* terebinths of Mamre; as he sat at the door of his tent in the heat of the day,

²He lifted up his eyes and looked, and behold, three men stood at a little distance from him. He ran from the tent door to meet them and bowed himself to the ground

³And said, My lord, if now I have found favor in your sight, do not pass by your servant, I beg of you.

⁴Let a little water be brought, and you may wash your feet and recline *and* rest yourselves under the tree.

⁵And I will bring a morsel (mouthful) of bread to refresh *and* sustain your hearts before you go on further—for that is why you have come to your servant. And they replied, Do as you have said.

⁶So Abraham hastened into the tent to Sarah and said, Quickly get ready three measures of fine meal, knead it, and bake cakes.

⁷And Abraham ran to the herd and brought a calf tender and good and gave it to the young man [to butcher]; then he [Abraham] hastened to prepare it.

⁸And he took curds and milk and the calf which he had made ready, and set it before [the men]; and he stood by them under the tree while they ate.

⁹And they said to him, Where is Sarah your wife? And he said, [She is here] in the tent.

¹⁰ⁱ[The Lord] said, I will surely return to you when the season comes round, and behold, Sarah your wife will have a son. And Sarah was listening *and* heard it at the tent door which was behind Him. [Rom. 9:9–12.]

¹¹Now Abraham and Sarah were old, well advanced in years; it had ceased to be with Sarah as with [young] women. [She was past the age of childbearing].

¹²Therefore Sarah laughed to herself, saying, After I have become aged shall I have pleasure *and* delight, my lord (husband), being old also? [I Pet. 3:6.]

¹³And the Lord asked Abraham, Why did Sarah laugh, saying, Shall I really bear a child when I am so old?

ⁱOne of the three guests was the Lord, and since God the Father was never seen in bodily form (John 1:18), only the "Angel of the covenant," Christ Himself, can be meant here; see especially Gen. 18:22 and also the footnote on Gen. 16:7.

^oHeb. *stay*   ^pHeb. *you have passed*   ^qHeb. *Hasten*

New American Standard

20"As for Ishmael, I have heard you; behold, I will bless him, and will make him fruitful and will multiply him exceedingly. He shall become the father of twelve princes, and I will make him a great nation.

21"But My covenant I will establish with Isaac, whom Sarah will bear to you at this season next year."

22 When He finished talking with him, God went up from Abraham.

23 ¶ Then Abraham took Ishmael his son, and all *the servants* who were born in his house and all who were bought with his money, every male among the men of Abraham's household, and circumcised the flesh of their foreskin in the very same day, as God had said to him.

24 Now Abraham was ninety-nine years old when he was circumcised in the flesh of his foreskin.

25 And Ishmael his son was thirteen years old when he was circumcised in the flesh of his foreskin.

26 In the very same day Abraham was circumcised, and Ishmael his son.

27 All the men of his household, who were born in the house or bought with money from a foreigner, were circumcised with him.

Birth of Isaac Promised

18 NOW THE LORD appeared to him by the oaks of Mamre, while he was sitting at the tent door in the heat of the day.

2 When he lifted up his eyes and looked, behold, three men were standing opposite him; and when he saw *them,* he ran from the tent door to meet them and bowed himself to the earth,

3 and said, "My lord, if now I have found favor in your sight, please do not pass your servant by.

4"Please let a little water be brought and wash your feet, and rest yourselves under the tree;

5 and I will bring a piece of bread, that you may refresh yourselves; after that you may go on, since you have visited your servant." And they said, "So do, as you have said."

6 So Abraham hurried into the tent to Sarah, and said, "Quickly, prepare three measures of fine flour, knead *it* and make bread cakes."

7 Abraham also ran to the herd, and took a tender and choice calf and gave *it* to the servant, and he hurried to prepare it.

8 He took curds and milk and the calf which he had prepared, and placed *it* before them; and he was standing by them under the tree as they ate.

9 ¶ Then they said to him, "Where is Sarah your wife?" And he said, "There, in the tent."

10 He said, "I will surely return to you at this time next year; and behold, Sarah your wife will have a son." And Sarah was listening at the tent door, which was behind him.

11 Now Abraham and Sarah were old, advanced in age; Sarah was past childbearing.

12 Sarah laughed to herself, saying, "After I have become old, shall I have pleasure, my lord being old also?"

13 And the LORD said to Abraham, "Why did Sarah laugh, saying, 'Shall I indeed bear *a child,* when I am *so* old?'

New International

descendants after him. 20And as for Ishmael, I have heard you: I will surely bless him; I will make him fruitful and will greatly increase his numbers. He will be the father of twelve rulers, and I will make him into a great nation. 21But my covenant I will establish with Isaac, whom Sarah will bear to you by this time next year." 22When he had finished speaking with Abraham, God went up from him.

23On that very day Abraham took his son Ishmael and all those born in his household or bought with his money, every male in his household, and circumcised them, as God told him. 24Abraham was ninety-nine years old when he was circumcised, 25and his son Ishmael was thirteen; 26Abraham and his son Ishmael were both circumcised on that same day. 27And every male in Abraham's household, including those born in his household or bought from a foreigner, was circumcised with him.

The Three Visitors

18 THE LORD appeared to Abraham near the great trees of Mamre while he was sitting at the entrance to his tent in the heat of the day. 2Abraham looked up and saw three men standing nearby. When he saw them, he hurried from the entrance of his tent to meet them and bowed low to the ground.

3He said, "If I have found favor in your eyes, my lord,*d* do not pass your servant by. 4Let a little water be brought, and then you may all wash your feet and rest under this tree. 5Let me get you something to eat, so you can be refreshed and then go on your way—now that you have come to your servant."

"Very well," they answered, "do as you say."

6So Abraham hurried into the tent to Sarah. "Quick," he said, "get three seahs*e* of fine flour and knead it and bake some bread."

7Then he ran to the herd and selected a choice, tender calf and gave it to a servant, who hurried to prepare it. 8He then brought some curds and milk and the calf that had been prepared, and set these before them. While they ate, he stood near them under a tree.

9"Where is your wife Sarah?" they asked him.

"There, in the tent," he said.

10Then the LORD*f* said, "I will surely return to you about this time next year, and Sarah your wife will have a son."

Now Sarah was listening at the entrance to the tent, which was behind him. 11Abraham and Sarah were already old and well advanced in years, and Sarah was past the age of childbearing. 12So Sarah laughed to herself as she thought, "After I am worn out and my master*g* is old, will I now have this pleasure?"

13Then the LORD said to Abraham, "Why did Sarah laugh and say, 'Will I really have a child, now that I am

d 3 Or *O Lord*   *e* 6 That is, probably about 20 quarts (about 22 liters)   *f* 10 Hebrew *Then he*   *g* 12 Or *husband*

King James

¹⁴Is any thing too hard for the LORD? At the time appointed I will return unto thee, according to the time of life, and Sarah shall have a son.

¹⁵Then Sarah denied, saying, I laughed not; for she was afraid. And he said, Nay; but thou didst laugh.

Abraham pleads for Sodom

¹⁶ ¶ And the men rose up from thence, and looked toward Sodom: and Abraham went with them to bring them on the way.

¹⁷And the LORD said, Shall I hide from Abraham that thing which I do;

¹⁸Seeing that Abraham shall surely become a great and mighty nation, and all the nations of the earth shall be blessed in him?

¹⁹For I know him, that he will command his children and his household after him, and they shall keep the way of the LORD, to do justice and judgment; that the LORD may bring upon Abraham that which he hath spoken of him.

²⁰And the LORD said, Because the cry of Sodom and Gomorrah is great, and because their sin is very grievous;

²¹I will go down now, and see whether they have done altogether according to the cry of it, which is come unto me; and if not, I will know.

²²And the men turned their faces from thence, and went toward Sodom: but Abraham stood yet before the LORD.

²³ ¶ And Abraham drew near, and said, Wilt thou also destroy the righteous with the wicked?

²⁴Peradventure there be fifty righteous within the city: wilt thou also destroy and not spare the place for the fifty righteous that *are* therein?

²⁵That be far from thee to do after this manner, to slay the righteous with the wicked: and that the righteous should be as the wicked, that be far from thee: Shall not the Judge of all the earth do right?

²⁶And the LORD said, If I find in Sodom fifty righteous within the city, then I will spare all the place for their sakes.

²⁷And Abraham answered and said, Behold now, I have taken upon me to speak unto the Lord, which *am but* dust and ashes:

²⁸Peradventure there shall lack five of the fifty righteous: wilt thou destroy all the city for *lack of* five? And he said, If I there forty and five, I will not destroy *it*.

²⁹And he spake unto him yet again, and said, Peradventure there shall be forty found there. And he said, I will not do *it* for forty's sake.

³⁰And he said *unto him,* Oh let not the Lord be angry, and I will speak: Peradventure there shall thirty be found there. And he said, I will not do *it,* if I find thirty there.

³¹And he said, Behold now, I have taken upon me to speak unto the Lord: Peradventure there shall be twenty found there. And he said, I will not destroy *it* for twenty's sake.

³²And he said, Oh let not the Lord be angry, and I will speak yet but this once: Peradventure ten shall be found there. And he said, I will not destroy *it* for ten's sake.

³³And the LORD went his way, as soon as he had left communing with Abraham: and Abraham returned unto his place.

Amplified

¹⁴Is anything too hard *or* too wonderful *j*for the Lord? At the appointed time, when the season [for her delivery] comes around, I will return to you and Sarah shall have borne a son. [Matt. 19:26.]

¹⁵Then Sarah denied it, saying, I did not laugh; for she was afraid. And He said, No, but you did laugh.

¹⁶The men rose up from there and faced toward Sodom, and Abraham went with them to bring them on the way.

¹⁷And the Lord said, Shall I hide from Abraham [My friend and servant] what I am going to do, [Gal. 3:8.]

¹⁸Since Abraham shall surely become a great and mighty nation, and all the nations of the earth shall be blessed through him *and* shall bless themselves by him? [Gen. 12:2–3.]

¹⁹For I have known (chosen, acknowledged) him [as My own], so that he may teach *and* command his children and the sons of his house after him to keep the way of the Lord and to do what is just and righteous, so that the Lord may bring Abraham what He has promised him.

²⁰And the Lord said, Because the shriek [of the sins] of Sodom and Gomorrah is great and their sin is exceedingly grievous,

²¹I will go down now and see whether they have done altogether [as vilely and wickedly] as is the cry of it which has come to Me; and if not, I will know.

²²Now the [two] men turned from there and went toward Sodom, but Abraham still stood before the Lord.

²³And Abraham came close and said, Will You destroy the righteous (those upright and in right standing with God) together with the wicked?

²⁴Suppose there are in the city fifty righteous; will You destroy the place and not spare it for [the sake of] the fifty righteous in it?

²⁵Far be it from You to do such a thing—to slay the righteous with the wicked, so that the righteous fare as do the wicked! Far be it from You! Shall not the Judge of all the earth execute judgment *and* do righteously?

²⁶And the Lord said, If I find in the city of Sodom fifty righteous (upright and in right standing with God), I will spare the whole place for their sake.

²⁷Abraham answered, Behold now, I who am but dust and ashes have taken upon myself to speak to the Lord.

²⁸If five of the fifty righteous should be lacking—will You destroy the whole city for lack of five? He said, If I find forty-five, I will not destroy it.

²⁹And [Abraham] spoke to Him yet again, and said, Suppose [only] forty shall be found there. And He said, I will not do it for forty's sake.

³⁰Then [Abraham] said to Him, Oh, let not the Lord be angry, and I will speak [again]. Suppose [only] thirty shall be found there. And He answered, I will not do it if I find thirty.

³¹And [Abraham] said, Behold now, I have taken upon myself to speak [again] to the Lord. Suppose [only] twenty shall be found there. And [the Lord] replied, I will not destroy it for twenty's sake.

³²And he said, Oh, let not the Lord be angry, and I will speak again only this once. Suppose ten [righteous people] shall be found there. And [the Lord] said, I will not destroy it for ten's sake.

³³And the Lord went His way when He had finished speaking with Abraham, and Abraham returned to his place.

Sodom and Gomorrah destroyed

19 AND THERE came two angels to Sodom at even; and Lot sat in the gate of Sodom: and Lot seeing *them* rose up to meet them; and he bowed himself with his face toward the ground;

19 IT WAS evening when the two angels came to Sodom. Lot was sitting at Sodom's [city] gate. Seeing them, Lot rose up to meet them and bowed to the ground.

*j*The word "Lord" as applied to God is obviously the most important word in the Bible, for it occurs oftener than any other important word—by actual count more than 5,000 times. **Nothing** is "too hard *or* too wonderful" for Him when He is truly made Lord.

New American Standard

14"Is anything too difficult for the LORD? At the appointed time I will return to you, at this time next year, and Sarah will have a son."

15 Sarah denied *it* however, saying, "I did not laugh"; for she was afraid. And He said, "No, but you did laugh."

16 ¶ Then the men rose up from there, and looked down toward Sodom; and Abraham was walking with them to send them off.

17 The LORD said, "Shall I hide from Abraham what I am about to do,

18 since Abraham will surely become a great and mighty nation, and in him all the nations of the earth will be blessed?

19"For I have chosen him, so that he may command his children and his household after him to keep the way of the LORD by doing righteousness and justice, so that the LORD may bring upon Abraham what He has spoken about him."

20 And the LORD said, "The outcry of Sodom and Gomorrah is indeed great, and their sin is exceedingly grave.

21"I will go down now, and see if they have done entirely according to its outcry, which has come to Me; and if not, I will know."

22 ¶ Then the men turned away from there and went toward Sodom, while Abraham was still standing before the LORD.

23 Abraham came near and said, "Will You indeed sweep away the righteous with the wicked?

24"Suppose there are fifty righteous within the city; will You indeed sweep *it* away and not spare the place for the sake of the fifty righteous who are in it?

25"Far be it from You to do such a thing, to slay the righteous with the wicked, so that the righteous and the wicked are *treated* alike. Far be it from You! Shall not the Judge of all the earth deal justly?"

26 So the LORD said, "If I find in Sodom fifty righteous within the city, then I will spare the whole place on their account."

27 And Abraham replied, "Now behold, I have ventured to speak to the Lord, although I am *but* dust and ashes.

28"Suppose the fifty righteous are lacking five, will You destroy the whole city because of five?" And He said, "I will not destroy *it* if I find forty-five there."

29 He spoke to Him yet again and said, "Suppose forty are found there?" And He said, "I will not do *it* on account of the forty."

30 Then he said, "Oh may the Lord not be angry, and I shall speak; suppose thirty are found there?" And He said, "I will not do *it* if I find thirty there."

31 And he said, "Now behold, I have ventured to speak to the Lord; suppose twenty are found there?" And He said, "I will not destroy *it* on account of the twenty."

32 Then he said, "Oh may the Lord not be angry, and I shall speak only this once; suppose ten are found there?" And He said, "I will not destroy *it* on account of the ten."

33 As soon as He had finished speaking to Abraham the LORD departed, and Abraham returned to his place.

The Doom of Sodom

19 NOW THE two angels came to Sodom in the evening as Lot was sitting in the gate of Sodom. When Lot saw *them*, he rose to meet them and bowed down *with his* face to the ground.

New International

old?' 14Is anything too hard for the LORD? I will return to you at the appointed time next year and Sarah will have a son."

15Sarah was afraid, so she lied and said, "I did not laugh."

But he said, "Yes, you did laugh."

Abraham Pleads for Sodom

16When the men got up to leave, they looked down toward Sodom, and Abraham walked along with them to see them on their way. 17Then the LORD said, "Shall I hide from Abraham what I am about to do? 18Abraham will surely become a great and powerful nation, and all nations on earth will be blessed through him. 19For I have chosen him, so that he will direct his children and his household after him to keep the way of the LORD by doing what is right and just, so that the LORD will bring about for Abraham what he has promised him."

20Then the LORD said, "The outcry against Sodom and Gomorrah is so great and their sin so grievous 21that I will go down and see if what they have done is as bad as the outcry that has reached me. If not, I will know."

22The men turned away and went toward Sodom, but Abraham remained standing before the LORD.[h] 23Then Abraham approached him and said: "Will you sweep away the righteous with the wicked? 24What if there are fifty righteous people in the city? Will you really sweep it away and not spare[i] the place for the sake of the fifty righteous people in it? 25Far be it from you to do such a thing—to kill the righteous with the wicked, treating the righteous and the wicked alike. Far be it from you! Will not the Judge[j] of all the earth do right?"

26The LORD said, "If I find fifty righteous people in the city of Sodom, I will spare the whole place for their sake."

27Then Abraham spoke up again: "Now that I have been so bold as to speak to the Lord, though I am nothing but dust and ashes, 28what if the number of the righteous is five less than fifty? Will you destroy the whole city because of five people?"

"If I find forty-five there," he said, "I will not destroy it."

29Once again he spoke to him, "What if only forty are found there?"

He said, "For the sake of forty, I will not do it."

30Then he said, "May the Lord not be angry, but let me speak. What if only thirty can be found there?"

He answered, "I will not do it if I find thirty there."

31Abraham said, "Now that I have been so bold as to speak to the Lord, what if only twenty can be found there?"

He said, "For the sake of twenty, I will not destroy it."

32Then he said, "May the Lord not be angry, but let me speak just once more. What if only ten can be found there?"

He answered, "For the sake of ten, I will not destroy it."

33When the LORD had finished speaking with Abraham, he left, and Abraham returned home.

Sodom and Gomorrah Destroyed

19 THE TWO angels arrived at Sodom in the evening, and Lot was sitting in the gateway of the city. When he saw them, he got up to meet them and bowed down with his face to the ground. 2"My lords," he said,

---

h 22 Masoretic Text; an ancient Hebrew scribal tradition *but the LORD remained standing before Abraham*   i 24 Or *forgive*; also in verse 26   j 25 Or *Ruler*

King James

²And he said, Behold now, my lords, turn in, I pray you, into your servant's house, and tarry all night, and wash your feet, and ye shall rise up early, and go on your ways. And they said, Nay; but we will abide in the street all night.

³And he pressed upon them greatly; and they turned in unto him, and entered into his house; and he made them a feast, and did bake unleavened bread, and they did eat.

4 ¶ But before they lay down, the men of the city, *even* the men of Sodom, compassed the house round, both old and young, all the people from every quarter:

⁵And they called unto Lot, and said unto him, Where *are* the men which came in to thee this night? bring them out unto us, that we may know them.

⁶And Lot went out at the door unto them, and shut the door after him,

⁷And said, I pray you, brethren, do not so wickedly.

⁸Behold now, I have two daughters which have not known man; let me, I pray you, bring them out unto you, and do ye to them as *is* good in your eyes: only unto these men do nothing; for therefore came they under the shadow of my roof.

⁹And they said, Stand back. And they said *again,* This one *fellow* came in to sojourn, and he will needs be a judge: now will we deal worse with thee, than with them. And they pressed sore upon the man, *even* Lot, and came near to break the door.

¹⁰But the men put forth their hand, and pulled Lot into the house to them, and shut to the door.

¹¹And they smote the men that *were* at the door of the house with blindness, both small and great: so that they wearied themselves to find the door.

12 ¶ And the men said unto Lot, Hast thou here any besides? son-in-law, and thy sons, and thy daughters, and whatsoever thou hast in the city, bring *them* out of this place:

¹³For we will destroy this place, because the cry of them is waxen great before the face of the LORD; and the LORD hath sent us to destroy it.

¹⁴And Lot went out, and spake unto his sons in law, which married his daughters, and said, Up, get you out of this place; for the LORD will destroy this city. But he seemed as one that mocked unto his sons in law.

15 ¶ And when the morning arose, then the angels hastened Lot, saying, Arise, take thy wife, and thy two daughters, which ʳare here; lest thou be consumed in the ˢiniquity of the city.

¹⁶And while he lingered, the men laid hold upon his hand, and upon the hand of his wife, and upon the hand of his two daughters; the LORD being merciful unto him: and they brought him forth, and set him without the city.

17 ¶ And it came to pass, when they had brought them forth abroad, that he said, Escape for thy life; look not behind thee, neither stay thou in all the plain; escape to the mountain, lest thou be consumed.

¹⁸And Lot said unto them, Oh, not so, my Lord:

¹⁹Behold now, thy servant hath found grace in thy sight, and thou hast magnified thy mercy, which thou hast shown unto me in saving my life; and I cannot escape to the mountain, lest some evil take me, and I die:

²⁰Behold now, this city *is* near to flee unto, and it *is* a little one: Oh, let me escape thither, (*is* it not a little one?) and my soul shall live.

²¹And he said unto him, See, I have accepted ᵗthee concerning this thing also, that I will not overthrow this city, for the which thou hast spoken.

²²Haste thee, escape thither; for I cannot do any thing till thou be come thither. Therefore the name of the city was called ᵘZoar.

23 ¶ The sun was ᵛrisen upon the earth when Lot entered into Zoar.

Amplified

²And he said, My lords, turn aside, I beg of you, into your servant's house and spend the night and bathe your feet. Then you can arise early and go on your way. But they said, No, we will spend the night in the square.

³[Lot] entreated *and* urged them greatly until they yielded and [with him] entered his house. And he made them a dinner [with drinking] and had unleavened bread which he baked, and they ate.

⁴But before they lay down, the men of the city of Sodom, both young and old, all the men from every quarter, surrounded the house.

⁵And they called to Lot and said, Where are the men who came to you tonight? Bring them out to us, that we may know (be intimate with) them.

⁶And Lot went out of the door to the men and shut the door after him

⁷And said, I beg of you, my brothers, do not behave so wickedly.

⁸Look now, I have two daughters who are virgins; let me, I beg of you, bring them out to you, and you can do as you please with them. But only do nothing to these men, for they have come under the protection of my roof.

⁹But they said, Stand back! And they said, This fellow came in to live here temporarily, and now he presumes to be [our] judge! Now we will deal worse with you than with them. So they rushed at *and* pressed violently against Lot and came close to breaking down the door.

¹⁰But the men [the angels] reached out and pulled Lot into the house to them and shut the door after him.

¹¹And they struck the men who were at the door of the house with blindness [which dazzled them], from the youths to the old men, so that they wearied themselves [groping] to find the door.

¹²And the [two] men asked Lot, Have you any others here—sons-in-law or your sons or your daughters? Whomever you have in the city, bring them out of this place,

¹³For we will spoil *and* destroy [Sodom]; for the outcry *and* shriek against its people has grown great before the Lord, and He has sent us to destroy it.

¹⁴And Lot went out and spoke to his sons-in-law, who were to marry his daughters, and said, Up, get out of this place, for the Lord will spoil *and* destroy this city! But he seemed to his sons-in-law to be [only] joking.

¹⁵When morning came, the angels urged Lot to hurry, saying, Arise, take your wife and two daughters who are here [and be off], lest you [too] be consumed *and* swept away in the iniquity *and* punishment of the city.

¹⁶But while he lingered, the men seized him and his wife and his two daughters by the hand, for the Lord was merciful to him; and they brought him forth and set him outside the city and left him there.

¹⁷And when they had brought them forth, they said, Escape for your life! Do not look behind you or stop anywhere in ᵏthe whole valley; escape to the mountains [of Moab], lest you be consumed.

¹⁸And Lot said to them, Oh, not that, my lords!

¹⁹Behold now, your servant has found favor in your sight, and you have magnified your kindness and mercy to me in saving my life; but I cannot escape to the mountains, lest the evil overtake me, and I die.

²⁰See now yonder city; it is near enough to flee to, and it is a little one. Oh, let me escape to it! Is it not a little one? And my life shall be saved!

²¹And [the angel] said to him, See, I have yielded to your entreaty concerning this thing also; I will not destroy this city of which you have spoken.

²²Make haste and take refuge there, for I cannot do anything until you arrive there. Therefore the name of the city was called Zoar [little].

²³The sun had risen over the earth when Lot entered Zoar.

ʳHeb. *are found*   ˢOr, *punishment*   ᵗHeb. *thy face*   ᵘi.e. *Little*   ᵛHeb. *gone forth*

ᵏThe valley which Lot had once so much coveted (Gen. 13:10, 11).

New American Standard

2 And he said, "Now behold, my lords, please turn aside into your servant's house, and spend the night, and wash your feet; then you may rise early and go on your way." They said however, "No, but we shall spend the night in the square."

3 Yet he urged them strongly, so they turned aside to him and entered his house; and he prepared a feast for them, and baked unleavened bread, and they ate.

4 Before they lay down, the men of the city, the men of Sodom, surrounded the house, both young and old, all the people from every quarter;

5 and they called to Lot and said to him, "Where are the men who came to you tonight? Bring them out to us that we may have relations with them."

6 But Lot went out to them at the doorway, and shut the door behind him,

7 and said, "Please, my brothers, do not act wickedly.

8 "Now behold, I have two daughters who have not had relations with man; please let me bring them out to you, and do to them whatever you like; only do nothing to these men, inasmuch as they have come under the shelter of my roof."

9 But they said, "Stand aside." Furthermore, they said, "This one came in as an alien, and already he is acting like a judge; now we will treat you worse than them." So they pressed hard against Lot and came near to break the door.

10 But the men reached out their hands and brought Lot into the house with them, and shut the door.

11 They struck the men who were at the doorway of the house with blindness, both small and great, so that they wearied *themselves trying* to find the doorway.

12 Then the *two* men said to Lot, "Whom else have you here? A son-in-law, and your sons, and your daughters, and whomever you have in the city, bring *them* out of the place;

13 for we are about to destroy this place, because their outcry has become so great before the LORD that the LORD has sent us to destroy it."

14 Lot went out and spoke to his sons-in-law, who were to marry his daughters, and said, "Up, get out of this place, for the LORD will destroy the city." But he appeared to his sons-in-law to be jesting.

15 When morning dawned, the angels urged Lot, saying, "Up, take your wife and your two daughters who are here, or you will be swept away in the punishment of the city."

16 But he hesitated. So the men seized his hand and the hand of his wife and the hands of his two daughters, for the compassion of the LORD *was* upon him; and they brought him out, and put him outside the city.

17 When they had brought them outside, one said, "Escape for your life! Do not look behind you, and do not stay anywhere in the valley; escape to the mountains, or you will be swept away."

18 But Lot said to them, "Oh no, my lords!

19 "Now behold, your servant has found favor in your sight, and you have magnified your lovingkindness, which you have shown me by saving my life; but I cannot escape to the mountains, for the disaster will overtake me and I will die;

20 now behold, this town is near *enough* to flee to, and it is small. Please, let me escape there (is it not small?) that my life may be saved."

21 He said to him, "Behold, I grant you this request also, not to overthrow the town of which you have spoken.

22 "Hurry, escape there, for I cannot do anything until you arrive there." Therefore the name of the town was called ᵛZoar.

23 ¶ The sun had risen over the earth when Lot came to Zoar.

ᵛI.e. small

New International

"please turn aside to your servant's house. You can wash your feet and spend the night and then go on your way early in the morning."

"No," they answered, "we will spend the night in the square."

3 But he insisted so strongly that they did go with him and entered his house. He prepared a meal for them, baking bread without yeast, and they ate. 4 Before they had gone to bed, all the men from every part of the city of Sodom—both young and old—surrounded the house. 5 They called to Lot, "Where are the men who came to you tonight? Bring them out to us so that we can have sex with them."

6 Lot went outside to meet them and shut the door behind him 7 and said, "No, my friends. Don't do this wicked thing. 8 Look, I have two daughters who have never slept with a man. Let me bring them out to you, and you can do what you like with them. But don't do anything to these men, for they have come under the protection of my roof."

9 "Get out of our way," they replied. And they said, "This fellow came here as an alien, and now he wants to play the judge! We'll treat you worse than them." They kept bringing pressure on Lot and moved forward to break down the door.

10 But the men inside reached out and pulled Lot back into the house and shut the door. 11 Then they struck the men who were at the door of the house, young and old, with blindness so that they could not find the door.

12 The two men said to Lot, "Do you have anyone else here—sons-in-law, sons or daughters, or anyone else in the city who belongs to you? Get them out of here, 13 because we are going to destroy this place. The outcry to the LORD against its people is so great that he has sent us to destroy it."

14 So Lot went out and spoke to his sons-in-law, who were pledged to marryᵏ his daughters. He said, "Hurry and get out of this place, because the LORD is about to destroy the city!" But his sons-in-law thought he was joking.

15 With the coming of dawn, the angels urged Lot, saying, "Hurry! Take your wife and your two daughters who are here, or you will be swept away when the city is punished."

16 When he hesitated, the men grasped his hand and the hands of his wife and of his two daughters and led them safely out of the city, for the LORD was merciful to them. 17 As soon as they had brought them out, one of them said, "Flee for your lives! Don't look back, and don't stop anywhere in the plain! Flee to the mountains or you will be swept away!"

18 But Lot said to them, "No, my lords,ˡ please! 19 Yourᵐ servant has found favor in yourᵐ eyes, and youᵐ have shown great kindness to me in sparing my life. But I can't flee to the mountains; this disaster will overtake me, and I'll die. 20 Look, here is a town near enough to run to, and it is small. Let me flee to it—it is very small, isn't it? Then my life will be spared."

21 He said to him, "Very well, I will grant this request too; I will not overthrow the town you speak of. 22 But flee there quickly, because I cannot do anything until you reach it." (That is why the town was called Zoar.ⁿ)

23 By the time Lot reached Zoar, the sun had risen over

ᵏ14 Or *were married to*   ˡ18 Or *No, Lord*; or *No, my lord*
ᵐ19 The Hebrew is singular.   ⁿ22 *Zoar* means *small*.

King James

²⁴Then the LORD rained upon Sodom and upon Gomorrah brimstone and fire from the LORD out of heaven;

²⁵And he overthrew those cities, and all the plain, and all the inhabitants of the cities, and that which grew upon the ground.

²⁶ ¶ But his wife looked back from behind him, and she became a pillar of salt.

²⁷ ¶ And Abraham gat up early in the morning to the place where he stood before the LORD:

²⁸And he looked toward Sodom and Gomorrah, and toward all the land of the plain, and beheld, and, lo, the smoke of the country went up as the smoke of a furnace.

²⁹ ¶ And it came to pass, when God destroyed the cities of the plain, that God remembered Abraham, and sent Lot out of the midst of the overthrow, when he overthrew the cities in the which Lot dwelt.

The sin of Lot's daughters

³⁰ ¶ And Lot went up out of Zoar, and dwelt in the mountain, and his two daughters with him; for he feared to dwell in Zoar: and he dwelt in a cave, he and his two daughters.

³¹And the firstborn said unto the younger, Our father *is* old, and *there is* not a man in the earth to come in unto us after the manner of all the earth:

³²Come, let us make our father drink wine, and we will lie with him, that we may preserve seed of our father.

³³And they made their father drink wine that night: and the firstborn went in, and lay with her father; and he perceived not when she lay down, nor when she arose.

³⁴And it came to pass on the morrow, that the firstborn said unto the younger, Behold, I lay yesternight with my father: let us make him drink wine this night also; and go thou in, *and* lie with him, that we may preserve seed of our father.

³⁵And they made their father drink wine that night also: and the younger arose, and lay with him; and he perceived not when she lay down, nor when she arose.

³⁶Thus were both the daughters of Lot with child by their father.

³⁷And the firstborn bare a son, and called his name Moab: the same *is* the father of the Moabites unto this day.

³⁸And the younger, she also bare a son, and called his name Ben-ammi: the same *is* the father of the children of Ammon unto this day.

Abraham and Abimelech

20 AND ABRAHAM journeyed from thence toward the south country, and dwelled between Kadesh and Shur, and sojourned in Gerar.

Amplified

²⁴Then the Lord rained on Sodom and on Gomorrah brimstone and fire from the Lord out of the heavens.

²⁵He overthrew, destroyed, *and* ended those cities, and all the valley and all the inhabitants of the cities, and what grew on the ground.

²⁶But [Lot's] wife looked back from behind him, and she *ˡ*became a pillar of salt.

²⁷Abraham went up early the next morning to the place where he [only the day before] had stood before the Lord.

²⁸And he looked toward Sodom and Gomorrah, and toward all the land of the valley, and saw, and behold, the smoke of *ᵐ*the country went up like the smoke of a furnace.

²⁹When God ravaged *and* destroyed the cities of the plain [of Siddim], He [earnestly] remembered Abraham [imprinted and fixed him indelibly on His mind], and He sent Lot out of the midst of the overthrow when He overthrew the cities where Lot lived.

³⁰And Lot went up out of Zoar and dwelt in the mountain, and his two daughters with him, for he feared to dwell in Zoar; and he lived in a cave, he and his two daughters.

³¹The elder said to the younger, Our father is aging, and there is not a man on earth to live with us in the customary way.

³²Come, let us make our father drunk with wine, and we will lie with him, so that we may preserve offspring (our race) through our father.

³³And they made their father drunk with wine that night, and the older went in and lay with her father; and he was not aware of it when she lay down or when she arose.

³⁴Then the next day the firstborn said to the younger, See here, I lay last night with my father; let us make him drunk with wine tonight also, and then you go in and lie with him, so that we may preserve offspring (our race) through our father.

³⁵And they made their father drunk with wine again that night, and the younger arose and lay with him; and he was not aware of it when she lay down or when she arose.

³⁶Thus both the daughters of Lot were with child by their father.

³⁷The older bore a son, and named him Moab [of a father]; he is the father of the Moabites to this day.

³⁸The younger also bore a son and named him Ben-ammi [son of my people]; he is the father of the Ammonites to this day.

20 NOW ABRAHAM journeyed from there toward the *ⁿ*South country (the Negeb) and dwelt between Kadesh and Shur; and he lived temporarily in Gerar.

*ˡ*Lot's wife not only "looked back" to where her heart's interests were, but she lingered behind; and probably overtaken by the fire and brimstone, her dead body became incrusted with salt, which, in that salt-packed area now the Dead Sea, grew larger with more incrustations—a veritable "pillar of salt." In fact, at the southern end of the Dead Sea there is a mountain of table salt called Jebel Usdum, "Mount of Sodom." It is about six miles long, three miles wide, and 1,000 feet high. It is covered with a crust of earth several feet thick, but the rest of the mountain is said to be solid salt (George T. B. Davis, *Rebuilding Palestine According to Prophecy*). Somewhere in this area Lot's wife looked back to where her treasures and her heart were, and "she became a pillar of salt." Jesus said, "Remember Lot's wife" (Luke 17:32). *ᵐ*Not only were Sodom and Gomorrah blazing ruins, but also Admah and Zeboiim (Deut. 29:23; Hos. 11:8), as well as all the towns in the Valley of Siddim; Zoar was the lone exception. *ⁿ*"Primitive geographic expressions such as 'the South country (the Negeb)' (Gen. 12:9; 13:1, 3; 20:1; 24:62) and 'the east country' (Gen. 25:6) are used in the time of Abraham . . . After the time of Genesis they have well-known and well-defined names; I submit that they were written down in early days, and that no writer after Moses could have used such archaic expressions as these" (P. J. Wiseman, *New Discoveries in Babylonia About Genesis*).

New American Standard

24 Then the LORD rained on Sodom and Gomorrah brimstone and fire from the LORD out of heaven,

25 and He overthrew those cities, and all the valley, and all the inhabitants of the cities, and what grew on the ground.

26 But his wife, from behind him, looked *back,* and she became a pillar of salt.

27 ¶ Now Abraham arose early in the morning *and went* to the place where he had stood before the LORD;

28 and he looked down toward Sodom and Gomorrah, and toward all the land of the valley, and he saw, and behold, the smoke of the land ascended like the smoke of a furnace.

29 ¶ Thus it came about, when God destroyed the cities of the valley, that God remembered Abraham, and sent Lot out of the midst of the overthrow, when He overthrew the cities in which Lot lived.

Lot Is Debased

30 ¶ Lot went up from Zoar, and stayed in the mountains, and his two daughters with him; for he was afraid to stay in Zoar; and he stayed in a cave, he and his two daughters.

31 Then the firstborn said to the younger, "Our father is old, and there is not a man on earth to come in to us after the manner of the earth.

32 "Come, let us make our father drink wine, and let us lie with him that we may preserve our family through our father."

33 So they made their father drink wine that night, and the firstborn went in and lay with her father; and he did not know when she lay down or when she arose.

34 On the following day, the firstborn said to the younger, "Behold, I lay last night with my father; let us make him drink wine tonight also; then you go in and lie with him, that we may preserve our family through our father."

35 So they made their father drink wine that night also, and the younger arose and lay with him; and he did not know when she lay down or when she arose.

36 Thus both the daughters of Lot were with child by their father.

37 The firstborn bore a son, and called his name Moab; he is the father of the Moabites to this day.

38 As for the younger, she also bore a son, and called his name Ben-ammi; he is the father of the sons of Ammon to this day.

Abraham's Treachery

20 NOW ABRAHAM journeyed from there toward the land of the ʷNegev, and settled between Kadesh and Shur; then he sojourned in Gerar.

New International

the land. 24Then the LORD rained down burning sulfur on Sodom and Gomorrah—from the LORD out of the heavens. 25Thus he overthrew those cities and the entire plain, including all those living in the cities—and also the vegetation in the land. 26But Lot's wife looked back, and she became a pillar of salt.

27Early the next morning Abraham got up and returned to the place where he had stood before the LORD. 28He looked down toward Sodom and Gomorrah, toward all the land of the plain, and he saw dense smoke rising from the land, like smoke from a furnace.

29So when God destroyed the cities of the plain, he remembered Abraham, and he brought Lot out of the catastrophe that overthrew the cities where Lot had lived.

Lot and His Daughters

30Lot and his two daughters left Zoar and settled in the mountains, for he was afraid to stay in Zoar. He and his two daughters lived in a cave. 31One day the older daughter said to the younger, "Our father is old, and there is no man around here to lie with us, as is the custom all over the earth. 32Let's get our father to drink wine and then lie with him and preserve our family line through our father."

33That night they got their father to drink wine, and the older daughter went in and lay with him. He was not aware of it when she lay down or when she got up.

34The next day the older daughter said to the younger, "Last night I lay with my father. Let's get him to drink wine again tonight, and you go in and lie with him so we can preserve our family line through our father." 35So they got their father to drink wine that night also, and the younger daughter went and lay with him. Again he was not aware of it when she lay down or when she got up.

36So both of Lot's daughters became pregnant by their father. 37The older daughter had a son, and she named him Moabᵒ; he is the father of the Moabites of today. 38The younger daughter also had a son, and she named him Ben-Ammiᵖ; he is the father of the Ammonites of today.

Abraham and Abimelech

20 NOW ABRAHAM moved on from there into the region of the Negev and lived between Kadesh and Shur. For a while he stayed in Gerar, 2and there Abraham

o37 *Moab* sounds like the Hebrew for *from father.*
p38 *Ben-Ammi* means *son of my people.*

ʷI.e. South country

King James

2And Abraham said of Sarah his wife, She *is* my sister: and Abimelech king of Gerar sent, and took Sarah.

3But God came to Abimelech in a dream by night, and said to him, Behold, thou *art but* a dead man, for the woman which thou hast taken; for she *is* ʷa man's wife.

4But Abimelech had not come near her: and he said, Lord, wilt thou slay also a righteous nation?

5Said he not unto me, She *is* my sister? and she, even she herself said, He *is* my brother: in the ˣintegrity of my heart and innocency of my hands have I done this.

6And God said unto him in a dream, Yea, I know that thou didst this in the integrity of thy heart; for I also withheld thee from sinning against me: therefore suffered I thee not to touch her.

7Now therefore restore the man *his* wife; for he *is* a prophet, and he shall pray for thee, and thou shalt live: and if thou restore *her* not, know thou that thou shalt surely die, thou, and all that *are* thine.

8Therefore Abimelech rose early in the morning, and called all his servants, and told all these things in their ears: and the men were sore afraid.

9Then Abimelech called Abraham, and said unto him, What hast thou done unto us? and what have I offended thee, that thou hast brought on me and on my kingdom a great sin? thou hast done deeds unto me that ought not to be done.

10And Abimelech said unto Abraham, What sawest thou, that thou hast done this thing?

11And Abraham said, Because I thought, Surely the fear of God *is* not in this place; and they will slay me for my wife's sake.

12And yet indeed *she is* my sister; she *is* the daughter of my father, but not the daughter of my mother; and she became my wife.

13And it came to pass, when God caused me to wander from my father's house, that I said unto her, This *is* thy kindness which thou shalt show unto me; at every place whither we shall come, say of me, He *is* my brother.

14And Abimelech took sheep, and oxen, and menservants, and womenservants, and gave *them* unto Abraham, and restored him Sarah his wife.

15And Abimelech said, Behold, my land *is* before thee: dwell ʸwhere it pleaseth thee.

16And unto Sarah he said, Behold, I have given thy brother a thousand *pieces* of silver: behold, he *is* to thee a covering of the eyes, unto all that *are* with thee, and with all *other:* thus she was reproved.

17 ¶ So Abraham prayed unto God: and God healed Abimelech, and his wife, and his maidservants; and they bare *children.*

18For the LORD had fast closed up all the wombs of the house of Abimelech, because of Sarah Abraham's wife.

The birth of Isaac

21 AND THE LORD visited Sarah as he had said, and the LORD did unto Sarah as he had spoken.

2For Sarah conceived, and bare Abraham a son in his old age, at the set time of which God had spoken to him.

3And Abraham called the name of his son that was born unto him, whom Sarah bare to him, Isaac.

4And Abraham circumcised his son Isaac being eight days old, as God had commanded him.

5And Abraham was an hundred years old, when his son Isaac was born unto him.

6 ¶ And Sarah said, God hath made me to laugh, *so that* all that hear will laugh with me.

7And she said, Who would have said unto Abraham, that Sarah should have given children suck? for I have born *him* a son in his old age.

Amplified

2And Abraham said of Sarah his wife, She is my sister. And Abimelech king of Gerar sent and took Sarah [into his harem].

3But God came to Abimelech in a dream by night and said, Behold, you are a dead man because of the woman whom you have taken [as your own], for she is a man's wife.

4But Abimelech had not come near her, so he said, Lord, will you slay a people who are just *and* innocent?

5Did not the man tell me, She is my sister? And she herself said, He is my brother. In integrity of heart and innocency of hands I have done this.

6Then God said to him in the dream, Yes, I know you did this in the integrity of your heart, for it was I Who kept you back *and* spared you from sinning against Me; therefore I did not give you occasion to touch her.

7So now restore to the man his wife, for he is a prophet, and he will pray for you and you will live. But if you do not restore her [to him], know that you shall surely die, you and all who are yours.

8So Abimelech rose early in the morning and called all his servants and told them all these things; and the men were exceedingly filled with reverence *and* fear.

9Then Abimelech called Abraham and said to him, What have you done to us? And how have I offended you that you have brought on me and my kingdom a great sin? You have done to me what ought not to be done [to anyone].

10And Abimelech said to Abraham, What did you see [in us] that [justified] you in doing such a thing as this?

11And Abraham said, Because I thought, Surely there is no reverence *or* fear of God at all in this place, and they will slay me because of my wife.

12But truly, she is my sister; she is the daughter of my father but not of my mother; and she became my wife.

13When God caused me to wander from my father's house, I said to her, This kindness you can show me: at every place we stop, say of me, He is my brother.

14Then Abimelech took sheep and oxen and male and female slaves and gave them to Abraham and restored to him Sarah his wife.

15And Abimelech said, Behold, my land is before you; dwell wherever it pleases you.

16And to Sarah he said, Behold, I have given this brother of yours a thousand pieces of silver; see, it is to compensate you [for all that has occurred] and to vindicate your honor before all who are with you; before all men you are cleared *and* compensated.

17So Abraham prayed to God, and God healed Abimelech and his wife and his female slaves, and they bore children,

18For the Lord had closed fast the wombs of all in Abimelech's household because of Sarah, Abraham's wife.

21 THE LORD visited Sarah as He had said, and the Lord did for her as He had promised.

2For Sarah became pregnant and bore Abraham a son in his old age, at the set time God had told him.

3Abraham ᵒnamed his son whom Sarah bore to him Isaac [laughter].

4And Abraham circumcised his son Isaac when he was eight days old, as God had commanded him.

5Abraham was a hundred years old when Isaac was born.

6And Sarah said, God has made me to laugh; all who hear will laugh with me.

7And she said, Who would have said to Abraham that Sarah would nurse children at the breast? For I have borne him a son in his old age! [Heb. 11:12.]

ʷHeb. *married to an husband*   ˣOr, *simplicity,* or, *sincerity*
ʸHeb. *as is good in thine eyes*

ᵒSee footnote on Gen. 16:15.

New American Standard

2 Abraham said of Sarah his wife, "She is my sister." So Abimelech king of Gerar sent and took Sarah.

3 But God came to Abimelech in a dream of the night, and said to him, "Behold, you are a dead man because of the woman whom you have taken, for she is married."

4 Now Abimelech had not come near her; and he said, "Lord, will You slay a nation, even *though* blameless?

5 "Did he not himself say to me, 'She is my sister'? And she herself said, 'He is my brother.' In the integrity of my heart and the innocence of my hands I have done this."

6 Then God said to him in the dream, "Yes, I know that in the integrity of your heart you have done this, and I also kept you from sinning against Me; therefore I did not let you touch her.

7 "Now therefore, restore the man's wife, for he is a prophet, and he will pray for you and you will live. But if you do not restore *her,* know that you shall surely die, you and all who are yours."

8 ¶ So Abimelech arose early in the morning and called all his servants and told all these things in their hearing; and the men were greatly frightened.

9 Then Abimelech called Abraham and said to him, "What have you done to us? And how have I sinned against you, that you have brought on me and on my kingdom a great sin? You have done to me things that ought not to be done."

10 And Abimelech said to Abraham, "What have you encountered, that you have done this thing?"

11 Abraham said, "Because I thought, surely there is no fear of God in this place, and they will kill me because of my wife.

12 "Besides, she actually is my sister, the daughter of my father, but not the daughter of my mother, and she became my wife;

13 and it came about, when God caused me to wander from my father's house, that I said to her, 'This is the kindness which you will show to me: everywhere we go, say of me, "He is my brother." ' "

14 Abimelech then took sheep and oxen and male and female servants, and gave them to Abraham, and restored his wife Sarah to him.

15 Abimelech said, "Behold, my land is before you; settle wherever you please."

16 To Sarah he said, "Behold, I have given your brother a thousand pieces of silver; behold, it is your vindication before all who are with you, and before all men you are cleared."

17 Abraham prayed to God, and God healed Abimelech and his wife and his maids, so that they bore *children.*

18 For the LORD had closed fast all the wombs of the household of Abimelech because of Sarah, Abraham's wife.

Isaac Is Born

21 THEN THE LORD took note of Sarah as He had said, and the LORD did for Sarah as He had promised.

2 So Sarah conceived and bore a son to Abraham in his old age, at the appointed time of which God had spoken to him.

3 Abraham called the name of his son who was born to him, whom Sarah bore to him, Isaac.

4 Then Abraham circumcised his son Isaac when he was eight days old, as God had commanded him.

5 Now Abraham was one hundred years old when his son Isaac was born to him.

6 Sarah said, "God has made laughter for me; everyone who hears will laugh with me."

7 And she said, "Who would have said to Abraham that Sarah would nurse children? Yet I have borne him a son in his old age."

New International

said of his wife Sarah, "She is my sister." Then Abimelech king of Gerar sent for Sarah and took her.

3 But God came to Abimelech in a dream one night and said to him, "You are as good as dead because of the woman you have taken; she is a married woman."

4 Now Abimelech had not gone near her, so he said, "Lord, will you destroy an innocent nation? 5 Did he not say to me, 'She is my sister,' and didn't she also say, 'He is my brother'? I have done this with a clear conscience and clean hands."

6 Then God said to him in the dream, "Yes, I know you did this with a clear conscience, and so I have kept you from sinning against me. That is why I did not let you touch her. 7 Now return the man's wife, for he is a prophet, and he will pray for you and you will live. But if you do not return her, you may be sure that you and all yours will die."

8 Early the next morning Abimelech summoned all his officials, and when he told them all that had happened, they were very much afraid. 9 Then Abimelech called Abraham in and said, "What have you done to us? How have I wronged you that you have brought such great guilt upon me and my kingdom? You have done things to me that should not be done." 10 And Abimelech asked Abraham, "What was your reason for doing this?"

11 Abraham replied, "I said to myself, 'There is surely no fear of God in this place, and they will kill me because of my wife.' 12 Besides, she really is my sister, the daughter of my father though not of my mother; and she became my wife. 13 And when God had me wander from my father's household, I said to her, 'This is how you can show your love to me: Everywhere we go, say of me, "He is my brother." ' "

14 Then Abimelech brought sheep and cattle and male and female slaves and gave them to Abraham, and he returned Sarah his wife to him. 15 And Abimelech said, "My land is before you; live wherever you like."

16 To Sarah he said, "I am giving your brother a thousand shekels*q* of silver. This is to cover the offense against you before all who are with you; you are completely vindicated."

17 Then Abraham prayed to God, and God healed Abimelech, his wife and his slave girls so they could have children again, 18 for the LORD had closed up every womb in Abimelech's household because of Abraham's wife Sarah.

The Birth of Isaac

21 NOW THE LORD was gracious to Sarah as he had said, and the LORD did for Sarah what he had promised. 2 Sarah became pregnant and bore a son to Abraham in his old age, at the very time God had promised him. 3 Abraham gave the name Isaac*r* to the son Sarah bore him. 4 When his son Isaac was eight days old, Abraham circumcised him, as God commanded him. 5 Abraham was a hundred years old when his son Isaac was born to him.

6 Sarah said, "God has brought me laughter, and everyone who hears about this will laugh with me." 7 And she added, "Who would have said to Abraham that Sarah would nurse children? Yet I have borne him a son in his old age."

q 16 That is, about 25 pounds (about 11.5 kilograms)   *r 3 Isaac means he laughs.*

King James

Amplified

Hagar and Ishmael cast out

8And the child grew, and was weaned: and Abraham made a great feast the *same* day that Isaac was weaned.

9 ¶ And Sarah saw the son of Hagar the Egyptian, which she had born unto Abraham, mocking.

10Wherefore she said unto Abraham, Cast out this bondwoman and her son: for the son of this bondwoman shall not be heir with my son, *even* with Isaac.

11And the thing was very grievous in Abraham's sight because of his son.

12 ¶ And God said unto Abraham, Let it not be grievous in thy sight because of the lad, and because of thy bondwoman; in all that Sarah hath said unto thee, hearken unto her voice; for in Isaac shall thy seed be called.

13And also of the son of the bondwoman will I make a nation, because he *is* thy seed.

14And Abraham rose up early in the morning, and took bread, and a bottle of water, and gave *it* unto Hagar, putting *it* on her shoulder, and the child, and sent her away: and she departed, and wandered in the wilderness of Beersheba.

15And the water was spent in the bottle, and she cast the child under one of the shrubs.

16And she went, and sat her down over against *him* a good way off, as it were a bowshot: for she said, Let me not see the death of the child. And she sat over against *him,* and lift up her voice, and wept.

17And God heard the voice of the lad; and the angel of God called to Hagar out of heaven, and said unto her, What aileth thee, Hagar? fear not; for God hath heard the voice of the lad where he *is.*

18Arise, lift up the lad, and hold him in thine hand; for I will make him a great nation.

19And God opened her eyes, and she saw a well of water; and she went, and filled the bottle with water, and gave the lad drink.

20And God was with the lad; and he grew, and dwelt in the wilderness, and became an archer.

21And he dwelt in the wilderness of Paran: and his mother took him a wife out of the land of Egypt.

Covenant with Abimelech

22 ¶ And it came to pass at that time, that Abimelech and Phichol the chief captain of his host spake unto Abraham, saying, God *is* with thee in all that thou doest:

23Now therefore swear unto me here by God *z*that thou wilt not deal falsely with me, nor with my son, nor with my son's son: *but* according to the kindness that I have done unto thee, thou shalt do unto me, and to the land wherein thou hast sojourned.

24And Abraham said, I will swear.

25And Abraham reproved Abimelech because of a well of water, which Abimelech's servants had violently taken away.

26And Abimelech said, I wot not who hath done this thing: neither didst thou tell me, neither yet heard I *of it,* but today.

27And Abraham took sheep and oxen, and gave them unto Abimelech; and both of them made a covenant.

28And Abraham set seven ewe lambs of the flock by themselves.

29And Abimelech said unto Abraham, What *mean* these seven ewe lambs which thou hast set by themselves?

30And he said, For *these* seven ewe lambs shalt thou take of my hand, that they may be a witness unto me, that I have digged this well.

31Wherefore he called that place *a*Beer-sheba; because there they sware both of them.

32Thus they made a covenant at Beer-sheba: then Abimelech rose up, and Phichol the chief captain of his host, and they returned into the land of the Philistines.

8And the child grew and was *p*weaned, and Abraham made a great feast the same day that Isaac was weaned.

9Now Sarah saw the son of Hagar the Egyptian, whom she had borne to Abraham, mocking [Isaac].

10Therefore she said to Abraham, Cast out this bondwoman and her son, for the son of this bondwoman shall not be an heir with my son Isaac. [Gal. 4:28–31.]

11And the thing was very grievous (serious, evil) in Abraham's sight on account of his son [Ishmael].

12God said to Abraham, Do not let it seem grievous *and* evil to you because of the youth and your bondwoman; in all that Sarah has said to you, do what she asks, for in Isaac shall your posterity be called. [Rom. 9:7.]

13And I will make a nation of the son of the bondwoman also, because he is your offspring.

14So Abraham rose early in the morning and took bread and a bottle of water and gave them to Hagar, putting them on her shoulders, and he sent her and the *q*youth away. And she wandered on [aimlessly] and lost her way in the wilderness of Beersheba.

15When the water in the bottle was all gone, Hagar caused the youth to lie down under one of the shrubs.

16Then she went and sat down opposite him a good way off, about a bowshot, for she said, Let me not see the death of the lad. And as she sat down opposite him, *r*he lifted up his voice and wept *and* she raised her voice and wept.

17And God heard the voice of the youth, and the angel of God called to Hagar out of heaven and said to her, What troubles you, Hagar? Fear not, for God has heard the voice of the youth where he is.

18Arise, raise up the youth and support him with your hand, for I intend to make him a great nation.

19Then God opened her eyes and she saw a well of water; and she went and filled the [empty] bottle with water and caused the youth to drink.

20And God was with the youth, and he developed; and he dwelt in the wilderness and became an archer.

21He dwelt in the Wilderness of Paran; and his mother took a wife for him out of the land of Egypt.

22At that time Abimelech and Phicol the commander of his army said to Abraham, God is with you in everything you do.

23So now, swear to me here by God that you will not deal falsely with me or with my son or with my posterity; but as I have dealt with you kindly, you will do the same with me and with the land in which you have sojourned.

24And Abraham said, I will swear.

25When Abraham complained to *and* reasoned with Abimelech about a well of water [Abimelech's] servants had violently seized,

26Abimelech said, I know not who did this thing; you did not tell me, and I did not hear of it until today.

27So Abraham took sheep and oxen and gave them to Abimelech, and the two men made a league *or* covenant.

28Abraham set apart seven ewe lambs of the flock,

29And Abimelech said to Abraham, What do these seven ewe lambs which you have set apart mean?

30He said, You are to accept these seven ewe lambs from me as a witness for me that I dug this well.

31Therefore that place was called Beersheba [well of the oath], because there both parties swore an oath.

32Thus they made a covenant at Beersheba; then Abimelech and Phicol the commander of his army returned to the land of the Philistines.

---

p This was probably when the child was about three years of age. Samuel served in the sanctuary from the time that he was weaned (I Sam. 1:22-28). A Hebrew mother is quoted in II Maccabees 7:27 as saying to her son that she gave him "suck three years."
q Ishmael was born when Abraham was eighty-six years old (Gen. 16:16), so Ishmael was fourteen years old when Isaac was born. Isaac was weaned (Gen. 21:8) at least three years later probably (II Chron. 31:16; II Maccabees 7:27).   *r* The Hebrew says, "she lifted up her voice." *The Septuagint* (Greek translation of the Old Testament) says "he . . ."—which the next verse seems to support. The circumstances allow either.

z Heb. *if thou shalt lie unto me*   *a* i.e. *The well of the oath*

New American Standard

8 ¶ The child grew and was weaned, and Abraham made a great feast on the day that Isaac was weaned.

Sarah Turns against Hagar

9 Now Sarah saw the son of Hagar the Egyptian, whom she had borne to Abraham, mocking.

10 Therefore she said to Abraham, "Drive out this maid and her son, for the son of this maid shall not be an heir with my son Isaac."

11 The matter distressed Abraham greatly because of his son.

12 But God said to Abraham, "Do not be distressed because of the lad and your maid; whatever Sarah tells you, listen to her, for through Isaac your descendants shall be named.

13 "And of the son of the maid I will make a nation also, because he is your descendant."

14 So Abraham rose early in the morning and took bread and a skin of water and gave *them* to Hagar, putting *them* on her shoulder, and *gave her* the boy, and sent her away. And she departed and wandered about in the wilderness of Beersheba.

15 ¶ When the water in the skin was used up, she left the boy under one of the bushes.

16 Then she went and sat down opposite him, about a bowshot away, for she said, "Do not let me see the boy die." And she sat opposite him, and lifted up her voice and wept.

17 God heard the lad crying; and the angel of God called to Hagar from heaven and said to her, "What is the matter with you, Hagar? Do not fear, for God has heard the voice of the lad where he is.

18 "Arise, lift up the lad, and hold him by the hand, for I will make a great nation of him."

19 Then God opened her eyes and she saw a well of water; and she went and filled the skin with water and gave the lad a drink.

20 ¶ God was with the lad, and he grew; and he lived in the wilderness and became an archer.

21 He lived in the wilderness of Paran, and his mother took a wife for him from the land of Egypt.

Covenant with Abimelech

22 ¶ Now it came about at that time that Abimelech and Phicol, the commander of his army, spoke to Abraham, saying, "God is with you in all that you do;

23 now therefore, swear to me here by God that you will not deal falsely with me or with my offspring or with my posterity, but according to the kindness that I have shown to you, you shall show to me and to the land in which you have sojourned."

24 Abraham said, "I swear it."

25 But Abraham complained to Abimelech because of the well of water which the servants of Abimelech had seized.

26 And Abimelech said, "I do not know who has done this thing; you did not tell me, nor did I hear of it until today."

27 ¶ Abraham took sheep and oxen and gave them to Abimelech, and the two of them made a covenant.

28 Then Abraham set seven ewe lambs of the flock by themselves.

29 Abimelech said to Abraham, "What do these seven ewe lambs mean, which you have set by themselves?"

30 He said, "You shall take these seven ewe lambs from my hand so that it may be a witness to me, that I dug this well."

31 Therefore he called that place Beersheba, because there the two of them took an oath.

32 So they made a covenant at Beersheba; and Abimelech and Phicol, the commander of his army, arose and returned to the land of the Philistines.

New International

Hagar and Ishmael Sent Away

8 The child grew and was weaned, and on the day Isaac was weaned Abraham held a great feast. 9 But Sarah saw that the son whom Hagar the Egyptian had borne to Abraham was mocking, 10 and she said to Abraham, "Get rid of that slave woman and her son, for that slave woman's son will never share in the inheritance with my son Isaac."

11 The matter distressed Abraham greatly because it concerned his son. 12 But God said to him, "Do not be so distressed about the boy and your maidservant. Listen to whatever Sarah tells you, because it is through Isaac that your offspring[s] will be reckoned. 13 I will make the son of the maidservant into a nation also, because he is your offspring."

14 Early the next morning Abraham took some food and a skin of water and gave them to Hagar. He set them on her shoulders and then sent her off with the boy. She went on her way and wandered in the desert of Beersheba.

15 When the water in the skin was gone, she put the boy under one of the bushes. 16 Then she went off and sat down nearby, about a bowshot away, for she thought, "I cannot watch the boy die." And as she sat there nearby, she[t] began to sob.

17 God heard the boy crying, and the angel of God called to Hagar from heaven and said to her, "What is the matter, Hagar? Do not be afraid; God has heard the boy crying as he lies there. 18 Lift the boy up and take him by the hand, for I will make him into a great nation."

19 Then God opened her eyes and she saw a well of water. So she went and filled the skin with water and gave the boy a drink.

20 God was with the boy as he grew up. He lived in the desert and became an archer. 21 While he was living in the Desert of Paran, his mother got a wife for him from Egypt.

The Treaty at Beersheba

22 At that time Abimelech and Phicol the commander of his forces said to Abraham, "God is with you in everything you do. 23 Now swear to me here before God that you will not deal falsely with me or my children or my descendants. Show to me and the country where you are living as an alien the same kindness I have shown to you."

24 Abraham said, "I swear it."

25 Then Abraham complained to Abimelech about a well of water that Abimelech's servants had seized. 26 But Abimelech said, "I don't know who has done this. You did not tell me, and I heard about it only today."

27 So Abraham brought sheep and cattle and gave them to Abimelech, and the two men made a treaty. 28 Abraham set apart seven ewe lambs from the flock, 29 and Abimelech asked Abraham, "What is the meaning of these seven ewe lambs you have set apart by themselves?"

30 He replied, "Accept these seven lambs from my hand as a witness that I dug this well."

31 So that place was called Beersheba,[u] because the two men swore an oath there.

32 After the treaty had been made at Beersheba, Abimelech and Phicol the commander of his forces returned to

---

s 12 Or *seed*   *t 16* Hebrew; Septuagint *the child*
u 31 Beersheba can mean *well of seven* or *well of the oath.*

King James

33 ¶ And *Abraham* planted a *b*grove in Beer-sheba, and called there on the name of the LORD, the everlasting God.

34And Abraham sojourned in the Philistines' land many days.

God tests Abraham

22 AND IT came to pass after these things, that God did tempt Abraham, and said unto him, Abraham: and he said, *c*Behold, *here* I *am,*

2And he said, Take now thy son, thine only *son* Isaac, whom thou lovest, and get thee into the land of Moriah; and offer him there for a burnt offering upon one of the mountains which I will tell thee of.

3 ¶ And Abraham rose up early in the morning, and saddled his ass, and took two of his young men with him, and Isaac his son, and clave the wood for the burnt offering, and rose up, and went unto the place of which God had told him.

4Then on the third day Abraham lifted up his eyes, and saw the place afar off.

5And Abraham said unto his young men, Abide ye here with the ass; and I and the lad will go yonder and worship, and come again to you.

6And Abraham took the wood of the burnt offering, and laid *it* upon Isaac his son; and he took the fire in his hand, and a knife; and they went both of them together.

7And Isaac spake unto Abraham his father, and said, My father; and he said, *c*Here *am* I, my son. And he said, Behold the fire and the wood: but where *is* the *d*lamb for a burnt offering?

8And Abraham said, My son, God will provide himself a lamb for a burnt offering: so they went both of them together.

9And they came to the place which God had told him of; and Abraham built an altar there, and laid the wood in order, and bound Isaac his son, and laid him on the altar upon the wood.

10And Abraham stretched forth his hand, and took the knife to slay his son.

11And the angel of the LORD called unto him out of heaven, and said, Abraham, Abraham: and he said, Here *am* I.

12And he said, Lay not thine hand upon the lad, neither do thou any thing unto him: for now I know that thou fearest God, seeing thou hast not withheld thy son, thine only *son* from me.

13And Abraham lifted up his eyes, and looked, and behold behind *him* a ram caught in a thicket by his horns: and Abraham went and took the ram, and offered him up for a burnt offering in the stead of his son.

14And Abraham called the name of that place *e*Jehovah-jireh: as it is said *to* this day, In the mount of the LORD it shall be seen.

15 ¶ And the angel of the LORD called unto Abraham out of heaven the second time,

16And said, By myself have I sworn, saith the LORD, for because thou hast done this thing, and hast not withheld thy son, thine only *son:*

33Abraham planted a tamarisk tree in Beersheba and called there on the name of the Lord, the Eternal God.

34And Abraham sojourned in Philistia many days.

22 AFTER THESE events, God tested *and* proved Abraham and said to him, Abraham! And he said, Here I am.

2[God] said, Take now your son, your only son Isaac, whom you love, and go to the region of Moriah; and offer him there as a burnt offering upon one of the mountains of which I will tell you.

3So Abraham rose early in the morning, saddled his donkey, and took two of his young men with him and his son Isaac; and he split the wood for the burnt offering, and then began the trip to the place of which God had told him.

4On the third day Abraham looked up and saw the place in the distance.

5And Abraham said to his servants, Settle down *and* stay here with the donkey, and I and the young man will go yonder and worship and *s*come again to you.

6Then Abraham took the wood for the burnt offering and laid it on [the shoulders of] Isaac his son, and he took the fire (the firepot) in his own hand, and a knife; and the two of them went on together.

7And Isaac said to Abraham, My father! And he said, Here I am, my son. [Isaac] said, See, here are the fire and the wood, but where is the lamb for the burnt sacrifice?

8Abraham said, My son, *t*God Himself will provide a lamb for the burnt offering. So the two went on together.

9When they came to the place of which God had told him, Abraham built an altar there; then he laid the wood in order and *u*bound Isaac his son and laid him on the altar on the wood. [Matt. 10:37.]

10And Abraham stretched forth his hand and took hold of the knife to slay his son. [Heb. 11:17–19.]

11But the *v*Angel of the Lord called to him from heaven and said, Abraham, Abraham! He answered, Here I am.

12And He said, Do not lay your hand on the lad or do anything to him; for now I know that you fear *and* revere God, since you have not held back from Me *or* begrudged giving Me your son, your only son.

13Then Abraham looked up *and* glanced around, and behold, behind him was a ram caught in a thicket by his horns. And Abraham went and took the ram and offered it up for a burnt offering *and* an ascending sacrifice instead of his son!

14So Abraham called the name of that place The Lord Will Provide. And it is said to this day, On the mount of the Lord it will be provided.

15The Angel of the Lord called to Abraham from heaven a second time

16And said, I have sworn by Myself, says the Lord, that since you have done this and have not withheld [from Me] *or* begrudged [giving Me] your son, your only son,

---

s Abraham was not lying to his servants or trying to deceive them. He believed God, Who had promised him that this young man's posterity was to inherit the promises made to Abraham (Gen. 12:2, 3).   *t* We must not suppose that this was the language merely of faith and obedience. Abraham spoke prophetically, and referred to that Lamb of God which He had provided for Himself, Who in the fullness of time would take away the sin of the world, and of Whom Isaac was a most expressive type (Adam Clarke, *The Holy Bible with A Commentary*). For Abraham was a prophet (Gen. 20:7). Jesus said Abraham hoped for "My day [My incarnation]; and he did see it and was delighted" (John 8:56).   *u* Isaac, who was perhaps twenty-five years old (according to the ancient historian Josephus), shared his father's confidence in God's promise. Was not his very existence the result of God keeping His word? (Gen. 17:15-17.)   *v* See footnote on Gen. 16:7.

---

b Or, *tree*   *c* Heb. *Behold me*   *d* Or, *kid*   *e* i.e. *The LORD will see,* or *provide*

New American Standard

[33] *Abraham* planted a tamarisk tree at Beersheba, and there he called on the name of the Lord, the Everlasting God.

[34] And Abraham sojourned in the land of the Philistines for many days.

The Offering of Isaac

22 NOW IT came about after these things, that God tested Abraham, and said to him, "Abraham!" And he said, "Here I am."

[2] He said, "Take now your son, your only son, whom you love, Isaac, and go to the land of Moriah, and offer him there as a burnt offering on one of the mountains of which I will tell you."

[3] So Abraham rose early in the morning and saddled his donkey, and took two of his young men with him and Isaac his son; and he split wood for the burnt offering, and arose and went to the place of which God had told him.

[4] On the third day Abraham raised his eyes and saw the place from a distance.

[5] Abraham said to his young men, "Stay here with the donkey, and I and the lad will go over there; and we will worship and return to you."

[6] Abraham took the wood of the burnt offering and laid it on Isaac his son, and he took in his hand the fire and the knife. So the two of them walked on together.

[7] Isaac spoke to Abraham his father and said, "My father!" And he said, "Here I am, my son." And he said, "Behold, the fire and the wood, but where is the lamb for the burnt offering?"

[8] Abraham said, "God will provide for Himself the lamb for the burnt offering, my son." So the two of them walked on together.

[9] ¶ Then they came to the place of which God had told him; and Abraham built the altar there and arranged the wood, and bound his son Isaac and laid him on the altar, on top of the wood.

[10] Abraham stretched out his hand and took the knife to slay his son.

[11] But the angel of the Lord called to him from heaven and said, "Abraham, Abraham!" And he said, "Here I am."

[12] He said, "Do not stretch out your hand against the lad, and do nothing to him; for now I know that you fear God, since you have not withheld your son, your only son, from Me."

[13] Then Abraham raised his eyes and looked, and behold, behind *him* a ram caught in the thicket by his horns; and Abraham went and took the ram and offered him up for a burnt offering in the place of his son.

[14] Abraham called the name of that place The Lord Will Provide, as it is said to this day, "In the mount of the Lord it will be provided."

[15] ¶ Then the angel of the Lord called to Abraham a second time from heaven,

[16] and said, "By Myself I have sworn, declares the Lord, because you have done this thing and have not withheld your son, your only son,

New International

the land of the Philistines. [33] Abraham planted a tamarisk tree in Beersheba, and there he called upon the name of the Lord, the Eternal God. [34] And Abraham stayed in the land of the Philistines for a long time.

Abraham Tested

22 SOME TIME later God tested Abraham. He said to him, "Abraham!"

"Here I am," he replied.

[2] Then God said, "Take your son, your only son, Isaac, whom you love, and go to the region of Moriah. Sacrifice him there as a burnt offering on one of the mountains I will tell you about."

[3] Early the next morning Abraham got up and saddled his donkey. He took with him two of his servants and his son Isaac. When he had cut enough wood for the burnt offering, he set out for the place God had told him about. [4] On the third day Abraham looked up and saw the place in the distance. [5] He said to his servants, "Stay here with the donkey while I and the boy go over there. We will worship and then we will come back to you."

[6] Abraham took the wood for the burnt offering and placed it on his son Isaac, and he himself carried the fire and the knife. As the two of them went on together, [7] Isaac spoke up and said to his father Abraham, "Father?"

"Yes, my son?" Abraham replied.

"The fire and wood are here," Isaac said, "but where is the lamb for the burnt offering?"

[8] Abraham answered, "God himself will provide the lamb for the burnt offering, my son." And the two of them went on together.

[9] When they reached the place God had told him about, Abraham built an altar there and arranged the wood on it. He bound his son Isaac and laid him on the altar, on top of the wood. [10] Then he reached out his hand and took the knife to slay his son. [11] But the angel of the Lord called out to him from heaven, "Abraham! Abraham!"

"Here I am," he replied.

[12] "Do not lay a hand on the boy," he said. "Do not do anything to him. Now I know that you fear God, because you have not withheld from me your son, your only son."

[13] Abraham looked up and there in a thicket he saw a ram[v] caught by its horns. He went over and took the ram and sacrificed it as a burnt offering instead of his son. [14] So Abraham called that place The Lord Will Provide. And to this day it is said, "On the mountain of the Lord it will be provided."

[15] The angel of the Lord called to Abraham from heaven a second time [16] and said, "I swear by myself, declares the Lord, that because you have done this and have not with-

---

v 13 Many manuscripts of the Masoretic Text, Samaritan Pentateuch, Septuagint and Syriac; most manuscripts of the Masoretic Text *a ram behind ⎣him⎦*

King James

Amplified

King James

¹⁷That in blessing I will bless thee, and in multiplying I will multiply thy seed as the stars of the heaven, and as the sand which *is* upon the sea *f*shore; and thy seed shall possess the gate of his enemies;

¹⁸And in thy seed shall all the nations of the earth be blessed; because thou hast obeyed my voice.

¹⁹So Abraham returned unto his young men, and they rose up and went together to Beer-sheba; and Abraham dwelt at Beer-sheba.

²⁰ ¶ And it came to pass after these things, that it was told Abraham, saying, Behold, Milcah, she hath also born children unto thy brother Nahor;

²¹Huz his firstborn, and Buz his brother, and Kemuel the father of Aram,

²²And Chesed, and Hazo, and Pildash, and Jidlaph, and Bethuel.

²³And Bethuel begat Rebekah: these eight Milcah did bear to Nahor, Abraham's brother.

²⁴And his concubine, whose name *was* Reumah, she bare also Tebah, and Gaham, and Thahash, and Maachah.

The death of Sarah

23 AND SARAH was an hundred and seven and twenty years old: *these were* the years of the life of Sarah.

²And Sarah died in Kirjath-arba; the same *is* Hebron in the land of Canaan: and Abraham came to mourn for Sarah, and to weep for her.

³ ¶ And Abraham stood up from before his dead, and spake unto the sons of Heth, saying,

⁴I *am* a stranger and a sojourner with you: give me a possession of a buryingplace with you, that I may bury my dead out of my sight.

⁵And the children of Heth answered Abraham, saying unto him,

⁶Hear us, my lord: thou *art* *g*a mighty prince among us: in the choice of our sepulchres bury thy dead; none of us shall withhold from thee his sepulchre, but that thou mayest bury thy dead.

⁷And Abraham stood up, and bowed himself to the people of the land, *even* to the children of Heth.

⁸And he communed with them, saying, If it be your mind that I should bury my dead out of my sight; hear me, and entreat for me to Ephron the son of Zohar,

⁹That he may give me the cave of Machpelah, which he hath, which *is* in the end of his field; for *h*as much money as it is worth he shall give it me for a possession of a buryingplace amongst you.

¹⁰And Ephron dwelt among the children of Heth: and Ephron the Hittite answered Abraham in the *i*audience of the children of Heth, *even* of all that went in at the gate of his city, saying,

¹¹Nay, my lord, hear me: the field give I thee, and the cave that *is* therein, I give it thee; in the presence of the sons of my people give I it thee: bury thy dead.

¹²And Abraham bowed down himself before the people of the land.

¹³And he spake unto Ephron in the audience of the people of the land, saying, But if thou *wilt give it,* I pray thee, hear me: I will give thee money for the field; take *it* of me, and I will bury my dead there.

¹⁴And Ephron answered Abraham, saying unto him,

Amplified

¹⁷In blessing I will bless you and in multiplying I will multiply your descendants like the stars of the heavens and like the sand on the seashore. And your Seed (Heir) will possess the gate of His enemies, [Heb. 6:13, 14; 11:12.]

¹⁸And in your Seed [*w*Christ] shall all the nations of the earth be blessed *and* [by Him] bless themselves, because you have heard *and* obeyed My voice. [Gen. 12:2–3; 13:16; 22:18; 26:4; 28:14; Acts 3:25, 26; Gal. 3:16.]

¹⁹So Abraham returned to his servants, and they rose up and went with him to Beersheba; there Abraham lived.

²⁰Now after these things, it was told Abraham, Milcah has also borne children to your brother Nahor:

²¹Uz the firstborn, Buz his brother, Kemuel the father of Aram,

²²Chesed, Hazo, Pildash, Jidlaph, and Bethuel.

²³Bethuel became the father of Rebekah. These eight Milcah bore to Nahor, Abraham's brother.

²⁴And his concubine, whose name was Reumah, bore Tebah, Gaham, Tahash, and Maacah.

23 SARAH LIVED 127 years; this was the length of the life of Sarah.

²And Sarah died in Kiriath-arba, *x*that is, Hebron, in the land of Canaan. And Abraham went to mourn for Sarah and to weep for her.

³And Abraham stood up from before his dead and said to the sons of Heth,

⁴I am a stranger and a sojourner with you; give me property for a burial place among you, that I may bury my dead out of my sight.

⁵And the Hittites replied to Abraham,

⁶Listen to us, my lord; you are a mighty prince among us. Bury your dead in any tomb *or* grave of ours that you choose; none of us will withhold from you his tomb or hinder you from burying your dead.

⁷And Abraham stood up and bowed himself to the people of the land, the Hittites.

⁸And he said to them, If you are willing to grant my dead a burial out of my sight, listen to me and ask Ephron son of Zohar for me,

⁹That he may give me the cave of Machpelah, which he owns—it is at the end of his field. For the full price let him give it to me here in your presence as a burial place which I may hold fast among you.

¹⁰Now Ephron was present there among the sons of Heth; so, in the hearing of all who went in at the gate of his city, Ephron the Hittite answered Abraham, saying,

¹¹No, my lord, hear me; I give you the field, and the cave that is in it I give you. In the presence of the sons of my people I give it to you. Bury your dead.

¹²Then Abraham bowed himself down before the people of the land.

¹³And he said to Ephron in the presence of the people of the land, But if you will give it, I beg of you, hear me. I will give you the price of the field; accept it from me, and I will bury my dead there.

¹⁴Ephron replied to Abraham, saying,

w We have the authority of the apostle Paul (Gal. 3:8, 16, 18) to restrict this promise to our blessed Lord, Who was the Seed through Whom alone all God's blessings of providence, mercy, grace, and glory should be conveyed to the nations of the earth (Adam Clarke, *The Holy Bible with A Commentary*).   *x* Surely this indicates that this detail was written at a very early date—before Israel had entered the land. No one in later times would need to be told where Hebron was. Not only was it conspicuous in Joshua's and Caleb's day, but it became a "city of refuge." Besides all this, David was king in Hebron for seven years. Obviously the Israelites had not yet entered Canaan and had to be told not only the name of the place where Abraham and Isaac had lived and were buried, but also its location (P. J. Wiseman, *New Discoveries in Babylonia About Genesis*).

f Heb. *lip*   *g* Heb. *a prince of God*   *h* Heb. *full money*
i Heb. *ears*

New American Standard

¹⁷ indeed I will greatly bless you, and I will greatly multiply your seed as the stars of the heavens and as the sand which is on the seashore; and your seed shall possess the gate of their enemies.

¹⁸"In your seed all the nations of the earth shall be blessed, because you have obeyed My voice."

¹⁹ So Abraham returned to his young men, and they arose and went together to Beersheba; and Abraham lived at Beersheba.

²⁰ ¶ Now it came about after these things, that it was told Abraham, saying, "Behold, Milcah also has borne children to your brother Nahor:

²¹ Uz his firstborn and Buz his brother and Kemuel the father of Aram

²² and Chesed and Hazo and Pildash and Jidlaph and Bethuel."

²³ Bethuel became the father of Rebekah; these eight Milcah bore to Nahor, Abraham's brother.

²⁴ His concubine, whose name was Reumah, also bore Tebah and Gaham and Tahash and Maachah.

Death and Burial of Sarah

23 NOW SARAH lived one hundred and twenty-seven years; *these were* the years of the life of Sarah.

² Sarah died in Kiriath-arba (that is, Hebron) in the land of Canaan; and Abraham went in to mourn for Sarah and to weep for her.

³ Then Abraham rose from before his dead, and spoke to the sons of Heth, saying,

⁴"I am a stranger and a sojourner among you; give me a burial site among you that I may bury my dead out of my sight."

⁵ The sons of Heth answered Abraham, saying to him,

⁶"Hear us, my lord, you are a mighty prince among us; bury your dead in the choicest of our graves; none of us will refuse you his grave for burying your dead."

⁷ So Abraham rose and bowed to the people of the land, the sons of Heth.

⁸ And he spoke with them, saying, "If it is your wish *for me* to bury my dead out of my sight, hear me, and approach Ephron the son of Zohar for me,

⁹ that he may give me the cave of Machpelah which he owns, which is at the end of his field; for the full price let him give it to me in your presence for a burial site."

¹⁰ Now Ephron was sitting among the sons of Heth; and Ephron the Hittite answered Abraham in the hearing of the sons of Heth; *even* of all who went in at the gate of his city, saying,

¹¹"No, my lord, hear me; I give you the field, and I give you the cave that is in it. In the presence of the sons of my people I give it to you; bury your dead."

¹² And Abraham bowed before the people of the land.

¹³ He spoke to Ephron in the hearing of the people of the land, saying, "If you will only please listen to me; I will give the price of the field, accept *it* from me that I may bury my dead there."

¹⁴ Then Ephron answered Abraham, saying to him,

New International

held your son, your only son, ¹⁷I will surely bless you and make your descendants as numerous as the stars in the sky and as the sand on the seashore. Your descendants will take possession of the cities of their enemies, ¹⁸and through your offspring^w all nations on earth will be blessed, because you have obeyed me."

¹⁹Then Abraham returned to his servants, and they set off together for Beersheba. And Abraham stayed in Beersheba.

Nahor's Sons

²⁰Some time later Abraham was told, "Milcah is also a mother; she has borne sons to your brother Nahor: ²¹Uz the firstborn, Buz his brother, Kemuel (the father of Aram), ²²Kesed, Hazo, Pildash, Jidlaph and Bethuel." ²³Bethuel became the father of Rebekah. Milcah bore these eight sons to Abraham's brother Nahor. ²⁴His concubine, whose name was Reumah, also had sons: Tebah, Gaham, Tahash and Maacah.

The Death of Sarah

23 SARAH LIVED to be a hundred and twenty-seven years old. ²She died at Kiriath Arba (that is, Hebron) in the land of Canaan, and Abraham went to mourn for Sarah and to weep over her.

³Then Abraham rose from beside his dead wife and spoke to the Hittites.^x He said, ⁴"I am an alien and a stranger among you. Sell me some property for a burial site here so I can bury my dead."

⁵The Hittites replied to Abraham, ⁶"Sir, listen to us. You are a mighty prince among us. Bury your dead in the choicest of our tombs. None of us will refuse you his tomb for burying your dead."

⁷Then Abraham rose and bowed down before the people of the land, the Hittites. ⁸He said to them, "If you are willing to let me bury my dead, then listen to me and intercede with Ephron son of Zohar on my behalf ⁹so he will sell me the cave of Machpelah, which belongs to him and is at the end of his field. Ask him to sell it to me for the full price as a burial site among you."

¹⁰Ephron the Hittite was sitting among his people and he replied to Abraham in the hearing of all the Hittites who had come to the gate of his city. ¹¹"No, my lord," he said. "Listen to me; I give^y you the field, and I give^y you the cave that is in it. I give^y it to you in the presence of my people. Bury your dead."

¹²Again Abraham bowed down before the people of the land ¹³and he said to Ephron in their hearing, "Listen to me, if you will. I will pay the price of the field. Accept it from me so I can bury my dead there."

w 18 Or seed   x 3 Or the sons of Heth; also in verses 5, 7, 10,
16, 18 and 20   y 11 Or sell

King James

Amplified

¹⁵My lord, hearken unto me: the land *is worth* four hundred shekels of silver; what *is* that betwixt me and thee? bury therefore thy dead.

¹⁶And Abraham hearkened unto Ephron; and Abraham weighed to Ephron the silver, which he had named in the audience of the sons of Heth, four hundred shekels of silver, current *money* with the merchant.

¹⁷ ¶ And the field of Ephron, which *was* in Machpelah, which *was* before Mamre, the field, and the cave which *was* therein, and all the trees that *were* in the field, that *were* in all the borders round about, were made sure

¹⁸Unto Abraham for a possession in the presence of the children of Heth, before all that went in at the gate of his city.

¹⁹And after this, Abraham buried Sarah his wife in the cave of the field of Machpelah before Mamre: the same *is* Hebron in the land of Canaan.

²⁰And the field, and the cave that *is* therein, were made sure unto Abraham for a possession of a buryingplace by the sons of Heth.

Isaac and Rebekah

24 AND ABRAHAM was old, *and* j well stricken in age: and the LORD had blessed Abraham in all things.

²And Abraham said unto his eldest servant of his house, that ruled over all that he had, Put, I pray thee, thy hand under my thigh:

³And I will make thee swear by the LORD, the God of heaven, and the God of the earth, that thou shalt not take a wife unto my son of the daughters of the Canaanites, among whom I dwell:

⁴But thou shalt go unto my country, and to my kindred, and take a wife unto my son Isaac.

⁵And the servant said unto him, Peradventure the woman will not be willing to follow me unto this land: must I needs bring thy son again unto the land from whence thou camest?

⁶And Abraham said unto him, Beware thou that thou bring not my son thither again.

⁷ ¶ The LORD God of heaven, which took me from my father's house, and from the land of my kindred, and which spake unto me, and that sware unto me, saying, Unto thy seed will I give this land; he shall send his angel before thee, and thou shalt take a wife unto my son from thence.

⁸And if the woman will not be willing to follow thee, then thou shalt be clear from this my oath: only bring not my son thither again.

⁹And the servant put his hand under the thigh of Abraham his master, and sware to him concerning that matter.

¹⁰ ¶ And the servant took ten camels of the camels of his master, and departed; k for all the goods of his master *were* in his hand: and he arose, and went to Mesopotamia, unto the city of Nahor.

¹¹And he made his camels to kneel down without the city by a well of water at the time of the evening, *even* the time *l* that women go out to draw *water.*

¹²And he said, O LORD God of my master Abraham, I pray thee, send me good speed this day, and show kindness unto my master Abraham.

¹³Behold, I stand *here* by the well of water; and the daughters of the men of the city come out to draw water:

¹⁵My lord, listen to me. The land is worth 400 shekels of silver; what is that between you and me? So bury your dead.

¹⁶So Abraham listened to what Ephron said *and* acted upon it. He weighed to Ephron the silver which he had named in the hearing of the Hittites: 400 shekels of silver, according to the weights current among the merchants.

¹⁷So the field of Ephron in Machpelah, which was to the east of Mamre [Hebron]—the field and the cave which was in it, and all the trees that were in the field and in all its borders round about—was made over

¹⁸As a possession to Abraham in the presence of the Hittites, before all who went in at his city gate.

¹⁹After this, Abraham buried Sarah his wife in the cave of the field of *y* Machpelah to the east of Mamre, that is, Hebron, in the land of Canaan.

²⁰The field and the cave in it were conveyed to Abraham for a permanent burial place by the sons of Heth.

24 NOW ABRAHAM was old, well advanced in years, and the Lord had blessed Abraham in all things.

²And Abraham said to the eldest servant of his house [Eliezer of Damascus], who ruled over all that he had, I beg of you, put your hand under my thigh; [Gen. 15:2.]

³And you shall swear by the Lord, the God of heaven and earth, that you will not take a wife for my son from the daughters of the Canaanites, among whom I have settled,

⁴But you shall go to my country and to my relatives and take *z* a wife for my son Isaac.

⁵The servant said to him, But perhaps the woman will not be willing to come along after me to this country. Must I take your son to the country from which you came?

⁶Abraham said to him, See to it that you do not take my son back there.

⁷The Lord, the God of heaven, Who took me from my father's house, from the land of my family *and* my birth, Who spoke to me and swore to me, saying, To your offspring I will give this land—He will send His *a* Angel before you, and you will take a wife from there for my son.

⁸And if the woman should *b* not be willing to go along after you, then you will be clear from this oath; only you must not take my son back there.

⁹So the servant put his hand under the thigh of Abraham his master and swore to him concerning this matter.

¹⁰And the servant took ten of his master's camels and departed, taking some of all his master's treasures with him; thus he journeyed to Mesopotamia [between the Tigris and the Euphrates], to the city of Nahor [Abraham's brother].

¹¹And he made his camels to kneel down outside the city by a well of water at the time of the evening when women go out to draw water.

¹²And he said, O Lord, God of my master Abraham, I pray You, cause me to meet with good success today, and show kindness to my master Abraham.

¹³See, I stand here by the well of water, and the daughters of the men of the city are coming to draw water.

^yHere were buried Abraham and Sarah, Isaac and Rebekah, and Jacob and Leah (Gen. 49:31; 50:13).   ^zThis chapter is highly illustrative of God the Father, Who sends forth His Holy Spirit to win the consent of the individual soul to become the bride of His Son. Keep these resemblances constantly in mind as you read and see how the story unfolds. First meet the Father and note His concern about His Son's bride. Then get acquainted with the Holy Spirit's great, selfless heart, Whose one purpose is to win the girl for His Master's Son. Then meet the Son and note His tenderness as He claims His bride. The longest chapter in Genesis is devoted to this important story.   ^aSee footnote on Gen. 16:7.   ^bThe Holy Spirit does not win unwilling souls, only "whosoever will."

^jHeb. *gone into days*   ^kOr, *and*   ^lHeb. *that women which draw* water *go forth*

New American Standard

15"My lord, listen to me; a piece of land worth four hundred shekels of silver, what is that between me and you? So bury your dead."

16 Abraham listened to Ephron; and Abraham weighed out for Ephron the silver which he had named in the hearing of the sons of Heth, four hundred shekels of silver, commercial standard.

17 ¶ So Ephron's field, which was in Machpelah, which faced Mamre, the field and cave which was in it, and all the trees which were in the field, that were within all the confines of its border, were deeded over

18 to Abraham for a possession in the presence of the sons of Heth, before all who went in at the gate of his city.

19 After this, Abraham buried Sarah his wife in the cave of the field at Machpelah facing Mamre (that is, Hebron) in the land of Canaan.

20 So the field and the cave that is in it, were deeded over to Abraham for a burial site by the sons of Heth.

A Bride for Isaac

24 NOW ABRAHAM was old, advanced in age; and the LORD had blessed Abraham in every way.

2 Abraham said to his servant, the oldest of his household, who had charge of all that he owned, "Please place your hand under my thigh,

3 and I will make you swear by the LORD, the God of heaven and the God of earth, that you shall not take a wife for my son from the daughters of the Canaanites, among whom I live,

4 but you will go to my country and to my relatives, and take a wife for my son Isaac."

5 The servant said to him, "Suppose the woman is not willing to follow me to this land; should I take your son back to the land from where you came?"

6 Then Abraham said to him, "Beware that you do not take my son back there!

7"The LORD, the God of heaven, who took me from my father's house and from the land of my birth, and who spoke to me and who swore to me, saying, 'To your descendants I will give this land,' He will send His angel before you, and you will take a wife for my son from there.

8"But if the woman is not willing to follow you, then you will be free from this my oath; only do not take my son back there."

9 So the servant placed his hand under the thigh of Abraham his master, and swore to him concerning this matter.

10 ¶ Then the servant took ten camels from the camels of his master, and set out with a variety of good things of his master's in his hand; and he arose and went to Mesopotamia, to the city of Nahor.

11 He made the camels kneel down outside the city by the well of water at evening time, the time when women go out to draw water.

12 He said, "O LORD, the God of my master Abraham, please grant me success today, and show lovingkindness to my master Abraham.

13"Behold, I am standing by the spring, and the daughters of the men of the city are coming out to draw water;

New International

14Ephron answered Abraham, 15"Listen to me, my lord; the land is worth four hundred shekelsᶻ of silver, but what is that between me and you? Bury your dead."

16Abraham agreed to Ephron's terms and weighed out for him the price he had named in the hearing of the Hittites: four hundred shekels of silver, according to the weight current among the merchants.

17So Ephron's field in Machpelah near Mamre—both the field and the cave in it, and all the trees within the borders of the field—was deeded 18to Abraham as his property in the presence of all the Hittites who had come to the gate of the city. 19Afterward Abraham buried his wife Sarah in the cave in the field of Machpelah near Mamre (which is at Hebron) in the land of Canaan. 20So the field and the cave in it were deeded to Abraham by the Hittites as a burial site.

Isaac and Rebekah

24 ABRAHAM WAS now old and well advanced in years, and the LORD had blessed Abraham in every way. 2He said to the chiefᵃ servant in his household, the one in charge of all that he had, "Put your hand under my thigh. 3I want you to swear by the LORD, the God of heaven and the God of earth, that you will not get a wife for my son from the daughters of the Canaanites, among whom I am living, 4but will go to my country and my own relatives and get a wife for my son Isaac."

5The servant asked him, "What if the woman is unwilling to come back with me to this land? Shall I then take your son back to the country you came from?"

6"Make sure that you do not take my son back there," Abraham said. 7"The LORD, the God of heaven, who brought me out of my father's household and my native land and who spoke to me and promised me on oath, saying, 'To your offspringᵇ I will give this land'—he will send his angel before you so that you can get a wife for my son from there. 8If the woman is unwilling to come back with you, then you will be released from this oath of mine. Only do not take my son back there." 9So the servant put his hand under the thigh of his master Abraham and swore an oath to him concerning this matter.

10Then the servant took ten of his master's camels and left, taking with him all kinds of good things from his master. He set out for Aram Naharaimᶜ and made his way to the town of Nahor. 11He had the camels kneel down near the well outside the town; it was toward evening, the time the women go out to draw water.

12Then he prayed, "O LORD, God of my master Abraham, give me success today, and show kindness to my master Abraham. 13See, I am standing beside this spring, and the daughters of the townspeople are coming out to

---

z 15　That is, about 10 pounds (about 4.5 kilograms)
a 2　Or oldest　　b 7　Or seed　　c 10　That is, Northwest Mesopotamia

King James

¹⁴And let it come to pass, that the damsel to whom I shall say, Let down thy pitcher, I pray thee, that I may drink; and she shall say, Drink, and I will give thy camels drink also: *let the same be* she *that* thou hast appointed for thy servant Isaac; and thereby shall I know that thou hast shown kindness unto my master.

¹⁵ ¶ And it came to pass, before he had done speaking, that, behold, Rebekah came out, who was born to Bethuel, son of Milcah, the wife of Nahor, Abraham's brother, with her pitcher upon her shoulder.

¹⁶And the damsel *was* ᵐvery fair to look upon, a virgin, neither had any man known her: and she went down to the well, and filled her pitcher, and came up.

¹⁷And the servant ran to meet her, and said, Let me, I pray thee, drink a little water of thy pitcher.

¹⁸And she said, Drink, my lord: and she hasted, and let down her pitcher upon her hand, and gave him drink.

¹⁹And when she had done giving him drink, she said, I will draw *water* for thy camels also, until they have done drinking.

²⁰And she hasted, and emptied her pitcher into the trough, and ran again unto the well to draw *water*, and drew for all his camels.

²¹And the man wondering at her held his peace, to wit whether the LORD had made his journey prosperous or not.

²²And it came to pass, as the camels had done drinking, that the man took a golden ⁿearring of half a shekel weight, and two bracelets for her hands of ten *shekels* weight of gold;

²³And said, Whose daughter *art* thou? tell me, I pray thee: is there room *in* thy father's house for us to lodge in?

²⁴And she said unto him, I *am* the daughter of Bethuel the son of Milcah, which she bare unto Nahor.

²⁵She said moreover unto him, We have both straw and provender enough, and room to lodge in.

²⁶And the man bowed down his head, and worshipped the LORD.

²⁷And he said, Blessed *be* the LORD God of my master Abraham, who hath not left destitute my master of his mercy and his truth: I *being* in the way, the LORD led me to the house of my master's brethren.

²⁸And the damsel ran, and told *them of* her mother's house these things.

²⁹ ¶ And Rebekah had a brother, and his name *was* Laban: and Laban ran out unto the man, unto the well.

³⁰And it came to pass, when he saw the earring and bracelets upon his sister's hands, and when he heard the words of Rebekah his sister, saying, Thus spake the man unto me; that he came unto the man; and, behold, he stood by the camels at the well.

³¹And he said, Come in, thou blessed of the LORD; wherefore standest thou without? for I have prepared the house, and room for the camels.

³² ¶ And the man came into the house: and he ungirded his camels, and gave straw and provender for the camels, and water to wash his feet, and the men's feet that *were* with him.

³³And there was set *meat* before him to eat: but he said, I will not eat, until I have told mine errand. And he said, Speak on.

³⁴And he said, I *am* Abraham's servant.

³⁵And the LORD hath blessed my master greatly; and he is become great: and he hath given him flocks, and herds, and silver, and gold, and menservants, and maidservants, and camels, and asses.

³⁶And Sarah my master's wife bare a son to my master when she was old: and unto him hath he given all that he hath.

³⁷And my master made me swear, saying, Thou shalt not take a wife to my son of the daughters of the Canaanites, in whose land I dwell:

Amplified

¹⁴And let it so be that the girl to whom I say, I pray you, let down your jar that I may drink, and she replies, Drink, and I will give your camels drink also—let her be the one whom You have selected *and* appointed *and* indicated for Your servant Isaac [to be a wife to him]; and by it I shall know that You have shown kindness *and* faithfulness to my master.

¹⁵Before he had finished speaking, behold, out came Rebekah, who was the daughter of Bethuel son of Milcah, who was the wife of Nahor the brother of Abraham, with her water jar on her shoulder.

¹⁶And the girl was very beautiful *and* attractive, chaste *and* modest, and unmarried. And she went down to the well, filled her water jar, and came up.

¹⁷And the servant ran to meet her, and said, I pray you, let me drink a little water from your water jar.

¹⁸And she said, Drink, my lord; and she quickly let down her jar onto her hand and gave him a drink.

¹⁹When she had given him a drink, she said, I will draw water for your camels also, until they finish drinking.

²⁰So she quickly emptied her jar into the trough and ran again to the well and drew water for all his camels.

²¹The man stood gazing at her in silence, waiting to know if the Lord had made his trip prosperous.

²²And when the camels had finished drinking, the man took a gold earring *or* nose ring of half a shekel in weight, and for her hands two bracelets of ten shekels in weight in gold,

²³And said, Whose daughter are you? I pray you, tell me: Is there room in your father's house for us to lodge there?

²⁴And she said to him, I am the daughter of Bethuel son of Milcah and [her husband] Nahor.

²⁵She said also to him, We have both straw and provender (fodder) enough, and also room in which to lodge.

²⁶The man bowed down his head and worshiped the Lord

²⁷And said, Blessed be the Lord, the God of my master Abraham, Who has not left my master bereft *and* destitute of His loving-kindness and steadfastness. As for me, going on the way [of obedience and faith] the Lord led me to the house of my master's kinsmen.

²⁸The girl related to her mother's household what had happened.

²⁹Now Rebekah had a brother whose name was Laban, and Laban ran out to the man at the well.

³⁰For when he saw the earring *or* nose ring, and the bracelets on his sister's arms, and when he heard Rebekah his sister saying, The man said this to me, he went to the man and found him standing by the camels at the well.

³¹He cried, Come in, you blessed of the Lord! Why do you stand outside? For I have made the house ready *and* have prepared a place for the camels.

³²So the man came into the house; and [Laban] ungirded his camels and gave straw and provender for the camels and water to bathe his feet and the feet of the men who were with him.

³³A meal was set before him, but he said, ᶜI will not eat until I have told of my errand. And [Laban] said, Speak on.

³⁴And he said, I am Abraham's servant.

³⁵And the Lord has blessed my master mightily, and he has become great; and He has given him flocks, herds, silver, gold, menservants, maidservants, camels, and asses.

³⁶And Sarah my master's wife bore a son to my master when she was old, and to him he has given all that he has.

³⁷And my master made me swear, saying, You must not take a wife for my son from the daughters of the Canaanites, in whose land I dwell,

ᶜThe characteristics of a model servant of God are pictured here: 1. He is dependable and trustworthy (Gen. 24:2); 2. He is a praying person (Gen. 24:12); 3. He is so in earnest that he refuses to eat before attending to his Master's business (Gen. 24:33); 4. He never speaks his own name but is always speaking about his Master (Gen. 24:35ff.); 5. He gives God all the glory (Gen. 24:48).

ᵐHeb. *good of countenance* ⁿOr, *jewel for the forehead*

New American Standard

14 now may it be that the girl to whom I say, 'Please let down your jar so that I may drink,' and who answers, 'Drink, and I will water your camels also'—*may she be the one* whom You have appointed for Your servant Isaac; and by this I will know that You have shown lovingkindness to my master."

Rebekah Is Chosen

15 ¶ Before he had finished speaking, behold, Rebekah who was born to Bethuel the son of Milcah, the wife of Abraham's brother Nahor, came out with her jar on her shoulder.

16 The girl was very beautiful, a virgin, and no man had had relations with her; and she went down to the spring and filled her jar and came up.

17 Then the servant ran to meet her, and said, "Please let me drink a little water from your jar."

18 She said, "Drink, my lord"; and she quickly lowered her jar to her hand, and gave him a drink.

19 Now when she had finished giving him a drink, she said, "I will draw also for your camels until they have finished drinking."

20 So she quickly emptied her jar into the trough, and ran back to the well to draw, and she drew for all his camels.

21 Meanwhile, the man was gazing at her in silence, to know whether the LORD had made his journey successful or not.

22 ¶ When the camels had finished drinking, the man took a gold ring weighing a half-shekel and two bracelets for her wrists weighing ten shekels in gold,

23 and said, "Whose daughter are you? Please tell me, is there room for us to lodge in your father's house?"

24 She said to him, "I am the daughter of Bethuel, the son of Milcah, whom she bore to Nahor."

25 Again she said to him, "We have plenty of both straw and feed, and room to lodge in."

26 Then the man bowed low and worshiped the LORD.

27 He said, "Blessed be the LORD, the God of my master Abraham, who has not forsaken His lovingkindness and His truth toward my master; as for me, the LORD has guided me in the way to the house of my master's brothers."

28 ¶ Then the girl ran and told her mother's household about these things.

29 Now Rebekah had a brother whose name was Laban; and Laban ran outside to the man at the spring.

30 When he saw the ring and the bracelets on his sister's wrists, and when he heard the words of Rebekah his sister, saying, "This is what the man said to me," he went to the man; and behold, he was standing by the camels at the spring.

31 And he said, "Come in, blessed of the LORD! Why do you stand outside since I have prepared the house, and a place for the camels?"

32 So the man entered the house. Then Laban unloaded the camels, and he gave straw and feed to the camels, and water to wash his feet and the feet of the men who were with him.

33 But when *food* was set before him to eat, he said, "I will not eat until I have told my business." And he said, "Speak on."

34 So he said, "I am Abraham's servant.

35 "The LORD has greatly blessed my master, so that he has become rich; and He has given him flocks and herds, and silver and gold, and servants and maids, and camels and donkeys.

36 "Now Sarah my master's wife bore a son to my master in her old age, and he has given him all that he has.

37 "My master made me swear, saying, 'You shall not take a wife for my son from the daughters of the Canaanites, in whose land I live;

New International

draw water. 14 May it be that when I say to a girl, 'Please let down your jar that I may have a drink,' and she says, 'Drink, and I'll water your camels too'—let her be the one you have chosen for your servant Isaac. By this I will know that you have shown kindness to my master."

15 Before he had finished praying, Rebekah came out with her jar on her shoulder. She was the daughter of Bethuel son of Milcah, who was the wife of Abraham's brother Nahor. 16 The girl was very beautiful, a virgin; no man had ever lain with her. She went down to the spring, filled her jar and came up again.

17 The servant hurried to meet her and said, "Please give me a little water from your jar."

18 "Drink, my lord," she said, and quickly lowered the jar to her hands and gave him a drink.

19 After she had given him a drink, she said, "I'll draw water for your camels too, until they have finished drinking." 20 So she quickly emptied her jar into the trough, ran back to the well to draw more water, and drew enough for all his camels. 21 Without saying a word, the man watched her closely to learn whether or not the LORD had made his journey successful.

22 When the camels had finished drinking, the man took out a gold nose ring weighing a beka[d] and two gold bracelets weighing ten shekels.[e] 23 Then he asked, "Whose daughter are you? Please tell me, is there room in your father's house for us to spend the night?"

24 She answered him, "I am the daughter of Bethuel, the son that Milcah bore to Nahor." 25 And she added, "We have plenty of straw and fodder, as well as room for you to spend the night."

26 Then the man bowed down and worshiped the LORD, 27 saying, "Praise be to the LORD, the God of my master Abraham, who has not abandoned his kindness and faithfulness to my master. As for me, the LORD has led me on the journey to the house of my master's relatives."

28 The girl ran and told her mother's household about these things. 29 Now Rebekah had a brother named Laban, and he hurried out to the man at the spring. 30 As soon as he had seen the nose ring, and the bracelets on his sister's arms, and had heard Rebekah tell what the man said to her, he went out to the man and found him standing by the camels near the spring. 31 "Come, you who are blessed by the LORD," he said. "Why are you standing out here? I have prepared the house and a place for the camels."

32 So the man went to the house, and the camels were unloaded. Straw and fodder were brought for the camels, and water for him and his men to wash their feet. 33 Then food was set before him, but he said, "I will not eat until I have told you what I have to say."

"Then tell us," ⌊Laban⌋ said.

34 So he said, "I am Abraham's servant. 35 The LORD has blessed my master abundantly, and he has become wealthy. He has given him sheep and cattle, silver and gold, menservants and maidservants, and camels and donkeys. 36 My master's wife Sarah has borne him a son in her[f] old age, and he has given him everything he owns. 37 And my master made me swear an oath, and said, 'You must not get a wife for my son from the daughters of the

---

d 22 That is, about 1/5 ounce (about 5.5 grams)   *e 22* That is, about 4 ounces (about 110 grams)   *f 36* Or *his*

King James

Amplified

38But thou shalt go unto my father's house, and to my kindred, and take a wife unto my son.

39And I said unto my master, Peradventure the woman will not follow me.

40And he said unto me, The LORD, before whom I walk, will send his angel with thee, and prosper thy way; and thou shalt take a wife for my son of my kindred, and of my father's house:

41Then shalt thou be clear from *this* my oath, when thou comest to my kindred; and if they give not thee *one*, thou shalt be clear from my oath.

42And I came this day unto the well, and said, O LORD God of my master Abraham, if now thou do prosper my way which I go:

43Behold, I stand by the well of water; and it shall come to pass, that when the virgin cometh forth to draw *water*, and I say to her, Give me, I pray thee, a little water of thy pitcher to drink;

44And she say to me, Both drink thou, and I will also draw for thy camels: *let* the same *be* the woman which the LORD hath appointed out for my master's son.

45And before I had done speaking in mine heart, behold, Rebekah came forth with her pitcher on her shoulder; and she went down unto the well, and drew *water*: and I said unto her, Let me drink, I pray thee.

46And she made haste, and let down her pitcher from her *shoulder*, and said, Drink, and I will give thy camels drink also: so I drank, and she made the camels drink also.

47And I asked her, and said, Whose daughter *art* thou? And she said, The daughter of Bethuel, Nahor's son, whom Milcah bare unto him: and I put the earring upon her face, and the bracelets upon her hands.

48And I bowed down my head, and worshipped the LORD, and blessed the LORD God of my master Abraham, which had led me in the right way to take my master's brother's daughter unto his son.

49And now if ye will deal kindly and truly with my master, tell me: and if not, tell me; that I may turn to the right hand, or to the left.

50Then Laban and Bethuel answered and said, The thing proceedeth from the LORD: we cannot speak unto thee bad or good.

51Behold, Rebekah *is* before thee, take *her*, and go, and let her be thy master's son's wife, as the LORD hath spoken.

52And it came to pass, that, when Abraham's servant heard their words, he worshipped the LORD, *bowing himself* to the earth.

53And the servant brought forth *o*jewels of silver, and jewels of gold, and raiment, and gave *them* to Rebekah: he gave also to her brother and to her mother precious things.

54And they did eat and drink, he and the men that *were* with him, and tarried all night; and they rose up in the morning, and he said, Send me away unto my master.

55And her brother and her mother said, Let the damsel abide with us *Pa few* days, at the least ten; after that she shall go.

56And he said unto them, Hinder me not, seeing the LORD hath prospered my way; send me away that I may go to my master.

57And they said, We will call the damsel, and inquire at her mouth.

58And they called Rebekah, and said unto her, Wilt thou go with this man? And she said, I will go.

59And they sent away Rebekah their sister, and her nurse, and Abraham's servant, and his men.

60And they blessed Rebekah, and said unto her, Thou *art* our sister, be thou *the mother* of thousands of millions, and let thy seed possess the gate of those which hate them.

61 ¶ And Rebekah arose, and her damsels, and they rode upon the camels, and followed the man: and the servant took Rebekah, and went his way.

38But you shall go to my father's house and to my family and take a wife for my son.

39And I said to my master, But suppose the woman will not follow me.

40And he said to me, The Lord, in Whose presence I walk [habitually], will send His *d*Angel with you and prosper your way, and you will take a wife for my son from my kindred and from my father's house.

41Then you shall be clear from my oath, when you come to my kindred; and if they do not give her to you, you shall be free *and* innocent of my oath.

42I came today to the well and said, O Lord, God of my master Abraham, if You are now causing me to go on my way prosperously—

43See, I am standing by the well of water; now let it be that when the maiden comes out to draw water and I say to her, I pray you, give me a little water from your [water] jar to drink,

44And if she says to me, You drink, and I will draw water for your camels also, let that same woman be the one whom the Lord has selected *and* indicated for my master's son.

45And before I had finished praying in my heart, behold, Rebekah came out with her [water] jar on her shoulder, and she went down to the well and drew water. And I said to her, I pray you, let me have a drink.

46And she quickly let down her [water] jar from her shoulder and said, Drink, and I will water your camels also. So I drank, and she gave the camels drink also.

47I asked her, Whose daughter are you? She said, The daughter of Bethuel, Nahor's son, whom Milcah bore to him. And I put the earring *or* nose ring on her face and the bracelets on her arms.

48And I bowed down my head and worshiped the Lord and blessed the Lord, the God of my master Abraham, Who had led me in the right way to take my master's brother's daughter to his son.

49And now if you will deal kindly and truly with my master [showing faithfulness to him], tell me; and if not, tell me, that I may turn to the right or to the left.

50Then Laban and Bethuel answered, The thing comes forth from the Lord; we cannot speak bad or good to you.

51Rebekah is before you; take her and go, and let her be the wife of your master's son, as the Lord has said.

52And when Abraham's servant heard their words, he bowed himself to the ground before the Lord.

53And the servant brought out jewels of silver, jewels of gold, and garments and gave them to Rebekah; he also gave precious things to her brother and her mother.

54Then they ate and drank, he and the men who were with him, and stayed there all night. And in the morning they arose, and he said, Send me away to my master.

55But [Rebekah's] brother and mother said, Let the girl stay with us a few days—at least ten; then she may go.

56But [the servant] said to them, Do not hinder *and* delay me, seeing that the Lord has caused me to go prosperously on my way. Send me away, that I may go to my master.

57And they said, We will call the girl and ask her [what is] her desire.

58So they called Rebekah and said to her, Will you go with this man? And she said, I will go.

59So they sent away Rebekah their sister and her nurse [Deborah] and Abraham's servant and his men.

60And they blessed Rebekah and said to her, You are our sister; may you become the mother of thousands of ten thousands, and let your posterity possess the gate of their enemies.

61And Rebekah and her maids arose and followed the man upon their camels. Thus the servant took Rebekah and went on his way.

---

o Heb. *vessels*   *P* Or, *a full year*, or, *ten* months   *d* See footnote on Gen. 16:7.

New American Standard

38 but you shall go to my father's house and to my relatives, and take a wife for my son.'
39"I said to my master, 'Suppose the woman does not follow me.'
40"He said to me, 'The LORD, before whom I have walked, will send His angel with you to make your journey successful, and you will take a wife for my son from my relatives and from my father's house;
41 then you will be free from my oath, when you come to my relatives; and if they do not give her to you, you will be free from my oath.'
42 ¶ "So I came today to the spring, and said, 'O LORD, the God of my master Abraham, if now You will make my journey on which I go successful;
43 behold, I am standing by the spring, and may it be that the maiden who comes out to draw, and to whom I say, "Please let me drink a little water from your jar";
44 and she will say to me, "You drink, and I will draw for your camels also"; let her be the woman whom the LORD has appointed for my master's son.'
45 ¶ "Before I had finished speaking in my heart, behold, Rebekah came out with her jar on her shoulder, and went down to the spring and drew, and I said to her, 'Please let me drink.'
46"She quickly lowered her jar from her *shoulder,* and said, 'Drink, and I will water your camels also'; so I drank, and she watered the camels also.
47"Then I asked her, and said, 'Whose daughter are you?' And she said, 'The daughter of Bethuel, Nahor's son, whom Milcah bore to him'; and I put the ring on her nose, and the bracelets on her wrists.
48"And I bowed low and worshiped the LORD, and blessed the LORD, the God of my master Abraham, who had guided me in the right way to take the daughter of my master's kinsman for his son.
49"So now if you are going to ˣdeal kindly and truly with my master, tell me; and if not, let me know, that I may turn to the right hand or the left."
50 ¶ Then Laban and Bethuel replied, "The matter comes from the LORD; *so* we cannot speak to you bad or good.
51"Here is Rebekah before you, take *her* and go, and let her be the wife of your master's son, as the LORD has spoken."
52 ¶ When Abraham's servant heard their words, he bowed himself to the ground before the LORD.
53 The servant brought out articles of silver and articles of gold, and garments, and gave them to Rebekah; he also gave precious things to her brother and to her mother.
54 Then he and the men who were with him ate and drank and spent the night. When they arose in the morning, he said, "Send me away to my master."
55 But her brother and her mother said, "Let the girl stay with us *a few* days, say ten; afterward she may go."
56 He said to them, "Do not delay me, since the LORD has prospered my way. Send me away that I may go to my master."
57 And they said, "We will call the girl and consult her wishes."
58 Then they called Rebekah and said to her, "Will you go with this man?" And she said, "I will go."
59 Thus they sent away their sister Rebekah and her nurse with Abraham's servant and his men.
60 They blessed Rebekah and said to her,
"May you, our sister,
   Become thousands of ten thousands,
   And may your descendants possess
   The gate of those who hate them."
61 Then Rebekah arose with her maids, and they mounted the camels and followed the man. So the servant took Rebekah and departed.

New International

Canaanites, in whose land I live, 38but go to my father's family and to my own clan, and get a wife for my son.'
39"Then I asked my master, 'What if the woman will not come back with me?'
40"He replied, 'The LORD, before whom I have walked, will send his angel with you and make your journey a success, so that you can get a wife for my son from my own clan and from my father's family. 41Then, when you go to my clan, you will be released from my oath even if they refuse to give her to you—you will be released from my oath.'
42"When I came to the spring today, I said, 'O LORD, God of my master Abraham, if you will, please grant success to the journey on which I have come. 43See, I am standing beside this spring; if a maiden comes out to draw water and I say to her, "Please let me drink a little water from your jar," 44and if she says to me, "Drink, and I'll draw water for your camels too," let her be the one the LORD has chosen for my master's son.'
45"Before I finished praying in my heart, Rebekah came out, with her jar on her shoulder. She went down to the spring and drew water, and I said to her, 'Please give me a drink.'
46"She quickly lowered her jar from her shoulder and said, 'Drink, and I'll water your camels too.' So I drank, and she watered the camels also.
47"I asked her, 'Whose daughter are you?'
"She said, 'The daughter of Bethuel son of Nahor, whom Milcah bore to him.'
"Then I put the ring in her nose and the bracelets on her arms, 48and I bowed down and worshiped the LORD. I praised the LORD, the God of my master Abraham, who had led me on the right road to get the granddaughter of my master's brother for his son. 49Now if you will show kindness and faithfulness to my master, tell me; and if not, tell me, so I may know which way to turn."
50Laban and Bethuel answered, "This is from the LORD; we can say nothing to you one way or the other. 51Here is Rebekah; take her and go, and let her become the wife of your master's son, as the LORD has directed."
52When Abraham's servant heard what they said, he bowed down to the ground before the LORD. 53Then the servant brought out gold and silver jewelry and articles of clothing and gave them to Rebekah; he also gave costly gifts to her brother and to her mother. 54Then he and the men who were with him ate and drank and spent the night there.
When they got up the next morning, he said, "Send me on my way to my master."
55But her brother and her mother replied, "Let the girl remain with us ten days or so; then youᵍ may go."
56But he said to them, "Do not detain me, now that the LORD has granted success to my journey. Send me on my way so I may go to my master."
57Then they said, "Let's call the girl and ask her about it." 58So they called Rebekah and asked her, "Will you go with this man?"
"I will go," she said.
59So they sent their sister Rebekah on her way, along with her nurse and Abraham's servant and his men. 60And they blessed Rebekah and said to her,

"Our sister, may you increase
   to thousands upon thousands;
may your offspring possess
   the gates of their enemies."

61Then Rebekah and her maids got ready and mounted their camels and went back with the man. So the servant took Rebekah and left.

ˣLit *show lovingkindness and truth*

ᵍ55 Or *she*

King James

62And Isaac came from the way of the well Lahai-roi; for he dwelt in the south country.

63And Isaac went out qto meditate in the field at the eventide: and he lifted up his eyes, and saw, and, behold, the camels *were* coming.

64And Rebekah lifted up her eyes, and when she saw Isaac, she lighted off the camel.

65For she *had* said unto the servant, What man *is* this that walketh in the field to meet us? And the servant *had* said, It *is* my master: therefore she took a veil, and covered herself.

66And the servant told Isaac all things that he had done.

67And Isaac brought her into his mother Sarah's tent, and took Rebekah, and she became his wife; and he loved her: and Isaac was comforted after his mother's *death.*

The death of Abraham

25 THEN AGAIN Abraham took a wife, and her name *was* Keturah.

2And she bare him Zimran, and Jokshan, and Medan, and Midian, and Ishbak, and Shuah.

3And Jokshan begat Sheba, and Dedan. And the sons of Dedan were Asshurim, and Letushim, and Leummim.

4And the sons of Midian; Ephah, and Epher, and Ha-noch, and Abidah, and Eldaah. All these *were* the children of Keturah.

5 ¶ And Abraham gave all that he had unto Isaac.

6But unto the sons of the concubines, which Abraham had, Abraham gave gifts, and sent them away from Isaac his son, while he yet lived, eastward, unto the east country.

7And these *are* the days of the years of Abraham's life which he lived, an hundred threescore and fifteen years.

8Then Abraham gave up the ghost, and died in a good old age, an old man, and full *of years;* and was gathered to his people.

9And his sons Isaac and Ishmael buried him in the cave of Machpelah, in the field of Ephron the son of Zohar the Hittite, which *is* before Mamre;

10The field which Abraham purchased of the sons of Heth: there was Abraham buried, and Sarah his wife.

11 ¶ And it came to pass after the death of Abraham, that God blessed his son Isaac; and Isaac dwelt by the well Lahai-roi.

The descendants of Ishmael

12 ¶ Now these *are* the generations of Ishmael, Abra-ham's son, whom Hagar the Egyptian, Sarah's handmaid, bare unto Abraham:

13And these *are* the names of the sons of Ishmael, by their names, according to their generations: the firstborn of Ishmael, Nebajoth; and Kedar, and Adbeel, and Mibsam,

14And Mishma, and Dumah, and Massa,

15rHadar, and Tema, Jetur, Naphish, and Kedemah:

16These *are* the sons of Ishmael, and these *are* their names, by their towns, and by their castles; twelve princes according to their nations.

17And these *are* the years of the life of Ishmael, an hundred and thirty and seven years: and he gave up the ghost and died; and was gathered unto his people.

18And they dwelt from Havilah unto Shur, that *is* before Egypt, as thou goest toward Assyria: *and* he sdied in the presence of all his brethren.

Jacob and Esau

19 ¶ And these *are* the generations of Isaac, Abraham's son: Abraham begat Isaac:

20And Isaac was forty years old when he took Rebekah to wife, the daughter of Bethuel the Syrian of Padan-aram, the sister to Laban the Syrian.

Amplified

62Now Isaac had returned from going to the well Beer-lahai-roi [A well to the Living One Who sees me], for he [now] dwelt in the South country (the Negeb).

63And Isaac went out to meditate *and* bow down [in prayer] in the open country in the evening; and he looked up and saw that, behold, the camels were coming.

64And Rebekah looked up, and when she saw Isaac, she dismounted from the camel.

65For she [had] said to the servant, Who is that man walking across the field to meet us? And the servant [had] said, He is my master. So she took a veil and concealed herself with it.

66And the servant told Isaac everything that he had done.

67And Isaac brought her into his mother Sarah's tent, and he took Rebekah and she became his wife, and he loved her; thus Isaac was comforted after his mother's death.

25 ABRAHAM TOOK another wife, and her name was Keturah.

2And she bore him Zimran, Jokshan, Medan, Midian, Ishbak, and Shuah.

3Jokshan was the father of Sheba and Dedan. The sons of Dedan were Asshurim, Letushim, and Leummim.

4The sons of Midian were Ephah, Epher, Hanoch, Abi-da, and Eldaah. All these were the children of Keturah.

5And Abraham gave all that he had to Isaac.

6But to the sons of his concubines [Hagar and Keturah] Abraham gave gifts, and while he was still living he sent them to the east country, away from Isaac his son [of promise].

7The days of Abraham's life were 175 years.

8Then Abraham's spirit was released, and he died at a good (ample, full) old age, an old man, satisfied *and* satiat-ed, and ewas gathered to his people. [Gen. 15:15.]

9And his sons fIsaac and Ishmael buried him in the cave of Machpelah, in the field of Ephron the son of Zohar the Hittite, which is east of Mamre,

10The field which Abraham purchased from the Hittites. There Abraham was buried with Sarah his wife.

11After the death of Abraham, God blessed his son Isaac, and Isaac dwelt at Beer-lahai-roi [A well to the Living One Who sees me].

12Now this is the history of the descendants of Ishmael, Abraham's son, whom Hagar the Egyptian, Sarah's hand-maid, bore to Abraham.

13These are the names of the sons of Ishmael, named in the order of their births: Nebaioth, the firstborn of Ishmael, and Kedar, Adbeel, Mibsam,

14Mishma, Dumah, Massa,

15Hadad, Tema, Jetur, Naphish, and Kedemah.

16These are the sons of Ishmael, and these are their names, by their villages and by their encampments (sheep-folds)—twelve princes according to their tribes. [Foretold in Gen. 17:20.]

17And Ishmael lived 137 years; then his spirit left him, and he died and was gathered to his kindred.

18And [Ishmael's sons] dwelt from Havilah to Shur, which is before Egypt in the direction of Assyria. [Ishma-el] dwelt close [to the lands] of all his brethren.

19And this is the history of the descendants of Isaac, Abraham's son: Abraham was the father of Isaac.

20Isaac was forty years old when he married Rebekah, the daughter of Bethuel the Aramean of Padan-aram, the sister of Laban the Aramean.

---

eThis often repeated expression forms a remarkable testimony to the Old Testament belief in a life beyond the grave and to our recognition and fellowship with our loved ones there.   fIsaac was seventy-five and Ishmael nearly ninety years of age when their father died. Jacob and Esau were fifteen, and may have been present.

New American Standard

Isaac Marries Rebekah

62 ¶ Now Isaac had come from going to Beer-lahai-roi; for he was living in the Negev.

63 Isaac went out to meditate in the field toward evening; and he lifted up his eyes and looked, and behold, camels were coming.

64 Rebekah lifted up her eyes, and when she saw Isaac she dismounted from the camel.

65 She said to the servant, "Who is that man walking in the field to meet us?" And the servant said, "He is my master." Then she took her veil and covered herself.

66 The servant told Isaac all the things that he had done.

67 Then Isaac brought her into his mother Sarah's tent, and he took Rebekah, and she became his wife, and he loved her; thus Isaac was comforted after his mother's death.

Abraham's Death

25 NOW ABRAHAM took another wife, whose name was Keturah.

2 She bore to him Zimran and Jokshan and Medan and Midian and Ishbak and Shuah.

3 Jokshan became the father of Sheba and Dedan. And the sons of Dedan were Asshurim and Letushim and Leummim.

4 The sons of Midian *were* Ephah and Epher and Hanoch and Abida and Eldaah. All these *were* the sons of Keturah.

5 Now Abraham gave all that he had to Isaac;

6 but to the sons of his concubines, Abraham gave gifts while he was still living, and sent them away from his son Isaac eastward, to the land of the east.

7 ¶ These are all the years of Abraham's life that he lived, one hundred and seventy-five years.

8 Abraham breathed his last and died in a ripe old age, an old man and satisfied *with life;* and he was gathered to his people.

9 Then his sons Isaac and Ishmael buried him in the cave of Machpelah, in the field of Ephron the son of Zohar the Hittite, facing Mamre,

10 the field which Abraham purchased from the sons of Heth; there Abraham was buried with Sarah his wife.

11 It came about after the death of Abraham, that God blessed his son Isaac; and Isaac lived by Beer-lahai-roi.

Descendants of Ishmael

12 ¶ Now these are *the records of* the generations of Ishmael, Abraham's son, whom Hagar the Egyptian, Sarah's maid, bore to Abraham;

13 and these are the names of the sons of Ishmael, by their names, in the order of their birth: Nebaioth, the firstborn of Ishmael, and Kedar and Adbeel and Mibsam

14 and Mishma and Dumah and Massa,

15 Hadad and Tema, Jetur, Naphish and Kedemah.

16 These are the sons of Ishmael and these are their names, by their villages, and by their camps; twelve princes according to their tribes.

17 These are the years of the life of Ishmael, one hundred and thirty-seven years; and he breathed his last and died, and was gathered to his people.

18 They settled from Havilah to Shur which is east of Egypt as one goes toward Assyria; he settled in defiance of all his relatives.

Isaac's Sons

19 ¶ Now these are *the records of* the generations of Isaac, Abraham's son: Abraham became the father of Isaac;

20 and Isaac was forty years old when he took Rebekah, the daughter of Bethuel the Aramean of Paddan-aram, the sister of Laban the Aramean, to be his wife.

New International

62 Now Isaac had come from Beer Lahai Roi, for he was living in the Negev. 63 He went out to the field one evening to meditate,[h] and as he looked up, he saw camels approaching. 64 Rebekah also looked up and saw Isaac. She got down from her camel 65 and asked the servant, "Who is that man in the field coming to meet us?"

"He is my master," the servant answered. So she took her veil and covered herself.

66 Then the servant told Isaac all he had done. 67 Isaac brought her into the tent of his mother Sarah, and he married Rebekah. So she became his wife, and he loved her; and Isaac was comforted after his mother's death.

The Death of Abraham

25 ABRAHAM TOOK[i] another wife, whose name was Keturah. 2 She bore him Zimran, Jokshan, Medan, Midian, Ishbak and Shuah. 3 Jokshan was the father of Sheba and Dedan; the descendants of Dedan were the Asshurites, the Letushites and the Leummites. 4 The sons of Midian were Ephah, Epher, Hanoch, Abida and Eldaah. All these were descendants of Keturah.

5 Abraham left everything he owned to Isaac. 6 But while he was still living, he gave gifts to the sons of his concubines and sent them away from his son Isaac to the land of the east.

7 Altogether, Abraham lived a hundred and seventy-five years. 8 Then Abraham breathed his last and died at a good old age, an old man and full of years; and he was gathered to his people. 9 His sons Isaac and Ishmael buried him in the cave of Machpelah near Mamre, in the field of Ephron son of Zohar the Hittite, 10 the field Abraham had bought from the Hittites.[j] There Abraham was buried with his wife Sarah. 11 After Abraham's death, God blessed his son Isaac, who then lived near Beer Lahai Roi.

Ishmael's Sons

12 This is the account of Abraham's son Ishmael, whom Sarah's maidservant, Hagar the Egyptian, bore to Abraham.

13 These are the names of the sons of Ishmael, listed in the order of their birth: Nebaioth the firstborn of Ishmael, Kedar, Adbeel, Mibsam, 14 Mishma, Dumah, Massa, 15 Hadad, Tema, Jetur, Naphish and Kedemah. 16 These were the sons of Ishmael, and these are the names of the twelve tribal rulers according to their settlements and camps. 17 Altogether, Ishmael lived a hundred and thirty-seven years. He breathed his last and died, and he was gathered to his people. 18 His descendants settled in the area from Havilah to Shur, near the border of Egypt, as you go toward Asshur. And they lived in hostility toward[k] all their brothers.

Jacob and Esau

19 This is the account of Abraham's son Isaac.

Abraham became the father of Isaac, 20 and Isaac was forty years old when he married Rebekah daughter of Bethuel the Aramean from Paddan Aram[l] and sister of Laban the Aramean.

---

[h]63 The meaning of the Hebrew for this word is uncertain.   [i]1 Or *had taken*   [j]10 Or *the sons of Heth*   [k]18 Or *lived to the east of*   [l]20 That is, Northwest Mesopotamia

King James

21And Isaac entreated the LORD for his wife, because she *was* barren: and the LORD was entreated of him, and Rebekah his wife conceived.

22And the children struggled together within her; and she said, If *it be* so, why *am* I thus? And she went to inquire of the LORD.

23And the LORD said unto her, Two nations *are* in thy womb, and two manner of people shall be separated from thy bowels; and *the one* people shall be stronger than *the other* people; and the elder shall serve the younger.

24 ¶ And when her days to be delivered were fulfilled, behold, *there were* twins in her womb.

25And the first came out red, all over like an hairy garment; and they called his name Esau.

26And after that came his brother out, and his hand took hold on Esau's heel; and his name was called Jacob: and Isaac *was* threescore years old when she bare them.

27And the boys grew: and Esau was a cunning hunter, a man of the field; and Jacob *was* a plain man, dwelling in tents.

28And Isaac loved Esau, because *t*he did eat of *his* venison: but Rebekah loved Jacob.

29 ¶ And Jacob sod pottage: and Esau came from the field, and he *was* faint:

30And Esau said to Jacob, Feed me, I pray thee, *u*with that same red *pottage;* for I *am* faint: therefore was his name called *v*Edom.

31And Jacob said, Sell me this day thy birthright.

32And Esau said, Behold, I *am w*at the point to die: and what profit shall this birthright do to me?

33And Jacob said, Swear to me this day; and he sware unto him: and he sold his birthright unto Jacob.

34Then Jacob gave Esau bread and pottage of lentiles; and he did eat and drink, and rose up, and went his way: thus Esau despised *his* birthright.

Isaac and Abimelech

26 AND THERE was a famine in the land, beside the first famine that was in the days of Abraham. And Isaac went unto Abimelech king of the Philistines unto Gerar.

2And the LORD appeared unto him, and said, Go not down into Egypt; dwell in the land which I shall tell thee of:

3Sojourn in this land, and I will be with thee, and will bless thee; for unto thee, and unto thy seed, I will give all these countries, and I will perform the oath which I sware unto Abraham thy father;

4And I will make thy seed to multiply as the stars of heaven, and will give unto thy seed all these countries; and in thy seed shall all the nations of the earth be blessed;

5Because that Abraham obeyed my voice, and kept my charge, my commandments, my statutes, and my laws.

6 ¶ And Isaac dwelt in Gerar:

7And the men of the place asked *him* of his wife; and he said, She *is* my sister: for he feared to say, *She is* my wife; lest, *said he,* the men of the place should kill me for Rebekah; because she *was* fair to look upon.

8And it came to pass, when he had been there a long time, that Abimelech king of the Philistines looked out at a window, and saw, and, behold, Isaac *was* sporting with Rebekah his wife.

9And Abimelech called Isaac, and said, Behold, of a surety she *is* thy wife: and how saidst thou, She *is* my sister? And Isaac said unto him, Because I said, Lest I die for her.

10And Abimelech said, What *is* this thou hast done unto us? one of the people might lightly have lain with thy wife, and thou shouldest have brought guiltiness upon us.

Amplified

21And Isaac prayed much to the Lord for his wife because she was unable to bear children; and the Lord granted his prayer, and Rebekah his wife became pregnant.

22[Two] children struggled together within her; and she said, If it is so [that the Lord has heard our prayer], why am I like this? And she went to inquire of the Lord.

23The Lord said to her, [The founders of] two nations are in your womb, and the separation of two peoples has begun in your body; the one people shall be stronger than the other, and the elder shall serve the younger.

24When her days to be delivered were fulfilled, behold, there were twins in her womb.

25The first came out all over like a hairy garment, and they named him Esau [hairy].

26Afterward his brother came forth, and his hand grasped Esau's heel; so he was named Jacob [supplanter]. Isaac was sixty years old when she gave birth to them.

27When the boys grew up, Esau was a cunning *and* skilled hunter, a man of the outdoors; but Jacob was a plain *and* quiet man, dwelling in tents.

28And Isaac loved [and was partial to] Esau, because he ate of Esau's game; but Rebekah loved Jacob.

29Jacob was boiling pottage (lentil stew) one day, when Esau came from the field and was faint [with hunger].

30And Esau said to Jacob, I beg of you, let me have some of that red lentil stew to eat, for I am faint *and* famished! That is why his name was called Edom [red].

31Jacob answered, Then sell me today your birthright (the rights of a firstborn).

32Esau said, See here, I am at the point of death; what good can this birthright do me?

33Jacob said, Swear to me today [that you are selling it to me]; and he swore to [Jacob] and sold him his birthright.

34Then Jacob gave Esau bread and stew of lentils, and he ate and drank and rose up and went his way. Thus Esau scorned his birthright as beneath his notice.

26 AND THERE was a famine in the land, other than the former famine that was in the days of Abraham. And Isaac went to Gerar, to Abimelech king of the Philistines.

2And the Lord appeared to him and said, Do not go down to Egypt; live in the land of which I will tell you.

3Dwell temporarily in this land, and I will be with you and will favor you with blessings; for to you and to your descendants I will give all these lands, and I will perform the oath which I swore to Abraham your father.

4And I will make your descendants to multiply as the stars of the heavens, and will give to your posterity all these lands (kingdoms); and by your Offspring shall all the nations of the earth be blessed, *or* by Him bless themselves, [Gen. 22:18; Acts 3:25, 26; Gal. 3:16.]

5For Abraham listened to *and* obeyed My voice and kept My charge, My commands, My statutes, and My laws.

6So Isaac stayed in Gerar.

7And the men of the place asked him about his wife, and he said, She is my sister; for he was afraid to say, She is my wife—[thinking], Lest the men of the place should kill me for Rebekah, because she is attractive *and* is beautiful to look upon.

8When he had been there a long time, Abimelech king of the Philistines looked out of a window and saw Isaac caressing Rebekah his wife.

9And Abimelech called Isaac and said, See here, she is certainly your wife! How did you [dare] say to me, She is my sister? And Isaac said to him, Because I thought, Lest I die on account of her.

10And Abimelech said, What is this you have done to us? One of the men might easily have lain with your wife, and you would have brought guilt *and* sin upon us.

---

*t*Heb. *venison* was *in his mouth*   *u*Heb. *with that red,* with that *red* pottage   *v*i.e. *Red*   *w*Heb. *going to die*

New American Standard

21 Isaac prayed to the LORD on behalf of his wife, because she was barren; and the LORD answered him and Rebekah his wife conceived.

22 But the children struggled together within her; and she said, "If it is so, why then am I *this way?*" So she went to inquire of the LORD.

23 The LORD said to her,
"Two nations are in your womb;
And two peoples will be separated from your
    body;
And one people shall be stronger than the other;
And the older shall serve the younger."

24 When her days to be delivered were fulfilled, behold, there were twins in her womb.

25 Now the first came forth red, all over like a hairy garment; and they named him Esau.

26 Afterward his brother came forth with his hand holding on to Esau's heel, so his name was called yJacob; and Isaac was sixty years old when she gave birth to them.

27 ¶ When the boys grew up, Esau became a skillful hunter, a man of the field, but Jacob was a peaceful man, living in tents.

28 Now Isaac loved Esau, because he had a taste for game, but Rebekah loved Jacob.

29 When Jacob had cooked stew, Esau came in from the field and he was famished;

30 and Esau said to Jacob, "Please let me have a swallow of that red stuff there, for I am famished." Therefore his name was called zEdom.

31 But Jacob said, "First sell me your birthright."

32 Esau said, "Behold, I am about to die; so of what *use* then is the birthright to me?"

33 And Jacob said, "First swear to me"; so he swore to him, and sold his birthright to Jacob.

34 Then Jacob gave Esau bread and lentil stew; and he ate and drank, and rose and went on his way. Thus Esau despised his birthright.

Isaac Settles in Gerar

26 NOW THERE was a famine in the land, besides the previous famine that had occurred in the days of Abraham. So Isaac went to Gerar, to Abimelech king of the Philistines.

2 The LORD appeared to him and said, "Do not go down to Egypt; stay in the land of which I shall tell you.

3 Sojourn in this land and I will be with you and bless you, for to you and to your descendants I will give all these lands, and I will establish the oath which I swore to your father Abraham.

4 "I will multiply your descendants as the stars of heaven, and will give your descendants all these lands; and by your descendants all the nations of the earth shall be blessed;

5 because Abraham obeyed Me and kept My charge, My commandments, My statutes and My laws."

6 ¶ So Isaac lived in Gerar.

7 When the men of the place asked about his wife, he said, "She is my sister," for he was afraid to say, "my wife," *thinking,* "the men of the place might kill me on account of Rebekah, for she is beautiful."

8 It came about, when he had been there a long time, that Abimelech king of the Philistines looked out through a window, and saw, and behold, Isaac was caressing his wife Rebekah.

9 Then Abimelech called Isaac and said, "Behold, certainly she is your wife! How then did you say, 'She is my sister'?" And Isaac said to him, "Because I said, 'I might die on account of her.'"

10 Abimelech said, "What is this you have done to us? One of the people might easily have lain with your wife, and you would have brought guilt upon us."

New International

21 Isaac prayed to the LORD on behalf of his wife, because she was barren. The LORD answered his prayer, and his wife Rebekah became pregnant. 22The babies jostled each other within her, and she said, "Why is this happening to me?" So she went to inquire of the LORD.

23 The LORD said to her,
"Two nations are in your womb,
    and two peoples from within you will be
    separated;
one people will be stronger than the other,
    and the older will serve the younger."

24 When the time came for her to give birth, there were twin boys in her womb. 25The first to come out was red, and his whole body was like a hairy garment; so they named him Esau.m 26After this, his brother came out, with his hand grasping Esau's heel; so he was named Jacob.n Isaac was sixty years old when Rebekah gave birth to them.

27 The boys grew up, and Esau became a skillful hunter, a man of the open country, while Jacob was a quiet man, staying among the tents. 28Isaac, who had a taste for wild game, loved Esau, but Rebekah loved Jacob.

29 Once when Jacob was cooking some stew, Esau came in from the open country, famished. 30He said to Jacob, "Quick, let me have some of that red stew! I'm famished!" (That is why he was also called Edom.o)

31 Jacob replied, "First sell me your birthright."

32 "Look, I am about to die," Esau said. "What good is the birthright to me?"

33 But Jacob said, "Swear to me first." So he swore an oath to him, selling his birthright to Jacob.

34 Then Jacob gave Esau some bread and some lentil stew. He ate and drank, and then got up and left.

So Esau despised his birthright.

Isaac and Abimelech

26 NOW THERE was a famine in the land—besides the earlier famine of Abraham's time—and Isaac went to Abimelech king of the Philistines in Gerar. 2The LORD appeared to Isaac and said, "Do not go down to Egypt; live in the land where I tell you to live. 3Stay in this land for a while, and I will be with you and will bless you. For to you and your descendants I will give all these lands and will confirm the oath I swore to your father Abraham. 4I will make your descendants as numerous as the stars in the sky and will give them all these lands, and through your offspringp all nations on earth will be blessed, 5because Abraham obeyed me and kept my requirements, my commands, my decrees and my laws." 6So Isaac stayed in Gerar.

7 When the men of that place asked him about his wife, he said, "She is my sister," because he was afraid to say, "She is my wife." He thought, "The men of this place might kill me on account of Rebekah, because she is beautiful."

8 When Isaac had been there a long time, Abimelech king of the Philistines looked down from a window and saw Isaac caressing his wife Rebekah. 9So Abimelech summoned Isaac and said, "She is really your wife! Why did you say, 'She is my sister'?"

Isaac answered him, "Because I thought I might lose my life on account of her."

10 Then Abimelech said, "What is this you have done to us? One of the men might well have slept with your wife, and you would have brought guilt upon us."

---

yI.e. one who takes by the heel or supplants   zI.e. red

m25 *Esau* may mean *hairy*; he was also called Edom, which means red.   n26 *Jacob* means *he grasps the heel* (figuratively, *he deceives*).   o30 *Edom* means red.   p4 Or *seed*

King James

11And Abimelech charged all *his* people, saying, He that toucheth this man or his wife shall surely be put to death.

12Then Isaac sowed in that land, and *x*received in the same year an hundredfold: and the LORD blessed him.

13And the man waxed great, and *y*went forward, and grew until he became very great:

14For he had possession of flocks, and possession of herds, and great store of *z*servants: and the Philistines envied him.

15For all the wells which his father's servants had digged in the days of Abraham his father, the Philistines had stopped them, and filled them with earth.

16And Abimelech said unto Isaac, Go from us; for thou art much mightier than we.

17 ¶ And Isaac departed thence, and pitched his tent in the valley of Gerar, and dwelt there.

18And Isaac digged again the wells of water, which they had digged in the days of Abraham his father; for the Philistines had stopped them after the death of Abraham: and he called their names after the names by which his father had called them.

19And Isaac's servants digged in the valley, and found there a well of *a*springing water.

20And the herdmen of Gerar did strive with Isaac's herdmen, saying, The water *is* ours: and he called the name of the well *b*Esek; because they strove with him.

21And they digged another well, and strove for that also: and he called the name of it *c*Sitnah.

22And he removed from thence, and digged another well; and for that they strove not: and he called the name of it *d*Rehoboth; and he said, For now the LORD hath made room for us, and we shall be fruitful in the land.

23And he went up from thence to Beer-sheba.

24And the LORD appeared unto him the same night, and said, I *am* the God of Abraham thy father: fear not, for I *am* with thee, and will bless thee, and multiply thy seed for my servant Abraham's sake.

25And he builded an altar there, and called upon the name of the LORD, and pitched his tent there: and there Isaac's servants digged a well.

26 ¶ Then Abimelech went to him from Gerar, and Ahuzzath one of his friends, and Phichol the chief captain of his army.

27And Isaac said unto them, Wherefore come ye to me, seeing ye hate me, and have sent me away from you?

28And they said, *e*We saw certainly that the LORD was with thee: and we said, Let there be now an oath betwixt us, *even* betwixt us and thee, and let us make a covenant with thee;

29*f*That thou wilt do us no hurt, as we have not touched thee, and as we have done unto thee nothing but good, and have sent thee away in peace: thou *art* now the blessed of the LORD.

30And he made them a feast, and they did eat and drink.

31And they rose up betimes in the morning, and sware one to another: and Isaac sent them away, and they departed from him in peace.

32And it came to pass the same day, that Isaac's servants came, and told him concerning the well which they had digged, and said unto him, We have found water.

33And he called it *g*Shebah: therefore the name of the city *is* *h*Beer-sheba unto this day.

34 ¶ And Esau was forty years old when he took to wife Judith the daughter of Beeri the Hittite, and Bashemath the daughter of Elon the Hittite:

35Which were *i*a grief of mind unto Isaac and to Rebekah.

Amplified

11Then Abimelech charged all his people, He who touches this man or his wife shall surely be put to death.

12Then Isaac sowed seed in that land and received in the same year a hundred times as much as he had planted, and the Lord favored him with blessings.

13And the man became great and gained more and more until he became very wealthy *and* distinguished;

14He owned flocks, herds, and a great supply of servants, and the Philistines envied him.

15Now all the wells which his father's servants had dug in the days of Abraham his father, the Philistines had closed and filled with earth.

16And Abimelech said to Isaac, Go away from us, for you are much mightier than we are.

17So Isaac went away from there and pitched his tent in the Valley of Gerar, and dwelt there.

18And Isaac dug again the wells of water which had been dug in the days of Abraham his father, for the Philistines had stopped them after the death of Abraham; and he gave them the names by which his father had called them.

19Now Isaac's servants dug in the valley and found there a well of living [spring] water.

20And the herdsmen of Gerar quarreled with Isaac's herdsmen, saying, The water is ours. And he named the well Esek [contention] because they quarreled with him.

21Then [his servants] dug another well, and they quarreled over that also; so he named it Sitnah [enmity].

22And he moved away from there and dug another well, and for that one they did not quarrel. He named it Rehoboth [room], saying, For now the Lord has made room for us, and we shall be fruitful in the land.

23Now he went up from there to Beersheba.

24And the Lord appeared to him the same night and said, I am the God of Abraham your father. Fear not, for I am with you and will favor you with blessings and multiply your descendants for the sake of My servant Abraham.

25And [Isaac] *g*built an altar there and called on the name of the Lord and pitched his tent there; and there Isaac's servants were digging a well.

26Then Abimelech went to him from Gerar with Ahuzzah, one of his friends, and Phicol, his army's commander.

27And Isaac said to them, Why have you come to me, seeing that you hate me and have sent me away from you?

28They said, We saw that the Lord was certainly with you; so we said, Let there be now an oath between us [carrying a curse with it to befall the one who breaks it], even between you and us, and let us make a covenant with you

29That you will do us no harm, inasmuch as we have not touched you and have done to you nothing but good and have sent you away in peace. You are now the blessed *or* favored of the Lord!

30And he made them a [formal] dinner, and they ate and drank.

31And they rose up early in the morning and took oaths [with a curse] with one another; and Isaac sent them on their way and they departed from him in peace.

32That same day Isaac's servants came and told him about the well they had dug, saying, We have found water!

33And he named [the well] Shibah; therefore the name of the city is Beersheba [well of the oath] to this day. [Gen. 21:31.]

34Now Esau was 40 years old when he took as wife Judith the daughter of Beeri the Hittite, and Basemath the daughter of Elon the Hittite.

35And they made life bitter *and* a grief of mind *and* spirit for Isaac and Rebekah [their parents-in-law].

---

*x*Heb. *found*   *y*Heb. *went going*   *z*Or, *husbandry*   *a*Heb.
living   *b*i.e. *Contention*   *c*i.e. *Hatred*   *d*i.e. *Room*
*e*Heb. *Seeing we saw*   *f*Heb. *If thou shalt*   *g*i.e. *An oath*
*h*i.e. *The well of the oath*   *i*Heb. *bitterness of spirit*

*g*With Isaac God came first. Before doing anything else in the new place, he built an altar and then waited there to call upon the Lord. Second came his home; he pitched his tent. Third came his business; his servants dug a well.

New American Standard

11 So Abimelech charged all the people, saying, "He who touches this man or his wife shall surely be put to death."

12 ¶ Now Isaac sowed in that land and reaped in the same year a hundredfold. And the LORD blessed him,

13 and the man became rich, and continued to grow richer until he became very wealthy;

14 for he had possessions of flocks and herds and a great household, so that the Philistines envied him.

15 Now all the wells which his father's servants had dug in the days of Abraham his father, the Philistines stopped up by filling them with earth.

16 Then Abimelech said to Isaac, "Go away from us, for you are too powerful for us."

17 And Isaac departed from there and camped in the valley of Gerar, and settled there.

Quarrel over the Wells

18 ¶ Then Isaac dug again the wells of water which had been dug in the days of his father Abraham, for the Philistines had stopped them up after the death of Abraham; and he gave them the same names which his father had given them.

19 But when Isaac's servants dug in the valley and found there a well of flowing water,

20 the herdsmen of Gerar quarreled with the herdsmen of Isaac, saying, "The water is ours!" So he named the well Esek, because they contended with him.

21 Then they dug another well, and they quarreled over it too, so he named it Sitnah.

22 He moved away from there and dug another well, and they did not quarrel over it; so he named it Rehoboth, for he said, "At last the LORD has made room for us, and we will be fruitful in the land."

23 ¶ Then he went up from there to Beersheba.

24 The LORD appeared to him the same night and said, "I am the God of your father Abraham;
Do not fear, for I am with you.
I will bless you, and multiply your descendants,
For the sake of My servant Abraham."

25 So he built an altar there and called upon the name of the LORD, and pitched his tent there; and there Isaac's servants dug a well.

Covenant with Abimelech

26 ¶ Then Abimelech came to him from Gerar with his adviser Ahuzzath and Phicol the commander of his army.

27 Isaac said to them, "Why have you come to me, since you hate me and have sent me away from you?"

28 They said, "We see plainly that the LORD has been with you; so we said, 'Let there now be an oath between us, *even* between you and us, and let us make a covenant with you,

29 that you will do us no harm, just as we have not touched you and have done to you nothing but good and have sent you away in peace. You are now the blessed of the LORD.' "

30 Then he made them a feast, and they ate and drank.

31 In the morning they arose early and exchanged oaths; then Isaac sent them away and they departed from him in peace.

32 Now it came about on the same day, that Isaac's servants came in and told him about the well which they had dug, and said to him, "We have found water."

33 So he called it Shibah; therefore the name of the city is Beersheba to this day.

34 ¶ When Esau was forty years old he married Judith the daughter of Beeri the Hittite, and Basemath the daughter of Elon the Hittite;

35 and they *a*brought grief to Isaac and Rebekah.

New International

11 So Abimelech gave orders to all the people: "Anyone who molests this man or his wife shall surely be put to death."

12 Isaac planted crops in that land and the same year reaped a hundredfold, because the LORD blessed him. 13 The man became rich, and his wealth continued to grow until he became very wealthy. 14 He had so many flocks and herds and servants that the Philistines envied him. 15 So all the wells that his father's servants had dug in the time of his father Abraham, the Philistines stopped up, filling them with earth.

16 Then Abimelech said to Isaac, "Move away from us; you have become too powerful for us."

17 So Isaac moved away from there and encamped in the Valley of Gerar and settled there. 18 Isaac reopened the wells that had been dug in the time of his father Abraham, which the Philistines had stopped up after Abraham died, and he gave them the same names his father had given them.

19 Isaac's servants dug in the valley and discovered a well of fresh water there. 20 But the herdsmen of Gerar quarreled with Isaac's herdsmen and said, "The water is ours!" So he named the well Esek,*q* because they disputed with him. 21 Then they dug another well, but they quarreled over that one also; so he named it Sitnah.*r* 22 He moved on from there and dug another well, and no one quarreled over it. He named it Rehoboth,*s* saying, "Now the LORD has given us room and we will flourish in the land."

23 From there he went up to Beersheba. 24 That night the LORD appeared to him and said, "I am the God of your father Abraham. Do not be afraid, for I am with you; I will bless you and will increase the number of your descendants for the sake of my servant Abraham."

25 Isaac built an altar there and called on the name of the LORD. There he pitched his tent, and there his servants dug a well.

26 Meanwhile, Abimelech had come to him from Gerar, with Ahuzzath his personal adviser and Phicol the commander of his forces. 27 Isaac asked them, "Why have you come to me, since you were hostile to me and sent me away?"

28 They answered, "We saw clearly that the LORD was with you; so we said, 'There ought to be a sworn agreement between us'—between us and you. Let us make a treaty with you 29 that you will do us no harm, just as we did not molest you but always treated you well and sent you away in peace. And now you are blessed by the LORD."

30 Isaac then made a feast for them, and they ate and drank. 31 Early the next morning the men swore an oath to each other. Then Isaac sent them on their way, and they left him in peace.

32 That day Isaac's servants came and told him about the well they had dug. They said, "We've found water!" 33 He called it Shibah,*t* and to this day the name of the town has been Beersheba.*u*

34 When Esau was forty years old, he married Judith daughter of Beeri the Hittite, and also Basemath daughter of Elon the Hittite. 35 They were a source of grief to Isaac and Rebekah.

---

*q*20 *Esek* means *dispute.*   *r*21 *Sitnah* means *opposition.*
*s*22 *Rehoboth* means *room.*   *t*33 *Shibah* can mean *oath* or *seven.*   *u*33 *Beersheba* can mean *well of the oath* or *well of seven.*

---

*a*Lit *were a bitterness of spirit to*

King James

Amplified

Jacob's stolen blessing

27 AND IT came to pass, that when Isaac was old, and his eyes were dim, so that he could not see, he called Esau his eldest son, and said unto him, My son: and he said unto him, Behold, *here am* I.

²And he said, Behold now, I am old, I know not the day of my death:

³Now therefore take, I pray thee, thy weapons, thy quiver and thy bow, and go out to the field, and *J* take me *some* venison;

⁴And make me savoury meat, such as I love, and bring *it* to me, that I may eat; that my soul may bless thee before I die.

⁵And Rebekah heard when Isaac spake to Esau his son. And Esau went to the field to hunt *for* venison, *and* to bring *it.*

⁶ ¶ And Rebekah spake unto Jacob her son, saying, Behold, I heard thy father speak unto Esau thy brother, saying,

⁷Bring me venison, and make me savoury meat, that I may eat, and bless thee before the LORD before my death.

⁸Now therefore, my son, obey my voice according to that which I command thee.

⁹Go now to the flock, and fetch me from thence two good kids of the goats; and I will make them savoury meat for thy father, such as he loveth:

¹⁰And thou shalt bring *it* to thy father, that he may eat, and that he may bless thee before his death.

¹¹And Jacob said to Rebekah his mother, Behold, Esau my brother *is* a hairy man, and I *am* a smooth man:

¹²My father peradventure will feel me, and I shall seem to him as a deceiver; and I shall bring a curse upon me, and not a blessing.

¹³And his mother said unto him, Upon me *be* thy curse, my son: only obey my voice, and go fetch me *them.*

¹⁴And he went, and fetched, and brought *them* to his mother: and his mother made savoury meat, such as his father loved.

¹⁵And Rebekah took *k* goodly raiment of her eldest son Esau, which *were* with her in the house, and put them upon Jacob her younger son:

¹⁶And she put the skins of the kids of the goats upon his hands, and upon the smooth of his neck:

¹⁷And she gave the savoury meat and the bread, which she had prepared, into the hand of her son Jacob.

¹⁸ ¶ And he came unto his father, and said, My father: and he said, Here *am* I; who *art* thou, my son?

¹⁹And Jacob said unto his father, I *am* Esau thy firstborn; I have done according as thou badest me: arise, I pray thee, sit and eat of my venison, that thy soul may bless me.

²⁰And Isaac said unto his son, How *is it* that thou hast found *it* so quickly, my son? And he said, Because the LORD thy God brought *it* *l* to me.

²¹And Isaac said unto Jacob, Come near, I pray thee, that I may feel thee, my son, whether thou *be* my very son Esau or not.

²²And Jacob went near unto Isaac his father; and he felt him, and said, The voice *is* Jacob's voice, but the hands *are* the hands of Esau.

²³And he discerned him not, because his hands were hairy, as his brother Esau's hands: so he blessed him.

²⁴And he said, *Art* thou my very son Esau? And he said, I *am.*

²⁵And he said, Bring *it* near to me, and I will eat of my son's venison, that my soul may bless thee. And he brought *it* near to him, and he did eat: and he brought him wine, and he drank.

²⁶And his father Isaac said unto him, Come near now, and kiss me, my son.

27 WHEN ISAAC was old and his eyes were dim so that he could not see, he called Esau his elder son, and said to him, My son! And he answered him, Here I am.

²He said, See here now; I am old, I do not know when I may die.

³So now, I pray you, take your weapons, your [arrows in a] quiver and your bow, and go out into the open country and hunt game for me,

⁴And prepare me appetizing meat, such as I love, and bring it to me, that I may eat of it, [preparatory] to giving you my blessing [as my firstborn] before I die.

⁵But Rebekah heard what Isaac said to Esau his son; and when Esau had gone to the open country to hunt for game that he might bring it,

⁶Rebekah said to Jacob her younger son, See here, I heard your father say to Esau your brother,

⁷Bring me game and make me appetizing meat, so that I may eat and declare my blessing upon you before the Lord before my death.

⁸So now, my son, do exactly as I command you.

⁹Go now to the flock, and from it bring me two good *and* suitable kids; and I will make them into appetizing meat for your father, such as he loves.

¹⁰And you shall bring it to your father, that he may eat and declare his blessing upon you before his death.

¹¹But Jacob said to Rebekah his mother, Listen, Esau my brother is a hairy man and I am a smooth man.

¹²Suppose my father feels me; I will seem to him to be a cheat *and* an imposter, and I will bring [his] curse on me and not [his] blessing.

¹³But his mother said to him, On me be your curse, my son; only obey my word and go, fetch them to me.

¹⁴So [Jacob] went, got [the kids], and brought them to his mother; and his mother prepared appetizing meat with a delightful odor, such as his father loved.

¹⁵Then Rebekah took her elder son Esau's best clothes which were with her in the house, and put them on Jacob her younger son.

¹⁶And she put the skins of the kids on his hands and on the smooth part of his neck.

¹⁷And she gave the savory meat and the bread which she had prepared into the hand of her son Jacob.

¹⁸So he went to his father and said, My father. And he said, Here I am; who are you, my son?

¹⁹And Jacob said to his father, I am Esau your firstborn; I have done what you told me to do. Now sit up and eat of my game, so that you may proceed to bless me.

²⁰And Isaac said to his son, How is it that you have found the game so quickly, my son? And he said, Because the Lord your God caused it to come to me.

²¹But Isaac said to Jacob, Come close to me, I beg of you, that I may feel you, my son, *and* know whether you really are my son Esau or not.

²²So Jacob went near to Isaac, and his father felt him and said, The voice is Jacob's voice, but the hands are the hands of Esau.

²³He could not identify him, because his hands were hairy like his brother Esau's hands; so he blessed him.

²⁴But he said, Are you really my son Esau? He answered, I am.

²⁵Then [Isaac] said, Bring it to me and I will eat of my son's game, that I may bless you. He brought it to him and he ate; and he brought him wine and he drank.

²⁶Then his father Isaac said, Come near and kiss me, my son.

J Heb. *hunt*   *k* Heb. *desirable*   *l* Heb. *before me*

New American Standard

Jacob's Deception

27 NOW IT came about, when Isaac was old and his eyes were too dim to see, that he called his older son Esau and said to him, "My son." And he said to him, "Here I am."

2 Isaac said, "Behold now, I am old *and* I do not know the day of my death.

3 "Now then, please take your gear, your quiver and your bow, and go out to the field and hunt game for me;

4 and prepare a savory dish for me such as I love, and bring it to me that I may eat, so that my soul may bless you before I die."

5 ¶ Rebekah was listening while Isaac spoke to his son Esau. So when Esau went to the field to hunt for game to bring *home,*

6 Rebekah said to her son Jacob, "Behold, I heard your father speak to your brother Esau, saying,

7 'Bring me *some* game and prepare a savory dish for me, that I may eat, and bless you in the presence of the LORD before my death.'

8 "Now therefore, my son, listen to me as I command you.

9 "Go now to the flock and bring me two choice young goats from there, that I may prepare them *as* a savory dish for your father, such as he loves.

10 "Then you shall bring *it* to your father, that he may eat, so that he may bless you before his death."

11 Jacob answered his mother Rebekah, "Behold, Esau my brother is a hairy man and I am a smooth man.

12 "Perhaps my father will feel me, then I will be as a deceiver in his sight, and I will bring upon myself a curse and not a blessing."

13 But his mother said to him, "Your curse be on me, my son; only obey my voice, and go, get *them* for me."

14 So he went and got *them,* and brought *them* to his mother; and his mother made savory food such as his father loved.

15 Then Rebekah took the best garments of Esau her elder son, which were with her in the house, and put them on Jacob her younger son.

16 And she put the skins of the young goats on his hands and on the smooth part of his neck.

17 She also gave the savory food and the bread, which she had made, to her son Jacob.

18 ¶ Then he came to his father and said, "My father." And he said, "Here I am. Who are you, my son?"

19 Jacob said to his father, "I am Esau your firstborn; I have done as you told me. Get up, please, sit and eat of my game, that you may bless me."

20 Isaac said to his son, "How is it that you have *it* so quickly, my son?" And he said, "Because the LORD your God caused *it* to happen to me."

21 Then Isaac said to Jacob, "Please come close, that I may feel you, my son, whether you are really my son Esau or not."

22 So Jacob came close to Isaac his father, and he felt him and said, "The voice is the voice of Jacob, but the hands are the hands of Esau."

23 He did not recognize him, because his hands were hairy like his brother Esau's hands; so he blessed him.

24 And he said, "Are you really my son Esau?" And he said, "I am."

25 So he said, "Bring *it* to me, and I will eat of my son's game, that I may bless you." And he brought *it* to him, and he ate; he also brought him wine and he drank.

26 Then his father Isaac said to him, "Please come close and kiss me, my son."

New International

Jacob Gets Isaac's Blessing

27 WHEN ISAAC was old and his eyes were so weak that he could no longer see, he called for Esau his older son and said to him, "My son."

"Here I am," he answered.

2 Isaac said, "I am now an old man and don't know the day of my death. 3 Now then, get your weapons—your quiver and bow—and go out to the open country to hunt some wild game for me. 4 Prepare me the kind of tasty food I like and bring it to me to eat, so that I may give you my blessing before I die."

5 Now Rebekah was listening as Isaac spoke to his son Esau. When Esau left for the open country to hunt game and bring it back, 6 Rebekah said to her son Jacob, "Look, I overheard your father say to your brother Esau, 7 'Bring me some game and prepare me some tasty food to eat, so that I may give you my blessing in the presence of the LORD before I die.' 8 Now, my son, listen carefully and do what I tell you: 9 Go out to the flock and bring me two choice young goats, so I can prepare some tasty food for your father, just the way he likes it. 10 Then take it to your father to eat, so that he may give you his blessing before he dies."

11 Jacob said to Rebekah his mother, "But my brother Esau is a hairy man, and I'm a man with smooth skin. 12 What if my father touches me? I would appear to be tricking him and would bring down a curse on myself rather than a blessing."

13 His mother said to him, "My son, let the curse fall on me. Just do what I say; go and get them for me."

14 So he went and got them and brought them to his mother, and she prepared some tasty food, just the way his father liked it. 15 Then Rebekah took the best clothes of Esau her older son, which she had in the house, and put them on her younger son Jacob. 16 She also covered his hands and the smooth part of his neck with the goatskins. 17 Then she handed to her son Jacob the tasty food and the bread she had made.

18 He went to his father and said, "My father."

"Yes, my son," he answered. "Who is it?"

19 Jacob said to his father, "I am Esau your firstborn. I have done as you told me. Please sit up and eat some of my game so that you may give me your blessing."

20 Isaac asked his son, "How did you find it so quickly, my son?"

"The LORD your God gave me success," he replied.

21 Then Isaac said to Jacob, "Come near so I can touch you, my son, to know whether you really are my son Esau or not."

22 Jacob went close to his father Isaac, who touched him and said, "The voice is the voice of Jacob, but the hands are the hands of Esau." 23 He did not recognize him, for his hands were hairy like those of his brother Esau; so he blessed him. 24 "Are you really my son Esau?" he asked.

"I am," he replied.

25 Then he said, "My son, bring me some of your game to eat, so that I may give you my blessing."

Jacob brought it to him and he ate; and he brought some wine and he drank. 26 Then his father Isaac said to him, "Come here, my son, and kiss me."

King James

27And he came near, and kissed him: and he smelled the smell of his raiment, and blessed him, and said, See, the smell of my son *is* as the smell of a field which the LORD hath blessed:

28Therefore God give thee of the dew of heaven, and the fatness of the earth, and plenty of corn and wine:

29Let people serve thee, and nations bow down to thee: be lord over thy brethren, and let thy mother's sons bow down to thee: cursed *be* every one that curseth thee, and blessed *be* he that blesseth thee.

30 ¶ And it came to pass, as soon as Isaac had made an end of blessing Jacob, and Jacob was yet scarce gone out from the presence of Isaac his father, that Esau his brother came in from his hunting.

31And he also had made savoury meat, and brought it unto his father, and said unto his father, Let my father arise, and eat of his son's venison, that thy soul may bless me.

32And Isaac his father said unto him, Who *art* thou? And he said, I *am* thy son, thy firstborn Esau.

33And Isaac *m*trembled very exceedingly, and said, Who? where *is* he that hath *n*taken venison, and brought *it* me, and I have eaten of all before thou camest, and have blessed him? yea, *and* he shall be blessed.

34And when Esau heard the words of his father, he cried with a great and exceeding bitter cry, and said unto his father, Bless me, *even* me also, O my father.

35And he said, Thy brother came with subtlety, and hath taken away thy blessing.

36And he said, Is not he rightly named *o*Jacob? for he hath supplanted me these two times: he took away my birthright; and, behold, now he hath taken away my blessing. And he said, Hast thou not reserved a blessing for me?

37And Isaac answered and said unto Esau, Behold, I have made him thy lord, and all his brethren have I given to him for servants; and with corn and wine have I *p*sustained him: and what shall I do now unto thee, my son?

38And Esau said unto his father, Hast thou but one blessing, my father? bless me, *even* me also, O my father. And Esau lifted up his voice, and wept.

39And Isaac his father answered and said unto him, Behold, thy dwelling shall be *q*the fatness of the earth, and of the dew of heaven from above;

40And by thy sword shalt thou live, and shalt serve thy brother; and it shall come to pass when thou shalt have the dominion, that thou shalt break his yoke from off thy neck.

Isaac sends Jacob to Laban

41 ¶ And Esau hated Jacob because of the blessing wherewith his father blessed him: and Esau said in his heart, The days of mourning for my father are at hand; then will I slay my brother Jacob.

42And these words of Esau her elder son were told to Rebekah: and she sent and called Jacob her younger son, and said unto him, Behold, thy brother Esau, as touching thee, doth comfort himself, *purposing* to kill thee.

43Now therefore, my son, obey my voice; and arise, flee thou to Laban my brother to Haran;

44And tarry with him a few days, until thy brother's fury turn away;

Amplified

27So he came near and kissed him; and [Isaac] smelled his clothing and blessed him and said, The scent of my son is as the odor of a field which the Lord has blessed.

28And may God give you of the dew of the heavens and of the fatness of the earth and abundance of grain and [new] wine;

29Let peoples serve you and nations bow down to you; be master over your brothers, and let your mother's sons bow down to you. Let everyone be cursed who curses you and favored with blessings who blesses you.

30As soon as Isaac had finished blessing Jacob and Jacob was scarcely gone out from the presence of Isaac his father, Esau his brother came in from his hunting.

31Esau had also prepared savory food and brought it to his father and said to him, Let my father arise and eat of his son's game, that you may bless me.

32And Isaac his father said to him, Who are you? And he replied, I am your son, your firstborn, Esau.

33Then Isaac trembled *and* shook violently, and he said, Who? Where is he who has hunted game and brought it to me, and I ate of it all before you came and I have blessed him? Yes, and he shall be blessed.

34When Esau heard the words of his father, he cried out with a great and bitter cry and said to his father, Bless me, even me also, O my father! [Heb. 12:16, 17.]

35[Isaac] said, Your brother came with crafty cunning *and* treacherous deceit and has taken your blessing.

36[Esau] replied, Is he not rightly named Jacob [the supplanter]? For he has supplanted me these two times: he took away my birthright, and now he has taken away my blessing! Have you not still a blessing reserved for me?

37And Isaac answered Esau, Behold, I have made [Jacob] your lord and master; I have given all his brethren to him for servants, and with corn and [new] wine have I sustained him. What then can I do for you, my son?

38Esau said to his father, Have you only one blessing, my father? Bless me, even me also, O my father! And Esau lifted up [could not control] his voice and wept aloud.

39Then Isaac his father answered, Your [blessing and] dwelling shall all come from the fruitfulness of the earth and from the dew of the heavens above;

40By your sword you shall live and serve your brother. But [the time shall come] when you will grow restive *and* break loose, and you shall tear his yoke from off your neck.

41And Esau hated Jacob because of the blessing with which his father blessed him; and Esau said in his heart, The days of mourning for my father are very near. When [he is gone] I will *h*kill my brother Jacob.

42These words of Esau her elder son were repeated to Rebekah. She sent for Jacob her younger son and said to him, See here, your brother Esau comforts himself concerning you [by intending] to kill you.

43So now, my son, do what I tell you; arise, flee to my brother Laban in Haran;

44Linger and dwell with him for a while until your brother's fury is spent.

h Here began a feud that was to cost countless lives throughout succeeding centuries. Esau's descendants, the Amalekites, were the first enemies to obstruct the flight of Jacob's descendants from Egypt (Exod. 17:8); and the Edomites even refused to let their uncle Jacob's children pass through their land (Num. 20:17-20). Doeg, an Edomite, all but caused the death of Christ's chosen ancestor David (I Sam. 21, 22). Bloody battles were fought between the two nations in the centuries that followed. It was Herod, of Esau's race (Josephus, *Antiquities of the Jews* 14:1, Section 3), who had the male infants of Bethlehem slain in an effort to destroy the Christ Child (Matt. 2:16). Satan needs no better medium for his evil plans than a family feud, a "mere quarrel" between two brothers.

---

*m*Heb. *trembled with a great trembling greatly*   *n*Heb. *hunted*
*o*i.e. *A supplanter*   *p*Or, *supported*   *q*Or, *of the fatness*

New American Standard

27 So he came close and kissed him; and when he smelled the smell of his garments, he blessed him and said,
"See, the smell of my son
  Is like the smell of a field which the LORD has
     blessed;
28 Now may God give you of the dew of heaven,
  And of the fatness of the earth,
  And an abundance of grain and new wine;
29 May peoples serve you,
  And nations bow down to you;
  Be master of your brothers,
  And may your mother's sons bow down to you.
  Cursed be those who curse you,
  And blessed be those who bless you."

The Stolen Blessing

30 ¶ Now it came about, as soon as Isaac had finished blessing Jacob, and Jacob had hardly gone out from the presence of Isaac his father, that Esau his brother came in from his hunting.
31 Then he also made savory food, and brought it to his father; and he said to his father, "Let my father arise and eat of his son's game, that you may bless me."
32 Isaac his father said to him, "Who are you?" And he said, "I am your son, your firstborn, Esau."
33 Then Isaac trembled violently, and said, "Who was he then that hunted game and brought *it* to me, so that I ate of all *of it* before you came, and blessed him? Yes, and he shall be blessed."
34 When Esau heard the words of his father, he cried out with an exceedingly great and bitter cry, and said to his father, "Bless me, *even* me also, O my father!"
35 And he said, "Your brother came deceitfully and has taken away your blessing."
36 Then he said, "Is he not rightly named Jacob, for he has supplanted me these two times? He took away my birthright, and behold, now he has taken away my blessing." And he said, "Have you not reserved a blessing for me?"
37 But Isaac replied to Esau, "Behold, I have made him your master, and all his relatives I have given to him as servants; and with grain and new wine I have sustained him. Now as for you then, what can I do, my son?"
38 Esau said to his father, "Do you have only one blessing, my father? Bless me, *even* me also, O my father." So Esau lifted his voice and wept.
39 ¶ Then Isaac his father answered and said to him,
"Behold, away from the fertility of the earth shall
     be your dwelling,
  And away from the dew of heaven from above.
40 "By your sword you shall live,
  And your brother you shall serve;
  But it shall come about when you become
     restless,
  That you will break his yoke from your neck."
41 ¶ So Esau bore a grudge against Jacob because of the blessing with which his father had blessed him; and Esau said to himself, "The days of mourning for my father are near; then I will kill my brother Jacob."
42 Now when the words of her elder son Esau were reported to Rebekah, she sent and called her younger son Jacob, and said to him, "Behold your brother Esau is consoling himself concerning you *by planning* to kill you.
43 "Now therefore, my son, obey my voice, and arise, flee to Haran, to my brother Laban!
44 "Stay with him a few days, until your brother's fury subsides,

New International

27 So he went to him and kissed him. When Isaac caught the smell of his clothes, he blessed him and said,

"Ah, the smell of my son
  is like the smell of a field
  that the LORD has blessed.
28 May God give you of heaven's dew
  and of earth's richness—
  an abundance of grain and new wine.
29 May nations serve you
  and peoples bow down to you.
  Be lord over your brothers,
  and may the sons of your mother bow down
     to you.
  May those who curse you be cursed
  and those who bless you be blessed."

30 After Isaac finished blessing him and Jacob had scarcely left his father's presence, his brother Esau came in from hunting. 31 He too prepared some tasty food and brought it to his father. Then he said to him, "My father, sit up and eat some of my game, so that you may give me your blessing."
32 His father Isaac asked him, "Who are you?"
"I am your son," he answered, "your firstborn, Esau."
33 Isaac trembled violently and said, "Who was it, then, that hunted game and brought it to me? I ate it just before you came and I blessed him—and indeed he will be blessed!"
34 When Esau heard his father's words, he burst out with a loud and bitter cry and said to his father, "Bless me—me too, my father!"
35 But he said, "Your brother came deceitfully and took your blessing."
36 Esau said, "Isn't he rightly named Jacob[v]? He has deceived me these two times: He took my birthright, and now he's taken my blessing!" Then he asked, "Haven't you reserved any blessing for me?"
37 Isaac answered Esau, "I have made him lord over you and have made all his relatives his servants, and I have sustained him with grain and new wine. So what can I possibly do for you, my son?"
38 Esau said to his father, "Do you have only one blessing, my father? Bless me too, my father!" Then Esau wept aloud.
39 His father Isaac answered him,

"Your dwelling will be
  away from the earth's richness,
  away from the dew of heaven above.
40 You will live by the sword
  and you will serve your brother.
  But when you grow restless,
  you will throw his yoke
  from off your neck."

Jacob Flees to Laban

41 Esau held a grudge against Jacob because of the blessing his father had given him. He said to himself, "The days of mourning for my father are near; then I will kill my brother Jacob."
42 When Rebekah was told what her older son Esau had said, she sent for her younger son Jacob and said to him, "Your brother Esau is consoling himself with the thought of killing you. 43 Now then, my son, do what I say: Flee at once to my brother Laban in Haran. 44 Stay with him for a

---

v 36 *Jacob* means *he grasps the heel* (figuratively, *he deceives*).

King James

45Until thy brother's anger turn away from thee, and he forget *that* which thou hast done to him: then I will send, and fetch thee from thence: why should I be deprived also of you both in one day?

46And Rebekah said to Isaac, I am weary of my life because of the daughters of Heth: if Jacob take a wife of the daughters of Heth, such as these *which are* of the daughters of the land, what good shall my life do me?

28 AND ISAAC called Jacob, and blessed him, and charged him, and said unto him, Thou shalt not take a wife of the daughters of Canaan.

2Arise, go to Padan-aram, to the house of Bethuel thy mother's father; and take thee a wife from thence of the daughters of Laban thy mother's brother.

3And God Almighty bless thee, and make thee fruitful, and multiply thee, that thou mayest be *r*a multitude of people;

4And give thee the blessing of Abraham, to thee, and to thy seed with thee; that thou mayest inherit the land *s*wherein thou art a stranger, which God gave unto Abraham.

5And Isaac sent away Jacob: and he went to Padan-aram unto Laban, son of Bethuel the Syrian, the brother of Rebekah, Jacob's and Esau's mother.

6 ¶ When Esau saw that Isaac had blessed Jacob, and sent him away to Padan-aram, to take him a wife from thence; and that as he blessed him he gave him a charge, saying, Thou shalt not take a wife of the daughters of Canaan;

7And that Jacob obeyed his father and his mother, and was gone to Padan-aram;

8And Esau seeing that the daughters of Canaan *t*pleased not Isaac his father;

9Then went Esau unto Ishmael, and took unto the wives which he had Mahalath the daughter of Ishmael Abraham's son, the sister of Nebajoth, to be his wife.

Jacob's dream at Beth-el

10 ¶ And Jacob went out from Beer-sheba, and went toward Haran.

11And he lighted upon a certain place, and tarried there all night, because the sun was set; and he took of the stones of that place, and put *them for* his pillows, and lay down in that place to sleep.

12And he dreamed, and behold a ladder set up on the earth, and the top of it reached to heaven: and behold the angels of God ascending and descending on it.

13And, behold, the LORD stood above it, and said, I *am* the LORD God of Abraham thy father, and the God of Isaac: the land whereon thou liest, to thee will I give it, and to thy seed;

14And thy seed shall be as the dust of the earth, and thou shalt *u*spread abroad to the west, and to the east, and to the north, and to the south: and in thee and in thy seed shall all the families of the earth be blessed.

15And, behold, I *am* with thee, and will keep thee in all *places* whither thou goest, and will bring thee again into this land; for I will not leave thee, until I have done *that* which I have spoken to thee of.

16 ¶ And Jacob awaked out of his sleep, and he said, Surely the LORD is in this place; and I knew *it* not.

17And he was afraid, and said, How dreadful *is* this place! this *is* none other but the house of God, and this *is* the gate of heaven.

Amplified

45When your brother's anger is diverted from you, he will forget [the wrong] that you have done him. Then *i*I will send and bring you back from there. Why should I be deprived of both of you in one day?

46Then Rebekah said to Isaac, I am weary of my life because of the daughters of Heth [these wives of Esau]! If Jacob takes a wife of the daughters of Heth such as these Hittite girls around here, what good will my life be to me?

28 SO ISAAC called Jacob and blessed him and commanded him, You shall not marry one of the women of Canaan.

2Arise, go to Padan-aram, to the house of Bethuel your mother's father, and take from there as a wife one of the daughters of Laban your mother's brother.

3May God Almighty bless you and make you fruitful and multiply you until you become a group of peoples.

4May He give the blessing [He gave to] Abraham to you and your descendants with you, that you may inherit the land He gave to Abraham, in which you are a sojourner.

5Thus Isaac sent Jacob away. He went to Padan-aram, to Laban son of Bethuel the Aramean, the brother of Rebekah, Jacob and Esau's mother.

6Now Esau saw that Isaac had blessed Jacob and sent him to Padan-aram to take him a wife from there, and that as he blessed him, he gave him a charge, saying, You shall not take a wife of the daughters of Canaan;

7And that Jacob obeyed his father and his mother and had gone to Padan-aram.

8Also Esau saw that the daughters of Canaan did not please Isaac his father.

9So Esau went to Ishmael and took to be his wife, [in addition] to the wives he [already] had, Mahalath daughter of Ishmael, Abraham's son, the sister of Nebaioth.

10And Jacob left Beersheba and went toward Haran.

11And he came to a certain place and stayed there overnight, because the sun was set. Taking one of the stones of the place, he put it under his head and lay down there to sleep.

12And he dreamed that there was a ladder set up on the earth, and the top of it reached to heaven; and the angels of God were ascending and descending on it!

13And behold, the Lord stood over *and* beside him and said, I am the Lord, the God of Abraham your father [forefather] and the God of Isaac; I will give to you and to your descendants the land on which you are lying.

14And your offspring shall be as [countless as] the dust *or* sand of the ground, and you shall spread abroad to the west and the east and the north and the south; and by you and your Offspring shall all the families of the earth be blessed *and* bless themselves. [Gen. 12:2–3; 13:16; 22:18; 26:4; Acts 3:25–26; Gal. 3:8, 16.]

15And behold, I am with you and will keep (watch over you with care, take notice of) you wherever you may go, and I will bring you back to this land; for I will not leave you until I have done all of which I have told you.

16And Jacob awoke from his sleep and he said, Surely the Lord is in this place and I did not know it.

17He was afraid and said, How to be feared *and* reverenced is this place! This is none other than the house of God, and *j*this is the gateway to heaven!

*i*But Rebekah never saw her son Jacob again. He was well over 40 and probably 57 years old when he fled from Esau to Haran, and he stayed there at least 20 years.   *j*"There is an open way between heaven and earth for each of us. The movement of the tide and the circulation of the blood are not more regular than the intercommunication between heaven and earth. Jacob may have thought that God was local; now he found Him to be omnipresent. Every lonely spot was His house, filled with angels" (F. B. Meyer, *Through the Bible Day by Day*). When Jacob found God in his own heart, he found Him everywhere.

---

*r*Heb. *an assembly of people*   *s*Heb. *of thy sojournings*
*t*Heb. *were evil in the eyes*   *u*Heb. *break forth*

New American Standard

45 until your brother's anger against you subsides and he forgets what you did to him. Then I will send and get you from there. Why should I be bereaved of you both in one day?"

46 ¶ Rebekah said to Isaac, "I am tired of living because of the daughters of Heth; if Jacob takes a wife from the daughters of Heth, like these, from the daughters of the land, what good will my life be to me?"

Jacob Is Sent Away

28 SO ISAAC called Jacob and blessed him and charged him, and said to him, "You shall not take a wife from the daughters of Canaan.

2 "Arise, go to Paddan-aram, to the house of Bethuel your mother's father; and from there take to yourself a wife from the daughters of Laban your mother's brother.

3 "May God Almighty bless you and make you fruitful and multiply you, that you may become a company of peoples.

4 "May He also give you the blessing of Abraham, to you and to your descendants with you, that you may possess the land of your sojournings, which God gave to Abraham."

5 Then Isaac sent Jacob away, and he went to Paddan-aram to Laban, son of Bethuel the Aramean, the brother of Rebekah, the mother of Jacob and Esau.

6 ¶ Now Esau saw that Isaac had blessed Jacob and sent him away to Paddan-aram to take to himself a wife from there, *and that* when he blessed him he charged him, saying, "You shall not take a wife from the daughters of Canaan,"

7 and that Jacob had obeyed his father and his mother and had gone to Paddan-aram.

8 So Esau saw that the daughters of Canaan displeased his father Isaac;

9 and Esau went to Ishmael, and married, besides the wives that he had, Mahalath the daughter of Ishmael, Abraham's son, the sister of Nebaioth.

Jacob's Dream

10 ¶ Then Jacob departed from Beersheba and went toward Haran.

11 He came to a certain place and spent the night there, because the sun had set; and he took one of the stones of the place and put it under his head, and lay down in that place.

12 He had a dream, and behold, a ladder was set on the earth with its top reaching to heaven; and behold, the angels of God were ascending and descending on it.

13 And behold, the LORD stood above it and said, "I am the LORD, the God of your father Abraham and the God of Isaac; the land on which you lie, I will give it to you and to your descendants.

14 "Your descendants will also be like the dust of the earth, and you will spread out to the west and to the east and to the north and to the south; and in you and in your descendants shall all the families of the earth be blessed.

15 "Behold, I am with you and will keep you wherever you go, and will bring you back to this land; for I will not leave you until I have done what I have promised you."

16 Then Jacob awoke from his sleep and said, "Surely the LORD is in this place, and I did not know it."

17 He was afraid and said, "How awesome is this place! This is none other than the house of God, and this is the gate of heaven."

New International

while until your brother's fury subsides. 45 When your brother is no longer angry with you and forgets what you did to him, I'll send word for you to come back from there. Why should I lose both of you in one day?"

46 Then Rebekah said to Isaac, "I'm disgusted with living because of these Hittite women. If Jacob takes a wife from among the women of this land, from Hittite women like these, my life will not be worth living."

28 SO ISAAC called for Jacob and blessed[w] him and commanded him: "Do not marry a Canaanite woman. 2 Go at once to Paddan Aram,[x] to the house of your mother's father Bethuel. Take a wife for yourself there, from among the daughters of Laban, your mother's brother. 3 May God Almighty[y] bless you and make you fruitful and increase your numbers until you become a community of peoples. 4 May he give you and your descendants the blessing given to Abraham, so that you may take possession of the land where you now live as an alien, the land God gave to Abraham." 5 Then Isaac sent Jacob on his way, and he went to Paddan Aram, to Laban son of Bethuel the Aramean, the brother of Rebekah, who was the mother of Jacob and Esau.

6 Now Esau learned that Isaac had blessed Jacob and had sent him to Paddan Aram to take a wife from there, and that when he blessed him he commanded him, "Do not marry a Canaanite woman," 7 and that Jacob had obeyed his father and mother and had gone to Paddan Aram. 8 Esau then realized how displeasing the Canaanite women were to his father Isaac; 9 so he went to Ishmael and married Mahalath, the sister of Nebaioth and daughter of Ishmael son of Abraham, in addition to the wives he already had.

Jacob's Dream at Bethel

10 Jacob left Beersheba and set out for Haran. 11 When he reached a certain place, he stopped for the night because the sun had set. Taking one of the stones there, he put it under his head and lay down to sleep. 12 He had a dream in which he saw a stairway[z] resting on the earth, with its top reaching to heaven, and the angels of God were ascending and descending on it. 13 There above it[a] stood the LORD, and he said: "I am the LORD, the God of your father Abraham and the God of Isaac. I will give you and your descendants the land on which you are lying. 14 Your descendants will be like the dust of the earth, and you will spread out to the west and to the east, to the north and to the south. All peoples on earth will be blessed through you and your offspring. 15 I am with you and will watch over you wherever you go, and I will bring you back to this land. I will not leave you until I have done what I have promised you."

16 When Jacob awoke from his sleep, he thought, "Surely the LORD is in this place, and I was not aware of it." 17 He was afraid and said, "How awesome is this place! This is none other than the house of God; this is the gate of heaven."

---

w 1 Or greeted   x 2 That is, Northwest Mesopotamia; also in
verses 5, 6 and 7   y 3 Hebrew El-Shaddai   z 12 Or ladder
a 13 Or There beside him

King James

18And Jacob rose up early in the morning, and took the stone that he had put *for* his pillows, and set it up *for* a pillar, and poured oil upon the top of it.

19And he called the name of that place vBeth-el: but the name of that city *was called* Luz at the first.

20And Jacob vowed a vow, saying, If God will be with me, and will keep me in this way that I go, and will give me bread to eat, and raiment to put on,

21So that I come again to my father's house in peace; then shall the LORD be my God:

22And this stone, which I have set *for* a pillar, shall be God's house: and of all that thou shalt give me I will surely give the tenth unto thee.

Jacob meets Rachel

29 THEN JACOB wwent on his journey, and came into the land of the xpeople of the east.

2And he looked, and behold a well in the field, and, lo, there *were* three flocks of sheep lying by it; for out of that well they watered the flocks: and a great stone *was* upon the well's mouth.

3And thither were all the flocks gathered: and they rolled the stone from the well's mouth, and watered the sheep, and put the stone again upon the well's mouth in his place.

4And Jacob said unto them, My brethren, whence *be* ye? And they said, Of Haran *are* we.

5And he said unto them, Know ye Laban the son of Nahor? And they said, We know *him.*

6And he said unto them, yIs he well? And they said, *He is* well: and, behold, Rachel his daughter cometh with the sheep.

7And he said, Lo, zit *is* yet high day, neither *is it* time that the cattle should be gathered together: water ye the sheep, and go *and* feed *them.*

8And they said, We cannot, until all the flocks be gathered together, and *till* they roll the stone from the well's mouth; then we water the sheep.

9 ¶And while he yet spake with them, Rachel came with her father's sheep: for she kept them.

10And it came to pass, when Jacob saw Rachel the daughter of Laban his mother's brother, and the sheep of Laban his mother's brother, that Jacob went near, and rolled the stone from the well's mouth, and watered the flock of Laban his mother's brother.

11And Jacob kissed Rachel, and lifted up his voice, and wept.

12And Jacob told Rachel that he *was* her father's brother, and that he *was* Rebekah's son: and she ran and told her father.

13And it came to pass, when Laban heard the *a*tidings of Jacob his sister's son, that he ran to meet him, and embraced him, and kissed him, and brought him to his house. And he told Laban all these things.

14And Laban said to him, Surely thou *art* my bone and my flesh. And he abode with him *b*the space of a month.

Jacob marries Leah and Rachel

15 ¶And Laban said unto Jacob, Because thou *art* my brother, shouldest thou therefore serve me for nought? tell me, what *shall* thy wages *be?*

16And Laban had two daughters: the name of the elder *was* Leah, and the name of the younger *was* Rachel.

17Leah *was* tender eyed; but Rachel was beautiful and wellfavoured.

18And Jacob loved Rachel; and said, I will serve thee seven years for Rachel thy younger daughter.

19And Laban said, *It is* better that I give her to thee, than that I should give her to another man: abide with me.

Amplified

18And Jacob rose early in the morning and took the stone he had put under his head, and he set it up for a pillar (a monument to the vision in his dream), and he poured oil on its top [in dedication].

19And he named that place Bethel [the house of God]; but the name of that city was Luz at first.

20Then Jacob made a vow, saying, If God will be with me and will keep me in this way that I go and will give me food to eat and clothing to wear,

21So that I may come again to my father's house in peace, then the Lord shall be my God;

22And this stone which I have set up as a pillar (monument) shall be God's house [a sacred place to me], and of all [the increase of possessions] that You give me I will give the tenth to You.

29 THEN JACOB went [briskly and cheerfully] on his way [400 miles] and came to the land of the people of the East.

2As he looked, he saw a well in the field; and behold, there were three flocks of sheep lying by it, for out of that well the flocks were watered. The stone on the well's mouth was a big one,

3And when all the flocks were gathered there, [the shepherds] would roll the stone from the well's mouth, water the sheep, and replace the stone on the well's mouth.

4And Jacob said to them, My brothers, where are you from? And they said, We are from Haran.

5[Jacob] said to them, Do you know Laban the grandson of Nahor? And they said, We know him.

6He said to them, Is it well with him? And they said, He is doing well; and behold, here comes his daughter Rachel with [his] sheep!

7He said, The sun is still high; it is a long time yet before the flocks need be gathered [in their folds]. [Why not] water the sheep and return them to their pasture?

8But they said, We cannot until all the flocks are gathered together; then [the shepherds] roll the stone from the well's mouth and we water the sheep.

9While he was still talking with them, Rachel came with her father's sheep, for she shepherded them.

10When Jacob saw Rachel daughter of Laban, his mother's brother, and the sheep of Laban his uncle, Jacob went near and rolled the stone from the well's mouth and watered the flock of his uncle Laban.

11Then Jacob kissed Rachel and he wept aloud.

12Jacob told Rachel he was her father's relative, Rebekah's son; and she ran and told her father.

13When Laban heard of the arrival of Jacob his sister's son, he ran to meet him, and embraced and kissed him and brought him to his house. And [Jacob] told Laban all these things.

14Then Laban said to him, Surely you are my bone and my flesh. And [Jacob] stayed with him a month.

15Then Laban said to Jacob, Just because you are my relative, should you work for me for nothing? Tell me, what shall your wages be?

16Now Laban had two daughters; the name of the elder was Leah and the name of the younger was Rachel.

17Leah's eyes were weak *and* dull looking, but Rachel was beautiful and attractive.

18And Jacob loved Rachel; so he said, I will work for you for seven years for Rachel your younger daughter.

19And Laban said, It is better that I give her to you than to another man. Stay *and* live with me.

---

vi.e. *The house of God*   wHeb. *lift up his feet*   xHeb. *children*   yHeb. Is there *peace to him?*   zHeb. *yet the day* is *great*   *a*Heb. *hearing*   *b*Heb. *a month of days*

New American Standard

18 ¶ So Jacob rose early in the morning, and took the stone that he had put under his head and set it up as a pillar and poured oil on its top.

19 He called the name of that place *b*Bethel; however, previously the name of the city had been Luz.

20 Then Jacob made a vow, saying, "If God will be with me and will keep me on this journey that I take, and will give me food to eat and garments to wear,

21 and I return to my father's house in safety, then the LORD will be my God.

22 "This stone, which I have set up as a pillar, will be God's house, and of all that You give me I will surely give a tenth to You."

Jacob Meets Rachel

29 THEN JACOB *c*went on his journey, and came to the land of the sons of the east.

2 He looked, and saw a well in the field, and behold, three flocks of sheep were lying there beside it, for from that well they watered the flocks. Now the stone on the mouth of the well was large.

3 When all the flocks were gathered there, they would then roll the stone from the mouth of the well and water the sheep, and put the stone back in its place on the mouth of the well.

4 ¶ Jacob said to them, "My brothers, where are you from?" And they said, "We are from Haran."

5 He said to them, "Do you know Laban the son of Nahor?" And they said, "We know *him*."

6 And he said to them, "Is it well with him?" And they said, "It is well, and here is Rachel his daughter coming with the sheep."

7 He said, "Behold, it is still high day; it is not time for the livestock to be gathered. Water the sheep, and go, pasture them."

8 But they said, "We cannot, until all the flocks are gathered, and they roll the stone from the mouth of the well; then we water the sheep."

9 ¶ While he was still speaking with them, Rachel came with her father's sheep, for she was a shepherdess.

10 When Jacob saw Rachel the daughter of Laban his mother's brother, and the sheep of Laban his mother's brother, Jacob went up and rolled the stone from the mouth of the well and watered the flock of Laban his mother's brother.

11 Then Jacob kissed Rachel, and lifted his voice and wept.

12 Jacob told Rachel that he was a relative of her father and that he was Rebekah's son, and she ran and told her father.

13 ¶ So when Laban heard the news of Jacob his sister's son, he ran to meet him, and embraced him and kissed him and brought him to his house. Then he related to Laban all these things.

14 Laban said to him, "Surely you are my bone and my flesh." And he stayed with him a month.

15 ¶ Then Laban said to Jacob, "Because you are my relative, should you therefore serve me for nothing? Tell me, what shall your wages be?"

16 Now Laban had two daughters; the name of the older was Leah, and the name of the younger was Rachel.

17 And Leah's eyes were weak, but Rachel was beautiful of form and face.

18 Now Jacob loved Rachel, so he said, "I will serve you seven years for your younger daughter Rachel."

19 Laban said, "It is better that I give her to you than to give her to another man; stay with me."

New International

18 Early the next morning Jacob took the stone he had placed under his head and set it up as a pillar and poured oil on top of it. 19 He called that place Bethel,*b* though the city used to be called Luz.

20 Then Jacob made a vow, saying, "If God will be with me and will watch over me on this journey I am taking and will give me food to eat and clothes to wear 21 so that I return safely to my father's house, then the LORD*c* will be my God 22 and*d* this stone that I have set up as a pillar will be God's house, and of all that you give me I will give you a tenth."

Jacob Arrives in Paddan Aram

29 THEN JACOB continued on his journey and came to the land of the eastern peoples. 2 There he saw a well in the field, with three flocks of sheep lying near it because the flocks were watered from that well. The stone over the mouth of the well was large. 3 When all the flocks were gathered there, the shepherds would roll the stone away from the well's mouth and water the sheep. Then they would return the stone to its place over the mouth of the well.

4 Jacob asked the shepherds, "My brothers, where are you from?"

"We're from Haran," they replied.

5 He said to them, "Do you know Laban, Nahor's grandson?"

"Yes, we know him," they answered.

6 Then Jacob asked them, "Is he well?"

"Yes, he is," they said, "and here comes his daughter Rachel with the sheep."

7 "Look," he said, "the sun is still high; it is not time for the flocks to be gathered. Water the sheep and take them back to pasture."

8 "We can't," they replied, "until all the flocks are gathered and the stone has been rolled away from the mouth of the well. Then we will water the sheep."

9 While he was still talking with them, Rachel came with her father's sheep, for she was a shepherdess. 10 When Jacob saw Rachel daughter of Laban, his mother's brother, and Laban's sheep, he went over and rolled the stone away from the mouth of the well and watered his uncle's sheep. 11 Then Jacob kissed Rachel and began to weep aloud. 12 He had told Rachel that he was a relative of her father and a son of Rebekah. So she ran and told her father.

13 As soon as Laban heard the news about Jacob, his sister's son, he hurried to meet him. He embraced him and kissed him and brought him to his home, and there Jacob told him all these things. 14 Then Laban said to him, "You are my own flesh and blood."

Jacob Marries Leah and Rachel

After Jacob had stayed with him for a whole month, 15 Laban said to him, "Just because you are a relative of mine, should you work for me for nothing? Tell me what your wages should be."

16 Now Laban had two daughters; the name of the older was Leah, and the name of the younger was Rachel. 17 Leah had weak*e* eyes, but Rachel was lovely in form, and beautiful. 18 Jacob was in love with Rachel and said, "I'll work for you seven years in return for your younger daughter Rachel."

19 Laban said, "It's better that I give her to you than to

---

*b*19 *Bethel* means *house of God.*   *c*20,21 Or *Since God . . .*
father's house, the LORD   *d*21,22 Or *house, and the* LORD *will be
my God,* 22*then*   *e*17 Or *delicate*

King James

²⁰And Jacob served seven years for Rachel; and they seemed unto him *but* a few days, for the love he had to her.

²¹ ¶ And Jacob said unto Laban, Give *me* my wife, for my days are fulfilled, that I may go in unto her.

²²And Laban gathered together all the men of the place, and made a feast.

²³And it came to pass in the evening, that he took Leah his daughter, and brought her to him; and he went in unto her.

²⁴And Laban gave unto his daughter Leah Zilpah his maid *for* an handmaid.

²⁵And it came to pass, that in the morning, behold, it *was* Leah: and he said to Laban, What *is* this thou hast done unto me? did not I serve with thee for Rachel? wherefore then hast thou beguiled me?

²⁶And Laban said, It must not be so done in our ᶜcountry, to give the younger before the firstborn.

²⁷Fulfil her week, and we will give thee this also for the service which thou shalt serve with me yet seven other years.

²⁸And Jacob did so, and fulfilled her week: and he gave him Rachel his daughter to wife also.

²⁹And Laban gave to Rachel his daughter Bilhah his handmaid to be her maid.

³⁰And he went in also unto Rachel, and he loved also Rachel more than Leah, and served with him yet seven other years.

The sons of Jacob

³¹ ¶ And when the LORD saw that Leah *was* hated, he opened her womb: but Rachel *was* barren.

³²And Leah conceived, and bare a son, and she called his name ᵈReuben: for she said, Surely the LORD hath looked upon my affliction; now therefore my husband will love me.

³³And she conceived again, and bare a son; and said, Because the LORD hath heard that I *was* hated, he hath therefore given me this *son* also: and she called his name ᵉSimeon.

³⁴And she conceived again, and bare a son; and said, Now this time will my husband be joined unto me, because I have born him three sons: therefore was his name called ᶠLevi.

³⁵And she conceived again, and bare a son: and she said, Now will I praise the LORD: therefore she called his name ᵍJudah; and ʰleft bearing.

30 AND WHEN Rachel saw that she bare Jacob no children, Rachel envied her sister; and said unto Jacob, Give me children, or else I die.

²And Jacob's anger was kindled against Rachel: and he said, Am I in God's stead, who hath withheld from thee the fruit of the womb?

³And she said, Behold my maid Bilhah, go in unto her; and she shall bear upon my knees, that I may also ⁱhave children by her.

⁴And she gave him Bilhah her handmaid to wife: and Jacob went in unto her.

⁵And Bilhah conceived, and bare Jacob a son.

⁶And Rachel said, God hath judged me, and hath also heard my voice, and hath given me a son: therefore called she his name ʲDan.

⁷And Bilhah Rachel's maid conceived again, and bare Jacob a second son.

⁸And Rachel said, With ᵏgreat wrestlings have I wrestled with my sister, and I have prevailed: and she called his name ˡNaphtali.

Amplified

²⁰And Jacob served seven years for Rachel; and they seemed to him but a few days because of the love he had for her.

²¹Finally, Jacob said to Laban, Give me my wife, for my time is completed, so that I may take her to me.

²²And Laban gathered together all the men of the place and made a feast [with drinking].

²³But when night came, he took Leah his daughter and brought her to [Jacob], who had intercourse with her.

²⁴And Laban gave Zilpah his maid to his daughter Leah to be her maid.

²⁵But in the morning [Jacob saw his wife, and] behold, it was Leah! And he said to Laban, What is this you have done to me? Did I not work for you [all those seven years] for Rachel? Why then have you deceived *and* cheated *and* thrown me down [like this]?

²⁶And Laban said, It is not permitted in our country to give the younger [in marriage] before the elder.

²⁷Finish the [wedding feast] week [for Leah]; then we will give you [Rachel] also, and you shall work for me yet seven more years in return.

²⁸So Jacob complied and fulfilled [Leah's] week; then [Laban] gave him Rachel his daughter as his wife.

²⁹(And Laban gave Bilhah his maid to Rachel his daughter to be her maid.)

³⁰And Jacob lived with Rachel also as his wife, and he loved Rachel more than Leah and served [Laban] another seven years [for her].

³¹And when the Lord saw that Leah was despised, He made her able to bear children, but Rachel was barren.

³²And Leah became pregnant and bore a son and named him Reuben [See, a son!]; for she said, Because the Lord has seen my humiliation *and* affliction; now my husband will love me.

³³[Leah] became pregnant again and bore a son and said, Because the Lord heard that I am despised, He has given me this son also; and she named him Simeon [God hears].

³⁴And she became pregnant again and bore a son and said, Now this time will my husband be a companion to me, for I have borne him three sons. Therefore he was named Levi [companion].

³⁵Again she conceived and bore a son, and she said, Now will I praise the Lord! So she called his name Judah [praise]; then [for a time] she ceased bearing.

30 WHEN RACHEL saw that she bore Jacob no children, she envied her sister, and said to Jacob, Give me children, or else I will die!

²And Jacob became very angry with Rachel and he said, Am I in God's stead, Who has denied you children?

³And she said, See here, take my maid Bilhah and have intercourse with her; and [when the baby comes] she shall deliver it upon my knees, that I by her may also have children.

⁴And she gave him Bilhah her maid as a [secondary] wife, and Jacob had intercourse with her.

⁵And Bilhah became pregnant and bore Jacob a son.

⁶And Rachel said, God has judged *and* vindicated me, and has heard my plea and has given me a son; so she named him Dan [judged].

⁷And Bilhah, Rachel's maid, conceived again and bore Jacob a second son.

⁸And Rachel said, With mighty wrestlings [in prayer to God] I have struggled with my sister and have prevailed; so she named him [this second son Bilhah bore] Naphtali [struggled].

ᶜHeb. *place*   ᵈi.e. *See a son*   ᵉi.e. *Hearing*   ᶠi.e. *Joined*
ᵍi.e. *Praise*   ʰHeb. *stood from bearing*   ⁱHeb. *be built by*
her   ʲi.e. *Judging*   ᵏHeb. *wrestlings of God*   ˡi.e. *My wrestling*

New American Standard

20 So Jacob served seven years for Rachel and they seemed to him but a few days because of his love for her.

Laban's Treachery

21 ¶ Then Jacob said to Laban, "Give *me* my wife, for my time is completed, that I may go in to her."

22 Laban gathered all the men of the place and made a feast.

23 Now in the evening he took his daughter Leah, and brought her to him; and *Jacob* went in to her.

24 Laban also gave his maid Zilpah to his daughter Leah as a maid.

25 So it came about in the morning that, behold, it was Leah! And he said to Laban, "What is this you have done to me? Was it not for Rachel that I served with you? Why then have you deceived me?"

26 But Laban said, "It is not the practice in our place to marry off the younger before the firstborn.

27 "Complete the week of this one, and we will give you the other also for the service which you shall serve with me for another seven years."

28 Jacob did so and completed her week, and he gave him his daughter Rachel as his wife.

29 Laban also gave his maid Bilhah to his daughter Rachel as her maid.

30 So *Jacob* went in to Rachel also, and indeed he loved Rachel more than Leah, and he served with Laban for another seven years.

31 ¶ Now the LORD saw that Leah was unloved, and He opened her womb, but Rachel was barren.

32 Leah conceived and bore a son and named him Reuben, for she said, "Because the LORD has seen my affliction; surely now my husband will love me."

33 Then she conceived again and bore a son and said, "Because the LORD has heard that I am unloved, He has therefore given me this *son* also." So she named him Simeon.

34 She conceived again and bore a son and said, "Now this time my husband will become attached to me, because I have borne him three sons." Therefore he was named Levi.

35 And she conceived again and bore a son and said, "This time I will praise the LORD." Therefore she named him Judah. Then she stopped bearing.

The Sons of Jacob

30 NOW WHEN Rachel saw that she bore Jacob no children, she became jealous of her sister; and she said to Jacob, "Give me children, or else I die."

2 Then Jacob's anger burned against Rachel, and he said, "Am I in the place of God, who has withheld from you the fruit of the womb?"

3 She said, "Here is my maid Bilhah, go in to her that she may bear on my knees, that through her I too may have children."

4 So she gave him her maid Bilhah as a wife, and Jacob went in to her.

5 Bilhah conceived and bore Jacob a son.

6 Then Rachel said, "God has vindicated me, and has indeed heard my voice and has given me a son." Therefore she named him Dan.

7 Rachel's maid Bilhah conceived again and bore Jacob a second son.

8 So Rachel said, "With mighty wrestlings I have wrestled with my sister, *and* I have indeed prevailed." And she named him Naphtali.

New International

some other man. Stay here with me." 20 So Jacob served seven years to get Rachel, but they seemed like only a few days to him because of his love for her.

21 Then Jacob said to Laban, "Give me my wife. My time is completed, and I want to lie with her."

22 So Laban brought together all the people of the place and gave a feast. 23 But when evening came, he took his daughter Leah and gave her to Jacob, and Jacob lay with her. 24 And Laban gave his servant girl Zilpah to his daughter as her maidservant.

25 When morning came, there was Leah! So Jacob said to Laban, "What is this you have done to me? I served you for Rachel, didn't I? Why have you deceived me?"

26 Laban replied, "It is not our custom here to give the younger daughter in marriage before the older one. 27 Finish this daughter's bridal week; then we will give you the younger one also, in return for another seven years of work."

28 And Jacob did so. He finished the week with Leah, and then Laban gave him his daughter Rachel to be his wife. 29 Laban gave his servant girl Bilhah to his daughter Rachel as her maidservant. 30 Jacob lay with Rachel also, and he loved Rachel more than Leah. And he worked for Laban another seven years.

Jacob's Children

31 When the LORD saw that Leah was not loved, he opened her womb, but Rachel was barren. 32 Leah became pregnant and gave birth to a son. She named him Reuben,*f* for she said, "It is because the LORD has seen my misery. Surely my husband will love me now."

33 She conceived again, and when she gave birth to a son she said, "Because the LORD heard that I am not loved, he gave me this one too." So she named him Simeon.*g*

34 Again she conceived, and when she gave birth to a son she said, "Now at last my husband will become attached to me, because I have borne him three sons." So he was named Levi.*h*

35 She conceived again, and when she gave birth to a son she said, "This time I will praise the LORD." So she named him Judah.*i* Then she stopped having children.

30 WHEN RACHEL saw that she was not bearing Jacob any children, she became jealous of her sister. So she said to Jacob, "Give me children, or I'll die!"

2 Jacob became angry with her and said, "Am I in the place of God, who has kept you from having children?"

3 Then she said, "Here is Bilhah, my maidservant. Sleep with her so that she can bear children for me and that through her I too can build a family."

4 So she gave him her servant Bilhah as a wife. Jacob slept with her, 5 and she became pregnant and bore him a son. 6 Then Rachel said, "God has vindicated me; he has listened to my plea and given me a son." Because of this she named him Dan.*j*

7 Rachel's servant Bilhah conceived again and bore Jacob a second son. 8 Then Rachel said, "I have had a great struggle with my sister, and I have won." So she named him Naphtali.*k*

---

f32 Reuben sounds like the Hebrew for *he has seen my misery;* the name means *see, a son.* *g33 Simeon* probably means *one who hears.* *h34 Levi* sounds like and may be derived from the Hebrew for *attached.* *i35 Judah* sounds like and may be derived from the Hebrew for *praise.* *j6 Dan* here means *he has vindicated.* *k8 Naphtali* means *my struggle.*

King James

9When Leah saw that she had left bearing, she took Zilpah her maid, and gave her Jacob to wife.

10And Zilpah Leah's maid bare Jacob a son.

11And Leah said, A troop cometh: and she called his name *m*Gad.

12And Zilpah Leah's maid bare Jacob a second son.

13And Leah said, *n*Happy am I, for the daughters will call me blessed: and she called his name *o*Asher.

14 ¶ And Reuben went in the days of wheat harvest, and found mandrakes in the field, and brought them unto his mother Leah. Then Rachel said to Leah, Give me, I pray thee, of thy son's mandrakes.

15And she said unto her, *Is it* a small matter that thou hast taken my husband? and wouldest thou take away my son's mandrakes also? And Rachel said, Therefore he shall lie with thee tonight for thy son's mandrakes.

16And Jacob came out of the field in the evening, and Leah went out to meet him, and said, Thou must come in unto me; for surely I have hired thee with my son's mandrakes. And he lay with her that night.

17And God hearkened unto Leah, and she conceived, and bare Jacob the fifth son.

18And Leah said, God hath given me my hire, because I have given my maiden to my husband: and she called his name *p*Issachar.

19And Leah conceived again, and bare Jacob the sixth son.

20And Leah said, God hath endued me *with* a good dowry; now will my husband dwell with me, because I have born him six sons: and she called his name *q*Zebulun.

21And afterwards she bare a daughter, and called her name *r*Dinah.

22 ¶ And God remembered Rachel, and God hearkened to her, and opened her womb.

23And she conceived, and bare a son; and said, God hath taken away my reproach:

24And she called his name *s*Joseph; and said, The LORD shall add to me another son.

Jacob's bargain with Laban

25 ¶ And it came to pass, when Rachel had born Joseph, that Jacob said unto Laban, Send me away, that I may go unto mine own place, and to my country.

26Give *me* my wives and my children, for whom I have served thee, and let me go: for thou knowest my service which I have done thee.

27And Laban said unto him, I pray thee, if I have found favour in thine eyes, *tarry: for* I have learned by experience that the LORD hath blessed me for thy sake.

28And he said, Appoint me thy wages, and I will give *it.*

29And he said unto him, Thou knowest how I have served thee, and how thy cattle was with me.

30For *it was* little which thou hadst before I *came,* and it is *now t*increased unto a multitude; and the LORD hath blessed thee *u*since my coming: and now when shall I provide for mine own house also?

31And he said, What shall I give thee? And Jacob said, Thou shalt not give me any thing: if thou wilt do this thing for me, I will again feed *and* keep thy flock.

32I will pass through all thy flock today, removing from thence all the speckled and spotted cattle, and all the brown cattle among the sheep, and the spotted and speckled among the goats: and *of such* shall be my hire.

33So shall my righteousness answer for me *v*in time to come, when it shall come for my hire before thy face: every one that *is* not speckled and spotted among the goats, and brown among the sheep, that shall be counted stolen with me.

Amplified

9When Leah saw that she had ceased to bear, she gave Zilpah her maid to Jacob as a [secondary] wife.

10And Zilpah, Leah's maid, bore Jacob a son.

11Then Leah said, Victory *and* good fortune have come; and she named him Gad [fortune].

12Zilpah, Leah's maid, bore Jacob [her] second son.

13And Leah said, I am happy, for women will call me blessed (happy, fortunate, to be envied); and she named him Asher [happy].

14Now Reuben went at the time of wheat harvest and found some mandrakes (love apples) in the field and brought them to his mother Leah. Then Rachel said to Leah, Give me, I pray you, some of your son's mandrakes.

15But [Leah] answered, Is it not enough that you have taken my husband without your taking away my son's *k*mandrakes also? And Rachel said, Jacob shall sleep with you tonight [in exchange] for your son's mandrakes.

16And Jacob came out of the field in the evening, and Leah went out to meet him and said, You must sleep with me [tonight], for I have certainly paid your hire with my son's mandrakes. So he slept with her that night.

17And God heeded Leah's [prayer], and she conceived and bore Jacob [her] fifth son.

18Leah said, God has given me my hire, because I have given my maid to my husband; and she called his name Issachar [hired].

19And Leah became pregnant again and bore Jacob [her] sixth son.

20Then Leah said, God has endowed me with a good marriage gift [for my husband]; now will he dwell with me [and regard me as his wife in reality], because I have borne him six sons; and she named him Zebulun [dwelling].

21Afterwards she bore a daughter and called her Dinah.

22Then God remembered Rachel and answered her pleading and made it possible for her to have children.

23And [now for the first time] she became pregnant and bore a son; and she said, God has taken away my reproach, disgrace, *and* humiliation.

24And she called his name Joseph [may he add] and said, May the Lord add to me another son.

25When Rachel had borne Joseph, Jacob said to Laban, Send me away, that I may go to my own place and country.

26Give me my wives and my children, for whom I have served you, and let me go; for you know the work which I have done for you.

27And Laban said to him, If I have found favor in your sight, I pray you [do not go]; for I have learned by experience *and* from the omens in divination that the Lord has favored me with blessings on your account.

28He said, State your salary and I will give it.

29Jacob answered him, You know how I have served you, and how your possessions, your cattle *and* sheep *and* goats, have fared with me.

30For you had little before I came, and it has increased *and* multiplied abundantly; and the Lord has favored you with blessings wherever I turned. But now, when shall I provide for my own house also?

31[Laban] said, What shall I give you? And Jacob said, You shall not give me anything, if you will do this one thing for me [of which I am about to tell you], and I will again feed *and* take care of your flock.

32Let me pass through all your flock today, removing from it every speckled and spotted animal and every black one among the sheep, and the spotted and speckled among the goats; and such shall be my wages.

33So later when the matter of my wages is brought before you, my fair dealing will be evident *and* answer for me. Every one that is not speckled and spotted among the goats and black among the sheep, if found with me, shall be counted as stolen.

---

m i.e. A troop, or, company   *n* Heb. In my happiness   *o* i.e. Happy   *p* i.e. An hire   *q* i.e. Dwelling   *r* i.e. Judgment   *s* i.e. Adding   *t* Heb. broken forth   *u* Heb. at my foot   *v* Heb. tomorrow

k Mandrakes were superstitiously supposed to excite and win love.

New American Standard

9 ¶ When Leah saw that she had stopped bearing, she took her maid Zilpah and gave her to Jacob as a wife.
10 Leah's maid Zilpah bore Jacob a son.
11 Then Leah said, "How fortunate!" So she named him Gad.
12 Leah's maid Zilpah bore Jacob a second son.
13 Then Leah said, "Happy am I! For women will call me happy." So she named him Asher.
14 ¶ Now in the days of wheat harvest Reuben went and found mandrakes in the field, and brought them to his mother Leah. Then Rachel said to Leah, "Please give me some of your son's mandrakes."
15 But she said to her, "Is it a small matter for you to take my husband? And would you take my son's mandrakes also?" So Rachel said, "Therefore he may lie with you tonight in return for your son's mandrakes."
16 When Jacob came in from the field in the evening, then Leah went out to meet him and said, "You must come in to me, for I have surely hired you with my son's mandrakes." So he lay with her that night.
17 God gave heed to Leah, and she conceived and bore Jacob a fifth son.
18 Then Leah said, "God has given me my wages because I gave my maid to my husband." So she named him Issachar.
19 Leah conceived again and bore a sixth son to Jacob.
20 Then Leah said, "God has endowed me with a good gift; now my husband will dwell with me, because I have borne him six sons." So she named him Zebulun.
21 Afterward she bore a daughter and named her Dinah.
22 ¶ Then God remembered Rachel, and God gave heed to her and opened her womb.
23 So she conceived and bore a son and said, "God has taken away my reproach."
24 She named him Joseph, saying, "May the LORD give me another son."

Jacob Prospers

25 ¶ Now it came about when Rachel had borne Joseph, that Jacob said to Laban, "Send me away, that I may go to my own place and to my own country.
26 "Give *me* my wives and my children for whom I have served you, and let me depart; for you yourself know my service which I have rendered you."
27 But Laban said to him, "If now *d*it pleases you, *stay with me;* I have divined that the LORD has blessed me on your account."
28 He continued, "Name me your wages, and I will give it."
29 But he said to him, "You yourself know how I have served you and how your cattle have fared with me.
30 "For you had little before I came and it has increased to a multitude, and the LORD has blessed you wherever I turned. But now, when shall I provide for my own household also?"
31 So he said, "What shall I give you?" And Jacob said, "You shall not give me anything. If you will do this *one* thing for me, I will again pasture *and* keep your flock:
32 let me pass through your entire flock today, removing from there every speckled and spotted sheep and every black one among the lambs and the spotted and speckled among the goats; and *such* shall be my wages.
33 "So my honesty will answer for me later, when you come concerning my wages. Every one that is not speckled and spotted among the goats and black among the lambs, *if found* with me, will be considered stolen."

New International

9 When Leah saw that she had stopped having children, she took her maidservant Zilpah and gave her to Jacob as a wife. 10 Leah's servant Zilpah bore Jacob a son. 11 Then Leah said, "What good fortune!"*l* So she named him Gad.*m*
12 Leah's servant Zilpah bore Jacob a second son. 13 Then Leah said, "How happy I am! The women will call me happy." So she named him Asher.*n*
14 During wheat harvest, Reuben went out into the fields and found some mandrake plants, which he brought to his mother Leah. Rachel said to Leah, "Please give me some of your son's mandrakes."
15 But she said to her, "Wasn't it enough that you took away my husband? Will you take my son's mandrakes too?"
"Very well," Rachel said, "he can sleep with you tonight in return for your son's mandrakes."
16 So when Jacob came in from the fields that evening, Leah went out to meet him. "You must sleep with me," she said. "I have hired you with my son's mandrakes." So he slept with her that night.
17 God listened to Leah, and she became pregnant and bore Jacob a fifth son. 18 Then Leah said, "God has rewarded me for giving my maidservant to my husband." So she named him Issachar.*o*
19 Leah conceived again and bore Jacob a sixth son. 20 Then Leah said, "God has presented me with a precious gift. This time my husband will treat me with honor, because I have borne him six sons." So she named him Zebulun.*p*
21 Some time later she gave birth to a daughter and named her Dinah.
22 Then God remembered Rachel; he listened to her and opened her womb. 23 She became pregnant and gave birth to a son and said, "God has taken away my disgrace." 24 She named him Joseph,*q* and said, "May the LORD add to me another son."

Jacob's Flocks Increase

25 After Rachel gave birth to Joseph, Jacob said to Laban, "Send me on my way so I can go back to my own homeland. 26 Give me my wives and children, for whom I have served you, and I will be on my way. You know how much work I've done for you."
27 But Laban said to him, "If I have found favor in your eyes, please stay. I have learned by divination that*r* the LORD has blessed me because of you." 28 He added, "Name your wages, and I will pay them."
29 Jacob said to him, "You know how I have worked for you and how your livestock has fared under my care. 30 The little you had before I came has increased greatly, and the LORD has blessed you wherever I have been. But now, when may I do something for my own household?"
31 "What shall I give you?" he asked.
"Don't give me anything," Jacob replied. "But if you will do this one thing for me, I will go on tending your flocks and watching over them: 32 Let me go through all your flocks today and remove from them every speckled or spotted sheep, every dark-colored lamb and every spotted or speckled goat. They will be my wages. 33 And my honesty will testify for me in the future, whenever you check on the wages you have paid me. Any goat in my possession that is not speckled or spotted, or any lamb that is not dark-colored, will be considered stolen."

---

l 11 Or "A troop is coming!"   *m 11 Gad can mean good fortune or a troop.*   *n 13 Asher means happy.*   *o 18 Issachar sounds like the Hebrew for reward.*   *p 20 Zebulun probably means honor.*   *q 24 Joseph means may he add.*   *r 27 Or possibly have become rich and*

d Lit *I have found favor in your eyes*

King James

³⁴And Laban said, Behold, I would it might be according to thy word.

³⁵And he removed that day the he goats that were ringstraked and spotted, and all the she goats that were speckled and spotted, *and* every one that had *some* white in it, and all the brown among the sheep, and gave *them* into the hand of his sons.

³⁶And he set three days' journey betwixt himself and Jacob: and Jacob fed the rest of Laban's flocks.

³⁷ ¶ And Jacob took him rods of green poplar, and of the hazel and chestnut tree; and pilled white strakes in them, and made the white appear which *was* in the rods.

³⁸And he set the rods which he had pilled before the flocks in the gutters in the watering troughs when the flocks came to drink, that they should conceive when they came to drink.

³⁹And the flocks conceived before the rods, and brought forth cattle ringstraked, speckled, and spotted.

⁴⁰And Jacob did separate the lambs, and set the faces of the flocks toward the ringstraked, and all the brown in the flock of Laban; and he put his own flocks by themselves, and put them not unto Laban's cattle.

⁴¹And it came to pass, whensoever the stronger cattle did conceive, that Jacob laid the rods before the eyes of the cattle in the gutters, that they might conceive among the rods.

⁴²But when the cattle were feeble, he put *them* not in: so the feebler were Laban's, and the stronger Jacob's.

⁴³And the man increased exceedingly, and had much cattle, and maidservants, and menservants, and camels, and asses.

Jacob flees from Laban

31 AND HE heard the words of Laban's sons, saying, Jacob hath taken away all that *was* our father's; and of *that* which *was* our father's hath he gotten all this glory.

²And Jacob beheld the countenance of Laban, and, behold, it *was* not toward him ʷas before.

³And the LORD said unto Jacob, Return unto the land of thy fathers, and to thy kindred; and I will be with thee.

⁴And Jacob sent and called Rachel and Leah to the field unto his flock,

⁵And said unto them, I see your father's countenance, that it *is* not toward me as before; but the God of my father hath been with me.

⁶And ye know that with all my power I have served your father.

⁷And your father hath deceived me, and changed my wages ten times; but God suffered him not to hurt me.

⁸If he said thus, The speckled shall be thy wages; then all the cattle bare speckled: and if he said thus, The ringstraked shall be thy hire; then bare all the cattle ringstraked.

⁹Thus God hath taken away the cattle of your father, and given *them* to me.

¹⁰And it came to pass at the time that the cattle conceived, that I lifted up mine eyes, and saw in a dream, and, behold, the ˣrams which leaped upon the cattle *were* ringstraked, speckled, and grisled.

¹¹And the angel of God spake unto me in a dream, *saying,* Jacob: And I said, Here *am* I.

¹²And he said, Lift up now thine eyes, and see, all the rams which leap upon the cattle *are* ringstraked, speckled, and grisled: for I have seen all that Laban doeth unto thee.

Amplified

³⁴And Laban said, Good; let it be done as you say.

³⁵But that same day [Laban] removed the he-goats that were streaked and spotted and all the she-goats that were speckled and spotted, every one that had white on it, and every black lamb, and put them in charge of his sons.

³⁶And he set [a distance of] three days' journey between himself and Jacob; and Jacob was then left in care of the rest of Laban's flock.

³⁷But Jacob took fresh rods of poplar and almond and plane trees and peeled white streaks in them, exposing the white in the rods.

³⁸He set the rods which he had peeled in front of the flocks in the watering troughs where the flocks came to drink. And since they bred *and* conceived when they came to drink,

³⁹The flocks bred *and* conceived in sight of the rods and brought forth lambs *and* kids streaked, speckled, and spotted.

⁴⁰Jacob separated the lambs, and [as he had done with the peeled rods] he also set the faces of the flocks toward the streaked and all the dark in the [new] flock of Laban; and he put his own droves by themselves and did not let them breed with Laban's flock.

⁴¹And whenever the stronger animals were breeding, Jacob laid the rods in the watering troughs before the eyes of the flock, that they might breed *and* conceive among the rods.

⁴²But when the sheep *and* goats were feeble, he omitted putting the rods there; so the feebler animals were Laban's and the stronger Jacob's.

⁴³Thus the man increased *and* became exceedingly rich, and had many sheep *and* goats, and maidservants, menservants, camels, and donkeys.

31 JACOB HEARD Laban's sons complaining, Jacob has taken away all that was our father's; he has acquired all this wealth *and* honor from what belonged to our father.

²And Jacob noticed that Laban looked at him less favorably than before.

³Then the Lord said to Jacob, Return to the land of your fathers and to your people, and I will be with you.

⁴So Jacob sent and called Rachel and Leah to the field to his flock,

⁵And he said to them, I see how your father looks at me, that he is not [friendly] toward me as before; but the God of my father has been with me.

⁶You know that I have served your father with all my might *and* power.

⁷But your father has deceived me and changed my wages ten times, but God did not allow him to hurt me.

⁸If he said, The speckled shall be your wages, then all the flock bore speckled; and if he said, The streaked shall be your hire, then all the flock bore streaked.

⁹Thus God has taken away the flocks of your father and given them to me.

¹⁰And I had a ˡdream at the time the flock conceived. I looked up and saw that the rams which mated with the she-goats were streaked, speckled, and spotted.

¹¹And the ᵐAngel of God said to me in the dream, Jacob. And I said, Here am I.

¹²And He said, Look up and see, all the rams which mate with the flock are streaked, speckled, and mottled; for I have seen all that Laban does to you.

ˡWe naturally wonder why we have not heard of this dream before and are tempted to question Jacob's truthfulness; but the Samaritan text removes all such doubt by recording the whole dream in the previous chapter (Gen. 30), right after Gen. 30:36 (Adam Clarke, *The Holy Bible with A Commentary*).   ᵐSee footnote on Gen. 16:7. Note especially Gen. 31:13, where the Angel says, "I am the God of Bethel."

ʷHeb. *as yesterday and the day before*   ˣOr, *he goats*

New American Standard

³⁴ Laban said, "Good, let it be according to your word." ³⁵ So he removed on that day the striped and spotted male goats and all the speckled and spotted female goats, every one with white in it, and all the black ones among the sheep, and gave them into the care of his sons.

³⁶ And he put *a distance of* three days' journey between himself and Jacob, and Jacob fed the rest of Laban's flocks.

³⁷ ¶ Then Jacob took fresh rods of poplar and almond and plane trees, and peeled white stripes in them, exposing the white which *was* in the rods.

³⁸ He set the rods which he had peeled in front of the flocks in the gutters, *even* in the watering troughs, where the flocks came to drink; and they mated when they came to drink.

³⁹ So the flocks mated by the rods, and the flocks brought forth striped, speckled, and spotted.

⁴⁰ Jacob separated the lambs, and made the flocks face toward the striped and all the black in the flock of Laban; and he put his own herds apart, and did not put them with Laban's flock.

⁴¹ Moreover, whenever the stronger of the flock were mating, Jacob would place the rods in the sight of the flock in the gutters, so that they might mate by the rods;

⁴² but when the flock was feeble, he did not put *them* in; so the feebler were Laban's and the stronger Jacob's.

⁴³ So the man became exceedingly prosperous, and had large flocks and female and male servants and camels and donkeys.

Jacob Leaves Secretly for Canaan

31 NOW JACOB heard the words of Laban's sons, saying, "Jacob has taken away all that was our father's, and from what belonged to our father he has made all this wealth."

² Jacob saw the ᵉattitude of Laban, and behold, it was not *friendly* toward him as formerly.

³ Then the LORD said to Jacob, "Return to the land of your fathers and to your relatives, and I will be with you."

⁴ So Jacob sent and called Rachel and Leah to his flock in the field,

⁵ and said to them, "I see your father's attitude, that it is not *friendly* toward me as formerly, but the God of my father has been with me.

⁶ "You know that I have served your father with all my strength.

⁷ "Yet your father has cheated me and changed my wages ten times; however, God did not allow him to hurt me.

⁸ "If he spoke thus, 'The speckled shall be your wages,' then all the flock brought forth speckled; and if he spoke thus, 'The striped shall be your wages,' then all the flock brought forth striped.

⁹ "Thus God has taken away your father's livestock and given *them* to me.

¹⁰ "And it came about at the time when the flock were mating that I lifted up my eyes and saw in a dream, and behold, the male goats which were mating *were* striped, speckled, and mottled.

¹¹ "Then the angel of God said to me in the dream, 'Jacob,' and I said, 'Here I am.'

¹² "He said, 'Lift up now your eyes and see *that* all the male goats which are mating are striped, speckled, and mottled; for I have seen all that Laban has been doing to you.

New International

³⁴ "Agreed," said Laban. "Let it be as you have said." ³⁵ That same day he removed all the male goats that were streaked or spotted, and all the speckled or spotted female goats (all that had white on them) and all the dark-colored lambs, and he placed them in the care of his sons. ³⁶ Then he put a three-day journey between himself and Jacob, while Jacob continued to tend the rest of Laban's flocks.

³⁷ Jacob, however, took fresh-cut branches from poplar, almond and plane trees and made white stripes on them by peeling the bark and exposing the white inner wood of the branches. ³⁸ Then he placed the peeled branches in all the watering troughs, so that they would be directly in front of the flocks when they came to drink. When the flocks were in heat and came to drink, ³⁹ they mated in front of the branches. And they bore young that were streaked or speckled or spotted. ⁴⁰ Jacob set apart the young of the flock by themselves, but made the rest face the streaked and dark-colored animals that belonged to Laban. Thus he made separate flocks for himself and did not put them with Laban's animals. ⁴¹ Whenever the stronger females were in heat, Jacob would place the branches in the troughs in front of the animals so they would mate near the branches, ⁴² but if the animals were weak, he would not place them there. So the weak animals went to Laban and the strong ones to Jacob. ⁴³ In this way the man grew exceedingly prosperous and came to own large flocks, and maidservants and menservants, and camels and donkeys.

Jacob Flees From Laban

31 JACOB HEARD that Laban's sons were saying, "Jacob has taken everything our father owned and has gained all this wealth from what belonged to our father." ² And Jacob noticed that Laban's attitude toward him was not what it had been.

³ Then the LORD said to Jacob, "Go back to the land of your fathers and to your relatives, and I will be with you."

⁴ So Jacob sent word to Rachel and Leah to come out to the fields where his flocks were. ⁵ He said to them, "I see that your father's attitude toward me is not what it was before, but the God of my father has been with me. ⁶ You know that I've worked for your father with all my strength, ⁷ yet your father has cheated me by changing my wages ten times. However, God has not allowed him to harm me. ⁸ If he said, 'The speckled ones will be your wages,' then all the flocks gave birth to speckled young; and if he said, 'The streaked ones will be your wages,' then all the flocks bore streaked young. ⁹ So God has taken away your father's livestock and has given them to me.

¹⁰ "In breeding season I once had a dream in which I looked up and saw that the male goats mating with the flock were streaked, speckled or spotted. ¹¹ The angel of God said to me in the dream, 'Jacob.' I answered, 'Here I am.' ¹² And he said, 'Look up and see that all the male goats mating with the flock are streaked, speckled or spotted, for I have seen all that Laban has been doing to you.

ᵉ Lit *face*

King James

¹³I *am* the God of Beth-el, where thou anointedst the pillar, *and* where thou vowedst a vow unto me: now arise, get thee out from this land, and return unto the land of thy kindred.

¹⁴And Rachel and Leah answered and said unto him, *Is there* yet any portion or inheritance for us in our father's house?

¹⁵Are we not counted of him strangers? for he hath sold us, and hath quite devoured also our money.

¹⁶For all the riches which God hath taken from our father, that *is* ours, and our children's: now then, whatsoever God hath said unto thee, do.

¹⁷ ¶ Then Jacob rose up, and set his sons and his wives upon camels;

¹⁸And he carried away all his cattle, and all his goods which he had gotten, the cattle of his getting, which he had gotten in Padan-aram, for to go to Isaac his father in the land of Canaan.

¹⁹And Laban went to shear his sheep: and Rachel had stolen the images ^ythat *were* her father's.

²⁰And Jacob stole away ^zunawares to Laban the Syrian, in that he told him not that he fled.

²¹So he fled with all that he had; and he rose up, and passed over the river, and set his face *toward* the mount Gilead.

²²And it was told Laban on the third day that Jacob was fled.

²³And he took his brethren with him, and pursued after him seven days' journey; and they overtook him in the mount Gilead.

²⁴And God came to Laban the Syrian in a dream by night, and said unto him, Take heed that thou speak not to Jacob ^aeither good or bad.

²⁵ ¶ Then Laban overtook Jacob. Now Jacob had pitched his tent in the mount: and Laban with his brethren pitched in the mount of Gilead.

²⁶And Laban said to Jacob, What hast thou done, that thou hast stolen away unawares to me, and carried away my daughters, as captives *taken* with the sword?

²⁷Wherefore didst thou flee away secretly, and ^bsteal away from me; and didst not tell me, that I might have sent thee away with mirth, and with songs, with tabret, and with harp?

²⁸And hast not suffered me to kiss my sons and my daughters? thou hast now done foolishly in *so* doing.

²⁹It is in the power of my hand to do you hurt: but the God of your father spake unto me yesternight, saying, Take thou heed that thou speak not to Jacob either good or bad.

³⁰And now, *though* thou wouldest needs be gone, because thou sore longedst after thy father's house, *yet* wherefore hast thou stolen my gods?

³¹And Jacob answered and said to Laban, Because I was afraid: for I said, Peradventure thou wouldest take by force thy daughters from me.

Amplified

¹³I am the God of Bethel, where you anointed the pillar and where you vowed a vow to Me. Now arise, get out from this land and return to your native land.

¹⁴And Rachel and Leah answered him, Is there any portion or inheritance for us in our father's house?

¹⁵Are we not counted by him as strangers? For he sold us and has also quite devoured our money [the price you paid for us].

¹⁶For all the riches which God has taken from our father are ours and our children's. Now then, whatever God has said to you, do it.

¹⁷Then Jacob rose up and set his sons and his wives upon the camels;

¹⁸And he drove away all his livestock and all his gain which he had gotten, the livestock he had obtained *and* accumulated in Padan-aram, to go to Isaac his father in the land of Canaan.

¹⁹Now Laban had gone to shear his sheep [possibly to the feast of sheepshearing], and Rachel stole her father's household gods.

²⁰And Jacob outwitted Laban the Syrian [Aramean] in that he did not tell him that he [intended] to flee *and* slip away secretly.

²¹So he fled with all that he had, and arose and crossed the river [Euphrates] and set his face toward the hill country of Gilead.

²²But on the third day Laban was told that Jacob had fled.

²³So he took his kinsmen with him and pursued after [Jacob] for seven days, and they overtook him in the hill country of Gilead.

²⁴But God came to Laban the Syrian [Aramean] in a dream by night and said to him, Be careful that you do not speak from good to bad to Jacob [peaceably, then violently].

²⁵Then Laban overtook Jacob. Now Jacob had pitched his tent on the hill, and Laban coming with his kinsmen pitched [his tents] on the same hill of Gilead.

²⁶And Laban said to Jacob, What do you mean stealing away *and* leaving like this without my knowing it, and carrying off my daughters as if captives of the sword?

²⁷Why did you flee secretly and cheat me and did not tell me, so that I might have sent you away with joy *and* gladness and with singing, with tambourine and lyre?

²⁸And why did you not permit me to kiss my sons [grandchildren] and my daughters good-bye? Now you have done foolishly [in behaving like this].

²⁹It is in my power to do you harm; but the God of your father spoke to me last night, saying, Be careful that you do not speak from good to bad to Jacob [peaceably, then violently].

³⁰And now you felt you must go because you were homesick for your father's house, but why did you steal my [household] ⁿgods?

³¹Jacob answered Laban, Because I was afraid; for I thought, Suppose you would take your daughters from me by force.

ⁿWhy was Laban making such a great commotion about some small idols? It had never been satisfactorily explained until the answer was found in the excavated Nuzi tablets (J. P. Free, *Archaeology Illuminates the Bible*), which showed that possession of the father's household gods played an important role in inheritance (W. F. Albright, "Recent Discoveries in Bible Lands," in *Young's Analytical Concordance to the Bible*). One of the Nuzi tablets indicated that in the region where Laban lived, a son-in-law who possessed the family images could appear in court and make claim to the estate of his father-in-law (various authors cited by Allan A. MacRae, "The Relation of Archaeology to the Bible," in American Scientific Affiliation, *Modern Science and Christian Faith*). Since Jacob's possession of the images implied the right to inheritance of Laban's wealth, one can understand why Laban organized his hurried expedition to recover the images (J. P. Free, *Archaeology and Bible History*).

^yHeb. *teraphim*   ^zHeb. *the heart of Laban*   ^aHeb. *from good to bad*   ^bHeb. *hast stolen me*

New American Standard

13 'I am the God *of* Bethel, where you anointed a pillar, where you made a vow to Me; now arise, leave this land, and return to the land of your birth.' "

14 Rachel and Leah said to him, "Do we still have any portion or inheritance in our father's house?

15 "Are we not reckoned by him as foreigners? For he has sold us, and has also entirely consumed our purchase price.

16 "Surely all the wealth which God has taken away from our father belongs to us and our children; now then, do whatever God has said to you."

17 ¶ Then Jacob arose and put his children and his wives upon camels;

18 and he drove away all his livestock and all his property which he had gathered, his acquired livestock which he had gathered in Paddan-aram, to go to the land of Canaan to his father Isaac.

19 When Laban had gone to shear his flock, then Rachel stole the household idols that were her father's.

20 And Jacob deceived Laban the Aramean by not telling him that he was fleeing.

21 So he fled with all that he had; and he arose and crossed the *Euphrates* River, and set his face toward the hill country of Gilead.

Laban Pursues Jacob

22 ¶ When it was told Laban on the third day that Jacob had fled,

23 then he took his kinsmen with him and pursued him *a distance of* seven days' journey, and he overtook him in the hill country of Gilead.

24 God came to Laban the Aramean in a dream of the night and said to him, "Be careful that you do not speak to Jacob either good or bad."

25 ¶ Laban caught up with Jacob. Now Jacob had pitched his tent in the hill country, and Laban with his kinsmen camped in the hill country of Gilead.

26 Then Laban said to Jacob, "What have you done by deceiving me and carrying away my daughters like captives of the sword?

27 "Why did you flee secretly and deceive me, and did not tell me so that I might have sent you away with joy and with songs, with timbrel and with lyre;

28 and did not allow me to kiss my sons and my daughters? Now you have done foolishly.

29 "It is in my power to do you harm, but the God of your father spoke to me last night, saying, 'Be careful not to speak either good or bad to Jacob.'

30 "Now you have indeed gone away because you longed greatly for your father's house; *but* why did you steal my gods?"

31 Then Jacob replied to Laban, "Because I was afraid, for I thought that you would take your daughters from me by force.

New International

13 I am the God of Bethel, where you anointed a pillar and where you made a vow to me. Now leave this land at once and go back to your native land.' "

14 Then Rachel and Leah replied, "Do we still have any share in the inheritance of our father's estate? 15 Does he not regard us as foreigners? Not only has he sold us, but he has used up what was paid for us. 16 Surely all the wealth that God took away from our father belongs to us and our children. So do whatever God has told you."

17 Then Jacob put his children and his wives on camels, 18 and he drove all his livestock ahead of him, along with all the goods he had accumulated in Paddan Aram,[s] to go to his father Isaac in the land of Canaan.

19 When Laban had gone to shear his sheep, Rachel stole her father's household gods. 20 Moreover, Jacob deceived Laban the Aramean by not telling him he was running away. 21 So he fled with all he had, and crossing the River,[t] he headed for the hill country of Gilead.

Laban Pursues Jacob

22 On the third day Laban was told that Jacob had fled. 23 Taking his relatives with him, he pursued Jacob for seven days and caught up with him in the hill country of Gilead. 24 Then God came to Laban the Aramean in a dream at night and said to him, "Be careful not to say anything to Jacob, either good or bad."

25 Jacob had pitched his tent in the hill country of Gilead when Laban overtook him, and Laban and his relatives camped there too. 26 Then Laban said to Jacob, "What have you done? You've deceived me, and you've carried off my daughters like captives in war. 27 Why did you run off secretly and deceive me? Why didn't you tell me, so I could send you away with joy and singing to the music of tambourines and harps? 28 You didn't even let me kiss my grandchildren and my daughters good-by. You have done a foolish thing. 29 I have the power to harm you; but last night the God of your father said to me, 'Be careful not to say anything to Jacob, either good or bad.' 30 Now you have gone off because you longed to return to your father's house. But why did you steal my gods?"

31 Jacob answered Laban, "I was afraid, because I thought you would take your daughters away from me by

King James

³²With whomsoever thou findest thy gods, let him not live: before our brethren discern thou what *is* thine with me, and take *it* to thee. For Jacob knew not that Rachel had stolen them.

³³And Laban went into Jacob's tent, and into Leah's tent, and into the two maidservants' tents; but he found *them* not. Then went he out of Leah's tent, and entered into Rachel's tent.

³⁴Now Rachel had taken the images, and put them in the camel's furniture, and sat upon them. And Laban ᶜsearched all the tent, but found *them* not.

³⁵And she said to her father, Let it not displease my lord that I cannot rise up before thee; for the custom of women *is* upon me. And he searched, but found not the images.

³⁶ ¶ And Jacob was wroth, and chode with Laban: and Jacob answered and said to Laban, What *is* my trespass? what *is* my sin, that thou hast so hotly pursued after me?

³⁷Whereas thou hast ᶜsearched all my stuff, what hast thou found of all thy household stuff? set *it* here before my brethren and thy brethren, that they may judge betwixt us both.

³⁸This twenty years *have* I *been* with thee; thy ewes and thy she goats have not cast their young, and the rams of thy flock have I not eaten.

³⁹That which was torn *of beasts* I brought not unto thee; I bare the loss of it; of my hand didst thou require it, *whether* stolen by day, or stolen by night.

⁴⁰*Thus* I was; in the day the drought consumed me, and the frost by night; and my sleep departed from mine eyes.

⁴¹Thus have I been twenty years in thy house; I served thee fourteen years for thy two daughters, and six years for thy cattle: and thou hast changed my wages ten times.

⁴²Except the God of my father, the God of Abraham, and the fear of Isaac, had been with me, surely thou hadst sent me away now empty. God hath seen mine affliction and the labour of my hands, and rebuked *thee* yesternight.

⁴³ ¶ And Laban answered and said unto Jacob, *These* daughters *are* my daughters, and *these* children *are* my children, and *these* cattle *are* my cattle, and all that thou seest *is* mine: and what can I do this day unto these my daughters, or unto their children which they have born?

⁴⁴Now therefore come thou, let us make a covenant, I and thou; and let it be for a witness between me and thee.

⁴⁵And Jacob took a stone, and set it up *for* a pillar.

⁴⁶And Jacob said unto his brethren, Gather stones; and they took stones, and made an heap: and they did eat there upon the heap.

⁴⁷And Laban called it ᵈJegar-sahadutha: but Jacob called it ᵉGaleed.

⁴⁸And Laban said, This heap *is* a witness between me and thee this day. Therefore was the name of it called Galeed;

⁴⁹And ᶠMizpah; for he said, The LORD watch between me and thee, when we are absent one from another.

⁵⁰If thou shalt afflict my daughters, or if thou shalt take *other* wives beside my daughters, no man *is* with us; see, God *is* witness betwixt me and thee.

⁵¹And Laban said to Jacob, Behold this heap, and behold *this* pillar, which I have cast betwixt me and thee;

⁵²This heap *be* witness, and *this* pillar *be* witness, that I will not pass over this heap to thee, and that thou shalt not pass over this heap and this pillar unto me, for harm.

Amplified

³²The one with whom you find those gods of yours, let him not live. Here before our kinsmen [search my possessions and] take whatever you find that belongs to you. For Jacob did not know that Rachel had stolen [the images].

³³So Laban went into Jacob's tent and into Leah's tent and the tent of the two maids, but he did not find them. Then he went from Leah's tent into Rachel's tent.

³⁴Now Rachel had taken the images (gods) and put them in the camel's saddle and sat on them. Laban searched *and* felt through all the tent, but did not find them.

³⁵And [Rachel] said to her father, Do not be displeased, my lord, that I cannot rise up before you, for the period of women is upon me *and* I am unwell. And he searched, but did not find the gods.

³⁶Then Jacob became angry and reproached *and* argued with Laban. And Jacob said to Laban, What is my fault? What is my sin, that you so hotly pursued me?

³⁷Although you have searched *and* felt through all my household possessions, what have you found of all your household goods? Put it here before my brethren and yours, that they may judge *and* decide between us.

³⁸These twenty years I have been with you; your ewes and your she-goats have not lost their young, and the rams of your flock have not been eaten by me.

³⁹I did not bring you [the carcasses of the animals] torn by wild beasts; I bore the loss of it; you required of me [to make good] all that was stolen, whether it occurred by day or by night.

⁴⁰This was [my lot]; by day the heat consumed me and by night the cold, and I could not sleep.

⁴¹I have been twenty years in your house. I served you fourteen years for your two daughters and six years for your flocks; and you have changed my wages ten times.

⁴²And if the God of my father, the God of Abraham and the Dread [lest he should fall] *and* Fear [lest he offend] of Isaac, had not been with me, surely you would have sent me away now empty-handed. God has seen my affliction *and* humiliation and the [wearying] labor of my hands and rebuked you last night.

⁴³Laban answered Jacob, These daughters are my daughters, these children are my children, these flocks are my flocks, and all that you see is mine. But what can I do today to my daughters or to their children whom they have borne?

⁴⁴So come now, let us make a covenant *or* league, you and I, and let it be for a witness between you and me.

⁴⁵So Jacob set up a stone for a pillar *or* monument.

⁴⁶And Jacob said to his brethren, Gather stones; and they took stones and made a heap, and they ate [together] there upon the heap. [Prov. 16:7.]

⁴⁷Laban called it Jegar-sahadutha [witness heap, *in Aramaic*], but Jacob called it Galeed [ᵒwitness heap, *in Hebrew*.]

⁴⁸And Laban said, This heap is a witness today between you and me. Therefore it was named Galeed.

⁴⁹And [the pillar or monument was called] Mizpah [watchpost], for he [Laban] said, May the Lord watch between you and me when we are absent *and* hidden one from another.

⁵⁰If you should afflict, humiliate, *or* lower [divorce] my daughters, or if you should take other wives beside my daughters, although no man is with us [to witness], see (remember), God is witness between you and me.

⁵¹And Laban said to Jacob, See this heap and this pillar, which I have set up between you and me.

⁵²This heap is a witness and this pillar is a witness, that I will not pass by this heap to you, and that you will not pass by this heap and this pillar to me, for harm.

ᶜHeb. *felt*   ᵈi.e. *The heap of witness* Chald.   ᵉi.e. *The heap of witness* Heb.   ᶠi.e. *A beacon,* or, *watchtower*

ᵒ*The Latin Vulgate* adds, "Each according to the idiom of his own tongue"—i.e., Laban in Aramaic and Jacob in Hebrew.

New American Standard

32"The one with whom you find your gods shall not live; in the presence of our kinsmen point out what is yours among my belongings and take it for yourself." For Jacob did not know that Rachel had stolen them.

33 ¶ So Laban went into Jacob's tent and into Leah's tent and into the tent of the two maids, but he did not find them. Then he went out of Leah's tent and entered Rachel's tent.

34 Now Rachel had taken the household idols and put them in the camel's saddle, and she sat on them. And Laban felt through all the tent but did not find them.

35 She said to her father, "Let not my lord be angry that I cannot rise before you, for the manner of women is upon me." So he searched but did not find the household idols.

36 ¶ Then Jacob became angry and contended with Laban; and Jacob said to Laban, "What is my transgression? What is my sin that you have hotly pursued me?

37"Though you have felt through all my goods, what have you found of all your household goods? Set it here before my kinsmen and your kinsmen, that they may decide between us two.

38"These twenty years I have been with you; your ewes and your female goats have not miscarried, nor have I eaten the rams of your flocks.

39"That which was torn of beasts I did not bring to you; I bore the loss of it myself. You required it of my hand whether stolen by day or stolen by night.

40"Thus I was: by day the heat consumed me and the frost by night, and my sleep fled from my eyes.

41"These twenty years I have been in your house; I served you fourteen years for your two daughters and six years for your flock, and you changed my wages ten times.

42"If the God of my father, the God of Abraham, and the fear of Isaac, had not been for me, surely now you would have sent me away empty-handed. God has seen my affliction and the toil of my hands, so He rendered judgment last night."

The Covenant of Mizpah

43 ¶ Then Laban replied to Jacob, "The daughters are my daughters, and the children are my children, and the flocks are my flocks, and all that you see is mine. But what can I do this day to these my daughters or to their children whom they have borne?

44"So now come, let us make a covenant, you and I, and let it be a witness between you and me."

45 Then Jacob took a stone and set it up as a pillar.

46 Jacob said to his kinsmen, "Gather stones." So they took stones and made a heap, and they ate there by the heap.

47 Now Laban called it ƒJegar-sahadutha, but Jacob called it gGaleed.

48 Laban said, "This heap is a witness between you and me this day." Therefore it was named Galeed,

49 and hMizpah, for he said, "May the LORD watch between you and me when we are absent one from the other.

50"If you mistreat my daughters, or if you take wives besides my daughters, although no man is with us, see, God is witness between you and me."

51 Laban said to Jacob, "Behold this heap and behold the pillar which I have set between you and me.

52"This heap is a witness, and the pillar is a witness, that I will not pass by this heap to you for harm, and you will not pass by this heap and this pillar to me, for harm.

New International

force. 32But if you find anyone who has your gods, he shall not live. In the presence of our relatives, see for yourself whether there is anything of yours here with me; and if so, take it." Now Jacob did not know that Rachel had stolen the gods.

33So Laban went into Jacob's tent and into Leah's tent and into the tent of the two maidservants, but he found nothing. After he came out of Leah's tent, he entered Rachel's tent.

34Now Rachel had taken the household gods and put them inside her camel's saddle and was sitting on them. Laban searched through everything in the tent but found nothing.

35Rachel said to her father, "Don't be angry, my lord, that I cannot stand up in your presence; I'm having my period." So he searched but could not find the household gods.

36Jacob was angry and took Laban to task. "What is my crime?" he asked Laban. "What sin have I committed that you hunt me down? 37Now that you have searched through all my goods, what have you found that belongs to your household? Put it here in front of your relatives and mine, and let them judge between the two of us.

38"I have been with you for twenty years now. Your sheep and goats have not miscarried, nor have I eaten rams from your flocks. 39I did not bring you animals torn by wild beasts; I bore the loss myself. And you demanded payment from me for whatever was stolen by day or night. 40This was my situation: The heat consumed me in the daytime and the cold at night, and sleep fled from my eyes. 41It was like this for the twenty years I was in your household. I worked for you fourteen years for your two daughters and six years for your flocks, and you changed my wages ten times. 42If the God of my father, the God of Abraham and the Fear of Isaac, had not been with me, you would surely have sent me away empty-handed. But God has seen my hardship and the toil of my hands, and last night he rebuked you."

43Laban answered Jacob, "The women are my daughters, the children are my children, and the flocks are my flocks. All you see is mine. Yet what can I do today about these daughters of mine, or about the children they have borne? 44Come now, let's make a covenant, you and I, and let it serve as a witness between us."

45So Jacob took a stone and set it up as a pillar. 46He said to his relatives, "Gather some stones." So they took stones and piled them in a heap, and they ate there by the heap. 47Laban called it Jegar Sahadutha,u and Jacob called it Galeed.v

48Laban said, "This heap is a witness between you and me today." That is why it was called Galeed. 49It was also called Mizpah,w because he said, "May the LORD keep watch between you and me when we are away from each other. 50If you mistreat my daughters or if you take any wives besides my daughters, even though no one is with us, remember that God is a witness between you and me."

51Laban also said to Jacob, "Here is this heap, and here is this pillar I have set up between you and me. 52This heap is a witness, and this pillar is a witness, that I will not go past this heap to your side to harm you and that you will not go past this heap and pillar to my side to harm me.

ƒI.e. the heap of witness, in Aram Heb   gI.e. the heap of witness, in Heb   hLit the Mizpah; i.e. the watchtower

u47 The Aramaic Jegar Sahadutha means witness heap.
v47 The Hebrew Galeed means witness heap.   w49 Mizpah means watchtower.

King James

⁵³The God of Abraham, and the God of Nahor, the God of their father, judge betwixt us. And Jacob sware by the fear of his father Isaac.

⁵⁴Then Jacob ᵍoffered sacrifice upon the mount, and called his brethren to eat bread: and they did eat bread, and tarried all night in the mount.

⁵⁵And early in the morning Laban rose up, and kissed his sons and his daughters, and blessed them: and Laban departed, and returned unto his place.

Jacob prepares to meet Esau

32 AND JACOB went on his way, and the angels of God met him.

²And when Jacob saw them, he said, This *is* God's host: and he called the name of that place ʰMahanaim.

³And Jacob sent messengers before him to Esau his brother unto the land of Seir, the ⁱcountry of Edom.

⁴And he commanded them, saying, Thus shall ye speak unto my lord Esau; Thy servant Jacob saith thus, I have sojourned with Laban, and stayed there until now:

⁵And I have oxen, and asses, flocks, and menservants, and womenservants: and I have sent to tell my lord, that I may find grace in thy sight.

⁶ ¶ And the messengers returned to Jacob, saying, We came to thy brother Esau, and also he cometh to meet thee, and four hundred men with him.

⁷Then Jacob was greatly afraid and distressed: and he divided the people that *was* with him, and the flocks, and herds, and the camels, into two bands;

⁸And said, If Esau come to the one company, and smite it, then the other company which is left shall escape.

⁹ ¶ And Jacob said, O God of my father Abraham, and God of my father Isaac, the LORD which saidst unto me, Return unto thy country, and to thy kindred, and I will deal well with thee:

¹⁰ʲI am not worthy of the least of all the mercies, and of all the truth, which thou hast shown unto thy servant; for with my staff I passed over this Jordan; and now I am become two bands.

¹¹Deliver me, I pray thee, from the hand of my brother, from the hand of Esau: for I fear him, lest he will come and smite me, *and* the mother ᵏwith the children.

¹²And thou saidst, I will surely do thee good, and make thy seed as the sand of the sea, which cannot be numbered for multitude.

¹³ ¶ And he lodged there that same night; and took of that which came to his hand a present for Esau his brother;

¹⁴Two hundred she goats, and twenty he goats, two hundred ewes, and twenty rams,

¹⁵Thirty milch camels with their colts, forty kine, and ten bulls, twenty she asses, and ten foals.

¹⁶And he delivered *them* into the hand of his servants, every drove by themselves; and said unto his servants, Pass over before me, and put a space betwixt drove and drove.

¹⁷And he commanded the foremost, saying, When Esau my brother meeteth thee, and asketh thee, saying, Whose *art* thou? and whither goest thou? and whose *are* these before thee?

¹⁸Then thou shalt say, *They be* thy servant Jacob's; it *is* a present sent unto my lord Esau: and, behold, also he *is* behind us.

¹⁹And so commanded he the second, and the third, and all that followed the droves, saying, On this manner shall ye speak unto Esau, when ye find him.

Amplified

⁵³The God of Abraham and the God of Nahor, and the god [the object of worship] of their father [Terah, an idolator], judge between us. But Jacob swore [only] by [the one true God] the Dread *and* Fear of his father Isaac. [Josh. 24:2.]

⁵⁴Then Jacob offered a sacrifice on the mountain and called his brethren to eat food; and they ate food and lingered all night on the mountain.

⁵⁵And early in the morning Laban rose up and kissed his grandchildren and his daughters and pronounced a blessing [asking God's favor] on them. Then Laban departed and returned to his home.

32 THEN JACOB went on his way, and God's angels met him.

²When Jacob saw them, he said, This is God's army! So he named that place Mahanaim [two armies]. [Gen. 32:7, 10.]

³And Jacob sent messengers before him to Esau his brother in the land of Seir, the country of Edom.

⁴And he commanded them, Say this to my lord Esau: Your servant Jacob says this: I have been living temporarily with Laban and have stayed there till now.

⁵And I have oxen, donkeys, flocks, menservants, and women servants; and I have sent to tell my lord, that I may find mercy *and* kindness in your sight.

⁶And the messengers returned to Jacob, saying, We came to your brother Esau; and now he is [on the way] to meet you, and four hundred men are with him.

⁷Then Jacob was greatly afraid and distressed; and he divided the people who were with him, and the flocks and herds and camels, into two groups,

⁸Thinking, If Esau comes to the one group and smites it, then the other group which is left will escape.

⁹Jacob said, O God of my father Abraham and God of my father Isaac, the Lord Who said to me, Return to your country and to your people and I will do you good,

¹⁰I am not worthy of the least of all the mercy *and* loving-kindness and all the faithfulness which You have shown to Your servant, for with [only] my staff I passed over this Jordan [long ago], and now I have become two companies.

¹¹Deliver me, I pray You, from the hand of my brother, from the hand of Esau; for I fear him, lest he come and smite [us all], the mothers with the children.

¹²And You said, I will surely do you good and make your descendants as the sand of the sea, which cannot be numbered for multitude.

¹³And Jacob lodged there that night and took from what he had with him as a present for his brother Esau:

¹⁴Two hundred she-goats, 20 he-goats, 200 ewes, 20 rams,

¹⁵Thirty milk camels with their colts, 40 cows, 10 bulls, 20 she-donkeys, and 10 [donkey] colts.

¹⁶And he put them into the charge of his servants, every drove by itself, and said to his servants, Pass over before me and put a space between drove and drove.

¹⁷And he commanded the first, When Esau my brother meets you and asks to whom you belong, where you are going, and whose are the animals before you,

¹⁸Then you shall say, They are your servant Jacob's; it is a present sent to my lord Esau; and moreover, he is behind us.

¹⁹And so he commanded the second and the third and all that followed the droves, saying, This is what you are to say to Esau when you meet him.

ᵍOr, *killed beasts*   ʰi.e. *Two hosts,* or, *camps*   ⁱHeb. *field*
ʲHeb. *I am less than all*   ᵏHeb. *upon*

New American Standard

53"The God of Abraham and the God of Nahor, the God of their father, judge between us." So Jacob swore by the fear of his father Isaac.

54 Then Jacob offered a sacrifice on the mountain, and called his kinsmen to the meal; and they ate the meal and spent the night on the mountain.

55 Early in the morning Laban arose, and kissed his sons and his daughters and blessed them. Then Laban departed and returned to his place.

Jacob's Fear of Esau

32 NOW AS Jacob went on his way, the angels of God met him.

2 Jacob said when he saw them, "This is God's *i*camp." So he named that place *j*Mahanaim.

3 ¶ Then Jacob sent messengers before him to his brother Esau in the land of Seir, the country of Edom.

4 He also commanded them saying, "Thus you shall say to my lord Esau: 'Thus says your servant Jacob, "I have sojourned with Laban, and stayed until now;

5 I have oxen and donkeys *and* flocks and male and female servants; and I have sent to tell my lord, that I may find favor in your sight." ' "

6 ¶ The messengers returned to Jacob, saying, "We came to your brother Esau, and furthermore he is coming to meet you, and four hundred men are with him."

7 Then Jacob was greatly afraid and distressed; and he divided the people who were with him, and the flocks and the herds and the camels, into two companies;

8 for he said, "If Esau comes to the one company and attacks it, then the company which is left will escape."

9 ¶ Jacob said, "O God of my father Abraham and God of my father Isaac, O LORD, who said to me, 'Return to your country and to your relatives, and I will prosper you,'

10 I am unworthy of all the lovingkindness and of all the faithfulness which You have shown to Your servant; for with my staff *only* I crossed this Jordan, and now I have become two companies.

11"Deliver me, I pray, from the hand of my brother, from the hand of Esau; for I fear him, that he will come and attack me *and* the mothers with the children.

12"For You said, 'I will surely prosper you and make your descendants as the sand of the sea, which is too great to be numbered.' "

13 ¶ So he spent the night there. Then he selected from what he had with him a present for his brother Esau:

14 two hundred female goats and twenty male goats, two hundred ewes and twenty rams,

15 thirty milking camels and their colts, forty cows and ten bulls, twenty female donkeys and ten male donkeys.

16 He delivered *them* into the hand of his servants, every drove by itself, and said to his servants, "Pass on before me, and put a space between droves."

17 He commanded the one in front, saying, "When my brother Esau meets you and asks you, saying, 'To whom do you belong, and where are you going, and to whom do these *animals* in front of you belong?'

18 then you shall say, '*These* belong to your servant Jacob; it is a present sent to my lord Esau. And behold, he also is behind us.' "

19 Then he commanded also the second and the third, and all those who followed the droves, saying, "After this manner you shall speak to Esau when you find him;

New International

53May the God of Abraham and the God of Nahor, the God of their father, judge between us."

So Jacob took an oath in the name of the Fear of his father Isaac. 54He offered a sacrifice there in the hill country and invited his relatives to a meal. After they had eaten, they spent the night there.

55Early the next morning Laban kissed his grandchildren and his daughters and blessed them. Then he left and returned home.

Jacob Prepares to Meet Esau

32 JACOB ALSO went on his way, and the angels of God met him. 2When Jacob saw them, he said, "This is the camp of God!" So he named that place Mahanaim.*x*

3Jacob sent messengers ahead of him to his brother Esau in the land of Seir, the country of Edom. 4He instructed them: "This is what you are to say to my master Esau: 'Your servant Jacob says, I have been staying with Laban and have remained there till now. 5I have cattle and donkeys, sheep and goats, menservants and maidservants. Now I am sending this message to my lord, that I may find favor in your eyes.' "

6When the messengers returned to Jacob, they said, "We went to your brother Esau, and now he is coming to meet you, and four hundred men are with him."

7In great fear and distress Jacob divided the people who were with him into two groups,*y* and the flocks and herds and camels as well. 8He thought, "If Esau comes and attacks one group,*z* the group*z* that is left may escape."

9Then Jacob prayed, "O God of my father Abraham, God of my father Isaac, O LORD, who said to me, 'Go back to your country and your relatives, and I will make you prosper,' 10I am unworthy of all the kindness and faithfulness you have shown your servant. I had only my staff when I crossed this Jordan, but now I have become two groups. 11Save me, I pray, from the hand of my brother Esau, for I am afraid he will come and attack me, and also the mothers with their children. 12But you have said, 'I will surely make you prosper and will make your descendants like the sand of the sea, which cannot be counted.' "

13He spent the night there, and from what he had with him he selected a gift for his brother Esau: 14two hundred female goats and twenty male goats, two hundred ewes and twenty rams, 15thirty female camels with their young, forty cows and ten bulls, and twenty female donkeys and ten male donkeys. 16He put them in the care of his servants, each herd by itself, and said to his servants, "Go ahead of me, and keep some space between the herds."

17He instructed the one in the lead: "When my brother Esau meets you and asks, 'To whom do you belong, and where are you going, and who owns all these animals in front of you?' 18then you are to say, 'They belong to your servant Jacob. They are a gift sent to my lord Esau, and he is coming behind us.' "

19He also instructed the second, the third and all the others who followed the herds: "You are to say the same

---

*i*Or *company*   *j*I.e. Two Camps, or Two Companies

*x*2 *Mahanaim* means *two camps.*   *y*7 Or *camps*; also in verse 10
*z*8 Or *camp*

King James

Amplified

²⁰And say ye moreover, Behold, thy servant Jacob *is* behind us. For he said, I will appease him with the present that goeth before me, and afterward I will see his face; peradventure he will accept *l*of me.

²¹So went the present over before him: and himself lodged that night in the company.

Jacob's wrestling at Peniel

²²And he rose up that night, and took his two wives, and his two womenservants, and his eleven sons, and passed over the ford Jabbok.

²³And he took them, and *m*sent them over the brook, and sent over that he had.

²⁴ ¶ And Jacob was left alone; and there wrestled a man with him until the *n*breaking of the day.

²⁵And when he saw that he prevailed not against him, he touched the hollow of his thigh; and the hollow of Jacob's thigh was out of joint, as he wrestled with him.

²⁶And he said, Let me go, for the day breaketh. And he said, I will not let thee go, except thou bless me.

²⁷And he said unto him, What *is* thy name? And he said, Jacob.

²⁸And he said, Thy name shall be called no more Jacob, but *o*Israel: for as a prince hast thou power with God and with men, and hast prevailed.

²⁹And Jacob asked *him,* and said, Tell *me,* I pray thee, thy name. And he said, Wherefore *is* it *that* thou dost ask after my name? And he blessed him there.

³⁰And Jacob called the name of the place *p*Peniel: for I have seen God face to face, and my life is preserved.

³¹And as he passed over Penuel the sun rose upon him, and he halted upon his thigh.

³²Therefore the children of Israel eat not *of* the sinew which shrank, which *is* upon the hollow of the thigh, unto this day; because he touched the hollow of Jacob's thigh in the sinew that shrank.

Jacob and Esau meet

33 AND JACOB lifted up his eyes, and looked, and, behold, Esau came, and with him four hundred men. And he divided the children unto Leah, and unto Rachel, and unto the two handmaids.

²And he put the handmaids and their children foremost, and Leah and her children after, and Rachel and Joseph hindermost.

³And he passed over before them, and bowed himself to the ground seven times, until he came near to his brother.

⁴And Esau ran to meet him, and embraced him, and fell on his neck, and kissed him: and they wept.

⁵And he lifted up his eyes, and saw the women and the children; and said, Who *are* those *q*with thee? And he said, The children which God hath graciously given thy servant.

⁶Then the handmaidens came near, they and their children, and they bowed themselves.

⁷And Leah also with her children came near, and bowed themselves: and after came Joseph near and Rachel, and they bowed themselves.

⁸And he said, *r*What *meanest* thou by all this drove which I met? And he said, *These are* to find grace in the sight of my lord.

⁹And Esau said, I have enough, my brother; *s*keep that thou hast unto thyself.

²⁰And say, Moreover, your servant Jacob is behind us. For he said, I will appease him with the present that goes before me, and afterward I will see his face; perhaps he will accept me.

²¹So the present went on before him, and he himself lodged that night in the camp.

²²But he rose up that [same] night and took his two wives, his two women servants, and his eleven sons and passed over the ford [of the] Jabbok.

²³And he took them and sent them across the brook; also he sent over all that he had.

²⁴And Jacob was left alone, and a Man wrestled with him until daybreak.

²⁵And when [the *p*Man] saw that He did not prevail against [Jacob], He touched the hollow of his thigh; and Jacob's thigh was put out of joint as he wrestled with Him.

²⁶Then He said, Let Me go, for day is breaking. But [Jacob] said, I will not let You go unless You declare a blessing upon me.

²⁷[The Man] asked him, What is your name? And [in shock of realization, whispering] he said, Jacob [supplanter, schemer, trickster, swindler]!

²⁸And He said, Your name shall be called no more Jacob [supplanter], but Israel [contender with God]; for you have contended *and* have power with God and with men and have prevailed. [Hos. 12:3–4.]

²⁹Then Jacob asked Him, Tell me, I pray You, what [in contrast] is Your name? But He said, Why is it that you ask My name? And *p*[the Angel of God declared] a blessing on [Jacob] there.

³⁰And Jacob called the name of the place Peniel [the face of God], saying, For I have seen God face to face, and my life is spared *and* not snatched away.

³¹And as he passed Penuel [Peniel], the sun rose upon him, and he was limping because of his thigh.

³²That is why to this day the Israelites do not eat the sinew of the hip which is on the hollow of the thigh, because [the Angel of the Lord] touched the hollow of Jacob's thigh on the sinew of the hip.

33 AND JACOB raised his eyes and looked, and behold, Esau was coming and with him 400 men. So he divided the children to Leah and to Rachel and to the two maids.

²And he put the maids and their children in front, Leah and her children after them, and Rachel and Joseph last of all.

³Then Jacob went over [the stream] before them and bowed himself to the ground seven times, until he came near to his brother.

⁴But Esau ran to meet him, and embraced him and fell on his neck and kissed him, and they wept. [Luke 15:20.]

⁵[Esau] looked up and saw the women and the children and said, Who are these with you? And [Jacob] replied, They are the children whom God has graciously given your servant.

⁶Then the maids came near, they and their children, and they bowed themselves.

⁷And Leah also with her children came near, and they bowed themselves. After them Joseph and Rachel came near, and they bowed themselves.

⁸Esau said, What do you mean by all this company which I met? And he said, These are that I might find favor in the sight of my lord.

⁹And Esau said, I have plenty, my brother; keep what you have for yourself.

---

^lHeb. *my face*   ^mHeb. *caused to pass over*   ⁿHeb. *ascending of the morning*   ^oi.e. *A prince of God*   ^pi.e. *The face of God*   ^qHeb. *to thee?*   ^rHeb. *What is all this band to thee?*   ^sHeb. *be that to thee that is thine*

^pThis is God Himself (as Jacob eventually realizes in Gen. 32:30) in the form of an angel. See footnote on Gen. 16:7, as well as Hos. 12:3-4.

New American Standard

20 and you shall say, 'Behold, your servant Jacob also is behind us.' " For he said, "I will appease him with the present that goes before me. Then afterward I will see his face; perhaps he will accept me."

21 So the present passed on before him, while he himself spent that night in the camp.

22 ¶ Now he arose that same night and took his two wives and his two maids and his eleven children, and crossed the ford of the Jabbok.

23 He took them and sent them across the stream. And he sent across whatever he had.

Jacob Wrestles

24 Then Jacob was left alone, and a man wrestled with him until daybreak.

25 When he saw that he had not prevailed against him, he touched the socket of his thigh; so the socket of Jacob's thigh was dislocated while he wrestled with him.

26 Then he said, "Let me go, for the dawn is breaking." But he said, "I will not let you go unless you bless me."

27 So he said to him, "What is your name?" And he said, "Jacob."

28 He said, "Your name shall no longer be Jacob, but kIsrael; for you have striven with God and with men and have prevailed."

29 Then Jacob asked him and said, "Please tell me your name." But he said, "Why is it that you ask my name?" And he blessed him there.

30 So Jacob named the place lPeniel, for *he said,* "I have seen God face to face, yet my life has been preserved."

31 Now the sun rose upon him just as he crossed over Penuel, and he was limping on his thigh.

32 Therefore, to this day the sons of Israel do not eat the sinew of the hip which is on the socket of the thigh, because he touched the socket of Jacob's thigh in the sinew of the hip.

Jacob Meets Esau

33 THEN JACOB lifted his eyes and looked, and behold, Esau was coming, and four hundred men with him. So he divided the children among Leah and Rachel and the two maids.

2 He put the maids and their children in front, and Leah and her children next, and Rachel and Joseph last.

3 But he himself passed on ahead of them and bowed down to the ground seven times, until he came near to his brother.

4 ¶ Then Esau ran to meet him and embraced him, and fell on his neck and kissed him, and they wept.

5 He lifted his eyes and saw the women and the children, and said, "Who are these with you?" So he said, "The children whom God has graciously given your servant."

6 Then the maids came near with their children, and they bowed down.

7 Leah likewise came near with her children, and they bowed down; and afterward Joseph came near with Rachel, and they bowed down.

8 And he said, "What do you mean by all this company which I have met?" And he said, "To find favor in the sight of my lord."

9 But Esau said, "I have plenty, my brother; let what you have be your own."

New International

thing to Esau when you meet him. 20And be sure to say, 'Your servant Jacob is coming behind us.' " For he thought, "I will pacify him with these gifts I am sending on ahead; later, when I see him, perhaps he will receive me." 21So Jacob's gifts went on ahead of him, but he himself spent the night in the camp.

Jacob Wrestles With God

22That night Jacob got up and took his two wives, his two maidservants and his eleven sons and crossed the ford of the Jabbok. 23After he had sent them across the stream, he sent over all his possessions. 24So Jacob was left alone, and a man wrestled with him till daybreak. 25When the man saw that he could not overpower him, he touched the socket of Jacob's hip so that his hip was wrenched as he wrestled with the man. 26Then the man said, "Let me go, for it is daybreak."

But Jacob replied, "I will not let you go unless you bless me."

27The man asked him, "What is your name?"

"Jacob," he answered.

28Then the man said, "Your name will no longer be Jacob, but Israel,a because you have struggled with God and with men and have overcome."

29Jacob said, "Please tell me your name."

But he replied, "Why do you ask my name?" Then he blessed him there.

30So Jacob called the place Peniel,b saying, "It is because I saw God face to face, and yet my life was spared."

31The sun rose above him as he passed Peniel,c and he was limping because of his hip. 32Therefore to this day the Israelites do not eat the tendon attached to the socket of the hip, because the socket of Jacob's hip was touched near the tendon.

Jacob Meets Esau

33 JACOB LOOKED up and there was Esau, coming with his four hundred men; so he divided the children among Leah, Rachel and the two maidservants. 2He put the maidservants and their children in front, Leah and her children next, and Rachel and Joseph in the rear. 3He himself went on ahead and bowed down to the ground seven times as he approached his brother.

4But Esau ran to meet Jacob and embraced him; he threw his arms around his neck and kissed him. And they wept. 5Then Esau looked up and saw the women and children. "Who are these with you?" he asked.

Jacob answered, "They are the children God has graciously given your servant."

6Then the maidservants and their children approached and bowed down. 7Next, Leah and her children came and bowed down. Last of all came Joseph and Rachel, and they too bowed down.

8Esau asked, "What do you mean by all these droves I met?"

"To find favor in your eyes, my lord," he said.

9But Esau said, "I already have plenty, my brother. Keep what you have for yourself."

---

kI.e. he who strives with God; or God strives God   lI.e. the face of God

a28 *Israel* means *he struggles with God.*   b30 *Peniel* means *face of God.*   c31 Hebrew *Penuel,* a variant of *Peniel*

King James

¹⁰And Jacob said, Nay, I pray thee, if now I have found grace in thy sight, then receive my present at my hand: for therefore I have seen thy face, as though I had seen the face of God, and thou wast pleased with me.

¹¹Take, I pray thee, my blessing that is brought to thee; because God hath dealt graciously with me, and because I have ^tenough. And he urged him, and he took *it*.

¹²And he said, Let us take our journey, and let us go, and I will go before thee.

¹³And he said unto him, My lord knoweth that the children *are* tender, and the flocks and herds with young *are* with me: and if men should overdrive them one day, all the flock will die.

¹⁴Let my lord, I pray thee, pass over before his servant: and I will lead on softly, ^uaccording as the cattle that goeth before me and the children be able to endure, until I come unto my lord unto Seir.

¹⁵And Esau said, Let me now ^vleave with thee *some* of the folk that *are* with me. And he said, ^wWhat needeth it? let me find grace in the sight of my lord.

¹⁶ ¶ So Esau returned that day on his way unto Seir.

¹⁷And Jacob journeyed to Succoth, and built him an house, and made booths for his cattle: therefore the name of the place is called ^xSuccoth.

¹⁸ ¶ And Jacob came to Shalem, a city of ^yShechem, which *is* in the land of Canaan, when he came from Padan-aram; and pitched his tent before the city.

¹⁹And he bought a parcel of a field, where he had spread his tent, at the hand of the children of ^zHamor, Shechem's father, for an hundred ^apieces of money.

²⁰And he erected there an altar, and called it ^bEl-elohe-Israel.

The defiling of Dinah

34 AND DINAH the daughter of Leah, which she bare unto Jacob, went out to see the daughters of the land.

²And when Shechem the son of Hamor the Hivite, prince of the country, saw her, he took her, and lay with her, and ^cdefiled her.

³And his soul clave unto Dinah the daughter of Jacob, and he loved the damsel, and spake kindly unto the damsel.

⁴And Shechem spake unto his father Hamor, saying, Get me this damsel to wife.

⁵And Jacob heard that he had defiled Dinah his daughter: now his sons were with his cattle in the field: and Jacob held his peace until they were come.

⁶ ¶ And Hamor the father of Shechem went out unto Jacob to commune with him.

⁷And the sons of Jacob came out of the field when they heard *it*: and the men were grieved, and they were very wroth, because he had wrought folly in Israel in lying with Jacob's daughter; which thing ought not to be done.

⁸And Hamor communed with them, saying, The soul of my son Shechem longeth for your daughter: I pray you give her him to wife.

⁹And make ye marriages with us, *and* give your daughters unto us, and take our daughters unto you.

¹⁰And ye shall dwell with us: and the land shall be before you; dwell and trade ye therein, and get you possessions therein.

¹¹And Shechem said unto her father and unto her brethren, Let me find grace in your eyes, and what ye shall say unto me I will give.

Amplified

¹⁰But Jacob replied, No, I beg of you, if now I have found favor in your sight, receive my gift that I am presenting; for truly to see your face is to me as if I had seen the face of God, and you have received me favorably.

¹¹Accept, I beg of you, my blessing *and* gift that I have brought to you; for God has dealt graciously with me and I have everything. And he kept urging him and he accepted it.

¹²Then [Esau] said, Let us get started on our journey, and I will go before you.

¹³But Jacob replied, You know, my lord, that the children are tender *and* delicate *and* need gentle care, and the flocks and herds with young are of concern to me; for if the men should overdrive them for a single day, the whole of the flocks would die.

¹⁴Let my lord, I pray you, pass over before his servant; and I will lead on slowly, governed by [consideration for] the livestock that set the pace before me and the endurance of the children, ^quntil I come to my lord in Seir.

¹⁵Then Esau said, Let me now leave with you some of the people who are with me. But [Jacob] said, What need is there for it? Let me find favor in the sight of my lord.

¹⁶So Esau turned back that day on his way to Seir.

¹⁷But Jacob journeyed to Succoth and built himself a house and made booths *or* places of shelter for his livestock; so the name of the place is called Succoth [booths].

¹⁸When Jacob came from Padan-aram, he arrived safely *and* in peace at the town of Shechem, in the land of Canaan, and pitched his tents before the [enclosed] town.

¹⁹Then he bought the piece of land on which he had encamped from the sons of Hamor, Shechem's father, for a hundred pieces of money.

²⁰There he erected an altar and called it El-Elohe-Israel [God, the God of Israel].

34 NOW DINAH daughter of Leah, whom she bore to Jacob, went out [unattended] to see the girls of the place.

²And when Shechem son of Hamor the Hivite, prince of the country, saw her, he seized her, lay with her, and humbled, defiled, *and* disgraced her.

³But his soul longed for *and* clung to Dinah daughter of Jacob, and he loved the girl and spoke comfortingly to her young heart's wishes.

⁴And Shechem said to his father Hamor, Get me this girl to be my wife.

⁵Jacob heard that [Shechem] had defiled Dinah his daughter. Now his sons were with his livestock in the field. So Jacob held his peace until they came.

⁶But Hamor father of Shechem went out to Jacob to have a talk with him.

⁷When Jacob's sons heard it, they came from the field; and they were distressed and grieved and very angry, for [Shechem] had done a vile thing to Israel in lying with Jacob's daughter, which ought not to be done.

⁸And Hamor conferred with them, saying, The soul of my son Shechem craves your daughter [and sister]. I beg of you give her to him to be his wife.

⁹And make marriages with us and give your daughters to us and take our daughters to you.

¹⁰You shall dwell with us; the country will be open to you; live and trade and get your possessions in it.

¹¹And Shechem said to [Dinah's] father and to her brothers, Let me find favor in your eyes, and I will give you whatever you ask of me.

---

^tHeb. *all things*   ^uHeb. *according to the foot of the work, &c.*
and according to the foot of the children   ^vHeb. *set, or, place*
^wHeb. *Wherefore is this?*   ^xi.e. *Booths*   ^yCalled *Sychem* in
Acts 7:16   ^zCalled *Emmor* in Acts 7:16   ^aOr, *lambs*
^bi.e. *God the God of Israel*   ^cHeb. *humbled her*

^qEver the deceiver, Jacob had no intention of following Esau to Seir. In fact, he heads in the opposite direction.

New American Standard

10 Jacob said, "No, please, if now I have found favor in your sight, then take my present from my hand, for I see your face as one sees the face of God, and you have received me favorably.

11 "Please take my gift which has been brought to you, because God has dealt graciously with me and because I have plenty." Thus he urged him and he took *it*.

12 ¶ Then Esau said, "Let us take our journey and go, and I will go before you."

13 But he said to him, "My lord knows that the children are frail and that the flocks and herds which are nursing are a care to me. And if they are driven hard one day, all the flocks will die.

14 "Please let my lord pass on before his servant, and I will proceed at my leisure, according to the pace of the cattle that are before me and according to the pace of the children, until I come to my lord at Seir."

15 ¶ Esau said, "Please let me leave with you some of the people who are with me." But he said, "*m*What need is there? Let me find favor in the sight of my lord."

16 So Esau returned that day on his way to Seir.

17 Jacob journeyed to *n*Succoth, and built for himself a house and made booths for his livestock; therefore the place is named Succoth.

Jacob Settles in Shechem

18 ¶ Now Jacob came safely to the city of Shechem, which is in the land of Canaan, when he came from Paddan-aram, and camped before the city.

19 He bought the piece of land where he had pitched his tent from the hand of the sons of Hamor, Shechem's father, for one hundred pieces of money.

20 Then he erected there an altar and called it *o*El-Elohe-Israel.

The Treachery of Jacob's Sons

34 NOW DINAH the daughter of Leah, whom she had borne to Jacob, went out to visit the daughters of the land.

2 When Shechem the son of Hamor the Hivite, the prince of the land, saw her, he took her and lay with her by force.

3 He was deeply attracted to Dinah the daughter of Jacob, and he loved the girl and spoke tenderly to her.

4 So Shechem spoke to his father Hamor, saying, "Get me this young girl for a wife."

5 Now Jacob heard that he had defiled Dinah his daughter; but his sons were with his livestock in the field, so Jacob kept silent until they came in.

6 Then Hamor the father of Shechem went out to Jacob to speak with him.

7 Now the sons of Jacob came in from the field when they heard *it;* and the men were grieved, and they were very angry because he had done a disgraceful thing in Israel by lying with Jacob's daughter, for such a thing ought not to be done.

8 ¶ But Hamor spoke with them, saying, "The soul of my son Shechem longs for your daughter; please give her to him in marriage.

9 "Intermarry with us; give your daughters to us and take our daughters for yourselves.

10 "Thus you shall live with us, and the land shall be *open* before you; live and trade in it and acquire property in it."

11 Shechem also said to her father and to her brothers, "If I find favor in your sight, then I will give whatever you say to me.

New International

10 "No, please!" said Jacob. "If I have found favor in your eyes, accept this gift from me. For to see your face is like seeing the face of God, now that you have received me favorably. 11 Please accept the present that was brought to you, for God has been gracious to me and I have all I need." And because Jacob insisted, Esau accepted it.

12 Then Esau said, "Let us be on our way; I'll accompany you."

13 But Jacob said to him, "My lord knows that the children are tender and that I must care for the ewes and cows that are nursing their young. If they are driven hard just one day, all the animals will die. 14 So let my lord go on ahead of his servant, while I move along slowly at the pace of the droves before me and that of the children, until I come to my lord in Seir."

15 Esau said, "Then let me leave some of my men with you."

"But why do that?" Jacob asked. "Just let me find favor in the eyes of my lord."

16 So that day Esau started on his way back to Seir. 17 Jacob, however, went to Succoth, where he built a place for himself and made shelters for his livestock. That is why the place is called Succoth.*d*

18 After Jacob came from Paddan Aram,*e* he arrived safely at the*f* city of Shechem in Canaan and camped within sight of the city. 19 For a hundred pieces of silver,*g* he bought from the sons of Hamor, the father of Shechem, the plot of ground where he pitched his tent. 20 There he set up an altar and called it El Elohe Israel.*h*

Dinah and the Shechemites

34 NOW DINAH, the daughter Leah had borne to Jacob, went out to visit the women of the land. 2 When Shechem son of Hamor the Hivite, the ruler of that area, saw her, he took her and violated her. 3 His heart was drawn to Dinah daughter of Jacob, and he loved the girl and spoke tenderly to her. 4 And Shechem said to his father Hamor, "Get me this girl as my wife."

5 When Jacob heard that his daughter Dinah had been defiled, his sons were in the fields with his livestock; so he kept quiet about it until they came home.

6 Then Shechem's father Hamor went out to talk with Jacob. 7 Now Jacob's sons had come in from the fields as soon as they heard what had happened. They were filled with grief and fury, because Shechem had done a disgraceful thing in*i* Israel by lying with Jacob's daughter—a thing that should not be done.

8 But Hamor said to them, "My son Shechem has his heart set on your daughter. Please give her to him as his wife. 9 Intermarry with us; give us your daughters and take our daughters for yourselves. 10 You can settle among us; the land is open to you. Live in it, trade*j* in it, and acquire property in it."

11 Then Shechem said to Dinah's father and brothers, "Let me find favor in your eyes, and I will give you

---

d 17 *Succoth* means *shelters.*   *e* 18 That is, Northwest Mesopotamia   *f* 18 Or *arrived at Shalem, a*   *g* 19 Hebrew *hundred kesitahs*; a kesitah was a unit of money of unknown weight and value.   *h* 20 *El Elohe Israel* can mean *God, the God of Israel* or *mighty is the God of Israel.*   *i* 7 Or *against* *j* 10 Or *move about freely*; also in verse 21

---

m Lit *Why this?*   *n* I.e. booths   *o* I.e. God, the God of Israel

King James

¹²Ask me never so much dowry and gift, and I will give according as ye shall say unto me: but give me the damsel to wife.

¹³And the sons of Jacob answered Shechem and Hamor his father deceitfully, and said, because he had defiled Dinah their sister:

¹⁴And they said unto them, We cannot do this thing, to give our sister to one that is uncircumcised; for that *were* a reproach unto us:

¹⁵But in this will we consent unto you: If ye will be as we *be*, that every male of you be circumcised;

¹⁶Then will we give our daughters unto you, and we will take your daughters to us, and we will dwell with you, and we will become one people.

¹⁷But if ye will not hearken unto us, to be circumcised; then will we take our daughter, and we will be gone.

¹⁸And their words pleased Hamor, and Shechem Hamor's son.

¹⁹And the young man deferred not to do the thing, because he had delight in Jacob's daughter: and he *was* more honourable than all the house of his father.

²⁰ ¶ And Hamor and Shechem his son came unto the gate of their city, and communed with the men of their city, saying,

²¹These men *are* peaceable with us; therefore let them dwell in the land, and trade therein; for the land, behold, *it is* large enough for them; let us take their daughters to us for wives, and let us give them our daughters.

²²Only herein will the men consent unto us for to dwell with us, to be one people, if every male among us be circumcised, as they *are* circumcised.

²³*Shall* not their cattle and their substance and every beast of theirs *be* ours? only let us consent unto them, and they will dwell with us.

²⁴And unto Hamor and unto Shechem his son hearkened all that went out of the gate of his city; and every male was circumcised, all that went out of the gate of his city.

²⁵ ¶ And it came to pass on the third day, when they were sore, that two of the sons of Jacob, Simeon and Levi, Dinah's brethren, took each man his sword, and came upon the city boldly, and slew all the males.

²⁶And they slew Hamor and Shechem his son with the ^dedge of the sword, and took Dinah out of Shechem's house, and went out.

²⁷The sons of Jacob came upon the slain, and spoiled the city, because they had defiled their sister.

²⁸They took their sheep, and their oxen, and their asses, and that which *was* in the city, and that which *was* in the field,

²⁹And all their wealth, and all their little ones, and their wives took they captive, and spoiled even all that *was* in the house.

³⁰And Jacob said to Simeon and Levi, Ye have troubled me to make me to stink among the inhabitants of the land, among the Canaanites and the Perizzites: and I *being* few in number, they shall gather themselves together against me, and slay me; and I shall be destroyed, I and my house.

³¹And they said, Should he deal with our sister as with an harlot?

Jacob returns to Beth-el

35 AND GOD said unto Jacob, Arise, go up to Bethel, and dwell there: and make there an altar unto God, that appeared unto thee when thou fleddest from the face of Esau thy brother.

²Then Jacob said unto his household, and to all that *were* with him, Put away the strange gods that *are* among you, and be clean, and change your garments:

^dHeb. *mouth*

Amplified

¹²Ask me ever so much dowry and [marriage] gift, and I will give according to what you tell me; only give me the girl to be my wife.

¹³The sons of Jacob answered Shechem and Hamor his father deceitfully, [justifying their intended action by saying, in effect, we are going to do this] because Shechem had defiled *and* disgraced their sister Dinah.

¹⁴They said to them, We cannot do this thing *and* give our sister to one who is not circumcised, for that would be a reproach *and* disgrace to us.

¹⁵But we do consent to do this: if you will become as we are and every male among you be circumcised,

¹⁶Then we will give our daughters to you and we will take your daughters to us, and we will dwell with you and become one people.

¹⁷But if you will not listen to us and consent to be circumcised, then we will take our daughter and go.

¹⁸Their words pleased Hamor and his son Shechem.

¹⁹And the young man did not delay to do the thing, for he delighted in Jacob's daughter. He was honored above all his family [so, ranking first, he acted first].

²⁰Then Hamor and Shechem his son came to the gate of their [enclosed] town and discussed the matter with the citizens, saying,

²¹These men are peaceable with us; so let them dwell in the land and trade in it; for the land is large enough [for us and] for them; let us take their daughters for wives and let us give them our daughters.

²²But the men will consent to our request that they live among us and be one people only on condition that every male among us be circumcised, as they are.

²³Shall not their cattle and their possessions and all their beasts be ours? Only let us consent to them, and they will dwell here with us.

²⁴And all the people who went out of the town gate listened *and* heeded what Hamor and Shechem said; and every male was circumcised who was a resident of that town.

²⁵But on the third day [after the circumcision] when [all the men] were sore, two of the sons of Jacob, Simeon and Levi, Dinah's [full] brothers, took their swords, boldly entered the city [without danger], and slew all the males.

²⁶And they killed Hamor and Shechem his son with the edge of the sword and took Dinah out of Shechem's house [where she had been all this time] and departed.

²⁷[Then the rest of] Jacob's [eleven] sons came upon the slain and plundered the town, because there their sister had been defiled *and* disgraced.

²⁸They took their flocks, their herds, their donkeys, and whatever was in the town and in the field;

²⁹All their wealth and all their little ones and their wives they took captive, making spoil even of all [they found] in the houses.

³⁰And Jacob said to Simeon and Levi, You have ruined me, making me infamous *and* embroiling me with the inhabitants of the land, the Canaanites and the Perizzites! And we are few in number, and they will gather together against me and attack me; and I shall be destroyed, I and my household.

³¹And they said, Should he [be permitted to] deal with our sister as with a harlot?

35 AND GOD said to Jacob, Arise, go up to Bethel and dwell there. And make there an altar to God Who appeared to you [in a distinct manifestation] when you fled from the presence of Esau your brother. [Gen. 28:11–22.]

²Then Jacob said to his household and to all who were with him, Put away the [images of] strange gods that are among you, and purify yourselves and change [into fresh] garments;

New American Standard

12"Ask me ever so much bridal payment and gift, and I will give according as you say to me; but give me the girl in marriage."

13 ¶ But Jacob's sons answered Shechem and his father Hamor with deceit, because he had defiled Dinah their sister.

14 They said to them, "We cannot do this thing, to give our sister to one who is uncircumcised, for that would be a disgrace to us.

15"Only on this *condition* will we consent to you: if you will become like us, in that every male of you be circumcised,

16 then we will give our daughters to you, and we will take your daughters for ourselves, and we will live with you and become one people.

17"But if you will not listen to us to be circumcised, then we will take our daughter and go."

18 ¶ Now their words seemed reasonable to Hamor and Shechem, Hamor's son.

19 The young man did not delay to do the thing, because he was delighted with Jacob's daughter. Now he was more respected than all the household of his father.

20 So Hamor and his son Shechem came to the gate of their city and spoke to the men of their city, saying,

21"These men are friendly with us; therefore let them live in the land and trade in it, for behold, the land is large enough for them. Let us take their daughters in marriage, and give our daughters to them.

22"Only on this *condition* will the men consent to us to live with us, to become one people: that every male among us be circumcised as they are circumcised.

23"Will not their livestock and their property and all their animals be ours? Only let us consent to them, and they will live with us."

24 All who went out of the gate of his city listened to Hamor and to his son Shechem, and every male was circumcised, all who went out of the gate of his city.

25 ¶ Now it came about on the third day, when they were in pain, that two of Jacob's sons, Simeon and Levi, Dinah's brothers, each took his sword and came upon the city unawares, and killed every male.

26 They killed Hamor and his son Shechem with the edge of the sword, and took Dinah from Shechem's house, and went forth.

27 Jacob's sons came upon the slain and looted the city, because they had defiled their sister.

28 They took their flocks and their herds and their donkeys, and that which was in the city and that which was in the field;

29 and they captured and looted all their wealth and all their little ones and their wives, even all that *was* in the houses.

30 Then Jacob said to Simeon and Levi, "You have brought trouble on me by making me odious among the inhabitants of the land, among the Canaanites and the Perizzites; and my men being few in number, they will gather together against me and attack me and I will be destroyed, I and my household."

31 But they said, "Should he treat our sister as a harlot?"

Jacob Moves to Bethel

35 THEN GOD said to Jacob, "Arise, go up to Bethel and live there, and make an altar there to God, who appeared to you when you fled from your brother Esau."

2 So Jacob said to his household and to all who were with him, "Put away the foreign gods which are among you, and purify yourselves and change your garments;

New International

whatever you ask. 12Make the price for the bride and the gift I am to bring as great as you like, and I'll pay whatever you ask me. Only give me the girl as my wife."

13Because their sister Dinah had been defiled, Jacob's sons replied deceitfully as they spoke to Shechem and his father Hamor. 14They said to them, "We can't do such a thing; we can't give our sister to a man who is not uncircumcised. That would be a disgrace to us. 15We will give our consent to you on one condition only: that you become like us by circumcising all your males. 16Then we will give you our daughters and take your daughters for ourselves. We'll settle among you and become one people with you. 17But if you will not agree to be circumcised, we'll take our sister[k] and go."

18Their proposal seemed good to Hamor and his son Shechem. 19The young man, who was the most honored of all his father's household, lost no time in doing what they said, because he was delighted with Jacob's daughter. 20So Hamor and his son Shechem went to the gate of their city to speak to their fellow townsmen. 21"These men are friendly toward us," they said. "Let them live in our land and trade in it; the land has plenty of room for them. We can marry their daughters and they can marry ours. 22But the men will consent to live with us as one people only on the condition that our males be circumcised, as they themselves are. 23Won't their livestock, their property and all their other animals become ours? So let us give our consent to them, and they will settle among us."

24All the men who went out of the city gate agreed with Hamor and his son Shechem, and every male in the city was circumcised.

25Three days later, while all of them were still in pain, two of Jacob's sons, Simeon and Levi, Dinah's brothers, took their swords and attacked the unsuspecting city, killing every male. 26They put Hamor and his son Shechem to the sword and took Dinah from Shechem's house and left. 27The sons of Jacob came upon the dead bodies and looted the city where[l] their sister had been defiled. 28They seized their flocks and herds and donkeys and everything else of theirs in the city and out in the fields. 29They carried off all their wealth and all their women and children, taking as plunder everything in the houses.

30Then Jacob said to Simeon and Levi, "You have brought trouble on me by making me a stench to the Canaanites and Perizzites, the people living in this land. We are few in number, and if they join forces against me and attack me, I and my household will be destroyed."

31But they replied, "Should he have treated our sister like a prostitute?"

Jacob Returns to Bethel

35 THEN GOD said to Jacob, "Go up to Bethel and settle there, and build an altar there to God, who appeared to you when you were fleeing from your brother Esau."

2So Jacob said to his household and to all who were with him, "Get rid of the foreign gods you have with you, and purify yourselves and change your clothes. 3Then come,

---

k 17 Hebrew *daughter*   *l 27* Or *because*

King James

³And let us arise, and go up to Beth-el; and I will make there an altar unto God, who answered me in the day of my distress, and was with me in the way which I went.

⁴And they gave unto Jacob all the strange gods which *were* in their hand, and *all their* earrings which *were* in their ears; and Jacob hid them under the oak which *was* by Shechem.

⁵And they journeyed: and the terror of God was upon the cities that *were* round about them, and they did not pursue after the sons of Jacob.

⁶ ¶ So Jacob came to Luz, which *is* in the land of Canaan, that *is*, Beth-el, he and all the people that *were* with him.

⁷And he built there an altar, and called the place ᵉEl-beth-el: because there God appeared unto him, when he fled from the face of his brother.

⁸But Deborah Rebekah's nurse died, and she was buried beneath Beth-el under an oak: and the name of it was called ᶠAllon-bachuth.

⁹ ¶ And God appeared unto Jacob again, when he came out of Padan-aram, and blessed him.

¹⁰And God said unto him, Thy name *is* Jacob: thy name shall not be called any more Jacob, but Israel shall be thy name: and he called his name Israel.

¹¹And God said unto him, I *am* God Almighty: be fruitful and multiply; a nation and a company of nations shall be of thee, and kings shall come out of thy loins;

¹²And the land which I gave Abraham and Isaac, to thee I will give it, and to thy seed after thee will I give the land.

¹³And God went up from him in the place where he talked with him.

¹⁴And Jacob set up a pillar in the place where he talked with him, *even* a pillar of stone: and he poured a drink offering thereon, and he poured oil thereon.

¹⁵And Jacob called the name of the place where God spake with him, Beth-el.

The deaths of Rachel and Isaac

¹⁶ ¶ And they journeyed from Beth-el; and there was but ᵍa little way to come to Ephrath: and Rachel travailed, and she had hard labour.

¹⁷And it came to pass, when she was in hard labour, that the midwife said unto her, Fear not; thou shalt have this son also.

¹⁸And it came to pass, as her soul was in departing, (for she died) that she called his name ʰBen-oni: but his father called him ⁱBenjamin.

¹⁹And Rachel died, and was buried in the way to Ephrath, which *is* Beth-lehem.

²⁰And Jacob set a pillar upon her grave: that *is* the pillar of Rachel's grave unto this day.

²¹ ¶ And Israel journeyed, and spread his tent beyond the tower of Edar.

²²And it came to pass, when Israel dwelt in that land, that Reuben went and lay with Bilhah his father's concubine: and Israel heard *it*. Now the sons of Jacob were twelve:

²³The sons of Leah; Reuben, Jacob's firstborn, and Simeon, and Levi, and Judah, and Issachar, and Zebulun:

²⁴The sons of Rachel; Joseph, and Benjamin:

²⁵And the sons of Bilhah, Rachel's handmaid; Dan, and Naphtali:

²⁶And the sons of Zilpah, Leah's handmaid; Gad, and Asher: these *are* the sons of Jacob, which were born to him in Padan-aram.

Amplified

³Then let us arise and go up to Bethel, and I will make there an altar to God Who answered me in the day of my distress and was with me wherever I went.

⁴So they [both young men and women] gave to Jacob all the strange gods they had and their earrings which were [worn as charms against evil] in their ears; and Jacob buried *and* hid them under the oak near Shechem.

⁵And they journeyed and a terror from God fell on the towns round about them, and they did not pursue the sons of Jacob.

⁶So Jacob came to Luz, that is, Bethel, which is in the land of Canaan, he and all the people with him.

⁷There he built an altar, and called the place El-bethel [God of Bethel], for there God revealed Himself to him when he fled from the presence of his brother.

⁸But Deborah, Rebekah's nurse, died and was buried below Bethel under an oak; and the name of it was called Allon-bacuth [oak of weeping].

⁹And God [in a distinctly visible manifestation] appeared to Jacob again when he came out of Padan-aram, and declared a blessing on him. [Gen. 32:28.]

¹⁰Again God said to him, Your name is Jacob [supplanter]; you shall not be called Jacob any longer, but Israel shall be your name. So He called him Israel [contender with God].

¹¹And God said to him, I am God Almighty. Be fruitful and multiply; a nation and a company of nations shall come from you and kings shall be born of your stock;

¹²The land which I gave Abraham and Isaac I will give to you, and to your descendants after you I will give the land.

¹³Then God ascended from him in the place where He talked with him.

¹⁴And Jacob set up a pillar (monument) in the place where he talked with [God], a pillar of stone; and he poured a drink offering on it and he poured oil on it.

¹⁵And Jacob called the name of the place where God had talked with him Bethel [house of God].

¹⁶And they journeyed from Bethel and had but a little way to go to Ephrath [Bethlehem] when Rachel suffered the pangs of childbirth and had hard labor.

¹⁷When she was in hard labor, the midwife said to her, Do not be afraid; you shall have this son also.

¹⁸And as her soul was departing, for she died, she called his name Ben-oni [son of my sorrow]; but his father called him Benjamin [son of the right hand].

¹⁹So Rachel died and was buried on the way to Ephrath, that is, Bethlehem.

²⁰And Jacob set a pillar (monument) on her grave; that is the pillar of Rachel's grave to this day.

²¹Then Israel journeyed on and spread his tent on the other side of the tower of Edar.

²²When Israel dwelt there, Reuben [his eldest son] went and lay with Bilhah his father's concubine; and Israel heard about it. Now Jacob's sons were twelve.

²³The sons of Leah: Reuben, Jacob's firstborn, Simeon, Levi, Judah, Issachar, and Zebulun.

²⁴The sons of Rachel: Joseph and Benjamin.

²⁵The sons of Bilhah, Rachel's maid: Dan and Naphtali.

²⁶And the sons of Zilpah, Leah's maid: Gad and Asher. These are the sons of Jacob born to him in Padan-aram.

New American Standard

3 and let us arise and go up to Bethel, and I will make an altar there to God, who answered me in the day of my distress and has been with me wherever I have gone."

4 So they gave to Jacob all the foreign gods which they had and the rings which were in their ears, and Jacob hid them under the oak which was near Shechem.

5 ¶ As they journeyed, there was a great terror upon the cities which were around them, and they did not pursue the sons of Jacob.

6 So Jacob came to Luz (that is, Bethel), which is in the land of Canaan, he and all the people who were with him.

7 He built an altar there, and called the place El-bethel, because there God had revealed Himself to him when he fled from his brother.

8 Now Deborah, Rebekah's nurse, died, and she was buried below Bethel under the oak; it was named *p*Allonbacuth.

Jacob Is Named Israel

9 ¶ Then God appeared to Jacob again when he came from Paddan-aram, and He blessed him.

10 God said to him,
"Your name is Jacob;
You shall no longer be called Jacob,
But Israel shall be your name."
Thus He called him Israel.

11 God also said to him,
"I am God Almighty;
Be fruitful and multiply;
A nation and a company of nations shall come
from you,
And kings shall come forth from you.

12 "The land which I gave to Abraham and Isaac,
I will give it to you,
And I will give the land to your descendants after
you."

13 Then God went up from him in the place where He had spoken with him.

14 Jacob set up a pillar in the place where He had spoken with him, a pillar of stone, and he poured out a drink offering on it; he also poured oil on it.

15 So Jacob named the place where God had spoken with him, *q*Bethel.

16 ¶ Then they journeyed from Bethel; and when there was still some distance to go to Ephrath, Rachel began to give birth and she suffered severe labor.

17 When she was in severe labor the midwife said to her, "Do not fear, for now you have another son."

18 It came about as her soul was departing (for she died), that she named him *r*Ben-oni; but his father called him *s*Benjamin.

19 So Rachel died and was buried on the way to Ephrath (that is, Bethlehem).

20 Jacob set up a pillar over her grave; that is the pillar of Rachel's grave to this day.

21 Then Israel journeyed on and pitched his tent beyond the tower of Eder.

22 ¶ It came about while Israel was dwelling in that land, that Reuben went and lay with Bilhah his father's concubine, and Israel heard *of it.*

The Sons of Israel

¶ Now there were twelve sons of Jacob—
23 the sons of Leah: Reuben, Jacob's firstborn, then Simeon and Levi and Judah and Issachar and Zebulun;
24 the sons of Rachel: Joseph and Benjamin;
25 and the sons of Bilhah, Rachel's maid: Dan and Naphtali;
26 and the sons of Zilpah, Leah's maid: Gad and Asher. These are the sons of Jacob who were born to him in Paddan-aram.

New International

let us go up to Bethel, where I will build an altar to God, who answered me in the day of my distress and who has been with me wherever I have gone." 4So they gave Jacob all the foreign gods they had and the rings in their ears, and Jacob buried them under the oak at Shechem. 5Then they set out, and the terror of God fell upon the towns all around them so that no one pursued them.

6Jacob and all the people with him came to Luz (that is, Bethel) in the land of Canaan. 7There he built an altar, and he called the place El Bethel,*m* because it was there that God revealed himself to him when he was fleeing from his brother.

8Now Deborah, Rebekah's nurse, died and was buried under the oak below Bethel. So it was named Allon Bacuth.*n*

9After Jacob returned from Paddan Aram,*o* God appeared to him again and blessed him. 10God said to him, "Your name is Jacob,*p* but you will no longer be called Jacob; your name will be Israel.*q*" So he named him Israel.

11And God said to him, "I am God Almighty*r*; be fruitful and increase in number. A nation and a community of nations will come from you, and kings will come from your body. 12The land I gave to Abraham and Isaac I also give to you, and I will give this land to your descendants after you." 13Then God went up from him at the place where he had talked with him.

14Jacob set up a stone pillar at the place where God had talked with him, and he poured out a drink offering on it; he also poured oil on it. 15Jacob called the place where God had talked with him Bethel.*s*

The Deaths of Rachel and Isaac

16Then they moved on from Bethel. While they were still some distance from Ephrath, Rachel began to give birth and had great difficulty. 17And as she was having great difficulty in childbirth, the midwife said to her, "Don't be afraid, for you have another son." 18As she breathed her last—for she was dying—she named her son Ben-Oni.*t* But his father named him Benjamin.*u*

19So Rachel died and was buried on the way to Ephrath (that is, Bethlehem). 20Over her tomb Jacob set up a pillar, and to this day that pillar marks Rachel's tomb.

21Israel moved on again and pitched his tent beyond Migdal Eder. 22While Israel was living in that region, Reuben went in and slept with his father's concubine Bilhah, and Israel heard of it.

Jacob had twelve sons:
23The sons of Leah:
Reuben the firstborn of Jacob,
Simeon, Levi, Judah, Issachar and Zebulun.
24The sons of Rachel:
Joseph and Benjamin.
25The sons of Rachel's maidservant Bilhah:
Dan and Naphtali.
26The sons of Leah's maidservant Zilpah:
Gad and Asher.
These were the sons of Jacob, who were born to him in Paddan Aram.

---

m 7 El Bethel means God of Bethel.   n 8 Allon Bacuth means oak of weeping.   o 9 That is, Northwest Mesopotamia; also in verse 26   p 10 Jacob means he grasps the heel (figuratively, he deceives).   q 10 Israel means he struggles with God.   r 11 Hebrew El-Shaddai   s 15 Bethel means house of God.   t 18 Ben-Oni means son of my trouble.   u 18 Benjamin means son of my right hand.

---

p I.e. oak of weeping   *q* I.e. the house of God   *r* I.e. the son of my sorrow   *s* I.e. the son of the right hand

King James

27 ¶ And Jacob came unto Isaac his father unto Mamre, unto the city of Arbah, which *is* Hebron, where Abraham and Isaac sojourned.

28 And the days of Isaac were an hundred and fourscore years.

29 And Isaac gave up the ghost, and died, and was gathered unto his people, *being* old and full of days: and his sons Esau and Jacob buried him.

The descendants of Esau

36 NOW THESE *are* the generations of Esau, who *is* Edom.

2 Esau took his wives of the daughters of Canaan; Adah the daughter of Elon the Hittite, and Aholibamah the daughter of Anah the daughter of Zibeon the Hivite;

3 And Bashemath Ishmael's daughter, sister of Nebajoth.

4 And Adah bare to Esau Eliphaz; and Bashemath bare Reuel;

5 And Aholibamah bare Jeush, and Jaalam, and Korah: these *are* the sons of Esau, which were born unto him in the land of Canaan.

6 And Esau took his wives, and his sons, and his daughters, and all the *j*persons of his house, and his cattle, and all his beasts, and all his substance, which he had got in the land of Canaan; and went into the country from the face of his brother Jacob.

7 For their riches were more than that they might dwell together; and the land wherein they were strangers could not bear them because of their cattle.

8 Thus dwelt Esau in mount Seir: Esau *is* Edom.

9 ¶ And these *are* the generations of Esau the father of *k*the Edomites in mount Seir:

10 These *are* the names of Esau's sons; Eliphaz the son of Adah the wife of Esau, Reuel the son of Bashemath the wife of Esau.

11 And the sons of Eliphaz were Teman, Omar, *l*Zepho, and Gatam, and Kenaz.

12 And Timna was concubine to Eliphaz Esau's son; and she bare to Eliphaz Amalek: these *were* the sons of Adah Esau's wife.

13 And these *are* the sons of Reuel; Nahath, and Zerah, Shammah, and Mizzah: these were the sons of Bashemath Esau's wife.

14 ¶ And these were the sons of Aholibamah, the daughter of Anah the daughter of Zibeon, Esau's wife: and she bare to Esau Jeush, and Jaalam, and Korah.

15 ¶ These *were* dukes of the sons of Esau: the sons of Eliphaz the firstborn *son* of Esau; duke Teman, duke Omar, duke Zepho, duke Kenaz,

16 Duke Korah, duke Gatam, *and* duke Amalek: these *are* the dukes *that came* of Eliphaz in the land of Edom; these *were* the sons of Adah.

17 ¶ And these *are* the sons of Reuel Esau's son; duke Nahath, duke Zerah, duke Shammah, duke Mizzah: these *are* the dukes *that came* of Reuel in the land of Edom; these *are* the sons of Bashemath Esau's wife.

18 ¶ And these are the sons of Aholibamah Esau's wife; duke Jeush, duke Jaalam, duke Korah: these *were* the dukes *that came* of Aholibamah the daughter of Anah, Esau's wife.

19 These *are* the sons of Esau, who *is* Edom, and these *are* their dukes.

20 ¶ These *are* the sons of Seir the Horite, who inhabited the land; Lotan, and Shobal, and Zibeon, and Anah,

21 And Dishon, and Ezer, and Dishan: these *are* the dukes of the Horites, the children of Seir in the land of Edom.

Amplified

27 And Jacob came to Isaac his father at Mamre or Kiriath-arba, that is, Hebron, where Abraham and Isaac had sojourned.

28 Now the days of Isaac were 180 years.

29 And Isaac's spirit departed; he died and was gathered to his people, being an old man, satisfied *and* satiated with days; his sons Esau and Jacob buried him.

36 NOW THIS is the history of the descendants of Esau, that is, Edom.

2 Esau took his wives from the women of Canaan: Adah daughter of Elon the Hittite, and Oholibamah daughter of Anah, the son of Zibeon the Hivite,

3 And Basemath, Ishmael's daughter, sister of Nebaioth.

4 Adah bore to Esau, Eliphaz; Basemath bore Reuel;

5 And Oholibamah bore Jeush, Jalam, and Korah. These are the sons of Esau born to him in Canaan.

6 Now Esau took his wives, his sons, his daughters, and all the members of his household, his cattle, all his beasts, and all his possessions which he had obtained in the land of Canaan, and he went into a land away from his brother Jacob.

7 For their great flocks *and* herds *and* possessions [which they had collected] made it impossible for them to dwell together; the land in which they were strangers could not support them because of their livestock.

8 So Esau dwelt in the hill country of Seir; Esau is Edom.

9 And this is the history of the descendants of Esau the father of the Edomites in the hill country of Seir.

10 These are the names of Esau's sons: Eliphaz, the son of Adah, Esau's wife, and Reuel, the son of Basemath, Esau's wife.

11 And the sons of Eliphaz were Teman, Omar, Zepho, Gatam, and Kenaz.

12 And Timna was a concubine of Eliphaz, Esau's son; and she bore Amalek to Eliphaz. These are the sons of Adah, Esau's wife.

13 These are the sons of Reuel: Nahath, Zerah, Shammah, and Mizzah. These are the sons of Basemath, Esau's wife.

14 And these are the sons of Oholibamah daughter of Anah, the son of Zibeon, Esau's wife. She bore to Esau: Jeush, Jalam, and Korah.

15 These are the chiefs of the sons of Esau: The sons of Eliphaz the firstborn of Esau: Chiefs Teman, Omar, Zepho, Kenaz,

16 Korah, Gatam, and Amalek. These are the chiefs of Eliphaz in the land of Edom; they are the sons of Adah.

17 These are the sons of Reuel, Esau's son: Chiefs Nahath, Zerah, Shammah, Mizzah. These are the chiefs of Reuel in the land of Edom; they are the sons of Basemath, Esau's wife.

18 These are the sons of Oholibamah, Esau's wife: Chiefs Jeush, Jalam, and Korah. These are the chiefs born of Oholibamah daughter of Anah, Esau's wife.

19 These are the sons of Esau, that is, Edom, and these are their chiefs.

20 These are the sons of Seir the Horite, the inhabitants of the land: Lotan, Shobal, Zibeon, Anah,

21 Dishon, Ezer, and Dishan. These are the chiefs of the *r*Horites, the sons of Seir in the land of Edom.

*r*Because of the similarity of the word 'Horites' to a Hebrew word for "cave," the term Horite was formerly interpreted as "cave dweller." But later archaeological discoveries have shown that the Horites are not to be explained as cave dwellers, but are to be identified with an important group in the Near East in patriarchal times (J. P. Free, *Archaeology and Bible History*). In fact, neither the Bible nor archaeology has any proof of aboriginal "cavemen." Cities of great antiquity have been unearthed with ever-increasing evidence that "when civilization appears it is already fully grown," and "pre-Semitic culture springs into view ready-made" (Hall, *History of the Near East*).

---

*j*Heb. *souls*   *k*Heb. *Edom*   *l*Or, *Zephi;* see 1 Chr. 1:36

New American Standard

27 ¶ Jacob came to his father Isaac at Mamre of Kiriath-arba (that is, Hebron), where Abraham and Isaac had sojourned.

28 ¶ Now the days of Isaac were one hundred and eighty years.

29 Isaac breathed his last and died and was gathered to his people, an old man of ripe age; and his sons Esau and Jacob buried him.

Esau Moves

36 NOW THESE are *the records of* the generations of Esau (that is, Edom).

2 ¶ Esau took his wives from the daughters of Canaan: Adah the daughter of Elon the Hittite, and Oholibamah the daughter of Anah and the granddaughter of Zibeon the Hivite;

3 also Basemath, Ishmael's daughter, the sister of Nebaioth.

4 Adah bore Eliphaz to Esau, and Basemath bore Reuel,

5 and Oholibamah bore Jeush and Jalam and Korah. These are the sons of Esau who were born to him in the land of Canaan.

6 ¶ Then Esau took his wives and his sons and his daughters and all his household, and his livestock and all his cattle and all his goods which he had acquired in the land of Canaan, and went to *another* land away from his brother Jacob.

7 For their property had become too great for them to live together, and the land where they sojourned could not sustain them because of their livestock.

8 So Esau lived in the hill country of Seir; Esau is Edom.

Descendants of Esau

9 ¶ These then are *the records of* the generations of Esau the father of the Edomites in the hill country of Seir.

10 These are the names of Esau's sons: Eliphaz the son of Esau's wife Adah, Reuel the son of Esau's wife Basemath.

11 The sons of Eliphaz were Teman, Omar, Zepho and Gatam and Kenaz.

12 Timna was a concubine of Esau's son Eliphaz and she bore Amalek to Eliphaz. These are the sons of Esau's wife Adah.

13 These are the sons of Reuel: Nahath and Zerah, Shammah and Mizzah. These were the sons of Esau's wife Basemath.

14 These were the sons of Esau's wife Oholibamah, the daughter of Anah and the granddaughter of Zibeon: she bore to Esau, Jeush and Jalam and Korah.

15 ¶ These are the chiefs of the sons of Esau. The sons of Eliphaz, the firstborn of Esau, are chief Teman, chief Omar, chief Zepho, chief Kenaz,

16 chief Korah, chief Gatam, chief Amalek. These are the chiefs descended from Eliphaz in the land of Edom; these are the sons of Adah.

17 These are the sons of Reuel, Esau's son: chief Nahath, chief Zerah, chief Shammah, chief Mizzah. These are the chiefs descended from Reuel in the land of Edom; these are the sons of Esau's wife Basemath.

18 These are the sons of Esau's wife Oholibamah: chief Jeush, chief Jalam, chief Korah. These are the chiefs descended from Esau's wife Oholibamah, the daughter of Anah.

19 These are the sons of Esau (that is, Edom), and these are their chiefs.

20 ¶ These are the sons of Seir the Horite, the inhabitants of the land: Lotan and Shobal and Zibeon and Anah,

21 and Dishon and Ezer and Dishan. These are the chiefs descended from the Horites, the sons of Seir in the land of Edom.

New International

27 Jacob came home to his father Isaac in Mamre, near Kiriath Arba (that is, Hebron), where Abraham and Isaac had stayed. 28 Isaac lived a hundred and eighty years. 29 Then he breathed his last and died and was gathered to his people, old and full of years. And his sons Esau and Jacob buried him.

Esau's Descendants

36 THIS IS the account of Esau (that is, Edom).

2 Esau took his wives from the women of Canaan: Adah daughter of Elon the Hittite, and Oholibamah daughter of Anah and granddaughter of Zibeon the Hivite— 3 also Basemath daughter of Ishmael and sister of Nebaioth.

4 Adah bore Eliphaz to Esau, Basemath bore Reuel, 5 and Oholibamah bore Jeush, Jalam and Korah. These were the sons of Esau, who were born to him in Canaan.

6 Esau took his wives and sons and daughters and all the members of his household, as well as his livestock and all his other animals and all the goods he had acquired in Canaan, and moved to a land some distance from his brother Jacob. 7 Their possessions were too great for them to remain together; the land where they were staying could not support them both because of their livestock. 8 So Esau (that is, Edom) settled in the hill country of Seir.

9 This is the account of Esau the father of the Edomites in the hill country of Seir.

10 These are the names of Esau's sons:

Eliphaz, the son of Esau's wife Adah, and Reuel, the son of Esau's wife Basemath.

11 The sons of Eliphaz:

Teman, Omar, Zepho, Gatam and Kenaz.

12 Esau's son Eliphaz also had a concubine named Timna, who bore him Amalek. These were grandsons of Esau's wife Adah.

13 The sons of Reuel:

Nahath, Zerah, Shammah and Mizzah. These were grandsons of Esau's wife Basemath.

14 The sons of Esau's wife Oholibamah daughter of Anah and granddaughter of Zibeon, whom she bore to Esau:

Jeush, Jalam and Korah.

15 These were the chiefs among Esau's descendants:

The sons of Eliphaz the firstborn of Esau:

Chiefs Teman, Omar, Zepho, Kenaz, 16 Korah,[v] Gatam and Amalek. These were the chiefs descended from Eliphaz in Edom; they were grandsons of Adah.

17 The sons of Esau's son Reuel:

Chiefs Nahath, Zerah, Shammah and Mizzah. These were the chiefs descended from Reuel in Edom; they were grandsons of Esau's wife Basemath.

18 The sons of Esau's wife Oholibamah:

Chiefs Jeush, Jalam and Korah. These were the chiefs descended from Esau's wife Oholibamah daughter of Anah.

19 These were the sons of Esau (that is, Edom), and these were their chiefs.

20 These were the sons of Seir the Horite, who were living in the region:

Lotan, Shobal, Zibeon, Anah, 21 Dishon, Ezer and Dishan. These sons of Seir in Edom were Horite chiefs.

---

v 16 Masoretic Text; Samaritan Pentateuch (see also Gen. 36:11 and 1 Chron. 1:36) does not have *Korah*.

King James

22 And the children of Lotan were Hori and [m]Hemam; and Lotan's sister *was* Timna.

23 And the children of Shobal *were* these; [n]Alvan, and Manahath, and Ebal, [o]Shepho, and Onam.

24 And these *are* the children of Zibeon; both Ajah, and Anah: this *was that* Anah that found the mules in the wilderness, as he fed the asses of Zibeon his father.

25 And the children of Anah *were* these; Dishon, and Aholibamah the daughter of Anah.

26 And these *are* the children of Dishon; [p]Hemdan, and Eshban, and Ithran, and Cheran.

27 The children of Ezer *are* these; Bilhan, and Zaavan, and [q]Akan.

28 The children of Dishan *are* these; Uz, and Aran.

29 These *are* the dukes *that came* of the Horites; duke Lotan, duke Shobal, duke Zibeon, duke Anah,

30 Duke Dishon, duke Ezer, duke Dishan: these *are* the dukes *that came* of Hori, among their dukes in the land of Seir.

The kings of Edom

31 ¶ And these *are* the kings that reigned in the land of Edom, before there reigned any king over the children of Israel.

32 And Bela the son of Beor reigned in Edom: and the name of his city *was* Dinhabah.

33 And Bela died, and Jobab the son of Zerah of Bozrah reigned in his stead.

34 And Jobab died, and Husham of the land of Temani reigned in his stead.

35 And Husham died, and Hadad the son of Bedad, who smote Midian in the field of Moab, reigned in his stead: and the name of his city *was* Avith.

36 And Hadad died, and Samlah of Masrekah reigned in his stead.

37 And Samlah died, and Saul of Rehoboth *by* the river reigned in his stead.

38 And Saul died, and Baal-hanan the son of Achbor reigned in his stead.

39 And Baal-hanan the son of Achbor died, and Hadar reigned in his stead: and the name of his city *was* Pau; and his wife's name *was* Mehetabel, the daughter of Matred, the daughter of Mezahab.

40 And these *are* the names of the dukes *that came* of Esau, according to their families, after their places, by their names; duke Timnah, duke [r]Alvah, duke Jetheth,

41 Duke Aholibamah, duke Elah, duke Pinon,

42 Duke Kenaz, duke Teman, duke Mibzar,

43 Duke Magdiel, duke Iram: these *be* the dukes of Edom, according to their habitations in the land of their possession: he *is* Esau the father of [s]the Edomites.

Joseph's dream

37 AND JACOB dwelt in the land [t]wherein his father was a stranger, in the land of Canaan.

2 These *are* the generations of Jacob. Joseph, *being* seventeen years old, was feeding the flock with his brethren; and the lad *was* with the sons of Bilhah, and with the sons of Zilpah, his father's wives: and Joseph brought unto his father their evil report.

3 Now Israel loved Joseph more than all his children, because he *was* the son of his old age: and he made him a coat of *many* [u]colours.

[m] Or, *Homam;* see 1 Chr. 1:39 [n] Or, *Alian;* see 1 Chr. 1:40
[o] Or, *Shephi;* see 1 Chr. 1:40 [p] Or, *Amram;* see 1 Chr. 1:41
[q] Or, *Jakan;* see 1 Chr. 1:42 [r] Or, *Aliah* [s] Heb. *Edom*
[t] Heb. *of his father's sojournings* [u] Or, *pieces,*

Amplified

22 The sons of Lotan are Hori and Hemam; and Lotan's sister is Timna.

23 The sons of Shobal are these: Alvan, Manahath, Ebal, Shepho, and Onam.

24 These are the sons of Zibeon: Aiah and Anah. This is the Anah who found the hot springs in the wilderness as he pastured the donkeys of Zibeon his father.

25 The children of Anah are these: Dishon and Oholibamah daughter of Anah [Esau's wife].

26 These are the sons of Dishon: Hemdan, Eshban, Ithran, and Cheran.

27 Ezer's sons are these: Bilhan, Zaavan, and Akan.

28 The sons of Dishan are these: Uz and Aran.

29 The Horite chiefs are these: Lotan, Shobal, Zibeon, Anah,

30 Dishon, Ezer, Dishan. These are the Horite chiefs, according to their clans, in the land of Seir.

31 And these are the kings who reigned in Edom before any king reigned over the Israelites:

32 Bela son of Beor reigned in Edom. And the name of his city was Dinhabah.

33 Now Bela died, and Jobab son of Zerah of Bozrah reigned in his stead.

34 Then Jobab died, and Husham of the land of the Temanites reigned in his stead.

35 And Husham died, and Hadad son of Bedad, who defeated Midian in the country of Moab, reigned in his stead. The name of his [enclosed] city was Avith.

36 Hadad died, and Samlah of Masrekah succeeded him.

37 Then Samlah died, and Shaul of Rehoboth on the river [Euphrates] reigned in his stead.

38 And Shaul died, and Baal-hanan son of Achbor reigned in his stead.

39 Baal-hanan son of Achbor died, and then Hadar reigned. His [enclosed] city was Pau; his wife's name was Mehetabel daughter of Matred, the daughter of Mezahab.

40 And these are the names of the chiefs of Esau, according to their families and places of residence, by their names: Chiefs Timna, Alvah, Jetheth,

41 Oholibamah, Elah, Pinon,

42 Kenaz, Teman, Mibzar,

43 Magdiel, and Iram. These are the chiefs of Edom [that is, of Esau the father of the Edomites], according to their dwelling places in their land.

37 SO JACOB dwelt in the land in which his father had been a stranger *and* sojourner, in the land of Canaan.

2 This is the history of the descendants of Jacob *and* this is Jacob's line. Joseph, when he was seventeen years old, was shepherding the flock with his brothers; the lad was with the sons of Bilhah and Zilpah, his father's [secondary] wives; and Joseph brought to his father a bad report of them.

3 Now Israel loved Joseph more than all his children because he was the son of his old age, and he made him a [distinctive] long tunic with sleeves.

New American Standard

22 The sons of Lotan were Hori and Hemam; and Lotan's sister was Timna.

23 These are the sons of Shobal: Alvan and Manahath and Ebal, Shepho and Onam.

24 These are the sons of Zibeon: Aiah and Anah—he is the Anah who found the hot springs in the wilderness when he was pasturing the donkeys of his father Zibeon.

25 These are the children of Anah: Dishon, and Oholibamah, the daughter of Anah.

26 These are the sons of Dishon: Hemdan and Eshban and Ithran and Cheran.

27 These are the sons of Ezer: Bilhan and Zaavan and Akan.

28 These are the sons of Dishan: Uz and Aran.

29 These are the chiefs descended from the Horites: chief Lotan, chief Shobal, chief Zibeon, chief Anah,

30 chief Dishon, chief Ezer, chief Dishan. These are the chiefs descended from the Horites, according to their *various* chiefs in the land of Seir.

31 ¶ Now these are the kings who reigned in the land of Edom before any king reigned over the sons of Israel.

32 Bela the son of Beor reigned in Edom, and the name of his city was Dinhabah.

33 Then Bela died, and Jobab the son of Zerah of Bozrah became king in his place.

34 Then Jobab died, and Husham of the land of the Temanites became king in his place.

35 Then Husham died, and Hadad the son of Bedad, who defeated Midian in the field of Moab, became king in his place; and the name of his city was Avith.

36 Then Hadad died, and Samlah of Masrekah became king in his place.

37 Then Samlah died, and Shaul of Rehoboth on the *Euphrates* River became king in his place.

38 Then Shaul died, and Baal-hanan the son of Achbor became king in his place.

39 Then Baal-hanan the son of Achbor died, and Hadar became king in his place; and the name of his city was Pau; and his wife's name was Mehetabel, the daughter of Matred, daughter of Mezahab.

40 ¶ Now these are the names of the chiefs descended from Esau, according to their families *and* their localities, by their names: chief Timna, chief Alvah, chief Jetheth,

41 chief Oholibamah, chief Elah, chief Pinon,

42 chief Kenaz, chief Teman, chief Mibzar,

43 chief Magdiel, chief Iram. These are the chiefs of Edom (that is, Esau, the father of the Edomites), according to their habitations in the land of their possession.

Joseph's Dream

37 NOW JACOB lived in the land where his father had sojourned, in the land of Canaan.

2 These are *the records of* the generations of Jacob.

¶ Joseph, when seventeen years of age, was pasturing the flock with his brothers while he was *still* a youth, along with the sons of Bilhah and the sons of Zilpah, his father's wives. And Joseph brought back a bad report about them to their father.

3 Now Israel loved Joseph more than all his sons, because he was the son of his old age; and he made him a *t*varicolored tunic.

New International

22The sons of Lotan:
Hori and Homam.*w* Timna was Lotan's sister.

23The sons of Shobal:
Alvan, Manahath, Ebal, Shepho and Onam.

24The sons of Zibeon:
Aiah and Anah. This is the Anah who discovered the hot springs*x* in the desert while he was grazing the donkeys of his father Zibeon.

25The children of Anah:
Dishon and Oholibamah daughter of Anah.

26The sons of Dishon*y*:
Hemdan, Eshban, Ithran and Keran.

27The sons of Ezer:
Bilhan, Zaavan and Akan.

28The sons of Dishan:
Uz and Aran.

29These were the Horite chiefs:
Lotan, Shobal, Zibeon, Anah, 30Dishon, Ezer and Dishan. These were the Horite chiefs, according to their divisions, in the land of Seir.

The Rulers of Edom

31These were the kings who reigned in Edom before any Israelite king reigned*z*:

32Bela son of Beor became king of Edom. His city was named Dinhabah.

33When Bela died, Jobab son of Zerah from Bozrah succeeded him as king.

34When Jobab died, Husham from the land of the Temanites succeeded him as king.

35When Husham died, Hadad son of Bedad, who defeated Midian in the country of Moab, succeeded him as king. His city was named Avith.

36When Hadad died, Samlah from Masrekah succeeded him as king.

37When Samlah died, Shaul from Rehoboth on the river*a* succeeded him as king.

38When Shaul died, Baal-Hanan son of Acbor succeeded him as king.

39When Baal-Hanan son of Acbor died, Hadad*b* succeeded him as king. His city was named Pau, and his wife's name was Mehetabel daughter of Matred, the daughter of Me-Zahab.

40These were the chiefs descended from Esau, by name, according to their clans and regions:
Timna, Alvah, Jetheth, 41Oholibamah, Elah, Pinon, 42Kenaz, Teman, Mibzar, 43Magdiel and Iram. These were the chiefs of Edom, according to their settlements in the land they occupied.

This was Esau the father of the Edomites.

Joseph's Dreams

37 JACOB LIVED in the land where his father had stayed, the land of Canaan.

2This is the account of Jacob.

Joseph, a young man of seventeen, was tending the flocks with his brothers, the sons of Bilhah and the sons of Zilpah, his father's wives, and he brought their father a bad report about them.

3Now Israel loved Joseph more than any of his other sons, because he had been born to him in his old age; and

---

w 22 Hebrew *Hemam,* a variant of *Homam* (see 1 Chron. 1:39)   *x 24* Vulgate; Syriac *discovered water;* the meaning of the Hebrew for this word is uncertain.   *y 26* Hebrew *Dishan,* a variant of *Dishon*   *z 31* Or *before an Israelite king reigned over them*   *a 37* Possibly the Euphrates   *b 39* Many manuscripts of the Masoretic Text, Samaritan Pentateuch and Syriac (see also 1 Chron. 1:50); most manuscripts of the Masoretic Text *Hadar*

---

*t*Or *full-length robe*

King James

⁴And when his brethren saw that their father loved him more than all his brethren, they hated him, and could not speak peaceably unto him.

⁵ ¶ And Joseph dreamed a dream, and he told *it* his brethren: and they hated him yet the more.

⁶And he said unto them, Hear, I pray you, this dream which I have dreamed:

⁷For, behold, we *were* binding sheaves in the field, and, lo, my sheaf arose, and also stood upright; and, behold, your sheaves stood round about, and made obeisance to my sheaf.

⁸And his brethren said to him, Shalt thou indeed reign over us? or shalt thou indeed have dominion over us? And they hated him yet the more for his dreams, and for his words.

⁹ ¶ And he dreamed yet another dream, and told it his brethren, and said, Behold, I have dreamed a dream more; and, behold, the sun and the moon and the eleven stars made obeisance to me.

¹⁰And he told *it* to his father, and to his brethren: and his father rebuked him, and said unto him, What *is* this dream that thou hast dreamed? Shall I and thy mother and thy brethren indeed come to bow down ourselves to thee to the earth?

¹¹And his brethren envied him; but his father observed the saying.

Joseph sold to merchants

¹² ¶ And his brethren went to feed their father's flock in Shechem.

¹³And Israel said unto Joseph, Do not thy brethren feed *the flock* in Shechem? come, and I will send thee unto them. And he said to him, Here *am* I.

¹⁴And he said to him, Go, I pray thee, ^vsee whether it be well with thy brethren, and well with the flocks; and bring me word again. So he sent him out of the vale of Hebron, and he came to Shechem.

¹⁵ ¶ And a certain man found him, and, behold, *he was* wandering in the field: and the man asked him, saying, What seekest thou?

¹⁶And he said, I seek my brethren: tell me, I pray thee, where they feed *their flocks*.

¹⁷And the man said, They are departed hence; for I heard them say, Let us go to Dothan. And Joseph went after his brethren, and found them in Dothan.

¹⁸And when they saw him afar off, even before he came near unto them, they conspired against him to slay him.

¹⁹And they said one to another, Behold, this ^wdreamer cometh.

²⁰Come now therefore, and let us slay him, and cast him into some pit, and we will say, Some evil beast hath devoured him: and we shall see what will become of his dreams.

²¹And Reuben heard *it,* and he delivered him out of their hands; and said, Let us not kill him.

²²And Reuben said unto them, Shed no blood, *but* cast him into this pit that *is* in the wilderness, and lay no hand upon him; that he might rid him out of their hands, to deliver him to his father again.

²³ ¶ And it came to pass, when Joseph was come unto his brethren, that they stripped Joseph out of his coat, *his* coat of *many* ^xcolours that *was* on him;

²⁴And they took him, and cast him into a pit: and the pit *was* empty, *there was* no water in it.

²⁵And they sat down to eat bread: and they lifted up their eyes and looked, and, behold, a company of Ishmeelites came from Gilead with their camels bearing spicery and balm and myrrh, going to carry *it* down to Egypt.

²⁶And Judah said unto his brethren, What profit *is it* if we slay our brother, and conceal his blood?

Amplified

⁴But when his brothers saw that their father loved [Joseph] more than all of his brothers, they hated him and could not say, Peace [in friendly greeting] to him *or* speak peaceably to him.

⁵Now Joseph had a dream and he told it to his brothers, and they hated him still more.

⁶And he said to them, Listen now *and* hear, I pray you, this dream that I have dreamed:

⁷We [brothers] were binding sheaves in the field, and behold, my sheaf arose and stood upright, and behold, your sheaves stood round about my sheaf and bowed down!

⁸His brothers said to him, Shall you indeed reign over us? Or are you going to have us as your subjects *and* dominate us? And they hated him all the more for his dreams and for what he said.

⁹But Joseph dreamed yet another dream and told it to his brothers [also]. He said, See here, I have dreamed again, and behold, [this time not only] eleven stars [but also] the sun and the moon bowed down *and* did reverence to me!

¹⁰And he told it to his father [as well as] his brethren. But his father rebuked him and said to him, What *is* the meaning of this dream that you have dreamed? Shall I and your mother and your brothers actually come to bow down ourselves to the earth *and* do homage to you?

¹¹Joseph's brothers envied him *and* were jealous of him, but his father observed the saying *and* pondered over it.

¹²Joseph's brothers went to shepherd *and* feed their father's flock near Shechem.

¹³[One day] Israel said to Joseph, Do not your brothers shepherd my flock at Shechem? Come, and I will send you to them. And he said, Here I am.

¹⁴And [Jacob] said to him, Go, I pray you, see whether everything is all right with your brothers and with the flock; then come back and bring me word. So he sent him out of the Hebron Valley, and he came to Shechem.

¹⁵And a certain man found him, and behold, he had lost his way *and* was wandering in the open country. The man asked him, What are you trying to find?

¹⁶And he said, I am looking for my brothers. Tell me, I pray you, where they are pasturing our flocks.

¹⁷But the man said, [They were here, but] they have gone. I heard them say, Let us go to Dothan. And Joseph went after his brothers and found them at Dothan.

¹⁸And when they saw him far off, even before he came near to them, they conspired to kill him.

¹⁹And they said one to another, See, here comes this dreamer *and* master of dreams.

²⁰So come on now, let us kill him and throw his body into some pit; then we will say [to our father], Some wild *and* ferocious animal has devoured him; and we shall see what will become of his dreams!

²¹Now Reuben heard it and he delivered him out of their hands by saying, Let us not kill him.

²²And Reuben said to them, Shed no blood, but cast him into this pit *or* well that is out here in the wilderness and lay no hand on him. He was trying to get Joseph out of their hands in order to rescue him *and* deliver him again to his father.

²³When Joseph had come to his brothers, they stripped him of his [distinctive] long garment which he was wearing;

²⁴Then they took him and cast him into the [well-like] pit which was empty; there was no water in it.

²⁵Then they sat down to eat their lunch. When they looked up, behold, they saw a caravan of Ishmaelites [mixed Arabians] coming from Gilead, with their camels bearing gum [of the styrax tree], balm (balsam), and myrrh *or* ladanum, going on their way to carry them down to Egypt.

²⁶And Judah said to his brothers, What do we gain if we slay our brother and conceal his blood?

---

^vHeb. *see the peace of thy brethren*   ^wHeb. *master of dreams*
^xOr, *pieces*

New American Standard

4 His brothers saw that their father loved him more than all his brothers; and so they hated him and could not speak to him *on friendly terms.

5 ¶ Then Joseph had a dream, and when he told it to his brothers, they hated him even more.

6 He said to them, "Please listen to this dream which I have had;

7 for behold, we were binding sheaves in the field, and lo, my sheaf rose up and also stood erect; and behold, your sheaves gathered around and bowed down to my sheaf."

8 Then his brothers said to him, "Are you actually going to reign over us? Or are you really going to rule over us?" So they hated him even more for his dreams and for his words.

9 ¶ Now he had still another dream, and related it to his brothers, and said, "Lo, I have had still another dream; and behold, the sun and the moon and eleven stars were bowing down to me."

10 He related it to his father and to his brothers; and his father rebuked him and said to him, "What is this dream that you have had? Shall I and your mother and your brothers actually come to bow ourselves down before you to the ground?"

11 His brothers were jealous of him, but his father kept the saying in mind.

12 ¶ Then his brothers went to pasture their father's flock in Shechem.

13 Israel said to Joseph, "Are not your brothers pasturing the flock in Shechem? Come, and I will send you to them." And he said to him, "I will go."

14 Then he said to him, "Go now and see about the welfare of your brothers and the welfare of the flock, and bring word back to me." So he sent him from the valley of Hebron, and he came to Shechem.

15 ¶ A man found him, and behold, he was wandering in the field; and the man asked him, "What are you looking for?"

16 He said, "I am looking for my brothers; please tell me where they are pasturing the flock."

17 Then the man said, "They have moved from here; for I heard them say, 'Let us go to Dothan.' " So Joseph went after his brothers and found them at Dothan.

The Plot against Joseph

18 ¶ When they saw him from a distance and before he came close to them, they plotted against him to put him to death.

19 They said to one another, "Here comes this dreamer!

20 "Now then, come and let us kill him and throw him into one of the pits; and we will say, 'A wild beast devoured him.' Then let us see what will become of his dreams!"

21 But Reuben heard this and rescued him out of their hands and said, "Let us not take his life."

22 Reuben further said to them, "Shed no blood. Throw him into this pit that is in the wilderness, but do not lay hands on him"—that he might rescue him out of their hands, to restore him to his father.

23 So it came about, when Joseph reached his brothers, that they stripped Joseph of his tunic, the varicolored tunic that was on him;

24 and they took him and threw him into the pit. Now the pit was empty, without any water in it.

25 ¶ Then they sat down to eat a meal. And as they raised their eyes and looked, behold, a caravan of Ishmaelites was coming from Gilead, with their camels bearing aromatic gum and balm and myrrh, on their way to bring them down to Egypt.

26 Judah said to his brothers, "What profit is it for us to kill our brother and cover up his blood?

*Lit in peace

New International

he made a richly ornamented[c] robe for him. 4When his brothers saw that their father loved him more than any of them, they hated him and could not speak a kind word to him.

5Joseph had a dream, and when he told it to his brothers, they hated him all the more. 6He said to them, "Listen to this dream I had: 7We were binding sheaves of grain out in the field when suddenly my sheaf rose and stood upright, while your sheaves gathered around mine and bowed down to it."

8His brothers said to him, "Do you intend to reign over us? Will you actually rule us?" And they hated him all the more because of his dream and what he had said.

9Then he had another dream, and he told it to his brothers. "Listen," he said, "I had another dream, and this time the sun and moon and eleven stars were bowing down to me."

10When he told his father as well as his brothers, his father rebuked him and said, "What is this dream you had? Will your mother and I and your brothers actually come and bow down to the ground before you?" 11His brothers were jealous of him, but his father kept the matter in mind.

Joseph Sold by His Brothers

12Now his brothers had gone to graze their father's flocks near Shechem, 13and Israel said to Joseph, "As you know, your brothers are grazing the flocks near Shechem. Come, I am going to send you to them."

"Very well," he replied.

14So he said to him, "Go and see if all is well with your brothers and with the flocks, and bring word back to me." Then he sent him off from the Valley of Hebron.

When Joseph arrived at Shechem, 15a man found him wandering around in the fields and asked him, "What are you looking for?"

16He replied, "I'm looking for my brothers. Can you tell me where they are grazing their flocks?"

17"They have moved on from here," the man answered. "I heard them say, 'Let's go to Dothan.' "

So Joseph went after his brothers and found them near Dothan. 18But they saw him in the distance, and before he reached them, they plotted to kill him.

19"Here comes that dreamer!" they said to each other. 20"Come now, let's kill him and throw him into one of these cisterns and say that a ferocious animal devoured him. Then we'll see what comes of his dreams."

21When Reuben heard this, he tried to rescue him from their hands. "Let's not take his life," he said. 22"Don't shed any blood. Throw him into this cistern here in the desert, but don't lay a hand on him." Reuben said this to rescue him from them and take him back to his father.

23So when Joseph came to his brothers, they stripped him of his robe—the richly ornamented robe he was wearing— 24and they took him and threw him into the cistern. Now the cistern was empty; there was no water in it.

25As they sat down to eat their meal, they looked up and saw a caravan of Ishmaelites coming from Gilead. Their camels were loaded with spices, balm and myrrh, and they were on their way to take them down to Egypt.

26Judah said to his brothers, "What will we gain if we

c 3 The meaning of the Hebrew for richly ornamented is uncertain; also in verses 23 and 32.

King James

27Come, and let us sell him to the Ishmeelites, and let not our hand be upon him; for he *is* our brother *and* our flesh. And his brethren *y*were content.

28Then there passed by Midianites merchantmen; and they drew and lifted up Joseph out of the pit, and sold Joseph to the Ishmeelites for twenty *pieces* of silver: and they brought Joseph into Egypt.

29¶ And Reuben returned unto the pit; and, behold, Joseph *was* not in the pit; and he rent his clothes.

30And he returned unto his brethren, and said, The child *is* not; and I, whither shall I go?

31And they took Joseph's coat, and killed a kid of the goats, and dipped the coat in the blood;

32And they sent the coat of *many* colours, and they brought *it* to their father; and said, This have we found: know now whether it *be* thy son's coat or no.

33And he knew it, and said, *It is* my son's coat; an evil beast hath devoured him; Joseph is without doubt rent in pieces.

34And Jacob rent his clothes, and put sackcloth upon his loins, and mourned for his son many days.

35And all his sons and all his daughters rose up to comfort him; but he refused to be comforted; and he said, For I will go down into the grave unto my son mourning. Thus his father wept for him.

36And the Midianites sold him into Egypt unto Potiphar, an *z*officer of Pharaoh's, *and* *a* *b*captain of the guard.

Judah and Tamar

38 AND IT came to pass at that time, that Judah went down from his brethren, and turned in to a certain Adullamite, whose name *was* Hirah.

2And Judah saw there a daughter of a certain Canaanite, whose name *was* Shuah; and he took her, and went in unto her.

3And she conceived, and bare a son; and he called his name Er.

4And she conceived again, and bare a son; and she called his name Onan.

5And she yet again conceived, and bare a son; and called his name Shelah: and he was at Chezib, when she bare him.

6And Judah took a wife for Er his firstborn, whose name *was* Tamar.

7And Er, Judah's firstborn, was wicked in the sight of the LORD; and the LORD slew him.

8And Judah said unto Onan, Go in unto thy brother's wife, and marry her, and raise up seed to thy brother.

9And Onan knew that the seed should not be his; and it came to pass, when he went in unto his brother's wife, that he spilled *it* on the ground, lest that he should give seed to his brother.

10And the thing which he did *c*displeased the LORD: wherefore he slew him also.

11Then said Judah to Tamar his daughter-in-law, Remain a widow at thy father's house, till Shelah my son be grown: for he said, Lest peradventure he die also, as his brethren *did.* And Tamar went and dwelt in her father's house.

12 ¶ And *d*in process of time the daughter of Shuah Judah's wife died; and Judah was comforted, and went up unto his sheepshearers to Timnath, he and his friend Hirah the Adullamite.

13And it was told Tamar, saying, Behold thy father-in-law goeth up to Timnath to shear his sheep.

Amplified

27Come, let us sell him to the Ishmaelites [and Midianites, these mixed Arabians who are approaching], and let not our hand be upon him, for he is our brother and our flesh. And his brothers consented.

28Then as the Midianite [and Ishmaelite] merchants were passing by, the brothers pulled Joseph up and lifted him out of the well. And they sold him for twenty pieces of silver to the Ishmaelites, who took Joseph [captive] into Egypt.

29Then Reuben [who had not been there when the brothers plotted to sell the lad] returned to the pit; and behold, Joseph was not in the pit, and he rent his clothes.

30He rejoined his brothers and said, The boy is not there! And I, where shall I go [to hide from my father]?

31Then they took Joseph's [distinctive] long garment, killed a young goat, and dipped the garment in the blood;

32And they sent the garment to their father, saying, We have found this! Examine *and* decide whether it is your son's tunic or not.

33He said, My son's long garment! An evil [wild] beast has devoured him; Joseph is without doubt rent in pieces.

34And Jacob tore his clothes, put on sackcloth, and mourned many days for his son.

35And all his sons and daughters attempted to console him, but he refused to be comforted and said, I will go down to Sheol (the place of the dead) to my son mourning. And his father wept for him.

36And the Midianites [and Ishmaelites] sold [Joseph] in Egypt to Potiphar, an officer of Pharaoh and the captain *and* chief executioner of the [royal] guard.

38 AT THAT time Judah withdrew from his brothers and went to [lodge with] a certain Adullamite named Hirah.

2There Judah saw *and* met a daughter of Shuah, a Canaanite; he took her as wife and lived with her.

3And she became pregnant and bore a son, and he called him Er.

4And she conceived again and bore a son and named him Onan.

5Again she conceived and bore a son and named him Shelah. [They were living] at Chezib when she bore him.

6Now Judah took a wife for Er, his firstborn; her name was Tamar.

7And Er, Judah's firstborn, was wicked in the sight of the Lord, and the Lord slew him.

8Then Judah told Onan, Marry your brother's widow; live with her and raise offspring for your brother.

9But Onan knew that the family would not be his, so when he cohabited with his brother's widow, he prevented conception, lest he should raise up a child for his brother.

10And the thing which he did displeased the Lord; therefore He slew him also.

11Then Judah said to Tamar, his daughter-in-law, Remain a widow at your father's house till Shelah my [youngest] son is grown; for he thought, Lest perhaps [if Shelah should marry her] he would die also, as his brothers did. So Tamar went and lived in her father's house.

12But later Judah's wife, the daughter of Shuah, died; and when Judah was comforted, he went up to his sheepshearers at Timnath with his friend Hirah the Adullamite.

13Then it was told Tamar, Listen, your father-in-law is going up to Timnath to shear his sheep.

---

*y*Heb. *hearkened*   *z*Heb. *eunuch:* But the word doth signify not only *eunuchs,* but also *chamberlains, courtiers,* and *officers*
*a*Heb. *chief of the slaughtermen,* or, *executioners*   *b*Or, *chief marshal*   *c*Heb. *was evil in the eyes of the LORD*   *d*Heb. *the days were multiplied*

New American Standard

27"Come and let us sell him to the Ishmaelites and not lay our hands on him, for he is our brother, our *own* flesh." And his brothers listened *to him.*

28 Then some Midianite traders passed by, so they pulled *him* up and lifted Joseph out of the pit, and sold him to the Ishmaelites for twenty *shekels* of silver. Thus they brought Joseph into Egypt.

29 ¶ Now Reuben returned to the pit, and behold, Joseph was not in the pit; so he tore his garments.

30 He returned to his brothers and said, "The boy is not *there;* as for me, where am I to go?"

31 So they took Joseph's tunic, and slaughtered a male goat and dipped the tunic in the blood;

32 and they sent the varicolored tunic and brought it to their father and said, "We found this; please examine *it* to *see* whether it is your son's tunic or not."

33 Then he examined it and said, "It is my son's tunic. A wild beast has devoured him; Joseph has surely been torn to pieces!"

34 So Jacob tore his clothes, and put sackcloth on his loins and mourned for his son many days.

35 Then all his sons and all his daughters arose to comfort him, but he refused to be comforted. And he said, "Surely I will go down to Sheol in mourning for my son." So his father wept for him.

36 Meanwhile, the Midianites sold him in Egypt to Potiphar, Pharaoh's officer, the captain of the bodyguard.

Judah and Tamar

38 AND IT came about at that time, that Judah departed from his brothers and visited a certain Adullamite, whose name was Hirah.

2 Judah saw there a daughter of a certain Canaanite whose name was Shua; and he took her and went in to her.

3 So she conceived and bore a son and he named him Er.

4 Then she conceived again and bore a son and named him Onan.

5 She bore still another son and named him Shelah; and it was at Chezib that she bore him.

6 ¶ Now Judah took a wife for Er his firstborn, and her name *was* Tamar.

7 But Er, Judah's firstborn, was evil in the sight of the LORD, so the LORD took his life.

8 Then Judah said to Onan, "Go in to your brother's wife, and perform your duty as a brother-in-law to her, and raise up offspring for your brother."

9 Onan knew that the offspring would not be his; so when he went in to his brother's wife, he wasted his seed on the ground in order not to give offspring to his brother.

10 But what he did was displeasing in the sight of the LORD; so He took his life also.

11 Then Judah said to his daughter-in-law Tamar, "Remain a widow in your father's house until my son Shelah grows up"; for he thought, "*I am afraid* that he too may die like his brothers." So Tamar went and lived in her father's house.

12 ¶ Now after a considerable time Shua's daughter, the wife of Judah, died; and when the time of mourning was ended, Judah went up to his sheepshearers at Timnah, he and his friend Hirah the Adullamite.

13 It was told to Tamar, "Behold, your father-in-law is going up to Timnah to shear his sheep."

New International

kill our brother and cover up his blood? 27Come, let's sell him to the Ishmaelites and not lay our hands on him; after all, he is our brother, our own flesh and blood." His brothers agreed.

28So when the Midianite merchants came by, his brothers pulled Joseph up out of the cistern and sold him for twenty shekels^d of silver to the Ishmaelites, who took him to Egypt.

29When Reuben returned to the cistern and saw that Joseph was not there, he tore his clothes. 30He went back to his brothers and said, "The boy isn't there! Where can I turn now?"

31Then they got Joseph's robe, slaughtered a goat and dipped the robe in the blood. 32They took the ornamented robe back to their father and said, "We found this. Examine it to see whether it is your son's robe."

33He recognized it and said, "It is my son's robe! Some ferocious animal has devoured him. Joseph has surely been torn to pieces."

34Then Jacob tore his clothes, put on sackcloth and mourned for his son many days. 35All his sons and daughters came to comfort him, but he refused to be comforted. "No," he said, "in mourning will I go down to the grave^e to my son." So his father wept for him.

36Meanwhile, the Midianites^f sold Joseph in Egypt to Potiphar, one of Pharaoh's officials, the captain of the guard.

Judah and Tamar

38 AT THAT time, Judah left his brothers and went down to stay with a man of Adullam named Hirah.

2There Judah met the daughter of a Canaanite man named Shua. He married her and lay with her; 3she became pregnant and gave birth to a son, who was named Er. 4She conceived again and gave birth to a son and named him Onan. 5She gave birth to still another son and named him Shelah. It was at Kezib that she gave birth to him.

6Judah got a wife for Er, his firstborn, and her name was Tamar. 7But Er, Judah's firstborn, was wicked in the LORD's sight; so the LORD put him to death.

8Then Judah said to Onan, "Lie with your brother's wife and fulfill your duty to her as a brother-in-law to produce offspring for your brother." 9But Onan knew that the offspring would not be his; so whenever he lay with his brother's wife, he spilled his semen on the ground to keep from producing offspring for his brother. 10What he did was wicked in the LORD's sight; so he put him to death also.

11Judah then said to his daughter-in-law Tamar, "Live as a widow in your father's house until my son Shelah grows up." For he thought, "He may die too, just like his brothers." So Tamar went to live in her father's house.

12After a long time Judah's wife, the daughter of Shua, died. When Judah had recovered from his grief, he went up to Timnah, to the men who were shearing his sheep, and his friend Hirah the Adullamite went with him.

13When Tamar was told, "Your father-in-law is on his

---

^{d}28 That is, about 8 ounces (about 0.2 kilogram) ^{e}35 Hebrew *Sheol* ^{f}36 Samaritan Pentateuch, Septuagint, Vulgate and Syriac (see also verse 28); Masoretic Text *Medanites*

King James

¹⁴And she put her widow's garments off from her, and covered her with a veil, and wrapped herself, and sat in ^ean open place, which *is* by the way to Timnath; for she saw that Shelah was grown, and she was not given unto him to wife.

¹⁵When Judah saw her, he thought her *to be* an harlot; because she had covered her face.

¹⁶And he turned unto her by the way, and said, Go to, I pray thee, let me come in unto thee; (for he knew not that she *was* his daughter-in-law.) And she said, What wilt thou give me, that thou mayest come in unto me?

¹⁷And he said, I will send *thee* f a kid from the flock. And she said, Wilt thou give *me* a pledge, till thou send *it?*

¹⁸And he said, What pledge shall I give thee? And she said, Thy signet, and thy bracelets, and thy staff that *is* in thine hand. And he gave *it* her, and came in unto her, and she conceived by him.

¹⁹And she arose, and went away, and laid by her veil from her, and put on the garments of her widowhood.

²⁰And Judah sent the kid by the hand of his friend the Adullamite, to receive *his* pledge from the woman's hand: but he found her not.

²¹Then he asked the men of that place, saying, Where *is* the harlot, that *was* ^gopenly by the way side? And they said, There was no harlot in this *place.*

²²And he returned to Judah, and said, I cannot find her; and also the men of the place said, *that* there was no harlot in this *place.*

²³And Judah said, Let her take *it* to her, lest we ^hbe shamed: behold, I sent this kid, and thou hast not found her.

²⁴ ¶ And it came to pass about three months after, that it was told Judah, saying, Tamar thy daughter-in-law hath played the harlot; and also, behold, she *is* with child by whoredom. And Judah said, Bring her forth, and let her be burnt.

²⁵When she *was* brought forth, she sent to her father-in-law, saying, By the man, whose these *are, am* I with child: and she said, Discern, I pray thee, whose *are* these, the signet, and bracelets, and staff.

²⁶And Judah acknowledged *them,* and said, She hath been more righteous than I; because that I gave her not to Shelah my son. And he knew her again no more.

²⁷ ¶ And it came to pass in the time of her travail, that, behold, twins *were* in her womb.

²⁸And it came to pass, when she travailed, that *the one* put out *his* hand: and the midwife took and bound upon his hand a scarlet thread, saying, This came out first.

²⁹And it came to pass, as he drew back his hand, that, behold, his brother came out: and she said, ⁱHow hast thou broken forth? *this* breach *be* upon thee: therefore his name was called ^jPharez.

³⁰And afterward came out his brother, that had the scarlet thread upon his hand: and his name was called Zerah.

Joseph and Potiphar's wife

39 AND JOSEPH was brought down to Egypt; and Potiphar, an officer of Pharaoh, captain of the guard, an Egyptian, bought him of the hands of the Ishmeelites, which had brought him down thither.

²And the LORD was with Joseph, and he was a prosperous man; and he was in the house of his master the Egyptian.

³And his master saw that the LORD *was* with him, and that the LORD made all that he did to prosper in his hand.

Amplified

¹⁴So she put off her widow's garments and covered herself with a veil, wrapped herself up [in disguise], and sat in the entrance of Enaim, which is by the road to Timnath; for she saw that Shelah was grown and she was not given to him as his wife.

¹⁵When Judah saw her, he thought she was a harlot *or* devoted prostitute [under a vow to her goddess], for she had covered her face [as such women did].

¹⁶He turned to her by the road and said, Come, let me have intercourse with you; for he did not know that she was his daughter-in-law. And she said, What will you give me that you may have intercourse with me?

¹⁷He answered, I will send you a kid from the flock. And she said, Will you give me a pledge (deposit) until you send it?

¹⁸And he said, What pledge shall I give you? She said, Your signet [seal], your [signet] cord, and your staff that is in your hand. And he gave them to her and came in to her, and she became pregnant by him.

¹⁹And she arose and went away and laid aside her veil and put on the garments of her widowhood.

²⁰And Judah sent the kid by the hand of his friend the Adullamite, to receive the pledge from the woman's hand; but he was unable to find her.

²¹He asked the men of that place, Where is the harlot *or* cult prostitute who was openly by the roadside? They said, There was no harlot *or* temple prostitute here.

²²So he returned to Judah and said, I cannot find her; and also the local men said, There was no harlot *or* temple prostitute around here.

²³And Judah said, Let her keep [the pledge articles] for herself, lest we be made ashamed. I sent this kid, but you have not found her.

²⁴But about three months later Judah was told, Tamar your daughter-in-law has played the harlot, and also she is with child by her lewdness. And Judah said, Bring her forth and let her be burned!

²⁵When she was brought forth, she [took the things he had given her in pledge and] sent [them] to her father-in-law, saying, I am with child by the man to whom these articles belong. Then she added, Make out clearly, I pray you, to whom these belong, the signet [seal], [signet] cord, and staff.

²⁶And Judah acknowledged them and said, She has been more righteous *and* just than I, because I did not give her to Shelah my son. And he did not cohabit with her again.

²⁷Now when the time came for her to be delivered, behold, there were twins in her womb.

²⁸And when she was in labor, one baby put out his hand; and the midwife took his hand and bound upon it a scarlet thread, saying, This baby was born first.

²⁹But he drew back his hand, and behold, his brother was born first. And she said, What a breaking forth you have made for yourself! Therefore his name was called Perez [breaking forth]. [Matt. 1:3.]

³⁰And afterward his brother who had the scarlet thread on his hand was born and was named Zerah [scarlet].

39 AND JOSEPH was brought down to Egypt; and Potiphar, an officer of Pharaoh, the captain *and* chief executioner of the [royal] guard, an Egyptian, bought him from the Ishmaelites who had brought him down there.

²But the Lord was with Joseph, and he [though a slave] was a successful *and* prosperous man; and he was in the house of his master the Egyptian.

³And his master saw that the Lord was with him and that the Lord made all that he did to flourish *and* succeed in his hand. [Gen. 21:22; 26:27, 28; 41:38, 39.]

---

^eHeb. *the door of eyes,* or, *of Enajim*   ^fHeb. *a kid of the goats*
^gOr, *in Enajim*   ^hHeb. *become a contempt*   ⁱOr, *Wherefore hast thou made* this *breach against thee?*   ^ji.e. *A breach*

New American Standard

14 So she removed her widow's garments and covered *herself* with a ᵛveil, and wrapped herself, and sat in the gateway of Enaim, which is on the road to Timnah; for she saw that Shelah had grown up, and she had not been given to him as a wife.

15 When Judah saw her, he thought she *was* a harlot, for she had covered her face.

16 So he turned aside to her by the road, and said, "Here now, let me come in to you"; for he did not know that she was his daughter-in-law. And she said, "What will you give me, that you may come in to me?"

17 He said, therefore, "I will send you a young goat from the flock." She said, moreover, "Will you give a pledge until you send *it?*"

18 He said, "What pledge shall I give you?" And she said, "Your seal and your cord, and your staff that is in your hand." So he gave *them* to her and went in to her, and she conceived by him.

19 Then she arose and departed, and removed her veil and put on her widow's garments.

20 ¶ When Judah sent the young goat by his friend the Adullamite, to receive the pledge from the woman's hand, he did not find her.

21 He asked the men of her place, saying, "Where is the temple prostitute who was by the road at Enaim?" But they said, "There has been no temple prostitute here."

22 So he returned to Judah, and said, "I did not find her; and furthermore, the men of the place said, 'There has been no temple prostitute here.' "

23 Then Judah said, "Let her keep them, otherwise we will become a laughingstock. After all, I sent this young goat, but you did not find her."

24 ¶ Now it was about three months later that Judah was informed, "Your daughter-in-law Tamar has played the harlot, and behold, she is also with child by harlotry." Then Judah said, "Bring her out and let her be burned!"

25 It was while she was being brought out that she sent to her father-in-law, saying, "I am with child by the man to whom these things belong." And she said, "Please examine and see, whose signet ring and cords and staff are these?"

26 Judah recognized *them,* and said, "She is more righteous than I, inasmuch as I did not give her to my son Shelah." And he did not have relations with her again.

27 ¶ It came about at the time she was giving birth, that behold, there were twins in her womb.

28 Moreover, it took place while she was giving birth, one put out a hand, and the midwife took and tied a scarlet *thread* on his hand, saying, "This one came out first."

29 But it came about as he drew back his hand, that behold, his brother came out. Then she said, "What a breach you have made for yourself!" So he was named ᵂPerez.

30 Afterward his brother came out who had the scarlet *thread* on his hand; and he was named ˣZerah.

Joseph's Success in Egypt

39 NOW JOSEPH had been taken down to Egypt; and Potiphar, an Egyptian officer of Pharaoh, the captain of the bodyguard, bought him from the Ishmaelites, who had taken him down there.

2 The LORD was with Joseph, so he became a successful man. And he was in the house of his master, the Egyptian.

3 Now his master saw that the LORD was with him and *how* the LORD caused all that he did to prosper in his hand.

New International

way to Timnah to shear his sheep," 14she took off her widow's clothes, covered herself with a veil to disguise herself, and then sat down at the entrance to Enaim, which is on the road to Timnah. For she saw that, though Shelah had now grown up, she had not been given to him as his wife.

15When Judah saw her, he thought she was a prostitute, for she had covered her face. 16Not realizing that she was his daughter-in-law, he went over to her by the roadside and said, "Come now, let me sleep with you."

"And what will you give me to sleep with you?" she asked.

17"I'll send you a young goat from my flock," he said.

"Will you give me something as a pledge until you send it?" she asked.

18He said, "What pledge should I give you?"

"Your seal and its cord, and the staff in your hand," she answered. So he gave them to her and slept with her, and she became pregnant by him. 19After she left, she took off her veil and put on her widow's clothes again.

20Meanwhile Judah sent the young goat by his friend the Adullamite in order to get his pledge back from the woman, but he did not find her. 21He asked the men who lived there, "Where is the shrine prostitute who was beside the road at Enaim?"

"There hasn't been any shrine prostitute here," they said.

22So he went back to Judah and said, "I didn't find her. Besides, the men who lived there said, 'There hasn't been any shrine prostitute here.' "

23Then Judah said, "Let her keep what she has, or we will become a laughingstock. After all, I did send her this young goat, but you didn't find her."

24About three months later Judah was told, "Your daughter-in-law Tamar is guilty of prostitution, and as a result she is now pregnant."

Judah said, "Bring her out and have her burned to death!"

25As she was being brought out, she sent a message to her father-in-law. "I am pregnant by the man who owns these," she said. And she added, "See if you recognize whose seal and cord and staff these are."

26Judah recognized them and said, "She is more righteous than I, since I wouldn't give her to my son Shelah." And he did not sleep with her again.

27When the time came for her to give birth, there were twin boys in her womb. 28As she was giving birth, one of them put out his hand; so the midwife took a scarlet thread and tied it on his wrist and said, "This one came out first." 29But when he drew back his hand, his brother came out, and she said, "So this is how you have broken out!" And he was named Perez.ᵍ 30Then his brother, who had the scarlet thread on his wrist, came out and he was given the name Zerah.ʰ

Joseph and Potiphar's Wife

39 NOW JOSEPH had been taken down to Egypt. Potiphar, an Egyptian who was one of Pharaoh's officials, the captain of the guard, bought him from the Ishmaelites who had taken him there.

2The LORD was with Joseph and he prospered, and he lived in the house of his Egyptian master. 3When his master saw that the LORD was with him and that the LORD gave

---

ᵛOr *shawl*   ᵂI.e. a breach   ˣI.e. a dawning or brightness

ᵍ29 *Perez* means *breaking out.*   ʰ30 *Zerah* can mean *scarlet* or *brightness.*

King James

⁴And Joseph found grace in his sight, and he served him: and he made him overseer over his house, and all *that* he had he put into his hand.

⁵And it came to pass from the time *that* he had made him overseer in his house, and over all that he had, that the LORD blessed the Egyptian's house for Joseph's sake; and the blessing of the LORD was upon all that he had in the house, and in the field.

⁶And he left all that he had in Joseph's hand; and he knew not aught he had, save the bread which he did eat. And Joseph was *a* goodly *person,* and wellfavoured.

⁷ ¶ And it came to pass after these things, that his master's wife cast her eyes upon Joseph; and she said, Lie with me.

⁸But he refused, and said unto his master's wife, Behold, my master wotteth not what *is* with me in the house, and he hath committed all that he hath to my hand;

⁹*There is* none greater in this house than I; neither hath he kept back any thing from me but thee, because thou *art* his wife: how then can I do this great wickedness, and sin against God?

¹⁰And it came to pass, as she spake to Joseph day by day, that he hearkened not unto her, to lie by her, *or* to be with her.

¹¹And it came to pass about this time, that *Joseph* went into the house to do his business; and *there was* none of the men of the house there within.

¹²And she caught him by his garment, saying, Lie with me: and he left his garment in her hand, and fled, and got him out.

¹³And it came to pass, when she saw that he had left his garment in her hand, and was fled forth,

¹⁴That she called unto the men of her house, and spake unto them, saying, See, he hath brought in an Hebrew unto us to mock us; he came in unto me to lie with me, and I cried with a ^kloud voice:

¹⁵And it came to pass, when he heard that I lifted up my voice and cried, that he left his garment with me, and fled, and got him out.

¹⁶And she laid up his garment by her, until his lord came home.

¹⁷And she spake unto him according to these words, saying, The Hebrew servant, which thou hast brought unto us, came in unto me to mock me:

¹⁸And it came to pass, as I lifted up my voice and cried, that he left his garment with me, and fled out.

¹⁹And it came to pass, when his master heard the words of his wife, which she spake unto him, saying, After this manner did thy servant to me; that his wrath was kindled.

²⁰And Joseph's master took him, and put him into the prison, a place where the king's prisoners *were* bound: and he was there in the prison.

²¹ ¶ But the LORD was with Joseph, and ^lshowed him mercy, and gave him favour in the sight of the keeper of the prison.

²²And the keeper of the prison committed to Joseph's hand all the prisoners that *were* in the prison; and whatsoever they did there, he was the doer *of it.*

²³The keeper of the prison looked not to any thing *that was* under his hand; because the LORD was with him, and *that* which he did, the LORD made *it* to prosper.

Amplified

⁴So Joseph pleased [Potiphar] *and* found favor in his sight, and he served him. And [his master] made him supervisor over his house and he put all that he had in his charge.

⁵From the time that he made him supervisor in his house and over all that he had, the Lord blessed the Egyptian's house for Joseph's sake; and the Lord's blessing was on all that he had in the house and in the field.

⁶And [Potiphar] left all that he had in Joseph's charge and paid no attention to anything he had except the food he ate. Now Joseph was an attractive person and fine-looking.

⁷Then after a time his master's wife cast her eyes upon Joseph, and she said, Lie with me.

⁸But he refused and said to his master's wife, See here, with me in the house my master has concern about nothing; he has put all that he has in my care.

⁹He is not greater in this house than I am; nor has he kept anything from me except you, for you are his wife. How then can I do this great evil and sin against God?

¹⁰She spoke to Joseph day after day, but he did not listen to her, to lie with her or to be with her.

¹¹Then it happened about this time that Joseph went into the house to attend to his duties, and none of the men of the house were indoors.

¹²And she caught him by his garment, saying, Lie with me! But he left his garment in her hand and fled and got out [of the house].

¹³And when she saw that he had left his garment in her hand and had fled away,

¹⁴She called to the men of her household and said to them, Behold, he [your master] has brought in a Hebrew to us to mock *and* insult us; he came in where I was to lie with me, and I screamed at the top of my voice.

¹⁵And when he heard me screaming and crying, he left his garment with me and fled and got out of the house.

¹⁶And she laid up his garment by her until his master came home.

¹⁷Then she told him the same story, saying, The Hebrew servant whom you brought among us came to me to mock *and* insult me.

¹⁸And when I screamed and cried, he left his garment with me and fled out [of the house].

¹⁹And when [Joseph's] master heard the words of his wife, saying to him, This is the way your servant treated me, his wrath was kindled.

²⁰And Joseph's master took him and put him in the prison, a place where the state prisoners were confined; so he was there in the prison.

²¹But the Lord was with Joseph, and showed him mercy *and* loving-kindness and gave him favor in the sight of the warden of the prison.

²²And the warden of the prison committed to Joseph's care all the prisoners who were in the prison; and whatsoever was done there, he was in charge of it.

²³The prison warden paid no attention to anything that was in [Joseph's] charge, for the Lord was with him and made whatever he did to prosper.

Joseph interprets dreams

40 AND IT came to pass after these things, *that* the butler of the king of Egypt and *his* baker had offended their lord the king of Egypt.

²And Pharaoh was wroth against two *of* his officers, against the chief of the butlers, and against the chief of the bakers.

40 NOW SOME time later the butler and the baker of the king of Egypt offended their lord, Egypt's king.

²And Pharaoh was angry with his officers, the chief of the butlers and the chief of the bakers.

---

^kHeb. *great*   ^lHeb. *extended kindness unto him*

New American Standard

4 So Joseph found favor in his sight and became his personal servant; and he made him overseer over his house, and all that he owned he put in his charge.

5 It came about that from the time he made him overseer in his house and over all that he owned, the LORD blessed the Egyptian's house on account of Joseph; thus the LORD's blessing was upon all that he owned, in the house and in the field.

6 So he left everything he owned in Joseph's charge; and with him *there* he did not concern himself with anything except the food which he ate.

¶ Now Joseph was handsome in form and appearance.

7 It came about after these events that his master's wife looked with desire at Joseph, and she said, "Lie with me."

8 But he refused and said to his master's wife, "Behold, with me *here*, my master does not concern himself with anything in the house, and he has put all that he owns in my charge.

9 "There is no one greater in this house than I, and he has withheld nothing from me except you, because you are his wife. How then could I do this great evil and sin against God?"

10 As she spoke to Joseph day after day, he did not listen to her to lie beside her *or* be with her.

11 Now it happened one day that he went into the house to do his work, and none of the men of the household was there inside.

12 She caught him by his garment, saying, "Lie with me!" And he left his garment in her hand and fled, and went outside.

13 When she saw that he had left his garment in her hand and had fled outside,

14 she called to the men of her household and said to them, "See, he has brought in a Hebrew to us to make sport of us; he came in to me to lie with me, and I screamed.

15 "When he heard that I raised my voice and yscreamed, he left his garment beside me and fled and went outside."

16 So she left his garment beside her until his master came home.

17 Then she spoke to him with these words, "The Hebrew slave, whom you brought to us, came in to me to make sport of me;

18 and as I raised my voice and screamed, he left his garment beside me and fled outside."

Joseph Imprisoned

19 ¶ Now when his master heard the words of his wife, which she spoke to him, saying, "This is what your slave did to me," his anger burned.

20 So Joseph's master took him and put him into the jail, the place where the king's prisoners were confined; and he was there in the jail.

21 But the LORD was with Joseph and extended kindness to him, and gave him favor in the sight of the chief jailer.

22 The chief jailer committed to Joseph's charge all the prisoners who were in the jail; so that whatever was done there, he was responsible *for it.*

23 The chief jailer did not supervise anything under Joseph's charge because the LORD was with him; and whatever he did, the LORD made to prosper.

Joseph Interprets a Dream

40 THEN IT came about after these things, the cupbearer and the baker for the king of Egypt offended their lord, the king of Egypt.

2 Pharaoh was furious with his two officials, the chief cupbearer and the chief baker.

New International

him success in everything he did, 4Joseph found favor in his eyes and became his attendant. Potiphar put him in charge of his household, and he entrusted to his care everything he owned. 5From the time he put him in charge of his household and of all that he owned, the LORD blessed the household of the Egyptian because of Joseph. The blessing of the LORD was on everything Potiphar had, both in the house and in the field. 6So he left in Joseph's care everything he had; with Joseph in charge, he did not concern himself with anything except the food he ate.

Now Joseph was well-built and handsome, 7and after a while his master's wife took notice of Joseph and said, "Come to bed with me!"

8But he refused. "With me in charge," he told her, "my master does not concern himself with anything in the house; everything he owns he has entrusted to my care. 9No one is greater in this house than I am. My master has withheld nothing from me except you, because you are his wife. How then could I do such a wicked thing and sin against God?" 10And though she spoke to Joseph day after day, he refused to go to bed with her or even be with her.

11One day he went into the house to attend to his duties, and none of the household servants was inside. 12She caught him by his cloak and said, "Come to bed with me!" But he left his cloak in her hand and ran out of the house.

13When she saw that he had left his cloak in her hand and had run out of the house, 14she called her household servants. "Look," she said to them, "this Hebrew has been brought to us to make sport of us! He came in here to sleep with me, but I screamed. 15When he heard me scream for help, he left his cloak beside me and ran out of the house."

16She kept his cloak beside her until his master came home. 17Then she told him this story: "That Hebrew slave you brought us came to me to make sport of me. 18But as soon as I screamed for help, he left his cloak beside me and ran out of the house."

19When his master heard the story his wife told him, saying, "This is how your slave treated me," he burned with anger. 20Joseph's master took him and put him in prison, the place where the king's prisoners were confined.

But while Joseph was there in the prison, 21the LORD was with him; he showed him kindness and granted him favor in the eyes of the prison warden. 22So the warden put Joseph in charge of all those held in the prison, and he was made responsible for all that was done there. 23The warden paid no attention to anything under Joseph's care, because the LORD was with Joseph and gave him success in whatever he did.

The Cupbearer and the Baker

40 SOME TIME later, the cupbearer and the baker of the king of Egypt offended their master, the king of Egypt. 2Pharaoh was angry with his two officials, the chief cupbearer and the chief baker, 3and put them in custody in

y Lit *called out*

King James

Amplified

³And he put them in ward in the house of the captain of the guard, into the prison, the place where Joseph *was* bound.

⁴And the captain of the guard charged Joseph with them, and he served them: and they continued a season in ward.

⁵ ¶ And they dreamed a dream both of them, each man his dream in one night, each man according to the interpretation of his dream, the butler and the baker of the king of Egypt, which *were* bound in the prison.

⁶And Joseph came in unto them in the morning, and looked upon them, and, behold, they *were* sad.

⁷And he asked Pharaoh's officers that *were* with him in the ward of his lord's house, saying, Wherefore ^mlook ye *so* sadly today?

⁸And they said unto him, We have dreamed a dream, and *there is* no interpreter of it. And Joseph said unto them, *Do* not interpretations *belong* to God? tell me *them*, I pray you.

⁹And the chief butler told his dream to Joseph, and said to him, In my dream, behold, a vine *was* before me;

¹⁰And in the vine *were* three branches: and it *was* as though it budded, *and* her blossoms shot forth; and the clusters thereof brought forth ripe grapes:

¹¹And Pharaoh's cup *was* in my hand: and I took the grapes, and pressed them into Pharaoh's cup, and I gave the cup into Pharaoh's hand.

¹²And Joseph said unto him, This *is* the interpretation of it: The three branches *are* three days:

¹³Yet within three days shall Pharaoh ⁿlift up thine head, and restore thee unto thy place: and thou shalt deliver Pharaoh's cup into his hand, after the former manner when thou wast his butler.

¹⁴But ^othink on me when it shall be well with thee, and show kindness, I pray thee, unto me, and make mention of me unto Pharaoh, and bring me out of this house:

¹⁵For indeed I was stolen away out of the land of the Hebrews: and here also have I done nothing that they should put me into the dungeon.

¹⁶When the chief baker saw that the interpretation was good, he said unto Joseph, I also *was* in my dream, and, behold, *I had* three white baskets on my head:

¹⁷And in the uppermost basket *there was* of all manner of ^pbakemeats for Pharaoh; and the birds did eat them out of the basket upon my head.

¹⁸And Joseph answered and said, This *is* the interpretation thereof: The three baskets *are* three days:

¹⁹Yet within three days shall Pharaoh ^qlift up thy head from off thee, and shall hang thee on a tree; and the birds shall eat thy flesh from off thee.

²⁰ ¶ And it came to pass the third day, *which was* Pharaoh's birthday, that he made a feast unto all his servants: and he ^rlifted up the head of the chief butler and of the chief baker among his servants.

²¹And he restored the chief butler unto his butlership again; and he gave the cup into Pharaoh's hand:

²²But he hanged the chief baker: as Joseph had interpreted to them.

²³Yet did not the chief butler remember Joseph, but forgat him.

³He put them in custody in the house of the captain of the guard, in the prison where Joseph was confined.

⁴And the captain of the guard put them in Joseph's charge, and he served them; and they continued in custody for some time.

⁵And they both dreamed a dream in the same night, each man according to [the personal significance of] the interpretation of his dream—the butler and the baker of the king of Egypt, who were confined in the prison.

⁶When Joseph came to them in the morning and looked at them, he saw that they were sad *and* depressed.

⁷So he asked Pharaoh's officers who were in custody with him in his master's house, Why do you look so dejected *and* sad today?

⁸And they said to him, We have dreamed dreams, and there is no one to interpret them. And Joseph said to them, Do not interpretations belong to God? Tell me [your dreams], I pray you.

⁹And the chief butler told his dream to Joseph and said to him, In my dream I saw a vine before me,

¹⁰And on the vine were three branches. Then it was as though it budded; its blossoms burst forth and the clusters of them brought forth ripe grapes [almost all at once].

¹¹And Pharaoh's cup was in my hand, and I took the grapes and pressed them into Pharaoh's cup; then I gave the cup into Pharaoh's hand.

¹²And Joseph said to him, This is the interpretation of it: The three branches are three days.

¹³Within three days Pharaoh will lift up your head and restore you to your position, and you will again put Pharaoh's cup into his hand, as when you were his butler.

¹⁴But think of me when it shall be well with you and show kindness, I beg of you, to me, and mention me to Pharaoh and get me out of this house.

¹⁵For truly I was carried away from the land of the Hebrews by unlawful force, and here too I have done nothing for which they should put me into the dungeon.

¹⁶When the chief baker saw that the interpretation was good, he said to Joseph, I also dreamed, and behold, I had three cake baskets on my head.

¹⁷And in the uppermost basket were some of all kinds of baked food for Pharaoh, but the birds [of prey] were eating out of the basket on my head.

¹⁸And Joseph answered, This is the interpretation of it: The three baskets are three days.

¹⁹Within three days Pharaoh will lift up your head but will have you beheaded and hung on a tree, and [you will not so much as be given burial, but] the birds will eat your flesh.

²⁰And on the third day, Pharaoh's birthday, he made a feast for all his servants; and he lifted up the heads of the chief butler and the chief baker [by inviting them also] among his servants.

²¹And he restored the chief butler to his butlership, and the butler gave the cup into Pharaoh's hand;

²²But [Pharaoh] hanged the chief baker, as Joseph had interpreted to them.

²³But [even after all that] the chief butler gave no thought to Joseph, but forgot [all about] him.

Pharaoh's dreams

41 AND IT came to pass at the end of two full years, that Pharaoh dreamed: and, behold, he stood by the river.

²And, behold, there came up out of the river seven well-favoured kine and fatfleshed; and they fed in a meadow.

41 AFTER TWO full years, Pharaoh dreamed that he stood by the river [Nile].

²And behold, there came up out of the river [Nile] seven well-favored cows, sleek *and* handsome and fat; and they grazed in the reed grass [in a marshy pasture].

---

^mHeb. are *your faces evil?*   ⁿOr, *reckon*   ^oHeb. *remember me with thee*   ^pHeb. *meat of Pharaoh, the work of a baker,* or, *cook*   ^qOr, *reckon thee,* and take thy office *from thee*   ^rOr, *reckoned*

New American Standard

3 So he put them in confinement in the house of the captain of the bodyguard, in the jail, the *same* place where Joseph was imprisoned.

4 The captain of the bodyguard put Joseph in charge of them, and he took care of them; and they were in confinement for some time.

5 Then the cupbearer and the baker for the king of Egypt, who were confined in jail, both had a dream the same night, each man with his *own* dream *and* each dream with its *own* interpretation.

6 When Joseph came to them in the morning and observed them, behold, they were dejected.

7 He asked Pharaoh's officials who were with him in confinement in his master's house, "Why are your faces so sad today?"

8 Then they said to him, "We have had a dream and there is no one to interpret it." Then Joseph said to them, "Do not interpretations belong to God? Tell *it* to me, please."

9 ¶ So the chief cupbearer told his dream to Joseph, and said to him, "In my dream, behold, *there was* a vine in front of me;

10 and on the vine *were* three branches. And as it was budding, its blossoms came out, *and* its clusters produced ripe grapes.

11 "Now Pharaoh's cup was in my hand; so I took the grapes and squeezed them into Pharaoh's cup, and I put the cup into Pharaoh's hand."

12 Then Joseph said to him, "This is the interpretation of it: the three branches are three days;

13 within three more days Pharaoh will [z]lift up your head and restore you to your office; and you will put Pharaoh's cup into his hand according to your former custom when you were his cupbearer.

14 "Only keep me in mind when it goes well with you, and please do me a kindness by mentioning me to Pharaoh and get me out of this house.

15 "For I was in fact kidnapped from the land of the Hebrews, and even here I have done nothing that they should have put me into the dungeon."

16 ¶ When the chief baker saw that he had interpreted favorably, he said to Joseph, "I also *saw* in my dream, and behold, *there were* three baskets of white bread on my head;

17 and in the top basket *there were* some of all sorts of baked food for Pharaoh, and the birds were eating them out of the basket on my head."

18 Then Joseph answered and said, "This is its interpretation: the three baskets are three days;

19 within three more days Pharaoh will lift up your head from you and will hang you on a tree, and the birds will eat your flesh off you."

20 ¶ Thus it came about on the third day, *which was* Pharaoh's birthday, that he made a feast for all his servants; and he lifted up the head of the chief cupbearer and the head of the chief baker among his servants.

21 He restored the chief cupbearer to his office, and he put the cup into Pharaoh's hand;

22 but he hanged the chief baker, just as Joseph had interpreted to them.

23 Yet the chief cupbearer did not remember Joseph, but forgot him.

Pharaoh's Dream

41 NOW IT happened at the end of two full years that Pharaoh had a dream, and behold, he was standing by the Nile.

2 And lo, from the Nile there came up seven cows, sleek and fat; and they grazed in the marsh grass.

New International

the house of the captain of the guard, in the same prison where Joseph was confined. [4]The captain of the guard assigned them to Joseph, and he attended them.

After they had been in custody for some time, [5]each of the two men—the cupbearer and the baker of the king of Egypt, who were being held in prison—had a dream the same night, and each dream had a meaning of its own.

[6]When Joseph came to them the next morning, he saw that they were dejected. [7]So he asked Pharaoh's officials who were in custody with him in his master's house, "Why are your faces so sad today?"

[8]"We both had dreams," they answered, "but there is no one to interpret them."

Then Joseph said to them, "Do not interpretations belong to God? Tell me your dreams."

[9]So the chief cupbearer told Joseph his dream. He said to him, "In my dream I saw a vine in front of me, [10]and on the vine were three branches. As soon as it budded, it blossomed, and its clusters ripened into grapes. [11]Pharaoh's cup was in my hand, and I took the grapes, squeezed them into Pharaoh's cup and put the cup in his hand."

[12]"This is what it means," Joseph said to him. "The three branches are three days. [13]Within three days Pharaoh will lift up your head and restore you to your position, and you will put Pharaoh's cup in his hand, just as you used to do when you were his cupbearer. [14]But when all goes well with you, remember me and show me kindness; mention me to Pharaoh and get me out of this prison. [15]For I was forcibly carried off from the land of the Hebrews, and even here I have done nothing to deserve being put in a dungeon."

[16]When the chief baker saw that Joseph had given a favorable interpretation, he said to Joseph, "I too had a dream: On my head were three baskets of bread.[i] [17]In the top basket were all kinds of baked goods for Pharaoh, but the birds were eating them out of the basket on my head."

[18]"This is what it means," Joseph said. "The three baskets are three days. [19]Within three days Pharaoh will lift off your head and hang you on a tree.[j] And the birds will eat away your flesh."

[20]Now the third day was Pharaoh's birthday, and he gave a feast for all his officials. He lifted up the heads of the chief cupbearer and the chief baker in the presence of his officials: [21]He restored the chief cupbearer to his position, so that he once again put the cup into Pharaoh's hand, [22]but he hanged[k] the chief baker, just as Joseph had said to them in his interpretation.

[23]The chief cupbearer, however, did not remember Joseph; he forgot him.

Pharaoh's Dreams

41 WHEN TWO full years had passed, Pharaoh had a dream: He was standing by the Nile, [2]when out of the river there came up seven cows, sleek and fat, and they grazed among the reeds. [3]After them, seven other cows,

---

[z]Or possibly forgive you

[i]16 Or three wicker baskets   *[j]19 Or and impale you on a pole*
[k]22 Or impaled

King James

³And, behold, seven other kine came up after them out of the river, ill favoured and leanfleshed; and stood by the *other* kine upon the brink of the river.

⁴And the ill favoured and leanfleshed kine did eat up the seven wellfavoured and fat kine. So Pharaoh awoke.

⁵And he slept and dreamed the second time: and, behold, seven ears of corn came up upon one stalk, ^srank and good.

⁶And, behold, seven thin ears and blasted with the east wind sprung up after them.

⁷And the seven thin ears devoured the seven rank and full ears. And Pharaoh awoke, and, behold, *it was* a dream.

⁸And it came to pass in the morning that his spirit was troubled; and he sent and called for all the magicians of Egypt, and all the wise men thereof: and Pharaoh told them his dream; but *there was* none that could interpret them unto Pharaoh.

⁹ ¶ Then spake the chief butler unto Pharaoh, saying, I do remember my faults this day:

¹⁰Pharaoh was wroth with his servants, and put me in ward in the captain of the guard's house, *both* me and the chief baker:

¹¹And we dreamed a dream in one night, I and he; we dreamed each man according to the interpretation of his dream.

¹²And *there was* there with us a young man, an Hebrew, servant to the captain of the guard; and we told him, and he interpreted to us our dreams; to each man according to his dream he did interpret.

¹³And it came to pass, as he interpreted to us, so it was; me he restored unto mine office, and him he hanged.

¹⁴ ¶ Then Pharaoh sent and called Joseph, and they ^tbrought him hastily out of the dungeon: and he shaved *himself,* and changed his raiment, and came in unto Pharaoh.

¹⁵And Pharaoh said unto Joseph, I have dreamed a dream, and *there is* none that can interpret it: and I have heard say of thee, *that* ^uthou canst understand a dream to interpret it.

¹⁶And Joseph answered Pharaoh, saying, *It is* not in me: God shall give Pharaoh an answer of peace.

¹⁷And Pharaoh said unto Joseph, In my dream, behold, I stood upon the bank of the river:

¹⁸And, behold, there came up out of the river seven kine, fatfleshed and wellfavoured; and they fed in a meadow:

¹⁹And, behold, seven other kine came up after them, poor and very ill favoured and leanfleshed, such as I never saw in all the land of Egypt for badness:

²⁰And the lean and the ill favoured kine did eat up the first seven fat kine:

²¹And when they had ^veaten them up, it could not be known that they had eaten them; but they *were* still ill favoured, as at the beginning. So I awoke.

²²And I saw in my dream, and, behold, seven ears came up in one stalk, full and good:

²³And, behold, seven ears, ^wwithered, thin, *and* blasted with the east wind, sprung up after them:

²⁴And the thin ears devoured the seven good ears: and I told *this* unto the magicians; but *there was* none that could declare *it* to me.

²⁵ ¶ And Joseph said unto Pharaoh, The dream of Pharaoh *is* one: God hath shown Pharaoh what he *is* about to do.

²⁶The seven good kine *are* seven years; and the seven good ears *are* seven years: the dream *is* one.

²⁷And the seven thin and ill favoured kine that came up after them *are* seven years; and the seven empty ears blasted with the east wind shall be seven years of famine.

²⁸This *is* the thing which I have spoken unto Pharaoh: What God *is* about to do he showeth unto Pharaoh.

Amplified

³And behold, seven other cows came up after them out of the river [Nile], ill favored and gaunt *and* ugly, and stood by the fat cows on the bank of the river [Nile].

⁴And the ill-favored, gaunt, *and* ugly cows ate up the seven well-favored *and* fat cows. Then Pharaoh awoke.

⁵But he slept and dreamed the second time; and behold, seven ears of grain came out on one stalk, plump and good.

⁶And behold, after them seven ears [of grain] sprouted, thin *and* blighted by the east wind.

⁷And the seven thin ears [of grain] devoured the seven plump and full ears. And Pharaoh awoke, and behold, it was a dream.

⁸So when morning came his spirit was troubled, and he sent and called for all the magicians and all the wise men of Egypt. And Pharaoh told them his dreams, but not one could interpret them to [him].

⁹Then the chief butler said to Pharaoh, I remember my faults today.

¹⁰When Pharaoh was angry with his servants and put me in custody in the captain of the guard's house, both me and the chief baker,

¹¹We dreamed a dream in the same night, he and I; we dreamed each of us according to [the significance of] the interpretation of his dream.

¹²And there was there with us a young man, a Hebrew, servant to the captain of the guard *and* chief executioner; and we told him our dreams, and he interpreted them to us, to each man according to the significance of his dream.

¹³And as he interpreted to us, so it came to pass; I was restored to my office [as chief butler], and the baker was hanged.

¹⁴Then Pharaoh sent and called Joseph, and they brought him hastily out of the dungeon. But Joseph [first] shaved himself, changed his clothes, *and* made himself presentable; then he came into Pharaoh's presence.

¹⁵And Pharaoh said to Joseph, I have dreamed a dream, and there is no one who can interpret it; and I have heard it said of you that you can understand a dream *and* interpret it.

¹⁶Joseph answered Pharaoh, It is not in me; God [not I] will give Pharaoh a [favorable] answer of peace.

¹⁷And Pharaoh said to Joseph, In my dream, behold, I stood on the bank of the river [Nile];

¹⁸And behold, there came up out of the river [Nile] seven fat, sleek, *and* handsome cows, and they grazed in the reed grass [of a marshy pasture].

¹⁹And behold, seven other cows came up after them, undernourished, gaunt, *and* ugly [just skin and bones; such emaciated animals] as I have never seen in all of Egypt.

²⁰And the lean and ill favored cows ate up the seven fat cows that had come first.

²¹And when they had eaten them up, it could not be detected *and* known that they had eaten them, for they were still as thin *and* emaciated as at the beginning. Then I awoke. [But again I fell asleep and dreamed.]

²²And I saw in my dream, and behold, seven ears [of grain] growing on one stalk, plump and good.

²³And behold, seven [other] ears, withered, thin, and blighted by the east wind, sprouted after them.

²⁴And the thin ears devoured the seven good ears. Now I told this to the magicians, but there was no one who could tell me what it meant.

²⁵Then Joseph said to Pharaoh, The [two] dreams are one; God has shown Pharaoh what He is about to do.

²⁶The seven good cows are seven years, and the seven good ears [of grain] are seven years; the [two] dreams are one [in their meaning].

²⁷And the seven thin and ill favored cows that came up after them are seven years, and also the seven empty ears [of grain], blighted *and* shriveled by the east wind; they are seven years of hunger *and* famine.

²⁸This is the message just as I have told Pharaoh: God has shown Pharaoh what He is about to do.

---

^sHeb. *fat*   ^tHeb. *made him run*   ^uOr, when *thou hearest a dream thou canst interpret it*   ^vHeb. *come to the inward parts of them*   ^wOr, *small*

New American Standard

3 Then behold, seven other cows came up after them from the Nile, ugly and gaunt, and they stood by the *other* cows on the bank of the Nile.

4 The ugly and gaunt cows ate up the seven sleek and fat cows. Then Pharaoh awoke.

5 He fell asleep and dreamed a second time; and behold, seven ears of grain came up on a single stalk, plump and good.

6 Then behold, seven ears, thin and scorched by the east wind, sprouted up after them.

7 The thin ears swallowed up the seven plump and full ears. Then Pharaoh awoke, and behold, *it was* a dream.

8 Now in the morning his spirit was troubled, so he sent and called for all the magicians of Egypt, and all its wise men. And Pharaoh told them his dreams, but there was no one who could interpret them to Pharaoh.

9 ¶ Then the chief cupbearer spoke to Pharaoh, saying, "I would make mention today of my *own* offenses.

10 "Pharaoh was furious with his servants, and he put me in confinement in the house of the captain of the bodyguard, *both* me and the chief baker.

11 "We had a dream on the same night, he and I; each of us dreamed according to the interpretation of his *own* dream.

12 "Now a Hebrew youth *was* with us there, a servant of the captain of the bodyguard, and we related *them* to him, and he interpreted our dreams for us. To each one he interpreted according to his *own* dream.

13 "And just as he interpreted for us, so it happened; he restored me in my office, but he hanged him."

Joseph Interprets

14 ¶ Then Pharaoh sent and called for Joseph, and they hurriedly brought him out of the dungeon; and when he had shaved himself and changed his clothes, he came to Pharaoh.

15 Pharaoh said to Joseph, "I have had a dream, but no one can interpret it; and I have heard it said about you, that when you hear a dream you can interpret it."

16 Joseph then answered Pharaoh, saying, "It is not in me; God will give Pharaoh a favorable answer."

17 So Pharaoh spoke to Joseph, "In my dream, behold, I was standing on the bank of the Nile;

18 and behold, seven cows, fat and sleek came up out of the Nile, and they grazed in the marsh grass.

19 "Lo, seven other cows came up after them, poor and very ugly and gaunt, such as I had never seen for ugliness in all the land of Egypt;

20 and the lean and ugly cows ate up the first seven fat cows.

21 "Yet when they had devoured them, it could not be detected that they had devoured them, for they were just as ugly as before. Then I awoke.

22 "I saw also in my dream, and behold, seven ears, full and good, came up on a single stalk;

23 and lo, seven ears, withered, thin, *and* scorched by the east wind, sprouted up after them;

24 and the thin ears swallowed the seven good ears. Then I told it to the magicians, but there was no one who could explain it to me."

25 ¶ Now Joseph said to Pharaoh, "Pharaoh's dreams are one *and the same;* God has told to Pharaoh what He is about to do.

26 "The seven good cows are seven years; and the seven good ears are seven years; the dreams are one *and the same.*

27 "The seven lean and ugly cows that came up after them are seven years, and the seven thin ears scorched by the east wind will be seven years of famine.

28 "It is as I have spoken to Pharaoh: God has shown to Pharaoh what He is about to do.

New International

ugly and gaunt, came up out of the Nile and stood beside those on the riverbank. 4And the cows that were ugly and gaunt ate up the seven sleek, fat cows. Then Pharaoh woke up.

5He fell asleep again and had a second dream: Seven heads of grain, healthy and good, were growing on a single stalk. 6After them, seven other heads of grain sprouted—thin and scorched by the east wind. 7The thin heads of grain swallowed up the seven healthy, full heads. Then Pharaoh woke up; it had been a dream.

8In the morning his mind was troubled, so he sent for all the magicians and wise men of Egypt. Pharaoh told them his dreams, but no one could interpret them for him.

9Then the chief cupbearer said to Pharaoh, "Today I am reminded of my shortcomings. 10Pharaoh was once angry with his servants, and he imprisoned me and the chief baker in the house of the captain of the guard. 11Each of us had a dream the same night, and each dream had a meaning of its own. 12Now a young Hebrew was there with us, a servant of the captain of the guard. We told him our dreams, and he interpreted them for us, giving each man the interpretation of his dream. 13And things turned out exactly as he interpreted them to us: I was restored to my position, and the other man was hanged.*l*"

14So Pharaoh sent for Joseph, and he was quickly brought from the dungeon. When he had shaved and changed his clothes, he came before Pharaoh.

15Pharaoh said to Joseph, "I had a dream, and no one can interpret it. But I have heard it said of you that when you hear a dream you can interpret it."

16"I cannot do it," Joseph replied to Pharaoh, "but God will give Pharaoh the answer he desires."

17Then Pharaoh said to Joseph, "In my dream I was standing on the bank of the Nile, 18when out of the river there came up seven cows, fat and sleek, and they grazed among the reeds. 19After them, seven other cows came up—scrawny and very ugly and lean. I had never seen such ugly cows in all the land of Egypt. 20The lean, ugly cows ate up the seven fat cows that came up first. 21But even after they ate them, no one could tell that they had done so; they looked just as ugly as before. Then I woke up.

22"In my dreams I also saw seven heads of grain, full and good, growing on a single stalk. 23After them, seven other heads sprouted—withered and thin and scorched by the east wind. 24The thin heads of grain swallowed up the seven good heads. I told this to the magicians, but none could explain it to me."

25Then Joseph said to Pharaoh, "The dreams of Pharaoh are one and the same. God has revealed to Pharaoh what he is about to do. 26The seven good cows are seven years, and the seven good heads of grain are seven years; it is one and the same dream. 27The seven lean, ugly cows that came up afterward are seven years, and so are the seven worthless heads of grain scorched by the east wind: They are seven years of famine.

28"It is just as I said to Pharaoh: God has shown Pharaoh

l13 Or impaled

King James

²⁹Behold, there come seven years of great plenty throughout all the land of Egypt:

³⁰And there shall arise after them seven years of famine; and all the plenty shall be forgotten in the land of Egypt; and the famine shall consume the land;

³¹And the plenty shall not be known in the land by reason of that famine following; for it *shall be* very *x*grievous.

³²And for that the dream was doubled unto Pharaoh twice; *it is* because the thing *is* *y*established by God, and God will shortly bring it to pass.

³³Now therefore let Pharaoh look out a man discreet and wise, and set him over the land of Egypt.

³⁴Let Pharaoh do *this,* and let him appoint *z*officers over the land, and take up the fifth part of the land of Egypt in the seven plenteous years.

³⁵And let them gather all the food of those good years that come, and lay up corn under the hand of Pharaoh, and let them keep food in the cities.

³⁶And that food shall be for store to the land against the seven years of famine, which shall be in the land of Egypt; that the land *a*perish not through the famine.

Pharaoh makes Joseph a ruler

³⁷ ¶ And the thing was good in the eyes of Pharaoh, and in the eyes of all his servants.

³⁸And Pharaoh said unto his servants, Can we find *such a one* as this *is,* a man in whom the spirit of God *is?*

³⁹And Pharaoh said unto Joseph, Forasmuch as God hath shown thee all this, *there is* none so discreet and wise as thou *art:*

⁴⁰Thou shalt be over my house, and according unto thy word shall all my people *b*be ruled: only in the throne will I be greater than thou.

⁴¹And Pharaoh said unto Joseph, See, I have set thee over all the land of Egypt.

⁴²And Pharaoh took off his ring from his hand, and put it upon Joseph's hand, and arrayed him in vestures of *c*fine linen, and put a gold chain about his neck;

⁴³And he made him to ride in the second chariot which he had; and they cried before him, *d* *e*Bow the knee: and he made him *ruler* over all the land of Egypt.

⁴⁴And Pharaoh said unto Joseph, I *am* Pharaoh, and without thee shall no man lift up his hand or foot in all the land of Egypt.

⁴⁵And Pharaoh called Joseph's name *f*Zaphnath-paaneah; and he gave him to wife Asenath the daughter of Poti-pherah *g*priest of On. And Joseph went out over *all* the land of Egypt.

⁴⁶ ¶ And Joseph *was* thirty years old when he stood before Pharaoh king of Egypt. And Joseph went out from the presence of Pharaoh, and went throughout all the land of Egypt.

⁴⁷And in the seven plenteous years the earth brought forth by handfuls.

⁴⁸And he gathered up all the food of the seven years, which were in the land of Egypt, and laid up the food in the cities: the food of the field, which *was* round about every city, laid he up in the same.

⁴⁹And Joseph gathered corn as the sand of the sea, very much, until he left numbering; for *it was* without number.

⁵⁰And unto Joseph were born two sons before the years of famine came, which Asenath the daughter of Poti-pherah *h*priest of On bare unto him.

⁵¹And Joseph called the name of the firstborn *i*Manasseh: For God, *said he,* hath made me forget all my toil, and all my father's house.

Amplified

²⁹Take note! Seven years of great plenty throughout all the land of Egypt are coming.

³⁰Then there will come seven years of hunger *and* famine, and [there will be so much want that] all the great abundance of the previous years will be forgotten in the land of Egypt; and hunger (destitution, starvation) will exhaust (consume, finish) the land.

³¹And the plenty will become quite unknown in the land because of that following famine, for it will be very woefully severe.

³²That the dream was sent twice to Pharaoh *and* in two forms indicates that this thing which God will very soon bring to pass is fully prepared *and* established by God.

³³So now let Pharaoh seek out *and* provide a man discreet, understanding, proficient, *and* wise and set him over the land of Egypt [as governor].

³⁴Let Pharaoh do this; then let him select and appoint officers over the land, and take one-fifth [of the produce] of the [whole] land of Egypt in the seven plenteous years [year by year].

³⁵And let them gather all the food of these good years that are coming and lay up grain under the direction *and* authority of Pharaoh, and let them retain food [in fortified granaries] in the cities.

³⁶And that food shall be put in store for the country against the seven years of hunger *and* famine that are to come upon the land of Egypt, so that the land may not be ruined *and* cut off by the famine.

³⁷And the plan seemed good in the eyes of Pharaoh and in the eyes of all his servants.

³⁸And Pharaoh said to his servants, Can we find this man's equal, a man in whom is the spirit of God?

³⁹And Pharaoh said to Joseph, Forasmuch as [your] God has shown you all this, there is nobody as intelligent *and* discreet *and* understanding and wise as you are.

⁴⁰You shall have charge over my house, and all my people shall be governed according to your word [with reverence, submission, and obedience]. Only in matters of the throne will I be greater than you are.

⁴¹Then Pharaoh said to Joseph, See, I have set you over all the land of Egypt.

⁴²And Pharaoh took off his [signet] ring from his hand and put it on Joseph's hand, and arrayed him in [official] vestments of fine linen, and put a gold chain about his neck;

⁴³He made him to ride in the second chariot which he had, and [officials] cried before him, Bow the knee! And he set him over all the land of Egypt.

⁴⁴And Pharaoh said to Joseph, I am Pharaoh, and without you shall no man lift up his hand or foot in all the land of Egypt.

⁴⁵And Pharaoh called Joseph's name Zaphenath-paneah and he gave him Asenath daughter of Potiphera, priest of On, to be his wife. And Joseph made an [inspection] tour of all the land of Egypt.

⁴⁶Joseph [who had been in Egypt thirteen years] was thirty years old when he stood before Pharaoh king of Egypt. Joseph went out from the presence of Pharaoh and went [about his duties] through all the land of Egypt.

⁴⁷In the seven abundant years the earth brought forth by handfuls [for each seed planted].

⁴⁸And he gathered up all the [surplus] food of the seven [good] years in the land of Egypt and stored up the food in the cities; he stored away in each city the food from the fields around it.

⁴⁹And Joseph gathered grain as the sand of the sea, very much, until he stopped counting, for it could not be measured.

⁵⁰Now to Joseph were born two sons before the years of famine came, whom Asenath daughter of Potiphera, the priest of On, bore to him.

⁵¹And Joseph called the firstborn Manasseh [making to forget]. For God, said he, has made me forget all my toil *and* hardship and all my father's house.

---

x Heb. *heavy*   *y* Or, *prepared of God*   *z* Or, *overseers*
a Heb. *be not cut off*   *b* Heb. *be armed,* or, *kiss*   *c* Or, *silk*
d Or, *Tender father*   *e* Heb. *Abrech*   *f* Which in the Coptic signifies, *A revealer of secrets,* or, *The man to whom secrets* are *revealed*   *g* Or, *prince;* see Ex. 2:16; 2 Sam. 8:18 & 20:26   *h* Or, *prince*   *i* i.e. *Forgetting*

New American Standard

29"Behold, seven years of great abundance are coming in all the land of Egypt;

30 and after them seven years of famine will come, and all the abundance will be forgotten in the land of Egypt, and the famine will ravage the land.

31"So the abundance will be unknown in the land because of that subsequent famine; for it *will be* very severe.

32"Now as for the repeating of the dream to Pharaoh twice, *it means* that the matter is determined by God, and God will quickly bring it about.

33"Now let Pharaoh look for a man discerning and wise, and set him over the land of Egypt.

34"Let Pharaoh take action to appoint overseers in charge of the land, and let him exact a fifth *of the produce* of the land of Egypt in the seven years of abundance.

35"Then let them gather all the food of these good years that are coming, and store up the grain for food in the cities under Pharaoh's authority, and let them guard *it.*

36"Let the food become as a reserve for the land for the seven years of famine which will occur in the land of Egypt, so that the land will not perish during the famine."

37 ¶ Now the proposal seemed good to Pharaoh and to all his servants.

Joseph Is Made a Ruler of Egypt

38 Then Pharaoh said to his servants, "Can we find a man like this, in whom is a divine spirit?"

39 So Pharaoh said to Joseph, "Since God has informed you of all this, there is no one so discerning and wise as you are.

40"You shall be over my house, and according to your command all my people shall do homage; only in the throne I will be greater than you."

41 Pharaoh said to Joseph, "See, I have set you over all the land of Egypt."

42 Then Pharaoh took off his signet ring from his hand and put it on Joseph's hand, and clothed him in garments of fine linen and put the gold necklace around his neck.

43 He had him ride in his second chariot; and they proclaimed before him, "Bow the knee!" And he set him over all the land of Egypt.

44 Moreover, Pharaoh said to Joseph, "*Though* I am Pharaoh, yet without your permission no one shall raise his hand or foot in all the land of Egypt."

45 Then Pharaoh named Joseph *a*Zaphenath-paneah; and he gave him Asenath, the daughter of Potiphera priest of On, as his wife. And Joseph went forth over the land of Egypt.

46 ¶ Now Joseph was thirty years old when he *b*stood before Pharaoh, king of Egypt. And Joseph went out from the presence of Pharaoh and went through all the land of Egypt.

47 During the seven years of plenty the land brought forth abundantly.

48 So he gathered all the food of *these* seven years which occurred in the land of Egypt and placed the food in the cities; he placed in every city the food from its own surrounding fields.

49 Thus Joseph stored up grain in great abundance like the sand of the sea, until he stopped measuring *it,* for it was beyond measure.

The Sons of Joseph

50 ¶ Now before the year of famine came, two sons were born to Joseph, whom Asenath, the daughter of Potiphera priest of *c*On, bore to him.

51 Joseph named the firstborn *d*Manasseh, "For," *he said,* "God has made me forget all my trouble and all my father's household."

New International

what he is about to do. 29Seven years of great abundance are coming throughout the land of Egypt, 30but seven years of famine will follow them. Then all the abundance in Egypt will be forgotten, and the famine will ravage the land. 31The abundance in the land will not be remembered, because the famine that follows it will be so severe. 32The reason the dream was given to Pharaoh in two forms is that the matter has been firmly decided by God, and God will do it soon.

33"And now let Pharaoh look for a discerning and wise man and put him in charge of the land of Egypt. 34Let Pharaoh appoint commissioners over the land to take a fifth of the harvest of Egypt during the seven years of abundance. 35They should collect all the food of these good years that are coming and store up the grain under the authority of Pharaoh, to be kept in the cities for food. 36This food should be held in reserve for the country, to be used during the seven years of famine that will come upon Egypt, so that the country may not be ruined by the famine."

37The plan seemed good to Pharaoh and to all his officials. 38So Pharaoh asked them, "Can we find anyone like this man, one in whom is the spirit of God*m*?"

39Then Pharaoh said to Joseph, "Since God has made all this known to you, there is no one so discerning and wise as you. 40You shall be in charge of my palace, and all my people are to submit to your orders. Only with respect to the throne will I be greater than you."

Joseph in Charge of Egypt

41So Pharaoh said to Joseph, "I hereby put you in charge of the whole land of Egypt." 42Then Pharaoh took his signet ring from his finger and put it on Joseph's finger. He dressed him in robes of fine linen and put a gold chain around his neck. 43He had him ride in a chariot as his second-in-command,*n* and men shouted before him, "Make way*o*!" Thus he put him in charge of the whole land of Egypt.

44Then Pharaoh said to Joseph, "I am Pharaoh, but without your word no one will lift hand or foot in all Egypt." 45Pharaoh gave Joseph the name Zaphenath-Paneah and gave him Asenath daughter of Potiphera, priest of On,*p* to be his wife. And Joseph went throughout the land of Egypt.

46Joseph was thirty years old when he entered the service of Pharaoh king of Egypt. And Joseph went out from Pharaoh's presence and traveled throughout Egypt. 47During the seven years of abundance the land produced plentifully. 48Joseph collected all the food produced in those seven years of abundance in Egypt and stored it in the cities. In each city he put the food grown in the fields surrounding it. 49Joseph stored up huge quantities of grain, like the sand of the sea; it was so much that he stopped keeping records because it was beyond measure.

50Before the years of famine came, two sons were born to Joseph by Asenath daughter of Potiphera, priest of On. 51Joseph named his firstborn Manasseh*q* and said, "It is because God has made me forget all my trouble and all my

---

m 38 Or *of the gods*   *n 43* Or *in the chariot of his second-in-command;* or *in his second chariot*   *o 43* Or *Bow down*   *p 45* That is, Heliopolis; also in verse 50
q 51 Manasseh sounds like and may be derived from the Hebrew for *forget.*

---

*a*Probably Egyptian for "God speaks; he lives"   *b*Or *entered the service of*   *c*Or *Heliopolis*   *d*I.e. *making to forget*

King James

52And the name of the second called he *j*Ephraim: For God hath caused me to be fruitful in the land of my affliction.

53 ¶ And the seven years of plenteousness, that was in the land of Egypt, were ended.

54And the seven years of dearth began to come, according as Joseph had said: and the dearth was in all lands; but in all the land of Egypt there was bread.

55And when all the land of Egypt was famished, the people cried to Pharaoh for bread: and Pharaoh said unto all the Egyptians, Go unto Joseph; what he saith to you, do.

56And the famine was over all the face of the earth: and Joseph opened *k*all the storehouses, and sold unto the Egyptians; and the famine waxed sore in the land of Egypt.

57And all countries came into Egypt to Joseph for to buy *corn;* because that the famine was *so* sore in all lands.

Joseph's brethren visit Egypt

42 NOW WHEN Jacob saw that there was corn in Egypt, Jacob said unto his sons, Why do ye look one upon another?

2And he said, Behold, I have heard that there is corn in Egypt: get you down thither, and buy for us from thence; that we may live, and not die.

3 ¶ And Joseph's ten brethren went down to buy corn in Egypt.

4But Benjamin, Joseph's brother, Jacob sent not with his brethren; for he said, Lest peradventure mischief befall him.

5And the sons of Israel came to buy *corn* among those that came: for the famine was in the land of Canaan.

6And Joseph *was* the governor over the land, *and he it was* that sold to all the people of the land: and Joseph's brethren came, and bowed down themselves before him *with* their faces to the earth.

7And Joseph saw his brethren, and he knew them, but made himself strange unto them, and spake *l*roughly unto them; and he said unto them, Whence come ye? And they said, From the land of Canaan to buy food.

8And Joseph knew his brethren, but they knew not him.

9And Joseph remembered the dreams which he dreamed of them, and said unto them, Ye *are* spies; to see the nakedness of the land ye are come.

10And they said unto him, Nay, my lord, but to buy food are thy servants come.

11We *are* all one man's sons; we *are* true *men,* thy servants are no spies.

12And he said unto them, Nay, but to see the nakedness of the land ye are come.

13And they said, Thy servants *are* twelve brethren, the sons of one man in the land of Canaan; and, behold, the youngest *is* this day with our father, and one *is* not.

14And Joseph said unto them, That *is it* that I spake unto you, saying, Ye *are* spies:

15Hereby ye shall be proved: By the life of Pharaoh ye shall not go forth hence, except your youngest brother come hither.

16Send one of you, and let him fetch your brother, and ye shall be *m*kept in prison, that your words may be proved, whether *there be any* truth in you: or else by the life of Pharaoh surely ye *are* spies.

17And he *n*put them all together into ward three days.

18And Joseph said unto them the third day, This do, and live; *for* I fear God:

Amplified

52And the second he called Ephraim [to be fruitful], For [he said] God has caused me to be fruitful in the land of my affliction.

53When the seven years of plenty were ended in the land of Egypt,

54The seven years of scarcity *and* famine began to come, as Joseph had said they would; the famine was in all [the surrounding] lands, but in all of Egypt there was food.

55But when all the land of Egypt was weakened with hunger, the people [there] cried to Pharaoh for food; and Pharaoh said to [them] all, Go to Joseph; what he says to you, do.

56When the famine was over all the land, Joseph opened all the storehouses and sold to the Egyptians; for the famine grew extremely distressing in the land of Egypt.

57And all countries came to Egypt to Joseph to buy grain, because the famine was severe over all [the known] earth.

42 NOW WHEN Jacob learned that there was grain in Egypt, he said to his sons, Why do you look at one another?

2For, he said, I have heard that there is grain in Egypt; get down there and buy [grain] for us, that we may live and not die.

3So ten of Joseph's brethren went to buy grain in Egypt.

4But Benjamin, Joseph's [full] brother, Jacob did not send with his brothers; for he said, Lest perhaps some harm *or* injury should befall him.

5So the sons of Israel came to buy grain among those who came, for there was hunger *and* general lack of food in the land of Canaan.

6Now Joseph was the governor over the land, and he it was who sold to all the people of the land; and Joseph's [half] brothers came and bowed themselves down before him with their faces to the ground.

7Joseph saw his brethren and he recognized them, but he treated them as if he were a stranger to them and spoke roughly to them. He said, Where do you come from? And they replied, From the land of Canaan to buy food.

8Joseph knew his brethren, but they did not know him.

9And Joseph remembered the dreams he had dreamed about them and said to them, You are spies *and* with unfriendly purpose you have come to observe [secretly] the nakedness of the land.

10But they said to him, No, my lord, but your servants have come [only] to buy food.

11We are all one man's sons; we are true men; your servants are not spies.

12And he said to them, No, but you have come to see the nakedness of the land.

13But they said, Your servants are twelve brothers, the sons of one man in the land of Canaan; the youngest is today with our father, and one is not.

14And Joseph said to them, It is as I said to you, You are spies.

15You shall be proved by this test: by the life of Pharaoh, you shall not go away from here unless your youngest brother comes here.

16Send one of you and let him bring your brother, and you will be kept in prison, that your words may be proved whether there is any truth in you; or else by the life of Pharaoh you certainly are spies.

17Then he put them all in custody for three days.

18And Joseph said to them on the third day, Do this and live! I reverence *and* fear God:

---

*j*i.e. *Fruitful*   *k*Heb. *all wherein* was   *l*Heb. *hard things with them*   *m*Heb. *bound*   *n*Heb. *gathered*

New American Standard

52 He named the second *e*Ephraim, "For," *he said,* "God has made me fruitful in the land of my affliction."

53 ¶ When the seven years of plenty which had been in the land of Egypt came to an end,

54 and the seven years of famine began to come, just as Joseph had said, then there was famine in all the lands, but in all the land of Egypt there was bread.

55 So when all the land of Egypt was famished, the people cried out to Pharaoh for bread; and Pharaoh said to all the Egyptians, "Go to Joseph; whatever he says to you, you shall do."

56 When the famine was *spread* over all the face of the earth, then Joseph opened all the storehouses, and sold to the Egyptians; and the famine was severe in the land of Egypt.

57 *The people of* all the earth came to Egypt to buy grain from Joseph, because the famine was severe in all the earth.

Joseph's Brothers Sent to Egypt

42 NOW JACOB saw that there was grain in Egypt, and Jacob said to his sons, "Why are you staring at one another?"

2 He said, "Behold, I have heard that there is grain in Egypt; go down there and buy *some* for us from that place, so that we may live and not die."

3 Then ten brothers of Joseph went down to buy grain from Egypt.

4 But Jacob did not send Joseph's brother Benjamin with his brothers, for he said, "I am afraid that harm may befall him."

5 So the sons of Israel came to buy grain among those who were coming, for the famine was in the land of Canaan *also.*

6 ¶ Now Joseph was the ruler over the land; he was the one who sold to all the people of the land. And Joseph's brothers came and bowed down to him with *their* faces to the ground.

7 When Joseph saw his brothers he recognized them, but he disguised himself to them and spoke to them harshly. And he said to them, "Where have you come from?" And they said, "From the land of Canaan, to buy food."

8 ¶ But Joseph had recognized his brothers, although they did not recognize him.

9 Joseph remembered the dreams which he had about them, and said to them, "You are spies; you have come to look at the undefended parts of our land."

10 Then they said to him, "No, my lord, but your servants have come to buy food.

11 "We are all sons of one man; we are honest men, your servants are not spies."

12 Yet he said to them, "No, but you have come to look at the undefended parts of our land!"

13 But they said, "Your servants are twelve brothers *in all,* the sons of one man in the land of Canaan; and behold, the youngest is with our father today, and one is no longer alive."

14 Joseph said to them, "It is as I said to you, you are spies;

15 by this you will be tested: by the life of Pharaoh, you shall not go from this place unless your youngest brother comes here!

16 "Send one of you that he may get your brother, while you remain confined, that your words may be tested, whether there is truth in you. But if not, by the life of Pharaoh, surely you are spies."

17 So he put them all together in prison for three days.

18 ¶ Now Joseph said to them on the third day, "Do this and live, for I fear God:

New International

father's household." 52The second son he named Ephraim[r] and said, "It is because God has made me fruitful in the land of my suffering."

53The seven years of abundance in Egypt came to an end, 54and the seven years of famine began, just as Joseph had said. There was famine in all the other lands, but in the whole land of Egypt there was food. 55When all Egypt began to feel the famine, the people cried to Pharaoh for food. Then Pharaoh told all the Egyptians, "Go to Joseph and do what he tells you."

56When the famine had spread over the whole country, Joseph opened the storehouses and sold grain to the Egyptians, for the famine was severe throughout Egypt. 57And all the countries came to Egypt to buy grain from Joseph, because the famine was severe in all the world.

Joseph's Brothers Go to Egypt

42 WHEN JACOB learned that there was grain in Egypt, he said to his sons, "Why do you just keep looking at each other?" 2He continued, "I have heard that there is grain in Egypt. Go down there and buy some for us, so that we may live and not die."

3Then ten of Joseph's brothers went down to buy grain from Egypt. 4But Jacob did not send Benjamin, Joseph's brother, with the others, because he was afraid that harm might come to him. 5So Israel's sons were among those who went to buy grain, for the famine was in the land of Canaan also.

6Now Joseph was the governor of the land, the one who sold grain to all its people. So when Joseph's brothers arrived, they bowed down to him with their faces to the ground. 7As soon as Joseph saw his brothers, he recognized them, but he pretended to be a stranger and spoke harshly to them. "Where do you come from?" he asked.

"From the land of Canaan," they replied, "to buy food."

8Although Joseph recognized his brothers, they did not recognize him. 9Then he remembered his dreams about them and said to them, "You are spies! You have come to see where our land is unprotected."

10"No, my lord," they answered. "Your servants have come to buy food. 11We are all the sons of one man. Your servants are honest men, not spies."

12"No!" he said to them. "You have come to see where our land is unprotected."

13But they replied, "Your servants were twelve brothers, the sons of one man, who lives in the land of Canaan. The youngest is now with our father, and one is no more."

14Joseph said to them, "It is just as I told you: You are spies! 15And this is how you will be tested: As surely as Pharaoh lives, you will not leave this place unless your youngest brother comes here. 16Send one of your number to get your brother; the rest of you will be kept in prison, so that your words may be tested to see if you are telling the truth. If you are not, then as surely as Pharaoh lives, you are spies!" 17And he put them all in custody for three days.

18On the third day, Joseph said to them, "Do this and

---

e I.e. fruitfulness

r 52 *Ephraim* sounds like the Hebrew for *twice fruitful.*

King James

¹⁹If ye *be* true *men,* let one of your brethren be bound in the house of your prison: go ye, carry corn for the famine of your houses:

²⁰But bring your youngest brother unto me; so shall your words be verified, and ye shall not die. And they did so.

²¹ ¶ And they said one to another, We *are* verily guilty concerning our brother, in that we saw the anguish of his soul, when he besought us, and we would not hear; therefore is this distress come upon us.

²²And Reuben answered them, saying, Spake I not unto you, saying, Do not sin against the child; and ye would not hear? therefore, behold, also his blood is required.

²³And they knew not that Joseph understood *them;* for ^ohe spake unto them by an interpreter.

²⁴And he turned himself about from them, and wept; and returned to them again, and communed with them, and took from them Simeon, and bound him before their eyes.

²⁵ ¶ Then Joseph commanded to fill their sacks with corn, and to restore every man's money into his sack, and to give them provision for the way: and thus did he unto them.

²⁶And they laded their asses with the corn, and departed thence.

²⁷And as one of them opened his sack to give his ass provender in the inn, he espied his money; for, behold, it *was* in his sack's mouth.

²⁸And he said unto his brethren, My money is restored; and, lo, *it is* even in my sack: and their heart ^pfailed *them,* and they were afraid, saying one to another, What *is* this *that* God hath done unto us?

²⁹ ¶ And they came unto Jacob their father unto the land of Canaan, and told him all that befell unto them; saying,

³⁰The man, *who is* the lord of the land, spake ^qroughly to us, and took us for spies of the country.

³¹And we said unto him, We *are* true *men;* we are no spies:

³²We *be* twelve brethren, sons of our father; one *is* not, and the youngest *is* this day with our father in the land of Canaan.

³³And the man, the lord of the country, said unto us, Hereby shall I know that ye *are* true *men;* leave one of your brethren *here* with me, and take *food for* the famine of your households, and be gone:

³⁴And bring your youngest brother unto me: then shall I know that ye *are* no spies, but *that* ye *are* true *men: so* will I deliver you your brother, and ye shall traffick in the land.

³⁵ ¶ And it came to pass as they emptied their sacks, that, behold, every man's bundle of money *was* in his sack: and when *both* they and their father saw the bundles of money, they were afraid.

³⁶And Jacob their father said unto them, Me have ye bereaved *of my children:* Joseph *is* not, and Simeon *is* not, and ye will take Benjamin *away:* all these things are against me.

³⁷And Reuben spake unto his father, saying, Slay my two sons, if I bring him not to thee: deliver him into my hand, and I will bring him to thee again.

³⁸And he said, My son shall not go down with you; for his brother is dead, and he is left alone: if mischief befall him by the way in the which ye go, then shall ye bring down my gray hairs with sorrow to the grave.

The second trip to Egypt

43 AND THE famine *was* sore in the land.
²And it came to pass, when they had eaten up the corn which they had brought out of Egypt, their father said unto them, Go again, buy us a little food.

Amplified

¹⁹If you are true men, let one of your brothers be bound in your prison, but [the rest of] you go and carry grain for those weakened with hunger in your households.

²⁰But bring your youngest brother to me, so your words will be verified and you shall live. And they did so.

²¹And they said one to another, We are truly guilty about our brother, for we saw the distress *and* anguish of his soul when he begged us [to let him go], and we would not hear. So this distress *and* difficulty has come upon us.

²²Reuben answered them, Did I not tell you, Do not sin against the boy, and you would not hear? Therefore, behold, his blood is required [of us].

²³But they did not know that Joseph understood them, for he spoke to them through an interpreter.

²⁴And he turned away from them and wept; then he returned to them and talked with them, and took from them Simeon and bound him before their eyes.

²⁵Then [privately] Joseph commanded that their sacks be filled with grain, every man's money be restored to his sack, and provisions be given to them for the journey. And this was done for them.

²⁶They loaded their donkeys with grain and left.

²⁷And as one of them opened his sack to give his donkey fodder at the lodging place, he caught sight of his money; for behold, it was in his sack's mouth.

²⁸And he said to his brothers, My money is restored! Here it is in my sack! And their hearts failed them and they were afraid *and* turned trembling one to another, saying, What is this that God has done to us?

²⁹When they came to Jacob their father in Canaan, they told him all that had befallen them, saying,

³⁰The man who is the lord of the land spoke roughly to us and took us for spies of the country.

³¹And we said to him, We are true men, not spies.

³²We are twelve brothers with the same father; one is no more, and the youngest is today with our father in the land of Canaan.

³³And the man, the lord of the country, said to us, By this test I will know whether or not you are honest men: leave one of your brothers here with me and take grain for your famishing households and be gone.

³⁴Bring your youngest brother to me; then I will know that you are not spies, but that you are honest men. And I will deliver to you your brother [whom I have kept bound in prison], and you may do business in the land.

³⁵When they emptied their sacks, behold, every man's parcel of money was in his sack! When both they and their father saw the bundles of money, they were afraid.

³⁶And Jacob their father said to them, You have bereaved me! Joseph is not, and Simeon is not, and you would take Benjamin from me. All these things are against me!

³⁷And Reuben said to his father, Slay my two sons if I do not bring [Benjamin] back to you. Deliver him into my keeping, and I will bring him back to you.

³⁸But [Jacob] said, My son shall not go down with you, for his brother is dead and he alone is left [of his mother's children]; if harm *or* accident should befall him on the journey you are to take, you would bring my hoary head down to Sheol (the place of the dead) with grief.

43 BUT THE hunger *and* destitution *and* starvation were very severe *and* extremely distressing in the land [Canaan].
²And when [the families of Jacob's sons] had eaten up the grain which the men had brought from Egypt, their father said to them, Go again; buy us a little food.

---

^oHeb. *an interpreter* was *between them*   ^pHeb. *went forth*
^qHeb. *with us hard things*

New American Standard

¹⁹ if you are honest men, let one of your brothers be confined in your prison; but as for *the rest of* you, go, carry grain for the famine of your households,

²⁰ and bring your youngest brother to me, so your words may be verified, and you will not die." And they did so.

²¹ Then they said to one another, "Truly we are guilty concerning our brother, because we saw the distress of his soul when he pleaded with us, yet we would not listen; therefore this distress has come upon us."

²² Reuben answered them, saying, "Did I not tell you, 'Do not sin against the boy'; and you would not listen? Now comes the reckoning for his blood."

²³ They did not know, however, that Joseph understood, for there was an interpreter between them.

²⁴ He turned away from them and wept. But when he returned to them and spoke to them, he took Simeon from them and bound him before their eyes.

²⁵ Then Joseph gave orders to fill their bags with grain and to restore every man's money in his sack, and to give them provisions for the journey. And thus it was done for them.

²⁶ ¶ So they loaded their donkeys with their grain and departed from there.

²⁷ As one *of them* opened his sack to give his donkey fodder at the lodging place, he saw his money; and behold, it was in the mouth of his sack.

²⁸ Then he said to his brothers, "My money has been returned, and behold, it is even in my sack." And their hearts sank, and they *turned* trembling to one another, saying, "What is this that God has done to us?"

Simeon Is Held Hostage

²⁹ ¶ When they came to their father Jacob in the land of Canaan, they told him all that had happened to them, saying,

³⁰ "The man, the lord of the land, spoke harshly with us, and took us for spies of the country.

³¹ "But we said to him, 'We are honest men; we are not spies.

³² 'We are twelve brothers, sons of our father; one is no longer alive, and the youngest is with our father today in the land of Canaan.'

³³ "The man, the lord of the land, said to us, 'By this I will know that you are honest men: leave one of your brothers with me and take *grain for* the famine of your households, and go.

³⁴ 'But bring your youngest brother to me that I may know that you are not spies, but honest men. I will give your brother to you, and you may trade in the land.' "

³⁵ ¶ Now it came about as they were emptying their sacks, that behold, every man's bundle of money was in his sack; and when they and their father saw their bundles of money, they were dismayed.

³⁶ Their father Jacob said to them, "You have bereaved me of my children: Joseph is no more, and Simeon is no more, and you would take Benjamin; all these things are against me."

³⁷ Then Reuben spoke to his father, saying, "You may put my two sons to death if I do not bring him *back* to you; put him in my care, and I will return him to you."

³⁸ But Jacob said, "My son shall not go down with you; for his brother is dead, and he alone is left. If harm should befall him on the journey you are taking, then you will bring my gray hair down to Sheol in sorrow."

The Return to Egypt

43 NOW THE famine was severe in the land. ² So it came about when they had finished eating the grain which they had brought from Egypt, that their father said to them, "Go back, buy us a little food."

New International

you will live, for I fear God: ¹⁹If you are honest men, let one of your brothers stay here in prison, while the rest of you go and take grain back for your starving households. ²⁰But you must bring your youngest brother to me, so that your words may be verified and that you may not die." This they proceeded to do.

²¹They said to one another, "Surely we are being punished because of our brother. We saw how distressed he was when he pleaded with us for his life, but we would not listen; that's why this distress has come upon us."

²²Reuben replied, "Didn't I tell you not to sin against the boy? But you wouldn't listen! Now we must give an accounting for his blood." ²³They did not realize that Joseph could understand them, since he was using an interpreter.

²⁴He turned away from them and began to weep, but then turned back and spoke to them again. He had Simeon taken from them and bound before their eyes.

²⁵Joseph gave orders to fill their bags with grain, to put each man's silver back in his sack, and to give them provisions for their journey. After this was done for them, ²⁶they loaded their grain on their donkeys and left.

²⁷At the place where they stopped for the night one of them opened his sack to get feed for his donkey, and he saw his silver in the mouth of his sack. ²⁸"My silver has been returned," he said to his brothers. "Here it is in my sack."

Their hearts sank and they turned to each other trembling and said, "What is this that God has done to us?"

²⁹When they came to their father Jacob in the land of Canaan, they told him all that had happened to them. They said, ³⁰"The man who is lord over the land spoke harshly to us and treated us as though we were spying on the land. ³¹But we said to him, 'We are honest men; we are not spies. ³²We were twelve brothers, sons of one father. One is no more, and the youngest is now with our father in Canaan.'

³³"Then the man who is lord over the land said to us, 'This is how I will know whether you are honest men: Leave one of your brothers here with me, and take food for your starving households and go. ³⁴But bring your youngest brother to me so I will know that you are not spies but honest men. Then I will give your brother back to you, and you can trade[s] in the land.' "

³⁵As they were emptying their sacks, there in each man's sack was his pouch of silver! When they and their father saw the money pouches, they were frightened. ³⁶Their father Jacob said to them, "You have deprived me of my children. Joseph is no more and Simeon is no more, and now you want to take Benjamin. Everything is against me!"

³⁷Then Reuben said to his father, "You may put both of my sons to death if I do not bring him back to you. Entrust him to my care, and I will bring him back."

³⁸But Jacob said, "My son will not go down there with you; his brother is dead and he is the only one left. If harm comes to him on the journey you are taking, you will bring my gray head down to the grave[t] in sorrow."

The Second Journey to Egypt

43 NOW THE famine was still severe in the land. ²So when they had eaten all the grain they had brought from Egypt, their father said to them, "Go back and buy us a little more food."

---

[s] 34 Or *move about freely*   [t] 38 Hebrew *Sheol*

King James

³And Judah spake unto him, saying, The man ʳdid solemnly protest unto us, saying, Ye shall not see my face, except your brother *be* with you.

⁴If thou wilt send our brother with us, we will go down and buy thee food:

⁵But if thou wilt not send *him,* we will not go down: for the man said unto us, Ye shall not see my face, except your brother *be* with you.

⁶And Israel said, Wherefore dealt ye *so* ill with me, *as* to tell the man whether ye had yet a brother?

⁷And they said, The man ˢasked us straitly of our state, and of our kindred, saying, *Is* your father yet alive? have ye *another* brother? and we told him according to the ᵗtenor of these words: ᵘcould we certainly know that he would say, Bring your brother down?

⁸And Judah said unto Israel his father, Send the lad with me, and we will arise and go; that we may live, and not die, both we, and thou, *and* also our little ones.

⁹I will be surety for him; of my hand shalt thou require him: if I bring him not unto thee, and set him before thee, then let me bear the blame for ever:

¹⁰For except we had lingered, surely now we had returned ᵛthis second time.

¹¹And their father Israel said unto them, If *it must be* so now, do this; take of the best fruits in the land in your vessels, and carry down the man a present, a little balm, and a little honey, spices, and myrrh, nuts, and almonds:

¹²And take double money in your hand; and the money that was brought again in the mouth of your sacks, carry *it* again in your hand; peradventure it *was* an oversight:

¹³Take also your brother, and arise, go again unto the man:

¹⁴And God Almighty give you mercy before the man, that he may send away your other brother, and Benjamin. ʷIf I be bereaved *of my children,* I am bereaved.

15 ¶ And the men took that present, and they took double money in their hand, and Benjamin; and rose up, and went down to Egypt, and stood before Joseph.

¹⁶And when Joseph saw Benjamin with them, he said to the ruler of his house, Bring *these* men home, and ˣslay, and make ready; for *these* men shall ʸdine with me at noon.

¹⁷And the man did as Joseph bade; and the man brought the men into Joseph's house.

¹⁸And the men were afraid, because they were brought into Joseph's house; and they said, Because of the money that was returned in our sacks at the first time are we brought in; that he may ᶻseek occasion against us, and fall upon us, and take us for bondmen, and our asses.

¹⁹And they came near to the steward of Joseph's house, and they communed with him at the door of the house,

²⁰And said, O sir, ᵃwe came indeed down at the first time to buy food:

²¹And it came to pass, when we came to the inn, that we opened our sacks, and, behold, *every* man's money *was* in the mouth of his sack, our money in full weight: and we have brought it again in our hand.

²²And other money have we brought down in our hands to buy food: we cannot tell who put our money in our sacks.

²³And he said, Peace *be* to you, fear not: your God, and the God of your father, hath given you treasure in your sacks: ᵇI had your money. And he brought Simeon out unto them.

²⁴And the man brought the men into Joseph's house, and gave *them* water, and they washed their feet; and he gave their asses provender.

²⁵And they made ready the present against Joseph came at noon: for they heard that they should eat bread there.

Amplified

³But Judah said to him, The man solemnly *and* sternly warned us, saying, You shall not see my face *again* unless your brother is with you.

⁴If you will send our brother with us, we will go down [to Egypt] and buy you food;

⁵But if you will not send him, we will not go down; for the man said to us, You shall not see my face unless your brother is with you.

⁶And Israel said, Why did you do me such a wrong *and* suffer this evil to come upon me by telling the man that you had another brother?

⁷And they said, The man asked us straightforward questions about ourselves and our relatives. He said, Is your father still alive? Have you another brother? And we answered him accordingly. How could we know that he would say, Bring your brother down here?

⁸And Judah said to Israel his father, Send the lad with me and we will arise and go, that we may live and not die, both we and you and also our little ones.

⁹I will be security for him; you shall require him of me [personally]; if I do not bring him back to you and put him before you, then let me bear the blame forever.

¹⁰For if we had not lingered like this, surely by now we would have returned the second time.

¹¹And their father Israel said to them, If it must be so, now do this; take of the choicest products in the land in your sacks and carry down a present to the man, a little balm (balsam) and a little honey, aromatic spices and gum (of rock rose) *or* ladanum, pistachio nuts, and almonds.

¹²And take double the [grain] money with you; and the money that was put back in the mouth of your sacks, carry it again with you; there is a possibility that [its being in your sacks] was an oversight.

¹³Take your brother and arise and return to the man;

¹⁴May God Almighty give you mercy *and* favor before the man, that he may release to you your other brother and Benjamin. If I am bereaved [of my sons], I am bereaved.

¹⁵Then the men took the present, and they took double the [grain] money with them, and Benjamin; and they arose and went down to Egypt and stood before Joseph.

¹⁶And when Joseph saw Benjamin with them, he said to the steward of his house, Bring the men into the house and kill an animal and make ready, for the men will dine with me at noon.

¹⁷And the man did as Joseph ordered and brought the men to Joseph's house.

¹⁸The men were afraid because they were brought to Joseph's house; and they said, We are brought in because of the money that was returned in our sacks the first time we came, so that he may find occasion to accuse and assail us, take us for slaves, and seize our donkeys.

¹⁹So they came near to the steward of Joseph's house and talked with him at the door of the house,

²⁰And said, O sir, we came down truly the first time to buy food;

²¹And when we came to the inn, we opened our sacks and there was each man's money, full weight, returned in the mouth of his sack. Now we have brought it back again.

²²And we have brought down with us other money to buy food; we do not know who put our money in our sacks.

²³But [the steward] said, Peace be to you, fear not; your God and the God of your father has given you treasure in your sacks. I received your money. And he brought Simeon out to them.

²⁴And the man brought the men into Joseph's house and gave them water, and they washed their feet; and he gave their donkeys provender.

²⁵And they made ready the present they had brought for Joseph before his coming at noon, for they heard that they were to dine there.

ʳHeb. *protesting protested*   ˢHeb. *asking asked us*   ᵗHeb. *mouth*   ᵘHeb. *knowing could we know*   ᵛOr, *twice by this* ʷOr, *And I, as I have been*   ˣHeb. *kill a killing*   ʸHeb. *eat* ᶻHeb. *roll himself upon us*   ᵃHeb. *coming down we came down* ᵇHeb. *your money came to me*

New American Standard

3 Judah spoke to him, however, saying, "The man solemnly warned us, 'You shall not see my face unless your brother is with you.'

4"If you send our brother with us, we will go down and buy you food.

5"But if you do not send *him*, we will not go down; for the man said to us, 'You will not see my face unless your brother is with you.' "

6 Then Israel said, "Why did you treat me so badly by telling the man whether you still had *another* brother?"

7 But they said, "The man questioned particularly about us and our relatives, saying, 'Is your father still alive? Have you *another* brother?' So we answered his questions. Could we possibly know that he would say, 'Bring your brother down'?"

8 Judah said to his father Israel, "Send the lad with me and we will arise and go, that we may live and not die, we as well as you and our little ones.

9"I myself will be surety for him; you may hold me responsible for him. If I do not bring him *back* to you and set him before you, then let me bear the blame before you forever.

10"For if we had not delayed, surely by now we could have returned twice."

11 ¶ Then their father Israel said to them, "If *it must be* so, then do this: take some of the best products of the land in your bags, and carry down to the man as a present, a little balm and a little honey, aromatic gum and myrrh, pistachio nuts and almonds.

12"Take double *the* money in your hand, and take back in your hand the money that was returned in the mouth of your sacks; perhaps it was a mistake.

13"Take your brother also, and arise, return to the man;

14 and may God Almighty grant you compassion in the sight of the man, so that he will release to you your other brother and Benjamin. And as for me, if I am bereaved of my children, I am bereaved."

15 So the men took this present, and they took double *the* money in their hand, and Benjamin; then they arose and went down to Egypt and stood before Joseph.

Joseph Sees Benjamin

16 ¶ When Joseph saw Benjamin with them, he said to his house steward, "Bring the men into the house, and slay an animal and make ready; for the men are to dine with me at noon."

17 So the man did as Joseph said, and brought the men to Joseph's house.

18 Now the men were afraid, because they were brought to Joseph's house; and they said, "*It is* because of the money that was returned in our sacks the first time that we are being brought in, that he may seek occasion against us and fall upon us, and take us for slaves with our donkeys."

19 So they came near to Joseph's house steward, and spoke to him at the entrance of the house,

20 and said, "Oh, my lord, we indeed came down the first time to buy food,

21 and it came about when we came to the lodging place, that we opened our sacks, and behold, each man's money was in the mouth of his sack, our money in full. So we have brought it back in our hand.

22"We have also brought down other money in our hand to buy food; we do not know who put our money in our sacks."

23 He said, "*f*Be at ease, do not be afraid. Your God and the God of your father has given you treasure in your sacks; I had your money." Then he brought Simeon out to them.

24 Then the man brought the men into Joseph's house and gave them water, and they washed their feet; and he gave their donkeys fodder.

25 So they prepared the present for Joseph's coming at noon; for they had heard that they were to eat a meal there.

New International

3But Judah said to him, "The man warned us solemnly, 'You will not see my face again unless your brother is with you.' 4If you will send our brother along with us, we will go down and buy food for you. 5But if you will not send him, we will not go down, because the man said to us, 'You will not see my face again unless your brother is with you.' "

6Israel asked, "Why did you bring this trouble on me by telling the man you had another brother?"

7They replied, "The man questioned us closely about ourselves and our family. 'Is your father still living?' he asked us. 'Do you have another brother?' We simply answered his questions. How were we to know he would say, 'Bring your brother down here'?"

8Then Judah said to Israel his father, "Send the boy along with me and we will go at once, so that we and you and our children may live and not die. 9I myself will guarantee his safety; you can hold me personally responsible for him. If I do not bring him back to you and set him here before you, I will bear the blame before you all my life. 10As it is, if we had not delayed, we could have gone and returned twice."

11Then their father Israel said to them, "If it must be, then do this: Put some of the best products of the land in your bags and take them down to the man as a gift—a little balm and a little honey, some spices and myrrh, some pistachio nuts and almonds. 12Take double the amount of silver with you, for you must return the silver that was put back into the mouths of your sacks. Perhaps it was a mistake. 13Take your brother also and go back to the man at once. 14And may God Almighty[u] grant you mercy before the man so that he will let your other brother and Benjamin come back with you. As for me, if I am bereaved, I am bereaved."

15So the men took the gifts and double the amount of silver, and Benjamin also. They hurried down to Egypt and presented themselves to Joseph. 16When Joseph saw Benjamin with them, he said to the steward of his house, "Take these men to my house, slaughter an animal and prepare dinner; they are to eat with me at noon."

17The man did as Joseph told him and took the men to Joseph's house. 18Now the men were frightened when they were taken to his house. They thought, "We were brought here because of the silver that was put back into our sacks the first time. He wants to attack us and overpower us and seize us as slaves and take our donkeys."

19So they went up to Joseph's steward and spoke to him at the entrance to the house. 20"Please, sir," they said, "we came down here the first time to buy food. 21But at the place where we stopped for the night we opened our sacks and each of us found his silver—the exact weight—in the mouth of his sack. So we have brought it back with us. 22We have also brought additional silver with us to buy food. We don't know who put our silver in our sacks."

23"It's all right," he said. "Don't be afraid. Your God, the God of your father, has given you treasure in your sacks; I received your silver." Then he brought Simeon out to them.

24The steward took the men into Joseph's house, gave them water to wash their feet and provided fodder for their donkeys. 25They prepared their gifts for Joseph's arrival at noon, because they had heard that they were to eat there.

---

*f*Lit *Peace be to you*   *u 14* Hebrew *El-Shaddai*

King James

²⁶ ¶ And when Joseph came home, they brought him the present which *was* in their hand into the house, and bowed themselves to him to the earth.

²⁷And he asked them of *their* ^cwelfare, and said, ^d*Is* your father well, the old man of whom ye spake? *Is* he yet alive?

²⁸And they answered, Thy servant our father *is* in good health, he *is* yet alive. And they bowed down their heads, and made obeisance.

²⁹And he lifted up his eyes, and saw his brother Benjamin, his mother's son, and said, *Is* this your younger brother, of whom ye spake unto me? And he said, God be gracious unto thee, my son.

³⁰And Joseph made haste; for his bowels did yearn upon his brother: and he sought *where* to weep; and he entered into *his* chamber, and wept there.

³¹And he washed his face, and went out, and refrained himself, and said, Set on bread.

³²And they set on for him by himself, and for them by themselves, and for the Egyptians, which did eat with him, by themselves: because the Egyptians might not eat bread with the Hebrews; for that *is* an abomination unto the Egyptians.

³³And they sat before him, the firstborn according to his birthright, and the youngest according to his youth: and the men marvelled one at another.

³⁴And he took *and sent* messes unto them from before him: but Benjamin's mess was five times so much as any of theirs. And they drank, and ^ewere merry with him.

The missing silver cup

44 AND HE commanded ^fthe steward of his house, saying, Fill the men's sacks *with* food, as much as they can carry, and put every man's money in his sack's mouth.

²And put my cup, the silver cup, in the sack's mouth of the youngest, and his corn money. And he did according to the word that Joseph had spoken.

³As soon as the morning was light, the men were sent away, they and their asses.

⁴*And* when they were gone out of the city, *and* not *yet* far off, Joseph said unto his steward, Up, follow after the men; and when thou dost overtake them, say unto them, Wherefore have ye rewarded evil for good?

⁵*Is* not this *it* in which my lord drinketh, and whereby indeed he ^gdivineth? ye have done evil in so doing.

⁶ ¶ And he overtook them, and he spake unto them these same words.

⁷And they said unto him, Wherefore saith my lord these words? God forbid that thy servants should do according to this thing:

⁸Behold, the money, which we found in our sacks' mouths, we brought again unto thee out of the land of Canaan: how then should we steal out of thy lord's house silver or gold?

⁹With whomsoever of thy servants it be found, both let him die, and we also will be my lord's bondmen.

¹⁰And he said, Now also *let* it *be* according unto your words: he with whom it is found shall be my servant; and ye shall be blameless.

¹¹Then they speedily took down every man his sack to the ground, and opened every man his sack.

¹²And he searched, *and* began at the eldest, and left at the youngest: and the cup was found in Benjamin's sack.

¹³Then they rent their clothes, and laded every man his ass, and returned to the city.

¹⁴ ¶ And Judah and his brethren came to Joseph's house; for he *was* yet there: and they fell before him on the ground.

Amplified

²⁶And when Joseph came home, they brought into the house to him the present which they had with them, and bowed themselves to him to the ground.

²⁷He asked them of their welfare and said, Is your old father well, of whom you spoke? Is he still alive?

²⁸And they answered, Your servant our father is in good health; he is still alive. And they bowed down their heads and made obeisance.

²⁹And he looked up and saw his [full] brother Benjamin, his mother's [only other] son, and said, Is this your youngest brother, of whom you spoke to me? And he said, God be gracious to you, my son!

³⁰And Joseph hurried from the room, for his heart yearned for his brother, and he sought privacy to weep; so he entered his chamber and wept there.

³¹And he washed his face and went out, and, restraining himself, said, Let dinner be served.

³²And [the servants] set out [the food] for [Joseph] by himself, and for [his brothers] by themselves, and for those Egyptians who ate with him by themselves, according to the Egyptian custom not to eat food with the Hebrews; for that is an abomination to the Egyptians.

³³And [Joseph's brothers] were given seats before him—the eldest according to his birthright and the youngest according to his youth; and the men looked at one another amazed [that so much was known about them].

³⁴[Joseph] took and sent helpings to them from before him, but Benjamin's portion was five times as much as any of theirs. And they drank freely and were merry with him.

44 AND HE commanded the steward of his house, saying, Fill the men's sacks with food, as much as they can carry, and put every man's money in his sack's mouth.

²And put my cup, the silver cup, in the sack's mouth of the youngest, with his grain money. And [the steward] did according to what Joseph had said.

³As soon as the morning was light, the men were sent away, they and their donkeys.

⁴When they had left the city and were not yet far away, Joseph said to his steward, Up, follow after the men; and when you overtake them, say to them, Why have you rewarded evil for good? [Why have you stolen the silver cup?]

⁵Is it not my master's drinking cup with which he divines [the future]? You have done wrong in doing this.

⁶And the steward overtook them, and he said to them these same words.

⁷They said to him, Why does my lord say these things? Far be it from your servants to do such a thing!

⁸Note that the money which we found in the mouths of our sacks we brought back to you from the land of Canaan. Is it likely that we would steal from your master's house silver or gold?

⁹With whomever of your servants [your master's cup] is found, not only let that one die, but the rest of us will be my lord's slaves.

¹⁰And the steward said, Now let it be as you say: he with whom [the cup] is found shall be my slave, but [the rest of] you shall be blameless.

¹¹Then quickly every man lowered his sack to the ground and every man opened his sack.

¹²And [the steward] searched, beginning with the eldest and stopping with the youngest; and the cup was found in Benjamin's sack.

¹³Then they rent their clothes; and after each man had loaded his donkey again, they returned to the city.

¹⁴Judah and his brethren came to Joseph's house, for he was still there; and they fell prostrate before him.

---

^cHeb. *peace, drank largely maketh trial?*   ^dHeb. Is there *peace to your father?*   ^eHeb.
^fHeb. him *that was over his house*   ^gOr,

New American Standard

26 ¶ When Joseph came home, they brought into the house to him the present which was in their hand and bowed to the ground before him.

27 Then he asked them about their welfare, and said, "Is your old father well, of whom you spoke? Is he still alive?"

28 They said, "Your servant our father is well; he is still alive." They bowed down in homage.

29 As he lifted his eyes and saw his brother Benjamin, his mother's son, he said, "Is this your youngest brother, of whom you spoke to me?" And he said, "May God be gracious to you, my son."

30 Joseph hurried *out* for he was deeply stirred over his brother, and he sought *a place* to weep; and he entered his chamber and wept there.

31 Then he washed his face and came out; and he controlled himself and said, "Serve the meal."

32 So they served him by himself, and them by themselves, and the Egyptians who ate with him by themselves, because the Egyptians could not eat bread with the Hebrews, for that is loathsome to the Egyptians.

33 Now they were seated before him, the firstborn according to his birthright and the youngest according to his youth, and the men looked at one another in astonishment.

34 He took portions to them from his own table, but Benjamin's portion was five times as much as any of theirs. So they feasted and drank freely with him.

The Brothers Are Brought Back

44 THEN HE commanded his house steward, saying, "Fill the men's sacks with food, as much as they can carry, and put each man's money in the mouth of his sack.

2 "Put my cup, the silver cup, in the mouth of the sack of the youngest, and his money for the grain." And he did as Joseph had told *him.*

3 As soon as it was light, the men were sent away, they with their donkeys.

4 They had *just* gone out of the city, *and* were not far off, when Joseph said to his house steward, "Up, follow the men; and when you overtake them, say to them, 'Why have you repaid evil for good?

5 'Is not this the one from which my lord drinks and which he indeed uses for divination? You have done wrong in doing this.' "

6 ¶ So he overtook them and spoke these words to them.

7 They said to him, "Why does my lord speak such words as these? Far be it from your servants to do such a thing.

8 "Behold, the money which we found in the mouth of our sacks we have brought back to you from the land of Canaan. How then could we steal silver or gold from your lord's house?

9 "With whomever of your servants it is found, let him die, and we also will be my lord's slaves."

10 So he said, "Now let it also be according to your words; he with whom it is found shall be my slave, and *the rest* of you shall be innocent."

11 Then they hurried, each man lowered his sack to the ground, and each man opened his sack.

12 He searched, beginning with the oldest and ending with the youngest, and the cup was found in Benjamin's sack.

13 Then they tore their clothes, and when each man loaded his donkey, they returned to the city.

14 ¶ When Judah and his brothers came to Joseph's house, he was still there, and they fell to the ground before him.

New International

26 When Joseph came home, they presented to him the gifts they had brought into the house, and they bowed down before him to the ground. 27 He asked them how they were, and then he said, "How is your aged father you told me about? Is he still living?"

28 They replied, "Your servant our father is still alive and well." And they bowed low to pay him honor.

29 As he looked about and saw his brother Benjamin, his own mother's son, he asked, "Is this your youngest brother, the one you told me about?" And he said, "God be gracious to you, my son." 30 Deeply moved at the sight of his brother, Joseph hurried out and looked for a place to weep. He went into his private room and wept there.

31 After he had washed his face, he came out and, controlling himself, said, "Serve the food."

32 They served him by himself, the brothers by themselves, and the Egyptians who ate with him by themselves, because Egyptians could not eat with Hebrews, for that is detestable to Egyptians. 33 The men had been seated before him in the order of their ages, from the firstborn to the youngest; and they looked at each other in astonishment. 34 When portions were served to them from Joseph's table, Benjamin's portion was five times as much as anyone else's. So they feasted and drank freely with him.

A Silver Cup in a Sack

44 NOW JOSEPH gave these instructions to the steward of his house: "Fill the men's sacks with as much food as they can carry, and put each man's silver in the mouth of his sack. 2 Then put my cup, the silver one, in the mouth of the youngest one's sack, along with the silver for his grain." And he did as Joseph said.

3 As morning dawned, the men were sent on their way with their donkeys. 4 They had not gone far from the city when Joseph said to his steward, "Go after those men at once, and when you catch up with them, say to them, 'Why have you repaid good with evil? 5 Isn't this the cup my master drinks from and also uses for divination? This is a wicked thing you have done.' "

6 When he caught up with them, he repeated these words to them. 7 But they said to him, "Why does my lord say such things? Far be it from your servants to do anything like that! 8 We even brought back to you from the land of Canaan the silver we found inside the mouths of our sacks. So why would we steal silver or gold from your master's house? 9 If any of your servants is found to have it, he will die; and the rest of us will become my lord's slaves."

10 "Very well, then," he said, "let it be as you say. Whoever is found to have it will become my slave; the rest of you will be free from blame."

11 Each of them quickly lowered his sack to the ground and opened it. 12 Then the steward proceeded to search, beginning with the oldest and ending with the youngest. And the cup was found in Benjamin's sack. 13 At this, they tore their clothes. Then they all loaded their donkeys and returned to the city.

14 Joseph was still in the house when Judah and his brothers came in, and they threw themselves to the ground

King James

¹⁵And Joseph said unto them, What deed *is* this that ye have done? wot ye not that such a man as I can certainly *^hdivine*?

¹⁶And Judah said, What shall we say unto my lord? what shall we speak? or how shall we clear ourselves? God hath found out the iniquity of thy servants: behold, we *are* my lord's servants, both we, and *he* also with whom the cup is found.

¹⁷And he said, God forbid that I should do so: *but* the man in whose hand the cup is found, he shall be my servant; and as for you, get you up in peace unto your father.

¹⁸ ¶ Then Judah came near unto him, and said, Oh my lord, let thy servant, I pray thee, speak a word in my lord's ears, and let not thine anger burn against thy servant: for thou *art* even as Pharaoh.

¹⁹My lord asked his servants, saying, Have ye a father, or a brother?

²⁰And we said unto my lord, We have a father, an old man, and a child of his old age, a little one; and his brother is dead, and he alone is left of his mother, and his father loveth him.

²¹And thou saidst unto thy servants, Bring him down unto me, that I may set mine eyes upon him.

²²And we said unto my lord, The lad cannot leave his father: for *if* he should leave his father, *his father* would die.

²³And thou saidst unto thy servants, Except your youngest brother come down with you, ye shall see my face no more.

²⁴And it came to pass when we came up unto thy servant my father, we told him the words of my lord.

²⁵And our father said, Go again, *and* buy us a little food.

²⁶And we said, We cannot go down: if our youngest brother be with us, then will we go down: for we may not see the man's face, except our youngest brother *be* with us.

²⁷And thy servant my father said unto us, Ye know that my wife bare me two *sons:*

²⁸And the one went out from me, and I said, Surely he is torn in pieces; and I saw him not since:

²⁹And if ye take this also from me, and mischief befall him, ye shall bring down my gray hairs with sorrow to the grave.

³⁰Now therefore when I come to thy servant my father, and the lad *be* not with us; seeing that his life is bound up in the lad's life;

³¹It shall come to pass, when he seeth that the lad *is* not *with us,* that he will die: and thy servants shall bring down the gray hairs of thy servant our father with sorrow to the grave.

³²For thy servant became surety for the lad unto my father, saying, If I bring him not unto thee, then I shall bear the blame to my father for ever.

³³Now therefore, I pray thee, let thy servant abide instead of the lad a bondman to my lord; and let the lad go up with his brethren.

³⁴For how shall I go up to my father, and the lad *be* not with me? lest peradventure I see the evil that shall *ⁱcome* on my father.

Joseph reveals his identity

45 THEN JOSEPH could not refrain himself before all them that stood by him; and he cried, Cause every man to go out from me. And there stood no man with him, while Joseph made himself known unto his brethren.

²And he wept aloud: and the Egyptians and the house of Pharaoh heard.

Amplified

¹⁵Joseph said to them, What is this thing that you have done? Do you not realize that such a man as I can certainly detect *and* know by divination [everything you do without other knowledge of it]?

¹⁶And Judah said, What shall we say to my lord? What shall we reply? Or how shall we clear ourselves, since God has found out *and* exposed the iniquity of your servants? Behold, we are my lord's slaves, the rest of us as well as he with whom the cup is found.

¹⁷But [Joseph] said, God forbid that I should do that; but the man in whose hand the cup is found, he shall be my servant; and as for [the rest of] you, arise *and* go in peace to your father.

¹⁸Then Judah came close to [Joseph] and said, O my lord, let your servant, I pray you, speak a word to you in private, and let not your anger blaze against your servant, for you are as Pharaoh [so I will speak as if directly to him].

¹⁹My lord asked his servants, saying, Have you a father or a brother?

²⁰And we said to my lord, We have a father—an old man—and a young [brother, the] child of his old age; and his brother is dead, and he alone is left of his mother's [offspring], and his father loves him.

²¹And you said to your servants, Bring him down to me, that I may set my eyes on him.

²²And we said to my lord, The lad cannot leave his father; for if he should do so, his father would die.

²³And you told your servants, Unless your youngest brother comes with you, you shall not see my face again.

²⁴And when we went back to your servant my father, we told him what my lord had said.

²⁵And our father said, Go again and buy us a little food.

²⁶But we said, We cannot go down. If our youngest brother is with us, then we will go down; for we may not see the man's face except our youngest brother is with us.

²⁷And your servant my father said to us, You know that [Rachel] my wife bore me two sons:

²⁸And the one went out from me, and I said, Surely he is torn to pieces, and I have never seen him since.

²⁹And if you take this son also from me, and harm *or* accident should befall him, you will bring down my gray hairs with sorrow *and* evil to Sheol (the place of the dead).

³⁰Now therefore, when I come to your servant my father and the lad is not with us, since his life is bound up in the lad's life *and* his soul knit with the lad's soul,

³¹When he sees that the lad is not with us, he will die; and your servants will be responsible for his death *and* will bring down the gray hairs of your servant our father with sorrow to Sheol.

³²For your servant became security for the lad to my father, saying, If I do not bring him to you, then I will bear the blame to my father forever.

³³Now therefore, I pray you, let your servant remain instead of the youth [to be] a slave to my lord, and let the young man go home with his [half] brothers.

³⁴For how can I go up to my father if the lad is not with me?—lest I witness the woe *and* the evil that will come upon my father.

45 THEN JOSEPH could not restrain himself [any longer] before all those who stood by him, and he called out, Cause every man to go out from me! So no one stood there with Joseph while he made himself known to his brothers.

²And he wept *and* sobbed aloud, and the Egyptians [who had just left him] heard it, and the household of Pharaoh heard about it.

---

^hOr, *make trial?; see ver. 5*   ⁱHeb. *find my father*

New American Standard

15 Joseph said to them, "What is this deed that you have done? Do you not know that such a man as I can indeed practice divination?"

16 So Judah said, "What can we say to my lord? What can we speak? And how can we justify ourselves? God has found out the iniquity of your servants; behold, we are my lord's slaves, both we and the one in whose possession the cup has been found."

17 But he said, "Far be it from me to do this. The man in whose possession the cup has been found, he shall be my slave; but as for you, go up in peace to your father."

18 ¶ Then Judah approached him, and said, "Oh my lord, may your servant please speak a word in my lord's ears, and do not be angry with your servant; for you are equal to Pharaoh.

19 "My lord asked his servants, saying, 'Have you a father or a brother?'

20 "We said to my lord, 'We have an old father and a little child of *his* old age. Now his brother is dead, so he alone is left of his mother, and his father loves him.'

21 "Then you said to your servants, 'Bring him down to me that I may set my eyes on him.'

22 "But we said to my lord, 'The lad cannot leave his father, for if he should leave his father, his father would die.'

23 "You said to your servants, however, 'Unless your youngest brother comes down with you, you will not see my face again.'

24 "Thus it came about when we went up to your servant my father, we told him the words of my lord.

25 "Our father said, 'Go back, buy us a little food.'

26 "But we said, 'We cannot go down. If our youngest brother is with us, then we will go down; for we cannot see the man's face unless our youngest brother is with us.'

27 "Your servant my father said to us, 'You know that my wife bore me two sons;

28 and the one went out from me, and I said, "Surely he is torn in pieces," and I have not seen him since.

29 'If you take this one also from me, and harm befalls him, you will bring my gray hair down to Sheol in sorrow.'

30 "Now, therefore, when I come to your servant my father, and the lad is not with us, since his life is bound up in the lad's life,

31 when he sees that the lad is not *with us,* he will die. Thus your servants will bring the gray hair of your servant our father down to Sheol in sorrow.

32 "For your servant became surety for the lad to my father, saying, 'If I do not bring him *back* to you, then let me bear the blame before my father forever.'

33 "Now, therefore, please let your servant remain instead of the lad a slave to my lord, and let the lad go up with his brothers.

34 "For how shall I go up to my father if the lad is not with me—for fear that I see the evil that would overtake my father?"

New International

before him. 15 Joseph said to them, "What is this you have done? Don't you know that a man like me can find things out by divination?"

16 "What can we say to my lord?" Judah replied. "What can we say? How can we prove our innocence? God has uncovered your servants' guilt. We are now my lord's slaves—we ourselves and the one who was found to have the cup."

17 But Joseph said, "Far be it from me to do such a thing! Only the man who was found to have the cup will become my slave. The rest of you, go back to your father in peace."

18 Then Judah went up to him and said: "Please, my lord, let your servant speak a word to my lord. Do not be angry with your servant, though you are equal to Pharaoh himself. 19 My lord asked his servants, 'Do you have a father or a brother?' 20 And we answered, 'We have an aged father, and there is a young son born to him in his old age. His brother is dead, and he is the only one of his mother's sons left, and his father loves him.'

21 "Then you said to your servants, 'Bring him down to me so I can see him for myself.' 22 And we said to my lord, 'The boy cannot leave his father; if he leaves him, his father will die.' 23 But you told your servants, 'Unless your youngest brother comes down with you, you will not see my face again.' 24 When we went back to your servant my father, we told him what my lord had said.

25 "Then our father said, 'Go back and buy a little more food.' 26 But we said, 'We cannot go down. Only if our youngest brother is with us will we go. We cannot see the man's face unless our youngest brother is with us.'

27 "Your servant my father said to us, 'You know that my wife bore me two sons. 28 One of them went away from me, and I said, "He has surely been torn to pieces." And I have not seen him since. 29 If you take this one from me too and harm comes to him, you will bring my gray head down to the grave[v29] in misery.'

30 "So now, if the boy is not with us when I go back to your servant my father and if my father, whose life is closely bound up with the boy's life, 31 sees that the boy isn't there, he will die. Your servants will bring the gray head of our father down to the grave in sorrow. 32 Your servant guaranteed the boy's safety to my father. I said, 'If I do not bring him back to you, I will bear the blame before you, my father, all my life!'

33 "Now then, please let your servant remain here as my lord's slave in place of the boy, and let the boy return with his brothers. 34 How can I go back to my father if the boy is not with me? No! Do not let me see the misery that would come upon my father."

Joseph Deals Kindly with His Brothers

45 THEN JOSEPH could not control himself before all those who stood by him, and he cried, "Have everyone go out from me." So there was no man with him when Joseph made himself known to his brothers.

2 He wept so loudly that the Egyptians heard *it,* and the household of Pharaoh heard *of it.*

Joseph Makes Himself Known

45 THEN JOSEPH could no longer control himself before all his attendants, and he cried out, "Have everyone leave my presence!" So there was no one with Joseph when he made himself known to his brothers. 2 And he wept so loudly that the Egyptians heard him, and Pharaoh's household heard about it.

v29 Hebrew Sheol; also in verse 31

King James

3And Joseph said unto his brethren, I *am* Joseph; doth my father yet live? And his brethren could not answer him; for they were *j*troubled at his presence.

4And Joseph said unto his brethren, Come near to me, I pray you. And they came near. And he said, I *am* Joseph your brother, whom ye sold into Egypt.

5Now therefore be not grieved, *k*nor angry with yourselves, that ye sold me hither: for God did send me before you to preserve life.

6For these two years *hath* the famine *been* in the land: and yet *there are* five years, in the which *there shall* neither *be* earing nor harvest.

7And God sent me before you *l*to preserve you a posterity in the earth, and to save your lives by a great deliverance.

8So now *it was* not you *that* sent me hither, but God: and he hath made me a father to Pharaoh, and lord of all his house, and a ruler throughout all the land of Egypt.

9Haste ye, and go up to my father, and say unto him, Thus saith thy son Joseph, God hath made me lord of all Egypt: come down unto me, tarry not:

10And thou shalt dwell in the land of Goshen, and thou shalt be near unto me, thou, and thy children, and thy children's children, and thy flocks, and thy herds, and all that thou hast:

11And there will I nourish thee; for yet *there are* five years of famine; lest thou, and thy household, and all that thou hast, come to poverty.

12And, behold, your eyes see, and the eyes of my brother Benjamin, that *it is* my mouth that speaketh unto you.

13And ye shall tell my father of all my glory in Egypt, and of all that ye have seen; and ye shall haste and bring down my father hither.

14And he fell upon his brother Benjamin's neck, and wept; and Benjamin wept upon his neck.

15Moreover he kissed all his brethren, and wept upon them: and after that his brethren talked with him.

16 ¶ And the fame thereof was heard in Pharaoh's house, saying, Joseph's brethren are come: and it *m*pleased Pharaoh well, and his servants.

17And Pharaoh said unto Joseph, Say unto thy brethren, This do ye; lade your beasts, and go, get you unto the land of Canaan;

18And take your father and your households, and come unto me: and I will give you the good of the land of Egypt, and ye shall eat the fat of the land.

19Now thou art commanded, this do ye; take you wagons out of the land of Egypt for your little ones, and for your wives, and bring your father, and come.

20Also *n*regard not your stuff; for the good of all the land of Egypt *is* yours.

21And the children of Israel did so: and Joseph gave them wagons, according to the *o*commandment of Pharaoh, and gave them provision for the way.

22To all of them he gave each man changes of raiment; but to Benjamin he gave three hundred *pieces* of silver, and five changes of raiment.

23And to his father he sent after this *manner;* ten asses *p*laden with the good things of Egypt, and ten she asses laden with corn and bread and meat for his father by the way.

24So he sent his brethren away, and they departed: and he said unto them, See that ye fall not out by the way.

25 ¶ And they went up out of Egypt, and came into the land of Canaan unto Jacob their father,

26And told him, saying, Joseph *is* yet alive, and he *is* governor over all the land of Egypt. And *q*Jacob's heart fainted, for he believed them not.

Amplified

3And Joseph said to his brothers, I am Joseph! Is my father still alive? And his brothers could not reply, for they were distressingly disturbed *and* dismayed at [the startling realization that they were in] his presence.

4And Joseph said to his brothers, Come near to me, I pray you. And they did so. And he said, I am Joseph your brother, whom you sold into Egypt!

5But now, do not be distressed *and* disheartened or vexed *and* angry with yourselves because you sold me here, for God sent me ahead of you to preserve life.

6For these two years the famine has been in the land, and there are still five years more in which there will be neither plowing nor harvest.

7God sent me before you to preserve for you a posterity *and* to continue a remnant on the earth, to save your lives by a great escape *and* save for you many survivors.

8So now it was not you who sent me here, but God; and He has made me a father to Pharaoh and lord of all his house and ruler over all the land of Egypt.

9Hurry and go up to my father and tell him, Your son Joseph says this to you: God has put me in charge of all Egypt. Come down to me; do not delay.

10You will live in the land of Goshen, and you will be close to me—you and your children and your grandchildren, your flocks, your herds, and all you have.

11And there I will sustain *and* provide for you, so that you and your household and all that are yours may not come to poverty *and* want, for there are yet five [more] years of [the scarcity, hunger, and starvation of] famine.

12Now notice! Your own eyes and the eyes of my brother Benjamin can see that I am talking to you personally [in your language and not through an interpreter].

13And you shall tell my father of all my glory in Egypt and of all that you have seen; and you shall hurry and bring my father down here.

14And he fell on his brother Benjamin's neck and wept, and Benjamin wept on his neck.

15Moreover, he kissed all his brothers and wept upon them; and after that his brothers conversed with him.

16When the report was heard in Pharaoh's house that Joseph's brothers had come, it pleased Pharaoh and his servants well.

17And Pharaoh said to Joseph, Tell your brothers this: Load your animals and return to the land of Canaan,

18And get your father and your households and come to me. And I will give you the best in the land of Egypt and you will live on the fat of the land.

19You therefore command them, saying, You do this: take wagons from the land of Egypt for your little ones and for your wives, and bring your father and come.

20Also do not look with regret *or* concern upon your goods, for the best of all the land of Egypt is yours.

21And the sons of Israel did so; and Joseph gave them wagons, as the order of Pharaoh permitted, and gave them provisions for the journey.

22To each of them he gave changes of raiment, but to Benjamin he gave 300 pieces of silver and five changes of raiment.

23And to his father he sent as follows: ten donkeys loaded with the good things of Egypt, and ten she-donkeys laden with grain, bread, and nourishing food *and* provision for his father [to supply all who were with him] on the way.

24So he sent his brothers away, and they departed, and he said to them, See that you do not disagree (get excited, quarrel) along the road.

25So they went up out of Egypt and came into the land of Canaan to Jacob their father,

26And they said to him, Joseph is still alive! And he is governor over all the land of Egypt! And Jacob's heart began to stop beating *and* [he almost] fainted, for he did not believe them.

---

*j*Or, *terrified*   *k*Heb. *neither let there be anger in your eyes*
*l*Heb. *to put for you a remnant*   *m*Heb. *was good in the eyes of Pharaoh*   *n*Heb. *let not your eye spare*   *o*Heb. *mouth*
*p*Heb. *carrying*   *q*Heb. *his*

New American Standard

3 Then Joseph said to his brothers, "I am Joseph! Is my father still alive?" But his brothers could not answer him, for they were dismayed at his presence.

4 ¶ Then Joseph said to his brothers, "Please come closer to me." And they came closer. And he said, "I am your brother Joseph, whom you sold into Egypt.

5 "Now do not be grieved or angry with yourselves, because you sold me here, for God sent me before you to preserve life.

6 "For the famine *has been* in the land these two years, and there are still five years in which there will be neither plowing nor harvesting.

7 "God sent me before you to preserve for you a remnant in the earth, and to keep you alive by a great deliverance.

8 "Now, therefore, it was not you who sent me here, but God; and He has made me a father to Pharaoh and lord of all his household and ruler over all the land of Egypt.

9 "Hurry and go up to my father, and say to him, 'Thus says your son Joseph, "God has made me lord of all Egypt; come down to me, do not delay.

10 "You shall live in the land of Goshen, and you shall be near me, and your children and your children's children and your flocks and your herds and all that you have.

11 "There I will also provide for you, for there are still five years of famine *to come*, and you and your household and all that you have would be impoverished."'

12 "Behold, your eyes see, and the eyes of my brother Benjamin *see*, that it is my mouth which is speaking to you.

13 "Now you must tell my father of all my splendor in Egypt, and all that you have seen; and you must hurry and bring my father down here."

14 Then he fell on his brother Benjamin's neck and wept, and Benjamin wept on his neck.

15 He kissed all his brothers and wept on them, and afterward his brothers talked with him.

16 ¶ Now when the news was heard in Pharaoh's house that Joseph's brothers had come, it pleased Pharaoh and his servants.

17 Then Pharaoh said to Joseph, "Say to your brothers, 'Do this: load your beasts and go to the land of Canaan,

18 and take your father and your households and come to me, and I will give you the best of the land of Egypt and you will eat the fat of the land.'

19 "Now you are ordered, 'Do this: take wagons from the land of Egypt for your little ones and for your wives, and bring your father and come.

20 'Do not concern yourselves with your goods, for the best of all the land of Egypt is yours.'"

21 ¶ Then the sons of Israel did so; and Joseph gave them wagons according to the command of Pharaoh, and gave them provisions for the journey.

22 To each of them he gave changes of garments, but to Benjamin he gave three hundred *pieces of* silver and five changes of garments.

23 To his father he sent as follows: ten donkeys loaded with the best things of Egypt, and ten female donkeys loaded with grain and bread and sustenance for his father on the journey.

24 ¶ So he sent his brothers away, and as they departed, he said to them, "Do not quarrel on the journey."

25 Then they went up from Egypt, and came to the land of Canaan to their father Jacob.

26 They told him, saying, "Joseph is still alive, and indeed he is ruler over all the land of Egypt." But he was stunned, for he did not believe them.

New International

3 Joseph said to his brothers, "I am Joseph! Is my father still living?" But his brothers were not able to answer him, because they were terrified at his presence.

4 Then Joseph said to his brothers, "Come close to me." When they had done so, he said, "I am your brother Joseph, the one you sold into Egypt! 5 And now, do not be distressed and do not be angry with yourselves for selling me here, because it was to save lives that God sent me ahead of you. 6 For two years now there has been famine in the land, and for the next five years there will not be plowing and reaping. 7 But God sent me ahead of you to preserve for you a remnant on earth and to save your lives by a great deliverance.[w]

8 "So then, it was not you who sent me here, but God. He made me father to Pharaoh, lord of his entire household and ruler of all Egypt. 9 Now hurry back to my father and say to him, 'This is what your son Joseph says: God has made me lord of all Egypt. Come down to me; don't delay. 10 You shall live in the region of Goshen and be near me—you, your children and grandchildren, your flocks and herds, and all you have. 11 I will provide for you there, because five years of famine are still to come. Otherwise you and your household and all who belong to you will become destitute.'

12 "You can see for yourselves, and so can my brother Benjamin, that it is really I who am speaking to you. 13 Tell my father about all the honor accorded me in Egypt and about everything you have seen. And bring my father down here quickly."

14 Then he threw his arms around his brother Benjamin and wept, and Benjamin embraced him, weeping. 15 And he kissed all his brothers and wept over them. Afterward his brothers talked with him.

16 When the news reached Pharaoh's palace that Joseph's brothers had come, Pharaoh and all his officials were pleased. 17 Pharaoh said to Joseph, "Tell your brothers, 'Do this: Load your animals and return to the land of Canaan, 18 and bring your father and your families back to me. I will give you the best of the land of Egypt and you can enjoy the fat of the land.'

19 "You are also directed to tell them, 'Do this: Take some carts from Egypt for your children and your wives, and get your father and come. 20 Never mind about your belongings, because the best of all Egypt will be yours.'"

21 So the sons of Israel did this. Joseph gave them carts, as Pharaoh had commanded, and he also gave them provisions for their journey. 22 To each of them he gave new clothing, but to Benjamin he gave three hundred shekels[x] of silver and five sets of clothes. 23 And this is what he sent to his father: ten donkeys loaded with the best things of Egypt, and ten female donkeys loaded with grain and bread and other provisions for his journey. 24 Then he sent his brothers away, and as they were leaving he said to them, "Don't quarrel on the way!"

25 So they went up out of Egypt and came to their father Jacob in the land of Canaan. 26 They told him, "Joseph is still alive! In fact, he is ruler of all Egypt." Jacob was

---

w 7 Or *save you as a great band of survivors*   *x* 22 That is,
about 7 1/2 pounds (about 3.5 kilograms)

King James

²⁷And they told him all the words of Joseph, which he had said unto them: and when he saw the wagons which Joseph had sent to carry him, the spirit of Jacob their father revived:

²⁸And Israel said, *It is* enough; Joseph my son *is* yet alive: I will go and see him before I die.

Jacob goes to Egypt

46 AND ISRAEL took his journey with all that he had, and came to Beer-sheba, and offered sacrifices unto the God of his father Isaac.

²And God spake unto Israel in the visions of the night, and said, Jacob, Jacob. And he said, Here *am* I.

³And he said, I *am* God, the God of thy father: fear not to go down into Egypt; for I will there make of thee a great nation:

⁴I will go down with thee into Egypt; and I will also surely bring thee up *again:* and Joseph shall put his hand upon thine eyes.

⁵And Jacob rose up from Beer-sheba: and the sons of Israel carried Jacob their father, and their little ones, and their wives, in the wagons which Pharaoh had sent to carry him.

⁶And they took their cattle, and their goods, which they had gotten in the land of Canaan, and came into Egypt, Jacob, and all his seed with him:

⁷His sons, and his sons' sons with him, his daughters, and his sons' daughters, and all his seed brought he with him into Egypt.

⁸ ¶ And these *are* the names of the children of Israel, which came into Egypt, Jacob and his sons: Reuben, Jacob's firstborn.

⁹And the sons of Reuben; Hanoch, and Phallu, and Hezron, and Carmi.

¹⁰ ¶ And the sons of Simeon; ^rJemuel, and Jamin, and Ohad, and ^sJachin, and ^tZohar, and Shaul the son of a Canaanitish woman.

¹¹ ¶ And the sons of Levi; ^uGershon, Kohath, and Merari.

¹² ¶ And the sons of Judah; Er, and Onan, and Shelah, and Pharez, and Zerah: but Er and Onan died in the land of Canaan. And the sons of Pharez were Hezron and Hamul.

¹³ ¶ And the sons of Issachar; Tola, and ^vPhuvah, and Job, and Shimron.

¹⁴ ¶ And the sons of Zebulun; Sered, and Elon, and Jahleel.

¹⁵These *be* the sons of Leah, which she bare unto Jacob in Padan-aram, with his daughter Dinah: all the souls of his sons and his daughters *were* thirty and three.

¹⁶ ¶ And the sons of Gad; Ziphion, and Haggi, Shuni, and ^wEzbon, Eri, and ^xArodi, and Areli.

¹⁷ ¶ And the sons of Asher; Jimnah, and Ishuah, and Isui, and Beriah, and Serah their sister: and the sons of Beriah; Heber, and Malchiel.

¹⁸These *are* the sons of Zilpah, whom Laban gave to Leah his daughter, and these she bare unto Jacob, *even* sixteen souls.

¹⁹The sons of Rachel Jacob's wife; Joseph, and Benjamin.

²⁰ ¶ And unto Joseph in the land of Egypt were born Manasseh and Ephraim, which Asenath the daughter of Poti-pherah ^ypriest of On bare unto him.

Amplified

²⁷But when they told him all the words of Joseph which he had said to them, and when he saw the wagons which Joseph had sent to carry him, the spirit of Jacob their father revived [and warmth and life returned].

²⁸And Israel said, It is enough! Joseph my son is still alive. I will go and see him before I die.

46 SO ISRAEL made his journey with all that he had and came to Beersheba [a place hallowed by sacred memories] and offered sacrifices to the God of his father Isaac. [Gen. 21:33; 26:23–25.]

²And God spoke to Israel in visions of the night, and said, Jacob! Jacob! And he said, Here am I.

³And He said, I am God, the God of your father; do not be afraid to go down to Egypt, for I will there make of you a great nation.

⁴I will go down with you to Egypt, and I will also surely bring you [your people Israel] up again; and Joseph will put his hand upon your eyes [when they are about to close in death].

⁵So Jacob arose *and* set out from Beersheba, and Israel's sons conveyed their father, their little ones, and their wives in the wagons that Pharaoh had sent to carry him.

⁶And they took their cattle and the gains which they had acquired in the land of Canaan and came into Egypt, Jacob and all his offspring with him:

⁷His sons and his sons' sons with him, his daughters and his sons' daughters—all his offspring he brought with him into Egypt.

⁸And these are the names of the descendants of Israel who came into Egypt, Jacob and his sons: Reuben, Jacob's firstborn.

⁹And the sons of Reuben: Hanoch, Pallu, Hezron, and Carmi.

¹⁰The sons of Simeon: Jemuel, Jamin, Ohad, Jachin, Zohar, and Shaul the son of a Canaanite woman.

¹¹The sons of Levi: Gershon, Kohath, and Merari.

¹²The sons of Judah: Er, Onan, Shelah, Perez, and Zerah; but Er and Onan died in the land of Canaan. And the sons of Perez were Hezron and Hamul.

¹³The sons of Issachar: Tola, Puvah, Iob, and Shimron.

¹⁴The sons of Zebulun: Sered, Elon, and Jahleel.

¹⁵These are the sons of Leah, whom she bore to Jacob in Padan-aram, together with his daughter Dinah. All of his sons and his daughters numbered thirty-three.

¹⁶The sons of Gad: Ziphion, Haggi, Shuni, Ezbon, Eri, Arodi, and Areli.

¹⁷The sons of Asher: Imnah, Ishvah, Ishvi, Beriah, and Serah their sister. And the sons of Beriah: Heber and Malchiel.

¹⁸These are the sons of Zilpah, [the maid] whom Laban gave to Leah his daughter. And these she bore to Jacob—sixteen persons all told.

¹⁹The sons of Rachel, Jacob's wife: Joseph and Benjamin.

²⁰And to Joseph in the land of Egypt were born Manasseh and Ephraim, whom Asenath daughter of Potiphera, priest of On, bore to him.

---

^rOr, *Nemuel*   ^sOr, *Jarib*   ^tOr, *Zerah;* see 1 Chr. 4:24
^uOr, *Gershom*   ^vOr, *Puah, and Jashub*   ^wOr, *Ozni*   ^xOr,
Arod   ^yOr, *prince*

New American Standard

27 When they told him all the words of Joseph that he had spoken to them, and when he saw the wagons that Joseph had sent to carry him, the spirit of their father Jacob revived.
28 Then Israel said, "It is enough; my son Joseph is still alive. I will go and see him before I die."

Jacob Moves to Egypt

46 SO ISRAEL set out with all that he had, and came to Beersheba, and offered sacrifices to the God of his father Isaac.
2 God spoke to Israel in visions of the night and said, "Jacob, Jacob." And he said, "Here I am."
3 He said, "I am God, the God of your father; do not be afraid to go down to Egypt, for I will make you a great nation there.
4 "I will go down with you to Egypt, and I will also surely bring you up again; and Joseph will close your eyes."
5 ¶ Then Jacob arose from Beersheba; and the sons of Israel carried their father Jacob and their little ones and their wives in the wagons which Pharaoh had sent to carry him.
6 They took their livestock and their property, which they had acquired in the land of Canaan, and came to Egypt, Jacob and all his descendants with him:
7 his sons and his grandsons with him, his daughters and his granddaughters, and all his descendants he brought with him to Egypt.

Those Who Came to Egypt

8 ¶ Now these are the names of the sons of Israel, Jacob and his sons, who went to Egypt: Reuben, Jacob's firstborn.
9 The sons of Reuben: Hanoch and Pallu and Hezron and Carmi.
10 The sons of Simeon: Jemuel and Jamin and Ohad and Jachin and Zohar and Shaul the son of a Canaanite woman.
11 The sons of Levi: Gershon, Kohath, and Merari.
12 The sons of Judah: Er and Onan and Shelah and Perez and Zerah (but Er and Onan died in the land of Canaan). And the sons of Perez were Hezron and Hamul.
13 The sons of Issachar: Tola and Puvvah and Iob and Shimron.
14 The sons of Zebulun: Sered and Elon and Jahleel.
15 These are the sons of Leah, whom she bore to Jacob in Paddan-aram, with his daughter Dinah; all his sons and his daughters *numbered* thirty-three.
16 The sons of Gad: Ziphion and Haggi, Shuni and Ezbon, Eri and Arodi and Areli.
17 The sons of Asher: Imnah and Ishvah and Ishvi and Beriah and their sister Serah. And the sons of Beriah: Heber and Malchiel.
18 These are the sons of Zilpah, whom Laban gave to his daughter Leah; and she bore to Jacob these sixteen persons.
19 The sons of Jacob's wife Rachel: Joseph and Benjamin.
20 Now to Joseph in the land of Egypt were born Manasseh and Ephraim, whom Asenath, the daughter of Potiphera, priest of On, bore to him.

New International

stunned; he did not believe them. 27But when they told him everything Joseph had said to them, and when he saw the carts Joseph had sent to carry him back, the spirit of their father Jacob revived. 28And Israel said, "I'm convinced! My son Joseph is still alive. I will go and see him before I die."

Jacob Goes to Egypt

46 SO ISRAEL set out with all that was his, and when he reached Beersheba, he offered sacrifices to the God of his father Isaac.
2And God spoke to Israel in a vision at night and said, "Jacob! Jacob!"
"Here I am," he replied.
3"I am God, the God of your father," he said. "Do not be afraid to go down to Egypt, for I will make you into a great nation there. 4I will go down to Egypt with you, and I will surely bring you back again. And Joseph's own hand will close your eyes."
5Then Jacob left Beersheba, and Israel's sons took their father Jacob and their children and their wives in the carts that Pharaoh had sent to transport him. 6They also took with them their livestock and the possessions they had acquired in Canaan, and Jacob and all his offspring went to Egypt. 7He took with him to Egypt his sons and grandsons and his daughters and granddaughters—all his offspring.

8These are the names of the sons of Israel (Jacob and his descendants) who went to Egypt:

Reuben the firstborn of Jacob.
9The sons of Reuben:
   Hanoch, Pallu, Hezron and Carmi.
10The sons of Simeon:
   Jemuel, Jamin, Ohad, Jakin, Zohar and Shaul the son of a Canaanite woman.
11The sons of Levi:
   Gershon, Kohath and Merari.
12The sons of Judah:
   Er, Onan, Shelah, Perez and Zerah (but Er and Onan had died in the land of Canaan).
   The sons of Perez:
   Hezron and Hamul.
13The sons of Issachar:
   Tola, Puah,y Jashubz and Shimron.
14The sons of Zebulun:
   Sered, Elon and Jahleel.
15These were the sons Leah bore to Jacob in Paddan Aram,a besides his daughter Dinah. These sons and daughters of his were thirty-three in all.

16The sons of Gad:
   Zephon,b Haggi, Shuni, Ezbon, Eri, Arodi and Areli.
17The sons of Asher:
   Imnah, Ishvah, Ishvi and Beriah.
   Their sister was Serah.
   The sons of Beriah:
   Heber and Malkiel.
18These were the children born to Jacob by Zilpah, whom Laban had given to his daughter Leah—sixteen in all.

19The sons of Jacob's wife Rachel:
   Joseph and Benjamin. 20In Egypt, Manasseh and Ephraim were born to Joseph by Asenath daughter of Potiphera, priest of On.c

y 13 Samaritan Pentateuch and Syriac (see also 1 Chron. 7:1); Masoretic Text *Puvah*　　z 13 Samaritan Pentateuch and some Septuagint manuscripts (see also Num. 26:24 and 1 Chron. 7:1); Masoretic Text *Iob*　　a 15 That is, Northwest Mesopotamia　　b 16 Samaritan Pentateuch and Septuagint (see also Num. 26:15); Masoretic Text *Ziphion*　　c 20 That is, Heliopolis

King James

²¹ ¶ And the sons of Benjamin *were* Belah, and Becher, and Ashbel, Gera, and Naaman, Ehi, and Rosh, Muppim, and ^zHuppim, and Ard.

²²These *are* the sons of Rachel, which were born to Jacob: all the souls *were* fourteen.

²³ ¶ And the sons of Dan; ^aHushim.

²⁴ ¶ And the sons of Naphtali; Jahzeel, and Guni, and Jezer, and Shillem.

²⁵These *are* the sons of Bilhah, which Laban gave unto Rachel his daughter, and she bare these unto Jacob: all the souls *were* seven.

²⁶All the souls that came with Jacob into Egypt, which came out of his ^bloins, besides Jacob's sons' wives, all the souls *were* threescore and six;

²⁷And the sons of Joseph, which were born him in Egypt, *were* two souls: all the souls of the house of Jacob, which came into Egypt, *were* threescore and ten.

²⁸ ¶ And he sent Judah before him unto Joseph, to direct his face unto Goshen; and they came into the land of Goshen.

²⁹And Joseph made ready his chariot, and went up to meet Israel his father, to Goshen, and presented himself unto him; and he fell on his neck, and wept on his neck a good while.

³⁰And Israel said unto Joseph, Now let me die, since I have seen thy face, because thou *art* yet alive.

³¹And Joseph said unto his brethren, and unto his father's house, I will go up, and show Pharaoh, and say unto him, My brethren, and my father's house, which *were* in the land of Canaan, are come unto me;

³²And the men *are* shepherds, for ^ctheir trade hath been to feed cattle; and they have brought their flocks, and their herds, and all that they have.

³³And it shall come to pass, when Pharaoh shall call you, and shall say, What *is* your occupation?

³⁴That ye shall say, Thy servants' trade hath been about cattle from our youth even until now, both we, *and* also our fathers: that ye may dwell in the land of Goshen; for every shepherd *is* an abomination unto the Egyptians.

47 THEN JOSEPH came and told Pharaoh, and said, My father and my brethren, and their flocks, and their herds, and all that they have, are come out of the land of Canaan; and, behold, they *are* in the land of Goshen.

²And he took some of his brethren, *even* five men, and presented them unto Pharaoh.

³And Pharaoh said unto his brethren, What *is* your occupation? And they said unto Pharaoh, Thy servants *are* shepherds, both we, *and* also our fathers.

⁴They said moreover unto Pharaoh, For to sojourn in the land are we come; for thy servants have no pasture for their flocks; for the famine *is* sore in the land of Canaan: now therefore, we pray thee, let thy servants dwell in the land of Goshen.

⁵And Pharaoh spake unto Joseph, saying, Thy father and thy brethren are come unto thee:

⁶The land of Egypt *is* before thee; in the best of the land make thy father and brethren to dwell; in the land of Goshen let them dwell: and if thou knowest *any* men of activity among them, then make them rulers over my cattle.

⁷And Joseph brought in Jacob his father, and set him before Pharaoh: and Jacob blessed Pharaoh.

⁸And Pharaoh said unto Jacob, ^dHow old *art* thou?

Amplified

²¹And the sons of ^sBenjamin: Bela, Becher, Ashbel, Gera, Naaman, Ehi, Rosh, Muppim, Huppim, and Ard.

²²These are the sons of Rachel, who were born to Jacob—fourteen persons in all.

²³The son of Dan: Hushim.

²⁴The sons of Naphtali: Jahzeel, Guni, Jezer, and Shillem.

²⁵These are the sons of Bilhah, [the maid] whom Laban gave to Rachel his daughter. And she bore these to Jacob—seven persons in all.

²⁶All the persons who came with Jacob into Egypt—who were his own offspring, not counting the wives of Jacob's sons—were sixty-six persons all told.

²⁷And the sons of Joseph, who were born to him in Egypt, were two persons. All the persons of the house of Jacob [including Joseph and Jacob himself], who came into Egypt, were seventy.

²⁸And he sent Judah before him to Joseph, to direct him to Goshen *and* meet him there; and they came into the land of Goshen.

²⁹Then Joseph made ready his chariot and went up to meet Israel his father in Goshen; and he presented himself *and* gave distinct evidence of himself to him [that he was Joseph], and [each] fell on the [other's] neck and wept on his neck a good while.

³⁰And Israel said to Joseph, Now let me die, since I have seen your face [and know] that you are still alive.

³¹Joseph said to his brothers and to his father's household, I will go up and tell Pharaoh and say to him, My brothers and my father's household, who were in the land of Canaan, have come to me.

³²And the men are shepherds, for their occupation has been keeping livestock, and they have brought their flocks and their herds and all that they have.

³³When Pharaoh calls you and says, What is your occupation?

³⁴You shall say, Your servants' occupation has been as keepers of livestock from our youth until now, both we and our fathers before us—in order that you may live in the land of Goshen, for every shepherd is an abomination to the Egyptians.

47 THEN JOSEPH came and told Pharaoh, My father and my brothers, with their flocks and their herds and all that they own, have come from the land of Canaan, and they are in the land of Goshen.

²And from among his brothers he took five men and presented them to Pharaoh.

³And Pharaoh said to his brothers, What is your occupation? And they said to Pharaoh, Your servants are shepherds, both we and our fathers before us.

⁴Moreover, they said to Pharaoh, We have come to sojourn in the land, for your servants have no pasture for our flocks, for the famine is very severe in Canaan. So now, we pray you, let your servants dwell in the land of Goshen.

⁵And Pharaoh spoke to Joseph, saying, Your father and your brothers have come to you.

⁶The land of Egypt is before you; make your father and your brothers dwell in the best of the land. Let them live in the land of Goshen. And if you know of any men of ability among them, put them in charge of my cattle.

⁷Then Joseph brought in Jacob his father and presented him before Pharaoh; and Jacob blessed Pharaoh.

⁸And Pharaoh asked Jacob, How old are you?

^sBenjamin, whom uninformed artists have frequently pictured as a mere youth when he met Joseph in Egypt, was in fact the father of 10 sons at this time. Joseph was 17 when his brothers sold him; he was in prison 13 years; he had been governor of Egypt during the 7 good years and through 2 years of the famine. So Joseph was 39 years of age at this time, and Benjamin was only a few years younger.

^z*Hupham;* see Num. 26:39   ^aOr, *Shuham;* see Num. 26:42
^bHeb. *thigh;* see ch. 35:11   ^cHeb. *they are men of cattle*
^dHeb. *How many are the days of the years of thy life?*

New American Standard

21 The sons of Benjamin: Bela and Becher and Ashbel, Gera and Naaman, Ehi and Rosh, Muppim and Huppim and Ard.

22 These are the sons of Rachel, who were born to Jacob; *there were* fourteen persons in all.

23 The sons of Dan: Hushim.

24 The sons of Naphtali: Jahzeel and Guni and Jezer and Shillem.

25 These are the sons of Bilhah, whom Laban gave to his daughter Rachel, and she bore these to Jacob; *there were* seven persons in all.

26 All the persons belonging to Jacob, who came to Egypt, his direct descendants, not including the wives of Jacob's sons, *were* sixty-six persons in all,

27 and the sons of Joseph, who were born to him in Egypt were two; all the persons of the house of Jacob, who came to Egypt, *were* seventy.

28 ¶ Now he sent Judah before him to Joseph, to point out *the way* before him to Goshen; and they came into the land of Goshen.

29 Joseph prepared his chariot and went up to Goshen to meet his father Israel; as soon as he appeared before him, he fell on his neck and wept on his neck a long time.

30 Then Israel said to Joseph, "Now let me die, since I have seen your face, that you are still alive."

31 Joseph said to his brothers and to his father's household, "I will go up and tell Pharaoh, and will say to him, 'My brothers and my father's household, who *were* in the land of Canaan, have come to me;

32 and the men are shepherds, for they have been keepers of livestock; and they have brought their flocks and their herds and all that they have.'

33 "When Pharaoh calls you and says, 'What is your occupation?'

34 you shall say, 'Your servants have been keepers of livestock from our youth even until now, both we and our fathers,' that you may live in the land of Goshen; for every shepherd is loathsome to the Egyptians."

Jacob's Family Settles in Goshen

47 THEN JOSEPH went in and told Pharaoh, and said, "My father and my brothers and their flocks and their herds and all that they have, have come out of the land of Canaan; and behold, they are in the land of Goshen."

2 He took five men from among his brothers and presented them to Pharaoh.

3 Then Pharaoh said to his brothers, "What is your occupation?" So they said to Pharaoh, "Your servants are shepherds, both we and our fathers."

4 They said to Pharaoh, "We have come to sojourn in the land, for there is no pasture for your servants' flocks, for the famine is severe in the land of Canaan. Now, therefore, please let your servants live in the land of Goshen."

5 Then Pharaoh said to Joseph, "Your father and your brothers have come to you.

6 "The land of Egypt is ᵍat your disposal; settle your father and your brothers in the best of the land, let them live in the land of Goshen; and if you know any capable men among them, then put them in charge of my livestock."

7 ¶ Then Joseph brought his father Jacob and presented him to Pharaoh; and Jacob blessed Pharaoh.

8 Pharaoh said to Jacob, "How many years have you lived?"

New International

21 The sons of Benjamin:
Bela, Beker, Ashbel, Gera, Naaman, Ehi, Rosh, Muppim, Huppim and Ard.

22 These were the sons of Rachel who were born to Jacob—fourteen in all.

23 The son of Dan:
Hushim.

24 The sons of Naphtali:
Jahziel, Guni, Jezer and Shillem.

25 These were the sons born to Jacob by Bilhah, whom Laban had given to his daughter Rachel—seven in all.

26 All those who went to Egypt with Jacob—those who were his direct descendants, not counting his sons' wives—numbered sixty-six persons. 27 With the two sonsᵈ who had been born to Joseph in Egypt, the members of Jacob's family, which went to Egypt, were seventyᵉ in all.

28 Now Jacob sent Judah ahead of him to Joseph to get directions to Goshen. When they arrived in the region of Goshen, 29 Joseph had his chariot made ready and went to Goshen to meet his father Israel. As soon as Joseph appeared before him, he threw his arms around his fatherᶠ and wept for a long time.

30 Israel said to Joseph, "Now I am ready to die, since I have seen for myself that you are still alive."

31 Then Joseph said to his brothers and to his father's household, "I will go up and speak to Pharaoh and will say to him, 'My brothers and my father's household, who were living in the land of Canaan, have come to me. 32 The men are shepherds; they tend livestock, and they have brought along their flocks and herds and everything they own.' 33 When Pharaoh calls you in and asks, 'What is your occupation?' 34 you should answer, 'Your servants have tended livestock from our boyhood on, just as our fathers did.' Then you will be allowed to settle in the region of Goshen, for all shepherds are detestable to the Egyptians."

47 JOSEPH WENT and told Pharaoh, "My father and brothers, with their flocks and herds and everything they own, have come from the land of Canaan and are now in Goshen." 2 He chose five of his brothers and presented them before Pharaoh.

3 Pharaoh asked the brothers, "What is your occupation?"

"Your servants are shepherds," they replied to Pharaoh, "just as our fathers were." 4 They also said to him, "We have come to live here awhile, because the famine is severe in Canaan and your servants' flocks have no pasture. So now, please let your servants settle in Goshen."

5 Pharaoh said to Joseph, "Your father and your brothers have come to you, 6 and the land of Egypt is before you; settle your father and your brothers in the best part of the land. Let them live in Goshen. And if you know of any among them with special ability, put them in charge of my own livestock."

7 Then Joseph brought his father Jacob in and presented him before Pharaoh. After Jacob blessedᵍ Pharaoh, 8 Pharaoh asked him, "How old are you?"

ᵍ Lit *before you*

ᵈ 27 Hebrew; Septuagint *the nine children*   ᵉ 27 Hebrew (see also Exodus 1:5 and footnote); Septuagint (see also Acts 7:14) *seventy-five*   ᶠ 29 Hebrew *around him*   ᵍ 7 Or *greeted*

King James

9And Jacob said unto Pharaoh, The days of the years of my pilgrimage *are* an hundred and thirty years: few and evil have the days of the years of my life been, and have not attained unto the days of the years of the life of my fathers in the days of their pilgrimage.

10And Jacob blessed Pharaoh, and went out from before Pharaoh.

11 ¶ And Joseph placed his father and his brethren, and gave them a possession in the land of Egypt, in the best of the land, in the land of Rameses, as Pharaoh had commanded.

12And Joseph nourished his father, and his brethren, and all his father's household, with bread, *ef*according to *their* families.

Joseph and the famine

13 ¶ And *there was* no bread in all the land; for the famine *was* very sore, so that the land of Egypt and *all* the land of Canaan fainted by reason of the famine.

14And Joseph gathered up all the money that was found in the land of Egypt, and in the land of Canaan, for the corn which they bought: and Joseph brought the money into Pharaoh's house.

15And when money failed in the land of Egypt, and in the land of Canaan, all the Egyptians came unto Joseph, and said, Give us bread: for why should we die in thy presence? for the money faileth.

16And Joseph said, Give your cattle; and I will give you for your cattle, if money fail.

17And they brought their cattle unto Joseph: and Joseph gave them bread *in exchange* for horses, and for the flocks, and for the cattle of the herds, and for the asses: and he *g*fed them with bread for all their cattle for that year.

18When that year was ended, they came unto him the second year, and said unto him, We will not hide *it* from my lord, how that our money is spent; my lord also hath our herds of cattle; there is not aught left in the sight of my lord, but our bodies, and our lands:

19Wherefore shall we die before thine eyes, both we and our land? buy us and our land for bread, and we and our land will be servants unto Pharaoh: and give *us* seed, that we may live, and not die, that the land be not desolate.

20And Joseph bought all the land of Egypt for Pharaoh; for the Egyptians sold every man his field, because the famine prevailed over them: so the land became Pharaoh's.

21And as for the people, he removed them to cities from *one* end of the borders of Egypt even to the *other* end thereof.

22Only the land of the *h*priests bought he not; for the priests had a portion *assigned them* of Pharaoh, and did eat their portion which Pharaoh gave them: wherefore they sold not their lands.

23Then Joseph said unto the people, Behold, I have bought you this day and your land for Pharaoh: lo, *here is* seed for you, and ye shall sow the land.

24And it shall come to pass in the increase, that ye shall give the fifth *part* unto Pharaoh, and four parts shall be your own, for seed of the field, and for your food, and for them of your households, and for food for your little ones.

25And they said, Thou hast saved our lives: let us find grace in the sight of my lord, and we will be Pharaoh's servants.

26And Joseph made it a law over the land of Egypt unto this day, *that* Pharaoh should have the fifth *part;* except the land of the *i*priests only, *which* became not Pharaoh's.

27 ¶ And Israel dwelt in the land of Egypt, in the country of Goshen; and they had possessions therein, and grew, and multiplied exceedingly.

Amplified

9Jacob said to Pharaoh, The days of the years of my pilgrimage are 130 years; few and evil have the days of the years of my life been, and they have *t*not attained to those of the life of my fathers in their pilgrimage.

10And Jacob blessed Pharaoh and went out from his presence.

11Joseph settled his father and brethren and gave them a possession in Egypt in the best of the land, in the land of Rameses (Goshen), as Pharaoh commanded.

12And Joseph supplied his father and his brethren and all his father's household with food, according to [the needs of] their families.

13[In the course of time] there was no food in all the land, for the famine was distressingly severe, so that the land of Egypt and all the land of Canaan hung in doubt and wavered by reason of the hunger (destitution, starvation) of the famine.

14And Joseph gathered up all the money that was found in the land of Egypt and in the land of Canaan [in payment] for the grain which they bought, and Joseph brought the money into Pharaoh's house.

15And when the money was exhausted in the land of Egypt and in the land of Canaan, all the Egyptians came to Joseph and said, Give us food! Why should we die before your very eyes? For we have no money left.

16Joseph said, Give up your livestock, and I will give you food in exchange for [them] if your money is gone.

17So they brought their livestock to Joseph, and [he] gave them food in exchange for the horses, flocks, cattle of the herds, and the donkeys; and he supplied them with food in exchange for all their livestock that year.

18When that year was ended, they came to [Joseph] the second year and said to him, We will not hide from my lord [the fact] that our money is spent; my lord also has our herds of livestock; there is nothing left in the sight of my lord but our bodies and our lands.

19Why should we perish before your eyes, both we and our land? Buy us and our land in exchange for food, and we and our land will be servants to Pharaoh. And give us seed [to plant], that we may live and not die, and that the land may not be desolate.

20And Joseph bought all the land of Egypt for Pharaoh; for the Egyptians sold every man his field because of the overwhelming severity of the famine upon them. The land became Pharaoh's,

21And as for the people, he removed them to cities *and* practically made slaves of them [at their own request], from one end of the borders of Egypt to the other.

22Only the priests' land he did not buy, for the priests had a fixed pension from Pharaoh and lived on the amount Pharaoh gave them. So they did not sell their land.

23Then Joseph said to the people, Behold, I have today bought you and your land for Pharaoh. Now here is seed for you, and you shall sow the land.

24At [harvest time when you reap] the increase, you shall give one-fifth of it to Pharaoh, and four-fifths shall be your own to use for seed for the field and as food for you and those of your households and for your little ones.

25And they said, You have saved our lives! Let us find favor in the sight of my lord; and we will be Pharaoh's servants.

26And Joseph made it a law over the land of Egypt—to this day—that Pharaoh should have the fifth part [of the crops]; it was the priests' land only which did not become Pharaoh's.

27And Israel dwelt in the land of Egypt, in the country of Goshen; and they gained possessions there and grew and multiplied exceedingly.

---

*t*Abraham, Jacob's grandfather, had lived to be 175 years old; Isaac, his father, lived to be 180. Jacob lived seventeen years after making this statement to Pharaoh, in which time he had an opportunity to get a much more optimistic view of God's treatment of him. He died at 147, having said, "The redeeming Angel . . . has redeemed me continually from every evil" (Gen. 48:16).

---

*e*Or, *as a little child is nourished*   *f*Heb. *according to the little ones*   *g*Heb. *led them*   *h*Or, *princes;* see ch. 41:45   *i*Or, *princes;* see ver. 22

New American Standard

9 So Jacob said to Pharaoh, "The years of my sojourning are one hundred and thirty; few and unpleasant have been the years of my life, nor have they attained the years that my fathers lived during the days of their sojourning."

10 And Jacob blessed Pharaoh, and went out from his presence.

11 So Joseph settled his father and his brothers and gave them a possession in the land of Egypt, in the best of the land, in the land of Rameses, as Pharaoh had ordered.

12 Joseph provided his father and his brothers and all his father's household with food, according to their little ones.

13 ¶ Now there was no food in all the land, because the famine was very severe, so that the land of Egypt and the land of Canaan languished because of the famine.

14 Joseph gathered all the money that was found in the land of Egypt and in the land of Canaan for the grain which they bought, and Joseph brought the money into Pharaoh's house.

15 When the money was all spent in the land of Egypt and in the land of Canaan, all the Egyptians came to Joseph and said, "Give us food, for why should we die in your presence? For *our* money is gone."

16 Then Joseph said, "Give up your livestock, and I will give you *food* for your livestock, since *your* money is gone."

17 So they brought their livestock to Joseph, and Joseph gave them food in exchange for the horses and the flocks and the herds and the donkeys; and he fed them with food in exchange for all their livestock that year.

18 When that year was ended, they came to him the next year and said to him, "We will not hide from my lord that our money is all spent, and the cattle are my lord's. There is nothing left for my lord except our bodies and our lands.

19 "Why should we die before your eyes, both we and our land? Buy us and our land for food, and we and our land will be slaves to Pharaoh. So give us seed, that we may live and not die, and that the land may not be desolate."

Result of the Famine

20 ¶ So Joseph bought all the land of Egypt for Pharaoh, for every Egyptian sold his field, because the famine was severe upon them. Thus the land became Pharaoh's.

21 As for the people, he removed them to the cities from one end of Egypt's border to the other.

22 Only the land of the priests he did not buy, for the priests had an allotment from Pharaoh, and they lived off the allotment which Pharaoh gave them. Therefore, they did not sell their land.

23 Then Joseph said to the people, "Behold, I have today bought you and your land for Pharaoh; now, *here* is seed for you, and you may sow the land.

24 "At the harvest you shall give a fifth to Pharaoh, and four-fifths shall be your own for seed of the field and for your food and for those of your households and as food for your little ones."

25 So they said, "You have saved our lives! Let us find favor in the sight of my lord, and we will be Pharaoh's slaves."

26 Joseph made it a statute concerning the land of Egypt *valid* to this day, that Pharaoh should have the fifth; only the land of the priests did not become Pharaoh's.

27 ¶ Now Israel lived in the land of Egypt, in Goshen, and they acquired property in it and were fruitful and became very numerous.

New International

9 And Jacob said to Pharaoh, "The years of my pilgrimage are a hundred and thirty. My years have been few and difficult, and they do not equal the years of the pilgrimage of my fathers." 10 Then Jacob blessed[h] Pharaoh and went out from his presence.

11 So Joseph settled his father and his brothers in Egypt and gave them property in the best part of the land, the district of Rameses, as Pharaoh directed. 12 Joseph also provided his father and his brothers and all his father's household with food, according to the number of their children.

Joseph and the Famine

13 There was no food, however, in the whole region because the famine was severe; both Egypt and Canaan wasted away because of the famine. 14 Joseph collected all the money that was to be found in Egypt and Canaan in payment for the grain they were buying, and he brought it to Pharaoh's palace. 15 When the money of the people of Egypt and Canaan was gone, all Egypt came to Joseph and said, "Give us food. Why should we die before your eyes? Our money is used up."

16 "Then bring your livestock," said Joseph. "I will sell you food in exchange for your livestock, since your money is gone." 17 So they brought their livestock to Joseph, and he gave them food in exchange for their horses, their sheep and goats, their cattle and donkeys. And he brought them through that year with food in exchange for all their livestock.

18 When that year was over, they came to him the following year and said, "We cannot hide from our lord the fact that since our money is gone and our livestock belongs to you, there is nothing left for our lord except our bodies and our land. 19 Why should we perish before your eyes—we and our land as well? Buy us and our land in exchange for food, and we with our land will be in bondage to Pharaoh. Give us seed so that we may live and not die, and that the land may not become desolate."

20 So Joseph bought all the land in Egypt for Pharaoh. The Egyptians, one and all, sold their fields, because the famine was too severe for them. The land became Pharaoh's, 21 and Joseph reduced the people to servitude,[i] from one end of Egypt to the other. 22 However, he did not buy the land of the priests, because they received a regular allotment from Pharaoh and had food enough from the allotment Pharaoh gave them. That is why they did not sell their land.

23 Joseph said to the people, "Now that I have bought you and your land today for Pharaoh, here is seed for you so you can plant the ground. 24 But when the crop comes in, give a fifth of it to Pharaoh. The other four-fifths you may keep as seed for the fields and as food for yourselves and your households and your children."

25 "You have saved our lives," they said. "May we find favor in the eyes of our lord; we will be in bondage to Pharaoh."

26 So Joseph established it as a law concerning land in Egypt—still in force today—that a fifth of the produce belongs to Pharaoh. It was only the land of the priests that did not become Pharaoh's.

27 Now the Israelites settled in Egypt in the region of Goshen. They acquired property there and were fruitful and increased greatly in number.

---

h 10 Or *said farewell to*   i 21 Samaritan Pentateuch and Septuagint (see also Vulgate); Masoretic Text *and he moved the people into the cities*

King James

[28] And Jacob lived in the land of Egypt seventeen years: so [j] the whole age of Jacob was an hundred forty and seven years.

[29] And the time drew nigh that Israel must die: and he called his son Joseph, and said unto him, If now I have found grace in thy sight, put, I pray thee, thy hand under my thigh, and deal kindly and truly with me; bury me not, I pray thee, in Egypt:

[30] But I will lie with my fathers, and thou shalt carry me out of Egypt, and bury me in their buryingplace. And he said, I will do as thou hast said.

[31] And he said, Swear unto me. And he sware unto him. And Israel bowed himself upon the bed's head.

Jacob blesses Joseph's sons

48 AND IT came to pass after these things, that *one* told Joseph, Behold, thy father *is* sick: and he took with him his two sons, Manasseh and Ephraim.

[2] And *one* told Jacob, and said, Behold, thy son Joseph cometh unto thee: and Israel strengthened himself, and sat upon the bed.

[3] And Jacob said unto Joseph, God Almighty appeared unto me at Luz in the land of Canaan, and blessed me,

[4] And said unto me, Behold, I will make thee fruitful, and multiply thee, and I will make of thee a multitude of people; and will give this land to thy seed after thee *for* an everlasting possession.

[5] ¶ And now thy two sons, Ephraim and Manasseh, which were born unto thee in the land of Egypt before I came unto thee into Egypt, *are* mine; as Reuben and Simeon, they shall be mine.

[6] And thy issue, which thou begettest after them, shall be thine, *and* shall be called after the name of their brethren in their inheritance.

[7] And as for me, when I came from Padan, Rachel died by me in the land of Canaan in the way, when yet *there was* but a little way to come unto Ephrath: and I buried her there in the way of Ephrath; the same *is* Bethlehem.

[8] And Israel beheld Joseph's sons, and said, Who *are* these?

[9] And Joseph said unto his father, They *are* my sons, whom God hath given me in this *place*. And he said, Bring them, I pray thee, unto me, and I will bless them.

[10] Now the eyes of Israel were [k] dim for age, *so that* he could not see. And he brought them near unto him; and he kissed them, and embraced them.

[11] And Israel said unto Joseph, I had not thought to see thy face: and, lo, God hath shown me also thy seed.

[12] And Joseph brought them out from between his knees, and he bowed himself with his face to the earth.

[13] And Joseph took them both, Ephraim in his right hand toward Israel's left hand, and Manasseh in his left hand toward Israel's right hand, and brought *them* near unto him.

[14] And Israel stretched out his right hand, and laid *it* upon Ephraim's head, who *was* the younger, and his left hand upon Manasseh's head, guiding his hands wittingly; for Manasseh *was* the firstborn.

[15] ¶ And he blessed Joseph, and said, God, before whom my fathers Abraham and Isaac did walk, the God which fed me all my life long unto this day,

Amplified

[28] And Jacob lived in the land of Egypt seventeen years; so Jacob reached the age of 147 years.

[29] When the time drew near that Israel must die, he called his son Joseph and said to him, If now I have found favor in your sight, [u] put your hand under my thigh and [promise to] deal loyally and faithfully with me. Do not bury me, I beg of you, in Egypt,

[30] But let me lie with my fathers; you shall carry me out of Egypt and bury me in their burying place. And [Joseph] said, I will do as you have directed.

[31] Then Jacob said, Swear to me [that you will do it]. And he swore to him. And Israel bowed himself upon the head of the bed.

48 SOME TIME after these things occurred, someone told Joseph, Behold, your father is sick. And he took with him his two sons, Manasseh and Ephraim [and went to Goshen].

[2] When Jacob was told, Your son Joseph has come to you, Israel collected his strength and sat up on the bed.

[3] And Jacob said to Joseph, God Almighty appeared to me at Luz [Bethel] in the land of Canaan and blessed me

[4] And said to me, Behold, I will make you fruitful and multiply you, and I will make you a multitude of people and will give this land to your descendants after you as an everlasting possession. [Gen. 28:13–22; 35:6–15.]

[5] And now your two sons, [Ephraim and Manasseh], who were born to you in the land of Egypt before I came to you in Egypt, are mine. [I am adopting them, and now] as Reuben and Simeon, [they] shall be mine.

[6] But other sons who may be born after them shall be your own; and they shall be called after the names of these [two] brothers *and* reckoned as belonging to them [when they come] into their inheritance.

[7] And as for me, when I came from Padan, Rachel died at my side in the land of Canaan on the way, when yet there was but a little way to come to Ephrath; and I buried her there on the way to Ephrath, that is, Bethlehem.

[8] When Israel [almost blind] saw Joseph's sons, he said, Who are these?

[9] And Joseph said to his father, They are my sons, whom God has given me in this place. And he said, Bring them to me, I pray you, that I may bless them.

[10] Now Israel's eyes were dim from age, so that he could not see. And Joseph brought them near to him, and he kissed and embraced them.

[11] Israel said to Joseph, I had not thought that I would see your face, but see, God has shown me your offspring also.

[12] Then Joseph took [the boys] from [his father's embrace] and he bowed [before him] with his face to the earth.

[13] Then Joseph took both [boys], Ephraim with his right hand toward Israel's left, and Manasseh with his left hand toward Israel's right, and brought them close to him.

[14] And Israel reached out his right hand and laid it on the head of Ephraim, who was the younger, and his left hand on Manasseh's head, [v] crossing his hands intentionally, for Manasseh was the firstborn.

[15] Then [Jacob] blessed Joseph and said, God [Himself], before Whom my fathers Abraham and Isaac lived *and* walked habitually, God [Himself], Who has [been my Shepherd and has led and] fed me from the time I came into being until this day,

[j] Heb. *the days of the years of his life*   [k] Heb. *heavy*

New American Standard

28 Jacob lived in the land of Egypt seventeen years; so the length of Jacob's life was one hundred and forty-seven years.

29 ¶ When the time for Israel to die drew near, he called his son Joseph and said to him, "Please, if I have found favor in your sight, place now your hand under my thigh and deal with me in kindness and [h]faithfulness. Please do not bury me in Egypt,

30 but when I lie down with my fathers, you shall carry me out of Egypt and bury me in their burial place." And he said, "I will do as you have said."

31 He said, "Swear to me." So he swore to him. Then Israel bowed *in worship* at the head of the bed.

Israel's Last Days

48 NOW IT came about after these things that Joseph was told, "Behold, your father is sick." So he took his two sons Manasseh and Ephraim with him.

2 When it was told to Jacob, "Behold, your son Joseph has come to you," Israel collected his strength and sat up in the bed.

3 Then Jacob said to Joseph, "God Almighty appeared to me at Luz in the land of Canaan and blessed me,

4 and He said to me, 'Behold, I will make you fruitful and numerous, and I will make you a company of peoples, and will give this land to your descendants after you for an everlasting possession.'

5 "Now your two sons, who were born to you in the land of Egypt before I came to you in Egypt, are mine; Ephraim and Manasseh shall be mine, as Reuben and Simeon are.

6 "But your offspring that have been born after them shall be yours; they shall be called by the names of their brothers in their inheritance.

7 "Now as for me, when I came from Paddan, Rachel died, to my sorrow, in the land of Canaan on the journey, when there was still some distance to go to Ephrath; and I buried her there on the way to Ephrath (that is, Bethlehem)."

8 ¶ When Israel saw Joseph's sons, he said, "Who are these?"

9 Joseph said to his father, "They are my sons, whom God has given me here." So he said, "Bring them to me, please, that I may bless them."

10 Now the eyes of Israel were *so* dim from age *that* he could not see. Then Joseph brought them close to him, and he kissed them and embraced them.

11 Israel said to Joseph, "I never expected to see your face, and behold, God has let me see your children as well."

12 Then Joseph took them from his knees, and bowed with his face to the ground.

13 Joseph took them both, Ephraim with his right hand toward Israel's left, and Manasseh with his left hand toward Israel's right, and brought them close to him.

14 But Israel stretched out his right hand and laid it on the head of Ephraim, who was the younger, and his left hand on Manasseh's head, crossing his hands, although Manasseh was the firstborn.

15 He blessed Joseph, and said,
"The God before whom my fathers Abraham and
Isaac walked,
The God who has been my shepherd all my life
to this day,

New International

28 Jacob lived in Egypt seventeen years, and the years of his life were a hundred and forty-seven. 29 When the time drew near for Israel to die, he called for his son Joseph and said to him, "If I have found favor in your eyes, put your hand under my thigh and promise that you will show me kindness and faithfulness. Do not bury me in Egypt, 30 but when I rest with my fathers, carry me out of Egypt and bury me where they are buried."

"I will do as you say," he said.

31 "Swear to me," he said. Then Joseph swore to him, and Israel worshiped as he leaned on the top of his staff.[j]

Manasseh and Ephraim

48 SOME TIME later Joseph was told, "Your father is ill." So he took his two sons Manasseh and Ephraim along with him. 2 When Jacob was told, "Your son Joseph has come to you," Israel rallied his strength and sat up on the bed.

3 Jacob said to Joseph, "God Almighty[k] appeared to me at Luz in the land of Canaan, and there he blessed me 4 and said to me, 'I am going to make you fruitful and will increase your numbers. I will make you a community of peoples, and I will give this land as an everlasting possession to your descendants after you.'

5 "Now then, your two sons born to you in Egypt before I came to you here will be reckoned as mine; Ephraim and Manasseh will be mine, just as Reuben and Simeon are mine. 6 Any children born to you after them will be yours; in the territory they inherit they will be reckoned under the names of their brothers. 7 As I was returning from Paddan,[l] to my sorrow Rachel died in the land of Canaan while we were still on the way, a little distance from Ephrath. So I buried her there beside the road to Ephrath" (that is, Bethlehem).

8 When Israel saw the sons of Joseph, he asked, "Who are these?"

9 "They are the sons God has given me here," Joseph said to his father.

Then Israel said, "Bring them to me so I may bless them."

10 Now Israel's eyes were failing because of old age, and he could hardly see. So Joseph brought his sons close to him, and his father kissed them and embraced them.

11 Israel said to Joseph, "I never expected to see your face again, and now God has allowed me to see your children too."

12 Then Joseph removed them from Israel's knees and bowed down with his face to the ground. 13 And Joseph took both of them, Ephraim on his right toward Israel's left hand and Manasseh on his left toward Israel's right hand, and brought them close to him. 14 But Israel reached out his right hand and put it on Ephraim's head, though he was the younger, and crossing his arms, he put his left hand on Manasseh's head, even though Manasseh was the firstborn.

15 Then he blessed Joseph and said,

"May the God before whom my fathers
Abraham and Isaac walked,
the God who has been my shepherd
all my life to this day,

j 31 Or *Israel bowed down at the head of his bed*   *k* 3 Hebrew *El-Shaddai*   *l* 7 That is, Northwest Mesopotamia

King James

[16]The Angel which redeemed me from all evil, bless the lads; and let my name be named on them, and the name of my fathers Abraham and Isaac; and let them [l]grow into a multitude in the midst of the earth.

[17]And when Joseph saw that his father laid his right hand upon the head of Ephraim, it [m]displeased him: and he held up his father's hand, to remove it from Ephraim's head unto Manasseh's head.

[18]And Joseph said unto his father, Not so, my father: for this *is* the firstborn; put thy right hand upon his head.

[19]And his father refused, and said, I know *it,* my son, I know *it:* he also shall become a people, and he also shall be great: but truly his younger brother shall be greater than he, and his seed shall become a [n]multitude of nations.

[20]And he blessed them that day, saying, In thee shall Israel bless, saying, God make thee as Ephraim and as Manasseh: and he set Ephraim before Manasseh.

[21]And Israel said unto Joseph, Behold, I die: but God shall be with you, and bring you again unto the land of your fathers.

[22]Moreover I have given to thee one portion above thy brethren, which I took out of the hand of the Amorite with my sword and with my bow.

Jacob blesses his sons

49 AND JACOB called unto his sons, and said, Gather yourselves together, that I may tell you *that* which shall befall you in the last days.

[2]Gather yourselves together, and hear, ye sons of Jacob; and hearken unto Israel your father.

[3] ¶ Reuben, thou *art* my firstborn, my might, and the beginning of my strength, the excellency of dignity, and the excellency of power:

[4]Unstable as water, [o]thou shalt not excel; because thou wentest up to thy father's bed; then defiledst thou *it:* [p]he went up to my couch.

[5] ¶ Simeon and Levi *are* brethren; [q]instruments of cruelty *are in* their habitations.

Amplified

[16]The [w]redeeming Angel [that is, the Angel the Redeemer—not a created being but the Lord Himself] Who has redeemed me continually from every evil, bless the lads! And let my name be perpetuated in them [may they be worthy of having their names coupled with mine], and the names of my fathers Abraham and Isaac; and let them become a multitude in the midst of the earth.

[17]When Joseph saw that his father laid his right hand on Ephraim's head, it displeased him; and he held up his father's hand to move it to Manasseh's head.

[18]And Joseph said, Not so, my father, for this is the firstborn; put your right hand upon his head.

[19]But his father refused and said, I know, my son, I know. He also shall become a people and shall be great; but his younger brother shall be [x]greater than he, and his offspring shall become a multitude of nations.

[20]And he blessed them that day, saying, By you shall Israel bless [one another], saying, May God make you like Ephraim and like Manasseh. And he set Ephraim before Manasseh.

[21]And Israel said to Joseph, Behold, I [am about to] die, but God will be with you and bring you again to the land of your fathers.

[22]Moreover, I have given to you [Joseph] one portion [Shechem, one mountain slope] more than any of your brethren, which I took [reclaiming it] out of the hand of the Amorites with my sword and with my bow. [Gen. 33:18, 19; Josh. 24:32, 33; John 4:5.]

49 AND JACOB called for his sons and said, Gather yourselves together [around me], that I may tell you what shall befall you [y]in the latter *or* last days.

[2]Gather yourselves together and hear, you sons of Jacob; and hearken to Israel your father.

[3]Reuben, you are my [z]firstborn, my might, the beginning (the firstfruits) of my manly strength *and* vigor; [your birthright gave you] the preeminence in dignity and the preeminence in power.

[4]But unstable *and* boiling over like water, you shall [a]not excel *and* have the preeminence [of the firstborn], because you went to your father's bed; you defiled it—he went to my couch! [Gen. 35:22.]

[5]Simeon and Levi are brothers [equally headstrong, deceitful, vindictive, and cruel]; their swords are weapons of violence. [Gen. 34:25–29.]

[w]The "Angel of the Lord" is here identified as Christ Himself. See also the footnote on Gen. 16:7.   [x]This prophecy begins to be fulfilled "from the days of the judges onward, as the tribe of Ephraim in power and compass so increased that it became the head of the northern ten tribes, and its name became of like significance with that of Israel; although, in the time of Moses, Manasseh still outnumbered Ephraim by 20,000" (Karl F. Keil and F. Delitzsch, *Biblical Commentary on the Old Testament*). Joshua, whom Israel so long regarded as their ruler, was an Ephraimite. The ark of the covenant was placed in Shiloh in the territory of Ephraim, which increased the tribe's prestige. How could Jacob have prophesied Ephraim's supremacy so positively except by divine inspiration? [y]See Deut. 33, where Moses blesses the same tribes in a similar prophetic way.   [z]Reuben was the eldest of Jacob's twelve sons and therefore entitled to the birthright, which would make him successor to his father as head of the family or tribe and inheritor of a double portion of his father's estate. But Reuben forfeited all this by his conduct with Bilhah, his father's concubine (Gen. 35:22). By adopting Joseph's two sons, Ephraim and Manasseh, and giving each of them a portion of the inheritance, Jacob virtually gave Joseph Reuben's extra portion of the land. And Judah became the tribal leader in Reuben's place (Gen. 49:8-10). [a]The whole fertile territory once occupied by the tribe of Reuben has long since been deserted by its settled inhabitants and given up to the nomad tribes of the desert. Reuben did "not excel," and even before Jacob's death he had lost his "preeminence of the firstborn" (John D. Davis, *A Dictionary of the Bible*).

[l]Heb. *as fishes do increase*   [m]*was evil in his eyes*   [n]Heb. *fulness*   [o]Heb. *do not thou excel*   [p]Or, *my couch is gone*   [q]Or, *their swords are weapons of violence*

New American Standard

16 The angel who has redeemed me from all evil,
Bless the lads;
And may my name live on in them,
And the names of my fathers Abraham and Isaac;
And may they grow into a multitude in the midst
of the earth."

17 ¶ When Joseph saw that his father laid his right hand
on Ephraim's head, it displeased him; and he grasped his
father's hand to remove it from Ephraim's head to Manasseh's head.

18 Joseph said to his father, "Not so, my father, for this
one is the firstborn. Place your right hand on his head."

19 But his father refused and said, "I know, my son, I
know; he also will become a people and he also will be
great. However, his younger brother shall be greater than
he, and his descendants shall become a multitude of nations."

20 He blessed them that day, saying,
"By you Israel will pronounce blessing, saying,
'May God make you like Ephraim and
Manasseh!' "
Thus he put Ephraim before Manasseh.

21 Then Israel said to Joseph, "Behold, I am about to
die, but God will be with you, and bring you back to the
land of your fathers.

22 "I give you one portion more than your brothers,
which I took from the hand of the Amorite with my sword
and my bow."

Israel's Prophecy concerning His Sons

49 THEN JACOB summoned his sons and said, "Assemble yourselves that I may tell you what will
befall you in the days to come.

2 "Gather together and hear, O sons of Jacob;
And listen to Israel your father.

3 ¶ "Reuben, you are my firstborn;
My might and the beginning of my strength,
Preeminent in dignity and preeminent in power.

4 "Uncontrolled as water, you shall not have
preeminence,
Because you went up to your father's bed;
Then you defiled it—he went up to my couch.

5 ¶ "Simeon and Levi are brothers;
Their swords are implements of violence.

New International

16 the Angel who has delivered me from all
harm
—may he bless these boys.
May they be called by my name
and the names of my fathers Abraham and
Isaac,
and may they increase greatly
upon the earth."

17 When Joseph saw his father placing his right hand on
Ephraim's head he was displeased; so he took hold of his
father's hand to move it from Ephraim's head to Manasseh's head. 18 Joseph said to him, "No, my father, this one
is the firstborn; put your right hand on his head."

19 But his father refused and said, "I know, my son, I
know. He too will become a people, and he too will become great. Nevertheless, his younger brother will be
greater than he, and his descendants will become a group
of nations." 20 He blessed them that day and said,

"In your[m] name will Israel pronounce this
blessing:
'May God make you like Ephraim and
Manasseh.' "

So he put Ephraim ahead of Manasseh.

21 Then Israel said to Joseph, "I am about to die, but God
will be with you[n] and take you[n] back to the land of
your[n] fathers. 22 And to you, as one who is over your
brothers, I give the ridge of land[o] I took from the Amorites with my sword and my bow."

Jacob Blesses His Sons

49 THEN JACOB called for his sons and said: "Gather around so I can tell you what will happen to you
in days to come.

2 "Assemble and listen, sons of Jacob;
listen to your father Israel.

3 "Reuben, you are my firstborn,
my might, the first sign of my strength,
excelling in honor, excelling in power.

4 Turbulent as the waters, you will no longer
excel,
for you went up onto your father's bed,
onto my couch and defiled it.

5 "Simeon and Levi are brothers—
their swords[p] are weapons of violence.

m 20 The Hebrew is singular.   n 21 The Hebrew is plural.
o 22 Or And to you I give one portion more than to your
brothers—the portion   p 5 The meaning of the Hebrew for this
word is uncertain.

King James

Amplified

King James

⁶O my soul, come not thou into their secret; unto their assembly, mine honour, be not thou united: for in their anger they slew a man, and in their selfwill they ʳdigged down a wall.

⁷Cursed *be* their anger, for *it was* fierce; and their wrath, for it was cruel: I will divide them in Jacob, and scatter them in Israel.

⁸ ¶ Judah, thou *art he* whom thy brethren shall praise: thy hand *shall be* in the neck of thine enemies; thy father's children shall bow down before thee.

⁹Judah *is* a lion's whelp: from the prey, my son, thou art gone up: he stooped down, he couched as a lion, and as an old lion; who shall rouse him up?

¹⁰The sceptre shall not depart from Judah, nor a lawgiver from between his feet, until Shiloh come; and unto him *shall* the gathering of the people *be.*

¹¹Binding his foal unto the vine, and his ass's colt unto the choice vine; he washed his garments in wine, and his clothes in the blood of grapes:

¹²His eyes *shall be* red with wine, and his teeth white with milk.

¹³ ¶ Zebulun shall dwell at the haven of the sea; and he *shall be* for an haven of ships; and his border *shall be* unto Zidon.

¹⁴ ¶ Issachar *is* a strong ass couching down between two burdens:

¹⁵And he saw that rest *was* good, and the land that *it was* pleasant; and bowed his shoulder to bear, and became a servant unto tribute.

¹⁶ ¶ Dan shall judge his people, as one of the tribes of Israel.

¹⁷Dan shall be a serpent by the way, ˢan adder in the path, that biteth the horse heels, so that his rider shall fall backward.

¹⁸I have waited for thy salvation, O LORD.

¹⁹ ¶ Gad, a troop shall overcome him: but he shall overcome at the last.

²⁰ ¶ Out of Asher his bread *shall be* fat, and he shall yield royal dainties.

²¹ ¶ Naphtali *is* a hind let loose: he giveth goodly words.

²² ¶ Joseph *is* a fruitful bough, *even* a fruitful bough by a well; *whose* ᵗbranches run over the wall:

²³The archers have sorely grieved him, and shot *at him,* and hated him:

²⁴But his bow abode in strength, and the arms of his hands were made strong by the hands of the mighty *God* of Jacob; (from thence *is* the shepherd, the stone of Israel:)

Amplified

⁶O my soul, come not into their secret council; unto their assembly let not my honor be united [for I knew nothing of their plot], because in their anger they slew men [an honored man, Shechem, and the Shechemites], and in their self-will they disabled oxen.

⁷Cursed be their anger, for it was fierce, and their wrath, for it was cruel. I will divide them in Jacob and ᵇscatter them in Israel.

⁸Judah, you are the one whom your brothers shall praise; your hand shall be on the neck of your enemies; your father's sons shall bow down to you.

⁹Judah, a lion's cub! With the prey, my son, you have gone high up [the mountain]. He stooped down, he crouched like a lion, and like a lioness—who dares provoke *and* rouse him? [Rev. 5:5.]

¹⁰The scepter *or* leadership shall not depart from Judah, nor the ruler's staff from between his feet, until Shiloh [the Messiah, the Peaceful One] comes to Whom it belongs, and to Whom shall be the obedience of the people. [Num. 24:17; Ps. 60:7.]

¹¹Binding His foal to the vine and His donkey's colt to the choice vine, He washes His garments in wine and His clothes in the blood of grapes. [Isa. 63:1–3; Zech. 9:9; Rev. 19:11–16.]

¹²His eyes are darker *and* more sparkling than wine, and His teeth whiter than milk.

¹³Zebulun shall live toward the seashore, and he shall be a haven *and* a landing place for ships; and his border shall be toward Sidon.

¹⁴Issachar is a strong-boned donkey crouching down between the sheepfolds.

¹⁵And he saw that rest was good and that the land was pleasant; and he bowed his shoulder to bear [his burdens] and became a servant to tribute [subjected to forced labor].

¹⁶Dan shall judge his people as one of the tribes of Israel.

¹⁷Dan shall be a serpent by the way, a horned snake in the path, that bites at the horse's heels, so that his rider falls backward.

¹⁸I wait for Your salvation, O Lord.

¹⁹Gad—a raiding troop shall raid him, but he shall raid at their heels *and* assault them [victoriously].

²⁰Asher's food [supply] shall be rich *and* fat, and he shall yield *and* deliver royal delights.

²¹Naphtali is a hind let loose which yields lovely fawns.

²²Joseph is a fruitful bough, a fruitful bough by a well (spring or fountain), whose branches run over the wall.

²³Skilled archers have bitterly attacked *and* sorely worried him; they have shot at him and persecuted him.

²⁴But his bow remained strong *and* steady *and* rested in the Strength that does not fail him, for the arms of his hands were made strong *and* active by the hands of the Mighty God of Jacob, by the name of the Shepherd, the Rock of Israel, [Gen. 48:15; Deut. 32:4; Isa. 9:6; 49:26.]

ᵇThis was literally fulfilled. Levi got no inheritance except 48 towns scattered throughout different parts of Canaan. As to Simeon, they were originally given only a few towns and villages in Judah's lot (Josh. 19:1). Afterward, needing more room, they formed colonies in districts which they conquered from the Idumeans and the Amalekites [I Chron. 4:39, 40]. (Adam Clarke, *The Holy Bible with A Commentary*).

ʳOr, *houghed oxen*   ˢHeb. *an arrow-snake*   ᵗHeb. *daughters*

New American Standard

6"Let my soul not enter into their council;
  Let not my glory be united with their assembly;
  Because in their anger they slew men,
  And in their self-will they lamed oxen.
7"Cursed be their anger, for it is fierce;
  And their wrath, for it is cruel.
  I will disperse them in Jacob,
  And scatter them in Israel.

8 ¶ "Judah, your brothers shall praise you;
  Your hand shall be on the neck of your enemies;
  Your father's sons shall bow down to you.
9"Judah is a lion's whelp;
  From the prey, my son, you have gone up.
  He couches, he lies down as a lion,
  And as a lion, who dares rouse him up?
10"The scepter shall not depart from Judah,
  Nor the ruler's staff from between his feet,
  *i*Until Shiloh comes,
  And to him *shall be* the obedience of the peoples.
11"He ties *his* foal to the vine,
  And his donkey's colt to the choice vine;
  He washes his garments in wine,
  And his robes in the blood of grapes.
12"His eyes are *j*dull from wine,
  And his teeth *k*white from milk.

13 ¶ "Zebulun will dwell at the seashore;
  And he *shall be* a haven for ships;
  And his flank *shall be* toward Sidon.

14 ¶ "Issachar is a strong donkey,
  Lying down between the sheepfolds.
15"When he saw that a resting place was good
  And that the land was pleasant,
  He bowed his shoulder to bear *burdens,*
  And became a slave at forced labor.

16 ¶ "Dan shall judge his people,
  As one of the tribes of Israel.
17"Dan shall be a serpent in the way,
  A horned snake in the path,
  That bites the horse's heels,
  So that his rider falls backward.
18"For Your salvation I wait, O LORD.

19 ¶ "As for Gad, raiders shall raid him,
  But he will raid *at* their heels.

20 ¶ "As for Asher, his food shall be rich,
  And he will yield royal dainties.

21 ¶ "Naphtali is a doe let loose,
  He gives beautiful words.

22 ¶ "Joseph is a fruitful *l*bough,
  A fruitful bough by a spring;
  Its *m*branches run over a wall.
23"The archers bitterly attacked him,
  And shot *at him* and harassed him;
24 But his bow remained firm,
  And his arms were agile,
  From the hands of the Mighty One of Jacob
  (From there is the Shepherd, the Stone of Israel),

New International

6Let me not enter their council,
  let me not join their assembly,
  for they have killed men in their anger
  and hamstrung oxen as they pleased.
7Cursed be their anger, so fierce,
  and their fury, so cruel!
  I will scatter them in Jacob
  and disperse them in Israel.

8"Judah,*q* your brothers will praise you;
  your hand will be on the neck of your
    enemies;
  your father's sons will bow down to you.
9You are a lion's cub, O Judah;
  you return from the prey, my son.
  Like a lion he crouches and lies down,
  like a lioness—who dares to rouse him?
10The scepter will not depart from Judah,
  nor the ruler's staff from between his feet,
  until he comes to whom it belongs*r*
  and the obedience of the nations is his.
11He will tether his donkey to a vine,
  his colt to the choicest branch;
  he will wash his garments in wine,
  his robes in the blood of grapes.
12His eyes will be darker than wine,
  his teeth whiter than milk.*s*

13"Zebulun will live by the seashore
  and become a haven for ships;
  his border will extend toward Sidon.

14"Issachar is a rawboned*t* donkey
  lying down between two saddlebags.*u*
15When he sees how good is his resting place
  and how pleasant is his land,
  he will bend his shoulder to the burden
  and submit to forced labor.

16"Dan*v* will provide justice for his people
  as one of the tribes of Israel.
17Dan will be a serpent by the roadside,
  a viper along the path,
  that bites the horse's heels
  so that its rider tumbles backward.

18"I look for your deliverance, O LORD.

19"Gad*w* will be attacked by a band of raiders,
  but he will attack them at their heels.

20"Asher's food will be rich;
  he will provide delicacies fit for a king.

21"Naphtali is a doe set free
  that bears beautiful fawns.*x*

22"Joseph is a fruitful vine,
  a fruitful vine near a spring,
  whose branches climb over a wall.*y*
23With bitterness archers attacked him;
  they shot at him with hostility.
24But his bow remained steady,
  his strong arms stayed*z* limber,
  because of the hand of the Mighty One of
    Jacob,
  because of the Shepherd, the Rock of Israel,

q 8 *Judah* sounds like and may be derived from the Hebrew for
praise.   *r* 10 Or *until Shiloh comes*; or *until he comes to whom*
tribute belongs   *s* 12 Or *will be dull from wine, / his teeth white*
from milk   *t* 14 Or *strong*   *u* 14 Or *campfires*   *v* 16 *Dan*
here means *he provides justice.*   *w* 19 *Gad* can mean *attack* and
band of raiders.   *x* 21 Or *free; / he utters beautiful words*
y 22 Or *Joseph is a wild colt, / a wild colt near a spring, / a wild*
donkey on a terraced hill   *z* 23,24 Or *archers will attack . . . will*
shoot . . . will remain . . . will stay

*i*Or *Until he comes to Shiloh;* or *Until he comes to whom it belongs*
*j*Or *darker than*   *k*Or *whiter than*   *l*Lit *son*   *m*Lit
daughters

King James

²⁵*Even* by the God of thy father, who shall help thee; and by the Almighty, who shall bless thee with blessings of heaven above, blessings of the deep that lieth under, blessings of the breasts, and of the womb:
²⁶The blessings of thy father have prevailed above the blessings of my progenitors unto the utmost bound of the everlasting hills: they shall be on the head of Joseph, and on the crown of the head of him that was separate from his brethren.
²⁷ ¶ Benjamin shall ravin *as* a wolf: in the morning he shall devour the prey, and at night he shall divide the spoil.

The death of Jacob

²⁸ ¶ All these *are* the twelve tribes of Israel: and this *is it* that their father spake unto them, and blessed them; every one according to his blessing he blessed them.
²⁹And he charged them, and said unto them, I am to be gathered unto my people: bury me with my fathers in the cave that *is* in the field of Ephron the Hittite,
³⁰In the cave that *is* in the field of Machpelah, which *is* before Mamre, in the land of Canaan, which Abraham bought with the field of Ephron the Hittite for a possession of a buryingplace.
³¹There they buried Abraham and Sarah his wife; there they buried Isaac and Rebekah his wife; and there I buried Leah.
³²The purchase of the field and of the cave that *is* therein *was* from the children of Heth.
³³And when Jacob had made an end of commanding his sons, he gathered up his feet into the bed, and yielded up the ghost, and was gathered unto his people.

50 AND JOSEPH fell upon his father's face, and wept upon him, and kissed him.
²And Joseph commanded his servants the physicians to embalm his father: and the physicians embalmed Israel.
³And forty days were fulfilled for him; for so are fulfilled the days of those which are embalmed: and the Egyptians ^umourned for him threescore and ten days.
⁴And when the days of his mourning were past, Joseph spake unto the house of Pharaoh, saying, If now I have found grace in your eyes, speak, I pray you, in the ears of Pharaoh, saying,
⁵My father made me swear, saying, Lo, I die: in my grave which I have digged for me in the land of Canaan, there shalt thou bury me. Now therefore let me go up, I pray thee, and bury my father, and I will come again.
⁶And Pharaoh said, Go up, and bury thy father, according as he made thee swear.
⁷ ¶ And Joseph went up to bury his father: and with him went up all the servants of Pharaoh, the elders of his house, and all the elders of the land of Egypt,
⁸And all the house of Joseph, and his brethren, and his father's house: only their little ones, and their flocks, and their herds, they left in the land of Goshen.
⁹And there went up with him both chariots and horsemen: and it was a very great company.

Amplified

²⁵By the God of your father, Who will help you, and by the Almighty, Who will bless you with blessings of the heavens above, blessings lying in the deep beneath, blessings of the breasts and of the womb.
²⁶The blessings of your father [on you] are greater than the blessings of my forefathers [Abraham and Isaac on me] *and* are as lasting as the bounties of the eternal hills; they shall be on the head of Joseph, and on the crown of the head of him who was the consecrated one *and* the one separated from his brethren *and* [the one who] is prince among them.
²⁷Benjamin is a ^cravenous wolf, in the morning devouring the prey and at night dividing the spoil.
²⁸All these are the twelve tribes of Israel, and this is what their father said to them as he blessed them, blessing each one according to the blessing suited to him.
²⁹He charged them and said to them, I am to be gathered to my [departed] people; bury me with my fathers in the cave that is in the field of Ephron the Hittite,
³⁰In the cave in the field at Machpelah, east of Mamre in the land of Canaan, that Abraham bought, along with the field of Ephron the Hittite, to possess as a cemetery. [Gen. 23:17–20.]
³¹There they buried Abraham and Sarah his wife, there they buried Isaac and Rebekah his wife, and there I buried Leah.
³²The purchase of the field and the cave that is in it was from the sons of Heth.
³³When Jacob had finished commanding his sons, he drew his feet up into the bed and breathed his last and was gathered to his [departed] people.

50 THEN JOSEPH fell upon his father's face and wept over him and kissed him.
²And Joseph ordered his servants the physicians to embalm his father. So the physicians embalmed Israel.
³Then forty days were devoted [to this purpose] for him, for that is the customary number of days required for those who are embalmed. And the Egyptians wept and bemoaned him [as they would for royalty] for seventy days.
⁴And when the days of his weeping *and* deep grief were past, Joseph said to [the nobles of] the house of Pharaoh, If now I have found grace in your eyes, speak, I pray you, to Pharaoh [for Joseph was dressed in mourning and could not do so himself], saying,
⁵My father made me swear, saying, I am about to die; in my tomb which I hewed out for myself in the land of Canaan, there you shall bury me. So now let me go up, I pray you, and bury my father, and I will come again.
⁶And Pharaoh said, Go up and bury your father, as he made you swear.
⁷And Joseph went up [to Canaan] to bury his father; and with him went all the officials of Pharaoh—the nobles of his court, *and* the elders of his house and all the nobles *and* elders of the land of Egypt—
⁸And all the household of Joseph and his brethren and his father's household. Only their little ones and their flocks and herds they left in the land of Goshen.
⁹And there went with [Joseph] both chariots and horsemen; and it was a very great company.

---

^cThe tribe of Benjamin is fitly compared to a ravenous wolf because of the rude courage and ferocity which they invariably displayed, particularly in their war with the other tribes, in which they killed more men than all of their own numbers combined (Adam Clarke, *The Holy Bible with A Commentary*). The tribe was absorbed by the tribe of Judah and is not mentioned after the return from the Babylonian captivity, except in connection with its former land or as the source of some individual person. Ehud, Saul, Jonathan, and the apostle Paul were Benjamites.

^uHeb. *wept*

New American Standard

25 From the God of your father who helps you,
And by the Almighty who blesses you
With blessings of heaven above,
Blessings of the deep that lies beneath,
Blessings of the breasts and of the womb.
26"The blessings of your father
Have surpassed the blessings of my ancestors
Up to the utmost bound of the everlasting hills;
May they be on the head of Joseph,
And on the crown of the head of the one
distinguished among his brothers.

27 ¶ "Benjamin is a ravenous wolf;
In the morning he devours the prey,
And in the evening he divides the spoil."

28 ¶ All these are the twelve tribes of Israel, and this is
what their father said to them when he blessed them. He
blessed them, every one with the blessing appropriate to
him.

29 Then he charged them and said to them, "I am about
to be gathered to my people; bury me with my fathers in
the cave that is in the field of Ephron the Hittite,
30 in the cave that is in the field of Machpelah, which is
before Mamre, in the land of Canaan, which Abraham
bought along with the field from Ephron the Hittite for a
burial site.
31"There they buried Abraham and his wife Sarah, there
they buried Isaac and his wife Rebekah, and there I buried
Leah—
32 the field and the cave that is in it, purchased from the
sons of Heth."
33 When Jacob finished charging his sons, he drew his
feet into the bed and breathed his last, and was gathered to
his people.

The Death of Israel

50 THEN JOSEPH fell on his father's face, and wept
over him and kissed him.
2 Joseph commanded his servants the physicians to
embalm his father. So the physicians embalmed Israel.
3 Now forty days were required for it, for such is the
period required for embalming. And the Egyptians wept
for him seventy days.
4 ¶ When the days of mourning for him were past,
Joseph spoke to the household of Pharaoh, saying, "If now
I have found favor in your sight, please speak to Pharaoh,
saying,
5 'My father made me swear, saying, "Behold, I am
about to die; in my grave which I dug for myself in the
land of Canaan, there you shall bury me." Now therefore,
please let me go up and bury my father; then I will return.' "
6 Pharaoh said, "Go up and bury your father, as he
made you swear."
7 ¶ So Joseph went up to bury his father, and with him
went up all the servants of Pharaoh, the elders of his
household and all the elders of the land of Egypt,
8 and all the household of Joseph and his brothers and
his father's household; they left only their little ones and
their flocks and their herds in the land of Goshen.
9 There also went up with him both chariots and horsemen; and it was a very great company.

New International

25because of your father's God, who helps you,
because of the Almighty,[a] who blesses you
with blessings of the heavens above,
blessings of the deep that lies below,
blessings of the breast and womb.
26Your father's blessings are greater
than the blessings of the ancient mountains,
than[b] the bounty of the age-old hills.
Let all these rest on the head of Joseph,
on the brow of the prince among[c] his
brothers.

27"Benjamin is a ravenous wolf;
in the morning he devours the prey,
in the evening he divides the plunder."

28All these are the twelve tribes of Israel, and this is
what their father said to them when he blessed them, giving each the blessing appropriate to him.

The Death of Jacob

29Then he gave them these instructions: "I am about to
be gathered to my people. Bury me with my fathers in the
cave in the field of Ephron the Hittite, 30the cave in the
field of Machpelah, near Mamre in Canaan, which Abraham bought as a burial place from Ephron the Hittite,
along with the field. 31There Abraham and his wife Sarah
were buried, there Isaac and his wife Rebekah were buried,
and there I buried Leah. 32The field and the cave in it were
bought from the Hittites.[d] "
33When Jacob had finished giving instructions to his
sons, he drew his feet up into the bed, breathed his last and
was gathered to his people.

50 JOSEPH THREW himself upon his father and
wept over him and kissed him. 2Then Joseph directed the physicians in his service to embalm his father
Israel. So the physicians embalmed him, 3taking a full
forty days, for that was the time required for embalming.
And the Egyptians mourned for him seventy days.
4When the days of mourning had passed, Joseph said to
Pharaoh's court, "If I have found favor in your eyes, speak
to Pharaoh for me. Tell him, 5'My father made me swear
an oath and said, "I am about to die; bury me in the tomb
I dug for myself in the land of Canaan." Now let me go up
and bury my father; then I will return.' "
6Pharaoh said, "Go up and bury your father, as he made
you swear to do."
7So Joseph went up to bury his father. All Pharaoh's
officials accompanied him—the dignitaries of his court
and all the dignitaries of Egypt— 8besides all the members
of Joseph's household and his brothers and those belonging to his father's household. Only their children and their
flocks and herds were left in Goshen. 9Chariots and horsemen[e] also went up with him. It was a very large company.

a 25 Hebrew *Shaddai*   b 26 Or *of my progenitors, / as great as*
c 26 Or *the one separated from*   d 32 Or *the sons of Heth*
e 9 Or *charioteers*

King James   # Amplified

10And they came to the threshingfloor of Atad, which *is* beyond Jordan, and there they mourned with a great and very sore lamentation: and he made a mourning for his father seven days.

11And when the inhabitants of the land, the Canaanites, saw the mourning in the floor of Atad, they said, This *is* a grievous mourning to the Egyptians: wherefore the name of it was called *v*Abel-mizraim, which *is* beyond Jordan.

12And his sons did unto him according as he commanded them:

13For his sons carried him into the land of Canaan, and buried him in the cave of the field of Machpelah, which Abraham bought with the field for a possession of a buryingplace of Ephron the Hittite, before Mamre.

14 ¶ And Joseph returned into Egypt, he, and his brethren, and all that went up with him to bury his father, after he had buried his father.

15 ¶ And when Joseph's brethren saw that their father was dead, they said, Joseph will peradventure hate us, and will certainly requite us all the evil which we did unto him.

16And they *w*sent a messenger unto Joseph, saying, Thy father did command before he died, saying,

17So shall ye say unto Joseph, Forgive, I pray thee now, the trespass of thy brethren, and their sin; for they did unto thee evil: and now, we pray thee, forgive the trespass of the servants of the God of thy father. And Joseph wept when they spake unto him.

18And his brethren also went and fell down before his face; and they said, Behold, we *be* thy servants.

19And Joseph said unto them, Fear not: for *am* I in the place of God?

20But as for you, ye thought evil against me; *but* God meant it unto good, to bring to pass, as *it is* this day, to save much people alive.

21Now therefore fear ye not: I will nourish you, and your little ones. And he comforted them, and spake *x*kindly unto them.

The death of Joseph

22 ¶ And Joseph dwelt in Egypt, he, and his father's house: and Joseph lived an hundred and ten years.

23And Joseph saw Ephraim's children of the third *generation*: the children also of Machir the son of Manasseh were *y*brought up upon Joseph's knees.

24And Joseph said unto his brethren, I die: and God will surely visit you, and bring you out of this land unto the land which he sware to Abraham, to Isaac, and to Jacob.

25And Joseph took an oath of the children of Israel, saying, God will surely visit you, and ye shall carry up my bones from hence.

26So Joseph died, *being* an hundred and ten years old: and they embalmed him, and he was put in a coffin in Egypt.

10And they came to the threshing floor of Atad, which is beyond [west of] the Jordan, and there they mourned with a great lamentation and extreme demonstrations of sorrow [according to Egyptian custom]; and [Joseph] made a mourning for his father seven days.

11When the inhabitants of the land, the Canaanites, saw the mourning at the floor of Atad, they said, This is a grievous mourning for the Egyptians. Therefore the place was called Abel-mizraim [mourning of Egypt]; it is west of the Jordan.

12Thus [Jacob's] sons did for him as he had commanded them.

13For his sons carried him to the land of Canaan and buried him in the cave of the field of Machpelah, east of Mamre, which Abraham bought, along with the field, for a possession as a burying place from Ephron the Hittite.

14After he had buried his father, Joseph returned to Egypt, he and his brethren and all who had gone up with him.

15When Joseph's brethren saw that their father was dead, they said, Perhaps now Joseph will hate us and will pay us back for all the evil we did to him.

16And they sent a messenger to Joseph, saying, Your father commanded before he died, saying,

17So shall you say to Joseph: Forgive (take up and away all resentment and all claim to requital concerning), I pray you now, the trespass of your brothers and their sin, for they did evil to you. Now, we pray you, forgive the trespass of the servants of your father's God. And Joseph wept when they spoke thus to him.

18Then his brothers went and fell down before him, saying, See, we are your servants (your slaves)!

19And Joseph said to them, Fear not; for am I in the place of God? [Vengeance is His, not mine.]

20As for you, you thought evil against me, but God meant it for good, to bring about that many people should be kept alive, as they are this day.

21Now therefore, do not be afraid. I will provide for *and* support you and your little ones. And he comforted them [imparting cheer, hope, strength] and spoke to their hearts [kindly].

22Joseph dwelt in Egypt, he and his father's household. And Joseph lived 110 years.

23And Joseph saw Ephraim's children of the third generation; the children also of Machir son of Manasseh were brought up on Joseph's knees.

24And Joseph said to his brethren, I am going to die. But God will surely visit you and bring you out of this land to the land He swore to Abraham, to Isaac, and to Jacob [to give you].

25And Joseph took an oath from the sons of Israel, saying, God will surely visit you, and you will carry up my bones from here.

26So Joseph died, being 110 years old; and they embalmed him, and he was put *d*in a coffin in Egypt.

---

*d*Joseph's body remained in Egypt until the exodus to the promised land of Canaan about 200 years later. Its final resting-place was Shechem, near Samaria, "in the parcel of ground which Jacob bought from the sons of Hamor, the father of Shechem" (Josh. 24:32). Here each of his brothers was also buried (Acts 7:15, 16).

New American Standard

10 When they came to the threshing floor of Atad, which is beyond the Jordan, they lamented there with a very great and sorrowful lamentation; and he observed seven days mourning for his father.

11 Now when the inhabitants of the land, the Canaanites, saw the mourning at the threshing floor of Atad, they said, "This is a grievous mourning for the Egyptians." Therefore it was named Abel-mizraim, which is beyond the Jordan.

Burial at Machpelah

12 Thus his sons did for him as he had charged them;
13 for his sons carried him to the land of Canaan and buried him in the cave of the field of Machpelah before Mamre, which Abraham had bought along with the field for a burial site from Ephron the Hittite.

14 After he had buried his father, Joseph returned to Egypt, he and his brothers, and all who had gone up with him to bury his father.

15 ¶ When Joseph's brothers saw that their father was dead, they said, "What if Joseph bears a grudge against us and pays us back in full for all the wrong which we did to him!"

16 So they sent *a message* to Joseph, saying, "Your father charged before he died, saying,

17 'Thus you shall say to Joseph, "Please forgive, I beg you, the transgression of your brothers and their sin, for they did you wrong." ' And now, please forgive the transgression of the servants of the God of your father." And Joseph wept when they spoke to him.

18 Then his brothers also came and fell down before him and said, "Behold, we are your servants."

19 But Joseph said to them, "Do not be afraid, for am I in God's place?

20 "As for you, you meant evil against me, *but* God meant it for good in order to bring about this present result, to preserve many people alive.

21 "So therefore, do not be afraid; I will provide for you and your little ones." So he comforted them and spoke kindly to them.

Death of Joseph

22 ¶ Now Joseph stayed in Egypt, he and his father's household, and Joseph lived one hundred and ten years.

23 Joseph saw the third generation of Ephraim's sons; also the sons of Machir, the son of Manasseh, were born on Joseph's knees.

24 Joseph said to his brothers, "I am about to die, but God will surely take care of you and bring you up from this land to the land which He promised on oath to Abraham, to Isaac and to Jacob."

25 Then Joseph made the sons of Israel swear, saying, "God will surely take care of you, and you shall carry my bones up from here."

26 So Joseph died at the age of one hundred and ten years; and he was embalmed and placed in a coffin in Egypt.

New International

10 When they reached the threshing floor of Atad, near the Jordan, they lamented loudly and bitterly; and there Joseph observed a seven-day period of mourning for his father. 11 When the Canaanites who lived there saw the mourning at the threshing floor of Atad, they said, "The Egyptians are holding a solemn ceremony of mourning." That is why that place near the Jordan is called Abel Mizraim.*f*

12 So Jacob's sons did as he had commanded them: 13 They carried him to the land of Canaan and buried him in the cave in the field of Machpelah, near Mamre, which Abraham had bought as a burial place from Ephron the Hittite, along with the field. 14 After burying his father, Joseph returned to Egypt, together with his brothers and all the others who had gone with him to bury his father.

Joseph Reassures His Brothers

15 When Joseph's brothers saw that their father was dead, they said, "What if Joseph holds a grudge against us and pays us back for all the wrongs we did to him?" 16 So they sent word to Joseph, saying, "Your father left these instructions before he died: 17 'This is what you are to say to Joseph: I ask you to forgive your brothers the sins and the wrongs they committed in treating you so badly.' Now please forgive the sins of the servants of the God of your father." When their message came to him, Joseph wept.

18 His brothers then came and threw themselves down before him. "We are your slaves," they said.

19 But Joseph said to them, "Don't be afraid. Am I in the place of God? 20 You intended to harm me, but God intended it for good to accomplish what is now being done, the saving of many lives. 21 So then, don't be afraid. I will provide for you and your children." And he reassured them and spoke kindly to them.

The Death of Joseph

22 Joseph stayed in Egypt, along with all his father's family. He lived a hundred and ten years 23 and saw the third generation of Ephraim's children. Also the children of Makir son of Manasseh were placed at birth on Joseph's knees.*g*

24 Then Joseph said to his brothers, "I am about to die. But God will surely come to your aid and take you up out of this land to the land he promised on oath to Abraham, Isaac and Jacob." 25 And Joseph made the sons of Israel swear an oath and said, "God will surely come to your aid, and then you must carry my bones up from this place."

26 So Joseph died at the age of a hundred and ten. And after they embalmed him, he was placed in a coffin in Egypt.

---

f 11 Abel Mizraim means *mourning of the Egyptians.*   *g 23 That* is, were counted as his

THE SECOND BOOK OF MOSES, CALLED

Exodus

THE SECOND BOOK OF MOSES, COMMONLY CALLED

Exodus

Israel's growth and bondage

1 NOW THESE *are* the names of the children of Israel, which came into Egypt; every man and his household came with Jacob.

2 Reuben, Simeon, Levi, and Judah,

3 Issachar, Zebulun, and Benjamin,

4 Dan, and Naphtali, Gad, and Asher.

5 And all the souls that came out of the *a*loins of Jacob were seventy souls: for Joseph was in Egypt *already*.

6 And Joseph died, and all his brethren, and all that generation.

7 ¶ And the children of Israel were fruitful, and increased abundantly, and multiplied, and waxed exceeding mighty; and the land was filled with them.

8 Now there arose up a new king over Egypt, which knew not Joseph.

9 And he said unto his people, Behold, the people of the children of Israel *are* more and mightier than we:

10 Come on, let us deal wisely with them; lest they multiply, and it come to pass, that, when there falleth out any war, they join also unto our enemies, and fight against us, and *so* get them up out of the land.

11 Therefore they did set over them taskmasters to afflict them with their burdens. And they built for Pharaoh treasure cities, Pithom and Raamses.

12 *b*But the more they afflicted them, the more they multiplied and grew. And they were grieved because of the children of Israel.

13 And the Egyptians made the children of Israel to serve with rigour:

14 And they made their lives bitter with hard bondage, in mortar, and in brick, and in all manner of service in the field: all their service, wherein they made them serve, *was* with rigour.

15 ¶ And the king of Egypt spake to the Hebrew midwives, of which the name of the one *was* Shiphrah, and the name of the other Puah:

16 And he said, When ye do the office of a midwife to the Hebrew women, and see *them* upon the stools; if it *be* a son, then ye shall kill him: but if it *be* a daughter, then she shall live.

17 But the midwives feared God, and did not as the king of Egypt commanded them, but saved the men children alive.

18 And the king of Egypt called for the midwives, and said unto them, Why have ye done this thing, and have saved the men children alive?

19 And the midwives said unto Pharaoh, Because the Hebrew women *are* not as the Egyptian women; for they *are* lively, and are delivered ere the midwives come in unto them.

20 Therefore God dealt well with the midwives: and the people multiplied, and waxed very mighty.

21 And it came to pass, because the midwives feared God, that he made them houses.

22 And Pharaoh charged all his people, saying, Every son that is born ye shall cast into the river, and every daughter ye shall save alive.

1 THESE ARE the names of the sons of Israel who came into Egypt with Jacob, each with his household:

2 Reuben, Simeon, Levi, and Judah,

3 Issachar, Zebulun, and Benjamin,

4 Dan and Naphtali, Gad and Asher.

5 All the offspring of Jacob were seventy persons; Joseph was already in Egypt.

6 Then Joseph died, and all his brothers and all that generation.

7 But the descendants of Israel were fruitful and increased abundantly; they multiplied and grew exceedingly strong, and the land was full of them.

8 Now a new king arose over Egypt who did not know Joseph.

9 He said to his people, Behold, the Israelites are too many and too mighty for us [and they *a*outnumber us both in people and in strength].

10 Come, let us deal shrewdly with them, lest they multiply more and, should war befall us, they join our enemies, fight against us, and escape out of the land.

11 So they set over [the Israelites] taskmasters to afflict *and* oppress them with [increased] burdens. And [the Israelites] built Pithom and Rameses as store cities for Pharaoh.

12 But the more [the Egyptians] oppressed them, the more they multiplied and expanded, so that [the Egyptians] were vexed *and* alarmed because of the Israelites.

13 And the Egyptians reduced the Israelites to severe slavery.

14 They made their lives bitter with hard service in mortar, brick, and all kinds of work in the field. All their service was with harshness *and* severity.

15 Then the king of Egypt said to the Hebrew midwives, of whom one was named Shiprah and the other Puah,

16 When you act as midwives to the Hebrew women and see them on the birthstool, if it is a son, you shall kill him; but if it is a daughter, she shall live.

17 But the midwives feared God and did not do as the king of Egypt commanded, but let the male babies live.

18 So the king of Egypt called for the midwives and said to them, Why have you done this thing and allowed the male children to live?

19 The midwives answered Pharaoh, Because the Hebrew women are not like the Egyptian women; they are vigorous and quickly delivered; their babies are born before the midwife comes to them.

20 So God dealt well with the midwives and the people multiplied and became very strong.

21 And because the midwives revered *and* feared God, He made them households [of their own].

22 Then Pharaoh charged all his people, saying, Every son born [to the Hebrews] you shall cast into the river [Nile], but every daughter you shall allow to live.

---

a Is there in all human history a more amazing spectacle than the exodus? A family of 70 immigrants grows into a people of slavery. Suddenly, according to God's detailed and preannounced plan, they are seen flinging away the shackles of generations of slavery and emigrating to a new country and a new life, with miraculous deliverances rescuing them from destruction again and again. The marvel of the exodus grows in wonder when, after more than 3,000 years, we see that same race, often persecuted almost to extinction, carrying out in startling detail God's predictions for their amazing national revitalization and prominence "in the last days" (adapted from many historians).

---

a Heb. *thigh*   *b* Heb. *And as they afflicted them, so they multiplied*

Exodus

Exodus

Israel Multiplies in Egypt

1 NOW THESE are the names of the sons of Israel who came to Egypt with Jacob; they came each one with his household:

2 Reuben, Simeon, Levi and Judah;

3 Issachar, Zebulun and Benjamin;

4 Dan and Naphtali, Gad and Asher.

5 All the persons who came from the loins of Jacob were seventy in number, but Joseph was *already* in Egypt.

6 Joseph died, and all his brothers and all that generation.

7 But the sons of Israel were fruitful and increased greatly, and multiplied, and became exceedingly mighty, so that the land was filled with them.

8 ¶ Now a new king arose over Egypt, who did not know Joseph.

9 He said to his people, "Behold, the people of the sons of Israel are more and mightier than we.

10 "Come, let us deal wisely with them, or else they will multiply and in the event of war, they will also join themselves to those who hate us, and fight against us and depart from the land."

11 So they appointed taskmasters over them to afflict them with hard labor. And they built for Pharaoh storage cities, Pithom and Raamses.

12 But the more they afflicted them, the more they multiplied and the more they spread out, so that they were in dread of the sons of Israel.

13 The Egyptians compelled the sons of Israel to labor rigorously;

14 and they made their lives bitter with hard labor in mortar and bricks and at all *kinds* of labor in the field, all their labors which they rigorously imposed on them.

15 ¶ Then the king of Egypt spoke to the Hebrew midwives, one of whom was named Shiphrah and the other was named Puah;

16 and he said, "When you are helping the Hebrew women to give birth and see *them* upon the birthstool, if it is a son, then you shall put him to death; but if it is a daughter, then she shall live."

17 But the midwives feared God, and did not do as the king of Egypt had commanded, but let the boys live.

18 So the king of Egypt called for the midwives and said to them, "Why have you done this thing, and let the boys live?"

19 The midwives said to Pharaoh, "Because the Hebrew women are not as the Egyptian women; for they are vigorous and give birth before the midwife can get to them."

20 So God was good to the midwives, and the people multiplied, and became very mighty.

21 Because the midwives feared God, He established households for them.

22 Then Pharaoh commanded all his people, saying, "Every son who is born *a*you are to cast into the Nile, and every daughter you are to keep alive."

The Israelites Oppressed

1 THESE ARE the names of the sons of Israel who went to Egypt with Jacob, each with his family: 2Reuben, Simeon, Levi and Judah; 3Issachar, Zebulun and Benjamin; 4Dan and Naphtali; Gad and Asher. 5The descendants of Jacob numbered seventy*a* in all; Joseph was already in Egypt.

6Now Joseph and all his brothers and all that generation died, 7but the Israelites were fruitful and multiplied greatly and became exceedingly numerous, so that the land was filled with them.

8Then a new king, who did not know about Joseph, came to power in Egypt. 9"Look," he said to his people, "the Israelites have become much too numerous for us. 10Come, we must deal shrewdly with them or they will become even more numerous and, if war breaks out, will join our enemies, fight against us and leave the country."

11So they put slave masters over them to oppress them with forced labor, and they built Pithom and Rameses as store cities for Pharaoh. 12But the more they were oppressed, the more they multiplied and spread; so the Egyptians came to dread the Israelites 13and worked them ruthlessly. 14They made their lives bitter with hard labor in brick and mortar and with all kinds of work in the fields; in all their hard labor the Egyptians used them ruthlessly.

15The king of Egypt said to the Hebrew midwives, whose names were Shiphrah and Puah, 16"When you help the Hebrew women in childbirth and observe them on the delivery stool, if it is a boy, kill him; but if it is a girl, let her live." 17The midwives, however, feared God and did not do what the king of Egypt had told them to do; they let the boys live. 18Then the king of Egypt summoned the midwives and asked them, "Why have you done this? Why have you let the boys live?"

19The midwives answered Pharaoh, "Hebrew women are not like Egyptian women; they are vigorous and give birth before the midwives arrive."

20So God was kind to the midwives and the people increased and became even more numerous. 21And because the midwives feared God, he gave them families of their own.

22Then Pharaoh gave this order to all his people: "Every boy that is born*b* you must throw into the Nile, but let every girl live."

---

*a*5 Masoretic Text (see also Gen. 46:27); Dead Sea Scrolls and Septuagint (see also Acts 7:14 and note at Gen. 46:27) *seventy-five*
*b*22 Masoretic Text; Samaritan Pentateuch, Septuagint and Targums *born to the Hebrews*

*a*Some versions insert *to the Hebrews*

Moses' birth

2 AND THERE went a man of the house of Levi, and took *to wife* a daughter of Levi.

2 And the woman conceived, and bare a son: and when she saw him that he *was a* goodly *child*, she hid him three months.

3 And when she could not longer hide him, she took for him an ark of bulrushes, and daubed it with slime and with pitch, and put the child therein; and she laid *it* in the flags by the river's brink.

4 And his sister stood afar off, to wit what would be done to him.

5 ¶And the daughter of Pharaoh came down to wash *herself* at the river; and her maidens walked along by the river's side; and when she saw the ark among the flags, she sent her maid to fetch it.

6 And when she had opened *it*, she saw the child: and, behold, the babe wept. And she had compassion on him, and said, This *is* one of the Hebrews' children.

7 Then said his sister to Pharaoh's daughter, Shall I go and call to thee a nurse of the Hebrew women, that she may nurse the child for thee?

8 And Pharaoh's daughter said to her, Go. And the maid went and called the child's mother.

9 And Pharaoh's daughter said unto her, Take this child away, and nurse it for me, and I will give *thee* thy wages. And the woman took the child, and nursed it.

10 And the child grew, and she brought him unto Pharaoh's daughter, and he became her son. And she called his name cMoses: and she said, Because I drew him out of the water.

Moses flees to Midian

11 ¶And it came to pass in those days, when Moses was grown, that he went out unto his brethren, and looked on their burdens: and he spied an Egyptian smiting an Hebrew, one of his brethren.

12 And he looked this way and that way, and when he saw that *there was* no man, he slew the Egyptian, and hid him in the sand.

13 And when he went out the second day, behold, two men of the Hebrews strove together: and he said to him that did the wrong, Wherefore smitest thou thy fellow?

14 And he said, Who made thee da prince and a judge over us? intendest thou to kill me, as thou killedst the Egyptian? And Moses feared, and said, Surely this thing is known.

15 Now when Pharaoh heard this thing, he sought to slay Moses. But Moses fled from the face of Pharaoh, and dwelt in the land of Midian: and he sat down by a well.

16 Now the epriest of Midian had seven daughters: and they came and drew *water*, and filled the troughs to water their father's flock.

17 And the shepherds came and drove them away: but Moses stood up and helped them, and watered their flock.

18 And when they came to Reuel their father, he said, How *is it that* ye are come so soon today?

19 And they said, An Egyptian delivered us out of the hand of the shepherds, and also drew *water* enough for us, and watered the flock.

20 And he said unto his daughters, And where *is* he? why *is* it *that* ye have left the man? call him, that he may eat bread.

21 And Moses was content to dwell with the man: and he gave Moses Zipporah his daughter.

2 NOW [AMRAM] a man of the house of Levi [the priestly tribe] went and took as his wife [Jochebed] a daughter of Levi. [Exod. 6:18, 20; Num. 26:59.]

2 And the woman became pregnant and bore a son; and when she saw that he was [exceedingly] beautiful, she hid him three months. [Acts 7:20; Heb. 11:23.]

3 And when she could no longer hide him, she took for him an ark *or* basket made of bulrushes *or* papyrus [making it watertight by] daubing it with bitumen and pitch. Then she put the child in it and laid it among the rushes by the brink of the river [Nile].

4 And his sister [Miriam] stood some distance away to blearn what would be done to him.

5 Now the daughter of Pharaoh came down to bathe at the river, and her maidens walked along the bank; she saw the ark among the rushes and sent her maid to fetch it.

6 When she opened it, she saw the child; and behold, the baby cried. And she took pity on him and said, This is one of the Hebrews' children!

7 Then his sister said to Pharaoh's daughter, Shall I go and call a nurse of the Hebrew women to nurse the child for you?

8 Pharaoh's daughter said to her, Go. And the girl went and called the child's mother.

9 Then Pharaoh's daughter said to her, Take this child away and nurse it for me, and I will give you your wages. So the woman took the child and nursed it.

10 And the child grew, and she brought him to Pharaoh's daughter and he became her son. And she called him Moses, for she said, Because I drew him out of the water.

11 One day, after Moses was grown, it happened that he went out to his brethren and looked at their burdens; and he saw an Egyptian beating a Hebrew, one of [Moses'] brethren.

12 He looked this way and that way, and when he saw no one, he killed the Egyptian and hid him in the sand.

13 He went out the second day and saw two Hebrew men quarreling *and* fighting; and he said to the unjust aggressor, Why are you striking your comrade?

14 And the man said, Who made you a prince and a judge over us? Do you intend to kill me as you killed the Egyptian? Then Moses was afraid and thought, Surely this thing is known.

15 When Pharaoh heard of it, he sought to slay Moses. But Moses fled from Pharaoh's presence and ctook refuge in the land of Midian, where he sat down by a well.

16 Now the priest of Midian had seven daughters, and they came and drew water and filled the troughs to water their father's flock.

17 The shepherds came and drove them away; but Moses stood up and helped them and watered their flock.

18 And when they came to Reuel [Jethro] their father, he said, How is it that you have come so soon today?

19 They said, An Egyptian delivered us from the shepherds; also he drew water for us and watered the flock.

20 He said to his daughters, Where is he? Why have you left the man? Call him, that he may eat bread.

21 And Moses was content to dwell with the man; and he gave Moses Zipporah his daughter.

---

b They launched the ark not only on the Nile but on God's providence. He would be Captain, Steersman, and Convoy of the tiny ark. Miriam stood to watch. There was no fear of fatal consequences, only the quiet expectancy that God would do something worthy of Himself. They reckoned on God's faithfulness and they were amply rewarded when the daughter of their greatest foe became the babe's patroness (F. B. Meyer, *Through the Bible Day by Day*).   c "There was true heroism in the act, when Moses stepped down from Pharaoh's throne to share the lot of his brethren. But it would take many a long year of lonely waiting and trial before this strong and radiant nature could be broken down, shaped into a vessel meet for the Master's use, and prepared for every good work. . . . One blow struck when God's time is fulfilled is worth a thousand struck in premature eagerness" (F. B. Meyer, *Moses, the Servant of God*).

---

c i.e. *Drawn out*   d Heb. *a man, a prince*; see Gen. 13:8   e Or, *prince*; see Gen. 41:45

New American Standard

The Birth of Moses

2 NOW A man from the house of Levi went and married a daughter of Levi.

2 The woman conceived and bore a son; and when she saw that he was beautiful, she hid him for three months.

3 But when she could hide him no longer, she got him a *b*wicker basket and covered it over with tar and pitch. Then she put the child into it and set *it* among the reeds by the bank of the Nile.

4 His sister stood at a distance to find out what would happen to him.

5 ¶ The daughter of Pharaoh came down to bathe at the Nile, with her maidens walking alongside the Nile; and she saw the basket among the reeds and sent her maid, and she brought it *to her.*

6 When she opened *it,* she saw the child, and behold, *the* boy was crying. And she had pity on him and said, "This is one of the Hebrews' children."

7 Then his sister said to Pharaoh's daughter, "Shall I go and call a nurse for you from the Hebrew women that she may nurse the child for you?"

8 Pharaoh's daughter said to her, "Go *ahead.*" So the girl went and called the child's mother.

9 Then Pharaoh's daughter said to her, "Take this child away and nurse him for me and I will give *you* your wages." So the woman took the child and nursed him.

10 The child grew, and she brought him to Pharaoh's daughter and he became her son. And she named him Moses, and said, "Because I drew him out of the water."

11 ¶ Now it came about in those days, when Moses had grown up, that he went out to his brethren and looked on their hard labors; and he saw an Egyptian beating a Hebrew, one of his brethren.

12 So he looked this way and that, and when he saw there was no one *around,* he struck down the Egyptian and hid him in the sand.

13 He went out the next day, and behold, two Hebrews were fighting with each other; and he said to the offender, "Why are you striking your companion?"

14 But he said, "Who made you a prince or a judge over us? Are you intending to kill me as you killed the Egyptian?" Then Moses was afraid and said, "Surely the matter has become known."

Moses Escapes to Midian

15 When Pharaoh heard of this matter, he tried to kill Moses. But Moses fled from the presence of Pharaoh and settled in the land of Midian, and he sat down by a well.

16 ¶ Now the priest of Midian had seven daughters; and they came to draw water and filled the troughs to water their father's flock.

17 Then the shepherds came and drove them away, but Moses stood up and helped them and watered their flock.

18 When they came to Reuel their father, he said, "Why have you come *back* so soon today?"

19 So they said, "An Egyptian delivered us from the hand of the shepherds, and what is more, he even drew the water for us and watered the flock."

20 He said to his daughters, "Where is he then? Why is it that you have left the man behind? Invite him to have something to eat."

21 Moses was willing to dwell with the man, and he gave his daughter Zipporah to Moses.

New International

The Birth of Moses

2 NOW A man of the house of Levi married a Levite woman, 2and she became pregnant and gave birth to a son. When she saw that he was a fine child, she hid him for three months. 3But when she could hide him no longer, she got a papyrus basket for him and coated it with tar and pitch. Then she placed the child in it and put it among the reeds along the bank of the Nile. 4His sister stood at a distance to see what would happen to him.

5Then Pharaoh's daughter went down to the Nile to bathe, and her attendants were walking along the river bank. She saw the basket among the reeds and sent her slave girl to get it. 6She opened it and saw the baby. He was crying, and she felt sorry for him. "This is one of the Hebrew babies," she said.

7Then his sister asked Pharaoh's daughter, "Shall I go and get one of the Hebrew women to nurse the baby for you?"

8"Yes, go," she answered. And the girl went and got the baby's mother. 9Pharaoh's daughter said to her, "Take this baby and nurse him for me, and I will pay you." So the woman took the baby and nursed him. 10When the child grew older, she took him to Pharaoh's daughter and he became her son. She named him Moses,*c* saying, "I drew him out of the water."

Moses Flees to Midian

11One day, after Moses had grown up, he went out to where his own people were and watched them at their hard labor. He saw an Egyptian beating a Hebrew, one of his own people. 12Glancing this way and that and seeing no one, he killed the Egyptian and hid him in the sand. 13The next day he went out and saw two Hebrews fighting. He asked the one in the wrong, "Why are you hitting your fellow Hebrew?"

14The man said, "Who made you ruler and judge over us? Are you thinking of killing me as you killed the Egyptian?" Then Moses was afraid and thought, "What I did must have become known."

15When Pharaoh heard of this, he tried to kill Moses, but Moses fled from Pharaoh and went to live in Midian, where he sat down by a well. 16Now a priest of Midian had seven daughters, and they came to draw water and fill the troughs to water their father's flock. 17Some shepherds came along and drove them away, but Moses got up and came to their rescue and watered their flock.

18When the girls returned to Reuel their father, he asked them, "Why have you returned so early today?"

19They answered, "An Egyptian rescued us from the shepherds. He even drew water for us and watered the flock."

20"And where is he?" he asked his daughters. "Why did you leave him? Invite him to have something to eat."

21Moses agreed to stay with the man, who gave his

---

b I.e. papyrus reeds

c 10 *Moses* sounds like the Hebrew for *draw out.*

King James

²²And she bare *him* a son, and he called his name *f*Gershom: for he said, I have been a stranger in a strange land.

²³ ¶ And it came to pass in process of time, that the king of Egypt died: and the children of Israel sighed by reason of the bondage, and they cried, and their cry came up unto God by reason of the bondage.

²⁴And God heard their groaning, and God remembered his covenant with Abraham, with Isaac, and with Jacob.

²⁵And God looked upon the children of Israel, and God *g*had respect unto *them*.

Moses and the burning bush

3 NOW MOSES kept the flock of Jethro his father-in-law, the priest of Midian: and he led the flock to the backside of the desert, and came to the mountain of God, *even* to Horeb.

²And the angel of the LORD appeared unto him in a flame of fire out of the midst of a bush: and he looked, and, behold, the bush burned with fire, and the bush *was* not consumed.

³And Moses said, I will now turn aside, and see this great sight, why the bush is not burnt.

⁴And when the LORD saw that he turned aside to see, God called unto him out of the midst of the bush, and said, Moses, Moses. And he said, Here *am* I.

⁵And he said, Draw not nigh hither: put off thy shoes from off thy feet, for the place whereon thou standest *is* holy ground.

⁶Moreover he said, I *am* the God of thy father, the God of Abraham, the God of Isaac, and the God of Jacob. And Moses hid his face; for he was afraid to look upon God.

⁷ ¶ And the LORD said, I have surely seen the affliction of my people which *are* in Egypt, and have heard their cry by reason of their taskmasters; for I know their sorrows;

⁸And I am come down to deliver them out of the hand of the Egyptians, and to bring them up out of that land unto a good land and a large, unto a land flowing with milk and honey; unto the place of the Canaanites, and the Hittites, and the Amorites, and the Perizzites, and the Hivites, and the Jebusites.

⁹Now therefore, behold, the cry of the children of Israel is come unto me: and I have also seen the oppression wherewith the Egyptians oppress them.

¹⁰Come now therefore, and I will send thee unto Pharaoh, that thou mayest bring forth my people the children of Israel out of Egypt.

¹¹ ¶ And Moses said unto God, Who *am* I, that I should go unto Pharaoh, and that I should bring forth the children of Israel out of Egypt?

¹²And he said, Certainly I will be with thee; and this *shall be* a token unto thee, that I have sent thee: When thou hast brought forth the people out of Egypt, ye shall serve God upon this mountain.

¹³And Moses said unto God, Behold, *when* I come unto the children of Israel, and shall say unto them, The God of your fathers hath sent me unto you; and they shall say to me, What *is* his name? what shall I say unto them?

¹⁴And God said unto Moses, I AM THAT I AM: and he said, Thus shalt thou say unto the children of Israel, I AM hath sent me unto you.

Amplified

²²And she bore a son, and he called his name Gershom [expulsion, or a stranger there]; for he said, I have been a stranger *and* a sojourner in a foreign land.

²³However, after a long time [nearly forty years] the king of Egypt died; and the Israelites were sighing *and* groaning because of the bondage. They kept crying, and their cry because of slavery ascended to God.

²⁴And God heard their sighing *and* groaning and [earnestly] remembered His covenant with Abraham, with Isaac, and with Jacob.

²⁵God saw the Israelites and took knowledge of them *and* concerned Himself about them [knowing all, understanding, remembering all]. [Ps. 56:8, 9; 139:2.]

3 NOW MOSES kept the flock of Jethro his father-in-law, the priest of Midian; and he led the flock to the back *or* west side of the wilderness and came to Horeb *or* Sinai, the mountain of God.

²The *d*Angel of the Lord appeared to him in a flame of fire out of the midst of a bush; and he looked, and behold, the bush burned with fire, yet was not consumed.

³And Moses said, I will now turn aside and see this great sight, why the bush is not burned.

⁴And when the Lord saw that he turned aside to see, God called to him out of the midst of the bush and said, Moses! Moses! And he said, Here am I.

⁵God said, Do not come near; put your shoes off your feet, for the place on which you stand is holy ground.

⁶Also He said, I am the God of your father, the God of Abraham, the God of Isaac, and the God of Jacob. And Moses hid his face, for he was afraid to look at God.

⁷And the Lord said, I have surely seen the affliction of My people who are in Egypt, and have heard their cry because of their taskmasters *and* oppressors; for I know their sorrows *and* sufferings *and* trials.

⁸And I have come down to deliver them out of the hand *and* power of the Egyptians and to bring them up out of that land to a land good and large, a land flowing with milk and honey [a land of plenty]—to the place of the Canaanite, the Hittite, the Amorite, the Perizzite, the Hivite, and the Jebusite.

⁹Now behold, the cry of the Israelites has come to Me, and I have also seen how the Egyptians oppress them.

¹⁰Come now therefore, and I will send you to Pharaoh, that you may bring forth My people, the Israelites, out of Egypt.

¹¹And Moses said to God, *e*Who am I, that I should go to Pharaoh and bring the Israelites out of Egypt?

¹²God said, I will surely be with you; and this shall be the sign to you that I have sent you: when you have brought the people out of Egypt, you shall serve God on this mountain [Horeb, or Sinai].

¹³And Moses said to God, Behold, when I come to the Israelites and say to them, The God of your fathers has sent me to you, and they say to me, What is His name? What shall I say to them?

¹⁴And God said to Moses, I AM WHO I AM *and* WHAT I AM, *and* I WILL BE WHAT I WILL BE; and He said, You shall say this to the Israelites: I AM has sent me to you!

^dIn this report of Moses and the burning bush, "the Angel of the Lord" is identified as the Lord Himself. See especially Exod. 3:4, 6. See also the footnote on Gen. 16:7.   ^e"There was something more than humility here; there was a tone of self-depreciation which was inconsistent with a true faith in God's selection and appointment. Surely it is God's business to choose His special instruments; and when we are persuaded that we are in the line of His purpose, we have no right to question the wisdom of His appointment. To do so is to depreciate His wisdom or to doubt His power and willingness to become **all that is necessary** to complete our need" (F. B. Meyer, *Moses, the Servant of God*).

^fi.e. A stranger here   ^gHeb. knew

New American Standard

22 Then she gave birth to a son, and he named him Gershom, for he said, "I have been a sojourner in a foreign land."

23 ¶ Now it came about in *the course of* those many days that the king of Egypt died. And the sons of Israel sighed because of the bondage, and they cried out; and their cry for help because of *their* bondage rose up to God. 24 So God heard their groaning; and God remembered His covenant with Abraham, Isaac, and Jacob. 25 God saw the sons of Israel, and God took notice *of them.*

The Burning Bush

3 NOW MOSES was pasturing the flock of Jethro his father-in-law, the priest of Midian; and he led the flock to the west side of the wilderness and came to Horeb, the mountain of God. 2 The angel of the LORD appeared to him in a blazing fire from the midst of a bush; and he looked, and behold, the bush was burning with fire, yet the bush was not consumed. 3 So Moses said, "I must turn aside now and see this marvelous sight, why the bush is not burned up." 4 When the LORD saw that he turned aside to look, God called to him from the midst of the bush and said, "Moses, Moses!" And he said, "Here I am." 5 Then He said, "Do not come near here; remove your sandals from your feet, for the place on which you are standing is holy ground." 6 He said also, "I am the God of your father, the God of Abraham, the God of Isaac, and the God of Jacob." Then Moses hid his face, for he was afraid to look at God. 7 ¶ The LORD said, "I have surely seen the affliction of My people who are in Egypt, and have given heed to their cry because of their taskmasters, for I am aware of their sufferings. 8 "So I have come down to deliver them from the power of the Egyptians, and to bring them up from that land to a good and spacious land, to a land flowing with milk and honey, to the place of the Canaanite and the Hittite and the Amorite and the Perizzite and the Hivite and the Jebusite. 9 "Now, behold, the cry of the sons of Israel has come to Me; furthermore, I have seen the oppression with which the Egyptians are oppressing them.

The Mission of Moses

10 "Therefore, come now, and I will send you to Pharaoh, so that you may bring My people, the sons of Israel, out of Egypt." 11 But Moses said to God, "Who am I, that I should go to Pharaoh, and that I should bring the sons of Israel out of Egypt?" 12 And He said, "Certainly I will be with you, and this shall be the sign to you that it is I who have sent you: when you have brought the people out of Egypt, you shall worship God at this mountain." 13 ¶ Then Moses said to God, "Behold, I am going to the sons of Israel, and I will say to them, 'The God of your fathers has sent me to you.' Now they may say to me, 'What is His name?' What shall I say to them?" 14 God said to Moses, "cI AM WHO cI AM"; and He said, "Thus you shall say to the sons of Israel, 'cI AM has sent me to you.' "

New International

daughter Zipporah to Moses in marriage. 22 Zipporah gave birth to a son, and Moses named him Gershom,d saying, "I have become an alien in a foreign land."

23 During that long period, the king of Egypt died. The Israelites groaned in their slavery and cried out, and their cry for help because of their slavery went up to God. 24 God heard their groaning and he remembered his covenant with Abraham, with Isaac and with Jacob. 25 So God looked on the Israelites and was concerned about them.

Moses and the Burning Bush

3 NOW MOSES was tending the flock of Jethro his father-in-law, the priest of Midian, and he led the flock to the far side of the desert and came to Horeb, the mountain of God. 2 There the angel of the LORD appeared to him in flames of fire from within a bush. Moses saw that though the bush was on fire it did not burn up. 3 So Moses thought, "I will go over and see this strange sight—why the bush does not burn up."

4 When the LORD saw that he had gone over to look, God called to him from within the bush, "Moses! Moses!"

And Moses said, "Here I am."

5 "Do not come any closer," God said. "Take off your sandals, for the place where you are standing is holy ground." 6 Then he said, "I am the God of your father, the God of Abraham, the God of Isaac and the God of Jacob." At this, Moses hid his face, because he was afraid to look at God.

7 The LORD said, "I have indeed seen the misery of my people in Egypt. I have heard them crying out because of their slave drivers, and I am concerned about their suffering. 8 So I have come down to rescue them from the hand of the Egyptians and to bring them up out of that land into a good and spacious land, a land flowing with milk and honey—the home of the Canaanites, Hittites, Amorites, Perizzites, Hivites and Jebusites. 9 And now the cry of the Israelites has reached me, and I have seen the way the Egyptians are oppressing them. 10 So now, go. I am sending you to Pharaoh to bring my people the Israelites out of Egypt."

11 But Moses said to God, "Who am I, that I should go to Pharaoh and bring the Israelites out of Egypt?"

12 And God said, "I will be with you. And this will be the sign to you that it is I who have sent you: When you have brought the people out of Egypt, youe will worship God on this mountain."

13 Moses said to God, "Suppose I go to the Israelites and say to them, 'The God of your fathers has sent me to you,' and they ask me, 'What is his name?' Then what shall I tell them?"

14 God said to Moses, "I AM WHO I AM.f This is what you are to say to the Israelites: 'I AM has sent me to you.' "

---

c Related to the name of God, *YHWH*, rendered *LORD*, which is derived from the verb *HAYAH, to be*

d 22 *Gershom* sounds like the Hebrew for *an alien there.*
e 12 The Hebrew is plural. f 14 Or *I WILL BE WHAT I WILL BE*

King James

¹⁵And God said moreover unto Moses, Thus shalt thou say unto the children of Israel, The LORD God of your fathers, the God of Abraham, the God of Isaac, and the God of Jacob, hath sent me unto you: this *is* my name for ever, and this *is* my memorial unto all generations.

¹⁶Go, and gather the elders of Israel together, and say unto them, The LORD God of your fathers, the God of Abraham, of Isaac, and of Jacob, appeared unto me, saying, I have surely visited you, and *seen* that which is done to you in Egypt:

¹⁷And I have said, I will bring you up out of the affliction of Egypt unto the land of the Canaanites, and the Hittites, and the Amorites, and the Perizzites, and the Hivites, and the Jebusites, unto a land flowing with milk and honey.

¹⁸And they shall hearken to thy voice: and thou shalt come, thou and the elders of Israel, unto the king of Egypt, and ye shall say unto him, The LORD God of the Hebrews hath met with us: and now let us go, we beseech thee, three days' journey into the wilderness, that we may sacrifice to the LORD our God.

¹⁹ ¶ And I am sure that the king of Egypt will not let you go, ^hno, not by a mighty hand.

²⁰And I will stretch out my hand, and smite Egypt with all my wonders which I will do in the midst thereof: and after that he will let you go.

²¹And I will give this people favour in the sight of the Egyptians: and it shall come to pass, that, when ye go, ye shall not go empty:

²²But every woman shall borrow of her neighbour, and of her that sojourneth in her house, jewels of silver, and jewels of gold, and raiment: and ye shall put *them* upon your sons, and upon your daughters; and ye shall spoil ⁱthe Egyptians.

God equips Moses

4 AND MOSES answered and said, But, behold, they will not believe me, nor hearken unto my voice: for they will say, The LORD hath not appeared unto thee.

²And the LORD said unto him, What *is* that in thine hand? And he said, A rod.

³And he said, Cast it on the ground. And he cast it on the ground, and it became a serpent; and Moses fled from before it.

⁴And the LORD said unto Moses, Put forth thine hand, and take it by the tail. And he put forth his hand, and caught it, and it became a rod in his hand:

⁵That they may believe that the LORD God of their fathers, the God of Abraham, the God of Isaac, and the God of Jacob, hath appeared unto thee.

⁶ ¶ And the LORD said furthermore unto him, Put now thine hand into thy bosom. And he put his hand into his bosom: and when he took it out, behold, his hand *was* leprous as snow.

⁷And he said, Put thine hand into thy bosom again. And he put his hand into his bosom again; and plucked it out of his bosom, and, behold, it was turned again as his *other* flesh.

⁸And it shall come to pass, if they will not believe thee, neither hearken to the voice of the first sign, that they will believe the voice of the latter sign.

Amplified

¹⁵God said also to Moses, This shall you say to the Israelites: The Lord, the God of your fathers, of Abraham, of Isaac, and of Jacob, has sent me to you! This is My ^fname forever, and by this name I am to be remembered to all generations.

¹⁶Go, gather the elders of Israel together [the mature teachers and tribal leaders], and say to them, The Lord God of your fathers, the God of Abraham, of Isaac, and of Jacob, appeared to me, saying, I have surely visited you and seen that which is done to you in Egypt:

¹⁷And I have declared that I will bring you up out of the affliction of Egypt to the land of the Canaanite, the Hittite, the Amorite, the Perizzite, the Hivite, and the Jebusite, to a land flowing with milk and honey.

¹⁸And [the elders] shall believe *and* obey your voice; and you shall go, you and the elders of Israel, to the king of Egypt and you shall say to him, The Lord, the God of the Hebrews, has met with us; and now let us go, we beseech you, three days' journey into the wilderness, that we may sacrifice to the Lord our God.

¹⁹And I know that the king of Egypt will not let you go [unless forced to do so], no, not by a mighty hand.

²⁰So I will stretch out My hand and smite Egypt with all My wonders which I will do in it; and after that he will let you go.

²¹And I will give this people favor *and* respect in the sight of the Egyptians; and it shall be that when you go, you shall not go empty-handed.

²²But every woman shall [insistently] solicit of her neighbor and of her that may be residing at her house jewels and articles of silver and gold, and garments, which you shall put on your sons and daughters; and you shall strip the Egyptians [of belongings due to you].

4 AND MOSES answered, ^gBut behold, they will not believe me or listen to *and* obey my voice; for they will say, The Lord has not appeared to you.

²And the Lord said to him, What is that in your hand? And he said, A rod.

³And He said, Cast it on the ground. And he did so and it became a serpent [the symbol of royal and divine power worn on the crown of the Pharaohs]; and Moses fled from before it.

⁴And the Lord said to Moses, Put forth your hand and take it by the tail. And he stretched out his hand and caught it, and it became a rod in his hand,

⁵[This you shall do, said the Lord] that the elders may believe that the Lord, the God of their fathers, of Abraham, of Isaac, and of Jacob, has indeed appeared to you.

⁶The Lord said also to him, Put your hand into your bosom. He put his hand into his bosom, and when he took it out, behold, his hand was leprous, as white as snow.

⁷[God] said, Put your hand into your bosom again. So he put his hand back into his bosom, and when he took it out, behold, it was restored as the rest of his flesh.

⁸[Then God said] If they will not believe you or heed the voice *or* the testimony of the first sign, they may believe the voice *or* the witness of the second sign.

---

^fTo know the **name** of God is to witness the manifestation of those attributes and apprehend that character which the name denotes (Exod. 6:3; I Kings 8:33ff.; Ps. 91:14; Isa. 52:6; 64:2; Jer. 16:21) (John D. Davis, *A Dictionary of the Bible*). God's name is His self-revelation (Charles Ellicott, *A Bible Commentary*). The name signifies the active presence of the person in the fullness of the revealed character (J.D. Douglas et al., eds., *The New Bible Dictionary*).   ^gThere need be no "buts" in our relationship to God's will. Nothing will take the Lord by surprise. The entire field has been surveyed and the preparations are complete. When the Lord says, "I will send thee," every provision has been made for the appointed task. "I will not fail thee." He who gives the command will also give the equipment (John Henry Jowett, *My Daily Meditation*).

^hOr, *but by strong hand*   ⁱOr, *Egypt*

New American Standard

15 God, furthermore, said to Moses, "Thus you shall say to the sons of Israel, 'The LORD, the God of your fathers, the God of Abraham, the God of Isaac, and the God of Jacob, has sent me to you.' This is My name forever, and this is My memorial-name to all generations.

16"Go and gather the elders of Israel together and say to them, 'The LORD, the God of your fathers, the God of Abraham, Isaac and Jacob, has appeared to me, saying, "I am indeed concerned about you and what has been done to you in Egypt.

17"So I said, I will bring you up out of the affliction of Egypt to the land of the Canaanite and the Hittite and the Amorite and the Perizzite and the Hivite and the Jebusite, to a land flowing with milk and honey."'

18"They will pay heed to what you say; and you with the elders of Israel will come to the king of Egypt and you will say to him, 'The LORD, the God of the Hebrews, has met with us. So now, please, let us go a three days' journey into the wilderness, that we may sacrifice to the LORD our God.'

19"But I know that the king of Egypt will not permit you to go, except under compulsion.

20"So I will stretch out My hand and strike Egypt with all My miracles which I shall do in the midst of it; and after that he will let you go.

21"I will grant this people favor in the sight of the Egyptians; and it shall be that when you go, you will not go empty-handed.

22"But every woman shall ask of her neighbor and the woman who lives in her house, articles of silver and articles of gold, and clothing; and you will put them on your sons and daughters. Thus you will plunder the Egyptians."

Moses Given Powers

4 THEN MOSES said, "What if they will not believe me or listen to what I say? For they may say, 'The LORD has not appeared to you.'"

2 The LORD said to him, "What is that in your hand?" And he said, "A staff."

3 Then He said, "Throw it on the ground." So he threw it on the ground, and it became a serpent; and Moses fled from it.

4 But the LORD said to Moses, "Stretch out your hand and grasp it by its tail"—so he stretched out his hand and caught it, and it became a staff in his hand—

5"that they may believe that the LORD, the God of their fathers, the God of Abraham, the God of Isaac, and the God of Jacob, has appeared to you."

6 ¶ The LORD furthermore said to him, "Now put your hand into your bosom." So he put his hand into his bosom, and when he took it out, behold, his hand was leprous like snow.

7 Then He said, "Put your hand into your bosom again." So he put his hand into his bosom again, and when he took it out of his bosom, behold, it was restored like the rest of his flesh.

8"If they will not believe you or heed the witness of the first sign, they may believe the witness of the last sign.

New International

15God also said to Moses, "Say to the Israelites, 'The LORD,[g] the God of your fathers—the God of Abraham, the God of Isaac and the God of Jacob—has sent me to you.' This is my name forever, the name by which I am to be remembered from generation to generation.

16"Go, assemble the elders of Israel and say to them, 'The LORD, the God of your fathers—the God of Abraham, Isaac and Jacob—appeared to me and said: I have watched over you and have seen what has been done to you in Egypt. 17And I have promised to bring you up out of your misery in Egypt into the land of the Canaanites, Hittites, Amorites, Perizzites, Hivites and Jebusites—a land flowing with milk and honey.'

18"The elders of Israel will listen to you. Then you and the elders are to go to the king of Egypt and say to him, 'The LORD, the God of the Hebrews, has met with us. Let us take a three-day journey into the desert to offer sacrifices to the LORD our God.' 19But I know that the king of Egypt will not let you go unless a mighty hand compels him. 20So I will stretch out my hand and strike the Egyptians with all the wonders that I will perform among them. After that, he will let you go.

21"And I will make the Egyptians favorably disposed toward this people, so that when you leave you will not go empty-handed. 22Every woman is to ask her neighbor and any woman living in her house for articles of silver and gold and for clothing, which you will put on your sons and daughters. And so you will plunder the Egyptians."

Signs for Moses

4 MOSES ANSWERED, "What if they do not believe me or listen to me and say, 'The LORD did not appear to you'?"

2Then the LORD said to him, "What is that in your hand?"

"A staff," he replied.

3The LORD said, "Throw it on the ground."

Moses threw it on the ground and it became a snake, and he ran from it. 4Then the LORD said to him, "Reach out your hand and take it by the tail." So Moses reached out and took hold of the snake and it turned back into a staff in his hand. 5"This," said the LORD, "is so that they may believe that the LORD, the God of their fathers—the God of Abraham, the God of Isaac and the God of Jacob—has appeared to you."

6Then the LORD said, "Put your hand inside your cloak." So Moses put his hand into his cloak, and when he took it out, it was leprous,[h] like snow.

7"Now put it back into your cloak," he said. So Moses put his hand back into his cloak, and when he took it out, it was restored, like the rest of his flesh.

8Then the LORD said, "If they do not believe you or pay attention to the first miraculous sign, they may believe the

---

g 15 The Hebrew for LORD sounds like and may be derived from the Hebrew for I AM in verse 14.   h 6 The Hebrew word was used for various diseases affecting the skin—not necessarily leprosy.

King James

⁹And it shall come to pass, if they will not believe also these two signs, neither hearken unto thy voice, that thou shalt take of the water of the river, and pour *it* upon the dry *land:* and the water which thou takest out of the river *J* shall become blood upon the dry *land.*

¹⁰ ¶ And Moses said unto the LORD, O my Lord, I *am* not *k*eloquent, neither *l*heretofore, nor since thou hast spoken unto thy servant: but I *am* slow of speech, and of a slow tongue.

¹¹And the LORD said unto him, Who hath made man's mouth? or who maketh the dumb, or deaf, or the seeing, or the blind? have not I the LORD?

¹²Now therefore go, and I will be with thy mouth, and teach thee what thou shalt say.

¹³And he said, O my Lord, send, I pray thee, by the hand *of him whom* thou *m*wilt send.

¹⁴And the anger of the LORD was kindled against Moses, and he said, *Is* not Aaron the Levite thy brother? I know that he can speak well. And also, behold, he cometh forth to meet thee: and when he seeth thee, he will be glad in his heart.

¹⁵And thou shalt speak unto him, and put words in his mouth: and I will be with thy mouth, and with his mouth, and will teach you what ye shall do.

¹⁶And he shall be thy spokesman unto the people: and he shall be, *even* he shall be to thee instead of a mouth, and thou shalt be to him instead of God.

¹⁷And thou shalt take this rod in thine hand, wherewith thou shalt do signs.

Moses returns to Egypt

¹⁸ ¶ And Moses went and returned to *n*Jethro his father-in-law, and said unto him, Let me go, I pray thee, and return unto my brethren which *are* in Egypt, and see whether they be yet alive. And Jethro said to Moses, Go in peace.

¹⁹And the LORD said unto Moses in Midian, Go, return into Egypt: for all the men are dead which sought thy life.

²⁰And Moses took his wife and his sons, and set them upon an ass, and he returned to the land of Egypt: and Moses took the rod of God in his hand.

²¹And the LORD said unto Moses, When thou goest to return into Egypt, see that thou do all those wonders before Pharaoh, which I have put in thine hand: but I will harden his heart, that he shall not let the people go.

²²And thou shalt say unto Pharaoh, Thus saith the LORD, Israel *is* my son, *even* my firstborn:

²³And I say unto thee, Let my son go, that he may serve me: and if thou refuse to let him go, behold, I will slay thy son, *even* thy firstborn.

²⁴ ¶ And it came to pass by the way in the inn, that the LORD met him, and sought to kill him.

²⁵Then Zipporah took a sharp *o*stone, and cut off the foreskin of her son, and *p*cast *it* at his feet, and said, Surely a bloody husband *art* thou to me.

²⁶So he let him go: then she said, A bloody husband *thou art,* because of the circumcision.

²⁷ ¶ And the LORD said to Aaron, Go into the wilderness to meet Moses. And he went, and met him in the mount of God, and kissed him.

²⁸And Moses told Aaron all the words of the LORD who had sent him, and all the signs which he had commanded him.

²⁹ ¶ And Moses and Aaron went and gathered together all the elders of the children of Israel:

³⁰And Aaron spake all the words which the LORD had spoken unto Moses, and did the signs in the sight of the people.

Amplified

⁹But if they will also not believe these two signs or heed your voice, you shall take some water of the river [Nile] and pour it upon the dry land; and the water which you take out of the river [Nile] shall become blood on the dry land.

¹⁰And Moses said to the Lord, O Lord, I am not eloquent *or* a man of words, neither before nor since You have spoken to Your servant; for I am slow of speech and have a heavy *and* awkward tongue.

¹¹And the Lord said to him, Who has made man's mouth? Or who makes the dumb, or the deaf, or the seeing, or the blind? Is it not I, the Lord?

¹²Now therefore go, and I will be with your mouth and will teach you what you shall say.

¹³And he said, Oh, my Lord, I pray You, send by the hand of [some other] whom You will [send].

¹⁴Then the anger of the Lord blazed against Moses; He said, Is there not Aaron your brother, the Levite? I know he can speak well. Also, he is coming out to meet you, and when he sees you, he will be overjoyed.

¹⁵You must speak to him and put the words in his mouth; and I will be with your mouth and with his mouth and will teach you what you shall do.

¹⁶He shall speak for you to the people, acting as a mouthpiece for you, and you shall be as God to him.

¹⁷And you shall take this rod in your hand with which you shall work the signs [that prove I sent you].

¹⁸And Moses went away and, returning to Jethro his father-in-law, said to him, Let me go back, I pray you, to my relatives in Egypt to see whether they are still alive. And Jethro said to Moses, Go in peace.

¹⁹The Lord said to Moses in Midian, Go back to Egypt; for all the men who were seeking your life [for killing the Egyptian] are dead. [Exod. 2:11, 12.]

²⁰And Moses took his wife and his sons and set them on donkeys, and he returned to the land of Egypt; and Moses took the rod of God in his hand.

²¹And the Lord said to Moses, When you return into Egypt, see that you do before Pharaoh all those miracles *and* wonders which I have put in your hand; but I will make him stubborn *and* harden his heart, so that he will not let the people go.

²²And you shall say to Pharaoh, Thus says the Lord, Israel is My son, even My firstborn.

²³And I say to you, Let My son go, that he may serve Me; and if you refuse to let him go, behold, I will slay your son, your firstborn.

²⁴Along the way at a [resting-] place, the Lord met [Moses] and sought to kill him [made him acutely and almost fatally ill].

²⁵[Now apparently he had *h*failed to circumcise one of his sons, his wife being opposed to it; but seeing his life in such danger] Zipporah took a flint knife and cut off the foreskin of her son and cast it to touch [Moses'] feet, and said, Surely a husband of blood you are to me!

²⁶When He let [Moses] alone [to recover], Zipporah said, A husband of blood are you because of the circumcision.

²⁷The Lord said to Aaron, Go into the wilderness to meet Moses. And he went, and met him in the mountain of God [Horeb, or Sinai] and kissed him.

²⁸Moses told Aaron all the words of the Lord with which He had sent him, and all the signs with which He had charged him.

²⁹Moses and Aaron went and gathered together [in Egypt] all the elders of the Israelites.

³⁰Aaron spoke all the words which the Lord had spoken to Moses, and did the signs in the sight of the people.

---

*h*He who is on his way to liberate the people of the circumcision has in Midian even neglected to circumcise his second son Eliezer (J.P. Lange, *A Commentary*). It was necessary that at this stage of Moses' experience he should learn that God is in earnest when He speaks, and will assuredly perform all that He has threatened (J.G. Murphy, *A Commentary on the Book of Exodus*).

*J*Heb. *shall be and shall be*   *k*Heb. *a man of words*   *l*Heb. *since yesterday, nor since the third day*   *m*Or, *shouldest*   *n*Heb. *Jether*   *o*Or, *knife*   *p*Heb. *made it touch*

New American Standard

9"But if they will not believe even these two signs or heed what you say, then you shall take some water from the Nile and pour it on the dry ground; and the water which you take from the Nile will become blood on the dry ground."

10 ¶ Then Moses said to the LORD, "Please, Lord, I have never been eloquent, neither recently nor in time past, nor since You have spoken to Your servant; for I am slow of speech and slow of tongue."

11 The LORD said to him, "Who has made man's mouth? Or who makes *him* mute or deaf, or seeing or blind? Is it not I, the LORD?

12"Now then go, and I, even I, will be with your mouth, and teach you what you are to say."

13 But he said, "Please, Lord, now send *the message* by whomever You will."

Aaron to Be Moses' Mouthpiece

14 Then the anger of the LORD burned against Moses, and He said, "Is there not your brother Aaron the Levite? I know that he speaks fluently. And moreover, behold, he is coming out to meet you; when he sees you, he will be glad in his heart.

15"You are to speak to him and put the words in his mouth; and I, even I, will be with your mouth and his mouth, and I will teach you what you are to do.

16"Moreover, he shall speak for you to the people; and he will be as a mouth for you and you will be as God to him.

17"You shall take in your hand this staff, with which you shall perform the signs."

18 ¶ Then Moses departed and returned to Jethro his father-in-law and said to him, "Please, let me go, that I may return to my brethren who are in Egypt, and see if they are still alive." And Jethro said to Moses, "Go in peace."

19 Now the LORD said to Moses in Midian, "Go back to Egypt, for all the men who were seeking your life are dead."

20 So Moses took his wife and his sons and mounted them on a donkey, and returned to the land of Egypt. Moses also took the staff of God in his hand.

21 ¶ The LORD said to Moses, "When you go back to Egypt see that you perform before Pharaoh all the wonders which I have put in your power; but I will harden his heart so that he will not let the people go.

22"Then you shall say to Pharaoh, 'Thus says the LORD, "Israel is My son, My firstborn.

23"So I said to you, 'Let My son go that he may serve Me'; but you have refused to let him go. Behold, I will kill your son, your firstborn." ' "

24 ¶ Now it came about at the lodging place on the way that the LORD met him and sought to put him to death.

25 Then Zipporah took a flint and cut off her son's foreskin and threw it at Moses' feet, and she said, "You are indeed a bridegroom of blood to me."

26 So He let him alone. At that time she said, "*You are a bridegroom of blood*"—because of the circumcision.

27 ¶ Now the LORD said to Aaron, "Go to meet Moses in the wilderness." So he went and met him at the mountain of God and kissed him.

28 Moses told Aaron all the words of the LORD with which He had sent him, and all the signs that He had commanded him *to do*.

29 Then Moses and Aaron went and assembled all the elders of the sons of Israel;

30 and Aaron spoke all the words which the LORD had spoken to Moses. He then performed the signs in the sight of the people.

New International

second. 9But if they do not believe these two signs or listen to you, take some water from the Nile and pour it on the dry ground. The water you take from the river will become blood on the ground."

10Moses said to the LORD, "O Lord, I have never been eloquent, neither in the past nor since you have spoken to your servant. I am slow of speech and tongue."

11The LORD said to him, "Who gave man his mouth? Who makes him deaf or mute? Who gives him sight or makes him blind? Is it not I, the LORD? 12Now go; I will help you speak and will teach you what to say."

13But Moses said, "O Lord, please send someone else to do it."

14Then the LORD's anger burned against Moses and he said, "What about your brother, Aaron the Levite? I know he can speak well. He is already on his way to meet you, and his heart will be glad when he sees you. 15You shall speak to him and put words in his mouth; I will help both of you speak and will teach you what to do. 16He will speak to the people for you, and it will be as if he were your mouth and as if you were God to him. 17But take this staff in your hand so you can perform miraculous signs with it."

Moses Returns to Egypt

18Then Moses went back to Jethro his father-in-law and said to him, "Let me go back to my own people in Egypt to see if any of them are still alive."

Jethro said, "Go, and I wish you well."

19Now the LORD had said to Moses in Midian, "Go back to Egypt, for all the men who wanted to kill you are dead." 20So Moses took his wife and sons, put them on a donkey and started back to Egypt. And he took the staff of God in his hand.

21The LORD said to Moses, "When you return to Egypt, see that you perform before Pharaoh all the wonders I have given you the power to do. But I will harden his heart so that he will not let the people go. 22Then say to Pharaoh, 'This is what the LORD says: Israel is my firstborn son, 23and I told you, "Let my son go, so he may worship me." But you refused to let him go; so I will kill your firstborn son.' "

24At a lodging place on the way, the LORD met ˌMosesˌ[i] and was about to kill him. 25But Zipporah took a flint knife, cut off her son's foreskin and touched ˌMoses'ˌ feet with it.[j] "Surely you are a bridegroom of blood to me," she said. 26So the LORD let him alone. (At that time she said "bridegroom of blood," referring to circumcision.)

27The LORD said to Aaron, "Go into the desert to meet Moses." So he met Moses at the mountain of God and kissed him. 28Then Moses told Aaron everything the LORD had sent him to say, and also about all the miraculous signs he had commanded him to perform.

29Moses and Aaron brought together all the elders of the Israelites, 30and Aaron told them everything the LORD had said to Moses. He also performed the signs before the

i 24 Or ˌMoses' sonˌ; Hebrew *him*   *j 25* Or *and drew near* ˌMoses'ˌ *feet*

King James

31And the people believed: and when they heard that the LORD had visited the children of Israel, and that he had looked upon their affliction, then they bowed their heads and worshipped.

Pharaoh oppresses Israel

5 AND AFTERWARD Moses and Aaron went in, and told Pharaoh, Thus saith the LORD God of Israel, Let my people go, that they may hold a feast unto me in the wilderness.

2And Pharaoh said, Who is the LORD, that I should obey his voice to let Israel go? I know not the LORD, neither will I let Israel go.

3And they said, The God of the Hebrews hath met with us: let us go, we pray thee, three days' journey into the desert, and sacrifice unto the LORD our God; lest he fall upon us with pestilence, or with the sword.

4And the king of Egypt said unto them, Wherefore do ye, Moses and Aaron, let the people from their works? get you unto your burdens.

5And Pharaoh said, Behold, the people of the land now are many, and ye make them rest from their burdens.

6And Pharaoh commanded the same day the taskmasters of the people, and their officers, saying,

7Ye shall no more give the people straw to make brick, as heretofore: let them go and gather straw for themselves.

8And the tale of the bricks, which they did make heretofore, ye shall lay upon them; ye shall not diminish aught thereof: for they be idle; therefore they cry, saying, Let us go and sacrifice to our God.

9qLet there more work be laid upon the men, that they may labour therein; and let them not regard vain words.

10 ¶ And the taskmasters of the people went out, and their officers, and they spake to the people, saying, Thus saith Pharaoh, I will not give you straw.

11Go ye, get you straw where ye can find it: yet not aught of your work shall be diminished.

12So the people were scattered abroad throughout all the land of Egypt to gather stubble instead of straw.

13And the taskmasters hasted them, saying, Fulfil your works, ryour daily tasks, as when there was straw.

14And the officers of the children of Israel, which Pharaoh's taskmasters had set over them, were beaten, and demanded, Wherefore have ye not fulfilled your task in making brick both yesterday and today, as heretofore?

15 ¶ Then the officers of the children of Israel came and cried unto Pharaoh, saying, Wherefore dealest thou thus with thy servants?

16There is no straw given unto thy servants, and they say to us, Make brick: and, behold, thy servants are beaten; but the fault is in thine own people.

17But he said, Ye are idle, ye are idle: therefore ye say, Let us go and do sacrifice to the LORD.

18Go therefore now, and work; for there shall no straw be given you, yet shall ye deliver the tale of bricks.

19And the officers of the children of Israel did see that they were in evil case, after it was said, Ye shall not minish aught from your bricks of your daily task.

20 ¶ And they met Moses and Aaron, who stood in the way, as they came forth from Pharaoh:

Amplified

31And the people believed; and when they heard that the Lord had visited the Israelites, and that He had looked [in compassion] upon their affliction, they bowed their heads and worshiped.

5 AFTERWARD MOSES and Aaron went in and told Pharaoh, Thus says the Lord, the God of Israel, Let My people go, that they may hold a feast to Me in the wilderness.

2But Pharaoh said, Who is the Lord, that I should obey His voice to let Israel go? I know not the Lord, neither will I let Israel go.

3And they said, The God of the Hebrews has met with us; let us go, we pray you, three days' journey into the desert and sacrifice to the Lord our God, lest He fall upon us with pestilence or with the sword.

4The king of Egypt said to Moses and Aaron, Why do you take the people from their jobs? Get to your burdens!

5Pharaoh said, Behold, the people of the land now are many, and you make them rest from their burdens!

6The very same day Pharaoh commanded the taskmasters of the people and their officers,

7You shall no more give the people straw to make brick; let them go and gather straw for themselves.

8But the number of the bricks which they made before you shall still require of them; you shall not diminish it in the least. For they are idle; that is why they cry, Let us go and sacrifice to our God.

9Let heavier work be laid upon the men that they may labor at it and pay no attention to lying words.

10The taskmasters of the people went out, and their officers, and they said to the people, Thus says Pharaoh, I will not give you straw.

11Go, get istraw where you can find it; but your work shall not be diminished in the least.

12So the people were scattered through all the land of Egypt to gather the short stubble instead of straw.

13And the taskmasters were urgent, saying, Finish your work, your daily quotas, as when there was straw.

14And the Hebrew foremen, whom Pharaoh's taskmasters had set over them, were beaten and were asked, Why have you not fulfilled all your quota of making bricks yesterday and today, as before?

15Then the Hebrew foremen came to Pharaoh and cried, Why do you deal like this with your servants?

16No straw is given to your servants, yet they say to us, Make bricks! And behold, your servants are beaten, but the fault is in your own people.

17But [Pharaoh] said, You are idle, lazy and idle! That is why you say, Let us go and sacrifice to the Lord.

18Get out now and get to work; for no straw shall be given you, yet you shall deliver the full quota of bricks.

19And the Hebrew foremen saw that they were in an evil situation when it was said, You shall not diminish in the least your full daily quota of bricks.

20And the foremen met Moses and Aaron, who were standing in the way as they came forth from Pharaoh.

---

iArchaeologists became interested early in examining Egyptian bricks of Moses' time to see if they contained straw. They found that, while many did contain straw, many also did not, leaving the impression that the Bible was wrong. But as usual in such cases, sooner or later it is shown that "the testimony of the Lord is sure, making wise the simple" (Ps. 19:7)—who know no better than to doubt the truth of God's Word. It is now known that oat straw boiled in water, when added to clay, makes the clay much easier to handle. Without the organic material obtained from the straw, the difficulty of making bricks was greatly increased. The fact that brickmakers of Egypt found the use of straw essential, whether visible evidence remains or not, is fully borne out, as various writers have asserted. (See Allan A. MacRae's, "The Relation of Archaeology to the Bible" in Modern Science and Christian Faith.)

qHeb. Let the work be heavy upon the men in his day   rHeb. a matter of a day in his day

New American Standard

31 So the people believed; and when they heard that the LORD was concerned about the sons of Israel and that He had seen their affliction, then they bowed low and worshiped.

Israel's Labor Increased

5 AND AFTERWARD Moses and Aaron came and said to Pharaoh, "Thus says the LORD, the God of Israel, 'Let My people go that they may celebrate a feast to Me in the wilderness.' "

2 But Pharaoh said, "Who is the LORD that I should obey His voice to let Israel go? I do not know the LORD, and besides, I will not let Israel go."

3 Then they said, "The God of the Hebrews has met with us. Please, let us go a three days' journey into the wilderness that we may sacrifice to the LORD our God, otherwise He will fall upon us with pestilence or with the sword."

4 But the king of Egypt said to them, "Moses and Aaron, why do you draw the people away from their work? Get *back* to your labors!"

5 Again Pharaoh said, "Look, the people of the land are now many, and you would have them cease from their labors!"

6 So the same day Pharaoh commanded the taskmasters over the people and their foremen, saying,

7 "You are no longer to give the people straw to make brick as previously; let them go and gather straw for themselves.

8 "But the quota of bricks which they were making previously, you shall impose on them; you are not to reduce any of it. Because they are lazy, therefore they cry out, 'Let us go and sacrifice to our God.'

9 "Let the labor be heavier on the men, and let them work at it so that they will pay no attention to false words."

10 ¶ So the taskmasters of the people and their foremen went out and spoke to the people, saying, "Thus says Pharaoh, 'I am not going to give you *any* straw.

11 'You go *and* get straw for yourselves wherever you can find *it*, but none of your labor will be reduced.' "

12 So the people scattered through all the land of Egypt to gather stubble for straw.

13 The taskmasters pressed them, saying, "Complete your work quota, *your* daily amount, just as when you had straw."

14 Moreover, the foremen of the sons of Israel, whom Pharaoh's taskmasters had set over them, were beaten and were asked, "Why have you not completed your required amount either yesterday or today in making brick as previously?"

15 ¶ Then the foremen of the sons of Israel came and cried out to Pharaoh, saying, "Why do you deal this way with your servants?

16 "There is no straw given to your servants, yet they keep saying to us, 'Make bricks!' And behold, your servants are being beaten; but it is the fault of your *own* people."

17 But he said, "You are lazy, *very* lazy; therefore you say, 'Let us go *and* sacrifice to the LORD.'

18 "So go now *and* work; for you will be given no straw, yet you must deliver the quota of bricks."

19 The foremen of the sons of Israel saw that they were in trouble because they were told, "You must not reduce *your* daily amount of bricks."

20 When they left Pharaoh's presence, they met Moses and Aaron as they were waiting for them.

New International

people, 31 and they believed. And when they heard that the LORD was concerned about them and had seen their misery, they bowed down and worshiped.

Bricks Without Straw

5 AFTERWARD Moses and Aaron went to Pharaoh and said, "This is what the LORD, the God of Israel, says: 'Let my people go, so that they may hold a festival to me in the desert.' "

2 Pharaoh said, "Who is the LORD, that I should obey him and let Israel go? I do not know the LORD and I will not let Israel go."

3 Then they said, "The God of the Hebrews has met with us. Now let us take a three-day journey into the desert to offer sacrifices to the LORD our God, or he may strike us with plagues or with the sword."

4 But the king of Egypt said, "Moses and Aaron, why are you taking the people away from their labor? Get back to your work!" 5 Then Pharaoh said, "Look, the people of the land are now numerous, and you are stopping them from working."

6 That same day Pharaoh gave this order to the slave drivers and foremen in charge of the people: 7 "You are no longer to supply the people with straw for making bricks; let them go and gather their own straw. 8 But require them to make the same number of bricks as before; don't reduce the quota. They are lazy; that is why they are crying out, 'Let us go and sacrifice to our God.' 9 Make the work harder for the men so that they keep working and pay no attention to lies."

10 Then the slave drivers and the foremen went out and said to the people, "This is what Pharaoh says: 'I will not give you any more straw. 11 Go and get your own straw wherever you can find it, but your work will not be reduced at all.' " 12 So the people scattered all over Egypt to gather stubble to use for straw. 13 The slave drivers kept pressing them, saying, "Complete the work required of you for each day, just as when you had straw." 14 The Israelite foremen appointed by Pharaoh's slave drivers were beaten and were asked, "Why didn't you meet your quota of bricks yesterday or today, as before?"

15 Then the Israelite foremen went and appealed to Pharaoh: "Why have you treated your servants this way? 16 Your servants are given no straw, yet we are told, 'Make bricks!' Your servants are being beaten, but the fault is with your own people."

17 Pharaoh said, "Lazy, that's what you are—lazy! That is why you keep saying, 'Let us go and sacrifice to the LORD.' 18 Now get to work. You will not be given any straw, yet you must produce your full quota of bricks."

19 The Israelite foremen realized they were in trouble when they were told, "You are not to reduce the number of bricks required of you for each day." 20 When they left Pharaoh, they found Moses and Aaron waiting to meet

King James

²¹And they said unto them, The LORD look upon you, and judge; because ye have made our savour *s*to be abhorred in the eyes of Pharaoh, and in the eyes of his servants, to put a sword in their hand to slay us.

God's promise of deliverance

²²And Moses returned unto the LORD, and said, Lord, wherefore hast thou *so* evil entreated this people? why *is* it *that* thou hast sent me?

²³For since I came to Pharaoh to speak in thy name, he hath done evil to this people; *t*neither hast thou delivered thy people at all.

6 THEN THE LORD said unto Moses, Now shalt thou see what I will do to Pharaoh: for with a strong hand shall he let them go, and with a strong hand shall he drive them out of his land.

²And God spake unto Moses, and said unto him, I *am* *u*the LORD:

³And I appeared unto Abraham, unto Isaac, and unto Jacob, by *the name of* God Almighty, but by my name JEHOVAH was I not known to them.

⁴And I have also established my covenant with them, to give them the land of Canaan, the land of their pilgrimage, wherein they were strangers.

⁵And I have also heard the groaning of the children of Israel, whom the Egyptians keep in bondage; and I have remembered my covenant.

⁶Wherefore say unto the children of Israel, I *am* the LORD, and I will bring you out from under the burdens of the Egyptians, and I will rid you out of their bondage, and I will redeem you with a stretched out arm, and with great judgments:

⁷And I will take you to me for a people, and I will be to you a God: and ye shall know that I *am* the LORD your God, which bringeth you out from under the burdens of the Egyptians.

⁸And I will bring you in unto the land, concerning the which I did *v*swear to give it to Abraham, to Isaac, and to Jacob; and I will give it you for an heritage: I *am* the LORD.

⁹ ¶ And Moses spake unto the children of Israel: but they hearkened not unto Moses for *w*anguish of spirit, and for cruel bondage.

¹⁰And the LORD spake unto Moses, saying,

¹¹Go in, speak unto Pharaoh king of Egypt, that he let the children of Israel go out of his land.

¹²And Moses spake before the LORD, saying, Behold, the children of Israel have not hearkened unto me; how then shall Pharaoh hear me, who *am* of uncircumcised lips?

¹³And the LORD spake unto Moses and unto Aaron, and gave them a charge unto the children of Israel, and unto Pharaoh king of Egypt, to bring the children of Israel out of the land of Egypt.

The descendants of Israel

¹⁴ ¶ These *be* the heads of their fathers' houses: The sons of Reuben the firstborn of Israel; Hanoch, and Pallu, Hezron, and Carmi: these *be* the families of Reuben.

¹⁵And the sons of Simeon; Jemuel, and Jamin, and Ohad, and Jachin, and Zohar, and Shaul the son of a Canaanitish woman: these *are* the families of Simeon.

¹⁶ ¶ And these *are* the names of the sons of Levi according to their generations; Gershon, and Kohath, and Merari: and the years of the life of Levi *were* an hundred thirty and seven years.

Amplified

²¹And the foremen said to them, The Lord look upon you and judge, because you have made us a rotten stench to be detested by Pharaoh and his servants and have put a sword in their hand to slay us.

²²Then Moses turned again to the Lord and said, O Lord, why have You dealt evil to this people? Why did You ever send me?

²³For since I came to Pharaoh to speak in Your name, he has done evil to this people, neither have You delivered Your people at all.

6 THEN THE Lord said to Moses, Now you shall see what I will do to Pharaoh; for [compelled] by a strong hand he will [not only] let them go, but he will drive them out of his land with a strong hand.

²And God said to Moses, I am the Lord.

³I appeared to Abraham, to Isaac, and to Jacob as God Almighty [El-Shaddai], but by My *j*name the Lord [Yahweh—the redemptive name of God] I did not make Myself known to them [in acts and great miracles]. [Gen. 17:1.]

⁴I have also established My covenant with them to give them the land of Canaan, the land of their temporary residence in which they were strangers.

⁵I have also heard the groaning of the Israelites whom the Egyptians have enslaved; and I have [earnestly] remembered My covenant [with Abraham, Isaac, and Jacob].

⁶Accordingly, say to the Israelites, I am the Lord, and I will bring you out from under the burdens of the Egyptians, and I will free you from their bondage, and I will rescue you with an outstretched arm [with special and vigorous action] and by mighty acts of judgment.

⁷And I will take you to Me for a people, and I will be to you a God; and you shall know that it is I, the Lord your God, Who brings you out from under the burdens of the Egyptians.

⁸And I will bring you into the land concerning which I lifted up My hand *and* swore that I would give it to Abraham, Isaac, and Jacob; and I will give it to you for a heritage. I am the Lord [you have the pledge of My changeless omnipotence and faithfulness].

⁹Moses told this to the Israelites, but they refused to listen to Moses because of their impatience *and* anguish of spirit and because of their cruel bondage.

¹⁰The Lord said to Moses,

¹¹Go in, tell Pharaoh king of Egypt to let the Israelites go out of his land.

¹²But Moses said to the Lord, Behold, [my own people] the Israelites have not listened to me; how then shall Pharaoh give heed to me, who am of deficient *and* impeded speech?

¹³But the Lord spoke to Moses and Aaron, and gave them a command for the Israelites and for Pharaoh king of Egypt, to bring the Israelites out of the land of Egypt.

¹⁴These are the heads of their clans. The sons of Reuben, Israel's firstborn: Hanoch, Pallu, Hezron, and Carmi; these are the families of Reuben.

¹⁵The sons of Simeon: Jemuel, Jamin, Ohad, Jachin, Zohar, and Shaul the son of a Canaanite woman; these are the families of Simeon.

¹⁶These are the names of the sons of Levi according to their births: Gershon, Kohath, and Merari; and Levi lived 137 years.

---

*s*Heb. *to stink;* see Gen. 34:30; 2 Sam. 10:6   *t*Heb. *delivering thou hast not delivered*   *u*Or, *JEHOVAH*   *v*Heb. *lift up my hand;* see Gen. 14:22; Deut. 32:40   *w*Heb. *shortness,* or, *straitness*

*j*See footnote on Exod. 3:15.

New American Standard

21 They said to them, "May the LORD look upon you and judge *you*, for you have made *d*us odious in Pharaoh's sight and in the sight of his servants, to put a sword in their hand to kill us."

22 ¶ Then Moses returned to the LORD and said, "O Lord, why have You brought harm to this people? Why did You ever send me?

23 "Ever since I came to Pharaoh to speak in Your name, he has done harm to this people, and You have not delivered Your people at all."

God Promises Action

6 THEN THE LORD said to Moses, "Now you shall see what I will do to Pharaoh; for under compulsion he will let them go, and under compulsion he will drive them out of his land."

2 ¶ God spoke further to Moses and said to him, "I am the LORD;

3 and I appeared to Abraham, Isaac, and Jacob, as God Almighty, but *by* My name, *e*LORD, I did not make Myself known to them.

4 "I also established My covenant with them, to give them the land of Canaan, the land in which they sojourned.

5 "Furthermore I have heard the groaning of the sons of Israel, because the Egyptians are holding them in bondage, and I have remembered My covenant.

6 "Say, therefore, to the sons of Israel, 'I am the LORD, and I will bring you out from under the burdens of the Egyptians, and I will deliver you from their bondage. I will also redeem you with an outstretched arm and with great judgments.

7 'Then I will take you for My people, and I will be your God; and you shall know that I am the LORD your God, who brought you out from under the burdens of the Egyptians.

8 'I will bring you to the land which I swore to give to Abraham, Isaac, and Jacob, and I will give it to you *for* a possession; I am the LORD.' "

9 So Moses spoke thus to the sons of Israel, but they did not listen to Moses on account of *their* despondency and cruel bondage.

10 ¶ Now the LORD spoke to Moses, saying,

11 "Go, tell Pharaoh king of Egypt to let the sons of Israel go out of his land."

12 But Moses spoke before the LORD, saying, "Behold, the sons of Israel have not listened to me; how then will Pharaoh listen to me, for I am unskilled in speech?"

13 Then the LORD spoke to Moses and to Aaron, and gave them a charge to the sons of Israel and to Pharaoh king of Egypt, to bring the sons of Israel out of the land of Egypt.

The Heads of Israel

14 ¶ These are the heads of their fathers' households. The sons of Reuben, Israel's firstborn: Hanoch and Pallu, Hezron and Carmi; these are the families of Reuben.

15 The sons of Simeon: Jemuel and Jamin and Ohad and Jachin and Zohar and Shaul the son of a Canaanite woman; these are the families of Simeon.

16 These are the names of the sons of Levi according to their generations: Gershon and Kohath and Merari; and the length of Levi's life was one hundred and thirty-seven years.

New International

them, 21 and they said, "May the LORD look upon you and judge you! You have made us a stench to Pharaoh and his officials and have put a sword in their hand to kill us."

God Promises Deliverance

22 Moses returned to the LORD and said, "O Lord, why have you brought trouble upon this people? Is this why you sent me? 23 Ever since I went to Pharaoh to speak in your name, he has brought trouble upon this people, and you have not rescued your people at all."

6 THEN THE LORD said to Moses, "Now you will see what I will do to Pharaoh: Because of my mighty hand he will let them go; because of my mighty hand he will drive them out of his country."

2 God also said to Moses, "I am the LORD. 3 I appeared to Abraham, to Isaac and to Jacob as God Almighty,*k* but by my name the LORD*l* I did not make myself known to them.*m* 4 I also established my covenant with them to give them the land of Canaan, where they lived as aliens. 5 Moreover, I have heard the groaning of the Israelites, whom the Egyptians are enslaving, and I have remembered my covenant.

6 "Therefore, say to the Israelites: 'I am the LORD, and I will bring you out from under the yoke of the Egyptians. I will free you from being slaves to them, and I will redeem you with an outstretched arm and with mighty acts of judgment. 7 I will take you as my own people, and I will be your God. Then you will know that I am the LORD your God, who brought you out from under the yoke of the Egyptians. 8 And I will bring you to the land I swore with uplifted hand to give to Abraham, to Isaac and to Jacob. I will give it to you as a possession. I am the LORD.' "

9 Moses reported this to the Israelites, but they did not listen to him because of their discouragement and cruel bondage.

10 Then the LORD said to Moses, 11 "Go, tell Pharaoh king of Egypt to let the Israelites go out of his country."

12 But Moses said to the LORD, "If the Israelites will not listen to me, why would Pharaoh listen to me, since I speak with faltering lips*n* ?"

Family Record of Moses and Aaron

13 Now the LORD spoke to Moses and Aaron about the Israelites and Pharaoh king of Egypt, and he commanded them to bring the Israelites out of Egypt.

14 These were the heads of their families*o*:

The sons of Reuben the firstborn son of Israel were Hanoch and Pallu, Hezron and Carmi. These were the clans of Reuben.

15 The sons of Simeon were Jemuel, Jamin, Ohad, Jakin, Zohar and Shaul the son of a Canaanite woman. These were the clans of Simeon.

16 These were the names of the sons of Levi according to their records: Gershon, Kohath and Merari. Levi lived 137 years.

---

k3 Hebrew *El-Shaddai*   *l3* See note at Exodus 3:15.
m3 Or *Almighty, and by my name the LORD did I not let myself be known to them?*   *n12* Hebrew *I am uncircumcised of lips*; also in verse 30   *o14* The Hebrew for *families* here and in verse 25 refers to units larger than clans.

---

*d*Lit *our savor to stink*   *e*Heb *YHWH,* usually rendered LORD

King James

17The sons of Gershon; Libni, and Shimi, according to their families.

18And the sons of Kohath; Amram, and Izhar, and Hebron, and Uzziel: and the years of the life of Kohath were an hundred thirty and three years.

19And the sons of Merari; Mahali and Mushi: these are the families of Levi according to their generations.

20And Amram took him Jochebed his father's sister to wife; and she bare him Aaron and Moses: and the years of the life of Amram were an hundred and thirty and seven years.

21 ¶ And the sons of Izhar; Korah, and Nepheg, and Zichri.

22And the sons of Uzziel; Mishael, and Elzaphan, and Zithri.

23And Aaron took him Elisheba, daughter of Amminadab, sister of Naashon, to wife; and she bare him Nadab, and Abihu, Eleazar, and Ithamar.

24And the sons of Korah; Assir, and Elkanah, and Abiasaph: these are the families of the Korhites.

25And Eleazar Aaron's son took him one of the daughters of Putiel to wife; and she bare him Phinehas: these are the heads of the fathers of the Levites according to their families.

26These are that Aaron and Moses, to whom the LORD said, Bring out the children of Israel from the land of Egypt according to their armies.

27These are they which spake to Pharaoh king of Egypt, to bring out the children of Israel from Egypt: these are that Moses and Aaron.

Aaron to speak for Moses

28 ¶ And it came to pass on the day when the LORD spake unto Moses in the land of Egypt,

29That the LORD spake unto Moses, saying, I am the LORD: speak thou unto Pharaoh king of Egypt all that I say unto thee.

30And Moses said before the LORD, Behold, I am of uncircumcised lips, and how shall Pharaoh hearken unto me?

7 AND THE LORD said unto Moses, See, I have made thee a god to Pharaoh: and Aaron thy brother shall be thy prophet.

2Thou shalt speak all that I command thee: and Aaron thy brother shall speak unto Pharaoh, that he send the children of Israel out of his land.

3And I will harden Pharaoh's heart, and multiply my signs and my wonders in the land of Egypt.

4But Pharaoh shall not hearken unto you, that I may lay my hand upon Egypt, and bring forth mine armies, and my people the children of Israel, out of the land of Egypt by great judgments.

5And the Egyptians shall know that I am the LORD, when I stretch forth mine hand upon Egypt, and bring out the children of Israel from among them.

6And Moses and Aaron did as the LORD commanded them, so did they.

7And Moses was fourscore years old, and Aaron fourscore and three years old, when they spake unto Pharaoh.

The rod becomes a serpent

8 ¶ And the LORD spake unto Moses and unto Aaron, saying,

9When Pharaoh shall speak unto you, saying, Show a miracle for you: then thou shalt say unto Aaron, Take thy rod, and cast it before Pharaoh, and it shall become a serpent.

10 ¶ And Moses and Aaron went in unto Pharaoh, and they did so as the LORD had commanded: and Aaron cast down his rod before Pharaoh, and before his servants, and it became a serpent.

Amplified

17The sons of Gershon: Libni and Shimi, by their families.

18The sons of Kohath: Amram, Izhar, Hebron, and Uzziel; and Kohath lived 133 years.

19The sons of Merari: Mahli and Mushi. These are the families of Levi according to their generations.

20Amram took Jochebed his father's sister as wife, and she bore him Aaron and Moses; and Amram lived 137 years.

21The sons of Izhar: Korah, Nepheg, and Zichri.

22The sons of Uzziel: Mishael, Elzaphan, and Sithri.

23Aaron took Elisheba, daughter of Amminadab and sister of Nahshon, as wife; she bore him Nadab, Abihu, Eleazar, and Ithamar.

24The sons of Korah: Assir, Elkanah, and Abiasaph. These are the families of the Korahites.

25Eleazar, Aaron's son, took one of the daughters of Putiel as wife; and she bore him Phinehas. These are the heads of the fathers' houses of the Levites by their families.

26These are the [same] Aaron and Moses to whom the Lord said, Bring out the Israelites from the land of Egypt by their hosts,

27And who spoke to [the] Pharaoh king of Egypt about bringing the Israelites out of Egypt; these are that Moses and Aaron.

28On the day when the Lord spoke to Moses in Egypt,

29The Lord said to Moses, I am the Lord; tell Pharaoh king of Egypt all that I say to you.

30But Moses said to the Lord, Behold, I am of deficient and impeded speech; how then shall Pharaoh listen to me?

7 THE LORD said to Moses, Behold, I make you as God to Pharaoh [to declare My will and purpose to him]; and Aaron your brother shall be your prophet.

2You shall speak all that I command you, and Aaron your brother shall tell Pharaoh to let the Israelites go out of his land.

3And I will make Pharaoh's heart stubborn and hard, and multiply My signs, My wonders, and miracles in the land of Egypt.

4But Pharaoh will not listen to you, and I will lay My hand upon Egypt and bring forth My hosts, My people the Israelites, out of the land of Egypt by great acts of judgment.

5The Egyptians shall know that I am the Lord when I stretch forth My hand upon Egypt and bring out the Israelites from among them.

6And Moses and Aaron did so, as the Lord commanded them.

7Now Moses was 80 years old and Aaron 83 years old when they spoke to Pharaoh.

8And the Lord said to Moses and Aaron,

9When Pharaoh says to you, Prove [your authority] by a miracle, then tell Aaron, Throw your rod down before Pharaoh, that it may become a serpent.

10So Moses and Aaron went to Pharaoh and did as the Lord had commanded; Aaron threw down his rod before Pharaoh and his servants, and it became a serpent.

New American Standard

17 The sons of Gershon: Libni and Shimei, according to their families.

18 The sons of Kohath: Amram and Izhar and Hebron and Uzziel; and the length of Kohath's life was one hundred and thirty-three years.

19 The sons of Merari: Mahli and Mushi. These are the families of the Levites according to their generations.

20 Amram married his father's sister Jochebed, and she bore him Aaron and Moses; and the length of Amram's life was one hundred and thirty-seven years.

21 The sons of Izhar: Korah and Nepheg and Zichri.

22 The sons of Uzziel: Mishael and Elzaphan and Sithri.

23 Aaron married Elisheba, the daughter of Amminadab, the sister of Nahshon, and she bore him Nadab and Abihu, Eleazar and Ithamar.

24 The sons of Korah: Assir and Elkanah and Abiasaph; these are the families of the Korahites.

25 Aaron's son Eleazar married one of the daughters of Putiel, and she bore him Phinehas. These are the heads of the fathers' *households* of the Levites according to their families.

26 It was *the same* Aaron and Moses to whom the LORD said, "Bring out the sons of Israel from the land of Egypt according to their hosts."

27 They were the ones who spoke to Pharaoh king of Egypt about bringing out the sons of Israel from Egypt; it was *the same* Moses and Aaron.

28 ¶ Now it came about on the day when the LORD spoke to Moses in the land of Egypt,

29 that the LORD spoke to Moses, saying, "I am the LORD; speak to Pharaoh king of Egypt all that I speak to you."

30 But Moses said before the LORD, "Behold, I am unskilled in speech; how then will Pharaoh listen to me?"

"I Will Stretch Out My Hand"

7 THEN THE LORD said to Moses, "See, I make you *as* God to Pharaoh, and your brother Aaron shall be your prophet.

2 "You shall speak all that I command you, and your brother Aaron shall speak to Pharaoh that he let the sons of Israel go out of his land.

3 "But I will harden Pharaoh's heart that I may multiply My signs and My wonders in the land of Egypt.

4 "When Pharaoh does not listen to you, then I will lay My hand on Egypt and bring out My hosts, My people the sons of Israel, from the land of Egypt by great judgments.

5 "The Egyptians shall know that I am the LORD, when I stretch out My hand on Egypt and bring out the sons of Israel from their midst."

6 So Moses and Aaron did *it;* as the LORD commanded them, thus they did.

7 Moses was eighty years old and Aaron eighty-three, when they spoke to Pharaoh.

Aaron's Rod Becomes a Serpent

8 ¶ Now the LORD spoke to Moses and Aaron, saying,

9 "When Pharaoh speaks to you, saying, 'Work a miracle,' then you shall say to Aaron, 'Take your staff and throw *it* down before Pharaoh, *that* it may become a serpent.' "

10 So Moses and Aaron came to Pharaoh, and thus they did just as the LORD had commanded; and Aaron threw his staff down before Pharaoh and his servants, and it became a serpent.

New International

17 The sons of Gershon, by clans, were Libni and Shimei.

18 The sons of Kohath were Amram, Izhar, Hebron and Uzziel. Kohath lived 133 years.

19 The sons of Merari were Mahli and Mushi.

These were the clans of Levi according to their records.

20 Amram married his father's sister Jochebed, who bore him Aaron and Moses. Amram lived 137 years.

21 The sons of Izhar were Korah, Nepheg and Zicri.

22 The sons of Uzziel were Mishael, Elzaphan and Sithri.

23 Aaron married Elisheba, daughter of Amminadab and sister of Nahshon, and she bore him Nadab and Abihu, Eleazar and Ithamar.

24 The sons of Korah were Assir, Elkanah and Abiasaph. These were the Korahite clans.

25 Eleazar son of Aaron married one of the daughters of Putiel, and she bore him Phinehas.

These were the heads of the Levite families, clan by clan.

26 It was this same Aaron and Moses to whom the LORD said, "Bring the Israelites out of Egypt by their divisions."

27 They were the ones who spoke to Pharaoh king of Egypt about bringing the Israelites out of Egypt. It was the same Moses and Aaron.

Aaron to Speak for Moses

28 Now when the LORD spoke to Moses in Egypt, 29 he said to him, "I am the LORD. Tell Pharaoh king of Egypt everything I tell you."

30 But Moses said to the LORD, "Since I speak with faltering lips, why would Pharaoh listen to me?"

7 THEN THE LORD said to Moses, "See, I have made you like God to Pharaoh, and your brother Aaron will be your prophet. 2 You are to say everything I command you, and your brother Aaron is to tell Pharaoh to let the Israelites go out of his country. 3 But I will harden Pharaoh's heart, and though I multiply my miraculous signs and wonders in Egypt, 4 he will not listen to you. Then I will lay my hand on Egypt and with mighty acts of judgment I will bring out my divisions, my people the Israelites. 5 And the Egyptians will know that I am the LORD when I stretch out my hand against Egypt and bring the Israelites out of it."

6 Moses and Aaron did just as the LORD commanded them. 7 Moses was eighty years old and Aaron eighty-three when they spoke to Pharaoh.

Aaron's Staff Becomes a Snake

8 The LORD said to Moses and Aaron, 9 "When Pharaoh says to you, 'Perform a miracle,' then say to Aaron, 'Take your staff and throw it down before Pharaoh,' and it will become a snake."

10 So Moses and Aaron went to Pharaoh and did just as the LORD commanded. Aaron threw his staff down in front

King James

[11]Then Pharaoh also called the wise men and the sorcerers: now the magicians of Egypt, they also did in like manner with their enchantments.

[12]For they cast down every man his rod, and they became serpents: but Aaron's rod swallowed up their rods.

[13]And he hardened Pharaoh's heart, that he hearkened not unto them; as the LORD had said.

The water becomes blood

[14] ¶ And the LORD said unto Moses, Pharaoh's heart is hardened, he refuseth to let the people go.

[15]Get thee unto Pharaoh in the morning; lo, he goeth out unto the water; and thou shalt stand by the river's brink against he come; and the rod which was turned to a serpent shalt thou take in thine hand.

[16]And thou shalt say unto him, The LORD God of the Hebrews hath sent me unto thee, saying, Let my people go, that they may serve me in the wilderness: and, behold, hitherto thou wouldest not hear.

[17]Thus saith the LORD, In this thou shalt know that I *am* the LORD: behold, I will smite with the rod that *is* in mine hand upon the waters which *are* in the river, and they shall be turned to blood.

[18]And the fish that *is* in the river shall die, and the river shall stink; and the Egyptians shall loathe to drink of the water of the river.

[19] ¶ And the LORD spake unto Moses, Say unto Aaron, Take thy rod, and stretch out thine hand upon the waters of Egypt, upon their streams, upon their rivers, and upon their ponds, and upon all their *x*pools of water, that they may become blood; and *that* there may be blood throughout all the land of Egypt, both in *vessels of* wood, and in *vessels of* stone.

[20]And Moses and Aaron did so, as the LORD commanded; and he lifted up the rod, and smote the waters that *were* in the river, in the sight of Pharaoh, and in the sight of his servants; and all the waters that *were* in the river were turned to blood.

[21]And the fish that *was* in the river died; and the river stank, and the Egyptians could not drink of the water of the river; and there was blood throughout all the land of Egypt.

[22]And the magicians of Egypt did so with their enchantments: and Pharaoh's heart was hardened, neither did he hearken unto them; as the LORD had said.

[23]And Pharaoh turned and went into his house, neither did he set his heart to this also.

[24]And all the Egyptians digged round about the river for water to drink; for they could not drink of the water of the river.

The plague of frogs

[25]And seven days were fulfilled, after that the LORD had smitten the river.

8 AND THE LORD spake unto Moses, Go unto Pharaoh, and say unto him, Thus saith the LORD, Let my people go, that they may serve me.

[2]And if thou refuse to let *them* go, behold, I will smite all thy borders with frogs:

[3]And the river shall bring forth frogs abundantly, which shall go up and come into thine house, and into thy bedchamber, and upon thy bed, and into the house of thy servants, and upon thy people, and into thine ovens, and into thy *y*kneadingtroughs:

[4]And the frogs shall come up both on thee, and upon thy people, and upon all thy servants.

Amplified

[11]Then Pharaoh called for the wise men [skilled in magic and divination] and the sorcerers (wizards and jugglers). And they also, these magicians of Egypt, did similar things with their enchantments *and* secret arts.

[12]For they cast down every man his rod and they became serpents; but Aaron's rod swallowed up their rods.

[13]But Pharaoh's heart was hardened *and* stubborn and he would not listen to them, just as the Lord had said.

[14]Then the Lord said to Moses, Pharaoh's heart is hard *and* stubborn; he refuses to let the people go.

[15]Go to Pharaoh in the morning; he will be going out to the water; wait for him by the river's brink; and the rod which was turned to a serpent you shall take in your hand.

[16]And say to him, The Lord, the God of the Hebrews has sent me to you, saying, Let My people go, that they may serve Me in the wilderness; and behold, heretofore you have not listened.

[17]Thus says the Lord, In this you shall know, recognize, *and* understand that I am the Lord: behold, I will smite with the rod in my hand the waters in the [Nile] River, and they shall be turned to blood.

[18]The fish in the river shall die, the river shall become foul smelling, and the Egyptians shall loathe to drink from it.

[19]And the Lord said to Moses, Say to Aaron, Take your rod and stretch out your hand over the waters of Egypt, over their streams, rivers, pools, and ponds of water, that they may become blood; and there shall be blood throughout all the land of Egypt, in containers both of wood and of stone.

[20]Moses and Aaron did as the Lord commanded; [Aaron] lifted up the rod and smote the waters in the river in the sight of Pharaoh and his servants, and all the waters in the river were turned to blood.

[21]And the fish in the river died; and the river became foul smelling, and the Egyptians could not drink its water, and there was blood throughout all the land of Egypt.

[22]But the magicians of Egypt did the same by their enchantments *and* secret arts; and Pharaoh's heart was made hard *and* obstinate, and he did not listen to Moses and Aaron, just as the Lord had said.

[23]And Pharaoh turned and went into his house; neither did he take even this to heart.

[24]And all the Egyptians dug round about the river for water to drink, for they could not drink the water of the [Nile].

[25]Seven days passed after the Lord had smitten the river.

8 THEN THE Lord said to Moses, Go to Pharaoh and say to him, Thus says the Lord, Let My people go, that they may serve Me.

[2]And if you refuse to let them go, behold, I will smite your entire land with frogs;

[3]And the river shall swarm with frogs which shall go up and come into your house, into your bedchamber and on your bed, and into the houses of your servants and upon your people, and into your ovens, your kneading bowls, *and* your dough.

[4]And the frogs shall come up on you and on your people and all your servants.

---

*x*Heb. *gathering of their waters* *y*Or, *dough*

New American Standard

11 Then Pharaoh also called for *the* wise men and *the* sorcerers, and they also, the magicians of Egypt, did the same with their secret arts.

12 For each one threw down his staff and they turned into serpents. But Aaron's staff swallowed up their staffs.

13 Yet Pharaoh's heart was hardened, and he did not listen to them, as the LORD had said.

Water Is Turned to Blood

14 ¶ Then the LORD said to Moses, "Pharaoh's heart is stubborn; he refuses to let the people go.

15"Go to Pharaoh in the morning as he is going out to the water, and station yourself to meet him on the bank of the Nile; and you shall take in your hand the staff that was turned into a serpent.

16"You shall say to him, 'The LORD, the God of the Hebrews, sent me to you, saying, "Let My people go, that they may serve Me in the wilderness. But behold, you have not listened until now."

17'Thus says the LORD, "By this you shall know that I am the LORD: behold, I will strike the water that is in the Nile with the staff that is in my hand, and it will be turned to blood.

18"The fish that are in the Nile will die, and the Nile will become foul, and the Egyptians will find difficulty in drinking water from the Nile."'"

19 Then the LORD said to Moses, "Say to Aaron, 'Take your staff and stretch out your hand over the waters of Egypt, over their rivers, over their streams, and over their pools, and over all their reservoirs of water, that they may become blood; and there will be blood throughout all the land of Egypt, both in *vessels of* wood and in *vessels of* stone.'"

20 ¶ So Moses and Aaron did even as the LORD had commanded. And he lifted up the staff and struck the water that *was* in the Nile, in the sight of Pharaoh and in the sight of his servants, and all the water that *was* in the Nile was turned to blood.

21 The fish that *were* in the Nile died, and the Nile became foul, so that the Egyptians could not drink water from the Nile. And the blood was through all the land of Egypt.

22 But the magicians of Egypt did the same with their secret arts; and Pharaoh's heart was hardened, and he did not listen to them, as the LORD had said.

23 Then Pharaoh turned and went into his house with no concern even for this.

24 So all the Egyptians dug around the Nile for water to drink, for they could not drink of the water of the Nile.

25 Seven days passed after the LORD had struck the Nile.

Frogs over the Land

8 THEN THE LORD said to Moses, "Go to Pharaoh and say to him, 'Thus says the LORD, "Let My people go, that they may serve Me.

2"But if you refuse to let *them* go, behold, I will smite your whole territory with frogs.

3"The Nile will swarm with frogs, which will come up and go into your house and into your bedroom and on your bed, and into the houses of your servants and on your people, and into your ovens and into your kneading bowls.

4"So the frogs will come up on you and your people and all your servants."'"

New International

of Pharaoh and his officials, and it became a snake. 11Pharaoh then summoned wise men and sorcerers, and the Egyptian magicians also did the same things by their secret arts: 12Each one threw down his staff and it became a snake. But Aaron's staff swallowed up their staffs. 13Yet Pharaoh's heart became hard and he would not listen to them, just as the LORD had said.

The Plague of Blood

14Then the LORD said to Moses, "Pharaoh's heart is unyielding; he refuses to let the people go. 15Go to Pharaoh in the morning as he goes out to the water. Wait on the bank of the Nile to meet him, and take in your hand the staff that was changed into a snake. 16Then say to him, 'The LORD, the God of the Hebrews, has sent me to say to you: Let my people go, so that they may worship me in the desert. But until now you have not listened. 17This is what the LORD says: By this you will know that I am the LORD: With the staff that is in my hand I will strike the water of the Nile, and it will be changed into blood. 18The fish in the Nile will die, and the river will stink; the Egyptians will not be able to drink its water.'"

19The LORD said to Moses, "Tell Aaron, 'Take your staff and stretch out your hand over the waters of Egypt—over the streams and canals, over the ponds and all the reservoirs'—and they will turn to blood. Blood will be everywhere in Egypt, even in the wooden buckets and stone jars."

20Moses and Aaron did just as the LORD had commanded. He raised his staff in the presence of Pharaoh and his officials and struck the water of the Nile, and all the water was changed into blood. 21The fish in the Nile died, and the river smelled so bad that the Egyptians could not drink its water. Blood was everywhere in Egypt.

22But the Egyptian magicians did the same things by their secret arts, and Pharaoh's heart became hard; he would not listen to Moses and Aaron, just as the LORD had said. 23Instead, he turned and went into his palace, and did not take even this to heart. 24And all the Egyptians dug along the Nile to get drinking water, because they could not drink the water of the river.

The Plague of Frogs

25Seven days passed after the LORD struck the Nile. 1Then the LORD said to Moses, "Go to Pharaoh and say to him, 'This is what the LORD says: Let my people go, so that they may worship me. 2If you refuse to let them go, I will plague your whole country with frogs. 3The Nile will teem with frogs. They will come up into your palace and your bedroom and onto your bed, into the houses of your officials and on your people, and into your ovens and kneading troughs. 4The frogs will go up on you and your people and all your officials.'"

King James

5 ¶ And the LORD spake unto Moses, Say unto Aaron, Stretch forth thine hand with thy rod over the streams, over the rivers, and over the ponds, and cause frogs to come up upon the land of Egypt.

6 And Aaron stretched out his hand over the waters of Egypt; and the frogs came up, and covered the land of Egypt.

7 And the magicians did so with their enchantments, and brought up frogs upon the land of Egypt.

8 ¶ Then Pharaoh called for Moses and Aaron, and said, Entreat the LORD, that he may take away the frogs from me, and from my people; and I will let the people go, that they may do sacrifice unto the LORD.

9 And Moses said unto Pharaoh, *z*Glory over me: *a*when shall I entreat for thee, and for thy servants, and for thy people, *b*to destroy the frogs from thee and thy houses, *that* they may remain in the river only?

10 And he said, *c*Tomorrow. And he said, *Be it* according to thy word: that thou mayest know that *there is* none like unto the LORD our God.

11 And the frogs shall depart from thee, and from thy houses, and from thy servants, and from thy people; they shall remain in the river only.

12 And Moses and Aaron went out from Pharaoh: and Moses cried unto the LORD because of the frogs which he had brought against Pharaoh.

13 And the LORD did according to the word of Moses; and the frogs died out of the houses, out of the villages, and out of the fields.

14 And they gathered them together upon heaps: and the land stank.

15 But when Pharaoh saw that there was respite, he hardened his heart, and hearkened not unto them; as the LORD had said.

The plague of lice

16 ¶ And the LORD said unto Moses, Say unto Aaron, Stretch out thy rod, and smite the dust of the land, that it may become lice throughout all the land of Egypt.

17 And they did so; for Aaron stretched out his hand with his rod, and smote the dust of the earth, and it became lice in man, and in beast; all the dust of the land became lice throughout all the land of Egypt.

18 And the magicians did so with their enchantments to bring forth lice, but they could not: so there were lice upon man, and upon beast.

19 Then the magicians said unto Pharaoh, This *is* the finger of God: and Pharaoh's heart was hardened, and he hearkened not unto them; as the LORD had said.

The swarms of flies

20 ¶ And the LORD said unto Moses, Rise up early in the morning, and stand before Pharaoh; lo, he cometh forth to the water; and say unto him, Thus saith the LORD, Let my people go, that they may serve me.

21 Else, if thou wilt not let my people go, behold, I will send *d*swarms *of flies* upon thee, and upon thy servants, and upon thy people, and into thy houses: and the houses of the Egyptians shall be full of swarms *of flies,* and also the ground whereon they *are.*

22 And I will sever in that day the land of Goshen, in which my people dwell, that no swarms *of flies* shall be there; to the end thou mayest know that I *am* the LORD in the midst of the earth.

23 And I will put *e*a division between my people and thy people: *f*tomorrow shall this sign be.

24 And the LORD did so; and there came a grievous swarm *of flies* into the house of Pharaoh, and *into* his servants' houses, and into all the land of Egypt: the land was *g*corrupted by reason of the swarm *of flies.*

Amplified

5 And the Lord said to Moses, Say to Aaron, Stretch out your hand with your rod over the rivers, the streams *and* canals, and over the pools, and cause frogs to come up on the land of Egypt.

6 So Aaron stretched out his hand over the waters of Egypt, and the frogs came up and covered the land.

7 But the magicians did the same thing with their enchantments *and* secret arts, and brought up [more] frogs upon the land of Egypt.

8 Then Pharaoh called for Moses and Aaron, and said, Entreat the Lord, that He may take away the frogs from me and my people; and I will let the people go that they may sacrifice to the Lord.

9 Moses said to Pharaoh, Glory over me in this: dictate when I shall pray [to the Lord] for you, your servants, and your people, that the frogs may be destroyed from you and your houses and remain only in the river.

10 And [Pharaoh] said, Tomorrow. [Moses] said, Let it be as you say, that you may know that there is no one like the Lord our God.

11 And the frogs shall depart from you and your houses and from your servants and your people; they shall remain in the river only.

12 So Moses and Aaron went out from Pharaoh, and Moses cried to the Lord [as he had agreed with Pharaoh] concerning the frogs which He had brought against him.

13 And the Lord did according to the word of Moses, and the frogs died out of the houses, out of the courtyards *and* villages, and out of the fields.

14 [The people] gathered them together in heaps, and the land was loathsome *and* stank.

15 But when Pharaoh saw that there was temporary relief, he made his heart stubborn *and* hard and would not listen *or* heed them, just as the Lord had said.

16 Then the Lord said to Moses, Say to Aaron, Stretch out your rod and strike the dust of the ground, that it may become biting gnats *or* mosquitoes throughout all the land of Egypt.

17 And they did so; Aaron stretched out his hand with his rod and struck the dust of the earth, and there came biting gnats *or* mosquitoes on man and beast; all the dust of the land became biting gnats *or* mosquitoes throughout all the land of Egypt.

18 The magicians tried by their enchantments *and* secret arts to bring forth gnats *or* mosquitoes, but they could not; and there were gnats *or* mosquitoes on man and beast.

19 Then the magicians said to Pharaoh, This is the finger of God! But Pharaoh's heart was hardened *and* strong and he would not listen to them, just as the Lord had said.

20 Then the Lord said to Moses, Rise up early in the morning and stand before Pharaoh as he comes forth to the water; and say to him, Thus says the Lord, Let My people go, that they may serve Me.

21 Else, if you will not let My people go, behold, I will send swarms [of bloodsucking gadflies] upon you, your servants, and your people, and into your houses; and the houses of the Egyptians shall be full of swarms [of bloodsucking gadflies], and also the ground on which they stand.

22 But on that day I will sever *and* set apart the land of Goshen in which My people dwell, that no swarms [of gadflies] shall be there, so that you may know that I am the Lord in the midst of the earth.

23 And I will put a division *and* a sign of deliverance between My people and your people. By tomorrow shall this sign be in evidence.

24 And the Lord did so; and there came heavy *and* oppressive swarms [of bloodsucking gadflies] into the house of Pharaoh and his servants' houses; and in all of Egypt the land was corrupted *and* ruined by reason of the great invasion [of gadflies].

z Or, *Have* this *honour over me*   *a* Or, *against when*   *b* Heb. *to cut off*   *c* Or, *Against tomorrow*   *d* Or, *a mixture of noisome beasts*   *e* Heb. *a redemption*   *f* Or, *by tomorrow*   *g* Or, *destroyed*

New American Standard

5 Then the LORD said to Moses, "Say to Aaron, 'Stretch out your hand with your staff over the rivers, over the streams and over the pools, and make frogs come up on the land of Egypt.' "

6 So Aaron stretched out his hand over the waters of Egypt, and the frogs came up and covered the land of Egypt.

7 The magicians did the same with their secret arts, making frogs come up on the land of Egypt.

8 ¶ Then Pharaoh called for Moses and Aaron and said, "Entreat the LORD that He remove the frogs from me and from my people; and I will let the people go, that they may sacrifice to the LORD."

9 Moses said to Pharaoh, "The honor is yours to tell me: when shall I entreat for you and your servants and your people, that the frogs be destroyed from you and your houses, *that* they may be left only in the Nile?"

10 ¶ Then he said, "Tomorrow." So he said, "*May it be* according to your word, that you may know that there is no one like the LORD our God.

11 "The frogs will depart from you and your houses and your servants and your people; they will be left only in the Nile."

12 Then Moses and Aaron went out from Pharaoh, and Moses cried to the LORD concerning the frogs which He had inflicted upon Pharaoh.

13 The LORD did according to the word of Moses, and the frogs died out of the houses, the courts, and the fields.

14 So they piled them in heaps, and the land became foul.

15 But when Pharaoh saw that there was relief, he hardened his heart and did not listen to them, as the LORD had said.

The Plague of Insects

16 ¶ Then the LORD said to Moses, "Say to Aaron, 'Stretch out your staff and strike the dust of the earth, that it may become ƒgnats through all the land of Egypt.' "

17 They did so; and Aaron stretched out his hand with his staff, and struck the dust of the earth, and there were gnats on man and beast. All the dust of the earth became gnats through all the land of Egypt.

18 The magicians tried with their secret arts to bring forth gnats, but they could not; so there were gnats on man and beast.

19 Then the magicians said to Pharaoh, "This is the finger of God." But Pharaoh's heart was hardened, and he did not listen to them, as the LORD had said.

20 ¶ Now the LORD said to Moses, "Rise early in the morning and present yourself before Pharaoh, as he comes out to the water, and say to him, 'Thus says the LORD, "Let My people go, that they may serve Me.

21 "For if you do not let My people go, behold, I will send swarms of insects on you and on your servants and on your people and into your houses; and the houses of the Egyptians will be full of swarms of insects, and also the ground on which they *dwell.*

22 "But on that day I will set apart the land of Goshen, where My people are living, so that no swarms of insects will be there, in order that you may know that I, the LORD, am in the midst of the land.

23 "I will ᵍput a division between My people and your people. Tomorrow this sign will occur.' " "

24 Then the LORD did so. And there came great swarms of insects into the house of Pharaoh and the houses of his servants and the land was laid waste because of the swarms of insects in all the land of Egypt.

New International

5 Then the LORD said to Moses, "Tell Aaron, 'Stretch out your hand with your staff over the streams and canals and ponds, and make frogs come up on the land of Egypt.' "

6 So Aaron stretched out his hand over the waters of Egypt, and the frogs came up and covered the land. 7 But the magicians did the same things by their secret arts; they also made frogs come up on the land of Egypt.

8 Pharaoh summoned Moses and Aaron and said, "Pray to the LORD to take the frogs away from me and my people, and I will let your people go to offer sacrifices to the LORD."

9 Moses said to Pharaoh, "I leave to you the honor of setting the time for me to pray for you and your officials and your people that you and your houses may be rid of the frogs, except for those that remain in the Nile."

10 "Tomorrow," Pharaoh said.

Moses replied, "It will be as you say, so that you may know there is no one like the LORD our God. 11 The frogs will leave you and your houses, your officials and your people; they will remain only in the Nile."

12 After Moses and Aaron left Pharaoh, Moses cried out to the LORD about the frogs he had brought on Pharaoh. 13 And the LORD did what Moses asked. The frogs died in the houses, in the courtyards and in the fields. 14 They were piled into heaps, and the land reeked of them. 15 But when Pharaoh saw that there was relief, he hardened his heart and would not listen to Moses and Aaron, just as the LORD had said.

The Plague of Gnats

16 Then the LORD said to Moses, "Tell Aaron, 'Stretch out your staff and strike the dust of the ground,' and throughout the land of Egypt the dust will become gnats." 17 They did this, and when Aaron stretched out his hand with the staff and struck the dust of the ground, gnats came upon men and animals. All the dust throughout the land of Egypt became gnats. 18 But when the magicians tried to produce gnats by their secret arts, they could not. And the gnats were on men and animals.

19 The magicians said to Pharaoh, "This is the finger of God." But Pharaoh's heart was hard and he would not listen, just as the LORD had said.

The Plague of Flies

20 Then the LORD said to Moses, "Get up early in the morning and confront Pharaoh as he goes to the water and say to him, 'This is what the LORD says: Let my people go, so that they may worship me. 21 If you do not let my people go, I will send swarms of flies on you and your officials, on your people and into your houses. The houses of the Egyptians will be full of flies, and even the ground where they are.

22 " 'But on that day I will deal differently with the land of Goshen, where my people live; no swarms of flies will be there, so that you will know that I, the LORD, am in this land. 23 I will make a distinctionᵖ between my people and your people. This miraculous sign will occur tomorrow.' "

24 And the LORD did this. Dense swarms of flies poured into Pharaoh's palace and into the houses of his officials, and throughout Egypt the land was ruined by the flies.

ƒOr *lice*   ᵍLit *set a ransom*   ᵖ23 Septuagint and Vulgate; Hebrew *will put a deliverance*

King James

25 ¶ And Pharaoh called for Moses and for Aaron, and said, Go ye, sacrifice to your God in the land.

26And Moses said, It is not meet so to do; for we shall sacrifice the abomination of the Egyptians to the LORD our God: lo, shall we sacrifice the abomination of the Egyptians before their eyes, and will they not stone us?

27We will go three days' journey into the wilderness, and sacrifice to the LORD our God, as he shall command us.

28And Pharaoh said, I will let you go, that ye may sacrifice to the LORD your God in the wilderness; only ye shall not go very far away: entreat for me.

29And Moses said, Behold, I go out from thee, and I will entreat the LORD that the swarms *of flies* may depart from Pharaoh, from his servants, and from his people, tomorrow: but let not Pharaoh deal deceitfully any more in not letting the people go to sacrifice to the LORD.

30And Moses went out from Pharaoh, and entreated the LORD.

31And the LORD did according to the word of Moses; and he removed the swarms *of flies* from Pharaoh, from his servants, and from his people; there remained not one.

32And Pharaoh hardened his heart at this time also, neither would he let the people go.

The death of Egyptian cattle

9 THEN THE LORD said unto Moses, Go in unto Pharaoh, and tell him, Thus saith the LORD God of the Hebrews, Let my people go, that they may serve me.

2For if thou refuse to let *them* go, and wilt hold them still,

3Behold, the hand of the LORD is upon thy cattle which *is* in the field, upon the horses, upon the asses, upon the camels, upon the oxen, and upon the sheep: *there shall be* a very grievous murrain.

4And the LORD shall sever between the cattle of Israel and the cattle of Egypt: and there shall nothing die of all *that is* the children's of Israel.

5And the LORD appointed a set time, saying, Tomorrow the LORD shall do this thing in the land.

6And the LORD did that thing on the morrow, and all the cattle of Egypt died: but of the cattle of the children of Israel died not one.

7And Pharaoh sent, and, behold, there was not one of the cattle of the Israelites dead. And the heart of Pharaoh was hardened, and he did not let the people go.

The plague of boils and blains

8 ¶ And the LORD said unto Moses and unto Aaron, Take to you handfuls of ashes of the furnace, and let Moses sprinkle it toward the heaven in the sight of Pharaoh.

9And it shall become small dust in all the land of Egypt, and shall be a boil breaking forth *with* blains upon man, and upon beast, throughout all the land of Egypt.

10And they took ashes of the furnace, and stood before Pharaoh; and Moses sprinkled it up toward heaven; and it became a boil breaking forth *with* blains upon man, and upon beast.

11And the magicians could not stand before Moses because of the boils; for the boil was upon the magicians, and upon all the Egyptians.

12And the LORD hardened the heart of Pharaoh, and he hearkened not unto them; as the LORD had spoken unto Moses.

The plague of hail and fire

13 ¶ And the LORD said unto Moses, Rise up early in the morning, and stand before Pharaoh, and say unto him, Thus saith the LORD God of the Hebrews, Let my people go, that they may serve me.

Amplified

25And Pharaoh called for Moses and Aaron, and said, Go, sacrifice to your God [here] in the land [of Egypt].

26And Moses said, It is not suitable *or* right to do that; for the animals the Egyptians hold sacred and will not permit to be slain are those which we are accustomed to sacrifice to the Lord our God; if we did this before the eyes of the Egyptians, would they not stone us?

27We will go a three days' journey into the wilderness and sacrifice to the Lord our God, as He will command us.

28So Pharaoh said, I will let you go, that you may sacrifice to the Lord your God in the wilderness; only you shall not go very far away. Entreat [your God] for me.

29Moses said, I go out from you, and I will entreat the Lord that the swarms [of bloodsucking gadflies] may depart from Pharaoh, his servants, and his people tomorrow; only let not Pharaoh deal deceitfully any more in not letting the people go to sacrifice to the Lord.

30So Moses went out from Pharaoh and entreated the Lord.

31And the Lord did as Moses had spoken: He removed the swarms [of attacking gadflies] from Pharaoh, from his servants, and his people; there remained not one.

32But Pharaoh hardened his heart *and* made it stubborn this time also, nor would he let the people go.

9 THEN THE Lord said to Moses, Go to Pharaoh and tell him, Thus says the Lord God of the Hebrews: Let My people go, that they may serve Me.

2If you refuse to let them go and still hold them,

3Behold, the hand of the Lord [will fall] upon your livestock which are out in the field, upon the horses, the donkeys, the camels, the herds and the flocks; there shall be a very severe plague.

4But the Lord shall make a distinction between the livestock of Israel and the livestock of Egypt, and nothing shall die of all that belongs to the Israelites.

5And the Lord set a time, saying, Tomorrow the Lord will do this thing in the land.

6And the Lord did that the next day, and all [kinds of] the livestock of Egypt died; but of the livestock of the Israelites not one died.

7Pharaoh sent to find out, and behold, there was not one of the cattle of the Israelites dead. But the heart of Pharaoh was hardened [his mind was set] and he did not let the people go.

8The Lord said to Moses and Aaron, Take handfuls of ashes *or* soot from the brickkiln and let Moses sprinkle them toward the heavens in the sight of Pharaoh.

9And it shall become small dust over all the land of Egypt, and become boils breaking out in sores on man and beast in all the land [occupied by the Egyptians].

10So they took ashes *or* soot of the kiln and stood before Pharaoh; and Moses threw them toward the sky, and it became boils erupting in sores on man and beast.

11And the magicians could not stand before Moses because of their boils; for the boils were on the magicians and all the Egyptians.

12But the Lord hardened the heart of Pharaoh, making it strong *and* obstinate, and he did not listen to them or heed them, just as the Lord had told Moses.

13Then the Lord said to Moses, Rise up early in the morning and stand before Pharaoh and say to him, Thus says the Lord, the God of the Hebrews, Let My people go, that they may serve Me.

New American Standard

25 ¶ Pharaoh called for Moses and Aaron and said, "Go, sacrifice to your God within the land."
26 But Moses said, "It is not right to do so, for we will sacrifice to the LORD our God what is an abomination to the Egyptians. If we sacrifice what is an abomination to the Egyptians before their eyes, will they not then stone us?
27 "We must go a three days' journey into the wilderness and sacrifice to the LORD our God as He commands us."
28 Pharaoh said, "I will let you go, that you may sacrifice to the LORD your God in the wilderness; only you shall not go very far away. Make supplication for me."
29 Then Moses said, "Behold, I am going out from you, and I shall make supplication to the LORD that the swarms of insects may depart from Pharaoh, from his servants, and from his people tomorrow; only do not let Pharaoh deal deceitfully again in not letting the people go to sacrifice to the LORD."
30 ¶ So Moses went out from Pharaoh and made supplication to the LORD.
31 The LORD did as Moses asked, and removed the swarms of insects from Pharaoh, from his servants and from his people; not one remained.
32 But Pharaoh hardened his heart this time also, and he did not let the people go.

Egyptian Cattle Die

9 THEN THE LORD said to Moses, "Go to Pharaoh and speak to him, 'Thus says the LORD, the God of the Hebrews, "Let My people go, that they may serve Me.
2 "For if you refuse to let *them* go and continue to hold them,
3 behold, the hand of the LORD will come *with* a very severe pestilence on your livestock which are in the field, on the horses, on the donkeys, on the camels, on the herds, and on the flocks.
4 "But the LORD will make a distinction between the livestock of Israel and the livestock of Egypt, so that nothing will die of all that belongs to the sons of Israel." ' "
5 The LORD set a definite time, saying, "Tomorrow the LORD will do this thing in the land."
6 So the LORD did this thing on the next day, and all the livestock of Egypt died; but of the livestock of the sons of Israel, not one died.
7 Pharaoh sent, and behold, there was not even one of the livestock of Israel dead. But the heart of Pharaoh was hardened, and he did not let the people go.

The Plague of Boils

8 ¶ Then the LORD said to Moses and Aaron, "Take for yourselves handfuls of soot from a kiln, and let Moses throw it toward the sky in the sight of Pharaoh.
9 "It will become fine dust over all the land of Egypt, and will become boils breaking out with sores on man and beast through all the land of Egypt."
10 So they took soot from a kiln, and stood before Pharaoh; and Moses threw it toward the sky, and it became boils breaking out with sores on man and beast.
11 The magicians could not stand before Moses because of the boils, for the boils were on the magicians as well as on all the Egyptians.
12 And the LORD hardened Pharaoh's heart, and he did not listen to them, just as the LORD had spoken to Moses.
13 ¶ Then the LORD said to Moses, "Rise up early in the morning and stand before Pharaoh and say to him, 'Thus says the LORD, the God of the Hebrews, "Let My people go, that they may serve Me.

New International

25 Then Pharaoh summoned Moses and Aaron and said, "Go, sacrifice to your God here in the land."
26 But Moses said, "That would not be right. The sacrifices we offer the LORD our God would be detestable to the Egyptians. And if we offer sacrifices that are detestable in their eyes, will they not stone us? 27 We must take a three-day journey into the desert to offer sacrifices to the LORD our God, as he commands us."
28 Pharaoh said, "I will let you go to offer sacrifices to the LORD your God in the desert, but you must not go very far. Now pray for me."
29 Moses answered, "As soon as I leave you, I will pray to the LORD, and tomorrow the flies will leave Pharaoh and his officials and his people. Only be sure that Pharaoh does not act deceitfully again by not letting the people go to offer sacrifices to the LORD."
30 Then Moses left Pharaoh and prayed to the LORD, 31 and the LORD did what Moses asked: The flies left Pharaoh and his officials and his people; not a fly remained.
32 But this time also Pharaoh hardened his heart and would not let the people go.

The Plague on Livestock

9 THEN THE LORD said to Moses, "Go to Pharaoh and say to him, 'This is what the LORD, the God of the Hebrews, says: "Let my people go, so that they may worship me." 2 If you refuse to let them go and continue to hold them back, 3 the hand of the LORD will bring a terrible plague on your livestock in the field—on your horses and donkeys and camels and on your cattle and sheep and goats. 4 But the LORD will make a distinction between the livestock of Israel and that of Egypt, so that no animal belonging to the Israelites will die.' "
5 The LORD set a time and said, "Tomorrow the LORD will do this in the land." 6 And the next day the LORD did it: All the livestock of the Egyptians died, but not one animal belonging to the Israelites died. 7 Pharaoh sent men to investigate and found that not even one of the animals of the Israelites had died. Yet his heart was unyielding and he would not let the people go.

The Plague of Boils

8 Then the LORD said to Moses and Aaron, "Take handfuls of soot from a furnace and have Moses toss it into the air in the presence of Pharaoh. 9 It will become fine dust over the whole land of Egypt, and festering boils will break out on men and animals throughout the land."
10 So they took soot from a furnace and stood before Pharaoh. Moses tossed it into the air, and festering boils broke out on men and animals. 11 The magicians could not stand before Moses because of the boils that were on them and on all the Egyptians. 12 But the LORD hardened Pharaoh's heart and he would not listen to Moses and Aaron, just as the LORD had said to Moses.

The Plague of Hail

13 Then the LORD said to Moses, "Get up early in the morning, confront Pharaoh and say to him, 'This is what the LORD, the God of the Hebrews, says: Let my people

King James

¹⁴For I will at this time send all my plagues upon thine heart, and upon thy servants, and upon thy people; that thou mayest know that *there is* none like me in all the earth.

¹⁵For now I will stretch out my hand, that I may smite thee and thy people with pestilence; and thou shalt be cut off from the earth.

¹⁶And in very deed for this *cause* have I ^hraised thee up, for to show *in* thee my power; and that my name may be declared throughout all the earth.

¹⁷As yet exaltest thou thyself against my people, that thou wilt not let them go?

¹⁸Behold, tomorrow about this time I will cause it to rain a very grievous hail, such as hath not been in Egypt since the foundation thereof even until now.

¹⁹Send therefore now, *and* gather thy cattle, and all that thou hast in the field; *for upon* every man and beast which shall be found in the field, and shall not be brought home, the hail shall come down upon them, and they shall die.

²⁰He that feared the word of the LORD among the servants of Pharaoh made his servants and his cattle flee into the houses:

²¹And he that regarded not the word of the LORD left his servants and his cattle in the field.

²²¶ And the LORD said unto Moses, Stretch forth thine hand toward heaven, that there may be hail in all the land of Egypt, upon man, and upon beast, and upon every herb of the field, throughout the land of Egypt.

²³And Moses stretched forth his rod toward heaven: and the LORD sent thunder and hail, and the fire ran along upon the ground; and the LORD rained hail upon the land of Egypt.

²⁴So there was hail, and fire mingled with the hail, very grievous, such as there was none like it in all the land of Egypt since it became a nation.

²⁵And the hail smote throughout all the land of Egypt all that *was* in the field, both man and beast; and the hail smote every herb of the field, and brake every tree of the field.

²⁶Only in the land of Goshen, where the children of Israel *were,* was there no hail.

²⁷¶ And Pharaoh sent, and called for Moses and Aaron, and said unto them, I have sinned this time: the LORD *is* righteous, and I and my people *are* wicked.

²⁸Entreat the LORD (for *it is* enough) that there be no *more* ⁱmighty thunderings and hail; and I will let you go, and ye shall stay no longer.

²⁹And Moses said unto him, As soon as I am gone out of the city, I will spread abroad my hands unto the LORD; *and* the thunder shall cease, neither shall there be any more hail; that thou mayest know how that the earth *is* the LORD'S.

³⁰But as for thee and thy servants, I know that ye will not yet fear the LORD God.

³¹And the flax and the barley was smitten: for the barley *was* in the ear, and the flax *was* bolled.

³²But the wheat and the rie were not smitten: for they *were* ^jnot grown up.

³³And Moses went out of the city from Pharaoh, and spread abroad his hands unto the LORD: and the thunders and hail ceased, and the rain was not poured upon the earth.

³⁴And when Pharaoh saw that the rain and the hail and the thunders were ceased, he sinned yet more, and hardened his heart, he and his servants.

³⁵And the heart of Pharaoh was hardened, neither would he let the children of Israel go; as the LORD had spoken ^kby Moses.

Amplified

¹⁴For this time I will send all My plagues upon your heart and upon your servants and your people, that you may recognize *and* know that there is none like Me in all the earth.

¹⁵For by now I could have put forth My hand and have struck you and your people with pestilence, and you would have been cut off from the earth.

¹⁶But for this very purpose have I let you live, that I might show you My power, and that My name may be declared throughout all the earth. [Rom. 9:17–24.]

¹⁷Since you are still exalting yourself [in haughty defiance] against My people by not letting them go,

¹⁸Behold, tomorrow about this time I will cause it to rain a very heavy *and* dreadful fall of hail, such as has not been in Egypt from its founding until now.

¹⁹Send therefore now and gather your cattle in hastily, and all that you have in the field; for every man and beast that is in the field and is not brought home shall be struck by the hail and shall die.

²⁰Then he who feared the word of the Lord among the servants of Pharaoh made his servants and his livestock flee into the houses *and* shelters.

²¹And he who ignored the word of the Lord left his servants and his livestock in the field.

²²The Lord said to Moses, Stretch forth your hand toward the heavens, that there may be hail in all the land of Egypt, upon man and beast, and upon all the vegetation of the field, throughout the land of Egypt.

²³Then Moses stretched forth his rod toward the heavens, and the Lord sent thunder and hail, and fire (lightning) ran down to *and* along the ground, and the Lord rained hail upon the land of Egypt.

²⁴So there was hail and fire flashing continually in the midst of the weighty hail, such as had not been in all the land of Egypt since it became a nation.

²⁵The hail struck down throughout all the land of Egypt everything that was in the field, both man and beast; and the hail beat down all the vegetation of the field and shattered every tree of the field.

²⁶Only in the land of Goshen, where the Israelites were, was there no hail.

²⁷And Pharaoh sent for Moses and Aaron, and said to them, I have sinned this time; the Lord is in the right and I and my people are in the wrong.

²⁸Entreat the Lord, for there has been enough of these mighty thunderings and hail [these voices of God]; I will let you go; you shall stay here no longer.

²⁹Moses said to him, As soon as I leave the city, I will stretch out my hands to the Lord; the thunder shall cease, neither shall there be any more hail, that you may know that the earth is the Lord's.

³⁰But as for you and your servants, I know that you do not yet [reverently] fear the Lord God.

³¹The flax and the barley were smitten *and* ruined, for the barley was in the ear and the flax in bloom.

³²But the wheat and spelt [another wheat] were not smitten, for they ripen late and were not grown up yet.

³³So Moses left the city and Pharaoh, and stretched forth his hands to the Lord; and the thunder and hail ceased, and rain was no longer poured upon the earth.

³⁴But when Pharaoh saw that the rain, the hail, and the thunder had ceased, he sinned yet more, and toughened *and* stiffened his hard heart, he and his servants.

³⁵So Pharaoh's heart was strong *and* obstinate; he would not let the Israelites go, just as the Lord had said by Moses. [Exod. 4:21.]

---

^hHeb. *made thee stand*   ⁱHeb. *voices of God*   ^jHeb. *hidden,* or, *dark*   ^kHeb. *by the hand of Moses*

New American Standard

14"For this time I will send all My plagues on you and your servants and your people, so that you may know that there is no one like Me in all the earth.

15"For if by now I had put forth My hand and struck you and your people with pestilence, you would then have been cut off from the earth.

16"But, indeed, for this reason I have allowed you to remain, in order to show you My power and in order to proclaim My name through all the earth.

17"Still you exalt yourself against My people by not letting them go.

The Plague of Hail

18"Behold, about this time tomorrow, I will send a very heavy hail, such as has not been *seen* in Egypt from the day it was founded until now.

19"Now therefore send, bring your livestock and whatever you have in the field to safety. Every man and beast that is found in the field and is not brought home, when the hail comes down on them, will die."'"

20 The one among the servants of Pharaoh who feared the word of the LORD made his servants and his livestock flee into the houses;

21 but he who paid no regard to the word of the LORD left his servants and his livestock in the field.

22 ¶ Now the LORD said to Moses, "Stretch out your hand toward the sky, that hail may fall on all the land of Egypt, on man and on beast and on every plant of the field, throughout the land of Egypt."

23 Moses stretched out his staff toward the sky, and the LORD sent thunder and hail, and fire ran down to the earth. And the LORD rained hail on the land of Egypt.

24 So there was hail, and fire flashing continually in the midst of the hail, very severe, such as had not been in all the land of Egypt since it became a nation.

25 The hail struck all that was in the field through all the land of Egypt, both man and beast; the hail also struck every plant of the field and shattered every tree of the field.

26 Only in the land of Goshen, where the sons of Israel *were*, there was no hail.

27 ¶ Then Pharaoh sent for Moses and Aaron, and said to them, "I have sinned this time; the LORD is the righteous one, and I and my people are the wicked ones.

28"Make supplication to the LORD, for there has been enough of God's thunder and hail; and I will let you go, and you shall stay no longer."

29 Moses said to him, "As soon as I go out of the city, I will spread out my hands to the LORD; the thunder will cease and there will be hail no longer, that you may know that the earth is the LORD's.

30"But as for you and your servants, I know that you do not yet fear the LORD God."

31 (Now the flax and the barley were ruined, for the barley was in the ear and the flax was in bud.

32 But the wheat and the spelt were not ruined, for they *ripen* late.)

33 So Moses went out of the city from Pharaoh, and spread out his hands to the LORD; and the thunder and the hail ceased, and rain no longer poured on the earth.

34 But when Pharaoh saw that the rain and the hail and the thunder had ceased, he sinned again and hardened his heart, he and his servants.

35 Pharaoh's heart was hardened, and he did not let the sons of Israel go, just as the LORD had spoken through Moses.

New International

go, so that they may worship me, 14or this time I will send the full force of my plagues against you and against your officials and your people, so you may know that there is no one like me in all the earth. 15For by now I could have stretched out my hand and struck you and your people with a plague that would have wiped you off the earth. 16But I have raised you up[q] for this very purpose, that I might show you my power and that my name might be proclaimed in all the earth. 17You still set yourself against my people and will not let them go. 18Therefore, at this time tomorrow I will send the worst hailstorm that has ever fallen on Egypt, from the day it was founded till now. 19Give an order now to bring your livestock and everything you have in the field to a place of shelter, because the hail will fall on every man and animal that has not been brought in and is still out in the field, and they will die.'"

20Those officials of Pharaoh who feared the word of the LORD hurried to bring their slaves and their livestock inside. 21But those who ignored the word of the LORD left their slaves and livestock in the field.

22Then the LORD said to Moses, "Stretch out your hand toward the sky so that hail will fall all over Egypt—on men and animals and on everything growing in the fields of Egypt." 23When Moses stretched out his staff toward the sky, the LORD sent thunder and hail, and lightning flashed down to the ground. So the LORD rained hail on the land of Egypt; 24hail fell and lightning flashed back and forth. It was the worst storm in all the land of Egypt since it had become a nation. 25Throughout Egypt hail struck everything in the fields—both men and animals; it beat down everything growing in the fields and stripped every tree. 26The only place it did not hail was the land of Goshen, where the Israelites were.

27Then Pharaoh summoned Moses and Aaron. "This time I have sinned," he said to them. "The LORD is in the right, and I and my people are in the wrong. 28Pray to the LORD, for we have had enough thunder and hail. I will let you go; you don't have to stay any longer."

29Moses replied, "When I have gone out of the city, I will spread out my hands in prayer to the LORD. The thunder will stop and there will be no more hail, so you may know that the earth is the LORD's. 30But I know that you and your officials still do not fear the LORD God."

31(The flax and barley were destroyed, since the barley had headed and the flax was in bloom. 32The wheat and spelt, however, were not destroyed, because they ripen later.)

33Then Moses left Pharaoh and went out of the city. He spread out his hands toward the LORD; the thunder and hail stopped, and the rain no longer poured down on the land. 34When Pharaoh saw that the rain and hail and thunder had stopped, he sinned again: He and his officials hardened their hearts. 35So Pharaoh's heart was hard and he would not let the Israelites go, just as the LORD had said through Moses.

q 16 Or *have spared you*

King James

The plague of locusts

10 AND THE LORD said unto Moses, Go in unto Pharaoh: for I have hardened his heart, and the heart of his servants, that I might show these my signs before him:

²And that thou mayest tell in the ears of thy son, and of thy son's son, what things I have wrought in Egypt, and my signs which I have done among them; that ye may know how that I *am* the LORD.

³And Moses and Aaron came in unto Pharaoh, and said unto him, Thus saith the LORD God of the Hebrews, How long wilt thou refuse to humble thyself before me? let my people go, that they may serve me.

⁴Else, if thou refuse to let my people go, behold, tomorrow will I bring the locusts into thy coast:

⁵And they shall cover the ᶦface of the earth, that one cannot be able to see the earth: and they shall eat the residue of that which is escaped, which remaineth unto you from the hail, and shall eat every tree which groweth for you out of the field:

⁶And they shall fill thy houses, and the houses of all thy servants, and the houses of all the Egyptians; which neither thy fathers, nor thy fathers' fathers have seen, since the day that they were upon the earth unto this day. And he turned himself, and went out from Pharaoh.

⁷And Pharaoh's servants said unto him, How long shall this man be a snare unto us? let the men go, that they may serve the LORD their God: knowest thou not yet that Egypt is destroyed?

⁸And Moses and Aaron were brought again unto Pharaoh: and he said unto them, Go, serve the LORD your God: *but* ᵐwho *are* they that shall go?

⁹And Moses said, We will go with our young and with our old, with our sons and with our daughters, with our flocks and with our herds will we go; for we *must hold* a feast unto the LORD.

¹⁰And he said unto them, Let the LORD be so with you, as I will let you go, and your little ones: look *to it;* for evil *is* before you.

¹¹Not so: go now ye *that are* men, and serve the LORD; for that ye did desire. And they were driven out from Pharaoh's presence.

¹² ¶ And the LORD said unto Moses, Stretch out thine hand over the land of Egypt for the locusts, that they may come up upon the land of Egypt, and eat every herb of the land, *even* all that the hail hath left.

¹³And Moses stretched forth his rod over the land of Egypt, and the LORD brought an east wind upon the land all that day, and all *that* night; *and* when it was morning, the east wind brought the locusts.

¹⁴And the locusts went up over all the land of Egypt, and rested in all the coasts of Egypt: very grievous *were they;* before them there were no such locusts as they, neither after them shall be such.

¹⁵For they covered the face of the whole earth, so that the land was darkened; and they did eat every herb of the land, and all the fruit of the trees which the hail had left: and there remained not any green thing in the trees, or in the herbs of the field, through all the land of Egypt.

¹⁶ ¶ Then Pharaoh ⁿcalled for Moses and Aaron in haste; and he said, I have sinned against the LORD your God, and against you.

¹⁷Now therefore forgive, I pray thee, my sin only this once, and entreat the LORD your God, that he may take away from me this death only.

¹⁸And he went out from Pharaoh, and entreated the LORD.

¹⁹And the LORD turned a mighty strong west wind, which took away the locusts, and ᵒcast them into the Red sea; there remained not one locust in all the coasts of Egypt.

Amplified

10 THE LORD said to Moses, Go to Pharaoh, for I have made his heart hard, and his servants' hearts, that I might show these My signs [of divine power] before him,

²And that you may recount in the ears of your son and of your grandson what I have done in derision of the Egyptians *and* what things I have [repeatedly] done there—My signs [of divine power] done among them— that you may recognize *and* know that I am the Lord.

³So Moses and Aaron went to Pharaoh, and said to him, Thus says the Lord, the God of the Hebrews, How long will you refuse to humble yourself before Me? Let My people go, that they may serve Me.

⁴For if you refuse to let My people go, behold, tomorrow I will bring locusts into your country.

⁵And they shall cover the land so that one cannot see the ground; and they shall eat the remainder of what escaped and is left to you from the hail, and they shall eat every tree of yours that grows in the field;

⁶The locusts shall fill your houses and those of all your servants and of all the Egyptians, as neither your fathers nor your fathers' fathers have seen from their birth until this day. Then Moses departed from Pharaoh.

⁷And Pharaoh's servants said to him, How long shall this man be a snare to us? Let the men go, that they may serve the Lord their God; do you not yet understand *and* know that Egypt is destroyed?

⁸So Moses and Aaron were brought again to Pharaoh; and he said to them, Go, serve the Lord your God; but just who are to go?

⁹And Moses said, We will go with our young and our old, with our sons and our daughters, with our flocks and our herds [all of us and all we have], for we must hold a feast to the Lord.

¹⁰Pharaoh said to them, Let the Lord be with you, if I ever let you go with your little ones! See, you have some evil purpose in mind.

¹¹Not so! You that are men, [without your families] go and serve the Lord, for that is what you want. And [Moses and Aaron] were driven from Pharaoh's presence.

¹²Then the Lord said to Moses, Stretch out your hand over the land of Egypt for the locusts, that they may come up on the land of Egypt and eat all the vegetation of the land, all that the hail has left.

¹³And Moses stretched forth his rod over the land of Egypt, and the Lord brought an east wind upon the land all that day and all that night; when it was morning, the east wind brought the locusts.

¹⁴And the locusts came up over all the land of Egypt and settled down on the whole country of Egypt, a very dreadful mass of them; never before were there such locusts as these, nor will there ever be again.

¹⁵For they covered the whole land, so that the ground was darkened, and they ate every bit of vegetation of the land and all the fruit of the trees which the hail had left; there remained not a green thing of the trees or the plants of the field in all the land of Egypt.

¹⁶Then Pharaoh sent for Moses and Aaron in haste. He said, I have sinned against the Lord your God and you.

¹⁷Now therefore forgive my sin, I pray you, only this once, and entreat the Lord your God only that He may remove from me this [plague of] death.

¹⁸Then Moses left Pharaoh and entreated the Lord.

¹⁹And the Lord turned a violent west wind, which lifted the locusts and drove them into the Red Sea; not one locust remained in all the country of Egypt.

ᶦHeb. *eye*   ᵐHeb. *who, and who*   ⁿHeb. *hastened to call*
ᵒHeb. *fastened*

New American Standard

The Plague of Locusts

10 THEN THE LORD said to Moses, "Go to Pharaoh, for I have *h*hardened his heart and the heart of his servants, that I may perform these signs of Mine among them, 2 and that you may tell in the hearing of your son, and of your grandson, how I made a mockery of the Egyptians and how I performed My signs among them, that you may know that I am the LORD."

3 ¶ Moses and Aaron went to Pharaoh and said to him, "Thus says the LORD, the God of the Hebrews, 'How long will you refuse to humble yourself before Me? Let My people go, that they may serve Me. 4 'For if you refuse to let My people go, behold, tomorrow I will bring locusts into your territory. 5 'They shall cover the surface of the land, so that no one will be able to see the land. They will also eat the rest of what has escaped—what is left to you from the hail—and they will eat every tree which sprouts for you out of the field. 6 'Then your houses shall be filled and the houses of all your servants and the houses of all the Egyptians, *something* which neither your fathers nor your grandfathers have seen, from the day that they came upon the earth until this day.' " And he turned and went out from Pharaoh.

7 Pharaoh's servants said to him, "How long will this man be a snare to us? Let the men go, that they may serve the LORD their God. Do you not realize that Egypt is destroyed?"

8 So Moses and Aaron were brought back to Pharaoh, and he said to them, "Go, serve the LORD your God! Who are the ones that are going?"

9 Moses said, "We shall go with our young and our old; with our sons and our daughters, with our flocks and our herds we shall go, for we must hold a feast to the LORD."

10 Then he said to them, "Thus may the LORD be with you, if ever I let you and your little ones go! Take heed, for evil is in your mind.

11 "Not so! Go now, the men *among you,* and serve the LORD, for that is what you desire." So they were driven out from Pharaoh's presence.

12 ¶ Then the LORD said to Moses, "Stretch out your hand over the land of Egypt for the locusts, that they may come up on the land of Egypt and eat every plant of the land, *even* all that the hail has left."

13 So Moses stretched out his staff over the land of Egypt, and the LORD directed an east wind on the land all that day and all that night; and when it was morning, the east wind brought the locusts.

14 The locusts came up over all the land of Egypt and settled in all the territory of Egypt; *they were* very numerous. There had never been so *many* locusts, nor would there be so *many* again.

15 For they covered the surface of the whole land, so that the land was darkened; and they ate every plant of the land and all the fruit of the trees that the hail had left. Thus nothing green was left on tree or plant of the field through all the land of Egypt.

16 Then Pharaoh hurriedly called for Moses and Aaron, and he said, "I have sinned against the LORD your God and against you.

17 "Now therefore, please forgive my sin only this once, and make supplication to the LORD your God, that He would only remove this death from me."

18 He went out from Pharaoh and made supplication to the LORD.

19 So the LORD shifted *the wind* to a very strong west wind which took up the locusts and drove them into the *i*Red Sea; not one locust was left in all the territory of Egypt.

New International

The Plague of Locusts

10 THEN THE LORD said to Moses, "Go to Pharaoh, for I have hardened his heart and the hearts of his officials so that I may perform these miraculous signs of mine among them 2 that you may tell your children and grandchildren how I dealt harshly with the Egyptians and how I performed my signs among them, and that you may know that I am the LORD."

3 So Moses and Aaron went to Pharaoh and said to him, "This is what the LORD, the God of the Hebrews, says: 'How long will you refuse to humble yourself before me? Let my people go, so that they may worship me. 4 If you refuse to let them go, I will bring locusts into your country tomorrow. 5 They will cover the face of the ground so that it cannot be seen. They will devour what little you have left after the hail, including every tree that is growing in your fields. 6 They will fill your houses and those of all your officials and all the Egyptians—something neither your fathers nor your forefathers have ever seen from the day they settled in this land till now.' " Then Moses turned and left Pharaoh.

7 Pharaoh's officials said to him, "How long will this man be a snare to us? Let the people go, so that they may worship the LORD their God. Do you not yet realize that Egypt is ruined?"

8 Then Moses and Aaron were brought back to Pharaoh. "Go, worship the LORD your God," he said. "But just who will be going?"

9 Moses answered, "We will go with our young and old, with our sons and daughters, and with our flocks and herds, because we are to celebrate a festival to the LORD."

10 Pharaoh said, "The LORD be with you—if I let you go, along with your women and children! Clearly you are bent on evil.*r* 11 No! Have only the men go; and worship the LORD, since that's what you have been asking for." Then Moses and Aaron were driven out of Pharaoh's presence.

12 And the LORD said to Moses, "Stretch out your hand over Egypt so that locusts will swarm over the land and devour everything growing in the fields, everything left by the hail."

13 So Moses stretched out his staff over Egypt, and the LORD made an east wind blow across the land all that day and all that night. By morning the wind had brought the locusts; 14 they invaded all Egypt and settled down in every area of the country in great numbers. Never before had there been such a plague of locusts, nor will there ever be again. 15 They covered all the ground until it was black. They devoured all that was left after the hail—everything growing in the fields and the fruit on the trees. Nothing green remained on tree or plant in all the land of Egypt.

16 Pharaoh quickly summoned Moses and Aaron and said, "I have sinned against the LORD your God and against you. 17 Now forgive my sin once more and pray to the LORD your God to take this deadly plague away from me."

18 Moses then left Pharaoh and prayed to the LORD. 19 And the LORD changed the wind to a very strong west wind, which caught up the locusts and carried them into the Red Sea.*s* Not a locust was left anywhere in Egypt.

---

h Lit *made heavy*   *i* Lit *Sea of Reeds*

r 10 Or *Be careful, trouble is in store for you!*   *s 19* Hebrew *Yam Suph;* that is, Sea of Reeds

King James

²⁰But the LORD hardened Pharaoh's heart, so that he would not let the children of Israel go.

The plague of darkness

²¹ ¶ And the LORD said unto Moses, Stretch out thine hand toward heaven, that there may be darkness over the land of Egypt, ᵖeven darkness *which* may be felt.

²²And Moses stretched forth his hand toward heaven; and there was a thick darkness in all the land of Egypt three days:

²³They saw not one another, neither rose any from his place for three days: but all the children of Israel had light in their dwellings.

²⁴ ¶ And Pharaoh called unto Moses, and said, Go ye, serve the LORD; only let your flocks and your herds be stayed: let your little ones also go with you.

²⁵And Moses said, Thou must give ᵠus also sacrifices and burnt offerings, that we may sacrifice unto the LORD our God.

²⁶Our cattle also shall go with us; there shall not an hoof be left behind; for thereof must we take to serve the LORD our God; and we know not with what we must serve the LORD, until we come thither.

²⁷ ¶ But the LORD hardened Pharaoh's heart, and he would not let them go.

²⁸And Pharaoh said unto him, Get thee from me, take heed to thyself, see my face no more; for in *that* day thou seest my face thou shalt die.

²⁹And Moses said, Thou hast spoken well, I will see thy face again no more.

The last plague

11 AND THE LORD said unto Moses, Yet will I bring one plague *more* upon Pharaoh, and upon Egypt; afterwards he will let you go hence: when he shall let *you* go, he shall surely thrust you out hence altogether.

²Speak now in the ears of the people, and let every man borrow of his neighbour, and every woman of her neighbour, jewels of silver, and jewels of gold.

³And the LORD gave the people favour in the sight of the Egyptians. Moreover the man Moses *was* very great in the land of Egypt, in the sight of Pharaoh's servants, and in the sight of the people.

⁴And Moses said, Thus saith the LORD, About midnight will I go out into the midst of Egypt:

⁵And all the firstborn in the land of Egypt shall die, from the firstborn of Pharaoh that sitteth upon *his* throne, even unto the firstborn of the maidservant that *is* behind the mill; and all the firstborn of beasts.

⁶And there shall be a great cry throughout all the land of Egypt, such as there was none like it, nor shall be like it any more.

⁷But against any of the children of Israel shall not a dog move his tongue, against man or beast: that ye may know how that the LORD doth put a difference between the Egyptians and Israel.

⁸And all these thy servants shall come down unto me, and bow down themselves unto me, saying, Get thee out, and all the people ʳthat follow thee: and after that I will go out. And he went out from Pharaoh in ˢa great anger.

⁹And the LORD said unto Moses, Pharaoh shall not hearken unto you; that my wonders may be multiplied in the land of Egypt.

¹⁰And Moses and Aaron did all these wonders before Pharaoh: and the LORD hardened Pharaoh's heart, so that he would not let the children of Israel go out of his land.

Amplified

²⁰But the Lord made Pharaoh's heart more strong *and* obstinate, and he would not let the Israelites go.

²¹And the Lord said to Moses, Stretch out your hand toward the heavens, that there may be darkness over the land of Egypt, a darkness which may be felt.

²²So Moses stretched out his hand toward the sky, and for three days a thick darkness was all over the land of Egypt.

²³The Egyptians could not see one another, nor did anyone rise from his place for three days; but all the Israelites had natural light in their dwellings.

²⁴And Pharaoh called to Moses, and said, Go, serve the Lord; let your little ones also go with you; it is only your flocks and your herds that must not go.

²⁵But Moses said, You must give into our hand also sacrifices and burnt offerings, that we may sacrifice to the Lord our God.

²⁶Our livestock also shall go with us; there shall not a hoof be left behind; for of them must we take to serve the Lord our God, and we know not with what we must serve the Lord until we arrive there.

²⁷But the Lord made Pharaoh's heart stronger *and* more stubborn, and he would not let them go.

²⁸And Pharaoh said to Moses, Get away from me! See that you never enter my presence again, for the day you see my face again you shall die!

²⁹And Moses said, You have spoken truly; I will never see your face again.

11 THEN THE Lord said to Moses, Yet will I bring one plague more on Pharaoh and on Egypt; afterwards he will let you go. When he lets you go from here, he will thrust you out altogether.

²Speak now in the hearing of the people, and let every man solicit *and* ask of his neighbor, and every woman of her neighbor, jewels of silver and jewels of gold.

³And the Lord gave the people favor in the sight of the Egyptians. Moreover, the man Moses was exceedingly great in the land of Egypt, in the sight of Pharaoh's servants and of the people.

⁴And Moses said, Thus says the Lord, About midnight I will go out into the midst of Egypt;

⁵And all the firstborn in the land [the pride, hope, and joy] of Egypt shall die, from the firstborn of Pharaoh, who sits on his throne, even to the firstborn of the maidservant who is behind the hand mill, and all the firstborn of beasts.

⁶There shall be a great cry in all the land of Egypt, such as has never been nor ever shall be again.

⁷But against any of the Israelites shall not so much as a dog move his tongue against man or beast, that you may know that the Lord makes a distinction between the Egyptians and Israel.

⁸And all these your servants shall come down to me and bow down to me, saying, Get out, and all the people who follow you! And after that I will go out. And he went out from Pharaoh in great anger.

⁹Then the Lord said to Moses, Pharaoh will not listen to you, that My wonders *and* miracles may be multiplied in the land of Egypt.

¹⁰Moses and Aaron did all these wonders *and* miracles before Pharaoh; and the Lord hardened Pharaoh's stubborn heart, and he did not let the Israelites go out of his land.

ᵖ Heb. *that one may feel darkness* ᵠ Heb. *into our hands*
ʳ Heb. *that is at thy feet;* see Judg. 4:10 & 8:5 ˢ Heb. *heat of anger*

New American Standard

20 But the LORD hardened Pharaoh's heart, and he did not let the sons of Israel go.

Darkness over the Land

21 ¶ Then the LORD said to Moses, "Stretch out your hand toward the sky, that there may be darkness over the land of Egypt, even a darkness which may be felt."

22 So Moses stretched out his hand toward the sky, and there was thick darkness in all the land of Egypt for three days.

23 They did not see one another, nor did anyone rise from his place for three days, but all the sons of Israel had light in their dwellings.

24 Then Pharaoh called to Moses, and said, "Go, serve the LORD; only let your flocks and your herds be detained. Even your little ones may go with you."

25 But Moses said, "You must also let us have sacrifices and burnt offerings, that we may sacrifice *them* to the LORD our God.

26"Therefore, our livestock too shall go with us; not a hoof shall be left behind, for we shall take some of them to serve the LORD our God. And until we arrive there, we ourselves do not know with what we shall serve the LORD."

27 But the LORD hardened Pharaoh's heart, and he was not willing to let them go.

28 Then Pharaoh said to him, "Get away from me! Beware, do not see my face again, for in the day you see my face you shall die!"

29 Moses said, "You are right; I shall never see your face again!"

The Last Plague

11 NOW THE LORD said to Moses, "One more plague I will bring on Pharaoh and on Egypt; after that he will let you go from here. When he lets you go, he will surely drive you out from here completely.

2"Speak now in the hearing of the people that each man ask from his neighbor and each woman from her neighbor for articles of silver and articles of gold."

3 The LORD gave the people favor in the sight of the Egyptians. Furthermore, the man Moses *himself* was greatly esteemed in the land of Egypt, *both* in the sight of Pharaoh's servants and in the sight of the people.

4 ¶ Moses said, "Thus says the LORD, 'About midnight I am going out into the midst of Egypt,

5 and all the firstborn in the land of Egypt shall die, from the firstborn of the Pharaoh who sits on his throne, even to the firstborn of the slave girl who is behind the millstones; all the firstborn of the cattle as well.

6 'Moreover, there shall be a great cry in all the land of Egypt, such as there has not been *before* and such as shall never be again.

7 'But against any of the sons of Israel a dog will not *even* bark, whether against man or beast, that you may understand how the LORD makes a distinction between Egypt and Israel.'

8"All these your servants will come down to me and bow themselves before me, saying, 'Go out, you and all the people who follow you,' and after that I will go out." And he went out from Pharaoh in hot anger.

9 ¶ Then the LORD said to Moses, "Pharaoh will not listen to you, so that My wonders will be multiplied in the land of Egypt."

10 Moses and Aaron performed all these wonders before Pharaoh; yet the LORD hardened Pharaoh's heart, and he did not let the sons of Israel go out of his land.

New International

20But the LORD hardened Pharaoh's heart, and he would not let the Israelites go.

The Plague of Darkness

21Then the LORD said to Moses, "Stretch out your hand toward the sky so that darkness will spread over Egypt—darkness that can be felt." 22So Moses stretched out his hand toward the sky, and total darkness covered all Egypt for three days. 23No one could see anyone else or leave his place for three days. Yet all the Israelites had light in the places where they lived.

24Then Pharaoh summoned Moses and said, "Go, worship the LORD. Even your women and children may go with you; only leave your flocks and herds behind."

25But Moses said, "You must allow us to have sacrifices and burnt offerings to present to the LORD our God. 26Our livestock too must go with us; not a hoof is to be left behind. We have to use some of them in worshiping the LORD our God, and until we get there we will not know what we are to use to worship the LORD."

27But the LORD hardened Pharaoh's heart, and he was not willing to let them go. 28Pharaoh said to Moses, "Get out of my sight! Make sure you do not appear before me again! The day you see my face you will die."

29"Just as you say," Moses replied, "I will never appear before you again."

The Plague on the Firstborn

11 NOW THE LORD had said to Moses, "I will bring one more plague on Pharaoh and on Egypt. After that, he will let you go from here, and when he does, he will drive you out completely. 2Tell the people that men and women alike are to ask their neighbors for articles of silver and gold." 3(The LORD made the Egyptians favorably disposed toward the people, and Moses himself was highly regarded in Egypt by Pharaoh's officials and by the people.)

4So Moses said, "This is what the LORD says: 'About midnight I will go throughout Egypt. 5Every firstborn son in Egypt will die, from the firstborn son of Pharaoh, who sits on the throne, to the firstborn son of the slave girl, who is at her hand mill, and all the firstborn of the cattle as well. 6There will be loud wailing throughout Egypt—worse than there has ever been or ever will be again. 7But among the Israelites not a dog will bark at any man or animal.' Then you will know that the LORD makes a distinction between Egypt and Israel. 8All these officials of yours will come to me, bowing down before me and saying, 'Go, you and all the people who follow you!' After that I will leave." Then Moses, hot with anger, left Pharaoh.

9The LORD had said to Moses, "Pharaoh will refuse to listen to you—so that my wonders may be multiplied in Egypt." 10Moses and Aaron performed all these wonders before Pharaoh, but the LORD hardened Pharaoh's heart, and he would not let the Israelites go out of his country.

King James

The Passover

12 AND THE LORD spake unto Moses and Aaron in the land of Egypt, saying,

2This month *shall be* unto you the beginning of months: it *shall be* the first month of the year to you.

3 ¶ Speak ye unto all the congregation of Israel, saying, In the tenth *day* of this month they shall take to them every man a *t*lamb, according to the house of *their* fathers, a lamb for an house:

4And if the household be too little for the lamb, let him and his neighbour next unto his house take *it* according to the number of the souls; every man according to his eating shall make your count for the lamb.

5Your lamb shall be without blemish, a male *u*of the first year: ye shall take *it* out from the sheep, or from the goats:

6And ye shall keep it up until the fourteenth day of the same month: and the whole assembly of the congregation of Israel shall kill it *v*in the evening.

7And they shall take of the blood, and strike *it* on the two side posts and on the upper door post of the houses, wherein they shall eat it.

8And they shall eat the flesh in that night, roast with fire, and unleavened bread; *and* with bitter *herbs* they shall eat it.

9Eat not of it raw, nor sodden at all with water, but roast *with* fire; his head with his legs, and with the purtenance thereof.

10And ye shall let nothing of it remain until the morning; and that which remaineth of it until the morning ye shall burn with fire.

11 ¶ And thus shall ye eat it; *with* your loins girded, your shoes on your feet, and your staff in your hand; and ye shall eat it in haste: it *is* the LORD'S passover.

12For I will pass through the land of Egypt this night, and will smite all the firstborn in the land of Egypt, both man and beast; and against all the *w*gods of Egypt I will execute judgment: I *am* the LORD.

13And the blood shall be to you for a token upon the houses where ye *are:* and when I see the blood, I will pass over you, and the plague shall not be upon you *x*to destroy *you,* when I smite the land of Egypt.

14And this day shall be unto you for a memorial; and ye shall keep it a feast to the LORD throughout your generations; ye shall keep it a feast by an ordinance for ever.

15Seven days shall ye eat unleavened bread; even the first day ye shall put away leaven out of your houses: for whosoever eateth leavened bread from the first day until the seventh day, that soul shall be cut off from Israel.

16And in the first day *there shall be* an holy convocation, and in the seventh day there shall be an holy convocation to you; no manner of work shall be done in them, save *that* which every *y*man must eat, that only may be done of you.

17And ye shall observe *the feast of* unleavened bread; for in this selfsame day have I brought your armies out of the land of Egypt: therefore shall ye observe this day in your generations by an ordinance for ever.

18 ¶ In the first *month,* on the fourteenth day of the month at even, ye shall eat unleavened bread, until the one and twentieth day of the month at even.

19Seven days shall there be no leaven found in your houses: for whosoever eateth that which is leavened, even that soul shall be cut off from the congregation of Israel, whether he be a stranger, or born in the land.

20Ye shall eat nothing leavened; in all your habitations shall ye eat unleavened bread.

21 ¶ Then Moses called for all the elders of Israel, and said unto them, Draw out and take you a *t*lamb according to your families, and kill the passover.

Amplified

12 THE LORD said to Moses and Aaron in the land of Egypt,

2This month shall be to you the beginning of months, the first month of the year to you.

3Tell all the congregation of Israel, On the tenth day of this month they shall take every man a lamb *or* kid, according to [the size of] the family of which he is the father, a lamb *or* kid for each house.

4And if the household is too small to consume the lamb, let him and his next door neighbor take it according to the number of persons, every man according to what each can eat shall make your count for the lamb.

5Your lamb *or* kid shall be without blemish, a male of the first year; you shall take it from the sheep or the goats. [I Pet. 1:19, 20.]

6And you shall keep it until the fourteenth day of the same month; and the whole assembly of the congregation of Israel shall [each] kill [his] lamb in the evening.

7They shall take of the blood and put it on the two side posts and on the lintel [above the door space] of the houses in which they shall eat [the Passover lamb]. [Matt. 26:28; John 1:29; Heb. 9:14.]

8They shall eat the flesh that night roasted; with unleavened bread and bitter herbs they shall eat it.

9Eat not of it raw nor boiled at all with water, but roasted—its head, its legs, and its inner parts.

10You shall let nothing of the meat remain until the morning; and the bones *and* unedible bits which remain of it until morning you shall burn with fire.

11And you shall eat it thus: [as fully prepared for a journey] your loins girded, your shoes on your feet, and your staff in your hand; and you shall eat it in haste. It is the Lord's Passover.

12For I will pass through the land of Egypt this night and will smite all the firstborn in the land of Egypt, both man and beast; and against all the gods of Egypt I will execute judgment [proving their helplessness]. I am the Lord.

13The blood shall be for a token *or* sign to you upon [the doorposts of] the houses where you are, [that] when I see the blood, I will pass over you, and no plague shall be upon you to destroy you when I smite the land of Egypt. [I Cor. 5:7; Heb. 11:28.]

14And this day shall be to you for a memorial. You shall keep it as a feast to the Lord throughout your generations, keep it as an ordinance forever.

15[In celebration of the Passover in future years] seven days shall you eat unleavened bread; even the first day you shall put away leaven [symbolic of corruption] out of your houses; for whoever eats leavened bread from the first day until the seventh day, that person shall be cut off from Israel.

16On the first day you shall hold a solemn *and* holy assembly, and on the seventh day there shall be a solemn *and* holy assembly; no kind of work shall be done in them, save [preparation of] that which every person must eat— that only may be done by you.

17And you shall observe the Feast of Unleavened Bread, for on this very day have I brought your hosts out of the land of Egypt; therefore shall you observe this day throughout your generations as an ordinance forever.

18In the first month, on the fourteenth day of the month at evening, you shall eat unleavened bread [and continue] until the twenty-first day of the month at evening.

19Seven days no leaven [symbolic of corruption] shall be found in your houses; whoever eats what is leavened shall be excluded from the congregation of Israel, whether a stranger or native-born. [I Cor. 5:6–8.]

20You shall eat nothing leavened; in all your dwellings you shall eat unleavened bread [during that week].

21Then Moses called for all the elders of Israel, and said to them, Go forth, select and take a lamb according to your families and kill the Passover [lamb].

---

*t*Or, kid evenings soul   *u*Heb. son of a year   *w*Or, princes   *v*Heb. between the two evenings   *x*Heb. for a destruction   *y*Heb.

New American Standard

The Passover Lamb

12 NOW THE LORD said to Moses and Aaron in the land of Egypt,

2 "This month shall be the beginning of months for you; it is to be the first month of the year to you.

3 "Speak to all the congregation of Israel, saying, 'On the tenth of this month they are each one to take a lamb for themselves, according to their fathers' households, a lamb for each household.

4 'Now if the household is too small for a lamb, then he and his neighbor nearest to his house are to take one according to the number of persons *in them;* according to what each man should eat, you are to divide the lamb.

5 'Your lamb shall be an unblemished male a year old; you may take it from the sheep or from the goats.

6 'You shall keep it until the fourteenth day of the same month, then the whole assembly of the congregation of Israel is to kill it at twilight.

7 'Moreover, they shall take some of the blood and put it on the two doorposts and on the lintel of the houses in which they eat it.

8 'They shall eat the flesh that *same* night, roasted with fire, and they shall eat it with unleavened bread and bitter herbs.

9 'Do not eat any of it raw or boiled at all with water, but rather roasted with fire, *both* its head and its legs along with its entrails.

10 'And you shall not leave any of it over until morning, but whatever is left of it until morning, you shall burn with fire.

11 'Now you shall eat it in this manner: *with* your loins girded, your sandals on your feet, and your staff in your hand; and you shall eat it in haste—it is the LORD'S Passover.

12 'For I will go through the land of Egypt on that night, and will strike down all the firstborn in the land of Egypt, both man and beast; and against all the gods of Egypt I will execute judgments—I am the LORD.

13 'The blood shall be a sign for you on the houses where you live; and when I see the blood I will pass over you, and no plague will befall you to destroy *you* when I strike the land of Egypt.

Feast of Unleavened Bread

14 ¶ 'Now this day will be a memorial to you, and you shall celebrate it *as* a feast to the LORD; throughout your generations you are to celebrate it *as* a permanent ordinance.

15 'Seven days you shall eat unleavened bread, but on the first day you shall remove leaven from your houses; for whoever eats anything leavened from the first day until the seventh day, that person shall be cut off from Israel.

16 'On the first day you shall have a holy assembly, and *another* holy assembly on the seventh day; no work at all shall be done on them, except what must be eaten by every person, that alone may be prepared by you.

17 'You shall also observe the *Feast of* Unleavened Bread, for on this very day I brought your hosts out of the land of Egypt; therefore you shall observe this day throughout your generations as a permanent ordinance.

18 'In the first *month,* on the fourteenth day of the month at evening, you shall eat unleavened bread, until the twenty-first day of the month at evening.

19 'Seven days there shall be no leaven found in your houses; for whoever eats what is leavened, that person shall be cut off from the congregation of Israel, whether *he is* an alien or a native of the land.

20 'You shall not eat anything leavened; in all your dwellings you shall eat unleavened bread.' "

21 ¶ Then Moses called for all the elders of Israel and said to them, "Go and take for yourselves lambs according to your families, and slay the Passover *lamb.*

New International

The Passover

12 THE LORD said to Moses and Aaron in Egypt, 2 "This month is to be for you the first month, the first month of your year. 3 Tell the whole community of Israel that on the tenth day of this month each man is to take a lamb[f] for his family, one for each household. 4 If any household is too small for a whole lamb, they must share one with their nearest neighbor, having taken into account the number of people there are. You are to determine the amount of lamb needed in accordance with what each person will eat. 5 The animals you choose must be year-old males without defect, and you may take them from the sheep or the goats. 6 Take care of them until the fourteenth day of the month, when all the people of the community of Israel must slaughter them at twilight. 7 Then they are to take some of the blood and put it on the sides and tops of the doorframes of the houses where they eat the lambs. 8 That same night they are to eat the meat roasted over the fire, along with bitter herbs, and bread made without yeast. 9 Do not eat the meat raw or cooked in water, but roast it over the fire—head, legs and inner parts. 10 Do not leave any of it till morning; if some is left till morning, you must burn it. 11 This is how you are to eat it: with your cloak tucked into your belt, your sandals on your feet and your staff in your hand. Eat it in haste; it is the LORD's Passover.

12 "On that same night I will pass through Egypt and strike down every firstborn—both men and animals—and I will bring judgment on all the gods of Egypt. I am the LORD. 13 The blood will be a sign for you on the houses where you are; and when I see the blood, I will pass over you. No destructive plague will touch you when I strike Egypt.

14 "This is a day you are to commemorate; for the generations to come you shall celebrate it as a festival to the LORD—a lasting ordinance. 15 For seven days you are to eat bread made without yeast. On the first day remove the yeast from your houses, for whoever eats anything with yeast in it from the first day through the seventh must be cut off from Israel. 16 On the first day hold a sacred assembly, and another one on the seventh day. Do no work at all on these days, except to prepare food for everyone to eat—that is all you may do.

17 "Celebrate the Feast of Unleavened Bread, because it was on this very day that I brought your divisions out of Egypt. Celebrate this day as a lasting ordinance for the generations to come. 18 In the first month you are to eat bread made without yeast, from the evening of the fourteenth day until the evening of the twenty-first day. 19 For seven days no yeast is to be found in your houses. And whoever eats anything with yeast in it must be cut off from the community of Israel, whether he is an alien or native-born. 20 Eat nothing made with yeast. Wherever you live, you must eat unleavened bread."

21 Then Moses summoned all the elders of Israel and said to them, "Go at once and select the animals for your fami-

---

3 The Hebrew word can mean *lamb* or *kid*; also in verse 4.

King James

Amplified

22And ye shall take a bunch of hyssop, and dip *it* in the blood that *is* in the basin, and strike the lintel and the two side posts with the blood that *is* in the basin; and none of you shall go out at the door of his house until the morning.

23For the LORD will pass through to smite the Egyptians; and when he seeth the blood upon the lintel, and on the two side posts, the LORD will pass over the door, and will not suffer the destroyer to come in unto your houses to smite *you*.

24And ye shall observe this thing for an ordinance to thee and to thy sons for ever.

25And it shall come to pass, when ye be come to the land which the LORD will give you, according as he hath promised, that ye shall keep this service.

26And it shall come to pass, when your children shall say unto you, What mean ye by this service?

27That ye shall say, It *is* the sacrifice of the LORD's passover, who passed over the houses of the children of Israel in Egypt, when he smote the Egyptians, and delivered our houses. And the people bowed the head and worshipped.

28And the children of Israel went away, and did as the LORD had commanded Moses and Aaron, so did they.

29 ¶ And it came to pass, that at midnight the LORD smote all the firstborn in the land of Egypt, from the firstborn of Pharaoh that sat on his throne unto the firstborn of the captive that *was* in the ᶻdungeon; and all the firstborn of cattle.

30And Pharaoh rose up in the night, he, and all his servants, and all the Egyptians; and there was a great cry in Egypt; for *there was* not a house where *there was* not one dead.

The exodus begins

31 ¶ And he called for Moses and Aaron by night, and said, Rise up, *and* get you forth from among my people, both ye and the children of Israel; and go, serve the LORD, as ye have said.

32Also take your flocks and your herds, as ye have said, and be gone; and bless me also.

33And the Egyptians were urgent upon the people, that they might send them out of the land in haste; for they said, We *be* all dead *men*.

34And the people took their dough before it was leavened, their ᵃkneadingtroughs being bound up in their clothes upon their shoulders.

35And the children of Israel did according to the word of Moses; and they borrowed of the Egyptians jewels of silver, and jewels of gold, and raiment:

36And the LORD gave the people favour in the sight of the Egyptians, so that they lent unto them *such things as they required*. And they spoiled the Egyptians.

37 ¶ And the children of Israel journeyed from Rameses to Succoth, about six hundred thousand on foot *that were* men, beside children.

38And ᵇa mixed multitude went up also with them; and flocks, and herds, *even* very much cattle.

39And they baked unleavened cakes of the dough which they brought forth out of Egypt, for it was not leavened; because they were thrust out of Egypt, and could not tarry, neither had they prepared for themselves any victual.

40 ¶ Now the sojourning of the children of Israel, who dwelt in Egypt, *was* four hundred and thirty years.

41And it came to pass at the end of the four hundred and thirty years, even the selfsame day it came to pass, that all the hosts of the LORD went out from the land of Egypt.

42It *is* a ᶜnight to be much observed unto the LORD for bringing them out from the land of Egypt: this *is* that night of the LORD to be observed of all the children of Israel in their generations.

22And you shall take a bunch of hyssop, dip it in the blood in the basin, and touch the lintel above the door and the two side posts with the blood; and none of you shall go out of his house until morning.

23For the Lord will pass through to slay the Egyptians; and when He sees the blood upon the lintel and the two side posts, the Lord will pass over the door and will not allow the destroyer to come into your houses to slay you.

24You shall observe this rite for an ordinance to you and to your sons forever.

25When you come to the land which the Lord will give you, as He has promised, you shall keep this service.

26When your children shall say to you, What do you mean by this service?

27You shall say, It is the sacrifice of the Lord's Passover, for He passed over the houses of the Israelites in Egypt when He slew the Egyptians but spared our houses. And the people bowed their heads and worshiped.

28The Israelites went and, as the Lord had commanded Moses and Aaron, so they did.

29At midnight the Lord slew every firstborn in the land of Egypt, from the firstborn of Pharaoh who sat on his throne to the firstborn of the prisoner in the dungeon, and all the firstborn of the livestock.

30Pharaoh rose up in the night, he, all his servants, and all the Egyptians; and there was a great cry in Egypt, for there was not a house where there was not one dead.

31He called for Moses and Aaron by night, and said, Rise up, get out from among my people, both you and the Israelites; and go, serve the Lord, as you said.

32Also take your flocks and your herds, as you have said, and be gone! And [ask your God to] bless me also.

33The Egyptians were urgent with the people to depart, that they might send them out of the land in haste; for they said, We are all dead men.

34The people took their dough before it was leavened, their kneading bowls being bound up in their clothes on their shoulders.

35The Israelites did according to the word of Moses; and they [urgently] asked of the Egyptians jewels of silver and of gold, and clothing.

36The Lord gave the people favor in the sight of the Egyptians, so that they gave them what they asked. And they stripped the Egyptians [of those things].

37The Israelites journeyed from Rameses to Succoth, about 600,000 men on foot, besides women and children.

38And a mixed multitude went also with them, and very much livestock, both flocks and herds.

39They baked unleavened cakes of the dough which they brought from Egypt; it was not leavened because they were driven from Egypt and could not delay, nor had they prepared for themselves any food.

40Now the time the Israelites dwelt in Egypt was 430 years. [Gen. 15:13, 14.]

41At the end of the 430 years, even that very day, all the hosts of the Lord went out of Egypt.

42It was a night of watching unto the Lord *and* to be much observed for bringing them out of Egypt; this same night of watching unto the Lord is to be observed by all the Israelites throughout their generations.

ᶻHeb. *house of the pit*   ᵃOr, *dough*   ᵇHeb. *a great mixture*
ᶜHeb. *a night of observations*

New American Standard

22"You shall take a bunch of hyssop and dip it in the blood which is in the basin, and apply some of the blood that is in the basin to the lintel and the two doorposts; and none of you shall go outside the door of his house until morning.

A Memorial of Redemption

23"For the LORD will pass through to smite the Egyptians; and when He sees the blood on the lintel and on the two doorposts, the LORD will pass over the door and will not allow the destroyer to come in to your houses to smite *you*.

24"And you shall observe this event as an ordinance for you and your children forever.

25"When you enter the land which the LORD will give you, as He has promised, you shall observe this rite.

26"And when your children say to you, 'What does this rite mean to you?'

27 you shall say, 'It is a Passover sacrifice to the LORD who passed over the houses of the sons of Israel in Egypt when He smote the Egyptians, but spared our homes.' " And the people bowed low and worshiped.

28 ¶ Then the sons of Israel went and did *so;* just as the LORD had commanded Moses and Aaron, so they did.

29 ¶ Now it came about at midnight that the LORD struck all the firstborn in the land of Egypt, from the firstborn of Pharaoh who sat on his throne to the firstborn of the captive who was in the dungeon, and all the firstborn of cattle.

30 Pharaoh arose in the night, he and all his servants and all the Egyptians, and there was a great cry in Egypt, for there was no home where there was not someone dead.

31 Then he called for Moses and Aaron at night and said, "Rise up, get out from among my people, both you and the sons of Israel; and go, worship the LORD, as you have said.

32"Take both your flocks and your herds, as you have said, and go, and bless me also."

Exodus of Israel

33 The Egyptians urged the people, to send them out of the land in haste, for they said, "We will all be dead."

34 So the people took their dough before it was leavened, *with* their kneading bowls bound up in the clothes on their shoulders.

35 ¶ Now the sons of Israel had done according to the word of Moses, for they had requested from the Egyptians articles of silver and articles of gold, and clothing;

36 and the LORD had given the people favor in the sight of the Egyptians, so that they let them have their request. Thus they plundered the Egyptians.

37 ¶ Now the sons of Israel journeyed from Rameses to Succoth, about six hundred thousand men on foot, aside from children.

38 A mixed multitude also went up with them, along with flocks and herds, a very large number of livestock.

39 They baked the dough which they had brought out of Egypt into cakes of unleavened bread. For it had not become leavened, since they were driven out of Egypt and could not delay, nor had they prepared any provisions for themselves.

40 ¶ Now the time that the sons of Israel lived in Egypt was four hundred and thirty years.

41 And at the end of four hundred and thirty years, to the very day, all the hosts of the LORD went out from the land of Egypt.

Ordinance of the Passover

42 It is a night to be observed for the LORD for having brought them out from the land of Egypt; this night is for the LORD, to be observed by all the sons of Israel throughout their generations.

New International

lies and slaughter the Passover lamb. 22Take a bunch of hyssop, dip it into the blood in the basin and put some of the blood on the top and on both sides of the doorframe. Not one of you shall go out the door of his house until morning. 23When the LORD goes through the land to strike down the Egyptians, he will see the blood on the top and sides of the doorframe and will pass over that doorway, and he will not permit the destroyer to enter your houses and strike you down.

24"Obey these instructions as a lasting ordinance for you and your descendants. 25When you enter the land that the LORD will give you as he promised, observe this ceremony. 26And when your children ask you, 'What does this ceremony mean to you?' 27then tell them, 'It is the Passover sacrifice to the LORD, who passed over the houses of the Israelites in Egypt and spared our homes when he struck down the Egyptians.' " Then the people bowed down and worshiped. 28The Israelites did just what the LORD commanded Moses and Aaron.

29At midnight the LORD struck down all the firstborn in Egypt, from the firstborn of Pharaoh, who sat on the throne, to the firstborn of the prisoner, who was in the dungeon, and the firstborn of all the livestock as well. 30Pharaoh and all his officials and all the Egyptians got up during the night, and there was loud wailing in Egypt, for there was not a house without someone dead.

The Exodus

31During the night Pharaoh summoned Moses and Aaron and said, "Up! Leave my people, you and the Israelites! Go, worship the LORD as you have requested. 32Take your flocks and herds, as you have said, and go. And also bless me."

33The Egyptians urged the people to hurry and leave the country. "For otherwise," they said, "we will all die!" 34So the people took their dough before the yeast was added, and carried it on their shoulders in kneading troughs wrapped in clothing. 35The Israelites did as Moses instructed and asked the Egyptians for articles of silver and gold and for clothing. 36The LORD had made the Egyptians favorably disposed toward the people, and they gave them what they asked for; so they plundered the Egyptians.

37The Israelites journeyed from Rameses to Succoth. There were about six hundred thousand men on foot, besides women and children. 38Many other people went up with them, as well as large droves of livestock, both flocks and herds. 39With the dough they had brought from Egypt, they baked cakes of unleavened bread. The dough was without yeast because they had been driven out of Egypt and did not have time to prepare food for themselves.

40Now the length of time the Israelite people lived in Egypt[u] was 430 years. 41At the end of the 430 years, to the very day, all the LORD's divisions left Egypt. 42Because the LORD kept vigil that night to bring them out of Egypt, on this night all the Israelites are to keep vigil to honor the LORD for the generations to come.

---

u40 Masoretic Text; Samaritan Pentateuch and Septuagint Egypt and Canaan

King James

The law of the Passover

43 ¶ And the LORD said unto Moses and Aaron, This *is* the ordinance of the passover: There shall no stranger eat thereof:

44But every man's servant that is bought for money, when thou hast circumcised him, then shall he eat thereof.

45A foreigner and an hired servant shall not eat thereof.

46In one house shall it be eaten; thou shalt not carry forth aught of the flesh abroad out of the house; neither shall ye break a bone thereof.

47All the congregation of Israel shall [d]keep it.

48And when a stranger shall sojourn with thee, and will keep the passover to the LORD, let all his males be circumcised, and then let him come near and keep it; and he shall be as one that is born in the land: for no uncircumcised person shall eat thereof.

49One law shall be to him that is homeborn, and unto the stranger that sojourneth among you.

50Thus did all the children of Israel; as the LORD commanded Moses and Aaron, so did they.

51And it came to pass the selfsame day, *that* the LORD did bring the children of Israel out of the land of Egypt by their armies.

The firstborn set apart

13 AND THE LORD spake unto Moses, saying,

2Sanctify unto me all the firstborn, whatsoever openeth the womb among the children of Israel, *both* of man and of beast: it *is* mine.

3 ¶ And Moses said unto the people, Remember this day, in which ye came out from Egypt, out of the house of [e]bondage; for by strength of hand the LORD brought you out from this *place:* there shall no leavened bread be eaten.

4This day came ye out in the month Abib.

5 ¶ And it shall be when the LORD shall bring thee into the land of the Canaanites, and the Hittites, and the Amorites, and the Hivites, and the Jebusites, which he sware unto thy fathers to give thee, a land flowing with milk and honey, that thou shalt keep this service in this month.

6Seven days thou shalt eat unleavened bread, and in the seventh day *shall be* a feast to the LORD.

7Unleavened bread shall be eaten seven days; and there shall no leavened bread be seen with thee, neither shall there be leaven seen with thee in all thy quarters.

8 ¶ And thou shalt show thy son in that day, saying, *This is done* because of that *which* the LORD did unto me when I came forth out of Egypt.

9And it shall be for a sign unto thee upon thine hand, and for a memorial between thine eyes, that the LORD's law may be in thy mouth: for with a strong hand hath the LORD brought thee out of Egypt.

10Thou shalt therefore keep this ordinance in his season from year to year.

11 ¶ And it shall be when the LORD shall bring thee into the land of the Canaanites, as he sware unto thee and to thy fathers, and shall give it thee,

12That thou shalt [f]set apart unto the LORD all that openeth the matrix, and every firstling that cometh of a beast which thou hast; the males *shall be* the LORD's.

13And every firstling of an ass thou shalt redeem with a [g]lamb; and if thou wilt not redeem it, then thou shalt break his neck: and all the firstborn of man among thy children shalt thou redeem.

14 ¶ And it shall be when thy son asketh thee [h]in time to come, saying, What *is* this? that thou shalt say unto him, By strength of hand the LORD brought us out from Egypt, from the house of bondage:

Amplified

43The Lord said to Moses and Aaron, This is the ordinance of the Passover: No foreigner shall eat of it;

44But every man's servant who is bought for money, when you have circumcised him, then may he eat of it.

45A foreigner or hired servant shall not eat of it.

46In one house shall it be eaten [by one company]; you shall not carry any of the flesh outside the house; neither shall you break a bone of it. [John 19:33, 36.]

47All the congregation of Israel shall keep it.

48When a stranger sojourning with you wishes to keep the Passover to the Lord, let all his males be circumcised, and then let him come near and keep it; and he shall be as one that is born in the land. But no uncircumcised person shall eat of it.

49There shall be one law for the native-born and for the stranger or foreigner who sojourns among you.

50Thus did all the Israelites; as the Lord commanded Moses and Aaron, so did they.

51And on that very day the Lord brought the Israelites out of the land of Egypt by their hosts.

13 THE LORD said to Moses,

2Sanctify (consecrate, set apart) to Me all the firstborn [males]; whatever is first to open the womb among the Israelites, both of man and of beast, is Mine.

3And Moses said to the people, [Earnestly] remember this day in which you came out from Egypt, out of the house of bondage *and* bondmen, for by strength of hand the Lord brought you out from this place; no leavened bread shall be eaten.

4This day you go forth in the month Abib.

5And when the Lord brings you into the land of the Canaanites, Hittites, Amorites, Hivites, and Jebusites, which He promised *and* swore to your fathers to give you, a land flowing with milk and honey [a land of plenty], you shall keep this service in this month.

6Seven days you shall eat unleavened bread and the seventh day shall be a feast to the Lord.

7Unleavened bread shall be eaten for seven days; no leavened bread shall be seen with you, neither shall there be leaven in all your territory.

8You shall explain to your son on that day, This is done because of what the Lord did for me when I came out of Egypt.

9It shall be as a sign to you upon your hand and as a memorial between your eyes, that the law of the Lord may be in your mouth; for with a strong hand the Lord has brought you out of Egypt.

10You shall therefore keep this ordinance at this time from year to year.

11And when the Lord brings you into the land of the Canaanites, as He promised *and* swore to you and your fathers, and shall give it to you,

12You shall set apart to the Lord all that first opens the womb. All the firstlings of your livestock that are males shall be the Lord's.

13Every firstborn of a donkey you shall redeem by [substituting for it] a lamb, or if you will not redeem it, then you shall break its neck; and every firstborn among your sons shall you redeem.

14And when, in time to come, your son asks you, What does this mean? You shall say to him, By strength of hand the Lord brought us out from Egypt, from the house of bondage *and* bondmen.

---

[d]Heb. *do it*   [e]Heb. *servants*   [f]Heb. *cause to pass over*
[g]Or, *kid*   [h]Heb. *tomorrow*

New American Standard

43 ¶ The LORD said to Moses and Aaron, "This is the ordinance of the Passover: no *j*foreigner is to eat of it;
44 but every man's slave purchased with money, after you have circumcised him, then he may eat of it.
45"A sojourner or a hired servant shall not eat of it.
46"It is to be eaten in a single house; you are not to bring forth any of the flesh outside of the house, nor are you to break any bone of it.
47"All the congregation of Israel are to celebrate this.
48"But if a stranger sojourns with you, and celebrates the Passover to the LORD, let all his males be circumcised, and then let him come near to celebrate it; and he shall be like a native of the land. But no uncircumcised person may eat of it.
49"The same law shall apply to the native as to the stranger who sojourns among you."
50 ¶ Then all the sons of Israel did *so;* they did just as the LORD had commanded Moses and Aaron.
51 And on that same day the LORD brought the sons of Israel out of the land of Egypt by their hosts.

Consecration of the Firstborn

13 THEN THE LORD spoke to Moses, saying,
2"Sanctify to Me every firstborn, the first offspring of every womb among the sons of Israel, both of man and beast; it belongs to Me."
3 ¶ Moses said to the people, "Remember this day in which you went out from Egypt, from the house of slavery; for by a powerful hand the LORD brought you out from this place. And nothing leavened shall be eaten.
4"On this day in the month of Abib, you are about to go forth.
5"It shall be when the LORD brings you to the land of the Canaanite, the Hittite, the Amorite, the Hivite and the Jebusite, which He swore to your fathers to give you, a land flowing with milk and honey, that you shall observe this rite in this month.
6"For seven days you shall eat unleavened bread, and on the seventh day there shall be a feast to the LORD.
7"Unleavened bread shall be eaten throughout the seven days; and nothing leavened shall be seen among you, nor shall any leaven be seen among you in all your borders.
8"You shall tell your son on that day, saying, 'It is because of what the LORD did for me when I came out of Egypt.'
9"And it shall serve as a sign to you on your hand, and as a reminder on your forehead, that the law of the LORD may be in your mouth; for with a powerful hand the LORD brought you out of Egypt.
10"Therefore, you shall keep this ordinance at its appointed time from year to year.
11 ¶ "Now when the LORD brings you to the land of the Canaanite, as He swore to you and to your fathers, and gives it to you,
12 you shall devote to the LORD the first offspring of every womb, and the first offspring of every beast that you own; the males belong to the LORD.
13"But every first offspring of a donkey you shall redeem with a lamb, but if you do not redeem *it,* then you shall break its neck; and every firstborn of man among your sons you shall redeem.
14"And it shall be when your son asks you in time to come, saying, 'What is this?' then you shall say to him, 'With a powerful hand the LORD brought us out of Egypt, from the house of slavery.

New International

Passover Restrictions

43The LORD said to Moses and Aaron, "These are the regulations for the Passover:
"No foreigner is to eat of it. 44Any slave you have bought may eat of it after you have circumcised him, 45but a temporary resident and a hired worker may not eat of it.
46"It must be eaten inside one house; take none of the meat outside the house. Do not break any of the bones. 47The whole community of Israel must celebrate it.
48"An alien living among you who wants to celebrate the LORD's Passover must have all the males in his household circumcised; then he may take part like one born in the land. No uncircumcised male may eat of it. 49The same law applies to the native-born and to the alien living among you."

50All the Israelites did just what the LORD had commanded Moses and Aaron. 51And on that very day the LORD brought the Israelites out of Egypt by their divisions.

Consecration of the Firstborn

13 THE LORD said to Moses, 2"Consecrate to me every firstborn male. The first offspring of every womb among the Israelites belongs to me, whether man or animal."
3Then Moses said to the people, "Commemorate this day, the day you came out of Egypt, out of the land of slavery, because the LORD brought you out of it with a mighty hand. Eat nothing containing yeast. 4Today, in the month of Abib, you are leaving. 5When the LORD brings you into the land of the Canaanites, Hittites, Amorites, Hivites and Jebusites—the land he swore to your forefathers to give you, a land flowing with milk and honey—you are to observe this ceremony in this month: 6For seven days eat bread made without yeast and on the seventh day hold a festival to the LORD. 7Eat unleavened bread during those seven days; nothing with yeast in it is to be seen among you, nor shall any yeast be seen anywhere within your borders. 8On that day tell your son, 'I do this because of what the LORD did for me when I came out of Egypt.' 9This observance will be for you like a sign on your hand and a reminder on your forehead that the law of the LORD is to be on your lips. For the LORD brought you out of Egypt with his mighty hand. 10You must keep this ordinance at the appointed time year after year.
11"After the LORD brings you into the land of the Canaanites and gives it to you, as he promised on oath to you and your forefathers, 12you are to give over to the LORD the first offspring of every womb. All the firstborn males of your livestock belong to the LORD. 13Redeem with a lamb every firstborn donkey, but if you do not redeem it, break its neck. Redeem every firstborn among your sons.
14"In days to come, when your son asks you, 'What does this mean?' say to him, 'With a mighty hand the LORD

King James

15And it came to pass, when Pharaoh would hardly let us go, that the LORD slew all the firstborn in the land of Egypt, both the firstborn of man, and the firstborn of beast: therefore I sacrifice to the LORD all that openeth the matrix, being males; but all the firstborn of my children I redeem.

16And it shall be for a token upon thine hand, and for frontlets between thine eyes: for by strength of hand the LORD brought us forth out of Egypt.

Crossing the Red sea

17 ¶ And it came to pass, when Pharaoh had let the people go, that God led them not *through* the way of the land of the Philistines, although that *was* near; for God said, Lest peradventure the people repent when they see war, and they return to Egypt:

18But God led the people about, *through* the way of the wilderness of the Red sea: and the children of Israel went up *i*harnessed out of the land of Egypt.

19And Moses took the bones of Joseph with him: for he had straitly sworn the children of Israel, saying, God will surely visit you; and ye shall carry up my bones away hence with you.

20 ¶ And they took their journey from Succoth, and encamped in Etham, in the edge of the wilderness.

21And the LORD went before them by day in a pillar of a cloud, to lead them the way; and by night in a pillar of fire, to give them light; to go by day and night:

22He took not away the pillar of the cloud by day, nor the pillar of fire by night, *from* before the people.

14 AND THE LORD spake unto Moses, saying,
2Speak unto the children of Israel, that they turn and encamp before Pi-hahiroth, between Migdol and the sea, over against Baal-zephon: before it shall ye encamp by the sea.

3For Pharaoh will say of the children of Israel, They *are* entangled in the land, the wilderness hath shut them in.

4And I will harden Pharaoh's heart, that he shall follow after them; and I will be honoured upon Pharaoh, and upon all his host; that the Egyptians may know that I *am* the LORD. And they did so.

5 ¶ And it was told the king of Egypt that the people fled: and the heart of Pharaoh and of his servants was turned against the people, and they said, Why have we done this, that we have let Israel go from serving us?

6And he made ready his chariot, and took his people with him:

7And he took six hundred chosen chariots, and all the chariots of Egypt, and captains over every one of them.

8And the LORD hardened the heart of Pharaoh king of Egypt, and he pursued after the children of Israel: and the children of Israel went out with an high hand.

9But the Egyptians pursued after them, all the horses *and* chariots of Pharaoh, and his horsemen, and his army, and overtook them encamping by the sea, beside Pi-hahiroth, before Baal-zephon.

10 ¶ And when Pharaoh drew nigh, the children of Israel lifted up their eyes, and, behold, the Egyptians marched after them; and they were sore afraid: and the children of Israel cried out unto the LORD.

11And they said unto Moses, Because *there were* no graves in Egypt, hast thou taken us away to die in the wilderness? wherefore hast thou dealt thus with us, to carry us forth out of Egypt?

12*Is* not this the word that we did tell thee in Egypt, saying, Let us alone, that we may serve the Egyptians? For *it had been* better for us to serve the Egyptians, than that we should die in the wilderness.

*i*Or, *by five in a rank*

Amplified

15For when Pharaoh stubbornly refused to let us go, the Lord slew all the firstborn in the land of Egypt, both firstborn of man and of livestock. Therefore I sacrifice to the Lord all the males that first open the womb; but all the firstborn of my sons I redeem.

16And it shall be as a reminder upon your hand or as frontlets between your eyes, for by a strong hand the Lord brought us out of Egypt.

17When Pharaoh let the people go, God led them not by way of the land of the Philistines, although that was nearer; for God said, Lest the people change their purpose when they see war and return to Egypt.

18But God led the people around by way of the wilderness toward the Red Sea. And the Israelites went up marshaled [in ranks] out of the land of Egypt.

19And Moses took the bones of Joseph with him, for [Joseph] had strictly sworn the Israelites, saying, Surely God will be with you, and you must carry my bones away from here with you. [Gen. 50:25.]

20They journeyed from Succoth and encamped at Etham on the edge of the wilderness.

21The Lord went before them by day in a pillar of cloud to lead them along the way and by night in a pillar of fire to give them light, that they might travel by day and by night.

22The pillar of cloud by day and the pillar of fire by night did not depart from before the people.

14 AND THE Lord said to Moses,
2Tell the Israelites to turn back and encamp before Pi-hahiroth, between Migdol and the [Red] Sea, before *k*Baal-zephon. You shall encamp opposite it by the sea.

3For Pharaoh will say of the Israelites, They are entangled in the land; the wilderness has shut them in.

4I will harden (make stubborn, strong) Pharaoh's heart, that he will pursue them, and I will gain honor *and* glory over Pharaoh and all his host, and the Egyptians shall know that I am the Lord. And they did so.

5It was told the king of Egypt that the people had fled; and the heart of Pharaoh and of his servants was changed toward the people, and they said, What is this we have done? We have let Israel go from serving us!

6And he made ready his chariots and took his army,

7And took 600 chosen chariots and all the other chariots of Egypt, with officers over all of them.

8The Lord made hard *and* strong the heart of Pharaoh king of Egypt, and he pursued the Israelites, for [they] left proudly *and* defiantly. [Acts 13:17.]

9The Egyptians pursued them, all the horses and chariots of Pharaoh and his horsemen and his army, and overtook them encamped at the [Red] Sea by Pi-hahiroth, in front of Baal-zephon.

10When Pharaoh drew near, the Israelites looked up, and behold, the Egyptians were marching after them; and the Israelites were exceedingly frightened and cried out to the Lord.

11And they said to Moses, Is it because there are no graves in Egypt that you have taken us away to die in the wilderness? Why have you treated us this way and brought us out of Egypt?

12Did we not tell you in Egypt, Let us alone; let us serve the Egyptians? For it would have been better for us to serve the Egyptians than to die in the wilderness.

*k*Melvin Grove Kyle has said that travelers who follow the coast of the Red Sea along the line of the exodus need no other guidebook than the Bible. The whole topography corresponds to that mentioned in the Biblical account (Floyd E. Hamilton, *The Basis of Christian Faith*).

New American Standard

15 'It came about, when Pharaoh was stubborn about letting us go, that the LORD killed every firstborn in the land of Egypt, both the firstborn of man and the firstborn of beast. Therefore, I sacrifice to the LORD the males, the first offspring of every womb, but every firstborn of my sons I redeem.'

16 "So it shall serve as a sign on your hand and as phylacteries on your forehead, for with a powerful hand the LORD brought us out of Egypt."

God Leads the People

17 ¶ Now when Pharaoh had let the people go, God did not lead them by the way of the land of the Philistines, even though it was near; for God said, "The people might change their minds when they see war, and return to Egypt."

18 Hence God led the people around by the way of the wilderness to the Red Sea; and the sons of Israel went up in martial array from the land of Egypt.

19 Moses took the bones of Joseph with him, for he had made the sons of Israel solemnly swear, saying, "God will surely take care of you, and you shall carry my bones from here with you."

20 Then they set out from Succoth and camped in Etham on the edge of the wilderness.

21 The LORD was going before them in a pillar of cloud by day to lead them on the way, and in a pillar of fire by night to give them light, that they might travel by day and by night.

22 He did not take away the pillar of cloud by day, nor the pillar of fire by night, from before the people.

Pharaoh in Pursuit

14 NOW THE LORD spoke to Moses, saying,

2 "Tell the sons of Israel to turn back and camp before Pi-hahiroth, between Migdol and the sea; you shall camp in front of Baal-zephon, opposite it, by the sea.

3 "For Pharaoh will say of the sons of Israel, 'They are wandering aimlessly in the land; the wilderness has shut them in.'

4 "Thus I will harden Pharaoh's heart, and he will chase after them; and I will be honored through Pharaoh and all his army, and the Egyptians will know that I am the LORD." And they did so.

5 ¶ When the king of Egypt was told that the people had fled, Pharaoh and his servants had a change of heart toward the people, and they said, "What is this we have done, that we have let Israel go from serving us?"

6 So he made his chariot ready and took his people with him;

7 and he took six hundred select chariots, and all the other chariots of Egypt with officers over all of them.

8 The LORD hardened the heart of Pharaoh, king of Egypt, and he chased after the sons of Israel as the sons of Israel were going out boldly.

9 Then the Egyptians chased after them with all the horses and chariots of Pharaoh, his horsemen and his army, and they overtook them camping by the sea, beside Pi-hahiroth, in front of Baal-zephon.

10 ¶ As Pharaoh drew near, the sons of Israel looked, and behold, the Egyptians were marching after them, and they became very frightened; so the sons of Israel cried out to the LORD.

11 Then they said to Moses, "Is it because there were no graves in Egypt that you have taken us away to die in the wilderness? Why have you dealt with us in this way, bringing us out of Egypt?

12 "Is this not the word that we spoke to you in Egypt, saying, 'Leave us alone that we may serve the Egyptians'? For it would have been better for us to serve the Egyptians than to die in the wilderness."

New International

brought us out of Egypt, out of the land of slavery. 15 When Pharaoh stubbornly refused to let us go, the LORD killed every firstborn in Egypt, both man and animal. This is why I sacrifice to the LORD the first male offspring of every womb and redeem each of my firstborn sons.' 16 And it will be like a sign on your hand and a symbol on your forehead that the LORD brought us out of Egypt with his mighty hand."

Crossing the Sea

17 When Pharaoh let the people go, God did not lead them on the road through the Philistine country, though that was shorter. For God said, "If they face war, they might change their minds and return to Egypt." 18 So God led the people around by the desert road toward the Red Sea.[v] The Israelites went up out of Egypt armed for battle.

19 Moses took the bones of Joseph with him because Joseph had made the sons of Israel swear an oath. He had said, "God will surely come to your aid, and then you must carry my bones up with you from this place."[w]

20 After leaving Succoth they camped at Etham on the edge of the desert. 21 By day the LORD went ahead of them in a pillar of cloud to guide them on their way and by night in a pillar of fire to give them light, so that they could travel by day or night. 22 Neither the pillar of cloud by day nor the pillar of fire by night left its place in front of the people.

14 THEN THE LORD said to Moses, 2 "Tell the Israelites to turn back and encamp near Pi Hahiroth, between Migdol and the sea. They are to encamp by the sea, directly opposite Baal Zephon. 3 Pharaoh will think, 'The Israelites are wandering around the land in confusion, hemmed in by the desert.' 4 And I will harden Pharaoh's heart, and he will pursue them. But I will gain glory for myself through Pharaoh and all his army, and the Egyptians will know that I am the LORD." So the Israelites did this.

5 When the king of Egypt was told that the people had fled, Pharaoh and his officials changed their minds about them and said, "What have we done? We have let the Israelites go and have lost their services!" 6 So he had his chariot made ready and took his army with him. 7 He took six hundred of the best chariots, along with all the other chariots of Egypt, with officers over all of them. 8 The LORD hardened the heart of Pharaoh king of Egypt, so that he pursued the Israelites, who were marching out boldly. 9 The Egyptians—all Pharaoh's horses and chariots, horsemen[x] and troops—pursued the Israelites and overtook them as they camped by the sea near Pi Hahiroth, opposite Baal Zephon.

10 As Pharaoh approached, the Israelites looked up, and there were the Egyptians, marching after them. They were terrified and cried out to the LORD. 11 They said to Moses, "Was it because there were no graves in Egypt that you brought us to the desert to die? What have you done to us by bringing us out of Egypt? 12 Didn't we say to you in Egypt, 'Leave us alone; let us serve the Egyptians'? It would have been better for us to serve the Egyptians than to die in the desert!"

---

[v]18 Hebrew *Yam Suph*; that is, Sea of Reeds   [w]19 See Gen. 50:25.   [x]9 Or *charioteers*; also in verses 17, 18, 23, 26 and 28

King James

¹³ ¶ And Moses said unto the people, Fear ye not, stand still, and see the salvation of the LORD, which he will show to you today: *j*for the Egyptians whom ye have seen today, ye shall see them again no more for ever.

¹⁴The LORD shall fight for you, and ye shall hold your peace.

¹⁵ ¶ And the LORD said unto Moses, Wherefore criest thou unto me? speak unto the children of Israel, that they go forward:

¹⁶But lift thou up thy rod, and stretch out thine hand over the sea, and divide it: and the children of Israel shall go on dry *ground* through the midst of the sea.

¹⁷And I, behold, I will harden the hearts of the Egyptians, and they shall follow them: and I will get me honour upon Pharaoh, and upon all his host, upon his chariots, and upon his horsemen.

¹⁸And the Egyptians shall know that I *am* the LORD, when I have gotten me honour upon Pharaoh, upon his chariots, and upon his horsemen.

¹⁹ ¶ And the angel of God, which went before the camp of Israel, removed and went behind them; and the pillar of the cloud went from before their face, and stood behind them:

²⁰And it came between the camp of the Egyptians and the camp of Israel; and it was a cloud and darkness *to them,* but it gave light by night *to these:* so that the one came not near the other all the night.

²¹And Moses stretched out his hand over the sea; and the LORD caused the sea to go *back* by a strong east wind all that night, and made the sea dry *land,* and the waters were divided.

²²And the children of Israel went into the midst of the sea upon the dry *ground:* and the waters *were* a wall unto them on their right hand, and on their left.

²³ ¶ And the Egyptians pursued, and went in after them to the midst of the sea, *even* all Pharaoh's horses, his chariots, and his horsemen.

²⁴And it came to pass, that in the morning watch the LORD looked unto the host of the Egyptians through the pillar of fire and of the cloud, and troubled the host of the Egyptians,

²⁵And took off their chariot wheels, *k*that they drave them heavily: so that the Egyptians said, Let us flee from the face of Israel; for the LORD fighteth for them against the Egyptians.

²⁶ ¶ And the LORD said unto Moses, Stretch out thine hand over the sea, that the waters may come again upon the Egyptians, upon their chariots, and upon their horsemen.

²⁷And Moses stretched forth his hand over the sea, and the sea returned to his strength when the morning appeared; and the Egyptians fled against it; and the LORD overthrew *l*the Egyptians in the midst of the sea.

²⁸And the waters returned, and covered the chariots, and the horsemen, *and* all the host of Pharaoh that came into the sea after them; there remained not so much as one of them.

²⁹But the children of Israel walked upon dry *land* in the midst of the sea; and the waters *were* a wall unto them on their right hand, and on their left.

³⁰Thus the LORD saved Israel that day out of the hand of the Egyptians; and Israel saw the Egyptians dead upon the sea shore.

³¹And Israel saw that great *m*work which the LORD did upon the Egyptians: and the people feared the LORD, and believed the LORD, and his servant Moses.

Amplified

¹³Moses told the people, Fear not; stand still (firm, confident, undismayed) and see the salvation of the Lord which He will work for you today. For the Egyptians you have seen today you shall never see again.

¹⁴The Lord will fight for you, and you shall hold your peace *and* remain at rest.

¹⁵The Lord said to Moses, Why do you cry to Me? Tell the people of Israel to go forward!

¹⁶Lift up your rod and stretch out your hand over the sea and divide it, and the Israelites shall go on dry ground through the midst of the sea.

¹⁷And I, behold, I will harden (make stubborn and strong) the hearts of the Egyptians, and they shall go [into the sea] after them; and I will gain honor over Pharaoh and all his host, his chariots, and horsemen.

¹⁸The Egyptians shall know *and* realize that I am the Lord when I have gained honor *and* glory over Pharaoh, his chariots, and his horsemen.

¹⁹And the *l*Angel of God Who went before the host of Israel moved and went behind them; and the pillar of the cloud went from before them and stood behind them,

²⁰Coming between the host of Egypt and the host of Israel. It was a cloud and darkness to the Egyptians, but it gave light by night to the Israelites; and the one host did not come near the other all night.

²¹Then Moses stretched out his hand over the sea, and the Lord caused the sea to go back by a strong east wind all that night and made the sea dry land; and the waters were divided.

²²And the Israelites went into the midst of the sea on dry ground, the waters being a wall to them on their right hand and on their left.

²³The Egyptians pursued and went in after them into the midst of the sea, even all Pharaoh's horses, his chariots, and his horsemen.

²⁴And in the morning watch the Lord through the pillar of fire and cloud looked down on the host of the Egyptians and discomfited [them],

²⁵And bound (clogged, took off) their chariot wheels, making them drive heavily; and the Egyptians said, Let us flee from the face of Israel, for the Lord fights for them against the Egyptians!

²⁶Then the Lord said to Moses, Stretch out your hand over the sea, that the waters may come again upon the Egyptians, upon their chariots and horsemen.

²⁷So Moses stretched forth his hand over the sea, and the sea returned to its strength *and* normal flow when the morning appeared; and the Egyptians fled into it [being met by it]; and the Lord overthrew the Egyptians *and* shook them off into the midst of the sea.

²⁸The waters returned and covered the chariots, the horsemen, and all the host of Pharaoh that pursued them; not even one of them remained.

²⁹But the Israelites walked on dry ground in the midst of the sea, the waters being a wall to them on their right hand and on their left.

³⁰Thus the Lord saved Israel that day from the hand of the Egyptians, and Israel saw the Egyptians dead upon the seashore.

³¹And Israel saw that great work which the Lord did against the Egyptians, and the people [reverently] feared the Lord and trusted in (relied on, remained steadfast to) the Lord and to His servant Moses.

---

*j*Or, *for whereas ye have seen the Egyptians today made them to go heavily*   *k*Or, *and*   *l*Heb. *shook off*   *m*Heb. *hand*

*l*See footnote on Gen. 16:7; here the "Angel of God" is associated with the cloud (Exod. 13:21).

New American Standard

The Sea Is Divided

13 But Moses said to the people, "Do not fear! Stand by and see the salvation of the LORD which He will accomplish for you today; for the Egyptians whom you have seen today, you will never see them again forever.
14"The LORD will fight for you while you keep silent."
15 ¶ Then the LORD said to Moses, "Why are you crying out to Me? Tell the sons of Israel to go forward.
16"As for you, lift up your staff and stretch out your hand over the sea and divide it, and the sons of Israel shall go through the midst of the sea on dry land.
17"As for Me, behold, I will harden the hearts of the Egyptians so that they will go in after them; and I will be honored through Pharaoh and all his army, through his chariots and his horsemen.
18"Then the Egyptians will know that I am the LORD, when I am honored through Pharaoh, through his chariots and his horsemen."
19 ¶ The angel of God, who had been going before the camp of Israel, moved and went behind them; and the pillar of cloud moved from before them and stood behind them.
20 So it came between the camp of Egypt and the camp of Israel; and there was the cloud along with the darkness, yet it gave light at night. Thus the one did not come near the other all night.
21 ¶ Then Moses stretched out his hand over the sea; and the LORD swept the sea *back* by a strong east wind all night and turned the sea into dry land, so the waters were divided.
22 The sons of Israel went through the midst of the sea on the dry land, and the waters *were like* a wall to them on their right hand and on their left.
23 Then the Egyptians took up the pursuit, and all Pharaoh's horses, his chariots and his horsemen went in after them into the midst of the sea.
24 At the morning watch, the LORD looked down on the army of the Egyptians through the pillar of fire and cloud and brought the army of the Egyptians into confusion.
25 He caused their chariot wheels to swerve, and He made them drive with difficulty; so the Egyptians said, "Let us flee from Israel, for the LORD is fighting for them against the Egyptians."
26 ¶ Then the LORD said to Moses, "Stretch out your hand over the sea so that the waters may come back over the Egyptians, over their chariots and their horsemen."
27 So Moses stretched out his hand over the sea, and the sea returned to its normal state at daybreak, while the Egyptians were fleeing right into it; then the LORD overthrew the Egyptians in the midst of the sea.
28 The waters returned and covered the chariots and the horsemen, even Pharaoh's entire army that had gone into the sea after them; not even one of them remained.
29 But the sons of Israel walked on dry land through the midst of the sea, and the waters *were like* a wall to them on their right hand and on their left.
30 ¶ Thus the LORD saved Israel that day from the hand of the Egyptians, and Israel saw the Egyptians dead on the seashore.
31 When Israel saw the great power which the LORD had used against the Egyptians, the people feared the LORD, and they believed in the LORD and in His servant Moses.

New International

13Moses answered the people, "Do not be afraid. Stand firm and you will see the deliverance the LORD will bring you today. The Egyptians you see today you will never see again. 14The LORD will fight for you; you need only to be still."
15Then the LORD said to Moses, "Why are you crying out to me? Tell the Israelites to move on. 16Raise your staff and stretch out your hand over the sea to divide the water so that the Israelites can go through the sea on dry ground. 17I will harden the hearts of the Egyptians so that they will go in after them. And I will gain glory through Pharaoh and all his army, through his chariots and his horsemen. 18The Egyptians will know that I am the LORD when I gain glory through Pharaoh, his chariots and his horsemen."
19Then the angel of God, who had been traveling in front of Israel's army, withdrew and went behind them. The pillar of cloud also moved from in front and stood behind them, 20coming between the armies of Egypt and Israel. Throughout the night the cloud brought darkness to the one side and light to the other side; so neither went near the other all night long.
21Then Moses stretched out his hand over the sea, and all that night the LORD drove the sea back with a strong east wind and turned it into dry land. The waters were divided, 22and the Israelites went through the sea on dry ground, with a wall of water on their right and on their left.
23The Egyptians pursued them, and all Pharaoh's horses and chariots and horsemen followed them into the sea. 24During the last watch of the night the LORD looked down from the pillar of fire and cloud at the Egyptian army and threw it into confusion. 25He made the wheels of their chariots come off[y] so that they had difficulty driving. And the Egyptians said, "Let's get away from the Israelites! The LORD is fighting for them against Egypt."
26Then the LORD said to Moses, "Stretch out your hand over the sea so that the waters may flow back over the Egyptians and their chariots and horsemen." 27Moses stretched out his hand over the sea, and at daybreak the sea went back to its place. The Egyptians were fleeing toward[z] it, and the LORD swept them into the sea. 28The water flowed back and covered the chariots and horsemen—the entire army of Pharaoh that had followed the Israelites into the sea. Not one of them survived.
29But the Israelites went through the sea on dry ground, with a wall of water on their right and on their left. 30That day the LORD saved Israel from the hands of the Egyptians, and Israel saw the Egyptians lying dead on the shore. 31And when the Israelites saw the great power the LORD displayed against the Egyptians, the people feared the LORD and put their trust in him and in Moses his servant.

King James

Amplified

The song of Moses

15 THEN SANG Moses and the children of Israel this song unto the LORD, and spake, saying, I will sing unto the LORD, for he hath triumphed gloriously: the horse and his rider hath he thrown into the sea.

²The LORD *is* my strength and song, and he is become my salvation: he *is* my God, and I will prepare him an habitation; my father's God, and I will exalt him.

³The LORD *is* a man of war: the LORD *is* his name.

⁴Pharaoh's chariots and his host hath he cast into the sea: his chosen captains also are drowned in the Red sea.

⁵The depths have covered them: they sank into the bottom as a stone.

⁶Thy right hand, O LORD, is become glorious in power: thy right hand, O LORD, hath dashed in pieces the enemy.

⁷And in the greatness of thine excellency thou hast overthrown them that rose up against thee: thou sentest forth thy wrath, *which* consumed them as stubble.

⁸And with the blast of thy nostrils the waters were gathered together, the floods stood upright as an heap, *and* the depths were congealed in the heart of the sea.

⁹The enemy said, I will pursue, I will overtake, I will divide the spoil; my lust shall be satisfied upon them; I will draw my sword, my hand shall ⁿdestroy them.

¹⁰Thou didst blow with thy wind, the sea covered them: they sank as lead in the mighty waters.

¹¹Who *is* like unto thee, O LORD, among the ᵒgods? who *is* like thee, glorious in holiness, fearful *in* praises, doing wonders?

¹²Thou stretchedst out thy right hand, the earth swallowed them.

¹³Thou in thy mercy hast led forth the people *which* thou hast redeemed: thou hast guided *them* in thy strength unto thy holy habitation.

¹⁴The people shall hear, *and* be afraid: sorrow shall take hold on the inhabitants of Palestina.

¹⁵Then the dukes of Edom shall be amazed; the mighty men of Moab, trembling shall take hold upon them; all the inhabitants of Canaan shall melt away.

¹⁶Fear and dread shall fall upon them; by the greatness of thine arm they shall be *as* still as a stone; till thy people pass over, O LORD, till the people pass over, *which* thou hast purchased.

15 THEN MOSES and the Israelites sang this song to the Lord, saying, I will sing to the Lord, for He has triumphed gloriously; the horse and his rider *or* its chariot has He thrown into the sea.

²The Lord is my Strength and my Song, and He has become my Salvation; this is my God, and I will praise Him, my father's God, and I will exalt Him.

³The Lord is a Man of War; the Lord is His name.

⁴Pharaoh's chariots and his host has He cast into the sea; his chosen captains also are sunk in the Red Sea.

⁵The floods cover them; they sank in the depths [clad in mail] like a stone.

⁶Your right hand, O Lord, is glorious in power; Your right hand, O Lord, shatters the enemy.

⁷In the greatness of Your majesty You overthrow those rising against You. You send forth Your fury; it consumes them like stubble.

⁸With the blast of Your nostrils the waters piled up, the floods stood fixed in a heap, the deeps congealed in the heart of the sea.

⁹The enemy said, I will pursue, I will overtake, I will divide the spoil; my desire shall be satisfied upon them; I will draw my sword, my hand shall destroy them.

¹⁰You [Lord] blew with Your wind, the sea covered them; [clad in mail] they sank as lead in the mighty waters.

¹¹Who is like You, O Lord, among the gods? Who is like You, glorious in holiness, awesome in splendor, doing wonders?

¹²You stretched out Your right hand, the earth's [sea] swallowed them.

¹³You in Your mercy *and* loving-kindness have led forth the people whom You have redeemed; You have guided them in Your strength to Your holy habitation.

¹⁴The peoples have heard of it; they tremble; pangs have taken hold on the inhabitants of Philistia.

¹⁵Now the chiefs of Edom are dismayed; the mighty men of Moab [renowned for strength], trembling takes hold of them; all the inhabitants of Canaan have melted away—little by little.

¹⁶Terror and dread fall upon them; because of the greatness of Your arm they are as still as a stone—till Your people pass by *and* over [into Canaan], O Lord, till the people pass by whom You have purchased.

ⁿOr, *repossess*   ᵒOr, *mighty ones?*

New American Standard

The Song of Moses and Israel

15 THEN MOSES and the sons of Israel sang this song to the LORD, and said,

"I will sing to the LORD, for He is highly exalted;
  The horse and its rider He has hurled into the sea.
2"The LORD is my strength and song,
  And He has become my salvation;
  This is my God, and I will praise Him;
  My father's God, and I will extol Him.
3"The LORD is a warrior;
  The LORD is His name.
4"Pharaoh's chariots and his army He has cast into the sea;
  And the choicest of his officers are drowned in the *k*Red Sea.
5"The deeps cover them;
  They went down into the depths like a stone.
6"Your right hand, O LORD, is majestic in power,
  Your right hand, O LORD, shatters the enemy.
7"And in the greatness of Your excellence You overthrow those who rise up against You;
  You send forth Your burning anger, *and* it consumes them as chaff.
8"At the blast of Your nostrils the waters were piled up,
  The flowing waters stood up like a heap;
  The deeps were congealed in the heart of the sea.
9"The enemy said, 'I will pursue, I will overtake, I will divide the spoil;
  My desire shall be gratified against them;
  I will draw out my sword, my hand will destroy them.'
10"You blew with Your wind, the sea covered them;
  They sank like lead in the mighty waters.
11"Who is like You among the gods, O LORD?
  Who is like You, majestic in holiness,
  Awesome in praises, working wonders?
12"You stretched out Your right hand,
  The earth swallowed them.
13"In Your lovingkindness You have led the people whom You have redeemed;
  In Your strength You have guided *them* to Your holy habitation.
14"The peoples have heard, they tremble;
  Anguish has gripped the inhabitants of Philistia.
15"Then the chiefs of Edom were dismayed;
  The leaders of Moab, trembling grips them;
  All the inhabitants of Canaan have melted away;
16"Terror and dread fall upon them;
  By the greatness of Your arm they are motionless as stone;
  Until Your people pass over, O LORD,
  Until the people pass over whom You have purchased.

New International

The Song of Moses and Miriam

15 THEN MOSES and the Israelites sang this song to the LORD:

"I will sing to the LORD,
  for he is highly exalted.
The horse and its rider
  he has hurled into the sea.
2The LORD is my strength and my song;
  he has become my salvation.
He is my God, and I will praise him,
  my father's God, and I will exalt him.
3The LORD is a warrior;
  the LORD is his name.
4Pharaoh's chariots and his army
  he has hurled into the sea.
The best of Pharaoh's officers
  are drowned in the Red Sea.*a*
5The deep waters have covered them;
  they sank to the depths like a stone.
6"Your right hand, O LORD,
  was majestic in power.
Your right hand, O LORD,
  shattered the enemy.
7In the greatness of your majesty
  you threw down those who opposed you.
You unleashed your burning anger;
  it consumed them like stubble.
8By the blast of your nostrils
  the waters piled up.
The surging waters stood firm like a wall;
  the deep waters congealed in the heart of the sea.
9"The enemy boasted,
  'I will pursue, I will overtake them.
I will divide the spoils;
  I will gorge myself on them.
I will draw my sword
  and my hand will destroy them.'
10But you blew with your breath,
  and the sea covered them.
They sank like lead
  in the mighty waters.
11"Who among the gods is like you, O LORD?
  Who is like you—
  majestic in holiness,
  awesome in glory,
  working wonders?
12You stretched out your right hand
  and the earth swallowed them.
13"In your unfailing love you will lead
  the people you have redeemed.
In your strength you will guide them
  to your holy dwelling.
14The nations will hear and tremble;
  anguish will grip the people of Philistia.
15The chiefs of Edom will be terrified,
  the leaders of Moab will be seized with trembling,
  the people*b* of Canaan will melt away;
16 terror and dread will fall upon them.
By the power of your arm
  they will be as still as a stone—
until your people pass by, O LORD,
  until the people you bought*c* pass by.

a4 Hebrew *Yam Suph*; that is, Sea of Reeds; also in verse 22
b15 Or *rulers*   *c16* Or *created*

k Lit *Sea of Reeds*

King James

¹⁷Thou shalt bring them in, and plant them in the mountain of thine inheritance, *in* the place, O LORD, *which* thou hast made for thee to dwell in, *in* the Sanctuary, O LORD, *which* thy hands have established.

¹⁸The LORD shall reign for ever and ever.

¹⁹For the horse of Pharaoh went in with his chariots and with his horsemen into the sea, and the LORD brought again the waters of the sea upon them; but the children of Israel went on dry *land* in the midst of the sea.

²⁰ ¶ And Miriam the prophetess, the sister of Aaron, took a timbrel in her hand; and all the women went out after her with timbrels and with dances.

²¹And Miriam answered them, Sing ye to the LORD, for he hath triumphed gloriously; the horse and his rider hath he thrown into the sea.

Bitter waters made sweet

²²So Moses brought Israel from the Red sea, and they went out into the wilderness of Shur; and they went three days in the wilderness, and found no water.

²³ ¶ And when they came to Marah, they could not drink of the waters of Marah, for they *were* bitter: therefore the name of it was called *p*Marah.

²⁴And the people murmured against Moses, saying, What shall we drink?

²⁵And he cried unto the LORD; and the LORD showed him a tree, *which* when he had cast into the waters, the waters were made sweet: there he made for them a statute and an ordinance, and there he proved them,

²⁶And said, If thou wilt diligently hearken to the voice of the LORD thy God, and wilt do that which is right in his sight, and wilt give ear to his commandments, and keep all his statutes, I will put none of these diseases upon thee, which I have brought upon the Egyptians: for I *am* the LORD that healeth thee.

²⁷ ¶ And they came to Elim, where *were* twelve wells of water, and threescore and ten palm trees: and they encamped there by the waters.

Quails and manna provided

16 AND THEY took their journey from Elim, and all the congregation of the children of Israel came unto the wilderness of Sin, which *is* between Elim and Sinai, on the fifteenth day of the second month after their departing out of the land of Egypt.

²And the whole congregation of the children of Israel murmured against Moses and Aaron in the wilderness:

³And the children of Israel said unto them, Would to God we had died by the hand of the LORD in the land of Egypt, when we sat by the flesh pots, *and* when we did eat bread to the full; for ye have brought us forth into this wilderness, to kill this whole assembly with hunger.

⁴ ¶ Then said the LORD unto Moses, Behold, I will rain bread from heaven for you; and the people shall go out and gather *q*a certain rate every day, that I may prove them, whether they will walk in my law, or no.

⁵And it shall come to pass, that on the sixth day they shall prepare *that* which they bring in; and it shall be twice as much as they gather daily.

⁶And Moses and Aaron said unto all the children of Israel, At even, then ye shall know that the LORD hath brought you out from the land of Egypt:

⁷And in the morning, then ye shall see the glory of the LORD; for that he heareth your murmurings against the LORD: and what *are* we, that ye murmur against us?

Amplified

¹⁷You will bring them in [to the land] and plant them on Your own mountain, the place, O Lord, You have made for Your dwelling, the sanctuary, O Lord, which Your hands have established.

¹⁸The Lord will reign forever and ever.

¹⁹For the horses of Pharaoh went with his chariots and horsemen into the sea, and the Lord brought back the waters of the sea upon them, but the Israelites walked on dry ground in the midst of the sea.

²⁰Then Miriam the prophetess, the sister of Aaron, took a timbrel in her hand, and all the women went out after her with timbrels and dancing.

²¹And Miriam responded to them, Sing to the Lord, for He has triumphed gloriously *and* is highly exalted; the horse and his rider He has thrown into the sea.

²²Then Moses led Israel onward from the Red Sea and they went into the Wilderness of Shur; they went three days [thirty-three miles] in the wilderness and found no water.

²³When they came to Marah, they could not drink its waters for they were bitter; therefore it was named Marah [bitterness].

²⁴The people murmured against Moses, saying, What shall we drink?

²⁵And he cried to the Lord, and the Lord showed him a tree which he cast into the waters, and the waters were made sweet. There [the Lord] made for them a statute and an ordinance, and there He proved them,

²⁶Saying, If you will diligently hearken to the voice of the Lord your God and will do what is right in His sight, and will listen to *and* obey His commandments and keep all His statutes, I will put none of the diseases upon you which I brought upon the Egyptians, for I am the Lord Who heals you.

²⁷And they came to Elim, where there were twelve springs of water and seventy palm trees; and they encamped there by the waters.

16 THEY SET out from Elim, and all the congregation of Israel came to the Wilderness of Sin, which is between Elim and Sinai, on the fifteenth day of the second month after they left the land of Egypt.

²And the whole congregation of Israel murmured against Moses and Aaron in the wilderness,

³And said to them, Would that we had died by the hand of the Lord in the land of Egypt, when we sat by the fleshpots and ate bread to the full; for you have brought us out into this wilderness to kill this whole assembly with hunger.

⁴Then the Lord said to Moses, Behold, I will rain bread from the heavens for you; and the people shall go out and gather a day's portion every day, that I may prove them, whether they will walk in My law or not.

⁵On the sixth day they shall prepare to bring in twice as much as they gather daily.

⁶So Moses and Aaron said to all Israel, At evening you shall know that the Lord has brought you out from the land of Egypt,

⁷And in the morning you shall see the glory of the Lord, for He hears your murmurings against the Lord. For what are we, that you murmur against us?

_{*p*} i.e. *Bitterness*   _{*q*} Heb. *the portion of a day in his day*

New American Standard

17"You will bring them and plant them in the
   mountain of Your inheritance,
The place, O LORD, which You have made for
   Your dwelling,
The sanctuary, O Lord, which Your hands have
   established.
18"The LORD shall reign forever and ever."
19 ¶ For the horses of Pharaoh with his chariots and his
horsemen went into the sea, and the LORD brought back
the waters of the sea on them, but the sons of Israel walked
on dry land through the midst of the sea.
20 ¶ Miriam the prophetess, Aaron's sister, took the timbrel in her hand, and all the women went out after her with
timbrels and with dancing.
21 Miriam answered them,
   "Sing to the LORD, for He is highly exalted;
   The horse and his rider He has hurled into the
     sea."

The LORD Provides Water

22 ¶ Then Moses led Israel from the Red Sea, and they
went out into the wilderness of Shur; and they went three
days in the wilderness and found no water.
23 When they came to Marah, they could not drink the
waters of Marah, for they were bitter; therefore it was
named *l*Marah.
24 So the people grumbled at Moses, saying, "What
shall we drink?"
25 Then he cried out to the LORD, and the LORD showed
him a tree; and he threw *it* into the waters, and the waters
became sweet.
   ¶ There He made for them a statute and regulation, and
there He tested them.
26 And He said, "If you will give earnest heed to the
voice of the LORD your God, and do what is right in His
sight, and give ear to His commandments, and keep all His
statutes, I will put none of the diseases on you which I
have put on the Egyptians; for I, the LORD, am your
healer."
27 ¶ Then they came to Elim where there *were* twelve
springs of water and seventy date palms, and they camped
there beside the waters.

The LORD Provides Manna

16 THEN THEY set out from Elim, and all the congregation of the sons of Israel came to the wilderness of Sin, which is between Elim and Sinai, on the
fifteenth day of the second month after their departure
from the land of Egypt.
2 The whole congregation of the sons of Israel grumbled against Moses and Aaron in the wilderness.
3 The sons of Israel said to them, "Would that we had
died by the LORD's hand in the land of Egypt, when we sat
by the pots of meat, when we ate bread to the full; for you
have brought us out into this wilderness to kill this whole
assembly with hunger."
4 ¶ Then the LORD said to Moses, "Behold, I will rain
bread from heaven for you; and the people shall go out and
gather a day's portion every day, that I may test them,
whether or not they will walk in My *m*instruction.
5"On the sixth day, when they prepare what they bring
in, it will be twice as much as they gather daily."
6 So Moses and Aaron said to all the sons of Israel, "At
evening you will know that the LORD has brought you out
of the land of Egypt;
7 and in the morning you will see the glory of the
LORD, for He hears your grumblings against the LORD; and
what are we, that you grumble against us?"

New International

17You will bring them in and plant them
   on the mountain of your inheritance—
the place, O LORD, you made for your
   dwelling,
the sanctuary, O Lord, your hands
   established.
18The LORD will reign
   for ever and ever."
19When Pharaoh's horses, chariots and horsemen*d*
went into the sea, the LORD brought the waters of the sea
back over them, but the Israelites walked through the sea
on dry ground. 20Then Miriam the prophetess, Aaron's
sister, took a tambourine in her hand, and all the women
followed her, with tambourines and dancing. 21Miriam
sang to them:

   "Sing to the LORD,
     for he is highly exalted.
   The horse and its rider
     he has hurled into the sea."

The Waters of Marah and Elim

22Then Moses led Israel from the Red Sea and they went
into the Desert of Shur. For three days they traveled in the
desert without finding water. 23When they came to Marah,
they could not drink its water because it was bitter. (That
is why the place is called Marah.*e*) 24So the people grumbled against Moses, saying, "What are we to drink?"
25Then Moses cried out to the LORD, and the LORD
showed him a piece of wood. He threw it into the water,
and the water became sweet.
   There the LORD made a decree and a law for them, and
there he tested them. 26He said, "If you listen carefully to
the voice of the LORD your God and do what is right in his
eyes, if you pay attention to his commands and keep all his
decrees, I will not bring on you any of the diseases I
brought on the Egyptians, for I am the LORD, who heals
you."
27Then they came to Elim, where there were twelve
springs and seventy palm trees, and they camped there
near the water.

Manna and Quail

16 THE WHOLE Israelite community set out from
Elim and came to the Desert of Sin, which is between Elim and Sinai, on the fifteenth day of the second
month after they had come out of Egypt. 2In the desert the
whole community grumbled against Moses and Aaron.
3The Israelites said to them, "If only we had died by the
LORD's hand in Egypt! There we sat around pots of meat
and ate all the food we wanted, but you have brought us
out into this desert to starve this entire assembly to death."
4Then the LORD said to Moses, "I will rain down bread
from heaven for you. The people are to go out each day
and gather enough for that day. In this way I will test them
and see whether they will follow my instructions. 5On the
sixth day they are to prepare what they bring in, and that
is to be twice as much as they gather on the other days."
6So Moses and Aaron said to all the Israelites, "In the
evening you will know that it was the LORD who brought
you out of Egypt, 7and in the morning you will see the
glory of the LORD, because he has heard your grumbling
against him. Who are we, that you should grumble against

---

*l*I.e. bitterness   *m*Or *law*   *d*19 Or *charioteers*   *e*23 *Marah* means *bitter*.

King James

8And Moses said, *This shall be,* when the LORD shall give you in the evening flesh to eat, and in the morning bread to the full; for that the LORD heareth your murmurings which ye murmur against him: and what *are* we? your murmurings *are* not against us, but against the LORD.

9 ¶ And Moses spake unto Aaron, Say unto all the congregation of the children of Israel, Come near before the LORD: for he hath heard your murmurings.

10And it came to pass, as Aaron spake unto the whole congregation of the children of Israel, that they looked toward the wilderness, and, behold, the glory of the LORD appeared in the cloud.

11 ¶ And the LORD spake unto Moses, saying,

12I have heard the murmurings of the children of Israel: speak unto them, saying, At even ye shall eat flesh, and in the morning ye shall be filled with bread; and ye shall know that I *am* the LORD your God.

13And it came to pass, that at even the quails came up, and covered the camp: and in the morning the dew lay round about the host.

14And when the dew that lay was gone up, behold, upon the face of the wilderness *there lay* a small round thing, *as* small as the hoar frost on the ground.

15And when the children of Israel saw *it,* they said one to another, rIt *is* manna: for they wist not what it *was.* And Moses said unto them, This *is* the bread which the LORD hath given you to eat.

16 ¶ This *is* the thing which the LORD hath commanded, Gather of it every man according to his eating, an omer sfor every man, *according to* the number of your tpersons; take ye every man for *them* which *are* in his tents.

17And the children of Israel did so, and gathered, some more, some less.

18And when they did mete *it* with an omer, he that gathered much had nothing over, and he that gathered little had no lack; they gathered every man according to his eating.

19And Moses said, Let no man leave of it till the morning.

20Notwithstanding they hearkened not unto Moses; but some of them left of it until the morning, and it bred worms, and stank: and Moses was wroth with them.

21And they gathered it every morning, every man according to his eating: and when the sun waxed hot, it melted.

22 ¶ And it came to pass, *that* on the sixth day they gathered twice as much bread, two omers for one *man:* and all the rulers of the congregation came and told Moses.

23And he said unto them, This *is that* which the LORD hath said, Tomorrow is the rest of the holy sabbath unto the LORD: bake *that* which ye will bake *today,* and seethe that ye will seethe; and that which remaineth over lay up for you to be kept until the morning.

24And they laid it up till the morning, as Moses bade: and it did not stink, neither was there any worm therein.

25And Moses said, Eat that today; for today *is* a sabbath unto the LORD: today ye shall not find it in the field.

26Six days ye shall gather it; but on the seventh day, *which is* the sabbath, in it there shall be none.

27 ¶ And it came to pass, *that* there went out *some* of the people on the seventh day for to gather, and they found none.

28And the LORD said unto Moses, How long refuse ye to keep my commandments and my laws?

29See, for that the LORD hath given you the sabbath, therefore he giveth you on the sixth day the bread of two days; abide ye every man in his place, let no man go out of his place on the seventh day.

30So the people rested on the seventh day.

Amplified

8And Moses said, [This will happen] when the Lord gives you in the evening flesh to eat and in the morning bread to the full, because the Lord has heard your grumblings which you murmur against Him; what are we? Your murmurings are not against us, but against the Lord.

9And Moses said to Aaron, Say to all the congregation of Israel, Come near before the Lord, for He has heard your murmurings.

10And as Aaron spoke to the whole congregation of Israel, they looked toward the wilderness, and behold, the glory of the Lord appeared in the cloud!

11The Lord said to Moses,

12I have heard the murmurings of the Israelites; speak to them, saying, At twilight you shall eat meat, and between the two evenings you shall be filled with bread; and you shall know that I am the Lord your God.

13In the evening quails came up and covered the camp; and in the morning the dew lay round about the camp.

14And when the dew had gone, behold, upon the face of the wilderness there lay a fine, round *and* flakelike thing, as fine as hoarfrost on the ground.

15When the Israelites saw it, they said one to another, Manna [What is it?]. For they did not know what it was. And Moses said to them, This is the bread which the Lord has given you to eat. [John 6:31, 33.]

16This is what the Lord has commanded: Let every man gather of it as much as he will need, an omer for each person, according to the number of your persons; take it, every man for those in his tent.

17The [people] did so, and gathered, some more, some less.

18When they measured it with an omer, he who gathered much had nothing over, and he who gathered little had no lack; each gathered according to his need.

19Moses said, Let none of it be left until morning.

20But they did not listen to Moses; some of them left of it until morning, and it bred worms, became foul, *and* stank; and Moses was angry with them.

21They gathered it every morning, each as much as he needed, for when the sun became hot it melted.

22And on the sixth day they gathered twice as much bread, two omers for each person; and all the leaders of the congregation came and told Moses.

23He said to them, The Lord has said, Tomorrow is a solemn rest, a holy Sabbath to the Lord; bake and boil what you will bake and boil today; and all that remains over put aside for you to keep until morning.

24They laid it aside till morning, as Moses told them; and it did not become foul, neither was it wormy.

25Moses said, Eat that today, for today is a Sabbath to the Lord. Today you shall find none in the field.

26Six days you shall gather it, but on the seventh day, the Sabbath, there shall be none.

27On the seventh day some of the people went out to gather, but they found none.

28The Lord said to Moses, How long do you [people] refuse to keep My commandments and My laws?

29See, the Lord has given you the Sabbath; therefore He gives you on the sixth day the bread for two days; let every man remain in his place; let no man leave his place on the seventh day.

30So the people rested on the seventh day.

---

rOr, *What is this?* or, *It is a portion*　　sHeb. *by the poll,* or, *head*
tHeb. *souls*

New American Standard

The LORD Provides Meat

8 Moses said, *"This will happen* when the LORD gives you meat to eat in the evening, and bread to the full in the morning; for the LORD hears your grumblings which you grumble against Him. And what are we? Your grumblings are not against us but against the LORD."

9 ¶ Then Moses said to Aaron, "Say to all the congregation of the sons of Israel, 'Come near before the LORD, for He has heard your grumblings.' "

10 It came about as Aaron spoke to the whole congregation of the sons of Israel, that they looked toward the wilderness, and behold, the glory of the LORD appeared in the cloud.

11 And the LORD spoke to Moses, saying,

12"I have heard the grumblings of the sons of Israel; speak to them, saying, 'At twilight you shall eat meat, and in the morning you shall be filled with bread; and you shall know that I am the LORD your God.' "

13 ¶ So it came about at evening that the quails came up and covered the camp, and in the morning there was a layer of dew around the camp.

14 When the layer of dew evaporated, behold, on the surface of the wilderness there was a fine flake-like thing, fine as the frost on the ground.

15 When the sons of Israel saw *it,* they said to one another, "What is it?" For they did not know what it was. And Moses said to them, "It is the bread which the LORD has given you to eat.

16"This is what the LORD has commanded, 'Gather of it every man as much as he should eat; you shall take an omer apiece according to the number of persons each of you has in his tent.' "

17 The sons of Israel did so, and *some* gathered much and *some* little.

18 When they measured it with an omer, he who had gathered much had no excess, and he who had gathered little had no lack; every man gathered as much as he should eat.

19 Moses said to them, "Let no man leave any of it until morning."

20 But they did not listen to Moses, and some left part of it until morning, and it bred worms and became foul; and Moses was angry with them.

21 They gathered it morning by morning, every man as much as he should eat; but when the sun grew hot, it would melt.

The Sabbath Observed

22 ¶ Now on the sixth day they gathered twice as much bread, two omers for each one. When all the leaders of the congregation came and told Moses,

23 then he said to them, "This is what the LORD meant: Tomorrow is a sabbath observance, a holy sabbath to the LORD. Bake what you will bake and boil what you will boil, and all that is left over put aside to be kept until morning."

24 So they put it aside until morning, as Moses had ordered, and it did not become foul nor was there any worm in it.

25 Moses said, "Eat it today, for today is a sabbath to the LORD; today you will not find it in the field.

26"Six days you shall gather it, but on the seventh day, *the* sabbath, there will be none."

27 ¶ It came about on the seventh day that some of the people went out to gather, but they found none.

28 Then the LORD said to Moses, "How long do you refuse to keep My commandments and My ⁿinstructions?

29"See, the LORD has given you the sabbath; therefore He gives you bread for two days on the sixth day. Remain every man in his place; let no man go out of his place on the seventh day."

30 So the people rested on the seventh day.

ⁿ Or *laws*

New International

us?" 8Moses also said, "You will know that it was the LORD when he gives you meat to eat in the evening and all the bread you want in the morning, because he has heard your grumbling against him. Who are we? You are not grumbling against us, but against the LORD."

9Then Moses told Aaron, "Say to the entire Israelite community, 'Come before the LORD, for he has heard your grumbling.' "

10While Aaron was speaking to the whole Israelite community, they looked toward the desert, and there was the glory of the LORD appearing in the cloud.

11The LORD said to Moses, 12"I have heard the grumbling of the Israelites. Tell them, 'At twilight you will eat meat, and in the morning you will be filled with bread. Then you will know that I am the LORD your God.' "

13That evening quail came and covered the camp, and in the morning there was a layer of dew around the camp. 14When the dew was gone, thin flakes like frost on the ground appeared on the desert floor. 15When the Israelites saw it, they said to each other, "What is it?" For they did not know what it was.

Moses said to them, "It is the bread the LORD has given you to eat. 16This is what the LORD has commanded: 'Each one is to gather as much as he needs. Take an omerᶠ for each person you have in your tent.' "

17The Israelites did as they were told; some gathered much, some little. 18And when they measured it by the omer, he who gathered much did not have too much, and he who gathered little did not have too little. Each one gathered as much as he needed.

19Then Moses said to them, "No one is to keep any of it until morning."

20However, some of them paid no attention to Moses; they kept part of it until morning, but it was full of maggots and began to smell. So Moses was angry with them.

21Each morning everyone gathered as much as he needed, and when the sun grew hot, it melted away. 22On the sixth day, they gathered twice as much—two omersᵍ for each person—and the leaders of the community came and reported this to Moses. 23He said to them, "This is what the LORD commanded: 'Tomorrow is to be a day of rest, a holy Sabbath to the LORD. So bake what you want to bake and boil what you want to boil. Save whatever is left and keep it until morning.' "

24So they saved it until morning, as Moses commanded, and it did not stink or get maggots in it. 25"Eat it today," Moses said, "because today is a Sabbath to the LORD. You will not find any of it on the ground today. 26Six days you are to gather it, but on the seventh day, the Sabbath, there will not be any."

27Nevertheless, some of the people went out on the seventh day to gather it, but they found none. 28Then the LORD said to Moses, "How long will you refuse to keep my commands and my instructions? 29Bear in mind that the LORD has given you the Sabbath; that is why on the sixth day he gives you bread for two days. Everyone is to stay where he is on the seventh day; no one is to go out." 30So the people rested on the seventh day.

ᶠ16 That is, probably about 2 quarts (about 2 liters); also in verses 18, 32, 33 and 36   ᵍ22 That is, probably about 4 quarts (about 4.5 liters)   ʰ28 The Hebrew is plural.

King James

[31]And the house of Israel called the name thereof Manna: and it *was* like coriander seed, white; and the taste of it *was* like wafers *made* with honey.

[32] ¶ And Moses said, This *is* the thing which the LORD commandeth, Fill an omer of it to be kept for your generations; that they may see the bread wherewith I have fed you in the wilderness, when I brought you forth from the land of Egypt.

[33]And Moses said unto Aaron, Take a pot, and put an omer full of manna therein, and lay it up before the LORD, to be kept for your generations.

[34]As the LORD commanded Moses, so Aaron laid it up before the Testimony, to be kept.

[35]And the children of Israel did eat manna forty years, until they came to a land inhabited; they did eat manna, until they came unto the borders of the land of Canaan.

[36]Now an omer *is* the tenth *part* of an ephah.

The water from the rock

17 AND ALL the congregation of the children of Israel journeyed from the wilderness of Sin, after their journeys, according to the commandment of the LORD, and pitched in Rephidim: and *there was* no water for the people to drink.

[2]Wherefore the people did chide with Moses, and said, Give us water that we may drink. And Moses said unto them, Why chide ye with me? wherefore do ye tempt the LORD?

[3]And the people thirsted there for water; and the people murmured against Moses, and said, Wherefore *is* this *that* thou hast brought us up out of Egypt, to kill us and our children and our cattle with thirst?

[4]And Moses cried unto the LORD, saying, What shall I do unto this people? they be almost ready to stone me.

[5]And the LORD said unto Moses, Go on before the people, and take with thee of the elders of Israel; and thy rod, wherewith thou smotest the river, take in thine hand, and go.

[6]Behold, I will stand before thee there upon the rock in Horeb; and thou shalt smite the rock, and there shall come water out of it, that the people may drink. And Moses did so in the sight of the elders of Israel.

[7]And he called the name of the place uMassah, and vMeribah, because of the chiding of the children of Israel, and because they tempted the LORD, saying, Is the LORD among us, or not?

The defeat of Amalek

[8] ¶ Then came Amalek, and fought with Israel in Rephidim.

[9]And Moses said unto Joshua, Choose us out men, and go out, fight with Amalek: tomorrow I will stand on the top of the hill with the rod of God in mine hand.

[10]So Joshua did as Moses had said to him, and fought with Amalek: and Moses, Aaron, and Hur went up to the top of the hill.

[11]And it came to pass, when Moses held up his hand, that Israel prevailed: and when he let down his hand, Amalek prevailed.

[12]But Moses' hands *were* heavy; and they took a stone, and put *it* under him, and he sat thereon; and Aaron and Hur stayed up his hands, the one on the one side, and the other on the other side; and his hands were steady until the going down of the sun.

[13]And Joshua discomfited Amalek and his people with the edge of the sword.

[14]And the LORD said unto Moses, Write this *for* a memorial in a book, and rehearse *it* in the ears of Joshua: for I will utterly put out the remembrance of Amalek from under heaven.

Amplified

[31]The house of Israel called the bread manna; it was like coriander seed, white, and it tasted like wafers made with honey.

[32]Moses said, This is what the Lord commands, Take an omer of it to be kept throughout your generations, that they may see the bread with which I fed you in the wilderness when I brought you out of the land of Egypt.

[33]And Moses said to Aaron, Take a pot and put an omer of manna in it, and lay it up before the Lord, to be kept throughout your generations.

[34]As the Lord commanded Moses, Aaron laid it up before the Testimony to be kept [in the ark]. [Heb. 9:4.]

[35]And the Israelites ate manna forty years, until they came to a habitable land; they ate the manna until they came to the border of the land of Canaan.

[36](Now an omer is the tenth of an ephah.)

17 ALL THE congregation of the Israelites moved on from the Wilderness of Sin by stages, according to the commandment of the Lord, and encamped at Rephidim; but there was no water for the people to drink.

[2]Therefore, the people contended with Moses, and said, Give us water that we may drink. And Moses said to them, Why do you find fault with me? Why do you tempt the Lord *and* try His patience?

[3]But the people thirsted there for water, and the people murmured against Moses, and said, Why did you bring us up out of Egypt to kill us and our children and livestock with thirst?

[4]So Moses cried to the Lord, What shall I do with this people? They are almost ready to stone me.

[5]And the Lord said to Moses, Pass on before the people, and take with you some of the elders of Israel; and take in your hand the rod with which you smote the river [Nile], and go.

[6]Behold, I will stand before you there on the rock at [Mount] Horeb; and you shall strike the rock, and water shall come out of it, that the people may drink. And Moses did so in the sight of the elders of Israel. [I Cor. 10:4.]

[7]He called the place Massah [proof] and Meribah [contention] because of the faultfinding of the Israelites and because they tempted *and* tried the patience of the Lord, saying, Is the Lord among us or not?

[8]Then came Amalek [descendants of Esau] and fought with Israel at Rephidim.

[9]And Moses said to Joshua, Choose us out men and go out, fight with Amalek. Tomorrow I will stand on the top of the hill with the rod of God in my hand.

[10]So Joshua did as Moses said and fought with Amalek; and Moses, Aaron, and Hur went up to the hilltop.

[11]When Moses held up his hand, Israel prevailed; and when he lowered his hand, Amalek prevailed.

[12]But Moses' hands were heavy *and* grew weary. So [the other men] took a stone and put it under him and he sat on it. Then Aaron and Hur held up his hands, one on one side and one on the other side; so his hands were steady until the going down of the sun.

[13]And Joshua mowed down *and* disabled Amalek and his people with the sword.

[14]And the Lord said to Moses, Write this for a memorial in the book and rehearse it in the ears of Joshua, that I will utterly blot out the remembrance of Amalek from under the heavens. [I Sam. 15:2–8.]

---

ui.e. *Temptation*   vi.e. *Chiding,* or, *Strife*

New American Standard

31 ¶ The house of Israel named it manna, and it was like coriander seed, white, and its taste was like wafers with honey.
32 Then Moses said, "This is what the LORD has commanded, 'Let an omerful of it be kept throughout your generations, that they may see the bread that I fed you in the wilderness, when I brought you out of the land of Egypt.'"
33 Moses said to Aaron, "Take a jar and put an omerful of manna in it, and place it before the LORD to be kept throughout your generations."
34 As the LORD commanded Moses, so Aaron placed it before the Testimony, to be kept.
35 The sons of Israel ate the manna forty years, until they came to an inhabited land; they ate the manna until they came to the border of the land of Canaan.
36 (Now an omer is a tenth of an ephah.)

Water in the Rock

17 THEN ALL the congregation of the sons of Israel journeyed by stages from the wilderness of Sin, according to the command of the LORD, and camped at Rephidim, and there was no water for the people to drink.
2 Therefore the people quarreled with Moses and said, "Give us water that we may drink." And Moses said to them, "Why do you quarrel with me? Why do you test the LORD?"
3 But the people thirsted there for water; and they grumbled against Moses and said, "Why, now, have you brought us up from Egypt, to kill us and our children and our livestock with thirst?"
4 So Moses cried out to the LORD, saying, "What shall I do to this people? A little more and they will stone me."
5 Then the LORD said to Moses, "Pass before the people and take with you some of the elders of Israel; and take in your hand your staff with which you struck the Nile, and go.
6 "Behold, I will stand before you there on the rock at Horeb; and you shall strike the rock, and water will come out of it, that the people may drink." And Moses did so in the sight of the elders of Israel.
7 He named the place oMassah and pMeribah because of the quarrel of the sons of Israel, and because they tested the LORD, saying, "Is the LORD among us, or not?"

Amalek Fought

8 ¶ Then Amalek came and fought against Israel at Rephidim.
9 So Moses said to Joshua, "Choose men for us and go out, fight against Amalek. Tomorrow I will station myself on the top of the hill with the staff of God in my hand."
10 Joshua did as Moses told him, and fought against Amalek; and Moses, Aaron, and Hur went up to the top of the hill.
11 So it came about when Moses held his hand up, that Israel prevailed, and when he let his hand down, Amalek prevailed.
12 But Moses' hands were heavy. Then they took a stone and put it under him, and he sat on it; and Aaron and Hur supported his hands, one on one side and one on the other. Thus his hands were steady until the sun set.
13 So Joshua overwhelmed Amalek and his people with the edge of the sword.
14 ¶ Then the LORD said to Moses, "Write this in a book as a memorial and recite it to Joshua, that I will utterly blot out the memory of Amalek from under heaven."

New International

31 The people of Israel called the bread manna.i It was white like coriander seed and tasted like wafers made with honey. 32 Moses said, "This is what the LORD has commanded: 'Take an omer of manna and keep it for the generations to come, so they can see the bread I gave you to eat in the desert when I brought you out of Egypt.'"
33 So Moses said to Aaron, "Take a jar and put an omer of manna in it. Then place it before the LORD to be kept for the generations to come."
34 As the LORD commanded Moses, Aaron put the manna in front of the Testimony, that it might be kept. 35 The Israelites ate manna forty years, until they came to a land that was settled; they ate manna until they reached the border of Canaan.
36 (An omer is one tenth of an ephah.)

Water From the Rock

17 THE WHOLE Israelite community set out from the Desert of Sin, traveling from place to place as the LORD commanded. They camped at Rephidim, but there was no water for the people to drink. 2 So they quarreled with Moses and said, "Give us water to drink."
Moses replied, "Why do you quarrel with me? Why do you put the LORD to the test?"
3 But the people were thirsty for water there, and they grumbled against Moses. They said, "Why did you bring us up out of Egypt to make us and our children and livestock die of thirst?"
4 Then Moses cried out to the LORD, "What am I to do with these people? They are almost ready to stone me."
5 The LORD answered Moses, "Walk on ahead of the people. Take with you some of the elders of Israel and take in your hand the staff with which you struck the Nile, and go. 6 I will stand there before you by the rock at Horeb. Strike the rock, and water will come out of it for the people to drink." So Moses did this in the sight of the elders of Israel. 7 And he called the place Massahj and Meribahk because the Israelites quarreled and because they tested the LORD saying, "Is the LORD among us or not?"

The Amalekites Defeated

8 The Amalekites came and attacked the Israelites at Rephidim. 9 Moses said to Joshua, "Choose some of our men and go out to fight the Amalekites. Tomorrow I will stand on top of the hill with the staff of God in my hands."
10 So Joshua fought the Amalekites as Moses had ordered, and Moses, Aaron and Hur went to the top of the hill. 11 As long as Moses held up his hands, the Israelites were winning, but whenever he lowered his hands, the Amalekites were winning. 12 When Moses' hands grew tired, they took a stone and put it under him and he sat on it. Aaron and Hur held his hands up—one on one side, one on the other—so that his hands remained steady till sunset. 13 So Joshua overcame the Amalekite army with the sword.
14 Then the LORD said to Moses, "Write this on a scroll as something to be remembered and make sure that Joshua hears it, because I will completely blot out the memory of Amalek from under heaven."

---

i31 Manna means What is it? (see verse 15).   j7 Massah means testing.   k7 Meribah means quarreling.

o I.e. test   p I.e. quarrel

King James

Amplified

¹⁵And Moses built an altar, and called the name of it ^wJehovah-nissi:

¹⁶For he said, ^xBecause ^ythe LORD hath sworn *that* the LORD *will have* war with Amalek from generation to generation.

The coming of Jethro

18 WHEN JETHRO, the priest of Midian, Moses' father-in-law, heard of all that God had done for Moses, and for Israel his people, *and* that the LORD had brought Israel out of Egypt;

²Then Jethro, Moses' father-in-law, took Zipporah, Moses' wife, after he had sent her back,

³And her two sons; of which the name of the one *was* ^zGershom; for he said, I have been an alien in a strange land:

⁴And the name of the other *was* ^aEliezer; for the God of my father, *said he, was* mine help, and delivered me from the sword of Pharaoh:

⁵And Jethro, Moses' father-in-law, came with his sons and his wife unto Moses into the wilderness, where he encamped at the mount of God:

⁶And he said unto Moses, I thy father-in-law Jethro am come unto thee, and thy wife, and her two sons with her.

⁷ ¶ And Moses went out to meet his father-in-law, and did obeisance, and kissed him; and they asked each other of *their* ^bwelfare; and they came into the tent.

⁸And Moses told his father-in-law all that the LORD had done unto Pharaoh and to the Egyptians for Israel's sake, *and* all the travail that had ^ccome upon them by the way, and *how* the LORD delivered them.

⁹And Jethro rejoiced for all the goodness which the LORD had done to Israel, whom he had delivered out of the hand of the Egyptians.

¹⁰And Jethro said, Blessed *be* the LORD, who hath delivered you out of the hand of the Egyptians, and out of the hand of Pharaoh, who hath delivered the people from under the hand of the Egyptians.

¹¹Now I know that the LORD *is* greater than all gods: for in the thing wherein they dealt proudly *he was* above them.

¹²And Jethro, Moses' father-in-law, took a burnt offering and sacrifices for God: and Aaron came, and all the elders of Israel, to eat bread with Moses' father-in-law before God.

¹³ ¶ And it came to pass on the morrow, that Moses sat to judge the people: and the people stood by Moses from the morning unto the evening.

¹⁴And when Moses' father-in-law saw all that he did to the people, he said, What *is* this thing that thou doest to the people? why sittest thou thyself alone, and all the people stand by thee from morning unto even?

¹⁵And Moses said unto his father-in-law, Because the people come unto me to inquire of God:

¹⁶When they have a matter, they come unto me; and I judge between ^done and another, and I do make *them* know the statutes of God, and his laws.

¹⁷And Moses' father-in-law said unto him, The thing that thou doest *is* not good.

^{18e}Thou wilt surely wear away, both thou, and this people that *is* with thee: for this thing *is* too heavy for thee; thou art not able to perform it thyself alone.

¹⁹Hearken now unto my voice, I will give thee counsel, and God shall be with thee: Be thou for the people to God-ward, that thou mayest bring the causes unto God:

²⁰And thou shalt teach them ordinances and laws, and shalt show them the way wherein they must walk, and the work that they must do.

¹⁵And Moses built an altar and called the name of it, The Lord is my Banner;

¹⁶And he said, Because [theirs] is a hand against the throne of the Lord, the Lord will have war with Amalek from generation to generation.

18 NOW JETHRO [Reuel], the priest of Midian, Moses' father-in-law, heard of all that God had done for Moses and for Israel His people, and that the Lord had brought Israel out of Egypt.

²Then Jethro, Moses' father-in-law, took Zipporah, Moses' wife, after Moses had sent her back [to her father],

³And her two sons, of whom the name of the one was Gershom [expulsion, or a stranger there], for Moses said, I have been an alien in a strange land;

⁴And the name of the other was Eliezer [God is help], for the God of my father, said Moses, was my help, and delivered me from the sword of Pharaoh.

⁵And Jethro, Moses' father-in-law, came with Moses' sons and his wife to the wilderness where he was encamped at the mount of God [Horeb, or Sinai].

⁶And he said [in a message] to Moses, I, your father-in-law Jethro, am come to you and your wife and her two sons with her.

⁷And Moses went out to meet his father-in-law and bowed in homage and kissed him; and each asked the other of his welfare and they came into the tent.

⁸Moses told his father-in-law all the Lord had done to Pharaoh and the Egyptians for Israel's sake and all the hardships that had come upon them by the way and how the Lord delivered them.

⁹Jethro rejoiced for all the goodness the Lord had done to Israel in that He had delivered them out of the hand of the Egyptians.

¹⁰Jethro said, Blessed be the Lord, Who has delivered you out of the hand of the Egyptians and out of the hand of Pharaoh, Who has delivered the people [Israel] from under the hand of the Egyptians.

¹¹Now I know that the Lord is greater than all gods. Yes, in the [very] thing in which they dealt proudly [He showed Himself infinitely superior to all their gods].

¹²And Jethro, Moses' father-in-law, took a burnt offering and sacrifices [to offer] to God, and Aaron came with all the elders of Israel to eat bread with Moses' father-in-law before God.

¹³Next day Moses sat to judge the people, and the people stood around Moses from morning till evening.

¹⁴When Moses' father-in-law saw all that he was doing for the people, he said, What is this that you do for the people? Why do you sit alone, and all the people stand around you from morning till evening?

¹⁵Moses said to his father-in-law, Because the people come to me to inquire of God.

¹⁶When they have a dispute they come to me, and I judge between a man and his neighbor, and I make them know the statutes of God and His laws.

¹⁷Moses' father-in-law said to him, The thing that you are doing is not good.

¹⁸You will surely wear out both yourself and this people with you, for the thing is too heavy for you; you are not able to perform it all by yourself.

¹⁹Listen now to [me]; I will counsel you, and God will be with you. You shall represent the people before God, bringing their cases *and* causes to Him,

²⁰Teaching them the decrees and laws, showing them the way they must walk and the work they must do.

---

^wi.e. *The LORD my banner*   ^xOr, *Because the hand* of Amalek is *against the throne of the LORD*, therefore   ^yHeb. *the hand upon the throne of the LORD*   ^zi.e. *A stranger there*   ^ai.e. *My God is an help*   ^bHeb. *peace*   ^cHeb. *found them*   ^dHeb. *a man and his fellow*   ^eHeb. *Fading thou wilt fade*

New American Standard

15 Moses built an altar and named it The LORD is My Banner;

16 and he said, "The LORD has sworn; the LORD will have war against Amalek from generation to generation."

Jethro, Moses' Father-in-law

18 NOW JETHRO, the priest of Midian, Moses' father-in-law, heard of all that God had done for Moses and for Israel His people, how the LORD had brought Israel out of Egypt.

2 Jethro, Moses' father-in-law, took Moses' wife Zipporah, after he had sent her away,

3 and her two sons, of whom one was named Gershom, for Moses said, "I have been a sojourner in a foreign land."

4 The other was named Eliezer, for he said, "The God of my father was my help, and delivered me from the sword of Pharaoh."

5 ¶ Then Jethro, Moses' father-in-law, came with his sons and his wife to Moses in the wilderness where he was camped, at the mount of God.

6 He sent word to Moses, "I, your father-in-law Jethro, am coming to you with your wife and her two sons with her."

7 Then Moses went out to meet his father-in-law, and he bowed down and kissed him; and they asked each other of their welfare and went into the tent.

8 Moses told his father-in-law all that the LORD had done to Pharaoh and to the Egyptians for Israel's sake, all the hardship that had befallen them on the journey, and how the LORD had delivered them.

9 Jethro rejoiced over all the goodness which the LORD had done to Israel, in delivering them from the hand of the Egyptians.

10 So Jethro said, "Blessed be the LORD who delivered you from the hand of the Egyptians and from the hand of Pharaoh, and who delivered the people from under the hand of the Egyptians.

11 "Now I know that the LORD is greater than all the gods; indeed, it was proven when they dealt proudly against the people."

12 Then Jethro, Moses' father-in-law, took a burnt offering and sacrifices for God, and Aaron came with all the elders of Israel to eat a meal with Moses' father-in-law before God.

13 ¶ It came about the next day that Moses sat to judge the people, and the people stood about Moses from the morning until the evening.

14 Now when Moses' father-in-law saw all that he was doing for the people, he said, "What is this thing that you are doing for the people? Why do you alone sit as judge and all the people stand about you from morning until evening?"

15 Moses said to his father-in-law, "Because the people come to me to inquire of God.

16 "When they have a dispute, it comes to me, and I judge between a man and his neighbor and make known the statutes of God and His laws."

Jethro Counsels Moses

17 Moses' father-in-law said to him, "The thing that you are doing is not good.

18 "You will surely wear out, both yourself and these people who are with you, for the task is too heavy for you; you cannot do it alone.

19 "Now listen to me: I will give you counsel, and God be with you. You be the people's representative before God, and you bring the disputes to God,

20 then teach them the statutes and the laws, and make known to them the way in which they are to walk and the work they are to do.

New International

15 Moses built an altar and called it The LORD is my Banner. 16 He said, "For hands were lifted up to the throne of the LORD. The[j] LORD will be at war against the Amalekites from generation to generation."

Jethro Visits Moses

18 NOW JETHRO, the priest of Midian and father-in-law of Moses, heard of everything God had done for Moses and for his people Israel, and how the LORD had brought Israel out of Egypt.

2 After Moses had sent away his wife Zipporah, his father-in-law Jethro received her 3 and her two sons. One son was named Gershom,[m] for Moses said, "I have become an alien in a foreign land"; 4 and the other was named Eliezer,[n] for he said, "My father's God was my helper; he saved me from the sword of Pharaoh."

5 Jethro, Moses' father-in-law, together with Moses' sons and wife, came to him in the desert, where he was camped near the mountain of God. 6 Jethro had sent word to him, "I, your father-in-law Jethro, am coming to you with your wife and her two sons."

7 So Moses went out to meet his father-in-law and bowed down and kissed him. They greeted each other and then went into the tent. 8 Moses told his father-in-law about everything the LORD had done to Pharaoh and the Egyptians for Israel's sake and about all the hardships they had met along the way and how the LORD had saved them.

9 Jethro was delighted to hear about all the good things the LORD had done for Israel in rescuing them from the hand of the Egyptians. 10 He said, "Praise be to the LORD, who rescued you from the hand of the Egyptians and of Pharaoh, and who rescued the people from the hand of the Egyptians. 11 Now I know that the LORD is greater than all other gods, for he did this to those who had treated Israel arrogantly." 12 Then Jethro, Moses' father-in-law, brought a burnt offering and other sacrifices to God, and Aaron came with all the elders of Israel to eat bread with Moses' father-in-law in the presence of God.

13 The next day Moses took his seat to serve as judge for the people, and they stood around him from morning till evening. 14 When his father-in-law saw all that Moses was doing for the people, he said, "What is this you are doing for the people? Why do you alone sit as judge, while all these people stand around you from morning till evening?"

15 Moses answered him, "Because the people come to me to seek God's will. 16 Whenever they have a dispute, it is brought to me, and I decide between the parties and inform them of God's decrees and laws."

17 Moses' father-in-law replied, "What you are doing is not good. 18 You and these people who come to you will only wear yourselves out. The work is too heavy for you; you cannot handle it alone. 19 Listen now to me and I will give you some advice, and may God be with you. You must be the people's representative before God and bring their disputes to him. 20 Teach them the decrees and laws, and show them the way to live and the duties they are to

l 16 Or "Because a hand was against the throne of the LORD, the
m 3 Gershom sounds like the Hebrew for an alien there.
n 4 Eliezer means my God is helper.

King James

²¹Moreover thou shalt provide out of all the people able men, such as fear God, men of truth, hating covetousness; and place *such* over them, *to be* rulers of thousands, *and* rulers of hundreds, rulers of fifties, and rulers of tens:

²²And let them judge the people at all seasons: and it shall be, *that* every great matter they shall bring unto thee, but every small matter they shall judge: so shall it be easier for thyself, and they shall bear *the burden* with thee.

²³If thou shalt do this thing, and God command thee *so,* then thou shalt be able to endure, and all this people shall also go to their place in peace.

²⁴So Moses hearkened to the voice of his father-in-law, and did all that he had said.

²⁵And Moses chose able men out of all Israel, and made them heads over the people, rulers of thousands, rulers of hundreds, rulers of fifties, and rulers of tens.

²⁶And they judged the people at all seasons: the hard causes they brought unto Moses, but every small matter they judged themselves.

²⁷ ¶ And Moses let his father-in-law depart; and he went his way into his own land.

At mount Sinai

19 IN THE third month, when the children of Israel were gone forth out of the land of Egypt, the same day came they *into* the wilderness of Sinai.

²For they were departed from Rephidim, and were come *to* the desert of Sinai, and had pitched in the wilderness; and there Israel camped before the mount.

³And Moses went up unto God, and the LORD called unto him out of the mountain, saying, Thus shalt thou say to the house of Jacob, and tell the children of Israel;

⁴Ye have seen what I did unto the Egyptians, and *how* I bare you on eagles' wings, and brought you unto myself.

⁵Now therefore, if ye will obey my voice indeed, and keep my covenant, then ye shall be a peculiar treasure unto me above all people: for all the earth *is* mine:

⁶And ye shall be unto me a kingdom of priests, and an holy nation. These *are* the words which thou shalt speak unto the children of Israel.

⁷ ¶ And Moses came and called for the elders of the people, and laid before their faces all these words which the LORD commanded him.

⁸And all the people answered together, and said, All that the LORD hath spoken we will do. And Moses returned the words of the people unto the LORD.

⁹And the LORD said unto Moses, Lo, I come unto thee in a thick cloud, that the people may hear when I speak with thee, and believe thee for ever. And Moses told the words of the people unto the LORD.

¹⁰ ¶ And the LORD said unto Moses, Go unto the people, and sanctify them today and tomorrow, and let them wash their clothes,

¹¹And be ready against the third day: for the third day the LORD will come down in the sight of all the people upon mount Sinai.

¹²And thou shalt set bounds unto the people round about, saying, Take heed to yourselves, *that ye* go *not* up into the mount, or touch the border of it: whosoever toucheth the mount shall be surely put to death:

¹³There shall not an hand touch it, but he shall surely be stoned, or shot through; whether *it be* beast or man, it shall not live: when the *f*trumpet soundeth long, they shall come up to the mount.

¹⁴ ¶ And Moses went down from the mount unto the people, and sanctified the people; and they washed their clothes.

¹⁵And he said unto the people, Be ready against the third day: come not at *your* wives.

Amplified

²¹Moreover, you shall choose able men from all the people—God-fearing men of truth who hate unjust gain—and place them over thousands, hundreds, fifties, and tens, to be their rulers.

²²And let them judge the people at all times; every great matter they shall bring to you, but every small matter they shall judge. So it will be easier for you, and they will bear the burden with you.

²³If you will do this, and God so commands you, you will be able to endure [the strain], and all these people also will go to their [tents] in peace.

²⁴So Moses listened to *and* heeded the voice of his father-in-law and did all that he had said.

²⁵Moses chose able men out of all Israel and made them heads over the people, rulers of thousands, of hundreds, of fifties, and of tens.

²⁶And they judged the people at all times; the hard cases they brought to Moses, but every small matter they decided themselves.

²⁷Then Moses let his father-in-law depart, and he went his way into his own land.

19 IN THE third month after the Israelites left the land of Egypt, the same day, they came into the Wilderness of Sinai.

²When they had departed from Rephidim and had come to the Wilderness of Sinai, they encamped there before the mountain.

³And Moses went up to God, and the Lord called to him out of the mountain, Say this to the house of Jacob and tell the Israelites:

⁴You have seen what I did to the Egyptians, and how I bore you on eagles' wings and brought you to Myself.

⁵Now therefore, if you will obey My voice in truth and keep My covenant, then you shall be My own peculiar possession *and* treasure from among *and* above all peoples; for all the earth is Mine.

⁶And you shall be to Me a kingdom of priests, a holy nation [consecrated, set apart to the worship of God]. These are the words you shall speak to the Israelites.

⁷So Moses called for the elders of the people and told them all these words which the Lord commanded him.

⁸And all the people answered together, and said, All that the Lord has spoken we will do. And Moses reported the words of the people to the Lord.

⁹And the Lord said to Moses, Behold, I come to you in a thick cloud, that the people may hear when I speak with you and believe you *and* remain steadfast forever. Then Moses told the words of the people to the Lord.

¹⁰And the Lord said to Moses, Go and sanctify the people [set them apart for God] today and tomorrow, and let them wash their clothes

¹¹And be ready by the third day, for the third day the Lord will come down upon Mount Sinai [in the cloud] in the sight of all the people.

¹²And you shall set bounds for the people round about, saying, Take heed that you go not up into the mountain or touch the border of it. Whoever touches the mountain shall surely be put to death.

¹³No hand shall touch it [or the offender], but he shall surely be stoned or shot [with arrows]; whether beast or man, he shall not live. When the trumpet sounds a long blast, they shall come up to the mountain. [Num. 24:8.]

¹⁴So Moses went down from the mountain to the people and sanctified them [set them apart for God], and they washed their clothes.

¹⁵And he said to the people, Be ready by the day after tomorrow; do not go near a woman.

^fOr, *cornet*

New American Standard

21"Furthermore, you shall select out of all the people able men who fear God, men of truth, those who hate dishonest gain; and you shall place *these* over them *as* leaders of thousands, of hundreds, of fifties and of tens.

22"Let them judge the people at all times; and let it be that every major dispute they will bring to you, but every minor dispute they themselves will judge. So it will be easier for you, and they will bear *the burden* with you.

23"If you do this thing and God *so* commands you, then you will be able to endure, and all these people also will go to their place in peace."

24 ¶ So Moses listened to his father-in-law and did all that he had said.

25 Moses chose able men out of all Israel and made them heads over the people, leaders of thousands, of hundreds, of fifties and of tens.

26 They judged the people at all times; the difficult dispute they would bring to Moses, but every minor dispute they themselves would judge.

27 Then Moses bade his father-in-law farewell, and he went his way into his own land.

Moses on Sinai

19 IN THE third month after the sons of Israel had gone out of the land of Egypt, on that very day they came into the wilderness of Sinai.

2 When they set out from Rephidim, they came to the wilderness of Sinai and camped in the wilderness; and there Israel camped in front of the mountain.

3 Moses went up to God, and the LORD called to him from the mountain, saying, "Thus you shall say to the house of Jacob and tell the sons of Israel:

4 'You yourselves have seen what I did to the Egyptians, and *how* I bore you on eagles' wings, and brought you to Myself.

5 'Now then, if you will indeed obey My voice and keep My covenant, then you shall be My qown possession among all the peoples, for all the earth is Mine;

6 and you shall be to Me a kingdom of priests and a holy nation.' These are the words that you shall speak to the sons of Israel."

7 ¶ So Moses came and called the elders of the people, and set before them all these words which the LORD had commanded him.

8 All the people answered together and said, "All that the LORD has spoken we will do!" And Moses brought back the words of the people to the LORD.

9 The LORD said to Moses, "Behold, I will come to you in a thick cloud, so that the people may hear when I speak with you and may also believe in you forever." Then Moses told the words of the people to the LORD.

10 ¶ The LORD also said to Moses, "Go to the people and consecrate them today and tomorrow, and let them wash their garments;

11 and let them be ready for the third day, for on the third day the LORD will come down on Mount Sinai in the sight of all the people.

12"You shall set bounds for the people all around, saying, 'Beware that you do not go up on the mountain or touch the border of it; whoever touches the mountain shall surely be put to death.

13 'No hand shall touch him, but he shall surely be stoned or rshot through; whether beast or man, he shall not live.' When the ram's horn sounds a long blast, they shall come up to the mountain."

14 So Moses went down from the mountain to the people and consecrated the people, and they washed their garments.

15 He said to the people, "Be ready for the third day; do not go near a woman."

New International

perform. 21But select capable men from all the people— men who fear God, trustworthy men who hate dishonest gain—and appoint them as officials over thousands, hundreds, fifties and tens. 22Have them serve as judges for the people at all times, but have them bring every difficult case to you; the simple cases they can decide themselves. That will make your load lighter, because they will share it with you. 23If you do this and God so commands, you will be able to stand the strain, and all these people will go home satisfied."

24Moses listened to his father-in-law and did everything he said. 25He chose capable men from all Israel and made them leaders of the people, officials over thousands, hundreds, fifties and tens. 26They served as judges for the people at all times. The difficult cases they brought to Moses, but the simple ones they decided themselves.

27Then Moses sent his father-in-law on his way, and Jethro returned to his own country.

At Mount Sinai

19 IN THE third month after the Israelites left Egypt—on the very day—they came to the Desert of Sinai. 2After they set out from Rephidim, they entered the Desert of Sinai, and Israel camped there in the desert in front of the mountain.

3Then Moses went up to God, and the LORD called to him from the mountain and said, "This is what you are to say to the house of Jacob and what you are to tell the people of Israel: 4'You yourselves have seen what I did to Egypt, and how I carried you on eagles' wings and brought you to myself. 5Now if you obey me fully and keep my covenant, then out of all nations you will be my treasured possession. Although the whole earth is mine, 6youₒ will be for me a kingdom of priests and a holy nation.' These are the words you are to speak to the Israelites."

7So Moses went back and summoned the elders of the people and set before them all the words the LORD had commanded him to speak. 8The people all responded together, "We will do everything the LORD has said." So Moses brought their answer back to the LORD.

9The LORD said to Moses, "I am going to come to you in a dense cloud, so that the people will hear me speaking with you and will always put their trust in you." Then Moses told the LORD what the people had said.

10And the LORD said to Moses, "Go to the people and consecrate them today and tomorrow. Have them wash their clothes 11and be ready by the third day, because on that day the LORD will come down on Mount Sinai in the sight of all the people. 12Put limits for the people around the mountain and tell them, 'Be careful that you do not go up the mountain or touch the foot of it. Whoever touches the mountain shall surely be put to death. 13He shall surely be stoned or shot with arrows; not a hand is to be laid on him. Whether man or animal, he shall not be permitted to live.' Only when the ram's horn sounds a long blast may they go up to the mountain."

14After Moses had gone down the mountain to the people, he consecrated them, and they washed their clothes. 15Then he said to the people, "Prepare yourselves for the third day. Abstain from sexual relations."

---

qOr *special treasure*   rI.e. with arrows   ₒ5,6 Or *possession, for the whole earth is mine.* 6You

King James

¹⁶ ¶ And it came to pass on the third day in the morning, that there were thunders and lightnings, and a thick cloud upon the mount, and the voice of the trumpet exceeding loud; so that all the people that *was* in the camp trembled.

¹⁷And Moses brought forth the people out of the camp to meet with God; and they stood at the nether part of the mount.

¹⁸And mount Sinai was altogether on a smoke, because the LORD descended upon it in fire: and the smoke thereof ascended as the smoke of a furnace, and the whole mount quaked greatly.

¹⁹And when the voice of the trumpet sounded long, and waxed louder and louder, Moses spake, and God answered him by a voice.

²⁰And the LORD came down upon mount Sinai, on the top of the mount: and the LORD called Moses *up* to the top of the mount; and Moses went up.

²¹And the LORD said unto Moses, Go down, ᵍcharge the people, lest they break through unto the LORD to gaze, and many of them perish.

²²And let the priests also, which come near to the LORD, sanctify themselves, lest the LORD break forth upon them.

²³And Moses said unto the LORD, The people cannot come up to mount Sinai: for thou chargedst us, saying, Set bounds about the mount, and sanctify it.

²⁴And the LORD said unto him, Away, get thee down, and thou shalt come up, thou, and Aaron with thee: but let not the priests and the people break through to come up unto the LORD, lest he break forth upon them.

²⁵So Moses went down unto the people, and spake unto them.

The Ten Commandments

20 AND GOD spake all these words, saying, ²I *am* the LORD thy God, which have brought thee out of the land of Egypt, out of the house of ʰbondage.

³Thou shalt have no other gods before me.

⁴Thou shalt not make unto thee any graven image, or any likeness *of any thing* that *is* in heaven above, or that *is* in the earth beneath, or that *is* in the water under the earth:

⁵Thou shalt not bow down thyself to them, nor serve them: for I the LORD thy God *am* a jealous God, visiting the iniquity of the fathers upon the children unto the third and fourth *generation* of them that hate me;

⁶And showing mercy unto thousands of them that love me, and keep my commandments.

⁷Thou shalt not take the name of the LORD thy God in vain; for the LORD will not hold him guiltless that taketh his name in vain.

⁸Remember the sabbath day, to keep it holy.

⁹Six days shalt thou labour, and do all thy work:

¹⁰But the seventh day *is* the sabbath of the LORD thy God: *in it* thou shalt not do any work, thou, nor thy son, nor thy daughter, thy manservant, nor thy maidservant, nor thy cattle, nor thy stranger that *is* within thy gates:

¹¹For *in* six days the LORD made heaven and earth, the sea, and all that in them *is,* and rested the seventh day: wherefore the LORD blessed the sabbath day, and hallowed it.

¹² ¶ Honour thy father and thy mother: that thy days may be long upon the land which the LORD thy God giveth thee.

¹³Thou shalt not kill.

Amplified

¹⁶The third morning there were thunders and lightnings, and a thick cloud upon the mountain, and a very loud trumpet blast, so that all the people in the camp trembled.

¹⁷Then Moses brought the people from the camp to meet God, and they stood at the foot of the mountain.

¹⁸Mount Sinai was wrapped in smoke, for the Lord descended upon it in fire; its smoke ascended like that of a furnace, and the whole mountain quaked greatly.

¹⁹As the trumpet blast grew louder and louder, Moses spoke and God answered him with a voice. [Deut. 4:12.]

²⁰The Lord came down upon Mount Sinai to the top of the mountain, and the Lord called Moses to the top of mountain, and Moses went up.

²¹The Lord said to Moses, Go down and warn the people, lest they break through to the Lord to gaze and many of them perish.

²²And also let the priests, who come near to the Lord, sanctify (set apart) themselves [for God], lest the Lord break forth against them.

²³And Moses said to the Lord, The people cannot come up to Mount Sinai, for You Yourself charged us, saying, Set bounds about the mountain and sanctify it [set it apart for God].

²⁴Then the Lord said to him, Go, get down and you shall come up, you and Aaron with you; but let not the priests and the people break through to come up to the Lord, lest He break forth against them.

²⁵So Moses went down to the people and told them.

20 THEN GOD spoke all these words: ²I am the Lord your God, Who has brought you out of the land of Egypt, out of the house of bondage.

³You shall have no other gods before *or* besides Me.

⁴You shall not make yourself any graven image [to worship it] or any likeness of anything that is in the heavens above, or that is in the earth beneath, or that is in the water under the earth;

⁵You shall not bow down yourself to them or serve them; for I the Lord your God am a jealous God, visiting the iniquity of the fathers upon the children to the third and fourth generation of those who hate Me, [Isa. 42:8; 48:11.]

⁶But showing mercy *and* steadfast love to a thousand generations of those who love Me and keep My commandments.

⁷You shall not use *or* repeat the name of the Lord your God in vain [that is, lightly or frivolously, in false affirmations or profanely]; for the Lord will not hold him guiltless who takes His name in vain.

⁸[Earnestly] remember the Sabbath day, to keep it holy (withdrawn from common employment and dedicated to God).

⁹Six days you shall labor and do all your work,

¹⁰But the seventh day is a Sabbath to the Lord your God; in it you shall not do any work, you, or your son, your daughter, your manservant, your maidservant, your domestic animals, or the sojourner within your gates.

¹¹For in six days the Lord made the heavens and the earth, the sea, and all that is in them, and rested the seventh day. That is why the Lord blessed the Sabbath day and hallowed it [set it apart for His purposes].

¹²Regard (treat with honor, due obedience, and courtesy) your father and mother, that your days may be long in the land the Lord your God gives you.

¹³You shall not commit murder.

ᵍ Heb. *contest*   ʰ Heb. *servants*

New American Standard

16 ¶ So it came about on the third day, when it was morning, that there were thunder and lightning flashes and a thick cloud upon the mountain and a very loud trumpet sound, so that all the people who *were* in the camp trembled.

17 And Moses brought the people out of the camp to meet God, and they stood at the foot of the mountain.

The LORD Visits Sinai

18 Now Mount Sinai *was* all in smoke because the LORD descended upon it in fire; and its smoke ascended like the smoke of a furnace, and the whole mountain quaked violently.

19 When the sound of the trumpet grew louder and louder, Moses spoke and God answered him with thunder.

20 The LORD came down on Mount Sinai, to the top of the mountain; and the LORD called Moses to the top of the mountain, and Moses went up.

21 Then the LORD spoke to Moses, "Go down, warn the people, so that they do not break through to the LORD to gaze, and many of them perish.

22 "Also let the priests who come near to the LORD consecrate themselves, or else the LORD will break out against them."

23 Moses said to the LORD, "The people cannot come up to Mount Sinai, for You warned us, saying, 'Set bounds about the mountain and consecrate it.' "

24 Then the LORD said to him, "Go down and come up *again,* you and Aaron with you; but do not let the priests and the people break through to come up to the LORD, or He will break forth upon them."

25 So Moses went down to the people and told them.

The Ten Commandments

20 THEN GOD spoke all these words, saying,

2 ¶ "I am the LORD your God, who brought you out of the land of Egypt, out of the house of slavery.

3 ¶ "You shall have no other gods s before Me.

4 ¶ "You shall not make for yourself t an idol, or any likeness of what is in heaven above or on the earth beneath or in the water under the earth.

5 "You shall not worship them or serve them; for I, the LORD your God, am a jealous God, visiting the iniquity of the fathers on the children, on the third and the fourth generations of those who hate Me,

6 but showing lovingkindness to thousands, to those who love Me and keep My commandments.

7 ¶ "You shall not take the name of the LORD your God in vain, for the LORD will not leave him unpunished who takes His name in vain.

8 ¶ "Remember the sabbath day, to keep it holy.

9 "Six days you shall labor and do all your work,

10 but the seventh day is a sabbath of the LORD your God; *in it* you shall not do any work, you or your son or your daughter, your male or your female servant or your cattle or your sojourner who stays with you.

11 "For in six days the LORD made the heavens and the earth, the sea and all that is in them, and rested on the seventh day; therefore the LORD blessed the sabbath day and made it holy.

12 ¶ "Honor your father and your mother, that your days may be prolonged in the land which the LORD your God gives you.

13 ¶ "You shall not murder.

New International

16 On the morning of the third day there was thunder and lightning, with a thick cloud over the mountain, and a very loud trumpet blast. Everyone in the camp trembled. 17 Then Moses led the people out of the camp to meet with God, and they stood at the foot of the mountain. 18 Mount Sinai was covered with smoke, because the LORD descended on it in fire. The smoke billowed up from it like smoke from a furnace, the whole mountain p trembled violently, 19 and the sound of the trumpet grew louder and louder. Then Moses spoke and the voice of God answered him. q

20 The LORD descended to the top of Mount Sinai and called Moses to the top of the mountain. So Moses went up 21 and the LORD said to him, "Go down and warn the people so they do not force their way through to see the LORD and many of them perish. 22 Even the priests, who approach the LORD, must consecrate themselves, or the LORD will break out against them."

23 Moses said to the LORD, "The people cannot come up Mount Sinai, because you yourself warned us, 'Put limits around the mountain and set it apart as holy.' "

24 The LORD replied, "Go down and bring Aaron up with you. But the priests and the people must not force their way through to come up to the LORD, or he will break out against them."

25 So Moses went down to the people and told them.

The Ten Commandments

20 AND GOD spoke all these words:

2 "I am the LORD your God, who brought you out of Egypt, out of the house of slavery.

3 "You shall have no other gods before r me.

4 "You shall not make for yourself an idol in the form of anything in heaven above or on the earth beneath or in the waters below. 5 You shall not bow down to them or worship them; for I, the LORD your God, am a jealous God, punishing the children for the sin of the fathers to the third and fourth generation of those who hate me, 6 but showing love to a thousand ⌊generations⌋ of those who love me and keep my commandments.

7 "You shall not misuse the name of the LORD your God, for the LORD will not hold anyone guiltless who misuses his name.

8 "Remember the Sabbath day by keeping it holy. 9 Six days you shall labor and do all your work, 10 but the seventh day is a Sabbath to the LORD your God. On it you shall not do any work, neither you, nor your son or daughter, nor your manservant or maidservant, nor your animals, nor the alien within your gates. 11 For in six days the LORD made the heavens and the earth, the sea, and all that is in them, but he rested on the seventh day. Therefore the LORD blessed the Sabbath day and made it holy.

12 Honor your father and your mother, so that you may live long in the land the LORD your God is giving you.

13 "You shall not murder.

---

p 18 Most Hebrew manuscripts; a few Hebrew manuscripts and Septuagint *all the people*   q 19 Or *and God answered him with thunder*   r 3 Or *besides*

---

s Or *besides Me*   t Or *a graven image*

King James

¹⁴Thou shalt not commit adultery.

¹⁵Thou shalt not steal.

¹⁶Thou shalt not bear false witness against thy neighbour.

¹⁷Thou shalt not covet thy neighbour's house, thou shalt not covet thy neighbour's wife, nor his manservant, nor his maidservant, nor his ox, nor his ass, nor any thing that is thy neighbour's.

¹⁸ ¶ And all the people saw the thunderings, and the lightnings, and the noise of the trumpet, and the mountain smoking: and when the people saw it, they removed, and stood afar off.

¹⁹And they said unto Moses, Speak thou with us, and we will hear: but let not God speak with us, lest we die.

²⁰And Moses said unto the people, Fear not: for God is come to prove you, and that his fear may be before your faces, that ye sin not.

Making an altar of earth

²¹And the people stood afar off, and Moses drew near unto the thick darkness where God was.

²² ¶ And the LORD said unto Moses, Thus thou shalt say unto the children of Israel, Ye have seen that I have talked with you from heaven.

²³Ye shall not make with me gods of silver, neither shall ye make unto you gods of gold.

²⁴ ¶ An altar of earth thou shalt make unto me, and shalt sacrifice thereon thy burnt offerings, and thy peace offerings, thy sheep, and thine oxen: in all places where I record my name I will come unto thee, and I will bless thee.

²⁵And if thou wilt make me an altar of stone, thou shalt not ⁱbuild it of hewn stone: for if thou lift up thy tool upon it, thou hast polluted it.

²⁶Neither shalt thou go up by steps unto mine altar, that thy nakedness be not discovered thereon.

Laws about servants

21 NOW THESE are the judgments which thou shalt set before them.

²If thou buy an Hebrew servant, six years he shall serve: and in the seventh he shall go out free for nothing.

³If he came in ^jby himself, he shall go out by himself: if he were married, then his wife shall go out with him.

⁴If his master have given him a wife, and she have born him sons or daughters; the wife and her children shall be her master's, and he shall go out by himself.

⁵And if the servant ^kshall plainly say, I love my master, my wife, and my children; I will not go out free:

⁶Then his master shall bring him unto the judges; he shall also bring him to the door, or unto the door post; and his master shall bore his ear through with an awl; and he shall serve him for ever.

⁷ ¶ And if a man sell his daughter to be a maidservant, she shall not go out as the menservants do.

⁸If she ^lplease not her master, who hath betrothed her to himself, then shall he let her be redeemed: to sell her unto a strange nation he shall have no power, seeing he hath dealt deceitfully with her.

⁹And if he have betrothed her unto his son, he shall deal with her after the manner of daughters.

Amplified

¹⁴You shall not commit ^madultery. [Prov. 6:25, 26; Matt. 5:28; Rom. 1:24; Eph. 5:3.]

¹⁵You shall not steal. [Prov. 11:1; 16:8; 21:6; 22:16; Jer. 17:11; Mal. 3:8.]

¹⁶You shall not witness falsely against your neighbor. [Exod. 23:1; Prov. 19:9; 24:28.]

¹⁷You shall not covet your neighbor's house, your neighbor's wife, or his manservant, or his maidservant, or his ox, or his donkey, or anything that is your neighbor's. [Luke 12:15; Col. 3:5.]

¹⁸Now all the people perceived the thunderings and the lightnings and the noise of the trumpet and the smoking mountain, and as [they] looked they trembled with fear and fell back and stood afar off.

¹⁹And they said to Moses, You speak to us and we will listen, but let not God speak to us, lest we die.

²⁰And Moses said to the people, Fear not; for God has come to prove you, so that the [reverential] fear of Him may be before you, that you may not sin.

²¹And the people stood afar off, but Moses drew near to the thick darkness where God was.

²²And the Lord said to Moses, Thus shall you say to the Israelites, You have seen for yourselves that I have talked with you from heaven.

²³You shall not make [gods to share] with Me [My glory and your worship]; gods of silver or gods of gold you shall not make for yourselves.

²⁴An altar of earth you shall make to Me and sacrifice on it your burnt offerings and your peace offerings, your sheep and your oxen. In every place where I record My name and cause it to be remembered I will come to you and bless you.

²⁵And if you will make Me an altar of stone, you shall not build it of hewn stone, for if you lift up a tool upon it you have polluted it.

²⁶Neither shall you go up by steps to My altar, that your nakedness be not exposed upon it.

21 NOW THESE are the ordinances you [Moses] shall set before [the Israelites].

²If you buy a Hebrew servant [as the result of debt or theft], he shall serve six years, and in the seventh he shall go out free, paying nothing. [Lev. 25:39.]

³If he came [to you] by himself, he shall go out by himself; if he came married, then his wife shall go out with him.

⁴If his master has given him a wife and she has borne him sons or daughters, the wife and her children shall be her master's, and he shall go out [of your service] alone.

⁵But if the servant shall plainly say, I love my master, my wife, and my children; I will not go free,

⁶Then his master shall bring him to God [the judges as His agents]; he shall bring him to the door or doorpost and shall pierce his ear with an awl; and he shall serve him for life.

⁷If a man sells his daughter to be a maidservant or bondwoman, she shall not go out [in six years] as menservants do.

⁸If she does not please her master who has not espoused her to himself, he shall let her be redeemed. To sell her to a foreign people he shall have no power, for he has dealt faithlessly with her.

⁹And if he espouses her to his son, he shall deal with her as with a daughter.

---

^mObserve here the expansion of the meaning of the seventh commandment in many catechisms to include whoredom in all its forms, as well as unchastity [premarital relations, sexual impurity, and lustful desire under whatever name] (J.P. Lange, *A Commentary*). Not only is adultery forbidden here, but also fornication and all kinds of mental and sensual uncleanness. All impure books, songs, pictures, etc., which tend to inflame and debauch the mind are against this law (Adam Clarke, *The Holy Bible with A Commentary*).

ⁱHeb. *build them* with *hewing*   ^jHeb. *with his body*   ^kHeb. *saying shall say*   ^lHeb. *be evil in the eyes of*

New American Standard

14 ¶ "You shall not commit adultery.

15 ¶ "You shall not steal.

16 ¶ "You shall not bear false witness against your neighbor.

17 ¶ "You shall not covet your neighbor's house; you shall not covet your neighbor's wife or his male servant or his female servant or his ox or his donkey or anything that belongs to your neighbor."

18 ¶ All the people perceived the thunder and the lightning flashes and the sound of the trumpet and the mountain smoking; and when the people saw *it*, they trembled and stood at a distance.

19 Then they said to Moses, "Speak to us yourself and we will listen; but let not God speak to us, or we will die."

20 Moses said to the people, "Do not be afraid; for God has come in order to test you, and in order that the fear of Him may remain with you, so that you may not sin."

21 So the people stood at a distance, while Moses approached the thick cloud where God *was*.

22 ¶ Then the LORD said to Moses, "Thus you shall say to the sons of Israel, 'You yourselves have seen that I have spoken to you from heaven.

23 'You shall not make *other gods* besides Me; gods of silver or gods of gold, you shall not make for yourselves.

24 'You shall make an altar of earth for Me, and you shall sacrifice on it your burnt offerings and your peace offerings, your sheep and your oxen; in every place where I cause My name to be remembered, I will come to you and bless you.

25 'If you make an altar of stone for Me, you shall not build it of cut stones, for if you wield your tool on it, you will profane it.

26 'And you shall not go up by steps to My altar, so that your nakedness will not be exposed on it.'

Ordinances for the People

21 "NOW THESE are the ordinances which you are to set before them:

2 ¶ "If you buy a Hebrew slave, he shall serve for six years; but on the seventh he shall go out as a free man without payment.

3 "If he comes alone, he shall go out alone; if he is the husband of a wife, then his wife shall go out with him.

4 "If his master gives him a wife, and she bears him sons or daughters, the wife and her children shall belong to her master, and he shall go out alone.

5 "But if the slave plainly says, 'I love my master, my wife and my children; I will not go out as a free man,'

6 then his master shall bring him to "God, then he shall bring him to the door or the doorpost. And his master shall pierce his ear with an awl; and he shall serve him permanently.

7 ¶ "If a man sells his daughter as a female slave, she is not to go free as the male slaves do.

8 "If she is displeasing in the eyes of her master who designated her for himself, then he shall let her be redeemed. He does not have authority to sell her to a foreign people because of his unfairness to her.

9 "If he designates her for his son, he shall deal with her according to the custom of daughters.

New International

14 "You shall not commit adultery.

15 "You shall not steal.

16 "You shall not give false testimony against your neighbor.

17 "You shall not covet your neighbor's house. You shall not covet your neighbor's wife, or his manservant or maidservant, his ox or donkey, or anything that belongs to your neighbor."

18 When the people saw the thunder and lightning and heard the trumpet and saw the mountain in smoke, they trembled with fear. They stayed at a distance 19 and said to Moses, "Speak to us yourself and we will listen. But do not have God speak to us or we will die."

20 Moses said to the people, "Do not be afraid. God has come to test you, so that the fear of God will be with you to keep you from sinning."

21 The people remained at a distance, while Moses approached the thick darkness where God was.

Idols and Altars

22 Then the LORD said to Moses, "Tell the Israelites this: 'You have seen for yourselves that I have spoken to you from heaven: 23 Do not make any gods to be alongside me; do not make for yourselves gods of silver or gods of gold.

24 " 'Make an altar of earth for me and sacrifice on it your burnt offerings and fellowship offerings,ˢ your sheep and goats and your cattle. Wherever I cause my name to be honored, I will come to you and bless you. 25 If you make an altar of stones for me, do not build it with dressed stones, for you will defile it if you use a tool on it. 26 And do not go up to my altar on steps, lest your nakedness be exposed on it.'

21 "THESE ARE the laws you are to set before them:

Hebrew Servants

2 "If you buy a Hebrew servant, he is to serve you for six years. But in the seventh year, he shall go free, without paying anything. 3 If he comes alone, he is to go free alone; but if he has a wife when he comes, she is to go with him. 4 If his master gives him a wife and she bears him sons or daughters, the woman and her children shall belong to her master, and only the man shall go free.

5 "But if the servant declares, 'I love my master and my wife and children and do not want to go free,' 6 then his master must take him before the judges.ᵗ He shall take him to the door or the doorpost and pierce his ear with an awl. Then he will be his servant for life.

7 "If a man sells his daughter as a servant, she is not to go free as menservants do. 8 If she does not please the master who has selected her for himself,ᵘ he must let her be redeemed. He has no right to sell her to foreigners, because he has broken faith with her. 9 If he selects her for

King James

Amplified

¹⁰If he take him another *wife;* her food, her raiment, and her duty of marriage, shall he not diminish.

¹¹And if he do not these three unto her, then shall she go out free without money.

Laws about murder and strife

¹² ¶ He that smiteth a man, so that he die, shall be surely put to death.

¹³And if a man lie not in wait, but God deliver *him* into his hand; then I will appoint thee a place whither he shall flee:

¹⁴But if a man come presumptuously upon his neighbour, to slay him with guile; thou shalt take him from mine altar, that he may die.

¹⁵ ¶ And he that smiteth his father, or his mother, shall be surely put to death.

¹⁶ ¶ And he that stealeth a man, and selleth him, or if he be found in his hand, he shall surely be put to death.

¹⁷ ¶ And he that ^mcurseth his father, or his mother, shall surely be put to death.

¹⁸ ¶ And if men strive together, and one smite ⁿanother with a stone, or with *his* fist, and he die not, but keepeth *his* bed:

¹⁹If he rise again, and walk abroad upon his staff, then shall he that smote *him* be quit: only he shall pay *for* ^othe loss of his time, and shall cause *him* to be thoroughly healed.

²⁰ ¶ And if a man smite his servant, or his maid, with a rod, and he die under his hand; he shall be surely ^ppunished.

²¹Notwithstanding, if he continue a day or two, he shall not be punished: for he *is* his money.

²² ¶ If men strive, and hurt a woman with child, so that her fruit depart *from her,* and yet no mischief follow: he shall be surely punished, according as the woman's husband will lay upon him; and he shall pay as the judges *determine.*

²³And if *any* mischief follow, then thou shalt give life for life,

²⁴Eye for eye, tooth for tooth, hand for hand, foot for foot,

²⁵Burning for burning, wound for wound, stripe for stripe.

²⁶ ¶ And if a man smite the eye of his servant, or the eye of his maid, that it perish; he shall let him go free for his eye's sake.

²⁷And if he smite out his manservant's tooth, or his maidservant's tooth; he shall let him go free for his tooth's sake.

²⁸ ¶ If an ox gore a man or a woman, that they die: then the ox shall be surely stoned, and his flesh shall not be eaten; but the owner of the ox *shall be* quit.

²⁹But if the ox were wont to push with his horn in time past, and it hath been testified to his owner, and he hath not kept him in, but that he hath killed a man or a woman; the ox shall be stoned, and his owner also shall be put to death.

³⁰If there be laid on him a sum of money, then he shall give for the ransom of his life whatsoever is laid upon him.

³¹Whether he have gored a son, or have gored a daughter, according to this judgment shall it be done unto him.

³²If the ox shall push a manservant or a maidservant; he shall give unto their master thirty shekels of silver, and the ox shall be stoned.

³³ ¶ And if a man shall open a pit, or if a man shall dig a pit, and not cover it, and an ox or an ass fall therein;

³⁴The owner of the pit shall make *it* good, *and* give money unto the owner of them; and the dead *beast* shall be his.

³⁵ ¶ And if one man's ox hurt another's, that he die; then they shall sell the live ox, and divide the money of it; and the dead *ox* also they shall divide.

¹⁰If he marries again, her food, clothing, and privilege as a wife shall he not diminish.

¹¹And if he does not do these three things for her, then shall she go out free, without payment of money.

¹²Whoever strikes a man so that he dies shall be surely put to death.

¹³But if he did not lie in wait for him, but God allowed him to fall into his hand, then I will appoint you a place to which he may flee [for protection until duly tried]. [Num. 35:22–28.]

¹⁴But if a man comes willfully upon another to slay him craftily, you shall take him from My altar [to which he may have fled for protection], that he may die.

¹⁵Whoever strikes his father or his mother shall surely be put to death.

¹⁶Whoever kidnaps a man, whether he sells him or is found with him in his possession, shall surely be put to death.

¹⁷Whoever curses his father or his mother shall surely be put to death.

¹⁸If men quarrel and one strikes another with a stone or with his fist and he does not die but keeps his bed,

¹⁹If he rises again and walks about leaning upon his staff, then he that struck him shall be clear, except he must pay for the loss of his time and shall cause him to be thoroughly healed.

²⁰And if a man strikes his servant or his maid with a rod and he [or she] dies under his hand, he shall surely be punished.

²¹But if the servant lives on for a day or two, the offender shall not be punished, for he [has injured] his own property.

²²If men contend with each other, and a pregnant woman [interfering] is hurt so that she has a miscarriage, yet no further damage follows, [the one who hurt her] shall surely be punished with a fine [paid] to the woman's husband, as much as the judges determine.

²³But if any damage follows, then you shall give life for life,

²⁴Eye for eye, tooth for tooth, hand for hand, foot for foot,

²⁵Burn for burn, wound for wound, and lash for lash.

²⁶And if a man hits the eye of his servant or the eye of his maid so that it is destroyed, he shall let him go free for his eye's sake.

²⁷And if he knocks out his manservant's tooth or his maidservant's tooth, he shall let him go free for his tooth's sake.

²⁸If an ox gores a man or a woman to death, then the ox shall surely be stoned, and its flesh shall not be eaten; but the owner of the ox shall be clear.

²⁹But if the ox has tried to gore before, and its owner has been warned but has not kept it closed in and it kills a man or a woman, the ox shall be stoned and its owner also put to death.

³⁰If a ransom is put on [the man's] life, then he shall give for the redemption of his life whatever is laid upon him.

³¹If the [man's ox] has gored another's son or daughter, he shall be dealt with according to this same rule.

³²If the ox gores a manservant or a maidservant, the owner shall give to their master thirty shekels of silver, and the ox shall be stoned.

³³If a man leaves a pit open or digs a pit and does not cover it and an ox or a donkey falls into it,

³⁴The owner of the pit shall make it good; he shall give money to the animal's owner, but the dead beast shall be his.

³⁵If one man's ox hurts another's so that it dies, they shall sell the live ox and divide the price of it; the dead ox also they shall divide between them.

---

^mOr, *revileth*   ⁿOr, *his neighbour*   ^oHeb. *his ceasing*
^pHeb. *avenged*

New American Standard

10"If he takes to himself another woman, he may not reduce her food, her clothing, or her conjugal rights.

11"If he will not do these three *things* for her, then she shall go out for nothing, without *payment of* money.

Personal Injuries

12 ¶ "He who strikes a man so that he dies shall surely be put to death.

13"But if he did not lie in wait *for him,* but God let *him* fall into his hand, then I will appoint you a place to which he may flee.

14"If, however, a man acts presumptuously toward his neighbor, so as to kill him craftily, you are to take him *even* from My altar, that he may die.

15 ¶ "He who strikes his father or his mother shall surely be put to death.

16 ¶ "He who kidnaps a man, whether he sells him or he is found in his possession, shall surely be put to death.

17 ¶ "He who curses his father or his mother shall surely be put to death.

18 ¶ "If men have a quarrel and one strikes the other with a stone or with *his* fist, and he does not die but remains in bed,

19 if he gets up and walks around outside on his staff, then he who struck him shall go unpunished; he shall only pay for his loss of time, and shall take care of him until he is completely healed.

20 ¶ "If a man strikes his male or female slave with a rod and he dies at his hand, he shall be punished.

21"If, however, he survives a day or two, no vengeance shall be taken; for he is his property.

22 ¶ "If men struggle with each other and strike a woman with child so that she gives birth prematurely, yet there is no injury, he shall surely be fined as the woman's husband may demand of him, and he shall pay as the judges *decide.*

23"But if there is *any further* injury, then you shall appoint *as a penalty* life for life,

24 eye for eye, tooth for tooth, hand for hand, foot for foot,

25 burn for burn, wound for wound, bruise for bruise.

26 ¶ "If a man strikes the eye of his male or female slave, and destroys it, he shall let him go free on account of his eye.

27"And if he knocks out a tooth of his male or female slave, he shall let him go free on account of his tooth.

28 ¶ "If an ox gores a man or a woman to death, the ox shall surely be stoned and its flesh shall not be eaten; but the owner of the ox shall go unpunished.

29"If, however, an ox was previously in the habit of goring and its owner has been warned, yet he does not confine it and it kills a man or a woman, the ox shall be stoned and its owner also shall be put to death.

30"If a ransom is demanded of him, then he shall give for the redemption of his life whatever is demanded of him.

31"Whether it gores a son or a daughter, it shall be done to him according to the same rule.

32"If the ox gores a male or female slave, the owner shall give his *or her* master thirty shekels of silver, and the ox shall be stoned.

33 ¶ "If a man opens a pit, or digs a pit and does not cover it over, and an ox or a donkey falls into it,

34 the owner of the pit shall make restitution; he shall give money to its owner, and the dead *animal* shall become his.

35 ¶ "If one man's ox hurts another's so that it dies, then they shall sell the live ox and divide its price equally; and also they shall divide the dead *ox.*

New International

his son, he must grant her the rights of a daughter. 10If he marries another woman, he must not deprive the first one of her food, clothing and marital rights. 11If he does not provide her with these three things, she is to go free, without any payment of money.

Personal Injuries

12"Anyone who strikes a man and kills him shall surely be put to death. 13However, if he does not do it intentionally, but God lets it happen, he is to flee to a place I will designate. 14But if a man schemes and kills another man deliberately, take him away from my altar and put him to death.

15"Anyone who attacksv his father or his mother must be put to death.

16"Anyone who kidnaps another and either sells him or still has him when he is caught must be put to death.

17"Anyone who curses his father or mother must be put to death.

18"If men quarrel and one hits the other with a stone or with his fistw and he does not die but is confined to bed, 19the one who struck the blow will not be held responsible if the other gets up and walks around outside with his staff; however, he must pay the injured man for the loss of his time and see that he is completely healed.

20"If a man beats his male or female slave with a rod and the slave dies as a direct result, he must be punished, 21but he is not to be punished if the slave gets up after a day or two, since the slave is his property.

22"If men who are fighting hit a pregnant woman and she gives birth prematurelyx but there is no serious injury, the offender must be fined whatever the woman's husband demands and the court allows. 23But if there is serious injury, you are to take life for life, 24eye for eye, tooth for tooth, hand for hand, foot for foot, 25burn for burn, wound for wound, bruise for bruise.

26"If a man hits a manservant or maidservant in the eye and destroys it, he must let the servant go free to compensate for the eye. 27And if he knocks out the tooth of a manservant or maidservant, he must let the servant go free to compensate for the tooth.

28"If a bull gores a man or a woman to death, the bull must be stoned to death, and its meat must not be eaten. But the owner of the bull will not be held responsible. 29If, however, the bull has had the habit of goring and the owner has been warned but has not kept it penned up and it kills a man or woman, the bull must be stoned and the owner also must be put to death. 30However, if payment is demanded of him, he may redeem his life by paying whatever is demanded. 31This law also applies if the bull gores a son or daughter. 32If the bull gores a male or female slave, the owner must pay thirty shekelsy of silver to the master of the slave, and the bull must be stoned.

33"If a man uncovers a pit or digs one and fails to cover it and an ox or a donkey falls into it, 34the owner of the pit must pay for the loss; he must pay its owner, and the dead animal will be his.

35"If a man's bull injures the bull of another and it dies, they are to sell the live one and divide both the money and

---

v 15 Or kills   w 18 Or *with a tool*   x 22 Or *she has a*
miscarriage   y 32 That is, about 12 ounces (about 0.3 kilogram)

King James

36Or if it be known that the ox hath used to push in time past, and his owner hath not kept him in; he shall surely pay ox for ox; and the dead shall be his own.

Laws about property

22 IF A man shall steal an ox, or a qsheep, and kill it, or sell it; he shall restore five oxen for an ox, and four sheep for a sheep.

2 ¶ If a thief be found breaking up, and be smitten that he die, *there shall* no blood *be shed* for him.

3If the sun be risen upon him, *there shall be* blood *shed* for him; *for* he should make full restitution; if he have nothing, then he shall be sold for his theft.

4If the theft be certainly found in his hand alive, whether it be ox, or ass, or sheep; he shall restore double.

5 ¶ If a man shall cause a field or vineyard to be eaten, and shall put in his beast, and shall feed in another man's field; of the best of his own field, and of the best of his own vineyard, shall he make restitution.

6 ¶ If fire break out, and catch in thorns, so that the stacks of corn, or the standing corn, or the field, be consumed *therewith;* he that kindled the fire shall surely make restitution.

7 ¶ If a man shall deliver unto his neighbour money or stuff to keep, and it be stolen out of the man's house; if the thief be found, let him pay double.

8If the thief be not found, then the master of the house shall be brought unto the judges, *to see* whether he have put his hand unto his neighbour's goods.

9For all manner of trespass, *whether it be* for ox, for ass, for sheep, for raiment, *or* for any manner of lost thing, which *another* challengeth to be his, the cause of both parties shall come before the judges; *and* whom the judges shall condemn, he shall pay double unto his neighbour.

10If a man deliver unto his neighbour an ass, or an ox, or a sheep, or any beast, to keep; and it die, or be hurt, or driven away, no man seeing *it:*

11*Then* shall an oath of the LORD be between them both, that he hath not put his hand unto his neighbour's goods; and the owner of it shall accept *thereof,* and he shall not make *it* good.

12And if it be stolen from him, he shall make restitution unto the owner thereof.

13If it be torn in pieces, *then* let him bring it *for* witness, *and* he shall not make good that which was torn.

14 ¶ And if a man borrow *aught* of his neighbour, and it be hurt, or die, the owner thereof *being* not with it, he shall surely make *it* good.

15*But* if the owner thereof *be* with it, he shall not make *it* good: if it *be* an hired *thing,* it came for his hire.

Laws about personal actions

16 ¶ And if a man entice a maid that is not betrothed, and lie with her, he shall surely endow her to be his wife.

17If her father utterly refuse to give her unto him, he shall rpay money according to the dowry of virgins.

18 ¶ Thou shalt not suffer a witch to live.

19 ¶ Whosoever lieth with a beast shall surely be put to death.

20 ¶ He that sacrificeth unto *any* god, save unto the LORD only, he shall be utterly destroyed.

21 ¶ Thou shalt neither vex a stranger, nor oppress him: for ye were strangers in the land of Egypt.

22 ¶ Ye shall not afflict any widow, or fatherless child.

23If thou afflict them in any wise, and they cry at all unto me, I will surely hear their cry;

24And my wrath shall wax hot, and I will kill you with the sword; and your wives shall be widows, and your children fatherless.

Amplified

36Or if it is known that the ox has gored in the past, and its owner has not kept it closed in, he shall surely pay ox for ox, and the dead beast shall be his.

22 IF A man steals an ox or sheep and kills or sells it, he shall pay five oxen for an ox, or four sheep for a sheep.

2If a thief is found breaking in and is struck so that he dies, there shall be no blood shed for him.

3But if the sun has risen [so he can be seen], blood must be shed for slaying him. The thief [if he lives] must make full restitution; if he has nothing, then he shall be sold for his theft.

4If the beast which he stole is found in his possession alive, whether it is ox or ass or sheep, he shall restore double.

5If a man causes a field or vineyard to be grazed over or lets his beast loose and it feeds in another man's field, he shall make restitution of the best of his own field or his own vineyard.

6If fire breaks out and catches so that the stacked grain or standing grain or the field be consumed, he who kindled the fire shall make full restitution.

7If a man delivers to his neighbor money or goods to keep and it is stolen out of the neighbor's house, then, if the thief is found, he shall pay double.

8But if the thief is not found, the house owner shall appear before God [the judges as His agents] to find whether he stole his neighbor's goods.

9For every unlawful deed, whether it concerns ox, donkey, sheep, clothing, or any lost thing at all, which another identifies as his, the cause of both parties shall come before God [the judges]. Whomever [they] shall condemn shall pay his neighbor double.

10If a man delivers to his neighbor a donkey or an ox or a sheep or any beast to keep and it dies or is hurt or driven away, no man seeing it,

11Then an oath before the Lord shall be required between the two that the man has not taken his neighbor's property; and the owner of it shall accept his word and not require him to make good the loss.

12But if it is stolen when in his care, he shall make restitution to its owner.

13If it be torn in pieces [by some wild beast or by accident], let him bring it [the mangled carcass] for witness; he shall not make good what was torn.

14And if a man borrows anything of his neighbor and it gets hurt or dies without its owner being with it, the borrower shall make full restitution.

15But if the owner is with it [when the damage is done], the borrower shall not make it good. If it is a hired thing, the damage is included in its hire.

16If a man seduces a virgin not betrothed and lies with her, he shall surely pay a dowry for her to become his wife.

17If her father utterly refuses to give her to him, he shall pay money equivalent to the dowry of virgins.

18You shall not allow a woman to live who practices sorcery.

19Whoever lies carnally with a beast shall surely be put to death.

20He who sacrifices to any god but the Lord only shall be utterly destroyed.

21You shall not wrong a stranger or oppress him; for you were strangers in the land of Egypt.

22You shall not afflict any widow or fatherless child.

23If you afflict them in any way and they cry at all to Me, I will surely hear their cry;

24And My wrath shall burn; I will kill you with the sword, and your wives shall be widows and your children fatherless.

---

qOr, goat   rHeb. weigh; see Gen. 23:16

New American Standard

36"Or *if* it is known that the ox was previously in the habit of goring, yet its owner has not confined it, he shall surely pay ox for ox, and the dead *animal* shall become his.

Property Rights

22 "IF A man steals an ox or a sheep and slaughters it or sells it, he shall pay five oxen for the ox and four sheep for the sheep.

2 ¶ "If the thief is caught while breaking in and is struck so that he dies, there will be no bloodguiltiness on his account.

3"*But* if the sun has risen on him, there will be bloodguiltiness on his account. He shall surely make restitution; if he owns nothing, then he shall be sold for his theft.

4"If what he stole is actually found alive in his possession, whether an ox or a donkey or a sheep, he shall pay double.

5 ¶ "If a man lets a field or vineyard be grazed *bare* and lets his animal loose so that it grazes in another man's field, he shall make restitution from the best of his own field and the best of his own vineyard.

6 ¶ "If a fire breaks out and spreads to thorn bushes, so that stacked grain or the standing grain or the field *itself* is consumed, he who started the fire shall surely make restitution.

7 ¶ "If a man gives his neighbor money or goods to keep *for him* and it is stolen from the man's house, if the thief is caught, he shall pay double.

8"If the thief is not caught, then the owner of the house shall appear before the judges, *to* determine whether he laid his hands on his neighbor's property.

9"For every breach of trust, *whether it is* for ox, for donkey, for sheep, for clothing, *or* for any lost thing about which one says, 'This is it,' the case of both parties shall come before the judges; he whom the judges condemn shall pay double to his neighbor.

10 ¶ "If a man gives his neighbor a donkey, an ox, a sheep, or any animal to keep *for him,* and it dies or is hurt or is driven away while no one is looking,

11 an oath before the LORD shall be made by the two of them that he has not laid hands on his neighbor's property; and its owner shall accept *it,* and he shall not make restitution.

12"But if it is actually stolen from him, he shall make restitution to its owner.

13"If it is all torn to pieces, let him bring it as evidence; he shall not make restitution for what has been torn to pieces.

14 ¶ "If a man borrows *anything* from his neighbor, and it is injured or dies while its owner is not with it, he shall make full restitution.

15"If its owner is with it, he shall not make restitution; if it is hired, it came for its hire.

Sundry Laws

16 ¶ "If a man seduces a virgin who is not engaged, and lies with her, he must pay a dowry for her *to be* his wife.

17"If her father absolutely refuses to give her to him, he shall pay money equal to the dowry for virgins.

18 ¶ "You shall not allow a sorceress to live.

19 ¶ "Whoever lies with an animal shall surely be put to death.

20 ¶ "He who sacrifices to any god, other than to the LORD alone, shall be utterly destroyed.

21 ¶ "You shall not wrong a stranger or oppress him, for you were strangers in the land of Egypt.

22"You shall not afflict any widow or orphan.

23"If you afflict him at all, *and* if he does cry out to Me, I will surely hear his cry;

24 and My anger will be kindled, and I will kill you with the sword, and your wives shall become widows and your children fatherless.

New International

the dead animal equally. 36However, if it was known that the bull had the habit of goring, yet the owner did not keep it penned up, the owner must pay, animal for animal, and the dead animal will be his.

Protection of Property

22 "IF A man steals an ox or a sheep and slaughters it or sells it, he must pay back five head of cattle for the ox and four sheep for the sheep.

2"If a thief is caught breaking in and is struck so that he dies, the defender is not guilty of bloodshed; 3but if it happens[z] after sunrise, he is guilty of bloodshed.

"A thief must certainly make restitution, but if he has nothing, he must be sold to pay for his theft.

4"If the stolen animal is found alive in his possession—whether ox or donkey or sheep—he must pay back double.

5"If a man grazes his livestock in a field or vineyard and lets them stray and they graze in another man's field, he must make restitution from the best of his own field or vineyard.

6"If a fire breaks out and spreads into thornbushes so that it burns shocks of grain or standing grain or the whole field, the one who started the fire must make restitution.

7"If a man gives his neighbor silver or goods for safekeeping and they are stolen from the neighbor's house, the thief, if he is caught, must pay back double. 8But if the thief is not found, the owner of the house must appear before the judges[a] to determine whether he has laid his hands on the other man's property. 9In all cases of illegal possession of an ox, a donkey, a sheep, a garment, or any other lost property about which somebody says, 'This is mine,' both parties are to bring their cases before the judges. The one whom the judges declare[b] guilty must pay back double to his neighbor.

10"If a man gives a donkey, an ox, a sheep or any other animal to his neighbor for safekeeping and it dies or is injured or is taken away while no one is looking, 11the issue between them will be settled by the taking of an oath before the LORD that the neighbor did not lay hands on the other person's property. The owner is to accept this, and no restitution is required. 12But if the animal was stolen from the neighbor, he must make restitution to the owner. 13If it was torn to pieces by a wild animal, he shall bring in the remains as evidence and he will not be required to pay for the torn animal.

14"If a man borrows an animal from his neighbor and it is injured or dies while the owner is not present, he must make restitution. 15But if the owner is with the animal, the borrower will not have to pay. If the animal was hired, the money paid for the hire covers the loss.

Social Responsibility

16"If a man seduces a virgin who is not pledged to be married and sleeps with her, he must pay the bride-price, and she shall be his wife. 17If her father absolutely refuses to give her to him, he must still pay the bride-price for virgins.

18"Do not allow a sorceress to live.

19"Anyone who has sexual relations with an animal must be put to death.

20"Whoever sacrifices to any god other than the LORD must be destroyed.[c]

21"Do not mistreat an alien or oppress him, for you were aliens in Egypt.

22"Do not take advantage of a widow or an orphan. 23If you do and they cry out to me, I will certainly hear their cry. 24My anger will be aroused, and I will kill you with the sword; your wives will become widows and your children fatherless.

z 3 Or *if he strikes him*   *a 8* Or *before God*; also in verse 9
b 9 Or *whom God declares*   *c 20* The Hebrew term refers to the irrevocable giving over of things or persons to the LORD, often by totally destroying them.

King James

²⁵ ¶ If thou lend money to *any of* my people *that is* poor by thee, thou shalt not be to him as an usurer, neither shalt thou lay upon him usury.

²⁶If thou at all take thy neighbour's raiment to pledge, thou shalt deliver it unto him by that the sun goeth down:

²⁷For that *is* his covering only, it *is* his raiment for his skin: wherein shall he sleep? and it shall come to pass, when he crieth unto me, that I will hear; for I *am* gracious.

²⁸ ¶ Thou shalt not revile the ^sgods, nor curse the ruler of thy people.

²⁹ ¶ Thou shalt not delay *to offer* ^tthe first of thy ripe fruits, and of thy ^uliquors: the firstborn of thy sons shalt thou give unto me.

³⁰Likewise shalt thou do with thine oxen, *and* with thy sheep: seven days it shall be with his dam; on the eighth day thou shalt give it me.

³¹ ¶ And ye shall be holy men unto me: neither shall ye eat *any* flesh *that is* torn of beasts in the field; ye shall cast it to the dogs.

23 THOU SHALT not ^vraise a false report: put not thine hand with the wicked to be an unrighteous witness.

² ¶ Thou shalt not follow a multitude to *do* evil; neither shalt thou ^wspeak in a cause to decline after many to wrest *judgment:*

³ ¶ Neither shalt thou countenance a poor man in his cause.

⁴ ¶ If thou meet thine enemy's ox or his ass going astray, thou shalt surely bring it back to him again.

⁵If thou see the ass of him that hateth thee lying under his burden, ^xand wouldest forbear to help him, thou shalt surely help with him.

⁶Thou shalt not wrest the judgment of thy poor in his cause.

⁷Keep thee far from a false matter; and the innocent and righteous slay thou not: for I will not justify the wicked.

⁸ ¶ And thou shalt take no gift: for the gift blindeth ^ythe wise, and perverteth the words of the righteous.

⁹ ¶ Also thou shalt not oppress a stranger: for ye know the ^zheart of a stranger, seeing ye were strangers in the land of Egypt.

The law about the Sabbath

¹⁰And six years thou shalt sow thy land, and shalt gather in the fruits thereof:

¹¹But the seventh *year* thou shalt let it rest and lie still; that the poor of thy people may eat: and what they leave the beasts of the field shall eat. In like manner thou shalt deal with thy vineyard, *and* with thy ^aoliveyard.

¹²Six days thou shalt do thy work, and on the seventh day thou shalt rest: that thine ox and thine ass may rest, and the son of thy handmaid, and the stranger, may be refreshed.

¹³And in all *things* that I have said unto you be circumspect: and make no mention of the name of other gods, neither let it be heard out of thy mouth.

Laws about appointed feasts

¹⁴ ¶ Three times thou shalt keep a feast unto me in the year.

¹⁵Thou shalt keep the feast of unleavened bread: (thou shalt eat unleavened bread seven days, as I commanded thee, in the time appointed of the month Abib; for in it thou camest out from Egypt: and none shall appear before me empty:)

Amplified

²⁵If you lend money to any of My people with you who is poor, you shall not be to him as a creditor, neither shall you require interest from him.

²⁶If you ever take your neighbor's garment in pledge, you shall give it back to him before the sun goes down;

²⁷For that is his only covering, his clothing for his body. In what shall he sleep? When he cries to Me, I will hear, for I am gracious *and* merciful.

²⁸You shall not revile God [the judges as His agents] or esteem lightly *or* curse a ruler of your people.

²⁹You shall not delay to bring to Me from the fullness [of your harvested grain] and the outflow [of your grape juice *and* olive oil]; give Me the firstborn of your sons [or redeem them]. [Exod. 34:19, 20.]

³⁰Likewise shall you do with your oxen *and* your sheep. Seven days the firstborn [beast] shall be with its mother; on the eighth day you shall give it to Me.

³¹And you shall be holy men [consecrated] to Me; therefore you shall not eat any flesh that is torn by beasts in the field; you shall throw it to the dogs.

23 YOU SHALL not repeat *or* raise a false report; you shall not join with the wicked to be an unrighteous witness.

²You shall not follow a crowd to do evil; nor shall you bear witness at a trial so as to side with a multitude to pervert justice.

³Neither shall you be partial to a poor man in his trial [just because he is poor].

⁴If you meet your enemy's ox or his donkey going astray, you shall surely bring it back to him again.

⁵If you see the donkey of one who hates you lying [helpless] under his load, you shall refrain from leaving the man to cope with it alone; you shall help him to release the animal.

⁶You shall not pervert the justice due to your poor in his cause.

⁷Keep far from a false matter and [be very careful] not to condemn to death the innocent and the righteous, for I will not justify *and* acquit the wicked.

⁸You shall take no bribe, for the bribe blinds those who have sight and perverts the testimony *and* the cause of the righteous.

⁹Also you shall not oppress a temporary resident, for you know the heart of a stranger *and* sojourner, seeing you were strangers *and* sojourners in Egypt.

¹⁰Six years you shall sow your land and reap its yield.

¹¹But the seventh year you shall release it *and* let it rest and lie fallow, that the poor of your people may eat [what the land voluntarily yields], and what they leave the wild beasts shall eat. In like manner you shall deal with your vineyard and olive grove.

¹²Six days you shall do your work, but the seventh day you shall rest and keep Sabbath, that your ox and your donkey may rest, and the son of your bondwoman, and the alien, may be refreshed.

¹³In all I have said to you take heed; do not mention the name of other gods [either in blessing or cursing]; do not let such speech be heard from your mouth.

¹⁴Three times in the year you shall keep a feast to Me.

¹⁵You shall keep the Feast of Unleavened Bread; seven days you shall eat unleavened bread as I commanded you, at the time appointed in the month of Abib, for in it you came out of Egypt. None shall appear before Me empty-handed.

---

^sOr, *judges*   ^tHeb. *thy fulness*   ^uHeb. *tear*   ^vOr, *receive* ^wHeb. *answer*   ^xOr, *wilt thou cease to help him?* or, *and wouldest cease to leave* thy business *for him; thou shalt surely leave* it to join *with him*   ^yHeb. *the seeing*   ^zHeb. *soul*   ^aOr, olive trees

New American Standard

25 ¶ "If you lend money to My people, to the poor among you, you are not to act as a creditor to him; you shall not charge him interest.

26 "If you ever take your neighbor's cloak as a pledge, you are to return it to him before the sun sets,

27 for that is his only covering; it is his cloak for his body. What else shall he sleep in? And it shall come about that when he cries out to Me, I will hear him, for I am gracious.

28 ¶ "You shall not curse God, nor curse a ruler of your people.

29 ¶ "You shall not delay the offering from your harvest and your vintage. The firstborn of your sons you shall give to Me.

30 "You shall do the same with your oxen and with your sheep. It shall be with its mother seven days; on the eighth day you shall give it to Me.

31 ¶ "You shall be holy men to Me, therefore you shall not eat any flesh torn to pieces in the field; you shall throw it to the dogs.

Sundry Laws

23 "YOU SHALL not bear a false report; do not join your hand with a wicked man to be a malicious witness.

2 "You shall not follow the masses in doing evil, nor shall you testify in a dispute so as to turn aside after a multitude in order to pervert justice;

3 nor shall you be partial to a poor man in his dispute.

4 ¶ "If you meet your enemy's ox or his donkey wandering away, you shall surely return it to him.

5 "If you see the donkey of one who hates you lying helpless under its load, you shall refrain from leaving it to him, you shall surely release it with him.

6 ¶ "You shall not pervert the justice due to your needy brother in his dispute.

7 "Keep far from a false charge, and do not kill the innocent or the righteous, for I will not acquit the guilty.

8 ¶ "You shall not take a bribe, for a bribe blinds the clear-sighted and subverts the cause of the just.

9 ¶ "You shall not oppress a stranger, since you yourselves know the feelings of a stranger, for you also were strangers in the land of Egypt.

The Sabbath and Land

10 ¶ "You shall sow your land for six years and gather in its yield,

11 but on the seventh year you shall let it rest and lie fallow, so that the needy of your people may eat; and whatever they leave the beast of the field may eat. You are to do the same with your vineyard and your olive grove.

12 ¶ "Six days you are to do your work, but on the seventh day you shall cease from labor so that your ox and your donkey may rest, and the son of your female slave, as well as your stranger, may refresh themselves.

13 "Now concerning everything which I have said to you, be on your guard; and do not mention the name of other gods, nor let them be heard from your mouth.

Three National Feasts

14 ¶ "Three times a year you shall celebrate a feast to Me.

15 "You shall observe the Feast of Unleavened Bread; for seven days you are to eat unleavened bread, as I commanded you, at the appointed time in the month Abib, for in it you came out of Egypt. And none shall appear before Me empty-handed.

New International

25 "If you lend money to one of my people among you who is needy, do not be like a moneylender; charge him no interest.[d] 26 If you take your neighbor's cloak as a pledge, return it to him by sunset, 27 because his cloak is the only covering he has for his body. What else will he sleep in? When he cries out to me, I will hear, for I am compassionate.

28 "Do not blaspheme God[e] or curse the ruler of your people.

29 "Do not hold back offerings from your granaries or your vats.[f]

"You must give me the firstborn of your sons. 30 Do the same with your cattle and your sheep. Let them stay with their mothers for seven days, but give them to me on the eighth day.

31 "You are to be my holy people. So do not eat the meat of an animal torn by wild beasts; throw it to the dogs.

Laws of Justice and Mercy

23 "DO NOT spread false reports. Do not help a wicked man by being a malicious witness.

2 "Do not follow the crowd in doing wrong. When you give testimony in a lawsuit, do not pervert justice by siding with the crowd, 3 and do not show favoritism to a poor man in his lawsuit.

4 "If you come across your enemy's ox or donkey wandering off, be sure to take it back to him. 5 If you see the donkey of someone who hates you fallen down under its load, do not leave it there; be sure you help him with it.

6 "Do not deny justice to your poor people in their lawsuits. 7 Have nothing to do with a false charge and do not put an innocent or honest person to death, for I will not acquit the guilty.

8 "Do not accept a bribe, for a bribe blinds those who see and twists the words of the righteous.

9 "Do not oppress an alien; you yourselves know how it feels to be aliens, because you were aliens in Egypt.

Sabbath Laws

10 "For six years you are to sow your fields and harvest the crops, 11 but during the seventh year let the land lie unplowed and unused. Then the poor among your people may get food from it, and the wild animals may eat what they leave. Do the same with your vineyard and your olive grove.

12 "Six days do your work, but on the seventh day do not work, so that your ox and your donkey may rest and the slave born in your household, and the alien as well, may be refreshed.

13 "Be careful to do everything I have said to you. Do not invoke the names of other gods; do not let them be heard on your lips.

The Three Annual Festivals

14 "Three times a year you are to celebrate a festival to me.

15 "Celebrate the Feast of Unleavened Bread; for seven days eat bread made without yeast, as I commanded you. Do this at the appointed time in the month of Abib, for in that month you came out of Egypt.

"No one is to appear before me empty-handed.

---

d 25 Or excessive interest   e 28 Or Do not revile the judges
f 29 The meaning of the Hebrew for this phrase is uncertain.

King James

¹⁶And the feast of harvest, the firstfruits of thy labours, which thou hast sown in the field: and the feast of ingathering, *which is* in the end of the year, when thou hast gathered in thy labours out of the field.

¹⁷Three times in the year all thy males shall appear before the Lord GOD.

¹⁸Thou shalt not offer the blood of my sacrifice with leavened bread; neither shall the fat of my *b*sacrifice remain until the morning.

¹⁹The first of the firstfruits of thy land thou shalt bring into the house of the LORD thy God. Thou shalt not seethe a kid in his mother's milk.

Promise of God's protection

²⁰ ¶ Behold, I send an Angel before thee, to keep thee in the way, and to bring thee into the place which I have prepared.

²¹Beware of him, and obey his voice, provoke him not; for he will not pardon your transgressions: for my name *is* in him.

²²But if thou shalt indeed obey his voice, and do all that I speak; then I will be an enemy unto thine enemies, and *c*an adversary unto thine adversaries.

²³For mine Angel shall go before thee, and bring thee in unto the Amorites, and the Hittites, and the Perizzites, and the Canaanites, the Hivites, and the Jebusites: and I will cut them off.

²⁴Thou shalt not bow down to their gods, nor serve them, nor do after their works: but thou shalt utterly overthrow them, and quite break down their images.

²⁵And ye shall serve the LORD your God, and he shall bless thy bread, and thy water; and I will take sickness away from the midst of thee.

²⁶ ¶ There shall nothing cast their young, nor be barren, in thy land: the number of thy days I will fulfil.

²⁷I will send my fear before thee, and will destroy all the people to whom thou shalt come, and I will make all thine enemies turn their *d*backs unto thee.

²⁸And I will send hornets before thee, which shall drive out the Hivite, the Canaanite, and the Hittite, from before thee.

²⁹I will not drive them out from before thee in one year; lest the land become desolate, and the beast of the field multiply against thee.

³⁰By little and little I will drive them out from before thee, until thou be increased, and inherit the land.

³¹And I will set thy bounds from the Red sea even unto the sea of the Philistines, and from the desert unto the river: for I will deliver the inhabitants of the land into your hand; and thou shalt drive them out before thee.

³²Thou shalt make no covenant with them, nor with their gods.

³³They shall not dwell in thy land, lest they make thee sin against me: for if thou serve their gods, it will surely be a snare unto thee.

The covenant affirmed

24 AND HE said unto Moses, Come up unto the LORD, thou, and Aaron, Nadab, and Abihu, and seventy of the elders of Israel; and worship ye afar off.

²And Moses alone shall come near the LORD: but they shall not come nigh; neither shall the people go up with him.

³ ¶ And Moses came and told the people all the words of the LORD, and all the judgments: and all the people answered with one voice, and said, All the words which the LORD hath said will we do.

Amplified

¹⁶Also you shall keep the Feast of Harvest [Pentecost], [acknowledging] the firstfruits of your toil, of what you sow in the field. And [third] you shall keep the Feast of Ingathering [Booths or Tabernacles] at the end of the year, when you gather in the fruit of your labors from the field.

¹⁷Three times in the year all your males shall appear before the Lord God.

¹⁸You shall not offer the blood of My sacrifice with leavened bread [but keep it unmixed], neither shall the fat of My feast remain all night until morning.

¹⁹The first of the firstfruits of your ground you shall bring into the house of the Lord your God. You shall not boil a kid in its mother's milk.

²⁰Behold, I send an *n*Angel before you to keep *and* guard you on the way and to bring you to the place I have prepared.

²¹Give heed to Him, listen to *and* obey His voice; be not rebellious before Him *or* provoke Him, for He will not pardon your transgression; for My *o*Name is in Him. [Exod. 32:34; 33:14; Isa. 63:9.]

²²But if you will indeed listen to and obey His voice and all that I speak, then I will be an enemy to your enemies and an adversary to your adversaries.

²³When My Angel goes before you and brings you to the Amorites, the Hittites, the Perizzites, the Canaanites, the Hivites, and the Jebusites, and I reject them *and* blot them out,

²⁴You shall not bow down to their gods or serve them or do after their works; but you shall utterly overthrow them and break down their pillars *and* images.

²⁵You shall serve the Lord your God; He shall bless your bread and water, and I will take sickness from your midst.

²⁶None shall lose her young by miscarriage or be barren in your land; I will fulfill the number of your days.

²⁷I will send My terror before you and will throw into confusion all the people to whom you shall come, and I will make all your foes turn from you [in flight].

²⁸And I will send hornets before you which shall drive out the Hivite, Canaanite, and Hittite from before you.

²⁹I will not drive them out from before you in one year, lest the land become desolate [for lack of attention] and the wild beasts multiply against you.

³⁰Little by little I will drive them out from before you, until you have increased *and* are numerous enough to take possession of the land.

³¹I will set your borders from the Red Sea to the Sea of the Philistines, and from the wilderness to the river [Euphrates]; for I will deliver the inhabitants of the land into your hand and you shall drive them out before you.

³²You shall make no covenant with them or with their gods.

³³They shall not dwell in your land, lest they make you sin against Me; for if you serve their gods, it will surely be a snare to you.

24 GOD SAID to Moses, Come up to the Lord, you and Aaron, Nadab and Abihu [Aaron's sons], and seventy of Israel's elders, and worship at a distance.

²Moses alone shall come near the Lord; the others shall not come near, and neither shall the people come up with him.

³Moses came and told the people all that the Lord had said and all the ordinances; and all the people answered with one voice, All that the Lord has spoken we will do.

---

b Or, *feast neck*   *c* Or, *I will afflict them that afflict thee*   *d* Heb.

n See footnote on Gen. 16:7.   *o* Representing God's presence.

New American Standard

16"Also *you shall observe* the Feast of the Harvest *of* the first fruits of your labors *from* what you sow in the field; also the Feast of the Ingathering at the end of the year when you gather in *the fruit of* your labors from the field.

17"Three times a year all your males shall appear before the Lord GOD.

18 ¶ "You shall not offer the blood of My sacrifice with leavened bread; nor is the fat of My feast to remain overnight until morning.

19 ¶ "You shall bring the choice first fruits of your soil into the house of the LORD your God.

¶ "You are not to boil a young goat in the milk of its mother.

Conquest of the Land

20 ¶ "Behold, I am going to send an angel before you to guard you along the way and to bring you into the place which I have prepared.

21"Be on your guard before him and obey his voice; do not be rebellious toward him, for he will not pardon your transgression, since My name is in him.

22"But if you truly obey his voice and do all that I say, then I will be an enemy to your enemies and an adversary to your adversaries.

23"For My angel will go before you and bring you in to *the land of* the Amorites, the Hittites, the Perizzites, the Canaanites, the Hivites and the Jebusites; and I will completely destroy them.

24"You shall not worship their gods, nor serve them, nor do according to their deeds; but you shall utterly overthrow them and break their *sacred* pillars in pieces.

25"But you shall serve the LORD your God, and He will bless your bread and your water; and I will remove sickness from your midst.

26"There shall be no one miscarrying or barren in your land; I will fulfill the number of your days.

27"I will send My terror ahead of you, and throw into confusion all the people among whom you come, and I will make all your enemies turn *their* backs to you.

28"I will send hornets ahead of you so that they will drive out the Hivites, the Canaanites, and the Hittites before you.

29"I will not drive them out before you in a single year, that the land may not become desolate and the beasts of the field become too numerous for you.

30"I will drive them out before you little by little, until you become fruitful and take possession of the land.

31"I will fix your boundary from the Red Sea to the sea of the Philistines, and from the wilderness to the River *Euphrates;* for I will deliver the inhabitants of the land into your hand, and you will drive them out before you.

32"You shall make no covenant with them or with their gods.

33"They shall not live in your land, because they will make you sin against Me; for *if* you serve their gods, it will surely be a snare to you."

People Affirm Their Covenant with God

24 THEN HE said to Moses, "Come up to the LORD, you and Aaron, Nadab and Abihu and seventy of the elders of Israel, and you shall worship at a distance.

2"Moses alone, however, shall come near to the LORD, but they shall not come near, nor shall the people come up with him."

3 ¶ Then Moses came and recounted to the people all the words of the LORD and all the ordinances; and all the people answered with one voice and said, "All the words which the LORD has spoken we will do!"

New International

16"Celebrate the Feast of Harvest with the firstfruits of the crops you sow in your field.

"Celebrate the Feast of Ingathering at the end of the year, when you gather in your crops from the field.

17"Three times a year all the men are to appear before the Sovereign LORD.

18"Do not offer the blood of a sacrifice to me along with anything containing yeast.

"The fat of my festival offerings must not be kept until morning.

19"Bring the best of the firstfruits of your soil to the house of the LORD your God.

"Do not cook a young goat in its mother's milk.

God's Angel to Prepare the Way

20"See, I am sending an angel ahead of you to guard you along the way and to bring you to the place I have prepared. 21Pay attention to him and listen to what he says. Do not rebel against him; he will not forgive your rebellion, since my Name is in him. 22If you listen carefully to what he says and do all that I say, I will be an enemy to your enemies and will oppose those who oppose you. 23My angel will go ahead of you and bring you into the land of the Amorites, Hittites, Perizzites, Canaanites, Hivites and Jebusites, and I will wipe them out. 24Do not bow down before their gods or worship them or follow their practices. You must demolish them and break their sacred stones to pieces. 25Worship the LORD your God, and his blessing will be on your food and water. I will take away sickness from among you, 26and none will miscarry or be barren in your land. I will give you a full life span.

27"I will send my terror ahead of you and throw into confusion every nation you encounter. I will make all your enemies turn their backs and run. 28I will send the hornet ahead of you to drive the Hivites, Canaanites and Hittites out of your way. 29But I will not drive them out in a single year, because the land would become desolate and the wild animals too numerous for you. 30Little by little I will drive them out before you, until you have increased enough to take possession of the land.

31"I will establish your borders from the Red Sea[g] to the Sea of the Philistines,[h] and from the desert to the River.[i] I will hand over to you the people who live in the land and you will drive them out before you. 32Do not make a covenant with them or with their gods. 33Do not let them live in your land, or they will cause you to sin against me, because the worship of their gods will certainly be a snare to you."

The Covenant Confirmed

24 THEN HE said to Moses, "Come up to the LORD, you and Aaron, Nadab and Abihu, and seventy of the elders of Israel. You are to worship at a distance, 2but Moses alone is to approach the LORD; the others must not come near. And the people may not come up with him."

3When Moses went and told the people all the LORD's words and laws, they responded with one voice, "Every-

---

g 31 Hebrew *Yam Suph*; that is, Sea of Reeds   h 31 That is, the
Mediterranean   i 31 That is, the Euphrates

King James

4And Moses wrote all the words of the LORD, and rose up early in the morning, and builded an altar under the hill, and twelve pillars, according to the twelve tribes of Israel.

5And he sent young men of the children of Israel, which offered burnt offerings, and sacrificed peace offerings of oxen unto the LORD.

6And Moses took half of the blood, and put *it* in basins; and half of the blood he sprinkled on the altar.

7And he took the book of the covenant, and read in the audience of the people: and they said, All that the LORD hath said will we do, and be obedient.

8And Moses took the blood, and sprinkled *it* on the people, and said, Behold the blood of the covenant, which the LORD hath made with you concerning all these words.

9 ¶ Then went up Moses, and Aaron, Nadab, and Abihu, and seventy of the elders of Israel:

10And they saw the God of Israel: and *there was* under his feet as it were a paved work of a sapphire stone, and as it were the body of heaven in *his* clearness.

11And upon the nobles of the children of Israel he laid not his hand: also they saw God, and did eat and drink.

12 ¶ And the LORD said unto Moses, Come up to me into the mount, and be there: and I will give thee tables of stone, and a law, and commandments which I have written; that thou mayest teach them.

13And Moses rose up, and his minister Joshua: and Moses went up into the mount of God.

14And he said unto the elders, Tarry ye here for us, until we come again unto you: and, behold, Aaron and Hur *are* with you: if any man have any matters to do, let him come unto them.

15And Moses went up into the mount, and a cloud covered the mount.

16And the glory of the LORD abode upon mount Sinai, and the cloud covered it six days: and the seventh day he called unto Moses out of the midst of the cloud.

17And the sight of the glory of the LORD *was* like devouring fire on the top of the mount in the eyes of the children of Israel.

18And Moses went into the midst of the cloud, and gat him up into the mount: and Moses was in the mount forty days and forty nights.

Offerings for the tabernacle

25 AND THE LORD spake unto Moses, saying,

2Speak unto the children of Israel, that they [e]bring me an [f]offering: of every man that giveth it willingly with his heart ye shall take my offering.

3And this *is* the offering which ye shall take of them; gold, and silver, and brass,

4And blue, and purple, and scarlet, and [g]fine linen, and goats' *hair,*

5And rams' skins dyed red, and badgers' skins, and shittim wood,

6Oil for the light, spices for anointing oil, and for sweet incense,

[e]Heb. *take for me* [f]Or, *heave offering* [g]Or, *silk*

Amplified

4Moses [p]wrote all the words of the Lord. He rose up early in the morning and built an altar at the foot of the mountain and set up twelve pillars representing Israel's twelve tribes.

5And he sent young Israelite men, who offered burnt offerings and sacrificed peace offerings of oxen to the Lord.

6And Moses took half of the blood and put it in basins, and half of the blood he dashed against the altar.

7Then he took the Book of the Covenant and read in the hearing of the people; and they said, All that the Lord has said we will do, and we will be obedient.

8And Moses took the [remaining half of the] blood and sprinkled it on the people, and said, Behold the blood of the covenant which the Lord has made with you in accordance with all these words. [I Cor. 11:25; Heb. 8:6; 10:28, 29.]

9Then Moses, Aaron, Nadab, and Abihu, and seventy of the elders of Israel went up [the mountainside].

10And they saw the God of Israel [that is, a convincing manifestation of His presence], and under His feet it was like pavement of bright sapphire stone, like the very heavens in clearness. [Exod. 33:20–23; Deut. 4:12; Ezek. 28:14]

11And upon the nobles of the Israelites He laid not His hand [to conceal Himself from them, to rebuke their daring, or to harm them]; but they saw [the manifestation of the presence of] God, and ate and drank. [Exod. 19:21.]

12And the Lord said to Moses, Come up to Me into the mountain and be there, and I will give you tables of stone, with the law and the commandments which [q]I have written that you may teach them. [II Cor. 3:2, 3.]

13So Moses rose up with Joshua his attendant; and Moses went up into the mountain of God.

14And he said to the elders, Tarry here for us until we come back to you; remember, Aaron and Hur are with you; whoever has a cause, let him go to them.

15Then Moses went up into the mountain, and the cloud covered the mountain.

16The glory of the Lord rested on Mount Sinai, and the cloud covered it for six days. On the seventh day [God] called to Moses out of the midst of the cloud.

17And the glory of the Lord appeared to the Israelites like devouring fire on the top of the mountain.

18Moses entered into the midst of the cloud and went up the mountain, and Moses was on the mountain forty days and nights.

25 AND THE Lord said to Moses,

2Speak to the Israelites, that they take for Me an offering. From every man who gives it willingly *and* ungrudgingly with his heart you shall take My offering.

3This is the offering you shall receive from them: gold, silver, and bronze,

4Blue, purple, and scarlet [stuff] and fine twined linen and goats' hair,

5Rams' skins tanned red, goatskins, dolphin *or* porpoise skins, acacia wood,

6Oil for the light, spices for anointing oil and for sweet incense,

[p]The contemporary evidence, supplied by archaeology, that writing had long been in common use before the time of Moses now makes conjectures about the contents of the earlier books of the Old Testament being handed down **orally** look absurd. Not only is much of the misleading criticism of the Bible now recognized as unjustified, it is out of harmony with the scientific outlook of the present day (Sir Charles Marston, *New Bible Evidence*). [q]The two tables were "written with the finger of God" (Exod. 31:18), and "the tables were the work of God" (Exod. 32:16). A man may be said to write what a secretary writes at his dictation; but if he expressly states that certain things are written with his own hand, it is unreasonable to suppose that they were written by the hand of another (J.P. Lange, *A Commentary*).

New American Standard

4 Moses wrote down all the words of the LORD. Then he arose early in the morning, and built an altar at the foot of the mountain with twelve pillars for the twelve tribes of Israel.

5 He sent young men of the sons of Israel, and they offered burnt offerings and sacrificed young bulls as peace offerings to the LORD.

6 Moses took half of the blood and put *it* in basins, and the *other* half of the blood he sprinkled on the altar.

7 Then he took the book of the covenant and read *it* in the hearing of the people; and they said, "All that the LORD has spoken we will do, and we will be obedient!"

8 So Moses took the blood and sprinkled *it* on the people, and said, "Behold the blood of the covenant, which the LORD has made with you in accordance with all these words."

9 ¶ Then Moses went up with Aaron, Nadab and Abihu, and seventy of the elders of Israel,

10 and they saw the God of Israel; and under His feet there appeared to be a pavement of sapphire, as clear as the sky itself.

11 Yet He did not stretch out His hand against the nobles of the sons of Israel; and they saw God, and they ate and drank.

12 ¶ Now the LORD said to Moses, "Come up to Me on the mountain and remain there, and I will give you the stone tablets with the law and the commandment which I have written for their instruction."

13 So Moses arose with Joshua his servant, and Moses went up to the mountain of God.

14 But to the elders he said, "Wait here for us until we return to you. And behold, Aaron and Hur are with you; whoever has a legal matter, let him approach them."

15 Then Moses went up to the mountain, and the cloud covered the mountain.

16 The glory of the LORD rested on Mount Sinai, and the cloud covered it for six days; and on the seventh day He called to Moses from the midst of the cloud.

17 And to the eyes of the sons of Israel the appearance of the glory of the LORD was like a consuming fire on the mountain top.

18 Moses entered the midst of the cloud as he went up to the mountain; and Moses was on the mountain forty days and forty nights.

Offerings for the Sanctuary

25 THEN THE LORD spoke to Moses, saying, 2"Tell the sons of Israel to raise a contribution for Me; from every man whose heart moves him you shall raise My contribution.

3"This is the contribution which you are to raise from them: gold, silver and bronze,

4 blue, purple and scarlet *material,* fine linen, goat *hair,*

5 rams' skins dyed red, porpoise skins, acacia wood,

6 oil for lighting, spices for the anointing oil and for the fragrant incense,

New International

thing the LORD has said we will do." 4Moses then wrote down everything the LORD had said.

He got up early the next morning and built an altar at the foot of the mountain and set up twelve stone pillars representing the twelve tribes of Israel. 5Then he sent young Israelite men, and they offered burnt offerings and sacrificed young bulls as fellowship offerings[j] to the LORD. 6Moses took half of the blood and put it in bowls, and the other half he sprinkled on the altar. 7Then he took the Book of the Covenant and read it to the people. They responded, "We will do everything the LORD has said; we will obey."

8Moses then took the blood, sprinkled it on the people and said, "This is the blood of the covenant that the LORD has made with you in accordance with all these words."

9Moses and Aaron, Nadab and Abihu, and the seventy elders of Israel went up 10and saw the God of Israel. Under his feet was something like a pavement made of sapphire,[k] clear as the sky itself. 11But God did not raise his hand against these leaders of the Israelites; they saw God, and they ate and drank.

12The LORD said to Moses, "Come up to me on the mountain and stay here, and I will give you the tablets of stone, with the law and commands I have written for their instruction."

13Then Moses set out with Joshua his aide, and Moses went up on the mountain of God. 14He said to the elders, "Wait here for us until we come back to you. Aaron and Hur are with you, and anyone involved in a dispute can go to them."

15When Moses went up on the mountain, the cloud covered it, 16and the glory of the LORD settled on Mount Sinai. For six days the cloud covered the mountain, and on the seventh day the LORD called to Moses from within the cloud. 17To the Israelites the glory of the LORD looked like a consuming fire on top of the mountain. 18Then Moses entered the cloud as he went on up the mountain. And he stayed on the mountain forty days and forty nights.

Offerings for the Tabernacle

25 THE LORD said to Moses, 2"Tell the Israelites to bring me an offering. You are to receive the offering for me from each man whose heart prompts him to give. 3These are the offerings you are to receive from them: gold, silver and bronze; 4blue, purple and scarlet yarn and fine linen; goat hair; 5ram skins dyed red and hides of sea cows[l]; acacia wood; 6olive oil for the light; spices for the anointing oil and for the fragrant incense;

---

j 5 Traditionally *peace offerings*   k 10 Or *lapis lazuli*
l 5 That is, dugongs

King James

7Onyx stones, and stones to be set in the ephod, and in the breastplate.

8And let them make me a sanctuary; that I may dwell among them.

9According to all that I show thee, *after* the pattern of the tabernacle, and the pattern of all the instruments thereof, even so shall ye make *it*.

The ark

10 ¶ And they shall make an ark *of* shittim wood: two cubits and a half *shall be* the length thereof, and a cubit and a half the breadth thereof, and a cubit and a half the height thereof.

11And thou shalt overlay it with pure gold, within and without shalt thou overlay it, and shalt make upon it a crown of gold round about.

12And thou shalt cast four rings of gold for it, and put *them* in the four corners thereof; and two rings *shall be* in the one side of it, and two rings in the other side of it.

13And thou shalt make staves *of* shittim wood, and overlay them with gold.

14And thou shalt put the staves into the rings by the sides of the ark, that the ark may be borne with them.

15The staves shall be in the rings of the ark: they shall not be taken from it.

16And thou shalt put into the ark the testimony which I shall give thee.

17And thou shalt make a mercy seat *of* pure gold: two cubits and a half *shall be* the length thereof, and a cubit and a half the breadth thereof.

18And thou shalt make two cherubims *of* gold, *of* beaten work shalt thou make them, in the two ends of the mercy seat.

19And make one cherub on the one end, and the other cherub on the other end: *even* hof the mercy seat shall ye make the cherubims on the two ends thereof.

20And the cherubims shall stretch forth *their* wings on high, covering the mercy seat with their wings, and their faces *shall look* one to another; toward the mercy seat shall the faces of the cherubims be.

21And thou shalt put the mercy seat above upon the ark; and in the ark thou shalt put the testimony that I shall give thee.

22And there I will meet with thee, and I will commune with thee from above the mercy seat, from between the two cherubims which *are* upon the ark of the testimony, of all *things* which I will give thee in commandment unto the children of Israel.

The table

23 ¶ Thou shalt also make a table *of* shittim wood: two cubits *shall be* the length thereof, and a cubit the breadth thereof, and a cubit and a half the height thereof.

24And thou shalt overlay it with pure gold, and make thereto a crown of gold round about.

25And thou shalt make unto it a border of an handbreadth round about, and thou shalt make a golden crown to the border thereof round about.

26And thou shalt make for it four rings of gold, and put the rings in the four corners that *are* on the four feet thereof.

27Over against the border shall the rings be for places of the staves to bear the table.

28And thou shalt make the staves *of* shittim wood, and overlay them with gold, that the table may be borne with them.

29And thou shalt make the dishes thereof, and spoons thereof, and covers thereof, and bowls thereof, ito cover withal: *of* pure gold shalt thou make them.

30And thou shalt set upon the table showbread before me always.

Amplified

7Onyx stones, and stones for setting in the ephod and in the breastplate.

8Let them make Me a sanctuary, that I may dwell among them. [Heb. 8:1, 2; 10:1.]

9And you shall make it according to all that I show you, the pattern of the tabernacle *or* dwelling and the pattern of all the furniture of it.

10They shall make an ark of acacia wood: two and a half cubits long, a cubit and a half wide, and a cubit and a half high.

11You shall overlay the ark with pure gold, inside and out, and make a gold crown, a rim *or* border, around its top.

12You shall cast four gold rings and attach them to the four lower corners of it, two rings on either side.

13You shall make poles of acacia wood and overlay them with gold,

14And put the poles through the rings on the ark's sides, by which to carry it.

15The poles shall remain in the rings of the ark; they shall not be removed from it [that the ark be not touched].

16And you shall put inside the ark the Testimony [the Ten Commandments] which I will give you.

17And you shall make a mercy seat (a covering) of pure gold, two cubits and a half long and a cubit and a half wide.

18And you shall make two cherubim (winged angelic figures) of [solid] hammered gold on the two ends of the mercy seat.

19Make one cherub on each end, making the cherubim of one piece with the mercy seat, on the two ends of it.

20And the cherubim shall spread out their wings above, covering the mercy seat with their wings, facing each other and looking down toward the mercy seat.

21You shall put the mercy seat on the top of the ark, and in the ark you shall put the Testimony [the Ten Commandments] that I will give you.

22There I will meet with you and, from above the mercy seat, from between the two cherubim that are upon the ark of the Testimony, I will speak intimately with you of all which I will give you in commandment to the Israelites.

23Also, make a table of acacia wood, two cubits long, one cubit wide, and a cubit and a half high [for the showbread].

24You shall overlay it with pure gold and make a crown, a rim *or* molding, of gold around the top of it;

25And make a frame of a handbreadth around *and* below the top of it and put around it a gold molding as a border.

26You shall make for it four rings of gold and fasten them at the four corners that are on the table's four legs.

27Close against the frame shall the rings be as places for the poles to pass to carry the table [of showbread].

28You shall make the poles of acacia wood and overlay them with gold, that the table may be carried with them.

29And you shall make its plates [for showbread] and cups [for incense], and its flagons and bowls [for liquids in sacrifice]; make them of pure gold.

30And you shall set the showbread (the bread of the Presence) on the table before Me always. [John 6:58.]

---

hOr, *of the* matter *of the mercy seat*   iOr, *to pour out withal*

New American Standard

7 onyx stones and setting stones for the ephod and for the breastpiece.

8 "Let them construct a sanctuary for Me, that I may dwell among them.

9 "According to all that I am going to show you, *as* the pattern of the tabernacle and the pattern of all its furniture, just so you shall construct *it.*

Ark of the Covenant

10 ¶ "They shall construct an ark of acacia wood two and a half cubits long, and one and a half cubits wide, and one and a half cubits high.

11 "You shall overlay it with pure gold, inside and out you shall overlay it, and you shall make a gold molding around it.

12 "You shall cast four gold rings for it and fasten them on its four feet, and two rings shall be on one side of it and two rings on the other side of it.

13 "You shall make poles of acacia wood and overlay them with gold.

14 "You shall put the poles into the rings on the sides of the ark, to carry the ark with them.

15 "The poles shall remain in the rings of the ark; they shall not be removed from it.

16 "You shall put into the ark the testimony which I shall give you.

17 ¶ "You shall make a [v]mercy seat of pure gold, two and a half cubits long and one and a half cubits wide.

18 "You shall make two cherubim of gold, make them of hammered work at the two ends of the mercy seat.

19 "Make one cherub at one end and one cherub at the other end; you shall make the cherubim *of one piece* with the mercy seat at its two ends.

20 "The cherubim shall have *their* wings spread upward, covering the mercy seat with their wings and facing one another; the faces of the cherubim are to be *turned* toward the mercy seat.

21 "You shall put the mercy seat on top of the ark, and in the ark you shall put the testimony which I will give to you.

22 "There I will meet with you; and from above the mercy seat, from between the two cherubim which are upon the ark of the testimony, I will speak to you about all that I will give you in commandment for the sons of Israel.

The Table of Showbread

23 ¶ "You shall make a table of acacia wood, two cubits long and one cubit wide and one and a half cubits high.

24 "You shall overlay it with pure gold and make a gold border around it.

25 "You shall make for it a rim of a handbreadth around *it;* and you shall make a gold border for the rim around it.

26 "You shall make four gold rings for it and put rings on the four corners which are on its four feet.

27 "The rings shall be close to the rim as holders for the poles to carry the table.

28 "You shall make the poles of acacia wood and overlay them with gold, so that with them the table may be carried.

29 "You shall make its dishes and its pans and its jars and its bowls with which to pour drink offerings; you shall make them of pure gold.

30 "You shall set the bread of the Presence on the table before Me at all times.

[v]Lit *propitiatory,* and so through v 22

New International

7 and onyx stones and other gems to be mounted on the
ephod and breastpiece.
8 "Then have them make a sanctuary for me, and I will
dwell among them. 9 Make this tabernacle and all its furnishings exactly like the pattern I will show you.

The Ark

10 "Have them make a chest of acacia wood—two and a
half cubits long, a cubit and a half wide, and a cubit and
a half high.[m] 11 Overlay it with pure gold, both inside and
out, and make a gold molding around it. 12 Cast four gold
rings for it and fasten them to its four feet, with two rings
on one side and two rings on the other. 13 Then make poles
of acacia wood and overlay them with gold. 14 Insert the
poles into the rings on the sides of the chest to carry it.
15 The poles are to remain in the rings of this ark; they are
not to be removed. 16 Then put in the ark the Testimony,
which I will give you.
17 "Make an atonement cover[n] of pure gold—two and
a half cubits long and a cubit and a half wide.[o] 18 And
make two cherubim out of hammered gold at the ends of
the cover. 19 Make one cherub on one end and the second
cherub on the other; make the cherubim of one piece with
the cover, at the two ends. 20 The cherubim are to have
their wings spread upward, overshadowing the cover with
them. The cherubim are to face each other, looking toward
the cover. 21 Place the cover on top of the ark and put in the
ark the Testimony, which I will give you. 22 There, above
the cover between the two cherubim that are over the ark
of the Testimony, I will meet with you and give you all my
commands for the Israelites.

The Table

23 "Make a table of acacia wood—two cubits long, a
cubit wide and a cubit and a half high.[p] 24 Overlay it with
pure gold and make a gold molding around it. 25 Also make
around it a rim a handbreadth[q] wide and put a gold molding on the rim. 26 Make four gold rings for the table and
fasten them to the four corners, where the four legs are.
27 The rings are to be close to the rim to hold the poles used
in carrying the table. 28 Make the poles of acacia wood,
overlay them with gold and carry the table with them.
29 And make its plates and dishes of pure gold, as well as
its pitchers and bowls for the pouring out of offerings.
30 Put the bread of the Presence on this table to be before
me at all times.

[m] *10* That is, about 3 3/4 feet (about 1.1 meters) long and 2 1/4 feet (about 0.7 meter) wide and high [n] *17* Traditionally *a mercy seat* [o] *17* That is, about 3 3/4 feet (about 1.1 meters) long and 2 1/4 feet (about 0.7 meter) wide [p] *23* That is, about 3 feet (about 0.9 meter) long and 1 1/2 feet (about 0.5 meter) wide and 2 1/4 feet (about 0.7 meter) high [q] *25* That is, about 3 inches (about 8 centimeters)

King James

The candlestick

31 ¶ And thou shalt make a candlestick *of* pure gold: *of* beaten work shall the candlestick be made: his shaft, and his branches, his bowls, his knobs, and his flowers, shall be of the same.

32 And six branches shall come out of the sides of it; three branches of the candlestick out of the one side, and three branches of the candlestick out of the other side:

33 Three bowls made like unto almonds, *with* a knob and a flower in one branch; and three bowls made like almonds in the other branch, *with* a knob and a flower: so in the six branches that come out of the candlestick.

34 And in the candlestick *shall be* four bowls made like unto almonds, *with* their knobs and their flowers.

35 And *there shall be* a knob under two branches of the same, and a knob under two branches of the same, and a knob under two branches of the same, according to the six branches that proceed out of the candlestick.

36 Their knobs and their branches shall be of the same: all it *shall be* one beaten work *of* pure gold.

37 And thou shalt make the seven lamps thereof: and they shall *j*light the lamps thereof, that they may give light over against *k*it.

38 And the tongs thereof, and the snuffdishes thereof, *shall be of* pure gold.

39 *Of* a talent of pure gold shall he make it, with all these vessels.

40 And look that thou make *them* after their pattern, *l*which was shown thee in the mount.

The tabernacle

26 MOREOVER THOU shalt make the tabernacle *with* ten curtains *of* fine twined linen, and blue, and purple, and scarlet: *with* cherubims *m*of cunning work shalt thou make them.

2 The length of one curtain *shall be* eight and twenty cubits, and the breadth of one curtain four cubits: and every one of the curtains shall have one measure.

3 The five curtains shall be coupled together one to another; and *other* five curtains *shall be* coupled one to another.

4 And thou shalt make loops of blue upon the edge of the one curtain from the selvedge in the coupling; and likewise shalt thou make in the uttermost edge of *another* curtain, in the coupling of the second.

5 Fifty loops shalt thou make in the one curtain, and fifty loops shalt thou make in the edge of the curtain that *is* in the coupling of the second; that the loops may take hold one of another.

6 And thou shalt make fifty taches of gold, and couple the curtains together with the taches: and it shall be one tabernacle.

7 ¶ And thou shalt make curtains *of* goats' *hair* to be a covering upon the tabernacle: eleven curtains shalt thou make.

8 The length of one curtain *shall be* thirty cubits, and the breadth of one curtain four cubits: and the eleven curtains *shall be all* of one measure.

9 And thou shalt couple five curtains by themselves, and six curtains by themselves, and shalt double the sixth curtain in the forefront of the tabernacle.

10 And thou shalt make fifty loops on the edge of the one curtain *that is* outmost in the coupling, and fifty loops in the edge of the curtain which coupleth the second.

Amplified

31 You shall make a lampstand of pure gold. Of beaten *and* turned work shall the lampstand be made, both its base and its shaft; its cups, its knobs, and its flowers shall be of one piece with it.

32 Six branches shall come out of the sides of it; three branches of the lampstand out of the one side and three branches out of its other side;

33 Three cups made like almond blossoms, each with a knob and a flower on one branch, and three cups made like almond blossoms on the other branch with a knob and a flower; so for the six branches coming out of the lampstand.

34 And on the [center shaft] itself you shall [make] four cups like almond blossoms with their knobs and their flowers.

35 Also make a knob [on the shaft] under each pair of the six branches going out from the lampstand and one piece with it;

36 Their knobs and their branches shall be of one piece with it; the whole of it one beaten work of pure gold.

37 And you shall make the lamps of the [lampstand] to include a *r*seventh one [at the top of the shaft]. [The priests] shall set up the [seven] lamps of it so they may give light in front of it.

38 Its snuffers and its ashtrays shall be of pure gold.

39 Use a talent of pure gold for it, including all these utensils.

40 And see to it that you copy [exactly] their pattern which was shown you on the mountain. [Heb. 8:5, 6.]

26 MOREOVER, YOU shall make the tabernacle with ten curtains; of fine twined linen, and blue and purple and scarlet [stuff], with cherubim skillfully embroidered shall you make them.

2 The length of one curtain shall be twenty-eight cubits and the breadth of one curtain four cubits; each of the curtains shall measure the same.

3 The five curtains shall be coupled to one another, and the other five curtains shall be coupled to one another.

4 And you shall make loops of blue on the edge of the last curtain in the first set, and likewise in the second set.

5 Fifty loops you shall make on the one curtain and fifty loops on the edge of the last curtain that is in the second coupling *or* set, so that the loops on one correspond to the loops on the other.

6 And you shall make fifty clasps of gold and fasten the curtains together with the clasps; then the tabernacle shall be one whole.

7 And make curtains of goats' hair to be a [second] covering over the tabernacle; eleven curtains shall you make.

8 One curtain shall be thirty cubits long and four cubits wide; and the eleven curtains shall all measure the same.

9 You shall join together five curtains by themselves and six curtains by themselves, and shall double over the sixth curtain in the front of the tabernacle [to make a closed door].

10 And make fifty loops on the edge of the outmost curtain in the one set and fifty loops on the edge of the outmost curtain in the second set.

*r*Certain Biblical critics in the past doubted the existence of the tabernacle and asserted that the concept of a sevenfold lamp was unknown until hundreds of years later, in Babylonian times (600 B.C.). The first objective evidence to the contrary came to light in W. F. Albright's excavation of Tell Beit Mirsim, south of Jerusalem, where he found seven-sprouted lamps from about 1200 B.C. The seventh season at Dothan yielded three sevenfold lamps from the period 1200-1400 B.C., showing again that this was not a late idea (Joseph P. Free, *Near Eastern Archaeology*).

*j*Or, *cause to ascend wast caused to see embroiderer*   *k*Heb. *the face of it*   *l*Heb. *which thou*   *m*Heb. *the work of a cunning workman,* or,

New American Standard

The Golden Lampstand

31 ¶ "Then you shall make a lampstand of pure gold. The lampstand *and* its base and its shaft are to be made of hammered work; its cups, its bulbs and its flowers shall be *of one piece* with it.

32"Six branches shall go out from its sides; three branches of the lampstand from its one side and three branches of the lampstand from its other side.

33"Three cups *shall be* shaped like almond *blossoms* in the one branch, a *w*bulb and a flower, and three cups shaped like almond *blossoms* in the other branch, a bulb and a flower—so for six branches going out from the lampstand;

34 and in the lampstand four cups shaped like almond *blossoms,* its bulbs and its flowers.

35"A bulb shall be under the *first* pair of branches *coming* out of it, and a bulb under the *second* pair of branches *coming* out of it, and a bulb under the *third* pair of branches *coming* out of it, for the six branches coming out of the lampstand.

36"Their bulbs and their branches *shall be of one piece* with it; all of it shall be one piece of hammered work of pure gold.

37"Then you shall make its lamps seven *in number;* and they shall mount its lamps so as to shed light on the space in front of it.

38"Its snuffers and their trays *shall be* of pure gold.

39"It shall be made from a talent of pure gold, with all these utensils.

40"See that you make *them* after the pattern for them, which was shown to you on the mountain.

Curtains of Linen

26 "MOREOVER YOU shall make the tabernacle with ten curtains of fine twisted linen and *x*blue and purple and scarlet *material;* you shall make them with cherubim, the work of a skillful workman.

2"The length of each curtain shall be twenty-eight cubits, and the width of each curtain four cubits; all the curtains shall have the same measurements.

3"Five curtains shall be joined to one another, and *the other* five curtains *shall be* joined to one another.

4"You shall make loops of blue on the edge of the outermost curtain in the *first* set, and likewise you shall make *them* on the edge of the curtain that is outermost in the second set.

5"You shall make fifty loops in the one curtain, and you shall make fifty loops on the edge of the curtain that is in the second set; the loops shall be opposite each other.

6"You shall make fifty clasps of gold, and join the curtains to one another with the clasps so that the *y*tabernacle will be a unit.

Curtains of Goats' Hair

7 ¶ "Then you shall make curtains of goats' *hair* for a tent over the tabernacle; you shall make eleven curtains in all.

8"The length of each curtain *shall be* thirty cubits, and the width of each curtain four cubits; the eleven curtains shall have the same measurements.

9"You shall join five curtains by themselves and the *other* six curtains by themselves, and you shall double over the sixth curtain at the front of the tent.

10"You shall make fifty loops on the edge of the curtain that is outermost in the *first* set, and fifty loops on the edge of the curtain *that is outermost in* the second set.

New International

The Lampstand

31"Make a lampstand of pure gold and hammer it out, base and shaft; its flowerlike cups, buds and blossoms shall be of one piece with it. 32Six branches are to extend from the sides of the lampstand—three on one side and three on the other. 33Three cups shaped like almond flowers with buds and blossoms are to be on one branch, three on the next branch, and the same for all six branches extending from the lampstand. 34And on the lampstand there are to be four cups shaped like almond flowers with buds and blossoms. 35One bud shall be under the first pair of branches extending from the lampstand, a second bud under the second pair, and a third bud under the third pair—six branches in all. 36The buds and branches shall all be of one piece with the lampstand, hammered out of pure gold.

37"Then make its seven lamps and set them up on it so that they light the space in front of it. 38Its wick trimmers and trays are to be of pure gold. 39A talent*r* of pure gold is to be used for the lampstand and all these accessories. 40See that you make them according to the pattern shown you on the mountain.

The Tabernacle

26 "MAKE THE tabernacle with ten curtains of finely twisted linen and blue, purple and scarlet yarn, with cherubim worked into them by a skilled craftsman. 2All the curtains are to be the same size—twenty-eight cubits long and four cubits wide.*s* 3Join five of the curtains together, and do the same with the other five. 4Make loops of blue material along the edge of the end curtain in one set, and do the same with the end curtain in the other set. 5Make fifty loops on one curtain and fifty loops on the end curtain of the other set, with the loops opposite each other. 6Then make fifty gold clasps and use them to fasten the curtains together so that the tabernacle is a unit.

7"Make curtains of goat hair for the tent over the tabernacle—eleven altogether. 8All eleven curtains are to be the same size—thirty cubits long and four cubits wide.*t* 9Join five of the curtains together into one set and the other six into another set. Fold the sixth curtain double at the front of the tent. 10Make fifty loops along the edge of the end curtain in one set and also along the edge of the end

King James

¹¹And thou shalt make fifty taches of brass, and put the taches into the loops, and couple the *n*tent together, that it may be one.

¹²And the remnant that remaineth of the curtains of the tent, the half curtain that remaineth, shall hang over the backside of the tabernacle.

¹³And a cubit on the one side, and a cubit on the other side *o*of that which remaineth in the length of the curtains of the tent, it shall hang over the sides of the tabernacle on this side and on that side, to cover it.

¹⁴And thou shalt make a covering for the tent *of* rams' skins dyed red, and a covering above *of* badgers' skins.

¹⁵ ¶ And thou shalt make boards for the tabernacle *of* shittim wood standing up.

¹⁶Ten cubits *shall be* the length of a board, and a cubit and a half *shall be* the breadth of one board.

¹⁷Two *p*tenons *shall there be* in one board, set in order one against another: thus shalt thou make for all the boards of the tabernacle.

¹⁸And thou shalt make the boards for the tabernacle, twenty boards on the south side southward.

¹⁹And thou shalt make forty sockets of silver under the twenty boards; two sockets under one board for his two tenons, and two sockets under another board for his two tenons.

²⁰And for the second side of the tabernacle on the north side *there shall be* twenty boards:

²¹And their forty sockets *of* silver; two sockets under one board, and two sockets under another board.

²²And for the sides of the tabernacle westward thou shalt make six boards.

²³And two boards shalt thou make for the corners of the tabernacle in the two sides.

²⁴And they shall be *q*coupled together beneath, and they shall be coupled together above the head of it unto one ring: thus shall it be for them both; they shall be for the two corners.

²⁵And they shall be eight boards, and their sockets *of* silver, sixteen sockets; two sockets under one board, and two sockets under another board.

²⁶ ¶ And thou shalt make bars *of* shittim wood; five for the boards of the one side of the tabernacle,

²⁷And five bars for the boards of the other side of the tabernacle, and five bars for the boards of the side of the tabernacle, for the two sides westward.

²⁸And the middle bar in the midst of the boards shall reach from end to end.

²⁹And thou shalt overlay the boards with gold, and make their rings *of* gold *for* places for the bars: and thou shalt overlay the bars with gold.

³⁰And thou shalt rear up the tabernacle according to the fashion thereof which was shown thee in the mount.

³¹ ¶ And thou shalt make a veil *of* blue, and purple, and scarlet, and fine twined linen of cunning work: with cherubims shall it be made:

³²And thou shalt hang it upon four pillars of shittim *wood* overlaid with gold: their hooks *shall be of* gold, upon the four sockets of silver.

³³ ¶ And thou shalt hang up the veil under the taches, that thou mayest bring in thither within the veil the ark of the testimony: and the veil shall divide unto you between the holy *place* and the most holy.

³⁴And thou shalt put the mercy seat upon the ark of the testimony in the most holy *place*.

³⁵And thou shalt set the table without the veil, and the candlestick over against the table on the side of the tabernacle toward the south: and thou shalt put the table on the north side.

Amplified

¹¹You shall make fifty clasps of bronze and put the clasps into the loops and couple the tent together, that it may be one whole.

¹²The surplus that remains of the tent curtains, the half curtain that remains, shall hang over the back of the tabernacle.

¹³And the cubit on the one side and the cubit on the other side of what remains in the length of the curtains of the tent shall hang over the sides of the tabernacle, on this side and that side, to cover it.

¹⁴You shall make a [third] covering for the tent of rams' skins tanned red, and a [fourth] covering above that of dolphin *or* porpoise skins.

¹⁵And you shall make the upright frame for the tabernacle of boards of acacia wood.

¹⁶Ten cubits shall be the length of a board and a cubit and a half shall be the breadth of one board.

¹⁷Make two tenons in each board for dovetailing *and* fitting together; so shall you do for all the tabernacle boards.

¹⁸And make the boards for the tabernacle: twenty boards for the south side;

¹⁹And you shall make forty silver sockets under the twenty boards, two sockets under each board for its two tenons.

²⁰And for the north side of the tabernacle there shall be twenty boards

²¹And their forty silver sockets, two sockets under each board.

²²For the back or west side of the tabernacle you shall make six boards.

²³Make two boards for the corners of the tabernacle in the rear on both sides.

²⁴They shall be coupled down below and coupled together on top with one ring. Thus shall it be for both of them; they shall form the two corners.

²⁵And that will be eight boards and their sockets of silver, sixteen sockets, two sockets under each board.

²⁶And you shall make bars of acacia wood: five for the boards of one side,

²⁷And five bars for the boards of the other side of the tabernacle, and five bars for the boards of the rear end of the tabernacle, for the back wall to the west.

²⁸And the middle bar halfway up the boards shall pass through from end to end.

²⁹You shall overlay the boards with gold and make their rings of gold to hold the bars and overlay the bars with gold.

³⁰You shall erect the tabernacle after the plan of it shown you on the mountain.

³¹And make a veil of blue, purple, and scarlet [stuff] and fine twined linen, skillfully worked with cherubim on it.

³²You shall hang it on four pillars of acacia wood overlaid with gold, with gold hooks, on four sockets of silver.

³³And you shall hang the veil from the clasps and bring the ark of the Testimony into place within the veil; and the veil shall separate for you the Holy Place from the Most Holy Place.

³⁴And you shall put the mercy seat on the ark of the Testimony in the Most Holy Place.

³⁵And you shall set the table [for the showbread] outside the veil [in the Holy Place] on the north side and the lampstand opposite the table on the south side of the tabernacle.

n Or, *covering*   *o* Heb. *in the remainder,* or, *surplusage*
p Heb. *hands*   *q* Heb. *twinned*

New American Standard

11 ¶ "You shall make fifty clasps of ᶻbronze, and you shall put the clasps into the loops and join the tent together so that it will be a unit.

12"The overlapping part that is left over in the curtains of the tent, the half curtain that is left over, shall lap over the back of the tabernacle.

13"The cubit on one side and the cubit on the other, of what is left over in the length of the curtains of the tent, shall lap over the sides of the tabernacle on one side and on the other, to cover it.

14"You shall make a covering for the tent of rams' skins dyed red and a covering of porpoise skins above.

Boards and Sockets

15 ¶ "Then you shall make the boards for the tabernacle of acacia wood, standing upright.

16"Ten cubits *shall be* the length of each board and one and a half cubits the width of each board.

17"*There shall be* two tenons for each board, fitted to one another; thus you shall do for all the boards of the tabernacle.

18"You shall make the boards for the tabernacle: twenty boards for the south side.

19"You shall make forty ᵃsockets of silver under the twenty boards, two sockets under one board for its two tenons and two sockets under another board for its two tenons;

20 and for the second side of the tabernacle, on the north side, twenty boards,

21 and their forty sockets of silver; two sockets under one board and two sockets under another board.

22"For the rear of the tabernacle, to the west, you shall make six boards.

23"You shall make two boards for the corners of the tabernacle at the rear.

24"They shall be double beneath, and together they shall be complete to its top to the first ring; thus it shall be with both of them: they shall form the two corners.

25"There shall be eight boards with their sockets of silver, sixteen sockets; two sockets under one board and two sockets under another board.

26 ¶ "Then you shall make bars of acacia wood, five for the boards of one side of the tabernacle,

27 and five bars for the boards of the other side of the tabernacle, and five bars for the boards of the side of the tabernacle for the rear *side* to the west.

28"The middle bar in the center of the boards shall pass through from end to end.

29"You shall overlay the boards with gold and make their rings of gold *as* holders for the bars; and you shall overlay the bars with gold.

30"Then you shall erect the tabernacle according to its plan which you have been shown in the mountain.

The Veil and Screen

31 ¶ "You shall make a veil of blue and purple and scarlet *material* and fine twisted linen; it shall be made with cherubim, the work of a skillful workman.

32"You shall hang it on four pillars of acacia overlaid with gold, their hooks *also being of* gold, on four sockets of silver.

33"You shall hang up the veil under the clasps, and shall bring in the ark of the testimony there within the veil; and the veil shall serve for you as a partition between the holy place and the holy of holies.

34"You shall put the mercy seat on the ark of the testimony in the holy of holies.

35"You shall set the table outside the veil, and the lampstand opposite the table on the side of the tabernacle toward the south; and you shall put the table on the north side.

New International

curtain in the other set. 11Then make fifty bronze clasps and put them in the loops to fasten the tent together as a unit. 12As for the additional length of the tent curtains, the half curtain that is left over is to hang down at the rear of the tabernacle. 13The tent curtains will be a cubitᵘ longer on both sides; what is left will hang over the sides of the tabernacle so as to cover it. 14Make for the tent a covering of ram skins dyed red, and over that a covering of hides of sea cows.ᵛ

15"Make upright frames of acacia wood for the tabernacle. 16Each frame is to be ten cubits long and a cubit and a half wide,ʷ 17with two projections set parallel to each other. Make all the frames of the tabernacle in this way. 18Make twenty frames for the south side of the tabernacle 19and make forty silver bases to go under them—two bases for each frame, one under each projection. 20For the other side, the north side of the tabernacle, make twenty frames 21and forty silver bases—two under each frame. 22Make six frames for the far end, that is, the west end of the tabernacle, 23and make two frames for the corners at the far end. 24At these two corners they must be double from the bottom all the way to the top, and fitted into a single ring; both shall be like that. 25So there will be eight frames and sixteen silver bases—two under each frame.

26"Also make crossbars of acacia wood: five for the frames on one side of the tabernacle, 27five for those on the other side, and five for the frames on the west, at the far end of the tabernacle. 28The center crossbar is to extend from end to end at the middle of the frames. 29Overlay the frames with gold and make gold rings to hold the crossbars. Also overlay the crossbars with gold.

30"Set up the tabernacle according to the plan shown you on the mountain.

31"Make a curtain of blue, purple and scarlet yarn and finely twisted linen, with cherubim worked into it by a skilled craftsman. 32Hang it with gold hooks on four posts of acacia wood overlaid with gold and standing on four silver bases. 33Hang the curtain from the clasps and place the ark of the Testimony behind the curtain. The curtain will separate the Holy Place from the Most Holy Place. 34Put the atonement cover on the ark of the Testimony in the Most Holy Place. 35Place the table outside the curtain on the north side of the tabernacle and put the lampstand opposite it on the south side.

ᵘ 13 That is, about 1 1/2 feet (about 0.5 meter)   ᵛ 14 That is, dugongs   ʷ 16 That is, about 15 feet (about 4.5 meters) long and 2 1/4 feet (about 0.7 meter) wide

ᶻ Or *copper*   ᵃ Or *bases*

King James

36And thou shalt make an hanging for the door of the tent, *of* blue, and purple, and scarlet, and fine twined linen, wrought with needlework.

37And thou shalt make for the hanging five pillars *of* shittim *wood*, and overlay them with gold, *and* their hooks *shall be of* gold: and thou shalt cast five sockets of brass for them.

The altar

27 AND THOU shalt make an altar *of* shittim wood, five cubits long, and five cubits broad; the altar shall be foursquare: and the height thereof *shall be* three cubits.

2And thou shalt make the horns of it upon the four corners thereof: his horns shall be of the same: and thou shalt overlay it with brass.

3And thou shalt make his pans to receive his ashes, and his shovels, and his basins, and his fleshhooks, and his firepans: all the vessels thereof thou shalt make *of* brass.

4And thou shalt make for it a grate of network *of* brass; and upon the net shalt thou make four brasen rings in the four corners thereof.

5And thou shalt put it under the compass of the altar beneath, that the net may be even to the midst of the altar.

6And thou shalt make staves for the altar, staves *of* shittim wood, and overlay them with brass.

7And the staves shall be put into the rings, and the staves shall be upon the two sides of the altar, to bear it.

8Hollow with boards shalt thou make it: as *r*it was shown thee in the mount, so shall they make *it*.

The court of the tabernacle

9 ¶ And thou shalt make the court of the tabernacle: for the south side southward *there shall be* hangings for the court *of* fine twined linen of an hundred cubits long for one side:

10And the twenty pillars thereof and their twenty sockets *shall be of* brass; the hooks of the pillars and their fillets *shall be of* silver.

11And likewise for the north side in length *there shall be* hangings of an hundred *cubits* long, and his twenty pillars and their twenty sockets *of* brass; the hooks of the pillars and their fillets *of* silver.

12 ¶ And *for* the breadth of the court on the west side *shall be* hangings of fifty cubits: their pillars ten, and their sockets ten.

13And the breadth of the court on the east side eastward *shall be* fifty cubits.

14The hangings of one side *of the gate shall be* fifteen cubits: their pillars three, and their sockets three.

15And on the other side *shall be* hangings fifteen *cubits:* their pillars three, and their sockets three.

16 ¶ And for the gate of the court *shall be* an hanging of twenty cubits, *of* blue, and purple, and scarlet, and fine twined linen, wrought with needlework: *and* their pillars *shall be* four, and their sockets four.

17All the pillars round about the court *shall be* filleted with silver; their hooks *shall be of* silver, and their sockets *of* brass.

18 ¶ The length of the court *shall be* an hundred cubits, and the breadth *s*fifty every where, and the height five cubits *of* fine twined linen, and their sockets *of* brass.

19All the vessels of the tabernacle in all the service thereof, and all the pins thereof, and all the pins of the court, *shall be of* brass.

Oil for the lamp

20 ¶ And thou shalt command the children of Israel, that they bring thee pure oil olive beaten for the light, to cause the lamp *t*to burn always.

Amplified

36You shall make a hanging [to form a screen] for the door of the tent of blue, purple, and scarlet [stuff] and fine twined linen, embroidered. [John 10:9.]

37You shall make five pillars of acacia wood to support the hanging curtain and overlay them with gold; their hooks shall be of gold, and you shall cast five [base] sockets of bronze for them.

27 AND MAKE the altar of acacia wood, five cubits square and three cubits high [within reach of all].

2Make horns for it on its four corners; they shall be of one piece with it, and you shall overlay it with bronze.

3You shall make pots to take away its ashes, and shovels, basins, forks, and firepans; make all its utensils of bronze.

4Also make for it a grate, a network of bronze; and on the net you shall make four bronze rings at its four corners.

5And you shall put it under the ledge of the altar, so that the net will extend halfway down the altar.

6And make poles for the altar, poles of acacia wood overlaid with bronze.

7The poles shall be put through the rings on the two sides of the altar, with which to carry it. [Num. 4:14, 15.]

8You shall make [the altar] hollow with slabs *or* planks; as shown you on the mountain, so shall it be made.

9And you shall make the court of the tabernacle. On the south side the court shall have hangings of fine twined linen, a hundred cubits long for one side;

10Their pillars shall be twenty and their sockets twenty, of bronze, but the hooks of the pillars and their joinings shall be of silver;

11Likewise for the north side hangings, a hundred cubits long, and their twenty pillars and their twenty sockets of bronze, but the hooks of the pillars and their joinings shall be of silver.

12And for the breadth of the court on the west side there shall be hangings of fifty cubits, with ten pillars and ten sockets.

13The breadth of the court to the front, the east side, shall be fifty cubits.

14The hangings for one side of the gate shall be fifteen cubits, with three pillars and three sockets.

15On the other side the hangings shall be fifteen cubits, with three pillars and three sockets.

16And for the gate of the court there shall be a hanging [for a screen] twenty cubits long, of blue, purple, and scarlet [stuff] and fine twined linen, embroidered. It shall have four pillars and four sockets for them.

17All the pillars round about the court shall be joined together with silver rods; their hooks shall be of silver and their sockets of bronze.

18The length of the court shall be a hundred cubits and the breadth fifty and the height five cubits, [with hangings of] fine twined linen and sockets of bronze.

19All the tabernacle's utensils *and* instruments used in all its service, and all its pegs and all the pegs for the court, shall be of bronze.

20You shall command the Israelites to provide you with pure oil of crushed olives for the light, to cause it to burn continually [every night].

---

*r*Heb. *he showed*   *s*Heb. *fifty by fifty*   *t*Heb. *to ascend up*

New American Standard

36 ¶ "You shall make a screen for the doorway of the tent of blue and purple and scarlet *material* and fine twisted linen, the work of a weaver.

37 "You shall make five pillars of acacia for the screen and overlay them with gold, their hooks *also being of* gold; and you shall cast five sockets of bronze for them.

The Bronze Altar

27 "AND YOU shall make the altar of acacia wood, five cubits long and five cubits wide; the altar shall be square, and its height shall be three cubits.

2 "You shall make its horns on its four corners; its horns shall be of one piece with it, and you shall overlay it with bronze.

3 "You shall make its pails for removing its ashes, and its shovels and its basins and its forks and its firepans; you shall make all its utensils of bronze.

4 "You shall make for it a grating of network of bronze, and on the net you shall make four bronze rings at its four corners.

5 "You shall put it beneath, under the ledge of the altar, so that the net will reach halfway up the altar.

6 "You shall make poles for the altar, poles of acacia wood, and overlay them with bronze.

7 "Its poles shall be inserted into the rings, so that the poles shall be on the two sides of the altar when it is carried.

8 "You shall make it hollow with planks; as it was shown to you in the mountain, so they shall make *it*.

Court of the Tabernacle

9 ¶ "You shall make the court of the tabernacle. On the south side *there shall be* hangings for the court of fine twisted linen one hundred cubits long for one side;

10 and its pillars *shall be* twenty, with their twenty sockets of bronze; the hooks of the pillars and their bands *shall be* of silver.

11 "Likewise for the north side in length *there shall be* hangings one hundred *cubits* long, and its twenty pillars with their twenty sockets of bronze; the hooks of the pillars and their bands *shall be* of silver.

12 "*For* the width of the court on the west side *shall be* hangings of fifty cubits *with* their ten pillars and their ten sockets.

13 "The width of the court on the east side *shall be* fifty cubits.

14 "The hangings for the *one* side *of the gate shall be* fifteen cubits *with* their three pillars and their three sockets.

15 "And for the other side *shall be* hangings of fifteen cubits *with* their three pillars and their three sockets.

16 "For the gate of the court *there shall be* a screen of twenty cubits, of blue and purple and scarlet *material* and fine twisted linen, the work of a weaver, *with* their four pillars and their four sockets.

17 "All the pillars around the court shall be furnished with silver bands *with* their hooks of silver and their sockets of bronze.

18 "The length of the court *shall be* one hundred cubits, and the width fifty throughout, and the height five cubits of fine twisted linen, and their sockets of bronze.

19 "All the utensils of the tabernacle *used* in all its service, and all its pegs, and all the pegs of the court, *shall be* of bronze.

20 ¶ "You shall charge the sons of Israel, that they bring you clear oil of beaten olives for the light, to make a lamp burn continually.

New International

36 "For the entrance to the tent make a curtain of blue, purple and scarlet yarn and finely twisted linen—the work of an embroiderer. 37 Make gold hooks for this curtain and five posts of acacia wood overlaid with gold. And cast five bronze bases for them.

The Altar of Burnt Offering

27 "BUILD AN altar of acacia wood, three cubits[x] high; it is to be square, five cubits long and five cubits wide.[y] 2 Make a horn at each of the four corners, so that the horns and the altar are of one piece, and overlay the altar with bronze. 3 Make all its utensils of bronze—its pots to remove the ashes, and its shovels, sprinkling bowls, meat forks and firepans. 4 Make a grating for it, a bronze network, and make a bronze ring at each of the four corners of the network. 5 Put it under the ledge of the altar so that it is halfway up the altar. 6 Make poles of acacia wood for the altar and overlay them with bronze. 7 The poles are to be inserted into the rings so they will be on two sides of the altar when it is carried. 8 Make the altar hollow, out of boards. It is to be made just as you were shown on the mountain.

The Courtyard

9 "Make a courtyard for the tabernacle. The south side shall be a hundred cubits[z] long and is to have curtains of finely twisted linen, 10 with twenty posts and twenty bronze bases and with silver hooks and bands on the posts. 11 The north side shall also be a hundred cubits long and is to have curtains, with twenty posts and twenty bronze bases and with silver hooks and bands on the posts.

12 "The west end of the courtyard shall be fifty cubits[a] wide and have curtains, with ten posts and ten bases. 13 On the east end, toward the sunrise, the courtyard shall also be fifty cubits wide. 14 Curtains fifteen cubits[b] long are to be on one side of the entrance, with three posts and three bases, 15 and curtains fifteen cubits long are to be on the other side, with three posts and three bases.

16 "For the entrance to the courtyard, provide a curtain twenty cubits[c] long, of blue, purple and scarlet yarn and finely twisted linen—the work of an embroiderer—with four posts and four bases. 17 All the posts around the courtyard are to have silver bands and hooks, and bronze bases. 18 The courtyard shall be a hundred cubits long and fifty cubits wide,[d] with curtains of finely twisted linen five cubits[e] high, and with bronze bases. 19 All the other articles used in the service of the tabernacle, whatever their function, including all the tent pegs for it and those for the courtyard, are to be of bronze.

Oil for the Lampstand

20 "Command the Israelites to bring you clear oil of pressed olives for the light so that the lamps may be kept

---

x 1 That is, about 4 1/2 feet (about 1.3 meters)   *y 1* That is, about 7 1/2 feet (about 2.3 meters) long and wide   *z 9* That is, about 150 feet (about 46 meters); also in verse 11   *a 12* That is, about 75 feet (about 23 meters); also in verse 13   *b 14* That is, about 22 1/2 feet (about 6.9 meters); also in verse 15   *c 16* That is, about 30 feet (about 9 meters)   *d 18* That is, about 150 feet (about 46 meters) long and 75 feet (about 23 meters) wide   *e 18* That is, about 7 1/2 feet (about 2.3 meters)

King James

²¹In the tabernacle of the congregation without the veil, which *is* before the testimony, Aaron and his sons shall order it from evening to morning before the LORD: *it shall be* a statute for ever unto their generations on the behalf of the children of Israel.

The priest's garments

28 AND TAKE thou unto thee Aaron thy brother, and his sons with him, from among the children of Israel, that he may minister unto me in the priest's office, *even* Aaron, Nadab and Abihu, Eleazar and Ithamar, Aaron's sons.

²And thou shalt make holy garments for Aaron thy brother for glory and for beauty.

³And thou shalt speak unto all *that are* wisehearted, whom I have filled with the spirit of wisdom, that they may make Aaron's garments to consecrate him, that he may minister unto me in the priest's office.

⁴And these *are* the garments which they shall make; a breastplate, and an ephod, and a robe, and a broidered coat, a mitre, and a girdle: and they shall make holy garments for Aaron thy brother, and his sons, that he may minister unto me in the priest's office.

⁵And they shall take gold, and blue, and purple, and scarlet, and fine linen.

⁶ ¶ And they shall make the ephod *of* gold, *of* blue, and *of* purple, *of* scarlet, and fine twined linen, with cunning work.

⁷It shall have the two shoulderpieces thereof joined at the two edges thereof; and *so* it shall be joined together.

⁸And the ^ucurious girdle of the ephod, which *is* upon it, shall be of the same, according to the work thereof; *even of* gold, *of* blue, and purple, and scarlet, and fine twined linen.

⁹And thou shalt take two onyx stones, and grave on them the names of the children of Israel:

¹⁰Six of their names on one stone, and *the other* six names of the rest on the other stone, according to their birth.

¹¹With the work of an engraver in stone, *like* the engravings of a signet, shalt thou engrave the two stones with the names of the children of Israel: thou shalt make them to be set in ouches of gold.

¹²And thou shalt put the two stones upon the shoulders of the ephod *for* stones of memorial unto the children of Israel: and Aaron shall bear their names before the LORD upon his two shoulders for a memorial.

¹³ ¶ And thou shalt make ouches *of* gold;

¹⁴And two chains *of* pure gold at the ends; *of* wreathen work shalt thou make them, and fasten the wreathen chains to the ouches.

The priest's breastplate

¹⁵ ¶ And thou shalt make the breastplate of judgment with cunning work; after the work of the ephod thou shalt make it; *of* gold, *of* blue, and *of* purple, and *of* scarlet, and *of* fine twined linen, shalt thou make it.

¹⁶Foursquare it shall be *being* doubled; a span *shall be* the length thereof, and a span *shall be* the breadth thereof.

¹⁷And thou shalt ^vset in it settings of stones, *even* four rows of stones: *the first* row *shall be* a ^wsardius, a topaz, and a carbuncle: *this shall be* the first row.

¹⁸And the second row *shall be* an emerald, a sapphire, and a diamond.

¹⁹And the third row a ligure, an agate, and an amethyst.

²⁰And the fourth row a beryl, and an onyx, and a jasper: they shall be set in gold in their ^xinclosings.

²¹And the stones shall be with the names of the children of Israel, twelve, according to their names, *like* the engravings of a signet; every one with his name shall they be according to the twelve tribes.

Amplified

²¹In the Tent of Meeting [of God with His people], outside the veil which sets apart the Testimony, Aaron and his sons shall keep it burning from evening to morning before the Lord. It shall be a statute to be observed on behalf of the Israelites throughout their generations.

28 FROM AMONG the Israelites take your brother Aaron and his sons with him, that he may minister to Me in the priest's office, even Aaron, Nadab and Abihu, Eleazar and Ithamar, Aaron's sons.

²And you shall make for Aaron your brother sacred garments [appointed official dress set apart for special holy services] for honor and for beauty.

³Tell all who are expert, whom I have endowed with skill *and* good judgment, that they shall make Aaron's garments to sanctify him for My priesthood.

⁴They shall make these garments: a breastplate, an ephod [a distinctive vestment to which the breastplate was to be attached], a robe, long *and* sleeved tunic of checkerwork, a turban, and a sash *or* band. They shall make sacred garments for Aaron your brother and his sons to minister to Me in the priest's office.

⁵They shall receive [from the people] *and* use gold, and blue, purple, and scarlet [stuff], and fine linen.

⁶And they shall make the ephod of gold, of blue, purple, and scarlet [stuff], and fine twined linen, skillfully woven *and* worked.

⁷It shall have two shoulder straps to join the two [back and front] edges, that it may be held together.

⁸The skillfully woven girding band which is on the ephod shall be made of the same, of gold, blue, purple, and scarlet [stuff], and fine twined linen.

⁹And you shall take two onyx *or* beryl stones and engrave on them the names of the twelve sons of Israel;

¹⁰Six of their names on one stone and the six names of the rest on the other stone, arranged in order of their birth.

¹¹With the work of a stone engraver, like the engravings of a signet, you shall engrave the two stones according to the names of the sons of Israel. You shall have them set in sockets *or* rosettes of gold.

¹²And you shall put the two stones upon the [two] shoulder straps of the ephod [of the high priest] as memorial stones for Israel; and Aaron shall bear their names upon his two shoulders as a memorial before the Lord.

¹³And you shall make sockets *or* rosettes of gold for settings,

¹⁴And two chains of pure gold, like cords shall you twist them, and fasten the corded chains to the settings.

¹⁵You shall make a breastplate of judgment, in skilled work; like the workmanship of the ephod shall you make it, of gold, blue, purple, and scarlet [stuff], and of fine twined linen.

¹⁶The breastplate shall be square *and* doubled; a span [nine inches] shall be its length and a span shall be its breadth.

¹⁷You shall set in it four rows of stones: a sardius, a topaz, and a carbuncle shall be the first row;

¹⁸The second row an emerald, a sapphire, and a diamond [so called at that time];

¹⁹The third row a jacinth, an agate, and an amethyst;

²⁰And the fourth row a beryl, an onyx, and a jasper; they shall be set in gold filigree.

²¹And the stones shall be twelve, according to the names of the sons of Israel, like the engravings of a signet, each with its name for the twelve tribes.

---

^uOr, *embroidered*   ^vHeb. *fill in it fillings of stone*   ^wOr, *ruby*   ^xHeb. *fillings*

New American Standard

21"In the tent of meeting, outside the veil which is before the testimony, Aaron and his sons shall keep it in order from evening to morning before the LORD; *it shall be* a perpetual statute throughout their generations for the sons of Israel.

Garments of the Priests

28 "THEN BRING near to yourself Aaron your brother, and his sons with him, from among the sons of Israel, to minister as priest to Me—Aaron, Nadab and Abihu, Eleazar and Ithamar, Aaron's sons.

2"You shall make holy garments for Aaron your brother, for glory and for beauty.

3"You shall speak to all the skillful persons whom I have endowed with the spirit of wisdom, that they make Aaron's garments to consecrate him, that he may minister as priest to Me.

4"These are the garments which they shall make: a bbreastpiece and an ephod and a robe and a tunic of checkered work, a turban and a sash, and they shall make holy garments for Aaron your brother and his sons, that he may minister as priest to Me.

5"They shall take the gold and the blue and the purple and the scarlet *material* and the fine linen.

6 ¶ "They shall also make the ephod of gold, of blue and purple *and* scarlet *material* and fine twisted linen, the work of the skillful workman.

7"It shall have two shoulder pieces joined to its two ends, that it may be joined.

8"The skillfully woven band, which is on it, shall be like its workmanship, of the same material: of gold, of blue and purple and scarlet *material* and fine twisted linen.

9"You shall take two onyx stones and engrave on them the names of the sons of Israel,

10 six of their names on the one stone and the names of the remaining six on the other stone, according to their birth.

11"As a jeweler engraves a signet, you shall engrave the two stones according to the names of the sons of Israel; you shall set them in filigree *settings* of gold.

12"You shall put the two stones on the shoulder pieces of the ephod, *as* stones of memorial for the sons of Israel, and Aaron shall bear their names before the LORD on his two shoulders for a memorial.

13"You shall make filigree *settings* of gold,

14 and two chains of pure gold; you shall make them of twisted cordage work, and you shall put the corded chains on the filigree *settings*.

15 ¶ "You shall make a breastpiece of judgment, the work of a skillful workman; like the work of the ephod you shall make it: of gold, of blue and purple and scarlet *material* and fine twisted linen you shall make it.

16"It shall be square *and* folded double, a span in length and a span in width.

17"You shall mount on it four rows of stones; the first row *shall be* a row of ruby, topaz and emerald;

18 and the second row a turquoise, a sapphire and a diamond;

19 and the third row a jacinth, an agate and an amethyst;

20 and the fourth row a beryl and an onyx and a jasper; they shall be set in gold filigree.

21"The stones shall be according to the names of the sons of Israel: twelve, according to their names; they shall be *like* the engravings of a seal, each according to his name for the twelve tribes.

New International

burning. 21In the Tent of Meeting, outside the curtain that is in front of the Testimony, Aaron and his sons are to keep the lamps burning before the LORD from evening till morning. This is to be a lasting ordinance among the Israelites for the generations to come.

The Priestly Garments

28 "HAVE AARON your brother brought to you from among the Israelites, along with his sons Nadab and Abihu, Eleazar and Ithamar, so they may serve me as priests. 2Make sacred garments for your brother Aaron, to give him dignity and honor. 3Tell all the skilled men to whom I have given wisdom in such matters that they are to make garments for Aaron, for his consecration, so he may serve me as priest. 4These are the garments they are to make: a breastpiece, an ephod, a robe, a woven tunic, a turban and a sash. They are to make these sacred garments for your brother Aaron and his sons, so they may serve me as priests. 5Have them use gold, and blue, purple and scarlet yarn, and fine linen.

The Ephod

6"Make the ephod of gold, and of blue, purple and scarlet yarn, and of finely twisted linen—the work of a skilled craftsman. 7It is to have two shoulder pieces attached to two of its corners, so it can be fastened. 8Its skillfully woven waistband is to be like it—of one piece with the ephod and made with gold, and with blue, purple and scarlet yarn, and with finely twisted linen.

9"Take two onyx stones and engrave on them the names of the sons of Israel 10in the order of their birth—six names on one stone and the remaining six on the other. 11Engrave the names of the sons of Israel on the two stones the way a gem cutter engraves a seal. Then mount the stones in gold filigree settings 12and fasten them on the shoulder pieces of the ephod as memorial stones for the sons of Israel. Aaron is to bear the names on his shoulders as a memorial before the LORD. 13Make gold filigree settings 14and two braided chains of pure gold, like a rope, and attach the chains to the settings.

The Breastpiece

15"Fashion a breastpiece for making decisions—the work of a skilled craftsman. Make it like the ephod: of gold, and of blue, purple and scarlet yarn, and of finely twisted linen. 16It is to be square—a span*f* long and a span wide—and folded double. 17Then mount four rows of precious stones on it. In the first row there shall be a ruby, a topaz and a beryl; 18in the second row a turquoise, a sapphire*g* and an emerald; 19in the third row a jacinth, an agate and an amethyst; 20in the fourth row a chrysolite, an onyx and a jasper.*h* Mount them in gold filigree settings. 21There are to be twelve stones, one for each of the names of the sons of Israel, each engraved like a seal with the name of one of the twelve tribes.

---

f 16 That is, about 9 inches (about 22 centimeters)   *g 18* Or *lapis lazuli*   *h 20* The precise identification of some of these precious stones is uncertain.

bOr *pouch*

King James

22 ¶ And thou shalt make upon the breastplate chains at the ends *of* wreathen work *of* pure gold.

23And thou shalt make upon the breastplate two rings of gold, and shalt put the two rings on the two ends of the breastplate.

24And thou shalt put the two wreathen *chains* of gold in the two rings *which are* on the ends of the breastplate.

25And *the other* two ends of the two wreathen *chains* thou shalt fasten in the two ouches, and put *them* on the shoulderpieces of the ephod before it.

26 ¶ And thou shalt make two rings of gold, and thou shalt put them upon the two ends of the breastplate in the border thereof, which *is* in the side of the ephod inward.

27And two *other* rings of gold thou shalt make, and shalt put them on the two sides of the ephod underneath, toward the forepart thereof, over against the *other* coupling thereof, above the curious girdle of the ephod.

28And they shall bind the breastplate by the rings thereof unto the rings of the ephod with a lace of blue, that *it* may be above the curious girdle of the ephod, and that the breastplate be not loosed from the ephod.

29And Aaron shall bear the names of the children of Israel in the breastplate of judgment upon his heart, when he goeth in unto the holy *place*, for a memorial before the LORD continually.

30 ¶ And thou shalt put in the breastplate of judgment the Urim and the Thummim; and they shall be upon Aaron's heart, when he goeth in before the LORD: and Aaron shall bear the judgment of the children of Israel upon his heart before the LORD continually.

The priest's robe

31 ¶ And thou shalt make the robe of the ephod all *of* blue.

32And there shall be an hole in the top of it, in the midst thereof: it shall have a binding of woven work round about the hole of it, as it were the hole of an habergeon, that it be not rent.

33 ¶ And *beneath* upon the ʸhem of it thou shalt make pomegranates *of* blue, and *of* purple, and *of* scarlet, round about the hem thereof; and bells of gold between them round about:

34A golden bell and a pomegranate, a golden bell and a pomegranate, upon the hem of the robe round about.

35And it shall be upon Aaron to minister: and his sound shall be heard when he goeth in unto the holy *place* before the LORD, and when he cometh out, that he die not.

36 ¶ And thou shalt make a plate *of* pure gold, and grave upon it, *like* the engravings of a signet, HOLINESS TO THE LORD.

37And thou shalt put it on a blue lace, that it may be upon the mitre; upon the forefront of the mitre it shall be.

38And it shall be upon Aaron's forehead, that Aaron may bear the iniquity of the holy things, which the children of Israel shall hallow in all their holy gifts; and it shall be always upon his forehead, that they may be accepted before the LORD.

39 ¶ And thou shalt embroider the coat of fine linen, and thou shalt make the mitre *of* fine linen, and thou shalt make the girdle *of* needlework.

40 ¶ And for Aaron's sons thou shalt make coats, and thou shalt make for them girdles, and bonnets shalt thou make for them, for glory and for beauty.

41And thou shalt put them upon Aaron thy brother, and his sons with him; and shalt anoint them, and ᶻconsecrate them, and sanctify them, that they may minister unto me in the priest's office.

42And thou shalt make them linen breeches to cover ᵃtheir nakedness; from the loins even unto the thighs they shall ᵇreach:

Amplified

22You shall make for the breastplate chains of pure gold twisted like cords.

23You shall make on the breastplate two rings of gold and put [them] on the two edges of the breastplate.

24And you shall put the two twisted, cordlike chains of gold in the two rings which are on the edges of the breastplate.

25The other two ends of the two twisted, cordlike chains you shall fasten in the two sockets *or* rosettes in front, putting them on the shoulder straps of the ephod;

26And make two rings of gold and put them at the two ends of the breastplate on its inside edge next to the ephod.

27Two gold rings you shall make and attach them to the lower part of the two shoulder pieces of the ephod in front, close by where they join, above the skillfully woven girdle *or* band of the ephod.

28And they shall bind the breastplate by its rings to the rings of the ephod with a lace of blue, that it may be above the skillfully woven girding band of the ephod, and that the breastplate may not become loose from the ephod.

29So Aaron shall bear the names of the sons of Israel in the breastplate of judgment upon his heart when he goes into the Holy Place, to bring them in continual remembrance before the Lord.

30In the breastplate of judgment you shall put the Urim and the Thummim [unspecified articles used when the high priest asked God's counsel for all Israel]; they shall be upon Aaron's heart when he goes in before the Lord, and Aaron shall bear the judgment (rights, judicial decisions) of the Israelites upon his heart before the Lord continually.

31Make the robe [to be worn beneath] the ephod all of blue.

32There shall be a hole in the center of it [to slip over the head], with a binding of woven work around the hole, like the opening in a coat of mail *or* a garment, that it may not fray *or* tear.

33And you shall make pomegranates of blue, purple, and scarlet [stuff] around about its skirts, with gold bells between them;

34A gold bell and a pomegranate, a gold bell and a pomegranate, round about on the skirts of the robe.

35Aaron shall wear the robe when he ministers, and its sound shall be heard when he goes [alone] into the Holy of Holies before the Lord and when he comes out, lest he die there.

36And you shall make a plate of pure gold and engrave on it, like the engravings of a signet, HOLY TO THE LORD. [Exod. 39:30.]

37You shall fasten it on the front of the turban with a blue cord.

38It shall be upon Aaron's forehead, that Aaron may take upon himself *and* bear [any] iniquity [connected with] the holy things which the Israelites shall give *and* dedicate; and it shall always be upon his forehead, that they may be accepted before the Lord [in the priest's person]. [Luke 24:44; Heb. 8:1, 2.]

39And you shall weave the long *and* sleeved tunic of checkerwork of fine linen *or* silk and make a turban of fine linen *or* silk; and you shall make a girdle, the work of the embroiderer.

40For Aaron's sons you shall make long *and* sleeved tunics and belts *or* sashes and caps, for glory *and* honor and beauty.

41And you shall put them on Aaron your brother and his sons with him, and shall anoint them and ordain and sanctify them [set them apart for God], that they may serve Me as priests.

42You shall make for them [white] linen trunks to cover their naked flesh, reaching from the waist to the thighs.

ʸ Or, *skirts*   ᶻHeb. *fill their hand*   ᵃHeb. *flesh of their*
nakedness   ᵇHeb. *be*

New American Standard

22"You shall make on the breastpiece chains of twisted cordage work in pure gold.

23"You shall make on the breastpiece two rings of gold, and shall put the two rings on the two ends of the breastpiece.

24"You shall put the two cords of gold on the two rings at the ends of the breastpiece.

25"You shall put the *other* two ends of the two cords on the two filigree *settings,* and put them on the shoulder pieces of the ephod, at the front of it.

26"You shall make two rings of gold and shall place them on the two ends of the breastpiece, on the edge of it, which is toward the inner side of the ephod.

27"You shall make two rings of gold and put them on the bottom of the two shoulder pieces of the ephod, on the front of it close to the place where it is joined, above the skillfully woven band of the ephod.

28"They shall bind the breastpiece by its rings to the rings of the ephod with a blue cord, so that it will be on the skillfully woven band of the ephod, and that the breastpiece will not come loose from the ephod.

29"Aaron shall carry the names of the sons of Israel in the breastpiece of judgment over his heart when he enters the holy place, for a memorial before the LORD continually.

30"You shall put in the breastpiece of judgment the cUrim and the Thummim, and they shall be over Aaron's heart when he goes in before the LORD; and Aaron shall carry the judgment of the sons of Israel over his heart before the LORD continually.

31 ¶ "You shall make the robe of the ephod all of blue.

32"There shall be an opening at its top in the middle of it; around its opening there shall be a binding of woven work, as like the opening of a coat of mail, so that it will not be torn.

33"You shall make on its hem pomegranates of blue and purple and scarlet *material,* all around on its hem, and bells of gold between them all around:

34 a golden bell and a pomegranate, a golden bell and a pomegranate, all around on the hem of the robe.

35"It shall be on Aaron when he ministers; and its tinkling shall be heard when he enters and leaves the holy place before the LORD, so that he will not die.

36 ¶ "You shall also make a plate of pure gold and shall engrave on it, like the engravings of a seal, 'Holy to the LORD.'

37"You shall fasten it on a blue cord, and it shall be on the turban; it shall be at the front of the turban.

38"It shall be on Aaron's forehead, and Aaron shall take away the iniquity of the holy things which the sons of Israel consecrate, with regard to all their holy gifts; and it shall always be on his forehead, that they may be accepted before the LORD.

39 ¶ "You shall weave the tunic of checkered work of fine linen, and shall make a turban of fine linen, and you shall make a sash, the work of a weaver.

40 ¶ "For Aaron's sons you shall make tunics; you shall also make sashes for them, and you shall make caps for them, for glory and for beauty.

41"You shall put them on Aaron your brother and on his sons with him; and you shall anoint them and ordain them and consecrate them, that they may serve Me as priests.

42"You shall make for them linen breeches to cover *their* bare flesh; they shall reach from the loins even to the thighs.

New International

22"For the breastpiece make braided chains of pure gold, like a rope. 23Make two gold rings for it and fasten them to two corners of the breastpiece. 24Fasten the two gold chains to the rings at the corners of the breastpiece, 25and the other ends of the chains to the two settings, attaching them to the shoulder pieces of the ephod at the front. 26Make two gold rings and attach them to the other two corners of the breastpiece on the inside edge next to the ephod. 27Make two more gold rings and attach them to the bottom of the shoulder pieces on the front of the ephod, close to the seam just above the waistband of the ephod. 28The rings of the breastpiece are to be tied to the rings of the ephod with blue cord, connecting it to the waistband, so that the breastpiece will not swing out from the ephod.

29"Whenever Aaron enters the Holy Place, he will bear the names of the sons of Israel over his heart on the breastpiece of decision as a continuing memorial before the LORD. 30Also put the Urim and the Thummim in the breastpiece, so they may be over Aaron's heart whenever he enters the presence of the LORD. Thus Aaron will always bear the means of making decisions for the Israelites over his heart before the LORD.

Other Priestly Garments

31"Make the robe of the ephod entirely of blue cloth, 32with an opening for the head in its center. There shall be a woven edge like a collar*i* around this opening, so that it will not tear. 33Make pomegranates of blue, purple and scarlet yarn around the hem of the robe, with gold bells between them. 34The gold bells and the pomegranates are to alternate around the hem of the robe. 35Aaron must wear it when he ministers. The sound of the bells will be heard when he enters the Holy Place before the LORD and when he comes out, so that he will not die.

36"Make a plate of pure gold and engrave on it as on a seal: HOLY TO THE LORD. 37Fasten a blue cord to it to attach it to the turban; it is to be on the front of the turban. 38It will be on Aaron's forehead, and he will bear the guilt involved in the sacred gifts the Israelites consecrate, whatever their gifts may be. It will be on Aaron's forehead continually so that they will be acceptable to the LORD.

39"Weave the tunic of fine linen and make the turban of fine linen. The sash is to be the work of an embroiderer. 40Make tunics, sashes and headbands for Aaron's sons, to give them dignity and honor. 41After you put these clothes on your brother Aaron and his sons, anoint and ordain them. Consecrate them so they may serve me as priests.

42"Make linen undergarments as a covering for the

---

c I.e. lights and perfections

i 32 The meaning of the Hebrew for this word is uncertain.

King James

43And they shall be upon Aaron, and upon his sons, when they come in unto the tabernacle of the congregation, or when they come near unto the altar to minister in the holy *place;* that they bear not iniquity, and die: *it shall be* a statute for ever unto him and his seed after him.

Consecrating the priests

29 AND THIS *is* the thing that thou shalt do unto them to hallow them, to minister unto me in the priest's office: Take one young bullock, and two rams without blemish,

2And unleavened bread, and cakes unleavened tempered with oil, and wafers unleavened anointed with oil: *of* wheaten flour shalt thou make them.

3And thou shalt put them into one basket, and bring them in the basket, with the bullock and the two rams.

4And Aaron and his sons thou shalt bring unto the door of the tabernacle of the congregation, and shalt wash them with water.

5And thou shalt take the garments, and put upon Aaron the coat, and the robe of the ephod, and the ephod, and the breastplate, and gird him with the curious girdle of the ephod:

6And thou shalt put the mitre upon his head, and put the holy crown upon the mitre.

7Then shalt thou take the anointing oil, and pour *it* upon his head, and anoint him.

8And thou shalt bring his sons, and put coats upon them.

9And thou shalt gird them with girdles, Aaron and his sons, and *c*put the bonnets on them: and the priest's office shall be theirs for a perpetual statute: and thou shalt *d*consecrate Aaron and his sons.

10And thou shalt cause a bullock to be brought before the tabernacle of the congregation: and Aaron and his sons shall put their hands upon the head of the bullock.

11And thou shalt kill the bullock before the LORD, *by* the door of the tabernacle of the congregation.

12And thou shalt take of the blood of the bullock, and put *it* upon the horns of the altar with thy finger, and pour all the blood beside the bottom of the altar.

13And thou shalt take all the fat that covereth the inwards, and *e*the caul *that is* above the liver, and the two kidneys, and the fat that *is* upon them, and burn *them* upon the altar.

14But the flesh of the bullock, and his skin, and his dung, shalt thou burn with fire without the camp: it *is* a sin offering.

15 ¶ Thou shalt also take one ram; and Aaron and his sons shall put their hands upon the head of the ram.

16And thou shalt slay the ram, and thou shalt take his blood, and sprinkle *it* round about upon the altar.

17And thou shalt cut the ram in pieces, and wash the inwards of him, and his legs, and put *them* unto his pieces, and *f*unto his head.

18And thou shalt burn the whole ram upon the altar: it *is* a burnt offering unto the LORD: it *is* a sweet savour, an offering made by fire unto the LORD.

19 ¶ And thou shalt take the other ram; and Aaron and his sons shall put their hands upon the head of the ram.

20Then shalt thou kill the ram, and take of his blood, and put *it* upon the tip of the right ear of Aaron, and upon the tip of the right ear of his sons, and upon the thumb of their right hand, and upon the great toe of their right foot, and sprinkle the blood upon the altar round about.

21And thou shalt take of the blood that *is* upon the altar, and of the anointing oil, and sprinkle *it* upon Aaron, and upon his garments, and upon his sons, and upon the garments of his sons with him: and he shall be hallowed, and his garments, and his sons, and his sons' garments with him.

Amplified

43And they shall be on Aaron and his sons when they go into the Tent of Meeting or when they come near to the altar to minister in the Holy Place, lest they bring iniquity upon themselves and die; it shall be a statute forever to Aaron and to his descendants after him.

29 THIS IS what you shall do to consecrate (set them apart) that they may serve Me as priests. Take one young bull and two rams, all without blemish,

2And unleavened bread and unleavened cakes mixed with oil and unleavened wafers spread with oil; of fine flour shall you make them.

3You shall put them in one basket and bring them in [it], and bring also the bull and the two rams;

4And bring Aaron and his sons to the door of the Tent of Meeting [out where the laver is] and wash them with water.

5Then take the garments and put on Aaron the long *and* sleeved tunic and the robe of the ephod and the ephod and the breastplate, and gird him with the skillfully woven girding band of the ephod.

6And you shall put the turban *or* miter upon his head and put the holy crown upon the turban.

7Then take the anointing oil and pour it on his head and anoint him.

8And bring his sons and put long *and* sleeved tunics on them.

9And you shall gird them with sashes *or* belts, Aaron and his sons, and bind caps on them; and the priest's office shall be theirs by a perpetual statute. Thus you shall ordain *and* consecrate Aaron and his sons.

10Then bring the bull before the Tent of Meeting, and Aaron and his sons shall lay their hands upon its head.

11And you shall kill the bull before the Lord by the door of the Tent of Meeting.

12And you shall take of the blood of the bull and put it on the horns of the altar with your finger, and pour out all the blood at the base of the altar.

13And take all the fat that covers the entrails, and the appendage that is on the liver, and the two kidneys, and the fat that is on them, and burn them on the altar.

14But the flesh of the bull, its hide, and the contents of its entrails you shall burn with fire outside the camp; it is a sin offering. [Heb. 13:11–13.]

15You shall also take one of the rams, and Aaron and his sons shall lay their hands upon the head of the ram.

16And you shall kill the ram and you shall take its blood and throw it against the altar round about.

17And you shall cut the ram in pieces and wash its entrails and legs and put them with its pieces and its head,

18And you shall burn the whole ram upon the altar. It is a burnt offering to the Lord; it is a sweet *and* satisfying fragrance, an offering made by fire to the Lord.

19And you shall take the other ram, and Aaron and his sons shall lay their hands upon the head of the ram;

20Then you shall kill the ram and take part of its blood and put it on the tip of the right ears of Aaron and his sons and on the thumb of their right hands and on the great toe of their right feet, and dash the rest of the blood against the altar round about.

21Then you shall take part of the blood that is on the altar, and of the anointing oil, and sprinkle it upon Aaron and his garments and on his sons and their garments; and he and his garments and his sons and their garments shall be sanctified *and* made holy.

---

*c*Heb. *bind*   *d*Heb. *fill the hand of*   *e*It seemeth by anatomy, and the Hebrew doctors, to be *the midriff*   *f*Or, *upon*

New American Standard

43"They shall be on Aaron and on his sons when they enter the tent of meeting, or when they approach the altar to minister in the holy place, so that they do not incur guilt and die. It *shall be* a statute forever to him and to his descendants after him.

Consecration of the Priests

29 "NOW THIS is what you shall do to them to consecrate them to minister as priests to Me: take one young bull and two rams without blemish,

2 and unleavened bread and unleavened cakes mixed with oil, and unleavened wafers spread with oil; you shall make them of fine wheat flour.

3"You shall put them in one basket, and present them in the basket along with the bull and the two rams.

4"Then you shall bring Aaron and his sons to the doorway of the tent of meeting and wash them with water.

5"You shall take the garments, and put on Aaron the tunic and the robe of the ephod and the ephod and the breastpiece, and gird him with the skillfully woven band of the ephod;

6 and you shall set the turban on his head and put the holy crown on the turban.

7"Then you shall take the anointing oil and pour it on his head and anoint him.

8"You shall bring his sons and put tunics on them.

9"You shall gird them with sashes, Aaron and his sons, and bind caps on them, and they shall have the priesthood by a perpetual statute. So you shall ordain Aaron and his sons.

The Sacrifices

10 ¶ "Then you shall bring the bull before the tent of meeting, and Aaron and his sons shall lay their hands on the head of the bull.

11"You shall slaughter the bull before the LORD at the doorway of the tent of meeting.

12"You shall take some of the blood of the bull and put *it* on the horns of the altar with your finger; and you shall pour out all the blood at the base of the altar.

13"You shall take all the fat that covers the entrails and the lobe of the liver, and the two kidneys and the fat that is on them, and offer them up in smoke on the altar.

14"But the flesh of the bull and its hide and its refuse, you shall burn with fire outside the camp; it is a sin offering.

15 ¶ "You shall also take the one ram, and Aaron and his sons shall lay their hands on the head of the ram;

16 and you shall slaughter the ram and shall take its blood and sprinkle it around on the altar.

17"Then you shall cut the ram into its pieces, and wash its entrails and its legs, and put *them* with its pieces and its head.

18"You shall offer up in smoke the whole ram on the altar; it is a burnt offering to the LORD: it is a soothing aroma, an offering by fire to the LORD.

19 ¶ "Then you shall take the other ram, and Aaron and his sons shall lay their hands on the head of the ram.

20"You shall slaughter the ram, and take some of its blood and put *it* on the lobe of Aaron's right ear and on the lobes of his sons' right ears and on the thumbs of their right hands and on the big toes of their right feet, and sprinkle the *rest of the* blood around on the altar.

21"Then you shall take some of the blood that is on the altar and some of the anointing oil, and sprinkle *it* on Aaron and on his garments and on his sons and on his sons' garments with him; so he and his garments shall be consecrated, as well as his sons and his sons' garments with him.

New International

body, reaching from the waist to the thigh. 43Aaron and his sons must wear them whenever they enter the Tent of Meeting or approach the altar to minister in the Holy Place, so that they will not incur guilt and die.

"This is to be a lasting ordinance for Aaron and his descendants.

Consecration of the Priests

29 "THIS IS what you are to do to consecrate them, so they may serve me as priests: Take a young bull and two rams without defect. 2And from fine wheat flour, without yeast, make bread, and cakes mixed with oil, and wafers spread with oil. 3Put them in a basket and present them in it—along with the bull and the two rams. 4Then bring Aaron and his sons to the entrance to the Tent of Meeting and wash them with water. 5Take the garments and dress Aaron with the tunic, the robe of the ephod, the ephod itself and the breastpiece. Fasten the ephod on him by its skillfully woven waistband. 6Put the turban on his head and attach the sacred diadem to the turban. 7Take the anointing oil and anoint him by pouring it on his head. 8Bring his sons and dress them in tunics 9and put headbands on them. Then tie sashes on Aaron and his sons.*j* The priesthood is theirs by a lasting ordinance. In this way you shall ordain Aaron and his sons.

10"Bring the bull to the front of the Tent of Meeting, and Aaron and his sons shall lay their hands on its head. 11Slaughter it in the LORD's presence at the entrance to the Tent of Meeting. 12Take some of the bull's blood and put it on the horns of the altar with your finger, and pour out the rest of it at the base of the altar. 13Then take all the fat around the inner parts, the covering of the liver, and both kidneys with the fat on them, and burn them on the altar. 14But burn the bull's flesh and its hide and its offal outside the camp. It is a sin offering.

15"Take one of the rams, and Aaron and his sons shall lay their hands on its head. 16Slaughter it and take the blood and sprinkle it against the altar on all sides. 17Cut the ram into pieces and wash the inner parts and the legs, putting them with the head and the other pieces. 18Then burn the entire ram on the altar. It is a burnt offering to the LORD, a pleasing aroma, an offering made to the LORD by fire.

19"Take the other ram, and Aaron and his sons shall lay their hands on its head. 20Slaughter it, take some of its blood and put it on the lobes of the right ears of Aaron and his sons, on the thumbs of their right hands, and on the big toes of their right feet. Then sprinkle blood against the altar on all sides. 21And take some of the blood on the altar and some of the anointing oil and sprinkle it on Aaron and his garments and on his sons and their garments. Then he and his sons and their garments will be consecrated.

j9 Hebrew; Septuagint on them

King James

22Also thou shalt take of the ram the fat and the rump, and the fat that covereth the inwards, and the caul *above* the liver, and the two kidneys, and the fat that *is* upon them, and the right shoulder; for it *is* a ram of consecration:

23And one loaf of bread, and one cake of oiled bread, and one wafer out of the basket of the unleavened bread that *is* before the LORD:

24And thou shalt put all in the hands of Aaron, and in the hands of his sons; and shalt gwave them *for* a wave offering before the LORD.

25And thou shalt receive them of their hands, and burn *them* upon the altar for a burnt offering, for a sweet savour before the LORD: it *is* an offering made by fire unto the LORD.

26And thou shalt take the breast of the ram of Aaron's consecration, and wave it *for* a wave offering before the LORD: and it shall be thy part.

27And thou shalt sanctify the breast of the wave offering, and the shoulder of the heave offering, which is waved, and which is heaved up, of the ram of the consecration, *even* of *that* which *is* for Aaron, and of *that* which is for his sons:

28And it shall be Aaron's and his sons' by a statute for ever from the children of Israel: for it *is* an heave offering: and it shall be an heave offering from the children of Israel of the sacrifice of their peace offerings, *even* their heave offering unto the LORD.

29 ¶ And the holy garments of Aaron shall be his sons' after him, to be anointed therein, and to be consecrated in them.

30And hthat son that is priest in his stead shall put them on seven days, when he cometh into the tabernacle of the congregation to minister in the holy *place*.

31 ¶ And thou shalt take the ram of the consecration, and seethe his flesh in the holy place.

32And Aaron and his sons shall eat the flesh of the ram, and the bread that *is* in the basket, *by* the door of the tabernacle of the congregation.

33And they shall eat those things wherewith the atonement was made, to consecrate *and* to sanctify them: but a stranger shall not eat *thereof*, because they *are* holy.

34And if aught of the flesh of the consecrations, or of the bread, remain unto the morning, then thou shalt burn the remainder with fire: it shall not be eaten, because it *is* holy.

35And thus shalt thou do unto Aaron, and to his sons, according to all *things* which I have commanded thee: seven days shalt thou consecrate them.

36And thou shalt offer every day a bullock *for* a sin offering for atonement: and thou shalt cleanse the altar, when thou hast made an atonement for it, and thou shalt anoint it, to sanctify it.

37Seven days thou shalt make an atonement for the altar, and sanctify it; and it shall be an altar most holy: whatsoever toucheth the altar shall be holy.

38 ¶ Now this *is that* which thou shalt offer upon the altar; two lambs of the first year day by day continually.

39The one lamb thou shalt offer in the morning; and the other lamb thou shalt offer at even:

40And with the one lamb a tenth deal of flour mingled with the fourth part of an hin of beaten oil; and the fourth part of an hin of wine *for* a drink offering.

41And the other lamb thou shalt offer at even, and shalt do thereto according to the meat offering of the morning, and according to the drink offering thereof, for a sweet savour, an offering made by fire unto the LORD.

42*This shall be* a continual burnt offering throughout your generations *at* the door of the tabernacle of the congregation before the LORD: where I will meet you, to speak there unto thee.

43And there I will meet with the children of Israel, and *the tabernacle* shall be sanctified by my glory.

Amplified

22Also you shall take the fat of the ram, the fat tail, the fat that covers the entrails, the appendage on the liver, the two kidneys with the fat that is on them, and the right thigh; for it is a ram of consecration *and* ordination.

23Take also one loaf of bread, and one cake of oiled bread, and one wafer out of the basket of the unleavened bread that is before the Lord.

24And put all these in the hands of Aaron and his sons and they shall wave them for a wave offering before the Lord.

25Then you shall take them from their hands, add them to the burnt offering, and burn them on the altar for a sweet *and* satisfying fragrance before the Lord; it is an offering made by fire to the Lord.

26And take the breast of the ram of Aaron's consecration *and* ordination and wave it for a wave offering before the Lord; and it shall be your portion [Moses].

27And you shall sanctify (set apart for God) the waved breast of the ram used in the ordination and the waved thigh of the priests' portion, since it is for Aaron and his sons.

28It shall be for Aaron and his sons as their due portion from the Israelites perpetually, an offering from the Israelites of their peace *and* thanksgiving sacrifices, their offering to the Lord.

29The holy garments of Aaron shall pass to his descendants who succeed him, to be anointed in them and to be consecrated *and* ordained in them.

30And that son who is [high] priest in his stead shall put them on [each day for] seven days when he comes into the Tent of Meeting to minister in the Holy Place.

31You shall take the ram of the consecration *and* ordination and boil its flesh in a holy *and* set-apart place.

32Aaron and his sons shall eat the flesh of the ram and the bread in the basket, at the door of the Tent of Meeting.

33They shall eat those things with which atonement was made, to ordain and consecrate them; but a stranger (layman) shall not eat of them because they are holy (set apart to the worship of God).

34And if any of the flesh or bread for the ordination remains until morning, you shall burn it with fire; it shall not be eaten, because it is holy (set apart to the worship of God).

35Thus shall you do to Aaron and to his sons according to all I have commanded you; during seven days shall you ordain them.

36You shall offer every day a bull as a sin offering for atonement. And you shall cleanse the altar by making atonement for it, and anoint it to consecrate it.

37Seven days you shall make atonement for the altar and sanctify it [set it apart for God]; and the altar shall be most holy; whoever *or* whatever touches the altar must be holy (set apart for God's service).

38Now this is what you shall offer on the altar: two lambs a year old shall be offered day by day continually.

39One lamb you shall offer in the morning and the other lamb in the evening;

40And with the one lamb a tenth measure of fine flour mixed with a fourth of a hin of beaten oil, and a fourth of a hin of wine for a drink offering [to be poured out].

41And the other lamb you shall offer at evening, and do with it as with the cereal offering of the morning and with the drink offering, for a sweet *and* satisfying fragrance, an offering made by fire to the Lord.

42This shall be a continual burnt offering throughout your generations at the door of the Tent of Meeting before the Lord, where I will meet with you to speak there to you.

43There I will meet with the Israelites, and the Tent of Meeting shall be sanctified by My glory [the Shekinah, God's visible presence].

---

gOr, *shake to and fro*   hHeb. he *of his sons*   iOr, Israel

New American Standard

22 ¶ "You shall also take the fat from the ram and the fat tail, and the fat that covers the entrails and the lobe of the liver, and the two kidneys and the fat that is on them and the right thigh (for it is a ram of ordination),

23 and one cake of bread and one cake of bread *mixed with* oil and one wafer from the basket of unleavened bread which is *set* before the LORD;

24 and you shall put all these in the hands of Aaron and in the hands of his sons, and shall wave them as a wave offering before the LORD.

25 "You shall take them from their hands, and offer them up in smoke on the altar on the burnt offering for a soothing aroma before the LORD; it is an offering by fire to the LORD.

26 ¶ "Then you shall take the breast of Aaron's ram of ordination, and wave it as a wave offering before the LORD; and it shall be your portion.

27 "You shall consecrate the breast of the wave offering and the thigh of the heave offering which was waved and which was offered from the ram of ordination, from the one which was for Aaron and from the one which was for his sons.

28 "It shall be for Aaron and his sons as *their* portion forever from the sons of Israel, for it is a heave offering; and it shall be a heave offering from the sons of Israel from the sacrifices of their peace offerings, *even* their heave offering to the LORD.

29 ¶ "The holy garments of Aaron shall be for his sons after him, that in them they may be anointed and ordained.

30 "For seven days the one of his sons who is priest in his stead shall put them on when he enters the tent of meeting to minister in the holy place.

Food of the Priests

31 ¶ "You shall take the ram of ordination and boil its flesh in a holy place.

32 "Aaron and his sons shall eat the flesh of the ram and the bread that is in the basket, at the doorway of the tent of meeting.

33 "Thus they shall eat those things by which atonement was made at their ordination *and* consecration; but a layman shall not eat *them,* because they are holy.

34 "If any of the flesh of ordination or any of the bread remains until morning, then you shall burn the remainder with fire; it shall not be eaten, because it is holy.

35 ¶ "Thus you shall do to Aaron and to his sons, according to all that I have commanded you; you shall ordain them through seven days.

36 "Each day you shall offer a bull as a sin offering for atonement, and you shall purify the altar when you make atonement for it, and you shall anoint it to consecrate it.

37 "For seven days you shall make atonement for the altar and consecrate it; then the altar shall be most holy, *and* whatever touches the altar shall be holy.

38 ¶ "Now this is what you shall offer on the altar: two one year old lambs each day, continuously.

39 "The one lamb you shall offer in the morning and the other lamb you shall offer at twilight;

40 and there *shall be* one-tenth *of an ephah* of fine flour mixed with one-fourth of a hin of beaten oil, and one-fourth of a hin of wine for a drink offering with one lamb.

41 "The other lamb you shall offer at twilight, and shall offer with it the same grain offering and the same drink offering as in the morning, for a soothing aroma, an offering by fire to the LORD.

42 "It shall be a continual burnt offering throughout your generations at the doorway of the tent of meeting before the LORD, where I will meet with you, to speak to you there.

43 "I will meet there with the sons of Israel, and it shall be consecrated by My glory.

New International

22 "Take from this ram the fat, the fat tail, the fat around the inner parts, the covering of the liver, both kidneys with the fat on them, and the right thigh. (This is the ram for the ordination.) 23 From the basket of bread made without yeast, which is before the LORD, take a loaf, and a cake made with oil, and a wafer. 24 Put all these in the hands of Aaron and his sons and wave them before the LORD as a wave offering. 25 Then take them from their hands and burn them on the altar along with the burnt offering for a pleasing aroma to the LORD, an offering made to the LORD by fire. 26 After you take the breast of the ram for Aaron's ordination, wave it before the LORD as a wave offering, and it will be your share.

27 "Consecrate those parts of the ordination ram that belong to Aaron and his sons: the breast that was waved and the thigh that was presented. 28 This is always to be the regular share from the Israelites for Aaron and his sons. It is the contribution the Israelites are to make to the LORD from their fellowship offerings.[k]

29 "Aaron's sacred garments will belong to his descendants so that they can be anointed and ordained in them. 30 The son who succeeds him as priest and comes to the Tent of Meeting to minister in the Holy Place is to wear them seven days.

31 "Take the ram for the ordination and cook the meat in a sacred place. 32 At the entrance to the Tent of Meeting, Aaron and his sons are to eat the meat of the ram and the bread that is in the basket. 33 They are to eat these offerings by which atonement was made for their ordination and consecration. But no one else may eat them, because they are sacred. 34 And if any of the meat of the ordination ram or any bread is left over till morning, burn it up. It must not be eaten, because it is sacred.

35 "Do for Aaron and his sons everything I have commanded you, taking seven days to ordain them. 36 Sacrifice a bull each day as a sin offering to make atonement. Purify the altar by making atonement for it, and anoint it to consecrate it. 37 For seven days make atonement for the altar and consecrate it. Then the altar will be most holy, and whatever touches it will be holy.

38 "This is what you are to offer on the altar regularly each day: two lambs a year old. 39 Offer one in the morning and the other at twilight. 40 With the first lamb offer a tenth of an ephah[l] of fine flour mixed with a quarter of a hin[m] of oil from pressed olives, and a quarter of a hin of wine as a drink offering. 41 Sacrifice the other lamb at twilight with the same grain offering and its drink offering as in the morning—a pleasing aroma, an offering made to the LORD by fire.

42 "For the generations to come this burnt offering is to be made regularly at the entrance to the Tent of Meeting before the LORD. There I will meet you and speak to you; 43 there also I will meet with the Israelites, and the place will be consecrated by my glory.

k 28 Traditionally *peace offerings* l 40 That is, probably about 2 quarts (about 2 liters) m 40 That is, probably about 1 quart (about 1 liter)

King James

Amplified

44And I will sanctify the tabernacle of the congregation, and the altar: I will sanctify also both Aaron and his sons, to minister to me in the priest's office.

45 ¶ And I will dwell among the children of Israel, and will be their God.

46And they shall know that I *am* the LORD their God, that brought them forth out of the land of Egypt, that I may dwell among them: I *am* the LORD their God.

The altar of incense

30 AND THOU shalt make an altar to burn incense upon: *of* shittim wood shalt thou make it.

2A cubit *shall be* the length thereof, and a cubit the breadth thereof; foursquare shall it be: and two cubits *shall be* the height thereof: the horns thereof *shall be* of the same.

3And thou shalt overlay it with pure gold, the *j*top thereof, and the *k*sides thereof round about, and the horns thereof; and thou shalt make unto it a crown of gold round about.

4And two golden rings shalt thou make to it under the crown of it, by the two *l*corners thereof, upon the two sides of it shalt thou make *it;* and they shall be for places for the staves to bear it withal.

5And thou shalt make the staves *of* shittim wood, and overlay them with gold.

6And thou shalt put it before the veil that *is* by the ark of the testimony, before the mercy seat that *is* over the testimony, where I will meet with thee.

7And Aaron shall burn thereon *m*sweet incense every morning: when he dresseth the lamps, he shall burn incense upon it.

8And when Aaron *n*lighteth the lamps *o*at even, he shall burn incense upon it, a perpetual incense before the LORD throughout your generations.

9Ye shall offer no strange incense thereon, nor burnt sacrifice, nor meat offering; neither shall ye pour drink offering thereon.

10And Aaron shall make an atonement upon the horns of it once in a year with the blood of the sin offering of atonements: once in the year shall he make atonement upon it throughout your generations: it *is* most holy unto the LORD.

The offerings for the tabernacle

11 ¶ And the LORD spake unto Moses, saying,

12When thou takest the sum of the children of Israel after *p*their number, then shall they give every man a ransom for his soul unto the LORD, when thou numberest them; that there be no plague among them, when *thou* numberest them.

13This they shall give, every one that passeth among them that are numbered, half a shekel after the shekel of the sanctuary: (a shekel *is* twenty gerahs:) an half shekel *shall be* the offering of the LORD.

14Every one that passeth among them that are numbered, from twenty years old and above, shall give an offering unto the LORD.

15The rich shall not *q*give more, and the poor shall not *r*give less than half a shekel, when *they* give an offering unto the LORD, to make an atonement for your souls.

16And thou shalt take the atonement money of the children of Israel, and shalt appoint it for the service of the tabernacle of the congregation; that it may be a memorial unto the children of Israel before the LORD, to make an atonement for your souls.

The laver, oil and perfume

17 ¶ And the LORD spake unto Moses, saying,

44And I will sanctify the Tent of Meeting and the altar; I will sanctify also both Aaron and his sons to minister to Me in the priest's office.

45And I will dwell among the Israelites and be their God.

46And they shall know [from personal experience] that I am the Lord their God, Who brought them forth out of the land of Egypt that I might dwell among them; I am the Lord their God.

30 AND YOU shall make an altar to burn incense upon; of acacia wood you shall make it.

2A cubit shall be its length and a cubit its breadth; its top shall be square and it shall be two cubits high. Its horns shall be of one piece with it.

3And you shall overlay it with pure gold, its top and its sides round about and its horns, and you shall make a crown (a rim or molding) of gold around it.

4You shall make two golden rings under the rim of it, on the two ribs on the two opposite sides of it; and they shall be holders for the poles with which to carry it.

5And you shall make the poles of acacia wood, overlaid with gold.

6You shall put the altar [of incense] in front *and* outside of the veil that screens the ark of the Testimony, before the mercy seat that is over the Testimony (the Law, the tables of stone), where I will meet with you.

7And Aaron shall burn on it incense of sweet spices; every morning when he trims *and* fills the lamps he shall burn it. [Ps. 141:2; Rev. 5:8; 8:3, 4.]

8And when Aaron lights the lamps in the evening, he shall burn it, a perpetual incense before the Lord throughout your generations.

9You shall offer no unholy incense on the altar nor burnt sacrifice nor cereal offering; and you shall pour no libation (drink offering) on it.

10Aaron shall make atonement upon the horns of it once a year; with the blood of the sin offering of atonement once in the year shall he make atonement upon *and* for it throughout your generations. It is most holy to the Lord.

11And the Lord said to Moses,

12When you take the census of the Israelites, every man shall give a ransom for himself to the Lord when you number them, that no plague may fall upon them when you number them. [Rom. 8:1–4.]

13This is what everyone shall give as he joins those already numbered: a half shekel, in terms of the sanctuary shekel, a shekel being twenty gerahs; a half shekel as an offering to the Lord.

14Everyone from twenty years old and upward, as he joins those already numbered, shall give this offering to the Lord. [Matt. 10:24; I Pet. 1:18, 19.]

15The rich shall not give more and the poor shall not give less than half a shekel when [you] give this offering to the Lord to make atonement for yourselves.

16And you shall take the atonement money of the Israelites and use it [exclusively] for the service of the Tent of Meeting, that it may bring the Israelites to remembrance before the Lord, to make atonement for yourselves.

17And the Lord said to Moses,

---

*j*Heb. *roof*   *k*Heb. *walls*   *l*Heb. *ribs*   *m*Heb. *incense of spices*   *n*Or, setteth up Heb. *causeth to ascend*   *o*Heb. *between the two evens*   *p*Heb. *them that are to be numbered*   *q*Heb. *multiply*   *r*Heb. *diminish*

New American Standard

44"I will consecrate the tent of meeting and the altar; I will also consecrate Aaron and his sons to minister as priests to Me.

45"I will dwell among the sons of Israel and will be their God.

46"They shall know that I am the LORD their God who brought them out of the land of Egypt, that I might dwell among them; I am the LORD their God.

The Altar of Incense

30 "MOREOVER, YOU shall make an altar as a place for burning incense; you shall make it of acacia wood.

2"Its length *shall be* a cubit, and its width a cubit, it shall be square, and its height *shall be* two cubits; its horns *shall be* of one piece with it.

3"You shall overlay it with pure gold, its top and its sides all around, and its horns; and you shall make a gold molding all around for it.

4"You shall make two gold rings for it under its molding; you shall make *them* on its two side walls—on opposite sides—and they shall be holders for poles with which to carry it.

5"You shall make the poles of acacia wood and overlay them with gold.

6"You shall put this altar in front of the veil that is near the ark of the testimony, in front of the mercy seat that is over *the ark of* the testimony, where I will meet with you.

7"Aaron shall burn fragrant incense on it; he shall burn it every morning when he trims the lamps.

8"When Aaron trims the lamps at twilight, he shall burn incense. *There shall be* perpetual incense before the LORD throughout your generations.

9"You shall not offer any strange incense on this altar, or burnt offering or meal offering; and you shall not pour out a drink offering on it.

10"Aaron shall make atonement on its horns once a year; he shall make atonement on it with the blood of the sin offering of atonement once a year throughout your generations. It is most holy to the LORD."

11 ¶ The LORD also spoke to Moses, saying,

12"When you take a census of the sons of Israel to number them, then each one of them shall give a ransom for himself to the LORD, when you number them, so that there will be no plague among them when you number them.

13"This is what everyone who is numbered shall give: half a shekel according to the shekel of the sanctuary (the shekel is twenty gerahs), half a shekel as a contribution to the LORD.

14"Everyone who is numbered, from twenty years old and over, shall give the contribution to the LORD.

15"The rich shall not pay more and the poor shall not pay less than the half shekel, when you give the contribution to the LORD to make atonement for yourselves.

16"You shall take the atonement money from the sons of Israel and shall give it for the service of the tent of meeting, that it may be a memorial for the sons of Israel before the LORD, to make atonement for yourselves."

17 ¶ The LORD spoke to Moses, saying,

New International

44"So I will consecrate the Tent of Meeting and the altar and will consecrate Aaron and his sons to serve me as priests. 45Then I will dwell among the Israelites and be their God. 46They will know that I am the LORD their God, who brought them out of Egypt so that I might dwell among them. I am the LORD their God.

The Altar of Incense

30 "MAKE AN altar of acacia wood for burning incense. 2It is to be square, a cubit long and a cubit wide, and two cubits high[n]—its horns of one piece with it. 3Overlay the top and all the sides and the horns with pure gold, and make a gold molding around it. 4Make two gold rings for the altar below the molding—two on opposite sides—to hold the poles used to carry it. 5Make the poles of acacia wood and overlay them with gold. 6Put the altar in front of the curtain that is before the ark of the Testimony—before the atonement cover that is over the Testimony—where I will meet with you.

7"Aaron must burn fragrant incense on the altar every morning when he tends the lamps. 8He must burn incense again when he lights the lamps at twilight so incense will burn regularly before the LORD for the generations to come. 9Do not offer on this altar any other incense or any burnt offering or grain offering, and do not pour a drink offering on it. 10Once a year Aaron shall make atonement on its horns. This annual atonement must be made with the blood of the atoning sin offering for the generations to come. It is most holy to the LORD."

Atonement Money

11Then the LORD said to Moses, 12"When you take a census of the Israelites to count them, each one must pay the LORD a ransom for his life at the time he is counted. Then no plague will come on them when you number them. 13Each one who crosses over to those already counted is to give a half shekel,[o] according to the sanctuary shekel, which weighs twenty gerahs. This half shekel is an offering to the LORD. 14All who cross over, those twenty years old or more, are to give an offering to the LORD. 15The rich are not to give more than a half shekel and the poor are not to give less when you make the offering to the LORD to atone for your lives. 16Receive the atonement money from the Israelites and use it for the service of the Tent of Meeting. It will be a memorial for the Israelites before the LORD, making atonement for your lives."

Basin for Washing

17Then the LORD said to Moses, 18"Make a bronze basin,

n 2 That is, about 1 1/2 feet (about 0.5 meter) long and wide and about 3 feet (about 0.9 meter) high   o 13 That is, about 1/5 ounce (about 6 grams); also in verse 15

King James	Amplified

King James

18Thou shalt also make a laver *of* brass, and his foot *also of* brass, to wash *withal:* and thou shalt put it between the tabernacle of the congregation and the altar, and thou shalt put water therein.

19For Aaron and his sons shall wash their hands and their feet thereat:

20When they go into the tabernacle of the congregation, they shall wash with water, that they die not; or when they come near to the altar to minister, to burn offering made by fire unto the LORD:

21So they shall wash their hands and their feet, that they die not: and it shall be a statute for ever to them, *even* to him and to his seed throughout their generations.

22 ¶ Moreover the LORD spake unto Moses, saying,

23Take thou also unto thee principal spices, of pure myrrh five hundred *shekels,* and of sweet cinnamon half so much, *even* two hundred and fifty *shekels,* and of sweet calamus two hundred and fifty *shekels,*

24And of cassia five hundred *shekels,* after the shekel of the sanctuary, and of oil olive an hin:

25And thou shalt make it an oil of holy ointment, an ointment compound after the art of the *s*apothecary: it shall be an holy anointing oil.

26And thou shalt anoint the tabernacle of the congregation therewith, and the ark of the testimony,

27And the table and all his vessels, and the candlestick and his vessels, and the altar of incense,

28And the altar of burnt offering with all his vessels, and the laver and his foot.

29And thou shalt sanctify them, that they may be most holy: whatsoever toucheth them shall be holy.

30And thou shalt anoint Aaron and his sons, and consecrate them, that *they* may minister unto me in the priest's office.

31And thou shalt speak unto the children of Israel, saying, This shall be an holy anointing oil unto me throughout your generations.

32Upon man's flesh shall it not be poured, neither shall ye make *any other* like it, after the composition of it: it *is* holy, *and* it shall be holy unto you.

33Whosoever compoundeth *any* like it, or whosoever putteth *any* of it upon a stranger, shall even be cut off from his people.

34 ¶ And the LORD said unto Moses, Take unto thee sweet spices, stacte, and onycha, and galbanum; *these* sweet spices with pure frankincense: of each shall there be a like *weight:*

35And thou shalt make it a perfume, a confection after the art of the apothecary, *t*tempered together, pure *and* holy:

36And thou shalt beat *some* of it very small, and put of it before the testimony in the tabernacle of the congregation, where I will meet with thee: it shall be unto you most holy.

37And *as for* the perfume which thou shalt make, ye shall not make to yourselves according to the composition thereof: it shall be unto thee holy for the LORD.

38Whosoever shall make like unto that, to smell thereto, shall even be cut off from his people.

The appointment of the workmen

31 AND THE LORD spake unto Moses, saying, 2See, I have called by name Bezaleel the son of Uri, the son of Hur, of the tribe of Judah:

3And I have filled him with the spirit of God, in wisdom, and in understanding, and in knowledge, and in all manner of workmanship,

4To devise cunning works, to work in gold, and in silver, and in brass,

5And in cutting of stones, to set *them,* and in carving of timber, to work in all manner of workmanship.

Amplified

18You shall also make a laver *or* large basin of bronze, and its base of bronze, for washing; and you shall put it [outside in the court] between the Tent of Meeting and the altar [of burnt offering], and you shall put water in it;

19There Aaron and his sons shall wash their hands and their feet. [Tit. 3:5.]

20When they go into the Tent of Meeting, they shall wash with water, that they die not; or when they come near to the altar to minister, to burn an offering made by fire to the Lord, [John 13:6–8.]

21So they shall wash their hands and their feet, lest they die; it shall be a perpetual statute for [Aaron] and his descendants throughout their generations.

22Moreover, the Lord said to Moses,

23Take the best spices: of liquid myrrh 500 shekels, of sweet-scented cinnamon half as much, 250 shekels, of fragrant calamus 250 shekels,

24And of cassia 500 shekels, in terms of the sanctuary shekel, and of olive oil a hin.

25And you shall make of these a holy anointing oil, a perfume compounded after the art of the perfumer; it shall be a sacred anointing oil.

26And you shall anoint the Tent of Meeting with it, and the ark of the Testimony,

27And the [showbread] table and all its utensils, and the lampstand and its utensils, and the altar of incense,

28And the altar of burnt offering with all its utensils, and the laver [for cleansing] and its base.

29You shall sanctify (separate) them, that they may be most holy; whoever *and* whatever touches them must be holy (set apart to God).

30And you shall anoint Aaron and his sons and sanctify (separate) them, that they may minister to Me as priests.

31And say to the Israelites, This is a holy anointing oil [symbol of the Holy Spirit], sacred to Me alone throughout your generations. [Rom. 8:9; I Cor. 12:3.]

32It shall not be poured upon a layman's body, nor shall you make any other like it in composition; it is holy, and you shall hold it sacred.

33Whoever compounds any like it or puts any of it upon an outsider shall be cut off from his people.

34Then the Lord said to Moses, Take sweet spices—stacte, onycha, and galbanum, sweet spices with pure frankincense, an equal amount of each—

35And make of them incense, a perfume after the perfumer's art, seasoned with salt *and* mixed, pure and sacred.

36You shall beat some of it very small and put some of it before the Testimony in the Tent of Meeting, where I will meet with you; it shall be to you most holy.

37And the incense which you shall make according to its composition you shall not make for yourselves; it shall be to you holy to the Lord.

38Whoever makes any like it for perfume shall be cut off from his people.

31 AND THE Lord said to Moses, 2See, I have called by name Bezalel son of Uri, the son of Hur, of the tribe of Judah:

3And I have filled him with the Spirit of God, in wisdom *and* ability, in understanding *and* intelligence, and in knowledge, and in all kinds of craftsmanship,

4To devise skillful works, to work in gold, and in silver, and in bronze,

5And in cutting of stones for setting, and in carving of wood, to work in all kinds of craftsmanship.

*s*Or, *perfumer*   *t*Heb. *salted*

New American Standard

18"You shall also make a laver of bronze, with its base of bronze, for washing; and you shall put it between the tent of meeting and the altar, and you shall put water in it.

19"Aaron and his sons shall wash their hands and their feet from it;

20, when they enter the tent of meeting, they shall wash with water, so that they will not die; or when they approach the altar to minister, by offering up in smoke a fire sacrifice to the LORD.

21"So they shall wash their hands and their feet, so that they will not die; and it shall be a perpetual statute for them, for Aaron and his descendants throughout their generations."

The Anointing Oil

22 ¶ Moreover, the LORD spoke to Moses, saying,

23"Take also for yourself the finest of spices: of flowing myrrh five hundred *shekels,* and of fragrant cinnamon half as much, two hundred and fifty, and of fragrant cinnamon cane two hundred and fifty,

24 and of cassia five hundred, according to the shekel of the sanctuary, and of olive oil a hin.

25"You shall make of these a holy anointing oil, a perfume mixture, the work of a perfumer; it shall be a holy anointing oil.

26"With it you shall anoint the tent of meeting and the ark of the testimony,

27 and the table and all its utensils, and the lampstand and its utensils, and the altar of incense,

28 and the altar of burnt offering and all its utensils, and the laver and its stand.

29"You shall also consecrate them, that they may be most holy; whatever touches them shall be holy.

30"You shall anoint Aaron and his sons, and consecrate them, that they may minister as priests to Me.

31"You shall speak to the sons of Israel, saying, 'This shall be a holy anointing oil to Me throughout your generations.

32 'It shall not be poured on anyone's body, nor shall you make *any* like it in the same proportions; it is holy, *and* it shall be holy to you.

33 'Whoever shall mix *any* like it or whoever puts any of it on a layman shall be cut off from his people.' "

The Incense

34 ¶ Then the LORD said to Moses, "Take for yourself spices, stacte and onycha and galbanum, spices with pure frankincense; there shall be an equal part of each.

35"With it you shall make incense, a perfume, the work of a perfumer, salted, pure, *and* holy.

36"You shall beat some of it very fine, and put part of it before the testimony in the tent of meeting where I will meet with you; it shall be most holy to you.

37"The incense which you shall make, you shall not make in the same proportions for yourselves; it shall be holy to you for the LORD.

38"Whoever shall make *any* like it, to use as perfume, shall be cut off from his people."

The Skilled Craftsmen

31 NOW THE LORD spoke to Moses, saying,
2"See, I have called by name Bezalel, the son of Uri, the son of Hur, of the tribe of Judah.

3"I have filled him with the Spirit of God in wisdom, in understanding, in knowledge, and in all *kinds of* craftsmanship,

4 to make artistic designs for work in gold, in silver, and in bronze,

5 and in the cutting of stones for settings, and in the carving of wood, that he may work in all *kinds of* craftsmanship.

New International

with its bronze stand, for washing. Place it between the Tent of Meeting and the altar, and put water in it. 19Aaron and his sons are to wash their hands and feet with water from it. 20Whenever they enter the Tent of Meeting, they shall wash with water so that they will not die. Also, when they approach the altar to minister by presenting an offering made to the LORD by fire, 21they shall wash their hands and feet so that they will not die. This is to be a lasting ordinance for Aaron and his descendants for the generations to come."

Anointing Oil

22Then the LORD said to Moses, 23"Take the following fine spices: 500 shekelsp of liquid myrrh, half as much (that is, 250 shekels) of fragrant cinnamon, 250 shekels of fragrant cane, 24500 shekels of cassia—all according to the sanctuary shekel—and a hinq of olive oil. 25Make these into a sacred anointing oil, a fragrant blend, the work of a perfumer. It will be the sacred anointing oil. 26Then use it to anoint the Tent of Meeting, the ark of the Testimony, 27the table and all its articles, the lampstand and its accessories, the altar of incense, 28the altar of burnt offering and all its utensils, and the basin with its stand. 29You shall consecrate them so they will be most holy, and whatever touches them will be holy.

30"Anoint Aaron and his sons and consecrate them so they may serve me as priests. 31Say to the Israelites, 'This is to be my sacred anointing oil for the generations to come. 32Do not pour it on men's bodies and do not make any oil with the same formula. It is sacred, and you are to consider it sacred. 33Whoever makes perfume like it and whoever puts it on anyone other than a priest must be cut off from his people.' "

Incense

34Then the LORD said to Moses, "Take fragrant spices—gum resin, onycha and galbanum—and pure frankincense, all in equal amounts, 35and make a fragrant blend of incense, the work of a perfumer. It is to be salted and pure and sacred. 36Grind some of it to powder and place it in front of the Testimony in the Tent of Meeting, where I will meet with you. It shall be most holy to you. 37Do not make any incense with this formula for yourselves; consider it holy to the LORD. 38Whoever makes any like it to enjoy its fragrance must be cut off from his people."

Bezalel and Oholiab

31 THEN THE LORD said to Moses, 2"See, I have chosen Bezalel son of Uri, the son of Hur, of the tribe of Judah, 3and I have filled him with the Spirit of God, with skill, ability and knowledge in all kinds of crafts— 4to make artistic designs for work in gold, silver and bronze, 5to cut and set stones, to work in wood, and

---

p 23 That is, about 12 1/2 pounds (about 6 kilograms)   q 24 That is, probably about 4 quarts (about 4 liters)

King James

⁶And I, behold, I have given with him Aholiab, the son of Ahisamach, of the tribe of Dan: and in the hearts of all that are wisehearted I have put wisdom, that they may make all that I have commanded thee;

⁷The tabernacle of the congregation, and the ark of the testimony, and the mercy seat that *is* thereupon, and all the *u*furniture of the tabernacle,

⁸And the table and his furniture, and the pure candlestick with all his furniture, and the altar of incense,

⁹And the altar of burnt offering with all his furniture, and the laver and his foot,

¹⁰And the cloths of service, and the holy garments for Aaron the priest, and the garments of his sons, to minister in the priest's office,

¹¹And the anointing oil, and sweet incense for the holy *place:* according to all that I have commanded thee shall they do.

The Sabbath

¹² ¶ And the LORD spake unto Moses, saying,

¹³Speak thou also unto the children of Israel, saying, Verily my sabbaths ye shall keep: for it *is* a sign between me and you throughout your generations; that *ye* may know that I *am* the LORD that doth sanctify you.

¹⁴Ye shall keep the sabbath therefore; for it *is* holy unto you: every one that defileth it shall surely be put to death: for whosoever doeth *any* work therein, that soul shall be cut off from among his people.

¹⁵Six days may work be done; but in the seventh *is* the sabbath of rest, *v*holy to the LORD: whosoever doeth *any* work in the sabbath day, he shall surely be put to death.

¹⁶Wherefore the children of Israel shall keep the sabbath, to observe the sabbath throughout their generations, *for* a perpetual covenant.

¹⁷It *is* a sign between me and the children of Israel for ever: for *in* six days the LORD made heaven and earth, and on the seventh day he rested, and was refreshed.

¹⁸ ¶ And he gave unto Moses, when he had made an end of communing with him upon mount Sinai, two tables of testimony, tables of stone, written with the finger of God.

The golden calf

32 AND WHEN the people saw that Moses delayed to come down out of the mount, the people gathered themselves together unto Aaron, and said unto him, Up, make us gods, which shall go before us; for *as for* this Moses, the man that brought us up out of the land of Egypt, we wot not what is become of him.

²And Aaron said unto them, Break off the golden earrings, which *are* in the ears of your wives, of your sons, and of your daughters, and bring *them* unto me.

³And all the people brake off the golden earrings which *were* in their ears, and brought *them* unto Aaron.

⁴And he received *them* at their hand, and fashioned it with a graving tool, after he had made it a molten calf: and they said, These *be* thy gods, O Israel, which brought thee up out of the land of Egypt.

⁵And when Aaron saw *it,* he built an altar before it; and Aaron made proclamation, and said, Tomorrow *is* a feast to the LORD.

⁶And they rose up early on the morrow, and offered burnt offerings, and brought peace offerings; and the people sat down to eat and to drink, and rose up to play.

⁷ ¶ And the LORD said unto Moses, Go, get thee down; for thy people, which thou broughtest out of the land of Egypt, have corrupted *themselves:*

⁸They have turned aside quickly out of the way which I commanded them: they have made them a molten calf, and have worshipped it, and have sacrificed thereunto, and said, These *be* thy gods, O Israel, which have brought thee up out of the land of Egypt.

Amplified

⁶And behold, I have appointed with him Aholiab son of Ahisamach, of the tribe of Dan; and to all who are wisehearted I have given wisdom *and* ability to make all that I have commanded you:

⁷The Tent of Meeting, the ark of the Testimony, the mercy seat that is on it, all the furnishings of the tent—

⁸The table [of the showbread] and its utensils, the pure lampstand with all its utensils, the altar of incense,

⁹The altar of burnt offering with all its utensils, the laver and its base—

¹⁰The finely worked garments, the holy garments for Aaron the [high] priest and for his sons to minister as priests,

¹¹And the anointing oil and incense of sweet spices for the Holy Place. According to all that I have commanded you they shall do.

¹²And the Lord said to Moses,

¹³Say to the Israelites, Truly you shall keep My Sabbaths, for it is a sign between Me and you throughout your generations, that you may know that I, the Lord, sanctify you [set you apart for Myself].

¹⁴You shall keep the Sabbath therefore, for it is holy to you; everyone who profanes it shall surely be put to death; for whoever does work on the Sabbath shall be cut off from among his people.

¹⁵Six days may work be done, but the seventh is the Sabbath of rest, sacred to the Lord; whoever does work on the Sabbath day shall surely be put to death.

¹⁶Wherefore the Israelites shall keep the Sabbath to observe it throughout their generations, a perpetual covenant.

¹⁷It is a sign between Me and the Israelites forever; for in six days the Lord made the heavens and earth, and on the seventh day He ceased and was refreshed.

¹⁸And He gave to Moses, when He had ceased communing with him on Mount Sinai, the two tables of the Testimony, tables of stone, written with the finger of God.

32 WHEN THE people saw that Moses delayed to come down from the mountain, [they] gathered together to Aaron, and said to him, Up, make us gods to go before us; as for this Moses, the man who brought us up out of the land of Egypt, we do not know what has become of him.

²So Aaron replied, Take the gold rings from the ears of your wives, your sons, and daughters, and bring them to me.

³So all the people took the gold rings from their ears and brought them to Aaron.

⁴And he received the gold at their hand and fashioned it with a graving tool and made it a molten calf; and they said, These are your gods, O Israel, which brought you up out of the land of Egypt!

⁵And when Aaron saw the molten calf, he built an altar before it; and Aaron made proclamation, and said, Tomorrow shall be a feast to the Lord.

⁶And they rose up early the next day and offered burnt offerings and brought peace offerings; and the people sat down to eat and drink and rose up to play.

⁷The Lord said to Moses, Go down, for your people, whom you brought out of the land of Egypt, have corrupted themselves;

⁸They have turned aside quickly out of the way which I commanded them; they have made them a molten calf and have worshiped it and sacrificed to it, and said, These are your gods, O Israel, that brought you up out of the land of Egypt!

---

*u*Heb. *vessels*   *v*Heb. *holiness*

New American Standard

6"And behold, I Myself have appointed with him Oholiab, the son of Ahisamach, of the tribe of Dan; and in the hearts of all who are skillful I have put skill, that they may make all that I have commanded you: 7 the tent of meeting, and the ark of testimony, and the mercy seat upon it, and all the furniture of the tent, 8 the table also and its utensils, and the pure *gold* lampstand with all its utensils, and the altar of incense, 9 the altar of burnt offering also with all its utensils, and the laver and its stand, 10 the woven garments as well, and the holy garments for Aaron the priest, and the garments of his sons, *with which* to carry on their priesthood; 11 the anointing oil also, and the fragrant incense for the holy place, they are to make *them* according to all that I have commanded you."

The Sign of the Sabbath

12 ¶ The LORD spoke to Moses, saying, 13"But as for you, speak to the sons of Israel, saying, 'You shall surely observe My sabbaths; for *this* is a sign between Me and you throughout your generations, that you may know that I am the LORD who sanctifies you. 14 'Therefore you are to observe the sabbath, for it is holy to you. Everyone who profanes it shall surely be put to death; for whoever does any work on it, that person shall be cut off from among his people. 15 'For six days work may be done, but on the seventh day there is a sabbath of complete rest, holy to the LORD; whoever does any work on the sabbath day shall surely be put to death. 16 'So the sons of Israel shall observe the sabbath, to celebrate the sabbath throughout their generations as a perpetual covenant.' 17"It is a sign between Me and the sons of Israel forever; for in six days the LORD made heaven and earth, but on the seventh day He ceased *from labor,* and was refreshed." 18 ¶ When He had finished speaking with him upon Mount Sinai, He gave Moses the two tablets of the testimony, tablets of stone, written by the finger of God.

The Golden Calf

32 NOW WHEN the people saw that Moses delayed to come down from the mountain, the people assembled about Aaron and said to him, "Come, make us a god who will go before us; as for this Moses, the man who brought us up from the land of Egypt, we do not know what has become of him." 2 Aaron said to them, "Tear off the gold rings which are in the ears of your wives, your sons, and your daughters, and bring *them* to me." 3 Then all the people tore off the gold rings which were in their ears and brought *them* to Aaron. 4 He took *this* from their hand, and fashioned it with a graving tool and made it into a molten calf; and they said, "This is your god, O Israel, who brought you up from the land of Egypt." 5 Now when Aaron saw *this,* he built an altar before it; and Aaron made a proclamation and said, "Tomorrow *shall be* a feast to the LORD." 6 So the next day they rose early and offered burnt offerings, and brought peace offerings; and the people sat down to eat and to drink, and rose up to play. 7 ¶ Then the LORD spoke to Moses, "Go down at once, for your people, whom you brought up from the land of Egypt, have corrupted *themselves.* 8"They have quickly turned aside from the way which I commanded them. They have made for themselves a molten calf, and have worshiped it and have sacrificed to it and said, 'This is your god, O Israel, who brought you up from the land of Egypt!' "

New International

to engage in all kinds of craftsmanship. 6Moreover, I have appointed Oholiab son of Ahisamach, of the tribe of Dan, to help him. Also I have given skill to all the craftsmen to make everything I have commanded you: 7the Tent of Meeting, the ark of the Testimony with the atonement cover on it, and all the other furnishings of the tent— 8the table and its articles, the pure gold lampstand and all its accessories, the altar of incense, 9the altar of burnt offering and all its utensils, the basin with its stand— 10and also the woven garments, both the sacred garments for Aaron the priest and the garments for his sons when they serve as priests, 11and the anointing oil and fragrant incense for the Holy Place. They are to make them just as I commanded you."

The Sabbath

12Then the LORD said to Moses, 13"Say to the Israelites, 'You must observe my Sabbaths. This will be a sign between me and you for the generations to come, so you may know that I am the LORD, who makes you holy.*r* 14" 'Observe the Sabbath, because it is holy to you. Anyone who desecrates it must be put to death; whoever does any work on that day must be cut off from his people. 15For six days, work is to be done, but the seventh day is a Sabbath of rest, holy to the LORD. Whoever does any work on the Sabbath day must be put to death. 16The Israelites are to observe the Sabbath, celebrating it for the generations to come as a lasting covenant. 17It will be a sign between me and the Israelites forever, for in six days the LORD made the heavens and the earth, and on the seventh day he abstained from work and rested.' " 18When the LORD finished speaking to Moses on Mount Sinai, he gave him the two tablets of the Testimony, the tablets of stone inscribed by the finger of God.

The Golden Calf

32 WHEN THE people saw that Moses was so long in coming down from the mountain, they gathered around Aaron and said, "Come, make us gods*s* who will go before us. As for this fellow Moses who brought us up out of Egypt, we don't know what has happened to him." 2Aaron answered them, "Take off the gold earrings that your wives, your sons and your daughters are wearing, and bring them to me." 3So all the people took off their earrings and brought them to Aaron. 4He took what they handed him and made it into an idol cast in the shape of a calf, fashioning it with a tool. Then they said, "These are your gods,*t* O Israel, who brought you up out of Egypt." 5When Aaron saw this, he built an altar in front of the calf and announced, "Tomorrow there will be a festival to the LORD." 6So the next day the people rose early and sacrificed burnt offerings and presented fellowship offerings.*u* Afterward they sat down to eat and drink and got up to indulge in revelry.

7Then the LORD said to Moses, "Go down, because your people, whom you brought up out of Egypt, have become corrupt. 8They have been quick to turn away from what I commanded them and have made themselves an idol cast in the shape of a calf. They have bowed down to it and sacrificed to it and have said, 'These are your gods, O Israel, who brought you up out of Egypt.'

r13 Or *who sanctifies you;* or *who sets you apart as holy*
s1 Or *a god*; also in verses 23 and 31   *t4* Or *This is your god*;
also in verse 8   *u6* Traditionally *peace offerings*

King James

9And the LORD said unto Moses, I have seen this people, and, behold, it *is* a stiffnecked people:

10Now therefore let me alone, that my wrath may wax hot against them, and that I may consume them: and I will make of thee a great nation.

11And Moses besought wthe LORD his God, and said, LORD, why doth thy wrath wax hot against thy people, which thou hast brought forth out of the land of Egypt with great power, and with a mighty hand?

12Wherefore should the Egyptians speak, and say, For mischief did he bring them out, to slay them in the mountains, and to consume them from the face of the earth? Turn from thy fierce wrath, and repent of this evil against thy people.

13Remember Abraham, Isaac, and Israel, thy servants, to whom thou swarest by thine own self, and saidst unto them, I will multiply your seed as the stars of heaven, and all this land that I have spoken of will I give unto your seed, and they shall inherit *it* for ever.

14And the LORD repented of the evil which he thought to do unto his people.

15 ¶ And Moses turned, and went down from the mount, and the two tables of the testimony *were* in his hand: the tables *were* written on both their sides; on the one side and on the other *were* they written.

16And the tables *were* the work of God, and the writing *was* the writing of God, graven upon the tables.

17And when Joshua heard the noise of the people as they shouted, he said unto Moses, *There is* a noise of war in the camp.

18And he said, *It is* not the voice of *them that* shout for mastery, neither *is it* the voice of *them that* cry for xbeing overcome: *but* the noise of *them that* sing do I hear.

19 ¶ And it came to pass, as soon as he came nigh unto the camp, that he saw the calf, and the dancing: and Moses' anger waxed hot, and he cast the tables out of his hands, and brake them beneath the mount.

20And he took the calf which they had made, and burnt *it* in the fire, and ground *it* to powder, and strawed *it* upon the water, and made the children of Israel drink *of it.*

21And Moses said unto Aaron, What did this people unto thee, that thou hast brought so great a sin upon them?

22And Aaron said, Let not the anger of my lord wax hot: thou knowest the people, that they *are* set on mischief.

23For they said unto me, Make us gods, which shall go before us: for *as for* this Moses, the man that brought us up out of the land of Egypt, we wot not what is become of him.

24And I said unto them, Whosoever hath any gold, let them break *it* off. So they gave *it* me: then I cast it into the fire, and there came out this calf.

25 ¶ And when Moses saw that the people *were* naked; (for Aaron had made them naked unto *their* shame among ytheir enemies:)

26Then Moses stood in the gate of the camp, and said, Who *is* on the LORD's side? *let him come* unto me. And all the sons of Levi gathered themselves together unto him.

27And he said unto them, Thus saith the LORD God of Israel, Put every man his sword by his side, *and* go in and out from gate to gate throughout the camp, and slay every man his brother, and every man his companion, and every man his neighbour.

28And the children of Levi did according to the word of Moses: and there fell of the people that day about three thousand men.

29zFor Moses had said, aConsecrate yourselves today to the LORD, even every man upon his son, and upon his brother; that he may bestow upon you a blessing this day.

Amplified

9And the Lord said to Moses, I have seen this people, and behold, it is a stiff-necked people;

10Now therefore let Me alone, that My wrath may burn hot against them and that I may destroy them; but I will make of you a great nation.

11But Moses besought the Lord his God, and said, Lord, why does Your wrath blaze hot against Your people, whom You have brought forth out of the land of Egypt with great power and a mighty hand?

12Why should the Egyptians say, For evil He brought them forth, to slay them in the mountains and consume them from the face of the earth? Turn from Your fierce wrath, and change Your mind concerning this evil against Your people.

13[Earnestly] remember Abraham, Isaac, and Israel, Your servants, to whom You swore by Your own self and said to them, I will multiply your seed as the stars of the heavens, and all this land that I have spoken of will I give to your seed, and they shall inherit it forever.

14Then the Lord turned from the evil which He had thought to do to His people.

15And Moses turned and went down from the mountain with the two tables of the Testimony in his hand, tables *or* tablets that were written on both sides.

16The tables were the work of God; the writing was the writing of God, graven upon the tables.

17And when Joshua heard the noise of the people as they shouted, he said to Moses, There is a noise of war in the camp.

18But Moses said, It is not the sound of shouting for victory, neither is it the sound of the cry of the defeated, but the sound of singing that I hear.

19And as soon as he came near to the camp he saw the calf and the dancing. And Moses' anger blazed hot and he cast the tables out of his hands and broke them at the foot of the mountain.

20And he took the calf they had made and burned it in the fire, and ground it to powder and scattered it on the water and made the Israelites drink it.

21And Moses said to Aaron, What did this people do to you, that you have brought so great a sin upon them?

22And Aaron said, Let not the anger of my lord blaze hot; you know the people, that they are set on evil.

23For they said to me, Make us gods which shall go before us; as for this Moses, the man who brought us up out of the land of Egypt, we do not know what has become of him.

24I said to them, Those who have any gold, let them take it off. So they gave it to me; then I cast it into the fire, and there came out this calf.

25And when Moses saw that the people were unruly *and* unrestrained (for Aaron had let them get out of control, so that they were a derision *and* object of shame among their enemies),

26Then Moses stood in the gate of the camp, and said, Whoever is on the Lord's side, let him come to me. And all the Levites [the priestly tribe] gathered together to him.

27And he said to them, Thus says the Lord God of Israel, Every man put his sword on his side and go in and out from gate to gate throughout the camp and slay every man his brother, and every man his companion, and every man his neighbor.

28And the sons of Levi did according to the word of Moses; and there fell of the people that day about 3000 men.

29And Moses said [to the Levites, By your obedience to God's command] you have consecrated yourselves today [as priests] to the Lord, each man [at the cost of being] against his own son and his own brother, that the Lord may restore *and* bestow His blessing upon *you* this day.

---

wHeb. *the face of the LORD*   xHeb. *weakness*   yHeb. *those that rose up against them*   zOr, *And Moses said, Consecrate yourselves today to the LORD, because every man hath been against his son, and against his brother*   aHeb. *Fill your hands*

New American Standard

9 The LORD said to Moses, "I have seen this people, and behold, they are an obstinate people.

10 "Now then let Me alone, that My anger may burn against them and that I may destroy them; and I will make of you a great nation."

Moses' Entreaty

11 ¶ Then Moses entreated the LORD his God, and said, "O LORD, why does Your anger burn against Your people whom You have brought out from the land of Egypt with great power and with a mighty hand?

12 "Why should the Egyptians speak, saying, 'With evil *intent* He brought them out to kill them in the mountains and to destroy them from the face of the earth'? Turn from Your burning anger and change Your mind about *doing* harm to Your people.

13 "Remember Abraham, Isaac, and Israel, Your servants to whom You swore by Yourself, and said to them, 'I will multiply your descendants as the stars of the heavens, and all this land of which I have spoken I will give to your descendants, and they shall inherit *it* forever.' "

14 So the LORD changed His mind about the harm which He said He would do to His people.

15 ¶ Then Moses turned and went down from the mountain with the two tablets of the testimony in his hand, tablets which were written on both sides; they were written on one *side* and the other.

16 The tablets were God's work, and the writing was God's writing engraved on the tablets.

17 Now when Joshua heard the sound of the people as they shouted, he said to Moses, "There is a sound of war in the camp."

18 But he said,
"It is not the sound of the cry of triumph,
Nor is it the sound of the cry of defeat;
But the sound of singing I hear."

Moses' Anger

19 It came about, as soon as Moses came near the camp, that he saw the calf and *the* dancing; and Moses' anger burned, and he threw the tablets from his hands and shattered them at the foot of the mountain.

20 He took the calf which they had made and burned *it* with fire, and ground it to powder, and scattered it over the surface of the water and made the sons of Israel drink *it.*

21 ¶ Then Moses said to Aaron, "What did this people do to you, that you have brought *such* great sin upon them?"

22 Aaron said, "Do not let the anger of my lord burn; you know the people yourself, that they are prone to evil.

23 "For they said to me, 'Make a god for us who will go before us; for this Moses, the man who brought us up from the land of Egypt, we do not know what has become of him.'

24 "I said to them, 'Whoever has any gold, let them tear it off.' So they gave *it* to me, and I threw it into the fire, and out came this calf."

25 ¶ Now when Moses saw that the people were out of control—for Aaron had let them get out of control to be a derision among their enemies—

26 then Moses stood in the gate of the camp, and said, "Whoever is for the LORD, *come* to me!" And all the sons of Levi gathered together to him.

27 He said to them, "Thus says the LORD, the God of Israel, 'Every man *of you* put his sword upon his thigh, and go back and forth from gate to gate in the camp, and kill every man his brother, and every man his friend, and every man his neighbor.' "

28 So the sons of Levi did as Moses instructed, and about three thousand men of the people fell that day.

29 Then Moses said, "Dedicate yourselves today to the LORD—for every man has been against his son and against his brother—in order that He may bestow a blessing upon you today."

New International

9 "I have seen these people," the LORD said to Moses, "and they are a stiff-necked people. 10 Now leave me alone so that my anger may burn against them and that I may destroy them. Then I will make you into a great nation."

11 But Moses sought the favor of the LORD his God. "O LORD," he said, "why should your anger burn against your people, whom you brought out of Egypt with great power and a mighty hand? 12 Why should the Egyptians say, 'It was with evil intent that he brought them out, to kill them in the mountains and to wipe them off the face of the earth'? Turn from your fierce anger; relent and do not bring disaster on your people. 13 Remember your servants Abraham, Isaac and Israel, to whom you swore by your own self: 'I will make your descendants as numerous as the stars in the sky and I will give your descendants all this land I promised them, and it will be their inheritance forever.' " 14 Then the LORD relented and did not bring on his people the disaster he had threatened.

15 Moses turned and went down the mountain with the two tablets of the Testimony in his hands. They were inscribed on both sides, front and back. 16 The tablets were the work of God; the writing was the writing of God, engraved on the tablets.

17 When Joshua heard the noise of the people shouting, he said to Moses, "There is the sound of war in the camp."

18 Moses replied:

"It is not the sound of victory,
    it is not the sound of defeat;
    it is the sound of singing that I hear."

19 When Moses approached the camp and saw the calf and the dancing, his anger burned and he threw the tablets out of his hands, breaking them to pieces at the foot of the mountain. 20 And he took the calf they had made and burned it in the fire; then he ground it to powder, scattered it on the water and made the Israelites drink it.

21 He said to Aaron, "What did these people do to you, that you led them into such great sin?"

22 "Do not be angry, my lord," Aaron answered. "You know how prone these people are to evil. 23 They said to me, 'Make us gods who will go before us. As for this fellow Moses who brought us up out of Egypt, we don't know what has happened to him.' 24 So I told them, 'Whoever has any gold jewelry, take it off.' Then they gave me the gold, and I threw it into the fire, and out came this calf!"

25 Moses saw that the people were running wild and that Aaron had let them get out of control and so become a laughingstock to their enemies. 26 So he stood at the entrance to the camp and said, "Whoever is for the LORD, come to me." And all the Levites rallied to him.

27 Then he said to them, "This is what the LORD, the God of Israel, says: 'Each man strap a sword to his side. Go back and forth through the camp from one end to the other, each killing his brother and friend and neighbor.' " 28 The Levites did as Moses commanded, and that day about three thousand of the people died. 29 Then Moses said, "You have been set apart to the LORD today, for you were against your own sons and brothers, and he has blessed you this day."

King James

30 ¶ And it came to pass on the morrow, that Moses said unto the people, Ye have sinned a great sin: and now I will go up unto the LORD; peradventure I shall make an atonement for your sin.

31 And Moses returned unto the LORD, and said, Oh, this people have sinned a great sin, and have made them gods of gold.

32 Yet now, if thou wilt forgive their sin—; and if not, blot me, I pray thee, out of thy book which thou hast written.

33 And the LORD said unto Moses, Whosoever hath sinned against me, him will I blot out of my book.

34 Therefore now go, lead the people unto *the place* of which I have spoken unto thee: behold, mine Angel shall go before thee: nevertheless in the day when I visit I will visit their sin upon them.

35 And the LORD plagued the people, because they made the calf, which Aaron made.

The renewal of the covenant

33 AND THE LORD said unto Moses, Depart, *and* go up hence, thou and the people which thou hast brought up out of the land of Egypt, unto the land which I sware unto Abraham, to Isaac, and to Jacob, saying, Unto thy seed will I give it:

2 And I will send an angel before thee; and I will drive out the Canaanite, the Amorite, and the Hittite, and the Perizzite, the Hivite, and the Jebusite:

3 Unto a land flowing with milk and honey: for I will not go up in the midst of thee; for thou *art* a stiffnecked people: lest I consume thee in the way.

4 ¶ And when the people heard these evil tidings, they mourned: and no man did put on him his ornaments.

5 For the LORD had said unto Moses, Say unto the children of Israel, Ye *are* a stiffnecked people: I will come up into the midst of thee in a moment, and consume thee: therefore now put off thy ornaments from thee, that I may know what to do unto thee.

6 And the children of Israel stripped themselves of their ornaments by the mount Horeb.

7 And Moses took the tabernacle, and pitched it without the camp, afar off from the camp, and called it the Tabernacle of the congregation. And it came to pass, *that* every one which sought the LORD went out unto the tabernacle of the congregation, which *was* without the camp.

8 And it came to pass, when Moses went out unto the tabernacle, *that* all the people rose up, and stood every man *at* his tent door, and looked after Moses, until he was gone into the tabernacle.

9 And it came to pass, as Moses entered into the tabernacle, the cloudy pillar descended, and stood *at* the door of the tabernacle, and *the* LORD *talked with Moses.*

10 And all the people saw the cloudy pillar stand *at* the tabernacle door: and all the people rose up and worshipped, every man *in* his tent door.

11 And the LORD spake unto Moses face to face, as a man speaketh unto his friend. And he turned again into the camp: but his servant Joshua, the son of Nun, a young man, departed not out of the tabernacle.

12 ¶ And Moses said unto the LORD, See, thou sayest unto me, Bring up this people: and thou hast not let me know whom thou wilt send with me. Yet thou hast said, I know thee by name, and thou hast also found grace in my sight.

13 Now therefore, I pray thee, if I have found grace in thy sight, show me now thy way, that I may know thee, that I may find grace in thy sight: and consider that this nation *is* thy people.

14 And he said, My presence shall go *with thee,* and I will give thee rest.

Amplified

30 The next day Moses said to the people, You have sinned a great sin. And now I will go up to the Lord; perhaps I can make atonement for your sin.

31 So Moses returned to the Lord, and said, Oh, these people have sinned a great sin and have made themselves gods of gold!

32 Yet now, if You will forgive their sin—and if not, blot me, I pray You, out of Your book which You have written!

33 But the Lord said to Moses, Whoever has sinned against Me, I will blot him [not you] out of My book. [Dan. 12:1; Phil. 4:3; Rev. 3:5.]

34 But now go, lead the people to the place of which I have told you. Behold, My [s]Angel shall go before you. Nevertheless, in the day when I punish I will visit their sin upon them! [Exod. 23:20; 33:2, 3.]

35 And the Lord sent a plague upon the people because they made the calf which Aaron fashioned for them.

33 THE LORD said to Moses, Depart, go up from here, you and the people whom you have brought from the land of Egypt, to the land which I swore to Abraham, Isaac, and Jacob, saying, To your descendants I will give it.

2 I will send an [s]Angel before you, and I will drive out the Canaanite, Amorite, Hittite, Perizzite, Hivite, and Jebusite. [Exod. 23:23; 34:11.]

3 Go up to a land flowing with milk and honey; but I will not go up among you, for you are a stiff-necked people, lest I destroy you on the way.

4 When the people heard these evil tidings, they mourned and no man put on his ornaments.

5 For the Lord had said to Moses, Say to the Israelites, You are a stiff-necked people! If I should come among you for one moment, I would consume *and* destroy you. Now therefore [penitently] leave off your ornaments, that I may know what to do with you.

6 And the Israelites left off all their ornaments, from Mount Horeb onward.

7 Now Moses used to take [his own] tent and pitch it outside the camp, far off from the camp, and he called it the tent of meeting [of God with His own people]. And everyone who sought the Lord went out to [that temporary] tent of meeting which was outside the camp.

8 When Moses went out to the tent of meeting, all the people rose and stood, every man at his tent door, and looked after Moses until he had gone into the tent.

9 When Moses entered the tent, the pillar of cloud would descend and stand at the door of the tent, and the Lord would talk with Moses.

10 And all the people saw the pillar of cloud stand at the tent door, and all the people rose up and worshiped, every man at his tent door.

11 And the Lord spoke to Moses face to face, as a man speaks to his friend. Moses returned to the camp, but his minister Joshua son of Nun, a young man, did not depart from the [temporary prayer] tent.

12 Moses said to the Lord, See, You say to me, Bring up this people, but You have not let me know whom You will send with me. Yet You said, I know you by name and you have also found favor in My sight.

13 Now therefore, I pray You, if I have found favor in Your sight, show me now Your way, that I may know You [progressively become more deeply and intimately acquainted with You, perceiving and recognizing and understanding more strongly and clearly] and that I may find favor in Your sight. And [Lord, do] consider that this nation is Your people.

14 And the Lord said, My Presence shall go with you, and I will give you rest.

_____
s See footnote on Gen. 16:7.

New American Standard

30 ¶ On the next day Moses said to the people, "You yourselves have committed a great sin; and now I am going up to the LORD, perhaps I can make atonement for your sin."

31 Then Moses returned to the LORD, and said, "Alas, this people has committed a great sin, and they have made a god of gold for themselves.

32 "But now, if You will, forgive their sin—and if not, please blot me out from Your book which You have written!"

33 The LORD said to Moses, "Whoever has sinned against Me, I will blot him out of My book.

34 "But go now, lead the people where I told you. Behold, My angel shall go before you; nevertheless in the day when I punish, I will punish them for their sin."

35 Then the LORD smote the people, because of what they did with the calf which Aaron had made.

The Journey Resumed

33 THEN THE LORD spoke to Moses, "Depart, go up from here, you and the people whom you have brought up from the land of Egypt, to the land of which I swore to Abraham, Isaac, and Jacob, saying, 'To your descendants I will give it.'

2 "I will send an angel before you and I will drive out the Canaanite, the Amorite, the Hittite, the Perizzite, the Hivite and the Jebusite.

3 "*Go up* to a land flowing with milk and honey; for I will not go up in your midst, because you are an obstinate people, and I might destroy you on the way."

4 ¶ When the people heard this sad word, they went into mourning, and none of them put on his ornaments.

5 For the LORD had said to Moses, "Say to the sons of Israel, 'You are an obstinate people; should I go up in your midst for one moment, I would destroy you. Now therefore, put off your ornaments from you, that I may know what I shall do with you.'"

6 So the sons of Israel stripped themselves of their ornaments, from Mount Horeb *onward.*

7 ¶ Now Moses used to take the tent and pitch it outside the camp, a good distance from the camp, and he called it the tent of meeting. And everyone who sought the LORD would go out to the tent of meeting which was outside the camp.

8 And it came about, whenever Moses went out to the tent, that all the people would arise and stand, each at the entrance of his tent, and gaze after Moses until he entered the tent.

9 Whenever Moses entered the tent, the pillar of cloud would descend and stand at the entrance of the tent; and the LORD would speak with Moses.

10 When all the people saw the pillar of cloud standing at the entrance of the tent, all the people would arise and worship, each at the entrance of his tent.

11 Thus the LORD used to speak to Moses face to face, just as a man speaks to his friend. When Moses returned to the camp, his servant Joshua, the son of Nun, a young man, would not depart from the tent.

Moses Intercedes

12 ¶ Then Moses said to the LORD, "See, You say to me, 'Bring up this people!' But You Yourself have not let me know whom You will send with me. Moreover, You have said, 'I have known you by name, and you have also found favor in My sight.'

13 "Now therefore, I pray You, if I have found favor in Your sight, let me know Your ways that I may know You, so that I may find favor in Your sight. Consider too, that this nation is Your people."

14 And He said, "My presence shall go *with you,* and I will give you rest."

New International

30 The next day Moses said to the people, "You have committed a great sin. But now I will go up to the LORD; perhaps I can make atonement for your sin."

31 So Moses went back to the LORD and said, "Oh, what a great sin these people have committed! They have made themselves gods of gold. 32 But now, please forgive their sin—but if not, then blot me out of the book you have written."

33 The LORD replied to Moses, "Whoever has sinned against me I will blot out of my book. 34 Now go, lead the people to the place I spoke of, and my angel will go before you. However, when the time comes for me to punish, I will punish them for their sin."

35 And the LORD struck the people with a plague because of what they did with the calf Aaron had made.

33 THEN THE LORD said to Moses, "Leave this place, you and the people you brought up out of Egypt, and go up to the land I promised on oath to Abraham, Isaac and Jacob, saying, 'I will give it to your descendants.' 2 I will send an angel before you and drive out the Canaanites, Amorites, Hittites, Perizzites, Hivites and Jebusites. 3 Go up to the land flowing with milk and honey. But I will not go with you, because you are a stiff-necked people and I might destroy you on the way."

4 When the people heard these distressing words, they began to mourn and no one put on any ornaments. 5 For the LORD had said to Moses, "Tell the Israelites, 'You are a stiff-necked people. If I were to go with you even for a moment, I might destroy you. Now take off your ornaments and I will decide what to do with you.'" 6 So the Israelites stripped off their ornaments at Mount Horeb.

The Tent of Meeting

7 Now Moses used to take a tent and pitch it outside the camp some distance away, calling it the "tent of meeting." Anyone inquiring of the LORD would go to the tent of meeting outside the camp. 8 And whenever Moses went out to the tent, all the people rose and stood at the entrances to their tents, watching Moses until he entered the tent. 9 As Moses went into the tent, the pillar of cloud would come down and stay at the entrance, while the LORD spoke with Moses. 10 Whenever the people saw the pillar of cloud standing at the entrance to the tent, they all stood and worshiped, each at the entrance to his tent. 11 The LORD would speak to Moses face to face, as a man speaks with his friend. Then Moses would return to the camp, but his young aide Joshua son of Nun did not leave the tent.

Moses and the Glory of the LORD

12 Moses said to the LORD, "You have been telling me, 'Lead these people,' but you have not let me know whom you will send with me. You have said, 'I know you by name and you have found favor with me.' 13 If you are pleased with me, teach me your ways so I may know you and continue to find favor with you. Remember that this nation is your people."

14 The LORD replied, "My Presence will go with you, and I will give you rest."

King James

Amplified

15And he said unto him, If thy presence go not *with me*, carry us not up hence.

16For wherein shall it be known here that I and thy people have found grace in thy sight? *is it* not in that thou goest with us? so shall we be separated, I and thy people, from all the people that *are* upon the face of the earth.

Moses beholds God's glory

17And the LORD said unto Moses, I will do this thing also that thou hast spoken: for thou hast found grace in my sight, and I know thee by name.

18And he said, I beseech thee, shew me thy glory.

19And he said, I will make all my goodness pass before thee, and I will proclaim the name of the LORD before thee: and will be gracious to whom I will be gracious, and will show mercy on whom I will show mercy.

20And he said, Thou canst not see my face: for there shall no man see me, and live.

21And the LORD said, Behold, *there is* a place by me, and thou shalt stand upon a rock:

22And it shall come to pass, while my glory passeth by, that I will put thee in a cleft of the rock, and will cover thee with my hand while I pass by:

23And I will take away mine hand, and thou shalt see my back parts: but my face shall not be seen.

The second tables of stone

34 AND THE LORD said unto Moses, Hew thee two tables of stone like unto the first: and I will write upon *these* tables the words that were in the first tables, which thou brakest.

2And be ready in the morning, and come up in the morning unto mount Sinai, and present thyself there to me in the top of the mount.

3And no man shall come up with thee, neither let any man be seen throughout all the mount; neither let the flocks nor herds feed before that mount.

4 ¶ And he hewed two tables of stone like unto the first; and Moses rose up early in the morning, and went up unto mount Sinai, as the LORD had commanded him, and took in his hand the two tables of stone.

5And the LORD descended in the cloud, and stood with him there, and proclaimed the name of the LORD.

6And the LORD passed by before him, and proclaimed, The LORD, The LORD God, merciful and gracious, longsuffering, and abundant in goodness and truth,

7Keeping mercy for thousands, forgiving iniquity and transgression and sin, and that will by no means clear *the guilty;* visiting the iniquity of the fathers upon the children, and upon the children's children, unto the third and to the fourth *generation.*

8And Moses made haste, and bowed his head toward the earth, and worshipped.

9And he said, If now I have found grace in thy sight, O Lord, let my Lord, I pray thee, go among us; for it *is* a stiffnecked people; and pardon our iniquity and our sin, and take us for thine inheritance.

10 ¶ And he said, Behold, I make a covenant: before all thy people I will do marvels, such as have not been done in all the earth, nor in any nation: and all the people among which thou *art* shall see the work of the LORD: for it *is* a terrible thing that I will do with thee.

11Observe thou that which I command thee this day: behold, I drive out before thee the Amorite, and the Canaanite, and the Hittite, and the Perizzite, and the Hivite, and the Jebusite.

15And Moses said to the Lord, If Your Presence does not go with me, do not carry us up from here!

16For by what shall it be known that I and Your people have found favor in Your sight? Is it not in Your going with us so that we are distinguished, I and Your people, from all the other people upon the face of the earth?

17And the Lord said to Moses, I will do this thing also that you have asked, for you have found favor, lovingkindness, *and* mercy in My sight and I know you personally by name. [Rev. 2:17.]

18And Moses said, I beseech You, show me Your glory.

19And God said, I will make all My goodness pass before you, and I will proclaim My name, THE LORD, before you; for I will be gracious to whom I will be gracious, and will show mercy *and* loving-kindness on whom I will show mercy *and* loving-kindness. [Rom. 9:15, 16.]

20But, He said, You can not see My face, for no man shall see Me and live.

21And the Lord said, Behold, there is a place beside Me, and you shall stand upon the rock,

22And while My glory passes by, I will put you in a cleft of the rock and cover you with My hand until I have passed by.

23Then I will take away My hand and you shall see My back; but My face shall not be seen.

34 THE LORD said to Moses, Cut two tables of stone like the first, and I will write upon these tables the words that were on the first tables, which you broke.

2Be ready and come up in the morning to Mount Sinai, and present yourself there to Me on the top of the mountain.

3And no man shall come up with you, neither let any man be seen throughout all the mountain; neither let flocks or herds feed before that mountain.

4So Moses cut two tables of stone like the first, and he rose up early in the morning and went up on Mount Sinai, as the Lord had commanded him, and took [1]in his hand two tables of stone.

5And the Lord descended in the cloud and stood with him there and proclaimed the name of the Lord.

6And the Lord passed by before him, and proclaimed, The Lord! the Lord! a God merciful and gracious, slow to anger, and abundant in loving-kindness and truth,

7Keeping mercy *and* loving-kindness for thousands, forgiving iniquity and transgression and sin, but Who will by no means clear the guilty, visiting the iniquity of the fathers upon the children and the children's children, to the third and fourth generation.

8And Moses made haste to bow his head toward the earth and worshiped.

9And he said, If now I have found favor *and* lovingkindness in Your sight, O Lord, let the Lord, I pray You, go in the midst of us, although it is a stiff-necked people, and pardon our iniquity and our sin, and take us for Your inheritance.

10And the Lord said, Behold, I lay down [afresh the terms of the mutual agreement between Israel and Me] a covenant. Before all your people I will do marvels (wonders, miracles) such as have not been wrought *or* created in all the earth or in any nation; and all the people among whom you are shall see the work of the Lord; for it is a terrible thing [fearful and full of awe] that I will do with you.

11Observe what I command you this day. Behold, I drive out before you the Amorite, Canaanite, Hittite, Perizzite, Hivite, and Jebusite.

---

[1]The two tables of stone are believed to have been pocket-size, easily carried in one hand. The pictures of Moses carrying tombstone-size tables are the result of the misconception of artists, and are not supported by the Bible.

New American Standard

15 Then he said to Him, "If Your presence does not go *with us,* do not lead us up from here.

16 "For how then can it be known that I have found favor in Your sight, I and Your people? Is it not by Your going with us, so that we, I and Your people, may be distinguished from all the *other* people who are upon the face of the earth?"

17 ¶ The LORD said to Moses, "I will also do this thing of which you have spoken; for you have found favor in My sight and I have known you by name."

18 Then Moses said, "I pray You, show me Your glory!"

19 And He said, "I Myself will make all My goodness pass before you, and will proclaim the name of the LORD before you; and I will be gracious to whom I will be gracious, and will show compassion on whom I will show compassion."

20 But He said, "You cannot see My face, for no man can see Me and live!"

21 Then the LORD said, "Behold, there is a place by Me, and you shall stand *there* on the rock;

22 and it will come about, while My glory is passing by, that I will put you in the cleft of the rock and cover you with My hand until I have passed by.

23 "Then I will take My hand away and you shall see My back, but My face shall not be seen."

The Two Tablets Replaced

34 NOW THE LORD said to Moses, "Cut out for yourself two stone tablets like the former ones, and I will write on the tablets the words that were on the former tablets which you shattered.

2 "So be ready by morning, and come up in the morning to Mount Sinai, and present yourself there to Me on the top of the mountain.

3 "No man is to come up with you, nor let any man be seen anywhere on the mountain; even the flocks and the herds may not graze in front of that mountain."

4 So he cut out two stone tablets like the former ones, and Moses rose up early in the morning and went up to Mount Sinai, as the LORD had commanded him, and he took two stone tablets in his hand.

5 The LORD descended in the cloud and stood there with him as he called upon the name of the LORD.

6 Then the LORD passed by in front of him and proclaimed, "The LORD, the LORD God, compassionate and gracious, slow to anger, and abounding in lovingkindness and truth;

7 who keeps lovingkindness for thousands, who forgives iniquity, transgression and sin; yet He will by no means leave *the guilty* unpunished, visiting the iniquity of fathers on the children and on the grandchildren to the third and fourth generations."

8 Moses made haste to bow low toward the earth and worship.

9 He said, "If now I have found favor in Your sight, O Lord, I pray, let the Lord go along in our midst, even though the people are so obstinate, and pardon our iniquity and our sin, and take us as Your own possession."

The Covenant Renewed

10 ¶ Then God said, "Behold, I am going to make a covenant. Before all your people I will perform miracles which have not been produced in all the earth nor among any of the nations; and all the people among whom you live will see the working of the LORD, for it is a fearful thing that I am going to perform with you.

11 ¶ "Be sure to observe what I am commanding you this day; behold, I am going to drive out the Amorite before you, and the Canaanite, the Hittite, the Perizzite, the Hivite and the Jebusite.

New International

15 Then Moses said to him, "If your Presence does not go with us, do not send us up from here. 16 How will anyone know that you are pleased with me and with your people unless you go with us? What else will distinguish me and your people from all the other people on the face of the earth?"

17 And the LORD said to Moses, "I will do the very thing you have asked, because I am pleased with you and I know you by name."

18 Then Moses said, "Now show me your glory."

19 And the LORD said, "I will cause all my goodness to pass in front of you, and I will proclaim my name, the LORD, in your presence. I will have mercy on whom I will have mercy, and I will have compassion on whom I will have compassion. 20 But," he said, "you cannot see my face, for no one may see me and live."

21 Then the LORD said, "There is a place near me where you may stand on a rock. 22 When my glory passes by, I will put you in a cleft in the rock and cover you with my hand until I have passed by. 23 Then I will remove my hand and you will see my back; but my face must not be seen."

The New Stone Tablets

34 THE LORD said to Moses, "Chisel out two stone tablets like the first ones, and I will write on them the words that were on the first tablets, which you broke. 2 Be ready in the morning, and then come up on Mount Sinai. Present yourself to me there on top of the mountain. 3 No one is to come with you or be seen anywhere on the mountain; not even the flocks and herds may graze in front of the mountain."

4 So Moses chiseled out two stone tablets like the first ones and went up Mount Sinai early in the morning, as the LORD had commanded him; and he carried the two stone tablets in his hands. 5 Then the LORD came down in the cloud and stood there with him and proclaimed his name, the LORD. 6 And he passed in front of Moses, proclaiming, "The LORD, the LORD, the compassionate and gracious God, slow to anger, abounding in love and faithfulness, 7 maintaining love to thousands, and forgiving wickedness, rebellion and sin. Yet he does not leave the guilty unpunished; he punishes the children and their children for the sin of the fathers to the third and fourth generation."

8 Moses bowed to the ground at once and worshiped. 9 "O Lord, if I have found favor in your eyes," he said, "then let the Lord go with us. Although this is a stiff-necked people, forgive our wickedness and our sin, and take us as your inheritance."

10 Then the LORD said: "I am making a covenant with you. Before all your people I will do wonders never before done in any nation in all the world. The people you live among will see how awesome is the work that I, the LORD, will do for you. 11 Obey what I command you today. I will drive out before you the Amorites, Canaanites, Hittites,

King James

Amplified

¹²Take heed to thyself, lest thou make a covenant with the inhabitants of the land whither thou goest, lest it be for a snare in the midst of thee:

¹³But ye shall destroy their altars, break their *b*images, and cut down their groves:

¹⁴For thou shalt worship no other god: for the LORD, whose name *is* Jealous, *is* a jealous God:

¹⁵Lest thou make a covenant with the inhabitants of the land, and they go a-whoring after their gods, and do sacrifice unto their gods, and *one* call thee, and thou eat of his sacrifice;

¹⁶And thou take of their daughters unto thy sons, and their daughters go a-whoring after their gods, and make thy sons go a-whoring after their gods.

¹⁷Thou shalt make thee no molten gods.

¹⁸ ¶ The feast of unleavened bread shalt thou keep. Seven days thou shalt eat unleavened bread, as I commanded thee, in the time of the month Abib: for in the month Abib thou camest out from Egypt.

¹⁹All that openeth the matrix *is* mine; and every firstling among thy cattle, *whether* ox or sheep, *that is male.*

²⁰But the firstling of an ass thou shalt redeem with a *c*lamb: and if thou redeem *him* not, then shalt thou break his neck. All the firstborn of thy sons thou shalt redeem. And none shall appear before me empty.

²¹ ¶ Six days thou shalt work, but on the seventh day thou shalt rest: in earing time and in harvest thou shalt rest.

²² ¶ And thou shalt observe the feast of weeks, of the firstfruits of wheat harvest, and the feast of ingathering at the *d*year's end.

²³ ¶ Thrice in the year shall all your menchildren appear before the Lord GOD, the God of Israel.

²⁴For I will cast out the nations before thee, and enlarge thy borders: neither shall any man desire thy land, when thou shalt go up to appear before the LORD thy God thrice in the year.

²⁵Thou shalt not offer the blood of my sacrifice with leaven; neither shall the sacrifice of the feast of the passover be left unto the morning.

²⁶The first of the firstfruits of thy land thou shalt bring unto the house of the LORD thy God. Thou shalt not seethe a kid in his mother's milk.

²⁷And the LORD said unto Moses, Write thou these words: for after the tenor of these words I have made a covenant with thee and with Israel.

²⁸And he was there with the LORD forty days and forty nights; he did neither eat bread, nor drink water. And he wrote upon the tables the words of the covenant, the ten *e*commandments.

Moses' shining face

²⁹ ¶ And it came to pass, when Moses came down from mount Sinai with the two tables of testimony in Moses' hand, when he came down from the mount, that Moses wist not that the skin of his face shone while he talked with him.

³⁰And when Aaron and all the children of Israel saw Moses, behold, the skin of his face shone; and they were afraid to come nigh him.

³¹And Moses called unto them; and Aaron and all the rulers of the congregation returned unto him: and Moses talked with them.

³²And afterward all the children of Israel came nigh: and he gave them in commandment all that the LORD had spoken with him in mount Sinai.

³³And *till* Moses had done speaking with them, he put a veil on his face.

¹²Take heed to yourself, lest you make a covenant *or* mutual agreement with the inhabitants of the land to which you go, lest it become a snare in the midst of you.

¹³But you shall destroy their altars, dash in pieces their pillars (obelisks, images), and cut down their Asherim [symbols of the goddess Asherah];

¹⁴For you shall worship no other god; for the Lord, Whose name is Jealous, is a jealous (impassioned) God,

¹⁵Lest you make a covenant with the inhabitants of the land, and when they play the harlot after their gods and sacrifice to their gods and one invites you, you eat of his food sacrificed to idols,

¹⁶And you take of their daughters for your sons, and their daughters play the harlot after their gods and make your sons play the harlot after their gods.

¹⁷You shall make for yourselves no molten gods.

¹⁸The Feast of Unleavened Bread you shall keep. Seven days you shall eat unleavened bread, as I commanded you, in the time of the month of Abib; for in the month of Abib you came out of Egypt.

¹⁹All the males that first open the womb among your livestock are Mine, whether ox or sheep.

²⁰But the firstling of a donkey [an unclean beast] you shall redeem with a lamb *or* kid, and if you do not redeem it, then you shall break its neck. All the firstborn of your sons you shall redeem. And none of you shall appear before Me empty-handed.

²¹Six days you shall work, but on the seventh day you shall rest; even in plowing time and in harvest you shall rest [on the Sabbath].

²²You shall observe the Feast of Weeks, the firstfruits of the wheat harvest, and the Feast of Ingathering at the year's end.

²³Three times in the year shall all your males appear before the Lord God, the God of Israel.

²⁴For I will cast out the nations before you and enlarge your borders; neither shall any man desire [and molest] your land when you go up to appear before the Lord your God three times in the year.

²⁵You shall not offer the blood of My sacrifice with leaven; neither shall the sacrifice of the Feast of the Passover be left until morning.

²⁶The first of the firstfruits of your ground you shall bring to the house of the Lord your God. You shall not boil a kid in his mother's milk.

²⁷And the Lord said to Moses, Write these words, for after the purpose *and* character of these words I have made a covenant with you and with Israel.

²⁸Moses was there with the Lord forty days and forty nights; he ate no bread and drank no water. And he wrote upon the tables the words of the covenant, the Ten Commandments.

²⁹When Moses came down from Mount Sinai with the two tables of the Testimony in his hand, he did not know that the skin of his face shone *and* sent forth beams by reason of his speaking with the Lord.

³⁰When Aaron and all the Israelites saw Moses, behold, the skin of his face shone, and they feared to come near him.

³¹But Moses called to them; and Aaron and all the leaders of the congregation returned to him, and [he] talked with them.

³²Afterward all the Israelites came near, and he gave them in commandment all the Lord had said to him in Mount Sinai.

³³And when Moses had finished speaking with them, he put a veil on his face.

b Heb. *statues*   *c* Or, *kid*   *d* Heb. *revolution of the year*
e Heb. *words*

New American Standard

12"Watch yourself that you make no covenant with the inhabitants of the land into which you are going, or it will become a snare in your midst.

13"But *rather*, you are to tear down their altars and smash their *sacred* pillars and cut down their [d] Asherim

14 —for you shall not worship any other god, for the LORD, whose name is Jealous, is a jealous God—

15 otherwise you might make a covenant with the inhabitants of the land and they would play the harlot with their gods and sacrifice to their gods, and someone might invite you to eat of his sacrifice,

16 and you might take some of his daughters for your sons, and his daughters might play the harlot with their gods and cause your sons *also* to play the harlot with their gods.

17"You shall make for yourself no molten gods.

18 ¶ "You shall observe the Feast of Unleavened Bread. For seven days you are to eat unleavened bread, as I commanded you, at the appointed time in the month of Abib, for in the month of Abib you came out of Egypt.

19 ¶ "The first offspring from every womb belongs to Me, and all your male livestock, the first offspring from cattle and sheep.

20"You shall redeem with a lamb the first offspring from a donkey; and if you do not redeem *it*, then you shall break its neck. You shall redeem all the firstborn of your sons. None shall appear before Me empty-handed.

21 ¶ "You shall work six days, but on the seventh day you shall rest; *even* during plowing time and harvest you shall rest.

22"You shall celebrate the Feast of Weeks, *that is*, the first fruits of the wheat harvest, and the Feast of Ingathering at the turn of the year.

23"Three times a year all your males are to appear before the Lord GOD, the God of Israel.

24"For I will drive out nations before you and enlarge your borders, and no man shall covet your land when you go up three times a year to appear before the LORD your God.

25 ¶ "You shall not offer the blood of My sacrifice with leavened bread, nor is the sacrifice of the Feast of the Passover to be left over until morning.

26 ¶ "You shall bring the very first of the first fruits of your soil into the house of the LORD your God.

¶ "You shall not boil a young goat in its mother's milk."

27 ¶ Then the LORD said to Moses, "Write down these words, for in accordance with these words I have made a covenant with you and with Israel."

28 So he was there with the LORD forty days and forty nights; he did not eat bread or drink water. And he wrote on the tablets the words of the covenant, the Ten Commandments.

Moses' Face Shines

29 ¶ It came about when Moses was coming down from Mount Sinai (and the two tablets of the testimony *were* in Moses' hand as he was coming down from the mountain), that Moses did not know that the skin of his face shone because of his speaking with Him.

30 So when Aaron and all the sons of Israel saw Moses, behold, the skin of his face shone, and they were afraid to come near him.

31 Then Moses called to them, and Aaron and all the rulers in the congregation returned to him; and Moses spoke to them.

32 Afterward all the sons of Israel came near, and he commanded them *to do* everything that the LORD had spoken to him on Mount Sinai.

33 When Moses had finished speaking with them, he put a veil over his face.

New International

Perizzites, Hivites and Jebusites. 12Be careful not to make a treaty with those who live in the land where you are going, or they will be a snare among you. 13Break down their altars, smash their sacred stones and cut down their Asherah poles.[v] 14Do not worship any other god, for the LORD, whose name is Jealous, is a jealous God.

15"Be careful not to make a treaty with those who live in the land; for when they prostitute themselves to their gods and sacrifice to them, they will invite you and you will eat their sacrifices. 16And when you choose some of their daughters as wives for your sons and those daughters prostitute themselves to their gods, they will lead your sons to do the same.

17"Do not make cast idols.

18"Celebrate the Feast of Unleavened Bread. For seven days eat bread made without yeast, as I commanded you. Do this at the appointed time in the month of Abib, for in that month you came out of Egypt.

19"The first offspring of every womb belongs to me, including all the firstborn males of your livestock, whether from herd or flock. 20Redeem the firstborn donkey with a lamb, but if you do not redeem it, break its neck. Redeem all your firstborn sons.

"No one is to appear before me empty-handed.

21"Six days you shall labor, but on the seventh day you shall rest; even during the plowing season and harvest you must rest.

22"Celebrate the Feast of Weeks with the firstfruits of the wheat harvest, and the Feast of Ingathering at the turn of the year.[w] 23Three times a year all your men are to appear before the Sovereign LORD, the God of Israel. 24I will drive out nations before you and enlarge your territory, and no one will covet your land when you go up three times each year to appear before the LORD your God.

25"Do not offer the blood of a sacrifice to me along with anything containing yeast, and do not let any of the sacrifice from the Passover Feast remain until morning.

26"Bring the best of the firstfruits of your soil to the house of the LORD your God.

"Do not cook a young goat in its mother's milk."

27Then the LORD said to Moses, "Write down these words, for in accordance with these words I have made a covenant with you and with Israel." 28Moses was there with the LORD forty days and forty nights without eating bread or drinking water. And he wrote on the tablets the words of the covenant—the Ten Commandments.

The Radiant Face of Moses

29When Moses came down from Mount Sinai with the two tablets of the Testimony in his hands, he was not aware that his face was radiant because he had spoken with the LORD. 30When Aaron and all the Israelites saw Moses, his face was radiant, and they were afraid to come near him. 31But Moses called to them; so Aaron and all the leaders of the community came back to him, and he spoke to them. 32Afterward all the Israelites came near him, and he gave them all the commands the LORD had given him on Mount Sinai.

33When Moses finished speaking to them, he put a veil

---

[d]I.e. wooden symbols of a female deity

[v] 13 That is, symbols of the goddess Asherah   [w] 22 That is, in the fall

King James

³⁴But when Moses went in before the LORD to speak with him, he took the veil off, until he came out. And he came out, and spake unto the children of Israel *that* which he was commanded.

³⁵And the children of Israel saw the face of Moses, that the skin of Moses' face shone: and Moses put the veil upon his face again, until he went in to speak with him.

Sabbath regulations

35 AND MOSES gathered all the congregation of the children of Israel together, and said unto them, These *are* the words which the LORD hath commanded, that *ye* should do them.

²Six days shall work be done, but on the seventh day there shall be to you ⨍an holy day, a sabbath of rest to the LORD: whosoever doeth work therein shall be put to death.

³Ye shall kindle no fire throughout your habitations upon the sabbath day.

⁴ ¶ And Moses spake unto all the congregation of the children of Israel, saying, This *is* the thing which the LORD commanded, saying,

⁵Take ye from among you an offering unto the LORD: whosoever *is* of a willing heart, let him bring it, an offering of the LORD; gold, and silver, and brass,

⁶And blue, and purple, and scarlet, and fine linen, and goats' *hair,*

⁷And rams' skins dyed red, and badgers' skins, and shittim wood,

⁸And oil for the light, and spices for anointing oil, and for the sweet incense,

⁹And onyx stones, and stones to be set for the ephod, and for the breastplate.

¹⁰And every wisehearted among you shall come, and make all that the LORD hath commanded;

¹¹The tabernacle, his tent, and his covering, his taches, and his boards, his bars, his pillars, and his sockets,

¹²The ark, and the staves thereof, *with* the mercy seat, and the veil of the covering,

¹³The table, and his staves, and all his vessels, and the showbread,

¹⁴The candlestick also for the light, and his furniture, and his lamps, with the oil for the light,

¹⁵And the incense altar, and his staves, and the anointing oil, and the sweet incense, and the hanging for the door at the entering in of the tabernacle,

¹⁶The altar of burnt offering, with his brasen grate, his staves, and all his vessels, the laver and his foot,

¹⁷The hangings of the court, his pillars, and their sockets, and the hanging for the door of the court,

¹⁸The pins of the tabernacle, and the pins of the court, and their cords,

¹⁹The cloths of service, to do service in the holy *place,* the holy garments for Aaron the priest, and the garments of his sons, to minister in the priest's office.

Offerings for the tabernacle

²⁰ ¶ And all the congregation of the children of Israel departed from the presence of Moses.

²¹And they came, every one whose heart stirred him up, and every one whom his spirit made willing, *and* they brought the LORD'S offering to the work of the tabernacle of the congregation, and for all his service, and for the holy garments.

²²And they came, both men and women, as many as were willing-hearted, *and* brought bracelets, and earrings, and rings, and tablets, all jewels of gold: and every man that offered *offered* an offering of gold unto the LORD.

²³And every man, with whom was found blue, and purple, and scarlet, and fine linen, and goats' *hair,* and red skins of rams, and badgers' skins, brought *them.*

⨍Heb. *holiness*

Amplified

³⁴But when Moses went in before the Lord to speak with Him, ᵘhe took the veil off until he came out. And he came out and told the Israelites what he was commanded.

³⁵The Israelites saw the face of Moses, how the skin of it shone; and Moses put the veil on his face again until he went in to speak with God.

35 MOSES GATHERED all the congregation of the Israelites together and said to them, These are the things which the Lord has commanded that you do:

²Six days shall work be done, but the seventh day shall be to you a holy day, a Sabbath of rest to the Lord; whoever works [on that day] shall be put to death.

³You shall kindle no fire in all your dwellings on the Sabbath day.

⁴And Moses said to all the congregation of the Israelites, This is what the Lord commanded:

⁵Take from among you an offering to the Lord. Whoever is of a willing *and* generous heart, let him bring the Lord's offering: gold, silver, and bronze;

⁶Blue, purple, and scarlet [stuff], fine linen; goats' hair;

⁷And rams' skins tanned red, and skins of dolphins *or* porpoises; and acacia wood;

⁸And oil for the light; and spices for anointing oil and for fragrant incense;

⁹And onyx stones and other stones to be set for the ephod and the breastplate.

¹⁰And let every able *and* wisehearted man among you come and make all that the Lord has commanded:

¹¹The tabernacle, its tent and its covering, its hooks, its boards, its bars, its pillars, and its sockets *or* bases;

¹²The ark and its poles, with the mercy seat, and the veil of the screen;

¹³The table and its poles and all its utensils, and the showbread (the bread of the Presence);

¹⁴The lampstand also for the light, and its utensils and its lamps, and the oil for the light;

¹⁵And the incense altar and its poles, the anointing oil and the fragrant incense, the hanging *or* screen for the door at the entrance of the tabernacle;

¹⁶The altar of burnt offering, with its bronze grating, its poles and all its utensils, the laver and its base;

¹⁷The court's hangings, its pillars and their sockets *or* bases, and the hanging *or* screen for the gate of the court;

¹⁸The pegs of the tabernacle and of the court, and their cords,

¹⁹The finely wrought garments for ministering in the Holy Place, the holy garments for Aaron the [high] priest and for his sons to minister as priests.

²⁰Then all the congregation of the Israelites left Moses' presence.

²¹And they came, each one whose heart stirred him up and whose spirit made him willing, and brought the Lord's offering to be used for the [new] Tent of Meeting, for all its service, and the holy garments.

²²They came, both men and women, all who were willinghearted, and brought brooches, earrings *or* nose rings, signet rings, and armlets *or* necklaces, all jewels of gold, everyone bringing an offering of gold to the Lord.

²³And everyone with whom was found blue or purple or scarlet [stuff], or fine linen, or goats' hair, or rams' skins made red [in tanning], or dolphin *or* porpoise skins brought them.

ᵘThe apostle Paul expressly refers to this incident when he says that we all may, with unveiled faces, behold the glory of the Lord, and be transformed (II Cor. 3:13-18). That blessed vision, which of old was given only to the great leader of Israel, is now within reach of each individual believer. The Gospel has no fences to keep the crowd off the mount of vision; the lowliest and most unworthy of its children may pass upward where the shining glory is to be seen. "We **all** . . . are changed" (F. B. Meyer, *Moses, the Servant of God*).

New American Standard

34 But whenever Moses went in before the LORD to speak with Him, he would take off the veil until he came out; and whenever he came out and spoke to the sons of Israel what he had been commanded,

35 the sons of Israel would see the face of Moses, that the skin of Moses' face shone. So Moses would replace the veil over his face until he went in to speak with Him.

The Sabbath Emphasized

35 THEN MOSES assembled all the congregation of the sons of Israel, and said to them, "These are the things that the LORD has commanded *you* to do:

2 ¶ "For six days work may be done, but on the seventh day you shall have a holy *day*, a sabbath of complete rest to the LORD; whoever does any work on it shall be put to death.

3 "You shall not kindle a fire in any of your dwellings on the sabbath day."

4 ¶ Moses spoke to all the congregation of the sons of Israel, saying, "This is the thing which the LORD has commanded, saying,

5 'Take from among you a contribution to the LORD; whoever is of a willing heart, let him bring it as the LORD's contribution: gold, silver, and bronze,

6 and blue, purple and scarlet *material*, fine linen, goats' *hair*,

7 and rams' skins dyed red, and porpoise skins, and acacia wood,

8 and oil for lighting, and spices for the anointing oil, and for the fragrant incense,

9 and onyx stones and setting stones for the ephod and for the breastpiece.

Tabernacle Workmen

10 ¶ 'Let every skillful man among you come, and make all that the LORD has commanded:

11 the tabernacle, its tent and its covering, its hooks and its boards, its bars, its pillars, and its sockets;

12 the ark and its poles, the mercy seat, and the curtain of the screen;

13 the table and its poles, and all its utensils, and the bread of the ᵉPresence;

14 the lampstand also for the light and its utensils and its lamps and the oil for the light;

15 and the altar of incense and its poles, and the anointing oil and the fragrant incense, and the screen for the doorway at the entrance of the tabernacle;

16 the altar of burnt offering with its bronze grating, its poles, and all its utensils, the basin and its stand;

17 the hangings of the court, its pillars and its sockets, and the screen for the gate of the court;

18 the pegs of the tabernacle and the pegs of the court and their cords;

19 the woven garments for ministering in the holy place, the holy garments for Aaron the priest and the garments of his sons, to minister as priests.'"

Gifts Received

20 ¶ Then all the congregation of the sons of Israel departed from Moses' presence.

21 Everyone whose heart stirred him and everyone whose spirit moved him came *and* brought the LORD's contribution for the work of the tent of meeting and for all its service and for the holy garments.

22 Then all whose hearts moved them, both men and women, came *and* brought brooches and earrings and signet rings and bracelets, all articles of gold; so *did* every man who presented an offering of gold to the LORD.

23 Every man, who had in his possession blue and purple and scarlet *material* and fine linen and goats' *hair* and rams' skins dyed red and porpoise skins, brought them.

New International

over his face. 34But whenever he entered the LORD's presence to speak with him, he removed the veil until he came out. And when he came out and told the Israelites what he had been commanded, 35they saw that his face was radiant. Then Moses would put the veil back over his face until he went in to speak with the LORD.

Sabbath Regulations

35 MOSES ASSEMBLED the whole Israelite community and said to them, "These are the things the LORD has commanded you to do: 2For six days, work is to be done, but the seventh day shall be your holy day, a Sabbath of rest to the LORD. Whoever does any work on it must be put to death. 3Do not light a fire in any of your dwellings on the Sabbath day."

Materials for the Tabernacle

4Moses said to the whole Israelite community, "This is what the LORD has commanded: 5From what you have, take an offering for the LORD. Everyone who is willing is to bring to the LORD an offering of gold, silver and bronze; 6blue, purple and scarlet yarn and fine linen; goat hair; 7ram skins dyed red and hides of sea cowsˣ; acacia wood; 8olive oil for the light; spices for the anointing oil and for the fragrant incense; 9and onyx stones and other gems to be mounted on the ephod and breastpiece.

10"All who are skilled among you are to come and make everything the LORD has commanded: 11the tabernacle with its tent and its covering, clasps, frames, crossbars, posts and bases; 12the ark with its poles and the atonement cover and the curtain that shields it; 13the table with its poles and all its articles and the bread of the Presence; 14the lampstand that is for light with its accessories, lamps and oil for the light; 15the altar of incense with its poles, the anointing oil and the fragrant incense; the curtain for the doorway at the entrance to the tabernacle; 16the altar of burnt offering with its bronze grating, its poles and all its utensils; the bronze basin with its stand; 17the curtains of the courtyard with its posts and bases, and the curtain for the entrance to the courtyard; 18the tent pegs for the tabernacle and for the courtyard, and their ropes; 19the woven garments worn for ministering in the sanctuary—both the sacred garments for Aaron the priest and the garments for his sons when they serve as priests."

20Then the whole Israelite community withdrew from Moses' presence, 21and everyone who was willing and whose heart moved him came and brought an offering to the LORD for the work on the Tent of Meeting, for all its service, and for the sacred garments. 22All who were willing, men and women alike, came and brought gold jewelry of all kinds: brooches, earrings, rings and ornaments. They all presented their gold as a wave offering to the LORD. 23Everyone who had blue, purple or scarlet yarn or fine linen, or goat hair, ram skins dyed red or hides of sea cows

---

ᵉLit *Face*

ˣ7 That is, dugongs; also in verse 23

King James

²⁴Every one that did offer an offering of silver and brass brought the LORD's offering: and every man, with whom was found shittim wood for any work of the service, brought *it*.

²⁵And all the women that were wisehearted did spin with their hands, and brought that which they had spun, *both* of blue, and of purple, *and* of scarlet, and of fine linen.

²⁶And all the women whose heart stirred them up in wisdom spun goats' *hair*.

²⁷And the rulers brought onyx stones, and stones to be set, for the ephod, and for the breastplate;

²⁸And spice, and oil for the light, and for the anointing oil, and for the sweet incense.

²⁹The children of Israel brought a willing offering unto the LORD, every man and woman, whose heart made them willing to bring for all manner of work, which the LORD had commanded to be made by the hand of Moses.

The workmen gathered

³⁰ ¶ And Moses said unto the children of Israel, See, the LORD hath called by name Bezaleel the son of Uri, the son of Hur, of the tribe of Judah;

³¹And he hath filled him with the spirit of God, in wisdom, in understanding, and in knowledge, and in all manner of workmanship;

³²And to devise curious works, to work in gold, and in silver, and in brass,

³³And in the cutting of stones, to set *them*, and in carving of wood, to make any manner of cunning work.

³⁴And he hath put in his heart that he may teach, *both* he, and Aholiab, the son of Ahisamach, of the tribe of Dan.

³⁵Them hath he filled with wisdom of heart, to work all manner of work, of the engraver, and of the cunning workman, and of the embroiderer, in blue, and in purple, in scarlet, and in fine linen, and of the weaver, *even* of them that do any work, and of those that devise cunning work.

36 THEN WROUGHT Bezaleel and Aholiab, and every wisehearted man, in whom the LORD put wisdom and understanding to know how to work all manner of work for the service of the sanctuary, according to all that the LORD had commanded.

²And Moses called Bezaleel and Aholiab, and every wisehearted man, in whose heart the LORD had put wisdom, *even* every one whose heart stirred him up to come unto the work to do it:

³And they received of Moses all the offering, which the children of Israel had brought for the work of the service of the sanctuary, to make it *withal*. And they brought yet unto him free offerings every morning.

⁴And all the wise men, that wrought all the work of the sanctuary, came every man from his work which they made;

⁵ ¶ And they spake unto Moses, saying, The people bring much more than enough for the service of the work, which the LORD commanded to make.

⁶And Moses gave commandment, and they caused it to be proclaimed throughout the camp, saying, Let neither man nor woman make any more work for the offering of the sanctuary. So the people were restrained from bringing.

⁷For the stuff they had was sufficient for all the work to make it, and too much.

The work for the tabernacle

⁸ ¶ And every wisehearted man among them that wrought the work of the tabernacle made ten curtains *of* fine twined linen, and blue, and purple, and scarlet: *with* cherubims of cunning work made he them.

Amplified

²⁴Everyone who could make an offering of silver or bronze brought it as the Lord's offering, and every man with whom was found any acacia wood for any work of the service brought it.

²⁵All the women who had ability *and* were wisehearted spun with their hands and brought what they had spun of blue and purple and scarlet [stuff] and fine linen;

²⁶And all the women who had ability *and* whose hearts stirred them up in wisdom spun the goats' hair.

²⁷The leaders brought onyx stones and stones to be set for the ephod and for the breastplate,

²⁸And spice, and oil for the light and for the anointing oil and for the fragrant incense.

²⁹The Israelites brought a freewill offering to the Lord, all men and women whose hearts made them willing *and* moved them to bring anything for any of the work which the Lord had commanded by Moses to be done.

³⁰And Moses said to the Israelites, See, the Lord called by name Bezalel son of Uri, the son of Hur, of the tribe of Judah;

³¹And He has filled him with the Spirit of God, with ability *and* wisdom, with intelligence *and* understanding, and with knowledge and all craftsmanship,

³²To devise artistic designs, to work in gold, silver, and bronze,

³³In cutting of stones for setting, and in carving of wood, for work in every skilled craft.

³⁴And God has put in Bezalel's heart that he may teach, both he and Aholiab son of Ahisamach, of the tribe of Dan.

³⁵He has filled them with wisdom of heart *and* ability to do all manner of craftsmanship, of the engraver, of the skillful workman, of the embroiderer in blue, purple, and scarlet [stuff] and in fine linen, and of the weaver, even of those who do or design any skilled work.

36 BEZALEL AND Aholiab and every wisehearted man in whom the Lord has put wisdom and understanding to know how to do all the work for the service of the sanctuary shall work according to all that the Lord has commanded.

²And Moses called Bezalel and Aholiab and every able *and* wisehearted man in whose mind the Lord had put wisdom *and* ability, everyone whose heart stirred him up to come to do the work;

³And they received from Moses all the freewill offerings which the Israelites had brought for doing the work of the sanctuary, to prepare it for service. And they continued to bring him freewill offerings every morning.

⁴And all the wise *and* able men who were doing the work on the sanctuary came, every man from the work he was doing,

⁵And they said to Moses, The people bring much more than enough for doing the work which the Lord commanded to do.

⁶So Moses commanded and it was proclaimed in all the camp, Let no man or woman do anything more for the sanctuary offering. So the people were restrained from bringing,

⁷For the stuff they had was sufficient to do all the work and more.

⁸And all the able *and* wisehearted men among them who did the work on the tabernacle made ten curtains of fine twined linen and blue, purple, and scarlet [stuff], with cherubim skillfully worked on them.

New American Standard

24 Everyone who could make a contribution of silver and bronze brought the LORD'S contribution; and every man who had in his possession acacia wood for any work of the service brought it.

25 All the skilled women spun with their hands, and brought what they had spun, *in* blue and purple *and* scarlet *material* and *in* fine linen.

26 All the women whose heart stirred with a skill spun the goats' *hair.*

27 The rulers brought the onyx stones and the stones for setting for the ephod and for the breastpiece;

28 and the spice and the oil for the light and for the anointing oil and for the fragrant incense.

29 The Israelites, all the men and women, whose heart moved them to bring *material* for all the work, which the LORD had commanded through Moses to be done, brought a freewill offering to the LORD.

30 ¶ Then Moses said to the sons of Israel, "See, the LORD has called by name Bezalel the son of Uri, the son of Hur, of the tribe of Judah.

31 "And He has filled him with the Spirit of God, in wisdom, in understanding and in knowledge and in all craftsmanship;

32 to make designs for working in gold and in silver and in bronze,

33 and in the cutting of stones for settings and in the carving of wood, so as to perform in every inventive work.

34 "He also has put in his heart to teach, both he and Oholiab, the son of Ahisamach, of the tribe of Dan.

35 "He has filled them with skill to perform every work of an engraver and of a designer and of an embroiderer, in blue and in purple *and* in scarlet *material,* and in fine linen, and of a weaver, as performers of every work and makers of designs.

The Tabernacle Underwritten

36 "NOW BEZALEL and Oholiab, and every skillful person in whom the LORD has put skill and understanding to know how to perform all the work in the construction of the sanctuary, shall perform in accordance with all that the LORD has commanded."

2 ¶ Then Moses called Bezalel and Oholiab and every skillful person in whom the LORD had put skill, everyone whose heart stirred him, to come to the work to perform it.

3 They received from Moses all the contributions which the sons of Israel had brought to perform the work in the construction of the sanctuary. And they still *continued* bringing to him freewill offerings every morning.

4 And all the skillful men who were performing all the work of the sanctuary came, each from the work which he was performing,

5 and they said to Moses, "The people are bringing much more than enough for the construction work which the LORD commanded *us* to perform."

6 So Moses issued a command, and a proclamation was circulated throughout the camp, saying, "Let no man or woman any longer perform work for the contributions of the sanctuary." Thus the people were restrained from bringing *any more.*

7 For the material they had was sufficient and more than enough for all the work, to perform it.

Construction Proceeds

8 ¶ All the skillful men among those who were performing the work made the tabernacle with ten curtains; of fine twisted linen and blue and purple and scarlet *material,* with cherubim, the work of a skillful workman, Bezalel made them.

New International

brought them. 24 Those presenting an offering of silver or bronze brought it as an offering to the LORD, and everyone who had acacia wood for any part of the work brought it. 25 Every skilled woman spun with her hands and brought what she had spun—blue, purple or scarlet yarn or fine linen. 26 And all the women who were willing and had the skill spun the goat hair. 27 The leaders brought onyx stones and other gems to be mounted on the ephod and breastpiece. 28 They also brought spices and olive oil for the light and for the anointing oil and for the fragrant incense. 29 All the Israelite men and women who were willing brought to the LORD freewill offerings for all the work the LORD through Moses had commanded them to do.

Bezalel and Oholiab

30 Then Moses said to the Israelites, "See, the LORD has chosen Bezalel son of Uri, the son of Hur, of the tribe of Judah, 31 and he has filled him with the Spirit of God, with skill, ability and knowledge in all kinds of crafts— 32 to make artistic designs for work in gold, silver and bronze, 33 to cut and set stones, to work in wood and to engage in all kinds of artistic craftsmanship. 34 And he has given both him and Oholiab son of Ahisamach, of the tribe of Dan, the ability to teach others. 35 He has filled them with skill to do all kinds of work as craftsmen, designers, embroiderers in blue, purple and scarlet yarn and fine linen, and weavers—all of them master craftsmen and designers.

36 1 SO BEZALEL, Oholiab and every skilled person to whom the LORD has given skill and ability to know how to carry out all the work of constructing the sanctuary are to do the work just as the LORD has commanded."

2 Then Moses summoned Bezalel and Oholiab and every skilled person to whom the LORD had given ability and who was willing to come and do the work. 3 They received from Moses all the offerings the Israelites had brought to carry out the work of constructing the sanctuary. And the people continued to bring freewill offerings morning after morning. 4 So all the skilled craftsmen who were doing all the work on the sanctuary left their work 5 and said to Moses, "The people are bringing more than enough for doing the work the LORD commanded to be done."

6 Then Moses gave an order and they sent this word throughout the camp: "No man or woman is to make anything else as an offering for the sanctuary." And so the people were restrained from bringing more, 7 because what they already had was more than enough to do all the work.

The Tabernacle

8 All the skilled men among the workmen made the tabernacle with ten curtains of finely twisted linen and blue, purple and scarlet yarn, with cherubim worked into them

King James

[9]The length of one curtain *was* twenty and eight cubits, and the breadth of one curtain four cubits: the curtains *were* all of one size.

[10]And he coupled the five curtains one unto another: and *the other* five curtains he coupled one unto another.

[11]And he made loops of blue on the edge of one curtain from the selvedge in the coupling: likewise he made in the uttermost side of *another* curtain, in the coupling of the second.

[12]Fifty loops made he in one curtain, and fifty loops made he in the edge of the curtain which *was* in the coupling of the second: the loops held one *curtain* to another.

[13]And he made fifty taches of gold, and coupled the curtains one unto another with the taches: so it became one tabernacle.

[14] ¶ And he made curtains *of* goats' *hair* for the tent over the tabernacle: eleven curtains he made them.

[15]The length of one curtain *was* thirty cubits, and four cubits *was* the breadth of one curtain: the eleven curtains *were* of one size.

[16]And he coupled five curtains by themselves, and six curtains by themselves.

[17]And he made fifty loops upon the uttermost edge of the curtain in the coupling, and fifty loops made he upon the edge of the curtain which coupleth the second.

[18]And he made fifty taches *of* brass to couple the tent together, that it might be one.

[19]And he made a covering for the tent *of* rams' skins dyed red, and a covering *of* badgers' skins above *that*.

[20] ¶ And he made boards for the tabernacle *of* shittim wood, standing up.

[21]The length of a board *was* ten cubits, and the breadth of a board one cubit and a half.

[22]One board had two tenons, equally distant one from another: thus did he make for all the boards of the tabernacle.

[23]And he made boards for the tabernacle; twenty boards for the south side southward:

[24]And forty sockets of silver he made under the twenty boards; two sockets under one board for his two tenons, and two sockets under another board for his two tenons.

[25]And for the other side of the tabernacle, *which is* toward the north corner, he made twenty boards,

[26]And their forty sockets of silver; two sockets under one board, and two sockets under another board.

[27]And for the sides of the tabernacle westward he made six boards.

[28]And two boards made he for the corners of the tabernacle in the two sides.

[29]And they were [g]coupled beneath, and coupled together at the head thereof, to one ring: thus he did to both of them in both the corners.

[30]And there were eight boards; and their sockets *were* sixteen sockets of silver, [h]under every board two sockets.

[31] ¶ And he made bars of shittim wood; five for the boards of the one side of the tabernacle,

[32]And five bars for the boards of the other side of the tabernacle, and five bars for the boards of the tabernacle for the sides westward.

[33]And he made the middle bar to shoot through the boards from the one end to the other.

[34]And he overlaid the boards with gold, and made rings *of* gold *to be* places for the bars, and overlaid the bars with gold.

Amplified

[9]The length of each curtain was twenty-eight cubits and its breadth four cubits; all the curtains were one size.

[10][Bezalel] coupled five curtains one to another and the other five curtains he coupled one to another.

[11]And he made loops of blue on the outer edge of the last curtain in the first set; this he did also on the inner edge of the first curtain in the second set.

[12]Fifty loops he made in the one curtain and fifty loops in the edge of the curtain which was the second set; the loops were opposite one another.

[13]And he made fifty clasps of gold and coupled the curtains together with the clasps so that the tabernacle became one unit.

[14]And he made eleven curtains of goats' hair for a tent over the tabernacle.

[15]The length of one curtain was thirty cubits and four cubits was the breadth; the eleven curtains were of equal size.

[16]And he coupled five curtains by themselves and the other six curtains by themselves.

[17]And he made fifty loops on the outmost edge of curtain to be coupled and fifty loops he made on the inner edge of the second curtain to be coupled.

[18]He made fifty clasps of bronze to couple the tent together into one whole.

[19]He made a covering for the tent of [v]rams' skins tanned red, and above it a covering of dolphin *or* porpoise skins.

[20]He made boards of acacia wood for the upright framework of the tabernacle.

[21]The length of a board was ten cubits and the breadth one cubit and a half.

[22]Each board had two tenons (projections) to fit into a mortise to form a clutch; he did this for all the boards of the tabernacle.

[23]And he made thus the boards [for frames] for the tabernacle: twenty boards for the south side,

[24]And he made under the twenty boards forty sockets *or* bases of silver, two sockets under one board for its two tenons *or* hands, and two sockets under another board for its two tenons.

[25]For the other side of the tabernacle, the north side, he made twenty boards

[26]And their forty sockets *or* bases of silver, two sockets under [the end of] each board.

[27]And for the rear or west side of the tabernacle he made six [frame] boards.

[28]And two boards he made for each corner of the tabernacle in the rear.

[29]They were separate below but linked together at the top with one ring; thus he made both of them in both corners.

[30]There were eight boards with sixteen sockets *or* bases of silver, and under [the end of] each board two sockets.

[31]He made bars of acacia wood, five for the [frame] boards of the one side of the tabernacle,

[32]And five bars for the boards of its other side, and five bars for the boards at the rear or west side.

[33]And he made the middle bar pass through halfway up the boards from one end to the other.

[34]He overlaid the boards and the bars with gold and made their rings of gold as places for the bars.

[v]The final coverings of the tabernacle tent are not to be confused with the second one of goats' hair (Exod. 36:14). There were **four distinct coverings** of the tabernacle tent: 1. A covering of fine twined linen woven with blue, purple, and scarlet, with figures of cherubim upon it. It was made of two long pieces, one running from north to south, the other from east to west [and overlapping for the ceiling] (Exod. 26:1, 6; 36:8ff.). 2. Over this a covering of woven goats' hair was thrown (Exod. 26:7; 36:14). 3. A third covering of rams' skins made red (Exod. 26:14; 36:19). 4. And "above it" another covering of dolphin or porpoise skins, weighing the others down and giving perfect protection from the weather (Exod. 26:14; 36:19).

[g]Heb. *twinned*　　　[h]Heb. *two sockets, two sockets under one board*

New American Standard

9 The length of each curtain was twenty-eight cubits and the width of each curtain four cubits; all the curtains had the same measurements.

10 He joined five curtains to one another and *the other* five curtains he joined to one another.

11 He made loops of blue on the edge of the outermost curtain in the first set; he did likewise on the edge of the curtain that was outermost in the second set.

12 He made fifty loops in the one curtain and he made fifty loops on the edge of the curtain that was in the second set; the loops were opposite each other.

13 He made fifty clasps of gold and joined the curtains to one another with the clasps, so the tabernacle was a unit.

14 ¶ Then he made curtains of goats' *hair* for a tent over the tabernacle; he made eleven curtains in all.

15 The length of each curtain *was* thirty cubits and four cubits the width of each curtain; the eleven curtains had the same measurements.

16 He joined five curtains by themselves and *the other* six curtains by themselves.

17 Moreover, he made fifty loops on the edge of the curtain that was outermost in the *first* set, and he made fifty loops on the edge of the curtain *that was outermost in* the second set.

18 He made fifty clasps of bronze to join the tent together so that it would be a unit.

19 He made a covering for the tent of rams' skins dyed red, and a covering of porpoise skins above.

20 ¶ Then he made the boards for the tabernacle of acacia wood, standing upright.

21 Ten cubits *was* the length of each board and one and a half cubits the width of each board.

22 *There were* two tenons for each board, fitted to one another; thus he did for all the boards of the tabernacle.

23 He made the boards for the tabernacle: twenty boards for the south side;

24 and he made forty sockets of silver under the twenty boards; two sockets under one board for its two tenons and two sockets under another board for its two tenons.

25 Then for the second side of the tabernacle, on the north side, he made twenty boards,

26 and their forty sockets of silver; two sockets under one board and two sockets under another board.

27 For the rear of the tabernacle, to the west, he made six boards.

28 He made two boards for the corners of the tabernacle at the rear.

29 They were double beneath, and together they were complete to its top to the first ring; thus he did with both of them for the two corners.

30 There were eight boards with their sockets of silver, sixteen sockets, two under every board.

31 ¶ Then he made bars of acacia wood, five for the boards of one side of the tabernacle,

32 and five bars for the boards of the other side of the tabernacle, and five bars for the boards of the tabernacle for the rear *side* to the west.

33 He made the middle bar to pass through in the center of the boards from end to end.

34 He overlaid the boards with gold and made their rings of gold *as* holders for the bars, and overlaid the bars with gold.

New International

by a skilled craftsman. 9All the curtains were the same size—twenty-eight cubits long and four cubits wide.*y* 10They joined five of the curtains together and did the same with the other five. 11Then they made loops of blue material along the edge of the end curtain in one set, and the same was done with the end curtain in the other set. 12They also made fifty loops on one curtain and fifty loops on the end curtain of the other set, with the loops opposite each other. 13Then they made fifty gold clasps and used them to fasten the two sets of curtains together so that the tabernacle was a unit.

14They made curtains of goat hair for the tent over the tabernacle—eleven altogether. 15All eleven curtains were the same size—thirty cubits long and four cubits wide.*z* 16They joined five of the curtains into one set and the other six into another set. 17Then they made fifty loops along the edge of the end curtain in one set and also along the edge of the end curtain in the other set. 18They made fifty bronze clasps to fasten the tent together as a unit. 19Then they made for the tent a covering of rams' skins dyed red, and over that a covering of hides of sea cows.*a*

20They made upright frames of acacia wood for the tabernacle. 21Each frame was ten cubits long and a cubit and a half wide,*b* 22with two projections set parallel to each other. They made all the frames of the tabernacle in this way. 23They made twenty frames for the south side of the tabernacle 24and made forty silver bases to go under them—two bases for each frame, one under each projection. 25For the other side, the north side of the tabernacle, they made twenty frames 26and forty silver bases—two under each frame. 27They made six frames for the far end, that is, the west end of the tabernacle, 28and two frames were made for the corners of the tabernacle at the far end. 29At these two corners the frames were double from the bottom all the way to the top and fitted into a single ring; both were made alike. 30So there were eight frames and sixteen silver bases—two under each frame.

31They also made crossbars of acacia wood: five for the frames on one side of the tabernacle, 32five for those on the other side, and five for the frames on the west, at the far end of the tabernacle. 33They made the center crossbar so that it extended from end to end at the middle of the frames. 34They overlaid the frames with gold and made gold rings to hold the crossbars. They also overlaid the crossbars with gold.

y 9 That is, about 42 feet (about 12.5 meters) long and 6 feet (about 1.8 meters) wide   *z 15* That is, about 45 feet (about 13.5 meters) long and 6 feet (about 1.8 meters) wide   *a 19* That is, dugongs *b 21* That is, about 15 feet (about 4.5 meters) long and 2 1/4 feet (about 0.7 meter) wide

King James

³⁵ ¶ And he made a veil *of* blue, and purple, and scarlet, and fine twined linen: *with* cherubims made he it of cunning work.

³⁶And he made thereunto four pillars *of* shittim *wood,* and overlaid them with gold: their hooks *were of* gold; and he cast for them four sockets of silver.

³⁷ ¶ And he made an hanging for the tabernacle door *of* blue, and purple, and scarlet, and fine twined linen, *i* of needlework;

³⁸And the five pillars of it with their hooks: and he overlaid their chapiters and their fillets with gold: but their five sockets *were of* brass.

The construction of the ark

37 AND BEZALEEL made the ark *of* shittim wood: two cubits and a half *was* the length of it, and a cubit and a half the breadth of it, and a cubit and a half the height of it:

²And he overlaid it with pure gold within and without, and made a crown of gold to it round about.

³And he cast for it four rings of gold, *to be set* by the four corners of it; even two rings upon the one side of it, and two rings upon the other side of it.

⁴And he made staves *of* shittim wood, and overlaid them with gold.

⁵And he put the staves into the rings by the sides of the ark, to bear the ark.

⁶ ¶ And he made the mercy seat *of* pure gold: two cubits and a half *was* the length thereof, and one cubit and a half the breadth thereof.

⁷And he made two cherubims *of* gold, beaten out of one piece made he them, on the two ends of the mercy seat;

⁸One cherub *j* on the end on this side, and another cherub *j* on the *other* end on that side: out of the mercy seat made he the cherubims on the two ends thereof.

⁹And the cherubims spread out *their* wings on high, *and* covered with their wings over the mercy seat, with their faces one to another; *even* to the mercy seatward were the faces of the cherubims.

The table and the candlestick

¹⁰ ¶ And he made the table *of* shittim wood: two cubits *was* the length thereof, and a cubit the breadth thereof, and a cubit and a half the height thereof:

¹¹And he overlaid it with pure gold, and made thereunto a crown of gold round about.

¹²Also he made thereunto a border of an handbreadth round about; and made a crown of gold for the border thereof round about.

¹³And he cast for it four rings of gold, and put the rings upon the four corners that *were* in the four feet thereof.

¹⁴Over against the border were the rings, the places for the staves to bear the table.

¹⁵And he made the staves *of* shittim wood, and overlaid them with gold, to bear the table.

¹⁶And he made the vessels which *were* upon the table, his dishes, and his spoons, and his bowls, and his covers *k* to cover withal, *of* pure gold.

¹⁷ ¶ And he made the candlestick *of* pure gold: *of* beaten work made he the candlestick; his shaft, and his branch, his bowls, his knobs, and his flowers, were of the same:

¹⁸And six branches going out of the sides thereof; three branches of the candlestick out of the one side thereof, and three branches of the candlestick out of the other side thereof:

¹⁹Three bowls made after the fashion of almonds in one branch, a knob and a flower; and three bowls made like almonds in another branch, a knob and a flower: so throughout the six branches going out of the candlestick.

²⁰And in the candlestick *were* four bowls made like almonds, his knobs, and his flowers:

Amplified

³⁵And he made the veil of blue, purple, and scarlet [stuff] and fine twined linen, with cherubim skillfully worked. [Matt. 27:50, 51; Heb. 10:19–22.]

³⁶For [the veil] he made four pillars of acacia [wood] and overlaid them with gold; their hooks were of gold, and he cast for them four sockets *or* bases of silver.

³⁷And he made a screen for the tent door of blue, purple, and scarlet [stuff] and fine twined linen, embroidered,

³⁸And he made the five pillars of it with their hooks, and overlaid their ornamental tops and joinings with gold, but their five sockets were of bronze.

37 BEZALEL MADE the ark of acacia wood—two cubits and a half was the length of it, a cubit and a half the breadth of it, and a cubit and a half the height of it.

²He overlaid it with pure gold within and without and made a molding *or* crown of gold to go around the top of it.

³He cast four rings of gold for its four corners, two rings on either side.

⁴He made poles of acacia wood and overlaid them with gold.

⁵He put the poles through the rings at the sides of the ark to carry it.

⁶[Bezalel] made the mercy seat of pure gold, two cubits and a half its length and one cubit and a half its breadth.

⁷And he made two cherubim of beaten gold; on the two ends of the mercy seat he made them,

⁸One cherub at one end and one at the other end; of one piece with the mercy seat he made the cherubim at its two ends.

⁹And the cherubim spread out their wings on high, covering the mercy seat with their wings, with their faces to each other, looking down to the mercy seat. [Heb. 9:23–26.]

¹⁰Bezalel made the [showbread] table of acacia wood; it was two cubits long, a cubit wide, and a cubit and a half high.

¹¹He overlaid it with pure gold and made a molding of gold around its top.

¹²And he made a border around it [just under the top] a handbreadth wide, and a molding of gold around the border.

¹³And he cast for it four rings of gold and fastened the rings on the four corners that were at its four legs.

¹⁴Close to the border were the rings, the places for the poles to pass through to carry the [showbread] table.

¹⁵[Bezalel] made the poles of acacia wood to carry the [showbread] table and overlaid them with gold.

¹⁶He made of pure gold the vessels which were to be on the table, its plates and dishes [for bread], its bowls and flagons for pouring [liquid sacrifices].

¹⁷And he made the lampstand of pure gold; its base and shaft were made of hammered work; its cups, its knobs, and its flowers were of one piece with it.

¹⁸There were six branches going out of the sides of the lampstand, three branches out of one side of it and three branches out of the other side of it;

¹⁹Three cups made like almond blossoms in one branch, each with a [calyx] knob and a flower, and three cups made like almond blossoms in the [opposite] branch, each with a [calyx] knob and a flower; and so for the six branches going out of the lampstand.

²⁰On [the shaft of] the lampstand were four cups made like almond blossoms, with knobs and flowers [one at the top].

i Heb. *the work of a needleworker,* or, *embroiderer*   *j* Or, *out of*
k Or, *to pour out withal*

New American Standard

35 ¶ Moreover, he made the veil of blue and purple and scarlet *material,* and fine twisted linen; he made it with cherubim, the work of a skillful workman.
36 He made four pillars of acacia for it, and overlaid them with gold, with their hooks of gold; and he cast four sockets of silver for them.
37 He made a screen for the doorway of the tent, of blue and purple and scarlet *material,* and fine twisted linen, the work of a weaver;
38 and *he made* its five pillars with their hooks, and he overlaid their tops and their bands with gold; but their five sockets were of bronze.

Construction Continues

37 NOW BEZALEL made the ark of acacia wood; its length was two and a half cubits, and its width one and a half cubits, and its height one and a half cubits;
2 and he overlaid it with pure gold inside and out, and made a gold molding for it all around.
3 He cast four rings of gold for it on its four feet; even two rings on one side of it, and two rings on the other side of it.
4 He made poles of acacia wood and overlaid them with gold.
5 He put the poles into the rings on the sides of the ark, to carry it.
6 He made a mercy seat of pure gold, two and a half cubits long and one and a half cubits wide.
7 He made two cherubim of gold; he made them of hammered work at the two ends of the mercy seat;
8 one cherub at the one end and one cherub at the other end; he made the cherubim *of one piece* with the mercy seat at the two ends.
9 The cherubim had *their* wings spread upward, covering the mercy seat with their wings, with their faces toward each other; the faces of the cherubim were toward the mercy seat.
10 ¶ Then he made the table of acacia wood, two cubits long and a cubit wide and one and a half cubits high.
11 He overlaid it with pure gold, and made a gold molding for it all around.
12 He made a rim for it of a handbreadth all around, and made a gold molding for its rim all around.
13 He cast four gold rings for it and put the rings on the four corners that were on its four feet.
14 Close by the rim were the rings, the holders for the poles to carry the table.
15 He made the poles of acacia wood and overlaid them with gold, to carry the table.
16 He made the utensils which were on the table, its dishes and its pans and its bowls and its jars, with which to pour out drink offerings, of pure gold.
17 ¶ Then he made the lampstand of pure gold. He made the lampstand of hammered work, its base and its shaft; its cups, its bulbs and its flowers were *of one piece* with it.
18 There were six branches going out of its sides; three branches of the lampstand from the one side of it and three branches of the lampstand from the other side of it;
19 three cups shaped like almond *blossoms,* a bulb and a flower in one branch, and three cups shaped like almond *blossoms,* a bulb and a flower in the other branch—so for the six branches going out of the lampstand.
20 In the lampstand *there were* four cups shaped like almond *blossoms,* its bulbs and its flowers;

New International

35 They made the curtain of blue, purple and scarlet yarn and finely twisted linen, with cherubim worked into it by a skilled craftsman. 36 They made four posts of acacia wood for it and overlaid them with gold. They made gold hooks for them and cast their four silver bases. 37 For the entrance to the tent they made a curtain of blue, purple and scarlet yarn and finely twisted linen—the work of an embroiderer; 38 and they made five posts with hooks for them. They overlaid the tops of the posts and their bands with gold and made their five bases of bronze.

The Ark

37 BEZALEL MADE the ark of acacia wood—two and a half cubits long, a cubit and a half wide, and a cubit and a half high.[c] 2 He overlaid it with pure gold, both inside and out, and made a gold molding around it. 3 He cast four gold rings for it and fastened them to its four feet, with two rings on one side and two rings on the other. 4 Then he made poles of acacia wood and overlaid them with gold. 5 And he inserted the poles into the rings on the sides of the ark to carry it.
6 He made the atonement cover of pure gold—two and a half cubits long and a cubit and a half wide.[d] 7 Then he made two cherubim out of hammered gold at the ends of the cover. 8 He made one cherub on one end and the second cherub on the other; at the two ends he made them of one piece with the cover. 9 The cherubim had their wings spread upward, overshadowing the cover with them. The cherubim faced each other, looking toward the cover.

The Table

10 They[e] made the table of acacia wood—two cubits long, a cubit wide, and a cubit and a half high.[f] 11 Then they overlaid it with pure gold and made a gold molding around it. 12 They also made around it a rim a handbreadth[g] wide and put a gold molding on the rim. 13 They cast four gold rings for the table and fastened them to the four corners, where the four legs were. 14 The rings were put close to the rim to hold the poles used in carrying the table. 15 The poles for carrying the table were made of acacia wood and were overlaid with gold. 16 And they made from pure gold the articles for the table—its plates and dishes and bowls and its pitchers for the pouring out of drink offerings.

The Lampstand

17 They made the lampstand of pure gold and hammered it out, base and shaft; its flowerlike cups, buds and blossoms were of one piece with it. 18 Six branches extended from the sides of the lampstand—three on one side and three on the other. 19 Three cups shaped like almond flowers with buds and blossoms were on one branch, three on the next branch and the same for all six branches extending from the lampstand. 20 And on the lampstand were four cups shaped like almond flowers with buds and blossoms.

c 1 That is, about 3 3/4 feet (about 1.1 meters) long and 2 1/4 feet (about 0.7 meter) wide and high   d 6 That is, about 3 3/4 feet (about 1.1 meters) long and 2 1/4 feet (about 0.7 meter) wide   e 10 Or *He;* also in verses 11-29   f 10 That is, about 3 feet (about 0.9 meter) long, 1 1/2 feet (about 0.5 meter) wide, and 2 1/4 feet (about 0.7 meter) high   g 12 That is, about 3 inches (about 8 centimeters)

King James

²¹And a knob under two branches of the same, and a knob under two branches of the same, and a knob under two branches of the same, according to the six branches going out of it.

²²Their knobs and their branches were of the same: all of it *was* one beaten work *of* pure gold.

²³And he made his seven lamps, and his snuffers, and his snuffdishes, *of* pure gold.

²⁴*Of* a talent of pure gold made he it, and all the vessels thereof.

The altar of incense

25 ¶ And he made the incense altar *of* shittim wood: the length of it *was* a cubit, and the breadth of it a cubit; *it was* foursquare; and two cubits *was* the height of it; the horns thereof were of the same.

²⁶And he overlaid it with pure gold, *both* the top of it, and the sides thereof round about, and the horns of it: also he made unto it a crown of gold round about.

²⁷And he made two rings of gold for it under the crown thereof, by the two corners of it, upon the two sides thereof, to be places for the staves to bear it withal.

²⁸And he made the staves *of* shittim wood, and overlaid them with gold.

29 ¶ And he made the holy anointing oil, and the pure incense of sweet spices, according to the work of the apothecary.

The altar of burnt offering

38 AND HE made the altar of burnt offering *of* shittim wood: five cubits *was* the length thereof, and five cubits the breadth thereof; *it was* foursquare; and three cubits the height thereof.

²And he made the horns thereof on the four corners of it; the horns thereof were of the same: and he overlaid it with brass.

³And he made all the vessels of the altar, the pots, and the shovels, and the basins, *and* the fleshhooks, and the firepans: all the vessels thereof made he *of* brass.

⁴And he made for the altar a brasen grate of network under the compass thereof beneath unto the midst of it.

⁵And he cast four rings for the four ends of the grate of brass, *to be* places for the staves.

⁶And he made the staves *of* shittim wood, and overlaid them with brass.

⁷And he put the staves into the rings on the sides of the altar, to bear it withal; he made the altar hollow with boards.

8 ¶ And he made the laver *of* brass, and the foot of it *of* brass, of the *l*looking glasses of *the women* *m*assembling, which assembled *at* the door of the tabernacle of the congregation.

The court of the tabernacle

9 ¶ And he made the court: on the south side southward the hangings of the court *were* of fine twined linen, an hundred cubits:

¹⁰Their pillars *were* twenty, and their brasen sockets twenty; the hooks of the pillars and their fillets *were of* silver.

¹¹And for the north side *the hangings were* an hundred cubits, their pillars *were* twenty, and their sockets of brass twenty; the hooks of the pillars and their fillets *of* silver.

¹²And for the west side *were* hangings of fifty cubits, their pillars ten, and their sockets ten; the hooks of the pillars and their fillets *of* silver.

¹³And for the east side eastward fifty cubits.

¹⁴The hangings of the one side *of the gate were* fifteen cubits; their pillars three, and their sockets three.

Amplified

²¹And a knob under each pair of branches, of one piece with the lampstand, for the six branches going out of it.

²²Their knobs and their branches were of one piece with it, all of it hammered work of pure gold.

²³And he made of pure gold its seven lamps, its snuffers, and its ashtrays.

²⁴A talent of pure gold he made the lampstand and all its utensils. [John 1:4, 5, 9; II Cor. 4:6.]

²⁵And [Bezalel] made the incense altar of acacia wood; its top was a cubit square and it was two cubits high; the horns were one piece with it.

²⁶He overlaid it with pure gold, its top, its sides round about, and its horns; also he made a rim around it of gold.

²⁷And he made two rings of gold for it under its rim, on its two opposite sides, as places for the poles [to pass through] to carry it.

²⁸And he made the poles of acacia wood and overlaid them with gold.

²⁹He also made the holy anointing oil [symbol of the Holy Spirit] and the pure, fragrant incense, after the perfumer's art.

38 BEZALEL MADE the burnt offering altar of acacia wood; its top was five cubits square and it was three cubits high.

²He made its horns on the four corners of it; the horns were of one piece with it, and he overlaid it with bronze.

³He made all the utensils *and* vessels of the altar, the pots, shovels, basins, forks *or* fleshhooks, and firepans; all its utensils *and* vessels he made of bronze.

⁴And he made for the altar a bronze grate of network under its ledge, extending halfway down it.

⁵He cast four rings for the four corners of the bronze grating to be places for the poles [with which to carry it].

⁶He made the poles of acacia wood and overlaid them with bronze.

⁷And he put the poles through the rings on the altar's sides with which to carry it; he made it hollow with planks.

⁸He made the laver and its base of bronze from the mirrors of the women who ministered at the door of the Tent of Meeting.

⁹And he made the court: for the south side the hangings of the court were of fine twined linen, a hundred cubits.

¹⁰Their pillars and their bronze sockets *or* bases were twenty; the hooks of the pillars and their joinings were silver.

¹¹And for the north side the hangings were [also] a hundred cubits; their pillars and their sockets *or* bases of bronze were twenty; the hooks of the pillars and their joinings were of silver.

¹²But for the west side were hangings of fifty cubits; their pillars and their sockets *or* bases were ten; the hooks of the pillars and their joinings were of silver.

¹³And for the front, the east side, fifty cubits.

¹⁴The hangings for one side of the gate were fifteen cubits; their pillars three and their sockets *or* bases three.

---

*l*Or, *brasen glasses*   *m*Heb. *assembling by troops* as 1 Sam. 2:22

New American Standard

21 and a bulb was under the *first* pair of branches *coming* out of it, and a bulb under the *second* pair of branches *coming* out of it, and a bulb under the *third* pair of branches *coming* out of it, for the six branches coming out of the lampstand.

22 Their bulbs and their branches were *of one piece* with it; the whole of it *was* a single hammered work of pure gold.

23 He made its seven lamps with its snuffers and its trays of pure gold.

24 He made it and all its utensils from a talent of pure gold.

25 ¶ Then he made the altar of incense of acacia wood: a cubit long and a cubit wide, square, and two cubits high; its horns were *of one piece* with it.

26 He overlaid it with pure gold, its top and its sides all around, and its horns; and he made a gold molding for it all around.

27 He made two golden rings for it under its molding, on its two sides—on opposite sides—as holders for poles with which to carry it.

28 He made the poles of acacia wood and overlaid them with gold.

29 And he made the holy anointing oil and the pure, fragrant incense of spices, the work of a perfumer.

The Tabernacle Completed

38 THEN HE made the altar of burnt offering of acacia wood, five cubits long, and five cubits wide, square, and three cubits high.

2 He made its horns on its four corners, its horns being *of one piece* with it, and he overlaid it with bronze.

3 He made all the utensils of the altar, the pails and the shovels and the basins, the flesh hooks and the firepans; he made all its utensils of bronze.

4 He made for the altar a grating of bronze network beneath, under its ledge, reaching halfway up.

5 He cast four rings on the four ends of the bronze grating *as* holders for the poles.

6 He made the poles of acacia wood and overlaid them with bronze.

7 He inserted the poles into the rings on the sides of the altar, with which to carry it. He made it hollow with planks.

8 ¶ Moreover, he made the laver of bronze with its base of bronze, from the mirrors of the serving women who served at the doorway of the tent of meeting.

9 ¶ Then he made the court: for the south side the hangings of the court were of fine twisted linen, one hundred cubits;

10 their twenty pillars, and their twenty sockets, *made* of bronze; the hooks of the pillars and their bands *were* of silver.

11 For the north side *there were* one hundred cubits; their twenty pillars and their twenty sockets *were* of bronze, the hooks of the pillars and their bands *were* of silver.

12 For the west side *there were* hangings of fifty cubits *with* their ten pillars and their ten sockets; the hooks of the pillars and their bands *were* of silver.

13 For the east side fifty cubits.

14 The hangings for the *one* side *of the gate were* fifteen cubits, *with* their three pillars and their three sockets,

New International

21 One bud was under the first pair of branches extending from the lampstand, a second bud under the second pair, and a third bud under the third pair—six branches in all. 22 The buds and the branches were all of one piece with the lampstand, hammered out of pure gold.

23 They made its seven lamps, as well as its wick trimmers and trays, of pure gold. 24 They made the lampstand and all its accessories from one talent[h] of pure gold.

The Altar of Incense

25 They made the altar of incense out of acacia wood. It was square, a cubit long and a cubit wide, and two cubits high[i]—its horns of one piece with it. 26 They overlaid the top and all the sides and the horns with pure gold, and made a gold molding around it. 27 They made two gold rings below the molding—two on opposite sides—to hold the poles used to carry it. 28 They made the poles of acacia wood and overlaid them with gold.

29 They also made the sacred anointing oil and the pure, fragrant incense—the work of a perfumer.

The Altar of Burnt Offering

38 THEY[j] BUILT the altar of burnt offering of acacia wood, three cubits[k] high; it was square, five cubits long and five cubits wide.[l] 2 They made a horn at each of the four corners, so that the horns and the altar were of one piece, and they overlaid the altar with bronze. 3 They made all its utensils of bronze—its pots, shovels, sprinkling bowls, meat forks and firepans. 4 They made a grating for the altar, a bronze network, to be under its ledge, halfway up the altar. 5 They cast bronze rings to hold the poles for the four corners of the bronze grating. 6 They made the poles of acacia wood and overlaid them with bronze. 7 They inserted the poles into the rings so they would be on the sides of the altar for carrying it. They made it hollow, out of boards.

Basin for Washing

8 They made the bronze basin and its bronze stand from the mirrors of the women who served at the entrance to the Tent of Meeting.

The Courtyard

9 Next they made the courtyard. The south side was a hundred cubits[m] long and had curtains of finely twisted linen, 10 with twenty posts and twenty bronze bases, and with silver hooks and bands on the posts. 11 The north side was also a hundred cubits long and had twenty posts and twenty bronze bases, with silver hooks and bands on the posts.

12 The west end was fifty cubits[n] wide and had curtains, with ten posts and ten bases, with silver hooks and bands on the posts. 13 The east end, toward the sunrise, was also fifty cubits wide. 14 Curtains fifteen cubits[o] long were on one side of the entrance, with three posts and three bases,

---

h 24 That is, about 75 pounds (about 34 kilograms) *i 25* That is, about 1 1/2 feet (about 0.5 meter) long and wide, and about 3 feet (about 0.9 meter) high *j 1* Or *He*; also in verses 2-9
k 1 That is, about 4 1/2 feet (about 1.3 meters) *l 1* That is, about 7 1/2 feet (about 2.3 meters) long and wide *m 9* That is, about 150 feet (about 46 meters) *n 12* That is, about 75 feet (about 23 meters) *o 14* That is, about 22 1/2 feet (about 6.9 meters)

King James

15And for the other side of the court gate, on this hand and that hand, *were* hangings of fifteen cubits; their pillars three, and their sockets three.

16All the hangings of the court round about *were* of fine twined linen.

17And the sockets for the pillars *were of* brass; the hooks of the pillars and their fillets *of* silver; and the overlaying of their chapiters *of* silver; and all the pillars of the court *were* filleted with silver.

18And the hanging for the gate of the court *was* needle-work, *of* blue, and purple, and scarlet, and fine twined linen: and twenty cubits *was* the length, and the height in the breadth *was* five cubits, answerable to the hangings of the court.

19And their pillars *were* four, and their sockets *of* brass four; their hooks *of* silver, and the overlaying of their chapiters and their fillets *of* silver.

20And all the pins of the tabernacle, and of the court round about, *were of* brass.

21 ¶ This is the sum of the tabernacle, *even* of the tabernacle of testimony, as it was counted, according to the commandment of Moses, *for* the service of the Levites, by the hand of Ithamar, son to Aaron the priest.

22And Bezaleel the son of Uri, the son of Hur, of the tribe of Judah, made all that the LORD commanded Moses.

23And with him *was* Aholiab, son of Ahisamach, of the tribe of Dan, an engraver, and a cunning workman, and an embroiderer in blue, and in purple, and in scarlet, and fine linen.

The valuable metals used

24All the gold that was occupied for the work in all the work of the holy *place,* even the gold of the offering, was twenty and nine talents, and seven hundred and thirty shekels, after the shekel of the sanctuary.

25And the silver of them that were numbered of the congregation *was* an hundred talents, and a thousand seven hundred and threescore and fifteen shekels, after the shekel of the sanctuary:

26A bekah for *n*every man, *that is,* half a shekel, after the shekel of the sanctuary, for every one that went to be numbered, from twenty years old and upward, for six hundred thousand and three thousand and five hundred and fifty *men.*

27And of the hundred talents of silver were cast the sockets of the sanctuary, and the sockets of the veil; an hundred sockets of the hundred talents, a talent for a socket.

28And of the thousand seven hundred seventy and five *shekels* he made hooks for the pillars, and overlaid their chapiters, and filleted them.

29And the brass of the offering *was* seventy talents, and two thousand and four hundred shekels.

30And therewith he made the sockets to the door of the tabernacle of the congregation, and the brasen altar, and the brasen grate for it, and all the vessels of the altar,

31And the sockets of the court round about, and the sockets of the court gate, and all the pins of the tabernacle, and all the pins of the court round about.

The garments of the priesthood

39 AND OF the blue, and purple, and scarlet, they made cloths of service, to do service in the holy *place,* and made the holy garments for Aaron; as the LORD commanded Moses.

Amplified

15Also for the other side of the court gate, left and right, were hangings of fifteen cubits; their pillars three and their sockets *or* bases three.

16All the hangings around the court were of fine twined linen.

17The sockets for the pillars were of bronze, the hooks of the pillars and their joinings of silver, the overlaying of their tops of silver, and all the pillars of the court were joined with silver.

18The hanging *or* screen for the gate of the court was embroidered in blue, purple, and scarlet [stuff], and fine twined linen; the length was twenty cubits and the height in the breadth was five cubits, corresponding to the hangings of the court.

19Their pillars were four and their sockets of bronze four; their hooks were of silver, and the overlaying of their tops and their joinings were of silver.

20All the pegs for the tabernacle and around the court were of bronze.

21This is the sum of the things for the tabernacle of the Testimony, as counted at the command of Moses, for the work of the Levites under the direction of Ithamar son of Aaron, the [high] priest.

22Bezalel son of Uri, the son of Hur, of the tribe of Judah, made all that the Lord commanded Moses.

23With him was Aholiab son of Ahisamach, of the tribe of Dan, an engraver, a skillful craftsman, and embroiderer in blue, purple, and scarlet [stuff], and in fine linen.

24All the gold that was used for the work in all the building *and* furnishing of the sanctuary, the gold from the offering, was 29 talents and 730 shekels, by the shekel of the sanctuary.

25And the silver from those numbered of the congregation was 100 talents and 1,775 shekels, by sanctuary standards:

26A beka for each man, that is, half a shekel, by the sanctuary shekel, for everyone who was counted, from twenty years old and upward, for 603,550 men.

27The 100 talents of silver were for casting the sockets *or* bases of the sanctuary and of the veil; 100 sockets for the 100 talents, a talent for a socket.

28Of the 1,775 shekels he made hooks for the pillars, and overlaid their tops, and made joinings for them.

29The bronze of the offering was 70 talents and 2,400 shekels.

30With it Bezalel made the sockets for the door of the Tent of Meeting, and the bronze altar and the bronze grate for it, and all the utensils of the altar,

31The sockets of the court round about and of the court gate, and all the pegs of the tabernacle and around the court.

39 AND OF the blue and purple and scarlet [stuff] they made finely wrought garments for serving in the Holy Place; they made the holy garments for Aaron, as the Lord had commanded Moses.

---

*n*Heb. *a poll*

New American Standard

15 and so for the other side. On both sides of the gate of the court *were* hangings of fifteen cubits, *with* their three pillars and their three sockets.
16 All the hangings of the court all around *were* of fine twisted linen.
17 The sockets for the pillars *were* of bronze, the hooks of the pillars and their bands, of silver; and the overlaying of their tops, of silver, and all the pillars of the court were furnished with silver bands.
18 The screen of the gate of the court was the work of the weaver, of blue and purple and scarlet *material* and fine twisted linen. And the length *was* twenty cubits and the height *was* five cubits, corresponding to the hangings of the court.
19 Their four pillars and their four sockets *were* of bronze; their hooks *were* of silver, and the overlaying of their tops and their bands *were* of silver.
20 All the pegs of the tabernacle and of the court all around *were* of bronze.

The Cost of the Tabernacle

21 ¶ This is the number of the things for the tabernacle, the tabernacle of the testimony, as they were numbered according to the command of Moses, for the service of the Levites, by the hand of Ithamar the son of Aaron the priest.
22 Now Bezalel the son of Uri, the son of Hur, of the tribe of Judah, made all that the LORD had commanded Moses.
23 With him *was* Oholiab the son of Ahisamach, of the tribe of Dan, an engraver and a skillful workman and a weaver in blue and in purple and in scarlet *material,* and fine linen.
24 ¶ All the gold that was used for the work, in all the work of the sanctuary, even the gold of the wave offering, was 29 talents and 730 shekels, according to the shekel of the sanctuary.
25 The silver of those of the congregation who were numbered was 100 talents and 1,775 shekels, according to the shekel of the sanctuary;
26 a beka a head (*that is,* half a shekel according to the shekel of the sanctuary), for each one who passed over to those who were numbered, from twenty years old and upward, for 603,550 men.
27 The hundred talents of silver were for casting the sockets of the sanctuary and the sockets of the veil; one hundred sockets for the hundred talents, a talent for a socket.
28 Of the 1,775 *shekels,* he made hooks for the pillars and overlaid their tops and made bands for them.
29 The bronze of the wave offering was 70 talents and 2,400 shekels.
30 With it he made the sockets to the doorway of the tent of meeting, and the bronze altar and its bronze grating, and all the utensils of the altar,
31 and the sockets of the court all around and the sockets of the gate of the court, and all the pegs of the tabernacle and all the pegs of the court all around.

The Priestly Garments

39 MOREOVER, FROM the blue and purple and scarlet *material,* they made finely woven garments for ministering in the holy place as well as the holy garments which were for Aaron, just as the LORD had commanded Moses.

New International

15and curtains fifteen cubits long were on the other side of the entrance to the courtyard, with three posts and three bases. 16All the curtains around the courtyard were of finely twisted linen. 17The bases for the posts were bronze. The hooks and bands on the posts were silver, and their tops were overlaid with silver; so all the posts of the courtyard had silver bands.
18The curtain for the entrance to the courtyard was of blue, purple and scarlet yarn and finely twisted linen—the work of an embroiderer. It was twenty cubits*p* long and, like the curtains of the courtyard, five cubits*q* high, 19with four posts and four bronze bases. Their hooks and bands were silver, and their tops were overlaid with silver. 20All the tent pegs of the tabernacle and of the surrounding courtyard were bronze.

The Materials Used

21These are the amounts of the materials used for the tabernacle, the tabernacle of the Testimony, which were recorded at Moses' command by the Levites under the direction of Ithamar son of Aaron, the priest. 22(Bezalel son of Uri, the son of Hur, of the tribe of Judah, made everything the LORD commanded Moses; 23with him was Oholiab son of Ahisamach, of the tribe of Dan—a craftsman and designer, and an embroiderer in blue, purple and scarlet yarn and fine linen.) 24The total amount of the gold from the wave offering used for all the work on the sanctuary was 29 talents and 730 shekels,*r* according to the sanctuary shekel.
25The silver obtained from those of the community who were counted in the census was 100 talents and 1,775 shekels,*s* according to the sanctuary shekel— 26one beka per person, that is, half a shekel,*t* according to the sanctuary shekel, from everyone who had crossed over to those counted, twenty years old or more, a total of 603,550 men. 27The 100 talents*u* of silver were used to cast the bases for the sanctuary and for the curtain—100 bases from the 100 talents, one talent for each base. 28They used the 1,775 shekels*v* to make the hooks for the posts, to overlay the tops of the posts, and to make their bands.
29The bronze from the wave offering was 70 talents and 2,400 shekels.*w* 30They used it to make the bases for the entrance to the Tent of Meeting, the bronze altar with its bronze grating and all its utensils, 31the bases for the surrounding courtyard and those for its entrance and all the tent pegs for the tabernacle and those for the surrounding courtyard.

The Priestly Garments

39 FROM THE blue, purple and scarlet yarn they made woven garments for ministering in the sanctuary. They also made sacred garments for Aaron, as the LORD commanded Moses.

p 18 That is, about 30 feet (about 9 meters)   *q 18* That is, about 7 1/2 feet (about 2.3 meters)   *r 24* The weight of the gold was a little over one ton (about 1 metric ton).   *s 25* The weight of the silver was a little over 3 3/4 tons (about 3.4 metric tons).   *t 26* That is, about 1/5 ounce (about 5.5 grams)   *u 27* That is, about 3 3/4 tons (about 3.4 metric tons)   *v 28* That is, about 45 pounds (about 20 kilograms)   *w 29* The weight of the bronze was about 2 1/2 tons (about 2.4 metric tons).

King James

²And he made the ephod *of* gold, blue, and purple, and scarlet, and fine twined linen.

³And they did beat the gold into thin plates, and cut *it into* wires, to work *it* in the blue, and in the purple, and in the scarlet, and in the fine linen, *with* cunning work.

⁴They made shoulderpieces for it, to couple *it* together: by the two edges was it coupled together.

⁵And the curious girdle of his ephod, that *was* upon it, *was* of the same, according to the work thereof; *of* gold, blue, and purple, and scarlet, and fine twined linen; as the LORD commanded Moses.

⁶ ¶ And they wrought onyx stones enclosed in ouches of gold, graven, as signets are graven, with the names of the children of Israel.

⁷And he put them on the shoulders of the ephod, *that they should be* stones for a memorial to the children of Israel; as the LORD commanded Moses.

The priest's breastplate

⁸ ¶ And he made the breastplate *of* cunning work, like the work of the ephod; *of* gold, and blue, and purple, and scarlet, and fine twined linen.

⁹It was foursquare; they made the breastplate double: a span *was* the length thereof, and a span the breadth thereof, *being* doubled.

¹⁰And they set in it four rows of stones: *the first* row *was* a °sardius, a topaz, and a carbuncle: this *was* the first row.

¹¹And the second row, an emerald, a sapphire, and a diamond.

¹²And the third row, a ligure, an agate, and an amethyst.

¹³And the fourth row, a beryl, an onyx, and a jasper: *they were* enclosed in ouches of gold in their enclosings.

¹⁴And the stones *were* according to the names of the children of Israel, twelve, according to their names, *like* the engravings of a signet, every one with his name, according to the twelve tribes.

¹⁵And they made upon the breastplate chains at the ends, *of* wreathen work *of* pure gold.

¹⁶And they made two ouches *of* gold, and two gold rings; and put the two rings in the two ends of the breastplate.

¹⁷And they put the two wreathen chains of gold in the two rings on the ends of the breastplate.

¹⁸And the two ends of the two wreathen chains they fastened in the two ouches, and put them on the shoulderpieces of the ephod, before it.

¹⁹And they made two rings of gold, and put *them* on the two ends of the breastplate, upon the border of it, which *was* on the side of the ephod inward.

²⁰And they made two *other* golden rings, and put them on the two sides of the ephod underneath, toward the forepart of it, over against the *other* coupling thereof, above the curious girdle of the ephod.

²¹And they did bind the breastplate by his rings unto the rings of the ephod with a lace of blue, that it might be above the curious girdle of the ephod, and that the breastplate might not be loosed from the ephod; as the LORD commanded Moses.

The robe of the ephod

²² ¶ And he made the robe of the ephod *of* woven work, all *of* blue.

²³And *there was* an hole in the midst of the robe, as the hole of an habergeon, *with* a band round about the hole, that it should not rend.

²⁴And they made upon the hems of the robe pomegranates *of* blue, and purple, and scarlet, *and* twined *linen*.

²⁵And they made bells *of* pure gold, and put the bells between the pomegranates upon the hem of the robe, round about between the pomegranates;

Amplified

²And Bezalel made the ephod of gold, blue, purple, and scarlet [stuff], and fine twined linen.

³And they beat the gold into thin sheets and cut it into wires to work into the blue, purple, and scarlet [stuff] and the fine linen, in skilled design.

⁴They made shoulder pieces for the ephod, joined to it at its two edges.

⁵And the skillfully woven band on it, to gird it on, was of the same piece and workmanship with it, of gold, blue, purple, and scarlet [stuff], and fine twined linen, as the Lord had commanded Moses.

⁶And they prepared the onyx stones enclosed in settings of gold filigree and engraved as signets are engraved with the names of the sons of Israel.

⁷And he put them on the shoulder pieces of the ephod to be stones of memorial *or* remembrance for the Israelites, as the Lord had commanded Moses.

⁸And [Bezalel] made the breastplate skillfully, like the work of the ephod, of gold, blue, purple, and scarlet [stuff], and fine twined linen.

⁹The breastplate was a [hand's] span square when doubled over.

¹⁰And they set in it four rows of stones; a sardius, a topaz, and a carbuncle made the first row;

¹¹The second row an emerald, a sapphire, and a diamond;

¹²The third row a jacinth, an agate, and an amethyst;

¹³And the fourth row a beryl, an onyx, and a jasper; they were enclosed in settings of gold filigree.

¹⁴There were twelve stones with their names according to those of the sons of Israel, engraved like a signet, each with its name, according to the twelve tribes.

¹⁵And they made [at the ends] of the breastplate twisted chains like cords, of pure gold.

¹⁶And they made two settings of gold filigree and two gold rings which they put on the two ends of the breastplate.

¹⁷And they put the two twisted cords *or* woven chains of gold in the two rings on the end edges of the breastplate.

¹⁸And the other two ends of the twisted cords *or* chains of gold they put on the two settings and put them on the shoulder pieces of the ephod, in front.

¹⁹They made two rings of gold and put them on the two ends of the breastplate, on the inside edge of it next to the ephod.

²⁰And they made two [other] gold rings and attached them to the two shoulder pieces of the ephod underneath, in front, at its joining above the skillfully woven band of the ephod.

²¹They bound the breastplate by its rings to those of the ephod with a blue lace, that it might lie upon the skillfully woven band of the ephod and that the breastplate might not be loosed from the ephod, as the Lord commanded Moses.

²²And he made the robe of the ephod of woven work all of blue.

²³And there was an opening [for the head] in the middle of the robe like the hole in a coat of mail, with a binding around it, that it should not be torn.

²⁴On the skirts of the robe they made pomegranates of blue and purple and scarlet [stuff] and twined linen.

²⁵And they made bells of pure gold and put [them] between the pomegranates around the skirts of the robe;

°Or, *ruby*

New American Standard

2 ¶ He made the ephod of gold, *and* of blue and purple and scarlet *material,* and fine twisted linen.
3 Then they hammered out gold sheets and cut *them* into threads to be woven in *with* the blue and the purple and the scarlet *material,* and the fine linen, the work of a skillful workman.
4 They made attaching shoulder pieces for the ephod; it was attached at its two *upper* ends.
5 The skillfully woven band which was on it was like its workmanship, of the same material: of gold *and* of blue and purple and scarlet *material,* and fine twisted linen, just as the LORD had commanded Moses.
6 ¶ They made the onyx stones, set in gold filigree *settings;* they were engraved *like* the engravings of a signet, according to the names of the sons of Israel.
7 And he placed them on the shoulder pieces of the ephod, *as* memorial stones for the sons of Israel, just as the LORD had commanded Moses.
8 ¶ He made the breastpiece, the work of a skillful workman, like the workmanship of the ephod: of gold *and* of blue and purple and scarlet *material* and fine twisted linen.
9 It was square; they made the breastpiece folded double, a span long and a span wide when folded double.
10 And they mounted four rows of stones on it. The first row *was* a row of ruby, topaz, and emerald;
11 and the second row, a turquoise, a sapphire and a diamond;
12 and the third row, a jacinth, an agate, and an amethyst;
13 and the fourth row, a beryl, an onyx, and a jasper. They were set in gold filigree *settings* when they were mounted.
14 The stones were corresponding to the names of the sons of Israel; they were twelve, corresponding to their names, *engraved with* the engravings of a signet, each with its name for the twelve tribes.
15 They made on the breastpiece chains like cords, of twisted cordage work in pure gold.
16 They made two gold filigree *settings* and two gold rings, and put the two rings on the two ends of the breastpiece.
17 Then they put the two gold cords in the two rings at the ends of the breastpiece.
18 They put the *other* two ends of the two cords on the two filigree *settings,* and put them on the shoulder pieces of the ephod at the front of it.
19 They made two gold rings and placed *them* on the two ends of the breastpiece, on its inner edge which was next to the ephod.
20 Furthermore, they made two gold rings and placed them on the bottom of the two shoulder pieces of the ephod, on the front of it, close to the place where it joined, above the woven band of the ephod.
21 They bound the breastpiece by its rings to the rings of the ephod with a blue cord, so that it would be on the woven band of the ephod, and that the breastpiece would not come loose from the ephod, just as the LORD had commanded Moses.
22 ¶ Then he made the robe of the ephod of woven work, all of blue;
23 and the opening of the robe was *at the top* in the center, as the opening of a coat of mail, with a binding all around its opening, so that it would not be torn.
24 They made pomegranates of blue and purple and scarlet *material and* twisted *linen* on the hem of the robe.
25 They also made bells of pure gold, and put the bells between the pomegranates all around on the hem of the robe,

New International

The Ephod

2They[x] made the ephod of gold, and of blue, purple and scarlet yarn, and of finely twisted linen. 3They hammered out thin sheets of gold and cut strands to be worked into the blue, purple and scarlet yarn and fine linen—the work of a skilled craftsman. 4They made shoulder pieces for the ephod, which were attached to two of its corners, so it could be fastened. 5Its skillfully woven waistband was like it—of one piece with the ephod and made with gold, and with blue, purple and scarlet yarn, and with finely twisted linen, as the LORD commanded Moses.

6They mounted the onyx stones in gold filigree settings and engraved them like a seal with the names of the sons of Israel. 7Then they fastened them on the shoulder pieces of the ephod as memorial stones for the sons of Israel, as the LORD commanded Moses.

The Breastpiece

8They fashioned the breastpiece—the work of a skilled craftsman. They made it like the ephod: of gold, and of blue, purple and scarlet yarn, and of finely twisted linen. 9It was square—a span[y] long and a span wide—and folded double. 10Then they mounted four rows of precious stones on it. In the first row there was a ruby, a topaz and a beryl; 11in the second row a turquoise, a sapphire[z] and an emerald; 12in the third row a jacinth, an agate and an amethyst; 13in the fourth row a chrysolite, an onyx and a jasper.[a] They were mounted in gold filigree settings. 14There were twelve stones, one for each of the names of the sons of Israel, each engraved like a seal with the name of one of the twelve tribes.

15For the breastpiece they made braided chains of pure gold, like a rope. 16They made two gold filigree settings and two gold rings, and fastened the rings to two of the corners of the breastpiece. 17They fastened the two gold chains to the rings at the corners of the breastpiece, 18and the other ends of the chains to the two settings, attaching them to the shoulder pieces of the ephod at the front. 19They made two gold rings and attached them to the other two corners of the breastpiece on the inside edge next to the ephod. 20Then they made two more gold rings and attached them to the bottom of the shoulder pieces on the front of the ephod, close to the seam just above the waistband of the ephod. 21They tied the rings of the breastpiece to the rings of the ephod with blue cord, connecting it to the waistband so that the breastpiece would not swing out from the ephod—as the LORD commanded Moses.

Other Priestly Garments

22They made the robe of the ephod entirely of blue cloth—the work of a weaver— 23with an opening in the center of the robe like the opening of a collar,[b] and a band around this opening, so that it would not tear. 24They made pomegranates of blue, purple and scarlet yarn and finely twisted linen around the hem of the robe. 25And they made bells of pure gold and attached them around the hem

King James

26A bell and a pomegranate, a bell and a pomegranate, round about the hem of the robe to minister *in;* as the LORD commanded Moses.

27 ¶ And they made coats *of* fine linen *of* woven work for Aaron, and for his sons,

28And a mitre *of* fine linen, and goodly bonnets *of* fine linen, and linen breeches *of* fine twined linen,

29And a girdle *of* fine twined linen, and blue, and purple, and scarlet, *of* needlework; as the LORD commanded Moses.

30 ¶ And they made the plate of the holy crown *of* pure gold, and wrote upon it a writing, *like to* the engravings of a signet, HOLINESS TO THE LORD.

31And they tied unto it a lace of blue, to fasten *it* on high upon the mitre; as the LORD commanded Moses.

The tabernacle finished

32 ¶ Thus was all the work of the tabernacle of the tent of the congregation finished: and the children of Israel did according to all that the LORD commanded Moses, so did they.

33 ¶ And they brought the tabernacle unto Moses, the tent, and all his furniture, his taches, his boards, his bars, and his pillars, and his sockets,

34And the covering of rams' skins dyed red, and the covering of badgers' skins, and the veil of the covering,

35The ark of the testimony, and the staves thereof, and the mercy seat,

36The table, *and* all the vessels thereof, and the showbread,

37The pure candlestick, *with* the lamps thereof, *even with* the lamps to be set in order, and all the vessels thereof, and the oil for light,

38And the golden altar, and the anointing oil, and *P*sweet incense, and the hanging for the tabernacle door,

39The brasen altar, and his grate of brass, his staves, and all his vessels, the laver and his foot,

40The hangings of the court, his pillars, and his sockets, and the hanging for the court gate, his cords, and his pins, and all the vessels of the service of the tabernacle, for the tent of the congregation,

41The cloths of service to do service in the holy *place,* and the holy garments for Aaron the priest, and his sons' garments, to minister in the priest's office.

42According to all that the LORD commanded Moses, so the children of Israel made all the work.

43And Moses did look upon all the work, and, behold, they had done it as the LORD had commanded, even so had they done it: and Moses blessed them.

Assembling the tabernacle

40 AND THE LORD spake unto Moses, saying, 2On the first day of the first month shalt thou set up the tabernacle of the tent of the congregation.

3And thou shalt put therein the ark of the testimony, and cover the ark with the veil.

4And thou shalt bring in the table, and set in order *q*the things that are to be set in order upon it; and thou shalt bring in the candlestick, and light the lamps thereof.

5And thou shalt set the altar of gold for the incense before the ark of the testimony, and put the hanging of the door to the tabernacle.

6And thou shalt set the altar of the burnt offering before the door of the tabernacle of the tent of the congregation.

Amplified

26A bell and a pomegranate, a bell and a pomegranate, round about on the skirts of the robe for ministering, as the Lord commanded Moses.

27And they made the long *and* sleeved tunics woven of fine linen for Aaron and his sons,

28And the turban, and the ornamental caps of fine linen, and the breeches of fine twined linen,

29The girdle *or* sash of fine twined linen, and blue, purple, and scarlet embroidery, as the Lord commanded Moses.

30And they made the plate of the holy crown of pure gold and wrote upon it an inscription, like the engravings of a signet, HOLY TO THE LORD. [Exod. 28:36.]

31They tied to it a lace of blue to fasten it on the turban above, as the Lord commanded Moses.

32Thus all the work of the tabernacle of the Tent of Meeting was finished; according to all that the Lord commanded Moses, so the Israelites had done.

33And they brought the tabernacle to Moses: the tent and all its furnishings, its clasps, its [frame] boards, its bars, its pillars, its sockets *or* bases;

34And the covering of rams' skins made red, and the covering of dolphin *or* porpoise skins, and the veil of the screen;

35The ark of the Testimony, its poles, and the mercy seat;

36The table and all its utensils, and the showbread (bread of the Presence);

37The pure [gold] lampstand and its lamps, with the lamps set in order, all its utensils, and the oil for the light;

38The golden altar, the anointing oil, the fragrant incense, and the hanging for the door of the tent;

39The bronze altar and its grate of bronze, its poles and all its utensils; the laver and its base;

40The hangings of the court, its pillars and sockets *or* bases, and the screen for the court gate, its cords, and pegs, and all the utensils for the service of the tabernacle, for the Tent of Meeting [of God with His people]; [Exod. 29:42, 43.]

41The finely worked vestments for ministering in the Holy Place, the holy garments for Aaron the priest, and the garments of his sons to minister as priests.

42According to all that the Lord had commanded Moses, so the Israelites had done all the work.

43And Moses inspected all the work, and behold, they had done it; as the Lord had commanded, so had they done it. And Moses blessed them.

40 AND THE Lord said to Moses, 2On the first day of the first month you shall set up the tabernacle of the Tent of Meeting [of God with you].

3And you shall put in it the ark of the Testimony and screen the ark [of God's Presence] with the veil. [Heb. 10:19–23.]

4You shall bring in the [showbread] table and set in order the things that are to be upon it; and you shall bring in the lampstand and set up *and* light its lamps. [Rev. 21:23–25.]

5You shall set the golden altar for the incense before the ark of the Testimony [outside the veil] and put the hanging *or* screen at the tabernacle door.

6You shall set the altar of the burnt offering before the door of the Tent of Meeting.

P Heb. *the incense of sweet spices*   *q* Heb. *the order thereof*

New American Standard

26 alternating a bell and a pomegranate all around on the hem of the robe for the service, just as the LORD had commanded Moses.

27 ¶ They made the tunics of finely woven linen for Aaron and his sons,

28 and the turban of fine linen, and the decorated caps of fine linen, and the linen breeches of fine twisted linen,

29 and the sash of fine twisted linen, and blue and purple and scarlet *material,* the work of the weaver, just as the LORD had commanded Moses.

30 ¶ They made the plate of the holy crown of pure gold, and inscribed it like the engravings of a signet, "Holy to the LORD."

31 They fastened a blue cord to it, to fasten it on the turban above, just as the LORD had commanded Moses.

32 ¶ Thus all the work of the tabernacle of the tent of meeting was completed; and the sons of Israel did according to all that the LORD had commanded Moses; so they did.

33 They brought the tabernacle to Moses, the tent and all its *f*furnishings: its clasps, its boards, its bars, and its pillars and its sockets;

34 and the covering of rams' skins dyed red, and the covering of porpoise skins, and the screening veil;

35 the ark of the testimony and its poles and the mercy seat;

36 the table, all its utensils, and the bread of the Presence;

37 the pure *gold* lampstand, with its arrangement of lamps and all its utensils, and the oil for the light;

38 and the gold altar, and the anointing oil and the fragrant incense, and the veil for the doorway of the tent;

39 the bronze altar and its bronze grating, its poles and all its utensils, the laver and its stand;

40 the hangings for the court, its pillars and its sockets, and the screen for the gate of the court, its cords and its pegs and all the equipment for the service of the tabernacle, for the tent of meeting;

41 the woven garments for ministering in the holy place and the holy garments for Aaron the priest and the garments of his sons, to minister as priests.

42 So the sons of Israel did all the work according to all that the LORD had commanded Moses.

43 And Moses examined all the work and behold, they had done it; just as the LORD had commanded, this they had done. So Moses blessed them.

The Tabernacle Erected

40 THEN THE LORD spoke to Moses, saying, 2"On the first day of the first month you shall set up the tabernacle of the tent of meeting.

3"You shall place the ark of the testimony there, and you shall screen the ark with the veil.

4"You shall bring in the table and arrange what belongs on it; and you shall bring in the lampstand and mount its lamps.

5"Moreover, you shall set the gold altar of incense before the ark of the testimony, and set up the veil for the doorway to the tabernacle.

6"You shall set the altar of burnt offering in front of the doorway of the tabernacle of the tent of meeting.

New International

between the pomegranates. 26The bells and pomegranates alternated around the hem of the robe to be worn for ministering, as the LORD commanded Moses.

27For Aaron and his sons, they made tunics of fine linen—the work of a weaver— 28and the turban of fine linen, the linen headbands and the undergarments of finely twisted linen. 29The sash was of finely twisted linen and blue, purple and scarlet yarn—the work of an embroiderer—as the LORD commanded Moses.

30They made the plate, the sacred diadem, out of pure gold and engraved on it, like an inscription on a seal: HOLY TO THE LORD. 31Then they fastened a blue cord to it to attach it to the turban, as the LORD commanded Moses.

Moses Inspects the Tabernacle

32So all the work on the tabernacle, the Tent of Meeting, was completed. The Israelites did everything just as the LORD commanded Moses. 33Then they brought the tabernacle to Moses: the tent and all its furnishings, its clasps, frames, crossbars, posts and bases; 34the covering of ram skins dyed red, the covering of hides of sea cows*c* and the shielding curtain; 35the ark of the Testimony with its poles and the atonement cover; 36the table with all its articles and the bread of the Presence; 37the pure gold lampstand with its row of lamps and all its accessories, and the oil for the light; 38the gold altar, the anointing oil, the fragrant incense, and the curtain for the entrance to the tent; 39the bronze altar with its bronze grating, its poles and all its utensils; the basin with its stand; 40the curtains of the courtyard with its posts and bases, and the curtain for the entrance to the courtyard; the ropes and tent pegs for the courtyard; all the furnishings for the tabernacle, the Tent of Meeting; 41and the woven garments worn for ministering in the sanctuary, both the sacred garments for Aaron the priest and the garments for his sons when serving as priests.

42The Israelites had done all the work just as the LORD had commanded Moses. 43Moses inspected the work and saw that they had done it just as the LORD had commanded. So Moses blessed them.

Setting Up the Tabernacle

40 THEN THE LORD said to Moses: 2"Set up the tabernacle, the Tent of Meeting, on the first day of the first month. 3Place the ark of the Testimony in it and shield the ark with the curtain. 4Bring in the table and set out what belongs on it. Then bring in the lampstand and set up its lamps. 5Place the gold altar of incense in front of the ark of the Testimony and put the curtain at the entrance to the tabernacle.

6"Place the altar of burnt offering in front of the en-

---

f Or *utensils*   *c 34* That is, dugongs

King James

7And thou shalt set the laver between the tent of the congregation and the altar, and shalt put water therein.

8And thou shalt set up the court round about, and hang up the hanging at the court gate.

9And thou shalt take the anointing oil, and anoint the tabernacle, and all that is therein, and shalt hallow it, and all the vessels thereof: and it shall be holy.

10And thou shalt anoint the altar of the burnt offering, and all his vessels, and sanctify the altar: and it shall be an altar rmost holy.

11And thou shalt anoint the laver and his foot, and sanctify it.

12And thou shalt bring Aaron and his sons unto the door of the tabernacle of the congregation, and wash them with water.

13And thou shalt put upon Aaron the holy garments, and anoint him, and sanctify him; that he may minister unto me in the priest's office.

14And thou shalt bring his sons, and clothe them with coats:

15And thou shalt anoint them, as thou didst anoint their father, that they may minister unto me in the priest's office: for their anointing shall surely be an everlasting priesthood throughout their generations.

16Thus did Moses: according to all that the LORD commanded him, so did he.

17 ¶ And it came to pass in the first month in the second year, on the first day of the month, that the tabernacle was reared up.

18And Moses reared up the tabernacle, and fastened his sockets, and set up the boards thereof, and put in the bars thereof, and reared up his pillars.

19And he spread abroad the tent over the tabernacle, and put the covering of the tent above upon it; as the LORD commanded Moses.

20 ¶ And he took and put the testimony into the ark, and set the staves on the ark, and put the mercy seat above upon the ark:

21And he brought the ark into the tabernacle, and set up the veil of the covering, and covered the ark of the testimony; as the LORD commanded Moses.

22 ¶ And he put the table in the tent of the congregation, upon the side of the tabernacle northward, without the veil.

23And he set the bread in order upon it before the LORD; as the LORD had commanded Moses.

24 ¶ And he put the candlestick in the tent of the congregation, over against the table, on the side of the tabernacle southward.

25And he lighted the lamps before the LORD; as the LORD commanded Moses.

26 ¶ And he put the golden altar in the tent of the congregation before the veil:

27And he burnt sweet incense thereon; as the LORD commanded Moses.

28 ¶ And he set up the hanging at the door of the tabernacle.

29And he put the altar of burnt offering by the door of the tabernacle of the tent of the congregation, and offered upon it the burnt offering and the meat offering; as the LORD commanded Moses.

30 ¶ And he set the laver between the tent of the congregation and the altar, and put water there, to wash withal.

Amplified

7And you shall wset the laver between the Tent of Meeting and the altar and put water in it.

8And you shall set up the court [curtains] round about and hang up the hanging or screen at the court gate.

9You shall take the anointing oil and anoint the tabernacle and all that is in it, and shall consecrate it and all its furniture, and it shall be holy.

10You shall anoint the altar of burnt offering and all its utensils; and consecrate (set apart for God) the altar, and the altar shall be most holy.

11And you shall anoint the laver and its base and consecrate it.

12You shall bring Aaron and his sons to the door of the Tent of Meeting and wash them with water. [John 17:17–19.]

13You shall put on Aaron the holy garments, and anoint and consecrate him, so he may serve Me as priest.

14And you shall bring his sons and put long and sleeved tunics on them,

15And you shall anoint them as you anointed their father, that they may minister to Me as priests; for their anointing shall be to them for an everlasting priesthood throughout their generations.

16Thus did Moses; according to all that the Lord commanded him, so he did.

17And on the first day of the first month in the second year the tabernacle was erected.

18Moses set up the tabernacle, laid its sockets, set up its boards, put in its bars, and erected its pillars.

19[Moses] spread the tent over the tabernacle and put the covering of the tent over it, as the Lord had commanded him.

20He took the Testimony [the Ten Commandments] and put it into the ark, and set the poles [in the rings] on the ark, and put the mercy seat on top of the ark.

21[Moses] brought the ark into the tabernacle and set up the veil of the screen and screened the ark of the Testimony, as the Lord had commanded him.

22Moses put the table [of showbread] in the Tent of Meeting on the north side of the tabernacle outside the veil;

23He set the bread [of the Presence] in order on it before the Lord, as the Lord had commanded him. [John 6:32–35.]

24And he put the lampstand in the Tent of Meeting opposite the table on the south side of the tabernacle.

25Moses set up and lighted the lamps before the Lord, as the Lord commanded him.

26He put the golden altar [of incense] in the Tent of Meeting before the veil;

27He burned sweet incense [symbol of prayer] upon it, as the Lord commanded him. [Ps. 141:2; Rev. 8:3.]

28And he set up the hanging or screen at the door of the tabernacle.

29[Moses] put the altar of burnt offering at the door of the tabernacle of the Tent of Meeting and offered on it the burnt offering and the cereal offering, as the Lord commanded him.

30And Moses set the laver between the Tent of Meeting and the altar and put water in it for washing.

---

w Why was it necessary for one exact position for the laver to be demanded of Moses by God? Those who have published charts of the tabernacle furniture arrangement, with the laver off to one side or the other of the door into the sanctuary, have missed a point here. The laver was to be placed directly "between [the doors of] the Tent of Meeting and the altar [of burnt offering]," thus completing the "cross" made by the arrangement of the furniture, from the ark to the altar. It could have no significance to the Jews of that time, but the One Who planned it had those in mind to whom Christ would one day say, "And these [very Scriptures] testify about Me!" (John 5:39.) How fitting that at the foot of that "cross" there should be the altar, picturing our complete surrender, and then the laver, picturing our cleansing, that we may enter in through Him Who alone is "the Door" to the eternal Holy of Holies (John 10:1-9).

---

r Heb. holiness of holinesses

New American Standard

7"You shall set the laver between the tent of meeting and the altar and put water in it.

8"You shall set up the court all around and hang up the veil for the gateway of the court.

9"Then you shall take the anointing oil and anoint the tabernacle and all that is in it, and shall consecrate it and all its furnishings; and it shall be holy.

10"You shall anoint the altar of burnt offering and all its utensils, and consecrate the altar, and the altar shall be most holy.

11"You shall anoint the laver and its stand, and consecrate it.

12"Then you shall bring Aaron and his sons to the doorway of the tent of meeting and wash them with water.

13"You shall put the holy garments on Aaron and anoint him and consecrate him, that he may minister as a priest to Me.

14"You shall bring his sons and put tunics on them;

15 and you shall anoint them even as you have anointed their father, that they may minister as priests to Me; and their anointing will qualify them for a perpetual priesthood throughout their generations."

16 Thus Moses did; according to all that the LORD had commanded him, so he did.

17 ¶ Now in the first month of the second year, on the first *day* of the month, the tabernacle was erected.

18 Moses erected the tabernacle and laid its sockets, and set up its boards, and inserted its bars and erected its pillars.

19 He spread the tent over the tabernacle and put the covering of the tent on top of it, just as the LORD had commanded Moses.

20 Then he took the testimony and put *it* into the ark, and attached the poles to the ark, and put the mercy seat on top of the ark.

21 He brought the ark into the tabernacle, and set up a veil for the screen, and screened off the ark of the testimony, just as the LORD had commanded Moses.

22 Then he put the table in the tent of meeting on the north side of the tabernacle, outside the veil.

23 He set the arrangement of bread in order on it before the LORD, just as the LORD had commanded Moses.

24 Then he placed the lampstand in the tent of meeting, opposite the table, on the south side of the tabernacle.

25 He lighted the lamps before the LORD, just as the LORD had commanded Moses.

26 Then he placed the gold altar in the tent of meeting in front of the veil;

27 and he burned fragrant incense on it, just as the LORD had commanded Moses.

28 Then he set up the veil for the doorway of the tabernacle.

29 He set the altar of burnt offering *before* the doorway of the tabernacle of the tent of meeting, and offered on it the burnt offering and the meal offering, just as the LORD had commanded Moses.

30 He placed the laver between the tent of meeting and the altar and put water in it for washing.

New International

trance to the tabernacle, the Tent of Meeting; 7place the basin between the Tent of Meeting and the altar and put water in it. 8Set up the courtyard around it and put the curtain at the entrance to the courtyard.

9"Take the anointing oil and anoint the tabernacle and everything in it; consecrate it and all its furnishings, and it will be holy. 10Then anoint the altar of burnt offering and all its utensils; consecrate the altar, and it will be most holy. 11Anoint the basin and its stand and consecrate them.

12"Bring Aaron and his sons to the entrance to the Tent of Meeting and wash them with water. 13Then dress Aaron in the sacred garments, anoint him and consecrate him so he may serve me as priest. 14Bring his sons and dress them in tunics. 15Anoint them just as you anointed their father, so they may serve me as priests. Their anointing will be to a priesthood that will continue for all generations to come." 16Moses did everything just as the LORD commanded him.

17So the tabernacle was set up on the first day of the first month in the second year. 18When Moses set up the tabernacle, he put the bases in place, erected the frames, inserted the crossbars and set up the posts. 19Then he spread the tent over the tabernacle and put the covering over the tent, as the LORD commanded him.

20He took the Testimony and placed it in the ark, attached the poles to the ark and put the atonement cover over it. 21Then he brought the ark into the tabernacle and hung the shielding curtain and shielded the ark of the Testimony, as the LORD commanded him.

22Moses placed the table in the Tent of Meeting on the north side of the tabernacle outside the curtain 23and set out the bread on it before the LORD, as the LORD commanded him.

24He placed the lampstand in the Tent of Meeting opposite the table on the south side of the tabernacle 25and set up the lamps before the LORD, as the LORD commanded him.

26Moses placed the gold altar in the Tent of Meeting in front of the curtain 27and burned fragrant incense on it, as the LORD commanded him. 28Then he put up the curtain at the entrance to the tabernacle.

29He set the altar of burnt offering near the entrance to the tabernacle, the Tent of Meeting, and offered on it burnt offerings and grain offerings, as the LORD commanded him.

30He placed the basin between the Tent of Meeting and

King James

³¹And Moses and Aaron and his sons washed their hands and their feet thereat:

³²When they went into the tent of the congregation, and when they came near unto the altar, they washed; as the LORD commanded Moses.

³³And he reared up the court round about the tabernacle and the altar, and set up the hanging of the court gate. So Moses finished the work.

The glory of the LORD

³⁴ ¶ Then a cloud covered the tent of the congregation, and the glory of the LORD filled the tabernacle.

³⁵And Moses was not able to enter into the tent of the congregation, because the cloud abode thereon, and the glory of the LORD filled the tabernacle.

³⁶And when the cloud was taken up from over the tabernacle, the children of Israel *went onward in all their journeys:

³⁷But if the cloud were not taken up, then they journeyed not till the day that it was taken up.

³⁸For the cloud of the LORD *was* upon the tabernacle by day, and fire was on it by night, in the sight of all the house of Israel, throughout all their journeys.

Amplified

³¹And Moses and Aaron and his sons washed their hands and their feet there.

³²When they went into the Tent of Meeting or came near the altar, they washed, as the Lord commanded Moses.

³³And he erected the court round about the tabernacle and the altar and set up the hanging *or* screen at the court gate. So Moses finished the work.

³⁴Then the cloud [the Shekinah, God's visible presence] covered the Tent of Meeting, and the glory of the Lord filled the tabernacle! [Rev. 15:8.]

³⁵And Moses was not able to enter the Tent of Meeting because the cloud remained upon it, and the glory of the Lord filled the tabernacle.

³⁶In all their journeys, whenever the cloud was taken up from over the tabernacle, the Israelites went onward;

³⁷But if the cloud was not taken up, they did not journey on till the day that it was taken up.

³⁸For throughout all their journeys the cloud of the Lord was upon the tabernacle by day, and fire was in it by night, in the sight of all the house of Israel.

---

^sHeb. *journeyed*

New American Standard

³¹ From it Moses and Aaron and his sons washed their hands and their feet.

³² When they entered the tent of meeting, and when they approached the altar, they washed, just as the LORD had commanded Moses.

³³ He erected the court all around the tabernacle and the altar, and hung up the veil for the gateway of the court. Thus Moses finished the work.

The Glory of the LORD

³⁴ ¶ Then the cloud covered the tent of meeting, and the glory of the LORD filled the tabernacle.

³⁵ Moses was not able to enter the tent of meeting because the cloud had settled on it, and the glory of the LORD filled the tabernacle.

³⁶ Throughout all their journeys whenever the cloud was taken up from over the tabernacle, the sons of Israel would set out;

³⁷ but if the cloud was not taken up, then they did not set out until the day when it was taken up.

³⁸ For throughout all their journeys, the cloud of the LORD was on the tabernacle by day, and there was fire in it by night, in the sight of all the house of Israel.

New International

the altar and put water in it for washing, ³¹and Moses and Aaron and his sons used it to wash their hands and feet. ³²They washed whenever they entered the Tent of Meeting or approached the altar, as the LORD commanded Moses.

³³Then Moses set up the courtyard around the tabernacle and altar and put up the curtain at the entrance to the courtyard. And so Moses finished the work.

The Glory of the LORD

³⁴Then the cloud covered the Tent of Meeting, and the glory of the LORD filled the tabernacle. ³⁵Moses could not enter the Tent of Meeting because the cloud had settled upon it, and the glory of the LORD filled the tabernacle.

³⁶In all the travels of the Israelites, whenever the cloud lifted from above the tabernacle, they would set out; ³⁷but if the cloud did not lift, they did not set out—until the day it lifted. ³⁸So the cloud of the LORD was over the tabernacle by day, and fire was in the cloud by night, in the sight of all the house of Israel during all their travels.

THE THIRD BOOK OF MOSES, CALLED

Leviticus

THE THIRD BOOK OF MOSES, CALLED

Leviticus

The law of burnt offering

1 AND THE LORD called unto Moses, and spake unto him out of the tabernacle of the congregation, saying,

2Speak unto the children of Israel, and say unto them, If any man of you bring an offering unto the LORD, ye shall bring your offering of the cattle, *even* of the herd, and of the flock.

3If his offering *be* a burnt sacrifice of the herd, let him offer a male without blemish: he shall offer it of his own voluntary will at the door of the tabernacle of the congregation before the LORD.

4And he shall put his hand upon the head of the burnt offering; and it shall be accepted for him to make atonement for him.

5And he shall kill the bullock before the LORD: and the priests, Aaron's sons, shall bring the blood, and sprinkle the blood round about upon the altar that *is by* the door of the tabernacle of the congregation.

6And he shall flay the burnt offering, and cut it into his pieces.

7And the sons of Aaron the priest shall put fire upon the altar, and lay the wood in order upon the fire:

8And the priests, Aaron's sons, shall lay the parts, the head, and the fat, in order upon the wood that *is* on the fire which *is* upon the altar:

9But his inwards and his legs shall he wash in water: and the priest shall burn all on the altar, *to be* a burnt sacrifice, an offering made by fire, of a sweet savour unto the LORD.

10 ¶ And if his offering *be* of the flocks, *namely,* of the sheep, or of the goats, for a burnt sacrifice; he shall bring it a male without blemish.

11And he shall kill it on the side of the altar northward before the LORD: and the priests, Aaron's sons, shall sprinkle his blood round about upon the altar.

12And he shall cut it into his pieces, with his head and his fat: and the priest shall lay them in order on the wood that *is* on the fire which *is* upon the altar:

13But he shall wash the inwards and the legs with water: and the priest shall bring *it* all, and burn *it* upon the altar: it *is* a burnt sacrifice, an offering made by fire, of a sweet savour unto the LORD.

14 ¶ And if the burnt sacrifice for his offering to the LORD *be* of fowls, then he shall bring his offering of turtledoves, or of young pigeons.

15And the priest shall bring it unto the altar, and awring off his head, and burn *it* on the altar; and the blood thereof shall be wrung out at the side of the altar:

1 THE LORD acalled to Moses out of the Tent of Meeting, and said to him,

2Say to the Israelites, When any man of you brings an offering to the Lord, you shall bring your offering of [domestic] animals from the herd or from the flock.

3If his offering is a burnt offering from the herd, he shall offer a male without blemish; he shall offer it at the door of the Tent of Meeting, that he may be accepted before the Lord. [Rom. 12:1; Phil. 1:20.]

4And he shall lay [both] his hands upon the head of the burnt offering [transferring symbolically his guilt to the victim], and it shall be ban acceptable atonement for him. [Heb. 13:15, 16; I Pet. 1:2.]

5The man shall kill the young bull before the Lord, and the priests, Aaron's sons, shall present the blood and dash [it] round about upon the altar that is at the door of the Tent of Meeting.

6And he shall skin the burnt offering and cut it into pieces.

7And the sons of Aaron the priest shall put fire on the altar and lay wood in order on the fire;

8And Aaron's sons the priests shall lay the pieces, the head and the fat, in order on the wood on the fire on the altar.

9But its entrails and its legs he shall wash with water. And the priest shall burn all of it on the altar for a burnt offering, an offering made by fire, a sweet and satisfying odor to the Lord. [Eph. 5:2; Phil. 4:18; I Pet. 2:5.]

10And if the man's offering is of the flock, from the sheep or the goats, for a burnt offering, he shall offer a male without blemish.

11And he shall kill it on the north side of the altar before the Lord, and Aaron's sons the priests shall dash its blood round about against the altar.

12And [the man] shall cut it into pieces, with its head and its fat, and the priest shall lay them in order on the wood that is on the fire on the altar.

13But he shall wash the entrails and legs with water. The priest shall offer all of it and burn it on the altar; it is a burnt offering, an offering made by fire, a sweet *and* satisfying fragrance to the Lord.

14And if the offering to the Lord is a burnt offering of birds, then [the man] shall bring turtledoves or young pigeons.

15And the priest shall bring it to the altar, and wring off its head, and burn it on the altar; and its blood shall be drained out on the side of the altar.

aThe first step toward understanding the message of Leviticus is to appreciate its viewpoint indicated here—"The Lord called to Moses out of the Tent of Meeting," and talked to him. Before this a forbidding God had spoken from the burning mountain. But now the tabernacle is erected according to the God-given pattern, and the God Who dwells among His people in fellowship with them talks with His servant Moses "out of the Tent of Meeting." The people, therefore, are not treated as sinners alienated from God, "but as being already brought into a new relationship, even that of fellowship, on the ground of a blood-sealed covenant" (J. Sidlow Baxter, *Explore the Book*).   bTo render the self-sacrifice perfect, it was necessary that the offerer should spiritually die, sinking it as it were into the death of the sacrifice that had died for him, so that through the mediator of his salvation he should put his soul into a living fellowship with the Lord and bring his bodily members within the operations of the gracious Spirit of God. Thereby he would be renewed and sanctified [separated for holy use], both body and soul, and enter into union with God (Karl Keil and F. Delitzsch, *Biblical Commentary on the Old Testament*).

aOr, *pinch off the head with the nail*

New American Standard

Leviticus

The Law of Burnt Offerings

1 THEN THE LORD called to Moses and spoke to him from the tent of meeting, saying,
2 "Speak to the sons of Israel and say to them, 'When any man of you brings an offering to the LORD, you shall bring your offering of animals from the herd or the flock.
3 'If his offering is a burnt offering from the herd, he shall offer it, a male without defect; he shall offer it at the doorway of the tent of meeting, that he may be accepted before the LORD.
4 'He shall lay his hand on the head of the burnt offering, that it may be accepted for him to make atonement on his behalf.
5 'He shall slay the young bull before the LORD; and Aaron's sons the priests shall offer up the blood and sprinkle the blood around on the altar that is at the doorway of the tent of meeting.
6 'He shall then skin the burnt offering and cut it into its pieces.
7 'The sons of Aaron the priest shall put fire on the altar and arrange wood on the fire.
8 'Then Aaron's sons the priests shall arrange the pieces, the head and the suet over the wood which is on the fire that is on the altar.
9 'Its entrails, however, and its legs he shall wash with water. And the priest shall offer up in smoke all of it on the altar for a burnt offering, an offering by fire of a soothing aroma to the LORD.
10 ¶ 'But if his offering is from the flock, of the sheep or of the goats, for a burnt offering, he shall offer it a male without defect.
11 'He shall slay it on the side of the altar northward before the LORD, and Aaron's sons the priests shall sprinkle its blood around on the altar.
12 'He shall then cut it into its pieces with its head and its suet, and the priest shall arrange them on the wood which is on the fire that is on the altar.
13 'The entrails, however, and the legs he shall wash with water. And the priest shall offer all of it, and offer it up in smoke on the altar; it is a burnt offering, an offering by fire of a soothing aroma to the LORD.
14 ¶ 'But if his offering to the LORD is a burnt offering of birds, then he shall bring his offering from the turtledoves or from young pigeons.
15 'The priest shall bring it to the altar, and wring off its head and offer it up in smoke on the altar; and its blood is to be drained out on the side of the altar.

New International

Leviticus

The Burnt Offering

1 THE LORD called to Moses and spoke to him from the Tent of Meeting. He said, 2 "Speak to the Israelites and say to them: 'When any of you brings an offering to the LORD, bring as your offering an animal from either the herd or the flock.
3 "'If the offering is a burnt offering from the herd, he is to offer a male without defect. He must present it at the entrance to the Tent of Meeting so that it[a] will be acceptable to the LORD. 4 He is to lay his hand on the head of the burnt offering, and it will be accepted on his behalf to make atonement for him. 5 He is to slaughter the young bull before the LORD, and then Aaron's sons the priests shall bring the blood and sprinkle it against the altar on all sides at the entrance to the Tent of Meeting. 6 He is to skin the burnt offering and cut it into pieces. 7 The sons of Aaron the priest are to put fire on the altar and arrange wood on the fire. 8 Then Aaron's sons the priests shall arrange the pieces, including the head and the fat, on the burning wood that is on the altar. 9 He is to wash the inner parts and the legs with water, and the priest is to burn all of it on the altar. It is a burnt offering, an offering made by fire, an aroma pleasing to the LORD.
10 "'If the offering is a burnt offering from the flock, from either the sheep or the goats, he is to offer a male without defect. 11 He is to slaughter it at the north side of the altar before the LORD, and Aaron's sons the priests shall sprinkle its blood against the altar on all sides. 12 He is to cut it into pieces, and the priest shall arrange them, including the head and the fat, on the burning wood that is on the altar. 13 He is to wash the inner parts and the legs with water, and the priest is to bring all of it and burn it on the altar. It is a burnt offering, an offering made by fire, an aroma pleasing to the LORD.
14 "'If the offering to the LORD is a burnt offering of birds, he is to offer a dove or a young pigeon. 15 The priest shall bring it to the altar, wring off the head and burn it on the altar; its blood shall be drained out on the side of the

King James

¹⁶And he shall pluck away his crop with ^bhis feathers, and cast it beside the altar on the east part, by the place of the ashes:

¹⁷And he shall cleave it with the wings thereof, *but* shall not divide *it* asunder: and the priest shall burn it upon the altar, upon the wood that *is* upon the fire: it *is* a burnt sacrifice, an offering made by fire, of a sweet savour unto the LORD.

The law of meat offerings

2 AND WHEN any will offer a meat offering unto the LORD, his offering shall be *of* fine flour; and he shall pour oil upon it, and put frankincense thereon:

²And he shall bring it to Aaron's sons the priests: and he shall take thereout his handful of the flour thereof, and of the oil thereof, with all the frankincense thereof; and the priest shall burn the memorial of it upon the altar, *to be* an offering made by fire, of a sweet savour unto the LORD:

³And the remnant of the meat offering *shall be* Aaron's and his sons': *it is* a thing most holy of the offerings of the LORD made by fire.

⁴ ¶ And if thou bring an oblation of a meat offering baked in the oven, *it shall be* unleavened cakes of fine flour mingled with oil, or unleavened wafers anointed with oil.

⁵ ¶ And if thy oblation *be* a meat offering *baked* ^cin a pan, it shall be *of* fine flour unleavened, mingled with oil.

⁶Thou shalt part it in pieces, and pour oil thereon: it *is* a meat offering.

⁷ ¶ And if thy oblation *be* a meat offering *baked* in the fryingpan, it shall be made *of* fine flour with oil.

⁸And thou shalt bring the meat offering that is made of these things unto the LORD: and when it is presented unto the priest, he shall bring it unto the altar.

⁹And the priest shall take from the meat offering a memorial thereof, and shall burn *it* upon the altar: *it is* an offering made by fire, of a sweet savour unto the LORD.

¹⁰And that which is left of the meat offering *shall be* Aaron's and his sons': *it is* a thing most holy of the offerings of the LORD made by fire.

¹¹No meat offering, which ye shall bring unto the LORD, shall be made with leaven: for ye shall burn no leaven, nor any honey, in any offering of the LORD made by fire.

¹² ¶ As for the oblation of the firstfruits, ye shall offer them unto the LORD: but they shall not ^dbe burnt on the altar for a sweet savour.

¹³And every oblation of thy meat offering shalt thou season with salt; neither shalt thou suffer the salt of the covenant of thy God to be lacking from thy meat offering: with all thine offerings thou shalt offer salt.

¹⁴And if thou offer a meat offering of thy firstfruits unto the LORD, thou shalt offer for the meat offering of thy firstfruits green ears of corn dried by the fire, *even* corn beaten out of full ears.

¹⁵And thou shalt put oil upon it, and lay frankincense thereon: it *is* a meat offering.

¹⁶And the priest shall burn the memorial of it, *part* of the beaten corn thereof, and *part* of the oil thereof, with all the frankincense thereof: *it is* an offering made by fire unto the LORD.

The law of peace offerings

3 AND IF his oblation *be* a sacrifice of peace offering, if he offer *it* of the herd; whether *it be* a male or female, he shall offer it without blemish before the LORD.

Amplified

¹⁶And he shall take away its crop with its feathers and cast it beside the altar on the east side, in the place for ashes.

¹⁷And he shall split it open [holding it] by its wings, but shall not cut it in two. And the priest shall burn it on the altar, on the wood that is on the fire; it is a burnt offering, an offering made by fire, a sweet *and* satisfying odor to the Lord.

2 WHEN ANYONE offers a cereal offering to the Lord, it shall be of fine flour; and he shall pour oil over it and lay frankincense on it.

²And he shall bring it to Aaron's sons the priests. Out of it he shall take a handful of the fine flour and oil, with all its frankincense, and the priest shall burn this on the altar as the memorial portion of it, an offering made by fire, of a sweet *and* satisfying fragrance to the Lord.

³What is left of the cereal offering shall be Aaron's and his sons'; it is a most holy part of the offerings made to the Lord by fire.

⁴When you bring as an offering cereal baked in the oven, it shall be unleavened cakes of fine flour mixed with oil, or unleavened wafers spread with oil.

⁵If your offering is cereal baked on a griddle, it shall be of fine flour unleavened, mixed with oil.

⁶You shall break it in pieces and pour oil on it; it is a cereal offering.

⁷And if your offering is cereal cooked in the frying pan, it shall be made of fine flour with oil.

⁸And you shall bring the cereal offering that is made of these things to the Lord; it shall be presented to the priest, and he shall bring it to the [bronze] altar.

⁹The priest shall take from the cereal offering its memorial portion and burn it on the altar, an offering made by fire, a sweet *and* satisfying fragrance to the Lord.

¹⁰What is left of the cereal offering shall be Aaron's and his sons'; it is a most holy part of the offerings made to the Lord by fire.

¹¹No cereal offering that you bring to the Lord shall be made with leaven, for you shall burn no leaven or honey in any offering made by fire to the Lord. [I Cor. 5:8.]

¹²As an offering of firstfruits you may offer leaven and honey to the Lord, but ^cthey shall not be burned on the altar for a sweet odor [to the Lord, for their aid to fermentation is symbolic of corruption in the human heart].

¹³Every cereal offering you shall season with salt [symbol of preservation]; neither shall you allow the salt of the covenant of your God to be lacking from your cereal offering; with all your offerings you shall offer salt. [Mark 9:49, 50.]

¹⁴If you offer a cereal offering of your firstfruits to the Lord, you shall offer for it of your firstfruits grain in the ear parched with fire, bruised *and* crushed grain out of the fresh *and* fruitful ear.

¹⁵And you shall put oil on it and lay frankincense on it; it is a cereal offering.

¹⁶The priest shall burn as its memorial portion part of the bruised *and* crushed grain of it and part of the oil of it, with all its frankincense; it is an offering made by fire to the Lord.

3 IF A man's offering is a sacrifice of peace offering, if he offers an animal from the herd, whether male or female, he shall offer it without blemish before the Lord.

---

^bOr, *the filth thereof ascend*   ^cOr, *on a flat plate*, or, *slice*   ^dHeb.   ^cThere is to be no division between one's spiritual life and one's secular life, but the whole of one's life is to be of the nature of a sacrament (Col. 3:23, 24).

New American Standard

16 'He shall also take away its crop with its feathers and cast it beside the altar eastward, to the place of the ashes.

17 'Then he shall tear it by its wings, *but* shall not sever *it*. And the priest shall offer it up in smoke on the altar on the wood which is on the fire; it is a burnt offering, an offering by fire of a soothing aroma to the LORD.

The Law of Grain Offerings

2 'NOW WHEN anyone presents a grain offering as an offering to the LORD, his offering shall be of fine flour, and he shall pour oil on it and put frankincense on it.

2 'He shall then bring it to Aaron's sons the priests; and shall take from it his handful of its fine flour and of its oil with all of its frankincense. And the priest shall offer *it* up in smoke *as* its memorial portion on the altar, an offering by fire of a soothing aroma to the LORD.

3 'The remainder of the grain offering belongs to Aaron and his sons: a thing most holy, of the offerings to the LORD by fire.

4 ¶ 'Now when you bring an offering of a grain offering baked in an oven, *it shall be* unleavened cakes of fine flour mixed with oil, or unleavened wafers spread with oil.

5 'If your offering is a grain offering *made* on the griddle, *it shall be* of fine flour, unleavened, mixed with oil;

6 you shall break it into bits and pour oil on it; it is a grain offering.

7 'Now if your offering is a grain offering *made* in a pan, it shall be made of fine flour with oil.

8 'When you bring in the grain offering which is made of these things to the LORD, it shall be presented to the priest and he shall bring it to the altar.

9 'The priest then shall take up from the grain offering its memorial portion, and shall offer *it* up in smoke on the altar *as* an offering by fire of a soothing aroma to the LORD.

10 'The remainder of the grain offering belongs to Aaron and his sons: a thing most holy of the offerings to the LORD by fire.

11 ¶ 'No grain offering, which you bring to the LORD, shall be made with leaven, for you shall not offer up in smoke any leaven or any honey as an offering by fire to the LORD.

12 'As an offering of first fruits you shall bring them to the LORD, but they shall not ascend for a soothing aroma on the altar.

13 'Every grain offering of yours, moreover, you shall season with salt, so that the salt of the covenant of your God shall not be lacking from your grain offering; with all your offerings you shall offer salt.

14 ¶ 'Also if you bring a grain offering of early ripened things to the LORD, you shall bring fresh heads of grain roasted in the fire, grits of new growth, for the grain offering of your early ripened things.

15 'You shall then put oil on it and lay incense on it; it is a grain offering.

16 'The priest shall offer up in smoke its memorial portion, part of its grits and its oil with all its incense as an offering by fire to the LORD.

The Law of Peace Offerings

3 'NOW IF his offering is a sacrifice of peace offerings, if he is going to offer out of the herd, whether male or female, he shall offer it without defect before the LORD.

New International

altar. 16He is to remove the crop with its contents[b] and throw it to the east side of the altar, where the ashes are. 17He shall tear it open by the wings, not severing it completely, and then the priest shall burn it on the wood that is on the fire on the altar. It is a burnt offering, an offering made by fire, an aroma pleasing to the LORD.

The Grain Offering

2 " 'WHEN SOMEONE brings a grain offering to the LORD, his offering is to be of fine flour. He is to pour oil on it, put incense on it 2and take it to Aaron's sons the priests. The priest shall take a handful of the fine flour and oil, together with all the incense, and burn this as a memorial portion on the altar, an offering made by fire, an aroma pleasing to the LORD. 3The rest of the grain offering belongs to Aaron and his sons; it is a most holy part of the offerings made to the LORD by fire.

4" 'If you bring a grain offering baked in an oven, it is to consist of fine flour: cakes made without yeast and mixed with oil, or[c] wafers made without yeast and spread with oil. 5If your grain offering is prepared on a griddle, it is to be made of fine flour mixed with oil, and without yeast. 6Crumble it and pour oil on it; it is a grain offering. 7If your grain offering is cooked in a pan, it is to be made of fine flour and oil. 8Bring the grain offering made of these things to the LORD; present it to the priest, who shall take it to the altar. 9He shall take out the memorial portion from the grain offering and burn it on the altar as an offering made by fire, an aroma pleasing to the LORD. 10The rest of the grain offering belongs to Aaron and his sons; it is a most holy part of the offerings made to the LORD by fire.

11" 'Every grain offering you bring to the LORD must be made without yeast, for you are not to burn any yeast or honey in an offering made to the LORD by fire. 12You may bring them to the LORD as an offering of the firstfruits, but they are not to be offered on the altar as a pleasing aroma. 13Season all your grain offerings with salt. Do not leave the salt of the covenant of your God out of your grain offerings; add salt to all your offerings.

14" 'If you bring a grain offering of firstfruits to the LORD, offer crushed heads of new grain roasted in the fire. 15Put oil and incense on it; it is a grain offering. 16The priest shall burn the memorial portion of the crushed grain and the oil, together with all the incense, as an offering made to the LORD by fire.

The Fellowship Offering

3 " 'IF SOMEONE'S offering is a fellowship offering,[d] and he offers an animal from the herd, whether male or female, he is to present before the LORD an animal without defect. 2He is to lay his hand on the head of his

---

b 16 Or *crop and the feathers*; the meaning of the Hebrew for this word is uncertain.   *c* 4 Or *and*   *d* 1 Traditionally *peace offering*; also in verses 3, 6 and 9

King James

²And he shall lay his hand upon the head of his offering, and kill it *at* the door of the tabernacle of the congregation: and Aaron's sons the priests shall sprinkle the blood upon the altar round about.

³And he shall offer of the sacrifice of the peace offering an offering made by fire unto the LORD; the *e*fat that covereth the inwards, and all the fat that *is* upon the inwards,

⁴And the two kidneys, and the fat that *is* on them, which *is* by the flanks, and the *f*caul above the liver, with the kidneys, it shall he take away.

⁵And Aaron's sons shall burn it on the altar upon the burnt sacrifice, which *is* upon the wood that *is* on the fire: *it is* an offering made by fire, of a sweet savour unto the LORD.

⁶ ¶ And if his offering for a sacrifice of peace offering unto the LORD *be* of the flock; male or female, he shall offer it without blemish.

⁷If he offer a lamb for his offering, then shall he offer it before the LORD.

⁸And he shall lay his hand upon the head of his offering, and kill it before the tabernacle of the congregation: and Aaron's sons shall sprinkle the blood thereof round about upon the altar.

⁹And he shall offer of the sacrifice of the peace offering an offering made by fire unto the LORD; the fat thereof, *and* the whole rump, it shall he take off hard by the backbone; and the fat that covereth the inwards, and all the fat that *is* upon the inwards,

¹⁰And the two kidneys, and the fat that *is* upon them, which *is* by the flanks, and the caul above the liver, with the kidneys, it shall he take away.

¹¹And the priest shall burn it upon the altar: *it is* the food of the offering made by fire unto the LORD.

¹² ¶ And if his offering *be* a goat, then he shall offer it before the LORD.

¹³And he shall lay his hand upon the head of it, and kill it before the tabernacle of the congregation: and the sons of Aaron shall sprinkle the blood thereof upon the altar round about.

¹⁴And he shall offer thereof his offering, *even* an offering made by fire unto the LORD; the fat that covereth the inwards, and all the fat that *is* upon the inwards,

¹⁵And the two kidneys, and the fat that *is* upon them, which *is* by the flanks, and the caul above the liver, with the kidneys, it shall he take away.

¹⁶And the priest shall burn them upon the altar: *it is* the food of the offering made by fire for a sweet savour: all the fat *is* the LORD'S.

¹⁷*It shall be* a perpetual statute for your generations throughout all your dwellings, that ye eat neither fat nor blood.

The sin offering

4 AND THE LORD spake unto Moses, saying,
²Speak unto the children of Israel, saying, If a soul shall sin through ignorance against any of the commandments of the LORD *concerning things* which ought not to be done, and shall do against any of them:

³If the priest that is anointed do sin according to the sin of the people; then let him bring for his sin, which he hath sinned, a young bullock without blemish unto the LORD for a sin offering.

⁴And he shall bring the bullock unto the door of the tabernacle of the congregation before the LORD; and shall lay his hand upon the bullock's head, and kill the bullock before the LORD.

⁵And the priest that is anointed shall take of the bullock's blood, and bring it to the tabernacle of the congregation:

Amplified

²He shall lay [both] his *d*hands upon the head of his offering and kill it at the door of the Tent of Meeting; and Aaron's sons the priests shall throw the blood against the altar round about.

³And from the sacrifice of the peace offering, an offering made by fire to the Lord, he shall offer the fat that covers and is upon the entrails,

⁴And the two kidneys with the fat that is on them at the loins, and the appendage of the liver which he shall take away with the kidneys.

⁵Aaron's sons shall burn it all on the altar upon the burnt offering which is on the wood on the fire, an offering made by fire, of a sweet *and* satisfying odor to the Lord.

⁶If his peace offering to the Lord is an animal from the flock, male or female, he shall offer it without blemish.

⁷If he offers a lamb, then he shall offer it before the Lord.

⁸He shall lay [both] his hands on the head of his offering and kill it before the Tent of Meeting; and Aaron's sons shall throw its blood around against the altar.

⁹And he shall offer from the peace offering as an offering made by fire to the Lord: the fat of it, the fat tail as a whole, taking it off close to the backbone, and the fat that covers and is upon the entrails,

¹⁰And the two kidneys, and the fat on them at the loins, and the appendage of the liver, which he shall take away with the kidneys.

¹¹The priest shall burn it upon the altar, a food offering made by fire to the Lord.

¹²If [a man's] offering is a goat, he shall offer it before the Lord,

¹³And lay his hands upon its head, and kill it before the Tent of Meeting; and the sons of Aaron shall throw its blood against the altar round about.

¹⁴Then he shall offer from it as his offering made by fire to the Lord: the fat that covers and is on the entrails,

¹⁵And the two kidneys and the fat that is on them at the loins, and the appendage of the liver which he shall take away with the kidneys.

¹⁶The priest shall burn them on the altar as food, offered by fire, for a sweet *and* satisfying fragrance. All the fat is the Lord's.

¹⁷It shall be a perpetual statute for your generations in all your dwelling places, that you eat neither fat nor blood.

4 AND THE Lord said to Moses,
²Say to the Israelites, If anyone shall sin through error *or* unwittingly in any of the things which the Lord has commanded not to be done, and shall do any one of them—

³If it is the anointed priest who sins, thus bringing guilt on the people, then let him offer for his sin which he has committed a young bull without blemish to the Lord as a sin offering. [Heb. 7:27, 28.]

⁴He shall bring the bull to the door of the Tent of Meeting before the Lord, and shall lay [both] his hands on the bull's head and kill [it] before the Lord.

⁵And the anointed priest shall take some of the bull's blood and bring it into the Tent of Meeting;

---

*e*Or, *suet*   *f*Or, *midriff over the liver,* and *over the kidneys*   *d*The Septuagint (Greek translation of the Old Testament) so reads.

New American Standard

2 'He shall lay his hand on the head of his offering and slay it at the doorway of the tent of meeting, and Aaron's sons the priests shall sprinkle the blood around on the altar.

3 'From the sacrifice of the peace offerings he shall present an offering by fire to the LORD, the fat that covers the entrails and all the fat that is on the entrails,

4 and the two kidneys with the fat that is on them, which is on the loins, and the lobe of the liver, which he shall remove with the kidneys.

5 'Then Aaron's sons shall offer *it* up in smoke on the altar on the burnt offering, which is on the wood that is on the fire; it is an offering by fire of a soothing aroma to the LORD.

6 'But if his offering for a sacrifice of peace offerings to the LORD is from the flock, he shall offer it, male or female, without defect.

7 'If he is going to offer a lamb for his offering, then he shall offer it before the LORD,

8 and he shall lay his hand on the head of his offering and slay it before the tent of meeting, and Aaron's sons shall sprinkle its blood around on the altar.

9 'From the sacrifice of peace offerings he shall bring as an offering by fire to the LORD, its fat, the entire fat tail which he shall remove close to the backbone, and the fat that covers the entrails and all the fat that is on the entrails,

10 and the two kidneys with the fat that is on them, which is on the loins, and the lobe of the liver, which he shall remove with the kidneys.

11 'Then the priest shall offer *it* up in smoke on the altar *as* food, an offering by fire to the LORD.

12 ¶ 'Moreover, if his offering is a goat, then he shall offer it before the LORD,

13 and he shall lay his hand on its head and slay it before the tent of meeting, and the sons of Aaron shall sprinkle its blood around on the altar.

14 'From it he shall present his offering as an offering by fire to the LORD, the fat that covers the entrails and all the fat that is on the entrails,

15 and the two kidneys with the fat that is on them, which is on the loins, and the lobe of the liver, which he shall remove with the kidneys.

16 'The priest shall offer them up in smoke on the altar *as* food, an offering by fire for a soothing aroma; all fat is the LORD'S.

17 'It is a perpetual statute throughout your generations in all your dwellings: you shall not eat any fat or any blood.' "

The Law of Sin Offerings

4 THEN THE LORD spoke to Moses, saying,
2 "Speak to the sons of Israel, saying, 'If a person sins unintentionally in any of the things which the LORD has commanded not to be done, and commits any of them,

3 if the anointed priest sins so as to bring guilt on the people, then let him offer to the LORD a bull without defect as a sin offering for the sin he has committed.

4 'He shall bring the bull to the doorway of the tent of meeting before the LORD, and he shall lay his hand on the head of the bull and slay the bull before the LORD.

5 'Then the anointed priest is to take some of the blood of the bull and bring it to the tent of meeting,

New International

offering and slaughter it at the entrance to the Tent of Meeting. Then Aaron's sons the priests shall sprinkle the blood against the altar on all sides. 3From the fellowship offering he is to bring a sacrifice made to the LORD by fire: all the fat that covers the inner parts or is connected to them, 4both kidneys with the fat on them near the loins, and the covering of the liver, which he will remove with the kidneys. 5Then Aaron's sons are to burn it on the altar on top of the burnt offering that is on the burning wood, as an offering made by fire, an aroma pleasing to the LORD.

6" 'If he offers an animal from the flock as a fellowship offering to the LORD, he is to offer a male or female without defect. 7If he offers a lamb, he is to present it before the LORD. 8He is to lay his hand on the head of his offering and slaughter it in front of the Tent of Meeting. Then Aaron's sons shall sprinkle its blood against the altar on all sides. 9From the fellowship offering he is to bring a sacrifice made to the LORD by fire: its fat, the entire fat tail cut off close to the backbone, all the fat that covers the inner parts or is connected to them, 10both kidneys with the fat on them near the loins, and the covering of the liver, which he will remove with the kidneys. 11The priest shall burn them on the altar as food, an offering made to the LORD by fire.

12" 'If his offering is a goat, he is to present it before the LORD. 13He is to lay his hand on its head and slaughter it in front of the Tent of Meeting. Then Aaron's sons shall sprinkle its blood against the altar on all sides. 14From what he offers he is to make this offering to the LORD by fire: all the fat that covers the inner parts or is connected to them, 15both kidneys with the fat on them near the loins, and the covering of the liver, which he will remove with the kidneys. 16The priest shall burn them on the altar as food, an offering made by fire, a pleasing aroma. All the fat is the LORD'S.

17" 'This is a lasting ordinance for the generations to come, wherever you live: You must not eat any fat or any blood.' "

The Sin Offering

4 THE LORD said to Moses, 2"Say to the Israelites: 'When anyone sins unintentionally and does what is forbidden in any of the LORD's commands—

3" 'If the anointed priest sins, bringing guilt on the people, he must bring to the LORD a young bull without defect as a sin offering for the sin he has committed. 4He is to present the bull at the entrance to the Tent of Meeting before the LORD. He is to lay his hand on its head and slaughter it before the LORD. 5Then the anointed priest shall take some of the bull's blood and carry it into the

King James

⁶And the priest shall dip his finger in the blood, and sprinkle of the blood seven times before the LORD, before the veil of the sanctuary.

⁷And the priest shall put *some* of the blood upon the horns of the altar of sweet incense before the LORD, which *is* in the tabernacle of the congregation; and shall pour all the blood of the bullock at the bottom of the altar of the burnt offering, which *is at* the door of the tabernacle of the congregation.

⁸And he shall take off from it all the fat of the bullock for the sin offering; the fat that covereth the inwards, and all the fat that *is* upon the inwards,

⁹And the two kidneys, and the fat that *is* upon them, which *is* by the flanks, and the caul above the liver, with the kidneys, it shall he take away,

¹⁰As it was taken off from the bullock of the sacrifice of peace offerings: and the priest shall burn them upon the altar of the burnt offering.

¹¹And the skin of the bullock, and all his flesh, with his head, and with his legs, and his inwards, and his dung,

¹²Even the whole bullock shall he carry forth *s*without the camp unto a clean place, where the ashes are poured out, and burn him on the wood with fire: *h*where the ashes are poured out shall he be burnt.

¹³ ¶ And if the whole congregation of Israel sin through ignorance, and the thing be hid from the eyes of the assembly, and they have done *somewhat against* any of the commandments of the LORD *concerning things* which should not be done, and are guilty;

¹⁴When the sin, which they have sinned against it, is known, then the congregation shall offer a young bullock for the sin, and bring him before the tabernacle of the congregation.

¹⁵And the elders of the congregation shall lay their hands upon the head of the bullock before the LORD: and the bullock shall be killed before the LORD.

¹⁶And the priest that is anointed shall bring of the bullock's blood to the tabernacle of the congregation:

¹⁷And the priest shall dip his finger *in some* of the blood, and sprinkle *it* seven times before the LORD, *even* before the veil.

¹⁸And he shall put *some* of the blood upon the horns of the altar which *is* before the LORD, that *is* in the tabernacle of the congregation, and shall pour out all the blood at the bottom of the altar of the burnt offering, which *is at* the door of the tabernacle of the congregation.

¹⁹And he shall take all his fat from him, and burn *it* upon the altar.

²⁰And he shall do with the bullock as he did with the bullock for a sin offering, so shall he do with this: and the priest shall make an atonement for them, and it shall be forgiven them.

²¹And he shall carry forth the bullock without the camp, and burn him as he burned the first bullock: it *is* a sin offering for the congregation.

²² ¶ When a ruler hath sinned, and done *somewhat* through ignorance *against* any of the commandments of the LORD his God *concerning things* which should not be done, and is guilty;

²³Or if his sin, wherein he hath sinned, come to his knowledge; he shall bring his offering, a kid of the goats, a male without blemish.

²⁴And he shall lay his hand upon the head of the goat, and kill it in the place where they kill the burnt offering before the LORD: it *is* a sin offering.

²⁵And the priest shall take of the blood of the sin offering with his finger, and put *it* upon the horns of the altar of burnt offering, and shall pour out his blood at the bottom of the altar of burnt offering.

Amplified

⁶And the priest shall dip his finger in the blood and sprinkle some of [it] seven times before the Lord before the veil of the sanctuary.

⁷And the priest shall put some of the blood on the horns of the altar of sweet incense before the Lord which is in the Tent of Meeting; and all the rest of the blood of the bull shall he pour out at the base of the altar of the burnt offering at the door of the Tent of Meeting.

⁸And all the fat of the bull for the sin offering he shall take off of it—the fat that covers and is on the entrails,

⁹And the two kidneys and the fat that is on them at the loins, and the appendage of the liver, which he shall take away with the kidneys—

¹⁰Just as these are taken off of the bull of the sacrifice of the peace offerings; and the priest shall burn them on the altar of burnt offering.

¹¹But the hide of the bull and all its flesh, its head, its legs, its entrails, and its dung,

¹²Even the whole bull shall he carry forth without the camp to a clean place, where the ashes are poured out, and burn it on a fire of wood, there where the ashes are poured out. [Heb. 13:11–13.]

¹³If the whole congregation of Israel sins unintentionally, and it be hidden from the eyes of the assembly, and they have done what the Lord has commanded not to be done and are guilty,

¹⁴When the sin which they have committed becomes known, then the congregation shall offer a young bull for a sin offering and bring it before the Tent of Meeting.

¹⁵The elders of the congregation shall lay their hands upon the head of the bull before the Lord, and the bull shall be killed before the Lord.

¹⁶The anointed priest shall bring some of the bull's blood to the Tent of Meeting,

¹⁷And shall dip his finger in the blood, and sprinkle it seven times before the Lord, before the veil [which screens the ark of the covenant].

¹⁸He shall put some of the blood on the horns of the altar [of incense] which is before the Lord in the Tent of Meeting, and he shall pour out all the blood at the base of the altar of burnt offering near the door of the Tent of Meeting.

¹⁹And he shall take all its fat from the bull and burn it on the altar.

²⁰Thus shall he do with the bull; as he did with the bull for a sin offering, so shall he do with this; and the priest shall make atonement for [the people], and they shall be forgiven.

²¹And he shall carry forth the bull outside the camp and burn it as he burned the first bull; it is the sin offering for the congregation.

²²When a ruler *or* leader sins and unwittingly does any one of the things the Lord his God has forbidden, and is guilty,

²³If his sin which he has committed be known to him, he shall bring as his offering a goat, a male without blemish.

²⁴He shall lay his hand on the head of the goat and kill it in the place where they kill the burnt offering before the Lord; it is a sin offering.

²⁵The priest shall take some of the blood of the sin offering with his finger and put it on the horns of the altar of burnt offering and pour the rest of its blood at the base of the altar of burnt offering.

---

*g*Heb. *to without the camp ashes*   *h*Heb. *at the pouring out of the*

New American Standard

6 and the priest shall dip his finger in the blood and sprinkle some of the blood seven times before the LORD, in front of the veil of the sanctuary.

7 'The priest shall also put some of the blood on the horns of the altar of fragrant incense which is before the LORD in the tent of meeting; and all the blood of the bull he shall pour out at the base of the altar of burnt offering which is at the doorway of the tent of meeting.

8 'He shall remove from it all the fat of the bull of the sin offering: the fat that covers the entrails, and all the fat which is on the entrails,

9 and the two kidneys with the fat that is on them, which is on the loins, and the lobe of the liver, which he shall remove with the kidneys

10 (just as it is removed from the ox of the sacrifice of peace offerings), and the priest is to offer them up in smoke on the altar of burnt offering.

11 'But the hide of the bull and all its flesh with its head and its legs and its entrails and its refuse,

12 that is, all *the rest of* the bull, he is to bring out to a clean place outside the camp where the ashes are poured out, and burn it on wood with fire; where the ashes are poured out it shall be burned.

13 ¶ 'Now if the whole congregation of Israel commits error and the matter escapes the notice of the assembly, and they commit any of the things which the LORD has commanded not to be done, and they become guilty;

14 when the sin which they have committed becomes known, then the assembly shall offer a bull of the herd for a sin offering and bring it before the tent of meeting.

15 'Then the elders of the congregation shall lay their hands on the head of the bull before the LORD, and the bull shall be slain before the LORD.

16 'Then the anointed priest is to bring some of the blood of the bull to the tent of meeting;

17 and the priest shall dip his finger in the blood and sprinkle *it* seven times before the LORD, in front of the veil.

18 'He shall put some of the blood on the horns of the altar which is before the LORD in the tent of meeting; and all the blood he shall pour out at the base of the altar of burnt offering which is at the doorway of the tent of meeting.

19 'He shall remove all its fat from it and offer it up in smoke on the altar.

20 'He shall also do with the bull just as he did with the bull of the sin offering; thus he shall do with it. So the priest shall make atonement for them, and they will be forgiven.

21 'Then he is to bring out the bull to *a place* outside the camp and burn it as he burned the first bull; it is the sin offering for the assembly.

22 ¶ 'When a leader sins and unintentionally does any one of all the things which the LORD his God has commanded not to be done, and he becomes guilty,

23 if his sin which he has committed is made known to him, he shall bring for his offering a goat, a male without defect.

24 'He shall lay his hand on the head of the male goat and slay it in the place where they slay the burnt offering before the LORD; it is a sin offering.

25 'Then the priest is to take some of the blood of the sin offering with his finger and put it on the horns of the altar of burnt offering; and *the rest of* its blood he shall pour out at the base of the altar of burnt offering.

New International

Tent of Meeting. 6He is to dip his finger into the blood and sprinkle some of it seven times before the LORD, in front of the curtain of the sanctuary. 7The priest shall then put some of the blood on the horns of the altar of fragrant incense that is before the LORD in the Tent of Meeting. The rest of the bull's blood he shall pour out at the base of the altar of burnt offering at the entrance to the Tent of Meeting. 8He shall remove all the fat from the bull of the sin offering—the fat that covers the inner parts or is connected to them, 9both kidneys with the fat on them near the loins, and the covering of the liver, which he will remove with the kidneys— 10just as the fat is removed from the ox[e] sacrificed as a fellowship offering.[f] Then the priest shall burn them on the altar of burnt offering. 11But the hide of the bull and all its flesh, as well as the head and legs, the inner parts and offal— 12that is, all the rest of the bull—he must take outside the camp to a place ceremonially clean, where the ashes are thrown, and burn it in a wood fire on the ash heap.

13" 'If the whole Israelite community sins unintentionally and does what is forbidden in any of the LORD's commands, even though the community is unaware of the matter, they are guilty. 14When they become aware of the sin they committed, the assembly must bring a young bull as a sin offering and present it before the Tent of Meeting. 15The elders of the community are to lay their hands on the bull's head before the LORD, and the bull shall be slaughtered before the LORD. 16Then the anointed priest is to take some of the bull's blood into the Tent of Meeting. 17He shall dip his finger into the blood and sprinkle it before the LORD seven times in front of the curtain. 18He is to put some of the blood on the horns of the altar that is before the LORD in the Tent of Meeting. The rest of the blood he shall pour out at the base of the altar of burnt offering at the entrance to the Tent of Meeting. 19He shall remove all the fat from it and burn it on the altar, 20and do with this bull just as he did with the bull for the sin offering. In this way the priest will make atonement for them, and they will be forgiven. 21Then he shall take the bull outside the camp and burn it as he burned the first bull. This is the sin offering for the community.

22" 'When a leader sins unintentionally and does what is forbidden in any of the commands of the LORD his God, he is guilty. 23When he is made aware of the sin he committed, he must bring as his offering a male goat without defect. 24He is to lay his hand on the goat's head and slaughter it at the place where the burnt offering is slaughtered before the LORD. It is a sin offering. 25Then the priest shall take some of the blood of the sin offering with his finger and put it on the horns of the altar of burnt offering and pour out the rest of the blood at the base of the altar.

---

e 10 The Hebrew word can include both male and female.
f 10 Traditionally *peace offering*; also in verses 26, 31 and 35

King James

26And he shall burn all his fat upon the altar, as the fat of the sacrifice of peace offerings: and the priest shall make an atonement for him as concerning his sin, and it shall be forgiven him.

27 ¶ And if *i*any one of the *j*common people sin through ignorance, while he doeth *somewhat against* any of the commandments of the LORD *concerning things* which ought not to be done, and be guilty;

28Or if his sin, which he hath sinned, come to his knowledge: then he shall bring his offering, a kid of the goats, a female without blemish, for his sin which he hath sinned.

29And he shall lay his hand upon the head of the sin offering, and slay the sin offering in the place of the burnt offering.

30And the priest shall take of the blood thereof with his finger, and put *it* upon the horns of the altar of burnt offering, and shall pour out all the blood thereof at the bottom of the altar.

31And he shall take away all the fat thereof, as the fat is taken away from off the sacrifice of peace offerings; and the priest shall burn *it* upon the altar for a sweet savour unto the LORD; and the priest shall make an atonement for him, and it shall be forgiven him.

32And if he bring a lamb for a sin offering, he shall bring it a female without blemish.

33And he shall lay his hand upon the head of the sin offering, and slay it for a sin offering in the place where they kill the burnt offering.

34And the priest shall take of the blood of the sin offering with his finger, and put *it* upon the horns of the altar of burnt offering, and shall pour out all the blood thereof at the bottom of the altar:

35And he shall take away all the fat thereof, as the fat of the lamb is taken away from the sacrifice of the peace offerings; and the priest shall burn them upon the altar, according to the offerings made by fire unto the LORD: and the priest shall make an atonement for his sin that he hath committed, and it shall be forgiven him.

5 AND IF a soul sin, and hear the voice of swearing, and *is* a witness, whether he hath seen or known *of it;* if he do not utter *it,* then he shall bear his iniquity.

2Or if a soul touch any unclean thing, whether *it be* a carcase of an unclean beast, or a carcase of unclean cattle, or the carcase of unclean creeping things, and *if* it be hidden from him; he also shall be unclean, and guilty.

3Or if he touch the uncleanness of man, whatsoever uncleanness *it be* that a man shall be defiled withal, and it be hid from him; when he knoweth *of it,* then he shall be guilty.

4Or if a soul swear, pronouncing with *his* lips to do evil, or to do good, whatsoever *it be* that a man shall pronounce with an oath, and it be hid from him; when he knoweth *of it,* then he shall be guilty in one of these.

5And it shall be, when he shall be guilty in one of these *things,* that he shall confess that he hath sinned in that *thing:*

6And he shall bring his trespass offering unto the LORD for his sin which he hath sinned, a female from the flock, a lamb or a kid of the goats, for a sin offering; and the priest shall make an atonement for him concerning his sin.

7And if *k*he be not able to bring a lamb, then he shall bring for his trespass, which he hath committed, two turtledoves, or two young pigeons, unto the LORD; one for a sin offering, and the other for a burnt offering.

8And he shall bring them unto the priest, who shall offer *that* which *is* for the sin offering first, and wring off his head from his neck, but shall not divide *it* asunder:

Amplified

26And he shall burn all its fat upon the altar like the fat of the sacrifice of peace offerings; so the priest shall make atonement for him for his sin, and it shall be forgiven him.

27If any one of the common people sins unwittingly in doing anything the Lord has commanded not to be done, and is guilty,

28When the sin which he has committed is made known to him, he shall bring for his offering a goat, a female without blemish, for his sin which he has committed.

29The offender shall lay his hand on the head of the sin offering and kill [it] at the place of the burnt offering.

30And the priest shall take some of its blood with his finger and put it on the horns of the altar of burnt offering and shall pour out the rest of its blood at the base of the altar.

31And all the fat of it he shall take away, as the fat is taken away from off the sacrifice of peace offerings; and the priest shall burn it on the altar for a sweet *and* satisfying fragrance to the Lord; and the priest shall make atonement for [the man], and he shall be forgiven.

32If he brings a lamb as his sin offering, he shall bring a female without blemish.

33He shall lay his hand upon the head of the sin offering and kill it in the place where they kill the burnt offering.

34And the priest shall take some of the blood of the sin offering with his finger and put it on the horns of the altar of burnt offering and all the rest of the blood of the lamb he shall pour out at the base of the altar.

35And he shall take away all the fat of it, just as the fat of the lamb is removed from the sacrifice of the peace offerings; and the priest shall burn it on the altar upon the offerings made by fire to the Lord; and the priest shall make atonement for the sin which the man has committed, and he shall be forgiven. [Heb. 9:13, 14.]

5 IF ANYONE sins in that he is sworn to testify and has knowledge of the matter, either by seeing or hearing of it, but fails to report it, then he shall bear his iniquity *and* willfulness.

2Or if anyone touches an unclean thing, whether the carcass of an unclean wild beast or of an unclean domestic animal or of unclean creeping things that multiply prolifically, even if he is unaware of it, and he has become unclean, he is guilty.

3Or if he touches human uncleanness, of whatever kind the uncleanness may be with which he becomes defiled, and he is unaware of it, when he does know it, then he shall be guilty.

4Or if anyone unthinkingly swears he will do something, whether to do evil or good, whatever it may be that a man shall pronounce rashly taking an oath, then, when he becomes aware of it, he shall be guilty in either of these. [Mark 6:23.]

5When a man is guilty in one of these, he shall confess the sin he has committed.

6He shall bring his guilt *or* trespass offering to the Lord for the sin which he has committed, a female from the flock, a lamb or a goat, for a sin offering; and the priest shall make atonement for his sin.

7But if he cannot afford a lamb, then he shall bring for his guilt offering to the Lord two turtledoves or two young pigeons, one for a sin offering and the other for a burnt offering.

8He shall bring them to the priest, who shall offer the one for the sin offering first, and wring its head from its neck, but shall not sever it;

---

i Heb. *any soul*   *j* Heb. *people of the land*   *k* Heb. *his hand cannot reach to the sufficiency of a lamb*

New American Standard

26 'All its fat he shall offer up in smoke on the altar as *in the case of* the fat of the sacrifice of peace offerings. Thus the priest shall make atonement for him in regard to his sin, and he will be forgiven.

27 ¶ 'Now if anyone of the common people sins unintentionally in doing any of the things which the LORD has commanded not to be done, and becomes guilty,

28 if his sin which he has committed is made known to him, then he shall bring for his offering a goat, a female without defect, for his sin which he has committed.

29 'He shall lay his hand on the head of the sin offering and slay the sin offering at the place of the burnt offering.

30 'The priest shall take some of its blood with his finger and put it on the horns of the altar of burnt offering; and all *the rest of* its blood he shall pour out at the base of the altar.

31 'Then he shall remove all its fat, just as the fat was removed from the sacrifice of peace offerings; and the priest shall offer it up in smoke on the altar for a soothing aroma to the LORD. Thus the priest shall make atonement for him, and he will be forgiven.

32 ¶ 'But if he brings a lamb as his offering for a sin offering, he shall bring it, a female without defect.

33 'He shall lay his hand on the head of the sin offering and slay it for a sin offering in the place where they slay the burnt offering.

34 'The priest is to take some of the blood of the sin offering with his finger and put it on the horns of the altar of burnt offering, and all *the rest of* its blood he shall pour out at the base of the altar.

35 'Then he shall remove all its fat, just as the fat of the lamb is removed from the sacrifice of the peace offerings, and the priest shall offer them up in smoke on the altar, on the offerings by fire to the LORD. Thus the priest shall make atonement for him in regard to his sin which he has committed, and he will be forgiven.

The Law of Guilt Offerings

5 'NOW IF a person sins after he hears a public adjuration *to testify* when he is a witness, whether he has seen or *otherwise* known, if he does not tell *it*, then he will bear his guilt.

2 'Or if a person touches any unclean thing, whether a carcass of an unclean beast or the carcass of unclean cattle or a carcass of unclean swarming things, though it is hidden from him and he is unclean, then he will be guilty.

3 'Or if he touches human uncleanness, of whatever *sort* his uncleanness *may* be with which he becomes unclean, and it is hidden from him, and then he comes to know *it*, he will be guilty.

4 'Or if a person swears thoughtlessly with his lips to do evil or to do good, in whatever matter a man may speak thoughtlessly with an oath, and it is hidden from him, and then he comes to know *it*, he will be guilty in one of these.

5 'So it shall be when he becomes guilty in one of these, that he shall confess that in which he has sinned.

6 'He shall also bring his guilt offering to the LORD for his sin which he has committed, a female from the flock, a lamb or a goat as a sin offering. So the priest shall make atonement on his behalf for his sin.

7 ¶ 'But if he cannot afford a lamb, then he shall bring to the LORD his guilt offering for that in which he has sinned, two turtledoves or two young pigeons, one for a sin offering and the other for a burnt offering.

8 'He shall bring them to the priest, who shall offer first that which is for the sin offering and shall nip its head at the front of its neck, but he shall not sever *it*.

New International

26He shall burn all the fat on the altar as he burned the fat of the fellowship offering. In this way the priest will make atonement for the man's sin, and he will be forgiven.

27" 'If a member of the community sins unintentionally and does what is forbidden in any of the LORD's commands, he is guilty. 28When he is made aware of the sin he committed, he must bring as his offering for the sin he committed a female goat without defect. 29He is to lay his hand on the head of the sin offering and slaughter it at the place of the burnt offering. 30Then the priest is to take some of the blood with his finger and put it on the horns of the altar of burnt offering and pour out the rest of the blood at the base of the altar. 31He shall remove all the fat, just as the fat is removed from the fellowship offering, and the priest shall burn it on the altar as an aroma pleasing to the LORD. In this way the priest will make atonement for him, and he will be forgiven.

32" 'If he brings a lamb as his sin offering, he is to bring a female without defect. 33He is to lay his hand on its head and slaughter it for a sin offering at the place where the burnt offering is slaughtered. 34Then the priest shall take some of the blood of the sin offering with his finger and put it on the horns of the altar of burnt offering and pour out the rest of the blood at the base of the altar. 35He shall remove all the fat, just as the fat is removed from the lamb of the fellowship offering, and the priest shall burn it on the altar on top of the offerings made to the LORD by fire. In this way the priest will make atonement for him for the sin he has committed, and he will be forgiven.

5 " 'IF A person sins because he does not speak up when he hears a public charge to testify regarding something he has seen or learned about, he will be held responsible.

2" 'Or if a person touches anything ceremonially unclean—whether the carcasses of unclean wild animals or of unclean livestock or of unclean creatures that move along the ground—even though he is unaware of it, he has become unclean and is guilty.

3" 'Or if he touches human uncleanness—anything that would make him unclean—even though he is unaware of it, when he learns of it he will be guilty.

4" 'Or if a person thoughtlessly takes an oath to do anything, whether good or evil—in any matter one might carelessly swear about—even though he is unaware of it, in any case when he learns of it he will be guilty.

5" 'When anyone is guilty in any of these ways, he must confess in what way he has sinned 6and, as a penalty for the sin he has committed, he must bring to the LORD a female lamb or goat from the flock as a sin offering; and the priest shall make atonement for him for his sin.

7" 'If he cannot afford a lamb, he is to bring two doves or two young pigeons to the LORD as a penalty for his sin—one for a sin offering and the other for a burnt offering. 8He is to bring them to the priest, who shall first offer the one for the sin offering. He is to wring its head from

King James

⁹And he shall sprinkle of the blood of the sin offering upon the side of the altar; and the rest of the blood shall be wrung out at the bottom of the altar: it *is* a sin offering.

¹⁰And he shall offer the second *for* a burnt offering, according to the *ˡ*manner: and the priest shall make an atonement for him for his sin which he hath sinned, and it shall be forgiven him.

¹¹ ¶ But if he be not able to bring two turtledoves, or two young pigeons, then he that sinned shall bring for his offering the tenth part of an ephah of fine flour for a sin offering; he shall put no oil upon it, neither shall he put *any* frankincense thereon: for it *is* a sin offering.

¹²Then shall he bring it to the priest, and the priest shall take his handful of it, *even* a memorial thereof, and burn *it* on the altar, according to the offerings made by fire unto the LORD: it *is* a sin offering.

¹³And the priest shall make an atonement for him as touching his sin that he hath sinned in one of these, and it shall be forgiven him: and *the remnant* shall be the priest's, as a meat offering.

¹⁴ ¶ And the LORD spake unto Moses, saying,

¹⁵If a soul commit a trespass, and sin through ignorance, in the holy things of the LORD; then he shall bring for his trespass unto the LORD a ram without blemish out of the flocks, with thy estimation by shekels of silver, after the shekel of the sanctuary, for a trespass offering:

¹⁶And he shall make amends for the harm that he hath done in the holy thing, and shall add the fifth part thereto, and give it unto the priest: and the priest shall make an atonement for him with the ram of the trespass offering, and it shall be forgiven him.

¹⁷ ¶ And if a soul sin, and commit any of these things which are forbidden to be done by the commandments of the LORD; though he wist *it* not, yet is he guilty, and shall bear his iniquity.

¹⁸And he shall bring a ram without blemish out of the flock, with thy estimation, for a trespass offering, unto the priest: and the priest shall make an atonement for him concerning his ignorance wherein he erred and wist *it* not, and it shall be forgiven him.

¹⁹It *is* a trespass offering: he hath certainly trespassed against the LORD.

6 AND THE LORD spake unto Moses, saying,
²If a soul sin, and commit a trespass against the LORD, and lie unto his neighbour in that which was delivered him to keep, or in *ᵐ*fellowship, or in a thing taken away by violence, or hath deceived his neighbour;

³Or have found that which was lost, and lieth concerning it, and sweareth falsely; in any of all these that a man doeth, sinning therein:

⁴Then it shall be, because he hath sinned, and is guilty, that he shall restore that which he took violently away, or the thing which he hath deceitfully gotten, or that which was delivered him to keep, or the lost thing which he found,

⁵Or all that about which he hath sworn falsely; he shall even restore it in the principal, and shall add the fifth part more thereto, *and* give it unto him to whom it appertaineth, *ᵒᵖ*in the day of his trespass offering.

⁶And he shall bring his trespass offering unto the LORD, a ram without blemish out of the flock, with thy estimation, for a trespass offering, unto the priest:

⁷And the priest shall make an atonement for him before the LORD: and it shall be forgiven him for any thing of all that he hath done in trespassing therein.

Amplified

⁹And he shall sprinkle some of the blood of the sin offering on the side of the altar, and the rest of the blood shall be drained out at the base of the altar; it is a sin offering.

¹⁰And he shall prepare the second bird for a burnt offering, according to the ordinance; and the priest shall make atonement for him for his sin which he has committed, and he shall be forgiven.

¹¹But if the offender cannot afford to bring two turtledoves or two young pigeons, then he shall bring for his offering the tenth part of an ephah of fine flour for a sin offering; he shall put no oil or frankincense on it, for it is a sin offering.

¹²He shall bring it to the priest, who shall take a handful of it as a memorial portion and burn it on the altar, on the offerings made by fire to the Lord; it is a sin offering.

¹³Thus the priest shall make atonement for him for the sin that he has committed in any of these things, and he shall be forgiven; and the remainder shall be for the priest, as in the cereal offering.

¹⁴And the Lord said to Moses,

¹⁵If anyone commits a breach of faith and sins unwittingly in the holy things of the Lord, he shall bring his trespass *or* guilt offering to the Lord, a ram without blemish out of the flock, valued by you in shekels of silver, that is, the shekel of the sanctuary, for a trespass *or* guilt offering.

¹⁶And he shall make restitution for what he has done amiss in the holy thing, and shall add a fifth to it, and give it to the priest; and the priest shall make atonement for him with the ram of the trespass *or* guilt offering, and he shall be forgiven.

¹⁷If anyone sins and does any of the things the Lord has forbidden, though he was not aware of it, yet he is guilty and shall bear his iniquity. [Luke 12:48.]

¹⁸He shall bring [to the priest] a ram without blemish out of the flock, estimated by you to the amount [of the trespass], for a guilt *or* trespass offering; and the priest shall make atonement for him for the error which he committed unknowingly, and he shall be forgiven.

¹⁹It is a trespass *or* guilt offering; he is certainly guilty before the Lord.

6 AND THE Lord said to Moses,
²If anyone sins and commits a trespass against the Lord and deals falsely with his neighbor in a matter of deposit given him to keep, or of bargain *or* pledge, or of robbery, or has oppressed his neighbor,

³Or has found what was lost and lied about it, or swears falsely, in any of all the things which men do and sin in so doing,

⁴Then if he has sinned and is guilty, he shall restore what he took by robbery, or what he secured by oppression *or* extortion, or what was delivered him to keep in trust, or the lost thing which he found,

⁵Or anything about which he has sworn falsely; he shall not only restore it in full, but shall add to it one fifth more and give it to him to whom it belongs on the day of his trespass *or* guilt offering.

⁶And he shall bring to the priest his trespass *or* guilt offering to the Lord, a ram without blemish out of the flock, valued by you to the amount of his trespass;

⁷And the priest shall make atonement for him before the Lord, and he shall be forgiven for anything of all that he may have done by which he has become guilty.

---

*ˡ*Or, *ordinance*   *ᵐ*Or, *in dealing*   *ⁿ*Heb. *putting of the hand*
*ᵒ*Or, *in the day of his being found guilty*   *ᵖ*Heb. *in the day of his trespass*

New American Standard

9 'He shall also sprinkle some of the blood of the sin offering on the side of the altar, while the rest of the blood shall be drained out at the base of the altar: it is a sin offering.

10 'The second he shall then prepare as a burnt offering according to the ordinance. So the priest shall make atonement on his behalf for his sin which he has committed, and it will be forgiven him.

11 ¶ 'But if his means are insufficient for two turtledoves or two young pigeons, then for his offering for that which he has sinned, he shall bring the tenth of an *ephah of fine flour for a sin offering; he shall not put oil on it or place incense on it, for it is a sin offering.

12 'He shall bring it to the priest, and the priest shall take his handful of it as its memorial portion and offer *it* up in smoke on the altar, with the offerings of the LORD by fire: it is a sin offering.

13 'So the priest shall make atonement for him concerning his sin which he has committed from one of these, and it will be forgiven him; then *the rest* shall become the priest's, like the grain offering.' "

14 ¶ Then the LORD spoke to Moses, saying,

15 "If a person acts unfaithfully and sins unintentionally against the LORD's holy things, then he shall bring his guilt offering to the LORD: a ram without defect from the flock, according to your valuation in silver by shekels, in *terms of* the shekel of the sanctuary, for a guilt offering.

16 "He shall make restitution for that which he has sinned against the holy thing, and shall add to it a fifth part of it and give it to the priest. The priest shall then make atonement for him with the ram of the guilt offering, and it will be forgiven him.

17 ¶ "Now if a person sins and does any of the things which the LORD has commanded not to be done, though he was unaware, still he is guilty and shall bear his punishment.

18 "He is then to bring to the priest a ram without defect from the flock, according to your valuation, for a guilt offering. So the priest shall make atonement for him concerning his error in which he sinned unintentionally and did not know *it,* and it will be forgiven him.

19 "It is a guilt offering; he was certainly guilty before the LORD."

Guilt Offering

6 THEN THE LORD spoke to Moses, saying,

2 "When a person sins and acts unfaithfully against the LORD, and deceives his companion in regard to a deposit or a security entrusted *to him,* or through robbery, or *if* he has extorted from his companion,

3 or has found what was lost and lied about it and sworn falsely, so that he sins in regard to any one of the things a man may do;

4 then it shall be, when he sins and becomes guilty, that he shall restore what he took by robbery or what he got by extortion, or the deposit which was entrusted to him or the lost thing which he found,

5 or anything about which he swore falsely; he shall make restitution for it in full and add to it one-fifth more. He shall give it to the one to whom it belongs on the day *he presents* his guilt offering.

6 "Then he shall bring to the priest his guilt offering to the LORD, a ram without defect from the flock, according to your valuation, for a guilt offering,

7 and the priest shall make atonement for him before the LORD, and he will be forgiven for any one of the things which he may have done to incur guilt."

New International

its neck, not severing it completely, 9and is to sprinkle some of the blood of the sin offering against the side of the altar; the rest of the blood must be drained out at the base of the altar. It is a sin offering. 10The priest shall then offer the other as a burnt offering in the prescribed way and make atonement for him for the sin he has committed, and he will be forgiven.

11 'If, however, he cannot afford two doves or two young pigeons, he is to bring as an offering for his sin a tenth of an ephah^g of fine flour for a sin offering. He must not put oil or incense on it, because it is a sin offering. 12He is to bring it to the priest, who shall take a handful of it as a memorial portion and burn it on the altar on top of the offerings made to the LORD by fire. It is a sin offering. 13In this way the priest will make atonement for him for any of these sins he has committed, and he will be forgiven. The rest of the offering will belong to the priest, as in the case of the grain offering.' "

The Guilt Offering

14The LORD said to Moses: 15"When a person commits a violation and sins unintentionally in regard to any of the LORD's holy things, he is to bring to the LORD as a penalty a ram from the flock, one without defect and of the proper value in silver, according to the sanctuary shekel.^h It is a guilt offering. 16He must make restitution for what he has failed to do in regard to the holy things, add a fifth of the value to that and give it all to the priest, who will make atonement for him with the ram as a guilt offering, and he will be forgiven.

17"If a person sins and does what is forbidden in any of the LORD's commands, even though he does not know it, he is guilty and will be held responsible. 18He is to bring to the priest as a guilt offering a ram from the flock, one without defect and of the proper value. In this way the priest will make atonement for him for the wrong he has committed unintentionally, and he will be forgiven. 19It is a guilt offering; he has been guilty of^i wrongdoing against the LORD."

6 THE LORD said to Moses: 2"If anyone sins and is unfaithful to the LORD by deceiving his neighbor about something entrusted to him or left in his care or stolen, or if he cheats him, 3or if he finds lost property and lies about it, or if he swears falsely, or if he commits any such sin that people may do— 4when he thus sins and becomes guilty, he must return what he has stolen or taken by extortion, or what was entrusted to him, or the lost property he found, 5or whatever it was he swore falsely about. He must make restitution in full, add a fifth of the value to it and give it all to the owner on the day he presents his guilt offering. 6And as a penalty he must bring to the priest, that is, to the LORD, his guilt offering, a ram from the flock, one without defect and of the proper value. 7In this way the priest will make atonement for him before the LORD, and he will be forgiven for any of these things he did that made him guilty."

---

^g 11 That is, probably about 2 quarts (about 2 liters)   ^h 15 That is, about 2/5 ounce (about 11.5 grams)   ^i 19 Or *has made full expiation for his*

^a I.e. Approx one bu

King James

The burnt offering

8 ¶ And the LORD spake unto Moses, saying,

9Command Aaron and his sons, saying, This *is* the law of the burnt offering: It *is* the burnt offering, qbecause of the burning upon the altar all night unto the morning, and the fire of the altar shall be burning in it.

10And the priest shall put on his linen garment, and his linen breeches shall he put upon his flesh, and take up the ashes which the fire hath consumed with the burnt offering on the altar, and he shall put them beside the altar.

11And he shall put off his garments, and put on other garments, and carry forth the ashes without the camp unto a clean place.

12And the fire upon the altar shall be burning in it; it shall not be put out: and the priest shall burn wood on it every morning, and lay the burnt offering in order upon it; and he shall burn thereon the fat of the peace offerings.

13The fire shall ever be burning upon the altar; it shall never go out.

The meat offering

14 ¶ And this *is* the law of the meat offering: the sons of Aaron shall offer it before the LORD, before the altar.

15And he shall take of it his handful, of the flour of the meat offering, and of the oil thereof, and all the frankincense which *is* upon the meat offering, and shall burn *it* upon the altar *for* a sweet savour, *even* the memorial of it, unto the LORD.

16And the remainder thereof shall Aaron and his sons eat: with unleavened bread shall it be eaten in the holy place; in the court of the tabernacle of the congregation they shall eat it.

17It shall not be baken with leaven. I have given it *unto them for* their portion of my offerings made by fire; it *is* most holy, as *is* the sin offering, and as the trespass offering.

18All the males among the children of Aaron shall eat of it. *It shall be* a statute for ever in your generations concerning the offerings of the LORD made by fire: every one that toucheth them shall be holy.

19 ¶ And the LORD spake unto Moses, saying,

20This *is* the offering of Aaron and of his sons, which they shall offer unto the LORD in the day when he is anointed; the tenth part of an ephah of fine flour for a meat offering perpetual, half of it in the morning, and half thereof at night.

21In a pan it shall be made with oil; *and when it is* baked, thou shalt bring it in: *and* the baken pieces of the meat offering shalt thou offer *for* a sweet savour unto the LORD.

22And the priest of his sons that is anointed in his stead shall offer it: *it is* a statute for ever unto the LORD; it shall be wholly burnt.

23For every meat offering for the priest shall be wholly burnt: it shall not be eaten.

The sin offering

24 ¶ And the LORD spake unto Moses, saying,

25Speak unto Aaron and to his sons, saying, This *is* the law of the sin offering: In the place where the burnt offering is killed shall the sin offering be killed before the LORD: it *is* most holy.

26The priest that offereth it for sin shall eat it: in the holy place shall it be eaten, in the court of the tabernacle of the congregation.

27Whatsoever shall touch the flesh thereof shall be holy: and when there is sprinkled of the blood thereof upon any garment, thou shalt wash that whereon it was sprinkled in the holy place.

28But the earthen vessel wherein it is sodden shall be broken: and if it be sodden in a brasen pot, it shall be both scoured, and rinsed in water.

Amplified

8And the Lord said to Moses,

9Command Aaron and his sons, saying, This is the law of the burnt offering: The burnt offering shall remain on the altar all night until morning; the fire shall be kept burning on the altar.

10And the priest shall put on his linen garment and put his linen breeches on his body, and take up the ashes of what the fire has consumed with the burnt offering on the altar and put them beside the altar.

11And he shall put off his garments and put on other garments, and carry the ashes outside the camp to a clean place.

12And the fire upon the altar shall be kept burning on it; it shall not be allowed to go out. The priest shall burn wood on it every morning and lay the burnt offering in order upon it and he shall burn on it the fat of the peace offerings.

13The fire shall be burning continually upon the altar; it shall not go out.

14And this is the law of the cereal offering: The sons of Aaron shall offer it before the Lord, in front of the altar.

15One of them shall take his handful of the fine flour of the cereal offering, the oil of it, and all the frankincense which is upon the cereal offering, and burn it on the altar as the memorial of it, a sweet *and* satisfying fragrance to the Lord.

16And the remainder of it shall Aaron and his sons eat, without leaven in a holy place; in the court of the Tent of Meeting shall they eat it. [I Cor. 9:13, 14.]

17It shall not be baked with leaven. I have given it as their portion of My offerings made by fire; it is most holy, like the sin offering and the guilt offering.

18Every male among the children of Aaron may eat of it, as his portion forever throughout your generations, from the Lord's offerings made by fire; whoever touches them shall [first] be holy (consecrated and ceremonially clean).

19And the Lord said to Moses,

20This is the offering which Aaron and his sons shall offer to the Lord on the day when one is anointed (and consecrated): the tenth of an ephah of fine flour for a regular cereal offering, half of it in the morning and half of it at night.

21On a griddle *or* baking pan it shall be made with oil; and when it is fried you shall bring it in; in broken *and* fried pieces shall you offer the cereal offering as a sweet *and* satisfying odor to the Lord.

22And the priest among Aaron's sons who is consecrated *and* anointed in his stead shall offer it; by a statute forever it shall be entirely burned to the Lord.

23For every cereal offering of the priest shall be wholly burned, and not be eaten.

24And the Lord said to Moses,

25Say to Aaron and his sons: This is the law of the sin offering: In the place where the burnt offering is killed shall the sin offering be killed before the Lord; it is most holy.

26The priest who offers it for sin shall eat it; in a sacred place shall it be eaten, in the court of the Tent of Meeting.

27Whoever *or* whatever touches its flesh shall [first] be dedicated and made clean, and when any of its blood is sprinkled on a garment, you shall wash that garment in a place set apart to God's worship.

28But the earthen vessel in which it is boiled shall be broken, and if it is boiled in a bronze vessel, that vessel shall be scoured and rinsed in water.

q Or, *for the burning*

New American Standard

The Priest's Part in the Offerings

8 ¶ Then the LORD spoke to Moses, saying,

9 "Command Aaron and his sons, saying, 'This is the law for the burnt offering: the burnt offering itself *shall remain* on the hearth on the altar all night until the morning, and the fire on the altar is to be kept burning on it.

10 'The priest is to put on his linen robe, and he shall put on undergarments next to his flesh; and he shall take up the ashes *to* which the fire reduces the burnt offering on the altar and place them beside the altar.

11 'Then he shall take off his garments and put on other garments, and carry the ashes outside the camp to a clean place.

12 'The fire on the altar shall be kept burning on it. It shall not go out, but the priest shall burn wood on it every morning; and he shall lay out the burnt offering on it, and offer up in smoke the fat portions of the peace offerings on it.

13 'Fire shall be kept burning continually on the altar; it is not to go out.

14 ¶ 'Now this is the law of the grain offering: the sons of Aaron shall present it before the LORD in front of the altar.

15 'Then one *of them* shall lift up from it a handful of the fine flour of the grain offering, with its oil and all the incense that is on the grain offering, and he shall offer *it* up in smoke on the altar, a soothing aroma, as its memorial offering to the LORD.

16 'What is left of it Aaron and his sons are to eat. It shall be eaten as unleavened cakes in a holy place; they are to eat it in the court of the tent of meeting.

17 'It shall not be baked with leaven. I have given it as their share from My offerings by fire; it is most holy, like the sin offering and the guilt offering.

18 'Every male among the sons of Aaron may eat it; it is a permanent ordinance throughout your generations, from the offerings by fire to the LORD. Whoever touches them will become consecrated.' "

19 ¶ Then the LORD spoke to Moses, saying,

20 "This is the offering which Aaron and his sons are to present to the LORD on the day when he is anointed; the tenth of an ephah of fine flour as a regular grain offering, half of it in the morning and half of it in the evening.

21 "It shall be prepared with oil on a griddle. When it is *well* stirred, you shall bring it. You shall present the grain offering in baked pieces as a soothing aroma to the LORD.

22 "The anointed priest who will be in his place among his sons shall offer it. By a permanent ordinance it shall be entirely offered up in smoke to the LORD.

23 "So every grain offering of the priest shall be burned entirely. It shall not be eaten."

24 ¶ Then the LORD spoke to Moses, saying,

25 "Speak to Aaron and to his sons, saying, 'This is the law of the sin offering: in the place where the burnt offering is slain the sin offering shall be slain before the LORD; it is most holy.

26 'The priest who offers it for sin shall eat it. It shall be eaten in a holy place, in the court of the tent of meeting.

27 'Anyone who touches its flesh will become consecrated; and when any of its blood splashes on a garment, in a holy place you shall wash what was splashed on.

28 'Also the earthenware vessel in which it was boiled shall be broken; and if it was boiled in a bronze vessel, then it shall be scoured and rinsed in water.

New International

The Burnt Offering

8 The LORD said to Moses: 9 "Give Aaron and his sons this command: 'These are the regulations for the burnt offering: The burnt offering is to remain on the altar hearth throughout the night, till morning, and the fire must be kept burning on the altar. 10 The priest shall then put on his linen clothes, with linen undergarments next to his body, and shall remove the ashes of the burnt offering that the fire has consumed on the altar and place them beside the altar. 11 Then he is to take off these clothes and put on others, and carry the ashes outside the camp to a place that is ceremonially clean. 12 The fire on the altar must be kept burning; it must not go out. Every morning the priest is to add firewood and arrange the burnt offering on the fire and burn the fat of the fellowship offerings*j* on it. 13 The fire must be kept burning on the altar continuously; it must not go out.

The Grain Offering

14 " 'These are the regulations for the grain offering: Aaron's sons are to bring it before the LORD, in front of the altar. 15 The priest is to take a handful of fine flour and oil, together with all the incense on the grain offering, and burn the memorial portion on the altar as an aroma pleasing to the LORD. 16 Aaron and his sons shall eat the rest of it, but it is to be eaten without yeast in a holy place; they are to eat it in the courtyard of the Tent of Meeting. 17 It must not be baked with yeast; I have given it as their share of the offerings made to me by fire. Like the sin offering and the guilt offering, it is most holy. 18 Any male descendant of Aaron may eat it. It is his regular share of the offerings made to the LORD by fire for the generations to come. Whatever touches them will become holy.*k* ' "

19 The LORD also said to Moses, 20 "This is the offering Aaron and his sons are to bring to the LORD on the day he*l* is anointed: a tenth of an ephah*m* of fine flour as a regular grain offering, half of it in the morning and half in the evening. 21 Prepare it with oil on a griddle; bring it well-mixed and present the grain offering broken*n* in pieces as an aroma pleasing to the LORD. 22 The son who is to succeed him as anointed priest shall prepare it. It is the LORD's regular share and is to be burned completely. 23 Every grain offering of a priest shall be burned completely; it must not be eaten."

The Sin Offering

24 The LORD said to Moses, 25 "Say to Aaron and his sons: 'These are the regulations for the sin offering: The sin offering is to be slaughtered before the LORD in the place the burnt offering is slaughtered; it is most holy. 26 The priest who offers it shall eat it; it is to be eaten in a holy place, in the courtyard of the Tent of Meeting. 27 Whatever touches any of the flesh will become holy, and if any of the blood is spattered on a garment, you must wash it in a holy place. 28 The clay pot the meat is cooked in must be broken; but if it is cooked in a bronze pot, the

---

j 12 Traditionally *peace offerings must be holy*; similarly in verse 27 *l 20* Or *each* is, probably about 2 quarts (about 2 liters) the Hebrew for this word is uncertain.   *k 18* Or *Whoever touches them must be holy*   *m 20* That   *n 21* The meaning of

King James

²⁹All the males among the priests shall eat thereof: it *is* most holy.

³⁰And no sin offering, whereof *any* of the blood is brought into the tabernacle of the congregation to reconcile *withal* in the holy *place,* shall be eaten: it shall be burnt in the fire.

The trespass offering

7 LIKEWISE THIS *is* the law of the trespass offering: it *is* most holy.

²In the place where they kill the burnt offering shall they kill the trespass offering: and the blood thereof shall he sprinkle round about upon the altar.

³And he shall offer of it all the fat thereof; the rump, and the fat that covereth the inwards.

⁴And the two kidneys, and the fat that *is* on them, which *is* by the flanks, and the caul *that is* above the liver, with the kidneys, it shall he take away:

⁵And the priest shall burn them upon the altar *for* an offering made by fire unto the LORD: it *is* a trespass offering.

⁶Every male among the priests shall eat thereof: it shall be eaten in the holy place: it *is* most holy.

⁷As the sin offering *is,* so *is* the trespass offering: *there is* one law for them: the priest that maketh atonement therewith shall have *it.*

⁸And the priest that offereth any man's burnt offering, *even* the priest shall have to himself the skin of the burnt offering which he hath offered.

⁹And all the meat offering that is baken in the oven, and all that is dressed in the fryingpan, and ʳin the pan, shall be the priest's that offereth it.

¹⁰And every meat offering, mingled with oil, and dry, shall all the sons of Aaron have, one *as much* as another.

The peace offering

¹¹And this *is* the law of the sacrifice of peace offerings, which he shall offer unto the LORD.

¹²If he offer it for a thanksgiving, then he shall offer with the sacrifice of thanksgiving unleavened cakes mingled with oil, and unleavened wafers anointed with oil, and cakes mingled with oil, of fine flour, fried.

¹³Besides the cakes, he shall offer *for* his offering leavened bread with the sacrifice of thanksgiving of his peace offerings.

¹⁴And of it he shall offer one out of the whole oblation *for* an heave offering unto the LORD, *and* it shall be the priest's that sprinkleth the blood of the peace offerings.

¹⁵And the flesh of the sacrifice of his peace offerings for thanksgiving shall be eaten the same day that it is offered; he shall not leave any of it until the morning.

¹⁶But if the sacrifice of his offering *be* a vow, or a voluntary offering, it shall be eaten the same day that he offereth his sacrifice: and on the morrow also the remainder of it shall be eaten:

¹⁷But the remainder of the flesh of the sacrifice on the third day shall be burnt with fire.

¹⁸And if *any* of the flesh of the sacrifice of his peace offerings be eaten at all on the third day, it shall not be accepted, neither shall it be imputed unto him that offereth it: it shall be an abomination, and the soul that eateth of it shall bear his iniquity.

¹⁹And the flesh that toucheth any unclean *thing* shall not be eaten; it shall be burnt with fire: and as for the flesh, all that be clean shall eat thereof.

²⁰But the soul that eateth *of* the flesh of the sacrifice of peace offerings, that *pertain* unto the LORD, having his uncleanness upon him, even that soul shall be cut off from his people.

Amplified

²⁹Every male among the priests may eat of this offering; it is most holy.

³⁰But no sin offering shall be eaten of which any of the blood is brought into the Tent of Meeting to make atonement in the Holy Place; it shall be [wholly] burned with fire. [Heb. 13:11–13.]

7 THIS IS the law of the guilt *or* trespass offering; it is most holy *or* sacred:

²In the place where they kill the burnt offering shall they kill the guilt *or* trespass offering; the blood of it shall the priest dash against the altar round about.

³And he shall offer all its fat, the fat tail and the fat that covers the entrails,

⁴And the two kidneys and the fat that is on them at the loins, and the lobe *or* appendage of the liver, which he shall take away with the kidneys.

⁵And the priest shall burn them on the altar for an offering made by fire to the Lord; it is a guilt *or* trespass offering.

⁶Every male among the priests may eat of it; it shall be eaten in a sacred place; it is most holy.

⁷As is the sin offering, so is the guilt *or* trespass offering; there is one law for them: the priest who makes atonement with it shall have it.

⁸And the priest who offers any man's burnt offering, that priest shall have for himself the hide of the burnt offering which he has offered.

⁹And every cereal offering that is baked in the oven and all that is prepared in a pan or on a griddle shall belong to the priest who offered it.

¹⁰And every cereal offering, mixed with oil or dry, all the sons of Aaron may have, one as well as another.

¹¹And this is the law of the sacrifice of peace offerings which shall be offered to the Lord:

¹²If one offers it for a thanksgiving, then he shall offer with the thank offering unleavened cakes mixed with oil, and unleavened wafers spread with oil, and cakes of fine flour mixed with oil.

¹³With cakes of leavened bread he shall offer his sacrifice of thanksgiving with the sacrifice of his peace offerings.

¹⁴And of it he shall offer one cake from each offering as an offering to the Lord; it shall belong to the priest who dashes the blood of the peace offerings.

¹⁵The flesh of the sacrifice of thanksgiving presented as a peace offering shall be eaten on the day that it is offered; none of it shall be left until morning.

¹⁶But if the sacrifice of the worshiper's offering is a vow or a freewill offering, it shall be eaten the same day that he offers his sacrifice, and on the morrow that which remains of it shall be eaten;

¹⁷But the remainder of the flesh of the sacrifice on the third day shall be [wholly] burned with fire.

¹⁸If any of the flesh of the sacrifice of his peace offerings be eaten at all on the third day, then the one who brought it shall not be credited with it; it shall not be accepted. It shall be an abomination *and* an abhorred thing; the one who eats of it shall bear his iniquity *and* answer for it.

¹⁹The flesh that comes in contact with anything that is not clean shall not be eaten; it shall be burned with fire. As for the meat, everyone who is clean [ceremonially] may eat of it.

²⁰But the one who eats of the flesh of the sacrifice of peace offerings that belong to the Lord when he is [ceremonially] unclean, that person shall be cut off from his people [deprived of the privileges of association with them].

ʳOr, *on the flat plate,* or, *slice*

New American Standard

29 'Every male among the priests may eat of it; it is most holy.

30 'But no sin offering of which any of the blood is brought into the tent of meeting to make atonement in the holy place shall be eaten; it shall be burned with fire.

The Priest's Part in the Offerings

7 'NOW THIS is the law of the guilt offering; it is most holy.

2 'In the place where they slay the burnt offering they are to slay the guilt offering, and he shall sprinkle its blood around on the altar.

3 'Then he shall offer from it all its fat: the fat tail and the fat that covers the entrails,

4 and the two kidneys with the fat that is on them, which is on the loins, and the lobe on the liver he shall remove with the kidneys.

5 'The priest shall offer them up in smoke on the altar as an offering by fire to the LORD; it is a guilt offering.

6 'Every male among the priests may eat of it. It shall be eaten in a holy place; it is most holy.

7 'The guilt offering is like the sin offering, there is one law for them; the priest who makes atonement with it shall have it.

8 'Also the priest who presents any man's burnt offering, that priest shall have for himself the skin of the burnt offering which he has presented.

9 'Likewise, every grain offering that is baked in the oven and everything prepared in a pan or on a griddle shall belong to the priest who presents it.

10 'Every grain offering, mixed with oil or dry, shall belong to all the sons of Aaron, to all alike.

11 ¶ 'Now this is the law of the sacrifice of peace offerings which shall be presented to the LORD.

12 'If he offers it by way of thanksgiving, then along with the sacrifice of thanksgiving he shall offer unleavened cakes mixed with oil, and unleavened wafers spread with oil, and cakes of *well* stirred fine flour mixed with oil.

13 'With the sacrifice of his peace offerings for thanksgiving, he shall present his offering with cakes of leavened bread.

14 'Of this he shall present one of every offering as a contribution to the LORD; it shall belong to the priest who sprinkles the blood of the peace offerings.

15 ¶ 'Now *as for* the flesh of the sacrifice of his thanksgiving peace offerings, it shall be eaten on the day of his offering; he shall not leave any of it over until morning.

16 'But if the sacrifice of his offering is a votive or a freewill offering, it shall be eaten on the day that he offers his sacrifice, and on the next day what is left of it may be eaten;

17 but what is left over from the flesh of the sacrifice on the third day shall be burned with fire.

18 'So if any of the flesh of the sacrifice of his peace offerings should *ever* be eaten on the third day, he who offers it will not be accepted, *and* it will not be reckoned to his *benefit*. It shall be an offensive thing, and the person who eats of it will bear his *own* iniquity.

19 ¶ 'Also the flesh that touches anything unclean shall not be eaten; it shall be burned with fire. As for *other* flesh, anyone who is clean may eat *such* flesh.

20 'But the person who eats the flesh of the sacrifice of peace offerings which belong to the LORD, in his uncleanness, that person shall be cut off from his people.

New International

pot is to be scoured and rinsed with water. 29 Any male in a priest's family may eat it; it is most holy. 30 But any sin offering whose blood is brought into the Tent of Meeting to make atonement in the Holy Place must not be eaten; it must be burned.

The Guilt Offering

7 " 'THESE ARE the regulations for the guilt offering, which is most holy: 2 The guilt offering is to be slaughtered in the place where the burnt offering is slaughtered, and its blood is to be sprinkled against the altar on all sides. 3 All its fat shall be offered: the fat tail and the fat that covers the inner parts, 4 both kidneys with the fat on them near the loins, and the covering of the liver, which is to be removed with the kidneys. 5 The priest shall burn them on the altar as an offering made to the LORD by fire. It is a guilt offering. 6 Any male in a priest's family may eat it, but it must be eaten in a holy place; it is most holy.

7 " 'The same law applies to both the sin offering and the guilt offering: They belong to the priest who makes atonement with them. 8 The priest who offers a burnt offering for anyone may keep its hide for himself. 9 Every grain offering baked in an oven or cooked in a pan or on a griddle belongs to the priest who offers it, 10 and every grain offering, whether mixed with oil or dry, belongs equally to all the sons of Aaron.

The Fellowship Offering

11 " 'These are the regulations for the fellowship offering*o* a person may present to the LORD:

12 " 'If he offers it as an expression of thankfulness, then along with this thank offering he is to offer cakes of bread made without yeast and mixed with oil, wafers made without yeast and spread with oil, and cakes of fine flour well-kneaded and mixed with oil. 13 Along with his fellowship offering of thanksgiving he is to present an offering with cakes of bread made with yeast. 14 He is to bring one of each kind as an offering, a contribution to the LORD; it belongs to the priest who sprinkles the blood of the fellowship offerings. 15 The meat of his fellowship offering of thanksgiving must be eaten on the day it is offered; he must leave none of it till morning.

16 " 'If, however, his offering is the result of a vow or is a freewill offering, the sacrifice shall be eaten on the day he offers it, but anything left over may be eaten on the next day. 17 Any meat of the sacrifice left over till the third day must be burned up. 18 If any meat of the fellowship offering is eaten on the third day, it will not be accepted. It will not be credited to the one who offered it, for it is impure; the person who eats any of it will be held responsible.

19 " 'Meat that touches anything ceremonially unclean must not be eaten; it must be burned up. As for other meat, anyone ceremonially clean may eat it. 20 But if anyone who is unclean eats any meat of the fellowship offering belonging to the LORD, that person must be cut off from his

---

o 11 Traditionally *peace offering*; also in verses 13-37

King James

21Moreover the soul that shall touch any unclean *thing, as* the uncleanness of man, or *any* unclean beast, or any abominable unclean *thing,* and eat of the flesh of the sacrifice of peace offerings, which *pertain* unto the LORD, even that soul shall be cut off from his people.

Forbidden portions

22 ¶ And the LORD spake unto Moses, saying,

23Speak unto the children of Israel, saying, Ye shall eat no manner of fat, of ox, or of sheep, or of goat.

24And the fat of the *[s]*beast that dieth of itself, and the fat of that which is torn with beasts, may be used in any other use: but ye shall in no wise eat of it.

25For whosoever eateth the fat of the beast, of which men offer an offering made by fire unto the LORD, even the soul that eateth *it* shall be cut off from his people.

26Moreover ye shall eat no manner of blood, *whether it be* of fowl or of beast, in any of your dwellings.

27Whatsoever soul *it be* that eateth any manner of blood, even that soul shall be cut off from his people.

The portion for priests

28 ¶ And the LORD spake unto Moses, saying,

29Speak unto the children of Israel, saying, He that offereth the sacrifice of his peace offerings unto the LORD shall bring his oblation unto the LORD of the sacrifice of his peace offerings.

30His own hands shall bring the offerings of the LORD made by fire, the fat with the breast, it shall he bring, that the breast may be waved *for* a wave offering before the LORD.

31And the priest shall burn the fat upon the altar: but the breast shall be Aaron's and his sons'.

32And the right shoulder shall ye give unto the priest *for* an heave offering of the sacrifices of your peace offerings.

33He among the sons of Aaron, that offereth the blood of the peace offerings, and the fat, shall have the right shoulder for *his* part.

34For the wave breast and the heave shoulder have I taken of the children of Israel from off the sacrifices of their peace offerings, and have given them unto Aaron the priest and unto his sons by a statute for ever from among the children of Israel.

35 ¶ This *is the portion* of the anointing of Aaron, and of the anointing of his sons, out of the offerings of the LORD made by fire, in the day *when* he presented them to minister unto the LORD in the priest's office;

36Which the LORD commanded to be given them of the children of Israel, in the day that he anointed them, *by* a statute for ever throughout their generations.

37This *is* the law of the burnt offering, of the meat offering, and of the sin offering, and of the trespass offering, and of the consecrations, and of the sacrifice of the peace offerings;

38Which the LORD commanded Moses in mount Sinai, in the day that he commanded the children of Israel to offer their oblations unto the LORD, in the wilderness of Sinai.

The anointing of priests

8 AND THE LORD spake unto Moses, saying,
2Take Aaron and his sons with him, and the garments, and the anointing oil, and a bullock for the sin offering, and two rams, and a basket of unleavened bread;

3And gather thou all the congregation together unto the door of the tabernacle of the congregation.

4And Moses did as the LORD commanded him; and the assembly was gathered together unto the door of the tabernacle of the congregation.

5And Moses said unto the congregation, This *is* the thing which the LORD commanded to be done.

[s] Heb. *carcase*

Amplified

21And if anyone touches any unclean thing—the uncleanness of man or an unclean beast or any unclean abomination—and then eats of the flesh of the sacrifice of the Lord's peace offerings, that person shall be cut off from his people.

22And the Lord said to Moses,

23Say to the Israelites, You shall eat no kind of fat, of ox, or sheep, or goat.

24The fat of the beast that dies of itself and the fat of one that is torn with beasts may be put to any other use, but under no circumstances are you to eat of it.

25For whoever eats the fat of the beast from which men offer an offering made by fire to the Lord, that person shall be cut off from his people.

26Moreover, you shall eat no blood of any kind, whether of bird or of beast, in any of your dwellings.

27Whoever eats any kind of blood, that person shall be cut off from his people.

28And the Lord said to Moses,

29Tell the Israelites, He who offers the sacrifice of his peace offerings to the Lord shall bring his offering to the Lord; from the sacrifice of his peace offerings

30He shall bring with his own hands the offerings made by fire to the Lord; he shall bring the fat with the breast, that the breast may be waved as a wave offering before the Lord.

31The priest shall burn the fat on the altar, but the breast shall be for Aaron and his sons.

32And the right thigh you shall give to the priest for an offering from the sacrifices of your peace offerings.

33The son of Aaron who offers the blood of the peace offerings and the fat shall have the right thigh for his portion.

34For I have taken the breast that was waved and the thigh that was offered from the Israelites, out of the sacrifices of their peace offerings, and have given them to Aaron the priest and to his sons as their perpetual due from the Israelites.

35This is the anointing portion of Aaron and his sons out of the offerings to the Lord made by fire on the day when they were presented to minister to the Lord in the priest's office.

36The Lord commanded this to be given them of the Israelites on the day when they were anointed. It is their portion perpetually throughout their generations.

37This is the law of the burnt offering, the cereal offering, the sin offering, the guilt *or* trespass offering, the consecration offering, and the sacrifice of peace offerings,

38Which the Lord ordered Moses on Mount Sinai on the day He commanded the Israelites to offer their sacrifices to the Lord, in the Wilderness of Sinai.

8 AND THE Lord said to Moses,
2Take Aaron and his sons with him, and the garments [symbols of their office], and the anointing oil, and the bull of the sin offering, and the two rams, and the basket of unleavened bread;

3And assemble all the congregation at the door of the Tent of Meeting.

4Moses did as the Lord commanded him, and the congregation was assembled at the door of the Tent of Meeting.

5Moses told the congregation, This is what the Lord has commanded to be done.

New American Standard

21 'When anyone touches anything unclean, whether human uncleanness, or an unclean animal, or any unclean *b*detestable thing, and eats of the flesh of the sacrifice of peace offerings which belong to the LORD, that person shall be cut off from his people.' "

22 ¶ Then the LORD spoke to Moses, saying,

23"Speak to the sons of Israel, saying, 'You shall not eat any fat *from* an ox, a sheep or a goat.

24 'Also the fat of *an animal* which dies and the fat of an animal torn *by beasts* may be put to any other use, but you must certainly not eat it.

25 'For whoever eats the fat of the animal from which an offering by fire is offered to the LORD, even the person who eats shall be cut off from his people.

26 'You are not to eat any blood, either of bird or animal, in any of your dwellings.

27 'Any person who eats any blood, even that person shall be cut off from his people.' "

28 ¶ Then the LORD spoke to Moses, saying,

29"Speak to the sons of Israel, saying, 'He who offers the sacrifice of his peace offerings to the LORD shall bring his offering to the LORD from the sacrifice of his peace offerings.

30 'His own hands are to bring offerings by fire to the LORD. He shall bring the fat with the breast, that the breast may be presented as a wave offering before the LORD.

31 'The priest shall offer up the fat in smoke on the altar, but the breast shall belong to Aaron and his sons.

32 'You shall give the right thigh to the priest as a contribution from the sacrifices of your peace offerings.

33 'The one among the sons of Aaron who offers the blood of the peace offerings and the fat, the right thigh shall be his as *his* portion.

34 'For I have taken the breast of the wave offering and the thigh of the contribution from the sons of Israel from the sacrifices of their peace offerings, and have given them to Aaron the priest and to his sons as *their* due forever from the sons of Israel.

35 ¶ 'This is that which is consecrated to Aaron and that which is consecrated to his sons from the offerings by fire to the LORD, in that day when he presented them to serve as priests to the LORD.

36 'These the LORD had commanded to be given them from the sons of Israel in the day that He anointed them. It is *their* due forever throughout their generations.' "

37 ¶ This is the law of the burnt offering, the grain offering and the sin offering and the guilt offering and the ordination offering and the sacrifice of peace offerings,

38 which the LORD commanded Moses at Mount Sinai in the day that He commanded the sons of Israel to present their offerings to the LORD in the wilderness of Sinai.

The Consecration of Aaron and His Sons

8 THEN THE LORD spoke to Moses, saying,

2"Take Aaron and his sons with him, and the garments and the anointing oil and the bull of the sin offering, and the two rams and the basket of unleavened bread,

3 and assemble all the congregation at the doorway of the tent of meeting."

4 So Moses did just as the LORD commanded him. When the congregation was assembled at the doorway of the tent of meeting,

5 Moses said to the congregation, "This is the thing which the LORD has commanded to do."

New International

people. 21If anyone touches something unclean—whether human uncleanness or an unclean animal or any unclean, detestable thing—and then eats any of the meat of the fellowship offering belonging to the LORD, that person must be cut off from his people.' "

Eating Fat and Blood Forbidden

22The LORD said to Moses, 23"Say to the Israelites: 'Do not eat any of the fat of cattle, sheep or goats. 24The fat of an animal found dead or torn by wild animals may be used for any other purpose, but you must not eat it. 25Anyone who eats the fat of an animal from which an offering by fire may be*p* made to the LORD must be cut off from his people. 26And wherever you live, you must not eat the blood of any bird or animal. 27If anyone eats blood, that person must be cut off from his people.' "

The Priests' Share

28The LORD said to Moses, 29"Say to the Israelites: 'Anyone who brings a fellowship offering to the LORD is to bring part of it as his sacrifice to the LORD. 30With his own hands he is to bring the offering made to the LORD by fire; he is to bring the fat, together with the breast, and wave the breast before the LORD as a wave offering. 31The priest shall burn the fat on the altar, but the breast belongs to Aaron and his sons. 32You are to give the right thigh of your fellowship offerings to the priest as a contribution. 33The son of Aaron who offers the blood and the fat of the fellowship offering shall have the right thigh as his share. 34From the fellowship offerings of the Israelites, I have taken the breast that is waved and the thigh that is presented and have given them to Aaron the priest and his sons as their regular share from the Israelites.' "

35This is the portion of the offerings made to the LORD by fire that were allotted to Aaron and his sons on the day they were presented to serve the LORD as priests. 36On the day they were anointed, the LORD commanded that the Israelites give this to them as their regular share for the generations to come.

37These, then, are the regulations for the burnt offering, the grain offering, the sin offering, the guilt offering, the ordination offering and the fellowship offering, 38which the LORD gave Moses on Mount Sinai on the day he commanded the Israelites to bring their offerings to the LORD, in the Desert of Sinai.

The Ordination of Aaron and His Sons

8 THE LORD said to Moses, 2"Bring Aaron and his sons, their garments, the anointing oil, the bull for the sin offering, the two rams and the basket containing bread made without yeast, 3and gather the entire assembly at the entrance to the Tent of Meeting." 4Moses did as the LORD commanded him, and the assembly gathered at the entrance to the Tent of Meeting.

5Moses said to the assembly, "This is what the LORD has

---

b Some mss read *swarming thing*   *p* 25 Or *fire is*

King James

Amplified

⁶And Moses brought Aaron and his sons, and washed them with water.

⁷And he put upon him the coat, and girded him with the girdle, and clothed him with the robe, and put the ephod upon him, and he girded him with the curious girdle of the ephod, and bound *it* unto him therewith.

⁸And he put the breastplate upon him: also he put in the breastplate the Urim and the Thummim.

⁹And he put the mitre upon his head; also upon the mitre, *even* upon his forefront, did he put the golden plate, the holy crown; as the LORD commanded Moses.

¹⁰And Moses took the anointing oil, and anointed the tabernacle and all that *was* therein, and sanctified them.

¹¹And he sprinkled thereof upon the altar seven times, and anointed the altar and all his vessels, both the laver and his foot, to sanctify them.

¹²And he poured of the anointing oil upon Aaron's head, and anointed him, to sanctify him.

¹³And Moses brought Aaron's sons, and put coats upon them, and girded them with girdles, and ¹put bonnets upon them; as the LORD commanded Moses.

¹⁴And he brought the bullock for the sin offering: and Aaron and his sons laid their hands upon the head of the bullock for the sin offering.

¹⁵And he slew *it;* and Moses took the blood, and put *it* upon the horns of the altar round about with his finger, and purified the altar, and poured the blood at the bottom of the altar, and sanctified it, to make reconciliation upon it.

¹⁶And he took all the fat that *was* upon the inwards, and the caul *above* the liver, and the two kidneys, and their fat, and Moses burned *it* upon the altar.

¹⁷But the bullock, and his hide, his flesh, and his dung, he burnt with fire without the camp; as the LORD commanded Moses.

¹⁸ ¶ And he brought the ram for the burnt offering: and Aaron and his sons laid their hands upon the head of the ram.

¹⁹And he killed *it;* and Moses sprinkled the blood upon the altar round about.

²⁰And he cut the ram into pieces; and Moses burnt the head, and the pieces, and the fat.

²¹And he washed the inwards and the legs in water; and Moses burnt the whole ram upon the altar: it *was* a burnt sacrifice for a sweet savour, *and* an offering made by fire unto the LORD; as the LORD commanded Moses.

²² ¶ And he brought the other ram, the ram of consecration: and Aaron and his sons laid their hands upon the head of the ram.

²³And he slew *it;* and Moses took of the blood of it, and put *it* upon the tip of Aaron's right ear, and upon the thumb of his right hand, and upon the great toe of his right foot.

²⁴And he brought Aaron's sons, and Moses put of the blood upon the tip of their right ear, and upon the thumbs of their right hands, and upon the great toes of their right feet: and Moses sprinkled the blood upon the altar round about.

²⁵And he took the fat, and the rump, and all the fat that *was* upon the inwards, and the caul *above* the liver, and the two kidneys, and their fat, and the right shoulder:

²⁶And out of the basket of unleavened bread, that *was* before the LORD, he took one unleavened cake, and a cake of oiled bread, and one wafer, and put *them* on the fat, and upon the right shoulder:

²⁷And he put all upon Aaron's hands, and upon his sons' hands, and waved them *for* a wave offering before the LORD.

²⁸And Moses took them from off their hands, and burnt *them* on the altar upon the burnt offering: they *were* consecrations for a sweet savour: it *is* an offering made by fire unto the LORD.

⁶Moses brought Aaron and his sons and washed them with water.

⁷He put on Aaron the long undertunic, girded him with the long sash, clothed him with the robe, put the ephod (an upper vestment) upon him, and girded him with the skillfully woven cords attached to the ephod, binding it to him.

⁸And Moses put upon Aaron the breastplate; also he put in the breastplate the Urim and the Thummim [articles upon which the high priest put his hand when seeking the divine will concerning the nation].

⁹And he put the turban *or* miter on his head; on it, in front, Moses put the shining gold plate, the holy diadem, as the Lord commanded him.

¹⁰And Moses took the anointing oil and anointed the tabernacle and all that was in it, and consecrated them.

¹¹And he sprinkled some of the oil on the altar seven times and anointed the altar and all its utensils, and the laver and its base, to consecrate them.

¹²And he poured some of the anointing oil upon Aaron's head and anointed him to consecrate him.

¹³And Moses brought Aaron's sons and put undertunics on them and girded them with sashes and wound turbans on them, as the Lord commanded Moses.

¹⁴Then he brought the bull of the sin offering, and Aaron and his sons laid their hands on the head of the bull of the sin offering.

¹⁵Moses killed it and took the blood and put it on the horns of the altar round about with his finger and poured the blood at the base of the altar and purified and consecrated the altar to make atonement for it.

¹⁶He took all the fat that was on the entrails, and the lobe of the liver, and the two kidneys with their fat, and Moses burned them on the altar.

¹⁷But the bull [the sin offering] and its hide, its flesh, and its dung he burned with fire outside the camp, as the Lord commanded Moses.

¹⁸He brought the ram for the burnt offering, and Aaron and his sons laid their hands on the head of the ram.

¹⁹And Moses killed it and dashed the blood upon the altar round about.

²⁰He cut the ram into pieces and Moses burned the head, the pieces, and the fat.

²¹And he washed the entrails and the legs in water; then Moses burned the whole ram on the altar; it was a burnt sacrifice, for a sweet *and* satisfying fragrance, an offering made by fire to the Lord, as the Lord commanded Moses.

²²And he brought the other ram, the ram of consecration *and* ordination, and Aaron and his sons laid their hands upon the head of the ram.

²³And Moses killed it and took some of its blood and put it on the tip of Aaron's right ear, and on the thumb of his right hand, and on the great toe of his right foot.

²⁴And he brought Aaron's sons and Moses put some of the blood on the tips of their right ears, and the thumbs of their right hands, and the great toes of their right feet; and Moses dashed the blood upon the altar round about.

²⁵And he took the fat, the fat tail, all the fat that was on the entrails, the lobe of the liver, and the two kidneys and their fat, and the right thigh;

²⁶And out of the basket of unleavened bread, that was before the Lord, he took one unleavened cake, a cake of oiled bread, and one wafer and put them on the fat and on the right thigh;

²⁷And he put all these in Aaron's hands and his sons' hands and waved them for a wave offering before the Lord.

²⁸Then Moses took these things from their hands and burned them on the altar with the burnt offering as an ordination offering, for a sweet *and* satisfying fragrance, an offering made by fire to the Lord.

¹Heb. *bound*

New American Standard

6 ¶ Then Moses had Aaron and his sons come near and washed them with water.

7. He put the tunic on him and girded him with the sash, and clothed him with the robe and put the ephod on him; and he girded him with the artistic band of the ephod, with which he tied *it* to him.

8 He then placed the breastpiece on him, and in the breastpiece he put *c*the Urim and the Thummim.

9 He also placed the turban on his head, and on the turban, at its front, he placed the golden plate, the holy crown, just as the LORD had commanded Moses.

10 ¶ Moses then took the anointing oil and anointed the tabernacle and all that was in it, and consecrated them.

11 He sprinkled some of it on the altar seven times and anointed the altar and all its utensils, and the basin and its stand, to consecrate them.

12 Then he poured some of the anointing oil on Aaron's head and anointed him, to consecrate him.

13 Next Moses had Aaron's sons come near and clothed them with tunics, and girded them with sashes and bound caps on them, just as the LORD had commanded Moses.

14 ¶ Then he brought the bull of the sin offering, and Aaron and his sons laid their hands on the head of the bull of the sin offering.

15 Next Moses slaughtered *it* and took the blood and with his finger put *some of it* around on the horns of the altar, and purified the altar. Then he poured out *the rest of* the blood at the base of the altar and consecrated it, to make atonement for it.

16 He also took all the fat that was on the entrails and the lobe of the liver, and the two kidneys and their fat; and Moses offered it up in smoke on the altar.

17 But the bull and its hide and its flesh and its refuse he burned in the fire outside the camp, just as the LORD had commanded Moses.

18 ¶ Then he presented the ram of the burnt offering, and Aaron and his sons laid their hands on the head of the ram.

19 Moses slaughtered *it* and sprinkled the blood around on the altar.

20 When he had cut the ram into its pieces, Moses offered up the head and the pieces and the suet in smoke.

21 After he had washed the entrails and the legs with water, Moses offered up the whole ram in smoke on the altar. It was a burnt offering for a soothing aroma; it was an offering by fire to the LORD, just as the LORD had commanded Moses.

22 ¶ Then he presented the second ram, the ram of *d*ordination, and Aaron and his sons laid their hands on the head of the ram.

23 Moses slaughtered *it* and took some of its blood and put it on the lobe of Aaron's right ear, and on the thumb of his right hand and on the big toe of his right foot.

24 He also had Aaron's sons come near; and Moses put some of the blood on the lobe of their right ear, and on the thumb of their right hand and on the big toe of their right foot. Moses then sprinkled *the rest of* the blood around on the altar.

25 He took the fat, and the fat tail, and all the fat that was on the entrails, and the lobe of the liver and the two kidneys and their fat and the right thigh.

26 From the basket of unleavened bread that was before the LORD, he took one unleavened cake and one cake of bread *mixed with* oil and one wafer, and placed *them* on the portions of fat and on the right thigh.

27 He then put all *these* on the hands of Aaron and on the hands of his sons and presented them as a wave offering before the LORD.

28 Then Moses took them from their hands and offered them up in smoke on the altar with the burnt offering. They were an ordination offering for a soothing aroma; it was an offering by fire to the LORD.

New International

commanded to be done." 6Then Moses brought Aaron and his sons forward and washed them with water. 7He put the tunic on Aaron, tied the sash around him, clothed him with the robe and put the ephod on him. He also tied the ephod to him by its skillfully woven waistband; so it was fastened on him. 8He placed the breastpiece on him and put the Urim and Thummim in the breastpiece. 9Then he placed the turban on Aaron's head and set the gold plate, the sacred diadem, on the front of it, as the LORD commanded Moses.

10Then Moses took the anointing oil and anointed the tabernacle and everything in it, and so consecrated them. 11He sprinkled some of the oil on the altar seven times, anointing the altar and all its utensils and the basin with its stand, to consecrate them. 12He poured some of the anointing oil on Aaron's head and anointed him to consecrate him. 13Then he brought Aaron's sons forward, put tunics on them, tied sashes around them and put headbands on them, as the LORD commanded Moses.

14He then presented the bull for the sin offering, and Aaron and his sons laid their hands on its head. 15Moses slaughtered the bull and took some of the blood, and with his finger he put it on all the horns of the altar to purify the altar. He poured out the rest of the blood at the base of the altar. So he consecrated it to make atonement for it. 16Moses also took all the fat around the inner parts, the covering of the liver, and both kidneys and their fat, and burned it on the altar. 17But the bull with its hide and its flesh and its offal he burned up outside the camp, as the LORD commanded Moses.

18He then presented the ram for the burnt offering, and Aaron and his sons laid their hands on its head. 19Then Moses slaughtered the ram and sprinkled the blood against the altar on all sides. 20He cut the ram into pieces and burned the head, the pieces and the fat. 21He washed the inner parts and the legs with water and burned the whole ram on the altar as a burnt offering, a pleasing aroma, an offering made to the LORD by fire, as the LORD commanded Moses.

22He then presented the other ram, the ram for the ordination, and Aaron and his sons laid their hands on its head. 23Moses slaughtered the ram and took some of its blood and put it on the lobe of Aaron's right ear, on the thumb of his right hand and on the big toe of his right foot. 24Moses also brought Aaron's sons forward and put some of the blood on the lobes of their right ears, on the thumbs of their right hands and on the big toes of their right feet. Then he sprinkled blood against the altar on all sides. 25He took the fat, the fat tail, all the fat around the inner parts, the covering of the liver, both kidneys and their fat and the right thigh. 26Then from the basket of bread made without yeast, which was before the LORD, he took a cake of bread, and one made with oil, and a wafer; he put these on the fat portions and on the right thigh. 27He put all these in the hands of Aaron and his sons and waved them before the LORD as a wave offering. 28Then Moses took them from their hands and burned them on the altar on top of the burnt offering as an ordination offering, a pleasing aroma,

c I.e. the lights and perfections   *d* Lit *filling,* and so throughout
the ch

King James

29And Moses took the breast, and waved it *for* a wave offering before the LORD: *for* of the ram of consecration it was Moses' part; as the LORD commanded Moses.

30And Moses took of the anointing oil, and of the blood which *was* upon the altar, and sprinkled *it* upon Aaron, *and* upon his garments, and upon his sons, and upon his sons' garments with him; and sanctified Aaron, *and* his garments, and his sons, and his sons' garments with him.

31 ¶ And Moses said unto Aaron and to his sons, Boil the flesh *at* the door of the tabernacle of the congregation: and there eat it with the bread that *is* in the basket of consecrations, as I commanded, saying, Aaron and his sons shall eat it.

32And that which remaineth of the flesh and of the bread shall ye burn with fire.

33And ye shall not go out of the door of the tabernacle of the congregation *in* seven days, until the days of your consecration be at an end: for seven days shall he consecrate you.

34As he hath done this day, *so* the LORD hath commanded to do, to make an atonement for you.

35Therefore shall ye abide *at* the door of the tabernacle of the congregation day and night seven days, and keep the charge of the LORD, that ye die not: for so I am commanded.

36So Aaron and his sons did all things which the LORD commanded by the hand of Moses.

The offerings of Aaron

9 AND IT came to pass on the eighth day, *that* Moses called Aaron and his sons, and the elders of Israel;

2And he said unto Aaron, Take thee a young calf for a sin offering, and a ram for a burnt offering, without blemish, and offer *them* before the LORD.

3And unto the children of Israel thou shalt speak, saying, Take ye a kid of the goats for a sin offering; and a calf and a lamb, *both* of the first year, without blemish, for a burnt offering;

4Also a bullock and a ram for peace offerings, to sacrifice before the LORD; and a meat offering mingled with oil: for today the LORD will appear unto you.

5 ¶ And they brought *that* which Moses commanded before the tabernacle of the congregation: and all the congregation drew near and stood before the LORD.

6And Moses said, This *is* the thing which the LORD commanded that ye should do: and the glory of the LORD shall appear unto you.

7And Moses said unto Aaron, Go unto the altar, and offer thy sin offering, and thy burnt offering, and make an atonement for thyself, and for the people: and offer the offering of the people, and make an atonement for them; as the LORD commanded.

8 ¶ Aaron therefore went unto the altar, and slew the calf of the sin offering, which *was* for himself.

9And the sons of Aaron brought the blood unto him: and he dipped his finger in the blood, and put *it* upon the horns of the altar, and poured out the blood at the bottom of the altar:

10But the fat, and the kidneys, and the caul above the liver of the sin offering, he burnt upon the altar; as the LORD commanded Moses.

11And the flesh and the hide he burnt with fire without the camp.

Amplified

29And Moses took the breast and waved it for a wave offering before the Lord; for of the ram of consecration *and* ordination it was Moses' portion, as the Lord commanded Moses.

30And Moses took some of the anointing oil and some of the blood which was on the altar and sprinkled it on Aaron and his garments, and upon his sons and their garments also; so Moses consecrated Aaron and his garments, and his sons and his sons' garments.

31And Moses said to Aaron and his sons, Boil the flesh at the door of the Tent of Meeting and there eat it with the bread that is in the basket of consecration *and* ordination, as I commanded, saying, Aaron and his sons shall eat it.

32And what remains of the flesh and of the bread you shall burn with fire.

33And you shall not go out of the door of the Tent of Meeting for seven days, until the days of your consecration *and* ordination are ended; for it will take seven days to consecrate *and* ordain you.

34As has been done this day, so the Lord has commanded to do for your atonement.

35At the door of the Tent of Meeting you shall remain day and night for seven days, eedoing what the Lord has charged you to do, that you die not; for so I am commanded.

36So Aaron and his sons did all the things which the Lord commanded through Moses.

9 ON THE eighth day Moses called Aaron and his sons and the elders of Israel;

2And he said to Aaron, Take a young calf for a sin offering and a ram for a burnt offering, [each] without blemish, and offer them before the Lord. [Heb. 10:10–12.]

3And say to the Israelites, Take a male goat for a sin offering, and a calf and a lamb, both a year old, without blemish, for a burnt offering,

4Also a bull and a ram for peace offerings to sacrifice before the Lord, and a cereal offering mixed with oil, for today the Lord will appear to you.

5They brought before the Tent of Meeting what Moses [had] commanded; all the congregation drew near and stood before the Lord.

6And Moses said, This is the thing which the Lord commanded you to do, and the glory of the Lord will appear to you.

7And Moses said to Aaron, Draw near to the altar and offer your sin offering and your burnt offering and make atonement for yourself and for the people; and offer the offering of the people and make atonement for them, as the Lord commanded. [Heb. 5:1–5; 7:27.]

8So Aaron drew near to the altar and killed the calf of the sin offering, which was designated for himself.

9The sons of Aaron presented the blood to him; he dipped his finger in the blood and put it on the horns of the altar and poured out the blood at the altar's base;

10But the fat, the kidneys, and the lobe of the liver from the sin offering he burned on the altar, as the Lord had commanded Moses.

11And the flesh and the hide Aaron burned with fire outside the camp.

eeWe have, every one of us, a charge to keep, an eternal God to glorify, an immortal soul to provide for, needful duty to be done, our generation to serve; and it must be our daily care to keep this charge, for it is the charge of the Lord our Master (Matthew Henry, *Commentary on the Holy Bible*). The laws contained in this book, for the most part ceremonial, had an important spiritual bearing, the study of which is highly instructive (Robert Jamieson, A.R. Fausset and David Brown, *A Commentary*). The Scripture references recorded within the text are intended to be a guide to its spiritual implications.

New American Standard

29 Moses also took the breast and presented it for a wave offering before the LORD; it was Moses' portion of the ram of ordination, just as the LORD had commanded Moses.

30 ¶ So Moses took some of the anointing oil and some of the blood which was on the altar and sprinkled it on Aaron, on his garments, on his sons, and on the garments of his sons with him; and he consecrated Aaron, his garments, and his sons, and the garments of his sons with him.

31 ¶ Then Moses said to Aaron and to his sons, "Boil the flesh at the doorway of the tent of meeting, and eat it there together with the bread which is in the basket of the ordination offering, just as I commanded, saying, 'Aaron and his sons shall eat it.'

32 "The remainder of the flesh and of the bread you shall burn in the fire.

33 "You shall not go outside the doorway of the tent of meeting for seven days, until the day that the period of your ordination is fulfilled; for he will ordain you through seven days.

34 "The LORD has commanded to do as has been done this day, to make atonement on your behalf.

35 "At the doorway of the tent of meeting, moreover, you shall remain day and night for seven days and keep the charge of the LORD, so that you will not die, for so I have been commanded."

36 Thus Aaron and his sons did all the things which the LORD had commanded through Moses.

Aaron Offers Sacrifices

9 NOW IT came about on the eighth day that Moses called Aaron and his sons and the elders of Israel; 2 and he said to Aaron, "Take for yourself a calf, a bull, for a sin offering and a ram for a burnt offering, both without defect, and offer *them* before the LORD.

3 "Then to the sons of Israel you shall speak, saying, 'Take a male goat for a sin offering, and a calf and a lamb, both one year old, without defect, for a burnt offering, 4 and an ox and a ram for peace offerings, to sacrifice before the LORD, and a grain offering mixed with oil; for today the LORD will appear to you.' "

5 So they took what Moses had commanded to the front of the tent of meeting, and the whole congregation came near and stood before the LORD.

6 Moses said, "This is the thing which the LORD has commanded you to do, that the glory of the LORD may appear to you."

7 Moses then said to Aaron, "Come near to the altar and offer your sin offering and your burnt offering, that you may make atonement for yourself and for the people; then make the offering for the people, that you may make atonement for them, just as the LORD has commanded."

8 ¶ So Aaron came near to the altar and slaughtered the calf of the sin offering which was for himself.

9 Aaron's sons presented the blood to him; and he dipped his finger in the blood and put *some* on the horns of the altar, and poured out *the rest of* the blood at the base of the altar.

10 The fat and the kidneys and the lobe of the liver of the sin offering, he then offered up in smoke on the altar just as the LORD had commanded Moses.

11 The flesh and the skin, however, he burned with fire outside the camp.

New International

an offering made to the LORD by fire. 29 He also took the breast—Moses' share of the ordination ram—and waved it before the LORD as a wave offering, as the LORD commanded Moses.

30 Then Moses took some of the anointing oil and some of the blood from the altar and sprinkled them on Aaron and his garments and on his sons and their garments. So he consecrated Aaron and his garments and his sons and their garments.

31 Moses then said to Aaron and his sons, "Cook the meat at the entrance to the Tent of Meeting and eat it there with the bread from the basket of ordination offerings, as I commanded, saying,*q* 'Aaron and his sons are to eat it.'

32 Then burn up the rest of the meat and the bread. 33 Do not leave the entrance to the Tent of Meeting for seven days, until the days of your ordination are completed, for your ordination will last seven days. 34 What has been done today was commanded by the LORD to make atonement for you. 35 You must stay at the entrance to the Tent of Meeting day and night for seven days and do what the LORD requires, so you will not die; for that is what I have been commanded." 36 So Aaron and his sons did everything the LORD commanded through Moses.

The Priests Begin Their Ministry

9 ON THE eighth day Moses summoned Aaron and his sons and the elders of Israel. 2 He said to Aaron, "Take a bull calf for your sin offering and a ram for your burnt offering, both without defect, and present them before the LORD. 3 Then say to the Israelites: 'Take a male goat for a sin offering, a calf and a lamb—both a year old and without defect—for a burnt offering, 4 and an ox*r* and a ram for a fellowship offering*s* to sacrifice before the LORD, together with a grain offering mixed with oil. For today the LORD will appear to you.' "

5 They took the things Moses commanded to the front of the Tent of Meeting, and the entire assembly came near and stood before the LORD. 6 Then Moses said, "This is what the LORD has commanded you to do, so that the glory of the LORD may appear to you."

7 Moses said to Aaron, "Come to the altar and sacrifice your sin offering and your burnt offering and make atonement for yourself and the people; sacrifice the offering that is for the people and make atonement for them, as the LORD has commanded."

8 So Aaron came to the altar and slaughtered the calf as a sin offering for himself. 9 His sons brought the blood to him, and he dipped his finger into the blood and put it on the horns of the altar; the rest of the blood he poured out at the base of the altar. 10 On the altar he burned the fat, the kidneys and the covering of the liver from the sin offering, as the LORD commanded Moses; 11 the flesh and the hide he burned up outside the camp.

q 31 Or *I was commanded:*   *r 4* The Hebrew word can include both male and female; also in verses 18 and 19.
s 4 Traditionally *peace offering;* also in verses 18 and 22

King James

12And he slew the burnt offering; and Aaron's sons presented unto him the blood, which he sprinkled round about upon the altar.

13And they presented the burnt offering unto him, with the pieces thereof, and the head: and he burnt *them* upon the altar.

14And he did wash the inwards and the legs, and burnt *them* upon the burnt offering on the altar.

15 ¶ And he brought the people's offering, and took the goat, which *was* the sin offering for the people, and slew it, and offered it for sin, as the first.

16And he brought the burnt offering, and offered it according to the *u*manner.

17And he brought the meat offering, and *v*took an handful thereof, and burnt *it* upon the altar, beside the burnt sacrifice of the morning.

18He slew also the bullock and the ram *for* a sacrifice of peace offerings, which *was* for the people: and Aaron's sons presented unto him the blood, which he sprinkled upon the altar round about,

19And the fat of the bullock and of the ram, the rump, and that which covereth *the inwards,* and the kidneys, and the caul *above* the liver:

20And they put the fat upon the breasts, and he burnt the fat upon the altar:

21And the breasts and the right shoulder Aaron waved *for* a wave offering before the LORD; as Moses commanded.

22And Aaron lifted up his hand toward the people, and blessed them, and came down from offering of the sin offering, and the burnt offering, and peace offerings.

23And Moses and Aaron went into the tabernacle of the congregation, and came out, and blessed the people: and the glory of the LORD appeared unto all the people.

24And there came a fire out from before the LORD, and consumed upon the altar the burnt offering and the fat: *which* when all the people saw, they shouted, and fell on their faces.

The death of Nadab and Abihu

10 AND NADAB and Abihu, the sons of Aaron, took either of them his censer, and put fire therein, and put incense thereon, and offered strange fire before the LORD, which he commanded them not.

2And there went out fire from the LORD, and devoured them, and they died before the LORD.

3Then Moses said unto Aaron, This *is it* that the LORD spake, saying, I will be sanctified in them that come nigh me, and before all the people I will be glorified. And Aaron held his peace.

Amplified

12He killed the burnt offering, and Aaron's sons delivered to him the blood, which he dashed round about upon the altar.

13And they brought the burnt offering to him piece by piece, and the head, and Aaron burned them upon the altar.

14And he washed the entrails and the legs and burned them with the burnt offering on the altar.

15Then Aaron presented the people's offering, and took the goat of the sin offering which was for the people and killed it and offered it for sin as he did the first sin offering. [Heb. 2:16, 17.]

16And he presented the burnt offering and offered it according to the ordinance.

17And Aaron presented the cereal offering and took a handful of it and burned it on the altar in addition to the burnt offering of the morning.

18He also killed the bull and the ram, the sacrifice of peace offerings, for the people; and Aaron's sons presented to him the blood, which he dashed upon the altar round about,

19And the fat of the bull and of the ram, the fat tail and that which covers the entrails, and the kidneys, and the lobe of the liver.

20And they put the fat upon the breasts, and Aaron burned the fat upon the altar;

21But the breasts and the right thigh Aaron waved for a wave offering before the Lord, as Moses commanded.

22Then Aaron lifted his hands toward the people and blessed them, and came down [from the altar] after offering the sin offering, the burnt offering, and the peace offerings.

23Moses and Aaron went into the Tent of Meeting, and when they came out they blessed the people, and the glory of the Lord [the Shekinah cloud] appeared to all the people [as promised]. [Lev. 9:6.]

24Then there came a fire out from before the Lord and consumed the burnt offering and the fat on the altar; and when all the people saw it, they shouted and fell on their faces.

10 AND NADAB and Abihu, the sons of Aaron, each took his censer and put fire in it, and put incense on it, and offered strange *and* unholy fire before the Lord, as He had not commanded them.

2And there came forth fire from before the Lord and killed them, and they died before the Lord.

3Then Moses said to Aaron, This is what the Lord meant when He said, I *f*[and My will, not their own] will be acknowledged as hallowed by those who come near Me, and before all the people I will be honored. And Aaron said nothing.

*f*Perhaps few believers have ever identified themselves with Nadab and Abihu, and yet few, if any, of us have not done exactly what they did in principle. Their sin, which God took so seriously and which proved fatal to them, was not a mere matter of failing to obey the letter of God's law for priests. Their inexcusable folly was in trying to please the Lord **their** way instead of **His** way. Who of us cannot recognize himself as the offerer of this prayer, with only the details lacking: "O Lord, make me rich! Then I will make large donations to Your interests!" Yet our very poverty may be the means to the end which He has in love and wisdom planned for us, the ultimate purpose of our creation, perhaps, which substitution of our will for His will would utterly defeat. No wonder God removed Nadab and Abihu from the earth! They, like ourselves, had acted like the child of a great painter who attempted to work on his father's priceless canvas instead of on the tablet assigned to him. They, like the child, were banished from the father's presence. And every believer does well to recognize the importance of being entirely surrendered to "God's will; nothing more; nothing less; nothing else; at any cost." And that does not mean first making an unholy alliance in marriage, or in business, or in thought, and then adjusting it to God's will. Remember Nadab and Abihu, who "offered strange *and* unholy fire before the Lord." It does not pay.

*u*Or, *ordinance*   *v*Heb. *filled his hand out of it*

New American Standard

12 ¶ Then he slaughtered the burnt offering; and Aaron's sons handed the blood to him and he sprinkled it around on the altar.

13 They handed the burnt offering to him in pieces, with the head, and he offered *them* up in smoke on the altar.

14 He also washed the entrails and the legs, and offered *them* up in smoke with the burnt offering on the altar.

15 ¶ Then he presented the people's offering, and took the goat of the sin offering which was for the people, and slaughtered it and offered it for sin, like the first.

16 He also presented the burnt offering, and offered it according to the ordinance.

17 Next he presented the grain offering, and filled his hand with some of it and offered *it* up in smoke on the altar, besides the burnt offering of the morning.

18 ¶ Then he slaughtered the ox and the ram, the sacrifice of peace offerings which was for the people; and Aaron's sons handed the blood to him and he sprinkled it around on the altar.

19 As for the portions of fat from the ox and from the ram, the fat tail, and the *fat* covering, and the kidneys and the lobe of the liver,

20 they now placed the portions of fat on the breasts; and he offered them up in smoke on the altar.

21 But the breasts and the right thigh Aaron presented as a wave offering before the LORD, just as Moses had commanded.

22 ¶ Then Aaron lifted up his hands toward the people and blessed them, and he stepped down after making the sin offering and the burnt offering and the peace offerings.

23 Moses and Aaron went into the tent of meeting. When they came out and blessed the people, the glory of the LORD appeared to all the people.

24 Then fire came out from before the LORD and consumed the burnt offering and the portions of fat on the altar; and when all the people saw *it,* they shouted and fell on their faces.

The Sin of Nadab and Abihu

10 NOW NADAB and Abihu, the sons of Aaron, took their respective firepans, and after putting fire in them, placed incense on it and offered strange fire before the LORD, which He had not commanded them.

2 And fire came out from the presence of the LORD and consumed them, and they died before the LORD.

3 Then Moses said to Aaron, "It is what the LORD spoke, saying,
'By those who come near Me I will be treated as holy,
And before all the people I will be honored.' "
So Aaron, therefore, kept silent.

New International

12Then he slaughtered the burnt offering. His sons handed him the blood, and he sprinkled it against the altar on all sides. 13They handed him the burnt offering piece by piece, including the head, and he burned them on the altar. 14He washed the inner parts and the legs and burned them on top of the burnt offering on the altar.

15Aaron then brought the offering that was for the people. He took the goat for the people's sin offering and slaughtered it and offered it for a sin offering as he did with the first one.

16He brought the burnt offering and offered it in the prescribed way. 17He also brought the grain offering, took a handful of it and burned it on the altar in addition to the morning's burnt offering.

18He slaughtered the ox and the ram as the fellowship offering for the people. His sons handed him the blood, and he sprinkled it against the altar on all sides. 19But the fat portions of the ox and the ram—the fat tail, the layer of fat, the kidneys and the covering of the liver— 20these they laid on the breasts, and then Aaron burned the fat on the altar. 21Aaron waved the breasts and the right thigh before the LORD as a wave offering, as Moses commanded.

22Then Aaron lifted his hands toward the people and blessed them. And having sacrificed the sin offering, the burnt offering and the fellowship offering, he stepped down.

23Moses and Aaron then went into the Tent of Meeting. When they came out, they blessed the people; and the glory of the LORD appeared to all the people. 24Fire came out from the presence of the LORD and consumed the burnt offering and the fat portions on the altar. And when all the people saw it, they shouted for joy and fell facedown.

The Death of Nadab and Abihu

10 AARON'S SONS Nadab and Abihu took their censers, put fire in them and added incense; and they offered unauthorized fire before the LORD, contrary to his command. 2So fire came out from the presence of the LORD and consumed them, and they died before the LORD. 3Moses then said to Aaron, "This is what the LORD spoke of when he said:

" 'Among those who approach me
I will show myself holy;
in the sight of all the people
I will be honored.' "

Aaron remained silent.

King James

4And Moses called Mishael and Elzaphan, the sons of Uzziel the uncle of Aaron, and said unto them, Come near, carry your brethren from before the sanctuary out of the camp.

5So they went near, and carried them in their coats out of the camp; as Moses had said.

6And Moses said unto Aaron, and unto Eleazar and unto Ithamar, his sons, Uncover not your heads, neither rend your clothes; lest ye die, and lest wrath come upon all the people: but let your brethren, the whole house of Israel, bewail the burning which the LORD hath kindled.

7And ye shall not go out from the door of the tabernacle of the congregation, lest ye die: for the anointing oil of the LORD is upon you. And they did according to the word of Moses.

8 ¶ And the LORD spake unto Aaron, saying,

9Do not drink wine nor strong drink, thou, nor thy sons with thee, when ye go into the tabernacle of the congregation, lest ye die: it shall be a statute for ever throughout your generations:

10And that ye may put difference between holy and unholy, and between unclean and clean;

11And that ye may teach the children of Israel all the statutes which the LORD hath spoken unto them by the hand of Moses.

12 ¶ And Moses spake unto Aaron, and unto Eleazar and unto Ithamar, his sons that were left, Take the meat offering that remaineth of the offerings of the LORD made by fire, and eat it without leaven beside the altar: for it is most holy:

13And ye shall eat it in the holy place, because it is thy due, and thy sons' due, of the sacrifices of the LORD made by fire: for so I am commanded.

14And the wave breast and heave shoulder shall ye eat in a clean place; thou, and thy sons, and thy daughters with thee: for they be thy due, and thy sons' due, which are given out of the sacrifices of peace offerings of the children of Israel.

15The heave shoulder and the wave breast shall they bring with the offerings made by fire of the fat, to wave it for a wave offering before the LORD; and it shall be thine, and thy sons' with thee, by a statute for ever; as the LORD hath commanded.

16 ¶ And Moses diligently sought the goat of the sin offering, and, behold, it was burnt: and he was angry with Eleazar and Ithamar, the sons of Aaron which were left alive, saying,

17Wherefore have ye not eaten the sin offering in the holy place, seeing it is most holy, and God hath given it you to bear the iniquity of the congregation, to make atonement for them before the LORD?

18Behold, the blood of it was not brought in within the holy place: ye should indeed have eaten it in the holy place, as I commanded.

19And Aaron said unto Moses, Behold, this day have they offered their sin offering and their burnt offering before the LORD; and such things have befallen me: and if I had eaten the sin offering today, should it have been accepted in the sight of the LORD?

20And when Moses heard that, he was content.

Amplified

4Moses called Mishael and Elzaphan, sons of Uzziel uncle of Aaron, and said to them, Come near, carry your brethren from before the sanctuary out of the camp.

5So they drew near and carried them in their undertunics [stripped of their priestly vestments] out of the camp, as Moses had said.

6And Moses said to Aaron and Eleazar and Ithamar, his sons [the father and brothers of the two priests whom God had slain for offering false fire], Do not uncover your heads or let your hair go loose or tear your clothes, lest you die [also] and lest God's wrath should come upon all the congregation; but let your brethren, the whole house of Israel, bewail the burning which the Lord has kindled.

7And you shall not go out from the door of the Tent of Meeting, lest you die, for the Lord's anointing oil is upon you. And they did according to Moses' word.

8And the Lord said to Aaron,

9Do not drink wine or strong drink, you or your sons, when you go into the Tent of Meeting, lest you die; it shall be a statute forever in all your generations.

10You shall make a distinction and recognize a difference between the holy and the common or unholy, and between the unclean and the clean;

11And you are to teach the Israelites all the statutes which the Lord has spoken to them by Moses.

12And Moses said to Aaron and to Eleazar and Ithamar, his sons who were left, Take the cereal offering that remains of the offerings of the Lord made by fire and eat it without leaven beside the altar, for it is most holy.

13You shall eat it in a sacred place, because it is your due and your sons' due, from the offerings made by fire to the Lord; for so I am commanded.

14But the breast that is waved and the thigh that is offered you shall eat in a clean place, you and your sons and daughters with you; for they are your due and your sons' due, given out of the sacrifices of the peace offerings of the Israelites.

15The thigh that is offered and the breast that is waved they shall bring with the offerings made by fire of the fat, to wave for a wave offering before the Lord; and it shall be yours and your sons' with you as a portion or due perpetually, as the Lord has commanded.

16And Moses diligently tried to find [what had become of] the goat [that had been offered] for the sin offering, and behold, it was burned up [as waste]! And he was angry with Eleazar and Ithamar, the sons of Aaron who were left alive, and said,

17Why have you not eaten the sin offering in the Holy Place? It is most holy; and God has given it to you to bear and take away the iniquity of the congregation, to make atonement for them before the Lord.

18Behold, the blood of it was not brought within the Holy Place; you should indeed have eaten [the flesh of it] in the Holy Place, as I commanded.

19But Aaron said to Moses, Behold, this very day in which they have [obediently] offered their sin offering and their burnt offering before the Lord, such [terrible calamities] have befallen me [and them]! If I [and they] had eaten the most holy sin offering today [humbled as we have been by the sin of our kinsmen and God's judgment upon them], would it have been acceptable in the sight of the Lord? [Hos. 9:4.]

20And when Moses heard that, he was pacified.

New American Standard

4 ¶ Moses called also to Mishael and Elzaphan, the sons of Aaron's uncle Uzziel, and said to them, "Come forward, carry your relatives away from the front of the sanctuary to the outside of the camp."

5 So they came forward and carried them still in their tunics to the outside of the camp, as Moses had said.

6 Then Moses said to Aaron and to his sons Eleazar and Ithamar, "Do not *uncover your heads nor tear your clothes, so that you will not die and that He will not become wrathful against all the congregation. But your kinsmen, the whole house of Israel, shall bewail the burning which the LORD has brought about.

7 "You shall not even go out from the doorway of the tent of meeting, or you will die; for the LORD'S anointing oil is upon you." So they did according to the word of Moses.

8 ¶ The LORD then spoke to Aaron, saying,

9 "Do not drink wine or strong drink, neither you nor your sons with you, when you come into the tent of meeting, so that you will not die—it is a perpetual statute throughout your generations—

10 and so as to make a distinction between the holy and the profane, and between the unclean and the clean,

11 and so as to teach the sons of Israel all the statutes which the LORD has spoken to them through Moses."

12 ¶ Then Moses spoke to Aaron, and to his surviving sons, Eleazar and Ithamar, "Take the grain offering that is left over from the LORD'S offerings by fire and eat it unleavened beside the altar, for it is most holy.

13 "You shall eat it, moreover, in a holy place, because it is your due and your sons' due out of the LORD'S offerings by fire; for thus I have been commanded.

14 "The breast of the wave offering, however, and the thigh of the offering you may eat in a clean place, you and your sons and your daughters with you; for they have been given as your due and your sons' due out of the sacrifices of the peace offerings of the sons of Israel.

15 "The thigh offered by lifting up and the breast offered by waving they shall bring along with the offerings by fire of the portions of fat, to present as a wave offering before the LORD; so it shall be a thing perpetually due you and your sons with you, just as the LORD has commanded."

16 ¶ But Moses searched carefully for the goat of the sin offering, and behold, it had been burned up! So he was angry with Aaron's surviving sons Eleazar and Ithamar, saying,

17 "Why did you not eat the sin offering at the holy place? For it is most holy, and He gave it to you to bear away the guilt of the congregation, to make atonement for them before the LORD.

18 "Behold, since its blood had not been brought inside, into the sanctuary, you should certainly have eaten it in the sanctuary, just as I commanded."

19 But Aaron spoke to Moses, "Behold, this very day they presented their sin offering and their burnt offering before the LORD. When things like these happened to me, if I had eaten a sin offering today, would it have been good in the sight of the LORD?"

20 When Moses heard *that*, it seemed good in his sight.

New International

4 Moses summoned Mishael and Elzaphan, sons of Aaron's uncle Uzziel, and said to them, "Come here; carry your cousins outside the camp, away from the front of the sanctuary." 5 So they came and carried them, still in their tunics, outside the camp, as Moses ordered.

6 Then Moses said to Aaron and his sons Eleazar and Ithamar, "Do not let your hair become unkempt,[f] and do not tear your clothes, or you will die and the LORD will be angry with the whole community. But your relatives, all the house of Israel, may mourn for those the LORD has destroyed by fire. 7 Do not leave the entrance to the Tent of Meeting or you will die, because the LORD's anointing oil is on you." So they did as Moses said.

8 Then the LORD said to Aaron, 9 "You and your sons are not to drink wine or other fermented drink whenever you go into the Tent of Meeting, or you will die. This is a lasting ordinance for the generations to come. 10 You must distinguish between the holy and the common, between the unclean and the clean, 11 and you must teach the Israelites all the decrees the LORD has given them through Moses."

12 Moses said to Aaron and his remaining sons, Eleazar and Ithamar, "Take the grain offering left over from the offerings made to the LORD by fire and eat it prepared without yeast beside the altar, for it is most holy. 13 Eat it in a holy place, because it is your share and your sons' share of the offerings made to the LORD by fire; for so I have been commanded. 14 But you and your sons and your daughters may eat the breast that was waved and the thigh that was presented. Eat them in a ceremonially clean place; they have been given to you and your children as your share of the Israelites' fellowship offerings.[u] 15 The thigh that was presented and the breast that was waved must be brought with the fat portions of the offerings made by fire, to be waved before the LORD as a wave offering. This will be the regular share for you and your children, as the LORD has commanded."

16 When Moses inquired about the goat of the sin offering and found that it had been burned up, he was angry with Eleazar and Ithamar, Aaron's remaining sons, and asked, 17 "Why didn't you eat the sin offering in the sanctuary area? It is most holy; it was given to you to take away the guilt of the community by making atonement for them before the LORD. 18 Since its blood was not taken into the Holy Place, you should have eaten the goat in the sanctuary area, as I commanded."

19 Aaron replied to Moses, "Today they sacrificed their sin offering and their burnt offering before the LORD, but such things as this have happened to me. Would the LORD have been pleased if I had eaten the sin offering today?" 20 When Moses heard this, he was satisfied.

e Lit unbind

f 6 Or Do not uncover your heads   *u* 14 Traditionally peace offerings

King James

Amplified

Clean and unclean animals

11 AND THE LORD spake unto Moses and to Aaron, saying unto them,

2Speak unto the children of Israel, saying, These *are* the beasts which ye shall eat among all the beasts that *are* on the earth.

3Whatsoever parteth the hoof, and is clovenfooted, *and* cheweth the cud, among the beasts, that shall ye eat.

4Nevertheless these shall ye not eat of them that chew the cud, or of them that divide the hoof: *as* the camel, because he cheweth the cud, but divideth not the hoof; he *is* unclean unto you.

5And the coney, because he cheweth the cud, but divideth not the hoof; he *is* unclean unto you.

6And the hare, because he cheweth the cud, but divideth not the hoof; he *is* unclean unto you.

7And the swine, though he divide the hoof, and be clovenfooted, yet he cheweth not the cud; he *is* unclean to you.

8Of their flesh shall ye not eat, and their carcase shall ye not touch; they *are* unclean to you.

9 ¶ These shall ye eat of all that *are* in the waters: whatsoever hath fins and scales in the waters, in the seas, and in the rivers, them shall ye eat.

10And all that have not fins and scales in the seas, and in the rivers, of all that move in the waters, and of any living thing which *is* in the waters, they *shall be* an abomination unto you:

11They shall be even an abomination unto you; ye shall not eat of their flesh, but ye shall have their carcases in abomination.

12Whatsoever hath no fins nor scales in the waters, that *shall be* an abomination unto you.

13 ¶ And these *are they which* ye shall have in abomination among the fowls; they shall not be eaten, they *are* an abomination: the eagle, and the ossifrage, and the ospray,

14And the vulture, and the kite after his kind;

15Every raven after his kind;

16And the owl, and the night hawk, and the cuckoo, and the hawk after his kind,

17And the little owl, and the cormorant, and the great owl,

18And the swan, and the pelican, and the gier eagle,

19And the stork, the heron after her kind, and the lapwing, and the bat.

20All fowls that creep, going upon *all* four, *shall be* an abomination unto you.

21Yet these may ye eat of every flying creeping thing that goeth upon *all* four, which have legs above their feet, to leap withal upon the earth;

22*Even* these of them ye may eat; the locust after his kind, and the bald locust after his kind, and the beetle after his kind, and the grasshopper after his kind.

23But all *other* flying creeping things, which have four feet, *shall be* an abomination unto you.

24And for these ye shall be unclean: whosoever toucheth the carcase of them shall be unclean until the even.

25And whosoever beareth *aught* of the carcase of them shall wash his clothes, and be unclean until the even.

26*The carcases* of every beast which divideth the hoof, and *is* not clovenfooted, nor cheweth the cud, *are* unclean unto you: every one that toucheth them shall be unclean.

11 AND THE Lord said to Moses and Aaron, 2Say to the Israelites: These are the animals gwhich you may eat among all the beasts that are on the earth. [Mark 7:15–19.]

3Whatever parts the hoof and is cloven-footed and chews the cud, any of these animals you may eat.

4Nevertheless these you shall not eat of those that chew the cud or divide the hoof: the camel, because it chews the cud but does not divide the hoof; it is unclean to you.

5And the coney *or* rock badger, because it chews the cud but does not divide the hoof; it is unclean to you.

6And the hare, because it chews the cud but does not divide the hoof; it is unclean to you.

7And the swine, because it divides the hoof and is cloven-footed but does not chew the cud; it is unclean to you.

8Of their flesh you shall not eat, and their carcasses you shall not touch; they are unclean to you.

9These you may eat of all that are in the waters: whatever has fins and scales in the waters, in the seas, and in the rivers, these you may eat;

10But all that have not fins and scales in the seas and in the rivers, of all the creeping things in the waters, and of all the living creatures which are in the waters, they are [to be considered] an abomination and abhorrence to you. [I Cor. 8:8–13.]

11They shall continue to be an abomination to you; you shall not eat of their flesh, but you shall detest their carcasses.

12Everything in the waters that has not fins or scales shall be abhorrent *and* detestable to you.

13These you shall have in abomination among the birds; they shall not be eaten, for they are detestable: the eagle, the ossifrage, the ospray,

14The kite, the whole species of falcon,

15Every kind of raven,

16The ostrich, the nighthawk, the sea gull, every species of hawk,

17The owl, the cormorant, the ibis,

18The swan, the pelican, the vulture,

19The stork, all kinds of heron, the hoopoe, and the bat.

20All winged insects that go upon all fours are to be an abomination to you;

21Yet of all winged insects that go upon all fours you may eat those which have legs above their feet with which to leap upon the ground.

22Of these you may eat: the whole species of locust, of bald locust, of cricket, and of grasshopper. [Matt. 3:4.]

23But all other winged insects which have four feet shall be detestable to you.

24And by [contact with] these you shall become unclean; whoever touches the carcass of them shall be unclean until the evening.

25And whoever carries any part of their carcass shall wash his clothes and be unclean until the evening.

26Every beast which parts the hoof but is not cloven-footed or does not chew the cud is unclean to you; everyone who touches them shall be unclean.

gAt first thought the laws given here seem only to have been made obsolete by Jesus. He taught that it is not what goes into the mouth but what comes out of it that defiles a man (Matt. 15:17-20), and Paul said that when the complete and perfect came, the incomplete and imperfect would become void and superseded (I Cor. 13:9, 10), for "there is nothing unclean of itself" (Rom. 14:14 KJV). But while all these specific laws have become void, we must not lose sight of the fact that they are "superseded" by the underlying spiritual principle, which is just as binding. Christ's teaching relates to the whole area of our living, including our eating and drinking, and is dominated by the principle, "Whatever you may do, do all for the honor *and* glory of God" (I Cor. 10:31). We do well to remember that it was Jesus Christ Himself who said, "Do not think that I have come to do away with *or* undo the Law . . .; I have come not to do away with *or* undo but to complete *and* fulfill" it (Matt. 5:17).

New American Standard

Laws about Animals for Food

11 THE LORD spoke again to Moses and to Aaron, saying to them,

2"Speak to the sons of Israel, saying, 'These are the creatures which you may eat from all the animals that are on the earth.

3 'Whatever divides a hoof, thus making split hoofs, *and* chews the cud, among the animals, that you may eat.

4 'Nevertheless, you are not to eat of these, among those which chew the cud, or among those which divide the hoof: the camel, for though it chews cud, it does not divide the hoof, it is unclean to you.

5 'Likewise, the shaphan, for though it chews cud, it does not divide the hoof, it is unclean to you;

6 the rabbit also, for though it chews cud, it does not divide the hoof, it is unclean to you;

7 and the pig, for though it divides the hoof, thus making a split hoof, it does not chew cud, it is unclean to you.

8 'You shall not eat of their flesh nor touch their carcasses; they are unclean to you.

9 ¶ 'These you may eat, whatever is in the water: all that have fins and scales, those in the water, in the seas or in the rivers, you may eat.

10 'But whatever is in the seas and in the rivers that does not have fins and scales among all the teeming life of the water, and among all the living creatures that are in the water, they are detestable things to you;

11 and they shall be *f*abhorrent to you; you may not eat of their flesh, and their carcasses you shall detest.

12 'Whatever in the water does not have fins and scales is abhorrent to you.

Avoid the Unclean

13 ¶ 'These, moreover, you shall detest among the birds; they are abhorrent, not to be eaten: the eagle and the vulture and the buzzard,

14 and the kite and the falcon in its kind,

15 every raven in its kind,

16 and the ostrich and the owl and the sea gull and the hawk in its kind,

17 and the little owl and the cormorant and the great owl,

18 and the white owl and the pelican and the carrion vulture,

19 and the stork, the heron in its kinds, and the hoopoe, and the bat.

20 ¶ 'All the winged insects that walk on *all* fours are detestable to you.

21 'Yet these you may eat among all the winged insects which walk on *all* fours: those which have above their feet jointed legs with which to jump on the earth.

22 'These of them you may eat: the locust in its kinds, and the devastating locust in its kinds, and the cricket in its kinds, and the grasshopper in its kinds.

23 'But all other winged insects which are four-footed are detestable to you.

24 ¶ 'By these, moreover, you will be made unclean: whoever touches their carcasses becomes unclean until evening,

25 and whoever picks up any of their carcasses shall wash his clothes and be unclean until evening.

26 'Concerning all the animals which divide the hoof but do not make a split *hoof,* or which do not chew cud, they are unclean to you: whoever touches them becomes unclean.

New International

Clean and Unclean Food

11 THE LORD said to Moses and Aaron, 2"Say to the Israelites: 'Of all the animals that live on land, these are the ones you may eat: 3You may eat any animal that has a split hoof completely divided and that chews the cud.

4" 'There are some that only chew the cud or only have a split hoof, but you must not eat them. The camel, though it chews the cud, does not have a split hoof; it is ceremonially unclean for you. 5The coney,*v* though it chews the cud, does not have a split hoof; it is unclean for you. 6The rabbit, though it chews the cud, does not have a split hoof; it is unclean for you. 7And the pig, though it has a split hoof completely divided, does not chew the cud; it is unclean for you. 8You must not eat their meat or touch their carcasses; they are unclean for you.

9" 'Of all the creatures living in the water of the seas and the streams, you may eat any that have fins and scales. 10But all creatures in the seas or streams that do not have fins and scales—whether among all the swarming things or among all the other living creatures in the water—you are to detest. 11And since you are to detest them, you must not eat their meat and you must detest their carcasses. 12Anything living in the water that does not have fins and scales is to be detestable to you.

13" 'These are the birds you are to detest and not eat because they are detestable: the eagle, the vulture, the black vulture, 14the red kite, any kind of black kite, 15any kind of raven, 16the horned owl, the screech owl, the gull, any kind of hawk, 17the little owl, the cormorant, the great owl, 18the white owl, the desert owl, the osprey, 19the stork, any kind of heron, the hoopoe and the bat.*w*

20" 'All flying insects that walk on all fours are to be detestable to you. 21There are, however, some winged creatures that walk on all fours that you may eat: those that have jointed legs for hopping on the ground. 22Of these you may eat any kind of locust, katydid, cricket or grasshopper. 23But all other winged creatures that have four legs you are to detest.

24" 'You will make yourselves unclean by these; whoever touches their carcasses will be unclean till evening. 25Whoever picks up one of their carcasses must wash his clothes, and he will be unclean till evening.

26" 'Every animal that has a split hoof not completely divided or that does not chew the cud is unclean for you; whoever touches ⌞the carcass of⌟ any of them will be un-

---

*f*Lit *detestable things*

v 5 That is, the hyrax or rock badger   *w 19* The precise identification of some of the birds, insects and animals in this chapter is uncertain.

King James

²⁷And whatsoever goeth upon his paws, among all manner of beasts that go on *all* four, those *are* unclean unto you: whoso toucheth their carcase shall be unclean until the even.
²⁸And he that beareth the carcase of them shall wash his clothes, and be unclean until the even: they *are* unclean unto you.
²⁹ ¶ These also *shall be* unclean unto you among the creeping things that creep upon the earth; the weasel, and the mouse, and the tortoise after his kind,
³⁰And the ferret, and the chameleon, and the lizard, and the snail, and the mole.
³¹These *are* unclean to you among all that creep: whosoever doth touch them, when they be dead, shall be unclean until the even.
³²And upon whatsoever *any* of them, when they are dead, doth fall, it shall be unclean; whether *it be* any vessel of wood, or raiment, or skin, or sack, whatsoever vessel *it be,* wherein *any* work is done, it must be put into water, and it shall be unclean until the even; so it shall be cleansed.
³³And every earthen vessel, whereinto *any* of them falleth, whatsoever *is* in it shall be unclean; and ye shall break it.
³⁴Of all meat which may be eaten, *that* on which *such* water cometh shall be unclean: and all drink that may be drunk in every *such* vessel shall be unclean.
³⁵And every *thing* whereupon *any part* of their carcase falleth shall be unclean; *whether it be* oven, or ranges for pots, they shall be broken down: *for* they *are* unclean, and shall be unclean unto you.
³⁶Nevertheless a fountain or pit, *wherein there is* plenty of water, shall be clean: but that which toucheth their carcase shall be unclean.
³⁷And if *any part* of their carcase fall upon any sowing seed which is to be sown, it *shall be* clean.
³⁸But if *any* water be put upon the seed, and *any part* of their carcase fall thereon, it *shall be* unclean unto you.
³⁹And if any beast, of which ye may eat, die; he that toucheth the carcase thereof shall be unclean until the even.
⁴⁰And he that eateth of the carcase of it shall wash his clothes, and be unclean until the even: he also that beareth the carcase of it shall wash his clothes, and be unclean until the even.
⁴¹And every creeping thing that creepeth upon the earth *shall be* an abomination; it shall not be eaten.
⁴²Whatsoever goeth upon the belly, and whatsoever goeth upon *all* four, or whatsoever ^xhath more feet among all creeping things that creep upon the earth, them ye shall not eat; for they *are* an abomination.
⁴³Ye shall not make your ^yselves abominable with any creeping thing that creepeth, neither shall ye make yourselves unclean with them, that ye should be defiled thereby.
⁴⁴For I *am* the LORD your God: ye shall therefore sanctify yourselves, and ye shall be holy; for I *am* holy: neither shall ye defile yourselves with any manner of creeping thing that creepeth upon the earth.
⁴⁵For I *am* the LORD that bringeth you up out of the land of Egypt, to be your God: ye shall therefore be holy, for I *am* holy.
⁴⁶This *is* the law of the beasts, and of the fowl, and of every living creature that moveth in the waters, and of every creature that creepeth upon the earth:
⁴⁷To make a difference between the unclean and the clean, and between the beast that may be eaten and the beast that may not be eaten.

Amplified

²⁷And all that go on their paws, among all kinds of four-footed beasts, are unclean to you; whoever touches their carcass shall be unclean until the evening,
²⁸And he who carries their carcass shall wash his clothes and be unclean until the evening; they are unclean to you.
²⁹These also are unclean to you among the creeping things [that multiply greatly] *and* creep upon the ground: the weasel, the mouse, any kind of great lizard,
³⁰The gecko, the land crocodile, the lizard, the sand lizard, and the chameleon.
³¹These are unclean to you among all that creep; whoever touches them when they are dead shall be unclean until the evening.
³²And upon whatever they may fall when they are dead, it shall be unclean, whether it is an article of wood or clothing or skin (bottle) or sack, any vessel in which work is done; it must be put in water, and it shall be unclean until the evening; so it shall be cleansed.
³³And every earthen vessel into which any of these [creeping things] falls, whatever may be in it shall be unclean, and you shall break the vessel.
³⁴Of all the food [in one of these unclean vessels] which may be eaten, that on which such water comes shall be unclean, and all drink that may be drunk from every such vessel shall be unclean.
³⁵And everything upon which any part of their carcass falls shall be unclean; whether an oven, *or* pan with a lid, or hearth for pots, it shall be broken in pieces; they are unclean, and shall be unclean to you.
³⁶Yet a spring or a cistern *or* reservoir of water shall be clean; but whoever touches their carcass shall be unclean.
³⁷If a part of their carcass falls on seed which is to be sown, it shall be clean;
³⁸But if any water be put on the seed and any part of their carcass falls on it, it shall be unclean to you.
³⁹If any animal of which you may eat dies [unslaughtered], he who touches its carcass shall be unclean until the evening.
⁴⁰And he who eats of its carcass [ignorantly] shall wash his clothes, and be unclean until the evening; he also who carries its carcass shall wash his clothes, and be unclean until the evening.
⁴¹And everything that creeps on the ground *and* [multiplies in] swarms shall be an abomination; it shall not be eaten.
⁴²Whatever goes on its belly, and whatever goes on all fours, or whatever has more [than four] feet among all things that creep on the ground *and* swarm you shall not eat; for they are detestable.
⁴³You shall not make yourselves loathsome *and* abominable [by eating] any swarming thing that [multiplies by] swarms, neither shall you make yourselves unclean with them, that you should be defiled by them.
⁴⁴For I am the Lord your God; so consecrate yourselves and be holy, for I am holy; neither defile yourselves with any manner of thing that multiplies in large numbers *or* swarms. [I Thess. 4:7, 8.]
⁴⁵For I am the Lord Who brought you up out of the land of Egypt to be your God; therefore you shall be holy, for I am holy. [I Pet. 1:14–16.]
⁴⁶This is the law of the beast, and of the bird, and of every living creature that moves in the waters, and creeps on the earth *and* multiplies in large numbers,
⁴⁷To make a difference (a distinction) between the unclean and the clean, and between the animal that may be eaten and the animal that may not be eaten.

---

^wHeb. *a gathering together of waters*   ^xHeb. *doth multiply feet*
^yHeb. *souls*

New American Standard

27 'Also whatever walks on its paws, among all the creatures that walk on *all* fours, are unclean to you; whoever touches their carcasses becomes unclean until evening,

28 and the one who picks up their carcasses shall wash his clothes and be unclean until evening; they are unclean to you.

29 ¶ 'Now these are to you the unclean among the swarming things which swarm on the earth: the mole, and the mouse, and the great lizard in its kinds,

30 and the gecko, and the crocodile, and the lizard, and the sand reptile, and the chameleon.

31 'These are to you the unclean among all the swarming things; whoever touches them when they are dead becomes unclean until evening.

32 'Also anything on which one of them may fall when they are dead becomes unclean, including any wooden article, or clothing, or a skin, or a sack—any article of which use is made—it shall be put in the water and be unclean until evening, then it becomes clean.

33 'As for any earthenware vessel into which one of them may fall, whatever is in it becomes unclean and you shall break the vessel.

34 'Any of the food which may be eaten, on which water comes, shall become unclean, and any liquid which may be drunk in every vessel shall become unclean.

35 'Everything, moreover, on which part of their carcass may fall becomes unclean; an oven or a *g*stove shall be smashed; they are unclean and shall continue as unclean to you.

36 'Nevertheless a spring or a cistern collecting water shall be clean, though the one who touches their carcass shall be unclean.

37 'If a part of their carcass falls on any seed for sowing which is to be sown, it is clean.

38 'Though if water is put on the seed and a part of their carcass falls on it, it is unclean to you.

39 ¶ 'Also if one of the animals dies which you have for food, the one who touches its carcass becomes unclean until evening.

40 'He too, who eats some of its carcass shall wash his clothes and be unclean until evening, and the one who picks up its carcass shall wash his clothes and be unclean until evening.

41 ¶ 'Now every swarming thing that swarms on the earth is detestable, not to be eaten.

42 'Whatever crawls on its belly, and whatever walks on *all* fours, whatever has many feet, in respect to every swarming thing that swarms on the earth, you shall not eat them, for they are detestable.

43 'Do not render yourselves detestable through any of the swarming things that swarm; and you shall not make yourselves unclean with them so that you become unclean.

44 'For I am the LORD your God. Consecrate yourselves therefore, and be holy, for I am holy. And you shall not make yourselves unclean with any of the swarming things that swarm on the earth.

45 'For I am the LORD who brought you up from the land of Egypt to be your God; thus you shall be holy, for I am holy.' "

46 ¶ This is the law regarding the animal and the bird, and every living thing that moves in the waters and everything that swarms on the earth,

47 to make a distinction between the unclean and the clean, and between the edible creature and the creature which is not to be eaten.

New International

clean. 27Of all the animals that walk on all fours, those that walk on their paws are unclean for you; whoever touches their carcasses will be unclean till evening. 28Anyone who picks up their carcasses must wash his clothes, and he will be unclean till evening. They are unclean for you.

29" 'Of the animals that move about on the ground, these are unclean for you: the weasel, the rat, any kind of great lizard, 30the gecko, the monitor lizard, the wall lizard, the skink and the chameleon. 31Of all those that move along the ground, these are unclean for you. Whoever touches them when they are dead will be unclean till evening. 32When one of them dies and falls on something, that article, whatever its use, will be unclean, whether it is made of wood, cloth, hide or sackcloth. Put it in water; it will be unclean till evening, and then it will be clean. 33If one of them falls into a clay pot, everything in it will be unclean, and you must break the pot. 34Any food that could be eaten but has water on it from such a pot is unclean, and any liquid that could be drunk from it is unclean. 35Anything that one of their carcasses falls on becomes unclean; an oven or cooking pot must be broken up. They are unclean, and you are to regard them as unclean. 36A spring, however, or a cistern for collecting water remains clean, but anyone who touches one of these carcasses is unclean. 37If a carcass falls on any seeds that are to be planted, they remain clean. 38But if water has been put on the seed and a carcass falls on it, it is unclean for you.

39" 'If an animal that you are allowed to eat dies, anyone who touches the carcass will be unclean till evening. 40Anyone who eats some of the carcass must wash his clothes, and he will be unclean till evening. Anyone who picks up the carcass must wash his clothes, and he will be unclean till evening.

41" 'Every creature that moves about on the ground is detestable; it is not to be eaten. 42You are not to eat any creature that moves about on the ground, whether it moves on its belly or walks on all fours or on many feet; it is detestable. 43Do not defile yourselves by any of these creatures. Do not make yourselves unclean by means of them or be made unclean by them. 44I am the LORD your God; consecrate yourselves and be holy, because I am holy. Do not make yourselves unclean by any creature that moves about on the ground. 45I am the LORD who brought you up out of Egypt to be your God; therefore be holy, because I am holy.

46" 'These are the regulations concerning animals, birds, every living thing that moves in the water and every creature that moves about on the ground. 47You must distinguish between the unclean and the clean, between living creatures that may be eaten and those that may not be eaten.' "

g Lit *hearth for supporting (two) pots*

King James

Purification after childbirth

12 AND THE LORD spake unto Moses, saying, [2]Speak unto the children of Israel, saying, If a woman have conceived seed, and born a man child: then she shall be unclean seven days; according to the days of the separation for her infirmity shall she be unclean.

[3]And in the eighth day the flesh of his foreskin shall be circumcised.

[4]And she shall then continue in the blood of her purifying three and thirty days; she shall touch no hallowed thing, nor come into the sanctuary, until the days of her purifying be fulfilled.

[5]But if she bear a maid child, then she shall be unclean two weeks, as in her separation: and she shall continue in the blood of her purifying threescore and six days.

[6]And when the days of her purifying are fulfilled, for a son, or for a daughter, she shall bring a lamb [z]of the first year for a burnt offering, and a young pigeon, or a turtledove, for a sin offering, unto the door of the tabernacle of the congregation, unto the priest:

[7]Who shall offer it before the LORD, and make an atonement for her; and she shall be cleansed from the issue of her blood. This *is* the law for her that hath born a male or a female.

[8]And if [a]she be not able to bring a lamb, then she shall bring two turtles, or two young pigeons; the one for the burnt offering, and the other for a sin offering: and the priest shall make an atonement for her, and she shall be clean.

Laws about skin plagues

13 AND THE LORD spake unto Moses and Aaron, saying, [2]When a man shall have in the skin of his flesh a [b]rising, a scab, or bright spot, and it be in the skin of his flesh *like* the plague of leprosy; then he shall be brought unto Aaron the priest, or unto one of his sons the priests:

[3]And the priest shall look on the plague in the skin of the flesh: and *when* the hair in the plague is turned white, and the plague in sight *be* deeper than the skin of his flesh, it *is* a plague of leprosy: and the priest shall look on him, and pronounce him unclean.

[4]If the bright spot *be* white in the skin of his flesh, and in sight *be* not deeper than the skin, and the hair thereof be not turned white; then the priest shall shut up *him that hath* the plague seven days:

[5]And the priest shall look on him the seventh day: and, behold, *if* the plague in his sight be at a stay, *and* the plague spread not in the skin; then the priest shall shut him up seven days more:

[6]And the priest shall look on him again the seventh day: and, behold, *if* the plague *be* somewhat dark, *and* the plague spread not in the skin, the priest shall pronounce him clean: it *is but* a scab: and he shall wash his clothes, and be clean.

[7]But if the scab spread much abroad in the skin, after that he hath been seen of the priest for his cleansing, he shall be seen of the priest again:

[8]And *if* the priest see that, behold, the scab spreadeth in the skin, then the priest shall pronounce him unclean: it *is* a leprosy.

[9] ¶ When the plague of leprosy is in a man, then he shall be brought unto the priest;

Amplified

12 AND THE Lord said to Moses, [2]Say to the Israelites, If a woman conceives and bears a male child, she shall be unclean seven days, unclean as during her monthly discomfort.

[3]And on the eighth day the child shall be circumcised.

[4]Then she shall remain [separated] thirty-three days to be purified [from her loss] of blood; she shall touch no hallowed thing nor come into the [court of the] sanctuary until the days of her purifying are over.

[5]But if the child she bears is a girl, then she shall be unclean two weeks, as in her periodic impurity, and she shall remain separated sixty-six days to be purified [from her loss] of blood.

[6]When the days of her purifying are completed, whether for a son or for a daughter, she shall bring a lamb a year old for a burnt offering and a young pigeon or a turtledove for a sin offering to the door of the Tent of Meeting to the priest;

[7]And he shall offer it before the Lord and make atonement for her, and she shall be cleansed from the flow of her blood. This is the law for her who has borne a male or a female child.

[8]If she is unable to bring a lamb [for lack of means] then she shall bring two turtledoves or young pigeons, one for a burnt offering, the other for a sin offering; the priest shall make atonement for her, and she shall be clean. [Luke 2:22, 24.]

13 AND THE Lord said to Moses and Aaron, [2]When a man has a swelling on his skin, a scab, or a bright spot, and it becomes the disease of [h]leprosy in his skin, then he shall be brought to the priest, to Aaron or one of his sons.

[3]The priest shall look at the diseased spot on his skin, and if the hair in it has turned white and the disease appears depressed *and* deeper than his skin, it is a leprous disease; and the priest shall examine him, and pronounce him unclean.

[4]If the bright spot is white on his skin, not depressed, and the hair on it not turned white, the priest shall quarantine the person *or* bind up the spot for seven days.

[5]And the priest shall examine him on the seventh day, and if the disease in his estimation is at a standstill *and* has not spread in the skin, then the priest shall quarantine the person *or* bind up the spot seven more days.

[6]And the priest shall examine him again the seventh day, and if the diseased part has a more normal color and the disease has not spread in the skin, the priest shall pronounce him clean; it is only an eruption *or* a scab; and he shall wash his clothes and be clean.

[7]But if the eruption *or* scab spreads farther in the skin after he has shown himself to the priest for his cleansing, he shall be seen by the priest again.

[8]If the priest sees that the eruption *or* scab is spreading in the skin, then he shall pronounce him unclean; it is leprosy.

[9]When the disease of leprosy is in a man, he shall be brought to the priest;

---

[h] Authorities are generally agreed that there certainly was true leprosy as it is known today in the Near East in New Testament times. But from the details of the disease in Lev. 13, it is believed that other very serious skin disorders were also included under the heading of "leprosy" in earlier times. Leprosy in the Old Testament, therefore, is not to be considered as confined to the traits by which it is known today, but rather defined by the symptoms, the treatment, and the history of individual cases as recorded in Leviticus and elsewhere. That it was worse than death is implied by the words of Aaron when his sister Miriam was stricken with it: "Alas, my lord [Moses], . . . Let her not be as one dead, of whom the flesh is half consumed when he cometh out of his mother's womb" (Num. 12:11, 12 KJV).

---

[z] Heb. *a son of his year*   [a] Heb. *her hand find not sufficiency of*
[b] Or, *swelling*

New American Standard

Laws of Motherhood

12 THEN THE LORD spoke to Moses, saying, 2 "Speak to the sons of Israel, saying:

¶ 'When a woman gives birth and bears a male *child,* then she shall be unclean for seven days, as in the days of her menstruation she shall be unclean.

3 'On the eighth day the flesh of his foreskin shall be circumcised.

4 'Then she shall remain in the blood of *her* purification for thirty-three days; she shall not touch any consecrated thing, nor enter the sanctuary until the days of her purification are completed.

5 'But if she bears a female *child,* then she shall be unclean for two weeks, as in her menstruation; and she shall remain in the blood of *her* purification for sixty-six days.

6 ¶ 'When the days of her purification are completed, for a son or for a daughter, she shall bring to the priest at the doorway of the tent of meeting a one year old lamb for a burnt offering and a young pigeon or a turtledove for a sin offering.

7 'Then he shall offer it before the LORD and make atonement for her, and she shall be cleansed from the flow of her blood. This is the law for her who bears *a child, whether* a male or a female.

8 'But if she cannot afford a lamb, then she shall take two turtledoves or two young pigeons, the one for a burnt offering and the other for a sin offering; and the priest shall make atonement for her, and she will be clean.' "

The Test for Leprosy

13 THEN THE LORD spoke to Moses and to Aaron, saying,

2 "When a man has on the skin of his body a swelling or a scab or a bright spot, and it becomes *ʰ*an infection of leprosy on the skin of his body, then he shall be brought to Aaron the priest or to one of his sons the priests.

3 "The priest shall look at the mark on the skin of the body, and if the hair in the infection has turned white and the infection appears to be deeper than the skin of his body, it is an infection of leprosy; when the priest has looked at him, he shall pronounce him unclean.

4 "But if the bright spot is white on the skin of his body, and it does not appear to be deeper than the skin, and the hair on it has not turned white, then the priest shall isolate *him who has* the infection for seven days.

5 "The priest shall look at him on the seventh day, and if in his eyes the infection has not changed *and* the infection has not spread on the skin, then the priest shall isolate him for seven more days.

6 "The priest shall look at him again on the seventh day, and if the infection has faded and the mark has not spread on the skin, then the priest shall pronounce him clean; it is *only* a scab. And he shall wash his clothes and be clean.

7 ¶ "But if the scab spreads farther on the skin after he has shown himself to the priest for his cleansing, he shall appear again to the priest.

8 "The priest shall look, and if the scab has spread on the skin, then the priest shall pronounce him unclean; it is leprosy.

9 ¶ "When the infection of leprosy is on a man, then he shall be brought to the priest.

New International

Purification After Childbirth

12 THE LORD said to Moses, 2 "Say to the Israelites: 'A woman who becomes pregnant and gives birth to a son will be ceremonially unclean for seven days, just as she is unclean during her monthly period. 3 On the eighth day the boy is to be circumcised. 4 Then the woman must wait thirty-three days to be purified from her bleeding. She must not touch anything sacred or go to the sanctuary until the days of her purification are over. 5 If she gives birth to a daughter, for two weeks the woman will be unclean, as during her period. Then she must wait sixty-six days to be purified from her bleeding.

6 " 'When the days of her purification for a son or daughter are over, she is to bring to the priest at the entrance to the Tent of Meeting a year-old lamb for a burnt offering and a young pigeon or a dove for a sin offering. 7 He shall offer them before the LORD to make atonement for her, and then she will be ceremonially clean from her flow of blood.

" 'These are the regulations for the woman who gives birth to a boy or a girl. 8 If she cannot afford a lamb, she is to bring two doves or two young pigeons, one for a burnt offering and the other for a sin offering. In this way the priest will make atonement for her, and she will be clean.' "

Regulations About Infectious Skin Diseases

13 THE LORD said to Moses and Aaron, 2 "When anyone has a swelling or a rash or a bright spot on his skin that may become an infectious skin disease,*ˣ* he must be brought to Aaron the priest or to one of his sons*ʸ* who is a priest. 3 The priest is to examine the sore on his skin, and if the hair in the sore has turned white and the sore appears to be more than skin deep,*ᶻ* it is an infectious skin disease. When the priest examines him, he shall pronounce him ceremonially unclean. 4 If the spot on his skin is white but does not appear to be more than skin deep and the hair in it has not turned white, the priest is to put the infected person in isolation for seven days. 5 On the seventh day the priest is to examine him, and if he sees that the sore is unchanged and has not spread in the skin, he is to keep him in isolation another seven days. 6 On the seventh day the priest is to examine him again, and if the sore has faded and has not spread in the skin, the priest shall pronounce him clean; it is only a rash. The man must wash his clothes, and he will be clean. 7 But if the rash does spread in his skin after he has shown himself to the priest to be pronounced clean, he must appear before the priest again. 8 The priest is to examine him, and if the rash has spread in the skin, he shall pronounce him unclean; it is an infectious skin disease.

9 "When anyone has an infectious skin disease, he must

ʰ Lit *a mark, stroke,* and so throughout the ch

*ˣ*2 Traditionally *leprosy*; the Hebrew word was used for various diseases affecting the skin—not necessarily leprosy; also elsewhere in this chapter.   *ʸ*2 Or *descendants*   *ᶻ*3 Or *be lower than the rest of the skin*; also elsewhere in this chapter

King James

¹⁰And the priest shall see *him:* and, behold, *if* the rising *be* white in the skin, and it have turned the hair white, and *there be* ᶜquick raw flesh in the rising;

¹¹It *is* an old leprosy in the skin of his flesh, and the priest shall pronounce him unclean, and shall not shut him up: for he *is* unclean.

¹²And if a leprosy break out abroad in the skin, and the leprosy cover all the skin of *him that hath* the plague from his head even to his foot, wheresoever the priest looketh;

¹³Then the priest shall consider: and, behold, *if* the leprosy have covered all his flesh, he shall pronounce *him* clean *that hath* the plague: it is all turned white: he *is* clean.

¹⁴But when raw flesh appeareth in him, he shall be unclean.

¹⁵And the priest shall see the raw flesh, and pronounce him to be unclean: *for* the raw flesh *is* unclean: it *is* a leprosy.

¹⁶Or if the raw flesh turn again, and be changed unto white, he shall come unto the priest;

¹⁷And the priest shall see him: and, behold, *if* the plague be turned into white; then the priest shall pronounce *him* clean *that hath* the plague: he *is* clean.

¹⁸ ¶ The flesh also, in which, *even* in the skin thereof, was a boil, and is healed,

¹⁹And in the place of the boil there be a white rising, or a bright spot, white, and somewhat reddish, and it be shown to the priest;

²⁰And if, when the priest seeth it, behold, it *be* in sight lower than the skin, and the hair thereof be turned white; the priest shall pronounce him unclean: it *is* a plague of leprosy broken out of the boil.

²¹But if the priest look on it, and, behold, *there be* no white hairs therein, and *if* it *be* not lower than the skin, but *be* somewhat dark; then the priest shall shut him up seven days:

²²And if it spread much abroad in the skin, then the priest shall pronounce him unclean: it *is* a plague.

²³But if the bright spot stay in his place, *and* spread not, it *is* a burning boil; and the priest shall pronounce him clean.

²⁴ ¶ Or if there be *any* flesh, in the skin whereof *there is* ᵈa hot burning, and the quick *flesh* that burneth have a white bright spot, somewhat reddish, or white;

²⁵Then the priest shall look upon it: and, behold, *if* the hair in the bright spot be turned white, and it *be in* sight deeper than the skin; *it is* a leprosy broken out of the burning: wherefore the priest shall pronounce him unclean: it *is* the plague of leprosy.

²⁶But if the priest look on it, and, behold, *there be* no white hair in the bright spot, and it *be* no lower than the *other* skin, but *be* somewhat dark; then the priest shall shut him up seven days:

²⁷And the priest shall look upon him the seventh day: *and* if it be spread much abroad in the skin, then the priest shall pronounce him unclean: it *is* the plague of leprosy.

²⁸And if the bright spot stay in his place, *and* spread not in the skin, but *be* somewhat dark; *it is* a rising of the burning, and the priest shall pronounce him clean: for it *is* an inflammation of the burning.

²⁹ ¶ If a man or woman have a plague upon the head or the beard;

³⁰Then the priest shall see the plague: and, behold, if it *be* in sight deeper than the skin; *and there be* in it a yellow thin hair; then the priest shall pronounce him unclean: it *is* a dry scall, *even* a leprosy upon the head or beard.

³¹And if the priest look on the plague of the scall, and, behold, it *be* not in sight deeper than the skin, and *that there is* no black hair in it; then the priest shall shut up *him that hath* the plague of the scall seven days:

Amplified

¹⁰And the priest shall examine him, and if there is a white swelling in the skin and the hair on it has turned white and there is quick raw flesh in the swelling,

¹¹It is a chronic leprosy in the skin of his body, and the priest shall pronounce him unclean; he shall not bind the spot up, for he is unclean.

¹²But if [supposed] leprosy breaks out in the skin, and it covers all the skin of him who has the disease from head to foot, wherever the priest looks,

¹³The priest shall examine him; if the [supposed] leprosy covers all his body, he shall pronounce him clean of the disease; it is all turned white, and he is clean.

¹⁴But when the raw flesh appears on him, he shall be unclean.

¹⁵And the priest shall examine the raw flesh and pronounce him unclean; for the raw flesh is unclean; it is leprosy.

¹⁶But if the raw flesh turns again and becomes white, he shall come to the priest,

¹⁷And the priest shall examine him, and if the diseased part is turned to white again, then the priest shall pronounce him clean who had the disease; he is clean.

¹⁸And when there is in the skin of the body [the scar of] a boil that is healed,

¹⁹And in the place of the boil there is a white swelling or a bright spot, reddish white, and it is shown to the priest,

²⁰And if when the priest examines it it looks lower than the skin and the hair on it is turned white, the priest shall pronounce him unclean; it is the disease of leprosy; it has broken out in the boil.

²¹But if the priest examines it and finds no white hair in it and it is not lower than the skin but appears darker, then the priest shall bind it up for seven days.

²²If it spreads in the skin, [he] shall pronounce him unclean; it is diseased.

²³But if the bright spot does not spread, it is the scar of the boil, and the priest shall pronounce him clean.

²⁴Or if there is any flesh in the skin of which there is a burn by fire and the quick flesh of the burn becomes a bright spot, reddish white or white,

²⁵Then the priest shall examine it, and if the hair in the bright spot is turned white, and it appears deeper than the skin, it is leprosy broken out in the burn. Therefore the priest shall pronounce him unclean; it is the disease of leprosy.

²⁶But if the priest examines it and there is no white hair in the bright spot and it is not lower than the rest of the skin but is darker, then the priest shall bind it up for seven days.

²⁷And the priest shall examine him on the seventh day; if it is spreading in the skin, then the priest shall pronounce him unclean; it is leprosy.

²⁸But if the bright spot has not spread but is darker, it is a swelling from the burn, and the priest shall pronounce him clean; for it is the scar of the burn.

²⁹When a man or woman has a disease upon the head or in the beard,

³⁰The priest shall examine the diseased place; if it appears to be deeper than the skin, with yellow, thin hair in it, the priest shall pronounce him unclean; it is a mangelike leprosy of the head or beard.

³¹If the priest examines the spot infected by the mangelike disease, and it does not appear deeper than the skin and there is no black hair in it, the priest shall bind up the spot for seven days.

ᶜHeb. *the quickening of living flesh*   ᵈHeb. a *burning of fire*

New American Standard

10"The priest shall then look, and if there is a white swelling in the skin, and it has turned the hair white, and there is quick raw flesh in the swelling,

11 it is a chronic leprosy on the skin of his body, and the priest shall pronounce him unclean; he shall not isolate him, for he is unclean.

12"If the leprosy breaks out farther on the skin, and the leprosy covers all the skin of *him who has* the infection from his head even to his feet, as far as the priest can see,

13 then the priest shall look, and behold, *if* the leprosy has covered all his body, he shall pronounce clean *him who has* the infection; it has all turned white *and* he is clean.

14"But whenever raw flesh appears on him, he shall be unclean.

15"The priest shall look at the raw flesh, and he shall pronounce him unclean; the raw flesh is unclean, it is leprosy.

16"Or if the raw flesh turns again and is changed to white, then he shall come to the priest,

17 and the priest shall look at him, and behold, *if* the infection has turned to white, then the priest shall pronounce clean *him who has* the infection; he is clean.

18 ¶ "When the body has a boil on its skin and it is healed,

19 and in the place of the boil there is a white swelling or a reddish-white, bright spot, then it shall be shown to the priest;

20 and the priest shall look, and behold, *if* it appears to be lower than the skin, and the hair on it has turned white, then the priest shall pronounce him unclean; it is the infection of leprosy, it has broken out in the boil.

21"But if the priest looks at it, and behold, there are no white hairs in it and it is not lower than the skin and is faded, then the priest shall isolate him for seven days;

22 and if it spreads farther on the skin, then the priest shall pronounce him unclean; it is an infection.

23"But if the bright spot remains in its place and does not spread, it is *only* the scar of the boil; and the priest shall pronounce him clean.

24 ¶ "Or if the body sustains in its skin a burn by fire, and the raw *flesh* of the burn becomes a bright spot, reddish-white, or white,

25 then the priest shall look at it. And if the hair in the bright spot has turned white and it appears to be deeper than the skin, it is leprosy; it has broken out in the burn. Therefore, the priest shall pronounce him unclean; it is an infection of leprosy.

26"But if the priest looks at it, and indeed, there is no white hair in the bright spot and it is no deeper than the skin, but is dim, then the priest shall isolate him for seven days;

27 and the priest shall look at him on the seventh day. If it spreads farther in the skin, then the priest shall pronounce him unclean; it is an infection of leprosy.

28"But if the bright spot remains in its place and has not spread in the skin, but is dim, it is the swelling from the burn; and the priest shall pronounce him clean, for it is *only* the scar of the burn.

29 ¶ "Now if a man or woman has an infection on the head or on the beard,

30 then the priest shall look at the infection, and if it appears to be deeper than the skin and there is thin yellowish hair in it, then the priest shall pronounce him unclean; it is a scale, it is leprosy of the head or of the beard.

31"But if the priest looks at the infection of the scale, and indeed, it appears to be no deeper than the skin and there is no black hair in it, then the priest shall isolate *the person* with the scaly infection for seven days.

New International

be brought to the priest. 10The priest is to examine him, and if there is a white swelling in the skin that has turned the hair white and if there is raw flesh in the swelling, 11it is a chronic skin disease and the priest shall pronounce him unclean. He is not to put him in isolation, because he is already unclean.

12"If the disease breaks out all over his skin and, so far as the priest can see, it covers all the skin of the infected person from head to foot, 13the priest is to examine him, and if the disease has covered his whole body, he shall pronounce that person clean. Since it has all turned white, he is clean. 14But whenever raw flesh appears on him, he will be unclean. 15When the priest sees the raw flesh, he shall pronounce him unclean. The raw flesh is unclean; he has an infectious disease. 16Should the raw flesh change and turn white, he must go to the priest. 17The priest is to examine him, and if the sores have turned white, the priest shall pronounce the infected person clean; then he will be clean.

18"When someone has a boil on his skin and it heals, 19and in the place where the boil was, a white swelling or reddish-white spot appears, he must present himself to the priest. 20The priest is to examine it, and if it appears to be more than skin deep and the hair in it has turned white, the priest shall pronounce him unclean. It is an infectious skin disease that has broken out where the boil was. 21But if, when the priest examines it, there is no white hair in it and it is not more than skin deep and has faded, then the priest is to put him in isolation for seven days. 22If it is spreading in the skin, the priest shall pronounce him unclean; it is infectious. 23But if the spot is unchanged and has not spread, it is only a scar from the boil, and the priest shall pronounce him clean.

24"When someone has a burn on his skin and a reddish-white or white spot appears in the raw flesh of the burn, 25the priest is to examine the spot, and if the hair in it has turned white, and it appears to be more than skin deep, it is an infectious disease that has broken out in the burn. The priest shall pronounce him unclean; it is an infectious skin disease. 26But if the priest examines it and there is no white hair in the spot and if it is not more than skin deep and has faded, then the priest is to put him in isolation for seven days. 27On the seventh day the priest is to examine him, and if it is spreading in the skin, the priest shall pronounce him unclean; it is an infectious skin disease. 28If, however, the spot is unchanged and has not spread in the skin but has faded, it is a swelling from the burn, and the priest shall pronounce him clean; it is only a scar from the burn.

29"If a man or woman has a sore on the head or on the chin, 30the priest is to examine the sore, and if it appears to be more than skin deep and the hair in it is yellow and thin, the priest shall pronounce that person unclean; it is an itch, an infectious disease of the head or chin. 31But if, when the priest examines this kind of sore, it does not seem to be more than skin deep and there is no black hair in it, then the priest is to put the infected person in isola-

King James

³²And in the seventh day the priest shall look on the plague: and, behold, *if* the scall spread not, and there be in it no yellow hair, and the scall *be* not in sight deeper than the skin;

³³He shall be shaven, but the scall shall he not shave; and the priest shall shut up *him that hath* the scall seven days more:

³⁴And in the seventh day the priest shall look on the scall: and, behold, *if* the scall be not spread in the skin, nor *be* in sight deeper than the skin; then the priest shall pronounce him clean: and he shall wash his clothes, and be clean.

³⁵But if the scall spread much in the skin after his cleansing;

³⁶Then the priest shall look on him: and, behold, if the scall be spread in the skin, the priest shall not seek for yellow hair; he *is* unclean.

³⁷But if the scall be in his sight at a stay, and *that* there is black hair grown up therein; the scall is healed, he *is* clean: and the priest shall pronounce him clean.

³⁸ ¶ If a man also or a woman have in the skin of their flesh bright spots, *even* white bright spots;

³⁹Then the priest shall look: and, behold, *if* the bright spots in the skin of their flesh *be* darkish white; it *is* a freckled spot *that* groweth in the skin; he *is* clean.

⁴⁰And the man whose ^ehair is fallen off his head, he *is* bald; *yet is* he clean.

⁴¹And he that hath his hair fallen off from the part of his head toward his face, he *is* forehead bald: *yet is* he clean.

⁴²And if there be in the bald head, or bald forehead, a white reddish sore; it *is* a leprosy sprung up in his bald head, or his bald forehead.

⁴³Then the priest shall look upon it: and, behold, *if* the rising of the sore *be* white reddish in his bald head, or in his bald forehead, as the leprosy appeareth in the skin of the flesh;

⁴⁴He is a leprous man, he *is* unclean: the priest shall pronounce him utterly unclean; his plague *is* in his head.

⁴⁵And the leper in whom the plague *is,* his clothes shall be rent, and his head bare, and he shall put a covering upon his upper lip, and shall cry, Unclean, unclean.

⁴⁶All the days wherein the plague *shall be* in him he shall be defiled; he *is* unclean: he shall dwell alone; without the camp *shall* his habitation *be.*

Leprosy in garments

⁴⁷ ¶ The garment also that the plague of leprosy is in, *whether it be* a woollen garment, or a linen garment;

⁴⁸Whether *it be* in the warp, or woof; of linen, or of woollen; whether in a skin, or in any ^fthing made of skin;

⁴⁹And if the plague be greenish or reddish in the garment, or in the skin, either in the warp, or in the woof, or in any ^gthing of skin; it *is* a plague of leprosy, and shall be shown unto the priest:

⁵⁰And the priest shall look upon the plague, and shut up *it that hath* the plague seven days:

⁵¹And he shall look on the plague on the seventh day: if the plague be spread in the garment, either in the warp, or in the woof, or in a skin, *or* in any work that is made of skin; the plague *is* a fretting leprosy; it *is* unclean.

⁵²He shall therefore burn that garment, whether warp or woof, in woollen or in linen, or any thing of skin, wherein the plague is: for it *is* a fretting leprosy; it shall be burnt in the fire.

⁵³And if the priest shall look, and, behold, the plague be not spread in the garment, either in the warp, or in the woof, or in any thing of skin;

⁵⁴Then the priest shall command that they wash *the thing* wherein the plague *is,* and he shall shut it up seven days more:

Amplified

³²On the seventh day the priest shall examine the diseased spot; if the mange has not spread and has no yellow hair in it and does not look deeper than the skin,

³³Then the patient shall be shaved, except the mangelike spot; and the priest shall bind up the spot seven days.

³⁴On the seventh day the priest shall look at the mangelike spot; if the mange has not spread and looks no deeper than the skin, he shall pronounce the patient clean; he shall wash his clothes and be clean.

³⁵But if the mangelike spot spreads in the skin after his cleansing,

³⁶Then the priest shall examine him, and if the mangelike spot is spread in the skin, the priest need not look for the yellow hair; the patient is unclean.

³⁷But if in his estimation the mange is at a standstill and has black hair in it, the mangelike disease is healed; he is clean; the priest shall pronounce him clean.

³⁸When a man or a woman has on the skin bright spots, even white bright spots,

³⁹Then the priest shall look, and if the bright spots in the skin are a dull white, it is a harmless eruption; he is clean.

⁴⁰If a man's hair has fallen from his head, he is bald, but he is clean.

⁴¹And if his hair has fallen out from the front of his head, he has baldness of the forehead, but he is clean.

⁴²But if there is on the bald head or forehead a reddish white diseased spot, it is leprosy breaking out on his baldness.

⁴³Then the priest shall examine him, and if the diseased swelling is reddish white on his bald head or forehead like the appearance of leprosy in the skin of the body,

⁴⁴He is a leprous man; he is unclean; the priest shall surely pronounce him unclean; his disease is on his head.

⁴⁵And the leper's clothes shall be rent, and the hair of his head shall hang loose, and he shall cover his upper lip and cry, Unclean, unclean!

⁴⁶He shall remain unclean as long as the disease is in him; he is unclean; he shall live alone [and] his dwelling shall be outside the camp.

⁴⁷The garment also that the disease of leprosy [symbolic of sin] is in, whether a wool or a linen garment, [Jude 23; Rev. 3:4.]

⁴⁸Whether it be in woven or knitted stuff *or* in the warp or woof of linen or of wool, or in a skin or anything made of skin,

⁴⁹If the disease is greenish or reddish in the garment, or in a skin or in the warp or woof or in anything made of skin, it is the plague of leprosy; show it to the priest.

⁵⁰The priest shall examine the diseased article and shut it up for seven days.

⁵¹He shall examine the disease on the seventh day; if [it] is spread in the garment, or in the article, whatever service it may be used for, the disease is a rotting *or* corroding leprosy; it is unclean.

⁵²He shall burn the garment, whether diseased in warp or woof, in wool or linen, or anything made of skin; for it is a rotting *or* corroding leprosy, to be burned in the fire.

⁵³But if the priest finds the disease has not spread in the garment, in the warp or the woof, or in anything made of skin,

⁵⁴Then the priest shall command that they wash the thing in which the plague is, and he shall shut it up seven days more.

^eHeb. *head is pilled instrument*   ^fHeb. *work of*   ^gHeb. *vessel,* or,

New American Standard

32"On the seventh day the priest shall look at the infection, and if the scale has not spread and no yellowish hair has grown in it, and the appearance of the scale is no deeper than the skin,
33 then he shall shave himself, but he shall not shave the scale; and the priest shall isolate *the person* with the scale seven more days.
34"Then on the seventh day the priest shall look at the scale, and if the scale has not spread in the skin and it appears to be no deeper than the skin, the priest shall pronounce him clean; and he shall wash his clothes and be clean.
35"But if the scale spreads farther in the skin after his cleansing,
36 then the priest shall look at him, and if the scale has spread in the skin, the priest need not seek for the yellowish hair; he is unclean.
37"If in his sight the scale has remained, however, and black hair has grown in it, the scale has healed, he is clean; and the priest shall pronounce him clean.
38 ¶ "When a man or a woman has bright spots on the skin of the body, *even* white bright spots,
39 then the priest shall look, and if the bright spots on the skin of their bodies are a faint white, it is eczema that has broken out on the skin; he is clean.
40 ¶ "Now if a man loses the hair of his head, he is bald; he is clean.
41"If his head becomes bald at the front and sides, he is bald on the forehead; he is clean.
42"But if on the bald head or the bald forehead, there occurs a reddish-white infection, it is leprosy breaking out on his bald head or on his bald forehead.
43"Then the priest shall look at him; and if the swelling of the infection is reddish-white on his bald head or on his bald forehead, like the appearance of leprosy in the skin of the body,
44 he is a leprous man, he is unclean. The priest shall surely pronounce him unclean; his infection is on his head.
45 ¶ "As for the leper who has the infection, his clothes shall be torn, and the hair of his head shall be uncovered, and he shall cover his mustache and cry, 'Unclean! Unclean!'
46"He shall remain unclean all the days during which he has the infection; he is unclean. He shall live alone; his dwelling shall be outside the camp.
47 ¶ "When a garment has a mark of leprosy in it, whether it is a wool garment or a linen garment,
48 whether in warp or woof, of linen or of wool, whether in leather or in any article made of leather,
49 if the mark is greenish or reddish in the garment or in the leather, or in the warp or in the woof, or in any article of leather, it is a leprous mark and shall be shown to the priest.
50"Then the priest shall look at the mark and shall quarantine the article with the mark for seven days.
51"He shall then look at the mark on the seventh day; if the mark has spread in the garment, whether in the warp or in the woof, or in the leather, whatever the purpose for which the leather is used, the mark is a leprous malignancy, it is unclean.
52"So he shall burn the garment, whether the warp or the woof, in wool or in linen, or any article of leather in which the mark occurs, for it is a leprous malignancy; it shall be burned in the fire.
53 ¶ "But if the priest shall look, and indeed the mark has not spread in the garment, either in the warp or in the woof, or in any article of leather,
54 then the priest shall order them to wash the thing in which the mark occurs and he shall quarantine it for seven more days.

New International

tion for seven days. 32On the seventh day the priest is to examine the sore, and if the itch has not spread and there is no yellow hair in it and it does not appear to be more than skin deep, 33he must be shaved except for the diseased area, and the priest is to keep him in isolation another seven days. 34On the seventh day the priest is to examine the itch, and if it has not spread in the skin and appears to be no more than skin deep, the priest shall pronounce him clean. He must wash his clothes, and he will be clean. 35But if the itch does spread in the skin after he is pronounced clean, 36the priest is to examine him, and if the itch has spread in the skin, the priest does not need to look for yellow hair; the person is unclean. 37If, however, in his judgment it is unchanged and black hair has grown in it, the itch is healed. He is clean, and the priest shall pronounce him clean.
38"When a man or woman has white spots on the skin, 39the priest is to examine them, and if the spots are dull white, it is a harmless rash that has broken out on the skin; that person is clean.
40"When a man has lost his hair and is bald, he is clean. 41If he has lost his hair from the front of his scalp and has a bald forehead, he is clean. 42But if he has a reddish-white sore on his bald head or forehead, it is an infectious disease breaking out on his head or forehead. 43The priest is to examine him, and if the swollen sore on his head or forehead is reddish-white like an infectious skin disease, 44the man is diseased and is unclean. The priest shall pronounce him unclean because of the sore on his head.
45"The person with such an infectious disease must wear torn clothes, let his hair be unkempt,[a] cover the lower part of his face and cry out, 'Unclean! Unclean!' 46As long as he has the infection he remains unclean. He must live alone; he must live outside the camp.

Regulations About Mildew

47"If any clothing is contaminated with mildew—any woolen or linen clothing, 48any woven or knitted material of linen or wool, any leather or anything made of leather— 49and if the contamination in the clothing, or leather, or woven or knitted material, or any leather article, is greenish or reddish, it is a spreading mildew and must be shown to the priest. 50The priest is to examine the mildew and isolate the affected article for seven days. 51On the seventh day he is to examine it, and if the mildew has spread in the clothing, or the woven or knitted material, or the leather, whatever its use, it is a destructive mildew; the article is unclean. 52He must burn up the clothing, or the woven or knitted material of wool or linen, or any leather article that has the contamination in it, because the mildew is destructive; the article must be burned up.
53"But if, when the priest examines it, the mildew has not spread in the clothing, or the woven or knitted material, or the leather article, 54he shall order that the contaminated article be washed. Then he is to isolate it for another

a 45 Or clothes, uncover his head

King James

⁵⁵And the priest shall look on the plague, after that it is washed: and, behold, *if* the plague have not changed his colour, and the plague be not spread; it *is* unclean; thou shalt burn it in the fire; it *is* fret inward, *whether it be* bare within or without.

⁵⁶And if the priest look, and, behold, the plague *be* somewhat dark after the washing of it; then he shall rend it out of the garment, or out of the skin, or out of the warp, or out of the woof:

⁵⁷And if it appear still in the garment, either in the warp, or in the woof, or in any thing of skin; it *is* a spreading *plague*: thou shalt burn that wherein the plague *is* with fire.

⁵⁸And the garment, either warp, or woof, or whatsoever thing of skin *it be,* which thou shalt wash, if the plague be departed from them, then it shall be washed the second time, and shall be clean.

⁵⁹This *is* the law of the plague of leprosy in a garment of woollen or linen, either in the warp, or woof, or any thing of skins, to pronounce it clean, or to pronounce it unclean.

The cleansing of lepers

14 AND THE LORD spake unto Moses, saying, ²This shall be the law of the leper in the day of his cleansing: He shall be brought unto the priest:

³And the priest shall go forth out of the camp; and the priest shall look, and, behold, *if* the plague of leprosy be healed in the leper;

⁴Then shall the priest command to take for him that is to be cleansed two *birds alive *and* clean, and cedar wood, and scarlet, and hyssop:

⁵And the priest shall command that one of the birds be killed in an earthen vessel over running water:

⁶As for the living bird, he shall take it, and the cedar wood, and the scarlet, and the hyssop, and shall dip them and the living bird in the blood of the bird *that was* killed over the running water:

⁷And he shall sprinkle upon him that is to be cleansed from the leprosy seven times, and shall pronounce him clean, and shall let the living bird loose *into the open field.

⁸And he that is to be cleansed shall wash his clothes, and shave off all his hair, and wash himself in water, that he may be clean: and after that he shall come into the camp, and shall tarry abroad out of his tent seven days.

⁹But it shall be on the seventh day, that he shall shave all his hair off his head and his beard and his eyebrows, even all his hair he shall shave off: and he shall wash his clothes, also he shall wash his flesh in water, and he shall be clean.

¹⁰And on the eighth day he shall take two he lambs without blemish, and one ewe lamb *of the first year without blemish, and three tenth deals of fine flour *for a meat offering, mingled with oil, and one log of oil.

¹¹And the priest that maketh *him* clean shall present the man that is to be made clean, and those things, before the LORD, *at* the door of the tabernacle of the congregation.

¹²And the priest shall take one he lamb, and offer him for a trespass offering, and the log of oil, and wave them *for a wave offering before the LORD:

¹³And he shall slay the lamb in the place where he shall kill the sin offering and the burnt offering, in the holy place: for as the sin offering *is* the priest's, *so is* the trespass offering: it *is* most holy:

¹⁴And the priest shall take *some* of the blood of the trespass offering, and the priest shall put *it* upon the tip of the right ear of him that is to be cleansed, and upon the thumb of his right hand, and upon the great toe of his right foot:

Amplified

⁵⁵And the priest shall examine the diseased article after it has been washed, and if the diseased portion has not changed color, though the disease has not spread, it is unclean; you shall burn it in the fire; it is a rotting *or* corroding [disease], whether the leprous spot be inside or outside.

⁵⁶If the priest looks and the diseased portion is less noticeable after it is washed, he shall tear it out of the garment, or the skin (leather), or out of the warp or woof.

⁵⁷If it appears still in the garment, either in the warp or in the woof, or in anything made of skin, it is spreading; you shall burn the diseased part with fire.

⁵⁸But the garment, or the woven or knitted stuff *or* warp or woof, or anything made of skin from which the disease departs when you have washed it, shall then be washed a second time, and be clean.

⁵⁹This is the law for a leprous disease in a garment of wool or linen, either in the warp or woof, or in anything made of skin, to pronounce it clean or unclean.

14 AND THE Lord said to Moses, ²This shall be the law of the leper on the day when he is to be pronounced clean: he shall be brought to the priest [at a meeting place outside the camp];

³The priest shall go out of the camp [to meet him]; and [he] shall examine him, and if the disease is healed in the leper,

⁴Then the priest shall command to take for him who is to be cleansed two living clean birds and cedar wood and scarlet [material] and hyssop. [Heb. 9:19–22.]

⁵And the priest shall command to kill one of the birds in an earthen vessel over fresh, running water.

⁶As for the living bird, he shall take it, the cedar wood, and the scarlet [material], and the hyssop, and shall dip them and the living bird in the blood of the bird killed over the running water;

⁷And he shall sprinkle [the blood] on him who is to be cleansed from the leprosy seven times and shall pronounce him clean, and shall let go the living bird into the open field. [Heb. 9:13–15.]

⁸He who is to be cleansed shall wash his clothes, shave off all his hair, and bathe himself in water; and he shall be clean. After that he shall come into the camp, but stay outside his tent seven days.

⁹But on the seventh day he shall shave all his hair off his head, his beard, his eyebrows, and his [body]; and he shall wash his clothes and bathe his body in water, and be clean.

¹⁰On the eighth day he shall take two he-lambs without blemish and one ewe lamb a year old without blemish, and three-tenths of an ephah of fine flour for a cereal offering, mixed with oil, and one log of oil.

¹¹And the priest who cleanses him shall set the man who is to be cleansed and these things before the Lord at the door of the Tent of Meeting;

¹²The priest shall take one of the male lambs and offer it for a guilt *or* trespass offering, and the log of oil, and wave them for a wave offering before the Lord.

¹³He shall kill the lamb in the place where they kill the sin offering and the burnt offering, in the sacred place [the court of the tabernacle]; for as the sin offering is the priest's, so is the guilt *or* trespass offering; it is most holy;

¹⁴And the priest shall take some of the blood of the guilt *or* trespass offering and put it on the tip of the right ear of him who is to be cleansed, and on the thumb of his right hand, and on the great toe of his right foot.

---

^hHeb. whether *it be bald in the head thereof,* or *in the forehead thereof*   ⁱOr, *sparrows*   ^jHeb. *upon the face of the field*   ^kHeb. *the daughter of her year*

New American Standard

55"After the article with the mark has been washed, the priest shall again look, and if the mark has not changed its appearance, even though the mark has not spread, it is unclean; you shall burn it in the fire, whether an eating away has produced bareness on the top or on the front of it.

56 ¶ "Then if the priest looks, and if the mark has faded after it has been washed, then he shall tear it out of the garment or out of the leather, whether from the warp or from the woof;

57 and if it appears again in the garment, whether in the warp or in the woof, or in any article of leather, it is an outbreak; the article with the mark shall be burned in the fire.

58"The garment, whether the warp or the woof, or any article of leather from which the mark has departed when you washed it, it shall then be washed a second time and will be clean."

59 ¶ This is the law for the mark of leprosy in a garment of wool or linen, whether in the warp or in the woof, or in any article of leather, for pronouncing it clean or unclean.

Law of Cleansing a Leper

14 THEN THE LORD spoke to Moses, saying, 2"This shall be the law of the leper in the day of his cleansing. Now he shall be brought to the priest,

3 and the priest shall go out to the outside of the camp. Thus the priest shall look, and if the infection of leprosy has been healed in the leper,

4 then the priest shall give orders to take two live clean birds and cedar wood and a scarlet string and hyssop for the one who is to be cleansed.

5"The priest shall also give orders to slay the one bird in an earthenware vessel over running water.

6"*As for* the live bird, he shall take it together with the cedar wood and the scarlet string and the hyssop, and shall dip them and the live bird in the blood of the bird that was slain over the running water.

7"He shall then sprinkle seven times the one who is to be cleansed from the leprosy and shall pronounce him clean, and shall let the live bird go free over the open field.

8"The one to be cleansed shall then wash his clothes and shave off all his hair and bathe in water and be clean. Now afterward, he may enter the camp, but he shall stay outside his tent for seven days.

9"It will be on the seventh day that he shall shave off all his hair: he shall shave his head and his beard and his eyebrows, even all his hair. He shall then wash his clothes and bathe his body in water and be clean.

10 ¶ "Now on the eighth day he is to take two male lambs without defect, and a yearling ewe lamb without defect, and three-tenths *of an ephah* of fine flour mixed with oil for a grain offering, and one *i*log of oil;

11 and the priest who pronounces him clean shall present the man to be cleansed and the aforesaid before the LORD at the doorway of the tent of meeting.

12"Then the priest shall take the one male lamb and bring it for a guilt offering, with the log of oil, and present them as a wave offering before the LORD.

13"Next he shall slaughter the male lamb in the place where they slaughter the sin offering and the burnt offering, at the place of the sanctuary—for the guilt offering, like the sin offering, belongs to the priest; it is most holy.

14"The priest shall then take some of the blood of the guilt offering, and the priest shall put *it* on the lobe of the right ear of the one to be cleansed, and on the thumb of his right hand and on the big toe of his right foot.

New International

seven days. 55After the affected article has been washed, the priest is to examine it, and if the mildew has not changed its appearance, even though it has not spread, it is unclean. Burn it with fire, whether the mildew has affected one side or the other. 56If, when the priest examines it, the mildew has faded after the article has been washed, he is to tear the contaminated part out of the clothing, or the leather, or the woven or knitted material. 57But if it reappears in the clothing, or in the woven or knitted material, or in the leather article, it is spreading, and whatever has the mildew must be burned with fire. 58The clothing, or the woven or knitted material, or any leather article that has been washed and is rid of the mildew, must be washed again, and it will be clean."

59These are the regulations concerning contamination by mildew in woolen or linen clothing, woven or knitted material, or any leather article, for pronouncing them clean or unclean.

Cleansing From Infectious Skin Diseases

14 THE LORD said to Moses, 2"These are the regulations for the diseased person at the time of his ceremonial cleansing, when he is brought to the priest: 3The priest is to go outside the camp and examine him. If the person has been healed of his infectious skin disease,*b* 4the priest shall order that two live clean birds and some cedar wood, scarlet yarn and hyssop be brought for the one to be cleansed. 5Then the priest shall order that one of the birds be killed over fresh water in a clay pot. 6He is then to take the live bird and dip it, together with the cedar wood, the scarlet yarn and the hyssop, into the blood of the bird that was killed over the fresh water. 7Seven times he shall sprinkle the one to be cleansed of the infectious disease and pronounce him clean. Then he is to release the live bird in the open fields.

8"The person to be cleansed must wash his clothes, shave off all his hair and bathe with water; then he will be ceremonially clean. After this he may come into the camp, but he must stay outside his tent for seven days. 9On the seventh day he must shave off all his hair; he must shave his head, his beard, his eyebrows and the rest of his hair. He must wash his clothes and bathe himself with water, and he will be clean.

10"On the eighth day he must bring two male lambs and one ewe lamb a year old, each without defect, along with three-tenths of an ephah*c* of fine flour mixed with oil for a grain offering, and one log*d* of oil. 11The priest who pronounces him clean shall present both the one to be cleansed and his offerings before the LORD at the entrance to the Tent of Meeting.

12"Then the priest is to take one of the male lambs and offer it as a guilt offering, along with the log of oil; he shall wave them before the LORD as a wave offering. 13He is to slaughter the lamb in the holy place where the sin offering and the burnt offering are slaughtered. Like the sin offering, the guilt offering belongs to the priest; it is most holy. 14The priest is to take some of the blood of the guilt offering and put it on the lobe of the right ear of the one to be cleansed, on the thumb of his right hand and on

---

b 3 Traditionally *leprosy*; the Hebrew word was used for various diseases affecting the skin—not necessarily leprosy; also elsewhere in this chapter.　　*c 10* That is, probably about 6 quarts (about 6.5 liters)　　*d 10* That is, probably about 2/3 pint (about 0.3 liter); also in verses 12, 15, 21 and 24

*i*I.e. Approx one pt

King James

¹⁵And the priest shall take *some* of the log of oil, and pour *it* into the palm of his own left hand:

¹⁶And the priest shall dip his right finger in the oil that *is* in his left hand, and shall sprinkle of the oil with his finger seven times before the LORD:

¹⁷And of the rest of the oil that *is* in his hand shall the priest put upon the tip of the right ear of him that is to be cleansed, and upon the thumb of his right hand, and upon the great toe of his right foot, upon the blood of the trespass offering:

¹⁸And the remnant of the oil that *is* in the priest's hand he shall pour upon the head of him that is to be cleansed: and the priest shall make an atonement for him before the LORD.

¹⁹And the priest shall offer the sin offering, and make an atonement for him that is to be cleansed from his uncleanness; and afterward he shall kill the burnt offering:

²⁰And the priest shall offer the burnt offering and the meat offering upon the altar: and the priest shall make an atonement for him, and he shall be clean.

²¹And if he *be* poor, and *l*cannot get so much; then he shall take one lamb *for* a trespass offering *m*to be waved, to make an atonement for him, and one tenth deal of fine flour mingled with oil for a meat offering, and a log of oil;

²²And two turtledoves, or two young pigeons, such as he is able to get; and the one shall be a sin offering, and the other a burnt offering.

²³And he shall bring them on the eighth day for his cleansing unto the priest, unto the door of the tabernacle of the congregation, before the LORD.

²⁴And the priest shall take the lamb of the trespass offering, and the log of oil, and the priest shall wave them *for* a wave offering before the LORD:

²⁵And he shall kill the lamb of the trespass offering, and the priest shall take *some* of the blood of the trespass offering, and put *it* upon the tip of the right ear of him that is to be cleansed, and upon the thumb of his right hand, and upon the great toe of his right foot:

²⁶And the priest shall pour of the oil into the palm of his own left hand:

²⁷And the priest shall sprinkle with his right finger *some* of the oil that *is* in his left hand seven times before the LORD:

²⁸And the priest shall put of the oil that *is* in his hand upon the tip of the right ear of him that is to be cleansed, and upon the thumb of his right hand, and upon the great toe of his right foot, upon the place of the blood of the trespass offering:

²⁹And the rest of the oil that *is* in the priest's hand he shall put upon the head of him that is to be cleansed, to make an atonement for him before the LORD.

³⁰And he shall offer the one of the turtledoves, or of the young pigeons, such as he can get;

³¹*Even* such as he is able to get, the one *for* a sin offering, and the other *for* a burnt offering, with the meat offering: and the priest shall make an atonement for him that is to be cleansed before the LORD.

³²This *is* the law *of him* in whom *is* the plague of leprosy, whose hand is not able to get *that which pertaineth* to his cleansing.

Leprosy in houses

³³ ¶ And the LORD spake unto Moses and unto Aaron, saying,

³⁴When ye be come into the land of Canaan, which I give to you for a possession, and I put the plague of leprosy in a house of the land of your possession;

³⁵And he that owneth the house shall come and tell the priest, saying, It seemeth to me *there is* as it were a plague in the house:

Amplified

¹⁵And the priest shall take some of the log of oil and pour it into the palm of his own left hand;

¹⁶And the priest shall dip his right finger in the oil that is in his left hand and shall sprinkle some of the oil with his finger seven times before the Lord;

¹⁷And of the rest of the oil that is in his hand shall the priest put some on the tip of the right ear of him who is to be cleansed, and on the thumb of his right hand, and on the great toe of his right foot, on the blood of the guilt *or* trespass offering [which he has previously placed in each of these places].

¹⁸And the rest of the oil that is in the priest's hand he shall pour upon the head of him who is to be cleansed and make atonement for him before the Lord.

¹⁹And the priest shall offer the sin offering and make atonement for him who is to be cleansed from his uncleanness, and afterward kill the burnt offering [victim].

²⁰And the priest shall offer the burnt offering and the cereal offering on the altar; and he shall make atonement for him, and he shall be clean.

²¹If the cleansed leper is poor and cannot afford so much, he shall take one lamb for a guilt *or* trespass offering to be waved to make atonement for him, and one tenth of an ephah of fine flour mixed with oil for a cereal offering, and a log of oil,

²²And two turtledoves or two young pigeons, such as he can afford, one for a sin offering, the other for a burnt offering.

²³He shall bring them on the eighth day for his cleansing to the priest at the door of the Tent of Meeting, before the Lord.

²⁴And the priest shall take the lamb of the guilt *or* trespass offering, and the log of oil, and shall wave them for a wave offering before the Lord.

²⁵And he shall kill the lamb of the guilt *or* trespass offering, and the priest shall take some of the blood of the offering and put it on the tip of the right ear of him who is to be cleansed, and on the thumb of his right hand, and on the great toe of his right foot.

²⁶And the priest shall pour some of the oil into the palm of his own left hand,

²⁷And shall sprinkle with his right finger some of the oil that is in his left hand seven times before the Lord.

²⁸The priest shall put some of the oil in his hand on the tip of the right ear of the one to be cleansed, and on the thumb of his right hand, and on the great toe of his right foot, on the places where he has put the blood of the guilt offering.

²⁹The rest of the oil that is in the priest's hand he shall put on the head of the one to be cleansed, to make atonement for him before the Lord.

³⁰And he shall offer one of the turtledoves or of the young pigeons, such as he is able to get,

³¹As he can afford, one for a sin offering and the other for a burnt offering, together with the cereal offering; and the priest shall make atonement for him who is to be cleansed before the Lord.

³²This is the law of him in whom is the plague of leprosy, who is not able to get what is required for his cleansing.

³³And the Lord said to Moses and Aaron,

³⁴When you have come into the land of Canaan, which I give to you for a possession, and I put the disease of leprosy in a house of the land of your possession,

³⁵Then he who owns the house shall come and tell the priest, It seems to me there is some sort of disease in my house.

---

*l*Heb. *his hand reach not*   *m*Heb. *for a waving*

New American Standard

15"The priest shall also take some of the log of oil, and pour *it* into his left palm;

16 the priest shall then dip his right-hand finger into the oil that is in his left palm, and with his finger sprinkle some of the oil seven times before the LORD.

17"Of the remaining oil which is in his palm, the priest shall put some on the right ear lobe of the one to be cleansed, and on the thumb of his right hand, and on the big toe of his right foot, on the blood of the guilt offering;

18 while the rest of the oil that is in the priest's palm, he shall put on the head of the one to be cleansed. So the priest shall make atonement on his behalf before the LORD.

19"The priest shall next offer the sin offering and make atonement for the one to be cleansed from his uncleanness. Then afterward, he shall slaughter the burnt offering.

20"The priest shall offer up the burnt offering and the grain offering on the altar. Thus the priest shall make atonement for him, and he will be clean.

21 ¶ "But if he is poor and his means are insufficient, then he is to take one male lamb for a guilt offering as a wave offering to make atonement for him, and one-tenth *of an ephah* of fine flour mixed with oil for a grain offering, and a log of oil,

22 and two turtledoves or two young pigeons which are within his means, the one shall be a sin offering and the other a burnt offering.

23"Then the eighth day he shall bring them for his cleansing to the priest, at the doorway of the tent of meeting, before the LORD.

24"The priest shall take the lamb of the guilt offering and the log of oil, and the priest shall offer them for a wave offering before the LORD.

25"Next he shall slaughter the lamb of the guilt offering; and the priest is to take some of the blood of the guilt offering and put *it* on the lobe of the right ear of the one to be cleansed and on the thumb of his right hand and on the big toe of his right foot.

26"The priest shall also pour some of the oil into his left palm;

27 and with his right-hand finger the priest shall sprinkle some of the oil that is in his left palm seven times before the LORD.

28"The priest shall then put some of the oil that is in his palm on the lobe of the right ear of the one to be cleansed, and on the thumb of his right hand and on the big toe of his right foot, on the place of the blood of the guilt offering.

29"Moreover, the rest of the oil that is in the priest's palm he shall put on the head of the one to be cleansed, to make atonement on his behalf before the LORD.

30"He shall then offer one of the turtledoves or young pigeons, which are within his means.

31"*He shall offer* what he can afford, the one for a sin offering and the other for a burnt offering, together with the grain offering. So the priest shall make atonement before the LORD on behalf of the one to be cleansed.

32"This is the law *for him* in whom there is an infection of leprosy, whose means are limited for his cleansing."

Cleansing a Leprous House

33 ¶ The LORD further spoke to Moses and to Aaron, saying:

34 ¶ "When you enter the land of Canaan, which I give you for a possession, and I put a mark of leprosy on a house in the land of your possession,

35 then the one who owns the house shall come and tell the priest, saying, '*Something* like a mark *of leprosy* has become visible to me in the house.'

New International

the big toe of his right foot. 15The priest shall then take some of the log of oil, pour it in the palm of his own left hand, 16dip his right forefinger into the oil in his palm, and with his finger sprinkle some of it before the LORD seven times. 17The priest is to put some of the oil remaining in his palm on the lobe of the right ear of the one to be cleansed, on the thumb of his right hand and on the big toe of his right foot, on top of the blood of the guilt offering. 18The rest of the oil in his palm the priest shall put on the head of the one to be cleansed and make atonement for him before the LORD.

19"Then the priest is to sacrifice the sin offering and make atonement for the one to be cleansed from his uncleanness. After that, the priest shall slaughter the burnt offering 20and offer it on the altar, together with the grain offering, and make atonement for him, and he will be clean.

21"If, however, he is poor and cannot afford these, he must take one male lamb as a guilt offering to be waved to make atonement for him, together with a tenth of an ephah[e] of fine flour mixed with oil for a grain offering, a log of oil, 22and two doves or two young pigeons, which he can afford, one for a sin offering and the other for a burnt offering.

23"On the eighth day he must bring them for his cleansing to the priest at the entrance to the Tent of Meeting, before the LORD. 24The priest is to take the lamb for the guilt offering, together with the log of oil, and wave them before the LORD as a wave offering. 25He shall slaughter the lamb for the guilt offering and take some of its blood and put it on the lobe of the right ear of the one to be cleansed, on the thumb of his right hand and on the big toe of his right foot. 26The priest is to pour some of the oil into the palm of his own left hand, 27and with his right forefinger sprinkle some of the oil from his palm seven times before the LORD. 28Some of the oil in his palm he is to put on the same places he put the blood of the guilt offering— on the lobe of the right ear of the one to be cleansed, on the thumb of his right hand and on the big toe of his right foot. 29The rest of the oil in his palm the priest shall put on the head of the one to be cleansed, to make atonement for him before the LORD. 30Then he shall sacrifice the doves or the young pigeons, which the person can afford, 31one[f] as a sin offering and the other as a burnt offering, together with the grain offering. In this way the priest will make atonement before the LORD on behalf of the one to be cleansed."

32These are the regulations for anyone who has an infectious skin disease and who cannot afford the regular offerings for his cleansing.

Cleansing From Mildew

33The LORD said to Moses and Aaron, 34"When you enter the land of Canaan, which I am giving you as your possession, and I put a spreading mildew in a house in that land, 35the owner of the house must go and tell the priest, 'I have seen something that looks like mildew in my

---

e 21 That is, probably about 2 quarts (about 2 liters)
f 31 Septuagint and Syriac; Hebrew *31such as the person can afford, one*

King James

36Then the priest shall command that they [n]empty the
house, before the priest go *into it* to see the plague, that all
that *is* in the house be not made unclean: and afterward the
priest shall go in to see the house:
37And he shall look on the plague, and, behold, *if* the
plague *be* in the walls of the house with hollow strakes,
greenish or reddish, which in sight *are* lower than the wall;
38Then the priest shall go out of the house to the door of
the house, and shut up the house seven days:
39And the priest shall come again the seventh day, and
shall look: and, behold, *if* the plague be spread in the walls
of the house;
40Then the priest shall command that they take away the
stones in which the plague *is,* and they shall cast them into
an unclean place without the city:
41And he shall cause the house to be scraped within
round about, and they shall pour out the dust that they
scrape off without the city into an unclean place:
42And they shall take other stones, and put *them* in the
place of those stones; and he shall take other mortar, and
shall plaster the house.
43And if the plague come again, and break out in the
house, after that he hath taken away the stones, and after
he hath scraped the house, and after it is plastered;
44Then the priest shall come and look, and, behold, *if* the
plague be spread in the house, it *is* a fretting leprosy in the
house: it *is* unclean.
45And he shall break down the house, the stones of it,
and the timber thereof, and all the mortar of the house; and
he shall carry *them* forth out of the city into an unclean
place.
46Moreover he that goeth into the house all the while
that it is shut up shall be unclean until the even.
47And he that lieth in the house shall wash his clothes;
and he that eateth in the house shall wash his clothes.
48And if the priest [o]shall come in, and look *upon it,*
and, behold, the plague hath not spread in the house, after
the house was plastered: then the priest shall pronounce
the house clean, because the plague is healed.
49And he shall take to cleanse the house two birds, and
cedar wood, and scarlet, and hyssop:
50And he shall kill the one of the birds in an earthen
vessel over running water:
51And he shall take the cedar wood, and the hyssop, and
the scarlet, and the living bird, and dip them in the blood
of the slain bird, and in the running water, and sprinkle the
house seven times:
52And he shall cleanse the house with the blood of the
bird, and with the running water, and with the living bird,
and with the cedar wood, and with the hyssop, and with
the scarlet:
53But he shall let go the living bird out of the city into
the open fields, and make an atonement for the house: and
it shall be clean.
54This *is* the law for all manner of plague of leprosy, and
scall,
55And for the leprosy of a garment, and of a house,
56And for a rising, and for a scab, and for a bright spot:
57To teach [p]when *it is* unclean, and when *it is* clean:
this *is* the law of leprosy.

Laws about uncleanness

15 AND THE LORD spake unto Moses and to Aaron,
saying,
2Speak unto the children of Israel, and say unto them,
When any man hath a [q]running issue out of his flesh,
because of his issue he *is* unclean.

[n]Or, *prepare* [o]Heb. *in coming in shall come in* [p]Heb. *in the day of the unclean, and in the day of the clean* [q]Or, *running of the reins*

Amplified

36Then the priest shall command that they empty the
house before [he] goes in to examine the disease, so that
all that is in the house may not be declared unclean; afterward [he] shall go in to see the house.
37He shall examine the disease, and if it is in the walls
of the house with depressed spots of dark green or dark red
appearing beneath [the surface of] the wall,
38Then the priest shall go out of the door and shut up the
house seven days.
39The priest shall come again on the seventh day and
shall look; and if the disease has spread in the walls of the
house,
40He shall command that they take out the diseased
stones and cast them into an unclean place outside the city.
41He shall cause the house to be scraped within round
about and the plaster *or* mortar that is scraped off to be
emptied out in an unclean place outside the city.
42And they shall put other stones in the place of those
stones, and he shall plaster the house with fresh mortar.
43If the disease returns, breaking out in the house after
he has removed the stones and has scraped and plastered
the house,
44Then the priest shall come and look, and if the disease
is spreading in the house, it is a rotting *or* corroding leprosy in the house; it is unclean.
45He shall tear down the house—its stones and its timber and all the plaster *or* mortar of the house—and shall
carry them forth out of the city to an unclean place.
46Moreover, he who enters the house during the whole
time that it is shut up shall be unclean until the evening.
47And he who lies down or eats in the house shall wash
his clothes.
48But if the priest inspects it and the disease has not
spread after the house was plastered, he shall pronounce
the house clean, because the disease is healed.
49He shall take to cleanse the house two birds, cedar
wood, scarlet [material], and hyssop;
50And he shall kill one of the birds in an earthen vessel
over running water,
51And he shall take the cedar wood, and the hyssop, and
the scarlet [material], and the living bird, and dip them in
the blood of the slain bird and in the running water, and
sprinkle the house seven times.
52And he shall cleanse the house with the blood of the
bird, the running water, the living bird, the cedar wood, the
hyssop, and the scarlet [material].
53But he shall let the living bird go out of the city into
the open field; so he shall make atonement for the house,
and it shall be clean.
54This is the law for all kinds of leprous diseases, and
mangelike conditions,
55For the leprosy of a garment or of a house,
56And for a swelling or an eruption *or* a scab or a bright
spot,
57To teach when it is unclean and when it is clean. This
is the law of leprosy.

15 AND THE Lord said to Moses and Aaron,
2Say to the Israelites, When any man has a running
discharge from his body, because of his discharge he is
unclean.

New American Standard

36"The priest shall then command that they empty the house before the priest goes in to look at the mark, so that everything in the house need not become unclean; and afterward the priest shall go in to look at the house.

37"So he shall look at the mark, and if the mark on the walls of the house has greenish or reddish depressions and appears deeper than the surface,

38 then the priest shall come out of the house, to the doorway, and quarantine the house for seven days.

39"The priest shall return on the seventh day and make an inspection. If the mark has indeed spread in the walls of the house,

40 then the priest shall order them to tear out the stones with the mark in them and throw them away at an unclean place outside the city.

41"He shall have the house scraped all around inside, and they shall dump the plaster that they scrape off at an unclean place outside the city.

42"Then they shall take other stones and replace *those* stones, and he shall take other plaster and replaster the house.

43 ¶ "If, however, the mark breaks out again in the house after he has torn out the stones and scraped the house, and after it has been replastered,

44 then the priest shall come in and make an inspection. If he sees that the mark has indeed spread in the house, it is a malignant mark in the house; it is unclean.

45"He shall therefore tear down the house, its stones and its timbers, and all the plaster of the house, and he shall take *them* outside the city to an unclean place.

46"Moreover, whoever goes into the house during the time that he has quarantined it, becomes unclean until evening.

47"Likewise, whoever lies down in the house shall wash his clothes, and whoever eats in the house shall wash his clothes.

48 ¶ "If, on the other hand, the priest comes in and makes an inspection and the mark has not indeed spread in the house after the house has been replastered, then the priest shall pronounce the house clean because the mark has not reappeared.

49"To cleanse the house then, he shall take two birds and cedar wood and a scarlet string and hyssop,

50 and he shall slaughter the one bird in an earthenware vessel over running water.

51"Then he shall take the cedar wood and the hyssop and the scarlet string, with the live bird, and dip them in the blood of the slain bird as well as in the running water, and sprinkle the house seven times.

52"He shall thus cleanse the house with the blood of the bird and with the running water, along with the live bird and with the cedar wood and with the hyssop and with the scarlet string.

53"However, he shall let the live bird go free outside the city into the open field. So he shall make atonement for the house, and it will be clean."

54 ¶ This is the law for any mark of leprosy—even for a scale,

55 and for the leprous garment or house,

56 and for a swelling, and for a scab, and for a bright spot—

57 to teach when they are unclean and when they are clean. This is the law of leprosy.

Cleansing Unhealthiness

15 THE LORD also spoke to Moses and to Aaron, saying,

2"Speak to the sons of Israel, and say to them, 'When any man has a discharge from his body, his discharge is unclean.

New International

house.' 36The priest is to order the house to be emptied before he goes in to examine the mildew, so that nothing in the house will be pronounced unclean. After this the priest is to go in and inspect the house. 37He is to examine the mildew on the walls, and if it has greenish or reddish depressions that appear to be deeper than the surface of the wall, 38the priest shall go out the doorway of the house and close it up for seven days. 39On the seventh day the priest shall return to inspect the house. If the mildew has spread on the walls, 40he is to order that the contaminated stones be torn out and thrown into an unclean place outside the town. 41He must have all the inside walls of the house scraped and the material that is scraped off dumped into an unclean place outside the town. 42Then they are to take other stones to replace these and take new clay and plaster the house.

43"If the mildew reappears in the house after the stones have been torn out and the house scraped and plastered, 44the priest is to go and examine it and, if the mildew has spread in the house, it is a destructive mildew; the house is unclean. 45It must be torn down—its stones, timbers and all the plaster—and taken out of the town to an unclean place.

46"Anyone who goes into the house while it is closed up will be unclean till evening. 47Anyone who sleeps or eats in the house must wash his clothes.

48"But if the priest comes to examine it and the mildew has not spread after the house has been plastered, he shall pronounce the house clean, because the mildew is gone. 49To purify the house he is to take two birds and some cedar wood, scarlet yarn and hyssop. 50He shall kill one of the birds over fresh water in a clay pot. 51Then he is to take the cedar wood, the hyssop, the scarlet yarn and the live bird, dip them into the blood of the dead bird and the fresh water, and sprinkle the house seven times. 52He shall purify the house with the bird's blood, the fresh water, the live bird, the cedar wood, the hyssop and the scarlet yarn. 53Then he is to release the live bird in the open fields outside the town. In this way he will make atonement for the house, and it will be clean."

54These are the regulations for any infectious skin disease, for an itch, 55for mildew in clothing or in a house, 56and for a swelling, a rash or a bright spot, 57to determine when something is clean or unclean.

These are the regulations for infectious skin diseases and mildew.

Discharges Causing Uncleanness

15 THE LORD said to Moses and Aaron, 2"Speak to the Israelites and say to them: 'When any man has a bodily discharge, the discharge is unclean. 3Whether it

King James

³And this shall be his uncleanness in his issue: whether his flesh run with his issue, or his flesh be stopped from his issue, it *is* his uncleanness.

⁴Every bed, whereon he lieth that hath the issue, is unclean: and every ʳthing, whereon he sitteth, shall be unclean.

⁵And whosoever toucheth his bed shall wash his clothes, and bathe *himself* in water, and be unclean until the even.

⁶And he that sitteth on *any* thing whereon he sat that hath the issue shall wash his clothes, and bathe *himself* in water, and be unclean until the even.

⁷And he that toucheth the flesh of him that hath the issue shall wash his clothes, and bathe *himself* in water, and be unclean until the even.

⁸And if he that hath the issue spit upon him that is clean; then he shall wash his clothes, and bathe *himself* in water, and be unclean until the even.

⁹And what saddle soever he rideth upon that hath the issue shall be unclean.

¹⁰And whosoever toucheth any thing that was under him shall be unclean until the even: and he that beareth *any of* those things shall wash his clothes, and bathe *himself* in water, and be unclean until the even.

¹¹And whomsoever he toucheth that hath the issue, and hath not rinsed his hands in water, he shall wash his clothes, and bathe *himself* in water, and be unclean until the even.

¹²And the vessel of earth, that he toucheth which hath the issue, shall be broken: and every vessel of wood shall be rinsed in water.

¹³And when he that hath an issue is cleansed of his issue; then he shall number to himself seven days for his cleansing, and wash his clothes, and bathe his flesh in running water, and shall be clean.

¹⁴And on the eighth day he shall take to him two turtledoves, or two young pigeons, and come before the LORD unto the door of the tabernacle of the congregation, and give them unto the priest:

¹⁵And the priest shall offer them, the one *for* a sin offering, and the other *for* a burnt offering; and the priest shall make an atonement for him before the LORD for his issue.

¹⁶And if any man's seed of copulation go out from him, then he shall wash all his flesh in water, and be unclean until the even.

¹⁷And every garment, and every skin, whereon is the seed of copulation, shall be washed with water, and be unclean until the even.

¹⁸The woman also with whom man shall lie *with* seed of copulation, they shall *both* bathe *themselves* in water, and be unclean until the even.

¹⁹ ¶ And if a woman have an issue, *and* her issue in her flesh be blood, she shall be ˢput apart seven days: and whosoever toucheth her shall be unclean until the even.

²⁰And every thing that she lieth upon in her separation shall be unclean: every thing also that she sitteth upon shall be unclean.

²¹And whosoever toucheth her bed shall wash his clothes, and bathe *himself* in water, and be unclean until the even.

²²And whosoever toucheth any thing that she sat upon shall wash his clothes, and bathe *himself* in water, and be unclean until the even.

²³And if it *be* on *her* bed, or on any thing whereon she sitteth, when he toucheth it, he shall be unclean until the even.

²⁴And if any man lie with her at all, and her flowers be upon him, he shall be unclean seven days; and all the bed whereon he lieth shall be unclean.

Amplified

³This shall be [the law concerning] his uncleanness in his discharge: whether his body runs with his discharge or has stopped [running], it is uncleanness in him.

⁴Every bed on which the one who has the discharge lies is unclean, and everything on which he sits shall be unclean.

⁵Whoever touches that person's bed shall wash his clothes, and bathe himself in water, and be unclean until the evening.

⁶And whoever sits on anything on which he who has the discharge has sat shall wash his clothes and bathe himself in water, and be unclean until the evening.

⁷And he who touches the flesh of him who has the discharge shall wash his clothes and bathe himself in water, and be unclean until the evening.

⁸And if he who has the discharge spits on him who is clean, then he shall wash his clothes and bathe himself in water, and be unclean until the evening.

⁹And any saddle on which he who has the discharge rides shall be unclean.

¹⁰Whoever touches anything that has been under him shall be unclean until evening; and he who carries those things shall wash his clothes and bathe himself in water, and be unclean until evening.

¹¹Whomever he who has the discharge touches without rinsing his hands in water shall wash his clothes and bathe himself in water, and be unclean until evening.

¹²The earthen vessel that he with the discharge touches shall be broken, and every vessel of wood shall be rinsed in water.

¹³When he who has a discharge is cleansed of it, he shall count seven days for his purification, then wash his clothes, bathe in running water, and be clean.

¹⁴On the eighth day he shall take two turtledoves or two young pigeons and come before the Lord to the door of the Tent of Meeting and give them to the priest;

¹⁵And the priest shall offer them, one for a sin offering and the other for a burnt offering; and [he] shall make atonement for the man before the Lord for his discharge.

¹⁶And if any man has a discharge of semen, he shall wash all his body in water, and be unclean until evening.

¹⁷And every garment and every skin on which the sperm comes shall be washed with water, and be unclean until evening.

¹⁸The woman also with whom a man with emission of semen shall lie, they shall both bathe themselves in water, and be unclean until evening.

¹⁹And if a woman has a discharge, her [regular] discharge of blood of her body, she shall be in her impurity or separation for seven days, and whoever touches her shall be unclean until evening.

²⁰And everything that she lies on in her separation shall be unclean; everything also that she sits on shall be unclean.

²¹And whoever touches her bed shall wash his clothes and bathe himself in water, and be unclean until evening.

²²Whoever touches anything she sat on shall wash his clothes and bathe himself in water, and be unclean until evening.

²³And if her flow has stained her bed or anything on which she sat, when he touches it, he shall be unclean until evening.

²⁴And if any man lie with her and her impurity be upon him, he shall be unclean seven days; and every bed on which he lies shall be unclean.

ʳHeb. *vessel*   ˢHeb. *in her separation*

New American Standard

3 'This, moreover, shall be his uncleanness in his discharge: it is his uncleanness whether his body allows its discharge to flow or whether his body obstructs its discharge.

4 'Every bed on which the person with the discharge lies becomes unclean, and everything on which he sits becomes unclean.

5 'Anyone, moreover, who touches his bed shall wash his clothes and bathe in water and be unclean until evening;

6 and whoever sits on the thing on which the man with the discharge has been sitting, shall wash his clothes and bathe in water and be unclean until evening.

7 'Also whoever touches the person with the discharge shall wash his clothes and bathe in water and be unclean until evening.

8 'Or if the man with the discharge spits on one who is clean, he too shall wash his clothes and bathe in water and be unclean until evening.

9 'Every saddle on which the person with the discharge rides becomes unclean.

10 'Whoever then touches any of the things which were under him shall be unclean until evening, and he who carries them shall wash his clothes and bathe in water and be unclean until evening.

11 'Likewise, whomever the one with the discharge touches without having rinsed his hands in water shall wash his clothes and bathe in water and be unclean until evening.

12 'However, an earthenware vessel which the person with the discharge touches shall be broken, and every wooden vessel shall be rinsed in water.

13 ¶ 'Now when the man with the discharge becomes cleansed from his discharge, then he shall count off for himself seven days for his cleansing; he shall then wash his clothes and bathe his body in running water and will become clean.

14 'Then on the eighth day he shall take for himself two turtledoves or two young pigeons, and come before the LORD to the doorway of the tent of meeting and give them to the priest;

15 and the priest shall offer them, one for a sin offering and the other for a burnt offering. So the priest shall make atonement on his behalf before the LORD because of his discharge.

16 ¶ 'Now if a man has a seminal emission, he shall bathe all his body in water and be unclean until evening.

17 'As for any garment or any leather on which there is seminal emission, it shall be washed with water and be unclean until evening.

18 'If a man lies with a woman *so that* there is a seminal emission, they shall both bathe in water and be unclean until evening.

19 ¶ 'When a woman has a discharge, *if* her discharge in her body is blood, she shall continue in her menstrual impurity for seven days; and whoever touches her shall be unclean until evening.

20 'Everything also on which she lies during her menstrual impurity shall be unclean, and everything on which she sits shall be unclean.

21 'Anyone who touches her bed shall wash his clothes and bathe in water and be unclean until evening.

22 'Whoever touches any thing on which she sits shall wash his clothes and bathe in water and be unclean until evening.

23 'Whether it be on the bed or on the thing on which she is sitting, when he touches it, he shall be unclean until evening.

24 'If a man actually lies with her so that her menstrual impurity is on him, he shall be unclean seven days, and every bed on which he lies shall be unclean.

New International

continues flowing from his body or is blocked, it will make him unclean. This is how his discharge will bring about uncleanness:

4 "'Any bed the man with a discharge lies on will be unclean, and anything he sits on will be unclean. 5Anyone who touches his bed must wash his clothes and bathe with water, and he will be unclean till evening. 6Whoever sits on anything that the man with a discharge sat on must wash his clothes and bathe with water, and he will be unclean till evening.

7 "'Whoever touches the man who has a discharge must wash his clothes and bathe with water, and he will be unclean till evening.

8 "'If the man with the discharge spits on someone who is clean, that person must wash his clothes and bathe with water, and he will be unclean till evening.

9 "'Everything the man sits on when riding will be unclean, 10and whoever touches any of the things that were under him will be unclean till evening; whoever picks up those things must wash his clothes and bathe with water, and he will be unclean till evening.

11 "'Anyone the man with a discharge touches without rinsing his hands with water must wash his clothes and bathe with water, and he will be unclean till evening.

12 "'A clay pot that the man touches must be broken, and any wooden article is to be rinsed with water.

13 "'When a man is cleansed from his discharge, he is to count off seven days for his ceremonial cleansing; he must wash his clothes and bathe himself with fresh water, and he will be clean. 14On the eighth day he must take two doves or two young pigeons and come before the LORD to the entrance to the Tent of Meeting and give them to the priest. 15The priest is to sacrifice them, the one for a sin offering and the other for a burnt offering. In this way he will make atonement before the LORD for the man because of his discharge.

16 "'When a man has an emission of semen, he must bathe his whole body with water, and he will be unclean till evening. 17Any clothing or leather that has semen on it must be washed with water, and it will be unclean till evening. 18When a man lies with a woman and there is an emission of semen, both must bathe with water, and they will be unclean till evening.

19 "'When a woman has her regular flow of blood, the impurity of her monthly period will last seven days, and anyone who touches her will be unclean till evening.

20 "'Anything she lies on during her period will be unclean, and anything she sits on will be unclean. 21Whoever touches her bed must wash his clothes and bathe with water, and he will be unclean till evening. 22Whoever touches anything she sits on must wash his clothes and bathe with water, and he will be unclean till evening. 23Whether it is the bed or anything she was sitting on, when anyone touches it, he will be unclean till evening.

24 "'If a man lies with her and her monthly flow touches him, he will be unclean for seven days; any bed he lies on will be unclean.

King James

25And if a woman have an issue of her blood many days out of the time of her separation, or if it run beyond the time of her separation; all the days of the issue of her uncleanness shall be as the days of her separation: she *shall be* unclean.

26Every bed whereon she lieth all the days of her issue shall be unto her as the bed of her separation: and whatsoever she sitteth upon shall be unclean, as the uncleanness of her separation.

27And whosoever toucheth those things shall be unclean, and shall wash his clothes, and bathe *himself* in water, and be unclean until the even.

28But if she be cleansed of her issue, then she shall number to herself seven days, and after that she shall be clean.

29And on the eighth day she shall take unto her two turtles, or two young pigeons, and bring them unto the priest, to the door of the tabernacle of the congregation.

30And the priest shall offer the one *for* a sin offering, and the other *for* a burnt offering; and the priest shall make an atonement for her before the LORD for the issue of her uncleanness.

31Thus shall ye separate the children of Israel from their uncleanness; that they die not in their uncleanness, when they defile my tabernacle that *is* among them.

32This *is* the law of him that hath an issue, and *of him* whose seed goeth from him, and is defiled therewith;

33And of her that is sick of her flowers, and of him that hath an issue, of the man, and of the woman, and of him that lieth with her that is unclean.

The day of Atonement

16 AND THE LORD spake unto Moses after the death of the two sons of Aaron, when they offered before the LORD, and died;

2And the LORD said unto Moses, Speak unto Aaron thy brother, that he come not at all times into the holy *place* within the veil before the mercy seat, which *is* upon the ark; that he die not: for I will appear in the cloud upon the mercy seat.

3Thus shall Aaron come into the holy *place:* with a young bullock for a sin offering, and a ram for a burnt offering.

4He shall put on the holy linen coat, and he shall have the linen breeches upon his flesh, and shall be girded with a linen girdle, and with the linen mitre shall he be attired: these *are* holy garments; therefore shall he wash his flesh in water, and *so* put them on.

5And he shall take of the congregation of the children of Israel two kids of the goats for a sin offering, and one ram for a burnt offering.

6And Aaron shall offer his bullock of the sin offering, which *is* for himself, and make an atonement for himself, and for his house.

7And he shall take the two goats, and present them before the LORD *at* the door of the tabernacle of the congregation.

8And Aaron shall cast lots upon the two goats; one lot for the LORD, and the other lot for the *scapegoat.

*Heb. *Azazel*

Amplified

25And if a woman has an issue of blood for many days, not during the time of her separation, or if she has a discharge beyond the time of her [regular] impurity, all the days of the issue of her uncleanness shall be as in the days of her impurity; she shall be unclean. [Matt. 9:20.]

26Every bed on which she lies all the days of her discharge shall be as the bed of her impurity, and whatever she sits on shall be unclean, as in her impurity.

27And whoever touches those things shall be unclean, and shall wash his clothes and bathe himself in water, and be unclean until evening.

28But if she is cleansed of her discharge, then she shall wait seven days, and after that she shall be clean.

29And on the eighth day she shall take two turtledoves or two young pigeons and bring them to the priest at the door of the Tent of Meeting;

30He shall offer one for a sin offering and the other for a burnt offering; and he shall make atonement for her before the Lord for her unclean discharge.

31Thus you shall separate the Israelites from their uncleanness, lest they die in their uncleanness by defiling My tabernacle that is in the midst of them.

32This is the law for him who has a discharge and for him who has emissions of sperm, being made unclean by it;

33And for her who is sick with her impurity, and for any person who has a discharge, whether man or woman, and for him who lies with her who is unclean.

16 AFTER THE death of Aaron's two sons, when they drew near before the Lord [offered false fire] and died, [Lev. 10:1, 2.]

2The Lord said to Moses, Tell Aaron your brother he [i]must not come at all times into the Holy of Holies within the veil before the mercy seat upon the ark, lest he die; for I will appear in the cloud on the mercy seat. [Heb. 9:7–15, 25–28.]

3But Aaron shall come into the holy enclosure in this way: with a young bull for a sin offering and a ram for a burnt offering.

4He shall put on the holy linen undergarment, and he shall have the linen breeches upon his body, and be girded with the linen girdle *or* sash, and with the linen turban *or* miter shall he be attired; these are the holy garments; he shall bathe his body in water and then put them on.

5He shall take [at the expense] of the congregation of the Israelites two male goats for a sin offering and one ram for a burnt offering.

6And Aaron shall present the bull as the sin offering for himself and make atonement for himself and for his house [the other priests].

7He shall take the two goats and present them before the Lord at the door of the Tent of Meeting.

8Aaron shall cast lots on the two goats—one lot for the Lord, the other lot for Azazel *or* removal.

[i]Since the priests have been warned by the death of Nadab and Abihu to approach God with reverence and godly fear, directions are here given how the nearest approach might be made .... Within the veil none must ever come but the high priest only, and he but one day in the year. But see what a blessed change is made by the Gospel of Christ; all good Christians now have boldness to enter into the Holy of Holies, through the veil, every day (Heb. 10:19, 20); and we come **boldly** (not as Aaron must, with fear and trembling) to the throne of grace, or mercy seat (Heb. 4:16) ... Now therefore we are welcome to come at all times into the Holy Place "not made with hands." In the past Aaron could not come near "at all times," lest he die; we now must come near "at all times," that we may live. It is [keeping our] distance only that is our death (Matthew Henry, *A Commentary*).

New American Standard

25 ¶ 'Now if a woman has a discharge of her blood many days, not at the period of her menstrual impurity, or if she has a discharge beyond that period, all the days of her impure discharge she shall continue as though in her menstrual impurity; she is unclean.
26 'Any bed on which she lies all the days of her discharge shall be to her like her bed at menstruation; and every thing on which she sits shall be unclean, like her uncleanness at that time.
27 'Likewise, whoever touches them shall be unclean and shall wash his clothes and bathe in water and be unclean until evening.
28 'When she becomes clean from her discharge, she shall count off for herself seven days; and afterward she will be clean.
29 'Then on the eighth day she shall take for herself two turtledoves or two young pigeons and bring them in to the priest, to the doorway of the tent of meeting.
30 'The priest shall offer the one for a sin offering and the other for a burnt offering. So the priest shall make atonement on her behalf before the LORD because of her impure discharge.'
31 ¶ "Thus you shall keep the sons of Israel separated from their uncleanness, so that they will not die in their uncleanness by their defiling My tabernacle that is among them."
32 This is the law for the one with a discharge, and for the man who has a seminal emission so that he is unclean by it,
33 and for the woman who is ill because of menstrual impurity, and for the one who has a discharge, whether a male or a female, or a man who lies with an unclean woman.

Law of Atonement

16 NOW THE LORD spoke to Moses after the death of the two sons of Aaron, when they had approached the presence of the LORD and died.
2 The LORD said to Moses:
¶ "Tell your brother Aaron that he shall not enter at any time into the holy place inside the veil, before the [j]mercy seat which is on the ark, or he will die; for I will appear in the cloud over the mercy seat.
3 "Aaron shall enter the holy place with this: with a bull for a sin offering and a ram for a burnt offering.
4 "He shall put on the holy linen tunic, and the linen undergarments shall be next to his body, and he shall be girded with the linen sash and attired with the linen turban (these are holy garments). Then he shall bathe his body in water and put them on.
5 "He shall take from the congregation of the sons of Israel two male goats for a sin offering and one ram for a burnt offering.
6 "Then Aaron shall offer the bull for the sin offering which is for himself, that he may make atonement for himself and for his household.
7 "He shall take the two goats and present them before the LORD at the doorway of the tent of meeting.
8 "Aaron shall cast lots for the two goats, one lot for the LORD and the other lot for the [k]scapegoat.

New International

25 'When a woman has a discharge of blood for many days at a time other than her monthly period or has a discharge that continues beyond her period, she will be unclean as long as she has the discharge, just as in the days of her period. 26 Any bed she lies on while her discharge continues will be unclean, as is her bed during her monthly period, and anything she sits on will be unclean, as during her period. 27 Whoever touches them will be unclean; he must wash his clothes and bathe with water, and he will be unclean till evening.
28 'When she is cleansed from her discharge, she must count off seven days, and after that she will be ceremonially clean. 29 On the eighth day she must take two doves or two young pigeons and bring them to the priest at the entrance to the Tent of Meeting. 30 The priest is to sacrifice one for a sin offering and the other for a burnt offering. In this way he will make atonement for her before the LORD for the uncleanness of her discharge.
31 'You must keep the Israelites separate from things that make them unclean, so they will not die in their uncleanness for defiling my dwelling place,[g] which is among them.' "
32 These are the regulations for a man with a discharge, for anyone made unclean by an emission of semen, 33 for a woman in her monthly period, for a man or a woman with a discharge, and for a man who lies with a woman who is ceremonially unclean.

The Day of Atonement

16 THE LORD spoke to Moses after the death of the two sons of Aaron who died when they approached the LORD. 2 The LORD said to Moses: "Tell your brother Aaron not to come whenever he chooses into the Most Holy Place behind the curtain in front of the atonement cover on the ark, or else he will die, because I appear in the cloud over the atonement cover.
3 "This is how Aaron is to enter the sanctuary area: with a young bull for a sin offering and a ram for a burnt offering. 4 He is to put on the sacred linen tunic, with linen undergarments next to his body; he is to tie the linen sash around him and put on the linen turban. These are sacred garments; so he must bathe himself with water before he puts them on. 5 From the Israelite community he is to take two male goats for a sin offering and a ram for a burnt offering.
6 "Aaron is to offer the bull for his own sin offering to make atonement for himself and his household. 7 Then he is to take the two goats and present them before the LORD at the entrance to the Tent of Meeting. 8 He is to cast lots for the two goats—one lot for the LORD and the other for

---

[j]Lit propitiatory   [k]Lit goat of removal, or else a name: Azazel   [g]31 Or my tabernacle

King James

⁹And Aaron shall bring the goat upon which the LORD's lot ᵘfell, and offer him *for* a sin offering.

¹⁰But the goat, on which the lot fell to be the scapegoat, shall be presented alive before the LORD, to make an atonement with him, *and* to let him go for a scapegoat into the wilderness.

¹¹And Aaron shall bring the bullock of the sin offering, which *is* for himself, and shall make an atonement for himself, and for his house, and shall kill the bullock of the sin offering which *is* for himself:

¹²And he shall take a censer full of burning coals of fire from off the altar before the LORD, and his hands full of sweet incense beaten small, and bring *it* within the veil:

¹³And he shall put the incense upon the fire before the LORD, that the cloud of the incense may cover the mercy seat that *is* upon the testimony, that he die not:

¹⁴And he shall take of the blood of the bullock, and sprinkle *it* with his finger upon the mercy seat eastward; and before the mercy seat shall he sprinkle of the blood with his finger seven times.

¹⁵ ¶ Then shall he kill the goat of the sin offering, that *is* for the people, and bring his blood within the veil, and do with that blood as he did with the blood of the bullock, and sprinkle it upon the mercy seat, and before the mercy seat:

¹⁶And he shall make an atonement for the holy *place*, because of the uncleanness of the children of Israel, and because of their transgressions in all their sins: and so shall he do for the tabernacle of the congregation, that ᵛremaineth among them in the midst of their uncleanness.

¹⁷And there shall be no man in the tabernacle of the congregation when he goeth in to make an atonement in the holy *place*, until he come out, and have made an atonement for himself, and for his household, and for all the congregation of Israel.

¹⁸And he shall go out unto the altar that *is* before the LORD, and make an atonement for it; and shall take of the blood of the bullock, and of the blood of the goat, and put *it* upon the horns of the altar round about.

¹⁹And he shall sprinkle of the blood upon it with his finger seven times, and cleanse it, and hallow it from the uncleanness of the children of Israel.

²⁰ ¶ And when he hath made an end of reconciling the holy *place*, and the tabernacle of the congregation, and the altar, he shall bring the live goat:

²¹And Aaron shall lay both his hands upon the head of the live goat, and confess over him all the iniquities of the children of Israel, and all their transgressions in all their sins, putting them upon the head of the goat, and shall send *him* away by the hand of ʷa fit man into the wilderness:

²²And the goat shall bear upon him all their iniquities unto a land ˣnot inhabited: and he shall let go the goat in the wilderness.

²³And Aaron shall come into the tabernacle of the congregation, and shall put off the linen garments, which he put on when he went into the holy *place*, and shall leave them there:

²⁴And he shall wash his flesh with water in the holy place, and put on his garments, and come forth, and offer his burnt offering, and the burnt offering of the people, and make an atonement for himself, and for the people.

²⁵And the fat of the sin offering shall he burn upon the altar.

Amplified

⁹And Aaron shall bring the goat on which the Lord's lot fell and offer him as a sin offering.

¹⁰But the goat on which the lot fell for Azazel *or* removal shall be presented alive before the Lord to make atonement over him, that he may be let go into the wilderness for Azazel (for dismissal).

¹¹Aaron shall present the bull as the sin offering for his own sins and shall make atonement for himself and for his house [the other priests], and shall kill the bull as the sin offering for himself.

¹²He shall take a censer full of burning coals of fire from off the [bronze] altar before the Lord, and his two hands full of sweet incense beaten small, and bring it within the veil [into the Holy of Holies],

¹³And put the incense on the fire [in the censer] before the Lord, that the cloud of the incense may cover the mercy seat that is upon [the ark of] the Testimony, lest he die.

¹⁴He shall take of the bull's blood and sprinkle it with his finger on the front [the east side] of the mercy seat, and before the mercy seat he shall sprinkle of the blood with his finger seven times.

¹⁵Then shall he kill the goat of the sin offering that is for [the sins of] the people and bring its blood within the veil [into the Holy of Holies] and do with that blood as he did with the blood of the bull, and sprinkle it on the mercy seat and before the mercy seat. [Heb. 2:17.]

¹⁶Thus he shall make atonement for the Holy Place because of the uncleanness of the Israelites and because of their transgressions, even all their sins; and so shall he do for the Tent of Meeting, that remains among them in the midst of their uncleanness. [Heb. 9:22-24.]

¹⁷There shall be no man in the Tent of Meeting when the high priest goes in to make atonement in the Holy of Holies [within the veil] until he comes out and has made atonement for his own sins and those of his house [the other priests] and of all the congregation of Israel.

¹⁸And he shall go out to the altar [of burnt offering in the court] which is before the Lord and make atonement for it, and shall take some of the blood of the bull and of the goat and put it on the horns of the altar round about.

¹⁹And he shall sprinkle some of the blood on it with his fingers seven times and cleanse it and hallow it from the uncleanness of the Israelites.

²⁰And when he has finished atoning for the Holy of Holies and the Tent of Meeting and the altar [of burnt offering], he shall present the live goat;

²¹And Aaron shall lay both his hands upon the head of the live goat and confess over him all the iniquities of the Israelites and all their transgressions, all their sins; and he shall put them upon the head of the goat [the sin-bearer], and send him away into the wilderness by the hand of a man ʲwho is timely (ready, fit).

²²The goat shall bear upon himself all their iniquities, carrying them to a land cut off (a land of forgetfulness *and* separation, not inhabited)! And the man leading it shall let the goat go in the wilderness. [Ps. 103:12; Isa. 53:11, 12; John 1:29.]

²³Aaron shall come into the Tent of Meeting and put off the linen garments which he put on when he went into the Holy of Holies, and leave them there;

²⁴And he shall bathe his body with water in a sacred place and put on his garments, and come forth and offer his burnt offering and that of the people, and make atonement for himself and for them.

²⁵And the fat of the sin offering he shall burn upon the altar.

ʲThis is suggestive of the part the personal worker has to play in showing the sinner that Christ the great Sin-bearer has made full substitution for him, if he will accept it. Notice the qualifications of this man, sent along to complete the picture of the transaction between the sinner and his only sin-bearer. He is to be a man, says the Hebrew, "timely (ready, fit)" to do such a task.

ᵘHeb. *went up*   ᵛHeb. *dwelleth*   ʷHeb. *a man of opportunity*
ˣHeb. *of separation*

New American Standard

9"Then Aaron shall offer the goat on which the lot for the LORD fell, and make it a sin offering.

10"But the goat on which the lot for the scapegoat fell shall be presented alive before the LORD, to make atonement upon it, to send it into the wilderness as the scapegoat.

11 ¶ "Then Aaron shall offer the bull of the sin offering which is for himself and make atonement for himself and for his household, and he shall slaughter the bull of the sin offering which is for himself.

12"He shall take a firepan full of coals of fire from upon the altar before the LORD and two handfuls of finely ground sweet incense, and bring *it* inside the veil.

13"He shall put the incense on the fire before the LORD, that the cloud of incense may cover the mercy seat that is on *the ark of* the testimony, otherwise he will die.

14"Moreover, he shall take some of the blood of the bull and sprinkle *it* with his finger on the mercy seat on the east *side;* also in front of the mercy seat he shall sprinkle some of the blood with his finger seven times.

15 ¶ "Then he shall slaughter the goat of the sin offering which is for the people, and bring its blood inside the veil and do with its blood as he did with the blood of the bull, and sprinkle it on the mercy seat and in front of the mercy seat.

16"He shall make atonement for the holy place, because of the impurities of the sons of Israel and because of their transgressions in regard to all their sins; and thus he shall do for the tent of meeting which abides with them in the midst of their impurities.

17"When he goes in to make atonement in the holy place, no one shall be in the tent of meeting until he comes out, that he may make atonement for himself and for his household and for all the assembly of Israel.

18"Then he shall go out to the altar that is before the LORD and make atonement for it, and shall take some of the blood of the bull and of the blood of the goat and put it on the horns of the altar on all sides.

19"With his finger he shall sprinkle some of the blood on it seven times and cleanse it, and from the impurities of the sons of Israel consecrate it.

20 ¶ "When he finishes atoning for the holy place and the tent of meeting and the altar, he shall offer the live goat.

21"Then Aaron shall lay both of his hands on the head of the live goat, and confess over it all the iniquities of the sons of Israel and all their transgressions in regard to all their sins; and he shall lay them on the head of the goat and send *it* away into the wilderness by the hand of a man who *stands* in readiness.

22"The goat shall bear on itself all their iniquities to a solitary land; and he shall release the goat in the wilderness.

23 ¶ "Then Aaron shall come into the tent of meeting and take off the linen garments which he put on when he went into the holy place, and shall leave them there.

24"He shall bathe his body with water in a holy place and put on his clothes, and come forth and offer his burnt offering and the burnt offering of the people and make atonement for himself and for the people.

25"Then he shall offer up in smoke the fat of the sin offering on the altar.

New International

the scapegoat.*h* 9Aaron shall bring the goat whose lot falls to the LORD and sacrifice it for a sin offering. 10But the goat chosen by lot as the scapegoat shall be presented alive before the LORD to be used for making atonement by sending it into the desert as a scapegoat.

11"Aaron shall bring the bull for his own sin offering to make atonement for himself and his household, and he is to slaughter the bull for his own sin offering. 12He is to take a censer full of burning coals from the altar before the LORD and two handfuls of finely ground fragrant incense and take them behind the curtain. 13He is to put the incense on the fire before the LORD, and the smoke of the incense will conceal the atonement cover above the Testimony, so that he will not die. 14He is to take some of the bull's blood and with his finger sprinkle it on the front of the atonement cover; then he shall sprinkle some of it with his finger seven times before the atonement cover.

15"He shall then slaughter the goat for the sin offering for the people and take its blood behind the curtain and do with it as he did with the bull's blood: He shall sprinkle it on the atonement cover and in front of it. 16In this way he will make atonement for the Most Holy Place because of the uncleanness and rebellion of the Israelites, whatever their sins have been. He is to do the same for the Tent of Meeting, which is among them in the midst of their uncleanness. 17No one is to be in the Tent of Meeting from the time Aaron goes in to make atonement in the Most Holy Place until he comes out, having made atonement for himself, his household and the whole community of Israel.

18"Then he shall come out to the altar that is before the LORD and make atonement for it. He shall take some of the bull's blood and some of the goat's blood and put it on all the horns of the altar. 19He shall sprinkle some of the blood on it with his finger seven times to cleanse it and to consecrate it from the uncleanness of the Israelites.

20"When Aaron has finished making atonement for the Most Holy Place, the Tent of Meeting and the altar, he shall bring forward the live goat. 21He is to lay both hands on the head of the live goat and confess over it all the wickedness and rebellion of the Israelites—all their sins—and put them on the goat's head. He shall send the goat away into the desert in the care of a man appointed for the task. 22The goat will carry on itself all their sins to a solitary place; and the man shall release it in the desert.

23"Then Aaron is to go into the Tent of Meeting and take off the linen garments he put on before he entered the Most Holy Place, and he is to leave them there. 24He shall bathe himself with water in a holy place and put on his regular garments. Then he shall come out and sacrifice the burnt offering for himself and the burnt offering for the people, to make atonement for himself and for the people. 25He shall also burn the fat of the sin offering on the altar.

h 8 That is, the goat of removal; Hebrew *azazel*; also in verses 10 and 26

King James

26And he that let go the goat for the scapegoat shall wash his clothes, and bathe his flesh in water, and afterward come into the camp.

27And the bullock *for* the sin offering, and the goat *for* the sin offering, whose blood was brought in to make atonement in the holy *place*, shall *one* carry forth without the camp; and they shall burn in the fire their skins, and their flesh, and their dung.

28And he that burneth them shall wash his clothes, and bathe his flesh in water, and afterward he shall come into the camp.

29 ¶ And *this* shall be a statute for ever unto you: *that* in the seventh month, on the tenth *day* of the month, ye shall afflict your souls, and do no work at all, *whether it be* one of your own country, or a stranger that sojourneth among you:

30For on that day shall *the priest* make an atonement for you, to cleanse you, *that* ye may be clean from all your sins before the LORD.

31It *shall be* a sabbath of rest unto you, and ye shall afflict your souls, by a statute for ever.

32And the priest, whom he shall anoint, and whom he shall *y*consecrate to minister in the priest's office in his father's stead, shall make the atonement, and shall put on the linen clothes, *even* the holy garments:

33And he shall make an atonement for the holy sanctuary, and he shall make an atonement for the tabernacle of the congregation, and for the altar, and he shall make an atonement for the priests, and for all the people of the congregation.

34And this shall be an everlasting statute unto you, to make an atonement for the children of Israel for all their sins once a year. And he did as the LORD commanded Moses.

Laws about special sacrifices

17 AND THE LORD spake unto Moses, saying,
2Speak unto Aaron, and unto his sons, and unto all the children of Israel, and say unto them; This *is* the thing which the LORD hath commanded, saying,

3What man soever *there be* of the house of Israel, that killeth an ox, or lamb, or goat, in the camp, or that killeth *it* out of the camp,

4And bringeth it not unto the door of the tabernacle of the congregation, to offer an offering unto the LORD before the tabernacle of the LORD; blood shall be imputed unto that man; he hath shed blood; and that man shall be cut off from among his people:

5To the end that the children of Israel may bring their sacrifices, which they offer in the open field, even that they may bring them unto the LORD, unto the door of the tabernacle of the congregation, unto the priest, and offer them *for* peace offerings unto the LORD.

6And the priest shall sprinkle the blood upon the altar of the LORD *at* the door of the tabernacle of the congregation, and burn the fat for a sweet savour unto the LORD.

7And they shall no more offer their sacrifices unto devils, after whom they have gone a-whoring. This shall be a statute for ever unto them throughout their generations.

8 ¶ And thou shalt say unto them, Whatsoever man *there be* of the house of Israel, or of the strangers which sojourn among you, that offereth a burnt offering or sacrifice,

9And bringeth it not unto the door of the tabernacle of the congregation, to offer it unto the LORD; even that man shall be cut off from among his people.

Amplified

26The man who led the sin-bearing goat out and let him go for Azazel *or* removal shall wash his clothes and bathe his body, and afterward he may come into the camp.

27The bull and the goat for the sin offering, whose blood was brought in to make atonement in the Holy of Holies, shall be carried forth without the camp; their skins, their flesh, and their dung shall be burned with fire. [Heb. 13:11–13.]

28And he who burns them shall wash his clothes and bathe his body in water, and afterward he may come into the camp.

29It shall be a statute to you forever that in the seventh month [nearly October] on the tenth day of the month you shall afflict yourselves [by fasting with penitence and humiliation] and do no work at all, either the native-born or the stranger who dwells temporarily among you.

30For on this day atonement shall be made for you, to cleanse you; from all your sins you shall be clean before the Lord. [Heb. 10:1, 2; I John 1:7, 9.]

31It is a sabbath of [solemn] rest to you, and you shall afflict yourselves [by fasting with penitence and humiliation]; it is a statute forever.

32And the priest who shall be anointed and consecrated to minister in the priest's office in his father's stead shall make atonement, wearing the holy linen garments;

33He shall make atonement for the Holy Sanctuary, for the Tent of Meeting, and for the altar [of burnt offering in the court], and shall make atonement for the priests and for all the people of the assembly.

34This shall be an everlasting statute for you, that atonement may be made for the Israelites for all their sins once a year. And Moses did as the Lord commanded him.

17 AND THE Lord said to Moses,
2Tell Aaron, his sons, and all the Israelites, This is what the Lord has commanded:

3If any man of the house of Israel kills an ox or lamb or goat in the camp or kills it outside the camp

4And does not bring it to the door of the Tent of Meeting to offer it as an offering to the Lord before the Lord's tabernacle, [guilt for shedding] *k*blood shall be imputed to that man; he has shed blood and shall be cut off from among his people.

5This is so that the Israelites, rather than offer their sacrifices [to idols] in the open field [where they slew them], may bring them to the Lord at the door of the Tent of Meeting, to the priest, to offer them as peace offerings to the Lord.

6And the priest shall dash the blood on the altar of the Lord at the door of the Tent of Meeting and burn the fat for a sweet *and* satisfying fragrance to the Lord.

7So they shall no more offer their sacrifices to goatlike gods *or* demons *or* field spirits after which they have played the harlot. This shall be a statute forever to them throughout their generations.

8And you shall say to them, Whoever of the house of Israel or of the strangers who dwell temporarily among you offers a burnt offering or sacrifice

9And does not bring it to the door of the Tent of Meeting to offer it to the Lord shall be cut off from among his people.

---

y Heb. *fill his hand*

k This requirement, that an animal to be killed was to be brought as an offering to the Lord, was no privation for the owner, for after offering it on the altar of burnt offering he received most of it back as a gift from God.

New American Standard

26"The one who released the goat as the scapegoat shall wash his clothes and bathe his body with water; then afterward he shall come into the camp.

27"But the bull of the sin offering and the goat of the sin offering, whose blood was brought in to make atonement in the holy place, shall be taken outside the camp, and they shall burn their hides, their flesh, and their refuse in the fire.

28"Then the one who burns them shall wash his clothes and bathe his body with water, then afterward he shall come into the camp.

An Annual Atonement

29 ¶ "This shall be a permanent statute for you: in the seventh month, on the tenth day of the month, you shall humble your souls and not do any work, whether the native, or the alien who sojourns among you;

30 for it is on this day that atonement shall be made for you to cleanse you; you will be clean from all your sins before the LORD.

31"It is to be a sabbath of solemn rest for you, that you may humble your souls; it is a permanent statute.

32"So the priest who is anointed and ordained to serve as priest in his father's place shall make atonement: he shall thus put on the linen garments, the holy garments,

33 and make atonement for the holy sanctuary, and he shall make atonement for the tent of meeting and for the altar. He shall also make atonement for the priests and for all the people of the assembly.

34"Now you shall have this as a permanent statute, to make atonement for the sons of Israel for all their sins once every year." And just as the LORD had commanded Moses, so he did.

Blood for Atonement

17 THEN THE LORD spoke to Moses, saying, 2"Speak to Aaron and to his sons and to all the sons of Israel and say to them, 'This is what the LORD has commanded, saying,

3"Any man from the house of Israel who slaughters an ox or a lamb or a goat in the camp, or who slaughters it outside the camp,

4 and has not brought it to the doorway of the tent of meeting to present it as an offering to the LORD before the tabernacle of the LORD, bloodguiltiness is to be reckoned to that man. He has shed blood and that man shall be cut off from among his people.

5"The reason is so that the sons of Israel may bring their sacrifices which they were sacrificing in the open field, that they may bring them in to the LORD, at the doorway of the tent of meeting to the priest, and sacrifice them as sacrifices of peace offerings to the LORD.

6"The priest shall sprinkle the blood on the altar of the LORD at the doorway of the tent of meeting, and offer up the fat in smoke as a soothing aroma to the LORD.

7"They shall no longer sacrifice their sacrifices to the goat demons with which they play the harlot. This shall be a permanent statute to them throughout their generations.' '

8 ¶ "Then you shall say to them, 'Any man from the house of Israel, or from the aliens who sojourn among them, who offers a burnt offering or sacrifice,

9 and does not bring it to the doorway of the tent of meeting to offer it to the LORD, that man also shall be cut off from his people.

New International

26"The man who releases the goat as a scapegoat must wash his clothes and bathe himself with water; afterward he may come into the camp. 27The bull and the goat for the sin offerings, whose blood was brought into the Most Holy Place to make atonement, must be taken outside the camp; their hides, flesh and offal are to be burned up. 28The man who burns them must wash his clothes and bathe himself with water; afterward he may come into the camp.

29"This is to be a lasting ordinance for you: On the tenth day of the seventh month you must deny yourselves[i] and not do any work—whether native-born or an alien living among you— 30because on this day atonement will be made for you, to cleanse you. Then, before the LORD, you will be clean from all your sins. 31It is a sabbath of rest, and you must deny yourselves; it is a lasting ordinance. 32The priest who is anointed and ordained to succeed his father as high priest is to make atonement. He is to put on the sacred linen garments 33and make atonement for the Most Holy Place, for the Tent of Meeting and the altar, and for the priests and all the people of the community.

34"This is to be a lasting ordinance for you: Atonement is to be made once a year for all the sins of the Israelites."

And it was done, as the LORD commanded Moses.

Eating Blood Forbidden

17 THE LORD said to Moses, 2"Speak to Aaron and his sons and to all the Israelites and say to them: 'This is what the LORD has commanded: 3Any Israelite who sacrifices an ox,[j] a lamb or a goat in the camp or outside of it 4instead of bringing it to the entrance to the Tent of Meeting to present it as an offering to the LORD in front of the tabernacle of the LORD—that man shall be considered guilty of bloodshed; he has shed blood and must be cut off from his people. 5This is so the Israelites will bring to the LORD the sacrifices they are now making in the open fields. They must bring them to the priest, that is, to the LORD, at the entrance to the Tent of Meeting and sacrifice them as fellowship offerings.[k] 6The priest is to sprinkle the blood against the altar of the LORD at the entrance to the Tent of Meeting and burn the fat as an aroma pleasing to the LORD. 7They must no longer offer any of their sacrifices to the goat idols[l] to whom they prostitute themselves. This is to be a lasting ordinance for them and for the generations to come.'

8"Say to them: 'Any Israelite or any alien living among them who offers a burnt offering or sacrifice 9and does not bring it to the entrance to the Tent of Meeting to sacrifice it to the LORD—that man must be cut off from his people.

---

i 29 Or must fast; also in verse 31 j 3 The Hebrew word can include both male and female. k 5 Traditionally peace offerings l 7 Or demons

King James

10 ¶ And whatsoever man *there be* of the house of Israel, or of the strangers that sojourn among you, that eateth any manner of blood; I will even set my face against that soul that eateth blood, and will cut him off from among his people.

11For the life of the flesh *is* in the blood: and I have given it to you upon the altar to make an atonement for your souls: for it *is* the blood *that* maketh an atonement for the soul.

12Therefore I said unto the children of Israel, No soul of you shall eat blood, neither shall any stranger that sojourneth among you eat blood.

13And whatsoever man *there be* of the children of Israel, or of the strangers that sojourn among you, ᶻwhich hunteth and catcheth any beast or fowl that may be eaten; he shall even pour out the blood thereof, and cover it with dust.

14For *it is* the life of all flesh; the blood of it *is* for the life thereof: therefore I said unto the children of Israel, Ye shall eat the blood of no manner of flesh: for the life of all flesh *is* the blood thereof: whosoever eateth it shall be cut off.

15And every soul that eateth ᵃthat which died *of itself*, or that which was torn *with beasts, whether it be* one of your own country, or a stranger, he shall both wash his clothes, and bathe *himself* in water, and be unclean until the even: then shall he be clean.

16But if he wash *them* not, nor bathe his flesh; then he shall bear his iniquity.

Unlawful sexual relations

18 AND THE LORD spake unto Moses, saying, 2Speak unto the children of Israel, and say unto them, I am the LORD your God.

3After the doings of the land of Egypt, wherein ye dwelt, shall ye not do: and after the doings of the land of Canaan, whither I bring you, shall ye not do: neither shall ye walk in their ordinances.

4Ye shall do my judgments, and keep mine ordinances, to walk therein: I *am* the LORD your God.

5Ye shall therefore keep my statutes, and my judgments: which if a man do, he shall live in them: I *am* the LORD.

6 ¶ None of you shall approach to any that is ᵇnear of kin to him, to uncover *their* nakedness: I *am* the LORD.

7The nakedness of thy father, or the nakedness of thy mother, shalt thou not uncover: she *is* thy mother; thou shalt not uncover her nakedness.

8The nakedness of thy father's wife shalt thou not uncover: it *is* thy father's nakedness.

9The nakedness of thy sister, the daughter of thy father, or daughter of thy mother, *whether she be* born at home, or born abroad, *even* their nakedness thou shalt not uncover.

10The nakedness of thy son's daughter, or of thy daughter's daughter, *even* their nakedness thou shalt not uncover: for theirs *is* thine own nakedness.

11The nakedness of thy father's wife's daughter, begotten of thy father, she *is* thy sister, thou shalt not uncover her nakedness.

12Thou shalt not uncover the nakedness of thy father's sister: she *is* thy father's near kinswoman.

13Thou shalt not uncover the nakedness of thy mother's sister: for she *is* thy mother's near kinswoman.

14Thou shalt not uncover the nakedness of thy father's brother, thou shalt not approach to his wife: she *is* thine aunt.

15Thou shalt not uncover the nakedness of thy daughter-in-law: she *is* thy son's wife; thou shalt not uncover her nakedness.

16Thou shalt not uncover the nakedness of thy brother's wife: it *is* thy brother's nakedness.

Amplified

10Any one of the house of Israel or of the strangers who dwell temporarily among them who eats any kind of blood, against that person I will set My face and I will cut him off from among his people [that he may not be included in the atonement made for them]. [Ezek. 33:25.]

11For the life (the animal soul) is in the blood, and I have given it for you upon the altar to make atonement for your souls; for it is the blood that makes atonement, by reason of the life [which it represents]. [Rom. 3:24–26.]

12Therefore I have said to the Israelites, No person among you shall eat blood, neither shall any stranger who dwells temporarily among you eat blood.

13And any of the Israelites or of the strangers who sojourn among them who takes in hunting any clean beast or bird shall pour out its blood and cover it with dust.

14As for the life of all flesh, the blood of it represents the life of it; therefore I said to the Israelites, You shall partake of the blood of no kind of flesh, for the life of all flesh is its blood. Whoever eats of it shall be cut off.

15And every person who eats what dies of itself or was torn by beasts, whether he be native-born or a temporary resident, shall wash his clothes and bathe himself in water, and be unclean until evening; then shall he be clean. [Acts 15:20.]

16But if he does not wash his clothes or bathe his body, he shall bear his own iniquity [for it shall not be borne by the sacrifice of atonement].

18 AND THE Lord said to Moses, 2Say to the Israelites, I am the Lord your God.

3You shall not do as was done in the land of Egypt in which you dwelt, nor shall you do as is done in the land of Canaan to which I am bringing you; neither shall you walk in their statutes.

4You shall do My ordinances and keep My statutes and walk in them. I am the Lord your God.

5You shall therefore keep My statutes and My ordinances which, if a man does, he shall live by them. I am the Lord. [Luke 10:25–28; Rom. 10:4, 5; Gal. 3:12.]

6None of you shall approach anyone close of kin to him to have sexual relations. I am the Lord.

7The nakedness of your father, which is the nakedness of your mother, you shall not uncover; she is your mother; you shall not have intercourse with her.

8The nakedness of your father's wife you shall not uncover; it is your father's nakedness.

9You shall not have intercourse with *or* uncover the nakedness of your sister, the daughter of your father or of your mother, whether born at home or born abroad.

10You must not have sexual relations with your son's daughter or your daughter's daughter; their nakedness you shall not uncover, for they are your own flesh.

11You must not have intercourse with your father's wife's daughter; begotten by your father, she is your sister; you shall not uncover her nakedness.

12You shall not have intercourse with your father's sister; she is your father's near kinswoman.

13You shall not have sexual relations with your mother's sister, for she is your mother's near kinswoman.

14You shall not have intercourse with your father's brother's wife; you shall not approach his wife; she is your aunt.

15You shall not uncover the nakedness of your daughter-in-law; she is your son's wife; you shall not have intercourse with her.

16You shall not have intercourse with your brother's wife; she belongs to your brother.

ᶻHeb. *that hunteth any hunting remainder of his flesh*   ᵃHeb. *a carcase*   ᵇHeb.

New American Standard

10 ¶ 'And any man from the house of Israel, or from the aliens who sojourn among them, who eats any blood, I will set My face against that person who eats blood and will cut him off from among his people.

11 'For the life of the flesh is in the blood, and I have given it to you on the altar to make atonement for your souls; for it is the blood by reason of the life that makes atonement.'

12"Therefore I said to the sons of Israel, 'No person among you may eat blood, nor may any alien who sojourns among you eat blood.'

13"So when any man from the sons of Israel, or from the aliens who sojourn among them, in hunting catches a beast or a bird which may be eaten, he shall pour out its blood and cover it with earth.

14 ¶ "For *as for the* life of all flesh, its blood is *identified* with its life. Therefore I said to the sons of Israel, 'You are not to eat the blood of any flesh, for the life of all flesh is its blood; whoever eats it shall be cut off.'

15"When any person eats *an animal* which dies or is torn *by beasts,* whether he is a native or an alien, he shall wash his clothes and bathe in water, and remain unclean until evening; then he will become clean.

16"But if he does not wash *them* or bathe his body, then he shall bear his guilt."

Laws on Immoral Relations

18 THEN THE LORD spoke to Moses, saying, 2"Speak to the sons of Israel and say to them, 'I am the LORD your God.

3 'You shall not do what is done in the land of Egypt where you lived, nor are you to do what is done in the land of Canaan where I am bringing you; you shall not walk in their statutes.

4 'You are to perform My judgments and keep My statutes, to live in accord with them; I am the LORD your God.

5 'So you shall keep My statutes and My judgments, by which a man may live if he does them; I am the LORD.

6 ¶ 'None of you shall approach any blood relative of his to uncover nakedness; I am the LORD.

7 'You shall not uncover the nakedness of your father, that is, the nakedness of your mother. She is your mother; you are not to uncover her nakedness.

8 'You shall not uncover the nakedness of your father's wife; it is your father's nakedness.

9 'The nakedness of your sister, *either* your father's daughter or your mother's daughter, whether born at home or born outside, their nakedness you shall not uncover.

10 'The nakedness of your son's daughter or your daughter's daughter, their nakedness you shall not uncover; for their nakedness is yours.

11 'The nakedness of your father's wife's daughter, born to your father, she is your sister, you shall not uncover her nakedness.

12 'You shall not uncover the nakedness of your father's sister; she is your father's blood relative.

13 'You shall not uncover the nakedness of your mother's sister, for she is your mother's blood relative.

14 'You shall not uncover the nakedness of your father's brother; you shall not approach his wife, she is your aunt.

15 'You shall not uncover the nakedness of your daughter-in-law; she is your son's wife, you shall not uncover her nakedness.

16 'You shall not uncover the nakedness of your brother's wife; it is your brother's nakedness.

New International

10" 'Any Israelite or any alien living among them who eats any blood—I will set my face against that person who eats blood and will cut him off from his people. 11For the life of a creature is in the blood, and I have given it to you to make atonement for yourselves on the altar; it is the blood that makes atonement for one's life. 12Therefore I say to the Israelites, "None of you may eat blood, nor may an alien living among you eat blood."

13" 'Any Israelite or any alien living among you who hunts any animal or bird that may be eaten must drain out the blood and cover it with earth, 14because the life of every creature is its blood. That is why I have said to the Israelites, "You must not eat the blood of any creature, because the life of every creature is its blood; anyone who eats it must be cut off."

15" 'Anyone, whether native-born or alien, who eats anything found dead or torn by wild animals must wash his clothes and bathe with water, and he will be ceremonially unclean till evening; then he will be clean. 16But if he does not wash his clothes and bathe himself, he will be held responsible.' "

Unlawful Sexual Relations

18 THE LORD said to Moses, 2"Speak to the Israelites and say to them: 'I am the LORD your God. 3You must not do as they do in Egypt, where you used to live, and you must not do as they do in the land of Canaan, where I am bringing you. Do not follow their practices. 4You must obey my laws and be careful to follow my decrees. I am the LORD your God. 5Keep my decrees and laws, for the man who obeys them will live by them. I am the LORD.

6" 'No one is to approach any close relative to have sexual relations. I am the LORD.

7" 'Do not dishonor your father by having sexual relations with your mother. She is your mother; do not have relations with her.

8" 'Do not have sexual relations with your father's wife; that would dishonor your father.

9" 'Do not have sexual relations with your sister, either your father's daughter or your mother's daughter, whether she was born in the same home or elsewhere.

10" 'Do not have sexual relations with your son's daughter or your daughter's daughter; that would dishonor you.

11" 'Do not have sexual relations with the daughter of your father's wife, born to your father; she is your sister.

12" 'Do not have sexual relations with your father's sister; she is your father's close relative.

13" 'Do not have sexual relations with your mother's sister, because she is your mother's close relative.

14" 'Do not dishonor your father's brother by approaching his wife to have sexual relations; she is your aunt.

15" 'Do not have sexual relations with your daughter-in-law. She is your son's wife; do not have relations with her.

16" 'Do not have sexual relations with your brother's wife; that would dishonor your brother.

King James

¹⁷Thou shalt not uncover the nakedness of a woman and her daughter, neither shalt thou take her son's daughter, or her daughter's daughter, to uncover her nakedness; *for* they *are* her near kinswomen: it *is* wickedness.

¹⁸Neither shalt thou take ^ca wife to her sister, to vex *her*, to uncover her nakedness, beside the other in her life *time*.

¹⁹Also thou shalt not approach unto a woman to uncover her nakedness, as long as she is put apart for her uncleanness.

²⁰Moreover thou shalt not lie carnally with thy neighbour's wife, to defile thyself with her.

²¹And thou shalt not let any of thy seed pass through *the fire* to Molech, neither shalt thou profane the name of thy God: I *am* the LORD.

²²Thou shalt not lie with mankind, as with womankind: it *is* abomination.

²³Neither shalt thou lie with any beast to defile thyself therewith: neither shall any woman stand before a beast to lie down thereto: it *is* confusion.

²⁴Defile not ye yourselves in any of these things: for in all these the nations are defiled which I cast out before you:

²⁵And the land is defiled: therefore I do visit the iniquity thereof upon it, and the land itself vomiteth out her inhabitants.

²⁶Ye shall therefore keep my statutes and my judgments, and shall not commit *any* of these abominations; *neither* any of your own nation, nor any stranger that sojourneth among you:

²⁷(For all these abominations have the men of the land done, which *were* before you, and the land is defiled;)

²⁸That the land spew not you out also, when ye defile it, as it spewed out the nations that *were* before you.

²⁹For whosoever shall commit any of these abominations, even the souls that commit *them* shall be cut off from among their people.

³⁰Therefore shall ye keep mine ordinance, that *ye* commit not *any one* of these abominable customs, which were committed before you, and that ye defile not yourselves therein: I *am* the LORD your God.

Personal conduct

19 AND THE LORD spake unto Moses, saying, ²Speak unto all the congregation of the children of Israel, and say unto them, Ye shall be holy: for I the LORD your God *am* holy.

³ ¶ Ye shall fear every man his mother, and his father, and keep my sabbaths: I *am* the LORD your God.

⁴ ¶ Turn ye not unto idols, nor make to yourselves molten gods: I *am* the LORD your God.

⁵ ¶ And if ye offer a sacrifice of peace offerings unto the LORD, ye shall offer it at your own will.

⁶It shall be eaten the same day ye offer it, and on the morrow: and if aught remain until the third day, it shall be burnt in the fire.

⁷And if it be eaten at all on the third day, it *is* abominable; it shall not be accepted.

⁸Therefore *every one* that eateth it shall bear his iniquity, because he hath profaned the hallowed thing of the LORD: and that soul shall be cut off from among his people.

⁹ ¶ And when ye reap the harvest of your land, thou shalt not wholly reap the corners of thy field, neither shalt thou gather the gleanings of thy harvest.

¹⁰And thou shalt not glean thy vineyard, neither shalt thou gather *every* grape of thy vineyard; thou shalt leave them for the poor and stranger: I *am* the LORD your God.

¹¹ ¶ Ye shall not steal, neither deal falsely, neither lie one to another.

Amplified

¹⁷You shall not marry a woman and her daughter, nor shall you take her son's daughter or her daughter's daughter to have intercourse; they are [her] near kinswomen; it is wickedness *and* an outrageous offense.

¹⁸You must not marry a woman in addition to her sister, to be a rival to her, having sexual relations with the second sister when the first one is alive.

¹⁹Also you shall not have intercourse with a woman during her [menstrual period or similar] uncleanness.

²⁰Moreover, you shall not lie carnally with your neighbor's wife, to defile yourself with her.

²¹You shall not give any of your children to pass through the fire *and* sacrifice them to Molech [the fire god], nor shall you profane the name of your God [by giving it to false gods]. I am the Lord.

²²You shall not lie with a man as with a woman; it is an abomination. [I Cor. 6:9, 10.]

²³Neither shall you lie with any beast and defile yourself with it; neither shall any woman yield herself to a beast to lie with it; it is confusion, perversion, *and* degradedly carnal.

²⁴Do not defile yourselves in any of these ways, for in all these things the nations are defiled which I am casting out before you.

²⁵And the land is defiled; therefore I visit the iniquity of it upon it, and the land itself vomits out her inhabitants.

²⁶So you shall keep My statutes and My ordinances and shall not commit any of these abominations, neither the native-born nor any stranger who sojourns among you,

²⁷For all these abominations have the men of the land done who were before you, and the land is defiled—

²⁸[Do none of these things] lest the land spew you out when you defile it as it spewed out the nation that was before you.

²⁹Whoever commits any of these abominations shall be cut off from among [his] people.

³⁰So keep My charge: do not practice any of these abominable customs which were practiced before you and defile yourselves by them. I am the Lord your God.

19 AND THE Lord said to Moses, ²Say to all the assembly of the Israelites, You shall be holy, for I the Lord your God am holy. [I Pet. 1:15.]

³Each of you shall give due respect to his mother and his father, and keep My Sabbaths holy. I the Lord am your God.

⁴Do not turn to idols *and* things of nought or make for yourselves molten gods. I the Lord am your God.

⁵And when you offer a sacrifice of peace offering to the Lord, you shall offer it so that you may be accepted.

⁶It shall be eaten the same day you offer it and on the day following; and if anything remains until the third day, it shall be burned in the fire.

⁷If it is eaten at all the third day, it is loathsome; it will not be accepted.

⁸But everyone who eats it shall bear his iniquity, for he has profaned a holy thing of the Lord; and that soul shall be cut off from his people [and not be included in the atonement made for them].

⁹And when you reap the harvest of your land, you shall not reap your field to its very corners, neither shall you gather the fallen ears *or* gleanings of your harvest.

¹⁰And you shall not glean your vineyard bare, neither shall you gather its fallen grapes; you shall leave them for the poor and the stranger. I am the Lord your God.

¹¹You shall not steal, or deal falsely, or lie one to another. [Col. 3:9, 10.]

---

^cOr, one *wife to another*

New American Standard

17 'You shall not uncover the nakedness of a woman and of her daughter, nor shall you take her son's daughter or her daughter's daughter, to uncover her nakedness; they are blood relatives. It is lewdness.

18 'You shall not marry a woman in addition to her sister as a rival while she is alive, to uncover her nakedness.

19 ¶ 'Also you shall not approach a woman to uncover her nakedness during her menstrual impurity.

20 'You shall not have intercourse with your neighbor's wife, to be defiled with her.

21 'You shall not give any of your offspring to offer them to Molech, nor shall you profane the name of your God; I am the LORD.

22 'You shall not lie with a male as one lies with a female; it is an abomination.

23 'Also you shall not have intercourse with any animal to be defiled with it, nor shall any woman stand before an animal to mate with it; it is a perversion.

24 ¶ 'Do not defile yourselves by any of these things; for by all these the nations which I am casting out before you have become defiled.

25 'For the land has become defiled, therefore I have brought its punishment upon it, so the land has spewed out its inhabitants.

26 'But as for you, you are to keep My statutes and My judgments and shall not do any of these abominations, *neither* the native, nor the alien who sojourns among you

27 (for the men of the land who have been before you have done all these abominations, and the land has become defiled);

28 so that the land will not spew you out, should you defile it, as it has spewed out the nation which has been before you.

29 'For whoever does any of these abominations, those persons who do *so* shall be cut off from among their people.

30 'Thus you are to keep My charge, that you do not practice any of the abominable customs which have been practiced before you, so as not to defile yourselves with them; I am the LORD your God.' "

Idolatry Forbidden

19 THEN THE LORD spoke to Moses, saying:
2 ¶ "Speak to all the congregation of the sons of Israel and say to them, 'You shall be holy, for I the LORD your God am holy.

3 'Every one of you shall reverence his mother and his father, and you shall keep My sabbaths; I am the LORD your God.

4 'Do not turn to idols or make for yourselves molten gods; I am the LORD your God.

5 ¶ 'Now when you offer a sacrifice of peace offerings to the LORD, you shall offer it so that you may be accepted.

6 'It shall be eaten the same day you offer *it,* and the next day; but what remains until the third day shall be burned with fire.

7 'So if it is eaten at all on the third day, it is an offense; it will not be accepted.

8 'Everyone who eats it will bear his iniquity, for he has profaned the holy thing of the LORD; and that person shall be cut off from his people.

Sundry Laws

9 ¶ 'Now when you reap the harvest of your land, you shall not reap to the very corners of your field, nor shall you gather the gleanings of your harvest.

10 'Nor shall you glean your vineyard, nor shall you gather the fallen fruit of your vineyard; you shall leave them for the needy and for the stranger. I am the LORD your God.

11 ¶ 'You shall not steal, nor deal falsely, nor lie to one another.

New International

17 'Do not have sexual relations with both a woman and her daughter. Do not have sexual relations with either her son's daughter or her daughter's daughter; they are her close relatives. That is wickedness.

18 'Do not take your wife's sister as a rival wife and have sexual relations with her while your wife is living.

19 'Do not approach a woman to have sexual relations during the uncleanness of her monthly period.

20 'Do not have sexual relations with your neighbor's wife and defile yourself with her.

21 'Do not give any of your children to be sacrificed[m] to Molech, for you must not profane the name of your God. I am the LORD.

22 'Do not lie with a man as one lies with a woman; that is detestable.

23 'Do not have sexual relations with an animal and defile yourself with it. A woman must not present herself to an animal to have sexual relations with it; that is a perversion.

24 'Do not defile yourselves in any of these ways, because this is how the nations that I am going to drive out before you became defiled. 25 Even the land was defiled; so I punished it for its sin, and the land vomited out its inhabitants. 26 But you must keep my decrees and my laws. The native-born and the aliens living among you must not do any of these detestable things, 27 for all these things were done by the people who lived in the land before you, and the land became defiled. 28 And if you defile the land, it will vomit you out as it vomited out the nations that were before you.

29 'Everyone who does any of these detestable things— such persons must be cut off from their people. 30 Keep my requirements and do not follow any of the detestable customs that were practiced before you came and do not defile yourselves with them. I am the LORD your God.' "

Various Laws

19 THE LORD said to Moses, 2 "Speak to the entire assembly of Israel and say to them: 'Be holy because I, the LORD your God, am holy.

3 'Each of you must respect his mother and father, and you must observe my Sabbaths. I am the LORD your God.

4 'Do not turn to idols or make gods of cast metal for yourselves. I am the LORD your God.

5 'When you sacrifice a fellowship offering[n] to the LORD, sacrifice it in such a way that it will be accepted on your behalf. 6 It shall be eaten on the day you sacrifice it or on the next day; anything left over until the third day must be burned up. 7 If any of it is eaten on the third day, it is impure and will not be accepted. 8 Whoever eats it will be held responsible because he has desecrated what is holy to the LORD; that person must be cut off from his people.

9 'When you reap the harvest of your land, do not reap to the very edges of your field or gather the gleanings of your harvest. 10 Do not go over your vineyard a second time or pick up the grapes that have fallen. Leave them for the poor and the alien. I am the LORD your God.

11 'Do not steal.

" 'Do not lie.

" 'Do not deceive one another.

m 21 Or *to be passed through* ⸤*the fire*⸥   n 5 Traditionally *peace offering*

King James

Amplified

12 ¶ And ye shall not swear by my name falsely, neither shalt thou profane the name of thy God: I *am* the LORD.

13 ¶ Thou shalt not defraud thy neighbour, neither rob *him:* the wages of him that is hired shall not abide with thee all night until the morning.

14 ¶ Thou shalt not curse the deaf, nor put a stumbling-block before the blind, but shalt fear thy God: I *am* the LORD.

15 ¶ Ye shall do no unrighteousness in judgment: thou shalt not respect the person of the poor, nor honour the person of the mighty: *but* in righteousness shalt thou judge thy neighbour.

16 ¶ Thou shalt not go up and down *as* a talebearer among thy people: neither shalt thou stand against the blood of thy neighbour: I *am* the LORD.

17 ¶ Thou shalt not hate thy brother in thine heart: thou shalt in any wise rebuke thy neighbour, *d* and not suffer sin upon him.

18 ¶ Thou shalt not avenge, nor bear any grudge against the children of thy people, but thou shalt love thy neighbour as thyself: I *am* the LORD.

19 ¶ Ye shall keep my statutes. Thou shalt not let thy cattle gender with a diverse kind: thou shalt not sow thy field with mingled seed: neither shall a garment mingled of linen and woollen come upon thee.

20 ¶ And whosoever lieth carnally with a woman, that *is* a bondmaid, *ef* betrothed to an husband, and not at all redeemed, nor freedom given her; *gh* she shall be scourged; they shall not be put to death, because she was not free.

21 And he shall bring his trespass offering unto the LORD, unto the door of the tabernacle of the congregation, *even* a ram for a trespass offering.

22 And the priest shall make an atonement for him with the ram of the trespass offering before the LORD for his sin which he hath done: and the sin which he hath done shall be forgiven him.

23 ¶ And when ye shall come into the land, and shall have planted all manner of trees for food, then ye shall count the fruit thereof as uncircumcised: three years shall it be as uncircumcised unto you: it shall not be eaten of.

24 But in the fourth year all the fruit thereof shall be *i* holy to praise the LORD *withal.*

25 And in the fifth year shall ye eat of the fruit thereof, that it may yield unto you the increase thereof: I *am* the LORD your God.

26 ¶ Ye shall not eat *any thing* with the blood: neither shall ye use enchantment, nor observe times.

27 Ye shall not round the corners of your heads, neither shalt thou mar the corners of thy beard.

28 Ye shall not make any cuttings in your flesh for the dead, nor print any marks upon you: I *am* the LORD.

29 ¶ Do not *j* prostitute thy daughter, to cause her to be a whore; lest the land fall to whoredom, and the land become full of wickedness.

30 ¶ Ye shall keep my sabbaths, and reverence my sanctuary: I *am* the LORD.

31 ¶ Regard not them that have familiar spirits, neither seek after wizards, to be defiled by them: I *am* the LORD your God.

32 ¶ Thou shalt rise up before the hoary head, and honour the face of the old man, and fear thy God: I *am* the LORD.

33 ¶ And if a stranger sojourn with thee in your land, ye shall not *k* vex him.

34 *But* the stranger that dwelleth with you shall be unto you as one born among you, and thou shalt love him as thyself; for ye were strangers in the land of Egypt: I *am* the LORD your God.

---

12 And you shall not swear by My name falsely, neither shall you profane the name of your God. I am the Lord.

13 You shall not defraud *or* oppress your neighbor or rob him; the wages of a hired servant shall not remain with you all night until morning.

14 You shall not curse the deaf or put a stumbling block before the blind, but you shall [reverently] fear your God. I am the Lord.

15 You shall do no injustice in judging a case; you shall not be partial to the poor or show a preference for the mighty, but in righteousness *and* according to the merits of the case judge your neighbor.

16 You shall not go up and down as a dispenser of gossip *and* scandal among your people, nor shall you [secure yourself by false testimony or by silence and] endanger the life of your neighbor. I am the Lord.

17 You shall not hate your brother in your heart; but you shall surely rebuke your neighbor, lest you incur sin because of him. [Gal. 6:1; I John 2:9, 11; 3:15.]

18 You shall not take revenge or bear any grudge against the sons of your people, but you shall love your neighbor as yourself. I am the Lord. [Matt. 5:43–46; Rom. 12:17, 19.]

19 You shall keep My statutes. You shall not let your domestic animals breed with a different kind [of animal]; you shall not sow your field with mixed seed, neither wear a garment of linen mixed with wool.

20 And if a man lies carnally with a woman who is a slave betrothed to a husband and not yet ransomed or given her freedom, they shall be punished [after investigation]; they shall not be put to death, because she was not free;

21 But he shall bring his guilt *or* trespass offering to the Lord to the door of the Tent of Meeting, a ram for a guilt *or* trespass offering.

22 The priest shall make atonement for him with the ram of the guilt *or* trespass offering before the Lord for his sin, and he shall be forgiven for committing the sin.

23 And when you come into the land and have planted all kinds of trees for food, then you shall count the fruit of them as inedible *and* forbidden to you for three years; it shall not be eaten.

24 In the fourth year all their fruit shall be holy for giving praise to the Lord.

25 But in the fifth year you may eat of the fruit [of the trees], that their produce may enrich you; I am the Lord your God.

26 You shall not eat anything with the blood; neither shall you use magic, omens, *or* witchcraft [or predict events by horoscope or signs and lucky days].

27 You shall not round the corners of the hair of your heads nor trim the corners of your beard [as some idolaters do].

28 You shall not make any cuttings in your flesh for the dead nor print *or* tattoo any marks upon you; I am the Lord.

29 Do not profane your daughter by causing her to be a harlot, lest the land fall into harlotry and become full of wickedness.

30 You shall keep My Sabbaths and reverence My sanctuary. I am the Lord.

31 Turn not to those [mediums] who have familiar spirits or to wizards; do not seek them out to be defiled by them. I am the Lord your God.

32 You shall rise up before the hoary head and honor the face of the old man and [reverently] fear your God. I am the Lord.

33 And if a stranger dwells temporarily with you in your land, you shall not suppress *and* mistreat him.

34 But the stranger who dwells with you shall be to you as one born among you; and you shall love him as yourself, for you were strangers in the land of Egypt. I am the Lord your God.

---

d Or, *that thou bear not sin for him*   *e* Or, *abused by any*
f Heb. *reproached by,* or, *for man*   *g* Or, *they*   *h* Heb. *there shall be a scourging*   *i* Heb. *holiness of praises to the LORD*
j Heb. *profane*   *k* Or, *oppress*

New American Standard

12 'You shall not swear falsely by My name, so as to profane the name of your God; I am the LORD.

13 ¶ 'You shall not oppress your neighbor, nor rob *him*. The wages of a hired man are not to remain with you all night until morning.

14 'You shall not curse a deaf man, nor place a stumbling block before the blind, but you shall revere your God; I am the LORD.

15 ¶ 'You shall do no injustice in judgment; you shall not be partial to the poor nor defer to the great, but you are to judge your neighbor fairly.

16 'You shall not go about as a slanderer among your people, and you are not to act against the life of your neighbor; I am the LORD.

17 ¶ 'You shall not hate your fellow countryman in your heart; you may surely reprove your neighbor, but shall not incur sin because of him.

18 'You shall not take vengeance, nor bear any grudge against the sons of your people, but you shall love your neighbor as yourself; I am the LORD.

19 ¶ 'You are to keep My statutes. You shall not breed together two kinds of your cattle; you shall not sow your field with two kinds of seed, nor wear a garment upon you of two kinds of material mixed together.

20 ¶ 'Now if a man lies carnally with a woman who is a slave acquired for *another* man, but who has in no way been redeemed nor given her freedom, there shall be punishment; they shall not, *however*, be put to death, because she was not free.

21 'He shall bring his guilt offering to the LORD to the doorway of the tent of meeting, a ram for a guilt offering.

22 'The priest shall also make atonement for him with the ram of the guilt offering before the LORD for his sin which he has committed, and the sin which he has committed will be forgiven him.

23 ¶ 'When you enter the land and plant all kinds of trees for food, then you shall count their fruit as forbidden. Three years it shall be forbidden to you; *it* shall not be eaten.

24 'But in the fourth year all its fruit shall be holy, an offering of praise to the LORD.

25 'In the fifth year you are to eat of its fruit, that its yield may increase for you; I am the LORD your God.

26 ¶ 'You shall not eat *anything* with the blood, nor practice divination or soothsaying.

27 'You shall not round off the side-growth of your heads nor harm the edges of your beard.

28 'You shall not make any cuts in your body for the dead nor make any tattoo marks on yourselves: I am the LORD.

29 ¶ 'Do not profane your daughter by making her a harlot, so that the land will not fall to harlotry and the land become full of lewdness.

30 'You shall keep My sabbaths and revere My sanctuary; I am the LORD.

31 ¶ 'Do not turn to mediums or spiritists; do not seek them out to be defiled by them. I am the LORD your God.

32 ¶ 'You shall rise up before the grayheaded and honor the aged, and you shall revere your God; I am the LORD.

33 ¶ 'When a stranger resides with you in your land, you shall not do him wrong.

34 'The stranger who resides with you shall be to you as the native among you, and you shall love him as yourself, for you were aliens in the land of Egypt; I am the LORD your God.

New International

12 'Do not swear falsely by my name and so profane the name of your God. I am the LORD.

13 'Do not defraud your neighbor or rob him.

" 'Do not hold back the wages of a hired man overnight.

14 'Do not curse the deaf or put a stumbling block in front of the blind, but fear your God. I am the LORD.

15 'Do not pervert justice; do not show partiality to the poor or favoritism to the great, but judge your neighbor fairly.

16 'Do not go about spreading slander among your people.

" 'Do not do anything that endangers your neighbor's life. I am the LORD.

17 'Do not hate your brother in your heart. Rebuke your neighbor frankly so you will not share in his guilt.

18 'Do not seek revenge or bear a grudge against one of your people, but love your neighbor as yourself. I am the LORD.

19 'Keep my decrees.

" 'Do not mate different kinds of animals.

" 'Do not plant your field with two kinds of seed.

" 'Do not wear clothing woven of two kinds of material.

20 'If a man sleeps with a woman who is a slave girl promised to another man but who has not been ransomed or given her freedom, there must be due punishment. Yet they are not to be put to death, because she had not been freed. 21 The man, however, must bring a ram to the entrance to the Tent of Meeting for a guilt offering to the LORD. 22 With the ram of the guilt offering the priest is to make atonement for him before the LORD for the sin he has committed, and his sin will be forgiven.

23 " 'When you enter the land and plant any kind of fruit tree, regard its fruit as forbidden.*o* For three years you are to consider it forbidden*o*; it must not be eaten. 24 In the fourth year all its fruit will be holy, an offering of praise to the LORD. 25 But in the fifth year you may eat its fruit. In this way your harvest will be increased. I am the LORD your God.

26 " 'Do not eat any meat with the blood still in it.

" 'Do not practice divination or sorcery.

27 " 'Do not cut the hair at the sides of your head or clip off the edges of your beard.

28 " 'Do not cut your bodies for the dead or put tattoo marks on yourselves. I am the LORD.

29 " 'Do not degrade your daughter by making her a prostitute, or the land will turn to prostitution and be filled with wickedness.

30 " 'Observe my Sabbaths and have reverence for my sanctuary. I am the LORD.

31 " 'Do not turn to mediums or seek out spiritists, for you will be defiled by them. I am the LORD your God.

32 " 'Rise in the presence of the aged, show respect for the elderly and revere your God. I am the LORD.

33 " 'When an alien lives with you in your land, do not mistreat him. 34 The alien living with you must be treated as one of your native-born. Love him as yourself, for you were aliens in Egypt. I am the LORD your God.

---

o 23 Hebrew *uncircumcised*

King James

³⁵ ¶ Ye shall do no unrighteousness in judgment, in meteyard, in weight, or in measure.

³⁶Just balances, just *¹weights*, a just ephah, and a just hin, shall ye have: I *am* the LORD your God, which brought you out of the land of Egypt.

³⁷Therefore shall ye observe all my statutes, and all my judgments, and do them: I *am* the LORD.

Punishments for sin

20 AND THE LORD spake unto Moses, saying, ²Again, thou shalt say to the children of Israel, Whosoever *he be* of the children of Israel, or of the strangers that sojourn in Israel, that giveth *any* of his seed unto Molech; he shall surely be put to death: the people of the land shall stone him with stones.

³And I will set my face against that man, and will cut him off from among his people; because he hath given of his seed unto Molech, to defile my sanctuary, and to profane my holy name.

⁴And if the people of the land do any ways hide their eyes from the man, when he giveth of his seed unto Molech, and kill him not:

⁵Then I will set my face against that man, and against his family, and will cut him off, and all that go a-whoring after him, to commit whoredom with Molech, from among their people.

⁶ ¶ And the soul that turneth after such as have familiar spirits, and after wizards, to go a-whoring after them, I will even set my face against that soul, and will cut him off from among his people.

⁷ ¶ Sanctify yourselves therefore, and be ye holy: for I *am* the LORD your God.

⁸And ye shall keep my statutes, and do them: I *am* the LORD which sanctify you.

⁹ ¶ For every one that curseth his father or his mother shall be surely put to death: he hath cursed his father or his mother; his blood *shall be* upon him.

¹⁰ ¶ And the man that committeth adultery with *another* man's wife, *even he* that committeth adultery with his neighbour's wife, the adulterer and the adulteress shall surely be put to death.

¹¹And the man that lieth with his father's wife hath uncovered his father's nakedness: both of them shall surely be put to death; their blood *shall be* upon them.

¹²And if a man lie with his daughter-in-law, both of them shall surely be put to death: they have wrought confusion; their blood *shall be* upon them.

¹³If a man also lie with mankind, as he lieth with a woman, both of them have committed an abomination: they shall surely be put to death; their blood *shall be* upon them.

¹⁴And if a man take a wife and her mother, it *is* wickedness: they shall be burnt with fire, both he and they; that there be no wickedness among you.

¹⁵And if a man lie with a beast, he shall surely be put to death: and ye shall slay the beast.

¹⁶And if a woman approach unto any beast, and lie down thereto, thou shalt kill the woman, and the beast: they shall surely be put to death; their blood *shall be* upon them.

¹⁷And if a man shall take his sister, his father's daughter, or his mother's daughter, and see her nakedness, and she see his nakedness; it *is* a wicked thing; and they shall be cut off in the sight of their people; he hath uncovered his sister's nakedness; he shall bear his iniquity.

Amplified

³⁵You shall do no unrighteousness in judgment, in measures of length or weight or quantity.

³⁶You shall have accurate *and* just balances, just weights, just ephah and hin measures. I am the Lord your God, Who brought you out of the land of Egypt.

³⁷You shall observe all My statutes and ordinances and do them. I am the Lord.

20 AND THE Lord said to Moses, ²Moreover, you shall say to the Israelites, Any one of the Israelites or of the strangers that sojourn in Israel who gives any of his children to Molech [the fire god worshiped with human sacrifices] shall surely be put to death; the people of the land shall stone him with stones.

³I also will set My face against that man [opposing him, withdrawing My protection from him, and excluding him from My covenant] and will cut him off from among his people, because he has given of his children to Molech, defiling My sanctuary and profaning My holy name.

⁴And if the people of the land do at all hide their eyes from the man when he gives one of his children [as a burnt offering] to Molech [the fire god] *and* they overlook it *or* neglect to take legal action to punish him, winking at his sin, and do not kill him [as My law requires],

⁵Then I will set My face against that man and against his family and will cut him off from among their people, him and all who follow him to [unfaithfulness to Me, and thus] play the harlot after Molech.

⁶The person who turns to those who have familiar spirits and to wizards, [being unfaithful to Israel's Maker Who is her Husband, and thus] playing the harlot after them, I will set My face against that person and will cut him off from among his people [that he may not be included in the atonement made for them]. [Isa. 54:5.]

⁷Consecrate yourselves therefore, and be holy; for I am the Lord your God.

⁸And you shall keep My statutes and do them. I am the Lord Who sanctifies you.

⁹Everyone who curses his father or mother shall surely be put to death; he has cursed his father or mother; his bloodguilt is upon him.

¹⁰The man who commits adultery with another's wife, even his neighbor's wife, the adulterer and the adulteress shall surely be put to death. [John 8:4–11.]

¹¹And the man who lies carnally with his father's wife has uncovered his father's nakedness; both of the guilty ones shall surely be put to death; their blood shall be upon their own heads.

¹²And if a man lies carnally with his daughter-in-law, both of them shall surely be put to death; they have wrought confusion, perversion, *and* defilement; their blood shall be upon their own heads.

¹³If a man lies with a male as if he were a woman, both men have committed an offense (something perverse, unnatural, abhorrent, and detestable); they shall surely be put to death; their blood shall be upon them.

¹⁴And if a man takes a wife and her mother, it is wickedness *and* an outrageous offense; all three shall be burned with fire, both he and they [after being stoned to death], that there be no wickedness among you. [Josh. 7:15, 25.]

¹⁵And if a man lies carnally with a beast, he shall surely be [stoned] to death, and you shall slay the beast.

¹⁶If a woman approaches any beast and lies carnally with it, you shall [stone] the woman and the beast; they shall surely be put to death; their blood is upon them.

¹⁷If a man takes his sister, his father's or his mother's daughter, and sees her nakedness and she sees his nakedness, it is a wicked *and* shameful thing; and they shall be cut off in the sight of their people; he has had sexual relations with his sister; he shall bear his iniquity.

¹Heb. *stones*

New American Standard

35 ¶ 'You shall do no wrong in judgment, in measurement of weight, or capacity.
36 'You shall have just balances, just weights, a just *l*ephah, and a just *m*hin; I am the LORD your God, who brought you out from the land of Egypt.
37 'You shall thus observe all My statutes and all My ordinances and do them; I am the LORD.' "

On Human Sacrifice and Immoralities

20 THEN THE LORD spoke to Moses, saying,
2 "You shall also say to the sons of Israel:
¶ 'Any man from the sons of Israel or from the aliens sojourning in Israel who gives any of his offspring to Molech, shall surely be put to death; the people of the land shall stone him with stones.
3 'I will also set My face against that man and will cut him off from among his people, because he has given some of his offspring to Molech, so as to defile My sanctuary and to profane My holy name.
4 'If the people of the land, however, should ever disregard that man when he gives any of his offspring to Molech, so as not to put him to death,
5 then I Myself will set My face against that man and against his family, and I will cut off from among their people both him and all those who play the harlot after him, by playing the harlot after Molech.
6 ¶ 'As for the person who turns to mediums and to spiritists, to play the harlot after them, I will also set My face against that person and will cut him off from among his people.
7 'You shall consecrate yourselves therefore and be holy, for I am the LORD your God.
8 'You shall keep My statutes and practice them; I am the LORD who sanctifies you.
9 ¶ 'If *there is* anyone who curses his father or his mother, he shall surely be put to death; he has cursed his father or his mother, his bloodguiltiness is upon him.
10 ¶ 'If *there is* a man who commits adultery with another man's wife, one who commits adultery with his friend's wife, the adulterer and the adulteress shall surely be put to death.
11 'If *there is* a man who lies with his father's wife, he has uncovered his father's nakedness; both of them shall surely be put to death, their bloodguiltiness is upon them.
12 'If *there is* a man who lies with his daughter-in-law, both of them shall surely be put to death; they have committed incest, their bloodguiltiness is upon them.
13 'If *there is* a man who lies with a male as those who lie with a woman, both of them have committed a detestable act; they shall surely be put to death. Their bloodguiltiness is upon them.
14 'If *there is* a man who marries a woman and her mother, it is immorality; both he and they shall be burned with fire, so that there will be no immorality in your midst.
15 'If *there is* a man who lies with an animal, he shall surely be put to death; you shall also kill the animal.
16 'If *there is* a woman who approaches any animal to mate with it, you shall kill the woman and the animal; they shall surely be put to death. Their bloodguiltiness is upon them.
17 ¶ 'If *there is* a man who takes his sister, his father's daughter or his mother's daughter, so that he sees her nakedness and she sees his nakedness, it is a disgrace; and they shall be cut off in the sight of the sons of their people. He has uncovered his sister's nakedness; he bears his guilt.

New International

35 " 'Do not use dishonest standards when measuring length, weight or quantity. 36 Use honest scales and honest weights, an honest ephah*p* and an honest hin.*q* I am the LORD your God, who brought you out of Egypt.
37 " 'Keep all my decrees and all my laws and follow them. I am the LORD.' "

Punishments for Sin

20 THE LORD said to Moses, 2 "Say to the Israelites: 'Any Israelite or any alien living in Israel who gives*r* any of his children to Molech must be put to death. The people of the community are to stone him. 3 I will set my face against that man and I will cut him off from his people; for by giving his children to Molech, he has defiled my sanctuary and profaned my holy name. 4 If the people of the community close their eyes when that man gives one of his children to Molech and they fail to put him to death, 5 I will set my face against that man and his family and will cut off from their people both him and all who follow him in prostituting themselves to Molech.
6 " 'I will set my face against the person who turns to mediums and spiritists to prostitute himself by following them, and I will cut him off from his people.
7 " 'Consecrate yourselves and be holy, because I am the LORD your God. 8 Keep my decrees and follow them. I am the LORD, who makes you holy.*s*
9 " 'If anyone curses his father or mother, he must be put to death. He has cursed his father or his mother, and his blood will be on his own head.
10 " 'If a man commits adultery with another man's wife—with the wife of his neighbor—both the adulterer and the adulteress must be put to death.
11 " 'If a man sleeps with his father's wife, he has dishonored his father. Both the man and the woman must be put to death; their blood will be on their own heads.
12 " 'If a man sleeps with his daughter-in-law, both of them must be put to death. What they have done is a perversion; their blood will be on their own heads.
13 " 'If a man lies with a man as one lies with a woman, both of them have done what is detestable. They must be put to death; their blood will be on their own heads.
14 " 'If a man marries both a woman and her mother, it is wicked. Both he and they must be burned in the fire, so that no wickedness will be among you.
15 " 'If a man has sexual relations with an animal, he must be put to death, and you must kill the animal.
16 " 'If a woman approaches an animal to have sexual relations with it, kill both the woman and the animal. They must be put to death; their blood will be on their own heads.
17 " 'If a man marries his sister, the daughter of either his father or his mother, and they have sexual relations, it is a disgrace. They must be cut off before the eyes of their people. He has dishonored his sister and will be held responsible.

---

l I.e. Approx one bu   *m* I.e. Approx one gal.

p 36 An ephah was a dry measure.   *q 36* A hin was a liquid measure.   *r 2* Or *sacrifices*; also in verses 3 and 4
s 8 Or *who sanctifies you*; or *who sets you apart as holy*

King James

18And if a man shall lie with a woman having her sickness, and shall uncover her nakedness; he hath *m*discovered her fountain, and she hath uncovered the fountain of her blood: and both of them shall be cut off from among their people.

19And thou shalt not uncover the nakedness of thy mother's sister, nor of thy father's sister: for he uncovereth his near kin: they shall bear their iniquity.

20And if a man shall lie with his uncle's wife, he hath uncovered his uncle's nakedness: they shall bear their sin; they shall die childless.

21And if a man shall take his brother's wife, it *is* *n*an unclean thing: he hath uncovered his brother's nakedness; they shall be childless.

22 ¶ Ye shall therefore keep all my statutes, and all my judgments, and do them: that the land, whither I bring you to dwell therein, spew you not out.

23And ye shall not walk in the manners of the nation, which I cast out before you: for they committed all these things, and therefore I abhorred them.

24But I have said unto you, Ye shall inherit their land, and I will give it unto you to possess it, a land that floweth with milk and honey: I *am* the LORD your God, which have separated you from *other* people.

25Ye shall therefore put difference between clean beasts and unclean, and between unclean fowls and clean: and ye shall not make your souls abominable by beast, or by fowl, or by any manner of living thing that *o*creepeth on the ground, which I have separated from you as unclean.

26And ye shall be holy unto me: for I the LORD *am* holy, and have severed you from *other* people, that ye should be mine.

27 ¶ A man also or woman that hath a familiar spirit, or that is a wizard, shall surely be put to death: they shall stone them with stones: their blood *shall be* upon them.

The sanctity of the priesthood

21 AND THE LORD said unto Moses, Speak unto the priests the sons of Aaron, and say unto them, There shall none be defiled for the dead among his people:

2But for his kin, that is near unto him, *that is,* for his mother, and for his father, and for his son, and for his daughter, and for his brother,

3And for his sister a virgin, that is nigh unto him, which hath had no husband; for her may he be defiled.

4But *p*he shall not defile himself, *being* a chief man among his people, to profane himself.

5They shall not make baldness upon their head, neither shall they shave off the corner of their beard, nor make any cuttings in their flesh.

6They shall be holy unto their God, and not profane the name of their God: for the offerings of the LORD made by fire, *and* the bread of their God, they do offer: therefore they shall be holy.

7They shall not take a wife *that is* a whore, or profane; neither shall they take a woman put away from her husband: for he *is* holy unto his God.

8Thou shalt sanctify him therefore; for he offereth the bread of thy God: he shall be holy unto thee: for I the LORD, which sanctify you, *am* holy.

9 ¶ And the daughter of any priest, if she profane herself by playing the whore, she profaneth her father: she shall be burnt with fire.

10And *he that is* the high priest among his brethren, upon whose head the anointing oil was poured, and that is consecrated to put on the garments, shall not uncover his head, nor rend his clothes;

*m*Heb. *made naked*   *n*Heb. *a separation*   *o*Or, *moveth*
*p*Or, *being an husband among his people, he shall not defile himself*
for his wife; see Ezek. 24:16,17

Amplified

18And if a man shall lie with a woman having her menstrual pains and shall uncover her nakedness, he has made naked her fountain, and she has uncovered the fountain of her blood; and both of them shall be cut off from among their people.

19You shall not uncover the nakedness of your mother's sister or of your father's sister, for that is to make naked his close kin; they shall bear their iniquity.

20And if a man shall lie carnally with his uncle's wife, he has uncovered his uncle's nakedness; they shall bear their sin; they shall die childless [not literally, but in a legal sense].

21And if a man shall take his brother's wife, it is impurity; he has uncovered his brother's nakedness; they shall be childless [not literally, but in a legal sense].

22You shall therefore keep all My statutes and all My ordinances and do them, that the land where I am bringing you to dwell may not vomit you out [as it did those before you]. [Lev. 18:28.]

23You shall not walk in the customs of the nation which I am casting out before you; for they did all these things, and therefore I was wearied *and* grieved by them.

24But I have said to you, You shall inherit their land, and I will give it to you to possess, a land flowing with milk and honey. I am the Lord your God, Who has separated you from the peoples.

25You shall therefore make a distinction between the clean beast and the unclean, and between the unclean fowl and the clean; and you shall not make yourselves detestable with beast or with bird or with anything with which the ground teems *or* that creeps, which I have set apart from you as unclean.

26And you shall be holy to Me; for I the Lord am holy, and have separated you from the peoples, that you should be Mine.

27A man or woman who is a medium *and* has a familiar spirit or is a wizard shall surely be put to death, be stoned with stones; their blood shall be upon them.

21 THE LORD said to Moses, Speak to the priests [exclusive of the high priest], the sons of Aaron, and say to them that none of them shall defile himself for the dead among his people [by touching a corpse or assisting in preparing it for burial],

2Except for his near [blood] kin, for his mother, father, son, daughter, brother,

3And for his sister, a virgin, who is near to him because she has had no husband; for her he may be defiled.

4He shall not even defile himself, being a [bereaved] husband [his wife not being his blood kin] *or* being a chief man among his people, and so profane himself.

5The priests [like the other Israelite men] shall not shave the crown of their heads or clip off the corners of their beard or make any cuttings in their flesh.

6They shall be holy to their God and not profane the name of their God; for they offer the offerings made by fire to the Lord, the bread of their God; therefore they shall be holy.

7They shall not take a wife who is a harlot or polluted *or* profane or divorced, for [the priest] is holy to his God.

8You shall consecrate him therefore, for he offers the bread of your God; he shall be holy to you, for I the Lord Who sanctifies you am holy.

9The daughter of any priest who profanes herself by playing the harlot profanes her father; she shall be burned with fire [after being stoned]. [Josh. 7:15, 25.]

10But he who is the high priest among his brethren, upon whose head the anointing oil was poured and who is consecrated to put on the [sacred] garments, shall not let the hair of his head hang loose or rend his clothes [in mourning],

New American Standard

18 'If *there is* a man who lies with a menstruous woman and uncovers her nakedness, he has laid bare her flow, and she has exposed the flow of her blood; thus both of them shall be cut off from among their people.

19 'You shall also not uncover the nakedness of your mother's sister or of your father's sister, for such a one has made naked his blood relative; they will bear their guilt.

20 'If *there is* a man who lies with his uncle's wife he has uncovered his uncle's nakedness; they will bear their sin. They will die childless.

21 'If *there is* a man who takes his brother's wife, it is abhorrent; he has uncovered his brother's nakedness. They will be childless.

22 ¶ 'You are therefore to keep all My statutes and all My ordinances and do them, so that the land to which I am bringing you to live will not spew you out.

23 'Moreover, you shall not follow the customs of the nation which I will drive out before you, for they did all these things, and therefore I have abhorred them.

24 'Hence I have said to you, "You are to possess their land, and I Myself will give it to you to possess it, a land flowing with milk and honey." I am the LORD your God, who has separated you from the peoples.

25 'You are therefore to make a distinction between the clean animal and the unclean, and between the unclean bird and the clean; and you shall not make yourselves detestable by animal or by bird or by anything that creeps on the ground, which I have separated for you as unclean.

26 'Thus you are to be holy to Me, for I the LORD am holy; and I have set you apart from the peoples to be Mine.

27 ¶ 'Now a man or a woman who is a medium or a spiritist shall surely be put to death. They shall be stoned with stones, their bloodguiltiness is upon them.' "

Regulations concerning Priests

21 THEN THE LORD said to Moses, "Speak to the priests, the sons of Aaron, and say to them:

¶ 'No one shall defile himself for a *dead* person among his people,

2 except for his relatives who are nearest to him, his mother and his father and his son and his daughter and his brother,

3 also for his virgin sister, who is near to him because she has had no husband; for her he may defile himself.

4 'He shall not defile himself as a relative by marriage among his people, and so profane himself.

5 'They shall not make any baldness on their heads, nor shave off the edges of their beards, nor make any cuts in their flesh.

6 'They shall be holy to their God and not profane the name of their God, for they present the offerings by fire to the LORD, the food of their God; so they shall be holy.

7 'They shall not take a woman who is profaned by harlotry, nor shall they take a woman divorced from her husband; for he is holy to his God.

8 'You shall consecrate him, therefore, for he offers the food of your God; he shall be holy to you; for I the LORD, who sanctifies you, am holy.

9 'Also the daughter of any priest, if she profanes herself by harlotry, she profanes her father; she shall be burned with fire.

10 ¶ 'The priest who is the highest among his brothers, on whose head the anointing oil has been poured and who has been consecrated to wear the garments, shall not uncover his head nor tear his clothes;

New International

18 " 'If a man lies with a woman during her monthly period and has sexual relations with her, he has exposed the source of her flow, and she has also uncovered it. Both of them must be cut off from their people.

19 " 'Do not have sexual relations with the sister of either your mother or your father, for that would dishonor a close relative; both of you would be held responsible.

20 " 'If a man sleeps with his aunt, he has dishonored his uncle. They will be held responsible; they will die childless.

21 " 'If a man marries his brother's wife, it is an act of impurity; he has dishonored his brother. They will be childless.

22 " 'Keep all my decrees and laws and follow them, so that the land where I am bringing you to live may not vomit you out. 23You must not live according to the customs of the nations I am going to drive out before you. Because they did all these things, I abhorred them. 24But I said to you, "You will possess their land; I will give it to you as an inheritance, a land flowing with milk and honey." I am the LORD your God, who has set you apart from the nations.

25 " 'You must therefore make a distinction between clean and unclean animals and between unclean and clean birds. Do not defile yourselves by any animal or bird or anything that moves along the ground—those which I have set apart as unclean for you. 26You are to be holy to me[t] because I, the LORD, am holy, and I have set you apart from the nations to be my own.

27 " 'A man or woman who is a medium or spiritist among you must be put to death. You are to stone them; their blood will be on their own heads.' "

Rules for Priests

21 THE LORD said to Moses, "Speak to the priests, the sons of Aaron, and say to them: 'A priest must not make himself ceremonially unclean for any of his people who die, 2except for a close relative, such as his mother or father, his son or daughter, his brother, 3or an unmarried sister who is dependent on him since she has no husband—for her he may make himself unclean. 4He must not make himself unclean for people related to him by marriage,[u] and so defile himself.

5 " 'Priests must not shave their heads or shave off the edges of their beards or cut their bodies. 6They must be holy to their God and must not profane the name of their God. Because they present the offerings made to the LORD by fire, the food of their God, they are to be holy.

7 " 'They must not marry women defiled by prostitution or divorced from their husbands, because priests are holy to their God. 8Regard them as holy, because they offer up the food of your God. Consider them holy, because I the LORD am holy—I who make you holy.[v]

9 " 'If a priest's daughter defiles herself by becoming a prostitute, she disgraces her father; she must be burned in the fire.

10 " 'The high priest, the one among his brothers who has had the anointing oil poured on his head and who has been ordained to wear the priestly garments, must not let his

---

t26 Or be my holy ones   u4 Or unclean as a leader among his people   v8 Or who sanctify you; or who set you apart as holy

King James

¹¹Neither shall he go in to any dead body, nor defile himself for his father, or for his mother;

¹²Neither shall he go out of the sanctuary, nor profane the sanctuary of his God; for the crown of the anointing oil of his God *is* upon him: I *am* the LORD.

¹³And he shall take a wife in her virginity.

¹⁴A widow, or a divorced woman, or profane, *or* an harlot, these shall he not take: but he shall take a virgin of his own people to wife.

¹⁵Neither shall he profane his seed among his people: for I the LORD do sanctify him.

¹⁶ ¶ And the LORD spake unto Moses, saying,

¹⁷Speak unto Aaron, saying, Whosoever *he be* of thy seed in their generations that hath *any* blemish, let him not approach to offer the �q bread of his God.

¹⁸For whatsoever man *he be* that hath a blemish, he shall not approach: a blind man, or a lame, or he that hath a flat nose, or any thing superfluous,

¹⁹Or a man that is brokenfooted, or brokenhanded,

²⁰Or crookbacked, or ʳa dwarf, or that hath a blemish in his eye, or be scurvy, or scabbed, or hath his stones broken;

²¹No man that hath a blemish of the seed of Aaron the priest shall come nigh to offer the offerings of the LORD made by fire: he hath a blemish; he shall not come nigh to offer the bread of his God.

²²He shall eat the bread of his God, *both* of the most holy, and of the holy.

²³Only he shall not go in unto the veil, nor come nigh unto the altar, because he hath a blemish; that he profane not my sanctuaries: for I the LORD do sanctify them.

²⁴And Moses told *it* unto Aaron, and to his sons, and unto all the children of Israel.

22 AND THE LORD spake unto Moses, saying,

²Speak unto Aaron and to his sons, that they separate themselves from the holy things of the children of Israel, and that they profane not my holy name *in those things* which they hallow unto me: I *am* the LORD.

³Say unto them, Whosoever *he be* of all your seed among your generations, that goeth unto the holy things, which the children of Israel hallow unto the LORD, having his uncleanness upon him, that soul shall be cut off from my presence: I *am* the LORD.

⁴What man soever of the seed of Aaron *is* a leper, or hath a ˢrunning issue; he shall not eat of the holy things, until he be clean. And whoso toucheth any thing *that is* unclean *by* the dead, or a man whose seed goeth from him;

⁵Or whosoever toucheth any creeping thing, whereby he may be made unclean, or a man of whom he may take uncleanness, whatsoever uncleanness he hath;

⁶The soul which hath touched any such shall be unclean until even, and shall not eat of the holy things, unless he wash his flesh with water.

⁷And when the sun is down, he shall be clean, and shall afterward eat of the holy things; because it *is* his food.

⁸That which dieth of itself, or is torn *with beasts,* he shall not eat to defile himself therewith: I *am* the LORD.

⁹They shall therefore keep mine ordinance, lest they bear sin for it, and die therefore, if they profane it: I the LORD do sanctify them.

Amplified

¹¹Neither shall he go in where any dead body lies nor defile himself [by doing so, even] for his father or for his mother;

¹²Neither shall he go out of the sanctuary nor desecrate *or* make ceremonially unclean the sanctuary of his God, for the crown *or* consecration of the anointing oil of his God is upon him. I am the Lord.

¹³He shall take a wife in her virginity.

¹⁴A widow or a divorced woman or a woman who is polluted *or* profane or a harlot, these he shall not marry, but he shall take as his wife a virgin of his own people, [I Tim. 3:2–7; Tit. 1:7–9.]

¹⁵That he may not profane *or* dishonor his children among his people; for I the Lord do sanctify the high priest.

¹⁶And the Lord said to Moses,

¹⁷Say to Aaron, Any one of your sons in their successive generations who has any blemish, let him not come near to offer the bread of his God.

¹⁸For no man who has a blemish shall approach [God's altar to serve as priest], a man blind or lame, or he who has a disfigured face or a limb too long,

¹⁹Or who has a fractured foot or hand,

²⁰Or is a hunchback, or a dwarf, or has a defect in his eye, or has scurvy *or* itch, or scabs *or* skin trouble, or has damaged testicles.

²¹No man of the offspring of Aaron the priest who has a blemish *and* is disfigured *or* deformed shall come near [the altar] to offer the offerings of the Lord made by fire. He has a blemish; he shall not come near to offer the bread of his God.

²²He may eat the bread of his God, both of the most holy and of the holy things,

²³But he shall not come within the veil or come near the altar [of incense], because he has a blemish, that he may not desecrate *and* make unclean My sanctuaries *and* hallowed things; for I the Lord do sanctify them. [Heb. 7:28.]

²⁴And Moses told it to Aaron and to his sons and to all the Israelites.

22 AND THE Lord said to Moses,

²Say to Aaron and his sons that they shall stay away from the holy things which the Israelites dedicate to Me, that they may not profane My holy name; I am the Lord.

³Tell them, Any one of your offspring throughout your generations who goes to the holy things which the Israelites dedicate to the Lord when he is unclean, that [priest] shall be cut off from My presence *and* excluded from the sanctuary; I am the Lord.

⁴No man of the offspring of Aaron who is a leper or has a discharge shall eat of the holy things [the offerings and the showbread] until he is clean. And whoever touches any person *or* thing made unclean by contact with a corpse or a man who has had a discharge of semen,

⁵Or whoever touches any dead creeping thing by which he may be made unclean, or a man from whom he may acquire uncleanness, whatever it may be, [Lev. 11:24–28.]

⁶The priest who has touched any such thing shall be unclean until evening and shall not eat of the holy things unless he has bathed with water. [Heb. 10:22.]

⁷When the sun is down, he shall be clean, and afterward may eat of the holy things, for they are his food.

⁸That which dies of itself or is torn by beasts he shall not eat, defiling himself with it. I am the Lord.

⁹The priests therefore shall observe My ordinance, lest they bear sin for it and die thereby if they profane it. I am the Lord, Who sanctifies them.

�q Or, *food*   ʳ Or, *too slender*   ˢ Heb. *running of the reins*

New American Standard

11 nor shall he approach any dead person, nor defile himself *even* for his father or his mother;

12 nor shall he go out of the sanctuary nor profane the sanctuary of his God, for the consecration of the anointing oil of his God is on him; I am the LORD.

13 'He shall take a wife in her virginity.

14 'A widow, or a divorced woman, or one who is profaned by harlotry, these he may not take; but rather he is to marry a virgin of his own people,

15 so that he will not profane his offspring among his people; for I am the LORD who sanctifies him.' "

16 ¶ Then the LORD spoke to Moses, saying,

17 "Speak to Aaron, saying, 'No man of your offspring throughout their generations who has a defect shall approach to offer the food of his God.

18 'For no one who has a defect shall approach: a blind man, or a lame man, or he who has a disfigured *face,* or any deformed *limb,*

19 or a man who has a broken foot or broken hand,

20 or a hunchback or a dwarf, or *one who has* a defect in his eye or eczema or scabs or crushed testicles.

21 'No man among the descendants of Aaron the priest who has a defect is to come near to offer the LORD's offerings by fire; *since* he has a defect, he shall not come near to offer the food of his God.

22 'He may eat the food of his God, *both* of the most holy and of the holy,

23 only he shall not go in to the veil or come near the altar because he has a defect, so that he will not profane My sanctuaries. For I am the LORD who sanctifies them.' "

24 So Moses spoke to Aaron and to his sons and to all the sons of Israel.

Sundry Rules for Priests

22 THEN THE LORD spoke to Moses, saying,
2 "Tell Aaron and his sons to be careful with the holy *gifts* of the sons of Israel, which they dedicate to Me, so as not to profane My holy name; I am the LORD.

3 "Say to them, 'If any man among all your descendants throughout your generations approaches the holy *gifts* which the sons of Israel dedicate to the LORD, while he has an uncleanness, that person shall be cut off from before Me; I am the LORD.

4 'No man of the descendants of Aaron, who is a leper or who has a discharge, may eat of the holy *gifts* until he is clean. And if one touches anything made unclean by a corpse or if a man has a seminal emission,

5 or if a man touches any teeming things by which he is made unclean, or any man by whom he is made unclean, whatever his uncleanness;

6 a person who touches any such shall be unclean until evening, and shall not eat of the holy *gifts* unless he has bathed his body in water.

7 'But when the sun sets, he will be clean, and afterward he shall eat of the holy *gifts,* for it is his food.

8 'He shall not eat *an animal* which dies or is torn *by beasts,* becoming unclean by it; I am the LORD.

9 'They shall therefore keep My charge, so that they will not bear sin because of it and die thereby because they profane it; I am the LORD who sanctifies them.

New International

hair become unkempt[w] or tear his clothes. 11He must not enter a place where there is a dead body. He must not make himself unclean, even for his father or mother, 12nor leave the sanctuary of his God or desecrate it, because he has been dedicated by the anointing oil of his God. I am the LORD.

13 'The woman he marries must be a virgin. 14He must not marry a widow, a divorced woman, or a woman defiled by prostitution, but only a virgin from his own people, 15so he will not defile his offspring among his people. I am the LORD, who makes him holy.[x] '

16The LORD said to Moses, 17"Say to Aaron: 'For the generations to come none of your descendants who has a defect may come near to offer the food of his God. 18No man who has any defect may come near: no man who is blind or lame, disfigured or deformed; 19no man with a crippled foot or hand, 20or who is hunchbacked or dwarfed, or who has any eye defect, or who has festering or running sores or damaged testicles. 21No descendant of Aaron the priest who has any defect is to come near to present the offerings made to the LORD by fire. He has a defect; he must not come near to offer the food of his God. 22He may eat the most holy food of his God, as well as the holy food; 23yet because of his defect, he must not go near the curtain or approach the altar, and so desecrate my sanctuary. I am the LORD, who makes them holy.[y] ' "

24So Moses told this to Aaron and his sons and to all the Israelites.

22 THE LORD said to Moses, 2"Tell Aaron and his sons to treat with respect the sacred offerings the Israelites consecrate to me, so they will not profane my holy name. I am the LORD.

3 "Say to them: 'For the generations to come, if any of your descendants is ceremonially unclean and yet comes near the sacred offerings that the Israelites consecrate to the LORD, that person must be cut off from my presence. I am the LORD.

4 'If a descendant of Aaron has an infectious skin disease[z] or a bodily discharge, he may not eat the sacred offerings until he is cleansed. He will also be unclean if he touches something defiled by a corpse or by anyone who has an emission of semen, 5or if he touches any crawling thing that makes him unclean, or any person who makes him unclean, whatever the uncleanness may be. 6The one who touches any such thing will be unclean till evening. He must not eat any of the sacred offerings unless he has bathed himself with water. 7When the sun goes down, he will be clean, and after that he may eat the sacred offerings, for they are his food. 8He must not eat anything found dead or torn by wild animals, and so become unclean through it. I am the LORD.

9 'The priests are to keep my requirements so that they do not become guilty and die for treating them with contempt. I am the LORD, who makes them holy.[a]

---

w10 Or *not uncover his head*   x15 Or *who sanctifies him*; or *who sets him apart as holy*   y23 Or *who sanctifies them*; or *who sets them apart as holy*   z4 Traditionally *leprosy*; the Hebrew word was used for various diseases affecting the skin—not necessarily leprosy.   a9 Or *who sanctifies them*; or *who sets them apart as holy*; also in verse 16

King James

¹⁰There shall no stranger eat *of* the holy thing: a sojourner of the priest, or an hired servant, shall not eat *of* the holy thing.

¹¹But if the priest buy *any* soul *t*with his money, he shall eat of it, and he that is born in his house: they shall eat of his meat.

¹²If the priest's daughter also be *married* unto *u*a stranger, she may not eat of an offering of the holy things.

¹³But if the priest's daughter be a widow, or divorced, and have no child, and is returned unto her father's house, as in her youth, she shall eat of her father's meat: but there shall no stranger eat thereof.

¹⁴ ¶ And if a man eat *of* the holy thing unwittingly, then he shall put the fifth *part* thereof unto it, and shall give *it* unto the priest with the holy thing.

¹⁵And they shall not profane the holy things of the children of Israel, which they offer unto the LORD;

¹⁶Or *v*suffer them to bear the iniquity of trespass, when they eat their holy things: for I the LORD do sanctify them.

Sacrifices of blemished animals

¹⁷ ¶ And the LORD spake unto Moses, saying,

¹⁸Speak unto Aaron, and to his sons, and unto all the children of Israel, and say unto them, Whatsoever *he be* of the house of Israel, or of the strangers in Israel, that will offer his oblation for all his vows, and for all his freewill offerings, which they will offer unto the LORD for a burnt offering;

¹⁹*Ye shall offer* at your own will a male without blemish, of the beeves, of the sheep, or of the goats.

²⁰*But* whatsoever hath a blemish, *that* shall ye not offer: for it shall not be acceptable for you.

²¹And whosoever offereth a sacrifice of peace offerings unto the LORD to accomplish *his* vow, or a freewill offering in beeves or *w*sheep, it shall be perfect to be accepted; there shall be no blemish therein.

²²Blind, or broken, or maimed, or having a wen, or scurvy, or scabbed, ye shall not offer these unto the LORD, nor make an offering by fire of them upon the altar unto the LORD.

²³Either a bullock or a *x*lamb that hath any thing superfluous or lacking in his parts, that mayest thou offer *for* a freewill offering; but for a vow it shall not be accepted.

²⁴Ye shall not offer unto the LORD that which is bruised, or crushed, or broken, or cut; neither shall ye make *any* offering thereof in your land.

²⁵Neither from a stranger's hand shall ye offer the bread of your God of any of these; because their corruption *is* in them, *and* blemishes *be* in them: they shall not be accepted for you.

²⁶ ¶ And the LORD spake unto Moses, saying,

²⁷When a bullock, or a sheep, or a goat, is brought forth, then it shall be seven days under the dam; and from the eighth day and thenceforth it shall be accepted for an offering made by fire unto the LORD.

²⁸And *whether it be* cow or *y*ewe, ye shall not kill it and her young both in one day.

²⁹And when ye will offer a sacrifice of thanksgiving unto the LORD, offer *it* at your own will.

³⁰On the same day it shall be eaten up; ye shall leave none of it until the morrow: I *am* the LORD.

³¹Therefore shall ye keep my commandments, and do them: I *am* the LORD.

³²Neither shall ye profane my holy name; but I will be hallowed among the children of Israel: I *am* the LORD which hallow you,

³³That brought you out of the land of Egypt, to be your God: I *am* the LORD.

Amplified

¹⁰No outsider [not of the family of Aaron] shall eat of the holy thing [which has been offered to God]; a sojourner with the priest or a hired servant shall not eat of the holy thing.

¹¹But if a priest buys a slave with his money, the slave may eat of the holy thing, and he also who is born in the priest's house; they may eat of his food.

¹²If a priest's daughter is married to an outsider [not of the priestly tribe], she shall not eat of the offering of the holy things.

¹³But if a priest's daughter is a widow or divorced, and has no child, and returns to her father's house as in her youth, she shall eat of her father's food; but no stranger shall eat of it.

¹⁴And if a man eats unknowingly of the holy thing [which has been offered to God], then he shall add one-fifth of its value to it and repay that amount to the priest for the holy thing.

¹⁵The priests shall not profane the holy things the Israelites offer to the Lord,

¹⁶And so cause them [by neglect of any essential observance] to bear the iniquity when they eat their holy things; for I the Lord sanctify them.

¹⁷And the Lord said to Moses,

¹⁸Say to Aaron and his sons and to all the Israelites, Whoever of the house of Israel and of the foreigners in Israel brings his offering, whether to pay a vow or as a freewill offering which is offered to the Lord for a burnt offering

¹⁹That you may be accepted, you shall offer a male without blemish of the young bulls, the sheep, or the goats.

²⁰But you shall not offer anything which has a blemish, for it will not be acceptable for you. [I Pet. 1:19.]

²¹And whoever offers a sacrifice of peace offering to the Lord to make a special vow to the Lord or for a freewill offering from the herd or from the flock must bring what is perfect to be accepted; there shall be no blemish in it.

²²Animals blind or made infirm *and* weak or maimed, or having sores *or* a wen or an itch or scabs, you shall not offer to the Lord or make an offering of them by fire upon the altar to the Lord.

²³For a freewill offering you may offer either a bull or a lamb which has some part too long or too short, but for [the payment of] a vow it shall not be accepted.

²⁴You shall not offer to the Lord any animal which has its testicles bruised or crushed or broken or cut, neither sacrifice it in your land.

²⁵Neither shall you offer as the bread of your God any such animals obtained from a foreigner [who may wish to pay respect to the true God], because their defects render them unfit; there is a blemish in them; they will not be accepted for you.

²⁶And the Lord said to Moses,

²⁷When a bull or a sheep or a goat is born, it shall remain for seven days with its mother; and from the eighth day on it shall be accepted for an offering made by fire to the Lord.

²⁸And whether [the mother] is a cow or a ewe, you shall not kill her and her young both in one day.

²⁹And when you sacrifice an offering of thanksgiving to the Lord, sacrifice it so that you may be accepted.

³⁰It shall be eaten on the same day; you shall leave none of it until the next day. I am the Lord.

³¹So shall you heartily accept My commandments *and* conform your life and conduct to them. I am the Lord.

³²Neither shall you profane My holy name [applying it to an idol, or treating it with irreverence or contempt or as a byword]; but I will be hallowed among the Israelites. I am the Lord, Who consecrates *and* makes you holy,

³³Who brought you out of the land of Egypt to be your God. I am the Lord.

*t*Heb. *with the purchase of his money*   *u*Heb. *a man a stranger*
*v*Or, *lade themselves with the iniquity of trespass in their eating*
*w*Or, *goats*   *x*Or, *kid*   *y*Or, *she goat*

New American Standard

10 ¶ 'No [n]layman, however, is to eat the holy *gift;* a sojourner with the priest or a hired man shall not eat of the holy *gift.*

11 'But if a priest buys a slave as *his* property with his money, that one may eat of it, and those who are born in his house may eat of his food.

12 'If a priest's daughter is married to a layman, she shall not eat of the offering of the *gifts.*

13 'But if a priest's daughter becomes a widow or divorced, and has no child and returns to her father's house as in her youth, she shall eat of her father's food; but no layman shall eat of it.

14 'But if a man eats a holy *gift* unintentionally, then he shall add to it a fifth of it and shall give the holy *gift* to the priest.'

15 'They shall not profane the holy *gifts* of the sons of Israel which they offer to the LORD,

16 and *so* cause them to bear punishment for guilt by eating their holy *gifts;* for I am the LORD who sanctifies them.' "

Flawless Animals for Sacrifice

17 ¶ Then the LORD spoke to Moses, saying,

18 "Speak to Aaron and to his sons and to all the sons of Israel and say to them, 'Any man of the house of Israel or of the aliens in Israel who presents his offering, whether it is any of their votive or any of their freewill offerings, which they present to the LORD for a burnt offering—

19 for you to be accepted—*it must be* a male without defect from the cattle, the sheep, or the goats.

20 'Whatever has a defect, you shall not offer, for it will not be accepted for you.

21 'When a man offers a sacrifice of peace offerings to the LORD to fulfill a special vow or for a freewill offering, of the herd or of the flock, it must be perfect to be accepted; there shall be no defect in it.

22 'Those *that are* blind or fractured or maimed or having a running sore or eczema or scabs, you shall not offer to the LORD, nor make of them an offering by fire on the altar to the LORD.

23 'In respect to an ox or a lamb which has an overgrown or stunted *member,* you may present it for a freewill offering, but for a vow it will not be accepted.

24 'Also anything *with its testicles* bruised or crushed or torn or cut, you shall not offer to the LORD, or sacrifice in your land,

25 nor shall you accept any such from the hand of a foreigner for offering as the food of your God; for their corruption is in them, they have a defect, they shall not be accepted for you.' "

26 ¶ Then the LORD spoke to Moses, saying,

27 "When an ox or a sheep or a goat is born, it shall remain seven days with its mother, and from the eighth day on it shall be accepted as a sacrifice of an offering by fire to the LORD.

28 "But, *whether* it is an ox or a sheep, you shall not kill *both* it and its young in one day.

29 "When you sacrifice a sacrifice of thanksgiving to the LORD, you shall sacrifice it so that you may be accepted.

30 "It shall be eaten on the same day, you shall leave none of it until morning; I am the LORD.

31 "So you shall keep My commandments, and do them; I am the LORD.

32 ¶ "You shall not profane My holy name, but I will be sanctified among the sons of Israel; I am the LORD who sanctifies you,

33 who brought you out from the land of Egypt, to be your God; I am the LORD."

[n] Lit *stranger*

New International

10 " 'No one outside a priest's family may eat the sacred offering, nor may the guest of a priest or his hired worker eat it. 11 But if a priest buys a slave with money, or if a slave is born in his household, that slave may eat his food. 12 If a priest's daughter marries anyone other than a priest, she may not eat any of the sacred contributions. 13 But if a priest's daughter becomes a widow or is divorced, yet has no children, and she returns to live in her father's house as in her youth, she may eat of her father's food. No unauthorized person, however, may eat any of it.

14 " 'If anyone eats a sacred offering by mistake, he must make restitution to the priest for the offering and add a fifth of the value to it. 15 The priests must not desecrate the sacred offerings the Israelites present to the LORD 16 by allowing them to eat the sacred offerings and so bring upon them guilt requiring payment. I am the LORD, who makes them holy.' "

Unacceptable Sacrifices

17 The LORD said to Moses, 18 "Speak to Aaron and his sons and to all the Israelites and say to them: 'If any of you—either an Israelite or an alien living in Israel—presents a gift for a burnt offering to the LORD, either to fulfill a vow or as a freewill offering, 19 you must present a male without defect from the cattle, sheep or goats in order that it may be accepted on your behalf. 20 Do not bring anything with a defect, because it will not be accepted on your behalf. 21 When anyone brings from the herd or flock a fellowship offering[b] to the LORD to fulfill a special vow or as a freewill offering, it must be without defect or blemish to be acceptable. 22 Do not offer to the LORD the blind, the injured or the maimed, or anything with warts or festering or running sores. Do not place any of these on the altar as an offering made to the LORD by fire. 23 You may, however, present as a freewill offering an ox[c] or a sheep that is deformed or stunted, but it will not be accepted in fulfillment of a vow. 24 You must not offer to the LORD an animal whose testicles are bruised, crushed, torn or cut. You must not do this in your own land, 25 and you must not accept such animals from the hand of a foreigner and offer them as the food of your God. They will not be accepted on your behalf, because they are deformed and have defects.' "

26 The LORD said to Moses, 27 "When a calf, a lamb or a goat is born, it is to remain with its mother for seven days. From the eighth day on, it will be acceptable as an offering made to the LORD by fire. 28 Do not slaughter a cow or a sheep and its young on the same day.

29 "When you sacrifice a thank offering to the LORD, sacrifice it in such a way that it will be accepted on your behalf. 30 It must be eaten that same day; leave none of it till morning. I am the LORD.

31 "Keep my commands and follow them. I am the LORD. 32 Do not profane my holy name. I must be acknowledged as holy by the Israelites. I am the LORD, who makes[d] you holy[e] 33 and who brought you out of Egypt to be your God. I am the LORD."

b 21 Traditionally *peace offering*　　*c 23* The Hebrew word can include both male and female.　　*d 32* Or *made sanctifies you; or who sets you apart as holy*　　*e 32* Or *who*

King James

Amplified

Feasts of the LORD

23 AND THE LORD spake unto Moses, saying, ²Speak unto the children of Israel, and say unto them, *Concerning* the feasts of the LORD, which ye shall proclaim *to be* holy convocations, *even* these *are* my feasts.

³Six days shall work be done: but the seventh day *is* the sabbath of rest, an holy convocation; ye shall do no work *therein:* it *is* the sabbath of the LORD in all your dwellings.

4 ¶ These *are* the feasts of the LORD, *even* holy convocations, which ye shall proclaim in their seasons.

⁵In the fourteenth *day* of the first month at even *is* the LORD'S passover.

⁶And on the fifteenth day of the same month *is* the feast of unleavened bread unto the LORD: seven days ye must eat unleavened bread.

⁷In the first day ye shall have an holy convocation: ye shall do no servile work therein.

⁸But ye shall offer an offering made by fire unto the LORD seven days: in the seventh day *is* an holy convocation: ye shall do no servile work *therein.*

9 ¶ And the LORD spake unto Moses, saying,

¹⁰Speak unto the children of Israel, and say unto them, When ye be come into the land which I give unto you, and shall reap the harvest thereof, then ye shall bring a ᶻᵃsheaf of the firstfruits of your harvest unto the priest:

¹¹And he shall wave the sheaf before the LORD, to be accepted for you: on the morrow after the sabbath the priest shall wave it.

¹²And ye shall offer that day when ye wave the sheaf an he lamb without blemish of the first year for a burnt offering unto the LORD.

¹³And the meat offering thereof *shall be* two tenth deals of fine flour mingled with oil, an offering made by fire unto the LORD *for* a sweet savour: and the drink offering thereof *shall be* of wine, the fourth *part* of an hin.

¹⁴And ye shall eat neither bread, nor parched corn, nor green ears, until the selfsame day that ye have brought an offering unto your God: *it shall be* a statute for ever throughout your generations in all your dwellings.

15 ¶ And ye shall count unto you from the morrow after the sabbath, from the day that ye brought the sheaf of the wave offering; seven sabbaths shall be complete:

¹⁶Even unto the morrow after the seventh sabbath shall ye number fifty days; and ye shall offer a new meat offering unto the LORD.

¹⁷Ye shall bring out of your habitations two wave loaves of two tenth deals: they shall be of fine flour; they shall be baked with leaven; *they are* the firstfruits unto the LORD.

¹⁸And ye shall offer with the bread seven lambs without blemish of the first year, and one young bullock, and two rams: they shall be *for* a burnt offering unto the LORD, with their meat offering, and their drink offerings, *even* an offering made by fire, of sweet savour unto the LORD.

¹⁹Then ye shall sacrifice one kid of the goats for a sin offering, and two lambs of the first year for a sacrifice of peace offerings.

²⁰And the priest shall wave them with the bread of the firstfruits *for* a wave offering before the LORD, with the two lambs: they shall be holy to the LORD for the priest.

²¹And ye shall proclaim on the selfsame day, *that* it may be an holy convocation unto you: ye shall do no servile work *therein: it shall be* a statute for ever in all your dwellings throughout your generations.

22 ¶ And when ye reap the harvest of your land, thou shalt not make clean riddance of the corners of thy field when thou reapest, neither shalt thou gather any gleaning of thy harvest: thou shalt leave them unto the poor, and to the stranger: I *am* the LORD your God.

23 ¶ And the LORD spake unto Moses, saying,

23 THE LORD said to Moses, ²Say to the Israelites, The set feasts *or* appointed seasons of the Lord which you shall proclaim as holy convocations, even My set feasts, are these:

³Six days shall work be done, but the seventh day is the Sabbath of rest, a holy convocation *or* assembly by summons. You shall do no work on that day; it is the Sabbath of the Lord in all your dwellings.

⁴These are the set feasts *or* appointed seasons of the Lord, holy convocations you shall proclaim at their stated times:

⁵On the fourteenth day of the first month at twilight is the Lord's Passover.

⁶On the fifteenth day of the same month is the Feast of Unleavened Bread to the Lord; for seven days you shall eat unleavened bread. [I Cor. 5:7, 8.]

⁷On the first day you shall have a holy "calling together;" you shall do no servile *or* laborious work on that day.

⁸But you shall offer an offering made by fire to the Lord for seven days; on the seventh day is a holy convocation; you shall do no servile *or* laborious work on that day.

⁹And the Lord said to Moses,

¹⁰Tell the Israelites, When you have come into the land I give you and reap its harvest, you shall bring the sheaf of the firstfruits of your harvest to the priest.

¹¹And he shall wave the sheaf before the Lord, that you may be accepted; on the next day after the Sabbath the priest shall wave it [before the Lord].

¹²You shall offer on the day when you wave the sheaf a male lamb a year old without blemish for a burnt offering to the Lord.

¹³Its cereal offering shall be two-tenths of an ephah of fine flour mixed with oil, an offering made by fire to the Lord for a sweet, pleasing, *and* satisfying fragrance; and the drink offering of it [to be poured out] shall be of wine, a fourth of a hin.

¹⁴And you shall eat neither bread nor parched grain nor green ears, until this same day when you have brought the offering of your God; it is a statute forever throughout your generations in all your houses.

¹⁵And you shall count from the day after the Sabbath, from the day that you brought the sheaf of the wave offering, seven Sabbaths; [seven full weeks] shall they be.

¹⁶Count fifty days to the day after the seventh Sabbath; then you shall present a cereal offering of new grain to the Lord.

¹⁷You shall bring from your dwellings two loaves of bread to be waved, made from two-tenths of an ephah of fine flour; they shall be baked with leaven, for firstfruits to the Lord.

¹⁸And you shall offer with the bread seven lambs, a year old and without blemish, and one young bull and two rams. They shall be a burnt offering to the Lord, with their cereal offering and their drink offerings, an offering made by fire, of a sweet *and* satisfying fragrance to the Lord.

¹⁹Then you shall sacrifice one he-goat for a sin offering and two he-lambs, a year old, for a sacrifice of peace offering.

²⁰The priest shall wave the two lambs, together with the bread of the firstfruits, for a wave offering before the Lord. They shall be holy to the Lord for the priest.

²¹You shall make proclamation the same day, summoning a holy assembly; you shall do no servile work that day. It shall be a statute forever in all your dwellings throughout your generations.

²²And when you reap the harvest of your land, you shall not wholly reap the corners of your field, neither shall you gather the gleanings of your harvest; you shall leave them for the poor and the stranger. I am the Lord your God.

²³And the Lord said to Moses,

ᶻ Or, *handful*   ᵃ Heb. *omer*

New American Standard

Laws of Religious Festivals

23 THE LORD spoke again to Moses, saying,
2"Speak to the sons of Israel and say to them,
'The LORD's appointed times which you shall proclaim as
holy convocations—My appointed times are these:
3 ¶ 'For six days work may be done, but on the seventh
day there is a sabbath of complete rest, a holy convocation.
You shall not do any work; it is a sabbath to the LORD in
all your dwellings.
4 ¶ 'These are the appointed times of the LORD, holy
convocations which you shall proclaim at the times appointed for them.
5 'In the first month, on the fourteenth day of the month
at twilight is the LORD's Passover.
6 'Then on the fifteenth day of the same month there is
the Feast of Unleavened Bread to the LORD; for seven days
you shall eat unleavened bread.
7 'On the first day you shall have a holy convocation;
you shall not do any laborious work.
8 'But for seven days you shall present an offering by
fire to the LORD. On the seventh day is a holy convocation;
you shall not do any laborious work.' "
9 ¶ Then the LORD spoke to Moses, saying,
10"Speak to the sons of Israel and say to them, 'When
you enter the land which I am going to give to you and
reap its harvest, then you shall bring in the sheaf of the
first fruits of your harvest to the priest.
11 'He shall wave the sheaf before the LORD for you to
be accepted; on the day after the sabbath the priest shall
wave it.
12 'Now on the day when you wave the sheaf, you shall
offer a male lamb one year old without defect for a burnt
offering to the LORD.
13 'Its grain offering shall then be two-tenths *of an ephah*
of fine flour mixed with oil, an offering by fire to the LORD
for a soothing aroma, with its drink offering, a fourth of a
*o*hin of wine.
14 'Until this same day, until you have brought in the
offering of your God, you shall eat neither bread nor roasted grain nor new growth. It is to be a perpetual statute
throughout your generations in all your dwelling places.
15 ¶ 'You shall also count for yourselves from the day
after the sabbath, from the day when you brought in the
sheaf of the wave offering; there shall be seven complete
sabbaths.
16 'You shall count fifty days to the day after the seventh
sabbath; then you shall present a new grain offering to the
LORD.
17 'You shall bring in from your dwelling places two
loaves of bread for a wave offering, made of two-tenths *of
an ephah;* they shall be of a fine flour, baked with leaven
as first fruits to the LORD.
18 'Along with the bread you shall present seven one
year old male lambs without defect, and a bull of the herd
and two rams; they are to be a burnt offering to the LORD,
with their grain offering and their drink offerings, an offering by fire of a soothing aroma to the LORD.
19 'You shall also offer one male goat for a sin offering
and two male lambs one year old for a sacrifice of peace
offerings.
20 'The priest shall then wave them with the bread of the
first fruits for a wave offering with two lambs before the
LORD; they are to be holy to the LORD for the priest.
21 'On this same day you shall make a proclamation as
well; you are to have a holy convocation. You shall do no
laborious work. It is to be a perpetual statute in all your
dwelling places throughout your generations.
22 ¶ 'When you reap the harvest of your land, moreover,
you shall not reap to the very corners of your field nor
gather the gleaning of your harvest; you are to leave them
for the needy and the alien. I am the LORD your God.' "
23 ¶ Again the LORD spoke to Moses, saying,

*o*I.e. Approx one gal.

New International

23 THE LORD said to Moses, 2"Speak to the Israelites and say to them: 'These are my appointed
feasts, the appointed feasts of the LORD, which you are to
proclaim as sacred assemblies.

The Sabbath

3" 'There are six days when you may work, but the
seventh day is a Sabbath of rest, a day of sacred assembly.
You are not to do any work; wherever you live, it is a
Sabbath to the LORD.

The Passover and Unleavened Bread

4" 'These are the LORD's appointed feasts, the sacred
assemblies you are to proclaim at their appointed times:
5The LORD's Passover begins at twilight on the fourteenth
day of the first month. 6On the fifteenth day of that month
the LORD's Feast of Unleavened Bread begins; for seven
days you must eat bread made without yeast. 7On the first
day hold a sacred assembly and do no regular work. 8For
seven days present an offering made to the LORD by fire.
And on the seventh day hold a sacred assembly and do no
regular work.' "

Firstfruits

9The LORD said to Moses, 10"Speak to the Israelites and
say to them: 'When you enter the land I am going to give
you and you reap its harvest, bring to the priest a sheaf of
the first grain you harvest. 11He is to wave the sheaf before
the LORD so it will be accepted on your behalf; the priest
is to wave it on the day after the Sabbath. 12On the day you
wave the sheaf, you must sacrifice as a burnt offering to
the LORD a lamb a year old without defect, 13together with
its grain offering of two-tenths of an ephah*f* of fine flour
mixed with oil—an offering made to the LORD by fire, a
pleasing aroma—and its drink offering of a quarter of a
hin*g* of wine. 14You must not eat any bread, or roasted or
new grain, until the very day you bring this offering to
your God. This is to be a lasting ordinance for the generations to come, wherever you live.

Feast of Weeks

15" 'From the day after the Sabbath, the day you brought
the sheaf of the wave offering, count off seven full weeks.
16Count off fifty days up to the day after the seventh
Sabbath, and then present an offering of new grain to the
LORD. 17From wherever you live, bring two loaves made
of two-tenths of an ephah of fine flour, baked with yeast,
as a wave offering of firstfruits to the LORD. 18Present with
this bread seven male lambs, each a year old and without
defect, one young bull and two rams. They will be a burnt
offering to the LORD, together with their grain offerings
and drink offerings—an offering made by fire, an aroma
pleasing to the LORD. 19Then sacrifice one male goat for
a sin offering and two lambs, each a year old, for a fellowship offering.*h* 20The priest is to wave the two lambs
before the LORD as a wave offering, together with the
bread of the firstfruits. They are a sacred offering to the
LORD for the priest. 21On that same day you are to proclaim a sacred assembly and do no regular work. This is
to be a lasting ordinance for the generations to come,
wherever you live.

22" 'When you reap the harvest of your land, do not reap
to the very edges of your field or gather the gleanings of
your harvest. Leave them for the poor and the alien. I am
the LORD your God.' "

Feast of Trumpets

23The LORD said to Moses, 24"Say to the Israelites: 'On

f 13 That is, probably about 4 quarts (about 4.5 liters); also in
verse 17   *g 13* That is, probably about 1 quart (about 1 liter)
h 19 Traditionally *peace offering*

King James

24Speak unto the children of Israel, saying, In the seventh month, in the first *day* of the month, shall ye have a sabbath, a memorial of blowing of trumpets, an holy convocation.

25Ye shall do no servile work *therein:* but ye shall offer an offering made by fire unto the LORD.

26 ¶ And the LORD spake unto Moses, saying,

27Also on the tenth *day* of this seventh month *there shall be* a day of atonement: it shall be an holy convocation unto you; and ye shall afflict your souls, and offer an offering made by fire unto the LORD.

28And ye shall do no work in that same day: for it *is* a day of atonement, to make an atonement for you before the LORD your God.

29For whatsoever soul *it be* that shall not be afflicted in that same day, he shall be cut off from among his people.

30And whatsoever soul *it be* that doeth any work in that same day, the same soul will I destroy from among his people.

31Ye shall do no manner of work: *it shall be* a statute for ever throughout your generations in all your dwellings.

32It *shall be* unto you a sabbath of rest, and ye shall afflict your souls: in the ninth *day* of the month at even, from even unto even, shall ye *b*celebrate your sabbath.

33 ¶ And the LORD spake unto Moses, saying,

34Speak unto the children of Israel, saying, The fifteenth day of this seventh month *shall be* the feast of tabernacles *for* seven days unto the LORD.

35On the first day *shall be* an holy convocation: ye shall do no servile work *therein.*

36Seven days ye shall offer an offering made by fire unto the LORD: on the eighth day shall be an holy convocation unto you; and ye shall offer an offering made by fire unto the LORD: it *is* a *c*solemn assembly; *and* ye shall do no servile work *therein.*

37These *are* the feasts of the LORD, which ye shall proclaim *to be* holy convocations, to offer an offering made by fire unto the LORD, a burnt offering, and a meat offering, a sacrifice, and drink offerings, every thing upon his day:

38Beside the sabbaths of the LORD, and beside your gifts, and beside all your vows, and beside all your freewill offerings, which ye give unto the LORD.

39Also in the fifteenth day of the seventh month, when ye have gathered in the fruit of the land, ye shall keep a feast unto the LORD seven days: on the first day *shall be* a sabbath, and on the eighth day *shall be* a sabbath.

40And ye shall take you on the first day the *d*boughs of goodly trees, branches of palm trees, and the boughs of thick trees, and willows of the brook; and ye shall rejoice before the LORD your God seven days.

41And ye shall keep it a feast unto the LORD seven days in the year. *It shall be* a statute for ever in your generations: ye shall celebrate it in the seventh month.

42Ye shall dwell in booths seven days; all that are Israelites born shall dwell in booths:

43That your generations may know that I made the children of Israel to dwell in booths, when I brought them out of the land of Egypt: I *am* the LORD your God.

44And Moses declared unto the children of Israel the feasts of the LORD.

The oil and the showbread

24 AND THE LORD spake unto Moses, saying, 2Command the children of Israel, that they bring unto thee pure oil olive beaten for the light, *e*to cause the lamps to burn continually.

Amplified

24Say to the Israelites, On the first day of the seventh month [almost October], you shall observe a day of solemn [sabbatical] rest, a memorial day announced by blowing of trumpets, a holy [called] assembly.

25You shall do no servile work on it, but you shall present an offering made by fire to the Lord.

26And the Lord said to Moses,

27Also the tenth day of this seventh month is the Day of Atonement; it shall be a holy [called] assembly, and you shall afflict yourselves [by fasting in penitence and humility] and present an offering made by fire to the Lord.

28And you shall do no work on this day, for it is the Day of Atonement, to make atonement for you before the Lord your God.

29For whoever is not afflicted [by fasting in penitence and humility] on this day shall be cut off from among his people [that he may not be included in the atonement made for them].

30And whoever does any work on that same day I will destroy from among his people.

31You shall do no kind of work [on that day]. It is a statute forever throughout your generations in all your dwellings.

32It shall be to you a sabbath of rest, and you shall afflict yourselves [by fasting in penitence and humility]. On the ninth day of the month from evening to evening you shall keep your sabbath.

33And the Lord said to Moses,

34Say to the Israelites, The fifteenth day of this seventh month, and for seven days, is the Feast of Tabernacles *or* Booths to the Lord.

35On the first day shall be a holy convocation; you shall do no servile work on that day.

36For seven days you shall offer an offering made by fire to the Lord; on the eighth day shall be a holy convocation and you shall present an offering made by fire to the Lord. It is a solemn assembly; you shall do no laborious work on that day.

37These are the set feasts *or* appointed seasons of the Lord, which you shall proclaim to be holy convocations, to present an offering made by fire to the Lord, a burnt offering and a cereal offering, sacrifices and drink offerings, each on its own day.

38This is in addition to the Sabbaths of the Lord and besides your gifts and all your vowed offerings and all your freewill offerings which you give to the Lord.

39Also on the fifteenth day of the seventh month [nearly October], when you have gathered in the fruit of the land, you shall keep the feast of the Lord for seven days, the first day and the eighth day each a Sabbath.

40And on the first day you shall take the fruit of pleasing trees [and make booths of them], branches of palm trees, and boughs of thick (leafy) trees, and willows of the brook; and you shall rejoice before the Lord your God for seven days.

41You shall keep it as a feast to the Lord for seven days in the year, a statute forever throughout your generations; you shall keep it in the seventh month.

42You shall dwell in booths (shelters) for seven days: All native Israelites shall dwell in booths,

43That your generations may know that I made the Israelites dwell in booths when I brought them out of the land of Egypt. I am the Lord your God.

44Thus Moses declared to the Israelites the set *or* appointed feasts of the Lord.

24 AND THE Lord said to Moses, 2Command the Israelites that they bring to you pure oil from beaten olives for the light [of the golden lampstand] to cause a lamp to burn continually.

---

*b*Heb. *rest*   *c*Heb. day of *restraint*   *d*Heb. *fruit*   *e*Heb. *to cause to ascend*

New American Standard

24"Speak to the sons of Israel, saying, 'In the seventh month on the first of the month you shall have a rest, a reminder by blowing *of trumpets,* a holy convocation.
25'You shall not do any laborious work, but you shall present an offering by fire to the LORD.' "

The Day of Atonement

26 ¶ The LORD spoke to Moses, saying,
27"On exactly the tenth day of this seventh month is the day of atonement; it shall be a holy convocation for you, and you shall humble your souls and present an offering by fire to the LORD.
28"You shall not do any work on this same day, for it is a day of atonement, to make atonement on your behalf before the LORD your God.
29"If there is any person who will not humble himself on this same day, he shall be cut off from his people.
30"As for any person who does any work on this same day, that person I will destroy from among his people.
31"You shall do no work at all. It is to be a perpetual statute throughout your generations in all your dwelling places.
32"It is to be a sabbath of complete rest to you, and you shall humble your souls; on the ninth of the month at evening, from evening until evening you shall keep your sabbath."
33 ¶ Again the LORD spoke to Moses, saying,
34"Speak to the sons of Israel, saying, 'On the fifteenth of this seventh month is the Feast of Booths for seven days to the LORD.
35'On the first day is a holy convocation; you shall do no laborious work of any kind.
36'For seven days you shall present an offering by fire to the LORD. On the eighth day you shall have a holy convocation and present an offering by fire to the LORD; it is an assembly. You shall do no laborious work.
37 ¶ 'These are the appointed times of the LORD which you shall proclaim as holy convocations, to present offerings by fire to the LORD—burnt offerings and grain offerings, sacrifices and drink offerings, *each* day's matter on its own day—
38 besides *those of* the sabbaths of the LORD, and besides your gifts and besides all your votive and freewill offerings, which you give to the LORD.
39 ¶ 'On exactly the fifteenth day of the seventh month, when you have gathered in the crops of the land, you shall celebrate the feast of the LORD for seven days, with a rest on the first day and a rest on the eighth day.
40 'Now on the first day you shall take for yourselves the foliage of beautiful trees, palm branches and boughs of leafy trees and willows of the brook, and you shall rejoice before the LORD your God for seven days.
41 'You shall thus celebrate it *as* a feast to the LORD for seven days in the year. It *shall be* a perpetual statute throughout your generations; you shall celebrate it in the seventh month.
42 'You shall live in booths for seven days; all the native-born in Israel shall live in booths,
43 so that your generations may know that I had the sons of Israel live in booths when I brought them out from the land of Egypt. I am the LORD your God.' "
44 So Moses declared to the sons of Israel the appointed times of the LORD.

The Lamp and the Bread of the Sanctuary

24 THEN THE LORD spoke to Moses, saying, 2"Command the sons of Israel that they bring to you clear oil from beaten olives for the light, to make a lamp burn continually.

New International

the first day of the seventh month you are to have a day of rest, a sacred assembly commemorated with trumpet blasts. 25Do no regular work, but present an offering made to the LORD by fire.' "

Day of Atonement

26The LORD said to Moses, 27"The tenth day of this seventh month is the Day of Atonement. Hold a sacred assembly and deny yourselves,[i] and present an offering made to the LORD by fire. 28Do no work on that day, because it is the Day of Atonement, when atonement is made for you before the LORD your God. 29Anyone who does not deny himself on that day must be cut off from his people. 30I will destroy from among his people anyone who does any work on that day. 31You shall do no work at all. This is to be a lasting ordinance for the generations to come, wherever you live. 32It is a sabbath of rest for you, and you must deny yourselves. From the evening of the ninth day of the month until the following evening you are to observe your sabbath."

Feast of Tabernacles

33The LORD said to Moses, 34"Say to the Israelites: 'On the fifteenth day of the seventh month the LORD's Feast of Tabernacles begins, and it lasts for seven days. 35The first day is a sacred assembly; do no regular work. 36For seven days present offerings made to the LORD by fire, and on the eighth day hold a sacred assembly and present an offering made to the LORD by fire. It is the closing assembly; do no regular work.
37(" 'These are the LORD's appointed feasts, which you are to proclaim as sacred assemblies for bringing offerings made to the LORD by fire—the burnt offerings and grain offerings, sacrifices and drink offerings required for each day. 38These offerings are in addition to those for the LORD's Sabbaths and[j] in addition to your gifts and whatever you have vowed and all the freewill offerings you give to the LORD.)
39" 'So beginning with the fifteenth day of the seventh month, after you have gathered the crops of the land, celebrate the festival to the LORD for seven days; the first day is a day of rest, and the eighth day also is a day of rest. 40On the first day you are to take choice fruit from the trees, and palm fronds, leafy branches and poplars, and rejoice before the LORD your God for seven days. 41Celebrate this as a festival to the LORD for seven days each year. This is to be a lasting ordinance for the generations to come; celebrate it in the seventh month. 42Live in booths for seven days: All native-born Israelites are to live in booths 43so your descendants will know that I had the Israelites live in booths when I brought them out of Egypt. I am the LORD your God.' "
44So Moses announced to the Israelites the appointed feasts of the LORD.

Oil and Bread Set Before the LORD

24 THE LORD said to Moses, 2"Command the Israelites to bring you clear oil of pressed olives for the light so that the lamps may be kept burning continually.

---

i 27 Or and fast; also in verses 29 and 32   *j 38 Or These feasts are in addition to the LORD's Sabbaths, and these offerings are*

King James

³Without the veil of the testimony, in the tabernacle of the congregation, shall Aaron order it from the evening unto the morning before the LORD continually: *it shall be* a statute for ever in your generations.

⁴He shall order the lamps upon the pure candlestick before the LORD continually.

⁵ ¶ And thou shalt take fine flour, and bake twelve cakes thereof: two tenth deals shall be in one cake.

⁶And thou shalt set them in two rows, six on a row, upon the pure table before the LORD.

⁷And thou shalt put pure frankincense upon *each* row, that it may be on the bread for a memorial, *even* an offering made by fire unto the LORD.

⁸Every sabbath he shall set it in order before the LORD continually, *being taken* from the children of Israel by an everlasting covenant.

⁹And it shall be Aaron's and his sons'; and they shall eat it in the holy place: for it *is* most holy unto him of the offerings of the LORD made by fire by a perpetual statute.

Death for blasphemy

¹⁰ ¶ And the son of an Israelitish woman, whose father *was* an Egyptian, went out among the children of Israel: and this son of the Israelitish *woman* and a man of Israel strove together in the camp;

¹¹And the Israelitish woman's son blasphemed the name *of the* LORD, and cursed. And they brought him unto Moses: (and his mother's name *was* Shelomith, the daughter of Dibri, of the tribe of Dan:)

¹²And they put him in ward, ᶠthat the mind of the LORD might be shown them.

¹³And the LORD spake unto Moses, saying,

¹⁴Bring forth him that hath cursed without the camp; and let all that heard *him* lay their hands upon his head, and let all the congregation stone *him*.

¹⁵And thou shalt speak unto the children of Israel, saying, Whosoever curseth his God shall bear his sin.

¹⁶And he that blasphemeth the name of the LORD, he shall surely be put to death, *and* all the congregation shall certainly stone him: as well the stranger, as he that is born in the land, when he blasphemeth the name *of the* LORD, shall be put to death.

¹⁷ ¶ And he that ᵍkilleth any man shall surely be put to death.

¹⁸And he that killeth a beast shall make it good; ʰbeast for beast.

¹⁹And if a man cause a blemish in his neighbour; as he hath done, so shall it be done to him;

²⁰Breach for breach, eye for eye, tooth for tooth: as he hath caused a blemish in a man, so shall it be done to him *again*.

²¹And he that killeth a beast, he shall restore it: and he that killeth a man, he shall be put to death.

²²Ye shall have one manner of law, as well for the stranger, as for one of your own country: for I *am* the LORD your God.

²³ ¶ And Moses spake to the children of Israel, that they should bring forth him that had cursed out of the camp, and stone him with stones. And the children of Israel did as the LORD commanded Moses.

Sabbath and jubilee years

25 AND THE LORD spake unto Moses in mount Sinai, saying,

²Speak unto the children of Israel, and say unto them, When ye come into the land which I give you, then shall the land ⁱkeep a sabbath unto the LORD.

³Six years thou shalt sow thy field, and six years thou shalt prune thy vineyard, and gather in the fruit thereof;

Amplified

³Outside the veil of the Testimony [between the Holy and the Most Holy Places] in the Tent of Meeting, Aaron shall keep it in order from evening to morning before the Lord continually; it shall be a statute forever throughout your generations.

⁴He shall keep the lamps in order upon the lampstand of pure gold before the Lord continually. [Rev. 1:12–18.]

⁵And you shall take fine flour and bake twelve cakes with it; two-tenths of an ephah shall be in each cake [of the showbread *or* bread of the Presence].

⁶And you shall set them in two rows, six in a row, upon the table of pure gold before the Lord.

⁷You shall put pure frankincense [in a bowl or spoon] beside each row, that it may be with the bread as a memorial portion, an offering to be made by fire to the Lord.

⁸Every Sabbath day Aaron shall set the showbread in order before the Lord continually; it is on behalf of the Israelites, an everlasting covenant.

⁹And the bread shall be for Aaron and his sons, and they shall eat it in a sacred place, for it is for [Aaron] a most holy portion of the offerings to the Lord made by fire, a perpetual due [to the high priest].

¹⁰Now the son of an Israelite woman, whose father was an Egyptian, went out among the Israelites, and he and a man of Israel quarreled *and* strove together in the camp.

¹¹The Israelite woman's son blasphemed the Name [of the Lord] and cursed. They brought him to Moses—his mother was Shelomith, the daughter of Dibri, of the tribe of Dan.

¹²And they put him in custody until the will of the Lord might be declared to them.

¹³And the Lord said to Moses,

¹⁴Bring him who has cursed out of the camp, and let all who heard him lay their hands upon his head; then let all the congregation stone him.

¹⁵And you shall say to the Israelites, Whoever curses his God shall bear his sin.

¹⁶And he who blasphemes the Name of the Lord, he shall surely be put to death, and all the congregation shall certainly stone him; the stranger as well as he who was born in the land shall be put to death when he blasphemes the Name [of the Lord].

¹⁷And he who kills any man shall surely be put to death.

¹⁸And he who kills a beast shall make it good, beast for beast.

¹⁹And if a man causes a blemish *or* disfigurement on his neighbor, it shall be done to him as he has done:

²⁰Fracture for fracture, eye for eye, tooth for tooth; as he has caused a blemish *or* disfigurement on a man, so shall it be done to him. [Matt. 5:38–42; 7:2.]

²¹He who kills a beast shall replace it; he who kills a man shall be put to death.

²²You shall have the same law for the sojourner among you as for one of your own nationality, for I am the Lord your God.

²³Moses spoke to the Israelites, and they brought him who had cursed out of the camp and stoned him with stones. Thus the Israelites did as the Lord commanded Moses.

25 THE LORD said to Moses on Mount Sinai,

²Say to the Israelites, When you come into the land which I give you, then shall the land keep a sabbath to the Lord.

³For six years you shall sow your field, and for six years you shall prune your vineyard and gather in its fruits.

ᶠHeb. *to expound unto them according to the mouth of the LORD*
ᵍHeb. *smiteth the life of a man*   ʰHeb. *life for life*   ⁱHeb. *rest*

New American Standard

3"Outside the veil of testimony in the tent of meeting, Aaron shall keep it in order from evening to morning before the LORD continually; *it shall be* a perpetual statute throughout your generations.

4"He shall keep the lamps in order on the pure *gold* lampstand before the LORD continually.

5 ¶ "Then you shall take fine flour and bake twelve cakes with it; two-tenths *of an ephah* shall be *in* each cake.

6"You shall set them *in* two rows, six *to* a row, on the pure *gold* table before the LORD.

7"You shall put pure frankincense on each row that it may be a memorial portion for the bread, *even* an offering by fire to the LORD.

8"Every sabbath day he shall set it in order before the LORD continually; it is an everlasting covenant for the sons of Israel.

9"It shall be for Aaron and his sons, and they shall eat it in a holy place; for it is most holy to him from the LORD's offerings by fire, *his* portion forever."

10 ¶ Now the son of an Israelite woman, whose father was an Egyptian, went out among the sons of Israel; and the Israelite woman's son and a man of Israel struggled with each other in the camp.

11 The son of the Israelite woman blasphemed the Name and cursed. So they brought him to Moses. (Now his mother's name was Shelomith, the daughter of Dibri, of the tribe of Dan.)

12 They put him in custody so that the command of the LORD might be made clear to them.

13 ¶ Then the LORD spoke to Moses, saying,

14"Bring the one who has cursed outside the camp, and let all who heard him lay their hands on his head; then let all the congregation stone him.

15"You shall speak to the sons of Israel, saying, 'If anyone curses his God, then he will bear his sin.

16 'Moreover, the one who blasphemes the name of the LORD shall surely be put to death; all the congregation shall certainly stone him. The alien as well as the native, when he blasphemes the Name, shall be put to death.

"An Eye for an Eye"

17 ¶ 'If a man takes the life of any human being, he shall surely be put to death.

18 'The one who takes the life of an animal shall make it good, life for life.

19 'If a man injures his neighbor, just as he has done, so it shall be done to him:

20 fracture for fracture, eye for eye, tooth for tooth; just as he has injured a man, so it shall be inflicted on him.

21 'Thus the one who kills an animal shall make it good, but the one who kills a man shall be put to death.

22 'There shall be one standard for you; it shall be for the stranger as well as the native, for I am the LORD your God.' "

23 Then Moses spoke to the sons of Israel, and they brought the one who had cursed outside the camp and stoned him with stones. Thus the sons of Israel did, just as the LORD had commanded Moses.

The Sabbatic Year and Year of Jubilee

25 THE LORD then spoke to Moses at Mount Sinai, saying,

2"Speak to the sons of Israel and say to them, 'When you come into the land which I shall give you, then the land shall have a sabbath to the LORD.

3 'Six years you shall sow your field, and six years you shall prune your vineyard and gather in its crop,

New International

3Outside the curtain of the Testimony in the Tent of Meeting, Aaron is to tend the lamps before the LORD from evening till morning, continually. This is to be a lasting ordinance for the generations to come. 4The lamps on the pure gold lampstand before the LORD must be tended continually.

5"Take fine flour and bake twelve loaves of bread, using two-tenths of an ephah[k] for each loaf. 6Set them in two rows, six in each row, on the table of pure gold before the LORD. 7Along each row put some pure incense as a memorial portion to represent the bread and to be an offering made to the LORD by fire. 8This bread is to be set out before the LORD regularly, Sabbath after Sabbath, on behalf of the Israelites, as a lasting covenant. 9It belongs to Aaron and his sons, who are to eat it in a holy place, because it is a most holy part of their regular share of the offerings made to the LORD by fire."

A Blasphemer Stoned

10Now the son of an Israelite mother and an Egyptian father went out among the Israelites, and a fight broke out in the camp between him and an Israelite. 11The son of the Israelite woman blasphemed the Name with a curse; so they brought him to Moses. (His mother's name was Shelomith, the daughter of Dibri the Danite.) 12They put him in custody until the will of the LORD should be made clear to them.

13Then the LORD said to Moses: 14"Take the blasphemer outside the camp. All those who heard him are to lay their hands on his head, and the entire assembly is to stone him. 15Say to the Israelites: 'If anyone curses his God, he will be held responsible; 16anyone who blasphemes the name of the LORD must be put to death. The entire assembly must stone him. Whether an alien or native-born, when he blasphemes the Name, he must be put to death.

17" 'If anyone takes the life of a human being, he must be put to death. 18Anyone who takes the life of someone's animal must make restitution—life for life. 19If anyone injures his neighbor, whatever he has done must be done to him: 20fracture for fracture, eye for eye, tooth for tooth. As he has injured the other, so he is to be injured. 21Whoever kills an animal must make restitution, but whoever kills a man must be put to death. 22You are to have the same law for the alien and the native-born. I am the LORD your God.' "

23Then Moses spoke to the Israelites, and they took the blasphemer outside the camp and stoned him. The Israelites did as the LORD commanded Moses.

The Sabbath Year

25 THE LORD said to Moses on Mount Sinai, 2"Speak to the Israelites and say to them: 'When you enter the land I am going to give you, the land itself must observe a sabbath to the LORD. 3For six years sow your fields, and for six years prune your vineyards and

---

k 5 That is, probably about 4 quarts (about 4.5 liters)

King James

4But in the seventh year shall be a sabbath of rest unto the land, a sabbath for the LORD: thou shalt neither sow thy field, nor prune thy vineyard.

5That which groweth of its own accord of thy harvest thou shalt not reap, neither gather the grapes *j*of thy vine undressed: *for* it is a year of rest unto the land.

6And the sabbath of the land shall be meat for you; for thee, and for thy servant, and for thy maid, and for thy hired servant, and for thy stranger that sojourneth with thee,

7And for thy cattle, and for the beast that *are* in thy land, shall all the increase thereof be meat.

8 ¶ And thou shalt number seven sabbaths of years unto thee, seven times seven years; and the space of the seven sabbaths of years shall be unto thee forty and nine years.

9Then shalt thou cause the trumpet *k*of the jubilee to sound on the tenth *day* of the seventh month, in the day of atonement shall ye make the trumpet sound throughout all your land.

10And ye shall hallow the fiftieth year, and proclaim liberty throughout *all* the land unto all the inhabitants thereof: it shall be a jubilee unto you; and ye shall return every man unto his possession, and ye shall return every man unto his family.

11A jubilee shall that fiftieth year be unto you: ye shall not sow, neither reap that which groweth of itself in it, nor gather *the grapes* in it of thy vine undressed.

12For it *is* the jubilee; it shall be holy unto you: ye shall eat the increase thereof out of the field.

13In the year of this jubilee ye shall return every man unto his possession.

14And if thou sell aught unto thy neighbour, or buyest *aught* of thy neighbour's hand, ye shall not oppress one another:

15According to the number of years after the jubilee thou shalt buy of thy neighbour, *and* according to the number of years of the fruits he shall sell unto thee:

16According to the multitude of years thou shalt increase the price thereof, and according to the fewness of years thou shalt diminish the price of it: for *according* to the number *of the years* of the fruits doth he sell unto thee.

17Ye shall not therefore oppress one another; but thou shalt fear thy God: for I *am* the LORD your God.

18 ¶ Wherefore ye shall do my statutes, and keep my judgments, and do them; and ye shall dwell in the land in safety.

19And the land shall yield her fruit, and ye shall eat your fill, and dwell therein in safety.

20And if ye shall say, What shall we eat the seventh year? behold, we shall not sow, nor gather in our increase:

21Then I will command my blessing upon you in the sixth year, and it shall bring forth fruit for three years.

22And ye shall sow the eighth year, and eat *yet* of old fruit until the ninth year; until her fruits come in ye shall eat *of* the old *store.*

23 ¶ The land shall not be sold *l m*for ever: for the land *is* mine; for ye *are* strangers and sojourners with me.

24And in all the land of your possession ye shall grant a redemption for the land.

25 ¶ If thy brother be waxen poor, and hath sold away *some* of his possession, and if any of his kin come to redeem it, then shall he redeem that which his brother sold.

26And if the man have none to redeem it, and *n*himself be able to redeem it;

27Then let him count the years of the sale thereof, and restore the overplus unto the man to whom he sold it; that he may return unto his possession.

Amplified

4But in the seventh year there shall be a sabbath of solemn rest for the land, a sabbath to the Lord; you shall neither sow your field nor prune your vineyard.

5What grows of itself in your harvest you shall not reap and the grapes on your uncultivated vine you shall not gather, for it is a year of rest to the land.

6And the sabbath rest of the [untilled] land shall [in its increase] furnish food for you, for your male and female slaves, your hired servant, and the temporary resident who lives with you,

7For your domestic animals also and for the [wild] beasts in your land; all its yield shall be for food.

8And you shall number seven sabbaths *or* weeks of years for you, seven times seven years, so the total time of the seven weeks of years shall be forty-nine years.

9Then you shall sound abroad the loud trumpet on the tenth day of the seventh month [almost October]; on the Day of Atonement blow the trumpet in all your land.

10And you shall hallow the fiftieth year and proclaim liberty throughout all the land to all its inhabitants. It shall be a jubilee for you; and each of you shall return to his ancestral possession [which through poverty he was compelled to sell], and each of you shall return to his family [from whom he was separated in bond service].

11That fiftieth year shall be a jubilee for you; in it you shall not sow, or reap and store what grows of itself, or gather the grapes of the uncultivated vines.

12For it is a jubilee; it shall be holy to you; you shall eat the [sufficient] increase of it out of the field.

13In this Year of Jubilee each of you shall return to his ancestral property.

14And if you sell anything to your neighbor or buy from your neighbor, you shall not wrong one another.

15According to the number of years after the Jubilee, you shall buy from your neighbor. And he shall sell to you according to the number of years [remaining in which you may gather] the crops [before you must restore the property to him].

16If the years [to the next Jubilee] are many, you may increase the price, and if the years remaining are few, you shall diminish the price, for the number of the crops is what he is selling to you.

17You shall not oppress *and* wrong one another, but you shall [reverently] fear your God. For I am the Lord your God.

18Therefore you shall do *and* give effect to My statutes and keep My ordinances and perform them, and you will dwell in the land in safety.

19The land shall yield its fruit; you shall eat your fill and dwell there in safety.

20And if you say, What shall we eat in the seventh year if we are not to sow or gather in our increase?

21Then [this is My answer:] I will command My [special] blessings on you in the sixth year, so that it shall bring forth [sufficient] fruit for three years.

22And you shall sow in the eighth year, but eat of the old store of produce; until the crops of the ninth year come in you shall eat of the old supply.

23The land shall not be sold into perpetual ownership, for the land is Mine; you are [only] strangers and temporary residents with Me. [Heb. 11:13; I Pet. 2:11–17.]

24And in all the country you possess you shall grant a redemption for the land [in the Year of Jubilee].

25If your brother has become poor and has sold some of his property, if any of his kin comes to redeem it, he shall [be allowed to] redeem what his brother has sold.

26And if the man has no one to redeem his property, and he himself has become more prosperous *and* has enough to redeem it,

27Then let him count the years since he sold it and restore the overpayment to the man to whom he sold it, and return to his ancestral possession. [I Kings 21:2, 3.]

---

*j*Heb. *of thy separation*   *k*Heb. *loud of sound*   *l*Or, *to be quite cut off*   *m*Heb. *for cutting off*   *n*Heb. *his hand hath attained and found sufficiency*

New American Standard

4 but during the seventh year the land shall have a sabbath rest, a sabbath to the LORD; you shall not sow your field nor prune your vineyard.

5 'Your harvest's *p*aftergrowth you shall not reap, and your grapes of untrimmed vines you shall not gather; the land shall have a sabbatical year.

6 'All of you shall have the sabbath *products* of the land for food; yourself, and your male and female slaves, and your hired man and your foreign resident, those who live as aliens with you.

7 'Even your cattle and the animals that are in your land shall have all its crops to eat.

8 ¶ 'You are also to count off seven sabbaths of years for yourself, seven times seven years, so that you have the time of the seven sabbaths of years, *namely,* forty-nine years.

9 'You shall then sound a ram's horn abroad on the tenth day of the seventh month; on the day of atonement you shall sound a horn all through your land.

10 'You shall thus consecrate the fiftieth year and proclaim *q*a release through the land to all its inhabitants. It shall be a jubilee for you, and each of you shall return to his own property, and each of you shall return to his family.

11 'You shall have the fiftieth year as a jubilee; you shall not sow, nor reap its aftergrowth, nor gather in *from* its untrimmed vines.

12 'For it is a jubilee; it shall be holy to you. You shall eat its crops out of the field.

13 ¶ 'On this year of jubilee each of you shall return to his own property.

14 'If you make a sale, moreover, to your friend or buy from your friend's hand, you shall not wrong one another.

15 'Corresponding to the number of years after the jubilee, you shall buy from your friend; he is to sell to you according to the number of years of crops.

16 'In proportion to the extent of the years you shall increase its price, and in proportion to the fewness of the years you shall diminish its price, for *it is* a number of crops he is selling to you.

17 'So you shall not wrong one another, but you shall fear your God; for I am the LORD your God.

18 ¶ 'You shall thus observe My statutes and keep My judgments, so as to carry them out, that you may live securely on the land.

19 'Then the land will yield its produce, so that you can eat your fill and live securely on it.

20 'But if you say, "What are we going to eat on the seventh year if we do not sow or gather in our crops?"

21 then I will so order My blessing for you in the sixth year that it will bring forth the crop for three years.

22 'When you are sowing the eighth year, you can still eat old things from the crop, eating *the old* until the ninth year when its crop comes in.

The Law of Redemption

23 ¶ 'The land, moreover, shall not be sold permanently, for the land is Mine; for you are *but* aliens and sojourners with Me.

24 'Thus for every piece of your property, you are to provide for the redemption of the land.

25 ¶ 'If a fellow countryman of yours becomes so poor he has to sell part of his property, then his nearest kinsman is to come and buy back what his relative has sold.

26 'Or in case a man has no kinsman, but so recovers his means as to find sufficient for its redemption,

27 then he shall calculate the years since its sale and refund the balance to the man to whom he sold it, and so return to his property.

New International

gather their crops. 4But in the seventh year the land is to have a sabbath of rest, a sabbath to the LORD. Do not sow your fields or prune your vineyards. 5Do not reap what grows of itself or harvest the grapes of your untended vines. The land is to have a year of rest. 6Whatever the land yields during the sabbath year will be food for you—for yourself, your manservant and maidservant, and the hired worker and temporary resident who live among you, 7as well as for your livestock and the wild animals in your land. Whatever the land produces may be eaten.

The Year of Jubilee

8" 'Count off seven sabbaths of years—seven times seven years—so that the seven sabbaths of years amount to a period of forty-nine years. 9Then have the trumpet sounded everywhere on the tenth day of the seventh month; on the Day of Atonement sound the trumpet throughout your land. 10Consecrate the fiftieth year and proclaim liberty throughout the land to all its inhabitants. It shall be a jubilee for you; each one of you is to return to his family property and each to his own clan. 11The fiftieth year shall be a jubilee for you; do not sow and do not reap what grows of itself or harvest the untended vines. 12For it is a jubilee and is to be holy for you; eat only what is taken directly from the fields.

13" 'In this Year of Jubilee everyone is to return to his own property.

14" 'If you sell land to one of your countrymen or buy any from him, do not take advantage of each other. 15You are to buy from your countryman on the basis of the number of years since the Jubilee. And he is to sell to you on the basis of the number of years left for harvesting crops. 16When the years are many, you are to increase the price, and when the years are few, you are to decrease the price, because what he is really selling you is the number of crops. 17Do not take advantage of each other, but fear your God. I am the LORD your God.

18" 'Follow my decrees and be careful to obey my laws, and you will live safely in the land. 19Then the land will yield its fruit, and you will eat your fill and live there in safety. 20You may ask, "What will we eat in the seventh year if we do not plant or harvest our crops?" 21I will send you such a blessing in the sixth year that the land will yield enough for three years. 22While you plant during the eighth year, you will eat from the old crop and will continue to eat from it until the harvest of the ninth year comes in.

23" 'The land must not be sold permanently, because the land is mine and you are but aliens and my tenants. 24Throughout the country that you hold as a possession, you must provide for the redemption of the land.

25" 'If one of your countrymen becomes poor and sells some of his property, his nearest relative is to come and redeem what his countryman has sold. 26If, however, a man has no one to redeem it for him but he himself prospers and acquires sufficient means to redeem it, 27he is to determine the value for the years since he sold it and refund the balance to the man to whom he sold it; he can

---

p Lit growth from spilled kernels   *q Or liberty*

King James

28 But if he be not able to restore *it* to him, then that which is sold shall remain in the hand of him that hath bought it until the year of jubilee: and in the jubilee it shall go out, and he shall return unto his possession.

29 And if a man sell a dwelling house in a walled city, then he may redeem it within a whole year after it is sold; *within* a full year may he redeem it.

30 And if it be not redeemed within the space of a full year, then the house that *is* in the walled city shall be established for ever to him that bought it throughout his generations: it shall not go out in the jubilee.

31 But the houses of the villages which have no wall round about them shall be counted as the fields of the country: [o]they may be redeemed, and they shall go out in the jubilee.

32 Notwithstanding the cities of the Levites, *and* the houses of the cities of their possession, may the Levites redeem at any time.

33 And if [p]a man purchase of the Levites, then the house that was sold, and the city of his possession, shall go out in *the year of* jubilee: for the houses of the cities of the Levites *are* their possession among the children of Israel.

34 But the field of the suburbs of their cities may not be sold; for it *is* their perpetual possession.

35 ¶ And if thy brother be waxen poor, and [q]fallen in decay with thee; then thou shalt [r]relieve him: *yea, though he be* a stranger, or a sojourner; that he may live with thee.

36 Take thou no usury of him, or increase: but fear thy God; that thy brother may live with thee.

37 Thou shalt not give him thy money upon usury, nor lend him thy victuals for increase.

38 I *am* the LORD your God, which brought you forth out of the land of Egypt, to give you the land of Canaan, *and* to be your God.

39 ¶ And if thy brother *that dwelleth* by thee be waxen poor, and be sold unto thee; thou shalt not [s]compel him to serve as a bondservant:

40 *But* as an hired servant, *and* as a sojourner, he shall be with thee, *and* shall serve thee unto the year of jubilee:

41 And *then* shall he depart from thee, *both* he and his children with him, and shall return unto his own family, and unto the possession of his fathers shall he return.

42 For they *are* my servants, which I brought forth out of the land of Egypt: they shall not be sold [t]as bondmen.

43 Thou shalt not rule over him with rigour; but shalt fear thy God.

44 Both thy bondmen, and thy bondmaids, which thou shalt have, *shall be* of the heathen that are round about you; of them shall ye buy bondmen and bondmaids.

45 Moreover of the children of the strangers that do sojourn among you, of them shall ye buy, and of their families that *are* with you, which they begat in your land: and they shall be your possession.

46 And ye shall take them as an inheritance for your children after you, to inherit *them for* a possession; [u]they shall be your bondmen for ever: but over your brethren the children of Israel, ye shall not rule one over another with rigour.

47 ¶ And if a sojourner or stranger [v]wax rich by thee, and thy brother *that dwelleth* by him wax poor, and sell himself unto the stranger *or* sojourner by thee, or to the stock of the stranger's family:

48 After that he is sold he may be redeemed again; one of his brethren may redeem him:

49 Either his uncle, or his uncle's son, may redeem him, or *any* that is nigh of kin unto him of his family may redeem him; or if he be able, he may redeem himself.

[o] Heb. *redemption belongeth unto it* [p] Or, one *of the Levites redeem* them [q] Heb. *his hand faileth* [r] Heb. *strengthen* [s] Heb. *serve thyself with him with the service;* see ver. 46 [t] Heb. *with the sale of a bondman* [u] Heb. *ye shall serve yourselves with them;* see ver. 39 [v] Heb. *his hand obtain*

Amplified

28 But if he is unable to redeem it, it shall remain in the buyer's possession until the Year of Jubilee, when it shall be set free and he may return to it.

29 If a man sells a dwelling house in a fortified city, he may redeem it within a whole year after it is sold; for a full year he may have the right of redemption.

30 And if it is not redeemed within a full year, then the house that is in the fortified city shall be made sure, permanently *and* without limitations, for him who bought it, throughout his generations. It shall not go free in the Year of Jubilee.

31 But the houses of the unwalled villages shall be counted with the fields of the country. They may be redeemed, and they shall go free in the Year of Jubilee.

32 Nevertheless, the cities of the Levites, the houses in the cities of their possession, the Levites may redeem at any time.

33 But if a house is not redeemed by a Levite, the sold house in the city they possess shall go free in the Year of Jubilee, for the houses in the Levite cities are their ancestral possession among the Israelites.

34 But the field of unenclosed *or* pasture lands of their cities may not be sold; it is their perpetual possession.

35 And if your [Israelite] brother has become poor and his hand wavers [from poverty, sickness, or age and he is unable to support himself], then you shall uphold (strengthen, relieve) him, [treating him with the courtesy and consideration that you would] a stranger or a temporary resident with you [without property], so that he may live [along] with you. [I John 3:17.]

36 Charge him no interest or [portion of] increase, but fear your God, so your brother may [continue to] live along with you.

37 You shall not give him your money at interest nor lend him food at a profit.

38 I am the Lord your God, Who brought you forth out of the land of Egypt to give you the land of Canaan and to be your God.

39 And if your brother becomes poor beside you and sells himself to you, you shall not compel him to serve as a bondman (a slave not eligible for redemption),

40 But as a hired servant and as a temporary resident he shall be with you; he shall serve you till the Year of Jubilee,

41 And then he shall depart from you, he and his children with him, and shall go back to his own family and return to the possession of his fathers.

42 For the Israelites are My servants; I brought them out of the land of Egypt; they shall not be sold as bondmen. [I Cor. 7:23.]

43 You shall not rule over him with harshness (severity, oppression), but you shall [reverently] fear your God. [Eph. 6:9; Col. 4:1.]

44 As for your bondmen and your bondmaids whom you may have, they shall be from the nations round about you, of whom you may buy bondmen and bondmaids.

45 Moreover, of the children of the strangers who sojourn among you, of them you may buy and of their families that are with you which they have begotten in your land, and they shall be your possession.

46 And you shall make them an inheritance for your children after you, to hold for a possession; of them shall you take your bondmen always, but over your brethren the Israelites you shall not rule one over another with harshness (severity, oppression).

47 And if a sojourner or stranger with you becomes rich and your [Israelite] brother becomes poor beside him and sells himself to the stranger or sojourner with you or to a member of the stranger's family,

48 After he is sold he may be redeemed. One of his brethren may redeem him:

49 Either his uncle or his uncle's son may redeem him, or a near kinsman may redeem him; or if he has enough *and* is able, he may redeem himself.

New American Standard

28 'But if he has not found sufficient means to get it back for himself, then what he has sold shall remain in the hands of its purchaser until the year of jubilee; but at the jubilee it shall revert, that he may return to his property.

29 ¶ 'Likewise, if a man sells a dwelling house in a walled city, then his redemption right remains valid until a full year from its sale; his right of redemption lasts a full year.

30 'But if it is not bought back for him within the space of a full year, then the house that is in the walled city passes permanently to its purchaser throughout his generations; it does not revert in the jubilee.

31 'The houses of the villages, however, which have no surrounding wall shall be considered as open fields; they have redemption rights and revert in the jubilee.

32 'As for cities of the Levites, the Levites have a permanent right of redemption for the houses of the cities which are their possession.

33 'What, therefore, belongs to the Levites may be redeemed and a house sale in the city of this possession reverts in the jubilee, for the houses of the cities of the Levites are their possession among the sons of Israel.

34 'But pasture fields of their cities shall not be sold, for that is their perpetual possession.

Of Poor Countrymen

35 ¶ 'Now in case a countryman of yours becomes poor and his means with regard to you falter, then you are to sustain him, like a stranger or a sojourner, that he may live with you.

36 'Do not take usurious interest from him, but revere your God, that your countryman may live with you.

37 'You shall not give him your silver at interest, nor your food for gain.

38 'I am the LORD your God, who brought you out of the land of Egypt to give you the land of Canaan *and* to be your God.

39 ¶ 'If a countryman of yours becomes so poor with regard to you that he sells himself to you, you shall not subject him to a slave's service.

40 'He shall be with you as a hired man, as if he were a sojourner; he shall serve with you until the year of jubilee.

41 'He shall then go out from you, he and his sons with him, and shall go back to his family, that he may return to the property of his forefathers.

42 'For they are My servants whom I brought out from the land of Egypt; they are not to be sold *in* a slave sale.

43 'You shall not rule over him with severity, but are to revere your God.

44 'As for your male and female slaves whom you may have—you may acquire male and female slaves from the pagan nations that are around you.

45 'Then, too, *it is* out of the sons of the sojourners who live as aliens among you that you may gain acquisition, and out of their families who are with you, whom they will have produced in your land; they also may become your possession.

46 'You may even bequeath them to your sons after you, to receive as a possession; you can use them as permanent slaves. But in respect to your countrymen, the sons of Israel, you shall not rule with severity over one another.

Of Redeeming a Poor Man

47 ¶ 'Now if the means of a stranger or of a sojourner with you becomes sufficient, and a countryman of yours becomes so poor with regard to him as to sell himself to a stranger who is sojourning with you, or to the descendants of a stranger's family,

48 then he shall have redemption right after he has been sold. One of his brothers may redeem him,

49 or his uncle, or his uncle's son, may redeem him, or one of his blood relatives from his family may redeem him; or if he prospers, he may redeem himself.

New International

then go back to his own property. 28But if he does not acquire the means to repay him, what he sold will remain in the possession of the buyer until the Year of Jubilee. It will be returned in the Jubilee, and he can then go back to his property.

29 'If a man sells a house in a walled city, he retains the right of redemption a full year after its sale. During that time he may redeem it. 30If it is not redeemed before a full year has passed, the house in the walled city shall belong permanently to the buyer and his descendants. It is not to be returned in the Jubilee. 31But houses in villages without walls around them are to be considered as open country. They can be redeemed, and they are to be returned in the Jubilee.

32 'The Levites always have the right to redeem their houses in the Levitical towns, which they possess. 33So the property of the Levites is redeemable—that is, a house sold in any town they hold—and is to be returned in the Jubilee, because the houses in the towns of the Levites are their property among the Israelites. 34But the pastureland belonging to their towns must not be sold; it is their permanent possession.

35 'If one of your countrymen becomes poor and is unable to support himself among you, help him as you would an alien or a temporary resident, so he can continue to live among you. 36Do not take interest of any kind[l] from him, but fear your God, so that your countryman may continue to live among you. 37You must not lend him money at interest or sell him food at a profit. 38I am the LORD your God, who brought you out of Egypt to give you the land of Canaan and to be your God.

39 'If one of your countrymen becomes poor among you and sells himself to you, do not make him work as a slave. 40He is to be treated as a hired worker or a temporary resident among you; he is to work for you until the Year of Jubilee. 41Then he and his children are to be released, and he will go back to his own clan and to the property of his forefathers. 42Because the Israelites are my servants, whom I brought out of Egypt, they must not be sold as slaves. 43Do not rule over them ruthlessly, but fear your God.

44 'Your male and female slaves are to come from the nations around you; from them you may buy slaves. 45You may also buy some of the temporary residents living among you and members of their clans born in your country, and they will become your property. 46You can will them to your children as inherited property and can make them slaves for life, but you must not rule over your fellow Israelites ruthlessly.

47 'If an alien or a temporary resident among you becomes rich and one of your countrymen becomes poor and sells himself to the alien living among you or to a member of the alien's clan, 48he retains the right of redemption after he has sold himself. One of his relatives may redeem him: 49An uncle or a cousin or any blood relative in his clan may redeem him. Or if he prospers, he may redeem

---

l 36 Or take excessive interest; similarly in verse 37

King James

50And he shall reckon with him that bought him from the year that he was sold to him unto the year of jubilee: and the price of his sale shall be according unto the number of years, according to the time of an hired servant shall it be with him.

51If *there be* yet many years *behind,* according unto them he shall give again the price of his redemption out of the money that he was bought for.

52And if there remain but few years unto the year of jubilee, then he shall count with him, *and* according unto his years shall he give him again the price of his redemption.

53*And* as a yearly hired servant shall he be with him: *and the other* shall not rule with rigour over him in thy sight.

54And if he be not redeemed *w*in these *years,* then he shall go out in the year of jubilee, *both* he, and his children with him.

55For unto me the children of Israel *are* servants; they *are* my servants whom I brought forth out of the land of Egypt: I *am* the LORD your God.

The blessings for obedience

26 YE SHALL make you no idols nor graven image, neither rear you up a *x*standing image, neither shall ye set up *any yz*image of stone in your land, to bow down unto it: for I *am* the LORD your God.

2 ¶ Ye shall keep my sabbaths, and reverence my sanctuary: I *am* the LORD.

3 ¶ If ye walk in my statutes, and keep my commandments, and do them;

4Then I will give you rain in due season, and the land shall yield her increase, and the trees of the field shall yield their fruit.

5And your threshing shall reach unto the vintage, and the vintage shall reach unto the sowing time: and ye shall eat your bread to the full, and dwell in your land safely.

6And I will give peace in the land, and ye shall lie down, and none shall make *you* afraid: and I will *a*rid evil beasts out of the land, neither shall the sword go through your land.

7And ye shall chase your enemies, and they shall fall before you by the sword.

8And five of you shall chase an hundred, and an hundred of you shall put ten thousand to flight: and your enemies shall fall before you by the sword.

9For I will have respect unto you, and make you fruitful, and multiply you, and establish my covenant with you.

10And ye shall eat old store, and bring forth the old because of the new.

11And I will set my tabernacle among you: and my soul shall not abhor you.

12And I will walk among you, and will be your God, and ye shall be my people.

13I *am* the LORD your God, which brought you forth out of the land of Egypt, that ye should not be their bondmen; and I have broken the bands of your yoke, and made you go upright.

The punishments for disobedience

14 ¶ But if ye will not hearken unto me, and will not do all these commandments;

15And if ye shall despise my statutes, or if your soul abhor my judgments, so that ye will not do all my commandments, *but* that ye break my covenant:

16I also will do this unto you; I will even appoint *b*over you terror, consumption, and the burning ague, that shall consume the eyes, and cause sorrow of heart: and ye shall sow your seed in vain, for your enemies shall eat it.

Amplified

50And [the redeemer] shall reckon with the purchaser of the servant from the year when he sold himself to the purchaser to the Year of Jubilee, and the price of his release shall be adjusted according to the number of years. The time he was with his owner shall be counted as that of a hired servant.

51If there remain many years [before the Year of Jubilee], in proportion to them he must refund [to the purchaser] for his release [the overpayment] for his acquisition.

52And if little time remains until the Year of Jubilee, he shall count it over with him and he shall refund the proportionate amount for his release.

53And as a servant hired year by year shall he deal with him; he shall not rule over him with harshness (severity, oppression) in your sight [make sure of that].

54And if he is not redeemed during these years *and* by these means, then he shall go free in the Year of Jubilee, he and his children with him.

55For to Me the Israelites are servants, My servants, whom I brought forth out of the land of Egypt. I am the Lord your God.

26 YOU SHALL make for yourselves no idols nor shall you erect a graven image, pillar, *or* obelisk, nor shall you place any figured stone in your land to which *or* on which to bow down; for I am the Lord your God.

2You shall keep My Sabbaths and reverence My sanctuary. I am the Lord.

3If you walk in My statutes and keep My commandments and do them,

4I will give you rain in due season, and the land shall yield her increase and the trees of the field yield their fruit.

5And your threshing [time] shall reach to the vintage and the vintage [time] shall reach to the sowing time, and you shall eat your bread to the full and dwell in your land securely.

6I will give peace in the land; you shall lie down and none shall fill you with dread *or* make you afraid; and I will clear ferocious (wild) beasts out of the land, and no sword shall go through your land.

7And you shall chase your enemies, and they shall fall before you by the sword.

8Five of you shall chase a hundred, and a hundred of you shall put ten thousand to flight; your enemies shall fall before you by the sword.

9For I will be leaning toward you with favor *and* regard for you, rendering you fruitful, multiplying you, and establishing *and* ratifying My covenant with you. [II Kings 13:23.]

10And you shall eat the [abundant] old store of produce long kept, and clear out the old [to make room] for the new.

11I will set My dwelling in *and* among you, and My soul shall not despise *or* reject *or* separate itself from you.

12And I will walk in *and* with *and* among you and will be your God, and you shall be My people.

13I am the Lord your God, Who brought you forth out of the land of Egypt, that you should no more be slaves; and I have broken the bars of your yoke and made you walk erect [as free men].

14But if you will not hearken to Me and will not do all these commandments,

15And if you spurn *and* despise My statutes, and if your soul despises *and* rejects My ordinances, so that you will not do all My commandments, but break My covenant,

16I will do this: I will appoint over you [sudden] terror (trembling, trouble), even consumption and fever that consume *and* waste the eyes and make the [physical] life pine away. You shall sow your seed in vain, for your enemies shall eat it.

---

w Or, *by these* means   *x* Or, *pillar*   *y* Or, *figured stone*
z Heb. *a stone of picture*   *a* Heb. *cause to cease*
b Heb. *upon you*

New American Standard

⁵⁰'He then with his purchaser shall calculate from the year when he sold himself to him up to the year of jubilee; and the price of his sale shall correspond to the number of years. *It is* like the days of a hired man *that* he shall be with him.

⁵¹'If there are still many years, he shall refund part of his purchase price in proportion to them for his own redemption;

⁵²'and if few years remain until the year of jubilee, he shall so calculate with him. In proportion to his years he is to refund *the amount for* his redemption.

⁵³'Like a man hired year by year he shall be with him; he shall not rule over him with severity in your sight.

⁵⁴'Even if he is not redeemed by these *means*, he shall still go out in the year of jubilee, he and his sons with him.

⁵⁵'For the sons of Israel are My servants; they are My servants whom I brought out from the land of Egypt. I am the LORD your God.

Blessings of Obedience

26 'YOU SHALL not make for yourselves idols, nor shall you set up for yourselves an image or a *sacred* pillar, nor shall you place a figured stone in your land to bow down to it; for I am the LORD your God.

²'You shall keep My sabbaths and reverence My sanctuary; I am the LORD.

³'If you walk in My statutes and keep My commandments so as to carry them out,

⁴then I shall give you rains in their season, so that the land will yield its produce and the trees of the field will bear their fruit.

⁵'Indeed, your threshing will last for you until grape gathering, and grape gathering will last until sowing time. You will thus eat your food to the full and live securely in your land.

⁶'I shall also grant peace in the land, so that you may lie down with no one making *you* tremble. I shall also eliminate harmful beasts from the land, and no sword will pass through your land.

⁷'But you will chase your enemies and they will fall before you by the sword;

⁸five of you will chase a hundred, and a hundred of you will chase ten thousand, and your enemies will fall before you by the sword.

⁹'So I will turn toward you and make you fruitful and multiply you, and I will confirm My covenant with you.

¹⁰'You will eat the old supply and clear out the old because of the new.

¹¹'Moreover, I will make My dwelling among you, and My soul will not reject you.

¹²'I will also walk among you and be your God, and you shall be My people.

¹³'I am the LORD your God, who brought you out of the land of Egypt so that *you* would not be their slaves, and I broke the bars of your yoke and made you walk erect.

Penalties of Disobedience

¹⁴¶'But if you do not obey Me and do not carry out all these commandments,

¹⁵if, instead, you reject My statutes, and if your soul abhors My ordinances so as not to carry out all My commandments, *and* so break My covenant,

¹⁶I, in turn, will do this to you: I will appoint over you a sudden terror, consumption and fever that will waste away the eyes and cause the soul to pine away; also, you will sow your seed uselessly, for your enemies will eat it up.

New International

himself. ⁵⁰He and his buyer are to count the time from the year he sold himself up to the Year of Jubilee. The price for his release is to be based on the rate paid to a hired man for that number of years. ⁵¹If many years remain, he must pay for his redemption a larger share of the price paid for him. ⁵²If only a few years remain until the Year of Jubilee, he is to compute that and pay for his redemption accordingly. ⁵³He is to be treated as a man hired from year to year; you must see to it that his owner does not rule over him ruthlessly.

⁵⁴"'Even if he is not redeemed in any of these ways, he and his children are to be released in the Year of Jubilee, ⁵⁵for the Israelites belong to me as servants. They are my servants, whom I brought out of Egypt. I am the LORD your God.

Reward for Obedience

26 "'DO NOT make idols or set up an image or a sacred stone for yourselves, and do not place a carved stone in your land to bow down before it. I am the LORD your God.

²"'Observe my Sabbaths and have reverence for my sanctuary. I am the LORD.

³"'If you follow my decrees and are careful to obey my commands, ⁴I will send you rain in its season, and the ground will yield its crops and the trees of the field their fruit. ⁵Your threshing will continue until grape harvest and the grape harvest will continue until planting, and you will eat all the food you want and live in safety in your land.

⁶"'I will grant peace in the land, and you will lie down and no one will make you afraid. I will remove savage beasts from the land, and the sword will not pass through your country. ⁷You will pursue your enemies, and they will fall by the sword before you. ⁸Five of you will chase a hundred, and a hundred of you will chase ten thousand, and your enemies will fall by the sword before you.

⁹"'I will look on you with favor and make you fruitful and increase your numbers, and I will keep my covenant with you. ¹⁰You will still be eating last year's harvest when you will have to move it out to make room for the new. ¹¹I will put my dwelling place*m* among you, and I will not abhor you. ¹²I will walk among you and be your God, and you will be my people. ¹³I am the LORD your God, who brought you out of Egypt so that you would no longer be slaves to the Egyptians; I broke the bars of your yoke and enabled you to walk with heads held high.

Punishment for Disobedience

¹⁴"'But if you will not listen to me and carry out all these commands, ¹⁵and if you reject my decrees and abhor my laws and fail to carry out all my commands and so violate my covenant, ¹⁶then I will do this to you: I will bring upon you sudden terror, wasting diseases and fever that will destroy your sight and drain away your life. You

m 11 Or my tabernacle

King James

17And I will set my face against you, and ye shall be slain before your enemies: they that hate you shall reign over you; and ye shall flee when none pursueth you.

18And if ye will not yet for all this hearken unto me, then I will punish you seven times more for your sins.

19And I will break the pride of your power; and I will make your heaven as iron, and your earth as brass:

20And your strength shall be spent in vain: for your land shall not yield her increase, neither shall the trees of the land yield their fruits.

21 ¶ And if ye walk ccontrary unto me, and will not hearken unto me; I will bring seven times more plagues upon you according to your sins.

22I will also send wild beasts among you, which shall rob you of your children, and destroy your cattle, and make you few in number; and your *high* ways shall be desolate.

23And if ye will not be reformed by me by these things, but will walk contrary unto me;

24Then will I also walk contrary unto you, and will punish you yet seven times for your sins.

25And I will bring a sword upon you, that shall avenge the quarrel of *my* covenant: and when ye are gathered together within your cities, I will send the pestilence among you; and ye shall be delivered into the hand of the enemy.

26*And* when I have broken the staff of your bread, ten women shall bake your bread in one oven, and they shall deliver *you* your bread again by weight: and ye shall eat, and not be satisfied.

27And if ye will not for all this hearken unto me, but walk contrary unto me;

28Then I will walk contrary unto you also in fury; and I, even I, will chastise you seven times for your sins.

29And ye shall eat the flesh of your sons, and the flesh of your daughters shall ye eat.

30And I will destroy your high places, and cut down your images, and cast your carcases upon the carcases of your idols, and my soul shall abhor you.

31And I will make your cities waste, and bring your sanctuaries unto desolation, and I will not smell the savour of your sweet odours.

32And I will bring the land into desolation: and your enemies which dwell therein shall be astonished at it.

33And I will scatter you among the heathen, and will draw out a sword after you: and your land shall be desolate, and your cities waste.

34Then shall the land enjoy her sabbaths, as long as it lieth desolate, and ye *be* in your enemies' land; *even* then shall the land rest, and enjoy her sabbaths.

35As long as it lieth desolate it shall rest; because it did not rest in your sabbaths, when ye dwelt upon it.

36And upon them that are left *alive* of you I will send a faintness into their hearts in the lands of their enemies; and the sound of a *d*shaken leaf shall chase them; and they shall flee, as fleeing from a sword; and they shall fall when none pursueth.

Amplified

17I [the Lord] will set My face against you and *l*you shall be defeated *and* slain before your enemies; they who hate you shall rule over you; you shall flee when no one pursues you. [I Sam. 4:10; 31:1.]

18And if in spite of all this you still will not listen *and* be obedient to Me, then I will chastise *and* discipline you seven times more for your sins.

19And I will break *and* humble your pride in your power, and I will make your heavens as iron [yielding no answer, no blessing, no rain] and your earth [as sterile] as brass. [I Kings 17:1.]

20And your strength shall be spent in vain, for your land shall not yield its increase, neither shall the trees of the land yield their fruit.

21If you walk contrary to Me and will not heed Me, I will bring seven times more plagues upon you, according to your sins.

22I will loose the wild beasts of the field among you, which shall rob you of your children, destroy your livestock, and make you few so that your roads shall be deserted *and* desolate. [II Kings 17:25, 26.]

23If by these means you are not turned to Me but determine to walk contrary to Me,

24I also will walk contrary to you, and I will smite you seven times for your sins.

25And I will bring a sword upon you that shall execute the vengeance [for the breaking] of My covenant; and you shall be gathered together within your cities, and I will send the pestilence among you, and you shall be delivered into the hands of the enemy. [Num. 16:49; II Sam. 24:15.]

26When I break your staff of bread *and* cut off your supply of food, ten women shall bake your bread in one oven, and they shall ration your bread *and* deliver it again by weight; and you shall eat, and not be satisfied. [Hag. 1:6.]

27And if in spite of all this you will not listen *and* give heed to Me but walk contrary to Me,

28Then I will walk contrary to you in wrath, and I also will chastise you seven times for your sins.

29You shall eat the flesh of your sons *and* of your daughters. [II Kings 6:28, 29.]

30And I will destroy your high places [devoted to idolatrous worship], and cut down your sun-images, and throw your dead bodies upon the [wrecked] bodies of your idols, and My soul shall abhor you [with deep and unutterable loathing]. [II Kings 23:8, 20.]

31I will lay your cities waste, bring your sanctuaries to desolation, and I will not smell the fragrance of your sweet *and* soothing odors [of offerings made by fire]. [II Kings 25:4–10; II Chron. 36:19.]

32And I will bring the land into desolation, and your enemies who dwell in it shall be astonished at it.

33I will scatter you among the nations and draw out [your enemies'] sword after you; and your land shall be desolate and your cities a waste. [Ps. 44:11–14.]

34Then shall the land [of Israel have the opportunity to] enjoy its sabbaths as long as it lies desolate and you are in your enemies' land; then shall the land rest, to enjoy *and* receive payments for its sabbaths [divinely ordained for it].

35As long as it lies desolate *and* waste, it shall have rest, the rest it did not have in your sabbaths when you dwelt upon it. [II Chron. 36:21.]

36As for those who are left of you, I will send dejection (lack of courage, a faintness) into their hearts in the lands of their enemies; the sound of a driven leaf shall put them to hasty *and* tumultuous flight, and they shall flee as if from the sword, and fall when no one pursues them.

---

*l*This chapter abounds in prophecies of what God would do for, or against, His people if they did, or did not, meet His conditions. Each of these prophecies was literally fulfilled in succeeding centuries. The Scripture references indicate where these fulfillments are recorded; there are at least a dozen of them. Yet some people do not seem to have awakened to the fact that God **keeps His word,** whether for us or against us. It all depends on us.

---

c Or, *at all adventures with me;* see ver. 24   *d*Heb. *driven*

New American Standard

17 'I will set My face against you so that you will be struck down before your enemies; and those who hate you will rule over you, and you will flee when no one is pursuing you.

18 'If also after these things you do not obey Me, then I will punish you seven times more for your sins.

19 'I will also break down your pride of power; I will also make your sky like iron and your earth like bronze.

20 'Your strength will be spent uselessly, for your land will not yield its produce and the trees of the land will not yield their fruit.

21 ¶ 'If then, you act with hostility against Me and are unwilling to obey Me, I will increase the plague on you seven times according to your sins.

22 'I will let loose among you the beasts of the field, which will bereave you of your children and destroy your cattle and reduce your number so that your roads lie deserted.

23 ¶ 'And if by these things you are not turned to Me, but act with hostility against Me,

24 then I will act with hostility against you; and I, even I, will strike you seven times for your sins.

25 'I will also bring upon you a sword which will execute vengeance for the covenant; and when you gather together into your cities, I will send pestilence among you, so that you shall be delivered into enemy hands.

26 'When I break your staff of bread, ten women will bake your bread in one oven, and they will bring back your bread ʳin rationed amounts, so that you will eat and not be satisfied.

27 ¶ 'Yet if in spite of this you do not obey Me, but act with hostility against Me,

28 then I will act with wrathful hostility against you, and I, even I, will punish you seven times for your sins.

29 'Further, you will eat the flesh of your sons and the flesh of your daughters you will eat.

30 'I then will destroy your high places, and cut down your incense altars, and heap your remains on the remains of your idols, for My soul shall abhor you.

31 'I will lay waste your cities as well and will make your sanctuaries desolate, and I will not smell your soothing aromas.

32 'I will make the land desolate so that your enemies who settle in it will be appalled over it.

33 'You, however, I will scatter among the nations and will draw out a sword after you, as your land becomes desolate and your cities become waste.

34 ¶ 'Then the land will enjoy its sabbaths all the days of the desolation, while you are in your enemies' land; then the land will rest and enjoy its sabbaths.

35 'All the days of *its* desolation it will observe the rest which it did not observe on your sabbaths, while you were living on it.

36 'As for those of you who may be left, I will also bring weakness into their hearts in the lands of their enemies. And the sound of a driven leaf will chase them, and even when no one is pursuing they will flee as though from the sword, and they will fall.

New International

will plant seed in vain, because your enemies will eat it. 17I will set my face against you so that you will be defeated by your enemies; those who hate you will rule over you, and you will flee even when no one is pursuing you.

18 'If after all this you will not listen to me, I will punish you for your sins seven times over. 19I will break down your stubborn pride and make the sky above you like iron and the ground beneath you like bronze. 20Your strength will be spent in vain, because your soil will not yield its crops, nor will the trees of the land yield their fruit.

21 'If you remain hostile toward me and refuse to listen to me, I will multiply your afflictions seven times over, as your sins deserve. 22I will send wild animals against you, and they will rob you of your children, destroy your cattle and make you so few in number that your roads will be deserted.

23 'If in spite of these things you do not accept my correction but continue to be hostile toward me, 24I myself will be hostile toward you and will afflict you for your sins seven times over. 25And I will bring the sword upon you to avenge the breaking of the covenant. When you withdraw into your cities, I will send a plague among you, and you will be given into enemy hands. 26When I cut off your supply of bread, ten women will be able to bake your bread in one oven, and they will dole out the bread by weight. You will eat, but you will not be satisfied.

27 'If in spite of this you still do not listen to me but continue to be hostile toward me, 28then in my anger I will be hostile toward you, and I myself will punish you for your sins seven times over. 29You will eat the flesh of your sons and the flesh of your daughters. 30I will destroy your high places, cut down your incense altars and pile your dead bodies on the lifeless forms of your idols, and I will abhor you. 31I will turn your cities into ruins and lay waste your sanctuaries, and I will take no delight in the pleasing aroma of your offerings. 32I will lay waste the land, so that your enemies who live there will be appalled. 33I will scatter you among the nations and will draw out my sword and pursue you. Your land will be laid waste, and your cities will lie in ruins. 34Then the land will enjoy its sabbath years all the time that it lies desolate and you are in the country of your enemies; then the land will rest and enjoy its sabbaths. 35All the time that it lies desolate, the land will have the rest it did not have during the sabbaths you lived in it.

36 'As for those of you who are left, I will make their hearts so fearful in the lands of their enemies that the sound of a windblown leaf will put them to flight. They will run as though fleeing from the sword, and they will

ʳLit *by weight*

King James

³⁷And they shall fall one upon another, as it were before a sword, when none pursueth: and ye shall have no power to stand before your enemies.

³⁸And ye shall perish among the heathen, and the land of your enemies shall eat you up.

³⁹And they that are left of you shall pine away in their iniquity in your enemies' lands; and also in the iniquities of their fathers shall they pine away with them.

⁴⁰If they shall confess their iniquity, and the iniquity of their fathers, with their trespass which they trespassed against me, and that also they have walked contrary unto me;

⁴¹And *that* I also have walked contrary unto them, and have brought them into the land of their enemies; if then their uncircumcised hearts be humbled, and they then accept of the punishment of their iniquity:

⁴²Then will I remember my covenant with Jacob, and also my covenant with Isaac, and also my covenant with Abraham will I remember; and I will remember the land.

⁴³The land also shall be left of them, and shall enjoy her sabbaths, while she lieth desolate without them: and they shall accept of the punishment of their iniquity: because, even because they despised my judgments, and because their soul abhorred my statutes.

⁴⁴And yet for all that, when they be in the land of their enemies, I will not cast them away, neither will I abhor them, to destroy them utterly, and to break my covenant with them: for I *am* the LORD their God.

⁴⁵But I will for their sakes remember the covenant of their ancestors, whom I brought forth out of the land of Egypt in the sight of the heathen, that I might be their God: I *am* the LORD.

⁴⁶These *are* the statutes and judgments and laws, which the LORD made between him and the children of Israel in mount Sinai by the hand of Moses.

Vows and tithes to the LORD

27 AND THE LORD spake unto Moses, saying, ²Speak unto the children of Israel, and say unto them, When a man shall make a singular vow, the persons *shall be* for the LORD by thy estimation.

³And thy estimation shall be of the male from twenty years old even unto sixty years old, even thy estimation shall be fifty shekels of silver, after the shekel of the sanctuary.

⁴And if *it be* a female, then thy estimation shall be thirty shekels.

⁵And if *it be* from five years old even unto twenty years old, then thy estimation shall be of the male twenty shekels, and for the female ten shekels.

⁶And if *it be* from a month old even unto five years old, then thy estimation shall be of the male five shekels of silver, and for the female thy estimation *shall be* three shekels of silver.

⁷And if *it be* from sixty years old and above; if *it be* a male, then thy estimation shall be fifteen shekels, and for the female ten shekels.

⁸But if he be poorer than thy estimation, then he shall present himself before the priest, and the priest shall value him; according to his ability that vowed shall the priest value him.

⁹And if *it be* a beast, whereof men bring an offering unto the LORD, all that *any man* giveth of such unto the LORD shall be holy.

Amplified

³⁷They shall stumble over one another as if to escape a sword when no one pursues them; and you shall have no power to stand before your enemies.

³⁸You shall perish among the nations; the land of your enemies shall eat you up.

³⁹And those of you who are left shall pine away in their iniquity in your enemies' lands; also in the iniquities of their fathers they shall pine away like them.

⁴⁰But if they confess their own and their fathers' iniquity in their treachery which they committed against Me—and also that because they walked contrary to Me

⁴¹I also walked contrary to them and brought them into the land of their enemies—if then their uncircumcised hearts are humbled and they then accept the punishment for their iniquity, [II Kings 24:10–14; Dan. 9:11–14.]

⁴²Then will I [earnestly] remember My covenant with Jacob, My covenant with Isaac, and My covenant with Abraham, and [earnestly] remember the land. [Ps. 106:44–46.]

⁴³But the land shall be left behind them and shall enjoy its sabbaths while it lies desolate without them; and they shall accept the punishment for their sins *and* make amends because they despised *and* rejected My ordinances and their soul scorned *and* rejected My statutes.

⁴⁴And ᵐyet for all that, when they are in the land of their enemies, I will not spurn *and* cast them away, neither will I despise *and* abhor them to destroy them utterly and to break My covenant with them, for I am the Lord their God. [Deut. 4:31–35; Jer. 33:4, 5, 23–26; Rom. 11:2–5.]

⁴⁵But I will for their sake [earnestly] remember the covenant with their forefathers whom I brought forth out of the land of Egypt in the sight of the nations, that I might be their God. I am the Lord.

⁴⁶These are the statutes, ordinances, and laws which the Lord made between Him and the Israelites on Mount Sinai through Moses.

27 AND THE Lord said to Moses, ²Say to the Israelites, When a man shall make a special vow of persons to the Lord at your valuation,

³Then your valuation of a male from twenty years old to sixty years old shall be fifty shekels of silver, according to the shekel of the sanctuary.

⁴And if the person is a female, your valuation shall be thirty shekels.

⁵And if the person is from five years old up to twenty years old, then your valuation shall be for the male twenty shekels and for the female ten shekels.

⁶And if a child is from a month up to five years old, then your valuation shall be for the male five shekels of silver and for the female three shekels.

⁷And if the person is from sixty years old and above, if it be a male, then your valuation shall be fifteen shekels and for the female ten shekels.

⁸But if the man is too poor to pay your valuation, then he shall be set before the priest, and the priest shall value him; according to the ability of him who vowed shall the priest value him.

⁹If it is a beast of which men offer an offering to the Lord, all that any man gives of such to the Lord shall be holy.

ᵐNo greater evidence that God keeps His word is available than the fact of the existence today of the Jews as a nation. Scattered for twenty-five centuries throughout the world with powerful forces determined to wipe them out, yet they are restored to their homeland because, in spite of all their sins against Him, God refuses to break His covenant with their forefathers and with them. The presence of even a small number of Jews in the world, after all the centuries of diabolical effort to exterminate them, would alone be sufficient assurance that God will keep His promises, whether good or bad, to individuals or to nations.

New American Standard

37 'They will therefore stumble over each other as if *running* from the sword, although no one is pursuing; and you will have *no strength* to stand up before your enemies.
38 'But you will perish among the nations, and your enemies' land will consume you.
39 'So those of you who may be left will rot away because of their iniquity in the lands of your enemies; and also because of the iniquities of their forefathers they will rot away with them.
40 ¶ 'If they confess their iniquity and the iniquity of their forefathers, in their unfaithfulness which they committed against Me, and also in their acting with hostility against Me—
41 I also was acting with hostility against them, to bring them into the land of their enemies—or if their uncircumcised heart becomes humbled so that they then make amends for their iniquity,
42 then I will remember My covenant with Jacob, and I will remember also My covenant with Isaac, and My covenant with Abraham as well, and I will remember the land.
43 'For the land will be abandoned by them, and will make up for its sabbaths while it is made desolate without them. They, meanwhile, will be making amends for their iniquity, because they rejected My ordinances and their soul abhorred My statutes.
44 'Yet in spite of this, when they are in the land of their enemies, I will not reject them, nor will I so abhor them as to destroy them, breaking My covenant with them; for I am the LORD their God.
45 'But I will remember for them the covenant with their ancestors, whom I brought out of the land of Egypt in the sight of the nations, that I might be their God. I am the LORD.' "
46 ¶ These are the statutes and ordinances and laws which the LORD established between Himself and the sons of Israel through Moses at Mount Sinai.

Rules concerning Valuations

27 AGAIN, THE LORD spoke to Moses, saying, 2"Speak to the sons of Israel and say to them, 'When a man makes a difficult vow, he *shall be valued* according to your valuation of persons belonging to the LORD.
3 'If your valuation is of the male from twenty years even to sixty years old, then your valuation shall be fifty shekels of silver, after the shekel of the sanctuary.
4 'Or if it is a female, then your valuation shall be thirty shekels.
5 'If it be from five years even to twenty years old then your valuation for the male shall be twenty shekels and for the female ten shekels.
6 'But if *they are* from a month even up to five years old, then your valuation shall be five shekels of silver for the male, and for the female your valuation shall be three shekels of silver.
7 'If *they are* from sixty years old and upward, if it is a male, then your valuation shall be fifteen shekels, and for the female ten shekels.
8 'But if he is poorer than your valuation, then he shall be placed before the priest and the priest shall value him; according to the means of the one who vowed, the priest shall value him.
9 ¶ 'Now if it is an animal of the kind which men can present as an offering to the LORD, any such that one gives to the LORD shall be holy.

New International

fall, even though no one is pursuing them. 37They will stumble over one another as though fleeing from the sword, even though no one is pursuing them. So you will not be able to stand before your enemies. 38You will perish among the nations; the land of your enemies will devour you. 39Those of you who are left will waste away in the lands of their enemies because of their sins; also because of their fathers' sins they will waste away.
40" 'But if they will confess their sins and the sins of their fathers—their treachery against me and their hostility toward me, 41which made me hostile toward them so that I sent them into the land of their enemies—then when their uncircumcised hearts are humbled and they pay for their sin, 42I will remember my covenant with Jacob and my covenant with Isaac and my covenant with Abraham, and I will remember the land. 43For the land will be deserted by them and will enjoy its sabbaths while it lies desolate without them. They will pay for their sins because they rejected my laws and abhorred my decrees. 44Yet in spite of this, when they are in the land of their enemies, I will not reject them or abhor them so as to destroy them completely, breaking my covenant with them. I am the LORD their God. 45But for their sake I will remember the covenant with their ancestors whom I brought out of Egypt in the sight of the nations to be their God. I am the LORD.' "

46These are the decrees, the laws and the regulations that the LORD established on Mount Sinai between himself and the Israelites through Moses.

Redeeming What Is the LORD's

27 THE LORD said to Moses, 2"Speak to the Israelites and say to them: 'If anyone makes a special vow to dedicate persons to the LORD by giving equivalent values, 3set the value of a male between the ages of twenty and sixty at fifty shekels[n] of silver, according to the sanctuary shekel[o]; 4and if it is a female, set her value at thirty shekels.[p] 5If it is a person between the ages of five and twenty, set the value of a male at twenty shekels[q] and of a female at ten shekels.[r] 6If it is a person between one month and five years, set the value of a male at five shekels[s] of silver and that of a female at three shekels[t] of silver. 7If it is a person sixty years old or more, set the value of a male at fifteen shekels[u] and of a female at ten shekels. 8If anyone making the vow is too poor to pay the specified amount, he is to present the person to the priest, who will set the value for him according to what the man making the vow can afford.
9" 'If what he vowed is an animal that is acceptable as an offering to the LORD, such an animal given to the LORD

---

n 3 That is, about 1 1/4 pounds (about 0.6 kilogram); also in verse 16   *o 3* That is, about 2/5 ounce (about 11.5 grams); also in verse 25   *p 4* That is, about 12 ounces (about 0.3 kilogram)   *q 5* That is, about 8 ounces (about 0.2 kilogram)   *r 5* That is, about 4 ounces (about 110 grams); also in verse 7   *s 6* That is, about 2 ounces (about 55 grams)   *t 6* That is, about 1 1/4 ounces (about 35 grams)   *u 7* That is, about 6 ounces (about 170 grams)

King James

10 He shall not alter it, nor change it, a good for a bad, or a bad for a good: and if he shall at all change beast for beast, then it and the exchange thereof shall be holy.

11 And if *it be* any unclean beast, of which they do not offer a sacrifice unto the LORD, then he shall present the beast before the priest:

12 And the priest shall value it, whether it be good or bad: [e]as thou valuest it, *who art* the priest, so shall it be.

13 But if he will at all redeem it, then he shall add a fifth *part* thereof unto thy estimation.

14 ¶ And when a man shall sanctify his house *to be* holy unto the LORD, then the priest shall estimate it, whether it be good or bad: as the priest shall estimate it, so shall it stand.

15 And if he that sanctified it will redeem his house, then he shall add the fifth *part* of the money of thy estimation unto it, and it shall be his.

16 And if a man shall sanctify unto the LORD *some part* of a field of his possession, then thy estimation shall be according to the seed thereof: [f]an homer of barley seed *shall be valued* at fifty shekels of silver.

17 If he sanctify his field from the year of jubilee, according to thy estimation it shall stand.

18 But if he sanctify his field after the jubilee, then the priest shall reckon unto him the money according to the years that remain, even unto the year of the jubilee, and it shall be abated from thy estimation.

19 And if he that sanctified the field will in any wise redeem it, then he shall add the fifth *part* of the money of thy estimation unto it, and it shall be assured to him.

20 And if he will not redeem the field, or if he have sold the field to another man, it shall not be redeemed any more.

21 But the field, when it goeth out in the jubilee, shall be holy unto the LORD, as a field devoted; the possession thereof shall be the priest's.

22 And if *a man* sanctify unto the LORD a field which he hath bought, which *is* not of the fields of his possession;

23 Then the priest shall reckon unto him the worth of thy estimation, *even* unto the year of the jubilee: and he shall give thine estimation in that day, *as* a holy thing unto the LORD.

24 In the year of the jubilee the field shall return unto him of whom it was bought, *even* to him to whom the possession of the land *did belong*.

25 And all thy estimations shall be according to the shekel of the sanctuary: twenty gerahs shall be the shekel.

26 ¶ Only the [g]firstling of the beasts, which should be the LORD'S firstling, no man shall sanctify it; whether *it be* ox, or sheep: it *is* the LORD'S.

27 And if *it be* of an unclean beast, then he shall redeem *it* according to thine estimation, and shall add a fifth *part* of it thereto: or if it be not redeemed, then it shall be sold according to thy estimation.

28 Notwithstanding no devoted thing, that a man shall devote unto the LORD of all that he hath, *both* of man and beast, and of the field of his possession, shall be sold or redeemed: every devoted thing *is* most holy unto the LORD.

29 None devoted, which shall be devoted of men, shall be redeemed; *but* shall surely be put to death.

30 And all the tithe of the land, *whether* of the seed of the land, *or* of the fruit of the tree, *is* the LORD'S: *it is* holy unto the LORD.

31 And if a man will at all redeem *aught* of his tithes, he shall add thereto the fifth *part* thereof.

32 And concerning the tithe of the herd, or of the flock, *even* of whatsoever passeth under the rod, the tenth shall be holy unto the LORD.

Amplified

10 He shall not replace it or exchange it, a good for a bad, or a bad for a good; and if he makes any exchange of a beast for a beast, then both the original offering and that exchanged for it shall be holy.

11 If it is an unclean animal, such as is not offered as an offering to the Lord, he shall bring the animal before the priest,

12 And the priest shall value it, whether it be good or bad; as you, the priest, value it, so shall it be.

13 But if he wishes to redeem it, he shall add a fifth to your valuation.

14 If a man dedicates his house to be sacred to the Lord, the priest shall appraise it, whether it be good or bad; as the priest appraises it, so shall it stand.

15 If he who dedicates his house wants to redeem it, he shall add a fifth of your valuation to it, and it shall be his.

16 And if a man shall dedicate to the Lord some part of a field of his possession, then your valuation shall be according to the seed [required] for it; [a sowing of] a homer of barley shall be valued at fifty shekels of silver.

17 If he dedicates his field during the Year of Jubilee, it shall stand according to your full valuation.

18 But if he dedicates his field after the Jubilee, then the priest shall count the money value in proportion to the years that remain until the Year of Jubilee, and it shall be deducted from your valuation.

19 If he who dedicates the field wishes to redeem it, then he shall add a fifth of the money of your appraisal to it, and it shall remain his.

20 But if he does not want to redeem the field, or if he has sold it to another man, it shall not be redeemed any more.

21 But the field, when it is released in the Jubilee, shall be holy to the Lord, as a field devoted [to God or destruction]; the priest shall have possession of it.

22 And if a man dedicates to the Lord a field he has bought, which is not of the fields of his [ancestral] possession,

23 The priest shall compute the amount of your valuation for it up to the Year of Jubilee; the man shall give that amount on that day as a holy thing to the Lord.

24 In the Year of Jubilee the field shall return to him of whom it was bought, to him to whom the land belonged [as his ancestral inheritance].

25 And all your valuations shall be according to the sanctuary shekel; twenty gerahs shall make a shekel.

26 But the firstling of the animals, since a firstling belongs to the Lord, no man may dedicate, whether it be ox or sheep. It is the Lord's [already].

27 If it be of an unclean animal, the owner may redeem it according to your valuation, and shall add a fifth to it; or if it is not redeemed, then it shall be sold according to your valuation.

28 But nothing that a man shall devote to the Lord of all that he has, whether of man or beast or of the field of his possession, shall be sold or redeemed; every devoted thing is most holy to the Lord.

29 No one doomed to death [under the claim of divine justice], who is to be completely destroyed from among men, shall be ransomed [from suffering the death penalty]; he shall surely be put to death.

30 And all the tithe of the land, whether of the seed of the land or of the fruit of the tree, is the Lord's; it is holy to the Lord. [I Cor. 9:11; Gal. 6:6.]

31 And if a man wants to redeem any of his tithe, he shall add a fifth to it.

32 And all the tithe of the herd or of the flock, whatever passes under the herdsman's staff [by means of which each tenth animal as it passes through a small door is selected and marked], the tenth shall be holy to the Lord. [II Cor. 9:7–9.]

[e] Heb. *according to thy estimation, O priest* [f] Or, *the land of an homer* [g] Heb. *firstborn*

New American Standard

10 'He shall not replace it or exchange it, a good for a bad, or a bad for a good; or if he does exchange animal for animal, then both it and its substitute shall become holy.

11 'If, however, it is any unclean animal of the kind which men do not present as an offering to the LORD, then he shall place the animal before the priest.

12 'The priest shall value it as either good or bad; as you, the priest, value it, so it shall be.

13 'But if he should ever *wish to* redeem it, then he shall add one-fifth of it to your valuation.

14 ¶ 'Now if a man consecrates his house as holy to the LORD, then the priest shall value it as either good or bad; as the priest values it, so it shall stand.

15 'Yet if the one who consecrates it should *wish to* redeem his house, then he shall add one-fifth of your valuation price to it, so that it may be his.

16 ¶ 'Again, if a man consecrates to the LORD part of the fields of his own property, then your valuation shall be proportionate to the seed needed for it: a homer of barley seed at fifty shekels of silver.

17 'If he consecrates his field as of the year of jubilee, according to your valuation it shall stand.

18 'If he consecrates his field after the jubilee, however, then the priest shall calculate the price for him proportionate to the years that are left until the year of jubilee; and it shall be deducted from your valuation.

19 'If the one who consecrates it should ever wish to redeem the field, then he shall add one-fifth of your valuation price to it, so that it may pass to him.

20 'Yet if he will not redeem the field, but has sold the field to another man, it may no longer be redeemed;

21 and when it reverts in the jubilee, the field shall be holy to the LORD, like a field set apart; it shall be for the priest as his property.

22 'Or if he consecrates to the LORD a field which he has bought, which is not a part of the field of his own property,

23 then the priest shall calculate for him the amount of your valuation up to the year of jubilee; and he shall on that day give your valuation as holy to the LORD.

24 'In the year of jubilee the field shall return to the one from whom he bought it, to whom the possession of the land belongs.

25 'Every valuation of yours, moreover, shall be after the shekel of the sanctuary. The shekel shall be twenty gerahs.

26 ¶ 'However, a firstborn among animals, which as a firstborn belongs to the LORD, no man may consecrate it; whether ox or sheep, it is the LORD'S.

27 'But if *it is* among the unclean animals, then he shall redeem it according to your valuation and add to it one-fifth of it; and if it is not redeemed, then it shall be sold according to your valuation.

28 ¶ 'Nevertheless, anything which a man *s*sets apart to the LORD out of all that he has, of man or animal or of the fields of his own property, shall not be sold or redeemed. Anything devoted to destruction is most holy to the LORD.

29 'No one who may have been set apart among men shall be ransomed; he shall surely be put to death.

30 ¶ 'Thus all the tithe of the land, of the seed of the land or of the fruit of the tree, is the LORD'S; it is holy to the LORD.

31 'If, therefore, a man wishes to redeem part of his tithe, he shall add to it one-fifth of it.

32 'For every tenth part of herd or flock, whatever passes under the rod, the tenth one shall be holy to the LORD.

New International

becomes holy. 10He must not exchange it or substitute a good one for a bad one, or a bad one for a good one; if he should substitute one animal for another, both it and the substitute become holy. 11If what he vowed is a ceremonially unclean animal—one that is not acceptable as an offering to the LORD—the animal must be presented to the priest, 12who will judge its quality as good or bad. Whatever value the priest then sets, that is what it will be. 13If the owner wishes to redeem the animal, he must add a fifth to its value.

14'If a man dedicates his house as something holy to the LORD, the priest will judge its quality as good or bad. Whatever value the priest then sets, so it will remain. 15If the man who dedicates his house redeems it, he must add a fifth to its value, and the house will again become his.

16'If a man dedicates to the LORD part of his family land, its value is to be set according to the amount of seed required for it—fifty shekels of silver to a homer*v* of barley seed. 17If he dedicates his field during the Year of Jubilee, the value that has been set remains. 18But if he dedicates his field after the Jubilee, the priest will determine the value according to the number of years that remain until the next Year of Jubilee, and its set value will be reduced. 19If the man who dedicates the field wishes to redeem it, he must add a fifth to its value, and the field will again become his. 20If, however, he does not redeem the field, or if he has sold it to someone else, it can never be redeemed. 21When the field is released in the Jubilee, it will become holy, like a field devoted to the LORD; it will become the property of the priests.*w*

22"'If a man dedicates to the LORD a field he has bought, which is not part of his family land, 23the priest will determine its value up to the Year of Jubilee, and the man must pay its value on that day as something holy to the LORD. 24In the Year of Jubilee the field will revert to the person from whom he bought it, the one whose land it was. 25Every value is to be set according to the sanctuary shekel, twenty gerahs to the shekel.

26"'No one, however, may dedicate the firstborn of an animal, since the firstborn already belongs to the LORD; whether an ox*x* or a sheep, it is the LORD's. 27If it is one of the unclean animals, he may buy it back at its set value, adding a fifth of the value to it. If he does not redeem it, it is to be sold at its set value.

28"'But nothing that a man owns and devotes*y* to the LORD—whether man or animal or family land—may be sold or redeemed; everything so devoted is most holy to the LORD.

29"'No person devoted to destruction*z* may be ransomed; he must be put to death.

30"'A tithe of everything from the land, whether grain from the soil or fruit from the trees, belongs to the LORD; it is holy to the LORD. 31If a man redeems any of his tithe, he must add a fifth of the value to it. 32The entire tithe of the herd and flock—every tenth animal that passes under

---

v 16 That is, probably about 6 bushels (about 220 liters)
w 21 Or *priest*   *x 26* The Hebrew word can include both male and female.   *y 28* The Hebrew term refers to the irrevocable giving over of things or persons to the LORD.   *z 29* The Hebrew term refers to the irrevocable giving over of things or persons to the LORD, often by totally destroying them.

*s*Lit *anything devoted;* or *banned*

King James

33He shall not search whether it be good or bad, neither shall he change it: and if he change it at all, then both it and the change thereof shall be holy; it shall not be redeemed.

34These *are* the commandments, which the LORD commanded Moses for the children of Israel in mount Sinai.

Amplified

33The man shall not examine whether the animal is good or bad nor shall he exchange it. If he does exchange it, then both it and the animal substituted for it shall be holy; it shall not be redeemed.

34These are the commandments which the Lord commanded Moses on Mount Sinai for the Israelites. [Rom. 10:4; Heb. 4:2; 12:18–29.]

New American Standard

33 'He is not to be concerned whether *it is* good or bad, nor shall he exchange it; or if he does exchange it, then both it and its substitute shall become holy. It shall not be redeemed.' "

34 ¶ These are the commandments which the LORD commanded Moses for the sons of Israel at Mount Sinai.

New International

the shepherd's rod—will be holy to the LORD. 33He must not pick out the good from the bad or make any substitution. If he does make a substitution, both the animal and its substitute become holy and cannot be redeemed.' "

34These are the commands the LORD gave Moses on Mount Sinai for the Israelites.

THE FOURTH BOOK OF MOSES, CALLED

Numbers

THE FOURTH BOOK OF MOSES, CALLED

Numbers

The census of the people

1 AND THE LORD spake unto Moses in the wilderness of Sinai, in the tabernacle of the congregation, on the first *day* of the second month, in the second year after they were come out of the land of Egypt, saying,

²Take ye the sum of all the congregation of the children of Israel, after their families, by the house of their fathers, with the number of *their* names, every male by their polls;

³From twenty years old and upward, all that are able to go forth to war in Israel: thou and Aaron shall number them by their armies.

⁴And with you there shall be a man of every tribe; every one head of the house of his fathers.

⁵ ¶ And these *are* the names of the men that shall stand with you: of *the tribe of* Reuben; Elizur the son of Shedeur.

⁶Of Simeon; Shelumiel the son of Zurishaddai.

⁷Of Judah; *ª*Nahshon the son of Amminadab.

⁸Of Issachar; Nethaneel the son of Zuar.

⁹Of Zebulun; Eliab the son of Helon.

¹⁰Of the children of Joseph: of Ephraim; Elishama the son of Ammihud: of Manasseh; Gamaliel the son of Pedahzur.

¹¹Of Benjamin; Abidan the son of Gideoni.

¹²Of Dan; Ahiezer the son of Ammishaddai.

¹³Of Asher; Pagiel the son of Ocran.

¹⁴Of Gad; Eliasaph the son of *ᵇ*Deuel.

¹⁵Of Naphtali; Ahira the son of Enan.

¹⁶These *were* the renowned of the congregation, princes of the tribes of their fathers, heads of thousands in Israel.

¹⁷ ¶ And Moses and Aaron took these men which are expressed by *their* names:

¹⁸And they assembled all the congregation together on the first *day* of the second month, and they declared their pedigrees after their families, by the house of their fathers, according to the number of the names, from twenty years old and upward, by their polls.

¹⁹As the LORD commanded Moses, so he numbered them in the wilderness of Sinai.

²⁰And the children of Reuben, Israel's eldest son, by their generations, after their families, by the house of their fathers, according to the number of the names, by their polls, every male from twenty years old and upward, all that were able to go forth to war;

²¹Those that were numbered of them, *even* of the tribe of Reuben, *were* forty and six thousand and five hundred.

²² ¶ Of the children of Simeon, by their generations, after their families, by the house of their fathers, those that were numbered of them, according to the number of the names, by their polls, every male from twenty years old and upward, all that were able to go forth to war;

²³Those that were numbered of them, *even* of the tribe of Simeon, *were* fifty and nine thousand and three hundred.

²⁴ ¶ Of the children of Gad, by their generations, after their families, by the house of their fathers, according to the number of the names, from twenty years old and upward, all that were able to go forth to war;

²⁵Those that were numbered of them, *even* of the tribe of Gad, *were* forty and five thousand six hundred and fifty.

1 THE LORD spoke to Moses in the Wilderness of Sinai in the Tent of Meeting on the first day of the second month in the second year after they came out of the land of Egypt, saying,

²Take a census of all the males of the congregation of the Israelites by families, by their fathers' houses, according to the number of names, head by head.

³From twenty years old and upward, all in Israel who are able to go forth to war you and Aaron shall number, company by company.

⁴And with you there shall be a man [to assist you] from each tribe, each being the head of his father's house.

⁵And these are the names of the men who shall attend you: Of Reuben, Elizur son of Shedeur;

⁶Of Simeon, Shelumiel son of Zurishaddai;

⁷Of Judah, Nahshon son of Amminadab;

⁸Of Issachar, Nethanel son of Zuar;

⁹Of Zebulun, Eliab son of Helon;

¹⁰Of the sons of Joseph: of Ephraim, Elishama son of Ammihud; of Manasseh, Gamaliel son of Pedahzur;

¹¹Of Benjamin, Abidan son of Gideoni;

¹²Of Dan, Ahiezer son of Ammishaddai;

¹³Of Asher, Pagiel son of Ochran;

¹⁴Of Gad, Eliasaph son of Deuel;

¹⁵Of Naphtali, Ahira son of Enan.

¹⁶These were those chosen from the congregation, the leaders of their ancestral tribes, heads of thousands [the highest class of officers] in Israel.

¹⁷And Moses and Aaron took these men who have been named,

¹⁸And assembled all the congregation on the first day of the second month, and they declared their ancestry after their families, by their fathers' houses, according to the number of names from twenty years old and upward, head by head,

¹⁹As the Lord commanded Moses. So he numbered them in the Wilderness of Sinai.

²⁰The sons of Reuben, Israel's firstborn, their generations, by their families, by their fathers' houses, according to the number of names, head by head, every male from twenty years old and upward, all who were able to go to war:

²¹Those of the tribe of Reuben numbered 46,500.

²²Of the sons of Simeon, their generations, by their families, by their fathers' houses, those numbered of them according to the number of names, head by head, every male from twenty years old and upward, all who were able to go to war:

²³Those of the tribe of Simeon numbered 59,300.

²⁴Of the sons of Gad, their generations, by their families, by their fathers' houses, according to the number of names, from twenty years old and upward, all who were able to go to war:

²⁵Those of the tribe of Gad numbered 45,650.

ª Called *Naasson* in Mat. 1:4   *ᵇ* ch. 2:14 he is called *Reuel*

Numbers

Numbers

The Census of Israel's Warriors

1 THEN THE LORD spoke to Moses in the wilderness of Sinai, in the tent of meeting, on the first of the second month, in the second year after they had come out of the land of Egypt, saying,

2"Take a *a*census of all the congregation of the sons of Israel, by their families, by their fathers' households, according to the number of names, every male, head by head

3 from twenty years old and upward, whoever *is able to* go out to war in Israel, you and Aaron shall *b*number them by their armies.

4"With you, moreover, there shall be a man of each tribe, each one head of his father's household.

5"These then are the names of the men who shall stand with you: of Reuben, Elizur the son of Shedeur;

6 of Simeon, Shelumiel the son of Zurishaddai;

7 of Judah, Nahshon the son of Amminadab;

8 of Issachar, Nethanel the son of Zuar;

9 of Zebulun, Eliab the son of Helon;

10 of the sons of Joseph: of Ephraim, Elishama the son of Ammihud; of Manasseh, Gamaliel the son of Pedahzur;

11 of Benjamin, Abidan the son of Gideoni;

12 of Dan, Ahiezer the son of Ammishaddai;

13 of Asher, Pagiel the son of Ochran;

14 of Gad, Eliasaph the son of Deuel;

15 of Naphtali, Ahira the son of Enan.

16"These are they who were called of the congregation, the leaders of their fathers' tribes; they were the heads of *c*divisions of Israel."

17 ¶ So Moses and Aaron took these men who had been designated by name,

18 and they assembled all the congregation together on the first of the second month. Then they registered by ancestry in their families, by their fathers' households, according to the number of names, from twenty years old and upward, head by head,

19 just as the LORD had commanded Moses. So he numbered them in the wilderness of Sinai.

20 ¶ Now the sons of Reuben, Israel's firstborn, their genealogical registration by their families, by their fathers' households, according to the number of names, head by head, every male from twenty years old and upward, whoever *was able to* go out to war,

21 their numbered men of the tribe of Reuben *were* 46,500.

22 ¶ Of the sons of Simeon, their genealogical registration by their families, by their fathers' households, their numbered men, according to the number of names, head by head, every male from twenty years old and upward, whoever *was able to* go out to war,

23 their numbered men of the tribe of Simeon *were* 59,300.

24 ¶ Of the sons of Gad, their genealogical registration by their families, by their fathers' households, according to the number of names, from twenty years old and upward, whoever *was able to* go out to war,

25 their numbered men of the tribe of Gad *were* 45,650.

The Census

1 THE LORD spoke to Moses in the Tent of Meeting in the Desert of Sinai on the first day of the second month of the second year after the Israelites came out of Egypt. He said: 2"Take a census of the whole Israelite community by their clans and families, listing every man by name, one by one. 3You and Aaron are to number by their divisions all the men in Israel twenty years old or more who are able to serve in the army. 4One man from each tribe, each the head of his family, is to help you. 5These are the names of the men who are to assist you:

from Reuben, Elizur son of Shedeur;

6from Simeon, Shelumiel son of Zurishaddai;

7from Judah, Nahshon son of Amminadab;

8from Issachar, Nethanel son of Zuar;

9from Zebulun, Eliab son of Helon;

10from the sons of Joseph:

from Ephraim, Elishama son of Ammihud;

from Manasseh, Gamaliel son of Pedahzur;

11from Benjamin, Abidan son of Gideoni;

12from Dan, Ahiezer son of Ammishaddai;

13from Asher, Pagiel son of Ocran;

14from Gad, Eliasaph son of Deuel;

15from Naphtali, Ahira son of Enan."

16These were the men appointed from the community, the leaders of their ancestral tribes. They were the heads of the clans of Israel.

17Moses and Aaron took these men whose names had been given, 18and they called the whole community together on the first day of the second month. The people indicated their ancestry by their clans and families, and the men twenty years old or more were listed by name, one by one, 19as the LORD commanded Moses. And so he counted them in the Desert of Sinai:

20From the descendants of Reuben the firstborn son of Israel:

All the men twenty years old or more who were able to serve in the army were listed by name, one by one, according to the records of their clans and families. 21The number from the tribe of Reuben was 46,500.

22From the descendants of Simeon:

All the men twenty years old or more who were able to serve in the army were counted and listed by name, one by one, according to the records of their clans and families. 23The number from the tribe of Simeon was 59,300.

24From the descendants of Gad:

All the men twenty years old or more who were able to serve in the army were listed by name, according to the records of their clans and families. 25The number from the tribe of Gad was 45,650.

---

*a*Lit *sum*   *b*Lit *muster,* and so throughout the ch   *c*Lit *thousands;* or *clans*

King James

26 ¶ Of the children of Judah, by their generations, after their families, by the house of their fathers, according to the number of the names, from twenty years old and upward, all that were able to go forth to war;

27Those that were numbered of them, *even* of the tribe of Judah, *were* threescore and fourteen thousand and six hundred.

28 ¶ Of the children of Issachar, by their generations, after their families, by the house of their fathers, according to the number of the names, from twenty years old and upward, all that were able to go forth to war;

29Those that were numbered of them, *even* of the tribe of Issachar, *were* fifty and four thousand and four hundred.

30 ¶ Of the children of Zebulun, by their generations, after their families, by the house of their fathers, according to the number of the names, from twenty years old and upward, all that were able to go forth to war;

31Those that were numbered of them, *even* of the tribe of Zebulun, *were* fifty and seven thousand and four hundred.

32 ¶ Of the children of Joseph, *namely,* of the children of Ephraim, by their generations, after their families, by the house of their fathers, according to the number of the names, from twenty years old and upward, all that were able to go forth to war;

33Those that were numbered of them, *even* of the tribe of Ephraim, *were* forty thousand and five hundred.

34 ¶ Of the children of Manasseh, by their generations, after their families, by the house of their fathers, according to the number of the names, from twenty years old and upward, all that were able to go forth to war;

35Those that were numbered of them, *even* of the tribe of Manasseh, *were* thirty and two thousand and two hundred.

36 ¶ Of the children of Benjamin, by their generations, after their families, by the house of their fathers, according to the number of the names, from twenty years old and upward, all that were able to go forth to war;

37Those that were numbered of them, *even* of the tribe of Benjamin, *were* thirty and five thousand and four hundred.

38 ¶ Of the children of Dan, by their generations, after their families, by the house of their fathers, according to the number of the names, from twenty years old and upward, all that were able to go forth to war;

39Those that were numbered of them, *even* of the tribe of Dan, *were* threescore and two thousand and seven hundred.

40 ¶ Of the children of Asher, by their generations, after their families, by the house of their fathers, according to the number of the names, from twenty years old and upward, all that were able to go forth to war;

41Those that were numbered of them, *even* of the tribe of Asher, *were* forty and one thousand and five hundred.

42 ¶ Of the children of Naphtali, throughout their generations, after their families, by the house of their fathers, according to the number of the names, from twenty years old and upward, all that were able to go forth to war;

43Those that were numbered of them, *even* of the tribe of Naphtali, *were* fifty and three thousand and four hundred.

44These *are* those that were numbered, which Moses and Aaron numbered, and the princes of Israel, *being* twelve men: each one was for the house of his fathers.

45So were all those that were numbered of the children of Israel, by the house of their fathers, from twenty years old and upward, all that were able to go forth to war in Israel;

46Even all they that were numbered were six hundred thousand and three thousand and five hundred and fifty.

47 ¶ But the Levites after the tribe of their fathers were not numbered among them.

48For the LORD had spoken unto Moses, saying,

Amplified

26Of the sons of Judah, their generations, by their families, by their fathers' houses, according to the number of names, from twenty years old and upward, all able to go to war:

27Those of the tribe of Judah numbered 74,600.

28Of the sons of Issachar, their generations, by their families, by their fathers' houses, according to the number of names, from twenty years old and upward, all able to go to war:

29Those of the tribe of Issachar numbered 54,400.

30Of the sons of Zebulun, their generations, by their families, by their fathers' houses, according to the number of names, from twenty years old and upward, all able to go to war:

31Those of the tribe of Zebulun numbered 57,400.

32Of the sons of Joseph: the sons of Ephraim, their generations, by their families, by their fathers' houses, according to the number of names, from twenty years old and upward, all able to go to war:

33Those of the tribe of Ephraim numbered 40,500.

34Of the sons of Manasseh, their generations, by their families, by their fathers' houses, according to the number of names, from twenty years old and upward, all able to go to war:

35Those of the tribe of Manasseh numbered 32,200.

36Of the sons of Benjamin, their generations, by their families, by their fathers' houses, according to the number of names, from twenty years old and upward, all able to go to war:

37Those of the tribe of Benjamin numbered 35,400.

38Of the sons of Dan, their generations, by their families, by their fathers' houses, according to the number of names, from twenty years old and upward, all able to go to war:

39Those of the tribe of Dan numbered 62,700.

40Of the sons of Asher, their generations, by their families, by their fathers' houses, according to the number of names, from twenty years old and upward, all able to go to war:

41Those of the tribe of Asher numbered 41,500.

42Of the sons of Naphtali, their generations, by their families, by their fathers' houses, according to the number of names, from twenty years old and upward, all able to go to war:

43Those of the tribe of Naphtali numbered 53,400.

44These were numbered by Moses and Aaron, and the leaders of Israel, twelve men, each representing his father's house.

45So all those numbered of the Israelites, by their fathers' houses, from twenty years old and upward, able to go to war in Israel,

46All who were numbered were 603,550.

47But the Levites by their fathers' tribe were not numbered with them.

48For the Lord had said to Moses,

New American Standard

26 ¶ Of the sons of Judah, their genealogical registration by their families, by their fathers' households, according to the number of names, from twenty years old and upward, whoever *was able to* go out to war, 27 their numbered men of the tribe of Judah *were* 74,600.

28 ¶ Of the sons of Issachar, their genealogical registration by their families, by their fathers' households, according to the number of names, from twenty years old and upward, whoever *was able to* go out to war, 29 their numbered men of the tribe of Issachar *were* 54,400.

30 ¶ Of the sons of Zebulun, their genealogical registration by their families, by their fathers' households, according to the number of names, from twenty years old and upward, whoever *was able to* go out to war, 31 their numbered men of the tribe of Zebulun *were* 57,400.

32 ¶ Of the sons of Joseph, *namely,* of the sons of Ephraim, their genealogical registration by their families, by their fathers' households, according to the number of names, from twenty years old and upward, whoever *was able to* go out to war, 33 their numbered men of the tribe of Ephraim *were* 40,500.

34 ¶ Of the sons of Manasseh, their genealogical registration by their families, by their fathers' households, according to the number of names, from twenty years old and upward, whoever *was able to* go out to war, 35 their numbered men of the tribe of Manasseh *were* 32,200.

36 ¶ Of the sons of Benjamin, their genealogical registration by their families, by their fathers' households, according to the number of names, from twenty years old and upward, whoever *was able to* go out to war, 37 their numbered men of the tribe of Benjamin *were* 35,400.

38 ¶ Of the sons of Dan, their genealogical registration by their families, by their fathers' households, according to the number of names, from twenty years old and upward, whoever *was able to* go out to war, 39 their numbered men of the tribe of Dan *were* 62,700.

40 ¶ Of the sons of Asher, their genealogical registration by their families, by their fathers' households, according to the number of names, from twenty years old and upward, whoever *was able to* go out to war, 41 their numbered men of the tribe of Asher *were* 41,500.

42 ¶ Of the sons of Naphtali, their genealogical registration by their families, by their fathers' households, according to the number of names, from twenty years old and upward, whoever *was able to* go out to war, 43 their numbered men of the tribe of Naphtali *were* 53,400.

44 ¶ These are the ones who were numbered, whom Moses and Aaron numbered, with the leaders of Israel, twelve men, each of whom was of his father's household.

45 So all the numbered men of the sons of Israel by their fathers' households, from twenty years old and upward, whoever *was able to* go out to war in Israel, 46 even all the numbered men were 603,550.

Levites Exempted

47 ¶ The Levites, however, were not numbered among them by their fathers' tribe. 48 For the LORD had spoken to Moses, saying,

New International

26From the descendants of Judah:

All the men twenty years old or more who were able to serve in the army were listed by name, according to the records of their clans and families. 27The number from the tribe of Judah was 74,600.

28From the descendants of Issachar:

All the men twenty years old or more who were able to serve in the army were listed by name, according to the records of their clans and families. 29The number from the tribe of Issachar was 54,400.

30From the descendants of Zebulun:

All the men twenty years old or more who were able to serve in the army were listed by name, according to the records of their clans and families. 31The number from the tribe of Zebulun was 57,400.

32From the sons of Joseph:

From the descendants of Ephraim:

All the men twenty years old or more who were able to serve in the army were listed by name, according to the records of their clans and families. 33The number from the tribe of Ephraim was 40,500.

34From the descendants of Manasseh:

All the men twenty years old or more who were able to serve in the army were listed by name, according to the records of their clans and families. 35The number from the tribe of Manasseh was 32,200.

36From the descendants of Benjamin:

All the men twenty years old or more who were able to serve in the army were listed by name, according to the records of their clans and families. 37The number from the tribe of Benjamin was 35,400.

38From the descendants of Dan:

All the men twenty years old or more who were able to serve in the army were listed by name, according to the records of their clans and families. 39The number from the tribe of Dan was 62,700.

40From the descendants of Asher:

All the men twenty years old or more who were able to serve in the army were listed by name, according to the records of their clans and families. 41The number from the tribe of Asher was 41,500.

42From the descendants of Naphtali:

All the men twenty years old or more who were able to serve in the army were listed by name, according to the records of their clans and families. 43The number from the tribe of Naphtali was 53,400.

44These were the men counted by Moses and Aaron and the twelve leaders of Israel, each one representing his family. 45All the Israelites twenty years old or more who were able to serve in Israel's army were counted according to their families. 46The total number was 603,550.

47The families of the tribe of Levi, however, were not counted along with the others. 48The LORD had said to

King James

⁴⁹Only thou shalt not number the tribe of Levi, neither take the sum of them among the children of Israel:

⁵⁰But thou shalt appoint the Levites over the tabernacle of testimony, and over all the vessels thereof, and over all things that *belong* to it: they shall bear the tabernacle, and all the vessels thereof; and they shall minister unto it, and shall encamp round about the tabernacle.

⁵¹And when the tabernacle setteth forward, the Levites shall take it down: and when the tabernacle is to be pitched, the Levites shall set it up: and the stranger that cometh nigh shall be put to death.

⁵²And the children of Israel shall pitch their tents, every man by his own camp, and every man by his own standard, throughout their hosts.

⁵³But the Levites shall pitch round about the tabernacle of testimony, that there be no wrath upon the congregation of the children of Israel: and the Levites shall keep the charge of the tabernacle of testimony.

⁵⁴And the children of Israel did according to all that the Lord commanded Moses, so did they.

The camps and tribal captains

2 AND THE Lord spake unto Moses and unto Aaron, saying,

²Every man of the children of Israel shall pitch by his own standard, with the ensign of their father's house: ᶜfar off about the tabernacle of the congregation shall they pitch.

³And on the east side toward the rising of the sun shall they of the standard of the camp of Judah pitch throughout their armies: and Nahshon the son of Amminadab *shall be* captain of the children of Judah.

⁴And his host, and those that were numbered of them, *were* threescore and fourteen thousand and six hundred.

⁵And those that do pitch next unto him *shall be* the tribe of Issachar: and Nethaneel the son of Zuar *shall be* captain of the children of Issachar.

⁶And his host, and those that were numbered thereof, *were* fifty and four thousand and four hundred.

⁷*Then* the tribe of Zebulun: and Eliab the son of Helon *shall be* captain of the children of Zebulun.

⁸And his host, and those that were numbered thereof, *were* fifty and seven thousand and four hundred.

⁹All that were numbered in the camp of Judah *were* an hundred thousand and fourscore thousand and six thousand and four hundred, throughout their armies. These shall first set forth.

¹⁰ ¶ On the south side *shall be* the standard of the camp of Reuben according to their armies: and the captain of the children of Reuben *shall be* Elizur the son of Shedeur.

¹¹And his host, and those that were numbered thereof, *were* forty and six thousand and five hundred.

¹²And those which pitch by him *shall be* the tribe of Simeon: and the captain of the children of Simeon *shall be* Shelumiel the son of Zurishaddai.

¹³And his host, and those that were numbered of them, *were* fifty and nine thousand and three hundred.

¹⁴Then the tribe of Gad: and the captain of the sons of Gad *shall be* Eliasaph the son of ᵈReuel.

¹⁵And his host, and those that were numbered of them, *were* forty and five thousand and six hundred and fifty.

¹⁶All that were numbered in the camp of Reuben *were* an hundred thousand and fifty and one thousand and four hundred and fifty, throughout their armies. And they shall set forth in the second rank.

¹⁷ ¶ Then the tabernacle of the congregation shall set forward with the camp of the Levites in the midst of the camp: as they encamp, so shall they set forward, every man in his place by their standards.

Amplified

⁴⁹Only the tribe of Levi you shall not number in the census of the Israelites.

⁵⁰But appoint the Levites over the tabernacle of the Testimony, and over all its vessels and furnishings and all things that belong to it. They shall carry the tabernacle [when journeying] and all its furnishings, and they shall minister to it and encamp around it.

⁵¹When the tabernacle is to go forward, the Levites shall take it down, and when the tabernacle is to be pitched, the Levites shall set it up. And the excluded [any not of the tribe of Levi] who approach the tabernacle shall be put to death.

⁵²The Israelites shall pitch their tents by their companies, every man by his own camp and every man by his own [tribal] standard.

⁵³But the Levites shall encamp around the tabernacle of the Testimony, that there may be no wrath upon the congregation of the Israelites; and the Levites shall keep charge of the tabernacle of the Testimony.

⁵⁴Thus did the Israelites; according to all that the Lord commanded Moses, so they did.

2 THE LORD said to Moses and Aaron,

²The Israelites shall encamp, each by his own [tribal] standard *or* banner with the ensign of his father's house, opposite the Tent of Meeting *and* facing it on every side.

³On the east side toward the sunrise shall they of the standard of the camp of Judah encamp by their companies; Nahshon son of Amminadab being the leader of the sons of Judah.

⁴Judah's host as numbered totaled 74,600.

⁵Next to Judah the tribe of Issachar shall encamp, Nethanel son of Zuar being the leader of the sons of Issachar.

⁶Issachar's host as numbered totaled 54,400.

⁷Then the tribe of Zebulun, Eliab son of Helon being the leader of the sons of Zebulun.

⁸Zebulun's host as numbered totaled 57,400.

⁹All these [three tribes] numbered in the camp of Judah totaled 186,400. They shall set forth first [on the march].

¹⁰On the south side shall be the standard of the camp of Reuben by their companies, the leader of the sons of Reuben being Elizur son of Shedeur.

¹¹Reuben's host as numbered totaled 46,500.

¹²Those who encamp next to Reuben shall be the tribe of Simeon, the leader of the sons of Simeon being Shelumiel son of Zurishaddai.

¹³Simeon's host as numbered totaled 59,300.

¹⁴Then the tribe of Gad, the leader of the sons of Gad being Eliasaph son of Reuel (Deuel).

¹⁵Gad's host as numbered totaled 45,650.

¹⁶The whole number in [the three tribes of] the camp of Reuben was 151,450. They shall take second place [on the march].

¹⁷Then the Tent of Meeting shall set out, with the camp of the Levites in the midst of the camps; as they encamp so shall they set forward, every man in his place, standard after standard.

ᶜHeb. *over against*   ᵈDeuel; see ch. 1:14 & 7:42,47 & 10:20

New American Standard

49"Only the tribe of Levi you shall not number, nor shall you take their census among the sons of Israel.
50"But you shall appoint the Levites over the [d]tabernacle of the testimony, and over all its furnishings and over all that belongs to it. They shall carry the tabernacle and all its furnishings, and they shall take care of it; they shall also camp around the tabernacle.
51"So when the tabernacle is to set out, the Levites shall take it down; and when the tabernacle encamps, the Levites shall set it up. But the [e]layman who comes near shall be put to death.
52"The sons of Israel shall camp, each man by his own camp, and each man by his own standard, according to their armies.
53"But the Levites shall camp around the tabernacle of the testimony, so that there will be no wrath on the congregation of the sons of Israel. So the Levites shall keep charge of the tabernacle of the testimony."
54 Thus the sons of Israel did; according to all which the LORD had commanded Moses, so they did.

Arrangement of the Camps

2 NOW THE LORD spoke to Moses and to Aaron, saying,
2"The sons of Israel shall camp, each by his own standard, with the banners of their fathers' households; they shall camp around the tent of meeting at a distance.
3"Now those who camp on the east side toward the sunrise *shall be* of the standard of the camp of Judah, by their armies, and the leader of the sons of Judah: Nahshon the son of Amminadab,
4 and his army, even their numbered men, 74,600.
5"Those who camp next to him *shall be* the tribe of Issachar, and the leader of the sons of Issachar: Nethanel the son of Zuar,
6 and his army, even their numbered men, 54,400.
7"*Then comes* the tribe of Zebulun, and the leader of the sons of Zebulun: Eliab the son of Helon,
8 and his army, even his numbered men, 57,400.
9"The total of the numbered men of the camp of Judah: 186,400, by their armies. They shall set out first.
10 ¶ "On the south side *shall be* the standard of the camp of Reuben by their armies, and the leader of the sons of Reuben: Elizur the son of Shedeur,
11 and his army, even their numbered men, 46,500.
12"Those who camp next to him *shall be* the tribe of Simeon, and the leader of the sons of Simeon: Shelumiel the son of Zurishaddai,
13 and his army, even their numbered men, 59,300.
14"Then *comes* the tribe of Gad, and the leader of the sons of Gad: Eliasaph the son of Deuel,
15 and his army, even their numbered men, 45,650.
16"The total of the numbered men of the camp of Reuben: 151,450 by their armies. And they shall set out second.
17 ¶ "Then the tent of meeting shall set out *with* the camp of the Levites in the midst of the camps; just as they camp, so they shall set out, every man in his place by their standards.

New International

Moses: 49"You must not count the tribe of Levi or include them in the census of the other Israelites. 50Instead, appoint the Levites to be in charge of the tabernacle of the Testimony—over all its furnishings and everything belonging to it. They are to carry the tabernacle and all its furnishings; they are to take care of it and encamp around it. 51Whenever the tabernacle is to move, the Levites are to take it down, and whenever the tabernacle is to be set up, the Levites shall do it. Anyone else who goes near it shall be put to death. 52The Israelites are to set up their tents by divisions, each man in his own camp under his own standard. 53The Levites, however, are to set up their tents around the tabernacle of the Testimony so that wrath will not fall on the Israelite community. The Levites are to be responsible for the care of the tabernacle of the Testimony."
54The Israelites did all this just as the LORD commanded Moses.

The Arrangement of the Tribal Camps

2 THE LORD said to Moses and Aaron: 2"The Israelites are to camp around the Tent of Meeting some distance from it, each man under his standard with the banners of his family."

3On the east, toward the sunrise, the divisions of the camp of Judah are to encamp under their standard. The leader of the people of Judah is Nahshon son of Amminadab. 4His division numbers 74,600.
5The tribe of Issachar will camp next to them. The leader of the people of Issachar is Nethanel son of Zuar. 6His division numbers 54,400.
7The tribe of Zebulun will be next. The leader of the people of Zebulun is Eliab son of Helon. 8His division numbers 57,400.
9All the men assigned to the camp of Judah, according to their divisions, number 186,400. They will set out first.

10On the south will be the divisions of the camp of Reuben under their standard. The leader of the people of Reuben is Elizur son of Shedeur. 11His division numbers 46,500.
12The tribe of Simeon will camp next to them. The leader of the people of Simeon is Shelumiel son of Zurishaddai. 13His division numbers 59,300.
14The tribe of Gad will be next. The leader of the people of Gad is Eliasaph son of Deuel.[a] 15His division numbers 45,650.
16All the men assigned to the camp of Reuben, according to their divisions, number 151,450. They will set out second.

17Then the Tent of Meeting and the camp of the Levites will set out in the middle of the camps. They will set out in the same order as they encamp, each in his own place under his standard.

---

a 14 Many manuscripts of the Masoretic Text, Samaritan Pentateuch and Vulgate (see also Num. 1:14); most manuscripts of the Masoretic Text *Reuel*

*d*Lit *dwelling place,* and so throughout the ch   *e*Lit *stranger*

| King James | Amplified |

King James

18 ¶ On the west side *shall be* the standard of the camp of Ephraim according to their armies: and the captain of the sons of Ephraim *shall be* Elishama the son of Ammihud.

19 And his host, and those that were numbered of them, *were* forty thousand and five hundred.

20 And by him *shall be* the tribe of Manasseh: and the captain of the children of Manasseh *shall be* Gamaliel the son of Pedahzur.

21 And his host, and those that were numbered of them, *were* thirty and two thousand and two hundred.

22 Then the tribe of Benjamin: and the captain of the sons of Benjamin *shall be* Abidan the son of Gideoni.

23 And his host, and those that were numbered of them, *were* thirty and five thousand and four hundred.

24 All that were numbered of the camp of Ephraim *were* an hundred thousand and eight thousand and an hundred, throughout their armies. And they shall go forward in the third rank.

25 ¶ The standard of the camp of Dan *shall be* on the north side by their armies: and the captain of the children of Dan *shall be* Ahiezer the son of Ammishaddai.

26 And his host, and those that were numbered of them, *were* threescore and two thousand and seven hundred.

27 And those that encamp by him *shall be* the tribe of Asher: and the captain of the children of Asher *shall be* Pagiel the son of Ocran.

28 And his host, and those that were numbered of them, *were* forty and one thousand and five hundred.

29 ¶ Then the tribe of Naphtali: and the captain of the children of Naphtali *shall be* Ahira the son of Enan.

30 And his host, and those that were numbered of them, *were* fifty and three thousand and four hundred.

31 All they that were numbered in the camp of Dan *were* an hundred thousand and fifty and seven thousand and six hundred. They shall go hindmost with their standards.

32 ¶ These *are* those which were numbered of the children of Israel by the house of their fathers: all those that were numbered of the camps throughout their hosts *were* six hundred thousand and three thousand and five hundred and fifty.

33 But the Levites were not numbered among the children of Israel; as the LORD commanded Moses.

34 And the children of Israel did according to all that the LORD commanded Moses: so they pitched by their standards, and so they set forward, every one after their families, according to the house of their fathers.

The Levites

3 THESE ALSO *are* the generations of Aaron and Moses in the day *that* the LORD spake with Moses in mount Sinai.

2 And these *are* the names of the sons of Aaron; Nadab the firstborn, and Abihu, Eleazar, and Ithamar.

3 These *are* the names of the sons of Aaron, the priests which were anointed, *e*whom he consecrated to minister in the priest's office.

4 And Nadab and Abihu died before the LORD, when they offered strange fire before the LORD, in the wilderness of Sinai, and they had no children: and Eleazar and Ithamar ministered in the priest's office in the sight of Aaron their father.

5 ¶ And the LORD spake unto Moses, saying,

6 Bring the tribe of Levi near, and present them before Aaron the priest, that they may minister unto him.

7 And they shall keep his charge, and the charge of the whole congregation before the tabernacle of the congregation, to do the service of the tabernacle.

8 And they shall keep all the instruments of the tabernacle of the congregation, and the charge of the children of Israel, to do the service of the tabernacle.

Amplified

18 On the west side shall be the standard of the camp of Ephraim by their companies, the leader of the sons of Ephraim being Elishama son of Ammihud.

19 Ephraim's host as numbered totaled 40,500.

20 Beside Ephraim shall be the tribe of Manasseh, the leader of the sons of Manasseh being Gamaliel son of Pedahzur.

21 Manasseh's host as numbered totaled 32,200.

22 Then the tribe of Benjamin, the leader of the sons of Benjamin being Abidan son of Gideoni.

23 Benjamin's host as numbered totaled 35,400.

24 The whole number [of the three tribes] in the camp of Ephraim totaled 108,100. They shall go forward in third place.

25 The standard of the camp of Dan shall be on the north side [of the tabernacle] by their companies, the leader of the sons of Dan being Ahiezer son of Ammishaddai.

26 Dan's host as numbered totaled 62,700.

27 Encamped next to Dan shall be the tribe of Asher, the leader of the sons of Asher being Pagiel son of Ochran.

28 Asher's host as numbered totaled 41,500.

29 Then the tribe of Naphtali, the leader of the sons of Naphtali being Ahira son of Enan.

30 Naphtali's host as numbered totaled 53,400.

31 The whole number [of the three tribes] in the camp of Dan totaled 157,600. They shall set out last, standard after standard.

32 These are the Israelites as numbered by their fathers' houses. All in the camps who were numbered by their companies were 603,550.

33 But the Levites were not numbered with the Israelites, for so the Lord commanded Moses.

34 Thus the Israelites did according to all the Lord commanded Moses; so they encamped by their standards, and so they set forward, everyone with his [tribal] families, according to his father's house.

3 NOW THESE are the generations of Aaron and Moses when the Lord spoke with Moses on Mount Sinai.

2 These are the names of the sons of Aaron: Nadab the firstborn, Abihu, Eleazar, and Ithamar.

3 These are the names of the sons of Aaron, the priests who were anointed, whom Aaron consecrated *and* ordained to minister in the priest's office.

4 But Nadab and Abihu died before the Lord when they offered strange fire before the Lord in the Wilderness of Sinai; and they had no children. So Eleazar and Ithamar ministered in the priest's office in the presence *and* under the supervision of Aaron their father. [Lev. 10:1–4.]

5 And the Lord said to Moses,

6 Bring the tribe of Levi near and set them before Aaron the priest, that they may minister to him.

7 And they shall carry out his instructions and the duties connected with the whole assembly before the Tent of Meeting, doing the service of the tabernacle.

8 And they shall keep all the instruments *and* furnishings of the Tent of Meeting and take charge of [attending] the Israelites, to serve in the tabernacle.

e Heb. *whose hand he filled*

New American Standard

18 ¶ "On the west side *shall be* the standard of the camp of Ephraim by their armies, and the leader of the sons of Ephraim *shall be* Elishama the son of Ammihud,
19 and his army, even their numbered men, 40,500.
20"Next to him *shall be* the tribe of Manasseh, and the leader of the sons of Manasseh: Gamaliel the son of Pedahzur,
21 and his army, even their numbered men, 32,200.
22"Then *comes* the tribe of Benjamin, and the leader of the sons of Benjamin: Abidan the son of Gideoni,
23 and his army, even their numbered men, 35,400.
24"The total of the numbered men of the camp of Ephraim: 108,100, by their armies. And they shall set out third.
25 ¶ "On the north side *shall be* the standard of the camp of Dan by their armies, and the leader of the sons of Dan: Ahiezer the son of Ammishaddai,
26 and his army, even their numbered men, 62,700.
27"Those who camp next to him *shall be* the tribe of Asher, and the leader of the sons of Asher: Pagiel the son of Ochran,
28 and his army, even their numbered men, 41,500.
29"Then *comes* the tribe of Naphtali, and the leader of the sons of Naphtali: Ahira the son of Enan,
30 and his army, even their numbered men, 53,400.
31"The total of the numbered men of the camp of Dan *was* 157,600. They shall set out last by their standards."
32 ¶ These are the numbered men of the sons of Israel by their fathers' households; the total of the numbered men of the camps by their armies, 603,550.
33 The Levites, however, were not numbered among the sons of Israel, just as the LORD had commanded Moses.
34 Thus the sons of Israel did; according to all that the LORD commanded Moses, so they camped by their standards, and so they set out, every one by his family according to his father's household.

Levites to Be Priesthood

3 NOW THESE are *the records of* the generations of Aaron and Moses at the time when the LORD spoke with Moses on Mount Sinai.
2 These then are the names of the sons of Aaron: Nadab the firstborn, and Abihu, Eleazar and Ithamar.
3 These are the names of the sons of Aaron, the anointed priests, whom he ordained to serve as priests.
4 But Nadab and Abihu died before the LORD when they offered strange fire before the LORD in the wilderness of Sinai; and they had no children. So Eleazar and Ithamar served as priests in the lifetime of their father Aaron.
5 ¶ Then the LORD spoke to Moses, saying,
6"Bring the tribe of Levi near and set them before Aaron the priest, that they may serve him.
7"They shall perform the duties for him and for the whole congregation before the tent of meeting, to do the service of the tabernacle.
8"They shall also keep all the furnishings of the tent of meeting, along with the duties of the sons of Israel, to do the service of the tabernacle.

New International

18On the west will be the divisions of the camp of Ephraim under their standard. The leader of the people of Ephraim is Elishama son of Ammihud. 19His division numbers 40,500.
20The tribe of Manasseh will be next to them. The leader of the people of Manasseh is Gamaliel son of Pedahzur. 21His division numbers 32,200.
22The tribe of Benjamin will be next. The leader of the people of Benjamin is Abidan son of Gideoni. 23His division numbers 35,400.
24All the men assigned to the camp of Ephraim, according to their divisions, number 108,100. They will set out third.

25On the north will be the divisions of the camp of Dan, under their standard. The leader of the people of Dan is Ahiezer son of Ammishaddai. 26His division numbers 62,700.
27The tribe of Asher will camp next to them. The leader of the people of Asher is Pagiel son of Ocran. 28His division numbers 41,500.
29The tribe of Naphtali will be next. The leader of the people of Naphtali is Ahira son of Enan. 30His division numbers 53,400.
31All the men assigned to the camp of Dan number 157,600. They will set out last, under their standards.

32These are the Israelites, counted according to their families. All those in the camps, by their divisions, number 603,550. 33The Levites, however, were not counted along with the other Israelites, as the LORD commanded Moses.

34So the Israelites did everything the LORD commanded Moses; that is the way they encamped under their standards, and that is the way they set out, each with his clan and family.

The Levites

3 THIS IS the account of the family of Aaron and Moses at the time the LORD talked with Moses on Mount Sinai.
2The names of the sons of Aaron were Nadab the firstborn and Abihu, Eleazar and Ithamar. 3Those were the names of Aaron's sons, the anointed priests, who were ordained to serve as priests. 4Nadab and Abihu, however, fell dead before the LORD when they made an offering with unauthorized fire before him in the Desert of Sinai. They had no sons; so only Eleazar and Ithamar served as priests during the lifetime of their father Aaron.
5The LORD said to Moses, 6"Bring the tribe of Levi and present them to Aaron the priest to assist him. 7They are to perform duties for him and for the whole community at the Tent of Meeting by doing the work of the tabernacle. 8They are to take care of all the furnishings of the Tent of Meeting, fulfilling the obligations of the Israelites by do-

King James

Amplified

⁹And thou shalt give the Levites unto Aaron and to his sons: they *are* wholly given unto him out of the children of Israel.

¹⁰And thou shalt appoint Aaron and his sons, and they shall wait on their priest's office: and the stranger that cometh nigh shall be put to death.

¹¹And the LORD spake unto Moses, saying,

¹²And I, behold, I have taken the Levites from among the children of Israel instead of all the firstborn that openeth the matrix among the children of Israel: therefore the Levites shall be mine;

¹³Because all the firstborn *are* mine; *for* on the day that I smote all the firstborn in the land of Egypt I hallowed unto me all the firstborn in Israel, both man and beast: mine shall they be: I *am* the LORD.

¹⁴ ¶ And the LORD spake unto Moses in the wilderness of Sinai, saying,

¹⁵Number the children of Levi after the house of their fathers, by their families: every male from a month old and upward shalt thou number them.

¹⁶And Moses numbered them according to the ⸕word of the LORD, as he was commanded.

¹⁷And these were the sons of Levi by their names; Gershon, and Kohath, and Merari.

¹⁸And these *are* the names of the sons of Gershon by their families; Libni, and Shimei.

¹⁹And the sons of Kohath by their families; Amram, and Izehar, Hebron, and Uzziel.

²⁰And the sons of Merari by their families; Mahli, and Mushi. These *are* the families of the Levites according to the house of their fathers.

²¹Of Gershon *was* the family of the Libnites, and the family of the Shimites: these *are* the families of the Gershonites.

²²Those that were numbered of them, according to the number of all the males, from a month old and upward, *even* those that were numbered of them *were* seven thousand and five hundred.

²³The families of the Gershonites shall pitch behind the tabernacle westward.

²⁴And the chief of the house of the father of the Gershonites *shall be* Eliasaph the son of Lael.

²⁵And the charge of the sons of Gershon in the tabernacle of the congregation *shall be* the tabernacle, and the tent, the covering thereof, and the hanging for the door of the tabernacle of the congregation,

²⁶And the hangings of the court, and the curtain for the door of the court, which *is* by the tabernacle, and by the altar round about, and the cords of it for all the service thereof.

²⁷ ¶ And of Kohath *was* the family of the Amramites, and the family of the Izeharites, and the family of the Hebronites, and the family of the Uzzielites: these *are* the families of the Kohathites.

²⁸In the number of all the males, from a month old and upward, *were* eight thousand and six hundred, keeping the charge of the sanctuary.

²⁹The families of the sons of Kohath shall pitch on the side of the tabernacle southward.

³⁰And the chief of the house of the father of the families of the Kohathites *shall be* Elizaphan the son of Uzziel.

³¹And their charge *shall be* the ark, and the table, and the candlestick, and the altars, and the vessels of the sanctuary wherewith they minister, and the hanging, and all the service thereof.

³²And Eleazar the son of Aaron the priest *shall be* chief over the chief of the Levites, *and have* the oversight of them that keep the charge of the sanctuary.

³³ ¶ Of Merari *was* the family of the Mahlites, and the family of the Mushites: these *are* the families of Merari.

³⁴And those that were numbered of them, according to the number of all the males, from a month old and upward, *were* six thousand and two hundred.

⁹And you shall give the Levites [as servants and helpers] to Aaron and his sons; they are wholly given to him from among the Israelites.

¹⁰And you shall appoint Aaron and his sons, and they shall observe *and* attend to their priest's office; but the excluded [anyone daring to assume priestly duties or privileges who is not of the house of Aaron and called of God] who comes near [the holy things] shall be put to death.

¹¹And the Lord said to Moses,

¹²Behold, I have taken the Levites from among the Israelites instead of every firstborn who opens the womb among the Israelites; and the Levites shall be Mine,

¹³For all the firstborn are Mine. On the day that I slew all the firstborn in the land of Egypt, I consecrated for Myself all the firstborn in Israel, both man and beast; Mine they shall be. I am the Lord.

¹⁴And the Lord said to Moses in the Wilderness of Sinai,

¹⁵Number the sons of Levi by their fathers' houses and by families. Every male from a month old and upward you shall number.

¹⁶So Moses numbered them as he was commanded by the word of the Lord.

¹⁷These were the sons of Levi by their names: Gershon, Kohath, and Merari.

¹⁸And these are the names of the sons of Gershon by their families: Libni and Shimei.

¹⁹The sons of Kohath by their families: Amram, Izhar, Hebron, and Uzziel.

²⁰The sons of Merari by their families: Mahli and Mushi. These are the families of the Levites by their fathers' houses.

²¹Of Gershon were the families of the Libnites and of the Shimeites. These are the families of the Gershonites.

²²The males who were numbered of them from a month old and upward totaled 7,500.

²³The families of the Gershonites were to encamp behind the tabernacle on the west,

²⁴The leader of the fathers' houses of the Gershonites being Eliasaph son of Lael.

²⁵And the responsibility of the sons of Gershon in the Tent of Meeting was to be the tabernacle, the tent, its covering, and the hangings for the door of the Tent of Meeting,

²⁶And the hangings of the court, the curtain for the door of the court which is around the tabernacle and the altar, its cords, and all the service pertaining to them.

²⁷Of Kohath were the families of the Amramites, the Izharites, the Hebronites, and the Uzzielites; these are the families of the Kohathites.

²⁸The number of all the males from a month old and upward totaled 8,600, attending to the duties of the sanctuary.

²⁹The families of the sons of Kohath were to encamp on the south side of the tabernacle,

³⁰The chief of the fathers' houses of the families of the Kohathites being Elizaphan son of Uzziel.

³¹Their charge was to be the ark, the table, the lampstand, the altars, and the utensils of the sanctuary with which the priests minister, and the screen, and all the service having to do with these.

³²Eleazar son of Aaron the priest was to be chief over the leaders of the Levites, and have the oversight of those who had charge of the sanctuary.

³³Of Merari were the families of the Mahlites and the Mushites; these are the families of Merari.

³⁴Their number of all the males from a month old and upward totaled 6,200.

⸕Heb. mouth

New American Standard

9"You shall thus give the Levites to Aaron and to his sons; they are wholly given to him from among the sons of Israel.

10"So you shall appoint Aaron and his sons that they may keep their priesthood, but the layman who comes near shall be put to death."

11 ¶ Again the LORD spoke to Moses, saying,

12"Now, behold, I have taken the Levites from among the sons of Israel instead of every firstborn, the first issue of the womb among the sons of Israel. So the Levites shall be Mine.

13"For all the firstborn are Mine; on the day that I struck down all the firstborn in the land of Egypt, I sanctified to Myself all the firstborn in Israel, from man to beast. They shall be Mine; I am the LORD."

14 ¶ Then the LORD spoke to Moses in the wilderness of Sinai, saying,

15"Number the sons of Levi by their fathers' households, by their families; every male from a month old and upward you shall number."

16 So Moses numbered them according to the word of the LORD, just as he had been commanded.

17 These then are the sons of Levi by their names: Gershon and Kohath and Merari.

18 These are the names of the sons of Gershon by their families: Libni and Shimei;

19 and the sons of Kohath by their families: Amram and Izhar, Hebron and Uzziel;

20 and the sons of Merari by their families: Mahli and Mushi. These are the families of the Levites according to their fathers' households.

21 ¶ Of Gershon *was* the family of the Libnites and the family of the Shimeites; these *were* the families of the Gershonites.

22 Their numbered men, in the numbering of every male from a month old and upward, *even* their numbered men *were* 7,500.

23 The families of the Gershonites were to camp behind the tabernacle westward,

24 and the leader of the fathers' households of the Gershonites *was* Eliasaph the son of Lael.

Duties of the Priests

25 Now the duties of the sons of Gershon in the tent of meeting *involved* the tabernacle and the tent, its covering, and the screen for the doorway of the tent of meeting,

26 and the hangings of the court, and the screen for the doorway of the court which is around the tabernacle and the altar, and its cords, according to all the service concerning them.

27 ¶ Of Kohath *was* the family of the Amramites and the family of the Izharites and the family of the Hebronites and the family of the Uzzielites; these were the families of the Kohathites.

28 In the numbering of every male from a month old and upward, *there were* 8,600, performing the duties of the sanctuary.

29 The families of the sons of Kohath were to camp on the southward side of the tabernacle,

30 and the leader of the fathers' households of the Kohathite families was Elizaphan the son of Uzziel.

31 Now their duties *involved* the ark, the table, the lampstand, the altars, and the utensils of the sanctuary with which they minister, and the screen, and all the service concerning them;

32 and Eleazar the son of Aaron the priest *was* the chief of the leaders of Levi, *and had* the oversight of those who perform the duties of the sanctuary.

33 ¶ Of Merari *was* the family of the Mahlites and the family of the Mushites; these *were* the families of Merari.

34 Their numbered men in the numbering of every male from a month old and upward, *were* 6,200.

New International

ing the work of the tabernacle. 9Give the Levites to Aaron and his sons; they are the Israelites who are to be given wholly to him.[b] 10Appoint Aaron and his sons to serve as priests; anyone else who approaches the sanctuary must be put to death."

11The LORD also said to Moses, 12"I have taken the Levites from among the Israelites in place of the first male offspring of every Israelite woman. The Levites are mine, 13for all the firstborn are mine. When I struck down all the firstborn in Egypt, I set apart for myself every firstborn in Israel, whether man or animal. They are to be mine. I am the LORD."

14The LORD said to Moses in the Desert of Sinai, 15"Count the Levites by their families and clans. Count every male a month old or more." 16So Moses counted them, as he was commanded by the word of the LORD.

17These were the names of the sons of Levi:
  Gershon, Kohath and Merari.

18These were the names of the Gershonite clans:
  Libni and Shimei.

19The Kohathite clans:
  Amram, Izhar, Hebron and Uzziel.

20The Merarite clans:
  Mahli and Mushi.

These were the Levite clans, according to their families.

21To Gershon belonged the clans of the Libnites and Shimeites; these were the Gershonite clans. 22The number of all the males a month old or more who were counted was 7,500. 23The Gershonite clans were to camp on the west, behind the tabernacle. 24The leader of the families of the Gershonites was Eliasaph son of Lael. 25At the Tent of Meeting the Gershonites were responsible for the care of the tabernacle and tent, its coverings, the curtain at the entrance to the Tent of Meeting, 26the curtains of the courtyard, the curtain at the entrance to the courtyard surrounding the tabernacle and altar, and the ropes—and everything related to their use.

27To Kohath belonged the clans of the Amramites, Izharites, Hebronites and Uzzielites; these were the Kohathite clans. 28The number of all the males a month old or more was 8,600.[c] The Kohathites were responsible for the care of the sanctuary. 29The Kohathite clans were to camp on the south side of the tabernacle. 30The leader of the families of the Kohathite clans was Elizaphan son of Uzziel. 31They were responsible for the care of the ark, the table, the lampstand, the altars, the articles of the sanctuary used in ministering, the curtain, and everything related to their use. 32The chief leader of the Levites was Eleazar son of Aaron, the priest. He was appointed over those who were responsible for the care of the sanctuary.

33To Merari belonged the clans of the Mahlites and the Mushites; these were the Merarite clans. 34The number of all the males a month old or more who were counted

b 9 Most manuscripts of the Masoretic Text; some manuscripts of the Masoretic Text, Samaritan Pentateuch and Septuagint (see also Num. 8:16) *to me*   c 28 Hebrew; some Septuagint manuscripts *8,300*

King James

35And the chief of the house of the father of the families of Merari *was* Zuriel the son of Abihail: *these* shall pitch on the side of the tabernacle northward.

36And *under* the custody and charge of the sons of Merari *shall be* the boards of the tabernacle, and the bars thereof, and the pillars thereof, and the sockets thereof, and all the vessels thereof, and all that serveth thereto,

37And the pillars of the court round about, and their sockets, and their pins, and their cords.

38 ¶ But those that encamp before the tabernacle toward the east, *even* before the tabernacle of the congregation eastward, *shall be* Moses, and Aaron and his sons, keeping the charge of the sanctuary for the charge of the children of Israel; and the stranger that cometh nigh shall be put to death.

39All that were numbered of the Levites, which Moses and Aaron numbered at the commandment of the LORD, throughout their families, all the males from a month old and upward, *were* twenty and two thousand.

40 ¶ And the LORD said unto Moses, Number all the firstborn of the males of the children of Israel from a month old and upward, and take the number of their names.

41And thou shalt take the Levites for me (I *am* the LORD) instead of all the firstborn among the children of Israel; and the cattle of the Levites instead of all the firstlings among the cattle of the children of Israel.

42And Moses numbered, as the LORD commanded him, all the firstborn among the children of Israel.

43And all the firstborn males by the number of names, from a month old and upward, of those that were numbered of them, were twenty and two thousand two hundred and threescore and thirteen.

44 ¶ And the LORD spake unto Moses, saying,

45Take the Levites instead of all the firstborn among the children of Israel, and the cattle of the Levites instead of their cattle; and the Levites shall be mine: I *am* the LORD.

46And for those that are to be redeemed of the two hundred and threescore and thirteen of the firstborn of the children of Israel, which are more than the Levites;

47Thou shalt even take five shekels apiece by the poll, after the shekel of the sanctuary shalt thou take *them*: (the shekel *is* twenty gerahs:)

48And thou shalt give the money, wherewith the odd number of them is to be redeemed, unto Aaron and to his sons.

49And Moses took the redemption money of them that were over and above them that were redeemed by the Levites:

50Of the firstborn of the children of Israel took he the money; a thousand three hundred and threescore and five *shekels,* after the shekel of the sanctuary:

51And Moses gave the money of them that were redeemed unto Aaron and to his sons, according to the word of the LORD, as the LORD commanded Moses.

Amplified

35And the head of the fathers' houses of the families of Merari was Zuriel son of Abihail; the Merarites were to encamp on the north side of the tabernacle.

36And the appointed charge of the sons of Merari was the boards or frames of the tabernacle, and its bars, pillars, sockets or bases, and all the accessories or instruments of it, and all the work connected with them,

37And the pillars of the surrounding court and their sockets or bases, with their pegs and their cords.

38But those to encamp before the tabernacle toward the east, before the Tent of Meeting, toward the sunrise, were to be Moses and Aaron and his sons, keeping the full charge of the rites of the sanctuary in whatever was required for the Israelites; and the [a]excluded [one not a descendant of Aaron and called of God] who came near [the sanctuary] was to be put to death.

39All the Levites whom Moses and Aaron numbered at the command of the Lord, by their families, all the males from a month old and upward, were 22,000.

40And the Lord said to Moses, Number all the firstborn of the males of the Israelites from a month old and upward, and take the number of their names.

41You shall take the Levites for Me instead of all the firstborn among the Israelites. I am the Lord; and you shall take the cattle of the Levites for Me instead of all the firstlings among the cattle of the Israelites.

42So Moses numbered, as the Lord commanded him, all the firstborn Israelites.

43But all the firstborn males from a month old and upward as numbered were 22,273 [273 more than the Levites].

44And the Lord said to Moses,

45Take the Levites [for Me] instead of all the firstborn Israelites, and the Levites' cattle instead of their cattle; and the Levites shall be Mine. I am the Lord.

46And for those 273 who are to be redeemed of the firstborn of the Israelites who outnumber the Levites,

47You shall take five shekels apiece, reckoning by the sanctuary shekel of twenty gerahs; you shall collect them,

48And you shall give the ransom silver from the excess number [over the Levites] to be redeemed to Aaron and his sons.

49So Moses took the redemption money from those who were left over from the number who were redeemed by the Levites.

50From the firstborn of the Israelites he took the money, 1,365 shekels, after the shekel of the sanctuary.

51And Moses gave the money from those who were ransomed to Aaron and his sons, as the Lord commanded Moses.

a This ban against "the excluded" from coming near the sanctuary (the sacred tent, the tabernacle proper) is not to be construed as discrimination against people who were not Israelites. It included everyone except the ordained descendants of Levi of the house of Aaron. The tabernacle proper was made up of two small rooms which no one except the priest or priests who had the assignment was ever to enter. The congregation entered the outside enclosure only. This was true also of the later temples. Neither Jesus nor any of his disciples or Paul ever entered the sanctuary. When Jesus "taught in the temple" or "entered into the temple," the Greek word invariably indicates that He was in the temple enclosure (*hieron*) and not in the sanctuary (*naos*). (For more information, see Richard Trench, *Synonyms of The New Testament*). For a violation of this ban see II Chron. 26:16-21, which tells of King Uzziah, who attempted to enter the sanctuary to burn incense and while being forcibly put out by eighty priests became a leper—for the rest of his life.

g Heb. *the office of the charge*

New American Standard

35 The leader of the fathers' households of the families of Merari *was* Zuriel the son of Abihail. They *were* to camp on the northward side of the tabernacle.

36 Now the appointed duties of the sons of Merari *involved* the frames of the tabernacle, its bars, its pillars, its sockets, all its equipment, and the service concerning them,

37 and the pillars around the court with their sockets and their pegs and their cords.

38 ¶ Now those who were to camp before the tabernacle eastward, before the tent of meeting toward the sunrise, are Moses and Aaron and his sons, performing the duties of the sanctuary for the obligation of the sons of Israel; but the layman coming near was to be put to death.

39 All the numbered men of the Levites, whom Moses and Aaron numbered at the command of the LORD by their families, every male from a month old and upward, *were* 22,000.

Firstborn Redeemed

40 ¶ Then the LORD said to Moses, "Number every firstborn male of the sons of Israel from a month old and upward, and make a list of their names.

41 "You shall take the Levites for Me, I am the LORD, instead of all the firstborn among the sons of Israel, and the cattle of the Levites instead of all the firstborn among the cattle of the sons of Israel."

42 So Moses numbered all the firstborn among the sons of Israel, just as the LORD had commanded him;

43 and all the firstborn males by the number of names from a month old and upward, for their numbered men were 22,273.

44 ¶ Then the LORD spoke to Moses, saying,

45 "Take the Levites instead of all the firstborn among the sons of Israel and the cattle of the Levites. And the Levites shall be Mine; I am the LORD.

46 "For the ransom of the 273 of the firstborn of the sons of Israel who are in excess beyond the Levites,

47 you shall take five shekels apiece, per head; you shall take *them* in terms of the shekel of the sanctuary (the shekel is twenty *f* gerahs),

48 and give the money, the ransom of those who are in excess among them, to Aaron and to his sons."

49 So Moses took the ransom money from those who were in excess, beyond those ransomed by the Levites;

50 from the firstborn of the sons of Israel he took the money in terms of the shekel of the sanctuary, 1,365.

51 Then Moses gave the ransom money to Aaron and to his sons, at the command of the LORD, just as the LORD had commanded Moses.

New International

was 6,200. 35 The leader of the families of the Merarite clans was Zuriel son of Abihail; they were to camp on the north side of the tabernacle. 36 The Merarites were appointed to take care of the frames of the tabernacle, its crossbars, posts, bases, all its equipment, and everything related to their use, 37 as well as the posts of the surrounding courtyard with their bases, tent pegs and ropes.

38 Moses and Aaron and his sons were to camp to the east of the tabernacle, toward the sunrise, in front of the Tent of Meeting. They were responsible for the care of the sanctuary on behalf of the Israelites. Anyone else who approached the sanctuary was to be put to death.

39 The total number of Levites counted at the LORD's command by Moses and Aaron according to their clans, including every male a month old or more, was 22,000.

40 The LORD said to Moses, "Count all the firstborn Israelite males who are a month old or more and make a list of their names. 41 Take the Levites for me in place of all the firstborn of the Israelites, and the livestock of the Levites in place of all the firstborn of the livestock of the Israelites. I am the LORD."

42 So Moses counted all the firstborn of the Israelites, as the LORD commanded him. 43 The total number of firstborn males a month old or more, listed by name, was 22,273.

44 The LORD also said to Moses, 45 "Take the Levites in place of all the firstborn of Israel, and the livestock of the Levites in place of their livestock. The Levites are to be mine. I am the LORD. 46 To redeem the 273 firstborn Israelites who exceed the number of the Levites, 47 collect five shekels*d* for each one, according to the sanctuary shekel, which weighs twenty gerahs. 48 Give the money for the redemption of the additional Israelites to Aaron and his sons."

49 So Moses collected the redemption money from those who exceeded the number redeemed by the Levites. 50 From the firstborn of the Israelites he collected silver weighing 1,365 shekels,*e* according to the sanctuary shekel. 51 Moses gave the redemption money to Aaron and his sons, as he was commanded by the word of the LORD.

---

f I.e. A gerah equals approx one-fortieth oz

d 47 That is, about 2 ounces (about 55 grams)   *e* 50 That is, about 35 pounds (about 15.5 kilograms)

<table>
<tr><td>

King James

</td><td>

Amplified

</td></tr>
</table>

<table>
<tr><td>

The descendants of Kohath

4 AND THE Lord spake unto Moses and unto Aaron, saying,

²Take the sum of the sons of Kohath from among the sons of Levi, after their families, by the house of their fathers,

³From thirty years old and upward even until fifty years old, all that enter into the host, to do the work in the tabernacle of the congregation.

⁴This *shall be* the service of the sons of Kohath in the tabernacle of the congregation, *about* the most holy things:

5 ¶ And when the camp setteth forward, Aaron shall come, and his sons, and they shall take down the covering veil, and cover the ark of testimony with it:

⁶And shall put thereon the covering of badgers' skins, and shall spread over *it* a cloth wholly of blue, and shall put in the staves thereof.

⁷And upon the table of showbread they shall spread a cloth of blue, and put thereon the dishes, and the spoons, and the bowls, and covers to ʰcover withal: and the continual bread shall be thereon:

⁸And they shall spread upon them a cloth of scarlet, and cover the same with a covering of badgers' skins, and shall put in the staves thereof.

⁹And they shall take a cloth of blue, and cover the candlestick of the light, and his lamps, and his tongs, and his snuffdishes, and all the oil vessels thereof, wherewith they minister unto it:

¹⁰And they shall put it and all the vessels thereof within a covering of badgers' skins, and shall put *it* upon a bar.

¹¹And upon the golden altar they shall spread a cloth of blue, and cover it with a covering of badgers' skins, and shall put to the staves thereof:

¹²And they shall take all the instruments of ministry, wherewith they minister in the sanctuary, and put *them* in a cloth of blue, and cover them with a covering of badgers' skins, and shall put *them* on a bar:

¹³And they shall take away the ashes from the altar, and spread a purple cloth thereon:

¹⁴And they shall put upon it all the vessels thereof, wherewith they minister about it, *even* the censers, the fleshhooks, and the shovels, and the ⁱbasins, all the vessels of the altar; and they shall spread upon it a covering of badgers' skins, and put to the staves of it.

¹⁵And when Aaron and his sons have made an end of covering the sanctuary, and all the vessels of the sanctuary, as the camp is to set forward; after that the sons of Kohath shall come to bear *it*: but they shall not touch *any* holy thing, lest they die. These *things are* the burden of the sons of Kohath in the tabernacle of the congregation.

16 ¶ And to the office of Eleazar the son of Aaron the priest *pertaineth* the oil for the light, and the sweet incense, and the daily meat offering, and the anointing oil, *and* the oversight of all the tabernacle, and of all that therein *is,* in the sanctuary, and in the vessels thereof.

17 ¶ And the LORD spake unto Moses and unto Aaron, saying,

¹⁸Cut ye not off the tribe of the families of the Kohathites from among the Levites:

¹⁹But thus do unto them, that they may live, and not die, when they approach unto the most holy things: Aaron and his sons shall go in, and appoint them every one to his service and to his burden:

²⁰But they shall not go in to see when the holy things are covered, lest they die.

The descendants of Gershon

21 ¶ And the LORD spake unto Moses, saying,

²²Take also the sum of the sons of Gershon, throughout the houses of their fathers, by their families;

</td><td>

4 AND THE Lord said to Moses and Aaron,

²Take a census of the Kohathite division among the sons of Levi, by their families, by their fathers' houses,

³From thirty years old and up to fifty years old, all who can enter the service to do the work in the Tent of Meeting.

⁴This shall be the responsibility of the sons of Kohath in the Tent of Meeting: the most holy things.

⁵When the camp prepares to set forward, Aaron and his sons shall take down the veil [screening the Holy of Holies] and cover the ark of the Testimony with it,

⁶And shall put on it the covering of dolphin *or* porpoise skin, and shall spread over that a cloth wholly of blue, and shall put in place the poles of the ark.

⁷And upon the table of showbread they shall spread a cloth of blue and put on it the plates, the dishes for incense, the bowls, the flagons for the drink offering, and also the continual showbread.

⁸And they shall spread over them a cloth of scarlet, and put over that a covering of dolphin *or* porpoise skin, and put in place the poles [for carrying].

⁹And they shall take a cloth of blue and cover the lampstand for the light and its lamps, its snuffers, its ashtrays, and all the oil vessels from which it is supplied.

¹⁰And they shall put the lampstand and all its utensils within a covering of dolphin *or* porpoise skin and shall put it upon the frame [for carrying].

¹¹And upon the golden [incense] altar they shall spread a cloth of blue, and cover it with a covering of dolphin *or* porpoise skin, and shall put in place its poles [for carrying].

¹²And they shall take all the utensils of the service with which they minister in the sanctuary, and put them in a cloth of blue, and cover them with a covering of dolphin *or* porpoise skin, and shall put them on the frame [for carrying].

¹³And they shall take away the ashes from the altar [of burnt offering] and spread a purple cloth over it.

¹⁴And they shall put upon it all its vessels *and* utensils with which they minister there, the firepans, the fleshhooks *or* forks, the shovels, the basins, and all the vessels *and* utensils of the altar, and they shall spread over it all a covering of dolphin *or* porpoise skin, and shall put in its poles [for carrying].

¹⁵When Aaron and his sons have finished covering the sanctuary and all its furniture, as the camp sets out, after all that [is done but not before], the sons of Kohath shall come to carry them. But they shall not touch the holy things, lest they die. These are the things of the Tent of Meeting which the sons of Kohath are to carry.

¹⁶And Eleazar son of Aaron the priest shall have charge of the oil for the light, the fragrant incense, the continual cereal offering, and the anointing oil, with the oversight of all the tabernacle and of all that is in it, of the sanctuary and its utensils.

¹⁷And the Lord said to Moses and Aaron,

¹⁸[Since] the tribe of the families of the Kohathites [are only Levites and not priests], do not [by exposing them to the sin of touching the most holy things] cut them off from among the Levites.

¹⁹But deal thus with them, that they may live and not die when they approach the most holy things: Aaron and his sons shall go in and appoint them each to his work and to his burden [to be carried on the march].

²⁰But [the Kohathites] shall not go in to see the sanctuary [the Holy Place and the Holy of Holies] *or* its holy things, even for an instant, lest they die.

²¹And the Lord said to Moses,

²²Take a census of the sons of Gershon, by their fathers' houses, by their families.

</td></tr>
</table>

ʰ Or, *pour out withal*   ⁱ Or, *bowls*

New American Standard

Duties of the Kohathites

4 THEN THE LORD spoke to Moses and to Aaron, saying,

2 "Take a census of the descendants of Kohath from among the sons of Levi, by their families, by their fathers' households,

3 from thirty years and upward, even to fifty years old, all who enter the service to do the work in the tent of meeting.

4 "This is the work of the descendants of Kohath in the tent of meeting, *concerning* the most holy things.

5 ¶ "When the camp sets out, Aaron and his sons shall go in and they shall take down the veil of the screen and cover the ark of the testimony with it;

6 and they shall lay a covering of porpoise skin on it, and shall spread over *it* a cloth of pure blue, and shall insert its poles.

7 "Over the table of the bread of the Presence they shall also spread a cloth of blue and put on it the dishes and the pans and the sacrificial bowls and the jars for the drink offering, and the continual bread shall be on it.

8 "They shall spread over them a cloth of scarlet *material*, and cover the same with a covering of porpoise skin, and they shall insert its poles.

9 "Then they shall take a blue cloth and cover the lampstand for the light, along with its lamps and its snuffers, and its trays and all its oil vessels, by which they serve it;

10 and they shall put it and all its utensils in a covering of porpoise skin, and shall put it on the carrying bars.

11 "Over the golden altar they shall spread a blue cloth and cover it with a covering of porpoise skin, and shall insert its poles;

12 and they shall take all the utensils of service, with which they serve in the sanctuary, and put them in a blue cloth and cover them with a covering of porpoise skin, and put them on the carrying bars.

13 "Then they shall take away the ashes from the altar, and spread a purple cloth over it.

14 "They shall also put on it all its utensils by which they serve in connection with it: the firepans, the forks and shovels and the basins, all the utensils of the altar; and they shall spread a cover of porpoise skin over it and insert its poles.

15 "When Aaron and his sons have finished covering the holy *objects* and all the furnishings of the sanctuary, when the camp is to set out, after that the sons of Kohath shall come to carry *them,* so that they will not touch the holy *objects* and die. These are the things in the tent of meeting which the sons of Kohath are to carry.

16 ¶ "The responsibility of Eleazar the son of Aaron the priest is the oil for the light and the fragrant incense and the continual grain offering and the anointing oil—the responsibility of all the tabernacle and of all that is in it, with the sanctuary and its furnishings."

17 ¶ Then the LORD spoke to Moses and to Aaron, saying,

18 "Do not let the tribe of the families of the Kohathites be cut off from among the Levites.

19 "But do this to them that they may live and not die when they approach the most holy *objects:* Aaron and his sons shall go in and assign each of them to his work and to his load;

20 but they shall not go in to see the holy *objects* even for a moment, or they will die."

Duties of the Gershonites

21 ¶ Then the LORD spoke to Moses, saying,

22 "Take a census of the sons of Gershon also, by their fathers' households, by their families;

New International

The Kohathites

4 THE LORD said to Moses and Aaron: 2 "Take a census of the Kohathite branch of the Levites by their clans and families. 3 Count all the men from thirty to fifty years of age who come to serve in the work in the Tent of Meeting.

4 "This is the work of the Kohathites in the Tent of Meeting: the care of the most holy things. 5 When the camp is to move, Aaron and his sons are to go in and take down the shielding curtain and cover the ark of the Testimony with it. 6 Then they are to cover this with hides of sea cows,[f] spread a cloth of solid blue over that and put the poles in place.

7 "Over the table of the Presence they are to spread a blue cloth and put on it the plates, dishes and bowls, and the jars for drink offerings; the bread that is continually there is to remain on it. 8 Over these they are to spread a scarlet cloth, cover that with hides of sea cows and put its poles in place.

9 "They are to take a blue cloth and cover the lampstand that is for light, together with its lamps, its wick trimmers and trays, and all its jars for the oil used to supply it. 10 Then they are to wrap it and all its accessories in a covering of hides of sea cows and put it on a carrying frame.

11 "Over the gold altar they are to spread a blue cloth and cover that with hides of sea cows and put its poles in place.

12 "They are to take all the articles used for ministering in the sanctuary, wrap them in a blue cloth, cover that with hides of sea cows and put them on a carrying frame.

13 "They are to remove the ashes from the bronze altar and spread a purple cloth over it. 14 Then they are to place on it all the utensils used for ministering at the altar, including the firepans, meat forks, shovels and sprinkling bowls. Over it they are to spread a covering of hides of sea cows and put its poles in place.

15 "After Aaron and his sons have finished covering the holy furnishings and all the holy articles, and when the camp is ready to move, the Kohathites are to come to do the carrying. But they must not touch the holy things or they will die. The Kohathites are to carry those things that are in the Tent of Meeting.

16 "Eleazar son of Aaron, the priest, is to have charge of the oil for the light, the fragrant incense, the regular grain offering and the anointing oil. He is to be in charge of the entire tabernacle and everything in it, including its holy furnishings and articles."

17 The LORD said to Moses and Aaron, 18 "See that the Kohathite tribal clans are not cut off from the Levites. 19 So that they may live and not die when they come near the most holy things, do this for them: Aaron and his sons are to go into the sanctuary and assign to each man his work and what he is to carry. 20 But the Kohathites must not go in to look at the holy things, even for a moment, or they will die."

The Gershonites

21 The LORD said to Moses, 22 "Take a census also of the

---

f 6 That is, dugongs; also in verses 8, 10, 11, 12, 14 and 25

King James

²³From thirty years old and upward until fifty years old shalt thou number them; all that enter in *j*to perform the service, to do the work in the tabernacle of the congregation.

²⁴This *is* the service of the families of the Gershonites, to serve, and for *k*burdens:

²⁵And they shall bear the curtains of the tabernacle, and the tabernacle of the congregation, his covering, and the covering of the badgers' skins that *is* above upon it, and the hanging for the door of the tabernacle of the congregation,

²⁶And the hangings of the court, and the hanging for the door of the gate of the court, which *is* by the tabernacle and by the altar round about, and their cords, and all the instruments of their service, and all that is made for them: so shall they serve.

²⁷At the *l*appointment of Aaron and his sons shall be all the service of the sons of the Gershonites, in all their burdens, and in all their service: and ye shall appoint unto them in charge all their burdens.

²⁸This *is* the service of the families of the sons of Gershon in the tabernacle of the congregation: and their charge *shall be* under the hand of Ithamar the son of Aaron the priest.

The descendants of Merari

²⁹ ¶ As for the sons of Merari, thou shalt number them after their families, by the house of their fathers;

³⁰From thirty years old and upward even unto fifty years old shalt thou number them, every one that entereth into the *m*service, to do the work of the tabernacle of the congregation.

³¹And this *is* the charge of their burden, according to all their service in the tabernacle of the congregation; the boards of the tabernacle, and the bars thereof, and the pillars thereof, and sockets thereof,

³²And the pillars of the court round about, and their sockets, and their pins, and their cords, with all their instruments, and with all their service: and by name ye shall reckon the instruments of the charge of their burden.

³³This *is* the service of the families of the sons of Merari, according to all their service, in the tabernacle of the congregation, under the hand of Ithamar the son of Aaron the priest.

The results of the census

³⁴ ¶ And Moses and Aaron and the chief of the congregation numbered the sons of the Kohathites after their families, and after the house of their fathers,

³⁵From thirty years old and upward even unto fifty years old, every one that entereth into the service, for the work in the tabernacle of the congregation:

³⁶And those that were numbered of them by their families were two thousand seven hundred and fifty.

³⁷These *were* they that were numbered of the families of the Kohathites, all that might do service in the tabernacle of the congregation, which Moses and Aaron did number according to the commandment of the LORD by the hand of Moses.

³⁸And those that were numbered of the sons of Gershon, throughout their families, and by the house of their fathers,

³⁹From thirty years old and upward even unto fifty years old, every one that entereth into the service, for the work in the tabernacle of the congregation,

⁴⁰Even those that were numbered of them, throughout their families, by the house of their fathers, were two thousand and six hundred and thirty.

⁴¹These *are* they that were numbered of the families of the sons of Gershon, of all that might do service in the tabernacle of the congregation, whom Moses and Aaron did number according to the commandment of the LORD.

Amplified

²³From thirty years old and up to fifty years old you shall number them, all who enter for service to do the work in the Tent of Meeting.

²⁴This is the service of the families of the Gershonites, in serving and in bearing burdens [when on the march]:

²⁵And they shall carry the curtains of the tabernacle, and the Tent of Meeting, its covering, and the covering of dolphin *or* porpoise skin that is on top of it, and the hanging *or* screen for the door of the Tent of Meeting,

²⁶And the hangings of the court, and the hanging *or* screen for the entrance of the gate of the court which is around the tabernacle and the altar [of burnt offering], and their cords, and all the equipment for their service; whatever needs to be done with them, that they shall do.

²⁷Under the direction of Aaron and his sons shall be all the service of the sons of the Gershonites, in all they have to carry and in all they have to do; and you shall assign to their charge all that they are to carry [on the march].

²⁸This is the service of the families of the sons of Gershon in the Tent of Meeting; and their work shall be under the direction of Ithamar son of Aaron, the [high] priest.

²⁹As for the sons of Merari, you shall number them by their families and their fathers' houses;

³⁰From thirty years old up to fifty years old you shall number them, everyone who enters the service to do the work of the Tent of Meeting.

³¹And this is what they are assigned to carry *and* to guard [on the march], according to all their service in the Tent of Meeting: the boards *or* frames of the tabernacle, and its bars, and its pillars, and its sockets *or* bases,

³²And the pillars of the court round about with their sockets *or* bases, and pegs, and cords, with all their equipment and all their accessories for service; and you shall assign to them by name the articles which they are to carry [on the march].

³³This is the work of the families of the sons of Merari, according to all their tasks in the Tent of Meeting, under the direction of Ithamar son of Aaron, the [high] priest.

³⁴And Moses and Aaron and the leaders of the congregation numbered the sons of the Kohathites by their families and their fathers' houses,

³⁵From thirty years old up to fifty years old, everyone who enters the service to do the work of the Tent of Meeting;

³⁶And those who were numbered of them by their families were 2,750.

³⁷These were numbered of the families of the Kohathites, all who did service in the Tent of Meeting, whom Moses and Aaron numbered according to the command of the Lord through Moses.

³⁸And those that were numbered of the sons of Gershon, by their families, and by their fathers' houses,

³⁹From thirty years old up to fifty years old, everyone who entered the service to do the work of the Tent of Meeting,

⁴⁰Those who were enrolled of them, by their families, by their fathers' houses, were 2,630.

⁴¹These were numbered of the families of the sons of Gershon, all who served in the Tent of Meeting, whom Moses and Aaron numbered as the Lord commanded.

---

^jHeb. *to war the warfare*   ^kOr, *carriage*   ^lHeb. *mouth*
^mHeb. *warfare*

New American Standard

23 from thirty years and upward to fifty years old, you shall number them; all who enter to perform the service to do the work in the tent of meeting.

24"This is the service of the families of the Gershonites, in serving and in carrying:

25 they shall carry the curtains of the tabernacle and the tent of meeting *with* its covering and the covering of porpoise skin that is on top of it, and the screen for the doorway of the tent of meeting,

26 and the hangings of the court, and the screen for the doorway of the gate of the court which is around the tabernacle and the altar, and their cords and all the equipment for their service; and all that is to be done, they shall perform.

27"All the service of the sons of the Gershonites, in all their loads and in all their work, shall be *performed* at the command of Aaron and his sons; and you shall assign to them as a duty all their loads.

28"This is the service of the families of the sons of the Gershonites in the tent of meeting, and their duties *shall be* under the direction of Ithamar the son of Aaron the priest.

Duties of the Merarites

29 ¶ "*As for* the sons of Merari, you shall number them by their families, by their fathers' households;

30 from thirty years and upward even to fifty years old, you shall number them, everyone who enters the service to do the work of the tent of meeting.

31"Now this is the duty of their loads, for all their service in the tent of meeting: the boards of the tabernacle and its bars and its pillars and its sockets,

32 and the pillars around the court and their sockets and their pegs and their cords, with all their equipment and with all their service; and you shall assign *each man* by name the items he is to carry.

33"This is the service of the families of the sons of Merari, according to all their service in the tent of meeting, under the direction of Ithamar the son of Aaron the priest."

34 ¶ So Moses and Aaron and the leaders of the congregation numbered the sons of the Kohathites by their families and by their fathers' households,

35 from thirty years and upward even to fifty years old, everyone who entered the service for work in the tent of meeting.

36 Their numbered men by their families were 2,750.

37 These are the numbered men of the Kohathite families, everyone who was serving in the tent of meeting, whom Moses and Aaron numbered according to the commandment of the LORD through Moses.

38 ¶ The numbered men of the sons of Gershon by their families and by their fathers' households,

39 from thirty years and upward even to fifty years old, everyone who entered the service for work in the tent of meeting.

40 Their numbered men by their families, by their fathers' households, were 2,630.

41 These are the numbered men of the families of the sons of Gershon, everyone who was serving in the tent of meeting, whom Moses and Aaron numbered according to the commandment of the LORD.

New International

Gershonites by their families and clans. 23Count all the men from thirty to fifty years of age who come to serve in the work at the Tent of Meeting.

24"This is the service of the Gershonite clans as they work and carry burdens: 25They are to carry the curtains of the tabernacle, the Tent of Meeting, its covering and the outer covering of hides of sea cows, the curtains for the entrance to the Tent of Meeting, 26the curtains of the courtyard surrounding the tabernacle and altar, the curtain for the entrance, the ropes and all the equipment used in its service. The Gershonites are to do all that needs to be done with these things. 27All their service, whether carrying or doing other work, is to be done under the direction of Aaron and his sons. You shall assign to them as their responsibility all they are to carry. 28This is the service of the Gershonite clans at the Tent of Meeting. Their duties are to be under the direction of Ithamar son of Aaron, the priest.

The Merarites

29"Count the Merarites by their clans and families. 30Count all the men from thirty to fifty years of age who come to serve in the work at the Tent of Meeting. 31This is their duty as they perform service at the Tent of Meeting: to carry the frames of the tabernacle, its crossbars, posts and bases, 32as well as the posts of the surrounding courtyard with their bases, tent pegs, ropes, all their equipment and everything related to their use. Assign to each man the specific things he is to carry. 33This is the service of the Merarite clans as they work at the Tent of Meeting under the direction of Ithamar son of Aaron, the priest."

The Numbering of the Levite Clans

34Moses, Aaron and the leaders of the community counted the Kohathites by their clans and families. 35All the men from thirty to fifty years of age who came to serve in the work in the Tent of Meeting, 36counted by clans, were 2,750. 37This was the total of all those in the Kohathite clans who served in the Tent of Meeting. Moses and Aaron counted them according to the LORD's command through Moses.

38The Gershonites were counted by their clans and families. 39All the men from thirty to fifty years of age who came to serve in the work at the Tent of Meeting, 40counted by their clans and families, were 2,630. 41This was the total of those in the Gershonite clans who served at the Tent of Meeting. Moses and Aaron counted them according to the LORD's command.

King James

42 ¶ And those that were numbered of the families of the sons of Merari, throughout their families, by the house of their fathers,

43From thirty years old and upward even unto fifty years old, every one that entereth into the service, for the work in the tabernacle of the congregation,

44Even those that were numbered of them after their families, were three thousand and two hundred.

45These be those that were numbered of the families of the sons of Merari, whom Moses and Aaron numbered according to the word of the LORD by the hand of Moses.

46All those that were numbered of the Levites, whom Moses and Aaron and the chief of Israel numbered, after their families, and after the house of their fathers,

47From thirty years old and upward even unto fifty years old, every one that came to do the service of the ministry, and the service of the burden in the tabernacle of the congregation,

48Even those that were numbered of them, were eight thousand and five hundred and fourscore.

49According to the commandment of the LORD they were numbered by the hand of Moses, every one according to his service, and according to his burden: thus were they numbered of him, as the LORD commanded Moses.

Concerning the unclean

5 AND THE LORD spake unto Moses, saying,
2Command the children of Israel, that they put out of the camp every leper, and every one that hath an issue, and whosoever is defiled by the dead:

3Both male and female shall ye put out, without the camp shall ye put them; that they defile not their camps, in the midst whereof I dwell.

4And the children of Israel did so, and put them out without the camp: as the LORD spake unto Moses, so did the children of Israel.

Suspected adultery

5 ¶ And the LORD spake unto Moses, saying,

6Speak unto the children of Israel, When a man or woman shall commit any sin that men commit, to do a trespass against the LORD, and that person be guilty;

7Then they shall confess their sin which they have done: and he shall recompense his trespass with the principal thereof, and add unto it the fifth *part* thereof, and give *it* unto *him* against whom he hath trespassed.

8But if the man have no kinsman to recompense the trespass unto, let the trespass be recompensed unto the LORD, *even* to the priest; beside the ram of the atonement, whereby an atonement shall be made for him.

9And every [n]offering of all the holy things of the children of Israel, which they bring unto the priest, shall be his.

10And every man's hallowed things shall be his: whatsoever any man giveth the priest, it shall be his.

11 ¶ And the LORD spake unto Moses, saying,

12Speak unto the children of Israel, and say unto them, If any man's wife go aside, and commit a trespass against him,

13And a man lie with her carnally, and it be hid from the eyes of her husband, and be kept close, and she be defiled, and *there be* no witness against her, neither she be taken *with the manner;*

14And the spirit of jealousy come upon him, and he be jealous of his wife, and she be defiled: or if the spirit of jealousy come upon him, and he be jealous of his wife, and she be not defiled:

Amplified

42And those numbered of the families of the sons of Merari, by their families, by their fathers' houses,

43From thirty years old up to fifty years old, everyone who entered into the service for work in the Tent of Meeting,

44Even those who were numbered of them by their families, were 3,200.

45These are those who were numbered of the families of the sons of Merari, whom Moses and Aaron numbered according to the command of the Lord by Moses.

46All those who were numbered of the Levites, whom Moses and Aaron and the leaders of Israel counted by their families and by their fathers' houses,

47From thirty years old up to fifty years old, everyone who could enter to do the work of service and of burden bearing in the Tent of Meeting,

48Those that were numbered of them were 8,580.

49According to the command of the Lord through Moses, they were assigned each to his work of serving and carrying. Thus they were numbered by him, as the Lord had commanded Moses.

5 THE LORD said to Moses,
2Command the Israelites that they put outside the camp every leper and everyone who has a discharge, and whoever is defiled by [coming in contact with] the dead.

3Both male and female you shall put out; without the camp you shall put them, that they may not defile their camp, in the midst of which I dwell.

4The Israelites did so, and put them outside the camp; as the Lord said to Moses, so the Israelites did.

5And the Lord said to Moses,

6Say to the Israelites, When a man or woman commits any sin that men commit by breaking faith with the Lord, and that person is guilty,

7Then he shall confess the sin which he has committed, and he shall make restitution for his wrong in full, and add a fifth to it, and give it to him whom he has wronged.

8But if the man [wronged] has no kinsman to whom the restitution may be made, let it be given to the Lord for the priest, besides the ram of atonement with which atonement shall be made for the offender.

9And every offering of all the holy things of the Israelites which they bring to the priest shall be his.

10And every man's hallowed things shall be the priest's; whatever any man gives the priest shall be his.

11And the Lord said to Moses,

12Say to the Israelites, If any man's wife goes astray and commits an offense of guilt against him,

13And a man lies with her carnally, and it is hidden from the eyes of her husband and it is kept secret though she is defiled, and there is no witness against her nor was she taken in the act,

14And if the spirit of jealousy comes upon him and he is jealous *and* suspicious of his wife who has defiled herself—or if the spirit of jealousy comes upon him and he is jealous *and* suspicious of his wife though she has not defiled herself—

[n] Or, heave offering

New American Standard

42 ¶ The numbered men of the families of the sons of Merari by their families, by their fathers' households,

43 from thirty years and upward even to fifty years old, everyone who entered the service for work in the tent of meeting.

44 Their numbered men by their families were 3,200.

45 These are the numbered men of the families of the sons of Merari, whom Moses and Aaron numbered according to the commandment of the LORD through Moses.

46 ¶ All the numbered men of the Levites, whom Moses and Aaron and the leaders of Israel numbered, by their families and by their fathers' households,

47 from thirty years and upward even to fifty years old, everyone who could enter to do the work of service and the work of carrying in the tent of meeting.

48 Their numbered men were 8,580.

49 According to the commandment of the LORD through Moses, they were numbered, everyone by his serving or carrying; thus *these were* his numbered men, just as the LORD had commanded Moses.

On Defilement

5 THEN THE LORD spoke to Moses, saying,
2"Command the sons of Israel that they send away from the camp every leper and everyone having a discharge and everyone who is unclean because of a *dead* person.

3"You shall send away both male and female; you shall send them outside the camp so that they will not defile their camp where I dwell in their midst."

4 The sons of Israel did so and sent them outside the camp; just as the LORD had spoken to Moses, thus the sons of Israel did.

5 ¶ Then the LORD spoke to Moses, saying,
6"Speak to the sons of Israel, 'When a man or woman commits any of the sins of mankind, acting unfaithfully against the LORD, and that person is guilty,

7 then he shall confess his sins which he has committed, and he shall make restitution in full for his wrong and add to it one-fifth of it, and give *it* to him whom he has wronged.

8 'But if the man has no ʰrelative to whom restitution may be made for the wrong, the restitution which is made for the wrong *must go* to the LORD for the priest, besides the ram of atonement, by which atonement is made for him.

9 'Also every contribution pertaining to all the holy *gifts* of the sons of Israel, which they offer to the priest, shall be his.

10 'So every man's holy *gifts* shall be his; whatever any man gives to the priest, it becomes his.' "

The Adultery Test

11 ¶ Then the LORD spoke to Moses, saying,
12"Speak to the sons of Israel and say to them, 'If any man's wife goes astray and is unfaithful to him,

13 and a man has intercourse with her and it is hidden from the eyes of her husband and she is undetected, although she has defiled herself, and there is no witness against her and she has not been caught in the act,

14 if a spirit of jealousy comes over him and he is jealous of his wife when she has defiled herself, or if a spirit of jealousy comes over him and he is jealous of his wife when she has not defiled herself,

New International

42The Merarites were counted by their clans and families. 43All the men from thirty to fifty years of age who came to serve in the work at the Tent of Meeting, 44counted by their clans, were 3,200. 45This was the total of those in the Merarite clans. Moses and Aaron counted them according to the LORD's command through Moses.

46So Moses, Aaron and the leaders of Israel counted all the Levites by their clans and families. 47All the men from thirty to fifty years of age who came to do the work of serving and carrying the Tent of Meeting 48numbered 8,580. 49At the LORD's command through Moses, each was assigned his work and told what to carry.

Thus they were counted, as the LORD commanded Moses.

The Purity of the Camp

5 THE LORD said to Moses, 2"Command the Israelites to send away from the camp anyone who has an infectious skin diseaseᵍ or a discharge of any kind, or who is ceremonially unclean because of a dead body. 3Send away male and female alike; send them outside the camp so they will not defile their camp, where I dwell among them." 4The Israelites did this; they sent them outside the camp. They did just as the LORD had instructed Moses.

Restitution for Wrongs

5The LORD said to Moses, 6"Say to the Israelites: 'When a man or woman wrongs another in any wayʰ and so is unfaithful to the LORD, that person is guilty 7and must confess the sin he has committed. He must make full restitution for his wrong, add one fifth to it and give it all to the person he has wronged. 8But if that person has no close relative to whom restitution can be made for the wrong, the restitution belongs to the LORD and must be given to the priest, along with the ram with which atonement is made for him. 9All the sacred contributions the Israelites bring to a priest will belong to him. 10Each man's sacred gifts are his own, but what he gives to the priest will belong to the priest.' "

The Test for an Unfaithful Wife

11Then the LORD said to Moses, 12"Speak to the Israelites and say to them: 'If a man's wife goes astray and is unfaithful to him 13by sleeping with another man, and this is hidden from her husband and her impurity is undetected (since there is no witness against her and she has not been caught in the act), 14and if feelings of jealousy come over her husband and he suspects his wife and she is impure— or if he is jealous and suspects her even though she is not

---

ᵍLit *redeemer*

ᵍ2 Traditionally *leprosy*; the Hebrew word was used for various diseases affecting the skin—not necessarily leprosy.
ʰ6 Or *woman commits any wrong common to mankind*

King James

¹⁵Then shall the man bring his wife unto the priest, and he shall bring her offering for her, the tenth *part* of an ephah of barley meal; he shall pour no oil upon it, nor put frankincense thereon; for it *is* an offering of jealousy, an offering of memorial, bringing iniquity to remembrance.

¹⁶And the priest shall bring her near, and set her before the LORD:

¹⁷And the priest shall take holy water in an earthen vessel; and of the dust that is in the floor of the tabernacle the priest shall take, and put *it* into the water:

¹⁸And the priest shall set the woman before the LORD, and uncover the woman's head, and put the offering of memorial in her hands, which *is* the jealousy offering: and the priest shall have in his hand the bitter water that causeth the curse:

¹⁹And the priest shall charge her by an oath, and say unto the woman, If no man have lain with thee, and if thou hast not gone aside to uncleanness *ᵒᵖwith another* instead of thy husband, be thou free from this bitter water that causeth the curse:

²⁰But if thou hast gone aside *to another* instead of thy husband, and if thou be defiled, and some man have lain with thee beside thine husband:

²¹Then the priest shall charge the woman with an oath of cursing, and the priest shall say unto the woman, The LORD make thee a curse and an oath among thy people, when the LORD doth make thy thigh to ᵠrot, and thy belly to swell;

²²And this water that causeth the curse shall go into thy bowels, to make *thy* belly to swell, and *thy* thigh to rot: And the woman shall say, Amen, amen.

²³And the priest shall write these curses in a book, and he shall blot *them* out with the bitter water:

²⁴And he shall cause the woman to drink the bitter water that causeth the curse: and the water that causeth the curse shall enter into her, *and become* bitter.

²⁵Then the priest shall take the jealousy offering out of the woman's hand, and shall wave the offering before the LORD, and offer it upon the altar:

²⁶And the priest shall take an handful of the offering, *even* the memorial thereof, and burn *it* upon the altar, and afterward shall cause the woman to drink the water.

²⁷And when he hath made her to drink the water, then it shall come to pass, *that,* if she be defiled, and have done trespass against her husband, that the water that causeth the curse shall enter into her, *and become* bitter, and her belly shall swell, and her thigh shall rot: and the woman shall be a curse among her people.

²⁸And if the woman be not defiled, but be clean; then she shall be free, and shall conceive seed.

²⁹This *is* the law of jealousies, when a wife goeth aside *to another* instead of her husband, and is defiled;

³⁰Or when the spirit of jealousy cometh upon him, and he be jealous over his wife, and shall set the woman before the LORD, and the priest shall execute upon her all this law.

³¹Then shall the man be guiltless from iniquity, and this woman shall bear her iniquity.

Amplified

¹⁵Then shall the man bring his wife to the priest, and he shall bring the offering required of her, a tenth of an ephah of barley meal; but he shall pour no oil upon it nor put frankincense on it [symbols of favor and joy], for it is a cereal offering of jealousy *and* suspicion, a memorial offering bringing iniquity to remembrance.

¹⁶And the priest shall bring her near and set her before the Lord.

¹⁷And the priest shall take holy water [probably from the sacred laver] in an earthen vessel and take some of the dust that is on the floor of the tabernacle and put it in the water.

¹⁸And the priest shall set the woman before the Lord, and let the hair of the woman's head hang loose, and put the meal offering of remembrance in her hands, which is the jealousy *and* suspicion offering. And the priest shall have in his hand the water of bitterness that brings the curse.

¹⁹Then the priest shall make her take an oath, and say to the woman, If no man has lain with you and if you have not gone astray to uncleanness with another instead of your husband, then be free from any effect of this water of bitterness which brings the curse.

²⁰But if you have gone astray and you are defiled, some man having lain with you beside your husband,

²¹Then the priest shall make the woman take the oath of the curse, and say to the woman, The Lord make you a curse and an oath among your people when the Lord makes your thigh fall away and your body swell.

²²May this water that brings the curse go into your bowels and make your body swell and your thigh fall away. And the woman shall say, So let it be, so let it be.

²³The priest shall then write these curses in a book and shall wash them off into the water of bitterness;

²⁴And he shall cause the woman to drink the water of bitterness that brings the curse, and the water that brings the curse shall enter into her [to try her] bitterly.

²⁵Then the priest shall take the cereal offering of jealousy *and* suspicion out of the woman's hand and shall wave the offering before the Lord and offer it upon the altar.

²⁶And the priest shall take a handful of the cereal offering as the memorial portion of it and burn it on the altar, and afterward shall cause the woman to drink the water.

²⁷And when he has made her drink the water, then if she is defiled and has committed a trespass against her husband, the curse water which she drank shall be bitterness and cause her body to swell and her thigh to fall away, and the woman shall be a curse among her people.

²⁸But if the woman is not defiled and is clean, then she shall be free [from the curse] and be able to have children.

²⁹This is the law of jealousy *and* suspicion when a wife goes aside to another instead of her husband and is defiled,

³⁰Or when the spirit of jealousy *and* suspicion comes upon a man and he is jealous *and* suspicious of his wife; then shall he set the woman before the Lord, and the priest shall execute on her all this law.

³¹The [husband] shall be free from iniquity *and* guilt, and that woman [if guilty] shall bear her iniquity.

The law of a Nazarite

6 AND THE LORD spake unto Moses, saying,
²Speak unto the children of Israel, and say unto them, When either man or woman shall ʳseparate *themselves* to vow a vow of a Nazarite, to separate *themselves* unto the LORD:

6 AND THE Lord said to Moses,
²Say to the Israelites, When either a man or a woman shall make a special vow, the vow of a Nazirite, that is, one separated *and* consecrated to the Lord,

---

ᵒOr, being *in the power of thy husband*   ᵖHeb. *under thy husband*   ᵠHeb. *fall*   ʳOr, *make* themselves Nazarites

New American Standard

15 the man shall then bring his wife to the priest, and shall bring *as* an offering for her one-tenth of an ephah of barley meal; he shall not pour oil on it nor put frankincense on it, for it is a grain offering of jealousy, a grain offering of memorial, a reminder of iniquity.

16 ¶ 'Then the priest shall bring her near and have her stand before the LORD,

17 and the priest shall take holy water in an earthenware vessel; and he shall take some of the dust that is on the floor of the tabernacle and put *it* into the water.

18 'The priest shall then have the woman stand before the LORD and let *the hair of* the woman's head go loose, and place the grain offering of memorial in her hands, which is the grain offering of jealousy, and in the hand of the priest is to be the water of bitterness that brings a curse.

19 'The priest shall have her take an oath and shall say to the woman, "If no man has lain with you and if you have not gone astray into uncleanness, *being* under *the authority of* your husband, be immune to this water of bitterness that brings a curse;

20 if you, however, have gone astray, *being* under *the authority of* your husband, and if you have defiled yourself and a man other than your husband has had intercourse with you"

21 (then the priest shall have the woman swear with the oath of the curse, and the priest shall say to the woman), "the LORD make you a curse and an oath among your people by the LORD's making your thigh waste away and your abdomen swell;

22 and this water that brings a curse shall go into your stomach, and make your abdomen swell and your thigh waste away." And the woman shall say, "Amen. Amen."

23 ¶ 'The priest shall then write these curses on a scroll, and he shall wash them off into the water of bitterness.

24 'Then he shall make the woman drink the water of bitterness that brings a curse, so that the water which brings a curse will go into her and *cause* bitterness.

25 'The priest shall take the grain offering of jealousy from the woman's hand, and he shall wave the grain offering before the LORD and bring it to the altar;

26 and the priest shall take a handful of the grain offering as its memorial offering and offer *it* up in smoke on the altar, and afterward he shall make the woman drink the water.

27 'When he has made her drink the water, then it shall come about, if she has defiled herself and has been unfaithful to her husband, that the water which brings a curse will go into her and *cause* bitterness, and her abdomen will swell and her thigh will waste away, and the woman will become a curse among her people.

28 'But if the woman has not defiled herself and is clean, she will then be free and conceive children.

29 ¶ 'This is the law of jealousy: when a wife, *being* under *the authority of* her husband, goes astray and defiles herself,

30 or when a spirit of jealousy comes over a man and he is jealous of his wife, he shall then make the woman stand before the LORD, and the priest shall apply all this law to her.

31 'Moreover, the man will be free from guilt, but that woman shall bear her guilt.'"

Law of the Nazirites

6 AGAIN THE LORD spoke to Moses, saying, 2"Speak to the sons of Israel and say to them, 'When a man or woman makes a special vow, the vow of a [h]Nazirite, to dedicate himself to the LORD,

New International

impure— 15then he is to take his wife to the priest. He must also take an offering of a tenth of an ephah[i] of barley flour on her behalf. He must not pour oil on it or put incense on it, because it is a grain offering for jealousy, a reminder offering to draw attention to guilt.

16" 'The priest shall bring her and have her stand before the LORD. 17Then he shall take some holy water in a clay jar and put some dust from the tabernacle floor into the water. 18After the priest has had the woman stand before the LORD, he shall loosen her hair and place in her hands the reminder offering, the grain offering for jealousy, while he himself holds the bitter water that brings a curse. 19Then the priest shall put the woman under oath and say to her, "If no other man has slept with you and you have not gone astray and become impure while married to your husband, may this bitter water that brings a curse not harm you. 20But if you have gone astray while married to your husband and you have defiled yourself by sleeping with a man other than your husband"— 21here the priest is to put the woman under this curse of the oath—"may the LORD cause your people to curse and denounce you when he causes your thigh to waste away and your abdomen to swell.[j] 22May this water that brings a curse enter your body so that your abdomen swells and your thigh wastes away.[k]"

" 'Then the woman is to say, "Amen. So be it."

23" 'The priest is to write these curses on a scroll and then wash them off into the bitter water. 24He shall have the woman drink the bitter water that brings a curse, and this water will enter her and cause bitter suffering. 25The priest is to take from her hands the grain offering for jealousy, wave it before the LORD and bring it to the altar. 26The priest is then to take a handful of the grain offering as a memorial offering and burn it on the altar; after that, he is to have the woman drink the water. 27If she has defiled herself and been unfaithful to her husband, when she is made to drink the water that brings a curse, it will go into her and cause bitter suffering; her abdomen will swell and her thigh waste away,[l] and she will become accursed among her people. 28If, however, the woman has not defiled herself and is free from impurity, she will be cleared of guilt and will be able to have children.

29" 'This, then, is the law of jealousy when a woman goes astray and defiles herself while married to her husband, 30or when feelings of jealousy come over a man because he suspects his wife. The priest is to have her stand before the LORD and is to apply this entire law to her. 31The husband will be innocent of any wrongdoing, but the woman will bear the consequences of her sin.'"

The Nazirite

6 THE LORD said to Moses, 2"Speak to the Israelites and say to them: 'If a man or woman wants to make a special vow, a vow of separation to the LORD as a Nazirite, 3he must abstain from wine and other fermented

---

i 15 That is, probably about 2 quarts (about 2 liters)
j 21 Or *causes you to have a miscarrying womb and barrenness*
k 22 Or *body and cause you to be barren and have a miscarrying womb* l 27 Or *suffering; she will have barrenness and a miscarrying womb*

---

h I.e. one separated

King James

³He shall separate *himself* from wine and strong drink, and shall drink no vinegar of wine, or vinegar of strong drink, neither shall he drink any liquor of grapes, nor eat moist grapes, or dried.

⁴All the days of his ^sseparation shall he eat nothing that is made of the ^tvine tree, from the kernels even to the husk.

⁵All the days of the vow of his separation there shall no razor come upon his head: until the days be fulfilled, in the which he separateth *himself* unto the LORD, he shall be holy, *and* shall let the locks of the hair of his head grow.

⁶All the days that he separateth *himself* unto the LORD he shall come at no dead body.

⁷He shall not make himself unclean for his father, or for his mother, for his brother, or for his sister, when they die: because the ^uconsecration of his God *is* upon his head.

⁸All the days of his separation he *is* holy unto the LORD.

⁹And if any man die very suddenly by him, and he hath defiled the head of his consecration; then he shall shave his head in the day of his cleansing, on the seventh day shall he shave it.

¹⁰And on the eighth day he shall bring two turtles, or two young pigeons, to the priest, to the door of the tabernacle of the congregation:

¹¹And the priest shall offer the one for a sin offering, and the other for a burnt offering, and make an atonement for him, for that he sinned by the dead, and shall hallow his head that same day.

¹²And he shall consecrate unto the LORD the days of his separation, and shall bring a lamb of the first year for a trespass offering: but the days that were before shall ^vbe lost, because his separation was defiled.

¹³ ¶ And this *is* the law of the Nazarite, when the days of his separation are fulfilled: he shall be brought unto the door of the tabernacle of the congregation:

¹⁴And he shall offer his offering unto the LORD, one he lamb of the first year without blemish for a burnt offering, and one ewe lamb of the first year without blemish for a sin offering, and one ram without blemish for peace offerings,

¹⁵And a basket of unleavened bread, cakes of fine flour mingled with oil, and wafers of unleavened bread anointed with oil, and their meat offering, and their drink offerings.

¹⁶And the priest shall bring *them* before the LORD, and shall offer his sin offering, and his burnt offering:

¹⁷And he shall offer the ram *for* a sacrifice of peace offerings unto the LORD, with the basket of unleavened bread: the priest shall offer also his meat offering, and his drink offering.

¹⁸And the Nazarite shall shave the head of his separation *at* the door of the tabernacle of the congregation, and shall take the hair of the head of his separation, and put *it* in the fire which *is* under the sacrifice of the peace offerings.

¹⁹And the priest shall take the sodden shoulder of the ram, and one unleavened cake out of the basket, and one unleavened wafer, and shall put *them* upon the hands of the Nazarite, after *the hair of* his separation is shaven:

²⁰And the priest shall wave them *for* a wave offering before the LORD: this *is* holy for the priest, with the wave breast and heave shoulder: and after that the Nazarite may drink wine.

²¹This *is* the law of the Nazarite who hath vowed, *and of* his offering unto the LORD for his separation, beside *that* that his hand shall get: according to the vow which he vowed, so he must do after the law of his separation.

The Aaronic benediction

²² ¶ And the LORD spake unto Moses, saying,

²³Speak unto Aaron and unto his sons, saying, On this wise ye shall bless the children of Israel, saying unto them,

²⁴The LORD bless thee, and keep thee:

Amplified

³He shall separate himself from wine and strong drink; he shall drink no vinegar of wine or of strong drink, and shall drink no grape juice, or eat grapes, fresh or dried. [Luke 1:15.]

⁴All the days of his separation he shall eat nothing produced from the grapevine, not even the seeds or the skins.

⁵All the days of the vow of his separation *and* abstinence there shall no razor come upon his head. Until the time is completed for which he separates himself to the Lord, he shall be holy, and shall let the locks of the hair of his head grow long.

⁶All the days that he separates himself to the Lord he shall not go near a dead body.

⁷He shall not make himself unclean for his father, mother, brother, or sister, when they die, because his separation *and* abstinence to his God is upon his head.

⁸All the days of his separation *and* abstinence he is holy to the Lord.

⁹And if any man dies very suddenly beside him, and he has defiled his consecrated head, then he shall shave his head on the day of his cleansing; on the seventh day shall he shave it.

¹⁰On the eighth day he shall bring two turtledoves or two young pigeons to the priest to the door of the Tent of Meeting,

¹¹And the priest shall offer the one for a sin offering and the other for a burnt offering and make atonement for him because he sinned by reason of the dead body. He shall consecrate his head the same day,

¹²And he shall consecrate *and* separate himself to the Lord for the days of his separation and shall bring a male lamb a year old for a trespass *or* guilt offering; but the previous days shall be void *and* lost, because his separation was defiled.

¹³And this is the law of the Nazirite when the days of his separation *and* abstinence are fulfilled. He shall be brought to the door of the Tent of Meeting,

¹⁴And he shall offer his gift to the Lord, one he-lamb a year old without blemish for a burnt offering, and one ewe lamb a year old without blemish for a sin offering, and one ram without blemish for a peace offering,

¹⁵And a basket of unleavened bread, cakes of fine flour mingled with oil, and wafers of unleavened bread spread with oil, and their cereal offering, and their drink offering.

¹⁶And the priest shall present them before the Lord and shall offer the person's sin offering and his burnt offering.

¹⁷And he shall offer the ram for a sacrifice of peace offering to the Lord, with the basket of unleavened bread; the priest shall offer also its cereal offering and its drink offering.

¹⁸And the Nazirite shall shave his consecrated head at the door of the Tent of Meeting, and shall take the hair and put it on the fire which is under the sacrifice of the peace offerings.

¹⁹And the priest shall take the boiled shoulder of the ram, and one unleavened cake out of the basket, and one unleavened wafer and shall put them upon the hands of the Nazirite, after he has shaven the hair of his separation *and* abstinence.

²⁰And the priest shall wave them for a wave offering before the Lord; they are a holy portion for the priest, with the breast that is waved and the thigh *or* shoulder that is offered; and after that the Nazirite may drink wine.

²¹This is the law for the Nazirite who has made a vow. His offering to the Lord, besides what else he is able to afford, shall be according to the vow which he has vowed; so shall he do according to the law for his separation *and* abstinence [as a Nazirite]. [Acts 21:24, 26.]

²²And the Lord said to Moses.

²³Say to Aaron and his sons, This is the way you shall bless the Israelites. Say to them,

²⁴The Lord bless you and watch, guard, *and* keep you;

---

^sOr, *Nazariteship*   ^tHeb. *vine of the wine*   ^uHeb. *separation*
^vHeb. *fall*

New American Standard

³ he shall abstain from wine and strong drink; he shall drink no vinegar, whether made from wine or strong drink, nor shall he drink any grape juice nor eat fresh or dried grapes.

⁴ 'All the days of his *i*separation he shall not eat anything that is produced by the grape vine, from *the* seeds even to *the* skin.

⁵ ¶ 'All the days of his vow of separation no razor shall pass over his head. He shall be holy until the days are fulfilled for which he separated himself to the LORD; he shall let the locks of hair on his head grow long.

⁶ ¶ 'All the days of his separation to the LORD he shall not go near to a dead person.

⁷ 'He shall not make himself unclean for his father or for his mother, for his brother or for his sister, when they die, because his separation to God is on his head.

⁸ 'All the days of his separation he is holy to the LORD.

⁹ ¶ 'But if a man dies very suddenly beside him and he defiles his dedicated head *of hair,* then he shall shave his head on the day when he becomes clean; he shall shave it on the seventh day.

¹⁰ 'Then on the eighth day he shall bring two turtledoves or two young pigeons to the priest, to the doorway of the tent of meeting.

¹¹ 'The priest shall offer one for a sin offering and *the* other for a burnt offering, and make atonement for him concerning his sin because of the *dead* person. And that same day he shall consecrate his head,

¹² and shall dedicate to the LORD his days as a Nazirite, and shall bring a male lamb a year old for a guilt offering; but the former days will be void because his separation was defiled.

¹³ ¶ 'Now this is the law of the Nazirite when the days of his separation are fulfilled, he shall bring the offering to the doorway of the tent of meeting.

¹⁴ 'He shall present his offering to the LORD: one male lamb a year old without defect for a burnt offering and one ewe-lamb a year old without defect for a sin offering and one ram without defect for a peace offering,

¹⁵ and a basket of unleavened cakes of fine flour mixed with oil and unleavened wafers spread with oil, along with their grain offering and their drink offering.

¹⁶ 'Then the priest shall present *them* before the LORD and shall offer his sin offering and his burnt offering.

¹⁷ 'He shall also offer the ram for a sacrifice of peace offerings to the LORD, together with the basket of unleavened cakes; the priest shall likewise offer its grain offering and its drink offering.

¹⁸ 'The Nazirite shall then shave his dedicated head *of hair* at the doorway of the tent of meeting, and take the dedicated hair of his head and put *it* on the fire which is under the sacrifice of peace offerings.

¹⁹ 'The priest shall take the ram's shoulder *when it has been* boiled, and one unleavened cake out of the basket and one unleavened wafer, and shall put *them* on the hands of the Nazirite after he has shaved his dedicated *hair.*

²⁰ 'Then the priest shall wave them for a wave offering before the LORD. It is holy for the priest, together with the breast offered by waving and the thigh offered by lifting up; and afterward the Nazirite may drink wine.'

²¹ ¶ "This is the law of the Nazirite who vows his offering to the LORD according to his separation, in addition to what *else* he can afford; according to his vow which he takes, so he shall do according to the law of his separation."

Aaron's Benediction

²² ¶ Then the LORD spoke to Moses, saying,

²³ "Speak to Aaron and to his sons, saying, 'Thus you shall bless the sons of Israel. You shall say to them:

²⁴ ¶ The LORD bless you, and keep you;

New International

drink and must not drink vinegar made from wine or from other fermented drink. He must not drink grape juice or eat grapes or raisins. As long as he is a Nazirite, he must not eat anything that comes from the grapevine, not even the seeds or skins.

⁵" 'During the entire period of his vow of separation no razor may be used on his head. He must be holy until the period of his separation to the LORD is over; he must let the hair of his head grow long. ⁶Throughout the period of his separation to the LORD he must not go near a dead body. ⁷Even if his own father or mother or brother or sister dies, he must not make himself ceremonially unclean on account of them, because the symbol of his separation to God is on his head. ⁸Throughout the period of his separation he is consecrated to the LORD.

⁹" 'If someone dies suddenly in his presence, thus defiling the hair he has dedicated, he must shave his head on the day of his cleansing—the seventh day. ¹⁰Then on the eighth day he must bring two doves or two young pigeons to the priest at the entrance to the Tent of Meeting. ¹¹The priest is to offer one as a sin offering and the other as a burnt offering to make atonement for him because he sinned by being in the presence of the dead body. That same day he is to consecrate his head. ¹²He must dedicate himself to the LORD for the period of his separation and must bring a year-old male lamb as a guilt offering. The previous days do not count, because he became defiled during his separation.

¹³" 'Now this is the law for the Nazirite when the period of his separation is over. He is to be brought to the entrance to the Tent of Meeting. ¹⁴There he is to present his offerings to the LORD: a year-old male lamb without defect for a burnt offering, a year-old ewe lamb without defect for a sin offering, a ram without defect for a fellowship offering,*m* ¹⁵together with their grain offerings and drink offerings, and a basket of bread made without yeast— cakes of fine flour mixed with oil, and wafers spread with oil.

¹⁶" 'The priest is to present them before the LORD and make the sin offering and the burnt offering. ¹⁷He is to present the basket of unleavened bread and is to sacrifice the ram as a fellowship offering to the LORD, together with its grain offering and drink offering.

¹⁸" 'Then at the entrance to the Tent of Meeting, the Nazirite must shave off the hair that he dedicated. He is to take the hair and put it in the fire that is under the sacrifice of the fellowship offering.

¹⁹" 'After the Nazirite has shaved off the hair of his dedication, the priest is to place in his hands a boiled shoulder of the ram, and a cake and a wafer from the basket, both made without yeast. ²⁰The priest shall then wave them before the LORD as a wave offering; they are holy and belong to the priest, together with the breast that was waved and the thigh that was presented. After that, the Nazirite may drink wine.

²¹" 'This is the law of the Nazirite who vows his offering to the LORD in accordance with his separation, in addition to whatever else he can afford. He must fulfill the vow he has made, according to the law of the Nazirite.' "

The Priestly Blessing

²²The LORD said to Moses, ²³"Tell Aaron and his sons, 'This is how you are to bless the Israelites. Say to them:

²⁴" ' "The LORD bless you
    and keep you;

---

*i*Or *living as a Nazirite,* and so through v 21

m 14 Traditionally *peace offering*; also in verses 17 and 18

King James

25The LORD make his face shine upon thee, and be gracious unto thee:

26The LORD lift up his countenance upon thee, and give thee peace.

27And they shall put my name upon the children of Israel; and I will bless them.

The dedication offerings

7 AND IT came to pass on the day that Moses had fully set up the tabernacle, and had anointed it, and sanctified it, and all the instruments thereof, both the altar and all the vessels thereof, and had anointed them, and sanctified them;

2That the princes of Israel, heads of the house of their fathers, who *were* the princes of the tribes, *w*and were over them that were numbered, offered:

3And they brought their offering before the LORD, six covered wagons, and twelve oxen; a wagon for two of the princes, and for each one an ox: and they brought them before the tabernacle.

4And the LORD spake unto Moses, saying,

5Take *it* of them, that they may be to do the service of the tabernacle of the congregation; and thou shalt give them unto the Levites, to every man according to his service.

6And Moses took the wagons and the oxen, and gave them unto the Levites.

7Two wagons and four oxen he gave unto the sons of Gershon, according to their service:

8And four wagons and eight oxen he gave unto the sons of Merari, according unto their service, under the hand of Ithamar the son of Aaron the priest.

9But unto the sons of Kohath he gave none: because the service of the sanctuary belonging unto them *was that* they should bear upon their shoulders.

10 ¶ And the princes offered for dedicating of the altar in the day that it was anointed, even the princes offered their offering before the altar.

11And the LORD said unto Moses, They shall offer their offering, each prince on his day, for the dedicating of the altar.

12 ¶ And he that offered his offering the first day was Nahshon the son of Amminadab, of the tribe of Judah:

13And his offering *was* one silver charger, the weight thereof *was* an hundred and thirty *shekels,* one silver bowl of seventy shekels, after the shekel of the sanctuary; both of them *were* full of fine flour mingled with oil for a meat offering:

14One spoon of ten *shekels* of gold, full of incense:

15One young bullock, one ram, one lamb of the first year, for a burnt offering:

Amplified

25The Lord make His face to shine upon *and* enlighten you and be gracious (kind, merciful, and giving favor) to you;

26The Lord lift up His [approving] countenance upon you and give you peace (tranquility of heart and life continually).

27And they shall put My name upon the Israelites, and I will bless them.

7 ON THE day that Moses had fully completed setting up the tabernacle and had anointed and consecrated it and all its furniture, and the altar and all its utensils, and had anointed and set them apart for holy use,

2The princes *or* leaders of Israel, heads of their fathers' houses, made offerings. These were the leaders of the tribes and were over those who were numbered.

3And they brought their offering before the Lord, six covered wagons and twelve oxen; a wagon for each two of the princes *or* leaders and an ox for each one; and they brought them before the tabernacle.

4Then the Lord said to Moses,

5Accept the things from them, that they may be used in doing the service of the Tent of Meeting, and give them to the Levites, to each man according to his service.

6So Moses took the wagons and the oxen and gave them to the Levites.

7Two wagons and four oxen he gave to the sons of Gershon, according to their service;

8And four wagons and eight oxen he gave to the sons of Merari, according to their service, under the supervision of Ithamar son of Aaron, the [high] priest.

9But to the sons of Kohath he gave none, because they were assigned the care of the sanctuary *and* the holy things which had to be carried on their shoulders.

10And the princes *or* leaders offered sacrifices for the dedication of the altar [of burnt offering] on the day that it was anointed; and they offered their sacrifice before the altar.

11And the Lord said to Moses, They shall offer their offerings, each prince *or* leader on his day, for the dedication of the altar.

12He who offered his offering on the first day was Nahshon son of Amminadab, of the tribe of Judah.

13And his offering was one silver platter, the weight of which was 130 shekels, one silver basin of seventy shekels, according to the shekel of the sanctuary, both of them full of fine flour mixed with oil for a cereal offering;

14One golden bowl of ten shekels, full of incense;

15One young bull, one ram, one male lamb a year old, for a burnt offering;

*w*Heb. *who stood*

New American Standard

²⁵ ¶ The LORD make His face shine on you,
And be gracious to you;
²⁶ ¶ The LORD lift up His countenance on you,
And give you peace.'
²⁷ "So they shall invoke My name on the sons of Israel,
and I *then* will bless them."

Offerings of the Leaders

7 NOW ON the day that Moses had finished setting up
the tabernacle, he anointed it and consecrated it with
all its furnishings and the altar and all its utensils; he
anointed them and consecrated them also.
² Then the leaders of Israel, the heads of their fathers'
households, made an offering (they were the leaders of
the tribes; they were the ones who were over the numbered men).
³ When they brought their offering before the LORD,
six covered carts and twelve oxen, a cart for *every* two of
the leaders and an ox for each one, then they presented
them before the tabernacle.
⁴ Then the LORD spoke to Moses, saying,
⁵ "Accept *these things* from them, that they may be used
in the service of the tent of meeting, and you shall give
them to the Levites, *to* each man according to his service."
⁶ So Moses took the carts and the oxen and gave them
to the Levites.
⁷ Two carts and four oxen he gave to the sons of Ger-
shon, according to their service,
⁸ and four carts and eight oxen he gave to the sons of
Merari, according to their service, under the direction of
Ithamar the son of Aaron the priest.
⁹ But he did not give *any* to the sons of Kohath because
theirs *was* the service of the holy *objects, which* they carried on the shoulder.
¹⁰ ¶ The leaders offered the dedication *offering* for the
altar when it was anointed, so the leaders offered their
offering before the altar.
¹¹ Then the LORD said to Moses, "Let them present their
offering, one leader each day, for the dedication of the
altar."
¹² ¶ Now the one who presented his offering on the first
day was Nahshon the son of Amminadab, of the tribe of
Judah;
¹³ and his offering *was* one silver *j* dish whose weight
was one hundred and thirty *shekels,* one silver bowl of
seventy shekels, according to *k* the shekel of the sanctuary, both of them full of fine flour mixed with oil for a
grain offering;
¹⁴ one gold pan of ten *shekels,* full of incense;
¹⁵ one bull, one ram, one male lamb one year old, for a
burnt offering;

New International

²⁵ the LORD make his face shine upon you
and be gracious to you;
²⁶ the LORD turn his face toward you
and give you peace." '

²⁷ "So they will put my name on the Israelites, and I will
bless them."

Offerings at the Dedication of the Tabernacle

7 WHEN MOSES finished setting up the tabernacle, he
anointed it and consecrated it and all its furnishings.
He also anointed and consecrated the altar and all its utensils. ² Then the leaders of Israel, the heads of families who
were the tribal leaders in charge of those who were counted, made offerings. ³ They brought as their gifts before the
LORD six covered carts and twelve oxen—an ox from each
leader and a cart from every two. These they presented
before the tabernacle.
⁴ The LORD said to Moses, ⁵ "Accept these from them,
that they may be used in the work at the Tent of Meeting.
Give them to the Levites as each man's work requires."
⁶ So Moses took the carts and oxen and gave them to the
Levites. ⁷ He gave two carts and four oxen to the Gershonites, as their work required, ⁸ and he gave four carts and
eight oxen to the Merarites, as their work required. They
were all under the direction of Ithamar son of Aaron, the
priest. ⁹ But Moses did not give any to the Kohathites,
because they were to carry on their shoulders the holy
things, for which they were responsible.
¹⁰ When the altar was anointed, the leaders brought their
offerings for its dedication and presented them before the
altar. ¹¹ For the LORD had said to Moses, "Each day one
leader is to bring his offering for the dedication of the
altar."

¹² The one who brought his offering on the first day was
Nahshon son of Amminadab of the tribe of Judah.
¹³ His offering was one silver plate weighing a hun-
dred and thirty shekels,ⁿ and one silver sprinkling
bowl weighing seventy shekels,^o both according to
the sanctuary shekel, each filled with fine flour mixed
with oil as a grain offering; ¹⁴ one gold dish weighing
ten shekels,^p filled with incense; ¹⁵ one young bull,
one ram and one male lamb a year old, for a burnt

j Or *platter,* and so through v 85   *k* I.e. Approx one-half oz, and
so through v 86

n 13 That is, about 3 1/4 pounds (about 1.5 kilograms); also
elsewhere in this chapter   *o 13* That is, about 1 3/4 pounds
(about 0.8 kilogram); also elsewhere in this chapter   *p 14* That
is, about 4 ounces (about 110 grams); also elsewhere in this chapter

King James

16One kid of the goats for a sin offering:

17And for a sacrifice of peace offerings, two oxen, five rams, five he goats, five lambs of the first year: this *was* the offering of Nahshon the son of Amminadab.

18 ¶ On the second day Nethaneel the son of Zuar, prince of Issachar, did offer:

19He offered *for* his offering one silver charger, the weight whereof *was* an hundred and thirty *shekels*, one silver bowl of seventy shekels, after the shekel of the sanctuary; both of them full of fine flour mingled with oil for a meat offering:

20One spoon of gold of ten *shekels,* full of incense:

21One young bullock, one ram, one lamb of the first year, for a burnt offering:

22One kid of the goats for a sin offering:

23And for a sacrifice of peace offerings, two oxen, five rams, five he goats, five lambs of the first year: this *was* the offering of Nethaneel the son of Zuar.

24 ¶ On the third day Eliab the son of Helon, prince of the children of Zebulun, *did offer:*

25His offering *was* one silver charger, the weight whereof *was* an hundred and thirty *shekels,* one silver bowl of seventy shekels, after the shekel of the sanctuary; both of them full of fine flour mingled with oil for a meat offering:

26One golden spoon of ten *shekels,* full of incense:

27One young bullock, one ram, one lamb of the first year, for a burnt offering:

28One kid of the goats for a sin offering:

29And for a sacrifice of peace offerings, two oxen, five rams, five he goats, five lambs of the first year: this *was* the offering of Eliab the son of Helon.

30 ¶ On the fourth day Elizur the son of Shedeur, prince of the children of Reuben, *did offer:*

31His offering *was* one silver charger of the weight of an hundred and thirty *shekels,* one silver bowl of seventy shekels, after the shekel of the sanctuary; both of them full of fine flour mingled with oil for a meat offering:

32One golden spoon of ten *shekels,* full of incense:

33One young bullock, one ram, one lamb of the first year, for a burnt offering:

34One kid of the goats for a sin offering:

35And for a sacrifice of peace offerings, two oxen, five rams, five he goats, five lambs of the first year: this *was* the offering of Elizur the son of Shedeur.

36 ¶ On the fifth day Shelumiel the son of Zurishaddai, prince of the children of Simeon, *did offer:*

37His offering *was* one silver charger, the weight whereof *was* an hundred and thirty *shekels,* one silver bowl of seventy shekels, after the shekel of the sanctuary; both of them full of fine flour mingled with oil for a meat offering:

38One golden spoon of ten *shekels,* full of incense:

39One young bullock, one ram, one lamb of the first year, for a burnt offering:

40One kid of the goats for a sin offering:

41And for a sacrifice of peace offerings, two oxen, five rams, five he goats, five lambs of the first year: this *was* the offering of Shelumiel the son of Zurishaddai.

Amplified

16One male goat for a sin offering;

17And *b*for the sacrifice of peace offerings, two oxen, five rams, five male goats, five male lambs a year old. This was the offering of Nahshon son of Amminadab.

18The second day Nethanel son of Zuar, leader [of the tribe] of Issachar, offered.

19He gave for his offering one silver platter, the weight of which was 130 shekels, one silver basin of seventy shekels, after the shekel of the sanctuary, both of them full of fine flour mixed with oil for a cereal offering;

20One golden bowl of ten shekels, full of incense;

21One young bull, one ram, one male lamb a year old, for a burnt offering;

22One male goat for a sin offering;

23And for the sacrifice of peace offerings, two oxen, five rams, five male goats, five male lambs a year old. This was the offering of Nethanel son of Zuar.

24The third day Eliab son of Helon, leader of the sons of Zebulun, offered.

25His offering was one silver platter, the weight of which was 130 shekels, one silver basin of seventy shekels, after the shekel of the sanctuary, both of them full of fine flour mixed with oil for a cereal offering;

26One golden bowl of ten shekels, full of incense;

27One young bull, one ram, one male lamb a year old, for a burnt offering;

28One male goat for a sin offering;

29And for the sacrifice of peace offerings, two oxen, five rams, five male goats, five male lambs a year old. This was the offering of Eliab son of Helon.

30The fourth day Elizur son of Shedeur, leader of the sons of Reuben, offered.

31His offering was one silver platter of the weight of 130 shekels, one silver basin of seventy shekels, after the shekel of the sanctuary, both of them full of fine flour mixed with oil for a cereal offering;

32One golden bowl of ten shekels, full of incense;

33One young bull, one ram, one male lamb a year old, for a burnt offering;

34One male goat for a sin offering;

35And for the sacrifice of peace offerings, two oxen, five rams, five male goats, five male lambs a year old. This was the offering of Elizur son of Shedeur.

36The fifth day Shelumiel son of Zurishaddai, leader of the sons of Simeon, offered.

37His offering was one silver platter, the weight of which was 130 shekels, one silver basin of seventy shekels, after the shekel of the sanctuary, both of them full of fine flour mixed with oil for a cereal offering;

38One golden bowl of ten shekels, full of incense;

39One young bull, one ram, one male lamb a year old, for a burnt offering;

40One male goat for a sin offering;

41And for the sacrifice of peace offerings, two oxen, five rams, five male goats, five male lambs a year old. This was the offering of Shelumiel son of Zurishaddai.

b Verses 12 to 17 give the detailed description of one tribe leader's offering. Then, instead of saying that the gifts of the other tribe leaders were exactly like this one and naming the leaders, the record goes on for **seventy** verses repeating what has already been said **eleven** more times! Why? These things "were written for our learning" (Rom. 15:4 KJV). Let us seek the answer. Other commentators give Matthew Henry credit for giving the correct view. He says that both in dictating that each tribal leader have a separate day for his gift and in giving the reports equal space, regardless of the contrast in the tribe's strength and rank in the camp, God had a definite purpose: "that an equal honor might thereby be put on each several tribe . . . Thus it was intimated that all the tribes of Israel had an equal share in the altar and an equal share in the sacrifices that were offered upon it. Though one tribe was posted more honorably in the camp than another, yet they and their services were all alike acceptable to God . . . Rich and poor meet together before God . . . He was letting us know that what is given is lent to the Lord, and He carefully records it, with everyone's name prefixed to his gift, because what is so given as a labor of love (Heb. 6:10 KJV) He will repay. Christ took particular notice of what was cast into the treasury (Mark 12:41)" (Matthew Henry, *A Commentary*).

New American Standard

16 one male goat for a sin offering;

17 and for the sacrifice of peace offerings, two oxen, five rams, five male goats, five male lambs one year old. This *was* the offering of Nahshon the son of Amminadab.

18 ¶ On the second day Nethanel the son of Zuar, leader of Issachar, presented *an offering;*

19 he presented as his offering one silver dish whose weight *was* one hundred and thirty *shekels,* one silver bowl of seventy shekels, according to the shekel of the sanctuary, both of them full of fine flour mixed with oil for a grain offering;

20 one gold pan of ten *shekels,* full of incense;

21 one bull, one ram, one male lamb one year old, for a burnt offering;

22 one male goat for a sin offering;

23 and for the sacrifice of peace offerings, two oxen, five rams, five male goats, five male lambs one year old. This *was* the offering of Nethanel the son of Zuar.

24 ¶ On the third day *it was* Eliab the son of Helon, leader of the sons of Zebulun;

25 his offering *was* one silver dish whose weight *was* one hundred and thirty *shekels,* one silver bowl of seventy shekels, according to the shekel of the sanctuary, both of them full of fine flour mixed with oil for a grain offering;

26 one gold pan of ten *shekels,* full of incense;

27 one young bull, one ram, one male lamb one year old, for a burnt offering;

28 one male goat for a sin offering;

29 and for the sacrifice of peace offerings, two oxen, five rams, five male goats, five male lambs one year old. This *was* the offering of Eliab the son of Helon.

30 ¶ On the fourth day *it was* Elizur the son of Shedeur, leader of the sons of Reuben;

31 his offering *was* one silver dish whose weight *was* one hundred and thirty *shekels,* one silver bowl of seventy shekels, according to the shekel of the sanctuary, both of them full of fine flour mixed with oil for a grain offering;

32 one gold pan of ten *shekels,* full of incense;

33 one bull, one ram, one male lamb one year old, for a burnt offering;

34 one male goat for a sin offering;

35 and for the sacrifice of peace offerings, two oxen, five rams, five male goats, five male lambs one year old. This *was* the offering of Elizur the son of Shedeur.

36 ¶ On the fifth day *it was* Shelumiel the son of Zurishaddai, leader of the children of Simeon;

37 his offering *was* one silver dish whose weight *was* one hundred and thirty *shekels,* one silver bowl of seventy shekels, according to the shekel of the sanctuary, both of them full of fine flour mixed with oil for a grain offering;

38 one gold pan of ten *shekels,* full of incense;

39 one bull, one ram, one male lamb one year old, for a burnt offering;

40 one male goat for a sin offering;

41 and for the sacrifice of peace offerings, two oxen, five rams, five male goats, five male lambs one year old. This *was* the offering of Shelumiel the son of Zurishaddai.

New International

offering; 16one male goat for a sin offering; 17and two oxen, five rams, five male goats and five male lambs a year old, to be sacrificed as a fellowship offering.*q* This was the offering of Nahshon son of Amminadab.

18On the second day Nethanel son of Zuar, the leader of Issachar, brought his offering.

19The offering he brought was one silver plate weighing a hundred and thirty shekels, and one silver sprinkling bowl weighing seventy shekels, both according to the sanctuary shekel, each filled with fine flour mixed with oil as a grain offering; 20one gold dish weighing ten shekels, filled with incense; 21one young bull, one ram and one male lamb a year old, for a burnt offering; 22one male goat for a sin offering; 23and two oxen, five rams, five male goats and five male lambs a year old, to be sacrificed as a fellowship offering. This was the offering of Nethanel son of Zuar.

24On the third day, Eliab son of Helon, the leader of the people of Zebulun, brought his offering.

25His offering was one silver plate weighing a hundred and thirty shekels, and one silver sprinkling bowl weighing seventy shekels, both according to the sanctuary shekel, each filled with fine flour mixed with oil as a grain offering; 26one gold dish weighing ten shekels, filled with incense; 27one young bull, one ram and one male lamb a year old, for a burnt offering; 28one male goat for a sin offering; 29and two oxen, five rams, five male goats and five male lambs a year old, to be sacrificed as a fellowship offering. This was the offering of Eliab son of Helon.

30On the fourth day Elizur son of Shedeur, the leader of the people of Reuben, brought his offering.

31His offering was one silver plate weighing a hundred and thirty shekels, and one silver sprinkling bowl weighing seventy shekels, both according to the sanctuary shekel, each filled with fine flour mixed with oil as a grain offering; 32one gold dish weighing ten shekels, filled with incense; 33one young bull, one ram and one male lamb a year old, for a burnt offering; 34one male goat for a sin offering; 35and two oxen, five rams, five male goats and five male lambs a year old, to be sacrificed as a fellowship offering. This was the offering of Elizur son of Shedeur.

36On the fifth day Shelumiel son of Zurishaddai, the leader of the people of Simeon, brought his offering.

37His offering was one silver plate weighing a hundred and thirty shekels, and one silver sprinkling bowl weighing seventy shekels, both according to the sanctuary shekel, each filled with fine flour mixed with oil as a grain offering; 38one gold dish weighing ten shekels, filled with incense; 39one young bull, one ram and one male lamb a year old, for a burnt offering; 40one male goat for a sin offering; 41and two oxen, five rams, five male goats and five male lambs a year old, to be sacrificed as a fellowship offering. This was the offering of Shelumiel son of Zurishaddai.

q 17 Traditionally *peace offering*; also elsewhere in this chapter

King James

42 ¶ On the sixth day Eliasaph the son of ˣDeuel, prince of the children of Gad, *offered:*

43His offering *was* one silver charger of the weight of an hundred and thirty *shekels,* a silver bowl of seventy shekels, after the shekel of the sanctuary; both of them full of fine flour mingled with oil for a meat offering:

44One golden spoon of ten *shekels,* full of incense:

45One young bullock, one ram, one lamb of the first year, for a burnt offering:

46One kid of the goats for a sin offering:

47And for a sacrifice of peace offerings, two oxen, five rams, five he goats, five lambs of the first year: this *was* the offering of Eliasaph the son of Deuel.

48 ¶ On the seventh day Elishama the son of Ammihud, prince of the children of Ephraim, *offered:*

49His offering *was* one silver charger, the weight whereof *was* an hundred and thirty *shekels,* one silver bowl of seventy shekels, after the shekel of the sanctuary; both of them full of fine flour mingled with oil for a meat offering:

50One golden spoon of ten *shekels,* full of incense:

51One young bullock, one ram, one lamb of the first year, for a burnt offering:

52One kid of the goats for a sin offering:

53And for a sacrifice of peace offerings, two oxen, five rams, five he goats, five lambs of the first year: this *was* the offering of Elishama the son of Ammihud.

54 ¶ On the eighth day *offered* Gamaliel the son of Pedahzur, prince of the children of Manasseh:

55His offering *was* one silver charger of the weight of an hundred and thirty *shekels,* one silver bowl of seventy shekels, after the shekel of the sanctuary; both of them full of fine flour mingled with oil for a meat offering:

56One golden spoon of ten *shekels,* full of incense:

57One young bullock, one ram, one lamb of the first year, for a burnt offering:

58One kid of the goats for a sin offering:

59And for a sacrifice of peace offerings, two oxen, five rams, five he goats, five lambs of the first year: this *was* the offering of Gamaliel the son of Pedahzur.

60 ¶ On the ninth day Abidan the son of Gideoni, prince of the children of Benjamin, *offered:*

61His offering *was* one silver charger, the weight whereof *was* an hundred and thirty *shekels,* one silver bowl of seventy shekels, after the shekel of the sanctuary; both of them full of fine flour mingled with oil for a meat offering:

62One golden spoon of ten *shekels,* full of incense:

63One young bullock, one ram, one lamb of the first year, for a burnt offering:

64One kid of the goats for a sin offering:

65And for a sacrifice of peace offerings, two oxen, five rams, five he goats, five lambs of the first year: this *was* the offering of Abidan the son of Gideoni.

66 ¶ On the tenth day Ahiezer the son of Ammishaddai, prince of the children of Dan, *offered:*

67His offering *was* one silver charger, the weight whereof *was* an hundred and thirty *shekels,* one silver bowl of seventy shekels, after the shekel of the sanctuary; both of them full of fine flour mingled with oil for a meat offering:

68One golden spoon of ten *shekels,* full of incense:

69One young bullock, one ram, one lamb of the first year, for a burnt offering:

70One kid of the goats for a sin offering:

71And for a sacrifice of peace offerings, two oxen, five rams, five he goats, five lambs of the first year: this *was* the offering of Ahiezer the son of Ammishaddai.

72 ¶ On the eleventh day Pagiel the son of Ocran, prince of the children of Asher, *offered:*

73His offering *was* one silver charger, the weight whereof *was* an hundred and thirty *shekels,* one silver bowl of seventy shekels, after the shekel of the sanctuary; both of them full of fine flour mingled with oil for a meat offering:

74One golden spoon of ten *shekels,* full of incense:

Amplified

42The sixth day Eliasaph son of Deuel, leader of the sons of Gad, offered.

43His offering was one silver platter of the weight of 130 shekels, a silver basin of seventy shekels, after the shekel of the sanctuary, both of them full of fine flour mixed with oil for a cereal offering;

44One golden bowl of ten shekels, full of incense;

45One young bull, one ram, one male lamb a year old, for a burnt offering;

46One male goat for a sin offering;

47And for the sacrifice of peace offerings, two oxen, five rams, five male goats, [and] five male lambs a year old. This was the offering of Eliasaph son of Deuel.

48The seventh day Elishama son of Ammihud, leader of the sons of Ephraim, offered.

49His offering was one silver platter, the weight of which was 130 shekels, one silver basin of seventy shekels, after the shekel of the sanctuary, both of them full of fine flour mixed with oil for a cereal offering;

50One golden bowl of ten shekels, full of incense;

51One young bull, one ram, one male lamb a year old, for a burnt offering;

52One male goat for a sin offering;

53And for the sacrifice of peace offerings, two oxen, five rams, five male goats, [and] five male lambs a year old. This was the offering of Elishama son of Ammihud.

54The eighth day Gamaliel son of Pedahzur, leader of the sons of Manasseh, offered.

55His offering was one silver platter of the weight of 130 shekels, one silver basin of seventy shekels, after the shekel of the sanctuary, both of them full of fine flour mixed with oil for a cereal offering;

56One golden bowl of ten shekels, full of incense;

57One young bull, one ram, one male lamb a year old, for a burnt offering;

58One male goat for a sin offering;

59And for the sacrifice of peace offerings, two oxen, five rams, five male goats, five male lambs a year old. This was the offering of Gamaliel son of Pedahzur.

60The ninth day Abidan son of Gideoni, prince *or* leader of the sons of Benjamin, offered.

61His offering was one silver platter, the weight of which was 130 shekels, one silver basin of seventy shekels, after the shekel of the sanctuary, both of them full of fine flour mixed with oil for a cereal offering;

62One golden bowl of ten shekels, full of incense;

63One young bull, one ram, one male lamb a year old, for a burnt offering;

64One male goat for a sin offering;

65And for the sacrifice of peace offerings, two oxen, five rams, five male goats, five male lambs a year old. This was the offering of Abidan son of Gideoni.

66The tenth day Ahiezer son of Ammishaddai, leader of the sons of Dan, offered.

67His offering was one silver platter, the weight of which was 130 shekels, one silver basin of seventy shekels, after the shekel of the sanctuary, both of them full of fine flour mixed with oil for a cereal offering;

68One golden bowl of ten shekels, full of incense;

69One young bull, one ram, one male lamb a year old, for a burnt offering;

70One male goat for a sin offering;

71And for the sacrifice of peace offerings, two oxen, five rams, five male goats, five male lambs a year old. This was the offering of Ahiezer son of Ammishaddai.

72The eleventh day Pagiel son of Ochran, leader of the sons of Asher, offered.

73His offering was one silver platter, the weight of which was 130 shekels, one silver basin of seventy shekels, after the shekel of the sanctuary, both of them full of fine flour mixed with oil for a cereal offering;

74One golden bowl of ten shekels, full of incense;

ˣOr, *Reuel*

New American Standard

42 ¶ On the sixth day *it was* Eliasaph the son of Deuel, leader of the sons of Gad;

43 his offering *was* one silver dish whose weight *was* one hundred and thirty *shekels,* one silver bowl of seventy shekels, according to the shekel of the sanctuary, both of them full of fine flour mixed with oil for a grain offering;

44 one gold pan of ten *shekels,* full of incense;

45 one bull, one ram, one male lamb one year old, for a burnt offering;

46 one male goat for a sin offering;

47 and for the sacrifice of peace offerings, two oxen, five rams, five male goats, five male lambs one year old. This *was* the offering of Eliasaph the son of Deuel.

48 ¶ On the seventh day *it was* Elishama the son of Ammihud, leader of the sons of Ephraim;

49 his offering *was* one silver dish whose weight *was* one hundred and thirty *shekels,* one silver bowl of seventy shekels, according to the shekel of the sanctuary, both of them full of fine flour mixed with oil for a grain offering;

50 one gold pan of ten *shekels,* full of incense;

51 one bull, one ram, one male lamb one year old, for a burnt offering;

52 one male goat for a sin offering;

53 and for the sacrifice of peace offerings, two oxen, five rams, five male goats, five male lambs one year old. This *was* the offering of Elishama the son of Ammihud.

54 ¶ On the eighth day *it was* Gamaliel the son of Pedahzur, leader of the sons of Manasseh;

55 his offering *was* one silver dish whose weight *was* one hundred and thirty *shekels,* one silver bowl of seventy shekels, according to the shekel of the sanctuary, both of them full of fine flour mixed with oil for a grain offering;

56 one gold pan of ten *shekels,* full of incense;

57 one bull, one ram, one male lamb one year old, for a burnt offering;

58 one male goat for a sin offering;

59 and for the sacrifice of peace offerings, two oxen, five rams, five male goats, five male lambs one year old. This *was* the offering of Gamaliel the son of Pedahzur.

60 ¶ On the ninth day *it was* Abidan the son of Gideoni, leader of the sons of Benjamin;

61 his offering *was* one silver dish whose weight *was* one hundred and thirty *shekels,* one silver bowl of seventy shekels, according to the shekel of the sanctuary, both of them full of fine flour mixed with oil for a grain offering;

62 one gold pan of ten *shekels,* full of incense;

63 one bull, one ram, one male lamb one year old, for a burnt offering;

64 one male goat for a sin offering;

65 and for the sacrifice of peace offerings, two oxen, five rams, five male goats, five male lambs one year old. This *was* the offering of Abidan the son of Gideoni.

66 ¶ On the tenth day *it was* Ahiezer the son of Ammishaddai, leader of the sons of Dan;

67 his offering *was* one silver dish whose weight *was* one hundred and thirty *shekels,* one silver bowl of seventy shekels, according to the shekel of the sanctuary, both of them full of fine flour mixed with oil for a grain offering;

68 one gold pan of ten *shekels,* full of incense;

69 one bull, one ram, one male lamb one year old, for a burnt offering;

70 one male goat for a sin offering;

71 and for the sacrifice of peace offerings, two oxen, five rams, five male goats, five male lambs one year old. This *was* the offering of Ahiezer the son of Ammishaddai.

72 ¶ On the eleventh day *it was* Pagiel the son of Ochran, leader of the sons of Asher;

73 his offering *was* one silver dish whose weight *was* one hundred and thirty *shekels,* one silver bowl of seventy shekels, according to the shekel of the sanctuary, both of them full of fine flour mixed with oil for a grain offering;

74 one gold pan of ten *shekels,* full of incense;

New International

42 On the sixth day Eliasaph son of Deuel, the leader of the people of Gad, brought his offering.

43 His offering was one silver plate weighing a hundred and thirty shekels, and one silver sprinkling bowl weighing seventy shekels, both according to the sanctuary shekel, each filled with fine flour mixed with oil as a grain offering; 44 one gold dish weighing ten shekels, filled with incense; 45 one young bull, one ram and one male lamb a year old, for a burnt offering; 46 one male goat for a sin offering; 47 and two oxen, five rams, five male goats and five male lambs a year old, to be sacrificed as a fellowship offering. This was the offering of Eliasaph son of Deuel.

48 On the seventh day Elishama son of Ammihud, the leader of the people of Ephraim, brought his offering.

49 His offering was one silver plate weighing a hundred and thirty shekels, and one silver sprinkling bowl weighing seventy shekels, both according to the sanctuary shekel, each filled with fine flour mixed with oil as a grain offering; 50 one gold dish weighing ten shekels, filled with incense; 51 one young bull, one ram and one male lamb a year old, for a burnt offering; 52 one male goat for a sin offering; 53 and two oxen, five rams, five male goats and five male lambs a year old, to be sacrificed as a fellowship offering. This was the offering of Elishama son of Ammihud.

54 On the eighth day Gamaliel son of Pedahzur, the leader of the people of Manasseh, brought his offering.

55 His offering was one silver plate weighing a hundred and thirty shekels, and one silver sprinkling bowl weighing seventy shekels, both according to the sanctuary shekel, each filled with fine flour mixed with oil as a grain offering; 56 one gold dish weighing ten shekels, filled with incense; 57 one young bull, one ram and one male lamb a year old, for a burnt offering; 58 one male goat for a sin offering; 59 and two oxen, five rams, five male goats and five male lambs a year old, to be sacrificed as a fellowship offering. This was the offering of Gamaliel son of Pedahzur.

60 On the ninth day Abidan son of Gideoni, the leader of the people of Benjamin, brought his offering.

61 His offering was one silver plate weighing a hundred and thirty shekels, and one silver sprinkling bowl weighing seventy shekels, both according to the sanctuary shekel, each filled with fine flour mixed with oil as a grain offering; 62 one gold dish weighing ten shekels, filled with incense; 63 one young bull, one ram and one male lamb a year old, for a burnt offering; 64 one male goat for a sin offering; 65 and two oxen, five rams, five male goats and five male lambs a year old, to be sacrificed as a fellowship offering. This was the offering of Abidan son of Gideoni.

66 On the tenth day Ahiezer son of Ammishaddai, the leader of the people of Dan, brought his offering.

67 His offering was one silver plate weighing a hundred and thirty shekels, and one silver sprinkling bowl weighing seventy shekels, both according to the sanctuary shekel, each filled with fine flour mixed with oil as a grain offering; 68 one gold dish weighing ten shekels, filled with incense; 69 one young bull, one ram and one male lamb a year old, for a burnt offering; 70 one male goat for a sin offering; 71 and two oxen, five rams, five male goats and five male lambs a year old, to be sacrificed as a fellowship offering. This was the offering of Ahiezer son of Ammishaddai.

72 On the eleventh day Pagiel son of Ocran, the leader of the people of Asher, brought his offering.

73 His offering was one silver plate weighing a hundred and thirty shekels, and one silver sprinkling bowl weighing seventy shekels, both according to the sanctuary shekel, each filled with fine flour mixed with oil as a grain offering; 74 one gold dish weighing ten shek-

King James

75One young bullock, one ram, one lamb of the first year, for a burnt offering:

76One kid of the goats for a sin offering:

77And for a sacrifice of peace offerings, two oxen, five rams, five he goats, five lambs of the first year: this *was* the offering of Pagiel the son of Ocran.

78 ¶ On the twelfth day Ahira the son of Enan, prince of the children of Naphtali, *offered:*

79His offering *was* one silver charger, the weight whereof *was* an hundred and thirty *shekels,* one silver bowl of seventy shekels, after the shekel of the sanctuary; both of them full of fine flour mingled with oil for a meat offering:

80One golden spoon of ten *shekels,* full of incense:

81One young bullock, one ram, one lamb of the first year, for a burnt offering:

82One kid of the goats for a sin offering:

83And for a sacrifice of peace offerings, two oxen, five rams, five he goats, five lambs of the first year: this *was* the offering of Ahira the son of Enan.

84This *was* the dedication of the altar, in the day when it was anointed, by the princes of Israel: twelve chargers of silver, twelve silver bowls, twelve spoons of gold:

85Each charger of silver *weighing* an hundred and thirty *shekels,* each bowl seventy: all the silver vessels *weighed* two thousand and four hundred *shekels,* after the shekel of the sanctuary:

86The golden spoons *were* twelve, full of incense, *weighing* ten *shekels* apiece, after the shekel of the sanctuary: all the gold of the spoons *was* an hundred and twenty *shekels.*

87All the oxen for the burnt offering *were* twelve bullocks, the rams twelve, the lambs of the first year twelve, with their meat offering: and the kids of the goats for sin offering twelve.

88And all the oxen for the sacrifice of the peace offerings *were* twenty and four bullocks, the rams sixty, the he goats sixty, the lambs of the first year sixty. This *was* the dedication of the altar, after that it was anointed.

89And when Moses was gone into the tabernacle of the congregation to speak with [y]him, then he heard the voice of one speaking unto him from off the mercy seat that *was* upon the ark of testimony, from between the two cherubims: and he spake unto him.

The candlestick

8 AND THE Lord spake unto Moses, saying, 2Speak unto Aaron, and say unto him, When thou lightest the lamps, the seven lamps shall give light over against the candlestick.

3And Aaron did so; he lighted the lamps thereof over against the candlestick, as the Lord commanded Moses.

4And this work of the candlestick *was of* beaten gold, unto the shaft thereof, unto the flowers thereof, *was* beaten work: according unto the pattern which the Lord had shown Moses, so he made the candlestick.

Purification of the Levites

5 ¶ And the Lord spake unto Moses, saying,

6Take the Levites from among the children of Israel, and cleanse them.

Amplified

75One young bull, one ram, one male lamb a year old, for a burnt offering;

76One male goat for a sin offering;

77And for the sacrifice of peace offerings, two oxen, five rams, five male goats, five male lambs a year old. This was the offering of Pagiel son of Ochran.

78The twelfth day Ahira son of Enan, leader of the sons of Naphtali, offered.

79His offering was one silver platter, the weight of which was 130 shekels, one silver basin of seventy shekels, after the shekel of the sanctuary, both of them full of fine flour mixed with oil for a cereal offering;

80One golden bowl of ten shekels, full of incense;

81One young bull, one ram, one male lamb a year old, for a burnt offering;

82One male goat for a sin offering;

83And for the sacrifice of peace offerings, two oxen, five rams, five male goats, five male lambs a year old. This was the offering of Ahira son of Enan.

84This was the dedication offering for the altar [of burnt offering] from the leaders of Israel on the day when it was anointed: twelve platters of silver, twelve silver basins, twelve golden bowls;

85Each platter of silver weighing 130 shekels, each basin seventy; all the silver vessels weighed 2,400 shekels, after the shekel of the sanctuary.

86The twelve golden bowls full of incense, weighing ten shekels apiece, after the shekel of the sanctuary, all the gold of the bowls being 120 shekels.

87All the oxen for the burnt offering were twelve bulls, the rams twelve, the male lambs a year old twelve, together with their cereal offering; and the male goats for a sin offering twelve.

88And all the oxen for the sacrifice of the peace offerings were twenty-four bulls, the rams sixty, the male goats sixty, the male lambs a year old sixty. This was the dedication of the altar [of burnt offering] after it was anointed.

89And when Moses went into the Tent of Meeting to speak with the Lord, he heard the voice speaking to him from above the mercy seat that was upon the ark of the Testimony from between the two cherubim; and He spoke to [Moses].

8 AND THE Lord said to Moses, 2Say to Aaron, When you set up *and* light the lamps, the seven lamps shall be made to give light in front of the lampstand.

3And Aaron did so; he lighted the lamps of the lampstand to give light in front of it, as the Lord commanded Moses.

4And this was the workmanship of the candlestick: beaten *or* turned gold, beaten work [of gold] from its base to its flowers; according to the pattern which the Lord had shown Moses, so he made the lampstand.

5And the Lord said to Moses,

6Take the cLevites from among the Israelites and cleanse them.

---

cThere are many lessons for the Christian in this section (Num. 8:5-22). He sees here the importance of each member of God's family having his own particular task (I Cor. 12). It is necessary that special men be designated for particular duties in order that the work of God's kingdom shall be done in orderly fashion. Those who do the work of God must be cleansed from all defilement of flesh and spirit. No one is fit in himself to serve God. It is only as we see ourselves as guilty sinners saved through the sacrifice of the Lord Jesus Christ at Calvary that we can do anything that is worthwhile in God's sight. Apart from Him, "all our righteousnesses *are* as filthy rags" (Isa. 64:6 KJV). (F. Davidson, ed., *The New Bible Commentary*).

[y]i.e. *God*

New American Standard

75 one bull, one ram, one male lamb one year old, for a burnt offering;

76 one male goat for a sin offering;

77 and for the sacrifice of peace offerings, two oxen, five rams, five male goats, five male lambs one year old. This *was* the offering of Pagiel the son of Ochran.

78 ¶ On the twelfth day *it was* Ahira the son of Enan, leader of the sons of Naphtali;

79 his offering *was* one silver dish whose weight *was* one hundred and thirty *shekels,* one silver bowl of seventy shekels, according to the shekel of the sanctuary, both of them full of fine flour mixed with oil for a grain offering;

80 one gold pan of ten *shekels,* full of incense;

81 one bull, one ram, one male lamb one year old, for a burnt offering;

82 one male goat for a sin offering;

83 and for the sacrifice of peace offerings, two oxen, five rams, five male goats, five male lambs one year old. This *was* the offering of Ahira the son of Enan.

84 ¶ This *was* the dedication *offering* for the altar from the leaders of Israel when it was anointed: twelve silver dishes, twelve silver bowls, twelve gold pans,

85 each silver dish *weighing* one hundred and thirty *shekels* and each bowl seventy; all the silver of the utensils *was* 2,400 *shekels,* according to the shekel of the sanctuary;

86 the twelve gold pans, full of incense, *weighing* ten *shekels* apiece, according to the shekel of the sanctuary, all the gold of the pans 120 *shekels;*

87 all the oxen for the burnt offering twelve bulls, *all* the rams twelve, the male lambs one year old with their grain offering twelve, and the male goats for a sin offering twelve;

88 and all the oxen for the sacrifice of peace offerings 24 bulls, *all* the rams 60, the male goats 60, the male lambs one year old 60. This *was* the dedication *offering* for the altar after it was anointed.

89 ¶ Now when Moses went into the tent of meeting to speak with Him, he heard the voice speaking to him from above the mercy seat that was on the ark of the testimony, from between the two cherubim, so He spoke to him.

The Seven Lamps

8 THEN THE LORD spoke to Moses, saying, 2"Speak to Aaron and say to him, 'When you mount the lamps, the seven lamps will give light in the front of the lampstand.'"

3 Aaron therefore did so; he mounted its lamps at the front of the lampstand, just as the LORD had commanded Moses.

4 Now this was the workmanship of the lampstand, hammered work of gold; from its base to its flowers it was hammered work; according to the pattern which the LORD had showed Moses, so he made the lampstand.

Cleansing the Levites

5 ¶ Again the LORD spoke to Moses, saying,

6"Take the Levites from among the sons of Israel and cleanse them.

New International

els, filled with incense; 75one young bull, one ram and one male lamb a year old, for a burnt offering; 76one male goat for a sin offering; 77and two oxen, five rams, five male goats and five male lambs a year old, to be sacrificed as a fellowship offering. This was the offering of Pagiel son of Ocran.

78On the twelfth day Ahira son of Enan, the leader of the people of Naphtali, brought his offering.

79His offering was one silver plate weighing a hundred and thirty shekels, and one silver sprinkling bowl weighing seventy shekels, both according to the sanctuary shekel, each filled with fine flour mixed with oil as a grain offering; 80one gold dish weighing ten shekels, filled with incense; 81one young bull, one ram and one male lamb a year old, for a burnt offering; 82one male goat for a sin offering; 83and two oxen, five rams, five male goats and five male lambs a year old, to be sacrificed as a fellowship offering. This was the offering of Ahira son of Enan.

84These were the offerings of the Israelite leaders for the dedication of the altar when it was anointed: twelve silver plates, twelve silver sprinkling bowls and twelve gold dishes. 85Each silver plate weighed a hundred and thirty shekels, and each sprinkling bowl seventy shekels. Altogether, the silver dishes weighed two thousand four hundred shekels,^{r} according to the sanctuary shekel. 86The twelve gold dishes filled with incense weighed ten shekels each, according to the sanctuary shekel. Altogether, the gold dishes weighed a hundred and twenty shekels.^{s} 87The total number of animals for the burnt offering came to twelve young bulls, twelve rams and twelve male lambs a year old, together with their grain offering. Twelve male goats were used for the sin offering. 88The total number of animals for the sacrifice of the fellowship offering came to twenty-four oxen, sixty rams, sixty male goats and sixty male lambs a year old. These were the offerings for the dedication of the altar after it was anointed.

89When Moses entered the Tent of Meeting to speak with the LORD, he heard the voice speaking to him from between the two cherubim above the atonement cover on the ark of the Testimony. And he spoke with him.

Setting Up the Lamps

8 THE LORD said to Moses, 2"Speak to Aaron and say to him, 'When you set up the seven lamps, they are to light the area in front of the lampstand.'"

3Aaron did so; he set up the lamps so that they faced forward on the lampstand, just as the LORD commanded Moses. 4This is how the lampstand was made: It was made of hammered gold—from its base to its blossoms. The lampstand was made exactly like the pattern the LORD had shown Moses.

The Setting Apart of the Levites

5The LORD said to Moses: 6"Take the Levites from among the other Israelites and make them ceremonially

---

^{r} 85 That is, about 60 pounds (about 28 kilograms) ^{s} 86 That is, about 3 pounds (about 1.4 kilograms)

King James

7And thus shalt thou do unto them, to cleanse them: Sprinkle water of purifying upon them, and zlet them shave all their flesh, and let them wash their clothes, and so make themselves clean.

8Then let them take a young bullock with his meat offering, even fine flour mingled with oil, and another young bullock shalt thou take for a sin offering.

9And thou shalt bring the Levites before the tabernacle of the congregation: and thou shalt gather the whole assembly of the children of Israel together:

10And thou shalt bring the Levites before the LORD: and the children of Israel shall put their hands upon the Levites:

11And Aaron shall aoffer the Levites before the LORD for an boffering of the children of Israel, that cthey may execute the service of the LORD.

12And the Levites shall lay their hands upon the heads of the bullocks: and thou shalt offer the one for a sin offering, and the other for a burnt offering, unto the LORD, to make an atonement for the Levites.

13And thou shalt set the Levites before Aaron, and before his sons, and offer them for an offering unto the LORD.

14Thus shalt thou separate the Levites from among the children of Israel: and the Levites shall be mine.

15And after that shall the Levites go in to do the service of the tabernacle of the congregation: and thou shalt cleanse them, and offer them for an offering.

16For they are wholly given unto me from among the children of Israel; instead of such as open every womb, even instead of the firstborn of all the children of Israel, have I taken them unto me.

17For all the firstborn of the children of Israel are mine, both man and beast: on the day that I smote every firstborn in the land of Egypt I sanctified them for myself.

18And I have taken the Levites for all the firstborn of the children of Israel.

19And I have given the Levites as da gift to Aaron and to his sons from among the children of Israel, to do the service of the children of Israel in the tabernacle of the congregation, and to make an atonement for the children of Israel: that there be no plague among the children of Israel, when the children of Israel come nigh unto the sanctuary.

20And Moses, and Aaron, and all the congregation of the children of Israel, did to the Levites according unto all that the LORD commanded Moses concerning the Levites, so did the children of Israel unto them.

21And the Levites were purified, and they washed their clothes; and Aaron offered them as an offering before the LORD; and Aaron made an atonement for them to cleanse them.

22And after that went the Levites in to do their service in the tabernacle of the congregation before Aaron, and before his sons: as the LORD had commanded Moses concerning the Levites, so did they unto them.

23 ¶ And the LORD spake unto Moses, saying,

24This is it that belongeth unto the Levites: from twenty and five years old and upward they shall go in to wait upon the service of the tabernacle of the congregation:

25And from the age of fifty years they shall ecease waiting upon the service thereof, and shall serve no more:

26But shall minister with their brethren in the tabernacle of the congregation, to keep the charge, and shall do no service. Thus shalt thou do unto the Levites touching their charge.

Amplified

7And thus you shall do to them to cleanse them: sprinkle the water of purification [water to be used in case of sin] upon them, and let them pass a razor over all their flesh and wash their clothes and cleanse themselves. [Num. 19:17, 18.]

8Then let them take a young bull and its cereal offering of fine flour mixed with oil, and another young bull you shall take for a sin offering.

9You shall present the Levites before the Tent of Meeting, and you shall assemble the whole Israelite congregation.

10And you shall present the Levites before the Lord, and the Israelites shall put their hands upon the Levites,

11And Aaron shall offer the Levites before the Lord as a wave offering from the Israelites and on their behalf, that they may do the service of the Lord.

12Then the Levites shall lay their hands upon the heads of the bulls, and you shall offer the one for a sin offering and the other for a burnt offering to the Lord, to make atonement for the Levites.

13And you shall present the Levites before Aaron and his sons and offer them as a wave offering to the Lord.

14Thus you shall separate the Levites from among the Israelites, and the Levites shall be Mine [in a very special sense].

15And after that the Levites shall go in to do service at the Tent of Meeting, when you have cleansed them and offered them as a wave offering.

16For they are wholly given to Me from among the Israelites; instead of all who open the womb, the firstborn of all the Israelites, I have taken the Levites for Myself.

17For all the firstborn of the Israelites are Mine, both of man and beast; on the day that I smote every firstborn in the land of Egypt [not of Israel], I consecrated them and set them apart for Myself.

18And I have taken the Levites instead of all the firstborn of the Israelites.

19And I have given the Levites as a gift to Aaron and to his sons from among the Israelites to do the service of the Israelites at the Tent of Meeting and to make atonement for them, that there may be no plague among the Israelites if they should come near the sanctuary.

20So Moses and Aaron and all the congregation of the Israelites did thus to the Levites; according to all that the Lord commanded Moses concerning [them], so did the Israelites to them.

21The Levites cleansed and purified themselves and they washed their clothes; and Aaron offered them as a wave offering before the Lord and Aaron made atonement for them to cleanse them.

22And after that the Levites went in to do their service in the Tent of Meeting with the attendance of Aaron and his sons; as the Lord had commanded Moses concerning the Levites, so did they to them.

23And the Lord said to Moses,

24This is what applies to the Levites: from twenty-five years old and upward they shall go in to perform the work of the service of the Tent of Meeting,

25And at the age of fifty years, they shall retire from the warfare of the service and serve no more,

26But shall help their brethren in the Tent of Meeting [attend to protecting the sacred things from being profaned], but shall do no regular or heavy service. Thus shall you direct the Levites in regard to their duties.

---

zHeb. let them cause a razor to pass over   aHeb. wave
bHeb. wave offering   cHeb. they may be to execute   dHeb.
given   eHeb. return from the warfare of the service

New American Standard

7"Thus you shall do to them, for their cleansing: *sprinkle* purifying water on them, and let them use a razor over their whole body and wash their clothes, and they will be clean.

8"Then let them take a bull with its grain offering, fine flour mixed with oil; and a second bull you shall take for a sin offering.

9"So you shall present the Levites before the tent of meeting. You shall also assemble the whole congregation of the sons of Israel,

10 and present the Levites before the LORD; and the sons of Israel shall lay their hands on the Levites.

11"Aaron then shall present the Levites before the LORD as a wave offering from the sons of Israel, that they may qualify to perform the service of the LORD.

12"Now the Levites shall lay their hands on the heads of the bulls; then offer the one for a sin offering and the other for a burnt offering to the LORD, to make atonement for the Levites.

13"You shall have the Levites stand before Aaron and before his sons so as to present them as a wave offering to the LORD.

14 ¶ "Thus you shall separate the Levites from among the sons of Israel, and the Levites shall be Mine.

15"Then after that the Levites may go in to serve the tent of meeting. But you shall cleanse them and present them as a wave offering;

16 for they are wholly given to Me from among the sons of Israel. I have taken them for Myself instead of every first issue of the womb, the firstborn of all the sons of Israel.

17"For every firstborn among the sons of Israel is Mine, among the men and among the animals; on the day that I struck down all the firstborn in the land of Egypt I sanctified them for Myself.

18"But I have taken the Levites instead of every firstborn among the sons of Israel.

19"I have given the Levites as a gift to Aaron and to his sons from among the sons of Israel, to perform the service of the sons of Israel at the tent of meeting and to make atonement on behalf of the sons of Israel, so that there will be no plague among the sons of Israel by their coming near to the sanctuary."

20 ¶ Thus did Moses and Aaron and all the congregation of the sons of Israel to the Levites; according to all that the LORD had commanded Moses concerning the Levites, so the sons of Israel did to them.

21 The Levites, too, purified themselves from sin and washed their clothes; and Aaron presented them as a wave offering before the LORD. Aaron also made atonement for them to cleanse them.

22 Then after that the Levites went in to perform their service in the tent of meeting before Aaron and before his sons; just as the LORD had commanded Moses concerning the Levites, so they did to them.

Retirement

23 ¶ Now the LORD spoke to Moses, saying,

24"This is what *applies* to the Levites: from twenty-five years old and upward they shall enter to perform service in the work of the tent of meeting.

25"But at the age of fifty years they shall retire from service in the work and not work any more.

26"They may, however, assist their brothers in the tent of meeting, to keep an obligation, but they *themselves* shall do no work. Thus you shall deal with the Levites concerning their obligations."

New International

clean. 7To purify them, do this: Sprinkle the water of cleansing on them; then have them shave their whole bodies and wash their clothes, and so purify themselves. 8Have them take a young bull with its grain offering of fine flour mixed with oil; then you are to take a second young bull for a sin offering. 9Bring the Levites to the front of the Tent of Meeting and assemble the whole Israelite community. 10You are to bring the Levites before the LORD, and the Israelites are to lay their hands on them. 11Aaron is to present the Levites before the LORD as a wave offering from the Israelites, so that they may be ready to do the work of the LORD.

12"After the Levites lay their hands on the heads of the bulls, use the one for a sin offering to the LORD and the other for a burnt offering, to make atonement for the Levites. 13Have the Levites stand in front of Aaron and his sons and then present them as a wave offering to the LORD. 14In this way you are to set the Levites apart from the other Israelites, and the Levites will be mine.

15"After you have purified the Levites and presented them as a wave offering, they are to come to do their work at the Tent of Meeting. 16They are the Israelites who are to be given wholly to me. I have taken them as my own in place of the firstborn, the first male offspring from every Israelite woman. 17Every firstborn male in Israel, whether man or animal, is mine. When I struck down all the firstborn in Egypt, I set them apart for myself. 18And I have taken the Levites in place of all the firstborn sons in Israel. 19Of all the Israelites, I have given the Levites as gifts to Aaron and his sons to do the work at the Tent of Meeting on behalf of the Israelites and to make atonement for them so that no plague will strike the Israelites when they go near the sanctuary."

20Moses, Aaron and the whole Israelite community did with the Levites just as the LORD commanded Moses. 21The Levites purified themselves and washed their clothes. Then Aaron presented them as a wave offering before the LORD and made atonement for them to purify them. 22After that, the Levites came to do their work at the Tent of Meeting under the supervision of Aaron and his sons. They did with the Levites just as the LORD commanded Moses.

23The LORD said to Moses, 24"This applies to the Levites: Men twenty-five years old or more shall come to take part in the work at the Tent of Meeting, 25but at the age of fifty, they must retire from their regular service and work no longer. 26They may assist their brothers in performing their duties at the Tent of Meeting, but they themselves must not do the work. This, then, is how you are to assign the responsibilities of the Levites."

King James

The Passover command

9 AND THE LORD spake unto Moses in the wilderness of Sinai, in the first month of the second year after they were come out of the land of Egypt, saying,

²Let the children of Israel also keep the passover at his appointed season.

³In the fourteenth day of this month, ƒat even, ye shall keep it in his appointed season: according to all the rites of it, and according to all the ceremonies thereof, shall ye keep it.

⁴And Moses spake unto the children of Israel, that they should keep the passover.

⁵And they kept the passover on the fourteenth day of the first month at even in the wilderness of Sinai: according to all that the LORD commanded Moses, so did the children of Israel.

⁶ ¶ And there were certain men, who were defiled by the dead body of a man, that they could not keep the passover on that day: and they came before Moses and before Aaron on that day:

⁷And those men said unto him, We *are* defiled by the dead body of a man: wherefore are we kept back, that we may not offer an offering of the LORD in his appointed season among the children of Israel?

⁸And Moses said unto them, Stand still, and I will hear what the LORD will command concerning you.

⁹ ¶ And the LORD spake unto Moses, saying,

¹⁰Speak unto the children of Israel, saying, If any man of you or of your posterity shall be unclean by reason of a dead body, or *be* in a journey afar off, yet he shall keep the passover unto the LORD.

¹¹The fourteenth day of the second month at even they shall keep it, *and* eat it with unleavened bread and bitter *herbs.*

¹²They shall leave none of it unto the morning, nor break any bone of it: according to all the ordinances of the passover they shall keep it.

¹³But the man that *is* clean, and is not in a journey, and forbeareth to keep the passover, even the same soul shall be cut off from among his people: because he brought not the offering of the LORD in his appointed season, that man shall bear his sin.

¹⁴And if a stranger shall sojourn among you, and will keep the passover unto the LORD; according to the ordinance of the passover, and according to the manner thereof, so shall he do: ye shall have one ordinance, both for the stranger, and for him that was born in the land.

The cloud of guidance

15 ¶ And on the day that the tabernacle was reared up the cloud covered the tabernacle, *namely,* the tent of the testimony: and at even there was upon the tabernacle as it were the appearance of fire, until the morning.

¹⁶So it was always: the cloud covered it *by day,* and the appearance of fire by night.

¹⁷And when the cloud was taken up from the tabernacle, then after that the children of Israel journeyed: and in the place where the cloud abode, there the children of Israel pitched their tents.

¹⁸At the commandment of the LORD the children of Israel journeyed, and at the commandment of the LORD they pitched: as long as the cloud abode upon the tabernacle they rested in their tents.

¹⁹And when the cloud ᵍtarried long upon the tabernacle many days, then the children of Israel kept the charge of the LORD, and journeyed not.

²⁰And *so* it was, when the cloud was a few days upon the tabernacle; according to the commandment of the LORD they abode in their tents, and according to the commandment of the LORD they journeyed.

Amplified

9 THE LORD said to Moses in the Wilderness of Sinai in the first month of the second year after they had come out of the land of Egypt,

²Let the Israelites keep the Passover at its appointed time.

³On the fourteenth day of this month in the evening, you shall keep it at its appointed time; according to all its statutes and ordinances you shall keep it.

⁴So Moses told the Israelites they should keep the Passover.

⁵And they kept the Passover on the fourteenth day of the first month in the evening in the Wilderness of Sinai; according to all that the Lord commanded Moses, so the Israelites did.

⁶And there were certain men who were defiled by touching the dead body of a man, so they could not keep the Passover on that day; and they came before Moses and Aaron on that day.

⁷Those men said to [Moses], We are defiled by touching the dead body. Why are we prevented from offering the Lord's offering at its appointed time among the Israelites?

⁸And Moses said to them, Stand still, and I will hear what the Lord will command concerning you.

⁹And the Lord said to Moses,

¹⁰Say to the Israelites, If any man of you or of your posterity shall be unclean by reason of touching a dead body or is far off on a journey, still he shall keep the Passover to the Lord.

¹¹On the fourteenth day of the second month in the evening they shall keep it, and eat it with unleavened bread and bitter herbs.

¹²They shall leave none of it until the morning nor break any bone of it; according to all the statutes for the Passover they shall keep it. [John 19:36.]

¹³But the man who is clean and is not on a journey, yet does not keep the Passover, that person shall be cut off from among his people because he did not bring the Lord's offering at its appointed time; that man shall bear [the penalty of] his sin.

¹⁴And if a stranger sojourns among you and will keep the Passover to the Lord, according to [its] statutes and its ordinances, so shall he do; you shall have one statute both for the temporary resident and for him who was born in the land.

¹⁵And on the day that the tabernacle was erected, the cloud [of God's presence] covered the tabernacle, that is, the Tent of the Testimony; and at evening it was over the tabernacle, having the appearance of [a pillar of] fire until the morning. [Exod. 13:21.]

¹⁶So it was constantly; the cloud covered it by day, and the appearance of fire by night.

¹⁷Whenever the cloud was taken up from over the Tent, after that the Israelites journeyed; and in the place where the cloud rested, there the Israelites encamped.

¹⁸At the Lord's command the Israelites journeyed, and at [His] command they encamped. As long as the cloud rested upon the tabernacle they remained encamped.

¹⁹Even when the cloud tarried upon the tabernacle many days, the Israelites kept the Lord's charge and did not set out.

²⁰And sometimes the cloud was only a few days upon the tabernacle, but according to the command of the Lord they remained encamped, and at His command they journeyed.

ƒHeb. *between the two evenings*   ᵍHeb. *prolonged*

New American Standard

The Passover

9 THUS THE LORD spoke to Moses in the wilderness of Sinai, in the first month of the second year after they had come out of the land of Egypt, saying, 2"Now, let the sons of Israel observe the Passover at its appointed time. 3"On the fourteenth day of this month, at twilight, you shall observe it at its appointed time; you shall observe it according to all its statutes and according to all its ordinances."

4 So Moses told the sons of Israel to observe the Passover.

5 They observed the Passover in the first *month,* on the fourteenth day of the month, at twilight, in the wilderness of Sinai; according to all that the LORD had commanded Moses, so the sons of Israel did. 6 But there were *some* men who were unclean because of *the* dead person, so that they could not observe Passover on that day; so they came before Moses and Aaron on that day. 7 Those men said to him, "*Though* we are unclean because of *the* dead person, why are we restrained from presenting the offering of the LORD at its appointed time among the sons of Israel?"

8 Moses therefore said to them, "Wait, and I will listen to what the LORD will command concerning you."

9 ¶ Then the LORD spoke to Moses, saying, 10"Speak to the sons of Israel, saying, 'If any one of you or of your generations becomes unclean because of a *dead* person, or is on a distant journey, he may, however, observe the Passover to the LORD.

11 'In the second month on the fourteenth day at twilight, they shall observe it; they shall eat it with unleavened bread and bitter herbs.

12 'They shall leave none of it until morning, nor break a bone of it; according to all the statute of the Passover they shall observe it.

13 'But the man who is clean and is not on a journey, and yet neglects to observe the Passover, that person shall then be cut off from his people, for he did not present the offering of the LORD at its appointed time. That man will bear his sin.

14 'If an alien sojourns among you and observes the Passover to the LORD, according to the statute of the Passover and according to its ordinance, so he shall do; you shall have one statute, both for the alien and for the native of the land.' "

The Cloud on the Tabernacle

15 ¶ Now on the day that the tabernacle was erected the cloud covered the tabernacle, the tent of the testimony, and in the evening it was like the appearance of fire over the tabernacle, until morning. 16 So it was continuously; the cloud would cover it *by day,* and the appearance of fire by night. 17 Whenever the cloud was lifted from over the tent, afterward the sons of Israel would then set out; and in the place where the cloud settled down, there the sons of Israel would camp. 18 At the command of the LORD the sons of Israel would set out, and at the command of the LORD they would camp; as long as the cloud settled over the tabernacle, they remained camped. 19 Even when the cloud lingered over the tabernacle for many days, the sons of Israel would keep the LORD'S charge and not set out. 20 If sometimes the cloud remained a few days over the tabernacle, according to the command of the LORD they remained camped. Then according to the command of the LORD they set out.

New International

The Passover

9 THE LORD spoke to Moses in the Desert of Sinai in the first month of the second year after they came out of Egypt. He said, 2"Have the Israelites celebrate the Passover at the appointed time. 3Celebrate it at the appointed time, at twilight on the fourteenth day of this month, in accordance with all its rules and regulations."

4So Moses told the Israelites to celebrate the Passover, 5and they did so in the Desert of Sinai at twilight on the fourteenth day of the first month. The Israelites did everything just as the LORD commanded Moses.

6But some of them could not celebrate the Passover on that day because they were ceremonially unclean on account of a dead body. So they came to Moses and Aaron that same day 7and said to Moses, "We have become unclean because of a dead body, but why should we be kept from presenting the LORD's offering with the other Israelites at the appointed time?"

8Moses answered them, "Wait until I find out what the LORD commands concerning you."

9Then the LORD said to Moses, 10"Tell the Israelites: 'When any of you or your descendants are unclean because of a dead body or are away on a journey, they may still celebrate the LORD's Passover. 11They are to celebrate it on the fourteenth day of the second month at twilight. They are to eat the lamb, together with unleavened bread and bitter herbs. 12They must not leave any of it till morning or break any of its bones. When they celebrate the Passover, they must follow all the regulations. 13But if a man who is ceremonially clean and not on a journey fails to celebrate the Passover, that person must be cut off from his people because he did not present the LORD's offering at the appointed time. That man will bear the consequences of his sin.

14" 'An alien living among you who wants to celebrate the LORD's Passover must do so in accordance with its rules and regulations. You must have the same regulations for the alien and the native-born.' "

The Cloud Above the Tabernacle

15On the day the tabernacle, the Tent of the Testimony, was set up, the cloud covered it. From evening till morning the cloud above the tabernacle looked like fire. 16That is how it continued to be; the cloud covered it, and at night it looked like fire. 17Whenever the cloud lifted from above the Tent, the Israelites set out; wherever the cloud settled, the Israelites encamped. 18At the LORD's command the Israelites set out, and at his command they encamped. As long as the cloud stayed over the tabernacle, they remained in camp. 19When the cloud remained over the tabernacle a long time, the Israelites obeyed the LORD's order and did not set out. 20Sometimes the cloud was over the tabernacle only a few days; at the LORD's command they would encamp, and then at his command they would set out.

King James

²¹And *so* it was, when the cloud *h*abode from even unto the morning, and *that* the cloud was taken up in the morning, then they journeyed: whether *it was* by day or by night that the cloud was taken up, they journeyed.

²²Or *whether it were* two days, or a month, or a year, that the cloud tarried upon the tabernacle, remaining thereon, the children of Israel abode in their tents, and journeyed not: but when it was taken up, they journeyed.

²³At the commandment of the LORD they rested in the tents, and at the commandment of the LORD they journeyed: they kept the charge of the LORD, at the commandment of the LORD by the hand of Moses.

The two silver trumpets

10

AND THE LORD spake unto Moses, saying, ²Make thee two trumpets of silver; of a whole piece shalt thou make them: that thou mayest use them for the calling of the assembly, and for the journeying of the camps.

³And when they shall blow with them, all the assembly shall assemble themselves to thee at the door of the tabernacle of the congregation.

⁴And if they blow *but* with one *trumpet,* then the princes, *which are* heads of the thousands of Israel, shall gather themselves unto thee.

⁵When ye blow an alarm, then the camps that lie on the east parts shall go forward.

⁶When ye blow an alarm the second time, then the camps that lie on the south side shall take their journey: they shall blow an alarm for their journeys.

⁷But when the congregation is to be gathered together, ye shall blow, but ye shall not sound an alarm.

⁸And the sons of Aaron, the priests, shall blow with the trumpets; and they shall be to you for an ordinance for ever throughout your generations.

⁹And if ye go to war in your land against the enemy that oppresseth you, then ye shall blow an alarm with the trumpets; and ye shall be remembered before the LORD your God, and ye shall be saved from your enemies.

¹⁰Also in the day of your gladness, and in your solemn days, and in the beginnings of your months, ye shall blow with the trumpets over your burnt offerings, and over the sacrifices of your peace offerings; that they may be to you for a memorial before your God: I *am* the LORD your God.

The departure from Sinai

¹¹ ¶ And it came to pass on the twentieth *day* of the second month, in the second year, that the cloud was taken up from off the tabernacle of the testimony.

¹²And the children of Israel took their journeys out of the wilderness of Sinai; and the cloud rested in the wilderness of Paran.

¹³And they first took their journey according to the commandment of the LORD by the hand of Moses.

¹⁴ ¶ In the first *place* went the standard of the camp of the children of Judah according to their armies: and over his host *was* Nahshon the son of Amminadab.

¹⁵And over the host of the tribe of the children of Issachar *was* Nethaneel the son of Zuar.

¹⁶And over the host of the tribe of the children of Zebulun *was* Eliab the son of Helon.

¹⁷And the tabernacle was taken down; and the sons of Gershon and the sons of Merari set forward, bearing the tabernacle.

¹⁸ ¶ And the standard of the camp of Reuben set forward according to their armies: and over his host *was* Elizur the son of Shedeur.

¹⁹And over the host of the tribe of the children of Simeon *was* Shelumiel the son of Zurishaddai.

²⁰And over the host of the tribe of the children of Gad *was* Eliasaph the son of Deuel.

Amplified

²¹And sometimes the cloud remained [over the tabernacle] from evening only until morning, but when the cloud was taken up, they journeyed; whether it was taken up by day or by night, they journeyed.

²²Whether it was two days or a month or a longer time that the cloud tarried upon the tabernacle, dwelling on it, the Israelites remained encamped; but when it was taken up, they journeyed.

²³At the command of the Lord they remained encamped, and at [His] command they journeyed; they kept the charge of the Lord, at the command of the Lord through Moses.

10

AND THE Lord said to Moses, ²Make two trumpets of silver; of hammered *or* turned work you shall make them, that you may use them to call the congregation and for breaking camp.

³When they both are blown, all the congregation shall assemble before you at the door of the Tent of Meeting.

⁴And if one blast on a single trumpet is blown, then the princes *or* leaders, heads of the tribes of Israel, shall gather themselves to you.

⁵When you blow an alarm, the camps on the east side [of the tabernacle] shall set out.

⁶When you blow an alarm the second time, then the camps on the south side shall set out. An alarm shall be blown whenever they are to set out on their journeys.

⁷When the congregation is to be assembled, you shall blow [the trumpets in short, sharp tones], but not the blast of an alarm.

⁸And the sons of Aaron, the priests, shall blow the trumpets, and the trumpets shall be to you for a perpetual statute throughout your generations.

⁹When you go to war in your land against the enemy that oppresses you, then blow an alarm with the trumpets, that you may be remembered before the Lord your God, and you shall be saved from your enemies.

¹⁰Also in the day of rejoicing, and in your set feasts, and at the beginnings of your months, you shall blow the trumpets over your burnt offerings and your peace offerings; thus they may be a remembrance before your God. I am the Lord your God.

¹¹On the twentieth day of the second month in the second year [since leaving Egypt], the cloud [of the Lord's presence] was taken up from over the tabernacle of the Testimony,

¹²And the Israelites took their journey by stages out of the Wilderness of Sinai, and the [guiding] cloud rested in the Wilderness of Paran.

¹³When the journey was to begin, at the command of the Lord through Moses,

¹⁴In the first place went the standard of the camp of the sons of Judah by their companies; and over their host was Nahshon son of Amminadab.

¹⁵And over the host of the tribe of the sons of Issachar was Nethanel son of Zuar.

¹⁶And over the host of the tribe of the sons of Zebulun was Eliab son of Helon.

¹⁷When the tabernacle was taken down, the sons of Gershon and Merari, bearing [it] on their shoulders, set out.

¹⁸The standard of the camp of Reuben set forward by their companies; and over Reuben's host was Elizur son of Shedeur.

¹⁹And over the host of the tribe of the sons of Simeon was Shelumiel son of Zurishaddai.

²⁰And over the host of the tribe of the sons of Gad was Eliasaph son of Deuel.

---

h Heb. *was*

New American Standard

21 If sometimes the cloud remained from evening until morning, when the cloud was lifted in the morning, they would move out; or *if it remained* in the daytime and at night, whenever the cloud was lifted, they would set out. 22 Whether it was two days or a month or a year that the cloud lingered over the tabernacle, staying above it, the sons of Israel remained camped and did not set out; but when it was lifted, they did set out. 23 At the command of the LORD they camped, and at the command of the LORD they set out; they kept the LORD's charge, according to the command of the LORD through Moses.

The Silver Trumpets

10 THE LORD spoke further to Moses, saying, 2 "Make yourself two trumpets of silver, of hammered work you shall make them; and you shall use them for summoning the congregation and for having the camps set out. 3 "When both are blown, all the congregation shall gather themselves to you at the doorway of the tent of meeting. 4 "Yet if *only* one is blown, then the leaders, the heads of the divisions of Israel, shall assemble before you. 5 "But when you blow an alarm, the camps that are pitched on the east side shall set out. 6 "When you blow an alarm the second time, the camps that are pitched on the south side shall set out; an alarm is to be blown for them to set out. 7 "When convening the assembly, however, you shall blow without sounding an alarm. 8 "The priestly sons of Aaron, moreover, shall blow the trumpets; and this shall be for you a perpetual statute throughout your generations. 9 "When you go to war in your land against the adversary who attacks you, then you shall sound an alarm with the trumpets, that you may be remembered before the LORD your God, and be saved from your enemies. 10 "Also in the day of your gladness and in your appointed feasts, and on the first *days* of your months, you shall blow the trumpets over your burnt offerings, and over the sacrifices of your peace offerings; and they shall be as a reminder of you before your God. I am the LORD your God."

The Tribes Leave Sinai

11 ¶ Now in the second year, in the second month, on the twentieth of the month, the cloud was lifted from over the tabernacle of the testimony; 12 and the sons of Israel set out on their journeys from the wilderness of Sinai. Then the cloud settled down in the wilderness of Paran. 13 So they moved out for the first time according to the commandment of the LORD through Moses. 14 The standard of the camp of the sons of Judah, according to their armies, set out first, with Nahshon the son of Amminadab, over its army, 15 and Nethanel the son of Zuar, over the tribal army of the sons of Issachar; 16 and Eliab the son of Helon over the tribal army of the sons of Zebulun. 17 ¶ Then the tabernacle was taken down; and the sons of Gershon and the sons of Merari, who were carrying the tabernacle, set out. 18 Next the standard of the camp of Reuben, according to their armies, set out with Elizur the son of Shedeur, over its army, 19 and Shelumiel the son of Zurishaddai over the tribal army of the sons of Simeon, 20 and Eliasaph the son of Deuel was over the tribal army of the sons of Gad.

New International

21 Sometimes the cloud stayed only from evening till morning, and when it lifted in the morning, they set out. Whether by day or by night, whenever the cloud lifted, they set out. 22 Whether the cloud stayed over the tabernacle for two days or a month or a year, the Israelites would remain in camp and not set out; but when it lifted, they would set out. 23 At the LORD's command they encamped, and at the LORD's command they set out. They obeyed the LORD's order, in accordance with his command through Moses.

The Silver Trumpets

10 THE LORD said to Moses: 2 "Make two trumpets of hammered silver, and use them for calling the community together and for having the camps set out. 3 When both are sounded, the whole community is to assemble before you at the entrance to the Tent of Meeting. 4 If only one is sounded, the leaders—the heads of the clans of Israel—are to assemble before you. 5 When a trumpet blast is sounded, the tribes camping on the east are to set out. 6 At the sounding of a second blast, the camps on the south are to set out. The blast will be the signal for setting out. 7 To gather the assembly, blow the trumpets, but not with the same signal.

8 "The sons of Aaron, the priests, are to blow the trumpets. This is to be a lasting ordinance for you and the generations to come. 9 When you go into battle in your own land against an enemy who is oppressing you, sound a blast on the trumpets. Then you will be remembered by the LORD your God and rescued from your enemies. 10 Also at your times of rejoicing—your appointed feasts and New Moon festivals—you are to sound the trumpets over your burnt offerings and fellowship offerings,[t] and they will be a memorial for you before your God. I am the LORD your God."

The Israelites Leave Sinai

11 On the twentieth day of the second month of the second year, the cloud lifted from above the tabernacle of the Testimony. 12 Then the Israelites set out from the Desert of Sinai and traveled from place to place until the cloud came to rest in the Desert of Paran. 13 They set out, this first time, at the LORD's command through Moses. 14 The divisions of the camp of Judah went first, under their standard. Nahshon son of Amminadab was in command. 15 Nethanel son of Zuar was over the division of the tribe of Issachar, 16 and Eliab son of Helon was over the division of the tribe of Zebulun. 17 Then the tabernacle was taken down, and the Gershonites and Merarites, who carried it, set out. 18 The divisions of the camp of Reuben went next, under their standard. Elizur son of Shedeur was in command. 19 Shelumiel son of Zurishaddai was over the division of the tribe of Simeon, 20 and Eliasaph son of Deuel was over

---

t 10 Traditionally *peace offerings*

King James

²¹And the Kohathites set forward, bearing the sanctuary: and *the other* did set up the tabernacle against they came.

²² ¶ And the standard of the camp of the children of Ephraim set forward according to their armies: and over his host *was* Elishama the son of Ammihud.

²³And over the host of the tribe of the children of Manasseh *was* Gamaliel the son of Pedahzur.

²⁴And over the host of the tribe of the children of Benjamin *was* Abidan the son of Gideoni.

²⁵ ¶ And the standard of the camp of the children of Dan set forward, *which was* the rearward of all the camps throughout their hosts: and over his host *was* Ahiezer the son of Ammishaddai.

²⁶And over the host of the tribe of the children of Asher *was* Pagiel the son of Ocran.

²⁷And over the host of the tribe of the children of Naphtali *was* Ahira the son of Enan.

²⁸ʲThus *were* the journeyings of the children of Israel according to their armies, when they set forward.

²⁹ ¶ And Moses said unto Hobab, the son of Raguel the Midianite, Moses' father-in-law, We are journeying unto the place of which the LORD said, I will give it you: come thou with us, and we will do thee good: for the LORD hath spoken good concerning Israel.

³⁰And he said unto him, I will not go; but I will depart to mine own land, and to my kindred.

³¹And he said, Leave us not, I pray thee; forasmuch as thou knowest how we are to encamp in the wilderness, and thou mayest be to us instead of eyes.

³²And it shall be, if thou go with us, yea, it shall be, that what goodness the LORD shall do unto us, the same will we do unto thee.

³³ ¶ And they departed from the mount of the LORD three days' journey: and the ark of the covenant of the LORD went before them in the three days' journey, to search out a resting place for them.

³⁴And the cloud of the LORD *was* upon them by day, when they went out of the camp.

³⁵And it came to pass, when the ark set forward, that Moses said, Rise up, LORD, and let thine enemies be scattered; and let them that hate thee flee before thee.

³⁶And when it rested, he said, Return, O LORD, unto the ᵏmany thousands of Israel.

The people complain

11 AND *WHEN* the people ˡcomplained, ᵐit displeased the LORD: and the LORD heard *it;* and his anger was kindled; and the fire of the LORD burnt among them, and consumed *them that were* in the uttermost parts of the camp.

²And the people cried unto Moses; and when Moses prayed unto the LORD, the fire ⁿwas quenched.

³And he called the name of the place ᵒTaberah: because the fire of the LORD burnt among them.

God sends quail

⁴ ¶ And the mixed multitude that *was* among them ᵖfell a-lusting: and the children of Israel also qwept again, and said, Who shall give us flesh to eat?

⁵We remember the fish, which we did eat in Egypt freely; the cucumbers, and the melons, and the leeks, and the onions, and the garlic:

⁶But now our soul *is* dried away: *there is* nothing at all, beside this manna, *before* our eyes.

⁷And the manna *was* as coriander seed, and the ʳcolour thereof as the colour of bdellium.

Amplified

²¹Then the Kohathites set forward, bearing the holy things, and the tabernacle was set up before they arrived.

²²And the standard of the camp of the sons of Ephraim set forward according to their companies; and over Ephraim's host was Elishama son of Ammihud.

²³Over the host of the tribe of the sons of Manasseh was Gamaliel son of Pedahzur.

²⁴And over the host of the tribe of the sons of Benjamin was Abidan son of Gideoni.

²⁵Then the standard of the camp of the sons of Dan, which was the rear guard of all the camps, set forward according to their companies; and over Dan's host was Ahiezer son of Ammishaddai.

²⁶And over the host of the tribe of the sons of Asher was Pagiel son of Ochran.

²⁷And over the host of the tribe of the sons of Naphtali was Ahira son of Enan.

²⁸This was the Israelites' order of march by their hosts when they set out.

²⁹And Moses said to Hobab son of Reuel the Midianite, Moses' father-in-law, We are journeying to the place of which the Lord said, I will give it to you. Come with us, and we will do you good, for the Lord has promised good concerning Israel.

³⁰And Hobab said to him, I will not go; I will depart to my own land and to my family.

³¹And Moses said, ᵈDo not leave us, I pray you; for you know how we are to encamp in the wilderness, and you will serve as eyes for us.

³²And if you will go with us, it shall be that whatever good the Lord does to us, the same we will do to you.

³³They departed from the mountain of the Lord [Mount Sinai] three days' journey; and the ark of the covenant of the Lord went before them during the three days' journey to seek out a resting-place for them.

³⁴The cloud of the Lord was over them by day when they went forward from the camp.

³⁵Whenever the ark set out, Moses said, Rise up, Lord; let Your enemies be scattered; and let those who hate You flee before You. [Ps. 68:1, 2.]

³⁶And when it rested, he said, Return, O Lord, to the ten thousand thousands in Israel.

11 AND THE people grumbled *and* deplored their hardships, which was evil in the ears of the Lord, and when the Lord heard it, His anger was kindled; and the fire of the Lord burned among them and devoured those in the outlying parts of the camp.

²The people cried to Moses, and when Moses prayed to the Lord, the fire subsided.

³He called the name of the place Taberah [burning], because the fire of the Lord burned among them.

⁴And the mixed multitude among them [the rabble who followed Israel from Egypt] began to lust greatly [for familiar and dainty food], and the Israelites wept again and said, Who will give us meat to eat?

⁵We remember the fish we ate freely in Egypt *and* without cost, the cucumbers, melons, leeks, onions, and garlic.

⁶But now our soul (our strength) is dried up; there is nothing at all [in the way of food] to be seen but this manna.

⁷The manna was like coriander seed and its appearance was like that of bdellium [perhaps a precious stone].

ⁱi.e. *the Gershonites and the Merarites; see ver. 17; ch. 1:51*
ʲHeb. *These*   ᵏHeb. *ten thousand thousands*   ˡOr, *were as it were complainers*   ᵐHeb. *it was evil in the ears of*   ⁿHeb. *sunk*   ᵒi.e. *A burning*   ᵖHeb. *lusted a lust*   qHeb. *returned and wept*   ʳHeb. *eye of it as the eye of*

ᵈThe record does not say so, but Hobab seems to have remained with the Israelites, for later history shows that his descendants lived in Canaan (Judg. 1:16; I Sam. 15:6).

New American Standard

21 ¶ Then the Kohathites set out, carrying the holy *objects;* and the tabernacle was set up before their arrival.
22 Next the standard of the camp of the sons of Ephraim, according to their armies, was set out, with Elishama the son of Ammihud over its army,
23 and Gamaliel the son of Pedahzur over the tribal army of the sons of Manasseh;
24 and Abidan the son of Gideoni over the tribal army of the sons of Benjamin.
25 ¶ Then the standard of the camp of the sons of Dan, according to their armies, *which formed* the rear guard for all the camps, set out, with Ahiezer the son of Ammishaddai over its army,
26 and Pagiel the son of Ochran over the tribal army of the sons of Asher;
27 and Ahira the son of Enan over the tribal army of the sons of Naphtali.
28 This was the order of march of the sons of Israel by their armies as they set out.
29 ¶ Then Moses said to Hobab the son of Reuel the Midianite, Moses' father-in-law, "We are setting out to the place of which the LORD said, 'I will give it to you'; come with us and we will do you good, for the LORD has promised good concerning Israel."
30 But he said to him, "I will not come, but rather will go to my *own* land and relatives."
31 Then he said, "Please do not leave us, inasmuch as you know where we should camp in the wilderness, and you will be as eyes for them.
32 "So it will be, if you go with us, that whatever good the LORD does for us, we will do for you."
33 ¶ Thus they set out from the mount of the LORD three days' journey, with the ark of the covenant of the LORD journeying in front of them for the three days, to seek out a resting place for them.
34 The cloud of the LORD was over them by day when they set out from the camp.
35 ¶ Then it came about when the ark set out that Moses said,

"Rise up, O LORD!
And let Your enemies be scattered,
And let those who hate You flee *l*before You."

36 When it came to rest, he said,

"Return, O LORD,
To the myriad thousands of Israel."

The People Complain

11 NOW THE people became like those who complain of adversity in the hearing of the LORD; and when the LORD heard *it,* His anger was kindled, and the fire of the LORD burned among them and consumed *some* of the outskirts of the camp.
2 The people therefore cried out to Moses, and Moses prayed to the LORD and the fire died out.
3 So the name of that place was called *m*Taberah, because the fire of the LORD burned among them.
4 ¶ The rabble who were among them had greedy desires; and also the sons of Israel wept again and said, "Who will give us meat to eat?
5 "We remember the fish which we used to eat free in Egypt, the cucumbers and the melons and the leeks and the onions and the garlic,
6 but now our *n*appetite is gone. There is nothing at all to look at except this manna."
7 ¶ Now the manna was like coriander seed, and its appearance like that of bdellium.

the division of the tribe of Gad. 21Then the Kohathites set out, carrying the holy things. The tabernacle was to be set up before they arrived.
22The divisions of the camp of Ephraim went next, under their standard. Elishama son of Ammihud was in command. 23Gamaliel son of Pedahzur was over the division of the tribe of Manasseh, 24and Abidan son of Gideoni was over the division of the tribe of Benjamin.
25Finally, as the rear guard for all the units, the divisions of the camp of Dan set out, under their standard. Ahiezer son of Ammishaddai was in command. 26Pagiel son of Ocran was over the division of the tribe of Asher, 27and Ahira son of Enan was over the division of the tribe of Naphtali. 28This was the order of march for the Israelite divisions as they set out.
29Now Moses said to Hobab son of Reuel the Midianite, Moses' father-in-law, "We are setting out for the place about which the LORD said, 'I will give it to you.' Come with us and we will treat you well, for the LORD has promised good things to Israel."
30He answered, "No, I will not go; I am going back to my own land and my own people."
31But Moses said, "Please do not leave us. You know where we should camp in the desert, and you can be our eyes. 32If you come with us, we will share with you whatever good things the LORD gives us."
33So they set out from the mountain of the LORD and traveled for three days. The ark of the covenant of the LORD went before them during those three days to find them a place to rest. 34The cloud of the LORD was over them by day when they set out from the camp.
35Whenever the ark set out, Moses said,

"Rise up, O LORD!
May your enemies be scattered;
may your foes flee before you."

36Whenever it came to rest, he said,

"Return, O LORD,
to the countless thousands of Israel."

Fire From the LORD

11 NOW THE people complained about their hardships in the hearing of the LORD, and when he heard them his anger was aroused. Then fire from the LORD burned among them and consumed some of the outskirts of the camp. 2When the people cried out to Moses, he prayed to the LORD and the fire died down. 3So that place was called Taberah,*u* because fire from the LORD had burned among them.

Quail From the LORD

4The rabble with them began to crave other food, and again the Israelites started wailing and said, "If only we had meat to eat! 5We remember the fish we ate in Egypt at no cost—also the cucumbers, melons, leeks, onions and garlic. 6But now we have lost our appetite; we never see anything but this manna!"
7The manna was like coriander seed and looked like

---

*l*Or *from Your presence*　　*m*I.e. *burning*　　*n*Lit *soul is dried up*　　*u*3 *Taberah* means *burning.*

King James

⁸*And* the people went about, and gathered *it,* and ground *it* in mills, or beat *it* in a mortar, and baked *it* in pans, and made cakes of it: and the taste of it was as the taste of fresh oil.

⁹And when the dew fell upon the camp in the night, the manna fell upon it.

¹⁰ ¶ Then Moses heard the people weep throughout their families, every man in the door of his tent: and the anger of the LORD was kindled greatly; Moses also was displeased.

¹¹And Moses said unto the LORD, Wherefore hast thou afflicted thy servant? and wherefore have I not found favour in thy sight, that thou layest the burden of all this people upon me?

¹²Have I conceived all this people? have I begotten them, that thou shouldest say unto me, Carry them in thy bosom, as a nursing father beareth the sucking child, unto the land which thou swarest unto their fathers?

¹³Whence should I have flesh to give unto all this people? for they weep unto me, saying, Give us flesh, that we may eat.

¹⁴I am not able to bear all this people alone, because *it is* too heavy for me.

¹⁵And if thou deal thus with me, kill me, I pray thee, out of hand, if I have found favour in thy sight; and let me not see my wretchedness.

¹⁶ ¶ And the LORD said unto Moses, Gather unto me seventy men of the elders of Israel, whom thou knowest to be the elders of the people, and officers over them; and bring them unto the tabernacle of the congregation, that they may stand there with thee.

¹⁷And I will come down and talk with thee there: and I will take of the spirit which *is* upon thee, and will put *it* upon them; and they shall bear the burden of the people with thee, that thou bear *it* not thyself alone.

¹⁸And say thou unto the people, Sanctify yourselves against tomorrow, and ye shall eat flesh: for ye have wept in the ears of the LORD, saying, Who shall give us flesh to eat? for *it was* well with us in Egypt: therefore the LORD will give you flesh, and ye shall eat.

¹⁹Ye shall not eat one day, nor two days, nor five days, neither ten days, nor twenty days;

²⁰*But* even a ^swhole month, until it come out at your nostrils, and it be loathsome unto you: because that ye have despised the LORD which *is* among you, and have wept before him, saying, Why came we forth out of Egypt?

²¹And Moses said, The people, among whom I *am, are* six hundred thousand footmen; and thou hast said, I will give them flesh, that they may eat a whole month.

²²Shall the flocks and the herds be slain for them, to suffice them? or shall all the fish of the sea be gathered together for them, to suffice them?

²³And the LORD said unto Moses, Is the LORD's hand waxed short? thou shalt see now whether my word shall come to pass unto thee or not.

²⁴ ¶ And Moses went out, and told the people the words of the LORD, and gathered the seventy men of the elders of the people, and set them round about the tabernacle.

²⁵And the LORD came down in a cloud, and spake unto him, and took of the spirit that *was* upon him, and gave *it* unto the seventy elders: and it came to pass, *that,* when the spirit rested upon them, they prophesied, and did not cease.

²⁶But there remained two *of the* men in the camp, the name of the one *was* Eldad, and the name of the other Medad: and the spirit rested upon them; and they *were* of them that were written, but went not out unto the tabernacle: and they prophesied in the camp.

Amplified

⁸The people went about and gathered it, and ground it in mills or beat it in mortars, and boiled it in pots, and made cakes of it; and it tasted like cakes baked with fresh oil.

⁹And when the dew fell on the camp in the night, the manna fell with it.

¹⁰And Moses heard the people weeping throughout their families, every man at the door of his tent; and the anger of the Lord blazed hotly, and in the eyes of Moses it was evil.

¹¹And Moses said to the Lord, Why have You dealt ill with Your servants? And why have I not found favor in Your sight, that You lay the burden of all this people on me?

¹²Have I conceived all this people? Have I brought them forth, that You should say to me, Carry them in your bosom, as a nursing father carries the sucking child, to the land which You swore to their fathers [to give them]?

¹³Where should I get meat to give to all these people? For they weep before me and say, Give us meat, that we may eat.

¹⁴I am not able to carry all these people alone, because the burden is too heavy for me.

¹⁵And if this is the way You deal with me, kill me, I pray You, at once, and be granting me a favor and let me not see my wretchedness [in the failure of all my efforts].

¹⁶And the Lord said to Moses, Gather for Me ^eseventy men of the elders of Israel whom you know to be the elders of the people and officers over them; and bring them to the Tent of Meeting and let them stand there with you.

¹⁷And I will come down and talk with you there; and I will take of the Spirit which is upon you and will put It upon them; and they shall bear the burden of the people with you, so that you may not have to bear it yourself alone.

¹⁸And say to the people, Consecrate yourselves for tomorrow, and you shall eat meat; for you have wept in the hearing of the Lord, saying, Who will give us meat to eat? For it was well with us in Egypt. Therefore the Lord will give you meat, and you shall eat.

¹⁹You shall not eat one day, or two, or five, or ten, or twenty days,

²⁰But a whole month—until [you are satiated and vomit it up violently] it comes out at your nostrils and is disgusting to you—because you have rejected *and* despised the Lord Who is among you, and have wept before Him, saying, Why did we come out of Egypt? [Ps. 106:13–15.]

²¹But Moses said, The people among whom I am are 600,000 footmen [besides all the women and children], and You have said, I will give them meat, that they may eat a whole month!

²²Shall flocks and herds be killed to suffice them? Or shall all the fish of the sea be collected to satisfy them?

²³The Lord said to Moses, Has the Lord's hand (His ability and power) become short (thwarted and inadequate)? You shall see now whether My word shall come to pass for you or not. [Isa. 50:2.]

²⁴So Moses went out and told the people the words of the Lord, and he gathered seventy men of the elders of the people and set them round about the Tent.

²⁵And the Lord came down in the cloud and spoke to him, and took of the Spirit that was upon him and put It upon the seventy elders; and when the Spirit rested upon them, they prophesied [sounding forth the praises of God and declaring His will]. Then they did so no more. [Num. 11:29.]

²⁶But there remained two men in the camp named Eldad and Medad. The Spirit rested upon them, and they were of those who were selected *and* listed, yet they did not go out to the Tent [as told to do], but they prophesied in the camp.

^e A council of seventy elders had existed the year before this (Exod. 24:9). It appears to be the source of the Sanhedrin, the highest Jewish assembly for government in the time of our Lord—usually translated "council."

^s Heb. *month of days*

New American Standard

8 The people would go about and gather *it* and grind *it* between two millstones or beat *it* in the mortar, and boil *it* in the pot and make cakes with it; and its taste was as the taste of cakes baked with oil.

9 When the dew fell on the camp at night, the manna would fall with it.

The Complaint of Moses

10 ¶ Now Moses heard the people weeping throughout their families, each man at the doorway of his tent; and the anger of the LORD was kindled greatly, and Moses was displeased.

11 So Moses said to the LORD, "Why have You *o*been so hard on Your servant? And why have I not found favor in Your sight, that You have laid the burden of all this people on me?

12"Was it I who conceived all this people? Was it I who brought them forth, that You should say to me, 'Carry them in your bosom as a nurse carries a nursing infant, to the land which You swore to their fathers'?

13"Where am I to get meat to give to all this people? For they weep before me, saying, 'Give us meat that we may eat!'

14"I alone am not able to carry all this people, because it is too burdensome for me.

15"So if You are going to deal thus with me, please kill me at once, if I have found favor in Your sight, and do not let me see my wretchedness."

Seventy Elders to Assist

16 ¶ The LORD therefore said to Moses, "Gather for Me seventy men from the elders of Israel, whom you know to be the elders of the people and their officers and bring them to the tent of meeting, and let them take their stand there with you.

17"Then I will come down and speak with you there, and I will take of the Spirit who is upon you, and will put *Him* upon them; and they shall bear the burden of the people with you, so that you will not bear *it* all alone.

18"Say to the people, 'Consecrate yourselves for tomorrow, and you shall eat meat; for you have wept in the ears of the LORD, saying, "Oh that someone would give us meat to eat! For we were well-off in Egypt." Therefore the LORD will give you meat and you shall eat.

19'You shall eat, not one day, nor two days, nor five days, nor ten days, nor twenty days,

20 but a whole month, until it comes out of your nostrils and becomes loathsome to you; because you have rejected the LORD who is among you and have wept before Him, saying, "Why did we ever leave Egypt?" '"

21 But Moses said, "The people, among whom I am, are 600,000 on foot; yet You have said, 'I will give them meat, so that they may eat for a whole month.'

22"Should flocks and herds be slaughtered for them, to be sufficient for them? Or should all the fish of the sea be gathered together for them, to be sufficient for them?"

23 The LORD said to Moses, "Is the LORD's power limited? Now you shall see whether My word will come true for you or not."

24 ¶ So Moses went out and told the people the words of the LORD. Also, he gathered seventy men of the elders of the people, and stationed them around the tent.

25 Then the LORD came down in the cloud and spoke to him; and He took of the Spirit who was upon him and placed *Him* upon the seventy elders. And when the Spirit rested upon them, they prophesied. But they did not do *it* again.

26 ¶ But two men had remained in the camp; the name of one was Eldad and the name of the other Medad. And the Spirit rested upon them (now they were among those who had been registered, but had not gone out to the tent), and they prophesied in the camp.

New International

resin. 8The people went around gathering it, and then ground it in a handmill or crushed it in a mortar. They cooked it in a pot or made it into cakes. And it tasted like something made with olive oil. 9When the dew settled on the camp at night, the manna also came down.

10Moses heard the people of every family wailing, each at the entrance to his tent. The LORD became exceedingly angry, and Moses was troubled. 11He asked the LORD, "Why have you brought this trouble on your servant? What have I done to displease you that you put the burden of all these people on me? 12Did I conceive all these people? Did I give them birth? Why do you tell me to carry them in my arms, as a nurse carries an infant, to the land you promised on oath to their forefathers? 13Where can I get meat for all these people? They keep wailing to me, 'Give us meat to eat!' 14I cannot carry all these people by myself; the burden is too heavy for me. 15If this is how you are going to treat me, put me to death right now—if I have found favor in your eyes—and do not let me face my own ruin."

16The LORD said to Moses: "Bring me seventy of Israel's elders who are known to you as leaders and officials among the people. Have them come to the Tent of Meeting, that they may stand there with you. 17I will come down and speak with you there, and I will take of the Spirit that is on you and put the Spirit on them. They will help you carry the burden of the people so that you will not have to carry it alone.

18"Tell the people: 'Consecrate yourselves in preparation for tomorrow, when you will eat meat. The LORD heard you when you wailed, "If only we had meat to eat! We were better off in Egypt!" Now the LORD will give you meat, and you will eat it. 19You will not eat it for just one day, or two days, or five, ten or twenty days, 20but for a whole month—until it comes out of your nostrils and you loathe it—because you have rejected the LORD, who is among you, and have wailed before him, saying, "Why did we ever leave Egypt?" ' "

21But Moses said, "Here I am among six hundred thousand men on foot, and you say, 'I will give them meat to eat for a whole month!' 22Would they have enough if flocks and herds were slaughtered for them? Would they have enough if all the fish in the sea were caught for them?"

23The LORD answered Moses, "Is the LORD's arm too short? You will now see whether or not what I say will come true for you."

24So Moses went out and told the people what the LORD had said. He brought together seventy of their elders and had them stand around the Tent. 25Then the LORD came down in the cloud and spoke with him, and he took of the Spirit that was on him and put the Spirit on the seventy elders. When the Spirit rested on them, they prophesied, but they did not do so again.*v*

26However, two men, whose names were Eldad and Medad, had remained in the camp. They were listed among the elders, but did not go out to the Tent. Yet the Spirit

*o*Lit *dealt ill with*   *v*25 Or *prophesied and continued to do so*

King James

²⁷And there ran a young man, and told Moses, and said, Eldad and Medad do prophesy in the camp.

²⁸And Joshua the son of Nun, the servant of Moses, *one* of his young men, answered and said, My lord Moses, forbid them.

²⁹And Moses said unto him, Enviest thou for my sake? would God that all the LORD's people were prophets, *and* that the LORD would put his spirit upon them!

³⁰And Moses gat him into the camp, he and the elders of Israel.

³¹ ¶ And there went forth a wind from the LORD, and brought quails from the sea, and let *them* fall by the camp, *t* as it were a day's journey on this side, and as it were a day's journey on the other side, round about the camp, and as it were two cubits *high* upon the face of the earth.

³²And the people stood up all that day, and all *that* night, and all the next day, and they gathered the quails: he that gathered least gathered ten homers: and they spread *them* all abroad for themselves round about the camp.

³³And while the flesh *was* yet between their teeth, ere it was chewed, the wrath of the LORD was kindled against the people, and the LORD smote the people with a very great plague.

³⁴And he called the name of that place *u*Kibroth-hattaavah: because there they buried the people that lusted.

³⁵*And* the people journeyed from Kibroth-hattaavah unto Hazeroth; and *v*abode at Hazeroth.

Miriam and Aaron

12 AND MIRIAM and Aaron spake against Moses because of the *w*Ethiopian woman whom he had married: for he had *x*married an Ethiopian woman.

²And they said, Hath the LORD indeed spoken only by Moses? hath he not spoken also by us? And the LORD heard *it*.

³(Now the man Moses *was* very meek, above all the men which *were* upon the face of the earth.)

⁴And the LORD spake suddenly unto Moses, and unto Aaron, and unto Miriam, Come out ye three unto the tabernacle of the congregation. And they three came out.

⁵And the LORD came down in the pillar of the cloud, and stood *in* the door of the tabernacle, and called Aaron and Miriam: and they both came forth.

⁶And he said, Hear now my words: If there be a prophet among you, *I* the LORD will make myself known unto him in a vision, *and* will speak unto him in a dream.

⁷My servant Moses *is* not so, who *is* faithful in all mine house.

⁸With him will I speak mouth to mouth, even apparently, and not in dark speeches; and the similitude of the LORD shall he behold: wherefore then were ye not afraid to speak against my servant Moses?

⁹And the anger of the LORD was kindled against them; and he departed.

¹⁰And the cloud departed from off the tabernacle; and, behold, Miriam *became* leprous, *white* as snow: and Aaron looked upon Miriam, and, behold, *she was* leprous.

¹¹And Aaron said unto Moses, Alas, my lord, I beseech thee, lay not the sin upon us, wherein we have done foolishly, and wherein we have sinned.

¹²Let her not be as one dead, of whom the flesh is half consumed when he cometh out of his mother's womb.

Amplified

²⁷And a young man ran to Moses and said, Eldad and Medad are prophesying [sounding forth the praises of God and declaring His will] in the camp.

²⁸Joshua son of Nun, the minister of Moses, one of his chosen men, said, My lord Moses, forbid them!

²⁹But Moses said to him, Are you *f*envious or jealous for my sake? Would that all the Lord's people were prophets and that the Lord would put His Spirit upon them! [Luke 9:49, 50.]

³⁰And Moses went back into the camp, he and the elders of Israel.

³¹And there went forth a wind from the Lord and brought quails from the sea, and let them fall [so they flew low] beside the camp, about a day's journey on this side and on the other side, all around the camp, about two cubits above the ground.

³²And the people rose all that day and all night and all the next day and caught *and* gathered the quails. He who gathered least gathered ten homers; and they spread them out for themselves round about the camp [to cure them by drying].

³³While the meat was yet between their teeth, before it was consumed, the anger of the Lord was kindled against the people, and the Lord smote them with a very great plague.

³⁴That place was called Kibroth-hattaavah [the graves of sensuous desire], because there they buried the people who lusted, whose physical appetite caused them to sin. [I Cor. 10:1–13.]

³⁵The Israelites journeyed from Kibroth-hattaavah to Hazeroth, where they remained.

12 NOW MIRIAM and Aaron talked against Moses [their brother] because of his *g*Cushite wife, for he had married a Cushite woman.

²And they said, Has the Lord indeed spoken only by Moses? Has He not spoken also by us? And the Lord heard it.

³Now the man Moses was very meek (gentle, kind, and humble) *or* above all the men on the face of the earth.

⁴Suddenly the Lord said to Moses, Aaron, and Miriam, Come out, you three, to the Tent of Meeting. And the three of them came out.

⁵The Lord came down in a pillar of cloud, and stood at the Tent door and called Aaron and Miriam, and they came forward.

⁶And He said, Hear now My words: If there is a prophet among you, I the Lord make Myself known to him in a vision and speak to him in a dream.

⁷But not so with My servant Moses; he is entrusted *and* faithful in all My house. [Heb. 3:2, 5, 6.]

⁸With him I speak mouth to mouth [directly], clearly and not in dark speeches; and he beholds the form of the Lord. Why then were you not afraid to speak against My servant Moses?

⁹And the anger of the Lord was kindled against them, and He departed.

¹⁰And when the cloud departed from over the Tent, behold, Miriam was leprous, as white as snow. And Aaron looked at Miriam, and, behold, she was leprous!

¹¹And Aaron said to Moses, Oh, my lord, I plead with you, lay not the sin upon us in which we have done foolishly and in which we have sinned.

¹²Let her not be as one dead, already half decomposed when he comes out of his mother's womb.

---

f"Moses, the minister of God, rebukes our partial love, / Who envy at the gifts bestow'd on those we disapprove. / We do not our own spirit know, who wish to see suppressed, / The men that Jesus' spirit show, the men whom God hath blest" (Charles Wesley).
*g*Zipporah, Moses' wife, seems to have died some time before. Marriage with a Canaanite was forbidden, but not with an Egyptian or Cushite. Joseph's wife was an Egyptian (Gen. 41:45).

---

*t*Heb. *as it were the way of a day*   *u*i.e. *The graves of lust*
*v*Heb. *they were in*   *w*Or, *Cushite*   *x*Heb. *taken*

New American Standard

27 So a young man ran and told Moses and said, "Eldad and Medad are prophesying in the camp."

28 Then Joshua the son of Nun, the attendant of Moses from his youth, said, "Moses, my lord, restrain them."

29 But Moses said to him, "Are you jealous for my sake? Would that all the LORD's people were prophets, that the LORD would put His Spirit upon them!"

30 Then Moses returned to the camp, *both* he and the elders of Israel.

The Quail and the Plague

31 ¶ Now there went forth a wind from the LORD and it brought quail from the sea, and let *them* fall beside the camp, about a day's journey on this side and a day's journey on the other side, all around the camp and about two cubits *deep* on the surface of the ground.

32 The people spent all day and all night and all the next day, and gathered the quail (he who gathered least gathered ten homers) and they spread *them* out for themselves all around the camp.

33 While the meat was still between their teeth, before it was chewed, the anger of the LORD was kindled against the people, and the LORD struck the people with a very severe plague.

34 So the name of that place was called ᴾKibroth-hattaavah, because there they buried the people who had been greedy.

35 From Kibroth-hattaavah the people set out for Hazeroth, and they remained at Hazeroth.

The Murmuring of Miriam and Aaron

12 THEN MIRIAM and Aaron spoke against Moses because of the Cushite woman whom he had married (for he had married a Cushite woman);

2 and they said, "Has the LORD indeed spoken only through Moses? Has He not spoken through us as well?" And the LORD heard it.

3 (Now the man Moses was very humble, more than any man who was on the face of the earth.)

4 Suddenly the LORD said to Moses and Aaron and to Miriam, "You three come out to the tent of meeting." So the three of them came out.

5 Then the LORD came down in a pillar of cloud and stood at the doorway of the tent, and He called Aaron and Miriam. When they had both come forward,

6 He said,
"Hear now My words:
If there is a prophet among you,
I, the LORD, shall make Myself known to him in
   a vision.
I shall speak with him in a dream.

7"Not so, with My servant Moses,
He is faithful in all My household;

8 With him I speak mouth to mouth,
Even openly, and not in dark sayings,
And he beholds the form of the LORD.
Why then were you not afraid
To speak against My servant, against Moses?"

9 ¶ So the anger of the LORD burned against them and He departed.

10 But when the cloud had withdrawn from over the tent, behold, Miriam *was* leprous, as *white as* snow. As Aaron turned toward Miriam, behold, she *was* leprous.

11 Then Aaron said to Moses, "Oh, my lord, I beg you, do not account *this* sin to us, in which we have acted foolishly and in which we have sinned.

12"Oh, do not let her be like one dead, whose flesh is half eaten away when he comes from their mother's womb!"

ᴾ I.e. the graves of greediness

New International

also rested on them, and they prophesied in the camp. 27A young man ran and told Moses, "Eldad and Medad are prophesying in the camp."

28Joshua son of Nun, who had been Moses' aide since youth, spoke up and said, "Moses, my lord, stop them!"

29But Moses replied, "Are you jealous for my sake? I wish that all the LORD's people were prophets and that the LORD would put his Spirit on them!" 30Then Moses and the elders of Israel returned to the camp.

31Now a wind went out from the LORD and drove quail in from the sea. It brought themʷ down all around the camp to about three feetˣ above the ground, as far as a day's walk in any direction. 32All that day and night and all the next day the people went out and gathered quail. No one gathered less than ten homers.ʸ Then they spread them out all around the camp. 33But while the meat was still between their teeth and before it could be consumed, the anger of the LORD burned against the people, and he struck them with a severe plague. 34Therefore the place was named Kibroth Hattaavah,ᶻ because there they buried the people who had craved other food.

35From Kibroth Hattaavah the people traveled to Hazeroth and stayed there.

Miriam and Aaron Oppose Moses

12 MIRIAM AND Aaron began to talk against Moses because of his Cushite wife, for he had married a Cushite. 2"Has the LORD spoken only through Moses?" they asked. "Hasn't he also spoken through us?" And the LORD heard this.

3(Now Moses was a very humble man, more humble than anyone else on the face of the earth.)

4At once the LORD said to Moses, Aaron and Miriam, "Come out to the Tent of Meeting, all three of you." So the three of them came out. 5Then the LORD came down in a pillar of cloud; he stood at the entrance to the Tent and summoned Aaron and Miriam. When both of them stepped forward, 6he said, "Listen to my words:

"When a prophet of the LORD is among you,
    I reveal myself to him in visions,
    I speak to him in dreams.
7But this is not true of my servant Moses;
    he is faithful in all my house.
8With him I speak face to face,
    clearly and not in riddles;
    he sees the form of the LORD.
Why then were you not afraid
    to speak against my servant Moses?"

9The anger of the LORD burned against them, and he left them.

10When the cloud lifted from above the Tent, there stood Miriam—leprous,ᵃ like snow. Aaron turned toward her and saw that she had leprosy; 11and he said to Moses, "Please, my lord, do not hold against us the sin we have so foolishly committed. 12Do not let her be like a stillborn infant coming from its mother's womb with its flesh half eaten away."

ʷ *31* Or *They flew*   ˣ *31* Hebrew *two cubits* (about 1 meter)
ʸ *32* That is, probably about 60 bushels (about 2.2 kiloliters)
ᶻ *34 Kibroth Hattaavah* means *graves of craving.*
ᵃ *10* The Hebrew word was used for various diseases affecting the skin—not necessarily leprosy.

King James

13And Moses cried unto the LORD, saying, Heal her now, O God, I beseech thee.

14 ¶ And the LORD said unto Moses, If her father had but spit in her face, should she not be ashamed seven days? let her be shut out from the camp seven days, and after that let her be received in *again.*

15And Miriam was shut out from the camp seven days: and the people journeyed not till Miriam was brought in *again.*

16And afterward the people removed from Hazeroth, and pitched in the wilderness of Paran.

Twelve spies sent to Canaan

13 AND THE LORD spake unto Moses, saying,
2Send thou men, that they may search the land of Canaan, which I give unto the children of Israel: of every tribe of their fathers shall ye send a man, every one a ruler among them.

3And Moses by the commandment of the LORD sent them from the wilderness of Paran: all those men *were* heads of the children of Israel.

4And these *were* their names: of the tribe of Reuben, Shammua the son of Zaccur.

5Of the tribe of Simeon, Shaphat the son of Hori.

6Of the tribe of Judah, Caleb the son of Jephunneh.

7Of the tribe of Issachar, Igal the son of Joseph.

8Of the tribe of Ephraim, Oshea the son of Nun.

9Of the tribe of Benjamin, Palti the son of Raphu.

10Of the tribe of Zebulun, Gaddiel the son of Sodi.

11Of the tribe of Joseph, *namely,* of the tribe of Manasseh, Gaddi the son of Susi.

12Of the tribe of Dan, Ammiel the son of Gemalli.

13Of the tribe of Asher, Sethur the son of Michael.

14Of the tribe of Naphtali, Nahbi the son of Vophsi.

15Of the tribe of Gad, Geuel the son of Machi.

16These *are* the names of the men which Moses sent to spy out the land. And Moses called Oshea the son of Nun Jehoshua.

17 ¶ And Moses sent them to spy out the land of Canaan, and said unto them, Get you up this *way* southward, and go up into the mountain:

18And see the land, what it *is;* and the people that dwelleth therein, whether they *be* strong or weak, few or many;

19And what the land *is* that they dwell in, whether it *be* good or bad; and what cities *they be* that they dwell in, whether in tents, or in strong holds;

20And what the land *is,* whether it *be* fat or lean, whether there be wood therein, or not. And be ye of good courage, and bring of the fruit of the land. Now the time *was* the time of the firstripe grapes.

21 ¶ So they went up, and searched the land from the wilderness of Zin unto Rehob, as men come to Hamath.

22And they ascended by the south, and came unto Hebron; where Ahiman, Sheshai, and Talmai, the children of Anak, *were.* (Now Hebron was built seven years before Zoan in Egypt.)

23And they came unto the ybrook of Eshcol, and cut down from thence a branch with one cluster of grapes, and they bare it between two upon a staff; and *they brought* of the pomegranates, and of the figs.

24The place was called the ybrook zEshcol, because of the cluster of grapes which the children of Israel cut down from thence.

The spies return

25And they returned from searching of the land after forty days.

Amplified

13And Moses cried to the Lord, saying, Heal her now, O God, I beseech You!

14And the Lord said to Moses, If her father had but spit in her face, should she not be ashamed for seven days? Let her be shut up outside the camp for seven days, and after that let her be brought in again.

15So Miriam was shut up without the camp for seven days, and the people did not journey on until Miriam was brought in again.

16Afterward [they] removed from Hazeroth and encamped in the Wilderness of Paran.

13 AND THE Lord said to Moses,
2Send men to explore *and* scout out [for yourselves] the land of Canaan, which I give to the Israelites. From each tribe of their fathers you shall send a man, every one a leader *or* head among them.

3So Moses by the command of the Lord sent scouts from the Wilderness of Paran, all of them men who were heads of the Israelites.

4These were their names: of the tribe of Reuben, Shammua son of Zaccur;

5Of the tribe of Simeon, Shaphat son of Hori;

6Of the tribe of Judah, Caleb son of Jephunneh;

7Of the tribe of Issachar, Igal son of Joseph;

8Of the tribe of Ephraim, Hoshea [that is, Joshua] son of Nun;

9Of the tribe of Benjamin, Palti son of Raphu;

10Of the tribe of Zebulun, Gaddiel son of Sodi;

11Of the tribe of Joseph, that is, of the tribe of Manasseh, Gaddi son of Susi;

12Of the tribe of Dan, Ammiel son of Gemalli;

13Of the tribe of Asher, Sethur son of Michael;

14Of the tribe of Naphtali, Nahbi son of Vophsi;

15Of the tribe of Gad, Geuel son of Machi.

16These are the names of the men whom Moses sent to explore *and* scout out the land. And Moses called Hoshea son of Nun, Joshua.

17Moses sent them to scout out the land of Canaan, and said to them, Get up this way by the South (the Negeb) and go up into the hill country,

18And see what the land is and whether the people who dwell there are strong or weak, few or many,

19And whether the land they live in is good or bad, and whether the cities they dwell in are camps or strongholds,

20And what the land is, whether it is fat or lean, whether there is timber on it or not. And be of good courage and bring some of the fruit of the land. Now the time was the time of the first ripe grapes.

21So they went up and scouted through the land from the Wilderness of Zin to Rehob, to the entrance of Hamath.

22And then went up into the South (the Negeb) and came to Hebron; and Ahiman, Sheshai, and Talmai [probably three tribes of] the sons of Anak were there. (Hebron was built seven years before Zoan in Egypt.)

23And they came to the Valley of Eshcol, and cut down from there a branch with one cluster of grapes, and they carried it on a pole between two [of them]; they brought also some pomegranates and figs.

24That place was called the Valley of Eshcol [cluster] because of the cluster which the Israelites cut down there.

25And they returned from scouting out the land after forty days.

yOr, *valley*   zi.e. A *cluster of grapes.*

New American Standard

13 Moses cried out to the LORD, saying, "O God, heal
her, I pray!"
14 But the LORD said to Moses, "If her father had but
spit in her face, would she not bear her shame for seven
days? Let her be shut up for seven days outside the camp,
and afterward she may be received again."
15 So Miriam was shut up outside the camp for seven
days, and the people did not move on until Miriam was
received again.
16 ¶ Afterward, however, the people moved out from
Hazeroth and camped in the wilderness of Paran.

Spies View the Land

13 THEN THE LORD spoke to Moses saying,
2 "Send out for yourself men so that they may spy
out the land of Canaan, which I am going to give to the
sons of Israel; you shall send a man from each of their
fathers' tribes, every one a leader among them."
3 So Moses sent them from the wilderness of Paran at
the command of the LORD, all of them men who were
heads of the sons of Israel.
4 These then *were* their names: from the tribe of Reuben, Shammua the son of Zaccur;
5 from the tribe of Simeon, Shaphat the son of Hori;
6 from the tribe of Judah, Caleb the son of Jephunneh;
7 from the tribe of Issachar, Igal the son of Joseph;
8 from the tribe of Ephraim, Hoshea the son of Nun;
9 from the tribe of Benjamin, Palti the son of Raphu;
10 from the tribe of Zebulun, Gaddiel the son of Sodi;
11 from the tribe of Joseph, from the tribe of Manasseh,
Gaddi the son of Susi;
12 from the tribe of Dan, Ammiel the son of Gemalli;
13 from the tribe of Asher, Sethur the son of Michael;
14 from the tribe of Naphtali, Nahbi the son of Vophsi;
15 from the tribe of Gad, Geuel the son of Machi.
16 These are the names of the men whom Moses sent to
spy out the land; but Moses called Hoshea the son of Nun,
Joshua.
17 ¶ When Moses sent them to spy out the land of Canaan, he said to them, "Go up there into the [q]Negev; then
go up into the hill country.
18 "See what the land is like, and whether the people who
live in it are strong *or* weak, whether they are few or many.
19 "How is the land in which they live, is it good or bad?
And how are the cities in which they live, are *they* like
open camps or with fortifications?
20 "How is the land, is it fat or lean? Are there trees in
it or not? Make an effort then to get some of the fruit of
the land." Now the time was the time of the first ripe
grapes.
21 ¶ So they went up and spied out the land from the
wilderness of Zin as far as Rehob, at Lebo-hamath.
22 When they had gone up into the Negev, they came to
Hebron where Ahiman, Sheshai and Talmai, the descendants of Anak were. (Now Hebron was built seven years
before Zoan in Egypt.)
23 ¶ Then they came to the valley of [r]Eshcol and from
there cut down a branch with a single cluster of grapes;
and they carried it on a pole between two *men,* with some
of the pomegranates and the figs.
24 That place was called the valley of Eshcol, because of
the cluster which the sons of Israel cut down from there.

The Spies' Reports

25 ¶ When they returned from spying out the land, at the
end of forty days,

[q] I.e. South country, and so throughout the ch [r] I.e. cluster

New International

13 So Moses cried out to the LORD, "O God, please heal
her!"
14 The LORD replied to Moses, "If her father had spit in
her face, would she not have been in disgrace for seven
days? Confine her outside the camp for seven days; after
that she can be brought back." 15 So Miriam was confined
outside the camp for seven days, and the people did not
move on till she was brought back.
16 After that, the people left Hazeroth and encamped in
the Desert of Paran.

Exploring Canaan

13 THE LORD said to Moses, 2 "Send some men to
explore the land of Canaan, which I am giving to
the Israelites. From each ancestral tribe send one of its
leaders."
3 So at the LORD's command Moses sent them out from
the Desert of Paran. All of them were leaders of the Israelites. 4 These are their names:
from the tribe of Reuben, Shammua son of Zaccur;
5 from the tribe of Simeon, Shaphat son of Hori;
6 from the tribe of Judah, Caleb son of Jephunneh;
7 from the tribe of Issachar, Igal son of Joseph;
8 from the tribe of Ephraim, Hoshea son of Nun;
9 from the tribe of Benjamin, Palti son of Raphu;
10 from the tribe of Zebulun, Gaddiel son of Sodi;
11 from the tribe of Manasseh (a tribe of Joseph), Gaddi
son of Susi;
12 from the tribe of Dan, Ammiel son of Gemalli;
13 from the tribe of Asher, Sethur son of Michael;
14 from the tribe of Naphtali, Nahbi son of Vophsi;
15 from the tribe of Gad, Geuel son of Maki.
16 These are the names of the men Moses sent to explore
the land. (Moses gave Hoshea son of Nun the name
Joshua.)
17 When Moses sent them to explore Canaan, he said,
"Go up through the Negev and on into the hill country.
18 See what the land is like and whether the people who
live there are strong or weak, few or many. 19 What kind of
land do they live in? Is it good or bad? What kind of towns
do they live in? Are they unwalled or fortified? 20 How is
the soil? Is it fertile or poor? Are there trees on it or not?
Do your best to bring back some of the fruit of the land."
(It was the season for the first ripe grapes.)
21 So they went up and explored the land from the Desert
of Zin as far as Rehob, toward Lebo[b] Hamath. 22 They
went up through the Negev and came to Hebron, where
Ahiman, Sheshai and Talmai, the descendants of Anak,
lived. (Hebron had been built seven years before Zoan in
Egypt.) 23 When they reached the Valley of Eshcol,[c] they
cut off a branch bearing a single cluster of grapes. Two of
them carried it on a pole between them, along with some
pomegranates and figs. 24 That place was called the Valley
of Eshcol because of the cluster of grapes the Israelites cut
off there. 25 At the end of forty days they returned from
exploring the land.

[b] 21 Or *toward the entrance to* [c] 23 *Eshcol* means *cluster*; also in verse 24.

King James

²⁶ ¶ And they went and came to Moses, and to Aaron, and to all the congregation of the children of Israel, unto the wilderness of Paran, to Kadesh; and brought back word unto them, and unto all the congregation, and showed them the fruit of the land.

²⁷And they told him, and said, We came unto the land whither thou sentest us, and surely it floweth with milk and honey; and this *is* the fruit of it.

²⁸Nevertheless the people *be* strong that dwell in the land, and the cities *are* walled, *and* very great: and moreover we saw the children of Anak there.

²⁹The Amalekites dwell in the land of the south: and the Hittites, and the Jebusites, and the Amorites, dwell in the mountains: and the Canaanites dwell by the sea, and by the coast of Jordan.

³⁰And Caleb stilled the people before Moses, and said, Let us go up at once, and possess it; for we are well able to overcome it.

³¹But the men that went up with him said, We be not able to go up against the people; for they *are* stronger than we.

³²And they brought up an evil report of the land which they had searched unto the children of Israel, saying, The land, through which we have gone to search it, *is* a land that eateth up the inhabitants thereof; and all the people that we saw in it *are* ^amen of a great stature.

³³And there we saw the giants, the sons of Anak, *which come* of the giants: and we were in our own sight as grasshoppers, and so we were in their sight.

The rebellion of Israel

14 AND ALL the congregation lifted up their voice, and cried; and the people wept that night.

²And all the children of Israel murmured against Moses and against Aaron: and the whole congregation said unto them, Would God that we had died in the land of Egypt! or would God we had died in this wilderness!

³And wherefore hath the LORD brought us unto this land, to fall by the sword, that our wives and our children should be a prey? were it not better for us to return into Egypt?

⁴And they said one to another, Let us make a captain, and let us return into Egypt.

⁵Then Moses and Aaron fell on their faces before all the assembly of the congregation of the children of Israel.

⁶ ¶ And Joshua the son of Nun, and Caleb the son of Jephunneh, *which were* of them that searched the land, rent their clothes:

⁷And they spake unto all the company of the children of Israel, saying, The land, which we passed through to search it, *is* an exceeding good land.

⁸If the LORD delight in us, then he will bring us into this land, and give it us; a land which floweth with milk and honey.

⁹Only rebel not ye against the LORD, neither fear ye the people of the land; for they *are* bread for us: their ^bdefence is departed from them, and the LORD *is* with us: fear them not.

¹⁰But all the congregation bade stone them with stones. And the glory of the LORD appeared in the tabernacle of the congregation before all the children of Israel.

¹¹ ¶ And the LORD said unto Moses, How long will this people provoke me? and how long will it be ere they believe me, for all the signs which I have shown among them?

¹²I will smite them with the pestilence, and disinherit them, and will make of thee a greater nation and mightier than they.

Amplified

²⁶They came to Moses and Aaron and to all the Israelite congregation in the Wilderness of Paran at Kadesh, and brought them word, and showed them the land's fruit.

²⁷They told Moses, We came to the land to which you sent us; surely it flows with milk and honey. This is its fruit.

²⁸But the people who dwell there are strong, and the cities are ^hfortified *and* very large; moreover, there we saw the sons of Anak [of great stature and courage].

²⁹Amalek dwells in the land of the South (the Negeb); the Hittite, the Jebusite, and the Amorite dwell in the hill country; and the Canaanite dwells by the sea and along by the side of the Jordan [River].

³⁰Caleb quieted the people before Moses, and said, Let us go up at once and possess it; we are well able to conquer it.

³¹But his fellow scouts said, We are not able to go up against the people [of Canaan], for they are stronger than we are.

³²So they brought the Israelites an evil report of the land which they had scouted out, saying, The land through which we went to spy it out is a land that devours its inhabitants. And all the people that we saw in it are men of great stature.

³³There we saw the Nephilim [or giants], the sons of Anak, who come from the giants; and we were in our own sight as grasshoppers, and so we were in their sight.

14 AND ALL the congregation cried out with a loud voice, and [they] wept that night.

²All the Israelites grumbled *and* deplored their situation, accusing Moses and Aaron, to whom the whole congregation said, Would that we had died in Egypt! Or that we had died in this wilderness!

³Why does the Lord bring us to this land to fall by the sword? Our wives and little ones will be a prey. Is it not better for us to return to Egypt? [Acts 7:37–39.]

⁴And they said one to another, Let us choose a captain and return to Egypt.

⁵Then Moses and Aaron fell on their faces before all the assembly of Israelites.

⁶And Joshua son of Nun and Caleb son of Jephunneh, who were among the scouts who had searched the land, rent their clothes,

⁷And they said to all the company of Israelites, The land through which we passed as scouts is an exceedingly good land.

⁸If the Lord delights in us, then He will bring us into this land and give it to us, a land flowing with milk and honey.

⁹Only do not rebel against the Lord, neither fear the people of the land, for they are bread for us. Their defense *and* the shadow [of protection] is removed from over them, but the Lord is with us. Fear them not.

¹⁰But all the congregation said to stone [Joshua and Caleb] with stones. But the glory of the Lord appeared at the Tent of Meeting before all the Israelites.

¹¹And the Lord said to Moses, How long will this people provoke (spurn, despise) Me? And how long will it be before they believe Me [trusting in, relying on, clinging to Me], for all the signs which I have performed among them?

¹²I will smite them with the pestilence and disinherit them, and will make of you [Moses] a nation greater and mightier than they.

---

^h The scouts probably had not seen walled cities before, having lived their childhood in Goshen in Egypt. Those who forgot God's power to help them naturally found the situation formidable, as happens in the lives of most people. " 'But God' makes all the difference between cowards and Calebs."

^aHeb. *men of statures*   ^bHeb. *shadow*

New American Standard

26 they proceeded to come to Moses and Aaron and to all the congregation of the sons of Israel in the wilderness of Paran, at Kadesh; and they brought back word to them and to all the congregation and showed them the fruit of the land.

27 Thus they told him, and said, "We went in to the land where you sent us; and it certainly does flow with milk and honey, and this is its fruit.

28"Nevertheless, the people who live in the land are strong, and the cities are fortified *and* very large; and moreover, we saw the descendants of Anak there.

29"Amalek is living in the land of the Negev and the Hittites and the Jebusites and the Amorites are living in the hill country, and the Canaanites are living by the sea and by the side of the Jordan."

30 ¶ Then Caleb quieted the people before Moses and said, "We should by all means go up and take possession of it, for we will surely overcome it."

31 But the men who had gone up with him said, "We are not able to go up against the people, for they are too strong for us."

32 So they gave out to the sons of Israel a bad report of the land which they had spied out, saying, "The land through which we have gone, in spying it out, is a land that devours its inhabitants; and all the people whom we saw in it are men of *great* size.

33"There also we saw the Nephilim (the sons of Anak are part of the Nephilim); and we became like grasshoppers in our own sight, and so we were in their sight."

The People Rebel

14 THEN ALL the congregation lifted up their voices and cried, and the people wept that night.

2 All the sons of Israel grumbled against Moses and Aaron; and the whole congregation said to them, "Would that we had died in the land of Egypt! Or would that we had died in this wilderness!

3"Why is the LORD bringing us into this land, to fall by the sword? Our wives and our little ones will become plunder; would it not be better for us to return to Egypt?"

4 So they said to one another, "Let us appoint a leader and return to Egypt."

5 ¶ Then Moses and Aaron fell on their faces in the presence of all the assembly of the congregation of the sons of Israel.

6 Joshua the son of Nun and Caleb the son of Jephunneh, of those who had spied out the land, tore their clothes;

7 and they spoke to all the congregation of the sons of Israel, saying, "The land which we passed through to spy out is an exceedingly good land.

8"If the LORD is pleased with us, then He will bring us into this land and give it to us—a land which flows with milk and honey.

9"Only do not rebel against the LORD; and do not fear the people of the land, for they will be our prey. Their protection has been removed from them, and the LORD is with us; do not fear them."

10 But all the congregation said to stone them with stones. Then the glory of the LORD appeared in the tent of meeting to all the sons of Israel.

Moses Pleads for the People

11 ¶ The LORD said to Moses, "How long will this people spurn Me? And how long will they not believe in Me, despite all the signs which I have performed in their midst?

12"I will smite them with pestilence and dispossess them, and I will make you into a nation greater and mightier than they."

New International

Report on the Exploration

26They came back to Moses and Aaron and the whole Israelite community at Kadesh in the Desert of Paran. There they reported to them and to the whole assembly and showed them the fruit of the land. 27They gave Moses this account: "We went into the land to which you sent us, and it does flow with milk and honey! Here is its fruit. 28But the people who live there are powerful, and the cities are fortified and very large. We even saw descendants of Anak there. 29The Amalekites live in the Negev; the Hittites, Jebusites and Amorites live in the hill country; and the Canaanites live near the sea and along the Jordan."

30Then Caleb silenced the people before Moses and said, "We should go up and take possession of the land, for we can certainly do it."

31But the men who had gone up with him said, "We can't attack those people; they are stronger than we are." 32And they spread among the Israelites a bad report about the land they had explored. They said, "The land we explored devours those living in it. All the people we saw there are of great size. 33We saw the Nephilim there (the descendants of Anak come from the Nephilim). We seemed like grasshoppers in our own eyes, and we looked the same to them."

The People Rebel

14 THAT NIGHT all the people of the community raised their voices and wept aloud. 2All the Israelites grumbled against Moses and Aaron, and the whole assembly said to them, "If only we had died in Egypt! Or in this desert! 3Why is the LORD bringing us to this land only to let us fall by the sword? Our wives and children will be taken as plunder. Wouldn't it be better for us to go back to Egypt?" 4And they said to each other, "We should choose a leader and go back to Egypt."

5Then Moses and Aaron fell facedown in front of the whole Israelite assembly gathered there. 6Joshua son of Nun and Caleb son of Jephunneh, who were among those who had explored the land, tore their clothes 7and said to the entire Israelite assembly, "The land we passed through and explored is exceedingly good. 8If the LORD is pleased with us, he will lead us into that land, a land flowing with milk and honey, and will give it to us. 9Only do not rebel against the LORD. And do not be afraid of the people of the land, because we will swallow them up. Their protection is gone, but the LORD is with us. Do not be afraid of them."

10But the whole assembly talked about stoning them. Then the glory of the LORD appeared at the Tent of Meeting to all the Israelites. 11The LORD said to Moses, "How long will these people treat me with contempt? How long will they refuse to believe in me, in spite of all the miraculous signs I have performed among them? 12I will strike them down with a plague and destroy them, but I will make you into a nation greater and stronger than they."

King James

13 ¶ And Moses said unto the LORD, Then the Egyptians shall hear *it*, (for thou broughtest up this people in thy might from among them;)

14And they will tell *it* to the inhabitants of this land: *for* they have heard that thou LORD *art* among this people, that thou LORD art seen face to face, and *that* thy cloud standeth over them, and *that* thou goest before them, by day time in a pillar of a cloud, and in a pillar of fire by night.

15 ¶ Now *if* thou shalt kill *all* this people as one man, then the nations which have heard the fame of thee will speak, saying,

16Because the LORD was not able to bring this people into the land which he sware unto them, therefore he hath slain them in the wilderness.

17And now, I beseech thee, let the power of my LORD be great, according as thou hast spoken, saying,

18The LORD *is* longsuffering, and of great mercy, forgiving iniquity and transgression, and by no means clearing *the guilty*, visiting the iniquity of the fathers upon the children unto the third and fourth *generation*.

19Pardon, I beseech thee, the iniquity of this people according unto the greatness of thy mercy, and as thou hast forgiven this people, from Egypt even ᶜuntil now.

20And the LORD said, I have pardoned according to thy word:

21But *as* truly *as* I live, all the earth shall be filled with the glory of the LORD.

22Because all those men which have seen my glory, and my miracles, which I did in Egypt and in the wilderness, and have tempted me now these ten times, and have not hearkened to my voice;

23ᵈ Surely they shall not see the land which I sware unto their fathers, neither shall any of them that provoked me see it:

24But my servant Caleb, because he had another spirit with him, and hath followed me fully, him will I bring into the land whereinto he went; and his seed shall possess it.

25(Now the Amalekites and the Canaanites dwelt in the valley.) Tomorrow turn you, and get you into the wilderness by the way of the Red sea.

26 ¶ And the LORD spake unto Moses and unto Aaron, saying,

27How long *shall I bear with* this evil congregation, which murmur against me? I have heard the murmurings of the children of Israel, which they murmur against me.

28Say unto them, *As truly as* I live, saith the LORD, as ye have spoken in mine ears, so will I do to you:

29Your carcases shall fall in this wilderness; and all that were numbered of you, according to your whole number, from twenty years old and upward, which have murmured against me,

30Doubtless ye shall not come into the land, *concerning* which I ᵉsware to make you dwell therein, save Caleb the son of Jephunneh, and Joshua the son of Nun.

31But your little ones, which ye said should be a prey, them will I bring in, and they shall know the land which ye have despised.

32But *as for* you, your carcases, they shall fall in this wilderness.

33And your children shall ᶠwander in the wilderness forty years, and bear your whoredoms, until your carcases be wasted in the wilderness.

34After the number of the days in which ye searched the land, *even* forty days, each day for a year, shall ye bear your iniquities, *even* forty years, and ye shall know my ᵍbreach of promise.

35I the LORD have said, I will surely do it unto all this evil congregation, that are gathered together against me: in this wilderness they shall be consumed, and there they shall die.

Amplified

13But Moses said to the Lord, Then the Egyptians will hear of it, for You brought up this people in Your might from among them.

14And they will tell it to the inhabitants of this land. They have heard that You, Lord, are in the midst of this people [of Israel], that You, Lord, are seen face to face, and that Your cloud stands over them, and that You go before them in a pillar of cloud by day and in a pillar of fire by night.

15Now if You kill all this people as one man, then the nations that have heard Your fame will say,

16Because the Lord was not able to bring this people into the land which He swore to give to them, therefore He has slain them in the wilderness.

17And now, I pray You, let the power of my Lord be great, as You have promised, saying,

18The Lord is long-suffering *and* slow to anger, and abundant in mercy *and* loving-kindness, forgiving iniquity and transgression; but He will by no means clear the guilty, visiting the iniquity of the fathers upon the children, upon the third and fourth generation. [Exod. 34:6, 7.]

19Pardon, I pray You, the iniquity of this people according to the greatness of Your mercy *and* loving-kindness, just as You have forgiven [them] from Egypt until now.

20And the Lord said, I have pardoned according to your word.

21But truly as I live and as all the earth shall be filled with the glory of the Lord, [Isa. 6:3; 11:9.]

22Because all those men who have seen My glory and My [miraculous] signs which I performed in Egypt and in the wilderness, yet have tested *and* proved Me these ten times and have not heeded My voice,

23Surely they shall not see the land which I swore to give to their fathers; nor shall any who provoked (spurned, despised) Me see it. [Heb. 6:4–11.]

24But My servant Caleb, because he has a different spirit and has followed Me fully, I will bring into the land into which he went, and his descendants shall possess it.

25Now because the Amalekites and the Canaanites dwell in the valley, tomorrow turn and go into the wilderness by way of the Red Sea.

26And the Lord said to Moses and Aaron,

27How long will this evil congregation murmur against Me? I have heard the complaints the Israelites murmur against Me.

28Tell them, As I live, says the Lord, what you have said in My hearing I will do to you:

29Your dead bodies shall fall in this wilderness—of all who were numbered of you, from twenty years old and upward, who have murmured against Me, [Heb. 3:17–19.]

30Surely none shall come into the land in which I swore to make you dwell, except Caleb son of Jephunneh and Joshua son of Nun.

31But your little ones whom you said would be a prey, them will I bring in and they shall know the land which you have despised *and* rejected.

32But as for you, your dead bodies shall fall in this wilderness.

33And your children shall be wanderers *and* shepherds in the wilderness for forty years and shall suffer for your whoredoms (your infidelity to your espoused God), until your corpses are consumed in the wilderness.

34After the number of the days in which you spied out the land [of Canaan], even forty days, for each day a year shall you bear *and* suffer for your iniquities, even for forty years, and you shall know My displeasure [the revoking of My promise and My estrangement].

35I the Lord have spoken; surely this will I do to all this evil congregation who is gathered together against Me. In this wilderness they shall be consumed [by war, disease, plagues], and here they shall die. [I Cor. 10:10, 11.]

ᶜOr, *hitherto*   ᵈHeb. *If they see the land*   ᵉHeb. *lifted up my hand*   ᶠOr, *feed*   ᵍOr, *altering of my purpose*

New American Standard

13 ¶ But Moses said to the Lord, "Then the Egyptians will hear of it, for by Your strength You brought up this people from their midst,

14 and they will tell *it* to the inhabitants of this land. They have heard that You, O Lord, are in the midst of this people, for You, O Lord, are seen eye to eye, while Your cloud stands over them; and You go before them in a pillar of cloud by day and in a pillar of fire by night.

15 "Now if You slay this people as one man, then the nations who have heard of Your fame will say,

16 'Because the Lord could not bring this people into the land which He promised them by oath, therefore He slaughtered them in the wilderness.'

17 "But now, I pray, let the power of the Lord be great, just as You have declared,

18 'The Lord is slow to anger and abundant in lovingkindness, forgiving iniquity and transgression; but He will by no means clear *the guilty,* visiting the iniquity of the fathers on the children to the third and the fourth *generations.*'

19 "Pardon, I pray, the iniquity of this people according to the greatness of Your lovingkindness, just as You also have forgiven this people, from Egypt even until now."

The Lord Pardons and Rebukes

20 ¶ So the Lord said, "I have pardoned *them* according to your word;

21 but indeed, as I live, all the earth will be filled with the glory of the Lord.

22 "Surely all the men who have seen My glory and My signs which I performed in Egypt and in the wilderness, yet have put Me to the test these ten times and have not listened to My voice,

23 shall by no means see the land which I swore to their fathers, nor shall any of those who spurned Me see it.

24 "But My servant Caleb, because he has had a different spirit and has followed Me fully, I will bring into the land which he entered, and his descendants shall take possession of it.

25 "Now the Amalekites and the Canaanites live in the valleys; turn tomorrow and set out to the wilderness by the way of the Red Sea."

26 ¶ The Lord spoke to Moses and Aaron, saying,

27 "How long *shall I bear* with this evil congregation who are grumbling against Me? I have heard the complaints of the sons of Israel, which they are making against Me.

28 "Say to them, 'As I live,' says the Lord, 'just as you have spoken in My hearing, so I will surely do to you;

29 your corpses will fall in this wilderness, even all your numbered men, according to your complete number from twenty years old and upward, who have grumbled against Me.

30 'Surely you shall not come into the land in which I swore to settle you, except Caleb the son of Jephunneh and Joshua the son of Nun.

31 'Your children, however, whom you said would become a prey—I will bring them in, and they will know the land which you have rejected.

32 'But as for you, your corpses will fall in this wilderness.

33 'Your sons shall be shepherds for forty years in the wilderness, and they will suffer *for* your unfaithfulness, until your corpses lie in the wilderness.

34 'According to the number of days which you spied out the land, forty days, for every day you shall bear your guilt a year, *even* forty years, and you will know My opposition.

35 'I, the Lord, have spoken, surely this I will do to all this evil congregation who are gathered together against Me. In this wilderness they shall be destroyed, and there they will die.' "

New International

13 Moses said to the Lord, "Then the Egyptians will hear about it! By your power you brought these people up from among them. 14 And they will tell the inhabitants of this land about it. They have already heard that you, O Lord, are with these people and that you, O Lord, have been seen face to face, that your cloud stays over them, and that you go before them in a pillar of cloud by day and a pillar of fire by night. 15 If you put these people to death all at one time, the nations who have heard this report about you will say, 16 'The Lord was not able to bring these people into the land he promised them on oath; so he slaughtered them in the desert.'

17 "Now may the Lord's strength be displayed, just as you have declared: 18 'The Lord is slow to anger, abounding in love and forgiving sin and rebellion. Yet he does not leave the guilty unpunished; he punishes the children for the sin of the fathers to the third and fourth generation.' 19 In accordance with your great love, forgive the sin of these people, just as you have pardoned them from the time they left Egypt until now."

20 The Lord replied, "I have forgiven them, as you asked. 21 Nevertheless, as surely as I live and as surely as the glory of the Lord fills the whole earth, 22 not one of the men who saw my glory and the miraculous signs I performed in Egypt and in the desert but who disobeyed me and tested me ten times— 23 not one of them will ever see the land I promised on oath to their forefathers. No one who has treated me with contempt will ever see it. 24 But because my servant Caleb has a different spirit and follows me wholeheartedly, I will bring him into the land he went to, and his descendants will inherit it. 25 Since the Amalekites and Canaanites are living in the valleys, turn back tomorrow and set out toward the desert along the route to the Red Sea.*d*"

26 The Lord said to Moses and Aaron: 27 "How long will this wicked community grumble against me? I have heard the complaints of these grumbling Israelites. 28 So tell them, 'As surely as I live, declares the Lord, I will do to you the very things I heard you say: 29 In this desert your bodies will fall—every one of you twenty years old or more who was counted in the census and who has grumbled against me. 30 Not one of you will enter the land I swore with uplifted hand to make your home, except Caleb son of Jephunneh and Joshua son of Nun. 31 As for your children that you said would be taken as plunder, I will bring them in to enjoy the land you have rejected. 32 But you—your bodies will fall in this desert. 33 Your children will be shepherds here for forty years, suffering for your unfaithfulness, until the last of your bodies lies in the desert. 34 For forty years—one year for each of the forty days you explored the land—you will suffer for your sins and know what it is like to have me against you.' 35 I, the Lord, have spoken, and I will surely do these things to this whole wicked community, which has banded together against me. They will meet their end in this desert; here they will die."

*d*25 Hebrew *Yam Suph*; that is, Sea of Reeds

King James

³⁶And the men, which Moses sent to search the land, who returned, and made all the congregation to murmur against him, by bringing up a slander upon the land,

³⁷Even those men that did bring up the evil report upon the land, died by the plague before the LORD.

³⁸But Joshua the son of Nun, and Caleb the son of Jephunneh, *which were* of the men that went to search the land, lived *still*.

³⁹And Moses told these sayings unto all the children of Israel: and the people mourned greatly.

⁴⁰ ¶ And they rose up early in the morning, and gat them up into the top of the mountain, saying, Lo, we *be here*, and will go up unto the place which the LORD hath promised: for we have sinned.

⁴¹And Moses said, Wherefore now do ye transgress the commandment of the LORD? but it shall not prosper.

⁴²Go not up, for the LORD *is* not among you; that ye be not smitten before your enemies.

⁴³For the Amalekites and the Canaanites *are* there before you, and ye shall fall by the sword: because ye are turned away from the LORD, therefore the LORD will not be with you.

⁴⁴But they presumed to go up unto the hill top: nevertheless the ark of the covenant of the LORD, and Moses, departed not out of the camp.

⁴⁵Then the Amalekites came down, and the Canaanites which dwelt in that hill, and smote them, and discomfited them, *even* unto Hormah.

Offerings required of Israel

15 AND THE LORD spake unto Moses, saying,
²Speak unto the children of Israel, and say unto them, When ye be come into the land of your habitations, which I give unto you,

³And will make an offering by fire unto the LORD, a burnt offering, or a sacrifice in ^hperforming a vow, or in a freewill offering, or in your solemn feasts, to make a sweet savour unto the LORD, of the herd, or of the flock:

⁴Then shall he that offereth his offering unto the LORD bring a meat offering of a tenth deal of flour mingled with the fourth *part* of an hin of oil.

⁵And the fourth *part* of an hin of wine for a drink offering shalt thou prepare with the burnt offering or sacrifice, for one lamb.

⁶Or for a ram, thou shalt prepare *for* a meat offering two tenth deals of flour mingled with the third *part* of an hin of oil.

⁷And for a drink offering thou shalt offer the third *part* of an hin of wine, *for* a sweet savour unto the LORD.

⁸And when thou preparest a bullock *for* a burnt offering, or *for* a sacrifice in performing a vow, or peace offerings unto the LORD:

⁹Then shall he bring with a bullock a meat offering of three tenth deals of flour mingled with half an hin of oil.

¹⁰And thou shalt bring for a drink offering half an hin of wine, *for* an offering made by fire, of a sweet savour unto the LORD.

¹¹Thus shall it be done for one bullock, or for one ram, or for a lamb, or a kid.

¹²According to the number that ye shall prepare, so shall ye do to every one according to their number.

¹³All that are born of the country shall do these things after this manner, in offering an offering made by fire, of a sweet savour unto the LORD.

Amplified

³⁶And the men whom Moses sent to search the land, who returned and made all the congregation grumble *and* complain against him by bringing back a slanderous report of the land,

³⁷Even those men who brought the evil report of the land died by a plague before the Lord. [Heb. 3:17–19; Jude 5–7.]

³⁸But Joshua son of Nun and Caleb son of Jephunneh, who were among the men who went to search the land, lived still.

³⁹Moses told [the Lord's] words to all the Israelites, and [they] mourned greatly.

⁴⁰And they rose early in the morning and went up to the top of the mountain, saying, Behold, we are here, and we intend to go up to the place which the Lord has promised, for we have sinned.

⁴¹But Moses said, Why now do you transgress the command of the Lord [to turn back by way of the Red Sea], since it will not succeed?

⁴²Go not up, for the Lord is not among you, that you be not struck down before your enemies.

⁴³For the Amalekites and the Canaanites are there before you, and you shall fall by the sword. Because you have turned away from following after the Lord, therefore the Lord will not be with you.

⁴⁴But they presumed to go up to the heights of the hill country; however, neither the ark of the covenant of the Lord nor Moses departed out of the camp.

⁴⁵Then the Amalekites came down and the Canaanites who dwelt in that hill country and smote them and beat them back, even as far as Hormah.

15 AND THE Lord said to Moses,
²Say to the Israelites, When you come into the land where you are to live, which I am giving you,

³And will make an offering by fire to the Lord from the herd or from the flock, a burnt offering or a sacrifice to fulfill a special vow or as a freewill offering or in your set feasts, to make a pleasant *and* soothing fragrance to the Lord,

⁴Then shall he who brings his offering to the Lord bring a cereal offering of a tenth of an ephah of fine flour mixed with a fourth of a hin of oil.

⁵And a fourth of a hin of wine for the drink offering you shall prepare with the burnt offering or for the sacrifice, for each lamb.

⁶Or for a ram you shall prepare for a cereal offering two tenths of an ephah of fine flour mixed with a third of a hin of oil.

⁷And for the drink offering you shall offer a third of a hin of wine, for a sweet *and* pleasing odor to the Lord. of the night.

⁸And when you prepare a bull for a burnt offering or for a sacrifice, in fulfilling a special vow or peace offering to the Lord,

⁹Then shall one offer with the bull a cereal offering of three tenths of an ephah of fine flour mixed with half a hin of oil.

¹⁰And you shall bring for the drink offering half a hin of wine for an offering made by fire, of a pleasant *and* soothing fragrance to the Lord.

¹¹Thus shall it be done for each bull or for each ram, or for each of the male lambs or of the kids.

¹²According to the number that you shall prepare, so shall you do to everyone according to their number.

¹³All who are native-born shall do these things in this way in bringing an offering made by fire of a sweet *and* pleasant odor to the Lord.

---

^hHeb. *separating*

New American Standard

³⁶ ¶ As for the men whom Moses sent to spy out the land and who returned and made all the congregation grumble against him by bringing out a bad report concerning the land,

³⁷ even those men who brought out the very bad report of the land died by a plague before the LORD.

³⁸ But Joshua the son of Nun and Caleb the son of Jephunneh remained alive out of those men who went to spy out the land.

Israel Repulsed

³⁹ ¶ When Moses spoke these words to all the sons of Israel, the people mourned greatly.

⁴⁰ In the morning, however, they rose up early and went up to the ridge of the hill country, saying, "Here we are; we have indeed sinned, but we will go up to the place which the LORD has promised."

⁴¹ But Moses said, "Why then are you transgressing the commandment of the LORD, when it will not succeed?

⁴²"Do not go up, or you will be struck down before your enemies, for the LORD is not among you.

⁴³"For the Amalekites and the Canaanites will be there in front of you, and you will fall by the sword, inasmuch as you have turned back from following the LORD. And the LORD will not be with you."

⁴⁴ But they went up heedlessly to the ridge of the hill country; neither the ark of the covenant of the LORD nor Moses left the camp.

⁴⁵ Then the Amalekites and the Canaanites who lived in that hill country came down, and struck them and beat them down as far as Hormah.

Laws for Canaan

15 NOW THE LORD spoke to Moses, saying, ²"Speak to the sons of Israel and say to them, 'When you enter the land where you are to live, which I am giving you,

³ then make an offering by fire to the LORD, a burnt offering or a sacrifice to fulfill a special vow, or as a freewill offering or in your appointed times, to make a soothing aroma to the LORD, from the herd or from the flock.

⁴ 'The one who presents his offering shall present to the LORD a grain offering of one-tenth *of an ephah* of fine flour mixed with one-fourth of a ^shin of oil,

⁵ and you shall prepare wine for the drink offering, one-fourth of a hin, with the burnt offering or for the sacrifice, for each lamb.

⁶ 'Or for a ram you shall prepare as a grain offering two-tenths *of an ephah* of fine flour mixed with one-third of a hin of oil;

⁷ and for the drink offering you shall offer one-third of a hin of wine as a soothing aroma to the LORD.

⁸ 'When you prepare a bull as a burnt offering or a sacrifice, to fulfill a special vow, or for peace offerings to the LORD,

⁹ then you shall offer with the bull a grain offering of three-tenths *of an ephah* of fine flour mixed with one-half a hin of oil;

¹⁰ and you shall offer as the drink offering one-half a hin of wine as an offering by fire, as a soothing aroma to the LORD.

¹¹ ¶ 'Thus it shall be done for each ox, or for each ram, or for each of the male lambs, or of the goats.

¹² 'According to the number that you prepare, so you shall do for everyone according to their number.

¹³ 'All who are native shall do these things in this manner, in presenting an offering by fire, as a soothing aroma to the LORD.

New International

³⁶So the men Moses had sent to explore the land, who returned and made the whole community grumble against him by spreading a bad report about it— ³⁷these men responsible for spreading the bad report about the land were struck down and died of a plague before the LORD. ³⁸Of the men who went to explore the land, only Joshua son of Nun and Caleb son of Jephunneh survived.

³⁹When Moses reported this to all the Israelites, they mourned bitterly. ⁴⁰Early the next morning they went up toward the high hill country. "We have sinned," they said. "We will go up to the place the LORD promised."

⁴¹But Moses said, "Why are you disobeying the LORD's command? This will not succeed! ⁴²Do not go up, because the LORD is not with you. You will be defeated by your enemies, ⁴³for the Amalekites and Canaanites will face you there. Because you have turned away from the LORD, he will not be with you and you will fall by the sword."

⁴⁴Nevertheless, in their presumption they went up toward the high hill country, though neither Moses nor the ark of the LORD's covenant moved from the camp. ⁴⁵Then the Amalekites and Canaanites who lived in that hill country came down and attacked them and beat them down all the way to Hormah.

Supplementary Offerings

15 THE LORD said to Moses, ²"Speak to the Israelites and say to them: 'After you enter the land I am giving you as a home ³and you present to the LORD offerings made by fire, from the herd or the flock, as an aroma pleasing to the LORD—whether burnt offerings or sacrifices, for special vows or freewill offerings or festival offerings— ⁴then the one who brings his offering shall present to the LORD a grain offering of a tenth of an ephah^e of fine flour mixed with a quarter of a hin^f of oil. ⁵With each lamb for the burnt offering or the sacrifice, prepare a quarter of a hin of wine as a drink offering.

⁶" 'With a ram prepare a grain offering of two-tenths of an ephah^g of fine flour mixed with a third of a hin^h of oil, ⁷and a third of a hin of wine as a drink offering. Offer it as an aroma pleasing to the LORD.

⁸" 'When you prepare a young bull as a burnt offering or sacrifice, for a special vow or a fellowship offeringⁱ to the LORD, ⁹bring with the bull a grain offering of three-tenths of an ephah^j of fine flour mixed with half a hin^k of oil. ¹⁰Also bring half a hin of wine as a drink offering. It will be an offering made by fire, an aroma pleasing to the LORD. ¹¹Each bull or ram, each lamb or young goat, is to be prepared in this manner. ¹²Do this for each one, for as many as you prepare.

¹³" 'Everyone who is native-born must do these things in this way when he brings an offering made by fire as an

---

^e4 That is, probably about 2 quarts (about 2 liters)   ^f4 That is, probably about 1 quart (about 1 liter); also in verse 5   ^g6 That is, probably about 4 quarts (about 4.5 liters)   ^h6 That is, probably about 1 1/4 quarts (about 1.2 liters); also in verse 7   ⁱ8 Traditionally *peace offering*   ^j9 That is, probably about 6 quarts (about 6.5 liters)   ^k9 That is, probably about 2 quarts (about 2 liters); also in verse 10

---

^sI.e. Approx one gal., and so through v 10

King James

14And if a stranger sojourn with you, or whosoever *be* among you in your generations, and will offer an offering made by fire, of a sweet savour unto the LORD; as ye do, so he shall do.

15One ordinance *shall be both* for you of the congregation, and also for the stranger that sojourneth *with you,* an ordinance for ever in your generations: as ye *are,* so shall the stranger be before the LORD.

16One law and one manner shall be for you, and for the stranger that sojourneth with you.

17 ¶ And the LORD spake unto Moses, saying,

18Speak unto the children of Israel, and say unto them, When ye come into the land whither I bring you,

19Then it shall be, that, when ye eat of the bread of the land, ye shall offer up an heave offering unto the LORD.

20Ye shall offer up a cake of the first of your dough *for* an heave offering: as *ye do* the heave offering of the threshingfloor, so shall ye heave it.

21Of the first of your dough ye shall give unto the LORD an heave offering in your generations.

Offering for unintentional sins

22 ¶ And if ye have erred, and not observed all these commandments, which the LORD hath spoken unto Moses,

23*Even* all that the LORD hath commanded you by the hand of Moses, from the day that the LORD commanded *Moses,* and henceforward among your generations;

24Then it shall be, if *aught* be committed by ignorance *i*without the knowledge of the congregation, that all the congregation shall offer one young bullock for a burnt offering, for a sweet savour unto the LORD, with his meat offering, and his drink offering, according to the *j*manner, and one kid of the goats for a sin offering.

25And the priest shall make an atonement for all the congregation of the children of Israel, and it shall be forgiven them; for it *is* ignorance: and they shall bring their offering, a sacrifice made by fire unto the LORD, and their sin offering before the LORD, for their ignorance:

26And it shall be forgiven all the congregation of the children of Israel, and the stranger that sojourneth among them; seeing all the people *were* in ignorance.

27 ¶ And if any soul sin through ignorance, then he shall bring a she goat of the first year for a sin offering.

28And the priest shall make an atonement for the soul that sinneth ignorantly, when he sinneth by ignorance before the LORD, to make an atonement for him; and it shall be forgiven him.

29Ye shall have one law for him that *k*sinneth through ignorance, *both for* him that is born among the children of Israel, and for the stranger that sojourneth among them.

30 ¶ But the soul that doeth *aught* *l*presumptuously, *whether he be* born in the land, or a stranger, the same reproacheth the LORD; and that soul shall be cut off from among his people.

31Because he hath despised the word of the LORD, and hath broken his commandment, that soul shall utterly be cut off; his iniquity *shall be* upon him.

Stoning the sabbath breaker

32 ¶ And while the children of Israel were in the wilderness, they found a man that gathered sticks upon the sabbath day.

33And they that found him gathering sticks brought him unto Moses and Aaron, and unto all the congregation.

34And they put him in ward, because it was not declared what should be done to him.

35And the LORD said unto Moses, The man shall be surely put to death: all the congregation shall stone him with stones without the camp.

36And all the congregation brought him without the camp, and stoned him with stones, and he died; as the LORD commanded Moses.

Amplified

14And if a stranger sojourns with you or whoever may be among you throughout your generations, and he wishes to offer an offering made by fire, of a pleasing *and* soothing fragrance to the Lord, as you do, so shall he do.

15There shall be one [and the same] statute [both] for you [of the congregation] and for the stranger who is a temporary resident with you, a statute forever throughout your generations: as you are, so shall the stranger be before the Lord.

16One law and one ordinance shall be for you and for the stranger who sojourns with you.

17And the Lord said to Moses,

18Say to the Israelites, When you come into the land to which I am bringing you,

19Then, when you eat of the food of the land, you shall set apart a portion for a gift to the Lord [called a heave or taken-out offering].

20You shall set apart a cake made of the first of your coarse meal as a gift [to the Lord]; as an offering set apart from the threshing floor, so shall you lift it out *or* heave it.

21Of the first of your coarse meal you shall give to the Lord a portion for a gift throughout your generations [your heave or lifted-out offering].

22When you have erred and have not observed all these commandments which the Lord has spoken to Moses,

23Even all that the Lord has commanded you through Moses, from the day that the Lord gave commandment and onward throughout your generations,

24Then it shall be, if it was done unwittingly *or* in error without the knowledge of the congregation, that all the congregation shall offer one young bull for a burnt offering, for a pleasant *and* soothing fragrance to the Lord, with its cereal offering and its drink offering, according to the ordinance, and one male goat for a sin offering.

25And the priest shall make atonement for all the congregation of the Israelites, and they shall be forgiven, for it was an error and they have brought their offering, an offering made by fire to the Lord, and their sin offering before the Lord for their error.

26And all the congregation of the Israelites shall be forgiven and the stranger who lives temporarily among them, because all the people were involved in the error.

27And if any person sins unknowingly *or* unintentionally, he shall offer a female goat a year old for a sin offering.

28And the priest shall make atonement before the Lord for the person who commits an error when he sins unknowingly *or* unintentionally, to make atonement for him; and he shall be forgiven.

29You shall have one law for him who sins unknowingly *or* unintentionally, whether he is native born among the Israelites or a stranger who is sojourning among them.

30But the person who does anything [wrong] willfully *and* openly, whether he is native-born or a stranger, that one reproaches, reviles, *and* blasphemes the Lord, and that person shall be cut off from among his people [that the atonement made for them may not include him].

31Because he has despised and rejected the word of the Lord, and has broken His commandment, that person shall be utterly cut off; his iniquity shall be upon him.

32While the Israelites were in the wilderness, they found a man who was gathering sticks on the Sabbath day.

33Those who found him gathering sticks brought him to Moses and Aaron and to all the congregation.

34They put him in custody, because it was not certain *or* clear what should be done to him.

35And the Lord said to Moses, The man shall surely be put to death. All the congregation shall stone him with stones without the camp.

36And all the congregation brought him without the camp and stoned him to death with stones, as the Lord commanded Moses.

---

*i*Heb. *from the eyes*   *j*Or, *ordinance*   *k*Heb. *doth*   *l*Heb. *with an high hand*

New American Standard

Law of the Sojourner

14 'If an alien sojourns with you, or one who may be among you throughout your generations, and he *wishes to* make an offering by fire, as a soothing aroma to the LORD, just as you do so he shall do.

15 '*As for* the assembly, there shall be one statute for you and for the alien who sojourns *with you,* a perpetual statute throughout your generations; as you are, so shall the alien be before the LORD.

16 'There is to be one law and one ordinance for you and for the alien who sojourns with you.' "

17 ¶ Then the LORD spoke to Moses, saying,

18 "Speak to the sons of Israel and say to them, 'When you enter the land where I bring you,

19 then it shall be, that when you eat of the food of the land, you shall lift up an offering to the LORD.

20 'Of the first of your ʳdough you shall lift up a cake as an offering; as the offering of the threshing floor, so you shall lift it up.

21 'From the first of your ʳdough you shall give to the LORD an offering throughout your generations.

22 ¶ 'But when you unwittingly fail and do not observe all these commandments, which the LORD has spoken to Moses,

23 *even* all that the LORD has commanded you through Moses, from the day when the LORD gave commandment and onward throughout your generations,

24 then it shall be, if it is done unintentionally, without the knowledge of the congregation, that all the congregation shall offer one bull for a burnt offering, as a soothing aroma to the LORD, with its grain offering and its drink offering, according to the ordinance, and one male goat for a sin offering.

25 'Then the priest shall make atonement for all the congregation of the sons of Israel, and they will be forgiven; for it was an error, and they have brought their offering, an offering by fire to the LORD, and their sin offering before the LORD, for their error.

26 'So all the congregation of the sons of Israel will be forgiven, with the alien who sojourns among them, for *it happened* to all the people through error.

27 ¶ 'Also if one person sins unintentionally, then he shall offer a one year old female goat for a sin offering.

28 'The priest shall make atonement before the LORD for the person who goes astray when he sins unintentionally, making atonement for him that he may be forgiven.

29 'You shall have one law for him who does *anything* unintentionally, for him who is native among the sons of Israel and for the alien who sojourns among them.

30 'But the person who does *anything* defiantly, whether he is native or an alien, that one is blaspheming the LORD; and that person shall be cut off from among his people.

31 'Because he has despised the word of the LORD and has broken His commandment, that person shall be completely cut off; his guilt *will be* on him.' "

Sabbath-breaking Punished

32 ¶ Now while the sons of Israel were in the wilderness, they found a man gathering wood on the sabbath day.

33 Those who found him gathering wood brought him to Moses and Aaron and to all the congregation;

34 and they put him in custody because it had not been declared what should be done to him.

35 Then the LORD said to Moses, "The man shall surely be put to death; all the congregation shall stone him with stones outside the camp."

36 So all the congregation brought him outside the camp and stoned him to death with stones, just as the LORD had commanded Moses.

New International

aroma pleasing to the LORD. 14For the generations to come, whenever an alien or anyone else living among you presents an offering made by fire as an aroma pleasing to the LORD, he must do exactly as you do. 15The community is to have the same rules for you and for the alien living among you; this is a lasting ordinance for the generations to come. You and the alien shall be the same before the LORD: 16The same laws and regulations will apply both to you and to the alien living among you.' "

17The LORD said to Moses, 18"Speak to the Israelites and say to them: 'When you enter the land to which I am taking you 19and you eat the food of the land, present a portion as an offering to the LORD. 20Present a cake from the first of your ground meal and present it as an offering from the threshing floor. 21Throughout the generations to come you are to give this offering to the LORD from the first of your ground meal.

Offerings for Unintentional Sins

22" 'Now if you unintentionally fail to keep any of these commands the LORD gave Moses— 23any of the LORD's commands to you through him, from the day the LORD gave them and continuing through the generations to come— 24and if this is done unintentionally without the community being aware of it, then the whole community is to offer a young bull for a burnt offering as an aroma pleasing to the LORD, along with its prescribed grain offering and drink offering, and a male goat for a sin offering. 25The priest is to make atonement for the whole Israelite community, and they will be forgiven, for it was not intentional and they have brought to the LORD for their wrong an offering made by fire and a sin offering. 26The whole Israelite community and the aliens living among them will be forgiven, because all the people were involved in the unintentional wrong.

27" 'But if just one person sins unintentionally, he must bring a year-old female goat for a sin offering. 28The priest is to make atonement before the LORD for the one who erred by sinning unintentionally, and when atonement has been made for him, he will be forgiven. 29One and the same law applies to everyone who sins unintentionally, whether he is a native-born Israelite or an alien.

30" 'But anyone who sins defiantly, whether native-born or alien, blasphemes the LORD, and that person must be cut off from his people. 31Because he has despised the LORD's word and broken his commands, that person must surely be cut off; his guilt remains on him.' "

The Sabbath-Breaker Put to Death

32While the Israelites were in the desert, a man was found gathering wood on the Sabbath day. 33Those who found him gathering wood brought him to Moses and Aaron and the whole assembly, 34and they kept him in custody, because it was not clear what should be done to him. 35Then the LORD said to Moses, "The man must die. The whole assembly must stone him outside the camp." 36So the assembly took him outside the camp and stoned him to death, as the LORD commanded Moses.

ʳOr *coarse meal*

King James

The fringes of remembrance

37 ¶ And the LORD spake unto Moses, saying,

38Speak unto the children of Israel, and bid them that they make them fringes in the borders of their garments throughout their generations, and that they put upon the fringe of the borders a ribband of blue:

39And it shall be unto you for a fringe, that ye may look upon it, and remember all the commandments of the LORD, and do them; and that ye seek not after your own heart and your own eyes, after which ye use to go a-whoring:

40That ye may remember, and do all my commandments, and be holy unto your God.

41I am the LORD your God, which brought you out of the land of Egypt, to be your God: I am the LORD your God.

The rebellion of Korah

16 NOW KORAH, the son of Izhar, the son of Kohath, the son of Levi, and Dathan and Abiram, the sons of Eliab, and On, the son of Peleth, sons of Reuben, took men:

2And they rose up before Moses, with certain of the children of Israel, two hundred and fifty princes of the assembly, famous in the congregation, men of renown:

3And they gathered themselves together against Moses and against Aaron, and said unto them, *mYe take* too much upon you, seeing all the congregation *are* holy, every one of them, and the LORD *is* among them: wherefore then lift ye up yourselves above the congregation of the LORD?

4And when Moses heard *it*, he fell upon his face:

5And he spake unto Korah and unto all his company, saying, Even tomorrow the LORD will show who *are* his, and *who is* holy; and will cause *him* to come near unto him: even *him* whom he hath chosen will he cause to come near unto him.

6This do; Take you censers, Korah, and all his company;

7And put fire therein, and put incense in them before the LORD tomorrow: and it shall be *that* the man whom the LORD doth choose, he *shall be* holy: ye take too much upon you, ye sons of Levi.

8And Moses said unto Korah, Hear, I pray you, ye sons of Levi:

9*Seemeth it but* a small thing unto you, that the God of Israel hath separated you from the congregation of Israel, to bring you near to himself to do the service of the tabernacle of the LORD, and to stand before the congregation to minister unto them?

10And he hath brought thee near *to him,* and all thy brethren the sons of Levi with thee: and seek ye the priesthood also?

11For which cause *both* thou and all thy company *are* gathered together against the LORD: and what *is* Aaron, that ye murmur against him?

12 ¶ And Moses sent to call Dathan and Abiram, the sons of Eliab: which said, We will not come up:

13*Is it* a small thing that thou hast brought us up out of a land that floweth with milk and honey, to kill us in the wilderness, except thou make thyself altogether a prince over us?

14Moreover thou hast not brought us into a land that floweth with milk and honey, or given us inheritance of fields and vineyards: wilt thou *n*put out the eyes of these men? we will not come up.

15And Moses was very wroth, and said unto the LORD, Respect not thou their offering: I have not taken one ass from them, neither have I hurt one of them.

16And Moses said unto Korah, Be thou and all thy company before the LORD, thou, and they, and Aaron, tomorrow:

Amplified

37And the Lord said to Moses,

38Speak to the Israelites and bid them make fringes *or* tassels on the corners in the borders of their garments throughout their generations, and put upon the fringe of the borders *or* upon the tassel of each corner a cord of blue.

39And it shall be to you a fringe *or* tassel that you may look upon and remember all the commandments of the Lord and do them, that you may not spy out *and* follow after [the desires of] your own heart and your own eyes, after which you used to follow *and* play the harlot [spiritually, if not physically],

40That you may remember and do all My commandments and be holy to your God.

41I am the Lord your God, Who brought you out of the land of Egypt to be your God. I am the Lord your God.

16 NOW KORAH son of Izhar, the son of Kohath, the son of Levi, with Dathan and Abiram sons of Eliab, and On son of Peleth, sons of Reuben, took men.

2And they rose up before Moses, with certain of the Israelites, 250 princes *or* leaders of the congregation called to the assembly, men well known *and* of distinction.

3And they gathered together against Moses and Aaron, and said to them, [Enough of you!] You take too much upon yourselves, seeing that all the congregation is holy, every one of them, and the Lord is among them. Why then do you lift yourselves up above the assembly of the Lord?

4And when Moses heard it, he fell upon his face.

5And he said to Korah and all his company, In the morning the Lord will show who are His and who is holy, and will cause him to come near to Him; him whom He has chosen will He cause to come near to Him. [II Tim. 2:19.]

6Do this: Take censers, Korah and all your company,

7And put fire in them and put incense upon them before the Lord tomorrow; and the man whom the Lord chooses shall be holy. You take too much upon yourselves, you sons of Levi.

8And Moses said to Korah, Hear, I pray you, you sons of Levi:

9Does it seem but a small thing to you that the God of Israel has separated you from the congregation of Israel, to bring you near to Himself to do the service of the tabernacle of the Lord and to stand before the congregation to minister to them,

10And that He has brought you near to Him, and all your brethren the sons of Levi with you? Would you seek the priesthood also?

11Therefore you and all your company are gathered together against the Lord. And Aaron, what is he that you murmur against him?

12And Moses sent to call Dathan and Abiram, the sons of Eliab, and they said, We will not come up.

13Is it a small thing that you have brought us up out of a land flowing with milk and honey to kill us in the wilderness, but you must also make yourself a prince over us?

14Moreover, you have not brought us into a land that flows with milk and honey or given us an inheritance of fields and vineyards. Will you bore out the eyes of these men? We will not come up!

15And Moses was very angry and said to the Lord, Do not respect their offering! I have not taken one donkey from them, nor have I hurt one of them.

16And Moses said to Korah, You and all your company be before the Lord tomorrow, you and they and Aaron.

---

*m*Heb. It is *much for you*   *n*Heb. *bore out*

New American Standard

37 ¶ The LORD also spoke to Moses, saying,
38"Speak to the sons of Israel, and tell them that they shall make for themselves tassels on the corners of their garments throughout their generations, and that they shall put on the tassel of each corner a cord of blue.
39"It shall be a tassel for you to look at and remember all the commandments of the LORD, so as to do them and not follow after your own heart and your own eyes, after which you played the harlot,
40 so that you may remember to do all My commandments and be holy to your God.
41"I am the LORD your God who brought you out from the land of Egypt to be your God; I am the LORD your God."

Korah's Rebellion

16 NOW KORAH the son of Izhar, the son of Kohath, the son of Levi, with Dathan and Abiram, the sons of Eliab, and On the son of Peleth, sons of Reuben, took *action,*
2 and they rose up before Moses, together with some of the sons of Israel, two hundred and fifty leaders of the congregation, chosen in the assembly, men of renown.
3 They assembled together against Moses and Aaron, and said to them, "You have gone far enough, for all the congregation are holy, every one of them, and the LORD is in their midst; so why do you exalt yourselves above the assembly of the LORD?"
4 ¶ When Moses heard *this,* he fell on his face;
5 and he spoke to Korah and all his company, saying, "Tomorrow morning the LORD will show who is His, and who is holy, and will bring *him* near to Himself; even the one whom He will choose, He will bring near to Himself.
6"Do this: take censers for yourselves, Korah and all your company,
7 and put fire in them, and lay incense upon them in the presence of the LORD tomorrow; and the man whom the LORD chooses *shall be* the one who is holy. You have gone far enough, you sons of Levi!"
8 ¶ Then Moses said to Korah, "Hear now, you sons of Levi,
9 is it not enough for you that the God of Israel has separated you from the *rest of* the congregation of Israel, to bring you near to Himself, to do the service of the tabernacle of the LORD, and to stand before the congregation to minister to them;
10 and that He has brought you near, *Korah,* and all your brothers, sons of Levi, with you? And are you seeking for the priesthood also?
11"Therefore you and all your company are gathered together against the LORD; but as for Aaron, who is he that you grumble against him?"
12 ¶ Then Moses sent a summons to Dathan and Abiram, the sons of Eliab; but they said, "We will not come up.
13"Is it not enough that you have brought us up out of a land flowing with milk and honey to have us die in the wilderness, but you would also lord it over us?
14"Indeed, you have not brought us into a land flowing with milk and honey, nor have you given us an inheritance of fields and vineyards. Would you put out the eyes of these men? We will not come up!"
15 ¶ Then Moses became very angry and said to the LORD, "Do not regard their offering! I have not taken a single donkey from them, nor have I done harm to any of them."
16 Moses said to Korah, "You and all your company be present before the LORD tomorrow, both you and they along with Aaron.

New International

Tassels on Garments

37The LORD said to Moses, 38"Speak to the Israelites and say to them: 'Throughout the generations to come you are to make tassels on the corners of your garments, with a blue cord on each tassel. 39You will have these tassels to look at and so you will remember all the commands of the LORD, that you may obey them and not prostitute yourselves by going after the lusts of your own hearts and eyes. 40Then you will remember to obey all my commands and will be consecrated to your God. 41I am the LORD your God, who brought you out of Egypt to be your God. I am the LORD your God.' "

Korah, Dathan and Abiram

16 KORAH SON of Izhar, the son of Kohath, the son of Levi, and certain Reubenites—Dathan and Abiram, sons of Eliab, and On son of Peleth—became insolent[1] 2and rose up against Moses. With them were 250 Israelite men, well-known community leaders who had been appointed members of the council. 3They came as a group to oppose Moses and Aaron and said to them, "You have gone too far! The whole community is holy, every one of them, and the LORD is with them. Why then do you set yourselves above the LORD's assembly?"
4When Moses heard this, he fell facedown. 5Then he said to Korah and all his followers: "In the morning the LORD will show who belongs to him and who is holy, and he will have that person come near him. The man he chooses he will cause to come near him. 6You, Korah, and all your followers are to do this: Take censers 7and tomorrow put fire and incense in them before the LORD. The man the LORD chooses will be the one who is holy. You Levites have gone too far!"
8Moses also said to Korah, "Now listen, you Levites! 9Isn't it enough for you that the God of Israel has separated you from the rest of the Israelite community and brought you near himself to do the work at the LORD's tabernacle and to stand before the community and minister to them? 10He has brought you and all your fellow Levites near himself, but now you are trying to get the priesthood too. 11It is against the LORD that you and all your followers have banded together. Who is Aaron that you should grumble against him?"
12Then Moses summoned Dathan and Abiram, the sons of Eliab. But they said, "We will not come! 13Isn't it enough that you have brought us up out of a land flowing with milk and honey to kill us in the desert? And now you also want to lord it over us? 14Moreover, you haven't brought us into a land flowing with milk and honey or given us an inheritance of fields and vineyards. Will you gouge out the eyes of[m] these men? No, we will not come!"
15Then Moses became very angry and said to the LORD, "Do not accept their offering. I have not taken so much as a donkey from them, nor have I wronged any of them."
16Moses said to Korah, "You and all your followers are to appear before the LORD tomorrow—you and they and

---

l 1 Or *Peleth—took ₍men₎*   *m* 14 Or *you make slaves of*; or *you deceive*

King James

¹⁷And take every man his censer, and put incense in them, and bring ye before the LORD every man his censer, two hundred and fifty censers; thou also, and Aaron, each *of you* his censer.

¹⁸And they took every man his censer, and put fire in them, and laid incense thereon, and stood in the door of the tabernacle of the congregation with Moses and Aaron.

¹⁹And Korah gathered all the congregation against them unto the door of the tabernacle of the congregation: and the glory of the LORD appeared unto all the congregation.

²⁰And the LORD spake unto Moses and unto Aaron, saying,

²¹Separate yourselves from among this congregation, that I may consume them in a moment.

²²And they fell upon their faces, and said, O God, the God of the spirits of all flesh, shall one man sin, and wilt thou be wroth with all the congregation?

²³ ¶ And the LORD spake unto Moses, saying,

²⁴Speak unto the congregation, saying, Get you up from about the tabernacle of Korah, Dathan, and Abiram.

²⁵And Moses rose up and went unto Dathan and Abiram; and the elders of Israel followed him.

²⁶And he spake unto the congregation, saying, Depart, I pray you, from the tents of these wicked men, and touch nothing of theirs, lest ye be consumed in all their sins.

²⁷So they gat up from the tabernacle of Korah, Dathan, and Abiram, on every side: and Dathan and Abiram came out, and stood in the door of their tents, and their wives, and their sons, and their little children.

²⁸And Moses said, Hereby ye shall know that the LORD hath sent me to do all these works; for *I have* not *done them* of mine own mind.

²⁹If these men die ^othe common death of all men, or if they be visited after the visitation of all men; *then* the LORD hath not sent me.

³⁰But if the LORD ^pmake a new thing, and the earth open her mouth, and swallow them up, with all that *appertain* unto them, and they go down quick into the pit; then ye shall understand that these men have provoked the LORD.

³¹ ¶ And it came to pass, as he had made an end of speaking all these words, that the ground clave asunder that *was* under them:

³²And the earth opened her mouth, and swallowed them up, and their houses, and all the men that *appertained* unto Korah, and all *their* goods.

³³They, and all that *appertained* to them, went down alive into the pit, and the earth closed upon them: and they perished from among the congregation.

³⁴And all Israel that *were* round about them fled at the cry of them: for they said, Lest the earth swallow us up *also.*

³⁵And there came out a fire from the LORD, and consumed the two hundred and fifty men that offered incense.

³⁶ ¶ And the LORD spake unto Moses, saying,

³⁷Speak unto Eleazar the son of Aaron the priest, that he take up the censers out of the burning, and scatter thou the fire yonder; for they are hallowed.

³⁸The censers of these sinners against their own souls, let them make them broad plates *for* a covering of the altar: for they offered them before the LORD, therefore they are hallowed: and they shall be a sign unto the children of Israel.

³⁹And Eleazar the priest took the brasen censers, wherewith they that were burnt had offered; and they were made broad *plates for* a covering of the altar:

⁴⁰*To be* a memorial unto the children of Israel, that no stranger, which *is* not of the seed of Aaron, come near to offer incense before the LORD; that he be not as Korah, and as his company: as the LORD said to him by the hand of Moses.

Amplified

¹⁷And let every man take his censer and put incense upon it and bring before the Lord every man his censer, 250 censers; you also and Aaron, each his censer.

¹⁸So they took every man his censer, and they put fire in them and laid incense upon it, and they stood at the entrance of the Tent of Meeting with Moses and Aaron.

¹⁹Then Korah assembled all the congregation against Moses and Aaron before the entrance of the Tent of Meeting, and the glory of the Lord appeared to all the congregation.

²⁰And the Lord said to Moses and Aaron,

²¹Separate yourselves from among this congregation, that I may consume them in a moment.

²²And they fell upon their faces, and said, O God, the God of the spirits of all flesh, shall one man sin and will You be angry with all the congregation?

²³And the Lord said to Moses,

²⁴Say to the congregation, Get away from around the tents of Korah, Dathan, and Abiram.

²⁵Then Moses rose up and went to Dathan and Abiram, and the elders of Israel followed him.

²⁶And he said to the congregation, Depart, I pray you, from the tents of these wicked men, and touch nothing of theirs, lest you be consumed in all their sins.

²⁷So they got away from around the tents of Korah, Dathan, and Abiram. And Dathan and Abiram came out and stood in the door of their tents with their wives, and their sons, and their little ones.

²⁸And Moses said, By this you shall know that the Lord has sent me to do all these works, for I do not act of my own accord:

²⁹If these men die the common death of all men or if [only] what happens to everyone happens to them, then the Lord has not sent me.

³⁰But if the Lord causes a new thing [to happen], and the earth opens its mouth and swallows them up, with all that belongs to them, and they go down alive into Sheol (the place of the dead), then you shall understand that these men have provoked (spurned, despised) the Lord!

³¹As soon as he stopped speaking, the ground under the offenders split apart

³²And the earth opened its mouth and swallowed them and their households and [Korah and] all [his] men and all their possessions. [Num. 26:10, 11.]

³³They and all that belonged to them went down alive into Sheol (the place of the dead); and the earth closed upon them, and they perished from among the assembly.

³⁴And all Israel who were round about them fled at their cry, for they said, Lest the earth swallow us up also.

³⁵And fire came forth from the Lord and devoured the 250 men who offered the incense.

³⁶And the Lord said to Moses,

³⁷Speak to Eleazar son of Aaron, the priest, that he take up the censers out of the burning and scatter the fire at a distance. For the censers are hallowed—

³⁸The censers of these men who have sinned against themselves *and* at the cost of their own lives. Let the censers be made into hammered plates for a covering of the altar [of burnt offering], for they were used in offering before the Lord and therefore they are sacred. They shall be a sign [of warning] to the Israelites.

³⁹Eleazar the priest took the bronze censers with which the Levites who were burned had offered incense, and they were hammered into broad sheets for a covering of the [brazen] altar [of burnt offering],

⁴⁰To be a memorial [a warning forever] to the Israelites, so that no outsider, that is, no one not of the descendants of Aaron, should come near to offer incense before the Lord, lest he become as Korah and as his company, as the Lord said to Eleazar through Moses.

---

^oHeb. *as every man dieth*   ^pHeb. *create a creature*

New American Standard

17"Each of you take his firepan and put incense on it, and each of you bring his censer before the LORD, two hundred and fifty firepans; also you and Aaron *shall* each *bring* his firepan."

18 So they each took his *own* censer and put fire on it, and laid incense on it; and they stood at the doorway of the tent of meeting, with Moses and Aaron.

19 Thus Korah assembled all the congregation against them at the doorway of the tent of meeting. And the glory of the LORD appeared to all the congregation.

20 ¶ Then the LORD spoke to Moses and Aaron, saying,

21"Separate yourselves from among this congregation, that I may consume them instantly."

22 But they fell on their faces and said, "O God, God of the spirits of all flesh, when one man sins, will You be angry with the entire congregation?"

23 ¶ Then the LORD spoke to Moses, saying,

24"Speak to the congregation, saying, 'Get back from around the dwellings of Korah, Dathan and Abiram.' "

25 ¶ Then Moses arose and went to Dathan and Abiram, with the elders of Israel following him,

26 and he spoke to the congregation, saying, "Depart now from the tents of these wicked men, and touch nothing that belongs to them, or you will be swept away in all their sin."

27 So they got back from around the dwellings of Korah, Dathan and Abiram; and Dathan and Abiram came out *and* stood at the doorway of their tents, along with their wives and their sons and their little ones.

28 Moses said, "By this you shall know that the LORD has sent me to do all these deeds; for this is not my doing.

29"If these men die the death of all men or if they suffer the fate of all men, *then* the LORD has not sent me.

30"But if the LORD brings about an entirely new thing and the ground opens its mouth and swallows them up with all that is theirs, and they descend alive into Sheol, then you will understand that these men have spurned the LORD."

31 ¶ As he finished speaking all these words, the ground that was under them split open;

32 and the earth opened its mouth and swallowed them up, and their households, and all the men who belonged to Korah with *their* possessions.

33 So they and all that belonged to them went down alive to Sheol; and the earth closed over them, and they perished from the midst of the assembly.

34 All Israel who *were* around them fled at their outcry, for they said, "The earth may swallow us up!"

35 Fire also came forth from the LORD and consumed the two hundred and fifty men who were offering the incense.

36 ¶ Then the LORD spoke to Moses, saying,

37"Say to Eleazar, the son of Aaron the priest, that he shall take up the censers out of the midst of the blaze, for they are holy; and you scatter the burning coals abroad."

38"As for the censers of these men who have sinned at the cost of their lives, let them be made into hammered sheets for a plating of the altar, since they did present them before the LORD and they are holy; and they shall be for a sign to the sons of Israel."

39 So Eleazar the priest took the bronze censers which the men who were burned had offered, and they hammered them out as a plating for the altar,

40 as a reminder to the sons of Israel that no layman who is not of the descendants of Aaron should come near to burn incense before the LORD; so that he will not become like Korah and his company—just as the LORD had spoken to him through Moses.

New International

Aaron. 17Each man is to take his censer and put incense in it—250 censers in all—and present it before the LORD. You and Aaron are to present your censers also." 18So each man took his censer, put fire and incense in it, and stood with Moses and Aaron at the entrance to the Tent of Meeting. 19When Korah had gathered all his followers in opposition to them at the entrance to the Tent of Meeting, the glory of the LORD appeared to the entire assembly. 20The LORD said to Moses and Aaron, 21"Separate yourselves from this assembly so I can put an end to them at once."

22But Moses and Aaron fell facedown and cried out, "O God, God of the spirits of all mankind, will you be angry with the entire assembly when only one man sins?"

23Then the LORD said to Moses, 24"Say to the assembly, 'Move away from the tents of Korah, Dathan and Abiram.' "

25Moses got up and went to Dathan and Abiram, and the elders of Israel followed him. 26He warned the assembly, "Move back from the tents of these wicked men! Do not touch anything belonging to them, or you will be swept away because of all their sins." 27So they moved away from the tents of Korah, Dathan and Abiram. Dathan and Abiram had come out and were standing with their wives, children and little ones at the entrances to their tents.

28Then Moses said, "This is how you will know that the LORD has sent me to do all these things and that it was not my idea: 29If these men die a natural death and experience only what usually happens to men, then the LORD has not sent me. 30But if the LORD brings about something totally new, and the earth opens its mouth and swallows them, with everything that belongs to them, and they go down alive into the grave,[n] then you will know that these men have treated the LORD with contempt."

31As soon as he finished saying all this, the ground under them split apart 32and the earth opened its mouth and swallowed them, with their households and all Korah's men and all their possessions. 33They went down alive into the grave, with everything they owned; the earth closed over them, and they perished and were gone from the community. 34At their cries, all the Israelites around them fled, shouting, "The earth is going to swallow us too!"

35And fire came out from the LORD and consumed the 250 men who were offering the incense.

36The LORD said to Moses, 37"Tell Eleazar son of Aaron, the priest, to take the censers out of the smoldering remains and scatter the coals some distance away, for the censers are holy— 38the censers of the men who sinned at the cost of their lives. Hammer the censers into sheets to overlay the altar, for they were presented before the LORD and have become holy. Let them be a sign to the Israelites."

39So Eleazar the priest collected the bronze censers brought by those who had been burned up, and he had them hammered out to overlay the altar, 40as the LORD directed him through Moses. This was to remind the Israelites that no one except a descendant of Aaron should come to burn incense before the LORD, or he would become like Korah and his followers.

---

[n]30 Hebrew *Sheol*; also in verse 33

King James

41 ¶ But on the morrow all the congregation of the children of Israel murmured against Moses and against Aaron, saying, Ye have killed the people of the LORD.

42And it came to pass, when the congregation was gathered against Moses and against Aaron, that they looked toward the tabernacle of the congregation: and, behold, the cloud covered it, and the glory of the LORD appeared.

43And Moses and Aaron came before the tabernacle of the congregation.

44 ¶ And the LORD spake unto Moses, saying,

45Get you up from among this congregation, that I may consume them as in a moment. And they fell upon their faces.

46 ¶ And Moses said unto Aaron, Take a censer, and put fire therein from off the altar, and put on incense, and go quickly unto the congregation, and make an atonement for them: for there is wrath gone out from the LORD; the plague is begun.

47And Aaron took as Moses commanded, and ran into the midst of the congregation; and, behold, the plague was begun among the people: and he put on incense, and made an atonement for the people.

48And he stood between the dead and the living; and the plague was stayed.

49Now they that died in the plague were fourteen thousand and seven hundred, beside them that died about the matter of Korah.

50And Aaron returned unto Moses unto the door of the tabernacle of the congregation: and the plague was stayed.

The budding of Aaron's rod

17 AND THE LORD spake unto Moses, saying,
2Speak unto the children of Israel, and take of every one of them a rod according to the house of *their* fathers, of all their princes according to the house of their fathers twelve rods: write thou every man's name upon his rod.

3And thou shalt write Aaron's name upon the rod of Levi: for one rod *shall be* for the head of the house of their fathers.

4And thou shalt lay them up in the tabernacle of the congregation before the testimony, where I will meet with you.

5And it shall come to pass, *that* the man's rod, whom I shall choose, shall blossom: and I will make to cease from me the murmurings of the children of Israel, whereby they murmur against you.

6 ¶ And Moses spake unto the children of Israel, and every one of their princes gave him qa rod apiece, for each prince one, according to their fathers' houses, *even* twelve rods: and the rod of Aaron *was* among their rods.

7And Moses laid up the rods before the LORD in the tabernacle of witness.

8And it came to pass, that on the morrow Moses went into the tabernacle of witness; and, behold, the rod of Aaron for the house of Levi was budded, and brought forth buds, and bloomed blossoms, and yielded almonds.

9And Moses brought out all the rods from before the LORD unto all the children of Israel: and they looked, and took every man his rod.

10 ¶ And the LORD said unto Moses, Bring Aaron's rod again before the testimony, to be kept for a token against the rrebels; and thou shalt quite take away their murmurings from me, that they die not.

11And Moses did *so:* as the LORD commanded him, so did he.

12And the children of Israel spake unto Moses, saying, Behold, we die, we perish, we all perish.

13Whosoever cometh any thing near unto the tabernacle of the LORD shall die: shall we be consumed with dying?

Amplified

41But on the morrow all the congregation of the Israelites murmured against Moses and Aaron, saying, You have killed the people of the Lord.

42When the congregation was gathered against Moses and Aaron, they looked at the Tent of Meeting, and behold, the cloud covered it and they saw the Lord's glory.

43And Moses and Aaron came to the front of the Tent of Meeting.

44And the Lord said to Moses,

45Get away from among this congregation, that I may consume them in a moment. And Moses and Aaron fell on their faces.

46And Moses said to Aaron, Take a censer and put fire in it from off the altar and lay incense on it, and carry it quickly to the congregation and make atonement for them. For there is wrath gone out from the Lord; the plague has begun!

47So Aaron took the burning censer as Moses commanded, and ran into the midst of the congregation; and behold, the plague was begun among the people; and he put on the incense and made atonement for the people.

48And he stood between the dead and the living, and the plague was stayed.

49Now those who died in the plague were 14,700, besides those who died in the matter of Korah.

50And Aaron returned to Moses to the door of the Tent of Meeting, since the plague was stayed.

17 AND THE Lord said to Moses,
2Speak to the Israelites and get from them rods *or* staves, one for each father's house, from all their leaders according to their father's houses, twelve rods. Write every man's name on his rod.

3And you shall write Aaron's name on the rod of Levi [his great-grandfather]. For there shall be one rod for the head of each father's house.

4You shall lay them up in the Tent of Meeting before [the ark of] the Testimony, where I meet with you.

5And the rod of the man whom I choose shall bud, and I will make to cease from Me the murmurings of the Israelites, which they murmur against you.

6And Moses spoke to the Israelites, and every one of their leaders gave him a rod *or* staff, one for each leader according to their fathers' houses, twelve rods, and the rod of Aaron was among their rods.

7And Moses deposited the rods before the Lord in the Tent of the Testimony.

8And the next day Moses went into the Tent of the Testimony, and behold, the rod of Aaron for the house of Levi had sprouted and brought forth buds and produced blossoms and yielded [ripe] almonds.

9Moses brought out all the rods from before the Lord to all the Israelites; and they looked, and each man took his rod.

10And the Lord told Moses, Put Aaron's rod back before the Testimony [in the ark], to be kept as a [warning] sign for the rebels; and you shall make an end of their murmurings against Me, lest they die.

11And Moses did so; as the Lord commanded him, so he did.

12The Israelites said to Moses, Behold, we perish, we are undone, all undone!

13Everyone who comes near, who comes near the tabernacle of the Lord, dies *or* shall die! Are we all to perish?

q Heb. *a rod for one prince, a rod for one prince*   r Heb. *children of rebellion*

New American Standard

Murmuring and Plague

41 ¶ But on the next day all the congregation of the sons of Israel grumbled against Moses and Aaron, saying, "You are the ones who have caused the death of the LORD's people."

42 It came about, however, when the congregation had assembled against Moses and Aaron, that they turned toward the tent of meeting, and behold, the cloud covered it and the glory of the LORD appeared.

43 Then Moses and Aaron came to the front of the tent of meeting,

44 and the LORD spoke to Moses, saying,

45 "Get away from among this congregation, that I may consume them instantly." Then they fell on their faces.

46 Moses said to Aaron, "Take your censer and put in it fire from the altar, and lay incense *on it;* then bring it quickly to the congregation and make atonement for them, for wrath has gone forth from the LORD, the plague has begun!"

47 Then Aaron took *it* as Moses had spoken, and ran into the midst of the assembly, for behold, the plague had begun among the people. So he put *on* the incense and made atonement for the people.

48 He took his stand between the dead and the living, so that the plague was checked.

49 But those who died by the plague were 14,700, besides those who died on account of Korah.

50 Then Aaron returned to Moses at the doorway of the tent of meeting, for the plague had been checked.

Aaron's Rod Buds

17 THEN THE LORD spoke to Moses, saying,

2 "Speak to the sons of Israel, and get from them a rod for each father's household: twelve rods, from all their leaders according to their fathers' households. You shall write each name on his rod,

3 and write Aaron's name on the rod of Levi; for there is one rod for the head *of each* of their fathers' households.

4 "You shall then deposit them in the tent of meeting in front of the testimony, where I meet with you.

5 "It will come about that the rod of the man whom I choose will sprout. Thus I will lessen from upon Myself the grumblings of the sons of Israel, who are grumbling against you."

6 Moses therefore spoke to the sons of Israel, and all their leaders gave him a rod apiece, for each leader according to their fathers' households, twelve rods, with the rod of Aaron among their rods.

7 So Moses deposited the rods before the LORD in the tent of the testimony.

8 ¶ Now on the next day Moses went into the tent of the testimony; and behold, the rod of Aaron for the house of Levi had sprouted and put forth buds and produced blossoms, and it bore ripe almonds.

9 Moses then brought out all the rods from the presence of the LORD to all the sons of Israel; and they looked, and each man took his rod.

10 But the LORD said to Moses, "Put back the rod of Aaron before the testimony to be kept as a sign against the rebels, that you may put an end to their grumblings against Me, so that they will not die."

11 Thus Moses did; just as the LORD had commanded him, so he did.

12 ¶ Then the sons of Israel spoke to Moses, saying, "Behold, we perish, we are dying, we are all dying!

13 "Everyone who comes near, who comes near to the tabernacle of the LORD, must die. Are we to perish completely?"

New International

41 The next day the whole Israelite community grumbled against Moses and Aaron. "You have killed the LORD's people," they said.

42 But when the assembly gathered in opposition to Moses and Aaron and turned toward the Tent of Meeting, suddenly the cloud covered it and the glory of the LORD appeared. 43 Then Moses and Aaron went to the front of the Tent of Meeting, 44 and the LORD said to Moses, 45 "Get away from this assembly so I can put an end to them at once." And they fell facedown.

46 Then Moses said to Aaron, "Take your censer and put incense in it, along with fire from the altar, and hurry to the assembly to make atonement for them. Wrath has come out from the LORD; the plague has started." 47 So Aaron did as Moses said, and ran into the midst of the assembly. The plague had already started among the people, but Aaron offered the incense and made atonement for them. 48 He stood between the living and the dead, and the plague stopped. 49 But 14,700 people died from the plague, in addition to those who had died because of Korah. 50 Then Aaron returned to Moses at the entrance to the Tent of Meeting, for the plague had stopped.

The Budding of Aaron's Staff

17 THE LORD said to Moses, 2 "Speak to the Israelites and get twelve staffs from them, one from the leader of each of their ancestral tribes. Write the name of each man on his staff. 3 On the staff of Levi write Aaron's name, for there must be one staff for the head of each ancestral tribe. 4 Place them in the Tent of Meeting in front of the Testimony, where I meet with you. 5 The staff belonging to the man I choose will sprout, and I will rid myself of this constant grumbling against you by the Israelites."

6 So Moses spoke to the Israelites, and their leaders gave him twelve staffs, one for the leader of each of their ancestral tribes, and Aaron's staff was among them. 7 Moses placed the staffs before the LORD in the Tent of the Testimony.

8 The next day Moses entered the Tent of the Testimony and saw that Aaron's staff, which represented the house of Levi, had not only sprouted but had budded, blossomed and produced almonds. 9 Then Moses brought out all the staffs from the LORD's presence to all the Israelites. They looked at them, and each man took his own staff.

10 The LORD said to Moses, "Put back Aaron's staff in front of the Testimony, to be kept as a sign to the rebellious. This will put an end to their grumbling against me, so that they will not die." 11 Moses did just as the LORD commanded him.

12 The Israelites said to Moses, "We will die! We are lost, we are all lost! 13 Anyone who even comes near the tabernacle of the LORD will die. Are we all going to die?"

King James

Duties of priests and Levites

18 AND THE LORD said unto Aaron, Thou and thy sons and thy father's house with thee shall bear the iniquity of the sanctuary: and thou and thy sons with thee shall bear the iniquity of your priesthood.

2And thy brethren also of the tribe of Levi, the tribe of thy father, bring thou with thee, that they may be joined unto thee, and minister unto thee: but thou and thy sons with thee *shall minister* before the tabernacle of witness.

3And they shall keep thy charge, and the charge of all the tabernacle: only they shall not come nigh the vessels of the sanctuary and the altar, that neither they, nor ye also, die.

4And they shall be joined unto thee, and keep the charge of the tabernacle of the congregation, for all the service of the tabernacle: and a stranger shall not come nigh unto you.

5And ye shall keep the charge of the sanctuary, and the charge of the altar: that there be no wrath any more upon the children of Israel.

6And I, behold, I have taken your brethren the Levites from among the children of Israel: to you *they are* given *as* a gift for the LORD, to do the service of the tabernacle of the congregation.

7Therefore thou and thy sons with thee shall keep your priest's office for every thing of the altar, and within the veil; and ye shall serve: I have given your priest's office *unto you as* a service of gift: and the stranger that cometh nigh shall be put to death.

Tithes and offerings

8 ¶ And the LORD spake unto Aaron, Behold, I also have given thee the charge of mine heave offerings of all the hallowed things of the children of Israel; unto thee have I given them by reason of the anointing, and to thy sons, by an ordinance for ever.

9This shall be thine of the most holy things, *reserved* from the fire: every oblation of theirs, every meat offering of theirs, and every sin offering of theirs, and every trespass offering of theirs, which they shall render unto me, *shall* be most holy for thee and for thy sons.

10In the most holy *place* shalt thou eat it; every male shall eat it: it shall be holy unto thee.

11And this *is* thine; the heave offering of their gift, with all the wave offerings of the children of Israel: I have given them unto thee, and to thy sons and to thy daughters with thee, by a statute for ever: every one that is clean in thy house shall eat of it.

12All the *s*best of the oil, and all the best of the wine, and of the wheat, the firstfruits of them which they shall offer unto the LORD, them have I given thee.

13*And* whatsoever is first ripe in the land, which they shall bring unto the LORD, shall be thine; every one that is clean in thine house shall eat *of* it.

14Every thing devoted in Israel shall be thine.

15Every thing that openeth the matrix in all flesh, which they bring unto the LORD, *whether it be* of men or beasts, shall be thine: nevertheless the firstborn of man shalt thou surely redeem, and the firstling of unclean beasts shalt thou redeem.

Amplified

18 AND THE Lord said to Aaron, You and your sons and your father's house with you shall bear *and* remove the iniquity of the sanctuary [that is, the guilt for the offenses which the people unknowingly commit when brought into contact with the manifestations of God's presence]. And you and your sons with you shall bear *and* remove the iniquity of your priesthood [your own unintentional offenses].

2And your brethren also of the tribe of Levi, the tribe of your [fore]father, bring with you, that they may be joined to you and minister to you; but only you and your sons with you shall come before the Tent of the Testimony [into the Holy Place where only priests may go and into the Most Holy Place which only the high priest dares enter].

3And the Levites shall attend you [as servants] and attend to all the duties of the Tent; only they shall not come near the sacred vessels of the sanctuary or to the brazen altar, that they also and you [Aaron] die not.

4And they shall be joined to you and attend to the duties of the Tent of Meeting—all the [menial] service of the Tent—and no stranger [no layman, anyone who is not a Levite] shall come near you [Aaron and your sons].

5And you shall attend to the duties of the sanctuary and attend to the altar [of burnt offering and the altar of incense], that there be no wrath any more upon the Israelites [as in the incident of Korah, Dathan, and Abiram]. [Num. 16:42–50.]

6And I, behold, I have taken your brethren the Levites from among the Israelites; to you they are a gift, given to the Lord, to do the [menial] service of the Tent of Meeting.

7Therefore you and your sons with you shall attend to your priesthood for everything of the altar [of burnt offering and the altar of incense] and [of the Holy of Holies] within the veil, and you shall serve. I give you your priesthood as a service of gift. And the stranger [anyone other than Moses or your sons, Aaron] who comes near shall be put to death. [Exod. 40:18, 20, 26.]

8And the Lord said to Aaron, And I, behold, I have given you the charge of My heave offerings [whatever is taken out and kept of the offerings made to Me], all the dedicated *and* consecrated things of the Israelites; to you have I given them [as your portion] and to your sons as a continual allowance forever by reason of your anointing as priests. [Lev. 7:35.]

9This shall be yours of the most holy things, reserved from the fire: every offering of the people, every cereal offering and sin offering and trespass offering of theirs, which they shall render to Me, shall be most holy for you [Aaron] and for your sons.

10As the most holy thing *and* in a sacred place shall you eat of it; every male [of your house] shall eat of it. It shall be holy to you. [Lev. 22:10–16.]

11And this also is yours: the heave offering of their gift, with all the wave offerings of the Israelites. I have given them to you and to your sons and to your daughters with you as a continual allowance forever; everyone in your house who is [ceremonially] clean may eat of it.

12All the best of the oil, and all the best of the [fresh] wine and of the grain, the firstfruits of what they give to the Lord, to you have I given them.

13Whatever is first ripe in the land, which they bring to the Lord, shall be yours. Everyone who is [ceremonially] clean in your house may eat of it.

14Every devoted thing in Israel [everything that has been vowed to the Lord] shall be yours.

15Everything that first opens the womb in all flesh, which they bring to the Lord, whether it be of men or beasts, shall be yours. Nevertheless the firstborn of man you shall surely redeem, and the firstling of unclean beasts you shall redeem.

---

s Heb. *fat*

New American Standard

Duties of Levites

18 SO THE LORD said to Aaron, "You and your sons and your father's household with you shall bear the guilt in connection with the sanctuary, and you and your sons with you shall bear the guilt in connection with your priesthood.

2"But bring with you also your brothers, the tribe of Levi, the tribe of your father, that they may be joined with you and serve you, while you and your sons with you are before the tent of the testimony.

3"And they shall thus attend to your obligation and the obligation of all the tent, but they shall not come near to the furnishings of the sanctuary and the altar, or both they and you will die.

4"They shall be joined with you and attend to the obligations of the tent of meeting, for all the service of the tent; but an outsider may not come near you.

5"So you shall attend to the obligations of the sanctuary and the obligations of the altar, so that there will no longer be wrath on the sons of Israel.

6"Behold, I Myself have taken your fellow Levites from among the sons of Israel; they are a gift to you, dedicated to the LORD, to perform the service for the tent of meeting.

7"But you and your sons with you shall attend to your priesthood for everything concerning the altar and inside the veil, and you are to perform service. I am giving you the priesthood as a bestowed service, but the outsider who comes near shall be put to death."

The Priests' Portion

8 ¶ Then the LORD spoke to Aaron, "Now behold, I Myself have given you charge of My offerings, even all the holy gifts of the sons of Israel I have given them to you as a portion and to your sons as a perpetual allotment.

9"This shall be yours from the most holy *gifts reserved* from the fire; every offering of theirs, even every grain offering and every sin offering and every guilt offering, which they shall render to Me, shall be most holy for you and for your sons.

10"As the most holy *gifts* you shall eat it; every male shall eat it. It shall be holy to you.

11"This also is yours, the offering of their gift, even all the wave offerings of the sons of Israel; I have given them to you and to your sons and daughters with you as a perpetual allotment. Everyone of your household who is clean may eat it.

12"All the best of the fresh oil and all the best of the fresh wine and of the grain, the first fruits of those which they give to the LORD, I give them to you.

13"The first ripe fruits of all that is in their land, which they bring to the LORD, shall be yours; everyone of your household who is clean may eat it.

14"Every devoted thing in Israel shall be yours.

15"Every first issue of the womb of all flesh, whether man or animal, which they offer to the LORD, shall be yours; nevertheless the firstborn of man you shall surely redeem, and the firstborn of unclean animals you shall redeem.

New International

Duties of Priests and Levites

18 THE LORD said to Aaron, "You, your sons and your father's family are to bear the responsibility for offenses against the sanctuary, and you and your sons alone are to bear the responsibility for offenses against the priesthood. 2Bring your fellow Levites from your ancestral tribe to join you and assist you when you and your sons minister before the Tent of the Testimony. 3They are to be responsible to you and are to perform all the duties of the Tent, but they must not go near the furnishings of the sanctuary or the altar, or both they and you will die. 4They are to join you and be responsible for the care of the Tent of Meeting—all the work at the Tent—and no one else may come near where you are.

5"You are to be responsible for the care of the sanctuary and the altar, so that wrath will not fall on the Israelites again. 6I myself have selected your fellow Levites from among the Israelites as a gift to you, dedicated to the LORD to do the work at the Tent of Meeting. 7But only you and your sons may serve as priests in connection with everything at the altar and inside the curtain. I am giving you the service of the priesthood as a gift. Anyone else who comes near the sanctuary must be put to death."

Offerings for Priests and Levites

8Then the LORD said to Aaron, "I myself have put you in charge of the offerings presented to me; all the holy offerings the Israelites give me I give to you and your sons as your portion and regular share. 9You are to have the part of the most holy offerings that is kept from the fire. From all the gifts they bring me as most holy offerings, whether grain or sin or guilt offerings, that part belongs to you and your sons. 10Eat it as something most holy; every male shall eat it. You must regard it as holy.

11"This also is yours: whatever is set aside from the gifts of all the wave offerings of the Israelites. I give this to you and your sons and daughters as your regular share. Everyone in your household who is ceremonially clean may eat it.

12"I give you all the finest olive oil and all the finest new wine and grain they give the LORD as the firstfruits of their harvest. 13All the land's firstfruits that they bring to the LORD will be yours. Everyone in your household who is ceremonially clean may eat it.

14"Everything in Israel that is devoted[o] to the LORD is yours. 15The first offspring of every womb, both man and animal, that is offered to the LORD is yours. But you must redeem every firstborn son and every firstborn male of

---

o 14 The Hebrew term refers to the irrevocable giving over of things or persons to the LORD.

King James

Amplified

¹⁶And those that are to be redeemed from a month old shalt thou redeem, according to thine estimation, for the money of five shekels, after the shekel of the sanctuary, which *is* twenty gerahs.

¹⁷But the firstling of a cow, or the firstling of a sheep, or the firstling of a goat, thou shalt not redeem; they *are* holy: thou shalt sprinkle their blood upon the altar, and shalt burn their fat *for* an offering made by fire, for a sweet savour unto the LORD.

¹⁸And the flesh of them shall be thine, as the wave breast and as the right shoulder are thine.

¹⁹All the heave offerings of the holy things, which the children of Israel offer unto the LORD, have I given thee, and thy sons and thy daughters with thee, by a statute for ever: it *is* a covenant of salt for ever before the LORD unto thee and to thy seed with thee.

²⁰ ¶ And the LORD spake unto Aaron, Thou shalt have no inheritance in their land, neither shalt thou have any part among them: I *am* thy part and thine inheritance among the children of Israel.

²¹And, behold, I have given the children of Levi all the tenth in Israel for an inheritance, for their service which they serve, *even* the service of the tabernacle of the congregation.

²²Neither must the children of Israel henceforth come nigh the tabernacle of the congregation, lest they bear sin, *t* and die.

²³But the Levites shall do the service of the tabernacle of the congregation, and they shall bear their iniquity: it *shall be* a statute for ever throughout your generations, that among the children of Israel they have no inheritance.

²⁴But the tithes of the children of Israel, which they offer *as* an heave offering unto the LORD, I have given to the Levites to inherit: therefore I have said unto them, Among the children of Israel they shall have no inheritance.

²⁵ ¶ And the LORD spake unto Moses, saying,

²⁶Thus speak unto the Levites, and say unto them, When ye take of the children of Israel the tithes which I have given you from them for your inheritance, then ye shall offer up an heave offering of it for the LORD, *even* a tenth *part* of the tithe.

²⁷And *this* your heave offering shall be reckoned unto you, as though *it were* the corn of the threshingfloor, and as the fulness of the winepress.

²⁸Thus ye also shall offer an heave offering unto the LORD of all your tithes, which ye receive of the children of Israel; and ye shall give thereof the LORD'S heave offering to Aaron the priest.

²⁹Out of all your gifts ye shall offer every heave offering of the LORD, of all the *u* best thereof, *even* the hallowed part thereof out of it.

³⁰Therefore thou shalt say unto them, When ye have heaved the best thereof from it, then it shall be counted unto the Levites as the increase of the threshingfloor, and as the increase of the winepress.

³¹And ye shall eat it in every place, ye and your households: for it *is* your reward for your service in the tabernacle of the congregation.

³²And ye shall bear no sin by reason of it, when ye have heaved from it the best of it: neither shall ye pollute the holy things of the children of Israel, lest ye die.

¹⁶And those that are to be redeemed of them, from a month old shall you redeem, according to your estimate [of their age], for the fixed price of five shekels in silver, according to the shekel of the sanctuary, which is twenty gerahs.

¹⁷But the firstling of a cow or of a sheep or of a goat you shall not redeem. They [as the firstborn of clean beasts belong to God and] are holy. You shall sprinkle their blood upon the altar and shall burn their fat for an offering made by fire, for a sweet *and* soothing odor to the Lord.

¹⁸And the flesh of them shall be yours, as the wave breast and as the right shoulder are yours.

¹⁹All the heave offerings [the lifted-out and kept portions] of the holy things which the Israelites give to the Lord I give to you and to your sons and your daughters with you, as a continual debt forever. It is a covenant of salt [that cannot be dissolved or violated] forever before the Lord for you [Aaron] and for your posterity with you.

²⁰And the Lord said to Aaron, You shall have no inheritance in the land [of the Israelites], neither shall you have any part among them. I am your portion and your inheritance among the Israelites.

²¹And, behold, I have given the Levites all the tithes in Israel for an inheritance in return for their service which they serve, the [menial] service of the Tent of Meeting.

²²Henceforth the Israelites shall not come near the Tent of Meeting [the covered sanctuary, the Holy Place, and the Holy of Holies], lest they incur guilt and die.

²³But the Levites shall do the [menial] service of the Tent of Meeting, and they shall bear and remove the iniquity of the people [that is, be answerable for the legal pollutions of the holy things and offer the necessary atonements for unintentional offenses in these matters]. It shall be a statute forever in all your generations, that among the Israelites the Levites have no inheritance [of land].

²⁴But the tithes of the Israelites, which they present as an offering to the Lord, I have given to the Levites to inherit; therefore I have said to them, Among the Israelites they shall have no inheritance. [They have homes and cities and pasturage to use but not to possess as their personal inheritance.]

²⁵And the Lord said to Moses,

²⁶Moreover, you shall say to the Levites, When you take from the Israelites the tithe which I have given you from them for your inheritance, then you shall present an offering from it to the Lord, even a tenth of the tithe [paid by the people].

²⁷And what you lift out and keep [your heave offering] shall be credited to you as though it were the grain of the threshing floor or as the fully ripe produce of the vine.

²⁸Likewise you shall also present an offering to the Lord of all your tithes which you receive from the Israelites; and therefore you shall give this heave offering [lifted out and kept] for the Lord to Aaron the priest.

²⁹Out of all the gifts to you, you shall present every offering due to the Lord, of all the best of it, even the hallowed part lifted out *and* held back out of it [for the Levites].

³⁰Therefore you shall say to them, When you have lifted out *and* held back the best from it [and presented it to the Lord by giving it to yourselves, the Levites], then it shall be counted to [you] the Levites just as if it were the increase of the threshing floor or of the winepress.

³¹And you may eat it in every place, you and your households, for it is your reward for your service in the Tent of Meeting.

³²And you shall be guilty of no sin by reason of it when you have lifted out *and* held back the best of it; neither shall you have polluted the holy things of the Israelites, neither shall you die [because of it].

^t Heb. *to die*   ^u Heb. *fat;* see ver. 12

New American Standard

16"As to their redemption price, from a month old you shall redeem them, by your valuation, five "shekels in silver, according to the shekel of the sanctuary, which is twenty gerahs.

17"But the firstborn of an ox or the firstborn of a sheep or the firstborn of a goat, you shall not redeem; they are holy. You shall sprinkle their blood on the altar and shall offer up their fat in smoke *as* an offering by fire, for a soothing aroma to the LORD.

18"Their meat shall be yours; it shall be yours like the breast of a wave offering and like the right thigh.

19"All the offerings of the holy *gifts*, which the sons of Israel offer to the LORD, I have given to you and your sons and your daughters with you, as a perpetual allotment. It is an everlasting covenant of salt before the LORD to you and your descendants with you."

20 Then the LORD said to Aaron, "You shall have no inheritance in their land nor own any portion among them; I am your portion and your inheritance among the sons of Israel.

21 ¶ "To the sons of Levi, behold, I have given all the tithe in Israel for an inheritance, in return for their service which they perform, the service of the tent of meeting.

22"The sons of Israel shall not come near the tent of meeting again, or they will bear sin and die.

23"Only the Levites shall perform the service of the tent of meeting, and they shall bear their iniquity; it shall be a perpetual statute throughout your generations, and among the sons of Israel they shall have no inheritance.

24"For the tithe of the sons of Israel, which they offer as an offering to the LORD, I have given to the Levites for an inheritance; therefore I have said concerning them, 'They shall have no inheritance among the sons of Israel.' "

25 ¶ Then the LORD spoke to Moses, saying,

26"Moreover, you shall speak to the Levites and say to them, 'When you take from the sons of Israel the tithe which I have given you from them for your inheritance, then you shall present an offering from it to the LORD, a tithe of the tithe.

27 'Your offering shall be reckoned to you as the grain from the threshing floor or the full produce from the wine vat.

28 'So you shall also present an offering to the LORD from your tithes, which you receive from the sons of Israel; and from it you shall give the LORD's offering to Aaron the priest.

29 'Out of all your gifts you shall present every offering due to the LORD, from all the best of them, the sacred part from them.'

30"You shall say to them, 'When you have offered from it the best of it, then *the rest* shall be reckoned to the Levites as the product of the threshing floor, and as the product of the wine vat.

31 'You may eat it anywhere, you and your households, for it is your compensation in return for your service in the tent of meeting.

32 'You will bear no sin by reason of it when you have offered the best of it. But you shall not profane the sacred gifts of the sons of Israel, or you will die.' "

New International

unclean animals. 16When they are a month old, you must redeem them at the redemption price set at five shekels*p* of silver, according to the sanctuary shekel, which weighs twenty gerahs.

17"But you must not redeem the firstborn of an ox, a sheep or a goat; they are holy. Sprinkle their blood on the altar and burn their fat as an offering made by fire, an aroma pleasing to the LORD. 18Their meat is to be yours, just as the breast of the wave offering and the right thigh are yours. 19Whatever is set aside from the holy offerings the Israelites present to the LORD I give to you and your sons and daughters as your regular share. It is an everlasting covenant of salt before the LORD for both you and your offspring."

20The LORD said to Aaron, "You will have no inheritance in their land, nor will you have any share among them; I am your share and your inheritance among the Israelites.

21"I give to the Levites all the tithes in Israel as their inheritance in return for the work they do while serving at the Tent of Meeting. 22From now on the Israelites must not go near the Tent of Meeting, or they will bear the consequences of their sin and will die. 23It is the Levites who are to do the work at the Tent of Meeting and bear the responsibility for offenses against it. This is a lasting ordinance for the generations to come. They will receive no inheritance among the Israelites. 24Instead, I give to the Levites as their inheritance the tithes that the Israelites present as an offering to the LORD. That is why I said concerning them: 'They will have no inheritance among the Israelites.' "

25The LORD said to Moses, 26"Speak to the Levites and say to them: 'When you receive from the Israelites the tithe I give you as your inheritance, you must present a tenth of that tithe as the LORD's offering. 27Your offering will be reckoned to you as grain from the threshing floor or juice from the winepress. 28In this way you also will present an offering to the LORD from all the tithes you receive from the Israelites. From these tithes you must give the LORD's portion to Aaron the priest. 29You must present as the LORD's portion the best and holiest part of everything given to you.'

30"Say to the Levites: 'When you present the best part, it will be reckoned to you as the product of the threshing floor or the winepress. 31You and your households may eat the rest of it anywhere, for it is your wages for your work at the Tent of Meeting. 32By presenting the best part of it you will not be guilty in this matter; then you will not defile the holy offerings of the Israelites, and you will not die.' "

"I.e. A shekel equals approx one-half oz

p 16 That is, about 2 ounces (about 55 grams)

King James	Amplified

Purification of the unclean

19 AND THE LORD spake unto Moses and unto Aaron, saying,

²This *is* the ordinance of the law which the LORD hath commanded, saying, Speak unto the children of Israel, that they bring thee a red heifer without spot, wherein *is* no blemish, *and* upon which never came yoke:

³And ye shall give her unto Eleazar the priest, that he may bring her forth without the camp, and *one* shall slay her before his face:

⁴And Eleazar the priest shall take of her blood with his finger, and sprinkle of her blood directly before the tabernacle of the congregation seven times:

⁵And *one* shall burn the heifer in his sight; her skin, and her flesh, and her blood, with her dung, shall he burn:

⁶And the priest shall take cedar wood, and hyssop, and scarlet, and cast *it* into the midst of the burning of the heifer.

⁷Then the priest shall wash his clothes, and he shall bathe his flesh in water, and afterward he shall come into the camp, and the priest shall be unclean until the even.

⁸And he that burneth her shall wash his clothes in water, and bathe his flesh in water, and shall be unclean until the even.

⁹And a man *that is* clean shall gather up the ashes of the heifer, and lay *them* up without the camp in a clean place, and it shall be kept for the congregation of the children of Israel for a water of separation: it *is* a purification for sin.

¹⁰And he that gathereth the ashes of the heifer shall wash his clothes, and be unclean until the even: and it shall be unto the children of Israel, and unto the stranger that sojourneth among them, for a statute for ever.

¹¹ ¶ He that toucheth the dead body of any ᵛman shall be unclean seven days.

¹²He shall purify himself with it on the third day, and on the seventh day he shall be clean: but if he purify not himself the third day, then the seventh day he shall not be clean.

¹³Whosoever toucheth the dead body of any man that is dead, and purifieth not himself, defileth the tabernacle of the LORD; and that soul shall be cut off from Israel: because the water of separation was not sprinkled upon him, he shall be unclean; his uncleanness *is* yet upon him.

¹⁴This *is* the law, when a man dieth in a tent: all that come into the tent, and all that *is* in the tent, shall be unclean seven days.

¹⁵And every open vessel, which hath no covering bound upon it, *is* unclean.

¹⁶And whosoever toucheth one that is slain with a sword in the open fields, or a dead body, or a bone of a man, or a grave, shall be unclean seven days.

¹⁷And for an unclean *person* they shall take of the ʷashes of the burnt heifer of purification for sin, and ˣrunning water shall be put thereto in a vessel:

¹⁸And a clean person shall take hyssop, and dip *it* in the water, and sprinkle *it* upon the tent, and upon all the vessels, and upon the persons that were there, and upon him that touched a bone, or one slain, or one dead, or a grave:

¹⁹And the clean *person* shall sprinkle upon the unclean on the third day, and on the seventh day: and on the seventh day he shall purify himself, and wash his clothes, and bathe himself in water, and shall be clean at even.

²⁰But the man that shall be unclean, and shall not purify himself, that soul shall be cut off from among the congregation, because he hath defiled the sanctuary of the LORD: the water of separation hath not been sprinkled upon him; he *is* unclean.

²¹And it shall be a perpetual statute unto them, that he that sprinkleth the water of separation shall wash his clothes; and he that toucheth the water of separation shall be unclean until even.

19 AND THE Lord said to Moses and Aaron,

²This is the ritual of the law which the Lord has commanded: Tell the Israelites to bring you a red heifer without spot, in which is no blemish, upon which a yoke has never come.

³And you shall give her to Eleazar the priest, and he shall bring her outside the camp, and she shall be slaughtered before him.

⁴Eleazar the priest shall take some of her blood with his finger and sprinkle it toward the front of the Tent of Meeting seven times.

⁵The heifer shall be burned in his sight, her skin, flesh, blood, and dung.

⁶And the priest shall take cedar wood, and hyssop, and scarlet [stuff] and cast them into the midst of the burning heifer.

⁷Then the priest shall wash his clothes and bathe his body in water; afterward he shall come into the camp, but he shall be unclean until evening.

⁸He who burns the heifer shall wash his clothes and bathe his body in water, and shall be unclean until evening.

⁹And a man who is clean shall collect the ashes of the heifer and put them outside the camp in a clean place, and they shall be kept for the congregation of the Israelites for the water for impurity; it is a sin offering.

¹⁰And he who gathers the ashes of the heifer shall wash his clothes, and be unclean until evening. This shall be to the Israelites and to the stranger who sojourns among them a perpetual statute.

¹¹He who touches the dead body of any person shall be unclean for seven days.

¹²He shall purify himself with the water for impurity [made with the ashes of the burned heifer] on the third day, and on the seventh day he shall be clean. But if he does not purify himself the third day, then the seventh day he shall not be clean.

¹³Whoever touches the corpse of any who has died and does not purify himself defiles the tabernacle of the Lord, and that person shall be cut off from Israel. Because the water for impurity was not sprinkled upon him, he shall be unclean; his uncleanness is still upon him.

¹⁴This is the law when a man dies in a tent: all who come into the tent and all who are in the tent shall be unclean for seven days.

¹⁵And every open vessel, which has no covering fastened upon it, is unclean.

¹⁶And whoever in the open field touches one who is slain with a sword, or a dead body, or a bone of a dead man, or a grave, shall be unclean for seven days.

¹⁷And for the unclean, they shall take of the ashes of the burning of the sin offering, and the running water shall be put with it in a vessel.

¹⁸And a clean person shall take hyssop and dip it in the water and sprinkle it upon the tent, and upon all the vessels, and upon the persons who were there, and upon him who touched the bone, or the slain, or the naturally dead, or the grave.

¹⁹And the clean person shall sprinkle [the water for purification] upon the unclean person on the third day and on the seventh day, and on the seventh day the unclean man shall purify himself, and wash his clothes and bathe himself in water, and shall be clean at evening.

²⁰But the man who is unclean and does not purify himself, that person shall be cut off from among the congregation, because he has defiled the sanctuary of the Lord. The water for purification has not been sprinkled upon him; he is unclean.

²¹And it shall be a perpetual statute to them. He who sprinkles the water for impurity [upon another] shall wash his clothes, and he who touches the water for impurity shall be unclean until evening.

ᵛHeb. *soul of man*   ʷHeb. *dust*   ˣHeb. *living waters shall be given*

New American Standard

Ordinance of the Red Heifer

19 THEN THE LORD spoke to Moses and Aaron, saying,

2 "This is the statute of the law which the LORD has commanded, saying, 'Speak to the sons of Israel that they bring you an unblemished red heifer in which is no defect *and* on which a yoke has never been placed.

3 'You shall give it to Eleazar the priest, and it shall be brought outside the camp and be slaughtered in his presence.

4 'Next Eleazar the priest shall take some of its blood with his finger and sprinkle some of its blood toward the front of the tent of meeting seven times.

5 'Then the heifer shall be burned in his sight; its hide and its flesh and its blood, with its refuse, shall be burned.

6 'The priest shall take cedar wood and hyssop and scarlet *material* and cast it into the midst of the burning heifer.

7 'The priest shall then wash his clothes and bathe his body in water, and afterward come into the camp, but the priest shall be unclean until evening.

8 'The one who burns it shall also wash his clothes in water and bathe his body in water, and shall be unclean until evening.

9 'Now a man who is clean shall gather up the ashes of the heifer and deposit them outside the camp in a clean place, and the congregation of the sons of Israel shall keep it as water to remove impurity; it is purification from sin.

10 'The one who gathers the ashes of the heifer shall wash his clothes and be unclean until evening; and it shall be a perpetual statute to the sons of Israel and to the alien who sojourns among them.

11 ¶ 'The one who touches the corpse of any person shall be unclean for seven days.

12 'That one shall purify himself from uncleanness with the water on the third day and on the seventh day, *and then* he will be clean; but if he does not purify himself on the third day and on the seventh day, he will not be clean.

13 'Anyone who touches a corpse, the body of a man who has died, and does not purify himself, defiles the tabernacle of the LORD; and that person shall be cut off from Israel. Because the water for impurity was not sprinkled on him, he shall be unclean; his uncleanness is still on him.

14 ¶ 'This is the law when a man dies in a tent: everyone who comes into the tent and everyone who is in the tent shall be unclean for seven days.

15 'Every open vessel, which has no covering tied down on it, shall be unclean.

16 'Also, anyone who in the open field touches one who has been slain with a sword or who has died *naturally,* or a human bone or a grave, shall be unclean for seven days.

17 'Then for the unclean *person* they shall take some of the ashes of the burnt purification from sin and flowing water shall be added to them in a vessel.

18 'A clean person shall take hyssop and dip *it* in the water, and sprinkle *it* on the tent and on all the furnishings and on the persons who were there, and on the one who touched the bone or the one slain or the one dying *naturally* or the grave.

19 'Then the clean *person* shall sprinkle on the unclean on the third day and on the seventh day; and on the seventh day he shall purify him from uncleanness, and he shall wash his clothes and bathe *himself* in water and shall be clean by evening.

20 ¶ 'But the man who is unclean and does not purify himself from uncleanness, that person shall be cut off from the midst of the assembly, because he has defiled the sanctuary of the LORD; the water for impurity has not been sprinkled on him, he is unclean.

21 'So it shall be a perpetual statute for them. And he who sprinkles the water for impurity shall wash his clothes, and he who touches the water for impurity shall be unclean until evening.

New International

The Water of Cleansing

19 THE LORD said to Moses and Aaron: 2 "This is a requirement of the law that the LORD has commanded: Tell the Israelites to bring you a red heifer without defect or blemish and that has never been under a yoke. 3 Give it to Eleazar the priest; it is to be taken outside the camp and slaughtered in his presence. 4 Then Eleazar the priest is to take some of its blood on his finger and sprinkle it seven times toward the front of the Tent of Meeting. 5 While he watches, the heifer is to be burned— its hide, flesh, blood and offal. 6 The priest is to take some cedar wood, hyssop and scarlet wool and throw them onto the burning heifer. 7 After that, the priest must wash his clothes and bathe himself with water. He may then come into the camp, but he will be ceremonially unclean till evening. 8 The man who burns it must also wash his clothes and bathe with water, and he too will be unclean till evening.

9 "A man who is clean shall gather up the ashes of the heifer and put them in a ceremonially clean place outside the camp. They shall be kept by the Israelite community for use in the water of cleansing; it is for purification from sin. 10 The man who gathers up the ashes of the heifer must also wash his clothes, and he too will be unclean till evening. This will be a lasting ordinance both for the Israelites and for the aliens living among them.

11 "Whoever touches the dead body of anyone will be unclean for seven days. 12 He must purify himself with the water on the third day and on the seventh day; then he will be clean. But if he does not purify himself on the third and seventh days, he will not be clean. 13 Whoever touches the dead body of anyone and fails to purify himself defiles the LORD's tabernacle. That person must be cut off from Israel. Because the water of cleansing has not been sprinkled on him, he is unclean; his uncleanness remains on him.

14 "This is the law that applies when a person dies in a tent: Anyone who enters the tent and anyone who is in it will be unclean for seven days, 15 and every open container without a lid fastened on it will be unclean.

16 "Anyone out in the open who touches someone who has been killed with a sword or someone who has died a natural death, or anyone who touches a human bone or a grave, will be unclean for seven days.

17 "For the unclean person, put some ashes from the burned purification offering into a jar and pour fresh water over them. 18 Then a man who is ceremonially clean is to take some hyssop, dip it in the water and sprinkle the tent and all the furnishings and the people who were there. He must also sprinkle anyone who has touched a human bone or a grave or someone who has been killed or someone who has died a natural death. 19 The man who is clean is to sprinkle the unclean person on the third and seventh days, and on the seventh day he is to purify him. The person being cleansed must wash his clothes and bathe with water, and that evening he will be clean. 20 But if a person who is unclean does not purify himself, he must be cut off from the community, because he has defiled the sanctuary of the LORD. The water of cleansing has not been sprinkled on him, and he is unclean. 21 This is a lasting ordinance for them.

"The man who sprinkles the water of cleansing must also wash his clothes, and anyone who touches the water

King James

²²And whatsoever the unclean *person* toucheth shall be unclean; and the soul that toucheth *it* shall be unclean until even.

20 THEN CAME the children of Israel, *even* the whole congregation, into the desert of Zin in the first month: and the people abode in Kadesh; and Miriam died there, and was buried there.

Water from the rock

²And there was no water for the congregation: and they gathered themselves together against Moses and against Aaron.

³And the people chode with Moses, and spake, saying, Would God that we had died when our brethren died before the LORD!

⁴And why have ye brought up the congregation of the LORD into this wilderness, that we and our cattle should die there?

⁵And wherefore have ye made us to come up out of Egypt, to bring us in unto this evil place? it *is* no place of seed, or of figs, or of vines, or of pomegranates; neither *is* there any water to drink.

⁶And Moses and Aaron went from the presence of the assembly unto the door of the tabernacle of the congregation, and they fell upon their faces: and the glory of the LORD appeared unto them.

⁷ ¶ And the LORD spake unto Moses, saying,

⁸Take the rod, and gather thou the assembly together, thou, and Aaron thy brother, and speak ye unto the rock before their eyes; and it shall give forth his water, and thou shalt bring forth to them water out of the rock: so thou shalt give the congregation and their beasts drink.

⁹And Moses took the rod from before the LORD, as he commanded him.

¹⁰And Moses and Aaron gathered the congregation together before the rock, and he said unto them, Hear now, ye rebels; must we fetch you water out of this rock?

¹¹And Moses lifted up his hand, and with his rod he smote the rock twice: and the water came out abundantly, and the congregation drank, and their beasts *also.*

¹² ¶ And the LORD spake unto Moses and Aaron, Because ye believed me not, to sanctify me in the eyes of the children of Israel, therefore ye shall not bring this congregation into the land which I have given them.

¹³This *is* the water of ᵞMeribah; because the children of Israel strove with the LORD, and he was sanctified in them.

Edom refuses Israel passage

¹⁴ ¶ And Moses sent messengers from Kadesh unto the king of Edom, Thus saith thy brother Israel, Thou knowest all the travail that hath ᶻbefallen us:

¹⁵How our fathers went down into Egypt, and we have dwelt in Egypt a long time; and the Egyptians vexed us, and our fathers:

¹⁶And when we cried unto the LORD, he heard our voice, and sent an angel, and hath brought us forth out of Egypt: and, behold, we *are* in Kadesh, a city in the uttermost of thy border:

¹⁷Let us pass, I pray thee, through thy country: we will not pass through the fields, or through the vineyards, neither will we drink *of* the water of the wells: we will go by the king's *high* way, we will not turn to the right hand nor to the left, until we have passed thy borders.

¹⁸And Edom said unto him, Thou shalt not pass by me, lest I come out against thee with the sword.

Amplified

²²And whatever the unclean person touches shall be unclean, and anyone who touches it shall be unclean until evening.

20 AND THE Israelites, the whole congregation, came into the Wilderness of Zin in the first month. And the people dwelt in Kadesh. Miriam died and was buried there.

²Now there was no water for the congregation, and they assembled together against Moses and Aaron.

³And the people contended with Moses, and said, Would that we had died when our brethren died [in the plague] before the Lord! [Num. 16:49.]

⁴And why have you brought up the congregation of the Lord into this wilderness, that we should die here, we and our livestock?

⁵And why have you made us come up out of Egypt to bring us into this evil place? It is no place of grain or of figs or of vines or of pomegranates. And there is no water to drink.

⁶Then Moses and Aaron went from the presence of the assembly to the door of the Tent of Meeting and fell on their faces. Then the glory of the Lord appeared to them.

⁷And the Lord said to Moses,

⁸Take the rod, and assemble the congregation, you and Aaron your brother, and tell the rock before their eyes to give forth its water, and you shall bring forth to them water out of the rock; so you shall give the congregation and their livestock drink.

⁹So Moses took the rod from before the Lord, as He commanded him.

¹⁰And Moses and Aaron assembled the congregation before the rock and Moses said to them, Hear now, you rebels; must we bring you water out of this rock?

¹¹And Moses lifted up his hand and with his rod he smote the rock ⁱtwice. And the water came out abundantly, and the congregation drank, and their livestock.

¹²And the Lord said to Moses and Aaron, Because you did not believe in (rely on, cling to) Me to sanctify Me in the eyes of the Israelites, you therefore ʲshall not bring this congregation into the land which I have given them. [Ps. 106:32, 33.]

¹³These are the waters of Meribah [strife], where the Israelites contended with the Lord and He showed Himself holy among them.

¹⁴And Moses sent messengers from Kadesh to the king of Edom, saying, Thus says your kinsman Israel: You know all the adversity *and* birth pangs that have come upon us [as a nation]:

¹⁵How our fathers went down to Egypt; we dwelt there a long time, and the Egyptians dealt evilly with us and our fathers.

¹⁶But when we cried to the Lord, He heard us and sent an angel and brought us forth out of Egypt. Now behold, we are in Kadesh, a city on your country's edge.

¹⁷Let us pass, I pray you, through your country. We will not pass through field or vineyard, or drink of the water of the wells; we will go along the king's highway; we will not turn aside to the right hand or to the left until we have passed your borders.

¹⁸But Edom said to him, You shall not go through, lest I come out against you with the sword.

ⁱ"And the Rock was Christ," as I Cor. 10:4 explains. Once smitten at Rephidim (Exod. 17:6ff.), He did not need to be smitten, crucified, again. To smite the rock twice was to imply that Christ's death on the cross was not effectual or sufficient for time and eternity. ʲPossibly Moses was not aware of the significance of what he had been ordered to do, but nevertheless God held him responsible for not obeying Him exactly. Obedience to His will is vitally important, whether we understand His purpose or not. The motto "God's will: nothing more; nothing less; nothing else; at any cost" would have been priceless to Moses and Aaron that day, if they had only followed it.

ᵞi.e. *Strife*   ᶻHeb. *found us*

New American Standard

22 'Furthermore, anything that the unclean *person*
touches shall be unclean; and the person who touches *it*
shall be unclean until evening.' "

Death of Miriam

20 THEN THE sons of Israel, the whole congregation, came to the wilderness of Zin in the first
month; and the people stayed at Kadesh. Now Miriam died
there and was buried there.
2 ¶ There was no water for the congregation, and they
assembled themselves against Moses and Aaron.
3 The people thus contended with Moses and spoke,
saying, "If only we had perished when our brothers perished before the LORD!
4 "Why then have you brought the LORD'S assembly
into this wilderness, for us and our beasts to die here?
5 "Why have you made us come up from Egypt, to bring
us in to this wretched place? It is not a place of grain or
figs or vines or pomegranates, nor is there water to drink."
6 Then Moses and Aaron came in from the presence of
the assembly to the doorway of the tent of meeting and fell
on their faces. Then the glory of the LORD appeared to
them;
7 and the LORD spoke to Moses, saying,

The Water of Meribah

8 "Take the rod; and you and your brother Aaron assemble the congregation and speak to the rock before their
eyes, that it may yield its water. You shall thus bring forth
water for them out of the rock and let the congregation and
their beasts drink."
9 ¶ So Moses took the rod from before the LORD, just
as He had commanded him;
10 and Moses and Aaron gathered the assembly before
the rock. And he said to them, "Listen now, you rebels;
shall we bring forth water for you out of this rock?"
11 Then Moses lifted up his hand and struck the rock
twice with his rod; and water came forth abundantly, and
the congregation and their beasts drank.
12 But the LORD said to Moses and Aaron, "Because
you have not believed Me, to treat Me as holy in the sight
of the sons of Israel, therefore you shall not bring this
assembly into the land which I have given them."
13 Those *were* the waters of [v]Meribah, because the
sons of Israel contended with the LORD, and He proved
Himself holy among them.
14 ¶ From Kadesh Moses then sent messengers to the
king of Edom: "Thus your brother Israel has said, 'You
know all the hardship that has befallen us;
15 that our fathers went down to Egypt, and we stayed
in Egypt a long time, and the Egyptians treated us and our
fathers badly.
16 'But when we cried out to the LORD, He heard our
voice and sent an angel and brought us out from Egypt;
now behold, we are at Kadesh, a town on the edge of your
territory.
17 'Please let us pass through your land. We will not pass
through field or through vineyard; we will not even drink
water from a well. We will go along the king's highway,
not turning to the right or left, until we pass through your
territory.' "
18 ¶ Edom, however, said to him, "You shall not pass
through us, or I will come out with the sword against you."

[v] I.e. contention

New International

of cleansing will be unclean till evening. 22 Anything that
an unclean person touches becomes unclean, and anyone
who touches it becomes unclean till evening."

Water From the Rock

20 IN THE first month the whole Israelite community
arrived at the Desert of Zin, and they stayed at
Kadesh. There Miriam died and was buried.
2 Now there was no water for the community, and the
people gathered in opposition to Moses and Aaron. 3 They
quarreled with Moses and said, "If only we had died when
our brothers fell dead before the LORD! 4 Why did you
bring the LORD's community into this desert, that we and
our livestock should die here? 5 Why did you bring us up
out of Egypt to this terrible place? It has no grain or figs,
grapevines or pomegranates. And there is no water to
drink!"
6 Moses and Aaron went from the assembly to the entrance to the Tent of Meeting and fell facedown, and the
glory of the LORD appeared to them. 7 The LORD said to
Moses, 8 "Take the staff, and you and your brother Aaron
gather the assembly together. Speak to that rock before
their eyes and it will pour out its water. You will bring
water out of the rock for the community so they and their
livestock can drink."
9 So Moses took the staff from the LORD's presence, just
as he commanded him. 10 He and Aaron gathered the assembly together in front of the rock and Moses said to
them, "Listen, you rebels, must we bring you water out of
this rock?" 11 Then Moses raised his arm and struck the
rock twice with his staff. Water gushed out, and the community and their livestock drank.
12 But the LORD said to Moses and Aaron, "Because you
did not trust in me enough to honor me as holy in the sight
of the Israelites, you will not bring this community into the
land I give them."
13 These were the waters of Meribah,[q] where the Israelites quarreled with the LORD and where he showed himself
holy among them.

Edom Denies Israel Passage

14 Moses sent messengers from Kadesh to the king of
Edom, saying:

> "This is what your brother Israel says: You know
> about all the hardships that have come upon us. 15 Our
> forefathers went down into Egypt, and we lived there
> many years. The Egyptians mistreated us and our fa-
> thers, 16 but when we cried out to the LORD, he heard
> our cry and sent an angel and brought us out of Egypt.
> "Now we are here at Kadesh, a town on the edge of
> your territory. 17 Please let us pass through your coun-
> try. We will not go through any field or vineyard, or
> drink water from any well. We will travel along the
> king's highway and not turn to the right or to the left
> until we have passed through your territory."

18 But Edom answered:

> "You may not pass through here; if you try, we will
> march out and attack you with the sword."

[q] 13 *Meribah* means *quarreling*.

King James

19And the children of Israel said unto him, We will go by the high way: and if I and my cattle drink of thy water, then I will pay for it: I will only, without *doing* any thing *else*, go through on my feet.

20And he said, Thou shalt not go through. And Edom came out against him with much people, and with a strong hand.

21Thus Edom refused to give Israel passage through his border: wherefore Israel turned away from him.

The death of Aaron

22 ¶ And the children of Israel, *even* the whole congregation, journeyed from Kadesh, and came unto mount Hor.

23And the LORD spake unto Moses and Aaron in mount Hor, by the coast of the land of Edom, saying,

24Aaron shall be gathered unto his people: for he shall not enter into the land which I have given unto the children of Israel, because ye rebelled against my ^aword at the water of Meribah.

25Take Aaron and Eleazar his son, and bring them up unto mount Hor:

26And strip Aaron of his garments, and put them upon Eleazar his son: and Aaron shall be gathered *unto his people*, and shall die there.

27And Moses did as the LORD commanded: and they went up into mount Hor in the sight of all the congregation.

28And Moses stripped Aaron of his garments, and put them upon Eleazar his son; and Aaron died there in the top of the mount: and Moses and Eleazar came down from the mount.

29And when all the congregation saw that Aaron was dead, they mourned for Aaron thirty days, *even* all the house of Israel.

21 AND *WHEN* king Arad the Canaanite, which dwelt in the south, heard tell that Israel came by the way of the spies; then he fought against Israel, and took *some* of them prisoners.

The serpent of brass

2And Israel vowed a vow unto the LORD, and said, If thou wilt indeed deliver this people into my hand, then I will utterly destroy their cities.

3And the LORD hearkened to the voice of Israel, and delivered up the Canaanites; and they utterly destroyed them and their cities: and he called the name of the place ^bHormah.

4 ¶ And they journeyed from mount Hor by the way of the Red sea, to compass the land of Edom: and the soul of the people was much ^{c d}discouraged because of the way.

5And the people spake against God, and against Moses, Wherefore have ye brought us up out of Egypt to die in the wilderness? for *there is* no bread, neither *is there any* water; and our soul loatheth this light bread.

6And the LORD sent fiery serpents among the people, and they bit the people; and much people of Israel died.

7 ¶ Therefore the people came to Moses, and said, We have sinned, for we have spoken against the LORD, and against thee; pray unto the LORD, that he take away the serpents from us. And Moses prayed for the people.

8And the LORD said unto Moses, Make thee a fiery serpent, and set it upon a pole: and it shall come to pass, that every one that is bitten, when he looketh upon it, shall live.

Amplified

19And the Israelites said to him, We will go by the highway, and if I and my livestock drink of your water, I will pay for it. Only let me pass through on foot, nothing else.

20But Edom said, You shall not go through. And Edom came out against Israel with many people and a strong hand.

21Thus Edom refused to give Israel passage through his territory, ^kso Israel turned away from him.

22They journeyed from Kadesh, and the Israelites, even the whole congregation, came to Mount Hor.

23And the Lord said to Moses and Aaron at Mount Hor, on the border of the land of Edom,

24Aaron shall be gathered to his people. For he shall not enter the land which I have given to the Israelites, because you both rebelled against My instructions at the waters of Meribah.

25Take Aaron and Eleazar his son and bring them up to Mount Hor.

26Strip Aaron of his vestments and put them on Eleazar his son, and Aaron shall be gathered to his people, and shall die there.

27And Moses did as the Lord commanded; and they went up Mount Hor in the sight of all the congregation.

28And Moses stripped Aaron of his [priestly] garments and put them on Eleazar his son. And Aaron died there on the mountain top; and Moses and Eleazar came down from the mountain.

29When all the congregation saw that Aaron was dead, they wept *and* mourned for him thirty days, all the house of Israel.

21 WHEN THE Canaanite king of Arad, who dwelt in the South (the Negeb), heard that Israel was coming by the way of Atharim [the route traveled by the spies sent out by Moses], he fought against Israel and took some of them captive.

2And Israel vowed a vow to the Lord, and said, If You will indeed deliver this people into my hand, then I will utterly destroy their cities.

3And the Lord hearkened to Israel and gave over the Canaanites. And they utterly destroyed them and their cities; and the name of the place was called Hormah [a banned or devoted thing].

4And they journeyed from Mount Hor by the way to the Red Sea, to go around the land of Edom, and the people became impatient (depressed, much discouraged), because [of the trials] of the way.

5And the people spoke against God and against Moses, Why have you brought us out of Egypt to die in the wilderness? For there is no bread, neither is there any water, and we loathe this light (contemptible, unsubstantial) manna.

6Then the Lord sent fiery (burning) serpents among the people; and they bit the people, and many Israelites died.

7And the people came to Moses, and said, We have sinned, for we have spoken against the Lord and against you; pray to the Lord, that He may take away the serpents from us. So Moses prayed for the people.

8And the Lord said to Moses, Make a fiery serpent [of bronze] and set it on a pole; and everyone who is bitten, when he looks at it, shall live.

^k Israel (Jacob's offspring) did not fight Edom, the offspring of Jacob's brother Esau, because of the Lord's warning, later conveyed in definite instructions (Deut. 23:7). But what had begun as only a quarrel between twin brothers (Gen. 27:41) had now been passed on for generations and was to cost countless lives, extending throughout the Old Testament and into the New, where Herod, remotely related to Esau, tried to take the life of the Babe of Bethlehem, a descendant of Jacob. "See how much wood *or* how great a forest a tiny spark can set ablaze!" (James 3:5).

---

^aHeb. *mouth*   ^bi.e. *Utter destruction*   ^cOr, *grieved*
^dHeb. *shortened*

New American Standard

19 Again, the sons of Israel said to him, "We will go up by the highway, and if I and my livestock do drink any of your water, then I will pay its price. Let me only pass through on my feet, nothing *else.*"

20 But he said, "You shall not pass through." And Edom came out against him with a heavy force and with a strong hand.

21 Thus Edom refused to allow Israel to pass through his territory; so Israel turned away from him.

22 ¶ Now when they set out from Kadesh, the sons of Israel, the whole congregation, came to Mount Hor.

Death of Aaron

23 Then the LORD spoke to Moses and Aaron at Mount Hor by the border of the land of Edom, saying,

24 "Aaron will be gathered to his people; for he shall not enter the land which I have given to the sons of Israel, because you rebelled against My command at the waters of Meribah.

25 "Take Aaron and his son Eleazar and bring them up to Mount Hor;

26 and strip Aaron of his garments and put them on his son Eleazar. So Aaron will be gathered *to his people,* and will die there."

27 So Moses did just as the LORD had commanded, and they went up to Mount Hor in the sight of all the congregation.

28 After Moses had stripped Aaron of his garments and put them on his son Eleazar, Aaron died there on the mountain top. Then Moses and Eleazar came down from the mountain.

29 When all the congregation saw that Aaron had died, all the house of Israel wept for Aaron thirty days.

Arad Conquered

21 WHEN THE Canaanite, the king of Arad, who lived in the ʷNegev, heard that Israel was coming by the way of ˣAtharim, then he fought against Israel and took some of them captive.

2 So Israel made a vow to the LORD and said, "If You will indeed deliver this people into my hand, then I will utterly destroy their cities."

3 The LORD heard the voice of Israel and delivered up the Canaanites; then they utterly destroyed them and their cities. Thus the name of the place was called ʸHormah.

4 ¶ Then they set out from Mount Hor by the way of the Red Sea, to go around the land of Edom; and the people became impatient because of the journey.

5 The people spoke against God and Moses, "Why have you brought us up out of Egypt to die in the wilderness? For there is no food and no water, and we loathe this miserable food."

The Bronze Serpent

6 The LORD sent fiery serpents among the people and they bit the people, so that many people of Israel died.

7 So the people came to Moses and said, "We have sinned, because we have spoken against the LORD and you; intercede with the LORD, that He may remove the serpents from us." And Moses interceded for the people.

8 Then the LORD said to Moses, "Make a fiery *serpent,* and set it on a standard; and it shall come about, that everyone who is bitten, when he looks at it, he will live."

New International

19 The Israelites replied:

"We will go along the main road, and if we or our livestock drink any of your water, we will pay for it. We only want to pass through on foot—nothing else."

20 Again they answered:

"You may not pass through."

Then Edom came out against them with a large and powerful army. 21 Since Edom refused to let them go through their territory, Israel turned away from them.

The Death of Aaron

22 The whole Israelite community set out from Kadesh and came to Mount Hor. 23 At Mount Hor, near the border of Edom, the LORD said to Moses and Aaron, 24 "Aaron will be gathered to his people. He will not enter the land I give the Israelites, because both of you rebelled against my command at the waters of Meribah. 25 Get Aaron and his son Eleazar and take them up Mount Hor. 26 Remove Aaron's garments and put them on his son Eleazar, for Aaron will be gathered to his people; he will die there."

27 Moses did as the LORD commanded: They went up Mount Hor in the sight of the whole community. 28 Moses removed Aaron's garments and put them on his son Eleazar. And Aaron died there on top of the mountain. Then Moses and Eleazar came down from the mountain, 29 and when the whole community learned that Aaron had died, the entire house of Israel mourned for him thirty days.

Arad Destroyed

21 WHEN THE Canaanite king of Arad, who lived in the Negev, heard that Israel was coming along the road to Atharim, he attacked the Israelites and captured some of them. 2 Then Israel made this vow to the LORD: "If you will deliver these people into our hands, we will totally destroyʳ their cities." 3 The LORD listened to Israel's plea and gave the Canaanites over to them. They completely destroyed them and their towns; so the place was named Hormah.ˢ

The Bronze Snake

4 They traveled from Mount Hor along the route to the Red Sea,ᵗ to go around Edom. But the people grew impatient on the way; 5 they spoke against God and against Moses, and said, "Why have you brought us up out of Egypt to die in the desert? There is no bread! There is no water! And we detest this miserable food!"

6 Then the LORD sent venomous snakes among them; they bit the people and many Israelites died. 7 The people came to Moses and said, "We sinned when we spoke against the LORD and against you. Pray that the LORD will take the snakes away from us." So Moses prayed for the people.

8 The LORD said to Moses, "Make a snake and put it up

ʷ I.e. South country   ˣ Or *the spies*   ʸ I.e. a devoted thing; or Destruction

ʳ 2 The Hebrew term refers to the irrevocable giving over of things or persons to the LORD, often by totally destroying them; also in verse 3.   ˢ 3 *Hormah* means *destruction.*   ᵗ 4 Hebrew *Yam Suph;* that is, Sea of Reeds

King James

Amplified

9And Moses made a serpent of brass, and put it upon a pole, and it came to pass, that if a serpent had bitten any man, when he beheld the serpent of brass, he lived.

Israel moves on

10 ¶ And the children of Israel set forward, and pitched in Oboth.

11And they journeyed from Oboth, and pitched at eIjeabarim, in the wilderness which is before Moab, toward the sunrising.

12 ¶ From thence they removed, and pitched in the valley of Zared.

13From thence they removed, and pitched on the other side of Arnon, which is in the wilderness that cometh out of the coasts of the Amorites: for Arnon is the border of Moab, between Moab and the Amorites.

14Wherefore it is said in the book of the wars of the LORD, fWhat he did in the Red sea, and in the brooks of Arnon,

15And at the stream of the brooks that goeth down to the dwelling of Ar, and glieth upon the border of Moab.

16And from thence they went to Beer: that is the well whereof the LORD spake unto Moses, Gather the people together, and I will give them water.

17 ¶ Then Israel sang this song, hSpring up, O well; ising ye unto it:

18The princes digged the well, the nobles of the people digged it, by the direction of the lawgiver, with their staves. And from the wilderness they went to Mattanah:

19And from Mattanah to Nahaliel: and from Nahaliel to Bamoth:

20And from Bamoth in the valley, that is in the jcountry of Moab, to the top of kPisgah, which looketh toward lJeshimon.

Defeat of Sihon and Og

21 ¶ And Israel sent messengers unto Sihon king of the Amorites, saying,

22Let me pass through thy land: we will not turn into the fields, or into the vineyards; we will not drink of the waters of the well: but we will go along by the king's high way, until we be past thy borders.

23And Sihon would not suffer Israel to pass through his border: but Sihon gathered all his people together, and went out against Israel into the wilderness: and he came to Jahaz, and fought against Israel.

24And Israel smote him with the edge of the sword, and possessed his land from Arnon unto Jabbok, even unto the children of Ammon: for the border of the children of Ammon was strong.

25And Israel took all these cities: and Israel dwelt in all the cities of the Amorites, in Heshbon, and in all the mvillages thereof.

26For Heshbon was the city of Sihon the king of the Amorites, who had fought against the former king of Moab, and taken all his land out of his hand, even unto Arnon.

27Wherefore they that speak in proverbs say, Come into Heshbon, let the city of Sihon be built and prepared:

28For there is a fire gone out of Heshbon, a flame from the city of Sihon: it hath consumed Ar of Moab, and the lords of the high places of Arnon.

9And Moses made a serpent of bronze and put it on a pole, and if a serpent had bitten any man, when he looked to the serpent of bronze [lattentively, expectantly, with a steady and absorbing gaze], he lived.

10And the Israelites journeyed on and encamped at Oboth.

11They journeyed from Oboth and encamped at Iyeabarim, in the wilderness opposite Moab, toward the sunrise.

12From there they journeyed and encamped in the Valley of Zared.

13From there they journeyed and encamped on the other side of [the river] Arnon, which is in the desert or wilderness that extends from the frontier of the Amorites; for [the river] Arnon is the boundary of Moab, between Moab and the Amorites.

14That is why it is said in the Book of the Wars of the Lord: Waheb in Suphah, and the valleys of [the branches of] the Arnon [River],

15And the slope of the valleys that stretch toward the site of Ar and find support on the border of Moab.

16From there the Israelites went on to Beer [a well], the well of which the Lord had said to Moses, Assemble the people together and I will give them water. [John 7:37–39.]

17Then Israel sang this song, Spring up, O well! Let all sing to it, [Rom. 14:17.]

18The fountain that the princes opened, that the nobles of the people hollowed out from their staves. And from the wilderness or desert [Israel journeyed] to Mattanah,

19And from Mattanah to Nahaliel, and from Nahaliel to Bamoth,

20And from Bamoth to the valley that is in the field of Moab, to the top of Pisgah which looks down upon Jeshimon and the desert.

21And Israel sent messengers to Sihon king of the Amorites, saying,

22Let me pass through your land. We will not turn aside into field or vineyard; we will not drink the water of the wells. We will go by the king's highway until we have passed your border.

23But Sihon would not allow Israel to pass through his border. Instead Sihon gathered all his people together and went out against Israel into the wilderness, and came to Jahaz, and he fought against Israel.

24And Israel smote the king of the Amorites with the edge of the sword and possessed his land from the river Arnon to the river Jabbok, as far as the Ammonites, for the boundary of the Ammonites was strong.

25And Israel took all these cities and dwelt in all the cities of the Amorites, in Heshbon and in all its towns.

26For Heshbon was the city of Sihon king of the Amorites, who had fought against the former king of Moab and taken all his land out of his hand, as far as [the river] Arnon.

27That is why those who sing ballads say, Come to Heshbon, let the city of Sihon be built and established.

28For fire has gone out of Heshbon, a flame from the city of Sihon; it has devoured Ar of Moab and the lords of the heights of the Arnon.

lJesus said that as Moses lifted up the serpent in the wilderness, so must the Son of Man be lifted up, "that everyone who believes in Him [who cleaves to Him, trusts Him and relies on Him] may not perish, but have eternal life and [actually] live forever!" (John 3:14, 15). Obviously this implies that the look that caused the victim of a fiery serpent to be healed was something far more than a casual glance. A "look" would save, but what kind of a look? The Hebrew text here means "look attentively, expectantly, with a steady and absorbing gaze." Or, as Jesus said in the last verse of the chapter quoted above (John 3:36), "He who believes in (has faith in, clings to, relies on) the Son has (now possesses) eternal life." But whoever does not so believe in, cling to, and rely on the Son "will never see . . . life." The look that saves is not just a fleeting glance; it is a God-honoring, God-answered, fixed, and absorbing gaze!

eOr, Heaps of Abarim   fOr, Vaheb in Suphah   gHeb. leaneth
hHeb. Ascend   iOr, answer   jHeb. field   kOr, The hill
lOr, The wilderness   mHeb. daughters

New American Standard

⁹ And Moses made a bronze serpent and set it on the standard; and it came about, that if a serpent bit any man, when he looked to the bronze serpent, he lived.

¹⁰ ¶ Now the sons of Israel moved out and camped in Oboth.

¹¹ They journeyed from Oboth and camped at Iyeabarim, in the wilderness which is opposite Moab, to the east.

¹² From there they set out and camped in ᶻWadi Zered.

¹³ From there they journeyed and camped on the other side of the Arnon, which is in the wilderness that comes out of the border of the Amorites, for the Arnon is the border of Moab, between Moab and the Amorites.

¹⁴ Therefore it is said in the Book of the Wars of the LORD,

"Waheb in Suphah,
    And the wadis of the Arnon,
¹⁵ And the slope of the wadis
    That extends to the site of Ar,
    And leans to the border of Moab."

¹⁶ ¶ From there *they continued* to Beer, that is the well where the LORD said to Moses, "Assemble the people, that I may give them water."

¹⁷ ¶ Then Israel sang this song:
"Spring up, O well! Sing to it!
¹⁸ The well, which the leaders sank,
    Which the nobles of the people dug,
    With the scepter *and* with their staffs."
And from the wilderness *they continued* to Mattanah,
¹⁹ and from Mattanah to Nahaliel, and from Nahaliel to Bamoth,
²⁰ and from Bamoth to the valley that is in the land of Moab, at the top of Pisgah which overlooks the wasteland.

Two Victories

²¹ ¶ Then Israel sent messengers to Sihon, king of the Amorites, saying,

²² "Let me pass through your land. We will not turn off into field or vineyard; we will not drink water from wells. We will go by the king's highway until we have passed through your border."

²³ But Sihon would not permit Israel to pass through his border. So Sihon gathered all his people and went out against Israel in the wilderness, and came to Jahaz and fought against Israel.

²⁴ Then Israel struck him with the edge of the sword, and took possession of his land from the Arnon to the Jabbok, as far as the sons of Ammon; for the border of the sons of Ammon *was* Jazer.

²⁵ Israel took all these cities and Israel lived in all the cities of the Amorites, in Heshbon, and in all her villages.

²⁶ For Heshbon was the city of Sihon, king of the Amorites, who had fought against the former king of Moab and had taken all his land out of his hand, as far as the Arnon.

²⁷ Therefore those who use proverbs say,
"Come to Heshbon! Let it be built!
So let the city of Sihon be established.
²⁸ For a fire went forth from Heshbon,
    A flame from the town of Sihon;
    It devoured Ar of Moab,
    The dominant heights of the Arnon.

New International

on a pole; anyone who is bitten can look at it and live." ⁹So Moses made a bronze snake and put it up on a pole. Then when anyone was bitten by a snake and looked at the bronze snake, he lived.

The Journey to Moab

¹⁰The Israelites moved on and camped at Oboth. ¹¹Then they set out from Oboth and camped in Iye Abarim, in the desert that faces Moab toward the sunrise. ¹²From there they moved on and camped in the Zered Valley. ¹³They set out from there and camped alongside the Arnon, which is in the desert extending into Amorite territory. The Arnon is the border of Moab, between Moab and the Amorites. ¹⁴That is why the Book of the Wars of the LORD says:

". . . Waheb in Suphahᵘ and the ravines,
    the Arnon ¹⁵andᵛ the slopes of the ravines
    that lead to the site of Ar
    and lie along the border of Moab."

¹⁶From there they continued on to Beer, the well where the LORD said to Moses, "Gather the people together and I will give them water."

¹⁷Then Israel sang this song:

"Spring up, O well!
    Sing about it,
¹⁸about the well that the princes dug,
    that the nobles of the people sank—
    the nobles with scepters and staffs."

Then they went from the desert to Mattanah, ¹⁹from Mattanah to Nahaliel, from Nahaliel to Bamoth, ²⁰and from Bamoth to the valley in Moab where the top of Pisgah overlooks the wasteland.

Defeat of Sihon and Og

²¹Israel sent messengers to say to Sihon king of the Amorites:

²² "Let us pass through your country. We will not turn aside into any field or vineyard, or drink water from any well. We will travel along the king's highway until we have passed through your territory."

²³But Sihon would not let Israel pass through his territory. He mustered his entire army and marched out into the desert against Israel. When he reached Jahaz, he fought with Israel. ²⁴Israel, however, put him to the sword and took over his land from the Arnon to the Jabbok, but only as far as the Ammonites, because their border was fortified. ²⁵Israel captured all the cities of the Amorites and occupied them, including Heshbon and all its surrounding settlements. ²⁶Heshbon was the city of Sihon king of the Amorites, who had fought against the former king of Moab and had taken from him all his land as far as the Arnon.

²⁷That is why the poets say:

"Come to Heshbon and let it be rebuilt;
    let Sihon's city be restored.

²⁸ "Fire went out from Heshbon,
    a blaze from the city of Sihon.
    It consumed Ar of Moab,
    the citizens of Arnon's heights.

ᶻI.e. a dry ravine except during rainy season

ᵘ14 The meaning of the Hebrew for this phrase is uncertain.
ᵛ14,15 Or "I have been given from Suphah and the ravines / of the Arnon ¹⁵to

King James

²⁹Woe to thee, Moab! thou art undone, O people of Chemosh: he hath given his sons that escaped, and his daughters, into captivity unto Sihon king of the Amorites.

³⁰We have shot at them; Heshbon is perished even unto Dibon, and we have laid them waste even unto Nophah, which *reacheth* unto Medeba.

³¹ ¶ Thus Israel dwelt in the land of the Amorites.

³²And Moses sent to spy out Jaazer, and they took the villages thereof, and drove out the Amorites that *were* there.

³³ ¶ And they turned and went up by the way of Bashan: and Og the king of Bashan went out against them, he, and all his people, to the battle at Edrei.

³⁴And the LORD said unto Moses, Fear him not: for I have delivered him into thy hand, and all his people, and his land; and thou shalt do to him as thou didst unto Sihon king of the Amorites, which dwelt at Heshbon.

³⁵So they smote him, and his sons, and all his people, until there was none left him alive: and they possessed his land.

Balak sends for Balaam

22 AND THE children of Israel set forward, and pitched in the plains of Moab on this side Jordan *by* Jericho.

² ¶ And Balak the son of Zippor saw all that Israel had done to the Amorites.

³And Moab was sore afraid of the people, because they *were* many: and Moab was distressed because of the children of Israel.

⁴And Moab said unto the elders of Midian, Now shall this company lick up all *that are* round about us, as the ox licketh up the grass of the field. And Balak the son of Zippor *was* king of the Moabites at that time.

⁵He sent messengers therefore unto Balaam the son of Beor to Pethor, which *is* by the river of the land of the children of his people, to call him, saying, Behold, there is a people come out from Egypt: behold, they cover the ⁿface of the earth, and they abide over against me:

⁶Come now therefore, I pray thee, curse me this people; for they *are* too mighty for me: peradventure I shall prevail, *that* we may smite them, and *that* I may drive them out of the land: for I wot that he whom thou blessest *is* blessed, and he whom thou cursest is cursed.

⁷And the elders of Moab and the elders of Midian departed with the rewards of divination in their hand; and they came unto Balaam, and spake unto him the words of Balak.

⁸And he said unto them, Lodge here this night, and I will bring you word again, as the LORD shall speak unto me: and the princes of Moab abode with Balaam.

⁹And God came unto Balaam, and said, What men *are* these with thee?

¹⁰And Balaam said unto God, Balak the son of Zippor, king of Moab, hath sent unto me, *saying,*

¹¹Behold, *there is* a people come out of Egypt, which covereth the face of the earth: come now, curse me them; peradventure ^oI shall be able to overcome them, and drive them out.

¹²And God said unto Balaam, Thou shalt not go with them; thou shalt not curse the people: for they *are* blessed.

¹³And Balaam rose up in the morning, and said unto the princes of Balak, Get you into your land: for the LORD refuseth to give me leave to go with you.

¹⁴And the princes of Moab rose up, and they went unto Balak, and said, Balaam refuseth to come with us.

Amplified

²⁹Woe to you, Moab! You are undone, O people of [the god] Chemosh! Moab has given his sons as fugitives and his daughters into captivity to Sihon king of the Amorites.

³⁰We have shot them down; Heshbon has perished as far as Dibon, and we have laid them waste as far as Nophah, which reaches to Medeba.

³¹Thus Israel dwelt in the land of the Amorites.

³²And Moses sent to spy out Jazer, and they took its villages and dispossessed the Amorites who were there.

³³Then they turned and went up by the way of Bashan; and Og the king of Bashan went out against them, he and all his people, to battle at Edrei.

³⁴But the Lord said to Moses, Do not fear him, for I have delivered him and all his people and his land into your hand; and you shall do to him as you did to Sihon king of the Amorites, who dwelt at Heshbon.

³⁵So the Israelites slew Og and his sons and all his people until there was not one left alive, And they possessed his land.

22 THE ISRAELITES journeyed and encamped in the plains of Moab, on the east side of the Jordan [River] at Jericho.

²And Balak [the king of Moab] son of Zippor saw all that Israel had done to the Amorites.

³And Moab was terrified at the people *and* full of dread, because they were many. Moab was distressed *and* overcome with fear because of the Israelites.

⁴And Moab said to the elders of Midian, Now will this multitude lick up all that is round about us, as the ox licks up the grass of the field. So Balak son of Zippor, the king of the Moabites at that time,

⁵Sent messengers to Balaam [a foreteller of events] son of Beor at Pethor, which is by the [Euphrates] River, even to the land of the children of his people, to say to him, There is a people come out from Egypt; behold, they cover the face of the earth and they have settled down *and* dwell opposite me.

⁶Now come, I beg of you, curse this people for me, for they are too powerful for me. Perhaps I may be able to defeat them and drive them out of the land, for I know that he whom you bless is blessed, and he whom you curse is cursed.

⁷And the elders of Moab and of Midian departed with the rewards of foretelling in their hands; and they came to Balaam and told him the words of Balak.

⁸And he said to them, Lodge here tonight and I will bring you word as the Lord may speak to me. And the princes of Moab abode with Balaam [that night].

⁹And God came to Balaam, and said, What men are these with you?

¹⁰And Balaam said to God, Balak son of Zippor, king of Moab, has sent to me, saying,

¹¹Behold, the people who came out of Egypt cover the face of the earth; come now, curse them for me. Perhaps I shall be able to fight against them and drive them out.

¹²And God said to Balaam, You shall not go with them; you shall not curse the people, for they are blessed.

¹³And Balaam rose up in the morning, and said to the princes of Balak, Go back to your own land, for the Lord refuses to permit me to go with you.

¹⁴So the princes of Moab rose up and went to Balak, and said, Balaam refuses to come with us.

ⁿHeb. *eye*   ^oHeb. *I shall prevail in fighting against him*

New American Standard

29"Woe to you, O Moab!
   You are ruined, O people of Chemosh!
   He has given his sons as fugitives,
   And his daughters into captivity,
   To an Amorite king, Sihon.
30"But we have cast them down,
   Heshbon is ruined as far as Dibon,
   Then we have laid waste even to Nophah,
   Which *reaches* to Medeba."
31 ¶ Thus Israel lived in the land of the Amorites.
32 Moses sent to spy out Jazer, and they captured its villages and dispossessed the Amorites who *were* there.
33 ¶ Then they turned and went up by the way of Bashan, and Og the king of Bashan went out with all his people, for battle at Edrei.
34 But the LORD said to Moses, "Do not fear him, for I have given him into your hand, and all his people and his land; and you shall do to him as you did to Sihon, king of the Amorites, who lived at Heshbon."
35 So they killed him and his sons and all his people, until there was no remnant left him; and they possessed his land.

Balak Sends for Balaam

22 THEN THE sons of Israel journeyed, and camped in the plains of Moab beyond the Jordan *opposite* Jericho.
2 ¶ Now Balak the son of Zippor saw all that Israel had done to the Amorites.
3 So Moab was in great fear because of the people, for they were numerous; and Moab was in dread of the sons of Israel.
4 Moab said to the elders of Midian, "Now this horde will lick up all that is around us, as the ox licks up the grass of the field." And Balak the son of Zippor was king of Moab at that time.
5 So he sent messengers to Balaam the son of Beor, at Pethor, which is near the *a*River, *in* the land of the sons of his people, to call him, saying, "Behold, a people came out of Egypt; behold, they cover the surface of the land, and they are living opposite me.
6"Now, therefore, please come, curse this people for me since they are too mighty for me; perhaps I may be able to defeat them and drive them out of the land. For I know that he whom you bless is blessed, and he whom you curse is cursed."
7 ¶ So the elders of Moab and the elders of Midian departed with the *fees for* divination in their hand; and they came to Balaam and repeated Balak's words to him.
8 He said to them, "Spend the night here, and I will bring word back to you as the LORD may speak to me." And the leaders of Moab stayed with Balaam.
9 Then God came to Balaam and said, "Who are these men with you?"
10 Balaam said to God, "Balak the son of Zippor, king of Moab, has sent *word* to me,
11 'Behold, there is a people who came out of Egypt and they cover the surface of the land; now come, curse them for me; perhaps I may be able to fight against them and drive them out.' "
12 God said to Balaam, "Do not go with them; you shall not curse the people, for they are blessed."
13 So Balaam arose in the morning and said to Balak's leaders, "Go back to your land, for the LORD has refused to let me go with you."
14 The leaders of Moab arose and went to Balak and said, "Balaam refused to come with us."

New International

29Woe to you, O Moab!
   You are destroyed, O people of Chemosh!
   He has given up his sons as fugitives
   and his daughters as captives
   to Sihon king of the Amorites.

30"But we have overthrown them;
   Heshbon is destroyed all the way to Dibon.
   We have demolished them as far as Nophah,
   which extends to Medeba."

31So Israel settled in the land of the Amorites.
32After Moses had sent spies to Jazer, the Israelites captured its surrounding settlements and drove out the Amorites who were there. 33Then they turned and went up along the road toward Bashan, and Og king of Bashan and his whole army marched out to meet them in battle at Edrei.
34The LORD said to Moses, "Do not be afraid of him, for I have handed him over to you, with his whole army and his land. Do to him what you did to Sihon king of the Amorites, who reigned in Heshbon."
35So they struck him down, together with his sons and his whole army, leaving them no survivors. And they took possession of his land.

Balak Summons Balaam

22 THEN THE Israelites traveled to the plains of Moab and camped along the Jordan across from Jericho.*w*
2Now Balak son of Zippor saw all that Israel had done to the Amorites, 3and Moab was terrified because there were so many people. Indeed, Moab was filled with dread because of the Israelites.
4The Moabites said to the elders of Midian, "This horde is going to lick up everything around us, as an ox licks up the grass of the field."

So Balak son of Zippor, who was king of Moab at that time, 5sent messengers to summon Balaam son of Beor, who was at Pethor, near the River,*x* in his native land. Balak said:

   "A people has come out of Egypt; they cover the face of the land and have settled next to me. 6Now come and put a curse on these people, because they are too powerful for me. Perhaps then I will be able to defeat them and drive them out of the country. For I know that those you bless are blessed, and those you curse are cursed."

7The elders of Moab and Midian left, taking with them the fee for divination. When they came to Balaam, they told him what Balak had said.
8"Spend the night here," Balaam said to them, "and I will bring you back the answer the LORD gives me." So the Moabite princes stayed with him.
9God came to Balaam and asked, "Who are these men with you?"
10Balaam said to God, "Balak son of Zippor, king of Moab, sent me this message: 11'A people that has come out of Egypt covers the face of the land. Now come and put a curse on them for me. Perhaps then I will be able to fight them and drive them away.' "
12But God said to Balaam, "Do not go with them. You must not put a curse on those people, because they are blessed."
13The next morning Balaam got up and said to Balak's princes, "Go back to your own country, for the LORD has refused to let me go with you."
14So the Moabite princes returned to Balak and said, "Balaam refused to come with us."

*a*I.e. Euphrates

*w*1 Hebrew *Jordan of Jericho*; possibly an ancient name for the Jordan River   *x*5 That is, the Euphrates

King James

Amplified

15 ¶ And Balak sent yet again princes, more, and more honourable than they.

16 And they came to Balaam, and said to him, Thus saith Balak the son of Zippor, *p*Let nothing, I pray thee, hinder thee from coming unto me:

17 For I will promote thee unto very great honour, and I will do whatsoever thou sayest unto me: come therefore, I pray thee, curse me this people.

18 And Balaam answered and said unto the servants of Balak, If Balak would give me his house full of silver and gold, I cannot go beyond the word of the LORD my God, to do less or more.

19 Now therefore, I pray you, tarry ye also here this night, that I may know what the LORD will say unto me more.

20 And God came unto Balaam at night, and said unto him, If the men come to call thee, rise up, *and* go with them; but yet the word which I shall say unto thee, that shalt thou do.

Balaam's ass speaks

21 And Balaam rose up in the morning, and saddled his ass, and went with the princes of Moab.

22 ¶ And God's anger was kindled because he went: and the angel of the LORD stood in the way for an adversary against him. Now he was riding upon his ass, and his two servants *were* with him.

23 And the ass saw the angel of the LORD standing in the way, and his sword drawn in his hand: and the ass turned aside out of the way, and went into the field: and Balaam smote the ass, to turn her into the way.

24 But the angel of the LORD stood in a path of the vineyards, a wall *being* on this side, and a wall on that side.

25 And when the ass saw the angel of the LORD, she thrust herself unto the wall, and crushed Balaam's foot against the wall: and he smote her again.

26 And the angel of the LORD went further, and stood in a narrow place, where *was* no way to turn either to the right hand or to the left.

27 And when the ass saw the angel of the LORD, she fell down under Balaam: and Balaam's anger was kindled, and he smote the ass with a staff.

28 And the LORD opened the mouth of the ass, and she said unto Balaam, What have I done unto thee, that thou hast smitten me these three times?

29 And Balaam said unto the ass, Because thou hast mocked me: I would there were a sword in mine hand, for now would I kill thee.

30 And the ass said unto Balaam, *Am* not I thine ass, *q*upon which thou hast ridden *r*ever since *I was* thine unto this day? was I ever wont to do so unto thee? And he said, Nay.

31 Then the LORD opened the eyes of Balaam, and he saw the angel of the LORD standing in the way, and his sword drawn in his hand: and he bowed down his head, and *s*fell flat on his face.

32 And the angel of the LORD said unto him, Wherefore hast thou smitten thine ass these three times? behold, I went out *t*to withstand thee, because *thy* way is perverse before me:

33 And the ass saw me, and turned from me these three times: unless she had turned from me, surely now also I had slain thee, and saved her alive.

34 And Balaam said unto the angel of the LORD, I have sinned; for I knew not that thou stoodest in the way against me: now therefore, if it *u*displease thee, I will get me back again.

35 And the angel of the LORD said unto Balaam, Go with the men: but only the word that I shall speak unto thee, that thou shalt speak. So Balaam went with the princes of Balak.

Amplified

15 Then Balak again sent princes, more of them and more honorable than the first ones.

16 And they came to Balaam, and said to him, Thus says Balak son of Zippor, I beg of you, let nothing hinder you from coming to me;

17 For I will promote you to very great honor and I will do whatever you tell me; so come, I beg of you, curse this people for me.

18 And Balaam answered the servants of Balak, If Balak would give me his house full of silver and gold, I cannot go beyond the word of the Lord my God, to do less or more.

19 Now therefore, I pray you, tarry here again tonight that I may know what more the Lord will say to me.

20 And God came to Balaam at night, and said to him, If the men come to call you, rise up and go with them, but still only what I tell you may you do.

21 And Balaam rose up in the morning and saddled his donkey and went with the princes of Moab.

22 And God's anger was kindled because he went, and the *m*Angel of the Lord stood in the way as an adversary against him. Now he was riding upon his donkey, and his two servants were with him.

23 And the donkey saw the Angel of the Lord standing in the way and His sword drawn in His hand, and the donkey turned aside out of the way and went into the field. And Balaam struck the donkey to turn her into the way.

24 But the Angel of the Lord stood in a path of the vineyards, a wall on this side and a wall on that side.

25 And when the donkey saw the Angel of the Lord, she thrust herself against the wall and crushed Balaam's foot against it, and he struck her again.

26 And the Angel of the Lord went further and stood in a narrow place where there was no room to turn, either to the right hand or to the left.

27 And when the donkey saw the Angel of the Lord, she fell down under Balaam, and Balaam's anger was kindled and he struck the donkey with his staff.

28 And the Lord opened the mouth of the donkey, and she said to Balaam, What have I done to you that you should strike me these three times?

29 And Balaam said to the donkey, Because you have ridiculed *and* provoked me! I wish there were a sword in my hand, for now I would kill you!

30 And the donkey said to Balaam, Am not I your donkey, upon which you have ridden all your life long until this day? Was I ever accustomed to do so to you? And he said, No.

31 Then the Lord opened Balaam's eyes, and he saw the Angel of the Lord standing in the way with His sword drawn in His hand; and he bowed his head and fell on his face.

32 And the Angel of the Lord said to him, Why have you struck your donkey these three times? See, I came out to stand against *and* resist you, for your behavior is willfully obstinate *and* contrary before Me.

33 And the ass saw Me and turned from Me these three times. If she had not turned from Me, surely I would have slain you and saved her alive.

34 Balaam said to the Angel of the Lord, I have sinned, for I did not know You stood in the way against me. But now, if my going displeases You, I will return.

35 The Angel of the Lord said to Balaam, Go with the men, but you shall speak only what I tell you. So Balaam went with the princes of Balak.

---

p Heb. *Be not thou letted from*   *q* Heb. *who hast ridden upon me*
r Or, *ever since thou wast*   *s* Or, *bowed himself*   *t* Heb. *to be an adversary unto thee*   *u* Heb. *be evil in thine eyes*   *m* See footnote on Gen. 16:7.

New American Standard

15 ¶ Then Balak again sent leaders, more numerous and more distinguished than the former.
16 They came to Balaam and said to him, "Thus says Balak the son of Zippor, 'Let nothing, I beg you, hinder you from coming to me;
17 for I will indeed honor you richly, and I will do whatever you say to me. Please come then, curse this people for me.' "
18 Balaam replied to the servants of Balak, "Though Balak were to give me his house full of silver and gold, I could not do anything, either small or great, contrary to the command of the LORD my God.
19 "Now please, you also stay here tonight, and I will find out what else the LORD will speak to me."
20 God came to Balaam at night and said to him, "If the men have come to call you, rise up *and* go with them; but only the word which I speak to you shall you do."
21 ¶ So Balaam arose in the morning, and saddled his donkey and went with the leaders of Moab.

The Angel and Balaam

22 But God was angry because he was going, and the angel of the LORD took his stand in the way as an adversary against him. Now he was riding on his donkey and his two servants were with him.
23 When the donkey saw the angel of the LORD standing in the way with his drawn sword in his hand, the donkey turned off from the way and went into the field; but Balaam struck the donkey to turn her back into the way.
24 Then the angel of the LORD stood in a narrow path of the vineyards, *with* a wall on this side and a wall on that side.
25 When the donkey saw the angel of the LORD, she pressed herself to the wall and pressed Balaam's foot against the wall, so he struck her again.
26 The angel of the LORD went further, and stood in a narrow place where there was no way to turn to the right hand or the left.
27 When the donkey saw the angel of the LORD, she lay down under Balaam; so Balaam was angry and struck the donkey with his stick.
28 And the LORD opened the mouth of the donkey, and she said to Balaam, "What have I done to you, that you have struck me these three times?"
29 Then Balaam said to the donkey, "Because you have made a mockery of me! If there had been a sword in my hand, I would have killed you by now."
30 The donkey said to Balaam, "Am I not your donkey on which you have ridden all your life to this day? Have I ever been accustomed to do so to you?" And he said, "No."
31 ¶ Then the LORD opened the eyes of Balaam, and he saw the angel of the LORD standing in the way with his drawn sword in his hand; and he bowed all the way to the ground.
32 The angel of the LORD said to him, "Why have you struck your donkey these three times? Behold, I have come out as an adversary, because your way was contrary to me.
33 "But the donkey saw me and turned aside from me these three times. If she had not turned aside from me, I would surely have killed you just now, and let her live."
34 Balaam said to the angel of the LORD, "I have sinned, for I did not know that you were standing in the way against me. Now then, if it is displeasing to you, I will turn back."
35 But the angel of the LORD said to Balaam, "Go with the men, but you shall speak only the word which I tell you." So Balaam went along with the leaders of Balak.

New International

15 Then Balak sent other princes, more numerous and more distinguished than the first. 16 They came to Balaam and said:

"This is what Balak son of Zippor says: Do not let anything keep you from coming to me, 17 because I will reward you handsomely and do whatever you say. Come and put a curse on these people for me."

18 But Balaam answered them, "Even if Balak gave me his palace filled with silver and gold, I could not do anything great or small to go beyond the command of the LORD my God. 19 Now stay here tonight as the others did, and I will find out what else the LORD will tell me."

20 That night God came to Balaam and said, "Since these men have come to summon you, go with them, but do only what I tell you."

Balaam's Donkey

21 Balaam got up in the morning, saddled his donkey and went with the princes of Moab. 22 But God was very angry when he went, and the angel of the LORD stood in the road to oppose him. Balaam was riding on his donkey, and his two servants were with him. 23 When the donkey saw the angel of the LORD standing in the road with a drawn sword in his hand, she turned off the road into a field. Balaam beat her to get her back on the road.

24 Then the angel of the LORD stood in a narrow path between two vineyards, with walls on both sides. 25 When the donkey saw the angel of the LORD, she pressed close to the wall, crushing Balaam's foot against it. So he beat her again.

26 Then the angel of the LORD moved on ahead and stood in a narrow place where there was no room to turn, either to the right or to the left. 27 When the donkey saw the angel of the LORD, she lay down under Balaam, and he was angry and beat her with his staff. 28 Then the LORD opened the donkey's mouth, and she said to Balaam, "What have I done to you to make you beat me these three times?"

29 Balaam answered the donkey, "You have made a fool of me! If I had a sword in my hand, I would kill you right now."

30 The donkey said to Balaam, "Am I not your own donkey, which you have always ridden, to this day? Have I been in the habit of doing this to you?"

"No," he said.

31 Then the LORD opened Balaam's eyes, and he saw the angel of the LORD standing in the road with his sword drawn. So he bowed low and fell facedown.

32 The angel of the LORD asked him, "Why have you beaten your donkey these three times? I have come here to oppose you because your path is a reckless one before me.[y] 33 The donkey saw me and turned away from me these three times. If she had not turned away, I would certainly have killed you by now, but I would have spared her."

34 Balaam said to the angel of the LORD, "I have sinned. I did not realize you were standing in the road to oppose me. Now if you are displeased, I will go back."

35 The angel of the LORD said to Balaam, "Go with the men, but speak only what I tell you." So Balaam went with the princes of Balak.

y 32 The meaning of the Hebrew for this clause is uncertain.

King James

36 ¶ And when Balak heard that Balaam was come, he went out to meet him unto a city of Moab, which *is* in the border of Arnon, which *is* in the utmost coast.

37 And Balak said unto Balaam, Did I not earnestly send unto thee to call thee? wherefore camest thou not unto me? am I not able indeed to promote thee to honour?

38 And Balaam said unto Balak, Lo, I am come unto thee: have I now any power at all to say any thing? the word that God putteth in my mouth, that shall I speak.

39 And Balaam went with Balak, and they came unto ᵛKirjath-huzoth.

40 And Balak offered oxen and sheep, and sent to Balaam, and to the princes that *were* with him.

41 And it came to pass on the morrow, that Balak took Balaam, and brought him up into the high places of Baal, that thence he might see the utmost *part* of the people.

Balaam's parables

23 AND BALAAM said unto Balak, Build me here seven altars, and prepare me here seven oxen and seven rams.

2 And Balak did as Balaam had spoken; and Balak and Balaam offered on *every* altar a bullock and a ram.

3 And Balaam said unto Balak, Stand by thy burnt offering, and I will go: peradventure the LORD will come to meet me: and whatsoever he showeth me I will tell thee. And ʷhe went to an high place.

4 And God met Balaam: and he said unto him, I have prepared seven altars, and I have offered upon *every* altar a bullock and a ram.

5 And the LORD put a word in Balaam's mouth, and said, Return unto Balak, and thus thou shalt speak.

6 And he returned unto him, and, lo, he stood by his burnt sacrifice, he, and all the princes of Moab.

7 And he took up his parable, and said, Balak the king of Moab hath brought me from Aram, out of the mountains of the east, *saying,* Come, curse me Jacob, and come, defy Israel.

8 How shall I curse, whom God hath not cursed? or how shall I defy, *whom* the LORD hath not defied?

9 For from the top of the rocks I see him, and from the hills I behold him: lo, the people shall dwell alone, and shall not be reckoned among the nations.

10 Who can count the dust of Jacob, and the number of the fourth *part* of Israel? Let ˣme die the death of the righteous, and let my last end be like his!

11 And Balak said unto Balaam, What hast thou done unto me? I took thee to curse mine enemies, and, behold, thou hast blessed *them* altogether.

12 And he answered and said, Must I not take heed to speak that which the LORD hath put in my mouth?

13 And Balak said unto him, Come, I pray thee, with me unto another place, from whence thou mayest see them: thou shalt see but the utmost part of them, and shalt not see them all: and curse me them from thence.

14 ¶ And he brought him into the field of Zophim, to the top of ʸPisgah, and built seven altars, and offered a bullock and a ram on *every* altar.

15 And he said unto Balak, Stand here by thy burnt offering, while I meet *the* LORD yonder.

16 And the LORD met Balaam, and put a word in his mouth, and said, Go again unto Balak, and say thus.

Amplified

36 When Balak heard that Balaam had come, he went out to meet him at the city of Moab on the border formed by the Arnon [River], at the farthest end of the boundary.

37 Balak said to Balaam, Did I not [earnestly] send to you to ask you [to come] to me? Why did you not come? Am not I able to promote you to honor?

38 And Balaam said to Balak, Indeed I have come to you, but do I now have any power at all to say anything? The word that God puts in my mouth, that shall I speak.

39 And Balaam went with Balak, and they came to Kiriath-huzoth.

40 And Balak offered oxen and sheep, and sent [portions] to Balaam and to the princes who were with him.

41 And on the following day Balak took Balaam and brought him up into the high places of Bamoth-baal; from there he saw the nearest of the Israelites.

23 AND BALAAM said to Balak, Build me here seven altars, and prepare me here seven oxen and seven rams.

2 And Balak did as Balaam had spoken, and Balak and Balaam offered on each altar a bull and a ram.

3 And Balaam said to Balak, Stand by your burnt offering and I will go. Perhaps the Lord will come to meet me; and whatever He shows me I will tell you. And he went to a bare height.

4 God met Balaam, who said to Him, I have prepared seven altars, and I have offered on each altar a bull and a ram.

5 And the Lord put a speech in Balaam's mouth, and said, Return to Balak and thus shall you speak.

6 Balaam returned to Balak, who was standing by his burnt sacrifice, he and all the princes of Moab.

7 Balaam took up his [figurative] speech and said: Balak, the king of Moab, has brought me from Aram, out of the mountains of the east, saying, Come, curse Jacob for me; and come, violently denounce Israel.

8 How can I curse those God has not cursed? Or how can I [violently] denounce those the Lord has not denounced?

9 For from the top of the rocks I see Israel, and from the hills I behold him. Behold, the people [of Israel] shall ⁿdwell alone and shall not be reckoned *and* esteemed among the nations.

10 Who can count the dust (the descendants) of Jacob and the number of the fourth part of Israel? Let me die the death of the righteous [those who are upright and in right standing with God], and let my last end be like theirs! [Ps. 37:37; Rev. 14:13.]

11 And Balak said to Balaam, What have you done to me? I brought you to curse my enemies, and here you have [thoroughly] blessed them instead!

12 And Balaam answered, Must I not be obedient *and* speak what the Lord has put in my mouth?

13 Balak said to him, Come with me, I implore you, to another place from which you can see them, though you will see only the nearest and not all of them; and curse them for me from there.

14 So he took Balaam into the field of Zophim to the top of [Mount] Pisgah, and built seven altars, and offered a bull and a ram on each altar.

15 Balaam said to Balak, Stand here by your burnt offering while I go to meet the Lord yonder.

16 And the Lord met Balaam and put a speech in his mouth, and said, Go again to Balak and speak thus.

ⁿThe literal fulfillment of this prophecy has been obvious during the more than thirty-four centuries since it was spoken. The Jews have always been separate as a nation from other peoples. Though conquered many times, they have never been absorbed by their conquerors or lost their identity. The prophecy had to become true, for "the Lord put [it] . . . in Balaam's mouth" (Num. 23:5).

ᵛOr, *A city of streets*   ʷOr, *he went solitary*   ˣHeb. *my soul,* or, *my life*   ʸOr, *The hill*

New American Standard

36 ¶ When Balak heard that Balaam was coming, he went out to meet him at the city of Moab, which is on the Arnon border, at the extreme end of the border.

37 Then Balak said to Balaam, "Did I not urgently send to you to call you? Why did you not come to me? Am I really unable to honor you?"

38 So Balaam said to Balak, "Behold, I have come now to you! Am I able to speak anything at all? The word that God puts in my mouth, that I shall speak."

39 And Balaam went with Balak, and they came to Kiriath-huzoth.

40 Balak sacrificed oxen and sheep, and sent *some* to Balaam and the leaders who were with him.

41 ¶ Then it came about in the morning that Balak took Balaam and brought him up to the high places of Baal, and he saw from there a portion of the people.

The Prophecies of Balaam

23 THEN BALAAM said to Balak, "Build seven altars for me here, and prepare seven bulls and seven rams for me here."

2 Balak did just as Balaam had spoken, and Balak and Balaam offered up a bull and a ram on each altar.

3 Then Balaam said to Balak, "Stand beside your burnt offering, and I will go; perhaps the LORD will come to meet me, and whatever He shows me I will tell you." So he went to a bare hill.

4 ¶ Now God met Balaam, and he said to Him, "I have set up the seven altars, and I have offered up a bull and a ram on each altar."

5 Then the LORD put a word in Balaam's mouth and said, "Return to Balak, and you shall speak thus."

6 So he returned to him, and behold, he was standing beside his burnt offering, he and all the leaders of Moab.

7 He took up his [b]discourse and said,
"From Aram Balak has brought me,
Moab's king from the mountains of the East,
'Come curse Jacob for me,
And come, denounce Israel!'

8 "How shall I curse whom God has not cursed?
And how can I denounce whom the LORD has not denounced?

9 "As I see him from the top of the rocks,
And I look at him from the hills;
Behold, a people *who* dwells apart,
And will not be reckoned among the nations.

10 "Who can count the dust of Jacob,
Or number the fourth part of Israel?
Let me die the death of the upright,
And let my end be like his!"

11 ¶ Then Balak said to Balaam, "What have you done to me? I took you to curse my enemies, but behold, you have actually blessed them!"

12 He replied, "Must I not be careful to speak what the LORD puts in my mouth?"

13 ¶ Then Balak said to him, "Please come with me to another place from where you may see them, although you will only see the extreme end of them and will not see all of them; and curse them for me from there."

14 So he took him to the field of Zophim, to the top of Pisgah, and built seven altars and offered a bull and a ram on *each* altar.

15 And he said to Balak, "Stand here beside your burnt offering while I myself meet *the LORD* over there."

16 Then the LORD met Balaam and put a word in his mouth and said, "Return to Balak, and thus you shall speak."

New International

36 When Balak heard that Balaam was coming, he went out to meet him at the Moabite town on the Arnon border, at the edge of his territory. 37 Balak said to Balaam, "Did I not send you an urgent summons? Why didn't you come to me? Am I really not able to reward you?"

38 "Well, I have come to you now," Balaam replied. "But can I say just anything? I must speak only what God puts in my mouth."

39 Then Balaam went with Balak to Kiriath Huzoth. 40 Balak sacrificed cattle and sheep, and gave some to Balaam and the princes who were with him. 41 The next morning Balak took Balaam up to Bamoth Baal, and from there he saw part of the people.

Balaam's First Oracle

23 BALAAM SAID, "Build me seven altars here, and prepare seven bulls and seven rams for me." 2 Balak did as Balaam said, and the two of them offered a bull and a ram on each altar.

3 Then Balaam said to Balak, "Stay here beside your offering while I go aside. Perhaps the LORD will come to meet with me. Whatever he reveals to me I will tell you." Then he went off to a barren height.

4 God met with him, and Balaam said, "I have prepared seven altars, and on each altar I have offered a bull and a ram."

5 The LORD put a message in Balaam's mouth and said, "Go back to Balak and give him this message."

6 So he went back to him and found him standing beside his offering, with all the princes of Moab. 7 Then Balaam uttered his oracle:

"Balak brought me from Aram,
the king of Moab from the eastern
mountains.
'Come,' he said, 'curse Jacob for me;
come, denounce Israel.'

8 How can I curse
those whom God has not cursed?
How can I denounce
those whom the LORD has not denounced?

9 From the rocky peaks I see them,
from the heights I view them.
I see a people who live apart
and do not consider themselves one of the
nations.

10 Who can count the dust of Jacob
or number the fourth part of Israel?
Let me die the death of the righteous,
and may my end be like theirs!"

11 Balak said to Balaam, "What have you done to me? I brought you to curse my enemies, but you have done nothing but bless them!"

12 He answered, "Must I not speak what the LORD puts in my mouth?"

Balaam's Second Oracle

13 Then Balak said to him, "Come with me to another place where you can see them; you will see only a part but not all of them. And from there, curse them for me." 14 So he took him to the field of Zophim on the top of Pisgah, and there he built seven altars and offered a bull and a ram on each altar.

15 Balaam said to Balak, "Stay here beside your offering while I meet with him over there."

16 The LORD met with Balaam and put a message in his mouth and said, "Go back to Balak and give him this message."

[b]Lit *parable*

King James

¹⁷And when he came to him, behold, he stood by his burnt offering, and the princes of Moab with him. And Balak said unto him, What hath the LORD spoken?

¹⁸And he took up his parable, and said, Rise up, Balak, and hear; hearken unto me, thou son of Zippor:

¹⁹God *is* not a man, that he should lie; neither the son of man, that he should repent: hath he said, and shall he not do *it?* or hath he spoken, and shall he not make it good?

²⁰Behold, I have received *commandment* to bless: and he hath blessed; and I cannot reverse it.

²¹He hath not beheld iniquity in Jacob, neither hath he seen perverseness in Israel; the LORD his God *is* with him, and the shout of a king *is* among them.

²²God brought them out of Egypt; he hath as it were the strength of an unicorn.

²³Surely *there is* no enchantment ^zagainst Jacob, neither *is there* any divination against Israel: according to this time it shall be said of Jacob and of Israel, What hath God wrought!

²⁴Behold, the people shall rise up as a great lion, and lift up himself as a young lion: he shall not lie down until he eat *of* the prey, and drink the blood of the slain.

²⁵ ¶ And Balak said unto Balaam, Neither curse them at all, nor bless them at all.

²⁶But Balaam answered and said unto Balak, Told not I thee, saying, All that the LORD speaketh, that I must do?

²⁷ ¶ And Balak said unto Balaam, Come, I pray thee, I will bring thee unto another place; peradventure it will please God that thou mayest curse me them from thence.

²⁸And Balak brought Balaam unto the top of Peor, that looketh toward Jeshimon.

²⁹And Balaam said unto Balak, Build me here seven altars, and prepare me here seven bullocks and seven rams.

³⁰And Balak did as Balaam had said, and offered a bullock and a ram on *every* altar.

24 AND WHEN Balaam saw that it pleased the LORD to bless Israel, he went not, as at other times, ^ato seek for enchantments, but he set his face toward the wilderness.

²And Balaam lifted up his eyes, and he saw Israel abiding *in his tents* according to their tribes; and the spirit of God came upon him.

³And he took up his parable, and said, Balaam the son of Beor hath said, and the man ^bwhose eyes are open hath said:

⁴He hath said, which heard the words of God, which saw the vision of the Almighty, falling *into a trance,* but having his eyes open:

⁵How goodly are thy tents, O Jacob, *and* thy tabernacles, O Israel!

⁶As the valleys are they spread forth, as gardens by the river's side, as the trees of lign aloes which the LORD hath planted, *and* as cedar trees beside the waters.

⁷He shall pour the water out of his buckets, and his seed *shall be* in many waters, and his king shall be higher than Agag, and his kingdom shall be exalted.

Amplified

¹⁷And when he returned to Balak, he was standing beside his burnt offering, and the princes of Moab with him. And Balak said to him, What has the Lord said?

¹⁸Balaam took up his [figurative] discourse and said: Rise up, Balak, and hear; listen [closely] to me, son of Zippor.

¹⁹God is not a man, that He should tell *or* act a lie, neither the son of man, that He should feel repentance *or* compunction [for what He has promised]. Has He said and shall He not do it? Or has He spoken and shall He not make it good?

²⁰You see, I have received His command to bless Israel. He has blessed, and I cannot reverse *or* qualify it.

²¹[God] has not beheld iniquity in Jacob [for he is forgiven], neither has He seen mischief *or* perverseness in Israel [for the same reason]. The Lord their God is with Israel, and the shout of praise to their King is among the people. [Rom. 4:7, 8; I John 3:1, 2.]

²²God brought them forth out of Egypt; they have as it were the strength of a wild ox.

²³Surely there is no enchantment with *or* against Jacob, neither is there any divination with *or* against Israel. [In due season and even] now it shall be said of Jacob and of Israel, What has God wrought!

²⁴Behold, a people! They rise up as a lioness and lift themselves up as a lion; he shall not lie down until he devours the prey and drinks the blood of the slain.

²⁵And Balak said to Balaam, Neither curse them at all nor bless them at all.

²⁶But Balaam answered Balak, Did I not say to you, All the Lord speaks, that I must do?

²⁷And Balak said to Balaam, Come, I implore you; I will take you to another place. Perhaps it will please God to let you curse them for me from there.

²⁸So Balak brought Balaam to the top of [Mount] Peor, that overlooks [the wilderness or desert] Jeshimon.

²⁹And Balaam said to Balak, Build me here seven altars, and prepare me here seven bulls and seven rams.

³⁰And Balak did as Balaam had said, and offered a bull and a ram on each altar.

24 WHEN BALAAM saw that it pleased the Lord to bless Israel, he did not go as he had done each time before [superstitiously] to meet with omens *and* signs in the natural world, but he set his face toward the wilderness *or* desert.

²And Balaam lifted up his eyes and he saw Israel abiding in their tents according to their tribes. And the Spirit of God came upon him

³And he took up his [figurative] discourse and said: Balaam son of Beor, the man whose eye is opened [at last, to see clearly the purposes and will of God],

⁴He [Balaam] who hears the words of God, who sees the vision of the Almighty, falling down, but having his eyes open *and* uncovered, he says:

⁵How attractive *and* considerable are your tents, O Jacob, *and* your tabernacles, O Israel!

⁶As valleys are they spread forth, as gardens by the riverside, as [rare spice] of lignaloes which the Lord has planted, and as cedar trees beside the waters. [Ps. 1:3.]

⁷[Israel] shall pour water out of his own buckets [have his own sources of rich blessing and plenty], and his offspring shall dwell by many waters, and his king shall be higher than ^oAgag, and his kingdom shall be exalted.

---

^zOr, *in had his eyes shut,* but now opened   ^aHeb. *to the meeting of enchantments*   ^bHeb. *who*

^o"Agag" was the title of the Amalekite kings, and it represents here the kingdom of the Gentiles. The Amalekites at that time were the most powerful of all the desert tribes (Num. 24:20).

New American Standard

17 He came to him, and behold, he was standing beside his burnt offering, and the leaders of Moab with him. And Balak said to him, "What has the LORD spoken?"
18 Then he took up his ᶜdiscourse and said,
"Arise, O Balak, and hear;
    Give ear to me, O son of Zippor!
19"God is not a man, that He should lie,
    Nor a son of man, that He should repent;
    Has He said, and will He not do it?
    Or has He spoken, and will He not make it good?
20"Behold, I have received *a command* to bless;
    When He has blessed, then I cannot revoke it.
21"He has not observed misfortune in Jacob;
    Nor has He seen trouble in Israel;
    The LORD his God is with him,
    And the shout of a king is among them.
22"God brings them out of Egypt,
    He is for them like the horns of the wild ox.
23"For there is no omen against Jacob,
    Nor is there any divination against Israel;
    At the proper time it shall be said to Jacob
    And to Israel, what God has done!
24"Behold, a people rises like a lioness,
    And as a lion it lifts itself;
    It will not lie down until it devours the prey,
    And drinks the blood of the slain."
25 ¶ Then Balak said to Balaam, "Do not curse them at all nor bless them at all!"
26 But Balaam replied to Balak, "Did I not tell you, 'Whatever the LORD speaks, that I must do'?"
27 ¶ Then Balak said to Balaam, "Please come, I will take you to another place; perhaps it will be agreeable with God that you curse them for me from there."
28 So Balak took Balaam to the top of Peor which overlooks the wasteland.
29 Balaam said to Balak, "Build seven altars for me here and prepare seven bulls and seven rams for me here."
30 Balak did just as Balaam had said, and offered up a bull and a ram on *each* altar.

The Prophecy from Peor

24 WHEN BALAAM saw that it pleased the LORD to bless Israel, he did not go as at other times to seek omens but he set his face toward the wilderness.
2 And Balaam lifted up his eyes and saw Israel camping tribe by tribe; and the Spirit of God came upon him.
3 He took up his discourse and said,
"The oracle of Balaam the son of Beor,
    And the oracle of the man whose eye is opened;
4 The oracle of him who hears the words of God,
    Who sees the vision of the Almighty,
    Falling down, yet having his eyes uncovered,
5 How fair are your tents, O Jacob,
    Your dwellings, O Israel!
6"Like valleys that stretch out,
    Like gardens beside the river,
    Like aloes planted by the LORD,
    Like cedars beside the waters.
7"Water will flow from his buckets,
    And his seed *will be* by many waters,
    And his king shall be higher than Agag,
    And his kingdom shall be exalted.

New International

17So he went to him and found him standing beside his offering, with the princes of Moab. Balak asked him, "What did the LORD say?"
18Then he uttered his oracle:

"Arise, Balak, and listen;
    hear me, son of Zippor.
19God is not a man, that he should lie,
    nor a son of man, that he should change his mind.
Does he speak and then not act?
    Does he promise and not fulfill?
20I have received a command to bless;
    he has blessed, and I cannot change it.

21"No misfortune is seen in Jacob,
    no misery observed in Israel.ᶻ
The LORD their God is with them;
    the shout of the King is among them.
22God brought them out of Egypt;
    they have the strength of a wild ox.
23There is no sorcery against Jacob,
    no divination against Israel.
It will now be said of Jacob
    and of Israel, 'See what God has done!'
24The people rise like a lioness;
    they rouse themselves like a lion
that does not rest till he devours his prey
    and drinks the blood of his victims."

25Then Balak said to Balaam, "Neither curse them at all nor bless them at all!"
26Balaam answered, "Did I not tell you I must do whatever the LORD says?"

Balaam's Third Oracle

27Then Balak said to Balaam, "Come, let me take you to another place. Perhaps it will please God to let you curse them for me from there." 28And Balak took Balaam to the top of Peor, overlooking the wasteland.
29Balaam said, "Build me seven altars here, and prepare seven bulls and seven rams for me." 30Balak did as Balaam had said, and offered a bull and a ram on each altar.

24 NOW WHEN Balaam saw that it pleased the LORD to bless Israel, he did not resort to sorcery as at other times, but turned his face toward the desert. 2When Balaam looked out and saw Israel encamped tribe by tribe, the Spirit of God came upon him 3and he uttered his oracle:

"The oracle of Balaam son of Beor,
    the oracle of one whose eye sees clearly,
4the oracle of one who hears the words of God,
    who sees a vision from the Almighty,ᵃ
    who falls prostrate, and whose eyes are opened:

5"How beautiful are your tents, O Jacob,
    your dwelling places, O Israel!

6"Like valleys they spread out,
    like gardens beside a river,
like aloes planted by the LORD,
    like cedars beside the waters.
7Water will flow from his buckets;
    their seed will have abundant water.

"Their king will be greater than Agag;
    their kingdom will be exalted.

ᶜLit *parable*

ᶻ*21 Or He has not looked on Jacob's offenses / or on the wrongs found in Israel.*   ᵃ*4 Hebrew Shaddai; also in verse 16*

King James	Amplified

⁸God brought him forth out of Egypt; he hath as it were the strength of an unicorn: he shall eat up the nations his enemies, and shall break their bones, and pierce *them* through with his arrows.

⁹He couched, he lay down as a lion, and as a great lion: who shall stir him up? Blessed *is* he that blesseth thee, and cursed *is* he that curseth thee.

¹⁰ ¶ And Balak's anger was kindled against Balaam, and he smote his hands together: and Balak said unto Balaam, I called thee to curse mine enemies, and, behold, thou hast altogether blessed *them* these three times.

¹¹Therefore now flee thou to thy place: I thought to promote thee unto great honour; but, lo, the LORD hath kept thee back from honour.

¹²And Balaam said unto Balak, Spake I not also to thy messengers which thou sentest unto me, saying,

¹³If Balak would give me his house full of silver and gold, I cannot go beyond the commandment of the LORD, to do *either* good or bad of mine own mind; *but* what the LORD saith, that will I speak?

¹⁴And now, behold, I go unto my people: come *therefore, and* I will advertise thee what this people shall do to thy people in the latter days.

¹⁵ ¶ And he took up his parable, and said, Balaam the son of Beor hath said, and the man whose eyes are open hath said:

¹⁶He hath said, which heard the words of God, and knew the knowledge of the most High, *which* saw the vision of the Almighty, falling *into a trance,* but having his eyes open:

¹⁷I shall see him, but not now: I shall behold him, but not nigh: there shall come a Star out of Jacob, and a Sceptre shall rise out of Israel, and shall ^csmite the corners of Moab, and destroy all the children of Sheth.

¹⁸And Edom shall be a possession, Seir also shall be a possession for his enemies; and Israel shall do valiantly.

¹⁹Out of Jacob shall come he that shall have dominion, and shall destroy him that remaineth of the city.

²⁰ ¶ And when he looked on Amalek, he took up his parable, and said, Amalek *was* ^dthe first of the nations; but his latter end *shall* ^ebe that he perish for ever.

²¹And he looked on the Kenites, and took up his parable, and said, Strong is thy dwellingplace, and thou puttest thy nest in a rock.

²²Nevertheless ^fthe Kenite shall be wasted, ^guntil Asshur shall carry thee away captive.

²³And he took up his parable, and said, Alas, who shall live when God doeth this!

⁸God brought [Israel] forth out of Egypt; [Israel] has strength like the wild ox; he shall eat up the nations, his enemies, crushing their bones and piercing them through with his arrows.

⁹He couched, he lay down as a lion; and as a lioness, who shall rouse him? Blessed [of God] is he who blesses you [who prays for and contributes to your welfare] and cursed [of God] is he who curses you [who in word, thought, or deed would bring harm upon you]. [Matt. 25:40.]

¹⁰Then Balak's anger was kindled against Balaam, and he smote his hands together; and Balak said to Balaam, I called you to curse my enemies, and, behold, you have done nothing but bless them these three times.

¹¹Therefore now go back where you belong *and* do it in a hurry! I had intended to promote you to great honor, but behold, the Lord has held you back from honor.

¹²Balaam said to Balak, Did I not say to your messengers whom you sent to me,

¹³If Balak would give me his house full of silver and gold, I cannot go beyond the command of the Lord, to do either good or bad of my own will, but what the Lord says, that will I speak?

¹⁴And now, behold, I am going to my people; come, I will tell you what this people [Israel] will do to your people [Moab] in the latter days.

¹⁵And he took up his [figurative] discourse, and said: Balaam son of Beor speaks, the man whose eye is opened speaks,

¹⁶He speaks, who heard the words of God and knew the knowledge of the Most High, who saw the vision of the Almighty, falling down, but having his eyes open *and* uncovered:

¹⁷I see Him, but not now; I behold Him, but He is not near. A ^pstar (Star) shall come forth out of Jacob, and a scepter (Scepter) shall rise out of Israel and shall crush all the corners of Moab and break down all the sons of Sheth [Moab's sons of tumult]. [Matt. 2:2; Rom. 15:12.]

¹⁸And Edom shall be [taken as] a possession, [Mount] Seir also shall be dispossessed, who were Israel's enemies, while Israel does valiantly.

¹⁹Out of Jacob shall one (One) come having dominion and shall destroy the remnant from the city.

²⁰[Balaam] looked at Amalek and took up his [prophetic] utterance, and said: Amalek is the foremost of the [neighboring] nations, but in his latter end he shall ^qcome to destruction.

²¹And he looked at the Kenites and took up his [prophetic] utterance, and said: Strong is your dwelling place, and you set your nest in the rock.

²²Nevertheless the Kenites shall be wasted. How long shall Asshur (Assyria) take you away captive?

²³And he took up his [prophetic] speech, and said: Alas, who shall live when God does this *and* establishes [Assyria]?

^p "This imagery in the hieroglyphic language of the East denotes some eminent ruler—primarily David, but secondarily and preeminently the Messiah" (Robert Jamieson, A.R. Fausset and David Brown, *A Commentary*). Notice that the principal time for these events is set in the prophecy for "the latter days" (Num. 24:14). "The prophecy [concerning Moab] was partially, or typically, fulfilled in the time of David (II Sam. 8:2). Moab and Edom represented symbolically the enemies of Christ and His church, and as such will eventually be subdued by the King of kings (see Ps. 60:8)" (Charles J. Ellicott, *A Bible Commentary*). "The star which the wise men from the East saw, and which led them in the way to the newborn 'King of the Jews,' refers clearly to the prophecy of Balaam (Matt. 2:1, 2)" (J.P. Lange, *A Commentary*). ^qAfter the time of David (who was forced to rescue two of his wives from Amalekite bandits, I Sam. 30:18), the Amalekites are mentioned again only in Hezekiah's time (I Chron. 4:43), before "they disappear from the field of history . . . So that the word of God here also stood fast; and the first of the surrounding tribes who impiously sought to measure their strength with the cause and people of God were likewise the first to lose their national existence" (Patrick Fairbairn, ed., *The Imperial Bible-dictionary*).

^cOr, *smite through the princes of Moab*   ^dOr, *the first of the nations that warred against Israel*   ^eOr, shall be *even to destruction*   ^fHeb. *Kain*   ^gOr, *how long* shall it be ere Asshur carry thee away captive?

New American Standard

8"God brings him out of Egypt,
He is for him like the horns of the wild ox.
He will devour the nations *who are* his
  adversaries,
And will crush their bones in pieces,
And shatter *them* with his arrows.
9"He couches, he lies down as a lion,
And as a lion, who dares rouse him?
Blessed is everyone who blesses you,
And cursed is everyone who curses you."

10 ¶ Then Balak's anger burned against Balaam, and he struck his hands together; and Balak said to Balaam, "I called you to curse my enemies, but behold, you have persisted in blessing them these three times! 11"Therefore, flee to your place now. I said I would honor you greatly, but behold, the LORD has held you back from honor."

12 Balaam said to Balak, "Did I not tell your messengers whom you had sent to me, saying, 13 'Though Balak were to give me his house full of silver and gold, I could not do anything contrary to the command of the LORD, either good or bad, of my own accord. What the LORD speaks, that I will speak'? 14"And now, behold, I am going to my people; come, *and* I will advise you what this people will do to your people in the days to come."

15 ¶ He took up his discourse and said,
"The oracle of Balaam the son of Beor,
And the oracle of the man whose eye is opened.
16 The oracle of him who hears the words of God,
And knows the knowledge of the Most High,
Who sees the vision of the Almighty,
Falling down, yet having his eyes uncovered.
17"I see him, but not now;
I behold him, but not near;
A star shall come forth from Jacob,
A scepter shall rise from Israel,
And shall crush through the forehead of Moab,
And tear down all the sons of *d*Sheth.
18"Edom shall be a possession,
Seir, its enemies, also will be a possession,
While Israel performs valiantly.
19"One from Jacob shall have dominion,
And will destroy the remnant from the city."

20 ¶ And he looked at Amalek and took up his discourse and said,
"Amalek was the first of the nations,
But his end *shall be* destruction."
21 ¶ And he looked at the Kenite, and took up his discourse and said,
"Your dwelling place is enduring,
And your nest is set in the cliff.
22"Nevertheless Kain will be consumed;
How long will Asshur keep you captive?"
23 ¶ Then he took up his discourse and said,
"Alas, who can live except God has ordained it?

New International

8"God brought them out of Egypt;
they have the strength of a wild ox.
They devour hostile nations
and break their bones in pieces;
with their arrows they pierce them.
9Like a lion they crouch and lie down,
like a lioness—who dares to rouse them?

"May those who bless you be blessed
and those who curse you be cursed!"

10Then Balak's anger burned against Balaam. He struck his hands together and said to him, "I summoned you to curse my enemies, but you have blessed them these three times. 11Now leave at once and go home! I said I would reward you handsomely, but the LORD has kept you from being rewarded."

12Balaam answered Balak, "Did I not tell the messengers you sent me, 13'Even if Balak gave me his palace filled with silver and gold, I could not do anything of my own accord, good or bad, to go beyond the command of the LORD—and I must say only what the LORD says'? 14Now I am going back to my people, but come, let me warn you of what this people will do to your people in days to come."

Balaam's Fourth Oracle

15Then he uttered his oracle:

"The oracle of Balaam son of Beor,
the oracle of one whose eye sees clearly,
16the oracle of one who hears the words of God,
who has knowledge from the Most High,
who sees a vision from the Almighty,
who falls prostrate, and whose eyes are
  opened:

17"I see him, but not now;
I behold him, but not near.
A star will come out of Jacob;
a scepter will rise out of Israel.
He will crush the foreheads of Moab,
the skulls*b* of*c* all the sons of Sheth.*d*
18Edom will be conquered;
Seir, his enemy, will be conquered,
but Israel will grow strong.
19A ruler will come out of Jacob
and destroy the survivors of the city."

Balaam's Final Oracles

20Then Balaam saw Amalek and uttered his oracle:

"Amalek was first among the nations,
but he will come to ruin at last."

21Then he saw the Kenites and uttered his oracle:

"Your dwelling place is secure,
your nest is set in a rock;
22yet you Kenites will be destroyed
when Asshur takes you captive."

23Then he uttered his oracle:

"Ah, who can live when God does this?*e*

---

d I.e. tumult

b 17 Samaritan Pentateuch (see also Jer. 48:45); the meaning of the word in the Masoretic Text is uncertain.   *c* 17 Or possibly *Moab, / batter*   *d* 17 Or *all the noisy boasters*   *e* 23 Masoretic Text; with a different word division of the Hebrew *A people will gather from the north.*

King James

Amplified

24And ships *shall come* from the coast of Chittim, and shall afflict Asshur, and shall afflict Eber, and he also shall perish for ever.

25And Balaam rose up, and went and returned to his place: and Balak also went his way.

Israel's idolatry in Shittim

25 AND ISRAEL abode in Shittim, and the people began to commit whoredom with the daughters of Moab.

2And they called the people unto the sacrifices of their gods: and the people did eat, and bowed down to their gods.

3And Israel joined himself unto Baal-peor: and the anger of the LORD was kindled against Israel.

4And the LORD said unto Moses, Take all the heads of the people, and hang them up before the LORD against the sun, that the fierce anger of the LORD may be turned away from Israel.

5And Moses said unto the judges of Israel, Slay ye every one his men that were joined unto Baal-peor.

6 ¶ And, behold, one of the children of Israel came and brought unto his brethren a Midianitish woman in the sight of Moses, and in the sight of all the congregation of the children of Israel, who *were* weeping *before* the door of the tabernacle of the congregation.

7And when Phinehas, the son of Eleazar, the son of Aaron the priest, saw *it,* he rose up from among the congregation, and took a javelin in his hand;

8And he went after the man of Israel into the tent, and thrust both of them through, the man of Israel, and the woman through her belly. So the plague was stayed from the children of Israel.

9And those that died in the plague were twenty and four thousand.

10 ¶ And the LORD spake unto Moses, saying,

11Phinehas, the son of Eleazar, the son of Aaron the priest, hath turned my wrath away from the children of Israel, while he was zealous *h*for my sake among them, that I consumed not the children of Israel in my jealousy.

12Wherefore say, Behold, I give unto him my covenant of peace:

13And he shall have it, and his seed after him, *even* the covenant of an everlasting priesthood; because he was zealous for his God, and made an atonement for the children of Israel.

14Now the name of the Israelite that was slain, *even that* was slain with the Midianitish woman, *was* Zimri, the son of Salu, a prince of a *i*chief house among the Simeonites.

15And the name of the Midianitish woman that was slain *was* Cozbi, the daughter of Zur; he *was* head over a people, *and* of a chief house in Midian.

16 ¶ And the LORD spake unto Moses, saying,

17Vex the Midianites, and smite them:

18For they vex you with their wiles, wherewith they have beguiled you in the matter of Peor, and in the matter of Cozbi, the daughter of a prince of Midian, their sister, which was slain in the day of the plague for Peor's sake.

24But ships shall come from Kittim [Cyprus and the greater part of the Mediterranean's east coast] and shall afflict Assyria and Eber [the Hebrews, certain Arabs, and descendants of Nahor], and he [the victor] also shall come to destruction.

25And Balaam rose up, returned to his place, and Balak also went his way.

25 ISRAEL SETTLED down *and* remained in Shittim, and the people began to play the harlot with the daughters of Moab,

2Who invited the [Israelites] to the sacrifices of their gods, and [they] ate and bowed down to Moab's gods.

3So Israel joined himself to [the god] Baal of Peor. And the anger of the Lord was kindled against Israel.

4And the Lord said to Moses, Take all the leaders *or* chiefs of the people, and hang them before the Lord in the sun [after killing them], that the fierce anger of the Lord may turn away from Israel.

5And Moses said to the judges of Israel, Each one of you slay his men who joined themselves to Baal of Peor.

6And behold, one of the Israelites came and brought to his brethren a Midianite woman in the sight of Moses and of all the congregation of Israel while they were weeping at the door of the Tent of Meeting [over the divine judgment and the punishment].

7And when Phinehas son of Eleazar, the son of Aaron the priest, saw it, he rose up from the midst of the congregation and took a spear in his hand

8And went after the man of Israel into the inner room and thrust both of them through, the man of Israel and the woman through her body. Then the [smiting] plague was stayed from the Israelites.

9Nevertheless those who died in the [smiting] plague were 24,000.

10And the Lord said to Moses,

11Phinehas son of Eleazar, the son of Aaron the priest, has turned my wrath away from the Israelites, in that he was jealous with My jealousy among them, so that I did not consume the Israelites in My jealousy.

12Therefore say, Behold, I give to Phinehas the priest My covenant of peace.

13And he shall have it, and his descendants after him, the covenant of an everlasting priesthood, because he was jealous for his God and made atonement for the Israelites. [Ps. 106:28–31.]

14Now the man of Israel who was slain with the Midianite woman was Zimri son of Salu, a head of a father's house among the Simeonites.

15And the Midianite woman who was slain was Cozbi daughter of Zur; he was head of a father's house in Midian.

16And the Lord said to Moses,

17Provoke hostilities with the Midianites and attack them,

18For they harass you with their wiles with which they have beguiled you in the matter of Peor, and of Cozbi, the daughter of the prince of Midian, their sister, who was slain on the day of the plague in the matter of Peor.

Israel's second census

26 AND IT came to pass after the plague, that the LORD spake unto Moses and unto Eleazar the son of Aaron the priest, saying,

2Take the sum of all the congregation of the children of Israel, from twenty years old and upward, throughout their fathers' house, all that are able to go to war in Israel.

26 AFTER THE plague the Lord said to Moses and Eleazar son of Aaron, the priest,

2Take a census of all the [male] congregation of the Israelites from twenty years old and upward, by their fathers' houses, all in Israel able to go to war.

---

h Heb. *with my zeal*   *i* Heb. *house of a father*

New American Standard

24"But ships *shall come* from the coast of Kittim,
And they shall afflict Asshur and will afflict
Eber;
So they also *will come* to destruction."
25 ¶ Then Balaam arose and departed and returned to
his place, and Balak also went his way.

The Sin of Peor

25 WHILE ISRAEL remained at Shittim, the people
began to play the harlot with the daughters of
Moab.
2 For they invited the people to the sacrifices of their
gods, and the people ate and bowed down to their gods.
3 So Israel joined themselves to Baal of Peor, and the
LORD was angry against Israel.
4 The LORD said to Moses, "Take all the leaders of the
people and execute them in broad daylight before the
LORD, so that the fierce anger of the LORD may turn away
from Israel."
5 So Moses said to the judges of Israel, "Each of you
slay his men who have joined themselves to Baal of Peor."
6 ¶ Then behold, one of the sons of Israel came and
brought to his relatives a Midianite woman, in the sight of
Moses and in the sight of all the congregation of the sons
of Israel, while they were weeping at the doorway of the
tent of meeting.
7 When Phinehas the son of Eleazar, the son of Aaron
the priest, saw it, he arose from the midst of the congregation and took a spear in his hand,
8 and he went after the man of Israel into the tent and
pierced both of them through, the man of Israel and the
woman, through the body. So the plague on the sons of
Israel was checked.
9 Those who died by the plague were 24,000.

The Zeal of Phinehas

10 ¶ Then the LORD spoke to Moses, saying,
11"Phinehas the son of Eleazar, the son of Aaron the
priest, has turned away My wrath from the sons of Israel
in that he was jealous with My jealousy among them, so
that I did not destroy the sons of Israel in My jealousy.
12"Therefore say, 'Behold, I give him My covenant of
peace;
13 and it shall be for him and his descendants after him,
a covenant of a perpetual priesthood, because he was jealous for his God and made atonement for the sons of Israel.' "
14 ¶ Now the name of the slain man of Israel who was
slain with the Midianite woman, was Zimri the son of
Salu, a leader of a father's household among the Simeonites.
15 The name of the Midianite woman who was slain was
Cozbi the daughter of Zur, who was head of the people of
a father's household in Midian.
16 ¶ Then the LORD spoke to Moses, saying,
17"Be hostile to the Midianites and strike them;
18 for they have been hostile to you with their tricks,
with which they have deceived you in the affair of Peor
and in the affair of Cozbi, the daughter of the leader of
Midian, their sister who was slain on the day of the plague
because of Peor."

Census of a New Generation

26 THEN IT came about after the plague, that the
LORD spoke to Moses and to Eleazar the son of
Aaron the priest, saying,
2"Take a census of all the congregation of the sons of
Israel from twenty years old and upward, by their fathers'
households, whoever is able to go out to war in Israel."

New International

24 Ships will come from the shores of Kittim;
they will subdue Asshur and Eber,
but they too will come to ruin."
25Then Balaam got up and returned home and Balak
went his own way.

Moab Seduces Israel

25 WHILE ISRAEL was staying in Shittim, the men
began to indulge in sexual immorality with Moabite women, 2who invited them to the sacrifices to their
gods. The people ate and bowed down before these gods.
3So Israel joined in worshiping the Baal of Peor. And the
LORD's anger burned against them.
4The LORD said to Moses, "Take all the leaders of these
people, kill them and expose them in broad daylight before
the LORD, so that the LORD's fierce anger may turn away
from Israel."
5So Moses said to Israel's judges, "Each of you must put
to death those of your men who have joined in worshiping
the Baal of Peor."
6Then an Israelite man brought to his family a Midianite
woman right before the eyes of Moses and the whole
assembly of Israel while they were weeping at the entrance
to the Tent of Meeting. 7When Phinehas son of Eleazar,
the son of Aaron, the priest, saw this, he left the assembly,
took a spear in his hand 8and followed the Israelite into the
tent. He drove the spear through both of them—through
the Israelite and into the woman's body. Then the plague
against the Israelites was stopped; 9but those who died in
the plague numbered 24,000.
10The LORD said to Moses, 11"Phinehas son of Eleazar,
the son of Aaron, the priest, has turned my anger away
from the Israelites; for he was as zealous as I am for my
honor among them, so that in my zeal I did not put an end
to them. 12Therefore tell him I am making my covenant of
peace with him. 13He and his descendants will have a
covenant of a lasting priesthood, because he was zealous
for the honor of his God and made atonement for the
Israelites."
14The name of the Israelite who was killed with the
Midianite woman was Zimri son of Salu, the leader of a
Simeonite family. 15And the name of the Midianite woman
who was put to death was Cozbi daughter of Zur, a tribal
chief of a Midianite family.
16The LORD said to Moses, 17"Treat the Midianites as
enemies and kill them, 18because they treated you as enemies when they deceived you in the affair of Peor and their
sister Cozbi, the daughter of a Midianite leader, the woman who was killed when the plague came as a result of
Peor."

The Second Census

26 AFTER THE plague the LORD said to Moses and
Eleazar son of Aaron, the priest, 2"Take a census
of the whole Israelite community by families—all those
twenty years old or more who are able to serve in the army
of Israel." 3So on the plains of Moab by the Jordan across

King James

³And Moses and Eleazar the priest spake with them in the plains of Moab by Jordan *near* Jericho, saying,

⁴*Take the sum of the people,* from twenty years old and upward; as the LORD commanded Moses and the children of Israel, which went forth out of the land of Egypt.

⁵ ¶ Reuben, the eldest son of Israel: the children of Reuben; Hanoch, *of whom cometh* the family of the Hanochites: of Pallu, the family of the Palluites:

⁶Of Hezron, the family of the Hezronites: of Carmi, the family of the Carmites.

⁷These *are* the families of the Reubenites: and they that were numbered of them were forty and three thousand and seven hundred and thirty.

⁸And the sons of Pallu; Eliab.

⁹And the sons of Eliab; Nemuel, and Dathan, and Abiram. This *is that* Dathan and Abiram, *which were* famous in the congregation, who strove against Moses and against Aaron in the company of Korah, when they strove against the LORD:

¹⁰And the earth opened her mouth, and swallowed them up together with Korah, when that company died, what time the fire devoured two hundred and fifty men: and they became a sign.

¹¹Notwithstanding the children of Korah died not.

¹² ¶ The sons of Simeon after their families: of Nemuel, the family of the Nemuelites: of Jamin, the family of the Jaminites: of Jachin, the family of the Jachinites:

¹³Of Zerah, the family of the Zarhites: of Shaul, the family of the Shaulites.

¹⁴These *are* the families of the Simeonites, twenty and two thousand and two hundred.

¹⁵ ¶ The children of Gad after their families: of Zephon, the family of the Zephonites: of Haggi, the family of the Haggites: of Shuni, the family of the Shunites:

¹⁶Of ʲOzni, the family of the Oznites: of Eri, the family of the Erites:

¹⁷Of Arod, the family of the Arodites: of Areli, the family of the Arelites.

¹⁸These *are* the families of the children of Gad according to those that were numbered of them, forty thousand and five hundred.

¹⁹ ¶ The sons of Judah *were* Er and Onan: and Er and Onan died in the land of Canaan.

²⁰And the sons of Judah after their families were; of Shelah, the family of the Shelanites: of Pharez, the family of the Pharzites: of Zerah, the family of the Zarhites.

²¹And the sons of Pharez were; of Hezron, the family of the Hezronites: of Hamul, the family of the Hamulites.

²²These *are* the families of Judah according to those that were numbered of them, threescore and sixteen thousand and five hundred.

²³ ¶ *Of* the sons of Issachar after their families: *of* Tola, the family of the Tolaites: of ᵏPua, the family of the Punites:

²⁴Of ˡJashub, the family of the Jashubites: of Shimron, the family of the Shimronites.

²⁵These *are* the families of Issachar according to those that were numbered of them, threescore and four thousand and three hundred.

²⁶ ¶ *Of* the sons of Zebulun after their families: of Sered, the family of the Sardites: of Elon, the family of the Elonites: of Jahleel, the family of the Jahleelites.

²⁷These *are* the families of the Zebulunites according to those that were numbered of them, threescore thousand and five hundred.

²⁸ ¶ The sons of Joseph after their families *were* Manasseh and Ephraim.

Amplified

³And Moses and Eleazar the priest told [the people] in the plains of Moab by the Jordan at Jericho,

⁴A census of the people shall be taken from twenty years old and upward, as the Lord commanded Moses. And the Israelites who came forth out of the land of Egypt were:

⁵Reuben, the firstborn of Israel, the sons of Reuben: of Hanoch, the family of the Hanochites; of Pallu, the family of the Palluites;

⁶Of Hezron, the family of the Hezronites; of Carmi, the family of the Carmites.

⁷These are the families of the Reubenites; and their number was 43,730.

⁸And the son of Pallu: Eliab.

⁹The sons of Eliab: Nemuel, Dathan, and Abiram. These are the Dathan and Abiram chosen from the congregation who contended against Moses and Aaron in the company of Korah when they contended against the Lord.

¹⁰And the earth opened its mouth and swallowed them up together with Korah, when that company died and the fire devoured 250 men; and they became a [warning] sign.

¹¹But Korah's sons did not die.

¹²The sons of Simeon according to their families: of Nemuel, the family of the Nemuelites; of Jamin, the family of the Jaminites; of Jachin, the family of the Jachinites;

¹³Of Zerah, the family of the Zerahites; of Shaul, the family of the Shaulites.

¹⁴These are the families of the Simeonites, 22,200.

¹⁵The sons of Gad after their families: of Zephon, the family of the Zephonites; of Haggi, the family of the Haggites; of Shuni, the family of the Shunites;

¹⁶Of Ozni, the family of the Oznites; of Eri, the family of the Erites;

¹⁷Of Arod, the family of the Arodites; of Areli, the family of the Arelites.

¹⁸These, the families of the sons of Gad according to their numbering, totaled 40,500.

¹⁹The sons of Judah were Er and Onan, but Er and Onan died in the land of Canaan.

²⁰And the sons of Judah according to their families were: of Shelah, the family of the Shelanites; of Perez, the family of the Perezites; of Zerah, the family of the Zerahites.

²¹And the sons of Perez were: of Hezron, the family of the Hezronites; of Hamul, the family of the Hamulites.

²²These, the families of Judah according to their numbering, totaled 76,500.

²³The sons of Issachar after their families: of Tola, the family of the Tolaites; of Puvah, the family of the Punites;

²⁴Of Jashub, the family of the Jashubites; of Shimron, the family of the Shimronites.

²⁵These, the families of Issachar according to their numbering, totaled 64,300.

²⁶The sons of Zebulun after their families: of Sered, the family of the Seredites; of Elon, the family of the Elonites; of Jahleel, the family of the Jahleelites.

²⁷These, the families of the Zebulunites according to their numbering, totaled 60,500.

²⁸The sons of Joseph after their families were Manasseh and Ephraim.

New American Standard

3 So Moses and Eleazar the priest spoke with them in the plains of Moab by the Jordan at Jericho, saying,

4 *"Take a census of the people* from twenty years old and upward, as the LORD has commanded Moses."

¶ Now the sons of Israel who came out of the land of Egypt *were:*

5 ¶ Reuben, Israel's firstborn, the sons of Reuben: *of* Hanoch, the family of the Hanochites; of Pallu, the family of the Palluites;

6 of Hezron, the family of the Hezronites; of Carmi, the family of the Carmites.

7 These are the families of the Reubenites, and those who were numbered of them were 43,730.

8 The son of Pallu: Eliab.

9 The sons of Eliab: Nemuel and Dathan and Abiram. These are the Dathan and Abiram who were called by the congregation, who contended against Moses and against Aaron in the company of Korah, when they contended against the LORD,

10 and the earth opened its mouth and swallowed them up along with Korah, when that company died, when the fire devoured 250 men, so that they became a warning.

11 The sons of Korah, however, did not die.

12 ¶ The sons of Simeon according to their families: of Nemuel, the family of the Nemuelites; of Jamin, the family of the Jaminites; of Jachin, the family of the Jachinites;

13 of Zerah, the family of the Zerahites; of Shaul, the family of the Shaulites.

14 These are the families of the Simeonites, 22,200.

15 ¶ The sons of Gad according to their families: of Zephon, the family of the Zephonites; of Haggi, the family of the Haggites; of Shuni, the family of the Shunites;

16 of Ozni, the family of the Oznites; of Eri, the family of the Erites;

17 of Arod, the family of the Arodites; of Areli, the family of the Arelites.

18 These are the families of the sons of Gad according to those who were numbered of them, 40,500.

19 ¶ The sons of Judah *were* Er and Onan, but Er and Onan died in the land of Canaan.

20 The sons of Judah according to their families were: of Shelah, the family of the Shelanites; of Perez, the family of the Perezites; of Zerah, the family of the Zerahites.

21 The sons of Perez were: of Hezron, the family of the Hezronites; of Hamul, the family of the Hamulites.

22 These are the families of Judah according to those who were numbered of them, 76,500.

23 ¶ The sons of Issachar according to their families: *of* Tola, the family of the Tolaites; of Puvah, the family of the Punites;

24 of Jashub, the family of the Jashubites; of Shimron, the family of the Shimronites.

25 These are the families of Issachar according to those who were numbered of them, 64,300.

26 ¶ The sons of Zebulun according to their families: of Sered, the family of the Seredites; of Elon, the family of the Elonites; of Jahleel, the family of the Jahleelites.

27 These are the families of the Zebulunites according to those who were numbered of them, 60,500.

28 ¶ The sons of Joseph according to their families: Manasseh and Ephraim.

New International

from Jericho,*f* Moses and Eleazar the priest spoke with them and said, 4 "Take a census of the men twenty years old or more, as the LORD commanded Moses."

These were the Israelites who came out of Egypt:

5 The descendants of Reuben, the firstborn son of Israel, were:

    through Hanoch, the Hanochite clan;

    through Pallu, the Palluite clan;

6 through Hezron, the Hezronite clan;

    through Carmi, the Carmite clan.

7 These were the clans of Reuben; those numbered were 43,730.

8 The son of Pallu was Eliab, 9 and the sons of Eliab were Nemuel, Dathan and Abiram. The same Dathan and Abiram were the community officials who rebelled against Moses and Aaron and were among Korah's followers when they rebelled against the LORD. 10 The earth opened its mouth and swallowed them along with Korah, whose followers died when the fire devoured the 250 men. And they served as a warning sign. 11 The line of Korah, however, did not die out.

12 The descendants of Simeon by their clans were:

    through Nemuel, the Nemuelite clan;

    through Jamin, the Jaminite clan;

    through Jakin, the Jakinite clan;

13 through Zerah, the Zerahite clan;

    through Shaul, the Shaulite clan.

14 These were the clans of Simeon; there were 22,200 men.

15 The descendants of Gad by their clans were:

    through Zephon, the Zephonite clan;

    through Haggi, the Haggite clan;

    through Shuni, the Shunite clan;

16 through Ozni, the Oznite clan;

    through Eri, the Erite clan;

17 through Arodi,*g* the Arodite clan;

    through Areli, the Arelite clan.

18 These were the clans of Gad; those numbered were 40,500.

19 Er and Onan were sons of Judah, but they died in Canaan.

20 The descendants of Judah by their clans were:

    through Shelah, the Shelanite clan;

    through Perez, the Perezite clan;

    through Zerah, the Zerahite clan.

21 The descendants of Perez were:

    through Hezron, the Hezronite clan;

    through Hamul, the Hamulite clan.

22 These were the clans of Judah; those numbered were 76,500.

23 The descendants of Issachar by their clans were:

    through Tola, the Tolaite clan;

    through Puah, the Puite*h* clan;

24 through Jashub, the Jashubite clan;

    through Shimron, the Shimronite clan.

25 These were the clans of Issachar; those numbered were 64,300.

26 The descendants of Zebulun by their clans were:

    through Sered, the Seredite clan;

    through Elon, the Elonite clan;

    through Jahleel, the Jahleelite clan.

27 These were the clans of Zebulun; those numbered were 60,500.

28 The descendants of Joseph by their clans through Manasseh and Ephraim were:

---

f 3 Hebrew *Jordan of Jericho;* possibly an ancient name for the Jordan River; also in verse 63   *g* 17 Samaritan Pentateuch and Syriac (see also Gen. 46:16); Masoretic Text *Arod*   *h* 23 Samaritan Pentateuch, Septuagint, Vulgate and Syriac (see also 1 Chron. 7:1); Masoretic Text *through Puvah, the Punite*

King James

²⁹Of the sons of Manasseh: of Machir, the family of the Machirites: and Machir begat Gilead: of Gilead *come* the family of the Gileadites.

³⁰These *are* the sons of Gilead: *of* Jeezer, the family of the Jeezerites: of Helek, the family of the Helekites:

³¹And *of* Asriel, the family of the Asrielites: and *of* Shechem, the family of the Shechemites:

³²And *of* Shemida, the family of the Shemidaites: and *of* Hepher, the family of the Hepherites.

³³ ¶ And Zelophehad the son of Hepher had no sons, but daughters: and the names of the daughters of Zelophehad *were* Mahlah, and Noah, Hoglah, Milcah, and Tirzah.

³⁴These *are* the families of Manasseh, and those that were numbered of them, fifty and two thousand and seven hundred.

³⁵ ¶ These *are* the sons of Ephraim after their families: of Shuthelah, the family of the Shuthalhites: of Becher, the family of the Bachrites: of Tahan, the family of the Tahanites.

³⁶And these *are* the sons of Shuthelah: of Eran, the family of the Eranites.

³⁷These *are* the families of the sons of Ephraim according to those that were numbered of them, thirty and two thousand and five hundred. These *are* the sons of Joseph after their families.

³⁸ ¶ The sons of Benjamin after their families: of Bela, the family of the Belaites: of Ashbel, the family of the Ashbelites: of Ahiram, the family of the Ahiramites:

³⁹Of Shupham, the family of the Shuphamites: of Hupham, the family of the Huphamites.

⁴⁰And the sons of Bela were Ard and Naaman: *of Ard,* the family of the Ardites: *and* of Naaman, the family of the Naamites.

⁴¹These *are* the sons of Benjamin after their families: and they that were numbered of them *were* forty and five thousand and six hundred.

⁴² ¶ These *are* the sons of Dan after their families: of ^mShuham, the family of the Shuhamites. These *are* the families of Dan after their families.

⁴³All the families of the Shuhamites, according to those that were numbered of them, *were* threescore and four thousand and four hundred.

⁴⁴ ¶ *Of* the children of Asher after their families: of Jimna, the family of the Jimnites: of Jesui, the family of the Jesuites: of Beriah, the family of the Beriites.

⁴⁵Of the sons of Beriah: of Heber, the family of the Heberites: of Malchiel, the family of the Malchielites.

⁴⁶And the name of the daughter of Asher *was* Sarah.

⁴⁷These *are* the families of the sons of Asher according to those that were numbered of them; *who were* fifty and three thousand and four hundred.

⁴⁸ ¶ *Of* the sons of Naphtali after their families: of Jahzeel, the family of the Jahzeelites: of Guni, the family of the Gunites:

⁴⁹Of Jezer, the family of the Jezerites: of Shillem, the family of the Shillemites.

⁵⁰These *are* the families of Naphtali according to their families: and they that were numbered of them *were* forty and five thousand and four hundred.

⁵¹These *were* the numbered of the children of Israel, six hundred thousand and a thousand seven hundred and thirty.

⁵² ¶ And the LORD spake unto Moses, saying,

⁵³Unto these the land shall be divided for an inheritance according to the number of names.

⁵⁴To many thou shalt ⁿgive the more inheritance, and to few thou shalt ^ogive the less inheritance: to every one shall his inheritance be given according to those that were numbered of him.

Amplified

²⁹The sons of Manasseh: of Machir, the family of the Machirites (and Machir was the father of Gilead); of Gilead, the family of the Gileadites.

³⁰These are the sons of Gilead: of Iezer, the family of the Iezerites; of Helek, the family of the Helekites;

³¹Of Asriel, the family of the Asrielites; of Shechem, the family of the Shechemites;

³²Of Shemida, the family of the Shemidaites; and of Hepher, the family of the Hepherites.

³³Zelophehad son of Hepher had no sons, but only daughters, and their names were Mahlah, Noah, Hoglah, Milcah, and Tirzah.

³⁴These are the families of Manasseh, and their number was 52,700.

³⁵These are the sons of Ephraim according to their families: of Shuthelah, the family of the Shuthelahites; of Becher, the family of the Becherites; of Tahan, the family of the Tahanites.

³⁶And these are the sons of Shuthelah: of Eran, the family of the Eranites.

³⁷These, the families of the sons of Ephraim according to their number, totaled 32,500. These are the sons of Joseph after their families.

³⁸The sons of Benjamin according to their families: of Bela, the family of the Belaites; of Ashbel, the family of the Ashbelites; of Ahiram, the family of the Ahiramites;

³⁹Of Shephupham, the family of the Shuphamites; of Hupham, the family of the Huphamites.

⁴⁰And the sons of Bela were Ard and Naaman; of Ard, the family of the Ardites; of Naaman, the family of the Naamites.

⁴¹These are the sons of Benjamin according to their families; and their number was 45,600.

⁴²These are the sons of Dan according to their families: of Shuham, the family of the Shuhamites. These are the families of Dan according to their families.

⁴³All the families of the Shuhamites according to their number were 64,400.

⁴⁴Of the sons of Asher according to their families: of Imnah, the family of the Imnites; of Ishvi, the family of the Ishvites; of Beriah, the family of the Beriites.

⁴⁵Of the sons of Beriah: of Heber, the family of the Heberites; of Malchiel, the family of the Malchielites.

⁴⁶And the name of the daughter of Asher was Serah.

⁴⁷These, the families of the sons of Asher according to their number, totaled 53,400.

⁴⁸Of the sons of Naphtali after their families: of Jahzeel, the family of the Jahzeelites; of Guni, the family of the Gunites;

⁴⁹Of Jezer, the family of the Jezerites; of Shillem, the family of the Shillemites.

⁵⁰These are the families of Naphtali according to their families; and their number totaled 45,400.

⁵¹This was the number of the Israelites, 601,730.

⁵²And the Lord said to Moses,

⁵³To these the land shall be divided for inheritance according to the number of names.

⁵⁴To a larger tribe you shall give the greater inheritance, and to a small tribe the less inheritance; to each tribe shall its inheritance be given according to its numbers.

---

^mOr, *Hushim*   ⁿHeb. *multiply his inheritance*   ^oHeb. *diminish his inheritance*

New American Standard

²⁹ The sons of Manasseh: of Machir, the family of the Machirites; and Machir became the father of Gilead: of Gilead, the family of the Gileadites.
³⁰ These are the sons of Gilead: *of* Iezer, the family of the Iezerites; of Helek, the family of the Helekites;
³¹ and *of* Asriel, the family of the Asrielites; and *of* Shechem, the family of the Shechemites;
³² and *of* Shemida, the family of the Shemidaites; and *of* Hepher, the family of the Hepherites.
³³ Now Zelophehad the son of Hepher had no sons, but only daughters; and the names of the daughters of Zelophehad were Mahlah, Noah, Hoglah, Milcah and Tirzah.
³⁴ These are the families of Manasseh; and those who were numbered of them were 52,700.
³⁵ ¶ These are the sons of Ephraim according to their families: of Shuthelah, the family of the Shuthelahites; of Becher, the family of the Becherites; of Tahan, the family of the Tahanites.
³⁶ These are the sons of Shuthelah: of Eran, the family of the Eranites.
³⁷ These are the families of the sons of Ephraim according to those who were numbered of them, 32,500. These are the sons of Joseph according to their families.
³⁸ ¶ The sons of Benjamin according to their families: of Bela, the family of the Belaites; of Ashbel, the family of the Ashbelites; of Ahiram, the family of the Ahiramites;
³⁹ of Shephupham, the family of the Shuphamites; of Hupham, the family of the Huphamites.
⁴⁰ The sons of Bela were Ard and Naaman: *of Ard,* the family of the Ardites; of Naaman, the family of the Naamites.
⁴¹ These are the sons of Benjamin according to their families; and those who were numbered of them were 45,600.
⁴² ¶ These are the sons of Dan according to their families: of Shuham, the family of the Shuhamites. These are the families of Dan according to their families.
⁴³ All the families of the Shuhamites, according to those who were numbered of them, were 64,400.
⁴⁴ ¶ The sons of Asher according to their families: of Imnah, the family of the Imnites; of Ishvi, the family of the Ishvites; of Beriah, the family of the Beriites.
⁴⁵ Of the sons of Beriah: of Heber, the family of the Heberites; of Malchiel, the family of the Malchielites.
⁴⁶ The name of the daughter of Asher *was* Serah.
⁴⁷ These are the families of the sons of Asher according to those who were numbered of them, 53,400.
⁴⁸ ¶ The sons of Naphtali according to their families: of Jahzeel, the family of the Jahzeelites; of Guni, the family of the Gunites;
⁴⁹ of Jezer, the family of the Jezerites; of Shillem, the family of the Shillemites.
⁵⁰ These are the families of Naphtali according to their families; and those who were numbered of them were 45,400.
⁵¹ ¶ These are those who were numbered of the sons of Israel, 601,730.
⁵² ¶ Then the LORD spoke to Moses, saying,
⁵³"Among these the land shall be divided for an inheritance according to the number of names.
⁵⁴"To the larger *group* you shall increase their inheritance, and to the smaller *group* you shall diminish their inheritance; each shall be given their inheritance according to those who were numbered of them.

New International

²⁹The descendants of Manasseh:
  through Makir, the Makirite clan (Makir was the father of Gilead);
  through Gilead, the Gileadite clan.
³⁰These were the descendants of Gilead:
  through Iezer, the Iezerite clan;
  through Helek, the Helekite clan;
³¹through Asriel, the Asrielite clan;
  through Shechem, the Shechemite clan;
³²through Shemida, the Shemidaite clan;
  through Hepher, the Hepherite clan.
³³(Zelophehad son of Hepher had no sons; he had only daughters, whose names were Mahlah, Noah, Hoglah, Milcah and Tirzah.)
³⁴These were the clans of Manasseh; those numbered were 52,700.

³⁵These were the descendants of Ephraim by their clans:
  through Shuthelah, the Shuthelahite clan;
  through Beker, the Bekerite clan;
  through Tahan, the Tahanite clan.
³⁶These were the descendants of Shuthelah:
  through Eran, the Eranite clan.
³⁷These were the clans of Ephraim; those numbered were 32,500.

These were the descendants of Joseph by their clans.

³⁸The descendants of Benjamin by their clans were:
  through Bela, the Belaite clan;
  through Ashbel, the Ashbelite clan;
  through Ahiram, the Ahiramite clan;
³⁹through Shupham,ⁱ the Shuphamite clan;
  through Hupham, the Huphamite clan.
⁴⁰The descendants of Bela through Ard and Naaman were:
  through Ard,ʲ the Ardite clan;
  through Naaman, the Naamite clan.
⁴¹These were the clans of Benjamin; those numbered were 45,600.

⁴²These were the descendants of Dan by their clans:
  through Shuham, the Shuhamite clan.
These were the clans of Dan: ⁴³All of them were Shuhamite clans; and those numbered were 64,400.

⁴⁴The descendants of Asher by their clans were:
  through Imnah, the Imnite clan;
  through Ishvi, the Ishvite clan;
  through Beriah, the Beriite clan;
⁴⁵and through the descendants of Beriah:
  through Heber, the Heberite clan;
  through Malkiel, the Malkielite clan.
⁴⁶(Asher had a daughter named Serah.)
⁴⁷These were the clans of Asher; those numbered were 53,400.

⁴⁸The descendants of Naphtali by their clans were:
  through Jahzeel, the Jahzeelite clan;
  through Guni, the Gunite clan;
⁴⁹through Jezer, the Jezerite clan;
  through Shillem, the Shillemite clan.
⁵⁰These were the clans of Naphtali; those numbered were 45,400.

⁵¹The total number of the men of Israel was 601,730.

⁵²The LORD said to Moses, ⁵³"The land is to be allotted to them as an inheritance based on the number of names. ⁵⁴To a larger group give a larger inheritance, and to a smaller group a smaller one; each is to receive its inheri-

---

ⁱ39 A few manuscripts of the Masoretic Text, Samaritan Pentateuch, Vulgate and Syriac (see also Septuagint); most manuscripts of the Masoretic Text *Shephupham*   ʲ40 Samaritan Pentateuch and Vulgate (see also Septuagint); Masoretic Text does not have *through Ard.*

King James

55Notwithstanding the land shall be divided by lot: according to the names of the tribes of their fathers they shall inherit.

56According to the lot shall the possession thereof be divided between many and few.

57 ¶ And these *are* they that were numbered of the Levites after their families: of Gershon, the family of the Gershonites: of Kohath, the family of the Kohathites: of Merari, the family of the Merarites.

58These *are* the families of the Levites: the family of the Libnites, the family of the Hebronites, the family of the Mahlites, the family of the Mushites, the family of the Korathites. And Kohath begat Amram.

59And the name of Amram's wife *was* Jochebed, the daughter of Levi, whom *her mother* bare to Levi in Egypt: and she bare unto Amram Aaron and Moses, and Miriam their sister.

60And unto Aaron was born Nadab, and Abihu, Eleazar, and Ithamar.

61And Nadab and Abihu died, when they offered strange fire before the LORD.

62And those that were numbered of them were twenty and three thousand, all males from a month old and upward: for they were not numbered among the children of Israel, because there was no inheritance given them among the children of Israel.

63 ¶ These *are* they that were numbered by Moses and Eleazar the priest, who numbered the children of Israel in the plains of Moab by Jordan *near* Jericho.

64But among these there was not a man of them whom Moses and Aaron the priest numbered, when they numbered the children of Israel in the wilderness of Sinai.

65For the LORD had said of them, They shall surely die in the wilderness. And there was not left a man of them, save Caleb the son of Jephunneh, and Joshua the son of Nun.

The daughters of Zelophehad

27 THEN CAME the daughters of Zelophehad, the son of Hepher, the son of Gilead, the son of Machir, the son of Manasseh, of the families of Manasseh the son of Joseph: and these *are* the names of his daughters; Mahlah, Noah, and Hoglah, and Milcah, and Tirzah.

2And they stood before Moses, and before Eleazar the priest, and before the princes and all the congregation, *by* the door of the tabernacle of the congregation, saying,

3Our father died in the wilderness, and he was not in the company of them that gathered themselves together against the LORD in the company of Korah; but died in his own sin, and had no sons.

4Why should the name of our father be *ᵖ*done away from among his family, because he hath no son? Give unto us *therefore* a possession among the brethren of our father.

5And Moses brought their cause before the LORD.

6 ¶ And the LORD spake unto Moses, saying,

7The daughters of Zelophehad speak right: thou shalt surely give them a possession of an inheritance among their father's brethren; and thou shalt cause the inheritance of their father to pass unto them.

8And thou shalt speak unto the children of Israel, saying, If a man die, and have no son, then ye shall cause his inheritance to pass unto his daughter.

9And if he have no daughter, then ye shall give his inheritance unto his brethren.

10And if he have no brethren, then ye shall give his inheritance unto his father's brethren.

11And if his father have no brethren, then ye shall give his inheritance unto his kinsman that is next to him of his family, and he shall possess it: and it shall be unto the children of Israel a statute of judgment, as the LORD commanded Moses.

Amplified

55But the land shall be divided by lot; according to the names of the tribes of their fathers they shall inherit.

56According to the lot shall their inheritance be divided between the larger and the smaller.

57And these were numbered of the Levites according to their families: of Gershon, the family of the Gershonites; of Kohath, the family of the Kohathites; of Merari, the family of the Merarites.

58These are the families of Levi: the family of the Libnites, the family of the Hebronites, the family of the Mahlites, the family of the Mushites, the family of the Korahites. And Kohath was the father of Amram.

59Amram's wife was Jochebed daughter of Levi, who was born to Levi in Egypt; and she bore to Amram Aaron, Moses, and Miriam their sister.

60And to Aaron were born Nadab, Abihu, Eleazar, and Ithamar.

61But Nadab and Abihu died when they offered strange *and* unholy fire before the Lord.

62And those numbered of them were 23,000, every male from a month old and upward; for they were not numbered among the Israelites, because there was no inheritance given them among the Israelites.

63These were those numbered by Moses and Eleazar the priest, who numbered the Israelites in the plains of Moab by the Jordan at Jericho.

64But among these there was not a man of those numbered by Moses and Aaron the priest when they numbered the Israelites in the Wilderness of Sinai.

65For the Lord had said of them, They shall surely die in the wilderness. There was not left a man of them except Caleb son of Jephunneh and Joshua son of Nun.

27 THEN CAME the daughters of Zelophehad son of Hepher, the son of Gilead, the son of Machir, the son of Manasseh, from the families of Manasseh son of Joseph. The names of his daughters: Mahlah, Noah, Hoglah, Milcah, and Tirzah.

2They stood before Moses, Eleazar the priest, and the leaders, and all the congregation at the door of the Tent of Meeting, saying,

3Our father died in the wilderness. He was not among those who assembled together against the Lord in the company of Korah, but died for his own sin [as did all those who rebelled at Kadesh], and he had no sons. [Num. 14:26–35.]

4Why should the name of our father be removed from his family because he had no son? Give to us a possession among our father's brethren.

5Moses brought their case before the Lord.

6And the Lord said to Moses,

7The daughters of Zelophehad are justified *and* speak correctly. You shall surely give them an inheritance among their father's brethren, and you shall cause their father's inheritance to pass to them.

8And say to the Israelites, If a man dies and has no son, you shall cause his inheritance to pass to his daughter.

9If he has no daughter, you shall give his inheritance to his brethren.

10If he has no brethren, give his inheritance to his father's brethren.

11And if his father has no brethren, then give his inheritance to his next of kin, and he shall possess it. It shall be to the Israelites a statute and ordinance, as the Lord commanded Moses.

*ᵖ*Heb. *diminished*

New American Standard

55"But the land shall be divided by lot. They shall receive their inheritance according to the names of the tribes of their fathers.

56"According to the selection by lot, their inheritance shall be divided between the larger and the smaller groups."

57 ¶ These are those who were numbered of the Levites according to their families: of Gershon, the family of the Gershonites; of Kohath, the family of the Kohathites; of Merari, the family of the Merarites.

58 These are the families of Levi: the family of the Libnites, the family of the Hebronites, the family of the Mahlites, the family of the Mushites, the family of the Korahites. Kohath became the father of Amram.

59 The name of Amram's wife was Jochebed, the daughter of Levi, who was born to Levi in Egypt; and she bore to Amram: Aaron and Moses and their sister Miriam.

60 To Aaron were born Nadab and Abihu, Eleazar and Ithamar.

61 But Nadab and Abihu died when they offered strange fire before the LORD.

62 Those who were numbered of them were 23,000, every male from a month old and upward, for they were not numbered among the sons of Israel since no inheritance was given to them among the sons of Israel.

63 ¶ These are those who were numbered by Moses and Eleazar the priest, who numbered the sons of Israel in the plains of Moab by the Jordan at Jericho.

64 But among these there was not a man of those who were numbered by Moses and Aaron the priest, who numbered the sons of Israel in the wilderness of Sinai.

65 For the LORD had said of them, "They shall surely die in the wilderness." And not a man was left of them, except Caleb the son of Jephunneh and Joshua the son of Nun.

A Law of Inheritance

27 THEN THE daughters of Zelophehad, the son of Hepher, the son of Gilead, the son of Machir, the son of Manasseh, of the families of Manasseh the son of Joseph, came near; and these are the names of his daughters: Mahlah, Noah and Hoglah and Milcah and Tirzah.

2 They stood before Moses and before Eleazar the priest and before the leaders and all the congregation, at the doorway of the tent of meeting, saying,

3"Our father died in the wilderness, yet he was not among the company of those who gathered themselves together against the LORD in the company of Korah; but he died in his own sin, and he had no sons.

4"Why should the name of our father be withdrawn from among his family because he had no son? Give us a possession among our father's brothers."

5 So Moses brought their case before the LORD.

6 ¶ Then the LORD spoke to Moses, saying,

7"The daughters of Zelophehad are right in *their* statements. You shall surely give them a hereditary possession among their father's brothers, and you shall transfer the inheritance of their father to them.

8"Further, you shall speak to the sons of Israel, saying, 'If a man dies and has no son, then you shall transfer his inheritance to his daughter.

9 'If he has no daughter, then you shall give his inheritance to his brothers.

10 'If he has no brothers, then you shall give his inheritance to his father's brothers.

11 'If his father has no brothers, then you shall give his inheritance to his nearest relative in his own family, and he shall possess it; and it shall be a statutory ordinance to the sons of Israel, just as the LORD commanded Moses.' "

New International

tance according to the number of those listed. 55Be sure that the land is distributed by lot. What each group inherits will be according to the names for its ancestral tribe. 56Each inheritance is to be distributed by lot among the larger and smaller groups."

57These were the Levites who were counted by their clans:
    through Gershon, the Gershonite clan;
    through Kohath, the Kohathite clan;
    through Merari, the Merarite clan.
58These also were Levite clans:
    the Libnite clan,
    the Hebronite clan,
    the Mahlite clan,
    the Mushite clan,
    the Korahite clan.
(Kohath was the forefather of Amram; 59the name of Amram's wife was Jochebed, a descendant of Levi, who was born to the Levites[k] in Egypt. To Amram she bore Aaron, Moses and their sister Miriam. 60Aaron was the father of Nadab and Abihu, Eleazar and Ithamar. 61But Nadab and Abihu died when they made an offering before the LORD with unauthorized fire.)

62All the male Levites a month old or more numbered 23,000. They were not counted along with the other Israelites because they received no inheritance among them.

63These are the ones counted by Moses and Eleazar the priest when they counted the Israelites on the plains of Moab by the Jordan across from Jericho. 64Not one of them was among those counted by Moses and Aaron the priest when they counted the Israelites in the Desert of Sinai. 65For the LORD had told those Israelites they would surely die in the desert, and not one of them was left except Caleb son of Jephunneh and Joshua son of Nun.

Zelophehad's Daughters

27 THE DAUGHTERS of Zelophehad son of Hepher, the son of Gilead, the son of Makir, the son of Manasseh, belonged to the clans of Manasseh son of Joseph. The names of the daughters were Mahlah, Noah, Hoglah, Milcah and Tirzah. They approached 2the entrance to the Tent of Meeting and stood before Moses, Eleazar the priest, the leaders and the whole assembly, and said, 3"Our father died in the desert. He was not among Korah's followers, who banded together against the LORD, but he died for his own sin and left no sons. 4Why should our father's name disappear from his clan because he had no son? Give us property among our father's relatives."

5So Moses brought their case before the LORD 6and the LORD said to him, 7"What Zelophehad's daughters are saying is right. You must certainly give them property as an inheritance among their father's relatives and turn their father's inheritance over to them.

8"Say to the Israelites, 'If a man dies and leaves no son, turn his inheritance over to his daughter. 9If he has no daughter, give his inheritance to his brothers. 10If he has no brothers, give his inheritance to his father's brothers. 11If his father had no brothers, give his inheritance to the nearest relative in his clan, that he may possess it. This is to be a legal requirement for the Israelites, as the LORD commanded Moses.' "

---

k 59 Or Jochebed, a daughter of Levi, who was born to Levi

King James

Amplified

Joshua to succeed Moses

12 ¶ And the LORD said unto Moses, Get thee up into this mount Abarim, and see the land which I have given unto the children of Israel.

13 And when thou hast seen it, thou also shalt be gathered unto thy people, as Aaron thy brother was gathered.

14 For ye rebelled against my commandment in the desert of Zin, in the strife of the congregation, to sanctify me at the water before their eyes: that *is* the water of Meribah in Kadesh in the wilderness of Zin.

15 ¶ And Moses spake unto the LORD, saying,

16 Let the LORD, the God of the spirits of all flesh, set a man over the congregation,

17 Which may go out before them, and which may go in before them, and which may lead them out, and which may bring them in; that the congregation of the LORD be not as sheep which have no shepherd.

18 ¶ And the LORD said unto Moses, Take thee Joshua the son of Nun, a man in whom *is* the spirit, and lay thine hand upon him;

19 And set him before Eleazar the priest, and before all the congregation; and give him a charge in their sight.

20 And thou shalt put *some* of thine honour upon him, that all the congregation of the children of Israel may be obedient.

21 And he shall stand before Eleazar the priest, who shall ask *counsel* for him after the judgment of Urim before the LORD: at his word shall they go out, and at his word they shall come in, *both* he, and all the children of Israel with him, even all the congregation.

22 And Moses did as the LORD commanded him: and he took Joshua, and set him before Eleazar the priest, and before all the congregation:

23 And he laid his hands upon him, and gave him a charge, as the LORD commanded by the hand of Moses.

12 And the Lord said to Moses, Go up into this mountain of Abarim and behold the land I have given to the Israelites.

13 And when you have seen it, you also shall be gathered to your [departed] people as Aaron your brother was gathered,

14 For you disobeyed My order in the Wilderness of Zin during the strife of the congregation to uphold My sanctity [by strict obedience to My authority] at the waters before their eyes. [These are the waters of Meribah in Kadesh in the Wilderness of Zin]. [Num. 20:10–12.]

15 And Moses said to the Lord,

16 Let the Lord, the God of the spirits of all flesh, set a man over the congregation

17 Who shall go out and come in before them, leading them out and bringing them in, that the congregation of the Lord may not be as sheep which have no shepherd.

18 The Lord said to Moses, Take Joshua son of Nun, a man in whom is the Spirit, and lay your hand upon him;

19 And set him before Eleazar the priest and all the congregation and give him a charge in their sight.

20 And put some of your honor *and* authority upon him, that all the congregation of the Israelites may obey him.

21 He shall stand before Eleazar the priest, who shall inquire for him before the Lord by the judgment of the Urim [one of two articles in the priest's breastplate worn when asking counsel of the Lord for the people]. At Joshua's word the people shall go out and come in, both he and all the Israelite congregation with him.

22 And Moses did as the Lord commanded him. He took Joshua and set him before Eleazar the priest and all the congregation,

23 And he laid his hands upon him and commissioned him, as the Lord commanded through Moses.

The daily burnt offering

28 AND THE LORD spake unto Moses, saying,
2 Command the children of Israel, and say unto them, My offering, *and* my bread for my sacrifices made by fire, *for* [q]a sweet savour unto me, shall ye observe to offer unto me in their due season.

3 And thou shalt say unto them, This *is* the offering made by fire which ye shall offer unto the LORD; two lambs of the first year without spot [r]day by day, *for* a continual burnt offering.

4 The one lamb shalt thou offer in the morning, and the other lamb shalt thou offer [s]at even;

5 And a tenth *part* of an ephah of flour for a meat offering, mingled with the fourth *part* of an hin of beaten oil.

6 *It is* a continual burnt offering, which was ordained in mount Sinai for a sweet savour, a sacrifice made by fire unto the LORD.

7 And the drink offering thereof *shall be* the fourth *part* of an hin for the one lamb: in the holy *place* shalt thou cause the strong wine to be poured unto the LORD *for* a drink offering.

8 And the other lamb shalt thou offer at even: as the meat offering of the morning, and as the drink offering thereof, thou shalt offer *it,* a sacrifice made by fire, of a sweet savour unto the LORD.

The offering on the Sabbath

9 ¶ And on the sabbath day two lambs of the first year without spot, and two tenth deals of flour *for* a meat offering, mingled with oil, and the drink offering thereof:

10 *This is* the burnt offering of every sabbath, beside the continual burnt offering, and his drink offering.

28 AND THE Lord said to Moses,
2 Command the Israelites, saying, My offering, My food for My offerings made by fire, My sweet *and* soothing odor you shall be careful to offer to Me at its proper time.

3 And you shall say to the people, This is the offering made by fire which you shall offer to the Lord: two male lambs a year old without spot *or* blemish, two day by day, for a continual burnt offering.

4 One lamb you shall offer in the morning and the other in the evening,

5 Also a tenth of an ephah of flour for a cereal offering, mixed with a fourth of a hin of beaten oil.

6 It is a continual burnt offering which was ordained in Mount Sinai for a sweet *and* soothing odor, an offering made by fire to the Lord.

7 Its drink offering shall be a fourth of a hin for each lamb; in the Holy Place you shall pour out a fermented drink offering to the Lord.

8 And the other lamb you shall offer in the evening; like the cereal offering of the morning and like its drink offering, you shall offer it, an offering made by fire, a sweet *and* soothing odor to the Lord.

9 And on the Sabbath day two male lambs a year old without spot *or* blemish, and two-tenths of an ephah of flour for a cereal offering, mixed with oil, and its drink offering.

10 This is the burnt offering of every Sabbath, besides the continual burnt offering and its drink offering.

[q]Heb. *a savour of my rest* [r]Heb. *in a day* [s]Heb. *between the two evenings*

New American Standard

12 ¶ Then the LORD said to Moses, "Go up to this mountain of Abarim, and see the land which I have given to the sons of Israel.
13"When you have seen it, you too will be gathered to your people, as Aaron your brother was;
14 for in the wilderness of Zin, during the strife of the congregation, you rebelled against My command to treat Me as holy before their eyes at the water." (These are the waters of Meribah of Kadesh in the wilderness of Zin.)

Joshua to Succeed Moses

15 ¶ Then Moses spoke to the LORD, saying,
16"May the LORD, the God of the spirits of all flesh, appoint a man over the congregation,
17 who will go out and come in before them, and who will lead them out and bring them in, so that the congregation of the LORD will not be like sheep which have no shepherd."
18 So the LORD said to Moses, "Take Joshua the son of Nun, a man in whom is the Spirit, and lay your hand on him;
19 and have him stand before Eleazar the priest and before all the congregation, and commission him in their sight.
20"You shall put some of your authority on him, in order that all the congregation of the sons of Israel may obey him.
21"Moreover, he shall stand before Eleazar the priest, who shall inquire for him by the judgment of the Urim before the LORD. At his command they shall go out and at his command they shall come in, both he and the sons of Israel with him, even all the congregation."
22 Moses did just as the LORD commanded him; and he took Joshua and set him before Eleazar the priest and before all the congregation.
23 Then he laid his hands on him and commissioned him, just as the LORD had spoken through Moses.

Laws for Offerings

28 THEN THE LORD spoke to Moses, saying,
2"Command the sons of Israel and say to them, 'You shall be careful to present My offering, My food for My offerings by fire, of a soothing aroma to Me, at their appointed time.'
3"You shall say to them, 'This is the offering by fire which you shall offer to the LORD: two male lambs one year old without defect as a continual burnt offering every day.
4 'You shall offer the one lamb in the morning and the other lamb you shall offer at twilight;
5 also a tenth of an ephah of fine flour for a grain offering, mixed with a fourth of a hin of beaten oil.
6 'It is a continual burnt offering which was ordained in Mount Sinai as a soothing aroma, an offering by fire to the LORD.
7 'Then the drink offering with it shall be a fourth of a hin for each lamb, in the holy place you shall pour out a drink offering of strong drink to the LORD.
8 'The other lamb you shall offer at twilight; as the grain offering of the morning and as its drink offering, you shall offer it, an offering by fire, a soothing aroma to the LORD.
9 ¶ 'Then on the sabbath day two male lambs one year old without defect, and two-tenths of an ephah of fine flour mixed with oil as a grain offering, and its drink offering:
10 'This is the burnt offering of every sabbath in addition to the continual burnt offering and its drink offering.

New International

Joshua to Succeed Moses

12Then the LORD said to Moses, "Go up this mountain in the Abarim range and see the land I have given the Israelites. 13After you have seen it, you too will be gathered to your people, as your brother Aaron was, 14for when the community rebelled at the waters in the Desert of Zin, both of you disobeyed my command to honor me as holy before their eyes." (These were the waters of Meribah Kadesh, in the Desert of Zin.)

15Moses said to the LORD, 16"May the LORD, the God of the spirits of all mankind, appoint a man over this community 17to go out and come in before them, one who will lead them out and bring them in, so the LORD's people will not be like sheep without a shepherd."

18So the LORD said to Moses, "Take Joshua son of Nun, a man in whom is the spirit,[l] and lay your hand on him. 19Have him stand before Eleazar the priest and the entire assembly and commission him in their presence. 20Give him some of your authority so the whole Israelite community will obey him. 21He is to stand before Eleazar the priest, who will obtain decisions for him by inquiring of the Urim before the LORD. At his command he and the entire community of the Israelites will go out, and at his command they will come in."

22Moses did as the LORD commanded him. He took Joshua and had him stand before Eleazar the priest and the whole assembly. 23Then he laid his hands on him and commissioned him, as the LORD instructed through Moses.

Daily Offerings

28 THE LORD said to Moses, 2"Give this command to the Israelites and say to them: 'See that you present to me at the appointed time the food for my offerings made by fire, as an aroma pleasing to me.' 3Say to them: 'This is the offering made by fire that you are to present to the LORD: two lambs a year old without defect, as a regular burnt offering each day. 4Prepare one lamb in the morning and the other at twilight, 5together with a grain offering of a tenth of an ephah[m] of fine flour mixed with a quarter of a hin[n] of oil from pressed olives. 6This is the regular burnt offering instituted at Mount Sinai as a pleasing aroma, an offering made to the LORD by fire. 7The accompanying drink offering is to be a quarter of a hin of fermented drink with each lamb. Pour out the drink offering to the LORD at the sanctuary. 8Prepare the second lamb at twilight, along with the same kind of grain offering and drink offering that you prepare in the morning. This is an offering made by fire, an aroma pleasing to the LORD.

Sabbath Offerings

9" 'On the Sabbath day, make an offering of two lambs a year old without defect, together with its drink offering and a grain offering of two-tenths of an ephah[o] of fine flour mixed with oil. 10This is the burnt offering for every Sabbath, in addition to the regular burnt offering and its drink offering.

---

l 18 Or Spirit   m 5 That is, probably about 2 quarts (about 2 liters); also in verses 13, 21 and 29   n 5 That is, probably about 1 quart (about 1 liter); also in verses 7 and 14   o 9 That is, probably about 4 quarts (about 4.5 liters); also in verses 12, 20 and 28

King James	Amplified

King James

The offering at the new moon

11 ¶ And in the beginnings of your months ye shall offer a burnt offering unto the LORD; two young bullocks, and one ram, seven lambs of the first year without spot;

12And three tenth deals of flour *for* a meat offering, mingled with oil, for one bullock; and two tenth deals of flour *for* a meat offering, mingled with oil, for one ram;

13And a several tenth deal of flour mingled with oil *for* a meat offering unto one lamb; *for* a burnt offering of a sweet savour, a sacrifice made by fire unto the LORD.

14And their drink offerings shall be half an hin of wine unto a bullock, and the third *part* of an hin unto a ram, and a fourth *part* of an hin unto a lamb: this *is* the burnt offering of every month throughout the months of the year.

15And one kid of the goats for a sin offering unto the LORD shall be offered, beside the continual burnt offering, and his drink offering.

The feast of unleavened bread

16And in the fourteenth day of the first month *is* the passover of the LORD.

17And in the fifteenth day of this month *is* the feast: seven days shall unleavened bread be eaten.

18In the first day *shall be* an holy convocation; ye shall do no manner of servile work *therein:*

19But ye shall offer a sacrifice made by fire *for* a burnt offering unto the LORD; two young bullocks, and one ram, and seven lambs of the first year: they shall be unto you without blemish:

20And their meat offering *shall be of* flour mingled with oil: three tenth deals shall ye offer for a bullock, and two tenth deals for a ram;

21A several tenth deal shalt thou offer for every lamb, throughout the seven lambs:

22And one goat *for* a sin offering, to make an atonement for you.

23Ye shall offer these beside the burnt offering in the morning, which *is* for a continual burnt offering.

24After this manner ye shall offer daily, throughout the seven days, the meat of the sacrifice made by fire, of a sweet savour unto the LORD: it shall be offered beside the continual burnt offering, and his drink offering.

25And on the seventh day ye shall have an holy convocation; ye shall do no servile work.

26 ¶ Also in the day of the firstfruits, when ye bring a new meat offering unto the LORD, after your weeks *be out,* ye shall have an holy convocation; ye shall do no servile work:

27But ye shall offer the burnt offering for a sweet savour unto the LORD; two young bullocks, one ram, seven lambs of the first year;

28And their meat offering of flour mingled with oil, three tenth deals unto one bullock, two tenth deals unto one ram,

29A several tenth deal unto one lamb, throughout the seven lambs;

30*And* one kid of the goats, to make an atonement for you.

31Ye shall offer *them* beside the continual burnt offering, and his meat offering, (they shall be unto you without blemish) and their drink offerings.

Feast of the trumpets offerings

29 AND IN the seventh month, on the first *day* of the month, ye shall have an holy convocation; ye shall do no servile work: it is a day of blowing the trumpets unto you.

2And ye shall offer a burnt offering for a sweet savour unto the LORD; one young bullock, one ram, *and* seven lambs of the first year without blemish:

Amplified

11And at the beginning of your months you shall offer a burnt offering to the Lord: two young bulls, one ram, seven male lambs a year old without spot *or* blemish;

12And three-tenths of an ephah of fine flour for a cereal offering, mixed with oil, for each bull; and two-tenths of an ephah of fine flour for a cereal offering, mixed with oil, for the one ram.

13And a tenth part of fine flour mixed with oil as a cereal offering, for each lamb, for a burnt offering of a sweet *and* pleasant fragrance, an offering made by fire to the Lord.

14And their drink offerings shall be half a hin of wine for a bull, and a third of a hin for a ram, and a fourth of a hin for a lamb. This is the burnt offering of each month throughout the months of the year.

15And one male goat for a sin offering to the Lord—it shall be offered in addition to the continual burnt offering and its drink offering.

16On the fourteenth day of the first month is the Lord's Passover.

17On the fifteenth day of this month is a feast; for seven days shall unleavened bread be eaten.

18On the first day there shall be a holy [summoned] assembly; you shall do no servile work that day.

19But you shall offer an offering made by fire, a burnt offering to the Lord: two young bulls, one ram, and seven male lambs a year old; they shall be without blemish to the best of your knowledge.

20And their cereal offering shall be of fine flour mixed with oil; three-tenths of an ephah shall you offer for a bull, and two-tenths for a ram;

21A tenth shall you offer for each of the seven male lambs,

22Also one male goat for a sin offering to make atonement for you.

23You shall offer these in addition to the burnt offering of the morning, which is for a continual burnt offering.

24In this way you shall offer daily for seven days the food of an offering made by fire, a sweet *and* soothing odor to the Lord; it shall be offered in addition to the continual burnt offering and its drink offering.

25And on the seventh day you shall have a holy [summoned] assembly; you shall do no work befitting a slave *or* a servant.

26Also in the day of the firstfruits, when you offer a cereal offering of new grain to the Lord at your Feast of Weeks, you shall have a holy [summoned] assembly; you shall do no servile work.

27But you shall offer the burnt offering for a sweet, pleasing, *and* soothing fragrance to the Lord: two young bulls, one ram, seven male lambs a year old,

28And their cereal offering of fine flour mixed with oil, three-tenths of an ephah for each bull, two-tenths for one ram,

29A tenth for each of the seven male lambs,

30And one male goat to make atonement for you.

31You shall offer them in addition to the continual burnt offering and its cereal offering and their drink offerings. See that they are without blemish.

29 ON THE first day of the seventh month [on New Year's Day of the civil year], you shall have a holy [summoned] assembly; you shall do no servile work. It is a day of blowing of trumpets for you [everyone blowing who wishes, proclaiming that the glad New Year has come and that the great Day of Atonement and the Feast of Tabernacles are now approaching].

2And you shall offer a burnt offering for a sweet *and* pleasing odor to the Lord: one young bull, one ram, and seven male lambs a year old without blemish.

New American Standard

¹¹ ¶ 'Then at the beginning of each of your months you shall present a burnt offering to the LORD: two bulls and one ram, seven male lambs one year old without defect;

¹² and three-tenths *of an ephah* of fine flour mixed with oil for a grain offering, for each bull; and two-tenths of fine flour mixed with oil for a grain offering, for the one ram;

¹³ and a tenth *of an ephah* of fine flour mixed with oil for a grain offering for each lamb, for a burnt offering of a soothing aroma, an offering by fire to the LORD.

¹⁴ 'Their drink offerings shall be half a hin of wine for a bull and a third of a hin for the ram and a fourth of a hin for a lamb; this is the burnt offering of each month throughout the months of the year.

¹⁵ 'And one male goat for a sin offering to the LORD; it shall be offered with its drink offering in addition to the continual burnt offering.

¹⁶ ¶ 'Then on the fourteenth day of the first month shall be the LORD'S Passover.

¹⁷ 'On the fifteenth day of this month *shall be* a feast, unleavened bread *shall be* eaten for seven days.

¹⁸ 'On the first day *shall be* a holy convocation; you shall do no laborious work.

¹⁹ 'You shall present an offering by fire, a burnt offering to the LORD: two bulls and one ram and seven male lambs one year old, having them without defect.

²⁰ 'For their grain offering, you shall offer fine flour mixed with oil: three-tenths *of an ephah* for a bull and two-tenths for the ram.

²¹ 'A tenth *of an ephah* you shall offer for each of the seven lambs;

²² and one male goat for a sin offering to make atonement for you.

²³ 'You shall present these besides the burnt offering of the morning, which is for a continual burnt offering.

²⁴ 'After this manner you shall present daily, for seven days, the food of the offering by fire, of a soothing aroma to the LORD; it shall be presented with its drink offering in addition to the continual burnt offering.

²⁵ 'On the seventh day you shall have a holy convocation; you shall do no laborious work.

²⁶ ¶ 'Also on the day of the first fruits, when you present a new grain offering to the LORD in your *Feast of Weeks*, you shall have a holy convocation; you shall do no laborious work.

²⁷ 'You shall offer a burnt offering for a soothing aroma to the LORD: two young bulls, one ram, seven male lambs one year old;

²⁸ and their grain offering, fine flour mixed with oil: three-tenths *of an ephah* for each bull, two-tenths for the one ram,

²⁹ a tenth for each of the seven lambs;

³⁰ *also* one male goat to make atonement for you.

³¹ 'Besides the continual burnt offering and its grain offering, you shall present *them* with their drink offerings. They shall be without defect.

Offerings of the Seventh Month

29 'NOW IN the seventh month, on the first day of the month, you shall also have a holy convocation; you shall do no laborious work. It will be to you a day for blowing trumpets.

² 'You shall offer a burnt offering as a soothing aroma to the LORD: one bull, one ram, *and* seven male lambs one year old without defect;

New International

Monthly Offerings

¹¹" 'On the first of every month, present to the LORD a burnt offering of two young bulls, one ram and seven male lambs a year old, all without defect. ¹²With each bull there is to be a grain offering of three-tenths of an ephah^p of fine flour mixed with oil; with the ram, a grain offering of two-tenths of an ephah of fine flour mixed with oil; ¹³and with each lamb, a grain offering of a tenth of an ephah of fine flour mixed with oil. This is for a burnt offering, a pleasing aroma, an offering made to the LORD by fire. ¹⁴With each bull there is to be a drink offering of half a hin^q of wine; with the ram, a third of a hin^r; and with each lamb, a quarter of a hin. This is the monthly burnt offering to be made at each new moon during the year. ¹⁵Besides the regular burnt offering with its drink offering, one male goat is to be presented to the LORD as a sin offering.

The Passover

¹⁶" 'On the fourteenth day of the first month the LORD'S Passover is to be held. ¹⁷On the fifteenth day of this month there is to be a festival; for seven days eat bread made without yeast. ¹⁸On the first day hold a sacred assembly and do no regular work. ¹⁹Present to the LORD an offering made by fire, a burnt offering of two young bulls, one ram and seven male lambs a year old, all without defect. ²⁰With each bull prepare a grain offering of three-tenths of an ephah of fine flour mixed with oil; with the ram, two-tenths; ²¹and with each of the seven lambs, one-tenth. ²²Include one male goat as a sin offering to make atonement for you. ²³Prepare these in addition to the regular morning burnt offering. ²⁴In this way prepare the food for the offering made by fire every day for seven days as an aroma pleasing to the LORD; it is to be prepared in addition to the regular burnt offering and its drink offering. ²⁵On the seventh day hold a sacred assembly and do no regular work.

Feast of Weeks

²⁶" 'On the day of firstfruits, when you present to the LORD an offering of new grain during the Feast of Weeks, hold a sacred assembly and do no regular work. ²⁷Present a burnt offering of two young bulls, one ram and seven male lambs a year old as an aroma pleasing to the LORD. ²⁸With each bull there is to be a grain offering of three-tenths of an ephah of fine flour mixed with oil; with the ram, two-tenths; ²⁹and with each of the seven lambs, one-tenth. ³⁰Include one male goat to make atonement for you. ³¹Prepare these together with their drink offerings, in addition to the regular burnt offering and its grain offering. Be sure the animals are without defect.

Feast of Trumpets

29 " 'ON THE first day of the seventh month hold a sacred assembly and do no regular work. It is a day for you to sound the trumpets. ²As an aroma pleasing to the LORD, prepare a burnt offering of one young bull, one ram and seven male lambs a year old, all without defect.

---

^p 12 That is, probably about 6 quarts (about 6.5 liters); also in verses 20 and 28   ^q 14 That is, probably about 2 quarts (about 2 liters)
^r 14 That is, probably about 1 1/4 quarts (about 1.2 liters)

King James

³And their meat offering *shall be of* flour mingled with oil, three tenth deals for a bullock, *and* two tenth deals for a ram,

⁴And one tenth deal for one lamb, throughout the seven lambs:

⁵And one kid of the goats *for* a sin offering, to make an atonement for you:

⁶Beside the burnt offering of the month, and his meat offering, and the daily burnt offering, and his meat offering, and their drink offerings, according unto their manner, for a sweet savour, a sacrifice made by fire unto the LORD.

Day of Atonement offerings

⁷ ¶ And ye shall have on the tenth *day* of this seventh month an holy convocation; and ye shall afflict your souls: ye shall not do any work *therein:*

⁸But ye shall offer a burnt offering unto the LORD *for* a sweet savour; one young bullock, one ram, *and* seven lambs of the first year; they shall be unto you without blemish:

⁹And their meat offering *shall be of* flour mingled with oil, three tenth deals to a bullock, *and* two tenth deals to one ram,

¹⁰A several tenth deal for one lamb, throughout the seven lambs:

¹¹One kid of the goats *for* a sin offering; beside the sin offering of atonement, and the continual burnt offering, and the meat offering of it, and their drink offerings.

Feast of tabernacles offerings

¹² ¶ And on the fifteenth day of the seventh month ye shall have an holy convocation; ye shall do no servile work, and ye shall keep a feast unto the LORD seven days:

¹³And ye shall offer a burnt offering, a sacrifice made by fire, of a sweet savour unto the LORD; thirteen young bullocks, two rams, *and* fourteen lambs of the first year; they shall be without blemish:

¹⁴And their meat offering *shall be of* flour mingled with oil, three tenth deals unto every bullock of the thirteen bullocks, two tenth deals to each ram of the two rams,

¹⁵And a several tenth deal to each lamb of the fourteen lambs:

¹⁶And one kid of the goats *for* a sin offering; beside the continual burnt offering, his meat offering, and his drink offering.

¹⁷ ¶ And on the second day *ye shall offer* twelve young bullocks, two rams, fourteen lambs of the first year without spot:

¹⁸And their meat offering and their drink offerings for the bullocks, for the rams, and for the lambs, *shall be* according to their number, after the manner:

¹⁹And one kid of the goats *for* a sin offering; beside the continual burnt offering, and the meat offering thereof, and their drink offerings.

²⁰ ¶ And on the third day eleven bullocks, two rams, fourteen lambs of the first year without blemish;

²¹And their meat offering and their drink offerings for the bullocks, for the rams, and for the lambs, *shall be* according to their number, after the manner:

²²And one goat *for* a sin offering; beside the continual burnt offering, and his meat offering, and his drink offering.

²³ ¶ And on the fourth day ten bullocks, two rams, *and* fourteen lambs of the first year without blemish:

²⁴Their meat offering and their drink offerings for the bullocks, for the rams, and for the lambs, *shall be* according to their number, after the manner:

²⁵And one kid of the goats *for* a sin offering; beside the continual burnt offering, his meat offering, and his drink offering.

²⁶ ¶ And on the fifth day nine bullocks, two rams, *and* fourteen lambs of the first year without spot:

Amplified

³Their cereal offering shall be of fine flour mixed with oil, three-tenths of an ephah for a bull, two-tenths for a ram;

⁴And one-tenth of an ephah for each of the seven lambs,

⁵And one male goat for a sin offering to make atonement for you.

⁶These are in addition to the burnt offering of the new moon and its cereal offering, and the daily burnt offering and its cereal offering, and their drink offerings, according to the ordinance for them, for a pleasant *and* soothing fragrance, an offering made by fire to the Lord.

⁷And you shall have on the tenth day of this seventh month a holy [summoned] assembly; [it is the great Day of Atonement, a day of humiliation] and you shall humble *and* abase yourselves; you shall not do any work in it.

⁸But you shall offer a burnt offering to the Lord for a sweet *and* soothing fragrance: one young bull, one ram, and seven male lambs a year old. See that they are without blemish.

⁹And their cereal offering shall be of fine flour mixed with oil, three-tenths of an ephah for the bull, two-tenths for the one ram,

¹⁰A tenth for each of the seven male lambs,

¹¹One male goat for a sin offering, in addition to the sin offering of atonement, and the continual burnt offering and its cereal offering, and their drink offerings.

¹²And on the fifteenth day of the seventh month you shall have a holy [summoned] assembly; you shall do no servile work, and you shall keep a feast to the Lord for seven days.

¹³And you shall offer a burnt offering, an offering made by fire, of a sweet *and* pleasing fragrance to the Lord: thirteen young bulls, two rams, and fourteen male lambs a year old; they shall be without blemish.

¹⁴And their cereal offering shall be of fine flour mixed with oil, three-tenths of an ephah for each of the thirteen bulls, two-tenths for each of the two rams,

¹⁵And a tenth part for each of the fourteen male lambs,

¹⁶Also one male goat for a sin offering, in addition to the continual burnt offering, its cereal offering, and its drink offering.

¹⁷And on the second day you shall offer twelve young bulls, two rams, fourteen male lambs a year old without spot *or* blemish,

¹⁸With their cereal offering and the drink offerings for the bulls, the rams, and the lambs, by number according to the ordinance,

¹⁹Also one male goat for a sin offering, besides the continual burnt offering, its cereal offering, and their drink offerings.

²⁰And on the third day eleven bulls, two rams, fourteen male lambs a year old without blemish,

²¹With their cereal offering and drink offerings for the bulls, the rams, and the lambs, by number according to the ordinance,

²²And one male goat for a sin offering, besides the continual burnt offering, its cereal offering, and its drink offerings.

²³On the fourth day ten bulls, two rams, and fourteen male lambs a year old without blemish,

²⁴Their cereal offering and their drink offerings for the bulls, the rams, and the lambs shall be by number according to the ordinance,

²⁵And one male goat for a sin offering, besides the continual burnt offering, its cereal offering, and its drink offerings.

²⁶And on the fifth day nine bulls, two rams, and fourteen male lambs a year old without spot *or* blemish,

New American Standard

3 also their grain offering, fine flour mixed with oil: three-tenths *of an ephah* for the bull, two-tenths for the ram,

4 and one-tenth for each of the seven lambs.

5 '*Offer* one male goat for a sin offering, to make atonement for you,

6 besides the burnt offering of the new moon and its grain offering, and the continual burnt offering and its grain offering, and their drink offerings, according to their ordinance, for a soothing aroma, an offering by fire to the LORD.

7 ¶ 'Then on the tenth day of this seventh month you shall have a holy convocation, and you shall humble yourselves; you shall not do any work.

8 'You shall present a burnt offering to the LORD *as a* soothing aroma: one bull, one ram, seven male lambs one year old, having them without defect;

9 and their grain offering, fine flour mixed with oil: three-tenths *of an ephah* for the bull, two-tenths for the one ram,

10 a tenth for each of the seven lambs;

11 one male goat for a sin offering, besides the sin offering of atonement and the continual burnt offering and its grain offering, and their drink offerings.

12 ¶ 'Then on the fifteenth day of the seventh month you shall have a holy convocation; you shall do no laborious work, and you shall observe a feast to the LORD for seven days.

13 'You shall present a burnt offering, an offering by fire as a soothing aroma to the LORD: thirteen bulls, two rams, fourteen male lambs one year old, which are without defect;

14 and their grain offering, fine flour mixed with oil: three-tenths *of an ephah* for each of the thirteen bulls, two-tenths for each of the two rams,

15 and a tenth for each of the fourteen lambs;

16 and one male goat for a sin offering, besides the continual burnt offering, its grain offering and its drink offering.

17 ¶ 'Then on the second day: twelve bulls, two rams, fourteen male lambs one year old without defect;

18 and their grain offering and their drink offerings for the bulls, for the rams and for the lambs, by their number according to the ordinance;

19 and one male goat for a sin offering, besides the continual burnt offering and its grain offering, and their drink offerings.

20 ¶ 'Then on the third day: eleven bulls, two rams, fourteen male lambs one year old without defect;

21 and their grain offering and their drink offerings for the bulls, for the rams and for the lambs, by their number according to the ordinance;

22 and one male goat for a sin offering, besides the continual burnt offering and its grain offering and its drink offering.

23 ¶ 'Then on the fourth day: ten bulls, two rams, fourteen male lambs one year old without defect;

24 their grain offering and their drink offerings for the bulls, for the rams and for the lambs, by their number according to the ordinance;

25 and one male goat for a sin offering, besides the continual burnt offering, its grain offering and its drink offering.

26 ¶ 'Then on the fifth day: nine bulls, two rams, fourteen male lambs one year old without defect;

New International

3With the bull prepare a grain offering of three-tenths of an ephah[s] of fine flour mixed with oil; with the ram, two-tenths[t]; 4and with each of the seven lambs, one-tenth.[u] 5Include one male goat as a sin offering to make atonement for you. 6These are in addition to the monthly and daily burnt offerings with their grain offerings and drink offerings as specified. They are offerings made to the LORD by fire—a pleasing aroma.

Day of Atonement

7" 'On the tenth day of this seventh month hold a sacred assembly. You must deny yourselves[v] and do no work. 8Present as an aroma pleasing to the LORD a burnt offering of one young bull, one ram and seven male lambs a year old, all without defect. 9With the bull prepare a grain offering of three-tenths of an ephah of fine flour mixed with oil; with the ram, two-tenths; 10and with each of the seven lambs, one-tenth. 11Include one male goat as a sin offering, in addition to the sin offering for atonement and the regular burnt offering with its grain offering, and their drink offerings.

Feast of Tabernacles

12" 'On the fifteenth day of the seventh month, hold a sacred assembly and do no regular work. Celebrate a festival to the LORD for seven days. 13Present an offering made by fire as an aroma pleasing to the LORD, a burnt offering of thirteen young bulls, two rams and fourteen male lambs a year old, all without defect. 14With each of the thirteen bulls prepare a grain offering of three-tenths of an ephah of fine flour mixed with oil; with each of the two rams, two-tenths; 15and with each of the fourteen lambs, one-tenth. 16Include one male goat as a sin offering, in addition to the regular burnt offering with its grain offering and drink offering.

17" 'On the second day prepare twelve young bulls, two rams and fourteen male lambs a year old, all without defect. 18With the bulls, rams and lambs, prepare their grain offerings and drink offerings according to the number specified. 19Include one male goat as a sin offering, in addition to the regular burnt offering with its grain offering, and their drink offerings.

20" 'On the third day prepare eleven bulls, two rams and fourteen male lambs a year old, all without defect. 21With the bulls, rams and lambs, prepare their grain offerings and drink offerings according to the number specified. 22Include one male goat as a sin offering, in addition to the regular burnt offering with its grain offering and drink offering.

23" 'On the fourth day prepare ten bulls, two rams and fourteen male lambs a year old, all without defect. 24With the bulls, rams and lambs, prepare their grain offerings and drink offerings according to the number specified. 25Include one male goat as a sin offering, in addition to the regular burnt offering with its grain offering and drink offering.

26" 'On the fifth day prepare nine bulls, two rams and

---

s 3 That is, probably about 6 quarts (about 6.5 liters); also in verses 9 and 14   *t* 3 That is, probably about 4 quarts (about 4.5 liters); also in verses 9 and 14   *u* 4 That is, probably about 2 quarts (about 2 liters); also in verses 10 and 15   *v* 7 Or *must fast*

King James

²⁷And their meat offering and their drink offerings for the bullocks, for the rams, and for the lambs, *shall be* according to their number, after the manner:

²⁸And one goat *for* a sin offering; beside the continual burnt offering, and his meat offering, and his drink offering.

²⁹ ¶ And on the sixth day eight bullocks, two rams, *and* fourteen lambs of the first year without blemish:

³⁰And their meat offering and their drink offerings for the bullocks, for the rams, and for the lambs, *shall be* according to their number, after the manner:

³¹And one goat *for* a sin offering; beside the continual burnt offering, his meat offering, and his drink offering.

³² ¶ And on the seventh day seven bullocks, two rams, *and* fourteen lambs of the first year without blemish:

³³And their meat offering and their drink offerings for the bullocks, for the rams, and for the lambs, *shall be* according to their number, after the manner:

³⁴And one goat *for* a sin offering; beside the continual burnt offering, his meat offering, and his drink offering.

³⁵ ¶ On the eighth day ye shall have a solemn assembly: ye shall do no servile work *therein*:

³⁶But ye shall offer a burnt offering, a sacrifice made by fire, of a sweet savour unto the LORD: one bullock, one ram, seven lambs of the first year without blemish:

³⁷Their meat offering and their drink offerings for the bullock, for the ram, and for the lambs, *shall be* according to their number, after the manner:

³⁸And one goat *for* a sin offering; beside the continual burnt offering, and his meat offering, and his drink offering.

³⁹These *things* ye shall ¹do unto the LORD in your set feasts, beside your vows, and your freewill offerings, for your burnt offerings, and for your meat offerings, and for your drink offerings, and for your peace offerings.

⁴⁰And Moses told the children of Israel according to all that the LORD commanded Moses.

The laws about vows

30 AND MOSES spake unto the heads of the tribes concerning the children of Israel, saying, This *is* the thing which the LORD hath commanded.

²If a man vow a vow unto the LORD, or swear an oath to bind his soul with a bond; he shall not ᵘbreak his word, he shall do according to all that proceedeth out of his mouth.

³If a woman also vow a vow unto the LORD, and bind *herself* by a bond, *being* in her father's house in her youth;

⁴And her father hear her vow, and her bond wherewith she hath bound her soul, and her father shall hold his peace at her: then all her vows shall stand, and every bond wherewith she hath bound her soul shall stand.

⁵But if her father disallow her in the day that he heareth; not any of her vows, or of her bonds wherewith she hath bound her soul, shall stand: and the LORD shall forgive her, because her father disallowed her.

⁶And if she had at all an husband, when ᵛshe vowed, or uttered aught out of her lips, wherewith she bound her soul;

⁷And her husband heard *it,* and held his peace at her in the day that he heard *it:* then her vows shall stand, and her bonds wherewith she bound her soul shall stand.

⁸But if her husband disallowed her on the day that he heard *it;* then he shall make her vow which she vowed, and that which she uttered with her lips, wherewith she bound her soul, of none effect: and the LORD shall forgive her.

Amplified

²⁷And their cereal offering and drink offerings for the bulls, the rams, and the lambs, by number according to the ordinance,

²⁸And one goat for a sin offering, besides the continual burnt offering, and its cereal offering, and its drink offerings.

²⁹And on the sixth day eight bulls, two rams, and fourteen male lambs a year old without blemish,

³⁰And their cereal offering and their drink offerings for the bulls, the rams, and the lambs, by number according to the ordinance,

³¹And one goat for a sin offering, besides the continual burnt offering, its cereal offering, and its drink offerings.

³²And on the seventh day seven bulls, two rams, and fourteen male lambs a year old without blemish,

³³And their cereal and drink offerings for the bulls, the rams, and the lambs, by number according to the ordinance,

³⁴And one male goat for a sin offering, besides the continual burnt offering, and its cereal offering, and its drink offerings.

³⁵On the eighth day you shall have a solemn assembly; you shall do no servile work.

³⁶You shall offer a burnt offering, an offering made by fire, of a sweet *and* pleasing fragrance to the Lord: one bull, one ram, seven male lambs a year old without blemish,

³⁷Their cereal offering and drink offerings for the bull, the ram, and the lambs shall be by number according to the ordinance,

³⁸And one male goat for a sin offering, besides the continual burnt offering, and its cereal offering, and its drink offerings.

³⁹These you shall offer to the Lord at your appointed feasts, besides the offerings you have vowed and your freewill offerings, for your burnt offerings, cereal offerings, drink offerings, and peace offerings.

⁴⁰And Moses told the Israelites all that the Lord commanded him.

30 AND MOSES said to the heads *or* leaders of the tribes of Israel, This is the thing which the Lord has commanded:

²If a man vows a vow to the Lord or swears an oath to bind himself by a pledge, he shall not break *and* profane his word; he shall do according to all that proceeds out of his mouth.

³Also when a woman vows a vow to the Lord and binds herself by a pledge, being in her father's house in her youth,

⁴And her father hears her vow and her pledge with which she has bound herself and he offers no objection, then all her vows shall stand and every pledge with which she has bound herself shall stand.

⁵But if her father refuses to allow her [to carry out her vow] on the day that he hears about it, not any of her vows or of her pledges with which she has bound herself shall stand. And the Lord will forgive her because her father refused to let her [carry out her purpose].

⁶And if she is married to a husband while her vows are upon her or she has bound herself by a rash utterance

⁷And her husband hears of it and holds his peace concerning it on the day that he hears it, then her vows shall stand and her pledge with which she bound herself shall stand.

⁸But if her husband refuses to allow her [to keep her vow or pledge] on the day that he hears of it, then he shall make void *and* annul her vow which is upon her and the rash utterance of her lips by which she bound herself, and the Lord will forgive her.

---

¹Or, *offer*   ᵘHeb. *profane*   ᵛHeb. *her vows* were *upon her*

New American Standard

27 and their grain offering and their drink offerings for the bulls, for the rams and for the lambs, by their number according to the ordinance;

28 and one male goat for a sin offering, besides the continual burnt offering and its grain offering and its drink offering.

29 ¶ 'Then on the sixth day: eight bulls, two rams, fourteen male lambs one year old without defect;

30 and their grain offering and their drink offerings for the bulls, for the rams and for the lambs, by their number according to the ordinance;

31 and one male goat for a sin offering, besides the continual burnt offering, its grain offering and its drink offerings.

32 ¶ 'Then on the seventh day: seven bulls, two rams, fourteen male lambs one year old without defect;

33 and their grain offering and their drink offerings for the bulls, for the rams and for the lambs, by their number according to the ordinance;

34 and one male goat for a sin offering, besides the continual burnt offering, its grain offering and its drink offering.

35 ¶ 'On the eighth day you shall have a solemn assembly; you shall do no laborious work.

36 'But you shall present a burnt offering, an offering by fire, as a soothing aroma to the LORD: one bull, one ram, seven male lambs one year old without defect;

37 their grain offering and their drink offerings for the bull, for the ram and for the lambs, by their number according to the ordinance;

38 and one male goat for a sin offering, besides the continual burnt offering and its grain offering and its drink offering.

39 ¶ 'You shall present these to the LORD at your appointed times, besides your votive offerings and your freewill offerings, for your burnt offerings and for your grain offerings and for your drink offerings and for your peace offerings.' "

40 Moses spoke to the sons of Israel in accordance with all that the LORD had commanded Moses.

The Law of Vows

30 THEN MOSES spoke to the heads of the tribes of the sons of Israel, saying, "This is the word which the LORD has commanded.

2 "If a man makes a vow to the LORD, or takes an oath to bind himself with a binding obligation, he shall not violate his word; he shall do according to all that proceeds out of his mouth.

3 ¶ "Also if a woman makes a vow to the LORD, and binds herself by an obligation in her father's house in her youth,

4 and her father hears her vow and her obligation by which she has bound herself, and her father says nothing to her, then all her vows shall stand and every obligation by which she has bound herself shall stand.

5 "But if her father should forbid her on the day he hears of it, none of her vows or her obligations by which she has bound herself shall stand; and the LORD will forgive her because her father had forbidden her.

6 ¶ "However, if she should marry while under her vows or the rash statement of her lips by which she has bound herself,

7 and her husband hears of it and says nothing to her on the day he hears it, then her vows shall stand and her obligations by which she has bound herself shall stand.

8 "But if on the day her husband hears of it, he forbids her, then he shall annul her vow which she is under and the rash statement of her lips by which she has bound herself; and the LORD will forgive her.

New International

fourteen male lambs a year old, all without defect. 27With the bulls, rams and lambs, prepare their grain offerings and drink offerings according to the number specified. 28Include one male goat as a sin offering, in addition to the regular burnt offering with its grain offering and drink offering.

29" 'On the sixth day prepare eight bulls, two rams and fourteen male lambs a year old, all without defect. 30With the bulls, rams and lambs, prepare their grain offerings and drink offerings according to the number specified. 31Include one male goat as a sin offering, in addition to the regular burnt offering with its grain offering and drink offering.

32" 'On the seventh day prepare seven bulls, two rams and fourteen male lambs a year old, all without defect. 33With the bulls, rams and lambs, prepare their grain offerings and drink offerings according to the number specified. 34Include one male goat as a sin offering, in addition to the regular burnt offering with its grain offering and drink offering.

35" 'On the eighth day hold an assembly and do no regular work. 36Present an offering made by fire as an aroma pleasing to the LORD, a burnt offering of one bull, one ram and seven male lambs a year old, all without defect. 37With the bull, the ram and the lambs, prepare their grain offerings and drink offerings according to the number specified. 38Include one male goat as a sin offering, in addition to the regular burnt offering with its grain offering and drink offering.

39" 'In addition to what you vow and your freewill offerings, prepare these for the LORD at your appointed feasts: your burnt offerings, grain offerings, drink offerings and fellowship offerings.w' "

40Moses told the Israelites all that the LORD commanded him.

Vows

30 MOSES SAID to the heads of the tribes of Israel: "This is what the LORD commands: 2When a man makes a vow to the LORD or takes an oath to obligate himself by a pledge, he must not break his word but must do everything he said.

3"When a young woman still living in her father's house makes a vow to the LORD or obligates herself by a pledge 4and her father hears about her vow or pledge but says nothing to her, then all her vows and every pledge by which she obligated herself will stand. 5But if her father forbids her when he hears about it, none of her vows or the pledges by which she obligated herself will stand; the LORD will release her because her father has forbidden her.

6"If she marries after she makes a vow or after her lips utter a rash promise by which she obligates herself 7and her husband hears about it but says nothing to her, then her vows or the pledges by which she obligated herself will stand. 8But if her husband forbids her when he hears about it, he nullifies the vow that obligates her or the rash promise by which she obligates herself, and the LORD will release her.

King James

Amplified

9But every vow of a widow, and of her that is divorced, wherewith they have bound their souls, shall stand against her.

10And if she vowed in her husband's house, or bound her soul by a bond with an oath;

11And her husband heard *it*, and held his peace at her, *and* disallowed her not: then all her vows shall stand, and every bond wherewith she bound her soul shall stand.

12But if her husband *w*hath utterly made them void on the day he heard *them; then* whatsoever proceeded out of her lips concerning her vows, or concerning the bond of her soul, shall not stand: her husband hath made them void; and the LORD shall forgive her.

13Every vow, and every binding oath to afflict the soul, her husband may establish it, or her husband may make it void.

14But if her husband altogether hold his peace at her from day to day; then he establisheth all her vows, or all her bonds, which *are* upon her: he confirmeth them, because he held his peace at her in the day that he heard *them.*

15But if he shall any ways make them void after that he hath heard *them;* then he shall bear her iniquity.

16These *are* the statutes, which the LORD commanded Moses, between a man and his wife, between the father and his daughter, *being yet* in her youth in her father's house.

The killing of the Midianites

31 AND THE LORD spake unto Moses, saying,
2Avenge the children of Israel of the Midianites: afterward shalt thou be gathered unto thy people.

3And Moses spake unto the people, saying, Arm some of yourselves unto the war, and let them go against the Midianites, and avenge the LORD of Midian.

4*x*Of every tribe a thousand, throughout all the tribes of Israel, shall ye send to the war.

5So there were delivered out of the thousands of Israel, a thousand of *every* tribe, twelve thousand armed for war.

6And Moses sent them to the war, a thousand of *every* tribe, them and Phinehas the son of Eleazar the priest, to the war, with the holy instruments, and the trumpets to blow in his hand.

7And they warred against the Midianites, as the LORD commanded Moses; and they slew all the males.

8And they slew the kings of Midian, beside the rest of them that were slain; *namely,* Evi, and Rekem, and Zur, and Hur, and Reba, five kings of Midian: Balaam also the son of Beor they slew with the sword.

9And the children of Israel took *all* the women of Midian captives, and their little ones, and took the spoil of all their cattle, and all their flocks, and all their goods.

10And they burnt all their cities wherein they dwelt, and all their goodly castles, with fire.

11And they took all the spoil, and all the prey, *both* of men and of beasts.

12And they brought the captives, and the prey, and the spoil, unto Moses, and Eleazar the priest, and unto the congregation of the children of Israel, unto the camp at the plains of Moab, which *are* by Jordan *near* Jericho.

Purification of those who killed

13 ¶ And Moses, and Eleazar the priest, and all the princes of the congregation, went forth to meet them without the camp.

14And Moses was wroth with the officers of the host, *with* the captains over thousands, and captains over hundreds, which came from the *y*battle.

15And Moses said unto them, Have ye saved all the women alive?

9But the vow of a widow or of a divorced woman, with which she has bound herself, shall stand against her.

10And if she vowed in her husband's house or bound herself by a pledge with an oath

11And her husband heard it and did not oppose or prohibit her, then all her vows and every pledge with which she bound herself shall stand.

12But if her husband positively made them void on the day he heard them, then whatever proceeded out of her lips concerning her vows or concerning her pledge of herself shall not stand. Her husband has annulled them, and the Lord will forgive her.

13Every vow and every binding oath to humble *or* afflict herself, her husband may establish it or her husband may annul it.

14But if her husband altogether holds his peace [concerning the matter] with her from day to day, then he establishes *and* confirms all her vows or all her pledges which are upon her. He establishes them because he said nothing to [restrain] her on the day he heard of them.

15But if he shall nullify them after he hears of them, then he shall be responsible for *and* bear her iniquity.

16These are the statutes which the Lord commanded Moses, between a man and his wife, and between a father and his daughter while in her youth in her father's house.

31 THE LORD said to Moses,
2Avenge the Israelites on the Midianites; afterward you shall be gathered to your [departed] people.

3And Moses said to the people, Arm men from among you for the war, that they may go against Midian and execute the Lord's vengeance on Midian [for seducing Israel]. [Num. 25:16–18.]

4From each of the tribes of Israel you shall send 1,000 to the war.

5So there were provided out of the thousands of Israel 1,000 from each tribe, 12,000 armed for war.

6And Moses sent them to the war, 1,000 from each tribe, together with Phinehas son of Eleazar, the priest, with the [sacred] vessels of the sanctuary and the trumpets to blow the alarm in his hand.

7They fought with Midian, as the Lord commanded Moses, and slew every male,

8Including the five kings of Midian: Evi, Rekem, Zur, Hur, and Reba; also Balaam son of Beor they slew with the sword. [Num. 22:31–35; Neh. 13:1, 2.]

9And the Israelites took captive the women of Midian and their little ones, and all their cattle, their flocks, and their goods as booty.

10They burned all the cities in which they dwelt, and all their encampments.

11And they took all the spoil and all the prey, both of man and of beast.

12Then they brought the captives, the prey, and the spoil to Moses and Eleazar the priest and to the congregation of the Israelites at the camp on the plains of Moab by Jordan at Jericho.

13Moses and Eleazar the priest and all the princes *or* leaders of the congregation went to meet them outside the camp.

14But Moses was angry with the officers of the army, the commanders of thousands and of hundreds, who served in the war.

15And Moses said to them, Have you let all the women live?

---

*w*Heb. *making void hath made them void*   *x*Heb. *A thousand of a tribe, a thousand of a tribe*   *y*Heb. *host of war*

New American Standard

9 ¶ "But the vow of a widow or of a divorced woman, everything by which she has bound herself, shall stand against her.

10"However, if she vowed in her husband's house, or bound herself by an obligation with an oath,

11 and her husband heard *it,* but said nothing to her *and* did not forbid her, then all her vows shall stand and every obligation by which she bound herself shall stand.

12"But if her husband indeed annuls them on the day he hears *them,* then whatever proceeds out of her lips concerning her vows or concerning the obligation of herself shall not stand; her husband has annulled them, and the LORD will forgive her.

13 ¶ "Every vow and every binding oath to humble herself, her husband may confirm it or her husband may annul it.

14"But if her husband indeed says nothing to her from day to day, then he confirms all her vows or all her obligations which are on her; he has confirmed them, because he said nothing to her on the day he heard them.

15"But if he indeed annuls them after he has heard them, then he shall bear her guilt."

16 ¶ These are the statutes which the LORD commanded Moses, *as* between a man and his wife, *and as* between a father and his daughter, *while she is* in her youth in her father's house.

The Slaughter of Midian

31 THEN THE LORD spoke to Moses, saying, 2"Take full vengeance for the sons of Israel on the Midianites; afterward you will be gathered to your people."

3 Moses spoke to the people, saying, "Arm men from among you for the war, that they may go against Midian to execute the LORD'S vengeance on Midian.

4"A thousand from each tribe of all the tribes of Israel you shall send to the war."

5 So there were furnished from the thousands of Israel, a thousand from each tribe, twelve thousand armed for war.

6 Moses sent them, a thousand from each tribe, to the war, and Phinehas the son of Eleazar the priest, to the war with them, and the holy vessels and the trumpets for the alarm in his hand.

7 So they made war against Midian, just as the LORD had commanded Moses, and they killed every male.

8 They killed the kings of Midian along with the *rest of* their slain: Evi and Rekem and Zur and Hur and Reba, the five kings of Midian; they also killed Balaam the son of Beor with the sword.

9 The sons of Israel captured the women of Midian and their little ones; and all their cattle and all their flocks and all their goods they plundered.

10 Then they burned all their cities where they lived and all their camps with fire.

11 They took all the spoil and all the prey, both of man and of beast.

12 They brought the captives and the prey and the spoil to Moses, and to Eleazar the priest and to the congregation of the sons of Israel, to the camp at the plains of Moab, which are by the Jordan *opposite* Jericho.

13 ¶ Moses and Eleazar the priest and all the leaders of the congregation went out to meet them outside the camp.

14 Moses was angry with the officers of the army, the captains of thousands and the captains of hundreds, who had come from service in the war.

15 And Moses said to them, "Have you spared all the women?

New International

9"Any vow or obligation taken by a widow or divorced woman will be binding on her.

10"If a woman living with her husband makes a vow or obligates herself by a pledge under oath 11and her husband hears about it but says nothing to her and does not forbid her, then all her vows or the pledges by which she obligated herself will stand. 12But if her husband nullifies them when he hears about them, then none of the vows or pledges that came from her lips will stand. Her husband has nullified them, and the LORD will release her. 13Her husband may confirm or nullify any vow she makes or any sworn pledge to deny herself. 14But if her husband says nothing to her about it from day to day, then he confirms all her vows or the pledges binding on her. He confirms them by saying nothing to her when he hears about them. 15If, however, he nullifies them some time after he hears about them, then he is responsible for her guilt."

16These are the regulations the LORD gave Moses concerning relationships between a man and his wife, and between a father and his young daughter still living in his house.

Vengeance on the Midianites

31 THE LORD said to Moses, 2"Take vengeance on the Midianites for the Israelites. After that, you will be gathered to your people."

3So Moses said to the people, "Arm some of your men to go to war against the Midianites and to carry out the LORD's vengeance on them. 4Send into battle a thousand men from each of the tribes of Israel." 5So twelve thousand men armed for battle, a thousand from each tribe, were supplied from the clans of Israel. 6Moses sent them into battle, a thousand from each tribe, along with Phinehas son of Eleazar, the priest, who took with him articles from the sanctuary and the trumpets for signaling.

7They fought against Midian, as the LORD commanded Moses, and killed every man. 8Among their victims were Evi, Rekem, Zur, Hur and Reba—the five kings of Midian. They also killed Balaam son of Beor with the sword. 9The Israelites captured the Midianite women and children and took all the Midianite herds, flocks and goods as plunder. 10They burned all the towns where the Midianites had settled, as well as all their camps. 11They took all the plunder and spoils, including the people and animals, 12and brought the captives, spoils and plunder to Moses and Eleazar the priest and the Israelite assembly at their camp on the plains of Moab, by the Jordan across from Jericho.*x*

13Moses, Eleazar the priest and all the leaders of the community went to meet them outside the camp. 14Moses was angry with the officers of the army—the commanders of thousands and commanders of hundreds—who returned from the battle.

15"Have you allowed all the women to live?" he asked

---

x 12 Hebrew *Jordan of Jericho;* possibly an ancient name for the Jordan River

King James

16Behold, these caused the children of Israel, through the counsel of Balaam, to commit trespass against the LORD in the matter of Peor, and there was a plague among the congregation of the LORD.

17Now therefore kill every male among the little ones, and kill every woman that hath known man by lying with zhim.

18But all the women children, that have not known a man by lying with him, keep alive for yourselves.

19And do ye abide without the camp seven days: whosoever hath killed any person, and whosoever hath touched any slain, purify *both* yourselves and your captives on the third day, and on the seventh day.

20And purify all *your* raiment, and all athat is made of skins, and all work of goats' *hair,* and all things made of wood.

21 ¶ And Eleazar the priest said unto the men of war which went to the battle, This *is* the ordinance of the law which the LORD commanded Moses;

22Only the gold, and the silver, the brass, the iron, the tin, and the lead,

23Every thing that may abide the fire, ye shall make *it* go through the fire, and it shall be clean: nevertheless it shall be purified with the water of separation: and all that abideth not the fire ye shall make go through the water.

24And ye shall wash your clothes on the seventh day, and ye shall be clean, and afterward ye shall come into the camp.

The division of the prey

25 ¶ And the LORD spake unto Moses, saying,

26Take the sum of the prey bthat was taken, *both* of man and of beast, thou, and Eleazar the priest, and the chief fathers of the congregation:

27And divide the prey into two parts; between them that took the war upon them, who went out to battle, and between all the congregation:

28And levy a tribute unto the LORD of the men of war which went out to battle: one soul of five hundred, *both* of the persons, and of the beeves, and of the asses, and of the sheep:

29Take *it* of their half, and give *it* unto Eleazar the priest, *for* an heave offering of the LORD.

30And of the children of Israel's half, thou shalt take one portion of fifty, of the persons, of the beeves, of the asses, and of the cflocks, of all manner of beasts, and give them unto the Levites, which keep the charge of the tabernacle of the LORD.

31And Moses and Eleazar the priest did as the LORD commanded Moses.

32And the booty, *being* the rest of the prey which the men of war had caught, was six hundred thousand and seventy thousand and five thousand sheep,

33And threescore and twelve thousand beeves,

34And threescore and one thousand asses,

35And thirty and two thousand persons in all, of women that had not known man by lying with him.

36And the half, *which was* the portion of them that went out to war, was in number three hundred thousand and seven and thirty thousand and five hundred sheep:

37And the LORD's tribute of the sheep was six hundred and threescore and fifteen.

38And the beeves *were* thirty and six thousand; of which the LORD's tribute *was* threescore and twelve.

39And the asses *were* thirty thousand and five hundred; of which the LORD's tribute *was* threescore and one.

40And the persons *were* sixteen thousand; of which the LORD's tribute *was* thirty and two persons.

41And Moses gave the tribute, *which was* the LORD's heave offering, unto Eleazar the priest, as the LORD commanded Moses.

Amplified

16Behold, these caused the Israelites by the counsel of Balaam to trespass *and* act treacherously against the Lord in the matter of Peor, and so a [smiting] plague came among the congregation of the Lord. [Num. 25:1–9; 31:8.]

17Now therefore, kill every male among the little ones, and kill every woman who is not a virgin.

18But all the young girls who have not known man by lying with him keep alive for yourselves.

19Encamp outside the camp seven days; whoever has killed any person and whoever has touched any slain, purify yourselves and your captives on the third day and on the seventh day.

20You shall purify every garment, all that is made of skins, all work of goats' hair, and every article of wood.

21And Eleazar the priest said to the men of war who had gone to battle, This is the statute of the law which the Lord has commanded Moses:

22Only the gold, the silver, the bronze, the iron, the tin, and the lead,

23Everything that can stand fire, you shall make go through fire, and it shall be clean. Nevertheless it shall also be purified with the water of impurity; and all that cannot stand fire [such as fabrics] you shall pass through water.

24And you shall wash your clothes on the seventh day and you shall be clean; then you shall come into the camp.

25And the Lord said to Moses,

26Take the count of the prey that was taken, both of man and of beast, you and Eleazar the priest and the heads of the fathers' houses of the congregation.

27Divide the booty into two [equal] parts between the warriors who went out to battle and all the congregation.

28And levy a tribute to the Lord from the warriors who went to battle, one out of every 500 of the persons, the oxen, the donkeys, and the flocks.

29Take [this tribute] from the warriors' half and give it to Eleazar the priest as an offering to the Lord.

30And from the Israelites' half [of the booty] you shall take one out of every fifty of the persons, the oxen, the donkeys, the flocks, and of all livestock, and give them to the Levites who have charge of the tabernacle of the Lord.

31And Moses and Eleazar the priest did as the Lord commanded Moses.

32The prey, besides the booty which the men of war took, was 675,000 sheep,

33And 72,000 cattle,

34And 61,000 donkeys,

35And 32,000 persons in all, of the women who were virgins.

36And the half share, the portion of those who went to war, was: 337,500 sheep,

37And the Lord's tribute of the sheep was 675;

38The cattle were 36,000, of which the Lord's tribute was 72;

39The donkeys were 30,500, of which the Lord's tribute was 61;

40The persons were 16,000, of whom the Lord's tribute was 32 persons.

41And Moses gave the tribute which was the Lord's offering to Eleazar the priest, as the Lord commanded Moses.

---

zHeb. *a male of the captivity*   aHeb. *instrument,* or, *vessel of skins*   cOr, *goats*   bHeb.

New American Standard

16"Behold, these caused the sons of Israel, through the counsel of Balaam, to trespass against the LORD in the matter of Peor, so the plague was among the congregation of the LORD.

17"Now therefore, kill every male among the little ones, and kill every woman who has known man intimately.

18"But all the girls who have not known man intimately, spare for yourselves.

19"And you, camp outside the camp seven days; whoever has killed any person and whoever has touched any slain, purify yourselves, you and your captives, on the third day and on the seventh day.

20"You shall purify for yourselves every garment and every article of leather and all the work of goats' *hair,* and all articles of wood."

21 ¶ Then Eleazar the priest said to the men of war who had gone to battle, "This is the statute of the law which the LORD has commanded Moses:

22 only the gold and the silver, the bronze, the iron, the tin and the lead,

23 everything that can stand the fire, you shall pass through the fire, and it shall be clean, but it shall be purified with water for impurity. But whatever cannot stand the fire you shall pass through the water.

24"And you shall wash your clothes on the seventh day and be clean, and afterward you may enter the camp."

Division of the Booty

25 ¶ Then the LORD spoke to Moses, saying,

26"You and Eleazar the priest and the heads of the fathers' *households* of the congregation take a count of the booty that was captured, both of man and of animal;

27 and divide the booty between the warriors who went out to battle and all the congregation.

28"Levy a tax for the LORD from the men of war who went out to battle, one in five hundred of the persons and of the cattle and of the donkeys and of the sheep;

29 take it from their half and give it to Eleazar the priest, as an offering to the LORD.

30"From the sons of Israel's half, you shall take one drawn out of every fifty of the persons, of the cattle, of the donkeys and of the sheep, from all the animals, and give them to the Levites who keep charge of the tabernacle of the LORD."

31 Moses and Eleazar the priest did just as the LORD had commanded Moses.

32 ¶ Now the booty that remained from the spoil which the men of war had plundered was 675,000 sheep,

33 and 72,000 cattle,

34 and 61,000 donkeys,

35 and of human beings, of the women who had not known man intimately, all the persons were 32,000.

36 ¶ The half, the portion of those who went out to war, was *as follows:* the number of sheep was 337,500,

37 and the LORD'S levy of the sheep was 675;

38 and the cattle were 36,000, from which the LORD'S levy was 72;

39 and the donkeys were 30,500, from which the LORD'S levy was 61;

40 and the human beings were 16,000, from whom the LORD'S levy was 32 persons.

41 Moses gave the levy *which was* the LORD'S offering to Eleazar the priest, just as the LORD had commanded Moses.

New International

them. 16"They were the ones who followed Balaam's advice and were the means of turning the Israelites away from the LORD in what happened at Peor, so that a plague struck the LORD'S people. 17Now kill all the boys. And kill every woman who has slept with a man, 18but save for yourselves every girl who has never slept with a man.

19"All of you who have killed anyone or touched anyone who was killed must stay outside the camp seven days. On the third and seventh days you must purify yourselves and your captives. 20Purify every garment as well as everything made of leather, goat hair or wood."

21Then Eleazar the priest said to the soldiers who had gone into battle, "This is the requirement of the law that the LORD gave Moses: 22Gold, silver, bronze, iron, tin, lead 23and anything else that can withstand fire must be put through the fire, and then it will be clean. But it must also be purified with the water of cleansing. And whatever cannot withstand fire must be put through that water. 24On the seventh day wash your clothes and you will be clean. Then you may come into the camp."

Dividing the Spoils

25The LORD said to Moses, 26"You and Eleazar the priest and the family heads of the community are to count all the people and animals that were captured. 27Divide the spoils between the soldiers who took part in the battle and the rest of the community. 28From the soldiers who fought in the battle, set apart as tribute for the LORD one out of every five hundred, whether persons, cattle, donkeys, sheep or goats. 29Take this tribute from their half share and give it to Eleazar the priest as the LORD'S part. 30From the Israelites' half, select one out of every fifty, whether persons, cattle, donkeys, sheep, goats or other animals. Give them to the Levites, who are responsible for the care of the LORD'S tabernacle." 31So Moses and Eleazar the priest did as the LORD commanded Moses.

32The plunder remaining from the spoils that the soldiers took was 675,000 sheep, 3372,000 cattle, 3461,000 donkeys 35and 32,000 women who had never slept with a man.

36The half share of those who fought in the battle was:

337,500 sheep, 37of which the tribute for the LORD was 675;

3836,000 cattle, of which the tribute for the LORD was 72;

3930,500 donkeys, of which the tribute for the LORD was 61;

4016,000 people, of which the tribute for the LORD was 32.

41Moses gave the tribute to Eleazar the priest as the LORD'S part, as the LORD commanded Moses.

King James

42And of the children of Israel's half, which Moses divided from the men that warred,

43(Now the half *that pertained unto* the congregation was three hundred thousand and thirty thousand *and* seven thousand and five hundred sheep,

44And thirty and six thousand beeves,

45And thirty thousand asses and five hundred,

46And sixteen thousand persons;)

47Even of the children of Israel's half, Moses took one portion of fifty, *both* of man and of beast, and gave them unto the Levites, which kept the charge of the tabernacle of the LORD; as the LORD commanded Moses.

48 ¶ And the officers which *were* over thousands of the host, the captains of thousands, and captains of hundreds, came near unto Moses:

49And they said unto Moses, Thy servants have taken the sum of the men of war which *are* under our dcharge, and there lacketh not one man of us.

50We have therefore brought an oblation for the LORD, what every man hath egotten, of jewels of gold, chains, and bracelets, rings, earrings, and tablets, to make an atonement for our souls before the LORD.

51And Moses and Eleazar the priest took the gold of them, *even* all wrought jewels.

52And all the gold of the foffering that they offered up to the LORD, of the captains of thousands, and of the captains of hundreds, was sixteen thousand seven hundred and fifty shekels.

53(For the men of war had taken spoil, every man for himself.)

54And Moses and Eleazar the priest took the gold of the captains of thousands and of hundreds, and brought it into the tabernacle of the congregation, *for* a memorial to the children of Israel before the LORD.

Tribes to possess Gilead

32 NOW THE children of Reuben and the children of Gad had a very great multitude of cattle: and when they saw the land of Jazer, and the land of Gilead, that, behold, the place *was* a place for cattle;

2The children of Gad and the children of Reuben came and spake unto Moses, and to Eleazar the priest, and unto the princes of the congregation, saying,

3Ataroth, and Dibon, and Jazer, and Nimrah, and Heshbon, and Elealeh, and Shebam, and Nebo, and Beon,

4*Even* the country which the LORD smote before the congregation of Israel, *is* a land for cattle, and thy servants have cattle:

5Wherefore, said they, if we have found grace in thy sight, let this land be given unto thy servants for a possession, *and* bring us not over Jordan.

6 ¶ And Moses said unto the children of Gad and to the children of Reuben, Shall your brethren go to war, and shall ye sit here?

7And wherefore gdiscourage ye the heart of the children of Israel from going over into the land which the LORD hath given them?

8Thus did your fathers, when I sent them from Kadeshbarnea to see the land.

9For when they went up unto the valley of Eshcol, and saw the land, they discouraged the heart of the children of Israel, that they should not go into the land which the LORD had given them.

10And the LORD'S anger was kindled the same time, and he sware, saying,

11Surely none of the men that came up out of Egypt, from twenty years old and upward, shall see the land which I sware unto Abraham, unto Isaac, and unto Jacob; because they have not hwholly followed me:

Amplified

42And the Israelites' half Moses separated from that of the warriors'—

43Now the congregation's half was 337,500 sheep,

44And 36,000 cattle,

45And 30,500 donkeys,

46And 16,000 persons—

47Even of the Israelites' half, Moses took one of every 50, both of persons and of beasts, and gave them to the Levites, who had charge of the tabernacle of the Lord, as the Lord commanded Moses.

48And the officers who were over the thousands of the army, the commanders of thousands and hundreds, came to Moses.

49They told [him], Your servants have counted the warriors under our command, and not one man of us is missing.

50We have brought as the Lord's offering what each man obtained—articles of gold, armlets, bracelets, signet rings, earrings, neck ornaments—to make atonement for ourselves before the Lord.

51Moses and Eleazar the priest took the gold from them, all the wrought articles.

52And all the gold of the offering that they offered to the Lord from the commanders of thousands and of hundreds was 16,750 shekels.

53For the men of war had taken booty, every man for himself.

54And Moses and Eleazar the priest received the gold from the commanders of thousands and of hundreds and brought it into the Tent of Meeting as a memorial for the Israelites before the Lord.

32 NOW THE sons of Reuben and of Gad had a very great multitude of cattle, and they saw the land of Jazer and the land of Gilead [on the east side of the Jordan], and behold, the place was suitable for cattle.

2So the sons of Gad and of Reuben came and said to Moses, Eleazar the priest, and the leaders of the congregation,

3[The country around] Ataroth, Dibon, Jazer, Nimrah, Heshbon, Elealeh, Sebam, Nebo, and Beon,

4The land the Lord smote before the congregation of Israel, is a land for cattle, and your servants have cattle.

5And they said, If we have found favor in your sight, let this land be given to your servants for a possession. Do not take us over the Jordan.

6And Moses said to the sons of Gad and of Reuben, Shall your brethren go to war while you sit here?

7Why do you discourage the hearts of the Israelites from going over into the land which the Lord has given them?

8Thus your fathers did when I sent them from Kadeshbarnea to see the land!

9For when they went up to the Valley of Eshcol and saw the land, they discouraged the hearts of the Israelites from going into the land the Lord had given them.

10And the Lord's anger was kindled on that day and He swore, saying,

11Surely none of the men who came up out of Egypt, from twenty years old and upward, shall see the land which I swore to Abraham, to Isaac, and to Jacob, because they have not wholly followed Me—

---

dHeb. *hand*   eHeb. *found*   fHeb. *heave offering*   gHeb. *break*   hHeb. *fulfilled after me*

New American Standard

42 ¶ As for the sons of Israel's half, which Moses separated from the men who had gone to war—

43 now the congregation's half was 337,500 sheep,

44 and 36,000 cattle,

45 and 30,500 donkeys,

46 and the human beings were 16,000—

47 and from the sons of Israel's half, Moses took one drawn out of every fifty, both of man and of animals, and gave them to the Levites, who kept charge of the tabernacle of the LORD, just as the LORD had commanded Moses.

48 ¶ Then the officers who were over the thousands of the army, the captains of thousands and the captains of hundreds, approached Moses,

49 and they said to Moses, "Your servants have taken a census of men of war who are in our charge, and no man of us is missing.

50 "So we have brought as an offering to the LORD what each man found, articles of gold, armlets and bracelets, signet rings, earrings and necklaces, to make atonement for ourselves before the LORD."

51 Moses and Eleazar the priest took the gold from them, all kinds of wrought articles.

52 All the gold of the offering which they offered up to the LORD, from the captains of thousands and the captains of hundreds, was 16,750 shekels.

53 The men of war had taken booty, every man for himself.

54 So Moses and Eleazar the priest took the gold from the captains of thousands and of hundreds, and brought it to the tent of meeting as a memorial for the sons of Israel before the LORD.

Reuben and Gad Settle in Gilead

32 NOW THE sons of Reuben and the sons of Gad had an exceedingly large number of livestock. So when they saw the land of Jazer and the land of Gilead, that it was indeed a place suitable for livestock,

2 the sons of Gad and the sons of Reuben came and spoke to Moses and to Eleazar the priest and to the leaders of the congregation, saying,

3 "Ataroth, Dibon, Jazer, Nimrah, Heshbon, Elealeh, Sebam, Nebo and Beon,

4 the land which the LORD conquered before the congregation of Israel, is a land for livestock, and your servants have livestock.

5 They said, "If we have found favor in your sight, let this land be given to your servants as a possession; do not take us across the Jordan."

6 ¶ But Moses said to the sons of Gad and to the sons of Reuben, "Shall your brothers go to war while you yourselves sit here?

7 "Now why are you discouraging the sons of Israel from crossing over into the land which the LORD has given them?

8 "This is what your fathers did when I sent them from Kadesh-barnea to see the land.

9 "For when they went up to the valley of Eshcol and saw the land, they discouraged the sons of Israel so that they did not go into the land which the LORD had given them.

10 "So the LORD's anger burned in that day, and He swore, saying,

11 'None of the men who came up from Egypt, from twenty years old and upward, shall see the land which I swore to Abraham, to Isaac and to Jacob; for they did not follow Me fully,

New International

42 The half belonging to the Israelites, which Moses set apart from that of the fighting men— 43 the community's half—was 337,500 sheep, 44 36,000 cattle, 45 30,500 donkeys 46 and 16,000 people. 47 From the Israelites' half, Moses selected one out of every fifty persons and animals, as the LORD commanded him, and gave them to the Levites, who were responsible for the care of the LORD's tabernacle.

48 Then the officers who were over the units of the army—the commanders of thousands and commanders of hundreds—went to Moses 49 and said to him, "Your servants have counted the soldiers under our command, and not one is missing. 50 So we have brought as an offering to the LORD the gold articles each of us acquired—armlets, bracelets, signet rings, earrings and necklaces—to make atonement for ourselves before the LORD."

51 Moses and Eleazar the priest accepted from them the gold—all the crafted articles. 52 All the gold from the commanders of thousands and commanders of hundreds that Moses and Eleazar presented as a gift to the LORD weighed 16,750 shekels.[y] 53 Each soldier had taken plunder for himself. 54 Moses and Eleazar the priest accepted the gold from the commanders of thousands and commanders of hundreds and brought it into the Tent of Meeting as a memorial for the Israelites before the LORD.

The Transjordan Tribes

32 THE REUBENITES and Gadites, who had very large herds and flocks, saw that the lands of Jazer and Gilead were suitable for livestock. 2 So they came to Moses and Eleazar the priest and to the leaders of the community, and said, 3 "Ataroth, Dibon, Jazer, Nimrah, Heshbon, Elealeh, Sebam, Nebo and Beon— 4 the land the LORD subdued before the people of Israel—are suitable for livestock, and your servants have livestock. 5 If we have found favor in your eyes," they said, "let this land be given to your servants as our possession. Do not make us cross the Jordan."

6 Moses said to the Gadites and Reubenites, "Shall your countrymen go to war while you sit here? 7 Why do you discourage the Israelites from going over into the land the LORD has given them? 8 This is what your fathers did when I sent them from Kadesh Barnea to look over the land. 9 After they went up to the Valley of Eshcol and viewed the land, they discouraged the Israelites from entering the land the LORD had given them. 10 The LORD's anger was aroused that day and he swore this oath: 11 'Because they have not followed me wholeheartedly, not one of the men twenty years old or more who came up out of Egypt will see the land I promised on oath to Abraham, Isaac and

y 52 That is, about 420 pounds (about 190 kilograms)

King James

¹²Save Caleb the son of Jephunneh the Kenezite, and Joshua the son of Nun: for they have wholly followed the LORD.

¹³And the LORD's anger was kindled against Israel, and he made them wander in the wilderness forty years, until all the generation, that had done evil in the sight of the LORD, was consumed.

¹⁴And, behold, ye are risen up in your fathers' stead, an increase of sinful men, to augment yet the fierce anger of the LORD toward Israel.

¹⁵For if ye turn away from after him, he will yet again leave them in the wilderness; and ye shall destroy all this people.

¹⁶ ¶ And they came near unto him, and said, We will build sheepfolds here for our cattle, and cities for our little ones:

¹⁷But we ourselves will go ready armed before the children of Israel, until we have brought them unto their place: and our little ones shall dwell in the fenced cities because of the inhabitants of the land.

¹⁸We will not return unto our houses, until the children of Israel have inherited every man his inheritance.

¹⁹For we will not inherit with them on yonder side Jordan, or forward; because our inheritance is fallen to us on this side Jordan eastward.

²⁰ ¶ And Moses said unto them, If ye will do this thing, if ye will go armed before the LORD to war,

²¹And will go all of you armed over Jordan before the LORD, until he hath driven out his enemies from before him,

²²And the land be subdued before the LORD: then afterward ye shall return, and be guiltless before the LORD, and before Israel; and this land shall be your possession before the LORD.

²³But if ye will not do so, behold, ye have sinned against the LORD: and be sure your sin will find you out.

²⁴Build you cities for your little ones, and folds for your sheep; and do that which hath proceeded out of your mouth.

²⁵And the children of Gad and the children of Reuben spake unto Moses, saying, Thy servants will do as my lord commandeth.

²⁶Our little ones, our wives, our flocks, and all our cattle, shall be there in the cities of Gilead:

²⁷But thy servants will pass over, every man armed for war, before the LORD to battle, as my lord saith.

²⁸So concerning them Moses commanded Eleazar the priest, and Joshua the son of Nun, and the chief fathers of the tribes of the children of Israel:

²⁹And Moses said unto them, If the children of Gad and the children of Reuben will pass with you over Jordan, every man armed to battle, before the LORD, and the land shall be subdued before you; then ye shall give them the land of Gilead for a possession:

³⁰But if they will not pass over with you armed, they shall have possessions among you in the land of Canaan.

³¹And the children of Gad and the children of Reuben answered, saying, As the LORD hath said unto thy servants, so will we do.

³²We will pass over armed before the LORD into the land of Canaan, that the possession of our inheritance on this side Jordan *may be* ours.

³³And Moses gave unto them, *even* to the children of Gad, and to the children of Reuben, and unto half the tribe of Manasseh the son of Joseph, the kingdom of Sihon king of the Amorites, and the kingdom of Og king of Bashan, the land, with the cities thereof in the coasts, *even* the cities of the country round about.

³⁴ ¶ And the children of Gad built Dibon, and Ataroth, and Aroer,

³⁵And Atroth, Shophan, and Jaazer, and Jogbehah,

Amplified

¹²Except Caleb son of Jephunneh the Kenizzite and Joshua son of Nun, for they have wholly followed the Lord.

¹³And the Lord's anger was kindled against Israel and He made them wander in the wilderness for forty years, until all the generation that had done evil in the sight of the Lord was consumed.

¹⁴And behold, you are risen up in your fathers' stead, a brood of sinful men, to increase still more the fierce anger of the Lord against Israel.

¹⁵For if you turn from following Him, He will again abandon them in the wilderness, and you will destroy all this people.

¹⁶But they came near to him and said, We will build sheepfolds here for our flocks and walled settlements for our little ones.

¹⁷But we will be armed and ready to go before the Israelites until we have brought them to their place. Our little ones shall dwell in the fortified settlements because of the people of the land.

¹⁸We will not return to our homes until the Israelites have inherited every man his inheritance.

¹⁹For we will not inherit with them on the [west] side of the Jordan and beyond, because our inheritance is fallen to us on this side of the Jordan eastward.

²⁰Moses replied, If you will do as you say, going armed before the Lord to war,

²¹And every armed man of you will pass over the Jordan before the Lord until He has driven out His enemies before Him

²²And the land is subdued before the Lord, then afterward you shall return and be guiltless [in this matter] before the Lord and before Israel, and this land shall be your possession before the Lord.

²³But if you will not do so, behold, you have sinned against the Lord; and be sure your sin will find you out.

²⁴Build settlements for your little ones, and folds for your sheep, and do that of which you have spoken.

²⁵And the sons of Gad and of Reuben said to Moses, Your servants will do as my lord commands.

²⁶Our little ones, our wives, our flocks, and all our cattle shall be there in the cities of Gilead.

²⁷But your servants will pass over, every man armed for war, before the Lord to battle, as my lord says.

²⁸So Moses gave command concerning them to Eleazar the priest and Joshua son of Nun and the heads of the fathers' houses of the tribes of Israel.

²⁹And Moses said to them, If the sons of Gad and Reuben will pass with you over the Jordan, every man armed to battle before the Lord, and the land shall be subdued before you, then you shall give them the land of Gilead for a possession.

³⁰But if they will not pass over with you armed, they shall have possessions among you in the land of Canaan.

³¹The sons of Gad and Reuben answered, As the Lord has said to your servants, so will we do.

³²We will pass over armed before the Lord into the land of Canaan, that the possession of our inheritance on this side of the Jordan may be ours.

³³Moses gave to them, to the sons of Gad and of Reuben and to half the tribe of Manasseh son of Joseph, the kingdom of Sihon king of the Amorites and the kingdom of Og king of Bashan—the land with its cities and their territories, even the cities round about the country.

³⁴And the sons of Gad built Dibon, Ataroth, Aroer,

³⁵Atroth-shophan, Jazer, Jogbehah,

New American Standard

12 except Caleb the son of Jephunneh the Kenizzite and Joshua the son of Nun, for they have followed the LORD fully.'

13 "So the LORD's anger burned against Israel, and He made them wander in the wilderness forty years, until the entire generation of those who had done evil in the sight of the LORD was destroyed.

14 "Now behold, you have risen up in your fathers' place, a brood of sinful men, to add still more to the burning anger of the LORD against Israel.

15 "For if you turn away from following Him, He will once more abandon them in the wilderness, and you will destroy all these people."

16 ¶ Then they came near to him and said, "We will build here sheepfolds for our livestock and cities for our little ones;

17 but we ourselves will be armed ready *to go* before the sons of Israel, until we have brought them to their place, while our little ones live in the fortified cities because of the inhabitants of the land.

18 "We will not return to our homes until every one of the sons of Israel has possessed his inheritance.

19 "For we will not have an inheritance with them on the other side of the Jordan and beyond, because our inheritance has fallen to us on this side of the Jordan toward the east."

20 ¶ So Moses said to them, "If you will do this, if you will arm yourselves before the LORD for the war,

21 and all of you armed men cross over the Jordan before the LORD until He has driven His enemies out from before Him,

22 and the land is subdued before the LORD, then afterward you shall return and be free of obligation toward the LORD and toward Israel, and this land shall be yours for a possession before the LORD.

23 "But if you will not do so, behold, you have sinned against the LORD, and be sure your sin will find you out.

24 "Build yourselves cities for your little ones, and sheepfolds for your sheep, and do what you have promised."

25 ¶ The sons of Gad and the sons of Reuben spoke to Moses, saying, "Your servants will do just as my lord commands.

26 "Our little ones, our wives, our livestock and all our cattle shall remain there in the cities of Gilead;

27 while your servants, everyone who is armed for war, will cross over in the presence of the LORD to battle, just as my lord says."

28 ¶ So Moses gave command concerning them to Eleazar the priest, and to Joshua the son of Nun, and to the heads of the fathers' *households* of the tribes of the sons of Israel.

29 Moses said to them, "If the sons of Gad and the sons of Reuben, everyone who is armed for battle, will cross with you over the Jordan in the presence of the LORD, and the land is subdued before you, then you shall give them the land of Gilead for a possession;

30 but if they will not cross over with you armed, they shall have possessions among you in the land of Canaan."

31 The sons of Gad and the sons of Reuben answered, saying, "As the LORD has said to your servants, so we will do.

32 "We ourselves will cross over armed in the presence of the LORD into the land of Canaan, and the possession of our inheritance *shall remain* with us across the Jordan."

33 ¶ So Moses gave to them, to the sons of Gad and to the sons of Reuben and to the half-tribe of Joseph's son Manasseh, the kingdom of Sihon, king of the Amorites and the kingdom of Og, the king of Bashan, the land with its cities with *their* territories, the cities of the surrounding land.

34 The sons of Gad built Dibon and Ataroth and Aroer,

35 and Atroth-shophan and Jazer and Jogbehah,

New International

Jacob— 12 not one except Caleb son of Jephunneh the Kenizzite and Joshua son of Nun, for they followed the LORD wholeheartedly.' 13 The LORD's anger burned against Israel and he made them wander in the desert forty years, until the whole generation of those who had done evil in his sight was gone.

14 "And here you are, a brood of sinners, standing in the place of your fathers and making the LORD even more angry with Israel. 15 If you turn away from following him, he will again leave all this people in the desert, and you will be the cause of their destruction."

16 Then they came up to him and said, "We would like to build pens here for our livestock and cities for our women and children. 17 But we are ready to arm ourselves and go ahead of the Israelites until we have brought them to their place. Meanwhile our women and children will live in fortified cities, for protection from the inhabitants of the land. 18 We will not return to our homes until every Israelite has received his inheritance. 19 We will not receive any inheritance with them on the other side of the Jordan, because our inheritance has come to us on the east side of the Jordan."

20 Then Moses said to them, "If you will do this—if you will arm yourselves before the LORD for battle, 21 and if all of you will go armed over the Jordan before the LORD until he has driven his enemies out before him— 22 then when the land is subdued before the LORD, you may return and be free from your obligation to the LORD and to Israel. And this land will be your possession before the LORD.

23 "But if you fail to do this, you will be sinning against the LORD; and you may be sure that your sin will find you out. 24 Build cities for your women and children, and pens for your flocks, but do what you have promised."

25 The Gadites and Reubenites said to Moses, "We your servants will do as our lord commands. 26 Our children and wives, our flocks and herds will remain here in the cities of Gilead. 27 But your servants, every man armed for battle, will cross over to fight before the LORD, just as our lord says."

28 Then Moses gave orders about them to Eleazar the priest and Joshua son of Nun and to the family heads of the Israelite tribes. 29 He said to them, "If the Gadites and Reubenites, every man armed for battle, cross over the Jordan with you before the LORD, then when the land is subdued before you, give them the land of Gilead as their possession. 30 But if they do not cross over with you armed, they must accept their possession with you in Canaan."

31 The Gadites and Reubenites answered, "Your servants will do what the LORD has said. 32 We will cross over before the LORD into Canaan armed, but the property we inherit will be on this side of the Jordan."

33 Then Moses gave to the Gadites, the Reubenites and the half-tribe of Manasseh son of Joseph the kingdom of Sihon king of the Amorites and the kingdom of Og king of Bashan—the whole land with its cities and the territory around them.

34 The Gadites built up Dibon, Ataroth, Aroer, 35 Atroth

King James

³⁶And Beth-nimrah, and Beth-haran, fenced cities: and folds for sheep.

³⁷And the children of Reuben built Heshbon, and Elealeh, and Kirjathaim,

³⁸And Nebo and Baal-meon, (their names being changed,) and Shibmah: and ⁱgave other names unto the cities which they builded.

³⁹And the children of Machir the son of Manasseh went to Gilead, and took it, and dispossessed the Amorite which *was* in it.

⁴⁰And Moses gave Gilead unto Machir the son of Manasseh; and he dwelt therein.

⁴¹And Jair the son of Manasseh went and took the small towns thereof, and called them Havoth-jair.

⁴²And Nobah went and took Kenath, and the villages thereof, and called it Nobah, after his own name.

Journey from Egypt to Canaan

33 THESE *ARE* the journeys of the children of Israel, which went forth out of the land of Egypt with their armies under the hand of Moses and Aaron.

²And Moses wrote their goings out according to their journeys by the commandment of the LORD: and these *are* their journeys according to their goings out.

³And they departed from Rameses in the first month, on the fifteenth day of the first month; on the morrow after the passover the children of Israel went out with an high hand in the sight of all the Egyptians.

⁴For the Egyptians buried all *their* firstborn, which the LORD had smitten among them: upon their gods also the LORD executed judgments.

⁵And the children of Israel removed from Rameses, and pitched in Succoth.

⁶And they departed from Succoth, and pitched in Etham, which *is* in the edge of the wilderness.

⁷And they removed from Etham, and turned again unto Pi-hahiroth, which *is* before Baal-zephon: and they pitched before Migdol.

⁸And they departed from before Pi-hahiroth, and passed through the midst of the sea into the wilderness, and went three days' journey in the wilderness of Etham, and pitched in Marah.

⁹And they removed from Marah, and came unto Elim: and in Elim *were* twelve fountains of water, and threescore and ten palm trees; and they pitched there.

¹⁰And they removed from Elim, and encamped by the Red sea.

¹¹And they removed from the Red sea, and encamped in the wilderness of Sin.

¹²And they took their journey out of the wilderness of Sin, and encamped in Dophkah.

¹³And they departed from Dophkah, and encamped in Alush.

¹⁴And they removed from Alush, and encamped at Rephidim, where was no water for the people to drink.

¹⁵And they departed from Rephidim, and pitched in the wilderness of Sinai.

¹⁶And they removed from the desert of Sinai, and pitched at ʲKibroth-hattaavah.

¹⁷And they departed from Kibroth-hattaavah, and encamped at Hazeroth.

¹⁸And they departed from Hazeroth, and pitched in Rithmah.

¹⁹And they departed from Rithmah, and pitched at Rimmon-parez.

²⁰And they departed from Rimmon-parez, and pitched in Libnah.

²¹And they removed from Libnah, and pitched at Rissah.

²²And they journeyed from Rissah, and pitched in Kehelathah.

Amplified

³⁶Beth-nimrah, and Beth-haran, fortified cities, and folds for sheep.

³⁷And the sons of Reuben built Heshbon, Elealeh, Kiriathaim,

³⁸Nebo, and Baal-meon—their names were to be changed—and Shibmah; and they gave other names to the cities they built.

³⁹And the sons of Machir son of Manasseh went to Gilead and took it and dispossessed the Amorites who were in it.

⁴⁰And Moses gave Gilead to Machir son of Manasseh, and he settled in it.

⁴¹Jair son of Manasseh took their villages and called them Havvoth-jair.

⁴²And Nobah took Kenath and its villages and called it Nobah after his own name.

33 THESE ARE the stages of the journeys of the Israelites by which they went out of the land of Egypt by their hosts under the leadership of Moses and Aaron.

²Moses recorded their starting places, as the Lord commanded, stage by stage; and these are their journeying stages from their starting places:

³They set out from Rameses on the fifteenth day of the first month; on the day after the Passover the Israelites went out [of Egypt] with a high hand *and* triumphantly in the sight of all the Egyptians,

⁴While the Egyptians were burying all their firstborn whom the Lord had struck down among them; upon their gods also the Lord executed judgments.

⁵The Israelites set out from Rameses and encamped in Succoth.

⁶And they departed from Succoth and encamped in Etham, which is at the edge of the wilderness.

⁷They set out from Etham and turned back to Pi-hahiroth, east of Baal-zephon, and they encamped before Migdol.

⁸And they journeyed from before Pi-hahiroth and passed through the midst of the [Red] Sea into the wilderness; and they went a three days' journey in the Wilderness of Etham and encamped at Marah.

⁹They journeyed from Marah and came to Elim; at Elim there were twelve springs of water and seventy palm trees, and they encamped there.

¹⁰They set out from Elim and encamped by the Red Sea.

¹¹They journeyed from the Red Sea and encamped in the Wilderness of Sin.

¹²And they traveled on from the Wilderness of Sin and encamped at Dophkah.

¹³And they departed from Dophkah and encamped at Alush.

¹⁴And they set out from Alush and encamped at Rephidim, where there was no water for the people to drink.

¹⁵And they departed from Rephidim and encamped in the Wilderness of Sinai.

¹⁶And they journeyed from the Wilderness of Sinai and encamped at Kibroth-hattaavah.

¹⁷And they traveled on from Kibroth-hattaavah and encamped at Hazeroth.

¹⁸And they journeyed from Hazeroth and encamped at Rithmah.

¹⁹And they departed from Rithmah and encamped at Rimmon-perez.

²⁰And they departed from Rimmon-perez and encamped at Libnah.

²¹And they removed from Libnah and encamped at Rissah.

²²And they journeyed from Rissah and encamped at Kehelathah.

ⁱHeb. *they called by names the names of the cities*   ʲi.e. *The graves of lust*

New American Standard

36 and Beth-nimrah and Beth-haran as fortified cities, and sheepfolds for sheep.

37 The sons of Reuben built Heshbon and Elealeh and Kiriathaim,

38 and Nebo and Baal-meon—*their* names being changed—and Sibmah, and they gave *other* names to the cities which they built.

39 The sons of Machir the son of Manasseh went to Gilead and took it, and dispossessed the Amorites who were in it.

40 So Moses gave Gilead to Machir the son of Manasseh, and he lived in it.

41 Jair the son of Manasseh went and took its towns, and called them Havvoth-jair.

42 Nobah went and took Kenath and its villages, and called it Nobah after his own name.

Review of the Journey from Egypt to Jordan

33 THESE ARE the journeys of the sons of Israel, by which they came out from the land of Egypt by their armies, under the leadership of Moses and Aaron.

2 Moses recorded their starting places according to their journeys by the command of the LORD, and these are their journeys according to their starting places.

3 They journeyed from Rameses in the first month, on the fifteenth day of the first month; on the next day after the Passover the sons of Israel started out boldly in the sight of all the Egyptians,

4 while the Egyptians were burying all their firstborn whom the LORD had struck down among them. The LORD had also executed judgments on their gods.

5 ¶ Then the sons of Israel journeyed from Rameses and camped in Succoth.

6 They journeyed from Succoth and camped in Etham, which is on the edge of the wilderness.

7 They journeyed from Etham and turned back to Pi-hahiroth, which faces Baal-zephon, and they camped before Migdol.

8 They journeyed from before Hahiroth and passed through the midst of the sea into the wilderness; and they went three days' journey in the wilderness of Etham and camped at Marah.

9 They journeyed from Marah and came to Elim; and in Elim there were twelve springs of water and seventy palm trees, and they camped there.

10 They journeyed from Elim and camped by the Red Sea.

11 They journeyed from the Red Sea and camped in the wilderness of Sin.

12 They journeyed from the wilderness of Sin and camped at Dophkah.

13 They journeyed from Dophkah and camped at Alush.

14 They journeyed from Alush and camped at Rephidim; now it was there that the people had no water to drink.

15 They journeyed from Rephidim and camped in the wilderness of Sinai.

16 They journeyed from the wilderness of Sinai and camped at Kibroth-hattaavah.

17 ¶ They journeyed from Kibroth-hattaavah and camped at Hazeroth.

18 They journeyed from Hazeroth and camped at Rithmah.

19 They journeyed from Rithmah and camped at Rimmon-perez.

20 They journeyed from Rimmon-perez and camped at Libnah.

21 They journeyed from Libnah and camped at Rissah.

22 They journeyed from Rissah and camped in Kehelathah.

New International

Shophan, Jazer, Jogbehah, 36Beth Nimrah and Beth Haran as fortified cities, and built pens for their flocks. 37And the Reubenites rebuilt Heshbon, Elealeh and Kiriathaim, 38as well as Nebo and Baal Meon (these names were changed) and Sibmah. They gave names to the cities they rebuilt.

39The descendants of Makir son of Manasseh went to Gilead, captured it and drove out the Amorites who were there. 40So Moses gave Gilead to the Makirites, the descendants of Manasseh, and they settled there. 41Jair, a descendant of Manasseh, captured their settlements and called them Havvoth Jair.z 42And Nobah captured Kenath and its surrounding settlements and called it Nobah after himself.

Stages in Israel's Journey

33 HERE ARE the stages in the journey of the Israelites when they came out of Egypt by divisions under the leadership of Moses and Aaron. 2At the LORD's command Moses recorded the stages in their journey. This is their journey by stages:

3The Israelites set out from Rameses on the fifteenth day of the first month, the day after the Passover. They marched out boldly in full view of all the Egyptians, 4who were burying all their firstborn, whom the LORD had struck down among them; for the LORD had brought judgment on their gods.

5The Israelites left Rameses and camped at Succoth.

6They left Succoth and camped at Etham, on the edge of the desert.

7They left Etham, turned back to Pi Hahiroth, to the east of Baal Zephon, and camped near Migdol.

8They left Pi Hahiroth[a] and passed through the sea into the desert, and when they had traveled for three days in the Desert of Etham, they camped at Marah.

9They left Marah and went to Elim, where there were twelve springs and seventy palm trees, and they camped there.

10They left Elim and camped by the Red Sea.[b]

11They left the Red Sea and camped in the Desert of Sin.

12They left the Desert of Sin and camped at Dophkah.

13They left Dophkah and camped at Alush.

14They left Alush and camped at Rephidim, where there was no water for the people to drink.

15They left Rephidim and camped in the Desert of Sinai.

16They left the Desert of Sinai and camped at Kibroth Hattaavah.

17They left Kibroth Hattaavah and camped at Hazeroth.

18They left Hazeroth and camped at Rithmah.

19They left Rithmah and camped at Rimmon Perez.

20They left Rimmon Perez and camped at Libnah.

21They left Libnah and camped at Rissah.

22They left Rissah and camped at Kehelathah.

---

z41 Or *them the settlements of Jair*   a8 Many manuscripts of the Masoretic Text, Samaritan Pentateuch and Vulgate; most manuscripts of the Masoretic Text *left from before Hahiroth* b10 Hebrew *Yam Suph*; that is, Sea of Reeds; also in verse 11

King James

²³And they went from Kehelathah, and pitched in mount Shapher.

²⁴And they removed from mount Shapher, and encamped in Haradah.

²⁵And they removed from Haradah, and pitched in Makheloth.

²⁶And they removed from Makheloth, and encamped in Tahath.

²⁷And they departed from Tahath, and pitched at Tarah.

²⁸And they removed from Tarah, and pitched in Mithcah.

²⁹And they went from Mithcah, and pitched in Hashmonah.

³⁰And they departed from Hashmonah, and encamped at Moseroth.

³¹And they departed from Moseroth, and pitched in Bene-jaakan.

³²And they removed from Bene-jaakan, and encamped at Hor-hagidgad.

³³And they went from Hor-hagidgad, and pitched in Jotbathah.

³⁴And they removed from Jotbathah, and encamped at Ebronah.

³⁵And they departed from Ebronah, and encamped at Ezion-geber.

³⁶And they removed from Ezion-geber, and pitched in the wilderness of Zin, which *is* Kadesh.

³⁷And they removed from Kadesh, and pitched in mount Hor, in the edge of the land of Edom.

³⁸And Aaron the priest went up into mount Hor at the commandment of the LORD, and died there, in the fortieth year after the children of Israel were come out of the land of Egypt, in the first *day* of the fifth month.

³⁹And Aaron *was* an hundred and twenty and three years old when he died in mount Hor.

⁴⁰And king Arad the Canaanite, which dwelt in the south in the land of Canaan, heard of the coming of the children of Israel.

⁴¹And they departed from mount Hor, and pitched in Zalmonah.

⁴²And they departed from Zalmonah, and pitched in Punon.

⁴³And they departed from Punon, and pitched in Oboth.

⁴⁴And they departed from Oboth, and pitched in *k*Ijeabarim, in the border of Moab.

⁴⁵And they departed from Iim, and pitched in Dibongad.

⁴⁶And they removed from Dibon-gad, and encamped in Almon-diblathaim.

⁴⁷And they removed from Almon-diblathaim, and pitched in the mountains of Abarim, before Nebo.

⁴⁸And they departed from the mountains of Abarim, and pitched in the plains of Moab by Jordan *near* Jericho.

⁴⁹And they pitched by Jordan, from Beth-jeshimoth *even* unto *l*Abel-shittim in the plains of Moab.

⁵⁰ ¶ And the LORD spake unto Moses in the plains of Moab by Jordan *near* Jericho, saying,

⁵¹Speak unto the children of Israel, and say unto them, When ye are passed over Jordan into the land of Canaan:

⁵²Then ye shall drive out all the inhabitants of the land from before you, and destroy all their pictures, and destroy all their molten images, and quite pluck down all their high places:

⁵³And ye shall dispossess *the inhabitants of* the land, and dwell therein: for I have given you the land to possess it.

⁵⁴And ye shall divide the land by lot for an inheritance among your families: *and* to the more ye shall *m*give the more inheritance, and to the fewer ye shall *n*give the less inheritance: every man's *inheritance* shall be in the place where his lot falleth; according to the tribes of your fathers ye shall inherit.

Amplified

²³And they went from Kehelathah and encamped at Mount Shepher.

²⁴And they removed from Mount Shepher and encamped at Haradah.

²⁵And they set out from Haradah and encamped at Makheloth.

²⁶And they removed from Makheloth and encamped at Tahath.

²⁷And they departed from Tahath and encamped at Terah.

²⁸And they removed from Terah and encamped at Mithkah.

²⁹And they set out from Mithkah and encamped at Hashmonah.

³⁰And they traveled on from Hashmonah and encamped at Moseroth.

³¹And they journeyed from Moseroth and pitched in Bene-jaakan.

³²And they set out from Bene-jaakan and encamped at Hor-haggidgad.

³³And they set out from Hor-haggidgad and encamped at Jotbathah.

³⁴And they journeyed from Jotbathah and encamped at Abronah.

³⁵And they traveled on from Abronah and encamped at Ezion-geber.

³⁶And they removed from Ezion-geber and encamped in the Wilderness of Zin, which is Kadesh.

³⁷And they removed from Kadesh and encamped at Mount Hor, on the edge of Edom.

³⁸Aaron the priest went up on Mount Hor at the command of the Lord, and died there in the fortieth year after the Israelites came out of Egypt, the first day of the fifth month. [Num. 20:23–29.]

³⁹Aaron was 123 years old when he died on Mount Hor.

⁴⁰The Canaanite king of Arad, who lived in the South (the Negeb) in the land of Canaan, heard of the coming of the Israelites.

⁴¹They set out from Mount Hor and encamped at Zalmonah.

⁴²And they set out from Zalmonah and encamped at Punon.

⁴³And they set out from Punon and encamped at Oboth.

⁴⁴And they traveled on from Oboth and encamped at Iye-abarim, on the border of Moab.

⁴⁵And they departed from Iyim and encamped at Dibongad.

⁴⁶And they set out from Dibon-gad and encamped in Almon-diblathaim.

⁴⁷And they traveled on from Almon-diblathaim and encamped in the mountains of Abarim, before Nebo.

⁴⁸And they departed from the mountains of Abarim and encamped in the plains of Moab by the Jordan at Jericho.

⁴⁹And they encamped by the Jordan from Bethjeshimoth as far as Abel-shittim in the plains of Moab.

⁵⁰And the Lord said to Moses in the plains of Moab by the Jordan at Jericho,

⁵¹Tell the Israelites, When you have passed over the Jordan into the land of Canaan,

⁵²Then you shall drive out all the inhabitants of the land before you and destroy all their figured stones and all their molten images and completely demolish all their [idolatrous] high places,

⁵³And you shall take possession of the land and dwell in it, for to you I have given the land to possess it.

⁵⁴You shall inherit the land by lot according to your families; to the large tribe you shall give a larger inheritance, and to the small tribe you shall give a smaller inheritance. Wherever the lot falls to any man, that shall be his. According to the tribes of your fathers you shall inherit.

---

*k*Or, *Heaps of Abarim*   *l*Or, *The plains of Shittim*   *m*Heb.
multiply his inheritance   *n*Heb. *diminish his inheritance*

New American Standard

23 They journeyed from Kehelathah and camped at Mount Shepher.

24 They journeyed from Mount Shepher and camped at Haradah.

25 They journeyed from Haradah and camped at Makheloth.

26 They journeyed from Makheloth and camped at Tahath.

27 They journeyed from Tahath and camped at Terah.

28 They journeyed from Terah and camped at Mithkah.

29 They journeyed from Mithkah and camped at Hashmonah.

30 They journeyed from Hashmonah and camped at Moseroth.

31 They journeyed from Moseroth and camped at Bene-jaakan.

32 They journeyed from Bene-jaakan and camped at Hor-haggidgad.

33 They journeyed from Hor-haggidgad and camped at Jotbathah.

34 They journeyed from Jotbathah and camped at Abronah.

35 They journeyed from Abronah and camped at Ezion-geber.

36 They journeyed from Ezion-geber and camped in the wilderness of Zin, that is, Kadesh.

37 They journeyed from Kadesh and camped at Mount Hor, at the edge of the land of Edom.

38 ¶ Then Aaron the priest went up to Mount Hor at the command of the LORD, and died there in the fortieth year after the sons of Israel had come from the land of Egypt, on the first *day* in the fifth month.

39 Aaron was one hundred twenty-three years old when he died on Mount Hor.

40 ¶ Now the Canaanite, the king of Arad who lived in the Negev in the land of Canaan, heard of the coming of the sons of Israel.

41 ¶ Then they journeyed from Mount Hor and camped at Zalmonah.

42 They journeyed from Zalmonah and camped at Punon.

43 They journeyed from Punon and camped at Oboth.

44 They journeyed from Oboth and camped at Iye-abarim, at the border of Moab.

45 They journeyed from Iyim and camped at Dibon-gad.

46 They journeyed from Dibon-gad and camped at Almon-diblathaim.

47 They journeyed from Almon-diblathaim and camped in the mountains of Abarim, before Nebo.

48 They journeyed from the mountains of Abarim and camped in the plains of Moab by the Jordan *opposite* Jericho.

49 They camped by the Jordan, from Beth-jeshimoth as far as Abel-shittim in the plains of Moab.

Law of Possessing the Land

50 ¶ Then the LORD spoke to Moses in the plains of Moab by the Jordan *opposite* Jericho, saying,

51 "Speak to the sons of Israel and say to them, 'When you cross over the Jordan into the land of Canaan,

52 then you shall drive out all the inhabitants of the land from before you, and destroy all their figured stones, and destroy all their molten images and demolish all their high places;

53 and you shall take possession of the land and live in it, for I have given the land to you to possess it.

54 'You shall inherit the land by lot according to your families; to the larger you shall give more inheritance, and to the smaller you shall give less inheritance. Wherever the lot falls to anyone, that shall be his. You shall inherit according to the tribes of your fathers.

New International

23 They left Kehelathah and camped at Mount Shepher.

24 They left Mount Shepher and camped at Haradah.

25 They left Haradah and camped at Makheloth.

26 They left Makheloth and camped at Tahath.

27 They left Tahath and camped at Terah.

28 They left Terah and camped at Mithcah.

29 They left Mithcah and camped at Hashmonah.

30 They left Hashmonah and camped at Moseroth.

31 They left Moseroth and camped at Bene Jaakan.

32 They left Bene Jaakan and camped at Hor Haggidgad.

33 They left Hor Haggidgad and camped at Jotbathah.

34 They left Jotbathah and camped at Abronah.

35 They left Abronah and camped at Ezion Geber.

36 They left Ezion Geber and camped at Kadesh, in the Desert of Zin.

37 They left Kadesh and camped at Mount Hor, on the border of Edom. 38At the LORD's command Aaron the priest went up Mount Hor, where he died on the first day of the fifth month of the fortieth year after the Israelites came out of Egypt. 39Aaron was a hundred and twenty-three years old when he died on Mount Hor.

40 The Canaanite king of Arad, who lived in the Negev of Canaan, heard that the Israelites were coming.

41 They left Mount Hor and camped at Zalmonah.

42 They left Zalmonah and camped at Punon.

43 They left Punon and camped at Oboth.

44 They left Oboth and camped at Iye Abarim, on the border of Moab.

45 They left Iyim*c* and camped at Dibon Gad.

46 They left Dibon Gad and camped at Almon Diblathaim.

47 They left Almon Diblathaim and camped in the mountains of Abarim, near Nebo.

48 They left the mountains of Abarim and camped on the plains of Moab by the Jordan across from Jericho.*d* 49There on the plains of Moab they camped along the Jordan from Beth Jeshimoth to Abel Shittim.

50 On the plains of Moab by the Jordan across from Jericho the LORD said to Moses, 51"Speak to the Israelites and say to them: 'When you cross the Jordan into Canaan, 52drive out all the inhabitants of the land before you. Destroy all their carved images and their cast idols, and demolish all their high places. 53Take possession of the land and settle in it, for I have given you the land to possess. 54Distribute the land by lot, according to your clans. To a larger group give a larger inheritance, and to a smaller group a smaller one. Whatever falls to them by lot will be theirs. Distribute it according to your ancestral tribes.

c45 That is, Iye Abarim   *d48* Hebrew *Jordan of Jericho;* possibly an ancient name for the Jordan River; also in verse 50

King James

⁵⁵But if ye will not drive out the inhabitants of the land from before you; then it shall come to pass, that those which ye let remain of them *shall be* pricks in your eyes, and thorns in your sides, and shall vex you in the land wherein ye dwell.

⁵⁶Moreover it shall come to pass, *that* I shall do unto you, as I thought to do unto them.

The borders of Canaan

34 AND THE LORD spake unto Moses, saying,
²Command the children of Israel, and say unto them, When ye come into the land of Canaan; (this *is* the land that shall fall unto you for an inheritance, *even* the land of Canaan with the coasts thereof:)

³Then your south quarter shall be from the wilderness of Zin along by the coast of Edom, and your south border shall be the outmost coast of the salt sea eastward:

⁴And your border shall turn from the south to the ascent of Akrabbim, and pass on to Zin: and the going forth thereof shall be from the south to Kadesh-barnea, and shall go on to Hazar-addar, and pass on to Azmon:

⁵And the border shall fetch a compass from Azmon unto the river of Egypt, and the goings out of it shall be at the sea.

⁶And *as for* the western border, ye shall even have the great sea for a border: this shall be your west border.

⁷And this shall be your north border: from the great sea ye shall point out for you mount Hor:

⁸From mount Hor ye shall point out *your border* unto the entrance of Hamath; and the goings forth of the border shall be to Zedad:

⁹ ¶ And the border shall go on to Ziphron, and the goings out of it shall be at Hazar-enan: this shall be your north border.

¹⁰And ye shall point out your east border from Hazar-enan to Shepham:

¹¹And the coast shall go down from Shepham to Riblah, on the east side of Ain: and the border shall descend, and shall reach unto the ^oside of the sea of Chinnereth eastward:

¹²And the border shall go down to Jordan, and the goings out of it shall be at the salt sea: this shall be your land with the coasts thereof round about.

¹³And Moses commanded the children of Israel, saying, This *is* the land which ye shall inherit by lot, which the LORD commanded to give unto the nine tribes, and to the half tribe:

¹⁴For the tribe of the children of Reuben according to the house of their fathers, and the tribe of the children of Gad according to the house of their fathers, have received *their inheritance;* and half the tribe of Manasseh have received their inheritance:

¹⁵The two tribes and the half tribe have received their inheritance on this side Jordan *near* Jericho eastward, toward the sunrising.

¹⁶And the LORD spake unto Moses, saying,

¹⁷These *are* the names of the men which shall divide the land unto you: Eleazar the priest, and Joshua the son of Nun.

¹⁸And ye shall take one prince of every tribe, to divide the land by inheritance.

¹⁹And the names of the men *are* these: Of the tribe of Judah, Caleb the son of Jephunneh.

²⁰And of the tribe of the children of Simeon, Shemuel the son of Ammihud.

²¹Of the tribe of Benjamin, Eliad the son of Chislon.

²²And the prince of the tribe of the children of Dan, Bukki the son of Jogli.

²³The prince of the children of Joseph, for the tribe of the children of Manasseh, Hanniel the son of Ephod.

Amplified

⁵⁵But if you will not drive out the inhabitants of the land from before you, then those you let remain of them shall be as pricks in your eyes and as thorns in your sides, and they shall vex you in the land in which you dwell.

⁵⁶And as I thought to do to them, so will I do to you.

34 AND THE Lord said to Moses,
²Command the Israelites, When you come into the land of Canaan (which is the land that shall be yours for an inheritance, the land of Canaan according to its boundaries),

³Your south side shall be from the Wilderness of Zin along the side of Edom, and your southern boundary from the end of the Salt [Dead] Sea eastward.

⁴Your boundary shall turn south of the ascent of Akrabbim, and pass on to Zin, and its end shall be south of Kadesh-barnea. Then it shall go on to Hazar-addar and pass on to Azmon.

⁵Then the boundary shall turn from Azmon to the Brook of Egypt, and it shall terminate at the [Mediterranean] Sea.

⁶For the western boundary you shall have the Great Sea and its coast.

⁷And this shall be your north border: from the Great Sea mark out your boundary line to Mount Hor;

⁸From Mount Hor you shall mark out your boundary to the entrance of Hamath, and its end shall be at Zedad;

⁹Then the northern boundary shall go on to Ziphron, and the end of it shall be at Hazar-enan.

¹⁰You shall mark out your eastern boundary from Hazar-enan to Shepham;

¹¹The boundary shall go down from Shepham to Riblah on the east side of Ain and shall descend and reach to the shoulder of the Sea of Chinnereth [the Sea of Galilee] on the east;

¹²And the boundary shall go down to the Jordan, and the end shall be at the Salt Sea. This shall be your land with its boundaries all around.

¹³Moses commanded the Israelites, This is the land you shall inherit by lot, which the Lord has commanded to give to the nine tribes and the half-tribe [of Manasseh],

¹⁴For the tribes of the sons of Reuben and of Gad by their fathers' houses have received their inheritance, and also the half-tribe of Manasseh.

¹⁵The two and a half tribes have received their inheritance east of the Jordan at Jericho, toward the sunrise.

¹⁶And the Lord said to Moses,

¹⁷These are the men who shall divide the land to you for inheritance: Eleazar the priest and Joshua son of Nun.

¹⁸And [with them] you shall take one head *or* prince of each tribe to divide the land for inheritance.

¹⁹The names of the men are: Of the tribe of Judah, Caleb son of Jephunneh;

²⁰Of the tribe of the sons of Simeon, Shemuel son of Ammihud;

²¹Of the tribe of Benjamin, Eliad son of Chislon;

²²Of the tribe of the sons of Dan a leader, Bukki son of Jogli;

²³Of the sons of Joseph: of the tribe of the sons of Manasseh a leader, Hanniel son of Ephod;

---

^oHeb. *shoulder*

New American Standard

55 'But if you do not drive out the inhabitants of the land from before you, then it shall come about that those whom you let remain of them *will become* as pricks in your eyes and as thorns in your sides, and they will trouble you in the land in which you live.

56 'And as I plan to do to them, so I will do to you.' "

Instruction for Apportioning Canaan

34 THEN THE LORD spoke to Moses, saying, 2 "Command the sons of Israel and say to them, 'When you enter the land of Canaan, this is the land that shall fall to you as an inheritance, *even the* land of Canaan according to its borders.

3 'Your southern sector shall extend from the wilderness of Zin along the side of Edom, and your southern border shall extend from the end of the Salt Sea eastward.

4 'Then your border shall turn *direction* from the south to the ascent of Akrabbim and continue to Zin, and its *e*termination shall be to the south of Kadesh-barnea; and it shall reach Hazaraddar and continue to Azmon.

5 'The border shall turn *direction* from Azmon to the brook of Egypt, and its termination shall be at the sea.

6 ¶ 'As for the western border, you shall have the Great Sea, that is, *its* coastline; this shall be your west border.

7 ¶ 'And this shall be your north border: you shall draw your *border* line from the Great Sea to Mount Hor.

8 'You shall draw a line from Mount Hor to the Lebo-hamath, and the termination of the border shall be at Zedad;

9 and the border shall proceed to Ziphron, and its termination shall be at Hazar-enan. This shall be your north border.

10 ¶ 'For your eastern border you shall also draw a line from Hazar-enan to Shepham,

11 and the border shall go down from Shepham to Riblah on the east side of Ain; and the border shall go down and reach to the *f*slope on the east side of the Sea of Chinnereth.

12 'And the border shall go down to the Jordan and its termination shall be at the Salt Sea. This shall be your land according to its borders all around.' "

13 ¶ So Moses commanded the sons of Israel, saying, "This is the land that you are to apportion by lot among you as a possession, which the LORD has commanded to give to the nine and a half tribes.

14 "For the tribe of the sons of Reuben have received *theirs* according to their fathers' households, and the tribe of the sons of Gad according to their fathers' households, and the half-tribe of Manasseh have received their possession.

15 "The two and a half tribes have received their possession across the Jordan opposite Jericho, eastward toward the sunrising."

16 ¶ Then the LORD spoke to Moses, saying,

17 "These are the names of the men who shall apportion the land to you for inheritance: Eleazar the priest and Joshua the son of Nun.

18 "You shall take one leader of every tribe to apportion the land for inheritance.

19 "These are the names of the men: of the tribe of Judah, Caleb the son of Jephunneh.

20 "Of the tribe of the sons of Simeon, Samuel the son of Ammihud.

21 "Of the tribe of Benjamin, Elidad the son of Chislon.

22 "Of the tribe of the sons of Dan a leader, Bukki the son of Jogli.

23 "Of the sons of Joseph: of the tribe of the sons of Manasseh a leader, Hanniel the son of Ephod.

New International

55 " 'But if you do not drive out the inhabitants of the land, those you allow to remain will become barbs in your eyes and thorns in your sides. They will give you trouble in the land where you will live. 56 And then I will do to you what I plan to do to them.' "

Boundaries of Canaan

34 THE LORD said to Moses, 2 "Command the Israelites and say to them: 'When you enter Canaan, the land that will be allotted to you as an inheritance will have these boundaries:

3 " 'Your southern side will include some of the Desert of Zin along the border of Edom. On the east, your southern boundary will start from the end of the Salt Sea,*e* 4 cross south of Scorpion*f* Pass, continue on to Zin and go south of Kadesh Barnea. Then it will go to Hazar Addar and over to Azmon, 5 where it will turn, join the Wadi of Egypt and end at the Sea.*g*

6 " 'Your western boundary will be the coast of the Great Sea. This will be your boundary on the west.

7 " 'For your northern boundary, run a line from the Great Sea to Mount Hor 8 and from Mount Hor to Lebo*h* Hamath. Then the boundary will go to Zedad, 9 continue to Ziphron and end at Hazar Enan. This will be your boundary on the north.

10 " 'For your eastern boundary, run a line from Hazar Enan to Shepham. 11 The boundary will go down from Shepham to Riblah on the east side of Ain and continue along the slopes east of the Sea of Kinnereth.*i* 12 Then the boundary will go down along the Jordan and end at the Salt Sea.

" 'This will be your land, with its boundaries on every side.' "

13 Moses commanded the Israelites: "Assign this land by lot as an inheritance. The LORD has ordered that it be given to the nine and a half tribes, 14 because the families of the tribe of Reuben, the tribe of Gad and the half-tribe of Manasseh have received their inheritance. 15 These two and a half tribes have received their inheritance on the east side of the Jordan of Jericho,*j* toward the sunrise."

16 The LORD said to Moses, 17 "These are the names of the men who are to assign the land for you as an inheritance: Eleazar the priest and Joshua son of Nun. 18 And appoint one leader from each tribe to help assign the land. 19 These are their names:

Caleb son of Jephunneh,
    from the tribe of Judah;
20 Shemuel son of Ammihud,
    from the tribe of Simeon;
21 Elidad son of Kislon,
    from the tribe of Benjamin;
22 Bukki son of Jogli,
    the leader from the tribe of Dan;
23 Hanniel son of Ephod,
    the leader from the tribe of Manasseh son of Joseph;

---

e 3 That is, the Dead Sea; also in verse 12   *f* 4 Hebrew *Akrabbim*   *g* 5 That is, the Mediterranean; also in verses 6 and 7   *h* 8 Or *to the entrance to*   *i* 11 That is, Galilee   *j* 15 *Jordan of Jericho* was possibly an ancient name for the Jordan River.

---

*e*Lit *goings out*, and so throughout the ch   *f*Lit *shoulder*

King James

24And the prince of the tribe of the children of Ephraim, Kemuel the son of Shiphtan.

25And the prince of the tribe of the children of Zebulun, Elizaphan the son of Parnach.

26And the prince of the tribe of the children of Issachar, Paltiel the son of Azzan.

27And the prince of the tribe of the children of Asher, Ahihud the son of Shelomi.

28And the prince of the tribe of the children of Naphtali, Pedahel the son of Ammihud.

29These *are they* whom the LORD commanded to divide the inheritance unto the children of Israel in the land of Canaan.

Cities for the Levites

35 AND THE LORD spake unto Moses in the plains of Moab by Jordan *near* Jericho, saying,

2Command the children of Israel, that they give unto the Levites of the inheritance of their possession cities to dwell in; and ye shall give *also* unto the Levites suburbs for the cities round about them.

3And the cities shall they have to dwell in; and the suburbs of them shall be for their cattle, and for their goods, and for all their beasts.

4And the suburbs of the cities, which ye shall give unto the Levites, *shall reach* from the wall of the city and outward a thousand cubits round about.

5And ye shall measure from without the city on the east side two thousand cubits, and on the south side two thousand cubits, and on the west side two thousand cubits, and on the north side two thousand cubits; and the city *shall be* in the midst: this shall be to them the suburbs of the cities.

6And among the cities which ye shall give unto the Levites *there shall be* six cities for refuge, which ye shall appoint for the manslayer, that he may flee thither: and *p*to them ye shall add forty and two cities.

7*So* all the cities which ye shall give to the Levites *shall be* forty and eight cities: them *shall ye give* with their suburbs.

8And the cities which ye shall give *shall be* of the possession of the children of Israel: from *them that have* many ye shall give many; but from *them that have* few ye shall give few: every one shall give of his cities unto the Levites according to his inheritance which *q*he inheriteth.

The cities of refuge

9 ¶ And the LORD spake unto Moses, saying,

10Speak unto the children of Israel, and say unto them, When ye be come over Jordan into the land of Canaan;

11Then ye shall appoint you cities to be cities of refuge for you; that the slayer may flee thither, which killeth any person *r*at unawares.

12And they shall be unto you cities for refuge from the avenger; that the manslayer die not, until he stand before the congregation in judgment.

13And of these cities which ye shall give six cities shall ye have for refuge.

14Ye shall give three cities on this side Jordan, and three cities shall ye give in the land of Canaan, *which* shall be cities of refuge.

15These six cities shall be a refuge, *both* for the children of Israel, and for the stranger, and for the sojourner among them: that every one that killeth any person unawares may flee thither.

16And if he smite him with an instrument of iron, so that he die, he *is* a murderer: the murderer shall surely be put to death.

17And if he smite him *s*with throwing a stone, wherewith he may die, and he die, he *is* a murderer: the murderer shall surely be put to death.

Amplified

24And of the tribe of the sons of Ephraim a leader, Kemuel son of Shiphtan;

25And of the tribe of the sons of Zebulun a leader, Elizaphan son of Parnach;

26And of the tribe of the sons of Issachar a leader, Paltiel son of Azzan;

27And of the tribe of the sons of Asher a leader, Ahihud son of Shelomi;

28And of the tribe of the sons of Naphtali a leader, Pedahel son of Ammihud.

29These are the men whom the Lord commanded to divide the inheritance to the Israelites in the land of Canaan.

35 AND THE Lord said to Moses in the plains of Moab by the Jordan at Jericho,

2Command the Israelites that they give to the Levites from the inheritance of their possession cities to dwell in; and [suburb] pasturelands round about the cities' walls you shall give to the Levites also.

3They shall have the cities to dwell in and their [suburb] pasturelands shall be for their cattle, for their wealth [in flocks], and for all their beasts.

4And the pasturelands of the cities which you shall give to the Levites shall reach from the wall of the city and outward 1,000 cubits round about.

5You shall measure from the wall of the city outward on the east, south, west, and north sides 2,000 cubits, the city being in the center. This shall belong to [the Levites] as [suburb] pasturelands for their cities.

6Of the cities which you shall give to the Levites there shall be the six cities of refuge, which you shall give for the manslayer to flee into; and in addition to them you shall give forty-two cities.

7So all the cities which you shall give to the Levites shall be forty-eight; you shall give them with their adjacent [suburb] pasturelands.

8As for the cities, you shall give from the possession of the Israelites, from the larger tribes you shall take many and from the smaller tribes few; each tribe shall give of its cities to the Levites in proportion to its inheritance.

9And the Lord said to Moses,

10Say to the Israelites, When you cross the Jordan into the land of Canaan,

11Then you shall select cities to be cities of refuge for you, that the slayer who kills any person unintentionally *and* unawares may flee there.

12And the cities shall be to you for refuge from the avenger, that the manslayer may not die until he has had a fair trial before the congregation.

13And of the cities which you give there shall be your six cities for refuge.

14You shall give three cities on this [east] side of the Jordan and three cities in the land of Canaan, to be cities of refuge.

15These six cities shall be a refuge for the Israelites and for the stranger and the temporary resident among them; that anyone who kills any person unintentionally *and* unawares may flee there.

16But if he struck him down with an instrument of iron so that he died, he is a murderer; the murderer shall surely be put to death.

17And if he struck him down by throwing a stone, by which a person may die, and he died, he is a murderer; the murderer shall surely be put to death.

---

*p*Heb. *above them ye shall give*   *q*Heb. *they inherit*   *r*Heb. *by error*   *s*Heb. *with a stone of the hand*

New American Standard

24"Of the tribe of the sons of Ephraim a leader, Kemuel the son of Shiphtan.
25"Of the tribe of the sons of Zebulun a leader, Elizaphan the son of Parnach.
26"Of the tribe of the sons of Issachar a leader, Paltiel the son of Azzan.
27"Of the tribe of the sons of Asher a leader, Ahihud the son of Shelomi.
28"Of the tribe of the sons of Naphtali a leader, Pedahel the son of Ammihud."
29 These are those whom the LORD commanded to apportion the inheritance to the sons of Israel in the land of Canaan.

Cities for the Levites

35 NOW THE LORD spoke to Moses in the plains of Moab by the Jordan *opposite* Jericho, saying,
2"Command the sons of Israel that they give to the Levites from the inheritance of their possession cities to live in; and you shall give to the Levites pasture lands around the cities.
3"The cities shall be theirs to live in; and their pasture lands shall be for their cattle and for their herds and for all their beasts.
4 ¶ "The pasture lands of the cities which you shall give to the Levites *shall extend* from the wall of the city outward a thousand cubits around.
5"You shall also measure outside the city on the east side two thousand cubits, and on the south side two thousand cubits, and on the west side two thousand cubits, and on the north side two thousand cubits, with the city in the center. This shall become theirs as pasture lands for the cities.

Cities of Refuge

6"The cities which you shall give to the Levites *shall be* the six cities of refuge, which you shall give for the manslayer to flee to; and in addition to them you shall give forty-two cities.
7"All the cities which you shall give to the Levites *shall be* forty-eight cities, together with their pasture lands.
8"As for the cities which you shall give from the possession of the sons of Israel, you shall take more from the larger and you shall take less from the smaller; each shall give some of his cities to the Levites in proportion to his possession which he inherits."
9 ¶ Then the LORD spoke to Moses, saying,
10"Speak to the sons of Israel and say to them, 'When you cross the Jordan into the land of Canaan,
11 then you shall select for yourselves cities to be your cities of refuge, that the manslayer who has killed any person unintentionally may flee there.
12 'The cities shall be to you as a refuge from the avenger, so that the manslayer will not die until he stands before the congregation for trial.
13 'The cities which you are to give shall be your six cities of refuge.
14 'You shall give three cities across the Jordan and three cities in the land of Canaan; they are to be cities of refuge.
15 'These six cities shall be for refuge for the sons of Israel, and for the alien and for the sojourner among them; that anyone who kills a person unintentionally may flee there.
16 ¶ 'But if he struck him down with an iron object, so that he died, he is a murderer; the murderer shall surely be put to death.
17 'If he struck him down with a stone in the hand, by which he will die, and *as a result* he died, he is a murderer; the murderer shall surely be put to death.

New International

24Kemuel son of Shiphtan,
    the leader from the tribe of Ephraim son of Joseph;
25Elizaphan son of Parnach,
    the leader from the tribe of Zebulun;
26Paltiel son of Azzan,
    the leader from the tribe of Issachar;
27Ahihud son of Shelomi,
    the leader from the tribe of Asher;
28Pedahel son of Ammihud,
    the leader from the tribe of Naphtali."
29These are the men the LORD commanded to assign the inheritance to the Israelites in the land of Canaan.

Towns for the Levites

35 ON THE plains of Moab by the Jordan across from Jericho,[k] the LORD said to Moses, 2"Command the Israelites to give the Levites towns to live in from the inheritance the Israelites will possess. And give them pasturelands around the towns. 3Then they will have towns to live in and pasturelands for their cattle, flocks and all their other livestock.
4"The pasturelands around the towns that you give the Levites will extend out fifteen hundred feet[l] from the town wall. 5Outside the town, measure three thousand feet[m] on the east side, three thousand on the south side, three thousand on the west and three thousand on the north, with the town in the center. They will have this area as pastureland for the towns.

Cities of Refuge

6"Six of the towns you give the Levites will be cities of refuge, to which a person who has killed someone may flee. In addition, give them forty-two other towns. 7In all you must give the Levites forty-eight towns, together with their pasturelands. 8The towns you give the Levites from the land the Israelites possess are to be given in proportion to the inheritance of each tribe: Take many towns from a tribe that has many, but few from one that has few."
9Then the LORD said to Moses: 10"Speak to the Israelites and say to them: 'When you cross the Jordan into Canaan, 11select some towns to be your cities of refuge, to which a person who has killed someone accidentally may flee. 12They will be places of refuge from the avenger, so that a person accused of murder may not die before he stands trial before the assembly. 13These six towns you give will be your cities of refuge. 14Give three on this side of the Jordan and three in Canaan as cities of refuge. 15These six towns will be a place of refuge for Israelites, aliens and any other people living among them, so that anyone who has killed another accidentally can flee there.
16" 'If a man strikes someone with an iron object so that he dies, he is a murderer; the murderer shall be put to death. 17Or if anyone has a stone in his hand that could kill, and he strikes someone so that he dies, he is a murder-

k 1 Hebrew *Jordan of Jericho*; possibly an ancient name for the Jordan River   l 4 Hebrew *a thousand cubits* (about 450 meters)
m 5 Hebrew *two thousand cubits* (about 900 meters)

| King James | Amplified |

King James

¹⁸Or *if* he smite him with an handweapon of wood, wherewith he may die, and he die, he *is* a murderer: the murderer shall surely be put to death.

¹⁹The revenger of blood himself shall slay the murderer: when he meeteth him, he shall slay him.

²⁰But if he thrust him of hatred, or hurl at him by laying of wait, that he die;

²¹Or in enmity smite him with his hand, that he die: he that smote *him* shall surely be put to death; *for* he *is* a murderer: the revenger of blood shall slay the murderer, when he meeteth him.

²²But if he thrust him suddenly without enmity, or have cast upon him any thing without laying of wait,

²³Or with any stone, wherewith a man may die, seeing *him* not, and cast *it* upon him, that he die, and *was* not his enemy, neither sought his harm:

²⁴Then the congregation shall judge between the slayer and the revenger of blood according to these judgments:

²⁵And the congregation shall deliver the slayer out of the hand of the revenger of blood, and the congregation shall restore him to the city of his refuge, whither he was fled: and he shall abide in it unto the death of the high priest, which was anointed with the holy oil.

²⁶But if the slayer shall at any time come without the border of the city of his refuge, whither he was fled;

²⁷And the revenger of blood find him without the borders of the city of his refuge, and the revenger of blood kill the slayer; *t*he shall not be guilty of blood:

²⁸Because he should have remained in the city of his refuge until the death of the high priest: but after the death of the high priest the slayer shall return into the land of his possession.

²⁹So these *things* shall be for a statute of judgment unto you throughout your generations in all your dwellings.

³⁰Whoso killeth any person, the murderer shall be put to death by the mouth of witnesses: but one witness shall not testify against any person *to cause him* to die.

³¹Moreover ye shall take no satisfaction for the life of a murderer, which *is* ᵘguilty of death: but he shall be surely put to death.

³²And ye shall take no satisfaction for him that is fled to the city of his refuge, that he should come again to dwell in the land, until the death of the priest.

³³So ye shall not pollute the land wherein ye *are:* for blood it defileth the land: and ᵛthe land cannot be cleansed of the blood that is shed therein, but by the blood of him that shed it.

³⁴Defile not therefore the land which ye shall inhabit, wherein I dwell: for I the LORD dwell among the children of Israel.

The marriage of heiresses

36 AND THE chief fathers of the families of the children of Gilead, the son of Machir, the son of Manasseh, of the families of the sons of Joseph, came near, and spake before Moses, and before the princes, the chief fathers of the children of Israel:

²And they said, The LORD commanded my lord to give the land for an inheritance by lot to the children of Israel: and my lord was commanded by the LORD to give the inheritance of Zelophehad our brother unto his daughters.

³And if they be married to any of the sons of the *other* tribes of the children of Israel, then shall their inheritance be taken from the inheritance of our fathers, and shall be put to the inheritance of the tribe ʷwhereunto they are received: so shall it be taken from the lot of our inheritance.

Amplified

¹⁸Or if he struck him down with a weapon of wood in his hand, by which one may die, and he died, the offender is a murderer; he shall surely be put to death.

¹⁹The avenger of blood shall himself slay the murderer; when he meets him, he shall slay him.

²⁰But if he stabbed him through hatred or hurled at him by lying in wait so that he died

²¹Or in enmity struck him down with his hand so that he died, he that smote him shall surely be put to death; he is a murderer. The avenger of blood shall slay the murderer when he meets him.

²²But if he stabbed him suddenly without enmity or threw anything at *or* upon him without lying in wait

²³Or with any stone with which a man may be killed, not seeing him, and threw it at him so that he died, and was not his enemy nor sought to harm him,

²⁴Then the congregation shall judge between the slayer and the avenger of blood according to these ordinances.

²⁵And the congregation shall rescue the manslayer from the hand of the avenger of blood and restore him to his city of refuge to which he had fled; and he shall live in it until the high priest dies, who was anointed with the sacred oil.

²⁶But if the slayer shall at any time come outside the limits of his city of refuge to which he had fled

²⁷And the avenger of blood finds him outside the limits of his city of refuge and kills the manslayer, he shall not be guilty of blood

²⁸Because the manslayer should have remained in his city of refuge until the death of the high priest. But after the high priest's death the manslayer shall return to the land of his possession.

²⁹And these things shall be for a statute *and* ordinance to you throughout your generations in all your dwellings.

³⁰Whoever kills any person [intentionally], the murderer shall be put to death on the testimony of witnesses; but no one shall be put to death on the testimony of one witness.

³¹Moreover, you shall take no ransom for the life of a murderer guilty of death; but he shall surely be put to death.

³²And you shall accept no ransom for him who has fled to his city of refuge, so that he may return to dwell in the land before the death of the high priest.

³³So you shall not pollute the land in which you live; for blood pollutes the land, and no atonement can be made for the land for the blood shed in it, but by the blood of him who shed it.

³⁴And you shall not defile the land in which you live, in the midst of which I dwell, for I, the Lord, dwell in the midst of the people of Israel.

36 THE HEADS of the fathers' houses of the families of the sons of Gilead son of Machir, the son of Manasseh, of the fathers' houses of the sons of Joseph, came near and spoke before Moses and the leaders, the heads of the fathers' houses of the Israelites.

²They said, The Lord commanded [you] my lord to give the land for inheritance by lot to the Israelites; and my lord was commanded by the Lord to give the inheritance of Zelophehad our brother to his daughters.

³But if they are married to any of the sons of the other tribes of the Israelites, then their inheritance will be taken from that of our fathers and added to the inheritance of the tribe to which they are received *and* belong; so it will be taken out of the lot of our inheritance.

---

*t*Heb. *no blood* shall be *to him*   ᵘHeb. *faulty to die*   ᵛHeb *there can be no expiation for the land*   ʷHeb. *unto whom they shall be*

New American Standard

18 'Or if he struck him with a wooden object in the hand, by which he might die, and *as a result* he died, he is a murderer; the murderer shall surely be put to death.
19 'The blood avenger himself shall put the murderer to death; he shall put him to death when he meets him.
20 'If he pushed him of hatred, or threw something at him lying in wait and *as a result* he died,
21 or if he struck him down with his hand in enmity, and *as a result* he died, the one who struck him shall surely be put to death, he is a murderer; the blood avenger shall put the murderer to death when he meets him.
22 ¶ 'But if he pushed him suddenly without enmity, or threw something at him without lying in wait,
23 or with any deadly object of stone, and without seeing it dropped on him so that he died, while he was not his enemy nor seeking his injury,
24 then the congregation shall judge between the slayer and the blood avenger according to these ordinances.
25 'The congregation shall deliver the manslayer from the hand of the blood avenger, and the congregation shall restore him to his city of refuge to which he fled; and he shall live in it until the death of the high priest who was anointed with the holy oil.
26 'But if the manslayer at any time goes beyond the border of his city of refuge to which he may flee,
27 and the blood avenger finds him outside the border of his city of refuge, and the blood avenger kills the manslayer, he will not be guilty of blood
28 because he should have remained in his city of refuge until the death of the high priest. But after the death of the high priest the manslayer shall return to the land of his possession.
29 ¶ 'These things shall be for a statutory ordinance to you throughout your generations in all your dwellings.
30 ¶ 'If anyone kills a person, the murderer shall be put to death at the evidence of witnesses, but no person shall be put to death on the testimony of one witness.
31 'Moreover, you shall not take ransom for the life of a murderer who is guilty of death, but he shall surely be put to death.
32 'You shall not take ransom for him who has fled to his city of refuge, that he may return to live in the land before the death of the priest.
33 'So you shall not pollute the land in which you are; for blood pollutes the land and no expiation can be made for the land for the blood that is shed on it, except by the blood of him who shed it.
34 'You shall not defile the land in which you live, in the midst of which I dwell; for I the LORD am dwelling in the midst of the sons of Israel.' "

Inheritance by Marriage

36 AND THE heads of the fathers' *households* of the family of the sons of Gilead, the son of Machir, the son of Manasseh, of the families of the sons of Joseph, came near and spoke before Moses and before the leaders, the heads of the fathers' *households* of the sons of Israel,
2 and they said, "The LORD commanded my lord to give the land by lot to the sons of Israel as an inheritance, and my lord was commanded by the LORD to give the inheritance of Zelophehad our brother to his daughters.
3 "But if they marry one of the sons of the *other* tribes of the sons of Israel, their inheritance will be withdrawn from the inheritance of our fathers and will be added to the inheritance of the tribe to which they belong; thus it will be withdrawn from our allotted inheritance.

New International

er; the murderer shall be put to death. 18Or if anyone has a wooden object in his hand that could kill, and he hits someone so that he dies, he is a murderer; the murderer shall be put to death. 19The avenger of blood shall put the murderer to death; when he meets him, he shall put him to death. 20If anyone with malice aforethought shoves another or throws something at him intentionally so that he dies 21or if in hostility he hits him with his fist so that he dies, that person shall be put to death; he is a murderer. The avenger of blood shall put the murderer to death when he meets him.
22 " 'But if without hostility someone suddenly shoves another or throws something at him unintentionally 23or, without seeing him, drops a stone on him that could kill him, and he dies, then since he was not his enemy and he did not intend to harm him, 24the assembly must judge between him and the avenger of blood according to these regulations. 25The assembly must protect the one accused of murder from the avenger of blood and send him back to the city of refuge to which he fled. He must stay there until the death of the high priest, who was anointed with the holy oil.
26 " 'But if the accused ever goes outside the limits of the city of refuge to which he has fled 27and the avenger of blood finds him outside the city, the avenger of blood may kill the accused without being guilty of murder. 28The accused must stay in his city of refuge until the death of the high priest; only after the death of the high priest may he return to his own property.
29 " 'These are to be legal requirements for you throughout the generations to come, wherever you live.
30 " 'Anyone who kills a person is to be put to death as a murderer only on the testimony of witnesses. But no one is to be put to death on the testimony of only one witness.
31 " 'Do not accept a ransom for the life of a murderer, who deserves to die. He must surely be put to death.
32 " 'Do not accept a ransom for anyone who has fled to a city of refuge and so allow him to go back and live on his own land before the death of the high priest.
33 " 'Do not pollute the land where you are. Bloodshed pollutes the land, and atonement cannot be made for the land on which blood has been shed, except by the blood of the one who shed it. 34Do not defile the land where you live and where I dwell, for I, the LORD, dwell among the Israelites.' "

Inheritance of Zelophehad's Daughters

36 THE FAMILY heads of the clan of Gilead son of Makir, the son of Manasseh, who were from the clans of the descendants of Joseph, came and spoke before Moses and the leaders, the heads of the Israelite families.
2They said, "When the LORD commanded my lord to give the land as an inheritance to the Israelites by lot, he ordered you to give the inheritance of our brother Zelophehad to his daughters. 3Now suppose they marry men from other Israelite tribes; then their inheritance will be taken from our ancestral inheritance and added to that of the tribe they marry into. And so part of the inheritance allot-

King James

4And when the jubilee of the children of Israel shall be, then shall their inheritance be put unto the inheritance of the tribe whereunto they are received: so shall their inheritance be taken away from the inheritance of the tribe of our fathers.

5And Moses commanded the children of Israel according to the word of the LORD, saying, The tribe of the sons of Joseph hath said well.

6This *is* the thing which the LORD doth command concerning the daughters of Zelophehad, saying, Let them xmarry to whom they think best; only to the family of the tribe of their father shall they marry.

7So shall not the inheritance of the children of Israel remove from tribe to tribe: for every one of the children of Israel shall ykeep himself to the inheritance of the tribe of his fathers.

8And every daughter, that possesseth an inheritance in any tribe of the children of Israel, shall be wife unto one of the family of the tribe of her father, that the children of Israel may enjoy every man the inheritance of his fathers.

9Neither shall the inheritance remove from *one* tribe to another tribe; but every one of the tribes of the children of Israel shall keep himself to his own inheritance.

10Even as the LORD commanded Moses, so did the daughters of Zelophehad:

11For Mahlah, Tirzah, and Hoglah, and Milcah, and Noah, the daughters of Zelophehad, were married unto their father's brothers' sons:

12*And* they were married zinto the families of the sons of Manasseh the son of Joseph, and their inheritance remained in the tribe of the family of their father.

13These *are* the commandments and the judgments, which the LORD commanded by the hand of Moses unto the children of Israel in the plains of Moab by Jordan *near* Jericho.

Amplified

4And when the Jubilee of the Israelites comes, then their inheritance will be added to that of the tribe to which they are received *and* belong; so will their inheritance be taken away from that of the tribe of our fathers.

5And Moses commanded the Israelites according to the word of the Lord, saying, The tribe of the sons of Joseph is right.

6This is what the Lord commands concerning the daughters of Zelophehad: Let them marry whom they think best; only they shall marry within the family of the tribe of their father.

7So shall no inheritance of the Israelites be transferred from tribe to tribe, for every one of the Israelites shall cling to the inheritance of the tribe of his fathers.

8And every daughter who possesses an inheritance in any tribe of the Israelites shall be wife to one of the family of the tribe of her father, so that the Israelites may each one possess the inheritance of his fathers.

9So shall no inheritance be transferred from one tribe to another, but each of the tribes of the Israelites shall cling to its own inheritance.

10The daughters of Zelophehad did as the Lord commanded Moses.

11For Mahlah, Tirzah, Hoglah, Milcah, and Noah, the daughters of Zelophehad, were married to sons of their father's brothers.

12They married into the families of the sons of Manasseh son of Joseph, and their inheritance remained in the tribe of the family of their father.

13These are the commandments and ordinances which the Lord commanded the Israelites through Moses in the plains of Moab by the Jordan [River] at Jericho.

---

xHeb. *be wives*   yHeb. *cleave to the*   zHeb. *to some that were of the families*

New American Standard

4"When the jubilee of the sons of Israel comes, then their inheritance will be added to the inheritance of the tribe to which they belong; so their inheritance will be withdrawn from the inheritance of the tribe of our fathers."

5 ¶ Then Moses commanded the sons of Israel according to the word of the LORD, saying, "The tribe of the sons of Joseph are right in *their* statements.

6"This is what the LORD has commanded concerning the daughters of Zelophehad, saying, 'Let them marry whom they wish; only they must marry within the family of the tribe of their father.'

7"Thus no inheritance of the sons of Israel shall be transferred from tribe to tribe, for the sons of Israel shall each hold to the inheritance of the tribe of his fathers.

8"Every daughter who comes into possession of an inheritance of any tribe of the sons of Israel shall be wife to one of the family of the tribe of her father, so that the sons of Israel each may possess the inheritance of his fathers.

9"Thus no inheritance shall be transferred from one tribe to another tribe, for the tribes of the sons of Israel shall each hold to his own inheritance."

10 ¶ Just as the LORD had commanded Moses, so the daughters of Zelophehad did:

11 Mahlah, Tirzah, Hoglah, Milcah and Noah, the daughters of Zelophehad married their uncles' sons.

12 They married *those* from the families of the sons of Manasseh the son of Joseph, and their inheritance remained with the tribe of the family of their father.

13 ¶ These are the commandments and the ordinances which the LORD commanded to the sons of Israel through Moses in the plains of Moab by the Jordan *opposite* Jericho.

New International

ted to us will be taken away. 4When the Year of Jubilee for the Israelites comes, their inheritance will be added to that of the tribe into which they marry, and their property will be taken from the tribal inheritance of our forefathers."

5Then at the LORD's command Moses gave this order to the Israelites: "What the tribe of the descendants of Joseph is saying is right. 6This is what the LORD commands for Zelophehad's daughters: They may marry anyone they please as long as they marry within the tribal clan of their father. 7No inheritance in Israel is to pass from tribe to tribe, for every Israelite shall keep the tribal land inherited from his forefathers. 8Every daughter who inherits land in any Israelite tribe must marry someone in her father's tribal clan, so that every Israelite will possess the inheritance of his fathers. 9No inheritance may pass from tribe to tribe, for each Israelite tribe is to keep the land it inherits."

10So Zelophehad's daughters did as the LORD commanded Moses. 11Zelophehad's daughters—Mahlah, Tirzah, Hoglah, Milcah and Noah—married their cousins on their father's side. 12They married within the clans of the descendants of Manasseh son of Joseph, and their inheritance remained in their father's clan and tribe.

13These are the commands and regulations the LORD gave through Moses to the Israelites on the plains of Moab by the Jordan across from Jericho.[n]

---

[n] 13 Hebrew *Jordan of Jericho*; possibly an ancient name for the Jordan River

THE FIFTH BOOK OF MOSES, CALLED

Deuteronomy

THE FIFTH BOOK OF MOSES, CALLED

Deuteronomy

King James

Moses tells of God's guidance

1 THESE *BE* the words which Moses spake unto all Israel on this side Jordan in the wilderness, in the plain over against *a*the Red *sea,* between Paran, and Tophel, and Laban, and Hazeroth, and Dizahab.

2(*There are* eleven days' *journey* from Horeb by the way of mount Seir unto Kadesh-barnea.)

3And it came to pass in the fortieth year, in the eleventh month, on the first *day* of the month, *that* Moses spake unto the children of Israel, according unto all that the LORD had given him in commandment unto them;

4After he had slain Sihon the king of the Amorites, which dwelt in Heshbon, and Og the king of Bashan, which dwelt at Astaroth in Edrei:

5On this side Jordan, in the land of Moab, began Moses to declare this law, saying,

6The LORD our God spake unto us in Horeb, saying, Ye have dwelt long enough in this mount:

7Turn you, and take your journey, and go to the mount of the Amorites, and unto *b*all *the places* nigh thereunto, in the plain, in the hills, and in the vale, and in the south, and by the sea side, to the land of the Canaanites, and unto Lebanon, unto the great river, the river Euphrates.

8Behold, I have *c*set the land before you: go in and possess the land which the LORD sware unto your fathers, Abraham, Isaac, and Jacob, to give unto them and to their seed after them.

The choice of leaders

9 ¶ And I spake unto you at that time, saying, I am not able to bear you myself alone:

10The LORD your God hath multiplied you, and, behold, ye *are* this day as the stars of heaven for multitude.

11(The LORD God of your fathers make you a thousand times so many more as ye *are,* and bless you, as he hath promised you!)

12How can I myself alone bear your cumbrance, and your burden, and your strife?

13*d*Take you wise men, and understanding, and known among your tribes, and I will make them rulers over you.

14And ye answered me, and said, The thing which thou hast spoken *is* good *for us* to do.

15So I took the chief of your tribes, wise men, and known, and *e*made them heads over you, captains over thousands, and captains over hundreds, and captains over fifties, and captains over tens, and officers among your tribes.

16And I charged your judges at that time, saying, Hear *the causes* between your brethren, and judge righteously between *every* man and his brother, and the stranger *that is* with him.

17Ye shall not *f*respect persons in judgment; *but* ye shall hear the small as well as the great; ye shall not be afraid of the face of man; for the judgment *is* God's: and the cause that is too hard for you, bring *it* unto me, and I will hear it.

18And I commanded you at that time all the things which ye should do.

Amplified

1 THESE ARE the words which Moses spoke to all Israel [still] on the [east] side of the Jordan [River] in the wilderness, in the Arabah [the deep valley running north and south from the eastern arm of the Red Sea to beyond the Dead Sea], over near Suph, between Paran and Tophel, Laban, Hazeroth, and Dizahab.

2It is [only] eleven days' journey from Horeb by the way of Mount Seir to Kadesh-barnea [on Canaan's border; yet Israel took forty years to get beyond it].

3And in the fortieth year, on the first day of the eleventh month, Moses spoke to the Israelites according to all that the Lord had given him in commandment to them,

4After He had defeated Sihon king of the Amorites, who lived in Heshbon, and Og king of Bashan, who lived in Ashtaroth [and] Edrei,

5Beyond (east of) the Jordan in the land of Moab, Moses began to explain this law, saying,

6The Lord our God said to us in Horeb, You have dwelt long enough on this mountain.

7Turn and take up your journey and go to the hill country of the Amorites, and to all their neighbors in the Arabah, in the hill country, in the lowland, in the South (the Negeb), and on the coast, the land of the Canaanites, and Lebanon, as far as the great river, the river Euphrates.

8Behold, I have set the land before you; go in and take possession of the land which the Lord swore to your fathers, to Abraham, to Isaac, and to Jacob, to give to them and to their descendants after them.

9I said to you at that time, I am not able to bear you alone.

10The Lord your God has multiplied you, and behold, you are this day as the stars of the heavens for multitude.

11May the Lord, the God of your fathers, make you a thousand times as many as you are and bless you as He has promised you!

12How can I bear alone the weariness *and* pressure and burden of you and your strife?

13Choose wise, understanding, experienced, *and* respected men according to your tribes, and I will make them heads over you.

14And you answered me, The thing which you have spoken is good for us to do.

15So I took the heads of your tribes, wise, experienced, *and* respected men, and made them heads over you, commanders of thousands, and hundreds, and fifties, and tens, and officers according to your tribes.

16And I charged your judges at that time: Hear the cases between your brethren and judge righteously between a man and his brother or the stranger *or* sojourner who is with him.

17You shall not be partial in judgment; but you shall hear the small as well as the great. You shall not be afraid of the face of man, for the judgment is God's. And the case that is too hard for you, you shall bring to me, and I will hear it.

18And I commanded you at that time all the things that you should do.

---

*a*Or, *Zuph*   *b*Heb. *all his neighbours*   *c*Heb. *given*
*d*Heb. *Give*   *e*Heb. *gave*   *f*Heb. *acknowledge faces*

Deuteronomy

New American Standard

New International

New American Standard

Israel's History after the Exodus

1 THESE ARE the words which Moses spoke to all Israel across the Jordan in the wilderness, in the Arabah opposite Suph, between Paran and Tophel and Laban and Hazeroth and Dizahab.

2 It is eleven days' *journey* from Horeb by the way of Mount Seir to Kadesh-barnea.

3 In the fortieth year, on the first *day* of the eleventh month, Moses spoke to the children of Israel, according to all that the LORD had commanded him *to give* to them,

4 after he had defeated Sihon the king of the Amorites, who lived in Heshbon, and Og the king of Bashan, who lived in Ashtaroth and Edrei.

5 Across the Jordan in the land of Moab, Moses undertook to expound this law, saying,

6 ¶ "The LORD our God spoke to us at Horeb, saying, 'You have stayed long enough at this mountain.

7 'Turn and set your journey, and go to the hill country of the Amorites, and to all their neighbors in the Arabah, in the hill country and in the lowland and in the *a*Negev and by the seacoast, the land of the Canaanites, and Lebanon, as far as the great river, the river Euphrates.

8 'See, I have placed the land before you; go in and possess the land which the LORD swore to give to your fathers, to Abraham, to Isaac, and to Jacob, to them and their descendants after them.'

9 ¶ "I spoke to you at that time, saying, 'I am not able to bear *the burden* of you alone.

10 'The LORD your God has multiplied you, and behold, you are this day like the stars of heaven in number.

11 'May the LORD, the God of your fathers, increase you a thousand-fold more than you are and bless you, just as He has promised you!

12 'How can I alone bear the load and burden of you and your strife?

13 'Choose wise and discerning and experienced men from your tribes, and I will appoint them as your heads.'

14 "You answered me and said, 'The thing which you have said to do is good.'

15 "So I took the heads of your tribes, wise and experienced men, and appointed them heads over you, leaders of thousands and of hundreds, of fifties and of tens, and officers for your tribes.

16 ¶ "Then I charged your judges at that time, saying, 'Hear *the cases* between your fellow countrymen, and judge righteously between a man and his fellow countryman, or the alien who is with him.

17 'You shall not show partiality in judgment; you shall hear the small and the great alike. You shall not fear man, for the judgment is God's. The case that is too hard for you, you shall bring to me, and I will hear it.'

18 "I commanded you at that time all the things that you should do.

New International

The Command to Leave Horeb

1 THESE ARE the words Moses spoke to all Israel in the desert east of the Jordan—that is, in the Arabah—opposite Suph, between Paran and Tophel, Laban, Hazeroth and Dizahab. 2(It takes eleven days to go from Horeb to Kadesh Barnea by the Mount Seir road.)

3In the fortieth year, on the first day of the eleventh month, Moses proclaimed to the Israelites all that the LORD had commanded him concerning them. 4This was after he had defeated Sihon king of the Amorites, who reigned in Heshbon, and at Edrei had defeated Og king of Bashan, who reigned in Ashtaroth.

5East of the Jordan in the territory of Moab, Moses began to expound this law, saying:

6The LORD our God said to us at Horeb, "You have stayed long enough at this mountain. 7Break camp and advance into the hill country of the Amorites; go to all the neighboring peoples in the Arabah, in the mountains, in the western foothills, in the Negev and along the coast, to the land of the Canaanites and to Lebanon, as far as the great river, the Euphrates. 8See, I have given you this land. Go in and take possession of the land that the LORD swore he would give to your fathers—to Abraham, Isaac and Jacob—and to their descendants after them."

The Appointment of Leaders

9At that time I said to you, "You are too heavy a burden for me to carry alone. 10The LORD your God has increased your numbers so that today you are as many as the stars in the sky. 11May the LORD, the God of your fathers, increase you a thousand times and bless you as he has promised! 12But how can I bear your problems and your burdens and your disputes all by myself? 13Choose some wise, understanding and respected men from each of your tribes, and I will set them over you."

14You answered me, "What you propose to do is good."

15So I took the leading men of your tribes, wise and respected men, and appointed them to have authority over you—as commanders of thousands, of hundreds, of fifties and of tens and as tribal officials. 16And I charged your judges at that time: Hear the disputes between your brothers and judge fairly, whether the case is between brother Israelites or between one of them and an alien. 17Do not show partiality in judging; hear both small and great alike. Do not be afraid of any man, for judgment belongs to God. Bring me any case too hard for you, and I will hear it. 18And at that time I told you everything you were to do.

---

a I.e. South country

King James

Amplified

The report of the spies

19 ¶ And when we departed from Horeb, we went through all that great and terrible wilderness, which ye saw by the way of the mountain of the Amorites, as the LORD our God commanded us; and we came to Kadesh-barnea.

20 And I said unto you, Ye are come unto the mountain of the Amorites, which the LORD our God doth give unto us.

21 Behold, the LORD thy God hath set the land before thee: go up *and* possess *it*, as the LORD God of thy fathers hath said unto thee; fear not, neither be discouraged.

22 ¶ And ye came near unto me every one of you, and said, We will send men before us, and they shall search us out the land, and bring us word again by what way we must go up, and into what cities we shall come.

23 And the saying pleased me well: and I took twelve men of you, one of a tribe:

24 And they turned and went up into the mountain, and came unto the valley of Eshcol, and searched it out.

25 And they took of the fruit of the land in their hands, and brought *it* down unto us, and brought us word again, and said, *It is* a good land which the LORD our God doth give us.

The murmuring of Israel

26 Notwithstanding ye would not go up, but rebelled against the commandment of the LORD your God:

27 And ye murmured in your tents, and said, Because the LORD hated us, he hath brought us forth out of the land of Egypt, to deliver us into the hand of the Amorites, to destroy us.

28 Whither shall we go up? our brethren have ⁸discouraged our heart, saying, The people *is* greater and taller than we; the cities *are* great and walled up to heaven; and moreover we have seen the sons of the Anakims there.

29 Then I said unto you, Dread not, neither be afraid of them.

30 The LORD your God which goeth before you, he shall fight for you, according to all that he did for you in Egypt before your eyes;

31 And in the wilderness, where thou hast seen how that the LORD thy God bare thee, as a man doth bear his son, in all the way that ye went, until ye came into this place.

32 Yet in this thing ye did not believe the LORD your God,

33 Who went in the way before you, to search you out a place to pitch your tents *in*, in fire by night, to show you by what way ye should go, and in a cloud by day.

34 And the LORD heard the voice of your words, and was wroth, and sware, saying,

35 Surely there shall not one of these men of this evil generation see that good land, which I sware to give unto your fathers,

36 Save Caleb the son of Jephunneh; he shall see it, and to him will I give the land that he hath trodden upon, and to his children, because he hath ʰwholly followed the LORD.

37 Also the LORD was angry with me for your sakes, saying, Thou also shalt not go in thither.

38 *But* Joshua the son of Nun, which standeth before thee, he shall go in thither: encourage him: for he shall cause Israel to inherit it.

39 Moreover your little ones, which ye said should be a prey, and your children, which in that day had no knowledge between good and evil, they shall go in thither, and unto them will I give it, and they shall possess it.

40 But *as for* you, turn you, and take your journey into the wilderness by the way of the Red sea.

19 And when we departed from Horeb, we went through all that great and terrible wilderness which you saw on the way to the hill country of the Amorites, as the Lord our God commanded us, and we came to Kadesh-barnea.

20 And I said to you, You have come to the hill country of the Amorites, which the Lord our God gives us.

21 Behold, the Lord your God has set the land before you; go up and possess it, as the Lord, the God of your fathers, has said to you. Fear not, neither be dismayed.

22 Then you all came near to me and said, Let us send men before us, that they may search out the land for us and bring us word again by what way we should go up and the cities into which we shall come.

23 The thing pleased me well, and I took twelve men of you, one for each tribe.

24 And they turned and went up into the hill country, and came to the Valley of Eshcol and spied it out.

25 And they took of the fruit of the land in their hands and brought it down to us and brought us word again, and said, It is a good land which the Lord our God gives us.

26 Yet you would not go up, but rebelled against the commandment of the Lord your God.

27 You were peevish *and* discontented in your tents, and said, Because the Lord hated us, He brought us forth out of the land of Egypt to deliver us into the hand of the Amorites to destroy us.

28 To what are we going up? Our brethren have made our hearts melt, saying, The people are bigger and taller than we are; the cities are great and fortified to the heavens. And moreover we have seen the [giantlike] sons of the Anakim there.

29 Then I said to you, Dread not, neither be afraid of them.

30 The Lord your God Who goes before you, He will fight for you just as He did for you in Egypt before your eyes,

31 And in the wilderness, where you have seen how the Lord your God bore you, as a man carries his son, in all the way that you went until you came to this place.

32 Yet in spite of this word you did not believe (trust, rely on, and remain steadfast to) the Lord your God,

33 Who went in the way before you to search out a place to pitch your tents, in fire by night, to show you by what way you should go, and in the cloud by day.

34 And the Lord heard your words, and was angered and He swore,

35 Not one of these men of this evil generation shall see that good land which I swore to give to your fathers,

36 Except [Joshua, of course, and] Caleb son of Jephunneh; he shall see it, and to him and to his children I will give the land upon which he has walked, because he has wholly followed the Lord.

37 The Lord was angry with me also for your sakes, and said, You also shall not enter Canaan.

38 But Joshua son of Nun, who stands before you, he shall enter there. Encourage him, for he shall cause Israel to inherit it.

39 Moreover, your little ones whom you said would become a prey, and your children who at this time cannot discern between good and evil, they shall enter Canaan, and to them I will give it and they shall possess it.

40 But as for you, turn and journey into the wilderness by way of the Red Sea.

---

⁸ Heb. *melted*　　ʰ Heb. *fulfilled* to go *after*

New American Standard

19 ¶ "Then we set out from Horeb, and went through all that great and terrible wilderness which you saw on the way to the hill country of the Amorites, just as the LORD our God had commanded us; and we came to Kadesh-barnea.

20"I said to you, 'You have come to the hill country of the Amorites which the LORD our God is about to give us.

21 'See, the LORD your God has placed the land before you; go up, take possession, as the LORD, the God of your fathers, has spoken to you. Do not fear or be dismayed.'

22 ¶ "Then all of you approached me and said, 'Let us send men before us, that they may search out the land for us, and bring back to us word of the way by which we should go up and the cities which we shall enter.'

23"The thing pleased me and I took twelve of your men, one man for each tribe.

24"They turned and went up into the hill country, and came to the valley of Eshcol and spied it out.

25"Then they took *some* of the fruit of the land in their hands and brought it down to us; and they brought us back a report and said, 'It is a good land which the LORD our God is about to give us.'

26 ¶ "Yet you were not willing to go up, but rebelled against the command of the LORD your God;

27 and you grumbled in your tents and said, 'Because the LORD hates us, He has brought us out of the land of Egypt to deliver us into the hand of the Amorites to destroy us.

28 'Where can we go up? Our brethren have made our hearts melt, saying, "The people are bigger and taller than we; the cities are large and fortified to heaven. And besides, we saw the sons of the Anakim there." '

29"Then I said to you, 'Do not be shocked, nor fear them.

30 'The LORD your God who goes before you will Himself fight on your behalf, just as He did for you in Egypt before your eyes,

31 and in the wilderness where you saw how the LORD your God carried you, just as a man carries his son, in all the way which you have walked until you came to this place.'

32"But for all this, you did not trust the LORD your God,

33 who goes before you on *your* way, to seek out a place for you to encamp, in fire by night and cloud by day, to show you the way in which you should go.

34 ¶ "Then the LORD heard the sound of your words, and He was angry and took an oath, saying,

35 'Not one of these men, this evil generation, shall see the good land which I swore to give your fathers,

36 except Caleb the son of Jephunneh; he shall see it, and to him and to his sons I will give the land on which he has set foot, because he has followed the LORD fully.'

37"The LORD was angry with me also on your account, saying, 'Not even you shall enter there.

38 'Joshua the son of Nun, who stands before you, he shall enter there; encourage him, for he will cause Israel to inherit it.

39 'Moreover, your little ones who you said would become a prey, and your sons, who this day have no knowledge of good or evil, shall enter there, and I will give it to them and they shall possess it.

40 'But as for you, turn around and set out for the wilderness by the way to the Red Sea.'

New International

Spies Sent Out

19Then, as the LORD our God commanded us, we set out from Horeb and went toward the hill country of the Amorites through all that vast and dreadful desert that you have seen, and so we reached Kadesh Barnea. 20Then I said to you, "You have reached the hill country of the Amorites, which the LORD our God is giving us. 21See, the LORD your God has given you the land. Go up and take possession of it as the LORD, the God of your fathers, told you. Do not be afraid; do not be discouraged."

22Then all of you came to me and said, "Let us send men ahead to spy out the land for us and bring back a report about the route we are to take and the towns we will come to."

23The idea seemed good to me; so I selected twelve of you, one man from each tribe. 24They left and went up into the hill country, and came to the Valley of Eshcol and explored it. 25Taking with them some of the fruit of the land, they brought it down to us and reported, "It is a good land that the LORD our God is giving us."

Rebellion Against the LORD

26But you were unwilling to go up; you rebelled against the command of the LORD your God. 27You grumbled in your tents and said, "The LORD hates us; so he brought us out of Egypt to deliver us into the hands of the Amorites to destroy us. 28Where can we go? Our brothers have made us lose heart. They say, 'The people are stronger and taller than we are; the cities are large, with walls up to the sky. We even saw the Anakites there.' "

29Then I said to you, "Do not be terrified; do not be afraid of them. 30The LORD your God, who is going before you, will fight for you, as he did for you in Egypt, before your very eyes, 31and in the desert. There you saw how the LORD your God carried you, as a father carries his son, all the way you went until you reached this place."

32In spite of this, you did not trust in the LORD your God, 33who went ahead of you on your journey, in fire by night and in a cloud by day, to search out places for you to camp and to show you the way you should go.

34When the LORD heard what you said, he was angry and solemnly swore: 35"Not a man of this evil generation shall see the good land I swore to give your forefathers, 36except Caleb son of Jephunneh. He will see it, and I will give him and his descendants the land he set his feet on, because he followed the LORD wholeheartedly."

37Because of you the LORD became angry with me also and said, "You shall not enter it, either. 38But your assistant, Joshua son of Nun, will enter it. Encourage him, because he will lead Israel to inherit it. 39And the little ones that you said would be taken captive, your children who do not yet know good from bad—they will enter the land. I will give it to them and they will take possession of it. 40But as for you, turn around and set out toward the desert along the route to the Red Sea.*a*"

a 40 Hebrew Yam Suph; that is, Sea of Reeds

King James

41Then ye answered and said unto me, We have sinned against the LORD, we will go up and fight, according to all that the LORD our God commanded us. And when ye had girded on every man his weapons of war, ye were ready to go up into the hill.

42And the LORD said unto me, Say unto them, Go not up, neither fight; for I *am* not among you; lest ye be smitten before your enemies.

43So I spake unto you; and ye would not hear, but rebelled against the commandment of the LORD, and *i*went presumptuously up into the hill.

44And the Amorites, which dwelt in that mountain, came out against you, and chased you, as bees do, and destroyed you in Seir, *even* unto Hormah.

45And ye returned and wept before the LORD; but the LORD would not hearken to your voice, nor give ear unto you.

46So ye abode in Kadesh many days, according unto the days that ye abode *there.*

The years in the wilderness

2 THEN WE turned, and took our journey into the wilderness by the way of the Red sea, as the LORD spake unto me: and we compassed mount Seir many days.

2And the LORD spake unto me, saying,

3Ye have compassed this mountain long enough: turn you northward.

4And command thou the people, saying, Ye *are* to pass through the coast of your brethren the children of Esau, which dwell in Seir; and they shall be afraid of you: take ye good heed unto yourselves therefore:

5Meddle not with them; for I will not give you of their land, *j*no, not so much as a footbreadth; because I have given mount Seir unto Esau *for* a possession.

6Ye shall buy meat of them for money, that ye may eat; and ye shall also buy water of them for money, that ye may drink.

7For the LORD thy God hath blessed thee in all the works of thy hand: he knoweth thy walking through this great wilderness: these forty years the LORD thy God *hath been* with thee; thou hast lacked nothing.

8And when we passed by from our brethren the children of Esau, which dwelt in Seir, through the way of the plain from Elath, and from Ezion-geber, we turned and passed by the way of the wilderness of Moab.

9And the LORD said unto me, *k*Distress not the Moabites, neither contend with them in battle: for I will not give thee of their land *for* a possession; because I have given Ar unto the children of Lot *for* a possession.

10The Emims dwelt therein in times past, a people great, and many, and tall, as the Anakims;

11Which also were accounted giants, as the Anakims; but the Moabites call them Emims.

12The Horims also dwelt in Seir beforetime; but the children of Esau *l*succeeded them, when they had destroyed them from before them, and dwelt in their *m*stead; as Israel did unto the land of his possession, which the LORD gave unto them.

13Now rise up, *said I,* and get you over the *n*brook Zered. And we went over the brook Zered.

14And the space in which we came from Kadesh-barnea, until we were come over the brook Zered, *was* thirty and eight years; until all the generation of the men of war were wasted out from among the host, as the LORD sware unto them.

15For indeed the hand of the LORD was against them, to destroy them from among the host, until they were consumed.

16 ¶ So it came to pass, when all the men of war were consumed and dead from among the people,

Amplified

41Then you said to me, We have sinned against the Lord. We will go up and fight, as the Lord our God commanded us. And you girded on every man his battle weapons, and thought it a simple matter to go up into the hill country.

42And the Lord said to me, Say to them, Do not go up or fight, for I am not among you—lest you be dangerously hurt by your enemies.

43So I spoke to you, and you would not hear, but rebelled against the commandment of the Lord, and were presumptuous and went up into the hill country.

44Then the Amorites who lived in that hill country came out against you and chased you as bees do and struck you down in Seir as far as Hormah.

45And you returned and wept before the Lord, but the Lord would not heed your voice or listen to you.

46So you remained in Kadesh; many days you remained there.

2 THEN WE turned, and took our journey into the wilderness by the way of the Red Sea, as the Lord directed me; and for many days we journeyed around Mount Seir.

2And the Lord spoke to me [Moses], saying,

3You have roamed around this mountain country long enough; turn northward.

4And command the Israelites, You are to pass through the territory of your kinsmen the sons of Esau, who live in Seir; and they will be afraid of you. So watch yourselves carefully.

5Do not provoke *or* stir them up, for I will not give you of their land, no, not enough for the sole of your foot to tread on, for I have given Mount Seir to Esau for a possession.

6You shall buy food from them for money, that you may eat, and you shall also buy water from them for money, that you may drink.

7For the Lord your God has blessed you in all the work of your hand. He knows your walking through this great wilderness. These forty years the Lord your God has been with you; you have lacked nothing.

8So we passed on from our brethren the sons of Esau, who dwelt in Seir, away from the Arabah (wilderness), and from Elath and from Ezion-geber. We turned and went by the way of the wilderness of Moab.

9And the Lord said to me, Do not trouble *or* assault Moab or contend with them in battle, for I will not give you any of their land for a possession, because I have given Ar to the sons of Lot for a possession.

10(The Emim dwelt there in times past, a people great and many, and tall as the Anakim.

11These also are known as Rephaim [of giant stature], as are the Anakim, but the Moabites call them Emim.

12The Horites also formerly lived in Seir, but the sons of Esau dispossessed them and destroyed them from before them and dwelt in their stead, as Israel did to the land of their possession which the Lord gave to them.)

13Now rise up and go over the brook Zered. So we went over the brook Zered.

14And the time from our leaving Kadesh-barnea until we had come over the brook Zered was thirty-eight years, until the whole generation of the men of war had perished from the camp, as the Lord had sworn to them.

15Moreover the hand of the Lord was against them to exterminate them from the midst of the camp, until they were all gone.

16So when all the men of war had died from among the people,

---

*i*Heb. *ye were presumptuous, and went up*   *j*Heb. *even to the treading of the sole of the foot*   *k*Or, *Use no hostility against Moab*   *l*Heb. *inherited them*   *m*Or, *room*   *n*Or, *valley*

New American Standard

41 ¶ "Then you said to me, 'We have sinned against the LORD; we will indeed go up and fight, just as the LORD our God commanded us.' And every man of you girded on his weapons of war, and regarded it as easy to go up into the hill country.

42 "And the LORD said to me, 'Say to them, "Do not go up nor fight, for I am not among you; otherwise you will be defeated before your enemies."'

43 "So I spoke to you, but you would not listen. Instead you rebelled against the command of the LORD, and acted presumptuously and went up into the hill country.

44 "The Amorites who lived in that hill country came out against you and chased you as bees do, and crushed you from Seir to Hormah.

45 "Then you returned and wept before the LORD; but the LORD did not listen to your voice nor give ear to you.

46 "So you remained in Kadesh many days, the days that you spent *there*.

Wanderings in the Wilderness

2 "THEN WE turned and set out for the wilderness by the way to the Red Sea, as the LORD spoke to me, and circled Mount Seir for many days.

2 "And the LORD spoke to me, saying,

3 'You have circled this mountain long enough. *Now* turn north,

4 and command the people, saying, "You will pass through the territory of your brothers the sons of Esau who live in Seir; and they will be afraid of you. So be very careful;

5 do not provoke them, for I will not give you any of their land, even *as little as* a footstep because I have given Mount Seir to Esau as a possession.

6 "You shall buy food from them with money so that you may eat, and you shall also purchase water from them with money so that you may drink.

7 "For the LORD your God has blessed you in all that you have done; He has known your wanderings through this great wilderness. These forty years the LORD your God has been with you; you have not lacked a thing."'

8 ¶ "So we passed beyond our brothers the sons of Esau, who live in Seir, away from the Arabah road, away from Elath and from Ezion-geber. And we turned and passed through by the way of the wilderness of Moab.

9 "Then the LORD said to me, 'Do not harass Moab, nor provoke them to war, for I will not give you any of their land as a possession, because I have given Ar to the sons of Lot as a possession.

10 (The Emim lived there formerly, a people as great, numerous, and tall as the Anakim.

11 Like the Anakim, they are also regarded as Rephaim, but the Moabites call them Emim.

12 The Horites formerly lived in Seir, but the sons of Esau dispossessed them and destroyed them from before them and settled in their place, just as Israel did to the land of their possession which the LORD gave to them.)

13 'Now arise and cross over the brook Zered yourselves.' So we crossed over the brook Zered.

14 "Now the time that it took for us to come from Kadesh-barnea until we crossed over the brook Zered was thirty-eight years, until all the generation of the men of war perished from within the camp, as the LORD had sworn to them.

15 "Moreover the hand of the LORD was against them, to destroy them from within the camp until they all perished.

16 ¶ "So it came about when all the men of war had finally perished from among the people,

New International

41 Then you replied, "We have sinned against the LORD. We will go up and fight, as the LORD our God commanded us." So every one of you put on his weapons, thinking it easy to go up into the hill country.

42 But the LORD said to me, "Tell them, 'Do not go up and fight, because I will not be with you. You will be defeated by your enemies.'"

43 So I told you, but you would not listen. You rebelled against the LORD's command and in your arrogance you marched up into the hill country. 44 The Amorites who lived in those hills came out against you; they chased you like a swarm of bees and beat you down from Seir all the way to Hormah. 45 You came back and wept before the LORD, but he paid no attention to your weeping and turned a deaf ear to you. 46 And so you stayed in Kadesh many days—all the time you spent there.

Wanderings in the Desert

2 THEN WE turned back and set out toward the desert along the route to the Red Sea,[b] as the LORD had directed me. For a long time we made our way around the hill country of Seir.

2 Then the LORD said to me, 3 "You have made your way around this hill country long enough; now turn north. 4 Give the people these orders: 'You are about to pass through the territory of your brothers the descendants of Esau, who live in Seir. They will be afraid of you, but be very careful. 5 Do not provoke them to war, for I will not give you any of their land, not even enough to put your foot on. I have given Esau the hill country of Seir as his own. 6 You are to pay them in silver for the food you eat and the water you drink.'"

7 The LORD your God has blessed you in all the work of your hands. He has watched over your journey through this vast desert. These forty years the LORD your God has been with you, and you have not lacked anything.

8 So we went on past our brothers the descendants of Esau, who live in Seir. We turned from the Arabah road, which comes up from Elath and Ezion Geber, and traveled along the desert road of Moab.

9 Then the LORD said to me, "Do not harass the Moabites or provoke them to war, for I will not give you any part of their land. I have given Ar to the descendants of Lot as a possession."

10 (The Emites used to live there—a people strong and numerous, and as tall as the Anakites. 11 Like the Anakites, they too were considered Rephaites, but the Moabites called them Emites. 12 Horites used to live in Seir, but the descendants of Esau drove them out. They destroyed the Horites from before them and settled in their place, just as Israel did in the land the LORD gave them as their possession.)

13 And the LORD said, "Now get up and cross the Zered Valley." So we crossed the valley.

14 Thirty-eight years passed from the time we left Kadesh Barnea until we crossed the Zered Valley. By then, that entire generation of fighting men had perished from the camp, as the LORD had sworn to them. 15 The LORD's hand was against them until he had completely eliminated them from the camp.

16 Now when the last of these fighting men among the

King James

¹⁷That the LORD spake unto me, saying,

¹⁸Thou art to pass over through Ar, the coast of Moab, this day:

¹⁹And *when* thou comest nigh over against the children of Ammon, distress them not, nor meddle with them: for I will not give thee of the land of the children of Ammon *any* possession; because I have given it unto the children of Lot *for* a possession.

²⁰(That also was accounted a land of giants: giants dwelt therein in old time; and the Ammonites call them Zamzummims;

²¹A people great, and many, and tall, as the Anakims; but the LORD destroyed them before them; and they succeeded them, and dwelt in their stead:

²²As he did to the children of Esau, which dwelt in Seir, when he destroyed the Horims from before them; and they succeeded them, and dwelt in their stead even unto this day:

²³And the Avims which dwelt in Hazerim, *even* unto Azzah, the Caphtorims, which came forth out of Caphtor, destroyed them, and dwelt in their stead.)

²⁴ ¶ Rise ye up, take your journey, and pass over the river Arnon: behold, I have given into thine hand Sihon the Amorite, king of Heshbon, and his land: *ᵒ*begin to possess *it*, and contend with him in battle.

²⁵This day will I begin to put the dread of thee and the fear of thee upon the nations *that are* under the whole heaven, who shall hear report of thee, and shall tremble, and be in anguish because of thee.

The victory over Sihon

²⁶ ¶ And I sent messengers out of the wilderness of Kedemoth unto Sihon king of Heshbon with words of peace, saying,

²⁷Let me pass through thy land: I will go along by the high way, I will neither turn unto the right hand nor to the left.

²⁸Thou shalt sell me meat for money, that I may eat; and give me water for money, that I may drink: only I will pass through on my feet;

²⁹(As the children of Esau which dwell in Seir, and the Moabites which dwell in Ar, did unto me;) until I shall pass over Jordan into the land which the LORD our God giveth us.

³⁰But Sihon king of Heshbon would not let us pass by him: for the LORD thy God hardened his spirit, and made his heart obstinate, that he might deliver him into thy hand, as *appeareth* this day.

³¹And the LORD said unto me, Behold, I have begun to give Sihon and his land before thee: begin to possess, that thou mayest inherit his land.

³²Then Sihon came out against us, he and all his people, to fight at Jahaz.

³³And the LORD our God delivered him before us; and we smote him, and his sons, and all his people.

³⁴And we took all his cities at that time, and utterly destroyed *ᵖ*the men, and the women, and the little ones, of every city, we left none to remain:

³⁵Only the cattle we took for a prey unto ourselves, and the spoil of the cities which we took.

³⁶From Aroer, which *is* by the brink of the river of Arnon, and *from* the city that *is* by the river, even unto Gilead, there was not one city too strong for us: the LORD our God delivered all unto us:

³⁷Only unto the land of the children of Ammon thou camest not, *nor* unto any place of the river Jabbok, nor unto the cities in the mountains, nor unto whatsoever the LORD our God forbad us.

Amplified

¹⁷The Lord spoke to me [Moses], saying,

¹⁸You are this day to pass through Ar, the border of Moab.

¹⁹But when you come near the territory of the sons of Ammon, do not trouble *or* assault them or provoke *or* stir them up, for I will not give you any of the land of the Ammonites for a possession, because I have given it to the sons of Lot for a possession.

²⁰(That also is known as a land of Rephaim [of giant stature]; Rephaim dwelt there formerly, but the Ammonites call them Zamzummim,

²¹A people great and many, and tall as the Anakim. But the Lord destroyed them before [Ammon], and they dispossessed them and settled in their stead,

²²As He did for the sons of Esau, who dwell in Seir, when He destroyed the Horites from before them, and they dispossessed them and settled in their stead even to this day.

²³As for the Avvim who dwelt in villages as far as Gaza, the Caphtorim who came from Caphtor destroyed them and dwelt in their stead.)

²⁴Rise up, take your journey, and pass over the Valley of the Arnon. Behold, I have given into your hand Sihon the Amorite, king of Heshbon, and his land; begin to possess it and contend with him in battle.

²⁵This day will I begin to put the dread and fear of you upon the peoples who are under the whole heavens, who shall hear the report of you and shall tremble and be in anguish because of you.

²⁶So I sent messengers from the wilderness of Kedemoth to Sihon king of Heshbon with words of peace, saying,

²⁷Let me pass through your land. I will go only by the road, turning aside neither to the right nor to the left.

²⁸You shall sell me food to eat and sell me water to drink; only let me walk through,

²⁹As the sons of Esau, who dwell in Seir, and the Moabites, who dwell in Ar, *ᵃ*did for me, until I go over the Jordan into the land which the Lord our God gives us.

³⁰But Sihon king of Heshbon would not let us pass by him; for the Lord your God hardened his spirit and made his heart obstinate, that He might give him into your hand, as at this day.

³¹And the Lord said to me [Moses], Behold, I have begun to give Sihon and his land over to you. Begin to take possession, that you may succeed him *and* occupy his land.

³²Then Sihon came out against us, he and all his people, to fight at Jahaz.

³³And the Lord our God gave him over to us, and we defeated him and his sons and all his people.

³⁴At the same time we took all his cities and utterly destroyed every city—men, women, and children. We left none to remain.

³⁵Only the cattle we took as booty for ourselves and the spoil of the cities which we had captured.

³⁶From Aroer, which is on the edge of the Arnon Valley, and from the city that is in the valley, as far as Gilead, there was no city too high *and* strong for us; the Lord our God delivered all to us.

³⁷Only you did not go near the land of the Ammonites, that is, to any bank of the river Jabbok and the cities of the hill country, and wherever the Lord our God had forbidden us.

ᵃ All that is said here is that the Edomites and Moabites sold Israel bread and water. There is no denial, expressed or implied, of their hostility to Israel and their desire for her destruction. The passage is in entire harmony with Num. 20:17, 21, and Deut. 23:3, 4 (J.P. Lange, *A Commentary*).

ᵒ Heb. *begin, possess*   *ᵖ* Heb. *every city of men, and women, and little ones*

New American Standard

17 that the LORD spoke to me, saying,

18 'Today you shall cross over Ar, the border of Moab.

19 'When you come opposite the sons of Ammon, do not harass them nor provoke them, for I will not give you any of the land of the sons of Ammon as a possession, because I have given it to the sons of Lot as a possession.'

20 (It is also regarded as the land of the Rephaim, *for* Rephaim formerly lived in it, but the Ammonites call them Zamzummin,

21 a people as great, numerous, and tall as the Anakim, but the LORD destroyed them before them. And they dispossessed them and lived in their place,

22 just as He did for the sons of Esau, who live in Seir, when He destroyed the Horites from before them; they dispossessed them and settled in their place even to this day.

23 And the Avvim, who lived in villages as far as Gaza, the *b*Caphtorim who came from *c*Caphtor, destroyed them and lived in their place.)

24 'Arise, set out, and pass through the valley of Arnon. Look! I have given Sihon the Amorite, king of Heshbon, and his land into your hand; begin to take possession and contend with him in battle.

25 'This day I will begin to put the dread and fear of you upon the peoples everywhere under the heavens, who, when they hear the report of you, will tremble and be in anguish because of you.'

26 ¶ "So I sent messengers from the wilderness of Kedemoth to Sihon king of Heshbon with words of peace, saying,

27 'Let me pass through your land, I will travel only on the highway; I will not turn aside to the right or to the left.

28 'You will sell me food for money so that I may eat, and give me water for money so that I may drink, only let me pass through on foot,

29 just as the sons of Esau who live in Seir and the Moabites who live in Ar did for me, until I cross over the Jordan into the land which the LORD our God is giving to us.'

30 "But Sihon king of Heshbon was not willing for us to pass through his land; for the LORD your God hardened his spirit and made his heart obstinate, in order to deliver him into your hand, as *he is* today.

31 "The LORD said to me, 'See, I have begun to deliver Sihon and his land over to you. Begin to occupy, that you may possess his land.'

32 ¶ "Then Sihon with all his people came out to meet us in battle at Jahaz.

33 "The LORD our God delivered him over to us, and we defeated him with his sons and all his people.

34 "So we captured all his cities at that time and utterly destroyed the men, women and children of every city. We left no survivor.

35 "We took only the animals as our booty and the spoil of the cities which we had captured.

36 "From Aroer which is on the edge of the valley of Arnon and *from* the city which is in the valley, even to Gilead, there was no city that was too high for us; the LORD our God delivered all over to us.

37 "Only you did not go near to the land of the sons of Ammon, all along the river Jabbok and the cities of the hill country, and wherever the LORD our God had commanded us.

New International

people had died, 17the LORD said to me, 18"Today you are to pass by the region of Moab at Ar. 19When you come to the Ammonites, do not harass them or provoke them to war, for I will not give you possession of any land belonging to the Ammonites. I have given it as a possession to the descendants of Lot."

20(That too was considered a land of the Rephaites, who used to live there; but the Ammonites called them Zamzummites. 21They were a people strong and numerous, and as tall as the Anakites. The LORD destroyed them from before the Ammonites, who drove them out and settled in their place. 22The LORD had done the same for the descendants of Esau, who lived in Seir, when he destroyed the Horites from before them. They drove them out and have lived in their place to this day. 23And as for the Avvites who lived in villages as far as Gaza, the Caphtorites coming out from Caphtor*c* destroyed them and settled in their place.)

Defeat of Sihon King of Heshbon

24"Set out now and cross the Arnon Gorge. See, I have given into your hand Sihon the Amorite, king of Heshbon, and his country. Begin to take possession of it and engage him in battle. 25This very day I will begin to put the terror and fear of you on all the nations under heaven. They will hear reports of you and will tremble and be in anguish because of you."

26From the desert of Kedemoth I sent messengers to Sihon king of Heshbon offering peace and saying, 27"Let us pass through your country. We will stay on the main road; we will not turn aside to the right or to the left. 28Sell us food to eat and water to drink for their price in silver. Only let us pass through on foot— 29as the descendants of Esau, who live in Seir, and the Moabites, who live in Ar, did for us—until we cross the Jordan into the land the LORD our God is giving us." 30But Sihon king of Heshbon refused to let us pass through. For the LORD your God had made his spirit stubborn and his heart obstinate in order to give him into your hands, as he has now done.

31The LORD said to me, "See, I have begun to deliver Sihon and his country over to you. Now begin to conquer and possess his land."

32When Sihon and all his army came out to meet us in battle at Jahaz, 33the LORD our God delivered him over to us and we struck him down, together with his sons and his whole army. 34At that time we took all his towns and completely destroyed*d* them—men, women and children. We left no survivors. 35But the livestock and the plunder from the towns we had captured we carried off for ourselves. 36From Aroer on the rim of the Arnon Gorge, and from the town in the gorge, even as far as Gilead, not one town was too strong for us. The LORD our God gave us all of them. 37But in accordance with the command of the LORD our God, you did not encroach on any of the land of the Ammonites, neither the land along the course of the Jabbok nor that around the towns in the hills.

c23 That is, Crete   *d34* The Hebrew term refers to the irrevocable giving over of things or persons to the LORD, often by totally destroying them.

b I.e. Philistines   *c* I.e. Crete

King James

The victory over Og

3 THEN WE turned, and went up the way to Bashan: and Og the king of Bashan came out against us, he and all his people, to battle at Edrei.

2And the LORD said unto me, Fear him not: for I will deliver him, and all his people, and his land, into thy hand; and thou shalt do unto him as thou didst unto Sihon king of the Amorites, which dwelt at Heshbon.

3So the LORD our God delivered into our hands Og also, the king of Bashan, and all his people: and we smote him until none was left to him remaining.

4And we took all his cities at that time, there was not a city which we took not from them, threescore cities, all the region of Argob, the kingdom of Og in Bashan.

5All these cities were fenced with high walls, gates, and bars; beside unwalled towns a great many.

6And we utterly destroyed them, as we did unto Sihon king of Heshbon, utterly destroying the men, women, and children, of every city.

7But all the cattle, and the spoil of the cities, we took for a prey to ourselves.

8And we took at that time out of the hand of the two kings of the Amorites the land that was on this side Jordan, from the river of Arnon unto mount Hermon;

9(Which Hermon the Sidonians call Sirion; and the Amorites call it Shenir;)

10All the cities of the plain, and all Gilead, and all Bashan, unto Salchah and Edrei, cities of the kingdom of Og in Bashan.

11For only Og king of Bashan remained of the remnant of giants; behold, his bedstead was a bedstead of iron; is it not in Rabbath of the children of Ammon? nine cubits was the length thereof, and four cubits the breadth of it, after the cubit of a man.

The distribution of the land

12And this land, which we possessed at that time, from Aroer, which is by the river Arnon, and half mount Gilead, and the cities thereof, gave I unto the Reubenites and to the Gadites.

13And the rest of Gilead, and all Bashan, being the kingdom of Og, gave I unto the half tribe of Manasseh; all the region of Argob, with all Bashan, which was called the land of giants.

14Jair the son of Manasseh took all the country of Argob unto the coasts of Geshuri and Maachathi; and called them after his own name, Bashan-havoth-jair, unto this day.

15And I gave Gilead unto Machir.

16And unto the Reubenites and unto the Gadites I gave from Gilead even unto the river Arnon half the valley, and the border even unto the river Jabbok, which is the border of the children of Ammon;

17The plain also, and Jordan, and the coast thereof, from Chinnereth even unto the sea of the plain, even the salt sea, qunder Ashdoth-pisgah eastward.

18 ¶ And I commanded you at that time, saying, The LORD your God hath given you this land to possess it: ye shall pass over armed before your brethren the children of Israel, all that are rmeet for the war.

19But your wives, and your little ones, and your cattle, (for I know that ye have much cattle,) shall abide in your cities which I have given you;

20Until the LORD have given rest unto your brethren, as well as unto you, and until they also possess the land which the LORD your God hath given them beyond Jordan: and then shall ye return every man unto his possession, which I have given you.

21 ¶ And I commanded Joshua at that time, saying, Thine eyes have seen all that the LORD your God hath done unto these two kings: so shall the LORD do unto all the kingdoms whither thou passest.

qOr, under the springs of Pisgah, or, the hill   rHeb. sons of
power.

Amplified

3 THEN WE turned and went up the road to Bashan, and Og king of Bashan came out against us, he and all his people, to battle at Edrei.

2And the Lord said to me, Do not fear him, for I have given him and all his people and his land into your hand; and you shall do to him as you did to Sihon king of the Amorites, who lived at Heshbon.

3So the Lord our God also gave into our hands Og king of Bashan and all his people, and we smote him until not one was left to him.

4And we took all his cities at that time; there was not a city which we did not take from them, sixty cities, the whole region of Argob, the kingdom of Og in Bashan.

5All these cities were fortified with high and haughty walls, gates, and bars, besides a great many unwalled villages.

6And we utterly destroyed them, as we did to Sihon king of Heshbon, utterly destroying every city—men, women, and children.

7But all the cattle and the spoil of the cities we took for booty for ourselves.

8So we took the land at that time out of the hand of the two kings of the Amorites who were beyond the Jordan, from the Valley of the Arnon to Mount Hermon

9(The Sidonians call Hermon, Sirion, and the Amorites call it Senir),

10All the cities of the plain, and all Gilead, and all Bashan as far as Salecah and Edrei, cities of the kingdom of Og in Bashan.

11For only Og king of Bashan remained of the remnant of the [gigantic] Rephaim. Behold, his bedstead was of iron; is it not in Rabbah of the Ammonites? Nine cubits was its length and four cubits its breadth, using the cubit of a man [the forearm to the end of the middle finger].

12When we took possession of this land, I gave to the Reubenites and the Gadites the territory from Aroer, which is on the edge of the Valley of the Arnon, and half the hill country of Gilead and its cities.

13The rest of Gilead and all of Bashan, the kingdom of Og, that is, all the region of Argob in Bashan, I gave to the half-tribe of Manasseh. It is called the land of Rephaim [of giant stature].

14Jair son of Manasseh took all the region of Argob, that is, Bashan, as far as the border of the Geshurites and the Maacathites, and called it after his own name, Havvoth-jair, so called to this day.

15And I gave Gilead to Machir [son of Manasseh].

16And to the Reubenites and Gadites I gave from Gilead even to the Valley of the Arnon, with the middle of the valley as the boundary of it, as far over as the river Jabbok, the boundary of the Ammonites,

17The Arabah also, with the Jordan as its boundary, from Chinnereth as far as the Sea of the Arabah, the Salt [Dead] Sea, under the cliffs [of the headlands] of Pisgah on the east.

18And I commanded you at that time, saying, The Lord your God has given you this land to possess it; you [Reuben, Gad, and the half-tribe of Manasseh] shall go over [the Jordan] armed before your brethren the other Israelites, all that are able for war.

19But your wives and your little ones and your cattle—I know that you have many cattle—shall remain in your cities which I have given you,

20Until the Lord has given rest to your brethren as to you, and until they also possess the land which the Lord your God has given them beyond the Jordan. Then shall you return every man to the possession which I have given you.

21And I commanded Joshua at that time, saying, Your own eyes have seen all that the Lord your God has done to these two kings [Sihon and Og]; so shall the Lord do to all the kingdoms into which you are going over [the Jordan].

New American Standard

Conquests Recounted

3 "THEN WE turned and went up the road to Bashan, and Og, king of Bashan, with all his people came out to meet us in battle at Edrei. ²"But the LORD said to me, 'Do not fear him, for I have delivered him and all his people and his land into your hand; and you shall do to him just as you did to Sihon king of the Amorites, who lived at Heshbon.' ³"So the LORD our God delivered Og also, king of Bashan, with all his people into our hand, and we smote them until no survivor was left.

⁴"We captured all his cities at that time; there was not a city which we did not take from them: sixty cities, all the region of Argob, the kingdom of Og in Bashan. ⁵"All these were cities fortified with high walls, gates and bars, besides a great many unwalled towns. ⁶"We utterly destroyed them, as we did to Sihon king of Heshbon, utterly destroying the men, women and children of every city. ⁷"But all the animals and the spoil of the cities we took as our booty.

8 ¶ "Thus we took the land at that time from the hand of the two kings of the Amorites who were beyond the Jordan, from the valley of Arnon to Mount Hermon 9 (Sidonians call Hermon Sirion, and the Amorites call it Senir): ¹⁰ all the cities of the plateau and all Gilead and all Bashan, as far as Salecah and Edrei, cities of the kingdom of Og in Bashan.

¹¹ (For only Og king of Bashan was left of the remnant of the Rephaim. Behold, his bedstead was an iron bedstead; it is in Rabbah of the sons of Ammon. Its length was nine cubits and its width four cubits by ordinary cubit.) ¹² ¶ "So we took possession of this land at that time. From Aroer, which is by the valley of Arnon, and half the hill country of Gilead and its cities I gave to the Reubenites and to the Gadites. ¹³"The rest of Gilead and all Bashan, the kingdom of Og, I gave to the half-tribe of Manasseh, all the region of Argob (concerning all Bashan, it is called the land of Rephaim.

¹⁴ Jair the son of Manasseh took all the region of Argob as far as the border of the Geshurites and the Maacathites, and called it, *that is,* Bashan, after his own name, Havvoth-jair, *as it is* to this day.) ¹⁵"To Machir I gave Gilead. ¹⁶"To the Reubenites and to the Gadites I gave from Gilead even as far as the valley of Arnon, the middle of the valley as a border and as far as the river Jabbok, the border of the sons of Ammon; ¹⁷ the Arabah also, with the Jordan as *a* border, from *d*Chinnereth even as far as the sea of the Arabah, the Salt Sea, at the foot of the slopes of Pisgah on the east.

18 ¶ "Then I commanded you at that time, saying, 'The LORD your God has given you this land to possess it; all you valiant men shall cross over armed before your brothers, the sons of Israel.

¹⁹ 'But your wives and your little ones and your livestock (I know that you have much livestock) shall remain in your cities which I have given you, ²⁰ until the LORD gives rest to your fellow countrymen as to you, and they also possess the land which the LORD your God will give them beyond the Jordan. Then you may return every man to his possession which I have given you.'

²¹"I commanded Joshua at that time, saying, 'Your eyes have seen all that the LORD your God has done to these two kings; so the LORD shall do to all the kingdoms into which you are about to cross.

*d*I.e. the Sea of Galilee

New International

Defeat of Og King of Bashan

3 NEXT WE turned and went up along the road toward Bashan, and Og king of Bashan with his whole army marched out to meet us in battle at Edrei. ²The LORD said to me, "Do not be afraid of him, for I have handed him over to you with his whole army and his land. Do to him what you did to Sihon king of the Amorites, who reigned in Heshbon."

³So the LORD our God also gave into our hands Og king of Bashan and all his army. We struck them down, leaving no survivors. ⁴At that time we took all his cities. There was not one of the sixty cities that we did not take from them— the whole region of Argob, Og's kingdom in Bashan. ⁵All these cities were fortified with high walls and with gates and bars, and there were also a great many unwalled villages. ⁶We completely destroyed*e* them, as we had done with Sihon king of Heshbon, destroying*e* every city— men, women and children. ⁷But all the livestock and the plunder from their cities we carried off for ourselves.

⁸So at that time we took from these two kings of the Amorites the territory east of the Jordan, from the Arnon Gorge as far as Mount Hermon. ⁹(Hermon is called Sirion by the Sidonians; the Amorites call it Senir.) ¹⁰We took all the towns on the plateau, and all Gilead, and all Bashan as far as Salecah and Edrei, towns of Og's kingdom in Bashan. ¹¹(Only Og king of Bashan was left of the remnant of the Rephaites. His bed*f* was made of iron and was more than thirteen feet long and six feet wide.*g* It is still in Rabbah of the Ammonites.)

Division of the Land

¹²Of the land that we took over at that time, I gave the Reubenites and the Gadites the territory north of Aroer by the Arnon Gorge, including half the hill country of Gilead, together with its towns. ¹³The rest of Gilead and also all of Bashan, the kingdom of Og, I gave to the half-tribe of Manasseh. (The whole region of Argob in Bashan used to be known as a land of the Rephaites. ¹⁴Jair, a descendant of Manasseh, took the whole region of Argob as far as the border of the Geshurites and the Maacathites; it was named after him, so that to this day Bashan is called Havvoth Jair.*h*) ¹⁵And I gave Gilead to Makir. ¹⁶But to the Reubenites and the Gadites I gave the territory extending from Gilead down to the Arnon Gorge (the middle of the gorge being the border) and out to the Jabbok River, which is the border of the Ammonites. ¹⁷Its western border was the Jordan in the Arabah, from Kinnereth to the Sea of the Arabah (the Salt Sea*i*), below the slopes of Pisgah.

¹⁸I commanded you at that time: "The LORD your God has given you this land to take possession of it. But all your able-bodied men, armed for battle, must cross over ahead of your brother Israelites. ¹⁹However, your wives, your children and your livestock (I know you have much livestock) may stay in the towns I have given you, ²⁰until the LORD gives rest to your brothers as he has to you, and they too have taken over the land that the LORD your God is giving them, across the Jordan. After that, each of you may go back to the possession I have given you."

Moses Forbidden to Cross the Jordan

²¹At that time I commanded Joshua: "You have seen with your own eyes all that the LORD your God has done to these two kings. The LORD will do the same to all the

e6 The Hebrew term refers to the irrevocable giving over of things or persons to the LORD, often by totally destroying them.
f11 Or *sarcophagus*   *g11* Hebrew *nine cubits long and four cubits wide* (about 4 meters long and 1.8 meters wide)
h14 Or *called the settlements of Jair*   *i17* That is, the Dead Sea

King James

²²Ye shall not fear them: for the LORD your God he shall fight for you.

Moses forbidden to cross Jordan

²³And I besought the LORD at that time, saying,

²⁴O Lord GOD, thou hast begun to show thy servant thy greatness, and thy mighty hand: for what God *is there* in heaven or in earth, that can do according to thy works, and according to thy might?

²⁵I pray thee, let me go over, and see the good land that *is* beyond Jordan, that goodly mountain, and Lebanon.

²⁶But the LORD was wroth with me for your sakes, and would not hear me: and the LORD said unto me, Let it suffice thee; speak no more unto me of this matter.

²⁷Get thee up into the top of ^sPisgah, and lift up thine eyes westward, and northward, and southward, and eastward, and behold *it* with thine eyes: for thou shalt not go over this Jordan.

²⁸But charge Joshua, and encourage him, and strengthen him: for he shall go over before this people, and he shall cause them to inherit the land which thou shalt see.

²⁹So we abode in the valley over against Beth-peor.

Moses commands obedience

4 NOW THEREFORE hearken, O Israel, unto the statutes and unto the judgments, which I teach you, for to do *them,* that ye may live, and go in and possess the land which the LORD God of your fathers giveth you.

²Ye shall not add unto the word which I command you, neither shall ye diminish *aught* from it, that ye may keep the commandments of the LORD your God which I command you.

³Your eyes have seen what the LORD did because of Baal-peor: for all the men that followed Baal-peor, the LORD thy God hath destroyed them from among you.

⁴But ye that did cleave unto the LORD your God *are* alive every one of you this day.

⁵Behold, I have taught you statutes and judgments, even as the LORD my God commanded me, that ye should do so in the land whither ye go to possess it.

⁶Keep therefore and do *them;* for this *is* your wisdom and your understanding in the sight of the nations, which shall hear all these statutes, and say, Surely this great nation *is* a wise and understanding people.

⁷For what nation *is there so* great, who *hath* God *so* nigh unto them, as the LORD our God *is* in all *things that* we call upon him *for?*

⁸And what nation *is there so* great, that hath statutes and judgments *so* righteous as all this law, which I set before you this day?

⁹Only take heed to thyself, and keep thy soul diligently, lest thou forget the things which thine eyes have seen, and lest they depart from thy heart all the days of thy life: but teach them thy sons, and thy sons' sons;

¹⁰*Specially* the day that thou stoodest before the LORD thy God in Horeb, when the LORD said unto me, Gather me the people together, and I will make them hear my words, that they may learn to fear me all the days that they shall live upon the earth, and *that* they may teach their children.

¹¹And ye came near and stood under the mountain; and the mountain burned with fire unto the ^tmidst of heaven, with darkness, clouds, and thick darkness.

¹²And the LORD spake unto you out of the midst of the fire: ye heard the voice of the words, but saw no similitude; ^uonly *ye heard* a voice.

¹³And he declared unto you his covenant, which he commanded you to perform, *even* ten commandments; and he wrote them upon two tables of stone.

Amplified

²²You shall not fear them, for the Lord your God shall fight for you.

²³And I besought the Lord at that time, saying,

²⁴O Lord God, You have only begun to show Your servant Your greatness and Your mighty hand; for what god is there in heaven or on earth that can do according to Your works and according to Your might?

²⁵I pray You, [will You not just] let me go over and see the good land that is beyond the Jordan, that goodly mountain country [with Hermon] and Lebanon?

²⁶But the Lord was angry with me on your account and would not listen to me; and the Lord said to me, That is enough! Say no more to Me about it.

²⁷Get up to the top of Pisgah and lift up your eyes westward and northward and southward and eastward, and behold it with your eyes, for you shall not go over this Jordan.

²⁸But charge Joshua, and encourage and strengthen him, for he shall go over before this people and he shall cause them to possess the land which you shall see.

²⁹So we remained in the valley opposite Beth-peor.

4 NOW LISTEN *and* give heed, O Israel, to the statutes and ordinances which I teach you, and do them, that you may live and go in and possess the land which the Lord, the God of your fathers, gives you.

²You shall not add to the word which I command you, neither shall you diminish it, that you may keep the commandments of the Lord your God which I command you.

³Your eyes still see what the Lord did because of Baal-peor; for all the men who followed the Baal of Peor the Lord your God has destroyed from among you, [Num. 25:1–9.]

⁴But you who clung fast to the Lord your God are alive, every one of you, this day.

⁵Behold, I have taught you statutes and ordinances as the Lord my God commanded me, that you should do them in the land which you are entering to possess.

⁶So keep them and do them, for that is your wisdom and your understanding in the sight of the peoples who, when they hear all these statutes, will say, Surely this great nation is a wise and understanding people.

⁷For what great nation is there who has a god so near to them as the Lord our God is to us in all things for which we call upon Him?

⁸And what large *and* important nation has statutes and ordinances so upright *and* just as all this law which I set before you today?

⁹Only take heed, and guard your life diligently, lest you forget the things which your eyes have seen and lest they depart from your [mind and] heart all the days of your life. Teach them to your children and your children's children—

¹⁰Especially how on the day that you stood before the Lord your God in Horeb, the Lord said to me, Gather the people together to Me and I will make them hear My words, that they may learn [reverently] to fear Me all the days they live upon the earth and that they may teach their children.

¹¹And you came near and stood at the foot of the mountain, and the mountain burned with fire to the heart of heaven, with darkness, cloud, and thick gloom.

¹²And the Lord spoke to you out of the midst of the fire. You heard the voice of the words, but saw no form; there was only a voice.

¹³And He declared to you His covenant, which He commanded you to perform, the Ten Commandments, and He wrote them on two tables of stone.

^sOr, *The hill*   ^tHeb. *heart*   ^uHeb. *save a voice*

New American Standard

22 'Do not fear them, for the LORD your God is the one fighting for you.'

23 ¶ "I also pleaded with the LORD at that time, saying, 24 'O Lord GOD, You have begun to show Your servant Your greatness and Your strong hand; for what god is there in heaven or on earth who can do such works and mighty acts as Yours? 25 'Let me, I pray, cross over and see the fair land that is beyond the Jordan, that good hill country and Lebanon.' 26 "But the LORD was angry with me on your account, and would not listen to me; and the LORD said to me, 'Enough! Speak to Me no more of this matter. 27 'Go up to the top of Pisgah and lift up your eyes to the west and north and south and east, and see *it* with your eyes, for you shall not cross over this Jordan. 28 'But charge Joshua and encourage him and strengthen him, for he shall go across at the head of this people, and he will give them as an inheritance the land which you will see.'

29 "So we remained in the valley opposite Beth-peor.

Israel Urged to Obey God's Law

4 "NOW, O Israel, listen to the statutes and the judgments which I am teaching you to perform, so that you may live and go in and take possession of the land which the LORD, the God of your fathers, is giving you. 2 "You shall not add to the word which I am commanding you, nor take away from it, that you may keep the commandments of the LORD your God which I command you. 3 "Your eyes have seen what the LORD has done in the case of Baal-peor, for all the men who followed Baal-peor, the LORD your God has destroyed them from among you. 4 "But you who held fast to the LORD your God are alive today, every one of you. 5 ¶ "See, I have taught you statutes and judgments just as the LORD my God commanded me, that you should do thus in the land where you are entering to possess it. 6 "So keep and do *them,* for that is your wisdom and your understanding in the sight of the peoples who will hear all these statutes and say, 'Surely this great nation is a wise and understanding people.' 7 "For what great nation is there that has a god so near to it as is the LORD our God whenever we call on Him? 8 "Or what great nation is there that has statutes and judgments as righteous as this whole law which I am setting before you today? 9 ¶ "Only give heed to yourself and keep your soul diligently, so that you do not forget the things which your eyes have seen and they do not depart from your heart all the days of your life; but make them known to your sons and your grandsons. 10 "*Remember* the day you stood before the LORD your God at Horeb, when the LORD said to me, 'Assemble the people to Me, that I may let them hear My words so they may learn to *e*fear Me all the days they live on the earth, and that they may teach their children.' 11 "You came near and stood at the foot of the mountain, and the mountain burned with fire to the *very* heart of the heavens: darkness, cloud and thick gloom. 12 "Then the LORD spoke to you from the midst of the fire; you heard the sound of words, but you saw no form—only a voice. 13 "So He declared to you His covenant which He commanded you to perform, *that is,* the Ten Commandments; and He wrote them on two tablets of stone.

New International

kingdoms over there where you are going. 22 Do not be afraid of them; the LORD your God himself will fight for you."

23 At that time I pleaded with the LORD: 24 "O Sovereign LORD, you have begun to show to your servant your greatness and your strong hand. For what god is there in heaven or on earth who can do the deeds and mighty works you do? 25 Let me go over and see the good land beyond the Jordan—that fine hill country and Lebanon." 26 But because of you the LORD was angry with me and would not listen to me. "That is enough," the LORD said. "Do not speak to me anymore about this matter. 27 Go up to the top of Pisgah and look west and north and south and east. Look at the land with your own eyes, since you are not going to cross this Jordan. 28 But commission Joshua, and encourage and strengthen him, for he will lead this people across and will cause them to inherit the land that you will see." 29 So we stayed in the valley near Beth Peor.

Obedience Commanded

4 HEAR NOW, O Israel, the decrees and laws I am about to teach you. Follow them so that you may live and may go in and take possession of the land that the LORD, the God of your fathers, is giving you. 2 Do not add to what I command you and do not subtract from it, but keep the commands of the LORD your God that I give you.

3 You saw with your own eyes what the LORD did at Baal Peor. The LORD your God destroyed from among you everyone who followed the Baal of Peor, 4 but all of you who held fast to the LORD your God are still alive today.

5 See, I have taught you decrees and laws as the LORD my God commanded me, so that you may follow them in the land you are entering to take possession of it. 6 Observe them carefully, for this will show your wisdom and understanding to the nations, who will hear about all these decrees and say, "Surely this great nation is a wise and understanding people." 7 What other nation is so great as to have their gods near them the way the LORD our God is near us whenever we pray to him? 8 And what other nation is so great as to have such righteous decrees and laws as this body of laws I am setting before you today?

9 Only be careful, and watch yourselves closely so that you do not forget the things your eyes have seen or let them slip from your heart as long as you live. Teach them to your children and to their children after them. 10 Remember the day you stood before the LORD your God at Horeb, when he said to me, "Assemble the people before me to hear my words so that they may learn to revere me as long as they live in the land and may teach them to their children." 11 You came near and stood at the foot of the mountain while it blazed with fire to the very heavens, with black clouds and deep darkness. 12 Then the LORD spoke to you out of the fire. You heard the sound of words but saw no form; there was only a voice. 13 He declared to you his covenant, the Ten Commandments, which he commanded you to follow and then wrote them on two stone

e Or *reverence*

King James

Amplified

14 ¶ And the LORD commanded me at that time to teach you statutes and judgments, that ye might do them in the land whither ye go over to possess it.

Idolatry forbidden

15Take ye therefore good heed unto yourselves; for ye saw no manner of similitude on the day *that* the LORD spake unto you in Horeb out of the midst of the fire:

16Lest ye corrupt *yourselves,* and make you a graven image, the similitude of any figure, the likeness of male or female,

17The likeness of any beast that *is* on the earth, the likeness of any winged fowl that flieth in the air,

18The likeness of any thing that creepeth on the ground, the likeness of any fish that *is* in the waters beneath the earth:

19And lest thou lift up thine eyes unto heaven, and when thou seest the sun, and the moon, and the stars, *even* all the host of heaven, shouldest be driven to worship them, and serve them, which the LORD thy God hath ᵛdivided unto all nations under the whole heaven.

20But the LORD hath taken you, and brought you forth out of the iron furnace, *even* out of Egypt, to be unto him a people of inheritance, as *ye are* this day.

21Furthermore the LORD was angry with me for your sakes, and sware that I should not go over Jordan, and that I should not go in unto that good land, which the LORD thy God giveth thee *for* an inheritance.

22But I must die in this land, I must not go over Jordan: but ye shall go over, and possess that good land.

23Take heed unto yourselves, lest ye forget the covenant of the LORD your God, which he made with you, and make you a graven image, *or* the likeness of any *thing,* which the LORD thy God hath forbidden thee.

24For the LORD thy God *is* a consuming fire, *even* a jealous God.

25 ¶ When thou shalt beget children, and children's children, and ye shall have remained long in the land, and shall corrupt *yourselves,* and make a graven image, *or* the likeness of any *thing,* and shall do evil in the sight of the LORD thy God, to provoke him to anger:

26I call heaven and earth to witness against you this day, that ye shall soon utterly perish from off the land whereunto ye go over Jordan to possess it; ye shall not prolong *your* days upon it, but shall utterly be destroyed.

27And the LORD shall scatter you among the nations, and ye shall be left few in number among the heathen, whither the LORD shall lead you.

28And there ye shall serve gods, the work of men's hands, wood and stone, which neither see, nor hear, nor eat, nor smell.

29But if from thence thou shalt seek the LORD thy God, thou shalt find *him,* if thou seek him with all thy heart and with all thy soul.

30When thou art in tribulation, and all these things ʷare come upon thee, *even* in the latter days, if thou turn to the LORD thy God, and shalt be obedient unto his voice;

31(For the LORD thy God *is* a merciful God;) he will not forsake thee, neither destroy thee, nor forget the covenant of thy fathers which he sware unto them.

Israel as a chosen nation

32For ask now of the days that are past, which were before thee, since the day that God created man upon the earth, and *ask* from the one side of heaven unto the other, whether there hath been *any such thing* as this great thing *is,* or hath been heard like it?

33Did *ever* people hear the voice of God speaking out of the midst of the fire, as thou hast heard, and live?

14And the Lord commanded me at that time to teach you the statutes and precepts, that you might do them in the land which you are going over to possess.

15Therefore take good heed to yourselves, since you saw no form of Him on the day the Lord spoke to you on Horeb out of the midst of the fire,

16Beware lest you become corrupt by making for yourselves [to worship] a graven image in the form of any figure, the likeness of male or female,

17The likeness of any beast that is on the earth, or of any winged fowl that flies in the air,

18The likeness of anything that creeps on the ground, or of any fish that is in the waters beneath the earth.

19And beware lest you lift up your eyes to the heavens, and when you see the sun, moon, and stars, even all the host of the heavens, you be drawn away and worship them and serve them, things which the Lord your God has allotted to all nations under the whole heaven.

20But the Lord has taken you and brought you forth out of the iron furnace, out of Egypt, to be to Him a people of His own possession, as you are this day.

21Furthermore the Lord was angry with me because of you, and He swore that I should not go over the Jordan and that I should not enter the good land which the Lord your God gives you for an inheritance.

22But I must die in this land; I must not cross the Jordan; but you shall go over and possess that good land.

23Take heed to yourselves, lest you forget the covenant of the Lord your God which He made with you, and make for yourselves a graven image in the form of anything which the Lord your God has forbidden you.

24For the Lord your God is a consuming fire, a jealous God.

25When children shall be born to you, and children's children, and you have grown old in the land, if you corrupt yourselves by making a graven image in the form of anything, and do evil in the sight of the Lord your God, provoking Him to anger,

26I call heaven and earth to witness against you this day that you shall soon utterly perish from the land which you are going over the Jordan to possess. You will not live long upon it but will be utterly destroyed.

27And the Lord will scatter you among the peoples, and you will be left few in number among the nations to which the Lord will drive you.

28There you will serve gods, the work of men's hands, wood and stone, which neither see nor hear nor eat nor smell.

29But if from there you will seek (inquire for and require as necessity) the Lord your God, you will find Him if you [truly] seek Him with all your heart [and mind] and soul and life.

30When you are in tribulation and all these things come upon you, in the latter days you will turn to the Lord your God and be obedient to His voice.

31For the Lord your God is a merciful God; He will not fail you or destroy you or forget the covenant of your fathers, which He swore to them.

32For ask now of the days that are past, which were before you, since the day that God created man upon the earth, and ask from one end of the heavens to the other, whether such a great thing as this has ever occurred or been heard of anywhere.

33Did ever people hear the voice of God speaking out of the midst of the fire, as you heard, and live?

ᵛ Or, *imparted*   ʷ Heb. *have found thee*

New American Standard

14"The LORD commanded me at that time to teach you statutes and judgments, that you might perform them in the land where you are going over to possess it.

15 ¶ "So watch yourselves carefully, since you did not see any form on the day the LORD spoke to you at Horeb from the midst of the fire,

16 so that you do not act corruptly and make a graven image for yourselves in the form of any figure, the likeness of male or female,

17 the likeness of any animal that is on the earth, the likeness of any winged bird that flies in the sky,

18 the likeness of anything that creeps on the ground, the likeness of any fish that is in the water below the earth.

19"And *beware* not to lift up your eyes to heaven and see the sun and the moon and the stars, all the host of heaven, and be drawn away and worship them and serve them, those which the LORD your God has allotted to all the peoples under the whole heaven.

20"But the LORD has taken you and brought you out of the iron furnace, from Egypt, to be a people for His own possession, as today.

21 ¶ "Now the LORD was angry with me on your account, and swore that I would not cross the Jordan, and that I would not enter the good land which the LORD your God is giving you as an inheritance.

22"For I will die in this land, I shall not cross the Jordan, but you shall cross and take possession of this good land.

23"So watch yourselves, that you do not forget the covenant of the LORD your God which He made with you, and make for yourselves a graven image in the form of anything *against* which the LORD your God has commanded you.

24"For the LORD your God is a consuming fire, a jealous God.

25 ¶ "When you become the father of children and children's children and have remained long in the land, and act corruptly, and make an idol in the form of anything, and do that which is evil in the sight of the LORD your God *so as* to provoke Him to anger,

26 I call heaven and earth to witness against you today, that you will surely perish quickly from the land where you are going over the Jordan to possess it. You shall not live long on it, but will be utterly destroyed.

27"The LORD will scatter you among the peoples, and you will be left few in number among the nations where the LORD drives you.

28"There you will serve gods, the work of man's hands, wood and stone, which neither see nor hear nor eat nor smell.

29"But from there you will seek the LORD your God, and you will find *Him* if you search for Him with all your heart and all your soul.

30"When you are in distress and all these things have come upon you, in the latter days you will return to the LORD your God and listen to His voice.

31"For the LORD your God is a compassionate God; He will not fail you nor destroy you nor forget the covenant with your fathers which He swore to them.

32 ¶ "Indeed, ask now concerning the former days which were before you, since the day that God created man on the earth, and *inquire* from one end of the heavens to the other. Has *anything* been done like this great thing, or has *anything* been heard like it?

33"Has *any* people heard the voice of God speaking from the midst of the fire, as you have heard *it*, and survived?

New International

tablets. 14And the LORD directed me at that time to teach you the decrees and laws you are to follow in the land that you are crossing the Jordan to possess.

Idolatry Forbidden

15You saw no form of any kind the day the LORD spoke to you at Horeb out of the fire. Therefore watch yourselves very carefully, 16so that you do not become corrupt and make for yourselves an idol, an image of any shape, whether formed like a man or a woman, 17or like any animal on earth or any bird that flies in the air, 18or like any creature that moves along the ground or any fish in the waters below. 19And when you look up to the sky and see the sun, the moon and the stars—all the heavenly array—do not be enticed into bowing down to them and worshiping things the LORD your God has apportioned to all the nations under heaven. 20But as for you, the LORD took you and brought you out of the iron-smelting furnace, out of Egypt, to be the people of his inheritance, as you now are.

21The LORD was angry with me because of you, and he solemnly swore that I would not cross the Jordan and enter the good land the LORD your God is giving you as your inheritance. 22I will die in this land; I will not cross the Jordan; but you are about to cross over and take possession of that good land. 23Be careful not to forget the covenant of the LORD your God that he made with you; do not make for yourselves an idol in the form of anything the LORD your God has forbidden. 24For the LORD your God is a consuming fire, a jealous God.

25After you have had children and grandchildren and have lived in the land a long time—if you then become corrupt and make any kind of idol, doing evil in the eyes of the LORD your God and provoking him to anger, 26I call heaven and earth as witnesses against you this day that you will quickly perish from the land that you are crossing the Jordan to possess. You will not live there long but will certainly be destroyed. 27The LORD will scatter you among the peoples, and only a few of you will survive among the nations to which the LORD will drive you. 28There you will worship man-made gods of wood and stone, which cannot see or hear or eat or smell. 29But if from there you seek the LORD your God, you will find him if you look for him with all your heart and with all your soul. 30When you are in distress and all these things have happened to you, then in later days you will return to the LORD your God and obey him. 31For the LORD your God is a merciful God; he will not abandon or destroy you or forget the covenant with your forefathers, which he confirmed to them by oath.

The LORD Is God

32Ask now about the former days, long before your time, from the day God created man on the earth; ask from one end of the heavens to the other. Has anything so great as this ever happened, or has anything like it ever been heard of? 33Has any other people heard the voice of God*j*

King James	Amplified

King James

³⁴Or hath God assayed to go *and* take him a nation from the midst of *another* nation, by temptations, by signs, and by wonders, and by war, and by a mighty hand, and by a stretched out arm, and by great terrors, according to all that the LORD your God did for you in Egypt before your eyes?

³⁵Unto thee it was shown, that thou mightest know that the LORD he *is* God; *there is* none else beside him.

³⁶Out of heaven he made thee to hear his voice, that he might instruct thee: and upon earth he showed thee his great fire; and thou heardest his words out of the midst of the fire.

³⁷And because he loved thy fathers, therefore he chose their seed after them, and brought thee out in his sight with his mighty power out of Egypt;

³⁸To drive out nations from before thee greater and mightier than thou *art,* to bring thee in, to give thee their land *for* an inheritance, as *it is* this day.

³⁹Know therefore this day, and consider *it* in thine heart, that the LORD he *is* God in heaven above, and upon the earth beneath: *there is* none else.

⁴⁰Thou shalt keep therefore his statutes, and his commandments, which I command thee this day, that it may go well with thee, and with thy children after thee, and that thou mayest prolong *thy* days upon the earth, which the LORD thy God giveth thee, for ever.

⁴¹ ¶ Then Moses severed three cities on this side Jordan toward the sunrising;

⁴²That the slayer might flee thither, which should kill his neighbour unawares, and hated him not in times past; and that fleeing unto one of these cities he might live:

⁴³*Namely,* Bezer in the wilderness, in the plain country, of the Reubenites; and Ramoth in Gilead, of the Gadites; and Golan in Bashan, of the Manassites.

⁴⁴ ¶ And this *is* the law which Moses set before the children of Israel:

⁴⁵These *are* the testimonies, and the statutes, and the judgments, which Moses spake unto the children of Israel, after they came forth out of Egypt,

⁴⁶On this side Jordan, in the valley over against Beth-peor, in the land of Sihon king of the Amorites, who dwelt at Heshbon, whom Moses and the children of Israel smote, after they were come forth out of Egypt:

⁴⁷And they possessed his land, and the land of Og king of Bashan, two kings of the Amorites, which *were* on this side Jordan toward the sunrising;

⁴⁸From Aroer, which *is* by the bank of the river Arnon, even unto mount Sion, which *is* Hermon,

⁴⁹And all the plain on this side Jordan eastward, even unto the sea of the plain, under the springs of Pisgah.

The Ten Commandments

5 AND MOSES called all Israel, and said unto them, Hear, O Israel, the statutes and judgments which I speak in your ears this day, that ye may learn them, and ˣkeep, and do them.

²The LORD our God made a covenant with us in Horeb.

³The LORD made not this covenant with our fathers, but with us, *even* us, who *are* all of us here alive this day.

⁴The LORD talked with you face to face in the mount out of the midst of the fire,

⁵(I stood between the LORD and you at that time, to show you the word of the LORD: for ye were afraid by reason of the fire, and went not up into the mount;) saying,

⁶ ¶ I *am* the LORD thy God, which brought thee out of the land of Egypt, from the house of ʸbondage.

⁷Thou shalt have none other gods before me.

Amplified

³⁴Or has God ever tried to go and take for Himself a nation from the midst of another nation, by trials, by signs, by wonders, by war, by a mighty hand, by an outstretched arm, and by great terrors, as the Lord your God did for you in Egypt before your eyes?

³⁵To you it was shown, that you might realize *and* have personal knowledge that the Lord is God; there is no other besides Him.

³⁶Out of heaven He made you hear His voice, that He might correct, discipline, *and* admonish you; and on earth He made you see His great fire, and you heard His words out of the midst of the fire.

³⁷And because He loved your fathers, He chose their descendants after them, and brought you out from Egypt with His own Presence, by His mighty power,

³⁸Driving out nations from before you, greater and mightier than yourselves, to bring you in, to give you their land for an inheritance, as it is this day;

³⁹Know, recognize, *and* understand therefore this day and turn your [mind and] heart to it that the Lord is God in the heavens above and upon the earth beneath; there is no other.

⁴⁰Therefore you shall keep His statutes and His commandments, which I command you this day, that it may go well with you and your children after you and that you may prolong your days in the land which the Lord your God gives you forever.

⁴¹Then Moses set apart three cities [of refuge] beyond the Jordan to the east,

⁴²That the manslayer might flee there, who slew his neighbor unintentionally and had not previously been at enmity with him, that fleeing to one of these cities he might save his life:

⁴³Bezer in the wilderness on the tableland, for the Reubenites; and Ramoth in Gilead, for the Gadites; and Golan in Bashan, for the Manassites.

⁴⁴This is the law which Moses set before the Israelites.

⁴⁵These are the testimonies and the laws and the precepts which Moses spoke to the Israelites when they came out of Egypt,

⁴⁶Beyond the Jordan in the valley opposite Beth-peor, in the land of Sihon king of the Amorites, who dwelt at Heshbon, whom Moses and the Israelites smote when they came out of Egypt.

⁴⁷And they took possession of his land and the land of Og king of Bashan, the two kings of the Amorites, who lived beyond the Jordan to the east,

⁴⁸From Aroer, which is on the edge of the Valley of the Arnon, as far as Mount Sirion (that is, Hermon),

⁴⁹And all the Arabah (lowlands) beyond the Jordan eastward, as far as the Sea of the Arabah [the Dead Sea], under the slopes *and* springs of Pisgah.

5 AND MOSES called all Israel, and said to them, Hear, O Israel, the statutes and ordinances which I speak in your hearing this day, that you may learn them and take heed and do them.

²The Lord our God made a covenant with us in Horeb.

³The Lord made this covenant not with our fathers, but with us, who are all of us here alive this day.

⁴The Lord spoke with you face to face at the mount out of the midst of the fire.

⁵I stood between the Lord and you at that time to show you the word of the Lord, for you were afraid because of the fire and went not up into the mount. He said,

⁶I am the Lord your God, Who brought you out of the land of Egypt, from the house of bondage.

⁷You shall have no other gods before Me *or* besides Me.

ˣHeb. *keep to do them*   ʸHeb. *servants*

New American Standard

34"Or has a god tried to go to take for himself a nation from within *another* nation by trials, by signs and wonders and by war and by a mighty hand and by an outstretched arm and by great terrors, as the LORD your God did for you in Egypt before your eyes?

35"To you it was shown that you might know that the LORD, He is God; there is no other besides Him.

36"Out of the heavens He let you hear His voice to discipline you; and on earth He let you see His great fire, and you heard His words from the midst of the fire.

37"Because He loved your fathers, therefore He chose their descendants after them. And He personally brought you from Egypt by His great power,

38 driving out from before you nations greater and mightier than you, to bring you in *and* to give you their land for an inheritance, as it is today.

39"Know therefore today, and take it to your heart, that the LORD, He is God in heaven above and on the earth below; there is no other.

40"So you shall keep His statutes and His commandments which I am giving you today, that it may go well with you and with your children after you, and that you may live long on the land which the LORD your God is giving you for all time."

41 ¶ Then Moses set apart three cities across the Jordan to the east,

42 that a manslayer might flee there, who unintentionally slew his neighbor without having enmity toward him in time past; and by fleeing to one of these cities he might live:

43 Bezer in the wilderness on the plateau for the Reubenites, and Ramoth in Gilead for the Gadites, and Golan in Bashan for the Manassites.

44 ¶ Now this is the law which Moses set before the sons of Israel;

45 these are the testimonies and the statutes and the ordinances which Moses spoke to the sons of Israel, when they came out from Egypt,

46 across the Jordan, in the valley opposite Beth-peor, in the land of Sihon king of the Amorites who lived at Heshbon, whom Moses and the sons of Israel defeated when they came out from Egypt.

47 They took possession of his land and the land of Og king of Bashan, the two kings of the Amorites, *who were* across the Jordan to the east,

48 from Aroer, which is on the edge of the valley of Arnon, even as far as Mount Sion (that is, Hermon),

49 with all the Arabah across the Jordan to the east, even as far as the sea of the Arabah, at the foot of the slopes of Pisgah.

The Ten Commandments Repeated

5 THEN MOSES summoned all Israel and said to them:

¶ "Hear, O Israel, the statutes and the ordinances which I am speaking today in your hearing, that you may learn them and observe them carefully.

2"The LORD our God made a covenant with us at Horeb.

3"The LORD did not make this covenant with our fathers, but with us, *with* all those of us alive here today.

4"The LORD spoke to you face to face at the mountain from the midst of the fire,

5 *while* I was standing between the LORD and you at that time, to declare to you the word of the LORD; for you were afraid because of the fire and did not go up the mountain. He said,

6 ¶ 'I am the LORD your God who brought you out of the land of Egypt, out of the house of slavery.

7 ¶ 'You shall have no other gods before Me.

New International

speaking out of fire, as you have, and lived? 34Has any god ever tried to take for himself one nation out of another nation, by testings, by miraculous signs and wonders, by war, by a mighty hand and an outstretched arm, or by great and awesome deeds, like all the things the LORD your God did for you in Egypt before your very eyes?

35You were shown these things so that you might know that the LORD is God; besides him there is no other. 36From heaven he made you hear his voice to discipline you. On earth he showed you his great fire, and you heard his words from out of the fire. 37Because he loved your forefathers and chose their descendants after them, he brought you out of Egypt by his Presence and his great strength, 38to drive out before you nations greater and stronger than you and to bring you into their land to give it to you for your inheritance, as it is today.

39Acknowledge and take to heart this day that the LORD is God in heaven above and on the earth below. There is no other. 40Keep his decrees and commands, which I am giving you today, so that it may go well with you and your children after you and that you may live long in the land the LORD your God gives you for all time.

Cities of Refuge

41Then Moses set aside three cities east of the Jordan, 42to which anyone who had killed a person could flee if he had unintentionally killed his neighbor without malice aforethought. He could flee into one of these cities and save his life. 43The cities were these: Bezer in the desert plateau, for the Reubenites; Ramoth in Gilead, for the Gadites; and Golan in Bashan, for the Manassites.

Introduction to the Law

44This is the law Moses set before the Israelites. 45These are the stipulations, decrees and laws Moses gave them when they came out of Egypt 46and were in the valley near Beth Peor east of the Jordan, in the land of Sihon king of the Amorites, who reigned in Heshbon and was defeated by Moses and the Israelites as they came out of Egypt. 47They took possession of his land and the land of Og king of Bashan, the two Amorite kings east of the Jordan. 48This land extended from Aroer on the rim of the Arnon Gorge to Mount Siyon[k] (that is, Hermon), 49and included all the Arabah east of the Jordan, as far as the Sea of the Arabah,[l] below the slopes of Pisgah.

The Ten Commandments

5 MOSES SUMMONED all Israel and said:
Hear, O Israel, the decrees and laws I declare in your hearing today. Learn them and be sure to follow them. 2The LORD our God made a covenant with us at Horeb. 3It was not with our fathers that the LORD made this covenant, but with us, with all of us who are alive here today. 4The LORD spoke to you face to face out of the fire on the mountain. 5(At that time I stood between the LORD and you to declare to you the word of the LORD, because you were afraid of the fire and did not go up the mountain.) And he said:

6"I am the LORD your God, who brought you out of Egypt, out of the land of slavery.
7"You shall have no other gods before[m] me.

---

k48 Hebrew; Syriac (see also Deut. 3:9) *Sirion*   *l49* That is, the Dead Sea   *m7 Or besides*

King James

8Thou shalt not make thee *any* graven image, *or* any likeness *of any thing* that *is* in heaven above, or that *is* in the earth beneath, or that *is* in the waters beneath the earth:

9Thou shalt not bow down thyself unto them, nor serve them: for I the LORD thy God *am* a jealous God, visiting the iniquity of the fathers upon the children unto the third and fourth *generation* of them that hate me,

10And showing mercy unto thousands of them that love me and keep my commandments.

11Thou shalt not take the name of the LORD thy God in vain: for the LORD will not hold *him* guiltless that taketh his name in vain.

12Keep the sabbath day to sanctify it, as the LORD thy God hath commanded thee.

13Six days thou shalt labour, and do all thy work:

14But the seventh day *is* the sabbath of the LORD thy God: *in it* thou shalt not do any work, thou, nor thy son, nor thy daughter, nor thy manservant, nor thy maidservant, nor thine ox, nor thine ass, nor any of thy cattle, nor thy stranger that *is* within thy gates; that thy manservant and thy maidservant may rest as well as thou.

15And remember that thou wast a servant in the land of Egypt, and *that* the LORD thy God brought thee out thence through a mighty hand and by a stretched out arm: therefore the LORD thy God commanded thee to keep the sabbath day.

16 ¶ Honour thy father and thy mother, as the LORD thy God hath commanded thee; that thy days may be prolonged, and that it may go well with thee, in the land which the LORD thy God giveth thee.

17Thou shalt not kill.

18Neither shalt thou commit adultery.

19Neither shalt thou steal.

20Neither shalt thou bear false witness against thy neighbour.

21Neither shalt thou desire thy neighbour's wife, neither shalt thou covet thy neighbour's house, his field, or his manservant, or his maidservant, his ox, or his ass, or any *thing* that *is* thy neighbour's.

22 ¶ These words the LORD spake unto all your assembly in the mount out of the midst of the fire, of the cloud, and of the thick darkness, with a great voice: and he added no more. And he wrote them in two tables of stone, and delivered them unto me.

23And it came to pass, when ye heard the voice out of the midst of the darkness, (for the mountain did burn with fire,) that ye came near unto me, *even* all the heads of your tribes, and your elders;

24And ye said, Behold, the LORD our God hath shown us his glory and his greatness, and we have heard his voice out of the midst of the fire: we have seen this day that God doth talk with man, and he liveth.

25Now therefore why should we die? for this great fire will consume us: if we ᶻhear the voice of the LORD our God any more, then we shall die.

26For who *is there of* all flesh, that hath heard the voice of the living God speaking out of the midst of the fire, as we *have*, and lived?

27Go thou near, and hear all that the LORD our God shall say: and speak thou unto us all that the LORD our God shall speak unto thee; and we will hear *it*, and do *it*.

28And the LORD heard the voice of your words, when ye spake unto me; and the LORD said unto me, I have heard the voice of the words of this people, which they have spoken unto thee: they have well said all that they have spoken.

29O that there were such an heart in them, that they would fear me, and keep all my commandments always, that it might be well with them, and with their children for ever!

30Go say to them, Get you into your tents again.

Amplified

8You shall not make for yourself [to worship] a graven image or any likeness of anything that is in the heavens above or that is in the earth beneath or that is in the water under the earth.

9You shall not bow down to them or serve them; for I, the Lord your God, am a jealous God, visiting the iniquity of the fathers upon the children to the third and fourth generations of those who hate Me,

10And showing mercy *and* steadfast love to thousands *and* to a thousand generations of those who love Me and keep My commandments.

11You shall not take the name of the Lord your God in vain, for the Lord will not hold him guiltless who takes His name in falsehood *or* without purpose.

12Observe the Sabbath day to keep it holy, as the Lord your God commanded you.

13Six days you shall labor and do all your work,

14But the seventh day is a Sabbath to the Lord your God; in it you shall not do any work, you or your son or your daughter, or your manservant or your maidservant, or your ox or your donkey or any of your livestock, or the stranger *or* sojourner who is within your gates, that your manservant and your maidservant may rest as well as you.

15And [earnestly] remember that you were a servant in the land of Egypt and that the Lord your God brought you out from there with a mighty hand and an outstretched arm; therefore the Lord your God commanded you to observe *and* take heed to the Sabbath day.

16Honor your father and your mother, as the Lord your God commanded you, that your days may be prolonged and that it may go well with you in the land which the Lord your God gives you.

17You shall not murder.

18Neither shall you commit adultery.

19Neither shall you act slyly *or* steal.

20Neither shall you witness falsely against your neighbor.

21Neither shall you covet your neighbor's wife, nor desire your neighbor's house, his field, his manservant or his maidservant, his ox or his donkey, or anything that is your neighbor's.

22These words the Lord spoke to all your assembly at the mountain out of the midst of the fire, the cloud, and the thick darkness, with a loud voice; and He spoke not again [added no more]. He wrote them on two tables of stone and gave them to me [Moses].

23And when you heard the voice out of the midst of the darkness, while the mountain was burning with fire, you came near me, all the heads of your tribes and your elders;

24And you said, Behold, the Lord our God has shown us His glory and His greatness, and we have heard His voice out of the midst of the fire; we have this day seen that God speaks with man and man still lives.

25Now therefore, why should we die? For this great fire will consume us; if we hear the voice of the Lord our God any longer, we shall die.

26For who is there of all flesh who has heard the voice of the living God speaking out of the midst of fire, as we have, and lived?

27Go near [Moses] and hear all that the Lord our God will say. And speak to us all that the Lord our God will speak to you; and we will hear and do it.

28And the Lord heard your words when you spoke to me and the Lord said to me, I have heard the words of this people which they have spoken to you. They have said well all that they have spoken.

29Oh, that they had such a [mind and] heart in them always [reverently] to fear Me and keep all My commandments, that it might go well with them and with their children forever!

30Go and say to them, Return to your tents.

ᶻHeb. *add to hear*

New American Standard

8 ¶ 'You shall not make for yourself an idol, *or* any likeness *of* what is in heaven above or on the earth beneath or in the water under the earth.

9 'You shall not worship them or serve them; for I, the LORD your God, am a jealous God, visiting the iniquity of the fathers on the children, and on the third and the fourth *generations* of those who hate Me,

10 but showing lovingkindness to thousands, to those who love Me and keep My commandments.

11 ¶ 'You shall not take the name of the LORD your God in vain, for the LORD will not leave him unpunished who takes His name in vain.

12 ¶ 'Observe the sabbath day to keep it holy, as the LORD your God commanded you.

13 'Six days you shall labor and do all your work,

14 but the seventh day is a sabbath of the LORD your God; *in it* you shall not do any work, you or your son or your daughter or your male servant or your female servant or your ox or your donkey or any of your cattle or your sojourner who stays with you, so that your male servant and your female servant may rest as well as you.

15 'You shall remember that you were a slave in the land of Egypt, and the LORD your God brought you out of there by a mighty hand and by an outstretched arm; therefore the LORD your God commanded you to observe the sabbath day.

16 ¶ 'Honor your father and your mother, as the LORD your God has commanded you, that your days may be prolonged and that it may go well with you on the land which the LORD your God gives you.

17 ¶ 'You shall not murder.

18 ¶ 'You shall not commit adultery.

19 ¶ 'You shall not steal.

20 ¶ 'You shall not bear false witness against your neighbor.

21 ¶ 'You shall not covet your neighbor's wife, and you shall not desire your neighbor's house or his field or his male servant or his female servant, his ox or his donkey or anything that belongs to your neighbor.'

Moses Interceded

22 ¶ "These words the LORD spoke to all your assembly at the mountain from the midst of the fire, *of* the cloud and *of* the thick gloom, with a great voice, and He added no more. He wrote them on two tablets of stone and gave them to me.

23"And when you heard the voice from the midst of the darkness, while the mountain was burning with fire, you came near to me, all the heads of your tribes and your elders.

24"You said, 'Behold, the LORD our God has shown us His glory and His greatness, and we have heard His voice from the midst of the fire; we have seen today that God speaks with man, yet he lives.

25 'Now then why should we die? For this great fire will consume us; if we hear the voice of the LORD our God any longer, then we will die.

26 'For who is there of all flesh who has heard the voice of the living God speaking from the midst of the fire, as we *have*, and lived?

27 'Go near and hear all that the LORD our God says; then speak to us all that the LORD our God speaks to you, and we will hear and do *it*.'

28 ¶ "The LORD heard the voice of your words when you spoke to me, and the LORD said to me, 'I have heard the voice of the words of this people which they have spoken to you. They have done well in all that they have spoken.

29 'Oh that they had such a heart in them, that they would fear Me and keep all My commandments always, that it may be well with them and with their sons forever!

30 'Go, say to them, "Return to your tents."

New International

8"You shall not make for yourself an idol in the form of anything in heaven above or on the earth beneath or in the waters below. 9You shall not bow down to them or worship them; for I, the LORD your God, am a jealous God, punishing the children for the sin of the fathers to the third and fourth generation of those who hate me, 10but showing love to a thousand ¡generations¡ of those who love me and keep my commandments.

11"You shall not misuse the name of the LORD your God, for the LORD will not hold anyone guiltless who misuses his name.

12"Observe the Sabbath day by keeping it holy, as the LORD your God has commanded you. 13Six days you shall labor and do all your work, 14but the seventh day is a Sabbath to the LORD your God. On it you shall not do any work, neither you, nor your son or daughter, nor your manservant or maidservant, nor your ox, your donkey or any of your animals, nor the alien within your gates, so that your manservant and maidservant may rest, as you do. 15Remember that you were slaves in Egypt and that the LORD your God brought you out of there with a mighty hand and an out-stretched arm. Therefore the LORD your God has commanded you to observe the Sabbath day.

16"Honor your father and your mother, as the LORD your God has commanded you, so that you may live long and that it may go well with you in the land the LORD your God is giving you.

17"You shall not murder.

18"You shall not commit adultery.

19"You shall not steal.

20"You shall not give false testimony against your neighbor.

21"You shall not covet your neighbor's wife. You shall not set your desire on your neighbor's house or land, his manservant or maidservant, his ox or donkey, or anything that belongs to your neighbor."

22These are the commandments the LORD proclaimed in a loud voice to your whole assembly there on the mountain from out of the fire, the cloud and the deep darkness; and he added nothing more. Then he wrote them on two stone tablets and gave them to me.

23When you heard the voice out of the darkness, while the mountain was ablaze with fire, all the leading men of your tribes and your elders came to me. 24And you said, "The LORD our God has shown us his glory and his majesty, and we have heard his voice from the fire. Today we have seen that a man can live even if God speaks with him. 25But now, why should we die? This great fire will consume us, and we will die if we hear the voice of the LORD our God any longer. 26For what mortal man has ever heard the voice of the living God speaking out of fire, as we have, and survived? 27Go near and listen to all that the LORD our God says. Then tell us whatever the LORD our God tells you. We will listen and obey."

28The LORD heard you when you spoke to me and the LORD said to me, "I have heard what this people said to you. Everything they said was good. 29Oh, that their hearts would be inclined to fear me and keep all my commands always, so that it might go well with them and their children forever!

King James

Amplified

[31]But as for thee, stand thou here by me, and I will speak unto thee all the commandments, and the statutes, and the judgments, which thou shalt teach them, that they may do *them* in the land which I give them to possess it.

[32]Ye shall observe to do therefore as the LORD your God hath commanded you: ye shall not turn aside to the right hand or to the left.

[33]Ye shall walk in all the ways which the LORD your God hath commanded you, that ye may live, and *that it may be* well with you, and *that* ye may prolong *your* days in the land which ye shall possess.

Love the LORD thy God

6 NOW THESE *are* the commandments, the statutes, and the judgments, which the LORD your God commanded to teach you, that ye might do *them* in the land whither ye [a]go to possess it:

[2]That thou mightest fear the LORD thy God, to keep all his statutes and his commandments, which I command thee, thou, and thy son, and thy son's son, all the days of thy life; and that thy days *may* be prolonged.

[3] ¶ Hear therefore, O Israel, and observe to do *it;* that it may be well with thee, and that ye may increase mightily, as the LORD God of thy fathers hath promised thee, in the land that floweth with milk and honey.

[4]Hear, O Israel: The LORD our God *is* one LORD:

[5]And thou shalt love the LORD thy God with all thine heart, and with all thy soul, and with all thy might.

[6]And these words, which I command thee this day, shall be in thine heart:

[7]And thou shalt [b]teach them diligently unto thy children, and shalt talk of them when thou sittest in thine house, and when thou walkest by the way, and when thou liest down, and when thou risest up.

[8]And thou shalt bind them for a sign upon thine hand, and they shall be as frontlets between thine eyes.

[9]And thou shalt write them upon the posts of thy house, and on thy gates.

[10]And it shall be, when the LORD thy God shall have brought thee into the land which he sware unto thy fathers, to Abraham, to Isaac, and to Jacob, to give thee great and goodly cities, which thou buildest not,

[11]And houses full of all good *things,* which thou filledst not, and wells digged, which thou diggedst not, vineyards and olive trees, which thou plantedst not; when thou shalt have eaten and be full;

[12]*Then* beware lest thou forget the LORD, which brought thee forth out of the land of Egypt, from the house of [c]bondage.

[13]Thou shalt fear the LORD thy God, and serve him, and shalt swear by his name.

[14]Ye shall not go after other gods, of the gods of the people which *are* round about you;

[15](For the LORD thy God *is* a jealous God among you) lest the anger of the LORD thy God be kindled against thee, and destroy thee from off the face of the earth.

[16] ¶ Ye shall not tempt the LORD your God, as ye tempted *him* in Massah.

[17]Ye shall diligently keep the commandments of the LORD your God, and his testimonies, and his statutes, which he hath commanded thee.

[18]And thou shalt do *that which is* right and good in the sight of the LORD: that it may be well with thee, and that thou mayest go in and possess the good land which the LORD sware unto thy fathers,

[19]To cast out all thine enemies from before thee, as the LORD hath spoken.

[31]But you [Moses], stand here by Me, and I will tell you all the commandments and the statutes and the precepts which you shall teach them, that they may do them in the land which I give them to possess.

[32]Therefore you people shall be watchful to do as the Lord your God has commanded you; you shall not turn aside to the right hand or to the left.

[33]You shall walk in all the ways which the Lord your God has commanded you, that you may live and that it may go well with you and that you may live long in the land which you shall possess.

6 NOW THIS is the instruction, the laws, and the precepts which the Lord your God commanded me to teach you, that you might do them in the land to which you go to possess it,

[2]That you may [reverently] fear the Lord your God, you and your son and your son's son, and keep all His statutes and His commandments which I command you all the days of your life, and that your days may be prolonged.

[3]Hear therefore, O Israel, and be watchful to do them, that it may be well with you and that you may increase exceedingly, as the Lord, the God of your fathers, has promised you, in a land flowing with milk and honey.

[4]Hear, O Israel: the Lord our God is one Lord [the only Lord].

[5]And you shall love the Lord your God with all your [mind and] heart and with your entire being and with all your might.

[6]And these words which I am commanding you this day shall be [first] in your [own] minds *and* hearts; [then]

[7]You shall whet *and* sharpen them so as to make them penetrate, *and* teach *and* impress them diligently upon the [minds and] hearts of your children, and shall talk of them when you sit in your house and when you walk by the way, and when you lie down and when you rise up.

[8]And you shall bind them as a sign upon your hand, and they shall be as frontlets (forehead bands) between your eyes.

[9]And you shall write them upon the doorposts of your house and on your gates.

[10]And when the Lord your God brings you into the land which He swore to your fathers, to Abraham, Isaac, and Jacob, to give you, with great and goodly cities which you did not build,

[11]And houses full of all good things which you did not fill, and cisterns hewn out which you did not hew, and vineyards and olive trees which you did not plant, and when you eat and are full,

[12]Then beware lest you forget the Lord, Who brought you out of the land of Egypt, out of the house of bondage.

[13]You shall [reverently] fear the Lord your God and serve Him and swear by His name [and presence].

[14]You shall not go after other gods, any of the gods of the peoples who are round about you;

[15]For the Lord your God in the midst of you is a jealous God; lest the anger of the Lord your God be kindled against you, and He destroy you from the face of the earth.

[16]You shall not tempt *and* try the Lord your God as you tempted *and* tried Him in Massah. [Exod. 17:7.]

[17]You shall diligently keep the commandments of the Lord your God and His exhortations and His statutes which He commanded you.

[18]And you shall do what is right and good in the sight of the Lord, that it may go well with you and that you may go in and possess the good land which the Lord swore to give to your fathers,

[19]To cast out all your enemies from before you, as the Lord has promised.

---

[a] Heb. *pass over* or, *servants*   [b] Heb. *whet,* or, *sharpen*   [c] Heb. *bondmen,*

New American Standard

31 'But as for you, stand here by Me, that I may speak to you all the commandments and the statutes and the judgments which you shall teach them, that they may observe *them* in the land which I give them to possess.'

32"So you shall observe to do just as the LORD your God has commanded you; you shall not turn aside to the right or to the left.

33"You shall walk in all the way which the LORD your God has commanded you, that you may live and that it may be well with you, and that you may prolong *your* days in the land which you will possess.

Obey God and Prosper

6 "NOW THIS is the commandment, the statutes and the judgments which the LORD your God has commanded *me* to teach you, that you might do *them* in the land where you are going over to possess it,

2 so that you and your son and your grandson might fear the LORD your God, to keep all His statutes and His commandments which I command you, all the days of your life, and that your days may be prolonged.

3"O Israel, you should listen and be careful to do *it*, that it may be well with you and that you may multiply greatly, just as the LORD, the God of your fathers, has promised you, *in* a land flowing with milk and honey.

4 ¶ "Hear, O Israel! The LORD is our God, the LORD is one!

5"You shall love the LORD your God with all your heart and with all your soul and with all your might.

6"These words, which I am commanding you today, shall be on your heart.

7 You shall teach them diligently to your sons and shall talk of them when you sit in your house and when you walk by the way and when you lie down and when you rise up.

8"You shall bind them as a sign on your hand and they shall be as frontals on your forehead.

9"You shall write them on the doorposts of your house and on your gates.

10 ¶ "Then it shall come about when the LORD your God brings you into the land which He swore to your fathers, Abraham, Isaac and Jacob, to give you, great and splendid cities which you did not build,

11 and houses full of all good things which you did not fill, and hewn cisterns which you did not dig, vineyards and olive trees which you did not plant, and you eat and are satisfied,

12 then watch yourself, that you do not forget the LORD who brought you from the land of Egypt, out of the house of slavery.

13"You shall *f*fear *only* the LORD your God; and you shall worship Him and swear by His name.

14"You shall not follow other gods, any of the gods of the peoples who surround you,

15 for the LORD your God in the midst of you is a jealous God; otherwise the anger of the LORD your God will be kindled against you, and He will wipe you off the face of the earth.

16 ¶ "You shall not put the LORD your God to the test, as you tested *Him* at Massah.

17"You should diligently keep the commandments of the LORD your God, and His testimonies and His statutes which He has commanded you.

18"You shall do what is right and good in the sight of the LORD, that it may be well with you and that you may go in and possess the good land which the LORD swore to *give* your fathers,

19 by driving out all your enemies from before you, as the LORD has spoken.

New International

30"Go, tell them to return to their tents. 31But you stay here with me so that I may give you all the commands, decrees and laws you are to teach them to follow in the land I am giving them to possess."

32So be careful to do what the LORD your God has commanded you; do not turn aside to the right or to the left. 33Walk in all the way that the LORD your God has commanded you, so that you may live and prosper and prolong your days in the land that you will possess.

Love the LORD Your God

6 THESE ARE the commands, decrees and laws the LORD your God directed me to teach you to observe in the land that you are crossing the Jordan to possess, 2so that you, your children and their children after them may fear the LORD your God as long as you live by keeping all his decrees and commands that I give you, and so that you may enjoy long life. 3Hear, O Israel, and be careful to obey so that it may go well with you and that you may increase greatly in a land flowing with milk and honey, just as the LORD, the God of your fathers, promised you.

4Hear, O Israel: The LORD our God, the LORD is one.*n* 5Love the LORD your God with all your heart and with all your soul and with all your strength. 6These commandments that I give you today are to be upon your hearts. 7Impress them on your children. Talk about them when you sit at home and when you walk along the road, when you lie down and when you get up. 8Tie them as symbols on your hands and bind them on your foreheads. 9Write them on the doorframes of your houses and on your gates.

10When the LORD your God brings you into the land he swore to your fathers, to Abraham, Isaac and Jacob, to give you—a land with large, flourishing cities you did not build, 11houses filled with all kinds of good things you did not provide, wells you did not dig, and vineyards and olive groves you did not plant—then when you eat and are satisfied, 12be careful that you do not forget the LORD, who brought you out of Egypt, out of the land of slavery.

13Fear the LORD your God, serve him only and take your oaths in his name. 14Do not follow other gods, the gods of the peoples around you; 15for the LORD your God, who is among you, is a jealous God and his anger will burn against you, and he will destroy you from the face of the land. 16Do not test the LORD your God as you did at Massah. 17Be sure to keep the commands of the LORD your God and the stipulations and decrees he has given you. 18Do what is right and good in the LORD's sight, so that it may go well with you and you may go in and take over the good land that the LORD promised on oath to your forefathers, 19thrusting out all your enemies before you, as the LORD said.

---

*f*Or *reverence*

*n*4 Or *The LORD our God is one LORD*; or *The LORD is our God, the LORD is one*; or *The LORD is our God, the LORD alone*

King James

²⁰*And* when thy son asketh thee ᵈin time to come, saying, What *mean* the testimonies, and the statutes, and the judgments, which the LORD our God hath commanded you?

²¹Then thou shalt say unto thy son, We were Pharaoh's bondmen in Egypt; and the LORD brought us out of Egypt with a mighty hand:

²²And the LORD showed signs and wonders, great and ᵉsore, upon Egypt, upon Pharaoh, and upon all his household, before our eyes:

²³And he brought us out from thence, that he might bring us in, to give us the land which he sware unto our fathers.

²⁴And the LORD commanded us to do all these statutes, to fear the LORD our God, for our good always, that he might preserve us alive, as *it is* at this day.

²⁵And it shall be our righteousness, if we observe to do all these commandments before the LORD our God, as he hath commanded us.

God will defeat the nations

7 WHEN THE LORD thy God shall bring thee into the land whither thou goest to possess it, and hath cast out many nations before thee, the Hittites, and the Girgashites, and the Amorites, and the Canaanites, and the Perizzites, and the Hivites, and the Jebusites, seven nations greater and mightier than thou;

²And when the LORD thy God shall deliver them before thee; thou shalt smite them, *and* utterly destroy them; thou shalt make no covenant with them, nor show mercy unto them:

³Neither shalt thou make marriages with them; thy daughter thou shalt not give unto his son, nor his daughter shalt thou take unto thy son.

⁴For they will turn away thy son from following me, that they may serve other gods: so will the anger of the LORD be kindled against you, and destroy thee suddenly.

⁵But thus shall ye deal with them; ye shall destroy their altars, and break down their ᶠimages, and cut down their groves, and burn their graven images with fire.

⁶For thou *art* an holy people unto the LORD thy God: the LORD thy God hath chosen thee to be a special people unto himself, above all people that *are* upon the face of the earth.

⁷The LORD did not set his love upon you, nor choose you, because ye were more in number than any people; for ye *were* the fewest of all people:

⁸But because the LORD loved you, and because he would keep the oath which he had sworn unto your fathers, hath the LORD brought you out with a mighty hand, and redeemed you out of the house of bondmen, from the hand of Pharaoh king of Egypt.

⁹Know therefore that the LORD thy God, he *is* God, the faithful God, which keepeth covenant and mercy with them that love him and keep his commandments to a thousand generations;

¹⁰And repayeth them that hate him to their face, to destroy them: he will not be slack to him that hateth him, he will repay him to his face.

¹¹Thou shalt therefore keep the commandments, and the statutes, and the judgments, which I command thee this day, to do them.

¹² ¶ Wherefore it shall come to pass, ᵍif ye hearken to these judgments, and keep, and do them, that the LORD thy God shall keep unto thee the covenant and the mercy which he sware unto thy fathers:

Amplified

²⁰When your son asks you in time to come, What is the meaning of the testimonies and statutes and precepts which the Lord our God has commanded you?

²¹Then you shall say to your son, We were Pharaoh's bondmen in Egypt, and the Lord brought us out of Egypt with a mighty hand.

²²And the Lord showed signs and wonders, great and evil, against Egypt, against Pharaoh, and all his household, before our eyes;

²³And He brought us out from there, that He might bring us in to give us the land which He swore to give our fathers.

²⁴And the Lord commanded us to do all these statutes, to [reverently] fear the Lord our God for our good always, that He might preserve us alive, as it is this day.

²⁵And it will be accounted as righteousness (conformity to God's will in word, thought, and action) for us if we are watchful to do all this commandment before the Lord our God, as He has commanded us.

7 WHEN THE Lord your God brings you into the land which you are entering to possess and has plucked away many nations before you, the Hittites, the Girgashites, the Amorites, the Canaanites, the Perizzites, the Hivites, and the Jebusites, seven nations greater and mightier than you,

²And when the Lord your God gives them over to you and you smite them, then you must utterly destroy them. You shall make no covenant with them, or show mercy to them.

³You shall not make marriages with them; your daughter you shall not give to his son nor shall you take his daughter for your son,

⁴For they will turn away your sons from following Me, that they may serve other gods; so will the anger of the Lord be kindled against you and He will destroy you quickly.

⁵But thus shall you deal with them: you shall break down their altars and dash in pieces their pillars and hew down their Asherim [symbols of the goddess Asherah] and burn their graven images with fire.

⁶For you are a holy *and* set-apart people to the Lord your God; the Lord your God has chosen you to be a special people to Himself out of all the peoples on the face of the earth.

⁷The Lord did not set His love upon you and choose you because you were more in number than any other people, for you were the fewest of all people.

⁸But because the Lord loves you and because He would keep the oath which He had sworn to your fathers, the Lord has brought you out with a mighty hand and redeemed you out of the house of bondage, from the hand of Pharaoh king of Egypt.

⁹Know, recognize, *and* understand therefore that the Lord your God, He is God, the faithful God, Who keeps covenant and steadfast love *and* mercy with those who love Him and keep His commandments, to a thousand generations,

¹⁰And repays those who hate Him to their face, by destroying them; He will not be slack to him who hates Him, but will requite him to his face.

¹¹You shall therefore keep and do the instruction, laws, and precepts which I command you this day.

¹²And if you hearken to these precepts and keep and do them, the Lord your God will keep with you the covenant and the steadfast love which He swore to your fathers.

ᵈHeb. *tomorrow*   ᵉHeb. *evil*   ᶠHeb. *statues,* or, *pillars*
ᵍHeb. *because*

New American Standard

20 ¶ "When your son asks you in time to come, saying, 'What *do* the testimonies and the statutes and the judgments *mean* which the LORD our God commanded you?'
21 then you shall say to your son, 'We were slaves to Pharaoh in Egypt, and the LORD brought us from Egypt with a mighty hand.
22 'Moreover, the LORD showed great and distressing signs and wonders before our eyes against Egypt, Pharaoh and all his household;
23 He brought us out from there in order to bring us in, to give us the land which He had sworn to our fathers.'
24 "So the LORD commanded us to observe all these statutes, to fear the LORD our God for our good always and for our survival, as *it is* today.
25 "It will be righteousness for us if we are careful to observe all this commandment before the LORD our God, just as He commanded us.

Warnings

7 "WHEN THE LORD your God brings you into the land where you are entering to possess it, and clears away many nations before you, the Hittites and the Girgashites and the Amorites and the Canaanites and the Perizzites and the Hivites and the Jebusites, seven nations greater and stronger than you,
2 and when the LORD your God delivers them before you and you defeat them, then you shall utterly destroy them. You shall make no covenant with them and show no favor to them.
3 "Furthermore, you shall not intermarry with them; you shall not give your daughters to their sons, nor shall you take their daughters for your sons.
4 "For they will turn your sons away from following Me to serve other gods; then the anger of the LORD will be kindled against you and He will quickly destroy you.
5 "But thus you shall do to them: you shall tear down their altars, and smash their *sacred* pillars, and hew down their *g*Asherim, and burn their graven images with fire.
6 "For you are a holy people to the LORD your God; the LORD your God has chosen you to be a people for His own possession out of all the peoples who are on the face of the earth.
7 ¶ "The LORD did not set His love on you nor choose you because you were more in number than any of the peoples, for you were the fewest of all peoples,
8 but because the LORD loved you and kept the oath which He swore to your forefathers, the LORD brought you out by a mighty hand and redeemed you from the house of slavery, from the hand of Pharaoh king of Egypt.
9 "Know therefore that the LORD your God, He is God, the faithful God, who keeps His covenant and His lovingkindness to a thousandth generation with those who love Him and keep His commandments;
10 but repays those who hate Him to their faces, to destroy them; He will not delay with him who hates Him, He will repay him to his face.
11 "Therefore, you shall keep the commandment and the statutes and the judgments which I am commanding you today, to do them.

Promises of God

12 ¶ "Then it shall come about, because you listen to these judgments and keep and do them, that the LORD your God will keep with you His covenant and His lovingkindness which He swore to your forefathers.

New International

20 In the future, when your son asks you, "What is the meaning of the stipulations, decrees and laws the LORD our God has commanded you?" 21 tell him: "We were slaves of Pharaoh in Egypt, but the LORD brought us out of Egypt with a mighty hand. 22 Before our eyes the LORD sent miraculous signs and wonders—great and terrible—upon Egypt and Pharaoh and his whole household. 23 But he brought us out from there to bring us in and give us the land that he promised on oath to our forefathers. 24 The LORD commanded us to obey all these decrees and to fear the LORD our God, so that we might always prosper and be kept alive, as is the case today. 25 And if we are careful to obey all this law before the LORD our God, as he has commanded us, that will be our righteousness."

Driving Out the Nations

7 WHEN THE LORD your God brings you into the land you are entering to possess and drives out before you many nations—the Hittites, Girgashites, Amorites, Canaanites, Perizzites, Hivites and Jebusites, seven nations larger and stronger than you— 2 and when the LORD your God has delivered them over to you and you have defeated them, then you must destroy them totally.*o* Make no treaty with them, and show them no mercy. 3 Do not intermarry with them. Do not give your daughters to their sons or take their daughters for your sons, 4 for they will turn your sons away from following me to serve other gods, and the LORD's anger will burn against you and will quickly destroy you. 5 This is what you are to do to them: Break down their altars, smash their sacred stones, cut down their Asherah poles*p* and burn their idols in the fire. 6 For you are a people holy to the LORD your God. The LORD your God has chosen you out of all the peoples on the face of the earth to be his people, his treasured possession.
7 The LORD did not set his affection on you and choose you because you were more numerous than other peoples, for you were the fewest of all peoples. 8 But it was because the LORD loved you and kept the oath he swore to your forefathers that he brought you out with a mighty hand and redeemed you from the land of slavery, from the power of Pharaoh king of Egypt. 9 Know therefore that the LORD your God is God; he is the faithful God, keeping his covenant of love to a thousand generations of those who love him and keep his commands. 10 But

> those who hate him he will repay to their face
>   by destruction;
> he will not be slow to repay to their face
>   those who hate him.

11 Therefore, take care to follow the commands, decrees and laws I give you today.
12 If you pay attention to these laws and are careful to follow them, then the LORD your God will keep his covenant of love with you, as he swore to your forefathers.

---

g I.e. wooden symbols of a female deity

o 2 The Hebrew term refers to the irrevocable giving over of things or persons to the LORD, often by totally destroying them; also in verse 26.   *p 5* That is, symbols of the goddess Asherah; here and elsewhere in Deuteronomy

King James

¹³And he will love thee, and bless thee, and multiply thee: he will also bless the fruit of thy womb, and the fruit of thy land, thy corn, and thy wine, and thine oil, the increase of thy kine, and the flocks of thy sheep, in the land which he sware unto thy fathers to give thee.

¹⁴Thou shalt be blessed above all people: there shall not be male or female barren among you, or among your cattle.

¹⁵And the LORD will take away from thee all sickness, and will put none of the evil diseases of Egypt, which thou knowest, upon thee; but will lay them upon all *them* that hate thee.

¹⁶And thou shalt consume all the people which the LORD thy God shall deliver thee; thine eye shall have no pity upon them: neither shalt thou serve their gods; for that *will be* a snare unto thee.

¹⁷If thou shalt say in thine heart, These nations *are* more than I; how can I dispossess them?

¹⁸Thou shalt not be afraid of them: *but* shalt well remember what the LORD thy God did unto Pharaoh, and unto all Egypt;

¹⁹The great temptations which thine eyes saw, and the signs, and the wonders, and the mighty hand, and the stretched out arm, whereby the LORD thy God brought thee out: so shall the LORD thy God do unto all the people of whom thou art afraid.

²⁰Moreover the LORD thy God will send the hornet among them, until they that are left, and hide themselves from thee, be destroyed.

²¹Thou shalt not be affrighted at them: for the LORD thy God *is* among you, a mighty God and terrible.

²²And the LORD thy God will ^hput out those nations before thee by little and little: thou mayest not consume them at once, lest the beasts of the field increase upon thee.

²³But the LORD thy God shall deliver them ⁱunto thee, and shall destroy them with a mighty destruction, until they be destroyed.

²⁴And he shall deliver their kings into thine hand, and thou shalt destroy their name from under heaven: there shall no man be able to stand before thee, until thou have destroyed them.

²⁵The graven images of their gods shall ye burn with fire: thou shalt not desire the silver or gold *that is* on them, nor take *it* unto thee, lest thou be snared therein: for it *is* an abomination to the LORD thy God.

²⁶Neither shalt thou bring an abomination into thine house, lest thou be a cursed thing like it: *but* thou shalt utterly detest it, and thou shalt utterly abhor it; for it *is* a cursed thing.

God's mercies in the wilderness

8 ALL THE commandments which I command thee this day shall ye observe to do, that ye may live, and multiply, and go in and possess the land which the LORD sware unto your fathers.

²And thou shalt remember all the way which the LORD thy God led thee these forty years in the wilderness, to humble thee, *and* to prove thee, to know what *was* in thine heart, whether thou wouldest keep his commandments, or no.

³And he humbled thee, and suffered thee to hunger, and fed thee with manna, which thou knewest not, neither did thy fathers know; that he might make thee know that man doth not live by bread only, but by every *word* that proceedeth out of the mouth of the LORD doth man live.

⁴Thy raiment waxed not old upon thee, neither did thy foot swell, these forty years.

Amplified

¹³And He will love you, bless you, and multiply you; He will also bless the fruit of your body and the fruit of your land, your grain, your new wine, and your oil, the increase of your cattle and the young of your flock in the land which He swore to your fathers to give you.

¹⁴You shall be blessed above all peoples; there shall not be male or female barren among you, or among your cattle.

¹⁵And the Lord will take away from you all sickness, and none of the evil diseases of Egypt which you knew will He put upon you, but will lay them upon all who hate you.

¹⁶And you shall consume all the peoples whom the Lord your God will give over to you; your eye shall not pity them, neither shall you serve their gods, for that would be a snare to you.

¹⁷If you say in your [minds and] hearts, These nations are greater than we are; how can we dispossess them?

¹⁸You shall not be afraid of them, but remember [earnestly] what the Lord your God did to Pharaoh and to all Egypt,

¹⁹The great trials which your eyes saw, the signs, the wonders, the mighty hand and the outstretched arm by which the Lord your God brought you out. So shall the Lord your God do to all the people of whom you are afraid.

²⁰Moreover, the Lord your God will send the ^bhornet among them until those who are left and hide themselves from you are destroyed.

²¹You shall not dread them, for the Lord your God is among you, a mighty and terrible God.

²²And the Lord your God will clear out those nations before you, little by little; you may not consume them quickly, lest the beasts of the field increase among you.

²³But the Lord your God will give them over to you and will confuse them with a mighty panic until they are destroyed.

²⁴And He will give their kings into your hand, and you shall make their name perish from under the heavens; there shall no man be able to stand before you, until you have destroyed them.

²⁵The graven images of their gods you shall burn with fire. You shall not desire the silver or gold that is on them, nor take it for yourselves, lest you be ensnared by it, for it is an abomination to the Lord your God.

²⁶Neither shall you bring an abomination (an idol) into your house, lest you become an accursed thing like it; but you shall utterly detest and abhor it, for it is an accursed thing.

8 ALL THE commandments which I command you this day you shall be watchful to do, that you may live and multiply and go in and possess the land which the Lord swore to give to your fathers.

²And you shall [earnestly] remember all the way which the Lord your God led you these forty years in the wilderness, to humble you and to prove you, to know what was in your [mind and] heart, whether you would keep His commandments or not.

³And He humbled you and allowed you to hunger and fed you with manna, which you did not know nor did your fathers know, that He might make you recognize *and* personally know that man does not live by bread only, but man lives by every word that proceeds out of the mouth of the Lord.

⁴Your clothing did not become old upon you nor did your feet swell these forty years.

---

^b" . . . the hornet" with the article, used in a collective sense as a species or kind, is thus evidently to be understood, as in Deut. 2:25, as the terrors of God which should go before Israel, with which also Josh. 24:12 and Ps. 44:2 fully agree (J.P. Lange, *A Commentary*).

---

^hHeb. *pluck off*   ⁱHeb. *before thy face*

New American Standard

13"He will love you and bless you and multiply you; He will also bless the fruit of your womb and the fruit of your ground, your grain and your new wine and your oil, the increase of your herd and the young of your flock, in the land which He swore to your forefathers to give you.

14"You shall be blessed above all peoples; there will be no male or female barren among you or among your cattle.

15"The LORD will remove from you all sickness; and He will not put on you any of the harmful diseases of Egypt which you have known, but He will lay them on all who hate you.

16"You shall consume all the peoples whom the LORD your God will deliver to you; your eye shall not pity them, nor shall you serve their gods, for that *would be* a snare to you.

17 ¶ "If you should say in your heart, 'These nations are greater than I; how can I dispossess them?'

18 you shall not be afraid of them; you shall well remember what the LORD your God did to Pharaoh and to all Egypt:

19 the great trials which your eyes saw and the signs and the wonders and the mighty hand and the outstretched arm by which the LORD your God brought you out. So shall the LORD your God do to all the peoples of whom you are afraid.

20"Moreover, the LORD your God will send the hornet against them, until those who are left and hide themselves from you perish.

21"You shall not dread them, for the LORD your God is in your midst, a great and awesome God.

22"The LORD your God will clear away these nations before you little by little; you will not be able to put an end to them quickly, for the wild beasts would grow too numerous for you.

23"But the LORD your God will deliver them before you, and will throw them into great confusion until they are destroyed.

24"He will deliver their kings into your hand so that you will make their name perish from under heaven; no man will be able to stand before you until you have destroyed them.

25"The graven images of their gods you are to burn with fire; you shall not covet the silver or the gold that is on them, nor take it for yourselves, or you will be snared by it, for it is an abomination to the LORD your God.

26"You shall not bring an abomination into your house, and like it come under the ban; you shall utterly detest it and you shall utterly abhor it, for it is something banned.

God's Gracious Dealings

8 "ALL THE commandments that I am commanding you today you shall be careful to do, that you may live and multiply, and go in and possess the land which the LORD swore *to give* to your forefathers.

2"You shall remember all the way which the LORD your God has led you in the wilderness these forty years, that He might humble you, testing you, to know what was in your heart, whether you would keep His commandments or not.

3"He humbled you and let you be hungry, and fed you with manna which you did not know, nor did your fathers know, that He might make you understand that man does not live by bread alone, but man lives by everything that proceeds out of the mouth of the LORD.

4"Your clothing did not wear out on you, nor did your foot swell these forty years.

New International

13He will love you and bless you and increase your numbers. He will bless the fruit of your womb, the crops of your land—your grain, new wine and oil—the calves of your herds and the lambs of your flocks in the land that he swore to your forefathers to give you. 14You will be blessed more than any other people; none of your men or women will be childless, nor any of your livestock without young. 15The LORD will keep you free from every disease. He will not inflict on you the horrible diseases you knew in Egypt, but he will inflict them on all who hate you. 16You must destroy all the peoples the LORD your God gives over to you. Do not look on them with pity and do not serve their gods, for that will be a snare to you.

17You may say to yourselves, "These nations are stronger than we are. How can we drive them out?" 18But do not be afraid of them; remember well what the LORD your God did to Pharaoh and to all Egypt. 19You saw with your own eyes the great trials, the miraculous signs and wonders, the mighty hand and outstretched arm, with which the LORD your God brought you out. The LORD your God will do the same to all the peoples you now fear. 20Moreover, the LORD your God will send the hornet among them until even the survivors who hide from you have perished. 21Do not be terrified by them, for the LORD your God, who is among you, is a great and awesome God. 22The LORD your God will drive out those nations before you, little by little. You will not be allowed to eliminate them all at once, or the wild animals will multiply around you. 23But the LORD your God will deliver them over to you, throwing them into great confusion until they are destroyed. 24He will give their kings into your hand, and you will wipe out their names from under heaven. No one will be able to stand up against you; you will destroy them. 25The images of their gods you are to burn in the fire. Do not covet the silver and gold on them, and do not take it for yourselves, or you will be ensnared by it, for it is detestable to the LORD your God. 26Do not bring a detestable thing into your house or you, like it, will be set apart for destruction. Utterly abhor and detest it, for it is set apart for destruction.

Do Not Forget the LORD

8 BE CAREFUL to follow every command I am giving you today, so that you may live and increase and may enter and possess the land that the LORD promised on oath to your forefathers. 2Remember how the LORD your God led you all the way in the desert these forty years, to humble you and to test you in order to know what was in your heart, whether or not you would keep his commands. 3He humbled you, causing you to hunger and then feeding you with manna, which neither you nor your fathers had known, to teach you that man does not live on bread alone but on every word that comes from the mouth of the LORD. 4Your clothes did not wear out and your feet did not swell

King James

⁵Thou shalt also consider in thine heart, that, as a man chasteneth his son, *so* the LORD thy God chasteneth thee.

⁶Therefore thou shalt keep the commandments of the LORD thy God, to walk in his ways, and to fear him.

⁷For the LORD thy God bringeth thee into a good land, a land of brooks of water, of fountains and depths that spring out of valleys and hills;

⁸A land of wheat, and barley, and vines, and fig trees, and pomegranates; a land *j* of oil olive, and honey;

⁹A land wherein thou shalt eat bread without scarceness, thou shalt not lack any *thing* in it; a land whose stones *are* iron, and out of whose hills thou mayest dig brass.

¹⁰When thou hast eaten and art full, then thou shalt bless the LORD thy God for the good land which he hath given thee.

Warning against pride

¹¹Beware that thou forget not the LORD thy God, in not keeping his commandments, and his judgments, and his statutes, which I command thee this day:

¹²Lest *when* thou hast eaten and art full, and hast built goodly houses, and dwelt *therein;*

¹³And *when* thy herds and thy flocks multiply, and thy silver and thy gold is multiplied, and all that thou hast is multiplied;

¹⁴Then thine heart be lifted up, and thou forget the LORD thy God, which brought thee forth out of the land of Egypt, from the house of bondage;

¹⁵Who led thee through that great and terrible wilderness, *wherein were* fiery serpents, and scorpions, and drought, where *there was* no water; who brought thee forth water out of the rock of flint;

¹⁶Who fed thee in the wilderness with manna, which thy fathers knew not, that he might humble thee, and that he might prove thee, to do thee good at thy latter end;

¹⁷And thou say in thine heart, My power and the might of *mine* hand hath gotten me this wealth.

¹⁸But thou shalt remember the LORD thy God: for *it is* he that giveth thee power to get wealth, that he may establish his covenant which he sware unto thy fathers, as *it is* this day.

¹⁹And it shall be, if thou do at all forget the LORD thy God, and walk after other gods, and serve them, and worship them, I testify against you this day that ye shall surely perish.

²⁰As the nations which the LORD destroyeth before your face, so shall ye perish; because ye would not be obedient unto the voice of the LORD your God.

9 HEAR, O Israel: Thou *art* to pass over Jordan this day, to go in to possess nations greater and mightier than thyself, cities great and fenced up to heaven,

²A people great and tall, the children of the Anakims, whom thou knowest, and *of whom* thou hast heard *say,* Who can stand before the children of Anak!

³Understand therefore this day, that the LORD thy God *is* he which goeth over before thee; *as* a consuming fire he shall destroy them, and he shall bring them down before thy face: so shalt thou drive them out, and destroy them quickly, as the LORD hath said unto thee.

⁴Speak not thou in thine heart, after that the LORD thy God hath cast them out from before thee, saying, For my righteousness the LORD hath brought me in to possess this land: but for the wickedness of these nations the LORD doth drive them out from before thee.

Amplified

⁵Know also in your [minds and] hearts that, as a man disciplines *and* instructs his son, so the Lord your God disciplines *and* instructs you.

⁶So you shall keep the commandments of the Lord your God, to walk in His ways and [reverently] fear Him. [Prov. 8:13.]

⁷For the Lord your God is bringing you into a good land, a land of brooks of water, of fountains and springs, flowing forth in valleys and hills;

⁸A land of wheat and barley, and vines and fig trees and pomegranates, a land of olive trees and honey;

⁹A land in which you shall eat food without shortage and lack nothing in it; a land whose stones are iron and out of whose hills you can dig copper.

¹⁰When you have eaten and are full, then you shall bless the Lord your God for all the good land which He has given you.

¹¹Beware that you do not forget the Lord your God by not keeping His commandments, His precepts, and His statutes which I command you today,

¹²Lest when you have eaten and are full, and have built goodly houses and live in them,

¹³And when your herds and flocks multiply and your silver and gold is multiplied and all you have is multiplied,

¹⁴Then your [minds and] hearts be lifted up and you forget the Lord your God, Who brought you out of the land of Egypt, out of the house of bondage,

¹⁵Who led you through the great and terrible wilderness, with its fiery serpents and scorpions and thirsty ground where there was no water, but Who brought you forth water out of the flinty rock,

¹⁶Who fed you in the wilderness with manna, which your fathers did not know, that He might humble you and test you, to do you good in the end.

¹⁷And beware lest you say in your [mind and] heart, My power and the might of my hand have gotten me this wealth.

¹⁸But you shall [earnestly] remember the Lord your God, for it is He Who gives you power to get wealth, that He may establish His covenant which He swore to your fathers, as it is this day.

¹⁹And if you forget the Lord your God and walk after other gods and serve them and worship them, I testify against you this day that you shall surely perish.

²⁰Like the nations which the Lord makes to perish before you, so shall you perish, because you would not obey the voice of the Lord your God.

9 HEAR, O Israel. You are to cross the Jordan today to go in to dispossess nations greater and mightier than you are, cities great and fortified up to the heavens,

²A people great and tall, the sons of the Anakim, whom you know and of whom you have heard it said, Who can stand before the sons of Anak?

³Know therefore this day that the Lord your God is He Who goes over before you as a devouring fire. He will destroy them and bring them down before you; so you shall dispossess them and make them perish quickly, as the Lord has promised you.

⁴Do not say in your [mind and] heart, after the Lord your God has thrust them out from before you, It is because of my righteousness that the Lord has brought me in to possess this land—whereas it is because of the wickedness of these nations that the Lord is dispossessing them before you.

---

*j*Heb. *of olive tree of oil*

New American Standard

5"Thus you are to know in your heart that the LORD your God was disciplining you just as a man disciplines his son.

6"Therefore, you shall keep the commandments of the LORD your God, to walk in His ways and to fear Him.

7"For the LORD your God is bringing you into a good land, a land of brooks of water, of fountains and springs, flowing forth in valleys and hills;

8 a land of wheat and barley, of vines and fig trees and pomegranates, a land of olive oil and honey;

9 a land where you will eat food without scarcity, in which you will not lack anything; a land whose stones are iron, and out of whose hills you can dig copper.

10"When you have eaten and are satisfied, you shall bless the LORD your God for the good land which He has given you.

11 ¶ "Beware that you do not forget the LORD your God by not keeping His commandments and His ordinances and His statutes which I am commanding you today;

12 otherwise, when you have eaten and are satisfied, and have built good houses and lived *in them,*

13 and when your herds and your flocks multiply, and your silver and gold multiply, and all that you have multiplies,

14 then your heart will become proud and you will forget the LORD your God who brought you out from the land of Egypt, out of the house of slavery.

15"He led you through the great and terrible wilderness, *with its* fiery serpents and scorpions and thirsty ground where there was no water; He brought water for you out of the rock of flint.

16"In the wilderness He fed you manna which your fathers did not know, that He might humble you and that He might test you, to do good for you in the end.

17"Otherwise, you may say in your heart, 'My power and the strength of my hand made me this wealth.'

18"But you shall remember the LORD your God, for it is He who is giving you power to make wealth, that He may confirm His covenant which He swore to your fathers, as *it is* this day.

19"It shall come about if you ever forget the LORD your God and go after other gods and serve them and worship them, I testify against you today that you will surely perish.

20"Like the nations that the LORD makes to perish before you, so you shall perish; because you would not listen to the voice of the LORD your God.

Israel Provoked God

9 "HEAR, O Israel! You are crossing over the Jordan today to go in to dispossess nations greater and mightier than you, great cities fortified to heaven,

2 a people great and tall, the sons of the Anakim, whom you know and of whom you have heard *it said,* 'Who can stand before the sons of Anak?'

3"Know therefore today that it is the LORD your God who is crossing over before you as a consuming fire. He will destroy them and He will subdue them before you, so that you may drive them out and destroy them quickly, just as the LORD has spoken to you.

4 ¶ "Do not say in your heart when the LORD your God has driven them out before you, 'Because of my righteousness the LORD has brought me in to possess this land,' but *it is* because of the wickedness of these nations *that the* LORD is dispossessing them before you.

New International

during these forty years. 5Know then in your heart that as a man disciplines his son, so the LORD your God disciplines you.

6Observe the commands of the LORD your God, walking in his ways and revering him. 7For the LORD your God is bringing you into a good land—a land with streams and pools of water, with springs flowing in the valleys and hills; 8a land with wheat and barley, vines and fig trees, pomegranates, olive oil and honey; 9a land where bread will not be scarce and you will lack nothing; a land where the rocks are iron and you can dig copper out of the hills.

10When you have eaten and are satisfied, praise the LORD your God for the good land he has given you. 11Be careful that you do not forget the LORD your God, failing to observe his commands, his laws and his decrees that I am giving you this day. 12Otherwise, when you eat and are satisfied, when you build fine houses and settle down, 13and when your herds and flocks grow large and your silver and gold increase and all you have is multiplied, 14then your heart will become proud and you will forget the LORD your God, who brought you out of Egypt, out of the land of slavery. 15He led you through the vast and dreadful desert, that thirsty and waterless land, with its venomous snakes and scorpions. He brought you water out of hard rock. 16He gave you manna to eat in the desert, something your fathers had never known, to humble and to test you so that in the end it might go well with you. 17You may say to yourself, "My power and the strength of my hands have produced this wealth for me." 18But remember the LORD your God, for it is he who gives you the ability to produce wealth, and so confirms his covenant, which he swore to your forefathers, as it is today.

19If you ever forget the LORD your God and follow other gods and worship and bow down to them, I testify against you today that you will surely be destroyed. 20Like the nations the LORD destroyed before you, so you will be destroyed for not obeying the LORD your God.

Not Because of Israel's Righteousness

9 HEAR, O Israel. You are now about to cross the Jordan to go in and dispossess nations greater and stronger than you, with large cities that have walls up to the sky. 2The people are strong and tall—Anakites! You know about them and have heard it said: "Who can stand up against the Anakites?" 3But be assured today that the LORD your God is the one who goes across ahead of you like a devouring fire. He will destroy them; he will subdue them before you. And you will drive them out and annihilate them quickly, as the LORD has promised you.

4After the LORD your God has driven them out before you, do not say to yourself, "The LORD has brought me here to take possession of this land because of my righteousness." No, it is on account of the wickedness of these nations that the LORD is going to drive them out before

King James

⁵Not for thy righteousness, or for the uprightness of thine heart, dost thou go to possess their land: but for the wickedness of these nations the LORD thy God doth drive them out from before thee, and that he may perform the word which the LORD sware unto thy fathers, Abraham, Isaac, and Jacob.

The golden calf

⁶Understand therefore, that the LORD thy God giveth thee not this good land to possess it for thy righteousness; for thou *art* a stiffnecked people.

⁷ ¶ Remember, *and* forget not, how thou provokedst the LORD thy God to wrath in the wilderness: from the day that thou didst depart out of the land of Egypt, until ye came unto this place, ye have been rebellious against the LORD.

⁸Also in Horeb ye provoked the LORD to wrath, so that the LORD was angry with you to have destroyed you.

⁹When I was gone up into the mount to receive the tables of stone, *even* the tables of the covenant which the LORD made with you, then I abode in the mount forty days and forty nights, I neither did eat bread nor drink water:

¹⁰And the LORD delivered unto me two tables of stone written with the finger of God; and on them *was written* according to all the words, which the LORD spake with you in the mount out of the midst of the fire in the day of the assembly.

¹¹And it came to pass at the end of forty days and forty nights, *that* the LORD gave me the two tables of stone, *even* the tables of the covenant.

¹²And the LORD said unto me, Arise, get thee down quickly from hence; for thy people which thou hast brought forth out of Egypt have corrupted *themselves;* they are quickly turned aside out of the way which I commanded them; they have made them a molten image.

¹³Furthermore the LORD spake unto me, saying, I have seen this people, and, behold, it *is* a stiffnecked people:

¹⁴Let me alone, that I may destroy them, and blot out their name from under heaven: and I will make of thee a nation mightier and greater than they.

¹⁵So I turned and came down from the mount, and the mount burned with fire: and the two tables of the covenant *were* in my two hands.

¹⁶And I looked, and, behold, ye had sinned against the LORD your God, *and* had made you a molten calf: ye had turned aside quickly out of the way which the LORD had commanded you.

¹⁷And I took the two tables, and cast them out of my two hands, and brake them before your eyes.

¹⁸And I fell down before the LORD, as at the first, forty days and forty nights: I did neither eat bread, nor drink water, because of all your sins which ye sinned, in doing wickedly in the sight of the LORD, to provoke him to anger.

¹⁹For I was afraid of the anger and hot displeasure, wherewith the LORD was wroth against you to destroy you. But the LORD hearkened unto me at that time also.

²⁰And the LORD was very angry with Aaron to have destroyed him: and I prayed for Aaron also the same time.

²¹And I took your sin, the calf which ye had made, and burnt it with fire, and stamped it, *and* ground *it* very small, *even* until it was as small as dust: and I cast the dust thereof into the brook that descended out of the mount.

²²And at Taberah, and at Massah, and at Kibrothhattaavah, ye provoked the LORD to wrath.

²³Likewise when the LORD sent you from Kadeshbarnea, saying, Go up and possess the land which I have given you; then ye rebelled against the commandment of the LORD your God, and ye believed him not, nor hearkened to his voice.

²⁴Ye have been rebellious against the LORD from the day that I knew you.

²⁵Thus I fell down before the LORD forty days and forty nights, as I fell down *at the first;* because the LORD had said he would destroy you.

Amplified

⁵Not for your righteousness or for the uprightness of your [minds and] hearts do you go to possess their land; but because of the wickedness of these nations the Lord your God is driving them out before you, and that He may fulfill the promise which the Lord swore to your fathers, Abraham, Isaac, and Jacob.

⁶Know therefore that the Lord your God does not give you this good land to possess because of your righteousness, for you are a hard *and* stubborn people.

⁷[Earnestly] remember and forget not how you provoked the Lord your God to wrath in the wilderness; from the day you left the land of Egypt until you came to this place, you have been rebellious against the Lord.

⁸Even in Horeb you provoked the Lord to wrath, and the Lord was so angry with you that He would have destroyed you.

⁹When I went up the mountain to receive the tables of stone, the tables of the covenant which the Lord made with you, I remained on the mountain forty days and forty nights; I neither ate food nor drank water.

¹⁰And the Lord delivered to me the two tables of stone written with the finger of God; and on them were all the words which the Lord spoke with you on the mountain out of the midst of the fire in the day of the assembly.

¹¹And at the end of forty days and forty nights the Lord gave me the two tables of stone, the tables of the covenant.

¹²And the Lord said to me, Arise, go down from here quickly, for your people whom you brought out of Egypt have corrupted themselves. They have quickly turned aside from the way which I commanded them; they have made for themselves a molten image.

¹³Furthermore the Lord said to me, I have seen this people, and behold, they are stubborn *and* hard.

¹⁴Let me alone, that I may destroy them and blot out their name from under the heavens; and I will make of you a nation mightier and greater than they.

¹⁵So I turned and came down from the mountain, and the mountain was burning with fire. And the two tables of the covenant were in my two hands.

¹⁶And I looked, and behold, you had sinned against the Lord your God; you had made for yourselves a molten calf. You had turned aside quickly from the way which the Lord had commanded you.

¹⁷I took the two tables, cast them out of my two hands, and broke them before your eyes.

¹⁸Then I fell down before the Lord as before, for forty days and forty nights; I neither ate food nor drank water, because of all the sin you had committed in doing wickedly in the sight of the Lord, to provoke Him to anger.

¹⁹For I was afraid of the anger and hot displeasure which the Lord held against you, enough to destroy you. But the Lord listened to me that time also.

²⁰And the Lord was very angry with Aaron, angry enough to have destroyed him, and I prayed for Aaron also at the same time.

²¹And I took your sin, the calf which you had made, and burned it with fire and crushed it, grinding it very small, until it was as fine as dust; and I cast the dust of it into the brook that came down out of the mountain.

²²At Taberah also and at Massah and at Kibrothhattaavah you provoked the Lord to wrath.

²³Likewise when the Lord sent you from Kadeshbarnea, saying, Go up and possess the land which I have given you, then you rebelled against the commandment of the Lord your God, and you did not believe Him *or* trust *and* rely on Him or obey His voice.

²⁴You have been rebellious against the Lord from the day that I knew you.

²⁵So I fell down *and* lay prostrate before the Lord forty days and nights because the Lord had said He would destroy you.

New American Standard

5"It is not for your righteousness or for the uprightness of your heart that you are going to possess their land, but *it is* because of the wickedness of these nations *that* the LORD your God is driving them out before you, in order to confirm the oath which the LORD swore to your fathers, to Abraham, Isaac and Jacob.

6 ¶ "Know, then, *it is* not because of your righteousness *that* the LORD your God is giving you this good land to possess, for you are a stubborn people.

7"Remember, do not forget how you provoked the LORD your God to wrath in the wilderness; from the day that you left the land of Egypt until you arrived at this place, you have been rebellious against the LORD.

8"Even at Horeb you provoked the LORD to wrath, and the LORD was so angry with you that He would have destroyed you.

9"When I went up to the mountain to receive the tablets of stone, the tablets of the covenant which the LORD had made with you, then I remained on the mountain forty days and nights; I neither ate bread nor drank water.

10"The LORD gave me the two tablets of stone written by the finger of God; and on them *were* all the words which the LORD had spoken with you at the mountain from the midst of the fire on the day of the assembly.

11"It came about at the end of forty days and nights that the LORD gave me the two tablets of stone, the tablets of the covenant.

12"Then the LORD said to me, 'Arise, go down from here quickly, for your people whom you brought out of Egypt have acted corruptly. They have quickly turned aside from the way which I commanded them; they have made a molten image for themselves.'

13"The LORD spoke further to me, saying, 'I have seen this people, and indeed, it is a stubborn people.

14'Let Me alone, that I may destroy them and blot out their name from under heaven; and I will make of you a nation mightier and greater than they.'

15 ¶ "So I turned and came down from the mountain while the mountain was burning with fire, and the two tablets of the covenant were in my two hands.

16"And I saw that you had indeed sinned against the LORD your God. You had made for yourselves a molten calf; you had turned aside quickly from the way which the LORD had commanded you.

17"I took hold of the two tablets and threw them from my hands and smashed them before your eyes.

18"I fell down before the LORD, as at the first, forty days and nights; I neither ate bread nor drank water, because of all your sin which you had committed in doing what was evil in the sight of the LORD to provoke Him to anger.

19"For I was afraid of the anger and hot displeasure with which the LORD was wrathful against you in order to destroy you, but the LORD listened to me that time also.

20"The LORD was angry enough with Aaron to destroy him; so I also prayed for Aaron at the same time.

21"I took your sinful *thing,* the calf which you had made, and burned it with fire and crushed it, grinding it very small until it was as fine as dust; and I threw its dust into the brook that came down from the mountain.

22 ¶ "Again at Taberah and at Massah and at Kibroth-hattaavah you provoked the LORD to wrath.

23"When the LORD sent you from Kadesh-barnea, saying, 'Go up and possess the land which I have given you,' then you rebelled against the command of the LORD your God; you neither believed Him nor listened to His voice.

24"You have been rebellious against the LORD from the day I knew you.

25 ¶ "So I fell down before the LORD the forty days and nights, which I did because the LORD had said He would destroy you.

New International

you. 5It is not because of your righteousness or your integrity that you are going in to take possession of their land; but on account of the wickedness of these nations, the LORD your God will drive them out before you, to accomplish what he swore to your fathers, to Abraham, Isaac and Jacob. 6Understand, then, that it is not because of your righteousness that the LORD your God is giving you this good land to possess, for you are a stiff-necked people.

The Golden Calf

7Remember this and never forget how you provoked the LORD your God to anger in the desert. From the day you left Egypt until you arrived here, you have been rebellious against the LORD. 8At Horeb you aroused the LORD's wrath so that he was angry enough to destroy you. 9When I went up on the mountain to receive the tablets of stone, the tablets of the covenant that the LORD had made with you, I stayed on the mountain forty days and forty nights; I ate no bread and drank no water. 10The LORD gave me two stone tablets inscribed by the finger of God. On them were all the commandments the LORD proclaimed to you on the mountain out of the fire, on the day of the assembly.

11At the end of the forty days and forty nights, the LORD gave me the two stone tablets, the tablets of the covenant. 12Then the LORD told me, "Go down from here at once, because your people whom you brought out of Egypt have become corrupt. They have turned away quickly from what I commanded them and have made a cast idol for themselves."

13And the LORD said to me, "I have seen this people, and they are a stiff-necked people indeed! 14Let me alone, so that I may destroy them and blot out their name from under heaven. And I will make you into a nation stronger and more numerous than they."

15So I turned and went down from the mountain while it was ablaze with fire. And the two tablets of the covenant were in my hands.*q* 16When I looked, I saw that you had sinned against the LORD your God; you had made for yourselves an idol cast in the shape of a calf. You had turned aside quickly from the way that the LORD had commanded you. 17So I took the two tablets and threw them out of my hands, breaking them to pieces before your eyes.

18Then once again I fell prostrate before the LORD for forty days and forty nights; I ate no bread and drank no water, because of all the sin you had committed, doing what was evil in the LORD's sight and so provoking him to anger. 19I feared the anger and wrath of the LORD, for he was angry enough with you to destroy you. But again the LORD listened to me. 20And the LORD was angry enough with Aaron to destroy him, but at that time I prayed for Aaron too. 21Also I took that sinful thing of yours, the calf you had made, and burned it in the fire. Then I crushed it and ground it to powder as fine as dust and threw the dust into a stream that flowed down the mountain.

22You also made the LORD angry at Taberah, at Massah and at Kibroth Hattaavah.

23And when the LORD sent you out from Kadesh Barnea, he said, "Go up and take possession of the land I have given you." But you rebelled against the command of the LORD your God. You did not trust him or obey him. 24You have been rebellious against the LORD ever since I have known you.

25I lay prostrate before the LORD those forty days and forty nights because the LORD had said he would destroy

q 15 Or *And I had the two tablets of the covenant with me, one in each hand*

King James

Amplified

26I prayed therefore unto the LORD, and said, O Lord GOD, destroy not thy people and thine inheritance, which thou hast redeemed through thy greatness, which thou hast brought forth out of Egypt with a mighty hand.

27Remember thy servants, Abraham, Isaac, and Jacob; look not unto the stubbornness of this people, nor to their wickedness, nor to their sin:

28Lest the land whence thou broughtest us out say, Because the LORD was not able to bring them into the land which he promised them, and because he hated them, he hath brought them out to slay them in the wilderness.

29Yet they *are* thy people and thine inheritance, which thou broughtest out by thy mighty power and by thy stretched out arm.

The second tables of stone

10 AT THAT time the LORD said unto me, Hew thee two tables of stone like unto the first, and come up unto me into the mount, and make thee an ark of wood.

2And I will write on the tables the words that were in the first tables which thou brakest, and thou shalt put them in the ark.

3And I made an ark of shittim wood, and hewed two tables of stone like unto the first, and went up into the mount, having the two tables in mine hand.

4And he wrote on the tables, according to the first writing, the ten kcommandments, which the LORD spake unto you in the mount out of the midst of the fire in the day of the assembly: and the LORD gave them unto me.

5And I turned myself and came down from the mount, and put the tables in the ark which I had made; and there they be, as the LORD commanded me.

6 ¶ And the children of Israel took their journey from Beeroth of the children of Jaakan to Mosera: there Aaron died, and there he was buried; and Eleazar his son ministered in the priest's office in his stead.

7From thence they journeyed unto Gudgodah; and from Gudgodah to Jotbath, a land of rivers of waters.

8 ¶ At that time the LORD separated the tribe of Levi, to bear the ark of the covenant of the LORD, to stand before the LORD to minister unto him, and to bless in his name, unto this day.

9Wherefore Levi hath no part nor inheritance with his brethren; the LORD *is* his inheritance, according as the LORD thy God promised him.

10And I stayed in the mount, according to the lfirst time, forty days and forty nights; and the LORD hearkened unto me at that time also, *and* the LORD would not destroy thee.

11And the LORD said unto me, Arise, mtake *thy* journey before the people, that they may go in and possess the land, which I sware unto their fathers to give unto them.

God's great requirement

12 ¶ And now, Israel, what doth the LORD thy God require of thee, but to fear the LORD thy God, to walk in all his ways, and to love him, and to serve the LORD thy God with all thy heart and with all thy soul,

13To keep the commandments of the LORD, and his statutes, which I command thee this day for thy good?

14Behold, the heaven and the heaven of heavens *is* the LORD'S thy God, the earth *also,* with all that therein *is.*

26And I prayed to the Lord, O Lord God, do not destroy Your people and Your heritage, whom You have redeemed through Your greatness, whom You have brought out of Egypt with a mighty hand.

27Remember [earnestly] Your servants, Abraham, Isaac, and Jacob; look not at the stubbornness of this people or at their wickedness or at their sin,

28Lest the land from which You brought us out say, Because the Lord was not able to bring them into the land which He promised them, and because He hated them, He has brought them out to slay them in the wilderness.

29Yet they are Your people and Your inheritance, whom You brought out by Your mighty power and by Your outstretched arm.

10 AT THAT time the Lord said to me, Hew two tables of stone like the first and come up to Me on the mountain and make an ark of wood.

2And I will write on the tables the words that were on the first tables which you broke, and you shall put them in the ark.

3So I [Moses] made an ark of acacia wood and hewed two tables of stone like the first, and went up the mountain cwith the two tables of stone in my [one] hand.

4And the Lord wrote on the tables as at the first writing, the Ten Commandments which the Lord had spoken to you on the mountain out of the midst of the fire on the day of the assembly; and the Lord gave them to me.

5And I turned and came down from the mountain and put the tables in the ark which I had made; and there they are, as the Lord commanded me.

6(The Israelites journeyed from the wells of the sons of Jaakan to Moserah. There Aaron died, and there he was buried, and Eleazar his son ministered in the priest's office in his stead.

7From there they journeyed to Gudgodah, and then to Jotbathah, a land of brooks [dividing the valley].

8At that time the Lord set apart the tribe of Levi to bear the ark of the covenant of the Lord, to stand before the Lord to minister to Him and to bless in His name unto this day.

9Therefore Levi has no part or inheritance with his brethren; the Lord is his inheritance, as the Lord your God promised him.)

10And I [Moses] stayed on the mountain, as the first time, forty days and nights, and the Lord listened to me at that time also; the Lord would not destroy you.

11And the Lord said to me, Arise, journey on before the people, that they may go in and possess the land which I swore to their fathers to give to them.

12And now, Israel, what does the Lord your God require of you but [reverently] to fear the Lord your God, [that is] to walk in all His ways, and to love Him, and to serve the Lord your God with all your [mind and] heart and with your entire being,

13To keep the commandments of the Lord and His statutes which I command you today for your good?

14Behold, the heavens and the heaven of heavens belong to the Lord your God, the earth also, with all that is in it *and* on it.

---

cOne of the many misconceptions of articles and events mentioned in the Bible, innocently perpetuated by artists without adequate knowledge, is that of the size of the two tables of stone on which the Ten Commandments were written. They were not great tombstone-sized slabs, but probably small rectangular plates, two of which could easily be carried in one hand. Dr. George L. Robinson brought from the Sinai area a pair of "tables of stone" believed comparable to those mentioned here, which he put in his coat pocket. Moses says here, "I . . . went up the mountain with the two tables of stone in my [one] hand," and he confirms it in Exod. 34:4.

---

kHeb. *words*　　　lOr, *former days*　　　mHeb. *go in journey*

New American Standard

26"I prayed to the LORD and said, 'O Lord GOD, do not destroy Your people, even Your inheritance, whom You have redeemed through Your greatness, whom You have brought out of Egypt with a mighty hand.

27 'Remember Your servants, Abraham, Isaac, and Jacob; do not look at the stubbornness of this people or at their wickedness or their sin.

28 'Otherwise the land from which You brought us may say, "Because the LORD was not able to bring them into the land which He had promised them and because He hated them He has brought them out to slay them in the wilderness."

29 'Yet they are Your people, even Your inheritance, whom You have brought out by Your great power and Your outstretched arm.'

The Tablets Rewritten

10 "AT THAT time the LORD said to me, 'Cut out for yourself two tablets of stone like the former ones, and come up to Me on the mountain, and make an ark of wood for yourself.

2 'I will write on the tablets the words that were on the former tablets which you shattered, and you shall put them in the ark.'

3"So I made an ark of acacia wood and cut out two tablets of stone like the former ones, and went up on the mountain with the two tablets in my hand.

4"He wrote on the tablets, like the former writing, the Ten Commandments which the LORD had spoken to you on the mountain from the midst of the fire on the day of the assembly; and the LORD gave them to me.

5"Then I turned and came down from the mountain and put the tablets in the ark which I had made; and there they are, as the LORD commanded me."

6 ¶ (Now the sons of Israel set out from Beeroth Bene-jaakan to Moserah. There Aaron died and there he was buried and Eleazar his son ministered as priest in his place.

7 From there they set out to Gudgodah, and from Gudgodah to Jotbathah, a land of brooks of water.

8 At that time the LORD set apart the tribe of Levi to carry the ark of the covenant of the LORD, to stand before the LORD to serve Him and to bless in His name until this day.

9 Therefore, Levi does not have a portion or inheritance with his brothers; the LORD is his inheritance, just as the LORD your God spoke to him.)

10 ¶ "I, moreover, stayed on the mountain forty days and forty nights like the first time, and the LORD listened to me that time also; the LORD was not willing to destroy you.

11"Then the LORD said to me, 'Arise, proceed on your journey ahead of the people, that they may go in and possess the land which I swore to their fathers to give them.'

12 ¶ "Now, Israel, what does the LORD your God require from you, but to fear the LORD your God, to walk in all His ways and love Him, and to serve the LORD your God with all your heart and with all your soul,

13 and to keep the LORD'S commandments and His statutes which I am commanding you today for your good?

14"Behold, to the LORD your God belong heaven and the highest heavens, the earth and all that is in it.

New International

you. 26I prayed to the LORD and said, "O Sovereign LORD, do not destroy your people, your own inheritance that you redeemed by your great power and brought out of Egypt with a mighty hand. 27Remember your servants Abraham, Isaac and Jacob. Overlook the stubbornness of this people, their wickedness and their sin. 28Otherwise, the country from which you brought us will say, 'Because the LORD was not able to take them into the land he had promised them, and because he hated them, he brought them out to put them to death in the desert.' 29But they are your people, your inheritance that you brought out by your great power and your outstretched arm."

Tablets Like the First Ones

10 AT THAT time the LORD said to me, "Chisel out two stone tablets like the first ones and come up to me on the mountain. Also make a wooden chest.ʳ 2I will write on the tablets the words that were on the first tablets, which you broke. Then you are to put them in the chest."

3So I made the ark out of acacia wood and chiseled out two stone tablets like the first ones, and I went up on the mountain with the two tablets in my hands. 4The LORD wrote on these tablets what he had written before, the Ten Commandments he had proclaimed to you on the mountain, out of the fire, on the day of the assembly. And the LORD gave them to me. 5Then I came back down the mountain and put the tablets in the ark I had made, as the LORD commanded me, and they are there now.

6(The Israelites traveled from the wells of the Jaakanites to Moserah. There Aaron died and was buried, and Eleazar his son succeeded him as priest. 7From there they traveled to Gudgodah and on to Jotbathah, a land with streams of water. 8At that time the LORD set apart the tribe of Levi to carry the ark of the covenant of the LORD, to stand before the LORD to minister and to pronounce blessings in his name, as they still do today. 9That is why the Levites have no share or inheritance among their brothers; the LORD is their inheritance, as the LORD your God told them.)

10Now I had stayed on the mountain forty days and nights, as I did the first time, and the LORD listened to me at this time also. It was not his will to destroy you. 11"Go," the LORD said to me, "and lead the people on their way, so that they may enter and possess the land that I swore to their fathers to give them."

Fear the LORD

12And now, O Israel, what does the LORD your God ask of you but to fear the LORD your God, to walk in all his ways, to love him, to serve the LORD your God with all your heart and with all your soul, 13and to observe the LORD's commands and decrees that I am giving you today for your own good?

14To the LORD your God belong the heavens, even the

ʳ 1 That is, an ark

King James

¹⁵Only the LORD had a delight in thy fathers to love them, and he chose their seed after them, *even* you above all people, as *it is* this day.

¹⁶Circumcise therefore the foreskin of your heart, and be no more stiffnecked.

¹⁷For the LORD your God *is* God of gods, and Lord of lords, a great God, a mighty, and a terrible, which regardeth not persons, nor taketh reward:

¹⁸He doth execute the judgment of the fatherless and widow, and loveth the stranger, in giving him food and raiment.

¹⁹Love ye therefore the stranger: for ye were strangers in the land of Egypt.

²⁰Thou shalt fear the LORD thy God; him shalt thou serve, and to him shalt thou cleave, and swear by his name.

²¹He *is* thy praise, and he *is* thy God, that hath done for thee these great and terrible things, which thine eyes have seen.

²²Thy fathers went down into Egypt with threescore and ten persons; and now the LORD thy God hath made thee as the stars of heaven for multitude.

Love and obey God

11 THEREFORE THOU shalt love the LORD thy God, and keep his charge, and his statutes, and his judgments, and his commandments, always.

²And know ye this day: for *I speak* not with your children which have not known, and which have not seen the chastisement of the LORD your God, his greatness, his mighty hand, and his stretched out arm,

³And his miracles, and his acts, which he did in the midst of Egypt unto Pharaoh the king of Egypt, and unto all his land;

⁴And what he did unto the army of Egypt, unto their horses, and to their chariots; how he made the water of the Red sea to overflow them as they pursued after you, and *how* the LORD hath destroyed them unto this day;

⁵And what he did unto you in the wilderness, until ye came into this place;

⁶And what he did unto Dathan and Abiram, the sons of Eliab, the son of Reuben: how the earth opened her mouth, and swallowed them up, and their households, and their tents, and all the ⁿsubstance that ^o*was* in their possession, in the midst of all Israel:

⁷But your eyes have seen all the great acts of the LORD which he did.

⁸Therefore shall ye keep all the commandments which I command you this day, that ye may be strong, and go in and possess the land, whither ye go to possess it;

⁹And that ye may prolong *your* days in the land, which the LORD sware unto your fathers to give unto them and to their seed, a land that floweth with milk and honey.

¹⁰ ¶ For the land, whither thou goest in to possess it, *is* not as the land of Egypt, from whence ye came out, where thou sowedst thy seed, and wateredst *it* with thy foot, as a garden of herbs:

¹¹But the land, whither ye go to possess it, *is* a land of hills and valleys, *and* drinketh water of the rain of heaven:

¹²A land which the LORD thy God ^pcareth for: the eyes of the LORD thy God *are* always upon it, from the beginning of the year even unto the end of the year.

¹³ ¶ And it shall come to pass, if ye shall hearken diligently unto my commandments which I command you this day, to love the LORD your God, and to serve him with all your heart and with all your soul,

¹⁴That I will give *you* the rain of your land in his due season, the first rain and the latter rain, that thou mayest gather in thy corn, and thy wine, and thine oil.

Amplified

¹⁵Yet the Lord had a delight in loving your fathers, and He chose their descendants after them, you above all peoples, as it is this day.

¹⁶So circumcise the foreskin of your [minds and] hearts; be no longer stubborn *and* hardened.

¹⁷For the Lord your God is God of gods and Lord of lords, the great, the mighty, the terrible God, Who is not partial and takes no bribe.

¹⁸He executes justice for the fatherless and the widow, and loves the stranger *or* temporary resident and gives him food and clothing.

¹⁹Therefore love the stranger *and* sojourner, for you were strangers *and* sojourners in the land of Egypt.

²⁰You shall [reverently] fear the Lord your God; you shall serve Him and cling to Him, and by His name *and* presence you shall swear.

²¹He is your praise; He is your God, Who has done for you these great and terrible things which your eyes have seen.

²²Your fathers went down to Egypt seventy persons in all, and now the Lord your God has made you as the stars of the heavens for multitude.

11 THEREFORE YOU shall love the Lord your God and keep His charge, His statutes, His precepts, and His commandments always.

²And know this day—for I am not speaking to your children who have not [personally] known and seen it—the instruction *and* discipline of the Lord your God: His greatness, His mighty hand, and His outstretched arm;

³His signs and His deeds which He did in Egypt to Pharaoh the king of Egypt and to all his land;

⁴And what He did to the army of Egypt, to their horses and chariots, how He made the waters of the Red Sea flow over them as they pursued you, and how the Lord has destroyed them to this day;

⁵And what He did to you in the wilderness until you came to this place;

⁶And what He did to Dathan and Abiram, sons of Eliab, the son of Reuben, how the earth opened its mouth and swallowed up them, their households, their tents, and every living thing that followed them, in the midst of all Israel. [Num. 26:9, 10.]

⁷For your eyes have seen all the great work of the Lord which He did.

⁸Therefore you shall keep all the commandments which I command you today, that you may be strong and go in and possess the land which you go across [the Jordan] to possess,

⁹And that you may live long in the land which the Lord swore to your fathers to give to them and to their descendants, a land flowing with milk and honey.

¹⁰For the land which you go in to possess is not like the land of Egypt, from which you came out, where you sowed your seed and watered it with your foot laboriously as in a garden of vegetables.

¹¹But the land which you enter to possess is a land of hills and valleys which drinks water of the rain of the heavens,

¹²A land for which the Lord your God cares; the eyes of the Lord your God are always upon it from the beginning of the year to the end of the year.

¹³And if you will diligently heed My commandments which I command you this day—to love the Lord your God and to serve Him with all your [mind and] heart and with your entire being—

¹⁴I will give the rain for your land in its season, the early rain and the latter rain, that you may gather in your grain, your new wine, and your oil.

ⁿOr, *living substance which followed them   ^o*Heb. *was at their feet*   ^pHeb. *seeketh*

New American Standard

¹⁵"Yet on your fathers did the LORD set His affection to love them, and He chose their descendants after them, *even* you above all peoples, as *it is* this day.

¹⁶"So circumcise your heart, and stiffen your neck no longer.

¹⁷"For the LORD your God is the God of gods and the Lord of lords, the great, the mighty, and the awesome God who does not show partiality nor take a bribe.

¹⁸"He executes justice for the orphan and the widow, and shows His love for the alien by giving him food and clothing.

¹⁹"So show your love for the alien, for you were aliens in the land of Egypt.

²⁰"You shall fear the LORD your God; you shall serve Him and cling to Him, and you shall swear by His name.

²¹"He is your praise and He is your God, who has done these great and awesome things for you which your eyes have seen.

²²"Your fathers went down to Egypt seventy persons *in all,* and now the LORD your God has made you as numerous as the stars of heaven.

Rewards of Obedience

11 "YOU SHALL therefore love the LORD your God, and always keep His charge, His statutes, His ordinances, and His commandments.

²"Know this day that I *am* not *speaking* with your sons who have not known and who have not seen the ʰdiscipline of the LORD your God—His greatness, His mighty hand and His outstretched arm,

³ and His signs and His works which He did in the midst of Egypt to Pharaoh the king of Egypt and to all his land;

⁴ and what He did to Egypt's army, to its horses and its chariots, when He made the water of the Red Sea to engulf them while they were pursuing you, and the LORD completely destroyed them;

⁵ and what He did to you in the wilderness until you came to this place;

⁶ and what He did to Dathan and Abiram, the sons of Eliab, the son of Reuben, when the earth opened its mouth and swallowed them, their households, their tents, and every living thing that followed them, among all Israel—

⁷ but your own eyes have seen all the great work of the LORD which He did.

⁸ ¶ "You shall therefore keep every commandment which I am commanding you today, so that you may be strong and go in and possess the land into which you are about to cross to possess it;

⁹ so that you may prolong *your* days on the land which the LORD swore to your fathers to give to them and to their descendants, a land flowing with milk and honey.

¹⁰"For the land, into which you are entering to possess it, is not like the land of Egypt from which you came, where you used to sow your seed and water it with your ⁱfoot like a vegetable garden.

¹¹"But the land into which you are about to cross to possess it, a land of hills and valleys, drinks water from the rain of heaven,

¹² a land for which the LORD your God cares; the eyes of the LORD your God are always on it, from the beginning even to the end of the year.

¹³ ¶ "It shall come about, if you listen obediently to my commandments which I am commanding you today, to love the LORD your God and to serve Him with all your heart and all your soul,

¹⁴ that He will give the rain for your land in its season, the ʲearly and late rain, that you may gather in your grain and your new wine and your oil.

highest heavens, the earth and everything in it. ¹⁵Yet the LORD set his affection on your forefathers and loved them, and he chose you, their descendants, above all the nations, as it is today. ¹⁶Circumcise your hearts, therefore, and do not be stiff-necked any longer. ¹⁷For the LORD your God is God of gods and Lord of lords, the great God, mighty and awesome, who shows no partiality and accepts no bribes. ¹⁸He defends the cause of the fatherless and the widow, and loves the alien, giving him food and clothing. ¹⁹And you are to love those who are aliens, for you yourselves were aliens in Egypt. ²⁰Fear the LORD your God and serve him. Hold fast to him and take your oaths in his name. ²¹He is your praise; he is your God, who performed for you those great and awesome wonders you saw with your own eyes. ²²Your forefathers who went down into Egypt were seventy in all, and now the LORD your God has made you as numerous as the stars in the sky.

Love and Obey the LORD

11 LOVE THE LORD your God and keep his requirements, his decrees, his laws and his commands always. ²Remember today that your children were not the ones who saw and experienced the discipline of the LORD your God: his majesty, his mighty hand, his outstretched arm; ³the signs he performed and the things he did in the heart of Egypt, both to Pharaoh king of Egypt and to his whole country; ⁴what he did to the Egyptian army, to its horses and chariots, how he overwhelmed them with the waters of the Red Seaˢ as they were pursuing you, and how the LORD brought lasting ruin on them. ⁵It was not your children who saw what he did for you in the desert until you arrived at this place, ⁶and what he did to Dathan and Abiram, sons of Eliab the Reubenite, when the earth opened its mouth right in the middle of all Israel and swallowed them up with their households, their tents and every living thing that belonged to them. ⁷But it was your own eyes that saw all these great things the LORD has done.

⁸Observe therefore all the commands I am giving you today, so that you may have the strength to go in and take over the land that you are crossing the Jordan to possess, ⁹and so that you may live long in the land that the LORD swore to your forefathers to give to them and their descendants, a land flowing with milk and honey. ¹⁰The land you are entering to take over is not like the land of Egypt, from which you have come, where you planted your seed and irrigated it by foot as in a vegetable garden. ¹¹But the land you are crossing the Jordan to take possession of is a land of mountains and valleys that drinks rain from heaven. ¹²It is a land the LORD your God cares for; the eyes of the LORD your God are continually on it from the beginning of the year to its end.

¹³So if you faithfully obey the commands I am giving you today—to love the LORD your God and to serve him with all your heart and with all your soul— ¹⁴then I will send rain on your land in its season, both autumn and spring rains, so that you may gather in your grain, new

---

ʰ Or *instruction*   ⁱ I.e. probably a treadmill   ʲ I.e. autumn   ˢ 4 Hebrew *Yam Suph*; that is, Sea of Reeds

King James

¹⁵And I will ᵠsend grass in thy fields for thy cattle, that thou mayest eat and be full.

¹⁶Take heed to yourselves, that your heart be not deceived, and ye turn aside, and serve other gods, and worship them;

¹⁷And *then* the LORD'S wrath be kindled against you, and he shut up the heaven, that there be no rain, and that the land yield not her fruit; and *lest* ye perish quickly from off the good land which the LORD giveth you.

¹⁸ ¶ Therefore shall ye lay up these my words in your heart and in your soul, and bind them for a sign upon your hand, that they may be as frontlets between your eyes.

¹⁹And ye shall teach them your children, speaking of them when thou sittest in thine house, and when thou walkest by the way, when thou liest down, and when thou risest up.

²⁰And thou shalt write them upon the door posts of thine house, and upon thy gates:

²¹That your days may be multiplied, and the days of your children, in the land which the LORD sware unto your fathers to give them, as the days of heaven upon the earth.

²² ¶ For if ye shall diligently keep all these commandments which I command you, to do them, to love the LORD your God, to walk in all his ways, and to cleave unto him;

²³Then will the LORD drive out all these nations from before you, and ye shall possess greater nations and mightier than yourselves.

²⁴Every place whereon the soles of your feet shall tread shall be yours: from the wilderness and Lebanon, from the river, the river Euphrates, even unto the uttermost sea shall your coast be.

²⁵There shall no man be able to stand before you: *for* the LORD your God shall lay the fear of you and the dread of you upon all the land that ye shall tread upon, as he hath said unto you.

²⁶ ¶ Behold, I set before you this day a blessing and a curse;

²⁷A blessing, if ye obey the commandments of the LORD your God, which I command you this day:

²⁸And a curse, if ye will not obey the commandments of the LORD your God, but turn aside out of the way which I command you this day, to go after other gods, which ye have not known.

²⁹And it shall come to pass, when the LORD thy God hath brought thee in unto the land whither thou goest to possess it, that thou shalt put the blessing upon mount Gerizim, and the curse upon mount Ebal.

³⁰*Are* they not on the other side Jordan, by the way where the sun goeth down, in the land of the Canaanites, which dwell in the champaign over against Gilgal, beside the plains of Moreh?

³¹For ye shall pass over Jordan to go in to possess the land which the LORD your God giveth you, and ye shall possess it, and dwell therein.

³²And ye shall observe to do all the statutes and judgments which I set before you this day.

Sacrifice at one altar only

12 THESE *ARE* the statutes and judgments, which ye shall observe to do in the land, which the LORD God of thy fathers giveth thee to possess it, all the days that ye live upon the earth.

²Ye shall utterly destroy all the places, wherein the nations which ye shall ʳpossess served their gods, upon the high mountains, and upon the hills, and under every green tree:

³And ye shall ˢoverthrow their altars, and break their pillars, and burn their groves with fire; and ye shall hew down the graven images of their gods, and destroy the names of them out of that place.

Amplified

¹⁵And I will give grass in your fields for your cattle, that you may eat and be full.

¹⁶Take heed to yourselves, lest your [minds and] hearts be deceived and you turn aside and serve other gods and worship them,

¹⁷And the Lord's anger be kindled against you, and He shut up the heavens so that there will be no rain and the land will not yield its fruit, and you perish quickly off the good land which the Lord gives you.

¹⁸Therefore you shall lay up these My words in your [minds and] hearts and in your [entire] being, and bind them for a sign upon your hands and as forehead bands between your eyes.

¹⁹And you shall teach them to your children, speaking of them when you sit in your house and when you walk along the road, when you lie down and when you rise up.

²⁰And you shall write them upon the doorposts of your house and on your gates,

²¹That your days and the days of your children may be multiplied in the land which the Lord swore to your fathers to give them, as long as the heavens are above the earth.

²²For if you diligently keep all this commandment which I command you to do, to love the Lord your God, to walk in all His ways, and to cleave to Him—

²³Then the Lord will drive out all these nations before you, and you shall dispossess nations greater and mightier than you.

²⁴Every place upon which the sole of your foot shall tread shall be yours: from the wilderness to Lebanon, and from the River, the river Euphrates, to the western sea [Mediterranean] your territory shall be.

²⁵There shall no man be able to stand before you; the Lord your God shall lay the fear and the dread of you upon all the land that you shall tread, as He has said to you.

²⁶Behold, I set before you this day a blessing and a curse—

²⁷The blessing if you obey the commandments of the Lord your God which I command you this day;

²⁸And the curse if you will not obey the commandments of the Lord your God, but turn aside from the way which I command you this day to go after other gods, which you have not known.

²⁹And when the Lord your God has brought you into the land which you go to possess, you shall set the blessing on Mount Gerizim and the curse on Mount Ebal. [Josh. 8:33.]

³⁰Are they not beyond the Jordan, west of the road, where the sun goes down, in the land of the Canaanites living in the Arabah opposite Gilgal, beside the oaks *or* terebinths of Moreh?

³¹For you are to cross over the Jordan to go in to possess the land which the Lord your God gives you, and you shall possess it and live in it.

³²And you shall be watchful to do all the statutes and ordinances which I set before you this day.

12 THESE ARE the statutes and ordinances which you shall be watchful to do in the land which the Lord, the God of your fathers, gives you to possess all the days you live on the earth.

²You shall surely destroy all the places where the nations you dispossess served their gods, upon the high mountains and the hills and under every green tree.

³You shall break down their altars and dash in pieces their pillars and burn their Asherim with fire; you shall hew down the graven images of their gods and destroy their name out of that place.

ᵠHeb. *give*   ʳOr, *inherit*   ˢHeb. *break down*

New American Standard

15"He will give grass in your fields for your cattle, and you will eat and be satisfied.

16"Beware that your hearts are not deceived, and that you do not turn away and serve other gods and worship them.

17"Or the anger of the LORD will be kindled against you, and He will shut up the heavens so that there will be no rain and the ground will not yield its fruit; and you will perish quickly from the good land which the LORD is giving you.

18 ¶ "You shall therefore impress these words of mine on your heart and on your soul; and you shall bind them as a sign on your hand, and they shall be as frontals on your forehead.

19"You shall teach them to your sons, talking of them when you sit in your house and when you walk along the road and when you lie down and when you rise up.

20"You shall write them on the doorposts of your house and on your gates,

21 so that your days and the days of your sons may be multiplied on the land which the LORD swore to your fathers to give them, as long as the heavens *remain* above the earth.

22"For if you are careful to keep all this commandment which I am commanding you to do, to love the LORD your God, to walk in all His ways and hold fast to Him,

23 then the LORD will drive out all these nations from before you, and you will dispossess nations greater and mightier than you.

24"Every place on which the sole of your foot treads shall be yours; your border will be from the wilderness to Lebanon, *and* from the river, the river Euphrates, as far as *k*the western sea.

25"No man will be able to stand before you; the LORD your God will lay the dread of you and the fear of you on all the land on which you set foot, as He has spoken to you.

26 ¶ "See, I am setting before you today a blessing and a curse:

27 the blessing, if you listen to the commandments of the LORD your God, which I am commanding you today;

28 and the curse, if you do not listen to the commandments of the LORD your God, but turn aside from the way which I am commanding you today, by following other gods which you have not known.

29 ¶ "It shall come about, when the LORD your God brings you into the land where you are entering to possess it, that you shall place the blessing on Mount Gerizim and the curse on Mount Ebal.

30"Are they not across the Jordan, west of the way toward the sunset, in the land of the Canaanites who live in the Arabah, opposite Gilgal, beside the oaks of Moreh?

31"For you are about to cross the Jordan to go in to possess the land which the LORD your God is giving you, and you shall possess it and live in it,

32 and you shall be careful to do all the statutes and the judgments which I am setting before you today.

Laws of the Sanctuary

12 "THESE ARE the statutes and the judgments which you shall carefully observe in the land which the LORD, the God of your fathers, has given you to possess as long as you live on the earth.

2"You shall utterly destroy all the places where the nations whom you shall dispossess serve their gods, on the high mountains and on the hills and under every green tree.

3"You shall tear down their altars and smash their *sacred* pillars and burn their *l*Asherim with fire, and you shall cut down the engraved images of their gods and obliterate their name from that place.

New International

wine and oil. 15I will provide grass in the fields for your cattle, and you will eat and be satisfied.

16Be careful, or you will be enticed to turn away and worship other gods and bow down to them. 17Then the LORD's anger will burn against you, and he will shut the heavens so that it will not rain and the ground will yield no produce, and you will soon perish from the good land the LORD is giving you. 18Fix these words of mine in your hearts and minds; tie them as symbols on your hands and bind them on your foreheads. 19Teach them to your children, talking about them when you sit at home and when you walk along the road, when you lie down and when you get up. 20Write them on the doorframes of your houses and on your gates, 21so that your days and the days of your children may be many in the land that the LORD swore to give your forefathers, as many as the days that the heavens are above the earth.

22If you carefully observe all these commands I am giving you to follow—to love the LORD your God, to walk in all his ways and to hold fast to him— 23then the LORD will drive out all these nations before you, and you will dispossess nations larger and stronger than you. 24Every place where you set your foot will be yours: Your territory will extend from the desert to Lebanon, and from the Euphrates River to the western sea.*t* 25No man will be able to stand against you. The LORD your God, as he promised you, will put the terror and fear of you on the whole land, wherever you go.

26See, I am setting before you today a blessing and a curse— 27the blessing if you obey the commands of the LORD your God that I am giving you today; 28the curse if you disobey the commands of the LORD your God and turn from the way that I command you today by following other gods, which you have not known. 29When the LORD your God has brought you into the land you are entering to possess, you are to proclaim on Mount Gerizim the blessings, and on Mount Ebal the curses. 30As you know, these mountains are across the Jordan, west of the road,*u* toward the setting sun, near the great trees of Moreh, in the territory of those Canaanites living in the Arabah in the vicinity of Gilgal. 31You are about to cross the Jordan to enter and take possession of the land the LORD your God is giving you. When you have taken it over and are living there, 32be sure that you obey all the decrees and laws I am setting before you today.

The One Place of Worship

12 THESE ARE the decrees and laws you must be careful to follow in the land that the LORD, the God of your fathers, has given you to possess—as long as you live in the land. 2Destroy completely all the places on the high mountains and on the hills and under every spreading tree where the nations you are dispossessing worship their gods. 3Break down their altars, smash their sacred stones and burn their Asherah poles in the fire; cut down the idols of their gods and wipe out their names from those places.

---

k I.e. the Mediterranean   *l* I.e. wooden symbols of a female deity   *t 24* That is, the Mediterranean   *u 30* Or *Jordan, westward*

King James

4Ye shall not do so unto the LORD your God.

5But unto the place which the LORD your God shall choose out of all your tribes to put his name there, *even* unto his habitation shall ye seek, and thither thou shalt come:

6And thither ye shall bring your burnt offerings, and your sacrifices, and your tithes, and heave offerings of your hand, and your vows, and your freewill offerings, and the firstlings of your herds and of your flocks:

7And there ye shall eat before the LORD your God, and ye shall rejoice in all that ye put your hand unto, ye and your households, wherein the LORD thy God hath blessed thee.

8Ye shall not do after all *the things* that we do here this day, every man whatsoever *is* right in his own eyes.

9For ye are not as yet come to the rest and to the inheritance, which the LORD your God giveth you.

10But *when* ye go over Jordan, and dwell in the land which the LORD your God giveth you to inherit, and *when* he giveth you rest from all your enemies round about, so that ye dwell in safety;

11Then there shall be a place which the LORD your God shall choose to cause his name to dwell there; thither shall ye bring all that I command you; your burnt offerings, and your sacrifices, your tithes, and the heave offering of your hand, and all *t*your choice vows which ye vow unto the LORD:

12And ye shall rejoice before the LORD your God, ye, and your sons, and your daughters, and your menservants, and your maidservants, and the Levite that *is* within your gates; forasmuch as he hath no part nor inheritance with you.

13Take heed to thyself that thou offer not thy burnt offerings in every place that thou seest:

14But in the place which the LORD shall choose in one of thy tribes, there thou shalt offer thy burnt offerings, and there thou shalt do all that I command thee.

15Notwithstanding thou mayest kill and eat flesh in all thy gates, whatsoever thy soul lusteth after, according to the blessing of the LORD thy God which he hath given thee: the unclean and the clean may eat thereof, as of the roebuck, and as of the hart.

16Only ye shall not eat the blood; ye shall pour it upon the earth as water.

17 ¶ Thou mayest not eat within thy gates the tithe of thy corn, or of thy wine, or of thy oil, or the firstlings of thy herds or of thy flock, nor any of thy vows which thou vowest, nor thy freewill offerings, or heave offering of thine hand:

18But thou must eat them before the LORD thy God in the place which the LORD thy God shall choose, thou, and thy son, and thy daughter, and thy manservant, and thy maidservant, and the Levite that *is* within thy gates: and thou shalt rejoice before the LORD thy God in all that thou puttest thine hands unto.

19Take heed to thyself that thou forsake not the Levite *u*as long as thou livest upon the earth.

20 ¶ When the LORD thy God shall enlarge thy border, as he hath promised thee, and thou shalt say, I will eat flesh, because thy soul longeth to eat flesh; thou mayest eat flesh, whatsoever thy soul lusteth after.

Amplified

4You shall not behave so toward the Lord your God.

5But you shall seek the place which the Lord your God shall choose out of all your tribes to put His *d*Name and make His dwelling place, and there shall you come;

6And there you shall bring your burnt offerings and your sacrifices, your tithes and the offering of your hands, and your vows and your freewill offerings, and the firstlings of your herd and of your flock.

7And there you shall eat before the Lord your God, and you shall rejoice in all to which you put your hand, you and your households, in which the Lord your God has blessed you.

8You *e*shall not do according to all we do here [in the camp] this day, every man doing whatever looks right in his own eyes.

9For you have not yet come to the rest and to the inheritance which the Lord your God gives you.

10But when you go over the Jordan and dwell in the land which the Lord your God causes you to inherit, and He gives you rest from all your enemies round about so that you dwell in safety,

11Then there shall be a place which the Lord your God shall choose to cause His Name [and His Presence] to dwell there; to it you shall bring all that I command you: your burnt offerings, your sacrifices, your tithes and what the hand presents [as a first gift from the fruits of the ground], and all your choicest offerings which you vow to the Lord.

12And you shall rejoice before the Lord your God, you and your sons and your daughters, and your menservants and your maidservants, and the Levite that is within your towns, since he has no part or inheritance with you.

13Be watchful not to offer your burnt offerings in every place you see.

14But in the place which the Lord shall choose in one of your tribes, there you shall offer your burnt offerings, and there you shall do all I command you.

15However, you may kill and eat flesh in any of your towns whenever you desire, according to the provision for the support of life with which the Lord your God has blessed you; those [ceremonially] unclean and the clean may eat of it, as of the gazelle and the hart.

16Only you shall not eat the blood; you shall pour it upon the ground as water.

17You may not eat within your towns the tithe of your grain or of your new wine or of your oil, or the firstlings of your herd or flock, or anything you have vowed, or your freewill offerings, or the offerings from your hand [of garden products].

18But you shall eat them before the Lord your God in the place which the Lord your God shall choose, you and your son and your daughter, your manservant and your maidservant, and the Levite that is within your towns; and you shall rejoice before the Lord your God in all that you undertake.

19Take heed not to forsake *or* neglect the Levite [God's minister] as long as you live in your land.

20When the Lord your God enlarges your territory, as He promised you, and you say, I will eat flesh, because you crave flesh, you may eat flesh whenever you desire.

---

*d*The "Name" of God is equivalent to His gracious presence in passages such as this one. The place where God puts His Name is the place where the Lord Himself chooses to dwell. When it stands for God's presence at the sanctuary, "Name" is capitalized. *e*"It has been too often overlooked that the Law of Moses had a prophetic side. It was given to him and to Israel when they were not in a position to keep it [fully]. It was the law of the land which God would give them. In many ways its observance depended on the completion of the conquest of the land and upon the quietness of the times in which they lived. This prophetic aspect was certainly not unrecognized by the Jews, or they would not (for example) have neglected to dwell in booths at the Feast of Tabernacles from the time of Joshua to Nehemiah (Neh. 8:17)" (Charles J. Ellicott, *A Bible Commentary*).

---

*t*Heb. *the choice of your vows*   *u*Heb. *all thy days*

New American Standard

4"You shall not act like this toward the LORD your God.

5"But you shall seek *the LORD* at the place which the LORD your God will choose from all your tribes, to establish His name there for His dwelling, and there you shall come.

6"There you shall bring your burnt offerings, your sacrifices, your tithes, the contribution of your hand, your votive offerings, your freewill offerings, and the firstborn of your herd and of your flock.

7"There also you and your households shall eat before the LORD your God, and rejoice in all your undertakings in which the LORD your God has blessed you.

8 ¶ "You shall not do at all what we are doing here today, every man *doing* whatever is right in his own eyes;

9 for you have not as yet come to the resting place and the inheritance which the LORD your God is giving you.

10"When you cross the Jordan and live in the land which the LORD your God is giving you to inherit, and He gives you rest from all your enemies around *you* so that you live in security,

11 then it shall come about that the place in which the LORD your God will choose for His name to dwell, there you shall bring all that I command you: your burnt offerings and your sacrifices, your tithes and the contribution of your hand, and all your choice votive offerings which you will vow to the LORD.

12"And you shall rejoice before the LORD your God, you and your sons and daughters, your male and female servants, and the Levite who is within your gates, since he has no portion or inheritance with you.

13 ¶ "Be careful that you do not offer your burnt offerings in every *cultic* place you see,

14 but in the place which the LORD chooses in one of your tribes, there you shall offer your burnt offerings, and there you shall do all that I command you.

15 ¶ "However, you may slaughter and eat meat within any of your gates, whatever you desire, according to the blessing of the LORD your God which He has given you; the unclean and the clean may eat of it, as of the gazelle and the deer.

16"Only you shall not eat the blood; you are to pour it out on the ground like water.

17"You are not allowed to eat within your gates the tithe of your grain or new wine or oil, or the firstborn of your herd or flock, or any of your votive offerings which you vow, or your freewill offerings, or the contribution of your hand.

18"But you shall eat them before the LORD your God in the place which the LORD your God will choose, you and your son and daughter, and your male and female servants, and the Levite who is within your gates; and you shall rejoice before the LORD your God in all your undertakings.

19"Be careful that you do not forsake the Levite as long as you live in your land.

20 ¶ "When the LORD your God extends your border as He has promised you, and you say, 'I will eat meat,' because you desire to eat meat, *then* you may eat meat, whatever you desire.

New International

4You must not worship the LORD your God in their way. 5But you are to seek the place the LORD your God will choose from among all your tribes to put his Name there for his dwelling. To that place you must go; 6there bring your burnt offerings and sacrifices, your tithes and special gifts, what you have vowed to give and your freewill offerings, and the firstborn of your herds and flocks. 7There, in the presence of the LORD your God, you and your families shall eat and shall rejoice in everything you have put your hand to, because the LORD your God has blessed you.

8You are not to do as we do here today, everyone as he sees fit, 9since you have not yet reached the resting place and the inheritance the LORD your God is giving you. 10But you will cross the Jordan and settle in the land the LORD your God is giving you as an inheritance, and he will give you rest from all your enemies around you so that you will live in safety. 11Then to the place the LORD your God will choose as a dwelling for his Name—there you are to bring everything I command you: your burnt offerings and sacrifices, your tithes and special gifts, and all the choice possessions you have vowed to the LORD. 12And there rejoice before the LORD your God, you, your sons and daughters, your menservants and maidservants, and the Levites from your towns, who have no allotment or inheritance of their own. 13Be careful not to sacrifice your burnt offerings anywhere you please. 14Offer them only at the place the LORD will choose in one of your tribes, and there observe everything I command you.

15Nevertheless, you may slaughter your animals in any of your towns and eat as much of the meat as you want, as if it were gazelle or deer, according to the blessing the LORD your God gives you. Both the ceremonially unclean and the clean may eat it. 16But you must not eat the blood; pour it out on the ground like water. 17You must not eat in your own towns the tithe of your grain and new wine and oil, or the firstborn of your herds and flocks, or whatever you have vowed to give, or your freewill offerings or special gifts. 18Instead, you are to eat them in the presence of the LORD your God at the place the LORD your God will choose—you, your sons and daughters, your menservants and maidservants, and the Levites from your towns—and you are to rejoice before the LORD your God in everything you put your hand to. 19Be careful not to neglect the Levites as long as you live in your land.

20When the LORD your God has enlarged your territory as he promised you, and you crave meat and say, "I would like some meat," then you may eat as much of it as you

King James

²¹If the place which the LORD thy God hath chosen to put his name there be too far from thee, then thou shalt kill of thy herd and of thy flock, which the LORD hath given thee, as I have commanded thee, and thou shalt eat in thy gates whatsoever thy soul lusteth after.

²²Even as the roebuck and the hart is eaten, so thou shalt eat them: the unclean and the clean shall eat *of* them alike.

²³Only ᵛbe sure that thou eat not the blood: for the blood *is* the life; and thou mayest not eat the life with the flesh.

²⁴Thou shalt not eat it; thou shalt pour it upon the earth as water.

²⁵Thou shalt not eat it; that it may go well with thee, and with thy children after thee, when thou shalt do *that which is* right in the sight of the LORD.

²⁶Only thy holy things which thou hast, and thy vows, thou shalt take, and go unto the place which the LORD shall choose:

²⁷And thou shalt offer thy burnt offerings, the flesh and the blood, upon the altar of the LORD thy God: and the blood of thy sacrifices shall be poured out upon the altar of the LORD thy God, and thou shalt eat the flesh.

²⁸Observe and hear all these words which I command thee, that it may go well with thee, and with thy children after thee for ever, when thou doest *that which is* good and right in the sight of the LORD thy God.

²⁹ ¶ When the LORD thy God shall cut off the nations from before thee, whither thou goest to possess them, and thou ʷsucceedest them, and dwellest in their land;

³⁰Take heed to thyself that thou be not snared ˣby following them, after that they be destroyed from before thee; and that thou inquire not after their gods, saying, How did these nations serve their gods? even so will I do likewise.

³¹Thou shalt not do so unto the LORD thy God: for every ʸabomination to the LORD, which he hateth, have they done unto their gods; for even their sons and their daughters they have burnt in the fire to their gods.

³²What thing soever I command you, observe to do it: thou shalt not add thereto, nor diminish from it.

Warning against idolatry

13 IF THERE arise among you a prophet, or a dreamer of dreams, and giveth thee a sign or a wonder,

²And the sign or the wonder come to pass, whereof he spake unto thee, saying, Let us go after other gods, which thou hast not known, and let us serve them;

³Thou shalt not hearken unto the words of that prophet, or that dreamer of dreams: for the LORD your God proveth you, to know whether ye love the LORD your God with all your heart and with all your soul.

⁴Ye shall walk after the LORD your God, and fear him, and keep his commandments, and obey his voice, and ye shall serve him, and cleave unto him.

⁵And that prophet, or that dreamer of dreams, shall be put to death; because he hath ᶻspoken to turn *you* away from the LORD your God, which brought you out of the land of Egypt, and redeemed you out of the house of bondage, to thrust thee out of the way which the LORD thy God commanded thee to walk in. So shalt thou put the evil away from the midst of thee.

⁶ ¶ If thy brother, the son of thy mother, or thy son, or thy daughter, or the wife of thy bosom, or thy friend, which *is* as thine own soul, entice thee secretly, saying, Let us go and serve other gods, which thou hast not known, thou, nor thy fathers;

⁷*Namely,* of the gods of the people which *are* round about you, nigh unto thee, or far off from thee, from the *one* end of the earth even unto the *other* end of the earth;

Amplified

²¹If the place where the Lord your God has chosen to put His Name [and Presence] is too far from you, then you shall kill from your herd or flock which the Lord has given you, as I [Moses] have commanded you; eat in your towns as much as you desire.

²²Just as the roebuck and the hart is eaten, so you may eat of it [but not offer it]; the unclean and the clean alike may eat of it.

²³Only be sure that you do not eat the blood, for the blood is the life, and you may not eat the life with the flesh.

²⁴You shall not eat it; you shall pour it out on the earth like water.

²⁵You shall not eat it, that all may go well with you and with your children after you, when you do what is right in the sight of the Lord.

²⁶Only your holy things which you have [to offer] and what you have vowed you shall take, and go to the place [before the sanctuary] which the Lord shall choose.

²⁷And offer your burnt offerings, the flesh and the blood, upon the altar of the Lord your God; and the blood of your sacrifices shall be poured out on the altar of the Lord your God, and you may eat the flesh.

²⁸Be watchful and obey all these words which I command you, that it may go well with you and with your children after you forever, when you do what is good and right in the sight of the Lord your God.

²⁹When the Lord your God cuts off before you the nations whom you go to dispossess, and you dispossess them and live in their land,

³⁰Be watchful that you are not ensnared into following them after they have been destroyed before you and that you do not inquire after their gods, saying, How did these nations serve their gods? We will do likewise.

³¹You shall not do so to the Lord your God, for every abominable thing which the Lord hates they have done for their gods. For even their sons and their daughters they have burned in the fire to their gods.

³²Whatever I command you, be watchful to do it; you shall not add to it or diminish it.

13 IF A prophet arises among you, or a dreamer of dreams, and gives you a sign or a wonder,

²And the sign or the wonder he foretells to you comes to pass, and if he says, Let us go after other gods—gods you have not known—and let us serve them,

³You shall not listen to the words of that prophet or to that dreamer of dreams. For the Lord your God is testing you to know whether you love the Lord your God with all your [mind and] heart and with your entire being.

⁴You shall walk after the Lord your God and [reverently] fear Him, and keep His commandments and obey His voice, and you shall serve Him and cling to Him.

⁵But that prophet or that dreamer of dreams shall be put to death, because he has talked rebellion *and* turning away from the Lord your God, Who brought you out of the land of Egypt and redeemed you out of the house of bondage; that man has tried to draw you aside from the way in which the Lord your God commanded you to walk. So shall you put the evil away from your midst.

⁶If your brother, the son of your mother, or your son or daughter, or the wife of your bosom, or your friend who is as your own life entices you secretly, saying, Let us go and serve other gods—gods you have not known, you nor your fathers,

⁷Of the gods of the peoples who are round about you, near you or far away from you, from one end of the earth to the other—

ᵛHeb. *be strong*   ʷHeb. *inheritest,* or, *possessest them*
ˣHeb. *after them*   ʸHeb. *abomination of the*   ᶻHeb. *spoken revolt against the LORD*

New American Standard

21"If the place which the LORD your God chooses to put His name is too far from you, then you may slaughter of your herd and flock which the LORD has given you, as I have commanded you; and you may eat within your gates whatever you desire.

22"Just as a gazelle or a deer is eaten, so you will eat it; the unclean and the clean alike may eat of it.

23"Only be sure not to eat the blood, for the blood is the life, and you shall not eat the life with the flesh.

24"You shall not eat it; you shall pour it out on the ground like water.

25"You shall not eat it, so that it may be well with you and your sons after you, for you will be doing what is right in the sight of the LORD.

26"Only your holy things which you may have and your votive offerings, you shall take and go to the place which the LORD chooses.

27"And you shall offer your burnt offerings, the flesh and the blood, on the altar of the LORD your God; and the blood of your sacrifices shall be poured out on the altar of the LORD your God, and you shall eat the flesh.

28 ¶ "Be careful to listen to all these words which I command you, so that it may be well with you and your sons after you forever, for you will be doing what is good and right in the sight of the LORD your God.

29 ¶ "When the LORD your God cuts off before you the nations which you are going in to dispossess, and you dispossess them and dwell in their land,

30 beware that you are not ensnared to follow them, after they are destroyed before you, and that you do not inquire after their gods, saying, 'How do these nations serve their gods, that I also may do likewise?'

31"You shall not behave thus toward the LORD your God, for every abominable act which the LORD hates they have done for their gods; for they even burn their sons and daughters in the fire to their gods.

32 ¶ "Whatever I command you, you shall be careful to do; you shall not add to nor take away from it.

Shun Idolatry

13 "IF A prophet or a dreamer of dreams arises among you and gives you a sign or a wonder,

2 and the sign or the wonder comes true, concerning which he spoke to you, saying, 'Let us go after other gods (whom you have not known) and let us serve them,'

3 you shall not listen to the words of that prophet or that dreamer of dreams; for the LORD your God is testing you to find out if you love the LORD your God with all your heart and with all your soul.

4"You shall follow the LORD your God and fear Him; and you shall keep His commandments, listen to His voice, serve Him, and cling to Him.

5"But that prophet or that dreamer of dreams shall be put to death, because he has counseled rebellion against the LORD your God who brought you from the land of Egypt and redeemed you from the house of slavery, to seduce you from the way in which the LORD your God commanded you to walk. So you shall purge the evil from among you.

6 ¶ "If your brother, your mother's son, or your son or daughter, or the wife you cherish, or your friend who is as your own soul, entice you secretly, saying, 'Let us go and serve other gods' (whom neither you nor your fathers have known,

7 of the gods of the peoples who are around you, near you or far from you, from one end of the earth to the other end),

New International

want. 21If the place where the LORD your God chooses to put his Name is too far away from you, you may slaughter animals from the herds and flocks the LORD has given you, as I have commanded you, and in your own towns you may eat as much of them as you want. 22Eat them as you would gazelle or deer. Both the ceremonially unclean and the clean may eat. 23But be sure you do not eat the blood, because the blood is the life, and you must not eat the life with the meat. 24You must not eat the blood; pour it out on the ground like water. 25Do not eat it, so that it may go well with you and your children after you, because you will be doing what is right in the eyes of the LORD.

26But take your consecrated things and whatever you have vowed to give, and go to the place the LORD will choose. 27Present your burnt offerings on the altar of the LORD your God, both the meat and the blood. The blood of your sacrifices must be poured beside the altar of the LORD your God, but you may eat the meat. 28Be careful to obey all these regulations I am giving you, so that it may always go well with you and your children after you, because you will be doing what is good and right in the eyes of the LORD your God.

29The LORD your God will cut off before you the nations you are about to invade and dispossess. But when you have driven them out and settled in their land, 30and after they have been destroyed before you, be careful not to be ensnared by inquiring about their gods, saying, "How do these nations serve their gods? We will do the same." 31You must not worship the LORD your God in their way, because in worshiping their gods, they do all kinds of detestable things the LORD hates. They even burn their sons and daughters in the fire as sacrifices to their gods.

32See that you do all I command you; do not add to it or take away from it.

Worshiping Other Gods

13 IF A prophet, or one who foretells by dreams, appears among you and announces to you a miraculous sign or wonder, 2and if the sign or wonder of which he has spoken takes place, and he says, "Let us follow other gods" (gods you have not known) "and let us worship them," 3you must not listen to the words of that prophet or dreamer. The LORD your God is testing you to find out whether you love him with all your heart and with all your soul. 4It is the LORD your God you must follow, and him you must revere. Keep his commands and obey him; serve him and hold fast to him. 5That prophet or dreamer must be put to death, because he preached rebellion against the LORD your God, who brought you out of Egypt and redeemed you from the land of slavery; he has tried to turn you from the way the LORD your God commanded you to follow. You must purge the evil from among you.

6If your very own brother, or your son or daughter, or the wife you love, or your closest friend secretly entices you, saying, "Let us go and worship other gods" (gods that neither you nor your fathers have known, 7gods of the peoples around you, whether near or far, from one end of

King James

8Thou shalt not consent unto him, nor hearken unto him; neither shall thine eye pity him, neither shalt thou spare, neither shalt thou conceal him:

9But thou shalt surely kill him; thine hand shall be first upon him to put him to death, and afterwards the hand of all the people.

10And thou shalt stone him with stones, that he die; because he hath sought to thrust thee away from the Lord thy God, which brought thee out of the land of Egypt, from the house of *a*bondage.

11And all Israel shall hear, and fear, and shall do no more any such wickedness as this is among you.

12 ¶ If thou shalt hear *say* in one of thy cities, which the Lord thy God hath given thee to dwell there, saying,

13*Certain* men, *b*the children of Belial, are gone out from among you, and have withdrawn the inhabitants of their city, saying, Let us go and serve other gods, which ye have not known;

14Then shalt thou inquire, and make search, and ask diligently; and, behold, *if it be* truth, *and* the thing certain, *that* such abomination is wrought among you;

15Thou shalt surely smite the inhabitants of that city with the edge of the sword, destroying it utterly, and all that *is* therein, and the cattle thereof, with the edge of the sword.

16And thou shalt gather all the spoil of it into the midst of the street thereof, and shalt burn with fire the city, and all the spoil thereof every whit, for the Lord thy God: and it shall be an heap for ever; it shall not be built again.

17And there shall cleave nought of the *c*cursed thing to thine hand: that the Lord may turn from the fierceness of his anger, and shew thee mercy, and have compassion upon thee, and multiply thee, as he hath sworn unto thy fathers;

18When thou shalt hearken to the voice of the Lord thy God, to keep all his commandments which I command thee this day, to do *that which is* right in the eyes of the Lord thy God.

14 YE *ARE* the children of the Lord your God: ye shall not cut yourselves, nor make any baldness between your eyes for the dead.

2For thou *art* an holy people unto the Lord thy God, and the Lord hath chosen thee to be a peculiar people unto himself, above all the nations that *are* upon the earth.

Clean and unclean animals

3 ¶ Thou shalt not eat any abominable thing.

4These *are* the beasts which ye shall eat: the ox, the sheep, and the goat,

5The hart, and the roebuck, and the fallow deer, and the wild goat, and the *d* *e*pygarg, and the wild ox, and the chamois.

6And every beast that parteth the hoof, and cleaveth the cleft into two claws, *and* cheweth the cud among the beasts, that ye shall eat.

7Nevertheless these ye shall not eat of them that chew the cud, or of them that divide the cloven hoof; *as* the camel, and the hare, and the coney: for they chew the cud, but divide not the hoof; *therefore* they *are* unclean unto you.

8And the swine, because it divideth the hoof, yet cheweth not the cud, it *is* unclean unto you: ye shall not eat of their flesh, nor touch their dead carcase.

9 ¶ These ye shall eat of all that *are* in the waters: all that have fins and scales shall ye eat:

10And whatsoever hath not fins and scales ye may not eat; it *is* unclean unto you.

11 ¶ *Of* all clean birds ye shall eat.

Amplified

8You shall not give consent to him or listen to him; nor shall your eye pity him, nor shall you spare him or conceal him.

9But you shall surely kill him; your hand shall be first upon him to put him to death, and afterwards the hands of all the people.

10And you shall stone him to death with stones, because he has tried to draw you away from the Lord your God, Who brought you out of the land of Egypt, from the house of bondage.

11And all Israel shall hear and [reverently] fear, and shall never again do any such wickedness as this among you.

12If you hear it said in one of your cities which the Lord your God has given you in which to dwell

13That certain base fellows have gone out from your midst and have enticed away the inhabitants of their city, saying, Let us go and serve other gods—gods you have not known—

14Then you shall inquire and make search and ask diligently. And behold, if it is true and certain that such an abominable thing has been done among you,

15You shall surely smite the inhabitants of that city with the edge of the sword, destroying it utterly and all who are in it and its beasts with the edge of the sword.

16And you shall collect all its spoil into the midst of its open square and shall burn the city with fire with every bit of its spoil [as a whole burnt offering] to the Lord your God. It shall be a heap [of ruins] forever; it shall not be built again.

17And nothing of the accursed thing shall cling to your hand, so that the Lord may turn from the fierceness of His anger, and show you mercy and have compassion on you and multiply you, as He swore to your fathers,

18If you obey the voice of the Lord your God, to keep all His commandments which I command you this day, to do what is right in the eyes of the Lord your God.

14 YOU ARE the sons of the Lord your God; you shall not cut yourselves or make any baldness on your foreheads for the dead,

2For you are a holy people [set apart] to the Lord your God; and the Lord has chosen you to be a peculiar people to Himself, above all the nations on the earth.

3You shall not eat anything that is abominable [to the Lord and so forbidden by Him].

4These are the beasts which you may eat: the ox, the sheep, and the goat,

5The hart, the gazelle, the roebuck, the wild goat, the ibex, the antelope, and the mountain sheep.

6And every beast that parts the hoof and has it divided into two and brings up *and* chews the cud among the beasts you may eat.

7Yet these you shall not eat of those that chew the cud or have the hoof split in two: the camel, the hare, and the coney, because they chew the cud but divide not the hoof; they are unclean for you.

8And the swine, because it parts the hoof but does not chew the cud; it is unclean to you. You shall not eat of their flesh or touch their dead bodies.

9These you may eat of all that are in the waters: whatever has fins and scales you may eat,

10And whatever has not fins and scales you may not eat; it is unclean for you.

11Of all clean birds you may eat.

---

a Heb. *bondmen*   *b* Or, *naughty men*   *c* Or, *devoted*   *d* Or, *bison*   *e* Heb. *dishon*

New American Standard

8 you shall not yield to him or listen to him; and your eye shall not pity him, nor shall you spare or conceal him.

9"But you shall surely kill him; your hand shall be first against him to put him to death, and afterwards the hand of all the people.

10"So you shall stone him to death because he has sought to seduce you from the LORD your God who brought you out from the land of Egypt, out of the house of slavery.

11"Then all Israel will hear and be afraid, and will never again do such a wicked thing among you.

12 ¶ "If you hear in one of your cities, which the LORD your God is giving you to live in, *anyone* saying *that*

13 some worthless men have gone out from among you and have seduced the inhabitants of their city, saying, 'Let us go and serve other gods' (whom you have not known),

14 then you shall investigate and search out and inquire thoroughly. If it is true *and* the matter established that this abomination has been done among you,

15 you shall surely strike the inhabitants of that city with the edge of the sword, utterly destroying it and all that is in it and its cattle with the edge of the sword.

16"Then you shall gather all its booty into the middle of its open square and burn the city and all its booty with fire as a whole burnt offering to the LORD your God; and it shall be a ruin forever. It shall never be rebuilt.

17"Nothing from that which is put under the ban shall cling to your hand, in order that the LORD may turn from His burning anger and show mercy to you, and have compassion on you and make you increase, just as He has sworn to your fathers,

18 if you will listen to the voice of the LORD your God, keeping all His commandments which I am commanding you today, and doing what is right in the sight of the LORD your God.

Clean and Unclean Animals

14 "YOU ARE the sons of the LORD your God; you shall not cut yourselves nor shave your forehead for the sake of the dead.

2"For you are a holy people to the LORD your God, and the LORD has chosen you to be a people for His own possession out of all the peoples who are on the face of the earth.

3 ¶ "You shall not eat any detestable thing.

4"These are the animals which you may eat: the ox, the sheep, the goat,

5 the deer, the gazelle, the roebuck, the wild goat, the ibex, the antelope and the mountain sheep.

6"Any animal that divides the hoof and has the hoof split in two *and* chews the cud, among the animals, that you may eat.

7"Nevertheless, you are not to eat of these among those which chew the cud, or among those that divide the hoof in two: the camel and the rabbit and the shaphan, for though they chew the cud, they do not divide the hoof; they are unclean for you.

8"The pig, because it divides the hoof but *does* not *chew* the cud, it is unclean for you. You shall not eat any of their flesh nor touch their carcasses.

9 ¶ "These you may eat of all that are in water: anything that has fins and scales you may eat,

10 but anything that does not have fins and scales you shall not eat; it is unclean for you.

11 ¶ "You may eat any clean bird.

New International

the land to the other), 8do not yield to him or listen to him. Show him no pity. Do not spare him or shield him. 9You must certainly put him to death. Your hand must be the first in putting him to death, and then the hands of all the people. 10Stone him to death, because he tried to turn you away from the LORD your God, who brought you out of Egypt, out of the land of slavery. 11Then all Israel will hear and be afraid, and no one among you will do such an evil thing again.

12If you hear it said about one of the towns the LORD your God is giving you to live in 13that wicked men have arisen among you and have led the people of their town astray, saying, "Let us go and worship other gods" (gods you have not known), 14then you must inquire, probe and investigate it thoroughly. And if it is true and it has been proved that this detestable thing has been done among you, 15you must certainly put to the sword all who live in that town. Destroy it completely,*v* both its people and its livestock. 16Gather all the plunder of the town into the middle of the public square and completely burn the town and all its plunder as a whole burnt offering to the LORD your God. It is to remain a ruin forever, never to be rebuilt. 17None of those condemned things*v* shall be found in your hands, so that the LORD will turn from his fierce anger; he will show you mercy, have compassion on you, and increase your numbers, as he promised on oath to your forefathers, 18because you obey the LORD your God, keeping all his commands that I am giving you today and doing what is right in his eyes.

Clean and Unclean Food

14 YOU ARE the children of the LORD your God. Do not cut yourselves or shave the front of your heads for the dead, 2for you are a people holy to the LORD your God. Out of all the peoples on the face of the earth, the LORD has chosen you to be his treasured possession.

3Do not eat any detestable thing. 4These are the animals you may eat: the ox, the sheep, the goat, 5the deer, the gazelle, the roe deer, the wild goat, the ibex, the antelope and the mountain sheep.*w* 6You may eat any animal that has a split hoof divided in two and that chews the cud. 7However, of those that chew the cud or that have a split hoof completely divided you may not eat the camel, the rabbit or the coney.*x* Although they chew the cud, they do not have a split hoof; they are ceremonially unclean for you. 8The pig is also unclean; although it has a split hoof, it does not chew the cud. You are not to eat their meat or touch their carcasses.

9Of all the creatures living in the water, you may eat any that has fins and scales. 10But anything that does not have fins and scales you may not eat; for you it is unclean.

---

v 15,17 The Hebrew term refers to the irrevocable giving over of things or persons to the LORD, often by totally destroying them.
w 5 The precise identification of some of the birds and animals in this chapter is uncertain.   *x 7* That is, the hyrax or rock badger

King James

12But these *are they* of which ye shall not eat: the eagle, and the ossifrage, and the ospray,

13And the glede, and the kite, and the vulture after his kind,

14And every raven after his kind,

15And the owl, and the night hawk, and the cuckoo, and the hawk after his kind,

16The little owl, and the great owl, and the swan,

17And the pelican, and the gier eagle, and the cormorant,

18And the stork, and the heron after her kind, and the lapwing, and the bat.

19And every creeping thing that flieth *is* unclean unto you: they shall not be eaten.

20*But* of all clean fowls ye may eat.

21 ¶ Ye shall not eat *of* any thing that dieth of itself: thou shalt give it unto the stranger that *is* in thy gates, that he may eat it; or thou mayest sell it unto an alien: for thou *art* an holy people unto the LORD thy God. Thou shalt not seethe a kid in his mother's milk.

Laws about tithes

22Thou shalt truly tithe all the increase of thy seed, that the field bringeth forth year by year.

23And thou shalt eat before the LORD thy God, in the place which he shall choose to place his name there, the tithe of thy corn, of thy wine, and of thine oil, and the firstlings of thy herds and of thy flocks; that thou mayest learn to fear the LORD thy God always.

24And if the way be too long for thee, so that thou art not able to carry it; *or* if the place be too far from thee, which the LORD thy God shall choose to set his name there, when the LORD thy God hath blessed thee:

25Then shalt thou turn *it* into money, and bind up the money in thine hand, and shalt go unto the place which the LORD thy God shall choose:

26And thou shalt bestow that money for whatsoever thy soul lusteth after, for oxen, or for sheep, or for wine, or for strong drink, or for whatsoever thy soul *f* desireth: and thou shalt eat there before the LORD thy God, and thou shalt rejoice, thou, and thine household,

27And the Levite that *is* within thy gates; thou shalt not forsake him; for he hath no part nor inheritance with thee.

28 ¶ At the end of three years thou shalt bring forth all the tithe of thine increase the same year, and shalt lay *it* up within thy gates:

29And the Levite, (because he hath no part nor inheritance with thee,) and the stranger, and the fatherless, and the widow, which *are* within thy gates, shall come, and shall eat and be satisfied; that the LORD thy God may bless thee in all the work of thine hand which thou doest.

The sabbath years of release

15 AT THE end of *every* seven years thou shalt make a release.

2And this *is* the manner of the release: Every *g* creditor that lendeth *aught* unto his neighbour shall release *it;* he shall not exact *it* of his neighbour, or of his brother; because it is called the LORD'S release.

3Of a foreigner thou mayest exact *it again:* but *that* which is thine with thy brother thine hand shall release;

4*h* Save when there shall be no poor among you; for the LORD shall greatly bless thee in the land which the LORD thy God giveth thee *for* an inheritance to possess it:

5Only if thou carefully hearken unto the voice of the LORD thy God, to observe to do all these commandments which I command thee this day.

6For the LORD thy God blesseth thee, as he promised thee: and thou shalt lend unto many nations, but thou shalt not borrow; and thou shalt reign over many nations, but they shall not reign over thee.

Amplified

12But these are the ones which you shall not eat: the eagle, the vulture, the ospray,

13The buzzard, the kite in its several species,

14The raven in all its species,

15The ostrich, the nighthawk, the sea gull, the hawk of any variety,

16The little owl, the great owl, the horned owl,

17The pelican, the carrion vulture, the cormorant,

18The stork, the heron of any variety, the hoopoe, and the bat.

19And all flying insects are unclean for you; they shall not be eaten.

20But of all clean winged things you may eat.

21You shall not eat of anything that dies of itself. You may give it to the stranger *or* the foreigner who is within your towns, that he may eat it, or you may sell it to an alien. [They are not under God's law in this matter] but you are a people holy to the Lord your God. You shall not [even] boil a kid in its mother's milk.

22You shall surely tithe all the yield of your seed produced by your field each year.

23And you shall eat before the Lord your God in the place in which He will cause His Name [and Presence] to dwell the tithe (tenth) of your grain, your new wine, your oil, and the firstlings of your herd and your flock, that you may learn [reverently] to fear the Lord your God always.

24And if the distance is too long for you to carry your tithe, or the place where the Lord your God chooses to set His Name [and Presence] is too far away for you, when the Lord your God has blessed you,

25Then you shall turn it into money, and bind up the money in your hand, and shall go to the place [of worship] which the Lord your God has chosen.

26And you may spend that money for whatever your appetite craves, for oxen, or sheep, or new wine or strong[er] drink, or whatever you desire; and you shall eat there before the Lord your God and you shall rejoice, you and your household.

27And you shall not forsake *or* neglect the Levite [God's minister] in your towns, for he has been given no share or inheritance with you.

28At the end of every three years you shall bring forth all the tithe of your increase the same year and lay it up within your towns.

29And the Levite [because he has no part or inheritance with you] and the stranger *or* temporary resident, and the fatherless and the widow who are in your towns shall come and eat and be satisfied, so that the Lord your God may bless you in all the work of your hands that you do.

15 AT THE end of every seven years you shall grant a release.

2And this is the manner of the release: every creditor shall release that which he has lent to his neighbor; he shall not exact it of his neighbor, his brother, for the Lord's release is proclaimed.

3Of a foreigner you may exact it, but whatever of yours is with your brother [Israelite] your hand shall release.

4But there will be no poor among you, for the Lord will surely bless you in the land which the Lord your God gives you for an inheritance to possess,

5If only you carefully listen to the voice of the Lord your God, to do watchfully all these commandments which I command you this day.

6When the Lord your God blesses you as He promised you, then you shall lend to many nations, but you shall not borrow; and you shall rule over many nations, but they shall not rule over you.

---

f Heb. *asketh of thee*   *g* Heb. *master of the lending of his hand*
h Or, *To the end that there be no poor among you*

New American Standard

12"But these are the ones which you shall not eat: the eagle and the vulture and the buzzard,

13 and the red kite, the falcon, and the kite in their kinds,

14 and every raven in its kind,

15 and the ostrich, the owl, the sea gull, and the hawk in their kinds,

16 the little owl, the great owl, the white owl,

17 the pelican, the carrion vulture, the cormorant,

18 the stork, and the heron in their kinds, and the hoopoe and the bat.

19"And all the teeming life with wings are unclean to you; they shall not be eaten.

20"You may eat any clean bird.

21 ¶ "You shall not eat anything which dies of itself. You may give it to the alien who is in your town, so that he may eat it, or you may sell it to a foreigner, for you are a holy people to the LORD your God. You shall not boil a young goat in its mother's milk.

22 ¶ "You shall surely tithe all the produce from what you sow, which comes out of the field every year.

23"You shall eat in the presence of the LORD your God, at the place where He chooses to establish His name, the tithe of your grain, your new wine, your oil, and the first-born of your herd and your flock, so that you may learn to fear the LORD your God always.

24"If the distance is so great for you that you are not able to bring the tithe, since the place where the LORD your God chooses to set His name is too far away from you when the LORD your God blesses you,

25 then you shall exchange it for money, and bind the money in your hand and go to the place which the LORD your God chooses.

26"You may spend the money for whatever your heart desires: for oxen, or sheep, or wine, or strong drink, or whatever your heart desires; and there you shall eat in the presence of the LORD your God and rejoice, you and your household.

27"Also you shall not neglect the Levite who is in your town, for he has no portion or inheritance among you.

28 ¶ "At the end of every third year you shall bring out all the tithe of your produce in that year, and shall deposit it in your town.

29"The Levite, because he has no portion or inheritance among you, and the alien, the orphan and the widow who are in your town, shall come and eat and be satisfied, in order that the LORD your God may bless you in all the work of your hand which you do.

The Sabbatic Year

15 "AT THE end of every seven years you shall ^mgrant a remission of debts.

2"This is the manner of remission: every creditor shall release what he has loaned to his neighbor; he shall not exact it of his neighbor and his brother, because the LORD's remission has been proclaimed.

3"From a foreigner you may exact it, but your hand shall release whatever of yours is with your brother.

4"However, there will be no poor among you, since the LORD will surely bless you in the land which the LORD your God is giving you as an inheritance to possess,

5 if only you listen obediently to the voice of the LORD your God, to observe carefully all this commandment which I am commanding you today.

6"For the LORD your God will bless you as He has promised you, and you will lend to many nations, but you will not borrow; and you will rule over many nations, but they will not rule over you.

New International

11You may eat any clean bird. 12But these you may not eat: the eagle, the vulture, the black vulture, 13the red kite, the black kite, any kind of falcon, 14any kind of raven, 15the horned owl, the screech owl, the gull, any kind of hawk, 16the little owl, the great owl, the white owl, 17the desert owl, the osprey, the cormorant, 18the stork, any kind of heron, the hoopoe and the bat.

19All flying insects that swarm are unclean to you; do not eat them. 20But any winged creature that is clean you may eat.

21Do not eat anything you find already dead. You may give it to an alien living in any of your towns, and he may eat it, or you may sell it to a foreigner. But you are a people holy to the LORD your God.

Do not cook a young goat in its mother's milk.

Tithes

22Be sure to set aside a tenth of all that your fields produce each year. 23Eat the tithe of your grain, new wine and oil, and the firstborn of your herds and flocks in the presence of the LORD your God at the place he will choose as a dwelling for his Name, so that you may learn to revere the LORD your God always. 24But if that place is too distant and you have been blessed by the LORD your God and cannot carry your tithe (because the place where the LORD will choose to put his Name is so far away), 25then exchange your tithe for silver, and take the silver with you and go to the place the LORD your God will choose. 26Use the silver to buy whatever you like: cattle, sheep, wine or other fermented drink, or anything you wish. Then you and your household shall eat there in the presence of the LORD your God and rejoice. 27And do not neglect the Levites living in your towns, for they have no allotment or inheritance of their own.

28At the end of every three years, bring all the tithes of that year's produce and store it in your towns, 29so that the Levites (who have no allotment or inheritance of their own) and the aliens, the fatherless and the widows who live in your towns may come and eat and be satisfied, and so that the LORD your God may bless you in all the work of your hands.

The Year for Canceling Debts

15 AT THE end of every seven years you must cancel debts. 2This is how it is to be done: Every creditor shall cancel the loan he has made to his fellow Israelite. He shall not require payment from his fellow Israelite or brother, because the LORD's time for canceling debts has been proclaimed. 3You may require payment from a foreigner, but you must cancel any debt your brother owes you. 4However, there should be no poor among you, for in the land the LORD your God is giving you to possess as your inheritance, he will richly bless you, 5if only you fully obey the LORD your God and are careful to follow all these commands I am giving you today. 6For the LORD your God will bless you as he has promised, and you will lend to many nations but will borrow from none. You will rule over many nations but none will rule over you.

---

^mLit make a release

King James

7 ¶ If there be among you a poor man of one of thy brethren within any of thy gates in thy land which the LORD thy God giveth thee, thou shalt not harden thine heart, nor shut thine hand from thy poor brother:

8But thou shalt open thine hand wide unto him, and shalt surely lend him sufficient for his need, *in that* which he wanteth.

9Beware that there be not a *i*thought in thy *j*wicked heart, saying, The seventh year, the year of release, is at hand; and thine eye be evil against thy poor brother, and thou givest him nought; and he cry unto the LORD against thee, and it be sin unto thee.

10Thou shalt surely give him, and thine heart shall not be grieved when thou givest unto him: because that for this thing the LORD thy God shall bless thee in all thy works, and in all that thou puttest thine hand unto.

11For the poor shall never cease out of the land: therefore I command thee, saying, Thou shalt open thine hand wide unto thy brother, to thy poor, and to thy needy, in thy land.

Hebrew slaves to be freed

12 ¶ *And* if thy brother, an Hebrew man, or an Hebrew woman, be sold unto thee, and serve thee six years; then in the seventh year thou shalt let him go free from thee.

13And when thou sendest him out free from thee, thou shalt not let him go away empty:

14Thou shalt furnish him liberally out of thy flock, and out of thy floor, and out of thy winepress: *of that* wherewith the LORD thy God hath blessed thee thou shalt give unto him.

15And thou shalt remember that thou wast a bondman in the land of Egypt, and the LORD thy God redeemed thee: therefore I command thee this thing today.

16And it shall be, if he say unto thee, I will not go away from thee; because he loveth thee and thine house, because he is well with thee;

17Then thou shalt take an awl, and thrust *it* through his ear unto the door, and he shall be thy servant for ever. And also unto thy maidservant thou shalt do likewise.

18It shall not seem hard unto thee, when thou sendest him away free from thee; for he hath been worth a double hired servant *to thee,* in serving thee six years: and the LORD thy God shall bless thee in all that thou doest.

Offering the firstlings

19 ¶ All the firstling males that come of thy herd and of thy flock thou shalt sanctify unto the LORD thy God: thou shalt do no work with the firstling of thy bullock, nor shear the firstling of thy sheep.

20Thou shalt eat *it* before the LORD thy God year by year in the place which the LORD shall choose, thou and thy household.

21And if there be *any* blemish therein, *as if it be* lame, or blind, *or have* any ill blemish, thou shalt not sacrifice it unto the LORD thy God.

22Thou shalt eat it within thy gates: the unclean and the clean *person shall eat it* alike, as the roebuck, and as the hart.

23Only thou shalt not eat the blood thereof; thou shalt pour it upon the ground as water.

The Passover

16 OBSERVE THE month of Abib, and keep the passover unto the LORD thy God: for in the month of Abib the LORD thy God brought thee forth out of Egypt by night.

2Thou shalt therefore sacrifice the passover unto the LORD thy God, of the flock and the herd, in the place which the LORD shall choose to place his name there.

Amplified

7If there is among you a poor man, one of your kinsmen in any of the towns of your land which the Lord your God gives you, you shall not harden your [minds and] hearts or close your hands to your poor brother;

8But you shall open your hands wide to him and shall surely lend him sufficient for his need in whatever he lacks.

9Beware lest there be a base thought in your [minds and] hearts, and you say, The seventh year, the year of release, is at hand, and your eye be evil against your poor brother and you give him nothing, and he cry to the Lord against you, and it be sin in you.

10You shall give to him freely without begrudging it; because of this the Lord will bless you in all your work and in all you undertake.

11For the poor will never cease out of the land; therefore I command you, You shall open wide your hands to your brother, to your needy, and to your poor in your land.

12And if your brother, a Hebrew man or a Hebrew woman, is sold to you and serves you six years, then in the seventh year you shall let him go free from you.

13And when you send him out free from you, you shall not let him go away empty-handed.

14You shall furnish him liberally out of your flock, your threshing floor, and your winepress; of what the Lord your God has blessed you, you shall give to him.

15And you shall [earnestly] remember that you were a bondman in the land of Egypt and the Lord your God redeemed you; therefore I give you this command today.

16But if the servant says to you, I will not go away from you, because he loves you and your household, since he does well with you,

17Then take an awl and pierce his ear through to the door, and he shall be your servant always. And also to your bondwoman you shall do likewise.

18It shall not seem hard to you when you let him go free from you, for at half the cost of a hired servant he has served you six years; and the Lord your God will bless you in all you do.

19All the firstling males that are born of your herd and flock you shall set apart for the Lord your God; you shall do no work with the firstling of your herd, nor shear the firstling of your flock.

20You shall eat it before the Lord your God annually in the place [for worship] which the Lord shall choose, you and your household.

21But if it has any blemish, if it is lame, blind, or has any bad blemish whatsoever, you shall not sacrifice it to the Lord your God.

22You shall eat it within your towns; the [ceremonially] unclean and the clean alike may eat it, as if it were a gazelle or a hart.

23Only you shall not eat its blood; you shall pour it on the ground like water.

16 OBSERVE THE month of Abib and keep the Passover to the Lord your God, for in the month of Abib the Lord your God brought you out of Egypt by night.

2You shall offer the Passover sacrifice to the Lord your God from the flock or the herd in the place where the Lord will choose to make His Name [and His Presence] dwell.

---

*i*Heb. *word*   *j*Heb. *Belial*

New American Standard

7 ¶ "If there is a poor man with you, one of your brothers, in any of your towns in your land which the LORD your God is giving you, you shall not harden your heart, nor close your hand from your poor brother;

8 but you shall freely open your hand to him, and shall generously lend him sufficient for his need *in* whatever he lacks.

9"Beware that there is no base thought in your heart, saying, 'The seventh year, the year of remission, is near,' and your eye is hostile toward your poor brother, and you give him nothing; then he may cry to the LORD against you, and it will be a sin in you.

10"You shall generously give to him, and your heart shall not be grieved when you give to him, because for this thing the LORD your God will bless you in all your work and in all your undertakings.

11"For the poor will never cease *to be* in the land; therefore I command you, saying, 'You shall freely open your hand to your brother, to your needy and poor in your land.'

12 ¶ "If your kinsman, a Hebrew man or woman, is sold to you, then he shall serve you six years, but in the seventh year you shall set him free.

13"When you set him free, you shall not send him away empty-handed.

14"You shall furnish him liberally from your flock and from your threshing floor and from your wine vat; you shall give to him as the LORD your God has blessed you.

15"You shall remember that you were a slave in the land of Egypt, and the LORD your God redeemed you; therefore I command you this today.

16"It shall come about if he says to you, 'I will not go out from you,' because he loves you and your household, since he fares well with you;

17 then you shall take an awl and pierce it through his ear into the door, and he shall be your servant forever. Also you shall do likewise to your maidservant.

18 ¶ "It shall not seem hard to you when you set him free, for he has given you six years *with* double the service of a hired man; so the LORD your God will bless you in whatever you do.

19 ¶ "You shall consecrate to the LORD your God all the firstborn males that are born of your herd and of your flock; you shall not work with the firstborn of your herd, nor shear the firstborn of your flock.

20"You and your household shall eat it every year before the LORD your God in the place which the LORD chooses.

21"But if it has any defect, *such as* lameness or blindness, *or* any serious defect, you shall not sacrifice it to the LORD your God.

22"You shall eat it within your gates; the unclean and the clean alike *may eat it,* as a gazelle or a deer.

23"Only you shall not eat its blood; you are to pour it out on the ground like water.

New International

7If there is a poor man among your brothers in any of the towns of the land that the LORD your God is giving you, do not be hardhearted or tightfisted toward your poor brother. 8Rather be openhanded and freely lend him whatever he needs. 9Be careful not to harbor this wicked thought: "The seventh year, the year for canceling debts, is near," so that you do not show ill will toward your needy brother and give him nothing. He may then appeal to the LORD against you, and you will be found guilty of sin. 10Give generously to him and do so without a grudging heart; then because of this the LORD your God will bless you in all your work and in everything you put your hand to. 11There will always be poor people in the land. Therefore I command you to be openhanded toward your brothers and toward the poor and needy in your land.

Freeing Servants

12If a fellow Hebrew, a man or a woman, sells himself to you and serves you six years, in the seventh year you must let him go free. 13And when you release him, do not send him away empty-handed. 14Supply him liberally from your flock, your threshing floor and your winepress. Give to him as the LORD your God has blessed you. 15Remember that you were slaves in Egypt and the LORD your God redeemed you. That is why I give you this command today.

16But if your servant says to you, "I do not want to leave you," because he loves you and your family and is well off with you, 17then take an awl and push it through his ear lobe into the door, and he will become your servant for life. Do the same for your maidservant.

18Do not consider it a hardship to set your servant free, because his service to you these six years has been worth twice as much as that of a hired hand. And the LORD your God will bless you in everything you do.

The Firstborn Animals

19Set apart for the LORD your God every firstborn male of your herds and flocks. Do not put the firstborn of your oxen to work, and do not shear the firstborn of your sheep. 20Each year you and your family are to eat them in the presence of the LORD your God at the place he will choose. 21If an animal has a defect, is lame or blind, or has any serious flaw, you must not sacrifice it to the LORD your God. 22You are to eat it in your own towns. Both the ceremonially unclean and the clean may eat it, as if it were gazelle or deer. 23But you must not eat the blood; pour it out on the ground like water.

The Feasts of Passover, of Weeks, and of Booths

16 "OBSERVE THE month of Abib and celebrate the Passover to the LORD your God, for in the month of Abib the LORD your God brought you out of Egypt by night.

2"You shall sacrifice the Passover to the LORD your God from the flock and the herd, in the place where the LORD chooses to establish His name.

Passover

16 OBSERVE THE month of Abib and celebrate the Passover of the LORD your God, because in the month of Abib he brought you out of Egypt by night. 2Sacrifice as the Passover to the LORD your God an animal from your flock or herd at the place the LORD will choose as a dwelling for his Name. 3Do not eat it with bread made

King James

3Thou shalt eat no leavened bread with it; seven days shalt thou eat unleavened bread therewith, *even* the bread of affliction; for thou camest forth out of the land of Egypt in haste: that thou mayest remember the day when thou camest forth out of the land of Egypt all the days of thy life.

4And there shall be no leavened bread seen with thee in all thy coast seven days; neither shall there *any thing* of the flesh, which thou sacrificedst the first day at even, remain all night until the morning.

5Thou mayest not ksacrifice the passover within any of thy gates, which the LORD thy God giveth thee:

6But at the place which the LORD thy God shall choose to place his name in, there thou shalt sacrifice the passover at even, at the going down of the sun, at the season that thou camest forth out of Egypt.

7And thou shalt roast and eat *it* in the place which the LORD thy God shall choose: and thou shalt turn in the morning, and go unto thy tents.

8Six days thou shalt eat unleavened bread: and on the seventh day *shall be* a lsolemn assembly to the LORD thy God: thou shalt do no work *therein*.

Feasts of weeks and tabernacles

9 ¶ Seven weeks shalt thou number unto thee: begin to number the seven weeks from *such time as* thou beginnest *to put* the sickle to the corn.

10And thou shalt keep the feast of weeks unto the LORD thy God with ma tribute of a freewill offering of thine hand, which thou shalt give *unto the LORD thy God,* according as the LORD thy God hath blessed thee:

11And thou shalt rejoice before the LORD thy God, thou, and thy son, and thy daughter, and thy manservant, and thy maidservant, and the Levite that *is* within thy gates, and the stranger, and the fatherless, and the widow, that *are* among you, in the place which the LORD thy God hath chosen to place his name there.

12And thou shalt remember that thou wast a bondman in Egypt: and thou shalt observe and do these statutes.

13 ¶ Thou shalt observe the feast of tabernacles seven days, after that thou hast gathered in thy ncorn and thy wine:

14And thou shalt rejoice in thy feast, thou, and thy son, and thy daughter, and thy manservant, and thy maidservant, and the Levite, the stranger, and the fatherless, and the widow, that *are* within thy gates.

15Seven days shalt thou keep a solemn feast unto the LORD thy God in the place which the LORD shall choose: because the LORD thy God shall bless thee in all thine increase, and in all the works of thine hands, therefore thou shalt surely rejoice.

16 ¶ Three times in a year shall all thy males appear before the LORD thy God in the place which he shall choose; in the feast of unleavened bread, and in the feast of weeks, and in the feast of tabernacles: and they shall not appear before the LORD empty:

17Every man *shall give* oas he is able, according to the blessing of the LORD thy God which he hath given thee.

Appointment of judges and officers

18 ¶ Judges and officers shalt thou make thee in all thy gates, which the LORD thy God giveth thee, throughout thy tribes: and they shall judge the people with just judgment.

19Thou shalt not wrest judgment; thou shalt not respect persons, neither take a gift: for a gift doth blind the eyes of the wise, and pervert the pwords of the righteous.

20qThat which is altogether just shalt thou follow, that thou mayest live, and inherit the land which the LORD thy God giveth thee.

Amplified

3You shall eat no leavened bread with it; for seven days you shall eat it with unleavened bread, the bread of affliction—for you fled from the land of Egypt in haste—that all the days of your life you may [earnestly] remember the day when you came out of Egypt.

4No leaven shall be seen with you in all your territory for seven days; nor shall any of the flesh which you sacrificed the first day at evening be left all night until the morning.

5You may not offer the Passover sacrifice within any of your towns which the Lord your God gives you,

6But at the place which the Lord your God will choose in which to make His Name [and His Presence] dwell, there you shall offer the Passover sacrifice in the evening at sunset, at the season that you came out of Egypt.

7And you shall roast *or* boil and eat it in the place which the Lord your God will choose. And in the morning you shall turn and go to your tents.

8For six days you shall eat unleavened bread, and on the seventh day there shall be a solemn assembly to the Lord your God; you shall do no work on it.

9You shall count seven weeks; begin to number the seven weeks from the time you begin to put the sickle to the standing grain.

10Then you shall keep the Feast of Weeks to the Lord your God with a tribute of a freewill offering from your hand, which you shall give to the Lord your God, as the Lord your God blesses you.

11And you shall rejoice before the Lord your God, you and your son and daughter, your manservant and maidservant, and the Levite who is within your towns, the stranger *or* temporary resident, the fatherless, and the widow who are among you, at the place in which the Lord your God chooses to make His Name [and His Presence] dwell.

12And you shall [earnestly] remember that you were a slave in Egypt, and you shall be watchful and obey these statutes.

13You shall observe the Feast of Tabernacles *or* Booths for seven days after you have gathered in from your threshing floor and wine vat.

14You shall rejoice in your Feast, you, your son and daughter, your manservant and maidservant, the Levite, the transient *and* the stranger, the fatherless, and the widow who are within your towns.

15For seven days you shall keep a solemn Feast to the Lord your God in the place which the Lord chooses; because the Lord your God will bless you in all your produce and in all the works of your hands, so that you will be altogether joyful.

16Three times a year shall all your males appear before the Lord your God in the place which He chooses: at the Feast of Unleavened Bread, at the Feast of Weeks, and at the Feast of Tabernacles *or* Booths. They shall not appear before the Lord empty-handed:

17Every man shall give as he is able, according to the blessing of the Lord your God which He has given you.

18You shall appoint judges and officers in all your towns which the Lord your God gives you, according to your tribes, and they shall judge the people with righteous judgment.

19You shall not misinterpret *or* misapply judgment; you shall not be partial, or take a bribe, for a bribe blinds the eyes of the wise and perverts the words of the righteous.

20Follow what is altogether just (uncompromisingly righteous), that you may live and inherit the land which your God gives you.

kOr, *kill*   lHeb. *restraint;* see Lev. 23:36   mOr, *sufficiency*
nHeb. *floor, and thy winepress*   oHeb. *according to the gift of his hand*   pOr, *matters*   qHeb. *Justice, justice*

New American Standard

3"You shall not eat leavened bread with it; seven days you shall eat with it unleavened bread, the bread of affliction (for you came out of the land of Egypt in haste), so that you may remember all the days of your life the day when you came out of the land of Egypt.

4"For seven days no leaven shall be seen with you in all your territory, and none of the flesh which you sacrifice on the evening of the first day shall remain overnight until morning.

5"You are not allowed to sacrifice the Passover in any of your towns which the LORD your God is giving you;

6 but at the place where the LORD your God chooses to establish His name, you shall sacrifice the Passover in the evening at sunset, at the time that you came out of Egypt.

7"You shall cook and eat *it* in the place which the LORD your God chooses. In the morning you are to return to your tents.

8"Six days you shall eat unleavened bread, and on the seventh day there shall be a solemn assembly to the LORD your God; you shall do no work *on it.*

9 ¶ "You shall count seven weeks for yourself; you shall begin to count seven weeks from the time you begin to put the sickle to the standing grain.

10"Then you shall celebrate the Feast of Weeks to the LORD your God with a tribute of a freewill offering of your hand, which you shall give just as the LORD your God blesses you;

11 and you shall rejoice before the LORD your God, you and your son and your daughter and your male and female servants and the Levite who is in your town, and the stranger and the orphan and the widow who are in your midst, in the place where the LORD your God chooses to establish His name.

12"You shall remember that you were a slave in Egypt, and you shall be careful to observe these statutes.

13 ¶ "You shall celebrate the Feast of Booths seven days after you have gathered in from your threshing floor and your wine vat;

14 and you shall rejoice in your feast, you and your son and your daughter and your male and female servants and the Levite and the stranger and the orphan and the widow who are in your towns.

15"Seven days you shall celebrate a feast to the LORD your God in the place which the LORD chooses, because the LORD your God will bless you in all your produce and in all the work of your hands, so that you will be altogether joyful.

16 ¶ "Three times in a year all your males shall appear before the LORD your God in the place which He chooses, at the Feast of Unleavened Bread and at the Feast of Weeks and at the Feast of Booths, and they shall not appear before the LORD empty-handed.

17"Every man shall give as he is able, according to the blessing of the LORD your God which He has given you.

18 ¶ "You shall appoint for yourself judges and officers in all your towns which the LORD your God is giving you, according to your tribes, and they shall judge the people with righteous judgment.

19"You shall not distort justice; you shall not be partial, and you shall not take a bribe, for a bribe blinds the eyes of the wise and perverts the words of the righteous.

20"Justice, *and only* justice, you shall pursue, that you may live and possess the land which the LORD your God is giving you.

New International

with yeast, but for seven days eat unleavened bread, the bread of affliction, because you left Egypt in haste—so that all the days of your life you may remember the time of your departure from Egypt. [4]Let no yeast be found in your possession in all your land for seven days. Do not let any of the meat you sacrifice on the evening of the first day remain until morning.

[5]You must not sacrifice the Passover in any town the LORD your God gives you [6]except in the place he will choose as a dwelling for his Name. There you must sacrifice the Passover in the evening, when the sun goes down, on the anniversary[y] of your departure from Egypt. [7]Roast it and eat it at the place the LORD your God will choose. Then in the morning return to your tents. [8]For six days eat unleavened bread and on the seventh day hold an assembly to the LORD your God and do no work.

Feast of Weeks

[9]Count off seven weeks from the time you begin to put the sickle to the standing grain. [10]Then celebrate the Feast of Weeks to the LORD your God by giving a freewill offering in proportion to the blessings the LORD your God has given you. [11]And rejoice before the LORD your God at the place he will choose as a dwelling for his Name—you, your sons and daughters, your menservants and maidservants, the Levites in your towns, and the aliens, the fatherless and the widows living among you, [12]Remember that you were slaves in Egypt, and follow carefully these decrees.

Feast of Tabernacles

[13]Celebrate the Feast of Tabernacles for seven days after you have gathered the produce of your threshing floor and your winepress. [14]Be joyful at your Feast—you, your sons and daughters, your menservants and maidservants, and the Levites, the aliens, the fatherless and the widows who live in your towns. [15]For seven days celebrate the Feast to the LORD your God at the place the LORD will choose. For the LORD your God will bless you in all your harvest and in all the work of your hands, and your joy will be complete.

[16]Three times a year all your men must appear before the LORD your God at the place he will choose: at the Feast of Unleavened Bread, the Feast of Weeks and the Feast of Tabernacles. No man should appear before the LORD empty-handed: [17]Each of you must bring a gift in proportion to the way the LORD your God has blessed you.

Judges

[18]Appoint judges and officials for each of your tribes in every town the LORD your God is giving you, and they shall judge the people fairly. [19]Do not pervert justice or show partiality. Do not accept a bribe, for a bribe blinds the eyes of the wise and twists the words of the righteous. [20]Follow justice and justice alone, so that you may live and possess the land the LORD your God is giving you.

---

y6 Or down, at the time of day

King James

²¹ ¶ Thou shalt not plant thee a grove of any trees near unto the altar of the LORD thy God, which thou shalt make thee.

²²Neither shalt thou set thee up *any* ^rimage; which the LORD thy God hateth.

17 THOU SHALT not sacrifice unto the LORD thy God *any* bullock, or ^ssheep, wherein is blemish, *or* any evilfavouredness: for that *is* an abomination unto the LORD thy God.

The administration of justice

² ¶ If there be found among you, within any of thy gates which the LORD thy God giveth thee, man or woman, that hath wrought wickedness in the sight of the LORD thy God, in transgressing his covenant,

³And hath gone and served other gods, and worshipped them, either the sun, or moon, or any of the host of heaven, which I have not commanded;

⁴And it be told thee, and thou hast heard *of it*, and inquired diligently, and, behold, *it be* true, *and* the thing certain, *that* such abomination is wrought in Israel:

⁵Then shalt thou bring forth that man or that woman, which have committed that wicked thing, unto thy gates, *even* that man or that woman, and shalt stone them with stones, till they die.

⁶At the mouth of two witnesses, or three witnesses, shall he that is worthy of death be put to death; *but* at the mouth of one witness he shall not be put to death.

⁷The hands of the witnesses shall be first upon him to put him to death, and afterward the hands of all the people. So thou shalt put the evil away from among you.

⁸ ¶ If there arise a matter too hard for thee in judgment, between blood and blood, between plea and plea, and between stroke and stroke, *being* matters of controversy within thy gates: then shalt thou arise, and get thee up into the place which the LORD thy God shall choose;

⁹And thou shalt come unto the priests the Levites, and unto the judge that shall be in those days, and inquire; and they shall show thee the sentence of judgment:

¹⁰And thou shalt do according to the sentence, which they of that place which the LORD shall choose shall show thee; and thou shalt observe to do according to all that they inform thee:

¹¹According to the sentence of the law which they shall teach thee, and according to the judgment which they shall tell thee, thou shalt do: thou shalt not decline from the sentence which they shall show thee, *to* the right hand, nor *to* the left.

¹²And the man that will do presumptuously, ^tand will not hearken unto the priest that standeth to minister there before the LORD thy God, or unto the judge, even that man shall die: and thou shalt put away the evil from Israel.

¹³And all the people shall hear, and fear, and do no more presumptuously.

The choice of a king

¹⁴ ¶ When thou art come unto the land which the LORD thy God giveth thee, and shalt possess it, and shalt dwell therein, and shalt say, I will set a king over me, like as all the nations that *are* about me;

¹⁵Thou shalt in any wise set *him* king over thee, whom the LORD thy God shall choose: *one* from among thy brethren shalt thou set king over thee: thou mayest not set a stranger over thee, which *is* not thy brother.

¹⁶But he shall not multiply horses to himself, nor cause the people to return to Egypt, to the end that he should multiply horses: forasmuch as the LORD hath said unto you, Ye shall henceforth return no more that way.

Amplified

²¹You shall not plant for yourselves any kind of tree dedicated to [the goddess] Asherah beside the altar of the Lord your God which you shall make.

²²Neither shall you set up an idolatrous stone *or* image, which the Lord your God hates.

17 YOU SHALL not sacrifice to the Lord your God an ox or sheep with a blemish or any defect whatsoever, for that is an abomination to the Lord your God.

²If there is found among you within any of your towns which the Lord your God gives you a man or woman who does what is wicked in the sight of the Lord your God by transgressing His covenant,

³Who has gone and served other gods and worshiped them, or the sun or moon or any of the host of the heavens, which I have forbidden,

⁴And it is told and you hear of it, then inquire diligently. And if it is certainly true that such an abomination has been committed in Israel,

⁵Then you shall bring forth to your town's gates that man or woman who has done that wicked thing and you shall stone that man or woman to death.

⁶On the evidence of two or three witnesses he who is worthy of death shall be put to death; he shall not be put to death on the evidence of one witness.

⁷The hands of the witnesses shall be the first against him to put him to death, and afterward the hands of all the people. So you shall purge the evil from among you.

⁸If there arises a matter too hard for you in judgment— between one kind of bloodshed and another, between one legality and another, between one kind of assault and another, matters of controversy within your towns—then arise and go to the place which the Lord your God chooses.

⁹And you shall come to the Levitical priests and to the judge who is in office in those days, and you shall consult them and they shall make clear to you the decision.

¹⁰And you shall do according to the decision which they declare to you from that place which the Lord chooses; and you shall be watchful to do according to all that they tell you;

¹¹According to the decision of the law which they shall teach you and the judgment which they shall announce to you, you shall do; you shall not turn aside from the verdict they give you, ^feither to the right hand or the left.

¹²The man who does presumptuously and will not listen to the priest who stands to minister there before the Lord your God or to the judge, that man shall die; so you shall purge the evil from Israel.

¹³And all the people shall hear and [reverently] fear, and not act presumptuously again.

¹⁴When you come to the land which the Lord your God gives you and you possess it and live there, and then say, We will set a king over us like all the nations that are about us,

¹⁵You shall surely set as king over you him whom the Lord your God will choose. One from among your brethren you shall set as king over you; you may not set a foreigner, who is not your brother, over you.

¹⁶But he shall not multiply horses to himself or cause the people to return to Egypt in order to multiply horses, since the Lord said to you, You shall never return that way.

---

^rOr, *statue,* or, *pillar*   ^sOr, *goat*   ^tHeb. *not to hearken*   ^fThe Hebrew is obscure.

New American Standard

21 ¶ "You shall not plant for yourself an Asherah of any kind of tree beside the altar of the LORD your God, which you shall make for yourself.
22"You shall not set up for yourself a *sacred* pillar which the LORD your God hates.

Administration of Justice

17 "YOU SHALL not sacrifice to the LORD your God an ox or a sheep which has a blemish *or* any defect, for that is a detestable thing to the LORD your God.
2 ¶ "If there is found in your midst, in any of your towns, which the LORD your God is giving you, a man or a woman who does what is evil in the sight of the LORD your God, by transgressing His covenant,
3 and has gone and served other gods and worshiped them, or the sun or the moon or any of the heavenly host, which I have not commanded,
4 and if it is told you and you have heard of it, then you shall inquire thoroughly. Behold, if it is true and the thing certain that this detestable thing has been done in Israel,
5 then you shall bring out that man or that woman who has done this evil deed to your gates, *that is,* the man or the woman, and you shall stone them to death.
6"On the evidence of two witnesses or three witnesses, he who is to die shall be put to death; he shall not be put to death on the evidence of one witness.
7"The hand of the witnesses shall be first against him to put him to death, and afterward the hand of all the people. So you shall purge the evil from your midst.
8 ¶ "If any case is too difficult for you to decide, between one kind of homicide or another, between one kind of lawsuit or another, and between one kind of assault or another, being cases of dispute in your courts, then you shall arise and go up to the place which the LORD your God chooses.
9"So you shall come to the Levitical priest or the judge who is *in office* in those days, and you shall inquire *of them* and they will declare to you the verdict in the case.
10"You shall do according to the terms of the verdict which they declare to you from that place which the LORD chooses; and you shall be careful to observe according to all that they teach you.
11"According to the terms of the law which they teach you, and according to the verdict which they tell you, you shall do; you shall not turn aside from the word which they declare to you, to the right or to the left.
12"The man who acts presumptuously by not listening to the priest who stands there to serve the LORD your God, nor to the judge, that man shall die; thus you shall purge the evil from Israel.
13"Then all the people will hear and be afraid, and will not act presumptuously again.
14 ¶ "When you enter the land which the LORD your God gives you, and you possess it and live in it, and you say, 'I will set a king over me like all the nations who are around me,'
15 you shall surely set a king over you whom the LORD your God chooses, *one* from among your countrymen you shall set as king over yourselves; you may not put a foreigner over yourselves who is not your countryman.
16"Moreover, he shall not multiply horses for himself, nor shall he cause the people to return to Egypt to multiply horses, since the LORD has said to you, 'You shall never again return that way.'

New International

Worshiping Other Gods

21Do not set up any wooden Asherah pole[z] beside the altar you build to the LORD your God, 22and do not erect a sacred stone, for these the LORD your God hates.

17 DO NOT sacrifice to the LORD your God an ox or a sheep that has any defect or flaw in it, for that would be detestable to him.
2If a man or woman living among you in one of the towns the LORD gives you is found doing evil in the eyes of the LORD your God in violation of his covenant, 3and contrary to my command has worshiped other gods, bowing down to them or to the sun or the moon or the stars of the sky, 4and this has been brought to your attention, then you must investigate it thoroughly. If it is true and it has been proved that this detestable thing has been done in Israel, 5take the man or woman who has done this evil deed to your city gate and stone that person to death. 6On the testimony of two or three witnesses a man shall be put to death, but no one shall be put to death on the testimony of only one witness. 7The hands of the witnesses must be the first in putting him to death, and then the hands of all the people. You must purge the evil from among you.

Law Courts

8If cases come before your courts that are too difficult for you to judge—whether bloodshed, lawsuits or assaults—take them to the place the LORD your God will choose. 9Go to the priests, who are Levites, and to the judge who is in office at that time. Inquire of them and they will give you the verdict. 10You must act according to the decisions they give you at the place the LORD will choose. Be careful to do everything they direct you to do. 11Act according to the law they teach you and the decisions they give you. Do not turn aside from what they tell you, to the right or to the left. 12The man who shows contempt for the judge or for the priest who stands ministering there to the LORD your God must be put to death. You must purge the evil from Israel. 13All the people will hear and be afraid, and will not be contemptuous again.

The King

14When you enter the land the LORD your God is giving you and have taken possession of it and settled in it, and you say, "Let us set a king over us like all the nations around us," 15be sure to appoint over you the king the LORD your God chooses. He must be from among your own brothers. Do not place a foreigner over you, one who is not a brother Israelite. 16The king, moreover, must not acquire great numbers of horses for himself or make the people return to Egypt to get more of them, for the LORD has told you, "You are not to go back that way again."

---

z21 Or *Do not plant any tree dedicated to Asherah*

King James

¹⁷Neither shall he multiply wives to himself, that his heart turn not away: neither shall he greatly multiply to himself silver and gold.

¹⁸And it shall be, when he sitteth upon the throne of his kingdom, that he shall write him a copy of this law in a book out of *that which is* before the priests the Levites:

¹⁹And it shall be with him, and he shall read therein all the days of his life: that he may learn to fear the LORD his God, to keep all the words of this law and these statutes, to do them:

²⁰That his heart be not lifted up above his brethren, and that he turn not aside from the commandment, *to* the right hand, or *to* the left: to the end that he may prolong *his* days in his kingdom, he, and his children, in the midst of Israel.

The portion for the priests

18 THE PRIESTS the Levites, *and* all the tribe of Levi, shall have no part nor inheritance with Israel: they shall eat the offerings of the LORD made by fire, and his inheritance.

²Therefore shall they have no inheritance among their brethren: the LORD *is* their inheritance, as he hath said unto them.

³ ¶ And this shall be the priest's due from the people, from them that offer a sacrifice, whether *it be* ox or sheep; and they shall give unto the priest the shoulder, and the two cheeks, and the maw.

⁴The firstfruit *also* of thy corn, of thy wine, and of thine oil, and the first of the fleece of thy sheep, shalt thou give him.

⁵For the LORD thy God hath chosen him out of all thy tribes, to stand to minister in the name of the LORD, him and his sons for ever.

⁶ ¶ And if a Levite come from any of thy gates out of all Israel, where he sojourned, and come with all the desire of his mind unto the place which the LORD shall choose;

⁷Then he shall minister in the name of the LORD his God, as all his brethren the Levites *do,* which stand there before the LORD.

⁸They shall have like portions to eat, beside ^uthat which cometh of the sale of his patrimony.

Forbidden pagan practices

⁹ ¶ When thou art come into the land which the LORD thy God giveth thee, thou shalt not learn to do after the abominations of those nations.

¹⁰There shall not be found among you *any one* that maketh his son or his daughter to pass through the fire, *or* that useth divination, *or* an observer of times, or an enchanter, or a witch,

¹¹Or a charmer, or a consulter with familiar spirits, or a wizard, or a necromancer.

¹²For all that do these things *are* an abomination unto the LORD: and because of these abominations the LORD thy God doth drive them out from before thee.

¹³Thou shalt be ^vperfect with the LORD thy God.

¹⁴For these nations, which thou shalt ^wpossess, hearkened unto observers of times, and unto diviners: but as for thee, the LORD thy God hath not suffered thee so *to do.*

Amplified

¹⁷And he shall not multiply wives to himself, that his [mind and] heart turn not away; neither shall he greatly multiply to himself silver and gold.

¹⁸And when he sits on his royal throne, he shall write for himself a copy of this law in a book, out of what is before the Levitical priests.

¹⁹And he shall keep it with him, and he shall read in it all the days of his life, that he may learn [reverently] to fear the Lord his God, by keeping all the words of this law and these statutes and doing them,

²⁰That his [mind and] heart may not be lifted up above his brethren and that he may not turn aside from the commandment to the right hand or to the left; so that he may continue long, he and his sons, in his kingdom in Israel.

18 THE LEVITICAL priests and all the tribe of Levi shall have no part or inheritance with Israel; they shall eat the offerings made by fire to the Lord, and His rightful dues.

²They shall have no inheritance among their brethren; the Lord is their inheritance, as He promised them.

³And this shall be the priest's due from the people, from those who offer a sacrifice, whether it be ox or sheep: they shall give to the priest the shoulder and the two cheeks and the stomach.

⁴The firstfruits of your grain, of your new wine, and of your oil, and the first *or* best of the fleece of your sheep you shall give him.

⁵For the Lord your God has chosen him out of all your tribes to stand to minister in the name [and presence] of the Lord, him and his sons forever.

⁶And if a Levite comes from any of your towns out of all Israel where he is a temporary resident, he may come whenever he desires to [the sanctuary] the place the Lord will choose;

⁷Then he may minister in the name [and presence of] the Lord his God like all his brethren the Levites who stand to minister there before the Lord.

⁸They shall have equal portions to eat, besides what may come of the sale of his patrimony. [Jer. 32:6–15.]

⁹When you come into the land which the Lord your God gives you, you shall not learn to follow the abominable practices of these nations.

¹⁰There shall not be found among you anyone who makes his son or daughter pass through the fire, or who uses divination, or is a soothsayer, or an augur, or a sorcerer,

¹¹Or a charmer, or a medium, or a wizard, or a necromancer.

¹²For all who do these things are an abomination to the Lord, and it is because of these abominable practices that the Lord your God is driving them out before you.

¹³You shall be blameless [and absolutely true] to the Lord your God.

¹⁴For these nations whom you shall dispossess listen to soothsayers and diviners. But as for you, the Lord your God has not allowed you to do so.

^uHeb. *his sales by the fathers*   ^vOr, *upright,* or, *sincere*
^wOr, *inherit*

New American Standard

17"He shall not multiply wives for himself, or else his heart will turn away; nor shall he greatly increase silver and gold for himself.

18 ¶ "Now it shall come about when he sits on the throne of his kingdom, he shall write for himself a copy of this law on a scroll in the presence of the Levitical priests.

19"It shall be with him and he shall read it all the days of his life, that he may learn to fear the LORD his God, by carefully observing all the words of this law and these statutes,

20 that his heart may not be lifted up above his countrymen and that he may not turn aside from the commandment, to the right or the left, so that he and his sons may continue long in his kingdom in the midst of Israel.

Portion of the Levites

18 "THE LEVITICAL priests, the whole tribe of Levi, shall have no portion or inheritance in Israel; they shall eat the LORD's offerings by fire and His portion.

2"They shall have no inheritance among their countrymen; the LORD is their inheritance, as He promised them.

3 ¶ "Now this shall be the priests' due from the people, from those who offer a sacrifice, either an ox or a sheep, of which they shall give to the priest the shoulder and the two cheeks and the stomach.

4"You shall give him the first fruits of your grain, your new wine, and your oil, and the first shearing of your sheep.

5"For the LORD your God has chosen him and his sons from all your tribes, to stand and serve in the name of the LORD forever.

6 ¶ "Now if a Levite comes from any of your towns throughout Israel where he resides, and comes whenever he desires to the place which the LORD chooses,

7 then he shall serve in the name of the LORD his God, like all his fellow Levites who stand there before the LORD.

8"They shall eat equal portions, except *what they receive* from the sale of their fathers' *estates*.

Spiritism Forbidden

9 ¶ "When you enter the land which the LORD your God gives you, you shall not learn to imitate the detestable things of those nations.

10"There shall not be found among you anyone who makes his son or his daughter pass through the fire, one who uses divination, one who practices witchcraft, or one who interprets omens, or a sorcerer,

11 or one who casts a spell, or a medium, or a spiritist, or one who calls up the dead.

12"For whoever does these things is detestable to the LORD; and because of these detestable things the LORD your God will drive them out before you.

13"You shall be blameless before the LORD your God.

14"For those nations, which you shall dispossess, listen to those who practice witchcraft and to diviners, but as for you, the LORD your God has not allowed you *to do* so.

New International

17He must not take many wives, or his heart will be led astray. He must not accumulate large amounts of silver and gold.

18When he takes the throne of his kingdom, he is to write for himself on a scroll a copy of this law, taken from that of the priests, who are Levites. 19It is to be with him, and he is to read it all the days of his life so that he may learn to revere the LORD his God and follow carefully all the words of this law and these decrees 20and not consider himself better than his brothers and turn from the law to the right or to the left. Then he and his descendants will reign a long time over his kingdom in Israel.

Offerings for Priests and Levites

18 THE PRIESTS, who are Levites—indeed the whole tribe of Levi—are to have no allotment or inheritance with Israel. They shall live on the offerings made to the LORD by fire, for that is their inheritance. 2They shall have no inheritance among their brothers; the LORD is their inheritance, as he promised them.

3This is the share due the priests from the people who sacrifice a bull or a sheep: the shoulder, the jowls and the inner parts. 4You are to give them the firstfruits of your grain, new wine and oil, and the first wool from the shearing of your sheep, 5for the LORD your God has chosen them and their descendants out of all your tribes to stand and minister in the LORD's name always.

6If a Levite moves from one of your towns anywhere in Israel where he is living, and comes in all earnestness to the place the LORD will choose, 7he may minister in the name of the LORD his God like all his fellow Levites who serve there in the presence of the LORD. 8He is to share equally in their benefits, even though he has received money from the sale of family possessions.

Detestable Practices

9When you enter the land the LORD your God is giving you, do not learn to imitate the detestable ways of the nations there. 10Let no one be found among you who sacrifices his son or daughter in*a* the fire, who practices divination or sorcery, interprets omens, engages in witchcraft, 11or casts spells, or who is a medium or spiritist or who consults the dead. 12Anyone who does these things is detestable to the LORD, and because of these detestable practices the LORD your God will drive out those nations before you. 13You must be blameless before the LORD your God.

The Prophet

14The nations you will dispossess listen to those who practice sorcery or divination. But as for you, the LORD

---

a 10 Or who makes his son or daughter pass through

King James

The promise of a prophet

15 ¶ The LORD thy God will raise up unto thee a Prophet from the midst of thee, of thy brethren, like unto me; unto him ye shall hearken;

16According to all that thou desiredst of the LORD thy God in Horeb in the day of the assembly, saying, Let me not hear again the voice of the LORD my God, neither let me see this great fire any more, that I die not.

17And the LORD said unto me, They have well *spoken that* which they have spoken.

18I will raise them up a Prophet from among their brethren, like unto thee, and will put my words in his mouth; and he shall speak unto them all that I shall command him.

19And it shall come to pass, *that* whosoever will not hearken unto my words which he shall speak in my name, I will require *it* of him.

20But the prophet, which shall presume to speak a word in my name, which I have not commanded him to speak, or that shall speak in the name of other gods, even that prophet shall die.

21And if thou say in thine heart, How shall we know the word which the LORD hath not spoken?

22When a prophet speaketh in the name of the LORD, if the thing follow not, nor come to pass, that *is* the thing which the LORD hath not spoken, *but* the prophet hath spoken it presumptuously: thou shalt not be afraid of him.

Cities of refuge for murderers

19 WHEN THE LORD thy God hath cut off the nations, whose land the LORD thy God giveth thee, and thou *x*succeedest them, and dwellest in their cities, and in their houses;

2Thou shalt separate three cities for thee in the midst of thy land, which the LORD thy God giveth thee to possess it.

3Thou shalt prepare thee a way, and divide the coasts of thy land, which the LORD thy God giveth thee to inherit, into three parts, that every slayer may flee thither.

4 ¶ And this *is* the case of the slayer, which shall flee thither, that he may live: Whoso killeth his neighbour ignorantly, whom he hated not *y*in time past;

5As when a man goeth into the wood with his neighbour to hew wood, and his hand fetcheth a stroke with the axe to cut down the tree, and the *z*head slippeth from the *a*helve, and *b*lighteth upon his neighbour, that he die; he shall flee unto one of those cities, and live:

6Lest the avenger of the blood pursue the slayer, while his heart is hot, and overtake him, because the way is long, and *c*slay him; whereas he *was* not worthy of death, inasmuch as he hated him not *y*in time past.

7Wherefore I command thee, saying, Thou shalt separate three cities for thee.

8And if the LORD thy God enlarge thy coast, as he hath sworn unto thy fathers, and give thee all the land which he promised to give unto thy fathers;

9If thou shalt keep all these commandments to do them, which I command thee this day, to love the LORD thy God, and to walk ever in his ways; then shalt thou add three cities more for thee, beside these three:

Amplified

15The Lord your God will raise up for you *g*a prophet (Prophet) from the midst of your brethren like me [Moses]; to him you shall listen. [Matt. 21:11; John 1:21.]

16This is what you desired [and asked] of the Lord your God at Horeb on the day of the assembly when you said, Let me not hear again the voice of the Lord my God or see this great fire any more, lest I die.

17And the Lord said to me, They have well said all that they have spoken.

18I will raise up for them a prophet (Prophet) from among their brethren like you, and will put My words in his mouth; and he shall speak to them all that I command him.

19And whoever will not hearken to My words which he shall speak in My name, I Myself will require it of him.

20But the prophet who presumes to speak a word in My name which I have not commanded him to speak, or who speaks in the name of other gods, that same prophet shall die.

21And if you say in your [minds and] hearts, How shall we know which words the Lord has not spoken?

22When a prophet speaks in the name of the Lord, if the word does not come to pass or prove true, that is a word which the Lord has not spoken. The prophet has spoken it presumptuously; you shall not be afraid of him.

19 WHEN THE Lord your God has cut off the nations whose land the Lord your God gives you, and you dispossess them and dwell in their cities and in their houses,

2You shall set apart three cities for yourselves in the land which the Lord your God gives you to possess.

3You shall prepare the road and divide into three parts the territory of your land which the Lord your God gives you to possess, so that any manslayer can flee to them.

4And this is the case of the slayer who shall flee there in order that he may live. Whoever kills his neighbor unintentionally, for whom he had no enmity in time past—

5As when a man goes into the wood with his neighbor to hew wood, and his hand strikes with the ax to cut down the tree, and the head slips off the handle and lights on his neighbor and kills him—he may flee to one of those cities and live;

6Lest the avenger of the blood pursue the slayer while his [mind and] heart are hot with anger and overtake him, because the way is long, and slay him even though the slayer was not worthy of death, since he had not been at enmity with him previously.

7Therefore I command you, You shall set apart three [refuge] cities.

8And if the Lord your God enlarges your territory, as He has sworn to your fathers to do, and gives you all the land which He promised to your fathers to give,

9If you keep all these commandments to do them, which I command you this day, to love the Lord your God and to walk always in His ways, then you shall add three other cities to these three,

---

g The insertion of this promise in connection with the preceding prohibition might warrant the application which some make of it to that order of true prophets whom God commissioned in unbroken succession to instruct, to direct, and warn His people; in this view the gist of it is, "there is no need to consult with diviners and soothsayers, for I shall afford you the benefit of divinely appointed prophets, for judging of whose identity a sure clue is given" (Deut. 18:20, 22). But the prophet here promised was preeminently the Messiah, for He alone was "like unto Moses in His mediatorial character; in the peculiar excellence of His ministry; in the number, variety, and magnitude of His miracles; in His close and familiar communion with God; and in His being the author of a new dispensation of religion." This prediction was fulfilled 1,500 years afterwards, and was expressly applied to Christ by Peter (Acts 3:22, 23) and by Stephen (Acts 7:37) (Robert Jamieson, A.R. Fausset and David Brown, *A Commentary*).

---

x Heb. *inheritest,* or, *possessest*   *y* Heb. *from yesterday the third day*   *z* Heb. *iron*   *a* Heb. *wood*   *b* Heb. *findeth*   *c* Heb. *smite him in life*

New American Standard

15 ¶ "The LORD your God will raise up for you a prophet like me from among you, from your countrymen, you shall listen to him.

16 "This is according to all that you asked of the LORD your God in Horeb on the day of the assembly, saying, 'Let me not hear again the voice of the LORD my God, let me not see this great fire anymore, or I will die.'

17 "The LORD said to me, 'They have spoken well.

18 'I will raise up a prophet from among their countrymen like you, and I will put My words in his mouth, and he shall speak to them all that I command him.

19 'It shall come about that whoever will not listen to My words which he shall speak in My name, I Myself will require it of him.

20 'But the prophet who speaks a word presumptuously in My name which I have not commanded him to speak, or which he speaks in the name of other gods, that prophet shall die.'

21 "You may say in your heart, 'How will we know the word which the LORD has not spoken?'

22 "When a prophet speaks in the name of the LORD, if the thing does not come about or come true, that is the thing which the LORD has not spoken. The prophet has spoken it presumptuously; you shall not be afraid of him.

Cities of Refuge

19 "WHEN THE LORD your God cuts off the nations, whose land the LORD your God gives you, and you dispossess them and settle in their cities and in their houses,

2 you shall set aside three cities for yourself in the midst of your land, which the LORD your God gives you to possess.

3 "You shall prepare the roads for yourself, and divide into three parts the territory of your land which the LORD your God will give you as a possession, so that any manslayer may flee there.

4 ¶ "Now this is the case of the manslayer who may flee there and live: when he kills his friend unintentionally, not hating him previously—

5 as when a man goes into the forest with his friend to cut wood, and his hand swings the axe to cut down the tree, and the iron head slips off the handle and strikes his friend so that he dies—he may flee to one of these cities and live;

6 otherwise the avenger of blood might pursue the manslayer in the heat of his anger, and overtake him, because the way is long, and take his life, though he was not deserving of death, since he had not hated him previously.

7 "Therefore, I command you, saying, 'You shall set aside three cities for yourself.'

8 ¶ "If the LORD your God enlarges your territory, just as He has sworn to your fathers, and gives you all the land which He promised to give your fathers—

9 if you carefully observe all this commandment which I command you today, to love the LORD your God, and to walk in His ways always—then you shall add three more cities for yourself, besides these three.

New International

your God has not permitted you to do so. 15 The LORD your God will raise up for you a prophet like me from among your own brothers. You must listen to him. 16 For this is what you asked of the LORD your God at Horeb on the day of the assembly when you said, "Let us not hear the voice of the LORD our God nor see this great fire anymore, or we will die."

17 The LORD said to me: "What they say is good. 18 I will raise up for them a prophet like you from among their brothers; I will put my words in his mouth, and he will tell them everything I command him. 19 If anyone does not listen to my words that the prophet speaks in my name, I myself will call him to account. 20 But a prophet who presumes to speak in my name anything I have not commanded him to say, or a prophet who speaks in the name of other gods, must be put to death."

21 You may say to yourselves, "How can we know when a message has not been spoken by the LORD?" 22 If what a prophet proclaims in the name of the LORD does not take place or come true, that is a message the LORD has not spoken. That prophet has spoken presumptuously. Do not be afraid of him.

Cities of Refuge

19 WHEN THE LORD your God has destroyed the nations whose land he is giving you, and when you have driven them out and settled in their towns and houses, 2 then set aside for yourselves three cities centrally located in the land the LORD your God is giving you to possess. 3 Build roads to them and divide into three parts the land the LORD your God is giving you as an inheritance, so that anyone who kills a man may flee there.

4 This is the rule concerning the man who kills another and flees there to save his life—one who kills his neighbor unintentionally, without malice aforethought. 5 For instance, a man may go into the forest with his neighbor to cut wood, and as he swings his ax to fell a tree, the head may fly off and hit his neighbor and kill him. That man may flee to one of these cities and save his life. 6 Otherwise, the avenger of blood might pursue him in a rage, overtake him if the distance is too great, and kill him even though he is not deserving of death, since he did it to his neighbor without malice aforethought. 7 This is why I command you to set aside for yourselves three cities.

8 If the LORD your God enlarges your territory, as he promised on oath to your forefathers, and gives you the whole land he promised them, 9 because you carefully follow all these laws I command you today—to love the LORD your God and to walk always in his ways—then you

King James

¹⁰That innocent blood be not shed in thy land, which the LORD thy God giveth thee *for* an inheritance, and *so* blood be upon thee.

¹¹ ¶ But if any man hate his neighbour, and lie in wait for him, and rise up against him, and smite him ^dmortally that he die, and fleeth into one of these cities:

¹²Then the elders of his city shall send and fetch him thence, and deliver him into the hand of the avenger of blood, that he may die.

¹³Thine eye shall not pity him, but thou shalt put away *the guilt of* innocent blood from Israel, that it may go well with thee.

¹⁴ ¶ Thou shalt not remove thy neighbour's landmark, which they of old time have set in thine inheritance, which thou shalt inherit in the land that the LORD thy God giveth thee to possess it.

Laws about witnesses

¹⁵ ¶ One witness shall not rise up against a man for any iniquity, or for any sin, in any sin that he sinneth: at the mouth of two witnesses, or at the mouth of three witnesses, shall the matter be established.

¹⁶ ¶ If a false witness rise up against any man to testify against him ^e*that which is* wrong;

¹⁷Then both the men, between whom the controversy *is,* shall stand before the LORD, before the priests and the judges, which shall be in those days;

¹⁸And the judges shall make diligent inquisition: and, behold, *if* the witness *be* a false witness, *and* hath testified falsely against his brother;

¹⁹Then shall ye do unto him, as he had thought to have done unto his brother: so shalt thou put the evil away from among you.

²⁰And those which remain shall hear, and fear, and shall henceforth commit no more any such evil among you.

²¹And thine eye shall not pity; *but* life *shall go* for life, eye for eye, tooth for tooth, hand for hand, foot for foot.

Laws about military service

20 WHEN THOU goest out to battle against thine enemies, and seest horses, and chariots, *and* a people more than thou, be not afraid of them: for the LORD thy God *is* with thee, which brought thee up out of the land of Egypt.

²And it shall be, when ye are come nigh unto the battle, that the priest shall approach and speak unto the people,

³And shall say unto them, Hear, O Israel, ye approach this day unto battle against your enemies: let not your hearts ^ffaint, fear not, and do not ^gtremble, neither be ye terrified because of them;

⁴For the LORD your God *is* he that goeth with you, to fight for you against your enemies, to save you.

⁵ ¶ And the officers shall speak unto the people, saying, What man *is there* that hath built a new house, and hath not dedicated it? let him go and return to his house, lest he die in the battle, and another man dedicate it.

⁶And what man *is he* that hath planted a vineyard, and hath not *yet* eaten of it? let him *also* go and return unto his house, lest he die in the battle, and another man eat of it.

⁷And what man *is there* that hath betrothed a wife, and hath not taken her? let him go and return unto his house, lest he die in the battle, and another man take her.

⁸And the officers shall speak further unto the people, and they shall say, What man *is there that is* fearful and fainthearted? let him go and return unto his house, lest his brethren's heart ^hfaint as well as his heart.

⁹And it shall be, when the officers have made an end of speaking unto the people, that they shall make captains of the armies ⁱto lead the people.

Amplified

¹⁰Lest innocent blood be shed in your land, which the Lord your God gives you as an inheritance, and so blood guilt be upon you.

¹¹But if any man hates his neighbor and lies in wait for him, and attacks him and wounds him mortally so that he dies, and the assailant flees into one of these cities,

¹²Then the elders of his own city shall send for him and fetch him from there and give him over to the avenger of blood, so that he may die.

¹³Your eyes shall not pity him, but you shall clear Israel of the guilt of innocent blood, that it may go well with you.

¹⁴You shall not remove your neighbor's landmark in the land which the Lord your God gives you to possess, which the men of old [the first dividers of the land] set.

¹⁵One witness shall not prevail against a man for any crime or any wrong in connection with any sin he commits; only on the testimony of two or three witnesses shall a charge be established.

¹⁶If a false witness rises up against any man to accuse him of wrongdoing,

¹⁷Then both parties to the controversy shall stand before the Lord, before the priests and the judges who are in office in those days.

¹⁸The judges shall inquire diligently, and if the witness is a false witness and has accused his brother falsely,

¹⁹Then you shall do to him as he had intended to do to his brother. So you shall put away the evil from among you.

²⁰And those who remain shall hear and [reverently] fear, and shall henceforth commit no such evil among you.

²¹Your eyes shall not pity: it shall be life for life, eye for eye, tooth for tooth, hand for hand, foot for foot.

20 WHEN YOU go forth to battle against your enemies and see horses and chariots and an army greater than your own, do not be afraid of them, for the Lord your God, Who brought you out of the land of Egypt, is with you.

²And when you come near to the battle, the priest shall approach and speak to the men,

³And shall say to them, Hear, O Israel, you draw near this day to battle against your enemies. Let not your [minds and] hearts faint; fear not, and do not tremble or be terrified [and in dread] because of them.

⁴For the Lord your God is He Who goes with you to fight for you against your enemies to save you. [I Sam. 17:45.]

⁵And the officers shall speak to the people, saying, What man is there who has built a new house and has not dedicated it? Let him return to his house, lest he die in the battle and another man dedicate it.

⁶And what man has planted a vineyard and has not used the fruit of it? Let him also return to his house, lest he die in the battle and another man use the fruit of it.

⁷And what man has betrothed a wife and has not taken her? Let him return to his house, lest he die in the battle and another man take her.

⁸And the officers shall speak further to the people, and say, What man is fearful and fainthearted? Let him return to his house, lest [because of him] his brethren's [minds and] hearts faint as does his own.

⁹And when the officers finish speaking to the people, they shall appoint commanders at the head of the people.

---

^dHeb. *in life make haste*   ^eOr, *falling away*   ^fHeb. *be tender*   ^gHeb. *melt*   ^hHeb. *melt*   ⁱHeb. to be *in the head of the people*

New American Standard

10"So innocent blood will not be shed in the midst of your land which the LORD your God gives you as an inheritance, and bloodguiltiness be on you.

11 ¶ "But if there is a man who hates his neighbor and lies in wait for him and rises up against him and strikes him so that he dies, and he flees to one of these cities,

12 then the elders of his city shall send and take him from there and deliver him into the hand of the avenger of blood, that he may die.

13"You shall not pity him, but you shall purge the blood of the innocent from Israel, that it may go well with you.

Laws of Landmark and Testimony

14 ¶ "You shall not move your neighbor's boundary mark, which the ancestors have set, in your inheritance which you will inherit in the land that the LORD your God gives you to possess.

15 ¶ "A single witness shall not rise up against a man on account of any iniquity or any sin which he has committed; on the evidence of two or three witnesses a matter shall be confirmed.

16"If a malicious witness rises up against a man to accuse him of wrongdoing,

17 then both the men who have the dispute shall stand before the LORD, before the priests and the judges who will be *in office* in those days.

18"The judges shall investigate thoroughly, and if the witness is a false witness *and* he has accused his brother falsely,

19 then you shall do to him just as he had intended to do to his brother. Thus you shall purge the evil from among you.

20"The rest will hear and be afraid, and will never again do such an evil thing among you.

21"Thus you shall not show pity: life for life, eye for eye, tooth for tooth, hand for hand, foot for foot.

Laws of Warfare

20 "WHEN YOU go out to battle against your enemies and see horses and chariots *and* people more numerous than you, do not be afraid of them; for the LORD your God, who brought you up from the land of Egypt, is with you.

2"When you are approaching the battle, the priest shall come near and speak to the people.

3"He shall say to them, 'Hear, O Israel, you are approaching the battle against your enemies today. Do not be fainthearted. Do not be afraid, or panic, or tremble before them,

4 for the LORD your God is the one who goes with you, to fight for you against your enemies, to save you.'

5"The officers also shall speak to the people, saying, 'Who is the man that has built a new house and has not dedicated it? Let him depart and return to his house, otherwise he might die in the battle and another man would dedicate it.

6 'Who is the man that has planted a vineyard and has not begun to use its fruit? Let him depart and return to his house, otherwise he might die in the battle and another man would begin to use its fruit.

7 'And who is the man that is engaged to a woman and has not married her? Let him depart and return to his house, otherwise he might die in the battle and another man would marry her.'

8"Then the officers shall speak further to the people and say, 'Who is the man that is afraid and fainthearted? Let him depart and return to his house, so that he might not make his brothers' hearts melt like his heart.'

9"When the officers have finished speaking to the people, they shall appoint commanders of armies at the head of the people.

New International

are to set aside three more cities. 10Do this so that innocent blood will not be shed in your land, which the LORD your God is giving you as your inheritance, and so that you will not be guilty of bloodshed.

11But if a man hates his neighbor and lies in wait for him, assaults and kills him, and then flees to one of these cities, 12the elders of his town shall send for him, bring him back from the city, and hand him over to the avenger of blood to die. 13Show him no pity. You must purge from Israel the guilt of shedding innocent blood, so that it may go well with you.

14Do not move your neighbor's boundary stone set up by your predecessors in the inheritance you receive in the land the LORD your God is giving you to possess.

Witnesses

15One witness is not enough to convict a man accused of any crime or offense he may have committed. A matter must be established by the testimony of two or three witnesses.

16If a malicious witness takes the stand to accuse a man of a crime, 17the two men involved in the dispute must stand in the presence of the LORD before the priests and the judges who are in office at the time. 18The judges must make a thorough investigation, and if the witness proves to be a liar, giving false testimony against his brother, 19then do to him as he intended to do to his brother. You must purge the evil from among you. 20The rest of the people will hear of this and be afraid, and never again will such an evil thing be done among you. 21Show no pity: life for life, eye for eye, tooth for tooth, hand for hand, foot for foot.

Going to War

20 WHEN YOU go to war against your enemies and see horses and chariots and an army greater than yours, do not be afraid of them, because the LORD your God, who brought you up out of Egypt, will be with you. 2When you are about to go into battle, the priest shall come forward and address the army. 3He shall say: "Hear, O Israel, today you are going into battle against your enemies. Do not be fainthearted or afraid; do not be terrified or give way to panic before them. 4For the LORD your God is the one who goes with you to fight for you against your enemies to give you victory."

5The officers shall say to the army: "Has anyone built a new house and not dedicated it? Let him go home, or he may die in battle and someone else may dedicate it. 6Has anyone planted a vineyard and not begun to enjoy it? Let him go home, or he may die in battle and someone else enjoy it. 7Has anyone become pledged to a woman and not married her? Let him go home, or he may die in battle and someone else marry her." 8Then the officers shall add, "Is any man afraid or fainthearted? Let him go home so that his brothers will not become disheartened too." 9When the officers have finished speaking to the army, they shall appoint commanders over it.

King James

¹⁰ ¶ When thou comest nigh unto a city to fight against it, then proclaim peace unto it.

¹¹And it shall be, if it make thee answer of peace, and open unto thee, then it shall be, *that* all the people *that is* found therein shall be tributaries unto thee, and they shall serve thee.

¹²And if it will make no peace with thee, but will make war against thee, then thou shalt besiege it:

¹³And when the Lord thy God hath delivered it into thine hands, thou shalt smite every male thereof with the edge of the sword:

¹⁴But the women, and the little ones, and the cattle, and all that is in the city, *even* all the spoil thereof, shalt thou *j*take unto thyself; and thou shalt eat the spoil of thine enemies, which the Lord thy God hath given thee.

¹⁵Thus shalt thou do unto all the cities *which are* very far off from thee, which *are* not of the cities of these nations.

¹⁶But of the cities of these people, which the Lord thy God doth give thee *for* an inheritance, thou shalt save alive nothing that breatheth:

¹⁷But thou shalt utterly destroy them; *namely,* the Hittites, and the Amorites, the Canaanites, and the Perizzites, the Hivites, and the Jebusites; as the Lord thy God hath commanded thee:

¹⁸That they teach you not to do after all their abominations, which they have done unto their gods; so should ye sin against the Lord your God.

¹⁹ ¶ When thou shalt besiege a city a long time, in making war against it to take it, thou shalt not destroy the trees thereof by forcing an axe against them: for thou mayest eat of them, and thou shalt not cut them down (*k*for the tree of the field *is* man's *life*) *l*to employ *them* in the siege:

²⁰Only the trees which thou knowest that they *be* not trees for meat, thou shalt destroy and cut them down; and thou shalt build bulwarks against the city that maketh war with thee, until *m*it be subdued.

Laws about unsolved murders

21 IF *ONE* be found slain in the land which the Lord thy God giveth thee to possess it, lying in the field, *and* it be not known who hath slain him:

²Then thy elders and thy judges shall come forth, and they shall measure unto the cities which *are* round about him that is slain:

³And it shall be, *that* the city *which is* next unto the slain man, even the elders of that city shall take an heifer, which hath not been wrought with, *and* which hath not drawn in the yoke;

⁴And the elders of that city shall bring down the heifer unto a rough valley, which is neither eared nor sown, and shall strike off the heifer's neck there in the valley:

⁵And the priests the sons of Levi shall come near; for them the Lord thy God hath chosen to minister unto him, and to bless in the name of the Lord; and by their *n*word shall every controversy and every stroke be *tried:*

⁶And all the elders of that city, *that are* next unto the slain *man,* shall wash their hands over the heifer that is beheaded in the valley:

⁷And they shall answer and say, Our hands have not shed this blood, neither have our eyes seen *it.*

⁸Be merciful, O Lord, unto thy people Israel, whom thou hast redeemed, and lay not innocent blood *o*unto thy people of Israel's charge. And the blood shall be forgiven them.

⁹So shalt thou put away the *guilt of* innocent blood from among you, when thou shalt do *that which is* right in the sight of the Lord.

Amplified

¹⁰When you draw near to a city to fight against it, then proclaim peace to it.

¹¹And if that city makes an answer of peace to you and opens to you, then all the people found in it shall be tributary to you and they shall serve you.

¹²But if it refuses to make peace with you and fights against you, then you shall besiege it.

¹³And when the Lord your God has given it into your hands, you shall smite every male there with the edge of the sword.

¹⁴But the women, the little ones, the beasts, and all that is in the city, all the spoil in it, you shall take for yourselves; and you shall use the spoil of your enemies which the Lord your God has given you.

¹⁵So shall you treat all the cities that are very far off from you, that do not belong to the cities of these nations.

¹⁶But in the cities of these people which the Lord your God gives you for an inheritance, you shall save alive nothing that breathes.

¹⁷But you shall utterly exterminate them, the Hittites, the Amorites, the Canaanites, the Perizzites, the Hivites, and the Jebusites, as the Lord your God has commanded you,

¹⁸So that they may not teach you all the abominable practices they have carried on for their gods, and so cause you to sin against the Lord your God.

¹⁹When you besiege a city for a long time, making war against it to take it, you shall not destroy its trees by using an ax on them, for you can eat their fruit; you must not cut them down, for is the tree of the field a man, that it should be besieged by you?

²⁰Only the trees which you know are not trees for food you may destroy and cut down, that you may build siege works against the city that makes war with you until it falls.

21 IF ONE is found slain in the land which the Lord your God gives you to possess, lying in the field, and it is not known who has killed him,

²Then your elders and judges shall come forth and measure the distance to the cities around him who is slain.

³And the city which is nearest to the slain man, the elders of that city shall take a heifer which has never been worked, never pulled in the yoke,

⁴And the elders of that city shall bring the heifer down to a valley with running water which is neither plowed nor sown, and shall break the heifer's neck there in the valley.

⁵And the priests, the sons of Levi, shall come near, for the Lord your God has chosen them to minister to Him and to bless in the name [and presence] of the Lord, and by their word shall every controversy and every assault be settled.

⁶And all the elders of that city nearest to the slain man shall wash their hands over the heifer whose neck was broken in the valley,

⁷And they shall testify, Our hands have not shed this blood, neither have our eyes seen it.

⁸Forgive, O Lord, Your people Israel, whom You have redeemed, and do not allow the shedding of innocent blood to be charged to Your people Israel. And the guilt of blood shall be forgiven them.

⁹So shall you purge the guilt of innocent blood from among you, when you do what is right in the sight of the Lord.

---

*j*Heb. spoil   *k*Or, *for, O man, the tree of the field* is to be employed in the siege   *l*Heb. *to go from before thee*   *m*Heb. it come down   *n*Heb. mouth   *o*Heb. *in the midst*

New American Standard

10 ¶ "When you approach a city to fight against it, you shall offer it terms of peace.

11"If it agrees to make peace with you and opens to you, then all the people who are found in it shall become your forced labor and shall serve you.

12"However, if it does not make peace with you, but makes war against you, then you shall besiege it.

13"When the LORD your God gives it into your hand, you shall strike all the men in it with the edge of the sword.

14"Only the women and the children and the animals and all that is in the city, all its spoil, you shall take as booty for yourself; and you shall use the spoil of your enemies which the LORD your God has given you.

15"Thus you shall do to all the cities that are very far from you, which are not of the cities of these nations nearby.

16"Only in the cities of these peoples that the LORD your God is giving you as an inheritance, you shall not leave alive anything that breathes.

17"But you shall utterly destroy them, the Hittite and the Amorite, the Canaanite and the Perizzite, the Hivite and the Jebusite, as the LORD your God has commanded you,

18 so that they may not teach you to do according to all their detestable things which they have done for their gods, so that you would sin against the LORD your God.

19 ¶ "When you besiege a city a long time, to make war against it in order to capture it, you shall not destroy its trees by swinging an axe against them; for you may eat from them, and you shall not cut them down. For is the tree of the field a man, that it should be besieged by you?

20"Only the trees which you know are not fruit trees you shall destroy and cut down, that you may construct siege-works against the city that is making war with you until it falls.

Expiation of a Crime

21 "IF A slain person is found lying in the open country in the land which the LORD your God gives you to possess, *and* it is not known who has struck him,

2 then your elders and your judges shall go out and measure *the distance* to the cities which are around the slain one.

3"It shall be that the city which is nearest to the slain man, that is, the elders of that city, shall take a heifer of the herd, which has not been worked and which has not pulled in a yoke;

4 and the elders of that city shall bring the heifer down to a valley with running water, which has not been plowed or sown, and shall break the heifer's neck there in the valley.

5"Then the priests, the sons of Levi, shall come near, for the LORD your God has chosen them to serve Him and to bless in the name of the LORD; and every dispute and every assault shall be settled by them.

6"All the elders of that city which is nearest to the slain man shall wash their hands over the heifer whose neck was broken in the valley;

7 and they shall answer and say, 'Our hands did not shed this blood, nor did our eyes see *it*.

8 '*n*Forgive Your people Israel whom You have redeemed, O LORD, and do not place the guilt of innocent blood in the midst of Your people Israel.' And the bloodguiltiness shall be forgiven them.

9"So you shall remove the guilt of innocent blood from your midst, when you do what is right in the eyes of the LORD.

New International

10When you march up to attack a city, make its people an offer of peace. 11If they accept and open their gates, all the people in it shall be subject to forced labor and shall work for you. 12If they refuse to make peace and they engage you in battle, lay siege to that city. 13When the LORD your God delivers it into your hand, put to the sword all the men in it. 14As for the women, the children, the livestock and everything else in the city, you may take these as plunder for yourselves. And you may use the plunder the LORD your God gives you from your enemies. 15This is how you are to treat all the cities that are at a distance from you and do not belong to the nations nearby.

16However, in the cities of the nations the LORD your God is giving you as an inheritance, do not leave alive anything that breathes. 17Completely destroy*b* them—the Hittites, Amorites, Canaanites, Perizzites, Hivites and Jebusites—as the LORD your God has commanded you. 18Otherwise, they will teach you to follow all the detestable things they do in worshiping their gods, and you will sin against the LORD your God.

19When you lay siege to a city for a long time, fighting against it to capture it, do not destroy its trees by putting an ax to them, because you can eat their fruit. Do not cut them down. Are the trees of the field people, that you should besiege them?*c* 20However, you may cut down trees that you know are not fruit trees and use them to build siege works until the city at war with you falls.

Atonement for an Unsolved Murder

21 IF A man is found slain, lying in a field in the land the LORD your God is giving you to possess, and it is not known who killed him, 2your elders and judges shall go out and measure the distance from the body to the neighboring towns. 3Then the elders of the town nearest the body shall take a heifer that has never been worked and has never worn a yoke 4and lead her down to a valley that has not been plowed or planted and where there is a flowing stream. There in the valley they are to break the heifer's neck. 5The priests, the sons of Levi, shall step forward, for the LORD your God has chosen them to minister and to pronounce blessings in the name of the LORD and to decide all cases of dispute and assault. 6Then all the elders of the town nearest the body shall wash their hands over the heifer whose neck was broken in the valley, 7and they shall declare: "Our hands did not shed this blood, nor did our eyes see it done. 8Accept this atonement for your people Israel, whom you have redeemed, O LORD, and do not hold your people guilty of the blood of an innocent man." And the bloodshed will be atoned for. 9So you will purge from yourselves the guilt of shedding innocent blood, since you have done what is right in the eyes of the LORD.

---

n Lit *Cover over, atone for*

b 17 The Hebrew term refers to the irrevocable giving over of things or persons to the LORD, often by totally destroying them.
c 19 Or *down to use in the siege, for the fruit trees are for the benefit of man.*

King James

Laws about captive wives

10 ¶ When thou goest forth to war against thine enemies, and the LORD thy God hath delivered them into thine hands, and thou hast taken them captive,

11 And seest among the captives a beautiful woman, and hast a desire unto her, that thou wouldest have her to thy wife;

12 Then thou shalt bring her home to thine house; and she shall shave her head, and *p*pare her nails;

13 And she shall put the raiment of her captivity from off her, and shall remain in thine house, and bewail her father and her mother a full month: and after that thou shalt go in unto her, and be her husband, and she shall be thy wife.

14 And it shall be, if thou have no delight in her, then thou shalt let her go whither she will; but thou shalt not sell her at all for money, thou shalt not make merchandise of her, because thou hast humbled her.

Laws concerning sons

15 ¶ If a man have two wives, one beloved, and another hated, and they have born him children, *both* the beloved and the hated; and *if* the firstborn son be hers that was hated:

16 Then it shall be, when he maketh his sons to inherit *that* which he hath, *that* he may not make the son of the beloved firstborn before the son of the hated, *which is indeed* the firstborn:

17 But he shall acknowledge the son of the hated *for* the firstborn, by giving him a double portion of all *r*that he hath: for he *is* the beginning of his strength; the right of the firstborn *is* his.

18 ¶ If a man have a stubborn and rebellious son, which will not obey the voice of his father, or the voice of his mother, and *that,* when they have chastened him, will not hearken unto them:

19 Then shall his father and his mother lay hold on him, and bring him out unto the elders of his city, and unto the gate of his place;

20 And they shall say unto the elders of his city, This our son *is* stubborn and rebellious, he will not obey our voice; *he is* a glutton, and a drunkard.

21 And all the men of his city shall stone him with stones, that he die: so shalt thou put evil away from among you; and all Israel shall hear, and fear.

Miscellaneous laws

22 ¶ And if a man have committed a sin worthy of death, and he be to be put to death, and thou hang him on a tree:

23 His body shall not remain all night upon the tree, but thou shalt in any wise bury him that day; (for he that is hanged *is* *s*accursed of God;) that thy land be not defiled, which the LORD thy God giveth thee *for* an inheritance.

22 THOU SHALT not see thy brother's ox or his sheep go astray, and hide thyself from them: thou shalt in any case bring them again unto thy brother.

2 And if thy brother *be* not nigh unto thee, or if thou know him not, then thou shalt bring it unto thine own house, and it shall be with thee until thy brother seek after it, and thou shalt restore it to him again.

3 In like manner shalt thou do with his ass; and so shalt thou do with his raiment; and with all lost thing of thy brother's, which he hath lost, and thou hast found, shalt thou do likewise: thou mayest not hide thyself.

4 ¶ Thou shalt not see thy brother's ass or his ox fall down by the way, and hide thyself from them: thou shalt surely help him to lift *them* up again.

Amplified

10 When you go forth to battle against your enemies and the Lord your God has given them into your hands and you carry them away captive,

11 And you see among the captives a beautiful woman and desire her, that you may have her as your wife,

12 Then you shall bring her home to your house, and she shall shave her head and pare her nails [in purification from heathenism]

13 And put off her prisoner's garb, and shall remain in your house and bewail her father and her mother a full month. After that you may go in to her and be her husband and she shall be your wife.

14 And if you have no delight in her, then you shall let her go absolutely free. You shall not sell her at all for money; you shall not deal with her as a slave *or* a servant, because you have humbled her.

15 If a man has two wives, one loved and the other disliked, and they both have borne him children, and if the firstborn son is the son of the one who is disliked,

16 Then on the day when he wills his possessions to his sons, he shall not put the firstborn of his loved wife in place of the [actual] firstborn of the disliked wife—her firstborn being older.

17 But he shall acknowledge the son of the disliked as the firstborn by giving him a double portion of all that he has, for he was the first issue of his strength; the right of the firstborn is his.

18 If a man has a stubborn and rebellious son who will not obey the voice of his father or his mother and though they chasten him will not listen to them,

19 Then his father and mother shall take hold of him and bring him out to the elders of his city at the gate of the place where he lives,

20 And they shall say to the elders of his city, This son of ours is stubborn and rebellious. He will not obey our voice. He is a glutton and a drunkard. [Prov. 23:20–22.]

21 Then all the men of his city shall stone him to death; so you shall cleanse out the evil from your midst, and all Israel shall hear and [reverently] fear.

22 And if a man has committed a sin worthy of death and he is put to death and [afterward] you hang him on a tree, [Josh. 10:26, 27.]

23 His body shall not remain all night upon the tree, but you shall surely bury him on the same day, for a hanged man is accursed by God. Thus you shall not defile your land which the Lord your God gives you for an inheritance. [Gal. 3:13.]

22 YOU SHALL not see your brother's ox or his sheep being driven away *or* stolen, and hide yourself from [your duty to help] them; you shall surely take them back to your brother. [Prov. 24:12.]

2 And if your brother [the owner] is not near you or if you do not know who he is, you shall bring the animal to your house and it shall be with you until your brother comes looking for it; then you shall restore it to him.

3 And so shall you do with his donkey or his garment or with anything which your brother has lost and you have found. You shall not hide from [your duty concerning] them.

4 You shall not see your brother's donkey or his ox fall down by the way, and hide from [your duty concerning] them; you shall surely help him to lift them up again.

New American Standard

Domestic Relations

10 ¶ "When you go out to battle against your enemies, and the LORD your God delivers them into your hands and you take them away captive,

11 and see among the captives a beautiful woman, and have a desire for her and would take her as a wife for yourself,

12 then you shall bring her home to your house, and she shall shave her head and trim her nails.

13 "She shall also remove the clothes of her captivity and shall remain in your house, and mourn her father and mother a full month; and after that you may go in to her and be her husband and she shall be your wife.

14 "It shall be, if you are not pleased with her, then you shall let her go wherever she wishes; but you shall certainly not sell her for money, you shall not mistreat her, because you have humbled her.

15 ¶ "If a man has two wives, the one loved and the other unloved, and *both* the loved and the unloved have borne him sons, if the firstborn son belongs to the unloved,

16 then it shall be in the day he wills what he has to his sons, he cannot make the son of the loved the firstborn before the son of the unloved, who is the firstborn.

17 "But he shall acknowledge the firstborn, the son of the unloved, by giving him a double portion of all that he has, for he is the beginning of his strength; to him belongs the right of the firstborn.

18 ¶ "If any man has a stubborn and rebellious son who will not obey his father or his mother, and when they chastise him, he will not even listen to them,

19 then his father and mother shall seize him, and bring him out to the elders of his city at the gateway of his hometown.

20 "They shall say to the elders of his city, 'This son of ours is stubborn and rebellious, he will not obey us, he is a glutton and a drunkard.'

21 "Then all the men of his city shall stone him to death; so you shall remove the evil from your midst, and all Israel will hear *of it* and fear.

22 ¶ "If a man has committed a sin worthy of death and he is put to death, and you hang him on a tree,

23 his corpse shall not hang all night on the tree, but you shall surely bury him on the same day (for he who is hanged is accursed of God), so that you do not defile your land which the LORD your God gives you as an inheritance.

Sundry Laws

22 "YOU SHALL not see your countryman's ox or his sheep straying away, and pay no attention to them; you shall certainly bring them back to your countryman.

2 "If your countryman is not near you, or if you do not know him, then you shall bring it home to your house, and it shall remain with you until your countryman looks for it; then you shall restore it to him.

3 "Thus you shall do with his donkey, and you shall do the same with his garment, and you shall do likewise with anything lost by your countryman, which he has lost and you have found. You are not allowed to neglect *them.*

4 "You shall not see your countryman's donkey or his ox fallen down on the way, and pay no attention to them; you shall certainly help him to raise *them* up.

New International

Marrying a Captive Woman

10 When you go to war against your enemies and the LORD your God delivers them into your hands and you take captives, 11 if you notice among the captives a beautiful woman and are attracted to her, you may take her as your wife. 12 Bring her into your home and have her shave her head, trim her nails 13 and put aside the clothes she was wearing when captured. After she has lived in your house and mourned her father and mother for a full month, then you may go to her and be her husband and she shall be your wife. 14 If you are not pleased with her, let her go wherever she wishes. You must not sell her or treat her as a slave, since you have dishonored her.

The Right of the Firstborn

15 If a man has two wives, and he loves one but not the other, and both bear him sons but the firstborn is the son of the wife he does not love, 16 when he wills his property to his sons, he must not give the rights of the firstborn to the son of the wife he loves in preference to his actual firstborn, the son of the wife he does not love. 17 He must acknowledge the son of his unloved wife as the firstborn by giving him a double share of all he has. That son is the first sign of his father's strength. The right of the firstborn belongs to him.

A Rebellious Son

18 If a man has a stubborn and rebellious son who does not obey his father and mother and will not listen to them when they discipline him, 19 his father and mother shall take hold of him and bring him to the elders at the gate of his town. 20 They shall say to the elders, "This son of ours is stubborn and rebellious. He will not obey us. He is a profligate and a drunkard." 21 Then all the men of his town shall stone him to death. You must purge the evil from among you. All Israel will hear of it and be afraid.

Various Laws

22 If a man guilty of a capital offense is put to death and his body is hung on a tree, 23 you must not leave his body on the tree overnight. Be sure to bury him that same day, because anyone who is hung on a tree is under God's curse. You must not desecrate the land the LORD your God is giving you as an inheritance.

22 IF YOU see your brother's ox or sheep straying, do not ignore it but be sure to take it back to him. 2 If the brother does not live near you or if you do not know who he is, take it home with you and keep it until he comes looking for it. Then give it back to him. 3 Do the same if you find your brother's donkey or his cloak or anything he loses. Do not ignore it.

4 If you see your brother's donkey or his ox fallen on the road, do not ignore it. Help him get it to its feet.

King James

5 ¶ The woman shall not wear that which pertaineth unto a man, neither shall a man put on a woman's garment: for all that do so *are* abomination unto the LORD thy God.

6 ¶ If a bird's nest chance to be before thee in the way in any tree, or on the ground, *whether they be* young ones, or eggs, and the dam sitting upon the young, or upon the eggs, thou shalt not take the dam with the young:

7*But* thou shalt in any wise let the dam go, and take the young to thee; that it may be well with thee, and *that* thou mayest prolong *thy* days.

8 ¶ When thou buildest a new house, then thou shalt make a battlement for thy roof, that thou bring not blood upon thine house, if any man fall from thence.

9 ¶ Thou shalt not sow thy vineyard with divers seeds: lest the *¹fruit of thy seed which thou hast sown, and the fruit of thy vineyard, be defiled.

10 ¶ Thou shalt not plow with an ox and an ass together.

11 ¶ Thou shalt not wear a garment of divers sorts, *as* of woollen and linen together.

12 ¶ Thou shalt make thee fringes upon the four *ᵘquarters of thy vesture, wherewith thou coverest *thyself.*

Laws about sexual conduct

13 ¶ If any man take a wife, and go in unto her, and hate her,

14And give occasions of speech against her, and bring up an evil name upon her, and say, I took this woman, and when I came to her, I found her not a maid:

15Then shall the father of the damsel, and her mother, take and bring forth *the tokens of* the damsel's virginity unto the elders of the city in the gate:

16And the damsel's father shall say unto the elders, I gave my daughter unto this man to wife, and he hateth her;

17And, lo, he hath given occasions of speech *against her,* saying, I found not thy daughter a maid; and yet these *are the tokens of* my daughter's virginity. And they shall spread the cloth before the elders of the city.

18And the elders of that city shall take that man and chastise him;

19And they shall amerce him in an hundred *shekels* of silver, and give *them* unto the father of the damsel, because he hath brought up an evil name upon a virgin of Israel: and she shall be his wife; he may not put her away all his days.

20But if this thing be true, *and the tokens of* virginity be not found for the damsel:

21Then they shall bring out the damsel to the door of her father's house, and the men of her city shall stone her with stones that she die: because she hath wrought folly in Israel, to play the whore in her father's house: so shalt thou put evil away from among you.

22 ¶ If a man be found lying with a woman married to an husband, then they shall both of them die, *both* the man that lay with the woman, and the woman: so shalt thou put away evil from Israel.

23 ¶ If a damsel *that is* a virgin be betrothed unto an husband, and a man find her in the city, and lie with her;

24Then ye shall bring them both out unto the gate of that city, and ye shall stone them with stones that they die; the damsel, because she cried not, *being* in the city; and the man, because he hath humbled his neighbour's wife: so thou shalt put away evil from among you.

25 ¶ But if a man find a betrothed damsel in the field, and the man ᵛforce her, and lie with her: then the man only that lay with her shall die:

26But unto the damsel thou shalt do nothing; *there is* in the damsel no sin *worthy* of death: for as when a man riseth against his neighbour, and slayeth him, even so *is* this matter:

27For he found her in the field, *and* the betrothed damsel cried, and *there was* none to save her.

Amplified

5The woman shall not wear that which pertains to a man, neither shall a man put on a woman's garment, for all that do so are an abomination to the Lord your God.

6If a bird's nest should chance to be before you in the way, in any tree or on the ground, with young ones or eggs, and the mother bird is sitting on the young or on the eggs, you shall not take the mother bird with the young.

7You shall surely let the mother bird go, and take only the young, that it may be well with you and that you may prolong your days.

8When you build a new house, then you shall put a railing around your [flat] roof, so that no one may fall from there and bring guilt of blood upon your house.

9You shall not plant your vineyard with two kinds of seed, lest the whole crop be forfeited [under this ban], the seed which you have sown and the yield of the vineyard forfeited to the sanctuary.

10You shall not plow with an ox [a clean animal] and a donkey [unclean] together. [II Cor. 6:14–16.]

11You shall not wear a garment of mingled stuff, wool and linen together. [Ezek. 44:18; Rev. 19:8.]

12You shall make yourself tassels on the four corners of your cloak with which you cover yourself. [Num. 15:37–40.]

13If any man takes a wife and goes in to her, and then scorns her

14And charges her with shameful things and gives her an evil reputation, and says, I took this woman, but when I came to her, I did not find in her the tokens of a virgin,

15Then the father of the young woman, and her mother, shall get and bring out the tokens of her virginity to the elders of the city at the gate.

16And her father shall say to the elders, I gave my daughter to this man as wife, but he hates *and* spurns her;

17And behold, he has made shameful charges against her, saying, I found not in your daughter the evidences of her virginity. And yet these are the tokens of my daughter's virginity. And they shall spread the garment before the elders of the city,

18And the elders of that city shall take the man and rebuke *and* whip him.

19And they shall fine him 100 shekels of silver and give them to the father of the young woman, because he has brought an evil name upon a virgin of Israel. And she shall be his wife; he may not divorce her all his days.

20But if it is true that the evidences of virginity were not found in the young woman,

21Then they shall bring her to the door of her father's house and the men of her city shall stone her to death, because she has wrought [criminal] folly in Israel by playing the harlot in her father's house. So you shall put away the evil from among you.

22If a man is found lying with another man's wife, they shall both die, the man who lay with the woman and the woman. So you shall purge the evil from Israel.

23If a maiden who is a virgin is engaged to be married, and a man finds her in the city and lies with her,

24Then you shall bring them both out to the gate of that city and shall stone them to death—the young woman because she did not cry for help though she was in the city, and the man because he has violated his neighbor's [promised] wife. So shall you put away evil from among you.

25But if a man finds the betrothed maiden in the open country and the man seizes her and lies with her, then only the man who lay with her shall die.

26But you shall do nothing to the young woman; she has committed no sin punishable by death, for this is as when a man attacks and slays his neighbor,

27For he came upon her in the open country, and the betrothed girl cried out, but there was no one to save her.

---

*¹Heb. *fulness of thy seed*   *ᵘHeb. *wings*   *ᵛOr, *take strong hold of her*

New American Standard

5 ¶ "A woman shall not wear man's clothing, nor shall a man put on a woman's clothing; for whoever does these things is an abomination to the LORD your God.

6 ¶ "If you happen to come upon a bird's nest along the way, in any tree or on the ground, with young ones or eggs, and the mother sitting on the young or on the eggs, you shall not take the mother with the young;

7 you shall certainly let the mother go, but the young you may take for yourself, in order that it may be well with you and that you may prolong your days.

8 ¶ "When you build a new house, you shall make a parapet for your roof, so that you will not bring bloodguilt on your house if anyone falls from it.

9 ¶ "You shall not sow your vineyard with two kinds of seed, or all the produce of the seed which you have sown and the increase of the vineyard will become defiled.

10 ¶ "You shall not plow with an ox and a donkey together.

11 ¶ "You shall not wear a material mixed of wool and linen together.

12 ¶ "You shall make yourself tassels on the four corners of your garment with which you cover yourself.

Laws on Morality

13 ¶ "If any man takes a wife and goes in to her and *then* turns against her,

14 and charges her with shameful deeds and publicly defames her, and says, 'I took this woman, *but* when I came near her, I did not find her a virgin,'

15 then the girl's father and her mother shall take and bring out the *evidence* of the girl's virginity to the elders of the city at the gate.

16 "The girl's father shall say to the elders, 'I gave my daughter to this man for a wife, but he turned against her;

17 and behold, he has charged her with shameful deeds, saying, "I did not find your daughter a virgin." But this is the evidence of my daughter's virginity.' And they shall spread the garment before the elders of the city.

18 "So the elders of that city shall take the man and chastise him,

19 and they shall fine him a hundred *shekels* of silver and give it to the girl's father, because he publicly defamed a virgin of Israel. And she shall remain his wife; he cannot divorce her all his days.

20 ¶ "But if this charge is true, that the girl was not found a virgin,

21 then they shall bring out the girl to the doorway of her father's house, and the men of her city shall stone her to death because she has committed an act of folly in Israel by playing the harlot in her father's house; thus you shall purge the evil from among you.

22 ¶ "If a man is found lying with a married woman, then both of them shall die, the man who lay with the woman, and the woman; thus you shall purge the evil from Israel.

23 ¶ "If there is a girl who is a virgin engaged to a man, and *another* man finds her in the city and lies with her,

24 then you shall bring them both out to the gate of that city and you shall stone them to death; the girl, because she did not cry out in the city, and the man, because he has violated his neighbor's wife. Thus you shall purge the evil from among you.

25 ¶ "But if in the field the man finds the girl who is engaged, and the man forces her and lies with her, then only the man who lies with her shall die.

26 "But you shall do nothing to the girl; there is no sin in the girl worthy of death, for just as a man rises against his neighbor and murders him, so is this case.

27 "When he found her in the field, the engaged girl cried out, but there was no one to save her.

New International

5 A woman must not wear men's clothing, nor a man wear women's clothing, for the LORD your God detests anyone who does this.

6 If you come across a bird's nest beside the road, either in a tree or on the ground, and the mother is sitting on the young or on the eggs, do not take the mother with the young. 7 You may take the young, but be sure to let the mother go, so that it may go well with you and you may have a long life.

8 When you build a new house, make a parapet around your roof so that you may not bring the guilt of bloodshed on your house if someone falls from the roof.

9 Do not plant two kinds of seed in your vineyard; if you do, not only the crops you plant but also the fruit of the vineyard will be defiled.[d]

10 Do not plow with an ox and a donkey yoked together.

11 Do not wear clothes of wool and linen woven together.

12 Make tassels on the four corners of the cloak you wear.

Marriage Violations

13 If a man takes a wife and, after lying with her, dislikes her 14 and slanders her and gives her a bad name, saying, "I married this woman, but when I approached her, I did not find proof of her virginity," 15 then the girl's father and mother shall bring proof that she was a virgin to the town elders at the gate. 16 The girl's father will say to the elders, "I gave my daughter in marriage to this man, but he dislikes her. 17 Now he has slandered her and said, 'I did not find your daughter to be a virgin.' But here is the proof of my daughter's virginity." Then her parents shall display the cloth before the elders of the town, 18 and the elders shall take the man and punish him. 19 They shall fine him a hundred shekels of silver[e] and give them to the girl's father, because this man has given an Israelite virgin a bad name. She shall continue to be his wife; he must not divorce her as long as he lives.

20 If, however, the charge is true and no proof of the girl's virginity can be found, 21 she shall be brought to the door of her father's house and there the men of her town shall stone her to death. She has done a disgraceful thing in Israel by being promiscuous while still in her father's house. You must purge the evil from among you.

22 If a man is found sleeping with another man's wife, both the man who slept with her and the woman must die. You must purge the evil from Israel.

23 If a man happens to meet in a town a virgin pledged to be married and he sleeps with her, 24 you shall take both of them to the gate of that town and stone them to death—the girl because she was in a town and did not scream for help, and the man because he violated another man's wife. You must purge the evil from among you.

25 But if out in the country a man happens to meet a girl pledged to be married and rapes her, only the man who has done this shall die. 26 Do nothing to the girl; she has committed no sin deserving death. This case is like that of someone who attacks and murders his neighbor, 27 for the man found the girl out in the country, and though the betrothed girl screamed, there was no one to rescue her.

d 9 Or *be forfeited to the sanctuary*   e 19 That is, about 2 1/2
pounds (about 1 kilogram)

King James

28 ¶ If a man find a damsel *that is* a virgin, which is not betrothed, and lay hold on her, and lie with her, and they be found;

29Then the man that lay with her shall give unto the damsel's father fifty *shekels* of silver, and she shall be his wife; because he hath humbled her, he may not put her away all his days.

30 ¶ A man shall not take his father's wife, nor discover his father's skirt.

Persons to be excluded

23 HE THAT is wounded in the stones, or hath his privy member cut off, shall not enter into the congregation of the LORD.

2A bastard shall not enter into the congregation of the LORD; even to his tenth generation shall he not enter into the congregation of the LORD.

3An Ammonite or Moabite shall not enter into the congregation of the LORD; even to their tenth generation shall they not enter into the congregation of the LORD for ever:

4Because they met you not with bread and with water in the way, when ye came forth out of Egypt; and because they hired against thee Balaam the son of Beor of Pethor of Mesopotamia, to curse thee.

5Nevertheless the LORD thy God would not hearken unto Balaam; but the LORD thy God turned the curse into a blessing unto thee, because the LORD thy God loved thee.

6Thou shalt not seek their peace nor their wprosperity all thy days for ever.

7 ¶ Thou shalt not abhor an Edomite; for he *is* thy brother: thou shalt not abhor an Egyptian; because thou wast a stranger in his land.

8The children that are begotten of them shall enter into the congregation of the LORD in their third generation.

Camp sanitation in wartime

9 ¶ When the host goeth forth against thine enemies, then keep thee from every wicked thing.

10 ¶ If there be among you any man, that is not clean by reason of uncleanness that chanceth him by night, then shall he go abroad out of the camp, he shall not come within the camp:

11But it shall be, when evening xcometh on, he shall wash *himself* with water: and when the sun is down, he shall come into the camp *again*.

12 ¶ Thou shalt have a place also without the camp, whither thou shalt go forth abroad:

13And thou shalt have a paddle upon thy weapon; and it shall be, when thou ywilt ease thyself abroad, thou shalt dig therewith, and shalt turn back and cover that which cometh from thee:

14For the LORD thy God walketh in the midst of thy camp, to deliver thee, and to give up thine enemies before thee; therefore shall thy camp be holy: that he see no zunclean thing in thee, and turn away from thee.

Various laws

15 ¶ Thou shalt not deliver unto his master the servant which is escaped from his master unto thee:

16He shall dwell with thee, *even* among you, in that place which he shall choose in one of thy gates, where it aliketh him best: thou shalt not oppress him.

17 ¶ There shall be no bwhore of the daughters of Israel, nor a sodomite of the sons of Israel.

18Thou shalt not bring the hire of a whore, or the price of a dog, into the house of the LORD thy God for any vow: for even both these *are* abomination unto the LORD thy God.

Amplified

28If a man finds a girl who is a virgin, who is not betrothed, and he seizes her and lies with her and they are found,

29Then the man who lay with her shall give to the girl's father fifty shekels of silver, and she shall be his wife, because he has violated her; he may not divorce her all his days.

30A man shall not take his father's former wife, nor shall he uncover her who belongs to his father.

23 HE WHO is wounded in the testicles, or has been made a eunuch, shall not enter into the congregation of the Lord.

2A person begotten out of wedlock shall not enter into the assembly of the Lord; even to his tenth generation shall his descendants not enter into the congregation of the Lord.

3An Ammonite or hMoabite shall not enter into the congregation of the Lord; even to their tenth generation their descendants shall not enter into the assembly of the Lord forever,

4Because they did not meet you with food and water on the way when you came forth out of Egypt, and because they hired Balaam son of Beor of Pethor of Mesopotamia against you to curse you.

5Nevertheless, the Lord your God would not listen to Balaam, but the Lord your God turned the curse into a blessing to you, because the Lord your God loves you.

6You shall not seek their peace or their prosperity all your days forever.

7You shall not abhor an Edomite, for he is your brother [Esau's descendant]. You shall not abhor an Egyptian, because you were a stranger *and* temporary resident in his land.

8Their children may enter into the congregation of the Lord in their third generation.

9When you go forth against your enemies and are in camp, you shall keep yourselves from every evil thing.

10If there is among you any man who is not clean by reason of what happens to him at night, then he shall go outside the camp; he shall not come within the camp;

11But when evening comes he shall bathe himself in water, and when the sun is down he may return to the camp.

12You shall have a place also outside the camp to which you shall go [as a comfort station];

13And you shall have a paddle *or* shovel among your weapons, and when you sit down outside [to relieve yourself], you shall dig a hole with it and turn back and cover up what has come from you.

14For the Lord your God walks in the midst of your camp to deliver you and to give up your enemies before you. Therefore shall your camp be holy, that He may see nothing indecent among you and turn away from you.

15You shall not give up to his master a servant who has escaped from his master to you.

16He shall dwell with you in your midst wherever he chooses in one of your towns where it pleases him best. You shall not defraud *or* oppress him.

17There shall be no cult prostitute among the daughters of Israel, neither shall there be a cult prostitute (a sodomite) among the sons of Israel.

18You shall not bring the hire of a harlot or the price of a dog (a sodomite) into the house of the Lord your God as payment of a vow, for both of these [the gift and the giver] are an abomination to the Lord your God.

hIt must be remembered that according to the Jewish law the children followed the father, not the mother. [Take the family of Boaz, for example. Although Boaz's wife Ruth was a Moabitess, his family was considered Israelite, including his wife]. The case of Ruth would not, therefore, be touched by this precept (Charles J. Ellicott, *A Bible Commentary*).

---

wHeb. *good*   xHeb. *turneth toward*   yHeb. *sittest down*   zHeb. *nakedness of anything*   aHeb. *is good for him*   bOr, *sodomitess*

New American Standard

28 ¶ "If a man finds a girl who is a virgin, who is not engaged, and seizes her and lies with her and they are discovered,

29 then the man who lay with her shall give to the girl's father fifty *shekels* of silver, and she shall become his wife because he has violated her; he cannot divorce her all his days.

30 ¶ "A man shall not take his father's wife so that he will not uncover his father's skirt.

Persons Excluded from the Assembly

23 "NO ONE who is emasculated or has his male organ cut off shall enter the assembly of the LORD.

2 "No one of illegitimate birth shall enter the assembly of the LORD; none of his *descendants*, even to the tenth generation, shall enter the assembly of the LORD.

3 "No Ammonite or Moabite shall enter the assembly of the LORD; none of their *descendants*, even to the tenth generation, shall ever enter the assembly of the LORD,

4 because they did not meet you with food and water on the way when you came out of Egypt, and because they hired against you Balaam the son of Beor from Pethor of Mesopotamia, to curse you.

5 "Nevertheless, the LORD your God was not willing to listen to Balaam, but the LORD your God turned the curse into a blessing for you because the LORD your God loves you.

6 "You shall never seek their peace or their prosperity all your days.

7 ¶ "You shall not detest an Edomite, for he is your brother; you shall not detest an Egyptian, because you were an alien in his land.

8 "The sons of the third generation who are born to them may enter the assembly of the LORD.

9 ¶ "When you go out as an army against your enemies, you shall keep yourself from every evil thing.

10 ¶ "If there is among you any man who is unclean because of a nocturnal emission, then he must go outside the camp; he may not reenter the camp.

11 "But it shall be when evening approaches, he shall bathe himself with water, and at sundown he may reenter the camp.

12 ¶ "You shall also have a place outside the camp and go out there,

13 and you shall have a spade among your tools, and it shall be when you sit down outside, you shall dig with it and shall turn to cover up your excrement.

14 "Since the LORD your God walks in the midst of your camp to deliver you and to defeat your enemies before you, therefore your camp must be holy; and He must not see anything indecent among you or He will turn away from you.

15 ¶ "You shall not hand over to his master a slave who has escaped from his master to you.

16 "He shall live with you in your midst, in the place which he shall choose in one of your towns where it pleases him; you shall not mistreat him.

17 ¶ "None of the daughters of Israel shall be a cult prostitute, nor shall any of the sons of Israel be a cult prostitute.

18 "You shall not bring the hire of a harlot or the wages of a *a*dog into the house of the LORD your God for any votive offering, for both of these are an abomination to the LORD your God.

New International

28 If a man happens to meet a virgin who is not pledged to be married and rapes her and they are discovered, 29 he shall pay the girl's father fifty shekels of silver.*f* He must marry the girl, for he has violated her. He can never divorce her as long as he lives.

30 A man is not to marry his father's wife; he must not dishonor his father's bed.

Exclusion From the Assembly

23 NO ONE who has been emasculated by crushing or cutting may enter the assembly of the LORD.

2 No one born of a forbidden marriage*g* nor any of his descendants may enter the assembly of the LORD, even down to the tenth generation.

3 No Ammonite or Moabite or any of his descendants may enter the assembly of the LORD, even down to the tenth generation. 4 For they did not come to meet you with bread and water on your way when you came out of Egypt, and they hired Balaam son of Beor from Pethor in Aram Naharaim*h* to pronounce a curse on you. 5 However, the LORD your God would not listen to Balaam but turned the curse into a blessing for you, because the LORD your God loves you. 6 Do not seek a treaty of friendship with them as long as you live.

7 Do not abhor an Edomite, for he is your brother. Do not abhor an Egyptian, because you lived as an alien in his country. 8 The third generation of children born to them may enter the assembly of the LORD.

Uncleanness in the Camp

9 When you are encamped against your enemies, keep away from everything impure. 10 If one of your men is unclean because of a nocturnal emission, he is to go outside the camp and stay there. 11 But as evening approaches he is to wash himself, and at sunset he may return to the camp.

12 Designate a place outside the camp where you can go to relieve yourself. 13 As part of your equipment have something to dig with, and when you relieve yourself, dig a hole and cover up your excrement. 14 For the LORD your God moves about in your camp to protect you and to deliver your enemies to you. Your camp must be holy, so that he will not see among you anything indecent and turn away from you.

Miscellaneous Laws

15 If a slave has taken refuge with you, do not hand him over to his master. 16 Let him live among you wherever he likes and in whatever town he chooses. Do not oppress him.

17 No Israelite man or woman is to become a shrine prostitute. 18 You must not bring the earnings of a female prostitute or of a male prostitute*i* into the house of the LORD your God to pay any vow, because the LORD your God detests them both.

---

f29 That is, about 1 1/4 pounds (about 0.6 kilogram)   g2 Or one of illegitimate birth   h4 That is, Northwest Mesopotamia   i18 Hebrew of a dog

*a*I.e. male prostitute, sodomite

King James

19 ¶ Thou shalt not lend upon usury to thy brother; usury of money, usury of victuals, usury of any thing that is lent upon usury:

20 Unto a stranger thou mayest lend upon usury; but unto thy brother thou shalt not lend upon usury: that the LORD thy God may bless thee in all that thou settest thine hand to in the land whither thou goest to possess it.

21 ¶ When thou shalt vow a vow unto the LORD thy God, thou shalt not slack to pay it: for the LORD thy God will surely require it of thee; and it would be sin in thee.

22 But if thou shalt forbear to vow, it shall be no sin in thee.

23 That which is gone out of thy lips thou shalt keep and perform; *even* a freewill offering, according as thou hast vowed unto the LORD thy God, which thou hast promised with thy mouth.

24 ¶ When thou comest into thy neighbour's vineyard, then thou mayest eat grapes thy fill at thine own pleasure; but thou shalt not put *any* in thy vessel.

25 When thou comest into the standing corn of thy neighbour, then thou mayest pluck the ears with thine hand; but thou shalt not move a sickle unto thy neighbour's standing corn.

24 WHEN A man hath taken a wife, and married her, and it come to pass that she find no favour in his eyes, because he hath found c some uncleanness in her: then let him write her a bill of d divorcement, and give *it* in her hand, and send her out of his house.

2 And when she is departed out of his house, she may go and be another man's *wife.*

3 And *if* the latter husband hate her, and write her a bill of divorcement, and giveth *it* in her hand, and sendeth her out of his house; or if the latter husband die, which took her *to be* his wife;

4 Her former husband, which sent her away, may not take her again to be his wife, after that she is defiled; for that *is* abomination before the LORD: and thou shalt not cause the land to sin, which the LORD thy God giveth thee *for* an inheritance.

5 ¶ When a man hath taken a new wife, he shall not go out to war, e neither shall he be charged with any business: *but* he shall be free at home one year, and shall cheer up his wife which he hath taken.

6 ¶ No man shall take the nether or the upper millstone to pledge: for he taketh *a man's* life to pledge.

7 ¶ If a man be found stealing any of his brethren of the children of Israel, and maketh merchandise of him, or selleth him; then that thief shall die; and thou shalt put evil away from among you.

8 ¶ Take heed in the plague of leprosy, that thou observe diligently, and do according to all that the priests the Levites shall teach you: as I commanded them, *so* ye shall observe to do.

9 Remember what the LORD thy God did unto Miriam by the way, after that ye were come forth out of Egypt.

10 ¶ When thou dost f lend thy brother any thing, thou shalt not go into his house to fetch his pledge.

11 Thou shalt stand abroad, and the man to whom thou dost lend shall bring out the pledge abroad unto thee.

12 And if the man *be* poor, thou shalt not sleep with his pledge:

13 In any case thou shalt deliver him the pledge again when the sun goeth down, that he may sleep in his own raiment, and bless thee: and it shall be righteousness unto thee before the LORD thy God.

14 ¶ Thou shalt not oppress an hired servant *that is* poor and needy, *whether he be* of thy brethren, or of thy strangers that *are* in thy land within thy gates:

Amplified

19 You shall not lend on interest to your brother—interest on money, on victuals, on anything that is lent for interest.

20 You may lend on interest to a foreigner, but to your brother you shall not lend on interest, that the Lord your God may bless you in all that you undertake in the land to which you go to possess it.

21 When you make a vow to the Lord your God, you shall not be slack in paying it, for the Lord your God will surely require it of you, and slackness would be sin in you.

22 But if you refrain from vowing, it will not be sin in you.

23 The vow which has passed your lips you shall be watchful to perform, a voluntary offering which you have made to the Lord your God, which you have promised with your mouth.

24 When you come into your neighbor's vineyard, you may eat your fill of grapes, as many as you please, but you shall not put any in your vessel.

25 When you come into the standing grain of your neighbor, you may pluck the ears with your hand, but you shall not put a sickle to your neighbor's standing grain.

24 WHEN A man takes a wife and marries her, if then she finds no favor in his eyes because he has found some indecency in her, and he writes her a bill of divorce, puts it in her hand, and sends her out of his house,

2 And when she departs out of his house she goes and marries another man,

3 And if the latter husband dislikes her and writes her a bill of divorce and puts it in her hand and sends her out of his house, or if the latter husband dies, who took her as his wife,

4 Then her former husband, who sent her away, may not take her again to be his wife after she is defiled. For that is an abomination before the Lord; and you shall not bring guilt upon the land which the Lord your God gives you as an inheritance.

5 When a man is newly married, he shall not go out with the army or be charged with any business; he shall be free at home one year and shall cheer his wife whom he has taken.

6 No man shall take a mill or an upper millstone in pledge, for he would be taking a life in pledge.

7 If a man is found kidnapping any of his brethren of the Israelites and treats him as a slave *or* a servant or sells him, then that thief shall die. So you shall put evil from among you.

8 Take heed in the plague of leprosy, that you watch diligently and do according to all that the Levitical priests shall teach you. As I commanded them, so you shall be watchful and do. [Lev. 13:14, 15.]

9 Remember [earnestly] what the Lord your God did to Miriam on the way after you had come out of Egypt. [Num. 12:10.]

10 When you lend your brother anything, you shall not go into his house to get his pledge.

11 You shall stand outside and the man to whom you lend shall bring the pledge out to you.

12 And if the man is poor, you shall not keep his pledge overnight.

13 You shall surely restore to him the pledge at sunset, that he may sleep in his garment and bless you; and it shall be credited to you as righteousness (rightness and justice) before the Lord your God.

14 You shall not oppress *or* extort from a hired servant who is poor and needy, whether he is of your brethren or of your strangers *and* sojourners who are in your land inside your towns.

---

c Heb. *matter of nakedness thing shall pass upon him*   d Heb. *cutting off*   e Heb. *not any*   f Heb. *lend the loan of any thing to*

New American Standard

19 ¶ "You shall not charge interest to your countrymen: interest on money, food, *or* anything that may be loaned at interest.

20"You may charge interest to a foreigner, but to your countrymen you shall not charge interest, so that the LORD your God may bless you in all that you undertake in the land which you are about to enter to possess.

21 ¶ "When you make a vow to the LORD your God, you shall not delay to pay it, for it would be sin in you, and the LORD your God will surely require it of you.

22"However, if you refrain from vowing, it would not be sin in you.

23"You shall be careful to perform what goes out from your lips, just as you have voluntarily vowed to the LORD your God, what you have promised.

24 ¶ "When you enter your neighbor's vineyard, then you may eat grapes until you are fully satisfied, but you shall not put any in your basket.

25 ¶ "When you enter your neighbor's standing grain, then you may pluck the heads with your hand, but you shall not wield a sickle in your neighbor's standing grain.

Law of Divorce

24 "WHEN A man takes a wife and marries her, and it happens that she finds no favor in his eyes because he has found some indecency in her, and he writes her a certificate of divorce and puts *it* in her hand and sends her out from his house,

2 and she leaves his house and goes and becomes another man's *wife,*

3 and if the latter husband turns against her and writes her a certificate of divorce and puts *it* in her hand and sends her out of his house, or if the latter husband dies who took her to be his wife,

4 *then* her former husband who sent her away is not allowed to take her again to be his wife, since she has been defiled; for that is an abomination before the LORD, and you shall not bring sin on the land which the LORD your God gives you as an inheritance.

5 ¶ "When a man takes a new wife, he shall not go out with the army nor be charged with any duty; he shall be free at home one year and shall give happiness to his wife whom he has taken.

Sundry Laws

6 ¶ "No one shall take a handmill or an upper millstone in pledge, for he would be taking a life in pledge.

7 ¶ "If a man is caught kidnapping any of his countrymen of the sons of Israel, and he deals with him violently or sells him, then that thief shall die; so you shall purge the evil from among you.

8 ¶ "Be careful against an infection of leprosy, that you diligently observe and do according to all that the Levitical priests teach you; as I have commanded them, so you shall be careful to do.

9"Remember what the LORD your God did to Miriam on the way as you came out of Egypt.

10 ¶ "When you make your neighbor a loan of any sort, you shall not enter his house to take his pledge.

11"You shall remain outside, and the man to whom you make the loan shall bring the pledge out to you.

12"If he is a poor man, you shall not sleep with his pledge.

13"When the sun goes down you shall surely return the pledge to him, that he may sleep in his cloak and bless you; and it will be righteousness for you before the LORD your God.

14 ¶ "You shall not oppress a hired servant *who is* poor and needy, whether *he is* one of your countrymen or one of your aliens who is in your land in your towns.

New International

19Do not charge your brother interest, whether on money or food or anything else that may earn interest. 20You may charge a foreigner interest, but not a brother Israelite, so that the LORD your God may bless you in everything you put your hand to in the land you are entering to possess.

21If you make a vow to the LORD your God, do not be slow to pay it, for the LORD your God will certainly demand it of you and you will be guilty of sin. 22But if you refrain from making a vow, you will not be guilty. 23Whatever your lips utter you must be sure to do, because you made your vow freely to the LORD your God with your own mouth.

24If you enter your neighbor's vineyard, you may eat all the grapes you want, but do not put any in your basket. 25If you enter your neighbor's grainfield, you may pick kernels with your hands, but you must not put a sickle to his standing grain.

24 IF A man marries a woman who becomes displeasing to him because he finds something indecent about her, and he writes her a certificate of divorce, gives it to her and sends her from his house, 2and if after she leaves his house she becomes the wife of another man, 3and her second husband dislikes her and writes her a certificate of divorce, gives it to her and sends her from his house, or if he dies, 4then her first husband, who divorced her, is not allowed to marry her again after she has been defiled. That would be detestable in the eyes of the LORD. Do not bring sin upon the land the LORD your God is giving you as an inheritance.

5If a man has recently married, he must not be sent to war or have any other duty laid on him. For one year he is to be free to stay at home and bring happiness to the wife he has married.

6Do not take a pair of millstones—not even the upper one—as security for a debt, because that would be taking a man's livelihood as security.

7If a man is caught kidnapping one of his brother Israelites and treats him as a slave or sells him, the kidnapper must die. You must purge the evil from among you.

8In cases of leprous[j] diseases be very careful to do exactly as the priests, who are Levites, instruct you. You must follow carefully what I have commanded them. 9Remember what the LORD your God did to Miriam along the way after you came out of Egypt.

10When you make a loan of any kind to your neighbor, do not go into his house to get what he is offering as a pledge. 11Stay outside and let the man to whom you are making the loan bring the pledge out to you. 12If the man is poor, do not go to sleep with his pledge in your possession. 13Return his cloak to him by sunset so that he may sleep in it. Then he will thank you, and it will be regarded as a righteous act in the sight of the LORD your God.

14Do not take advantage of a hired man who is poor and needy, whether he is a brother Israelite or an alien living

j 8 The Hebrew word was used for various diseases affecting the skin—not necessarily leprosy.

King James

¹⁵At his day thou shalt give *him* his hire, neither shall the sun go down upon it; for he *is* poor, and ^gsetteth his heart upon it: lest he cry against thee unto the LORD, and it be sin unto thee.

¹⁶The fathers shall not be put to death for the children, neither shall the children be put to death for the fathers: every man shall be put to death for his own sin.

¹⁷ ¶ Thou shalt not pervert the judgment of the stranger, *nor* of the fatherless; nor take a widow's raiment to pledge:

¹⁸But thou shalt remember that thou wast a bondman in Egypt, and the LORD thy God redeemed thee thence: therefore I command thee to do this thing.

¹⁹ ¶ When thou cuttest down thine harvest in thy field, and hast forgot a sheaf in the field, thou shalt not go again to fetch it: it shall be for the stranger, for the fatherless, and for the widow: that the LORD thy God may bless thee in all the work of thine hands.

²⁰When thou beatest thine olive tree, ^hthou shalt not go over the boughs again: it shall be for the stranger, for the fatherless, and for the widow.

²¹When thou gatherest the grapes of thy vineyard, thou shalt not glean *it* ⁱafterward: it shall be for the stranger, for the fatherless, and for the widow.

²²And thou shalt remember that thou wast a bondman in the land of Egypt: therefore I command thee to do this thing.

25 IF THERE be a controversy between men, and they come unto judgment, that *the judges* may judge them; then they shall justify the righteous, and condemn the wicked.

²And it shall be, if the wicked man *be* worthy to be beaten, that the judge shall cause him to lie down, and to be beaten before his face, according to his fault, by a certain number.

³Forty stripes he may give him, *and* not exceed: lest, *if* he should exceed, and beat him above these with many stripes, then thy brother should seem vile unto thee.

⁴ ¶ Thou shalt not muzzle the ox when he ^jtreadeth out *the corn.*

⁵ ¶ If brethren dwell together, and one of them die, and have no child, the wife of the dead shall not marry without unto a stranger: her ^khusband's brother shall go in unto her, and take her to him to wife, and perform the duty of an husband's brother unto her.

⁶And it shall be, *that* the firstborn which she beareth shall succeed in the name of his brother *which is* dead, that his name be not put out of Israel.

⁷And if the man like not to take his ^lbrother's wife, then let his brother's wife go up to the gate unto the elders, and say, My husband's brother refuseth to raise up unto his brother a name in Israel, he will not perform the duty of my husband's brother.

⁸Then the elders of his city shall call him, and speak unto him: and *if* he stand *to it,* and say, I like not to take her;

⁹Then shall his brother's wife come unto him in the presence of the elders, and loose his shoe from off his foot, and spit in his face, and shall answer and say, So shall it be done unto that man that will not build up his brother's house.

¹⁰And his name shall be called in Israel, The house of him that hath his shoe loosed.

¹¹ ¶ When men strive together one with another, and the wife of the one draweth near for to deliver her husband out of the hand of him that smiteth him, and putteth forth her hand, and taketh him by the secrets:

Amplified

¹⁵You shall give him his hire on the day he earns it before the sun goes down, for he is poor, and sets his heart upon it; lest he cry against you to the Lord, and it be sin to you.

¹⁶The fathers shall not be put to death for the children, neither shall the children be put to death for the fathers; only for his own sin shall anyone be put to death.

¹⁷You shall not pervert the justice due the stranger *or* the sojourner or the fatherless, or take a widow's garment in pledge.

¹⁸But you shall [earnestly] remember that you were a slave in Egypt and the Lord your God redeemed you from there; therefore I command you to do this.

¹⁹When you reap your harvest in your field and have forgotten a sheaf in the field, you shall not go back to get it; it shall be for the stranger *and* the sojourner, the fatherless, and the widow, that the Lord your God may bless you in all the work of your hands.

²⁰When you beat your olive tree, do not go over the boughs again; the leavings shall be for the stranger *and* the sojourner, the fatherless, and the widow.

²¹When you gather the grapes of your vineyard, you shall not glean it afterward; it shall be for the stranger *and* the sojourner, the fatherless, and the widow.

²²You shall [earnestly] remember that you were a slave in the land of Egypt; therefore I command you to do this.

25 IF THERE is a controversy between men, and they come into court and the judges decide between them, justifying the innocent and condemning the guilty,

²Then if the guilty man deserves to be beaten, the judge shall cause him to lie down and be beaten in his presence with a certain number of stripes according to his offense.

³Forty stripes may be given him but not more, lest, if he should be beaten with many stripes, your brother should [be treated like a beast and] seem low and worthless to you.

⁴You shall not muzzle the ox when he treads out the grain. [I Cor. 9:9, 10; I Tim. 5:17, 18.]

⁵If brothers live together and one of them dies and has no son, his wife shall not be married outside the family to a stranger [an excluded man]. Her husband's brother shall go in to her and take her as his wife and perform the duty of a husband's brother to her.

⁶And the firstborn son shall succeed to the name of the dead brother, that his name may not be blotted out of Israel.

⁷And if the man does not want to take his brother's wife, then let his brother's wife go up to the gate to the elders, and say, My husband's brother refuses to continue his brother's name in Israel; he will not perform the duty of my husband's brother.

⁸Then the elders of his city shall call him and speak to him. And if he stands firm and says, I do not want to take her,

⁹Then shall his brother's wife come to him in the presence of the elders and pull his shoe off his foot and spit in his face and shall answer, So shall it be done to that man who does not build up his brother's house.

¹⁰And his family shall be called in Israel, The House of Him Whose Shoe Was Loosed.

¹¹When men strive together one with another and the wife of the one draws near to rescue her husband out of the hand of him who is beating him, and puts out her hand and seizes the other man by the private parts,

---

^gHeb. *lifteth his soul unto it* ^hHeb. *thou shalt not bough* it *after thee* ⁱHeb. *after thee* ^jHeb. *thresheth* ^kOr, *next kinsman* ^lOr, *next kinsman's wife*

New American Standard

¹⁵"You shall give him his wages on his day before the sun sets, for he is poor and sets his heart on it; so that he will not cry against you to the LORD and it become sin in you.

¹⁶ ¶ "Fathers shall not be put to death for *their* sons, nor shall sons be put to death for *their* fathers; everyone shall be put to death for his own sin.

¹⁷ ¶ "You shall not pervert the justice due an alien *or* ᵖan orphan, nor take a widow's garment in pledge.

¹⁸"But you shall remember that you were a slave in Egypt, and that the LORD your God redeemed you from there; therefore I am commanding you to do this thing.

¹⁹ ¶ "When you reap your harvest in your field and have forgotten a sheaf in the field, you shall not go back to get it; it shall be for the alien, for the orphan, and for the widow, in order that the LORD your God may bless you in all the work of your hands.

²⁰"When you beat your olive tree, you shall not go over the boughs again; it shall be for the alien, for the orphan, and for the widow.

²¹ ¶ "When you gather the grapes of your vineyard, you shall not go over it again; it shall be for the alien, for the orphan, and for the widow.

²²"You shall remember that you were a slave in the land of Egypt; therefore I am commanding you to do this thing.

Sundry Laws

25 "IF THERE is a dispute between men and they go to court, and the judges decide their case, and they justify the righteous and condemn the wicked,

² then it shall be if the wicked man deserves to be beaten, the judge shall then make him lie down and be beaten in his presence with the number of stripes according to his guilt.

³"He may beat him forty times *but* no more, so that he does not beat him with many more stripes than these and your brother is not degraded in your eyes.

⁴ ¶ "You shall not muzzle the ox while he is threshing.

⁵ ¶ "When brothers live together and one of them dies and has no son, the wife of the deceased shall not be *married* outside *the family* to a strange man. Her husband's brother shall go in to her and take her to himself as wife and perform the duty of a husband's brother to her.

⁶"It shall be that the firstborn whom she bears shall assume the name of his dead brother, so that his name will not be blotted out from Israel.

⁷"But if the man does not desire to take his brother's wife, then his brother's wife shall go up to the gate to the elders and say, 'My husband's brother refuses to establish a name for his brother in Israel; he is not willing to perform the duty of a husband's brother to me.'

⁸"Then the elders of his city shall summon him and speak to him. And *if* he persists and says, 'I do not desire to take her,'

⁹ then his brother's wife shall come to him in the sight of the elders, and pull his sandal off his foot and spit in his face; and she shall declare, 'Thus it is done to the man who does not build up his brother's house.'

¹⁰"In Israel his name shall be called, 'The house of him whose sandal is removed.'

¹¹ ¶ "If *two* men, a man and his countryman, are struggling together, and the wife of one comes near to deliver her husband from the hand of the one who is striking him, and puts out her hand and seizes his genitals,

New International

in one of your towns. ¹⁵Pay him his wages each day before sunset, because he is poor and is counting on it. Otherwise he may cry to the LORD against you, and you will be guilty of sin.

¹⁶Fathers shall not be put to death for their children, nor children put to death for their fathers; each is to die for his own sin.

¹⁷Do not deprive the alien or the fatherless of justice, or take the cloak of the widow as a pledge. ¹⁸Remember that you were slaves in Egypt and the LORD your God redeemed you from there. That is why I command you to do this.

¹⁹When you are harvesting in your field and you overlook a sheaf, do not go back to get it. Leave it for the alien, the fatherless and the widow, so that the LORD your God may bless you in all the work of your hands. ²⁰When you beat the olives from your trees, do not go over the branches a second time. Leave what remains for the alien, the fatherless and the widow. ²¹When you harvest the grapes in your vineyard, do not go over the vines again. Leave what remains for the alien, the fatherless and the widow. ²²Remember that you were slaves in Egypt. That is why I command you to do this.

25 WHEN MEN have a dispute, they are to take it to court and the judges will decide the case, acquitting the innocent and condemning the guilty. ²If the guilty man deserves to be beaten, the judge shall make him lie down and have him flogged in his presence with the number of lashes his crime deserves, ³but he must not give him more than forty lashes. If he is flogged more than that, your brother will be degraded in your eyes.

⁴Do not muzzle an ox while it is treading out the grain.

⁵If brothers are living together and one of them dies without a son, his widow must not marry outside the family. Her husband's brother shall take her and marry her and fulfill the duty of a brother-in-law to her. ⁶The first son she bears shall carry on the name of the dead brother so that his name will not be blotted out from Israel.

⁷However, if a man does not want to marry his brother's wife, she shall go to the elders at the town gate and say, "My husband's brother refuses to carry on his brother's name in Israel. He will not fulfill the duty of a brother-in-law to me." ⁸Then the elders of his town shall summon him and talk to him. If he persists in saying, "I do not want to marry her," ⁹his brother's widow shall go up to him in the presence of the elders, take off one of his sandals, spit in his face and say, "This is what is done to the man who will not build up his brother's family line." ¹⁰That man's line shall be known in Israel as The Family of the Unsandaled.

¹¹If two men are fighting and the wife of one of them comes to rescue her husband from his assailant, and she

---

King James

Amplified

12Then thou shalt cut off her hand, thine eye shall not pity *her.*

13 ¶ Thou shalt not have in thy bag *m*divers weights, a great and a small.

14Thou shalt not have in thine house *n*divers measures, a great and a small.

15*But* thou shalt have a perfect and just weight, a perfect and just measure shalt thou have: that thy days may be lengthened in the land which the LORD thy God giveth thee.

16For all that do such things, *and* all that do unrighteously, *are* an abomination unto the LORD thy God.

17 ¶ Remember what Amalek did unto thee by the way, when ye were come forth out of Egypt;

18How he met thee by the way, and smote the hindmost of thee, *even* all *that were* feeble behind thee, when thou *wast* faint and weary; and he feared not God.

19Therefore it shall be, when the LORD thy God hath given thee rest from all thine enemies round about, in the land which the LORD thy God giveth thee *for* an inheritance to possess it, *that* thou shalt blot out the remembrance of Amalek from under heaven; thou shalt not forget *it.*

Firstfruits and tithes

26 AND IT shall be, when thou *art* come in unto the land which the LORD thy God giveth thee *for* an inheritance, and possessest it, and dwellest therein;

2That thou shalt take of the first of all the fruit of the earth, which thou shalt bring of thy land that the LORD thy God giveth thee, and shalt put *it* in a basket, and shalt go unto the place which the LORD thy God shall choose to place his name there.

3And thou shalt go unto the priest that shall be in those days, and say unto him, I profess this day unto the LORD thy God, that I am come unto the country which the LORD sware unto our fathers for to give us.

4And the priest shall take the basket out of thine hand, and set it down before the altar of the LORD thy God.

5And thou shalt speak and say before the LORD thy God, A Syrian ready to perish *was* my father, and he went down into Egypt, and sojourned there with a few, and became there a nation, great, mighty, and populous:

6And the Egyptians evil entreated us, and afflicted us, and laid upon us hard bondage:

7And when we cried unto the LORD God of our fathers, the LORD heard our voice, and looked on our affliction, and our labour, and our oppression;

8And the LORD brought us forth out of Egypt with a mighty hand, and with an outstretched arm, and with great terribleness, and with signs, and with wonders:

9And he hath brought us into this place, and hath given us this land, *even* a land that floweth with milk and honey.

10And now, behold, I have brought the firstfruits of the land, which thou, O LORD, hast given me. And thou shalt set it before the LORD thy God, and worship before the LORD thy God:

11And thou shalt rejoice in every good *thing* which the LORD thy God hath given unto thee, and unto thine house, thou, and the Levite, and the stranger that *is* among you.

12 ¶ When thou hast made an end of tithing all the tithes of thine increase the third year, *which is* the year of tithing, and hast given *it* unto the Levite, the stranger, the fatherless, and the widow, that they may eat within thy gates, and be filled;

12Then you shall cut off her hand; your eyes shall not pity her.

13You shall not have in your bag true and false weights, a large and a small.

14You shall not have in your house true and false measures, a large and a small.

15But you shall have a perfect and just weight and a perfect and just measure, that your days may be prolonged in the land which the Lord your God gives you.

16For all who do such things, all who do unrighteously, are an abomination to the Lord your God.

17Remember what Amalek did to you on the way when you had come forth from Egypt;

18How he did not fear God, but when you were faint and weary he attacked you along the way and cut off all the stragglers at your rear. [Exod. 17:14.]

19Therefore when the Lord your God has given you rest from all your enemies round about in the land which the Lord your God gives you to possess as an inheritance, you shall blot out the remembrance of Amalek from under the heavens; you must not forget.

26 WHEN YOU have come into the land which the Lord your God gives you as an inheritance and possess it and live in it,

2You shall take some of the first of all the produce of the soil which you harvest from the land the Lord your God gives you and put it in a basket, and go to the place [the sanctuary] which the Lord your God has chosen as the abiding place for His Name [and His Presence].

3And you shall go to the priest who is in office in those days, and say to him, I give thanks this day to the Lord your God that I have come to the land which the Lord swore to our fathers to give us.

4And the priest shall take the basket from your hand and set it down before the altar of the Lord your God.

5And you shall say before the Lord your God, A wandering *and* lost Aramean ready to perish was my father [Jacob], and he went down into Egypt and sojourned there, few in number, and he became there a nation, great, mighty, and numerous.

6And the Egyptians treated us very badly and afflicted us and laid upon us hard bondage.

7And when we cried to the Lord, the God of our fathers, the Lord heard our voice and looked on our affliction and our labor and our [cruel] oppression;

8And the Lord brought us forth out of Egypt with a mighty hand and with an outstretched arm, and with great (awesome) power and with signs and with wonders;

9And He brought us into this place and gave us this land, a land flowing with milk and honey.

10And now, behold, I bring the firstfruits of the ground which You, O Lord, have given me. And you shall set it down before the Lord your God and worship before the Lord your God;

11And you and the Levite and the stranger *and* the sojourner among you shall rejoice in all the good which the Lord your God has given you and your household.

12When you have finished paying all the tithe of the your produce the third year, which is the year of tithing, and have given it to the Levite, the stranger *and* the sojourner, the fatherless, and to the widow, that they may eat within your towns and be filled,

---

m Heb. *a stone and a stone*   *n* Heb. *an ephah and an ephah*

New American Standard

¹² then you shall cut off her hand; you shall not show pity.

¹³ ¶ "You shall not have in your bag differing weights, a large and a small.

¹⁴"You shall not have in your house differing measures, a large and a small.

¹⁵"You shall have a full and just weight; you shall have a full and just measure, that your days may be prolonged in the land which the LORD your God gives you.

¹⁶"For everyone who does these things, everyone who acts unjustly is an abomination to the LORD your God.

¹⁷ ¶ "Remember what Amalek did to you along the way when you came out from Egypt,

¹⁸ how he met you along the way and attacked among you all the stragglers at your rear when you were faint and weary; and he did not *q*fear God.

¹⁹"Therefore it shall come about when the LORD your God has given you rest from all your surrounding enemies, in the land which the LORD your God gives you as an inheritance to possess, you shall blot out the memory of Amalek from under heaven; you must not forget.

Offering First Fruits

26 "THEN IT shall be, when you enter the land which the LORD your God gives you as an inheritance, and you possess it and live in it,

² that you shall take some of the first of all the produce of the ground which you bring in from your land that the LORD your God gives you, and you shall put *it* in a basket and go to the place where the LORD your God chooses to establish His name.

³"You shall go to the priest who is in office at that time and say to him, 'I declare this day to the LORD my God that I have entered the land which the LORD swore to our fathers to give us.'

⁴"Then the priest shall take the basket from your hand and set it down before the altar of the LORD your God.

⁵"You shall answer and say before the LORD your God, 'My father was a wandering Aramean, and he went down to Egypt and sojourned there, few in number; but there he became a great, mighty and populous nation.

⁶ 'And the Egyptians treated us harshly and afflicted us, and imposed hard labor on us.

⁷ 'Then we cried to the LORD, the God of our fathers, and the LORD heard our voice and saw our affliction and our toil and our oppression;

⁸ and the LORD brought us out of Egypt with a mighty hand and an outstretched arm and with great terror and with signs and wonders;

⁹ and He has brought us to this place and has given us this land, a land flowing with milk and honey.

¹⁰ 'Now behold, I have brought the first of the produce of the ground which You, O LORD have given me.' And you shall set it down before the LORD your God, and worship before the LORD your God;

¹¹ and you and the Levite and the alien who is among you shall rejoice in all the good which the LORD your God has given you and your household.

¹² ¶ "When you have finished paying all the tithe of your increase in the third year, the year of tithing, then you shall give it to the Levite, to the stranger, to the orphan and to the widow, that they may eat in your towns and be satisfied.

New International

reaches out and seizes him by his private parts, ¹²you shall cut off her hand. Show her no pity.

¹³Do not have two differing weights in your bag—one heavy, one light. ¹⁴Do not have two differing measures in your house—one large, one small. ¹⁵You must have accurate and honest weights and measures, so that you may live long in the land the LORD your God is giving you. ¹⁶For the LORD your God detests anyone who does these things, anyone who deals dishonestly.

¹⁷Remember what the Amalekites did to you along the way when you came out of Egypt. ¹⁸When you were weary and worn out, they met you on your journey and cut off all who were lagging behind; they had no fear of God. ¹⁹When the LORD your God gives you rest from all the enemies around you in the land he is giving you to possess as an inheritance, you shall blot out the memory of Amalek from under heaven. Do not forget!

Firstfruits and Tithes

26 WHEN YOU have entered the land the LORD your God is giving you as an inheritance and have taken possession of it and settled in it, ²take some of the firstfruits of all that you produce from the soil of the land the LORD your God is giving you and put them in a basket. Then go to the place the LORD your God will choose as a dwelling for his Name ³and say to the priest in office at the time, "I declare today to the LORD your God that I have come to the land the LORD swore to our forefathers to give us." ⁴The priest shall take the basket from your hands and set it down in front of the altar of the LORD your God. ⁵Then you shall declare before the LORD your God: "My father was a wandering Aramean, and he went down into Egypt with a few people and lived there and became a great nation, powerful and numerous. ⁶But the Egyptians mistreated us and made us suffer, putting us to hard labor. ⁷Then we cried out to the LORD, the God of our fathers, and the LORD heard our voice and saw our misery, toil and oppression. ⁸So the LORD brought us out of Egypt with a mighty hand and an outstretched arm, with great terror and with miraculous signs and wonders. ⁹He brought us to this place and gave us this land, a land flowing with milk and honey; ¹⁰and now I bring the firstfruits of the soil that you, O LORD, have given me." Place the basket before the LORD your God and bow down before him. ¹¹And you and the Levites and the aliens among you shall rejoice in all the good things the LORD your God has given to you and your household.

¹²When you have finished setting aside a tenth of all your produce in the third year, the year of the tithe, you shall give it to the Levite, the alien, the fatherless and the widow, so that they may eat in your towns and be satisfied.

---

q Or *reverence*

King James

¹³Then thou shalt say before the LORD thy God, I have brought away the hallowed things out of *mine* house, and also have given them unto the Levite, and unto the stranger, to the fatherless, and to the widow, according to all thy commandments which thou hast commanded me: I have not transgressed thy commandments, neither have I forgotten *them:*

¹⁴I have not eaten thereof in my mourning, neither have I taken away *aught* thereof for *any* unclean *use*, nor given *aught* thereof for the dead: *but* I have hearkened to the voice of the LORD my God, *and* have done according to all that thou hast commanded me.

¹⁵Look down from thy holy habitation, from heaven, and bless thy people Israel, and the land which thou hast given us, as thou swarest unto our fathers, a land that floweth with milk and honey.

¹⁶ ¶ This day the LORD thy God hath commanded thee to do these statutes and judgments: thou shalt therefore keep and do them with all thine heart, and with all thy soul.

¹⁷Thou hast avouched the LORD this day to be thy God, and to walk in his ways, and to keep his statutes, and his commandments, and his judgments, and to hearken unto his voice:

¹⁸And the LORD hath avouched thee this day to be his peculiar people, as he hath promised thee, and that *thou* shouldest keep all his commandments;

¹⁹And to make thee high above all nations which he hath made, in praise, and in name, and in honour; and that thou mayest be an holy people unto the LORD thy God, as he hath spoken.

The altar at mount Ebal

27 AND MOSES with the elders of Israel commanded the people, saying, Keep all the commandments which I command you this day.

²And it shall be on the day when ye shall pass over Jordan unto the land which the LORD thy God giveth thee, that thou shalt set thee up great stones, and plaster them with plaster:

³And thou shalt write upon them all the words of this law, when thou art passed over, that thou mayest go in unto the land which the LORD thy God giveth thee, a land that floweth with milk and honey; as the LORD God of thy fathers hath promised thee.

⁴Therefore it shall be when ye be gone over Jordan, *that* ye shall set up these stones, which I command you this day, in mount Ebal, and thou shalt plaster them with plaster.

⁵And there shalt thou build an altar unto the LORD thy God, an altar of stones: thou shalt not lift up *any* iron *tool* upon them.

⁶Thou shalt build the altar of the LORD thy God of whole stones: and thou shalt offer burnt offerings thereon unto the LORD thy God:

⁷And thou shalt offer peace offerings, and shalt eat there, and rejoice before the LORD thy God.

⁸And thou shalt write upon the stones all the words of this law very plainly.

⁹ ¶ And Moses and the priests the Levites spake unto all Israel, saying, Take heed, and hearken, O Israel; this day thou art become the people of the LORD thy God.

¹⁰Thou shalt therefore obey the voice of the LORD thy God, and do his commandments and his statutes, which I command thee this day.

¹¹ ¶ And Moses charged the people the same day, saying,

¹²These shall stand upon mount Gerizim to bless the people, when ye are come over Jordan; Simeon, and Levi, and Judah, and Issachar, and Joseph, and Benjamin:

Amplified

¹³Then you shall say before the Lord your God, I have brought the hallowed things (the tithe) out of my house and moreover have given them to the Levite, to the stranger *and* the sojourner, to the fatherless, and to the widow, according to all Your commandments which You have commanded me; I have not transgressed any of Your commandments, neither have I forgotten them.

¹⁴I have not eaten of the tithe in my mourning [making the tithe unclean], nor have I handled any of it when I was unclean, nor given any of it to the dead. I have hearkened to the voice of the Lord my God; I have done according to all that You have commanded me.

¹⁵Look down from Your holy habitation, from heaven, and bless Your people Israel and the land which You have given us as You swore to our fathers, a land flowing with milk and honey.

¹⁶This day the Lord your God has commanded you to do these statutes and ordinances. Therefore you shall keep and do them with all your [mind and] heart and with all your being.

¹⁷You have [openly] declared the Lord this day to be your God, [pledging] to walk in His ways, to keep His statutes and His commandments and His precepts, and to hearken to His voice.

¹⁸And the Lord has declared this day that you are His peculiar people as He promised you, and you are to keep all His commandments;

¹⁹And He will make you high above all nations which He has made, in praise and in fame and in honor, and that you shall be a holy people to the Lord your God, as He has spoken.

27 AND MOSES with the elders of Israel commanded the people, Keep all the commandments with which I charge you today.

²And on the day when you pass over the Jordan to the land which the Lord your God gives you, you shall set up great stones and cover them with plaster.

³And you shall write on them all the words of this law when you have passed over, that you may go into the land which the Lord your God is giving you, a land flowing with milk and honey, as the Lord, the God of your fathers, has promised you.

⁴And when you have gone over the Jordan, you shall set up these stones, as I command you this day, on Mount Ebal, and coat them with plaster.

⁵And there you shall build an altar to the Lord your God, an altar of stones; you shall not lift up any iron tool upon them.

⁶You shall build the altar of the Lord your God of whole stones and offer burnt offerings on it to Him;

⁷And you shall offer peace offerings, and eat there and rejoice before the Lord your God.

⁸And you shall write upon the stones all the words of this law very plainly.

⁹And Moses and the Levitical priests said to all Israel, Keep silence and hear, O Israel! This day you have become the people of the Lord your God.

¹⁰So you shall obey the voice of the Lord your God and do His commandments and statutes which I command you today.

¹¹And Moses charged the people the same day, saying,

¹²These [tribes] shall stand on Mount Gerizim to bless the people, when you have passed over the Jordan: Simeon, Levi, Judah, Issachar, Joseph's [sons], and Benjamin.

New American Standard

13"You shall say before the LORD your God, 'I have removed the sacred *portion* from *my* house, and also have given it to the Levite and the alien, the orphan and the widow, according to all Your commandments which You have commanded me; I have not transgressed or forgotten any of Your commandments.

14'I have not eaten of it while mourning, nor have I removed any of it while I was unclean, nor offered any of it to the dead. I have listened to the voice of the LORD my God; I have done according to all that You have commanded me.

15'Look down from Your holy habitation, from heaven, and bless Your people Israel, and the ground which You have given us, a land flowing with milk and honey, as You swore to our fathers.'

16 ¶ "This day the LORD your God commands you to do these statutes and ordinances. You shall therefore be careful to do them with all your heart and with all your soul.

17"You have today declared the LORD to be your God, and that you would walk in His ways and keep His statutes, His commandments and His ordinances, and listen to His voice.

18"The LORD has today declared you to be His people, a treasured possession, as He promised you, and that you should keep all His commandments;

19 and that He will set you high above all nations which He has made, for praise, fame, and honor; and that you shall be a consecrated people to the LORD your God, as He has spoken."

The Curses of Mount Ebal

27 THEN MOSES and the elders of Israel charged the people, saying, "Keep all the commandments which I command you today.

2"So it shall be on the day when you cross the Jordan to the land which the LORD your God gives you, that you shall set up for yourself large stones and coat them with lime

3 and write on them all the words of this law, when you cross over, so that you may enter the land which the LORD your God gives you, a land flowing with milk and honey, as the LORD, the God of your fathers, promised you.

4"So it shall be when you cross the Jordan, you shall set up on Mount Ebal, these stones, as I am commanding you today, and you shall coat them with lime.

5"Moreover, you shall build there an altar to the LORD your God, an altar of stones; you shall not wield an iron *tool* on them.

6"You shall build the altar of the LORD your God of uncut stones, and you shall offer on it burnt offerings to the LORD your God;

7 and you shall sacrifice peace offerings and eat there, and rejoice before the LORD your God.

8"You shall write on the stones all the words of this law very distinctly."

9 ¶ Then Moses and the Levitical priests spoke to all Israel, saying, "Be silent and listen, O Israel! This day you have become a people for the LORD your God.

10"You shall therefore obey the LORD your God, and do His commandments and His statutes which I command you today."

11 ¶ Moses also charged the people on that day, saying,

12"When you cross the Jordan, these shall stand on Mount Gerizim to bless the people: Simeon, Levi, Judah, Issachar, Joseph, and Benjamin.

New International

13Then say to the LORD your God: "I have removed from my house the sacred portion and have given it to the Levite, the alien, the fatherless and the widow, according to all you commanded. I have not turned aside from your commands nor have I forgotten any of them. 14I have not eaten any of the sacred portion while I was in mourning, nor have I removed any of it while I was unclean, nor have I offered any of it to the dead. I have obeyed the LORD my God; I have done everything you commanded me. 15Look down from heaven, your holy dwelling place, and bless your people Israel and the land you have given us as you promised on oath to our forefathers, a land flowing with milk and honey."

Follow the LORD's Commands

16The LORD your God commands you this day to follow these decrees and laws; carefully observe them with all your heart and with all your soul. 17You have declared this day that the LORD is your God and that you will walk in his ways, that you will keep his decrees, commands and laws, and that you will obey him. 18And the LORD has declared this day that you are his people, his treasured possession as he promised, and that you are to keep all his commands. 19He has declared that he will set you in praise, fame and honor high above all the nations he has made and that you will be a people holy to the LORD your God, as he promised.

The Altar on Mount Ebal

27 MOSES AND the elders of Israel commanded the people: "Keep all these commands that I give you today. 2When you have crossed the Jordan into the land the LORD your God is giving you, set up some large stones and coat them with plaster. 3Write on them all the words of this law when you have crossed over to enter the land the LORD your God is giving you, a land flowing with milk and honey, just as the LORD, the God of your fathers, promised you. 4And when you have crossed the Jordan, set up these stones on Mount Ebal, as I command you today, and coat them with plaster. 5Build there an altar to the LORD your God, an altar of stones. Do not use any iron tool upon them. 6Build the altar of the LORD your God with fieldstones and offer burnt offerings on it to the LORD your God. 7Sacrifice fellowship offerings[k] there, eating them and rejoicing in the presence of the LORD your God. 8And you shall write very clearly all the words of this law on these stones you have set up."

Curses From Mount Ebal

9Then Moses and the priests, who are Levites, said to all Israel, "Be silent, O Israel, and listen! You have now become the people of the LORD your God. 10Obey the LORD your God and follow his commands and decrees that I give you today."

11On the same day Moses commanded the people:

12When you have crossed the Jordan, these tribes shall stand on Mount Gerizim to bless the people: Simeon, Levi,

---

k 7 Traditionally *peace offerings*

King James

13 And these shall stand upon mount Ebal [o]to curse; Reuben, Gad, and Asher, and Zebulun, Dan, and Naphtali.

14 ¶ And the Levites shall speak, and say unto all the men of Israel with a loud voice,

15 Cursed *be* the man that maketh *any* graven or molten image, an abomination unto the LORD, the work of the hands of the craftsman, and putteth *it* in *a* secret *place.* And all the people shall answer and say, Amen.

16 Cursed *be* he that setteth light by his father or his mother. And all the people shall say, Amen.

17 Cursed *be* he that removeth his neighbour's landmark. And all the people shall say, Amen.

18 Cursed *be* he that maketh the blind to wander out of the way. And all the people shall say, Amen.

19 Cursed *be* he that perverteth the judgment of the stranger, fatherless, and widow. And all the people shall say, Amen.

20 Cursed *be* he that lieth with his father's wife; because he uncovereth his father's skirt. And all the people shall say, Amen.

21 Cursed *be* he that lieth with any manner of beast. And all the people shall say, Amen.

22 Cursed *be* he that lieth with his sister, the daughter of his father, or the daughter of his mother. And all the people shall say, Amen.

23 Cursed *be* he that lieth with his mother-in-law. And all the people shall say, Amen.

24 Cursed *be* he that smiteth his neighbour secretly. And all the people shall say, Amen.

25 Cursed *be* he that taketh reward to slay an innocent person. And all the people shall say, Amen.

26 Cursed *be* he that confirmeth not *all* the words of this law to do them. And all the people shall say, Amen.

The blessings of obedience

28 AND IT shall come to pass, if thou shalt hearken diligently unto the voice of the LORD thy God, to observe *and* to do all his commandments which I command thee this day, that the LORD thy God will set thee on high above all nations of the earth:

2 And all these blessings shall come on thee, and overtake thee, if thou shalt hearken unto the voice of the LORD thy God.

3 Blessed *shalt* thou *be* in the city, and blessed *shalt* thou *be* in the field.

4 Blessed *shall be* the fruit of thy body, and the fruit of thy ground, and the fruit of thy cattle, the increase of thy kine, and the flocks of thy sheep.

5 Blessed *shall be* thy basket and thy [p]store.

6 Blessed *shalt* thou *be* when thou comest in, and blessed *shalt* thou *be* when thou goest out.

7 The LORD shall cause thine enemies that rise up against thee to be smitten before thy face: they shall come out against thee one way, and flee before thee seven ways.

8 The LORD shall command the blessing upon thee in thy [q]storehouses, and in all that thou settest thine hand unto; and he shall bless thee in the land which the LORD thy God giveth thee.

[o] Heb. *for a cursing* [p] Or, *dough,* or, *kneading-trough* [q] Or, *barns*

Amplified

13 And these [tribes] shall stand on Mount Ebal to pronounce the curse [for disobedience]: Reuben, Gad, Asher, Zebulun, Dan, and Naphtali.

14 And the Levites shall declare with a loud voice to all the men of Israel:

15 Cursed is the man who makes a graven or molten image, an abomination to the Lord, the work of the hands of the craftsman, and sets it up in secret. All the people shall answer, Amen.

16 Cursed is he who dishonors his father or his mother. All the people shall say, Amen.

17 Cursed is he who moves [back] his neighbor's landmark. All the people shall say, Amen.

18 Cursed is he who misleads a blind man on his way. All the people shall say, Amen.

19 Cursed is he who perverts the justice due to the sojourner *or* the stranger, the fatherless, and the widow. All the people shall say, Amen.

20 Cursed is he who lies with his father's wife, because he uncovers what belongs to his father. All the people shall say, Amen.

21 Cursed is he who lies with any beast. All the people shall say, Amen.

22 Cursed is he who lies with his half sister, whether his father's or his mother's daughter. All the people shall say, Amen.

23 Cursed is he who lies with his mother-in-law. All the people shall say, Amen.

24 Cursed is he who slays his neighbor secretly. All the people shall say, Amen.

25 Cursed is he who takes a bribe to slay an innocent person. All the people shall say, Amen.

26 Cursed is he who does not support *and* give assent to the words of this law to do them [as the rule of his life]. All the people shall say, Amen.

28 IF YOU will listen diligently to the voice of the Lord your God, being watchful to do all His commandments which I command you this day, the Lord your God will set you high above all the nations of the earth.

2 And all these blessings shall come upon you and overtake you if you heed the voice of the Lord your God.

3 Blessed shall you be in the city and blessed shall you be in the field.

4 Blessed shall be the fruit of your body and the fruit of your ground and the fruit of your beasts, the increase of your cattle and the young of your flock.

5 Blessed shall be your basket and your kneading trough.

6 Blessed shall you be when you come in and blessed shall you be when you go out.

7 The Lord shall cause your enemies who rise up against you to be defeated before your face; they shall come out against you one way and flee before you seven ways.

8 The Lord shall command the blessing upon you in your storehouse and in all that you undertake. And He will bless you in the land which the Lord your God gives you.

New American Standard

¹³"For the curse, these shall stand on Mount Ebal: Reuben, Gad, Asher, Zebulun, Dan, and Naphtali.

¹⁴"The Levites shall then answer and say to all the men of Israel with a loud voice,

¹⁵ ¶ 'Cursed is the man who makes an idol or a molten image, an abomination to the LORD, the work of the hands of the craftsman, and sets *it* up in secret.' And all the people shall answer and say, 'Amen.'

¹⁶ ¶ 'Cursed is he who dishonors his father or mother.' And all the people shall say, 'Amen.'

¹⁷ ¶ 'Cursed is he who moves his neighbor's boundary mark.' And all the people shall say, 'Amen.'

¹⁸ ¶ 'Cursed is he who misleads a blind *person* on the road.' And all the people shall say, 'Amen.'

¹⁹ ¶ 'Cursed is he who distorts the justice due an alien, orphan, and widow.' And all the people shall say, 'Amen.'

²⁰ ¶ 'Cursed is he who lies with his father's wife, because he has uncovered his father's skirt.' And all the people shall say, 'Amen.'

²¹ ¶ 'Cursed is he who lies with any animal.' And all the people shall say, 'Amen.'

²² ¶ 'Cursed is he who lies with his sister, the daughter of his father or of his mother.' And all the people shall say, 'Amen.'

²³ ¶ 'Cursed is he who lies with his mother-in-law.' And all the people shall say, 'Amen.'

²⁴ ¶ 'Cursed is he who strikes his neighbor in secret.' And all the people shall say, 'Amen.'

²⁵ ¶ 'Cursed is he who accepts a bribe to strike down an innocent person.' And all the people shall say, 'Amen.'

²⁶ ¶ 'Cursed is he who does not confirm the words of this law by doing them.' And all the people shall say, 'Amen.'

Blessings at Gerizim

28 "NOW IT shall be, if you diligently obey the LORD your God, being careful to do all His commandments which I command you today, the LORD your God will set you high above all the nations of the earth.

²"All these blessings will come upon you and overtake you if you obey the LORD your God:

³ ¶ "Blessed *shall* you *be* in the city, and blessed *shall* you *be* in the country.

⁴ ¶ "Blessed *shall be* the offspring of your body and the produce of your ground and the offspring of your beasts, the increase of your herd and the young of your flock.

⁵ ¶ "Blessed *shall be* your basket and your kneading bowl.

⁶ ¶ "Blessed *shall* you *be* when you come in, and blessed *shall* you *be* when you go out.

⁷ ¶ "The LORD shall cause your enemies who rise up against you to be defeated before you; they will come out against you one way and will flee before you seven ways.

⁸"The LORD will command the blessing upon you in your barns and in all that you put your hand to, and He will bless you in the land which the LORD your God gives you.

New International

Judah, Issachar, Joseph and Benjamin. ¹³And these tribes shall stand on Mount Ebal to pronounce curses: Reuben, Gad, Asher, Zebulun, Dan and Naphtali.

¹⁴The Levites shall recite to all the people of Israel in a loud voice:

¹⁵"Cursed is the man who carves an image or casts an idol—a thing detestable to the LORD, the work of the craftsman's hands—and sets it up in secret."

Then all the people shall say, "Amen!"

¹⁶"Cursed is the man who dishonors his father or his mother."

Then all the people shall say, "Amen!"

¹⁷"Cursed is the man who moves his neighbor's boundary stone."

Then all the people shall say, "Amen!"

¹⁸"Cursed is the man who leads the blind astray on the road."

Then all the people shall say, "Amen!"

¹⁹"Cursed is the man who withholds justice from the alien, the fatherless or the widow."

Then all the people shall say, "Amen!"

²⁰"Cursed is the man who sleeps with his father's wife, for he dishonors his father's bed."

Then all the people shall say, "Amen!"

²¹"Cursed is the man who has sexual relations with any animal."

Then all the people shall say, "Amen!"

²²"Cursed is the man who sleeps with his sister, the daughter of his father or the daughter of his mother."

Then all the people shall say, "Amen!"

²³"Cursed is the man who sleeps with his mother-in-law."

Then all the people shall say, "Amen!"

²⁴"Cursed is the man who kills his neighbor secretly."

Then all the people shall say, "Amen!"

²⁵"Cursed is the man who accepts a bribe to kill an innocent person."

Then all the people shall say, "Amen!"

²⁶"Cursed is the man who does not uphold the words of this law by carrying them out."

Then all the people shall say, "Amen!"

Blessings for Obedience

28 IF YOU fully obey the LORD your God and carefully follow all his commands I give you today, the LORD your God will set you high above all the nations on earth. ²All these blessings will come upon you and accompany you if you obey the LORD your God:

³You will be blessed in the city and blessed in the country.

⁴The fruit of your womb will be blessed, and the crops of your land and the young of your livestock—the calves of your herds and the lambs of your flocks.

⁵Your basket and your kneading trough will be blessed.

⁶You will be blessed when you come in and blessed when you go out.

⁷The LORD will grant that the enemies who rise up against you will be defeated before you. They will come at you from one direction but flee from you in seven.

⁸The LORD will send a blessing on your barns and on everything you put your hand to. The LORD your God will bless you in the land he is giving you.

King James

⁹The LORD shall establish thee an holy people unto himself, as he hath sworn unto thee, if thou shalt keep the commandments of the LORD thy God, and walk in his ways.

¹⁰And all people of the earth shall see that thou art called by the name of the LORD; and they shall be afraid of thee.

¹¹And the LORD shall make thee plenteous ^rin goods, in the fruit of thy ^sbody, and in the fruit of thy cattle, and in the fruit of thy ground, in the land which the LORD sware unto thy fathers to give thee.

¹²The LORD shall open unto thee his good treasure, the heaven to give the rain unto thy land in his season, and to bless all the work of thine hand: and thou shalt lend unto many nations, and thou shalt not borrow.

¹³And the LORD shall make thee the head, and not the tail; and thou shalt be above only, and thou shalt not be beneath; if that thou hearken unto the commandments of the LORD thy God, which I command thee this day, to observe and to do *them:*

¹⁴And thou shalt not go aside from any of the words which I command thee this day, *to* the right hand, or *to* the left, to go after other gods to serve them.

The curses of disobedience

¹⁵ ¶ But it shall come to pass, if thou wilt not hearken unto the voice of the LORD thy God, to observe to do all his commandments and his statutes which I command thee this day; that all these curses shall come upon thee, and overtake thee:

¹⁶Cursed *shalt thou be* in the city, and cursed *shalt thou be* in the field.

¹⁷Cursed *shall be* thy basket and thy store.

¹⁸Cursed *shall be* the fruit of thy body, and the fruit of thy land, the increase of thy kine, and the flocks of thy sheep.

¹⁹Cursed *shalt thou be* when thou comest in, and cursed *shalt thou be* when thou goest out.

²⁰The LORD shall send upon thee cursing, vexation, and rebuke, in all that thou settest thine hand unto ^tfor to do, until thou be destroyed, and until thou perish quickly; because of the wickedness of thy doings, whereby thou hast forsaken me.

²¹The LORD shall make the pestilence cleave unto thee, until he have consumed thee from off the land, whither thou goest to possess it.

²²The LORD shall smite thee with a consumption, and with a fever, and with an inflammation, and with an extreme burning, and with the ^usword, and with blasting, and with mildew; and they shall pursue thee until thou perish.

²³And thy heaven that *is* over thy head shall be brass, and the earth that *is* under thee *shall be* iron.

²⁴The LORD shall make the rain of thy land powder and dust: from heaven shall it come down upon thee, until thou be destroyed.

²⁵The LORD shall cause thee to be smitten before thine enemies: thou shalt go out one way against them, and flee seven ways before them: and shalt be ^vremoved into all the kingdoms of the earth.

²⁶And thy carcase shall be meat unto all fowls of the air, and unto the beasts of the earth, and no man shall fray *them* away.

²⁷The LORD will smite thee with the botch of Egypt, and with the emerods, and with the scab, and with the itch, whereof thou canst not be healed.

²⁸The LORD shall smite thee with madness, and blindness, and astonishment of heart:

²⁹And thou shalt grope at noonday, as the blind gropeth in darkness, and thou shalt not prosper in thy ways: and thou shalt be only oppressed and spoiled evermore, and no man shall save *thee.*

Amplified

⁹The Lord will establish you as a people holy to Himself, as He has sworn to you, if you keep the commandments of the Lord your God and walk in His ways.

¹⁰And all people of the earth shall see that you are called by the name [and in the presence of] the Lord, and they shall be afraid of you.

¹¹And the Lord shall make you have a surplus of prosperity, through the fruit of your body, of your livestock, and of your ground, in the land which the Lord swore to your fathers to give you.

¹²The Lord shall open to you His good treasury, the heavens, to give the rain of your land in its season and to bless all the work of your hands; and you shall lend to many nations, but you shall not borrow.

¹³And the Lord shall make you the head, and not the tail; and you shall be above only, and you shall not be beneath, if you heed the commandments of the Lord your God which I command you this day and are watchful to do them.

¹⁴And you shall not turn aside from any of the words which I command you this day, to the right hand or to the left, to go after other gods to serve them.

¹⁵But if you will not obey the voice of the Lord your God, being watchful to do all His commandments and His statutes which I command you this day, then all these curses shall come upon you and overtake you:

¹⁶Cursed shall you be in the city and cursed shall you be in the field.

¹⁷Cursed shall be your basket and your kneading trough.

¹⁸Cursed shall be the fruit of your body, of your land, of the increase of your cattle and the young of your sheep.

¹⁹Cursed shall you be when you come in and cursed shall you be when you go out.

²⁰The Lord shall send you curses, confusion, and rebuke in every enterprise to which you set your hand, until you are destroyed, perishing quickly because of the evil of your doings by which you have forsaken me [Moses and God as one].

²¹The Lord will make the pestilence cling to you until He has consumed you from the land into which you go to possess.

²²The Lord will smite you with consumption, with fever and inflammation, fiery heat, sword *and* drought, blasting and mildew; they shall pursue you until you perish.

²³The heavens over your head shall be brass and the earth under you shall be iron.

²⁴The Lord shall make the rain of your land powdered soil and dust; from the heavens it shall come down upon you until you are destroyed.

²⁵The Lord shall cause you to be struck down before your enemies; you shall go out one way against them and flee seven ways before them, and you shall be tossed to and fro *and* be a terror among all the kingdoms of the earth. [Fulfilled in II Chron. 29:8.]

²⁶And your dead body shall be food for all the birds of the air and the beasts of the earth, and there shall be no one to frighten them away.

²⁷The Lord will smite you with the boils of Egypt and the tumors, the scurvy and the itch, from which you cannot be healed.

²⁸The Lord will smite you with madness and blindness and dismay of [mind and] heart.

²⁹And you shall grope at noonday as the blind grope in darkness. And you shall not prosper in your ways; and you shall be only oppressed and robbed continually, and there shall be no one to save you.

---

^rOr, *for good*   ^sHeb. *belly*   ^tHeb. *which thou wouldest do*
^uOr, *drought*   ^vHeb. *for a removing*

New American Standard

9"The LORD will establish you as a holy people to Himself, as He swore to you, if you keep the commandments of the LORD your God and walk in His ways.

10"So all the peoples of the earth will see that you are called by the name of the LORD, and they will be afraid of you.

11"The LORD will make you abound in prosperity, in the offspring of your body and in the offspring of your beast and in the produce of your ground, in the land which the LORD swore to your fathers to give you.

12"The LORD will open for you His good storehouse, the heavens, to give rain to your land in its season and to bless all the work of your hand; and you shall lend to many nations, but you shall not borrow.

13"The LORD will make you the head and not the tail, and you only will be above, and you will not be underneath, if you listen to the commandments of the LORD your God, which I charge you today, to observe *them* carefully,

14 and do not turn aside from any of the words which I command you today, to the right or to the left, to go after other gods to serve them.

Consequences of Disobedience

15 ¶ "But it shall come about, if you do not obey the LORD your God, to observe to do all His commandments and His statutes with which I charge you today, that all these curses will come upon you and overtake you:

16 ¶ "Cursed *shall* you *be* in the city, and cursed *shall* you *be* in the country.

17 ¶ "Cursed *shall be* your basket and your kneading bowl.

18 ¶ "Cursed *shall be* the offspring of your body and the produce of your ground, the increase of your herd and the young of your flock.

19 ¶ "Cursed *shall* you *be* when you come in, and cursed *shall* you *be* when you go out.

20 ¶ "The LORD will send upon you curses, confusion, and rebuke, in all you undertake to do, until you are destroyed and until you perish quickly, on account of the evil of your deeds, because you have forsaken Me.

21"The LORD will make the pestilence cling to you until He has consumed you from the land where you are entering to possess it.

22"The LORD will smite you with consumption and with fever and with inflammation and with fiery heat and with ʳthe sword and with blight and with mildew, and they will pursue you until you perish.

23"The heaven which is over your head shall be bronze, and the earth which is under you, iron.

24"The LORD will make the rain of your land powder and dust; from heaven it shall come down on you until you are destroyed.

25 ¶ "The LORD shall cause you to be defeated before your enemies; you will go out one way against them, but you will flee seven ways before them, and you will be *an example of* terror to all the kingdoms of the earth.

26"Your carcasses will be food to all birds of the sky and to the beasts of the earth, and there will be no one to frighten *them* away.

27 ¶ "The LORD will smite you with the boils of Egypt and with tumors and with the scab and with the itch, from which you cannot be healed.

28"The LORD will smite you with madness and with blindness and with bewilderment of heart;

29 and you will grope at noon, as the blind man gropes in darkness, and you will not prosper in your ways; but you shall only be oppressed and robbed continually, with none to save you.

New International

9The LORD will establish you as his holy people, as he promised you on oath, if you keep the commands of the LORD your God and walk in his ways. 10Then all the peoples on earth will see that you are called by the name of the LORD, and they will fear you. 11The LORD will grant you abundant prosperity—in the fruit of your womb, the young of your livestock and the crops of your ground—in the land he swore to your forefathers to give you.

12The LORD will open the heavens, the storehouse of his bounty, to send rain on your land in season and to bless all the work of your hands. You will lend to many nations but will borrow from none. 13The LORD will make you the head, not the tail. If you pay attention to the commands of the LORD your God that I give you this day and carefully follow them, you will always be at the top, never at the bottom. 14Do not turn aside from any of the commands I give you today, to the right or to the left, following other gods and serving them.

Curses for Disobedience

15However, if you do not obey the LORD your God and do not carefully follow all his commands and decrees I am giving you today, all these curses will come upon you and overtake you:

16You will be cursed in the city and cursed in the country.

17Your basket and your kneading trough will be cursed.

18The fruit of your womb will be cursed, and the crops of your land, and the calves of your herds and the lambs of your flocks.

19You will be cursed when you come in and cursed when you go out.

20The LORD will send on you curses, confusion and rebuke in everything you put your hand to, until you are destroyed and come to sudden ruin because of the evil you have done in forsaking him.ˡ 21The LORD will plague you with diseases until he has destroyed you from the land you are entering to possess. 22The LORD will strike you with wasting disease, with fever and inflammation, with scorching heat and drought, with blight and mildew, which will plague you until you perish. 23The sky over your head will be bronze, the ground beneath you iron. 24The LORD will turn the rain of your country into dust and powder; it will come down from the skies until you are destroyed.

25The LORD will cause you to be defeated before your enemies. You will come at them from one direction but flee from them in seven, and you will become a thing of horror to all the kingdoms on earth. 26Your carcasses will be food for all the birds of the air and the beasts of the earth, and there will be no one to frighten them away. 27The LORD will afflict you with the boils of Egypt and with tumors, festering sores and the itch, from which you cannot be cured. 28The LORD will afflict you with madness, blindness and confusion of mind. 29At midday you will grope about like a blind man in the dark. You will be unsuccessful in everything you do; day after day you will be oppressed and robbed, with no one to rescue you.

ʳ Another reading is *drought*   ˡ20 Hebrew *me*

King James

³⁰Thou shalt betroth a wife, and another man shall lie with her: thou shalt build an house, and thou shalt not dwell therein: thou shalt plant a vineyard, and shalt not gather the grapes thereof.

³¹Thine ox *shall be* slain before thine eyes, and thou shalt not eat thereof: thine ass *shall be* violently taken away from before thy face, and ^wshall not be restored to thee: thy sheep *shall be* given unto thine enemies, and thou shalt have none to rescue *them.*

³²Thy sons and thy daughters *shall be* given unto another people, and thine eyes shall look, and fail *with longing* for them all the day long: and *there shall be* no might in thine hand.

³³The fruit of thy land, and all thy labours, shall a nation which thou knowest not eat up; and thou shalt be only oppressed and crushed always:

³⁴So that thou shalt be mad for the sight of thine eyes which thou shalt see.

³⁵The LORD shall smite thee in the knees, and in the legs, with a sore botch that cannot be healed, from the sole of thy foot unto the top of thy head.

³⁶The LORD shall bring thee, and thy king which thou shalt set over thee, unto a nation which neither thou nor thy fathers have known; and there shalt thou serve other gods, wood and stone.

³⁷And thou shalt become an astonishment, a proverb, and a byword, among all nations whither the LORD shall lead thee.

³⁸Thou shalt carry much seed out into the field, and shalt gather *but* little in; for the locust shall consume it.

³⁹Thou shalt plant vineyards, and dress *them,* but shalt neither drink *of* the wine, nor gather *the grapes;* for the worms shall eat them.

⁴⁰Thou shalt have olive trees throughout all thy coasts, but thou shalt not anoint *thyself* with the oil; for thine olive shall cast *his fruit.*

⁴¹Thou shalt beget sons and daughters, but ^xthou shalt not enjoy them; for they shall go into captivity.

⁴²All thy trees and fruit of thy land shall the locust ^yconsume.

⁴³The stranger that *is* within thee shall get up above thee very high; and thou shalt come down very low.

⁴⁴He shall lend to thee, and thou shalt not lend to him: he shall be the head, and thou shalt be the tail.

⁴⁵Moreover all these curses shall come upon thee, and shall pursue thee, and overtake thee, till thou be destroyed; because thou hearkenedst not unto the voice of the LORD thy God, to keep his commandments and his statutes which he commanded thee:

⁴⁶And they shall be upon thee for a sign and for a wonder, and upon thy seed for ever.

⁴⁷Because thou servedst not the LORD thy God with joyfulness, and with gladness of heart, for the abundance of all *things;*

⁴⁸Therefore shalt thou serve thine enemies which the LORD shall send against thee, in hunger, and in thirst, and in nakedness, and in want of all *things:* and he shall put a yoke of iron upon thy neck, until he have destroyed thee.

⁴⁹The LORD shall bring a nation against thee from far, from the end of the earth, *as swift* as the eagle flieth; a nation whose tongue thou shalt not ^zunderstand;

⁵⁰A nation ^aof fierce countenance, which shall not regard the person of the old, nor show favour to the young:

⁵¹And he shall eat the fruit of thy cattle, and the fruit of thy land, until thou be destroyed: which *also* shall not leave thee *either* corn, wine, or oil, *or* the increase of thy kine, or flocks of thy sheep, until he have destroyed thee.

Amplified

³⁰You shall betroth a wife, but another man shall lie with her; you shall build a house, but not live in it; you shall plant a vineyard, but not gather its grapes.

³¹Your ox shall be slain before your eyes, but you shall not eat of it; your donkey shall be violently taken away before your face and not be restored to you; your sheep shall be given to your enemies, and you shall have no one to help you.

³²Your sons and daughters shall be given to another people, and your eyes shall look and fail with longing for them all the day; and there shall be no power in your hands to prevent it. [Fulfilled in II Chron. 29:9.]

³³A nation which you have not known shall eat up the fruit of your land and of all your labors, and you shall be only oppressed and crushed continually, [Fulfilled in Judg. 6:1–6; 13:1.]

³⁴So that you shall be driven mad by the sights which your eyes shall see.

³⁵The Lord will smite you on the knees and on the legs with a sore boil that cannot be healed, from the sole of your foot to the top of your head.

³⁶The Lord shall bring you and your king whom you have set over you to a nation which neither you nor your fathers have known, and there you shall [be forced to] serve other gods, of wood and stone. [Fulfilled in II Kings 17:4, 6; 24:12, 14; 25:7, 11; Dan. 6:11, 12.]

³⁷And you shall become an amazement, a proverb, and a byword among all the peoples to which the Lord will lead you.

³⁸You shall carry much seed out into the field and shall gather little in, for the locust shall consume it. [Fulfilled in Hag. 1:6.]

³⁹You shall plant vineyards and dress them but shall neither drink of the wine nor gather the grapes, for the worm shall eat them.

⁴⁰You shall have olive trees throughout all your territory but you shall not anoint yourselves with the oil, for your olive trees shall drop their fruit.

⁴¹You shall beget sons and daughters but shall not enjoy them, for they shall go into captivity. [Fulfilled in Lam. 1:5.]

⁴²All your trees and the fruit of your ground shall the locust possess. [Fulfilled in Joel 1:4.]

⁴³The transient (stranger) among you shall mount up higher and higher above you, and you shall come down lower and lower.

⁴⁴He shall lend to you, but you shall not lend to him; he shall be the head, and you shall be the tail.

⁴⁵All these curses shall come upon you and shall pursue you and overtake you till you are destroyed, because you do not obey the voice of the Lord your God, to keep His commandments and His statutes which He commanded you.

⁴⁶They shall be upon you for a sign [of warning to other nations] and for a wonder, and upon your descendants forever.

⁴⁷Because you did not serve the Lord your God with joyfulness of [mind and] heart [in gratitude] for the abundance of all [with which He had blessed you],

⁴⁸Therefore you shall serve your enemies whom the Lord shall send against you, in hunger and thirst, in nakedness and in want of all things; and He will put a yoke of iron upon your neck until He has destroyed you.

⁴⁹The Lord will bring a nation against you from afar, from the end of the earth, as swift as the eagle flies, a nation whose language you shall not understand,

⁵⁰A nation of unyielding countenance who will not regard the person of the old or show favor to the young,

⁵¹And shall eat the fruit of your cattle and the fruit of your ground until you are destroyed, who also shall not leave you grain, new wine, oil, the increase of your cattle or the young of your sheep until they have caused you to perish.

^w Heb. *shall not return to thee*   ^x Heb. *they shall not be thine*
^y Or, *possess*   ^z Heb. *hear*   ^a Heb. *strong of face*

New American Standard

30"You shall betroth a wife, but another man will violate her; you shall build a house, but you will not live in it; you shall plant a vineyard, but you will not use its fruit.

31"Your ox shall be slaughtered before your eyes, but you will not eat of it; your donkey shall be torn away from you, and will not be restored to you; your sheep shall be given to your enemies, and you will have none to save you.

32"Your sons and your daughters shall be given to another people, while your eyes look on and yearn for them continually; but there will be nothing you can do.

33"A people whom you do not know shall eat up the produce of your ground and all your labors, and you will never be anything but oppressed and crushed continually.

34"You shall be driven mad by the sight of what you see.

35"The LORD will strike you on the knees and legs with sore boils, from which you cannot be healed, from the sole of your foot to the crown of your head.

36"The LORD will bring you and your king, whom you set over you, to a nation which neither you nor your fathers have known, and there you shall serve other gods, wood and stone.

37"You shall become a horror, a proverb, and a taunt among all the people where the LORD drives you.

38 ¶ "You shall bring out much seed to the field but you will gather in little, for the locust will consume it.

39"You shall plant and cultivate vineyards, but you will neither drink of the wine nor gather *the grapes,* for the worm will devour them.

40"You shall have olive trees throughout your territory but you will not anoint yourself with the oil, for your olives will drop off.

41"You shall have sons and daughters but they will not be yours, for they will go into captivity.

42"The cricket shall possess all your trees and the produce of your ground.

43"The alien who is among you shall rise above you higher and higher, but you will go down lower and lower.

44"He shall lend to you, but you will not lend to him; he shall be the head, and you will be the tail.

45 ¶ "So all these curses shall come on you and pursue you and overtake you until you are destroyed, because you would not obey the LORD your God by keeping His commandments and His statutes which He commanded you.

46"They shall become a sign and a wonder on you and your descendants forever.

47 ¶ "Because you did not serve the LORD your God with joy and a glad heart, for the abundance of all things;

48 therefore you shall serve your enemies whom the LORD will send against you, in hunger, in thirst, in nakedness, and in the lack of all things; and He will put an iron yoke on your neck until He has destroyed you.

49 ¶ "The LORD will bring a nation against you from afar, from the end of the earth, as the eagle swoops down, a nation whose language you shall not understand,

50 a nation of fierce countenance who will have no respect for the old, nor show favor to the young.

51"Moreover, it shall eat the offspring of your herd and the produce of your ground until you are destroyed, who also leaves you no grain, new wine, or oil, nor the increase of your herd or the young of your flock until they have caused you to perish.

New International

30You will be pledged to be married to a woman, but another will take her and ravish her. You will build a house, but you will not live in it. You will plant a vineyard, but you will not even begin to enjoy its fruit. 31Your ox will be slaughtered before your eyes, but you will eat none of it. Your donkey will be forcibly taken from you and will not be returned. Your sheep will be given to your enemies, and no one will rescue them. 32Your sons and daughters will be given to another nation, and you will wear out your eyes watching for them day after day, powerless to lift a hand. 33A people that you do not know will eat what your land and labor produce, and you will have nothing but cruel oppression all your days. 34The sights you see will drive you mad. 35The LORD will afflict your knees and legs with painful boils that cannot be cured, spreading from the soles of your feet to the top of your head.

36The LORD will drive you and the king you set over you to a nation unknown to you or your fathers. There you will worship other gods, gods of wood and stone. 37You will become a thing of horror and an object of scorn and ridicule to all the nations where the LORD will drive you.

38You will sow much seed in the field but you will harvest little, because locusts will devour it. 39You will plant vineyards and cultivate them but you will not drink the wine or gather the grapes, because worms will eat them. 40You will have olive trees throughout your country but you will not use the oil, because the olives will drop off. 41You will have sons and daughters but you will not keep them, because they will go into captivity. 42Swarms of locusts will take over all your trees and the crops of your land.

43The alien who lives among you will rise above you higher and higher, but you will sink lower and lower. 44He will lend to you, but you will not lend to him. He will be the head, but you will be the tail.

45All these curses will come upon you. They will pursue you and overtake you until you are destroyed, because you did not obey the LORD your God and observe the commands and decrees he gave you. 46They will be a sign and a wonder to you and your descendants forever. 47Because you did not serve the LORD your God joyfully and gladly in the time of prosperity, 48therefore in hunger and thirst, in nakedness and dire poverty, you will serve the enemies the LORD sends against you. He will put an iron yoke on your neck until he has destroyed you.

49The LORD will bring a nation against you from far away, from the ends of the earth, like an eagle swooping down, a nation whose language you will not understand, 50a fierce-looking nation without respect for the old or pity for the young. 51They will devour the young of your livestock and the crops of your land until you are destroyed. They will leave you no grain, new wine or oil, nor any calves of your herds or lambs of your flocks until you are

King James

Amplified

⁵²And he shall besiege thee in all thy gates, until thy high and fenced walls come down, wherein thou trustedst, throughout all thy land: and he shall besiege thee in all thy gates throughout all thy land, which the LORD thy God hath given thee.

⁵³And thou shalt eat the fruit of thine own *b*body, the flesh of thy sons and of thy daughters, which the LORD thy God hath given thee, in the siege, and in the straitness, wherewith thine enemies shall distress thee:

⁵⁴*So that* the man *that is* tender among you, and very delicate, his eye shall be evil toward his brother, and toward the wife of his bosom, and toward the remnant of his children which he shall leave:

⁵⁵So that he will not give to any of them of the flesh of his children whom he shall eat: because he hath nothing left him in the siege, and in the straitness, wherewith thine enemies shall distress thee in all thy gates.

⁵⁶The tender and delicate woman among you, which would not adventure to set the sole of her foot upon the ground for delicateness and tenderness, her eye shall be evil toward the husband of her bosom, and toward her son, and toward her daughter,

⁵⁷And toward her *c*young one that cometh out from between her feet, and toward her children which she shall bear: for she shall eat them for want of all *things* secretly in the siege and straitness, wherewith thine enemy shall distress thee in thy gates.

⁵⁸If thou wilt not observe to do all the words of this law that are written in this book, that thou mayest fear this glorious and fearful name, THE LORD THY GOD;

⁵⁹Then the LORD will make thy plagues wonderful, and the plagues of thy seed, *even* great plagues, and of long continuance, and sore sicknesses, and of long continuance.

⁶⁰Moreover he will bring upon thee all the diseases of Egypt, which thou wast afraid of; and they shall cleave unto thee.

⁶¹Also every sickness, and every plague, which *is* not written in the book of this law, them will the LORD *d*bring upon thee, until thou be destroyed.

⁶²And ye shall be left few in number, whereas ye were as the stars of heaven for multitude; because thou wouldest not obey the voice of the LORD thy God.

⁶³And it shall come to pass, *that* as the LORD rejoiced over you to do you good, and to multiply you; so the LORD will rejoice over you to destroy you, and to bring you to nought; and ye shall be plucked from off the land whither thou goest to possess it.

⁶⁴And the LORD shall scatter thee among all people, from the one end of the earth even unto the other; and there thou shalt serve other gods, which neither thou nor thy fathers have known, *even* wood and stone.

⁶⁵And among these nations shalt thou find no ease, neither shall the sole of thy foot have rest: but the LORD shall give thee there a trembling heart, and failing of eyes, and sorrow of mind:

⁶⁶And thy life shall hang in doubt before thee; and thou shalt fear day and night, and shalt have none assurance of thy life:

⁶⁷In the morning thou shalt say, Would God it were even! and at even thou shalt say, Would God it were morning! for the fear of thine heart wherewith thou shalt fear, and for the sight of thine eyes which thou shalt see.

⁵²They shall besiege you in all your towns until your high and fortified walls in which you trusted come down throughout all your land; and they shall besiege you in all your towns throughout all your land which the Lord your God has given you.

⁵³And you shall eat the fruit of your own body, the flesh of your sons and daughters whom the Lord your God has given you, in the siege and in the [pressing] misery with which your enemies shall distress you. [Fulfilled in II Kings 6:24–29.]

⁵⁴The man who is most tender among you and extremely particular *and* well-bred, his eye shall be cruel *and* grudging of food toward his brother and toward the wife of his bosom and toward those of his children still remaining,

⁵⁵So that he will not give to any of them any of the flesh of his children which he is eating, because he has nothing left to him in the siege and in the distress with which your enemies shall distress you in all your towns.

⁵⁶The most tender and daintily bred woman among you, who would not venture to set the sole of her foot upon the ground because she is so dainty and kind, will grudge to the husband of her bosom, to her son and to her daughter

⁵⁷Her afterbirth that comes out from her body and the children whom she shall bear. For she will eat them secretly for want of anything else in the siege and distress with which your enemies shall distress you in your towns.

⁵⁸If you will not be watchful to do all the words of this law that are written in this book, that you may [reverently] fear this glorious and fearful name [and presence]—THE LORD YOUR GOD—

⁵⁹Then the Lord will bring upon you and your descendants extraordinary strokes and blows, great plagues of long continuance, and grievous sicknesses of long duration.

⁶⁰Moreover, He will bring upon you all the diseases of Egypt of which you were afraid, and they shall cling to you.

⁶¹Also every sickness and every affliction which is not written in this Book of the Law the Lord will bring upon you until you are destroyed.

⁶²And you shall be *i*left few in number, whereas you had been as the stars of the heavens for multitude, because you would not obey the voice of the Lord your God.

⁶³And as the Lord rejoiced over you to do you good and to multiply you, so the Lord will rejoice to bring ruin upon you and to destroy you; and you shall be *j*plucked from the land into which you go to possess.

⁶⁴And the Lord shall scatter you among all peoples from one end of the earth to the other; and there you shall [be forced to] serve other gods, of wood and stone, which neither you nor your fathers have known. [Fulfilled in Dan. 3:6.]

⁶⁵And among these nations you shall find no ease and there shall be no rest for the sole of your foot; but the Lord will give you there a trembling heart, failing of eyes [from disappointment of hope], fainting of mind, *and* languishing of spirit.

⁶⁶Your life shall hang in doubt before you; day and night you shall be worried, and have no assurance of your life.

⁶⁷In the morning you shall say, Would that it were evening! and at evening you shall say, Would that it were morning!—because of the anxiety *and* dread of your [minds and] hearts and the sights which you shall see with your [own] eyes.

---

*i*The informed reader scarcely needs to be reminded of how literally fulfilled have been many of these predictions of evil made against the chosen people because of their idolatry and rebellion against God. Such verses as Deut. 28:25, 32, 33, 36, 38, 41, 42, and 53 foretell historical facts now recorded in Jewish history, both sacred and secular. Here Deut. 28:62 foretells how the Jewish race has been "thinned and kept down," again and again.   *j*The Roman emperor Hadrian issued a proclamation forbidding any Jews to reside in Judea, or even to approach its confines (James C. Gray and George M. Adams, *Bible Commentary*).

*b*Heb. *belly*   *c*Heb. *afterbirth*   *d*Heb. *cause to ascend*

New American Standard

52"It shall besiege you in all your towns until your high and fortified walls in which you trusted come down throughout your land, and it shall besiege you in all your towns throughout your land which the LORD your God has given you.

53"Then you shall eat the offspring of your own body, the flesh of your sons and of your daughters whom the LORD your God has given you, during the siege and the distress by which your enemy will oppress you.

54"The man who is refined and very delicate among you shall be hostile toward his brother and toward the wife he cherishes and toward the rest of his children who remain,

55 so that he will not give *even* one of them any of the flesh of his children which he will eat, since he has nothing *else* left, during the siege and the distress by which your enemy will oppress you in all your towns.

56"The refined and delicate woman among you, who would not venture to set the sole of her foot on the ground for delicateness and refinement, shall be hostile toward the husband she cherishes and toward her son and daughter,

57 and toward her afterbirth which issues from between her legs and toward her children whom she bears; for she will eat them secretly for lack of anything *else*, during the siege and the distress by which your enemy will oppress you in your towns.

58 ¶ "If you are not careful to observe all the words of this law which are written in this book, to fear this honored and awesome name, the LORD your God,

59 then the LORD will bring extraordinary plagues on you and your descendants, even severe and lasting plagues, and miserable and chronic sicknesses.

60"He will bring back on you all the diseases of Egypt of which you were afraid, and they will cling to you.

61"Also every sickness and every plague which, not written in the book of this law, the LORD will bring on you until you are destroyed.

62"Then you shall be left few in number, whereas you were as numerous as the stars of heaven, because you did not obey the LORD your God.

63"It shall come about that as the LORD delighted over you to prosper you, and multiply you, so the LORD will delight over you to make you perish and destroy you; and you will be torn from the land where you are entering to possess it.

64"Moreover, the LORD will scatter you among all peoples, from one end of the earth to the other end of the earth; and there you shall serve other gods, wood and stone, which you or your fathers have not known.

65"Among those nations you shall find no rest, and there will be no resting place for the sole of your foot; but there the LORD will give you a trembling heart, failing of eyes, and despair of soul.

66"So your life shall hang in doubt before you; and you will be in dread night and day, and shall have no assurance of your life.

67"In the morning you shall say, 'Would that it were evening!' And at evening you shall say, 'Would that it were morning!' because of the dread of your heart which you dread, and for the sight of your eyes which you will see.

New International

ruined. 52They will lay siege to all the cities throughout your land until the high fortified walls in which you trust fall down. They will besiege all the cities throughout the land the LORD your God is giving you.

53Because of the suffering that your enemy will inflict on you during the siege, you will eat the fruit of the womb, the flesh of the sons and daughters the LORD your God has given you. 54Even the most gentle and sensitive man among you will have no compassion on his own brother or the wife he loves or his surviving children, 55and he will not give to one of them any of the flesh of his children that he is eating. It will be all he has left because of the suffering your enemy will inflict on you during the siege of all your cities. 56The most gentle and sensitive woman among you—so sensitive and gentle that she would not venture to touch the ground with the sole of her foot—will begrudge the husband she loves and her own son or daughter 57the afterbirth from her womb and the children she bears. For she intends to eat them secretly during the siege and in the distress that your enemy will inflict on you in your cities.

58If you do not carefully follow all the words of this law, which are written in this book, and do not revere this glorious and awesome name—the LORD your God— 59the LORD will send fearful plagues on you and your descendants, harsh and prolonged disasters, and severe and lingering illnesses. 60He will bring upon you all the diseases of Egypt that you dreaded, and they will cling to you. 61The LORD will also bring on you every kind of sickness and disaster not recorded in this Book of the Law, until you are destroyed. 62You who were as numerous as the stars in the sky will be left but few in number, because you did not obey the LORD your God. 63Just as it pleased the LORD to make you prosper and increase in number, so it will please him to ruin and destroy you. You will be uprooted from the land you are entering to possess.

64Then the LORD will scatter you among all nations, from one end of the earth to the other. There you will worship other gods—gods of wood and stone, which neither you nor your fathers have known. 65Among those nations you will find no repose, no resting place for the sole of your foot. There the LORD will give you an anxious mind, eyes weary with longing, and a despairing heart. 66You will live in constant suspense, filled with dread both night and day, never sure of your life. 67In the morning you will say, "If only it were evening!" and in the evening, "If only it were morning!"—because of the terror that will

King James

68And the LORD shall bring thee into Egypt again with ships, by the way whereof I spake unto thee, Thou shalt see it no more again: and there ye shall be sold unto your enemies for bondmen and bondwomen, and no man shall buy *you.*

Keep the covenant

29 THESE *ARE* the words of the covenant, which the LORD commanded Moses to make with the children of Israel in the land of Moab, beside the covenant which he made with them in Horeb.

2 ¶ And Moses called unto all Israel, and said unto them, Ye have seen all that the LORD did before your eyes in the land of Egypt unto Pharaoh, and unto all his servants, and unto all his land;

3The great temptations which thine eyes have seen, the signs, and those great miracles:

4Yet the LORD hath not given you an heart to perceive, and eyes to see, and ears to hear, unto this day.

5And I have led you forty years in the wilderness: your clothes are not waxen old upon you, and thy shoe is not waxen old upon thy foot.

6Ye have not eaten bread, neither have ye drunk wine or strong drink: that ye might know that I *am* the LORD your God.

7And when ye came unto this place, Sihon the king of Heshbon, and Og the king of Bashan, came out against us unto battle, and we smote them:

8And we took their land, and gave it for an inheritance unto the Reubenites, and to the Gadites, and to the half tribe of Manasseh.

9Keep therefore the words of this covenant, and do them, that ye may prosper in all that ye do.

10 ¶ Ye stand this day all of you before the LORD your God; your captains of your tribes, your elders, and your officers, *with* all the men of Israel,

11Your little ones, your wives, and thy stranger that *is* in thy camp, from the hewer of thy wood unto the drawer of thy water:

12That thou shouldest *e*enter into covenant with the LORD thy God, and into his oath, which the LORD thy God maketh with thee this day:

13That he may establish thee today for a people unto himself, and *that* he may be unto thee a God, as he hath said unto thee, and as he hath sworn unto thy fathers, to Abraham, to Isaac, and to Jacob.

14Neither with you only do I make this covenant and this oath;

15But with *him* that standeth here with us this day before the LORD our God, and also with *him* that *is* not here with us this day:

16(For ye know how we have dwelt in the land of Egypt; and how we came through the nations which ye passed by;

17And ye have seen their abominations, and their *f*idols, wood and stone, silver and gold, which *were* among them:)

18Lest there should be among you man, or woman, or family, or tribe, whose heart turneth away this day from the LORD our God, to go *and* serve the gods of these nations; lest there should be among you a root that beareth *g h*gall and wormwood;

Amplified

68And the Lord shall *k*bring you into Egypt again with ships by the way about which I said to you, You shall never see it again. And there you shall be sold to your enemies as bondmen and bondwomen, but no man shall buy you. [Hos. 8:13.]

29 THESE ARE the words of the covenant which the Lord commanded Moses to make with the Israelites in the land of Moab, besides the covenant which He made with them in Horeb.

2Moses called to all Israel and said to them, You have seen all that the Lord did before your eyes in the land of Egypt to Pharaoh, to all his servants, and to all his land;

3The great trials which your eyes saw, the signs, and those great wonders.

4Yet the Lord has not given you a [mind and] heart to understand and eyes to see and ears to hear, to this day.

5I have led you forty years in the wilderness; your clothes have not worn out upon you, and your sandals have not worn off your feet.

6You have not eaten [grain] bread, nor have you drunk wine or strong drink, that you might recognize *and* know [your dependence on Him Who is saying], I am the Lord your God.

7And when you came to this place, Sihon king of Heshbon and Og king of Bashan came out against us to battle, but we defeated them.

8We took their land and gave it as an inheritance to the Reubenites, the Gadites, and the half-tribe of the Manassites.

9Therefore keep the words of this covenant and do them, that you may deal wisely *and* prosper in all that you do.

10All of you stand today before the Lord your God—your heads, your tribes, your elders, and your officers, even all the men of Israel,

11Your little ones, your wives, and the stranger *and* sojourner in your camp, from the hewer of your wood to the drawer of your water—

12That you may enter into the covenant of the Lord your God, and into His oath which He makes with you today,

13That He may establish you this day as a people for Himself, and that He may be to you a God as He said to you and as He swore to your fathers, Abraham, Isaac, and Jacob.

14It is not with you only that I make this sworn covenant

15But with future Israelites who do not stand here with us today before the Lord our God, as well as with those who are here with us this day.

16You know how we lived in the land of Egypt and how we came through the midst of the nations you crossed.

17And you have seen their abominations and their idols of wood and stone, of silver and gold, which were among them.

18Beware lest there should be among you a man or woman, or family or tribe, whose [mind and] heart turns away this day from the Lord our God to go and serve the gods of these nations; lest there should be among you a [poisonous] root that bears gall and wormwood,

---

k"Observe the contrast: you came out from bondage by God's high hand, monuments of His grace and power; you shall be carried back into bondage in men's slave ships. This was literally fulfilled under [the Roman emperor] Titus, and also under Hadrian" (James C. Gray and George M. Adams, *Bible Commentary*). The curses . . . were also fulfilled in a terrible manner during the Middle Ages, and are still in a course of fulfillment, though frequently less sensibly felt (J.P. Lange, *A Commentary*). "Here, then, are prophecies delivered above 3,000 years ago and yet being fulfilled in the world at this very time . . . I must acknowledge that they not only convince but amaze and astonish me beyond expression; they are truly as Moses foretold (Deut. 28:45, 46) they would be, 'a sign and a wonder forever'" (Bishop Thomas Newton, cited by Robert Jamieson, A.R. Fausset and David Brown, *A Commentary*).

---

e Heb. *pass*   *f* Heb. *dungy gods*   *g* Or, *a poisonful herb*
h Heb. *rosh*

New American Standard

68"The LORD will bring you back to Egypt in ships, by the way about which I spoke to you, 'You will never see it again!' And there you will offer yourselves for sale to your enemies as male and female slaves, but there will be no buyer."

The Covenant in Moab

29 THESE ARE the words of the covenant which the LORD commanded Moses to make with the sons of Israel in the land of Moab, besides the covenant which He had made with them at Horeb.

2 ¶ And Moses summoned all Israel and said to them, "You have seen all that the LORD did before your eyes in the land of Egypt to Pharaoh and all his servants and all his land;

3 the great trials which your eyes have seen, those great signs and wonders.

4"Yet to this day the LORD has not given you a heart to know, nor eyes to see, nor ears to hear.

5"I have led you forty years in the wilderness; your clothes have not worn out on you, and your sandal has not worn out on your foot.

6"You have not eaten bread, nor have you drunk wine or strong drink, in order that you might know that I am the LORD your God.

7"When you reached this place, Sihon the king of Heshbon and Og the king of Bashan came out to meet us for battle, but we defeated them;

8 and we took their land and gave it as an inheritance to the Reubenites, the Gadites, and the half-tribe of the Manassites.

9"So keep the words of this covenant to do them, that you may prosper in all that you do.

10 ¶ "You stand today, all of you, before the LORD your God: your chiefs, your tribes, your elders and your officers, even all the men of Israel,

11 your little ones, your wives, and the alien who is within your camps, from the one who chops your wood to the one who draws your water,

12 that you may enter into the covenant with the LORD your God, and into His oath which the LORD your God is making with you today,

13 in order that He may establish you today as His people and that He may be your God, just as He spoke to you and as He swore to your fathers, to Abraham, Isaac, and Jacob.

14 ¶ "Now not with you alone am I making this covenant and this oath,

15 but both with those who stand here with us today in the presence of the LORD our God and with those who are not with us here today

16 (for you know how we lived in the land of Egypt, and how we came through the midst of the nations through which you passed;

17 moreover, you have seen their abominations and their idols of wood, stone, silver, and gold, which they had with them);

18 so that there will not be among you a man or woman, or family or tribe, whose heart turns away today from the LORD our God, to go and serve the gods of those nations; that there will not be among you a root bearing poisonous fruit and wormwood.

New International

fill your hearts and the sights that your eyes will see. 68The LORD will send you back in ships to Egypt on a journey I said you should never make again. There you will offer yourselves for sale to your enemies as male and female slaves, but no one will buy you.

Renewal of the Covenant

29 THESE ARE the terms of the covenant the LORD commanded Moses to make with the Israelites in Moab, in addition to the covenant he had made with them at Horeb.

2Moses summoned all the Israelites and said to them:

Your eyes have seen all that the LORD did in Egypt to Pharaoh, to all his officials and to all his land. 3With your own eyes you saw those great trials, those miraculous signs and great wonders. 4But to this day the LORD has not given you a mind that understands or eyes that see or ears that hear. 5During the forty years that I led you through the desert, your clothes did not wear out, nor did the sandals on your feet. 6You ate no bread and drank no wine or other fermented drink. I did this so that you might know that I am the LORD your God.

7When you reached this place, Sihon king of Heshbon and Og king of Bashan came out to fight against us, but we defeated them. 8We took their land and gave it as an inheritance to the Reubenites, the Gadites and the half-tribe of Manasseh.

9Carefully follow the terms of this covenant, so that you may prosper in everything you do. 10All of you are standing today in the presence of the LORD your God—your leaders and chief men, your elders and officials, and all the other men of Israel, 11together with your children and your wives, and the aliens living in your camps who chop your wood and carry your water. 12You are standing here in order to enter into a covenant with the LORD your God, a covenant the LORD is making with you this day and sealing with an oath, 13to confirm you this day as his people, that he may be your God as he promised you and as he swore to your fathers, Abraham, Isaac and Jacob. 14I am making this covenant, with its oath, not only with you 15who are standing here with us today in the presence of the LORD our God but also with those who are not here today.

16You yourselves know how we lived in Egypt and how we passed through the countries on the way here. 17You saw among them their detestable images and idols of wood and stone, of silver and gold. 18Make sure there is no man or woman, clan or tribe among you today whose heart turns away from the LORD our God to go and worship the gods of those nations; make sure there is no root among you that produces such bitter poison.

King James

¹⁹And it come to pass, when he heareth the words of this curse, that he bless himself in his heart, saying, I shall have peace, though I walk in the ⁱimagination of mine heart, to add ^jdrunkenness to thirst:

²⁰The LORD will not spare him, but then the anger of the LORD and his jealousy shall smoke against that man, and all the curses that are written in this book shall lie upon him, and the LORD shall blot out his name from under heaven.

²¹And the LORD shall separate him unto evil out of all the tribes of Israel, according to all the curses of the covenant that ^kare written in this book of the law:

²²So that the generation to come of your children that shall rise up after you, and the stranger that shall come from a far land, shall say, when they see the plagues of that land, and the sicknesses ^lwhich the LORD hath laid upon it;

²³*And that* the whole land thereof *is* brimstone, and salt, *and* burning, *that* it is not sown, nor beareth, nor any grass groweth therein, like the overthrow of Sodom, and Gomorrah, Admah, and Zeboim, which the LORD overthrew in his anger, and in his wrath:

²⁴Even all nations shall say, Wherefore hath the LORD done thus unto this land? what *meaneth* the heat of this great anger?

²⁵Then men shall say, Because they have forsaken the covenant of the LORD God of their fathers, which he made with them when he brought them forth out of the land of Egypt:

²⁶For they went and served other gods, and worshipped them, gods whom they knew not, and ^mwhom he had not ⁿgiven unto them:

²⁷And the anger of the LORD was kindled against this land, to bring upon it all the curses that are written in this book:

²⁸And the LORD rooted them out of their land in anger, and in wrath, and in great indignation, and cast them into another land, as *it is* this day.

²⁹The secret *things belong* unto the LORD our God: but those *things which are* revealed *belong* unto us and to our children for ever, that *we* may do all the words of this law.

The rewards of repentance

30 AND IT shall come to pass, when all these things are come upon thee, the blessing and the curse, which I have set before thee, and thou shalt call *them* to mind among all the nations, whither the LORD thy God hath driven thee,

²And shalt return unto the LORD thy God, and shalt obey his voice according to all that I command thee this day, thou and thy children, with all thine heart, and with all thy soul;

³That then the LORD thy God will turn thy captivity, and have compassion upon thee, and will return and gather thee from all the nations, whither the LORD thy God hath scattered thee.

⁴If *any* of thine be driven out unto the outmost *parts* of heaven, from thence will the LORD thy God gather thee, and from thence will he fetch thee:

⁵And the LORD thy God will bring thee into the land which thy fathers possessed, and thou shalt possess it; and he will do thee good, and multiply thee above thy fathers.

Amplified

¹⁹And lest, when he hears the words of this curse *and* oath, he flatters *and* congratulates himself in his [mind and] heart, saying, I shall have peace *and* safety, ^lthough I walk in the stubbornness of my [mind and] heart [bringing down a hurricane of destruction] and sweep away the watered land with the dry.

²⁰The Lord will not pardon him, but then the anger of the Lord and His jealousy will smoke against that man, and all the curses that are written in this book shall settle on him; the Lord will blot out his very name from under the heavens.

²¹And the Lord will single him out for ruin *and* destruction from all the tribes of Israel, according to all the curses of the covenant that are written in this Book of the Law,

²²So that the next generation, your children who rise up after you, and the foreigner who shall come from a distant land, shall say, when they see the plagues of this land and the diseases with which the Lord has made it sick—

²³The whole land is brimstone and salt and a burned waste, not sown or bearing anything, where no grass can take root, like the overthrow of Sodom and Gomorrah with Admah and Zeboiim, which the Lord overthrew in His anger and wrath—

²⁴Even all the nations shall say, Why has the Lord done thus to this land? What does the heat of this great anger mean?

²⁵Then men shall say, Because they forsook the covenant of the Lord, the God of their fathers, which He made with them when He brought them forth out of the land of Egypt.

²⁶For they went and served other gods and worshiped them, gods they knew not and that He had not given to them.

²⁷So the anger of the Lord was kindled against this land, bringing upon it all the curses that are written in this book.

²⁸And the Lord rooted them out of their land in anger and in wrath and in great indignation and cast them into another land, as it is this day.

²⁹The secret things belong unto the Lord our God, but the things which are revealed belong to us and to our children forever, that we may do all of the words of this law.

30 AND WHEN all these things have come upon you, the blessings and the curses which I have set before you, and you shall call them to mind among all the nations where the Lord your God has driven you,

²And shall return to the Lord your God and obey His voice according to all that I command you today, you and your children, with all your [mind and] heart and with all your being,

³Then the Lord your God will restore your fortunes and have compassion upon you and will gather you again from all the nations where He has scattered you.

⁴Even if any of your dispersed are in the uttermost parts of the heavens, from there the Lord your God will gather you and from there will He bring you.

⁵And the Lord your God will bring you into the land which your fathers possessed, and you shall possess it; and He will do you good and multiply you above your fathers.

---

^lIt is on the strength of the Lord's oath to be Israel's God and so to protect them that this Israelite flatters himself into thinking he is secure, no matter how he may behave. In the history of religion such a delusion has been lamentably frequent, and persons depending upon the unlimited protection of election have presumed on this and recklessly indulged in evil (*The Cambridge Bible*). The Bible emphasizes the "security of the saints," but it is equally emphatic concerning the insecurity of those in conscious and continued indifference to God (Ezek. 3:20; 18:24, 26; Gal. 6:8; James 1:21; II Pet. 1:10, 11; Rev. 22:14).

ⁱOr, *stubbornness*   ^jHeb. *the drunken to the thirsty*   ^kHeb. *is written*   ^lHeb. *wherewith the LORD hath made it sick*   ^mOr, *who had not given to them* any portion   ⁿHeb. *divided*

New American Standard

19"It shall be when he hears the words of this curse, that he will boast, saying, 'I have peace though I walk in the stubbornness of my heart in order to destroy the watered *land* with the dry.'

20"The LORD shall never be willing to forgive him, but rather the anger of the LORD and His jealousy will burn against that man, and every curse which is written in this book will rest on him, and the LORD will blot out his name from under heaven.

21"Then the LORD will single him out for adversity from all the tribes of Israel, according to all the curses of the covenant which are written in this book of the law.

22 ¶ "Now the generation to come, your sons who rise up after you and the foreigner who comes from a distant land, when they see the plagues of the land and the diseases with which the LORD has afflicted it, will say,

23 'All its land is brimstone and salt, a burning waste, unsown and unproductive, and no grass grows in it, like the overthrow of Sodom and Gomorrah, Admah and Zeboiim, which the LORD overthrew in His anger and in His wrath.'

24"All the nations will say, 'Why has the LORD done thus to this land? Why this great outburst of anger?'

25"Then *men* will say, 'Because they forsook the covenant of the LORD, the God of their fathers, which He made with them when He brought them out of the land of Egypt.

26 'They went and served other gods and worshiped them, gods whom they have not known and whom He had not allotted to them.

27 'Therefore, the anger of the LORD burned against that land, to bring upon it every curse which is written in this book;

28 and the LORD uprooted them from their land in anger and in fury and in great wrath, and cast them into another land, as *it is* this day.'

29 ¶ "The secret things belong to the LORD our God, but the things revealed belong to us and to our sons forever, that we may observe all the words of this law.

Restoration Promised

30 "SO IT shall be when all of these things have come upon you, the blessing and the curse which I have set before you, and you call *them* to mind in all nations where the LORD your God has banished you,

2 and you return to the LORD your God and obey Him with all your heart and soul according to all that I command you today, you and your sons,

3 then the LORD your God will restore you from captivity, and have compassion on you, and will gather you again from all the peoples where the LORD your God has scattered you.

4"If your outcasts are at the ends of the earth, from there the LORD your God will gather you, and from there He will bring you back.

5"The LORD your God will bring you into the land which your fathers possessed, and you shall possess it; and He will prosper you and multiply you more than your fathers.

New International

19When such a person hears the words of this oath, he invokes a blessing on himself and therefore thinks, "I will be safe, even though I persist in going my own way." This will bring disaster on the watered land as well as the dry.*m*

20The LORD will never be willing to forgive him; his wrath and zeal will burn against that man. All the curses written in this book will fall upon him, and the LORD will blot out his name from under heaven. 21The LORD will single him out from all the tribes of Israel for disaster, according to all the curses of the covenant written in this Book of the Law.

22Your children who follow you in later generations and foreigners who come from distant lands will see the calamities that have fallen on the land and the diseases with which the LORD has afflicted it. 23The whole land will be a burning waste of salt and sulfur—nothing planted, nothing sprouting, no vegetation growing on it. It will be like the destruction of Sodom and Gomorrah, Admah and Zeboiim, which the LORD overthrew in fierce anger. 24All the nations will ask: "Why has the LORD done this to this land? Why this fierce, burning anger?"

25And the answer will be: "It is because this people abandoned the covenant of the LORD, the God of their fathers, the covenant he made with them when he brought them out of Egypt. 26They went off and worshiped other gods and bowed down to them, gods they did not know, gods he had not given them. 27Therefore the LORD's anger burned against this land, so that he brought on it all the curses written in this book. 28In furious anger and in great wrath the LORD uprooted them from their land and thrust them into another land, as it is now."

29The secret things belong to the LORD our God, but the things revealed belong to us and to our children forever, that we may follow all the words of this law.

Prosperity After Turning to the LORD

30 WHEN ALL these blessings and curses I have set before you come upon you and you take them to heart wherever the LORD your God disperses you among the nations, 2and when you and your children return to the LORD your God and obey him with all your heart and with all your soul according to everything I command you today, 3then the LORD your God will restore your fortunes*n* and have compassion on you and gather you again from all the nations where he scattered you. 4Even if you have been banished to the most distant land under the heavens, from there the LORD your God will gather you and bring you back. 5He will bring you to the land that belonged to your fathers, and you will take possession of it. He will make you more prosperous and numerous than your fathers.

---

m 19 Or *way, in order to add drunkenness to thirst.*   *n 3* Or *will bring you back from captivity*

King James

⁶And the LORD thy God will circumcise thine heart, and the heart of thy seed, to love the LORD thy God with all thine heart, and with all thy soul, that thou mayest live.

⁷And the LORD thy God will put all these curses upon thine enemies, and on them that hate thee, which persecuted thee.

⁸And thou shalt return and obey the voice of the LORD, and do all his commandments which I command thee this day.

⁹And the LORD thy God will make thee plenteous in every work of thine hand, in the fruit of thy body, and in the fruit of thy cattle, and in the fruit of thy land, for good: for the LORD will again rejoice over thee for good, as he rejoiced over thy fathers:

¹⁰If thou shalt hearken unto the voice of the LORD thy God, to keep his commandments and his statutes which are written in this book of the law, *and* if thou turn unto the LORD thy God with all thine heart, and with all thy soul.

Closing advice

¹¹ ¶ For this commandment which I command thee this day, it *is* not hidden from thee, neither *is* it far off.

¹²It *is* not in heaven, that thou shouldest say, Who shall go up for us to heaven, and bring it unto us, that we may hear it, and do it?

¹³Neither *is* it beyond the sea, that thou shouldest say, Who shall go over the sea for us, and bring it unto us, that we may hear it, and do it?

¹⁴But the word *is* very nigh unto thee, in thy mouth, and in thy heart, that thou mayest do it.

¹⁵ ¶ See, I have set before thee this day life and good, and death and evil;

¹⁶In that I command thee this day to love the LORD thy God, to walk in his ways, and to keep his commandments and his statutes and his judgments, that thou mayest live and multiply: and the LORD thy God shall bless thee in the land whither thou goest to possess it.

¹⁷But if thine heart turn away, so that thou wilt not hear, but shalt be drawn away, and worship other gods, and serve them;

¹⁸I denounce unto you this day, that ye shall surely perish, *and that* ye shall not prolong *your* days upon the land, whither thou passest over Jordan to go to possess it.

¹⁹I call heaven and earth to record this day against you, *that* I have set before you life and death, blessing and cursing: therefore choose life, that both thou and thy seed may live:

²⁰That thou mayest love the LORD thy God, *and* that thou mayest obey his voice, and that thou mayest cleave unto him: for he *is* thy life, and the length of thy days: that thou mayest dwell in the land which the LORD sware unto thy fathers, to Abraham, to Isaac, and to Jacob, to give them.

The appointment of Joshua

31 AND MOSES went and spake these words unto all Israel.

²And he said unto them, I *am* an hundred and twenty years old this day; I can no more go out and come in: also the LORD hath said unto me, Thou shalt not go over this Jordan.

³The LORD thy God, he will go over before thee, *and* he will destroy these nations from before thee, and thou shalt possess them: *and* Joshua, he shall go over before thee, as the LORD hath said.

⁴And the LORD shall do unto them as he did to Sihon and to Og, kings of the Amorites, and unto the land of them, whom he destroyed.

⁵And the LORD shall give them up before your face, that ye may do unto them according unto all the commandments which I have commanded you.

Amplified

⁶And the Lord your God will circumcise your hearts and the hearts of your descendants, to love the Lord your God with all your [mind and] heart and with all your being, that you may live.

⁷And the Lord your God will put all these curses upon your enemies and on those who hate you, who persecute you.

⁸And you shall return and obey the voice of the Lord and do all His commandments which I command you today.

⁹And the Lord your God will make you abundantly prosperous in every work of your hand, in the fruit of your body, of your cattle, of your land, for good; for the Lord will again delight in prospering you, as He took delight in your fathers,

¹⁰If you obey the voice of the Lord your God, to keep His commandments and His statutes which are written in this Book of the Law, and if you turn to the Lord your God with all your [mind and] heart and with all your being.

¹¹For this commandment which I command you this day is not too difficult for you, nor is it far off.

¹²It is not [a secret laid up] in heaven, that you should say, Who shall go up for us to heaven and bring it to us, that we may hear and do it?

¹³Neither is it beyond the sea, that you should say, Who shall go over the sea for us and bring it to us, that we may hear and do it?

¹⁴But the word is very near you, in your mouth and in your mind *and* in your heart, so that you can do it.

¹⁵See, I have set before you this day life and good, and death and evil.

¹⁶[If you obey the commandments of the Lord your God which] I command you today, to love the Lord your God, to walk in His ways, and to keep His commandments and His statutes and His ordinances, then you shall live and multiply, and the Lord your God will bless you in the land into which you go to possess.

¹⁷But if your [mind and] heart turn away and you will not hear, but are drawn away to worship other gods and serve them,

¹⁸I declare to you today that you shall surely perish, and you shall not live long in the land which you pass over the Jordan to enter and possess.

¹⁹I call heaven and earth to witness this day against you that I have set before you life and death, the blessings and the curses; therefore choose life, that you and your descendants may live

²⁰And may love the Lord your God, obey His voice, and cling to Him. For He is your life and the length of your days, that you may dwell in the land which the Lord swore to give to your fathers, to Abraham, Isaac, and Jacob.

31 AND MOSES went on speaking these words to all Israel:

²And he said to them, I am 120 years old this day; I can no more go out and come in. And the Lord has said to me, You shall not go over this Jordan.

³The Lord your God will Himself go over before you, and He will destroy these nations from before you, and you shall dispossess them. And Joshua shall go over before you, as the Lord has said.

⁴And the Lord will do to them as He did to Sihon and Og, the kings of the Amorites, and to their land, when He destroyed them.

⁵And the Lord will give them over to you, and you shall do to them according to all the commandments which I have commanded you.

New American Standard

6 ¶ "Moreover the LORD your God will circumcise your heart and the heart of your descendants, to love the LORD your God with all your heart and with all your soul, so that you may live.

7"The LORD your God will inflict all these curses on your enemies and on those who hate you, who persecuted you.

8"And you shall again obey the LORD, and observe all His commandments which I command you today.

9"Then the LORD your God will prosper you abundantly in all the work of your hand, in the offspring of your body and in the offspring of your cattle and in the produce of your ground, for the LORD will again rejoice over you for good, just as He rejoiced over your fathers;

10 if you obey the LORD your God to keep His commandments and His statutes which are written in this book of the law, if you turn to the LORD your God with all your heart and soul.

11 ¶ "For this commandment which I command you today is not too difficult for you, nor is it out of reach.

12"It is not in heaven, that you should say, 'Who will go up to heaven for us to get it for us and make us hear it, that we may observe it?'

13"Nor is it beyond the sea, that you should say, 'Who will cross the sea for us to get it for us and make us hear it, that we may observe it?'

14"But the word is very near you, in your mouth and in your heart, that you may observe it.

Choose Life

15 ¶ "See, I have set before you today life and prosperity, and death and adversity;

16 in that I command you today to love the LORD your God, to walk in His ways and to keep His commandments and His statutes and His judgments, that you may live and multiply, and that the LORD your God may bless you in the land where you are entering to possess it.

17"But if your heart turns away and you will not obey, but are drawn away and worship other gods and serve them,

18 I declare to you today that you shall surely perish. You will not prolong *your* days in the land where you are crossing the Jordan to enter and possess it.

19"I call heaven and earth to witness against you today, that I have set before you life and death, the blessing and the curse. So choose life in order that you may live, you and your descendants,

20 by loving the LORD your God, by obeying His voice, and by holding fast to Him; for this is your life and the length of your days, that you may live in the land which the LORD swore to your fathers, to Abraham, Isaac, and Jacob, to give them."

Moses' Last Counsel

31 SO MOSES went and spoke these words to all Israel.

2 And he said to them, "I am a hundred and twenty years old today; I am no longer able to come and go, and the LORD has said to me, 'You shall not cross this Jordan.'

3"It is the LORD your God who will cross ahead of you; He will destroy these nations before you, and you shall dispossess them. Joshua is the one who will cross ahead of you, just as the LORD has spoken.

4"The LORD will do to them just as He did to Sihon and Og, the kings of the Amorites, and to their land, when He destroyed them.

5"The LORD will deliver them up before you, and you shall do to them according to all the commandments which I have commanded you.

New International

6The LORD your God will circumcise your hearts and the hearts of your descendants, so that you may love him with all your heart and with all your soul, and live. 7The LORD your God will put all these curses on your enemies who hate and persecute you. 8You will again obey the LORD and follow all his commands I am giving you today. 9Then the LORD your God will make you most prosperous in all the work of your hands and in the fruit of your womb, the young of your livestock and the crops of your land. The LORD will again delight in you and make you prosperous, just as he delighted in your fathers, 10if you obey the LORD your God and keep his commands and decrees that are written in this Book of the Law and turn to the LORD your God with all your heart and with all your soul.

The Offer of Life or Death

11Now what I am commanding you today is not too difficult for you or beyond your reach. 12It is not up in heaven, so that you have to ask, "Who will ascend into heaven to get it and proclaim it to us so we may obey it?" 13Nor is it beyond the sea, so that you have to ask, "Who will cross the sea to get it and proclaim it to us so we may obey it?" 14No, the word is very near you; it is in your mouth and in your heart so you may obey it.

15See, I set before you today life and prosperity, death and destruction. 16For I command you today to love the LORD your God, to walk in his ways, and to keep his commands, decrees and laws; then you will live and increase, and the LORD your God will bless you in the land you are entering to possess.

17But if your heart turns away and you are not obedient, and if you are drawn away to bow down to other gods and worship them, 18I declare to you this day that you will certainly be destroyed. You will not live long in the land you are crossing the Jordan to enter and possess.

19This day I call heaven and earth as witnesses against you that I have set before you life and death, blessings and curses. Now choose life, so that you and your children may live 20and that you may love the LORD your God, listen to his voice, and hold fast to him. For the LORD is your life, and he will give you many years in the land he swore to give to your fathers, Abraham, Isaac and Jacob.

Joshua to Succeed Moses

31 THEN MOSES went out and spoke these words to all Israel: 2"I am now a hundred and twenty years old and I am no longer able to lead you. The LORD has said to me, 'You shall not cross the Jordan.' 3The LORD your God himself will cross over ahead of you. He will destroy these nations before you, and you will take possession of their land. Joshua also will cross over ahead of you, as the LORD said. 4And the LORD will do to them what he did to Sihon and Og, the kings of the Amorites, whom he destroyed along with their land. 5The LORD will deliver them to you, and you must do to them all that I have command-

King James

6Be strong and of a good courage, fear not, nor be afraid of them: for the LORD thy God, *it is* that doth go with thee; he will not fail thee, nor forsake thee.

7 ¶ And Moses called unto Joshua, and said unto him in the sight of all Israel, Be strong and of a good courage: for thou must go with this people unto the land which the LORD hath sworn unto their fathers to give them; and thou shalt cause them to inherit it.

8And the LORD, he *it is* that doth go before thee; he will be with thee, he will not fail thee, neither forsake thee: fear not, neither be dismayed.

Provision for teaching the law

9 ¶ And Moses wrote this law, and delivered it unto the priests the sons of Levi, which bare the ark of the covenant of the LORD, and unto all the elders of Israel.

10And Moses commanded them, saying, At the end of *every* seven years, in the solemnity of the year of release, in the feast of tabernacles,

11When all Israel is come to appear before the LORD thy God in the place which he shall choose, thou shalt read this law before all Israel in their hearing.

12Gather the people together, men, and women, and children, and thy stranger that *is* within thy gates, that they may hear, and that they may learn, and fear the LORD your God, and observe to do all the words of this law:

13And *that* their children, which have not known *any thing,* may hear, and learn to fear the LORD your God, as long as ye live in the land whither ye go over Jordan to possess it.

The LORD appears to Moses

14 ¶ And the LORD said unto Moses, Behold, thy days approach that thou must die: call Joshua, and present yourselves in the tabernacle of the congregation, that I may give him a charge. And Moses and Joshua went, and presented themselves in the tabernacle of the congregation.

15And the LORD appeared in the tabernacle in a pillar of a cloud: and the pillar of the cloud stood over the door of the tabernacle.

16 ¶ And the LORD said unto Moses, Behold, thou shalt osleep with thy fathers; and this people will rise up, and go a-whoring after the gods of the strangers of the land, whither they go *to be* among them, and will forsake me, and break my covenant which I have made with them.

17Then my anger shall be kindled against them in that day, and I will forsake them, and I will hide my face from them, and they shall be devoured, and many evils and troubles shall pbefall them; so that they will say in that day, Are not these evils come upon us, because our God *is* not among us?

18And I will surely hide my face in that day for all the evils which they shall have wrought, in that they are turned unto other gods.

19Now therefore write ye this song for you, and teach it the children of Israel: put it in their mouths, that this song may be a witness for me against the children of Israel.

20For when I shall have brought them into the land which I sware unto their fathers, that floweth with milk and honey; and they shall have eaten and filled themselves, and waxen fat; then will they turn unto other gods, and serve them, and provoke me, and break my covenant.

21And it shall come to pass, when many evils and troubles are befallen them, that this song shall testify qagainst them as a witness; for it shall not be forgotten out of the mouths of their seed: for I know their imagination which they rgo about, even now, before I have brought them into the land which I sware.

22 ¶ Moses therefore wrote this song the same day, and taught it the children of Israel.

Amplified

6Be strong, courageous, *and* firm; fear not nor be in terror before them, for it is the Lord your God Who goes with you; He will not fail you or forsake you.

7And Moses called to Joshua and said to him in the sight of all Israel, Be strong, courageous, *and* firm, for you shall go with this people into the land which the Lord has sworn to their fathers to give them, and you shall cause them to possess it.

8It is the Lord Who goes before you; He will [march] with you; He will not fail you *or* let you go or forsake you; [let there be no cowardice or flinching, but] fear not, neither become broken [in spirit—depressed, dismayed, and unnerved with alarm].

9And Moses wrote this law and delivered it to the Levitical priests, who carried the ark of the covenant of the Lord, and to all the elders of Israel.

10And Moses commanded them, At the end of every seven years, at the set time of the year of release [of debtors from their debts], at the Feast of Booths,

11When all Israel comes to appear before the Lord your God in the place which He chooses [for His sanctuary], you shall read this law before all Israel in their hearing.

12Assemble the people—men, women, and children, and the stranger *and* the sojourner within your towns—that they may hear and learn [reverently] to fear the Lord your God and be watchful to do all the words of this law,

13And that their children, who have not known it, may hear and learn [reverently] to fear the Lord your God as long as you live in the land which you go over the Jordan to possess.

14And the Lord said to Moses, Behold, your days are nearing when you must die. Call Joshua and present yourselves at the Tent of Meeting, that I may give him his charge. And Moses and Joshua went and presented themselves at the Tent of Meeting.

15And the Lord appeared in the Tent in a pillar of cloud, and the pillar of cloud stood over the door of the Tent.

16And the Lord said to Moses, Behold, you shall sleep with your fathers, and this people will rise up and play the harlot after the strange gods of the land where they go to be among them; and they will forsake Me and break My covenant which I have made with them.

17Then My anger will be kindled against them in that day, and I will forsake them and hide My face from them. And they shall be devoured, and many evils and troubles shall befall them, so that they will say in that day, Have not these evils come upon us because our God is not among us?

18And I will surely hide My face in that day because of all the evil which they have done in turning to other gods.

19And now write this song for yourselves and teach it to the Israelites; put it in their mouths, that this song may be a witness for Me against the Israelites.

20For when I have brought them into the land which I swore to their fathers, a land flowing with milk and honey, and they have eaten and filled themselves and become fat, then they will turn to other gods and serve them, and despise *and* scorn Me and break My covenant.

21And when many evils and troubles have befallen them, this [sacred] song will confront them as a witness, for it will never be forgotten from the mouths of their descendants. For I know their strong desire *and* the purposes which they are forming even now, before I have brought them into the land which I swore to give them.

22Moses wrote this song the same day and taught it to the Israelites. [Deut. 32:1–43.]

---

oHeb. *lie down*   pHeb. *find them*   qHeb. *before*
rHeb. *do*

New American Standard

6"Be strong and courageous, do not be afraid or tremble at them, for the LORD your God is the one who goes with you. He will not fail you or forsake you."

7 ¶ Then Moses called to Joshua and said to him in the sight of all Israel, "Be strong and courageous, for you shall go with this people into the land which the LORD has sworn to their fathers to give them, and you shall give it to them as an inheritance.

8"The LORD is the one who goes ahead of you; He will be with you. He will not fail you or forsake you. Do not fear or be dismayed."

9 ¶ So Moses wrote this law and gave it to the priests, the sons of Levi who carried the ark of the covenant of the LORD, and to all the elders of Israel.

10 Then Moses commanded them, saying, "At the end of *every* seven years, at the time of the year of remission of debts, at the Feast of Booths,

11 when all Israel comes to appear before the LORD your God at the place which He will choose, you shall read this law in front of all Israel in their hearing.

12"Assemble the people, the men and the women and children and the alien who is in your town, so that they may hear and learn and fear the LORD your God, and be careful to observe all the words of this law.

13"Their children, who have not known, will hear and learn to fear the LORD your God, as long as you live on the land which you are about to cross the Jordan to possess."

Israel Will Fall Away

14 ¶ Then the LORD said to Moses, "Behold, the time for you to die is near; call Joshua, and present yourselves at the tent of meeting, that I may commission him." So Moses and Joshua went and presented themselves at the tent of meeting.

15 The LORD appeared in the tent in a pillar of cloud, and the pillar of cloud stood at the doorway of the tent.

16 The LORD said to Moses, "Behold, you are about to lie down with your fathers; and this people will arise and play the harlot with the strange gods of the land, into the midst of which they are going, and will forsake Me and break My covenant which I have made with them.

17"Then My anger will be kindled against them in that day, and I will forsake them and hide My face from them, and they will be consumed, and many evils and troubles will come upon them; so that they will say in that day, 'Is it not because our God is not among us that these evils have come upon us?'

18"But I will surely hide My face in that day because of all the evil which they will do, for they will turn to other gods.

19 ¶ "Now therefore, write this song for yourselves, and teach it to the sons of Israel; put it on their lips, so that this song may be a witness for Me against the sons of Israel.

20"For when I bring them into the land flowing with milk and honey, which I swore to their fathers, and they have eaten and are satisfied and become prosperous, then they will turn to other gods and serve them, and spurn Me and break My covenant.

21"Then it shall come about, when many evils and troubles have come upon them, that this song will testify before them as a witness (for it shall not be forgotten from the lips of their descendants); for I know their intent which they are developing today, before I have brought them into the land which I swore."

22 So Moses wrote this song the same day, and taught it to the sons of Israel.

New International

ed you. 6Be strong and courageous. Do not be afraid or terrified because of them, for the LORD your God goes with you; he will never leave you nor forsake you."

7Then Moses summoned Joshua and said to him in the presence of all Israel, "Be strong and courageous, for you must go with this people into the land that the LORD swore to their forefathers to give them, and you must divide it among them as their inheritance. 8The LORD himself goes before you and will be with you; he will never leave you nor forsake you. Do not be afraid; do not be discouraged."

The Reading of the Law

9So Moses wrote down this law and gave it to the priests, the sons of Levi, who carried the ark of the covenant of the LORD, and to all the elders of Israel. 10Then Moses commanded them: "At the end of every seven years, in the year for canceling debts, during the Feast of Tabernacles, 11when all Israel comes to appear before the LORD your God at the place he will choose, you shall read this law before them in their hearing. 12Assemble the people—men, women and children, and the aliens living in your towns—so they can listen and learn to fear the LORD your God and follow carefully all the words of this law. 13Their children, who do not know this law, must hear it and learn to fear the LORD your God as long as you live in the land you are crossing the Jordan to possess."

Israel's Rebellion Predicted

14The LORD said to Moses, "Now the day of your death is near. Call Joshua and present yourselves at the Tent of Meeting, where I will commission him." So Moses and Joshua came and presented themselves at the Tent of Meeting.

15Then the LORD appeared at the Tent in a pillar of cloud, and the cloud stood over the entrance to the Tent. 16And the LORD said to Moses: "You are going to rest with your fathers, and these people will soon prostitute themselves to the foreign gods of the land they are entering. They will forsake me and break the covenant I made with them. 17On that day I will become angry with them and forsake them; I will hide my face from them, and they will be destroyed. Many disasters and difficulties will come upon them, and on that day they will ask, 'Have not these disasters come upon us because our God is not with us?' 18And I will certainly hide my face on that day because of all their wickedness in turning to other gods.

19"Now write down for yourselves this song and teach it to the Israelites and have them sing it, so that it may be a witness for me against them. 20When I have brought them into the land flowing with milk and honey, the land I promised on oath to their forefathers, and when they eat their fill and thrive, they will turn to other gods and worship them, rejecting me and breaking my covenant. 21And when many disasters and difficulties come upon them, this song will testify against them, because it will not be forgotten by their descendants. I know what they are disposed to do, even before I bring them into the land I promised them on oath." 22So Moses wrote down this song that day and taught it to the Israelites.

King James

²³And he gave Joshua the son of Nun a charge, and said, Be strong and of a good courage: for thou shalt bring the children of Israel into the land which I sware unto them: and I will be with thee.

²⁴ ¶ And it came to pass, when Moses had made an end of writing the words of this law in a book, until they were finished,

²⁵That Moses commanded the Levites, which bare the ark of the covenant of the LORD, saying,

²⁶Take this book of the law, and put it in the side of the ark of the covenant of the LORD your God, that it may be there for a witness against thee.

²⁷For I know thy rebellion, and thy stiff neck: behold, while I am yet alive with you this day, ye have been rebellious against the LORD; and how much more after my death?

²⁸ ¶ Gather unto me all the elders of your tribes, and your officers, that I may speak these words in their ears, and call heaven and earth to record against them.

²⁹For I know that after my death ye will utterly corrupt *yourselves,* and turn aside from the way which I have commanded you; and evil will befall you in the latter days; because ye will do evil in the sight of the LORD, to provoke him to anger through the work of your hands.

The song of Moses

³⁰And Moses spake in the ears of all the congregation of Israel the words of this song, until they were ended.

32 GIVE EAR, O ye heavens, and I will speak; and hear, O earth, the words of my mouth.

²My doctrine shall drop as the rain, my speech shall distil as the dew, as the small rain upon the tender herb, and as the showers upon the grass:

³Because I will publish the name of the LORD: ascribe ye greatness unto our God.

⁴*He is* the Rock, his work *is* perfect: for all his ways *are* judgment; a God of truth and without iniquity, just and right *is* he.

⁵^sThey have corrupted themselves, ^ttheir spot *is* not *the spot* of his children: *they are* a perverse and crooked generation.

⁶Do ye thus requite the LORD, O foolish people and unwise? *is* not he thy father *that* hath bought thee? hath he not made thee, and established thee?

⁷ ¶ Remember the days of old, consider the years of ^umany generations: ask thy father, and he will show thee; thy elders, and they will tell thee.

⁸When the Most High divided to the nations their inheritance, when he separated the sons of Adam, he set the bounds of the people according to the number of the children of Israel.

⁹For the LORD'S portion *is* his people; Jacob *is* the ^vlot of his inheritance.

¹⁰He found him in a desert land, and in the waste howling wilderness; he ^wled him about, he instructed him, he kept him as the apple of his eye.

Amplified

²³And [the Lord] charged Joshua son of Nun, Be strong and courageous *and* firm, for you shall bring the Israelites into the land which I swore to give them, and I will be with you.

²⁴And when Moses had finished writing the words of this law in a book to the very end,

²⁵He commanded the Levites who carried the ark of the covenant of the Lord,

²⁶Take this Book of the Law and put it by the side of the ark of the covenant of the Lord your God, that it may be there for a witness against you.

²⁷For I know your rebellion and stubbornness; behold, while I am yet alive with you today, you have been rebellious against the Lord; and how much more after my death!

²⁸Gather to me all the elders of your tribes and your officers, that I may speak these words in their ears and call heaven and earth to witness against them.

²⁹For I know that after my death you will utterly corrupt yourselves and turn aside from the way which I have commanded you; and evil will befall you in the latter days because you will do what is evil in the sight of the Lord, to provoke Him to anger through the work of your hands.

³⁰And Moses spoke in the hearing of all the congregation of Israel the words of this song until they were ended:

32 GIVE EAR, O heavens, and I [Moses] will speak; and let the earth hear the words of my mouth.

²My message shall drop as the rain, my speech shall distil as the dew, as the light rain upon the tender grass, and as the showers upon the herb.

³For I will proclaim the name [and presence] of the Lord. Concede *and* ascribe greatness to our God.

⁴He is the Rock, His work is perfect, for all His ways are law *and* justice. A God of faithfulness without breach *or* deviation, just and right is He.

⁵They [Israel] have spoiled themselves. They are not sons to Him, and that is their blemish—a perverse and crooked generation!

⁶Do you thus repay the Lord, you foolish and senseless people? Is not He your Father Who acquired you for His own, Who made and established you [as a nation]?

⁷Remember the days of old; consider the years of many generations. Ask your father and he will show you, your elders, and they will tell you.

⁸When the Most High gave to the nations their inheritance, when He separated the children of men, He set the bounds of the peoples according to the number of the Israelites.

⁹For the Lord's portion is His people; Jacob (Israel) is the lot of His inheritance.

¹⁰He found him in a desert land, in the howling void of the wilderness; He kept circling around him, He scanned him [penetratingly], He kept him as the pupil of His eye.

---

^sHeb. *He hath corrupted to himself*   ^tOr, that they are *not his children,* that is *their blot*   ^uHeb. *generation and generation*
^vHeb. *cord*   ^wOr, *compassed him about*

New American Standard

Joshua Is Commissioned

23 ¶ Then He commissioned Joshua the son of Nun, and said, "Be strong and courageous, for you shall bring the sons of Israel into the land which I swore to them, and I will be with you."

24 ¶ It came about, when Moses finished writing the words of this law in a book until they were complete,

25 that Moses commanded the Levites who carried the ark of the covenant of the LORD, saying,

26 "Take this book of the law and place it beside the ark of the covenant of the LORD your God, that it may remain there as a witness against you.

27 "For I know your rebellion and your stubbornness; behold, while I am still alive with you today, you have been rebellious against the LORD; how much more, then, after my death?

28 "Assemble to me all the elders of your tribes and your officers, that I may speak these words in their hearing and call the heavens and the earth to witness against them.

29 "For I know that after my death you will act corruptly and turn from the way which I have commanded you; and evil will befall you in the latter days, for you will do that which is evil in the sight of the LORD, provoking Him to anger with the work of your hands."

30 ¶ Then Moses spoke in the hearing of all the assembly of Israel the words of this song, until they were complete:

The Song of Moses

32 "GIVE EAR, O heavens, and let me speak;
And let the earth hear the words of my mouth.

2 "Let my teaching drop as the rain,
My speech distill as the dew,
As the droplets on the fresh grass
And as the showers on the herb.

3 "For I proclaim the name of the LORD;
Ascribe greatness to our God!

4 "The Rock! His work is perfect,
For all His ways are just;
A God of faithfulness and without injustice,
Righteous and upright is He.

5 "They have acted corruptly toward Him,
They are not His children, because of their defect;
But are a perverse and crooked generation.

6 "Do you thus repay the LORD,
O foolish and unwise people?
Is not He your Father who has bought you?
He has made you and established you.

7 "Remember the days of old,
Consider the years of all generations.
Ask your father, and he will inform you,
Your elders, and they will tell you.

8 "When the Most High gave the nations their
inheritance,
When He separated the sons of man,
He set the boundaries of the peoples
According to the number of the sons of Israel.

9 "For the LORD's portion is His people;
Jacob is the allotment of His inheritance.

10 "He found him in a desert land,
And in the howling waste of a wilderness;
He encircled him, He cared for him,
He guarded him as the pupil of His eye.

New International

23 The LORD gave this command to Joshua son of Nun: "Be strong and courageous, for you will bring the Israelites into the land I promised them on oath, and I myself will be with you."

24 After Moses finished writing in a book the words of this law from beginning to end, 25 he gave this command to the Levites who carried the ark of the covenant of the LORD: 26 "Take this Book of the Law and place it beside the ark of the covenant of the LORD your God. There it will remain as a witness against you. 27 For I know how rebellious and stiff-necked you are. If you have been rebellious against the LORD while I am still alive and with you, how much more will you rebel after I die! 28 Assemble before me all the elders of your tribes and all your officials, so that I can speak these words in their hearing and call heaven and earth to testify against them. 29 For I know that after my death you are sure to become utterly corrupt and to turn from the way I have commanded you. In days to come, disaster will fall upon you because you will do evil in the sight of the LORD and provoke him to anger by what your hands have made."

The Song of Moses

30 And Moses recited the words of this song from beginning to end in the hearing of the whole assembly of Israel:

32 LISTEN, O heavens, and I will speak;
hear, O earth, the words of my mouth.

2 Let my teaching fall like rain
and my words descend like dew,
like showers on new grass,
like abundant rain on tender plants.

3 I will proclaim the name of the LORD.
Oh, praise the greatness of our God!

4 He is the Rock, his works are perfect,
and all his ways are just.
A faithful God who does no wrong,
upright and just is he.

5 They have acted corruptly toward him;
to their shame they are no longer his
children,
but a warped and crooked generation.*o*

6 Is this the way you repay the LORD,
O foolish and unwise people?
Is he not your Father, your Creator,*p*
who made you and formed you?

7 Remember the days of old;
consider the generations long past.
Ask your father and he will tell you,
your elders, and they will explain to you.

8 When the Most High gave the nations their
inheritance,
when he divided all mankind,
he set up boundaries for the peoples
according to the number of the sons of
Israel.*q*

9 For the LORD's portion is his people,
Jacob his allotted inheritance.

10 In a desert land he found him,
in a barren and howling waste.
He shielded him and cared for him;
he guarded him as the apple of his eye,

---

o 5 Or *Corrupt are they and not his children, / a generation warped
and twisted to their shame*   *p* 6 Or *Father, who bought you*
q 8 Masoretic Text; Dead Sea Scrolls (see also Septuagint) *sons
of God*

King James

11As an eagle stirreth up her nest, fluttereth over her young, spreadeth abroad her wings, taketh them, beareth them on her wings:

12So the LORD alone did lead him, and *there was* no strange god with him.

13He made him ride on the high places of the earth, that he might eat the increase of the fields; and he made him to suck honey out of the rock, and oil out of the flinty rock;

14Butter of kine, and milk of sheep, with fat of lambs, and rams of the breed of Bashan, and goats, with the fat of kidneys of wheat; and thou didst drink the pure blood of the grape.

15 ¶ But Jeshurun waxed fat, and kicked: thou art waxen fat, thou art grown thick, thou art covered *with fatness;* then he forsook God *which* made him, and lightly esteemed the Rock of his salvation.

16They provoked him to jealousy with strange *gods,* with abominations provoked they him to anger.

17They sacrificed unto devils, xnot to God; to gods whom they knew not, to new *gods that* came newly up, whom your fathers feared not.

18Of the Rock *that* begat thee thou art unmindful, and hast forgotten God that formed thee.

19And when the LORD saw *it,* he yabhorred *them,* because of the provoking of his sons, and of his daughters.

20And he said, I will hide my face from them, I will see what their end *shall be:* for they *are* a very froward generation, children in whom *is* no faith.

21They have moved me to jealousy with *that which is* not God; they have provoked me to anger with their vanities: and I will move them to jealousy with *those which are* not a people; I will provoke them to anger with a foolish nation.

22For a fire is kindled in mine anger, and zshall burn unto the lowest hell, and ashall consume the earth with her increase, and set on fire the foundations of the mountains.

23I will heap mischiefs upon them; I will spend mine arrows upon them.

24*They shall be* burnt with hunger, and devoured with bburning heat, and with bitter destruction: I will also send the teeth of beasts upon them, with the poison of serpents of the dust.

25The sword without, and terror cwithin, shall ddestroy both the young man and the virgin, the suckling *also* with the man of gray hairs.

26I said, I would scatter them into corners, I would make the remembrance of them to cease from among men:

27Were it not that I feared the wrath of the enemy, lest their adversaries should behave themselves strangely, *and* lest they should say, eOur hand *is* high, and the LORD hath not done all this.

28For they *are* a nation void of counsel, neither *is there* any understanding in them.

Amplified

11As an eagle that stirs up her nest, that flutters over her young, He spread abroad His wings and He took them, He bore them on His pinions. [Luke 13:34.]

12So the Lord alone led him; there was no foreign god with Him.

13He made Israel ride on the high places of the earth, and he ate the increase of the field; and He made him suck honey out of the rock and oil out of the flinty rock,

14Butter *and* curds of the herd and milk of the flock, with fat of lambs, and rams of the breed of Bashan, and he-goats, with the finest of the wheat; and you drank wine of the blood of the grape.

15But Jeshurun (Israel) grew fat and kicked. You became fat, you grew thick, you were gorged *and* sleek! Then he forsook God Who made him and forsook *and* despised the Rock of his salvation.

16They provoked Him to jealousy with strange gods, with abominations they provoked Him to anger.

17They sacrificed to demons, not to God—to gods whom they knew not, to new gods lately come up, whom your fathers never knew or feared.

18Of the Rock Who bore you you were unmindful; you forgot the God Who travailed in your birth.

19And the Lord saw it and He spurned *and* rejected them, out of indignation with His sons and His daughters.

20And He said, I will hide My face from them, I will see what their end will be; for they are a perverse generation, children in whom is no faithfulness.

21They have moved Me to jealousy with what is not God; they have angered Me with their idols. So I will move them to jealousy with those who are not a people; I will anger them with a foolish nation.

22For a fire is kindled by My anger, and it burns to the depths of Sheol, devours the earth with its increase, and sets on fire the foundations of the mountains.

23And I will heap evils upon them; I will spend My arrows upon them.

24They shall be wasted with hunger and devoured with burning heat and poisonous pestilence; and the teeth of beasts will I send against them, with the poison of crawling things of the dust.

25From without the sword shall bereave, and in the chambers shall be terror, destroying both young man and virgin, the sucking child with the man of gray hairs.

26I said, I would scatter them afar and I would have made the remembrance of them to cease from among men,

27Had I not feared the provocation of the foe, lest their enemies misconstrue it and lest they should say, Our own hand has prevailed; all this was not the work of the Lord.

28For they are a nation void of counsel, and there is no understanding in them.

xOr, which were *not God;* see ver. 21 yOr, *despised* zOr, *hath burned* aOr, *hath consumed* bHeb. *burning coals* cHeb. *from the chambers* dHeb. *bereave* eOr, *Our high hand, and not the LORD, hath done all this*

New American Standard

11"Like an eagle that stirs up its nest,
　　That hovers over its young,
　　He spread His wings and caught them,
　　He carried them on His pinions.
12"The LORD alone guided him,
　　And there was no foreign god with him.
13"He made him ride on the high places of the earth,
　　And he ate the produce of the field;
　　And He made him suck honey from the rock,
　　And oil from the flinty rock,
14　Curds of cows, and milk of the flock,
　　With fat of lambs,
　　And rams, the breed of Bashan, and goats,
　　With the finest of the wheat—
　　And of the blood of grapes you drank wine.

15 ¶ "But ˢJeshurun grew fat and kicked—
　　You are grown fat, thick, and sleek—
　　Then he forsook God who made him,
　　And scorned the Rock of his salvation.
16"They made Him jealous with strange *gods;*
　　With abominations they provoked Him to anger.
17"They sacrificed to demons who were not God,
　　To gods whom they have not known,
　　New *gods* who came lately,
　　Whom your fathers did not dread.
18"You neglected the Rock who begot you,
　　And forgot the God who gave you birth.

19 ¶ "The LORD saw *this,* and spurned *them*
　　Because of the provocation of His sons and
　　　daughters.
20"Then He said, 'I will hide My face from them,
　　I will see what their end *shall be;*
　　For they are a perverse generation,
　　Sons in whom is no faithfulness.
21 'They have made Me jealous with *what* is not
　　　God;
　　They have provoked Me to anger with their idols.
　　So I will make them jealous with *those who* are
　　　not a people;
　　I will provoke them to anger with a foolish
　　　nation,
22　For a fire is kindled in My anger,
　　And burns to the lowest part of Sheol,
　　And consumes the earth with its yield,
　　And sets on fire the foundations of the mountains.

23 ¶ 'I will heap misfortunes on them;
　　I will use My arrows on them.
24 '*They will be* wasted by famine, and consumed by
　　　plague
　　And bitter destruction;
　　And the teeth of beasts I will send upon them,
　　With the venom of crawling things of the dust.
25 'Outside the sword will bereave,
　　And inside terror—
　　Both young man and virgin,
　　The nursling with the man of gray hair.
26 'I would have said, "I will cut them to pieces,
　　I will remove the memory of them from men,"
27　Had I not feared the provocation by the enemy,
　　That their adversaries would misjudge,
　　That they would say, "Our hand is triumphant,
　　And the LORD has not done all this." '

28 ¶ "For they are a nation lacking in counsel,
　　And there is no understanding in them.

New International

11like an eagle that stirs up its nest
　　and hovers over its young,
　　that spreads its wings to catch them
　　and carries them on its pinions.
12The LORD alone led him;
　　no foreign god was with him.
13He made him ride on the heights of the land
　　and fed him with the fruit of the fields.
　　He nourished him with honey from the rock,
　　and with oil from the flinty crag,
14with curds and milk from herd and flock
　　and with fattened lambs and goats,
　　with choice rams of Bashan
　　and the finest kernels of wheat.
　　You drank the foaming blood of the grape.

15Jeshurunʳ grew fat and kicked;
　　filled with food, he became heavy and
　　　sleek.
　　He abandoned the God who made him
　　and rejected the Rock his Savior.
16They made him jealous with their foreign
　　　gods
　　and angered him with their detestable idols.
17They sacrificed to demons, which are not
　　　God—
　　gods they had not known,
　　gods that recently appeared,
　　gods your fathers did not fear.
18You deserted the Rock, who fathered you;
　　you forgot the God who gave you birth.

19The LORD saw this and rejected them
　　because he was angered by his sons and
　　　daughters.
20"I will hide my face from them," he said,
　　"and see what their end will be;
　　for they are a perverse generation,
　　children who are unfaithful.
21They made me jealous by what is no god
　　and angered me with their worthless idols.
　　I will make them envious by those who are
　　　not a people;
　　I will make them angry by a nation that has
　　　no understanding.
22For a fire has been kindled by my wrath,
　　one that burns to the realm of deathˢ
　　　below.
　　It will devour the earth and its harvests
　　and set afire the foundations of the
　　　mountains.

23"I will heap calamities upon them
　　and spend my arrows against them.
24I will send wasting famine against them,
　　consuming pestilence and deadly plague;
　　I will send against them the fangs of wild
　　　beasts,
　　the venom of vipers that glide in the dust.
25In the street the sword will make them
　　　childless;
　　in their homes terror will reign.
　　Young men and young women will perish,
　　infants and gray-haired men.
26I said I would scatter them
　　and blot out their memory from mankind,
27but I dreaded the taunt of the enemy,
　　lest the adversary misunderstand
　　and say, 'Our hand has triumphed;
　　the LORD has not done all this.' "

28They are a nation without sense,
　　there is no discernment in them.

ʳ15 *Jeshurun* means *the upright one,* that is, Israel.
ˢ22 Hebrew *to Sheol*

ˢI.e. Israel

King James

²⁹O that they were wise, *that* they understood this, *that* they would consider their latter end!

³⁰How should one chase a thousand, and two put ten thousand to flight, except their Rock had sold them, and the LORD had shut them up?

³¹For their rock *is* not as our Rock, even our enemies themselves *being* judges.

³²For their vine *f is* of the vine of Sodom, and of the fields of Gomorrah: their grapes *are* grapes of gall, their clusters *are* bitter:

³³Their wine *is* the poison of dragons, and the cruel venom of asps.

³⁴*Is* not this laid up in store with me, *and* sealed up among my treasures?

³⁵To me *belongeth* vengeance, and recompence; their foot shall slide in *due* time: for the day of their calamity *is* at hand, and the things that shall come upon them make haste.

³⁶For the LORD shall judge his people, and repent himself for his servants, when he seeth that *their g*power is gone, and *there is* none shut up, or left.

³⁷And he shall say, Where *are* their gods, *their* rock in whom they trusted,

³⁸Which did eat the fat of their sacrifices, *and* drank the wine of their drink offerings? let them rise up and help you, *and* be *h*your protection.

³⁹See now that I, *even* I, *am* he, and *there is* no god with me: I kill, and I make alive; I wound, and I heal: neither *is there any* that can deliver out of my hand.

⁴⁰For I lift up my hand to heaven, and say, I live for ever.

⁴¹If I whet my glittering sword, and mine hand take hold on judgment; I will render vengeance to mine enemies, and will reward them that hate me.

⁴²I will make mine arrows drunk with blood, and my sword shall devour flesh; *and that* with the blood of the slain and of the captives, from the beginning of revengers upon the enemy.

⁴³*i*Rejoice, O ye nations, *with* his people: for he will avenge the blood of his servants, and will render vengeance to his adversaries, and will be merciful unto his land, *and* to his people.

⁴⁴ ¶ And Moses came and spake all the words of this song in the ears of the people, he, and *j*Hoshea the son of Nun.

⁴⁵And Moses made an end of speaking all these words to all Israel:

⁴⁶And he said unto them, Set your hearts unto all the words which I testify among you this day, which ye shall command your children to observe to do, all the words of this law.

⁴⁷For it *is* not a vain thing for you; because it *is* your life: and through this thing ye shall prolong *your* days in the land, whither ye go over Jordan to possess it.

Moses to die on mount Nebo

⁴⁸And the LORD spake unto Moses that selfsame day, saying,

⁴⁹Get thee up into this mountain Abarim, *unto* mount Nebo, which *is* in the land of Moab, that *is* over against Jericho; and behold the land of Canaan, which I give unto the children of Israel for a possession:

⁵⁰And die in the mount whither thou goest up, and be gathered unto thy people; as Aaron thy brother died in mount Hor, and was gathered unto his people:

Amplified

²⁹O that they were wise and would see through this [present triumph] to their ultimate fate!

³⁰How could one have chased a thousand, and two put ten thousand to flight, except their Rock had sold them, and the Lord had delivered them up?

³¹For their rock is not like our Rock, even our enemies themselves judge this.

³²For their vine comes from the vine of Sodom and from the fields of Gomorrah; their grapes are grapes of [poisonous] gall, their clusters are bitter.

³³Their wine is the [furious] venom of serpents, and the pitiless poison of vipers.

³⁴Is not this laid up in store with Me, sealed up in My treasuries?

³⁵Vengeance is Mine, and recompense, in the time when their foot shall slide; for the day of their disaster is at hand and their doom comes speedily.

³⁶For the Lord will revoke sentence for His people and relent for His servants' sake when He sees that their power is gone and none remains, whether bond or free.

³⁷And He will say, Where are their gods, the rock in which they took refuge,

³⁸Who ate the fat of their sacrifices and drank the wine of their drink offering? Let them rise up and help you, let them be your protection!

³⁹See now that I, I am He, and there is no god beside Me; I kill and I make alive, I wound and I heal, and there is none who can deliver out of My hand.

⁴⁰For I lift up My hand to heaven and swear, As I live forever,

⁴¹If I whet My lightning sword and My hand takes hold on judgment, I will wreak vengeance on My foes and recompense those who hate Me.

⁴²I will make My arrows drunk with blood, and My sword shall devour flesh, with the blood of the slain and the captives, from the long-haired heads of the foe.

⁴³Rejoice [with] His people, O you nations, for He avenges the blood of His servants, and vengeance He inflicts on His foes and clears guilt from the land of His people.

⁴⁴And Moses came and spoke all the words of this song in the ears of the people, he and Hoshea (Joshua) son of Nun.

⁴⁵And when Moses had finished speaking all these words to all Israel,

⁴⁶He said to them, Set your [minds and] hearts on all the words which I command you this day, that you may command them to your children, that they may be watchful to do all the words of this law.

⁴⁷For it is not an empty *and* worthless trifle for you; it is your [very] life. By it you shall live long in the land which you are going over the Jordan to possess.

⁴⁸And the Lord said to Moses that same day,

⁴⁹Get up into this mountain of the Abarim, Mount Nebo, which is in the land of Moab, opposite Jericho, and look at the land of Canaan which I give to the Israelites for a possession.

⁵⁰And die on the mountain which you ascend and be gathered to your people, as Aaron your brother died on Mount Hor and was gathered to his people,

---

*f*Or, is worse *than the vine of Sodom*   *g*Heb. *hand*   *h*Heb. *an hiding for you*   *i*Or, *Praise his people, ye nations:* or, *Sing ye* *j*Or, *Joshua*

New American Standard

29"Would that they were wise, that they understood
  this,
   That they would discern their future!
30"How could one chase a thousand,
   And two put ten thousand to flight,
   Unless their Rock had sold them,
   And the LORD had given them up?
31"Indeed their rock is not like our Rock,
   Even our enemies themselves judge this.
32"For their vine is from the vine of Sodom,
   And from the fields of Gomorrah;
   Their grapes are grapes of poison,
   Their clusters, bitter.
33"Their wine is the venom of serpents,
   And the deadly poison of cobras.

34 ¶ 'Is it not laid up in store with Me,
   Sealed up in My treasuries?
35 'Vengeance is Mine, and retribution,
   In due time their foot will slip;
   For the day of their calamity is near,
   And the impending things are hastening upon
     them.'
36"For the LORD will vindicate His people,
   And will have compassion on His servants,
   When He sees that *their* strength is gone,
   And there is none *remaining,* bond or free.
37"And He will say, 'Where are their gods,
   The rock in which they sought refuge?
38 'Who ate the fat of their sacrifices,
   And drank the wine of their drink offering?
   Let them rise up and help you,
   Let them be your hiding place!
39 'See now that I, I am He,
   And there is no god besides Me;
   It is I who put to death and give life.
   I have wounded and it is I who heal,
   And there is no one who can deliver from My
     hand.
40 'Indeed, I lift up My hand to heaven,
   And say, as I live forever,
41 If I sharpen My flashing sword,
   And My hand takes hold on justice,
   I will render vengeance on My adversaries,
   And I will repay those who hate Me.
42 'I will make My arrows drunk with blood,
   And My sword will devour flesh,
   With the blood of the slain and the captives,
   From the long-haired leaders of the enemy.'
43"Rejoice, O nations, *with* His people;
   For He will avenge the blood of His servants,
   And will render vengeance on His adversaries,
   And will atone for His land *and* His people."

44 ¶ Then Moses came and spoke all the words of this
song in the hearing of the people, he, with Joshua the son
of Nun.
45 When Moses had finished speaking all these words to
all Israel,
46 he said to them, "Take to your heart all the words
with which I am warning you today, which you shall command your sons to observe carefully, *even* all the words of
this law.
47"For it is not an idle word for you; indeed it is your
life. And by this word you will prolong your days in the
land, which you are about to cross the Jordan to possess."

48 ¶ The LORD spoke to Moses that very same day, saying,
49"Go up to this mountain of the Abarim, Mount Nebo,
which is in the land of Moab opposite Jericho, and look at
the land of Canaan, which I am giving to the sons of Israel
for a possession.
50"Then die on the mountain where you ascend, and be
gathered to your people, as Aaron your brother died on
Mount Hor and was gathered to his people,

New International

29If only they were wise and would understand
  this
   and discern what their end will be!
30How could one man chase a thousand,
   or two put ten thousand to flight,
   unless their Rock had sold them,
   unless the LORD had given them up?
31For their rock is not like our Rock,
   as even our enemies concede.
32Their vine comes from the vine of Sodom
   and from the fields of Gomorrah.
   Their grapes are filled with poison,
   and their clusters with bitterness.
33Their wine is the venom of serpents,
   the deadly poison of cobras.

34"Have I not kept this in reserve
   and sealed it in my vaults?
35It is mine to avenge; I will repay.
   In due time their foot will slip;
   their day of disaster is near
   and their doom rushes upon them."
36The LORD will judge his people
   and have compassion on his servants
   when he sees their strength is gone
   and no one is left, slave or free.
37He will say: "Now where are their gods,
   the rock they took refuge in,
38the gods who ate the fat of their sacrifices
   and drank the wine of their drink offerings?
   Let them rise up to help you!
   Let them give you shelter!
39"See now that I myself am He!
   There is no god besides me.
   I put to death and I bring to life,
   I have wounded and I will heal,
   and no one can deliver out of my hand.
40I lift my hand to heaven and declare:
   As surely as I live forever,
41when I sharpen my flashing sword
   and my hand grasps it in judgment,
   I will take vengeance on my adversaries
   and repay those who hate me.
42I will make my arrows drunk with blood,
   while my sword devours flesh:
   the blood of the slain and the captives,
   the heads of the enemy leaders."
43Rejoice, O nations, with his people,[t,u]
   for he will avenge the blood of his servants;
   he will take vengeance on his enemies
   and make atonement for his land and
     people.

44Moses came with Joshua[v] son of Nun and spoke all
the words of this song in the hearing of the people. 45When
Moses finished reciting all these words to all Israel, 46he
said to them, "Take to heart all the words I have solemnly
declared to you this day, so that you may command your
children to obey carefully all the words of this law. 47They
are not just idle words for you—they are your life. By
them you will live long in the land you are crossing the
Jordan to possess."

Moses to Die on Mount Nebo

48On that same day the LORD told Moses, 49"Go up into
the Abarim Range to Mount Nebo in Moab, across from
Jericho, and view Canaan, the land I am giving the Israelites as their own possession. 50There on the mountain that
you have climbed you will die and be gathered to your
people, just as your brother Aaron died on Mount Hor and

---

t43 Or *Make his people rejoice, O nations*   *u43* Masoretic Text;
Dead Sea Scrolls (see also Septuagint) *people, / and let all the
angels worship him /*   *v44* Hebrew *Hoshea,* a variant of *Joshua*

King James

⁵¹Because ye trespassed against me among the children of Israel at the waters of ^kMeribah-Kadesh, in the wilderness of Zin; because ye sanctified me not in the midst of the children of Israel.

⁵²Yet thou shalt see the land before *thee;* but thou shalt not go thither unto the land which I give the children of Israel.

Moses blesses the tribes

33 AND THIS *is* the blessing, wherewith Moses the man of God blessed the children of Israel before his death.

²And he said, The LORD came from Sinai, and rose up from Seir unto them; he shined forth from mount Paran, and he came with ten thousands of saints: from his right hand *went* ^la fiery law for them.

³Yea, he loved the people; all his saints *are* in thy hand: and they sat down at thy feet; *every one* shall receive of thy words.

⁴Moses commanded us a law, *even* the inheritance of the congregation of Jacob.

⁵And he was king in Jeshurun, when the heads of the people *and* the tribes of Israel were gathered together.

⁶ ¶ Let Reuben live, and not die; and let *not* his men be few.

⁷ ¶ And this *is the blessing* of Judah: and he said, Hear, LORD, the voice of Judah, and bring him unto his people: let his hands be sufficient for him; and be thou an help *to him* from his enemies.

⁸ ¶ And of Levi he said, *Let* thy Thummim and thy Urim *be* with thy holy one, whom thou didst prove at Massah, *and with* whom thou didst strive at the waters of Meribah;

⁹Who said unto his father and to his mother, I have not seen him; neither did he acknowledge his brethren, nor knew his own children: for they have observed thy word, and kept thy covenant.

¹⁰^mThey shall teach Jacob thy judgments, and Israel thy law: ⁿthey shall put incense ^obefore thee, and whole burnt sacrifice upon thine altar.

¹¹Bless, LORD, his substance, and accept the work of his hands: smite through the loins of them that rise against him, and of them that hate him, that they rise not again.

¹² ¶ *And* of Benjamin he said, The beloved of the LORD shall dwell in safety by him; *and the LORD* shall cover him all the day long, and he shall dwell between his shoulders.

¹³ ¶ And of Joseph he said, Blessed of the LORD *be* his land, for the precious things of heaven, for the dew, and for the deep that coucheth beneath,

Amplified

⁵¹Because you broke faith with Me in the midst of the Israelites at the waters of Meribah-kadesh in the Wilderness of Zin and because you did not set Me apart as holy in the midst of the Israelites.

⁵²For you shall see the land opposite you at a distance, but you shall not go there, into the land which I give the Israelites.

33 THIS IS the blessing with which Moses the man of God blessed the Israelites before his death.

²He said, The Lord came from Sinai and beamed upon us from Seir; He flashed forth from Mount Paran, from among ten thousands of holy ones, a flaming fire, a law, at His right hand.

³Yes, He loves [the tribes] His people; all those consecrated to Him are in Your hand. They followed in Your steps; they [accepted Your word and] received direction from You,

⁴When Moses commanded us a law, as a possession for the assembly of Jacob.

⁵[The Lord] was King in Jeshurun (Israel) when the heads of the people were gathered, all the tribes of Israel together.

⁶Let [the tribe of] Reuben live and not die out, but ^mlet his men be few.

⁷And this he [Moses] said of Judah: Hear, O Lord, the voice of Judah, and bring him to his people! With his hands he contended for himself; but may You be a help against his enemies.

⁸And of Levi he said: Your Thummim and Your Urim [by which the priest sought God's will for the nation] are for Your pious one [Aaron on behalf of the tribe], whom You tried *and* proved at Massah, with whom You contended at the waters of Meribah; [Num. 20:1–13.]

⁹[Aaron] who ⁿsaid of his father and mother, I do not regard them; nor did he acknowledge his brothers or openly recognize his own children. For the priests observed Your word and kept Your covenant [as to their limitations].

¹⁰[The priests] shall teach Jacob Your ordinances and Israel Your law. They shall put incense before You and whole burnt offerings upon Your altar.

¹¹Bless, O Lord, [Levi's] substance, and accept the work of his hands; crush the loins of his adversaries, and of those who hate him, that they arise no more.

¹²Of Benjamin he said: The beloved of the Lord shall ^odwell in safety by Him; He covers him all the day long, and makes His dwelling between his shoulders.

¹³And of Joseph he said: Blessed by the Lord be his land, with the precious gifts of heaven from the dew and from the deep that couches beneath,

^mThe earlier Bible translators could not believe that Moses meant to say of Reuben, "let his men be few," so they put "not" in italics: "let *not* his men be few." But Reuben had committed a grave offense (Gen. 49:3, 4) which cancelled his birthright, and God meant exactly what He directed Moses to say, as continuous fulfillment of the prophecy proves. "In Judg. 5:16 the tribe [of Reuben] is scorned for its failure to join the others against the Canaanites, and except for I Chron. 5:3-20 it does not again appear in Israel's history. Nor does Misha of Moab, ninth century, B.C., name it" (*The Cambridge Bible*). Furthermore, by A.D. 1951 no Jew was permitted to enter the territory once allotted to the tribe of Reuben. "The whole territory, which is . . . quite capable of cultivation, is now deserted by its settled inhabitants" (John D. Davis, *A Dictionary of the Bible*). It was then being restored not by Israelites but by Arabs.   ⁿThe law required that the high priest act just as impartially when one of his immediate family died, as if the departed were no kin to him (Lev. 21:10-12). This throws light on Christ's attitude toward His mother and brothers in Matt. 12:46-50 (see also Heb. 3:1-3; 8:1-6).   ^oThe temple in Jerusalem was located almost between the ridges of the territory of Benjamin, suggesting "between his shoulders" (see also Josh. 15:8). Moses sees it as a symbol of the Lord's presence covering Benjamin continually.

^kOr, *Strife at Kadesh*   ^lHeb. *a fire of law*   ^mOr, *Let them teach*   ⁿOr, *let them put incense*   ^oHeb. *at thy nose*

New American Standard

[51] because you broke faith with Me in the midst of the sons of Israel at the waters of Meribah-kadesh, in the wilderness of Zin, because you did not treat Me as holy in the midst of the sons of Israel.

[52]"For you shall see the land at a distance, but you shall not go there, into the land which I am giving the sons of Israel."

The Blessing of Moses

33 NOW THIS is the blessing with which Moses the man of God blessed the sons of Israel before his death.

[2] He said,

"The LORD came from Sinai,
And dawned on them from Seir;
He shone forth from Mount Paran,
And He came from the midst of ten thousand
holy ones;
At His right hand there was flashing lightning for
them.
[3]"Indeed, He loves the people;
All Your holy ones are in Your hand,
And they followed in Your steps;
Everyone receives of Your words.
[4]"Moses charged us with a law,
A possession for the assembly of Jacob.
[5]"And He was king in Jeshurun,
When the heads of the people were gathered,
The tribes of Israel together.

[6] ¶ "May Reuben live and not die,
Nor his men be few."

[7] ¶ And this regarding Judah; so he said,
"Hear, O LORD, the voice of Judah,
And bring him to his people.
With his hands he contended for them,
And may You be a help against his adversaries."

[8] ¶ Of Levi he said,
"*Let* Your Thummim and Your Urim *belong* to
Your godly man,
Whom You proved at Massah,
With whom You contended at the waters of
Meribah;
[9] Who said of his father and his mother,
'I did not consider them';
And he did not acknowledge his brothers,
Nor did he regard his own sons,
For they observed Your word,
And kept Your covenant.
[10]"They shall teach Your ordinances to Jacob,
And Your law to Israel.
They shall put incense before You,
And whole burnt offerings on Your altar.
[11]"O LORD, bless his substance,
And accept the work of his hands;
Shatter the loins of those who rise up against
him,
And those who hate him, so that they will not
rise *again*."

[12] ¶ Of Benjamin he said,
"May the beloved of the LORD dwell in security by
Him,
Who shields him all the day,
And he dwells between His shoulders."

[13] ¶ Of Joseph he said,
"Blessed of the LORD *be* his land,
With the choice things of heaven, with the dew,
And from the deep lying beneath,

New International

was gathered to his people. [51]This is because both of you broke faith with me in the presence of the Israelites at the waters of Meribah Kadesh in the Desert of Zin and because you did not uphold my holiness among the Israelites. [52]Therefore, you will see the land only from a distance; you will not enter the land I am giving to the people of Israel."

Moses Blesses the Tribes

33 THIS IS the blessing that Moses the man of God pronounced on the Israelites before his death. [2]He said:

"The LORD came from Sinai,
and dawned over them from Seir;
he shone forth from Mount Paran.
He came with[w] myriads of holy ones
from the south, from his mountain slopes.[x]
[3]Surely it is you who love the people;
all the holy ones are in your hand.
At your feet they all bow down,
and from you receive instruction,
[4]the law that Moses gave us,
the possession of the assembly of Jacob.
[5]He was king over Jeshurun[y]
when the leaders of the people assembled,
along with the tribes of Israel.

[6]"Let Reuben live and not die,
nor[z] his men be few."

[7]And this he said about Judah:

"Hear, O LORD, the cry of Judah;
bring him to his people.
With his own hands he defends his cause.
Oh, be his help against his foes!"

[8]About Levi he said:

"Your Thummim and Urim belong
to the man you favored.
You tested him at Massah;
you contended with him at the waters of
Meribah.
[9]He said of his father and mother,
'I have no regard for them.'
He did not recognize his brothers
or acknowledge his own children,
but he watched over your word
and guarded your covenant.
[10]He teaches your precepts to Jacob
and your law to Israel.
He offers incense before you
and whole burnt offerings on your altar.
[11]Bless all his skills, O LORD,
and be pleased with the work of his hands.
Smite the loins of those who rise up against
him;
strike his foes till they rise no more."

[12]About Benjamin he said:

"Let the beloved of the LORD rest secure in
him,
for he shields him all day long,
and the one the LORD loves rests between
his shoulders."

[13]About Joseph he said:

"May the LORD bless his land
with the precious dew from heaven above
and with the deep waters that lie below;

King James

¹⁴And for the precious fruits *brought forth* by the sun, and for the precious things *p*put forth by the *q*moon,

¹⁵And for the chief things of the ancient mountains, and for the precious things of the lasting hills,

¹⁶And for the precious things of the earth and fulness thereof, and *for* the good will of him that dwelt in the bush: let *the blessing* come upon the head of Joseph, and upon the top of the head of him *that was* separated from his brethren.

¹⁷His glory *is like* the firstling of his bullock, and his horns *are like* the horns of *r*unicorns: with them he shall push the people together to the ends of the earth: and they *are* the ten thousands of Ephraim, and they *are* the thousands of Manasseh.

¹⁸ ¶ And of Zebulun he said, Rejoice, Zebulun, in thy going out; and, Issachar, in thy tents.

¹⁹They shall call the people unto the mountain; there they shall offer sacrifices of righteousness: for they shall suck *of* the abundance of the seas, and *of* treasures hid in the sand.

²⁰ ¶ And of Gad he said, Blessed *be* he that enlargeth Gad: he dwelleth as a lion, and teareth the arm with the crown of the head.

²¹And he provided the first part for himself, because there, *in* a portion of the lawgiver, *was he* *s*seated; and he came with the heads of the people, he executed the justice of the LORD, and his judgments with Israel.

²² ¶ And of Dan he said, Dan *is* a lion's whelp: he shall leap from Bashan.

²³ ¶ And of Naphtali he said, O Naphtali, satisfied with favour, and full with the blessing of the LORD: possess thou the west and the south.

²⁴ ¶ And of Asher he said, *Let Asher be* blessed with children; let him be acceptable to his brethren, and let him dip his foot in oil.

²⁵*t*Thy shoes *shall be* iron and brass; and as thy days, *so shall* thy strength *be.*

²⁶ ¶ *There is* none like unto the God of Jeshurun, *who* rideth upon the heaven in thy help, and in his excellency on the sky.

²⁷The eternal God *is thy* refuge, and underneath *are* the everlasting arms: and he shall thrust out the enemy from before thee; and shall say, Destroy *them.*

²⁸Israel then shall dwell in safety alone: the fountain of Jacob *shall be* upon a land of corn and wine; also his heavens shall drop down dew.

Amplified

¹⁴With the precious things of the fruits of the sun and with the precious yield of the months,

¹⁵With the chief products of the ancient mountains and with the precious things of the everlasting hills,

¹⁶With the precious things of the earth and its fullness and the favor *and* goodwill of Him Who dwelt in the bush. Let these blessings come upon the head of Joseph, upon the crown of the head of him who was separate *and* prince among his brothers. [Exod. 3:4.]

¹⁷Like a firstling young bull his majesty is, and his horns like the horns of the wild ox; with them he shall push the peoples, all of them, to the ends of the earth. And they are the ten thousands of Ephraim, and they are the thousands of Manasseh.

¹⁸And of Zebulun he said: *p*Rejoice, Zebulun, in your interests abroad, and you, Issachar, in your tents [at home].

¹⁹They shall call the people unto Mount [Carmel]; there they shall offer sacrifices of righteousness, for *q*they shall suck the abundance of the seas and the treasures hid in the sand.

²⁰And of Gad he said: Blessed is He Who enlarges Gad! Gad lurks like a lioness, and tears the arm, yes, the crown of the head.

²¹He selected the best land for himself, for there was the leader's portion reserved; yet he came with the chiefs of the nation, and the righteous will of the Lord he performed, and His ordinances with Israel. [Num. 32:29–33.]

²²Of Dan he said: Dan is a lion's whelp that leaps forth from Bashan.

²³Of Naphtali he said: O Naphtali, *r*satisfied with favor and full of the blessing of the Lord, possess the Sea [of Galilee] and [its warm, sunny climate like] the south.

²⁴Of Asher he said: Blessed above sons is Asher; let him be acceptable to his brothers, and *s*let him dip his foot in oil.

²⁵Your castles and strongholds shall have bars of iron and bronze, and as your day, so shall your strength, your rest *and* security, be.

²⁶There is none like God, O Jeshurun [Israel], Who rides through the heavens to your help and in His majestic glory through the skies.

²⁷The eternal God is your refuge *and* dwelling place, and underneath are the everlasting arms; He drove the enemy before you *and* thrust them out, saying, Destroy!

²⁸And Israel dwells in safety, the fountain of Jacob alone in a land of grain and new wine; yes, His heavens drop dew.

*p*Not until 1934 was this prophecy notably in process of fulfillment, when Haifa's bay became one of the great harbors of the Mediterranean Sea, with commerce affecting the whole world. *q*The great oil pipeline path across Palestine was first opened in 1935. Until then this prophecy fell far short of fulfillment. But 3,400 years before, Moses sent out the inspired headlines, "Zebulun ... Issachar ... shall suck the abundance of the seas, and the treasures hid in the sand." Our omnipotent God was "declaring the end *and* the result from the beginning, and from ancient times the things that are not yet done, saying, My counsel shall stand" (Isa. 46:10). *r*For many centuries much of the territory of upper Naphtali was little more than a miasmic swamp, unfit for man or beast. But when the Jews returned to Palestine, they drained and redeemed the area, and by 1940 it was dotted over with irrigation colonies, as Moses had foretold, "satisfied with favor and full of the blessing of the Lord." *s*The maps of the territory of Asher sometimes suggest the shape of the sole of a foot, sometimes that of a leg and foot; but in either case the Great International Iraq-Petroleum Enterprise, opened in 1935, crossed the area just at the toe of Asher's "foot." Oil brought nearly 1,000 miles across the sands from Mesopotamia began pouring through pipes into the Haifa harbor, a million gallons of oil a day. Jacob had prophesied about Asher, " ... his bread *shall be* fat" (Gen. 49:20 KJV), and here Moses says of Asher, "Let him dip his foot in oil"!

New American Standard

14 And with the choice yield of the sun,
And with the choice produce of the months.
15"And with the best things of the ancient
mountains,
And with the choice things of the everlasting
hills,
16 And with the choice things of the earth and its
fullness,
And the favor of Him who dwelt in the bush.
Let it come to the head of Joseph,
And to the crown of the head of the one
distinguished among his brothers.
17"As the firstborn of his ox, majesty is his,
And his horns are the horns of the wild ox;
With them he will push the peoples,
All at once, to the ends of the earth.
And those are the ten thousands of Ephraim,
And those are the thousands of Manasseh."

18 ¶ Of Zebulun he said,
"Rejoice, Zebulun, in your going forth,
And, Issachar, in your tents.
19"They will call peoples to the mountain;
There they will offer righteous sacrifices;
For they will draw out the abundance of the seas,
And the hidden treasures of the sand."

20 ¶ Of Gad he said,
"Blessed is the one who enlarges Gad;
He lies down as a lion,
And tears the arm, also the crown of the head.
21"Then he provided the first part for himself,
For there the ruler's portion was reserved;
And he came with the leaders of the people;
He executed the justice of the LORD,
And His ordinances with Israel."

22 ¶ Of Dan he said,
"Dan is a lion's whelp,
That leaps forth from Bashan."

23 ¶ Of Naphtali he said,
"O Naphtali, satisfied with favor,
And full of the blessing of the LORD,
Take possession of the sea and the south."

24 ¶ Of Asher he said,
"More blessed than sons is Asher;
May he be favored by his brothers,
And may he dip his foot in oil.
25"Your locks will be iron and bronze,
And according to your days, so will your
leisurely walk be.

26 ¶ "There is none like the God of ¹Jeshurun,
Who rides the heavens to your help,
And through the skies in His majesty.
27"The eternal God is a dwelling place,
And underneath are the everlasting arms;
And He drove out the enemy from before you,
And said, 'Destroy!'
28"So Israel dwells in security,
The fountain of Jacob secluded,
In a land of grain and new wine;
His heavens also drop down dew.

New International

14with the best the sun brings forth
and the finest the moon can yield;
15with the choicest gifts of the ancient
mountains
and the fruitfulness of the everlasting hills;
16with the best gifts of the earth and its fullness
and the favor of him who dwelt in the
burning bush.
Let all these rest on the head of Joseph,
on the brow of the prince among^a his
brothers.
17In majesty he is like a firstborn bull;
his horns are the horns of a wild ox.
With them he will gore the nations,
even those at the ends of the earth.
Such are the ten thousands of Ephraim;
such are the thousands of Manasseh."

18About Zebulun he said:

"Rejoice, Zebulun, in your going out,
and you, Issachar, in your tents.
19They will summon peoples to the mountain
and there offer sacrifices of righteousness;
they will feast on the abundance of the seas,
on the treasures hidden in the sand."

20About Gad he said:

"Blessed is he who enlarges Gad's domain!
Gad lives there like a lion,
tearing at arm or head.
21He chose the best land for himself;
the leader's portion was kept for him.
When the heads of the people assembled,
he carried out the LORD's righteous will,
and his judgments concerning Israel."

22About Dan he said:

"Dan is a lion's cub,
springing out of Bashan."

23About Naphtali he said:

"Naphtali is abounding with the favor of the
LORD
and is full of his blessing;
he will inherit southward to the lake."

24About Asher he said:

"Most blessed of sons is Asher;
let him be favored by his brothers,
and let him bathe his feet in oil.
25The bolts of your gates will be iron and
bronze,
and your strength will equal your days.

26"There is no one like the God of Jeshurun,
who rides on the heavens to help you
and on the clouds in his majesty.
27The eternal God is your refuge,
and underneath are the everlasting arms.
He will drive out your enemy before you,
saying, 'Destroy him!'
28So Israel will live in safety alone;
Jacob's spring is secure
in a land of grain and new wine,
where the heavens drop dew.

¹ I.e. Israel   ^a 16 Or of the one separated from

King James

29Happy *art* thou, O Israel: who *is* like unto thee, O people saved by the LORD, the shield of thy help, and who *is* the sword of thy excellency! and thine enemies ushall be found liars unto thee; and thou shalt tread upon their high places.

The death of Moses

34 AND MOSES went up from the plains of Moab unto the mountain of Nebo, to the top of vPisgah, that *is* over against Jericho. And the LORD showed him all the land of Gilead, unto Dan,

2And all Naphtali, and the land of Ephraim, and Manasseh, and all the land of Judah, unto the utmost sea,

3And the south, and the plain of the valley of Jericho, the city of palm trees, unto Zoar.

4And the LORD said unto him, This *is* the land which I sware unto Abraham, unto Isaac, and unto Jacob, saying, I will give it unto thy seed: I have caused thee to see *it* with thine eyes, but thou shalt not go over thither.

5 ¶ So Moses the servant of the LORD died there in the land of Moab, according to the word of the LORD.

6And he buried him in a valley in the land of Moab, over against Beth-peor: but no man knoweth of his sepulchre unto this day.

7 ¶ And Moses *was* an hundred and twenty years old when he died: his eye was not dim, nor his wnatural force xabated.

8 ¶ And the children of Israel wept for Moses in the plains of Moab thirty days: so the days of weeping *and* mourning for Moses were ended.

9 ¶ And Joshua the son of Nun was full of the spirit of wisdom; for Moses had laid his hands upon him: and the children of Israel hearkened unto him, and did as the LORD commanded Moses.

10 ¶ And there arose not a prophet since in Israel like unto Moses, whom the LORD knew face to face,

11In all the signs and the wonders, which the LORD sent him to do in the land of Egypt to Pharaoh, and to all his servants, and to all his land,

12And in all that mighty hand, and in all the great terror which Moses showed in the sight of all Israel.

Amplified

29Happy are you, O Israel, *and* blessing is yours! Who is like you, a people saved by the Lord, the Shield of your help, the Sword that exalts you! Your enemies shall come fawning *and* cringing, *and* submit feigned obedience to you, and you shall march on their high places.

34 AND MOSES went up from the plains of Moab to Mount Nebo, to the top of Pisgah, that is opposite Jericho. And the Lord showed him all the land—from Gilead to Dan,

2And all Naphtali, and the land of Ephraim and Manasseh, and all the land of Judah to the western [Mediterranean] sea,

3And the South (the Negeb) and the plain, that is, the Valley of Jericho, the City of Palm Trees, as far as Zoar.

4And the Lord said to him, This is the land which I swore to Abraham, Isaac, and Jacob, saying, I will give it to your descendants. I have let you see it with your eyes, but you shall not go over there.

5So Moses the servant of the Lord died there in the land of Moab, according to the word of the Lord,

6And He buried him in the valley of the land of Moab opposite Beth-peor, but no man knows where his tomb is to this day.

7Moses was 120 years old when he died; his eye was not dim nor his natural force abated. [Deut. 31:2.]

8And the Israelites wept for Moses in the plains of Moab thirty days; then the days of weeping and mourning for Moses were ended.

9And Joshua son of Nun was full of the spirit of wisdom, for Moses had laid his hands upon him; so the Israelites listened to him and did as the Lord commanded Moses.

10And there arose not a prophet since in Israel like Moses, whom the Lord knew face to face,

11[None equal to him] in all the signs and wonders which the Lord sent him to do in the land of Egypt—to Pharaoh and to all his servants and to all his land,

12And in all the mighty power and all the great and terrible deeds which Moses wrought in the sight of all Israel.

---

uOr, *shall be subdued*   vOr, *The hill*   wHeb. *moisture*
xHeb. *fled*

New American Standard

29"Blessed are you, O Israel;
  Who is like you, a people saved by the LORD,
  Who is the shield of your help
  And the sword of your majesty!
  So your enemies will cringe before you,
  And you will tread upon their high places."

The Death of Moses

34 NOW MOSES went up from the plains of Moab to Mount Nebo, to the top of Pisgah, which is opposite Jericho. And the LORD showed him all the land, Gilead as far as Dan,

2 and all Naphtali and the land of Ephraim and Manasseh, and all the land of Judah as far as the *u*western sea,

3 and the Negev and the plain in the valley of Jericho, the city of palm trees, as far as Zoar.

4 Then the LORD said to him, "This is the land which I swore to Abraham, Isaac, and Jacob, saying, 'I will give it to your descendants'; I have let you see *it* with your eyes, but you shall not go over there."

5 So Moses the servant of the LORD died there in the land of Moab, according to the word of the LORD.

6 And He buried him in the valley in the land of Moab, opposite Beth-peor; but no man knows his burial place to this day.

7 Although Moses was one hundred and twenty years old when he died, his eye was not dim, nor his vigor abated.

8 So the sons of Israel wept for Moses in the plains of Moab thirty days; then the days of weeping *and* mourning for Moses came to an end.

9 ¶ Now Joshua the son of Nun was filled with the spirit of wisdom, for Moses had laid his hands on him; and the sons of Israel listened to him and did as the LORD had commanded Moses.

10 Since that time no prophet has risen in Israel like Moses, whom the LORD knew face to face,

11 for all the signs and wonders which the LORD sent him to perform in the land of Egypt against Pharaoh, all his servants, and all his land,

12 and for all the mighty power and for all the great terror which Moses performed in the sight of all Israel.

New International

29Blessed are you, O Israel!
  Who is like you,
  a people saved by the LORD?
He is your shield and helper
  and your glorious sword.
Your enemies will cower before you,
  and you will trample down their high
    places.*b*"

The Death of Moses

34 THEN MOSES climbed Mount Nebo from the plains of Moab to the top of Pisgah, across from Jericho. There the LORD showed him the whole land—from Gilead to Dan, 2all of Naphtali, the territory of Ephraim and Manasseh, all the land of Judah as far as the western sea,*c* 3the Negev and the whole region from the Valley of Jericho, the City of Palms, as far as Zoar. 4Then the LORD said to him, "This is the land I promised on oath to Abraham, Isaac and Jacob when I said, 'I will give it to your descendants.' I have let you see it with your eyes, but you will not cross over into it."

5And Moses the servant of the LORD died there in Moab, as the LORD had said. 6He buried him*d* in Moab, in the valley opposite Beth Peor, but to this day no one knows where his grave is. 7Moses was a hundred and twenty years old when he died, yet his eyes were not weak nor his strength gone. 8The Israelites grieved for Moses in the plains of Moab thirty days, until the time of weeping and mourning was over.

9Now Joshua son of Nun was filled with the spirit*e* of wisdom because Moses had laid his hands on him. So the Israelites listened to him and did what the LORD had commanded Moses.

10Since then, no prophet has risen in Israel like Moses, whom the LORD knew face to face, 11who did all those miraculous signs and wonders the LORD sent him to do in Egypt—to Pharaoh and to all his officials and to his whole land. 12For no one has ever shown the mighty power or performed the awesome deeds that Moses did in the sight of all Israel.

---

u I.e. Mediterranean Sea

b 29 Or *will tread upon their bodies*   *c* 2 That is, the Mediterranean   *d* 6 Or *He was buried*   *e* 9 Or *Spirit*

King James

THE BOOK OF
Joshua

The LORD instructs Joshua

1 NOW AFTER the death of Moses the servant of the LORD it came to pass, that the LORD spake unto Joshua the son of Nun, Moses' minister, saying,

2Moses my servant is dead; now therefore arise, go over this Jordan, thou, and all this people, unto the land which I do give to them, *even* to the children of Israel.

3Every place that the sole of your foot shall tread upon, that have I given unto you, as I said unto Moses.

4From the wilderness and this Lebanon even unto the great river, the river Euphrates, all the land of the Hittites, and unto the great sea toward the going down of the sun, shall be your coast.

5There shall not any man be able to stand before thee all the days of thy life: as I was with Moses, *so* I will be with thee: I will not fail thee, nor forsake thee.

6Be strong and of a good courage: for *a*unto this people shalt thou divide for an inheritance the land, which I sware unto their fathers to give them.

7Only be thou strong and very courageous, that thou mayest observe to do according to all the law, which Moses my servant commanded thee: turn not from it *to* the right hand or *to* the left, that thou mayest *b*prosper whithersoever thou goest.

8This book of the law shall not depart out of thy mouth; but thou shalt meditate therein day and night, that thou mayest observe to do according to all that is written therein: for then thou shalt make thy way prosperous, and then thou shalt *b*have good success.

9Have not I commanded thee? Be strong and of a good courage; be not afraid, neither be thou dismayed: for the LORD thy God *is* with thee whithersoever thou goest.

10 ¶ Then Joshua commanded the officers of the people, saying,

11Pass through the host, and command the people, saying, Prepare you victuals; for within three days ye shall pass over this Jordan, to go in to possess the land, which the LORD your God giveth you to possess it.

12 ¶ And to the Reubenites, and to the Gadites, and to half the tribe of Manasseh, spake Joshua, saying,

13Remember the word which Moses the servant of the LORD commanded you, saying, The LORD your God hath given you rest, and hath given you this land.

14Your wives, your little ones, and your cattle, shall remain in the land which Moses gave you on this side Jordan; but ye shall pass before your brethren *c*armed, all the mighty men of valour, and help them;

Amplified

THE BOOK OF
Joshua

1 AFTER THE death of Moses the servant of the Lord, the Lord said to Joshua son of Nun, Moses' minister, [Deut. 34:4–8.]

2Moses My servant is dead. So now arise [take his place], go over this Jordan, you and all this people, into the land which I am giving to them, the Israelites.

3Every place upon which the sole of your foot shall tread, that have I given to you, as I promised Moses.

4From the wilderness and this Lebanon to the great river Euphrates—all the land of the *a*Hittites [Canaan]—and to the Great [Mediterranean] Sea on the west shall be your territory.

5No man shall be able to stand before you all the days of your life. As I was with Moses, so I will be with you; I will not fail you or forsake you.

6Be strong (confident) and of good courage, for you shall cause this people to inherit the land which I swore to their fathers to give them.

7Only you be strong and very courageous, that you may do according to all the law which Moses My servant commanded you. Turn not from it to the right hand or to the left, that you may prosper wherever you go.

8This Book of the Law shall not depart out of your mouth, but you shall meditate on it day and night, that you may observe *and* do according to all that is written in it. For then you shall make your way prosperous, and then you shall deal wisely *and* have good *b*success.

9Have not I commanded you? Be strong, vigorous, and very courageous. Be not afraid, neither be dismayed, for the Lord your God is with you wherever you go.

10Then Joshua commanded the officers of the people, saying,

11Pass through the camp and command the people, Prepare your provisions, for within three days you shall pass over this Jordan to go in to take possession of the land which the Lord your God is giving you to possess.

12And to the Reubenites, the Gadites, and the half-tribe of Manasseh, Joshua said,

13Remember what Moses the servant of the Lord commanded you, saying, The Lord your God is giving you [of these two and a half tribes a place of] rest and will give you this land [east of the Jordan].

14Your wives, your little ones, and your cattle shall dwell in the land which Moses gave you on this side of the Jordan, but all your mighty men of valor shall pass on before your brethren [of the other tribes] armed, and help them [possess their land]

*a*Although the Hittites are mentioned forty-eight times in the Bible, some critics long refused to accept the possibility, or at least the probability, of the importance of such an ancient people. But archaeological discoveries of the twentieth century have confirmed the importance of the Hittites beyond all question. For instance, G. A. Barton in *Archaeology and the Bible* records the existence of an archive of clay tablets containing among other things a military treaty made by the Egyptians and the Hittites nearly thirteen centuries before the birth of Christ. *b*This is the only place in the early English versions where the word "success" is found. The secret of success is given in verses 5 through 9. Joshua accepted Moses' place of leadership without misgivings. God's will for him was his will, and he did not hesitate. To go "all out" for God was already habitual with him; it is the unfailing prerequisite of eternal success (Deut. 6:3-5; Ps. 1:1-3; Luke 10:25-28).

*a*Or, *thou shalt cause this people to inherit the land*   *b*Or, *do wisely*   *c*Heb. *marshalled by five* as Ex. 13:18

THE BOOK OF

Joshua

Joshua

God's Charge to Joshua

1 NOW IT came about after the death of Moses the servant of the LORD, that the LORD spoke to Joshua the son of Nun, Moses' [a]servant, saying,

2"Moses My servant is dead; now therefore arise, cross this Jordan, you and all this people, to the land which I am giving to them, to the sons of Israel.

3"Every place on which the sole of your foot treads, I have given it to you, just as I spoke to Moses.

4"From the wilderness and this Lebanon, even as far as the great river, the river Euphrates, all the land of the Hittites, and as far as the Great Sea toward the setting of the sun will be your territory.

5"No man will *be able to* stand before you all the days of your life. Just as I have been with Moses, I will be with you; I will not fail you or forsake you.

6"Be strong and courageous, for you shall give this people possession of the land which I swore to their fathers to give them.

7"Only be strong and very courageous; be careful to do according to all the law which Moses My servant commanded you; do not turn from it to the right or to the left, so that you may have success wherever you go.

8"This book of the law shall not depart from your mouth, but you shall meditate on it day and night, so that you may be careful to do according to all that is written in it; for then you will make your way prosperous, and then you will have success.

9"Have I not commanded you? Be strong and courageous! Do not tremble or be dismayed, for the LORD your God is with you wherever you go."

Joshua Assumes Command

10 ¶ Then Joshua commanded the officers of the people, saying,

11"Pass through the midst of the camp and command the people, saying, 'Prepare provisions for yourselves, for within three days you are to cross this Jordan, to go in to possess the land which the LORD your God is giving you, to possess it.' "

12 ¶ To the Reubenites and to the Gadites and to the half-tribe of Manasseh, Joshua said,

13"Remember the word which Moses the servant of the LORD commanded you, saying, 'The LORD your God gives you rest and will give you this land.'

14"Your wives, your little ones, and your cattle shall remain in the land which Moses gave you beyond the Jordan, but you shall cross before your brothers in battle array, all your valiant warriors, and shall help them,

The LORD Commands Joshua

1 AFTER THE death of Moses the servant of the LORD, the LORD said to Joshua son of Nun, Moses' aide:

2"Moses my servant is dead. Now then, you and all these people, get ready to cross the Jordan River into the land I am about to give to them—to the Israelites. 3I will give you every place where you set your foot, as I promised Moses. 4Your territory will extend from the desert to Lebanon, and from the great river, the Euphrates—all the Hittite country—to the Great Sea[a] on the west. 5No one will be able to stand up against you all the days of your life. As I was with Moses, so I will be with you; I will never leave you nor forsake you.

6"Be strong and courageous, because you will lead these people to inherit the land I swore to their forefathers to give them. 7Be strong and very courageous. Be careful to obey all the law my servant Moses gave you; do not turn from it to the right or to the left, that you may be successful wherever you go. 8Do not let this Book of the Law depart from your mouth; meditate on it day and night, so that you may be careful to do everything written in it. Then you will be prosperous and successful. 9Have I not commanded you? Be strong and courageous. Do not be terrified; do not be discouraged, for the LORD your God will be with you wherever you go."

10So Joshua ordered the officers of the people: 11"Go through the camp and tell the people, 'Get your supplies ready. Three days from now you will cross the Jordan here to go in and take possession of the land the LORD your God is giving you for your own.' "

12But to the Reubenites, the Gadites and the half-tribe of Manasseh, Joshua said, 13"Remember the command that Moses the servant of the LORD gave you: 'The LORD your God is giving you rest and has granted you this land.' 14Your wives, your children and your livestock may stay in the land that Moses gave you east of the Jordan, but all your fighting men, fully armed, must cross over ahead of

---

[a] Or *minister*

[a] 4 That is, the Mediterranean

King James

15Until the LORD have given your brethren rest, as *he hath given* you, and they also have possessed the land which the LORD your God giveth them: then ye shall return unto the land of your possession, and enjoy it, which Moses the LORD's servant gave you on this side Jordan toward the sunrising.

16 ¶ And they answered Joshua, saying, All that thou commandest us we will do, and whithersoever thou sendest us, we will go.

17According as we hearkened unto Moses in all things, so will we hearken unto thee: only the LORD thy God be with thee, as he was with Moses.

18Whosoever *he be* that doth rebel against thy commandment, and will not hearken unto thy words in all that thou commandest him, he shall be put to death: only be strong and of a good courage.

Two spies sent to Jericho

2 AND JOSHUA the son of Nun *d*sent out of Shittim two men to spy secretly, saying, Go view the land, even Jericho. And they went, and came into an harlot's house, named Rahab, and *e*lodged there.

2And it was told the king of Jericho, saying, Behold, there came men in hither tonight of the children of Israel to search out the country.

3And the king of Jericho sent unto Rahab, saying, Bring forth the men that are come to thee, which are entered into thine house: for they be come to search out all the country.

4And the woman took the two men, and hid them, and said thus, There came men unto me, but I wist not whence they *were*:

5And it came to pass *about the time* of shutting of the gate, when it was dark, that the men went out: whither the men went I wot not: pursue after them quickly; for ye shall overtake them.

6But she had brought them up to the roof of the house, and hid them with the stalks of flax, which she had laid in order upon the roof.

7And the men pursued after them the way to Jordan unto the fords: and as soon as they which pursued after them were gone out, they shut the gate.

8 ¶ And before they were laid down, she came up unto them upon the roof;

9And she said unto the men, I know that the LORD hath given you the land, and that your terror is fallen upon us, and that all the inhabitants of the land *f*faint because of you.

10For we have heard how the LORD dried up the water of the Red sea for you, when ye came out of Egypt; and what ye did unto the two kings of the Amorites, that *were* on the other side Jordan, Sihon and Og, whom ye utterly destroyed.

11And as soon as we had heard *these things,* our hearts did melt, neither *g*did there remain any more courage in any man, because of you: for the LORD your God, he *is* God in heaven above, and in earth beneath.

12Now therefore, I pray you, swear unto me by the LORD, since I have shown you kindness, that ye will also show kindness unto my father's house, and give me a true token:

13And *that* ye will save alive my father, and my mother, and my brethren, and my sisters, and all that they have, and deliver our lives from death.

14And the men answered her, Our life *h*for yours, if ye utter not this our business. And it shall be, when the LORD hath given us the land, that we will deal kindly and truly with thee.

Amplified

15Until the Lord gives your brethren rest, as He has given you, and they also possess the land the Lord your God is giving you. Then you shall return to the land of your possession and possess it, the land Moses the Lord's servant gave you on the sunrise side of the Jordan.

16They answered Joshua, All you command us we will do, and wherever you send us we will go.

17As we hearkened to Moses in all things, so will we hearken to you; only may the Lord your God be with you as He was with Moses.

18Whoever rebels against your commandment and will not hearken to all you command him shall be put to death. Only be strong, vigorous, *and* of good courage.

2 JOSHUA SON of Nun sent two men secretly from Shittim as scouts, saying, Go, view the land, especially Jericho. And they went and came to the house of a harlot named Rahab and lodged there.

2It was told the king of Jericho, Behold, there came men in here tonight of the Israelites to search out the country.

3And the king of Jericho sent to Rahab, saying, Bring forth the men who have come to you, who entered your house, for they have come to search out the land.

4But the woman had taken the two men and hidden them. So she said, Yes, two men came to me, but I did not know from where they had come.

5And at gate closing time, after dark, the men went out. Where they went I do not know. Pursue them quickly, for you will overtake them.

6But she had brought them up to the roof and hidden them under the stalks of flax which she had laid in order there.

7So the men pursued them to the Jordan as far as the fords. As soon as the pursuers had gone, the city's gate was shut.

8Before the two men had lain down, Rahab came up to them on the roof,

9And she said to the men, I know that the Lord has given you the land and that your terror is fallen upon us and that all the inhabitants of the land faint because of you.

10For we have heard how the Lord dried up the water of the Red Sea for you when you came out of Egypt, and what you did to the two kings of the Amorites who were on the [east] side of the Jordan, Sihon and Og, whom you utterly destroyed.

11When we heard it, our hearts melted, neither did spirit *or* courage remain any more in any man because of you, for the Lord your God, He is God in heaven above and on earth beneath. [Heb. 11:31.]

12Now then, I pray you, swear to me by the Lord, since I have shown you kindness, that you also will show kindness to my father's house, and give me a sure sign,

13And save alive my father and mother, my brothers and sisters, and all they have, and deliver us from death.

14And the men said to her, Our lives for yours! If you do not tell this business of ours, then when the Lord gives us the land we will deal kindly and faithfully with you.

---

*d*Or, *had sent*　　*e*Heb. *lay*　　*f*Heb. *melt*　　*g*Heb. *rose up*
*h*Heb. *instead of you to die*

New American Standard

15 until the LORD gives your brothers rest, as *He gives* you, and they also possess the land which the LORD your God is giving them. Then you shall return to your own land, and possess that which Moses the servant of the LORD gave you beyond the Jordan toward the sunrise."

16 ¶ They answered Joshua, saying, "All that you have commanded us we will do, and wherever you send us we will go.

17 "Just as we obeyed Moses in all things, so we will obey you; only may the LORD your God be with you as He was with Moses.

18 "Anyone who rebels against your command and does not obey your words in all that you command him, shall be put to death; only be strong and courageous."

Rahab Shelters Spies

2 THEN JOSHUA the son of Nun sent two men as spies secretly from Shittim, saying, "Go, view the land, especially Jericho." So they went and came into the house of a harlot whose name was Rahab, and lodged there.

2 It was told the king of Jericho, saying, "Behold, men from the sons of Israel have come here tonight to search out the land."

3 And the king of Jericho sent *word* to Rahab, saying, "Bring out the men who have come to you, who have entered your house, for they have come to search out all the land."

4 But the woman had taken the two men and hidden them, and she said, "Yes, the men came to me, but I did not know where they were from.

5 "It came about when *it was time* to shut the gate at dark, that the men went out; I do not know where the men went. Pursue them quickly, for you will overtake them."

6 But she had brought them up to the roof and hidden them in the stalks of flax which she had laid in order on the roof.

7 So the men pursued them on the road to the Jordan to the fords; and as soon as those who were pursuing them had gone out, they shut the gate.

8 ¶ Now before they lay down, she came up to them on the roof,

9 and said to the men, "I know that the LORD has given you the land, and that the terror of you has fallen on us, and that all the inhabitants of the land have melted away before you.

10 "For we have heard how the LORD dried up the water of the Red Sea before you when you came out of Egypt, and what you did to the two kings of the Amorites who were beyond the Jordan, to Sihon and Og, whom you utterly destroyed.

11 "When we heard *it,* our hearts melted and no courage remained in any man any longer because of you; for the LORD your God, He is God in heaven above and on earth beneath.

12 "Now therefore, please swear to me by the LORD, since I have dealt kindly with you, that you also will deal kindly with my father's household, and give me a pledge of truth,

13 and spare my father and my mother and my brothers and my sisters, with all who belong to them, and deliver our *b*lives from death."

14 So the men said to her, "Our life for yours if you do not tell this business of ours; and it shall come about when the LORD gives us the land that we will deal kindly and faithfully with you."

*b*Lit *souls*

New International

your brothers. You are to help your brothers 15until the LORD gives them rest, as he has done for you, and until they too have taken possession of the land that the LORD your God is giving them. After that, you may go back and occupy your own land, which Moses the servant of the LORD gave you east of the Jordan toward the sunrise."

16Then they answered Joshua, "Whatever you have commanded us we will do, and wherever you send us we will go. 17Just as we fully obeyed Moses, so we will obey you. Only may the LORD your God be with you as he was with Moses. 18Whoever rebels against your word and does not obey your words, whatever you may command them, will be put to death. Only be strong and courageous!"

Rahab and the Spies

2 THEN JOSHUA son of Nun secretly sent two spies from Shittim. "Go, look over the land," he said, "especially Jericho." So they went and entered the house of a prostitute*b* named Rahab and stayed there.

2The king of Jericho was told, "Look! Some of the Israelites have come here tonight to spy out the land." 3So the king of Jericho sent this message to Rahab: "Bring out the men who came to you and entered your house, because they have come to spy out the whole land."

4But the woman had taken the two men and hidden them. She said, "Yes, the men came to me, but I did not know where they had come from. 5At dusk, when it was time to close the city gate, the men left. I don't know which way they went. Go after them quickly. You may catch up with them." 6(But she had taken them up to the roof and hidden them under the stalks of flax she had laid out on the roof.) 7So the men set out in pursuit of the spies on the road that leads to the fords of the Jordan, and as soon as the pursuers had gone out, the gate was shut.

8Before the spies lay down for the night, she went up on the roof 9and said to them, "I know that the LORD has given this land to you and that a great fear of you has fallen on us, so that all who live in this country are melting in fear because of you. 10We have heard how the LORD dried up the water of the Red Sea*c* for you when you came out of Egypt, and what you did to Sihon and Og, the two kings of the Amorites east of the Jordan, whom you completely destroyed.*d* 11When we heard of it, our hearts melted and everyone's courage failed because of you, for the LORD your God is God in heaven above and on the earth below. 12Now then, please swear to me by the LORD that you will show kindness to my family, because I have shown kindness to you. Give me a sure sign 13that you will spare the lives of my father and mother, my brothers and sisters, and all who belong to them, and that you will save us from death."

14"Our lives for your lives!" the men assured her. "If you don't tell what we are doing, we will treat you kindly and faithfully when the LORD gives us the land."

b 1 Or possibly *an innkeeper*   *c 10* Hebrew *Yam Suph*; that is, Sea of Reeds   *d 10* The Hebrew term refers to the irrevocable giving over of things or persons to the LORD, often by totally destroying them.

King James

¹⁵Then she let them down by a cord through the window: for her house *was* upon the town wall, and she dwelt upon the wall.

¹⁶And she said unto them, Get you to the mountain, lest the pursuers meet you; and hide yourselves there three days, until the pursuers be returned: and afterward may ye go your way.

¹⁷And the men said unto her, We *will be* blameless of this thine oath which thou hast made us swear.

¹⁸Behold, *when* we come into the land, thou shalt bind this line of scarlet thread in the window which thou didst let us down by: and thou shalt *i*bring thy father, and thy mother, and thy brethren, and all thy father's household, home unto thee.

¹⁹And it shall be, *that* whosoever shall go out of the doors of thy house into the street, his blood *shall be* upon his head, and we *will be* guiltless: and whosoever shall be with thee in the house, his blood *shall be* on our head, if *any* hand be upon him.

²⁰And if thou utter this our business, then we will be quit of thine oath which thou hast made us to swear.

²¹And she said, According unto your words, so *be* it. And she sent them away, and they departed: and she bound the scarlet line in the window.

²²And they went, and came unto the mountain, and abode there three days, until the pursuers were returned: and the pursuers sought *them* throughout all the way, but found *them* not.

²³ ¶ So the two men returned, and descended from the mountain, and passed over, and came to Joshua the son of Nun, and told him all *things* that befell them:

²⁴And they said unto Joshua, Truly the LORD hath delivered into our hands all the land; for even all the inhabitants of the country do *i*faint because of us.

Israel crosses the Jordan

3 AND JOSHUA rose early in the morning; and they removed from Shittim, and came to Jordan, he and all the children of Israel, and lodged there before they passed over.

²And it came to pass after three days, that the officers went through the host;

³And they commanded the people, saying, When ye see the ark of the covenant of the LORD your God, and the priests the Levites bearing it, then ye shall remove from your place, and go after it.

⁴Yet there shall be a space between you and it, about two thousand cubits by measure: come not near unto it, that ye may know the way by which ye must go: for ye have not passed *this* way *k*heretofore.

⁵And Joshua said unto the people, Sanctify yourselves: for tomorrow the LORD will do wonders among you.

⁶And Joshua spake unto the priests, saying, Take up the ark of the covenant, and pass over before the people. And they took up the ark of the covenant, and went before the people.

⁷ ¶ And the LORD said unto Joshua, This day will I begin to magnify thee in the sight of all Israel, that they may know that, as I was with Moses, *so* I will be with thee.

⁸And thou shalt command the priests that bear the ark of the covenant, saying, When ye are come to the brink of the water of Jordan, ye shall stand still in Jordan.

⁹ ¶ And Joshua said unto the children of Israel, Come hither, and hear the words of the LORD your God.

Amplified

¹⁵Then she let them down by a rope through the window, for her house was built into the [town] wall so that she dwelt in the wall.

¹⁶And she said to them, Get to the mountain, lest the pursuers meet you; hide yourselves there three days until the pursuers have returned; and afterward you may go your way.

¹⁷The men said to her, We will be blameless of this oath you have made us swear. [The responsibility is now yours.]

¹⁸Behold, when we come into the land, you shall bind this scarlet cord in the window through which you let us down, and you shall bring your father and mother, your brothers, and all your father's household into your house.

¹⁹And if anyone goes out of the doors of your house into the street, his blood shall be upon his head, and we will be guiltless; but if a hand is laid upon anyone who is with you in the house, his blood shall be on our head.

²⁰But if you tell this business of ours, we shall be guiltless of your oath which you made us swear.

²¹And she said, According to your words, so it is. Then she sent them away and they departed; and she bound the *c*scarlet cord in the window.

²²They left and went to the mountain and stayed there three days, until the pursuers returned, who had searched all along the way without finding them.

²³So the two men descended from the mountain, passed over [the Jordan], and came to Joshua son of Nun, and told him all that had befallen them.

²⁴They said to Joshua, Truly the Lord has given all the land into our hands; for all the inhabitants of the country are faint because of us.

3 JOSHUA ROSE early in the morning and they removed from Shittim and came to the Jordan, he and all the Israelites, and lodged there before passing over.

²After three days the officers went through the camp,

³Commanding the people: When you see the ark of the covenant of the Lord your God being borne by the Levitical priests, set out from where you are and follow it.

⁴Yet a space must be kept between you and it, about 2,000 cubits by measure; come not near it, that you may [be able to see the ark and] know the way you must go, for you have not passed this way before.

⁵And Joshua said to the people, Sanctify yourselves [that is, separate yourselves for a special holy purpose], for tomorrow the Lord will do wonders among you.

⁶Joshua said to the priests, Take up the ark of the covenant and pass over before the people. And they took it up and went on before the people.

⁷The Lord said to Joshua, This day I will begin to magnify you in the sight of all Israel, so they may know that as I was with Moses, so I will be with you.

⁸You shall command the priests who bear the ark of the covenant, When you come to the brink of the waters of the Jordan, you shall stand still in the Jordan.

⁹Joshua said to the Israelites, Come near, hear the words of the Lord your God.

^cWhat the blood on the doorposts on the first Passover night in Egypt was to the houses of Israel (Exod. 12:13), the scarlet cord in the window was to the house of Rahab. Her sinful years of ignorance God ignored (Acts 17:30, 31); she became an ancestress, as did Ruth, of David and of Jesus Christ (Matt. 1:1, 5, 6).

ⁱHeb. *gather*   ^jHeb. *melt*   ^kHeb. *since yesterday, and the third day*

New American Standard

The Promise to Rahab

15 ¶ Then she let them down by a rope through the window, for her house was on the city wall, so that she was living on the wall.

16 She said to them, "Go to the hill country, so that the pursuers will not happen upon you, and hide yourselves there for three days until the pursuers return. Then afterward you may go on your way."

17 The men said to her, "We *shall be* free from this oath to you which you have made us swear,

18 unless, when we come into the land, you tie this cord of scarlet thread in the window through which you let us down, and gather to yourself into the house your father and your mother and your brothers and all your father's household.

19 "It shall come about that anyone who goes out of the doors of your house into the street, his blood *shall be* on his own head, and we *shall be* free; but anyone who is with you in the house, his blood *shall be* on our head if a hand is *laid* on him.

20 "But if you tell this business of ours, then we shall be free from the oath which you have made us swear."

21 She said, "According to your words, so be it." So she sent them away, and they departed; and she tied the scarlet cord in the window.

22 ¶ They departed and came to the hill country, and remained there for three days until the pursuers returned. Now the pursuers had sought *them* all along the road, but had not found *them*.

23 Then the two men returned and came down from the hill country and crossed over and came to Joshua the son of Nun, and they related to him all that had happened to them.

24 They said to Joshua, "Surely the LORD has given all the land into our hands; moreover, all the inhabitants of the land have melted away before us."

Israel Crosses the Jordan

3 THEN JOSHUA rose early in the morning; and he and all the sons of Israel set out from Shittim and came to the Jordan, and they lodged there before they crossed.

2 At the end of three days the officers went through the midst of the camp;

3 and they commanded the people, saying, "When you see the ark of the covenant of the LORD your God with the Levitical priests carrying it, then you shall set out from your place and go after it.

4 "However, there shall be between you and it a distance of about 2,000 cubits by measure. Do not come near it, that you may know the way by which you shall go, for you have not passed this way before."

5 ¶ Then Joshua said to the people, "Consecrate yourselves, for tomorrow the LORD will do wonders among you."

6 And Joshua spoke to the priests, saying, "Take up the ark of the covenant and cross over ahead of the people." So they took up the ark of the covenant and went ahead of the people.

7 ¶ Now the LORD said to Joshua, "This day I will begin to exalt you in the sight of all Israel, that they may know that just as I have been with Moses, I will be with you.

8 "You shall, moreover, command the priests who are carrying the ark of the covenant, saying, 'When you come to the edge of the waters of the Jordan, you shall stand *still* in the Jordan.' "

9 Then Joshua said to the sons of Israel, "Come here, and hear the words of the LORD your God."

New International

15 So she let them down by a rope through the window, for the house she lived in was part of the city wall. 16 Now she had said to them, "Go to the hills so the pursuers will not find you. Hide yourselves there three days until they return, and then go on your way."

17 The men said to her, "This oath you made us swear will not be binding on us 18 unless, when we enter the land, you have tied this scarlet cord in the window through which you let us down, and unless you have brought your father and mother, your brothers and all your family into your house. 19 If anyone goes outside your house into the street, his blood will be on his own head; we will not be responsible. As for anyone who is in the house with you, his blood will be on our head if a hand is laid on him. 20 But if you tell what we are doing, we will be released from the oath you made us swear."

21 "Agreed," she replied. "Let it be as you say." So she sent them away and they departed. And she tied the scarlet cord in the window.

22 When they left, they went into the hills and stayed there three days, until the pursuers had searched all along the road and returned without finding them. 23 Then the two men started back. They went down out of the hills, forded the river and came to Joshua son of Nun and told him everything that had happened to them. 24 They said to Joshua, "The LORD has surely given the whole land into our hands; all the people are melting in fear because of us."

Crossing the Jordan

3 EARLY IN the morning Joshua and all the Israelites set out from Shittim and went to the Jordan, where they camped before crossing over. 2 After three days the officers went throughout the camp, 3 giving orders to the people: "When you see the ark of the covenant of the LORD your God, and the priests, who are Levites, carrying it, you are to move out from your positions and follow it. 4 Then you will know which way to go, since you have never been this way before. But keep a distance of about a thousand yards[e] between you and the ark; do not go near it."

5 Joshua told the people, "Consecrate yourselves, for tomorrow the LORD will do amazing things among you."

6 Joshua said to the priests, "Take up the ark of the covenant and pass on ahead of the people." So they took it up and went ahead of them.

7 And the LORD said to Joshua, "Today I will begin to exalt you in the eyes of all Israel, so they may know that I am with you as I was with Moses. 8 Tell the priests who carry the ark of the covenant: 'When you reach the edge of the Jordan's waters, go and stand in the river.' "

9 Joshua said to the Israelites, "Come here and listen to

---

[e] 4 Hebrew *about two thousand cubits* (about 900 meters)

King James

¹⁰And Joshua said, Hereby ye shall know that the living God *is* among you, and *that* he will without fail drive out from before you the Canaanites, and the Hittites, and the Hivites, and the Perizzites, and the Girgashites, and the Amorites, and the Jebusites.

¹¹Behold, the ark of the covenant of the Lord of all the earth passeth over before you into Jordan.

¹²Now therefore take you twelve men out of the tribes of Israel, out of every tribe a man.

¹³And it shall come to pass, as soon as the soles of the feet of the priests that bear the ark of the LORD, the Lord of all the earth, shall rest in the waters of Jordan, *that* the waters of Jordan shall be cut off *from* the waters that come down from above; and they shall stand upon an heap.

¹⁴ ¶ And it came to pass, when the people removed from their tents, to pass over Jordan, and the priests bearing the ark of the covenant before the people;

¹⁵And as they that bare the ark were come unto Jordan, and the feet of the priests that bare the ark were dipped in the brim of the water, (for Jordan overfloweth all his banks all the time of harvest,)

¹⁶That the waters which came down from above stood *and* rose up upon an heap very far from the city Adam, that *is* beside Zaretan: and those that came down toward the sea of the plain, *even* the salt sea, failed, *and* were cut off: and the people passed over right against Jericho.

¹⁷And the priests that bare the ark of the covenant of the LORD stood firm on dry ground in the midst of Jordan, and all the Israelites passed over on dry ground, until all the people were passed clean over Jordan.

4 AND IT came to pass, when all the people were clean passed over Jordan, that the LORD spake unto Joshua, saying,

²Take you twelve men out of the people, out of every tribe a man,

³And command ye them, saying, Take you hence out of the midst of Jordan, out of the place where the priests' feet stood firm, twelve stones, and ye shall carry them over with you, and leave them in the lodging place, where ye shall lodge this night.

⁴Then Joshua called the twelve men, whom he had prepared of the children of Israel, out of every tribe a man:

⁵And Joshua said unto them, Pass over before the ark of the LORD your God into the midst of Jordan, and take you up every man of you a stone upon his shoulder, according unto the number of the tribes of the children of Israel:

⁶That this may be a sign among you, *that* when your children ask *their fathers* ^l in time to come, saying, What *mean* ye by these stones?

⁷Then ye shall answer them, That the waters of Jordan were cut off before the ark of the covenant of the LORD; when it passed over Jordan, the waters of Jordan were cut off: and these stones shall be for a memorial unto the children of Israel for ever.

⁸And the children of Israel did so as Joshua commanded, and took up twelve stones out of the midst of Jordan, as the LORD spake unto Joshua, according to the number of the tribes of the children of Israel, and carried them over with them unto the place where they lodged, and laid them down there.

Amplified

¹⁰Joshua said, Hereby you shall know that the living God is among you and that He will surely drive out from before you the Canaanites, Hittites, Hivites, Perizzites, Girgashites, Amorites, and Jebusites.

¹¹Behold, the ark of the covenant of the Lord of all the earth is passing over before you into the Jordan!

¹²So now take twelve men from the tribes of Israel, one from each tribe.

¹³When the soles of the feet of the priests who bear the ark of the Lord of all the earth shall rest in the Jordan, the waters of the Jordan coming down from above shall be cut off and they shall stand in one heap.

¹⁴So when the people set out from their tents to pass over the Jordan, with the priests bearing the ark of the covenant before the people,

¹⁵And when those who bore the ark had come to the Jordan and the feet of the priests bearing the ark were in the brink of the water—for the Jordan overflows all its banks throughout the time of harvest—

¹⁶Then the ^dwaters which came down from above stood and rose up in a heap far off, at Adam, the city that is beside Zarethan; and those flowing down toward the Sea of the Arabah, the Salt [Dead] Sea, were wholly cut off. And the people passed over opposite Jericho. [Ps. 114.]

¹⁷And while all Israel passed over on dry ground, the priests who bore the ark of the covenant of the Lord stood firm on dry ground in the midst of the Jordan, until all the nation finished passing over the Jordan.

4 WHEN ALL the nation had fully passed over the Jordan, the Lord said to Joshua,

²Take twelve men from among the people, one man out of every tribe,

³And command them, Take twelve stones out of the midst of the Jordan from the place where the priests' feet stood firm; carry them over with you and leave them at the place where you lodge tonight.

⁴Then Joshua called the twelve men of the Israelites whom he had appointed, a man from each tribe.

⁵And Joshua said to them, Pass over before the ark of the Lord your God in the midst of the Jordan, and take up every man of you a stone on his shoulder, as is the number of the tribes of the Israelites,

⁶That this may be a sign among you when your children ask in time to come, What do these stones mean to you?

⁷Then you shall tell them that the waters of the Jordan were cut off before the ark of the covenant of the Lord; when it passed over the Jordan, the waters of Jordan were cut off. So these stones shall be to the Israelites a memorial forever.

⁸And the Israelites did as Joshua commanded, and took up twelve stones out of the midst of the Jordan, according to the number of the tribes of the Israelites, as the Lord told Joshua, and carried them over with them to the place where they lodged and laid them down there.

---

^dThe city of Adam has been placed 16 miles up the river from Jericho, and it seems probable that a stretch of 20 or 30 miles of the riverbed was left dry. An interesting parallel of the event here recorded has been found in the pages of an Arabic historian telling how in A.D. 1266, near a place many experts have identified with Adam, the bed of the [Jordan] river was left dry for ten hours as the result of a landslide. John Garstang (*The Story of Jericho*) cites other parallels. But to accept this "natural" explanation of what happened centuries earlier does not detract in any way from the supernatural intervention which opened the way to Israel just at the moment when they needed to cross. The sight of the priests standing in the dry bed of the river as the whole nation passed over was the sign (Josh. 3:10) that this was the doing of the Lord (F. Davidson, ed., *The New Bible Commentary*).

^lHeb. *tomorrow*

New American Standard

[10] Joshua said, "By this you shall know that the living God is among you, and that He will assuredly dispossess from before you the Canaanite, the Hittite, the Hivite, the Perizzite, the Girgashite, the Amorite, and the Jebusite.

[11]"Behold, the ark of the covenant of the Lord of all the earth is crossing over ahead of you into the Jordan.

[12]"Now then, take for yourselves twelve men from the tribes of Israel, one man for each tribe.

[13]"It shall come about when the soles of the feet of the priests who carry the ark of the LORD, the Lord of all the earth, rest in the waters of the Jordan, the waters of the Jordan will be cut off, *and* the waters which are flowing down from above will stand in one heap."

[14] ¶ So when the people set out from their tents to cross the Jordan with the priests carrying the ark of the covenant before the people,

[15] and when those who carried the ark came into the Jordan, and the feet of the priests carrying the ark were dipped in the edge of the water (for the Jordan overflows all its banks all the days of harvest),

[16] the waters which were flowing down from above stood *and* rose up in one heap, a great distance away at Adam, the city that is beside Zarethan; and those which were flowing down toward the sea of the Arabah, the Salt Sea, were completely cut off. So the people crossed opposite Jericho.

[17] And the priests who carried the ark of the covenant of the LORD stood firm on dry ground in the middle of the Jordan while all Israel crossed on dry ground, until all the nation had finished crossing the Jordan.

Memorial Stones from Jordan

4 NOW WHEN all the nation had finished crossing the Jordan, the LORD spoke to Joshua, saying,

[2]"Take for yourselves twelve men from the people, one man from each tribe,

[3] and command them, saying, 'Take up for yourselves twelve stones from here out of the middle of the Jordan, from the place where the priests' feet are standing firm, and carry them over with you and lay them down in the lodging place where you will lodge tonight.' "

[4] So Joshua called the twelve men whom he had appointed from the sons of Israel, one man from each tribe;

[5] and Joshua said to them, "Cross again to the ark of the LORD your God into the middle of the Jordan, and each of you take up a stone on his shoulder, according to the number of the tribes of the sons of Israel.

[6]"Let this be a sign among you, so that when your children ask later, saying, 'What do these stones mean to you?'

[7] then you shall say to them, 'Because the waters of the Jordan were cut off before the ark of the covenant of the LORD; when it crossed the Jordan, the waters of the Jordan were cut off.' So these stones shall become a memorial to the sons of Israel forever."

[8] ¶ Thus the sons of Israel did as Joshua commanded, and took up twelve stones from the middle of the Jordan, just as the LORD spoke to Joshua, according to the number of the tribes of the sons of Israel; and they carried them over with them to the lodging place and put them down there.

New International

the words of the LORD your God. [10]This is how you will know that the living God is among you and that he will certainly drive out before you the Canaanites, Hittites, Hivites, Perizzites, Girgashites, Amorites and Jebusites. [11]See, the ark of the covenant of the Lord of all the earth will go into the Jordan ahead of you. [12]Now then, choose twelve men from the tribes of Israel, one from each tribe. [13]And as soon as the priests who carry the ark of the LORD—the Lord of all the earth—set foot in the Jordan, its waters flowing downstream will be cut off and stand up in a heap."

[14]So when the people broke camp to cross the Jordan, the priests carrying the ark of the covenant went ahead of them. [15]Now the Jordan is at flood stage all during harvest. Yet as soon as the priests who carried the ark reached the Jordan and their feet touched the water's edge, [16]the water from upstream stopped flowing. It piled up in a heap a great distance away, at a town called Adam in the vicinity of Zarethan, while the water flowing down to the Sea of the Arabah (the Salt Sea *f*) was completely cut off. So the people crossed over opposite Jericho. [17]The priests who carried the ark of the covenant of the LORD stood firm on dry ground in the middle of the Jordan, while all Israel passed by until the whole nation had completed the crossing on dry ground.

4 WHEN THE whole nation had finished crossing the Jordan, the LORD said to Joshua, [2]"Choose twelve men from among the people, one from each tribe, [3]and tell them to take up twelve stones from the middle of the Jordan from right where the priests stood and to carry them over with you and put them down at the place where you stay tonight."

[4]So Joshua called together the twelve men he had appointed from the Israelites, one from each tribe, [5]and said to them, "Go over before the ark of the LORD your God into the middle of the Jordan. Each of you is to take up a stone on his shoulder, according to the number of the tribes of the Israelites, [6]to serve as a sign among you. In the future, when your children ask you, 'What do these stones mean?' [7]tell them that the flow of the Jordan was cut off before the ark of the covenant of the LORD. When it crossed the Jordan, the waters of the Jordan were cut off. These stones are to be a memorial to the people of Israel forever."

[8]So the Israelites did as Joshua commanded them. They took twelve stones from the middle of the Jordan, according to the number of the tribes of the Israelites, as the LORD had told Joshua; and they carried them over with

King James

9And Joshua set up twelve stones in the midst of Jordan, in the place where the feet of the priests which bare the ark of the covenant stood: and they are there unto this day.

10 ¶ For the priests which bare the ark stood in the midst of Jordan, until every thing was finished that the LORD commanded Joshua to speak unto the people, according to all that Moses commanded Joshua: and the people hasted and passed over.

11And it came to pass, when all the people were clean passed over, that the ark of the LORD passed over, and the priests, in the presence of the people.

12And the children of Reuben, and the children of Gad, and half the tribe of Manasseh, passed over armed before the children of Israel, as Moses spake unto them:

13About forty thousand *m*prepared for war passed over before the LORD unto battle, to the plains of Jericho.

14 ¶ On that day the LORD magnified Joshua in the sight of all Israel; and they feared him, as they feared Moses, all the days of his life.

15And the LORD spake unto Joshua, saying,

16Command the priests that bear the ark of the testimony, that they come up out of Jordan.

17Joshua therefore commanded the priests, saying, Come ye up out of Jordan.

18And it came to pass, when the priests that bare the ark of the covenant of the LORD were come up out of the midst of Jordan, *and* the soles of the priests' feet were *n*lifted up unto the dry land, that the waters of Jordan returned unto their place, and *o*flowed over all his banks, as *they did* before.

19 ¶ And the people came up out of Jordan on the tenth *day* of the first month, and encamped in Gilgal, in the east border of Jericho.

20And those twelve stones, which they took out of Jordan, did Joshua pitch in Gilgal.

21And he spake unto the children of Israel, saying, When your children shall ask their fathers *p*in time to come, saying, What *mean* these stones?

22Then ye shall let your children know, saying, Israel came over this Jordan on dry land.

23For the LORD your God dried up the waters of Jordan from before you, until ye were passed over, as the LORD your God did to the Red sea, which he dried up from before us, until we were gone over:

24That all the people of the earth might know the hand of the LORD, that it *is* mighty: that ye might fear the LORD your God *q*for ever.

5 AND IT came to pass, when all the kings of the Amorites, which *were* on the side of Jordan westward, and all the kings of the Canaanites, which *were* by the sea, heard that the LORD had dried up the waters of the Jordan from before the children of Israel, until we were passed over, that their heart melted, neither was there spirit in them any more, because of the children of Israel.

Circumcising of the nation

2 ¶ At that time the LORD said unto Joshua, Make thee *r*sharp knives, and circumcise again the children of Israel the second time.

3And Joshua made him sharp knives, and circumcised the children of Israel at *s*the hill of the foreskins.

4And this *is* the cause why Joshua did circumcise: All the people that came out of Egypt, *that were* males, *even* all the men of war, died in the wilderness by the way, after they came out of Egypt.

Amplified

9And Joshua set up twelve stones in the midst of the Jordan in the place where the feet of the priests bearing the ark of the covenant had stood. And they are there to this day.

10For the priests who bore the ark stood in the midst of the Jordan until everything was finished that the Lord commanded Joshua to tell the people, according to all that Moses had commanded Joshua. The people passed over in haste.

11When all the people had passed over, the ark of the Lord and the priests went over in the presence of the people.

12And the sons of Reuben, Gad, and half the tribe of Manasseh passed over armed before the [other] Israelites, as Moses had bidden them;

13About 40,000 [of these] prepared for war passed over before the Lord to the plains of Jericho for battle.

14On that day the Lord magnified Joshua in the sight of all Israel; and they stood in awe of him, as they stood in awe of Moses, all the days of his life.

15And the Lord said to Joshua,

16Order the priests bearing the ark of the Testimony to come up out of the Jordan.

17So Joshua commanded the priests, Come up out of the Jordan.

18And when the priests who bore the ark of the covenant of the Lord had come up out of the midst of the Jordan, and the soles of their feet were lifted up to the dry land, the waters of the Jordan returned to their place and flowed over all its banks as they had before.

19And the people came up out of the Jordan on the tenth day of the first month and encamped in Gilgal on the east border of Jericho.

20And those twelve stones which they took out of the Jordan Joshua set up in Gilgal.

21And he said to the Israelites, When your children ask their fathers in time to come, What do these stones mean?

22You shall let your children know, Israel came over this Jordan on dry ground.

23For the Lord your God dried up the waters of the Jordan for you until you passed over, as the Lord your God did to the Red Sea, which He dried up for us until we passed over,

24That all the peoples of the earth may know that the hand of the Lord is mighty and that you may reverence *and* fear the Lord your God forever.

5 WHEN ALL the kings of the Amorites who were beyond the Jordan to the west and all the kings of the Canaanites who were by the sea heard that the Lord had dried up the waters of the Jordan before the Israelites until we had crossed over, their hearts melted and there was no spirit in them any more because of the Israelites.

2At that time the Lord said to Joshua, Make knives of flint and circumcise the [new generation of] Israelites as before.

3So Joshua made knives of flint and circumcised the sons of Israel at Gibeath-haaraloth.

4And this is the reason Joshua circumcised them: all the males of the people who came out of Egypt, all the men of war, had died in the wilderness on the way after they came out of Egypt.

---

*m*Or, *ready armed*   *n*Heb. *plucked up*   *o*Heb. *went*
*p*Heb. *tomorrow*   *q*Heb. *all days*   *r*Or, *knives of flints*
*s*Or, *Gibeah-haaraloth*

New American Standard

9 Then Joshua set up twelve stones in the middle of the Jordan at the place where the feet of the priests who carried the ark of the covenant were standing, and they are there to this day.

10 For the priests who carried the ark were standing in the middle of the Jordan until everything was completed that the LORD had commanded Joshua to speak to the people, according to all that Moses had commanded Joshua. And the people hurried and crossed;

11 and when all the people had finished crossing, the ark of the LORD and the priests crossed before the people.

12 The sons of Reuben and the sons of Gad and the half-tribe of Manasseh crossed over in battle array before the sons of Israel, just as Moses had spoken to them;

13 about 40,000 equipped for war, crossed for battle before the LORD to the desert plains of Jericho.

14 ¶ On that day the LORD exalted Joshua in the sight of all Israel; so that they ᶜrevered him, just as they had revered Moses all the days of his life.

15 ¶ Now the LORD said to Joshua,

16"Command the priests who carry the ark of the testimony that they come up from the Jordan."

17 So Joshua commanded the priests, saying, "Come up from the Jordan."

18 It came about when the priests who carried the ark of the covenant of the LORD had come up from the middle of the Jordan, and the soles of the priests' feet were lifted up to the dry ground, that the waters of the Jordan returned to their place, and went over all its banks as before.

19 ¶ Now the people came up from the Jordan on the tenth of the first month and camped at Gilgal on the eastern edge of Jericho.

20 Those twelve stones which they had taken from the Jordan, Joshua set up at Gilgal.

21 He said to the sons of Israel, "When your children ask their fathers in time to come, saying, 'What are these stones?'

22 then you shall inform your children, saying, 'Israel crossed this Jordan on dry ground.'

23"For the LORD your God dried up the waters of the Jordan before you until you had crossed, just as the LORD your God had done to the Red Sea, which He dried up before us until we had crossed;

24 that all the peoples of the earth may know that the hand of the LORD is mighty, so that you may fear the LORD your God forever."

Israel Is Circumcised

5 NOW IT came about when all the kings of the Amorites who *were* beyond the Jordan to the west, and all the kings of the Canaanites who *were* by the sea, heard how the LORD had dried up the waters of the Jordan before the sons of Israel until they had crossed, that their hearts melted, and there was no spirit in them any longer because of the sons of Israel.

2 ¶ At that time the LORD said to Joshua, "Make for yourself flint knives and circumcise again the sons of Israel the second time."

3 So Joshua made himself flint knives and circumcised the sons of Israel at ᵈGibeath-haaraloth.

4 This is the reason why Joshua circumcised them: all the people who came out of Egypt who were males, all the men of war, died in the wilderness along the way after they came out of Egypt.

New International

them to their camp, where they put them down. 9Joshua set up the twelve stones that had beenᵍ in the middle of the Jordan at the spot where the priests who carried the ark of the covenant had stood. And they are there to this day.

10Now the priests who carried the ark remained standing in the middle of the Jordan until everything the LORD had commanded Joshua was done by the people, just as Moses had directed Joshua. The people hurried over, 11and as soon as all of them had crossed, the ark of the LORD and the priests came to the other side while the people watched. 12The men of Reuben, Gad and the half-tribe of Manasseh crossed over, armed, in front of the Israelites, as Moses had directed them. 13About forty thousand armed for battle crossed over before the LORD to the plains of Jericho for war.

14That day the LORD exalted Joshua in the sight of all Israel; and they revered him all the days of his life, just as they had revered Moses.

15Then the LORD said to Joshua, 16"Command the priests carrying the ark of the Testimony to come up out of the Jordan."

17So Joshua commanded the priests, "Come up out of the Jordan."

18And the priests came up out of the river carrying the ark of the covenant of the LORD. No sooner had they set their feet on the dry ground than the waters of the Jordan returned to their place and ran at flood stage as before.

19On the tenth day of the first month the people went up from the Jordan and camped at Gilgal on the eastern border of Jericho. 20And Joshua set up at Gilgal the twelve stones they had taken out of the Jordan. 21He said to the Israelites, "In the future when your descendants ask their fathers, 'What do these stones mean?' 22tell them, 'Israel crossed the Jordan on dry ground.' 23For the LORD your God dried up the Jordan before you until you had crossed over. The LORD your God did to the Jordan just what he had done to the Red Seaʰ when he dried it up before us until we had crossed over. 24He did this so that all the peoples of the earth might know that the hand of the LORD is powerful and so that you might always fear the LORD your God."

Circumcision at Gilgal

5 NOW WHEN all the Amorite kings west of the Jordan and all the Canaanite kings along the coast heard how the LORD had dried up the Jordan before the Israelites until we had crossed over, their hearts melted and they no longer had the courage to face the Israelites.

2At that time the LORD said to Joshua, "Make flint knives and circumcise the Israelites again." 3So Joshua made flint knives and circumcised the Israelites at Gibeath Haaraloth.ⁱ

4Now this is why he did so: All those who came out of Egypt—all the men of military age—died in the desert on

---

ᶜOr *feared*   ᵈI.e. the hill of the foreskins

ᵍ9 Or *Joshua also set up twelve stones*   ʰ23 Hebrew *Yam Suph*; that is, Sea of Reeds   ⁱ3 *Gibeath Haaraloth* means *hill of foreskins.*

King James

[5] Now all the people that came out were circumcised: but all the people *that were* born in the wilderness by the way as they came forth out of Egypt, *them* they had not circumcised.

[6] For the children of Israel walked forty years in the wilderness, till all the people *that were* men of war, which came out of Egypt, were consumed, because they obeyed not the voice of the LORD: unto whom the LORD sware that he would not show them the land, which the LORD sware unto their fathers that he would give us, a land that floweth with milk and honey.

[7] And their children, *whom* he raised up in their stead, them Joshua circumcised: for they were uncircumcised, because they had not circumcised them by the way.

[8] And it came to pass, *[t]* when they had done circumcising all the people, that they abode in their places in the camp, till they were whole.

[9] And the LORD said unto Joshua, This day have I rolled away the reproach of Egypt from off you. Wherefore the name of the place is called *[u]* Gilgal unto this day.

[10] ¶ And the children of Israel encamped in Gilgal, and kept the passover on the fourteenth day of the month at even in the plains of Jericho.

[11] And they did eat of the old corn of the land on the morrow after the passover, unleavened cakes, and parched *corn* in the selfsame day.

[12] ¶ And the manna ceased on the morrow after they had eaten of the old corn of the land; neither had the children of Israel manna any more; but they did eat of the fruit of the land of Canaan that year.

The fall of Jericho

[13] ¶ And it came to pass, when Joshua was by Jericho, that he lifted up his eyes and looked, and, behold, there stood a man over against him with his sword drawn in his hand: and Joshua went unto him, and said unto him, *Art* thou for us, or for our adversaries?

[14] And he said, Nay; but *as* [v]captain of the host of the LORD am I now come. And Joshua fell on his face to the earth, and did worship, and said unto him, What saith my lord unto his servant?

[15] And the captain of the LORD's host said unto Joshua, Loose thy shoe from off thy foot; for the place whereon thou standest *is* holy. And Joshua did so.

6 NOW JERICHO [w]was straitly shut up because of the children of Israel: none went out, and none came in.

[2] And the LORD said unto Joshua, See, I have given into thine hand Jericho, and the king thereof, *and* the mighty men of valour.

[3] And ye shall compass the city, all *ye* men of war, *and* go round about the city once. Thus shalt thou do six days.

[4] And seven priests shall bear before the ark seven trumpets of rams' horns: and the seventh day ye shall compass the city seven times, and the priests shall blow with the trumpets.

[5] And it shall come to pass, that when they make a long *blast* with the ram's horn, *and* when ye hear the sound of the trumpet, all the people shall shout with a great shout; and the wall of the city shall fall down [x]flat, and the people shall ascend up every man straight before him.

Amplified

[5] Though all the people who came out were circumcised, yet all the people who were born in the wilderness on the way after Israel came out of Egypt had not been circumcised.

[6] For the Israelites walked forty years in the wilderness till all who were men of war who came out of Egypt perished, because they did not hearken to the voice of the Lord; to them the Lord swore that He would not let them see the land which the Lord swore to their fathers to give us, a land flowing with milk and honey.

[7] So it was their uncircumcised children whom He raised up in their stead whom Joshua circumcised, because the rite had not been performed on the way.

[8] When they finished circumcising all the males of the nation, they remained in their places in the camp till they were healed.

[9] And the Lord said to Joshua, This day have I rolled away the reproach of Egypt from you. So the name of the place is called Gilgal [rolling] to this day.

[10] And the Israelites encamped in Gilgal; and they kept the Passover on the fourteenth day of the month at evening in the plains of Jericho.

[11] And on that same day they ate the produce of the land: unleavened cakes and parched grain.

[12] And the manna ceased on the day after they ate of the produce of the land; and the Israelites had manna no more, but they ate of the fruit of the land of Canaan that year.

[13] When Joshua was by Jericho, he looked up, and behold, a Man stood near him with His drawn sword in His hand. And Joshua went to Him and said to Him, Are you for us or for our adversaries?

[14] And He said, No [neither]; but as Prince of the Lord's host have I now come. And Joshua fell on his face to the earth and worshiped, and said to Him, What says my Lord to His servant?

[15] And the Prince of the Lord's host said to Joshua, [e]Loose your shoes from off your feet, for the place where you stand is holy. And Joshua did so. [Exod. 3:5.]

6 NOW JERICHO [a fenced town with high walls] was tightly closed because of the Israelites; no one went out or came in.

[2] And the Lord said to Joshua, See, I have given Jericho, its king and mighty men of valor, into your hands.

[3] You shall march around the enclosure, all the men of war going around the city once. This you shall do for six days.

[4] And seven priests shall bear before the ark seven trumpets of rams' horns; and on the seventh day you shall march around the enclosure seven times, and the priests shall blow the trumpets.

[5] When they make a long blast with the ram's horn and you hear the sound of the trumpet, all the people shall shout with a great shout; and the wall of the enclosure shall fall down in its place and the people shall go up [over it], every man straight before him.

---

[e] "The real character of this personage was disclosed by His accepting the homage of worship (cf. Acts 10:25, 26; Rev. 19:10), and still further in the command, 'Loose thy shoe from off thy foot' " (KJV) (Robert Jamieson, A.R. Fausset and David Brown, *A Commentary*). *The New Bible Commentary* supports this position (as do J.P. Lange, *The Cambridge Bible,* Charles Ellicott, and many others) when it says, "We believe that this was the Son of God Himself."

---

[t] Heb. *when the people had made an end to be circumcised*   [u]i.e. *Rolling*   [v] Or, *prince; see Dan. 10:13,21*   [w] Heb. *did shut up, and was shut up*   [x] Heb. *under it*

New American Standard

5 For all the people who came out were circumcised, but all the people who were born in the wilderness along the way as they came out of Egypt had not been circumcised.

6 For the sons of Israel walked forty years in the wilderness, until all the nation, *that is*, the men of war who came out of Egypt, perished because they did not listen to the voice of the LORD, to whom the LORD had sworn that He would not let them see the land which the LORD had sworn to their fathers to give us, a land flowing with milk and honey.

7 Their children whom He raised up in their place, Joshua circumcised; for they were uncircumcised, because they had not circumcised them along the way.

8 ¶ Now when they had finished circumcising all the nation, they remained in their places in the camp until they were healed.

9 Then the LORD said to Joshua, "Today I have rolled away the reproach of Egypt from you." So the name of that place is called ᵉGilgal to this day.

10 ¶ While the sons of Israel camped at Gilgal they observed the Passover on the evening of the fourteenth day of the month on the desert plains of Jericho.

11 On the day after the Passover, on that very day, they ate some of the produce of the land, unleavened cakes and parched *grain*.

12 The manna ceased on the day after they had eaten some of the produce of the land, so that the sons of Israel no longer had manna, but they ate some of the yield of the land of Canaan during that year.

13 ¶ Now it came about when Joshua was by Jericho, that he lifted up his eyes and looked, and behold, a man was standing opposite him with his sword drawn in his hand, and Joshua went up to him and said to him, "Are you for us or for our adversaries?"

14 He said, "No; rather I indeed come now *as* captain of the host of the LORD." And Joshua fell on his face to the earth, and bowed down, and said to him, "What has my lord to say to his servant?"

15 The captain of the LORD'S host said to Joshua, "Remove your sandals from your feet, for the place where you are standing is holy." And Joshua did so.

The Conquest of Jericho

6 NOW JERICHO was tightly shut because of the sons of Israel; no one went out and no one came in.

2 The LORD said to Joshua, "See, I have given Jericho into your hand, with its king *and* the valiant warriors.

3 "You shall march around the city, all the men of war circling the city once. You shall do so for six days.

4 "Also seven priests shall carry seven trumpets of rams' horns before the ark; then on the seventh day you shall march around the city seven times, and the priests shall blow the trumpets.

5 "It shall be that when they make a long blast with the ram's horn, and when you hear the sound of the trumpet, all the people shall shout with a great shout; and the wall of the city will fall down flat, and the people will go up every man straight ahead."

New International

the way after leaving Egypt. 5All the people that came out had been circumcised, but all the people born in the desert during the journey from Egypt had not. 6The Israelites had moved about in the desert forty years until all the men who were of military age when they left Egypt had died, since they had not obeyed the LORD. For the LORD had sworn to them that they would not see the land that he had solemnly promised their fathers to give us, a land flowing with milk and honey. 7So he raised up their sons in their place, and these were the ones Joshua circumcised. They were still uncircumcised because they had not been circumcised on the way. 8And after the whole nation had been circumcised, they remained where they were in camp until they were healed.

9Then the LORD said to Joshua, "Today I have rolled away the reproach of Egypt from you." So the place has been called Gilgalʲ to this day.

10On the evening of the fourteenth day of the month, while camped at Gilgal on the plains of Jericho, the Israelites celebrated the Passover. 11The day after the Passover, that very day, they ate some of the produce of the land: unleavened bread and roasted grain. 12The manna stopped the day afterᵏ they ate this food from the land; there was no longer any manna for the Israelites, but that year they ate of the produce of Canaan.

The Fall of Jericho

13Now when Joshua was near Jericho, he looked up and saw a man standing in front of him with a drawn sword in his hand. Joshua went up to him and asked, "Are you for us or for our enemies?"

14"Neither," he replied, "but as commander of the army of the LORD I have now come." Then Joshua fell facedown to the ground in reverence, and asked him, "What message does my Lordˡ have for his servant?"

15The commander of the LORD's army replied, "Take off your sandals, for the place where you are standing is holy." And Joshua did so.

6 NOW JERICHO was tightly shut up because of the Israelites. No one went out and no one came in.

2Then the LORD said to Joshua, "See, I have delivered Jericho into your hands, along with its king and its fighting men. 3March around the city once with all the armed men. Do this for six days. 4Have seven priests carry trumpets of rams' horns in front of the ark. On the seventh day, march around the city seven times, with the priests blowing the trumpets. 5When you hear them sound a long blast on the trumpets, have all the people give a loud shout; then the wall of the city will collapse and the people will go up, every man straight in."

ʲ9 *Gilgal* sounds like the Hebrew for *roll.*   ᵏ12 Or *the day*
ˡ14 Or *lord*

King James

6 ¶ And Joshua the son of Nun called the priests, and said unto them, Take up the ark of the covenant, and let seven priests bear seven trumpets of rams' horns before the ark of the LORD.

7And he said unto the people, Pass on, and compass the city, and let him that is armed pass on before the ark of the LORD.

8 ¶ And it came to pass, when Joshua had spoken unto the people, that the seven priests bearing the seven trumpets of rams' horns passed on before the LORD, and blew with the trumpets: and the ark of the covenant of the LORD followed them.

9 ¶ And the armed men went before the priests that blew with the trumpets, and the ʸrearward came after the ark, *the priests* going on, and blowing with the trumpets.

10And Joshua had commanded the people, saying, Ye shall not shout, nor ᶻmake any noise with your voice, neither shall *any* word proceed out of your mouth, until the day I bid you shout; then shall ye shout.

11So the ark of the LORD compassed the city, going about *it* once: and they came into the camp, and lodged in the camp.

12 ¶ And Joshua rose early in the morning, and the priests took up the ark of the LORD.

13And seven priests bearing seven trumpets of rams' horns before the ark of the LORD went on continually, and blew with the trumpets: and the armed men went before them; but the rearward came after the ark of the LORD, *the priests* going on, and blowing with the trumpets.

14And the second day they compassed the city once, and returned into the camp: so they did six days.

15And it came to pass on the seventh day, that they rose early about the dawning of the day, and compassed the city after the same manner seven times: only on that day they compassed the city seven times.

16And it came to pass at the seventh time, when the priests blew with the trumpets, Joshua said unto the people, Shout; for the LORD hath given you the city.

17 ¶ And the city shall be ᵃaccursed, *even* it, and all that *are* therein, to the LORD: only Rahab the harlot shall live, she and all that *are* with her in the house, because she hid the messengers that we sent.

18And ye, in any wise keep *yourselves* from the accursed thing, lest ye make *yourselves* accursed, when ye take of the accursed thing, and make the camp of Israel a curse, and trouble it.

19But all the silver, and gold, and vessels of brass and iron, *are* ᵇconsecrated unto the LORD: they shall come into the treasury of the LORD.

20So the people shouted when *the priests* blew with the trumpets: and it came to pass, when the people heard the sound of the trumpet, and the people shouted with a great shout, that the wall fell down ᶜflat, so that the people went up into the city, every man straight before him, and they took the city.

21And they utterly destroyed all that *was* in the city, both man and woman, young and old, and ox, and sheep, and ass, with the edge of the sword.

22But Joshua had said unto the two men that had spied out the country, Go into the harlot's house, and bring out thence the woman, and all that she hath, as ye sware unto her.

Amplified

6So Joshua son of Nun called the priests and said to them, Take up the ark of the covenant and let seven priests bear seven trumpets of rams' horns before the ark of the Lord.

7He said to the people, Go on! March around the enclosure, and let the armed men pass on before the ark of the Lord.

8When Joshua had spoken to the people, the seven priests bearing the seven trumpets of rams' horns passed on before the Lord and blew the trumpets, and the ark of the covenant of the Lord followed them.

9The armed men went before the priests who blew the trumpets, and the rear guard came after the ark, the priests blowing the trumpets as they went.

10But Joshua commanded the people, You shall not shout or let your voice be heard, nor shall any word proceed out of your mouth until the day I tell you to shout. Then you shall shout!

11So he caused the ark of the Lord to go around the city once; and they came into the camp and lodged in the camp.

12Joshua rose early in the morning and the priests took up the ark of the Lord.

13And the seven priests bearing the seven trumpets of rams' horns before the ark of the Lord passed on, blowing the trumpets continually; and the armed men went before them and the rear guard came after the ark of the Lord, the priests blowing the trumpets as they went.

14On the second day they compassed the city enclosure once and returned to the camp. So they did for six days.

15On the seventh day they rose early at daybreak and marched around the city as usual, only on that day they compassed the city ᶠseven times.

16And the seventh time, when the priests had blown the trumpets, Joshua said to the people, Shout! For the Lord has given you the city.

17And the city and all that is in it shall be devoted to the Lord [for destruction]; only Rahab the harlot and all who are with her in her house shall live, because she hid the messengers whom we sent.

18But you, keep yourselves from the accursed *and* devoted things, lest when you have devoted it [to destruction], you take of the accursed thing, and so make the camp of Israel accursed and trouble it.

19But all the silver and gold and vessels of bronze and iron are consecrated to the Lord; they shall come into the treasury of the Lord.

20So the people shouted, and the trumpets were blown. When the people heard the sound of the trumpet, they raised a great shout, and [Jericho's] wall fell down in its place, so that the [Israelites] went up into the city, every man straight before him, and they took the city.

21Then they utterly destroyed all that was in the city, both man and woman, young and old, ox, sheep, and donkey, with the edge of the sword.

22But Joshua said to the two men who had spied out the land, Go into the harlot's house and bring out the woman and all she has, as you swore to her.

ᶠAny walled town was called a "city" and its headman was called "a king" in ancient times, but the fact that Joshua's army could march around the whole of Jericho seven times in one day shows that it was a very small place. Sir Charles Marston (*New Bible Evidence*) echoes the reports of other archaeologists when he says that the excavations of ancient Jericho do not confirm the conceptions of our youth. Though the walls were so formidable, the area they enclosed only measures seven acres. The whole circumference of the city was about 650 yards. Our disappointment is somewhat modified by the fact that Jebusite Jerusalem, which David captured, was about the same size. Schliemann experienced a similar disillusionment in 1873 when he excavated the city of Troy, which Homer tells us so long withstood the Grecian hosts. Indeed it would almost seem that these ancient cities were more in the nature of places of refuge resorted to when an enemy approached. Under peaceful conditions a large proportion of the inhabitants would dwell outside the city's walls (Sir Charles Marston, *New Bible Evidence*).

ʸHeb. *gathering host*   ᶻHeb. *make your voice to be heard*
ᵃOr, *devoted;* see Lev. 27:28   ᵇHeb. *holiness*   ᶜHeb. *under it*

New American Standard

6 ¶ So Joshua the son of Nun called the priests and said to them, "Take up the ark of the covenant, and let seven priests carry seven trumpets of rams' horns before the ark of the LORD."

7 Then he said to the people, "Go forward, and march around the city, and let the armed men go on before the ark of the LORD."

8 And it was *so,* that when Joshua had spoken to the people, the seven priests carrying the seven trumpets of rams' horns before the LORD went forward and blew the trumpets; and the ark of the covenant of the LORD followed them.

9 The armed men went before the priests who blew the trumpets, and the rear guard came after the ark, while they continued to blow the trumpets.

10 But Joshua commanded the people, saying, "You shall not shout nor let your voice be heard nor let a word proceed out of your mouth, until the day I tell you, 'Shout!' Then you shall shout!"

11 So he had the ark of the LORD taken around the city, circling *it* once; then they came into the camp and spent the night in the camp.

12 ¶ Now Joshua rose early in the morning, and the priests took up the ark of the LORD.

13 The seven priests carrying the seven trumpets of rams' horns before the ark of the LORD went on continually, and blew the trumpets; and the armed men went before them and the rear guard came after the ark of the LORD, while they continued to blow the trumpets.

14 Thus the second day they marched around the city once and returned to the camp; they did so for six days.

15 ¶ Then on the seventh day they rose early at the dawning of the day and marched around the city in the same manner seven times; only on that day they marched around the city seven times.

16 At the seventh time, when the priests blew the trumpets, Joshua said to the people, "Shout! For the LORD has given you the city.

17 "The city shall be under the ban, it and all that is in it belongs to the LORD; only Rahab the harlot and all who are with her in the house shall live, because she hid the messengers whom we sent.

18 "But as for you, only keep yourselves from the things under the ban, so that you do not covet *them* and take some of the things under the ban, and make the camp of Israel accursed and bring trouble on it.

19 "But all the silver and gold and articles of bronze and iron are holy to the LORD; they shall go into the treasury of the LORD."

20 So the people shouted, and *priests* blew the trumpets; and when the people heard the sound of the trumpet, the people shouted with a great shout and the wall fell down flat, so that the people went up into the city, every man straight ahead, and they took the city.

21 They utterly destroyed everything in the city, both man and woman, young and old, and ox and sheep and donkey, with the edge of the sword.

22 ¶ Joshua said to the two men who had spied out the land, "Go into the harlot's house and bring the woman and all she has out of there, as you have sworn to her."

New International

6 So Joshua son of Nun called the priests and said to them, "Take up the ark of the covenant of the LORD and have seven priests carry trumpets in front of it." 7 And he ordered the people, "Advance! March around the city, with the armed guard going ahead of the ark of the LORD."

8 When Joshua had spoken to the people, the seven priests carrying the seven trumpets before the LORD went forward, blowing their trumpets, and the ark of the LORD's covenant followed them. 9 The armed guard marched ahead of the priests who blew the trumpets, and the rear guard followed the ark. All this time the trumpets were sounding. 10 But Joshua had commanded the people, "Do not give a war cry, do not raise your voices, do not say a word until the day I tell you to shout. Then shout!" 11 So he had the ark of the LORD carried around the city, circling it once. Then the people returned to camp and spent the night there.

12 Joshua got up early the next morning and the priests took up the ark of the LORD. 13 The seven priests carrying the seven trumpets went forward, marching before the ark of the LORD and blowing the trumpets. The armed men went ahead of them and the rear guard followed the ark of the LORD, while the trumpets kept sounding. 14 So on the second day they marched around the city once and returned to the camp. They did this for six days.

15 On the seventh day, they got up at daybreak and marched around the city seven times in the same manner, except that on that day they circled the city seven times. 16 The seventh time around, when the priests sounded the trumpet blast, Joshua commanded the people, "Shout! For the LORD has given you the city! 17 The city and all that is in it are to be devoted*m* to the LORD. Only Rahab the prostitute*n* and all who are with her in her house shall be spared, because she hid the spies we sent. 18 But keep away from the devoted things, so that you will not bring about your own destruction by taking any of them. Otherwise you will make the camp of Israel liable to destruction and bring trouble on it. 19 All the silver and gold and the articles of bronze and iron are sacred to the LORD and must go into his treasury."

20 When the trumpets sounded, the people shouted, and at the sound of the trumpet, when the people gave a loud shout, the wall collapsed; so every man charged straight in, and they took the city. 21 They devoted the city to the LORD and destroyed with the sword every living thing in it—men and women, young and old, cattle, sheep and donkeys.

22 Joshua said to the two men who had spied out the land, "Go into the prostitute's house and bring her out and all who belong to her, in accordance with your oath to her."

---

m 17 The Hebrew term refers to the irrevocable giving over of things or persons to the LORD, often by totally destroying them; also in verses 18 and 21.   *n 17* Or possibly *innkeeper*; also in verses 22 and 25

King James

²³And the young men that were spies went in, and brought out Rahab, and her father, and her mother, and her brethren, and all that she had; and they brought out all her ^dkindred, and left them without the camp of Israel.

²⁴And they burnt the city with fire, and all that *was* therein: only the silver, and the gold, and the vessels of brass and of iron, they put into the treasury of the house of the LORD.

²⁵And Joshua saved Rahab the harlot alive, and her father's household, and all that she had; and she dwelleth in Israel *even* unto this day; because she hid the messengers, which Joshua sent to spy out Jericho.

²⁶ ¶ And Joshua adjured *them* at that time, saying, Cursed *be* the man before the LORD, that riseth up and buildeth this city Jericho: he shall lay the foundation thereof in his firstborn, and in his youngest *son* shall he set up the gates of it.

²⁷So the LORD was with Joshua; and his fame was *noised* throughout all the country.

Achan's sin

7 BUT THE children of Israel committed a trespass in the accursed thing: for *e*Achan, the son of Carmi, the son of *f*Zabdi, the son of Zerah, of the tribe of Judah, took of the accursed thing: and the anger of the LORD was kindled against the children of Israel.

²And Joshua sent men from Jericho to Ai, which *is* beside Beth-aven, on the east side of Beth-el, and spake unto them, saying, Go up and view the country. And the men went up and viewed Ai.

³And they returned to Joshua, and said unto him, Let not all the people go up; but let *g*about two or three thousand man go up and smite Ai; *and* make not all the people to labour thither; for they *are but* few.

⁴So there went up thither of the people about three thousand men: and they fled before the men of Ai.

⁵And the men of Ai smote of them about thirty and six men: for they chased them *from* before the gate *even* unto Shebarim, and smote them ^hin the going down: wherefore the hearts of the people melted, and became as water.

⁶ ¶ And Joshua rent his clothes, and fell to the earth upon his face before the ark of the LORD until the eventide, he and the elders of Israel, and put dust upon their heads.

⁷And Joshua said, Alas, O Lord GOD, wherefore hast thou at all brought this people over Jordan, to deliver us into the hand of the Amorites, to destroy us? would to God we had been content, and dwelt on the other side Jordan!

⁸O Lord, what shall I say, when Israel turneth their ⁱbacks before their enemies!

⁹For the Canaanites and all the inhabitants of the land shall hear *of it*, and shall environ us round, and cut off our name from the earth: and what wilt thou do unto thy great name?

¹⁰ ¶ And the LORD said unto Joshua, Get thee up; wherefore *j*liest thou thus upon thy face?

¹¹Israel hath sinned, and they have also transgressed my covenant which I commanded them: for they have even taken of the accursed thing, and have also stolen, and dissembled also, and they have put *it* even among their own stuff.

Amplified

²³So the young men, the spies, went in and brought out Rahab, her father and mother, her brethren, and all that she had; and they brought out all her kindred and set them outside the camp of Israel.

²⁴And they ^gburned the city with fire and all that was in it; only the silver, the gold, and the vessels of bronze and of iron they put into the treasury of the house of the Lord.

²⁵So Joshua saved Rahab the harlot, with her father's household and all that she had; and she lives in Israel even to this day, because she hid the messengers whom Joshua sent to spy out Jericho.

²⁶Then Joshua laid this oath on them, Cursed is the man before the Lord who rises up and rebuilds this city, Jericho. With the loss of his firstborn shall he lay its foundation, and with the loss of his youngest son shall he set up its gates. [I Kings 16:34.]

²⁷So the Lord was with Joshua, and his fame was in all the land.

7 BUT THE Israelites committed a trespass in regard to the devoted things; for Achan son of Carmi, the son of Zabdi, the son of Zerah, of the tribe of Judah, took some of the things devoted [for destruction]. And the anger of the Lord burned against Israel.

²Joshua sent men from Jericho to Ai, which is near Beth-aven, east of Bethel, and said to them, Go up and spy out the land. So the men went up and spied out Ai.

³And they returned to Joshua and said to him, Let not all the men go up; but let about two thousand or three thousand go up and attack Ai; do not make the whole army toil up there, for they of Ai are few.

⁴So about three thousand Israelites went up there, but they fled before the men of Ai.

⁵And the men of Ai killed about thirty-six of them, for they chased them from before the gate as far as Shebarim, and slew them at the descent. And the hearts of the people melted and became as water.

⁶Then Joshua rent his clothes and lay on the earth upon his face before the ark of the Lord until evening, he and the elders of Israel; and they put dust on their heads.

⁷Joshua said, Alas, O Lord God, why have You brought this people over the Jordan at all only to give us into the hands of the Amorites to destroy us? Would that we had been content to dwell beyond the Jordan!

⁸O Lord, what can I say, now that Israel has turned to flee before their enemies!

⁹For the Canaanites and all the inhabitants of the land will hear of it and will surround us and cut off our name from the earth. And what will You do for Your great name?

¹⁰The Lord said to Joshua, Get up! Why do you lie thus upon your face?

¹¹Israel has sinned; they have transgressed My covenant which I commanded them. They have taken some of the things devoted [for destruction]; they have stolen, and lied, and put them among their own baggage.

^g Important details of this story are fully substantiated by the findings of Dr. J. B. Garstang in his several excavations of Jericho: 1. The city was thoroughly burned by fire. 2. It had not been thoroughly plundered. Stored grain, for example, was found burned but undisturbed. 3. The "silver, the gold, and the vessels of bronze and of iron" were missing. 4. The walls had fallen, but the one gate had a tower left standing. 5. Well-supported houses had been built on the walls. 6. The gate tower was "an imposing edifice," 54 ft. by 24 ft., remarkably well built of gray brick. Its ruins still stand 16 ft. high. 7. Only on one side of Jericho is there a mountain, and that is a mountain ridge beginning a mile west of the city (John Garstang, *The Story of Jericho*, Joseph P. Free, *Archaeology and Bible History*, and other sources).

^dHeb. *families*   *e* 1 Chr. 2:7, *Achar*   *f* Or, *Zimri;* see 1 Chr. 2:6   *g* Heb. *about 2000 men, or about 3000 men*   ^h Or, *in Morad*   ⁱ Heb. *necks*   ^j Heb. *fallest*

New American Standard

23 So the young men who were spies went in and brought out Rahab and her father and her mother and her brothers and all she had; they also brought out all her relatives and placed them outside the camp of Israel. 24 They burned the city with fire, and all that was in it. Only the silver and gold, and articles of bronze and iron, they put into the treasury of the ƒhouse of the LORD. 25 However, Rahab the harlot and her father's household and all she had, Joshua spared; and she has lived in the midst of Israel to this day, for she hid the messengers whom Joshua sent to spy out Jericho.

26 ¶ Then Joshua made them take an oath at that time, saying, "Cursed before the LORD is the man who rises up and builds this city Jericho; with *the loss of* his firstborn he shall lay its foundation, and with *the loss of* his youngest son he shall set up its gates."

27 So the LORD was with Joshua, and his fame was in all the land.

Israel Is Defeated at Ai

7 BUT THE sons of Israel acted unfaithfully in regard to the things under the ban, for Achan, the son of Carmi, the son of Zabdi, the son of Zerah, from the tribe of Judah, took some of the things under the ban, therefore the anger of the LORD burned against the sons of Israel. 2 ¶ Now Joshua sent men from Jericho to Ai, which is near Beth-aven, east of Bethel, and said to them, "Go up and spy out the land." So the men went up and spied out Ai. 3 They returned to Joshua and said to him, "Do not let all the people go up; *only* about two or three thousand men need go up to Ai; do not make all the people toil up there, for they are few." 4 So about three thousand men from the people went up there, but they fled from the men of Ai. 5 The men of Ai struck down about thirty-six of their men, and pursued them from the gate as far as Shebarim and struck them down on the descent, so the hearts of the people melted and became as water. 6 ¶ Then Joshua tore his clothes and fell to the earth on his face before the ark of the LORD until the evening, *both* he and the elders of Israel; and they put dust on their heads. 7 Joshua said, "Alas, O Lord GOD, why did You ever bring this people over the Jordan, *only* to deliver us into the hand of the Amorites, to destroy us? If only we had been willing to dwell beyond the Jordan! 8 "O Lord, what can I say since Israel has turned *their* back before their enemies? 9 "For the Canaanites and all the inhabitants of the land will hear of it, and they will surround us and cut off our name from the earth. And what will You do for Your great name?"

10 ¶ So the LORD said to Joshua, "Rise up! Why is it that you have fallen on your face? 11 "Israel has sinned, and they have also transgressed My covenant which I commanded them. And they have even taken some of the things under the ban and have both stolen and deceived. Moreover, they have also put *them* among their own things.

New International

23So the young men who had done the spying went in and brought out Rahab, her father and mother and brothers and all who belonged to her. They brought out her entire family and put them in a place outside the camp of Israel. 24Then they burned the whole city and everything in it, but they put the silver and gold and the articles of bronze and iron into the treasury of the LORD's house. 25But Joshua spared Rahab the prostitute, with her family and all who belonged to her, because she hid the men Joshua had sent as spies to Jericho—and she lives among the Israelites to this day.

26At that time Joshua pronounced this solemn oath: "Cursed before the LORD is the man who undertakes to rebuild this city, Jericho:

> "At the cost of his firstborn son
> will he lay its foundations;
> at the cost of his youngest
> will he set up its gates."

27So the LORD was with Joshua, and his fame spread throughout the land.

Achan's Sin

7 BUT THE Israelites acted unfaithfully in regard to the devoted things*o*; Achan son of Carmi, the son of Zimri,*p* the son of Zerah, of the tribe of Judah, took some of them. So the LORD's anger burned against Israel. 2Now Joshua sent men from Jericho to Ai, which is near Beth Aven to the east of Bethel, and told them, "Go up and spy out the region." So the men went up and spied out Ai. 3When they returned to Joshua, they said, "Not all the people will have to go up against Ai. Send two or three thousand men to take it and do not weary all the people, for only a few men are there." 4So about three thousand men went up; but they were routed by the men of Ai, 5who killed about thirty-six of them. They chased the Israelites from the city gate as far as the stone quarries*q* and struck them down on the slopes. At this the hearts of the people melted and became like water.

6Then Joshua tore his clothes and fell facedown to the ground before the ark of the LORD, remaining there till evening. The elders of Israel did the same, and sprinkled dust on their heads. 7And Joshua said, "Ah, Sovereign LORD, why did you ever bring this people across the Jordan to deliver us into the hands of the Amorites to destroy us? If only we had been content to stay on the other side of the Jordan! 8O Lord, what can I say, now that Israel has been routed by its enemies? 9The Canaanites and the other people of the country will hear about this and they will surround us and wipe out our name from the earth. What then will you do for your own great name?"

10The LORD said to Joshua, "Stand up! What are you doing down on your face? 11Israel has sinned; they have violated my covenant, which I commanded them to keep. They have taken some of the devoted things; they have stolen, they have lied, they have put them with their own

---

*ƒ*I.e. tabernacle

o 1 The Hebrew term refers to the irrevocable giving over of things or persons to the LORD, often by totally destroying them; also in verses 11, 12, 13 and 15.   *p 1* See Septuagint and 1 Chron. 2:6; Hebrew *Zabdi*; also in verses 17 and 18.   *q 5* Or *as far as Shebarim*

King James

¹²Therefore the children of Israel could not stand before their enemies, *but* turned *their* backs before their enemies, because they were accursed: neither will I be with you any more, except ye destroy the accursed from among you.

¹³Up, sanctify the people, and say, Sanctify yourselves against tomorrow: for thus saith the LORD God of Israel, *There is* an accursed thing in the midst of thee, O Israel: thou canst not stand before thine enemies, until ye take away the accursed thing from among you.

¹⁴In the morning therefore ye shall be brought according to your tribes: and it shall be, *that* the tribe which the LORD taketh shall come according to the families *thereof;* and the family which the LORD shall take shall come by households; and the household which the LORD shall take shall come man by man.

¹⁵And it shall be, *that* he that is taken with the accursed thing shall be burnt with fire, he and all that he hath: because he hath transgressed the covenant of the LORD, and because he hath wrought *k*folly in Israel.

¹⁶ ¶ So Joshua rose up early in the morning, and brought Israel by their tribes; and the tribe of Judah was taken:

¹⁷And he brought the family of Judah; and he took the family of the Zarhites: and he brought the family of the Zarhites man by man; and Zabdi was taken:

¹⁸And he brought his household man by man; and Achan, the son of Carmi, the son of Zabdi, the son of Zerah, of the tribe of Judah, was taken.

¹⁹And Joshua said unto Achan, My son, give, I pray thee, glory to the LORD God of Israel, and make confession unto him; and tell me now what thou hast done; hide *it* not from me.

²⁰And Achan answered Joshua, and said, Indeed I have sinned against the LORD God of Israel, and thus and thus have I done:

²¹When I saw among the spoils a goodly Babylonish garment, and two hundred shekels of silver, and a *l*wedge of gold of fifty shekels weight, then I coveted them, and took them; and, behold, they *are* hid in the earth in the midst of my tent, and the silver under it.

²² ¶ So Joshua sent messengers, and they ran unto the tent; and, behold, *it was* hid in his tent, and the silver under it.

²³And they took them out of the midst of the tent, and brought them unto Joshua, and unto all the children of Israel, and *m*laid them out before the LORD.

²⁴And Joshua, and all Israel with him, took Achan the son of Zerah, and the silver, and the garment, and the wedge of gold, and his sons, and his daughters, and his oxen, and his asses, and his sheep, and his tent, and all that he had: and they brought them unto the valley of Achor.

²⁵And Joshua said, Why hast thou troubled us? the LORD shall trouble thee this day. And all Israel stoned him with stones, and burned them with fire, after they had stoned them with stones.

²⁶And they raised over him a great heap of stones unto this day. So the LORD turned from the fierceness of his anger. Wherefore the name of that place was called, The valley of *n*Achor, unto this day.

Amplified

¹²That is why the Israelites could not stand before their enemies, but fled before them; they are accursed *and* have become devoted [for destruction]. I will cease to be with you unless you destroy the accursed [devoted] things among you.

¹³Up, sanctify (set apart for a holy purpose) the people, and say, Sanctify yourselves for tomorrow; for thus says the Lord, the God of Israel: There are accursed things in the midst of you, O Israel. You can not stand before your enemies until you take away from among you the things devoted [to destruction].

¹⁴In the morning therefore, you shall present your tribes. And the tribe which the Lord takes shall come by families; and the family which the Lord takes shall come by households; and the household which the Lord takes shall come by persons.

¹⁵And he who is taken with the devoted things shall be [killed and his body] burned with fire, he and all he has, because he has transgressed the covenant of the Lord and because he has done a shameful *and* wicked thing in Israel. [Josh. 7:25.]

¹⁶So Joshua rose up early in the morning and brought Israel near by their tribes, and the tribe of Judah was taken.

¹⁷He brought near the family of Judah, and the family of the Zerahites was taken; and he brought near the family of the Zerahites man by man, and Zabdi was taken.

¹⁸He brought near his household man by man, and Achan son of Carmi, the son of Zabdi, the son of Zerah, of the tribe of Judah, was taken.

¹⁹And Joshua said to Achan, My son, give glory to the Lord, the God of Israel, and make confession to Him. And tell me now what you have done; do not hide it from me.

²⁰And Achan answered Joshua, In truth, I have sinned against the Lord, the God of Israel, and this have I done:

²¹When I saw among the spoils an attractive mantle from Shinar and two hundred shekels of silver and a bar of gold weighing fifty shekels, I coveted them and took them. Behold, they are hidden in the earth inside my tent, with the silver underneath.

²²So Joshua sent messengers, who ran to the tent, and behold, the spoil was hidden in his tent, with the silver underneath.

²³And they took them from the tent and brought them to Joshua and all the Israelites and laid them out before the Lord.

²⁴And Joshua and all Israel with him took Achan son of Zerah, and the silver, the garment, the wedge of gold, his sons, his daughters, his oxen, his donkeys, his sheep, his tent, and all that he had; and they brought them to the Valley of Achor.

²⁵And Joshua said, Why have you brought trouble on us? The Lord will trouble you this day. And all Israel stoned him and those with him with stones, and afterward burned their bodies with fire.

²⁶And they raised over him a great heap of stones that remains to this day. Then the Lord turned from the fierceness of His anger. Therefore the name of that place has been called the Valley of Achor *or* Troubling to this day.

The destruction of Ai

8 AND THE LORD said unto Joshua, Fear not, neither be thou dismayed: take all the people of war with thee, and arise, go up to Ai: see, I have given into thy hand the king of Ai, and his people, and his city, and his land:

8 AND THE Lord said to Joshua, Fear not nor be dismayed. Take all the men of war with you, and arise, go up to Ai; see, I have given into your hand the king of Ai, his people, his city, and his land.

---

*k*Or, *wickedness*   *l*Heb. *tongue*   *m*Heb. *poured*   *n*i.e. Trouble

New American Standard

12"Therefore the sons of Israel cannot stand before their enemies; they turn *their* backs before their enemies, for they have become accursed. I will not be with you any-more unless you destroy the things under the ban from your midst.

13"Rise up! Consecrate the people and say, 'Consecrate yourselves for tomorrow, for thus the LORD, the God of Israel, has said, "There are things under the ban in your midst, O Israel. You cannot stand before your enemies until you have removed the things under the ban from your midst."

14'In the morning then you shall come near by your tribes. And it shall be that the tribe which the LORD takes *by lot* shall come near by families, and the family which the LORD takes shall come near by households, and the household which the LORD takes shall come near man by man.

15'It shall be that the one who is taken with the things under the ban shall be burned with fire, he and all that belongs to him, because he has transgressed the covenant of the LORD, and because he has committed a disgraceful thing in Israel.' "

The Sin of Achan

16 ¶ So Joshua arose early in the morning and brought Israel near by tribes, and the tribe of Judah was taken.

17 He brought the family of Judah near, and he took the family of the Zerahites; and he brought the family of the Zerahites near man by man, and Zabdi was taken.

18 He brought his household near man by man; and Achan, son of Carmi, son of Zabdi, son of Zerah, from the tribe of Judah, was taken.

19 Then Joshua said to Achan, "My son, I implore you, give glory to the LORD, the God of Israel, and give praise to Him; and tell me now what you have done. Do not hide it from me."

20 So Achan answered Joshua and said, "Truly, I have sinned against the LORD, the God of Israel, and this is what I did:

21 when I saw among the spoil a beautiful mantle from Shinar and two hundred shekels of silver and a bar of gold fifty shekels in weight, then I coveted them and took them; and behold, they are concealed in the earth inside my tent with the silver underneath it."

22 ¶ So Joshua sent messengers, and they ran to the tent; and behold, it was concealed in his tent with the silver underneath it.

23 They took them from inside the tent and brought them to Joshua and to all the sons of Israel, and they poured them out before the LORD.

24 Then Joshua and all Israel with him, took Achan the son of Zerah, the silver, the mantle, the bar of gold, his sons, his daughters, his oxen, his donkeys, his sheep, his tent and all that belonged to him; and they brought them up to the valley of gAchor.

25 Joshua said, "Why have you troubled us? The LORD will trouble you this day." And all Israel stoned them with stones; and they burned them with fire after they had stoned them with stones.

26 They raised over him a great heap of stones that stands to this day, and the LORD turned from the fierceness of His anger. Therefore the name of that place has been called the valley of gAchor to this day.

The Conquest of Ai

8 NOW THE LORD said to Joshua, "Do not fear or be dismayed. Take all the people of war with you and arise, go up to Ai; see, I have given into your hand the king of Ai, his people, his city, and his land.

New International

possessions. 12That is why the Israelites cannot stand against their enemies; they turn their backs and run be-cause they have been made liable to destruction. I will not be with you anymore unless you destroy whatever among you is devoted to destruction.

13"Go, consecrate the people. Tell them, 'Consecrate yourselves in preparation for tomorrow; for this is what the LORD, the God of Israel, says: That which is devoted is among you, O Israel. You cannot stand against your enemies until you remove it.

14" 'In the morning, present yourselves tribe by tribe. The tribe that the LORD takes shall come forward clan by clan; the clan that the LORD takes shall come forward family by family; and the family that the LORD takes shall come forward man by man. 15He who is caught with the devoted things shall be destroyed by fire, along with all that belongs to him. He has violated the covenant of the LORD and has done a disgraceful thing in Israel!' "

16Early the next morning Joshua had Israel come for-ward by tribes, and Judah was taken. 17The clans of Judah came forward, and he took the Zerahites. He had the clan of the Zerahites come forward by families, and Zimri was taken. 18Joshua had his family come forward man by man, and Achan son of Carmi, the son of Zimri, the son of Zerah, of the tribe of Judah, was taken.

19Then Joshua said to Achan, "My son, give glory to the LORD,r the God of Israel, and give him the praise.s Tell me what you have done; do not hide it from me."

20Achan replied, "It is true! I have sinned against the LORD, the God of Israel. This is what I have done: 21When I saw in the plunder a beautiful robe from Babylonia,t two hundred shekelsu of silver and a wedge of gold weighing fifty shekels,v I coveted them and took them. They are hidden in the ground inside my tent, with the silver underneath."

22So Joshua sent messengers, and they ran to the tent, and there it was, hidden in his tent, with the silver under-neath. 23They took the things from the tent, brought them to Joshua and all the Israelites and spread them out before the LORD.

24Then Joshua, together with all Israel, took Achan son of Zerah, the silver, the robe, the gold wedge, his sons and daughters, his cattle, donkeys and sheep, his tent and all that he had, to the Valley of Achor. 25Joshua said, "Why have you brought this trouble on us? The LORD will bring trouble on you today."

Then all Israel stoned him, and after they had stoned the rest, they burned them. 26Over Achan they heaped up a large pile of rocks, which remains to this day. Then the LORD turned from his fierce anger. Therefore that place has been called the Valley of Achorw ever since.

Ai Destroyed

8 THEN THE LORD said to Joshua, "Do not be afraid; do not be discouraged. Take the whole army with you, and go up and attack Ai. For I have delivered into your hands the king of Ai, his people, his city and his land.

---

g I.e. trouble

r 19 A solemn charge to tell the truth   s 19 Or and confess to him   t 21 Hebrew Shinar   u 21 That is, about 5 pounds (about 2.3 kilograms)   v 21 That is, about 1 1/4 pounds (about 0.6 kilogram)   w 26 Achor means trouble.

King James

2And thou shalt do to Ai and her king as thou didst unto Jericho and her king: only the spoil thereof, and the cattle thereof, shall ye take for a prey unto yourselves: lay thee an ambush for the city behind it.

3 ¶ So Joshua arose, and all the people of war, to go up against Ai: and Joshua chose out thirty thousand mighty men of valour, and sent them away by night.

4And he commanded them, saying, Behold, ye shall lie in wait against the city, *even* behind the city: go not very far from the city, but be ye all ready:

5And I, and all the people that *are* with me, will approach unto the city: and it shall come to pass, when they come out against us, as at the first, that we will flee before them,

6(For they will come out after us) till we have *o*drawn them from the city; for they will say, They flee before us, as at the first: therefore we will flee before them.

7Then ye shall rise up from the ambush, and seize upon the city: for the LORD your God will deliver it into your hand.

8And it shall be, when ye have taken the city, *that* ye shall set the city on fire: according to the commandment of the LORD shall ye do. See, I have commanded you.

9 ¶ Joshua therefore sent them forth: and they went to lie in ambush, and abode between Beth-el and Ai, on the west side of Ai: but Joshua lodged that night among the people.

10And Joshua rose up early in the morning, and numbered the people, and went up, he and the elders of Israel, before the people to Ai.

11And all the people, *even the people* of war that *were* with him, went up, and drew nigh, and came before the city, and pitched on the north side of Ai: now *there was* a valley between them and Ai.

12And he took about five thousand men, and set them to lie in ambush between Beth-el and Ai, on the west side *p*of the city.

13And when they had set the people, *even* all the host that *was* on the north of the city, and their liers in wait on the west of the city, Joshua went that night into the midst of the valley.

14 ¶ And it came to pass, when the king of Ai saw *it*, that they hasted and rose up early, and the men of the city went out against Israel to battle, he and all his people, at a time appointed, before the plain; but he wist not that *there were* liers in ambush against him behind the city.

15And Joshua and all Israel made as if they were beaten before them, and fled by the way of the wilderness.

16And all the people that *were* in Ai were called together to pursue after them: and they pursued after Joshua, and were drawn away from the city.

17And there was not a man left in Ai or Beth-el, that went not out after Israel: and they left the city open, and pursued after Israel.

18And the LORD said unto Joshua, Stretch out the spear that *is* in thy hand toward Ai; for I will give it into thine hand. And Joshua stretched out the spear that *he had* in his hand toward the city.

19And the ambush arose quickly out of their place, and they ran as soon as he had stretched out his hand: and they entered into the city, and took it, and hasted and set the city on fire.

20And when the men of Ai looked behind them, they saw, and, behold, the smoke of the city ascended up to heaven, and they had no *q*power to flee this way or that way: and the people that fled to the wilderness turned back upon the pursuers.

21And when Joshua and all Israel saw that the ambush had taken the city, and that the smoke of the city ascended, then they turned again, and slew the men of Ai.

Amplified

2And you shall do to Ai and its king as you did to Jericho and its king, except that its spoil and its cattle [this time] you shall take as booty for yourselves. Lay an ambush against the city behind it.

3So Joshua arose, and all the people of war, to go up against Ai; [he] chose thirty thousand mighty men of strength and sent them forth by night.

4And he commanded them, Behold, you shall lie in wait against the city behind it. Do not go very far from the city, but all of you be ready.

5And I and all the people who are with me will approach the city. And when they come out against us, as the first time, we will flee before them.

6Till we have drawn them from the city, for they will say, They are fleeing from us as before. So we will flee before them.

7Then you shall rise up from the ambush and seize the city, for the Lord your God will deliver it into your hand.

8When you have taken the city, you shall set it afire; as the Lord commanded, you shall do. See, I have commanded you.

9So Joshua sent them forth, and they went to the place of ambush and remained between Bethel and Ai, on the west side of Ai; but Joshua lodged that night among the people.

10Joshua rose up early in the morning and mustered the men, and went up with the elders of Israel before the warriors to Ai.

11And all the fighting men who were with him went up and drew near before the city and encamped on the north side of [it], with a ravine between them and Ai.

12And he took about five thousand men and set them in ambush between Bethel and Ai, west of the city.

13So they stationed all the army—the main encampment that was north of the city and their men in ambush behind *and* on the west of the city—and Joshua went that night into the midst of the ravine.

14When the king of Ai saw it, they hastily rose early, and the men of the city went out against Israel to battle [at a time and place appointed] before the Arabah [plain]. But he did not know of the ambush against him behind the city.

15And Joshua and all Israel pretended to be beaten by them, and fled toward the wilderness.

16So all the people in Ai were called together to pursue them, and they pursued Joshua and were drawn away from the city.

17Not a man was left in Ai or Bethel who did not go out after Israel. Leaving the city open, they pursued Israel.

18Then the Lord said to Joshua, Stretch out the javelin that is in your hand toward Ai, for I will give it into your hand. So Joshua stretched out the javelin in his hand toward the city.

19The men in the ambush arose quickly out of their place and ran when he stretched out his hand; and they entered the city and took it, and they hastened and set it afire.

20When the men of Ai looked back, behold, the smoke of the city went up to the heavens, and they had no power to flee this way or that way. Then the Israelites who fled to the wilderness turned back upon the pursuers.

21When Joshua and all Israel saw that the ambush had taken the city and that the smoke of the city went up, they turned again and slew the men of Ai.

New American Standard

2"You shall do to Ai and its king just as you did to Jericho and its king; you shall take only its spoil and its cattle as plunder for yourselves. Set an ambush for the city behind it."

3 ¶ So Joshua rose with all the people of war to go up to Ai; and Joshua chose 30,000 men, valiant warriors, and sent them out at night.

4 He commanded them, saying, "See, you are going to ambush the city from behind it. Do not go very far from the city, but all of you be ready.

5"Then I and all the people who are with me will approach the city. And when they come out to meet us as at the first, we will flee before them.

6"They will come out after us until we have drawn them away from the city, for they will say, 'They are fleeing before us as at the first.' So we will flee before them.

7"And you shall rise from *your* ambush and take possession of the city, for the LORD your God will deliver it into your hand.

8"Then it will be when you have seized the city, that you shall set the city on fire. You shall do *it* according to the word of the LORD. See, I have commanded you."

9 So Joshua sent them away, and they went to the place of ambush and remained between Bethel and Ai, on the west side of Ai; but Joshua spent that night among the people.

10 ¶ Now Joshua rose early in the morning and mustered the people, and he went up with the elders of Israel before the people to Ai.

11 Then all the people of war who *were* with him went up and drew near and arrived in front of the city, and camped on the north side of Ai. Now *there was* a valley between him and Ai.

12 And he took about 5,000 men and set them in ambush between Bethel and Ai, on the west side of the city.

13 So they stationed the people, all the army that was on the north side of the city, and its rear guard on the west side of the city, and Joshua spent that night in the midst of the valley.

14 It came about when the king of Ai saw *it*, that the men of the city hurried and rose up early and went out to meet Israel in battle, he and all his people at the appointed place before the desert plain. But he did not know that *there was* an ambush against him behind the city.

15 Joshua and all Israel pretended to be beaten before them, and fled by the way of the wilderness.

16 And all the people who were in the city were called together to pursue them, and they pursued Joshua and were drawn away from the city.

17 So not a man was left in Ai or Bethel who had not gone out after Israel, and they left the city unguarded and pursued Israel.

18 ¶ Then the LORD said to Joshua, "Stretch out the javelin that is in your hand toward Ai, for I will give it into your hand." So Joshua stretched out the javelin that was in his hand toward the city.

19 The *men in* ambush rose quickly from their place, and when he had stretched out his hand, they ran and entered the city and captured it, and they quickly set the city on fire.

20 When the men of Ai turned back and looked, behold, the smoke of the city ascended to the sky, and they had no place to flee this way or that, for the people who had been fleeing to the wilderness turned against the pursuers.

21 When Joshua and all Israel saw that the *men in* ambush had captured the city and that the smoke of the city ascended, they turned back and slew the men of Ai.

New International

2You shall do to Ai and its king as you did to Jericho and its king, except that you may carry off their plunder and livestock for yourselves. Set an ambush behind the city."

3So Joshua and the whole army moved out to attack Ai. He chose thirty thousand of his best fighting men and sent them out at night 4with these orders: "Listen carefully. You are to set an ambush behind the city. Don't go very far from it. All of you be on the alert. 5I and all those with me will advance on the city, and when the men come out against us, as they did before, we will flee from them. 6They will pursue us until we have lured them away from the city, for they will say, 'They are running away from us as they did before.' So when we flee from them, 7you are to rise up from ambush and take the city. The LORD your God will give it into your hand. 8When you have taken the city, set it on fire. Do what the LORD has commanded. See to it; you have my orders."

9Then Joshua sent them off, and they went to the place of ambush and lay in wait between Bethel and Ai, to the west of Ai—but Joshua spent that night with the people.

10Early the next morning Joshua mustered his men, and he and the leaders of Israel marched before them to Ai. 11The entire force that was with him marched up and approached the city and arrived in front of it. They set up camp north of Ai, with the valley between them and the city. 12Joshua had taken about five thousand men and set them in ambush between Bethel and Ai, to the west of the city. 13They had the soldiers take up their positions—all those in the camp to the north of the city and the ambush to the west of it. That night Joshua went into the valley.

14When the king of Ai saw this, he and all the men of the city hurried out early in the morning to meet Israel in battle at a certain place overlooking the Arabah. But he did not know that an ambush had been set against him behind the city. 15Joshua and all Israel let themselves be driven back before them, and they fled toward the desert. 16All the men of Ai were called to pursue them, and they pursued Joshua and were lured away from the city. 17Not a man remained in Ai or Bethel who did not go after Israel. They left the city open and went in pursuit of Israel.

18Then the LORD said to Joshua, "Hold out toward Ai the javelin that is in your hand, for into your hand I will deliver the city." So Joshua held out his javelin toward Ai. 19As soon as he did this, the men in the ambush rose quickly from their position and rushed forward. They entered the city and captured it and quickly set it on fire.

20The men of Ai looked back and saw the smoke of the city rising against the sky, but they had no chance to escape in any direction, for the Israelites who had been fleeing toward the desert had turned back against their pursuers. 21For when Joshua and all Israel saw that the ambush had taken the city and that smoke was going up from the city, they turned around and attacked the men of

King James

²²And the other issued out of the city against them; so they were in the midst of Israel, some on this side, and some on that side: and they smote them, so that they let none of them remain or escape.

²³And the king of Ai they took alive, and brought him to Joshua.

²⁴And it came to pass, when Israel had made an end of slaying all the inhabitants of Ai in the field, in the wilderness wherein they chased them, and when they were all fallen on the edge of the sword, until they were consumed, that all the Israelites returned unto Ai, and smote it with the edge of the sword.

²⁵And so it was, that all that fell that day, both of men and women, were twelve thousand, even all the men of Ai.

²⁶For Joshua drew not his hand back, wherewith he stretched out the spear, until he had utterly destroyed all the inhabitants of Ai.

²⁷Only the cattle and the spoil of that city Israel took for a prey unto themselves, according unto the word of the LORD which he commanded Joshua.

²⁸And Joshua burnt Ai, and made it an heap for ever, even a desolation unto this day.

²⁹And the king of Ai he hanged on a tree until eventide: and as soon as the sun was down, Joshua commanded that they should take his carcase down from the tree, and cast it at the entering of the gate of the city, and raise thereon a great heap of stones, that remaineth unto this day.

An altar built in mount Ebal

³⁰ ¶ Then Joshua built an altar unto the LORD God of Israel in mount Ebal,

³¹As Moses the servant of the LORD commanded the children of Israel, as it is written in the book of the law of Moses, an altar of whole stones, over which no man hath lift up any iron: and they offered thereon burnt offerings unto the LORD, and sacrificed peace offerings.

³² ¶ And he wrote there upon the stones a copy of the law of Moses, which he wrote in the presence of the children of Israel.

³³And all Israel, and their elders, and officers, and their judges, stood on this side the ark and on that side before the priests the Levites, which bare the ark of the covenant of the LORD, as well the stranger, as he that was born among them; half of them over against mount Gerizim, and half of them over against mount Ebal; as Moses the servant of the LORD had commanded before, that they should bless the people of Israel.

³⁴And afterward he read all the words of the law, the blessings and cursings, according to all that is written in the book of the law.

³⁵There was not a word of all that Moses commanded, which Joshua read not before all the congregation of Israel, with the women, and the little ones, and the strangers that ʳwere conversant among them.

The trickery of the Gibeonites

9 AND IT came to pass, when all the kings which were on this side Jordan, in the hills, and in the valleys, and in all the coasts of the great sea over against Lebanon, the Hittite, and the Amorite, the Canaanite, the Perizzite, the Hivite, and the Jebusite, heard thereof;

²That they gathered themselves together, to fight with Joshua and with Israel, with one ˢaccord.

³ ¶ And when the inhabitants of Gibeon heard what Joshua had done unto Jericho and to Ai,

⁴They did work wilily, and went and made as if they had been ambassadors, and took old sacks upon their asses, and wine bottles, old, and rent, and bound up;

Amplified

²²And the others came forth out of the city against them [of Ai], so that they were in the midst of Israel, some on this side and some on that side. And [the Israelites] smote them, so that they let none of them remain or escape.

²³But they took the king of Ai alive and brought him to Joshua.

²⁴When Israel had finished slaying all the inhabitants of Ai in the field and in the wilderness into which they pursued them, and they were all fallen by the sword until they were consumed, then all the Israelites returned to Ai and smote it with the sword.

²⁵And all that fell that day, both men and women, were twelve thousand, including all the men of Ai.

²⁶For Joshua drew not back his hand with which he stretched out the javelin until he had utterly destroyed all the inhabitants of Ai.

²⁷Only the livestock and the spoil of that city Israel took as booty for themselves, according to the word of the Lord which He commanded Joshua.

²⁸So Joshua burned Ai and made it a heap of ruins for ever, even a desolation to this day.

²⁹And he hanged the king of Ai on a tree until evening; and at sunset, Joshua commanded and they took the body down from the tree and cast it at the entrance of the city gate and raised a great heap of stones over it that is there to this day.

³⁰Then Joshua built an altar to the Lord, the God of Israel, on Mount Ebal,

³¹As Moses the servant of the Lord commanded the Israelites, as it is written in the Book of the Law of Moses, an altar of unhewn stones, upon which no man has lifted up an iron tool; and they offered on it burnt offerings to the Lord and sacrificed peace offerings.

³²And there, in the presence of the Israelites, [Joshua] wrote on the stones a copy of the law of Moses.

³³And all Israel, sojourner as well as he who was born among them, with their elders, officers, and judges, stood on either side of the ark before the Levitical priests who carried the ark of the covenant of the Lord, half of them in front of Mount Gerizim and half of them in front of Mount Ebal, as Moses the servant of the Lord had commanded before that they should bless the Israelites.

³⁴Afterward, Joshua read all the words of the law, the blessings and cursings, all that is written in the Book of the Law.

³⁵There was not a word of all that Moses commanded which Joshua did not read before all the assembly of Israel, and the women, and little ones, and the foreigners who were living among them.

9 WHEN ALL the kings beyond the Jordan in the hill country and in the lowland and all along the coast of the Great [Mediterranean] Sea toward Lebanon, the Hittites, Amorites, Canaanites, Perizzites, Hivites, and Jebusites heard this,

²They gathered together with one accord to fight Joshua and Israel.

³But when the people of Gibeon heard what Joshua had done to Jericho and Ai,

⁴They worked cunningly, and went pretending to be ambassadors and took [provisions and] old sacks on their donkeys and wineskins, old, torn, and mended,

ʳHeb. *walked*   ˢHeb. *mouth*

New American Standard

22 The others came out from the city to encounter them, so that they were *trapped* in the midst of Israel, some on this side and some on that side; and they slew them until no one was left of those who survived or escaped.

23 But they took alive the king of Ai and brought him to Joshua.

24 ¶ Now when Israel had finished killing all the inhabitants of Ai in the field in the wilderness where they pursued them, and all of them were fallen by the edge of the sword until they were destroyed, then all Israel returned to Ai and struck it with the edge of the sword.

25 All who fell that day, both men and women, were 12,000—all the people of Ai.

26 For Joshua did not withdraw his hand with which he stretched out the javelin until he had utterly destroyed all the inhabitants of Ai.

27 Israel took only the cattle and the spoil of that city as plunder for themselves, according to the word of the LORD which He had commanded Joshua.

28 So Joshua burned Ai and made it a heap forever, a desolation until this day.

29 He hanged the king of Ai on a tree until evening; and at sunset Joshua gave command and they took his body down from the tree and threw it at the entrance of the city gate, and raised over it a great heap of stones *that stands* to this day.

30 ¶ Then Joshua built an altar to the LORD, the God of Israel, in Mount Ebal,

31 just as Moses the servant of the LORD had commanded the sons of Israel, as it is written in the book of the law of Moses, an altar of uncut stones on which no man had wielded an iron *tool;* and they offered burnt offerings on it to the LORD, and sacrificed peace offerings.

32 He wrote thereon the stones a copy of the law of Moses, which he had written, in the presence of the sons of Israel.

33 All Israel with their elders and officers and their judges were standing on both sides of the ark before the Levitical priests who carried the ark of the covenant of the LORD, the stranger as well as the native. Half of them *stood* in front of Mount Gerizim and half of them in front of Mount Ebal, just as Moses the servant of the LORD had given command at first to bless the people of Israel.

34 Then afterward he read all the words of the law, the blessing and the curse, according to all that is written in the book of the law.

35 There was not a word of all that Moses had commanded which Joshua did not read before all the assembly of Israel with the women and the little ones and the strangers who were living among them.

New International

Ai. 22The men of the ambush also came out of the city against them, so that they were caught in the middle, with Israelites on both sides. Israel cut them down, leaving them neither survivors nor fugitives. 23But they took the king of Ai alive and brought him to Joshua.

24When Israel had finished killing all the men of Ai in the fields and in the desert where they had chased them, and when every one of them had been put to the sword, all the Israelites returned to Ai and killed those who were in it. 25Twelve thousand men and women fell that day—all the people of Ai. 26For Joshua did not draw back the hand that held out his javelin until he had destroyed[x] all who lived in Ai. 27But Israel did carry off for themselves the livestock and plunder of this city, as the LORD had instructed Joshua.

28So Joshua burned Ai and made it a permanent heap of ruins, a desolate place to this day. 29He hung the king of Ai on a tree and left him there until evening. At sunset, Joshua ordered them to take his body from the tree and throw it down at the entrance of the city gate. And they raised a large pile of rocks over it, which remains to this day.

The Covenant Renewed at Mount Ebal

30Then Joshua built on Mount Ebal an altar to the LORD, the God of Israel, 31as Moses the servant of the LORD had commanded the Israelites. He built it according to what is written in the Book of the Law of Moses—an altar of uncut stones, on which no iron tool had been used. On it they offered to the LORD burnt offerings and sacrificed fellowship offerings.[y] 32There, in the presence of the Israelites, Joshua copied on stones the law of Moses, which he had written. 33All Israel, aliens and citizens alike, with their elders, officials and judges, were standing on both sides of the ark of the covenant of the LORD, facing those who carried it—the priests, who were Levites. Half of the people stood in front of Mount Gerizim and half of them in front of Mount Ebal, as Moses the servant of the LORD had formerly commanded when he gave instructions to bless the people of Israel.

34Afterward, Joshua read all the words of the law—the blessings and the curses—just as it is written in the Book of the Law. 35There was not a word of all that Moses had commanded that Joshua did not read to the whole assembly of Israel, including the women and children, and the aliens who lived among them.

Guile of the Gibeonites

9 NOW IT came about when all the kings who were beyond the Jordan, in the hill country and in the lowland and on all the coast of the Great Sea toward Lebanon, the Hittite and the Amorite, the Canaanite, the Perizzite, the Hivite and the Jebusite, heard of it,

2 that they gathered themselves together with one accord to fight with Joshua and with Israel.

3 ¶ When the inhabitants of Gibeon heard what Joshua had done to Jericho and to Ai,

4 they also acted craftily and set out as envoys, and took worn-out sacks on their donkeys, and wineskins worn-out and torn and mended,

The Gibeonite Deception

9 NOW WHEN all the kings west of the Jordan heard about these things—those in the hill country, in the western foothills, and along the entire coast of the Great Sea[z] as far as Lebanon (the kings of the Hittites, Amorites, Canaanites, Perizzites, Hivites and Jebusites)— 2they came together to make war against Joshua and Israel.

3However, when the people of Gibeon heard what Joshua had done to Jericho and Ai, 4they resorted to a ruse: They went as a delegation whose donkeys were loaded[a] with worn-out sacks and old wineskins, cracked and

---

x 26 The Hebrew term refers to the irrevocable giving over of things or persons to the LORD, often by totally destroying them.
y 31 Traditionally *peace offerings* z 1 That is, the Mediterranean
a 4 Most Hebrew manuscripts; some Hebrew manuscripts, Vulgate and Syriac (see also Septuagint) *They prepared provisions and loaded their donkeys*

King James

⁵And old shoes and clouted upon their feet, and old garments upon them; and all the bread of their provision was dry *and* mouldy.

⁶And they went to Joshua unto the camp at Gilgal, and said unto him, and to the men of Israel, We be come from a far country: now therefore make ye a league with us.

⁷And the men of Israel said unto the Hivites, Peradventure ye dwell among us; and how shall we make a league with you?

⁸And they said unto Joshua, We *are* thy servants. And Joshua said unto them, Who *are* ye? and from whence come ye?

⁹And they said unto him, From a very far country thy servants are come because of the name of the LORD thy God: for we have heard the fame of him, and all that he did in Egypt,

¹⁰And all that he did to the two kings of the Amorites, that *were* beyond Jordan, to Sihon king of Heshbon, and to Og king of Bashan, which *was* at Ashtaroth.

¹¹Wherefore our elders and all the inhabitants of our country spake to us, saying, Take victuals *t* with you for the journey, and go to meet them, and say unto them, We *are* your servants: therefore now make ye a league with us.

¹²This our bread we took hot *for* our provision out of our houses on the day we came forth to go unto you; but now, behold, it is dry, and it is mouldy:

¹³And these bottles of wine, which we filled, *were* new; and, behold, they be rent: and these our garments and our shoes are become old by reason of the very long journey.

¹⁴And *u* the men took of their victuals, and asked not *counsel* at the mouth of the LORD.

¹⁵And Joshua made peace with them, and made a league with them, to let them live: and the princes of the congregation sware unto them.

¹⁶ ¶ And it came to pass at the end of three days after they had made a league with them, that they heard that they *were* their neighbours, and *that* they dwelt among them.

¹⁷And the children of Israel journeyed, and came unto their cities on the third day. Now their cities *were* Gibeon, and Chephirah, and Beeroth, and Kirjath-jearim.

¹⁸And the children of Israel smote them not, because the princes of the congregation had sworn unto them by the LORD God of Israel. And all the congregation murmured against the princes.

¹⁹But all the princes said unto all the congregation, We have sworn unto them by the LORD God of Israel: now therefore we may not touch them.

²⁰This we will do to them; we will even let them live, lest wrath be upon us, because of the oath which we sware unto them.

²¹And the princes said unto them, Let them live; but let them be hewers of wood and drawers of water unto all the congregation; as the princes had promised them.

²² ¶ And Joshua called for them, and he spake unto them, saying, Wherefore have ye beguiled us, saying, We *are* very far from you; when ye dwell among us?

²³Now therefore ye *are* cursed, and there shall *v* none of you be freed from being bondmen, and hewers of wood and drawers of water for the house of my God.

²⁴And they answered Joshua, and said, Because it was certainly told thy servants, how that the LORD thy God commanded his servant Moses to give you all the land, and to destroy all the inhabitants of the land from before you, therefore we were sore afraid of our lives because of you, and have done this thing.

²⁵And now, behold, we *are* in thine hand: as it seemeth good and right unto thee to do unto us, do.

²⁶And so did he unto them, and delivered them out of the hand of the children of Israel, that they slew them not.

Amplified

⁵And old and patched shoes on their feet and wearing old garments; and all their supply of food was dry and moldy.

⁶And they went to Joshua in the camp at Gilgal and said to him and the men of Israel, We have come from a far country; so now, make a covenant with us.

⁷But the men of Israel said to the Hivites, Perhaps you live among us; how then can we make a covenant with you?

⁸They said to Joshua, We are your servants. And Joshua said to them, Who are you? From where have you come?

⁹They said to him, From a very far country your servants have come because of the name of the Lord your God. For we have heard the fame of Him, and all that He did in Egypt,

¹⁰And all that He did to the two kings of the Amorites who were beyond the Jordan, to Sihon king of Heshbon, and to Og king of Bashan, who lived in Ashtaroth.

¹¹So our elders and all the residents of our country said to us, Take provisions for the journey and go to meet [the Israelites] and say to them, We are your servants; and now make a covenant with us.

¹²This our bread we took hot for our provision out of our houses on the day we set out to go to you; but now behold, it is dry and has become moldy.

¹³These wineskins (bottles) which we filled were new, and behold, they are torn; and our garments and our shoes have become old because of the very long journey.

¹⁴So the [Israelite] men partook of their food and did not consult the Lord.

¹⁵Joshua made peace with them, covenanting with them to let them live, and the assembly's leaders swore to them.

¹⁶Then three days after they had made a covenant with [the strangers, the Israelites] heard that they were their neighbors and that they dwelt among them.

¹⁷And the Israelites set out and came to their cities on the third day. Now their cities were Gibeon, Chephirah, Beeroth, and Kiriath-jearim.

¹⁸But the Israelites did not slay them, because the leaders of the assembly had sworn to them by the Lord, the God of Israel, [to spare them]. And all the assembly murmured against the leaders.

¹⁹But all the leaders said to all the assembly, We have sworn to them by the Lord, the God of Israel, so now we may not touch them.

²⁰This we will do to them: we will let them live, lest wrath be upon us because of the oath which we swore to them.

²¹And the leaders said to them, Let them live [and be our slaves]. So they became hewers of wood and drawers of water for all the assembly, just as the leaders had said of them.

²²Joshua called the men and said, Why did you deceive us, saying, We live very far from you, when you dwell among us?

²³Now therefore you are cursed, and of you there shall always be slaves, hewers of wood and drawers of water for the house of my God.

²⁴They answered Joshua, Because it was surely told your servants that the Lord your God commanded His servant Moses to give you all the land and to destroy all the land's inhabitants from before you. So we feared greatly for our lives because of you, and have done this thing.

²⁵And now, behold, we are in your hand; do as it seems good and right in your sight to do to us.

²⁶So he did to them, and delivered them out of the hand of the Israelites, so that they did not kill them.

^tHeb. *in your hand.* ^uOr, *they received the men by reason of their victuals* ^vHeb. *not be cut off from you*

New American Standard

5 and worn-out and patched sandals on their feet, and worn-out clothes on themselves; and all the bread of their provision was dry *and* had become crumbled.

6 They went to Joshua to the camp at Gilgal and said to him and to the men of Israel, "We have come from a far country; now therefore, make a covenant with us."

7 The men of Israel said to the Hivites, "Perhaps you are living within our land; how then shall we make a covenant with you?"

8 But they said to Joshua, "We are your servants." Then Joshua said to them, "Who are you and where do you come from?"

9 They said to him, "Your servants have come from a very far country because of the fame of the LORD your God; for we have heard the report of Him and all that He did in Egypt,

10 and all that He did to the two kings of the Amorites who were beyond the Jordan, to Sihon king of Heshbon and to Og king of Bashan who was at Ashtaroth.

11 "So our elders and all the inhabitants of our country spoke to us, saying, 'Take provisions in your hand for the journey, and go to meet them and say to them, "We are your servants; now then, make a covenant with us." '

12 "This our bread *was* warm *when* we took it for our provisions out of our houses on the day that we left to come to you; but now behold, it is dry and has become crumbled.

13 "These wineskins which we filled were new, and behold, they are torn; and these our clothes and our sandals are worn out because of the very long journey."

14 So the men *of Israel* took some of their provisions, and did not ask for the counsel of the LORD.

15 Joshua made peace with them and made a covenant with them, to let them live; and the leaders of the congregation swore *an oath* to them.

16 ¶ It came about at the end of three days after they had made a covenant with them, that they heard that they were neighbors and that they were living within their land.

17 Then the sons of Israel set out and came to their cities on the third day. Now their cities *were* Gibeon and Chephirah and Beeroth and Kiriath-jearim.

18 The sons of Israel did not strike them because the leaders of the congregation had sworn to them by the LORD the God of Israel. And the whole congregation grumbled against the leaders.

19 But all the leaders said to the whole congregation, "We have sworn to them by the LORD, the God of Israel, and now we cannot touch them.

20 "This we will do to them, even let them live, so that wrath will not be upon us for the oath which we swore to them."

21 The leaders said to them, "Let them live." So they became hewers of wood and drawers of water for the whole congregation, just as the leaders had spoken to them.

22 ¶ Then Joshua called for them and spoke to them, saying, "Why have you deceived us, saying, 'We are very far from you,' when you are living within our land?

23 "Now therefore, you are cursed, and you shall never cease being slaves, both hewers of wood and drawers of water for the house of my God."

24 So they answered Joshua and said, "Because it was certainly told your servants that the LORD your God had commanded His servant Moses to give you all the land, and to destroy all the inhabitants of the land before you; therefore we feared greatly for our lives because of you, and have done this thing.

25 "Now behold, we are in your hands; do as it seems good and right in your sight to do to us."

26 Thus he did to them, and delivered them from the hands of the sons of Israel, and they did not kill them.

New International

mended. 5 The men put worn and patched sandals on their feet and wore old clothes. All the bread of their food supply was dry and moldy. 6 Then they went to Joshua in the camp at Gilgal and said to him and the men of Israel, "We have come from a distant country; make a treaty with us."

7 The men of Israel said to the Hivites, "But perhaps you live near us. How then can we make a treaty with you?"

8 "We are your servants," they said to Joshua.

But Joshua asked, "Who are you and where do you come from?"

9 They answered: "Your servants have come from a very distant country because of the fame of the LORD your God. For we have heard reports of him: all that he did in Egypt, 10 and all that he did to the two kings of the Amorites east of the Jordan—Sihon king of Heshbon, and Og king of Bashan, who reigned in Ashtaroth. 11 And our elders and all those living in our country said to us, 'Take provisions for your journey; go and meet them and say to them, "We are your servants; make a treaty with us." ' 12 This bread of ours was warm when we packed it at home on the day we left to come to you. But now see how dry and moldy it is. 13 And these wineskins that we filled were new, but see how cracked they are. And our clothes and sandals are worn out by the very long journey."

14 The men of Israel sampled their provisions but did not inquire of the LORD. 15 Then Joshua made a treaty of peace with them to let them live, and the leaders of the assembly ratified it by oath.

16 Three days after they made the treaty with the Gibeonites, the Israelites heard that they were neighbors, living near them. 17 So the Israelites set out and on the third day came to their cities: Gibeon, Kephirah, Beeroth and Kiriath Jearim. 18 But the Israelites did not attack them, because the leaders of the assembly had sworn an oath to them by the LORD, the God of Israel.

The whole assembly grumbled against the leaders, 19 but all the leaders answered, "We have given them our oath by the LORD, the God of Israel, and we cannot touch them now. 20 This is what we will do to them: We will let them live, so that wrath will not fall on us for breaking the oath we swore to them." 21 They continued, "Let them live, but let them be woodcutters and water carriers for the entire community." So the leaders' promise to them was kept.

22 Then Joshua summoned the Gibeonites and said, "Why did you deceive us by saying, 'We live a long way from you,' while actually you live near us? 23 You are now under a curse: You will never cease to serve as woodcutters and water carriers for the house of my God."

24 They answered Joshua, "Your servants were clearly told how the LORD your God had commanded his servant Moses to give you the whole land and to wipe out all its inhabitants from before you. So we feared for our lives because of you, and that is why we did this. 25 We are now in your hands. Do to us whatever seems good and right to you."

26 So Joshua saved them from the Israelites, and they did

King James

²⁷And Joshua ^wmade them that day hewers of wood and drawers of water for the congregation, and for the altar of the LORD, even unto this day, in the place which he should choose.

The sun stands still

10 NOW IT came to pass, when Adoni-zedec king of Jerusalem had heard how Joshua had taken Ai, and had utterly destroyed it; as he had done to Jericho and her king, so he had done to Ai and her king; and how the inhabitants of Gibeon had made peace with Israel, and were among them;

²That they feared greatly, because Gibeon *was* a great city, as one of the ^xroyal cities, and because it *was* greater than Ai, and all the men thereof *were* mighty.

³Wherefore Adoni-zedec king of Jerusalem sent unto Hoham king of Hebron, and unto Piram king of Jarmuth, and unto Japhia king of Lachish, and unto Debir king of Eglon, saying,

⁴Come up unto me, and help me, that we may smite Gibeon: for it hath made peace with Joshua and with the children of Israel.

⁵Therefore the five kings of the Amorites, the king of Jerusalem, the king of Hebron, the king of Jarmuth, the king of Lachish, the king of Eglon, gathered themselves together, and went up, they and all their hosts, and encamped before Gibeon, and made war against it.

⁶ ¶ And the men of Gibeon sent unto Joshua to the camp to Gilgal, saying, Slack not thy hand from thy servants; come up to us quickly, and save us, and help us: for all the kings of the Amorites that dwell in the mountains are gathered together against us.

⁷So Joshua ascended from Gilgal, he, and all the people of war with him, and all the mighty men of valour.

⁸ ¶ And the LORD said unto Joshua, Fear them not: for I have delivered them into thine hand; there shall not a man of them stand before thee.

⁹Joshua therefore came unto them suddenly, *and* went up from Gilgal all night.

¹⁰And the LORD discomfited them before Israel, and slew them with a great slaughter at Gibeon, and chased them along the way that goeth up to Beth-horon, and smote them to Azekah, and unto Makkedah.

¹¹And it came to pass, as they fled from before Israel, *and* were in the going down to Beth-horon, that the LORD cast down great stones from heaven upon them unto Azekah, and they died: *they were* more which died with hailstones than *they* whom the children of Israel slew with the sword.

¹² ¶ Then spake Joshua to the LORD in the day when the LORD delivered up the Amorites before the children of Israel, and he said in the sight of Israel, Sun, ^ystand thou still upon Gibeon; and thou, Moon, in the valley of Ajalon.

¹³And the sun stood still, and the moon stayed, until the people had avenged themselves upon their enemies. *Is* not this written in the book of ^zJasher? So the sun stood still in the midst of heaven, and hasted not to go down about a whole day.

¹⁴And there was no day like that before it or after it, that the LORD hearkened unto the voice of a man: for the LORD fought for Israel.

¹⁵ ¶ And Joshua returned, and all Israel with him, unto the camp to Gilgal.

¹⁶But these five kings fled, and hid themselves in a cave at Makkedah.

¹⁷And it was told Joshua, saying, The five kings are found hid in a cave at Makkedah.

¹⁸And Joshua said, Roll great stones upon the mouth of the cave, and set men by it for to keep them:

Amplified

²⁷But Joshua then made them hewers of wood and drawers of water for the congregation and for the altar of the Lord, to this day, in the place which He should choose.

10 WHEN ADONI-ZEDEK king of Jerusalem heard how Joshua had taken Ai and had utterly destroyed it, doing to Jericho and its king as he had done to Ai and its king, and how the residents of Gibeon had made peace with Israel and were among them,

²He feared greatly, because Gibeon was a great city, like one of the royal cities, and because it was greater than Ai, and all its men were mighty.

³So Adoni-zedek king of Jerusalem sent to Hoham king of Hebron, to Piram king of Jarmuth, to Japhia king of Lachish, and to Debir king of Eglon, saying,

⁴Come up to me and help me, and let us smite Gibeon, for it has made peace with Joshua and with the Israelites.

⁵Then the five kings of the Amorites—the kings of Jerusalem, Hebron, Jarmuth, Lachish, and Eglon—gathered their forces and went up with all their armies and encamped before Gibeon to fight against it.

⁶And the men of Gibeon sent to Joshua at the camp in Gilgal, saying, Do not relax your hand from your servants; come up to us quickly and save us and help us, for all the kings of the Amorites who dwell in the hill country are gathered against us.

⁷So Joshua went up from Gilgal, he and all the warriors with him and all the mighty men of valor.

⁸And the Lord said to Joshua, Do not fear them, for I have given them into your hand; there shall not a man of them stand before you.

⁹So Joshua came upon them suddenly, having gone up from Gilgal all night.

¹⁰And the Lord caused [the enemies] to panic before Israel, who slew them with a great slaughter at Gibeon and chased them along the way that goes up to Beth-horon and smote them as far as Azekah and Makkedah.

¹¹As they fled before Israel, while they were descending [the pass] to Beth-horon, the Lord cast great stones from the heavens on them as far as Azekah, killing them. More died because of the hailstones than the Israelites slew with the sword.

¹²Then Joshua spoke to the Lord on the day when the Lord gave the Amorites over to the Israelites, and he said in the sight of Israel, Sun, be silent *and* stand still at Gibeon, and you, moon, in the Valley of Ajalon!

¹³And the sun stood still, and the moon stayed, until the nation took vengeance upon their enemies. Is not this written in the Book of Jasher? So the sun stood still in the midst of the heavens and did not hasten to go down for about a whole day.

¹⁴There was no day like it before or since, when the Lord heeded the voice of a man. For the Lord fought for Israel.

¹⁵Then Joshua returned, and all Israel with him, to the camp at Gilgal.

¹⁶Those five kings fled and hid themselves in the cave of Makkedah.

¹⁷And it was told Joshua, The five kings are hidden in the cave at Makkedah.

¹⁸Joshua said, Roll great stones to the cave's mouth, and set men to guard them.

---

^wHeb. *gave, or, delivered to be*   ^xHeb. *cities of the kingdom*
^yHeb. *be silent*   ^zOr, *The upright?*

New American Standard

27 But Joshua made them that day hewers of wood and drawers of water for the congregation and for the altar of the LORD, to this day, in the place which He would choose.

Five Kings Attack Gibeon

10 NOW IT came about when Adoni-zedek king of Jerusalem heard that Joshua had captured Ai, and had utterly destroyed it (just as he had done to Jericho and its king, so he had done to Ai and its king), and that the inhabitants of Gibeon had made peace with Israel and were within their land,

2 that he feared greatly, because Gibeon *was* a great city, like one of the royal cities, and because it was greater than Ai, and all its men *were* mighty.

3 Therefore Adoni-zedek king of Jerusalem sent *word* to Hoham king of Hebron and to Piram king of Jarmuth and to Japhia king of Lachish and to Debir king of Eglon, saying,

4 "Come up to me and help me, and let us attack Gibeon, for it has made peace with Joshua and with the sons of Israel."

5 So the five kings of the Amorites, the king of Jerusalem, the king of Hebron, the king of Jarmuth, the king of Lachish, *and* the king of Eglon, gathered together and went up, they with all their armies, and camped by Gibeon and fought against it.

6 ¶ Then the men of Gibeon sent *word* to Joshua to the camp at Gilgal, saying, "Do not abandon your servants; come up to us quickly and save us and help us, for all the kings of the Amorites that live in the hill country have assembled against us."

7 So Joshua went up from Gilgal, he and all the people of war with him and all the valiant warriors.

8 The LORD said to Joshua, "Do not fear them, for I have given them into your hands; not one of them shall stand before you."

9 So Joshua came upon them suddenly by marching all night from Gilgal.

10 And the LORD confounded them before Israel, and He slew them with a great slaughter at Gibeon, and pursued them by the way of the ascent of Beth-horon and struck them as far as Azekah and Makkedah.

11 As they fled from before Israel, *while* they were at the descent of Beth-horon, the LORD threw large stones from heaven on them as far as Azekah, and they died; *there were* more who died from the hailstones than those whom the sons of Israel killed with the sword.

12 ¶ Then Joshua spoke to the LORD in the day when the LORD delivered up the Amorites before the sons of Israel, and he said in the sight of Israel,

"O sun, stand still at Gibeon,
And O moon in the valley of Aijalon."

13 So the sun stood still, and the moon stopped,
Until the nation avenged themselves of their enemies.

Is it not written in the book of Jashar? And the sun stopped in the middle of the sky and did not hasten to go *down* for about a whole day.

14 There was no day like that before it or after it, when the LORD listened to the voice of a man; for the LORD fought for Israel.

15 ¶ Then Joshua and all Israel with him returned to the camp to Gilgal.

Victory at Makkedah

16 ¶ Now these five kings had fled and hidden themselves in the cave at Makkedah.

17 It was told Joshua, saying, "The five kings have been found hidden in the cave at Makkedah."

18 Joshua said, "Roll large stones against the mouth of the cave, and assign men by it to guard them,

New International

not kill them. 27 That day he made the Gibeonites woodcutters and water carriers for the community and for the altar of the LORD at the place the LORD would choose. And that is what they are to this day.

The Sun Stands Still

10 NOW ADONI-ZEDEK king of Jerusalem heard that Joshua had taken Ai and totally destroyed[b] it, doing to Ai and its king as he had done to Jericho and its king, and that the people of Gibeon had made a treaty of peace with Israel and were living near them. 2 He and his people were very much alarmed at this, because Gibeon was an important city, like one of the royal cities; it was larger than Ai, and all its men were good fighters. 3 So Adoni-Zedek king of Jerusalem appealed to Hoham king of Hebron, Piram king of Jarmuth, Japhia king of Lachish and Debir king of Eglon. 4 "Come up and help me attack Gibeon," he said, "because it has made peace with Joshua and the Israelites."

5 Then the five kings of the Amorites—the kings of Jerusalem, Hebron, Jarmuth, Lachish and Eglon—joined forces. They moved up with all their troops and took up positions against Gibeon and attacked it.

6 The Gibeonites then sent word to Joshua in the camp at Gilgal: "Do not abandon your servants. Come up to us quickly and save us! Help us, because all the Amorite kings from the hill country have joined forces against us."

7 So Joshua marched up from Gilgal with his entire army, including all the best fighting men. 8 The LORD said to Joshua, "Do not be afraid of them; I have given them into your hand. Not one of them will be able to withstand you."

9 After an all-night march from Gilgal, Joshua took them by surprise. 10 The LORD threw them into confusion before Israel, who defeated them in a great victory at Gibeon. Israel pursued them along the road going up to Beth Horon and cut them down all the way to Azekah and Makkedah. 11 As they fled before Israel on the road down from Beth Horon to Azekah, the LORD hurled large hailstones down on them from the sky, and more of them died from the hailstones than were killed by the swords of the Israelites.

12 On the day the LORD gave the Amorites over to Israel, Joshua said to the LORD in the presence of Israel:

"O sun, stand still over Gibeon,
O moon, over the Valley of Aijalon."
13 So the sun stood still,
and the moon stopped,
till the nation avenged itself on[c] its enemies,

as it is written in the Book of Jashar.
The sun stopped in the middle of the sky and delayed going down about a full day. 14 There has never been a day like it before or since, a day when the LORD listened to a man. Surely the LORD was fighting for Israel!

15 Then Joshua returned with all Israel to the camp at Gilgal.

Five Amorite Kings Killed

16 Now the five kings had fled and hidden in the cave at Makkedah. 17 When Joshua was told that the five kings had been found hiding in the cave at Makkedah, 18 he said, "Roll large rocks up to the mouth of the cave, and post

b 1 The Hebrew term refers to the irrevocable giving over of things or persons to the LORD, often by totally destroying them; also in verses 28, 35, 37, 39 and 40.   *c 13* Or *nation triumphed over*

King James

¹⁹And stay ye not, *but* pursue after your enemies, and ªsmite the hindmost of them; suffer them not to enter into their cities: for the LORD your God hath delivered them into your hand.

²⁰And it came to pass, when Joshua and the children of Israel had made an end of slaying them with a very great slaughter, till they were consumed, that the rest *which* remained of them entered into fenced cities.

²¹And all the people returned to the camp to Joshua at Makkedah in peace: none moved his tongue against any of the children of Israel.

²²Then said Joshua, Open the mouth of the cave, and bring out those five kings unto me out of the cave.

²³And they did so, and brought forth those five kings unto him out of the cave, the king of Jerusalem, the king of Hebron, the king of Jarmuth, the king of Lachish, *and* the king of Eglon.

²⁴And it came to pass, when they brought out those kings unto Joshua, that Joshua called for all the men of Israel, and said unto the captains of the men of war which went with him, Come near, put your feet upon the necks of these kings. And they came near, and put their feet upon the necks of them.

²⁵And Joshua said unto them, Fear not, nor be dismayed, be strong and of good courage: for thus shall the LORD do to all your enemies against whom ye fight.

²⁶And afterward Joshua smote them, and slew them, and hanged them on five trees: and they were hanging upon the trees until the evening.

²⁷And it came to pass at the time of the going down of the sun, *that* Joshua commanded, and they took them down off the trees, and cast them into the cave wherein they had been hid, and laid great stones in the cave's mouth, *which remain* until this very day.

Conquest of the south

²⁸ ¶ And that day Joshua took Makkedah, and smote it with the edge of the sword, and the king thereof he utterly destroyed, them, and all the souls that *were* therein; he let none remain: and he did to the king of Makkedah as he did unto the king of Jericho.

²⁹Then Joshua passed from Makkedah, and all Israel with him, unto Libnah, and fought against Libnah:

³⁰And the LORD delivered it also, and the king thereof, into the hand of Israel; and he smote it with the edge of the sword, and all the souls that *were* therein; he let none remain in it; but did unto the king thereof as he did unto the king of Jericho.

³¹ ¶ And Joshua passed from Libnah, and all Israel with him, unto Lachish, and encamped against it, and fought against it:

³²And the LORD delivered Lachish into the hand of Israel, which took it on the second day, and smote it with the edge of the sword, and all the souls that *were* therein, according to all that he had done to Libnah.

³³ ¶ Then Horam king of Gezer came up to help Lachish; and Joshua smote him and his people, until he had left him none remaining.

³⁴ ¶ And from Lachish Joshua passed unto Eglon, and all Israel with him; and they encamped against it, and fought against it:

³⁵And they took it on that day, and smote it with the edge of the sword, and all the souls that *were* therein he utterly destroyed that day, according to all that he had done to Lachish.

³⁶And Joshua went up from Eglon, and all Israel with him, unto Hebron; and they fought against it:

³⁷And they took it, and smote it with the edge of the sword, and the king thereof, and all the cities thereof, and all the souls that *were* therein; he left none remaining, according to all that he had done to Eglon; but destroyed it utterly, and all the souls that *were* therein.

Amplified

¹⁹But do not stay. Pursue your enemies and fall upon their rear; do not allow them to enter their cities, for the Lord your God has given them into your hand.

²⁰When Joshua and the Israelites had ended slaying them until they were wiped out and the remnant remaining of them had entered into fortified cities,

²¹All the people returned to the camp to Joshua at Makkedah in peace; none moved his tongue against any of the Israelites.

²²Then said Joshua, Open the mouth of the cave and bring out those five kings to me from the cave.

²³They brought the five kings out of the cave to him—the kings of Jerusalem, Hebron, Jarmuth, Lachish, and Eglon.

²⁴When they brought out those kings to Joshua, [he] called for all the Israelites and told the commanders of the men of war who went with him, Come, put your feet on the necks of these kings. And they came and put their feet on the [kings'] necks.

²⁵Joshua said to them, Fear not nor be dismayed; be strong and of good courage. For thus shall the Lord do to all your enemies against whom you fight.

²⁶Afterward Joshua smote and slew them and hanged their bodies on five trees, and they hung on the trees until evening.

²⁷At sunset Joshua ordered and they took the bodies down from the trees and cast them into the cave where the kings had hidden and laid great stones on the cave's mouth, which remain to this very day.

²⁸Joshua took Makkedah that day and smote it and its king with the sword and utterly destroyed everyone in it. He left none remaining. And he did to the king of Makkedah as he had done to the king of Jericho. [Josh. 6:21.]

²⁹Then Joshua and all Israel went from Makkedah to Libnah and attacked Libnah.

³⁰And the Lord gave it also and its king into Israel's hands, and Joshua smote it with the sword, and all the people in it. He left none remaining in it. And he did to its king as he had done to the king of Jericho.

³¹And Joshua passed from Libnah, and all Israel with him, to Lachish and encamped against it and attacked it.

³²And the Lord delivered Lachish into the hands of Israel, and Joshua took it on the second day and smote it with the sword, and all the people in it, as he had done to Libnah.

³³Then Horam king of Gezer came up to help Lachish, and Joshua smote him and his people—until he had left none remaining.

³⁴From Lachish Joshua and all Israel went on to Eglon, laid siege to it, and attacked it.

³⁵And they took it that day and smote it with the sword and utterly destroyed all who were in it that day, as he had done to Lachish.

³⁶Then Joshua with all Israel went up from Eglon to Hebron, and they attacked it

³⁷And took it and smote it with the sword, and its king and all its towns and everyone in it. He left none remaining, as he had done to Eglon, and utterly destroyed it and all its people.

New American Standard

¹⁹ but do not stay *there* yourselves; pursue your enemies and attack them in the rear. Do not allow them to enter their cities, for the LORD your God has delivered them into your hand."

²⁰ It came about when Joshua and the sons of Israel had finished slaying them with a very great slaughter, until they were destroyed, and the survivors *who* remained of them had entered the fortified cities,

²¹ that all the people returned to the camp to Joshua at Makkedah in peace. No one uttered a word against any of the sons of Israel.

²² Then Joshua said, "Open the mouth of the cave and bring these five kings out to me from the cave."

²³ They did so, and brought these five kings out to him from the cave: the king of Jerusalem, the king of Hebron, the king of Jarmuth, the king of Lachish, *and* the king of Eglon.

²⁴ When they brought these kings out to Joshua, Joshua called for all the men of Israel, and said to the chiefs of the men of war who had gone with him, "Come near, put your feet on the necks of these kings." So they came near and put their feet on their necks.

²⁵ Joshua then said to them, "Do not fear or be dismayed! Be strong and courageous, for thus the LORD will do to all your enemies with whom you fight."

²⁶ So afterward Joshua struck them and put them to death, and he hanged them on five trees; and they hung on the trees until evening.

²⁷ It came about at sunset that Joshua gave a command, and they took them down from the trees and threw them into the cave where they had hidden themselves, and put large stones over the mouth of the cave, to this very day.

²⁸ ¶ Now Joshua captured Makkedah on that day, and struck it and its king with the edge of the sword; he utterly destroyed it and every ʰperson who was in it. He left no survivor. Thus he did to the king of Makkedah just as he had done to the king of Jericho.

Joshua's Conquest of Southern Palestine

²⁹ ¶ Then Joshua and all Israel with him passed on from Makkedah to Libnah, and fought against Libnah.

³⁰ The LORD gave it also with its king into the hands of Israel, and he struck it and every person who *was* in it with the edge of the sword. He left no survivor in it. Thus he did to its king just as he had done to the king of Jericho.

³¹ ¶ And Joshua and all Israel with him passed on from Libnah to Lachish, and they camped by it and fought against it.

³² The LORD gave Lachish into the hands of Israel; and he captured it on the second day, and struck it and every person who *was* in it with the edge of the sword, according to all that he had done to Libnah.

³³ ¶ Then Horam king of Gezer came up to help Lachish, and Joshua defeated him and his people until he had left him no survivor.

³⁴ ¶ And Joshua and all Israel with him passed on from Lachish to Eglon; and they camped by it and fought against it.

³⁵ They captured it on that day and struck it with the edge of the sword; and he utterly destroyed that day every person who *was* in it, according to all that he had done to Lachish.

³⁶ ¶ Then Joshua and all Israel with him went up from Eglon to Hebron, and they fought against it.

³⁷ They captured it and struck it and its king and all its cities and all the persons who *were* in it with the edge of the sword. He left no survivor, according to all that he had done to Eglon. And he utterly destroyed it and every person who *was* in it.

New International

some men there to guard it. ¹⁹But don't stop! Pursue your enemies, attack them from the rear and don't let them reach their cities, for the LORD your God has given them into your hand."

²⁰So Joshua and the Israelites destroyed them completely—almost to a man—but the few who were left reached their fortified cities. ²¹The whole army then returned safely to Joshua in the camp at Makkedah, and no one uttered a word against the Israelites.

²²Joshua said, "Open the mouth of the cave and bring those five kings out to me." ²³So they brought the five kings out of the cave—the kings of Jerusalem, Hebron, Jarmuth, Lachish and Eglon. ²⁴When they had brought these kings to Joshua, he summoned all the men of Israel and said to the army commanders who had come with him, "Come here and put your feet on the necks of these kings." So they came forward and placed their feet on their necks.

²⁵Joshua said to them, "Do not be afraid; do not be discouraged. Be strong and courageous. This is what the LORD will do to all the enemies you are going to fight." ²⁶Then Joshua struck and killed the kings and hung them on five trees, and they were left hanging on the trees until evening.

²⁷At sunset Joshua gave the order and they took them down from the trees and threw them into the cave where they had been hiding. At the mouth of the cave they placed large rocks, which are there to this day.

²⁸That day Joshua took Makkedah. He put the city and its king to the sword and totally destroyed everyone in it. He left no survivors. And he did to the king of Makkedah as he had done to the king of Jericho.

Southern Cities Conquered

²⁹Then Joshua and all Israel with him moved on from Makkedah to Libnah and attacked it. ³⁰The LORD also gave that city and its king into Israel's hand. The city and everyone in it Joshua put to the sword. He left no survivors there. And he did to its king as he had done to the king of Jericho.

³¹Then Joshua and all Israel with him moved on from Libnah to Lachish; he took up positions against it and attacked it. ³²The LORD handed Lachish over to Israel, and Joshua took it on the second day. The city and everyone in it he put to the sword, just as he had done to Libnah. ³³Meanwhile, Horam king of Gezer had come up to help Lachish, but Joshua defeated him and his army—until no survivors were left.

³⁴Then Joshua and all Israel with him moved on from Lachish to Eglon; they took up positions against it and attacked it. ³⁵They captured it that same day and put it to the sword and totally destroyed everyone in it, just as they had done to Lachish.

³⁶Then Joshua and all Israel with him went up from Eglon to Hebron and attacked it. ³⁷They took the city and put it to the sword, together with its king, its villages and everyone in it. They left no survivors. Just as at Eglon, they totally destroyed it and everyone in it.

ʰ Lit *soul,* and so throughout the ch

King James

38 ¶ And Joshua returned, and all Israel with him, to Debir; and fought against it:

39 And he took it, and the king thereof, and all the cities thereof; and they smote them with the edge of the sword, and utterly destroyed all the souls that *were* therein; he left none remaining: as he had done to Hebron, so he did to Debir, and to the king thereof; as he had done also to Libnah, and to her king.

40 ¶ So Joshua smote all the country of the hills, and of the south, and of the vale, and of the springs, and all their kings: he left none remaining, but utterly destroyed all that breathed, as the LORD God of Israel commanded.

41 And Joshua smote them from Kadesh-barnea even unto Gaza, and all the country of Goshen, even unto Gibeon.

42 And all these kings and their land did Joshua take at one time, because the LORD God of Israel fought for Israel.

43 And Joshua returned, and all Israel with him, unto the camp to Gilgal.

Conquest of the north

11 AND IT came to pass, when Jabin king of Hazor had heard *those things,* that he sent to Jobab king of Madon, and to the king of Shimron, and to the king of Achshaph,

2 And to the kings that *were* on the north of the mountains, and of the plains south of Chinneroth, and in the valley, and in the borders of Dor on the west,

3 *And to* the Canaanite on the east and on the west, and *to* the Amorite, and the Hittite, and the Perizzite, and the Jebusite in the mountains, and *to* the Hivite under Hermon in the land of Mizpeh.

4 And they went out, they and all their hosts with them, much people, even as the sand that *is* upon the sea shore in multitude, with horses and chariots very many.

5 And when all these kings were *b*met together, they came and pitched together at the waters of Merom, to fight against Israel.

6 ¶ And the LORD said unto Joshua, Be not afraid because of them: for tomorrow about this time will I deliver them up all slain before Israel: thou shalt hough their horses, and burn their chariots with fire.

7 So Joshua came, and all the people of war with him, against them by the waters of Merom suddenly; and they fell upon them.

8 And the LORD delivered them into the hand of Israel, who smote them, and chased them unto *c*great Zidon, and unto *d e*Misrephoth-maim, and unto the valley of Mizpeh eastward; and they smote them, until they left them none remaining.

9 And Joshua did unto them as the LORD bade him: he houghed their horses, and burnt their chariots with fire.

10 ¶ And Joshua at that time turned back, and took Hazor, and smote the king thereof with the sword: for Hazor beforetime was the head of all those kingdoms.

11 And they smote all the souls that *were* therein with the edge of the sword, utterly destroying *them:* there was not *f*any left to breathe: and he burnt Hazor with fire.

12 And all the cities of those kings, and all the kings of them, did Joshua take, and smote them with the edge of the sword, *and* he utterly destroyed them, as Moses the servant of the LORD commanded.

Amplified

38 And Joshua and all Israel with him returned to Debir and attacked it.

39 And he took it, with its king and all its towns, and they smote them with the sword and utterly destroyed everyone in it. He left none remaining. As he had done to Hebron and to Libnah and its king, so he did to Debir and its king.

40 So Joshua smote all the land, the hill country, the South, the lowland, and the slopes, and all their kings. He left none remaining, but utterly destroyed all that breathed, as the *h*Lord, the God of Israel, commanded. [Deut. 20:16.]

41 And Joshua smote them from Kadesh-barnea even to Gaza, and all the country of Goshen even to Gibeon.

42 Joshua took all these kings and their land at one time, because the Lord, the God of Israel, fought for Israel.

43 And Joshua returned, and all Israel with him, to the camp at Gilgal.

11 WHEN JABIN king of Hazor heard of this, he sent to Jobab king of Madon, and to the kings of Shimron and Achshaph,

2 And to the kings who were in the north in the hill country and in the Arabah south of Chinneroth and in the lowland and in the heights of Dor on the west;

3 To the Canaanites in the east and west; to the Amorites, the Hittites, the Perizzites, the Jebusites in the hill country; and to the Hivites below [Mount] Hermon in the land of Mizpah.

4 And they went out with all their hosts, much people, like the sand on the seashore in number, with very many horses and chariots.

5 And all these kings met and came and encamped together at the Waters of Merom, to fight against Israel.

6 But the Lord said to Joshua, Do not be afraid because of them; for tomorrow by this time I will give them up all slain to Israel; you shall hamstring their horses and burn their chariots with fire.

7 So Joshua and all the people of war with him came against them suddenly by the Waters of Merom and fell upon them.

8 And the Lord gave them into the hand of Israel, who smote them and chased them [toward] populous Sidon and Misrephoth-maim, and eastward as far as the Valley of Mizpah; they smote them until none remained.

9 And Joshua did to them as the Lord had commanded him: he hamstrung their horses and burned their chariots with fire.

10 And Joshua at that time turned back and took Hazor and smote its king with the sword; for Hazor previously was the head of all those kingdoms.

11 They smote all the people in it with the sword, utterly destroying them; none were left alive, and he burned Hazor with fire.

12 And Joshua took all the cities of those kings and all the kings and smote them with the sword, utterly destroying them, as Moses the servant of the Lord commanded. [Deut. 20:16.]

h As the presence of "the Prince of the Lord's host" (Josh. 5:13-15) indicates, the Lord will take part in this conflict not as an ally or an adversary but as Commander In Chief. It is not Israel's quarrel, in which they are to ask divine assistance. It is the Lord's own quarrel, and Israel and Joshua are but a division in His host. The wars of Israel in Canaan are always presented by the Old Testament as "the wars of the Lord." The conquest of Canaan is too often treated as an enterprise of the Israelites, carried out with great cruelties, for which they claimed divine sanction. The Old Testament presents the matter in an entirely different light. The Lord fights for His own right hand, and Israel is but a fragment of His army. "The sun stood still"(Josh. 10:13), the stars in their courses fought against His foes (Judg. 5:20) (Charles Ellicott, *A Bible Commentary*).

b Heb. *assembled by appointment*　*c* Or, *Zidon-rabbah*　*d* Or, *Salt pits*　*e* Heb. *Burnings*　*f* Heb. *any breath*

New American Standard

38 ¶ Then Joshua and all Israel with him returned to Debir, and they fought against it.
39 He captured it and its king and all its cities, and they struck them with the edge of the sword, and utterly destroyed every person *who was* in it. He left no survivor. Just as he had done to Hebron, so he did to Debir and its king, as he had also done to Libnah and its king.
40 ¶ Thus Joshua struck all the land, the hill country and the *i*Negev and the lowland and the slopes and all their kings. He left no survivor, but he utterly destroyed all who breathed, just as the LORD, the God of Israel, had commanded.
41 Joshua struck them from Kadesh-barnea even as far as Gaza, and all the country of Goshen even as far as Gibeon.
42 Joshua captured all these kings and their lands at one time, because the LORD, the God of Israel, fought for Israel.
43 So Joshua and all Israel with him returned to the camp at Gilgal.

Northern Palestine Taken

11 THEN IT came about, when Jabin king of Hazor heard *of it,* that he sent to Jobab king of Madon and to the king of Shimron and to the king of Achshaph,
2 and to the kings who were of the north in the hill country, and in the Arabah—south of *j*Chinneroth and in the lowland and on the heights of Dor on the west—
3 to the Canaanite on the east and on the west, and the Amorite and the Hittite and the Perizzite and the Jebusite in the hill country, and the Hivite at the foot of Hermon in the land of Mizpeh.
4 They came out, they and all their armies with them, *as* many people as the sand that is on the seashore, with very many horses and chariots.
5 So all of these kings having agreed to meet, came and encamped together at the waters of Merom, to fight against Israel.
6 ¶ Then the LORD said to Joshua, "Do not be afraid because of them, for tomorrow at this time I will deliver all of them slain before Israel; you shall hamstring their horses and burn their chariots with fire."
7 So Joshua and all the people of war with him came upon them suddenly by the waters of Merom, and attacked them.
8 The LORD delivered them into the hand of Israel, so that they defeated them, and pursued them as far as Great Sidon and Misrephoth-maim and the valley of Mizpeh to the east; and they struck them until no survivor was left to them.
9 Joshua did to them as the LORD had told him; he hamstrung their horses and burned their chariots with fire.
10 ¶ Then Joshua turned back at that time, and captured Hazor and struck its king with the sword; for Hazor formerly was the head of all these kingdoms.
11 They struck every person who was in it with the edge of the sword, utterly destroying *them;* there was no one left who breathed. And he burned Hazor with fire.
12 Joshua captured all the cities of these kings, and all their kings, and he struck them with the edge of the sword, *and* utterly destroyed them; just as Moses the servant of the LORD had commanded.

New International

38Then Joshua and all Israel with him turned around and attacked Debir. 39They took the city, its king and its villages, and put them to the sword. Everyone in it they totally destroyed. They left no survivors. They did to Debir and its king as they had done to Libnah and its king and to Hebron.
40So Joshua subdued the whole region, including the hill country, the Negev, the western foothills and the mountain slopes, together with all their kings. He left no survivors. He totally destroyed all who breathed, just as the LORD, the God of Israel, had commanded. 41Joshua subdued them from Kadesh Barnea to Gaza and from the whole region of Goshen to Gibeon. 42All these kings and their lands Joshua conquered in one campaign, because the LORD, the God of Israel, fought for Israel.
43Then Joshua returned with all Israel to the camp at Gilgal.

Northern Kings Defeated

11 WHEN JABIN king of Hazor heard of this, he sent word to Jobab king of Madon, to the kings of Shimron and Acshaph, 2and to the northern kings who were in the mountains, in the Arabah south of Kinnereth, in the western foothills and in Naphoth Dor*d* on the west; 3to the Canaanites in the east and west; to the Amorites, Hittites, Perizzites and Jebusites in the hill country; and to the Hivites below Hermon in the region of Mizpah. 4They came out with all their troops and a large number of horses and chariots—a huge army, as numerous as the sand on the seashore. 5All these kings joined forces and made camp together at the Waters of Merom, to fight against Israel.
6The LORD said to Joshua, "Do not be afraid of them, because by this time tomorrow I will hand all of them over to Israel, slain. You are to hamstring their horses and burn their chariots."
7So Joshua and his whole army came against them suddenly at the Waters of Merom and attacked them, 8and the LORD gave them into the hand of Israel. They defeated them and pursued them all the way to Greater Sidon, to Misrephoth Maim, and to the Valley of Mizpah on the east, until no survivors were left. 9Joshua did to them as the LORD had directed: He hamstrung their horses and burned their chariots.
10At that time Joshua turned back and captured Hazor and put its king to the sword. (Hazor had been the head of all these kingdoms.) 11Everyone in it they put to the sword. They totally destroyed*e* them, not sparing anything that breathed, and he burned up Hazor itself.
12Joshua took all these royal cities and their kings and put them to the sword. He totally destroyed them, as Mo-

---

*d*2 Or *in the heights of Dor*   *e*11 The Hebrew term refers to the irrevocable giving over of things or persons to the LORD, often by totally destroying them; also in verses 12, 20 and 21.

*i*I.e. South country   *j*I.e. Sea of Galilee

King James

13But *as for* the cities that stood still [g]in their strength, Israel burned none of them, save Hazor only; *that* did Joshua burn.

14And all the spoil of these cities, and the cattle, the children of Israel took for a prey unto themselves; but every man they smote with the edge of the sword, until they had destroyed them, neither left they any to breathe.

15 ¶ As the LORD commanded Moses his servant, so did Moses command Joshua, and so did Joshua; [h]he left nothing undone of all that the LORD commanded Moses.

16So Joshua took all that land, the hills, and all the south country, and all the land of Goshen, and the valley, and the plain, and the mountain of Israel, and the valley of the same;

17*Even* from [i]the mount Halak, that goeth up to Seir, even unto Baal-gad in the valley of Lebanon under mount Hermon: and all their kings he took, and smote them, and slew them.

18Joshua made war a long time with all those kings.

19There was not a city that made peace with the children of Israel, save the Hivites the inhabitants of Gibeon: all *other* they took in battle.

20For it was of the LORD to harden their hearts, that they should come against Israel in battle, that he might destroy them utterly, *and* that they might have no favour, but that he might destroy them, as the LORD commanded Moses.

21 ¶ And at that time came Joshua, and cut off the Anakims from the mountains, from Hebron, from Debir, from Anab, and from all the mountains of Judah, and from all the mountains of Israel: Joshua destroyed them utterly with their cities.

22There was none of the Anakims left in the land of the children of Israel: only in Gaza, in Gath, and in Ashdod, there remained.

23So Joshua took the whole land, according to all that the LORD said unto Moses; and Joshua gave it for an inheritance unto Israel according to their divisions by their tribes. And the land rested from war.

Defeated kings

12 NOW THESE *are* the kings of the land, which the children of Israel smote, and possessed their land on the other side Jordan toward the rising of the sun, from the river Arnon unto mount Hermon, and all the plain on the east:

2Sihon king of the Amorites, who dwelt in Heshbon, *and* ruled from Aroer, which *is* upon the bank of the river Arnon, and from the middle of the river, and from half Gilead, even unto the river Jabbok, *which is* the border of the children of Ammon;

3And from the plain to the sea of Chinneroth on the east, and unto the sea of the plain, *even* the salt sea on the east, the way to Beth-jeshimoth; and from [j]the south, under [k]Ashdoth-pisgah:

4 ¶ And the coast of Og king of Bashan, *which was* of the remnant of the giants, that dwelt at Ashtaroth and at Edrei,

5And reigned in mount Hermon, and in Salcah, and in all Bashan, unto the border of the Geshurites and the Maachathites, and half Gilead, the border of Sihon king of Heshbon.

Amplified

13But Israel burned none of the cities that stood [fortified] on their mounds—except Hazor only, which Joshua burned.

14And all the spoil of these cities and the livestock the Israelites took for their booty; but every man they smote with the sword until they had destroyed them, and they left none who breathed.

15As the Lord had commanded Moses His servant, so Moses commanded Joshua, and so Joshua did; he left nothing undone of all that the Lord commanded Moses.

16So Joshua took all that land: the hill country, all the South, all the land of Goshen, the lowland, the Arabah [plain], the hill country of Israel and its lowland,

17From Mount Halak, which rises toward Seir, as far as Baal-gad in the Valley of Lebanon below Mount Hermon. He captured all their kings and slew them.

18Joshua had waged war a long time [at least five years] with all those kings.

19Not a city made peace with the Israelites except the Hivites, the people of Gibeon; all the others they took in battle.

20For it was of the Lord to harden their hearts that they should come against Israel in battle, that [Israel] might [i]destroy them utterly, and that without favor *and* mercy, as the Lord commanded Moses.

21Joshua came at that time and cut off the Anakim [large in stature] from the hill country; from Hebron, from Debir, from Anab, and from all the hill country of Judah and the hill country of Israel. Joshua destroyed them utterly with their cities.

22None of the Anakim were left in the land of the Israelites; only in Gaza, Gath, and Ashdod [of Philistia] did some remain.

23So Joshua took the whole land, according to all that the Lord had spoken to Moses, and Joshua gave it for an inheritance to Israel according to their allotments by tribes. And the land had rest from war.

12 NOW THESE are the kings of the land whom the Israelites defeated and whose land they took possession of east of the Jordan, from the river Arnon to Mount Hermon, and all the Arabah eastward:

2Sihon king of the Amorites, who dwelt in Heshbon, and ruled from Aroer on the edge of the Valley of the [river] Arnon, and from the middle of the valley as far as the river Jabbok, the boundary of the Ammonites, including half of Gilead;

3And the Arabah to the Sea of Chinneroth eastward, and in the direction of Beth-jeshimoth, to the Sea of the Arabah, the Salt [or Dead] Sea, southward to the foot of the slopes of Pisgah.

4And Og king of Bashan, one of the remnant of the Rephaim, who lived at Ashtaroth and at Edrei,

5And ruled over Mount Hermon and Salecah and all of Bashan to the boundary of the Geshurites and the Maacathites, and over half of Gilead to the boundary of Sihon king of Heshbon.

---

i "Infidels say that it seems wholly inconsistent with what we should suppose to be the merciful character of God that He should thus command whole nations to be destroyed by the sword . . . [But] when we see juries in our own country bringing in a verdict of guilty, the judge pronouncing the sentence of death, and that sentence executed, we do not complain that there is anything unjust in the act. These Canaanites are proved to have polluted and stained the land with [intolerable] crimes; it was merely the holy Judge [the Lord] pronouncing the sentence on flagrant criminals and [Joshua] the righteous governor executing that sentence to the letter. It was not an act of arbitrary or private revenge, but the execution of the sentence of retributive justice, and as such had perhaps as great mercy to the innocent as justice to the guilty" (John Cumming, cited by James C. Gray and George M. Adams, *Bible Commentary*).

---

[g] Heb. *on their heap*　　[h] Heb. *he removed nothing*　　[i] Or, *the smooth mountain*　　[j] Or, *Teman*　　[k] Or, *The springs of Pisgah*, or, *The hill*

New American Standard

13 However, Israel did not burn any cities that stood on their mounds, except Hazor alone, *which* Joshua burned.

14 All the spoil of these cities and the cattle, the sons of Israel took as their plunder; but they struck every man with the edge of the sword, until they had destroyed them. They left no one who breathed.

15 Just as the LORD had commanded Moses his servant, so Moses commanded Joshua, and so Joshua did; he left nothing undone of all that the LORD had commanded Moses.

16 ¶ Thus Joshua took all that land: the hill country and all the Negev, all that land of Goshen, the lowland, the Arabah, the hill country of Israel and its lowland

17 from Mount Halak, that rises toward Seir, even as far as Baal-gad in the valley of Lebanon at the foot of Mount Hermon. And he captured all their kings and struck them down and put them to death.

18 Joshua waged war a long time with all these kings.

19 There was not a city which made peace with the sons of Israel except the Hivites living in Gibeon; they took them all in battle.

20 For it was of the LORD to harden their hearts, to meet Israel in battle in order that he might utterly destroy them, that they might receive no mercy, but that he might destroy them, just as the LORD had commanded Moses.

21 ¶ Then Joshua came at that time and cut off the Anakim from the hill country, from Hebron, from Debir, from Anab and from all the hill country of Judah and from all the hill country of Israel. Joshua utterly destroyed them with their cities.

22 There were no Anakim left in the land of the sons of Israel; only in Gaza, in Gath, and in Ashdod some remained.

23 So Joshua took the whole land, according to all that the LORD had spoken to Moses, and Joshua gave it for an inheritance to Israel according to their divisions by their tribes. Thus the land had rest from war.

Kings Defeated by Israel

12 NOW THESE are the kings of the land whom the sons of Israel defeated, and whose land they possessed beyond the Jordan toward the sunrise, from the valley of the Arnon as far as Mount Hermon, and all the Arabah to the east:

2 Sihon king of the Amorites, who lived in Heshbon, *and* ruled from Aroer, which is on the edge of the valley of the Arnon, both the middle of the valley and half of Gilead, even as far as the brook Jabbok, the border of the sons of Ammon;

3 and the Arabah as far as the Sea of *k*Chinneroth toward the east, and as far as the sea of the Arabah, *even* the Salt Sea, eastward toward Beth-jeshimoth, and on the south, at the foot of the slopes of Pisgah;

4 and the territory of Og king of Bashan, one of the remnant of Rephaim, who lived at Ashtaroth and at Edrei,

5 and ruled over Mount Hermon and Salecah and all Bashan, as far as the border of the Geshurites and the Maacathites, and half of Gilead, *as far as* the border of Sihon king of Heshbon.

New International

ses the servant of the LORD had commanded. 13 Yet Israel did not burn any of the cities built on their mounds—except Hazor, which Joshua burned. 14 The Israelites carried off for themselves all the plunder and livestock of these cities, but all the people they put to the sword until they completely destroyed them, not sparing anyone that breathed. 15 As the LORD commanded his servant Moses, so Moses commanded Joshua, and Joshua did it; he left nothing undone of all that the LORD commanded Moses.

16 So Joshua took this entire land: the hill country, all the Negev, the whole region of Goshen, the western foothills, the Arabah and the mountains of Israel with their foothills, 17 from Mount Halak, which rises toward Seir, to Baal Gad in the Valley of Lebanon below Mount Hermon. He captured all their kings and struck them down, putting them to death. 18 Joshua waged war against all these kings for a long time. 19 Except for the Hivites living in Gibeon, not one city made a treaty of peace with the Israelites, who took them all in battle. 20 For it was the LORD himself who hardened their hearts to wage war against Israel, so that he might destroy them totally, exterminating them without mercy, as the LORD had commanded Moses.

21 At that time Joshua went and destroyed the Anakites from the hill country: from Hebron, Debir and Anab, from all the hill country of Judah, and from all the hill country of Israel. Joshua totally destroyed them and their towns. 22 No Anakites were left in Israelite territory; only in Gaza, Gath and Ashdod did any survive. 23 So Joshua took the entire land, just as the LORD had directed Moses, and he gave it as an inheritance to Israel according to their tribal divisions.

Then the land had rest from war.

List of Defeated Kings

12 THESE ARE the kings of the land whom the Israelites had defeated and whose territory they took over east of the Jordan, from the Arnon Gorge to Mount Hermon, including all the eastern side of the Arabah:

2 Sihon king of the Amorites,
    who reigned in Heshbon. He ruled from Aroer on the rim of the Arnon Gorge—from the middle of the gorge—to the Jabbok River, which is the border of the Ammonites. This included half of Gilead. 3 He also ruled over the eastern Arabah from the Sea of Kinnereth*f* to the Sea of the Arabah (the Salt Sea*g*), to Beth Jeshimoth, and then southward below the slopes of Pisgah.

4 And the territory of Og king of Bashan,
    one of the last of the Rephaites, who reigned in Ashtaroth and Edrei. 5 He ruled over Mount Hermon, Salecah, all of Bashan to the border of the people of Geshur and Maacah, and half of Gilead to the border of Sihon king of Heshbon.

---

k I.e. Galilee

f 3 That is, Galilee   *g* 3 That is, the Dead Sea

King James

6Them did Moses the servant of the LORD and the children of Israel smite: and Moses the servant of the LORD gave it *for* a possession unto the Reubenites, and the Gadites, and the half tribe of Manasseh.

7 ¶ And these *are* the kings of the country which Joshua and the children of Israel smote on this side Jordan on the west, from Baal-gad in the valley of Lebanon even unto the mount Halak, that goeth up to Seir; which Joshua gave unto the tribes of Israel *for* a possession according to their divisions;

8In the mountains, and in the valleys, and in the plains, and in the springs, and in the wilderness, and in the south country; the Hittites, the Amorites, and the Canaanites, the Perizzites, the Hivites, and the Jebusites:

9 ¶ The king of Jericho, one; the king of Ai, which *is* beside Beth-el, one;

10The king of Jerusalem, one; the king of Hebron, one;
11The king of Jarmuth, one; the king of Lachish, one;
12The king of Eglon, one; the king of Gezer, one;
13The king of Debir, one; the king of Geder, one;
14The king of Hormah, one; the king of Arad, one;
15The king of Libnah, one; the king of Adullam, one;
16The king of Makkedah, one; the king of Beth-el, one;
17The king of Tappuah, one; the king of Hepher, one;
18The king of Aphek, one; the king of Lasharon, one;
19The king of Madon, one; the king of Hazor, one;
20The king of Shimron-meron, one; the king of Achshaph, one;
21The king of Taanach, one; the king of Megiddo, one;
22The king of Kedesh, one; the king of Jokneam of Carmel, one;
23The king of Dor in the coast of Dor, one; the king of the nations of Gilgal, one;
24The king of Tirzah, one: all the kings thirty and one.

Amplified

6These Moses the servant of the Lord and the Israelites defeated; and Moses the servant of the Lord gave their land for a possession to the Reubenites, the Gadites, and the half-tribe of Manasseh. [Num. 21; 32:33; Deut. 2; 3.]

7These are the kings of the land whom Joshua and the Israelites defeated on the west side of the Jordan, from Baal-gad in the Valley of Lebanon to Mount Halak, which rises toward Seir. Joshua gave their land to the tribes of Israel for a possession according to their allotments,

8In the hill country, in the lowland, in the Arabah, on the slopes, in the wilderness, and in the Negeb—the lands of the Hittites, Amorites, Canaanites, Perizzites, Hivites, and Jebusites:

9The king of Jericho, one; the king of Ai, which is beside Bethel, one;

10The king of Jerusalem, one; the king of Hebron, one;
11The king of Jarmuth, one; the king of Lachish, one;
12The king of Eglon, one; the king of Gezer, one;
13The king of Debir, one; the king of Geder, one;
14The king of Hormah, one; the king of Arad, one;
15The king of Libnah, one; the king of Adullam, one;
16The king of Makkedah, one; the king of Bethel, one;
17The king of Tappuah, one; the king of Hepher, one;
18The king of Aphek, one; the king of Lasharon, one;
19The king of Madon, one; the king of Hazor, one;
20The king of Shimron-meron, one; the king of Achshaph, one;
21The king of Taanach, one; the king of Megiddo, one;
22The king of Kedesh, one; the king of Jokneam in Carmel, one;
23The king of Dor in the heights of Dor, one; the king of Goiim in Gilgal, one;
24The king of Tirzah, one. In all, thirty-one kings.

Land yet to be conquered

13 NOW JOSHUA was old *and* stricken in years; and the LORD said unto him, Thou art old *and* stricken in years, and there remaineth yet very much land to be possessed.

2This *is* the land that yet remaineth: all the borders of the Philistines, and all Geshuri,

3From Sihor, which *is* before Egypt, even unto the borders of Ekron northward, *which is* counted to the Canaanite: five lords of the Philistines; the Gazathites, and the Ashdothites, the Eshkalonites, the Gittites, and the Ekronites; also the Avites:

4From the south, all the land of the Canaanites, and *1*Mearah that *is* beside the Sidonians, unto Aphek, to the borders of the Amorites:

5And the land of the Giblites, and all Lebanon, toward the sunrising, from Baal-gad under mount Hermon unto the entering into Hamath.

6All the inhabitants of the hill country from Lebanon unto Misrephoth-maim, *and* all the Sidonians, them will I drive out from before the children of Israel: only divide thou it by lot unto the Israelites for an inheritance, as I have commanded thee.

7Now therefore divide this land for an inheritance unto the nine tribes, and the half tribe of Manasseh,

13 NOW JOSHUA was old and gone far in years [over 100], and the Lord said to him, You have grown old and are gone far in years, and very much of the land still remains to be possessed.

2This is the land that yet remains: all the regions of the Philistines and all those of the Geshurites:

3From the Shihor [River] which is east of Egypt, northward to the boundary of Ekron, all of it counted as Canaanite; there are five rulers of the Philistines, those of Gaza, Ashdod, Ashkelon, Gath, and Ekron, and those of the Avvites;

4In the south, all the land of the Canaanites, and Mearah, which belongs to the Sidonians, to Aphek, to the boundary of the Amorites,

5And the land of the Gebalites; and all Lebanon toward the east, from Baal-gad below Mount Hermon to the gate of Hamath.

6As for all the inhabitants of the hill country from Lebanon to Misrephoth-maim, even all the Sidonians, I will Myself drive them out from before the Israelites; only allot the land to Israel for an inheritance, as I have commanded you.

7So now divide this land for an inheritance to the nine tribes and the half-tribe of Manasseh.

1Or, The cave

New American Standard

6. Moses the servant of the LORD and the sons of Israel defeated them; and Moses the servant of the LORD gave it to the Reubenites and the Gadites and the half-tribe of Manasseh as a possession.

7. ¶ Now these are the kings of the land whom Joshua and the sons of Israel defeated beyond the Jordan toward the west, from Baal-gad in the valley of Lebanon even as far as Mount Halak, which rises toward Seir; and Joshua gave it to the tribes of Israel as a possession according to their divisions,

8. in the hill country, in the lowland, in the Arabah, on the slopes, and in the wilderness, and in the Negev; the Hittite, the Amorite and the Canaanite, the Perizzite, the Hivite and the Jebusite:

9. the king of Jericho, one; the king of Ai, which is beside Bethel, one;

10. the king of Jerusalem, one; the king of Hebron, one;

11. the king of Jarmuth, one; the king of Lachish, one;

12. the king of Eglon, one; the king of Gezer, one;

13. the king of Debir, one; the king of Geder, one;

14. the king of Hormah, one; the king of Arad, one;

15. the king of Libnah, one; the king of Adullam, one;

16. the king of Makkedah, one; the king of Bethel, one;

17. the king of Tappuah, one; the king of Hepher, one;

18. the king of Aphek, one; the king of Lasharon, one;

19. the king of Madon, one; the king of Hazor, one;

20. the king of Shimron-meron, one; the king of Achshaph, one;

21. the king of Taanach, one; the king of Megiddo, one;

22. the king of Kedesh, one; the king of Jokneam in Carmel, one;

23. the king of Dor in the heights of Dor, one; the king of Goiim in Gilgal, one;

24. the king of Tirzah, one: in all, thirty-one kings.

Canaan Divided among the Tribes

13 NOW JOSHUA was old *and* advanced in years when the LORD said to him, "You are old *and* advanced in years, and very much of the land remains to be possessed.

2. "This is the land that remains: all the regions *of* the Philistines and all *those of* the Geshurites;

3. from the Shihor which is east of Egypt, even as far as the border of Ekron to the north (it is counted as Canaanite); the five lords of the Philistines: the Gazite, the Ashdodite, the Ashkelonite, the Gittite, the Ekronite; and the Avvite

4. to the south, all the land of the Canaanite, and Mearah that belongs to the Sidonians, as far as Aphek, to the border of the Amorite;

5. and the land of the Gebalite, and all of Lebanon, toward the east, from Baal-gad below Mount Hermon as far as Lebo-hamath.

6. "All the inhabitants of the hill country from Lebanon as far as Misrephoth-maim, all the Sidonians, I will drive them out from before the sons of Israel; only allot it to Israel for an inheritance as I have commanded you.

7. "Now therefore, apportion this land for an inheritance to the nine tribes and the half-tribe of Manasseh."

New International

6Moses, the servant of the LORD, and the Israelites conquered them. And Moses the servant of the LORD gave their land to the Reubenites, the Gadites and the half-tribe of Manasseh to be their possession.

7These are the kings of the land that Joshua and the Israelites conquered on the west side of the Jordan, from Baal Gad in the Valley of Lebanon to Mount Halak, which rises toward Seir (their lands Joshua gave as an inheritance to the tribes of Israel according to their tribal divisions— 8the hill country, the western foothills, the Arabah, the mountain slopes, the desert and the Negev—the lands of the Hittites, Amorites, Canaanites, Perizzites, Hivites and Jebusites):

9the king of Jericho	one
the king of Ai (near Bethel)	one
10the king of Jerusalem	one
the king of Hebron	one
11the king of Jarmuth	one
the king of Lachish	one
12the king of Eglon	one
the king of Gezer	one
13the king of Debir	one
the king of Geder	one
14the king of Hormah	one
the king of Arad	one
15the king of Libnah	one
the king of Adullam	one
16the king of Makkedah	one
the king of Bethel	one
17the king of Tappuah	one
the king of Hepher	one
18the king of Aphek	one
the king of Lasharon	one
19the king of Madon	one
the king of Hazor	one
20the king of Shimron Meron	one
the king of Acshaph	one
21the king of Taanach	one
the king of Megiddo	one
22the king of Kedesh	one
the king of Jokneam in Carmel	one
23the king of Dor (in Naphoth Dor*h*)	one
the king of Goyim in Gilgal	one
24the king of Tirzah	one

thirty-one kings in all.

Land Still to Be Taken

13 WHEN JOSHUA was old and well advanced in years, the LORD said to him, "You are very old, and there are still very large areas of land to be taken over.

2"This is the land that remains: all the regions of the Philistines and Geshurites: 3from the Shihor River on the east of Egypt to the territory of Ekron on the north, all of it counted as Canaanite (the territory of the five Philistine rulers in Gaza, Ashdod, Ashkelon, Gath and Ekron—that of the Avvites); 4from the south, all the land of the Canaanites, from Arah of the Sidonians as far as Aphek, the region of the Amorites, 5the area of the Gebalites*i*; and all Lebanon to the east, from Baal Gad below Mount Hermon to Lebo*j* Hamath.

6"As for all the inhabitants of the mountain regions from Lebanon to Misrephoth Maim, that is, all the Sidonians, I myself will drive them out before the Israelites. Be sure to allocate this land to Israel for an inheritance, as I have instructed you, 7and divide it as an inheritance among the nine tribes and half of the tribe of Manasseh."

*h*23 Or *in the heights of Dor*   *i*5 That is, the area of Byblos
*j*5 Or *to the entrance to*

King James

Land east of the Jordan

8With whom the Reubenites and the Gadites have received their inheritance, which Moses gave them, beyond Jordan eastward, *even* as Moses the servant of the LORD gave them;

9From Aroer, that *is* upon the bank of the river Arnon, and the city that *is* in the midst of the river, and all the plain of Medeba unto Dibon;

10And all the cities of Sihon king of the Amorites, which reigned in Heshbon, unto the border of the children of Ammon;

11And Gilead, and the border of the Geshurites and Maachathites, and all mount Hermon, and all Bashan unto Salcah;

12All the kingdom of Og in Bashan, which reigned in Ashtaroth and in Edrei, who remained of the remnant of the giants: for these did Moses smite, and cast them out.

13Nevertheless the children of Israel expelled not the Geshurites, nor the Maachathites: but the Geshurites and the Maachathites dwell among the Israelites until this day.

14Only unto the tribe of Levi he gave none inheritance; the sacrifices of the LORD God of Israel made by fire *are* their inheritance, as he said unto them.

15 ¶ And Moses gave unto the tribe of the children of Reuben *inheritance* according to their families.

16And their coast was from Aroer, that *is* on the bank of the river Arnon, and the city that *is* in the midst of the river, and all the plain by Medeba;

17Heshbon, and all her cities that *are* in the plain; Dibon, and *m*Bamoth-baal, and Beth-baal-meon,

18And Jahaza, and Kedemoth, and Mephaath,

19And Kirjathaim, and Sibmah, and Zareth-shahar in the mount of the valley,

20And Beth-peor, and *n*Ashdoth-pisgah, and Beth-jeshimoth,

21And all the cities of the plain, and all the kingdom of Sihon king of the Amorites, which reigned in Heshbon, whom Moses smote with the princes of Midian, Evi, and Rekem, and Zur, and Hur, and Reba, *which were* dukes of Sihon, dwelling in the country.

22 ¶ Balaam also the son of Beor, the *o*soothsayer, did the children of Israel slay with the sword among them that were slain by them.

23And the border of the children of Reuben was Jordan, and the border *thereof.* This *was* the inheritance of the children of Reuben after their families, the cities and the villages thereof.

24And Moses gave *inheritance* unto the tribe of Gad, *even* unto the children of Gad according to their families.

25And their coast was Jazer, and all the cities of Gilead, and half the land of the children of Ammon, unto Aroer that *is* before Rabbah;

26And from Heshbon unto Ramath-mizpeh, and Betonim; and from Mahanaim unto the border of Debir;

27And in the valley, Beth-aram, and Beth-nimrah, and Succoth, and Zaphon, the rest of the kingdom of Sihon king of Heshbon, Jordan and *his* border, *even* unto the edge of the sea of Chinnereth on the other side Jordan eastward.

28This *is* the inheritance of the children of Gad after their families, the cities, and their villages.

29 ¶ And Moses gave *inheritance* unto the half tribe of Manasseh: and *this* was the possession of the half tribe of the children of Manasseh by their families.

30And their coast was from Mahanaim, all Bashan, all the kingdom of Og king of Bashan, and all the towns of Jair, which *are* in Bashan, threescore cities:

31And half Gilead, and Ashtaroth, and Edrei, cities of the kingdom of Og in Bashan, *were pertaining* unto the children of Machir the son of Manasseh, *even* to the one half of the children of Machir by their families.

Amplified

8With the other half-tribe of Manasseh, the Reubenites and the Gadites received their inheritance beyond the Jordan eastward, as Moses the servant of the Lord gave them:

9From Aroer on the edge of the Valley of the [river] Arnon, and the city in the midst of the valley, and all the tableland of Medeba as far as Dibon;

10And all the cities of Sihon king of the Amorites, who ruled in Heshbon, as far as the boundary of the Ammonites;

11And Gilead, and the region of the Geshurites and Maacathites, and all Mount Hermon, and all Bashan to Salecah—

12All the kingdom of Og in Bashan, who reigned in Ashtaroth and Edrei and alone was left of the Rephaim [giants]; for these Moses had defeated and driven out.

13Yet the Israelites did not drive out the Geshurites or the Maacathites, but Geshur and Maacath dwell among [them] still.

14Only to the tribe of Levi Moses gave no inheritance; the sacrifices made by fire to the Lord, the God of Israel, are their inheritance, as He said to him.

15And Moses gave an inheritance to the tribe of the Reubenites according to their families:

16Their territory was from Aroer on the edge of the Valley of the [river] Arnon, and the city in the midst of the valley, and all the tableland by Medeba;

17With Heshbon and all its cities which are on the plain; Dibon, Bamoth-baal, and Beth-baal-meon,

18Jahaz, Kedemoth, Mephaath,

19Kiriathaim, Sibmah, and Zereth-shahar on the hill of the valley,

20Beth-peor, Pisgah's slopes, and Beth-jeshimoth,

21All the cities of the plain and all the kingdom of Sihon king of the Amorites, who ruled in Heshbon, whom Moses defeated along with the leaders of Midian, Evi, Rekem, Zur, Hur, and Reba, the princes of Sihon who lived in the land.

22Balaam son of Beor, the soothsayer, the Israelites also killed with the sword among the rest of their slain. [Num. 31:16.]

23And the border of the Reubenites was the Jordan. This was the inheritance of the Reubenites according to their families, with their cities and villages.

24Moses gave an inheritance also to the tribe of the Gadites according to their families.

25Their territory was Jazer, and all the cities of Gilead, and half the land of the Ammonites as far as Aroer east of Rabbah;

26And from Heshbon to Ramath-mizpeh and Betonim, and from Mahanaim to the territory of Debir;

27And in the valley, Beth-haram, Beth-nimrah, Succoth, and Zaphon, the rest of the realm of Sihon king of Heshbon, with the Jordan as a boundary, to the lower end of the Sea of Chinnereth east of the Jordan.

28This is the inheritance of the Gadites according to their families, with their cities and villages.

29And Moses gave an inheritance to the half-tribe of Manasseh; it was allotted to them according to their families.

30Their region extended from Mahanaim through all Bashan, the entire kingdom of Og king of Bashan, and all the towns of Jair, which are in Bashan, sixty cities;

31And half of Gilead, and Ashtaroth and Edrei, cities of the kingdom of Og in Bashan; these were allotted to the people of Machir son of Manasseh for half of the Machirites according to their families.

---

*m*Or, The high places of Baal, and house of Baal-meon   *n*Or, Springs of Pisgah, or, The hill   *o*Or, diviner

New American Standard

8 ¶ With the other half-tribe, the Reubenites and the Gadites received their inheritance which Moses gave them beyond the Jordan to the east, just as Moses the servant of the LORD gave to them;

9 from Aroer, which is on the edge of the valley of the Arnon, with the city which is in the middle of the valley, and all the plain of Medeba, as far as Dibon;

10 and all the cities of Sihon king of the Amorites, who reigned in Heshbon, as far as the border of the sons of Ammon;

11 and Gilead, and the territory of the Geshurites and Maacathites, and all Mount Hermon, and all Bashan as far as Salecah;

12 all the kingdom of Og in Bashan, who reigned in Ashtaroth and in Edrei (he alone was left of the remnant of the Rephaim); for Moses struck them and dispossessed them.

13 But the sons of Israel did not dispossess the Geshurites or the Maacathites; for Geshur and Maacath live among Israel until this day.

14 Only to the tribe of Levi he did not give an inheritance; the offerings by fire to the LORD, the God of Israel, are their inheritance, as He spoke to him.

15 ¶ So Moses gave an inheritance to the tribe of the sons of Reuben according to their families.

16 Their territory was from Aroer, which is on the edge of the valley of the Arnon, with the city which is in the middle of the valley and all the plain by Medeba;

17 Heshbon, and all its cities which are on the plain: Dibon and Bamoth-baal and Beth-baal-meon,

18 and Jahaz and Kedemoth and Mephaath,

19 and Kiriathaim and Sibmah and Zereth-shahar on the hill of the valley,

20 and Beth-peor and the slopes of Pisgah and Beth-jeshimoth,

21 even all the cities of the plain and all the kingdom of Sihon king of the Amorites who reigned in Heshbon, whom Moses struck with the chiefs of Midian, Evi and Rekem and Zur and Hur and Reba, the princes of Sihon, who lived in the land.

22 The sons of Israel also killed Balaam the son of Beor, the diviner, with the sword among the rest of their slain.

23 The border of the sons of Reuben was the Jordan. This was the inheritance of the sons of Reuben according to their families, the cities and their villages.

24 ¶ Moses also gave an inheritance to the tribe of Gad, to the sons of Gad, according to their families.

25 Their territory was Jazer, and all the cities of Gilead, and half the land of the sons of Ammon, as far as Aroer which is before Rabbah;

26 and from Heshbon as far as Ramath-mizpeh and Bet-onim, and from Mahanaim as far as the border of Debir;

27 and in the valley, Beth-haram and Beth-nimrah and Succoth and Zaphon, the rest of the kingdom of Sihon king of Heshbon, with the Jordan as a border, as far as the lower end of the Sea of Chinnereth beyond the Jordan to the east.

28 This is the inheritance of the sons of Gad according to their families, the cities and their villages.

29 ¶ Moses also gave an inheritance to the half-tribe of Manasseh; and it was for the half-tribe of the sons of Manasseh according to their families.

30 Their territory was from Mahanaim, all Bashan, all the kingdom of Og king of Bashan, and all the towns of Jair, which are in Bashan, sixty cities;

31 also half of Gilead, with Ashtaroth and Edrei, the cities of the kingdom of Og in Bashan, were for the sons of Machir the son of Manasseh, for half of the sons of Machir according to their families.

New International

Division of the Land East of the Jordan

8 The other half of Manasseh,[k] the Reubenites and the Gadites had received the inheritance that Moses had given them east of the Jordan, as he, the servant of the LORD, had assigned it to them.

9 It extended from Aroer on the rim of the Arnon Gorge, and from the town in the middle of the gorge, and included the whole plateau of Medeba as far as Dibon, 10 and all the towns of Sihon king of the Amorites, who ruled in Heshbon, out to the border of the Ammonites. 11 It also included Gilead, the territory of the people of Geshur and Maacah, all of Mount Hermon and all Bashan as far as Salecah— 12 that is, the whole kingdom of Og in Bashan, who had reigned in Ashtaroth and Edrei and had survived as one of the last of the Rephaites. Moses had defeated them and taken over their land. 13 But the Israelites did not drive out the people of Geshur and Maacah, so they continue to live among the Israelites to this day.

14 But to the tribe of Levi he gave no inheritance, since the offerings made by fire to the LORD, the God of Israel, are their inheritance, as he promised them.

15 This is what Moses had given to the tribe of Reuben, clan by clan:

16 The territory from Aroer on the rim of the Arnon Gorge, and from the town in the middle of the gorge, and the whole plateau past Medeba 17 to Heshbon and all its towns on the plateau, including Dibon, Bamoth Baal, Beth Baal Meon, 18 Jahaz, Kedemoth, Mephaath, 19 Kiriathaim, Sibmah, Zereth Shahar on the hill in the valley, 20 Beth Peor, the slopes of Pisgah, and Beth Jeshimoth 21—all the towns on the plateau and the entire realm of Sihon king of the Amorites, who ruled at Heshbon. Moses had defeated him and the Midianite chiefs, Evi, Rekem, Zur, Hur and Reba—princes allied with Sihon—who lived in that country. 22 In addition to those slain in battle, the Israelites had put to the sword Balaam son of Beor, who practiced divination. 23 The boundary of the Reubenites was the bank of the Jordan. These towns and their villages were the inheritance of the Reubenites, clan by clan.

24 This is what Moses had given to the tribe of Gad, clan by clan:

25 The territory of Jazer, all the towns of Gilead and half the Ammonite country as far as Aroer, near Rabbah; 26 and from Heshbon to Ramath Mizpah and Betonim, and from Mahanaim to the territory of Debir; 27 and in the valley, Beth Haram, Beth Nimrah, Succoth and Zaphon with the rest of the realm of Sihon king of Heshbon (the east side of the Jordan, the territory up to the end of the Sea of Kinnereth[l]). 28 These towns and their villages were the inheritance of the Gadites, clan by clan.

29 This is what Moses had given to the half-tribe of Manasseh, that is, to half the family of the descendants of Manasseh, clan by clan:

30 The territory extending from Mahanaim and including all of Bashan, the entire realm of Og king of Bashan—all the settlements of Jair in Bashan, sixty towns, 31 half of Gilead, and Ashtaroth and Edrei (the royal cities of Og in Bashan). This was for the descendants of Makir son of Manasseh—for half of the sons of Makir, clan by clan.

---

k 8 Hebrew With it (that is, with the other half of Manasseh)
l 27 That is, Galilee

King James	Amplified

King James

³²These *are the countries* which Moses did distribute for inheritance in the plains of Moab, on the other side Jordan, by Jericho, eastward.

³³But unto the tribe of Levi Moses gave not *any* inheritance: the Lᴏʀᴅ God of Israel *was* their inheritance, as he said unto them.

Land west of the Jordan

14 AND THESE *are the countries* which the children of Israel inherited in the land of Canaan, which Eleazar the priest, and Joshua the son of Nun, and the heads of the fathers of the tribes of the children of Israel, distributed for inheritance to them.

²By lot *was* their inheritance, as the Lᴏʀᴅ commanded by the hand of Moses, for the nine tribes, and *for* the half tribe.

³For Moses had given the inheritance of two tribes and an half tribe on the other side Jordan: but unto the Levites he gave none inheritance among them.

⁴For the children of Joseph were two tribes, Manasseh and Ephraim: therefore they gave no part unto the Levites in the land, save cities to dwell *in,* with their suburbs for their cattle and for their substance.

⁵As the Lᴏʀᴅ commanded Moses, so the children of Israel did, and they divided the land.

6 ¶ Then the children of Judah came unto Joshua in Gilgal: and Caleb the son of Jephunneh the Kenezite said unto him, Thou knowest the thing that the Lᴏʀᴅ said unto Moses the man of God concerning me and thee in Kadesh-barnea.

⁷Forty years old *was* I when Moses the servant of the Lᴏʀᴅ sent me from Kadesh-barnea to espy out the land; and I brought him word again as *it was* in mine heart.

⁸Nevertheless my brethren that went up with me made the heart of the people melt: but I wholly followed the Lᴏʀᴅ my God.

⁹And Moses sware on that day, saying, Surely the land whereon thy feet have trodden shall be thine inheritance, and thy children's for ever, because thou hast wholly followed the Lᴏʀᴅ my God.

¹⁰And now, behold, the Lᴏʀᴅ hath kept me alive, as he said, these forty and five years, even since the Lᴏʀᴅ spake this word unto Moses, while *the children of* Israel ᵖwandered in the wilderness: and now, lo, I *am* this day fourscore and five years old.

¹¹As yet I *am as* strong this day as *I was* in the day that Moses sent me: as my strength *was* then, even so *is* my strength now, for war, both to go out, and to come in.

¹²Now therefore give me this mountain, whereof the Lᴏʀᴅ spake in that day; for thou heardest in that day how the Anakims *were* there, and *that* the cities *were* great *and* fenced: if so be the Lᴏʀᴅ *will be* with me, then I shall be able to drive them out, as the Lᴏʀᴅ said.

¹³And Joshua blessed him, and gave unto Caleb the son of Jephunneh Hebron for an inheritance.

¹⁴Hebron therefore became the inheritance of Caleb the son of Jephunneh the Kenezite unto this day, because that he wholly followed the Lᴏʀᴅ God of Israel.

¹⁵And the name of Hebron before *was* Kirjath-arba; *which Arba was* a great man among the Anakims. And the land had rest from war.

The borders of Judah

15 THIS THEN was the lot of the tribe of the children of Judah by their families; *even* to the border of Edom the wilderness of Zin southward *was* the uttermost part of the south coast.

²And their south border was from the shore of the salt sea, from the ᵍbay that looketh southward:

Amplified

³²These are the inheritances which Moses distributed in the plains of Moab beyond the Jordan east of Jericho.

³³But to the tribe of Levi, Moses gave no inheritance; the Lord, the God of Israel, is their inheritance, as He told them.

14 THESE ARE the inheritances in the land of Canaan distributed to the Israelites by Eleazar the priest, Joshua son of Nun, and the heads of the fathers' houses of their tribes.

²Their inheritance was by lot, as the Lord commanded Moses, for the nine and one-half tribes.

³For Moses had given an inheritance to the two and one-half tribes beyond the Jordan, but to the Levites he gave no inheritance among them,

⁴For the people of Joseph were two tribes, Manasseh and Ephraim. And no part was given in the land to the Levites except cities in which to live, with their pasturelands for their livestock and for their possessions.

⁵As the Lord commanded Moses, so the Israelites did, and they divided the land.

⁶Then the people of Judah came to Joshua in Gilgal, and Caleb son of Jephunneh the Kenizzite said to him, You know what the Lord said to Moses the man of God concerning me and you in Kadesh-barnea.

⁷Forty years old was I when Moses the servant of the Lord sent me from Kadesh-barnea to scout out the land. And I brought him a report as it was in my heart.

⁸But my brethren who went up with me made the hearts of the people melt; yet I wholly followed the Lord my God.

⁹And Moses swore on that day, Surely the land on which your feet have walked shall be an inheritance to you and your children always, because you have wholly followed the Lord my God. [Deut. 1:35, 36.]

¹⁰And now, behold, the Lord has kept me alive, as He said, these forty-five years since the Lord spoke this word to Moses, while the Israelites wandered in the wilderness; and now, behold, I am this day eighty-five years old.

¹¹Yet I am as strong today as I was the day Moses sent me; as my strength was then, so is my strength now for war and to go out and to come in.

¹²So now give me this hill country of which the Lord spoke that day. For you heard then how the [giantlike] Anakim were there and that the cities were great and fortified; if the Lord will be with me, I shall drive them out just as the Lord said.

¹³Then Joshua blessed him and gave Hebron to Caleb son of Jephunneh for an inheritance.

¹⁴So Hebron became the inheritance of Caleb son of Jephunneh the Kenizzite to this day, because he wholly followed the Lord, the God of Israel.

¹⁵The name of Hebron before was Kiriath-arba [city of Arba]. This Arba was the greatest of the Anakim. And the land had rest from war.

15 THE LOT for the tribe of Judah according to its families reached southward to the boundary of Edom, to the Wilderness of Zin at its most southern part.

²And their south boundary was from the end of the Salt [Dead] Sea, from the bay that faces southward;

ᵖHeb. *walked*   ᵍHeb. *tongue*

New American Standard

32 ¶ These are *the territories* which Moses apportioned for an inheritance in the plains of Moab, beyond the Jordan at Jericho to the east.

33 But to the tribe of Levi, Moses did not give an inheritance; the LORD, the God of Israel, is their inheritance, as He had promised to them.

Caleb's Request

14 NOW THESE are *the territories* which the sons of Israel inherited in the land of Canaan, which Eleazar the priest, and Joshua the son of Nun, and the heads of the households of the tribes of the sons of Israel apportioned to them for an inheritance,

2 by the lot of their inheritance, as the LORD commanded through Moses, for the nine tribes and the half-tribe.

3 For Moses had given the inheritance of the two tribes and the half-tribe beyond the Jordan; but he did not give an inheritance to the Levites among them.

4 For the sons of Joseph were two tribes, Manasseh and Ephraim, and they did not give a portion to the Levites in the land, except cities to live in, with their pasture lands for their livestock and for their property.

5 Thus the sons of Israel did just as the LORD had commanded Moses, and they divided the land.

6 ¶ Then the sons of Judah drew near to Joshua in Gilgal, and Caleb the son of Jephunneh the Kenizzite said to him, "You know the word which the LORD spoke to Moses the man of God concerning you and me in Kadesh-barnea.

7 "I was forty years old when Moses the servant of the LORD sent me from Kadesh-barnea to spy out the land, and I brought word back to him as *it was* in my heart.

8 "Nevertheless my brethren who went up with me made the heart of the people melt with fear; but I followed the LORD my God fully.

9 "So Moses swore on that day, saying, 'Surely the land on which your foot has trodden will be an inheritance to you and to your children forever, because you have followed the LORD my God fully.'

10 "Now behold, the LORD has let me live, just as He spoke, these forty-five years, from the time that the LORD spoke this word to Moses, when Israel walked in the wilderness; and now behold, I am eighty-five years old today.

11 "I am still as strong today as I was in the day Moses sent me; as my strength was then, so my strength is now, for war and for going out and coming in.

12 "Now then, give me this hill country about which the LORD spoke on that day, for you heard on that day that Anakim *were* there, with great fortified cities; perhaps the LORD will be with me, and I will drive them out as the LORD has spoken."

13 ¶ So Joshua blessed him and gave Hebron to Caleb the son of Jephunneh for an inheritance.

14 Therefore, Hebron became the inheritance of Caleb the son of Jephunneh the Kenizzite until this day, because he followed the LORD God of Israel fully.

15 Now the name of Hebron was formerly Kiriath-arba; *for Arba* was the greatest man among the Anakim. Then the land had rest from war.

Territory of Judah

15 NOW THE lot for the tribe of the sons of Judah according to their families reached the border of Edom, southward to the wilderness of Zin at the extreme south.

2 Their south border was from the lower end of the Salt Sea, from the bay that turns to the south.

New International

32 This is the inheritance Moses had given when he was in the plains of Moab across the Jordan east of Jericho.

33 But to the tribe of Levi, Moses had given no inheritance; the LORD, the God of Israel, is their inheritance, as he promised them.

Division of the Land West of the Jordan

14 NOW THESE are the areas the Israelites received as an inheritance in the land of Canaan, which Eleazar the priest, Joshua son of Nun and the heads of the tribal clans of Israel allotted to them. 2 Their inheritances were assigned by lot to the nine-and-a-half tribes, as the LORD had commanded through Moses. 3 Moses had granted the two-and-a-half tribes their inheritance east of the Jordan but had not granted the Levites an inheritance among the rest, 4 for the sons of Joseph had become two tribes—Manasseh and Ephraim. The Levites received no share of the land but only towns to live in, with pasturelands for their flocks and herds. 5 So the Israelites divided the land, just as the LORD had commanded Moses.

Hebron Given to Caleb

6 Now the men of Judah approached Joshua at Gilgal, and Caleb son of Jephunneh the Kenizzite said to him, "You know what the LORD said to Moses the man of God at Kadesh Barnea about you and me. 7 I was forty years old when Moses the servant of the LORD sent me from Kadesh Barnea to explore the land. And I brought him back a report according to my convictions, 8 but my brothers who went up with me made the hearts of the people melt with fear. I, however, followed the LORD my God wholeheartedly. 9 So on that day Moses swore to me, 'The land on which your feet have walked will be your inheritance and that of your children forever, because you have followed the LORD my God wholeheartedly.'[m]

10 "Now then, just as the LORD promised, he has kept me alive for forty-five years since the time he said this to Moses, while Israel moved about in the desert. So here I am today, eighty-five years old! 11 I am still as strong today as the day Moses sent me out; I'm just as vigorous to go out to battle now as I was then. 12 Now give me this hill country that the LORD promised me that day. You yourself heard then that the Anakites were there and their cities were large and fortified, but, the LORD helping me, I will drive them out just as he said."

13 Then Joshua blessed Caleb son of Jephunneh and gave him Hebron as his inheritance. 14 So Hebron has belonged to Caleb son of Jephunneh the Kenizzite ever since, because he followed the LORD, the God of Israel, wholeheartedly. 15 (Hebron used to be called Kiriath Arba after Arba, who was the greatest man among the Anakites.)

Then the land had rest from war.

Allotment for Judah

15 THE ALLOTMENT for the tribe of Judah, clan by clan, extended down to the territory of Edom, to the Desert of Zin in the extreme south.

2 Their southern boundary started from the bay at the southern end of the Salt Sea,[n] 3 crossed south of Scor-

---

m 9 Deut. 1:36   *n 2* That is, the Dead Sea; also in verse 5

King James

³And it went out to the south side to ^rMaaleh-acrabbim, and passed along to Zin, and ascended up on the south side unto Kadesh-barnea, and passed along to Hezron, and went up to Adar, and fetched a compass to Karkaa:

⁴*From thence* it passed toward Azmon, and went out unto the river of Egypt; and the goings out of that coast were at the sea: this shall be your south coast.

⁵And the east border *was* the salt sea, *even* unto the end of Jordan. And *their* border in the north quarter *was* from the bay of the sea at the uttermost part of Jordan:

⁶And the border went up to Beth-hoglah, and passed along by the north by Beth-arabah; and the border went up to the stone of Bohan the son of Reuben:

⁷And the border went up toward Debir from the valley of Achor, and so northward, looking toward Gilgal, that *is* before the going up to Adummim, which *is* on the south side of the river: and the border passed toward the waters of En-shemesh, and the goings out thereof were at En-rogel:

⁸And the border went up by the valley of the son of Hinnom unto the south side of the Jebusite; the same *is* Jerusalem: and the border went up to the top of the mountain that *lieth* before the valley of Hinnom westward, which *is* at the end of the valley of the giants northward:

⁹And the border was drawn from the top of the hill unto the fountain of the water of Nephtoah, and went out to the cities of mount Ephron; and the border was drawn to Baalah, which *is* Kirjath-jearim:

¹⁰And the border compassed from Baalah westward unto mount Seir, and passed along unto the side of mount Jearim, which *is* Chesalon, on the north side, and went down to Beth-shemesh, and passed on to Timnah:

¹¹And the border went out unto the side of Ekron northward: and the border was drawn to Shicron, and passed along to mount Baalah, and went out unto Jabneel; and the goings out of the border were at the sea.

¹²And the west border *was* to the great sea, and the coast *thereof.* This *is* the coast of the children of Judah round about according to their families.

¹³ ¶ And unto Caleb the son of Jephunneh he gave a part among the children of Judah, according to the commandment of the LORD to Joshua, *even* ^sthe city of Arba the father of Anak, which *city is* Hebron.

¹⁴And Caleb drove thence the three sons of Anak, Sheshai, and Ahiman, and Talmai, the children of Anak.

¹⁵And he went up thence to the inhabitants of Debir: and the name of Debir before *was* Kirjath-sepher.

¹⁶ ¶ And Caleb said, He that smiteth Kirjath-sepher, and taketh it, to him will I give Achsah my daughter to wife.

¹⁷And Othniel the son of Kenaz, the brother of Caleb, took it: and he gave him Achsah his daughter to wife.

¹⁸And it came to pass, as she came *unto him,* that she moved him to ask of her father a field: and she lighted off *her* ass; and Caleb said unto her, What wouldest thou?

¹⁹Who answered, Give me a blessing; for thou hast given me a south land; give me also springs of water. And he gave her the upper springs, and the nether springs.

²⁰This *is* the inheritance of the tribe of the children of Judah according to their families.

²¹And the uttermost cities of the tribe of the children of Judah toward the coast of Edom southward were Kabzeel, and Eder, and Jagur,

²²And Kinah, and Dimonah, and Adadah,

²³And Kedesh, and Hazor, and Ithnan,

²⁴Ziph, and Telem, and Bealoth,

²⁵And Hazor, Hadattah, and Kerioth, *and* Hezron, which *is* Hazor,

²⁶Amam, and Shema, and Moladah,

²⁷And Hazar-gaddah, and Heshmon, and Beth-palet,

²⁸And Hazar-shual, and Beer-sheba, and Bizjothjah,

²⁹Baalah, and Iim, and Azem,

Amplified

³It went out south of the ascent of Akrabbim, passed along to Zin, and went up south of Kadesh-barnea, along by Hezron, up to Addar, and turned about to Karka.

⁴Passed along to Azmon, went out by the Brook of Egypt, and ended at the sea. This was their southern frontier.

⁵The eastern boundary was the Salt [Dead] Sea as far as the mouth of the Jordan. The northern boundary was from the bay of the sea at the mouth of the Jordan.

⁶And the boundary went up to Beth-hogla and passed along north of Beth-arabah and [it] went up to the [landmark] Stone of Bohan son of Reuben.

⁷And the boundary went up to Debir from the Valley of Achor, and so northward, turning toward Gilgal, which is opposite the ascent to Adummim on the south side of the valley; and it passed on to the waters of En-shemesh and ended at En-rogel.

⁸Then the boundary went up by the Valley of Ben-hinnom [son of Hinnom] at the southern shoulder of the Jebusite [city]—that is, Jerusalem; and the boundary went up to the top of the mountain that lies before the Valley of Hinnom on the west, at the northern end of the Valley of Rephaim.

⁹Then the boundary extended from the top of the mountain to the spring of the waters of Nephtoah and went on to the cities of Mount Ephron; then it bent round to Baalah, that is, Kiriath-jearim.

¹⁰And the boundary went around west of Baalah to Mount Seir, passed along to the northern side of Mount Jearim, which is Chesalon, went down to Beth-shemesh, and then passed on by Timnah.

¹¹And the boundary went out to the shoulder of the hill north of Ekron, then bent round to Shikkeron, and passed along to Mount Baalah, and went out to Jabneel. Then the boundary ended at the sea.

¹²And the west boundary was the Great Sea with its coastline. This is the boundary round about the people of Judah according to their families.

¹³And to Caleb son of Jephunneh, [Joshua] gave a part among the people of Judah, as the Lord commanded [him]; it was Kiriath-arba, which is Hebron, [named for] Arba the father of Anak.

¹⁴And Caleb drove from there the three sons of Anak—Sheshai and Ahiman and Talmai—the descendants of Anak.

¹⁵He went up from there against the people of Debir. Debir was formerly named Kiriath-sepher.

¹⁶Caleb said, He who smites Kiriath-sepher and takes it, to him will I give Achsah my daughter as wife.

¹⁷And Othniel son of Kenaz, Caleb's brother, took it; and he gave him Achsah his daughter as wife.

¹⁸When Achsah came to Othniel, she got his consent to ask her father for a field. Then she returned to Caleb and when she lighted off her donkey, Caleb said, What do you wish?

¹⁹Achsah answered, Give me a present. Since you have set me in the [dry] Negeb, give me also springs of water. And he gave her the [sloping field with] upper and lower springs.

²⁰This is the inheritance of the tribe of Judah according to their families.

²¹The cities of the tribe of Judah in the extreme south toward the boundary of Edom were: Kabzeel, Eder, Jagur,

²²Kinah, Dimonah, Adadah,

²³Kedesh, Hazor, Ithnan,

²⁴Ziph, Telem, Bealoth,

²⁵Hazor-hadattah, Kerioth-hezron (Hazor),

²⁶Amam, Shema, Moladah,

²⁷Hazar-gaddah, Heshmon, Beth-pelet,

²⁸Hazar-shual, Beersheba, Biziothiah,

²⁹Baalah, Iim, Ezem,

New American Standard

3 Then it proceeded southward to the ascent of Akrab-bim and continued to Zin, then went up by the south of Kadesh-barnea and continued to Hezron, and went up to Addar and turned about to Karka.

4 It continued to Azmon and proceeded to the brook of Egypt, and the border ended at the sea. This shall be your south border.

5 The east border *was* the Salt Sea, as far as the mouth of the Jordan. And the border of the north side was from the bay of the sea at the mouth of the Jordan.

6 Then the border went up to Beth-hoglah, and continued on the north of Beth-arabah, and the border went up to the stone of Bohan the son of Reuben.

7 The border went up to Debir from the valley of Achor, and turned northward toward Gilgal which is opposite the ascent of Adummim, which is on the south of the valley; and the border continued to the waters of En-shemesh and it ended at En-rogel.

8 Then the border went up the valley of Ben-hinnom to the slope of the Jebusite on the south (that is, Jerusalem); and the border went up to the top of the mountain which is before the valley of Hinnom to the west, which is at the end of the valley of Rephaim toward the north.

9 From the top of the mountain the border curved to the spring of the waters of Nephtoah and proceeded to the cities of Mount Ephron, then the border curved to Baalah (that is, Kiriath-jearim).

10 The border turned about from Baalah westward to Mount Seir, and continued to the slope of Mount Jearim on the north (that is, Chesalon), and went down to Beth-shemesh and continued through Timnah.

11 The border proceeded to the side of Ekron northward. Then the border curved to Shikkeron and continued to Mount Baalah and proceeded to Jabneel, and the border ended at the sea.

12 The west border *was* at the Great Sea, even *its* coastline. This is the border around the sons of Judah according to their families.

13 ¶ Now he gave to Caleb the son of Jephunneh a portion among the sons of Judah, according to the command of the LORD to Joshua, *namely,* Kiriath-arba, *Arba being* the father of Anak (that is, Hebron).

14 Caleb drove out from there the three sons of Anak: Sheshai and Ahiman and Talmai, the children of Anak.

15 Then he went up from there against the inhabitants of Debir; now the name of Debir formerly was Kiriath-sepher.

16 And Caleb said, "The one who attacks Kiriath-sepher and captures it, I will give him Achsah my daughter as a wife."

17 Othniel the son of Kenaz, the brother of Caleb, captured it; so he gave him Achsah his daughter as a wife.

18 It came about that when she came *to him,* she persuaded him to ask her father for a field. So she alighted from the donkey, and Caleb said to her, "What do you want?"

19 Then she said, "Give me a blessing; since you have given me the land of the Negev, give me also springs of water." So he gave her the upper springs and the lower springs.

20 ¶ This is the inheritance of the tribe of the sons of Judah according to their families.

21 ¶ Now the cities at the extremity of the tribe of the sons of Judah toward the border of Edom in the south were Kabzeel and Eder and Jagur,

22 and Kinah and Dimonah and Adadah,

23 and Kedesh and Hazor and Ithnan,

24 Ziph and Telem and Bealoth,

25 and Hazar-hadattah and Kerioth-hezron (that is, Hazor),

26 Amam and Shema and Moladah,

27 and Hazar-gaddah and Heshmon and Beth-pelet,

28 and Hazar-shual and Beersheba and Biziothiah,

29 Baalah and Iim and Ezem,

New International

pion[o] Pass, continued on to Zin and went over to the south of Kadesh Barnea. Then it ran past Hezron up to Addar and curved around to Karka. 4It then passed along to Azmon and joined the Wadi of Egypt, ending at the sea. This is their[p] southern boundary.

5The eastern boundary is the Salt Sea as far as the mouth of the Jordan.

The northern boundary started from the bay of the sea at the mouth of the Jordan, 6went up to Beth Hoglah and continued north of Beth Arabah to the Stone of Bohan son of Reuben. 7The boundary then went up to Debir from the Valley of Achor and turned north to Gilgal, which faces the Pass of Adummim south of the gorge. It continued along to the waters of En Shemesh and came out at En Rogel. 8Then it ran up the Valley of Ben Hinnom along the southern slope of the Jebusite city (that is, Jerusalem). From there it climbed to the top of the hill west of the Hinnom Valley at the northern end of the Valley of Rephaim. 9From the hilltop the boundary headed toward the spring of the waters of Nephtoah, came out at the towns of Mount Ephron and went down toward Baalah (that is, Kiriath Jearim). 10Then it curved westward from Baalah to Mount Seir, ran along the northern slope of Mount Jearim (that is, Kesalon), continued down to Beth Shemesh and crossed to Timnah. 11It went to the northern slope of Ekron, turned toward Shikkeron, passed along to Mount Baalah and reached Jabneel. The boundary ended at the sea.

12The western boundary is the coastline of the Great Sea.[q]

These are the boundaries around the people of Judah by their clans.

13In accordance with the LORD's command to him, Joshua gave to Caleb son of Jephunneh a portion in Judah—Kiriath Arba, that is, Hebron. (Arba was the forefather of Anak.) 14From Hebron Caleb drove out the three Anakites—Sheshai, Ahiman and Talmai—descendants of Anak. 15From there he marched against the people living in Debir (formerly called Kiriath Sepher). 16And Caleb said, "I will give my daughter Acsah in marriage to the man who attacks and captures Kiriath Sepher." 17Othniel son of Kenaz, Caleb's brother, took it; so Caleb gave his daughter Acsah to him in marriage.

18One day when she came to Othniel, she urged him[r] to ask her father for a field. When she got off her donkey, Caleb asked her, "What can I do for you?"

19She replied, "Do me a special favor. Since you have given me land in the Negev, give me also springs of water." So Caleb gave her the upper and lower springs.

20This is the inheritance of the tribe of Judah, clan by clan:

21The southernmost towns of the tribe of Judah in the Negev toward the boundary of Edom were:

Kabzeel, Eder, Jagur, 22Kinah, Dimonah, Adadah, 23Kedesh, Hazor, Ithnan, 24Ziph, Telem, Bealoth, 25Hazor Hadattah, Kerioth Hezron (that is, Hazor), 26Amam, Shema, Moladah, 27Hazar Gaddah, Heshmon, Beth Pelet, 28Hazar Shual, Beersheba, Biziothi-

King James

30And Eltolad, and Chesil, and Hormah,

31And Ziklag, and Madmannah, and Sansannah,

32And Lebaoth, and Shilhim, and Ain, and Rimmon: all the cities *are* twenty and nine, with their villages:

33*And* in the valley, Eshtaol, and Zoreah, and Ashnah,

34And Zanoah, and En-gannim, Tappuah, and Enam,

35Jarmuth, and Adullam, Socoh, and Azekah,

36And Sharaim, and Adithaim, and Gederah, *and* Gederothaim; fourteen cities with their villages:

37Zenan, and Hadashah, and Migdal-gad,

38And Dilean, and Mizpeh, and Joktheel,

39Lachish, and Bozkath, and Eglon,

40And Cabbon, and Lahmam, and Kithlish,

41And Gederoth, Beth-dagon, and Naamah, and Makkedah; sixteen cities with their villages:

42Libnah, and Ether, and Ashan,

43And Jiphtah, and Ashnah, and Nezib,

44And Keilah, and Achzib, and Mareshah; nine cities with their villages:

45Ekron, with her towns and her villages:

46From Ekron even unto the sea, all that *lay* unear Ashdod, with their villages:

47Ashdod with her towns and her villages, Gaza with her towns and her villages, unto the river of Egypt, and the great sea, and the border *thereof:*

48 ¶ And in the mountains, Shamir, and Jattir, and Socoh,

49And Dannah, and Kirjath-sannah, which *is* Debir,

50And Anab, and Eshtemoh, and Anim,

51And Goshen, and Holon, and Giloh; eleven cities with their villages:

52Arab, and Dumah, and Eshean,

53And vJanum, and Beth-tappuah, and Aphekah,

54And Humtah, and Kirjath-arba, which *is* Hebron, and Zior; nine cities with their villages:

55Maon, Carmel, and Ziph, and Juttah,

56And Jezreel, and Jokdeam, and Zanoah,

57Cain, Gibeah, and Timnah; ten cities with their villages:

58Halhul, Beth-zur, and Gedor,

59And Maarath, and Beth-anoth, and Eltekon; six cities with their villages:

60Kirjath-baal, which *is* Kirjath-jearim, and Rabbah; two cities with their villages:

61In the wilderness, Beth-arabah, Middin, and Secacah,

62And Nibshan, and the city of Salt, and En-gedi; six cities with their villages.

63 ¶ As for the Jebusites the inhabitants of Jerusalem, the children of Judah could not drive them out: but the Jebusites dwell with the children of Judah at Jerusalem unto this day.

Ephraim and Manasseh

16 AND THE lot of the children of Joseph wfell from Jordan by Jericho, unto the water of Jericho on the east, to the wilderness that goeth up from Jericho throughout mount Beth-el,

2And goeth out from Beth-el to Luz, and passeth along unto the borders of Archi to Ataroth,

3And goeth down westward to the coast of Japhleti, unto the coast of Beth-horon the nether, and to Gezer: and the goings out thereof are at the sea.

4So the children of Joseph, Manasseh and Ephraim, took their inheritance.

5 ¶ And the border of the children of Ephraim according to their families was *thus:* even the border of their inheritance on the east side was Ataroth-addar, unto Beth-horon the upper;

6And the border went out toward the sea to Michmethah on the north side; and the border went about eastward unto Taanath-shiloh, and passed by it on the east to Janohah;

Amplified

30Eltolad, Chesil, Hormah,

31Ziklag, Madmannah, Sansannah,

32Lebaoth, Shilhim, Ain, and Rimmon. All the cities were twenty-nine [later thirty-six] with their villages.

33In the lowland: Eshtaol, Zorah, Ashnah,

34Zanoah, En-gannim, Tappuah, Enam,

35Jarmuth, Adullam, Socoh, Azekah,

36Shaaraim, Adithaim, and Gederah and Gederothaim; fourteen cities with their villages.

37Zenan, Hadashah, Migdal-gad,

38Dilean, Mizpah, Joktheel,

39Lachish, Bozkath, Eglon,

40Cabbon, Lahmas, Chitlish,

41Gederoth, Beth-dagon, Naamah, and Makkedah; sixteen cities with their villages.

42Libnah, Ether, Ashan,

43Iphtah, Ashnah, Nezib,

44Keilah, Achzib, and Mareshah; nine cities with their villages.

45Ekron, with its towns and villages.

46From Ekron to the sea, all that lay beside Ashdod, with their villages;

47Ashdod, with its towns and its villages; Gaza, with its towns and its villages, as far as the Brook of Egypt, and the Great [Mediterranean] Sea with its coastline.

48In the hill country: Shamir, Jattir, Socoh,

49Dannah, Kiriath-sannah (that is, Debir),

50Anab, Eshtemoh, Anim,

51Goshen, Holon, and Giloh; eleven cities with their villages.

52Arab, Dumah, Eshan,

53Janim, Beth-tappuah, Aphekah,

54Humtah, Kiriath-arba (that is, Hebron), and Zior; nine cities with their villages.

55Maon, Carmel, Ziph, Juttah,

56Jezreel, Jokdeam, Zanoah,

57Kain, Gibeah, and Timnah; ten cities with their villages.

58Halhul, Beth-zur, Gedor,

59Maarath, Beth-anoth, and Eltekon; six cities with their villages.

60Kiriath-baal (that is, Kiriath-jearim) and Rabbah; two cities with their villages.

61In the wilderness: Beth-arabah, Middin, Secacah,

62Nibshan, the City of Salt, and En-gedi; six cities with their villages.

63But the Jebusites, the inhabitants of Jerusalem, the people of Judah could not drive out; so the Jebusites dwell with the people of Judah at Jerusalem to this day.

16 THE ALLOTMENT for the people of Joseph went from the Jordan by Jericho, east of the waters of Jericho, into the wilderness, going up from Jericho into the hill country to Bethel;

2Then it went from Bethel to Luz and passed on to Ataroth, the border of the Archites.

3And it went down westward to the territory of the Japhletites as far as the outskirts of Lower Beth-horon, then to Gezer, and ended at the sea.

4The descendants of Joseph, Manasseh and Ephraim, received their inheritance.

5The boundary of the Ephraimites according to their families was thus: on the east side their border was Ataroth-addar as far as Upper Beth-horon.

6Then the boundary went from there to the sea; on the north was Michmethath; then on the east the boundary went out to Taanath-shiloh, and eastward to Janoah,

---

tOr, *or* uHeb. *by the place of* vOr, *Janus* wHeb. *went forth*

New American Standard

30 and Eltolad and Chesil and Hormah,
31 and Ziklag and Madmannah and Sansannah,
32 and Lebaoth and Shilhim and Ain and Rimmon; in all, twenty-nine cities with their villages.
33 ¶ In the lowland: Eshtaol and Zorah and Ashnah,
34 and Zanoah and En-gannim, Tappuah and Enam,
35 Jarmuth and Adullam, Socoh and Azekah,
36 and Shaaraim and Adithaim and Gederah and Gederothaim; fourteen cities with their villages.
37 ¶ Zenan and Hadashah and Migdal-gad,
38 and Dilean and Mizpeh and Joktheel,
39 Lachish and Bozkath and Eglon,
40 and Cabbon and Lahmas and Chitlish,
41 and Gederoth, Beth-dagon and Naamah and Makkedah; sixteen cities with their villages.
42 ¶ Libnah and Ether and Ashan,
43 and Iphtah and Ashnah and Nezib,
44 and Keilah and Achzib and Mareshah; nine cities with their villages.
45 ¶ Ekron, with its towns and its villages;
46 from Ekron even to the sea, all that were by the side of Ashdod, with their villages.
47 ¶ Ashdod, its towns and its villages; Gaza, its towns and its villages; as far as the brook of Egypt and the Great Sea, even *its* coastline.
48 ¶ In the hill country: Shamir and Jattir and Socoh,
49 and Dannah and Kiriath-sannah (that is, Debir),
50 and Anab and Eshtemoh and Anim,
51 and Goshen and Holon and Giloh; eleven cities with their villages.
52 ¶ Arab and Dumah and Eshan,
53 and Janum and Beth-tappuah and Aphekah,
54 and Humtah and Kiriath-arba (that is, Hebron), and Zior; nine cities with their villages.
55 ¶ Maon, Carmel and Ziph and Juttah,
56 and Jezreel and Jokdeam and Zanoah,
57 Kain, Gibeah and Timnah; ten cities with their villages.
58 ¶ Halhul, Beth-zur and Gedor,
59 and Maarath and Beth-anoth and Eltekon; six cities with their villages.
60 ¶ Kiriath-baal (that is, Kiriath-jearim), and Rabbah; two cities with their villages.
61 ¶ In the wilderness: Beth-arabah, Middin and Secacah,
62 and Nibshan and the City of Salt and Engedi; six cities with their villages.
63 ¶ Now as for the Jebusites, the inhabitants of Jerusalem, the sons of Judah could not drive them out; so the Jebusites live with the sons of Judah at Jerusalem until this day.

Territory of Ephraim

16 THEN THE lot for the sons of Joseph went from the Jordan at Jericho to the waters of Jericho on the east into the wilderness, going up from Jericho through the hill country to Bethel.
2 It went from Bethel to Luz, and continued to the border of the Archites at Ataroth.
3 It went down westward to the territory of the Japhletites, as far as the territory of lower Beth-horon even to Gezer, and it ended at the sea.
4 ¶ The sons of Joseph, Manasseh and Ephraim, received their inheritance.
5 Now *this* was the territory of the sons of Ephraim according to their families: the border of their inheritance eastward was Ataroth-addar, as far as upper Beth-horon.
6 Then the border went westward at Michmethath on the north, and the border turned about eastward to Taanath-shiloh and continued *beyond* it to the east of Janoah.

New International

ah, 29Baalah, Iim, Ezem, 30Eltolad, Kesil, Hormah, 31Ziklag, Madmannah, Sansannah, 32Lebaoth, Shilhim, Ain and Rimmon—a total of twenty-nine towns and their villages.
33In the western foothills:
   Eshtaol, Zorah, Ashnah, 34Zanoah, En Gannim, Tappuah, Enam, 35Jarmuth, Adullam, Socoh, Azekah, 36Shaaraim, Adithaim and Gederah (or Gederothaim)*s*—fourteen towns and their villages.
37Zenan, Hadashah, Migdal Gad, 38Dilean, Mizpah, Joktheel, 39Lachish, Bozkath, Eglon, 40Cabbon, Lahmas, Kitlish, 41Gederoth, Beth Dagon, Naamah and Makkedah—sixteen towns and their villages.
42Libnah, Ether, Ashan, 43Iphtah, Ashnah, Nezib, 44Keilah, Aczib and Mareshah—nine towns and their villages.
45Ekron, with its surrounding settlements and villages; 46west of Ekron, all that were in the vicinity of Ashdod, together with their villages; 47Ashdod, its surrounding settlements and villages; and Gaza, its settlements and villages, as far as the Wadi of Egypt and the coastline of the Great Sea.
48In the hill country:
   Shamir, Jattir, Socoh, 49Dannah, Kiriath Sannah (that is, Debir), 50Anab, Eshtemoh, Anim, 51Goshen, Holon and Giloh—eleven towns and their villages.
52Arab, Dumah, Eshan, 53Janim, Beth Tappuah, Aphekah, 54Humtah, Kiriath Arba (that is, Hebron) and Zior—nine towns and their villages.
55Maon, Carmel, Ziph, Juttah, 56Jezreel, Jokdeam, Zanoah, 57Kain, Gibeah and Timnah—ten towns and their villages.
58Halhul, Beth Zur, Gedor, 59Maarath, Beth Anoth and Eltekon—six towns and their villages.
60Kiriath Baal (that is, Kiriath Jearim) and Rabbah—two towns and their villages.
61In the desert:
   Beth Arabah, Middin, Secacah, 62Nibshan, the City of Salt and En Gedi—six towns and their villages.
63Judah could not dislodge the Jebusites, who were living in Jerusalem; to this day the Jebusites live there with the people of Judah.

Allotment for Ephraim and Manasseh

16 THE ALLOTMENT for Joseph began at the Jordan of Jericho,*t* east of the waters of Jericho, and went up from there through the desert into the hill country of Bethel. 2It went on from Bethel (that is, Luz),*u* crossed over to the territory of the Arkites in Ataroth, 3descended westward to the territory of the Japhletites as far as the region of Lower Beth Horon and on to Gezer, ending at the sea.
4So Manasseh and Ephraim, the descendants of Joseph, received their inheritance.

5This was the territory of Ephraim, clan by clan:
   The boundary of their inheritance went from Ataroth Addar in the east to Upper Beth Horon 6and continued to the sea. From Micmethath on the north it curved eastward to Taanath Shiloh, passing by it to

---

s 36 Or *Gederah and Gederothaim*   *t 1 Jordan of Jericho* was possibly an ancient name for the Jordan River.   *u 2* Septuagint; Hebrew *Bethel to Luz*

<table>
<tr><td>

King James

</td><td>

Amplified

</td></tr>
</table>

King James

7And it went down from Janohah to Ataroth, and to Naarath, and came to Jericho, and went out at Jordan.

8The border went out from Tappuah westward unto the river Kanah; and the goings out thereof were at the sea. This *is* the inheritance of the tribe of the children of Ephraim by their families.

9And the separate cities for the children of Ephraim *were* among the inheritance of the children of Manasseh, all the cities with their villages.

10And they drave not out the Canaanites that dwelt in Gezer; but the Canaanites dwell among the Ephraimites unto this day, and serve under tribute.

17 THERE WAS also a lot for the tribe of Manasseh; for he *was* the firstborn of Joseph; *to wit,* for Machir the firstborn of Manasseh, the father of Gilead: because he was a man of war, therefore he had Gilead and Bashan.

2There was also *a lot* for the rest of the children of Manasseh by their families; for the children of ˣAbiezer, and for the children of Helek, and for the children of Asriel, and for the children of Shechem, and for the children of Hepher, and for the children of Shemida: these *were* the male children of Manasseh the son of Joseph by their families.

3 ¶ But Zelophehad, the son of Hepher, the son of Gilead, the son of Machir, the son of Manasseh, had no sons, but daughters: and these *are* the names of his daughters, Mahlah, and Noah, Hoglah, Milcah, and Tirzah.

4And they came near before Eleazar the priest, and before Joshua the son of Nun, and before the princes, saying, The LORD commanded Moses to give us an inheritance among our brethren. Therefore according to the commandment of the LORD he gave them an inheritance among the brethren of their father.

5And there fell ten portions to Manasseh, beside the land of Gilead and Bashan, which *were* on the other side Jordan;

6Because the daughters of Manasseh had an inheritance among his sons: and the rest of Manasseh's sons had the land of Gilead.

7 ¶ And the coast of Manasseh was from Asher to Michmethah, that *lieth* before Shechem; and the border went along on the right hand unto the inhabitants of Entappuah.

8*Now* Manasseh had the land of Tappuah: but Tappuah on the border of Manasseh *belonged* to the children of Ephraim;

9And the coast descended unto the ʸriver Kanah, southward of the river: these cities of Ephraim *are* among the cities of Manasseh: the coast of Manasseh also *was* on the north side of the river, and the outgoings of it were at the sea:

10Southward *it was* Ephraim's, and northward *it was* Manasseh's, and the sea is his border; and they met together in Asher on the north, and in Issachar on the east.

11And Manasseh had in Issachar and in Asher Bethshean and her towns, and Ibleam and her towns, and the inhabitants of Dor and her towns, and the inhabitants of En-dor and her towns, and the inhabitants of Taanach and her towns, and the inhabitants of Megiddo and her towns, *even* three countries.

12Yet the children of Manasseh could not drive out *the inhabitants of* those cities; but the Canaanites would dwell in that land.

13Yet it came to pass, when the children of Israel were waxen strong, that they put the Canaanites to tribute; but did not utterly drive them out.

Amplified

7Then it went down from Janoah to Ataroth and to Naarah, touched Jericho, and ended at the Jordan [River].

8The border went out from Tappuah westward to the brook Kanah and ended at the [Mediterranean] Sea. This is the inheritance of the Ephraimites by their families,

9With the towns set apart for the Ephraimites within the inheritance of the Manassites, all those towns with their villages.

10But they did not drive out the Canaanites who dwelt in Gezer; but the Canaanites dwell among the Ephraimites to this day, and they became slaves required to do forced labor.

17 ALLOTMENT WAS made for the tribe of Manasseh, for he was the firstborn of Joseph. To Machir the firstborn of Manasseh, the father of Gilead, were allotted Gilead and Bashan because he was a man of war.

2Allotment was also made for the other Manassites by their families—for the sons of Abiezer, of Helek, Asriel, Shechem, Hepher, and Shemida, the male offspring of Manasseh son of Joseph by their families.

3But Zelophehad son of Hepher, the son of Gilead, the son of Machir, the son of Manasseh, had no sons but only daughters; their names were Mahlah, Noah, Hoglah, Milcah, and Tirzah.

4They came before Eleazar the priest and Joshua son of Nun and the leaders and said, The Lord commanded Moses to give us an inheritance with our brethren. So according to the Lord's command, Joshua gave them an inheritance among their father's brethren.

5So there fell ten portions to Manasseh besides the land of Gilead and Bashan, which is on the other side of the Jordan,

6Because the [five] daughters of Manasseh received an inheritance among his [five] sons. The land of Gilead belonged to the other [half] of the Manassites.

7The territory of Manasseh reached from Asher to Michmethah east of Shechem; and the border went along southward to the inhabitants of En-tappuah.

8The land of Tappuah belonged to Manasseh, but the town of Tappuah on the border of Manasseh belonged to the Ephraimites.

9Then the boundary went down to the brook Kanah. The cities south of the brook lying among the cities of Manasseh belonged to Ephraim. But Manasseh's boundary went on north of the brook and ended at the sea.

10The land to the south was Ephraim's and that to the north was Manasseh's, and the sea was the boundary; on the north Asher was reached, and on the east Issachar.

11Also Manasseh had in Issachar and in Asher [these six towns], their inhabitants and their villages: Beth-shean, Ibleam, Dor, Endor, Taanach, and Megiddo.

12Yet the sons of Manasseh could not drive out the inhabitants of those cities, but the Canaanites persisted in dwelling in that land.

13When the Israelites became strong, they put the Canaanites to forced labor but did not utterly drive them out.

New American Standard

7 It went down from Janoah to Ataroth and to Naarah, then reached Jericho and came out at the Jordan. 8 From Tappuah the border continued westward to the brook of Kanah, and it ended at the sea. This is the inheritance of the tribe of the sons of Ephraim according to their families, 9 *together* with the cities which were set apart for the sons of Ephraim in the midst of the inheritance of the sons of Manasseh, all the cities with their villages. 10 But they did not drive out the Canaanites who lived in Gezer, so the Canaanites live in the midst of Ephraim to this day, and they became forced laborers.

Territory of Manasseh

17 NOW *THIS* was the lot for the tribe of Manasseh, for he was the firstborn of Joseph. To Machir the firstborn of Manasseh, the father of Gilead, were allotted Gilead and Bashan, because he was a man of war. 2 So *the lot* was *made* for the rest of the sons of Manasseh according to their families: for the sons of Abiezer and for the sons of Helek and for the sons of Asriel and for the sons of Shechem and for the sons of Hepher and for the sons of Shemida; these *were* the male descendants of Manasseh the son of Joseph according to their families.

3 ¶ However, Zelophehad, the son of Hepher, the son of Gilead, the son of Machir, the son of Manasseh, had no sons, only daughters; and these are the names of his daughters: Mahlah and Noah, Hoglah, Milcah and Tirzah. 4 They came near before Eleazar the priest and before Joshua the son of Nun and before the leaders, saying, "The LORD commanded Moses to give us an inheritance among our brothers." So according to the command of the LORD he gave them an inheritance among their father's brothers. 5 Thus there fell ten portions to Manasseh, besides the land of Gilead and Bashan, which is beyond the Jordan, 6 because the daughters of Manasseh received an inheritance among his sons. And the land of Gilead belonged to the rest of the sons of Manasseh.

7 ¶ The border of Manasseh ran from Asher to Michmethath which was east of Shechem; then the border went southward to the inhabitants of En-tappuah. 8 The land of Tappuah belonged to Manasseh, but Tappuah on the border of Manasseh *belonged* to the sons of Ephraim. 9 The border went down to the brook of Kanah, southward of the brook (these cities *belonged* to Ephraim among the cities of Manasseh), and the border of Manasseh *was* on the north side of the brook and it ended at the sea. 10 The south side *belonged* to Ephraim and the north side to Manasseh, and the sea was their border; and they reached to Asher on the north and to Issachar on the east. 11 In Issachar and in Asher, Manasseh had Beth-shean and its towns and Ibleam and its towns, and the inhabitants of Dor and its towns, and the inhabitants of En-dor and its towns, and the inhabitants of Taanach and its towns, and the inhabitants of Megiddo and its towns, the third is Napheth. 12 But the sons of Manasseh could not take possession of these cities, because the Canaanites persisted in living in that land. 13 It came about when the sons of Israel became strong, they put the Canaanites to forced labor, but they did not drive them out completely.

New International

Janoah on the east. 7 Then it went down from Janoah to Ataroth and Naarah, touched Jericho and came out at the Jordan. 8 From Tappuah the border went west to the Kanah Ravine and ended at the sea. This was the inheritance of the tribe of the Ephraimites, clan by clan. 9 It also included all the towns and their villages that were set aside for the Ephraimites within the inheritance of the Manassites. 10 They did not dislodge the Canaanites living in Gezer; to this day the Canaanites live among the people of Ephraim but are required to do forced labor.

17 THIS WAS the allotment for the tribe of Manasseh as Joseph's firstborn, that is, for Makir, Manasseh's firstborn. Makir was the ancestor of the Gileadites, who had received Gilead and Bashan because the Makirites were great soldiers. 2 So this allotment was for the rest of the people of Manasseh—the clans of Abiezer, Helek, Asriel, Shechem, Hepher and Shemida. These are the other male descendants of Manasseh son of Joseph by their clans.

3 Now Zelophehad son of Hepher, the son of Gilead, the son of Makir, the son of Manasseh, had no sons but only daughters, whose names were Mahlah, Noah, Hoglah, Milcah and Tirzah. 4 They went to Eleazar the priest, Joshua son of Nun, and the leaders and said, "The LORD commanded Moses to give us an inheritance among our brothers." So Joshua gave them an inheritance along with the brothers of their father, according to the LORD's command. 5 Manasseh's share consisted of ten tracts of land besides Gilead and Bashan east of the Jordan, 6 because the daughters of the tribe of Manasseh received an inheritance among the sons. The land of Gilead belonged to the rest of the descendants of Manasseh.

7 The territory of Manasseh extended from Asher to Micmethath east of Shechem. The boundary ran southward from there to include the people living at En Tappuah. 8 (Manasseh had the land of Tappuah, but Tappuah itself, on the boundary of Manasseh, belonged to the Ephraimites.) 9 Then the boundary continued south to the Kanah Ravine. There were towns belonging to Ephraim lying among the towns of Manasseh, but the boundary of Manasseh was the northern side of the ravine and ended at the sea. 10 On the south the land belonged to Ephraim, on the north to Manasseh. The territory of Manasseh reached the sea and bordered Asher on the north and Issachar on the east. 11 Within Issachar and Asher, Manasseh also had Beth Shan, Ibleam and the people of Dor, Endor, Taanach and Megiddo, together with their surrounding settlements (the third in the list is Naphoth[v]). 12 Yet the Manassites were not able to occupy these towns, for the Canaanites were determined to live in that region. 13 However, when the Israelites grew stronger, they subjected the Canaanites to forced labor but did not drive them out completely.

v 11 That is, Naphoth Dor

King James

¹⁴And the children of Joseph spake unto Joshua, saying, Why hast thou given me *but* one lot and one portion to inherit, seeing I *am* a great people, forasmuch as the LORD hath blessed me hitherto?

¹⁵And Joshua answered them, If thou *be* a great people, *then* get thee up to the wood *country,* and cut down for thyself there in the land of the Perizzites, and of the ^zgiants, if mount Ephraim be too narrow for thee.

¹⁶And the children of Joseph said, The hill is not enough for us: and all the Canaanites that dwell in the land of the valley have chariots of iron, *both they* who *are* of Beth-shean and her towns, and *they* who *are* of the valley of Jezreel.

¹⁷And Joshua spake unto the house of Joseph, *even* to Ephraim and to Manasseh, saying, Thou *art* a great people, and hast great power: thou shalt not have one lot *only:*

¹⁸But the mountain shall be thine; for it *is* a wood, and thou shalt cut it down: and the outgoings of it shall be thine: for thou shalt drive out the Canaanites, though they have iron chariots, *and* though they *be* strong.

Assigning the inherited land

18 AND THE whole congregation of the children of Israel assembled together at Shiloh, and set up the tabernacle of the congregation there. And the land was subdued before them.

²And there remained among the children of Israel seven tribes, which had not yet received their inheritance.

³And Joshua said unto the children of Israel, How long *are* ye slack to go to possess the land, which the LORD God of your fathers hath given you?

⁴Give out from among you three men for *each* tribe: and I will send them, and they shall rise, and go through the land, and describe it according to the inheritance of them; and they shall come *again* to me.

⁵And they shall divide it into seven parts: Judah shall abide in their coast on the south, and the house of Joseph shall abide in their coasts on the north.

⁶Ye shall therefore describe the land *into* seven parts, and bring *the description* hither to me, that I may cast lots for you here before the LORD our God.

⁷But the Levites have no part among you; for the priesthood of the LORD *is* their inheritance: and Gad, and Reuben, and half the tribe of Manasseh, have received their inheritance beyond Jordan on the east, which Moses the servant of the LORD gave them.

⁸ ¶ And the men arose, and went away: and Joshua charged them that went to describe the land, saying, Go and walk through the land, and describe it, and come again to me, that I may here cast lots for you before the LORD in Shiloh.

⁹And the men went and passed through the land, and described it by cities into seven parts in a book, and came *again* to Joshua to the host at Shiloh.

¹⁰ ¶ And Joshua cast lots for them in Shiloh before the LORD: and there Joshua divided the land unto the children of Israel according to their divisions.

The land of Benjamin

¹¹ ¶ And the lot of the tribe of the children of Benjamin came up according to their families: and the coast of their lot came forth between the children of Judah and the children of Joseph.

¹²And their border on the north side was from Jordan; and the border went up to the side of Jericho on the north side, and went up through the mountains westward; and the goings out thereof were at the wilderness of Beth-aven.

Amplified

¹⁴The tribe of Joseph spoke to Joshua, saying, Why have you given [us] but one lot and one portion as an inheritance when [we] are a great [abundant] people, for until now the Lord has blessed [us]?

¹⁵Joshua replied, If you are a great people, get up to the forest and clear ground for yourselves in the land of the Perizzites and the Rephaim, since the Ephraim hill country is too narrow for you.

¹⁶The Josephites said, The hill country is not enough for us, and all the Canaanites who dwell in the valley have iron chariots, both those in Beth-shean and its villages and in the Valley of Jezreel.

¹⁷And Joshua said to the house of Joseph, to Ephraim and to Manasseh, You are a great *and* numerous people and have great power; you shall not have only one lot

¹⁸But the hill country shall be yours; though it is a forest, you shall clear and possess it to its farthest borders, for you shall drive out the Canaanites, though they have iron chariots and are strong.

18 AND THE whole congregation of the Israelites assembled at Shiloh and set up the Tent of Meeting there; and the land was subdued before them.

²And there remained among the Israelites seven tribes who had not yet divided their inheritance.

³Joshua asked the Israelites, How long will you be slack to go in and possess the land which the Lord, the God of your fathers, has given you?

⁴Provide three men from each tribe, and I will send them to go through the land and write a description of it according to their [tribal] inheritances; then they shall return to me.

⁵And they shall divide it into seven parts. Judah shall remain in its territory on the south and the house of Joseph shall remain in its territory on the north.

⁶You shall describe the land in seven divisions, and bring the description here to me, that I may cast lots for you here before the Lord our God.

⁷But the Levites have no portion among you, for the priesthood of the Lord is their inheritance. Gad and Reuben and half the tribe of Manasseh have received their inheritance east of the Jordan, which Moses the servant of the Lord gave them.

⁸So the men arose and went, and Joshua charged them saying, Go and walk through the land and describe it and come again to me, and I will cast lots for you here before the Lord in Shiloh.

⁹And the men went and passed through the land and described it by cities in seven portions in a book; and they came again to Joshua to the camp at Shiloh.

¹⁰Joshua cast lots for them in Shiloh before the Lord, and there [he] divided the land to the Israelites, to each [tribe] his portion.

¹¹And the lot of the Benjamites came up according to their families; and the territory of their lot fell between the tribes of Judah and Joseph.

¹²On the north side their boundary began at the Jordan; then it went up to the shoulder of Jericho on the north and up through the hill country westward and ended at the Beth-aven wilderness.

---

^zOr, *Rephaims;* see Gen. 14:5 & 15:20

New American Standard

¹⁴ ¶ Then the sons of Joseph spoke to Joshua, saying, "Why have you given me only one lot and one portion for an inheritance, since I am a numerous people whom the LORD has thus far blessed?"

¹⁵ Joshua said to them, "If you are a numerous people, go up to the forest and clear a place for yourself there in the land of the Perizzites and of the Rephaim, since the hill country of Ephraim is too narrow for you."

¹⁶ The sons of Joseph said, "The hill country is not enough for us, and all the Canaanites who live in the valley land have chariots of iron, both those who are in Beth-shean and its towns and those who are in the valley of Jezreel."

¹⁷ Joshua spoke to the house of Joseph, to Ephraim and Manasseh, saying, "You are a numerous people and have great power; you shall not have one lot *only,*

¹⁸ but the hill country shall be yours. For though it is a forest, you shall clear it, and to its farthest borders it shall be yours; for you shall drive out the Canaanites, even though they have chariots of iron *and* though they are strong."

Rest of the Land Divided

18 THEN THE whole congregation of the sons of Israel assembled themselves at Shiloh, and set up the tent of meeting there; and the land was subdued before them.

² ¶ There remained among the sons of Israel seven tribes who had not divided their inheritance.

³ So Joshua said to the sons of Israel, "How long will you put off entering to take possession of the land which the LORD, the God of your fathers, has given you?

⁴"Provide for yourselves three men from each tribe that I may send them, and that they may arise and walk through the land and write a description of it according to their inheritance; then they shall return to me.

⁵"They shall divide it into seven portions; Judah shall stay in its territory on the south, and the house of Joseph shall stay in their territory on the north.

⁶"You shall describe the land in seven divisions, and bring *the description* here to me. I will cast lots for you here before the LORD our God.

⁷"For the Levites have no portion among you, because the priesthood of the LORD is their inheritance. Gad and Reuben and the half-tribe of Manasseh also have received their inheritance eastward beyond the Jordan, which Moses the servant of the LORD gave them."

⁸ ¶ Then the men arose and went, and Joshua commanded those who went to describe the land, saying, "Go and walk through the land and describe it, and return to me; then I will cast lots for you here before the LORD in Shiloh."

⁹ So the men went and passed through the land, and described it by cities in seven divisions in a book; and they came to Joshua to the camp at Shiloh.

¹⁰ And Joshua cast lots for them in Shiloh before the LORD, and there Joshua divided the land to the sons of Israel according to their divisions.

The Territory of Benjamin

¹¹ ¶ Now the lot of the tribe of the sons of Benjamin came up according to their families, and the territory of their lot lay between the sons of Judah and the sons of Joseph.

¹² Their border on the north side was from the Jordan, then the border went up to the side of Jericho on the north, and went up through the hill country westward, and ¹it ended at the wilderness of Beth-aven.

New International

¹⁴The people of Joseph said to Joshua, "Why have you given us only one allotment and one portion for an inheritance? We are a numerous people and the LORD has blessed us abundantly."

¹⁵"If you are so numerous," Joshua answered, "and if the hill country of Ephraim is too small for you, go up into the forest and clear land for yourselves there in the land of the Perizzites and Rephaites."

¹⁶The people of Joseph replied, "The hill country is not enough for us, and all the Canaanites who live in the plain have iron chariots, both those in Beth Shan and its settlements and those in the Valley of Jezreel."

¹⁷But Joshua said to the house of Joseph—to Ephraim and Manasseh—"You are numerous and very powerful. You will have not only one allotment ¹⁸but the forested hill country as well. Clear it, and its farthest limits will be yours; though the Canaanites have iron chariots and though they are strong, you can drive them out."

Division of the Rest of the Land

18 THE WHOLE assembly of the Israelites gathered at Shiloh and set up the Tent of Meeting there. The country was brought under their control, ²but there were still seven Israelite tribes who had not yet received their inheritance.

³So Joshua said to the Israelites: "How long will you wait before you begin to take possession of the land that the LORD, the God of your fathers, has given you? ⁴Appoint three men from each tribe. I will send them out to make a survey of the land and to write a description of it, according to the inheritance of each. Then they will return to me. ⁵You are to divide the land into seven parts. Judah is to remain in its territory on the south and the house of Joseph in its territory on the north. ⁶After you have written descriptions of the seven parts of the land, bring them here to me and I will cast lots for you in the presence of the LORD our God. ⁷The Levites, however, do not get a portion among you, because the priestly service of the LORD is their inheritance. And Gad, Reuben and the half-tribe of Manasseh have already received their inheritance on the east side of the Jordan. Moses the servant of the LORD gave it to them."

⁸As the men started on their way to map out the land, Joshua instructed them, "Go and make a survey of the land and write a description of it. Then return to me, and I will cast lots for you here at Shiloh in the presence of the LORD." ⁹So the men left and went through the land. They wrote its description on a scroll, town by town, in seven parts, and returned to Joshua in the camp at Shiloh. ¹⁰Joshua then cast lots for them in Shiloh in the presence of the LORD, and there he distributed the land to the Israelites according to their tribal divisions.

Allotment for Benjamin

¹¹The lot came up for the tribe of Benjamin, clan by clan. Their allotted territory lay between the tribes of Judah and Joseph:

¹²On the north side their boundary began at the Jordan, passed the northern slope of Jericho and headed west into the hill country, coming out at the desert

---

¹Lit *the goings out of it were*

King James

¹³And the border went over from thence toward Luz, to the side of Luz, which *is* Beth-el, southward; and the border descended to Ataroth-adar, near the hill that *lieth* on the south side of the nether Beth-horon.

¹⁴And the border was drawn *thence*, and compassed the corner of the sea southward, from the hill that *lieth* before Beth-horon southward; and the goings out thereof were at Kirjath-baal, which *is* Kirjath-jearim, a city of the children of Judah: this *was* the west quarter.

¹⁵And the south quarter *was* from the end of Kirjath-jearim, and the border went out on the west, and went out to the well of waters of Nephtoah:

¹⁶And the border came down to the end of the mountain that *lieth* before the valley of the son of Hinnom, *and* which *is* in the valley of the giants on the north, and descended to the valley of Hinnom, to the side of Jebusi on the south, and descended to En-rogel,

¹⁷And was drawn from the north, and went forth to En-shemesh, and went forth toward Geliloth, which *is* over against the going up of Adummim, and descended to the stone of Bohan the son of Reuben,

¹⁸And passed along toward the side over against ^aArabah northward, and went down unto Arabah:

¹⁹And the border passed along to the side of Beth-hoglah northward: and the outgoings of the border were at the north ^bbay of the salt sea at the south end of Jordan: this *was* the south coast.

²⁰And Jordan was the border of it on the east side. This *was* the inheritance of the children of Benjamin, by the coasts thereof round about, according to their families.

²¹Now the cities of the tribe of the children of Benjamin according to their families were Jericho, and Beth-hoglah, and the valley of Keziz,

²²And Beth-arabah, and Zemaraim, and Beth-el,

²³And Avim, and Parah, and Ophrah,

²⁴And Chephar-haammonai, and Ophni, and Gaba; twelve cities with their villages:

²⁵Gibeon, and Ramah, and Beeroth,

²⁶And Mizpeh, and Chephirah, and Mozah,

²⁷And Rekem, and Irpeel, and Taralah,

²⁸And Zelah, Eleph, and Jebusi, which *is* Jerusalem, Gibeath, *and* Kirjath; fourteen cities with their villages. This *is* the inheritance of the children of Benjamin according to their families.

The land of Simeon

19 AND THE second lot came forth to Simeon, *even* for the tribe of the children of Simeon according to their families: and their inheritance was within the inheritance of the children of Judah.

²And they had in their inheritance Beer-sheba, or Sheba, and Moladah,

³And Hazar-shual, and Balah, and Azem,

⁴And Eltolad, and Bethul, and Hormah,

⁵And Ziklag, and Beth-marcaboth, and Hazar-susah,

⁶And Beth-lebaoth, and Sharuhen; thirteen cities and their villages:

⁷Ain, Remmon, and Ether, and Ashan; four cities and their villages:

⁸And all the villages that *were* round about these cities to Baalath-beer, Ramath of the south. This *is* the inheritance of the tribe of the children of Simeon according to their families.

⁹Out of the portion of the children of Judah *was* the inheritance of the children of Simeon: for the part of the children of Judah was too much for them: therefore the children of Simeon had their inheritance within the inheritance of them.

Amplified

¹³Then the boundary passed over southward toward Luz, to the shoulder of Luz (that is, Bethel); then it went down to Ataroth-addar by the mountain that lies south of Lower Beth-horon.

¹⁴The boundary extended from there, and turning about on the western side southward from the mountain that lies to the south opposite Beth-horon, it ended at Kiriath-baal (that is, Kiriath-jearim), a city of the tribe of Judah. This formed the western side [of Benjamin's territory].

¹⁵The southern side began at the edge of Kiriath-jearim, and the boundary went on westward to the spring of the waters of Nephtoah.

¹⁶Then the boundary went down to the edge of the mountain overlooking the Valley of Ben-hinnom [son of Hinnom], which is at the north end of the Valley of Rephaim; and it descended to the Valley of Hinnom, south of the shoulder of the Jebusites, and went on down to En-rogel.

¹⁷Then it bent toward the north and went on to En-shemesh and on to Geliloth, which was opposite the ascent of Adummim, and went down to the Stone of Bohan son of Reuben.

¹⁸And it went on to the north of the shoulder [of Beth]-Arabah and down to the Arabah.

¹⁹Then the boundary passed along to the north of the shoulder of Beth-hoglah and ended at the northern bay of the Salt [Dead] Sea, at the south end of the Jordan. This was the southern border.

²⁰And the Jordan was its boundary on the east side. This was the inheritance of the sons of Benjamin by their boundaries round about, according to their families.

²¹Now the cities of the tribe of Benjamin according to [their] families were: Jericho, Beth-hoglah, Emek-keziz,

²²Beth-arabah, Zemaraim, Bethel,

²³Avvim, Parah, Ophrah,

²⁴Chephar-ammoni, Ophni, and Geba; twelve cities with their villages;

²⁵Gibeon, Ramah, Beeroth,

²⁶Mizpeh, Chephirah, Mozah,

²⁷Rekem, Irpeel, Taralah,

²⁸Zelah, Haeleph, the Jebusite [city]—that is, Jerusalem—Gibeah, and Kiriath-[jearim]; fourteen cities with their villages. This is the inheritance of the tribe of Benjamin according to their families.

19 THE SECOND lot fell to Simeon, to the tribe of the Simeonites according to their families; and their inheritance lay within that of the people of Judah.

²And they had for their inheritance: Beersheba or Sheba, Moladah,

³Hazarshual, Balah, Ezem,

⁴Eltolad, Bethul, Hormah,

⁵Ziklag, Beth-marcaboth, Hazar-susah,

⁶Beth-lebaoth, and Sharuhen; [making] thirteen cities and their villages;

⁷Ain [with] Rimmon, Ether, and Ashan; [making] four cities and their villages;

⁸And all the villages around these cities as far as Baalath-beer, or Ramah of the Negeb. This was the possession of the Simeonites according to their families.

⁹Out of the part assigned to the Judahites was the inheritance of the tribe of Simeon, for the portion of the tribe of Judah was too large for them. Therefore the tribe of Simeon had its inheritance in the midst of Judah's inheritance.

^aOr, *The plain*   ^bHeb. *tongue*

New American Standard

13 From there the border continued to Luz, to the side of Luz (that is, Bethel) southward; and the border went down to Ataroth-addar, near the hill which *lies* on the south of lower Beth-horon.

14 The border extended *from there* and turned round on the west side southward, from the hill which *lies* before Beth-horon southward; and *m*it ended at Kiriath-baal (that is, Kiriath-jearim), a city of the sons of Judah. This *was* the west side.

15 Then the south side *was* from the edge of Kiriath-jearim, and the border went westward and went to the fountain of the waters of Nephtoah.

16 The border went down to the edge of the hill which is in the valley of Ben-hinnom, which is in the valley of Rephaim northward; and it went down to the valley of Hinnom, to the slope of the Jebusite southward, and went down to En-rogel.

17 It extended northward and went to En-shemesh and went to Geliloth, which is opposite the ascent of Adummim, and it went down to the stone of Bohan the son of Reuben.

18 It continued to the side in front of the Arabah northward and went down to the Arabah.

19 The border continued to the side of Beth-hoglah northward; and the *n*border ended at the north bay of the Salt Sea, at the south end of the Jordan. This *was* the south border.

20 Moreover, the Jordan was its border on the east side. This *was* the inheritance of the sons of Benjamin, according to their families *and* according to its borders all around.

21 ¶ Now the cities of the tribe of the sons of Benjamin according to their families were Jericho and Beth-hoglah and Emek-keziz,

22 and Beth-arabah and Zemaraim and Bethel,

23 and Avvim and Parah and Ophrah,

24 and Chephar-ammoni and Ophni and Geba; twelve cities with their villages.

25 Gibeon and Ramah and Beeroth,

26 and Mizpeh and Chephirah and Mozah,

27 and Rekem and Irpeel and Taralah,

28 and Zelah, Haeleph and the Jebusite (that is, Jerusalem), Gibeah, Kiriath; fourteen cities with their villages. This is the inheritance of the sons of Benjamin according to their families.

Territory of Simeon

19 THEN THE second lot fell to Simeon, to the tribe of the sons of Simeon according to their families, and their inheritance was in the midst of the inheritance of the sons of Judah.

2 So they had as their inheritance Beersheba or Sheba and Moladah,

3 and Hazar-shual and Balah and Ezem,

4 and Eltolad and Bethul and Hormah,

5 and Ziklag and Beth-marcaboth and Hazar-susah,

6 and Beth-lebaoth and Sharuhen; thirteen cities with their villages;

7 Ain, Rimmon and Ether and Ashan; four cities with their villages;

8 and all the villages which *were* around these cities as far as Baalath-beer, Ramah of the Negev. This *was* the inheritance of the tribe of the sons of Simeon according to their families.

9 The inheritance of the sons of Simeon *was taken* from the portion of the sons of Judah, for the share of the sons of Judah was too large for them; so the sons of Simeon received *an* inheritance in the midst of Judah's inheritance.

New International

of Beth Aven. 13From there it crossed to the south slope of Luz (that is, Bethel) and went down to Ataroth Addar on the hill south of Lower Beth Horon.

14From the hill facing Beth Horon on the south the boundary turned south along the western side and came out at Kiriath Baal (that is, Kiriath Jearim), a town of the people of Judah. This was the western side.

15The southern side began at the outskirts of Kiriath Jearim on the west, and the boundary came out at the spring of the waters of Nephtoah. 16The boundary went down to the foot of the hill facing the Valley of Ben Hinnom, north of the Valley of Rephaim. It continued down the Hinnom Valley along the southern slope of the Jebusite city and so to En Rogel. 17It then curved north, went to En Shemesh, continued to Geliloth, which faces the Pass of Adummim, and ran down to the Stone of Bohan son of Reuben. 18It continued to the northern slope of Beth Arabah*w* and on down into the Arabah. 19It then went to the northern slope of Beth Hoglah and came out at the northern bay of the Salt Sea,*x* at the mouth of the Jordan in the south. This was the southern boundary.

20The Jordan formed the boundary on the eastern side.

These were the boundaries that marked out the inheritance of the clans of Benjamin on all sides.

21The tribe of Benjamin, clan by clan, had the following cities:

Jericho, Beth Hoglah, Emek Keziz, 22Beth Arabah, Zemaraim, Bethel, 23Avvim, Parah, Ophrah, 24Kephar Ammoni, Ophni and Geba—twelve towns and their villages.

25Gibeon, Ramah, Beeroth, 26Mizpah, Kephirah, Mozah, 27Rekem, Irpeel, Taralah, 28Zelah, Haeleph, the Jebusite city (that is, Jerusalem), Gibeah and Kiriath—fourteen towns and their villages.

This was the inheritance of Benjamin for its clans.

Allotment for Simeon

19 THE SECOND lot came out for the tribe of Simeon, clan by clan. Their inheritance lay within the territory of Judah. 2It included:

Beersheba (or Sheba),*y* Moladah, 3Hazar Shual, Balah, Ezem, 4Eltolad, Bethul, Hormah, 5Ziklag, Beth Marcaboth, Hazar Susah, 6Beth Lebaoth and Sharuhen—thirteen towns and their villages;

7Ain, Rimmon, Ether and Ashan—four towns and their villages— 8and all the villages around these towns as far as Baalath Beer (Ramah in the Negev).

This was the inheritance of the tribe of the Simeonites, clan by clan. 9The inheritance of the Simeonites was taken from the share of Judah, because Judah's portion was more than they needed. So the Simeonites received their inheritance within the territory of Judah.

---

m Lit *the goings out of it were*   *n* Lit *goings out of the border were*

w 18 Septuagint; Hebrew *slope facing the Arabah*   *x* 19 That is, the Dead Sea   *y* 2 Or *Beersheba, Sheba*; 1 Chron. 4:28 does not have *Sheba*.

King James

The land of Zebulun

10 ¶ And the third lot came up for the children of Zebulun according to their families: and the border of their inheritance was unto Sarid:

11And their border went up toward the sea, and Maralah, and reached to Dabbasheth, and reached to the river that *is* before Jokneam;

12And turned from Sarid eastward toward the sunrising unto the border of Chisloth-tabor, and then goeth out to Daberath, and goeth up to Japhia,

13And from thence passeth on along on the east to Gittah-hepher, to Ittah-kazin, and goeth out to Remmon-cmethoar to Neah;

14And the border compasseth it on the north side to Hannathon: and the outgoings thereof are in the valley of Jiphthah-el:

15And Kattath, and Nahallal, and Shimron, and Idalah, and Bethlehem: twelve cities with their villages.

16This *is* the inheritance of the children of Zebulun according to their families, these cities with their villages.

The land of Issachar

17 ¶ *And* the fourth lot came out to Issachar, for the children of Issachar according to their families.

18And their border was toward Jezreel, and Chesulloth, and Shunem,

19And Haphraim, and Shion, and Anaharath,

20And Rabbith, and Kishion, and Abez,

21And Remeth, and En-gannim, and En-haddah, and Beth-pazzez;

22And the coast reacheth to Tabor, and Shahazimah, and Beth-shemesh; and the outgoings of their border were at Jordan: sixteen cities with their villages.

23This *is* the inheritance of the tribe of the children of Issachar according to their families, the cities and their villages.

The land of Asher

24 ¶ And the fifth lot came out for the tribe of the children of Asher according to their families.

25And their border was Helkath, and Hali, and Beten, and Achshaph,

26And Alammelech, and Amad, and Misheal; and reacheth to Carmel westward, and to Shihor-libnath;

27And turneth toward the sunrising to Beth-dagon, and reacheth to Zebulun, and to the valley of Jiphthah-el toward the north side of Beth-emek, and Neiel, and goeth out to Cabul on the left hand,

28And Hebron, and Rehob, and Hammon, and Kanah, *even* unto great Zidon;

29And *then* the coast turneth to Ramah, and to the strong city Tyre; and the coast turneth to Hosah; and the outgoings thereof are at the sea from the coast to Achzib:

30Ummah also, and Aphek, and Rehob: twenty and two cities with their villages.

31This *is* the inheritance of the tribe of the children of Asher according to their families, these cities with their villages.

The land of Naphtali

32 ¶ The sixth lot came out to the children of Naphtali, *even* for the children of Naphtali according to their families.

33And their coast was from Heleph, from Allon to Zaanannim, and Adami, Nekeb, and Jabneel, unto Lakum; and the outgoings thereof were at Jordan:

34And *then* the coast turneth westward to Aznoth-tabor, and goeth out from thence to Hukkok, and reacheth to Zebulun on the south side, and reacheth to Asher on the west side, and to Judah upon Jordan toward the sunrising.

35And the fenced cities *are* Ziddim, Zer, and Hammath, Rakkath, and Chinnereth,

Amplified

10The third lot came up for the tribe of Zebulun according to their families. The border of its inheritance extended to Sarid.

11Then its boundary went up westward and on to Maralah and reached to Dabbesheth and to the brook east of Jokneam.

12And it turned from Sarid eastward to the border of Chisloth-tabor and it went out to Daberath and on up to Japhia,

13Then passed eastward to Gath-hepher [Jonah's birthplace] and to Eth-kazin, and went on to Rimmon bending toward Neah.

14The boundary circled on the north to Hannathon, ending at the Valley of Iphtah-el;

15Included were Kattath, Nahalal, Shimron, Idalah, and Bethlehem; twelve cities with their villages.

16This is the inheritance of the people of Zebulun according to their families, these cities with their villages.

17The fourth lot fell to Issachar, to its people according to their families.

18Their territory included: Jezreel, Chesulloth, Shunem,

19Hapharaim, Shion, Anaharath,

20Rabbith, Kishion, Ebez,

21Remeth, En-gannim, En-haddah, and Beth-pazzez.

22The boundary reached to Tabor, Shahazumah, and Beth-shemesh, and ended at the Jordan; sixteen cities with their villages.

23This is the inheritance of the tribe of Issachar according to their families, the cities and their villages.

24The fifth lot fell to the tribe of Asher according to their families.

25Their territory included: Helkath, Hali, Beten, Achshaph,

26Allammelech, Amad, and Mishal; and on the west it touched Carmel and Shihor-libnath,

27Then it turned eastward to Beth-dagon, touching Zebulun and the Valley of Iphtah-el northward to Beth-emek and Neiel, and continued in the north to Cabul,

28Ebron, Rehob, Hammon, and Kanah, even to populous Sidon.

29Then the boundary turned to Ramah, reaching to the fortified city of Tyre; and it turned to Hosah, and ended at the sea—Mahalab, Achzib,

30Ummah, Aphek, and Rehob; twenty-two cities with their villages.

31This is the inheritance of the tribe of Asher according to their families, these cities with their villages.

32The sixth lot fell to the tribe of Naphtali according to their families.

33Their boundary ran from Heleph, from the oak in Zaanannim and Adami-nekeb and Jabneel as far as Lakkum; and it ended at the Jordan.

34Then the boundary turned westward to Aznoth-tabor and went from there to Hukkok, touching Zebulun on the south, Asher on the west, and Judah on the east at the Jordan.

35The fortified cities included Ziddim, Zer, Hammath, Rakkath, Chinnereth,

---

cOr, *which is drawn*

New American Standard

Territory of Zebulun

10 ¶ Now the third lot came up for the sons of Zebulun according to their families. And the territory of their inheritance was as far as Sarid.

11 Then their border went up to the west and to Maralah, it then touched Dabbesheth and reached to the brook that is before Jokneam.

12 Then it turned from Sarid to the east toward the sunrise as far as the border of Chisloth-tabor, and it proceeded to Daberath and up to Japhia.

13 From there it continued eastward toward the sunrise to Gath-hepher, to Eth-kazin, and it proceeded to Rimmon which stretches to Neah.

14 The border circled around it on the north to Hannathon, and it ended at the valley of Iphtahel.

15 *Included* also *were* Kattah and Nahalal and Shimron and Idalah and Bethlehem; twelve cities with their villages.

16 This *was* the inheritance of the sons of Zebulun according to their families, these cities with their villages.

Territory of Issachar

17 ¶ The fourth lot fell to Issachar, to the sons of Issachar according to their families.

18 Their territory was to Jezreel and *included* Chesulloth and Shunem,

19 and Hapharaim and Shion and Anaharath,

20 and Rabbith and Kishion and Ebez,

21 and Remeth and En-gannim and En-haddah and Beth-pazzez.

22 The border reached to Tabor and Shahazumah and Beth-shemesh, and their border ended at the Jordan; sixteen cities with their villages.

23 This *was* the inheritance of the tribe of the sons of Issachar according to their families, the cities with their villages.

Territory of Asher

24 ¶ Now the fifth lot fell to the tribe of the sons of Asher according to their families.

25 Their territory was Helkath and Hali and Beten and Achshaph,

26 and Allammelech and Amad and Mishal; and it reached to Carmel on the west and to Shihor-libnath.

27 It turned toward the east to Beth-dagon and reached to Zebulun, and to the valley of Iphtahel northward to Beth-emek and Neiel; then it proceeded on north to Cabul,

28 and Ebron and Rehob and Hammon and Kanah, as far as Great Sidon.

29 The border turned to Ramah and to the fortified city of Tyre; then the border turned to Hosah, and it ended at the sea by the region of Achzib.

30 *Included* also *were* Ummah, and Aphek and Rehob; twenty-two cities with their villages.

31 This *was* the inheritance of the tribe of the sons of Asher according to their families, these cities with their villages.

Territory of Naphtali

32 ¶ The sixth lot fell to the sons of Naphtali; to the sons of Naphtali according to their families.

33 Their border was from Heleph, from the oak in Zaanannim and Adami-nekeb and Jabneel, as far as Lakkum, and it ended at the Jordan.

34 Then the border turned westward to Aznoth-tabor and proceeded from there to Hukkok; and it reached to Zebulun on the south and touched Asher on the west, and to Judah at the Jordan toward the east.

35 The fortified cities *were* Ziddim, Zer and Hammath, Rakkath and Chinnereth,

New International

Allotment for Zebulun

10The third lot came up for Zebulun, clan by clan:
The boundary of their inheritance went as far as Sarid. 11Going west it ran to Maralah, touched Dabbesheth, and extended to the ravine near Jokneam. 12It turned east from Sarid toward the sunrise to the territory of Kisloth Tabor and went on to Daberath and up to Japhia. 13Then it continued eastward to Gath Hepher and Eth Kazin; it came out at Rimmon and turned toward Neah. 14There the boundary went around on the north to Hannathon and ended at the Valley of Iphtah El. 15Included were Kattath, Nahalal, Shimron, Idalah and Bethlehem. There were twelve towns and their villages.

16These towns and their villages were the inheritance of Zebulun, clan by clan.

Allotment for Issachar

17The fourth lot came out for Issachar, clan by clan. 18Their territory included:
Jezreel, Kesulloth, Shunem, 19Hapharaim, Shion, Anaharath, 20Rabbith, Kishion, Ebez, 21Remeth, En Gannim, En Haddah and Beth Pazzez. 22The boundary touched Tabor, Shahazumah and Beth Shemesh, and ended at the Jordan. There were sixteen towns and their villages.

23These towns and their villages were the inheritance of the tribe of Issachar, clan by clan.

Allotment for Asher

24The fifth lot came out for the tribe of Asher, clan by clan. 25Their territory included:
Helkath, Hali, Beten, Acshaph, 26Allammelech, Amad and Mishal. On the west the boundary touched Carmel and Shihor Libnath. 27It then turned east toward Beth Dagon, touched Zebulun and the Valley of Iphtah El, and went north to Beth Emek and Neiel, passing Cabul on the left. 28It went to Abdon,*z* Rehob, Hammon and Kanah, as far as Greater Sidon. 29The boundary then turned back toward Ramah and went to the fortified city of Tyre, turned toward Hosah and came out at the sea in the region of Aczib, 30Ummah, Aphek and Rehob. There were twenty-two towns and their villages.

31These towns and their villages were the inheritance of the tribe of Asher, clan by clan.

Allotment for Naphtali

32The sixth lot came out for Naphtali, clan by clan:
33Their boundary went from Heleph and the large tree in Zaanannim, passing Adami Nekeb and Jabneel to Lakkum and ending at the Jordan. 34The boundary ran west through Aznoth Tabor and came out at Hukkok. It touched Zebulun on the south, Asher on the west and the Jordan*a* on the east. 35The fortified cities were Ziddim, Zer, Hammath, Rakkath, Kinnereth,

z 28 Some Hebrew manuscripts (see also Joshua 21:30); most Hebrew manuscripts *Ebron*   *a 34* Septuagint; Hebrew *west, and Judah, the Jordan,*

King James

36And Adamah, and Ramah, and Hazor,
37And Kedesh, and Edrei, and En-hazor,
38And Iron, and Migdal-el, Horem, and Beth-anath, and Beth-shemesh; nineteen cities with their villages.
39This *is* the inheritance of the tribe of the children of Naphtali according to their families, the cities and their villages.

The land of Dan

40 ¶ *And* the seventh lot came out for the tribe of the children of Dan according to their families.
41And the coast of their inheritance was Zorah, and Eshtaol, and Ir-shemesh,
42And Shaalabbin, and Ajalon, and Jethlah,
43And Elon, and Thimnathah, and Ekron,
44And Eltekeh, and Gibbethon, and Baalath,
45And Jehud, and Bene-berak, and Gath-rimmon,
46And Me-jarkon, and Rakkon, with the border *d*before *e*Japho.
47And the coast of the children of Dan went out *too little* for them: therefore the children of Dan went up to fight against Leshem, and took it, and smote it with the edge of the sword, and possessed it, and dwelt therein, and called Leshem, Dan, after the name of Dan their father.
48This *is* the inheritance of the tribe of the children of Dan according to their families, these cities with their villages.
49 ¶ When they had made an end of dividing the land for inheritance by their coasts, the children of Israel gave an inheritance to Joshua the son of Nun among them:
50According to the word of the LORD they gave him the city which he asked, *even* Timnath-serah in mount Ephraim: and he built the city, and dwelt therein.
51These *are* the inheritances, which Eleazar the priest, and Joshua the son of Nun, and the heads of the fathers of the tribes of the children of Israel, divided for an inheritance by lot in Shiloh before the LORD, at the door of the tabernacle of the congregation. So they made an end of dividing the country.

The six cities of refuge

20 THE LORD also spake unto Joshua, saying,
2Speak to the children of Israel, saying, Appoint out for you cities of refuge, whereof I spake unto you by the hand of Moses:
3That the slayer that killeth *any* person unawares and unwittingly may flee thither: and they shall be your refuge from the avenger of blood.
4And when he that doth flee unto one of those cities shall stand at the entering of the gate of the city, and shall declare his cause in the ears of the elders of that city, they shall take him into the city unto them, and give him a place, that he may dwell among them.
5And if the avenger of blood pursue after him, then they shall not deliver the slayer up into his hand; because he smote his neighbour unwittingly, and hated him not beforetime.
6And he shall dwell in that city, until he stand before the congregation for judgment, *and* until the death of the high priest that shall be in those days: then shall the slayer return, and come unto his own city, and unto his own house, unto the city from whence he fled.
7 ¶ And they *f*appointed Kedesh in Galilee in mount Naphtali, and Shechem in mount Ephraim, and Kirjath-arba, which *is* Hebron, in the mountain of Judah.
8And on the other side Jordan by Jericho eastward, they assigned Bezer in the wilderness upon the plain out of the tribe of Reuben, and Ramoth in Gilead out of the tribe of Gad, and Golan in Bashan out of the tribe of Manasseh.

Amplified

36Adamah, Ramah, Hazor,
37Kedesh, Edrei, En-hazor,
38Yiron, Migdal-el, Horem, Beth-anath, and Beth-shemesh; nineteen cities and their villages.
39This is the inheritance of the tribe of Naphtali according to their families, the cities and their villages.
40And the seventh lot fell to the tribe of Dan according to their families.
41The territory of their inheritance included: Zorah, Eshtaol, Ir-shemesh,
42Shaalabbin, Aijalon, Ithlah,
43Elon, Timnah, Ekron,
44Eltekeh, Gibbethon, Baalath,
45Jehud, Bene-berak, Gath-rimmon,
46Me-jarkon, and Rakkon, with the territory before Joppa.
47The territory of the tribe of Dan had to be extended [because of the crowding in of the Amorites and Philistines]; so the sons of Dan went up to fight against Leshem (Laish) and took it and smote it with the sword and possessed it and dwelt there, and they called Leshem (Laish) Dan after Dan their [forefather]. [Judg. 1:34; 18:7–10, 27.]
48This is the inheritance of the tribe of Dan according to their families, these cities with their villages.
49When they had finished dividing the land for inheritance by their boundaries, the Israelites gave an inheritance among them to Joshua son of Nun.
50According to the word of the Lord they gave him the city for which he asked—Timnath-serah in the hills of Ephraim. And he built the city and dwelt in it.
51These are the inheritances which Eleazar the priest, Joshua son of Nun, and the heads of the fathers' houses of the tribes of Israel distributed by lot in Shiloh before the Lord at the door of the Tent of Meeting. So they finished dividing the land.

20 THE LORD said also to Joshua,
2Say to the Israelites, Appoint among you cities of refuge, of which I spoke to you through Moses,
3That the slayer who kills anyone accidentally and unintentionally may flee there; and they shall be your refuge from the avenger of blood. [Num. 35:10ff.]
4He who flees to one of those cities shall stand at the entrance of the gate of the city and explain his case to the elders of that city; they shall receive him to [the protection of] that city and give him a place to dwell among them.
5If the avenger of blood pursues him, they shall not deliver the slayer into his hand, because he killed his neighbor unintentionally, having had no hatred for him previously.
6And he shall dwell in that city until he has been tried before the congregation and until the death of him who is the high priest in those days. Then the slayer shall return to his own city from which he fled and to his own house.
7And they set apart *and* consecrated Kedesh in Galilee in the hill country of Naphtali and Shechem in the hill country of Ephraim and Kiriath-arba (that is, Hebron) in the hill country of Judah.
8Beyond the Jordan east of Jericho they appointed Bezer in the wilderness tableland from the tribe of Reuben, and Ramoth in Gilead from the tribe of Gad, and Golan in Bashan from the tribe of Manasseh.

*d*Or, *over against*   *e*Or, *Joppa;* see Acts 9:36   *f*Heb. *sanctified*

New American Standard

36 and Adamah and Ramah and Hazor,
37 and Kedesh and Edrei and En-hazor,
38 and Yiron and Migdal-el, Horem and Beth-anath and Beth-shemesh; nineteen cities with their villages.
39 This *was* the inheritance of the tribe of the sons of Naphtali according to their families, the cities with their villages.

Territory of Dan

40 ¶ The seventh lot fell to the tribe of the sons of Dan according to their families.
41 The territory of their inheritance was Zorah and Eshtaol and Ir-shemesh,
42 and Shaalabbin and Aijalon and Ithlah,
43 and Elon and Timnah and Ekron,
44 and Eltekeh and Gibbethon and Baalath,
45 and Jehud and Bene-berak and Gath-rimmon,
46 and Me-jarkon and Rakkon, with the territory over against Joppa.
47 The territory of the sons of Dan proceeded beyond them; for the sons of Dan went up and fought with Leshem and captured it. Then they struck it with the edge of the sword and possessed it and settled in it; and they called Leshem Dan after the name of Dan their father.
48 This *was* the inheritance of the tribe of the sons of Dan according to their families, these cities with their villages.
49 ¶ When they finished apportioning the land for inheritance by its borders, the sons of Israel gave an inheritance in their midst to Joshua the son of Nun.
50 In accordance with the command of the LORD they gave him the city for which he asked, Timnath-serah in the hill country of Ephraim. So he built the city and settled in it.
51 ¶ These are the inheritances which Eleazar the priest, and Joshua the son of Nun, and the heads of the households of the tribes of the sons of Israel distributed by lot in Shiloh before the LORD at the doorway of the tent of meeting. So they finished dividing the land.

Six Cities of Refuge

20 THEN THE LORD spoke to Joshua, saying,
2 "Speak to the sons of Israel, saying, 'Designate the cities of refuge, of which I spoke to you through Moses,
3 that the manslayer who kills any person unintentionally, without premeditation, may flee there, and they shall become your refuge from the avenger of blood.
4 'He shall flee to one of these cities, and shall stand at the entrance of the gate of the city and state his case in the hearing of the elders of that city; and they shall take him into the city to them and give him a place, so that he may dwell among them.
5 'Now if the avenger of blood pursues him, then they shall not deliver the manslayer into his hand, because he struck his neighbor without premeditation and did not hate him beforehand.
6 'He shall dwell in that city until he stands before the congregation for judgment, until the death of the one who is high priest in those days. Then the manslayer shall return to his own city and to his own house, to the city from which he fled.' "
7 ¶ So they set apart Kedesh in Galilee in the hill country of Naphtali and Shechem in the hill country of Ephraim, and Kiriath-arba (that is, Hebron) in the hill country of Judah.
8 Beyond the Jordan east of Jericho, they designated Bezer in the wilderness on the plain from the tribe of Reuben, and Ramoth in Gilead from the tribe of Gad, and Golan in Bashan from the tribe of Manasseh.

New International

36 Adamah, Ramah, Hazor, 37 Kedesh, Edrei, En Hazor, 38 Iron, Migdal El, Horem, Beth Anath and Beth Shemesh. There were nineteen towns and their villages.
39 These towns and their villages were the inheritance of the tribe of Naphtali, clan by clan.

Allotment for Dan

40 The seventh lot came out for the tribe of Dan, clan by clan. 41 The territory of their inheritance included:
   Zorah, Eshtaol, Ir Shemesh, 42 Shaalabbin, Aijalon, Ithlah, 43 Elon, Timnah, Ekron, 44 Eltekeh, Gibbethon, Baalath, 45 Jehud, Bene Berak, Gath Rimmon, 46 Me Jarkon and Rakkon, with the area facing Joppa.
47 (But the Danites had difficulty taking possession of their territory, so they went up and attacked Leshem, took it, put it to the sword and occupied it. They settled in Leshem and named it Dan after their forefather.)
48 These towns and their villages were the inheritance of the tribe of Dan, clan by clan.

Allotment for Joshua

49 When they had finished dividing the land into its allotted portions, the Israelites gave Joshua son of Nun an inheritance among them, 50 as the LORD had commanded. They gave him the town he asked for—Timnath Serah[b] in the hill country of Ephraim. And he built up the town and settled there.
51 These are the territories that Eleazar the priest, Joshua son of Nun and the heads of the tribal clans of Israel assigned by lot at Shiloh in the presence of the LORD at the entrance to the Tent of Meeting. And so they finished dividing the land.

Cities of Refuge

20 THEN THE LORD said to Joshua: 2 "Tell the Israelites to designate the cities of refuge, as I instructed you through Moses, 3 so that anyone who kills a person accidentally and unintentionally may flee there and find protection from the avenger of blood.
4 "When he flees to one of these cities, he is to stand in the entrance of the city gate and state his case before the elders of that city. Then they are to admit him into their city and give him a place to live with them. 5 If the avenger of blood pursues him, they must not surrender the one accused, because he killed his neighbor unintentionally and without malice aforethought. 6 He is to stay in that city until he has stood trial before the assembly and until the death of the high priest who is serving at that time. Then he may go back to his own home in the town from which he fled."
7 So they set apart Kedesh in Galilee in the hill country of Naphtali, Shechem in the hill country of Ephraim, and Kiriath Arba (that is, Hebron) in the hill country of Judah. 8 On the east side of the Jordan of Jericho[c] they designated Bezer in the desert on the plateau in the tribe of Reuben, Ramoth in Gilead in the tribe of Gad, and Golan in Bashan

---

b 50 Also known as *Timnath Heres* (see Judges 2:9)   c 8 *Jordan of Jericho* was possibly an ancient name for the Jordan River.

King James

⁹These were the cities appointed for all the children of Israel, and for the stranger that sojourneth among them, that whosoever killeth *any* person at unawares might flee thither, and not die by the hand of the avenger of blood, until he stood before the congregation.

Cities for the Levites

21 THEN CAME near the heads of the fathers of the Levites unto Eleazar the priest, and unto Joshua the son of Nun, and unto the heads of the fathers of the tribes of the children of Israel;

²And they spake unto them at Shiloh in the land of Canaan, saying, The LORD commanded by the hand of Moses to give us cities to dwell in, with the suburbs thereof for our cattle.

³And the children of Israel gave unto the Levites out of their inheritance, at the commandment of the LORD, these cities and their suburbs.

⁴And the lot came out for the families of the Kohathites: and the children of Aaron the priest, *which were* of the Levites, had by lot out of the tribe of Judah, and out of the tribe of Simeon, and out of the tribe of Benjamin, thirteen cities.

⁵And the rest of the children of Kohath *had* by lot out of the families of the tribe of Ephraim, and out of the tribe of Dan, and out of the half tribe of Manasseh, ten cities.

⁶And the children of Gershon *had* by lot out of the families of the tribe of Issachar, and out of the tribe of Asher, and out of the tribe of Naphtali, and out of the half tribe of Manasseh in Bashan, thirteen cities.

⁷The children of Merari by their families *had* out of the tribe of Reuben, and out of the tribe of Gad, and out of the tribe of Zebulun, twelve cities.

⁸And the children of Israel gave by lot unto the Levites these cities with their suburbs, as the LORD commanded by the hand of Moses.

⁹ ¶ And they gave out of the tribe of the children of Judah, and out of the tribe of the children of Simeon, these cities which are *here* ^gmentioned by name,

¹⁰Which the children of Aaron, *being* of the families of the Kohathites, *who were* of the children of Levi, had: for their's was the first lot.

¹¹And they gave them ^hthe city of Arba the father of Anak, which *city is* Hebron, in the hill *country* of Judah, with the suburbs thereof round about it.

¹²But the fields of the city, and the villages thereof, gave they to Caleb the son of Jephunneh for his possession.

¹³ ¶ Thus they gave to the children of Aaron the priest Hebron with her suburbs, *to be* a city of refuge for the slayer; and Libnah with her suburbs,

¹⁴And Jattir with her suburbs, and Eshtemoa with her suburbs,

¹⁵And Holon with her suburbs, and Debir with her suburbs,

¹⁶And Ain with her suburbs, and Juttah with her suburbs, *and* Beth-shemesh with her suburbs; nine cities out of those two tribes.

¹⁷And out of the tribe of Benjamin, Gibeon with her suburbs, Geba with her suburbs,

¹⁸Anathoth with her suburbs, and Almon with her suburbs; four cities.

¹⁹All the cities of the children of Aaron, the priests, *were* thirteen cities with their suburbs.

²⁰ ¶ And the families of the children of Kohath, the Levites which remained of the children of Kohath, even they had the cities of their lot out of the tribe of Ephraim.

²¹For they gave them Shechem with her suburbs in mount Ephraim, *to be* a city of refuge for the slayer; and Gezer with her suburbs,

²²And Kibzaim with her suburbs, and Beth-horon with her suburbs; four cities.

Amplified

⁹These cities were for all the Israelites and the stranger sojourning among them, that whoever killed a person unintentionally might flee there and not be slain by the avenger of blood until he had been tried before the congregation.

21 THEN THE heads of the fathers' houses of the Levites came to Eleazar the priest and Joshua son of Nun and the heads of the fathers' houses of the Israelite tribes.

²They said to them at Shiloh in Canaan, The Lord commanded through Moses that we should be given cities to dwell in, with their pasturelands (suburbs) for our cattle.

³So the Israelites gave to the Levites out of their own inheritance, at the command of the Lord, these cities and their suburbs.

⁴The [first] lot came out for the families of the Kohathites. So those ^jLevites who were descendants of Aaron the priest received by lot from the tribes of Judah, Simeon, and Benjamin thirteen cities.

⁵And the rest of the Kohathites received by lot from the families of the tribes of Ephraim, Dan, and the half-tribe of Manasseh ten cities.

⁶The Gershonites received by lot from the families of the tribes of Issachar, Asher, Naphtali, and the half-tribe of Manasseh in Bashan thirteen cities.

⁷The Merarites received according to their families from the tribes of Reuben, Gad, and Zebulun twelve cities.

⁸The Israelites gave by lot to the Levites these cities with their pasturelands (suburbs), as the Lord commanded through Moses.

⁹They gave from the tribes of Judah and Simeon the cities here mentioned by name,

¹⁰Which went to the families of the descendants of Aaron, of the Kohathite branch of the Levites, for the lot fell to them first.

¹¹They gave them [the city of] Kiriath-arba, Arba being the father of Anak, which city is Hebron, in the hill country of Judah, with its pasturelands round about it.

¹²But the city's fields and villages they gave to Caleb son of Jephunneh as his own.

¹³Thus to the descendants of Aaron the priest they gave Hebron, the city of refuge for the slayer, with its pasturelands (suburbs), and together with their suburbs, Libnah,

¹⁴Jattir, Eshtemoa,

¹⁵Holon, Debir,

¹⁶Ain, Juttah, and Beth-shemesh; nine cities, each with its suburbs, out of those two tribes.

¹⁷Out of the tribe of Benjamin, Gibeon, Geba,

¹⁸Anathoth, and Almon; four cities, each with its suburbs.

¹⁹The cities of the sons of Aaron, the priests, were thirteen, with their suburbs.

²⁰The rest of the Kohathites belonging to the Levitical families were allotted cities out of the tribe of Ephraim.

²¹To them were given, each with its pasturelands (suburbs), Shechem in the hill country of Ephraim, as the city of refuge for the slayer, and Gezer,

²²And Kibzaim, and Beth-horon; four cities, each with its pasturelands (suburbs).

---

^jThe Levites were divided into three groups, the descendants of Levi's three sons, Gershon, Kohath, and Merari. But only those Israelites who were descendants of Levi through Kohath's grandson Aaron could be priests. The priesthood was made hereditary in the family of Aaron and restricted to it; however, even some of these were debarred by legal disabilities (Lev. 21:16ff.). The other families of Levi's descendants, the Gershonites and Merarites and those Kohathites who were not descended from Aaron, were charged with the care of the sanctuary. The priests ministered at the altar.

^gHeb. *called*   ^hOr, *Kirjath-arba;* see Gen. 23:2

New American Standard

9 These were the appointed cities for all the sons of Israel and for the stranger who sojourns among them, that whoever kills any person unintentionally may flee there, and not die by the hand of the avenger of blood until he stands before the congregation.

Forty-eight Cities of the Levites

21 THEN THE heads of households of the Levites approached Eleazar the priest, and Joshua the son of Nun, and the heads of households of the tribes of the sons of Israel.

2 They spoke to them at Shiloh in the land of Canaan, saying, "The LORD commanded through Moses to give us cities to live in, with their pasture lands for our cattle."

3 So the sons of Israel gave the Levites from their inheritance these cities with their pasture lands, according to the command of the LORD.

4 Then the lot came out for the families of the Kohathites. And the sons of Aaron the priest, who were of the Levites, received thirteen cities by lot from the tribe of Judah and from the tribe of the Simeonites and from the tribe of Benjamin.

5 ¶ The rest of the sons of Kohath received ten cities by lot from the families of the tribe of Ephraim and from the tribe of Dan and from the half-tribe of Manasseh.

6 ¶ The sons of Gershon received thirteen cities by lot from the families of the tribe of Issachar and from the tribe of Asher and from the tribe of Naphtali and from the half-tribe of Manasseh in Bashan.

7 ¶ The sons of Merari according to their families received twelve cities from the tribe of Reuben and from the tribe of Gad and from the tribe of Zebulun.

8 ¶ Now the sons of Israel gave by lot to the Levites these cities with their pasture lands, as the LORD had commanded through Moses.

9 ¶ They gave these cities which are *here* mentioned by name from the tribe of the sons of Judah and from the tribe of the sons of Simeon;

10 and they were for the sons of Aaron, one of the families of the Kohathites, of the sons of Levi, for the lot was theirs first.

11 Thus they gave them Kiriath-arba, *Arba being* the father of Anak (that is, Hebron), in the hill country of Judah, with its surrounding pasture lands.

12 But the fields of the city and its villages they gave to Caleb the son of Jephunneh as his possession.

13 ¶ So to the sons of Aaron the priest they gave Hebron, the city of refuge for the manslayer, with its pasture lands, and Libnah with its pasture lands,

14 and Jattir with its pasture lands and Eshtemoa with its pasture lands,

15 and Holon with its pasture lands and Debir with its pasture lands,

16 and Ain with its pasture lands and Juttah with its pasture lands *and* Beth-shemesh with its pasture lands; nine cities from these two tribes.

17 From the tribe of Benjamin, Gibeon with its pasture lands, Geba with its pasture lands,

18 Anathoth with its pasture lands and Almon with its pasture lands; four cities.

19 All the cities of the sons of Aaron, the priests, were thirteen cities with their pasture lands.

20 ¶ Then the cities from the tribe of Ephraim were allotted to the families of the sons of Kohath, the Levites, *even to* the rest of the sons of Kohath.

21 They gave them Shechem, the city of refuge for the manslayer, with its pasture lands, in the hill country of Ephraim, and Gezer with its pasture lands,

22 and Kibzaim with its pasture lands and Beth-horon with its pasture lands; four cities.

New International

in the tribe of Manasseh. 9Any of the Israelites or any alien living among them who killed someone accidentally could flee to these designated cities and not be killed by the avenger of blood prior to standing trial before the assembly.

Towns for the Levites

21 NOW THE family heads of the Levites approached Eleazar the priest, Joshua son of Nun, and the heads of the other tribal families of Israel 2at Shiloh in Canaan and said to them, "The LORD commanded through Moses that you give us towns to live in, with pasturelands for our livestock." 3So, as the LORD had commanded, the Israelites gave the Levites the following towns and pasturelands out of their own inheritance:

4The first lot came out for the Kohathites, clan by clan. The Levites who were descendants of Aaron the priest were allotted thirteen towns from the tribes of Judah, Simeon and Benjamin. 5The rest of Kohath's descendants were allotted ten towns from the clans of the tribes of Ephraim, Dan and half of Manasseh.

6The descendants of Gershon were allotted thirteen towns from the clans of the tribes of Issachar, Asher, Naphtali and the half-tribe of Manasseh in Bashan.

7The descendants of Merari, clan by clan, received twelve towns from the tribes of Reuben, Gad and Zebulun.

8So the Israelites allotted to the Levites these towns and their pasturelands, as the LORD had commanded through Moses.

9From the tribes of Judah and Simeon they allotted the following towns by name 10(these towns were assigned to the descendants of Aaron who were from the Kohathite clans of the Levites, because the first lot fell to them):

11They gave them Kiriath Arba (that is, Hebron), with its surrounding pastureland, in the hill country of Judah. (Arba was the forefather of Anak.) 12But the fields and villages around the city they had given to Caleb son of Jephunneh as his possession.

13So to the descendants of Aaron the priest they gave Hebron (a city of refuge for one accused of murder), Libnah, 14Jattir, Eshtemoa, 15Holon, Debir, 16Ain, Juttah and Beth Shemesh, together with their pasturelands—nine towns from these two tribes.

17And from the tribe of Benjamin they gave them Gibeon, Geba, 18Anathoth and Almon, together with their pasturelands—four towns.

19All the towns for the priests, the descendants of Aaron, were thirteen, together with their pasturelands.

20The rest of the Kohathite clans of the Levites were allotted towns from the tribe of Ephraim:

21In the hill country of Ephraim they were given Shechem (a city of refuge for one accused of murder) and Gezer, 22Kibzaim and Beth Horon, together with their pasturelands—four towns.

King James

23And out of the tribe of Dan, Eltekeh with her suburbs, Gibbethon with her suburbs,

24Aijalon with her suburbs, Gathrimmon with her suburbs; four cities.

25And out of the half tribe of Manasseh, Tanach with her suburbs, and Gath-rimmon with her suburbs; two cities.

26All the cities were ten with their suburbs for the families of the children of Kohath that remained.

27 ¶ And unto the children of Gershon, of the families of the Levites, out of the *other* half tribe of Manasseh *they gave* Golan in Bashan with her suburbs, *to be* a city of refuge for the slayer; and Beesh-terah with her suburbs; two cities.

28And out of the tribe of Issachar, Kishon with her suburbs, Dabareh with her suburbs,

29Jarmuth with her suburbs, En-gannim with her suburbs; four cities.

30And out of the tribe of Asher, Mishal with her suburbs, Abdon with her suburbs,

31Helkath with her suburbs, and Rehob with her suburbs; four cities.

32And out of the tribe of Naphtali, Kedesh in Galilee with her suburbs, *to be* a city of refuge for the slayer; and Hammoth-dor with her suburbs, and Kartan with her suburbs; three cities.

33All the cities of the Gershonites according to their families *were* thirteen cities with their suburbs.

34 ¶ And unto the families of the children of Merari, the rest of the Levites, out of the tribe of Zebulun, Jokneam with her suburbs, and Kartah with her suburbs,

35Dimnah with her suburbs, Nahalal with her suburbs; four cities.

36And out of the tribe of Reuben, Bezer with her suburbs, and Jahazah with her suburbs,

37Kedemoth with her suburbs, and Mephaath with her suburbs; four cities.

38And out of the tribe of Gad, Ramoth in Gilead with her suburbs, *to be* a city of refuge for the slayer; and Mahanaim with her suburbs,

39Heshbon with her suburbs, Jazer with her suburbs; four cities in all.

40So all the cities for the children of Merari by their families, which were remaining of the families of the Levites, were *by* their lot twelve cities.

41All the cities of the Levites within the possession of the children of Israel *were* forty and eight cities with their suburbs.

42These cities were every one with their suburbs round about them: thus *were* all these cities.

43 ¶ And the LORD gave unto Israel all the land which he sware to give unto their fathers; and they possessed it, and dwelt therein.

44And the LORD gave them rest round about, according to all that he sware unto their fathers: and there stood not a man of all their enemies before them; the LORD delivered all their enemies into their hand.

45There failed not aught of any good thing which the LORD had spoken unto the house of Israel; all came to pass.

Eastern tribes return home

22 THEN JOSHUA called the Reubenites, and the Gadites, and the half tribe of Manasseh,

2And said unto them, Ye have kept all that Moses the servant of the LORD commanded you, and have obeyed my voice in all that I commanded you:

3Ye have not left your brethren these many days unto this day, but have kept the charge of the commandment of the LORD your God.

Amplified

23And out of the tribe of Dan, each with its pasturelands (suburbs), Eltekeh, Gibbethon,

24Aijalon, and Gath-rimmon; four cities, each with its pasturelands (suburbs).

25And out of the half-tribe of Manasseh, Taanach, and [another] Gath-rimmon; two cities, each with its pasturelands (suburbs).

26All the cities for the families of the remaining Kohathites were ten, with their pasturelands (suburbs).

27And to the Gershonites of the families of the Levites they gave out of the other half-tribe of Manasseh the city of Golan in Bashan, as the city of refuge for the slayer, and Be-eshterah; two cities, each with its pasturelands.

28Out of the tribe of Issachar, Kishion, Daberath,

29Jarmuth, and En-gannim; four cities, each with its suburbs.

30Out of the tribe of Asher, Mishal, Abdon,

31Helkath, and Rehob; four cities, each with its pasturelands.

32And out of the tribe of Naphtali, Kedesh in Galilee, city of refuge for the slayer, and Hammoth-dor, and Kartan; three cities, each with its pasturelands.

33All the cities of the Gershonite families were thirteen, with their pasturelands (suburbs).

34And to the families of the Merarites, the rest of the Levites, out of the tribe of Zebulun were given Jokneam, Kartah,

35Dimnah, and Nahalal; four cities, each with its pasturelands (suburbs).

36And out of the tribe of Reuben, Bezer, Jahaz,

37Kedemoth, and Mephaath; four cities, each with its pasturelands (suburbs).

38And out of the tribe of Gad, Ramoth in Gilead, as the city of refuge for the slayer, and Mahanaim,

39Heshbon, and Jazer; four cities in all, each with its pasturelands (suburbs).

40So all the cities allotted to the Merarite families, that is, the remainder of the Levite families, were twelve cities.

41The cities of the Levites in the midst of the possession of the Israelites were forty-eight cities in all, with their pasturelands (suburbs).

42These cities all had their pasturelands (suburbs) around them.

43And the Lord gave to Israel all the land which He had sworn to give to their fathers, and they possessed it and dwelt in it.

44The Lord gave them rest round about, just as He had sworn to their fathers. Not one of all their enemies withstood them; the Lord delivered all their enemies into their hands.

45There failed no part of any good thing which the Lord had promised to the house of Israel; all came to pass.

22 THEN JOSHUA called the Reubenites, the Gadites, and the half-tribe of Manasseh,

2And said to them, You have kept all that Moses the servant of the Lord commanded you, and have obeyed my voice in all that I commanded you.

3You have not deserted your brethren [the other tribes] these many days to this day but have carefully kept the charge of the Lord your God.

New American Standard

23 From the tribe of Dan, Elteke with its pasture lands, Gibbethon with its pasture lands,

24 Aijalon with its pasture lands, Gath-rimmon with its pasture lands; four cities.

25 From the half-tribe of Manasseh, *they allotted* Taanach with its pasture lands and Gath-rimmon with its pasture lands; two cities.

26 All the cities with their pasture lands for the families of the rest of the sons of Kohath were ten.

27 ¶ To the sons of Gershon, one of the families of the Levites, from the half-tribe of Manasseh, *they gave* Golan in Bashan, the city of refuge for the manslayer, with its pasture lands, and Be-eshterah with its pasture lands; two cities.

28 From the tribe of Issachar, *they gave* Kishion with its pasture lands, Daberath with its pasture lands,

29 Jarmuth with its pasture lands, En-gannim with its pasture lands; four cities.

30 From the tribe of Asher, *they gave* Mishal with its pasture lands, Abdon with its pasture lands,

31 Helkath with its pasture lands and Rehob with its pasture lands; four cities.

32 From the tribe of Naphtali, *they gave* Kedesh in Galilee, the city of refuge for the manslayer, with its pasture lands and Hammoth-dor with its pasture lands and Kartan with its pasture lands; three cities.

33 All the cities of the Gershonites according to their families were thirteen cities with their pasture lands.

34 ¶ To the families of the sons of Merari, the rest of the Levites, *they gave* from the tribe of Zebulun, Jokneam with its pasture lands and Kartah with its pasture lands.

35 Dimnah with its pasture lands, Nahalal with its pasture lands; four cities.

36 From the tribe of Reuben, *they gave* Bezer with its pasture lands and Jahaz with its pasture lands,

37 Kedemoth with its pasture lands and Mephaath with its pasture lands; four cities.

38 From the tribe of Gad, *they gave* Ramoth in Gilead, the city of refuge for the manslayer, with its pasture lands and Mahanaim with its pasture lands,

39 Heshbon with its pasture lands, Jazer with its pasture lands; four cities in all.

40 All *these were* the cities of the sons of Merari according to their families, the rest of the families of the Levites; and their lot was twelve cities.

41 ¶ All the cities of the Levites in the midst of the possession of the sons of Israel were forty-eight cities with their pasture lands.

42 These cities each had its surrounding pasture lands; thus *it was* with all these cities.

43 ¶ So the LORD gave Israel all the land which He had sworn to give to their fathers, and they possessed it and lived in it.

44 And the LORD gave them rest on every side, according to all that He had sworn to their fathers, and no one of all their enemies stood before them; the LORD gave all their enemies into their hand.

45 Not one of the good promises which the LORD had made to the house of Israel failed; all came to pass.

Tribes beyond Jordan Return

22 THEN JOSHUA summoned the Reubenites and the Gadites and the half-tribe of Manasseh,

2 and said to them, "You have kept all that Moses the servant of the LORD commanded you, and have listened to my voice in all that I commanded you.

3 "You have not forsaken your brothers these many days to this day, but have kept the charge of the commandment of the LORD your God.

New International

23 Also from the tribe of Dan they received Eltekeh, Gibbethon, 24 Aijalon and Gath Rimmon, together with their pasturelands—four towns.

25 From half the tribe of Manasseh they received Taanach and Gath Rimmon, together with their pasturelands—two towns.

26 All these ten towns and their pasturelands were given to the rest of the Kohathite clans.

27 The Levite clans of the Gershonites were given:
from the half-tribe of Manasseh,
Golan in Bashan (a city of refuge for one accused of murder) and Be Eshtarah, together with their pasturelands—two towns;

28 from the tribe of Issachar,
Kishion, Daberath, 29 Jarmuth and En Gannim, together with their pasturelands—four towns;

30 from the tribe of Asher,
Mishal, Abdon, 31 Helkath and Rehob, together with their pasturelands—four towns;

32 from the tribe of Naphtali,
Kedesh in Galilee (a city of refuge for one accused of murder), Hammoth Dor and Kartan, together with their pasturelands—three towns.

33 All the towns of the Gershonite clans were thirteen, together with their pasturelands.

34 The Merarite clans (the rest of the Levites) were given:
from the tribe of Zebulun,
Jokneam, Kartah, 35 Dimnah and Nahalal, together with their pasturelands—four towns;

36 from the tribe of Reuben,
Bezer, Jahaz, 37 Kedemoth and Mephaath, together with their pasturelands—four towns;

38 from the tribe of Gad,
Ramoth in Gilead (a city of refuge for one accused of murder), Mahanaim, 39 Heshbon and Jazer, together with their pasturelands—four towns in all.

40 All the towns allotted to the Merarite clans, who were the rest of the Levites, were twelve.

41 The towns of the Levites in the territory held by the Israelites were forty-eight in all, together with their pasturelands. 42 Each of these towns had pasturelands surrounding it; this was true for all these towns.

43 So the LORD gave Israel all the land he had sworn to give their forefathers, and they took possession of it and settled there. 44 The LORD gave them rest on every side, just as he had sworn to their forefathers. Not one of their enemies withstood them; the LORD handed all their enemies over to them. 45 Not one of all the LORD's good promises to the house of Israel failed; every one was fulfilled.

Eastern Tribes Return Home

22 THEN JOSHUA summoned the Reubenites, the Gadites and the half-tribe of Manasseh 2 and said to them, "You have done all that Moses the servant of the LORD commanded, and you have obeyed me in everything I commanded. 3 For a long time now—to this very day—you have not deserted your brothers but have carried out

King James

⁴And now the LORD your God hath given rest unto your brethren, as he promised them: therefore now return ye, and get you unto your tents, *and* unto the land of your possession, which Moses the servant of the LORD gave you on the other side Jordan.

⁵But take diligent heed to do the commandment and the law, which Moses the servant of the LORD charged you, to love the LORD your God, and to walk in all his ways, and to keep his commandments, and to cleave unto him, and to serve him with all your heart and with all your soul.

⁶So Joshua blessed them, and sent them away: and they went unto their tents.

⁷ ¶ Now to the *one* half of the tribe of Manasseh Moses had given *possession* in Bashan: but unto the *other* half thereof gave Joshua among their brethren on this side Jordan westward. And when Joshua sent them away also unto their tents, then he blessed them,

⁸And he spake unto them, saying, Return with much riches unto your tents, and with very much cattle, with silver, and with gold, and with brass, and with iron, and with very much raiment: divide the spoil of your enemies with your brethren.

⁹ ¶ And the children of Reuben and the children of Gad and the half tribe of Manasseh returned, and departed from the children of Israel out of Shiloh, which *is* in the land of Canaan, to go unto the country of Gilead, to the land of their possession, whereof they were possessed, according to the word of the LORD by the hand of Moses.

¹⁰ ¶ And when they came unto the borders of Jordan, that *are* in the land of Canaan, the children of Reuben and the children of Gad and the half tribe of Manasseh built there an altar by Jordan, a great altar to see to.

¹¹ ¶ And the children of Israel heard say, Behold, the children of Reuben and the children of Gad and the half tribe of Manasseh have built an altar over against the land of Canaan, in the borders of Jordan, at the passage of the children of Israel.

¹²And when the children of Israel heard *of it,* the whole congregation of the children of Israel gathered themselves together at Shiloh, to go up to war against them.

¹³And the children of Israel sent unto the children of Reuben, and to the children of Gad, and to the half tribe of Manasseh, into the land of Gilead, Phinehas the son of Eleazar the priest,

¹⁴And with him ten princes, of each ⁱchief house a prince throughout all the tribes of Israel; and each one *was* an head of the house of their fathers among the thousands of Israel.

¹⁵ ¶ And they came unto the children of Reuben, and to the children of Gad, and to the half tribe of Manasseh, unto the land of Gilead, and they spake with them, saying,

¹⁶Thus saith the whole congregation of the LORD, What trespass *is* this that ye have committed against the God of Israel, to turn away this day from following the LORD, in that ye have builded you an altar, that ye might rebel this day against the LORD?

¹⁷*Is* the iniquity of Peor too little for us, from which we are not cleansed until this day, although there was a plague in the congregation of the LORD,

¹⁸But that ye must turn away this day from following the LORD? and it will be, *seeing* ye rebel today against the LORD, that tomorrow he will be wroth with the whole congregation of Israel.

¹⁹Notwithstanding, if the land of your possession *be* unclean, *then* pass ye over unto the land of the possession of the LORD, wherein the LORD's tabernacle dwelleth, and take possession among us: but rebel not against the LORD, nor rebel against us, in building you an altar beside the altar of the LORD our God.

²⁰Did not Achan the son of Zerah commit a trespass in the accursed thing, and wrath fell on all the congregation of Israel? and that man perished not alone in his iniquity.

ⁱHeb. *house of the father*

Amplified

⁴But now the Lord your God has given rest to your brethren, as He promised them; so now go, return to your homes in the land of your possession, which Moses the servant of the Lord gave you on the [east] side of the Jordan.

⁵But take diligent heed to do the commandment and the law which Moses the servant of the Lord charged you: to love the Lord your God and to walk in all His ways and to keep His commandments and to cling to *and* unite with Him and to serve Him with all your heart and soul [your very life].

⁶So Joshua blessed them and sent them away, and they went to their homes.

⁷Now to one-half of the tribe of Manasseh Moses had given a possession in Bashan, but to the other half Joshua gave a possession on the west side of the Jordan among their brethren. So when Joshua sent them away to their homes, he blessed them,

⁸And he said to them, Return with much riches to your tents and with very much livestock, with silver, gold, bronze, iron, and very much clothing. Divide the spoil of your enemies with your brethren.

⁹So the Reubenites, Gadites, and the half-tribe of Manasseh returned home, parting from the [other] Israelites at Shiloh in the land of Canaan to go to the land of Gilead, their own land of which they had been given possession by the command of the Lord through Moses.

¹⁰And when they came to the region of the Jordan in the land of Canaan, the Reubenites, Gadites, and the half-tribe of Manasseh built there an altar by the Jordan, an altar great to behold.

¹¹And the [other] Israelites heard it said, Behold, the Reubenites, Gadites, and the half-tribe of Manasseh have built an altar at the edge of the land of Canaan in the region [west] of the Jordan in the passage [belonging to us], the Israelites.

¹²When the Israelites heard of it, the whole congregation of the sons of Israel gathered at Shiloh to make war on them.

¹³And the [other] Israelites sent to the Reubenites, Gadites, and the half-tribe of Manasseh, in the land of Gilead, Phinehas son of Eleazar, the priest,

¹⁴And with him ten chiefs, one from each of the tribal families of Israel; and each one was a head of a father's house among the clans of Israel.

¹⁵And they came to the Reubenites, Gadites, and the half-tribe of Manasseh, in the land of Gilead, and they said to them,

¹⁶The whole congregation of the Lord says, What trespass is this that you have committed against the God of Israel, to turn away this day from following the Lord, in that you have built yourselves an altar to rebel this day against the Lord?

¹⁷Is the iniquity of Peor too little for us, from which we are not cleansed even now, although there came a plague [in which 24,000 died] in the congregation of the Lord, [Num. 25:1-9.]

¹⁸That you must turn away this day from following the Lord? The result will be, since you rebel today against the Lord, that tomorrow He will be angry with the whole congregation of Israel.

¹⁹But now, if your land is unclean, pass over into the Lord's land, where the Lord's tabernacle resides, and take for yourselves a possession among us. But do not rebel against the Lord or rebel against us by building for yourselves an altar other than the altar of the Lord our God.

²⁰Did not Achan son of Zerah commit a trespass in the matter of taking accursed things [devoted to destruction] and wrath fall on all the congregation of Israel? And he did not perish alone in his perversity *and* iniquity. [Josh. 7.]

New American Standard

4"And now the LORD your God has given rest to your brothers, as He spoke to them; therefore turn now and go to your tents, to the land of your possession, which Moses the servant of the LORD gave you beyond the Jordan.

5"Only be very careful to observe the commandment and the law which Moses the servant of the LORD commanded you, to love the LORD your God and walk in all His ways and keep His commandments and hold fast to Him and serve Him with all your heart and with all your soul."

6 So Joshua blessed them and sent them away, and they went to their tents.

7 ¶ Now to the one half-tribe of Manasseh Moses had given *a possession* in Bashan, but to the other half Joshua gave *a possession* among their brothers westward beyond the Jordan. So when Joshua sent them away to their tents, he blessed them,

8 and said to them, "Return to your tents with great riches and with very much livestock, with silver, gold, bronze, iron, and with very many clothes; divide the spoil of your enemies with your brothers."

9 The sons of Reuben and the sons of Gad and the half-tribe of Manasseh returned *home* and departed from the sons of Israel at Shiloh which is in the land of Canaan, to go to the land of Gilead, to the land of their possession which they had possessed, according to the command of the LORD through Moses.

The Offensive Altar

10 ¶ When they came to the region of the Jordan which is in the land of Canaan, the sons of Reuben and the sons of Gad and the half-tribe of Manasseh built an altar there by the Jordan, a large altar in appearance.

11 And the sons of Israel heard *it* said, "Behold, the sons of Reuben and the sons of Gad and the half-tribe of Manasseh have built an altar at the frontier of the land of Canaan, in the region of the Jordan, on the side *belonging to* the sons of Israel."

12 When the sons of Israel heard *of it,* the whole congregation of the sons of Israel gathered themselves at Shiloh to go up against them in war.

13 ¶ Then the sons of Israel sent to the sons of Reuben and to the sons of Gad and to the half-tribe of Manasseh, into the land of Gilead, Phinehas the son of Eleazar the priest,

14 and with him ten chiefs, one chief for each father's household from each of the tribes of Israel; and each one of them *was* the head of his father's household among the thousands of Israel.

15 They came to the sons of Reuben and to the sons of Gad and to the half-tribe of Manasseh, to the land of Gilead, and they spoke with them saying,

16"Thus says the whole congregation of the LORD, 'What is this unfaithful act which you have committed against the God of Israel, turning away from following the LORD this day, by building yourselves an altar, to rebel against the LORD this day?

17 'Is not the iniquity of Peor enough for us, from which we have not cleansed ourselves to this day, although a plague came on the congregation of the LORD,

18 that you must turn away this day from following the LORD? If you rebel against the LORD today, He will be angry with the whole congregation of Israel tomorrow.

19 'If, however, the land of your possession is unclean, then cross into the land of the possession of the LORD, where the LORD's tabernacle stands, and take possession among us. Only do not rebel against the LORD, or rebel against us by building an altar for yourselves, besides the altar of the LORD our God.

20 'Did not Achan the son of Zerah act unfaithfully in the things under the ban, and wrath fall on all the congregation of Israel? And that man did not perish alone in his iniquity.' "

New International

the mission the LORD your God gave you. 4Now that the LORD your God has given your brothers rest as he promised, return to your homes in the land that Moses the servant of the LORD gave you on the other side of the Jordan. 5But be very careful to keep the commandment and the law that Moses the servant of the LORD gave you: to love the LORD your God, to walk in all his ways, to obey his commands, to hold fast to him and to serve him with all your heart and all your soul."

6Then Joshua blessed them and sent them away, and they went to their homes. 7(To the half-tribe of Manasseh Moses had given land in Bashan, and to the other half of the tribe Joshua gave land on the west side of the Jordan with their brothers.) When Joshua sent them home, he blessed them, 8saying, "Return to your homes with your great wealth—with large herds of livestock, with silver, gold, bronze and iron, and a great quantity of clothing—and divide with your brothers the plunder from your enemies."

9So the Reubenites, the Gadites and the half-tribe of Manasseh left the Israelites at Shiloh in Canaan to return to Gilead, their own land, which they had acquired in accordance with the command of the LORD through Moses.

10When they came to Geliloth near the Jordan in the land of Canaan, the Reubenites, the Gadites and the half-tribe of Manasseh built an imposing altar there by the Jordan. 11And when the Israelites heard that they had built the altar on the border of Canaan at Geliloth near the Jordan on the Israelite side, 12the whole assembly of Israel gathered at Shiloh to go to war against them.

13So the Israelites sent Phinehas son of Eleazar, the priest, to the land of Gilead—to Reuben, Gad and the half-tribe of Manasseh. 14With him they sent ten of the chief men, one for each of the tribes of Israel, each the head of a family division among the Israelite clans.

15When they went to Gilead—to Reuben, Gad and the half-tribe of Manasseh—they said to them: 16"The whole assembly of the LORD says: 'How could you break faith with the God of Israel like this? How could you turn away from the LORD and build yourselves an altar in rebellion against him now? 17Was not the sin of Peor enough for us? Up to this very day we have not cleansed ourselves from that sin, even though a plague fell on the community of the LORD! 18And are you now turning away from the LORD?

" 'If you rebel against the LORD today, tomorrow he will be angry with the whole community of Israel. 19If the land you possess is defiled, come over to the LORD's land, where the LORD's tabernacle stands, and share the land with us. But do not rebel against the LORD or against us by building an altar for yourselves, other than the altar of the LORD our God. 20When Achan son of Zerah acted unfaithfully regarding the devoted things,*d* did not wrath come upon the whole community of Israel? He was not the only one who died for his sin.' "

---

d 20 The Hebrew term refers to the irrevocable giving over of things or persons to the LORD, often by totally destroying them.

King James

²¹ ¶ Then the children of Reuben and the children of Gad and the half tribe of Manasseh answered, and said unto the heads of the thousands of Israel,

²²The LORD God of gods, the LORD God of gods, he knoweth, and Israel he shall know; if *it be* in rebellion, or if in transgression against the LORD, (save us not this day,)

²³That we have built us an altar to turn from following the LORD, or if to offer thereon burnt offering or meat offering, or if to offer peace offerings thereon, let the LORD himself require *it;*

²⁴And if we have not *rather* done it for fear of *this* thing, saying, *ʲ*In time to come your children might speak unto our children, saying, What have ye to do with the LORD God of Israel?

²⁵For the LORD hath made Jordan a border between us and you, ye children of Reuben and children of Gad; ye have no part in the LORD: so shall your children make our children cease from fearing the LORD.

²⁶Therefore we said, Let us now prepare to build us an altar, not for burnt offering, nor for sacrifice:

²⁷But *that* it *may be* a witness between us, and you, and our generations after us, that we might do the service of the LORD before him with our burnt offerings, and with our sacrifices, and with our peace offerings; that your children may not say to our children in time to come, Ye have no part in the LORD.

²⁸Therefore said we, that it shall be, when they should *so* say to us or to our generations in time to come, that we may say *again,* Behold the pattern of the altar of the LORD, which our fathers made, not for burnt offerings, nor for sacrifices; but it *is* a witness between us and you.

²⁹God forbid that we should rebel against the LORD, and turn this day from following the LORD, to build an altar for burnt offerings, for meat offerings, or for sacrifices, beside the altar of the LORD our God that *is* before his tabernacle.

³⁰ ¶ And when Phinehas the priest, and the princes of the congregation and heads of the thousands of Israel which *were* with him, heard the words that the children of Reuben and the children of Gad and the children of Manasseh spake, ᵏit pleased them.

³¹And Phinehas the son of Eleazar the priest said unto the children of Reuben, and to the children of Gad, and to the children of Manasseh, This day we perceive that the LORD *is* among us, because ye have not committed this trespass against the LORD: *ˡ*now ye have delivered the children of Israel out of the hand of the LORD.

³² ¶ And Phinehas the son of Eleazar the priest, and the princes, returned from the children of Reuben, and from the children of Gad, out of the land of Gilead, unto the land of Canaan, to the children of Israel, and brought them word again.

³³And the thing pleased the children of Israel; and the children of Israel blessed God, and did not intend to go up against them in battle, to destroy the land wherein the children of Reuben and Gad dwelt.

³⁴And the children of Reuben and the children of Gad called the altar *ᵐEd:* for it *shall be* a witness between us that the LORD *is* God.

Joshua's address to Israel

23 AND IT came to pass a long time after that the LORD had given rest unto Israel from all their enemies round about, that Joshua waxed old *and* ⁿstricken in age.

²And Joshua called for all Israel, *and* for their elders, and for their heads, and for their judges, and for their officers, and said unto them, I am old *and* stricken in age:

³And ye have seen all that the LORD your God hath done unto all these nations because of you; for the LORD your God is he that hath fought for you.

Amplified

²¹Then the Reubenites, Gadites, and the half-tribe of Manasseh said to the heads of the clans of Israel,

²²The Mighty One, God, the Lord! The Mighty One, God, the Lord! He knows, and let Israel itself know! If it was in rebellion or in transgression against the Lord, spare us not today.

²³If we have built us an altar to turn away from following the Lord, or if we did so to offer on it burnt offerings or cereal offerings or peace offerings, may the Lord Himself take vengeance.

²⁴No! But we did it for fear that in time to come your children might say to our children, What have you to do with the Lord, the God of Israel?

²⁵For the Lord has made the Jordan a boundary between us and you, you Reubenites and Gadites; you have no part in the Lord. So your children might make our children cease from fearing the Lord.

²⁶So we said, Let us now prepare to build us an altar, not for burnt offering nor for sacrifice,

²⁷But to be a witness between us and you and between the generations after us, that we will perform the service of the Lord before Him with our burnt offerings and sacrifices and peace offerings; lest your children say to our children in time to come, You have no portion in the Lord.

²⁸So we thought, if that should be said to us or to our descendants in time to come, we can reply, Behold the copy of the altar of the Lord, which our fathers made, not for burnt offerings nor for sacrifices, but to be a witness between us and you.

²⁹Far be it from us that we should rebel against the Lord and turn away this day from following the Lord to build an altar for burnt offerings, for cereal offerings, or for sacrifices, besides the altar of the Lord our God that is before His tabernacle.

³⁰And when Phinehas the priest and the chiefs of the congregation and heads of the clans of Israel who were with him heard the words that the Reubenites, Gadites, and Manassites spoke, it pleased them.

³¹Phinehas son of Eleazar, the priest, said to the Reubenites, Gadites, and Manassites, Today we know the Lord is among us, because you have not committed this trespass *and* treachery against the Lord; now you have saved the Israelites from the Lord's hand.

³²Then Phinehas son of Eleazar, the priest, and the chiefs returned from the Reubenites and Gadites in the land of Gilead to the land of Canaan, to the [other] Israelites, and brought back word to them.

³³The report pleased the Israelites and they blessed God; and they spoke no more of going to war against them to destroy the land in which the Reubenites and Gadites dwelt.

³⁴The Reubenites and Gadites called the altar Ed [witness], saying, It shall be: A Witness Between Us that the Lord is God.

23 A LONG time after that, when the Lord had given Israel rest from all their enemies round about, and Joshua had grown old and advanced in years,

²Joshua summoned all Israel, their elders, heads, judges, and officers, and said to them, I am old and advanced in years,

³And you have seen all that the Lord your God has done to all these nations for your sake; for it is the Lord your God Who has fought for you. [Exod. 14:14.]

ʲHeb. *Tomorrow*   ᵏHeb. *it was good in their eyes*   ˡHeb.
then   ᵐi.e. A witness   ⁿHeb. *come into days*

New American Standard

21 ¶ Then the sons of Reuben and the sons of Gad and the half-tribe of Manasseh answered and spoke to the heads of the families of Israel.

22 "The Mighty One, God, the LORD, the Mighty One, God, the LORD! He knows, and may Israel itself know. If *it was* in rebellion, or if in an unfaithful act against the LORD do not save us this day!

23 "If we have built us an altar to turn away from following the LORD, or if to offer a burnt offering or grain offering on it, or if to offer sacrifices of peace offerings on it, may the LORD Himself require it.

24 "But truly we have done this out of concern, for a reason, saying, 'In time to come your sons may say to our sons, "What have you to do with the LORD, the God of Israel?

25 "For the LORD has made the Jordan a border between us and you, *you* sons of Reuben and sons of Gad; you have no portion in the LORD." So your sons may make our sons stop fearing the LORD.'

26 ¶ "Therefore we said, 'Let us build an altar, not for burnt offering or for sacrifice;

27 rather it shall be a witness between us and you and between our generations after us, that we are to perform the service of the LORD before Him with our burnt offerings, and with our sacrifices and with our peace offerings, so that your sons will not say to our sons in time to come, "You have no portion in the LORD." '

28 "Therefore we said, 'It shall also come about if they say *this* to us or to our generations in time to come, then we shall say, "See the copy of the altar of the LORD which our fathers made, not for burnt offering or for sacrifice; rather it is a witness between us and you." '

29 "Far be it from us that we should rebel against the LORD and turn away from following the LORD this day, by building an altar for burnt offering, for grain offering or for sacrifice, besides the altar of the LORD our God which is before His *o*tabernacle."

30 ¶ So when Phinehas the priest and the leaders of the congregation, even the heads of the families of Israel who *were* with him, heard the words which the sons of Reuben and the sons of Gad and the sons of Manasseh spoke, it pleased them.

31 And Phinehas the son of Eleazar the priest said to the sons of Reuben and to the sons of Gad and to the sons of Manasseh, "Today we know that the LORD is in our midst, because you have not committed this unfaithful act against the LORD; now you have delivered the sons of Israel from the hand of the LORD."

32 ¶ Then Phinehas the son of Eleazar the priest and the leaders returned from the sons of Reuben and from the sons of Gad, from the land of Gilead to the land of Canaan, to the sons of Israel, and brought back word to them.

33 The word pleased the sons of Israel, and the sons of Israel blessed God; and they did not speak of going up against them in war to destroy the land in which the sons of Reuben and the sons of Gad were living.

34 The sons of Reuben and the sons of Gad called the altar *Witness;* "For," *they said,* "it is a witness between us that the LORD is God."

Joshua's Farewell Address

23 NOW IT came about after many days, when the LORD had given rest to Israel from all their enemies on every side, and Joshua was old, advanced in years,

2 that Joshua called for all Israel, for their elders and their heads and their judges and their officers, and said to them, "I am old, advanced in years.

3 "And you have seen all that the LORD your God has done to all these nations because of you, for the LORD your God is He who has been fighting for you.

New International

21 Then Reuben, Gad and the half-tribe of Manasseh replied to the heads of the clans of Israel: 22 "The Mighty One, God, the LORD! The Mighty One, God, the LORD! He knows! And let Israel know! If this has been in rebellion or disobedience to the LORD, do not spare us this day. 23 If we have built our own altar to turn away from the LORD and to offer burnt offerings and grain offerings, or to sacrifice fellowship offerings*e* on it, may the LORD himself call us to account.

24 "No! We did it for fear that some day your descendants might say to ours, 'What do you have to do with the LORD, the God of Israel? 25 The LORD has made the Jordan a boundary between us and you—you Reubenites and Gadites! You have no share in the LORD.' So your descendants might cause ours to stop fearing the LORD.

26 "That is why we said, 'Let us get ready and build an altar—but not for burnt offerings or sacrifices.' 27 On the contrary, it is to be a witness between us and you and the generations that follow, that we will worship the LORD at his sanctuary with our burnt offerings, sacrifices and fellowship offerings. Then in the future your descendants will not be able to say to ours, 'You have no share in the LORD.'

28 "And we said, 'If they ever say this to us, or to our descendants, we will answer: Look at the replica of the LORD's altar, which our fathers built, not for burnt offerings and sacrifices, but as a witness between us and you.'

29 "Far be it from us to rebel against the LORD and turn away from him today by building an altar for burnt offerings, grain offerings and sacrifices, other than the altar of the LORD our God that stands before his tabernacle."

30 When Phinehas the priest and the leaders of the community—the heads of the clans of the Israelites—heard what Reuben, Gad and Manasseh had to say, they were pleased. 31 And Phinehas son of Eleazar, the priest, said to Reuben, Gad and Manasseh, "Today we know that the LORD is with us, because you have not acted unfaithfully toward the LORD in this matter. Now you have rescued the Israelites from the LORD's hand."

32 Then Phinehas son of Eleazar, the priest, and the leaders returned to Canaan from their meeting with the Reubenites and Gadites in Gilead and reported to the Israelites. 33 They were glad to hear the report and praised God. And they talked no more about going to war against them to devastate the country where the Reubenites and the Gadites lived.

34 And the Reubenites and the Gadites gave the altar this name: A Witness Between Us that the LORD is God.

Joshua's Farewell to the Leaders

23 AFTER A long time had passed and the LORD had given Israel rest from all their enemies around them, Joshua, by then old and well advanced in years, 2 summoned all Israel—their elders, leaders, judges and officials—and said to them: "I am old and well advanced in years. 3 You yourselves have seen everything the LORD your God has done to all these nations for your sake; it was

---

o Lit *dwelling place*

e 23 Traditionally *peace offerings*; also in verse 27

King James

⁴Behold, I have divided unto you by lot these nations that remain, to be an inheritance for your tribes, from Jordan, with all the nations that I have cut off, even unto the great sea ᵒwestward.

⁵And the LORD your God, he shall expel them from before you, and drive them from out of your sight; and ye shall possess their land, as the LORD your God hath promised unto you.

⁶Be ye therefore very courageous to keep and to do all that is written in the book of the law of Moses, that ye turn not aside therefrom *to* the right hand or *to* the left;

⁷That ye come not among these nations, these that remain among you; neither make mention of the name of their gods, nor cause to swear *by them,* neither serve them, nor bow yourselves unto them:

⁸ᵖBut cleave unto the LORD your God, as ye have done unto this day.

⁹ᑫFor the LORD hath driven out from before you great nations and strong: but *as for* you, no man hath been able to stand before you unto this day.

¹⁰One man of you shall chase a thousand: for the LORD your God, he *it is* that fighteth for you, as he hath promised you.

¹¹Take good heed therefore unto ʳyourselves, that ye love the LORD your God.

¹²Else if ye do in any wise go back, and cleave unto the remnant of these nations, *even* these that remain among you, and shall make marriages with them, and go in unto them, and they to you:

¹³Know for a certainty that the LORD your God will no more drive out *any of* these nations from before you; but they shall be snares and traps unto you, and scourges in your sides, and thorns in your eyes, until ye perish from off this good land which the LORD your God hath given you.

¹⁴And, behold, this day I *am* going the way of all the earth: and ye know in all your hearts and in all your souls, that not one thing hath failed of all the good things which the LORD your God spake concerning you; all are come to pass unto you, *and* not one thing hath failed thereof.

¹⁵Therefore it shall come to pass, *that* as all good things are come upon you, which the LORD your God promised you; so shall the LORD bring upon you all evil things, until he have destroyed you from off this good land which the LORD your God hath given you.

¹⁶When ye have transgressed the covenant of the LORD your God, which he commanded you, and have gone and served other gods, and bowed yourselves to them; then shall the anger of the LORD be kindled against you, and ye shall perish quickly from off the good land which he hath given unto you.

Israel renews the covenant

24 AND JOSHUA gathered all the tribes of Israel to Shechem, and called for the elders of Israel, and for their heads, and for their judges, and for their officers; and they presented themselves before God.

Amplified

⁴Behold, I have allotted to you as an inheritance for your tribes those nations that remain, with all the nations I have cut off, from the Jordan to the Great Sea on the west.

⁵The Lord your God will thrust them out from before you and drive them out of your sight, and you shall possess their land, as the Lord your God ᵏpromised you.

⁶So be very courageous *and* steadfast to keep and do all that is written in the Book of the Law of Moses, turning not aside from it to the right hand or the left,

⁷That you may not mix with these nations that remain among you, or make mention of the names of their gods or swear by them or serve them or bow down to them.

⁸But cling to the Lord your God as you have done to this day.

⁹For the Lord has driven out from before you great and strong nations; and as for you, no man has been able to withstand you to this day.

¹⁰One man of you shall put to flight a thousand, for it is the Lord your God Who fights for you, as He promised you.

¹¹Be very watchful of yourselves, therefore, to ˡlove the Lord your God.

¹²For if you turn back and adhere to the remnant of these nations left among you and make marriages with them, you marrying their women and they yours,

¹³Know with certainty that the Lord your God will not continue to drive these nations from before you; but they shall be a snare and trap to you, and a scourge in your sides and thorns in your eyes, until you perish from off this good land which the Lord your God has given you.

¹⁴And behold, this day I am going the way of all the earth. Know in all your hearts and in all your souls that not one thing has failed of all the good things which the Lord your God promised concerning you. All have come to pass for you; not one thing of them has failed.

¹⁵But just as all good things which the Lord promised you have come to you, so will the Lord carry out [His] every [warning of] evil upon you, until He has destroyed you from off this good land which the Lord your God has given you.

¹⁶If you transgress the covenant of the Lord your God, which He commanded you, if you serve other gods and bow down to them, then the anger of the Lord will be kindled against you, and you shall perish quickly from off the good land He has given you.

24 THEN JOSHUA gathered all the tribes of Israel to Shechem, and summoned the elders of Israel and their heads, their judges, and their officers; they presented themselves before God.

ᵏAll through the time of Joshua's leadership he kept giving as his warrant of faith the fact that the Lord had spoken, the Lord had promised. The word of God is the guaranty of faith. Genuine faith always advances on the authority expressed in Heb. 13:5, 6, "**He** [God] **Himself has said,** . . . So **we** take comfort *and* are encouraged *and* confidently *and* boldly say . . ." (emphasis added). ˡEverything depended on whether or not Israel would continue to be faithful to the covenant. Joshua's words do not conceal his apprehension. Seven times he refers to the idolatrous nations still left in Canaan. He knew the snare they would be to Israel, and he therefore prescribed three safeguards. First, there must be brave **adherence to God's word** (Josh. 23:6). Second, there must be a vigilantly continued **separation** from the Canaanite nations (Josh. 23:7). Finally, there must be a cleaving to the Lord with real and fervent **love** (Josh. 23:8-11) (J. Sidlow Baxter, *Explore the Book*).

ᵒHeb. *at the sunset*   ᵖOr, *For if ye will cleave*   ᑫOr, *Then* the LORD *will drive*   ʳHeb. *your souls*

New American Standard

⁴"See, I have apportioned to you these nations which remain as an inheritance for your tribes, with all the nations which I have cut off, from the Jordan even to the Great Sea toward the setting of the sun.

⁵"The LORD your God, He will thrust them out from before you and drive them from before you; and you will possess their land, just as the LORD your God promised you.

⁶"Be very firm, then, to keep and do all that is written in the book of the law of Moses, so that you may not turn aside from it to the right hand or to the left,

⁷ so that you will not associate with these nations, these which remain among you, or mention the name of their gods, or make *anyone* swear *by them,* or serve them, or bow down to them.

⁸"But you are to cling to the LORD your God, as you have done to this day.

⁹"For the LORD has driven out great and strong nations from before you; and as for you, no man has stood before you to this day.

¹⁰"One of your men puts to flight a thousand, for the LORD your God is He who fights for you, just as He promised you.

¹¹"So take diligent heed to yourselves to love the LORD your God.

¹²"For if you ever go back and cling to the rest of these nations, these which remain among you, and intermarry with them, so that you associate with them and they with you,

¹³ know with certainty that the LORD your God will not continue to drive these nations out from before you; but they will be a snare and a trap to you, and a whip on your sides and thorns in your eyes, until you perish from off this good land which the LORD your God has given you.

¹⁴ ¶ "Now behold, today I am going the way of all the earth, and you know in all your hearts and in all your souls that not one word of all the good words which the LORD your God spoke concerning you has failed; all have been fulfilled for you, not one of them has failed.

¹⁵"It shall come about that just as all the good words which the LORD your God spoke to you have come upon you, so the LORD will bring upon you all the threats, until He has destroyed you from off this good land which the LORD your God has given you.

¹⁶"When you transgress the covenant of the LORD your God, which He commanded you, and go and serve other gods and bow down to them, then the anger of the LORD will burn against you, and you will perish quickly from off the good land which He has given you."

Joshua Reviews Israel's History

24 THEN JOSHUA gathered all the tribes of Israel to Shechem, and called for the elders of Israel and for their heads and their judges and their officers; and they presented themselves before God.

New International

the LORD your God who fought for you. ⁴Remember how I have allotted as an inheritance for your tribes all the land of the nations that remain—the nations I conquered—between the Jordan and the Great Sea*f* in the west. ⁵The LORD your God himself will drive them out of your way. He will push them out before you, and you will take possession of their land, as the LORD your God promised you.

⁶"Be very strong; be careful to obey all that is written in the Book of the Law of Moses, without turning aside to the right or to the left. ⁷Do not associate with these nations that remain among you; do not invoke the names of their gods or swear by them. You must not serve them or bow down to them. ⁸But you are to hold fast to the LORD your God, as you have until now.

⁹"The LORD has driven out before you great and powerful nations; to this day no one has been able to withstand you. ¹⁰One of you routs a thousand, because the LORD your God fights for you, just as he promised. ¹¹So be very careful to love the LORD your God.

¹²"But if you turn away and ally yourselves with the survivors of these nations that remain among you and if you intermarry with them and associate with them, ¹³then you may be sure that the LORD your God will no longer drive out these nations before you. Instead, they will become snares and traps for you, whips on your backs and thorns in your eyes, until you perish from this good land, which the LORD your God has given you.

¹⁴"Now I am about to go the way of all the earth. You know with all your heart and soul that not one of all the good promises the LORD your God gave you has failed. Every promise has been fulfilled; not one has failed. ¹⁵But just as every good promise of the LORD your God has come true, so the LORD will bring on you all the evil he has threatened, until he has destroyed you from this good land he has given you. ¹⁶If you violate the covenant of the LORD your God, which he commanded you, and go and serve other gods and bow down to them, the LORD's anger will burn against you, and you will quickly perish from the good land he has given you."

The Covenant Renewed at Shechem

24 THEN JOSHUA assembled all the tribes of Israel at Shechem. He summoned the elders, leaders, judges and officials of Israel, and they presented themselves before God.

---

f4 That is, the Mediterranean

King James

²And Joshua said unto all the people, Thus saith the LORD God of Israel, Your fathers dwelt on the other side of the flood in old time, *even* Terah, the father of Abraham, and the father of Nachor: and they served other gods.

³And I took your father Abraham from the other side of the flood, and led him throughout all the land of Canaan, and multiplied his seed, and gave him Isaac.

⁴And I gave unto Isaac Jacob and Esau: and I gave unto Esau mount Seir, to possess it; but Jacob and his children went down into Egypt.

⁵I sent Moses also and Aaron, and I plagued Egypt, according to that which I did among them: and afterward I brought you out.

⁶And I brought your fathers out of Egypt: and ye came unto the sea; and the Egyptians pursued after your fathers with chariots and horsemen unto the Red sea.

⁷And when they cried unto the LORD, he put darkness between you and the Egyptians, and brought the sea upon them, and covered them; and your eyes have seen what I have done in Egypt: and ye dwelt in the wilderness a long season.

⁸And I brought you into the land of the Amorites, which dwelt on the other side Jordan; and they fought with you: and I gave them into your hand, that ye might possess their land; and I destroyed them from before you.

⁹Then Balak the son of Zippor, king of Moab, arose and warred against Israel, and sent and called Balaam the son of Beor to curse you:

¹⁰But I would not hearken unto Balaam; therefore he blessed you still: so I delivered you out of his hand.

¹¹And ye went over Jordan, and came unto Jericho: and the men of Jericho fought against you, the Amorites, and the Perizzites, and the Canaanites, and the Hittites, and the Girgashites, the Hivites, and the Jebusites; and I delivered them into your hand.

¹²And I sent the hornet before you, which drave them out from before you, *even* the two kings of the Amorites; *but* not with thy sword, nor with thy bow.

¹³And I have given you a land for which ye did not labour, and cities which ye built not, and ye dwell in them; of the vineyards and oliveyards which ye planted not do ye eat.

¹⁴ ¶ Now therefore fear the LORD, and serve him in sincerity and in truth: and put away the gods which your fathers served on the other side of the flood, and in Egypt; and serve ye the LORD.

¹⁵And if it seem evil unto you to serve the LORD, choose you this day whom ye will serve; whether the gods which your fathers served that *were* on the other side of the flood, or the gods of the Amorites, in whose land ye dwell: but as for me and my house, we will serve the LORD.

¹⁶And the people answered and said, God forbid that we should forsake the LORD, to serve other gods;

¹⁷For the LORD our God, he *it is* that brought us up and our fathers out of the land of Egypt, from the house of bondage, and which did those great signs in our sight, and preserved us in all the way wherein we went, and among all the people through whom we passed:

¹⁸And the LORD drave out from before us all the people, even the Amorites which dwelt in the land: *therefore* will we also serve the LORD; for he *is* our God.

¹⁹And Joshua said unto the people, Ye cannot serve the LORD: for he *is* an holy God; he *is* a jealous God; he will not forgive your transgressions nor your sins.

²⁰If ye forsake the LORD, and serve strange gods, then he will turn and do you hurt, and consume you, after that he hath done you good.

²¹And the people said unto Joshua, Nay; but we will serve the LORD.

Amplified

²Joshua said to all the people, Thus says the Lord, the God of Israel, Your fathers dwelt in olden times beyond the Euphrates River, including Terah the father of Abraham and Nahor, and they served other gods.

³And I took your father Abraham from beyond the Euphrates River and led him through all the land of Canaan and multiplied his offspring. I gave him Isaac,

⁴And I gave to Isaac Jacob and Esau. And I gave to Esau the hill country of Seir to possess, but Jacob and his children went down into Egypt.

⁵I sent Moses and Aaron, and I plagued Egypt with what I did in the midst of it; and afterward I brought you out.

⁶I brought your fathers out of Egypt, and you came to the sea; and the Egyptians pursued your fathers with chariots and horsemen to the Red Sea.

⁷When they cried to the Lord, He put darkness between you and the Egyptians, and brought the sea upon them and covered them; and your eyes saw what I did in Egypt. And you lived in the wilderness a long time [forty years]. [Josh. 5:6.]

⁸I brought you into the land of the Amorites who lived on the other side of the Jordan; they fought with you, and I gave them into your hand, and you possessed their land, and I destroyed them before you.

⁹Then Balak son of Zippor, king of Moab, arose and warred against Israel, and sent and called Balaam son of Beor to curse you.

¹⁰But I would not listen to Balaam; therefore he blessed you; so I delivered you out of Balak's hand. [Deut. 23:5.]

¹¹You went over the Jordan and came to Jericho; and the men of Jericho fought against you, as did the Amorites, Perizzites, Canaanites, Hittites, Girgashites, Hivites, and Jebusites, and I gave them into your hands.

¹²I sent the ᵐhornet [that is, the terror of you] before you, which drove the two kings of the Amorites out before you; but it was not by your sword or by your bow. [Exod. 23:27, 28; Deut. 2:25; 7:20.]

¹³I have given you a land for which you did not labor and cities you did not build, and you dwell in them; you eat from vineyards and olive yards you did not plant.

¹⁴Now therefore, [reverently] fear the Lord and serve Him in sincerity and in truth; put away the gods which your fathers served on the other side of the [Euphrates] River and in Egypt, and serve the Lord.

¹⁵And if it seems evil to you to serve the Lord, choose for yourselves this day whom you will serve, whether the gods which your fathers served on the other side of the River, or the gods of the Amorites, in whose land you dwell; but as for me and my house, we will serve the Lord.

¹⁶The people answered, Far be it from us to forsake the Lord to serve other gods;

¹⁷For it is the Lord our God Who brought us and our fathers up out of the land of Egypt, from the house of bondage, Who did those great signs in our sight and preserved us in all the way that we went and among all the peoples through whom we passed.

¹⁸And the Lord drove out before us all the people, the Amorites who dwelt in the land. Therefore we also will serve the Lord, for He is our God.

¹⁹And Joshua said to the people, You cannot serve the Lord, for He is a holy God; He is a jealous God. He will not forgive your transgressions or your sins.

²⁰If you forsake the Lord and ⁿserve strange gods, then He will turn and do you harm and consume you, after having done you good.

²¹And the people said to Joshua, No; but we will serve the Lord.

ᵐ See footnote on Deut. 7:20.   ⁿ Anything which we keep in our hearts in the place which God ought to have is an idol, whether it be an image of wood or stone or gold, or whether it be money, or desire for fame, or love of pleasure, or some secret sin which we will not give up. If God does not really occupy the highest place in our hearts, controlling all, something else does, and that something else is an idol (J. R. Miller, *Devotional Hours with the Bible*).

New American Standard

2 Joshua said to all the people, "Thus says the LORD, the God of Israel, 'From ancient times your fathers lived beyond the PRiver, *namely,* Terah, the father of Abraham and the father of Nahor, and they served other gods.

3 'Then I took your father Abraham from beyond the PRiver, and led him through all the land of Canaan, and multiplied his descendants and gave him Isaac.

4 'To Isaac I gave Jacob and Esau, and to Esau I gave Mount Seir to possess it; but Jacob and his sons went down to Egypt.

5 'Then I sent Moses and Aaron, and I plagued Egypt by what I did in its midst; and afterward I brought you out.

6 'I brought your fathers out of Egypt, and you came to the sea; and Egypt pursued your fathers with chariots and horsemen to the Red Sea.

7 'But when they cried out to the LORD, He put darkness between you and the Egyptians, and brought the sea upon them and covered them; and your own eyes saw what I did in Egypt. And you lived in the wilderness for a long time.

8 'Then I brought you into the land of the Amorites who lived beyond the Jordan, and they fought with you; and I gave them into your hand, and you took possession of their land when I destroyed them before you.

9 'Then Balak the son of Zippor, king of Moab, arose and fought against Israel, and he sent and summoned Balaam the son of Beor to curse you.

10 'But I was not willing to listen to Balaam. So he had to bless you, and I delivered you from his hand.

11 'You crossed the Jordan and came to Jericho; and the citizens of Jericho fought against you, *and* the Amorite and the Perizzite and the Canaanite and the Hittite and the Girgashite, the Hivite and the Jebusite. Thus I gave them into your hand.

12 'Then I sent the hornet before you and it drove out the two kings of the Amorites from before you, *but* not by your sword or your bow.

13 'I gave you a land on which you had not labored, and cities which you had not built, and you have lived in them; you are eating of vineyards and olive groves which you did not plant.'

"We Will Serve the LORD"

14 ¶ "Now, therefore, fear the LORD and serve Him in sincerity and truth; and put away the gods which your fathers served beyond the River and in Egypt, and serve the LORD.

15 "If it is disagreeable in your sight to serve the LORD, choose for yourselves today whom you will serve: whether the gods which your fathers served which were beyond the River, or the gods of the Amorites in whose land you are living; but as for me and my house, we will serve the LORD."

16 ¶ The people answered and said, "Far be it from us that we should forsake the LORD to serve other gods;

17 for the LORD our God is He who brought us and our fathers up out of the land of Egypt, from the house of bondage, and who did these great signs in our sight and preserved us through all the way in which we went and among all the peoples through whose midst we passed.

18 "The LORD drove out from before us all the peoples, even the Amorites who lived in the land. We also will serve the LORD, for He is our God."

19 ¶ Then Joshua said to the people, "You will not be able to serve the LORD, for He is a holy God. He is a jealous God; He will not forgive your transgression or your sins.

20 "If you forsake the LORD and serve foreign gods, then He will turn and do you harm and consume you after He has done good to you."

21 The people said to Joshua, "No, but we will serve the LORD."

New International

2 Joshua said to all the people, "This is what the LORD, the God of Israel, says: 'Long ago your forefathers, including Terah the father of Abraham and Nahor, lived beyond the River^g and worshiped other gods. 3 But I took your father Abraham from the land beyond the River and led him throughout Canaan and gave him many descendants. I gave him Isaac, 4 and to Isaac I gave Jacob and Esau. I assigned the hill country of Seir to Esau, but Jacob and his sons went down to Egypt.

5 " 'Then I sent Moses and Aaron, and I afflicted the Egyptians by what I did there, and I brought you out. 6 When I brought your fathers out of Egypt, you came to the sea, and the Egyptians pursued them with chariots and horsemen^h as far as the Red Sea.^{i} 7 But they cried to the LORD for help, and he put darkness between you and the Egyptians; he brought the sea over them and covered them. You saw with your own eyes what I did to the Egyptians. Then you lived in the desert for a long time.

8 " 'I brought you to the land of the Amorites who lived east of the Jordan. They fought against you, but I gave them into your hands. I destroyed them from before you, and you took possession of their land. 9 When Balak son of Zippor, the king of Moab, prepared to fight against Israel, he sent for Balaam son of Beor to put a curse on you. 10 But I would not listen to Balaam, so he blessed you again and again, and I delivered you out of his hand.

11 " 'Then you crossed the Jordan and came to Jericho. The citizens of Jericho fought against you, as did also the Amorites, Perizzites, Canaanites, Hittites, Girgashites, Hivites and Jebusites, but I gave them into your hands. 12 I sent the hornet ahead of you, which drove them out before you—also the two Amorite kings. You did not do it with your own sword and bow. 13 So I gave you a land on which you did not toil and cities you did not build; and you live in them and eat from vineyards and olive groves that you did not plant.'

14 "Now fear the LORD and serve him with all faithfulness. Throw away the gods your forefathers worshiped beyond the River and in Egypt, and serve the LORD. 15 But if serving the LORD seems undesirable to you, then choose for yourselves this day whom you will serve, whether the gods your forefathers served beyond the River, or the gods of the Amorites, in whose land you are living. But as for me and my household, we will serve the LORD."

16 Then the people answered, "Far be it from us to forsake the LORD to serve other gods! 17 It was the LORD our God himself who brought us and our fathers up out of Egypt, from that land of slavery, and performed those great signs before our eyes. He protected us on our entire journey and among all the nations through which we traveled. 18 And the LORD drove out before us all the nations, including the Amorites, who lived in the land. We too will serve the LORD, because he is our God."

19 Joshua said to the people, "You are not able to serve the LORD. He is a holy God; he is a jealous God. He will not forgive your rebellion and your sins. 20 If you forsake the LORD and serve foreign gods, he will turn and bring disaster on you and make an end of you, after he has been good to you."

21 But the people said to Joshua, "No! We will serve the LORD."

p I.e. Euphrates

g 2 That is, the Euphrates; also in verses 3, 14 and 15
h 6 Or *charioteers* i 6 Hebrew *Yam Suph;* that is, Sea of Reeds

King James

22And Joshua said unto the people, Ye *are* witnesses against yourselves that ye have chosen you the LORD, to serve him. And they said, *We are* witnesses.

23Now therefore put away, *said he*, the strange gods which *are* among you, and incline your heart unto the LORD God of Israel.

24And the people said unto Joshua, The LORD our God will we serve, and his voice will we obey.

25So Joshua made a covenant with the people that day, and set them a statute and an ordinance in Shechem.

26 And Joshua wrote these words in the book of the law of God, and took a great stone, and set it up there under an oak, that *was* by the sanctuary of the LORD.

27And Joshua said unto all the people, Behold, this stone shall be a witness unto us; for it hath heard all the words of the LORD which he spake unto us: it shall be therefore a witness unto you, lest ye deny your God.

28So Joshua let the people depart, every man unto his inheritance.

The death of Joshua

29 ¶ And it came to pass after these things, that Joshua the son of Nun, the servant of the LORD, died, *being* an hundred and ten years old.

30And they buried him in the border of his inheritance in Timnath-serah, which *is* in mount Ephraim, on the north side of the hill of Gaash.

31And Israel served the LORD all the days of Joshua, and all the days of the elders that *soverlived* Joshua, and which had known all the works of the LORD, that he had done for Israel.

32 ¶ And the bones of Joseph, which the children of Israel brought up out of Egypt, buried they in Shechem, in a parcel of ground which Jacob bought of the sons of Hamor the father of Shechem for an hundred *pieces of silver: and it became the inheritance of the children of Joseph.

33And Eleazar the son of Aaron died; and they buried him in a hill *that pertained to* Phinehas his son, which was given him in mount Ephraim.

Amplified

22Then Joshua said to the people, You are witnesses against yourselves that you have chosen the Lord, to serve Him. And they said, We are witnesses.

23Then put away, said he, the foreign gods that are among you and incline your hearts to the Lord, the God of Israel.

24The people said to Joshua, The Lord our God we will serve; His voice we will obey.

25So Joshua made a covenant with the people that day, and made statutes and ordinances for them at Shechem.

26And Joshua wrote these words in the Book of the Law of God; and he took a great stone and set it up there under an oak that was in [the court of] the sanctuary of the Lord.

27And Joshua said to all the people, See, this stone shall be a witness against us, for it has heard all the words the Lord spoke to us; so it shall be a witness against you, lest [afterward] you lie (pretend) *and* deny your God.

28So Joshua sent the people away, every man to his inheritance.

29After this, Joshua son of Nun, the servant of the Lord, died, being 110 years old.

30They buried him at the edge of his inheritance in Timnath-serah in the hill country of Ephraim, on the north side of the hill of Gaash.

31Israel served the Lord all the days of Joshua and of the elders who outlived Joshua and had known all the works the Lord had done for Israel.

32And the bones of Joseph, which the Israelites brought up out of Egypt, they buried in Shechem in the portion of ground Jacob bought from the sons of Hamor, the father of Shechem, for 100 pieces of money; and it became the inheritance of the Josephites.

33And Eleazar son of Aaron died; and they buried him at Gibeah [on the hill] of Phinehas his son, which was given him in the hill country of Ephraim.

---

s Heb. *prolonged* their *days after Joshua*   ¹Or, *lambs*

New American Standard

22 Joshua said to the people, "You are witnesses against yourselves that you have chosen for yourselves the LORD, to serve Him." And they said, "We are witnesses."

23 "Now therefore, put away the foreign gods which are in your midst, and incline your hearts to the LORD, the God of Israel."

24 The people said to Joshua, "We will serve the LORD our God and we will obey His voice."

25 So Joshua made a covenant with the people that day, and made for them a statute and an ordinance in Shechem.

26 And Joshua wrote these words in the book of the law of God; and he took a large stone and set it up there under the oak that was by the sanctuary of the LORD.

27 Joshua said to all the people, "Behold, this stone shall be for a witness against us, for it has heard all the words of the LORD which He spoke to us; thus it shall be for a witness against you, so that you do not deny your God."

28 Then Joshua dismissed the people, each to his inheritance.

Joshua's Death and Burial

29 ¶ It came about after these things that Joshua the son of Nun, the servant of the LORD, died, being one hundred and ten years old.

30 And they buried him in the territory of his inheritance in Timnath-serah, which is in the hill country of Ephraim, on the north of Mount Gaash.

31 ¶ Israel served the LORD all the days of Joshua and all the days of the elders who survived Joshua, and had known all the deeds of the LORD which He had done for Israel.

32 ¶ Now they buried the bones of Joseph, which the sons of Israel brought up from Egypt, at Shechem, in the piece of ground which Jacob had bought from the sons of Hamor the father of Shechem for one hundred pieces of money; and they became the inheritance of Joseph's sons.

33 And Eleazar the son of Aaron died; and they buried him at Gibeah of Phinehas his son, which was given him in the hill country of Ephraim.

New International

22 Then Joshua said, "You are witnesses against yourselves that you have chosen to serve the LORD."

"Yes, we are witnesses," they replied.

23 "Now then," said Joshua, "throw away the foreign gods that are among you and yield your hearts to the LORD, the God of Israel."

24 And the people said to Joshua, "We will serve the LORD our God and obey him."

25 On that day Joshua made a covenant for the people, and there at Shechem he drew up for them decrees and laws. 26 And Joshua recorded these things in the Book of the Law of God. Then he took a large stone and set it up there under the oak near the holy place of the LORD.

27 "See!" he said to all the people. "This stone will be a witness against us. It has heard all the words the LORD has said to us. It will be a witness against you if you are untrue to your God."

Buried in the Promised Land

28 Then Joshua sent the people away, each to his own inheritance.

29 After these things, Joshua son of Nun, the servant of the LORD, died at the age of a hundred and ten. 30 And they buried him in the land of his inheritance, at Timnath Serah[j] in the hill country of Ephraim, north of Mount Gaash.

31 Israel served the LORD throughout the lifetime of Joshua and of the elders who outlived him and who had experienced everything the LORD had done for Israel.

32 And Joseph's bones, which the Israelites had brought up from Egypt, were buried at Shechem in the tract of land that Jacob bought for a hundred pieces of silver[k] from the sons of Hamor, the father of Shechem. This became the inheritance of Joseph's descendants.

33 And Eleazar son of Aaron died and was buried at Gibeah, which had been allotted to his son Phinehas in the hill country of Ephraim.

---

[j]30 Also known as *Timnath Heres* (see Judges 2:9)
[k]32 Hebrew *hundred kesitahs*; a kesitah was a unit of money of unknown weight and value.

THE BOOK OF
Judges

THE BOOK OF
Judges

Fighting the Canaanites

1 NOW AFTER the death of Joshua it came to pass, that the children of Israel asked the LORD, saying, Who shall go up for us against the Canaanites first, to fight against them?

2 And the LORD said, Judah shall go up: behold, I have delivered the land into his hand.

3 And Judah said unto Simeon his brother, Come up with me into my lot, that we may fight against the Canaanites; and I likewise will go with thee into thy lot. So Simeon went with him.

4 And Judah went up; and the LORD delivered the Canaanites and the Perizzites into their hand: and they slew of them in Bezek ten thousand men.

5 And they found Adoni-bezek in Bezek: and they fought against him, and they slew the Canaanites and the Perizzites.

6 But Adoni-bezek fled; and they pursued after him, and caught him, and cut off his thumbs and his great toes.

7 And Adoni-bezek said, Threescore and ten kings, having *a*their thumbs and their great toes cut off, *b*gathered *their meat* under my table: as I have done, so God hath requited me. And they brought him to Jerusalem, and there he died.

8 Now the children of Judah had fought against Jerusalem, and had taken it, and smitten it with the edge of the sword, and set the city on fire.

9 ¶ And afterward the children of Judah went down to fight against the Canaanites, that dwelt in the mountain, and in the south, and in the *c*valley.

10 And Judah went against the Canaanites that dwelt in Hebron: (now the name of Hebron before *was* Kirjatharba:) and they slew Sheshai, and Ahiman, and Talmai.

11 And from thence he went against the inhabitants of Debir: and the name of Debir before *was* Kirjath-sepher:

12 And Caleb said, He that smiteth Kirjath-sepher, and taketh it, to him will I give Achsah my daughter to wife.

13 And Othniel the son of Kenaz, Caleb's younger brother, took it: and he gave him Achsah his daughter to wife.

14 And it came to pass, when she came *to him,* that she moved him to ask of her father a field: and she lighted from off *her* ass; and Caleb said unto her, What wilt thou?

15 And she said unto him, Give me a blessing: for thou hast given me a south land; give me also springs of water. And Caleb gave her the upper springs and the nether springs.

16 ¶ And the children of the Kenite, Moses' father-in-law, went up out of the city of palm trees with the children of Judah into the wilderness of Judah, which *lieth* in the south of Arad; and they went and dwelt among the people.

17 And Judah went with Simeon his brother, and they slew the Canaanites that inhabited Zephath, and utterly destroyed it. And the name of the city was called Hormah.

18 Also Judah took Gaza with the coast thereof, and Askelon with the coast thereof, and Ekron with the coast thereof.

19 And the LORD was with Judah; and *d*he drave out *the inhabitants of* the mountain; but could not drive out the inhabitants of the valley, because they had chariots of iron.

20 And they gave Hebron unto Caleb, as Moses said: and he expelled thence the three sons of Anak.

1 AFTER THE death of Joshua, the Israelites asked the Lord, Who shall go up first for us against the Canaanites to fight against them?

2 And the Lord said, Judah shall go up; behold, I have delivered the land into his hand.

3 And Judah [the tribe] said to [the tribe of] Simeon his brother, Come up with me into my allotted territory, so that we may fight against the Canaanites; and I likewise will go with you into your territory. So Simeon went with him.

4 Then Judah went up and the Lord delivered the Canaanites and the Perizzites into their hand, and they smote 10,000 of them in Bezek.

5 And they found Adoni-bezek in Bezek and fought against him, and they smote the Canaanites and the Perizzites.

6 Adoni-bezek fled, but they pursued him and caught him and cut off his thumbs and his big toes.

7 Adoni-bezek said, Seventy kings with their thumbs and big toes cut off used to gather their food under my table. As I have done, so God has repaid me. And they brought him to Jerusalem, and there he died.

8 And the men of Judah fought against [Jebusite] Jerusalem and took it, and smote it with the edge of the sword and set the city on fire.

9 Afterward the men of Judah went down to fight against the Canaanites who dwelt in the hill country, in the South (the Negeb), and in the lowland.

10 And Judah went against the Canaanites who dwelt in Hebron. The name of Hebron before was Kiriath-arba. And they defeated Sheshai and Ahiman and Talmai.

11 From there [Judah] went against the inhabitants of Debir. The name of Debir before was Kiriath-sepher [city of books and scribes].

12 And Caleb said, Whoever attacks Kiriath-sepher and takes it, to him will I give Achsah, my daughter, as wife.

13 And Othniel son of Kenaz, Caleb's younger brother, took it; and he gave him Achsah, his daughter, as wife.

14 And when she came to [Othniel], she got his consent to ask her father for a [sloping] field. And she alighted off her donkey, and Caleb said to her, What do you want?

15 And she said to him, Give me a present; since you have set me in the land of the South (the Negeb), give me also springs of water. And Caleb gave her the upper and lower springs.

16 And the descendants of the Kenite, Moses' father-in-law, went up with the Judahites from the City of Palms (Jericho) into the Wilderness of Judah, which lies in the South (the Negeb) near Arad; and they went and dwelt with the people.

17 And [the tribe of] Judah went with Simeon his brother, and they slew the Canaanites who inhabited Zephath and utterly destroyed it. So the city was called Hormah [destruction].

18 Also Judah took Gaza, Askelon, and Ekron—each with its territory.

19 The Lord was with Judah, and [Judah] drove out the inhabitants of the hill country, but he could not drive out those inhabiting the [difficult] valley basin because they had chariots of iron.

20 Hebron was given to Caleb as Moses said, and he expelled from there the three sons of Anak. [Josh. 14:6, 9.]

THE BOOK OF

Judges

Judges

Jerusalem Is Captured

1 NOW IT came about after the death of Joshua that the sons of Israel inquired of the LORD, saying, "Who shall go up first for us against the Canaanites, to fight against them?" 2 The LORD said, "Judah shall go up; behold, I have given the land into his hand." 3 Then Judah said to Simeon his brother, "Come up with me into the territory allotted me, that we may fight against the Canaanites; and I in turn will go with you into the territory allotted you." So Simeon went with him. 4 Judah went up, and the LORD gave the Canaanites and the Perizzites into their hands, and they defeated ten thousand men at Bezek. 5 They found Adoni-bezek in Bezek and fought against him, and they defeated the Canaanites and the Perizzites. 6 But Adoni-bezek fled; and they pursued him and caught him and cut off his thumbs and big toes. 7 Adoni-bezek said, "Seventy kings with their thumbs and their big toes cut off used to gather up *scraps* under my table; as I have done, so God has repaid me." So they brought him to Jerusalem and he died there.

8 ¶ Then the sons of Judah fought against Jerusalem and captured it and struck it with the edge of the sword and set the city on fire. 9 Afterward the sons of Judah went down to fight against the Canaanites living in the hill country and in the *a*Negev and in the lowland. 10 So Judah went against the Canaanites who lived in Hebron (now the name of Hebron formerly *was* Kiriath-arba); and they struck Sheshai and Ahiman and Talmai.

Capture of Other Cities

11 ¶ Then from there he went against the inhabitants of Debir (now the name of Debir formerly *was* Kiriath-sepher). 12 And Caleb said, "The one who attacks Kiriath-sepher and captures it, I will even give him my daughter Achsah for a wife." 13 Othniel the son of Kenaz, Caleb's younger brother, captured it; so he gave him his daughter Achsah for a wife. 14 Then it came about when she came *to him,* that she persuaded him to ask her father for a field. Then she alighted from her donkey, and Caleb said to her, "What do you want?" 15 She said to him, "Give me a blessing, since you have given me the land of the *a*Negev, give me also springs of water." So Caleb gave her the upper springs and the lower springs. 16 ¶ The descendants of the Kenite, Moses' father-in-law, went up from the city of palms with the sons of Judah, to the wilderness of Judah which is in the south of Arad; and they went and lived with the people. 17 Then Judah went with Simeon his brother, and they struck the Canaanites living in Zephath, and utterly destroyed it. So the name of the city was called Hormah. 18 And Judah took Gaza with its territory and Ashkelon with its territory and Ekron with its territory. 19 Now the LORD was with Judah, and they took possession of the hill country; but they could not drive out the inhabitants of the valley because they had iron chariots. 20 Then they gave Hebron to Caleb, as Moses had promised; and he drove out from there the three sons of Anak.

Israel Fights the Remaining Canaanites

1 AFTER THE death of Joshua, the Israelites asked the LORD, "Who will be the first to go up and fight for us against the Canaanites?"

2 The LORD answered, "Judah is to go; I have given the land into their hands."

3 Then the men of Judah said to the Simeonites their brothers, "Come up with us into the territory allotted to us, to fight against the Canaanites. We in turn will go with you into yours." So the Simeonites went with them.

4 When Judah attacked, the LORD gave the Canaanites and Perizzites into their hands and they struck down ten thousand men at Bezek. 5 It was there that they found Adoni-Bezek and fought against him, putting to rout the Canaanites and Perizzites. 6 Adoni-Bezek fled, but they chased him and caught him, and cut off his thumbs and big toes.

7 Then Adoni-Bezek said, "Seventy kings with their thumbs and big toes cut off have picked up scraps under my table. Now God has paid me back for what I did to them." They brought him to Jerusalem, and he died there.

8 The men of Judah attacked Jerusalem also and took it. They put the city to the sword and set it on fire.

9 After that, the men of Judah went down to fight against the Canaanites living in the hill country, the Negev and the western foothills. 10 They advanced against the Canaanites living in Hebron (formerly called Kiriath Arba) and defeated Sheshai, Ahiman and Talmai.

11 From there they advanced against the people living in Debir (formerly called Kiriath Sepher). 12 And Caleb said, "I will give my daughter Acsah in marriage to the man who attacks and captures Kiriath Sepher." 13 Othniel son of Kenaz, Caleb's younger brother, took it; so Caleb gave his daughter Acsah to him in marriage.

14 One day when she came to Othniel, she urged him*a* to ask her father for a field. When she got off her donkey, Caleb asked her, "What can I do for you?"

15 She replied, "Do me a special favor. Since you have given me land in the Negev, give me also springs of water." Then Caleb gave her the upper and lower springs.

16 The descendants of Moses' father-in-law, the Kenite, went up from the City of Palms*b* with the men of Judah to live among the people of the Desert of Judah in the Negev near Arad.

17 Then the men of Judah went with the Simeonites their brothers and attacked the Canaanites living in Zephath, and they totally destroyed*c* the city. Therefore it was called Hormah.*d* 18 The men of Judah also took*e* Gaza, Ashkelon and Ekron—each city with its territory.

19 The LORD was with the men of Judah. They took possession of the hill country, but they were unable to drive the people from the plains, because they had iron chariots. 20 As Moses had promised, Hebron was given to

---

a 14 Hebrew; Septuagint and Vulgate *Othniel, he urged her*
b 16 That is, Jericho   *c 17* The Hebrew term refers to the irrevocable giving over of things or persons to the LORD, often by totally destroying them.   *d 17* *Hormah* means *destruction.*
e 18 Hebrew; Septuagint *Judah did not take*

King James

²¹And the children of Benjamin did not drive out the Jebusites that inhabited Jerusalem; but the Jebusites dwell with the children of Benjamin in Jerusalem unto this day.

²² ¶ And the house of Joseph, they also went up against Beth-el: and the LORD *was* with them.

²³And the house of Joseph sent to descry Beth-el. (Now the name of the city before *was* Luz.)

²⁴And the spies saw a man come forth out of the city, and they said unto him, Show us, we pray thee, the entrance into the city, and we will show thee mercy.

²⁵And when he showed them the entrance into the city, they smote the city with the edge of the sword; but they let go the man and all his family.

²⁶And the man went into the land of the Hittites, and built a city, and called the name thereof Luz: which *is* the name thereof unto this day.

²⁷ ¶ Neither did Manasseh drive out *the inhabitants of* Beth-shean and her towns, nor Taanach and her towns, nor the inhabitants of Dor and her towns, nor the inhabitants of Ibleam and her towns, nor the inhabitants of Megiddo and her towns: but the Canaanites would dwell in that land.

²⁸And it came to pass, when Israel was strong, that they put the Canaanites to tribute, and did not utterly drive them out.

²⁹ ¶ Neither did Ephraim drive out the Canaanites that dwelt in Gezer; but the Canaanites dwelt in Gezer among them.

³⁰ ¶ Neither did Zebulun drive out the inhabitants of Kitron, nor the inhabitants of Nahalol; but the Canaanites dwelt among them, and became tributaries.

³¹ ¶ Neither did Asher drive out the inhabitants of Accho, nor the inhabitants of Zidon, nor of Ahlab, nor of Achzib, nor of Helbah, nor of Aphik, nor of Rehob:

³²But the Asherites dwelt among the Canaanites, the inhabitants of the land: for they did not drive them out.

³³ ¶ Neither did Naphtali drive out the inhabitants of Beth-shemesh, nor the inhabitants of Beth-anath; but he dwelt among the Canaanites, the inhabitants of the land: nevertheless the inhabitants of Beth-shemesh and of Beth-anath became tributaries unto them.

³⁴And the Amorites forced the children of Dan into the mountain: for they would not suffer them to come down to the valley:

³⁵But the Amorites would dwell in mount Heres in Aijalon, and in Shaalbim: yet the hand of the house of Joseph ᵉprevailed, so that they became tributaries.

³⁶And the coast of the Amorites *was* from ᶠthe going up to Akrabbim, from the rock, and upward.

Israel's disobedience

2 AND AN ᵍangel of the LORD came up from Gilgal to Bochim, and said, I made you to go up out of Egypt, and have brought you unto the land which I sware unto your fathers; and I said, I will never break my covenant with you.

²And ye shall make no league with the inhabitants of this land; ye shall throw down their altars: but ye have not obeyed my voice: why have ye done this?

³Wherefore I also said, I will not drive them out from before you; but they shall be *as thorns* in your sides, and their gods shall be a snare unto you.

⁴And it came to pass, when the angel of the LORD spake these words unto all the children of Israel, that the people lifted up their voice, and wept.

⁵And they called the name of that place ʰBochim: and they sacrificed there unto the LORD.

Amplified

²¹But the Benjamites did not drive out the Jebusites who inhabited Jerusalem; the Jebusites dwell with the Benjamites in Jerusalem to this day.

²²The house of Joseph also went up against Bethel, and the Lord was with them.

²³And the house of Joseph was sent to spy out Bethel. The name of the city formerly had been Luz.

²⁴And the spies saw a man coming out of the city and they said to him, Show us, we pray you, the way into the city and we will show you mercy.

²⁵When he showed them the entrance to the city, they smote the city with the sword, but they let the man and all his family go.

²⁶And the man went into the land of the Hittites and built a city and called it Luz, which is its name to this day.

²⁷Neither did Manasseh drive out the inhabitants of Beth-shean and its villages, or of Taanach or Dor or Ibleam or Megiddo and their villages, but the Canaanites remained in that land.

²⁸When Israel became strong, they put the Canaanites to forced labor but did not utterly drive them out.

²⁹Neither did Ephraim drive out the Canaanites who dwelt in Gezer, but the Canaanites dwelt in Gezer among them.

³⁰Neither did Zebulun drive out the inhabitants of Kitron or of Nahalol, but the Canaanites dwelt among them and were put to forced labor.

³¹Neither did Asher drive out the inhabitants of Acco or of Sidon or of Ahlab or of Achzib or of Helbah or of Aphik or of Rehob;

³²But the Asherites dwelt among the Canaanites, the inhabitants of the land, for they did not drive them out.

³³Neither did Naphtali drive out the inhabitants of Beth-shemesh or of Beth-anath, but dwelt among the Canaanites, the inhabitants of the land; but the inhabitants of Beth-shemesh and of Beth-anath became subject to forced labor for them.

³⁴The Amorites forced the Danites back into the hill country, for they would not allow them to come down into the plain;

³⁵The Amorites remained fixed in Mount Heres [mountain of the sun], in Aijalon, and in Shaalbim; yet the hand of the house of Joseph prevailed, so that they became subject to forced labor.

³⁶And the border of the Amorites was from the ascent of Akrabbim, from the rock Sela and onward.

2 NOW THE ᵃAngel of the Lord went up from Gilgal to Bochim. And He said, I brought you up from Egypt and have brought you to the land which I swore to give to your fathers, and I said, I will never break My covenant with you; [Exod. 20:2.]

²And you shall make no covenant with the inhabitants of this land; but you shall break down their altars. But you have not obeyed My voice. Why have you done this?

³So now I say, I will not drive them out from before you; but they shall be as thorns in your sides, and their gods shall be a snare to you.

⁴When the Angel of the Lord spoke these words to all the Israelites, the people lifted up their voice and wept.

⁵They named that place Bochim [weepers], and they sacrificed there to the Lord.

ᵉ Heb. *was heavy*   ᶠ Or, *Maaleh-akrabbim*   ᵍ Or, *messenger*
ʰ i.e. *Weepers*   ᵃ See footnote on Gen. 16:7.

New American Standard

21 But the sons of Benjamin did not drive out the Jebusites who lived in Jerusalem; so the Jebusites have lived with the sons of Benjamin in Jerusalem to this day.

22 ¶ Likewise the house of Joseph went up against Bethel, and the LORD was with them.

23 The house of Joseph spied out Bethel (now the name of the city was formerly Luz).

24 The spies saw a man coming out of the city and they said to him, "Please show us the entrance to the city and we will treat you kindly."

25 So he showed them the entrance to the city, and they struck the city with the edge of the sword, but they let the man and all his family go free.

26 The man went into the land of the Hittites and built a city and named it Luz which is its name to this day.

Places Not Conquered

27 ¶ But Manasseh did not take possession of Bethshean and its villages, or Taanach and its villages, or the inhabitants of Dor and its villages, or the inhabitants of Ibleam and its villages, or the inhabitants of Megiddo and its villages; so the Canaanites persisted in living in that land.

28 It came about when Israel became strong, that they put the Canaanites to forced labor, but they did not drive them out completely.

29 ¶ Ephraim did not drive out the Canaanites who were living in Gezer; so the Canaanites lived in Gezer among them.

30 ¶ Zebulun did not drive out the inhabitants of Kitron, or the inhabitants of *b*Nahalol; so the Canaanites lived among them and became subject to forced labor.

31 ¶ Asher did not drive out the inhabitants of Acco, or the inhabitants of Sidon, or of Ahlab, or of Achzib, or of Helbah, or of Aphik, or of Rehob.

32 So the Asherites lived among the Canaanites, the inhabitants of the land; for they did not drive them out.

33 ¶ Naphtali did not drive out the inhabitants of Bethshemesh, or the inhabitants of Beth-anath, but lived among the Canaanites, the inhabitants of the land; and the inhabitants of Beth-shemesh and Beth-anath became forced labor for them.

34 ¶ Then the Amorites forced the sons of Dan into the hill country, for they did not allow them to come down to the valley;

35 yet the Amorites persisted in living in Mount Heres, in Aijalon and in Shaalbim; but when the power of the house of Joseph grew strong, they became forced labor.

36 The border of the Amorites ran from the ascent of Akrabbim, from Sela and upward.

Israel Rebuked

2 NOW THE angel of the LORD came up from Gilgal to Bochim. And he said, "I brought you up out of Egypt and led you into the land which I have sworn to your fathers; and I said, 'I will never break My covenant with you,

2 and as for you, you shall make no covenant with the inhabitants of this land; you shall tear down their altars.' But you have not obeyed Me; what is this you have done?

3 "Therefore I also said, 'I will not drive them out before you; but they will *c*become *as thorns* in your sides and their gods will be a snare to you.' "

4 When the angel of the LORD spoke these words to all the sons of Israel, the people lifted up their voices and wept.

5 So they named that place *d*Bochim; and there they sacrificed to the LORD.

New International

Caleb, who drove from it the three sons of Anak. 21The Benjamites, however, failed to dislodge the Jebusites, who were living in Jerusalem; to this day the Jebusites live there with the Benjamites.

22Now the house of Joseph attacked Bethel, and the LORD was with them. 23When they sent men to spy out Bethel (formerly called Luz), 24the spies saw a man coming out of the city and they said to him, "Show us how to get into the city and we will see that you are treated well." 25So he showed them, and they put the city to the sword but spared the man and his whole family. 26He then went to the land of the Hittites, where he built a city and called it Luz, which is its name to this day.

27But Manasseh did not drive out the people of Beth Shan or Taanach or Dor or Ibleam or Megiddo and their surrounding settlements, for the Canaanites were determined to live in that land. 28When Israel became strong, they pressed the Canaanites into forced labor but never drove them out completely. 29Nor did Ephraim drive out the Canaanites living in Gezer, but the Canaanites continued to live there among them. 30Neither did Zebulun drive out the Canaanites living in Kitron or Nahalol, who remained among them; but they did subject them to forced labor. 31Nor did Asher drive out those living in Acco or Sidon or Ahlab or Aczib or Helbah or Aphek or Rehob, 32and because of this the people of Asher lived among the Canaanite inhabitants of the land. 33Neither did Naphtali drive out those living in Beth Shemesh or Beth Anath; but the Naphtalites too lived among the Canaanite inhabitants of the land, and those living in Beth Shemesh and Beth Anath became forced laborers for them. 34The Amorites confined the Danites to the hill country, not allowing them to come down into the plain. 35And the Amorites were determined also to hold out in Mount Heres, Aijalon and Shaalbim, but when the power of the house of Joseph increased, they too were pressed into forced labor. 36The boundary of the Amorites was from Scorpion*f* Pass to Sela and beyond.

The Angel of the LORD at Bokim

2 THE ANGEL of the LORD went up from Gilgal to Bokim and said, "I brought you up out of Egypt and led you into the land that I swore to give to your forefathers. I said, 'I will never break my covenant with you, 2and you shall not make a covenant with the people of this land, but you shall break down their altars.' Yet you have disobeyed me. Why have you done this? 3Now therefore I tell you that I will not drive them out before you; they will be ⌊thorns⌋ in your sides and their gods will be a snare to you."

4When the angel of the LORD had spoken these things to all the Israelites, the people wept aloud, 5and they called that place Bokim.*g* There they offered sacrifices to the LORD.

---

*b*Perhaps same as *Nahalal*   *c*Some ancient mss read *be adversaries, and*   *d*I.e. weepers

*f*36 Hebrew *Akrabbim*   *g*5 *Bokim* means *weepers.*

King James

6 ¶ And when Joshua had let the people go, the children of Israel went every man unto his inheritance to possess the land.

7And the people served the LORD all the days of Joshua, and all the days of the elders that *i*outlived Joshua, who had seen all the great works of the LORD, that he did for Israel.

8And Joshua the son of Nun, the servant of the LORD, died, *being* an hundred and ten years old.

9And they buried him in the border of his inheritance in Timnath-heres, in the mount of Ephraim, on the north side of the hill Gaash.

10And also all that generation were gathered unto their fathers: and there arose another generation after them, which knew not the LORD, nor yet the works which he had done for Israel.

11 ¶ And the children of Israel did evil in the sight of the LORD, and served Baalim:

12And they forsook the LORD God of their fathers, which brought them out of the land of Egypt, and followed other gods, of the gods of the people that *were* round about them, and bowed themselves unto them, and provoked the LORD to anger.

13And they forsook the LORD, and served Baal and Ashtaroth.

14 ¶ And the anger of the LORD was hot against Israel, and he delivered them into the hands of spoilers that spoiled them, and he sold them into the hands of their enemies round about, so that they could not any longer stand before their enemies.

15Whithersoever they went out, the hand of the LORD was against them for evil, as the LORD had said, and as the LORD had sworn unto them: and they were greatly distressed.

The LORD raises up judges

16 ¶ Nevertheless the LORD raised up judges, which *j*delivered them out of the hand of those that spoiled them.

17And yet they would not hearken unto their judges, but they went a-whoring after other gods, and bowed themselves unto them: they turned quickly out of the way which their fathers walked in, obeying the commandments of the LORD; *but* they did not so.

18And when the LORD raised them up judges, then the LORD was with the judge, and delivered them out of the hand of their enemies all the days of the judge: for it repented the LORD because of their groanings by reason of them that oppressed them and vexed them.

19And it came to pass, when the judge was dead, *that* they returned, and *k*corrupted *themselves* more than their fathers, in following other gods to serve them, and to bow down unto them; *l*they ceased not from their own doings, nor from their stubborn way.

20 ¶ And the anger of the LORD was hot against Israel; and he said, Because that this people hath transgressed my covenant which I commanded their fathers, and have not hearkened unto my voice;

21I also will not henceforth drive out any from before them of the nations which Joshua left when he died:

22That through them I may prove Israel, whether they will keep the way of the LORD to walk therein, as their fathers did keep *it*, or not.

23Therefore the LORD *m*left those nations, without driving them out hastily; neither delivered he them into the hand of Joshua.

3 NOW THESE *are* the nations which the LORD left, to prove Israel by them, *even* as many *of Israel* as had not known all the wars of Canaan;

Amplified

6And when Joshua had let the people go, the Israelites went every man to his inheritance to possess the land.

7And the people served the Lord all the days of Joshua and all the days of the elders who outlived Joshua, who had seen all the great works of the Lord which He did for Israel.

8And Joshua son of Nun, the servant of the Lord, died, being 110 years old.

9And they buried him within the boundary of his inheritance in Timnath-heres, in the hill country of Ephraim, north of Mount Gaash.

10And also all that generation were gathered to their fathers, and there arose another generation after them who did not know (recognize, understand) the Lord, or even the work which He had done for Israel.

11And the people of Israel did evil in the sight of the Lord and served the Baals.

12And they forsook the Lord, the God of their fathers, Who brought them out of the land of Egypt. They went after other gods of the peoples round about them, and bowed down to them, and provoked the Lord to anger.

13And they forsook the Lord and served Baal [the god worshiped by the Canaanites] and the Ashtaroth [female deities such as Ashtoreth and Asherah].

14So the anger of the Lord was kindled against Israel, and He gave them into the power of plunderers who robbed them; and He sold them into the hands of their enemies round about, so that they could no longer stand before their foes.

15Whenever they went out, the hand of the Lord was against them for evil as the Lord had said, and as the Lord had sworn to them; and they were bitterly distressed. [Lev. 26:14–46.]

16But the Lord raised up judges, who delivered them out of the hands of those who robbed them.

17And yet they did not listen to their judges, for they played the harlot after other gods and bowed down to them. They turned quickly out of the way in which their fathers had walked, who had obeyed the commandments of the Lord, and they did not so.

18When the Lord raised them up judges, then He was with the judge and delivered them out of the hands of their enemies all the days of the judge; for the Lord was moved to relent because of their groanings by reason of those who oppressed and vexed them.

19But when the judge was dead, they turned back and corrupted themselves more than their fathers, following and serving other gods, and bowing down to them. They did not cease from their practices or their stubborn way.

20So the anger of the Lord was kindled against Israel; and He said, Because this people have transgressed My covenant which I commanded their fathers and have not listened to My voice,

21I from now on will also not drive out from before them any of the nations which Joshua left when he died,

22That through them I may prove Israel, whether they will keep the way of the Lord to walk in it, as their fathers kept it, or not.

23So the Lord left those nations, without driving them out at once, nor had He delivered them into Joshua's power.

3 NOW THESE are the nations which the Lord left to prove Israel by them, that is, all in Israel who had not previously experienced war in Canaan;

---

*i*Heb. *prolonged days after Joshua*   *j*Heb. *saved*   *k*Or, *were corrupt*   *l*Heb. *they let nothing fall of their*   *m*Or, *suffered*

New American Standard

Joshua Dies

6 ¶ When Joshua had dismissed the people, the sons of Israel went each to his inheritance to possess the land.

7 The people served the LORD all the days of Joshua, and all the days of the elders who survived Joshua, who had seen all the great work of the LORD which He had done for Israel.

8 Then Joshua the son of Nun, the servant of the LORD, died at the age of one hundred and ten.

9 And they buried him in the territory of his inheritance in Timnath-heres, in the hill country of Ephraim, north of Mount Gaash.

10 All that generation also were gathered to their fathers; and there arose another generation after them who did not know the LORD, nor yet the work which He had done for Israel.

Israel Serves Baals

11 ¶ Then the sons of Israel did evil in the sight of the LORD and eserved the Baals,

12 and they forsook the LORD, the God of their fathers, who had brought them out of the land of Egypt, and followed other gods from *among* the gods of the peoples who were around them, and bowed themselves down to them; thus they provoked the LORD to anger.

13 So they forsook the LORD and served Baal and the Ashtaroth.

14 The anger of the LORD burned against Israel, and He gave them into the hands of plunderers who plundered them; and He sold them into the hands of their enemies around *them*, so that they could no longer stand before their enemies.

15 Wherever they went, the hand of the LORD was against them for evil, as the LORD had spoken and as the LORD had sworn to them, so that they were severely distressed.

16 ¶ Then the LORD raised up judges who delivered them from the hands of those who plundered them.

17 Yet they did not listen to their judges, for they played the harlot after other gods and bowed themselves down to them. They turned aside quickly from the way in which their fathers had walked in obeying the commandments of the LORD; they did not do as *their fathers*.

18 When the LORD raised up judges for them, the LORD was with the judge and delivered them from the hand of their enemies all the days of the judge; for the LORD was moved to pity by their groaning because of those who oppressed and afflicted them.

19 But it came about when the judge died, that they would turn back and act more corruptly than their fathers, in following other gods to serve them and bow down to them; they did not abandon their practices or their stubborn ways.

20 So the anger of the LORD burned against Israel, and He said, "Because this nation has transgressed My covenant which I commanded their fathers and has not listened to My voice,

21 I also will no longer drive out before them any of the nations which Joshua left when he died,

22 in order to test Israel by them, whether they will keep the way of the LORD to walk in it as their fathers did, or not."

23 So the LORD allowed those nations to remain, not driving them out quickly; and He did not give them into the hand of Joshua.

Idolatry Leads to Servitude

3 NOW THESE are the nations which the LORD left, to test Israel by them (*that is,* all who had not experienced any of the wars of Canaan;

---

e Or *worshiped*

New International

Disobedience and Defeat

6After Joshua had dismissed the Israelites, they went to take possession of the land, each to his own inheritance. 7The people served the LORD throughout the lifetime of Joshua and of the elders who outlived him and who had seen all the great things the LORD had done for Israel.

8Joshua son of Nun, the servant of the LORD, died at the age of a hundred and ten. 9And they buried him in the land of his inheritance, at Timnath Heresh in the hill country of Ephraim, north of Mount Gaash.

10After that whole generation had been gathered to their fathers, another generation grew up, who knew neither the LORD nor what he had done for Israel. 11Then the Israelites did evil in the eyes of the LORD and served the Baals. 12They forsook the LORD, the God of their fathers, who had brought them out of Egypt. They followed and worshiped various gods of the peoples around them. They provoked the LORD to anger 13because they forsook him and served Baal and the Ashtoreths. 14In his anger against Israel the LORD handed them over to raiders who plundered them. He sold them to their enemies all around, whom they were no longer able to resist. 15Whenever Israel went out to fight, the hand of the LORD was against them to defeat them, just as he had sworn to them. They were in great distress.

16Then the LORD raised up judges,i who saved them out of the hands of these raiders. 17Yet they would not listen to their judges but prostituted themselves to other gods and worshiped them. Unlike their fathers, they quickly turned from the way in which their fathers had walked, the way of obedience to the LORD's commands. 18Whenever the LORD raised up a judge for them, he was with the judge and saved them out of the hands of their enemies as long as the judge lived; for the LORD had compassion on them as they groaned under those who oppressed and afflicted them. 19But when the judge died, the people returned to ways even more corrupt than those of their fathers, following other gods and serving and worshiping them. They refused to give up their evil practices and stubborn ways.

20Therefore the LORD was very angry with Israel and said, "Because this nation has violated the covenant that I laid down for their forefathers and has not listened to me, 21I will no longer drive out before them any of the nations Joshua left when he died. 22I will use them to test Israel and see whether they will keep the way of the LORD and walk in it as their forefathers did." 23The LORD had allowed those nations to remain; he did not drive them out at once by giving them into the hands of Joshua.

3 THESE ARE the nations the LORD left to test all those Israelites who had not experienced any of the wars in Canaan 2(he did this only to teach warfare to the descen-

---

h 9 Also known as *Timnath Serah* (see Joshua 19:50 and 24:30)
i 16 Or *leaders*; similarly in verses 17–19

King James

2Only that the generations of the children of Israel might know, to teach them war, at the least such as before knew nothing thereof;

3*Namely,* five lords of the Philistines, and all the Canaanites, and the Sidonians, and the Hivites that dwelt in mount Lebanon, from mount Baal-hermon unto the entering in of Hamath.

4And they were to prove Israel by them, to know whether they would hearken unto the commandments of the LORD, which he commanded their fathers by the hand of Moses.

5 ¶ And the children of Israel dwelt among the Canaanites, Hittites, and Amorites, and Perizzites, and Hivites, and Jebusites:

6And they took their daughters to be their wives, and gave their daughters to their sons, and served their gods.

Othniel

7And the children of Israel did evil in the sight of the LORD, and forgat the LORD their God, and served Baalim and the groves.

8 ¶ Therefore the anger of the LORD was hot against Israel, and he sold them into the hand of Chushan-rishathaim king of [n]Mesopotamia: and the children of Israel served Chushan-rishathaim eight years.

9And when the children of Israel cried unto the LORD, the LORD raised up a [o]deliverer to the children of Israel, who delivered them, *even* Othniel the son of Kenaz, Caleb's younger brother.

10And the spirit of the LORD [p]came upon him, and he judged Israel, and went out to war: and the LORD delivered Chushan-rishathaim king of [q]Mesopotamia into his hand; and his hand prevailed against Chushan-rishathaim.

11And the land had rest forty years. And Othniel the son of Kenaz died.

Ehud

12 ¶ And the children of Israel did evil again in the sight of the LORD: and the LORD strengthened Eglon the king of Moab against Israel, because they had done evil in the sight of the LORD.

13And he gathered unto him the children of Ammon and Amalek, and went and smote Israel, and possessed the city of palm trees.

14So the children of Israel served Eglon the king of Moab eighteen years.

15But when the children of Israel cried unto the LORD, the LORD raised them up a deliverer, Ehud the son of Gera, [r]a Benjamite, a man lefthanded: and by him the children of Israel sent a present unto Eglon the king of Moab.

16But Ehud made him a dagger which had two edges, of a cubit length; and he did gird it under his raiment upon his right thigh.

17And he brought the present unto Eglon king of Moab: and Eglon *was* a very fat man.

18And when he had made an end to offer the present, he sent away the people that bare the present.

19But he himself turned again from the [s]quarries that *were* by Gilgal, and said, I have a secret errand unto thee, O king: who said, Keep silence. And all that stood by him went out from him.

20And Ehud came unto him; and he was sitting in a summer parlour, which he had for himself alone. And Ehud said, I have a message from God unto thee. And he arose out of *his* seat.

21And Ehud put forth his left hand, and took the dagger from his right thigh, and thrust it into his belly:

22And the haft also went in after the blade; and the fat closed upon the blade, so that he could not draw the dagger out of his belly; and [t]the dirt came out.

[n] Heb. *Aram-naharaim* [o] Heb. *saviour* [p] Heb. *was*
[q] Heb. *Aram* [r] Or, *the son of Jemini* [s] Or, *graven images*
[t] Or, *it came out at the fundament*

Amplified

2It was only that the generations of the Israelites might know and be taught war, at least those who previously knew nothing of it.

3The remaining nations are: the five lords of the Philistines, all the Canaanites, the Sidonians, and the Hivites who dwelt on Mount Lebanon from Mount Baal-hermon to the entrance of Hamath.

4They were for the testing *and* proving of Israel to know whether Israel would listen *and* obey the commandments of the Lord, which He commanded their fathers by Moses.

5And the Israelites dwelt among the Canaanites, Hittites, Amorites, Perizzites, Hivites, and Jebusites;

6And they married their daughters and gave their own daughters to their sons, and served their gods. [Exod. 34:12–16.]

7And the Israelites did evil in the sight of the Lord and forgot the Lord their God and served the Baals and the Ashtaroth. [Judg. 2:13.]

8So the anger of the Lord was kindled against Israel, and He sold them into the hand of Chushan-rishathaim king of Mesopotamia; and the Israelites served Chushan-rishathaim eight years.

9But when the Israelites cried to the Lord, the Lord raised up a deliverer for the people of Israel to deliver them, Othniel son of Kenaz, Caleb's younger brother.

10The Spirit of the Lord came upon him, and he judged Israel. He went out to war, and the Lord delivered Chushan-rishathaim king of Mesopotamia into his hand and his hand prevailed over Chushan-rishathaim.

11And the land had rest forty years. Then Othniel son of Kenaz died.

12And the Israelites again did evil in the sight of the Lord, and the Lord strengthened Eglon king of Moab against Israel because they had done what was evil in the sight of the Lord.

13And [Eglon] gathered to him the men of Ammon and Amalek, and went and smote Israel, and they possessed the City of Palm Trees (Jericho).

14And the Israelites served Eglon king of Moab eighteen years.

15But when the Israelites cried to the Lord, the Lord raised them up a deliverer, Ehud son of Gera, a Benjamite, a left-handed man; and by him the Israelites sent tribute to Eglon king of Moab.

16Ehud made for himself a sword, a cubit long, which had two edges, and he girded it on his right thigh under his clothing.

17And he brought the tribute to Eglon king of Moab. Now Eglon was a very fat man.

18And when Ehud had finished presenting the tribute, he sent away the people who had carried it.

19He himself went [with them] as far as the sculptured [boundary] stones near Gilgal, and then turned back and came to Eglon and said, I have a secret errand to you, O king. Eglon commanded silence, and all who stood by him went out from him.

20When Ehud had come [near] to him as he was sitting alone in his cool upper apartment, Ehud said, I have a commission from God to execute to you. And the king arose from his seat.

21Then Ehud put forth his left hand and took the sword from his right thigh and thrust it into Eglon's belly.

22And the hilt also went in after the blade, and the fat closed upon the blade, for [Ehud] did not draw the sword out of his belly, and the dirt came out.

New American Standard

2 only in order that the generations of the sons of Israel might be taught war, those who had not experienced it formerly).

3 *These nations are:* the five lords of the Philistines and all the Canaanites and the Sidonians and the Hivites who lived in Mount Lebanon, from Mount Baal-hermon as far as Lebo-hamath.

4 They were for testing Israel, to find out if they would obey the commandments of the LORD, which He had commanded their fathers through Moses.

5 The sons of Israel lived among the Canaanites, the Hittites, the Amorites, the Perizzites, the Hivites, and the Jebusites;

6 and they took their daughters for themselves as wives, and gave their own daughters to their sons, and served their gods.

7 ¶ The sons of Israel did what was evil in the sight of the LORD, and forgot the LORD their God and served the Baals and the *f*Asheroth.

8 Then the anger of the LORD was kindled against Israel, so that He sold them into the hands of Cushan-rishathaim king of Mesopotamia; and the sons of Israel served Cushan-rishathaim eight years.

The First Judge Delivers Israel

9 When the sons of Israel cried to the LORD, the LORD raised up a deliverer for the sons of Israel to deliver them, Othniel the son of Kenaz, Caleb's younger brother.

10 The Spirit of the LORD came upon him, and he judged Israel. When he went out to war, the LORD gave Cushan-rishathaim king of Mesopotamia into his hand, so that he prevailed over Cushan-rishathaim.

11 Then the land had rest forty years. And Othniel the son of Kenaz died.

12 ¶ Now the sons of Israel again did evil in the sight of the LORD. So the LORD strengthened Eglon the king of Moab against Israel, because they had done evil in the sight of the LORD.

13 And he gathered to himself the sons of Ammon and Amalek; and he went and defeated Israel, and they possessed the city of the palm trees.

14 The sons of Israel served Eglon the king of Moab eighteen years.

Ehud Delivers from Moab

15 ¶ But when the sons of Israel cried to the LORD, the LORD raised up a deliverer for them, Ehud the son of Gera, the Benjamite, a left-handed man. And the sons of Israel sent tribute by him to Eglon the king of Moab.

16 Ehud made himself a sword which had two edges, a cubit in length, and he bound it on his right thigh under his cloak.

17 He presented the tribute to Eglon king of Moab. Now Eglon was a very fat man.

18 It came about when he had finished presenting the tribute, that he sent away the people who had carried the tribute.

19 But he himself turned back from the idols which were at Gilgal, and said, "I have a secret message for you, O king." And he said, "Keep silence." And all who attended him left him.

20 Ehud came to him while he was sitting alone in his cool roof chamber. And Ehud said, "I have a message from God for you." And he arose from his seat.

21 Ehud stretched out his left hand, took the sword from his right thigh and thrust it into his belly.

22 The handle also went in after the blade, and the fat closed over the blade, for he did not draw the sword out of his belly; and the refuse came out.

New International

dants of the Israelites who had not had previous battle experience): [3]the five rulers of the Philistines, all the Canaanites, the Sidonians, and the Hivites living in the Lebanon mountains from Mount Baal Hermon to Lebo[j] Hamath. [4]They were left to test the Israelites to see whether they would obey the LORD's commands, which he had given their forefathers through Moses.

[5]The Israelites lived among the Canaanites, Hittites, Amorites, Perizzites, Hivites and Jebusites. [6]They took their daughters in marriage and gave their own daughters to their sons, and served their gods.

Othniel

[7]The Israelites did evil in the eyes of the LORD; they forgot the LORD their God and served the Baals and the Asherahs. [8]The anger of the LORD burned against Israel so that he sold them into the hands of Cushan-Rishathaim king of Aram Naharaim,[k] to whom the Israelites were subject for eight years. [9]But when they cried out to the LORD, he raised up for them a deliverer, Othniel son of Kenaz, Caleb's younger brother, who saved them. [10]The Spirit of the LORD came upon him, so that he became Israel's judge[l] and went to war. The LORD gave Cushan-Rishathaim king of Aram into the hands of Othniel, who overpowered him. [11]So the land had peace for forty years, until Othniel son of Kenaz died.

Ehud

[12]Once again the Israelites did evil in the eyes of the LORD, and because they did this evil the LORD gave Eglon king of Moab power over Israel. [13]Getting the Ammonites and Amalekites to join him, Eglon came and attacked Israel, and they took possession of the City of Palms.[m] [14]The Israelites were subject to Eglon king of Moab for eighteen years.

[15]Again the Israelites cried out to the LORD, and he gave them a deliverer—Ehud, a left-handed man, the son of Gera the Benjamite. The Israelites sent him with tribute to Eglon king of Moab. [16]Now Ehud had made a double-edged sword about a foot and a half[n] long, which he strapped to his right thigh under his clothing. [17]He presented the tribute to Eglon king of Moab, who was a very fat man. [18]After Ehud had presented the tribute, he sent on their way the men who had carried it. [19]At the idols[o] near Gilgal he himself turned back and said, "I have a secret message for you, O king."

The king said, "Quiet!" And all his attendants left him.

[20]Ehud then approached him while he was sitting alone in the upper room of his summer palace[p] and said, "I have a message from God for you." As the king rose from his seat, [21]Ehud reached with his left hand, drew the sword from his right thigh and plunged it into the king's belly. [22]Even the handle sank in after the blade, which came out his back. Ehud did not pull the sword out, and the fat

j 3 Or *to the entrance to*   *k* 8 That is, Northwest Mesopotamia
l 10 Or *leader*   *m* 13 That is, Jericho   *n* 16 Hebrew *a cubit*
(about 0.5 meter)   *o* 19 Or *the stone quarries*; also in verse 26
p 20 The meaning of the Hebrew for this phrase is uncertain.

f I.e. wooden symbol of a female deity

King James

Amplified

King James

23Then Ehud went forth through the porch, and shut the doors of the parlour upon him, and locked them.

24When he was gone out, his servants came; and when they saw that, behold, the doors of the parlour *were* locked, they said, Surely he *u*covereth his feet in his summer chamber.

25And they tarried till they were ashamed: and, behold, he opened not the doors of the parlour; therefore they took a key, and opened *them:* and, behold, their lord *was* fallen down dead on the earth.

26And Ehud escaped while they tarried, and passed beyond the quarries, and escaped unto Seirah.

27And it came to pass, when he was come, that he blew a trumpet in the mountain of Ephraim, and the children of Israel went down with him from the mount, and he before them.

28And he said unto them, Follow after me: for the LORD hath delivered your enemies the Moabites into your hand. And they went down after him, and took the fords of Jordan toward Moab, and suffered not a man to pass over.

29And they slew of Moab at that time about ten thousand men, all *v*lusty, and all men of valour; and there escaped not a man.

30So Moab was subdued that day under the hand of Israel. And the land had rest fourscore years.

31 ¶ And after him was Shamgar the son of Anath, which slew of the Philistines six hundred men with an ox goad: and he also delivered Israel.

Deborah

4 AND the children of Israel again did evil in the sight of the LORD, when Ehud was dead.

2And the LORD sold them into the hand of Jabin king of Canaan, that reigned in Hazor; the captain of whose host *was* Sisera, which dwelt in Harosheth of the Gentiles.

3And the children of Israel cried unto the LORD: for he had nine hundred chariots of iron; and twenty years he mightily oppressed the children of Israel.

4 ¶ And Deborah, a prophetess, the wife of Lapidoth, she judged Israel at that time.

5And she dwelt under the palm tree of Deborah between Ramah and Beth-el in mount Ephraim: and the children of Israel came up to her for judgment.

6And she sent and called Barak the son of Abinoam out of Kedesh-naphtali, and said unto him, Hath not the LORD God of Israel commanded, *saying,* Go and draw toward mount Tabor, and take with thee ten thousand men of the children of Naphtali and of the children of Zebulun?

7And I will draw unto thee to the river Kishon Sisera, the captain of Jabin's army, with his chariots and his multitude; and I will deliver him into thine hand.

8And Barak said unto her, If thou wilt go with me, then I will go: but if thou wilt not go with me, *then* I will not go.

Amplified

23Then Ehud went out into the vestibule and shut the doors of the upper room upon [Eglon] and locked them.

24When [Ehud] had gone out, [Eglon's] servants came. And when they saw the doors of the upper room were locked, they thought, Surely he [is seeking privacy while he] relieves himself in the closet of the cool chamber.

25They waited a long time until they became embarrassed *and* uneasy, but when he still did not open the doors of the upper room, they took the key and opened them, and there lay their master fallen to the floor, dead!

26Ehud escaped while they delayed and passed beyond the sculptured [boundary] stones (images) and escaped to Seirah.

27When he arrived, he blew a trumpet in the hill country of Ephraim, and the Israelites went down from the hill country, with him at their head.

28And he said to them, Follow me, for the Lord has delivered your enemies the Moabites into your hand. So they went down after him and seized the fords of Jordan against the Moabites and permitted not a man to pass over.

29They slew at that time about 10,000 Moabites, all strong, courageous men; not a man escaped.

30So Moab was subdued that day under the hand of Israel, and the land had peace *and* rest for eighty years.

31After [Ehud] was Shamgar son of Anath, who slew 600 Philistine men with an oxgoad. He also delivered Israel.

4 BUT AFTER Ehud died the Israelites again did evil in the sight of the Lord.

2So the Lord sold them into the hand of Jabin king of Canaan, who reigned in Hazor. The commander of his army was Sisera, who dwelt in Harosheth-hagoiim [fortress or city of the nations].

3Then the Israelites cried to the Lord, for [Jabin] had 900 chariots of iron and had severely oppressed the Israelites for twenty years.

4Now Deborah, a *b*prophetess, the wife of Lappidoth, judged Israel at that time.

5She sat under the palm tree of Deborah between Ramah and Bethel in the hill country of Ephraim, and the Israelites came up to her for judgment.

6And she sent and called Barak son of Abinoam from Kedesh in Naphtali and said to him, Has not the Lord, the God of Israel, commanded [you], Go, gather your men at Mount Tabor, taking 10,000 men from the tribes of Naphtali and Zebulun?

7And I will draw out Sisera, the general of Jabin's army, to meet you at the river Kishon with his chariots and his multitude, and I will deliver him into your hand?

8And Barak said to her, If you will go with me, then I will go; but if you will not go with me, I will not go.

b According to Num. 11:25, the prophetic gift has its source in the "Spirit of the Lord." The prophet is a spokesman of God and for God. Miriam was the first prophetess who praised God before all the people (Exod. 15:20). Deborah was not like Miriam, the sister of such men as Moses and Aaron. The objective Spirit of her God elevates her above her people, above heroes before and after her. Not only the ecstasy of enthusiasm, but also the calm wisdom of that Spirit Who informs the law dwells in her. Of no judge until Samuel [the last of the major judges] is it expressly said that he was a "prophet." Of none until him can it be said that he was possessed of the popular authority necessary for the office of judge. The position of Deborah in Israel is therefore a twofold testimony: it proves the relaxation of spiritual and manly energy, and, secondly, the undying might of divine truth, as delivered by Moses, comes brilliantly to view. History shows many instances where in times of distress, when men despaired, women arose and saved their nation; but in all such cases there must be an unextinguished spark of the old fire in the people themselves. Israel, formerly encouraged by the great exploit of a left-handed man—Ehud (Judg. 3:15), is now quickened by the glowing word of a noble woman (J.P. Lange, *A Commentary*).

u Or, *doeth his easement*   *v* Heb. *fat*

New American Standard

23 Then Ehud went out into the vestibule and shut the doors of the roof chamber behind him, and locked *them.* **24** ¶ When he had gone out, his servants came and looked, and behold, the doors of the roof chamber were locked; and they said, "He is only relieving himself in the cool room." **25** They waited until they became anxious; but behold, he did not open the doors of the roof chamber. Therefore they took the key and opened them, and behold, their master had fallen to the floor dead. **26** ¶ Now Ehud escaped while they were delaying, and he passed by the idols and escaped to Seirah. **27** It came about when he had arrived, that he blew the trumpet in the hill country of Ephraim; and the sons of Israel went down with him from the hill country, and he *was* in front of them. **28** He said to them, "Pursue *them,* for the LORD has given your enemies the Moabites into your hands." So they went down after him and seized the fords of the Jordan opposite Moab, and did not allow anyone to cross. **29** They struck down at that time about ten thousand Moabites, all robust and valiant men; and no one escaped. **30** So Moab was subdued that day under the hand of Israel. And the land was undisturbed for eighty years.

Shamgar Delivers from Philistines

31 ¶ After him came Shamgar the son of Anath, who struck down six hundred Philistines with an oxgoad; and he also saved Israel.

Deborah and Barak Deliver from Canaanites

4 THEN THE sons of Israel again did evil in the sight of the LORD, after Ehud died. **2** And the LORD sold them into the hand of Jabin king of Canaan, who reigned in Hazor; and the commander of his army was Sisera, who lived in Harosheth-hagoyim. **3** The sons of Israel cried to the LORD; for he had nine hundred iron chariots, and he oppressed the sons of Israel severely for twenty years. **4** ¶ Now Deborah, a prophetess, the wife of Lappidoth, was judging Israel at that time. **5** She used to sit under the palm tree of Deborah between Ramah and Bethel in the hill country of Ephraim; and the sons of Israel came up to her for judgment. **6** Now she sent and summoned Barak the son of Abinoam from Kedesh-naphtali, and said to him, "Behold, the LORD, the God of Israel, has commanded, 'Go and march to Mount Tabor, and take with you ten thousand men from the sons of Naphtali and from the sons of Zebulun. **7** 'I will draw out to you Sisera, the commander of Jabin's army, with his chariots and his many *troops* to the river Kishon, and I will give him into your hand.' " **8** Then Barak said to her, "If you will go with me, then I will go; but if you will not go with me, I will not go."

New International

closed in over it. **23** Then Ehud went out to the porch[q]; he shut the doors of the upper room behind him and locked them. **24** After he had gone, the servants came and found the doors of the upper room locked. They said, "He must be relieving himself in the inner room of the house." **25** They waited to the point of embarrassment, but when he did not open the doors of the room, they took a key and unlocked them. There they saw their lord fallen to the floor, dead. **26** While they waited, Ehud got away. He passed by the idols and escaped to Seirah. **27** When he arrived there, he blew a trumpet in the hill country of Ephraim, and the Israelites went down with him from the hills, with him leading them. **28** "Follow me," he ordered, "for the LORD has given Moab, your enemy, into your hands." So they followed him down and, taking possession of the fords of the Jordan that led to Moab, they allowed no one to cross over. **29** At that time they struck down about ten thousand Moabites, all vigorous and strong; not a man escaped. **30** That day Moab was made subject to Israel, and the land had peace for eighty years.

Shamgar

31 After Ehud came Shamgar son of Anath, who struck down six hundred Philistines with an oxgoad. He too saved Israel.

Deborah

4 AFTER EHUD died, the Israelites once again did evil in the eyes of the LORD. **2** So the LORD sold them into the hands of Jabin, a king of Canaan, who reigned in Hazor. The commander of his army was Sisera, who lived in Harosheth Haggoyim. **3** Because he had nine hundred iron chariots and had cruelly oppressed the Israelites for twenty years, they cried to the LORD for help. **4** Deborah, a prophetess, the wife of Lappidoth, was leading[r] Israel at that time. **5** She held court under the Palm of Deborah between Ramah and Bethel in the hill country of Ephraim, and the Israelites came to her to have their disputes decided. **6** She sent for Barak son of Abinoam from Kedesh in Naphtali and said to him, "The LORD, the God of Israel, commands you: 'Go, take with you ten thousand men of Naphtali and Zebulun and lead the way to Mount Tabor. **7** I will lure Sisera, the commander of Jabin's army, with his chariots and his troops to the Kishon River and give him into your hands.' " **8** Barak said to her, "If you go with me, I will go; but if you don't go with me, I won't go."

---

q 23 The meaning of the Hebrew for this word is uncertain.
r 4 Traditionally *judging*

King James

Amplified

9And she said, I will surely go with thee: notwithstanding the journey that thou takest shall not be for thine honour; for the LORD shall sell Sisera into the hand of a woman. And Deborah arose, and went with Barak to Kedesh.

10 ¶ And Barak called Zebulun and Naphtali to Kedesh; and he went up with ten thousand men at his feet: and Deborah went up with him.

11Now Heber the Kenite, *which was* of the children of Hobab the father-in-law of Moses, had severed himself from the Kenites, and pitched his tent unto the plain of Zaanaim, which *is* by Kedesh.

12And they showed Sisera that Barak the son of Abinoam was gone up to mount Tabor.

13And Sisera ʷgathered together all his chariots, *even* nine hundred chariots of iron, and all the people that *were* with him, from Harosheth of the Gentiles unto the river of Kishon.

14And Deborah said unto Barak, Up; for this *is* the day in which the LORD hath delivered Sisera into thine hand: is not the LORD gone out before thee? So Barak went down from mount Tabor, and ten thousand men after him.

15And the LORD discomfited Sisera, and all *his* chariots, and all *his* host, with the edge of the sword before Barak; so that Sisera lighted down off *his* chariot, and fled away on his feet.

16But Barak pursued after the chariots, and after the host, unto Harosheth of the Gentiles: and all the host of Sisera fell upon the edge of the sword; *and* there was not ˣa man left.

17Howbeit Sisera fled away on his feet to the tent of Jael the wife of Heber the Kenite: for *there was* peace between Jabin the king of Hazor and the house of Heber the Kenite.

18 ¶ And Jael went out to meet Sisera, and said unto him, Turn in, my lord, turn in to me; fear not. And when he had turned in unto her into the tent, she covered him with a ʸmantle.

19And he said unto her, Give me, I pray thee, a little water to drink; for I am thirsty. And she opened a bottle of milk, and gave him drink, and covered him.

20Again he said unto her, Stand in the door of the tent, and it shall be, when any man doth come and inquire of thee, and say, Is there any man here? that thou shalt say, No.

21Then Jael Heber's wife took a nail of the tent, and ᶻtook an hammer in her hand, and went softly unto him, and smote the nail into his temples, and fastened it into the ground: for he was fast asleep and weary. So he died.

22And, behold, as Barak pursued Sisera, Jael came out to meet him, and said unto him, Come, and I will show thee the man whom thou seekest. And when he came into her *tent,* behold, Sisera lay dead, and the nail *was* in his temples.

23So God subdued on that day Jabin the king of Canaan before the children of Israel.

24And the hand of the children of Israel ᵃprospered, and prevailed against Jabin the king of Canaan, until they had destroyed Jabin king of Canaan.

The song of Deborah

5 THEN SANG Deborah and Barak the son of Abinoam on that day, saying,

2Praise ye the LORD for the avenging of Israel, when the people willingly offered themselves.

9And she said, I will surely go with you; nevertheless, the trip you take will not be for your glory, for the Lord will sell Sisera into the hand of a woman. And Deborah arose and went with Barak to Kedesh. [Fulfilled in Judg. 4:22.]

10And Barak called Zebulun and Naphtali to Kedesh, and he went up with 10,000 men at his heels, and Deborah went up with him.

11Now Heber the Kenite, of the descendants of Hobab, the father-in-law of Moses, had separated from the Kenites and encamped as far away as the oak in Zaanannim, which is near Kedesh.

12When it was told Sisera that Barak son of Abinoam had gone up to Mount Tabor,

13Sisera gathered together all his chariots, even 900 chariots of iron, and all the men who were with him from Harosheth-hagoiim to the river Kishon.

14And Deborah said to Barak, Up! For this is the day when the Lord has given Sisera into your hand. Is not the Lord gone out before you? So Barak went down from Mount Tabor with 10,000 men following him.

15And the Lord confused *and* terrified Sisera and all his chariot drivers and all his army before Barak with the sword. And Sisera alighted from his chariot and fled on foot.

16But Barak pursued after the chariots and the army to Harosheth-hagoiim, and all the army of Sisera fell by the sword; not a man was left.

17But Sisera fled on foot to the tent of Jael, the wife of Heber the Kenite, for there was peace between Jabin the king of Hazor and the house of Heber the Kenite.

18And Jael went out to meet Sisera and said to him, Turn aside, my lord, turn aside to me; have no fear. So he turned aside to her into the tent, and she covered him with a rug.

19And he said to her, Give me, I pray you, a little water to drink for I am thirsty. And she opened a skin of milk and gave him a drink and covered him.

20And he said to her, Stand at the door of the tent, and if any man comes and asks you, Is there any man here? Tell him, No.

21But Jael, Heber's wife, took a tent pin and a hammer in her hand and went softly to him and drove the pin through his temple and into the ground; for he was in a deep sleep from weariness. So he died.

22And behold, as Barak pursued Sisera, Jael came out to meet him and said to him, Come, and I will show you the man you seek. And when he came into her tent, behold, Sisera lay dead, and the tent pin was in his temples.

23So God subdued on that day Jabin king of Canaan before the Israelites.

24And the hand of the Israelites bore more and more upon Jabin king of Canaan until they had destroyed [him].

5 THEN SANG Deborah and Barak son of Abinoam on that day, saying,

2For the leaders who took the lead in Israel, for the people who offered themselves willingly, bless the Lord!

ʷHeb. *gathered by cry,* or, *proclamation*   ˣHeb. *unto one*
ʸOr, *rug,* or, *blanket*   ᶻHeb. *put*   ᵃHeb. *going went and was hard*

New American Standard

9 She said, "I will surely go with you; nevertheless, the honor shall not be yours on the journey that you are about to take, for the LORD will sell Sisera into the hands of a woman." Then Deborah arose and went with Barak to Kedesh.

10 Barak called Zebulun and Naphtali together to Kedesh, and ten thousand men went up with him; Deborah also went up with him.

11 ¶ Now Heber the Kenite had separated himself from the Kenites, from the sons of Hobab the father-in-law of Moses, and had pitched his tent as far away as the oak in Zaanannim, which is near Kedesh.

12 ¶ Then they told Sisera that Barak the son of Abinoam had gone up to Mount Tabor.

13 Sisera called together all his chariots, nine hundred iron chariots, and all the people who *were* with him, from Harosheth-hagoyim to the river Kishon.

14 Deborah said to Barak, "Arise! For this is the day in which the LORD has given Sisera into your hand; [g]behold, the LORD has gone out before you." So Barak went down from Mount Tabor with ten thousand men following him.

15 The LORD routed Sisera and all *his* chariots and all *his* army with the edge of the sword before Barak; and Sisera alighted from *his* chariot and fled away on foot.

16 But Barak pursued the chariots and the army as far as Harosheth-hagoyim, and all the army of Sisera fell by the edge of the sword; not even one was left.

17 ¶ Now Sisera fled away on foot to the tent of Jael the wife of Heber the Kenite, for *there was* peace between Jabin the king of Hazor and the house of Heber the Kenite.

18 Jael went out to meet Sisera, and said to him, "Turn aside, my master, turn aside to me! Do not be afraid." And he turned aside to her into the tent, and she covered him with a rug.

19 He said to her, "Please give me a little water to drink, for I am thirsty." So she opened a [h]bottle of milk and gave him a drink; then she covered him.

20 He said to her, "Stand in the doorway of the tent, and it shall be if anyone comes and inquires of you, and says, 'Is there anyone here?' that you shall say, 'No.'"

21 But Jael, Heber's wife, took a tent peg and seized a hammer in her hand, and went secretly to him and drove the peg into his temple, and it went through into the ground; for he was sound asleep and exhausted. So he died.

22 And behold, as Barak pursued Sisera, Jael came out to meet him and said to him, "Come, and I will show you the man whom you are seeking." And he entered with her, and behold Sisera was lying dead with the tent peg in his temple.

23 ¶ So God subdued on that day Jabin the king of Canaan before the sons of Israel.

24 The hand of the sons of Israel pressed heavier and heavier upon Jabin the king of Canaan, until they had destroyed Jabin the king of Canaan.

The Song of Deborah and Barak

5 THEN DEBORAH and Barak the son of Abinoam sang on that day, saying,
2"That the leaders led in Israel,
That the people volunteered,
Bless the LORD!

New International

9"Very well," Deborah said, "I will go with you. But because of the way you are going about this,[s] the honor will not be yours, for the LORD will hand Sisera over to a woman." So Deborah went with Barak to Kedesh, 10where he summoned Zebulun and Naphtali. Ten thousand men followed him, and Deborah also went with him.

11Now Heber the Kenite had left the other Kenites, the descendants of Hobab, Moses' brother-in-law,[t] and pitched his tent by the great tree in Zaanannim near Kedesh.

12When they told Sisera that Barak son of Abinoam had gone up to Mount Tabor, 13Sisera gathered together his nine hundred iron chariots and all the men with him, from Harosheth Haggoyim to the Kishon River.

14Then Deborah said to Barak, "Go! This is the day the LORD has given Sisera into your hands. Has not the LORD gone ahead of you?" So Barak went down Mount Tabor, followed by ten thousand men. 15At Barak's advance, the LORD routed Sisera and all his chariots and army by the sword, and Sisera abandoned his chariot and fled on foot. 16But Barak pursued the chariots and army as far as Harosheth Haggoyim. All the troops of Sisera fell by the sword; not a man was left.

17Sisera, however, fled on foot to the tent of Jael, the wife of Heber the Kenite, because there were friendly relations between Jabin king of Hazor and the clan of Heber the Kenite.

18Jael went out to meet Sisera and said to him, "Come, my lord, come right in. Don't be afraid." So he entered her tent, and she put a covering over him.

19"I'm thirsty," he said. "Please give me some water." She opened a skin of milk, gave him a drink, and covered him up.

20"Stand in the doorway of the tent," he told her. "If someone comes by and asks you, 'Is anyone here?' say 'No.'"

21But Jael, Heber's wife, picked up a tent peg and a hammer and went quietly to him while he lay fast asleep, exhausted. She drove the peg through his temple into the ground, and he died.

22Barak came by in pursuit of Sisera, and Jael went out to meet him. "Come," she said, "I will show you the man you're looking for." So he went in with her, and there lay Sisera with the tent peg through his temple—dead.

23On that day God subdued Jabin, the Canaanite king, before the Israelites. 24And the hand of the Israelites grew stronger and stronger against Jabin, the Canaanite king, until they destroyed him.

The Song of Deborah

5 ON THAT day Deborah and Barak son of Abinoam sang this song:

2"When the princes in Israel take the lead,
when the people willingly offer
themselves—
praise the LORD!

---

[g] Or *has not the LORD gone...?*   [h] I.e. skin container

King James

Amplified

[3]Hear, O ye kings; give ear, O ye princes; I, *even* I, will sing unto the LORD; I will sing *praise* to the LORD God of Israel.

[4]LORD, when thou wentest out of Seir, when thou marchedst out of the field of Edom, the earth trembled, and the heavens dropped, the clouds also dropped water.

[5]The mountains *b*melted from before the LORD, *even* that Sinai from before the LORD God of Israel.

[6]In the days of Shamgar the son of Anath, in the days of Jael, the highways were unoccupied, and the *c*travellers walked through *d*byways.

[7]*The inhabitants of* the villages ceased, they ceased in Israel, until that I Deborah arose, that I arose a mother in Israel.

[8]They chose new gods; then *was* war in the gates: was there a shield or spear seen among forty thousand in Israel?

[9]My heart *is* toward the governors of Israel, that offered themselves willingly among the people. Bless ye the LORD.

[10]*e*Speak, ye that ride on white asses, ye that sit in judgment, and walk by the way.

[11]*They that are delivered* from the noise of archers in the places of drawing water, there shall they rehearse the *f*righteous acts of the LORD, *even* the righteous acts *toward the inhabitants* of his villages in Israel: then shall the people of the LORD go down to the gates.

[12]Awake, awake, Deborah: awake, awake, utter a song: arise, Barak, and lead thy captivity captive, thou son of Abinoam.

[13]Then he made him that remaineth have dominion over the nobles among the people: the LORD made me have dominion over the mighty.

[14]Out of Ephraim *was there* a root of them against Amalek; after thee, Benjamin, among thy people; out of Machir came down governors, and out of Zebulun they that *g*handle the pen of the writer.

[15]And the princes of Issachar *were* with Deborah; even Issachar, and also Barak: he was sent on *h*foot into the valley. *i*For the divisions of Reuben *there were* great *j*thoughts of heart.

[16]Why abodest thou among the sheepfolds, to hear the bleatings of the flocks? *k*For the divisions of Reuben *there were* great searchings of heart.

[17]Gilead abode beyond Jordan: and why did Dan remain in ships? Asher continued on the sea *l*shore, and abode in his *m*breaches.

[18]Zebulun and Naphtali *were* a people *that* *n*jeoparded their lives unto the death in the high places of the field.

[3]Hear, O kings; give ear, O princes; I will sing to the Lord, I will sing praise to the Lord, the God of Israel.

[4]Lord, when You went forth out of Seir, when You marched out of the field of Edom, the earth trembled and the heavens also dropped, yes, the clouds dropped water.

[5]The mountains quaked at the presence of the Lord, yes, yonder Sinai at the presence of the Lord, the God of Israel.

[6]After the days of Shamgar son of Anath, after the days of Jael [meaning here Ehud] the caravans ceased, travelers walked through byways.

[7]The villages were unoccupied *and* rulers ceased in Israel until *c*you arose—you, Deborah, arose—a mother in Israel.

[8][Formerly] they chose new gods; then war was in the gates. Was there a shield or spear seen among 40,000 in Israel?

[9]My heart goes out to the commanders of Israel who offered themselves willingly among the people. Bless the Lord!

[10]Tell of it—you who ride on white donkeys, you who sit on rich carpets, and you who walk by the way.

[11]Far from the noise of archers in the places of drawing water, there shall they rehearse the righteous acts of the Lord, even the righteous acts toward His villagers in Israel. Then the people of the Lord went down to the gates.

[12]Awake, awake, Deborah! Awake, awake, utter a song! Arise, Barak, and lead away your captives, you son of Abinoam.

[13]Then down marched the remnant of the nobles, the people of the Lord marched down for Me against the mighty.

[14]Out of Ephraim they came down whose root is in Amalek, after you, Benjamin, with your kinsmen. Out of Machir came down commanders *and* lawgivers, and out of Zebulun those who *d*handle the pen *or* stylus of the writer.

[15]And the princes of Issachar came with Deborah, and Issachar was faithful to Barak; into the valley they rushed forth at his heels. [But] among the clans of Reuben were great searchings of heart.

[16]Why [Reuben] did you linger among the sheepfolds listening to the piping for the flocks? Among the clans of Reuben there were great searchings of heart.

[17]Gilead remained beyond the Jordan, and why did Dan stay with the ships? Asher sat still on the seacoast and remained by his creeks. [These came not forth to battle for God's people.]

[18]But Zebulun was a people who endangered their lives to the death; Naphtali did also on the heights of the field.

---

b Heb. *flowed*   *c* Heb. *walkers of paths*   *d* Heb. *crooked ways*
e Or, *Meditate*   *f* Heb. *righteousnesses of the LORD*   *g* Heb.
draw with the pen   *h* Heb. *his feet*   *i* Or, *In the divisions*
j Heb. *impressions*   *k* Or, *In*   *l* Or, *port*   *m* Or, *creeks*
n Heb. *exposed to reproach*

c F. F. Bruce in *The New Bible Dictionary* calls attention to the fact that the repeated Hebrew verb here "may be understood not as the normal first person singular ('I arose') but as an archaic second person singular ('thou didst arise')."   *d* Reference at this date (about 1150 B.C.) to a writer is no more surprising than the mention of "the city of books" in Judg. 1:11. Writing, and alphabetical writing at that, had been practiced for some centuries along the Syrian Coast . . . Quantities of papyrus [the pith of papyrus was used for writing] were exported from Egypt to Phoenicia at around 1100 B.C. (Judg. 8:14) (F. Davidson, ed., *The New Bible Commentary*). "Zebulun, formerly known only for [its] experts with the ciphering-pencil, had now become a people courageous unto death" (J.P. Lange, *A Commentary*).

New American Standard

3"Hear, O kings; give ear, O rulers!
I—to the LORD, I will sing,
I will sing praise to the LORD, the God of Israel.
4"LORD, when You went out from Seir,
When You marched from the field of Edom,
The earth quaked, the heavens also dripped,
Even the clouds dripped water.
5"The mountains quaked at the presence of the LORD,
This Sinai, at the presence of the LORD, the God of Israel.

6 ¶ "In the days of Shamgar the son of Anath,
In the days of Jael, the highways were deserted,
And travelers went by roundabout ways.
7"The peasantry ceased, they ceased in Israel,
Until I, Deborah, arose,
Until I arose, a mother in Israel.
8"New gods were chosen;
Then war *was* in the gates.
Not a shield or a spear was seen
Among forty thousand in Israel.
9"My heart *goes out* to the commanders of Israel,
The volunteers among the people;
Bless the LORD!
10"You who ride on white donkeys,
You who sit on *rich* carpets,
And you who travel on the road—sing!
11"At the sound of those who divide *flocks* among
the watering places,
There they shall recount the righteous deeds of
the LORD,
The righteous deeds for His peasantry in Israel.
Then the people of the LORD went down to the
gates.

12 ¶ "Awake, awake, Deborah;
Awake, awake, sing a song!
Arise, Barak, and take away your captives, O son
of Abinoam.
13"Then survivors came down to the nobles;
The people of the LORD came down to me as
warriors.
14"From Ephraim those whose root is in Amalek
came down,
Following you, Benjamin, with your peoples;
From Machir commanders came down,
And from Zebulun those who wield the staff of
office.
15"And the princes of Issachar *were* with Deborah;
As *was* Issachar, so *was* Barak,
Into the valley they rushed at his heels;
Among the divisions of Reuben
There were great resolves of heart.
16"Why did you sit among the *sheepfolds,
To hear the piping for the flocks?
Among the divisions of Reuben
There were great searchings of heart.
17"Gilead remained across the Jordan;
And why did Dan stay in ships?
Asher sat at the seashore,
And remained by its landings.
18"Zebulun *was* a people who despised their lives
even to death,
And Naphtali also, on the high places of the field.

New International

3"Hear this, you kings! Listen, you rulers!
I will sing to*u* the LORD, I will sing;
I will make music to*v* the LORD, the God
of Israel.
4"O LORD, when you went out from Seir,
when you marched from the land of Edom,
the earth shook, the heavens poured,
the clouds poured down water.
5The mountains quaked before the LORD, the
One of Sinai,
before the LORD, the God of Israel.

6"In the days of Shamgar son of Anath,
in the days of Jael, the roads were
*abandoned;
travelers took to winding paths.
7Village life*w* in Israel ceased,
ceased until I,*x* Deborah, arose,
arose a mother in Israel.
8When they chose new gods,
war came to the city gates,
and not a shield or spear was seen
among forty thousand in Israel.
9My heart is with Israel's princes,
with the willing volunteers among the
people.
Praise the LORD!

10"You who ride on white donkeys,
sitting on your saddle blankets,
and you who walk along the road,
consider 11the voice of the singers*y* at the
watering places.
They recite the righteous acts of the LORD,
the righteous acts of his warriors*z* in Israel.

"Then the people of the LORD
went down to the city gates.
12'Wake up, wake up, Deborah!
Wake up, wake up, break out in song!
Arise, O Barak!
Take captive your captives, O son of
Abinoam.'

13"Then the men who were left
came down to the nobles;
the people of the LORD
came to me with the mighty.
14Some came from Ephraim, whose roots were
in Amalek;
Benjamin was with the people who followed
you.
From Makir captains came down,
from Zebulun those who bear a
commander's staff.
15The princes of Issachar were with Deborah;
yes, Issachar was with Barak,
rushing after him into the valley.
In the districts of Reuben
there was much searching of heart.
16Why did you stay among the campfires*a*
to hear the whistling for the flocks?
In the districts of Reuben
there was much searching of heart.
17Gilead stayed beyond the Jordan.
And Dan, why did he linger by the ships?
Asher remained on the coast
and stayed in his coves.
18The people of Zebulun risked their very lives;
so did Naphtali on the heights of the field.

*i*Or *saddlebags

*u*3 Or *of*   *v*3 Or *I* *with song I will praise*   *w*7 Or *Warriors*
*x*7 Or *you*   *y*11 Or *archers*; the meaning of the Hebrew for this
word is uncertain.   *z*11 Or *villagers*   *a*16 Or *saddlebags*

King James

19 The kings came *and* fought, then fought the kings of Canaan in Taanach by the waters of Megiddo; they took no gain of money.

20 They fought from heaven; the stars in their [o]courses fought against Sisera.

21 The river of Kishon swept them away, that ancient river, the river Kishon. O my soul, thou hast trodden down strength.

22 Then were the horsehoofs broken by the means of the [p]pransings, the pransings of their mighty ones.

23 Curse ye Meroz, said the angel of the LORD, curse ye bitterly the inhabitants thereof; because they came not to the help of the LORD, to the help of the LORD against the mighty.

24 Blessed above women shall Jael the wife of Heber the Kenite be, blessed shall she be above women in the tent.

25 He asked water, *and* she gave *him* milk; she brought forth butter in a lordly dish.

26 She put her hand to the nail, and her right hand to the workmen's hammer; and [q]with the hammer she smote Sisera, she smote off his head, when she had pierced and stricken through his temples.

27 [r]At her feet he bowed, he fell, he lay down: at her feet he bowed, he fell: where he bowed, there he fell down [s]dead.

28 The mother of Sisera looked out at a window, and cried through the lattice, Why is his chariot *so* long in coming? why tarry the wheels of his chariot?

29 Her wise ladies answered her, yea, she returned [t]answer to herself,

30 Have they not sped? have they *not* divided the prey; [u]to every man a damsel *or* two; to Sisera a prey of divers colours, a prey of divers colours of needlework, of divers colours of needlework on both sides, *meet* for the necks of *them that take* the spoil?

31 So let all thine enemies perish, O LORD: but *let* them that love him *be* as the sun when he goeth forth in his might. And the land had rest forty years.

Gideon

6 AND THE children of Israel did evil in the sight of the LORD: and the LORD delivered them into the hand of Midian seven years.

2 And the hand of Midian [v]prevailed against Israel: *and* because of the Midianites the children of Israel made them the dens which *are* in the mountains, and caves, and strong holds.

3 And *so* it was, when Israel had sown, that the Midianites came up, and the Amalekites, and the children of the east, even they came up against them;

4 And they encamped against them, and destroyed the increase of the earth, till thou come unto Gaza, and left no sustenance for Israel, neither [w]sheep, nor ox, nor ass.

5 For they came up with their cattle and their tents, and they came as grasshoppers for multitude; *for* both they and their camels were without number: and they entered into the land to destroy it.

[o] Heb. *paths* [p] Or, *tramplings*, or, *plungings* [q] Heb. *she hammered* [r] Heb. *Between* [s] Heb. *destroyed* [t] Heb. *her words* [u] Heb. *to the head of a man* [v] Heb. *was strong* [w] Or, *goat*

Amplified

19 The kings came and fought, then fought the kings of Canaan at Taanach by the waters of Megiddo. Gain of booty they did not obtain.

20 From the heavens the stars fought, from their courses they fought against Sisera.

21 The torrent Kishon swept [the foe] away, the onrushing torrent, the torrent Kishon. O my soul, march on with strength!

22 Then the horses' hoofs beat loudly because of the galloping of [fleeing] valiant riders.

23 Curse Meroz, said the messenger of the Lord. Curse bitterly its inhabitants, because they came not to the help of the Lord, to the help of the Lord against the mighty!

24 Blessed above women shall Jael, the wife of Heber the Kenite, be; blessed shall she be above women in the tent.

25 [Sisera] asked for water, and she gave [him] milk; she brought him curds in a lordly dish.

26 She put her [left] hand to the tent pin, and her right hand to the workmen's hammer. And with the wooden hammer she smote Sisera, she smote his head, yes, she struck and pierced his temple.

27 He sank, he fell, he lay still at her feet. At her feet he sank, he fell; where he sank, there he fell—dead!

28 The [e]mother of Sisera looked out at a window and wailed through the lattice, Why is his chariot so long in coming? Why do the hoofbeats of his chariots tarry?

29 Her wise ladies answered her, yet she repeated her words to herself,

30 Have they not found and been dividing the spoil? A maiden or two for every man, a spoil of dyed garments for Sisera, a spoil of dyed stuffs embroidered, two pieces of dyed work embroidered for my neck as spoil?

31 So let all Your enemies perish, O Lord! But let those who love Him be like the sun when it rises in its might. And the land had peace *and* rest for forty years.

6 BUT THE Israelites did evil in the sight of the Lord, and the Lord gave them into the hand of Midian for seven years.

2 And the hand of Midian prevailed against Israel. Because of Midian the Israelites made themselves the dens which are in the mountains and the caves and the strongholds.

3 For whenever Israel had sown their seed, the Midianites and the Amalekites and the people of the east came up against them.

4 They would encamp against them and destroy the crops as far as Gaza and leave no nourishment for Israel, and no ox or sheep or donkey.

5 For they came up with their cattle and their tents, and they came like locusts for multitude; both they and their camels could not be counted. So they wasted the land as they entered it.

[e] "Who should first suffer anxiety [in the palace of the women] if not the mother? Of a wife, nothing is said; such love thrives not in the harem of a prince. He is his mother's pride, the great hero, who had hitherto been invincible. What she has in him, and what she loses, concerns no other woman" (J.P. Lange, *A Commentary*).

New American Standard

19 ¶ "The kings came *and* fought;
  Then fought the kings of Canaan
  At Taanach near the waters of Megiddo;
  They took no plunder in silver.
20 "The stars fought from heaven,
  From their courses they fought against Sisera.
21 "The torrent of Kishon swept them away,
  The ancient torrent, the torrent Kishon.
  O my soul, march on with strength.
22 "Then the horses' hoofs beat
  From the dashing, the dashing of his valiant
    steeds.
23 'Curse Meroz,' said the angel of the LORD,
  'Utterly curse its inhabitants;
  Because they did not come to the help of the
    LORD,
  To the help of the LORD against the warriors.'

24 ¶ "Most blessed of women is Jael,
  The wife of Heber the Kenite;
  Most blessed is she of women in the tent.
25 "He asked for water *and* she gave him milk;
  In a magnificent bowl she brought him curds.
26 "She reached out her hand for the tent peg,
  And her right hand for the workmen's hammer.
  Then she struck Sisera, she smashed his head;
  And she shattered and pierced his temple.
27 "Between her feet he bowed, he fell, he lay;
  Between her feet he bowed, he fell;
  Where he bowed, there he fell dead.

28 ¶ "Out of the window she looked and lamented,
  The mother of Sisera through the lattice,
  'Why does his chariot delay in coming?
  Why do the hoofbeats of his chariots tarry?'
29 "Her wise princesses would answer her,
  Indeed she repeats her words to herself,
30 'Are they not finding, are they not dividing the
    spoil?
  A maiden, two maidens for every warrior;
  To Sisera a spoil of dyed work,
  A spoil of dyed work embroidered,
  Dyed work of double embroidery on the neck of
    the spoiler?'
31 "Thus let all Your enemies perish, O LORD;
  But let those who love Him be like the rising of
    the sun in its might."
And the land was undisturbed for forty years.

Israel Oppressed by Midian

6 THEN THE sons of Israel did what was evil in the
  sight of the LORD; and the LORD gave them into the
hands of Midian seven years.
2 The power of Midian prevailed against Israel. Because of Midian the sons of Israel made for themselves the
dens which were in the mountains and the caves and the
strongholds.
3 For it was when Israel had sown, that the Midianites
would come up with the Amalekites and the sons of the
east and go against them.
4 So they would camp against them and destroy the
produce of the earth as far as Gaza, and leave no sustenance in Israel as well as no sheep, ox, or donkey.
5 For they would come up with their livestock and their
tents, they would come in like locusts for number, both
they and their camels were innumerable; and they came
into the land to devastate it.

New International

19 "Kings came, they fought;
  the kings of Canaan fought
at Taanach by the waters of Megiddo,
  but they carried off no silver, no plunder.
20 From the heavens the stars fought,
  from their courses they fought against
    Sisera.
21 The river Kishon swept them away,
  the age-old river, the river Kishon.
  March on, my soul; be strong!
22 Then thundered the horses' hoofs—
  galloping, galloping go his mighty steeds.
23 'Curse Meroz,' said the angel of the LORD.
  'Curse its people bitterly,
because they did not come to help the LORD,
  to help the LORD against the mighty.'

24 "Most blessed of women be Jael,
  the wife of Heber the Kenite,
  most blessed of tent-dwelling women.
25 He asked for water, and she gave him milk;
  in a bowl fit for nobles she brought him
    curdled milk.
26 Her hand reached for the tent peg,
  her right hand for the workman's hammer.
  She struck Sisera, she crushed his head,
  she shattered and pierced his temple.
27 At her feet he sank,
  he fell; there he lay.
  At her feet he sank, he fell;
  where he sank, there he fell—dead.

28 "Through the window peered Sisera's mother;
  behind the lattice she cried out,
  'Why is his chariot so long in coming?
  Why is the clatter of his chariots delayed?'
29 The wisest of her ladies answer her;
  indeed, she keeps saying to herself,
30 'Are they not finding and dividing the spoils:
  a girl or two for each man,
  colorful garments as plunder for Sisera,
  colorful garments embroidered,
  highly embroidered garments for my neck—
all this as plunder?'

31 "So may all your enemies perish, O LORD!
  But may they who love you be like the sun
    when it rises in its strength."

Then the land had peace forty years.

Gideon

6 AGAIN THE Israelites did evil in the eyes of the
  LORD, and for seven years he gave them into the hands
of the Midianites. 2Because the power of Midian was so
oppressive, the Israelites prepared shelters for themselves
in mountain clefts, caves and strongholds. 3Whenever the
Israelites planted their crops, the Midianites, Amalekites
and other eastern peoples invaded the country. 4They
camped on the land and ruined the crops all the way to
Gaza and did not spare a living thing for Israel, neither
sheep nor cattle nor donkeys. 5They came up with their
livestock and their tents like swarms of locusts. It was
impossible to count the men and their camels; they invad-

King James

⁶And Israel was greatly impoverished because of the Midianites; and the children of Israel cried unto the LORD.

⁷ ¶ And it came to pass, when the children of Israel cried unto the LORD because of the Midianites,

⁸That the LORD sent *a prophet unto the children of Israel, which said unto them, Thus saith the LORD God of Israel, I brought you up from Egypt, and brought you forth out of the house of bondage;

⁹And I delivered you out of the hand of the Egyptians, and out of the hand of all that oppressed you, and drave them out from before you, and gave you their land;

¹⁰And I said unto you, I *am* the LORD your God; fear not the gods of the Amorites, in whose land ye dwell: but ye have not obeyed my voice.

¹¹ ¶ And there came an angel of the LORD, and sat under an oak which *was* in Ophrah, that *pertained* unto Joash the Abi-ezrite: and his son Gideon threshed wheat by the winepress, ^yto hide *it* from the Midianites.

¹²And the angel of the LORD appeared unto him, and said unto him, The LORD *is* with thee, thou mighty man of valour.

¹³And Gideon said unto him, Oh my Lord, if the LORD be with us, why then is all this befallen us? and where *be* all his miracles which our fathers told us of, saying, Did not the LORD bring us up from Egypt? but now the LORD hath forsaken us, and delivered us into the hands of the Midianites.

¹⁴And the LORD looked upon him, and said, Go in this thy might, and thou shalt save Israel from the hand of the Midianites: have not I sent thee?

¹⁵And he said unto him, Oh my Lord, wherewith shall I save Israel? behold, my family *is* poor in Manasseh, and I *am* the least in my father's house.

¹⁶And the LORD said unto him, Surely I will be with thee, and thou shalt smite the Midianites as one man.

¹⁷And he said unto him, If now I have found grace in thy sight, then show me a sign that thou talkest with me.

¹⁸Depart not hence, I pray thee, until I come unto thee, and bring forth my ^zpresent, and set *it* before thee. And he said, I will tarry until thou come again.

¹⁹ ¶ And Gideon went in, and made ready ^aa kid, and unleavened cakes of an ephah of flour: the flesh he put in a basket, and he put the broth in a pot, and brought *it* out unto him under the oak, and presented *it.*

²⁰And the angel of God said unto him, Take the flesh and the unleavened cakes, and lay *them* upon this rock, and pour out the broth. And he did so.

²¹ ¶ Then the angel of the LORD put forth the end of the staff that *was* in his hand, and touched the flesh and the unleavened cakes; and there rose up fire out of the rock, and consumed the flesh and the unleavened cakes. Then the angel of the LORD departed out of his sight.

²²And when Gideon perceived that he *was* an angel of the LORD, Gideon said, Alas, O Lord GOD! for because I have seen an angel of the LORD face to face.

²³And the LORD said unto him, Peace *be* unto thee; fear not: thou shalt not die.

²⁴Then Gideon built an altar there unto the LORD, and called it ^bJehovah-shalom: unto this day it *is* yet in Oph-rah of the Abi-ezrites.

²⁵ ¶ And it came to pass the same night, that the LORD said unto him, Take thy father's young bullock, ^ceven the second bullock of seven years old, and throw down the altar of Baal that thy father hath, and cut down the grove that *is* by it:

²⁶And build an altar unto the LORD thy God upon the top of this ^drock, ^ein the ordered place, and take the second bullock, and offer a burnt sacrifice with the wood of the grove which thou shalt cut down.

Amplified

⁶And Israel was greatly impoverished because of the Midianites, and the Israelites cried to the Lord.

⁷And when they cried to the Lord because of Midian,

⁸The Lord sent a prophet to the Israelites, who said to them, Thus says the Lord, the God of Israel, I brought you up from Egypt and brought you forth out of the house of bondage.

⁹And I delivered you out of the hand of the Egyptians and out of the hand of all who oppressed you, and drove them out from before you and gave you their land.

¹⁰And I said to you, I am the Lord your God; fear not the gods of the Amorites, in whose land you dwell. But you have not obeyed My voice.

¹¹Now the ^fAngel of the Lord came and sat under the oak (terebinth) at Ophrah, which belonged to Joash the Abiezrite, and his son Gideon was beating wheat in the winepress to hide it from the Midianites.

¹²And the Angel of the Lord appeared to him and said to him, The Lord is with you, you mighty man of [fearless] courage.

¹³And Gideon said to him, O sir, if the Lord is with us, why is all this befallen us? And where are all His won-drous works of which our fathers told us, saying, Did not the Lord bring us up from Egypt? But now the Lord has forsaken us and given us into the hand of Midian.

¹⁴The Lord turned to him and said, Go in this your might, and you shall save Israel from the hand of Midian. Have I not sent you?

¹⁵Gideon said to Him, Oh Lord, how can I deliver Isra-el? Behold, my clan is the poorest in Manasseh, and I am the least in my father's house.

¹⁶The Lord said to him, Surely I will be with you, and you shall smite the Midianites as one man.

¹⁷Gideon said to Him, If now I have found favor in Your sight, then show me a sign that it is You Who talks with me.

¹⁸Do not leave here, I pray You, until I return to You and bring my offering and set it before You. And He said, I will wait until you return.

¹⁹Then Gideon went in and prepared a kid and unleav-ened cakes of an ephah of flour. The meat he put in a basket and the broth in a pot, and brought them to Him under the oak and presented them.

²⁰And the Angel of God said to him, Take the meat and unleavened cakes and lay them on this rock and pour the broth over them. And he did so.

²¹Then the Angel of the Lord reached out the tip of the staff that was in His hand, and touched the meat and the unleavened cakes, and there flared up fire from the rock and consumed the meat and the unleavened cakes. Then the Angel of the Lord vanished from his sight.

²²And when Gideon perceived that He was the Angel of the Lord, Gideon said, Alas, O Lord God! For now I have seen the Angel of the Lord face to face!

²³The Lord said to him, Peace be to you, do not fear; you shall not die.

²⁴Then Gideon built an altar there to the Lord and called it, The Lord is Peace. To this day it still stands in Ophrah, which belongs to the Abiezrites.

²⁵That night the Lord said to Gideon, Take your father's bull, the second bull seven years old, and pull down the altar of Baal that your father has and cut down the Asherah [symbol of the goddess Asherah] that is beside it;

²⁶And build an altar to the Lord your God on top of this stronghold with stones laid in proper order. Then take the second bull and offer a burnt sacrifice with the wood of the Asherah which you shall cut down.

---

^xHeb. *a man a prophet*   ^yHeb. *to cause* it *to flee*   ^zOr, *meat offering*   ^aHeb. *a kid of the goats*   ^bi.e. *The LORD* send *peace*   ^cOr, *and*   ^dHeb. *strong place*   ^eOr, *in an orderly manner*

^fSee footnote on Gen. 16:7.

New American Standard

6 So Israel was brought very low because of Midian, and the sons of Israel cried to the LORD.

7 ¶ Now it came about when the sons of Israel cried to the LORD on account of Midian,

8 that the LORD sent a prophet to the sons of Israel, and he said to them, "Thus says the LORD, the God of Israel, 'It was I who brought you up from Egypt and brought you out from the house of slavery.

9 'I delivered you from the hands of the Egyptians and from the hands of all your oppressors, and dispossessed them before you and gave you their land,

10 and I said to you, "I am the LORD your God; you shall not fear the gods of the Amorites in whose land you live. But you have not obeyed Me." ' "

Gideon Is Visited

11 ¶ Then the angel of the LORD came and sat under the oak that was in Ophrah, which belonged to Joash the Abiezrite as his son Gideon was beating out wheat in the wine press in order to save *it* from the Midianites.

12 The angel of the LORD appeared to him and said to him, "The LORD is with you, O valiant warrior."

13 Then Gideon said to him, "O my lord, if the LORD is with us, why then has all this happened to us? And where are all His miracles which our fathers told us about, saying, 'Did not the LORD bring us up from Egypt?' But now the LORD has abandoned us and given us into the hand of Midian."

14 The LORD looked at him and said, "Go in this your strength and deliver Israel from the hand of Midian. Have I not sent you?"

15 He said to Him, "O Lord, how shall I deliver Israel? Behold, my family is the least in Manasseh, and I am the youngest in my father's house."

16 But the LORD said to him, "Surely I will be with you, and you shall defeat Midian as one man."

17 So Gideon said to Him, "If now I have found favor in Your sight, then show me a sign that it is You who speak with me.

18 "Please do not depart from here, until I come *back* to You, and bring out my offering and lay it before You." And He said, "I will remain until you return."

19 ¶ Then Gideon went in and prepared a young goat and unleavened bread from an *j* ephah of flour; he put the meat in a basket and the broth in a pot, and brought *them* out to him under the oak and presented *them*.

20 The angel of God said to him, "Take the meat and the unleavened bread and lay them on this rock, and pour out the broth." And he did so.

21 Then the angel of the LORD put out the end of the staff that was in his hand and touched the meat and the unleavened bread; and fire sprang up from the rock and consumed the meat and the unleavened bread. Then the angel of the LORD vanished from his sight.

22 When Gideon saw that he was the angel of the LORD, he said, "Alas, O Lord GOD! For now I have seen the angel of the LORD face to face."

23 The LORD said to him, "Peace to you, do not fear; you shall not die."

24 Then Gideon built an altar there to the LORD and named it The LORD is Peace. To this day it is still in Ophrah of the Abiezrites.

25 ¶ Now on the same night the LORD said to him, "Take your father's bull and a second bull seven years old, and pull down the altar of Baal which belongs to your father, and cut down the *k* Asherah that is beside it;

26 and build an altar to the LORD your God on the top of this stronghold in an orderly manner, and take a second bull and offer a burnt offering with the wood of the Asherah which you shall cut down."

New International

ed the land to ravage it. 6Midian so impoverished the Israelites that they cried out to the LORD for help.

7When the Israelites cried to the LORD because of Midian, 8he sent them a prophet, who said, "This is what the LORD, the God of Israel, says: I brought you up out of Egypt, out of the land of slavery. 9I snatched you from the power of Egypt and from the hand of all your oppressors. I drove them from before you and gave you their land. 10I said to you, 'I am the LORD your God; do not worship the gods of the Amorites, in whose land you live.' But you have not listened to me."

11The angel of the LORD came and sat down under the oak in Ophrah that belonged to Joash the Abiezrite, where his son Gideon was threshing wheat in a winepress to keep it from the Midianites. 12When the angel of the LORD appeared to Gideon, he said, "The LORD is with you, mighty warrior."

13"But sir," Gideon replied, "if the LORD is with us, why has all this happened to us? Where are all his wonders that our fathers told us about when they said, 'Did not the LORD bring us up out of Egypt?' But now the LORD has abandoned us and put us into the hand of Midian."

14The LORD turned to him and said, "Go in the strength you have and save Israel out of Midian's hand. Am I not sending you?"

15"But Lord,*b* " Gideon asked, "how can I save Israel? My clan is the weakest in Manasseh, and I am the least in my family."

16The LORD answered, "I will be with you, and you will strike down all the Midianites together."

17Gideon replied, "If now I have found favor in your eyes, give me a sign that it is really you talking to me. 18Please do not go away until I come back and bring my offering and set it before you."

And the LORD said, "I will wait until you return."

19Gideon went in, prepared a young goat, and from an ephah*c* of flour he made bread without yeast. Putting the meat in a basket and its broth in a pot, he brought them out and offered them to him under the oak.

20The angel of God said to him, "Take the meat and the unleavened bread, place them on this rock, and pour out the broth." And Gideon did so. 21With the tip of the staff that was in his hand, the angel of the LORD touched the meat and the unleavened bread. Fire flared from the rock, consuming the meat and the bread. And the angel of the LORD disappeared. 22When Gideon realized that it was the angel of the LORD, he exclaimed, "Ah, Sovereign LORD! I have seen the angel of the LORD face to face!"

23But the LORD said to him, "Peace! Do not be afraid. You are not going to die."

24So Gideon built an altar to the LORD there and called it The LORD is Peace. To this day it stands in Ophrah of the Abiezrites.

25That same night the LORD said to him, "Take the second bull from your father's herd, the one seven years old.*d* Tear down your father's altar to Baal and cut down the Asherah pole*e* beside it. 26Then build a proper kind of*f* altar to the LORD your God on the top of this height. Using the wood of the Asherah pole that you cut down, offer the second*g* bull as a burnt offering."

---

b 15 Or *sir*   *c 19* That is, probably about 3/5 bushel (about 22 liters)   *d 25* Or *Take a full-grown, mature bull from your father's herd*   *e 25* That is, a symbol of the goddess Asherah; here and elsewhere in Judges   *f 26* Or *build with layers of stone an*   *g 26* Or *full-grown*; also in verse 28

---

j I.e. Approx one bu also vv 26, 28, 30   *k* I.e. wooden symbol of a female deity,

King James

²⁷Then Gideon took ten men of his servants, and did as the LORD had said unto him: and *so* it was, because he feared his father's household, and the men of the city, that he could not do *it* by day, that he did *it* by night.

²⁸ ¶ And when the men of the city arose early in the morning, behold, the altar of Baal was cast down, and the grove was cut down that *was* by it, and the second bullock was offered upon the altar *that was* built.

²⁹And they said one to another, Who hath done this thing? And when they inquired and asked, they said, Gideon the son of Joash hath done this thing.

³⁰Then the men of the city said unto Joash, Bring out thy son, that he may die: because he hath cast down the altar of Baal, and because he hath cut down the grove that *was* by it.

³¹And Joash said unto all that stood against him, Will ye plead for Baal? will ye save him? he that will plead for him, let him be put to death whilst *it is yet* morning: if he *be* a god, let him plead for himself, because *one* hath cast down his altar.

³²Therefore on that day he called him ᶠJerubbaal, saying, Let Baal plead against him, because he hath thrown down his altar.

³³ ¶ Then all the Midianites and the Amalekites and the children of the east were gathered together, and went over, and pitched in the valley of Jezreel.

³⁴But the spirit of the LORD ᵍcame upon Gideon, and he blew a trumpet; and Abiezer ʰwas gathered after him.

³⁵And he sent messengers throughout all Manasseh; who also was gathered after him: and he sent messengers unto Asher, and unto Zebulun, and unto Naphtali; and they came up to meet them.

³⁶ ¶ And Gideon said unto God, If thou wilt save Israel by mine hand, as thou hast said,

³⁷Behold, I will put a fleece of wool in the floor; *and* if the dew be on the fleece only, and *it be* dry upon all the earth *beside,* then shall I know that thou wilt save Israel by mine hand, as thou hast said.

³⁸And it was so: for he rose up early on the morrow, and thrust the fleece together, and wringed the dew out of the fleece, a bowl full of water.

³⁹And Gideon said unto God, Let not thine anger be hot against me, and I will speak but this once: let me prove, I pray thee, but this once with the fleece; let it now be dry only upon the fleece, and upon all the ground let there be dew.

⁴⁰And God did so that night: for it was dry upon the fleece only, and there was dew on all the ground.

The defeat of the Midianites

7 THEN JERUBBAAL, who *is* Gideon, and all the people that *were* with him, rose up early, and pitched beside the well of Harod: so that the host of the Midianites were on the north side of them, by the hill of Moreh, in the valley.

²And the LORD said unto Gideon, The people that *are* with thee *are* too many for me to give the Midianites into their hands, lest Israel vaunt themselves against me, saying, Mine own hand hath saved me.

³Now therefore go to, proclaim in the ears of the people, saying, Whosoever *is* fearful and afraid, let him return and depart early from mount Gilead. And there returned of the people twenty and two thousand; and there remained ten thousand.

Amplified

²⁷Then Gideon took ten men of his servants and did as the Lord had told him, but because he was too afraid of his father's household and the men of the city to do it by day, he did it by night.

²⁸And when the men of the city arose early in the morning, behold, the altar of Baal was cast down, and the Asherah was cut down that was beside it, and the second bull was offered on the altar which had been built.

²⁹And they said to one another, Who has done this thing? And when they searched and asked, they were told, Gideon son of Joash has done this thing.

³⁰Then the men of the city commanded Joash, Bring out your son, that he may die, for he has pulled down the altar of Baal and cut down the Asherah beside it.

³¹But Joash said to all who stood against him, Will you contend for Baal? Or will you save him? He who will contend for Baal, let him be put to death while it is still morning. If Baal is a god, let him contend for himself because one has pulled down his altar.

³²Therefore on that day he called Gideon Jerubbaal, meaning, Let Baal contend against him, because he had pulled down his altar.

³³Then all the Midianites and the Amalekites and the people of the east came together and, crossing the Jordan, encamped in the Valley of Jezreel.

³⁴But the Spirit of the Lord clothed Gideon with Himself *and* took possession of him, and he blew a trumpet, and [the clan of] Abiezer was gathered to him.

³⁵And he sent messengers throughout all Manasseh, and the Manassites were called to follow him; and he sent messengers to Asher, to Zebulun, and to Naphtali, and they came up to meet them.

³⁶And Gideon said to God, If You will deliver Israel by my hand as You have said,

³⁷Behold, I will put a fleece of wool on the threshing floor. If there is dew on the fleece only and it is dry on all the ground, then I shall know that You will deliver Israel by my hand, as You have said.

³⁸And it was so. When he rose early next morning and squeezed the dew out of the fleece, he wrung from it a bowlful of water.

³⁹And Gideon said to God, Let not your anger be kindled against me, and I will speak but this once. Let me make trial only this once with the fleece, I pray you; let it now be dry only upon the fleece and upon all the ground let there be dew.

⁴⁰And God did so that night, for it was dry on the fleece only, and there was dew on all the ground.

7 THEN JERUBBAAL, that is, Gideon, and all the people who were with him rose early and encamped beside the spring of Harod; and the camp of Midian was north of them by the hill of Moreh in the valley.

²The Lord said to Gideon, The people who are with you are too many for Me to give the Midianites into their hands, lest Israel boast about themselves against Me, saying, My own hand has delivered me.

³So now proclaim in the ears of the men, saying, Whoever is fearful and trembling, let him turn back and depart from Mount Gilead. And 22,000 of the men returned, but 10,000 remained.

ᶠi.e. *Let Baal plead him*　　ᵍHeb. *clothed*　　ʰHeb. *was called after*

New American Standard

27 Then Gideon took ten men of his servants and did as the LORD had spoken to him; and because he was too afraid of his father's household and the men of the city to do it by day, he did it by night.

The Altar of Baal Destroyed

28 ¶ When the men of the city arose early in the morning, behold, the altar of Baal was torn down, and the Asherah which was beside it was cut down, and the second bull was offered on the altar which had been built.
29 They said to one another, "Who did this thing?" And when they searched about and inquired, they said, "Gideon the son of Joash did this thing."
30 Then the men of the city said to Joash, "Bring out your son, that he may die, for he has torn down the altar of Baal, and indeed, he has cut down the Asherah which was beside it."
31 But Joash said to all who stood against him, "Will you contend for Baal, or will you deliver him? Whoever will plead for him shall be put to death by morning. If he is a god, let him contend for himself, because someone has torn down his altar."
32 Therefore on that day he named him Jerubbaal, that is to say, "Let Baal contend against him," because he had torn down his altar.
33 ¶ Then all the Midianites and the Amalekites and the sons of the east assembled themselves; and they crossed over and camped in the valley of Jezreel.
34 So the Spirit of the LORD came upon Gideon; and he blew a trumpet, and the Abiezrites were called together to follow him.
35 He sent messengers throughout Manasseh, and they also were called together to follow him; and he sent messengers to Asher, Zebulun, and Naphtali, and they came up to meet them.

Sign of the Fleece

36 ¶ Then Gideon said to God, "If You will deliver Israel through me, as You have spoken,
37 behold, I will put a fleece of wool on the threshing floor. If there is dew on the fleece only, and it is dry on all the ground, then I will know that You will deliver Israel through me, as You have spoken."
38 And it was so. When he arose early the next morning and squeezed the fleece, he drained the dew from the fleece, a bowl full of water.
39 Then Gideon said to God, "Do not let Your anger burn against me that I may speak once more; please let me make a test once more with the fleece, let it now be dry only on the fleece, and let there be dew on all the ground."
40 God did so that night; for it was dry only on the fleece, and dew was on all the ground.

Gideon's 300 Chosen Men

7 THEN JERUBBAAL (that is, Gideon) and all the people who were with him, rose early and camped beside the spring of Harod; and the camp of Midian was on the north side of them by the hill of Moreh in the valley.
2 ¶ The LORD said to Gideon, "The people who are with you are too many for Me to give Midian into their hands, for Israel would become boastful, saying, 'My own power has delivered me.'
3 "Now therefore come, proclaim in the hearing of the people, saying, 'Whoever is afraid and trembling, let him return and depart from Mount Gilead.' " So 22,000 people returned, but 10,000 remained.

New International

27 So Gideon took ten of his servants and did as the LORD told him. But because he was afraid of his family and the men of the town, he did it at night rather than in the daytime.
28 In the morning when the men of the town got up, there was Baal's altar, demolished, with the Asherah pole beside it cut down and the second bull sacrificed on the newly built altar!
29 They asked each other, "Who did this?"
When they carefully investigated, they were told, "Gideon son of Joash did it."
30 The men of the town demanded of Joash, "Bring out your son. He must die, because he has broken down Baal's altar and cut down the Asherah pole beside it."
31 But Joash replied to the hostile crowd around him, "Are you going to plead Baal's cause? Are you trying to save him? Whoever fights for him shall be put to death by morning! If Baal really is a god, he can defend himself when someone breaks down his altar." 32 So that day they called Gideon "Jerub-Baal,[h]" saying, "Let Baal contend with him," because he broke down Baal's altar.
33 Now all the Midianites, Amalekites and other eastern peoples joined forces and crossed over the Jordan and camped in the Valley of Jezreel. 34 Then the Spirit of the LORD came upon Gideon, and he blew a trumpet, summoning the Abiezrites to follow him. 35 He sent messengers throughout Manasseh, calling them to arms, and also into Asher, Zebulun and Naphtali, so that they too went up to meet them.
36 Gideon said to God, "If you will save Israel by my hand as you have promised— 37 look, I will place a wool fleece on the threshing floor. If there is dew only on the fleece and all the ground is dry, then I will know that you will save Israel by my hand, as you said." 38 And that is what happened. Gideon rose early the next day; he squeezed the fleece and wrung out the dew—a bowlful of water.
39 Then Gideon said to God, "Do not be angry with me. Let me make just one more request. Allow me one more test with the fleece. This time make the fleece dry and the ground covered with dew." 40 That night God did so. Only the fleece was dry; all the ground was covered with dew.

Gideon Defeats the Midianites

7 EARLY IN the morning, Jerub-Baal (that is, Gideon) and all his men camped at the spring of Harod. The camp of Midian was north of them in the valley near the hill of Moreh. 2 The LORD said to Gideon, "You have too many men for me to deliver Midian into their hands. In order that Israel may not boast against me that her own strength has saved her, 3 announce now to the people, 'Anyone who trembles with fear may turn back and leave Mount Gilead.' " So twenty-two thousand men left, while ten thousand remained.

h 32 *Jerub-Baal* means *let Baal contend.*

King James

⁴And the LORD said unto Gideon, The people *are* yet *too* many; bring them down unto the water, and I will try them for thee there: and it shall be, *that* of whom I say unto thee, This shall go with thee, the same shall go with thee; and of whomsoever I say unto thee, This shall not go with thee, the same shall not go.

⁵So he brought down the people unto the water: and the LORD said unto Gideon, Every one that lappeth of the water with his tongue, as a dog lappeth, him shalt thou set by himself; likewise every one that boweth down upon his knees to drink.

⁶And the number of them that lapped, *putting* their hand to their mouth, were three hundred men: but all the rest of the people bowed down upon their knees to drink water.

⁷And the LORD said unto Gideon, By the three hundred men that lapped will I save you, and deliver the Midianites into thine hand: and let all the *other* people go every man unto his place.

⁸So the people took victuals in their hand, and their trumpets: and he sent all *the rest of* Israel every man unto his tent, and retained those three hundred men: and the host of Midian was beneath him in the valley.

⁹ ¶ And it came to pass the same night, that the LORD said unto him, Arise, get thee down unto the host; for I have delivered it into thine hand.

¹⁰But if thou fear to go down, go thou with Phurah thy servant down to the host:

¹¹And thou shalt hear what they say; and afterward shall thine hands be strengthened to go down unto the host. Then went he down with Phurah his servant unto the outside of the *i*armed men that *were* in the host.

¹²And the Midianites and the Amalekites and all the children of the east lay along in the valley like grasshoppers for multitude; and their camels *were* without number, as the sand by the sea side for multitude.

¹³And when Gideon was come, behold, *there was* a man that told a dream unto his fellow, and said, Behold, I dreamed a dream, and, lo, a cake of barley bread tumbled into the host of Midian, and came unto a tent, and smote it that it fell, and overturned it, that the tent lay along.

¹⁴And his fellow answered and said, This *is* nothing else save the sword of Gideon the son of Joash, a man of Israel: *for* into his hand hath God delivered Midian, and all the host.

¹⁵ ¶ And it was *so,* when Gideon heard the telling of the dream, and *j*the interpretation thereof, that he worshipped, and returned into the host of Israel, and said, Arise; for the LORD hath delivered into your hand the host of Midian.

¹⁶And he divided the three hundred men *into* three companies, and he put *k*a trumpet in every man's hand, with empty pitchers, and *l*lamps within the pitchers.

¹⁷And he said unto them, Look on me, and do likewise: and, behold, when I come to the outside of the camp, it shall be *that,* as I do, so shall ye do.

¹⁸When I blow with a trumpet, I and all that *are* with me, then blow ye the trumpets also on every side of all the camp, and say, The sword of the LORD, and of Gideon.

¹⁹ ¶ So Gideon, and the hundred men that *were* with him, came unto the outside of the camp in the beginning of the middle watch; and they had but newly set the watch: and they blew the trumpets, and brake the pitchers that *were* in their hands.

²⁰And the three companies blew the trumpets, and brake the pitchers, and held the lamps in their left hands, and the trumpets in their right hands to blow *withal:* and they cried, The sword of the LORD, and of Gideon.

²¹And they stood every man in his place round about the camp: and all the host ran, and cried, and fled.

Amplified

⁴And the Lord said to Gideon, The men are still too many; bring them down to the water, and I will test them for you there. And he of whom I say to you, This man shall go with you, shall go with you; and he of whom I say to you, This man shall not go with you, shall not go.

⁵So he brought the men down to the water, and the Lord said to Gideon, Everyone who laps up the water with his tongue as a dog laps it, you shall set by himself, likewise everyone who bows down on his knees to drink.

⁶And the number of those who lapped, putting their hand to their mouth, was 300 men, but all the rest of the people bowed down upon their knees to drink water.

⁷And the Lord said to Gideon, With the 300 men who lapped I will deliver you, and give the Midianites into your hand. Let all the others return every man to his home.

⁸So the people took provisions and their trumpets in their hands, and he sent all the rest of Israel every man to his home and retained those 300 men. And the host of Midian was below him in the valley.

⁹That same night the Lord said to Gideon, Arise, go down against their camp, for I have given it into your hand.

¹⁰But if you fear to go down, go with Purah your servant down to the camp

¹¹And you shall hear what they say, and afterward your hands shall be strengthened to go down against the camp. Then he went down with Purah his servant to the outposts of the camp of the armed men.

¹²And the Midianites and the Amalekites and all the sons of the east lay along the valley like locusts for multitude; and their camels were without number, as the sand on the seashore for multitude.

¹³When Gideon arrived, behold, a man was telling a dream to his comrade. And he said, Behold, I dreamed a dream, and behold, a cake of *g*barley bread tumbled into the camp of Midian and came to the tent and struck it so that it fell, and turned it upside down so that the tent lay flat.

¹⁴And his comrade replied, This is nothing else but the sword of Gideon son of Joash, a man of Israel. Into his hand God has given Midian and all the host.

¹⁵When Gideon heard the telling of the dream and its interpretation, he worshiped and returned to the camp of Israel and said, Arise, for the Lord has given into your hand the host of Midian.

¹⁶And he divided the 300 men into three companies, and he put into the hands of all of them trumpets and empty pitchers, with torches inside the pitchers.

¹⁷And he said to them, Look at me, then do likewise. When I come to the edge of their camp, do as I do.

¹⁸When I blow the trumpet, I and all who are with me, then you blow the trumpets also on every side of all the camp and shout, For the Lord and for Gideon!

¹⁹So Gideon and the 100 men who were with him came to the outskirts of the camp at the beginning of the middle watch, when the guards had just been changed, and they blew the trumpets and smashed the pitchers that were in their hands.

²⁰And the three companies blew the trumpets and shattered the pitchers, holding the torches in their left hands, and in their right hands the trumpets to blow [leaving no chance to use swords], and they cried, The sword for the Lord and Gideon!

²¹They stood every man in his place round about the camp, and all the [Midianite] army ran—they cried out and fled.

---

g Alluding to the insignificance of Gideon and his family, or perhaps his whole troop. Barley then, as it is still, was distinguished from "fine flour." "To heare himselfe but a Barly-cake, troubled him not. It matters not how base wee be thought, so wee be victorious" (Bishop Joseph Hall, cited by *The Cambridge Bible*).

---

i Or, *ranks by five*   *j* Heb. *the breaking thereof*   *k* Heb. *trumpets in the hand of all of them*   *l* Or, *firebrands,* or, *torches*

New American Standard

4 ¶ Then the LORD said to Gideon, "The people are still too many; bring them down to the water and I will test them for you there. Therefore it shall be that he of whom I say to you, 'This one shall go with you,' he shall go with you; but everyone of whom I say to you, 'This one shall not go with you,' he shall not go."

5 So he brought the people down to the water. And the LORD said to Gideon, "You shall separate everyone who laps the water with his tongue as a dog laps, as well as everyone who kneels to drink."

6 Now the number of those who lapped, putting their hand to their mouth, was 300 men; but all the rest of the people kneeled to drink water.

7 The LORD said to Gideon, "I will deliver you with the 300 men who lapped and will give the Midianites into your hands; so let all the *other* people go, each man to his home."

8 So the 300 men took the people's provisions and their trumpets into their hands. And Gideon sent all the *other* men of Israel, each to his tent, but retained the 300 men; and the camp of Midian was below him in the valley.

9 ¶ Now the same night it came about that the LORD said to him, "Arise, go down against the camp, for I have given it into your hands.

10 "But if you are afraid to go down, go with Purah your servant down to the camp,

11 and you will hear what they say; and afterward your hands will be strengthened that you may go down against the camp." So he went with Purah his servant down to the outposts of the army that was in the camp.

12 Now the Midianites and the Amalekites and all the sons of the east were lying in the valley as numerous as locusts; and their camels were without number, as numerous as the sand on the seashore.

13 When Gideon came, behold, a man was relating a dream to his friend. And he said, "Behold, I had a dream; a loaf of barley bread was tumbling into the camp of Midian, and it came to the tent and struck it so that it fell, and turned it upside down so that the tent lay flat."

14 His friend replied, "This is nothing less than the sword of Gideon the son of Joash, a man of Israel; God has given Midian and all the camp into his hand."

15 ¶ When Gideon heard the account of the dream and its interpretation, he bowed in worship. He returned to the camp of Israel and said, "Arise, for the LORD has given the camp of Midian into your hands."

16 He divided the 300 men into three companies, and he put trumpets and empty pitchers into the hands of all of them, with torches inside the pitchers.

17 He said to them, "Look at me and do likewise. And behold, when I come to the outskirts of the camp, do as I do.

18 "When I and all who are with me blow the trumpet, then you also blow the trumpets all around the camp and say, 'For the LORD and for Gideon.' "

Confusion of the Enemy

19 ¶ So Gideon and the hundred men who were with him came to the outskirts of the camp at the beginning of the middle watch, when they had just posted the watch; and they blew the trumpets and smashed the pitchers that were in their hands.

20 When the three companies blew the trumpets and broke the pitchers, they held the torches in their left hands and the trumpets in their right hands for blowing, and cried, "A sword for the LORD and for Gideon!"

21 Each stood in his place around the camp; and all the *l*army ran, crying out as they fled.

*l*Or *camp*

New International

4But the LORD said to Gideon, "There are still too many men. Take them down to the water, and I will sift them for you there. If I say, 'This one shall go with you,' he shall go; but if I say, 'This one shall not go with you,' he shall not go."

5So Gideon took the men down to the water. There the LORD told him, "Separate those who lap the water with their tongues like a dog from those who kneel down to drink." 6Three hundred men lapped with their hands to their mouths. All the rest got down on their knees to drink.

7The LORD said to Gideon, "With the three hundred men that lapped I will save you and give the Midianites into your hands. Let all the other men go, each to his own place." 8So Gideon sent the rest of the Israelites to their tents but kept the three hundred, who took over the provisions and trumpets of the others.

Now the camp of Midian lay below him in the valley. 9During that night the LORD said to Gideon, "Get up, go down against the camp, because I am going to give it into your hands. 10If you are afraid to attack, go down to the camp with your servant Purah 11and listen to what they are saying. Afterward, you will be encouraged to attack the camp." So he and Purah his servant went down to the outposts of the camp. 12The Midianites, the Amalekites and all the other eastern peoples had settled in the valley, thick as locusts. Their camels could no more be counted than the sand on the seashore.

13Gideon arrived just as a man was telling a friend his dream. "I had a dream," he was saying. "A round loaf of barley bread came tumbling into the Midianite camp. It struck the tent with such force that the tent overturned and collapsed."

14His friend responded, "This can be nothing other than the sword of Gideon son of Joash, the Israelite. God has given the Midianites and the whole camp into his hands."

15When Gideon heard the dream and its interpretation, he worshiped God. He returned to the camp of Israel and called out, "Get up! The LORD has given the Midianite camp into your hands." 16Dividing the three hundred men into three companies, he placed trumpets and empty jars in the hands of all of them, with torches inside.

17"Watch me," he told them. "Follow my lead. When I get to the edge of the camp, do exactly as I do. 18When I and all who are with me blow our trumpets, then from all around the camp blow yours and shout, 'For the LORD and for Gideon.' "

19Gideon and the hundred men with him reached the edge of the camp at the beginning of the middle watch, just after they had changed the guard. They blew their trumpets and broke the jars that were in their hands. 20The three companies blew the trumpets and smashed the jars. Grasping the torches in their left hands and holding in their right hands the trumpets they were to blow, they shouted, "A sword for the LORD and for Gideon!" 21While each man held his position around the camp, all the Midianites ran, crying out as they fled.

King James

22And the three hundred blew the trumpets, and the LORD set every man's sword against his fellow, even throughout all the host: and the host fled to Beth-shittah [m]in Zererath, *and* to the [n]border of Abel-meholah, unto Tabbath.

23And the men of Israel gathered themselves together out of Naphtali, and out of Asher, and out of all Manasseh, and pursued after the Midianites.

24 ¶ And Gideon sent messengers throughout all mount Ephraim, saying, Come down against the Midianites, and take before them the waters unto Beth-barah and Jordan. Then all the men of Ephraim gathered themselves together, and took the waters unto Beth-barah and Jordan.

25And they took two princes of the Midianites, Oreb and Zeeb; and they slew Oreb upon the rock Oreb, and Zeeb they slew at the winepress of Zeeb, and pursued Midian, and brought the heads of Oreb and Zeeb to Gideon on the other side Jordan.

8 AND THE men of Ephraim said unto him, [o]Why hast thou served us thus, that thou calledst us not, when thou wentest to fight with the Midianites? And they did chide with him [p]sharply.

2And he said unto them, What have I done now in comparison of you? *Is* not the gleaning of the grapes of Ephraim better than the vintage of Abiezer?

3God hath delivered into your hands the princes of Midian, Oreb and Zeeb: and what was I able to do in comparison of you? Then their [q]anger was abated toward him, when he had said that.

4 ¶ And Gideon came to Jordan, *and* passed over, he, and the three hundred men that *were* with him, faint, yet pursuing *them.*

5And he said unto the men of Succoth, Give, I pray you, loaves of bread unto the people that follow me; for they *be* faint, and I am pursuing after Zebah and Zalmunna, kings of Midian.

6 ¶ And the princes of Succoth said, *Are* the hands of Zebah and Zalmunna now in thine hand, that we should give bread unto thine army?

7And Gideon said, Therefore when the LORD hath delivered Zebah and Zalmunna into mine hand, then I will [r]tear your flesh with the thorns of the wilderness and with briers.

8 ¶ And he went up thence to Penuel, and spake unto them likewise: and the men of Penuel answered him as the men of Succoth had answered *him.*

9And he spake also unto the men of Penuel, saying, When I come again in peace, I will break down this tower.

10 ¶ Now Zebah and Zalmunna *were* in Karkor, and their hosts with them, about fifteen thousand *men,* all that were left of all the hosts of the children of the east: for there fell an hundred and twenty thousand men that drew sword.

11 ¶ And Gideon went up by the way of them that dwelt in tents on the east of Nobah and Jogbehah, and smote the host: for the host was secure.

12And when Zebah and Zalmunna fled, he pursued after them, and took the two kings of Midian, Zebah and Zalmunna, and [s]discomfited all the host.

13 ¶ And Gideon the son of Joash returned from battle before the sun *was up,*

[m]Or, *toward* [n]Heb. *lip* [o]Heb. *What thing* is *this thou hast done unto us* [p]Heb. *strongly* [q]Heb. *spirit* [r]Heb. *thresh* [s]Heb. *terrified*

Amplified

22When [Gideon's men] blew the 300 trumpets, the Lord set every [Midianite's] sword against his comrade and against all the army, and the army fled as far as Beth-shittah toward Zererah, as far as the border of Abel-meholah by Tabbath.

23And the men of Israel were called together out of Naphtali and Asher and all Manasseh, and they pursued Midian.

24And Gideon sent messengers throughout all the hill country of Ephraim, saying, Come down against the Midianites and take all the intervening fords as far as Beth-barah and also the Jordan. So all the men of Ephraim were gathered together and took all the fords as far as Beth-barah and also the Jordan.

25And [the men of Ephraim] took the two princes of Midian, Oreb and Zeeb, and they slew Oreb at the rock of Oreb, and Zeeb they slew at the winepress of Zeeb, and pursued Midian; and they brought the heads of Oreb and Zeeb to Gideon beyond the Jordan.

8 AND THE men of Ephraim said to Gideon, Why have you treated us like this, not calling us when you went to fight with Midian? And they quarreled with him furiously.

2And he said to them, What have I done now in comparison with you? Is not the gleaning of the grapes of [your big tribe of] Ephraim better than the vintage of [my little clan of] Abiezer?

3 [h]God has given into your hands the princes of Midian, Oreb and Zeeb, and what was I able to do in comparison with you? Then their anger toward him was abated when he had said that.

4And Gideon came to the Jordan and passed over, he and the 300 men with him, faint yet pursuing.

5And he said to the men of Succoth, Give, I pray you, loaves of bread to the people who follow me, for they are faint, and I am pursuing Zebah and Zalmunna, kings of Midian.

6And the princes of Succoth said, Are Zebah and Zalmunna already in your hand, that we should give bread to your army?

7And Gideon said, For that, when the Lord has delivered Zebah and Zalmunna into my hand, I will thresh your flesh with the thorns and briers of the wilderness!

8And he went from there up to Penuel and made the same request, and the men of Penuel answered him as the men of Succoth had done.

9And [Gideon] said to the men of Penuel, When I come again in peace, I will break down this tower.

10Now Zebah and Zalmunna were in Karkor with their army—about 15,000 men, all who were left of all the army of the sons of the east, for there had fallen 120,000 men who drew the sword.

11And Gideon went up by the route of those who dwelt in tents east of Nobah and Jogbehah and smote their camp [unexpectedly], for the army thought itself secure.

12And Zebah and Zalmunna fled, and he pursued them and took the two kings of Midian, Zebah and Zalmunna, and terrified all the army.

13Then Gideon son of Joash returned from the battle by the ascent of Heres.

[h]"Gideon's good words were as victorious as his sword" (Bishop Joseph Hall, cited by Charles Ellicott, *A Bible Commentary*). "He might have said that he could place but little dependence upon his brethren when, through faintheartedness, 22,000 left him at one time (Judg. 7:3), but he passed this by and took a more excellent way" (Adam Clarke, *The Holy Bible with A Commentary*). "The improving of a victory is often more honorable and of greater consequence than the winning of it . . . Humility of deportment is the . . . surest method of ending strife" (Matthew Henry, *Commentary on the Holy Bible*).

New American Standard

²² When they blew 300 trumpets, the LORD set the sword of one against another even throughout the whole army; and the army fled as far as Beth-shittah toward Zererah, as far as the edge of Abel-meholah, by Tabbath.

²³ The men of Israel were summoned from Naphtali and Asher and all Manasseh, and they pursued Midian.

²⁴ ¶ Gideon sent messengers throughout all the hill country of Ephraim, saying, "Come down against Midian and take the waters before them, as far as Beth-barah and the Jordan." So all the men of Ephraim were summoned and they took the waters as far as Beth-barah and the Jordan.

²⁵ They captured the two leaders of Midian, Oreb and Zeeb, and they killed Oreb at the rock of Oreb, and they killed Zeeb at the wine press of Zeeb, while they pursued Midian; and they brought the heads of Oreb and Zeeb to Gideon from across the Jordan.

Zebah and Zalmunna Routed

8 THEN THE men of Ephraim said to him, "What is this thing you have done to us, not calling us when you went to fight against Midian?" And they contended with him vigorously.

² But he said to them, "What have I done now in comparison with you? Is not the gleaning *of the grapes* of Ephraim better than the vintage of Abiezer?

³ "God has given the leaders of Midian, Oreb and Zeeb into your hands; and what was I able to do in comparison with you?" Then their anger toward him subsided when he said that.

⁴ ¶ Then Gideon and the 300 men who were with him came to the Jordan *and* crossed over, weary yet pursuing.

⁵ He said to the men of Succoth, "Please give loaves of bread to the people who are following me, for they are weary, and I am pursuing Zebah and Zalmunna, the kings of Midian."

⁶ The leaders of Succoth said, "Are the hands of Zebah and Zalmunna already in your hands, that we should give bread to your army?"

⁷ Gideon said, "All right, when the LORD has given Zebah and Zalmunna into my hand, then I will thrash your bodies with the thorns of the wilderness and with briers."

⁸ He went up from there to Penuel and spoke similarly to them; and the men of Penuel answered him just as the men of Succoth had answered.

⁹ So he spoke also to the men of Penuel, saying, "When I return safely, I will tear down this tower."

¹⁰ ¶ Now Zebah and Zalmunna were in Karkor, and their armies with them, about 15,000 men, all who were left of the entire army of the sons of the east; for the fallen were 120,000 swordsmen.

¹¹ Gideon went up by the way of those who lived in tents on the east of Nobah and Jogbehah, and attacked the camp when the camp was unsuspecting.

¹² When Zebah and Zalmunna fled, he pursued them and captured the two kings of Midian, Zebah and Zalmunna, and routed the whole army.

¹³ ¶ Then Gideon the son of Joash returned from the battle by the ascent of Heres.

New International

²²When the three hundred trumpets sounded, the LORD caused the men throughout the camp to turn on each other with their swords. The army fled to Beth Shittah toward Zererah as far as the border of Abel Meholah near Tabbath. ²³Israelites from Naphtali, Asher and all Manasseh were called out, and they pursued the Midianites. ²⁴Gideon sent messengers throughout the hill country of Ephraim, saying, "Come down against the Midianites and seize the waters of the Jordan ahead of them as far as Beth Barah."

So all the men of Ephraim were called out and they took the waters of the Jordan as far as Beth Barah. ²⁵They also captured two of the Midianite leaders, Oreb and Zeeb. They killed Oreb at the rock of Oreb, and Zeeb at the winepress of Zeeb. They pursued the Midianites and brought the heads of Oreb and Zeeb to Gideon, who was by the Jordan.

Zebah and Zalmunna

8 NOW THE Ephraimites asked Gideon, "Why have you treated us like this? Why didn't you call us when you went to fight Midian?" And they criticized him sharply.

²But he answered them, "What have I accomplished compared to you? Aren't the gleanings of Ephraim's grapes better than the full grape harvest of Abiezer? ³God gave Oreb and Zeeb, the Midianite leaders, into your hands. What was I able to do compared to you?" At this, their resentment against him subsided.

⁴Gideon and his three hundred men, exhausted yet keeping up the pursuit, came to the Jordan and crossed it. ⁵He said to the men of Succoth, "Give my troops some bread; they are worn out, and I am still pursuing Zebah and Zalmunna, the kings of Midian."

⁶But the officials of Succoth said, "Do you already have the hands of Zebah and Zalmunna in your possession? Why should we give bread to your troops?"

⁷Then Gideon replied, "Just for that, when the LORD has given Zebah and Zalmunna into my hand, I will tear your flesh with desert thorns and briers."

⁸From there he went up to Penielⁱ and made the same request of them, but they answered as the men of Succoth had. ⁹So he said to the men of Peniel, "When I return in triumph, I will tear down this tower."

¹⁰Now Zebah and Zalmunna were in Karkor with a force of about fifteen thousand men, all that were left of the armies of the eastern peoples; a hundred and twenty thousand swordsmen had fallen. ¹¹Gideon went up by the route of the nomads east of Nobah and Jogbehah and fell upon the unsuspecting army. ¹²Zebah and Zalmunna, the two kings of Midian, fled, but he pursued them and captured them, routing their entire army.

¹³Gideon son of Joash then returned from the battle by

ⁱ8 Hebrew *Penuel,* a variant of *Peniel;* also in verses 9 and 17

King James

¹⁴And caught a young man of the men of Succoth, and inquired of him: and he *described unto him the princes of Succoth, and the elders thereof, *even* threescore and seventeen men.

¹⁵And he came unto the men of Succoth, and said, Behold Zebah and Zalmunna, with whom ye did upbraid me, saying, *Are* the hands of Zebah and Zalmunna now in thine hand, that we should give bread unto thy men *that are* weary?

¹⁶And he took the elders of the city, and thorns of the wilderness and briers, and with them he ^utaught the men of Succoth.

¹⁷And he beat down the tower of Penuel, and slew the men of the city.

¹⁸ ¶ Then said he unto Zebah and Zalmunna, What manner of men *were they* whom ye slew at Tabor? And they answered, As thou *art*, so *were* they; each one ^vresembled the children of a king.

¹⁹And he said, they *were* my brethren, *even* the sons of my mother: *as* the LORD liveth, if ye had saved them alive, I would not slay you.

²⁰And he said unto Jether his firstborn, Up, *and* slay them. But the youth drew not his sword: for he feared, because he *was* yet a youth.

²¹Then Zebah and Zalmunna said, Rise thou, and fall upon us: for as the man *is, so is* his strength. And Gideon arose, and slew Zebah and Zalmunna, and took away the ^wornaments *that were* on their camels' necks.

Gideon refuses the kingship

²² ¶ Then the men of Israel said unto Gideon, Rule thou over us, both thou, and thy son, and thy son's son also: for thou hast delivered us from the hand of Midian.

²³And Gideon said unto them, I will not rule over you, neither shall my son rule over you: the LORD shall rule over you.

²⁴ ¶ And Gideon said unto them, I would desire a request of you, that ye would give me every man the earrings of his prey. (For they had golden earrings, because they *were* Ishmaelites.)

²⁵And they answered, We will willingly give *them*. And they spread a garment, and did cast therein every man the earrings of his prey.

²⁶And the weight of the golden earrings that he requested was a thousand and seven hundred *shekels* of gold; beside ornaments, and ^xcollars, and purple raiment that *was* on the kings of Midian, and beside the chains that *were* about their camels' necks.

²⁷And Gideon made an ephod thereof, and put it in his city, *even* in Ophrah: and all Israel went thither a-whoring after it: which thing became a snare unto Gideon, and to his house.

²⁸ ¶ Thus was Midian subdued before the children of Israel, so that they lifted up their heads no more. And the country was in quietness forty years in the days of Gideon.

Gideon's death

²⁹ ¶ And Jerubbaal the son of Joash went and dwelt in his own house.

³⁰And Gideon had threescore and ten sons ^yof his body begotten: for he had many wives.

³¹And his concubine that *was* in Shechem, she also bare him a son, whose name he ^zcalled Abimelech.

³² ¶ And Gideon the son of Joash died in a good old age, and was buried in the sepulchre of Joash his father, in Ophrah of the Abi-ezrites.

³³And it came to pass, as soon as Gideon was dead, that the children of Israel turned again, and went a-whoring after Baalim, and made Baal-berith their god.

Amplified

¹⁴And he caught a young man of Succoth and inquired of him, and [the youth] wrote down for him [the names of] the officials of Succoth and its elders, seventy-seven men.

¹⁵And he came to the men of Succoth and said, Behold Zebah and Zalmunna, about whom you scoffed at me, saying, Are Zebah and Zalmunna now in your hand, that we should give bread to your men who are faint?

¹⁶And he took the elders of the city and thorns of the wilderness and briers, and with them he taught the men of Succoth [a lesson].

¹⁷And he broke down the tower of Penuel and slew the men of the city.

¹⁸Then [Gideon] said to Zebah and Zalmunna, What kind of men were they whom you slew at Tabor? And they replied, They were like you, each of them resembled the son of a king.

¹⁹And he said, They were my brothers, the sons of my mother. As the Lord lives, if you had saved them alive, I would not slay you.

²⁰And [Gideon] said to Jether his firstborn [to embarrass them], Up, and slay them. But the youth drew not his sword, for he feared because he was yet a lad.

²¹Then Zebah and Zalmunna said, Rise yourself and fall on us; for as the man is, so is his strength. And Gideon arose and slew Zebah and Zalmunna and took the [crescent-shaped] ornaments that were on their camels' necks.

²²Then the men of Israel said to Gideon, Rule over us—you and your son and your son's son also—for you have delivered us from the hand of Midian.

²³And Gideon said to them, I will not rule over you, and my son will not rule over you; the Lord will rule over you.

²⁴And Gideon said to them, Let me make a request of you—every man of you give me the earrings of his spoil. For [the Midianites] had gold earrings because they were Ishmaelites [general term for all descendants of Keturah].

²⁵And they answered, We will willingly give them. And they spread a garment, and every man cast on it the earrings of his spoil.

²⁶And the weight of the golden earrings that he requested was 1,700 shekels of gold, besides the crescents and pendants and the purple garments worn by the kings of Midian, and the chains that were about their camels' necks.

²⁷And Gideon made an ephod [a sacred, high priest's garment] of it, and put it in his city of Ophrah, and all Israel paid homage to it there, and ⁱit became a snare to Gideon and to his family.

²⁸Thus was Midian subdued before the Israelites so that they lifted up their heads no more. And the land had peace *and* rest for forty years in the days of Gideon.

²⁹Jerubbaal (Gideon) son of Joash went and dwelt in his own house.

³⁰Now Gideon had seventy sons born to him, for he had many wives.

³¹And his concubine, who was in Shechem, also bore him a son, whom he named Abimelech.

³²Gideon son of Joash died at a good old age and was buried in the tomb of Joash his father in Ophrah of the Abiezrites.

³³As soon as Gideon was dead, the Israelites turned again and played the harlot after the Baals and made Baal-berith their god.

ⁱThe gold and purple of the spoil enabled Gideon to make an ephod, presumably on the pattern of that described in Exod. 28. It was not exactly an idol but a kind of fetish, and it diverted the thoughts of the people from Shiloh and the spiritual worship of the unseen and eternal God. So apt is the human heart to cling to some outward emblem—it may be a crucifix, a wafer, or a church—and miss that worship in spirit and in truth which the Father seeks (John 4:23) (F. B. Meyer, *Devotional Commentary on Joshua—II Kings*).

---

^tHeb. *writ*   ^uHeb. *made to know*   ^vHeb. *according to the form*   ^wOr, *ornaments like the moon*   ^xOr, *sweet jewels*   ^yHeb. *going out of his thigh*   ^zHeb. *set*

New American Standard

14 And he captured a youth from Succoth and questioned him. Then *the youth* wrote down for him the princes of Succoth and its elders, seventy-seven men.

15 He came to the men of Succoth and said, "Behold Zebah and Zalmunna, concerning whom you taunted me, saying, 'Are the hands of Zebah and Zalmunna already in your hand, that we should give bread to your men who are weary?'"

16 He took the elders of the city, and thorns of the wilderness and briers, and he disciplined the men of Succoth with them.

17 He tore down the tower of Penuel and killed the men of the city.

18 ¶ Then he said to Zebah and Zalmunna, "What kind of men *were* they whom you killed at Tabor?" And they said, "They were like you, each one resembling the son of a king."

19 He said, "They *were* my brothers, the sons of my mother. *As* the LORD lives, if only you had let them live, I would not kill you."

20 So he said to Jether his firstborn, "Rise, kill them." But the youth did not draw his sword, for he was afraid, because he was still a youth.

21 Then Zebah and Zalmunna said, "Rise up yourself, and fall on us; for as the man, so is his strength." So Gideon arose and killed Zebah and Zalmunna, and took the crescent ornaments which were on their camels' necks.

22 ¶ Then the men of Israel said to Gideon, "Rule over us, both you and your son, also your son's son, for you have delivered us from the hand of Midian."

23 But Gideon said to them, "I will not rule over you, nor shall my son rule over you; the LORD shall rule over you."

24 Yet Gideon said to them, "I would request of you, that each of you give me an earring from his spoil." (For they had gold earrings, because they were Ishmaelites.)

25 They said, "We will surely give *them*." So they spread out a garment, and every one of them threw an earring there from his spoil.

26 The weight of the gold earrings that he requested was 1,700 *shekels* of gold, besides the crescent ornaments and the pendants and the purple robes which *were* on the kings of Midian, and besides the neck bands that *were* on their camels' necks.

27 Gideon made it into an ephod, and placed it in his city, Ophrah, and all Israel played the harlot with it there, so that it became a snare to Gideon and his household.

Forty Years of Peace

28 So Midian was subdued before the sons of Israel, and they did not lift up their heads anymore. And the land was undisturbed for forty years in the days of Gideon.

29 ¶ Then Jerubbaal the son of Joash went and lived in his own house.

30 Now Gideon had seventy sons who were his direct descendants, for he had many wives.

31 His concubine who was in Shechem also bore him a son, and he named him Abimelech.

32 And Gideon the son of Joash died at a ripe old age and was buried in the tomb of his father Joash, in Ophrah of the Abiezrites.

33 ¶ Then it came about, as soon as Gideon was dead, that the sons of Israel again played the harlot with the Baals, and made Baal-berith their god.

New International

the Pass of Heres. 14He caught a young man of Succoth and questioned him, and the young man wrote down for him the names of the seventy-seven officials of Succoth, the elders of the town. 15Then Gideon came and said to the men of Succoth, "Here are Zebah and Zalmunna, about whom you taunted me by saying, 'Do you already have the hands of Zebah and Zalmunna in your possession? Why should we give bread to your exhausted men?'" 16He took the elders of the town and taught the men of Succoth a lesson by punishing them with desert thorns and briers. 17He also pulled down the tower of Peniel and killed the men of the town.

18Then he asked Zebah and Zalmunna, "What kind of men did you kill at Tabor?"

"Men like you," they answered, "each one with the bearing of a prince."

19Gideon replied, "Those were my brothers, the sons of my own mother. As surely as the LORD lives, if you had spared their lives, I would not kill you." 20Turning to Jether, his oldest son, he said, "Kill them!" But Jether did not draw his sword, because he was only a boy and was afraid.

21Zebah and Zalmunna said, "Come, do it yourself. 'As is the man, so is his strength.'" So Gideon stepped forward and killed them, and took the ornaments off their camels' necks.

Gideon's Ephod

22The Israelites said to Gideon, "Rule over us—you, your son and your grandson—because you have saved us out of the hand of Midian."

23But Gideon told them, "I will not rule over you, nor will my son rule over you. The LORD will rule over you." 24And he said, "I do have one request, that each of you give me an earring from your share of the plunder." (It was the custom of the Ishmaelites to wear gold earrings.)

25They answered, "We'll be glad to give them." So they spread out a garment, and each man threw a ring from his plunder onto it. 26The weight of the gold rings he asked for came to seventeen hundred shekels,*j* not counting the ornaments, the pendants and the purple garments worn by the kings of Midian or the chains that were on their camels' necks. 27Gideon made the gold into an ephod, which he placed in Ophrah, his town. All Israel prostituted themselves by worshiping it there, and it became a snare to Gideon and his family.

Gideon's Death

28Thus Midian was subdued before the Israelites and did not raise its head again. During Gideon's lifetime, the land enjoyed peace forty years.

29Jerub-Baal son of Joash went back home to live. 30He had seventy sons of his own, for he had many wives. 31His concubine, who lived in Shechem, also bore him a son, whom he named Abimelech. 32Gideon son of Joash died at a good old age and was buried in the tomb of his father Joash in Ophrah of the Abiezrites.

33No sooner had Gideon died than the Israelites again prostituted themselves to the Baals. They set up Baal-

j 26 That is, about 43 pounds (about 19.5 kilograms)

King James

³⁴And the children of Israel remembered not the LORD their God, who had delivered them out of the hands of all their enemies on every side:

³⁵Neither showed they kindness to the house of Jerubbaal, *namely,* Gideon, according to all the goodness which he had shown unto Israel.

Abimelech

9 AND ABIMELECH the son of Jerubbaal went to Shechem unto his mother's brethren, and communed with them, and with all the family of the house of his mother's father, saying,

²Speak, I pray you, in the ears of all the men of Shechem, ^aWhether *is* better for you, either that all the sons of Jerubbaal, *which are* threescore and ten persons, reign over you, or that one reign over you? remember also that I *am* your bone and your flesh.

³And his mother's brethren spake of him in the ears of all the men of Shechem all these words: and their hearts inclined ^bto follow Abimelech; for they said, He *is* our brother.

⁴And they gave him threescore and ten *pieces* of silver out of the house of Baal-berith, wherewith Abimelech hired vain and light persons, which followed him.

⁵And he went unto his father's house at Ophrah, and slew his brethren the sons of Jerubbaal, *being* threescore and ten persons, upon one stone: notwithstanding yet Jotham the youngest son of Jerubbaal was left; for he hid himself.

⁶And all the men of Shechem gathered together, and all the house of Millo, and went, and made Abimelech king, ^cby the plain of the pillar that *was* in Shechem.

⁷¶ And when they told *it* to Jotham, he went and stood in the top of mount Gerizim, and lifted up his voice, and cried, and said unto them, Hearken unto me, ye men of Shechem, that God may hearken unto you.

⁸The trees went forth *on a time* to anoint a king over them; and they said unto the olive tree, Reign thou over us.

⁹But the olive tree said unto them, Should I leave my fatness, wherewith by me they honour God and man, and ^dgo to be promoted over the trees?

¹⁰And the trees said to the fig tree, Come thou, *and* reign over us.

¹¹But the fig tree said unto them, Should I forsake my sweetness, and my good fruit, and go to be promoted over the trees?

¹²Then said the trees unto the vine, Come thou, *and* reign over us.

¹³And the vine said unto them, Should I leave my wine, which cheereth God and man, and go to be promoted over the trees?

¹⁴Then said all the trees unto the ^ebramble, Come thou, *and* reign over us.

¹⁵And the bramble said unto the trees, If in truth ye anoint me king over you, *then* come *and* put your trust in my shadow: and if not, let fire come out of the bramble, and devour the cedars of Lebanon.

¹⁶Now therefore, if ye have done truly and sincerely, in that ye have made Abimelech king, and if ye have dealt well with Jerubbaal and his house, and have done unto him according to the deserving of his hands;

¹⁷(For my father fought for you, and ^fadventured his life far, and delivered you out of the hand of Midian:

¹⁸And ye are risen up against my father's house this day, and have slain his sons, threescore and ten persons, upon one stone, and have made Abimelech, the son of his maidservant, king over the men of Shechem, because he *is* your brother;)

Amplified

³⁴And the Israelites did not remember the Lord their God, Who had delivered them out of the hand of all their enemies on every side;

³⁵Neither did they show kindness to the family of Jerubbaal, that is, Gideon, in return for all the good which he had done for Israel.

9 NOW ABIMELECH son of Jerubbaal (Gideon) went to Shechem to his mother's kinsmen and said to them and to the whole clan of his mother's family,

²Say, I pray you, in the hearing of all the men of Shechem, Which is better for you: that all seventy of the sons of Jerubbaal reign over you, or that one man rule over you? Remember also that I am your bone and your flesh.

³And his mother's kinsmen spoke all these words concerning him in the hearing of all the men of Shechem, and their hearts inclined to follow Abimelech, for they said, He is our brother.

⁴And they gave him seventy pieces of silver out of the house of Baal-berith, with which Abimelech hired worthless and foolhardy men who followed him.

⁵And he went to his father's house at Ophrah and slew his brothers the sons of Jerubbaal, seventy men, on one stone. But Jotham, the youngest son of Jerubbaal, was left, for he hid himself.

⁶And all the men of Shechem gathered together and all of Beth-millo, and they went and made Abimelech king by the oak (terebinth) of the pillar at Shechem.

⁷When it was told to Jotham, he went and stood at the top of Mount Gerizim and shouted to them, Hear me, men of Shechem, that God may hear you.

⁸One time the trees went forth to anoint a king over them, and they said to the olive tree, Reign over us.

⁹But the olive tree said to them, Should I leave my fatness, by which God and man are honored, and go to wave over the trees?

¹⁰Then the trees said to the fig tree, You come and reign over us.

¹¹But the fig tree said to them, Should I leave my sweetness and my good fruit and go to wave over the trees?

¹²Then the trees said to the vine (grapevine), You come and reign over us.

¹³And the vine (grapevine) replied, Should I leave my new wine, which rejoices God and man, and go to wave over the trees?

¹⁴Then all the trees said to the bramble, You come and reign over us.

¹⁵And the bramble said to the trees, If in good faith you are anointing me king over you, then come and take refuge in my shade; but if not, let fire come out of the bramble and devour the cedars of Lebanon.

¹⁶Now therefore, if you acted sincerely and honorably when you made Abimelech king, and if you have dealt well with Jerubbaal and his house and have done to him as his deeds deserved—

¹⁷For my father fought for you, jeopardized his life, and rescued you from the hand of Midian;

¹⁸And you have risen up against my father's house this day and have slain his sons, seventy men, on one stone and have made Abimelech, son of his maidservant, king over the people of Shechem because he is your kinsman—

---

^aHeb. *What is good? whether*   ^bHeb. *after*   ^cOr, *by the oak of the pillar;* see Josh. 24:26   ^dHeb. *go up and down for* other trees   ^eOr, *thistle*   ^fHeb. *cast his life*

New American Standard

34 Thus the sons of Israel did not remember the LORD their God, who had delivered them from the hands of all their enemies on every side;

35 nor did they show kindness to the household of Jerubbaal (*that is*, Gideon) in accord with all the good that he had done to Israel.

Abimelech's Conspiracy

9 AND ABIMELECH the son of Jerubbaal went to Shechem to his mother's relatives, and spoke to them and to the whole clan of the household of his mother's father, saying,

2"Speak, now, in the hearing of all the leaders of Shechem, 'Which is better for you, that seventy men, all the sons of Jerubbaal, rule over you, or that one man rule over you?' Also, remember that I am your bone and your flesh."

3 And his mother's relatives spoke all these words on his behalf in the hearing of all the leaders of Shechem; and they were inclined to follow Abimelech, for they said, "He is our relative."

4 They gave him seventy *pieces* of silver from the house of Baal-berith with which Abimelech hired worthless and reckless fellows, and they followed him.

5 Then he went to his father's house at Ophrah and killed his brothers the sons of Jerubbaal, seventy men, on one stone. But Jotham the youngest son of Jerubbaal was left, for he hid himself.

6 All the men of Shechem and all *m*Beth-millo assembled together, and they went and made Abimelech king, by the oak of the pillar which was in Shechem.

7 ¶ Now when they told Jotham, he went and stood on the top of Mount Gerizim, and lifted his voice and called out. Thus he said to them, "Listen to me, O men of Shechem, that God may listen to you.

8"Once the trees went forth to anoint a king over them, and they said to the olive tree, 'Reign over us!'

9"But the olive tree said to them, 'Shall I leave my fatness with which God and men are honored, and go to wave over the trees?'

10"Then the trees said to the fig tree, 'You come, reign over us!'

11"But the fig tree said to them, 'Shall I leave my sweetness and my good fruit, and go to wave over the trees?'

12"Then the trees said to the vine, 'You come, reign over us!'

13"But the vine said to them, 'Shall I leave my new wine, which cheers God and men, and go to wave over the trees?'

14"Finally all the trees said to the bramble, 'You come, reign over us!'

15"The bramble said to the trees, 'If in truth you are anointing me as king over you, come and take refuge in my shade; but if not, may fire come out from the bramble and consume the cedars of Lebanon.'

16 ¶ "Now therefore, if you have dealt in truth and integrity in making Abimelech king, and if you have dealt well with Jerubbaal and his house, and have dealt with him as he deserved—

17 for my father fought for you and risked his life and delivered you from the hand of Midian;

18 but you have risen against my father's house today and have killed his sons, seventy men, on one stone, and have made Abimelech, the son of his maidservant, king over the men of Shechem, because he is your relative—

New International

Berith as their god and 34did not remember the LORD their God, who had rescued them from the hands of all their enemies on every side. 35They also failed to show kindness to the family of Jerub-Baal (that is, Gideon) for all the good things he had done for them.

Abimelech

9 ABIMELECH SON of Jerub-Baal went to his mother's brothers in Shechem and said to them and to all his mother's clan, 2"Ask all the citizens of Shechem, 'Which is better for you: to have all seventy of Jerub-Baal's sons rule over you, or just one man?' Remember, I am your flesh and blood."

3When the brothers repeated all this to the citizens of Shechem, they were inclined to follow Abimelech, for they said, "He is our brother." 4They gave him seventy shekels*k* of silver from the temple of Baal-Berith, and Abimelech used it to hire reckless adventurers, who became his followers. 5He went to his father's home in Ophrah and on one stone murdered his seventy brothers, the sons of Jerub-Baal. But Jotham, the youngest son of Jerub-Baal, escaped by hiding. 6Then all the citizens of Shechem and Beth Millo gathered beside the great tree at the pillar in Shechem to crown Abimelech king.

7When Jotham was told about this, he climbed up on the top of Mount Gerizim and shouted to them, "Listen to me, citizens of Shechem, so that God may listen to you. 8One day the trees went out to anoint a king for themselves. They said to the olive tree, 'Be our king.'

9"But the olive tree answered, 'Should I give up my oil, by which both gods and men are honored, to hold sway over the trees?'

10"Next, the trees said to the fig tree, 'Come and be our king.'

11"But the fig tree replied, 'Should I give up my fruit, so good and sweet, to hold sway over the trees?'

12"Then the trees said to the vine, 'Come and be our king.'

13"But the vine answered, 'Should I give up my wine, which cheers both gods and men, to hold sway over the trees?'

14"Finally all the trees said to the thornbush, 'Come and be our king.'

15"The thornbush said to the trees, 'If you really want to anoint me king over you, come and take refuge in my shade; but if not, then let fire come out of the thornbush and consume the cedars of Lebanon!'

16"Now if you have acted honorably and in good faith when you made Abimelech king, and if you have been fair to Jerub-Baal and his family, and if you have treated him as he deserves— 17and to think that my father fought for you, risked his life to rescue you from the hand of Midian 18(but today you have revolted against my father's family, murdered his seventy sons on a single stone, and made Abimelech, the son of his slave girl, king over the citizens

---

m Or *the house of Millo*   *k 4* That is, about 1 3/4 pounds (about 0.8 kilogram)

King James

¹⁹If ye then have dealt truly and sincerely with Jerubbaal and with his house this day, *then* rejoice ye in Abimelech, and let him also rejoice in you:

²⁰But if not, let fire come out from Abimelech, and devour the men of Shechem, and the house of Millo; and let fire come out from the men of Shechem, and from the house of Millo, and devour Abimelech.

²¹And Jotham ran away, and fled, and went to Beer, and dwelt there, for fear of Abimelech his brother.

²² ¶ When Abimelech had reigned three years over Israel,

²³Then God sent an evil spirit between Abimelech and the men of Shechem; and the men of Shechem dealt treacherously with Abimelech:

²⁴That the cruelty *done* to the threescore and ten sons of Jerubbaal might come, and their blood be laid upon Abimelech their brother, which slew them; and upon the men of Shechem, which *g*aided him in the killing of his brethren.

²⁵And the men of Shechem set liers in wait for him in the top of the mountains, and they robbed all that came along that way by them: and it was told Abimelech.

²⁶And Gaal the son of Ebed came with his brethren, and went over to Shechem: and the men of Shechem put their confidence in him.

²⁷And they went out into the fields, and gathered their vineyards, and trode *the grapes,* and made merry, and went into the house of their god, and did eat and drink, and cursed Abimelech.

²⁸And Gaal the son of Ebed said, Who *is* Abimelech, and who *is* Shechem, that we should serve him? *is* not *he* the son of Jerubbaal? and Zebul his officer? serve the men of Hamor the father of Shechem: for why should we serve him?

²⁹And would to God this people were under my hand! then would I remove Abimelech. And he said to Abimelech, Increase thine army, and come out.

³⁰ ¶ And when Zebul the ruler of the city heard the words of Gaal the son of Ebed, his anger was *h*kindled.

³¹And he sent messengers unto Abimelech *i*privily, saying, Behold, Gaal the son of Ebed and his brethren be come to Shechem; and, behold, they fortify the city against thee.

³²Now therefore up by night, thou and the people that *is* with thee, and lie in wait in the field:

³³And it shall be, *that* in the morning, as soon as the sun is up, thou shalt rise early, and set upon the city: and, behold, *when* he and the people that *is* with him come out against thee, then mayest thou do to them *j*as thou shalt find occasion.

³⁴ ¶ And Abimelech rose up, and all the people that *were* with him, by night, and they laid wait against Shechem in four companies.

³⁵And Gaal the son of Ebed went out, and stood in the entering of the gate of the city: and Abimelech rose up, and the people that *were* with him, from lying in wait.

³⁶And when Gaal saw the people, he said to Zebul, Behold, there come people down from the top of the mountains. And Zebul said unto him, Thou seest the shadow of the mountains as *if they were* men.

³⁷And Gaal spake again and said, See there come people down by the *k*middle of the land, and another company come along by the plain of Meonenim.

³⁸Then said Zebul unto him, Where *is* now thy mouth, wherewith thou saidst, Who *is* Abimelech, that we should serve him? *is* not this the people that thou hast despised? go out, I pray now, and fight with them.

³⁹And Gaal went out before the men of Shechem, and fought with Abimelech.

⁴⁰And Abimelech chased him, and he fled before him, and many were overthrown *and* wounded, *even* unto the entering of the gate.

Amplified

¹⁹If you then have acted sincerely and honorably with Jerubbaal and his house this day, then rejoice in Abimelech, and let him also rejoice in you;

²⁰But if not, let fire come out from Abimelech and devour the people of Shechem and Beth-millo, and let fire come out from the people of Shechem and Beth-millo and devour Abimelech.

²¹And Jotham ran away and fled, and went to Beer and dwelt there for fear of Abimelech his brother.

²²Abimelech reigned three years over Israel.

²³And God sent an evil spirit between Abimelech and the men of Shechem, and the men of Shechem dealt treacherously with Abimelech,

²⁴That the violence done to the seventy sons of Jerubbaal might come, and that their blood might be laid upon Abimelech their brother, who slew them, and upon the men of Shechem, who strengthened his hands to slay his brothers.

²⁵And the men of Shechem set men in ambush against [Abimelech] on the mountaintops, and they robbed all who passed by them along that way; and it was told to Abimelech.

²⁶And Gaal son of Ebed came with his kinsmen and moved into Shechem, and the men of Shechem put confidence in him.

²⁷And they went out into the field, gathered their vineyard fruits and trod them, and held a festival; and going into the house of their god, they ate and drank and cursed Abimelech.

²⁸Gaal son of Ebed said, Who is Abimelech, and who are we of Shechem, that we should serve him? Were not the son of Jerubbaal and Zebul, his officer, servants of the men of Hamor the father *and* founder of Shechem? Then why should we serve him?

²⁹Would that this people were under my hand! Then would I remove Abimelech and say to him, Increase your army and come out.

³⁰When Zebul the city's mayor heard the words of Gaal son of Ebed, his anger was kindled.

³¹And he sent messengers to Abimelech slyly, saying, Behold, Gaal son of Ebed and his kinsmen have come to Shechem; and behold, they stir up the city to rise against you.

³²Now therefore, rise up by night, you and the men with you, and lie in wait in the field.

³³Then in the morning, as soon as the sun is up, rise early and set upon the city; and when Gaal and the men with him come out against you, do to them as opportunity permits.

³⁴And Abimelech rose up by night, and all the men with him, and they laid in wait against Shechem in four companies.

³⁵And Gaal son of Ebed came out and stood in the entrance of the city's gate. Then Abimelech and the men with him rose up from ambush.

³⁶When Gaal saw the men, he said to Zebul, Look, men are coming down from the mountaintops! Zebul said to him, The shadow of the mountains looks to you like men.

³⁷And Gaal spoke again and said, See, men are coming down from the center of the land, and one company is coming from the direction of the oak of Meonenim [the sorcerers].

³⁸Then said Zebul to Gaal, Where is your [big] mouth now, you who said, Who is Abimelech, that we should serve him? Are not these the men whom you have despised? Go out now and fight with them.

³⁹And Gaal went out ahead of the men of Shechem and fought with Abimelech.

⁴⁰And Abimelech chased him, and he fled before him; and many fell wounded—even to the entrance of the gate.

---

g Heb. *strengthened his hands to kill*   *h* Or, *hot*   *i* Heb.
craftily, or, *to Tormah*   *j* Heb. *as thine hand shall find*
k Heb. *navel*

New American Standard

19 if then you have dealt in truth and integrity with Jerubbaal and his house this day, rejoice in Abimelech, and let him also rejoice in you.

20 "But if not, let fire come out from Abimelech and consume the men of Shechem and Beth-millo; and let fire come out from the men of Shechem and from Beth-millo, and consume Abimelech."

21 Then Jotham escaped and fled, and went to Beer and remained there because of Abimelech his brother.

Shechem and Abimelech Fall

22 ¶ Now Abimelech ruled over Israel three years.

23 Then God sent an evil spirit between Abimelech and the men of Shechem; and the men of Shechem dealt treacherously with Abimelech,

24 so that the violence done to the seventy sons of Jerubbaal might come, and their blood might be laid on Abimelech their brother, who killed them, and on the men of Shechem, who strengthened his hands to kill his brothers.

25 The men of Shechem set men in ambush against him on the tops of the mountains, and they robbed all who might pass by them along the road; and it was told to Abimelech.

26 ¶ Now Gaal the son of Ebed came with his relatives, and crossed over into Shechem; and the men of Shechem put their trust in him.

27 They went out into the field and gathered *the grapes of* their vineyards and trod *them*, and held a festival; and they went into the house of their god, and ate and drank and cursed Abimelech.

28 Then Gaal the son of Ebed said, "Who is Abimelech, and who is Shechem, that we should serve him? Is he not the son of Jerubbaal, and *is* Zebul *not* his lieutenant? Serve the men of Hamor the father of Shechem; but why should we serve him?

29 "Would, therefore, that this people were under my authority! Then I would remove Abimelech." And he said to Abimelech, "Increase your army and come out."

30 ¶ When Zebul the ruler of the city heard the words of Gaal the son of Ebed, his anger burned.

31 He sent messengers to Abimelech deceitfully, saying, "Behold, Gaal the son of Ebed and his relatives have come to Shechem; and behold, they are stirring up the city against you.

32 "Now therefore, arise by night, you and the people who are with you, and lie in wait in the field.

33 "In the morning, as soon as the sun is up, you shall rise early and rush upon the city; and behold, when he and the people who are with him come out against you, you shall do to them whatever you can."

34 ¶ So Abimelech and all the people who *were* with him arose by night and lay in wait against Shechem in four companies.

35 Now Gaal the son of Ebed went out and stood in the entrance of the city gate; and Abimelech and the people who *were* with him arose from the ambush.

36 When Gaal saw the people, he said to Zebul, "Look, people are coming down from the tops of the mountains." But Zebul said to him, "You are seeing the shadow of the mountains as *if they were* men."

37 Gaal spoke again and said, "Behold, people are coming down from the highest part of the land, and one company comes by the way of the diviners' oak."

38 Then Zebul said to him, "Where is your boasting now with which you said, 'Who is Abimelech that we should serve him?' Is this not the people whom you despised? Go out now and fight with them!"

39 So Gaal went out before the leaders of Shechem and fought with Abimelech.

40 Abimelech chased him, and he fled before him; and many fell wounded up to the entrance of the gate.

New International

of Shechem because he is your brother)— 19 if then you have acted honorably and in good faith toward Jerub-Baal and his family today, may Abimelech be your joy, and may you be his, too! 20 But if you have not, let fire come out from Abimelech and consume you, citizens of Shechem and Beth Millo, and let fire come out from you, citizens of Shechem and Beth Millo, and consume Abimelech!"

21 Then Jotham fled, escaping to Beer, and he lived there because he was afraid of his brother Abimelech.

22 After Abimelech had governed Israel three years, 23 God sent an evil spirit between Abimelech and the citizens of Shechem, who acted treacherously against Abimelech. 24 God did this in order that the crime against Jerub-Baal's seventy sons, the shedding of their blood, might be avenged on their brother Abimelech and on the citizens of Shechem, who had helped him murder his brothers. 25 In opposition to him these citizens of Shechem set men on the hilltops to ambush and rob everyone who passed by, and this was reported to Abimelech.

26 Now Gaal son of Ebed moved with his brothers into Shechem, and its citizens put their confidence in him. 27 After they had gone out into the fields and gathered the grapes and trodden them, they held a festival in the temple of their god. While they were eating and drinking, they cursed Abimelech. 28 Then Gaal son of Ebed said, "Who is Abimelech, and who is Shechem, that we should be subject to him? Isn't he Jerub-Baal's son, and isn't Zebul his deputy? Serve the men of Hamor, Shechem's father! Why should we serve Abimelech? 29 If only this people were under my command! Then I would get rid of him. I would say to Abimelech, 'Call out your whole army!' "[l]

30 When Zebul the governor of the city heard what Gaal son of Ebed said, he was very angry. 31 Under cover he sent messengers to Abimelech, saying, "Gaal son of Ebed and his brothers have come to Shechem and are stirring up the city against you. 32 Now then, during the night you and your men should come and lie in wait in the fields. 33 In the morning at sunrise, advance against the city. When Gaal and his men come out against you, do whatever your hand finds to do."

34 So Abimelech and all his troops set out by night and took up concealed positions near Shechem in four companies. 35 Now Gaal son of Ebed had gone out and was standing at the entrance to the city gate just as Abimelech and his soldiers came out from their hiding place.

36 When Gaal saw them, he said to Zebul, "Look, people are coming down from the tops of the mountains!"

Zebul replied, "You mistake the shadows of the mountains for men."

37 But Gaal spoke up again: "Look, people are coming down from the center of the land, and a company is coming from the direction of the soothsayers' tree."

38 Then Zebul said to him, "Where is your big talk now, you who said, 'Who is Abimelech that we should be subject to him?' Aren't these the men you ridiculed? Go out and fight them!"

39 So Gaal led out[m] the citizens of Shechem and fought Abimelech. 40 Abimelech chased him, and many fell wounded in the flight—all the way to the entrance to the

---

King James

⁴¹And Abimelech dwelt at Arumah: and Zebul thrust out Gaal and his brethren, that they should not dwell in Shechem.

⁴²And it came to pass on the morrow, that the people went out into the field; and they told Abimelech.

⁴³And he took the people, and divided them into three companies, and laid wait in the field, and looked, and, behold, the people *were* come forth out of the city; and he rose up against them, and smote them.

⁴⁴And Abimelech, and the company that *was* with him, rushed forward, and stood in the entering of the gate of the city: and the two *other* companies ran upon all *the people* that *were* in the fields, and slew them.

⁴⁵And Abimelech fought against the city all that day; and he took the city, and slew the people that *was* therein, and beat down the city, and sowed it with salt.

⁴⁶ ¶ And when all the men of the tower of Shechem heard *that,* they entered into an hold of the house of the god Berith.

⁴⁷And it was told Abimelech, that all the men of the tower of Shechem were gathered together.

⁴⁸And Abimelech gat him up to mount Zalmon, he and all the people that *were* with him; and Abimelech took an axe in his hand, and cut down a bough from the trees, and took it, and laid *it* on his shoulder, and said unto the people that *were* with him, What ye have seen ¹me do, make haste, *and* do as I *have done.*

⁴⁹And all the people likewise cut down every man his bough, and followed Abimelech, and put *them* to the hold, and set the hold on fire upon them; so that all the men of the tower of Shechem died also, about a thousand men and women.

⁵⁰ ¶ Then went Abimelech to Thebez, and encamped against Thebez, and took it.

⁵¹But there was a strong tower within the city, and thither fled all the men and women, and all they of the city, and shut *it* to them, and gat them up to the top of the tower.

⁵²And Abimelech came unto the tower, and fought against it, and went hard unto the door of the tower to burn it with fire.

⁵³And a certain woman cast a piece of a millstone upon Abimelech's head, and all to brake his skull.

⁵⁴Then he called hastily unto the young man his armourbearer, and said unto him, Draw thy sword, and slay me, that men say not of me, A woman slew him. And his young man thrust him through, and he died.

⁵⁵And when the men of Israel saw that Abimelech was dead, they departed every man unto his place.

⁵⁶ ¶ Thus God rendered the wickedness of Abimelech, which he did unto his father, in slaying his seventy brethren:

⁵⁷And all the evil of the men of Shechem did God render upon their heads: and upon them came the curse of Jotham the son of Jerubbaal.

Amplified

⁴¹And Abimelech lodged at Arumah, and Zebul thrust out Gaal and his kinsmen so that they could not live in Shechem.

⁴²The next day the men went out into the fields, and Abimelech was told.

⁴³He took his men and divided them into three companies and laid in wait in the field; and he looked and behold, the people were coming out of the city. And he rose up against them and smote them.

⁴⁴And Abimelech and the company with him rushed forward and stood in the entrance of the city's gate, while the two other companies rushed upon all who were in the field and slew them.

⁴⁵And Abimelech fought against the city all that day. He took the city and slew the people who were in it. He demolished the city and ʲsowed it with salt.

⁴⁶And when all the men of the Tower of Shechem heard of it, they entered the stronghold of the house of El-berith [the god of Berith].

⁴⁷Abimelech was told that all the people of the Tower of Shechem were gathered together.

⁴⁸And Abimelech went up to Mount Zalmon, he and all the men with him; and Abimelech took an ax in his hand and cut down a bundle of brush, picked it up, and laid it on his shoulder. And he said to the men with him, What you have seen me do, make haste to do also.

⁴⁹So each of the men cut down his bundle and following Abimelech put it against the stronghold and set [the stronghold] on fire over the people in it, so that all the people of the Tower of Shechem also died, about 1,000 men and women.

⁵⁰Then Abimelech went to Thebez and encamped against Thebez and took it.

⁵¹But there was a strong tower in the city, and all the people of the city—men and women—fled to it, shut themselves in, and went to the roof of the tower.

⁵²And Abimelech came to the tower and fought against it and drew near the door of the tower to burn it with fire.

⁵³But a certain woman cast an upper millstone [down] upon Abimelech's head and broke his skull.

⁵⁴Then he called hastily to the young man, his armorbearer, and said to him, Draw your sword and slay me, so that men may not say of me, A woman slew him. And his young man thrust him through, and he died.

⁵⁵And when the men of Israel saw that Abimelech was dead, they departed each man to his home.

⁵⁶Thus God repaid the wickedness of Abimelech which he had done to his father [Gideon] by slaying his seventy brothers;

⁵⁷And all the wickedness of the men of Shechem God repaid upon their heads and caused to come upon them the curse of Jotham son of Jerubbaal. [Judg. 9:19, 20.]

ʲThis strewing of salt over Shechem was not intended (even if Abimelech had been able to supply enough salt) actually to make the ground unfruitful; but it was a symbol of perpetual desolation, and a sign that Shechem never would be rebuilt. However, such a forecast of a city's fate made by a true prophet of God, or by the Lord Himself, was one thing. This forecast, symbolized by the wicked usurper Abimelech, was quite another thing. For Shechem was later rebuilt (I Kings 12:25), and so was denounced Jericho (I Kings 16:34; see also Josh. 6). But this is not true of Samaria (Mic. 1:6), or Nineveh (Nah. 1:9-12), or Ashkelon (Zeph. 2:4), or the cities of Edom (Ezek. 35:9), or Tyre (Ezek. 26:3, 14), or Chorazin, or Bethsaida, or Capernaum (Matt. 11:20, 21, 23). That these cities, as such, would never be rebuilt permanently was foretold on the authority and by order of God Himself. "Sky and earth will pass away, but My words will not pass away" (Matt. 24:35).

¹Heb. *I have done*

New American Standard

41 Then Abimelech remained at Arumah, but Zebul drove out Gaal and his relatives so that they could not remain in Shechem.

42 ¶ Now it came about the next day, that the people went out to the field, and it was told to Abimelech.

43 So he took his people and divided them into three companies, and lay in wait in the field; when he looked and saw the people coming out from the city, he arose against them and slew them.

44 Then Abimelech and the company who was with him dashed forward and stood in the entrance of the city gate; the other two companies then dashed against all who *were* in the field and slew them.

45 Abimelech fought against the city all that day, and he captured the city and killed the people who *were* in it; then he razed the city and sowed it with salt.

46 ¶ When all the leaders of the tower of Shechem heard of *it,* they entered the inner chamber of the temple of El-berith.

47 It was told Abimelech that all the leaders of the tower of Shechem were gathered together.

48 So Abimelech went up to Mount Zalmon, he and all the people who *were* with him; and Abimelech took an axe in his hand and cut down a branch from the trees, lifted it and laid *it* on his shoulder. Then he said to the people who *were* with him, "What you have seen me do, hurry *and* do likewise."

49 All the people also cut down each one his branch and followed Abimelech, and put *them* on the inner chamber and set the inner chamber on fire over those *inside,* so that all the men of the tower of Shechem also died, about a thousand men and women.

50 ¶ Then Abimelech went to Thebez, and he camped against Thebez and captured it.

51 But there was a strong tower in the center of the city, and all the men and women with all the leaders of the city fled there and shut themselves in; and they went up on the roof of the tower.

52 So Abimelech came to the tower and fought against it, and approached the entrance of the tower to burn it with fire.

53 But a certain woman threw an upper millstone on Abimelech's head, crushing his skull.

54 Then he called quickly to the young man, his armor bearer, and said to him, "Draw your sword and kill me, so that it will not be said of me, 'A woman slew him.' " So the young man pierced him through, and he died.

55 When the men of Israel saw that Abimelech was dead, each departed to his home.

56 Thus God repaid the wickedness of Abimelech, which he had done to his father in killing his seventy brothers.

57 Also God returned all the wickedness of the men of Shechem on their heads, and the curse of Jotham the son of Jerubbaal came upon them.

New International

gate. 41Abimelech stayed in Arumah, and Zebul drove Gaal and his brothers out of Shechem.

42The next day the people of Shechem went out to the fields, and this was reported to Abimelech. 43So he took his men, divided them into three companies and set an ambush in the fields. When he saw the people coming out of the city, he rose to attack them. 44Abimelech and the companies with him rushed forward to a position at the entrance to the city gate. Then two companies rushed upon those in the fields and struck them down. 45All that day Abimelech pressed his attack against the city until he had captured it and killed its people. Then he destroyed the city and scattered salt over it.

46On hearing this, the citizens in the tower of Shechem went into the stronghold of the temple of El-Berith. 47When Abimelech heard that they had assembled there, 48he and all his men went up Mount Zalmon. He took an ax and cut off some branches, which he lifted to his shoulders. He ordered the men with him, "Quick! Do what you have seen me do!" 49So all the men cut branches and followed Abimelech. They piled them against the stronghold and set it on fire over the people inside. So all the people in the tower of Shechem, about a thousand men and women, also died.

50Next Abimelech went to Thebez and besieged it and captured it. 51Inside the city, however, was a strong tower, to which all the men and women—all the people of the city—fled. They locked themselves in and climbed up on the tower roof. 52Abimelech went to the tower and stormed it. But as he approached the entrance to the tower to set it on fire, 53a woman dropped an upper millstone on his head and cracked his skull.

54Hurriedly he called to his armor-bearer, "Draw your sword and kill me, so that they can't say, 'A woman killed him.' " So his servant ran him through, and he died. 55When the Israelites saw that Abimelech was dead, they went home.

56Thus God repaid the wickedness that Abimelech had done to his father by murdering his seventy brothers. 57God also made the men of Shechem pay for all their wickedness. The curse of Jotham son of Jerub-Baal came on them.

King James

Amplified

Israel cries for deliverance

10 AND AFTER Abimelech there arose to [m][n]defend Israel Tola the son of Puah, the son of Dodo, a man of Issachar; and he dwelt in Shamir in mount Ephraim.

2 And he judged Israel twenty and three years, and died, and was buried in Shamir.

3 ¶ And after him arose Jair, a Gileadite, and judged Israel twenty and two years.

4 And he had thirty sons that rode on thirty ass colts, and they had thirty cities, which are called [o]Havoth-jair unto this day, which *are* in the land of Gilead.

5 And Jair died, and was buried in Camon.

6 ¶ And the children of Israel did evil again in the sight of the LORD, and served Baalim, and Ashtaroth, and the gods of Syria, and the gods of Zidon, and the gods of Moab, and the gods of the children of Ammon, and the gods of the Philistines, and forsook the LORD, and served not him.

7 And the anger of the LORD was hot against Israel, and he sold them into the hands of the Philistines, and into the hands of the children of Ammon.

8 And that year they vexed and [p]oppressed the children of Israel: eighteen years, all the children of Israel that *were* on the other side Jordan in the land of the Amorites, which *is* in Gilead.

9 Moreover the children of Ammon passed over Jordan to fight also against Judah, and against Benjamin, and against the house of Ephraim; so that Israel was sore distressed.

10 ¶ And the children of Israel cried unto the LORD, saying, We have sinned against thee, both because we have forsaken our God, and also served Baalim.

11 And the LORD said unto the children of Israel, *Did* not *I deliver you* from the Egyptians, and from the Amorites, from the children of Ammon, and from the Philistines?

12 The Zidonians also, and the Amalekites, and the Maonites, did oppress you; and ye cried to me, and I delivered you out of their hand.

13 Yet ye have forsaken me, and served other gods: wherefore I will deliver you no more.

14 Go and cry unto the gods which ye have chosen; let them deliver you in the time of your tribulation.

15 ¶ And the children of Israel said unto the LORD, We have sinned: do thou unto us whatsoever [q]seemeth good unto thee; deliver us only, we pray thee, this day.

16 And they put away the [r]strange gods from among them, and served the LORD: and his soul [s]was grieved for the misery of Israel.

17 Then the children of Ammon were [t]gathered together, and encamped in Gilead. And the children of Israel assembled themselves together, and encamped in Mizpeh.

18 And the people *and* princes of Gilead said one to another, What man *is he* that will begin to fight against the children of Ammon? he shall be head over all the inhabitants of Gilead.

10 AFTER ABIMELECH there arose to rescue Israel, Tola son of Puah, the son of Dodo, a man of Issachar; and he lived at Shamir in the hill country of Ephraim.

2 He judged Israel twenty-three years; then he died and was buried in Shamir.

3 After him arose Jair the Gileadite, and he judged Israel twenty-two years.

4 And he had thirty sons who rode on thirty donkey colts, and they had thirty towns called Havvoth-jair [towns of Jair] which to this day are in the land of Gilead.

5 And Jair died and was buried in Kamon.

6 And the Israelites again did what was evil in the sight of the Lord, served the Baals, the Ashtaroth [female deities], the gods of Syria, the gods of Sidon, the gods of Moab, the gods of the Ammonites, and the gods of the Philistines. They forsook the Lord and did not serve Him.

7 And the anger of the Lord was kindled against Israel, and He sold them into the hands of the Philistines and the Ammonites,

8 And they oppressed and crushed *and* broke the Israelites that year. For eighteen years they oppressed all the Israelites beyond the Jordan in the land of the Amorites, which is in Gilead.

9 And the Ammonites passed over the Jordan to fight against Judah, Benjamin, and the house of Ephraim, so that Israel was sorely distressed.

10 And the Israelites cried to the Lord, saying, We have sinned against You, because we have forsaken our God and have served the Baals.

11 And the Lord said to the Israelites, Did I not deliver you from the Egyptians, the Amorites, the Ammonites, and the Philistines?

12 Also when the Sidonians, the Amalekites, and the Maonites oppressed *and* crushed you, you cried to Me, and I delivered you out of their hands.

13 Yet you have forsaken Me and served other gods; therefore I will deliver you no more.

14 Go, cry to the gods you have chosen; let them deliver you in your time of distress.

15 And the Israelites said to the Lord, We have sinned, do to us whatever seems good to You; only deliver us, we pray You, this day.

16 So they put away the foreign gods from among them and served the Lord, and His heart became impatient over the misery of Israel.

17 Then the Ammonites were gathered together and they encamped in Gilead. And the Israelites assembled and encamped at Mizpah.

18 And the leaders of Gilead [the Israelites] said one to another, Who is the man who will begin to fight against the Ammonites? He shall be head over all the inhabitants of Gilead.

Jephthah

11 NOW JEPHTHAH the Gileadite was a mighty man of valour, and he *was* the son of [u]an harlot: and Gilead begat Jephthah.

2 And Gilead's wife bare him sons; and his wife's sons grew up, and they thrust out Jephthah, and said unto him, Thou shalt not inherit in our father's house; for thou *art* the son of a strange woman.

3 Then Jephthah fled [v]from his brethren, and dwelt in the land of Tob: and there were gathered vain men to Jephthah, and went out with him.

11 NOW JEPHTHAH the Gileadite was a mighty warrior, but he was the son of a harlot. Gilead was Jephthah's father.

2 And Gilead's wife also bore him sons, and when his wife's sons grew up, they thrust Jephthah out and said to him, You shall not have an inheritance in our father's house, for you are the son of another woman.

3 Then Jephthah fled from his brothers and dwelt in the land of Tob; and worthless men gathered around Jephthah and went on raids with him.

---

[m]Or, *deliver*   [n]Heb. *save*   [o]Or, *The villages of Jair*
[p]Heb. *crushed*   [q]Heb. *is good in thine eyes*   [r]Heb. *gods of strangers*   [s]Heb. *was shortened*   [t]Heb. *cried together*
[u]Heb. *a woman an harlot*   [v]Heb. *from the face*

New American Standard

Oppression of Philistines and Ammonites

10 NOW AFTER Abimelech died, Tola the son of Puah, the son of Dodo, a man of Issachar, arose to save Israel; and he lived in Shamir in the hill country of Ephraim.

2 He judged Israel twenty-three years. Then he died and was buried in Shamir.

3 ¶ After him, Jair the Gileadite arose and judged Israel twenty-two years.

4 He had thirty sons who rode on thirty donkeys, and they had thirty cities in the land of Gilead that are called Havvoth-jair to this day.

5 And Jair died and was buried in Kamon.

6 ¶ Then the sons of Israel again did evil in the sight of the LORD, served the Baals and the Ashtaroth, the gods of Aram, the gods of Sidon, the gods of Moab, the gods of the sons of Ammon, and the gods of the Philistines; thus they forsook the LORD and did not serve Him.

7 The anger of the LORD burned against Israel, and He sold them into the hands of the Philistines and into the hands of the sons of Ammon.

8 They afflicted and crushed the sons of Israel that year; for eighteen years they *afflicted* all the sons of Israel who were beyond the Jordan in Gilead in the land of the Amorites.

9 The sons of Ammon crossed the Jordan to fight also against Judah, Benjamin, and the house of Ephraim, so that Israel was greatly distressed.

10 ¶ Then the sons of Israel cried out to the LORD, saying, "We have sinned against You, for indeed, we have forsaken our God and served the Baals."

11 The LORD said to the sons of Israel, "*Did I* not *deliver you* from the Egyptians, the Amorites, the sons of Ammon, and the Philistines?

12 "Also when the Sidonians, the Amalekites and the Maonites oppressed you, you cried out to Me, and I delivered you from their hands.

13 "Yet you have forsaken Me and served other gods; therefore I will no longer deliver you.

14 "Go and cry out to the gods which you have chosen; let them deliver you in the time of your distress."

15 The sons of Israel said to the LORD, "We have sinned, do to us whatever seems good to You; only please deliver us this day."

16 So they put away the foreign gods from among them and served the LORD; and He could bear the misery of Israel no longer.

17 ¶ Then the sons of Ammon were summoned and they camped in Gilead. And the sons of Israel gathered together and camped in Mizpah.

18 The people, the leaders of Gilead, said to one another, "Who is the man who will begin to fight against the sons of Ammon? He shall become head over all the inhabitants of Gilead."

Jephthah the Ninth Judge

11 NOW JEPHTHAH the Gileadite was a valiant warrior, but he was the son of a harlot. And Gilead was the father of Jephthah.

2 Gilead's wife bore him sons; and when his wife's sons grew up, they drove Jephthah out and said to him, "You shall not have an inheritance in our father's house, for you are the son of another woman."

3 So Jephthah fled from his brothers and lived in the land of Tob; and worthless fellows gathered themselves about Jephthah, and they went out with him.

New International

Tola

10 AFTER THE time of Abimelech a man of Issachar, Tola son of Puah, the son of Dodo, rose to save Israel. He lived in Shamir, in the hill country of Ephraim. 2He led[n] Israel twenty-three years; then he died, and was buried in Shamir.

Jair

3He was followed by Jair of Gilead, who led Israel twenty-two years. 4He had thirty sons, who rode thirty donkeys. They controlled thirty towns in Gilead, which to this day are called Havvoth Jair.[o] 5When Jair died, he was buried in Kamon.

Jephthah

6Again the Israelites did evil in the eyes of the LORD. They served the Baals and the Ashtoreths, and the gods of Aram, the gods of Sidon, the gods of Moab, the gods of the Ammonites and the gods of the Philistines. And because the Israelites forsook the LORD and no longer served him, 7he became angry with them. He sold them into the hands of the Philistines and the Ammonites, 8who that year shattered and crushed them. For eighteen years they oppressed all the Israelites on the east side of the Jordan in Gilead, the land of the Amorites. 9The Ammonites also crossed the Jordan to fight against Judah, Benjamin and the house of Ephraim; and Israel was in great distress. 10Then the Israelites cried out to the LORD, "We have sinned against you, forsaking our God and serving the Baals."

11The LORD replied, "When the Egyptians, the Amorites, the Ammonites, the Philistines, 12the Sidonians, the Amalekites and the Maonites[p] oppressed you and you cried to me for help, did I not save you from their hands? 13But you have forsaken me and served other gods, so I will no longer save you. 14Go and cry out to the gods you have chosen. Let them save you when you are in trouble!"

15But the Israelites said to the LORD, "We have sinned. Do with us whatever you think best, but please rescue us now." 16Then they got rid of the foreign gods among them and served the LORD. And he could bear Israel's misery no longer.

17When the Ammonites were called to arms and camped in Gilead, the Israelites assembled and camped at Mizpah. 18The leaders of the people of Gilead said to each other, "Whoever will launch the attack against the Ammonites will be the head of all those living in Gilead."

11 JEPHTHAH THE Gileadite was a mighty warrior. His father was Gilead; his mother was a prostitute. 2Gilead's wife also bore him sons, and when they were grown up, they drove Jephthah away. "You are not going to get any inheritance in our family," they said, "because you are the son of another woman." 3So Jephthah fled from his brothers and settled in the land of Tob, where a group of adventurers gathered around him and followed him.

---

n 2 Traditionally judged; also in verse 3   o 4 Or called the settlements of Jair   p 12 Hebrew; some Septuagint manuscripts Midianites

King James

4 ¶ And it came to pass ᵂin process of time, that the children of Ammon made war against Israel.

5And it was so, that when the children of Ammon made war against Israel, the elders of Gilead went to fetch Jephthah out of the land of Tob:

6And they said unto Jephthah, Come, and be our captain, that we may fight with the children of Ammon.

7And Jephthah said unto the elders of Gilead, Did not ye hate me, and expel me out of my father's house? and why are ye come unto me now when ye are in distress?

8And the elders of Gilead said unto Jephthah, Therefore we turn again to thee now, that thou mayest go with us, and fight against the children of Ammon, and be our head over all the inhabitants of Gilead.

9And Jephthah said unto the elders of Gilead, If ye bring me home again to fight against the children of Ammon, and the LORD deliver them before me, shall I be your head?

10And the elders of Gilead said unto Jephthah, The LORD ˣbe witness between us, if we do not so according to thy words.

11Then Jephthah went with the elders of Gilead, and the people made him head and captain over them: and Jephthah uttered all his words before the LORD in Mizpeh.

12 ¶ And Jephthah sent messengers unto the king of the children of Ammon, saying, What hast thou to do with me, that thou art come against me to fight in my land?

13And the king of the children of Ammon answered unto the messengers of Jephthah, Because Israel took away my land, when they came up out of Egypt, from Arnon even unto Jabbok, and unto Jordan: now therefore restore those *lands* again peaceably.

14And Jephthah sent messengers again unto the king of the children of Ammon:

15And said unto him, Thus saith Jephthah, Israel took not away the land of Moab, nor the land of the children of Ammon:

16But when Israel came up from Egypt, and walked through the wilderness unto the Red sea, and came to Kadesh;

17Then Israel sent messengers unto the king of Edom, saying, Let me, I pray thee, pass through thy land: but the king of Edom would not hearken *thereto.* And in like manner they sent unto the king of Moab: but he would not *consent:* and Israel abode in Kadesh.

18Then they went along through the wilderness, and compassed the land of Edom, and the land of Moab, and came by the east side of the land of Moab, and pitched on the other side of Arnon, but came not within the border of Moab: for Arnon *was* the border of Moab.

19And Israel sent messengers unto Sihon king of the Amorites, the king of Heshbon; and Israel said unto him, Let us pass, we pray thee, through thy land into my place.

20But Sihon trusted not Israel to pass through his coast: but Sihon gathered all his people together, and pitched in Jahaz, and fought against Israel.

21And the LORD God of Israel delivered Sihon and all his people into the hand of Israel, and they smote them: so Israel possessed all the land of the Amorites, the inhabitants of that country.

22And they possessed all the coasts of the Amorites, from Arnon even unto Jabbok, and from the wilderness even unto Jordan.

23So now the LORD God of Israel hath dispossessed the Amorites from before his people Israel, and shouldest thou possess it?

24Wilt not thou possess that which Chemosh thy god giveth thee to possess? So whomsoever the LORD our God shall drive out from before us, them will we possess.

25And now *art* thou any thing better than Balak the son of Zippor, king of Moab? did he ever strive against Israel, or did he ever fight against them,

Amplified

4And after a time, the Ammonites made war against Israel.

5And when the Ammonites made war against Israel, the elders of Gilead went to bring Jephthah out of the land of Tob;

6And they said to Jephthah, Come and be our leader, that we may fight with the Ammonites.

7But Jephthah said to the elders of Gilead, Did you not hate me and drive me out of my father's house? Why have you come to me now when you are in trouble?

8And the elders of Gilead said to Jephthah, This is why we have turned to you now, that you may go with us and fight the Ammonites and be our head over all the citizens of Gilead.

9Jephthah said to the elders of Gilead, If you bring me home again to fight against the Ammonites and the Lord gives them over to me, [understand that] I will be your head.

10And the elders of Gilead said to Jephthah, The Lord is witness between us, if we do not do as you have said.

11So Jephthah went with the elders of Gilead, and the people made him head and leader over them. And Jephthah repeated all he had promised before the Lord at Mizpah.

12And Jephthah sent messengers to the king of the Ammonites, saying, What have you to do with me, that you have come against me to fight in my land?

13The Ammonites' king replied to the messengers of Jephthah, Because Israel took away my land [which was not true] when they came up out of Egypt [300 years before], from the Arnon even to Jabbok and to the Jordan; now therefore, restore those lands peaceably.

14And Jephthah sent messengers again to the king of the Ammonites

15And said to him, Thus says Jephthah, Israel did not take the land of Moab or the land of the Ammonites.

16But when [Israel] came up from Egypt, [they] walked through the wilderness to the Red Sea and came to Kadesh.

17Then Israel sent messengers to the king of Edom, saying, Let us, we pray, pass through your land, but the king of Edom would not listen. Also they sent to the king of Moab, but he would not consent. So Israel remained at Kadesh.

18Then they went through the wilderness and went around the land of Edom and the land of Moab, and came by the east side of the land of Moab and camped on the other side of the Arnon; but they came not within the territory of Moab, for the Arnon was the boundary of Moab.

19Then Israel sent messengers to Sihon king of the Amorites, king of Heshbon, and Israel said to him, Let us pass, we pray you, through your land to our country.

20But Sihon did not trust Israel to pass through his territory; so Sihon gathered all his people together and encamped at Jahaz and fought with Israel.

21And the Lord, the God of Israel, gave Sihon and all his people into the hand of Israel, and they defeated them; so Israel took possession of all the land of the Amorites, the inhabitants of that country.

22They possessed all the territory of the Amorites, from the Arnon even to the Jabbok, and from the wilderness even to the Jordan.

23So now the Lord God of Israel has dispossessed the Amorites from before His people Israel, and should you possess them?

24Will you not possess what Chemosh your god gives you to possess? And all the Lord our God dispossessed before us, we will possess.

25Now are you any better than Balak son of Zippor, king of Moab? Did he ever strive against Israel or did he ever go to war with them?

ᵂHeb. *after days*   ˣHeb. *be the hearer between us*

New American Standard

4 ¶ It came about after a while that the sons of Ammon fought against Israel.

5 When the sons of Ammon fought against Israel, the elders of Gilead went to get Jephthah from the land of Tob;

6 and they said to Jephthah, "Come and be our chief that we may fight against the sons of Ammon."

7 Then Jephthah said to the elders of Gilead, "Did you not hate me and drive me from my father's house? So why have you come to me now when you are in trouble?"

8 The elders of Gilead said to Jephthah, "For this reason we have now returned to you, that you may go with us and fight with the sons of Ammon and become head over all the inhabitants of Gilead."

9 So Jephthah said to the elders of Gilead, "If you take me back to fight against the sons of Ammon and the LORD gives them up to me, will I become your head?"

10 The elders of Gilead said to Jephthah, "The LORD is witness between us; surely we will do as you have said."

11 Then Jephthah went with the elders of Gilead, and the people made him head and chief over them; and Jephthah spoke all his words before the LORD at Mizpah.

12 ¶ Now Jephthah sent messengers to the king of the sons of Ammon, saying, "What is between you and me, that you have come to me to fight against my land?"

13 The king of the sons of Ammon said to the messengers of Jephthah, "Because Israel took away my land when they came up from Egypt, from the Arnon as far as the Jabbok and the Jordan; therefore, return them peaceably now."

14 But Jephthah sent messengers again to the king of the sons of Ammon,

15 and they said to him, "Thus says Jephthah, 'Israel did not take away the land of Moab nor the land of the sons of Ammon.

16 'For when they came up from Egypt, and Israel went through the wilderness to the Red Sea and came to Kadesh,

17 then Israel sent messengers to the king of Edom, saying, "Please let us pass through your land," but the king of Edom would not listen. And they also sent to the king of Moab, but he would not consent. So Israel remained at Kadesh.

18 'Then they went through the wilderness and around the land of Edom and the land of Moab, and came to the east side of the land of Moab, and they camped beyond the Arnon; but they did not enter the territory of Moab, for the Arnon *was* the border of Moab.

19 'And Israel sent messengers to Sihon king of the Amorites, the king of Heshbon, and Israel said to him, "Please let us pass through your land to our place."

20 'But Sihon did not trust Israel to pass through his territory; so Sihon gathered all his people and camped in Jahaz and fought with Israel.

21 'The LORD, the God of Israel, gave Sihon and all his people into the hand of Israel, and they defeated them; so Israel possessed all the land of the Amorites, the inhabitants of that country.

22 'So they possessed all the territory of the Amorites, from the Arnon as far as the Jabbok, and from the wilderness as far as the Jordan.

23 'Since now the LORD, the God of Israel, drove out the Amorites from before His people Israel, are you then to possess it?

24 'Do you not possess what Chemosh your god gives you to possess? So whatever the LORD our God has driven out before us, we will possess it.

25 'Now are you any better than Balak the son of Zippor, king of Moab? Did he ever strive with Israel, or did he ever fight against them?

New International

4Some time later, when the Ammonites made war on Israel, 5the elders of Gilead went to get Jephthah from the land of Tob. 6"Come," they said, "be our commander, so we can fight the Ammonites."

7Jephthah said to them, "Didn't you hate me and drive me from my father's house? Why do you come to me now, when you're in trouble?"

8The elders of Gilead said to him, "Nevertheless, we are turning to you now; come with us to fight the Ammonites, and you will be our head over all who live in Gilead."

9Jephthah answered, "Suppose you take me back to fight the Ammonites and the LORD gives them to me—will I really be your head?"

10The elders of Gilead replied, "The LORD is our witness; we will certainly do as you say." 11So Jephthah went with the elders of Gilead, and the people made him head and commander over them. And he repeated all his words before the LORD in Mizpah.

12Then Jephthah sent messengers to the Ammonite king with the question: "What do you have against us that you have attacked our country?"

13The king of the Ammonites answered Jephthah's messengers, "When Israel came up out of Egypt, they took away my land from the Arnon to the Jabbok, all the way to the Jordan. Now give it back peaceably."

14Jephthah sent back messengers to the Ammonite king, 15saying:

"This is what Jephthah says: Israel did not take the land of Moab or the land of the Ammonites. 16But when they came up out of Egypt, Israel went through the desert to the Red Sea*q* and on to Kadesh. 17Then Israel sent messengers to the king of Edom, saying, 'Give us permission to go through your country,' but the king of Edom would not listen. They sent also to the king of Moab, and he refused. So Israel stayed at Kadesh.

18"Next they traveled through the desert, skirted the lands of Edom and Moab, passed along the eastern side of the country of Moab, and camped on the other side of the Arnon. They did not enter the territory of Moab, for the Arnon was its border.

19"Then Israel sent messengers to Sihon king of the Amorites, who ruled in Heshbon, and said to him, 'Let us pass through your country to our own place.' 20Sihon, however, did not trust Israel*r* to pass through his territory. He mustered all his men and encamped at Jahaz and fought with Israel.

21"Then the LORD, the God of Israel, gave Sihon and all his men into Israel's hands, and they defeated them. Israel took over all the land of the Amorites who lived in that country, 22capturing all of it from the Arnon to the Jabbok and from the desert to the Jordan.

23"Now since the LORD, the God of Israel, has driven the Amorites out before his people Israel, what right have you to take it over? 24Will you not take what your god Chemosh gives you? Likewise, whatever the LORD our God has given us, we will possess. 25Are you better than Balak son of Zippor, king of Moab? Did he ever quarrel with Israel or fight with

---

q 16 Hebrew *Yam Suph*; that is, Sea of Reeds   *r 20* Or *however, would not make an agreement for Israel*

King James

26While Israel dwelt in Heshbon and her towns, and in Aroer and her towns, and in all the cities that *be* along by the coasts of Arnon, three hundred years? why therefore did ye not recover *them* within that time?

27Wherefore I have not sinned against thee, but thou doest me wrong to war against me: the LORD the Judge be judge this day between the children of Israel and the children of Ammon.

28Howbeit the king of the children of Ammon hearkened not unto the words of Jephthah which he sent him.

29 ¶ Then the spirit of the LORD came upon ʸJephthah, and he passed over Gilead, and Manasseh, and passed over Mizpeh of Gilead, and from Mizpeh of Gilead he passed over *unto* the children of Ammon.

30And Jephthah vowed a vow unto the LORD, and said, If thou shalt without fail deliver the children of Ammon into mine hands,

31Then it shall be, that ᶻwhatsoever cometh forth of the doors of my house to meet me, when I return in peace from the children of Ammon, shall surely be the LORD'S, ᵃand I will offer it up for a burnt offering.

32 ¶ So Jephthah passed over unto the children of Ammon to fight against them; and the LORD delivered them into his hands.

33And he smote them from Aroer, even till thou come to Minnith, *even* twenty cities, and unto ᵇthe plain of the vineyards, with a very great slaughter. Thus the children of Ammon were subdued before the children of Israel.

34 ¶ And Jephthah came to Mizpeh unto his house, and, behold, his daughter came out to meet him with timbrels and with dances: and she *was his* only child; ᶜᵈbeside her he had neither son nor daughter.

35And it came to pass, when he saw her, that he rent his clothes, and said, Alas, my daughter! thou hast brought me very low, and thou art one of them that trouble me: for I have opened my mouth unto the LORD, and I cannot go back.

36And she said unto him, My father, *if* thou hast opened thy mouth unto the LORD, do to me according to that which hath proceeded out of thy mouth; forasmuch as the LORD hath taken vengeance for thee of thine enemies, *even* of the children of Ammon.

37And she said unto her father, Let this thing be done for me: let me alone two months, that I may ᵉgo up and down upon the mountains, and bewail my virginity, I and my fellows.

38And he said, Go. And he sent her away *for* two months: and she went with her companions, and bewailed her virginity upon the mountains.

39And it came to pass at the end of two months, that she returned unto her father, who did with her *according* to his vow which he had vowed: and she knew no man. And it was a ᶠcustom in Israel,

40*That* the daughters of Israel went ᵍyearly ʰto lament the daughter of Jephthah the Gileadite four days in a year.

Amplified

26While Israel dwelt in Heshbon and its villages, and in Aroer and its villages, and in all the cities along the banks of the Arnon for 300 years, why did you not recover [your lost lands] during that time?

27So I have not sinned against you, but you are doing me wrong to war against me. The Lord, the [righteous] Judge, judge this day between the Israelites and the Ammonites.

28But the king of the Ammonites did not listen to the message Jephthah sent him.

29Then the Spirit of the Lord came upon Jephthah, and he passed through Gilead and Manasseh, and Mizpah of Gilead, and from Mizpah of Gilead he passed on to the Ammonites.

30And Jephthah made a vow to the Lord and said, If You will indeed give the Ammonites into my hand,

31Then whatever *or* whoever comes forth from the doors of my house to meet me when I return in peace from the Ammonites, it shall be the Lord's, and I will offer it *or* him up as a burnt offering.

32Then Jephthah crossed over to the Ammonites to fight with them, and the Lord gave them into his hand.

33And from Aroer to Minnith he smote them, twenty cities, and as far as Abel-cheramim [the meadow of vineyards], with a very great slaughter. So the Ammonites were subdued before the Israelites.

34Then Jephthah came to Mizpah to his home, and behold, his daughter came out to meet him with timbrels and with dances! And she was his only child; beside her he had neither son nor daughter.

35And when he saw her, he rent his clothes and said, Alas, my daughter! You have brought me very low, and you are the cause of great trouble to me; for I have opened my mouth [in a vow] to the Lord, and I cannot take it back.

36And she said to him, My father, if you have opened your mouth to the Lord, do to me according to what you have vowed, since the Lord has taken vengeance for you on your enemies, the Ammonites.

37And she said to her father, Let this thing be done for me; let me alone two months, that I may go and wander upon the mountains and bewail my virginity, I and my companions.

38And he said, Go. And he sent her away for two months, and she went with her companions and bewailed her virginity upon the mountains.

39At the end of two months she returned to her father, who ᵏdid with her according to his vow which he had vowed. She never mated with a man. This became a custom in Israel—

40That the daughters of Israel went yearly to mourn the daughter of Jephthah the Gileadite four days in a year.

ᵏScholars fail to agree as to what Jephthah really did. For example, "This plain and restrained statement that 'he did with her according to his vow' is best taken as implying her actual sacrifice. Although human sacrifice was strictly forbidden to Israelites, we need not be surprised at a man of Jephthah's half-Canaanite antecedents following Canaanite usage in this matter" (F. Davidson, ed., *The New Bible Commentary*). And, "Although the lapse of two months might be supposed to have afforded time for reflection and a better sense of his duty, there is but too much reason to conclude that he was impelled to the fulfillment by the dictates of a pious but unenlightened conscience" (Robert Jamieson, A.R. Fausset and David Brown, *A Commentary*). And, "The religious system of Israel had fallen into suspension. From the days of Phinehas (Judg. 20:28) to the time of Samuel, we hear nothing of the high priest, the ark or the tabernacle" (*The Cambridge Bible*). On the other hand, J.P. Lange (*A Commentary*) articulates the position of many scholars when he calls attention to stories in Greek mythology in which the virginity of a goddess was celebrated by Greek maidens with song and dance. Summing up, Lange says, "At all events, it does not 'stand there in the text,' as Luther wrote, that she was offered in sacrifice." And the fact that the maidens mourned her virginity and not her death seems to prove that she did not die.

ʸJephthah seems to have been Judge only of Northeast *Israel*   ᶻHeb. *that which cometh forth, which shall come forth*   ᵃOr, *or I will offer it*   ᵇOr, *Abel*   ᶜOr, *he had not of his own either son or daughter*   ᵈHeb. *of himself*   ᵉHeb. *go and go down*   ᶠOr, *ordinance*   ᵍHeb. *from year to year*   ʰOr, *to talk with*

New American Standard

26 'While Israel lived in Heshbon and its villages, and in Aroer and its villages, and in all the cities that are on the banks of the Arnon, three hundred years, why did you not recover them within that time?

27 'I therefore have not sinned against you, but you are doing me wrong by making war against me; may the LORD, the Judge, judge today between the sons of Israel and the sons of Ammon.' "

28 But the king of the sons of Ammon disregarded the message which Jephthah sent him.

Jephthah's Tragic Vow

29 ¶ Now the Spirit of the LORD came upon Jephthah, so that he passed through Gilead and Manasseh; then he passed through Mizpah of Gilead, and from Mizpah of Gilead he went on to the sons of Ammon.

30 Jephthah made a vow to the LORD and said, "If You will indeed give the sons of Ammon into my hand,

31 then it shall be that whatever comes out of the doors of my house to meet me when I return in peace from the sons of Ammon, it shall be the LORD'S, and I will offer it up as a burnt offering."

32 So Jephthah crossed over to the sons of Ammon to fight against them; and the LORD gave them into his hand.

33 He struck them with a very great slaughter from Aroer to the entrance of Minnith, twenty cities, and as far as Abel-keramim. So the sons of Ammon were subdued before the sons of Israel.

34 ¶ When Jephthah came to his house at Mizpah, behold, his daughter was coming out to meet him with tambourines and with dancing. Now she was his one *and* only child; besides her he had no son or daughter.

35 When he saw her, he tore his clothes and said, "Alas, my daughter! You have brought me very low, and you are among those who trouble me; for I have given my word to the LORD, and I cannot take *it* back."

36 So she said to him, "My father, you have given your word to the LORD; do to me as you have said, since the LORD has avenged you of your enemies, the sons of Ammon."

37 She said to her father, "Let this thing be done for me; let me alone two months, that I may go to the mountains and weep because of my virginity, I and my companions."

38 Then he said, "Go." So he sent her away for two months; and she left with her companions, and wept on the mountains because of her virginity.

39 At the end of two months she returned to her father, who did to her according to the vow which he had made; and she had no relations with a man. Thus it became a custom in Israel,

40 that the daughters of Israel went yearly to commemorate the daughter of Jephthah the Gileadite four days in the year.

New International

them? 26For three hundred years Israel occupied Heshbon, Aroer, the surrounding settlements and all the towns along the Arnon. Why didn't you retake them during that time? 27I have not wronged you, but you are doing me wrong by waging war against me. Let the LORD, the Judge,[s] decide the dispute this day between the Israelites and the Ammonites."

28The king of Ammon, however, paid no attention to the message Jephthah sent him.

29Then the Spirit of the LORD came upon Jephthah. He crossed Gilead and Manasseh, passed through Mizpah of Gilead, and from there he advanced against the Ammonites. 30And Jephthah made a vow to the LORD: "If you give the Ammonites into my hands, 31whatever comes out of the door of my house to meet me when I return in triumph from the Ammonites will be the LORD'S, and I will sacrifice it as a burnt offering."

32Then Jephthah went over to fight the Ammonites, and the LORD gave them into his hands. 33He devastated twenty towns from Aroer to the vicinity of Minnith, as far as Abel Keramim. Thus Israel subdued Ammon.

34When Jephthah returned to his home in Mizpah, who should come out to meet him but his daughter, dancing to the sound of tambourines! She was an only child. Except for her he had neither son nor daughter. 35When he saw her, he tore his clothes and cried, "Oh! My daughter! You have made me miserable and wretched, because I have made a vow to the LORD that I cannot break."

36"My father," she replied, "you have given your word to the LORD. Do to me just as you promised, now that the LORD has avenged you of your enemies, the Ammonites. 37But grant me this one request," she said. "Give me two months to roam the hills and weep with my friends, because I will never marry."

38"You may go," he said. And he let her go for two months. She and the girls went into the hills and wept because she would never marry. 39After the two months, she returned to her father and he did to her as he had vowed. And she was a virgin.

From this comes the Israelite custom 40that each year the young women of Israel go out for four days to commemorate the daughter of Jephthah the Gileadite.

King James

Jephthah and Ephraim

12 AND THE men of Ephraim *i*gathered themselves together, and went northward, and said unto Jephthah, Wherefore passedst thou over to fight against the children of Ammon, and didst not call us to go with thee? we will burn thine house upon thee with fire.

2 And Jephthah said unto them, I and my people were at great strife with the children of Ammon; and when I called you, ye delivered me not out of their hands.

3 And when I saw that ye delivered *me* not, I put my life in my hands, and passed over against the children of Ammon, and the LORD delivered them into my hand: wherefore then are ye come up unto me this day, to fight against me?

4 Then Jephthah gathered together all the men of Gilead, and fought with Ephraim: and the men of Gilead smote Ephraim, because they said, Ye Gileadites *are* fugitives of Ephraim among the Ephraimites, *and* among the Manassites.

5 And the Gileadites took the passages of Jordan before the Ephraimites: and it was *so*, that when those Ephraimites which were escaped said, Let me go over; that the men of Gilead said unto him, *Art* thou an Ephraimite? If he said, Nay;

6 Then said they unto him, Say now *j*Shibboleth: and he said Sibboleth: for he could not frame to pronounce *it* right. Then they took him, and slew him at the passages of Jordan: and there fell at that time of the Ephraimites forty and two thousand.

7 And Jephthah judged Israel six years. Then died Jephthah the Gileadite, and was buried in *one of* the cities of Gilead.

Ibzan, Elon and Abdon

8 ¶ And after him *k*Ibzan of Bethlehem judged Israel.

9 And he had thirty sons, and thirty daughters, *whom* he sent abroad, and took in thirty daughters from abroad for his sons. And he judged Israel seven years.

10 Then died Ibzan, and was buried at Bethlehem.

11 ¶ And after him *l*Elon, a Zebulonite, judged Israel; and he judged Israel ten years.

12 And Elon the Zebulonite died, and was buried in Aijalon in the country of Zebulun.

13 ¶ And after him *m*Abdon the son of Hillel, a Pirathonite, judged Israel.

14 And he had forty sons and thirty *n*nephews, that rode on threescore and ten ass colts: and he judged Israel eight years.

15 And Abdon the son of Hillel the Pirathonite died, and was buried in Pirathon in the land of Ephraim, in the mount of the Amalekites.

13 AND THE children of Israel *o*did evil again in the sight of the LORD; *p*and the LORD delivered them into the hand of the Philistines forty years.

The birth of Samson

2 ¶ And there was a certain man of Zorah, of the family of the Danites, whose name *was* Manoah; and his wife *was* barren, and bare not.

3 And the angel of the LORD appeared unto the woman, and said unto her, Behold now, thou *art* barren, and bearest not: but thou shalt conceive, and bear a son.

4 Now therefore beware, I pray thee, and drink not wine nor strong drink, and eat not any unclean *thing*:

Amplified

12 THE MEN of Ephraim were summoned together and they crossed to Zaphon and said to Jephthah, Why did you cross over to fight with the Ammonites and did not summon us to go with you? We will burn your house over you with fire.

2 And Jephthah said to them, I and my people were in a severe conflict with the Ammonites, and I when I called you, you did not rescue me from their hands.

3 And when I saw that you would not rescue me, I put my life in my hands and crossed over against the Ammonites, and the Lord delivered them into my hand. Why then have you come up to me this day to fight against me?

4 Then Jephthah gathered all the men of Gilead and fought with Ephraim; and the men of Gilead smote Ephraim because they had said, You Gileadites are fugitives of Ephraim in the midst of Ephraim and Manasseh.

5 And the Gileadites took the fords of the Jordan before the Ephraimites; and when any of those Ephraimites who had escaped said, Let me go over, the men of Gilead said to him, Are you an Ephraimite? If he said, No,

6 They said to him, Then say Shibboleth; and he said, Sibboleth, for he could not pronounce it right. Then they seized him and slew him at the fords of the Jordan. And there fell at that time 42,000 of the Ephraimites.

7 Jephthah judged Israel six years. Then Jephthah the Gileadite died and was buried in one of the cities of Gilead.

8 And after him Ibzan of Bethlehem judged Israel.

9 And he had thirty sons and thirty daughters whom he gave [to husbands] outside his tribe, and thirty daughters [daughters-in-law] whom he brought in from outside his tribe for his sons. And he judged Israel seven years.

10 Then Ibzan died and was buried at Bethlehem.

11 After him Elon the Zebulunite judged Israel, and he judged Israel ten years.

12 Then Elon the Zebulunite died and was buried at Aijalon in the land of Zebulun.

13 And after him Abdon son of Hillel the Pirathonite judged Israel.

14 And he had forty sons and thirty grandsons who rode on seventy donkey colts; and he judged Israel eight years.

15 Then Abdon son of Hillel the Pirathonite died, and was buried at Pirathon in the land of Ephraim, in the hill country of the Amalekites.

13 AND THE Israelites again did what was evil in the sight of the Lord, and the Lord gave them into the hands of the Philistines for forty years.

2 And there was a certain man of Zorah, of the tribe of the Danites, whose name was Manoah; and his wife was barren and had no children.

3 And the *l*Angel of the Lord appeared to the woman and said to her, Behold, you are barren and have no children, but you shall become pregnant and bear a son.

4 Therefore beware and drink no wine or strong drink and eat nothing unclean.

---

*i*Heb. *were called*   *j*Which signifieth *a stream,* or, *flood*
*k*He seems to have been only a civil Judge to do justice in Northeast *Israel*   *l*A civil Judge in Northeast *Israel*
*m*A civil Judge also in Northeast *Israel*   *n*Heb. *sons' sons*
*o*Heb. *added to commit*   *p*This seems a partial captivity

*l*See footnote on Gen. 16:7. Note that in Judg. 13:22 the Angel of the Lord is identified with God.

New American Standard

Jephthah and His Successors

12 THEN THE men of Ephraim were summoned, and they crossed to Zaphon and said to Jephthah, "Why did you cross over to fight against the sons of Ammon without calling us to go with you? We will burn your house down on you."

2 Jephthah said to them, "I and my people were at great strife with the sons of Ammon; when I called you, you did not deliver me from their hand.

3 "When I saw that you would not deliver *me,* I took my life in my hands and crossed over against the sons of Ammon, and the LORD gave them into my hand. Why then have you come up to me this day to fight against me?"

4 Then Jephthah gathered all the men of Gilead and fought Ephraim; and the men of Gilead defeated Ephraim, because they said, "You are fugitives of Ephraim, O Gileadites, in the midst of Ephraim *and* in the midst of Manasseh."

5 The Gileadites captured the fords of the Jordan opposite Ephraim. And it happened when *any of* the fugitives of Ephraim said, "Let me cross over," the men of Gilead would say to him, "Are you an Ephraimite?" If he said, "No,"

6 then they would say to him, "Say now, 'Shibboleth.' " But he said, "Sibboleth," for he could not pronounce it correctly. Then they seized him and slew him at the fords of the Jordan. Thus there fell at that time 42,000 of Ephraim.

7 ¶ Jephthah judged Israel six years. Then Jephthah the Gileadite died and was buried in *one of* the cities of Gilead.

8 ¶ Now Ibzan of Bethlehem judged Israel after him.

9 He had thirty sons, and thirty daughters *whom* he gave in marriage outside *the family,* and he brought in thirty daughters from outside for his sons. And he judged Israel seven years.

10 Then Ibzan died and was buried in Bethlehem.

11 ¶ Now Elon the Zebulunite judged Israel after him; and he judged Israel ten years.

12 Then Elon the Zebulunite died and was buried at Aijalon in the land of Zebulun.

13 ¶ Now Abdon the son of Hillel the Pirathonite judged Israel after him.

14 He had forty sons and thirty grandsons who rode on seventy donkeys; and he judged Israel eight years.

15 Then Abdon the son of Hillel the Pirathonite died and was buried at Pirathon in the land of Ephraim, in the hill country of the Amalekites.

Philistines Oppress Again

13 NOW THE sons of Israel again did evil in the sight of the LORD, so that the LORD gave them into the hands of the Philistines forty years.

2 ¶ There was a certain man of Zorah, of the family of the Danites, whose name was Manoah; and his wife was barren and had borne no *children.*

3 Then the angel of the LORD appeared to the woman and said to her, "Behold now, you are barren and have borne no *children,* but you shall conceive and give birth to a son.

4 "Now therefore, be careful not to drink wine or strong drink, nor eat any unclean thing.

New International

Jephthah and Ephraim

12 THE MEN of Ephraim called out their forces, crossed over to Zaphon and said to Jephthah, "Why did you go to fight the Ammonites without calling us to go with you? We're going to burn down your house over your head."

2 Jephthah answered, "I and my people were engaged in a great struggle with the Ammonites, and although I called, you didn't save me out of their hands. 3 When I saw that you wouldn't help, I took my life in my hands and crossed over to fight the Ammonites, and the LORD gave me the victory over them. Now why have you come up today to fight me?"

4 Jephthah then called together the men of Gilead and fought against Ephraim. The Gileadites struck them down because the Ephraimites had said, "You Gileadites are renegades from Ephraim and Manasseh." 5 The Gileadites captured the fords of the Jordan leading to Ephraim, and whenever a survivor of Ephraim said, "Let me cross over," the men of Gilead asked him, "Are you an Ephraimite?" If he replied, "No," 6 they said, "All right, say 'Shibboleth.' " If he said, "Sibboleth," because he could not pronounce the word correctly, they seized him and killed him at the fords of the Jordan. Forty-two thousand Ephraimites were killed at that time.

7 Jephthah led[f] Israel six years. Then Jephthah the Gileadite died, and was buried in a town in Gilead.

Ibzan, Elon and Abdon

8 After him, Ibzan of Bethlehem led Israel. 9 He had thirty sons and thirty daughters. He gave his daughters away in marriage to those outside his clan, and for his sons he brought in thirty young women as wives from outside his clan. Ibzan led Israel seven years. 10 Then Ibzan died, and was buried in Bethlehem.

11 After him, Elon the Zebulunite led Israel ten years. 12 Then Elon died, and was buried in Aijalon in the land of Zebulun.

13 After him, Abdon son of Hillel, from Pirathon, led Israel. 14 He had forty sons and thirty grandsons, who rode on seventy donkeys. He led Israel eight years. 15 Then Abdon son of Hillel died, and was buried at Pirathon in Ephraim, in the hill country of the Amalekites.

The Birth of Samson

13 AGAIN THE Israelites did evil in the eyes of the LORD, so the LORD delivered them into the hands of the Philistines forty years.

2 A certain man of Zorah, named Manoah, from the clan of the Danites, had a wife who was sterile and remained childless. 3 The angel of the LORD appeared to her and said, "You are sterile and childless, but you are going to conceive and have a son. 4 Now see to it that you drink no wine or other fermented drink and that you do not eat anything

---

[f] 7 Traditionally *judged*; also in verses 8-14

King James

5For, lo, thou shalt conceive, and bear a son; and no razor shall come on his head: for the child shall be a Nazarite unto God from the womb: and he shall begin to deliver Israel out of the hand of the Philistines.

6 ¶ Then the woman came and told her husband, saying, A man of God came unto me, and his countenance *was* like the countenance of an angel of God, very terrible: but I asked him not whence he *was*, neither told he me his name:

7But he said unto me, Behold, thou shalt conceive, and bear a son; and now drink no wine nor strong drink, neither eat any unclean *thing:* for the child shall be a Nazarite to God from the womb to the day of his death.

8 ¶ Then Manoah entreated the LORD, and said, O my Lord, let the man of God which thou didst send come again unto us, and teach us what we shall do unto the child that shall be born.

9And God hearkened to the voice of Manoah; and the angel of God came again unto the woman as she sat in the field: but Manoah her husband *was* not with her.

10And the woman made haste, and ran, and showed her husband, and said unto him, Behold, the man hath appeared unto me, that came unto me the *other* day.

11And Manoah arose, and went after his wife, and came to the man, and said unto him, *Art* thou the man that spakest unto the woman? And he said, I *am.*

12And Manoah said, Now let thy words come to pass. *q*How shall we order the child, and *r*show shall we do unto him?

13And the angel of the LORD said unto Manoah, Of all that I said unto the woman let her beware.

14She may not eat of any *thing* that cometh of the vine, neither let her drink wine or strong drink, nor eat any unclean *thing:* all that I commanded her let her observe.

15 ¶ And Manoah said unto the angel of the LORD, I pray thee, let us detain thee, until we shall have made ready a kid *t*for thee.

16And the angel of the LORD said unto Manoah, Though thou detain me, I will not eat of thy bread: and if thou wilt offer a burnt offering, thou must offer it unto the LORD. For Manoah knew not that he *was* an angel of the LORD.

17And Manoah said unto the angel of the LORD, What *is* thy name, that when thy sayings come to pass we may do thee honour?

18And the angel of the LORD said unto him, Why askest thou thus after my name, seeing it *is* secret?

19So Manoah took a kid with a meat offering, and offered *it* upon a rock unto the LORD: and *the angel* did wondrously; and Manoah and his wife looked on.

20For it came to pass, when the flame went up toward heaven from off the altar, that the angel of the LORD ascended in the flame of the altar. And Manoah and his wife looked on *it,* and fell on their faces to the ground.

21But the angel of the LORD did no more appear to Manoah and to his wife. Then Manoah knew that he *was* an angel of the LORD.

22And Manoah said unto his wife, We shall surely die, because we have seen God.

23But his wife said unto him, If the LORD were pleased to kill us, he would not have received a burnt offering and a meat offering at our hands, neither would he have shown us all these *things,* nor would as at this time have told us *such things* as these.

24 ¶ And the woman bare a son, and called his name Samson: and the child grew, and the LORD blessed him.

25And the spirit of the LORD began to move him at times in *u*the camp of Dan between Zorah and Eshtaol.

Amplified

5For behold, you shall become pregnant and bear a son. No razor shall come upon his head, for the child shall be a Nazirite to God from birth, and he shall begin to deliver Israel out of the hands of the Philistines.

6Then the woman went and told her husband, saying, A *m*Man of God came to me and his face was like the face of the Angel of God, to be greatly and reverently feared. I did not ask him from where he came, and he did not tell me his name.

7But he said to me, Behold, you shall become pregnant and bear a son, and now drink no wine or strong drink and eat nothing unclean, for the child shall be a Nazirite to God from birth to the day of his death.

8Then Manoah entreated the Lord and said, O Lord, let the Man of God whom You sent come again to us and teach us what we shall do with the child that shall be born.

9And God listened to the voice of Manoah, and the Angel of God came again to the woman as she sat in the field; but Manoah her husband was not with her.

10And the woman ran in haste and told her husband and said to him, Behold, the Man who came to me the other day has appeared to me.

11And Manoah arose and went after his wife and came to the Man and said to him, Are you the Man who spoke to this woman? And he said, I am.

12And Manoah said, Now when your words come true, how shall we manage the child, and what is he to do?

13And the Angel of the Lord said to Manoah, Let the mother beware of all that I told her.

14She may not eat of anything that comes from the grapevine, nor drink wine or strong drink nor eat any unclean thing. All that I commanded her let her observe.

15And Manoah said to the Angel of the Lord, Pray, let us detain you that we may prepare a kid for you.

16And the Angel of the Lord said to Manoah, Though you detain me, I will not eat of your food, but if you make ready a burnt offering, offer it to the Lord. For Manoah did not know that he was the Angel of the Lord.

17And Manoah said to the Angel of the Lord, What is your name, so that when your words come true, we may do you honor?

18And the Angel of the Lord said to him, Why do you ask my name, seeing it is wonderful? [Isa. 9:6.]

19So Manoah took the kid with the cereal offering and offered it upon a rock to the Lord, the Angel working wonders, while Manoah and his wife looked on.

20For when the flame went up toward the heavens from the altar, the Angel of the Lord ascended in the altar flame. And Manoah and his wife looked on, and they fell on their faces to the ground.

21The Angel of the Lord did not appear again to Manoah or to his wife. Then Manoah knew that he was the Angel of the Lord.

22And Manoah said to his wife, We shall surely die, because we have seen God.

23But his [sensible] wife said to him, If the Lord were pleased to kill us, He would not have received a burnt offering and a cereal offering from our hands, nor have shown us all these things or now have announced such things as these.

24And the woman [in due time] bore a son and called his name Samson; and the child grew and the Lord blessed him.

25And the Spirit of the Lord began to move him at times in Mahaneh-dan [the camp of Dan] between Zorah and Eshtaol.

New American Standard

5"For behold, you shall conceive and give birth to a son, and no razor shall come upon his head, for the boy shall be a Nazirite to God from the womb; and he shall begin to deliver Israel from the hands of the Philistines."

6 Then the woman came and told her husband, saying, "A man of God came to me and his appearance was like the appearance of the angel of God, very awesome. And I did not ask him where he *came* from, nor did he tell me his name.

7"But he said to me, 'Behold, you shall conceive and give birth to a son, and now you shall not drink wine or strong drink nor eat any unclean thing, for the boy shall be a Nazirite to God from the womb to the day of his death.' "

8 ¶ Then Manoah entreated the LORD and said, "O Lord, please let the man of God whom You have sent come to us again that he may teach us what to do for the boy who is to be born."

9 God listened to the voice of Manoah; and the angel of God came again to the woman as she was sitting in the field, but Manoah her husband was not with her.

10 So the woman ran quickly and told her husband, "Behold, the man who came the *other* day has appeared to me."

11 Then Manoah arose and followed his wife, and when he came to the man he said to him, "Are you the man who spoke to the woman?" And he said, "I am."

12 Manoah said, "Now when your words come *to pass*, what shall be the boy's mode of life and his vocation?"

13 So the angel of the LORD said to Manoah, "Let the woman pay attention to all that I said.

14"She should not eat anything that comes from the vine nor drink wine or strong drink, nor eat any unclean thing; let her observe all that I commanded."

15 ¶ Then Manoah said to the angel of the LORD, "Please let us detain you so that we may prepare a young goat for you."

16 The angel of the LORD said to Manoah, "Though you detain me, I will not eat your food, but if you prepare a burnt offering, *then* offer it to the LORD." For Manoah did not know that he was the angel of the LORD.

17 Manoah said to the angel of the LORD, "What is your name, so that when your words come *to pass,* we may honor you?"

18 But the angel of the LORD said to him, "Why do you ask my name, seeing it is ⁿwonderful?"

19 So Manoah took the young goat with the grain offering and offered it on the rock to the LORD, and He performed wonders while Manoah and his wife looked on.

20 For it came about when the flame went up from the altar toward heaven, that the angel of the LORD ascended in the flame of the altar. When Manoah and his wife saw *this,* they fell on their faces to the ground.

21 ¶ Now the angel of the LORD did not appear to Manoah or his wife again. Then Manoah knew that he was the angel of the LORD.

22 So Manoah said to his wife, "We will surely die, for we have seen God."

23 But his wife said to him, "If the LORD had desired to kill us, He would not have accepted a burnt offering and a grain offering from our hands, nor would He have shown us all these things, nor would He have let us hear *things* like this at this time."

24 ¶ Then the woman gave birth to a son and named him Samson; and the child grew up and the LORD blessed him.

25 And the Spirit of the LORD began to stir him in ᵒMahaneh-dan, between Zorah and Eshtaol.

New International

unclean, 5because you will conceive and give birth to a son. No razor may be used on his head, because the boy is to be a Nazirite, set apart to God from birth, and he will begin the deliverance of Israel from the hands of the Philistines."

6Then the woman went to her husband and told him, "A man of God came to me. He looked like an angel of God, very awesome. I didn't ask him where he came from, and he didn't tell me his name. 7But he said to me, 'You will conceive and give birth to a son. Now then, drink no wine or other fermented drink and do not eat anything unclean, because the boy will be a Nazirite of God from birth until the day of his death.' "

8Then Manoah prayed to the LORD: "O Lord, I beg you, let the man of God you sent to us come again to teach us how to bring up the boy who is to be born."

9God heard Manoah, and the angel of God came again to the woman while she was out in the field; but her husband Manoah was not with her. 10The woman hurried to tell her husband, "He's here! The man who appeared to me the other day!"

11Manoah got up and followed his wife. When he came to the man, he said, "Are you the one who talked to my wife?"

"I am," he said.

12So Manoah asked him, "When your words are fulfilled, what is to be the rule for the boy's life and work?"

13The angel of the LORD answered, "Your wife must do all that I have told her. 14She must not eat anything that comes from the grapevine, nor drink any wine or other fermented drink nor eat anything unclean. She must do everything I have commanded her."

15Manoah said to the angel of the LORD, "We would like you to stay until we prepare a young goat for you."

16The angel of the LORD replied, "Even though you detain me, I will not eat any of your food. But if you prepare a burnt offering, offer it to the LORD." (Manoah did not realize that it was the angel of the LORD.)

17Then Manoah inquired of the angel of the LORD, "What is your name, so that we may honor you when your word comes true?"

18He replied, "Why do you ask my name? It is beyond understanding.ᵘ " 19Then Manoah took a young goat, together with the grain offering, and sacrificed it on a rock to the LORD. And the LORD did an amazing thing while Manoah and his wife watched: 20As the flame blazed up from the altar toward heaven, the angel of the LORD ascended in the flame. Seeing this, Manoah and his wife fell with their faces to the ground. 21When the angel of the LORD did not show himself again to Manoah and his wife, Manoah realized that it was the angel of the LORD.

22"We are doomed to die!" he said to his wife. "We have seen God!"

23But his wife answered, "If the LORD had meant to kill us, he would not have accepted a burnt offering and grain offering from our hands, nor shown us all these things or now told us this."

24The woman gave birth to a boy and named him Samson. He grew and the LORD blessed him, 25and the Spirit of the LORD began to stir him while he was in Mahaneh Dan, between Zorah and Eshtaol.

ⁿ I.e. incomprehensible   ᵒ I.e. the camp of Dan   ᵘ 18 Or *is wonderful*

King James

The marriage of Samson

14 AND SAMSON went down to Timnath, and saw a woman in Timnath of the daughters of the Philistines.

2And he came up, and told his father and his mother, and said, I have seen a woman in Timnath of the daughters of the Philistines: now therefore get her for me to wife.

3Then his father and his mother said unto him, *Is there* never a woman among the daughters of thy brethren, or among all my people, that thou goest to take a wife of the uncircumcised Philistines? And Samson said unto his father, Get her for me; for *v*she pleaseth me well.

4But his father and his mother knew not that it *was* of the LORD, that he sought an occasion against the Philistines: for at that time the Philistines had dominion over Israel.

5 ¶ Then went Samson down, and his father and his mother, to Timnath, and came to the vineyards of Timnath: and, behold, a young lion roared *w*against him.

6And the spirit of the LORD came mightily upon him, and he rent him as he would have rent a kid, and *he had* nothing in his hand: but he told not his father or his mother what he had done.

7And he went down, and talked with the woman; and she pleased Samson well.

8 ¶ And after a time he returned to take her, and he turned aside to see the carcase of the lion: and, behold, *there was* a swarm of bees and honey in the carcase of the lion.

9And he took thereof in his hands, and went on eating, and came to his father and mother, and he gave them, and they did eat: but he told not them that he had taken the honey out of the carcase of the lion.

10 ¶ So his father went down unto the woman: and Samson made there a feast; for so used the young men to do.

11And it came to pass, when they saw him, that they brought thirty companions to be with him.

12 ¶ And Samson said unto them, I will now put forth a riddle unto you: if ye can certainly declare it me within the seven days of the feast, and find *it* out, then I will give you thirty *x*sheets and thirty change of garments:

13But if ye cannot declare *it* me, then shall ye give me thirty sheets and thirty change of garments. And they said unto him, Put forth thy riddle, that we may hear it.

14And he said unto them, Out of the eater came forth meat, and out of the strong came forth sweetness. And they could not in three days expound the riddle.

15And it came to pass on the seventh day, that they said unto Samson's wife, Entice thy husband, that he may declare unto us the riddle, lest we burn thee and thy father's house with fire: have ye called us *y*to take that we have? *is it* not *so?*

16And Samson's wife wept before him, and said, Thou dost but hate me, and lovest me not: thou hast put forth a riddle unto the children of my people, and hast not told *it* me. And he said unto her, Behold, I have not told *it* my father nor my mother, and shall I tell *it* thee?

17And she wept before him *z*the seven days, while their feast lasted: and it came to pass on the seventh day, that he told her, because she lay sore upon him: and she told the riddle to the children of her people.

18And the men of the city said unto him on the seventh day before the sun went down, What *is* sweeter than honey? and what *is* stronger than a lion? And he said unto them, If ye had not plowed with my heifer, ye had not found out my riddle.

Amplified

14 SAMSON WENT down to Timnah and at Timnah saw one of the daughters of the Philistines.

2And he came up and told his father and mother, I saw one of the daughters of the Philistines at Timnah; now get her for me as my wife.

3But his father and mother said to him, Is there not a woman among the daughters of your kinsmen or among all our people, that you must go to take a wife from the uncircumcised Philistines? And Samson said to his father, Get her for me, for she is all right in my eyes.

4His father and mother did not know that it was of the Lord, and that He sought an occasion for assailing the Philistines. At that time the Philistines had dominion over Israel.

5Then Samson and his father and mother went down to Timnah and came to the vineyards of Timnah. And behold, a young lion roared against him.

6And the Spirit of the Lord came mightily upon him, and he tore the lion as he would have torn a kid, and he had nothing in his hand; but he did not tell his father or mother what he had done.

7And he went down and talked with the woman, and she pleased Samson well.

8And after a while he returned to take her, and he turned aside to see the body of the lion, and behold, a swarm of bees and honey were in the body of the lion.

9And he scraped some of the honey out into his hands and went along eating. And he came to his father and mother and gave them some, and they ate it; but he did not tell them he had taken the honey from the body of the lion.

10His father went down to the woman, and Samson made a feast there, for that was the customary thing for young men to do.

11And when the people saw him, they brought thirty companions to be with him.

12And Samson said to them, I will now put forth a riddle to you; if you can tell me what it is within the seven days of the feast, and find it out, then I will give you thirty linen undergarments and thirty changes of raiment.

13But if you cannot declare it to me, then shall you give me thirty linen undergarments and thirty changes of festive [costly] raiment. And they said to him, Put forth your riddle, that we may hear it.

14And he said to them, Out of the eater came forth food, and out of the strong came forth sweetness. And they could not solve the riddle in three days.

15And on the seventh day they said to Samson's wife, Entice your husband to declare to us the riddle, lest we burn you and your father's household with fire. Have you invited us to make us poor? Is this not true?

16And Samson's wife wept before him and said, You only hate me, you do not love me; you have put forth a riddle to my countrymen and have not told the answer to me. And he said to her, Behold, I have not told my father or my mother, and shall I tell you?

17And Samson's wife wept before him the seven days their feast lasted, and on the seventh day he told her because she pressed him with entreaties. Then she told the riddle to her countrymen.

18And the men of the city said to [Samson] on the seventh day before sundown, What is sweeter than honey? What is stronger than a lion? And he said to them, If you had not plowed with my heifer, you would not have solved my riddle.

---

*v*Heb. *she is right in mine eyes*   *w*Heb. *in meeting him*   *x*Or, *shirts*   *y*Heb. *to possess us,* or, *to impoverish us?*   *z*Or, the rest of *the seven days*

New American Standard

Samson's Marriage

14 THEN SAMSON went down to Timnah and saw a woman in Timnah, *one* of the daughters of the Philistines.

2 So he came back and told his father and mother, "I saw a woman in Timnah, *one* of the daughters of the Philistines; now therefore, get her for me as a wife."

3 Then his father and his mother said to him, "Is there no woman among the daughters of your relatives, or among all our people, that you go to take a wife from the uncircumcised Philistines?" But Samson said to his father, "Get her for me, for she looks good to me."

4 However, his father and mother did not know that it was of the LORD, for He was seeking an occasion against the Philistines. Now at that time the Philistines were ruling over Israel.

5 ¶ Then Samson went down to Timnah with his father and mother, and came as far as the vineyards of Timnah; and behold, a young lion *came* roaring toward him.

6 The Spirit of the LORD came upon him mightily, so that he tore him as one tears a young goat though he had nothing in his hand; but he did not tell his father or mother what he had done.

7 So he went down and talked to the woman; and she looked good to Samson.

8 When he returned later to take her, he turned aside to look at the carcass of the lion; and behold, a swarm of bees and honey were in the body of the lion.

9 So he scraped the honey into his hands and went on, eating as he went. When he came to his father and mother, he gave *some* to them and they ate *it;* but he did not tell them that he had scraped the honey out of the body of the lion.

10 ¶ Then his father went down to the woman; and Samson made a feast there, for the young men customarily did this.

11 When they saw him, they brought thirty companions to be with him.

Samson's Riddle

12 Then Samson said to them, "Let me now propound a riddle to you; if you will indeed tell it to me within the seven days of the feast, and find it out, then I will give you thirty linen wraps and thirty changes of clothes.

13"But if you are unable to tell me, then you shall give me thirty linen wraps and thirty changes of clothes." And they said to him, "Propound your riddle, that we may hear it."

14 So he said to them,

"Out of the eater came something to eat,
    And out of the strong came something sweet."

But they could not tell the riddle in three days.

15 ¶ Then it came about on the fourth day that they said to Samson's wife, "Entice your husband, so that he will tell us the riddle, or we will burn you and your father's house with fire. Have you invited us to impoverish us? Is this not *so?*"

16 Samson's wife wept before him and said, "You only hate me, and you do not love me; you have propounded a riddle to the sons of my people, and have not told *it* to me." And he said to her, "Behold, I have not told *it* to my father or mother; so should I tell you?"

17 However she wept before him seven days while their feast lasted. And on the seventh day he told her because she pressed him so hard. She then told the riddle to the sons of her people.

18 So the men of the city said to him on the seventh day before the sun went down,

"What is sweeter than honey?
    And what is stronger than a lion?"

And he said to them,

"If you had not plowed with my heifer,
    You would not have found out my riddle."

New International

Samson's Marriage

14 SAMSON WENT down to Timnah and saw there a young Philistine woman. 2When he returned, he said to his father and mother, "I have seen a Philistine woman in Timnah; now get her for me as my wife."

3His father and mother replied, "Isn't there an acceptable woman among your relatives or among all our people? Must you go to the uncircumcised Philistines to get a wife?"

But Samson said to his father, "Get her for me. She's the right one for me." 4(His parents did not know that this was from the LORD, who was seeking an occasion to confront the Philistines; for at that time they were ruling over Israel.) 5Samson went down to Timnah together with his father and mother. As they approached the vineyards of Timnah, suddenly a young lion came roaring toward him. 6The Spirit of the LORD came upon him in power so that he tore the lion apart with his bare hands as he might have torn a young goat. But he told neither his father nor his mother what he had done. 7Then he went down and talked with the woman, and he liked her.

8Some time later, when he went back to marry her, he turned aside to look at the lion's carcass. In it was a swarm of bees and some honey, 9which he scooped out with his hands and ate as he went along. When he rejoined his parents, he gave them some, and they too ate it. But he did not tell them that he had taken the honey from the lion's carcass.

10Now his father went down to see the woman. And Samson made a feast there, as was customary for bridegrooms. 11When he appeared, he was given thirty companions.

12"Let me tell you a riddle," Samson said to them. "If you can give me the answer within the seven days of the feast, I will give you thirty linen garments and thirty sets of clothes. 13If you can't tell me the answer, you must give me thirty linen garments and thirty sets of clothes."

"Tell us your riddle," they said. "Let's hear it."
14He replied,

"Out of the eater, something to eat;
    out of the strong, something sweet."

For three days they could not give the answer.

15On the fourth[v] day, they said to Samson's wife, "Coax your husband into explaining the riddle for us, or we will burn you and your father's household to death. Did you invite us here to rob us?"

16Then Samson's wife threw herself on him, sobbing, "You hate me! You don't really love me. You've given my people a riddle, but you haven't told me the answer."

"I haven't even explained it to my father or mother," he replied, "so why should I explain it to you?" 17She cried the whole seven days of the feast. So on the seventh day he finally told her, because she continued to press him. She in turn explained the riddle to her people.

18Before sunset on the seventh day the men of the town said to him,

"What is sweeter than honey?
    What is stronger than a lion?"

Samson said to them,

"If you had not plowed with my heifer,
    you would not have solved my riddle."

---

v 15 Some Septuagint manuscripts and Syriac; Hebrew *seventh*

King James

19 ¶ And the spirit of the LORD came upon him, and he went down to Ashkelon, and slew thirty men of them, and took their *a*spoil, and gave change of garments unto them which expounded the riddle. And his anger was kindled, and he went up to his father's house.

20 But Samson's wife was *given* to his companion, whom he had used as his friend.

The revenge of Samson

15 BUT IT came to pass within a while after, in the time of wheat harvest, that Samson visited his wife with a kid; and he said, I will go in to my wife into the chamber. But her father would not suffer him to go in.

2 And her father said, I verily thought that thou hadst utterly hated her; therefore I gave her to thy companion: *is* not her younger sister fairer than she? *b*take her, I pray thee, instead of her.

3 ¶ And Samson said concerning them, *c*Now shall I be more blameless than the Philistines, though I do them a displeasure.

4 And Samson went and caught three hundred foxes, and took *d*firebrands, and turned tail to tail, and put a firebrand in the midst between two tails.

5 And when he had set the brands on fire, he let *them* go into the standing corn of the Philistines, and burnt up both the shocks, and also the standing corn, with the vineyards *and* olives.

6 ¶ Then the Philistines said, Who hath done this? And they answered, Samson, the son-in-law of the Timnite, because he had taken his wife, and given her to his companion. And the Philistines came up, and burnt her and her father with fire.

7 ¶ And Samson said unto them, Though ye have done this, yet will I be avenged of you, and after that I will cease.

8 And he smote them hip and thigh with a great slaughter: and he went down and dwelt in the top of the rock Etam.

9 ¶ Then the Philistines went up, and pitched in Judah, and spread themselves in Lehi.

10 And the men of Judah said, Why are ye come up against us? And they answered, To bind Samson are we come up, to do to him as he hath done to us.

11 Then three thousand men of Judah *e*went to the top of the rock Etam, and said to Samson, Knowest thou not that the Philistines *are* rulers over us? what *is* this *that* thou hast done unto us? And he said unto them, As they did unto me, so have I done unto them.

12 And they said unto him, We are come down to bind thee, that we may deliver thee into the hand of the Philistines. And Samson said unto them, Swear unto me, that ye will not fall upon me yourselves.

13 And they spake unto him, saying, No; but we will bind thee fast, and deliver thee into their hand: but surely we will not kill thee. And they bound him with two new cords, and brought him up from the rock.

14 ¶ *And* when he came unto Lehi, the Philistines shouted against him: and the spirit of the LORD came mightily upon him, and the cords that *were* upon his arms became as flax that was burnt with fire, and his bands *f*loosed from off his hands.

15 And he found a *g*new jawbone of an ass, and put forth his hand, and took it, and slew a thousand men therewith.

16 And Samson said, With the jawbone of an ass, *h*heaps upon heaps, with the jaw of an ass have I slain a thousand men.

Amplified

19 And the Spirit of the Lord came upon him, and he went down to Ashkelon and slew thirty men of them and took their apparel [as spoil], and gave the changes of garments to those who explained the riddle. And his anger was kindled, and he went up to his father's house.

20 But Samson's wife was [given] to his companion who was his [best] friend.

15 BUT SOME days later, in the time of wheat harvest, Samson went to visit his wife, taking along a kid [as a token of reconciliation]; and he said, I will go unto my wife in the inner chamber. But her father would not allow him to go in.

2 And her father said, I truly thought you utterly hated her, so I gave her to your companion. Is her younger sister not fairer than she? Take her, I pray you, instead.

3 And Samson said of them, This time shall I be blameless as regards the Philistines, though I do them evil.

4 So Samson went and caught 300 foxes *or* jackals and took torches and turning the foxes tail to tail, he put a torch between each pair of tails.

5 And when he had set the torches ablaze, he let the foxes go into the standing grain of the Philistines, and he burned up the shocks and the standing grain, along with the olive orchards.

6 Then the Philistines said, Who has done this? And they were told, Samson, the son-in-law of the Timnite, because he [the Timnite] has taken his [Samson's] wife and has given her to his companion. And the Philistines came up and burned her and her father with fire.

7 And Samson said to them, If this is the way you act, surely I will take revenge on you, and after that I will quit.

8 And he smote them hip and thigh [unsparingly], a great slaughter; and he went down and dwelt in the cleft of the rock of Etam.

9 Then the Philistines came up and encamped in Judah and spread themselves in Lehi.

10 And the men of Judah said, Why have you come up against us? And they answered, We have come up to bind Samson, to do to him as he has done to us.

11 Then 3,000 men of Judah went down to the cleft of the rock Etam and said to Samson, Have you not known that the Philistines are rulers over us? What is this that you have done to us? He said to them, As they did to me, so have I done to them.

12 And they said to him, We have come down to bind you, that we may deliver you into the hands of the Philistines. And Samson said to them, Swear to me that you will not fall upon me yourselves.

13 And they said to him, No, we will bind you fast and give you into their hand; but surely we will not kill you. So they bound him with two new ropes and brought him up from the rock.

14 And when he came to Lehi, the Philistines came shouting to meet him. And the Spirit of the Lord came mightily upon [Samson], and the ropes on his arms became as flax that had caught fire, and his bonds melted off his hands.

15 And he found a still moist jawbone of a donkey and reached out and took it and slew 1,000 men with it.

16 And Samson said, With the jawbone of a donkey, heaps upon heaps, with the jawbone of a donkey I have slain 1,000 men!

---

*a*Or, *apparel*   *b*Heb. *let her be thine*   *c*Or, *Now shall I be blameless from the Philistines, though*   *d*Or, *torches*   *e*Heb. *went down*   *f*Heb. *were melted*   *g*Heb. *moist*   *h*Heb. *an heap, two heaps*

New American Standard

19 Then the Spirit of the LORD came upon him mightily, and he went down to Ashkelon and killed thirty of them and took their spoil and gave the changes of clothes to those who told the riddle. And his anger burned, and he went up to his father's house.

20 But Samson's wife was given to his companion who had been his friend.

Samson Burns Philistine Crops

15 BUT AFTER a while, in the time of wheat harvest, Samson visited his wife with a young goat, and said, "I will go in to my wife in her room." But her father did not let him enter.

2 Her father said, "I really thought that you hated her intensely; so I gave her to your companion. Is not her younger sister more beautiful than she? Please let her be yours instead."

3 Samson then said to them, "This time I shall be blameless in regard to the Philistines when I do them harm."

4 Samson went and caught three hundred foxes, and took torches, and turned the foxes tail to tail and put one torch in the middle between two tails.

5 When he had set fire to the torches, he released the foxes into the standing grain of the Philistines, thus burning up both the shocks and the standing grain, along with the vineyards and groves.

6 Then the Philistines said, "Who did this?" And they said, "Samson, the son-in-law of the Timnite, because he took his wife and gave her to his companion." So the Philistines came up and burned her and her father with fire.

7 Samson said to them, "Since you act like this, I will surely take revenge on you, but after that I will quit."

8 He struck them ruthlessly with a great slaughter; and he went down and lived in the cleft of the rock of Etam.

9 ¶ Then the Philistines went up and camped in Judah, and spread out in Lehi.

10 The men of Judah said, "Why have you come up against us?" And they said, "We have come up to bind Samson in order to do to him as he did to us."

11 Then 3,000 men of Judah went down to the cleft of the rock of Etam and said to Samson, "Do you not know that the Philistines are rulers over us? What then is this that you have done to us?" And he said to them, "As they did to me, so I have done to them."

12 They said to him, "We have come down to bind you so that we may give you into the hands of the Philistines." And Samson said to them, "Swear to me that you will not kill me."

13 So they said to him, "No, but we will bind you fast and give you into their hands; yet surely we will not kill you." Then they bound him with two new ropes and brought him up from the rock.

14 ¶ When he came to Lehi, the Philistines shouted as they met him. And the Spirit of the LORD came upon him mightily so that the ropes that were on his arms were as flax that is burned with fire, and his bonds dropped from his hands.

15 He found a fresh jawbone of a donkey, so he reached out and took it and killed a thousand men with it.

16 Then Samson said,

"With the jawbone of a donkey,
Heaps upon heaps,
With the jawbone of a donkey
I have killed a thousand men."

New International

19 Then the Spirit of the LORD came upon him in power. He went down to Ashkelon, struck down thirty of their men, stripped them of their belongings and gave their clothes to those who had explained the riddle. Burning with anger, he went up to his father's house. 20 And Samson's wife was given to the friend who had attended him at his wedding.

Samson's Vengeance on the Philistines

15 LATER ON, at the time of wheat harvest, Samson took a young goat and went to visit his wife. He said, "I'm going to my wife's room." But her father would not let him go in.

2 "I was so sure you thoroughly hated her," he said, "that I gave her to your friend. Isn't her younger sister more attractive? Take her instead."

3 Samson said to them, "This time I have a right to get even with the Philistines; I will really harm them." 4 So he went out and caught three hundred foxes and tied them tail to tail in pairs. He then fastened a torch to every pair of tails, 5 lit the torches and let the foxes loose in the standing grain of the Philistines. He burned up the shocks and standing grain, together with the vineyards and olive groves.

6 When the Philistines asked, "Who did this?" they were told, "Samson, the Timnite's son-in-law, because his wife was given to his friend."

So the Philistines went up and burned her and her father to death. 7 Samson said to them, "Since you've acted like this, I won't stop until I get my revenge on you." 8 He attacked them viciously and slaughtered many of them. Then he went down and stayed in a cave in the rock of Etam.

9 The Philistines went up and camped in Judah, spreading out near Lehi. 10 The men of Judah asked, "Why have you come to fight us?"

"We have come to take Samson prisoner," they answered, "to do to him as he did to us."

11 Then three thousand men from Judah went down to the cave in the rock of Etam and said to Samson, "Don't you realize that the Philistines are rulers over us? What have you done to us?"

He answered, "I merely did to them what they did to me."

12 They said to him, "We've come to tie you up and hand you over to the Philistines."

Samson said, "Swear to me that you won't kill me yourselves."

13 "Agreed," they answered. "We will only tie you up and hand you over to them. We will not kill you." So they bound him with two new ropes and led him up from the rock. 14 As he approached Lehi, the Philistines came toward him shouting. The Spirit of the LORD came upon him in power. The ropes on his arms became like charred flax, and the bindings dropped from his hands. 15 Finding a fresh jawbone of a donkey, he grabbed it and struck down a thousand men.

16 Then Samson said,

"With a donkey's jawbone
  I have made donkeys of them.[w]
With a donkey's jawbone
  I have killed a thousand men."

---

w 16 Or made a heap or two; the Hebrew for donkey sounds like the Hebrew for heap.

King James

17And it came to pass, when he had made an end of speaking, that he cast away the jawbone out of his hand, and called that place *i*Ramath-lehi.

18 ¶ And he was sore athirst, and called on the LORD, and said, Thou hast given this great deliverance into the hand of thy servant: and now shall I die for thirst, and fall into the hand of the uncircumcised?

19But God clave an hollow place that *was* in *j*the jaw, and there came water thereout; and when he had drunk, his spirit came again, and he revived: wherefore he called the name thereof *k*En-hakkore, which *is* in Lehi unto this day.

20*l*And he judged Israel in the days of the Philistines twenty years.

Samson and Delilah

16 THEN WENT Samson to Gaza, and saw there *m*an harlot, and went in unto her.

2*And it was told* the Gazites, saying, Samson is come hither. And they compassed *him* in, and laid wait for him all night in the gate of the city, and were *n*quiet all the night, saying, In the morning, when it is day, we shall kill him.

3And Samson lay till midnight, and arose at midnight, and took the doors of the gate of the city, and the two posts, and went away with them, *o*bar and all, and put *them* upon his shoulders, and carried them up to the top of an hill that *is* before Hebron.

4 ¶ And it came to pass afterward, that he loved a woman *p*in the valley of Sorek, whose name *was* Delilah.

5And the lords of the Philistines came up unto her, and said unto her, Entice him, and see wherein his great strength *lieth,* and by what *means* we may prevail against him, that we may bind him to *q*afflict him: and we will give thee every one of us eleven hundred *pieces* of silver.

6 ¶ And Delilah said to Samson, Tell me, I pray thee, wherein thy great strength *lieth,* and wherewith thou mightest be bound to afflict thee.

7And Samson said unto her, If they bind me with seven *rs*green withs that were never dried, then shall I be weak, and be as *t*another man.

8Then the lords of the Philistines brought up to her seven green withs which had not been dried, and she bound him with them.

9Now *there were* men lying in wait, abiding with her in the chamber. And she said unto him, The Philistines *be* upon thee, Samson. And he brake the withs, as a thread of tow is broken when it *u*toucheth the fire. So his strength was not known.

10And Delilah said unto Samson, Behold, thou hast mocked me, and told me lies: now tell me, I pray thee, wherewith thou mightest be bound.

11And he said unto her, If they bind me fast with new ropes *v*that never were occupied, then shall I be weak, and be as another man.

12Delilah therefore took new ropes, and bound him therewith, and said unto him, The Philistines *be* upon thee, Samson. And *there were* liers in wait abiding in the chamber. And he brake them from off his arms like a thread.

13And Delilah said unto Samson, Hitherto thou hast mocked me, and told me lies: tell me wherewith thou mightest be bound. And he said unto her, If thou weavest the seven locks of my head with the web.

Amplified

17And when he stopped speaking, he cast the jawbone from his hand; and that place was called Ramath-lehi [the hill of the jawbone].

18Samson was very thirsty, and he prayed to the Lord and said, You have given this great deliverance by the hand of Your servant, and now shall I die of thirst and fall into the hands of the uncircumcised?

19And God split open the hollow place that was at Lehi, and water came out of it. And when he drank, his spirit returned and he revived. Therefore the name of it was called En-hakkore [the spring of him who prayed], which is at Lehi to this day.

20And [Samson] judged (defended) Israel in the days of the Philistines twenty years. [Judg. 17:6.]

16 THEN SAMSON went to Gaza and saw a harlot there, and went in to her.

2The Gazites were told, Samson has come here. So they surrounded the place and lay in wait for him all night at the gate of the city. They were quiet all night, saying, In the morning, when it is light, we will kill him.

3But Samson lay until midnight, and [then] he arose and took hold of the doors of the city's gate and the two posts, and pulling them up, bar and all, he put them on his shoulders and carried them to the top of the hill that is before Hebron.

4After this he loved a woman in the Valley of Sorek whose name was Delilah.

5And the lords of the Philistines came to her and said to her, Entice him and see in what his great strength lies, and by what means we may overpower him that we may bind him to subdue him. And we will each give you 1,100 pieces of silver.

6And Delilah said to Samson, Tell me, I pray you, wherein your great strength lies, and with what you might be bound to subdue you.

7And Samson said to her, If they bind me with seven fresh, strong gutstrings, still moist, then shall I be weak and be like any other man.

8Then the Philistine lords brought to her seven fresh, strong bowstrings, still moist, and she bound him with them.

9Now she had men lying in wait in an inner room. And she said to him, The Philistines are upon you, Samson! And he broke the bowstrings as a string of tow breaks when it touches the fire. So the secret of his strength was not known.

10And Delilah said to Samson, Behold, you have mocked me and told me lies; now tell me, I pray you, how you might be bound.

11And he said to her, If they bind me fast with new ropes that have not been used, then I shall become weak and be like any other man.

12So Delilah took new ropes and bound him with them and said to him, The Philistines are upon you, Samson! And the men lying in wait were in the inner room. But he snapped the ropes off his arms like [sewing] thread.

13And Delilah said to Samson, Until now you have mocked me and told me lies; tell me with what you might be bound. And he said to her, If you weave the seven braids of [the hair of] my head with the web.

---

*i*i.e. *The lifting up of the jawbone,* or, *casting away of the jawbone*
*j*Or, *Lehi*   *k*i.e. *The well of him that called,* or, *cried*   *l*He
   ms to have judged Southwest Israel during twenty years of their
       de of the Philistines   *m*Heb. *a woman an harlot*
       ilent   *o*Heb. *with the bar*   *p*Or, *by the brook*
       le   *r*Or, *new cords*   *s*Heb. *moist*   *t*Heb. *one*
       th   *v*Heb. *wherewith work hath not been done*

New American Standard

17 When he had finished speaking, he threw the jaw-bone from his hand; and he named that place *p*Ramath-lehi.

18 Then he became very thirsty, and he called to the LORD and said, "You have given this great deliverance by the hand of Your servant, and now shall I die of thirst and fall into the hands of the uncircumcised?"

19 But God split the hollow place that is in Lehi so that water came out of it. When he drank, his strength returned and he revived. Therefore he named it En-hakkore, which is in Lehi to this day.

20 So he judged Israel twenty years in the days of the Philistines.

Samson's Weakness

16 NOW SAMSON went to Gaza and saw a harlot there, and went in to her.

2 *When it was told* to the Gazites, saying, "Samson has come here," they surrounded *the place* and lay in wait for him all night at the gate of the city. And they kept silent all night, saying, "*Let us wait* until the morning light, then we will kill him."

3 Now Samson lay until midnight, and at midnight he arose and took hold of the doors of the city gate and the two posts and pulled them up along with the bars; then he put them on his shoulders and carried them up to the top of the mountain which is opposite Hebron.

4 ¶ After this it came about that he loved a woman in the valley of Sorek, whose name was Delilah.

5 The lords of the Philistines came up to her and said to her, "Entice him, and see where his great strength *lies* and how we may overpower him that we may bind him to afflict him. Then we will each give you eleven hundred *pieces* of silver."

6 So Delilah said to Samson, "Please tell me where your great strength is and how you may be bound to afflict you."

7 Samson said to her, "If they bind me with seven fresh cords that have not been dried, then I will become weak and be like any *other* man."

8 Then the lords of the Philistines brought up to her seven fresh cords that had not been dried, and she bound him with them.

9 Now she had *men* lying in wait in an inner room. And she said to him, "The Philistines are upon you, Samson!" But he snapped the cords as a string of tow snaps when it touches fire. So his strength was not discovered.

10 ¶ Then Delilah said to Samson, "Behold, you have deceived me and told me lies; now please tell me how you may be bound."

11 He said to her, "If they bind me tightly with new ropes which have not been used, then I will become weak and be like any *other* man."

12 So Delilah took new ropes and bound him with them and said to him, "The Philistines are upon you, Samson!" For the *men* were lying in wait in the inner room. But he snapped the ropes from his arms like a thread.

13 ¶ Then Delilah said to Samson, "Up to now you have deceived me and told me lies; tell me how you may be bound." And he said to her, "If you weave the seven locks of my hair with the web *q*[and fasten it with a pin, then I will become weak and be like any other man.]"

New International

17When he finished speaking, he threw away the jawbone; and the place was called Ramath Lehi.*x*

18Because he was very thirsty, he cried out to the LORD, "You have given your servant this great victory. Must I now die of thirst and fall into the hands of the uncircumcised?" 19Then God opened up the hollow place in Lehi, and water came out of it. When Samson drank, his strength returned and he revived. So the spring was called En Hak-kore,*y* and it is still there in Lehi.

20Samson led*z* Israel for twenty years in the days of the Philistines.

Samson and Delilah

16 ONE DAY Samson went to Gaza, where he saw a prostitute. He went in to spend the night with her. 2The people of Gaza were told, "Samson is here!" So they surrounded the place and lay in wait for him all night at the city gate. They made no move during the night, saying, "At dawn we'll kill him."

3But Samson lay there only until the middle of the night. Then he got up and took hold of the doors of the city gate, together with the two posts, and tore them loose, bar and all. He lifted them to his shoulders and carried them to the top of the hill that faces Hebron.

4Some time later, he fell in love with a woman in the Valley of Sorek whose name was Delilah. 5The rulers of the Philistines went to her and said, "See if you can lure him into showing you the secret of his great strength and how we can overpower him so we may tie him up and subdue him. Each one of us will give you eleven hundred shekels*a* of silver."

6So Delilah said to Samson, "Tell me the secret of your great strength and how you can be tied up and subdued."

7Samson answered her, "If anyone ties me with seven fresh thongs*b* that have not been dried, I'll become as weak as any other man."

8Then the rulers of the Philistines brought her seven fresh thongs that had not been dried, and she tied him with them. 9With men hidden in the room, she called to him, "Samson, the Philistines are upon you!" But he snapped the thongs as easily as a piece of string snaps when it comes close to a flame. So the secret of his strength was not discovered.

10Then Delilah said to Samson, "You have made a fool of me; you lied to me. Come now, tell me how you can be tied."

11He said, "If anyone ties me securely with new ropes that have never been used, I'll become as weak as any other man."

12So Delilah took new ropes and tied him with them. Then, with men hidden in the room, she called to him, "Samson, the Philistines are upon you!" But he snapped the ropes off his arms as if they were threads.

13Delilah then said to Samson, "Until now, you have been making a fool of me and lying to me. Tell me how you can be tied."

He replied, "If you weave the seven braids of my head into the fabric ⌞on the loom⌟ and tighten it with the pin, I'll become as weak as any other man." So while he was sleeping, Delilah took the seven braids of his head,

---

King James

¹⁴And she fastened *it* with the pin, and said unto him, The Philistines *be* upon thee, Samson. And he awaked out of his sleep, and went away with the pin of the beam, and with the web.

¹⁵ ¶ And she said unto him, How canst thou say, I love thee, when thine heart *is* not with me? thou hast mocked me these three times, and hast not told me wherein thy great strength *lieth*.

¹⁶And it came to pass, when she pressed him daily with her words, and urged him, *so* that his soul was ^wvexed unto death;

¹⁷That he told her all his heart, and said unto her, There hath not come a razor upon mine head; for I *have been* a Nazarite unto God from my mother's womb: if I be shaven, then my strength will go from me, and I shall become weak, and be like any *other* man.

¹⁸And when Delilah saw that he had told her all his heart, she sent and called for the lords of the Philistines, saying, Come up this once, for he hath shown me all his heart. Then the lords of the Philistines came up unto her, and brought money in their hand.

¹⁹And she made him sleep upon her knees; and she called for a man, and she caused him to shave off the seven locks of his head; and she began to afflict him, and his strength went from him.

²⁰And she said, The Philistines *be* upon thee, Samson. And he awoke out of his sleep, and said, I will go out as at other times before, and shake myself. And he wist not that the LORD was departed from him.

²¹ ¶ But the Philistines took him, and ^xput out his eyes, and brought him down to Gaza, and bound him with fetters of brass; and he did grind in the prison house.

²²Howbeit the hair of his head began to grow again ^yafter he was shaven.

Samson's revenge and death

²³Then the lords of the Philistines gathered them together for to offer a great sacrifice unto Dagon their god, and to rejoice: for they said, Our god hath delivered Samson our enemy into our hand.

²⁴And when the people saw him, they praised their god: for they said, Our god hath delivered into our hands our enemy, and the destroyer of our country, ^zwhich slew many of us.

²⁵And it came to pass, when their hearts were merry, that they said, Call for Samson, that he may make us sport. And they called for Samson out of the prison house; and he made ^athem sport: and they set him between the pillars.

²⁶And Samson said unto the lad that held him by the hand, Suffer me that I may feel the pillars whereupon the house standeth, that I may lean upon them.

²⁷Now the house was full of men and women; and all the lords of the Philistines *were* there; and *there were* upon the roof about three thousand men and women, that beheld while Samson made sport.

²⁸And Samson called unto the LORD, and said, O Lord GOD, remember me, I pray thee, and strengthen me, I pray thee, only this once, O God, that I may be at once avenged of the Philistines for my two eyes.

²⁹And Samson took hold of the two middle pillars upon which the house stood, and ^bon which it was borne up, of the one with his right hand, and of the other with his left.

³⁰And Samson said, Let ^cme die with the Philistines. And he bowed himself with *all his* might; and the house fell upon the lords, and upon all the people that *were* therein. So the dead which he slew at his death were more than *they* which he slew in his life.

Amplified

¹⁴And she did so and fastened it with the pin and said to him, The Philistines are upon you, Samson! And he awoke out of his sleep and went away with the pin of the [weaver's] beam and with the web.

¹⁵And she said to him, How can you say, I love you, when your heart is not with me? You have mocked me these three times and have not told me in what your great strength lies.

¹⁶And when she pressed him day after day with her words and urged him, he was vexed to death.

¹⁷Then he told her all his mind and said to her, A razor has never come upon my head, for I have been a Nazirite to God from my birth. If I am shaved, then my strength will go from me, and I shall become weak and be like any other man.

¹⁸And when Delilah saw that he had told her all his mind, she went and called for the Philistine lords, saying, Come up this once, for he has told me all he knows. Then the Philistine lords came up to her and brought the money in their hands.

¹⁹And she made Samson sleep upon her knees, and she called a man and caused him to shave off the seven braids of his head. Then she began to torment [Samson], and his strength went from him.

²⁰She said, The Philistines are upon you, Samson! And he awoke out of his sleep and said, I will go out as I have time after time and shake myself free. For Samson did not know that the Lord had departed from him.

²¹But the Philistines laid hold of him, bored out his eyes, and brought him down to Gaza and bound him with [two] bronze fetters; and he ground at the mill in the prison.

²²But the hair of his head began to grow again after it had been shaved.

²³Then the Philistine lords gathered together to offer a great sacrifice to Dagon their god and to rejoice, for they said, Our god has given Samson our enemy into our hands.

²⁴And when the people saw Samson, they praised their god, for they said, Our god has delivered into our hands our enemy, the ravager of our country, who has slain many of us.

²⁵And when their hearts were merry, they said, Call for Samson, that he may make sport for us. So they called [blind] Samson out of the prison, and he made sport before them. They made him stand between the pillars.

²⁶And Samson said to the lad who held him by the hand, Allow me to feel the pillars upon which the house rests, that I may lean against them.

²⁷Now the house was full of men and women; all the Philistine princes were there, and on the roof were about 3,000 men and women who looked on while Samson made sport.

²⁸Then Samson called to the Lord and said, O Lord God, [earnestly] remember me, I pray You, and strengthen me, I pray You, only this once, O God, and let me have one vengeance upon the Philistines for both my eyes.

²⁹And Samson laid hold of the two middle pillars by which the house was borne up, one with his right hand and the other with his left.

³⁰And Samson cried, Let me die with the Philistines! And he bowed himself mightily, and the house fell upon the princes and upon all the people that were in it. So the dead whom he slew at his death were more than they whom he slew in his life.

New American Standard

14 So while he slept, Delilah took the seven locks of his hair and wove them into the web]. And she fastened *it* with the pin and said to him, "The Philistines are upon you, Samson!" But he awoke from his sleep and pulled out the pin of the loom and the web.

Delilah Extracts His Secret

15 ¶ Then she said to him, "How can you say, 'I love you,' when your heart is not with me? You have deceived me these three times and have not told me where your great strength is."

16 It came about when she pressed him daily with her words and urged him, that his soul was annoyed to death.

17 So he told her all *that was* in his heart and said to her, "A razor has never come on my head, for I have been a Nazirite to God from my mother's womb. If I am shaved, then my strength will leave me and I will become weak and be like any *other* man."

18 ¶ When Delilah saw that he had told her all *that was* in his heart, she sent and called the lords of the Philistines, saying, "Come up once more, for he has told me all *that is* in his heart." Then the lords of the Philistines came up to her and brought the money in their hands.

19 She made him sleep on her knees, and called for a man and had him shave off the seven locks of his hair. Then she began to afflict him, and his strength left him.

20 She said, "The Philistines are upon you, Samson!" And he awoke from his sleep and said, "I will go out as at other times and shake myself free." But he did not know that the LORD had departed from him.

21 Then the Philistines seized him and gouged out his eyes; and they brought him down to Gaza and bound him with bronze chains, and he was a grinder in the prison.

22 However, the hair of his head began to grow again after it was shaved off.

23 ¶ Now the lords of the Philistines assembled to offer a great sacrifice to Dagon their god, and to rejoice, for they said,

"Our god has given Samson our enemy into our hands."

24 When the people saw him, they praised their god, for they said,

"Our god has given Samson our enemy into our hands,
Even the destroyer of our country,
Who has slain many of us."

25 It so happened when they were in high spirits, that they said, "Call for Samson, that he may amuse us." So they called for Samson from the prison, and he entertained them. And they made him stand between the pillars.

26 Then Samson said to the boy who was holding his hand, "Let me feel the pillars on which the house rests, that I may lean against them."

27 Now the house was full of men and women, and all the lords of the Philistines were there. And about 3,000 men and women were on the roof looking on while Samson was amusing *them*.

Samson Is Avenged

28 ¶ Then Samson called to the LORD and said, "O Lord GOD, please remember me and please strengthen me just this time, O God, that I may at once be avenged of the Philistines for my two eyes."

29 Samson grasped the two middle pillars on which the house rested, and braced himself against them, the one with his right hand and the other with his left.

30 And Samson said, "Let me die with the Philistines!" And he bent with all his might so that the house fell on the lords and all the people who were in it. So the dead whom he killed at his death were more than those whom he killed in his life.

New International

wove them into the fabric [14]and[c] tightened it with the pin.

Again she called to him, "Samson, the Philistines are upon you!" He awoke from his sleep and pulled up the pin and the loom, with the fabric.

15 Then she said to him, "How can you say, 'I love you,' when you won't confide in me? This is the third time you have made a fool of me and haven't told me the secret of your great strength." 16 With such nagging she prodded him day after day until he was tired to death.

17 So he told her everything. "No razor has ever been used on my head," he said, "because I have been a Nazirite set apart to God since birth. If my head were shaved, my strength would leave me, and I would become as weak as any other man."

18 When Delilah saw that he had told her everything, she sent word to the rulers of the Philistines, "Come back once more; he has told me everything." So the rulers of the Philistines returned with the silver in their hands. 19 Having put him to sleep on her lap, she called a man to shave off the seven braids of his hair, and so began to subdue him.[d] And his strength left him.

20 Then she called, "Samson, the Philistines are upon you!"

He awoke from his sleep and thought, "I'll go out as before and shake myself free." But he did not know that the LORD had left him.

21 Then the Philistines seized him, gouged out his eyes and took him down to Gaza. Binding him with bronze shackles, they set him to grinding in the prison. 22 But the hair on his head began to grow again after it had been shaved.

The Death of Samson

23 Now the rulers of the Philistines assembled to offer a great sacrifice to Dagon their god and to celebrate, saying, "Our god has delivered Samson, our enemy, into our hands."

24 When the people saw him, they praised their god, saying,

"Our god has delivered our enemy
    into our hands,
the one who laid waste our land
    and multiplied our slain."

25 While they were in high spirits, they shouted, "Bring out Samson to entertain us." So they called Samson out of the prison, and he performed for them.

When they stood him among the pillars, 26 Samson said to the servant who held his hand, "Put me where I can feel the pillars that support the temple, so that I may lean against them." 27 Now the temple was crowded with men and women; all the rulers of the Philistines were there, and on the roof were about three thousand men and women watching Samson perform. 28 Then Samson prayed to the LORD, "O Sovereign LORD, remember me. O God, please strengthen me just once more, and let me with one blow get revenge on the Philistines for my two eyes." 29 Then Samson reached toward the two central pillars on which the temple stood. Bracing himself against them, his right hand on the one and his left hand on the other, 30 Samson said, "Let me die with the Philistines!" Then he pushed with all his might, and down came the temple on the rulers and all the people in it. Thus he killed many more when he died than while he lived.

---

c 13,14 Some Septuagint manuscripts; Hebrew *"I can, if you weave the seven braids of my head into the fabric on the loom."* *14So she*
d 19 Hebrew; some Septuagint manuscripts *and he began to weaken*

King James

³¹Then his brethren and all the house of his father came down, and took him, and brought *him* up, and buried him between Zorah and Eshtaol in the buryingplace of Manoah his father. And he judged Israel twenty years.

Micah's idols and priest

17 AND THERE was a man of mount Ephraim, whose name *was* Micah.

²And he said unto his mother, The eleven hundred *shekels* of silver that were taken from thee, about which thou cursedst, and spakest of also in mine ears, behold, the silver *is* with me; I took it. And his mother said, Blessed *be thou* of the LORD, my son.

³And when he had restored the eleven hundred *shekels* of silver to his mother, his mother said, I had wholly dedicated the silver unto the LORD from my hand for my son, to make a graven image and a molten image: now therefore I will restore it unto thee.

⁴Yet he restored the money unto his mother; and his mother took two hundred *shekels* of silver, and gave them to the founder, who made thereof a graven image and a molten image: and they were in the house of Micah.

⁵And the man Micah had an house of gods, and made an ephod, and teraphim, and ᵈconsecrated one of his sons, who became his priest.

⁶In those days *there was* no king in Israel, *but* every man did *that which was* right in his own eyes.

⁷ ¶ And there was a young man out of Bethlehem-judah of the family of Judah, who *was* a Levite, and he sojourned there.

⁸And the man departed out of the city from Bethlehem-judah to sojourn where he could find *a place:* and he came to mount Ephraim to the house of Micah, ᵉas he journeyed.

⁹And Micah said unto him, Whence comest thou? And he said unto him, I *am* a Levite of Bethlehem-judah, and I go to sojourn where I may find *a place.*

¹⁰And Micah said unto him, Dwell with me, and be unto me a father and a priest, and I will give thee ten *shekels* of silver by the year, and ᶠᵍa suit of apparel, and thy victuals. So the Levite went in.

¹¹And the Levite was content to dwell with the man; and the young man was unto him as one of his sons.

¹²And Micah consecrated the Levite; and the young man became his priest, and was in the house of Micah.

¹³Then said Micah, Now know I that the LORD will do me good, seeing I have a Levite to *my* priest.

Danites overtake Laish

18 IN THOSE days *there was* no king in Israel: and in those days the tribe of the Danites sought them an inheritance to dwell in; for unto that day *all their* inheritance had not fallen unto them among the tribes of Israel.

²And the children of Dan sent of their family five men from their coasts, ʰmen of valour, from Zorah, and from Eshtaol, to spy out the land, and to search it; and they said unto them, Go, search the land: who when they came to mount Ephraim, to the house of Micah, they lodged there.

³When they *were* by the house of Micah, they knew the voice of the young man the Levite: and they turned in thither, and said unto him, Who brought thee hither? and what makest thou in this *place?* and what hast thou here?

⁴And he said unto them, Thus and thus dealeth Micah with me, and hath hired me, and I am his priest.

Amplified

³¹Then his kinsmen and all the tribal family of his father came down, took his body, and brought it up; and they buried him between Zorah and Eshtaol in the burial place of Manoah his father. He had judged Israel [that is, had defended the Israelites] twenty years. [Judg. 17:6; Heb. 11:32.]

17 THERE WAS a man of the hill country of Ephraim whose name was Micah.

²And he said to his mother, The 1,100 shekels of silver that were taken from you, about which you cursed and also spoke about in my hearing, behold, I have the silver with me; I took it. And his mother said, Blessed be you by the Lord, my son!

³He restored the 1,100 shekels of silver to his mother, and she said, I had truly dedicated the silver to the Lord from my hand for my son to make a graven image and a molten image; now therefore, I will restore it to you.

⁴So when he restored the money to his mother, she took 200 pieces of silver and gave them to the silversmith, who made of it a graven image and a molten image; and they were in the house of Micah.

⁵And the man Micah had a house of gods, and he made an ephod and teraphim and dedicated one of his sons, who became his priest.

⁶In those days there was no king in Israel; every man did what was right in his own eyes.

⁷And there was a young man in Bethlehem of Judah, of the family of Judah, who was a Levite; and he sojourned there.

⁸And the man departed from the town of Bethlehem in Judah to sojourn where he could find a place, and as he journeyed he came to the hill country of Ephraim to the house of Micah.

⁹And Micah said to him, From where do you come? And he said to him, I am a Levite of Bethlehem in Judah, and I go to sojourn where I may find a place.

¹⁰And Micah said to him, Dwell with me and be to me a father and a priest, and I will give you ten pieces of silver each year, a suit of clothes, and your living. So the Levite went in.

¹¹And the Levite was content to dwell with the man, and the young man was to Micah as one of his sons.

¹²And Micah consecrated the Levite, and the young man became his priest and was in the house of Micah.

¹³Then said Micah, Now I know that the Lord will favor me, since I have a Levite to be my priest.

18 IN THOSE days there was no king in Israel. And in those days the tribe of the Danites sought for itself an inheritance to dwell in, for until then no [sufficient] inheritance had been acquired by them among the tribes of Israel.

²So the Danites sent from the whole number of their tribe five brave men from Zorah and Eshtaol to spy out the land and to explore it, and they said to them, Go, explore the land. They came to the hill country of Ephraim, to the house of Micah, and lodged there.

³When they went by the house of Micah, they recognized the voice of the young Levite, and they turned aside there and said to him, Who brought you here? And what do you do in this place? And what have you here?

⁴And he said to them, Thus and thus Micah deals with me and has hired me, and I am his priest.

ᵈ *the hand*   ᵉ Heb. *in making his way*   ᶠOr, *a*
ᵍ Heb. *an order of garments*   ʰ Heb. *sons*

New American Standard

31 Then his brothers and all his father's household came down, took him, brought him up and buried him between Zorah and Eshtaol in the tomb of Manoah his father. Thus he had judged Israel twenty years.

Micah's Idolatry

17 NOW THERE was a man of the hill country of Ephraim whose name was Micah.

2 He said to his mother, "The eleven hundred *pieces* of silver which were taken from you, about which you uttered a curse in my hearing, behold, the silver is with me; I took it." And his mother said, "Blessed be my son by the LORD."

3 He then returned the eleven hundred *pieces* of silver to his mother, and his mother said, "I wholly dedicate the silver from my hand to the LORD for my son to make a graven image and a molten image; now therefore, I will return them to you."

4 So when he returned the silver to his mother, his mother took two hundred *pieces* of silver and gave them to the silversmith who made them into a graven image and a molten image, and they were in the house of Micah.

5 And the man Micah had a ʳshrine and he made an ephod and household idols and consecrated one of his sons, that he might become his priest.

6 In those days there was no king in Israel; every man did what was right in his own eyes.

7 ¶ Now there was a young man from Bethlehem in Judah, of the family of Judah, who was a Levite; and he was staying there.

8 Then the man departed from the city, from Bethlehem in Judah, to stay wherever he might find *a place*; and as he made his journey, he came to the hill country of Ephraim to the house of Micah.

9 Micah said to him, "Where do you come from?" And he said to him, "I am a Levite from Bethlehem in Judah, and I am going to stay wherever I may find *a place*."

10 Micah then said to him, "Dwell with me and be a father and a priest to me, and I will give you ten *pieces* of silver a year, a suit of clothes, and your maintenance." So the Levite went *in*.

11 The Levite agreed to live with the man, and the young man became to him like one of his sons.

12 So Micah consecrated the Levite, and the young man became his priest and lived in the house of Micah.

13 Then Micah said, "Now I know that the LORD will prosper me, seeing I have a Levite as priest."

Danites Seek Territory

18 IN THOSE days there was no king of Israel; and in those days the tribe of the Danites was seeking an inheritance for themselves to live in, for until that day an inheritance had not been allotted to them as a possession among the tribes of Israel.

2 So the sons of Dan sent from their family five men out of their whole number, valiant men from Zorah and Eshtaol, to spy out the land and to search it; and they said to them, "Go, search the land." And they came to the hill country of Ephraim, to the house of Micah, and lodged there.

3 When they were near the house of Micah, they recognized the voice of the young man, the Levite; and they turned aside there and said to him, "Who brought you here? And what are you doing in this *place?* And what do you have here?"

4 He said to them, "Thus and so has Micah done to me, and he has hired me and I have become his priest."

ʳLit *house of gods*

New International

31 Then his brothers and his father's whole family went down to get him. They brought him back and buried him between Zorah and Eshtaol in the tomb of Manoah his father. He had ledᵉ Israel twenty years.

Micah's Idols

17 NOW A man named Micah from the hill country of Ephraim 2 said to his mother, "The eleven hundred shekelsᶠ of silver that were taken from you and about which I heard you utter a curse—I have that silver with me; I took it."

Then his mother said, "The LORD bless you, my son!"

3 When he returned the eleven hundred shekels of silver to his mother, she said, "I solemnly consecrate my silver to the LORD for my son to make a carved image and a cast idol. I will give it back to you."

4 So he returned the silver to his mother, and she took two hundred shekelsᵍ of silver and gave them to a silversmith, who made them into the image and the idol. And they were put in Micah's house.

5 Now this man Micah had a shrine, and he made an ephod and some idols and installed one of his sons as his priest. 6 In those days Israel had no king; everyone did as he saw fit.

7 A young Levite from Bethlehem in Judah, who had been living within the clan of Judah, 8 left that town in search of some other place to stay. On his wayʰ he came to Micah's house in the hill country of Ephraim.

9 Micah asked him, "Where are you from?"

"I'm a Levite from Bethlehem in Judah," he said, "and I'm looking for a place to stay."

10 Then Micah said to him, "Live with me and be my father and priest, and I'll give you ten shekelsⁱ of silver a year, your clothes and your food." 11 So the Levite agreed to live with him, and the young man was to him like one of his sons. 12 Then Micah installed the Levite, and the young man became his priest and lived in his house. 13 And Micah said, "Now I know that the LORD will be good to me, since this Levite has become my priest."

Danites Settle in Laish

18 IN THOSE days Israel had no king.

And in those days the tribe of the Danites was seeking a place of their own where they might settle, because they had not yet come into an inheritance among the tribes of Israel. 2 So the Danites sent five warriors from Zorah and Eshtaol to spy out the land and explore it. These men represented all their clans. They told them, "Go, explore the land."

The men entered the hill country of Ephraim and came to the house of Micah, where they spent the night. 3 When they were near Micah's house, they recognized the voice of the young Levite; so they turned in there and asked him, "Who brought you here? What are you doing in this place? Why are you here?"

4 He told them what Micah had done for him, and said, "He has hired me and I am his priest."

ᵉ31 Traditionally *judged*   ᶠ2 That is, about 28 pounds (about 13 kilograms)   ᵍ4 That is, about 5 pounds (about 2.3 kilograms)   ʰ8 Or *To carry on his profession*   ⁱ10 That is, about 4 ounces (about 110 grams)

King James

Amplified

⁵And they said unto him, Ask counsel, we pray thee, of God, that we may know whether our way which we go shall be prosperous.

⁶And the priest said unto them, Go in peace: before the LORD *is* your way wherein ye go.

⁷ ¶ Then the five men departed, and came to Laish, and saw the people that *were* therein, how they dwelt careless, after the manner of the Zidonians, quiet and secure; and *there was* no ⁱmagistrate in the land, that might put *them* to shame in *any* thing; and they *were* far from the Zidonians, and had no business with *any* man.

⁸And they came unto their brethren to Zorah and Eshtaol: and their brethren said unto them, What *say* ye?

⁹And they said, Arise, that we may go up against them: for we have seen the land, and, behold, it *is* very good: and *are* ye still? be not slothful to go, *and* to enter to possess the land.

¹⁰When ye go, ye shall come unto a people secure, and to a large land: for God hath given it into your hands; a place where *there is* no want of any thing that *is* in the earth.

¹¹ ¶ And there went from thence of the family of the Danites, out of Zorah and out of Eshtaol, six hundred men ʲappointed with weapons of war.

¹²And they went up, and pitched in Kirjath-jearim, in Judah: wherefore they called that place Mahaneh-dan unto this day: behold, *it is* behind Kirjath-jearim.

¹³And they passed thence unto mount Ephraim, and came unto the house of Micah.

¹⁴ ¶ Then answered the five men that went to spy out the country of Laish, and said unto their brethren, Do ye know that there is in these houses an ephod, and teraphim, and a graven image, and a molten image? now therefore consider what ye have to do.

¹⁵And they turned thitherward, and came to the house of the young man the Levite, *even* unto the house of Micah, and ᵏsaluted him.

¹⁶And the six hundred men appointed with their weapons of war, which *were* of the children of Dan, stood by the entering of the gate.

¹⁷And the five men that went to spy out the land went up, *and* came in thither, *and* took the graven image, and the ephod, and the teraphim, and the molten image: and the priest stood in the entering of the gate with the six hundred men *that were* appointed with weapons of war.

¹⁸And these went into Micah's house, and fetched the carved image, the ephod, and the teraphim, and the molten image. Then said the priest unto them, What do ye?

¹⁹And they said unto him, Hold thy peace, lay thine hand upon thy mouth, and go with us, and be to us a father and a priest: *is it* better for thee to be a priest unto the house of one man, or that thou be a priest unto a tribe and a family in Israel?

²⁰And the priest's heart was glad, and he took the ephod, and the teraphim, and the graven image, and went in the midst of the people.

²¹So they turned and departed, and put the little ones and the cattle and the carriage before them.

²² ¶ *And* when they were a good way from the house of Micah, the men that *were* in the houses near to Micah's house were gathered together, and overtook the children of Dan.

²³And they cried unto the children of Dan. And they turned their faces, and said unto Micah, What aileth thee, ˡthat thou comest with such a company?

²⁴And he said, Ye have taken away my gods which I made, and the priest, and ye are gone away: and what have I more? and what *is* this *that* ye say unto me, What aileth thee?

⁵And they said to him, Ask counsel, we pray you, of God that we may know whether our journey will be successful.

⁶And the priest said to them, Go in peace. The way in which you go is before (under the eye of) the Lord.

⁷Then the five men departed and came to Laish and saw the people who were there, how they dwelt securely after the manner of the Sidonians, quiet and feeling safe; and there was no magistrate in the land, who might put them to shame in anything *or* injure them; and they were far from the Sidonians and had no dealings with anyone.

⁸The five men came back to their brethren at Zorah and Eshtaol, and their brethren said to them, What do you say?

⁹They said, Arise, let us go up against them, for we have seen the land, and behold, it is very fertile. And will you do nothing? Do not be slow to go and enter in and possess the land.

¹⁰When you go, you will come to people [feeling] safe and secure. The land is broad [widely extended on all sides]; and God has given it into your hands—a place where there is no want of anything that is in the earth.

¹¹And there went from there of the tribe of the Danites, out of Zorah and Eshtaol, 600 men armed with weapons of war.

¹²And they went up and encamped at Kiriath-jearim in Judah. Therefore they called that place Mahaneh-dan [camp of Dan] to this day; it is west of Kiriath-jearim.

¹³And they passed from there to the hill country of Ephraim and came to Micah's house.

¹⁴Then the five men who had gone to spy out the country of Laish said to their brethren, Do you know that there are in these houses an ephod, teraphim, a graven image, and a molten image? Now therefore, consider what you have to do.

¹⁵And they turned in that direction and came to the house of the young Levite, at the home of Micah, and saluted him.

¹⁶Now the 600 Danites with their weapons of war stood at Micah's gate.

¹⁷And the five men who had gone to spy out the land went up and entered the house and took the graven image, the ephod, the teraphim, and the molten image, while the priest stood by the entrance of the gate with the 600 men armed with weapons of war.

¹⁸And when these went into Micah's house and took the carved image, the ephod, the teraphim, and the molten image, the priest said to them, What are you doing?

¹⁹And they said to him, Be still, put your hand over your mouth, and come with us, and be to us a father and a priest. Is it better for you to be a priest to the house of one man, or that you be a priest to a tribe and family in Israel?

²⁰And the priest's heart was glad, and he took the ephod, the teraphim, and the graven image, and went in the midst of the people.

²¹So they turned and departed and put the little ones, the cattle, and the baggage in front of them.

²²When they were a good way from the house of Micah, the men who were Micah's near neighbors were called out and overtook the Danites.

²³They shouted to the Danites, who turned and said to Micah, What ails you, that you come with such a company?

²⁴And he said, You take away my gods which I made and the priest, and go away; and what have I left? How can you say to me, What ails you?

ⁱ Heb. *possessor*, or, *heir of restraint*   ʲHeb. *girded*   ᵏHeb. *asked him of peace*   ˡHeb. *that thou art gathered together?*

New American Standard

5 They said to him, "Inquire of God, please, that we may know whether our way on which we are going will be prosperous."

6 The priest said to them, "Go in peace; your way in which you are going has the LORD'S approval."

7 ¶ Then the five men departed and came to Laish and saw the people who were in it living in security, after the manner of the Sidonians, quiet and secure; for there was no ruler humiliating *them* for anything in the land, and they were far from the Sidonians and had no dealings with anyone.

8 When they came back to their brothers at Zorah and Eshtaol, their brothers said to them, "What *do* you report?"

9 They said, "Arise, and let us go up against them; for we have seen the land, and behold, it is very good. And will you sit still? Do not delay to go, to enter, to possess the land.

10 "When you enter, you will come to a secure people with a spacious land; for God has given it into your hand, a place where there is no lack of anything that is on the earth."

11 ¶ Then from the family of the Danites, from Zorah and from Eshtaol, six hundred men armed with weapons of war set out.

12 They went up and camped at Kiriath-jearim in Judah. Therefore they called that place 𝑠Mahaneh-dan to this day; behold, it is west of Kiriath-jearim.

13 They passed from there to the hill country of Ephraim and came to the house of Micah.

Danites Take Micah's Idols

14 ¶ Then the five men who went to spy out the country of Laish said to their kinsmen, "Do you know that there are in these houses an ephod and 𝑡household idols and a graven image and a molten image? Now therefore, consider what you should do."

15 They turned aside there and came to the house of the young man, the Levite, to the house of Micah, and asked him of his welfare.

16 The six hundred men armed with their weapons of war, who were of the sons of Dan, stood by the entrance of the gate.

17 Now the five men who went to spy out the land went up *and* entered there, *and* took the graven image and the ephod and household idols and the molten image, while the priest stood by the entrance of the gate with the six hundred men armed with weapons of war.

18 When these went into Micah's house and took the graven image, the ephod and household idols and the molten image, the priest said to them, "What are you doing?"

19 They said to him, "Be silent, put your hand over your mouth and come with us, and be to us a father and a priest. Is it better for you to be a priest to the house of one man, or to be priest to a tribe and a family in Israel?"

20 The priest's heart was glad, and he took the ephod and household idols and the graven image and went among the people.

21 ¶ Then they turned and departed, and put the little ones and the livestock and the valuables in front of them.

22 When they had gone some distance from the house of Micah, the men who *were* in the houses near Micah's house assembled and overtook the sons of Dan.

23 They cried to the sons of Dan, who turned around and said to Micah, "What is *the matter* with you, that you have assembled together?"

24 He said, "You have taken away my gods which I made, and the priest, and have gone away, and what do I have besides? So how can you say to me, 'What is *the matter* with you?' "

New International

5 Then they said to him, "Please inquire of God to learn whether our journey will be successful."

6 The priest answered them, "Go in peace. Your journey has the LORD's approval."

7 So the five men left and came to Laish, where they saw that the people were living in safety, like the Sidonians, unsuspecting and secure. And since their land lacked nothing, they were prosperous.𝑗 Also, they lived a long way from the Sidonians and had no relationship with anyone else.𝑘

8 When they returned to Zorah and Eshtaol, their brothers asked them, "How did you find things?"

9 They answered, "Come on, let's attack them! We have seen that the land is very good. Aren't you going to do something? Don't hesitate to go there and take it over.

10 When you get there, you will find an unsuspecting people and a spacious land that God has put into your hands, a land that lacks nothing whatever."

11 Then six hundred men from the clan of the Danites, armed for battle, set out from Zorah and Eshtaol. 12 On their way they set up camp near Kiriath Jearim in Judah. This is why the place west of Kiriath Jearim is called Mahaneh Dan𝑙 to this day. 13 From there they went on to the hill country of Ephraim and came to Micah's house.

14 Then the five men who had spied out the land of Laish said to their brothers, "Do you know that one of these houses has an ephod, other household gods, a carved image and a cast idol? Now you know what to do." 15 So they turned in there and went to the house of the young Levite at Micah's place and greeted him. 16 The six hundred Danites, armed for battle, stood at the entrance to the gate. 17 The five men who had spied out the land went inside and took the carved image, the ephod, the other household gods and the cast idol while the priest and the six hundred armed men stood at the entrance to the gate.

18 When these men went into Micah's house and took the carved image, the ephod, the other household gods and the cast idol, the priest said to them, "What are you doing?"

19 They answered him, "Be quiet! Don't say a word. Come with us, and be our father and priest. Isn't it better that you serve a tribe and clan in Israel as priest rather than just one man's household?" 20 Then the priest was glad. He took the ephod, the other household gods and the carved image and went along with the people. 21 Putting their little children, their livestock and their possessions in front of them, they turned away and left.

22 When they had gone some distance from Micah's house, the men who lived near Micah were called together and overtook the Danites. 23 As they shouted after them, the Danites turned and said to Micah, "What's the matter with you that you called out your men to fight?"

24 He replied, "You took the gods I made, and my priest, and went away. What else do I have? How can you ask, 'What's the matter with you?' "

𝑗7 The meaning of the Hebrew for this clause is uncertain.
𝑘7 Hebrew; some Septuagint manuscripts *with the Arameans*
𝑙12 *Mahaneh Dan* means *Dan's camp*.

𝑠 I.e. the camp of Dan   𝑡 Heb *teraphim*

King James

Amplified

^{25}And the children of Dan said unto him, Let not thy voice be heard among us, lest ^{m}angry fellows run upon thee, and thou lose thy life, with the lives of thy household.

^{26}And the children of Dan went their way: and when Micah saw that they *were* too strong for him, he turned and went back unto his house.

^{27}And they took *the things* which Micah had made, and the priest which he had, and came unto Laish, unto a people *that were* at quiet and secure: and they smote them with the edge of the sword, and burnt the city with fire.

^{28}And *there was* no deliverer, because it *was* far from Zidon, and they had no business with *any* man; and it was in the valley that *lieth* by Beth-rehob. And they built a city, and dwelt therein.

^{29}And they called the name of the city Dan, after the name of Dan their father, who was born unto Israel: howbeit the name of the city *was* Laish at the first.

^{30} ¶ And the children of Dan set up the graven image: and Jonathan, the son of Gershom, the son of Manasseh, he and his sons were priests to the tribe of Dan until the day of the captivity of the land.

^{31}And they set them up Micah's graven image, which he made, all the time that the house of God was in Shiloh.

The Levite and his concubine

19 AND IT came to pass in those days, when *there was* no king in Israel, that there was a certain Levite sojourning on the side of mount Ephraim, who took to him ^{n}a concubine out of Bethlehem-judah.

^{2}And his concubine played the whore against him, and went away from him unto her father's house to Bethlehem-judah, and was there ^{op}four whole months.

^{3}And her husband arose, and went after her, to speak ^{q}friendly unto her, *and* to bring her again, having his servant with him, and a couple of asses: and she brought him into her father's house: and when the father of the damsel saw him, he rejoiced to meet him.

^{4}And his father-in-law, the damsel's father, retained him; and he abode with him three days: so they did eat and drink, and lodged there.

^{5} ¶ And it came to pass on the fourth day, when they arose early in the morning, that he rose up to depart: and the damsel's father said unto his son-in-law, ^{r}Comfort thine heart with a morsel of bread, and afterward go your way.

^{6}And they sat down, and did eat and drink both of them together: for the damsel's father had said unto the man, Be content, I pray thee, and tarry all night, and let thine heart be merry.

^{7}And when the man rose up to depart, his father-in-law urged him: therefore he lodged there again.

^{8}And he arose early in the morning on the fifth day to depart: and the damsel's father said, Comfort thine heart, I pray thee. And they tarried ^{s}until afternoon, and they did eat both of them.

^{9}And when the man rose up to depart, he, and his concubine, and his servant, his father-in-law, the damsel's father, said unto him, Behold, now the day ^{t}draweth toward evening, I pray you tarry all night: behold, ^{u}the day groweth to an end, lodge here, that thine heart may be merry; and tomorrow get you early on your way, that thou mayest go ^{v}home.

^{10}But the man would not tarry that night, but he rose up and departed, and came ^{w}over against Jebus, which *is* Jerusalem; and *there were* with him two asses saddled, his concubine also *was* with him.

^{25}And the men of Dan said to him, Let not your voice be heard among us, lest angry fellows fall upon you and you lose your life with the lives of your household.

^{26}And the Danites went their way; and when Micah saw that they were too strong for him, he turned and went back to his house.

^{27}And they took the things which Micah had made, and his priest, and came to Laish, to a people quiet and feeling secure, and they smote them with the sword and burned the city.

^{28}And there was no deliverer because it was far from Sidon, and they had no business with anyone. It was in the valley which belongs to Beth-rehob. And they rebuilt the city and dwelt in it.

^{29}They named the city Dan, after Dan their forefather who was born to Israel; however, the name of the city was Laish at first.

^{30}And the Danites set up the graven image for themselves; and Jonathan son of Gershom, the son of Moses, and his sons were priests to the tribe of Dan until the day of the captivity of the land.

^{31}So they set them up Micah's graven image which he made, as long as the house of God was at Shiloh.

19 IN THOSE days, when there was no king in Israel, a certain Levite was living temporarily in the most remote part of the hill district of Ephraim, who took to himself a concubine [of inferior status than a wife] from Bethlehem in Judah.

^{2}And his concubine was untrue to him and went away from him to her father's house at Bethlehem of Judah and stayed there the space of four months.

^{3}Then her husband arose and went after her to speak kindly to her [to her heart] and to bring her back, having with him his servant and a couple of donkeys. And she brought him into her father's house, and when her father saw him, he rejoiced to meet him.

^{4}And his father-in-law, the girl's father, [insistently] detained him, and he remained with him three days. So they ate and drank, and he lodged there.

^{5}On the fourth day they arose early in the morning, and the [Levite] prepared to leave, but the girl's father said to his son-in-law, Strengthen your heart with a morsel of bread and afterward go your way.

^{6}So both men sat down and ate and drank together, and the girl's father said to the man, Consent to stay all night and let your heart be merry.

^{7}And when the man rose up to depart, his father-in-law urged him; so he lodged there again.

^{8}And he arose early in the morning on the fifth day to depart, but the girl's father said, Strengthen your heart and tarry until toward evening. So they ate, both of them.

^{9}And when the man and his concubine and his servant rose up to leave, his father-in-law, the girl's father, said to him, Behold, now the day draws toward evening, I pray you stay all night. Behold, now the day grows to an end, lodge here and let your heart be merry, and tomorrow get early on your way and go home.

^{10}But the man would not stay that night; so he rose up and departed and came opposite to Jebus, which is Jerusalem. With him were two saddled donkeys [and his servant] and his concubine.

---

^{m}Heb. *bitter of soul* ^{n}Heb. *a woman a concubine,* or, *a wife a concubine* ^{o}Or, *a year* and *four months* ^{p}Heb. *days four months* ^{q}Heb. *to her heart* ^{r}Heb. *Strengthen* ^{s}Heb. *till the day declined* ^{t}Heb. *is weak* ^{u}Heb. *it is the pitching time of the day* ^{v}Heb. *to thy tent* ^{w}Heb. *to over against*

New American Standard

25 The sons of Dan said to him, "Do not let your voice be heard among us, or else fierce men will fall upon you and you will lose your life, with the lives of your household."

26 So the sons of Dan went on their way; and when Micah saw that they were too strong for him, he turned and went back to his house.

27 ¶ Then they took what Micah had made and the priest who had belonged to him, and came to Laish, to a people quiet and secure, and struck them with the edge of the sword; and they burned the city with fire.

28 And there was no one to deliver *them,* because it was far from Sidon and they had no dealings with anyone, and it was in the valley which is near Beth-rehob. And they rebuilt the city and lived in it.

29 They called the name of the city Dan, after the name of Dan their father who was born in Israel; however, the name of the city formerly was Laish.

30 The sons of Dan set up for themselves the graven image; and Jonathan, the son of Gershom, the son of uManasseh, he and his sons were priests to the tribe of the Danites until the day of the captivity of the land.

31 So they set up for themselves Micah's graven image which he had made, all the time that the house of God was at Shiloh.

A Levite's Concubine Degraded

19 NOW IT came about in those days, when there was no king in Israel, that there was a certain Levite staying in the remote part of the hill country of Ephraim, who took a concubine for himself from Bethlehem in Judah.

2 But his concubine played the harlot against him, and she went away from him to her father's house in Bethlehem in Judah, and was there for a period of four months.

3 Then her husband arose and went after her to speak tenderly to her in order to bring her back, taking with him his servant and a pair of donkeys. So she brought him into her father's house, and when the girl's father saw him, he was glad to meet him.

4 His father-in-law, the girl's father, detained him; and he remained with him three days. So they ate and drank and lodged there.

5 Now on the fourth day they got up early in the morning, and he prepared to go; and the girl's father said to his son-in-law, "Sustain yourself with a piece of bread, and afterward you may go."

6 So both of them sat down and ate and drank together; and the girl's father said to the man, "Please be willing to spend the night, and let your heart be merry."

7 Then the man arose to go, but his father-in-law urged him so that he spent the night there again.

8 On the fifth day he arose to go early in the morning, and the girl's father said, "Please sustain yourself, and wait until afternoon"; so both of them ate.

9 When the man arose to go along with his concubine and servant, his father-in-law, the girl's father, said to him, "Behold now, the day has drawn to a close; please spend the night. Lo, the day is coming to an end; spend the night here that your heart may be merry. Then tomorrow you may arise early for your journey so that you may go home."

10 ¶ But the man was not willing to spend the night, so he arose and departed and came to *a place* opposite Jebus (that is, Jerusalem). And there were with him a pair of saddled donkeys; his concubine also was with him.

New International

25The Danites answered, "Don't argue with us, or some hot-tempered men will attack you, and you and your family will lose your lives." 26So the Danites went their way, and Micah, seeing that they were too strong for him, turned around and went back home.

27Then they took what Micah had made, and his priest, and went on to Laish, against a peaceful and unsuspecting people. They attacked them with the sword and burned down their city. 28There was no one to rescue them because they lived a long way from Sidon and had no relationship with anyone else. The city was in a valley near Beth Rehob.

The Danites rebuilt the city and settled there. 29They named it Dan after their forefather Dan, who was born to Israel—though the city used to be called Laish. 30There the Danites set up for themselves the idols, and Jonathan son of Gershom, the son of Moses,m and his sons were priests for the tribe of Dan until the time of the captivity of the land. 31They continued to use the idols Micah had made, all the time the house of God was in Shiloh.

A Levite and His Concubine

19 IN THOSE days Israel had no king. Now a Levite who lived in a remote area in the hill country of Ephraim took a concubine from Bethlehem in Judah. 2But she was unfaithful to him. She left him and went back to her father's house in Bethlehem, Judah. After she had been there four months, 3her husband went to her to persuade her to return. He had with him his servant and two donkeys. She took him into her father's house, and when her father saw him, he gladly welcomed him. 4His father-in-law, the girl's father, prevailed upon him to stay; so he remained with him three days, eating and drinking, and sleeping there.

5On the fourth day they got up early and he prepared to leave, but the girl's father said to his son-in-law, "Refresh yourself with something to eat; then you can go." 6So the two of them sat down to eat and drink together. Afterward the girl's father said, "Please stay tonight and enjoy yourself." 7And when the man got up to go, his father-in-law persuaded him, so he stayed there that night. 8On the morning of the fifth day, when he rose to go, the girl's father said, "Refresh yourself. Wait till afternoon!" So the two of them ate together.

9Then when the man, with his concubine and his servant, got up to leave, his father-in-law, the girl's father, said, "Now look, it's almost evening. Spend the night here; the day is nearly over. Stay and enjoy yourself. Early tomorrow morning you can get up and be on your way home." 10But, unwilling to stay another night, the man left and went toward Jebus (that is, Jerusalem), with his two saddled donkeys and his concubine.

---

u Some ancient versions read *Moses*

m 30 An ancient Hebrew scribal tradition, some Septuagint manuscripts and Vulgate; Masoretic Text *Manasseh*

King James

¹¹*And* when they *were* by Jebus, the day was far spent; and the servant said unto his master, Come, I pray thee, and let us turn in into this city of the Jebusites, and lodge in it.

¹²And his master said unto him, We will not turn aside hither into the city of a stranger, that *is* not of the children of Israel; we will pass over to Gibeah.

¹³And he said unto his servant, Come, and let us draw near to one of these places to lodge all night, in Gibeah, or in Ramah.

¹⁴And they passed on and went their way; and the sun went down upon them *when they were* by Gibeah, which *belongeth* to Benjamin.

¹⁵And they turned aside thither, to go in *and* to lodge in Gibeah: and when he went in, he sat him down in a street of the city: for *there was* no man that took them into his house to lodging.

¹⁶ ¶ And, behold, there came an old man from his work out of the field at even, which *was* also of mount Ephraim; and he sojourned in Gibeah: but the men of the place *were* Benjamites.

¹⁷And when he had lifted up his eyes, he saw a wayfaring man in the street of the city: and the old man said, Whither goest thou? and whence comest thou?

¹⁸And he said unto him, We *are* passing from Bethlehem-judah toward the side of mount Ephraim; from thence *am* I: and I went to Bethlehem-judah, but I *am now* going to the house of the LORD; and there *is* no man that receiveth me to house.

¹⁹Yet there is both straw and provender for our asses; and there is bread and wine also for me, and for thy handmaid, and for the young man *which is* with thy servants: *there is* no want of any thing.

²⁰And the old man said, Peace *be* with thee; howsoever *let* all thy wants *lie* upon me; only lodge not in the street.

²¹So he brought him into his house, and gave provender unto the asses: and they washed their feet, and did eat and drink.

²² ¶ *Now* as they were making their hearts merry, behold, the men of the city, certain sons of Belial, beset the house round about, *and* beat at the door, and spake to the master of the house, the old man, saying, Bring forth the man that came into thine house, that we may know him.

²³And the man, the master of the house, went out unto them, and said unto them, Nay, my brethren, *nay,* I pray you, do not *so* wickedly; seeing that this man is come into mine house, do not this folly.

²⁴Behold, *here is* my daughter a maiden, and his concubine; them I will bring out now, and humble ye them, and do with them what seemeth good unto you: but unto this man do not ˣso vile a thing.

²⁵But the men would not hearken to him: so the man took his concubine, and brought her forth unto them; and they knew her, and abused her all the night until the morning: and when the day began to spring, they let her go.

²⁶Then came the woman in the dawning of the day, and fell down at the door of the man's house where her lord *was,* till it was light.

²⁷And her lord rose up in the morning, and opened the doors of the house, and went out to go his way: and, behold, the woman his concubine was fallen down *at* the door of the house, and her hands *were* upon the threshold.

²⁸And he said unto her, Up, and let us be going. But none answered. Then the man took her *up* upon an ass, and the man rose up, and gat him unto his place.

²⁹ ¶ And when he was come into his house, he took a knife, and laid hold on his concubine, and divided her, *together* with her bones, into twelve pieces, and sent her into all the coasts of Israel.

Amplified

¹¹When they were near Jebus, it was late, and the servant said to his master, Come I pray, and let us turn into this Jebusite city and lodge in it.

¹²His master said to him, We will not turn aside into the city of foreigners where there are no Israelites. We will go on to Gibeah.

¹³And he said to his servant, Come and let us go to one of these places and spend the night in Gibeah or in Ramah.

¹⁴So they passed on and went their way, and the sun went down on them near Gibeah, which belongs to Benjamin,

¹⁵And they turned aside there to go in and lodge at Gibeah. And the Levite went in and sat down in the open square of the city, for no man took them into his house to spend the night.

¹⁶And behold, an old man was coming from his work in the field at evening. He was from the hill country of Ephraim but was living temporarily in Gibeah, but the men of the place were Benjamites.

¹⁷And when he looked up, he saw the wayfarer in the city square, and the old man said, Where are you going? And from where did you come?

¹⁸The Levite replied, We are passing from Bethlehem of Judah to the rear side of the hill country of Ephraim; I am from there. I went to Bethlehem of Judah, but I am [now] going [home] to the house of the Lord [where I serve], and there is no man who receives me into his house.

¹⁹Yet we have both straw and provender for our donkeys and bread and wine also for me, your handmaid, and the young man who is with your servants; there is no lack of anything.

²⁰And the old man said, Peace be to you, but leave all your wants to me; only do not lodge in the street.

²¹So he brought him into his house and gave provender to the donkeys. And the guests washed their feet and ate and drank.

²²Now as they were making their hearts merry, behold, the men of the city, certain worthless fellows, beset the house round about, beat on the door, and said to the master of the house, the old man, Bring forth the man who came to your house, that we may have intercourse with him.

²³And the man, the master of the house, went out and said to them, No, my kinsmen, I pray you, do not act so wickedly; seeing that this man is my guest, do not do this [wicked] folly.

²⁴Behold, here are my virgin daughter and this man's concubine; them I will bring out now; debase them and do with them what seems good to you, but to this man do not so vile a thing.

²⁵But the men would not listen to him. So the man took his concubine and forced her forth to them, and they had intercourse with her and abused her all the night until morning. And when the dawn began to break, they let her go.

²⁶At daybreak the woman came and fell down and lay at the door of the man's house where her master was, till it was light.

²⁷And her master rose up in the morning and opened the doors of the house and went out to go his way; and behold, his concubine had fallen down at the door of the house, and her hands were upon the threshold.

²⁸And he said to her, Up, and let us be going. But there was no answer [for she was dead]. Then he put her [body] upon the donkey, and the man rose up and went home.

²⁹And when he came into his house, he took a knife, and took hold of his dead concubine and divided her [body] limb by limb into twelve pieces and sent her [body] throughout all the territory of Israel.

ˣHeb. *the matter of this folly*

New American Standard

11 When they *were* near Jebus, the day was almost gone; and the servant said to his master, "Please come, and let us turn aside into this city of the Jebusites and spend the night in it."

12 However, his master said to him, "We will not turn aside into the city of foreigners who are not of the sons of Israel; but we will go on as far as Gibeah."

13 He said to his servant, "Come and let us approach one of these places; and we will spend the night in Gibeah or Ramah."

14 So they passed along and went their way, and the sun set on them near Gibeah which belongs to Benjamin.

15 They turned aside there in order to enter *and* lodge in Gibeah. When they entered, they sat down in the open square of the city, for no one took them into *his* house to spend the night.

16 ¶ Then behold, an old man was coming out of the field from his work at evening. Now the man was from the hill country of Ephraim, and he was staying in Gibeah, but the men of the place were Benjamites.

17 And he lifted up his eyes and saw the traveler in the open square of the city; and the old man said, "Where are you going, and where do you come from?"

18 He said to him, "We are passing from Bethlehem in Judah to the remote part of the hill country of Ephraim, *for* I am from there, and I went to Bethlehem in Judah. But I am *now* going to my house, and no man will take me into his house.

19 "Yet there is both straw and fodder for our donkeys, and also bread and wine for me, your maidservant, and the young man who is with your servants; there is no lack of anything."

20 The old man said, "Peace to you. Only let me *take care of* all your needs; however, do not spend the night in the open square."

21 So he took him into his house and gave the donkeys fodder, and they washed their feet and ate and drank.

22 ¶ While they were celebrating, behold, the men of the city, certain worthless fellows, surrounded the house, pounding the door; and they spoke to the owner of the house, the old man, saying, "Bring out the man who came into your house that we may have relations with him."

23 Then the man, the owner of the house, went out to them and said to them, "No, my fellows, please do not act so wickedly; since this man has come into my house, do not commit this act of folly.

24 "Here is my virgin daughter and his concubine. Please let me bring them out that you may ravish them and do to them whatever you wish. But do not commit such an act of folly against this man."

25 But the men would not listen to him. So the man seized his concubine and brought *her* out to them; and they raped her and abused her all night until morning, then let her go at the approach of dawn.

26 As the day began to dawn, the woman came and fell down at the doorway of the man's house where her master was, until *full* daylight.

27 ¶ When her master arose in the morning and opened the doors of the house and went out to go on his way, then behold, his concubine was lying at the doorway of the house with her hands on the threshold.

28 He said to her, "Get up and let us go," but there was no answer. Then he placed her on the donkey; and the man arose and went to his home.

29 When he entered his house, he took a knife and laid hold of his concubine and cut her in twelve pieces, limb by limb, and sent her throughout the territory of Israel.

New International

11 When they were near Jebus and the day was almost gone, the servant said to his master, "Come, let's stop at this city of the Jebusites and spend the night."

12 His master replied, "No. We won't go into an alien city, whose people are not Israelites. We will go on to Gibeah." 13 He added, "Come, let's try to reach Gibeah or Ramah and spend the night in one of those places." 14 So they went on, and the sun set as they neared Gibeah in Benjamin. 15 There they stopped to spend the night. They went and sat in the city square, but no one took them into his home for the night.

16 That evening an old man from the hill country of Ephraim, who was living in Gibeah (the men of the place were Benjamites), came in from his work in the fields. 17 When he looked and saw the traveler in the city square, the old man asked, "Where are you going? Where did you come from?"

18 He answered, "We are on our way from Bethlehem in Judah to a remote area in the hill country of Ephraim where I live. I have been to Bethlehem in Judah and now I am going to the house of the LORD. No one has taken me into his house. 19 We have both straw and fodder for our donkeys and bread and wine for ourselves your servants—me, your maidservant, and the young man with us. We don't need anything."

20 "You are welcome at my house," the old man said. "Let me supply whatever you need. Only don't spend the night in the square." 21 So he took him into his house and fed his donkeys. After they had washed their feet, they had something to eat and drink.

22 While they were enjoying themselves, some of the wicked men of the city surrounded the house. Pounding on the door, they shouted to the old man who owned the house, "Bring out the man who came to your house so we can have sex with him."

23 The owner of the house went outside and said to them, "No, my friends, don't be so vile. Since this man is my guest, don't do this disgraceful thing. 24 Look, here is my virgin daughter, and his concubine. I will bring them out to you now, and you can use them and do to them whatever you wish. But to this man, don't do such a disgraceful thing."

25 But the men would not listen to him. So the man took his concubine and sent her outside to them, and they raped her and abused her throughout the night, and at dawn they let her go. 26 At daybreak the woman went back to the house where her master was staying, fell down at the door and lay there until daylight.

27 When her master got up in the morning and opened the door of the house and stepped out to continue on his way, there lay his concubine, fallen in the doorway of the house, with her hands on the threshold. 28 He said to her, "Get up; let's go." But there was no answer. Then the man put her on his donkey and set out for home.

29 When he reached home, he took a knife and cut up his concubine, limb by limb, into twelve parts and sent them

King James

³⁰And it was so, that all that saw it said, There was no such deed done nor seen from the day that the children of Israel came up out of the land of Egypt unto this day: consider of it, take advice, and speak *your minds.*

The rout of Benjamin

20 THEN ALL the children of Israel went out, and the congregation was gathered together as one man, from Dan even to Beer-sheba, with the land of Gilead, unto the LORD in Mizpeh.

²And the chief of all the people, *even* of all the tribes of Israel, presented themselves in the assembly of the people of God, four hundred thousand footmen that drew sword.

³(Now the children of Benjamin heard that the children of Israel were gone up to Mizpeh.) Then said the children of Israel, Tell *us,* how was this wickedness?

⁴And *y*the Levite, the husband of the woman that was slain, answered and said, I came into Gibeah that *belongeth* to Benjamin, I and my concubine, to lodge.

⁵And the men of Gibeah rose against me, and beset the house round about upon me by night, *and* thought to have slain me: and my concubine have they *z*forced, that she is dead.

⁶And I took my concubine, and cut her in pieces, and sent her throughout all the country of the inheritance of Israel: for they have committed lewdness and folly in Israel.

⁷Behold, ye *are* all children of Israel; give here your advice and counsel.

⁸ ¶ And all the people arose as one man, saying, We will not any *of us* go to his tent, neither will we any *of us* turn into his house.

⁹But now this *shall be* the thing which we will do to Gibeah; *we will go up* by lot against it;

¹⁰And we will take ten men of an hundred throughout all the tribes of Israel, and an hundred of a thousand, and a thousand out of ten thousand, to fetch victual for the people, that they may do, when they come to Gibeah of Benjamin, according to all the folly that they have wrought in Israel.

¹¹So all the men of Israel were gathered against the city, *a*knit together as one man.

¹² ¶ And the tribes of Israel sent men through all the tribe of Benjamin, saying, What wickedness *is* this that is done among you?

¹³Now therefore deliver *us* the men, the children of Belial, which *are* in Gibeah, that we may put them to death, and put away evil from Israel. But the children of Benjamin would not hearken to the voice of their brethren the children of Israel:

¹⁴But the children of Benjamin gathered themselves together out of the cities unto Gibeah, to go out to battle against the children of Israel.

¹⁵And the children of Benjamin were numbered at that time out of the cities twenty and six thousand men that drew sword, beside the inhabitants of Gibeah, which were numbered seven hundred chosen men.

¹⁶Among all this people *there were* seven hundred chosen men lefthanded; every one could sling stones at an hair *breadth,* and not miss.

¹⁷And the men of Israel, beside Benjamin, were numbered four hundred thousand men that drew sword: all these *were* men of war.

¹⁸ ¶ And the children of Israel arose, and went up to the house of God, and asked counsel of God, and said, Which of us shall go up first to the battle against the children of Benjamin? And the LORD said, Judah *shall go up* first.

¹⁹And the children of Israel rose up in the morning, and encamped against Gibeah.

Amplified

³⁰And all who saw it said, There was no such deed done or seen from the day that the Israelites came up out of the land of Egypt to this day; consider it, take counsel, and speak [your minds].

20 THEN ALL the Israelites came out, and the congregation assembled as one man to the Lord at Mizpah, from Dan even to Beersheba, including the land of Gilead.

²And the chiefs of all the people, of all the tribes of Israel, presented themselves in the assembly of the people of God, 400,000 men on foot who drew the sword.

³(Now the Benjamites [among whom the vile tragedy occurred] heard that the [other] Israelites had gone up to Mizpah.) There the Israelites asked, How did this wickedness happen?

⁴And the Levite, the husband of the woman who was murdered, replied, I came to Gibeah which belongs to Benjamin, I and my concubine, to spend the night.

⁵And the men of Gibeah rose against me and beset the house round about me by night; they meant to kill me and they raped my concubine, and she is dead.

⁶And I took my concubine and cut her in pieces and sent her throughout all the country of the inheritance of Israel, for they have committed abomination and [wicked] folly in Israel.

⁷Behold, you Israelites, all of you, give here your advice and counsel.

⁸And all the people arose as one man, saying, Not any of us will go to his tent, and none of us will return to his home.

⁹But now this we will do to Gibeah: we will go up by lot against it,

¹⁰And we will take ten men of 100 throughout all the tribes of Israel, and 100 of 1,000, and 1,000 out of 10,000, to bring provisions for the men, that when they come to Gibeah of Benjamin they may do to them according to all the [wicked] folly which they have committed in Israel.

¹¹So all the men of Israel gathered against the city, united as one man.

¹²And the tribes of Israel sent men through all the tribe of Benjamin, saying, What wickedness is this that has been done among you?

¹³Now therefore, give up the men [involved], the base fellows in Gibeah, that we may put them to death and put away evil from Israel. But the Benjamites would not listen to the voice of their kinsmen the Israelites.

¹⁴But the Benjamites out of the cities assembled at Gibeah to go out to battle against the other Israelites.

¹⁵And the Benjamites mustered out of their cities at that time 26,000 men who drew the sword, besides the inhabitants of Gibeah, who mustered 700 chosen men.

¹⁶Among all these were 700 chosen left-handed men; every one could sling stones at a hair and not miss.

¹⁷And the men of Israel, other than Benjamin, mustered 400,000 men who drew the sword; all these were men of war.

¹⁸The Israelites arose and went up to the house of God [Bethel] and asked counsel of God and said, Which of us shall take the lead to battle against the Benjamites? And the Lord said, Judah shall go up first.

¹⁹Then the Israelites rose in the morning and encamped against Gibeah.

---

*y*Heb. *the man the Levite*   *z*Heb. *humbled*   *a*Heb. *fellows*

New American Standard

30 All who saw *it* said, "Nothing like this has *ever* happened or been seen from the day when the sons of Israel came up from the land of Egypt to this day. Consider it, take counsel and speak up!"

Resolve to Punish the Guilty

20 THEN ALL the sons of Israel from Dan to Beersheba, including the land of Gilead, came out, and the congregation assembled as one man to the LORD at Mizpah.

2 The chiefs of all the people, *even* of all the tribes of Israel, took their stand in the assembly of the people of God, 400,000 foot soldiers who drew the sword.

3 (Now the sons of Benjamin heard that the sons of Israel had gone up to Mizpah.) And the sons of Israel said, "Tell *us*, how did this wickedness take place?"

4 So the Levite, the husband of the woman who was murdered, answered and said, "I came with my concubine to spend the night at Gibeah which belongs to Benjamin.

5 "But the men of Gibeah rose up against me and surrounded the house at night because of me. They intended to kill me; instead, they ravished my concubine so that she died.

6 "And I took hold of my concubine and cut her in pieces and sent her throughout the land of Israel's inheritance; for they have committed a lewd and disgraceful act in Israel.

7 "Behold, all you sons of Israel, give your advice and counsel here."

8 ¶ Then all the people arose as one man, saying, "Not one of us will go to his tent, nor will any of us return to his house.

9 "But now this is the thing which we will do to Gibeah; *we will go up* against it by lot.

10 "And we will take 10 men out of 100 throughout the tribes of Israel, and 100 out of 1,000, and 1,000 out of 10,000 to supply food for the people, that when they come to Gibeah of Benjamin, they may punish *them* for all the disgraceful acts that they have committed in Israel."

11 Thus all the men of Israel were gathered against the city, united as one man.

12 ¶ Then the tribes of Israel sent men through the entire tribe of Benjamin, saying, "What is this wickedness that has taken place among you?

13 "Now then, deliver up the men, the ᵛworthless fellows in Gibeah, that we may put them to death and remove *this* wickedness from Israel." But the sons of Benjamin would not listen to the voice of their brothers, the sons of Israel.

14 The sons of Benjamin gathered from the cities to Gibeah, to go out to battle against the sons of Israel.

15 From the cities on that day the sons of Benjamin were numbered, 26,000 men who draw the sword, besides the inhabitants of Gibeah who were numbered, 700 choice men.

16 Out of all these people 700 choice men were left-handed; each one could sling a stone at a hair and not miss.

17 ¶ Then the men of Israel besides Benjamin were numbered, 400,000 men who draw the sword; all these were men of war.

Civil War, Benjamin Defeated

18 ¶ Now the sons of Israel arose, went up to Bethel, and inquired of God and said, "Who shall go up first for us to battle against the sons of Benjamin?" Then the LORD said, "Judah *shall go up* first."

19 ¶ So the sons of Israel arose in the morning and camped against Gibeah.

New International

into all the areas of Israel. 30Everyone who saw it said, "Such a thing has never been seen or done, not since the day the Israelites came up out of Egypt. Think about it! Consider it! Tell us what to do!"

Israelites Fight the Benjamites

20 THEN ALL the Israelites from Dan to Beersheba and from the land of Gilead came out as one man and assembled before the LORD in Mizpah. 2The leaders of all the people of the tribes of Israel took their places in the assembly of the people of God, four hundred thousand soldiers armed with swords. 3(The Benjamites heard that the Israelites had gone up to Mizpah.) Then the Israelites said, "Tell us how this awful thing happened."

4So the Levite, the husband of the murdered woman, said, "I and my concubine came to Gibeah in Benjamin to spend the night. 5During the night the men of Gibeah came after me and surrounded the house, intending to kill me. They raped my concubine, and she died. 6I took my concubine, cut her into pieces and sent one piece to each region of Israel's inheritance, because they committed this lewd and disgraceful act in Israel. 7Now, all you Israelites, speak up and give your verdict."

8All the people rose as one man, saying, "None of us will go home. No, not one of us will return to his house. 9But now this is what we'll do to Gibeah: We'll go up against it as the lot directs. 10We'll take ten men out of every hundred from all the tribes of Israel, and a hundred from a thousand, and a thousand from ten thousand, to get provisions for the army. Then, when the army arrives at Gibeahⁿ in Benjamin, it can give them what they deserve for all this vileness done in Israel." 11So all the men of Israel got together and united as one man against the city.

12The tribes of Israel sent men throughout the tribe of Benjamin, saying, "What about this awful crime that was committed among you? 13Now surrender those wicked men of Gibeah so that we may put them to death and purge the evil from Israel."

But the Benjamites would not listen to their fellow Israelites. 14From their towns they came together at Gibeah to fight against the Israelites. 15At once the Benjamites mobilized twenty-six thousand swordsmen from their towns, in addition to seven hundred chosen men from those living in Gibeah. 16Among all these soldiers there were seven hundred chosen men who were left-handed, each of whom could sling a stone at a hair and not miss.

17Israel, apart from Benjamin, mustered four hundred thousand swordsmen, all of them fighting men.

18The Israelites went up to Bethelᵒ and inquired of God. They said, "Who of us shall go first to fight against the Benjamites?"

The LORD replied, "Judah shall go first."

19The next morning the Israelites got up and pitched

King James

Amplified

²⁰And the men of Israel went out to battle against Benjamin; and the men of Israel put themselves in array to fight against them at Gibeah.

²¹And the children of Benjamin came forth out of Gibeah, and destroyed down to the ground of the Israelites that day twenty and two thousand men.

²²And the people the men of Israel encouraged themselves, and set their battle again in array in the place where they put themselves in array the first day,

²³(And the children of Israel went up and wept before the LORD until even, and asked counsel of the LORD, saying, Shall I go up again to battle against the children of Benjamin my brother? And the LORD said, Go up against him.)

²⁴And the children of Israel came near against the children of Benjamin the second day.

²⁵And Benjamin went forth against them out of Gibeah the second day, and destroyed down to the ground of the children of Israel again eighteen thousand men; all these drew the sword.

²⁶ ¶ Then all the children of Israel, and all the people, went up, and came unto the house of God, and wept, and sat there before the LORD, and fasted that day until even, and offered burnt offerings and peace offerings before the LORD.

²⁷And the children of Israel inquired of the LORD, (for the ark of the covenant of God *was* there in those days,

²⁸And Phinehas, the son of Eleazar, the son of Aaron, stood before it in those days,) saying, Shall I yet again go out to battle against the children of Benjamin my brother, or shall I cease? And the LORD said, Go up; for tomorrow I will deliver them into thine hand.

²⁹And Israel set liers in wait round about Gibeah.

³⁰And the children of Israel went up against the children of Benjamin on the third day, and put themselves in array against Gibeah, as at other times.

³¹And the children of Benjamin went out against the people, *and* were drawn away from the city; and they began ^bto smite of the people, *and* kill, as at other times, in the highways, of which one goeth up to ^cthe house of God, and the other to Gibeah in the field, about thirty men of Israel.

³²And the children of Benjamin said, They *are* smitten down before us, as at the first. But the children of Israel said, Let us flee, and draw them from the city unto the highways.

³³And all the men of Israel rose up out of their place, and put themselves in array at Baal-tamar: and the liers in wait of Israel came forth out of their places, *even* out of the meadows of Gibeah.

³⁴And there came against Gibeah ten thousand chosen men out of all Israel, and the battle was sore: but they knew not that evil *was* near them.

³⁵And the LORD smote Benjamin before Israel: and the children of Israel destroyed of the Benjamites that day twenty and five thousand and an hundred men: all these drew the sword.

³⁶So the children of Benjamin saw that they were smitten: for the men of Israel gave place to the Benjamites, because they trusted unto the liers in wait which they had set beside Gibeah.

³⁷And the liers in wait hasted, and rushed upon Gibeah; and the liers in wait ^ddrew *themselves* along, and smote all the city with the edge of the sword.

³⁸Now there was an appointed ^esign between the men of Israel ^fand the liers in wait, that they should make a great ^gflame with smoke rise up out of the city.

³⁹And when the men of Israel retired in the battle, Benjamin began ^hto smite *and* kill of the men of Israel about thirty persons: for they said, Surely they are smitten down before us, as *in* the first battle.

²⁰And the men of Israel went out to battle against Benjamin and set the battle in array against them at Gibeah.

²¹The Benjamites came forth out of Gibeah and felled to the ground that day 22,000 men of the Israelites.

²²But the people, the men of Israel, took courage *and* strengthened themselves and again set their battle line in the same place where they formed it the first day.

²³And the Israelites went up and wept before the Lord until evening and asked of the Lord, Shall we go up again to battle against our brethren the Benjamites? And the Lord said, Go up against them.

²⁴So the Israelites came near against the Benjamites the second day.

²⁵And Benjamin went forth out of Gibeah against them the second day and felled to the ground the Israelites again, 18,000 men, all of whom were swordsmen.

²⁶Then all the Israelites, the whole army, went up and came to the house of God [Bethel] and wept; and they sat there before the Lord and fasted that day until evening and offered burnt offerings and peace offerings before the Lord.

²⁷And the Israelites inquired of the Lord—for the ark of the covenant of God was there [at Bethel] in those days,

²⁸And Phinehas son of Eleazar, the son of Aaron, ministered before it in those days—saying, Shall I yet again go out to battle against our brethren the Benjamites or shall we quit? And the Lord said, Go up, for tomorrow I will deliver them into your hand.

²⁹So Israel set men in ambush round about Gibeah.

³⁰And the Israelites went up against the Benjamites on the third day and set themselves in array against Gibeah as at other times.

³¹And the Benjamites went out against their army and were drawn away from the city; and they began to smite and kill some of the people as at other times, in the highways, one of which goes up to Bethel and the other to Gibeah, and in the open country—about thirty men of Israel.

³²And the Benjamites said, They are routed before us as at first. But the Israelites said, Let us flee and draw them from the city to the highways.

³³And all the men of Israel rose out of their places and set themselves in array at Baal-tamar, and the men of Israel in ambush rushed out of their place in the meadow of Geba.

³⁴And there came against Gibeah 10,000 chosen men out of all Israel, and the battle was hard; but the Benjamites did not know disaster was close upon them.

³⁵And the Lord overcame Benjamin before Israel, and the Israelites destroyed of the Benjamites that day 25,100 men, all of whom were swordsmen.

³⁶So the Benjamites saw that they were defeated. The men of Israel gave ground to the Benjamites, because they trusted in the men in ambush whom they had set against Gibeah.

³⁷And the men in ambush quickly rushed upon Gibeah, and the liers-in-wait moved out and smote all the city with the sword.

³⁸Now the appointed signal between the men of Israel and the men in ambush was that when they made a great cloud of smoke arise from the city,

³⁹The men of Israel should all turn back in battle. Now Benjamin had begun to smite and kill some of the men of Israel, about thirty persons. They said, Surely they are falling before us as in the first battle.

---

^bHeb. *to smite of the people wounded as at*   ^cOr, *Beth-el*
^dOr, *made a long* sound *with the trumpet*   ^eOr, *time*   ^fHeb.
with   ^gHeb. *elevation*   ^hHeb. *to smite the wounded*

New American Standard

New International

20 The men of Israel went out to battle against Benjamin, and the men of Israel arrayed for battle against them at Gibeah.

21 Then the sons of Benjamin came out of Gibeah and felled to the ground on that day 22,000 men of Israel.

22 But the people, the men of Israel, encouraged themselves and arrayed for battle again in the place where they had arrayed themselves the first day.

23 The sons of Israel went up and wept before the LORD until evening, and inquired of the LORD, saying, "Shall we again draw near for battle against the sons of my brother Benjamin?" And the LORD said, "Go up against him."

24 ¶ Then the sons of Israel came against the sons of Benjamin the second day.

25 Benjamin went out against them from Gibeah the second day and felled to the ground again 18,000 men of the sons of Israel; all these drew the sword.

26 Then all the sons of Israel and all the people went up and came to Bethel and wept; thus they remained there before the LORD and fasted that day until evening. And they offered burnt offerings and peace offerings before the LORD.

27 The sons of Israel inquired of the LORD (for the ark of the covenant of God *was* there in those days,

28 and Phinehas the son of Eleazar, Aaron's son, stood before it to *minister* in those days), saying, "Shall I yet again go out to battle against the sons of my brother Benjamin, or shall I cease?" And the LORD said, "Go up, for tomorrow I will deliver them into your hand."

29 ¶ So Israel set men in ambush around Gibeah.

30 The sons of Israel went up against the sons of Benjamin on the third day and arrayed themselves against Gibeah as at other times.

31 The sons of Benjamin went out against the people and were drawn away from the city, and they began to strike and kill some of the people as at other times, on the highways, one of which goes up to Bethel and the other to Gibeah, *and* in the field, about thirty men of Israel.

32 The sons of Benjamin said, "They are struck down before us, as at the first." But the sons of Israel said, "Let us flee that we may draw them away from the city to the highways."

33 Then all the men of Israel arose from their place and arrayed themselves at Baal-tamar; and the men of Israel in ambush broke out of their place, even out of Maareh-geba.

34 When ten thousand choice men from all Israel came against Gibeah, the battle became fierce; but Benjamin did not know that disaster was close to them.

35 And the LORD struck Benjamin before Israel, so that the sons of Israel destroyed 25,100 men of Benjamin that day, all who draw the sword.

36 ¶ So the sons of Benjamin saw that they were defeated. When the men of Israel gave ground to Benjamin because they relied on the men in ambush whom they had set against Gibeah,

37 the men in ambush hurried and rushed against Gibeah; the men in ambush also deployed and struck all the city with the edge of the sword.

38 Now the appointed sign between the men of Israel and the men in ambush was that they would make a great cloud of smoke rise from the city.

39 Then the men of Israel turned in the battle, and Benjamin began to strike and kill about thirty men of Israel, for they said, "Surely they are defeated before us, as in the first battle."

camp near Gibeah. **20**The men of Israel went out to fight the Benjamites and took up battle positions against them at Gibeah. **21**The Benjamites came out of Gibeah and cut down twenty-two thousand Israelites on the battlefield that day. **22**But the men of Israel encouraged one another and again took up their positions where they had stationed themselves the first day. **23**The Israelites went up and wept before the LORD until evening, and they inquired of the LORD. They said, "Shall we go up again to battle against the Benjamites, our brothers?"

The LORD answered, "Go up against them."

24Then the Israelites drew near to Benjamin the second day. **25**This time, when the Benjamites came out from Gibeah to oppose them, they cut down another eighteen thousand Israelites, all of them armed with swords.

26Then the Israelites, all the people, went up to Bethel, and there they sat weeping before the LORD. They fasted that day until evening and presented burnt offerings and fellowship offerings[p] to the LORD. **27**And the Israelites inquired of the LORD. (In those days the ark of the covenant of God was there, **28**with Phinehas son of Eleazar, the son of Aaron, ministering before it.) They asked, "Shall we go up again to battle with Benjamin our brother, or not?"

The LORD responded, "Go, for tomorrow I will give them into your hands."

29Then Israel set an ambush around Gibeah. **30**They went up against the Benjamites on the third day and took up positions against Gibeah as they had done before. **31**The Benjamites came out to meet them and were drawn away from the city. They began to inflict casualties on the Israelites as before, so that about thirty men fell in the open field and on the roads—the one leading to Bethel and the other to Gibeah.

32While the Benjamites were saying, "We are defeating them as before," the Israelites were saying, "Let's retreat and draw them away from the city to the roads."

33All the men of Israel moved from their places and took up positions at Baal Tamar, and the Israelite ambush charged out of its place on the west[r] of Gibeah.[r] **34**Then ten thousand of Israel's finest men made a frontal attack on Gibeah. The fighting was so heavy that the Benjamites did not realize how near disaster was. **35**The LORD defeated Benjamin before Israel, and on that day the Israelites struck down 25,100 Benjamites, all armed with swords. **36**Then the Benjamites saw that they were beaten.

Now the men of Israel had given way before Benjamin, because they relied on the ambush they had set near Gibeah. **37**The men who had been in ambush made a sudden dash into Gibeah, spread out and put the whole city to the sword. **38**The men of Israel had arranged with the ambush that they should send up a great cloud of smoke from the city, **39**and then the men of Israel would turn in the battle.

The Benjamites had begun to inflict casualties on the men of Israel (about thirty), and they said, "We are defeat-

King James

⁴⁰But when the flame began to arise up out of the city with a pillar of smoke, the Benjamites looked behind them, and, behold, ⁱthe flame of the city ascended up to heaven.

⁴¹And when the men of Israel turned again, the men of Benjamin were amazed: for they saw that evil ʲwas come upon them.

⁴²Therefore they turned *their backs* before the men of Israel unto the way of the wilderness; but the battle overtook them; and them which *came* out of the cities they destroyed in the midst of them.

⁴³*Thus* they inclosed the Benjamites round about, *and* chased them, *and* trode them down ᵏwith ease ˡover against Gibeah toward the sunrising.

⁴⁴And there fell of Benjamin eighteen thousand men; all these *were* men of valour.

⁴⁵And they turned and fled toward the wilderness unto the rock of Rimmon: and they gleaned of them in the highways five thousand men; and pursued hard after them unto Gidom, and slew two thousand men of them.

⁴⁶So that all which fell that day of Benjamin were twenty and five thousand men that drew the sword; all these *were* men of valour.

⁴⁷But six hundred men turned and fled to the wilderness unto the rock Rimmon, and abode in the rock Rimmon four months.

⁴⁸And the men of Israel turned again upon the children of Benjamin, and smote them with the edge of the sword, as well the men of *every* city, as the beast, and all that ᵐcame to hand: also they set on fire all the cities that ⁿthey came to.

Wives for the Benjaminites

21 NOW THE men of Israel had sworn in Mizpeh, saying, There shall not any of us give his daughter unto Benjamin to wife.

²And the people came to the house of God, and abode there till even before God, and lifted up their voices, and wept sore;

³And said, O LORD God of Israel, why is this come to pass in Israel, that there should be today one tribe lacking in Israel?

⁴And it came to pass on the morrow, that the people rose early, and built there an altar, and offered burnt offerings and peace offerings.

⁵And the children of Israel said, Who *is there* among all the tribes of Israel that came not up with the congregation unto the LORD? For they had made a great oath concerning him that came not up to the LORD to Mizpeh, saying, He shall surely be put to death.

⁶And the children of Israel repented them for Benjamin their brother, and said, There is one tribe cut off from Israel this day.

⁷How shall we do for wives for them that remain, seeing we have sworn by the LORD that we will not give them of our daughters to wives?

⁸ ¶ And they said, What one *is there* of the tribes of Israel that came not up to Mizpeh to the LORD? And, behold, there came none to the camp from Jabesh-gilead to the assembly.

⁹For the people were numbered, and, behold, *there were* none of the inhabitants of Jabesh-gilead there.

¹⁰And the congregation sent thither twelve thousand men of the valiantest, and commanded them, saying, Go and smite the inhabitants of Jabesh-gilead with the edge of the sword, with the women and the children.

¹¹And this *is* the thing that ye shall do, Ye shall utterly destroy every male, and every woman that ᵒhath lain by man.

Amplified

⁴⁰But when the [signal] cloud began to rise out of the city in a pillar of smoke, the Benjamites looked behind them, and behold, the whole of the city went up in smoke to the heavens.

⁴¹When the men of Israel turned back again, the men of Benjamin were dismayed, for they saw that disaster had come upon them.

⁴²Therefore they turned their backs before the men of Israel and fled toward the wilderness, but the battle followed close behind *and* overtook them; and the inhabitants of the cities destroyed those [Benjamites] who came through them in their midst.

⁴³They surrounded the Benjamites, pursued them, and overtook *and* trod them down at their resting-place as far as opposite Gibeah toward the east.

⁴⁴And there fell 18,000 men of Benjamin, all of them men of valor.

⁴⁵And [the Benjamites] turned and fled toward the wilderness to the rock of Rimmon, and Israel picked off on the highways 5,000 men of them; they pursued hard after them to Gidom and slew 2,000 more of them.

⁴⁶So that all of Benjamin who fell that day were 25,000 men who drew the sword, all of them men of valor.

⁴⁷But 600 men turned and fled to the wilderness to the rock Rimmon and remained at the rock Rimmon four months.

⁴⁸And the men of Israel turned back against the Benjamites and smote them with the sword, men and beasts and all that they found. Also they set on fire all the towns to which they came.

21 NOW THE men of Israel had sworn at Mizpah, None of us shall give his daughter in marriage to Benjamin.

²And the Israelites came to the house of God [Bethel] and sat there until evening before God and lifted up their voices and wept bitterly. [Judg. 20:27.]

³And they said, O Lord, the God of Israel, why has this come to pass in Israel, that there should be today one tribe lacking in Israel?

⁴And next morning the people rose early, and built there an altar, and offered burnt offerings and peace offerings.

⁵And the Israelites said, Which among all the tribes of Israel did not come up with the assembly to the Lord? For they had taken a great oath concerning him who did not come up to the Lord to Mizpah, saying, He shall surely die.

⁶And the Israelites changed their purpose [and had compassion] for the Benjamites their kinsmen and said, There is one tribe cut off from Israel today.

⁷What shall we do for wives for those who are left, seeing we have sworn by the Lord that we will not give them our daughters as wives?

⁸And they said, Which one is there of the tribes of Israel that did not come up to Mizpah to the Lord? And behold, no one had come to the camp from Jabesh-gilead, to the assembly.

⁹For when the people were mustered, behold, not one of the citizens of Jabesh-gilead was there.

¹⁰And the congregation sent there 12,000 of the bravest men, saying, Go and smite the inhabitants of Jabesh-gilead with the sword, also the women and the little ones.

¹¹And this is what you shall do; utterly destroy every male and every woman who is not a virgin.

ⁱHeb. *the whole consumption*   ʲHeb. *touched them*   ᵏOr, from *Menuchah*   ˡHeb. *unto over against*   ᵐHeb. *was found*   ⁿHeb. *were found*   ᵒHeb. *knoweth the lying* with *man*

New American Standard

40 But when the cloud began to rise from the city in a column of smoke, Benjamin looked behind them; and behold, the whole city was going up *in smoke* to heaven. **41** Then the men of Israel turned, and the men of Benjamin were terrified; for they saw that disaster was close to them.

42 Therefore, they turned their backs before the men of Israel toward the direction of the wilderness, but the battle overtook them while those who came out of the cities destroyed them in the midst of them.

43 They surrounded Benjamin, pursued them without rest *and* trod them down opposite Gibeah toward the east.

44 Thus 18,000 men of Benjamin fell; all these were valiant warriors.

45 The rest turned and fled toward the wilderness to the rock of Rimmon, but they caught 5,000 of them on the highways and overtook them at Gidom and killed 2,000 of them.

46 So all of Benjamin who fell that day were 25,000 men who draw the sword; all these were valiant warriors.

47 But 600 men turned and fled toward the wilderness to the rock of Rimmon, and they remained at the rock of Rimmon four months.

48 The men of Israel then turned back against the sons of Benjamin and struck them with the edge of the sword, both the entire city with the cattle and all that they found; they also set on fire all the cities which they found.

Mourning Lost Tribe

21 NOW THE men of Israel had sworn in Mizpah, saying, "None of us shall give his daughter to Benjamin in marriage."

2 So the people came to Bethel and sat there before God until evening, and lifted up their voices and wept bitterly.

3 They said, "Why, O LORD, God of Israel, has this come about in Israel, so that one tribe should be *missing* today in Israel?"

4 It came about the next day that the people arose early and built an altar there and offered burnt offerings and peace offerings.

5 ¶ Then the sons of Israel said, "Who is there among all the tribes of Israel who did not come up in the assembly to the LORD?" For they had taken a great oath concerning him who did not come up to the LORD at Mizpah, saying, "He shall surely be put to death."

6 And the sons of Israel were sorry for their brother Benjamin and said, "One tribe is cut off from Israel today.

7 "What shall we do for wives for those who are left, since we have sworn by the LORD not to give them any of our daughters in marriage?"

Provision for Their Survival

8 ¶ And they said, "What one is there of the tribes of Israel who did not come up to the LORD at Mizpah?" And behold, no one had come to the camp from Jabesh-gilead to the assembly.

9 For when the people were numbered, behold, not one of the inhabitants of Jabesh-gilead was there.

10 And the congregation sent 12,000 of the valiant warriors there, and commanded them, saying, "Go and strike the inhabitants of Jabesh-gilead with the edge of the sword, with the women and the little ones.

11 "This is the thing that you shall do: you shall utterly destroy every man and every woman who has lain with a man."

New International

ing them as in the first battle." **40** But when the column of smoke began to rise from the city, the Benjamites turned and saw the smoke of the whole city going up into the sky. **41** Then the men of Israel turned on them, and the men of Benjamin were terrified, because they realized that disaster had come upon them. **42** So they fled before the Israelites in the direction of the desert, but they could not escape the battle. And the men of Israel who came out of the towns cut them down there. **43** They surrounded the Benjamites, chased them and easily[s] overran them in the vicinity of Gibeah on the east. **44** Eighteen thousand Benjamites fell, all of them valiant fighters. **45** As they turned and fled toward the desert to the rock of Rimmon, the Israelites cut down five thousand men along the roads. They kept pressing after the Benjamites as far as Gidom and struck down two thousand more.

46 On that day twenty-five thousand Benjamite swordsmen fell, all of them valiant fighters. **47** But six hundred men turned and fled into the desert to the rock of Rimmon, where they stayed four months. **48** The men of Israel went back to Benjamin and put all the towns to the sword, including the animals and everything else they found. All the towns they came across they set on fire.

Wives for the Benjamites

21 THE MEN of Israel had taken an oath at Mizpah: "Not one of us will give his daughter in marriage to a Benjamite."

2 The people went to Bethel,[t] where they sat before God until evening, raising their voices and weeping bitterly. **3** "O LORD, the God of Israel," they cried, "why has this happened to Israel? Why should one tribe be missing from Israel today?"

4 Early the next day the people built an altar and presented burnt offerings and fellowship offerings.[u]

5 Then the Israelites asked, "Who from all the tribes of Israel has failed to assemble before the LORD?" For they had taken a solemn oath that anyone who failed to assemble before the LORD at Mizpah should certainly be put to death.

6 Now the Israelites grieved for their brothers, the Benjamites. "Today one tribe is cut off from Israel," they said. **7** "How can we provide wives for those who are left, since we have taken an oath by the LORD not to give them any of our daughters in marriage?" **8** Then they asked, "Which one of the tribes of Israel failed to assemble before the LORD at Mizpah?" They discovered that no one from Jabesh Gilead had come to the camp for the assembly. **9** For when they counted the people, they found that none of the people of Jabesh Gilead were there.

10 So the assembly sent twelve thousand fighting men with instructions to go to Jabesh Gilead and put to the sword those living there, including the women and children. **11** "This is what you are to do," they said. "Kill every

King James

12 And they found among the inhabitants of Jabesh-gilead four hundred [p]young virgins, that had known no man by lying with any male: and they brought them unto the camp to Shiloh, which *is* in the land of Canaan.

13 And the whole congregation sent *some* [q]to speak to the children of Benjamin that *were* in the rock Rimmon, and to [r]call peaceably unto them.

14 And Benjamin came again at that time; and they gave them wives which they had saved alive of the women of Jabesh-gilead: and yet so they sufficed them not.

15 And the people repented them for Benjamin, because that the LORD had made a breach in the tribes of Israel.

16 ¶ Then the elders of the congregation said, How shall we do for wives for them that remain, seeing the women are destroyed out of Benjamin?

17 And they said, *There must be* an inheritance for them that be escaped of Benjamin, that a tribe be not destroyed out of Israel.

18 Howbeit we may not give them wives of our daughters: for the children of Israel have sworn, saying, Cursed *be* he that giveth a wife to Benjamin.

19 Then they said, Behold, *there is* a feast of the LORD in Shiloh [s]yearly *in a place* which *is* on the north side of Beth-el, [t]on the east side [u]of the highway that goeth up from Beth-el to Shechem, and on the south of Lebonah.

20 Therefore they commanded the children of Benjamin, saying, Go and lie in wait in the vineyards;

21 And see, and, behold, if the daughters of Shiloh come out to dance in dances, then come ye out of the vineyards, and catch you every man his wife of the daughters of Shiloh, and go to the land of Benjamin.

22 And it shall be, when their fathers or their brethren come unto us to complain, that we will say unto them, [v]Be favourable unto them for our sakes: because we reserved not to each man his wife in the war: for ye did not give unto them at this time, *that* ye should be guilty.

23 And the children of Benjamin did so, and took *them* wives, according to their number, of them that danced, whom they caught: and they went and returned unto their inheritance, and repaired the cities, and dwelt in them.

24 And the children of Israel departed thence at that time, every man to his tribe and to his family, and they went out from thence every man to his inheritance.

25 In those days *there was* no king in Israel: every man did *that which was* right in his own eyes.

[p] Heb. *young women virgins* [q] Heb. *and spake and called* [r] Or, *proclaim peace* [s] Heb. *from year to year* [t] Or, *toward the sunrising* [u] Or, *on* [v] Or, *Gratify us in them*

Amplified

12 And they found among the inhabitants of Jabesh-gilead 400 young virgins, who had known no man by lying with him; and they brought them to the camp at Shiloh, which is in the land of Canaan.

13 And the whole congregation sent word to the Benjamites who were at the rock of Rimmon and invited them to be friendly with them.

14 And Benjamin returned at that time, and they gave them the women whom they had saved alive of the women of Jabesh-gilead; and yet there were not enough for them.

15 And the people had compassion on Benjamin, because the Lord had made a breach in the tribes of Israel.

16 Then the elders of the congregation said, What shall we do for wives for those who are left, since the women of Benjamin are destroyed?

17 And they said, There must be an inheritance for the survivors of Benjamin, so that a tribe shall not be wiped out of Israel.

18 But we cannot give them wives of our daughters, for the Israelites have sworn, Cursed be he who gives a wife to Benjamin.

19 So they said, Behold, there is the yearly feast of the Lord at Shiloh, which is north of Bethel, on the east of the highway that goes up from Bethel to Shechem and south of Lebonah.

20 So they commanded the Benjamites, Go and lie in wait in the vineyards,

21 And watch; if the daughters of Shiloh come out to dance in the dances, then come out of the vineyards and catch every man his wife from the daughters of Shiloh and go to the land of Benjamin.

22 And when their fathers or their brothers come to us to complain, we will say to them, Grant them graciously unto us, because we did not reserve a wife for each of them in battle, neither did you give wives to them, for that would have made you guilty [of breaking your oath].

23 And the Benjamites did so and took wives, according to their number, from the dancers whom they carried off; then they went and returned to their inheritance and repaired the towns and dwelt in them.

24 And the Israelites left there then, every man to his tribe and family, and they went out from there every man to his inheritance.

25 In those days [n]there was no king in Israel; every man did what was right in his own eyes.

[n] This statement is made three times in these latter chapters. All was well while Joshua and those who assisted him lived; then gradually came disorder. "What is the meaning of this? . . . There was no king [or counselor] in Israel because in Israel there was no God. The Lord is King. You cannot have a [true] king if you have not a God. There was no nominal renunciation of God, no public and blatant atheism, no boastful impiety; there was a deadlier heresy—namely, keeping God as a sign but paying no tribute to Him as a King, worshiping Him possibly in outward form but knowing nothing of the subduing and directing power of godliness. That is more to be dreaded than any intellectual difficulty of a theological kind . . . Dead consciences, prayerless prayers, mechanical formalities—these are the impediments which overturn . . . the chariots of progress. This was the case in Israel. Where God is, the king is not [merely] a man with a crown on, but a king in the sense of kingliness, sovereignty, authority, rule—the spirit of obligation and responsibility . . . You find the right monarch where you find the right God" (Joseph Parker, cited by James C. Gray and George M. Adams, *Bible Commentary*).

New American Standard

12 And they found among the inhabitants of Jabesh-gilead 400 young virgins who had not known a man by lying with him; and they brought them to the camp at Shiloh, which is in the land of Canaan.

13 ¶ Then the whole congregation sent *word* and spoke to the sons of Benjamin who were at the rock of Rimmon, and proclaimed peace to them.

14 Benjamin returned at that time, and they gave them the women whom they had kept alive from the women of Jabesh-gilead; yet they were not enough for them.

15 And the people were sorry for Benjamin because the LORD had made a breach in the tribes of Israel.

16 ¶ Then the elders of the congregation said, "What shall we do for wives for those who are left, since the women are destroyed out of Benjamin?"

17 They said, "*There must be* an inheritance for the survivors of Benjamin, so that a tribe will not be blotted out from Israel.

18 "But we cannot give them wives of our daughters." For the sons of Israel had sworn, saying, "Cursed is he who gives a wife to Benjamin."

19 ¶ So they said, "Behold, there is a feast of the LORD from year to year in Shiloh, which is on the north side of Bethel, on the east side of the highway that goes up from Bethel to Shechem, and on the south side of Lebonah."

20 And they commanded the sons of Benjamin, saying, "Go and lie in wait in the vineyards,

21 and watch; and behold, if the daughters of Shiloh come out to take part in the dances, then you shall come out of the vineyards and each of you shall catch his wife from the daughters of Shiloh, and go to the land of Benjamin.

22 "It shall come about, when their fathers or their brothers come to complain to us, that we shall say to them, 'Give them to us voluntarily, because we did not take for each man *of Benjamin* a wife in battle, nor did you give *them* to them, *else* you would now be guilty.' "

23 The sons of Benjamin did so, and took wives according to their number from those who danced, whom they carried away. And they went and returned to their inheritance and rebuilt the cities and lived in them.

24 The sons of Israel departed from there at that time, every man to his tribe and family, and each one of them went out from there to his inheritance.

25 ¶ In those days there was no king in Israel; everyone did what was right in his own eyes.

New International

male and every woman who is not a virgin." 12They found among the people living in Jabesh Gilead four hundred young women who had never slept with a man, and they took them to the camp at Shiloh in Canaan.

13Then the whole assembly sent an offer of peace to the Benjamites at the rock of Rimmon. 14So the Benjamites returned at that time and were given the women of Jabesh Gilead who had been spared. But there were not enough for all of them.

15The people grieved for Benjamin, because the LORD had made a gap in the tribes of Israel. 16And the elders of the assembly said, "With the women of Benjamin destroyed, how shall we provide wives for the men who are left? 17The Benjamite survivors must have heirs," they said, "so that a tribe of Israel will not be wiped out. 18We can't give them our daughters as wives, since we Israelites have taken this oath: 'Cursed be anyone who gives a wife to a Benjamite.' 19But look, there is the annual festival of the LORD in Shiloh, to the north of Bethel, and east of the road that goes from Bethel to Shechem, and to the south of Lebonah."

20So they instructed the Benjamites, saying, "Go and hide in the vineyards 21and watch. When the girls of Shiloh come out to join in the dancing, then rush from the vineyards and each of you seize a wife from the girls of Shiloh and go to the land of Benjamin. 22When their fathers or brothers complain to us, we will say to them, 'Do us a kindness by helping them, because we did not get wives for them during the war, and you are innocent, since you did not give your daughters to them.' "

23So that is what the Benjamites did. While the girls were dancing, each man caught one and carried her off to be his wife. Then they returned to their inheritance and rebuilt the towns and settled in them.

24At that time the Israelites left that place and went home to their tribes and clans, each to his own inheritance.

25In those days Israel had no king; everyone did as he saw fit.

THE BOOK OF

Ruth

THE BOOK OF

Ruth

Naomi and Ruth

1 NOW IT came to pass in the days when the judges *a*ruled, that there was a famine in the land. And a certain man of Bethlehem-judah went to sojourn in the country of Moab, he, and his wife, and his two sons.

2 And the name of the man *was* Elimelech, and the name of his wife Naomi, and the name of his two sons Mahlon and Chilion, Ephrathites of Bethlehem-judah. And they came into the country of Moab, and *b*continued there.

3 And Elimelech Naomi's husband died; and she was left, and her two sons.

4 And they took them wives of the women of Moab; the name of the one *was* Orpah, and the name of the other Ruth: and they dwelled there about ten years.

5 And Mahlon and Chilion died also both of them; and the woman was left of her two sons and her husband.

6 ¶ Then she arose with her daughters-in-law, that she might return from the country of Moab: for she had heard in the country of Moab how that the LORD had visited his people in giving them bread.

7 Wherefore she went forth out of the place where she was, and her two daughters-in-law with her; and they went on the way to return unto the land of Judah.

8 And Naomi said unto her two daughters-in-law, Go, return each to her mother's house: the LORD deal kindly with you, as ye have dealt with the dead, and with me.

9 The LORD grant you that ye may find rest, each *of you* in the house of her husband. Then she kissed them; and they lifted up their voice, and wept.

10 And they said unto her, Surely we will return with thee unto thy people.

11 And Naomi said, Turn again, my daughters: why will ye go with me? *are* there yet *any more* sons in my womb, that they may be your husbands?

12 Turn again, my daughters, go *your way;* for I am too old to have an husband. If I should say, I have hope, *c if* I should have an husband also tonight, and should also bear sons;

13 Would ye *d*tarry for them till they were grown? would ye stay for them from having husbands? nay, my daughters; for *e*it grieveth me much for your sakes that the hand of the LORD is gone out against me.

14 And they lifted up their voice, and wept again: and Orpah kissed her mother-in-law; but Ruth clave unto her.

15 And she said, Behold, thy sister-in-law is gone back unto her people, and unto her gods: return thou after thy sister-in-law.

1 IN THE days when the judges ruled, there was a famine in the land. And a certain man of Bethlehem of Judah went to sojourn in the country of Moab, he, his wife, and his two sons.

2 The man's name was Elimelech and his wife's name was Naomi and his two sons were named Mahlon [invalid] and Chilion [pining]; they were Ephrathites from Bethlehem of Judah. They went to the country of Moab and continued there.

3 But Elimelech, who Naomi's husband, died, and she was left with her two sons.

4 And they took wives of the women of Moab; the name of the one was Orpah and the name of the other Ruth. They dwelt there about ten years;

5 And Mahlon and Chilion died also, both of them, so the woman was bereft of her two sons and her husband.

6 Then she arose with her daughters-in-law to return from the country of Moab, for she had heard in Moab how the Lord had visited His people in giving them food.

7 So she left the place where she was, and her two daughters-in-law with her, and they started on the way back to Judah.

8 But Naomi said to her two daughters-in-law, Go, return each of you to her mother's house. May the Lord deal kindly with you, as you have dealt with the dead and with me.

9 The Lord grant that you may find a home *and* rest, each in the house of her husband! Then she kissed them and they wept aloud.

10 And they said to her, No, we will return with you to your people.

11 But Naomi said, Turn back, my daughters, why will you go with me? Have I yet sons in my womb that may become your husbands?

12 Turn back, my daughters, go; for I am too old to have a husband. If I should say I have hope, even if I should have a husband tonight and should bear sons,

13 Would you therefore wait till they were grown? Would you therefore refrain from marrying? No, my daughters; it is far more bitter for me than for you that the hand of the Lord is gone out against me.

14 Then they wept aloud again; and Orpah *a*kissed her mother-in-law [good-bye], but Ruth clung to her.

15 And Naomi said, See, your sister-in-law has gone back to her people and to her gods; return after your sister-in-law.

---

a "How many part with Christ at this crossway! Like Orpah they go a furlong or two with Christ, till He goes to take them off from their worldly hopes and bids them prepare for hardship, and then they fairly kiss and leave Him" (William Gurnall, cited by James C. Gray and George M. Adams, *Bible Commentary*).

a Heb. *judged*   *b* Heb. *were*   *c* Or, *if I were with an husband*
d Heb. *hope*   *e* Heb. *I have much bitterness*

THE BOOK OF

Ruth

Ruth

Naomi Widowed

1 NOW IT came about in the days when the judges governed, that there was a famine in the land. And a certain man of Bethlehem in Judah went to sojourn in the land of Moab with his wife and his two sons. ² The name of the man *was* Elimelech, and the name of his wife, Naomi; and the names of his two sons *were* Mahlon and Chilion, Ephrathites of Bethlehem in Judah. Now they entered the land of Moab and remained there. ³ Then Elimelech, Naomi's husband, died; and she was left with her two sons. ⁴ They took for themselves Moabite women *as* wives; the name of the one was Orpah and the name of the other Ruth. And they lived there about ten years. ⁵ Then both Mahlon and Chilion also died, and the woman was bereft of her two children and her husband.

⁶ ¶ Then she arose with her daughters-in-law that she might return from the land of Moab, for she had heard in the land of Moab that the LORD had visited His people in giving them food. ⁷ So she departed from the place where she was, and her two daughters-in-law with her; and they went on the way to return to the land of Judah. ⁸ And Naomi said to her two daughters-in-law, "Go, return each of you to her mother's house. May the LORD deal kindly with you as you have dealt with the dead and with me. ⁹"May the LORD grant that you may find rest, each in the house of her husband." Then she kissed them, and they lifted up their voices and wept. ¹⁰ And they said to her, "*No,* but we will surely return with you to your people." ¹¹ But Naomi said, "Return, my daughters. Why should you go with me? Have I yet sons in my womb, that they may be your husbands? ¹²"Return, my daughters! Go, for I am too old to have a husband. If I said I have hope, if I should even have a husband tonight and also bear sons, ¹³ would you therefore wait until they were grown? Would you therefore refrain from marrying? No, my daughters; for it is harder for me than for you, for the hand of the LORD has gone forth against me."

Ruth's Loyalty

¹⁴ And they lifted up their voices and wept again; and Orpah kissed her mother-in-law, but Ruth clung to her. ¹⁵ ¶ Then she said, "Behold, your sister-in-law has gone back to her people and her gods; return after your sister-in-law."

Naomi and Ruth

1 IN THE days when the judges ruled,*a* there was a famine in the land, and a man from Bethlehem in Judah, together with his wife and two sons, went to live for a while in the country of Moab. ²The man's name was Elimelech, his wife's name Naomi, and the names of his two sons were Mahlon and Kilion. They were Ephrathites from Bethlehem, Judah. And they went to Moab and lived there.

³Now Elimelech, Naomi's husband, died, and she was left with her two sons. ⁴They married Moabite women, one named Orpah and the other Ruth. After they had lived there about ten years, ⁵both Mahlon and Kilion also died, and Naomi was left without her two sons and her husband.

⁶When she heard in Moab that the LORD had come to the aid of his people by providing food for them, Naomi and her daughters-in-law prepared to return home from there. ⁷With her two daughters-in-law she left the place where she had been living and set out on the road that would take them back to the land of Judah.

⁸Then Naomi said to her two daughters-in-law, "Go back, each of you, to your mother's home. May the LORD show kindness to you, as you have shown to your dead and to me. ⁹May the LORD grant that each of you will find rest in the home of another husband."

Then she kissed them and they wept aloud ¹⁰and said to her, "We will go back with you to your people."

¹¹But Naomi said, "Return home, my daughters. Why would you come with me? Am I going to have any more sons, who could become your husbands? ¹²Return home, my daughters; I am too old to have another husband. Even if I thought there was still hope for me—even if I had a husband tonight and then gave birth to sons— ¹³would you wait until they grew up? Would you remain unmarried for them? No, my daughters. It is more bitter for me than for you, because the LORD's hand has gone out against me!"

¹⁴At this they wept again. Then Orpah kissed her mother-in-law good-by, but Ruth clung to her.

¹⁵"Look," said Naomi, "your sister-in-law is going back to her people and her gods. Go back with her."

---

a 1 Traditionally *judged*

King James

16And Ruth said, *f*Entreat me not to leave thee, *or* to return from following after thee: for whither thou goest, I will go; and where thou lodgest, I will lodge: thy people *shall be* my people, and thy God my God:

17Where thou diest, will I die, and there will I be buried: the LORD do so to me, and more also, *if aught* but death part thee and me.

18When she saw that she *g*was stedfastly minded to go with her, then she left speaking unto her.

19 ¶ So they two went until they came to Bethlehem. And it came to pass, when they were come to Bethlehem, that all the city was moved about them, and they said, *Is* this Naomi?

20And she said unto them, Call me not *h*Naomi, call me *i*Mara: for the Almighty hath dealt very bitterly with me.

21I went out full, and the LORD hath brought me home again empty: why *then* call ye me Naomi, seeing the LORD hath testified against me, and the Almighty hath afflicted me?

22So Naomi returned, and Ruth the Moabitess, her daughter-in-law, with her, which returned out of the country of Moab: and they came to Bethlehem in the beginning of barley harvest.

Boaz speaks with Ruth

2 AND NAOMI had a kinsman of her husband's, a mighty man of wealth, of the family of Elimelech; and his name *was j*Boaz.

2And Ruth the Moabitess said unto Naomi, Let me now go to the field, and glean ears of corn after *him* in whose sight I shall find grace. And she said unto her, Go, my daughter.

3And she went, and came, and gleaned in the field after the reapers: and her *k*hap was to light on a part of the field *belonging* unto Boaz, who *was* of the kindred of Elimelech.

4 ¶ And, behold, Boaz came from Bethlehem, and said unto the reapers, The LORD *be* with you. And they answered him, The LORD bless thee.

5Then said Boaz unto his servant that was set over the reapers, Whose damsel *is* this?

6And the servant that was set over the reapers answered and said, It *is* the Moabitish damsel that came back with Naomi out of the country of Moab:

7And she said, I pray you, let me glean and gather after the reapers among the sheaves: so she came, and hath continued even from the morning until now, that she tarried a little in the house.

8Then said Boaz unto Ruth, Hearest thou not, my daughter? Go not to glean in another field, neither go from hence, but abide here fast by my maidens:

9*Let* thine eyes *be* on the field that they do reap, and go thou after them: have I not charged the young men that they shall not touch thee? and when thou art athirst, go unto the vessels, and drink of *that* which the young men have drawn.

10Then she fell on her face, and bowed herself to the ground, and said unto him, Why have I found grace in thine eyes, that thou shouldest take knowledge of me, seeing I *am* a stranger?

Amplified

16And Ruth said, Urge me not to leave you or to turn back from following you; for where you go I will go, and where you lodge I will lodge. *b*Your people shall be my people and your God my God.

17Where you die I will die, and there will I be buried. The Lord do so to me, and more also, if anything but death parts me from you.

18When Naomi saw that Ruth was determined to go with her, she said no more.

19So they both went on until they came to Bethlehem. And when they arrived in Bethlehem, the whole town was stirred about them, and said, Is this Naomi?

20And she said to them, Call me not Naomi [pleasant]; call me Mara [bitter], for the Almighty has dealt very bitterly with me.

21I went out full, but the Lord has brought me home again empty. Why call me Naomi, since the Lord has testified against me, and the Almighty has afflicted me?

22So Naomi returned, and Ruth the Moabitess, her daughter-in-law, with her, who returned from the country of Moab. And they came to Bethlehem at the beginning of barley harvest.

2 NOW NAOMI had a kinsman of her husband's, a man of wealth, of the family of Elimelech, whose name was Boaz.

2And Ruth the Moabitess said to Naomi, Let me go to the field and glean among the ears of grain after him in whose sight I shall find favor. Naomi said to her, Go, my daughter.

3And [Ruth] went and gleaned in a field after the reapers; and she happened to stop at the part of the field belonging to Boaz, who was of the family of Elimelech.

4And behold, Boaz came from Bethlehem and said to the reapers, The Lord be with you! And they answered him, The Lord bless you!

5Then Boaz said to his servant who was set over the reapers, Whose maiden is this?

6And the servant set over the reapers answered, She is the Moabitish girl who came back with Naomi from the country of Moab.

7And she said, I pray you, let me glean and gather after the reapers among the sheaves. So she came and has continued from early morning until now, except when she rested a little in the house.

8Then Boaz said to Ruth, Listen, my daughter, do not go to glean in another field or leave this one, but stay here close by my maidens.

9Watch which field they reap, and follow them. Have I not charged the young men not to molest you? And when you are thirsty, go to the vessels and drink what the young men have drawn.

10Then she fell on her face, bowing to the ground, and said to him, Why have I found favor in your eyes that you should notice me, when I am a foreigner?

b "Ruth is a prophecy, than which none could be more beautiful and engaging, of the entrance of the heathen world into the kingdom of God. She comes forth out of Moab, an idolatrous people full of wantonness and sin, and is herself so tender and pure. In a land where dissolute sensuality formed one of the elements of idol worship, a woman appears, as wife and daughter, chaste as the rose of spring and unsurpassed in these relations by any other [human] character in Holy Writ.... Ruth's confession of God and His people originated in the home of her married life. It sprang from the love with which she was permitted to embrace Israelites .... The conduct of one Israelitish woman [Naomi] in a foreign land was able to call forth a love and a confession of God like that of Ruth .... Ruth loves a woman, and is thereby led to the God Whom that woman confesses" (J.P. Lange, *A Commentary*).

*f*Or, *Be not against me*   *g* Heb. *strengthened herself*   *h* i.e.
Pleasant   *i* i.e. *Bitter*   *j* Called *Booz* in Mat. 1:5   *k* Heb.
hap happened

New American Standard

16 But Ruth said, "Do not urge me to leave you *or* turn back from following you; for where you go, I will go, and where you lodge, I will lodge. Your people *shall be* my people, and your God, my God.

17"Where you die, I will die, and there I will be buried. Thus may the LORD do to me, and worse, if *anything but* death parts you and me."

18 When she saw that she was determined to go with her, she said no more to her.

19 ¶ So they both went until they came to Bethlehem. And when they had come to Bethlehem, all the city was stirred because of them, and the women said, "Is this Naomi?"

20 She said to them, "Do not call me *a*Naomi; call me *b*Mara, for the Almighty has dealt very bitterly with me.

21"I went out full, but the LORD has brought me back empty. Why do you call me Naomi, since the LORD has witnessed against me and the Almighty has afflicted me?"

22 ¶ So Naomi returned, and with her Ruth the Moabitess, her daughter-in-law, who returned from the land of Moab. And they came to Bethlehem at the beginning of barley harvest.

Ruth Gleans in Boaz' Field

2 NOW NAOMI had a kinsman of her husband, a man of great wealth, of the family of Elimelech, whose name was Boaz.

2 And Ruth the Moabitess said to Naomi, "Please let me go to the field and glean among the ears of grain after one in whose sight I may find favor." And she said to her, "Go, my daughter."

3 So she departed and went and gleaned in the field after the reapers; and she happened to come to the portion of the field belonging to Boaz, who was of the family of Elimelech.

4 Now behold, Boaz came from Bethlehem and said to the reapers, "May the LORD be with you." And they said to him, "May the LORD bless you."

5 Then Boaz said to his servant who was in charge of the reapers, "Whose young woman is this?"

6 The servant in charge of the reapers replied, "She is the young Moabite woman who returned with Naomi from the land of Moab.

7"And she said, 'Please let me glean and gather after the reapers among the sheaves.' Thus she came and has remained from the morning until now; she has been sitting in the house for a little while."

8 ¶ Then Boaz said to Ruth, "Listen carefully, my daughter. Do not go to glean in another field; furthermore, do not go on from this one, but stay here with my maids.

9"Let your eyes be on the field which they reap, and go after them. Indeed, I have commanded the servants not to touch you. When you are thirsty, go to the water jars and drink from what the servants draw."

10 Then she fell on her face, bowing to the ground and said to him, "Why have I found favor in your sight that you should take notice of me, since I am a foreigner?"

New International

16But Ruth replied, "Don't urge me to leave you or to turn back from you. Where you go I will go, and where you stay I will stay. Your people will be my people and your God my God. 17Where you die I will die, and there I will be buried. May the LORD deal with me, be it ever so severely, if anything but death separates you and me." 18When Naomi realized that Ruth was determined to go with her, she stopped urging her.

19So the two women went on until they came to Bethlehem. When they arrived in Bethlehem, the whole town was stirred because of them, and the women exclaimed, "Can this be Naomi?"

20"Don't call me Naomi,*b*" she told them. "Call me Mara,*c* because the Almighty*d* has made my life very bitter. 21I went away full, but the LORD has brought me back empty. Why call me Naomi? The LORD has afflicted*e* me; the Almighty has brought misfortune upon me."

22So Naomi returned from Moab accompanied by Ruth the Moabitess, her daughter-in-law, arriving in Bethlehem as the barley harvest was beginning.

Ruth Meets Boaz

2 NOW NAOMI had a relative on her husband's side, from the clan of Elimelech, a man of standing, whose name was Boaz.

2And Ruth the Moabitess said to Naomi, "Let me go to the fields and pick up the leftover grain behind anyone in whose eyes I find favor."

Naomi said to her, "Go ahead, my daughter." 3So she went out and began to glean in the fields behind the harvesters. As it turned out, she found herself working in a field belonging to Boaz, who was from the clan of Elimelech.

4Just then Boaz arrived from Bethlehem and greeted the harvesters, "The LORD be with you!"

"The LORD bless you!" they called back.

5Boaz asked the foreman of his harvesters, "Whose young woman is that?"

6The foreman replied, "She is the Moabitess who came back from Moab with Naomi. 7She said, 'Please let me glean and gather among the sheaves behind the harvesters.' She went into the field and has worked steadily from morning till now, except for a short rest in the shelter."

8So Boaz said to Ruth, "My daughter, listen to me. Don't go and glean in another field and don't go away from here. Stay here with my servant girls. 9Watch the field where the men are harvesting, and follow along after the girls. I have told the men not to touch you. And whenever you are thirsty, go and get a drink from the water jars the men have filled."

10At this, she bowed down with her face to the ground. She exclaimed, "Why have I found such favor in your eyes that you notice me—a foreigner?"

---

a I.e. pleasant   *b* I.e. bitter

b 20 Naomi means *pleasant*; also in verse 21.   *c 20 Mara* means *bitter.*   *d 20* Hebrew *Shaddai*; also in verse 21   *e 21* Or has *testified against*

King James

¹¹And Boaz answered and said unto her, It hath fully been shown me, all that thou hast done unto thy mother-in-law since the death of thine husband: and *how* thou hast left thy father and thy mother, and the land of thy nativity, and art come unto a people which thou knewest not heretofore.

¹²The LORD recompense thy work, and a full reward be given thee of the LORD God of Israel, under whose wings thou art come to trust.

¹³Then she said, *l*Let me find favour in thy sight, my lord; for that thou hast comforted me, and for that thou hast spoken *m*friendly unto thine handmaid, though I be not like unto one of thine handmaidens.

¹⁴And Boaz said unto her, At mealtime come thou hither, and eat of the bread, and dip thy morsel in the vinegar. And she sat beside the reapers: and he reached her parched *corn,* and she did eat, and was sufficed, and left.

¹⁵And when she was risen up to glean, Boaz commanded his young men, saying, Let her glean even among the sheaves, and *n*reproach her not:

¹⁶And let fall also *some* of the handfuls of purpose for her, and leave *them,* that she may glean *them,* and rebuke her not.

¹⁷So she gleaned in the field until even, and beat out that she had gleaned: and it was about an ephah of barley.

¹⁸ ¶ And she took *it* up, and went into the city: and her mother-in-law saw what she had gleaned: and she brought forth, and gave to her that she had reserved after she was sufficed.

¹⁹And her mother-in-law said unto her, Where hast thou gleaned today? and where wroughtest thou? blessed be he that did take knowledge of thee. And she showed her mother-in-law with whom she had wrought, and said, The man's name with whom I wrought today *is* Boaz.

²⁰And Naomi said unto her daughter-in-law, Blessed *be* he of the LORD, who hath not left off his kindness to the living and to the dead. And Naomi said unto her, The man *is* near of kin unto us, *o*one of our next kinsmen.

²¹And Ruth the Moabitess said, He said unto me also, Thou shalt keep fast by my young men, until they have ended all my harvest.

²²And Naomi said unto Ruth her daughter-in-law, *It is* good, my daughter, that thou go out with his maidens, that they *p*meet thee not in any other field.

²³So she kept fast by the maidens of Boaz to glean unto the end of barley harvest and of wheat harvest; and dwelt with her mother-in-law.

Ruth visits Boaz

3 THEN NAOMI her mother-in-law said unto her, My daughter, shall I not seek rest for thee, that it may be well with thee?

²And now *is* not Boaz of our kindred, with whose maidens thou wast? Behold, he winnoweth barley tonight in the threshingfloor.

³Wash thyself therefore, and anoint thee, and put thy raiment upon thee, and get thee down to the floor: *but* make not thyself known unto the man, until he shall have done eating and drinking.

⁴And it shall be, when he lieth down, that thou shalt mark the place where he shall lie, and thou shalt go in, and *q*uncover his feet, and lay thee down; and he will tell thee what thou shalt do.

⁵And she said unto her, All that thou sayest unto me I will do.

⁶ ¶ And she went down unto the floor, and did according to all that her mother-in-law bade her.

Amplified

¹¹And Boaz said to her, I have been made fully aware of all you have done for your mother-in-law since the death of your husband, and how you have left your father and mother and the land of your birth and have come to a people unknown to you before.

¹²The Lord recompense you for what you have done, and a full reward be given you by the Lord, the God of Israel, under Whose wings you have come to take refuge!

¹³Then she said, Let me find favor in your sight, my lord. For you have comforted me and have spoken to the heart of your maidservant, though I am not as one of your maidservants.

¹⁴And at mealtime Boaz said to her, Come here and eat of the bread and dip your morsel in the sour wine [mixed with oil]. And she sat beside the reapers; and he passed her some parched grain, and she ate until she was satisfied and she had some left [for Naomi].

¹⁵And when she got up to glean, Boaz ordered his young men, Let her glean even among the sheaves, and do not reproach her.

¹⁶And let fall some handfuls for her on purpose and let them lie there for her to glean, and do not rebuke her.

¹⁷So she gleaned in the field until evening. Then she beat out what she had gleaned. It was about an ephah of barley.

¹⁸And she took it up and went into the town; she showed her mother-in-law what she had gleaned, and she also brought forth and gave her the food she had reserved after she was satisfied.

¹⁹And her mother-in-law said to her, Where have you gleaned today? Where did you work? Blessed be the man who noticed you. So [Ruth] told [her], The name of him with whom I worked today is Boaz.

²⁰And Naomi said to her daughter-in-law, Blessed be he of the Lord who has not ceased his kindness to the living and to the dead. And Naomi said to her, The man is a near relative of ours, one who has the right to redeem us. [Lev. 25:25.]

²¹And Ruth the Moabitess said, He said to me also, Stay close to my young men until they have harvested my entire crop.

²²And Naomi said to Ruth, It is good, my daughter, for you to go out with his maidens, lest in any other field you be molested.

²³So she kept close to the maidens of Boaz, gleaning until the end of the barley and wheat harvests. And she lived with her mother-in-law.

3 THEN NAOMI her mother-in-law said to Ruth, My daughter, shall I not seek rest *or* a home for you, that you may prosper?

²And now is not Boaz, with whose maidens you were, our relative? See, he is winnowing barley tonight at the threshing floor.

³Wash and anoint yourself therefore, and put on your best clothes and go down to the threshing floor, but do not make yourself known to the man until he has finished eating and drinking.

⁴But when he lies down, notice the place where he lies; then go and uncover his feet and lie down. And he will tell you what to do.

⁵And Ruth said to her, All that you say to me I will do.

⁶So she went down to the threshing floor and did just as her mother-in-law had told her.

---

*l*Or, *I find favour*   *m*Heb. *to the heart*   *n*Heb. *shame her not*
*o*Or, *one that hath right to redeem*   *p*Or, *fall upon thee*
*q*Or, *lift up the clothes that are on his feet*

New American Standard

11 Boaz replied to her, "All that you have done for your mother-in-law after the death of your husband has been fully reported to me, and how you left your father and your mother and the land of your birth, and came to a people that you did not previously know.

12"May the LORD reward your work, and your wages be full from the LORD, the God of Israel, under whose wings you have come to seek refuge."

13 Then she said, "I have found favor in your sight, my lord, for you have comforted me and indeed have spoken kindly to your maidservant, though I am not like one of your maidservants."

14 ¶ At mealtime Boaz said to her, "Come here, that you may eat of the bread and dip your piece of bread in the vinegar." So she sat beside the reapers; and he served her roasted grain, and she ate and was satisfied and had some left.

15 When she rose to glean, Boaz commanded his servants, saying, "Let her glean even among the sheaves, and do not insult her.

16"Also you shall purposely pull out for her *some grain* from the bundles and leave *it* that she may glean, and do not rebuke her."

17 ¶ So she gleaned in the field until evening. Then she beat out what she had gleaned, and it was about an ephah of barley.

18 She took *it* up and went into the city, and her mother-in-law saw what she had gleaned. She also took *it* out and gave Naomi what she had left after she was satisfied.

19 Her mother-in-law then said to her, "Where did you glean today and where did you work? May he who took notice of you be blessed." So she told her mother-in-law with whom she had worked and said, "The name of the man with whom I worked today is Boaz."

20 Naomi said to her daughter-in-law, "May he be blessed of the LORD who has not withdrawn his kindness to the living and to the dead." Again Naomi said to her, "The man is our relative, he is one of our closest relatives."

21 Then Ruth the Moabitess said, "Furthermore, he said to me, 'You should stay close to my servants until they have finished all my harvest.' "

22 Naomi said to Ruth her daughter-in-law, "It is good, my daughter, that you go out with his maids, so that *others* do not fall upon you in another field."

23 So she stayed close by the maids of Boaz in order to glean until the end of the barley harvest and the wheat harvest. And she lived with her mother-in-law.

Boaz Will Redeem Ruth

3 THEN NAOMI her mother-in-law said to her, "My daughter, shall I not seek security for you, that it may be well with you?

2"Now is not Boaz our kinsman, with whose maids you were? Behold, he winnows barley at the threshing floor tonight.

3"Wash yourself therefore, and anoint yourself and put on your *best* clothes, and go down to the threshing floor; *but* do not make yourself known to the man until he has finished eating and drinking.

4"It shall be when he lies down, that you shall notice the place where he lies, and you shall go and uncover his feet and lie down; then he will tell you what you shall do."

5 She said to her, "All that you say I will do."

6 ¶ So she went down to the threshing floor and did according to all that her mother-in-law had commanded her.

New International

11Boaz replied, "I've been told all about what you have done for your mother-in-law since the death of your husband—how you left your father and mother and your homeland and came to live with a people you did not know before. 12May the LORD repay you for what you have done. May you be richly rewarded by the LORD, the God of Israel, under whose wings you have come to take refuge."

13"May I continue to find favor in your eyes, my lord," she said. "You have given me comfort and have spoken kindly to your servant—though I do not have the standing of one of your servant girls."

14At mealtime Boaz said to her, "Come over here. Have some bread and dip it in the wine vinegar."

When she sat down with the harvesters, he offered her some roasted grain. She ate all she wanted and had some left over. 15As she got up to glean, Boaz gave orders to his men, "Even if she gathers among the sheaves, don't embarrass her. 16Rather, pull out some stalks for her from the bundles and leave them for her to pick up, and don't rebuke her."

17So Ruth gleaned in the field until evening. Then she threshed the barley she had gathered, and it amounted to about an ephah.*f* 18She carried it back to town, and her mother-in-law saw how much she had gathered. Ruth also brought out and gave her what she had left over after she had eaten enough.

19Her mother-in-law asked her, "Where did you glean today? Where did you work? Blessed be the man who took notice of you!"

Then Ruth told her mother-in-law about the one at whose place she had been working. "The name of the man I worked with today is Boaz," she said.

20"The LORD bless him!" Naomi said to her daughter-in-law. "He has not stopped showing his kindness to the living and the dead." She added, "That man is our close relative; he is one of our kinsman-redeemers."

21Then Ruth the Moabitess said, "He even said to me, 'Stay with my workers until they finish harvesting all my grain.' "

22Naomi said to Ruth her daughter-in-law, "It will be good for you, my daughter, to go with his girls, because in someone else's field you might be harmed."

23So Ruth stayed close to the servant girls of Boaz to glean until the barley and wheat harvests were finished. And she lived with her mother-in-law.

Ruth and Boaz at the Threshing Floor

3 ONE DAY Naomi her mother-in-law said to her, "My daughter, should I not try to find a home*g* for you, where you will be well provided for? 2Is not Boaz, with whose servant girls you have been, a kinsman of ours? Tonight he will be winnowing barley on the threshing floor. 3Wash and perfume yourself, and put on your best clothes. Then go down to the threshing floor, but don't let him know you are there until he has finished eating and drinking. 4When he lies down, note the place where he is lying. Then go and uncover his feet and lie down. He will tell you what to do."

5"I will do whatever you say," Ruth answered. 6So she went down to the threshing floor and did everything her mother-in-law told her to do.

---

f17 That is, probably about 3/5 bushel (about 22 liters)
g1 Hebrew *find rest* (see Ruth 1:9)

King James

7And when Boaz had eaten and drunk, and his heart was merry, he went to lie down at the end of the heap of corn: and she came softly, and uncovered his feet, and laid her down.

8 ¶ And it came to pass at midnight, that the man was afraid, and ʳturned himself: and, behold, a woman lay at his feet.

9And he said, Who *art* thou? And she answered, I *am* Ruth thine handmaid: spread therefore thy skirt over thine handmaid; for thou *art* ˢa near kinsman.

10And he said, Blessed *be* thou of the LORD, my daughter: *for* thou hast shown more kindness in the latter end than at the beginning, inasmuch as thou followedst not young men, whether poor or rich.

11And now, my daughter, fear not; I will do to thee all that thou requirest: for all the ᵗcity of my people doth know that thou *art* a virtuous woman.

12And now it is true that I *am thy* near kinsman: howbeit there is a kinsman nearer than I.

13Tarry this night, and it shall be in the morning, *that* if he will perform unto thee the part of a kinsman, well; let him do the kinsman's part: but if he will not do the part of a kinsman to thee, then will I do the part of a kinsman to thee, *as* the LORD liveth: lie down until the morning.

14 ¶ And she lay ˡat his feet until the morning: and she rose up before one could know another. And he said, Let it not be known that a woman came into the floor.

15Also he said, Bring the ᵘveil that *thou hast* upon thee, and hold it. And when she held it, he measured six *measures* of barley, and laid *it* on her: and she went into the city.

16And when she came to her mother-in-law, she said, Who *art* thou, my daughter? And she told her all that the man had done to her.

17And she said, These six *measures* of barley gave he me; for he said to me, Go not empty unto thy mother-in-law.

18Then said she, Sit still, my daughter, until thou know how the matter will fall: for the man will not be in rest, until he have finished the thing this day.

Boaz and Ruth marry

4 THEN WENT Boaz up to the gate, and sat him down there: and, behold, the kinsman of whom Boaz spake came by; unto whom he said, Ho, such a one! turn aside, sit down here. And he turned aside, and sat down.

2And he took ten men of the elders of the city, and said, Sit ye down here. And they sat down.

3And he said unto the kinsman, Naomi, that is come again out of the country of Moab, selleth a parcel of land, which *was* our brother Elimelech's:

4And ʳI thought to advertise thee, saying, Buy *it* before the inhabitants, and before the elders of my people. If thou wilt redeem *it,* redeem *it:* but if thou wilt not redeem *it, then* tell me, that I may know: for *there is* none to redeem *it* beside thee; and I *am* after thee. And he said, I will redeem *it.*

5Then said Boaz, What day thou buyest the field of the hand of Naomi, thou must buy *it* also of Ruth the Moabitess, the wife of the dead, to raise up the name of the dead upon his inheritance.

6 ¶ And the kinsman said, I cannot redeem *it* for myself, lest I mar mine own inheritance: redeem thou my right to thyself; for I cannot redeem *it.*

7Now this *was the manner* in former time in Israel concerning redeeming and concerning changing, for to confirm all things; a man plucked off his shoe, and gave *it* to his neighbour: and this *was* a testimony in Israel.

Amplified

7And when Boaz had eaten and drunk and his heart was merry, he went to lie down at the end of the heap of grain. Then [Ruth] came softly and uncovered his feet and lay down.

8At midnight the man was startled, and he turned over, and behold, a woman lay at his feet!

9And he said, Who are you? And she answered, I am Ruth your maidservant. Spread your wing [of protection] over your maidservant, for you are a next of kin.

10And he said, Blessed be you of the Lord, my daughter. For you have made this last loving-kindness greater than the former, for you have not gone after young men, whether poor or rich.

11And now, my daughter, fear not. I will do for you all you require, for all my people in the city know that you are a woman of strength (worth, bravery, capability).

12It is true that I am your near kinsman; however, there is a kinsman nearer than I.

13Remain tonight, and in the morning if he will perform for you the part of a kinsman, good; let him do it. But if he will not do the part of a kinsman for you, then, as the Lord lives, I will do the part of a kinsman for you. Lie down until the morning.

14And she lay at his feet until the morning, but arose before one could recognize another; for he said, Let it not be known that the woman came to the threshing floor.

15Also he said, Bring the mantle you are wearing and hold it. So [Ruth] held it, and he measured out six measures of barley and laid it on her. And she went into the town.

16And when she came home, her mother-in-law said, How have you fared, my daughter? And Ruth told her all that the man had done for her.

17And she said, He gave me these six measures of barley, for he said to me, Do not go empty-handed to your mother-in-law.

18Then said she, Sit still, my daughter, until you learn how the matter turns out; for the man will not rest until he finishes the matter today.

4 THEN BOAZ went up to the city's gate and sat down there, and behold, the kinsman of whom Boaz had spoken came by. He said to him, Ho! Turn aside and sit down here. So he turned aside and sat down.

2And Boaz took ten men of the elders of the city and said, Sit down here. And they sat down.

3And he said to the kinsman, Naomi, who has returned from the country of Moab, has sold the parcel of land which belonged to our brother Elimelech.

4And I thought to let you hear of it, saying, Buy it in the presence of those sitting here and before the elders of my people. If you will redeem it, redeem it; but if you will not redeem it, then say so, that I may know; for there is no one besides you to redeem it, and I am [next of kin] after you. And he said, I will redeem it.

5Then Boaz said, The day you buy the field of Naomi, you must buy also Ruth the Moabitess, the widow of the dead man, to restore the name of the dead to his inheritance.

6And the kinsman said, I cannot redeem it for myself, lest [by marrying a Moabitess] I endanger my own inheritance. Take my right of redemption yourself, for I cannot redeem it. [Deut. 23:3, 4.]

7Now formerly in Israel this was the custom concerning redeeming and exchanging. To confirm a transaction, a man pulled off his sandal and gave it to the other. This was the way of attesting in Israel.

ʳOr, *took hold on* ˢOr, *one that hath right to redeem* ᵗHeb. *gate* ᵘOr, *sheet,* or *apron* ᵛHeb. *I said I will reveal* in *thine ear*

New American Standard

⁷ When Boaz had eaten and drunk and his heart was merry, he went to lie down at the end of the heap of grain; and she came secretly, and uncovered his feet and lay down.

⁸ It happened in the middle of the night that the man was startled and bent forward; and behold, a woman was lying at his feet.

⁹ He said, "Who are you?" And she answered, "I am Ruth your maid. So spread your covering over your maid, for you are a ^cclose relative."

¹⁰ Then he said, "May you be blessed of the LORD, my daughter. You have shown your last kindness to be better than the first by not going after young men, whether poor or rich.

¹¹"Now, my daughter, do not fear. I will do for you whatever you ask, for all my people in the city know that you are a woman of excellence.

¹²"Now it is true I am a close relative; however, there is a relative closer than I.

¹³"Remain this night, and when morning comes, if he will redeem you, good; let him redeem you. But if he does not wish to redeem you, then I will redeem you, as the LORD lives. Lie down until morning."

¹⁴ ¶ So she lay at his feet until morning and rose before one could recognize another; and he said, "Let it not be known that the woman came to the threshing floor."

¹⁵ Again he said, "Give me the cloak that is on you and hold it." So she held it, and he measured six *measures* of barley and laid *it* on her. Then she went into the city.

¹⁶ When she came to her mother-in-law, she said, "How did it go, my daughter?" And she told her all that the man had done for her.

¹⁷ She said, "These six *measures* of barley he gave to me, for he said, 'Do not go to your mother-in-law empty-handed.' "

¹⁸ Then she said, "Wait, my daughter, until you know how the matter turns out; for the man will not rest until he has settled it today."

The Marriage of Ruth

4 NOW BOAZ went up to the gate and sat down there, and behold, the close relative of whom Boaz spoke was passing by, so he said, "Turn aside, friend, sit down here." And he turned aside and sat down.

² He took ten men of the elders of the city and said, "Sit down here." So they sat down.

³ Then he said to the closest relative, "Naomi, who has come back from the land of Moab, has to sell the piece of land which belonged to our brother Elimelech.

⁴"So I thought to inform you, saying, 'Buy *it* before those who are sitting *here,* and before the elders of my people. If you will redeem *it,* redeem *it;* but if not, tell me that I may know; for there is no one but you to redeem *it,* and I am after you.' " And he said, "I will redeem *it.*"

⁵ Then Boaz said, "On the day you buy the field from the hand of Naomi, you must also acquire Ruth the Moab-itess, the widow of the deceased, in order to raise up the name of the deceased on his inheritance."

⁶ The closest relative said, "I cannot redeem *it* for myself, because I would jeopardize my own inheritance. Redeem *it* for yourself; you *may have* my right of redemption, for I cannot redeem *it.*"

⁷ ¶ Now this was *the custom* in former times in Israel concerning the redemption and the exchange *of land* to confirm any matter: a man removed his sandal and gave it to another; and this was the *manner of* attestation in Israel.

New International

⁷When Boaz had finished eating and drinking and was in good spirits, he went over to lie down at the far end of the grain pile. Ruth approached quietly, uncovered his feet and lay down. ⁸In the middle of the night something startled the man, and he turned and discovered a woman lying at his feet.

⁹"Who are you?" he asked.

"I am your servant Ruth," she said. "Spread the corner of your garment over me, since you are a kinsman-redeemer."

¹⁰"The LORD bless you, my daughter," he replied. "This kindness is greater than that which you showed earlier: You have not run after the younger men, whether rich or poor. ¹¹And now, my daughter, don't be afraid. I will do for you all you ask. All my fellow townsmen know that you are a woman of noble character. ¹²Although it is true that I am near of kin, there is a kinsman-redeemer nearer than I. ¹³Stay here for the night, and in the morning if he wants to redeem, good; let him redeem. But if he is not willing, as surely as the LORD lives I will do it. Lie here until morning."

¹⁴So she lay at his feet until morning, but got up before anyone could be recognized; and he said, "Don't let it be known that a woman came to the threshing floor."

¹⁵He also said, "Bring me the shawl you are wearing and hold it out." When she did so, he poured into it six measures of barley and put it on her. Then he^h went back to town.

¹⁶When Ruth came to her mother-in-law, Naomi asked, "How did it go, my daughter?"

Then she told her everything Boaz had done for her ¹⁷and added, "He gave me these six measures of barley, saying, 'Don't go back to your mother-in-law empty-handed.' "

¹⁸Then Naomi said, "Wait, my daughter, until you find out what happens. For the man will not rest until the matter is settled today."

Boaz Marries Ruth

4 MEANWHILE BOAZ went up to the town gate and sat there. When the kinsman-redeemer he had mentioned came along, Boaz said, "Come over here, my friend, and sit down." So he went over and sat down.

²Boaz took ten of the elders of the town and said, "Sit here," and they did so. ³Then he said to the kinsman-redeemer, "Naomi, who has come back from Moab, is selling the piece of land that belonged to our brother Elimelech. ⁴I thought I should bring the matter to your attention and suggest that you buy it in the presence of these seated here and in the presence of the elders of my people. If you will redeem it, do so. But if youⁱ will not, tell me, so I will know. For no one has the right to do it except you, and I am next in line."

"I will redeem it," he said.

⁵Then Boaz said, "On the day you buy the land from Naomi and from Ruth the Moabitess, you acquire^j the dead man's widow, in order to maintain the name of the dead with his property."

⁶At this, the kinsman-redeemer said, "Then I cannot redeem it because I might endanger my own estate. You redeem it yourself. I cannot do it."

⁷(Now in earlier times in Israel, for the redemption and transfer of property to become final, one party took off his sandal and gave it to the other. This was the method of legalizing transactions in Israel.)

King James

8Therefore the kinsman said unto Boaz, Buy *it* for thee. So he drew off his shoe.

9 ¶ And Boaz said unto the elders, and *unto* all the people, Ye *are* witnesses this day, that I have bought all that *was* Elimelech's, and all that *was* Chilion's and Mahlon's, of the hand of Naomi.

10Moreover Ruth the Moabitess, the wife of Mahlon, have I purchased to be my wife, to raise up the name of the dead upon his inheritance, that the name of the dead be not cut off from among his brethren, and from the gate of his place: ye *are* witnesses this day.

11And all the people that *were* in the gate, and the elders, said, *We are* witnesses. The LORD make the woman that is come into thine house like Rachel and like Leah, which two did build the house of Israel: and *w*do thou worthily in Ephratah, and *x*be famous in Bethlehem:

12And let thy house be like the house of Pharez, whom Tamar bare unto Judah, of the seed which the LORD shall give thee of this young woman.

Obed is born: the Davidic line

13 ¶ So Boaz took Ruth, and she was his wife: and when he went in unto her, the LORD gave her conception, and she bare a son.

14And the women said unto Naomi, Blessed *be* the LORD, which hath not *y*left thee this day without a *z*kinsman, that his name may be famous in Israel.

15And he shall be unto thee a restorer of *thy* life, and *a*a nourisher of *b*thine old age: for thy daughter-in-law, which loveth thee, which is better to thee than seven sons, hath borne him.

16And Naomi took the child, and laid it in her bosom, and became nurse unto it.

17And the women her neighbours gave it a name, saying, There is a son born to Naomi; and they called his name Obed: he *is* the father of Jesse, the father of David.

18 ¶ Now these *are* the generations of Pharez: Pharez begat Hezron,

19And Hezron begat Ram, and Ram begat Amminadab,

20And Amminadab begat Nahshon, and Nahshon begat *c*Salmon,

21And Salmon begat Boaz, and Boaz begat Obed,

22And Obed begat Jesse, and Jesse begat David.

Amplified

8Therefore, when the kinsman said to Boaz, Buy it for yourself, he pulled off his sandal.

9And Boaz said to the elders and to all the people, You are witnesses this day that I have bought all that was Elimelech's and all that was Chilion's and Mahlon's from the hand of Naomi.

10Also Ruth the Moabitess, the widow of Mahlon, I have bought to be my wife, to restore the name of the dead to his inheritance, that the name of the dead may not be cut off from among his brethren and from the gate of his birthplace. You are witnesses this day.

11And all the people at the gate and the elders said, We are witnesses. May the Lord make the woman who is coming into your house like Rachel and Leah, the two who built the household of Israel. May you do worthily *and* get wealth (power) in Ephratah and be famous in Bethlehem.

12And let your house be like the house of Perez, whom Tamar bore to Judah, because of the offspring which the Lord will give you by this young woman.

13So Boaz took Ruth and she became his wife. And he went in to her, and the Lord caused her to conceive, and she bore a son.

14And the women said to Naomi, Blessed be the Lord, Who has not left you this day without a close kinsman, and may his name be famous in Israel.

15And may he be to you a restorer of life and a nourisher *and* supporter in your old age, for your daughter-in-law who loves you, who is better to you than seven sons, has borne him.

16Then Naomi took the child and laid him in her bosom and became his nurse.

17And her neighbor women gave him a name, saying, A son is born to Naomi. They named him Obed. He was the father of Jesse, the father of David [the ancestor of Jesus Christ].

18Now these are the descendants of Perez: Perez was the father of Hezron,

19Hezron of Ram, Ram of Amminadab,

20Amminadab of Nahshon, Nahshon of Salmon,

21Salmon of Boaz, Boaz of Obed,

22Obed of Jesse, and Jesse of David [the ancestor of Jesus Christ].

---

*w*Or, *get thee riches*, or, *power*   *x*Heb. *proclaim* thy *name*
*y*Heb. *caused to cease unto thee*   *z*Or, *redeemer*   *a*Heb. *to*
nourish   *b*Heb. *thy gray hairs*   *c*Or, *Salmah*

New American Standard

8 So the closest relative said to Boaz, "Buy *it* for yourself." And he removed his sandal.

9 Then Boaz said to the elders and all the people, "You are witnesses today that I have bought from the hand of Naomi all that belonged to Elimelech and all that belonged to Chilion and Mahlon.

10 "Moreover, I have acquired Ruth the Moabitess, the widow of Mahlon, to be my wife in order to raise up the name of the deceased on his inheritance, so that the name of the deceased will not be cut off from his brothers or from the court of his *birth* place; you are witnesses today."

11 All the people who were in the court, and the elders, said, "*We are* witnesses. May the LORD make the woman who is coming into your home like Rachel and Leah, both of whom built the house of Israel; and may you achieve wealth in Ephrathah and become famous in Bethlehem.

12 "Moreover, may your house be like the house of Perez whom Tamar bore to Judah, through the offspring which the LORD will give you by this young woman."

13 ¶ So Boaz took Ruth, and she became his wife, and he went in to her. And the LORD enabled her to conceive, and she gave birth to a son.

14 Then the women said to Naomi, "Blessed is the LORD who has not left you without a redeemer today, and may his name become famous in Israel.

15 "May he also be to you a restorer of life and a sustainer of your old age; for your daughter-in-law, who loves you and is better to you than seven sons, has given birth to him."

The Line of David Began Here

16 Then Naomi took the child and laid him in her lap, and became his nurse.

17 The neighbor women gave him a name, saying, "A son has been born to Naomi!" So they named him Obed. He is the father of Jesse, the father of David.

18 ¶ Now these are the generations of Perez: to Perez was born Hezron,

19 and to Hezron was born Ram, and to Ram, Amminadab,

20 and to Amminadab was born Nahshon, and to Nahshon, Salmon,

21 and to Salmon was born Boaz, and to Boaz, Obed,

22 and to Obed was born Jesse, and to Jesse, David.

New International

8 So the kinsman-redeemer said to Boaz, "Buy it yourself." And he removed his sandal.

9 Then Boaz announced to the elders and all the people, "Today you are witnesses that I have bought from Naomi all the property of Elimelech, Kilion and Mahlon. 10 I have also acquired Ruth the Moabitess, Mahlon's widow, as my wife, in order to maintain the name of the dead with his property, so that his name will not disappear from among his family or from the town records. Today you are witnesses!"

11 Then the elders and all those at the gate said, "We are witnesses. May the LORD make the woman who is coming into your home like Rachel and Leah, who together built up the house of Israel. May you have standing in Ephrathah and be famous in Bethlehem. 12 Through the offspring the LORD gives you by this young woman, may your family be like that of Perez, whom Tamar bore to Judah."

The Genealogy of David

13 So Boaz took Ruth and she became his wife. Then he went to her, and the LORD enabled her to conceive, and she gave birth to a son. 14 The women said to Naomi: "Praise be to the LORD, who this day has not left you without a kinsman-redeemer. May he become famous throughout Israel! 15 He will renew your life and sustain you in your old age. For your daughter-in-law, who loves you and is better to you than seven sons, has given him birth."

16 Then Naomi took the child, laid him in her lap and cared for him. 17 The women living there said, "Naomi has a son." And they named him Obed. He was the father of Jesse, the father of David.

18 This, then, is the family line of Perez:

Perez was the father of Hezron,
19 Hezron the father of Ram,
   Ram the father of Amminadab,
20 Amminadab the father of Nahshon,
   Nahshon the father of Salmon,[k]
21 Salmon the father of Boaz,
   Boaz the father of Obed,
22 Obed the father of Jesse,
   and Jesse the father of David.

---

k 20 A few Hebrew manuscripts, some Septuagint manuscripts and Vulgate (see also verse 21 and Septuagint of 1 Chron. 2:11); most Hebrew manuscripts *Salma*

THE FIRST BOOK OF

Samuel

OTHERWISE CALLED THE FIRST BOOK OF THE KINGS

Samuel's birth

1 NOW THERE was a certain man of Ramathaim-zophim, of mount Ephraim, and his name *was* Elkanah, the son of Jeroham, the son of Elihu, the son of Tohu, the son of Zuph, an Ephrathite:

2 And he had two wives; the name of the one *was* Hannah, and the name of the other Peninnah: and Peninnah had children, but Hannah had no children.

3 And this man went up out of his city *a*yearly to worship and to sacrifice unto the LORD of hosts in Shiloh. And the two sons of Eli, Hophni and Phinehas, the priests of the LORD, *were* there.

4 ¶ And when the time was that Elkanah offered, he gave to Peninnah his wife, and to all her sons and her daughters, portions:

5 But unto Hannah he gave *b*a worthy portion; for he loved Hannah: but the LORD had shut up her womb.

6 And her adversary also *c*provoked her sore, for to make her fret, because the LORD had shut up her womb.

7 And *as* he did so year by year, *d e*when she went up to the house of the LORD, so she provoked her; therefore she wept, and did not eat.

8 Then said Elkanah her husband to her, Hannah, why weepest thou? and why eatest thou not? and why is thy heart grieved? *am* not I better to thee than ten sons?

9 ¶ So Hannah rose up after they had eaten in Shiloh, and after they had drunk. Now Eli the priest sat upon a seat by a post of the temple of the LORD.

10 And she *was* *f*in bitterness of soul, and prayed unto the LORD, and wept sore.

11 And she vowed a vow, and said, O LORD of hosts, if thou wilt indeed look on the affliction of thine handmaid, and remember me, and not forget thine handmaid, but wilt give unto thine handmaid *g*a man child, then I will give him unto the LORD all the days of his life, and there shall no razor come upon his head.

12 And it came to pass, as she *h*continued praying before the LORD, that Eli marked her mouth.

13 Now Hannah, she spake in her heart; only her lips moved, but her voice was not heard: therefore Eli thought she had been drunken.

14 And Eli said unto her, How long wilt thou be drunken? put away thy wine from thee.

15 And Hannah answered and said, No, my lord, I *am* a woman *i*of a sorrowful spirit: I have drunk neither wine nor strong drink, but have poured out my soul before the LORD.

16 Count not thine handmaid for a daughter of Belial: for out of the abundance of my *j*complaint and grief have I spoken hitherto.

17 Then Eli answered and said, Go in peace: and the God of Israel grant *thee* thy petition that thou hast asked of him.

18 And she said, Let thine handmaid find grace in thy sight. So the woman went her way, and did eat, and her countenance was no more *sad*.

19 ¶ And they rose up in the morning early, and worshipped before the LORD, and returned, and came to their house to Ramah: and Elkanah knew Hannah his wife; and the LORD remembered her.

THE FIRST BOOK OF

Samuel

1 THERE WAS a certain man of Ramathaim-zophim, of the hill country of Ephraim, named Elkanah son of Jeroham, the son of Elihu, the son of Tohu, the son of Zuph, an Ephraimite.

2 He had two wives, one named Hannah and the other named Peninnah. Peninnah had children, but Hannah had none.

3 This man went from his city year by year to worship and sacrifice to the Lord of hosts at Shiloh, where Hophni and Phinehas, the two sons of Eli, were the Lord's priests.

4 When the day came that Elkanah sacrificed, he would give to Peninnah his wife and all her sons and daughters portions [of the sacrificial meat].

5 But to Hannah he gave a double portion, for he loved Hannah, but the Lord had given her no children.

6 [This embarrassed and grieved Hannah] and her rival provoked her greatly to vex her, because the Lord had left her childless.

7 So it was year after year; whenever Hannah went up to the Lord's house, Peninnah provoked her, so she wept and did not eat.

8 Then Elkanah her husband said to her, Hannah, why do you cry? And why do you not eat? And why are you grieving? Am I not more to you than ten sons?

9 So Hannah rose after they had eaten and drunk in Shiloh. Now Eli the priest was sitting on his seat beside a post of the temple (tent) of the Lord.

10 And [Hannah] was in distress of soul, praying to the Lord and weeping bitterly.

11 She vowed, saying, O Lord of hosts, if You will indeed look on the affliction of Your handmaid and [earnestly] remember, and not forget Your handmaid but will give me a son, I will give him to the Lord all his life; no razor shall touch his head.

12 And as she continued praying before the Lord, Eli noticed her mouth.

13 Hannah was speaking in her heart; only her lips moved but her voice was not heard. So Eli thought she was drunk.

14 Eli said to her, How long will you be intoxicated? Put wine away from you.

15 But Hannah answered, No, my lord, I am a woman of a sorrowful spirit. I have drunk neither wine nor strong drink, but I was pouring out my soul before the Lord. [Gen. 19:34.]

16 Regard not your handmaid as a wicked woman; for out of my great complaint and bitter provocation I have been speaking.

17 Then Eli said, Go in peace, and may the God of Israel grant your petition which you have asked of Him.

18 Hannah said, Let your handmaid find grace in your sight. So [she] went her way and ate, her countenance no longer sad.

19 The family rose early the next morning, worshiped before the Lord, and returned to their home in Ramah. Elkanah knew Hannah his wife, and the Lord remembered her.

---

a Heb. *from year to year*   *b* Or, *a double portion*   *c* Heb. *angered her*   *d* Or, *from the time that she*   *e* Heb. *from her going up*   *f* Heb. *bitter of soul*   *g* Heb. *seed of men*   *h* Heb. *multiplied to pray*   *i* Heb. *hard of spirit*   *j* Or, *meditation*

THE FIRST BOOK OF

Samuel

1 Samuel

Elkanah and His Wives

1 NOW THERE was a certain man from Ramathaim-zophim from the hill country of Ephraim, and his name was Elkanah the son of Jeroham, the son of Elihu, the son of Tohu, the son of Zuph, an Ephraimite. ² He had two wives: the name of one was Hannah and the name of the other Peninnah; and Peninnah had children, but Hannah had no children.

³ ¶ Now this man would go up from his city yearly to worship and to sacrifice to the LORD of hosts in Shiloh. And the two sons of Eli, Hophni and Phinehas, were priests to the LORD there.

⁴ When the day came that Elkanah sacrificed, he would give portions to Peninnah his wife and to all her sons and her daughters;

⁵ but to Hannah he would give a double portion, for he loved Hannah, but the LORD had closed her womb.

⁶ Her rival, however, would provoke her bitterly to irritate her, because the LORD had closed her womb.

⁷ It happened year after year, as often as she went up to the house of the LORD, she would provoke her; so she wept and would not eat.

⁸ Then Elkanah her husband said to her, "Hannah, why do you weep and why do you not eat and why is your heart sad? Am I not better to you than ten sons?"

⁹ ¶ Then Hannah rose after eating and drinking in Shiloh. Now Eli the priest was sitting on the seat by the doorpost of the temple of the LORD.

¹⁰ She, greatly distressed, prayed to the LORD and wept bitterly.

¹¹ She made a vow and said, "O LORD of hosts, if You will indeed look on the affliction of Your maidservant and remember me, and not forget Your maidservant, but will give Your maidservant a son, then I will give him to the LORD all the days of his life, and a razor shall never come on his head."

¹² ¶ Now it came about, as she continued praying before the LORD, that Eli was watching her mouth.

¹³ As for Hannah, she was speaking in her heart, only her lips were moving, but her voice was not heard. So Eli thought she was drunk.

¹⁴ Then Eli said to her, "How long will you make yourself drunk? Put away your wine from you."

¹⁵ But Hannah replied, "No, my lord, I am a woman oppressed in spirit; I have drunk neither wine nor strong drink, but I have poured out my soul before the LORD.

¹⁶ "Do not consider your maidservant as a worthless woman, for I have spoken until now out of my great concern and provocation."

¹⁷ Then Eli answered and said, "Go in peace; and may the God of Israel grant your petition that you have asked of Him."

¹⁸ She said, "Let your maidservant find favor in your sight." So the woman went her way and ate, and her face was no longer sad.

Samuel Is Born to Hannah

¹⁹ ¶ Then they arose early in the morning and worshiped before the LORD, and returned again to their house in Ramah. And Elkanah had relations with Hannah his wife, and the LORD remembered her.

The Birth of Samuel

1 THERE WAS a certain man from Ramathaim, a Zuphite[a] from the hill country of Ephraim, whose name was Elkanah son of Jeroham, the son of Elihu, the son of Tohu, the son of Zuph, an Ephraimite. ² He had two wives; one was called Hannah and the other Peninnah. Peninnah had children, but Hannah had none.

³ Year after year this man went up from his town to worship and sacrifice to the LORD Almighty at Shiloh, where Hophni and Phinehas, the two sons of Eli, were priests of the LORD. ⁴ Whenever the day came for Elkanah to sacrifice, he would give portions of the meat to his wife Peninnah and to all her sons and daughters. ⁵ But to Hannah he gave a double portion because he loved her, and the LORD had closed her womb. ⁶ And because the LORD had closed her womb, her rival kept provoking her in order to irritate her. ⁷ This went on year after year. Whenever Hannah went up to the house of the LORD, her rival provoked her till she wept and would not eat. ⁸ Elkanah her husband would say to her, "Hannah, why are you weeping? Why don't you eat? Why are you downhearted? Don't I mean more to you than ten sons?"

⁹ Once when they had finished eating and drinking in Shiloh, Hannah stood up. Now Eli the priest was sitting on a chair by the doorpost of the LORD's temple.[b] ¹⁰ In bitterness of soul Hannah wept much and prayed to the LORD. ¹¹ And she made a vow, saying, "O LORD Almighty, if you will only look upon your servant's misery and remember me, and not forget your servant but give her a son, then I will give him to the LORD for all the days of his life, and no razor will ever be used on his head."

¹² As she kept on praying to the LORD, Eli observed her mouth. ¹³ Hannah was praying in her heart, and her lips were moving but her voice was not heard. Eli thought she was drunk ¹⁴ and said to her, "How long will you keep on getting drunk? Get rid of your wine."

¹⁵ "Not so, my lord," Hannah replied, "I am a woman who is deeply troubled. I have not been drinking wine or beer; I was pouring out my soul to the LORD. ¹⁶ Do not take your servant for a wicked woman; I have been praying here out of my great anguish and grief."

¹⁷ Eli answered, "Go in peace, and may the God of Israel grant you what you have asked of him."

¹⁸ She said, "May your servant find favor in your eyes." Then she went her way and ate something, and her face was no longer downcast.

¹⁹ Early the next morning they arose and worshiped before the LORD and then went back to their home at Ramah. Elkanah lay with Hannah his wife, and the LORD remem-

King James

²⁰Wherefore it came to pass, ^kwhen the time was come about after Hannah had conceived, that she bare a son, and called his name ^lSamuel, *saying,* Because I have asked him of the LORD.

Samuel dedicated

²¹And the man Elkanah, and all his house, went up to offer unto the LORD the yearly sacrifice, and his vow. ²²But Hannah went not up; for she said unto her husband, *I will not go up* until the child be weaned, and *then* I will bring him, that he may appear before the LORD, and there abide for ever. ²³And Elkanah her husband said unto her, Do what seemeth thee good; tarry until thou have weaned him; only the LORD establish his word. So the woman abode, and gave her son suck until she weaned him. ²⁴ ¶ And when she had weaned him, she took him up with her, with three bullocks, and one ephah of flour, and a bottle of wine, and brought him unto the house of the LORD in Shiloh: and the child *was* young. ²⁵And they slew a bullock, and brought the child to Eli. ²⁶And she said, Oh my lord, *as* thy soul liveth, my lord, I *am* the woman that stood by thee here, praying unto the LORD. ²⁷For this child I prayed; and the LORD hath given me my petition which I asked of him: ²⁸Therefore also I have ^mlent him to the LORD; as long as he liveth ⁿhe shall be lent to the LORD. And he worshipped the LORD there.

Hannah's song of praise

2 AND HANNAH prayed, and said, My heart rejoiceth in the LORD, mine horn is exalted in the LORD: my mouth is enlarged over mine enemies; because I rejoice in thy salvation. ²*There is* none holy as the LORD: for *there is* none beside thee: neither *is there* any rock like our God. ³Talk no more so exceeding proudly; let *not* ^oarrogancy come out of your mouth: for the LORD *is* a God of knowledge, and by him actions are weighed. ⁴The bows of the mighty men *are* broken, and they that stumbled are girded with strength. ⁵*They that were* full have hired out themselves for bread; and *they that were* hungry ceased: so that the barren hath born seven; and she that hath many children is waxed feeble. ⁶The LORD killeth, and maketh alive: he bringeth down to the grave, and bringeth up. ⁷The LORD maketh poor, and maketh rich: he bringeth low, and lifteth up. ⁸He raiseth up the poor out of the dust, *and* lifteth up the beggar from the dunghill, to set *them* among princes, and to make them inherit the throne of glory: for the pillars of the earth *are* the LORD'S, and he hath set the world upon them.

Amplified

²⁰Hannah became pregnant and in due time bore a son and named him Samuel [heard of God], Because, she said, I have asked him of the Lord.

²¹And Elkanah and all his house went up to offer to the Lord the yearly sacrifice and pay his vow. ²²But Hannah did not go, for she said to her husband, I will not go until the child is weaned, and then I will bring him, that he may appear before the Lord and remain there as long as he lives. ²³Elkanah her husband said to her, Do what seems best to you. Wait until you have weaned him; only may the Lord establish His word. So Hannah remained and nursed her son until she weaned him. ²⁴When she had ^aweaned him, she took him with her, with a three-year-old bull, an ephah of flour, and a skin bottle of wine [to pour over the burnt offering for a sweet odor], and brought Samuel to the Lord's house in Shiloh. The child was growing. ²⁵Then they slew the bull, and brought the child to Eli. ²⁶Hannah said, Oh, my lord! As your soul lives, my lord, I am the woman who stood by you here praying to the Lord. ²⁷For this child I prayed, and the Lord has granted my petition made to Him. ²⁸Therefore I have given him to the Lord; as long as he lives he is given to the Lord. And they worshiped the Lord there.

2 HANNAH PRAYED, and said, My heart exults *and* triumphs in the Lord; my horn (my strength) is lifted up in the Lord. My mouth is no longer silent, for it is opened wide over my enemies, because I rejoice in Your salvation. ²There is none holy like the Lord, there is none besides You; there is no Rock like our God. ³Talk no more so very proudly; let not arrogance go forth from your mouth, for the Lord is a God of knowledge, and by Him actions are weighed. ⁴The bows of the mighty are broken, and those who stumbled are girded with strength. ⁵Those who were full have hired themselves out for bread, but those who were hungry have ceased to hunger. The barren has borne seven, but she who has many children languishes *and* is forlorn. ⁶The Lord slays and makes alive; He brings down to Sheol and raises up. ⁷The Lord makes poor and makes rich; He brings low and He lifts up. ⁸He raises up the poor out of the dust and lifts up the needy from the ash heap, to make them sit with nobles and inherit the throne of glory. For the pillars of the earth are the Lord's, and He has set the world upon them.

---

^kHeb. *in revolution of days*   ^li.e. *Asked of God*   ^mOr, *returned him, whom I have obtained by petition, to the LORD* ⁿOr, *he whom I have obtained by petition shall be returned* ^oHeb. *hard*

^aHe would then be two or three years old. There were women engaged in tabernacle service to whose care he might have been committed. It was important that he should be dedicated as soon as possible. The earliest impressions of his boyhood were to be those of the house of God (*The Cambridge Bible*).

New American Standard

20 It came about in due time, after Hannah had conceived, that she gave birth to a son; and she named him Samuel, *saying,* "Because I have asked him of the LORD."

21 ¶ Then the man Elkanah went up with all his household to offer to the LORD the yearly sacrifice and *pay* his vow.

22 But Hannah did not go up, for she said to her husband, "*I will not go up* until the child is weaned; then I will bring him, that he may appear before the LORD and stay there forever."

23 Elkanah her husband said to her, "Do what seems best to you. Remain until you have weaned him; only may the LORD confirm His word." So the woman remained and nursed her son until she weaned him.

24 Now when she had weaned him, she took him up with her, with a three-year-old bull and one ephah of flour and a jug of wine, and brought him to the house of the LORD in Shiloh, although the child was young.

25 Then they slaughtered the bull, and brought the boy to Eli.

26 She said, "Oh, my lord! As your soul lives, my lord, I am the woman who stood here beside you, praying to the LORD.

27 "For this boy I prayed, and the LORD has given me my petition which I asked of Him.

28 "So I have also *a*dedicated him to the LORD; as long as he lives he is *a*dedicated to the LORD." And he worshiped the LORD there.

Hannah's Song of Thanksgiving

2 THEN HANNAH prayed and said,
"My heart exults in the LORD;
My horn is exalted in the LORD,
My mouth speaks boldly against my enemies,
Because I rejoice in Your salvation.
2 "There is no one holy like the LORD,
Indeed, there is no one besides You,
Nor is there any rock like our God.
3 "Boast no more so very proudly,
Do not let arrogance come out of your mouth;
For the LORD is a God of knowledge,
And with Him actions are weighed.
4 "The bows of the mighty are shattered,
But the feeble gird on strength.
5 "Those who were full hire themselves out for bread,
But those who were hungry cease *to hunger.*
Even the barren gives birth to seven,
But she who has many children languishes.
6 "The LORD kills and makes alive;
He brings down to Sheol and raises up.
7 "The LORD makes poor and rich;
He brings low, He also exalts.
8 "He raises the poor from the dust,
He lifts the needy from the ash heap
To make them sit with nobles,
And inherit a seat of honor;
For the pillars of the earth are the LORD'S,
And He set the world on them.

*a*Lit *lent*

New International

bered her. 20So in the course of time Hannah conceived and gave birth to a son. She named him Samuel,*c* saying, "Because I asked the LORD for him."

Hannah Dedicates Samuel

21 When the man Elkanah went up with all his family to offer the annual sacrifice to the LORD and to fulfill his vow, 22Hannah did not go. She said to her husband, "After the boy is weaned, I will take him and present him before the LORD, and he will live there always."

23 "Do what seems best to you," Elkanah her husband told her. "Stay here until you have weaned him; only may the LORD make good his*d* word." So the woman stayed at home and nursed her son until she had weaned him.

24 After he was weaned, she took the boy with her, young as he was, along with a three-year-old bull,*e* an ephah*f* of flour and a skin of wine, and brought him to the house of the LORD at Shiloh. 25When they had slaughtered the bull, they brought the boy to Eli, 26and she said to him, "As surely as you live, my lord, I am the woman who stood here beside you praying to the LORD. 27I prayed for this child, and the LORD has granted me what I asked of him. 28So now I give him to the LORD. For his whole life he will be given over to the LORD." And he worshiped the LORD there.

Hannah's Prayer

2 THEN HANNAH prayed and said:

"My heart rejoices in the LORD;
in the LORD my horn*g* is lifted high.
My mouth boasts over my enemies,
for I delight in your deliverance.

2 "There is no one holy*h* like the LORD;
there is no one besides you;
there is no Rock like our God.

3 "Do not keep talking so proudly
or let your mouth speak such arrogance,
for the LORD is a God who knows,
and by him deeds are weighed.

4 "The bows of the warriors are broken,
but those who stumbled are armed with strength.

5 Those who were full hire themselves out for food,
but those who were hungry hunger no more.
She who was barren has borne seven children,
but she who has had many sons pines away.

6 "The LORD brings death and makes alive;
he brings down to the grave*i* and raises up.

7 The LORD sends poverty and wealth;
he humbles and he exalts.

8 He raises the poor from the dust
and lifts the needy from the ash heap;
he seats them with princes
and has them inherit a throne of honor.

"For the foundations of the earth are the LORD's;
upon them he has set the world.

c20 Samuel sounds like the Hebrew for *heard of God.*
d23 Masoretic Text; Dead Sea Scrolls, Septuagint and Syriac *your*
e24 Dead Sea Scrolls, Septuagint and Syriac; Masoretic Text *with three bulls* *f24* That is, probably about 3/5 bushel (about 22 liters) *g1 Horn* here symbolizes strength; also in verse 10.
h2 Or *no Holy One* *i6* Hebrew *Sheol*

King James

9He will keep the feet of his saints, and the wicked shall be silent in darkness; for by strength shall no man prevail.

10The adversaries of the LORD shall be broken to pieces; out of heaven shall he thunder upon them: the LORD shall judge the ends of the earth; and he shall give strength unto his king, and exalt the horn of his anointed.

11And Elkanah went to Ramah to his house. And the child did minister unto the LORD before Eli the priest.

The sons of Eli

12 ¶ Now the sons of Eli *were* Psons of Belial; they knew not the LORD.

13And the priests' custom with the people *was, that,* when any man offered sacrifice, the priest's servant came, while the flesh was in seething, with a fleshhook of three teeth in his hand;

14And he struck *it* into the pan, or kettle, or caldron, or pot; all that the fleshhook brought up the priest took for himself. So they did in Shiloh unto all the Israelites that came thither.

15Also before they burnt the fat, the priest's servant came, and said to the man that sacrificed, Give flesh to roast for the priest; for he will not have sodden flesh of thee, but raw.

16And *if* any man said unto him, Let them not fail to burn the fat qpresently, and *then* take *as much* as thy soul desireth; then he would answer him, Nay; but thou shalt give *it me* now: and if not, I will take *it* by force.

17Wherefore the sin of the young men was very great before the LORD: for men abhorred the offering of the LORD.

18 ¶ But Samuel ministered before the LORD, *being* a child, girded with a linen ephod.

19Moreover his mother made him a little coat, and brought *it* to him from year to year, when she came up with her husband to offer the yearly sacrifice.

20 ¶ And Eli blessed Elkanah and his wife, and said, The LORD give thee seed of this woman for the rloan which is lent to the LORD. And they went unto their own home.

21And the LORD visited Hannah, so that she conceived, and bare three sons and two daughters. And the child Samuel grew before the LORD.

22 ¶ Now Eli was very old, and heard all that his sons did unto all Israel; and how they lay with the women that sassembled *at* the door of the tabernacle of the congregation.

23And he said unto them, Why do ye such things? for tI hear of your evil dealings by all this people.

24Nay, my sons; for *it is* no good report that I hear: ye make the LORD'S people uto transgress.

25If one man sin against another, the judge shall judge him: but if a man sin against the LORD, who shall entreat for him? Notwithstanding they hearkened not unto the voice of their father, because the LORD would slay them.

26And the child Samuel grew on, and was in favour both with the LORD, and also with men.

The prophecy of doom to Eli

27 ¶ And there came a man of God unto Eli, and said unto him, Thus saith the LORD, Did I plainly appear unto the house of thy father, when they were in Egypt in Pharaoh's house?

28And did I choose him out of all the tribes of Israel *to be* my priest, to offer upon mine altar, to burn incense, to wear an ephod before me? and did I give unto the house of thy father all the offerings made by fire of the children of Israel?

Amplified

9He will guard the feet of His godly ones, but the wicked shall be silenced *and* perish in darkness; for by strength shall no man prevail.

10The adversaries of the Lord shall be broken to pieces; against them will He thunder in heaven. The Lord will judge [all peoples] to the ends of the earth; and He will give strength to bHis king (King) and exalt the power of His anointed (Anointed cHis Christ). [Luke 1:46.]

11Elkanah and his wife Hannah returned to Ramah to his house. But the child ministered to the Lord before Eli the priest.

12The sons of Eli were base *and* worthless; they did not know *or* regard the Lord.

13And the custom of the priests with the people was this: when any man offered sacrifice, the priest's servant came while the flesh was boiling with a fleshhook of three prongs in his hand;

14And he thrust it into the pan or kettle or caldron or pot; all that the fleshhook brought up the priest took for himself. So they did in Shiloh with all the Israelites who came there.

15Also, before they burned the fat, the priest's servant came and said to the man who sacrificed, Give the priest meat to roast, for he will not accept boiled meat from you, but raw.

16And if the man said to him, Let them burn the fat first, and then you may take as much as you want, the priest's servant would say, No! Give it to me now or I will take it by force.

17So the sin of the [two] young men was very great before the Lord, for they despised the offering of the Lord.

18But Samuel ministered before the Lord, a child girded with a linen ephod.

19Moreover, his mother made him a little robe and brought it to him from year to year when she came up with her husband to offer the yearly sacrifice.

20And Eli would bless Elkanah and his wife and say, May the Lord give you children by this woman for the gift she asked for *and* gave to the Lord. Then they would go to their own home.

21And the Lord visited Hannah, so that she bore three sons and two daughters. And the child Samuel grew before the Lord.

22Now Eli was very old, and he heard all that his sons did to all Israel and how they lay with the women who served at the door of the Tent of Meeting.

23And he said to them, Why do you do such things? For I hear of your evil dealings from all the people.

24No, my sons; it is no good report which I hear the Lord's people spreading abroad.

25If one man wrongs another, God will mediate for him; but if a man wrongs the Lord, who shall intercede for him? Yet they did not listen to their father, for it was the Lord's will to slay them.

26Now the boy Samuel grew and was in favor both with the Lord and with men.

27A man of God came to Eli and said to him, Thus has the Lord said: I plainly revealed Myself to the house of your father [forefather Aaron] when they were in Egypt in bondage to Pharaoh's house.

28Moreover, I selected him out of all the tribes of Israel to be My priest, to offer on My altar, to burn incense, to wear an ephod before Me. And I gave [from then on] to the house of your father [forefather] all the offerings of the Israelites made by fire.

bHannah's prophetic prayer was but partially fulfilled in the king soon to be anointed by her son as the deliverer of Israel; it reaches forward to . . . the King Messiah, in Whom alone the lofty anticipations of the prophetess are to be completely realized (*The Cambridge Bible*). cBoth *The Septuagint* (Greek translation of the Old Testament) and *The Latin Vulgate* read "His Christ" (Luke 2:26).

pDeut. 13:13 qHeb. *as on the day* rOr, *petition which she asked* sHeb. *assembled by troops* tOr, *I hear evil words of you* uOr, *to cry out*

New American Standard

9"He keeps the feet of His godly ones,
   But the wicked ones are silenced in darkness;
   For not by might shall a man prevail.
10"Those who contend with the LORD will be
      shattered;
   Against them He will thunder in the heavens,
   The LORD will judge the ends of the earth;
   And He will give strength to His king,
   And will exalt the horn of His anointed."
11 ¶ Then Elkanah went to his home at Ramah. But the boy ministered to the LORD before Eli the priest.

The Sin of Eli's Sons

12 ¶ Now the sons of Eli were *b*worthless men; they did not know the LORD
13 and the custom of the priests with the people. When any man was offering a sacrifice, the priest's servant would come while the meat was boiling, with a three-pronged fork in his hand.
14 Then he would thrust it into the pan, or kettle, or caldron, or pot; all that the fork brought up the priest would take for himself. Thus they did in Shiloh to all the Israelites who came there.
15 Also, before they burned the fat, the priest's servant would come and say to the man who was sacrificing, "Give the priest meat for roasting, as he will not take boiled meat from you, only raw."
16 If the man said to him, "They must surely burn the fat first, and then take as much as you desire," then he would say, "No, but you shall give *it to me* now; and if not, I will take it by force."
17 Thus the sin of the young men was very great before the LORD, for the men despised the offering of the LORD.

Samuel before the LORD as a Boy

18 ¶ Now Samuel was ministering before the LORD, *as* a boy wearing a linen ephod.
19 And his mother would make him a little robe and bring it to him from year to year when she would come up with her husband to offer the yearly sacrifice.
20 Then Eli would bless Elkanah and his wife and say, "May the LORD give you children from this woman in place of the one she dedicated to the LORD." And they went to their own home.
21 ¶ The LORD visited Hannah; and she conceived and gave birth to three sons and two daughters. And the boy Samuel grew before the LORD.

Eli Rebukes His Sons

22 ¶ Now Eli was very old; and he heard all that his sons were doing to all Israel, and how they lay with the women who served at the doorway of the tent of meeting.
23 He said to them, "Why do you do such things, the evil things that I hear from all these people?
24"No, my sons; for the report is not good which I hear the LORD's people circulating.
25"If one man sins against another, God will mediate for him; but if a man sins against the LORD, who can intercede for him?" But they would not listen to the voice of their father, for the LORD desired to put them to death.
26 ¶ Now the boy Samuel was growing in stature and in favor both with the LORD and with men.
27 ¶ Then a man of God came to Eli and said to him, "Thus says the LORD, 'Did I *not* indeed reveal Myself to the house of your father when they were in Egypt *in bondage* to Pharaoh's house?
28 'Did I *not* choose them from all the tribes of Israel to be My priests, to go up to My altar, to burn incense, to carry an ephod before Me; and did I *not* give to the house of your father all the fire *offerings* of the sons of Israel?

New International

9He will guard the feet of his saints,
   but the wicked will be silenced in darkness.

   "It is not by strength that one prevails;
10 those who oppose the LORD will be
      shattered.
   He will thunder against them from heaven;
      the LORD will judge the ends of the earth.

   "He will give strength to his king
      and exalt the horn of his anointed."

11Then Elkanah went home to Ramah, but the boy ministered before the LORD under Eli the priest.

Eli's Wicked Sons

12Eli's sons were wicked men; they had no regard for the LORD. 13Now it was the practice of the priests with the people that whenever anyone offered a sacrifice and while the meat was being boiled, the servant of the priest would come with a three-pronged fork in his hand. 14He would plunge it into the pan or kettle or caldron or pot, and the priest would take for himself whatever the fork brought up. This is how they treated all the Israelites who came to Shiloh. 15But even before the fat was burned, the servant of the priest would come and say to the man who was sacrificing, "Give the priest some meat to roast; he won't accept boiled meat from you, but only raw."
16If the man said to him, "Let the fat be burned up first, and then take whatever you want," the servant would then answer, "No, hand it over now; if you don't, I'll take it by force."
17This sin of the young men was very great in the LORD's sight, for they*j* were treating the LORD's offering with contempt.
18But Samuel was ministering before the LORD—a boy wearing a linen ephod. 19Each year his mother made him a little robe and took it to him when she went up with her husband to offer the annual sacrifice. 20Eli would bless Elkanah and his wife, saying, "May the LORD give you children by this woman to take the place of the one she prayed for and gave to the LORD." Then they would go home. 21And the LORD was gracious to Hannah; she conceived and gave birth to three sons and two daughters. Meanwhile, the boy Samuel grew up in the presence of the LORD.
22Now Eli, who was very old, heard about everything his sons were doing to all Israel and how they slept with the women who served at the entrance to the Tent of Meeting. 23So he said to them, "Why do you do such things? I hear from all the people about these wicked deeds of yours. 24No, my sons; it is not a good report that I hear spreading among the LORD's people. 25If a man sins against another man, God*k* may mediate for him; but if a man sins against the LORD, who will intercede for him?" His sons, however, did not listen to their father's rebuke, for it was the LORD's will to put them to death.
26And the boy Samuel continued to grow in stature and in favor with the LORD and with men.

Prophecy Against the House of Eli

27Now a man of God came to Eli and said to him, "This is what the LORD says: 'Did I not clearly reveal myself to your father's house when they were in Egypt under Pharaoh? 28I chose your father out of all the tribes of Israel to be my priest, to go up to my altar, to burn incense, and to wear an ephod in my presence. I also gave your father's house all the offerings made with fire by the Israelites.

---

b Lit *sons of Belial*   *j* 17 Or *men*   *k* 25 Or *the judges*

King James

²⁹Wherefore kick ye at my sacrifice and at mine offering, which I have commanded *in my* habitation; and honourest thy sons above me, to make yourselves fat with the chiefest of all the offerings of Israel my people?

³⁰Wherefore the LORD God of Israel saith, I said indeed *that* thy house, and the house of thy father, should walk before me for ever: but now the LORD saith, Be it far from me; for them that honour me I will honour, and they that despise me shall be lightly esteemed.

³¹Behold, the days come, that I will cut off thine arm, and the arm of thy father's house, that there shall not be an old man in thine house.

³²And thou shalt see ^van enemy *in my* habitation, in all *the wealth* which *God* shall give Israel: and there shall not be an old man in thine house for ever.

³³And the man of thine, *whom* I shall not cut off from mine altar, *shall be* to consume thine eyes, and to grieve thine heart: and all the increase of thine house shall die ^win the flower of their age.

³⁴And this *shall be* a sign unto thee, that shall come upon thy two sons, on Hophni and Phinehas; in one day they shall die both of them.

³⁵And I will raise me up a faithful priest, *that* shall do according to *that* which *is* in mine heart and in my mind: and I will build him a sure house; and he shall walk before mine anointed for ever.

³⁶And it shall come to pass, *that* every one that is left in thine house shall come *and* crouch to him for a piece of silver and a morsel of bread, and shall say, ^xPut me, I pray thee, into ^yone of the priests' offices, that I may eat a piece of bread.

The LORD calls Samuel

3 AND THE child Samuel ministered unto the LORD before Eli. And the word of the LORD was precious in those days; *there was* no open vision.

²And it came to pass at that time, when Eli *was* laid down in his place, and his eyes began to wax dim, *that* he could not see;

³And ere the lamp of God went out in the temple of the LORD, where the ark of God *was,* and Samuel was laid down *to sleep;*

⁴That the LORD called Samuel: and he answered, Here *am* I.

⁵And he ran unto Eli, and said, Here *am* I; for thou calledst me. And he said, I called not; lie down again. And he went and lay down.

⁶And the LORD called yet again, Samuel. And Samuel arose and went to Eli, and said, Here *am* I; for thou didst call me. And he answered, I called not, my son; lie down again.

^{7z}Now Samuel did not yet know the LORD, neither was the word of the LORD yet revealed unto him.

⁸And the LORD called Samuel again the third time. And he arose and went to Eli, and said, Here *am* I; for thou didst call me. And Eli perceived that the LORD had called the child.

⁹Therefore Eli said unto Samuel, Go, lie down: and it shall be, if he call thee, that thou shalt say, Speak, LORD; for thy servant heareth. So Samuel went and lay down in his place.

¹⁰And the LORD came, and stood, and called as at other times, Samuel, Samuel. Then Samuel answered, Speak; for thy servant heareth.

¹¹ ¶ And the LORD said to Samuel, Behold, I will do a thing in Israel, at which both the ears of every one that heareth it shall tingle.

Amplified

²⁹Why then do you kick [trample upon, treat with contempt] My sacrifice and My offering which I commanded, and honor your sons above Me by fattening yourselves upon the choicest part of every offering of My people Israel?

³⁰Therefore the Lord, the God of Israel, says, I did promise that your house and that of your father [forefather Aaron] should go in and out before Me forever. But now the Lord says, Be it far from Me. For those who honor Me I will honor, and those who despise Me shall be lightly esteemed.

³¹Behold, the time is coming when I will cut off your strength and the strength of your own father's house, that there shall not be an old man in your house.

³²And you shall behold the distress of My house, even in all the prosperity which God will give Israel, and there shall not be an old man in your house forever.

³³Yet I will not cut off from My altar every man of yours; some shall survive to weep and mourn [over the family's ruin], but all the increase of your house shall die in their best years. [I Sam. 22:17–20.]

³⁴And what befalls your two sons, Hophni and Phinehas, shall be a sign to you—in one day they both shall die. [Fulfilled in I Sam. 4:17, 18.]

³⁵And I will raise up for Myself a ^dfaithful priest (Priest), who shall do according to what is in My heart and mind. And I will build him a sure house, and he shall walk before My anointed (Anointed) forever. [I Sam. 2:10.]

³⁶Everyone who is left in your house shall come crouching to him for a piece of silver and a bit of bread and say, Put me, I pray you, into a priest's office so I may have a piece of bread.

3 NOW THE boy Samuel ministered to the Lord before Eli. The word of the Lord was rare *and* precious in those days; there was no frequent *or* widely spread vision.

²At that time Eli, whose eyesight had dimmed so that he could not see, was lying down in his own place.

³The lamp of God had not yet gone out in the temple of the Lord, where the ark of God was, and Samuel was lying down

⁴When the Lord called, Samuel! And he answered, Here I am.

⁵He ran to Eli and said, Here I am, for you called me. Eli said, I did not call you; lie down again. So he went and lay down.

⁶And the Lord called again, Samuel! And Samuel arose and went to Eli and said, Here am I; you did call me. Eli answered, I did not call, my son; lie down again.

⁷Now Samuel did not yet know the Lord, and the word of the Lord was not yet revealed to him.

⁸And the Lord called Samuel the third time. And he went to Eli and said, Here I am, for you did call me. Then Eli perceived that the Lord was calling the boy.

⁹So Eli said to Samuel, Go, lie down. And if He calls you, you shall say, Speak, Lord, for Your servant is listening. So Samuel went and lay down in his place.

¹⁰And the Lord came and stood and called as at other times, Samuel! Samuel! Then Samuel answered, Speak, Lord, for Your servant is listening.

¹¹The Lord told Samuel, Behold, I am about to do a thing in Israel at which both ears of all who hear it shall tingle.

---

^vOr, *the affliction of the tabernacle, for all the wealth which God would have given Israel*   ^wHeb. *men*   ^xHeb. *Join*   ^yOr, *somewhat about the priesthood*   ^zOr, *Thus did Samuel before he knew the LORD, and before the word of the LORD was revealed unto him*

^dThis person is not identified, but this prophecy found its fulfillment from the standpoint of historical exposition in Samuel (J.P. Lange, *A Commentary*). Christian writers usually adopt also the Messianic interpretation. The text does not allow an exclusive reference to Christ, since it does look plainly to the then existing order of things; however, it also points to Christ as the consummation of the blessedness which it promises.

New American Standard

29 'Why do you kick at My sacrifice and at My offering which I have commanded *in My* dwelling, and honor your sons above Me, by making yourselves fat with the choicest of every offering of My people Israel?'

30"Therefore the LORD God of Israel declares, 'I did indeed say that your house and the house of your father should walk before Me forever'; but now the LORD declares, 'Far be it from Me—for those who honor Me I will honor, and those who despise Me will be lightly esteemed.

31 'Behold, the days are coming when I will break your strength and the strength of your father's house so that there will not be an old man in your house.

32 'You will see the distress of *My* dwelling, in *spite of* all the good that I do for Israel; and an old man will not be in your house forever.

33 'Yet I will not cut off every man of yours from My altar so that your eyes will fail *from weeping* and your soul grieve, and all the increase of your house will die in the prime of life.

34 'This will be the sign to you which will come concerning your two sons, Hophni and Phinehas: on the same day both of them will die.

35 'But I will raise up for Myself a faithful priest who will do according to what is in My heart and in My soul; and I will build him an enduring house, and he will walk before My anointed always.

36 'Everyone who is left in your house will come and bow down to him for a piece of silver or a loaf of bread and say, "Please assign me to one of the priest's offices so that I may eat a piece of bread." ' "

The Prophetic Call to Samuel

3 NOW THE boy Samuel was ministering to the LORD before Eli. And word from the LORD was rare in those days, visions were infrequent.

2 ¶ It happened at that time as Eli was lying down in his place (now his eyesight had begun to grow dim *and he could not see well*),

3 and the lamp of God had not yet gone out, and Samuel was lying down in the temple of the LORD where the ark of God *was,*

4 that the LORD called Samuel; and he said, "Here I am."

5 Then he ran to Eli and said, "Here I am, for you called me." But he said, "I did not call, lie down again." So he went and lay down.

6 The LORD called yet again, "Samuel!" So Samuel arose and went to Eli and said, "Here I am, for you called me." But he answered, "I did not call, my son, lie down again."

7 Now Samuel did not yet know the LORD, nor had the word of the LORD yet been revealed to him.

8 So the LORD called Samuel again for the third time. And he arose and went to Eli and said, "Here I am, for you called me." Then Eli discerned that the LORD was calling the boy.

9 And Eli said to Samuel, "Go lie down, and it shall be if He calls you, that you shall say, 'Speak, LORD, for Your servant is listening.' " So Samuel went and lay down in his place.

10 ¶ Then the LORD came and stood and called as at other times, "Samuel! Samuel!" And Samuel said, "Speak, for Your servant is listening."

11 The LORD said to Samuel, "Behold, I am about to do a thing in Israel at which both ears of everyone who hears it will tingle.

New International

29Why do you[l] scorn my sacrifice and offering that I prescribed for my dwelling? Why do you honor your sons more than me by fattening yourselves on the choice parts of every offering made by my people Israel?'

30"Therefore the LORD, the God of Israel, declares: 'I promised that your house and your father's house would minister before me forever.' But now the LORD declares: 'Far be it from me! Those who honor me I will honor, but those who despise me will be disdained. 31The time is coming when I will cut short your strength and the strength of your father's house, so that there will not be an old man in your family line 32and you will see distress in my dwelling. Although good will be done to Israel, in your family line there will never be an old man. 33Every one of you that I do not cut off from my altar will be spared only to blind your eyes with tears and to grieve your heart, and all your descendants will die in the prime of life.

34" 'And what happens to your two sons, Hophni and Phinehas, will be a sign to you—they will both die on the same day. 35I will raise up for myself a faithful priest, who will do according to what is in my heart and mind. I will firmly establish his house, and he will minister before my anointed one always. 36Then everyone left in your family line will come and bow down before him for a piece of silver and a crust of bread and plead, "Appoint me to some priestly office so I can have food to eat." ' "

The LORD Calls Samuel

3 THE BOY Samuel ministered before the LORD under Eli. In those days the word of the LORD was rare; there were not many visions.

2One night Eli, whose eyes were becoming so weak that he could barely see, was lying down in his usual place. 3The lamp of God had not yet gone out, and Samuel was lying down in the temple[m] of the LORD, where the ark of God was. 4Then the LORD called Samuel.

Samuel answered, "Here I am." 5And he ran to Eli and said, "Here I am; you called me."

But Eli said, "I did not call; go back and lie down." So he went and lay down.

6Again the LORD called, "Samuel!" And Samuel got up and went to Eli and said, "Here I am; you called me."

"My son," Eli said, "I did not call; go back and lie down."

7Now Samuel did not yet know the LORD: The word of the LORD had not yet been revealed to him.

8The LORD called Samuel a third time, and Samuel got up and went to Eli and said, "Here I am; you called me."

Then Eli realized that the LORD was calling the boy. 9So Eli told Samuel, "Go and lie down, and if he calls you, say, 'Speak, LORD, for your servant is listening.' " So Samuel went and lay down in his place.

10The LORD came and stood there, calling as at the other times, "Samuel! Samuel!"

Then Samuel said, "Speak, for your servant is listening."

11And the LORD said to Samuel: "See, I am about to do something in Israel that will make the ears of everyone

---

l 29 The Hebrew is plural.   *m* 3 That is, tabernacle

King James

¹²In that day I will perform against Eli all *things* which I have spoken concerning his house: *a*when I begin, I will also make an end.

¹³*b*For I have told him that I will judge his house for ever for the iniquity which he knoweth; because his sons made themselves *c*vile, and he *d*restrained them not.

¹⁴And therefore I have sworn unto the house of Eli, that the iniquity of Eli's house shall not be purged with sacrifice nor offering for ever.

¹⁵ ¶ And Samuel lay until the morning, and opened the doors of the house of the LORD. And Samuel feared to show Eli the vision.

¹⁶Then Eli called Samuel, and said, Samuel, my son. And he answered, Here *am* I.

¹⁷And he said, What *is* the thing that *the* LORD hath said unto thee? I pray thee hide *it* not from me: God do so to thee, and *e*more also, if thou hide *any f*thing from me of all the things that he said unto thee.

¹⁸And Samuel told him *g*every whit, and hid nothing from him. And he said, It *is* the LORD: let him do what seemeth him good.

¹⁹ ¶ And Samuel grew, and the LORD was with him, and did let none of his words fall to the ground.

²⁰And all Israel from Dan even to Beer-sheba knew that Samuel *was h*established *to be* a prophet of the LORD.

²¹And the LORD appeared again in Shiloh: for the LORD revealed himself to Samuel in Shiloh by the word of the LORD.

Israel defeated by the Philistines

4 AND THE word of Samuel *ij*came to all Israel. Now Israel went out against the Philistines to battle, and pitched beside Eben-ezer: and the Philistines pitched in Aphek.

²And the Philistines put themselves in array against Israel: and when *k*they joined battle, Israel was smitten before the Philistines: and they slew of *l*the army in the field about four thousand men.

³ ¶ And when the people were come into the camp, the elders of Israel said, Wherefore hath the LORD smitten us today before the Philistines? Let us *m*fetch the ark of the covenant of the LORD out of Shiloh unto us, that, when it cometh among us, it may save us out of the hand of our enemies.

⁴So the people sent to Shiloh, that they might bring from thence the ark of the covenant of the LORD of hosts, which dwelleth *between* the cherubims: and the two sons of Eli, Hophni and Phinehas, *were* there with the ark of the covenant of God.

⁵And when the ark of the covenant of the LORD came into the camp, all Israel shouted with a great shout, so that the earth rang again.

⁶And when the Philistines heard the noise of the shout, they said, What *meaneth* the noise of this great shout in the camp of the Hebrews? And they understood that the ark of the LORD was come into the camp.

⁷And the Philistines were afraid, for they said, God is come into the camp. And they said, Woe unto us! for there hath not been such a thing *n*heretofore.

⁸Woe unto us! who shall deliver us out of the hand of these mighty Gods? these *are* the Gods that smote the Egyptians with all the plagues in the wilderness.

⁹Be strong, and quit yourselves like men, O ye Philistines, that ye be not servants unto the Hebrews, as they have been to you: *o*quit yourselves like men, and fight.

Amplified

¹²On that day I will perform against Eli all that I have spoken concerning his house, from beginning to end.

¹³And I [now] announce to him that I will judge *and* punish his house forever for the iniquity of which he knew, for his sons were bringing a curse upon themselves [blaspheming God], and he did not restrain them.

¹⁴Therefore I have sworn to the house of Eli that the iniquity of Eli's house shall not be atoned for *or* purged with sacrifice or offering forever.

¹⁵Samuel lay until morning; then he opened the doors of the Lord's house. And [he] was afraid to tell the vision to Eli.

¹⁶But Eli called Samuel and said, Samuel, my son. And he answered, Here I am.

¹⁷Eli said, What is it He told you? Pray do not hide it from me. May God do so to you, and more also, if you hide anything from me of all that He said to you.

¹⁸And Samuel told him everything, hiding nothing. And Eli said, It is the Lord; let Him do what seems good to Him.

¹⁹Samuel grew; the Lord was with him and let none of his words fall to the ground. [Josh. 23:14.]

²⁰And all Israel from Dan to Beersheba knew that Samuel was established to be a prophet of the Lord.

²¹And the Lord continued to appear in Shiloh, for the Lord revealed Himself to Samuel in Shiloh through the word of the Lord.

4 AND THE word of [the Lord through] Samuel came to all Israel. Now Israel went out to battle against the Philistines and encamped beside Ebenezer; the Philistines encamped at Aphek.

²The Philistines drew up against Israel, and when the battle spread, Israel was smitten by the Philistines, who slew about 4,000 men on the battlefield.

³When the troops had come into the camp, the elders of Israel said, Why has the Lord smitten us today before the Philistines? Let us bring the ark of the covenant of the Lord here from Shiloh, that He may come among us and save us from the power of our enemies.

⁴So the people sent to Shiloh and brought from there the ark of the covenant of the Lord of hosts, Who dwells above the cherubim. And the two sons of Eli, Hophni and Phinehas, were with the ark of the covenant of God.

⁵And when the ark of the covenant of the Lord came into the camp, all Israel shouted with a great shout, so that the earth resounded.

⁶And when the Philistines heard the noise of the shout, they said, What does this great shout in the camp of the Hebrews mean? When they understood that the ark of the Lord had come into the camp,

⁷The Philistines were afraid, for they said, God has come into the camp. And they said, Woe to us! For such a thing has not happened before.

⁸Woe to us! Who shall deliver us out of the hand of these mighty gods? These are the gods that smote the Egyptians with every kind of plague in the wilderness.

⁹Be strong, and acquit yourselves like men, O you Philistines, that you may not become servants to the Hebrews, as they have been to you; behave yourselves like men, and fight!

---

a Heb. *beginning and ending*   *b* Or, *And I will tell him*   *c* Or, *accursed*   *d* Heb. *frowned not upon them*   *e* Heb. *so add*
f Or, *word*   *g* Heb. *all the things,* or, *words*   *h* Or, *faithful*
i Or, *came to pass*   *j* Heb. *was*   *k* Heb. *the battle was spread*
l Heb. *the array*   *m* Heb. *take unto us*   *n* Heb. *yesterday,* or, *the third day*   *o* Heb. *be men*

New American Standard

12"In that day I will carry out against Eli all that I have spoken concerning his house, from beginning to end.

13"For I have told him that I am about to judge his house forever for the iniquity which he knew, because his sons brought a curse on themselves and he did not rebuke them.

14"Therefore I have sworn to the house of Eli that the iniquity of Eli's house shall not be atoned for by sacrifice or offering forever."

15 ¶ So Samuel lay down until morning. Then he opened the doors of the house of the LORD. But Samuel was afraid to tell the vision to Eli.

16 Then Eli called Samuel and said, "Samuel, my son." And he said, "Here I am."

17 He said, "What is the word that He spoke to you? Please do not hide it from me. May God do so to you, and more also, if you hide anything from me of all the words that He spoke to you."

18 So Samuel told him everything and hid nothing from him. And he said, "It is the LORD; let Him do what seems good to Him."

19 ¶ Thus Samuel grew and the LORD was with him and let none of his words fail.

20 All Israel from Dan even to Beersheba knew that Samuel was confirmed as a prophet of the LORD.

21 And the LORD appeared again at Shiloh, because the LORD revealed Himself to Samuel at Shiloh by the word of the LORD.

Philistines Take the Ark in Victory

4 THUS THE word of Samuel came to all Israel. Now Israel went out to meet the Philistines in battle and camped beside Ebenezer while the Philistines camped in Aphek.

2 The Philistines drew up in battle array to meet Israel. When the battle spread, Israel was defeated before the Philistines who killed about four thousand men on the battlefield.

3 When the people came into the camp, the elders of Israel said, "Why has the LORD defeated us today before the Philistines? Let us take to ourselves from Shiloh the ark of the covenant of the LORD, that it may come among us and deliver us from the power of our enemies."

4 So the people sent to Shiloh, and from there they carried the ark of the covenant of the LORD of hosts who sits *above* the cherubim; and the two sons of Eli, Hophni and Phinehas, *were* there with the ark of the covenant of God.

5 ¶ As the ark of the covenant of the LORD came into the camp, all Israel shouted with a great shout, so that the earth resounded.

6 When the Philistines heard the noise of the shout, they said, "What *does* the noise of this great shout in the camp of the Hebrews *mean?*" Then they understood that the ark of the LORD had come into the camp.

7 The Philistines were afraid, for they said, "God has come into the camp." And they said, "Woe to us! For nothing like this has happened before.

8"Woe to us! Who shall deliver us from the hand of these mighty gods? These are the gods who smote the Egyptians with all *kinds of* plagues in the wilderness.

9"Take courage and be men, O Philistines, or you will become slaves to the Hebrews, as they have been slaves to you; therefore, be men and fight."

New International

who hears of it tingle. 12At that time I will carry out against Eli everything I spoke against his family—from beginning to end. 13For I told him that I would judge his family forever because of the sin he knew about; his sons made themselves contemptible,[n] and he failed to restrain them. 14Therefore, I swore to the house of Eli, 'The guilt of Eli's house will never be atoned for by sacrifice or offering.' "

15Samuel lay down until morning and then opened the doors of the house of the LORD. He was afraid to tell Eli the vision, 16but Eli called him and said, "Samuel, my son."

Samuel answered, "Here I am."

17"What was it he said to you?" Eli asked. "Do not hide it from me. May God deal with you, be it ever so severely, if you hide from me anything he told you." 18So Samuel told him everything, hiding nothing from him. Then Eli said, "He is the LORD; let him do what is good in his eyes."

19The LORD was with Samuel as he grew up, and he let none of his words fall to the ground. 20And all Israel from Dan to Beersheba recognized that Samuel was attested as a prophet of the LORD. 21The LORD continued to appear at Shiloh, and there he revealed himself to Samuel through his word.

The Philistines Capture the Ark

4 AND SAMUEL'S word came to all Israel.

Now the Israelites went out to fight against the Philistines. The Israelites camped at Ebenezer, and the Philistines at Aphek. 2The Philistines deployed their forces to meet Israel, and as the battle spread, Israel was defeated by the Philistines, who killed about four thousand of them on the battlefield. 3When the soldiers returned to camp, the elders of Israel asked, "Why did the LORD bring defeat upon us today before the Philistines? Let us bring the ark of the LORD's covenant from Shiloh, so that it[o] may go with us and save us from the hand of our enemies."

4So the people sent men to Shiloh, and they brought back the ark of the covenant of the LORD Almighty, who is enthroned between the cherubim. And Eli's two sons, Hophni and Phinehas, were there with the ark of the covenant of God.

5When the ark of the LORD's covenant came into the camp, all Israel raised such a great shout that the ground shook. 6Hearing the uproar, the Philistines asked, "What's all this shouting in the Hebrew camp?"

When they learned that the ark of the LORD had come into the camp, 7the Philistines were afraid. "A god has come into the camp," they said. "We're in trouble! Nothing like this has happened before. 8Woe to us! Who will deliver us from the hand of these mighty gods? They are the gods who struck the Egyptians with all kinds of plagues in the desert. 9Be strong, Philistines! Be men, or you will be subject to the Hebrews, as they have been to you. Be men, and fight!"

n 13 Masoretic Text; an ancient Hebrew scribal tradition and Septuagint *sons blasphemed God*   o 3 Or *he*

King James

¹⁰ ¶ And the Philistines fought, and Israel was smitten, and they fled every man into his tent: and there was a very great slaughter; for there fell of Israel thirty thousand footmen.

¹¹And the ark of God was taken; and the two sons of Eli, Hophni and Phinehas, ^pwere slain.

The death of Eli

¹² ¶ And there ran a man of Benjamin out of the army, and came to Shiloh the same day with his clothes rent, and with earth upon his head.

¹³And when he came, lo, Eli sat upon a seat by the wayside watching: for his heart trembled for the ark of God. And when the man came into the city, and told *it,* all the city cried out.

¹⁴And when Eli heard the noise of the crying, he said, What *meaneth* the noise of this tumult? And the man came in hastily, and told Eli.

¹⁵Now Eli was ninety and eight years old; and his eyes ^qwere dim, that he could not see.

¹⁶And the man said unto Eli, I *am* he that came out of the army, and I fled today out of the army. And he said, What ^ris there done, my son?

¹⁷And the messenger answered and said, Israel is fled before the Philistines, and there hath been also a great slaughter among the people, and thy two sons also, Hophni and Phinehas, are dead, and the ark of God is taken.

¹⁸And it came to pass, when he made mention of the ark of God, that he fell from off the seat backward by the side of the gate, and his neck brake, and he died: for he was an old man, and heavy. ^sAnd he had judged Israel forty years.

¹⁹ ¶ And his daughter-in-law, Phinehas' wife, was with child, *near* ^tto be delivered: and when she heard the tidings that the ark of God was taken, and that her father-in-law and her husband were dead, she bowed herself and travailed; for her pains ^ucame upon her.

²⁰And about the time of her death the women that stood by her said unto her, Fear not; for thou hast borne a son. But she answered not, ^vneither did she regard *it.*

²¹And she named the child ^wI-chabod, saying, The glory is departed from Israel: because the ark of God was taken, and because of her father-in-law and her husband.

²²And she said, The glory is departed from Israel: for the ark of God is taken.

The Philistines move the ark

5 AND THE Philistines took the ark of God, and brought it from Eben-ezer unto Ashdod.

²When the Philistines took the ark of God, they brought it into the house of Dagon, and set it by Dagon.

³ ¶ And when they of Ashdod arose early on the morrow, behold, Dagon *was* fallen upon his face to the earth before the ark of the Lord. And they took Dagon, and set him in his place again.

⁴And when they arose early on the morrow morning, behold, Dagon *was* fallen upon his face to the ground before the ark of the Lord; and the head of Dagon and both the palms of his hands *were* cut off upon the threshold; only ^xthe stump of Dagon was left to him.

⁵Therefore neither the priests of Dagon, nor any that come into Dagon's house, tread on the threshold of Dagon in Ashdod unto this day.

⁶But the hand of the Lord was heavy upon them of Ashdod, and he destroyed them, and smote them with emerods, *even* Ashdod and the coasts thereof.

Amplified

¹⁰And the Philistines fought; Israel was smitten and they fled every man to his own home. There was a very great slaughter; for 30,000 foot soldiers of Israel fell.

¹¹And the ark of God was taken, and the two sons of Eli, Hophni and Phinehas, were slain. [Foretold in I Sam. 2:34.]

¹²Now a man of Benjamin ran from the battle line and came to Shiloh that day, with his clothes torn and earth on his head.

¹³When he arrived, Eli was sitting by the road watching, for his heart trembled for the ark of God. When the man told the news in the city, all the city [people] cried out.

¹⁴When Eli heard the noise of the crying, he said, What is this uproar? And the man came hastily and told Eli.

¹⁵Now Eli was 98 years old; his eyes were dim so that he could not see.

¹⁶The man said to Eli, I have come from the battle; I fled from the battle today. Eli said, How did it go, my son?

¹⁷The messenger replied, Israel fled before the Philistines, and there has been a great slaughter among the people. Also your two sons, Hophni and Phinehas, are dead, and the ark of God is captured.

¹⁸And when he mentioned the ark of God, Eli fell off the seat backward by the side of the gate. His neck was broken and he died, for he was an old man and heavy. He had judged Israel forty years.

¹⁹Now his daughter-in-law, Phinehas' wife, was with child, about to be delivered. And when she heard that the ark of God was captured and that her father-in-law and her husband were dead, she bowed herself and gave birth, for her pains came upon her.

²⁰And about the time of her death the women attending her said to her, Fear not, for you have borne a son. But she did not answer or notice.

²¹And she named the child Ichabod, saying, The glory is departed from Israel!—because the ark of God had been captured and because of her father-in-law and her husband.

²²She said, The glory is gone from Israel, for the ark of God has been taken.

5 THE PHILISTINES brought the ark of God from Eb-enezer to Ashdod.

²They took the ark of God into the house of Dagon and set it beside Dagon [their idol].

³When they of Ashdod arose early on the morrow, behold, Dagon had fallen upon his face on the ground before the ark of the Lord. So they took Dagon and set him in his place again.

⁴But when they arose early the next morning, behold, Dagon had again fallen on his face on the ground before the ark of the Lord, and [his] head and both the palms of his hands were lying cut off on the threshold; only the trunk of Dagon was left him.

⁵This is the reason neither the priests of Dagon nor any who come into Dagon's house tread on the threshold of Dagon in Ashdod to this day.

⁶But the hand of the Lord was heavy upon the people of Ashdod, and He caused [mice to spring up and there was] very deadly destruction and He smote the people with [very painful] tumors *or* boils, both Ashdod and its territory.

---

^pHeb. *died*   ^qHeb. *stood*   ^rHeb. *is the thing*   ^sHe seems to have been a Judge to do justice only, and that in Southwest *Israel*   ^tOr, *to cry out*   ^uHeb. *were turned*   ^vHeb. *set not her heart*   ^wi.e. *Where is the glory?* or, There is *no glory*   ^xOr, *the fishy part*

New American Standard

10 ¶ So the Philistines fought and Israel was defeated, and every man fled to his tent; and the slaughter was very great, for there fell of Israel thirty thousand foot soldiers.

11 And the ark of God was taken; and the two sons of Eli, Hophni and Phinehas, died.

12 ¶ Now a man of Benjamin ran from the battle line and came to Shiloh the same day with his clothes torn and dust on his head.

13 When he came, behold, Eli was sitting on *his* seat by the road eagerly watching, because his heart was trembling for the ark of God. So the man came to tell *it* in the city, and all the city cried out.

14 When Eli heard the noise of the outcry, he said, "What *does* the noise of this commotion *mean?*" Then the man came hurriedly and told Eli.

15 Now Eli was ninety-eight years old, and his eyes were set so that he could not see.

16 The man said to Eli, "I am the one who came from the battle line. Indeed, I escaped from the battle line today." And he said, "How did things go, my son?"

17 Then the one who brought the news replied, "Israel has fled before the Philistines and there has also been a great slaughter among the people, and your two sons also, Hophni and Phinehas, are dead, and the ark of God has been taken."

18 When he mentioned the ark of God, Eli fell off the seat backward beside the gate, and his neck was broken and he died, for he was old and heavy. Thus he judged Israel forty years.

19 ¶ Now his daughter-in-law, Phinehas's wife, was pregnant and about to give birth; and when she heard the news that the ark of God was taken and that her father-in-law and her husband had died, she kneeled down and gave birth, for her pains came upon her.

20 And about the time of her death the women who stood by her said to her, "Do not be afraid, for you have given birth to a son." But she did not answer or pay attention.

21 And she called the boy cIchabod, saying, "The glory has departed from Israel," because the ark of God was taken and because of her father-in-law and her husband.

22 She said, "The glory has departed from Israel, for the ark of God was taken."

Capture of the Ark Provokes God

5 NOW THE Philistines took the ark of God and brought it from Ebenezer to Ashdod.

2 Then the Philistines took the ark of God and brought it to the house of Dagon and set it by Dagon.

3 When the Ashdodites arose early the next morning, behold, Dagon had fallen on his face to the ground before the ark of the LORD. So they took Dagon and set him in his place again.

4 But when they arose early the next morning, behold, Dagon had fallen on his face to the ground before the ark of the LORD. And the head of Dagon and both the palms of his hands *were* cut off on the threshold; only the trunk of Dagon was left to him.

5 Therefore neither the priests of Dagon nor all who enter Dagon's house tread on the threshold of Dagon in Ashdod to this day.

6 ¶ Now the hand of the LORD was heavy on the Ashdodites, and He ravaged them and smote them with tumors, both Ashdod and its territories.

New International

10 So the Philistines fought, and the Israelites were defeated and every man fled to his tent. The slaughter was very great; Israel lost thirty thousand foot soldiers. 11 The ark of God was captured, and Eli's two sons, Hophni and Phinehas, died.

Death of Eli

12 That same day a Benjamite ran from the battle line and went to Shiloh, his clothes torn and dust on his head. 13 When he arrived, there was Eli sitting on his chair by the side of the road, watching, because his heart feared for the ark of God. When the man entered the town and told what had happened, the whole town sent up a cry.

14 Eli heard the outcry and asked, "What is the meaning of this uproar?"

The man hurried over to Eli, 15 who was ninety-eight years old and whose eyes were set so that he could not see. 16 He told Eli, "I have just come from the battle line; I fled from it this very day."

Eli asked, "What happened, my son?"

17 The man who brought the news replied, "Israel fled before the Philistines, and the army has suffered heavy losses. Also your two sons, Hophni and Phinehas, are dead, and the ark of God has been captured."

18 When he mentioned the ark of God, Eli fell backward off his chair by the side of the gate. His neck was broken and he died, for he was an old man and heavy. He had ledᵖ Israel forty years.

19 His daughter-in-law, the wife of Phinehas, was pregnant and near the time of delivery. When she heard the news that the ark of God had been captured and that her father-in-law and her husband were dead, she went into labor and gave birth, but was overcome by her labor pains. 20 As she was dying, the women attending her said, "Don't despair; you have given birth to a son." But she did not respond or pay any attention.

21 She named the boy Ichabod,q saying, "The glory has departed from Israel"—because of the capture of the ark of God and the deaths of her father-in-law and her husband. 22 She said, "The glory has departed from Israel, for the ark of God has been captured."

The Ark in Ashdod and Ekron

5 AFTER THE Philistines had captured the ark of God, they took it from Ebenezer to Ashdod. 2 Then they carried the ark into Dagon's temple and set it beside Dagon. 3 When the people of Ashdod rose early the next day, there was Dagon, fallen on his face on the ground before the ark of the LORD! They took Dagon and put him back in his place. 4 But the following morning when they rose, there was Dagon, fallen on his face on the ground before the ark of the LORD! His head and hands had been broken off and were lying on the threshold; only his body remained. 5 That is why to this day neither the priests of Dagon nor any others who enter Dagon's temple at Ashdod step on the threshold.

6 The LORD's hand was heavy upon the people of Ashdod and its vicinity; he brought devastation upon them and

---

King James

7And when the men of Ashdod saw that *it was* so, they said, The ark of the God of Israel shall not abide with us: for his hand is sore upon us, and upon Dagon our god.

8They sent therefore and gathered all the lords of the Philistines unto them, and said, What shall we do with the ark of the God of Israel? And they answered, Let the ark of the God of Israel be carried about unto Gath. And they carried the ark of the God of Israel about *thither.*

9And it was *so,* that, after they had carried it about, the hand of the LORD was against the city with a very great destruction: and he smote the men of the city, both small and great, and they had emerods in their secret parts.

10 ¶ Therefore they sent the ark of God to Ekron. And it came to pass, as the ark of God came to Ekron, that the Ekronites cried out, saying, They have brought about the ark of the God of Israel to ʸus, to slay us and our people.

11So they sent and gathered together all the lords of the Philistines, and said, Send away the ark of the God of Israel, and let it go again to his own place, that it slay ᶻus not, and our people: for there was a deadly destruction throughout all the city; the hand of God was very heavy there.

12And the men that died not were smitten with the emerods: and the cry of the city went up to heaven.

The ark returned to Israel

6 AND THE ark of the LORD was in the country of the Philistines seven months.

2And the Philistines called for the priests and the diviners, saying, What shall we do to the ark of the LORD? tell us wherewith we shall send it to his place.

3And they said, If ye send away the ark of the God of Israel, send it not empty; but in any wise return him a trespass offering: then ye shall be healed, and it shall be known to you why his hand is not removed from you.

4Then said they, What *shall be* the trespass offering which we shall return to him? They answered, Five golden emerods, and five golden mice, *according to* the number of the lords of the Philistines: for one plague *was* on ᵃyou all, and on your lords.

5Wherefore ye shall make images of your emerods, and images of your mice that mar the land; and ye shall give glory unto the God of Israel: peradventure he will lighten his hand from off you, and from off your gods, and from off your land.

6Wherefore then do ye harden your hearts, as the Egyptians and Pharaoh hardened their hearts? when he had wrought ᵇwonderfully among them, did they not let ᵃthe people go, and they departed?

7Now therefore make a new cart, and take two milch kine, on which there hath come no yoke, and tie the kine to the cart, and bring their calves home from them:

8And take the ark of the LORD, and lay it upon the cart; and put the jewels of gold, which ye return him *for* a trespass offering, in a coffer by the side thereof; and send it away, that it may go.

9And see, if it goeth up by the way of his own coast to Beth-shemesh, *then* ᶜhe hath done us this great evil: but if not, then we shall know that *it is* not his hand *that* smote us; *it was* a chance *that* happened to us.

10 ¶ And the men did so; and took two milch kine, and tied them to the cart, and shut up their calves at home:

11And they laid the ark of the LORD upon the cart, and the coffer with the mice of gold and the images of their emerods.

12And the kine took the straight way to the way of Beth-shemesh, *and* went along the highway, lowing as they went, and turned not aside *to* the right hand or *to* the left; and the lords of the Philistines went after them unto the border of Beth-shemesh.

Amplified

7When the men of Ashdod saw that it was so, they said, The ark of the God of Israel must not remain with us, for His hand is heavy on us and on Dagon our god.

8So they sent and gathered all the lords of the Philistines to them and said, What shall we do with the ark of the God of Israel? They answered, Let [it] be carried around to Gath. So they carried the ark of the God of Israel there.

9But after they had carried it to Gath, the hand of the Lord was against the city, causing an exceedingly great panic [at the deaths from the plague], for He afflicted the people of the city, both small and great, and tumors *or* boils broke out on them.

10So they sent the ark of God to Ekron. And as [it] came, the people of Ekron cried out, They have brought the ark of the God of Israel to us to slay us and our people!

11So they sent and assembled all the lords of the Philistines and said, Send away the ark of the God of Israel; let it return to its own place, that it may not slay us and our people. For there was a deadly panic throughout all the city; the hand of God was very heavy there.

12The men who had not died were stricken with very painful tumors *or* boils, and the cry of the city went up to heaven.

6 THE ARK of the Lord was in the country of the Philistines seven months.

2And the Philistines called for the priests and the diviners, saying, What shall we do to the ark of the Lord? Tell us with what we shall send it to its place.

3And they said, If you send away the ark of the God of Israel, do not send it empty, but at least return to Him a guilt offering. Then you will be healed, and it will be known to you why His hand is not removed [and healing granted you].

4Then they said, What shall be the guilt offering which we shall return to Him? They answered, Five golden tumors and five golden mice, according to the number of the Philistine lords, for one plague was on you all, even on your lords.

5Therefore you must make images of your tumors and of your mice that destroy the land, and give glory to the God of Israel. Perhaps He will lighten His hand from off you and your gods and your land.

6Why then do you harden your hearts as the Egyptians and Pharaoh hardened their hearts? When He had done wonders *and* made a mock of them, did they not let the people go, and they departed?

7Now then, make and prepare a new cart and two milch cows on which no yoke has ever come; and yoke the cows to the cart, but take their calves home, away from them.

8And take the ark of the Lord and place it upon the cart, and put in a box at its side the figures of gold which you are returning to Him as a guilt offering. Then send it away and let it be gone.

9And watch. If it goes up by the way of its own land to Beth-shemesh, then He has done us this great evil. But if not, then we shall know that it was not His hand that struck us; it happened to us by chance.

10And the men did so, and took two milch cows and yoked them to the cart and shut up their calves at home.

11And they put the ark of the Lord on the cart and along with it the box with the mice of gold and the images of their tumors.

12And the cows went straight toward Beth-shemesh along the highway, lowing as they went, and turned not aside to the right or the left. And the Philistine lords followed them as far as the border of Beth-shemesh.

ʸHeb. *me, to slay me and my them*   ᵇOr, *reproachfully*   ᶻHeb. *me not, and my*   ᶜOr, *it*   ᵃHeb.

New American Standard

7 When the men of Ashdod saw that it was so, they said, "The ark of the God of Israel must not remain with us, for His hand is severe on us and on Dagon our god."

8 So they sent and gathered all the lords of the Philistines to them and said, "What shall we do with the ark of the God of Israel?" And they said, "Let the ark of the God of Israel be brought around to Gath." And they brought the ark of the God of Israel *around*.

9 After they had brought it around, the hand of the LORD was against the city with very great confusion; and He smote the men of the city, both young and old, so that tumors broke out on them.

10 So they sent the ark of God to Ekron. And as the ark of God came to Ekron the Ekronites cried out, saying, "They have brought the ark of the God of Israel around to us, to kill us and our people."

11 They sent therefore and gathered all the lords of the Philistines and said, "Send away the ark of the God of Israel, and let it return to its own place, so that it will not kill us and our people." For there was a deadly confusion throughout the city; the hand of God was very heavy there.

12 And the men who did not die were smitten with tumors and the cry of the city went up to heaven.

The Ark Returned to Israel

6 NOW THE ark of the LORD had been in the country of the Philistines seven months.

2 And the Philistines called for the priests and the diviners, saying, "What shall we do with the ark of the LORD? Tell us how we shall send it to its place."

3 They said, "If you send away the ark of the God of Israel, do not send it empty; but you shall surely return to Him a guilt offering. Then you will be healed and it will be known to you why His hand is not removed from you."

4 Then they said, "What shall be the guilt offering which we shall return to Him?" And they said, "Five golden tumors and five golden mice *according to* the number of the lords of the Philistines, for one plague was on all of you and on your lords.

5 "So you shall make likenesses of your tumors and likenesses of your mice that ravage the land, and you shall give glory to the God of Israel; perhaps He will ease His hand from you, your gods, and your land.

6 "Why then do you harden your hearts as the Egyptians and Pharaoh hardened their hearts? When He had severely dealt with them, did they not allow the people to go, and they departed?

7 "Now therefore, take and prepare a new cart and two milch cows on which there has never been a yoke; and hitch the cows to the cart and take their calves home, away from them.

8 "Take the ark of the LORD and place it on the cart; and put the articles of gold which you return to Him as a guilt offering in a box by its side. Then send it away that it may go.

9 "Watch, if it goes up by the way of its own territory to Beth-shemesh, then He has done us this great evil. But if not, then we will know that it was not His hand that struck us; it happened to us by chance."

10 ¶ Then the men did so, and took two milch cows and hitched them to the cart, and shut up their calves at home.

11 They put the ark of the LORD on the cart, and the box with the golden mice and the likenesses of their tumors.

12 And the cows took the straight way in the direction of Beth-shemesh; they went along the highway, lowing as they went, and did not turn aside to the right or to the left. And the lords of the Philistines followed them to the border of Beth-shemesh.

New International

afflicted them with tumors.[r] 7When the men of Ashdod saw what was happening, they said, "The ark of the god of Israel must not stay here with us, because his hand is heavy upon us and upon Dagon our god." 8So they called together all the rulers of the Philistines and asked them, "What shall we do with the ark of the god of Israel?"

They answered, "Have the ark of the god of Israel moved to Gath." So they moved the ark of the God of Israel.

9But after they had moved it, the LORD's hand was against that city, throwing it into a great panic. He afflicted the people of the city, both young and old, with an outbreak of tumors.[s] 10So they sent the ark of God to Ekron.

As the ark of God was entering Ekron, the people of Ekron cried out, "They have brought the ark of the god of Israel around to us to kill us and our people." 11So they called together all the rulers of the Philistines and said, "Send the ark of the god of Israel away; let it go back to its own place, or it[t] will kill us and our people." For death had filled the city with panic; God's hand was very heavy upon it. 12Those who did not die were afflicted with tumors, and the outcry of the city went up to heaven.

The Ark Returned to Israel

6 WHEN THE ark of the LORD had been in Philistine territory seven months, 2the Philistines called for the priests and the diviners and said, "What shall we do with the ark of the LORD? Tell us how we should send it back to its place."

3They answered, "If you return the ark of the god of Israel, do not send it away empty, but by all means send a guilt offering to him. Then you will be healed, and you will know why his hand has not been lifted from you."

4The Philistines asked, "What guilt offering should we send to him?"

They replied, "Five gold tumors and five gold rats, according to the number of the Philistine rulers, because the same plague has struck both you and your rulers. 5Make models of the tumors and of the rats that are destroying the country, and pay honor to Israel's god. Perhaps he will lift his hand from you and your gods and your land. 6Why do you harden your hearts as the Egyptians and Pharaoh did? When he[u] treated them harshly, did they not send the Israelites out so they could go on their way?

7"Now then, get a new cart ready, with two cows that have calved and have never been yoked. Hitch the cows to the cart, but take their calves away and pen them up. 8Take the ark of the LORD and put it on the cart, and in a chest beside it put the gold objects you are sending back to him as a guilt offering. Send it on its way, 9but keep watching it. If it goes up to its own territory, toward Beth Shemesh, then the LORD has brought this great disaster on us. But if it does not, then we will know that it was not his hand that struck us and that it happened to us by chance."

10So they did this. They took two such cows and hitched them to the cart and penned up their calves. 11They placed the ark of the LORD on the cart and along with it the chest containing the gold rats and the models of the tumors. 12Then the cows went straight up toward Beth Shemesh, keeping on the road and lowing all the way; they did not turn to the right or to the left. The rulers of the Philistines followed them as far as the border of Beth Shemesh.

---

r 6 Hebrew; Septuagint and Vulgate *tumors. And rats appeared in their land, and death and destruction were throughout the city*
s 9 Or *with tumors in the groin* (see Septuagint)   *t 11* Or *he*
u 6 That is, God

King James

¹³And *they of* Beth-shemesh *were* reaping their wheat harvest in the valley: and they lifted up their eyes, and saw the ark, and rejoiced to see *it.*

¹⁴And the cart came into the field of Joshua, a Beth-shemite, and stood there, where *there was* a great stone: and they clave the wood of the cart, and offered the kine a burnt offering unto the LORD.

¹⁵And the Levites took down the ark of the LORD, and the coffer that *was* with it, wherein the jewels of gold *were,* and put *them* on the great stone: and the men of Beth-shemesh offered burnt offerings and sacrificed sacrifices the same day unto the LORD.

¹⁶And when the five lords of the Philistines had seen *it,* they returned to Ekron the same day.

¹⁷And these *are* the golden emerods which the Philistines returned *for* a trespass offering unto the LORD; for Ashdod one, for Gaza one, for Askelon one, for Gath one, for Ekron one;

¹⁸And the golden mice, *according to* the number of all the cities of the Philistines *belonging* to the five lords, *both* of fenced cities, and of country villages, even unto the ^dgreat *stone of* Abel, whereon they set down the ark of the LORD: *which stone remaineth* unto this day in the field of Joshua, the Beth-shemite.

¹⁹ ¶ And he smote the men of Beth-shemesh, because they had looked into the ark of the LORD, even he smote of the people fifty thousand and threescore and ten men: and the people lamented, because the LORD had smitten *many* of the people with a great slaughter.

²⁰And the men of Beth-shemesh said, Who is able to stand before this holy LORD God? and to whom shall he go up from us?

²¹ ¶ And they sent messengers to the inhabitants of Kirjath-jearim, saying, The Philistines have brought again the ark of the LORD; come ye down, *and* fetch it up to you.

7 AND THE men of Kirjath-jearim came, and fetched up the ark of the LORD, and brought it into the house of Abinadab in the hill, and sanctified Eleazar his son to keep the ark of the LORD.

²And it came to pass, while the ark abode in Kirjath-jearim, that the time was long; for it was twenty years: and all the house of Israel lamented after the LORD.

Philistines defeated at Mizpah

³ ¶ And Samuel spake unto all the house of Israel, saying, If ye do return unto the LORD with all your hearts, *then* put away the strange gods and Ashtaroth from among you, and prepare your hearts unto the LORD, and serve him only: and he will deliver you out of the hand of the Philistines.

⁴Then the children of Israel did put away Baalim and Ashtaroth, and served the LORD only.

⁵And Samuel said, Gather all Israel to Mizpeh, and I will pray for you unto the LORD.

⁶And they gathered together to Mizpeh, and drew water, and poured *it* out before the LORD, and fasted on that day, and said there, We have sinned against the LORD. And Samuel judged the children of Israel in Mizpeh.

⁷And when the Philistines heard that the children of Israel were gathered together to Mizpeh, the lords of the Philistines went up against Israel. And when the children of Israel heard *it,* they were afraid of the Philistines.

⁸And the children of Israel said to Samuel, *e*Cease not to cry unto the LORD our God for us, that he will save us out of the hand of the Philistines.

⁹ ¶ And Samuel took a sucking lamb, and offered *it for* a burnt offering wholly unto the LORD: and Samuel cried unto the LORD for Israel; and the LORD *f*heard him.

Amplified

¹³Now the men of Beth-shemesh were reaping their wheat harvest in the valley, and they lifted up their eyes and saw the ark, and rejoiced to see it.

¹⁴The cart came into the field of Joshua of Beth-shemesh and stopped there. A great stone was there; and the men split up the wood of the cart and offered the cows as a burnt offering to the Lord.

¹⁵The Levites took down the ark of the Lord and the box beside it in which were the figures of gold and put them upon the great stone. And the men of Beth-shemesh offered burnt offerings and made sacrifices that day to the Lord.

¹⁶When the five lords of the Philistines saw it, they returned that day to Ekron.

¹⁷And these are the tumors of gold which the Philistines returned for a guilt offering to the Lord: one each for Ashdod, Gaza, Ashkelon, Gath and Ekron;

¹⁸Also the mice of gold was according to the number of all the cities of the Philistines belonging to the five lords, both fortified cities and country villages. The great stone, on which they set the ark of the Lord, remains as a witness to this day in the field of Joshua of Beth-shemesh.

¹⁹And the Lord slew some of the men of Beth-shemesh because they had looked into the ark of the Lord; He slew *e*seventy men of them, and the people mourned because the Lord had made a great slaughter among them.

²⁰And the men of Beth-shemesh said, Who is able to stand before the Lord, this holy God? And to whom shall He go away from us?

²¹And they sent messengers to the inhabitants of Kiriath-jearim, saying, The Philistines have returned the ark of the Lord. Come down and take it up to you.

7 SO THE men of Kiriath-jearim came and took the ark of the Lord and brought it into the house of Abinadab on the hill and consecrated Eleazar his son to have charge of the ark of the Lord.

²And the ark remained in Kiriath-jearim a very long time [nearly 100 years, through Samuel's entire judgeship, Saul's reign, and well into David's, when it was brought to Jerusalem]. For it was twenty years before all the house of Israel lamented after the Lord. [I Chron. 13:5–7.]

³Then Samuel said to all the house of Israel, If you are returning to the Lord with all your hearts, then put away the foreign gods and the Ashtaroth [female deities] from among you and direct your hearts to the Lord and serve Him only, and He will deliver you out of the hand of the Philistines.

⁴So the Israelites put away the Baals and the Ashtaroth, and served the Lord only.

⁵Samuel said, Gather all Israel to Mizpah and I will pray to the Lord for you.

⁶So they gathered at Mizpah and drew water and poured it out before the Lord and fasted on that day and said there, We have sinned against the Lord. And Samuel judged the Israelites at Mizpah.

⁷Now when the Philistines heard that the Israelites had gathered at Mizpah, the lords of the Philistines went up against Israel. And when the Israelites heard of it, they were afraid of the Philistines.

⁸And the Israelites said to Samuel, Do not cease to cry to the Lord our God for us, that He may save us from the hand of the Philistines.

⁹So Samuel took a sucking lamb and offered it as a whole burnt offering to the Lord; and Samuel cried to the Lord for Israel, and the Lord answered him.

---

^dOr, *great stone*   ^eHeb. *Be not silent from us from crying*
^fOr, *answered*

^eMost Hebrew manuscripts read 50,070.

New American Standard

13 ¶ Now *the people of* Beth-shemesh were reaping their wheat harvest in the valley, and they raised their eyes and saw the ark and were glad to see *it.*

14 The cart came into the field of Joshua the Beth-shemite and stood there where there *was* a large stone; and they split the wood of the cart and offered the cows as a burnt offering to the LORD.

15 The Levites took down the ark of the LORD and the box that was with it, in which were the articles of gold, and put them on the large stone; and the men of Beth-shemesh offered burnt offerings and sacrificed sacrifices that day to the LORD.

16 When the five lords of the Philistines saw it, they returned to Ekron that day.

17 ¶ These are the golden tumors which the Philistines returned for a guilt offering to the LORD: one for Ashdod, one for Gaza, one for Ashkelon, one for Gath, one for Ekron;

18 and the golden mice, *according* to the number of all the cities of the Philistines belonging to the five lords, both of fortified cities and of country villages. The large stone on which they set the ark of the LORD *is a witness* to this day in the field of Joshua the Beth-shemite.

19 ¶ He struck down some of the men of Beth-shemesh because they had looked into the ark of the LORD. He struck down of all the people, 50,070 men, and the people mourned because the LORD had struck the people with a great slaughter.

20 The men of Beth-shemesh said, "Who is able to stand before the LORD, this holy God? And to whom shall He go up from us?"

21 So they sent messengers to the inhabitants of Kiriath-jearim, saying, "The Philistines have brought back the ark of the LORD; come down and take it up to you."

Deliverance from the Philistines

7 AND THE men of Kiriath-jearim came and took the ark of the LORD and brought it into the house of Abinadab on the hill, and consecrated Eleazar his son to keep the ark of the LORD.

2 From the day that the ark remained at Kiriath-jearim, the time was long, for it was twenty years; and all the house of Israel lamented after the LORD.

3 ¶ Then Samuel spoke to all the house of Israel, saying, "If you return to the LORD with all your heart, remove the foreign gods and the Ashtaroth from among you and direct your hearts to the LORD and serve Him alone; and He will deliver you from the hand of the Philistines."

4 So the sons of Israel removed the Baals and the Ashtaroth and served the LORD alone.

5 ¶ Then Samuel said, "Gather all Israel to Mizpah and I will pray to the LORD for you."

6 They gathered to Mizpah, and drew water and poured it out before the LORD, and fasted on that day and said there, "We have sinned against the LORD." And Samuel judged the sons of Israel at Mizpah.

7 ¶ Now when the Philistines heard that the sons of Israel had gathered to Mizpah, the lords of the Philistines went up against Israel. And when the sons of Israel heard it, they were afraid of the Philistines.

8 Then the sons of Israel said to Samuel, "Do not cease to cry to the LORD our God for us, that He may save us from the hand of the Philistines."

9 Samuel took a suckling lamb and offered it for a whole burnt offering to the LORD; and Samuel cried to the LORD for Israel and the LORD answered him.

New International

13Now the people of Beth Shemesh were harvesting their wheat in the valley, and when they looked up and saw the ark, they rejoiced at the sight. 14The cart came to the field of Joshua of Beth Shemesh, and there it stopped beside a large rock. The people chopped up the wood of the cart and sacrificed the cows as a burnt offering to the LORD. 15The Levites took down the ark of the LORD, together with the chest containing the gold objects, and placed them on the large rock. On that day the people of Beth Shemesh offered burnt offerings and made sacrifices to the LORD. 16The five rulers of the Philistines saw all this and then returned that same day to Ekron.

17These are the gold tumors the Philistines sent as a guilt offering to the LORD—one each for Ashdod, Gaza, Ashkelon, Gath and Ekron. 18And the number of the gold rats was according to the number of Philistine towns belonging to the five rulers—the fortified towns with their country villages. The large rock, on which*v* they set the ark of the LORD, is a witness to this day in the field of Joshua of Beth Shemesh.

19But God struck down some of the men of Beth Shemesh, putting seventy*w* of them to death because they had looked into the ark of the LORD. The people mourned because of the heavy blow the LORD had dealt them, 20and the men of Beth Shemesh asked, "Who can stand in the presence of the LORD, this holy God? To whom will the ark go up from here?"

21Then they sent messengers to the people of Kiriath Jearim, saying, "The Philistines have returned the ark of the LORD. Come down and take it up to your place."

7 1SO THE men of Kiriath Jearim came and took up the ark of the LORD. They took it to Abinadab's house on the hill and consecrated Eleazar his son to guard the ark of the LORD.

Samuel Subdues the Philistines at Mizpah

2It was a long time, twenty years in all, that the ark remained at Kiriath Jearim, and all the people of Israel mourned and sought after the LORD. 3And Samuel said to the whole house of Israel, "If you are returning to the LORD with all your hearts, then rid yourselves of the foreign gods and the Ashtoreths and commit yourselves to the LORD and serve him only, and he will deliver you out of the hand of the Philistines." 4So the Israelites put away their Baals and Ashtoreths, and served the LORD only.

5Then Samuel said, "Assemble all Israel at Mizpah and I will intercede with the LORD for you." 6When they had assembled at Mizpah, they drew water and poured it out before the LORD. On that day they fasted and there they confessed, "We have sinned against the LORD." And Samuel was leader*x* of Israel at Mizpah.

7When the Philistines heard that Israel had assembled at Mizpah, the rulers of the Philistines came up to attack them. And when the Israelites heard of it, they were afraid because of the Philistines. 8They said to Samuel, "Do not stop crying out to the LORD our God for us, that he may rescue us from the hand of the Philistines." 9Then Samuel took a suckling lamb and offered it up as a whole burnt offering to the LORD. He cried out to the LORD on Israel's behalf, and the LORD answered him.

---

v 18 A few Hebrew manuscripts (see also Septuagint); most Hebrew manuscripts *villages as far as Greater Abel, where*   *w 19* A few Hebrew manuscripts; most Hebrew manuscripts and Septuagint *50,070*   *x 6* Traditionally *judge*

King James

10 And as Samuel was offering up the burnt offering, the
Philistines drew near to battle against Israel: but the LORD
thundered with a great thunder on that day upon the Philistines, and discomfited them; and they were smitten before
Israel.
11 And the men of Israel went out of Mizpeh, and pursued the Philistines, and smote them, until *they came* under Beth-car.
12 Then Samuel took a stone, and set *it* between Mizpeh
and Shen, and called the name of it [g]Eben-ezer, saying,
Hitherto hath the LORD helped us.
13 ¶ So the Philistines were subdued, and they came no
more into the coast of Israel: and the hand of the LORD was
against the Philistines all the days of Samuel.
14 And the cities which the Philistines had taken from
Israel were restored to Israel, from Ekron even unto Gath;
and the coasts thereof did Israel deliver out of the hands of
the Philistines. And there was peace between Israel and the
Amorites.
15 And Samuel judged Israel all the days of his life.
16 And he went from year to year [h]in circuit to Beth-el,
and Gilgal, and Mizpeh, and judged Israel in all those
places.
17 And his return *was* to Ramah; for there *was* his house;
and there he judged Israel; and there he built an altar unto
the LORD.

Israel demands a king

8 AND IT came to pass, when Samuel was old, that he
made his sons judges over Israel.
2 Now the name of his firstborn was [i]Joel; and the
name of his second, Abiah: *they were* judges in Beersheba.
3 And his sons walked not in his ways, but turned aside
after lucre, and took bribes, and perverted judgment.
4 Then all the elders of Israel gathered themselves together, and came to Samuel unto Ramah,
5 And said unto him, Behold, thou art old, and thy sons
walk not in thy ways: now make us a king to judge us like
all the nations.
6 ¶ But the thing [j]displeased Samuel, when they said,
Give us a king to judge us. And Samuel prayed unto the
LORD.
7 And the LORD said unto Samuel, Hearken unto the
voice of the people in all that they say unto thee: for they
have not rejected thee, but they have rejected me, that I
should not reign over them.
8 According to all the works which they have done since
the day that I brought them up out of Egypt even unto this
day, wherewith they have forsaken me, and served other
gods, so do they also unto thee.
9 Now therefore [k]hearken unto their voice: [l]howbeit
yet protest solemnly unto them, and show them the manner
of the king that shall reign over them.
10 ¶ And Samuel told all the words of the LORD unto the
people that asked of him a king.
11 And he said, This will be the manner of the king that
shall reign over you: He will take your sons, and appoint
them for himself, for his chariots, and *to be* his horsemen;
and *some* shall run before his chariots.
12 And he will appoint him captains over thousands, and
captains over fifties; and *will set them* to ear his ground,
and to reap his harvest, and to make his instruments of
war, and instruments of his chariots.
13 And he will take your daughters *to be* confectionaries,
and *to be* cooks, and *to be* bakers.

[g]i.e. *The stone of help* [h]Heb. *and he circuited* [i]*Vashni* in 1 Chr. 6:28 [j]Heb. *was evil in the eyes of Samuel* [k]Or, *obey* [l]Or, *notwithstanding when thou hast solemnly protested against them, then thou shalt show*

Amplified

10 As Samuel was offering up the burnt offering, the
Philistines drew near to attack Israel. But the Lord thundered with a great voice that day against the Philistines
and threw them into confusion, and they were defeated
before Israel.
11 And the men of Israel went out of Mizpah and pursued
the Philistines and smote them as far as below Beth-car.
12 Then Samuel took a stone and set it between Mizpah
and Shen, and he called the name of it Ebenezer [stone of
help], saying, Heretofore the Lord has helped us.
13 So the Philistines were subdued and came no more
into Israelite territory. And the hand of the Lord was
against the Philistines all the days of Samuel.
14 The cities the Philistines had taken from Israel were
restored to Israel, from Ekron to Gath, and Israel rescued
[the cities'] territory from the Philistines. There was peace
also between Israel and the Amorites.
15 And Samuel judged Israel all his days.
16 And he went from year to year on a circuit to Bethel,
Gilgal, and Mizpah, and was judge for Israel in all those
places.
17 Then he would return to Ramah, for his home was
there; there he judged Israel, and there he built an altar to
the Lord.

8 WHEN SAMUEL was old, he made his sons judges
over Israel.
2 Now the name of his firstborn was Joel and the name
of his second, Abijah. They were judges in Beersheba.
3 His sons did not walk in his ways, but turned aside after
gain, took bribes, and perverted justice.
4 All the elders of Israel assembled and came to Samuel
at Ramah
5 And said to him, Behold, you are old, and your sons do
not walk in your ways; now appoint us a king to rule over
us like all the other nations.
6 But it displeased Samuel when they said, Give us a
king to govern us. And Samuel prayed to the Lord.
7 And the Lord said to Samuel, Hearken to the voice of
the people in all they say to you; for they have not rejected
you, but they have rejected Me, that I should not be King
over them.
8 According to all the works which they have done since
I brought them up out of Egypt even to this day, forsaking
Me and serving other gods, so they also do to you.
9 So listen now to their voice; only solemnly warn them
and show them the ways of the king who shall reign over
them.
10 So Samuel told all the words of the Lord to the people
who asked of him a king.
11 And he said, These will be the ways of the king who
shall reign over you: he will take your sons and appoint
them to his chariots and to be his horsemen and to run
before his chariots.
12 He will appoint them for himself to be commanders
over thousands and over fifties, and some to plow his
ground and to reap his harvest and to make his implements
of war and equipment for his chariots.
13 He will take your daughters to be perfumers, cooks,
and bakers.

New American Standard

10 Now Samuel was offering up the burnt offering, and the Philistines drew near to battle against Israel. But the LORD thundered with a great thunder on that day against the Philistines and confused them, so that they were routed before Israel.

11 The men of Israel went out of Mizpah and pursued the Philistines, and struck them down as far as below Beth-car.

12 ¶ Then Samuel took a stone and set it between Mizpah and Shen, and named it dEbenezer, saying, "Thus far the LORD has helped us."

13 So the Philistines were subdued and they did not come anymore within the border of Israel. And the hand of the LORD was against the Philistines all the days of Samuel.

14 The cities which the Philistines had taken from Israel were restored to Israel, from Ekron even to Gath; and Israel delivered their territory from the hand of the Philistines. So there was peace between Israel and the Amorites.

Samuel's Ministry

15 ¶ Now Samuel judged Israel all the days of his life.

16 He used to go annually on circuit to Bethel and Gilgal and Mizpah, and he judged Israel in all these places.

17 Then his return *was* to Ramah, for his house *was* there, and there he judged Israel; and he built there an altar to the LORD.

Israel Demands a King

8 AND IT came about when Samuel was old that he appointed his sons judges over Israel.

2 Now the name of his firstborn was Joel, and the name of his second, Abijah; *they* were judging in Beersheba.

3 His sons, however, did not walk in his ways, but turned aside after dishonest gain and took bribes and perverted justice.

4 ¶ Then all the elders of Israel gathered together and came to Samuel at Ramah;

5 and they said to him, "Behold, you have grown old, and your sons do not walk in your ways. Now appoint a king for us to judge us like all the nations."

6 But the thing was displeasing in the sight of Samuel when they said, "Give us a king to judge us." And Samuel prayed to the LORD.

7 The LORD said to Samuel, "Listen to the voice of the people in regard to all that they say to you, for they have not rejected you, but they have rejected Me from being king over them.

8 "Like all the deeds which they have done since the day that I brought them up from Egypt even to this day—in that they have forsaken Me and served other gods—so they are doing to you also.

9 "Now then, listen to their voice; however, you shall solemnly warn them and tell them of the eprocedure of the king who will reign over them."

Warning concerning a King

10 ¶ So Samuel spoke all the words of the LORD to the people who had asked of him a king.

11 He said, "This will be the procedure of the king who will reign over you: he will take your sons and place *them* for himself in his chariots and among his horsemen and they will run before his chariots.

12 "He will appoint for himself commanders of thousands and of fifties, and *some* to do his plowing and to reap his harvest and to make his weapons of war and equipment for his chariots.

13 "He will also take your daughters for perfumers and cooks and bakers.

New International

10 While Samuel was sacrificing the burnt offering, the Philistines drew near to engage Israel in battle. But that day the LORD thundered with loud thunder against the Philistines and threw them into such a panic that they were routed before the Israelites. 11 The men of Israel rushed out of Mizpah and pursued the Philistines, slaughtering them along the way to a point below Beth Car.

12 Then Samuel took a stone and set it up between Mizpah and Shen. He named it Ebenezer,y saying, "Thus far has the LORD helped us." 13 So the Philistines were subdued and did not invade Israelite territory again.

Throughout Samuel's lifetime, the hand of the LORD was against the Philistines. 14 The towns from Ekron to Gath that the Philistines had captured from Israel were restored to her, and Israel delivered the neighboring territory from the power of the Philistines. And there was peace between Israel and the Amorites.

15 Samuel continued as judge over Israel all the days of his life. 16 From year to year he went on a circuit from Bethel to Gilgal to Mizpah, judging Israel in all those places. 17 But he always went back to Ramah, where his home was, and there he also judged Israel. And he built an altar there to the LORD.

Israel Asks for a King

8 WHEN SAMUEL grew old, he appointed his sons as judges for Israel. 2 The name of his firstborn was Joel and the name of his second was Abijah, and they served at Beersheba. 3 But his sons did not walk in his ways. They turned aside after dishonest gain and accepted bribes and perverted justice.

4 So all the elders of Israel gathered together and came to Samuel at Ramah. 5 They said to him, "You are old, and your sons do not walk in your ways; now appoint a king to leadz us, such as all the other nations have."

6 But when they said, "Give us a king to lead us," this displeased Samuel; so he prayed to the LORD. 7 And the LORD told him: "Listen to all that the people are saying to you; it is not you they have rejected, but they have rejected me as their king. 8 As they have done from the day I brought them up out of Egypt until this day, forsaking me and serving other gods, so they are doing to you. 9 Now listen to them; but warn them solemnly and let them know what the king who will reign over them will do."

10 Samuel told all the words of the LORD to the people who were asking him for a king. 11 He said, "This is what the king who will reign over you will do: He will take your sons and make them serve with his chariots and horses, and they will run in front of his chariots. 12 Some he will assign to be commanders of thousands and commanders of fifties, and others to plow his ground and reap his harvest, and still others to make weapons of war and equipment for his chariots. 13 He will take your daughters to be perfumers

---

d I.e. the stone of help   e Lit *custom*

y 12 *Ebenezer* means *stone of help.*   z 5 Traditionally *judge*; also in verses 6 and 20

King James

[14]And he will take your fields, and your vineyards, and your oliveyards, *even* the best *of them,* and give *them* to his servants.

[15]And he will take the tenth of your seed, and of your vineyards, and give to his [m]officers, and to his servants.

[16]And he will take your menservants, and your maidservants, and your goodliest young men, and your asses, and put *them* to his work.

[17]He will take the tenth of your sheep: and ye shall be his servants.

[18]And ye shall cry out in that day because of your king which ye shall have chosen you; and the LORD will not hear you in that day.

[19] ¶ Nevertheless the people refused to obey the voice of Samuel; and they said, Nay; but we will have a king over us;

[20]That we also may be like all the nations; and that our king may judge us, and go out before us, and fight our battles.

[21]And Samuel heard all the words of the people, and he rehearsed them in the ears of the LORD.

[22]And the LORD said to Samuel, Hearken unto their voice, and make them a king. And Samuel said unto the men of Israel, Go ye every man unto his city.

Saul anointed by Samuel

9 NOW THERE was a man of Benjamin, whose name *was* Kish, the son of Abiel, the son of Zeror, the son of Bechorath, the son of Aphiah, [n]a Benjamite, a mighty man of [o]power.

[2]And he had a son, whose name *was* Saul, a choice young man, and a goodly: and *there was* not among the children of Israel a goodlier person than he: from his shoulders and upward *he was* higher than any of the people.

[3]And the asses of Kish Saul's father were lost. And Kish said to Saul his son, Take now one of the servants with thee, and arise, go seek the asses.

[4]And he passed through mount Ephraim, and passed through the land of Shalisha, but they found *them* not: then they passed through the land of Shalim, and *there they were* not: and he passed through the land of the Benjamites, but they found *them* not.

[5]*And* when they were come to the land of Zuph, Saul said to his servant that *was* with him, Come, and let us return; lest my father leave *caring* for the asses, and take thought for us.

[6]And he said unto him, Behold now, *there is* in this city a man of God, and *he is* an honourable man; all that he saith cometh surely to pass: now let us go thither; peradventure he can show us our way that we should go.

[7]Then said Saul to his servant, But, behold, *if* we go, what shall we bring the man? for the bread [p]is spent in our vessels, and *there is* not a present to bring to the man of God: what [q]have we?

[8]And the servant answered Saul again, and said, Behold, [r]I have here at hand the fourth part of a shekel of silver: *that* will I give to the man of God, to tell us our way.

[9](Beforetime in Israel, when a man went to inquire of God, thus he spake, Come, and let us go to the seer: for *he that is* now *called* a Prophet was beforetime called a Seer.)

[10]Then said Saul to his servant, [s]Well said; come, let us go. So they went unto the city where the man of God *was.*

[11] ¶ *And* as they went up [t]the hill to the city, they found young maidens going out to draw water, and said unto them, Is the seer here?

Amplified

[14]He will take your fields, your vineyards, and your olive orchards, even the best of them, and give them to his servants.

[15]He will take a tenth of your grain and of your vineyards and give it to his officers and to his servants.

[16]He will take your men and women servants and the best of your cattle and your donkeys and put them to his work.

[17]He will take a tenth of your flocks, and you yourselves shall be his slaves.

[18]In that day you will cry out because of your king you have chosen for yourselves, but the Lord will not hear you then.

[19]Nevertheless, the people refused to listen to the voice of Samuel, and they said, No! We will have a king over us,

[20]That we also may be like all the nations, and that our king may govern us and go out before us and fight our battles.

[21]Samuel heard all the people's words and repeated them in the Lord's ears.

[22]And the Lord said to Samuel, Hearken to their voice and appoint them a king. And Samuel said to the men of Israel, Go every man to his city.

9 THERE WAS a man of Benjamin whose name was Kish son of Abiel, the son of Zeror, the son of Becorath, the son of Aphiah, a Benjamite, a mighty man of wealth *and* valor.

[2]Kish had a son named Saul, a choice young man and handsome; among all the Israelites there was not a man more handsome than he. He was a head taller than any of the people.

[3]The donkeys of Kish, Saul's father, were lost. Kish said to Saul, Take a servant with you and go, look for the donkeys.

[4]And they passed through the hill country of Ephraim and the land of Shalishah, but did not find them. Then they went through the land of Shaalim and the land of Benjamin, but did not find them.

[5]And when they came to the land of Zuph, Saul said to his servant, Come, let us return, lest my father stop worrying about the donkeys and become concerned about us.

[6]The servant said to him, Behold now, there is in this city a man of God, a man held in honor; all that he says surely comes true. Now let us go there. Perhaps he can show us where we should go.

[7]Then Saul said to his servant, But if we go, what shall we bring the man? The bread in our sacks is gone, and there is no gift for the man of God. What have we?

[8]The servant replied, I have here a quarter of a shekel of silver. I will give that to the man of God to tell us our way—

[9](Formerly in Israel, when a man went to inquire of God, he said, Come, let us go to the seer, for he that is now called a prophet was formerly called a seer.)

[10]Saul said to his servant, Well said; come, let us go. So they went to the city where the man of God was.

[11]As they went up the hill to the city, they met young maidens going out to draw water, and said to them, Is the seer here?

---

[m] Heb. *eunuchs;* see Gen. 37:36   [n] Or, *the son of a man of Jemini*   [o] Or, *substance*   [p] Heb. *is gone out of*   [q] Heb. *is with us*   [r] Heb. *there is found in my hand*   [s] Heb. *Thy word* is good   [t] Heb. *in the ascent of the city*

New American Standard

14"He will take the best of your fields and your vineyards and your olive groves and give *them* to his servants.

15"He will take a tenth of your seed and of your vineyards and give to his officers and to his servants.

16"He will also take your male servants and your female servants and your best young men and your donkeys and use *them* for his work.

17"He will take a tenth of your flocks, and you yourselves will become his servants.

18"Then you will cry out in that day because of your king whom you have chosen for yourselves, but the LORD will not answer you in that day."

19 ¶ Nevertheless, the people refused to listen to the voice of Samuel, and they said, "No, but there shall be a king over us,

20 that we also may be like all the nations, that our king may judge us and go out before us and fight our battles."

21 Now after Samuel had heard all the words of the people, he repeated them in the LORD's hearing.

22 The LORD said to Samuel, "Listen to their voice and appoint them a king." So Samuel said to the men of Israel, "Go every man to his city."

Saul's Search

9 NOW THERE was a man of Benjamin whose name was Kish the son of Abiel, the son of Zeror, the son of Becorath, the son of Aphiah, the son of a Benjamite, a mighty man of valor.

2 He had a son whose name was Saul, a choice and handsome *man,* and there was not a more handsome person than he among the sons of Israel; from his shoulders and up he was taller than any of the people.

3 ¶ Now the donkeys of Kish, Saul's father, were lost. So Kish said to his son Saul, "Take now with you one of the servants, and arise, go search for the donkeys."

4 He passed through the hill country of Ephraim and passed through the land of Shalishah, but they did not find *them.* Then they passed through the land of Shaalim, but *they were* not *there.* Then he passed through the land of the Benjamites, but they did not find *them.*

5 ¶ When they came to the land of Zuph, Saul said to his servant who was with him, "Come, and let us return, or else my father will cease *to be concerned* about the donkeys and will become anxious for us."

6 He said to him, "Behold now, there is a man of God in this city, and the man is held in honor; all that he says surely comes true. Now let us go there, perhaps he can tell us about our journey on which we have set out."

7 Then Saul said to his servant, "But behold, if we go, what shall we bring the man? For the bread is gone from our sack and there is no present to bring to the man of God. What do we have?"

8 The servant answered Saul again and said, "Behold, I have in my hand a fourth of a shekel of silver; I will give *it* to the man of God and he will tell us our way."

9 (Formerly in Israel, when a man went to inquire of God, he used to say, "Come, and let us go to the seer"; for *he who is called* a prophet now was formerly called a seer.)

10 Then Saul said to his servant, "Well said; come, let us go." So they went to the city where the man of God was.

11 ¶ As they went up the slope to the city, they found young women going out to draw water and said to them, "Is the seer here?"

New International

and cooks and bakers. 14He will take the best of your fields and vineyards and olive groves and give them to his attendants. 15He will take a tenth of your grain and of your vintage and give it to his officials and attendants. 16Your menservants and maidservants and the best of your cattle[a] and donkeys he will take for his own use. 17He will take a tenth of your flocks, and you yourselves will become his slaves. 18When that day comes, you will cry out for relief from the king you have chosen, and the LORD will not answer you in that day."

19But the people refused to listen to Samuel. "No!" they said. "We want a king over us. 20Then we will be like all the other nations, with a king to lead us and to go out before us and fight our battles."

21When Samuel heard all that the people said, he repeated it before the LORD. 22The LORD answered, "Listen to them and give them a king."

Then Samuel said to the men of Israel, "Everyone go back to his town."

Samuel Anoints Saul

9 THERE WAS a Benjamite, a man of standing, whose name was Kish son of Abiel, the son of Zeror, the son of Becorath, the son of Aphiah of Benjamin. 2He had a son named Saul, an impressive young man without equal among the Israelites—a head taller than any of the others.

3Now the donkeys belonging to Saul's father Kish were lost, and Kish said to his son Saul, "Take one of the servants with you and go and look for the donkeys." 4So he passed through the hill country of Ephraim and through the area around Shalisha, but they did not find them. They went on into the district of Shaalim, but the donkeys were not there. Then he passed through the territory of Benjamin, but they did not find them.

5When they reached the district of Zuph, Saul said to the servant who was with him, "Come, let's go back, or my father will stop thinking about the donkeys and start worrying about us."

6But the servant replied, "Look, in this town there is a man of God; he is highly respected, and everything he says comes true. Let's go there now. Perhaps he will tell us what way to take."

7Saul said to his servant, "If we go, what can we give the man? The food in our sacks is gone. We have no gift to take to the man of God. What do we have?"

8The servant answered him again. "Look," he said, "I have a quarter of a shekel[b] of silver. I will give it to the man of God so that he will tell us what way to take." 9(Formerly in Israel, if a man went to inquire of God, he would say, "Come, let us go to the seer," because the prophet of today used to be called a seer.)

10"Good," Saul said to his servant. "Come, let's go." So they set out for the town where the man of God was.

11As they were going up the hill to the town, they met some girls coming out to draw water, and they asked them, "Is the seer here?"

a 16 Septuagint; Hebrew *young men*   b 8 That is, about 1/10 ounce (about 3 grams)

King James

Amplified

¹²And they answered them, and said, He is; behold, *he is* before you: make haste now, for he came today to the city; for *there is* a ^usacrifice of the people today in the high place:

¹³As soon as ye be come into the city, ye shall straightway find him, before he go up to the high place to eat: for the people will not eat until he come, because he doth bless the sacrifice; *and* afterwards they eat that be bidden. Now therefore get you up; for about ^vthis time ye shall find him.

¹⁴And they went up into the city: *and* when they were come into the city, behold, Samuel came out against them, for to go up to the high place.

¹⁵ ¶ Now the Lord had told Samuel in his ear a day before Saul came, saying,

¹⁶Tomorrow about this time I will send thee a man out of the land of Benjamin, and thou shalt anoint him *to be* captain over my people Israel, that he may save my people out of the hand of the Philistines: for I have looked upon my people, because their cry is come unto me.

¹⁷And when Samuel saw Saul, the Lord said unto him, Behold the man whom I spake to thee of! this same shall ^wreign over my people.

¹⁸Then Saul drew near to Samuel in the gate, and said, Tell me, I pray thee, where the seer's house *is*.

¹⁹And Samuel answered Saul, and said, I *am* the seer: go up before me unto the high place; for ye shall eat with me today, and tomorrow I will let thee go, and will tell thee all that *is* in thine heart.

²⁰And as for thine asses that were lost ^xthree days ago, set not thy mind on them; for they are found. And on whom *is* all the desire of Israel? *Is it* not on thee, and on all thy father's house?

²¹And Saul answered and said, *Am* not I a Benjamite, of the smallest of the tribes of Israel? and my family the least of all the families of the tribe of Benjamin? wherefore then speakest thou ^yso to me?

²²And Samuel took Saul and his servant, and brought them into the parlour, and made them sit in the chiefest place among them that were bidden, which *were* about thirty persons.

²³And Samuel said unto the cook, Bring the portion which I gave thee, of which I said unto thee, Set it by thee.

²⁴And the cook took up the shoulder, and *that* which *was* upon it, and set *it* before Saul. And *Samuel* said, Behold that which is ^zleft! set *it* before thee, *and* eat: for unto this time hath it been kept for thee since I said, I have invited the people. So Saul did eat with Samuel that day.

²⁵ ¶ And when they were come down from the high place into the city, *Samuel* communed with Saul upon the top of the house.

²⁶And they arose early: and it came to pass about the spring of the day, that Samuel called Saul to the top of the house, saying, Up, that I may send thee away. And Saul arose, and they went out both of them, he and Samuel, abroad.

²⁷*And* as they were going down to the end of the city, Samuel said to Saul, Bid the servant pass on before us, (and he passed on,) but stand thou still ^va while, that I may show thee the word of God.

10 THEN SAMUEL took a vial of oil, and poured *it* upon his head, and kissed him, and said, *Is it* not because the Lord hath anointed thee *to be* captain over his inheritance?

¹²They answered, He is; behold, he is just beyond you. Hurry, for he came today to the city because the people have a sacrifice today on the high place.

¹³As you enter the city, you will find him before he goes up to the high place to eat. The people will not eat until he comes to ask the blessing on the sacrifice. Afterward, those who are invited eat. So go on up, for about now you will find him.

¹⁴So they went up to the city, and as they were entering, behold, Samuel came toward them, going up to the high place.

¹⁵Now a day before Saul came, the Lord had revealed to Samuel in his ear,

¹⁶Tomorrow about this time I will send you a man from the land of Benjamin, and you shall anoint him to be leader over My people Israel; and he shall save them out of the hand of the Philistines. For I have looked upon the distress of My people, because their cry has come to Me.

¹⁷When Samuel saw Saul, the Lord told him, There is the man of whom I told you. He shall have authority over My people.

¹⁸Then Saul came near to Samuel in the gate and said, Tell me where is the seer's house?

¹⁹Samuel answered Saul, I am the seer. Go up before me to the high place, for you shall eat with me today, and tomorrow I will let you go and will tell you all that is on your mind.

²⁰As for your donkeys that were lost three days ago, do not be thinking about them, for they are found. And for whom are all the desirable things of Israel? Are they not for you and for all your father's house?

²¹And Saul said, Am I not a Benjamite, of the smallest of the tribes of Israel? And is not my family the least of all the families of the clans of Benjamin? Why then do you speak this way to me?

²²Then Samuel took Saul and his servant and brought them into the guest room [at the high place] and had them sit in the chief place among the persons—about thirty of them—who were invited. [The other people feasted outside.]

²³And Samuel said to the cook, Bring the portion which I gave you, of which I said to you, Set it aside.

²⁴And the cook lifted high the shoulder and what was on it [indicating that it was the priest's honored portion] and set it before Saul. [Samuel] said, See what was reserved for you. Eat, for until the hour appointed it was kept for you, ever since I invited the people. So Saul ate that day with Samuel.

²⁵When they had come down from the high place into the city, Samuel conversed with Saul on the top of the house.

²⁶They arose early and about dawn Samuel called Saul [who was sleeping] on the top of the house, saying, Get up, that I may send you on your way. Saul arose, and both he and Samuel went out on the street.

²⁷And as they were going down to the outskirts of the city, Samuel said to Saul, Bid the servant pass on before us—and he passed on—but you stand still, first, that I may cause you to hear the word of God.

10 THEN SAMUEL took the vial of oil and poured it on Saul's head and kissed him and said, Has not the Lord anointed you to be prince over His heritage Israel?

^uOr, *feast*   ^vHeb. *today*   ^wHeb. *restrain in*   ^xHeb. *today* *three days*   ^yHeb. *according to this word?*   ^zOr, *reserved*

New American Standard

12 They answered them and said, "He is; see, *he is* ahead of you. Hurry now, for he has come into the city today, for the people have a sacrifice on the high place today.

13 "As soon as you enter the city you will find him before he goes up to the high place to eat, for the people will not eat until he comes, because he must bless the sacrifice; afterward those who are invited will eat. Now therefore, go up for you will find him at once."

14 So they went up to the city. As they came into the city, behold, Samuel was coming out toward them to go up to the high place.

God's Choice for King

15 ¶ Now a day before Saul's coming, the LORD had revealed *this* to Samuel saying,

16 "About this time tomorrow I will send you a man from the land of Benjamin, and you shall anoint him to be prince over My people Israel; and he will deliver My people from the hand of the Philistines. For I have regarded My people, because their cry has come to Me."

17 When Samuel saw Saul, the LORD said to him, "Behold, the man of whom I spoke to you! This one shall rule over My people."

18 Then Saul approached Samuel in the gate and said, "Please tell me where the seer's house is."

19 Samuel answered Saul and said, "I am the seer. Go up before me to the high place, for you shall eat with me today; and in the morning I will let you go, and will tell you all that is on your mind.

20 "As for your donkeys which were lost three days ago, do not set your mind on them, for they have been found. And for whom is all that is desirable in Israel? Is it not for you and for all your father's household?"

21 Saul replied, "Am I not a Benjamite, of the smallest of the tribes of Israel, and my family the least of all the families of the tribe of Benjamin? Why then do you speak to me in this way?"

22 ¶ Then Samuel took Saul and his servant and brought them into the hall and gave them a place at the head of those who were invited, who were about thirty men.

23 Samuel said to the cook, "Bring the portion that I gave you, concerning which I said to you, 'Set it aside.' "

24 Then the cook took up the leg with what was on it and set *it* before Saul. And *Samuel* said, "Here is what has been reserved! Set *it* before you *and* eat, because it has been kept for you until the appointed time, since I said I have invited the people." So Saul ate with Samuel that day.

25 ¶ When they came down from the high place into the city, *Samuel* spoke with Saul on the ʄroof.

26 And they arose early; and at daybreak Samuel called to Saul on the roof, saying, "Get up, that I may send you away." So Saul arose, and both he and Samuel went out into the street.

27 As they were going down to the edge of the city, Samuel said to Saul, "Say to the servant that he might go ahead of us and pass on, but you remain standing now, that I may proclaim the word of God to you."

Saul among Prophets

10 THEN SAMUEL took the flask of oil, poured it on his head, kissed him and said, "Has not the LORD anointed you a ruler over His inheritance?

New International

12 "He is," they answered. "He's ahead of you. Hurry now; he has just come to our town today, for the people have a sacrifice at the high place. 13 As soon as you enter the town, you will find him before he goes up to the high place to eat. The people will not begin eating until he comes, because he must bless the sacrifice; afterward, those who are invited will eat. Go up now; you should find him about this time."

14 They went up to the town, and as they were entering it, there was Samuel, coming toward them on his way up to the high place.

15 Now the day before Saul came, the LORD had revealed this to Samuel: 16 "About this time tomorrow I will send you a man from the land of Benjamin. Anoint him leader over my people Israel; he will deliver my people from the hand of the Philistines. I have looked upon my people, for their cry has reached me."

17 When Samuel caught sight of Saul, the LORD said to him, "This is the man I spoke to you about; he will govern my people."

18 Saul approached Samuel in the gateway and asked, "Would you please tell me where the seer's house is?"

19 "I am the seer," Samuel replied. "Go up ahead of me to the high place, for today you are to eat with me, and in the morning I will let you go and will tell you all that is in your heart. 20 As for the donkeys you lost three days ago, do not worry about them; they have been found. And to whom is all the desire of Israel turned, if not to you and all your father's family?"

21 Saul answered, "But am I not a Benjamite, from the smallest tribe of Israel, and is not my clan the least of all the clans of the tribe of Benjamin? Why do you say such a thing to me?"

22 Then Samuel brought Saul and his servant into the hall and seated them at the head of those who were invited—about thirty in number. 23 Samuel said to the cook, "Bring the piece of meat I gave you, the one I told you to lay aside."

24 So the cook took up the leg with what was on it and set it in front of Saul. Samuel said, "Here is what has been kept for you. Eat, because it was set aside for you for this occasion, from the time I said, 'I have invited guests.' " And Saul dined with Samuel that day.

25 After they came down from the high place to the town, Samuel talked with Saul on the roof of his house. 26 They rose about daybreak and Samuel called to Saul on the roof, "Get ready, and I will send you on your way." When Saul got ready, he and Samuel went outside together. 27 As they were going down to the edge of the town, Samuel said to Saul, "Tell the servant to go on ahead of us"—and the servant did so—"but you stay here awhile, so that I may give you a message from God."

10 THEN SAMUEL took a flask of oil and poured it on Saul's head and kissed him, saying, "Has not the LORD anointed you leader over his inheritance?ᶜ

ʄGr adds *and they spread a bed for Saul on the roof and he slept*

ᶜ1 Hebrew; Septuagint and Vulgate *over his people Israel? You will reign over the LORD's people and save them from the power of their enemies round about. And this will be a sign to you that the LORD has anointed you leader over his inheritance:*

King James

2When thou art departed from me today, then thou shalt find two men by Rachel's sepulchre in the border of Benjamin at Zelzah; and they will say unto thee, The asses which thou wentest to seek are found: and, lo, thy father hath left *a*the care of the asses, and sorroweth for you, saying, What shall I do for my son?

3Then shalt thou go on forward from thence, and thou shalt come to the plain of Tabor, and there shall meet thee three men going up to God to Beth-el, one carrying three kids, and another carrying three loaves of bread, and another carrying a bottle of wine:

4And they will *b*salute thee, and give thee two *loaves* of bread; which thou shalt receive of their hands.

5After that thou shalt come to the hill of God, where *is* the garrison of the Philistines: and it shall come to pass, when thou art come thither to the city, that thou shalt meet a company of prophets coming down from the high place with a psaltery, and a tabret, and a pipe, and a harp, before them; and they shall prophesy:

6And the spirit of the LORD will come upon thee, and thou shalt prophesy with them, and shalt be turned into another man.

7And *c*let it be, when these signs are come unto thee, *d*that thou do as occasion serve thee; for God *is* with thee.

8And thou shalt go down before me to Gilgal; and, behold, I will come down unto thee, to offer burnt offerings, *and* to sacrifice sacrifices of peace offerings: seven days shalt thou tarry, till I come to thee, and show thee what thou shalt do.

Saul becomes king of Israel

9 ¶ And it was *so,* that when he had turned his *e*back to go from Samuel, God *f*gave him another heart: and all those signs came to pass that day.

10And when they came thither to the hill, behold, a company of prophets met him; and the spirit of God came upon him, and he prophesied among them.

11And it came to pass, when all that knew him beforetime saw that, behold, he prophesied among the prophets, then the people said *g*one to another, What *is* this *that* is come unto the son of Kish? *Is* Saul also among the prophets?

12And one *h*of the same place answered and said, But who *is* their father? Therefore it became a proverb, *Is* Saul also among the prophets?

13And when he had made an end of prophesying, he came to the high place.

14 ¶ And Saul's uncle said unto him and to his servant, Whither went ye? And he said, To seek the asses: and when we saw that *they were* no where, we came to Samuel.

15And Saul's uncle said, Tell me, I pray thee, what Samuel said unto you.

16And Saul said unto his uncle, He told us plainly that the asses were found. But of the matter of the kingdom, whereof Samuel spake, he told him not.

17 ¶ And Samuel called the people together unto the LORD to Mizpeh;

18And said unto the children of Israel, Thus saith the LORD God of Israel, I brought up Israel out of Egypt, and delivered you out of the hand of the Egyptians, and out of the hand of all kingdoms, *and* of them that oppressed you:

19And ye have this day rejected your God, who himself saved you out of all your adversities and your tribulations; and ye have said unto him, *Nay,* but set a king over us. Now therefore present yourselves before the LORD by your tribes, and by your thousands.

20And when Samuel had caused all the tribes of Israel to come near, the tribe of Benjamin was taken.

Amplified

2When you have left me today, you will meet two men by Rachel's tomb in the territory of Benjamin at Zelzah, and they will say to you, The donkeys you sought are found. And your father has quit caring about them and is anxious for you, asking, What shall I do about my son?

3Then you will go on from there and you will come to the oak of Tabor, and three men going up to God at Bethel will meet you there, one carrying three kids, another carrying three loaves of bread, and another carrying a skin bottle of wine.

4They will greet you and give you two loaves of bread, which you shall accept from their hand.

5After that you will come to the hill of God, where the garrison of the Philistines is; and when you come to the city, you will meet a company of prophets coming down from the high place with harp, tambourine, flute, and lyre before them, prophesying.

6Then the Spirit of the Lord will come upon you mightily, and you will show yourself to be a prophet with them; and you will be turned into another man.

7When these signs meet you, do whatever you find to be done, for God is with you.

8You shall go down before me to Gilgal; and behold, I will come down to you to offer burnt offerings and to sacrifice peace offerings. You shall wait seven days until I come to you and show you what you shall do.

9And when [Saul] had turned his back to leave Samuel, God gave him another heart, and all these signs came to pass that day.

10When they came to the hill [Gibeah], behold, a band of prophets met him; and the Spirit of God came mightily upon him, and he spoke under divine inspiration among them.

11And when all who knew Saul before saw that he spoke by inspiration among the [schooled] prophets, the people said one to another, What has come over [him, who is nobody but] the son of Kish? Is Saul also among the prophets?

12One from that same place answered, But who is the father of the others? So it became a proverb, Is Saul also among the prophets?

13When [Saul] had ended his inspired speaking, he went to the high place.

14Saul's uncle said to him and to his servant, Where did you go? And Saul said, To look for the donkeys, and when we found them nowhere, we went to Samuel.

15Saul's uncle said, Tell me, what did Samuel say to you?

16And Saul said to his uncle, He told us plainly that the donkeys were found. But of the matter of the kingdom of which Samuel spoke he told him nothing.

17And Samuel called the people together to the Lord at Mizpah

18And said to the Israelites, Thus says the Lord, the God of Israel: It was I Who brought up Israel out of Egypt and delivered you out of the hands of the Egyptians and of all the kingdoms that oppressed you.

19But you have this day rejected your God, Who Himself saves you from all your calamities and distresses; and you have said to Him, No! Set a king over us. So now present yourselves before the Lord by your tribes and by your thousands.

20And when Samuel had caused all the tribes of Israel to come near, the tribe of Benjamin was taken [probably by lot].

---

a Heb. *the business*   *b* Heb. *ask thee of peace* as Judg. 18:15
c Heb. *it shall come to pass, that when these signs*   *d* Heb. *do for thee as thine hand shall find*   *e* Heb. *shoulder* *f* Heb. *turned*
g Heb. *a man to his neighbour*   *h* Heb. *from thence*

New American Standard

²"When you go from me today, then you will find two men close to Rachel's tomb in the territory of Benjamin at Zelzah; and they will say to you, 'The donkeys which you went to look for have been found. Now behold, your father has ceased to be concerned about the donkeys and is anxious for you, saying, "What shall I do about my son?"'

³"Then you will go on further from there, and you will come as far as the oak of Tabor, and there three men going up to God at Bethel will meet you, one carrying three young goats, another carrying three loaves of bread, and another carrying a jug of wine;

⁴ and they will greet you and give you two *loaves* of bread, which you will accept from their hand.

⁵"Afterward you will come to the hill of God where the Philistine garrison is; and it shall be as soon as you have come there to the city, that you will meet a group of prophets coming down from the high place with harp, tambourine, flute, and a lyre before them, and they will be prophesying.

⁶"Then the Spirit of the LORD will come upon you mightily, and you shall prophesy with them and be changed into another man.

⁷"It shall be when these signs come to you, do for yourself what the occasion requires, for God is with you.

⁸"And you shall go down before me to Gilgal; and behold, I will come down to you to offer burnt offerings and sacrifice peace offerings. You shall wait seven days until I come to you and show you what you should do."

⁹ ¶ Then it happened when he turned his back to leave Samuel, God changed his heart; and all those signs came about on that day.

¹⁰ When they came to the hill there, behold, a group of prophets met him; and the Spirit of God came upon him mightily, so that he prophesied among them.

¹¹ It came about, when all who knew him previously saw that he prophesied now with the prophets, that the people said to one another, "What has happened to the son of Kish? Is Saul also among the prophets?"

¹² A man there said, "Now, who is their father?" Therefore it became a proverb: "Is Saul also among the prophets?"

¹³ When he had finished prophesying, he came to the high place.

¹⁴ ¶ Now Saul's uncle said to him and his servant, "Where did you go?" And he said, "To look for the donkeys. When we saw that they could not be found, we went to Samuel."

¹⁵ Saul's uncle said, "Please tell me what Samuel said to you."

¹⁶ So Saul said to his uncle, "He told us plainly that the donkeys had been found." But he did not tell him about the matter of the kingdom which Samuel had mentioned.

Saul Publicly Chosen King

¹⁷ ¶ Thereafter Samuel called the people together to the LORD at Mizpah;

¹⁸ and he said to the sons of Israel, "Thus says the LORD, the God of Israel, 'I brought Israel up from Egypt, and I delivered you from the hand of the Egyptians and from the power of all the kingdoms that were oppressing you.'

¹⁹"But you have today rejected your God, who delivers you from all your calamities and your distresses; yet you have said, 'No, but set a king over us!' Now therefore, present yourselves before the LORD by your tribes and by your clans."

²⁰ ¶ Thus Samuel brought all the tribes of Israel near, and the tribe of Benjamin was taken by lot.

New International

²When you leave me today, you will meet two men near Rachel's tomb, at Zelzah on the border of Benjamin. They will say to you, 'The donkeys you set out to look for have been found. And now your father has stopped thinking about them and is worried about you. He is asking, "What shall I do about my son?"'

³"Then you will go on from there until you reach the great tree of Tabor. Three men going up to God at Bethel will meet you there. One will be carrying three young goats, another three loaves of bread, and another a skin of wine. ⁴They will greet you and offer you two loaves of bread, which you will accept from them.

⁵"After that you will go to Gibeah of God, where there is a Philistine outpost. As you approach the town, you will meet a procession of prophets coming down from the high place with lyres, tambourines, flutes and harps being played before them, and they will be prophesying. ⁶The Spirit of the LORD will come upon you in power, and you will prophesy with them; and you will be changed into a different person. ⁷Once these signs are fulfilled, do whatever your hand finds to do, for God is with you.

⁸"Go down ahead of me to Gilgal. I will surely come down to you to sacrifice burnt offerings and fellowship offerings,*d* but you must wait seven days until I come to you and tell you what you are to do."

Saul Made King

⁹As Saul turned to leave Samuel, God changed Saul's heart, and all these signs were fulfilled that day. ¹⁰When they arrived at Gibeah, a procession of prophets met him; the Spirit of God came upon him in power, and he joined in their prophesying. ¹¹When all those who had formerly known him saw him prophesying with the prophets, they asked each other, "What is this that has happened to the son of Kish? Is Saul also among the prophets?"

¹²A man who lived there answered, "And who is their father?" So it became a saying: "Is Saul also among the prophets?" ¹³After Saul stopped prophesying, he went to the high place.

¹⁴Now Saul's uncle asked him and his servant, "Where have you been?"

"Looking for the donkeys," he said. "But when we saw they were not to be found, we went to Samuel."

¹⁵Saul's uncle said, "Tell me what Samuel said to you."

¹⁶Saul replied, "He assured us that the donkeys had been found." But he did not tell his uncle what Samuel had said about the kingship.

¹⁷Samuel summoned the people of Israel to the LORD at Mizpah ¹⁸and said to them, "This is what the LORD, the God of Israel, says: 'I brought Israel up out of Egypt, and I delivered you from the power of Egypt and all the kingdoms that oppressed you.' ¹⁹But you have now rejected your God, who saves you out of all your calamities and distresses. And you have said, 'No, set a king over us.' So now present yourselves before the LORD by your tribes and clans."

²⁰When Samuel brought all the tribes of Israel near, the

---

d 8 Traditionally *peace offerings*

King James

21When he had caused the tribe of Benjamin to come near by their families, the family of Matri was taken, and Saul the son of Kish was taken: and when they sought him, he could not be found.

22Therefore they inquired of the LORD further, if the man should yet come thither. And the LORD answered, Behold, he hath hid himself among the stuff.

23And they ran and fetched him thence: and when he stood among the people, he was higher than any of the people from his shoulders and upward.

24And Samuel said to all the people, See ye him whom the LORD hath chosen, that *there is* none like him among all the people? And all the people shouted, and said, *i*God save the king.

25Then Samuel told the people the manner of the kingdom, and wrote *it* in a book, and laid *it* up before the LORD. And Samuel sent all the people away, every man to his house.

26 ¶ And Saul also went home to Gibeah; and there went with him a band of men, whose hearts God had touched.

27But the children of Belial said, How shall this man save us? And they despised him, and brought him no presents. But *j*he held his peace.

The Ammonites defeated

11 THEN NAHASH the Ammonite came up, and encamped against Jabesh-gilead: and all the men of Jabesh said unto Nahash, Make a covenant with us, and we will serve thee.

2And Nahash the Ammonite answered them, On this *condition* will I make *a covenant* with you, that I may thrust out all your right eyes, and lay *it for* a reproach upon all Israel.

3And the elders of Jabesh said unto him, *k*Give us seven days' respite, that we may send messengers unto all the coasts of Israel: and then, if *there be* no man to save us, we will come out to thee.

4 ¶ Then came the messengers to Gibeah of Saul, and told the tidings in the ears of the people: and all the people lifted up their voices, and wept.

5And, behold, Saul came after the herd out of the field; and Saul said, What *aileth* the people that they weep? And they told him the tidings of the men of Jabesh.

6And the spirit of God came upon Saul when he heard those tidings, and his anger was kindled greatly.

7And he took a yoke of oxen, and hewed them in pieces, and sent *them* throughout all the coasts of Israel by the hands of messengers, saying, Whosoever cometh not forth after Saul and after Samuel, so shall it be done to his oxen. And the fear of the LORD fell on the people, and they came out *l*with one consent.

8And when he numbered them in Bezek, the children of Israel were three hundred thousand, and the men of Judah thirty thousand.

9And they said unto the messengers that came, Thus shall ye say unto the men of Jabesh-gilead, Tomorrow, by *that time* the sun be hot, ye shall have *m*help. And the messengers came and showed *it* to the men of Jabesh; and they were glad.

10Therefore the men of Jabesh said, Tomorrow we will come out unto you, and ye shall do with us all that seemeth good unto you.

11And it was *so* on the morrow, that Saul put the people in three companies; and they came into the midst of the host in the morning watch, and slew the Ammonites until the heat of the day: and it came to pass, that they which remained were scattered, so that two of them were not left together.

Amplified

21When he had caused the tribe of Benjamin to come near by their families, the family of Matri was taken. And Saul son of Kish was taken. But when they looked for him, he could not be found.

22Therefore they inquired of the Lord further, if the man would yet come back. And the Lord answered, Behold, he has hidden himself among the baggage. [Exod. 28:30.]

23They ran and brought him from there. And when he stood among the people, he was a head taller than any of them.

24And Samuel said to all the people, Do you see him whom the Lord has chosen, that none like him is among all the people? And all the people shouted and said, Long live the king!

25Then Samuel told the people the manner of the kingdom [defining the position of the king in relation to God and to the people], and wrote it in a book and laid it up before the Lord. And Samuel sent all the people away, each one to his home.

26Saul also went home to Gibeah; and there went with him a band of valiant men whose hearts God had touched.

27But some worthless fellows said, How can this man save us? And they despised him and brought him no gift. But he held his peace *and* was as if deaf.

11 AND NAHASH the Ammonite went up and besieged Jabesh-gilead; and all the men of Jabesh said to Nahash, Make a treaty with us, and we will serve you.

2But Nahash the Ammonite told them, On this condition I will make a treaty with you, that I thrust out all your right eyes and thus lay disgrace on all Israel.

3The elders of Jabesh said to Nahash, Give us seven days' time, that we may send messengers through all the territory of Israel. Then, if there is no man to save us, we will come out to you.

4Then messengers came to Gibeah of Saul and told the news in the ears of the people; and all the people wept aloud.

5Now Saul came out of the field after the oxen, and [he] said, What ails the people that they are weeping? And they told him the words of the men of Jabesh.

6The Spirit of God came mightily upon Saul when he heard those tidings, and his anger was greatly kindled.

7And he took a yoke of oxen and cut them in pieces and sent them throughout all the territory of Israel by the hands of messengers, saying, Whoever does not come forth after Saul and Samuel, so shall it be done to his oxen! And terror from the Lord fell on the people, and they came out with one consent.

8And he numbered them at Bezek, and the Israelites were 300,000 and the men of Judah 30,000.

9The messengers who came were told, Say to the men of Jabesh-gilead, Tomorrow, by the time the sun is hot, you shall have help. The messengers came and reported to the men of Jabesh, and they were glad.

10So the men of Jabesh said to Nahash, Tomorrow we will come out to you, and you may do to us all that seems good to you.

11The next day Saul put the men in three companies; and they came into the midst of the enemy's camp in the [darkness of the] morning watch and slew the Ammonites until midday; and the survivors were scattered, so that no two of them remained together.

---

*i*Heb. *Let the king live*   *j*Or, *he was as though he had been deaf*
*k*Heb. *Forbear us*   *l*Heb. *as one man*   *m*Or, *deliverance*

New American Standard

²¹ Then he brought the tribe of Benjamin near by its families, and the Matrite family was taken. And Saul the son of Kish was taken; but when they looked for him, he could not be found.

²² Therefore they inquired further of the LORD, "Has the man come here yet?" So the LORD said, "Behold, he is hiding himself by the baggage."

²³ So they ran and took him from there, and when he stood among the people, he was taller than any of the people from his shoulders upward.

²⁴ Samuel said to all the people, "Do you see him whom the LORD has chosen? Surely there is no one like him among all the people." So all the people shouted and said, "*Long* live the king!"

²⁵ ¶ Then Samuel told the people the ordinances of the kingdom, and wrote *them* in the book and placed *it* before the LORD. And Samuel sent all the people away, each one to his house.

²⁶ Saul also went to his house at Gibeah; and the valiant *men* whose hearts God had touched went with him.

²⁷ But certain worthless men said, "How can this one deliver us?" And they despised him and did not bring him any present. But he kept silent.

Saul Defeats the Ammonites

11 NOW NAHASH the Ammonite came up and besieged Jabesh-gilead; and all the men of Jabesh said to Nahash, "Make a covenant with us and we will serve you."

² But Nahash the Ammonite said to them, "I will make *it* with you on this condition, that I will gouge out the right eye of every one of you, thus I will make it a reproach on all Israel."

³ The elders of Jabesh said to him, "Let us alone for seven days, that we may send messengers throughout the territory of Israel. Then, if there is no one to deliver us, we will come out to you."

⁴ Then the messengers came to Gibeah of Saul and spoke these words in the hearing of the people, and all the people lifted up their voices and wept.

⁵ ¶ Now behold, Saul was coming from the field behind the oxen, and he said, "What is *the matter* with the people that they weep?" So they related to him the words of the men of Jabesh.

⁶ Then the Spirit of God came upon Saul mightily when he heard these words, and he became very angry.

⁷ He took a yoke of oxen and cut them in pieces, and sent *them* throughout the territory of Israel by the hand of messengers, saying, "Whoever does not come out after Saul and after Samuel, so shall it be done to his oxen." Then the dread of the LORD fell on the people, and they came out as one man.

⁸ He numbered them in Bezek; and the sons of Israel were 300,000, and the men of Judah 30,000.

⁹ They said to the messengers who had come, "Thus you shall say to the men of Jabesh-gilead, 'Tomorrow, by the time the sun is hot, you will have deliverance.' " So the messengers went and told the men of Jabesh; and they were glad.

¹⁰ Then the men of Jabesh said, "Tomorrow we will come out to you, and you may do to us whatever seems good to you."

¹¹ The next morning Saul put the people in three companies; and they came into the midst of the camp at the morning watch and struck down the Ammonites until the heat of the day. Those who survived were scattered, so that no two of them were left together.

New International

tribe of Benjamin was chosen. ²¹Then he brought forward the tribe of Benjamin, clan by clan, and Matri's clan was chosen. Finally Saul son of Kish was chosen. But when they looked for him, he was not to be found. ²²So they inquired further of the LORD, "Has the man come here yet?"

And the LORD said, "Yes, he has hidden himself among the baggage."

²³They ran and brought him out, and as he stood among the people he was a head taller than any of the others. ²⁴Samuel said to all the people, "Do you see the man the LORD has chosen? There is no one like him among all the people."

Then the people shouted, "Long live the king!"

²⁵Samuel explained to the people the regulations of the kingship. He wrote them down on a scroll and deposited it before the LORD. Then Samuel dismissed the people, each to his own home.

²⁶Saul also went to his home in Gibeah, accompanied by valiant men whose hearts God had touched. ²⁷But some troublemakers said, "How can this fellow save us?" They despised him and brought him no gifts. But Saul kept silent.

Saul Rescues the City of Jabesh

11 NAHASH THE Ammonite went up and besieged Jabesh Gilead. And all the men of Jabesh said to him, "Make a treaty with us, and we will be subject to you."

²But Nahash the Ammonite replied, "I will make a treaty with you only on the condition that I gouge out the right eye of every one of you and so bring disgrace on all Israel."

³The elders of Jabesh said to him, "Give us seven days so we can send messengers throughout Israel; if no one comes to rescue us, we will surrender to you."

⁴When the messengers came to Gibeah of Saul and reported these terms to the people, they all wept aloud. ⁵Just then Saul was returning from the fields, behind his oxen, and he asked, "What is wrong with the people? Why are they weeping?" Then they repeated to him what the men of Jabesh had said.

⁶When Saul heard their words, the Spirit of God came upon him in power, and he burned with anger. ⁷He took a pair of oxen, cut them into pieces, and sent the pieces by messengers throughout Israel, proclaiming, "This is what will be done to the oxen of anyone who does not follow Saul and Samuel." Then the terror of the LORD fell on the people, and they turned out as one man. ⁸When Saul mustered them at Bezek, the men of Israel numbered three hundred thousand and the men of Judah thirty thousand.

⁹They told the messengers who had come, "Say to the men of Jabesh Gilead, 'By the time the sun is hot tomorrow, you will be delivered.' " When the messengers went and reported this to the men of Jabesh, they were elated. ¹⁰They said to the Ammonites, "Tomorrow we will surrender to you, and you can do to us whatever seems good to you."

¹¹The next day Saul separated his men into three divisions; during the last watch of the night they broke into the camp of the Ammonites and slaughtered them until the heat of the day. Those who survived were scattered, so that no two of them were left together.

King James

¹² ¶ And the people said unto Samuel, Who *is* he that said, Shall Saul reign over us? bring the men, that we may put them to death.

¹³And Saul said, There shall not a man be put to death this day: for today the LORD hath wrought salvation in Israel.

¹⁴Then said Samuel to the people, Come, and let us go to Gilgal, and renew the kingdom there.

¹⁵And all the people went to Gilgal; and there they made Saul king before the LORD in Gilgal; and there they sacrificed sacrifices of peace offerings before the LORD; and there Saul and all the men of Israel rejoiced greatly.

Samuel addresses the people

12 AND SAMUEL said unto all Israel, Behold, I have hearkened unto your voice in all that ye said unto me, and have made a king over you.

²And now, behold, the king walketh before you: and I am old and grayheaded; and, behold, my sons *are* with you: and I have walked before you from my childhood unto this day.

³Behold, here I *am:* witness against me before the LORD, and before his anointed: whose ox have I taken? or whose ass have I taken? or whom have I defrauded? whom have I oppressed? or of whose hand have I received *any* ⁿbribe ^oto blind mine eyes therewith? and I will restore it you.

⁴And they said, Thou hast not defrauded us, nor oppressed us, neither hast thou taken aught of any man's hand.

⁵And he said unto them, The LORD *is* witness against you, and his anointed *is* witness this day, that ye have not found aught in my hand. And they answered, *He is* witness.

⁶ ¶ And Samuel said unto the people, *It is* the LORD that ^padvanced Moses and Aaron, and that brought your fathers up out of the land of Egypt.

⁷Now therefore stand still, that I may reason with you before the LORD of all the ^qrighteous acts of the LORD, which he did ^rto you and to your fathers.

⁸When Jacob was come into Egypt, and your fathers cried unto the LORD, then the LORD sent Moses and Aaron, which brought forth your fathers out of Egypt, and made them dwell in this place.

⁹And when they forgat the LORD their God, he sold them into the hand of Sisera, captain of the host of Hazor, and into the hand of the Philistines, and into the hand of the king of Moab, and they fought against them.

¹⁰And they cried unto the LORD, and said, We have sinned, because we have forsaken the LORD, and have served Baalim and Ashtaroth: but now deliver us out of the hand of our enemies, and we will serve thee.

¹¹And the LORD sent Jerubbaal, and Bedan, and Jephthah, and Samuel, and delivered you out of the hand of your enemies on every side, and ye dwelled safe.

¹²And when ye saw that Nahash the king of the children of Ammon came against you, ye said unto me, Nay; but a king shall reign over us: when the LORD your God *was* your king.

¹³Now therefore behold the king whom ye have chosen, *and* whom ye have desired! and, behold, the LORD hath set a king over you.

¹⁴If ye will fear the LORD, and serve him, and obey his voice, and not rebel against the ^scommandment of the LORD, then shall both ye and also the king that reigneth over you ^tcontinue following the LORD your God:

¹⁵But if ye will not obey the voice of the LORD, but rebel against the commandment of the LORD, then shall the hand of the LORD be against you, as *it was* against your fathers.

Amplified

¹²The people said to Samuel, Who is he who said, Shall Saul reign over us? Bring the men, that we may put them to death.

¹³But Saul said, There shall not a man be put to death this day, for today the Lord has brought deliverance to Israel.

¹⁴Samuel said to the people, Come, let us go to Gilgal and there renew the kingdom.

¹⁵All the people went to Gilgal and there they made Saul king before the Lord. And there they sacrificed peace offerings before the Lord, and there Saul and all the men of Israel rejoiced greatly.

12 AND SAMUEL said to all Israel, I have listened to you in all that you have said to me and have made a king over you.

²And now, behold, the king walks before you. And I am old and gray, and behold, my sons are with you. And I have walked before you from my childhood to this day.

³Here I am; testify against me before the Lord and Saul His anointed. Whose ox or donkey have I taken? Or whom have I defrauded or oppressed? Or from whose hand have I received any bribe to blind my eyes? Tell me and I will restore it to you.

⁴And they said, You have not defrauded us or oppressed us or taken anything from any man's hand.

⁵And Samuel said to them, The Lord is witness against you, and His anointed is witness this day, that you have not found anything in my hand. And they answered, He is witness.

⁶And Samuel said to the people, It is the Lord Who appointed Moses and Aaron and brought your fathers up out of Egypt.

⁷Now present yourselves, that I may plead with you before the Lord concerning all the righteous acts of the Lord which He did for you and for your fathers.

⁸When Jacob and his sons had come into Egypt [and the Egyptians oppressed them], and your fathers cried to the Lord, then the Lord sent Moses and Aaron, who brought forth your fathers out of Egypt and made them dwell in this place.

⁹But when they forgot the Lord their God, He sold them into the hand of Sisera, commander of Hazor's army, and into the hands of the Philistines and of the king of Moab, and they fought those foes.

¹⁰And they cried to the Lord, saying, We have sinned because we have forsaken the Lord and have served the Baals and the Ashtaroth; but now deliver us from the hands of our enemies, and we will serve You.

¹¹And the Lord sent Jerubbaal and Barak and Jephthah and Samuel, and He delivered you out of the hands of your enemies on every side, and you dwelt safely.

¹²But when you saw that Nahash king of the Ammonites came against you, you said to me, No! A king shall reign over us—when the Lord your God was your King!

¹³Now see the king whom you have chosen and for whom you have asked; behold, the Lord has set a king over you.

¹⁴If you will revere *and* fear the Lord and serve Him and hearken to His voice and not rebel against His commandment, and if both you and your king will follow the Lord your God, it will be good!

¹⁵But if you will not hearken to the Lord's voice, but rebel against His commandment, then the hand of the Lord will be against you, as it was against your fathers.

ⁿ Heb. *ransom*   ^o Or, *that I should hide mine eyes at him*
^p Or, *made*   ^q Heb. *righteousnesses,* or, *benefits*   ^r Heb. *with*
^s Heb. *mouth*   ^t Heb. *be after*

New American Standard

¹² ¶ Then the people said to Samuel, "Who is he that said, 'Shall Saul reign over us?' Bring the men, that we may put them to death."

¹³ But Saul said, "Not a man shall be put to death this day, for today the LORD has accomplished deliverance in Israel."

¹⁴ ¶ Then Samuel said to the people, "Come and let us go to Gilgal and renew the kingdom there."

¹⁵ So all the people went to Gilgal, and there they made Saul king before the LORD in Gilgal. There they also offered sacrifices of peace offerings before the LORD; and there Saul and all the men of Israel rejoiced greatly.

Samuel Addresses Israel

12 THEN SAMUEL said to all Israel, "Behold, I have listened to your voice in all that you said to me and I have appointed a king over you.

²"Now, here is the king walking before you, but I am old and gray, and behold my sons are with you. And I have walked before you from my youth even to this day.

³"Here I am; bear witness against me before the LORD and His anointed. Whose ox have I taken, or whose donkey have I taken, or whom have I defrauded? Whom have I oppressed, or from whose hand have I taken a bribe to blind my eyes with it? I will restore *it* to you."

⁴ They said, "You have not defrauded us or oppressed us or taken anything from any man's hand."

⁵ He said to them, "The LORD is witness against you, and His anointed is witness this day that you have found nothing in my hand." And they said, "*He is* witness."

⁶ ¶ Then Samuel said to the people, "It is the LORD who appointed Moses and Aaron and who brought your fathers up from the land of Egypt.

⁷"So now, take your stand, that I may plead with you before the LORD concerning all the righteous acts of the LORD which He did for you and your fathers.

⁸"When Jacob went into Egypt and your fathers cried out to the LORD, then the LORD sent Moses and Aaron who brought your fathers out of Egypt and settled them in this place.

⁹"But they forgot the LORD their God, so He sold them into the hand of Sisera, captain of the army of Hazor, and into the hand of the Philistines and into the hand of the king of Moab, and they fought against them.

¹⁰"They cried out to the LORD and said, 'We have sinned because we have forsaken the LORD and have served the Baals and the Ashtaroth; but now deliver us from the hands of our enemies, and we will serve You.'

¹¹"Then the LORD sent Jerubbaal and ^gBedan and Jephthah and Samuel, and delivered you from the hands of your enemies all around, so that you lived in security.

The King Confirmed

¹²"When you saw that Nahash the king of the sons of Ammon came against you, you said to me, 'No, but a king shall reign over us,' although the LORD your God *was* your king.

¹³"Now therefore, here is the king whom you have chosen, whom you have asked for, and behold, the LORD has set a king over you.

¹⁴"If you will fear the LORD and serve Him, and listen to His voice and not rebel against the command of the LORD, then both you and also the king who reigns over you will follow the LORD your God.

¹⁵"If you will not listen to the voice of the LORD, but rebel against the command of the LORD, then the hand of the LORD will be against you, *as it was* against your fathers.

New International

Saul Confirmed as King

¹²The people then said to Samuel, "Who was it that asked, 'Shall Saul reign over us?' Bring these men to us and we will put them to death."

¹³But Saul said, "No one shall be put to death today, for this day the LORD has rescued Israel."

¹⁴Then Samuel said to the people, "Come, let us go to Gilgal and there reaffirm the kingship." ¹⁵So all the people went to Gilgal and confirmed Saul as king in the presence of the LORD. There they sacrificed fellowship offerings^e before the LORD, and Saul and all the Israelites held a great celebration.

Samuel's Farewell Speech

12 SAMUEL SAID to all Israel, "I have listened to everything you said to me and have set a king over you. ²Now you have a king as your leader. As for me, I am old and gray, and my sons are here with you. I have been your leader from my youth until this day. ³Here I stand. Testify against me in the presence of the LORD and his anointed. Whose ox have I taken? Whose donkey have I taken? Whom have I cheated? Whom have I oppressed? From whose hand have I accepted a bribe to make me shut my eyes? If I have done any of these, I will make it right."

⁴"You have not cheated or oppressed us," they replied. "You have not taken anything from anyone's hand."

⁵Samuel said to them, "The LORD is witness against you, and also his anointed is witness this day, that you have not found anything in my hand."

"He is witness," they said.

⁶Then Samuel said to the people, "It is the LORD who appointed Moses and Aaron and brought your forefathers up out of Egypt. ⁷Now then, stand here, because I am going to confront you with evidence before the LORD as to all the righteous acts performed by the LORD for you and your fathers.

⁸"After Jacob entered Egypt, they cried to the LORD for help, and the LORD sent Moses and Aaron, who brought your forefathers out of Egypt and settled them in this place.

⁹"But they forgot the LORD their God; so he sold them into the hand of Sisera, the commander of the army of Hazor, and into the hands of the Philistines and the king of Moab, who fought against them. ¹⁰They cried out to the LORD and said, 'We have sinned; we have forsaken the LORD and served the Baals and the Ashtoreths. But now deliver us from the hands of our enemies, and we will serve you.' ¹¹Then the LORD sent Jerub-Baal,^f Barak,^g Jephthah and Samuel,^h and he delivered you from the hands of your enemies on every side, so that you lived securely.

¹²"But when you saw that Nahash king of the Ammonites was moving against you, you said to me, 'No, we want a king to rule over us'—even though the LORD your God was your king. ¹³Now here is the king you have chosen, the one you asked for; see, the LORD has set a king over you. ¹⁴If you fear the LORD and serve and obey him and do not rebel against his commands, and if both you and the king who reigns over you follow the LORD your God—good! ¹⁵But if you do not obey the LORD, and if you rebel against his commands, his hand will be against you, as it was against your fathers.

---

^g Gr and Syr read *Barak*

^e 15 Traditionally *peace offerings*   ^f 11 Also called *Gideon*
^g 11 Some Septuagint manuscripts and Syriac; Hebrew *Bedan*
^h 11 Hebrew; some Septuagint manuscripts and Syriac *Samson*

King James

¹⁶ ¶ Now therefore stand and see this great thing, which the LORD will do before your eyes.

¹⁷*Is it* not wheat harvest today? I will call unto the LORD, and he shall send thunder and rain; that ye may perceive and see that your wickedness *is* great, which ye have done in the sight of the LORD, in asking you a king.

¹⁸So Samuel called unto the LORD; and the LORD sent thunder and rain that day: and all the people greatly feared the LORD and Samuel.

¹⁹And all the people said unto Samuel, Pray for thy servants unto the LORD thy God, that we die not: for we have added unto all our sins *this* evil, to ask us a king.

²⁰ ¶ And Samuel said unto the people, Fear not: ye have done all this wickedness: yet turn not aside from following the LORD, but serve the LORD with all your heart;

²¹And turn ye not aside: for *then should ye go* after vain *things,* which cannot profit nor deliver; for they *are* vain.

²²For the LORD will not forsake his people for his great name's sake: because it hath pleased the LORD to make you his people.

²³Moreover as for me, God forbid that I should sin against the LORD *u*in ceasing to pray for you: but I will teach you the good and the right way:

²⁴Only fear the LORD, and serve him in truth with all your heart: for consider *v*how great *things* he hath done for you.

²⁵But if ye shall still do wickedly, ye shall be consumed, both ye and your king.

Samuel rebukes Saul

13 SAUL *w*REIGNED one year; and when he had reigned two years over Israel,

²Saul chose him three thousand *men* of Israel; *whereof* two thousand were with Saul in Michmash and in mount Beth-el, and a thousand were with Jonathan in Gibeah of Benjamin: and the rest of the people he sent every man to his tent.

³And Jonathan smote the garrison of the Philistines that *was* in *x*Geba, and the Philistines heard *of it.* And Saul blew the trumpet throughout all the land, saying, Let the Hebrews hear.

⁴And all Israel heard say *that* Saul had smitten a garrison of the Philistines, and *that* Israel also *y*was had in abomination with the Philistines. And the people were called together after Saul to Gilgal.

⁵ ¶ And the Philistines gathered themselves together to fight with Israel, thirty thousand chariots, and six thousand horsemen, and people as the sand which *is* on the sea shore in multitude: and they came up, and pitched in Michmash, eastward from Beth-aven.

⁶When the men of Israel saw that they were in a strait, (for the people were distressed,) then the people did hide themselves in caves, and in thickets, and in rocks, and in high places, and in pits.

⁷And *some of* the Hebrews went over Jordan to the land of Gad and Gilead. As for Saul, he *was* yet in Gilgal, and all the people *z*followed him trembling.

⁸ ¶ And he tarried seven days, according to the set time that Samuel *had appointed:* but Samuel came not to Gilgal; and the people were scattered from him.

⁹And Saul said, Bring hither a burnt offering to me, and peace offerings. And he offered the burnt offering.

¹⁰And it came to pass, that as soon as he had made an end of offering the burnt offering, behold, Samuel came; and Saul went out to meet him, that he might *a*salute him.

Amplified

¹⁶So stand still and see this great thing the Lord will do before your eyes now.

¹⁷Is it not wheat harvest today? I will call to the Lord and He will send thunder and rain; then you shall know and see that your wickedness is great which you have done in the sight of the Lord in asking for a king for yourselves.

¹⁸So Samuel called to the Lord, and He sent thunder and rain that day; and all the people greatly feared the Lord and Samuel.

¹⁹And [they] all said to Samuel, Pray for your servants to the Lord your God, that we may not die, for we have added to all our sins this evil—to ask for a king.

²⁰And Samuel said to the people, Fear not. You have indeed done all this evil; yet turn not aside from following the Lord, but serve Him with all your heart.

²¹And turn not aside after vain *and* worthless things which cannot profit or deliver you, for they are empty *and* futile.

²²The Lord will not forsake His people for His great name's sake, for it has pleased Him to make you a people for Himself.

²³Moreover, as for me, far be it from me that I should sin against the Lord by ceasing to pray for you; but I will instruct you in the good and right way.

²⁴Only fear the Lord and serve Him faithfully with all your heart; for consider how great are the things He has done for you.

²⁵But if you still do wickedly, both you and your king shall be swept away.

13 SAUL WAS *f*[forty] years old when he began to reign; and when he had reigned two years over Israel,

²Saul chose 3,000 men of Israel; 2,000 were with [him] in Michmash and the hill country of Bethel, and 1,000 with Jonathan in Gibeah of Benjamin. The rest of the men he sent away, each one to his home.

³Jonathan smote the Philistine garrison at Geba, and the Philistines heard of it. And Saul blew the trumpet throughout all the land, saying, Let the Hebrews hear!

⁴All Israel heard that Saul had defeated the Philistine garrison and also that Israel had become an abomination to the Philistines. And the people were called out to join Saul at Gilgal.

⁵And the Philistines gathered to fight with Israel, 30,000 chariots and 6,000 horsemen and troops like sand on the seashore in multitude. They came up and encamped at Michmash, east of Beth-aven.

⁶When the men of Israel saw that they were in a tight situation—for their troops were hard pressed—they hid in caves, holes, rocks, tombs, and pits *or* cisterns.

⁷Some Hebrews had gone over the Jordan to the land of Gad and Gilead. As for Saul, he was still in Gilgal, and all the people followed him trembling.

⁸Saul waited seven days, according to the set time Samuel had appointed. But Samuel had not come to Gilgal, and the people were scattering from Saul.

⁹So Saul said, Bring me the burnt offering and the peace offerings. And he offered the burnt offering [which he was forbidden to do].

¹⁰And just as he finished offering the burnt offering, behold, Samuel came! Saul went out to meet and greet him.

---

^uHeb. *from ceasing*   ^vOr, *what a great* thing   ^wHeb. *the son of one year in his reigning*   ^xOr, *The hill*   ^yHeb. *did stink;* see Gen. 34:30; Ex. 5:21   ^zHeb. *trembled after him*   ^aHeb. *bless him*

^fThe complete numbers in this verse are missing in the Hebrew. The word "forty" is supplied by the best available estimate.

New American Standard

16"Even now, take your stand and see this great thing which the LORD will do before your eyes.

17"Is it not the wheat harvest today? I will call to the LORD, that He may send thunder and rain. Then you will know and see that your wickedness is great which you have done in the sight of the LORD by asking for yourselves a king."

18 So Samuel called to the LORD, and the LORD sent thunder and rain that day; and all the people greatly feared the LORD and Samuel.

19 ¶ Then all the people said to Samuel, "Pray for your servants to the LORD your God, so that we may not die, for we have added to all our sins this evil by asking for ourselves a king."

20 Samuel said to the people, "Do not fear. You have committed all this evil, yet do not turn aside from following the LORD, but serve the LORD with all your heart.

21"You must not turn aside, for *then you would go* after futile things which can not profit or deliver, because they are futile.

22"For the LORD will not abandon His people on account of His great name, because the LORD has been pleased to make you a people for Himself.

23"Moreover, as for me, far be it from me that I should sin against the LORD by ceasing to pray for you; but I will instruct you in the good and right way.

24"Only *h*fear the LORD and serve Him in truth with all your heart; for consider what great things He has done for you.

25"But if you still do wickedly, both you and your king will be swept away."

War with the Philistines

13 SAUL WAS *thirty* years old when he began to reign, and he reigned *forty* two years over Israel.

2 ¶ Now Saul chose for himself 3,000 men of Israel, of which 2,000 were with Saul in Michmash and in the hill country of Bethel, while 1,000 were with Jonathan at Gibeah of Benjamin. But he sent away the rest of the people, each to his tent.

3 Jonathan smote the garrison of the Philistines that was in Geba, and the Philistines heard of *it*. Then Saul blew the trumpet throughout the land, saying, "Let the Hebrews hear."

4 All Israel heard the news that Saul had smitten the garrison of the Philistines, and also that Israel had become odious to the Philistines. The people were then summoned to Saul at Gilgal.

5 ¶ Now the Philistines assembled to fight with Israel, 30,000 chariots and 6,000 horsemen, and people like the sand which is on the seashore in abundance; and they came up and camped in Michmash, east of Beth-aven.

6 When the men of Israel saw that they were in a strait (for the people were hard-pressed), then the people hid themselves in caves, in thickets, in cliffs, in cellars, and in pits.

7 Also *some of* the Hebrews crossed the Jordan into the land of Gad and Gilead. But as for Saul, he *was* still in Gilgal, and all the people followed him trembling.

8 ¶ Now he waited seven days, according to the appointed time set by Samuel, but Samuel did not come to Gilgal; and the people were scattering from him.

9 So Saul said, "Bring to me the burnt offering and the peace offerings." And he offered the burnt offering.

10 As soon as he finished offering the burnt offering, behold, Samuel came; and Saul went out to meet him *and* to greet him.

New International

16"Now then, stand still and see this great thing the LORD is about to do before your eyes! 17Is it not wheat harvest now? I will call upon the LORD to send thunder and rain. And you will realize what an evil thing you did in the eyes of the LORD when you asked for a king."

18Then Samuel called upon the LORD, and that same day the LORD sent thunder and rain. So all the people stood in awe of the LORD and of Samuel.

19The people all said to Samuel, "Pray to the LORD your God for your servants so that we will not die, for we have added to all our other sins the evil of asking for a king."

20"Do not be afraid," Samuel replied. "You have done all this evil; yet do not turn away from the LORD, but serve the LORD with all your heart. 21Do not turn away after useless idols. They can do you no good, nor can they rescue you, because they are useless. 22For the sake of his great name the LORD will not reject his people, because the LORD was pleased to make you his own. 23As for me, far be it from me that I should sin against the LORD by failing to pray for you. And I will teach you the way that is good and right. 24But be sure to fear the LORD and serve him faithfully with all your heart; consider what great things he has done for you. 25Yet if you persist in doing evil, both you and your king will be swept away."

Samuel Rebukes Saul

13 SAUL WAS ₍thirty₎*i* years old when he became king, and he reigned over Israel ₍forty-₎*j* two years.

2Saul*k* chose three thousand men from Israel; two thousand were with him at Micmash and in the hill country of Bethel, and a thousand were with Jonathan at Gibeah in Benjamin. The rest of the men he sent back to their homes.

3Jonathan attacked the Philistine outpost at Geba, and the Philistines heard about it. Then Saul had the trumpet blown throughout the land and said, "Let the Hebrews hear!" 4So all Israel heard the news: "Saul has attacked the Philistine outpost, and now Israel has become a stench to the Philistines." And the people were summoned to join Saul at Gilgal.

5The Philistines assembled to fight Israel, with three thousand*l* chariots, six thousand charioteers, and soldiers as numerous as the sand on the seashore. They went up and camped at Micmash, east of Beth Aven. 6When the men of Israel saw that their situation was critical and that their army was hard pressed, they hid in caves and thickets, among the rocks, and in pits and cisterns. 7Some Hebrews even crossed the Jordan to the land of Gad and Gilead.

Saul remained at Gilgal, and all the troops with him were quaking with fear. 8He waited seven days, the time set by Samuel; but Samuel did not come to Gilgal, and Saul's men began to scatter. 9So he said, "Bring me the burnt offering and the fellowship offerings.*m*" And Saul offered up the burnt offering. 10Just as he finished making the offering, Samuel arrived, and Saul went out to greet him.

---

i 1 A few late manuscripts of the Septuagint; Hebrew does not have *thirty*.   *j 1* See the round number in Acts 13:21; Hebrew does not have *forty-*.   *k 1,2* Or *and when he had reigned over Israel two years, 2he*   *l 5* Some Septuagint manuscripts and Syriac; Hebrew *thirty thousand*   *m 9* Traditionally *peace offerings*

hOr reverence

King James

Amplified

11 ¶ And Samuel said, What hast thou done? And Saul said, Because I saw that the people were scattered from me, and *that* thou camest not within the days appointed, and *that* the Philistines gathered themselves together at Michmash;

12 Therefore said I, The Philistines will come down now upon me to Gilgal, and I have not *b*made supplication unto the LORD: I forced myself therefore, and offered a burnt offering.

13 And Samuel said to Saul, Thou hast done foolishly: thou hast not kept the commandment of the LORD thy God, which he commanded thee: for now would the LORD have established thy kingdom upon Israel for ever.

14 But now thy kingdom shall not continue: the LORD hath sought him a man after his own heart, and the LORD hath commanded him *to be* captain over his people, because thou hast not kept *that* which the LORD commanded thee.

Saul's small army

15 And Samuel arose, and gat him up from Gilgal unto Gibeah of Benjamin. And Saul numbered the people *that were* *c*present with him, about six hundred men.

16 And Saul, and Jonathan his son, and the people *that were* present with them, abode in *d*Gibeah of Benjamin: but the Philistines encamped in Michmash.

17 ¶ And the spoilers came out of the camp of the Philistines in three companies: one company turned unto the way *that leadeth to* Ophrah, unto the land of Shual:

18 And another company turned the way *to* Beth-horon: and another company turned *to* the way of the border that looketh to the valley of Zeboim toward the wilderness.

19 ¶ Now there was no smith found throughout all the land of Israel: for the Philistines said, Lest the Hebrews make *them* swords or spears:

20 But all the Israelites went down to the Philistines, to sharpen every man his share, and his coulter, and his axe, and his mattock.

21 Yet they had *e*a file for the mattocks, and for the coulters, and for the forks, and for the axes, and *f*to sharpen the goads.

22 So it came to pass in the day of battle, that there was neither sword nor spear found in the hand of any of the people that *were* with Saul and Jonathan: but with Saul and with Jonathan his son was there found.

23 And the *g*garrison of the Philistines went out to the passage of Michmash.

Jonathan attacks the Philistines

14 NOW *h*IT came to pass upon a day, that Jonathan the son of Saul said unto the young man that bare his armour, Come, and let us go over to the Philistines' garrison, that *is* on the other side. But he told not his father.

2 And Saul tarried in the uttermost part of Gibeah under a pomegranate tree which *is* in Migron: and the people that *were* with him *were* about six hundred men;

3 And Ahiah, the son of Ahitub, Ichabod's brother, the son of Phinehas, the son of Eli, the LORD's priest in Shiloh, wearing an ephod. And the people knew not that Jonathan was gone.

4 ¶ And between the passages, by which Jonathan sought to go over unto the Philistines' garrison, *there was* a sharp rock on the one side, and a sharp rock on the other side: and the name of the one *was* Bozez, and the name of the other Seneh.

5 The *i*forefront of the one *was* situate northward over against Michmash, and the other southward over against Gibeah.

11 Samuel said, What have you done? Saul said, Because I saw that the people were scattering from me, and that you did not come within the days appointed, and that the Philistines were assembled at Michmash,

12 I thought, The Philistines will come down now upon me to Gilgal, and I have not made supplication to the Lord. So I forced myself to offer a burnt offering.

13 And Samuel said to Saul, You have done foolishly! You have not kept the commandment of the Lord your God which He commanded you; for the Lord would have established your kingdom over Israel forever;

14 But now your kingdom shall not continue; the Lord has sought out [David] a man after His own *g*heart, and the Lord has commanded him to be prince *and* ruler over His people, because you have not kept what the Lord commanded you.

15 And Samuel went up from Gilgal to Gibeah of Benjamin. And Saul numbered the people that were left with him, [only] about 600.

16 Saul and Jonathan his son and the people with them remained in Gibeah of Benjamin, but the Philistines encamped at Michmash.

17 And raiders came out of the Philistine camp in three companies; one company turned toward Ophrah, to the land of Shual,

18 Another turned toward Beth-horon, and another toward the border overlooking the Valley of Zeboim toward the wilderness.

19 Now there was no metal worker to be found throughout all the land of Israel, for the Philistines said, Lest the Hebrews make swords or spears.

20 But each of the Israelites had to go down to the Philistines to get his plowshare, mattock, axe, or sickle sharpened.

21 And the price for plowshares and mattocks was a pim, and a third of a shekel for axes and for setting goads [with resulting blunt edges on the sickles, mattocks, forks, axes, and goads.]

22 So on the day of battle neither sword nor spear was found in the hand of any of the men who were with Saul and Jonathan; but Saul and Jonathan his son had them.

23 And the garrison of the Philistines went out to the pass of Michmash.

14 ONE DAY Jonathan son of Saul said to his armor-bearer, Come, let us go over to the Philistine garrison on the other side. But he did not tell his father.

2 Saul was remaining in the outskirts of Gibeah under a pomegranate tree in Migron; and with him were about 600 men,

3 And Ahijah son of Ahitub, Ichabod's brother, the son of Phinehas, the son of Eli, the Lord's priest in Shiloh, was wearing the ephod. And the people did not know that Jonathan was gone.

4 Between the passes by which Jonathan sought to go over to the Philistine garrison there was a rocky crag on the one side and a rocky crag on the other side; one was named Bozez, and the other Seneh.

5 The one crag rose on the north in front of Michmash, and the other on the south in front of Geba.

---

b Heb. *entreated the face*   *c* Heb. *found*   *d* Heb. *Geba; see*
ver. 3   *e* Heb. *a file with mouths*   *f* Heb. *to set*   *g* Or,
standing camp   *h* Or, *there was a day*   *i* Heb. *tooth*

g See footnote on I Sam. 27:10.

New American Standard

11 But Samuel said, "What have you done?" And Saul said, "Because I saw that the people were scattering from me, and that you did not come within the appointed days, and that the Philistines were assembling at Michmash,

12 therefore I said, 'Now the Philistines will come down against me at Gilgal, and I have not asked the favor of the LORD.' So I forced myself and offered the burnt offering."

13 Samuel said to Saul, "You have acted foolishly; you have not kept the commandment of the LORD your God, which He commanded you, for now the LORD would have established your kingdom over Israel forever.

14 "But now your kingdom shall not endure. The LORD has sought out for Himself a man after His own heart, and the LORD has appointed him as ruler over His people, because you have not kept what the LORD commanded you."

15 ¶ Then Samuel arose and went up from Gilgal to Gibeah of Benjamin. And Saul numbered the people who were present with him, about six hundred men.

16 Now Saul and his son Jonathan and the people who were present with them were staying in Geba of Benjamin while the Philistines camped at Michmash.

17 And the raiders came from the camp of the Philistines in three companies: one company turned toward Ophrah, to the land of Shual,

18 and another company turned toward Beth-horon, and another company turned toward the border which overlooks the valley of Zeboim toward the wilderness.

19 ¶ Now no blacksmith could be found in all the land of Israel, for the Philistines said, "Otherwise the Hebrews will make swords or spears."

20 So all Israel went down to the Philistines, each to sharpen his plowshare, his mattock, his axe, and his hoe.

21 The charge was two-thirds of a shekel for the plowshares, the mattocks, the forks, and the axes, and to fix the hoes.

22 So it came about on the day of battle that neither sword nor spear was found in the hands of any of the people who *were* with Saul and Jonathan, but they were found with Saul and his son Jonathan.

23 And the garrison of the Philistines went out to the pass of Michmash.

Jonathan's Victory

14 NOW THE day came that Jonathan, the son of Saul, said to the young man who was carrying his armor, "Come and let us cross over to the Philistines' garrison that is on the other side." But he did not tell his father.

2 Saul was staying in the outskirts of Gibeah under the pomegranate tree which is in Migron. And the people who *were* with him *were* about six hundred men,

3 and Ahijah, the son of Ahitub, Ichabod's brother, the son of Phinehas, the son of Eli, the priest of the LORD at Shiloh, was wearing an ephod. And the people did not know that Jonathan had gone.

4 Between the passes by which Jonathan sought to cross over to the Philistines' garrison, there was a sharp crag on the one side and a sharp crag on the other side, and the name of the one was Bozez, and the name of the other Seneh.

5 The one crag rose on the north opposite Michmash, and the other on the south opposite Geba.

New International

11 "What have you done?" asked Samuel.

Saul replied, "When I saw that the men were scattering, and that you did not come at the set time, and that the Philistines were assembling at Micmash, 12 I thought, 'Now the Philistines will come down against me at Gilgal, and I have not sought the LORD's favor.' So I felt compelled to offer the burnt offering."

13 "You acted foolishly," Samuel said. "You have not kept the command the LORD your God gave you; if you had, he would have established your kingdom over Israel for all time. 14 But now your kingdom will not endure; the LORD has sought out a man after his own heart and appointed him leader of his people, because you have not kept the LORD's command."

15 Then Samuel left Gilgal[n] and went up to Gibeah in Benjamin, and Saul counted the men who were with him. They numbered about six hundred.

Israel Without Weapons

16 Saul and his son Jonathan and the men with them were staying in Gibeah[o] in Benjamin, while the Philistines camped at Micmash. 17 Raiding parties went out from the Philistine camp in three detachments. One turned toward Ophrah in the vicinity of Shual, 18 another toward Beth Horon, and the third toward the borderland overlooking the Valley of Zeboim facing the desert.

19 Not a blacksmith could be found in the whole land of Israel, because the Philistines had said, "Otherwise the Hebrews will make swords or spears!" 20 So all Israel went down to the Philistines to have their plowshares, mattocks, axes and sickles[p] sharpened. 21 The price was two thirds of a shekel[q] for sharpening plowshares and mattocks, and a third of a shekel[r] for sharpening forks and axes and for repointing goads.

22 So on the day of the battle not a soldier with Saul and Jonathan had a sword or spear in his hand; only Saul and his son Jonathan had them.

Jonathan Attacks the Philistines

23 Now a detachment of Philistines had gone out to the pass at Micmash. **14** ¹ One day Jonathan son of Saul said to the young man bearing his armor, "Come, let's go over to the Philistine outpost on the other side." But he did not tell his father.

2 Saul was staying on the outskirts of Gibeah under a pomegranate tree in Migron. With him were about six hundred men, 3 among whom was Ahijah, who was wearing an ephod. He was a son of Ichabod's brother Ahitub son of Phinehas, the son of Eli, the LORD's priest in Shiloh. No one was aware that Jonathan had left.

4 On each side of the pass that Jonathan intended to cross to reach the Philistine outpost was a cliff; one was called Bozez, and the other Seneh. 5 One cliff stood to the north toward Micmash, the other to the south toward Geba.

n 15 Hebrew; Septuagint *Gilgal and went his way; the rest of the people went after Saul to meet the army, and they went out of Gilgal*   *o 16* Two Hebrew manuscripts; most Hebrew manuscripts *Geba,* a variant of *Gibeah*   *p 20* Septuagint; Hebrew *plowshares*   *q 21* Hebrew *pim;* that is, about 1/4 ounce (about 8 grams)   *r 21* That is, about 1/8 ounce (about 4 grams)

King James

6And Jonathan said to the young man that bare his armour, Come, and let us go over unto the garrison of these uncircumcised: it may be that the LORD will work for us: for *there is* no restraint to the LORD to save by many or by few.

7And his armourbearer said unto him, Do all that *is* in thine heart: turn thee; behold, I *am* with thee according to thy heart.

8Then said Jonathan, Behold, we will pass over unto *these* men, and we will discover ourselves unto them.

9If they say thus unto us, *j*Tarry until we come to you; then we will stand still in our place, and will not go up unto them.

10But if they say thus, Come up unto us; then we will go up: for the LORD hath delivered them into our hand: and this *shall be* a sign unto us.

11And both of them discovered themselves unto the garrison of the Philistines: and the Philistines said, Behold, the Hebrews come forth out of the holes where they had hid themselves.

12And the men of the garrison answered Jonathan and his armourbearer, and said, Come up to us, and we will show you a thing. And Jonathan said unto his armourbearer, Come up after me: for the LORD hath delivered them into the hand of Israel.

13And Jonathan climbed up upon his hands and upon his feet, and his armourbearer after him: and they fell before Jonathan; and his armourbearer slew after him.

14And that first slaughter, which Jonathan and his armourbearer made, was about twenty men, within as it were *k*an half acre of land, *which* a yoke *of oxen might plow.*

15And there was trembling in the host, in the field, and among all the people: the garrison, and the spoilers, they also trembled, and the earth quaked: so it was *l*a very great trembling.

The Philistines flee

16And the watchmen of Saul in Gibeah of Benjamin looked; and, behold, the multitude melted away, and they went on beating down *one another.*

17Then said Saul unto the people that *were* with him, Number now, and see who is gone from us. And when they had numbered, behold, Jonathan and his armourbearer *were* not *there.*

18And Saul said unto Ahiah, Bring hither the ark of God. For the ark of God was at that time with the children of Israel.

19 ¶ And it came to pass, while Saul talked unto the priest, that the *m*noise that *was* in the host of the Philistines went on and increased: and Saul said unto the priest, Withdraw thine hand.

20And Saul and all the people that *were* with him *n*assembled themselves, and they came to the battle: and, behold, every man's sword was against his fellow, *and* there *was* a very great discomfiture.

21Moreover the Hebrews *that* were with the Philistines before that time, which went up with them into the camp *from the country* round about, even they also *turned* to be with the Israelites that *were* with Saul and Jonathan.

22Likewise all the men of Israel which had hid themselves in mount Ephraim, *when* they heard that the Philistines fled, even they also followed hard after them in the battle.

23So the LORD saved Israel that day: and the battle passed over unto Beth-aven.

Jonathan breaks Saul's oath

24 ¶ And the men of Israel were distressed that day: for Saul had adjured the people, saying, Cursed *be* the man that eateth *any* food until evening, that I may be avenged on mine enemies. So none of the people tasted *any* food.

Amplified

6And Jonathan said to his young armor-bearer, Come, and let us go over to the garrison of these uncircumcised; it may be that the Lord will work for us. For there is nothing to prevent the Lord from saving by many or by few.

7And his armor-bearer said to him, Do all that is in your mind; I am with you in whatever you think [best].

8Jonathan said, We will pass over to these men and we will let them see us.

9If they say to us, Wait until we come to you, then we will stand still in our place and will not go up to them.

10But if they say, Come up to us, we will go up, for the Lord has delivered them into our hand, and this will be our sign.

11So both of them let the Philistine garrison see them. And the Philistines said, Behold, the Hebrews are coming out of the holes where they have hidden themselves.

12The garrison men said to Jonathan and his armor-bearer, Come up to us and we will show you a thing. Jonathan said to his armor-bearer, Come up after me, for the Lord has given them into Israel's hand.

13Then Jonathan climbed up on his hands and feet, his armor-bearer after him; and the enemy fell before Jonathan, and his armor-bearer killed them after him.

14And that first slaughter which Jonathan and his armor-bearer made was about twenty men within about a half acre of land [which a yoke of oxen might plow].

15And there was trembling *and* panic in the [Philistine] camp, in the field, and among all the men; the garrison, and even the raiders trembled; the earth quaked, and it became a terror from God.

16Saul's watchmen in Gibeah of Benjamin looked, and behold, the multitude melted away and went hither and thither.

17Then Saul said to the men with him, Number and see who is gone from us. When they numbered, behold, Jonathan and his armor-bearer were missing.

18Saul said to Ahijah, Bring here the ark of God—for at that time the ark of God was with the children of Israel.

19While Saul talked to the priest, the tumult in the Philistine camp kept increasing. Then Saul said to the priest, Withdraw your hand.

20Then Saul and all the people with him rallied and went into the battle, and behold, every [Philistine's] sword was against his fellow in wild confusion.

21Moreover, the Hebrews who were with the Philistines before that time, who went up with them into the camp from the country round about, even they also turned to be with the Israelites who were with Saul and Jonathan.

22Likewise, all the men of Israel who had hid themselves in the hill country of Ephraim, when they heard that the Philistines fled, they also went after them in hot pursuit in the battle.

23So the Lord delivered Israel that day, and the battle passed beyond Beth-aven.

24But the men of Israel were distressed that day, for Saul had caused them to take an oath, saying, Cursed be the man who eats any food before evening and until I have taken vengeance on my enemies. So none of the men tasted any food.

New American Standard

6 ¶ Then Jonathan said to the young man who was carrying his armor, "Come and let us cross over to the garrison of these uncircumcised; perhaps the LORD will work for us, for the LORD is not restrained to save by many or by few."

7 His armor bearer said to him, "Do all that is in your heart; turn yourself, *and* here I am with you according to your desire."

8 Then Jonathan said, "Behold, we will cross over to the men and reveal ourselves to them.

9 "If they say to us, 'Wait until we come to you'; then we will stand in our place and not go up to them.

10 "But if they say, 'Come up to us,' then we will go up, for the LORD has given them into our hands; and this shall be the sign to us."

11 When both of them revealed themselves to the garrison of the Philistines, the Philistines said, "Behold, Hebrews are coming out of the holes where they have hidden themselves."

12 So the men of the garrison hailed Jonathan and his armor bearer and said, "Come up to us and we will tell you something." And Jonathan said to his armor bearer, "Come up after me, for the LORD has given them into the hands of Israel."

13 Then Jonathan climbed up on his hands and feet, with his armor bearer behind him; and they fell before Jonathan, and his armor bearer put some to death after him.

14 That first slaughter which Jonathan and his armor bearer made was about twenty men within about half a furrow in an acre of land.

15 And there was a trembling in the camp, in the field, and among all the people. Even the garrison and the raiders trembled, and the earth quaked so that it became a *i*great trembling.

16 ¶ Now Saul's watchmen in Gibeah of Benjamin looked, and behold, the multitude melted away; and they went here and *there.*

17 Saul said to the people who *were* with him, "Number now and see who has gone from us." And when they had numbered, behold, Jonathan and his armor bearer were not *there.*

18 Then Saul said to Ahijah, "Bring the ark of God here." For the ark of God was at that time with the sons of Israel.

19 While Saul talked to the priest, the commotion in the camp of the Philistines continued and increased; so Saul said to the priest, "Withdraw your hand."

20 Then Saul and all the people who *were* with him rallied and came to the battle; and behold, every man's sword was against his fellow, *and there was* very great confusion.

21 Now the Hebrews *who* were with the Philistines previously, who went up with them all around in the camp, even they also *turned* to be with the Israelites who *were* with Saul and Jonathan.

22 When all the men of Israel who had hidden themselves in the hill country of Ephraim heard that the Philistines had fled, even they also pursued them closely in the battle.

23 So the LORD delivered Israel that day, and the battle spread beyond Beth-aven.

Saul's Foolish Order

24 ¶ Now the men of Israel were hard-pressed on that day, for Saul had put the people under oath, saying, "Cursed be the man who eats food before evening, and until I have avenged myself on my enemies." So none of the people tasted food.

New International

6Jonathan said to his young armor-bearer, "Come, let's go over to the outpost of those uncircumcised fellows. Perhaps the LORD will act in our behalf. Nothing can hinder the LORD from saving, whether by many or by few."

7"Do all that you have in mind," his armor-bearer said. "Go ahead; I am with you heart and soul."

8Jonathan said, "Come, then; we will cross over toward the men and let them see us. 9If they say to us, 'Wait there until we come to you,' we will stay where we are and not go up to them. 10But if they say, 'Come up to us,' we will climb up, because that will be our sign that the LORD has given them into our hands."

11So both of them showed themselves to the Philistine outpost. "Look!" said the Philistines. "The Hebrews are crawling out of the holes they were hiding in." 12The men of the outpost shouted to Jonathan and his armor-bearer, "Come up to us and we'll teach you a lesson."

So Jonathan said to his armor-bearer, "Climb up after me; the LORD has given them into the hand of Israel."

13Jonathan climbed up, using his hands and feet, with his armor-bearer right behind him. The Philistines fell before Jonathan, and his armor-bearer followed and killed behind him. 14In that first attack Jonathan and his armor-bearer killed some twenty men in an area of about half an acre.*s*

Israel Routs the Philistines

15Then panic struck the whole army—those in the camp and field, and those in the outposts and raiding parties—and the ground shook. It was a panic sent by God.*t*

16Saul's lookouts at Gibeah in Benjamin saw the army melting away in all directions. 17Then Saul said to the men who were with him, "Muster the forces and see who has left us." When they did, it was Jonathan and his armor-bearer who were not there.

18Saul said to Ahijah, "Bring the ark of God." (At that time it was with the Israelites.)*u* 19While Saul was talking to the priest, the tumult in the Philistine camp increased more and more. So Saul said to the priest, "Withdraw your hand."

20Then Saul and all his men assembled and went to the battle. They found the Philistines in total confusion, striking each other with their swords. 21Those Hebrews who had previously been with the Philistines and had gone up with them to their camp went over to the Israelites who were with Saul and Jonathan. 22When all the Israelites who had hidden in the hill country of Ephraim heard that the Philistines were on the run, they joined the battle in hot pursuit. 23So the LORD rescued Israel that day, and the battle moved on beyond Beth Aven.

Jonathan Eats Honey

24Now the men of Israel were in distress that day, because Saul had bound the people under an oath, saying, "Cursed be any man who eats food before evening comes, before I have avenged myself on my enemies!" So none of the troops tasted food.

---

s 14 Hebrew *half a yoke*; a "yoke" was the land plowed by a yoke of oxen in one day.   *t* 15 Or *a terrible panic*   *u* 18 Hebrew; Septuagint *"Bring the ephod."* (At that time he wore the ephod before the Israelites.)

i Lit *trembling of God*

King James

²⁵And all *they of* the land came to a wood; and there was honey upon the ground.

²⁶And when the people were come into the wood, behold, the honey dropped; but no man put his hand to his mouth: for the people feared the oath.

²⁷But Jonathan heard not when his father charged the people with the oath: wherefore he put forth the end of the rod that *was* in his hand, and dipped it in an honeycomb, and put his hand to his mouth; and his eyes were enlightened.

²⁸Then answered one of the people, and said, Thy father straitly charged the people with an oath, saying, Cursed *be* the man that eateth *any* food this day. And the people were ᵒfaint.

²⁹Then said Jonathan, My father hath troubled the land: see, I pray you, how mine eyes have been enlightened, because I tasted a little of this honey.

³⁰How much more, if haply the people had eaten freely today of the spoil of their enemies which they found? for had there not been now a much greater slaughter among the Philistines?

³¹And they smote the Philistines that day from Michmash to Aijalon: and the people were very faint.

³²And the people flew upon the spoil, and took sheep, and oxen, and calves, and slew *them* on the ground: and the people did eat *them* with the blood.

³³ ¶ Then they told Saul, saying, Behold, the people sin against the LORD, in that they eat with the blood. And he said, Ye have ᵖtransgressed: roll a great stone unto me this day.

³⁴And Saul said, Disperse yourselves among the people, and say unto them, Bring me hither every man his ox, and every man his sheep, and slay *them* here, and eat; and sin not against the LORD in eating with the blood. And all the people brought every man his ox ᵍwith him that night, and slew *them* there.

³⁵And Saul built an altar unto the LORD: ʳthe same was the first altar that he built unto the LORD.

³⁶ ¶ And Saul said, Let us go down after the Philistines by night, and spoil them until the morning light, and let us not leave a man of them. And they said, Do whatsoever seemeth good unto thee. Then said the priest, Let us draw near hither unto God.

³⁷And Saul asked counsel of God, Shall I go down after the Philistines? wilt thou deliver them into the hand of Israel? But he answered him not that day.

³⁸And Saul said, Draw ye near hither, all the chief of the people: and know and see wherein this sin hath been this day.

³⁹For, *as* the LORD liveth, which saveth Israel, though it be in Jonathan my son, he shall surely die. But *there was* not a man among all the people *that* answered him.

⁴⁰Then said he unto all Israel, Be ye on one side, and I and Jonathan my son will be on the other side. And the people said unto Saul, Do what seemeth good unto thee.

⁴¹Therefore Saul said unto the LORD God of Israel, ˢGive a perfect *lot.* And Saul and Jonathan were taken: but the people ᵗescaped.

⁴²And Saul said, Cast *lots* between me and Jonathan my son. And Jonathan was taken.

⁴³Then Saul said to Jonathan, Tell me what thou hast done. And Jonathan told him, and said, I did but taste a little honey with the end of the rod that *was* in mine hand, *and,* lo, I must die.

⁴⁴And Saul answered, God do so and more also: for thou shalt surely die, Jonathan.

⁴⁵And the people said unto Saul, Shall Jonathan die, who hath wrought this great salvation in Israel? God forbid: *as* the LORD liveth, there shall not one hair of his head fall to the ground; for he hath wrought with God this day. So the people rescued Jonathan, that he died not.

Amplified

²⁵And all the people of the land came to a wood, and there was honey on the ground.

²⁶When the men entered the wood, behold, the honey was dripping, but no man tasted it, for the men feared the oath.

²⁷But Jonathan had not heard when his father charged the people with the oath. So he dipped the end of the rod in his hand into a honeycomb and put it to his mouth, and his [weary] eyes brightened.

²⁸Then one of the men told him, Your father strictly charged the men with an oath, saying, Cursed be the man who eats any food today. And the people were exhausted *and* faint.

²⁹Then Jonathan said, My father has troubled the land. See how my eyes have brightened because I tasted a little of this honey.

³⁰How much better if the men had eaten freely today of the spoil of their enemies which they found! For now the slaughter of the Philistines has not been great.

³¹They smote the Philistines that day from Michmash to Aijalon. And the people were very faint.

³²[When night came and the oath expired] the men flew upon the spoil. They took sheep, oxen, and calves, slew them on the ground, and ate them [raw] with the blood.

³³Then Saul was told, Behold, the men are sinning against the Lord by eating with the blood. And he said, You have transgressed; roll a great stone to me here.

³⁴Saul said, Disperse yourselves among the people and tell them, Bring me every man his ox or his sheep, and butcher them here and eat; and sin not against the Lord by eating the blood. So all the men brought each one his ox that night and butchered it there.

³⁵And Saul built an altar to the Lord; it was the first altar he built to the Lord.

³⁶Then Saul said, Let us go down after the Philistines by night and seize and plunder them until daylight, and let us not leave a man of them. They said, Do whatever seems good to you. Then the priest said, Let us draw near here to God.

³⁷And Saul asked counsel of God, Shall I go down after the Philistines? Will You deliver them into the hand of Israel? But He did not answer him that day.

³⁸Then Saul said, Draw near, all the chiefs of the people, and let us see how this sin [causing God's silence] arose today.

³⁹For as the Lord lives, Who delivers Israel, though it be in Jonathan my son, he shall surely die. But not a man among all the people answered him.

⁴⁰Then he said to all Israel, You be on one side; and I and Jonathan my son will be on the other side. The people said to Saul, Do what seems good to you.

⁴¹Therefore Saul said to the Lord, the God of Israel, Give a perfect lot *and* show the right. And Saul and Jonathan were taken [by lot], but the other men went free.

⁴²Saul said, Cast lots between me and Jonathan my son. And Jonathan was taken.

⁴³Saul said to Jonathan, Tell me what you have done. And Jonathan said, I tasted a little honey with the end of the rod that was in my hand. And behold, I must die.

⁴⁴Saul answered, May God do so, and more also, for you shall surely die, Jonathan.

⁴⁵But the people said to Saul, Shall Jonathan, who has wrought this great deliverance for Israel, die? God forbid! As the Lord lives, there shall not one hair of his head perish, for he has wrought this great deliverance with God this day. So the people rescued Jonathan, and he did not die.

ᵒOr, *weary*   ᵖOr, *dealt treacherously*   ᵍHeb. *in his hand*
ʳHeb. *that altar he began to build unto the LORD*   ˢOr, *Show the innocent*   ᵗHeb. *went forth*

New American Standard

25 All *the people of* the land entered the forest, and there was honey on the ground.

26 When the people entered the forest, behold, *there was* a flow of honey; but no man put his hand to his mouth, for the people feared the oath.

27 But Jonathan had not heard when his father put the people under oath; therefore, he put out the end of the staff that *was* in his hand and dipped it in the honeycomb, and put his hand to his mouth, and his eyes brightened.

28 Then one of the people said, "Your father strictly put the people under oath, saying, 'Cursed be the man who eats food today.' " And the people were weary.

29 Then Jonathan said, "My father has troubled the land. See now, how my eyes have brightened because I tasted a little of this honey.

30 "How much more, if only the people had eaten freely today of the spoil of their enemies which they found! For now the slaughter among the Philistines has not been great."

31 ¶ They struck among the Philistines that day from Michmash to Aijalon. And the people were very weary.

32 The people rushed greedily upon the spoil, and took sheep and oxen and calves, and slew *them* on the ground; and the people ate *them* with the blood.

33 Then they told Saul, saying, "Behold, the people are sinning against the LORD by eating with the blood." And he said, "You have acted treacherously; roll a great stone to me today."

34 Saul said, "Disperse yourselves among the people and say to them, 'Each one of you bring me his ox or his sheep, and slaughter *it* here and eat; and do not sin against the LORD by eating with the blood.' " So all the people that night brought each one his ox with him and slaughtered *it* there.

35 And Saul built an altar to the LORD; it was the first altar that he built to the LORD.

36 ¶ Then Saul said, "Let us go down after the Philistines by night and take spoil among them until the morning light, and let us not leave a man of them." And they said, "Do whatever seems good to you." So the priest said, "Let us draw near to God here."

37 Saul inquired of God, "Shall I go down after the Philistines? Will You give them into the hand of Israel?" But He did not answer him on that day.

38 Saul said, "Draw near here, all you chiefs of the people, and investigate and see how this sin has happened today.

39 "For as the LORD lives, who delivers Israel, though it is in Jonathan my son, he shall surely die." But not one of all the people answered him.

40 Then he said to all Israel, "You shall be on one side and I and Jonathan my son will be on the other side." And the people said to Saul, "Do what seems good to you."

41 Therefore, Saul said to the LORD, the God of Israel, "Give a perfect *lot*." And Jonathan and Saul were taken, but the people escaped.

42 Saul said, "Cast *lots* between me and Jonathan my son." And Jonathan was taken.

43 ¶ Then Saul said to Jonathan, "Tell me what you have done." So Jonathan told him and said, "I indeed tasted a little honey with the end of the staff that was in my hand. Here I am, I must die!"

44 Saul said, "May God do this *to me* and more also, for you shall surely die, Jonathan."

45 But the people said to Saul, "Must Jonathan die, who has brought about this great deliverance in Israel? Far from it! As the LORD lives, not one hair of his head shall fall to the ground, for he has worked with God this day." So the people rescued Jonathan and he did not die.

New International

25 The entire army[v] entered the woods, and there was honey on the ground. **26** When they went into the woods, they saw the honey oozing out, yet no one put his hand to his mouth, because they feared the oath. **27** But Jonathan had not heard that his father had bound the people with the oath, so he reached out the end of the staff that was in his hand and dipped it into the honeycomb. He raised his hand to his mouth, and his eyes brightened.[w] **28** Then one of the soldiers told him, "Your father bound the army under a strict oath, saying, 'Cursed be any man who eats food today!' That is why the men are faint."

29 Jonathan said, "My father has made trouble for the country. See how my eyes brightened[x] when I tasted a little of this honey. **30** How much better it would have been if the men had eaten today some of the plunder they took from their enemies. Would not the slaughter of the Philistines have been even greater?"

31 That day, after the Israelites had struck down the Philistines from Micmash to Aijalon, they were exhausted. **32** They pounced on the plunder and, taking sheep, cattle and calves, they butchered them on the ground and ate them, together with the blood. **33** Then someone said to Saul, "Look, the men are sinning against the LORD by eating meat that has blood in it."

"You have broken faith," he said. "Roll a large stone over here at once." **34** Then he said, "Go out among the men and tell them, 'Each of you bring me your cattle and sheep, and slaughter them here and eat them. Do not sin against the LORD by eating meat with blood still in it.' "

So everyone brought his ox that night and slaughtered it there. **35** Then Saul built an altar to the LORD; it was the first time he had done this.

36 Saul said, "Let us go down after the Philistines by night and plunder them till dawn, and let us not leave one of them alive."

"Do whatever seems best to you," they replied.

But the priest said, "Let us inquire of God here."

37 So Saul asked God, "Shall I go down after the Philistines? Will you give them into Israel's hand?" But God did not answer him that day.

38 Saul therefore said, "Come here, all you who are leaders of the army, and let us find out what sin has been committed today. **39** As surely as the LORD who rescues Israel lives, even if it lies with my son Jonathan, he must die." But not one of the men said a word.

40 Saul then said to all the Israelites, "You stand over there; I and Jonathan my son will stand over here."

"Do what seems best to you," the men replied.

41 Then Saul prayed to the LORD, the God of Israel, "Give me the right answer."[y] And Jonathan and Saul were taken by lot, and the men were cleared. **42** Saul said, "Cast the lot between me and Jonathan my son." And Jonathan was taken.

43 Then Saul said to Jonathan, "Tell me what you have done."

So Jonathan told him, "I merely tasted a little honey with the end of my staff. And now must I die?"

44 Saul said, "May God deal with me, be it ever so severely, if you do not die, Jonathan."

45 But the men said to Saul, "Should Jonathan die—he who has brought about this great deliverance in Israel? Never! As surely as the LORD lives, not a hair of his head will fall to the ground, for he did this today with God's help." So the men rescued Jonathan, and he was not put to death.

---

v 25 Or *Now all the people of the land*   *w 27* Or *his strength was renewed*   *x 29* Or *my strength was renewed*   *y 41* Hebrew; Septuagint *"Why have you not answered your servant today? If the fault is in me or my son Jonathan, respond with Urim, but if the men of Israel are at fault, respond with Thummim."*

King James

⁴⁶Then Saul went up from following the Philistines: and the Philistines went to their own place.

Saul wars against other nations

⁴⁷ ¶ So Saul took the kingdom over Israel, and fought against all his enemies on every side, against Moab, and against the children of Ammon, and against Edom, and against the kings of Zobah, and against the Philistines: and whithersoever he turned himself, he vexed *them*.

⁴⁸And he ^ugathered an host, and smote the Amalekites, and delivered Israel out of the hands of them that spoiled them.

⁴⁹Now the sons of Saul were Jonathan, and Ishui, and Melch-ishua: and the names of his two daughters *were these*; the name of the firstborn Merab, and the name of the younger Michal:

⁵⁰And the name of Saul's wife *was* Ahinoam, the daughter of Ahimaaz: and the name of the captain of his host *was* ^vAbner, the son of Ner, Saul's uncle.

⁵¹And Kish *was* the father of Saul; and Ner the father of Abner *was* the son of Abiel.

⁵²And there was sore war against the Philistines all the days of Saul: and when Saul saw any strong man, or any valiant man, he took him unto him.

Saul rejected as king

15 SAMUEL ALSO said unto Saul, The LORD sent me to anoint thee *to be* king over his people, over Israel: now therefore hearken thou unto the voice of the words of the LORD.

²Thus saith the LORD of hosts, I remember *that* which Amalek did to Israel, how he laid *wait* for him in the way, when he came up from Egypt.

³Now go and smite Amalek, and utterly destroy all that they have, and spare them not; but slay both man and woman, infant and suckling, ox and sheep, camel and ass.

⁴And Saul gathered the people together, and numbered them in Telaim, two hundred thousand footmen, and ten thousand men of Judah.

⁵And Saul came to a city of Amalek, and ^wlaid wait in the valley.

⁶ ¶ And Saul said unto the Kenites, Go, depart, get you down from among the Amalekites, lest I destroy you with them: for ye showed kindness to all the children of Israel, when they came up out of Egypt. So the Kenites departed from among the Amalekites.

⁷And Saul smote the Amalekites from Havilah *until* thou comest to Shur, that *is* over against Egypt.

⁸And he took Agag the king of the Amalekites alive, and utterly destroyed all the people with the edge of the sword.

⁹But Saul and the people spared Agag, and the best of the sheep, and of the oxen, and ^xof the fatlings, and the lambs, and all *that was* good, and would not utterly destroy them: but every thing *that was* vile and refuse, that they destroyed utterly.

¹⁰ ¶ Then came the word of the LORD unto Samuel, saying,

¹¹It repenteth me that I have set up Saul *to be* king: for he is turned back from following me, and hath not performed my commandments. And it grieved Samuel; and he cried unto the LORD all night.

¹²And when Samuel rose early to meet Saul in the morning, it was told Samuel, saying, Saul came to Carmel, and, behold, he set him up a place, and is gone about, and passed on, and gone down to Gilgal.

¹³And Samuel came to Saul: and Saul said unto him, Blessed *be* thou of the LORD: I have performed the commandment of the LORD.

Amplified

⁴⁶Then Saul ceased pursuing the Philistines, and they went to their own place.

⁴⁷When Saul took over the kingdom of Israel, he fought against all his enemies on every side: Moab, the Ammonites, Edom, the kings of Zobah, and the Philistines. Wherever he turned, he made it worse for them.

⁴⁸He did valiantly and smote the Amalekites, and delivered Israel out of the hands of those who plundered them.

⁴⁹Now Saul's sons were Jonathan, Ishvi, and Malchishua; and the names of his two daughters were, of the firstborn, Merab; and of the younger, Michal.

⁵⁰The name of Saul's wife was Ahinoam daughter of Ahimaaz. The commander of his army was Abner son of Ner, Saul's uncle.

⁵¹Kish the father of Saul and Ner the father of Abner were sons of Abiel.

⁵²There was severe war against the Philistines all the days of Saul, and whenever Saul saw any mighty or [outstandingly] courageous man, he attached him to himself.

15 SAMUEL TOLD Saul, The Lord sent me to anoint you king over His people Israel. Now listen and heed the words of the Lord.

²Thus says the Lord of hosts, I have considered *and* will punish what Amalek did to Israel, how he set himself against him in the way when [Israel] came out of Egypt.

³Now go and smite Amalek and utterly destroy all they have; do not spare them, but kill both man and woman, infant and suckling, ox and sheep, camel and donkey.

⁴So Saul assembled the men and numbered them at Telaim—200,000 men on foot and 10,000 men of Judah.

⁵And Saul came to the city of Amalek and laid wait in the valley.

⁶Saul warned the Kenites, Go, depart, get down from among the Amalekites, lest I destroy you with them; for you showed kindness to all the Israelites when they came up out of Egypt. So the Kenites departed from among the Amalekites.

⁷Saul smote the Amalekites from Havilah as far as Shur, which is east of Egypt.

⁸And he took Agag king of the Amalekites alive, though he utterly destroyed all the rest of the people with the sword.

⁹Saul and the people spared Agag and the best of the sheep, oxen, fatlings, lambs, and all that was good, and would not utterly destroy them; but all that was undesirable or worthless they destroyed utterly.

¹⁰Then the word of the Lord came to Samuel, saying,

¹¹I regret making Saul king, for he has turned back from following Me and has not performed My commands. And Samuel was grieved *and* angry [with Saul], and he cried to the Lord all night.

¹²When Samuel rose early to meet Saul in the morning, he was told, Saul came to Carmel, and behold, he set up for himself a monument or trophy [of his victory] and passed on and went down to Gilgal.

¹³And Samuel came to Saul, and Saul said to him, Blessed are you of the Lord. I have performed what the Lord ordered.

---

^uOr, *wrought mightily*   ^vHeb. *Abiner*   ^wOr, *fought*   ^xOr, *of the second sort*

New American Standard

46 Then Saul went up from pursuing the Philistines, and the Philistines went to their own place.

Constant Warfare

47 ¶ Now when Saul had taken the kingdom over Israel, he fought against all his enemies on every side, against Moab, the sons of Ammon, Edom, the kings of Zobah, and the Philistines; and wherever he turned, he inflicted punishment.

48 He acted valiantly and defeated the Amalekites, and delivered Israel from the hands of those who plundered them.

49 ¶ Now the sons of Saul were Jonathan and Ishvi and Malchi-shua; and the names of his two daughters *were these:* the name of the firstborn Merab and the name of the younger Michal.

50 The name of Saul's wife was Ahinoam the daughter of Ahimaaz. And the name of the captain of his army was Abner the son of Ner, Saul's uncle.

51 Kish *was* the father of Saul, and Ner the father of Abner *was* the son of Abiel.

52 ¶ Now the war against the Philistines was severe all the days of Saul; and when Saul saw any mighty man or any valiant man, he attached him to his staff.

Saul's Disobedience

15 THEN SAMUEL said to Saul, "The LORD sent me to anoint you as king over His people, over Israel; now therefore, listen to the words of the LORD.

2 "Thus says the LORD of hosts, 'I will punish Amalek *for* what he did to Israel, how he set himself against him on the way while he was coming up from Egypt.

3 'Now go and strike Amalek and utterly destroy all that he has, and do not spare him; but put to death both man and woman, child and infant, ox and sheep, camel and donkey.' "

4 ¶ Then Saul summoned the people and numbered them in Telaim, 200,000 foot soldiers and 10,000 men of Judah.

5 Saul came to the city of Amalek and set an ambush in the valley.

6 Saul said to the Kenites, "Go, depart, go down from among the Amalekites, so that I do not destroy you with them; for you showed kindness to all the sons of Israel when they came up from Egypt." So the Kenites departed from among the Amalekites.

7 So Saul defeated the Amalekites, from Havilah as you go to Shur, which is east of Egypt.

8 He captured Agag the king of the Amalekites alive, and utterly destroyed all the people with the edge of the sword.

9 But Saul and the people spared Agag and the best of the sheep, the oxen, the fatlings, the lambs, and all that was good, and were not willing to destroy them utterly; but everything despised and worthless, that they utterly destroyed.

Samuel Rebukes Saul

10 ¶ Then the word of the LORD came to Samuel, saying,

11 "I regret that I have made Saul king, for he has turned back from following Me and has not carried out My commands." And Samuel was distressed and cried out to the LORD all night.

12 Samuel rose early in the morning to meet Saul; and it was told Samuel, saying, "Saul came to Carmel, and behold, he set up a monument for himself, then turned and proceeded on down to Gilgal."

13 Samuel came to Saul, and Saul said to him, "Blessed are you of the LORD! I have carried out the command of the LORD."

New International

46 Then Saul stopped pursuing the Philistines, and they withdrew to their own land.

47 After Saul had assumed rule over Israel, he fought against their enemies on every side: Moab, the Ammonites, Edom, the kings*ᶻ* of Zobah, and the Philistines. Wherever he turned, he inflicted punishment on them.*ᵃ*
48 He fought valiantly and defeated the Amalekites, delivering Israel from the hands of those who had plundered them.

Saul's Family

49 Saul's sons were Jonathan, Ishvi and Malki-Shua. The name of his older daughter was Merab, and that of the younger was Michal. 50 His wife's name was Ahinoam daughter of Ahimaaz. The name of the commander of Saul's army was Abner son of Ner, and Ner was Saul's uncle. 51 Saul's father Kish and Abner's father Ner were sons of Abiel.

52 All the days of Saul there was bitter war with the Philistines, and whenever Saul saw a mighty or brave man, he took him into his service.

The LORD Rejects Saul as King

15 SAMUEL SAID to Saul, "I am the one the LORD sent to anoint you king over his people Israel; so listen now to the message from the LORD. 2 This is what the LORD Almighty says: 'I will punish the Amalekites for what they did to Israel when they waylaid them as they came up from Egypt. 3 Now go, attack the Amalekites and totally destroy*ᵇ* everything that belongs to them. Do not spare them; put to death men and women, children and infants, cattle and sheep, camels and donkeys.' "

4 So Saul summoned the men and mustered them at Telaim—two hundred thousand foot soldiers and ten thousand men from Judah. 5 Saul went to the city of Amalek and set an ambush in the ravine. 6 Then he said to the Kenites, "Go away, leave the Amalekites so that I do not destroy you along with them; for you showed kindness to all the Israelites when they came up out of Egypt." So the Kenites moved away from the Amalekites.

7 Then Saul attacked the Amalekites all the way from Havilah to Shur, to the east of Egypt. 8 He took Agag king of the Amalekites alive, and all his people he totally destroyed with the sword. 9 But Saul and the army spared Agag and the best of the sheep and cattle, the fat calves*ᶜ* and lambs—everything that was good. These they were unwilling to destroy completely, but everything that was despised and weak they totally destroyed.

10 Then the word of the LORD came to Samuel: 11 "I am grieved that I have made Saul king, because he has turned away from me and has not carried out my instructions." Samuel was troubled, and he cried out to the LORD all night.

12 Early in the morning Samuel got up and went to meet Saul, but he was told, "Saul has gone to Carmel. There he has set up a monument in his own honor and has turned and gone on down to Gilgal."

13 When Samuel reached him, Saul said, "The LORD bless you! I have carried out the LORD's instructions."

ᶻ47 Masoretic Text; Dead Sea Scrolls and Septuagint king
ᵃ47 Hebrew; Septuagint he was victorious   *ᵇ3 The Hebrew term refers to the irrevocable giving over of things or persons to the LORD, often by totally destroying them; also in verses 8, 9, 15, 18, 20 and 21.*   *ᶜ9 Or the grown bulls; the meaning of the Hebrew for this phrase is uncertain.*

King James

¹⁴And Samuel said, What *meaneth* then this bleating of the sheep in mine ears, and the lowing of the oxen which I hear?

¹⁵And Saul said, They have brought them from the Amalekites: for the people spared the best of the sheep and of the oxen, to sacrifice unto the LORD thy God; and the rest we have utterly destroyed.

¹⁶Then Samuel said unto Saul, Stay, and I will tell thee what the LORD hath said to me this night. And he said unto him, Say on.

¹⁷And Samuel said, When thou *wast* little in thine own sight, *wast* thou not *made* the head of the tribes of Israel, and the LORD anointed thee king over Israel?

¹⁸And the LORD sent thee on a journey, and said, Go and utterly destroy the sinners the Amalekites, and fight against them until *y*they be consumed.

¹⁹Wherefore then didst thou not obey the voice of the LORD, but didst fly upon the spoil, and didst evil in the sight of the LORD?

²⁰And Saul said unto Samuel, Yea, I have obeyed the voice of the LORD, and have gone the way which the LORD sent me, and have brought Agag the king of Amalek, and have utterly destroyed the Amalekites.

²¹But the people took of the spoil, sheep and oxen, the chief of the things which should have been utterly destroyed, to sacrifice unto the LORD thy God in Gilgal.

²²And Samuel said, Hath the LORD *as great* delight in burnt offerings and sacrifices, as in obeying the voice of the LORD? Behold, to obey *is* better than sacrifice, *and* to hearken than the fat of rams.

²³For rebellion *is as* the sin of *z*witchcraft, and stubbornness *is as* iniquity and idolatry. Because thou hast rejected the word of the LORD, he hath also rejected thee from *being* king.

²⁴ ¶ And Saul said unto Samuel, I have sinned: for I have transgressed the commandment of the LORD, and thy words: because I feared the people, and obeyed their voice.

²⁵Now therefore, I pray thee, pardon my sin, and turn again with me, that I may worship the LORD.

²⁶And Samuel said unto Saul, I will not return with thee: for thou hast rejected the word of the LORD, and the LORD hath rejected thee from being king over Israel.

²⁷And as Samuel turned about to go away, he laid hold upon the skirt of his mantle, and it rent.

²⁸And Samuel said unto him, The LORD hath rent the kingdom of Israel from thee this day, and hath given it to a neighbour of thine, *that is* better than thou.

²⁹And also the *a*Strength of Israel will not lie nor repent: for he *is* not a man, that he should repent.

³⁰Then he said, I have sinned: *yet* honour me now, I pray thee, before the elders of my people, and before Israel, and turn again with me, that I may worship the LORD thy God.

³¹So Samuel turned again after Saul; and Saul worshipped the LORD.

³² ¶ Then said Samuel, Bring ye hither to me Agag the king of the Amalekites. And Agag came unto him delicately. And Agag said, Surely the bitterness of death is past.

³³And Samuel said, As thy sword hath made women childless, so shall thy mother be childless among women. And Samuel hewed Agag in pieces before the LORD in Gilgal.

³⁴ ¶ Then Samuel went to Ramah; and Saul went up to his house to Gibeah of Saul.

³⁵And Samuel came no more to see Saul until the day of his death: nevertheless Samuel mourned for Saul: and the LORD repented that he had made Saul king over Israel.

Amplified

¹⁴And Samuel said, What then means this bleating of the sheep in my ears, and the lowing of the oxen which I hear?

¹⁵Saul said, They have brought them from the Amalekites; for the people spared the best of the sheep and oxen to sacrifice to the Lord your God, but the rest we have utterly destroyed.

¹⁶Then Samuel said to Saul, Stop! I will tell you what the Lord said to me tonight. Saul said to him, Say on.

¹⁷Samuel said, When you were small in your own sight, were you not made the head of the tribes of Israel, and the Lord anointed you king over Israel?

¹⁸And the Lord sent you on a mission and said, Go, utterly destroy the sinners, the Amalekites; and fight against them until they are consumed.

¹⁹Why then did you not obey the voice of the Lord, but swooped down upon the plunder and did evil in the Lord's sight?

²⁰Saul said to Samuel, Yes, I have obeyed the voice of the Lord and have gone the way which the Lord sent me, and have brought Agag king of Amalek and have utterly destroyed the Amalekites.

²¹But the people took from the spoil sheep and oxen, the chief of the things to be utterly destroyed, to sacrifice to the Lord your God in Gilgal.

²²Samuel said, Has the Lord as great a delight in burnt offerings and sacrifices as in obeying the voice of the Lord? Behold, to obey is better than sacrifice, and to hearken than the fat of rams.

²³For rebellion is as the sin of witchcraft, and stubbornness is as idolatry and teraphim (household good luck images). Because you have rejected the word of the Lord, He also has rejected you from being king.

²⁴And Saul said to Samuel, I have sinned; for I have transgressed the commandment of the Lord and your words, because I feared the people and obeyed their voice.

²⁵Now, I pray you, pardon my sin and go back with me, that I may worship the Lord.

²⁶And Samuel said to Saul, I will not return with you; for you have rejected the word of the Lord, and the Lord has rejected you from being king over Israel.

²⁷And as Samuel turned to go away, Saul seized the skirt of Samuel's mantle, and it tore.

²⁸And Samuel said to him, The Lord has torn the kingdom of Israel from you this day and has given it to a neighbor of yours who is better than you.

²⁹And also the Strength of Israel will not lie or repent; for He is not a man, that He should repent.

³⁰Saul said, I have sinned; yet honor me now, I pray you, before the elders of my people and before Israel, and return with me, that I may worship the Lord your God.

³¹So Samuel turned back after Saul, and Saul worshiped the Lord.

³²Then Samuel said, Bring here to me Agag king of the Amalekites. And Agag came to him cheerfully. And Agag said, Surely the bitterness of death is past.

³³Samuel said, As your sword has made women childless, so shall your mother be childless among women. And Samuel hewed Agag in pieces before the Lord in Gilgal.

³⁴Then Samuel went to Ramah, but Saul went up to his house in Gibeah of Saul.

³⁵And Samuel came no more to see Saul until the day of his death, though Samuel grieved over Saul. And the Lord repented that He had made Saul king over Israel.

---

^yHeb. *they consume them*   ^zHeb. *divination*   ^aOr, *Eternity,* or, *Victory*

New American Standard

14 But Samuel said, "What then is this bleating of the sheep in my ears, and the lowing of the oxen which I hear?"

15 Saul said, "They have brought them from the Amalekites, for the people spared the best of the sheep and oxen, to sacrifice to the LORD your God; but the rest we have utterly destroyed."

16 Then Samuel said to Saul, "Wait, and let me tell you what the LORD said to me last night." And he said to him, "Speak!"

17 ¶ Samuel said, "Is it not true, though you were little in your own eyes, you were *made* the head of the tribes of Israel? And the LORD anointed you king over Israel,

18 and the LORD sent you on a mission, and said, 'Go and utterly destroy the sinners, the Amalekites, and fight against them until they are exterminated.'

19 "Why then did you not obey the voice of the LORD, but rushed upon the spoil and did what was evil in the sight of the LORD?"

20 ¶ Then Saul said to Samuel, "I did obey the voice of the LORD, and went on the mission on which the LORD sent me, and have brought back Agag the king of Amalek, and have utterly destroyed the Amalekites.

21 "But the people took *some* of the spoil, sheep and oxen, the choicest of the things devoted to destruction, to sacrifice to the LORD your God at Gilgal."

22 Samuel said,
"Has the LORD as much delight in burnt offerings
    and sacrifices
As in obeying the voice of the LORD?
Behold, to obey is better than sacrifice,
And to heed than the fat of rams,

23 "For rebellion is as the sin of divination,
And insubordination is as iniquity and idolatry.
Because you have rejected the word of the LORD,
He has also rejected you from *being* king."

24 ¶ Then Saul said to Samuel, "I have sinned; I have indeed transgressed the command of the LORD and your words, because I feared the people and listened to their voice.

25 "Now therefore, please pardon my sin and return with me, that I may worship the LORD."

26 But Samuel said to Saul, "I will not return with you; for you have rejected the word of the LORD, and the LORD has rejected you from being king over Israel."

27 As Samuel turned to go, *Saul* seized the edge of his robe, and it tore.

28 So Samuel said to him, "The LORD has torn the kingdom of Israel from you today and has given it to your neighbor, who is better than you.

29 "Also the Glory of Israel will not lie or change His mind; for He is not a man that He should change His mind."

30 Then he said, "I have sinned; *but* please honor me now before the elders of my people and before Israel, and go back with me, that I may worship the LORD your God."

31 So Samuel went back following Saul, and Saul worshiped the LORD.

32 ¶ Then Samuel said, "Bring me Agag, the king of the Amalekites." And Agag came to him cheerfully. And Agag said, "Surely the bitterness of death is past."

33 But Samuel said, "As your sword has made women childless, so shall your mother be childless among women." And Samuel hewed Agag to pieces before the LORD at Gilgal.

34 ¶ Then Samuel went to Ramah, but Saul went up to his house at Gibeah of Saul.

35 Samuel did not see Saul again until the day of his death; for Samuel grieved over Saul. And the LORD regretted that He had made Saul king over Israel.

New International

14 But Samuel said, "What then is this bleating of sheep in my ears? What is this lowing of cattle that I hear?"

15 Saul answered, "The soldiers brought them from the Amalekites; they spared the best of the sheep and cattle to sacrifice to the LORD your God, but we totally destroyed the rest."

16 "Stop!" Samuel said to Saul. "Let me tell you what the LORD said to me last night."

"Tell me," Saul replied.

17 Samuel said, "Although you were once small in your own eyes, did you not become the head of the tribes of Israel? The LORD anointed you king over Israel. **18** And he sent you on a mission, saying, 'Go and completely destroy those wicked people, the Amalekites; make war on them until you have wiped them out.' **19** Why did you not obey the LORD? Why did you pounce on the plunder and do evil in the eyes of the LORD?"

20 "But I did obey the LORD," Saul said. "I went on the mission the LORD assigned me. I completely destroyed the Amalekites and brought back Agag their king. **21** The soldiers took sheep and cattle from the plunder, the best of what was devoted to God, in order to sacrifice them to the LORD your God at Gilgal."

22 But Samuel replied:

"Does the LORD delight in burnt offerings and
    sacrifices
  as much as in obeying the voice of the
    LORD?
To obey is better than sacrifice,
  and to heed is better than the fat of rams.
23 For rebellion is like the sin of divination,
  and arrogance like the evil of idolatry.
Because you have rejected the word of the
    LORD,
  he has rejected you as king."

24 Then Saul said to Samuel, "I have sinned. I violated the LORD's command and your instructions. I was afraid of the people and so I gave in to them. **25** Now I beg you, forgive my sin and come back with me, so that I may worship the LORD."

26 But Samuel said to him, "I will not go back with you. You have rejected the word of the LORD, and the LORD has rejected you as king over Israel!"

27 As Samuel turned to leave, Saul caught hold of the hem of his robe, and it tore. **28** Samuel said to him, "The LORD has torn the kingdom of Israel from you today and has given it to one of your neighbors—to one better than you. **29** He who is the Glory of Israel does not lie or change his mind; for he is not a man, that he should change his mind."

30 Saul replied, "I have sinned. But please honor me before the elders of my people and before Israel; come back with me, so that I may worship the LORD your God." **31** So Samuel went back with Saul, and Saul worshiped the LORD.

32 Then Samuel said, "Bring me Agag king of the Amalekites."

Agag came to him confidently,*d* thinking, "Surely the bitterness of death is past."

33 But Samuel said,

"As your sword has made women childless,
  so will your mother be childless among
    women."

And Samuel put Agag to death before the LORD at Gilgal.

34 Then Samuel left for Ramah, but Saul went up to his home in Gibeah of Saul. **35** Until the day Samuel died, he did not go to see Saul again, though Samuel mourned for him. And the LORD was grieved that he had made Saul king over Israel.

d 32 Or him trembling, yet

<table>
<tr><th>King James</th><th>Amplified</th></tr>
</table>

King James

David chosen to be king

16 AND THE LORD said unto Samuel, How long wilt thou mourn for Saul, seeing I have rejected him from reigning over Israel? fill thine horn with oil, and go, I will send thee to Jesse the Bethlehemite: for I have provided me a king among his sons.

2 And Samuel said, How can I go? if Saul hear *it,* he will kill me. And the LORD said, Take an heifer *b*with thee, and say, I am come to sacrifice to the LORD.

3 And call Jesse to the sacrifice, and I will show thee what thou shalt do: and thou shalt anoint unto me *him* whom I name unto thee.

4 And Samuel did that which the LORD spake, and came to Bethlehem. And the elders of the town trembled at his *c*coming, and said, Comest thou peaceably?

5 And he said, Peaceably: I am come to sacrifice unto the LORD: sanctify yourselves, and come with me to the sacrifice. And he sanctified Jesse and his sons, and called them to the sacrifice.

6 ¶ And it came to pass, when they were come, that he looked on Eliab, and said, Surely the LORD'S anointed *is* before him.

7 But the LORD said unto Samuel, Look not on his countenance, or on the height of his stature; because I have refused him: for *the LORD seeth* not as man seeth; for man looketh on the *d*outward appearance, but the LORD looketh on the heart.

8 Then Jesse called Abinadab, and made him pass before Samuel. And he said, Neither hath the LORD chosen this.

9 Then Jesse made *e*Shammah to pass by. And he said, Neither hath the LORD chosen this.

10 Again, Jesse made seven of his sons to pass before Samuel. And Samuel said unto Jesse, The LORD hath not chosen these.

11 And Samuel said unto Jesse, Are here all *thy* children? And he said, There remaineth yet the youngest, and, behold, he keepeth the sheep. And Samuel said unto Jesse, Send and fetch him: for we will not sit *f*down till he come hither.

12 And he sent, and brought him in. Now he *was* ruddy, *and* withal *g*of a beautiful countenance, and goodly to look to. And the LORD said, Arise, anoint him: for this *is* he.

13 Then Samuel took the horn of oil, and anointed him in the midst of his brethren: and the spirit of the LORD came upon David from that day forward. So Samuel rose up, and went to Ramah.

David plays the harp

14 ¶ But the spirit of the LORD departed from Saul, and an evil spirit from the LORD *h*troubled him.

15 And Saul's servants said unto him, Behold now, an evil spirit from God troubleth thee.

16 Let our lord now command thy servants, *which are* before thee, to seek out a man, *who is* a cunning player on an harp: and it shall come to pass, when the evil spirit from God is upon thee, that he shall play with his hand, and thou shalt be well.

17 And Saul said unto his servants, Provide me now a man that can play well, and bring *him* to me.

18 Then answered one of the servants, and said, Behold, I have seen a son of Jesse the Bethlehemite, *that is* cunning in playing, and a mighty valiant man, and a man of war, and prudent in *i*matters, and a comely person, and the LORD *is* with him.

19 ¶ Wherefore Saul sent messengers unto Jesse, and said, Send me David thy son, which *is* with the sheep.

20 And Jesse took an ass *laden* with bread, and a bottle of wine, and a kid, and sent *them* by David his son unto Saul.

Amplified

16 THE LORD said to Samuel, How long will you mourn for Saul, seeing I have rejected him from reigning over Israel? Fill your horn with oil; I will send you to Jesse the Bethlehemite. For I have provided for Myself a king among his sons.

2 Samuel said, How can I go? If Saul hears it, he will kill me. And the Lord said, Take a heifer with you and say, I have come to sacrifice to the Lord.

3 And invite Jesse to the sacrifice, and I will show you what you shall do; and you shall anoint for Me the one I name to you.

4 And Samuel did what the Lord said, and came to Bethlehem. And the elders of the town trembled at his coming and said, Have you come peaceably?

5 And he said, Peaceably; I have come to sacrifice to the Lord. Consecrate yourselves and come with me to the sacrifice. And he consecrated Jesse and his sons and called them to the sacrifice.

6 When they had come, he looked on Eliab [the eldest son] and said, Surely the Lord's anointed is before Him.

7 But the Lord said to Samuel, Look not on his appearance or at the height of his stature, for I have rejected him. For the Lord sees not as man sees; for man looks on the outward appearance, but the Lord looks on the heart.

8 Then Jesse called Abinadab and made him pass before Samuel. But Samuel said, Neither has the Lord chosen this one.

9 Then Jesse made Shammah pass by. Samuel said, Nor has the Lord chosen him.

10 Jesse made seven of his sons pass before Samuel. And Samuel said to Jesse, The Lord has not chosen any of these.

11 Then [he] said to Jesse, Are all your sons here? [Jesse] said, There is yet the youngest; he is tending the sheep. Samuel said to Jesse, Send for him; for we will not sit down to eat until he is here.

12 Jesse sent and brought him. David had a healthy reddish complexion and beautiful eyes, and was fine-looking. The Lord said [to Samuel], Arise, anoint him; this is he.

13 Then Samuel took the horn of oil and anointed David in the midst of his brothers; and the Spirit of the Lord came mightily upon David from that day forward. And Samuel arose and went to Ramah.

14 But the Spirit of the Lord departed from Saul, and an evil spirit from the Lord tormented *and* troubled him.

15 Saul's servants said to him, Behold, an evil spirit from God torments you.

16 Let our lord now command your servants here before you to find a man who plays skillfully on the lyre; and when the evil spirit from God is upon you, he will play it, and you will be well.

17 Saul told his servants, Find me a man who plays well and bring him to me.

18 One of the young men said, I have seen a son of Jesse the Bethlehemite who plays skillfully, a valiant man, a man of war, prudent in speech *and* eloquent, an attractive person; and the Lord is with him.

19 So Saul sent messengers to Jesse and said, Send me David your son, who is with the sheep.

20 And Jesse took a donkey loaded with bread, a skin of wine, and a kid and sent them by David his son to Saul.

---

*b*Heb. *in thine hand*   *c*Heb. *meeting*   *d*Heb. *eyes*
*e*Shimeah in 2 Sam. 13:3; *Shimma* in 1 Chr. 2:13   *f*Heb. *round*
*g*Heb. *fair of eyes*   *h*Or, *terrified*   *i*Or, *speech*

New American Standard

Samuel Goes to Bethlehem

16 NOW THE LORD said to Samuel, "How long will you grieve over Saul, since I have rejected him from being king over Israel? Fill your horn with oil and go; I will send you to Jesse the Bethlehemite, for I have selected a king for Myself among his sons."

2 But Samuel said, "How can I go? When Saul hears *of it,* he will kill me." And the LORD said, "Take a heifer with you and say, 'I have come to sacrifice to the LORD.'

3 "You shall invite Jesse to the sacrifice, and I will show you what you shall do; and you shall anoint for Me the one whom I designate to you."

4 So Samuel did what the LORD said, and came to Bethlehem. And the elders of the city came trembling to meet him and said, "Do you come in peace?"

5 He said, "In peace; I have come to sacrifice to the LORD. Consecrate yourselves and come with me to the sacrifice." He also consecrated Jesse and his sons and invited them to the sacrifice.

6 ¶ When they entered, he looked at Eliab and thought, "Surely the LORD's anointed is before Him."

7 But the LORD said to Samuel, "Do not look at his appearance or at the height of his stature, because I have rejected him; for God *sees* not as man sees, for man looks at the outward appearance, but the LORD looks at the heart."

8 Then Jesse called Abinadab and made him pass before Samuel. And he said, "The LORD has not chosen this one either."

9 Next Jesse made Shammah pass by. And he said, "The LORD has not chosen this one either."

10 Thus Jesse made seven of his sons pass before Samuel. But Samuel said to Jesse, "The LORD has not chosen these."

11 And Samuel said to Jesse, "Are these all the children?" And he said, "There remains yet the youngest, and behold, he is tending the sheep." Then Samuel said to Jesse, "Send and bring him; for we will not sit down until he comes here."

David Anointed

12 So he sent and brought him in. Now he was ruddy, with beautiful eyes and a handsome appearance. And the LORD said, "Arise, anoint him; for this is he."

13 Then Samuel took the horn of oil and anointed him in the midst of his brothers; and the Spirit of the LORD came mightily upon David from that day forward. And Samuel arose and went to Ramah.

14 ¶ Now the Spirit of the LORD departed from Saul, and an evil spirit from the LORD terrorized him.

15 Saul's servants then said to him, "Behold now, an evil spirit from God is terrorizing you.

16 "Let our lord now command your servants who are before you. Let them seek a man who is a skillful player on the harp; and it shall come about when the evil spirit from God is on you, that he shall play *the harp* with his hand, and you will be well."

17 So Saul said to his servants, "Provide for me now a man who can play well and bring *him* to me."

18 Then one of the young men said, "Behold, I have seen a son of Jesse the Bethlehemite who is a skillful musician, a mighty man of valor, a warrior, one prudent in speech, and a handsome man; and the LORD is with him."

19 So Saul sent messengers to Jesse and said, "Send me your son David who is with the flock."

20 Jesse took a donkey *loaded with* bread and a jug of wine and a young goat, and sent *them* to Saul by David his son.

New International

Samuel Anoints David

16 THE LORD said to Samuel, "How long will you mourn for Saul, since I have rejected him as king over Israel? Fill your horn with oil and be on your way; I am sending you to Jesse of Bethlehem. I have chosen one of his sons to be king."

2 But Samuel said, "How can I go? Saul will hear about it and kill me."

The LORD said, "Take a heifer with you and say, 'I have come to sacrifice to the LORD.' 3 Invite Jesse to the sacrifice, and I will show you what to do. You are to anoint for me the one I indicate."

4 Samuel did what the LORD said. When he arrived at Bethlehem, the elders of the town trembled when they met him. They asked, "Do you come in peace?"

5 Samuel replied, "Yes, in peace; I have come to sacrifice to the LORD. Consecrate yourselves and come to the sacrifice with me." Then he consecrated Jesse and his sons and invited them to the sacrifice.

6 When they arrived, Samuel saw Eliab and thought, "Surely the LORD's anointed stands here before the LORD."

7 But the LORD said to Samuel, "Do not consider his appearance or his height, for I have rejected him. The LORD does not look at the things man looks at. Man looks at the outward appearance, but the LORD looks at the heart."

8 Then Jesse called Abinadab and had him pass in front of Samuel. But Samuel said, "The LORD has not chosen this one either." 9 Jesse then had Shammah pass by, but Samuel said, "Nor has the LORD chosen this one." 10 Jesse had seven of his sons pass before Samuel, but Samuel said to him, "The LORD has not chosen these." 11 So he asked Jesse, "Are these all the sons you have?"

"There is still the youngest," Jesse answered, "but he is tending the sheep."

Samuel said, "Send for him; we will not sit down[e] until he arrives."

12 So he sent and had him brought in. He was ruddy, with a fine appearance and handsome features.

Then the LORD said, "Rise and anoint him; he is the one."

13 So Samuel took the horn of oil and anointed him in the presence of his brothers, and from that day on the Spirit of the LORD came upon David in power. Samuel then went to Ramah.

David in Saul's Service

14 Now the Spirit of the LORD had departed from Saul, and an evil[f] spirit from the LORD tormented him.

15 Saul's attendants said to him, "See, an evil spirit from God is tormenting you. 16 Let our lord command his servants here to search for someone who can play the harp. He will play when the evil spirit from God comes upon you, and you will feel better."

17 So Saul said to his attendants, "Find someone who plays well and bring him to me."

18 One of the servants answered, "I have seen a son of Jesse of Bethlehem who knows how to play the harp. He is a brave man and a warrior. He speaks well and is a fine-looking man. And the LORD is with him."

19 Then Saul sent messengers to Jesse and said, "Send me your son David, who is with the sheep." 20 So Jesse took a donkey loaded with bread, a skin of wine and a young goat and sent them with his son David to Saul.

---

e 11 Some Septuagint manuscripts; Hebrew *not gather around*
f 14 Or *injurious*; also in verses 15, 16 and 23

King James

21And David came to Saul, and stood before him: and he loved him greatly; and he became his armourbearer.

22And Saul sent to Jesse, saying, Let David, I pray thee, stand before me; for he hath found favour in my sight.

23And it came to pass, when the *evil* spirit from God was upon Saul, that David took an harp, and played with his hand: so Saul was refreshed, and was well, and the evil spirit departed from him.

David and Goliath

17 NOW THE Philistines gathered together their armies to battle, and were gathered together at Shochoh, which *belongeth* to Judah, and pitched between Shochoh and Azekah, in *j*Ephes-dammim.

2And Saul and the men of Israel were gathered together, and pitched by the valley of Elah, and *k*set the battle in array against the Philistines.

3And the Philistines stood on a mountain on the one side, and Israel stood on a mountain on the other side: and *there was* a valley between them.

4 ¶ And there went out a champion out of the camp of the Philistines, named Goliath, of Gath, whose height *was* six cubits and a span.

5And *he had* an helmet of brass upon his head, and he was *l*armed with a coat of mail; and the weight of the coat *was* five thousand shekels of brass.

6And *he had* greaves of brass upon his legs, and a *m*target of brass between his shoulders.

7And the staff of his spear *was* like a weaver's beam; and his spear's head *weighed* six hundred shekels of iron: and one bearing a shield went before him.

8And he stood and cried unto the armies of Israel, and said unto them, Why are ye come out to set *your* battle in array? *am* not I a Philistine, and ye servants to Saul? choose you a man for you, and let him come down to me.

9If he be able to fight with me, and to kill me, then will we be your servants: but if I prevail against him, and kill him, then shall ye be our servants, and serve us.

10And the Philistine said, I defy the armies of Israel this day; give me a man, that we may fight together.

11When Saul and all Israel heard those words of the Philistine, they were dismayed, and greatly afraid.

12 ¶ Now David *was* the son of that Ephrathite of Bethlehem-judah, whose name *was* Jesse; and he had eight sons: and the man went among men *for* an old man in the days of Saul.

13And the three eldest sons of Jesse went *and* followed Saul to the battle: and the names of his three sons that went to the battle *were* Eliab the firstborn, and next unto him Abinadab, and the third Shammah.

14And David *was* the youngest: and the three eldest followed Saul.

15But David went and returned from Saul to feed his father's sheep at Bethlehem.

16And the Philistine drew near morning and evening, and presented himself forty days.

17And Jesse said unto David his son, Take now for thy brethren an ephah of this parched *corn*, and these ten loaves, and run to the camp to thy brethren;

18And carry these ten *n*cheeses unto the *o*captain of *their* thousand, and look how thy brethren fare, and take their pledge.

19Now Saul, and they, and all the men of Israel, *were* in the valley of Elah, fighting with the Philistines.

20 ¶ And David rose up early in the morning, and left the sheep with a keeper, and took, and went, as Jesse had commanded him; and he came to the *p*trench, as the host was going forth to the *q*fight, and shouted for the battle.

Amplified

21And David came to Saul and served him. Saul became very fond of him, and he became his armor-bearer.

22Saul sent to Jesse, saying, Let David remain in my service, for he pleases me.

23And when the evil spirit from God was upon Saul, David took a lyre and played it; so Saul was refreshed and became well, and the evil spirit left him.

17 NOW THE Philistines gathered their armies for battle and were assembled at Socoh, which belongs to Judah, and encamped between Socoh and Azekah in Ephes-dammim.

2Saul and the men of Israel were encamped in the Valley of Elah and drew up in battle array against the Philistines.

3And the Philistines stood on a mountain on one side and Israel stood on a mountain on the other side, with the valley between them.

4And a champion went out of the camp of the Philistines named Goliath of Gath, whose height was six cubits and a span [almost ten feet].

5And he had a bronze helmet on his head and wore a coat of mail, and the coat weighed 5,000 shekels of bronze.

6He had bronze shin armor on his legs and a bronze javelin across his shoulders.

7And the shaft of his spear was like a weaver's beam; his spear's head weighed 600 shekels of iron. And a shield bearer went before him.

8Goliath stood and shouted to the ranks of Israel, Why have you come out to draw up for battle? Am I not a Philistine, and are you not servants of Saul? Choose a man for yourselves and let him come down to me.

9If he is able to fight with me and kill me, then we will be your servants; but if I prevail against him and kill him, then you shall be our servants and serve us.

10And the Philistine said, I defy the ranks of Israel this day; give me a man, that we may fight together.

11When Saul and all Israel heard those words of the Philistine, they were dismayed and greatly afraid.

12David was the son of an Ephrathite of Bethlehem in Judah named Jesse, who had eight sons. [Jesse] in the days of Saul was old, advanced in years.

13[His] three eldest sons had followed Saul into battle. Their names were Eliab the firstborn; next, Abinadab; and third, Shammah.

14David was the youngest. The three eldest followed Saul,

15But David went back and forth from Saul to feed his father's sheep at Bethlehem.

16The Philistine came out morning and evening, presenting himself for forty days.

17And Jesse said to David his son, Take for your brothers an ephah of this parched grain and these ten loaves and carry them quickly to your brothers at the camp.

18Also take these ten cheeses to the commander of their thousand. See how your brothers fare and bring some token from them.

19Now Saul and the brothers and all the men of Israel were in the Valley of Elah, fighting with the Philistines.

20So David rose up early next morning, left the sheep with a keeper, took the provisions and went, as Jesse had commanded him. And he came to the encampment as the host going forth to the battleground shouted the battle cry.

---

*j*Or, *The coast of Dammim,* called *Pas-dammim* in 1 Chr. 11:13
*k*Heb. *ranged the battle*   *l*Heb. *clothed*   *m*Or, *gorget*
*n*Heb. *cheeses of milk*   *o*Heb. *captain of a thousand*   *p*Or,
place of the carriage   *q*Or, *battle array,* or, *place of fight*

New American Standard

²¹ Then David came to Saul and attended him; and Saul loved him greatly, and he became his armor bearer. ²² Saul sent to Jesse, saying, "Let David now stand before me, for he has found favor in my sight." ²³ So it came about whenever the *evil* spirit from God came to Saul, David would take the harp and play *it* with his hand; and Saul would be refreshed and be well, and the evil spirit would depart from him.

Goliath's Challenge

17 NOW THE Philistines gathered their armies for battle; and they were gathered at Socoh which belongs to Judah, and they camped between Socoh and Azekah, in Ephes-dammim.
² Saul and the men of Israel were gathered and camped in the valley of Elah, and drew up in battle array to encounter the Philistines.
³ The Philistines stood on the mountain on one side while Israel stood on the mountain on the other side, with the valley between them.
⁴ Then a champion came out from the armies of the Philistines named Goliath, from Gath, whose height was six *j*cubits and a span.
⁵ *He had* a bronze helmet on his head, and he was clothed with scale-armor which weighed five thousand shekels of bronze.
⁶ *He* also *had* bronze *k*greaves on his legs and a bronze javelin *slung* between his shoulders.
⁷ The shaft of his spear was like a weaver's beam, and the head of his spear *weighed* six hundred shekels of iron; his shield-carrier also walked before him.
⁸ He stood and shouted to the ranks of Israel and said to them, "Why do you come out to draw up in battle array? Am I not the Philistine and you servants of Saul? Choose a man for yourselves and let him come down to me.
⁹"If he is able to fight with me and kill me, then we will become your servants; but if I prevail against him and kill him, then you shall become our servants and serve us."
¹⁰ Again the Philistine said, "I defy the ranks of Israel this day; give me a man that we may fight together."
¹¹ When Saul and all Israel heard these words of the Philistine, they were dismayed and greatly afraid.
¹² ¶ Now David was the son of the Ephrathite of Bethlehem in Judah, whose name was Jesse, and he had eight sons. And Jesse was old in the days of Saul, advanced *in years* among men.
¹³ The three older sons of Jesse had gone after Saul to the battle. And the names of his three sons who went to the battle were Eliab the firstborn, and the second to him Abinadab, and the third Shammah.
¹⁴ David was the youngest. Now the three oldest followed Saul,
¹⁵ but David went back and forth from Saul to tend his father's flock at Bethlehem.
¹⁶ The Philistine came forward morning and evening for forty days and took his stand.
¹⁷ ¶ Then Jesse said to David his son, "Take now for your brothers an ephah of this roasted grain and these ten loaves and run to the camp to your brothers.
¹⁸"Bring also these ten cuts of cheese to the commander of *their* thousand, and look into the welfare of your brothers, and bring back news of them.
¹⁹"For Saul and they and all the men of Israel are in the valley of Elah, fighting with the Philistines."

David Accepts the Challenge

²⁰ ¶ So David arose early in the morning and left the flock with a keeper and took *the supplies* and went as Jesse had commanded him. And he came to the circle of the camp while the army was going out in battle array shouting the war cry.

*j*I.e. One cubit equals approx 18 in.   *k*Or *shin guards*

New International

²¹David came to Saul and entered his service. Saul liked him very much, and David became one of his armor-bearers. ²²Then Saul sent word to Jesse, saying, "Allow David to remain in my service, for I am pleased with him."
²³Whenever the spirit from God came upon Saul, David would take his harp and play. Then relief would come to Saul; he would feel better, and the evil spirit would leave him.

David and Goliath

17 NOW THE Philistines gathered their forces for war and assembled at Socoh in Judah. They pitched camp at Ephes Dammim, between Socoh and Azekah. ²Saul and the Israelites assembled and camped in the Valley of Elah and drew up their battle line to meet the Philistines. ³The Philistines occupied one hill and the Israelites another, with the valley between them.
⁴A champion named Goliath, who was from Gath, came out of the Philistine camp. He was over nine feet*g* tall. ⁵He had a bronze helmet on his head and wore a coat of scale armor of bronze weighing five thousand shekels*h*; ⁶on his legs he wore bronze greaves, and a bronze javelin was slung on his back. ⁷His spear shaft was like a weaver's rod, and its iron point weighed six hundred shekels.*i* His shield bearer went ahead of him.
⁸Goliath stood and shouted to the ranks of Israel, "Why do you come out and line up for battle? Am I not a Philistine, and are you not the servants of Saul? Choose a man and have him come down to me. ⁹If he is able to fight and kill me, we will become your subjects; but if I overcome him and kill him, you will become our subjects and serve us." ¹⁰Then the Philistine said, "This day I defy the ranks of Israel! Give me a man and let us fight each other." ¹¹On hearing the Philistine's words, Saul and all the Israelites were dismayed and terrified.
¹²Now David was the son of an Ephrathite named Jesse, who was from Bethlehem in Judah. Jesse had eight sons, and in Saul's time he was old and well advanced in years. ¹³Jesse's three oldest sons had followed Saul to the war: The firstborn was Eliab; the second, Abinadab; and the third, Shammah. ¹⁴David was the youngest. The three oldest followed Saul, ¹⁵but David went back and forth from Saul to tend his father's sheep at Bethlehem.
¹⁶For forty days the Philistine came forward every morning and evening and took his stand.
¹⁷Now Jesse said to his son David, "Take this ephah*j* of roasted grain and these ten loaves of bread for your brothers and hurry to their camp. ¹⁸Take along these ten cheeses to the commander of their unit.*k* See how your brothers are and bring back some assurance*l* from them. ¹⁹They are with Saul and all the men of Israel in the Valley of Elah, fighting against the Philistines."
²⁰Early in the morning David left the flock with a shepherd, loaded up and set out, as Jesse had directed. He reached the camp as the army was going out to its battle

^g4 Hebrew *was six cubits and a span* (about 3 meters)   ^h5 That is, about 125 pounds (about 57 kilograms)   ⁱ7 That is, about 15 pounds (about 7 kilograms)   ^j17 That is, probably about 3/5 bushel (about 22 liters)   ^k18 Hebrew *thousand*   ^l18 Or *some token*; or *some pledge of spoils*

King James

21For Israel and the Philistines had put the battle in array, army against army.

22And David left *his carriage in the hand of the keeper of the carriage, and ran into the army, and came and saluted his brethren.

23And as he talked with them, behold, there came up the champion, the Philistine of Gath, Goliath by name, out of the armies of the Philistines, and spake according to the same words: and David heard *them.

24And all the men of Israel, when they saw the man, fled *from him, and were sore afraid.

25And the men of Israel said, Have ye seen this man that is come up? surely to defy Israel is he come up: and it shall be, *that the man who killeth him, the king will enrich him with great riches, and will give him his daughter, and make his father's house free in Israel.

26And David spake to the men that stood by him, saying, What shall be done to the man that killeth this Philistine, and taketh away the reproach from Israel? for who *is this uncircumcised Philistine, that he should defy the armies of the living God?

27And the people answered him after this manner, saying, So shall it be done to the man that killeth him.

28 ¶ And Eliab his eldest brother heard when he spake unto the men; and Eliab's anger was kindled against David, and he said, Why camest thou down hither? and with whom hast thou left those few sheep in the wilderness? I know thy pride, and the naughtiness of thine heart; for thou art come down that thou mightest see the battle.

29And David said, What have I now done? *Is there* not a cause?

30 ¶ And he turned from him toward another, and spake after the same *manner: and the people answered him again after the former manner.

31And when the words were heard which David spake, they rehearsed *them* before Saul: and he *sent for him.

32 ¶ And David said to Saul, Let no man's heart fail because of him; thy servant will go and fight with this Philistine.

33And Saul said to David, Thou art not able to go against this Philistine to fight with him: for thou *art but* a youth, and he a man of war from his youth.

34And David said unto Saul, Thy servant kept his father's sheep, and there came a lion, and a bear, and took a *lamb out of the flock:

35And I went out after him, and smote him, and delivered *it* out of his mouth: and when he arose against me, I caught *him* by his beard, and smote him, and slew him.

36Thy servant slew both the lion and the bear: and this uncircumcised Philistine shall be as one of them, seeing he hath defied the armies of the living God.

37David said moreover, The LORD that delivered me out of the paw of the lion, and out of the paw of the bear, he will deliver me out of the hand of this Philistine. And Saul said unto David, Go, and the LORD be with thee.

38 ¶ And Saul *armed David with his armour, and he put an helmet of brass upon his head; also he armed him with a coat of mail.

39And David girded his sword upon his armour, and he assayed to go; for he had not proved *it.* And David said unto Saul, I cannot go with these; for I have not proved *them.* And David put them off him.

40And he took his staff in his hand, and chose him five smooth stones out of the *brook, and put them in a shepherd's *bag which he had, even in a scrip; and his sling *was* in his hand: and he drew near to the Philistine.

41And the Philistine came on and drew near unto David; and the man that bare the shield *went* before him.

42And when the Philistine looked about, and saw David, he disdained him: for he was *but* a youth, and ruddy, and of a fair countenance.

Amplified

21And Israel and the Philistines put the battle in array, army against army.

22David left his packages in the care of the baggage keeper and ran into the ranks and came and greeted his brothers.

23As they talked, behold, Goliath, the champion, the Philistine of Gath, came forth from the Philistine ranks and spoke the same words as before, and David heard him.

24And all the men of Israel, when they saw the man, fled from him, terrified.

25And the Israelites said, Have you seen this man who has come out? Surely he has come out to defy Israel; and the man who kills him the king will enrich with great riches, and will give him his daughter and make his father's house free [from taxes and service] in Israel.

26And David said to the men standing by him, What shall be done for the man who kills this Philistine and takes away the reproach from Israel? For who is this uncircumcised Philistine that he should defy the armies of the living God?

27And the [men] told him, Thus shall it be done for the man who kills him.

28Now Eliab his eldest brother heard what he said to the men; and Eliab's anger was kindled against David and he said, Why did you come here? With whom have you left those few sheep in the wilderness? I know your presumption and evilness of heart; for you came down that you might see the battle.

29And David said, What have I done now? Was it not a harmless question?

30And David turned away from Eliab to another and he asked the same question, and again the men gave him the same answer.

31When David's words were heard, they were repeated to Saul, and he sent for him.

32David said to Saul, Let no man's heart fail because of this Philistine; your servant will go out and fight with him.

33And Saul said to David, You are not able to go to fight against this Philistine. You are only an adolescent, and he has been a warrior from his youth.

34And David said to Saul, Your servant kept his father's sheep. And when there came a lion or again a bear and took a lamb out of the flock,

35I went out after it and smote it and delivered the lamb out of its mouth; and when it arose against me, I caught it by its beard and smote it and killed it.

36Your servant killed both the lion and the bear; and this uncircumcised Philistine shall be like one of them, for he has defied the armies of the living God!

37David said, The Lord Who delivered me out of the paw of the lion and out of the paw of the bear, He will deliver me out of the hand of this Philistine. And Saul said to David, Go, and the Lord be with you!

38Then Saul clothed David with his armor; he put a bronze helmet on his head and clothed him with a coat of mail.

39And David girded his sword over his armor. Then he tried to go, but could not, for he was not used to it. And David said to Saul, I cannot go with these, for I am not used to them. And David took them off.

40Then he took his staff in his hand and chose five smooth stones out of the brook and put them in his shepherd's [lunch] bag [a whole kid's skin slung from his shoulder], in his pouch, and his sling was in his hand, and he drew near the Philistine.

41The Philistine came on and drew near to David, the man who bore the shield going before him.

42And when the Philistine looked around and saw David, he scorned *and* despised him, for he was but an adolescent, with a healthy reddish color and a fair face.

---

*Heb. *the vessels from upon him*   *Heb. *from his face*   *Heb.
word   *Heb. *took him*   *Or, *kid*   *Heb. *clothed David
with his clothes*   *Or, *valley*   *Heb. *vessel*

New American Standard

21 Israel and the Philistines drew up in battle array, army against army.

22 Then David left his baggage in the care of the baggage keeper, and ran to the battle line and entered in order to greet his brothers.

23 As he was talking with them, behold, the champion, the Philistine from Gath named Goliath, was coming up from the army of the Philistines, and he spoke these same words; and David heard *them*.

24 ¶ When all the men of Israel saw the man, they fled from him and were greatly afraid.

25 The men of Israel said, "Have you seen this man who is coming up? Surely he is coming up to defy Israel. And it will be that the king will enrich the man who kills him with great riches and will give him his daughter and make his father's house *l*free in Israel."

26 ¶ Then David spoke to the men who were standing by him, saying, "What will be done for the man who kills this Philistine and takes away the reproach from Israel? For who is this uncircumcised Philistine, that he should taunt the armies of the living God?"

27 The people answered him in accord with this word, saying, "Thus it will be done for the man who kills him."

28 ¶ Now Eliab his oldest brother heard when he spoke to the men; and Eliab's anger burned against David and he said, "Why have you come down? And with whom have you left those few sheep in the wilderness? I know your insolence and the wickedness of your heart; for you have come down in order to see the battle."

29 But David said, "What have I done now? Was it not just a question?"

30 Then he turned away from him to another and said the same thing; and the people answered the same thing as before.

David Kills Goliath

31 ¶ When the words which David spoke were heard, they told *them* to Saul, and he sent for him.

32 David said to Saul, "Let no man's heart fail on account of him; your servant will go and fight with this Philistine."

33 Then Saul said to David, "You are not able to go against this Philistine to fight with him; for you are *but* a youth while he has been a warrior from his youth."

34 But David said to Saul, "Your servant was tending his father's sheep. When a lion or a bear came and took a lamb from the flock,

35 I went out after him and attacked him, and rescued *it* from his mouth; and when he rose up against me, I seized *him* by his beard and struck him and killed him.

36 "Your servant has killed both the lion and the bear; and this uncircumcised Philistine will be like one of them, since he has taunted the armies of the living God."

37 And David said, "The LORD who delivered me from the paw of the lion and from the paw of the bear, He will deliver me from the hand of this Philistine." And Saul said to David, "Go, and may the LORD be with you."

38 Then Saul clothed David with his garments and put a bronze helmet on his head, and he clothed him with armor.

39 David girded his sword over his armor and tried to walk, for he had not tested *them*. So David said to Saul, "I cannot go with these, for I have not tested *them*." And David took them off.

40 He took his stick in his hand and chose for himself five smooth stones from the brook, and put them in the shepherd's bag which he had, even in *his* pouch, and his sling was in his hand; and he approached the Philistine.

41 ¶ Then the Philistine came on and approached David, with the shield-bearer in front of him.

42 When the Philistine looked and saw David, he disdained him; for he was *but* a youth, and ruddy, with a handsome appearance.

New International

positions, shouting the war cry. 21 Israel and the Philistines were drawing up their lines facing each other. 22 David left his things with the keeper of supplies, ran to the battle lines and greeted his brothers. 23 As he was talking with them, Goliath, the Philistine champion from Gath, stepped out from his lines and shouted his usual defiance, and David heard it. 24 When the Israelites saw the man, they all ran from him in great fear.

25 Now the Israelites had been saying, "Do you see how this man keeps coming out? He comes out to defy Israel. The king will give great wealth to the man who kills him. He will also give him his daughter in marriage and will exempt his father's family from taxes in Israel."

26 David asked the men standing near him, "What will be done for the man who kills this Philistine and removes this disgrace from Israel? Who is this uncircumcised Philistine that he should defy the armies of the living God?"

27 They repeated to him what they had been saying and told him, "This is what will be done for the man who kills him."

28 When Eliab, David's oldest brother, heard him speaking with the men, he burned with anger at him and asked, "Why have you come down here? And with whom did you leave those few sheep in the desert? I know how conceited you are and how wicked your heart is; you came down only to watch the battle."

29 "Now what have I done?" said David. "Can't I even speak?" 30 He then turned away to someone else and brought up the same matter, and the men answered him as before. 31 What David said was overheard and reported to Saul, and Saul sent for him.

32 David said to Saul, "Let no one lose heart on account of this Philistine; your servant will go and fight him."

33 Saul replied, "You are not able to go out against this Philistine and fight him; you are only a boy, and he has been a fighting man from his youth."

34 But David said to Saul, "Your servant has been keeping his father's sheep. When a lion or a bear came and carried off a sheep from the flock, 35 I went after it, struck it and rescued the sheep from its mouth. When it turned on me, I seized it by its hair, struck it and killed it. 36 Your servant has killed both the lion and the bear; this uncircumcised Philistine will be like one of them, because he has defied the armies of the living God. 37 The LORD who delivered me from the paw of the lion and the paw of the bear will deliver me from the hand of this Philistine."

Saul said to David, "Go, and the LORD be with you."

38 Then Saul dressed David in his own tunic. He put a coat of armor on him and a bronze helmet on his head. 39 David fastened on his sword over the tunic and tried walking around, because he was not used to them.

"I cannot go in these," he said to Saul, "because I am not used to them." So he took them off. 40 Then he took his staff in his hand, chose five smooth stones from the stream, put them in the pouch of his shepherd's bag and, with his sling in his hand, approached the Philistine.

41 Meanwhile, the Philistine, with his shield bearer in front of him, kept coming closer to David. 42 He looked David over and saw that he was only a boy, ruddy and

---

*l*I.e. free from taxes and public service

King James

⁴³And the Philistine said unto David, *Am* I a dog, that thou comest to me with staves? And the Philistine cursed David by his gods.

⁴⁴And the Philistine said to David, Come to me, and I will give thy flesh unto the fowls of the air, and to the beasts of the field.

⁴⁵Then said David to the Philistine, Thou comest to me with a sword, and with a spear, and with a shield: but I come to thee in the name of the LORD of hosts, the God of the armies of Israel, whom thou hast defied.

⁴⁶This day will the LORD ᶻdeliver thee into mine hand; and I will smite thee, and take thine head from thee; and I will give the carcases of the host of the Philistines this day unto the fowls of the air, and to the wild beasts of the earth; that all the earth may know that there is a God in Israel.

⁴⁷And all this assembly shall know that the LORD saveth not with sword and spear: for the battle *is* the LORD'S, and he will give you into our hands.

⁴⁸And it came to pass, when the Philistine arose, and came and drew nigh to meet David, that David hasted, and ran toward the army to meet the Philistine.

⁴⁹And David put his hand in his bag, and took thence a stone, and slang *it,* and smote the Philistine in his forehead, that the stone sunk into his forehead; and he fell upon his face to the earth.

⁵⁰So David prevailed over the Philistine with a sling and with a stone, and smote the Philistine, and slew him; but *there was* no sword in the hand of David.

⁵¹Therefore David ran, and stood upon the Philistine, and took his sword, and drew it out of the sheath thereof, and slew him, and cut off his head therewith. And when the Philistines saw their champion was dead, they fled.

⁵²And the men of Israel and of Judah arose, and shouted, and pursued the Philistines, until thou come to the valley, and to the gates of Ekron. And the wounded of the Philistines fell down by the way to Shaaraim, even unto Gath, and unto Ekron.

⁵³And the children of Israel returned from chasing after the Philistines, and they spoiled their tents.

⁵⁴And David took the head of the Philistine, and brought it to Jerusalem; but he put his armour in his tent.

⁵⁵ ¶ And when Saul saw David go forth against the Philistine, he said unto Abner, the captain of the host, Abner, whose son *is* this youth? And Abner said, *As* thy soul liveth, O king, I cannot tell.

⁵⁶And the king said, Inquire thou whose son the stripling *is.*

⁵⁷And as David returned from the slaughter of the Philistine, Abner took him, and brought him before Saul with the head of the Philistine in his hand.

⁵⁸And Saul said to him, Whose son *art* thou, *thou* young man? And David answered, *I am* the son of thy servant Jesse the Bethlehemite.

Saul's hatred of David

18

AND IT came to pass, when he had made an end of speaking unto Saul, that the soul of Jonathan was knit with the soul of David, and Jonathan loved him as his own soul.

²And Saul took him that day, and would let him go no more home to his father's house.

³Then Jonathan and David made a covenant, because he loved him as his own soul.

⁴And Jonathan stripped himself of the robe that *was* upon him, and gave it to David, and his garments, even to his sword, and to his bow, and to his girdle.

⁵ ¶ And David went out whithersoever Saul sent him, *and* ᵃbehaved himself wisely: and Saul set him over the men of war, and he was accepted in the sight of all the people, and also in the sight of Saul's servants.

Amplified

⁴³And the Philistine said to David, Am I a dog, that you should come to me with sticks? And the Philistine cursed David by his gods.

⁴⁴The Philistine said to David, Come to me, and I will give your flesh to the birds of the air and the beasts of the field.

⁴⁵Then said David to the Philistine, You come to me with a sword, a spear, and a javelin, but I come to you in the name of the Lord of hosts, the God of the ranks of Israel, Whom you have defied.

⁴⁶This day the Lord will deliver you into my hand, and I will smite you and cut off your head. And I will give the corpses of the army of the Philistines this day to the birds of the air and the wild beasts of the earth, that all the earth may know that there is a God in Israel.

⁴⁷And all this assembly shall know that the Lord saves not with sword and spear; for the battle is the Lord's, and He will give you into our hands.

⁴⁸When the Philistine came forward to meet David, David ran quickly toward the battle line to meet the Philistine.

⁴⁹David put his hand into his bag and took out a stone and slung it, and it struck the Philistine, sinking into his forehead, and he fell on his face to the earth.

⁵⁰So David prevailed over the Philistine with a sling and with a stone, and struck down the Philistine and slew him. But no sword was in David's hand.

⁵¹So he ran and stood over the Philistine, took his sword and drew it out of its sheath, and killed him, and cut off his head with it. When the Philistines saw that their mighty champion was dead, they fled.

⁵²And the men of Israel and Judah rose with a shout and pursued the Philistines as far as Gath and the gates of Ekron. So the wounded Philistines fell along the way from Shaaraim as far as Gath and Ekron.

⁵³The Israelites returned from their pursuit of the Philistines and plundered their tents.

⁵⁴David took the head of the Philistine and brought it to Jerusalem, but he put his armor in his tent.

⁵⁵When Saul saw David go out against the Philistine, he said to Abner, the captain of the host, Abner, whose son is this youth? And Abner said, As your soul lives, O king, I cannot tell.

⁵⁶And the king said, Inquire whose son the stripling is.

⁵⁷When David returned from killing Goliath the Philistine, Abner brought him before Saul with the head of the Philistine in his hand.

⁵⁸And Saul said to him, Whose son are you, young man? And David answered, I am the son of your servant Jesse of Bethlehem.

18

WHEN DAVID had finished speaking to Saul, the soul of Jonathan was knit with the soul of David, and Jonathan loved him as his own life.

²Saul took David that day and would not let him return to his father's house.

³Then Jonathan made a covenant with David, because he loved him as his own life.

⁴And Jonathan stripped himself of the robe that was on him and gave it to David, and his armor, even his sword, his bow, and his girdle.

⁵And David went out wherever Saul sent him, and prospered *and* behaved himself wisely; and Saul set him over the men of war. And it was satisfactory both to the people and to Saul's servants.

ᶻHeb. *shut thee up*   ᵃOr, *prospered;* see ver. 14,15,30

New American Standard

43 The Philistine said to David, "Am I a dog, that you come to me with sticks?" And the Philistine cursed David by his gods.

44 The Philistine also said to David, "Come to me, and I will give your flesh to the birds of the sky and the beasts of the field."

45 Then David said to the Philistine, "You come to me with a sword, a spear, and a javelin, but I come to you in the name of the LORD of hosts, the God of the armies of Israel, whom you have taunted.

46 "This day the LORD will deliver you up into my hands, and I will strike you down and remove your head from you. And I will give the dead bodies of the army of the Philistines this day to the birds of the sky and the wild beasts of the earth, that all the earth may know that there is a God in Israel,

47 and that all this assembly may know that the LORD does not deliver by sword or by spear; for the battle is the LORD's and He will give you into our hands."

48 ¶ Then it happened when the Philistine rose and came and drew near to meet David, that David ran quickly toward the battle line to meet the Philistine.

49 And David put his hand into his bag and took from it a stone and slung it, and struck the Philistine on his forehead. And the stone sank into his forehead, so that he fell on his face to the ground.

50 ¶ Thus David prevailed over the Philistine with a sling and a stone, and he struck the Philistine and killed him; but there was no sword in David's hand.

51 Then David ran and stood over the Philistine and took his sword and drew it out of its sheath and killed him, and cut off his head with it. When the Philistines saw that their champion was dead, they fled.

52 The men of Israel and Judah arose and shouted and pursued the Philistines as far as the valley, and to the gates of Ekron. And the slain Philistines lay along the way to Shaaraim, even to Gath and Ekron.

53 The sons of Israel returned from chasing the Philistines and plundered their camps.

54 Then David took the Philistine's head and brought it to Jerusalem, but he put his weapons in his tent.

55 ¶ Now when Saul saw David going out against the Philistine, he said to Abner the commander of the army, "Abner, whose son is this young man?" And Abner said, "By your life, O king, I do not know."

56 The king said, "You inquire whose son the youth is."

57 So when David returned from killing the Philistine, Abner took him and brought him before Saul with the Philistine's head in his hand.

58 Saul said to him, "Whose son are you, young man?" And David answered, "*I am* the son of your servant Jesse the Bethlehemite."

New International

handsome, and he despised him. 43He said to David, "Am I a dog, that you come at me with sticks?" And the Philistine cursed David by his gods. 44"Come here," he said, "and I'll give your flesh to the birds of the air and the beasts of the field!"

45David said to the Philistine, "You come against me with sword and spear and javelin, but I come against you in the name of the LORD Almighty, the God of the armies of Israel, whom you have defied. 46This day the LORD will hand you over to me, and I'll strike you down and cut off your head. Today I will give the carcasses of the Philistine army to the birds of the air and the beasts of the earth, and the whole world will know that there is a God in Israel. 47All those gathered here will know that it is not by sword or spear that the LORD saves; for the battle is the LORD's, and he will give all of you into our hands."

48As the Philistine moved closer to attack him, David ran quickly toward the battle line to meet him. 49Reaching into his bag and taking out a stone, he slung it and struck the Philistine on the forehead. The stone sank into his forehead, and he fell facedown on the ground.

50So David triumphed over the Philistine with a sling and a stone; without a sword in his hand he struck down the Philistine and killed him.

51David ran and stood over him. He took hold of the Philistine's sword and drew it from the scabbard. After he killed him, he cut off his head with the sword.

When the Philistines saw that their hero was dead, they turned and ran. 52Then the men of Israel and Judah surged forward with a shout and pursued the Philistines to the entrance of Gath[m] and to the gates of Ekron. Their dead were strewn along the Shaaraim road to Gath and Ekron. 53When the Israelites returned from chasing the Philistines, they plundered their camp. 54David took the Philistine's head and brought it to Jerusalem, and he put the Philistine's weapons in his own tent.

55As Saul watched David going out to meet the Philistine, he said to Abner, commander of the army, "Abner, whose son is that young man?"

Abner replied, "As surely as you live, O king, I don't know."

56The king said, "Find out whose son this young man is."

57As soon as David returned from killing the Philistine, Abner took him and brought him before Saul, with David still holding the Philistine's head.

58"Whose son are you, young man?" Saul asked him.

David said, "I am the son of your servant Jesse of Bethlehem."

Jonathan and David

18 NOW IT came about when he had finished speaking to Saul, that the soul of Jonathan was knit to the soul of David, and Jonathan loved him as himself.

2 Saul took him that day and did not let him return to his father's house.

3 Then Jonathan made a covenant with David because he loved him as himself.

4 Jonathan stripped himself of the robe that was on him and gave it to David, with his armor, including his sword and his bow and his belt.

5 So David went out wherever Saul sent him, *and* prospered; and Saul set him over the men of war. And it was pleasing in the sight of all the people and also in the sight of Saul's servants.

Saul's Jealousy of David

18 AFTER DAVID had finished talking with Saul, Jonathan became one in spirit with David, and he loved him as himself. 2From that day Saul kept David with him and did not let him return to his father's house. 3And Jonathan made a covenant with David because he loved him as himself. 4Jonathan took off the robe he was wearing and gave it to David, along with his tunic, and even his sword, his bow and his belt.

5Whatever Saul sent him to do, David did it so successfully[n] that Saul gave him a high rank in the army. This pleased all the people, and Saul's officers as well.

m 52 Some Septuagint manuscripts; Hebrew *a valley*
n 5 Or *wisely*

King James

⁶And it came to pass as they came, when David was returned from the slaughter of the ^bPhilistine, that the women came out of all cities of Israel, singing and dancing, to meet king Saul, with tabrets, with joy, and with ^cinstruments of music.

⁷And the women answered *one another* as they played, and said, Saul hath slain his thousands, and David his ten thousands.

⁸And Saul was very wroth, and the saying ^ddispleased him; and he said, They have ascribed unto David ten thousands, and to me they have ascribed *but* thousands: and *what* can he have more but the kingdom?

⁹And Saul eyed David from that day and forward.

¹⁰ ¶ And it came to pass on the morrow, that the evil spirit from God came upon Saul, and he prophesied in the midst of the house: and David played with his hand, as at other times: and *there was* a javelin in Saul's hand.

¹¹And Saul cast the javelin; for he said, I will smite David even to the wall *with it.* And David avoided out of his presence twice.

¹² ¶ And Saul was afraid of David, because the LORD was with him, and was departed from Saul.

¹³Therefore Saul removed him from him, and made him his captain over a thousand; and he went out and came in before the people.

¹⁴And David ^ebehaved himself wisely in all his ways; and the LORD *was* with him.

¹⁵Wherefore when Saul saw that he behaved himself very wisely, he was afraid of him.

¹⁶But all Israel and Judah loved David, because he went out and came in before them.

¹⁷ ¶ And Saul said to David, Behold my elder daughter Merab, her will I give thee to wife: only be thou ^fvaliant for me, and fight the LORD'S battles. For Saul said, Let not mine hand be upon him, but let the hand of the Philistines be upon him.

¹⁸And David said unto Saul, Who *am* I? and what *is* my life, *or* my father's family in Israel, that I should be son-in-law to the king?

¹⁹But it came to pass at the time when Merab Saul's daughter should have been given to David, that she was given unto Adriel the Meholathite to wife.

²⁰And Michal Saul's daughter loved David: and they told Saul, and the thing ^gpleased him.

²¹And Saul said, I will give him her, that she may be a snare to him, and that the hand of the Philistines may be against him. Wherefore Saul said to David, Thou shalt this day be my son-in-law in the one of the twain.

²² ¶ And Saul commanded his servants, *saying,* Commune with David secretly, and say, Behold, the king hath delight in thee, and all his servants love thee: now therefore be the king's son-in-law.

²³And Saul's servants spake those words in the ears of David. And David said, Seemeth it to you *a* light *thing* to be a king's son-in-law, seeing that I *am* a poor man, and lightly esteemed?

²⁴And the servants of Saul told him, saying, ^hOn this manner spake David.

²⁵And Saul said, Thus shall ye say to David, The king desireth not any dowry, but an hundred foreskins of the Philistines, to be avenged of the king's enemies. But Saul thought to make David fall by the hand of the Philistines.

²⁶And when his servants told David these words, it pleased David well to be the king's son-in-law: and the days were not ⁱexpired.

Amplified

⁶As they were coming home, when David returned from killing the Philistine, the women came out of all the Israelite towns, singing and dancing, to meet King Saul with timbrels, songs of joy, and instruments of music.

⁷And the women responded as they laughed *and* frolicked, saying, Saul has slain his thousands, and David his ten thousands.

⁸And Saul was very angry, for the saying displeased him; and he said, They have ascribed to David ten thousands, but to me they have ascribed only thousands. What more can he have but the kingdom?

⁹And Saul [jealously] eyed David from that day forward.

¹⁰The next day an evil spirit from God came mightily upon Saul, and he raved [madly] in his house, while David played [the lyre] with his hand, as at other times; and there was a javelin in Saul's hand.

¹¹And Saul cast the javelin, for he thought, I will pin David to the wall. And David evaded him twice.

¹²Saul was afraid of David, because the Lord was with him but had departed from Saul.

¹³So Saul removed David from him and made him his commander over a thousand; and he went out and came in before the people.

¹⁴David acted wisely in all his ways *and* succeeded, and the Lord was with him.

¹⁵When Saul saw how capable *and* successful David was, he stood in awe of him.

¹⁶But all Israel and Judah loved David, for he went out and came in before them.

¹⁷Saul said to David, My elder daughter Merab I will give you as wife; only serve me courageously and fight the Lord's battles. For Saul thought, Let not my hand, but the Philistines' hand, be upon him.

¹⁸David said to Saul, Who am I, and what is my life or my father's family in Israel, that I should be the king's son-in-law?

¹⁹But at the time when Merab, Saul's daughter, should have been given to David, she was given to Adriel the Meholathite as wife.

²⁰Now Michal, Saul's daughter, loved David; and they told Saul, and it pleased him.

²¹Saul thought, I will give her to him that she may be a snare to him and that the hand of the Philistines may be against him. So Saul said to David a second time, You shall now be my son-in-law.

²²And Saul commanded his servants to speak to David privately and say, The king delights in you, and all his servants love you; now then, become [his] son-in-law.

²³Saul's servants told those words to David. David said, Does it seem to you a light thing to be a king's son-in-law, seeing I am a poor man and lightly esteemed?

²⁴And the servants of Saul told him what David said.

²⁵Saul said, Say this to David, The king wants no dowry but a hundred foreskins of the Philistines, to avenge himself of the king's enemies. But Saul thought to make David fall by the Philistines' hands.

²⁶When his servants told David these words, it pleased [him] well to become the king's son-in-law. Before the days expired,

---

^bOr, *Philistines*   ^cHeb. *threestringed instruments*   ^dHeb. *was evil in his eyes*   ^eOr, *prospered; see ver. 5*   ^fHeb. *a son of valour*   ^gHeb. *was right in his eyes*   ^hHeb. *According to these words*   ⁱHeb. *fulfilled*

New American Standard

6 ¶ It happened as they were coming, when David returned from killing the Philistine, that the women came out of all the cities of Israel, singing and dancing, to meet King Saul, with tambourines, with joy and with ᵐmusical instruments.

7 The women sang as they played, and said,
"Saul has slain his thousands,
And David his ten thousands."

8 Then Saul became very angry, for this saying displeased him; and he said, "They have ascribed to David ten thousands, but to me they have ascribed thousands. Now what more can he have but the kingdom?"

9 Saul looked at David with suspicion from that day on.

Saul Turns against David

10 ¶ Now it came about on the next day that an evil spirit from God came mightily upon Saul, and he raved in the midst of the house, while David was playing *the harp* with his hand, as usual; and a spear *was* in Saul's hand.

11 Saul hurled the spear for he thought, "I will pin David to the wall." But David escaped from his presence twice.

12 ¶ Now Saul was afraid of David, for the LORD was with him but had departed from Saul.

13 Therefore Saul removed him from his presence and appointed him as his commander of a thousand; and he went out and came in before the people.

14 David was prospering in all his ways for the LORD *was* with him.

15 When Saul saw that he was prospering greatly, he dreaded him.

16 But all Israel and Judah loved David, and he went out and came in before them.

17 ¶ Then Saul said to David, "Here is my older daughter Merab; I will give her to you as a wife, only be a valiant man for me and fight the LORD'S battles." For Saul thought, "My hand shall not be against him, but let the hand of the Philistines be against him."

18 But David said to Saul, "Who am I, and what is my life *or* my father's family in Israel, that I should be the king's son-in-law?"

19 So it came about at the time when Merab, Saul's daughter, should have been given to David, that she was given to Adriel the Meholathite for a wife.

David Marries Saul's Daughter

20 ¶ Now Michal, Saul's daughter, loved David. When they told Saul, the thing was agreeable to him.

21 Saul thought, "I will give her to him that she may become a snare to him, and that the hand of the Philistines may be against him." Therefore Saul said to David, "For a second time you may be my son-in-law today."

22 Then Saul commanded his servants, "Speak to David secretly, saying, 'Behold, the king delights in you, and all his servants love you; now therefore, become the king's son-in-law.'"

23 So Saul's servants spoke these words to David. But David said, "Is it trivial in your sight to become the king's son-in-law, since I am a poor man and lightly esteemed?"

24 The servants of Saul reported to him according to these words *which* David spoke.

25 Saul then said, "Thus you shall say to David, 'The king does not desire any dowry except a hundred foreskins of the Philistines, to take vengeance on the king's enemies.'" Now Saul planned to make David fall by the hand of the Philistines.

26 When his servants told David these words, it pleased David to become the king's son-in-law. Before the days had expired

New International

6When the men were returning home after David had killed the Philistine, the women came out from all the towns of Israel to meet King Saul with singing and dancing, with joyful songs and with tambourines and lutes. 7As they danced, they sang:

"Saul has slain his thousands,
and David his tens of thousands."

8Saul was very angry; this refrain galled him. "They have credited David with tens of thousands," he thought, "but me with only thousands. What more can he get but the kingdom?" 9And from that time on Saul kept a jealous eye on David.

10The next day an evilᵒ spirit from God came forcefully upon Saul. He was prophesying in his house, while David was playing the harp, as he usually did. Saul had a spear in his hand 11and he hurled it, saying to himself, "I'll pin David to the wall." But David eluded him twice.

12Saul was afraid of David, because the LORD was with David but had left Saul. 13So he sent David away from him and gave him command over a thousand men, and David led the troops in his campaigns. 14In everything he did he had great success,ᵖ because the LORD was with him. 15When Saul saw how successfulᵍ he was, he was afraid of him. 16But all Israel and Judah loved David, because he led them in their campaigns.

17Saul said to David, "Here is my older daughter Merab. I will give her to you in marriage; only serve me bravely and fight the battles of the LORD." For Saul said to himself, "I will not raise a hand against him. Let the Philistines do that!"

18But David said to Saul, "Who am I, and what is my family or my father's clan in Israel, that I should become the king's son-in-law?" 19Soʳ when the time came for Merab, Saul's daughter, to be given to David, she was given in marriage to Adriel of Meholah.

20Now Saul's daughter Michal was in love with David, and when they told Saul about it, he was pleased. 21"I will give her to him," he thought, "so that she may be a snare to him and so that the hand of the Philistines may be against him." So Saul said to David, "Now you have a second opportunity to become my son-in-law."

22Then Saul ordered his attendants: "Speak to David privately and say, 'Look, the king is pleased with you, and his attendants all like you; now become his son-in-law.'"

23They repeated these words to David. But David said, "Do you think it is a small matter to become the king's son-in-law? I'm only a poor man and little known."

24When Saul's servants told him what David had said, 25Saul replied, "Say to David, 'The king wants no other price for the bride than a hundred Philistine foreskins, to take revenge on his enemies.'" Saul's plan was to have David fall by the hands of the Philistines.

26When the attendants told David these things, he was pleased to become the king's son-in-law. So before the

---

ᵐ I.e. triangles; or three-stringed instruments

o 10 Or *injurious*   *p 14* Or *he was very wise*   *q 15* Or *wise*
r 19 Or *However,*

King James

²⁷Wherefore David arose and went, he and his men, and slew of the Philistines two hundred men; and David brought their foreskins, and they gave them in full tale to the king, that he might be the king's son-in-law. And Saul gave him Michal his daughter to wife.

²⁸ ¶ And Saul saw and knew that the LORD *was* with David, and *that* Michal Saul's daughter loved him.

²⁹And Saul was yet the more afraid of David; and Saul became David's enemy continually.

³⁰Then the princes of the Philistines went forth: and it came to pass, after they went forth, *that* David behaved himself more wisely than all the servants of Saul; so that his name was much *j*set by.

Saul tries to kill David

19 AND SAUL spake to Jonathan his son, and to all his servants, that they should kill David.

²But Jonathan Saul's son delighted much in David: but Jonathan told David, saying, Saul my father seeketh to kill thee: now therefore, I pray thee, take heed to thyself until the morning, and abide in a secret *place,* and hide thyself:

³And I will go out and stand beside my father in the field where thou *art,* and I will commune with my father of thee; and what I see, that I will tell thee.

⁴ ¶ And Jonathan spake good of David unto Saul his father, and said unto him, Let not the king sin against his servant, against David; because he hath not sinned against thee, and because his works *have been* to thee-ward very good:

⁵For he did put his life in his hand, and slew the Philistine, and the LORD wrought a great salvation for all Israel: thou sawest *it,* and didst rejoice: wherefore then wilt thou sin against innocent blood, to slay David without a cause?

⁶And Saul hearkened unto the voice of Jonathan: and Saul sware, *As* the LORD liveth, he shall not be slain.

⁷And Jonathan called David, and Jonathan showed him all those things. And Jonathan brought David to Saul, and he was in his presence, as *k*in times past.

⁸ ¶ And there was war again: and David went out, and fought with the Philistines, and slew them with a great slaughter; and they fled from *l*him.

⁹And the evil spirit from the LORD was upon Saul, as he sat in his house with his javelin in his hand: and David played with *his* hand.

¹⁰And Saul sought to smite David even to the wall with the javelin; but he slipped away out of Saul's presence, and he smote the javelin into the wall: and David fled, and escaped that night.

¹¹Saul also sent messengers unto David's house, to watch him, and to slay him in the morning: and Michal David's wife told him, saying, If thou save not thy life tonight, tomorrow thou shalt be slain.

¹² ¶ So Michal let David down through a window: and he went, and fled, and escaped.

¹³And Michal took an *m*image, and laid *it* in the bed, and put a pillow of goats' *hair* for his bolster, and covered *it* with a cloth.

¹⁴And when Saul sent messengers to take David, she said, He *is* sick.

¹⁵And Saul sent the messengers *again* to see David, saying, Bring him up to me in the bed, that I may slay him.

¹⁶And when the messengers were come in, behold, *there was* an image in the bed, with a pillow of goats' *hair* for his bolster.

¹⁷And Saul said unto Michal, Why hast thou deceived me so, and sent away mine enemy, that he is escaped? And Michal answered Saul, He said unto me, Let me go; why should I kill thee?

¹⁸ ¶ So David fled, and escaped, and came to Samuel to Ramah, and told him all that Saul had done to him. And he and Samuel went and dwelt in Naioth.

Amplified

²⁷David went, he and his men, and slew two hundred Philistine men, and brought their foreskins and gave them in full number to the king, that he might become the king's son-in-law. And Saul gave him Michal his daughter as wife.

²⁸When Saul saw and knew that the Lord was with David and that Michal [his] daughter loved him,

²⁹Saul was still more afraid of David; and Saul became David's constant enemy.

³⁰Then the Philistine princes came out to battle, and when they did so, David had more success *and* behaved himself more wisely than all Saul's servants, so that his name was very dear *and* highly esteemed.

19 NOW SAUL told Jonathan his son and all his servants that they must kill David.

²But Jonathan, Saul's son, delighted much in David, and he told David, Saul my father is seeking to kill you. Now therefore, take heed to yourself in the morning, and stay in a secret place and hide yourself.

³And I will go out and stand beside my father in the field where you are; and I will converse with my father about you and if I learn anything, I will tell you.

⁴And Jonathan spoke well of David to Saul his father and said to him, Let not the king sin against his servant David, for he has not sinned against you, and his deeds have been of good service to you.

⁵For he took his life in his hands and slew the Philistine, and the Lord wrought a great deliverance for all Israel; you saw it and rejoiced. Why then will you sin against innocent blood and kill David without a cause?

⁶Saul heeded Jonathan and swore, As the Lord lives, David shall not be slain.

⁷So Jonathan called David and told him all these things. And Jonathan brought David to Saul, and he was in his presence as in times past.

⁸Then there was war again, and David went out and fought with the Philistines, and made a great slaughter among them and they fled before him.

⁹Then an evil spirit from the Lord came upon Saul as he sat in his house with his spear in his hand; and David was playing [the lyre] with his hand.

¹⁰Saul sought to pin David to the wall with the spear, but he slipped away, so that Saul struck the spear into the wall. Then David fled and escaped that night.

¹¹Saul sent messengers that night to David's house to watch him, that he might kill him in the morning. But Michal, David's wife, told him, If you do not save your life tonight, tomorrow you will be killed.

¹²So Michal let David down through the window, and he fled and escaped.

¹³And Michal took the teraph (household good luck image) and laid it in the bed, put a pillow of goats' hair at its head, and covered it with a bedspread.

¹⁴And when Saul sent messengers to take David, she said, He is sick.

¹⁵Then Saul sent the messengers again to see David, saying, Bring him up to me in the bed, that I may slay him.

¹⁶And when the messengers came in, behold, there was an image in the bed, with a pillow of goats' hair at its head.

¹⁷Saul said to Michal, Why have you deceived me so and sent away my enemy so that he has escaped? Michal answered Saul, He said to me, Let me go. Why should I kill you?

¹⁸So David fled and escaped and came to Samuel at Ramah and told him all that Saul had done to him. And he and Samuel went and dwelt in Naioth.

---

j Heb. *precious*   *k* Heb. *yesterday third day*   *l* Heb. *his face*
m Heb. *teraphim*

New American Standard

27 David rose up and went, he and his men, and struck down two hundred men among the Philistines. Then David brought their foreskins, and they gave them in full number to the king, that he might become the king's son-in-law. So Saul gave him Michal his daughter for a wife. 28 When Saul saw and knew that the LORD was with David, and *that* Michal, Saul's daughter, loved him, 29 then Saul was even more afraid of David. Thus Saul was David's enemy continually.

30 ¶ Then the commanders of the Philistines went out *to battle,* and it happened as often as they went out, that David behaved himself more wisely than all the servants of Saul. So his name was highly esteemed.

David Protected from Saul

19 NOW SAUL told Jonathan his son and all his servants to put David to death. But Jonathan, Saul's son, greatly delighted in David. 2 So Jonathan told David saying, "Saul my father is seeking to put you to death. Now therefore, please be on guard in the morning, and stay in a secret place and hide yourself. 3 "I will go out and stand beside my father in the field where you are, and I will speak with my father about you; if I find out anything, then I will tell you." 4 Then Jonathan spoke well of David to Saul his father and said to him, "Do not let the king sin against his servant David, since he has not sinned against you, and since his deeds *have been* very beneficial to you. 5 "For he took his life in his hand and struck the Philistine, and the LORD brought about a great deliverance for all Israel; you saw *it* and rejoiced. Why then will you sin against innocent blood by putting David to death without a cause?" 6 Saul listened to the voice of Jonathan, and Saul vowed, "As the LORD lives, he shall not be put to death." 7 Then Jonathan called David, and Jonathan told him all these words. And Jonathan brought David to Saul, and he was in his presence as formerly.

8 ¶ When there was war again, David went out and fought with the Philistines and defeated them with great slaughter, so that they fled before him. 9 Now there was an evil spirit from the LORD on Saul as he was sitting in his house with his spear in his hand, and David was playing *the harp* with *his* hand. 10 Saul tried to pin David to the wall with the spear, but he slipped away out of Saul's presence, so that he stuck the spear into the wall. And David fled and escaped that night.

11 ¶ Then Saul sent messengers to David's house to watch him, in order to put him to death in the morning. But Michal, David's wife, told him, saying, "If you do not save your life tonight, tomorrow you will be put to death." 12 So Michal let David down through a window, and he went out and fled and escaped. 13 Michal took the household idol and laid *it* on the bed, and put a quilt of goats' *hair* at its head, and covered *it* with clothes. 14 When Saul sent messengers to take David, she said, "He is sick." 15 Then Saul sent messengers to see David, saying, "Bring him up to me on his bed, that I may put him to death." 16 When the messengers entered, behold, the household idol *was* on the bed with the quilt of goats' *hair* at its head. 17 So Saul said to Michal, "Why have you deceived me like this and let my enemy go, so that he has escaped?" And Michal said to Saul, "He said to me, 'Let me go! Why should I put you to death?'"

18 ¶ Now David fled and escaped and came to Samuel at Ramah, and told him all that Saul had done to him. And he and Samuel went and stayed in Naioth.

New International

allotted time elapsed, 27 David and his men went out and killed two hundred Philistines. He brought their foreskins and presented the full number to the king so that he might become the king's son-in-law. Then Saul gave him his daughter Michal in marriage. 28 When Saul realized that the LORD was with David and that his daughter Michal loved David, 29 Saul became still more afraid of him, and he remained his enemy the rest of his days.

30 The Philistine commanders continued to go out to battle, and as often as they did, David met with more success[s] than the rest of Saul's officers, and his name became well known.

Saul Tries to Kill David

19 SAUL TOLD his son Jonathan and all the attendants to kill David. But Jonathan was very fond of David 2 and warned him, "My father Saul is looking for a chance to kill you. Be on your guard tomorrow morning; go into hiding and stay there. 3 I will go out and stand with my father in the field where you are. I'll speak to him about you and will tell you what I find out."

4 Jonathan spoke well of David to Saul his father and said to him, "Let not the king do wrong to his servant David; he has not wronged you, and what he has done has benefited you greatly. 5 He took his life in his hands when he killed the Philistine. The LORD won a great victory for all Israel, and you saw it and were glad. Why then would you do wrong to an innocent man like David by killing him for no reason?"

6 Saul listened to Jonathan and took this oath: "As surely as the LORD lives, David will not be put to death."

7 So Jonathan called David and told him the whole conversation. He brought him to Saul, and David was with Saul as before.

8 Once more war broke out, and David went out and fought the Philistines. He struck them with such force that they fled before him.

9 But an evil[t] spirit from the LORD came upon Saul as he was sitting in his house with his spear in his hand. While David was playing the harp, 10 Saul tried to pin him to the wall with his spear, but David eluded him as Saul drove the spear into the wall. That night David made good his escape.

11 Saul sent men to David's house to watch it and to kill him in the morning. But Michal, David's wife, warned him, "If you don't run for your life tonight, tomorrow you'll be killed." 12 So Michal let David down through a window, and he fled and escaped. 13 Then Michal took an idol[u] and laid it on the bed, covering it with a garment and putting some goats' hair at the head.

14 When Saul sent the men to capture David, Michal said, "He is ill."

15 Then Saul sent the men back to see David and told them, "Bring him up to me in his bed so that I may kill him." 16 But when the men entered, there was the idol in the bed, and at the head was some goats' hair.

17 Saul said to Michal, "Why did you deceive me like this and send my enemy away so that he escaped?"

Michal told him, "He said to me, 'Let me get away. Why should I kill you?'"

18 When David had fled and made his escape, he went to Samuel at Ramah and told him all that Saul had done to him. Then he and Samuel went to Naioth and stayed there.

---

s 30 Or *David acted more wisely*   *t 9* Or *injurious*
u 13 Hebrew *teraphim*; also in verse 16

King James

¹⁹And it was told Saul, saying, Behold, David is at Naioth in Ramah.

²⁰And Saul sent messengers to take David: and when they saw the company of the prophets prophesying, and Samuel standing as appointed over them, the spirit of God was upon the messengers of Saul, and they also prophesied.

²¹And when it was told Saul, he sent other messengers, and they prophesied likewise. And Saul sent messengers again the third time, and they prophesied also.

²²Then went he also to Ramah, and came to a great well that is in Sechu: and he asked and said, Where are Samuel and David? And one said, Behold, they be at Naioth in Ramah.

²³And he went thither to Naioth in Ramah: and the spirit of God was upon him also, and he went on, and prophesied, until he came to Naioth in Ramah.

²⁴And he stripped off his clothes also, and prophesied before Samuel in like manner, and ⁿlay down naked all that day and all that night. Wherefore they say, Is Saul also among the prophets?

David and Jonathan

20 AND DAVID fled from Naioth in Ramah, and came and said before Jonathan, What have I done? what is mine iniquity? and what is my sin before thy father, that he seeketh my life?

²And he said unto him, God forbid; thou shalt not die: behold, my father will do nothing either great or small, but that he will show it me: and why should my father hide this thing from me? it is not so.

³And David sware moreover, and said, Thy father certainly knoweth that I have found grace in thine eyes; and he saith, Let not Jonathan know this, lest he be grieved: but truly as the LORD liveth, and as thy soul liveth, there is but a step between me and death.

⁴Then said Jonathan unto David, ^oWhatsoever thy soul ^pdesireth, I will even do it for thee.

⁵And David said unto Jonathan, Behold, tomorrow is the new moon, and I should not fail to sit with the king at meat: but let me go, that I may hide myself in the field unto the third day at even.

⁶If thy father at all miss me, then say, David earnestly asked leave of me that he might run to Bethlehem his city: for there is a yearly ^qsacrifice there for all the family.

⁷If he say thus, It is well; thy servant shall have peace: but if he be very wroth, then be sure that evil is determined by him.

⁸Therefore thou shalt deal kindly with thy servant; for thou hast brought thy servant into a covenant of the LORD with thee: notwithstanding, if there be in me iniquity, slay me thyself; for why shouldest thou bring me to thy father?

⁹And Jonathan said, Far be it from thee: for if I knew certainly that evil were determined by my father to come upon thee, then would not I tell it thee?

¹⁰Then said David to Jonathan, Who shall tell me? or what if thy father answer thee roughly?

¹¹ ¶ And Jonathan said unto David, Come, and let us go out into the field. And they went out both of them into the field.

¹²And Jonathan said unto David, O LORD God of Israel, when I have ^rsounded my father about tomorrow any time, or the third day, and, behold, if there be good toward David, and I then send not unto thee, and ^sshow it thee;

¹³The LORD do so and much more to Jonathan: but if it please my father to do thee evil, then I will show it thee, and send thee away, that thou mayest go in peace: and the LORD be with thee, as he hath been with my father.

Amplified

¹⁹And it was told Saul, Behold, David is at Naioth in Ramah.

²⁰And Saul sent messengers to take David; and when they saw the company of the prophets prophesying, and Samuel standing as appointed head over them, the Spirit of God came upon the messengers of Saul and they also prophesied.

²¹When it was told Saul, he sent other messengers, and they also prophesied. And Saul sent messengers again the third time, and they also prophesied.

²²Then Saul himself went to Ramah and came to a great well that is in Secu; and he asked, Where are Samuel and David? And he was told, They are at Naioth in Ramah.

²³So he went on to Naioth in Ramah; and the Spirit of God came upon him also, and as he went on he prophesied until he came to Naioth in Ramah.

²⁴He took off his royal robes and prophesied before Samuel and lay down stripped thus all that day and night. So they say, Is Saul also among the prophets? [I Sam. 10:10.]

20 DAVID FLED from Naioth in Ramah and came and said to Jonathan, What have I done? Of what am I guilty? What is my sin before your father, that he seeks my life?

²Jonathan said, God forbid! You shall not die. My father does nothing great or small but what he tells me. And why should [he] hide this thing from me? It is not so.

³But David replied, Your father certainly knows that I have found favor in your eyes, and he thinks, Let not Jonathan know this, lest he be grieved. But truly as the Lord lives and as your soul lives, there is but a step between me and death.

⁴Then Jonathan said to David, Whatever you desire, I will do for you.

⁵David said to Jonathan, Tomorrow is the New Moon [festival], and I should not fail to sit at the table with the king; but let me go, that I may hide myself in the field till the third day at evening.

⁶If your father misses me at all, then say, David earnestly asked leave of me that he might run to Bethlehem, his city, for there is a yearly sacrifice there for all the family.

⁷If he says, All right, then it will be well with your servant; but if he is angry, then be sure that evil is determined by him.

⁸Therefore deal kindly with your servant, for you have brought [me] into a covenant of the Lord with you. But if there is guilt in me, kill me yourself; for why should you bring me to your father?

⁹And Jonathan said, Far be it from you! If I knew that evil was determined for you by my father, would I not tell you?

¹⁰Then said David to Jonathan, Who will tell me if your father answers you roughly?

¹¹Jonathan said, Come, let us go into the field. So they went into the field.

¹²Jonathan said to David, The Lord, the God of Israel, be witness. When I have sounded out my father about this time tomorrow, or the third day, behold, if he is well inclined toward David, and I do not send and let you know it,

¹³The Lord do so, and much more, to Jonathan. But if it please my father to do you harm, then I will disclose it to you and send you away, that you may go in safety. And may the Lord be with you as He has been with my father.

ⁿHeb. fell; see Num. 24:4   ^oOr, Say what is thy mind, and I will do   ^pHeb. speaketh, or, thinketh   ^qOr, feast   ^rHeb. searched   ^sHeb. uncover thine ear

New American Standard

19 It was told Saul, saying, "Behold, David is at Naioth in Ramah."

20 Then Saul sent messengers to take David, but when they saw the company of the prophets prophesying, with Samuel standing *and* presiding over them, the Spirit of God came upon the messengers of Saul; and they also prophesied.

21 When it was told Saul, he sent other messengers, and they also prophesied. So Saul sent messengers again the third time, and they also prophesied.

22 Then he himself went to Ramah and came as far as the large well that is in Secu; and he asked and said, "Where are Samuel and David?" And *someone* said, "Behold, they are at Naioth in Ramah."

23 He proceeded there to Naioth in Ramah; and the Spirit of God came upon him also, so that he went along prophesying continually until he came to Naioth in Ramah.

24 He also stripped off his clothes, and he too prophesied before Samuel and lay down naked all that day and all that night. Therefore they say, "Is Saul also among the prophets?"

David and Jonathan Covenant

20 THEN DAVID fled from Naioth in Ramah, and came and said to Jonathan, "What have I done? What is my iniquity? And what is my sin before your father, that he is seeking my life?"

2 He said to him, "Far from it, you shall not die. Behold, my father does nothing either great or small without disclosing it to me. So why should my father hide this thing from me? It is not so!"

3 Yet David vowed again, saying, "Your father knows well that I have found favor in your sight, and he has said, 'Do not let Jonathan know this, or he will be grieved.' But truly as the LORD lives and as your soul lives, there is hardly a step between me and death."

4 Then Jonathan said to David, "Whatever you say, I will do for you."

5 So David said to Jonathan, "Behold, tomorrow is the new moon, and I ought to sit down to eat with the king. But let me go, that I may hide myself in the field until the third evening.

6 "If your father misses me at all, then say, 'David earnestly asked *leave* of me to run to Bethlehem his city, because it is the yearly sacrifice there for the whole family.'

7 "If he says, 'It is good,' your servant *will be* safe; but if he is very angry, know that he has decided on evil.

8 "Therefore deal kindly with your servant, for you have brought your servant into a covenant of the LORD with you. But if there is iniquity in me, put me to death yourself; for why then should you bring me to your father?"

9 Jonathan said, "Far be it from you! For if I should indeed learn that evil has been decided by my father to come upon you, then would I not tell you about it?"

10 Then David said to Jonathan, "Who will tell me if your father answers you harshly?"

11 Jonathan said to David, "Come, and let us go out into the field." So both of them went out to the field.

12 ¶ Then Jonathan said to David, "The LORD, the God of Israel, *be witness!* When I have sounded out my father about this time tomorrow, *or* the third day, behold, if there is good *feeling* toward David, shall I not then send to you and make it known to you?

13 "If it please my father *to do* you harm, may the LORD do so to Jonathan and more also, if I do not make it known to you and send you away, that you may go in safety. And may the LORD be with you as He has been with my father.

New International

19 Word came to Saul: "David is in Naioth at Ramah"; 20 so he sent men to capture him. But when they saw a group of prophets prophesying, with Samuel standing there as their leader, the Spirit of God came upon Saul's men and they also prophesied. 21 Saul was told about it, and he sent more men, and they prophesied too. Saul sent men a third time, and they also prophesied. 22 Finally, he himself left for Ramah and went to the great cistern at Secu. And he asked, "Where are Samuel and David?"

"Over in Naioth at Ramah," they said.

23 So Saul went to Naioth at Ramah. But the Spirit of God came even upon him, and he walked along prophesying until he came to Naioth. 24 He stripped off his robes and also prophesied in Samuel's presence. He lay that way all that day and night. This is why people say, "Is Saul also among the prophets?"

David and Jonathan

20 THEN DAVID fled from Naioth at Ramah and went to Jonathan and asked, "What have I done? What is my crime? How have I wronged your father, that he is trying to take my life?"

2 "Never!" Jonathan replied. "You are not going to die! Look, my father doesn't do anything, great or small, without confiding in me. Why would he hide this from me? It's not so!"

3 But David took an oath and said, "Your father knows very well that I have found favor in your eyes, and he has said to himself, 'Jonathan must not know this or he will be grieved.' Yet as surely as the LORD lives and as you live, there is only a step between me and death."

4 Jonathan said to David, "Whatever you want me to do, I'll do for you."

5 So David said, "Look, tomorrow is the New Moon festival, and I am supposed to dine with the king; but let me go and hide in the field until the evening of the day after tomorrow. 6 If your father misses me at all, tell him, 'David earnestly asked my permission to hurry to Bethlehem, his hometown, because an annual sacrifice is being made there for his whole clan.' 7 If he says, 'Very well,' then your servant is safe. But if he loses his temper, you can be sure that he is determined to harm me. 8 As for you, show kindness to your servant, for you have brought him into a covenant with you before the LORD. If I am guilty, then kill me yourself! Why hand me over to your father?"

9 "Never!" Jonathan said. "If I had the least inkling that my father was determined to harm you, wouldn't I tell you?"

10 David asked, "Who will tell me if your father answers you harshly?"

11 "Come," Jonathan said, "let's go out into the field." So they went there together.

12 Then Jonathan said to David: "By the LORD, the God of Israel, I will surely sound out my father by this time the day after tomorrow! If he is favorably disposed toward you, will I not send you word and let you know? 13 But if my father is inclined to harm you, may the LORD deal with me, be it ever so severely, if I do not let you know and send you away safely. May the LORD be with you as he has

King James

¹⁴And thou shalt not only while yet I live show me the kindness of the LORD, that I die not:

¹⁵But *also* thou shalt not cut off thy kindness from my house for ever: no, not when the LORD hath cut off the enemies of David every one from the face of the earth.

¹⁶So Jonathan ^tmade *a covenant* with the house of David, *saying,* Let the LORD even require *it* at the hand of David's enemies.

¹⁷And Jonathan caused David to swear again, ^ubecause he loved him: for he loved him as he loved his own soul.

¹⁸Then Jonathan said to David, Tomorrow *is* the new moon: and thou shalt be missed, because thy seat will be ^vempty.

¹⁹And *when* thou hast stayed three days, *then* thou shalt go down ^{wx}quickly, and come to the place where thou didst hide thyself ^ywhen the business was *in hand,* and shalt remain by the stone ^zEzel.

²⁰And I will shoot three arrows on the side *thereof,* as though I shot at a mark.

²¹And, behold, I will send a lad, *saying,* Go, find out the arrows. If I expressly say unto the lad, Behold, the arrows *are* on this side of thee, take them; then come thou: for *there is* peace to thee, and ^ano hurt; *as* the LORD liveth.

²²But if I say thus unto the young man, Behold, the arrows *are* beyond thee; go thy way: for the LORD hath sent thee away.

²³And *as touching* the matter which thou and I have spoken of, behold, the LORD *be* between thee and me for ever.

²⁴ ¶ So David hid himself in the field: and when the new moon was come, the king sat him down to eat meat.

²⁵And the king sat upon his seat, as at other times, *even* upon a seat by the wall: and Jonathan arose, and Abner sat by Saul's side, and David's place was empty.

²⁶Nevertheless Saul spake not any thing that day: for he thought, Something hath befallen him, he *is* not clean; surely he *is* not clean.

²⁷And it came to pass on the morrow, *which was* the second *day* of the month, that David's place was empty: and Saul said unto Jonathan his son, Wherefore cometh not the son of Jesse to meat, neither yesterday, nor today?

²⁸And Jonathan answered Saul, David earnestly asked *leave* of me *to go* to Bethlehem:

²⁹And he said, Let me go, I pray thee; for our family hath a sacrifice in the city; and my brother, he hath commanded me *to be there:* and now, if I have found favour in thine eyes, let me get away, I pray thee, and see my brethren. Therefore he cometh not unto the king's table.

³⁰Then Saul's anger was kindled against Jonathan, and he said unto him, ^{bc}Thou son of the perverse rebellious *woman,* do not I know that thou hast chosen the son of Jesse to thine own confusion, and unto the confusion of thy mother's nakedness?

³¹For as long as the son of Jesse liveth upon the ground, thou shalt not be established, nor thy kingdom. Wherefore now send and fetch him unto me, for he ^dshall surely die.

³²And Jonathan answered Saul his father, and said unto him, Wherefore shall he be slain? what hath he done?

³³And Saul cast a javelin at him to smite him: whereby Jonathan knew that it was determined of his father to slay David.

³⁴So Jonathan arose from the table in fierce anger, and did eat no meat the second day of the month: for he was grieved for David, because his father had done him shame.

³⁵ ¶ And it came to pass in the morning, that Jonathan went out into the field at the time appointed with David, and a little lad with him.

Amplified

¹⁴While I am still alive you shall not only show me the loving-kindness of the Lord, so that I die not,

¹⁵But also you shall not cut off your kindness from my house forever—no, not even when the Lord has cut off every enemy of David from the face of the earth.

¹⁶So Jonathan made a covenant with the house of David, saying, And the Lord will require that this covenant be kept at the hands of David's enemies.

¹⁷And Jonathan caused David to swear again by his love for him, for Jonathan loved him as he loved his own life.

¹⁸Then Jonathan said to David, Tomorrow is the New Moon festival; and you will be missed, for your seat will be empty.

¹⁹On the third day you will go quickly and come to the place where you hid yourself when the matter was in hand, and remain by the stone Ezel.

²⁰And I will shoot three arrows on the side of it, as though I shot at a mark.

²¹And I will send a lad, saying, Go, find the arrows. If I expressly say to the lad, Look, the arrows are on this side of you, take them—then you are to come, for it is safe for you and there is no danger, as the Lord lives.

²²But if I say to the youth, Look, the arrows are beyond you—then go, for the Lord has sent you away.

²³And as touching the matter of which you and I have spoken, behold, the Lord is between you and me forever.

²⁴So David hid himself in the field, and when the New Moon [festival] came, the king sat down to eat food.

²⁵The king sat, as at other times, on his seat by the wall, and Jonathan sat opposite, and Abner sat by Saul's side, but David's place was empty.

²⁶Yet Saul said nothing that day, for he thought, Something has befallen him and he is not clean—surely he is not clean.

²⁷But on the morrow, the second day after the new moon, David's place was empty; and Saul said to Jonathan his son, Why has not the son of Jesse come to the meal, either yesterday or today?

²⁸And Jonathan answered, David earnestly asked leave of me to go to Bethlehem.

²⁹He said, Let me go, I pray, for our family holds a sacrifice in the city and my brother commanded me to be there. Now, if I have found favor in your eyes, let me get away and see my brothers. That is why he has not come to the king's table.

³⁰Then Saul's anger was kindled against Jonathan and he said to him, You son of a perverse, rebellious woman, do not I know that you have chosen the son of Jesse to your own shame and to the shame of your mother who bore you?

³¹For as long as the son of Jesse lives upon the earth, you shall not be established nor shall your kingdom. So now send and bring him to me, for he shall surely die.

³²Jonathan answered Saul his father, Why should he be killed? What has he done?

³³But Saul cast his spear at him to smite him, by which Jonathan knew that his father had determined to kill David.

³⁴So Jonathan arose from the table in fierce anger, and ate no food that second day of the month, for he grieved for David because his father had disgraced him.

³⁵In the morning Jonathan went out into the field at the time appointed with David, and a little lad was with him.

^tHeb. *cut*   ^uOr, *by his love toward him*   ^vHeb. *missed*
^wOr, *diligently*   ^xHeb. *greatly*   ^yHeb. *in the day of the*
business   ^zOr, *that showeth the way*   ^aHeb. *not any thing*
^bOr, *Thou perverse rebel*   ^cHeb. *Son of perverse rebellion*
^dHeb. *is the son of death*

New American Standard

14"If I am still alive, will you not show me the loving-kindness of the LORD, that I may not die?

15"You shall not cut off your lovingkindness from my house forever, not even when the LORD cuts off every one of the enemies of David from the face of the earth."

16 So Jonathan made a *covenant* with the house of David, *saying*, "May the LORD require *it* at the hands of David's enemies."

17 Jonathan made David vow again because of his love for him, because he loved him as he loved his own life.

18 ¶ Then Jonathan said to him, "Tomorrow is the new moon, and you will be missed because your seat will be empty.

19"When you have stayed for three days, you shall go down quickly and come to the place where you hid yourself on that eventful day, and you shall remain by the stone Ezel.

20"I will shoot three arrows to the side, as though I shot at a target.

21"And behold, I will send the lad, *saying*, 'Go, find the arrows.' If I specifically say to the lad, 'Behold, the arrows are on this side of you, get them,' then come; for there is safety for you and no harm, as the LORD lives.

22"But if I say to the youth, 'Behold, the arrows are beyond you,' go, for the LORD has sent you away.

23"As for the agreement of which you and I have spoken, behold, the LORD is between you and me forever."

24 ¶ So David hid in the field; and when the new moon came, the king sat down to eat food.

25 The king sat on his seat as usual, the seat by the wall; then Jonathan rose up and Abner sat down by Saul's side, but David's place was empty.

26 Nevertheless Saul did not speak anything that day, for he thought, "It is an accident, he is not clean, surely *he is* not clean."

27 It came about the next day, the second *day* of the new moon, that David's place was empty; so Saul said to Jonathan his son, "Why has the son of Jesse not come to the meal, either yesterday or today?"

28 Jonathan then answered Saul, "David earnestly asked leave of me *to go* to Bethlehem,

29 for he said, 'Please let me go, since our family has a sacrifice in the city, and my brother has commanded me to attend. And now, if I have found favor in your sight, please let me get away that I may see my brothers.' For this reason he has not come to the king's table."

Saul Is Angry with Jonathan

30 ¶ Then Saul's anger burned against Jonathan and he said to him, "You son of a perverse, rebellious woman! Do I not know that you are choosing the son of Jesse to your own shame and to the shame of your mother's nakedness?

31"For as long as the son of Jesse lives on the earth, neither you nor your kingdom will be established. Therefore now, send and bring him to me, for he must surely die."

32 But Jonathan answered Saul his father and said to him, "Why should he be put to death? What has he done?"

33 Then Saul hurled his spear at him to strike him down; so Jonathan knew that his father had decided to put David to death.

34 Then Jonathan arose from the table in fierce anger, and did not eat food on the second day of the new moon, for he was grieved over David because his father had dishonored him.

35 ¶ Now it came about in the morning that Jonathan went out into the field for the appointment with David, and a little lad *was* with him.

New International

been with my father. 14But show me unfailing kindness like that of the LORD as long as I live, so that I may not be killed, 15and do not ever cut off your kindness from my family—not even when the LORD has cut off every one of David's enemies from the face of the earth."

16So Jonathan made a covenant with the house of David, saying, "May the LORD call David's enemies to account." 17And Jonathan had David reaffirm his oath out of love for him, because he loved him as he loved himself.

18Then Jonathan said to David: "Tomorrow is the New Moon festival. You will be missed, because your seat will be empty. 19The day after tomorrow, toward evening, go to the place where you hid when this trouble began, and wait by the stone Ezel. 20I will shoot three arrows to the side of it, as though I were shooting at a target. 21Then I will send a boy and say, 'Go, find the arrows.' If I say to him, 'Look, the arrows are on this side of you; bring them here,' then come, because, as surely as the LORD lives, you are safe; there is no danger. 22But if I say to the boy, 'Look, the arrows are beyond you,' then you must go, because the LORD has sent you away. 23And about the matter you and I discussed—remember, the LORD is witness between you and me forever."

24So David hid in the field, and when the New Moon festival came, the king sat down to eat. 25He sat in his customary place by the wall, opposite Jonathan,v and Abner sat next to Saul, but David's place was empty. 26Saul said nothing that day, for he thought, "Something must have happened to David to make him ceremonially unclean—surely he is unclean." 27But the next day, the second day of the month, David's place was empty again. Then Saul said to his son Jonathan, "Why hasn't the son of Jesse come to the meal, either yesterday or today?"

28Jonathan answered, "David earnestly asked me for permission to go to Bethlehem. 29He said, 'Let me go, because our family is observing a sacrifice in the town and my brother has ordered me to be there. If I have found favor in your eyes, let me get away to see my brothers.' That is why he has not come to the king's table."

30Saul's anger flared up at Jonathan and he said to him, "You son of a perverse and rebellious woman! Don't I know that you have sided with the son of Jesse to your own shame and to the shame of the mother who bore you? 31As long as the son of Jesse lives on this earth, neither you nor your kingdom will be established. Now send and bring him to me, for he must die!"

32"Why should he be put to death? What has he done?" Jonathan asked his father. 33But Saul hurled his spear at him to kill him. Then Jonathan knew that his father intended to kill David.

34Jonathan got up from the table in fierce anger; on that second day of the month he did not eat, because he was grieved at his father's shameful treatment of David.

35In the morning Jonathan went out to the field for his

King James

36And he said unto his lad, Run, find out now the arrows which I shoot. *And* as the lad ran, he shot an arrow ebeyond him.

37And when the lad was come to the place of the arrow which Jonathan had shot, Jonathan cried after the lad, and said, *Is* not the arrow beyond thee?

38And Jonathan cried after the lad, Make speed, haste, stay not. And Jonathan's lad gathered up the arrows, and came to his master.

39But the lad knew not any thing: only Jonathan and David knew the matter.

40And Jonathan gave his ƒartillery unto ᵍhis lad, and said unto him, Go, carry *them* to the city.

41 ¶ *And* as soon as the lad was gone, David arose out of *a place* toward the south, and fell on his face to the ground, and bowed himself three times: and they kissed one another, and wept one with another, until David exceeded.

42And Jonathan said to David, Go in peace, ʰforasmuch as we have sworn both of us in the name of the LORD, saying, The LORD be between me and thee, and between my seed and thy seed for ever. And he arose and departed: and Jonathan went into the city.

David visits Ahimelech

21 THEN CAME David to Nob to Ahimelech the priest: and Ahimelech was afraid at the meeting of David, and said unto him, Why *art* thou alone, and no man with thee?

2And David said unto Ahimelech the priest, The king hath commanded me a business, and hath said unto me, Let no man know any thing of the business whereabout I send thee, and what I have commanded thee: and I have appointed *my* servants to such and such a place.

3Now therefore what is under thine hand? give *me* five *loaves of* bread in mine hand, or what there is ⁱpresent.

4And the priest answered David, and said, *There is* no common bread under mine hand, but there is hallowed bread; if the young men have kept themselves at least from women.

5And David answered the priest, and said unto him, Of a truth women *have been* kept from us about these three days, since I came out, and the vessels of the young men are holy, and *the bread is* in a manner common, ʲyea, though it were sanctified this day in the vessel.

6So the priest gave him hallowed *bread:* for there was no bread there but the showbread, that was taken from before the LORD, to put hot bread in the day when it was taken away.

7Now a certain man of the servants of Saul *was* there that day, detained before the LORD; and his name *was* Doeg, an Edomite, the chiefest of the herdmen that *belonged* to Saul.

David escapes to Gath

8 ¶ And David said unto Ahimelech, And is there not here under thine hand spear or sword? for I have neither brought my sword nor my weapons with me, because the king's business required haste.

9And the priest said, The sword of Goliath the Philistine, whom thou slewest in the valley of Elah, behold, it *is here* wrapped in a cloth behind the ephod: if thou wilt take that, take *it:* for *there is* no other save that here. And David said, *There is* none like that; give it me.

10 ¶ And David arose, and fled that day for fear of Saul, and went to ᵏAchish the king of Gath.

Amplified

36And he said to his lad, Run, find the arrows which I shoot. And as the lad ran, he shot an arrow beyond him.

37When the lad came to the place where Jonathan had shot the arrow, Jonathan called to [him], Is not the arrow beyond you?

38And Jonathan cried after the lad, Make speed, haste, stay not! The lad gathered up the arrow and came to his master.

39But the lad knew nothing; only Jonathan and David knew the matter.

40Jonathan gave his weapons to his lad and told him, Go, carry them to the city.

41And as soon as the lad was gone, David arose from beside the heap of stones and fell on his face to the ground and bowed himself three times. And they kissed one another and wept with one another until David got control of himself.

42And Jonathan told David, Go in peace, forasmuch as we have sworn to each other in the name of the Lord, saying, The Lord shall be between me and you, and between my descendants and yours forever. And Jonathan arose and departed into the city.

21 THEN DAVID went to Nob, to Ahimelech the priest; and Ahimelech was afraid at meeting David, and said to him, Why are you alone and no man with you?

2David said to Ahimelech the priest, The king has charged me with a matter and has told me, Let no man know anything of the mission on which I send you and with what I have charged you. I have appointed the young men to a certain place.

3Now what do you have on hand? Give me five loaves of bread, or whatever you may have.

4And the priest answered David, There is no common bread on hand, but there is hallowed bread—if the young men have kept themselves at least from women.

5And David told the priest, Truly women have been kept from us in these three days since I came out, and the food bags *and* utensils of the young men are clean, and although the bread will be used in a secular way, it will be set apart in the clean bags.

6So the priest gave him holy bread, for there was no bread there but the showbread which was taken from before the Lord to put hot bread in its place the day when it was taken away.

7Now a certain man of Saul's servants was there that day, detained before the Lord; his name was Doeg the Edomite, the chief of Saul's herdsmen.

8David said to Ahimelech, Do you have at hand a sword or spear? The king's business required haste, and I brought neither my sword nor my weapons with me.

9The priest said, The sword of Goliath the Philistine, whom you slew in the Valley of Elah, see, it is here wrapped in a cloth behind the ephod; if you will take that, do so, for there is no other here. And David said, There is none like that; give it to me.

10David arose and fled that day from Saul and went to Achish king of Gath.

ᵉHeb. *to pass over him*　　ƒHeb. *instruments*　　ᵍHeb. *that* was *his*　　ʰOr, the LORD *be witness of that which; see ver. 23*　　ⁱHeb. *found*　　ʲOr, *especially when this day there is other sanctified in the vessel*　　ᵏOr, *Abimelech; see Ps. 34, title*

New American Standard

36 He said to his lad, "Run, find now the arrows which I am about to shoot." As the lad was running, he shot an arrow past him.

37 When the lad reached the place of the arrow which Jonathan had shot, Jonathan called after the lad and said, "Is not the arrow beyond you?"

38 And Jonathan called after the lad, "Hurry, be quick, do not stay!" And Jonathan's lad picked up the arrow and came to his master.

39 But the lad was not aware of anything; only Jonathan and David knew about the matter.

40 Then Jonathan gave his weapons to his lad and said to him, "Go, bring *them* to the city."

41 When the lad was gone, David rose from the south side and fell on his face to the ground, and bowed three times. And they kissed each other and wept together, but David *wept* the more.

42 Jonathan said to David, "Go in safety, inasmuch as we have sworn to each other in the name of the LORD, saying, 'The LORD will be between me and you, and between my descendants and your descendants forever.' " Then he rose and departed, while Jonathan went into the city.

David Takes Consecrated Bread

21 THEN DAVID came to Nob to Ahimelech the priest; and Ahimelech came trembling to meet David and said to him, "Why are you alone and no one with you?"

2 David said to Ahimelech the priest, "The king has commissioned me with a matter and has said to me, 'Let no one know anything about the matter on which I am sending you and with which I have commissioned you; and I have directed the young men to a certain place.'

3 "Now therefore, what do you have on hand? Give me five loaves of bread, or whatever can be found."

4 The priest answered David and said, "There is no ordinary bread on hand, but there is consecrated bread; if only the young men have kept themselves from women."

5 David answered the priest and said to him, "Surely women have been kept from us as previously when I set out and the vessels of the young men were holy, though it was an ordinary journey; how much more then today will their vessels *be holy?*"

6 So the priest gave him consecrated *bread;* for there was no bread there but the bread of the Presence which was removed from before the LORD, in order to put hot bread *in its place* when it was taken away.

7 ¶ Now one of the servants of Saul was there that day, detained before the LORD; and his name was Doeg the Edomite, the chief of Saul's shepherds.

8 ¶ David said to Ahimelech, "Now is there not a spear or a sword on hand? For I brought neither my sword nor my weapons with me, because the king's matter was urgent."

9 Then the priest said, "The sword of Goliath the Philistine, whom you killed in the valley of Elah, behold, it is wrapped in a cloth behind the ephod; if you would take it for yourself, take *it.* For there is no other except it here." And David said, "There is none like it; give it to me."

10 ¶ Then David arose and fled that day from Saul, and went to Achish king of Gath.

New International

meeting with David. He had a small boy with him, 36and he said to the boy, "Run and find the arrows I shoot." As the boy ran, he shot an arrow beyond him. 37When the boy came to the place where Jonathan's arrow had fallen, Jonathan called out after him, "Isn't the arrow beyond you?" 38Then he shouted, "Hurry! Go quickly! Don't stop!" The boy picked up the arrow and returned to his master. 39(The boy knew nothing of all this; only Jonathan and David knew.) 40Then Jonathan gave his weapons to the boy and said, "Go, carry them back to town."

41After the boy had gone, David got up from the south side of the stone, and bowed down before Jonathan three times, with his face to the ground. Then they kissed each other and wept together—but David wept the most.

42Jonathan said to David, "Go in peace, for we have sworn friendship with each other in the name of the LORD, saying, 'The LORD is witness between you and me, and between your descendants and my descendants forever.' " Then David left, and Jonathan went back to the town.

David at Nob

21 DAVID WENT to Nob, to Ahimelech the priest. Ahimelech trembled when he met him, and asked, "Why are you alone? Why is no one with you?"

2David answered Ahimelech the priest, "The king charged me with a certain matter and said to me, 'No one is to know anything about your mission and your instructions.' As for my men, I have told them to meet me at a certain place. 3Now then, what do you have on hand? Give me five loaves of bread, or whatever you can find."

4But the priest answered David, "I don't have any ordinary bread on hand; however, there is some consecrated bread here—provided the men have kept themselves from women."

5David replied, "Indeed women have been kept from us, as usual whenever[w] I set out. The men's things[x] are holy even on missions that are not holy. How much more so today!" 6So the priest gave him the consecrated bread, since there was no bread there except the bread of the Presence that had been removed from before the LORD and replaced by hot bread on the day it was taken away.

7Now one of Saul's servants was there that day, detained before the LORD; he was Doeg the Edomite, Saul's head shepherd.

8David asked Ahimelech, "Don't you have a spear or a sword here? I haven't brought my sword or any other weapon, because the king's business was urgent."

9The priest replied, "The sword of Goliath the Philistine, whom you killed in the Valley of Elah, is here; it is wrapped in a cloth behind the ephod. If you want it, take it; there is no sword here but that one."

David said, "There is none like it; give it to me."

David at Gath

10That day David fled from Saul and went to Achish

---

[w] 5 Or *from us in the past few days since*   [x] 5 Or *bodies*

King James

11 And the servants of Achish said unto him, *Is* not this David the king of the land? did they not sing one to another of him in dances, saying, Saul hath slain his thousands, and David his ten thousands?

12 And David laid up these words in his heart, and was sore afraid of Achish the king of Gath.

13 And he changed his behaviour before them, and feigned himself mad in their hands, and [l]scrabbled on the doors of the gate, and let his spittle fall down upon his beard.

14 Then said Achish unto his servants, Lo, ye see the man [m]is mad: wherefore *then* have ye brought him to me?

15 Have I need of mad men, that ye have brought this *fellow* to play the mad man in my presence? shall this *fellow* come into my house?

David's flight continues

22 DAVID THEREFORE departed thence, and escaped to the cave Adullam: and when his brethren and all his father's house heard *it,* they went down thither to him.

2 And every one *that was* in distress, and every one that [n]*was* in debt, and every one *that was* [o]discontented, gathered themselves unto him; and he became a captain over them: and there were with him about four hundred men.

3 ¶ And David went thence to Mizpeh of Moab: and he said unto the king of Moab, Let my father and my mother, I pray thee, come forth, *and be* with you, till I know what God will do for me.

4 And he brought them before the king of Moab: and they dwelt with him all the while that David was in the hold.

5 ¶ And the prophet Gad said unto David, Abide not in the hold; depart, and get thee into the land of Judah. Then David departed, and came into the forest of Hareth.

6 ¶ When Saul heard that David was discovered, and the men that *were* with him, (now Saul abode in Gibeah under a [p]tree in Ramah, having his spear in his hand, and all his servants *were* standing about him;)

7 Then Saul said unto his servants that stood about him, Hear now, ye Benjamites; will the son of Jesse give every one of you fields and vineyards, *and* make you all captains of thousands, and captains of hundreds;

8 That all of you have conspired against me, and *there is* none that showeth me that my son hath made a league with the son of Jesse, and *there is* none of you that is sorry for me, or showeth unto me that my son hath stirred up my servant against me, to lie in wait, as at this day?

9 ¶ Then answered Doeg the Edomite, which was set over the servants of Saul, and said, I saw the son of Jesse coming to Nob, to Ahimelech the son of Ahitub.

10 And he inquired of the LORD for him, and gave him victuals, and gave him the sword of Goliath the Philistine.

Saul has Ahimelech killed

11 Then the king sent to call Ahimelech the priest, the son of Ahitub, and all his father's house, the priests that *were* in Nob: and they came all of them to the king.

12 And Saul said, Hear now, thou son of Ahitub. And he answered, [q]Here I *am,* my lord.

13 And Saul said unto him, Why have ye conspired against me, thou and the son of Jesse, in that thou hast given him bread, and a sword, and hast inquired of God for him, that he should rise against me, to lie in wait, as at this day?

14 Then Ahimelech answered the king, and said, And who *is so* faithful among all thy servants as David, which is the king's son-in-law, and goeth at thy bidding, and is honourable in thine house?

[l] Or, *made marks* [m] Or, *playeth the mad man* [n] Heb. *had a creditor* [o] Heb. *bitter of soul* [p] Or, *grove in a high place* [q] Heb. *Behold me*

Amplified

11 The servants of Achish said to him, Is not this David, the king of the land? Did they not sing one to another of him in their dances: Saul has slain his thousands, and David his ten thousands?

12 David took these words to heart and was much afraid of Achish king of Gath.

13 And he changed his behavior before them, and pretended to be insane in their [Philistine] hands, and scribbled on the gate doors, and drooled on his beard.

14 Then said Achish to his servants, You see the man is mad. Why then have you brought him to me?

15 Have I need of madmen, that you bring this fellow to play the madman in my presence? Shall this fellow come into my house?

22 SO DAVID departed and escaped to the cave of Adullam: and when his brothers and all his father's house heard it, they went down there to him.

2 And everyone in distress or in debt or discontented gathered to him, and he became a commander over them. And there were with him about 400 men.

3 And David went from there to Mizpah of Moab; and he said to the king of Moab, Let my father [of Moabite descent] and my mother, I pray you, come out [of Judah] and be with you till I know what God will do for me. [Ruth 4:13, 17.]

4 And he brought them before the king of Moab, and they dwelt with him all the while that David was in the stronghold [in Moab].

5 Then the prophet Gad said to David, Do not remain in the stronghold; leave, and get into the land of Judah. So David left and went into the forest of Hareth.

6 Saul heard that David was discovered, and the men that were with him. Saul was sitting in Gibeah under the tamarisk tree on the height, his spear in his hand and all his servants standing about him.

7 Saul said to his servants who stood about him, Hear now, you Benjamites! Will the son of Jesse give every one of you fields and vineyards and make you all commanders of thousands and hundreds,

8 That all of you have conspired against me? No one discloses to me when my son makes a league with the son of Jesse. None of you is sorry for me or discloses that my son has stirred up my servant against me to lie in wait, as he does this day?

9 Then Doeg the Edomite, who stood with Saul's servants, said, I saw the son of Jesse come to Nob, to Ahimelech son of Ahitub.

10 And [Ahimelech] inquired of the Lord for him, and gave him provisions and the sword of Goliath the Philistine.

11 Then the king sent to call Ahimelech the priest, the son of Ahitub, and all his father's house, the priests who were at Nob, and they all came to the king.

12 Saul said, Hear now, you son of Ahitub. He replied, Here I am, my lord.

13 Saul said to him, Why have you conspired against me, you and the son of Jesse, giving him bread and a sword and inquiring of God for him, so he could rise against me to lie in wait, as he does this day?

14 Then Ahimelech answered the king, And who is so faithful among all your servants as David, who is the king's son-in-law, and is taken into your council and honored in your house?

New American Standard

¹¹ But the servants of Achish said to him, "Is this not David the king of the land? Did they not sing of this one as they danced, saying,

'Saul has slain his thousands,
　And David his ten thousands'?"

¹² David took these words to heart and greatly feared Achish king of Gath.

¹³ So he disguised his sanity before them, and acted insanely in their hands, and scribbled on the doors of the gate, and let his saliva run down into his beard.

¹⁴ Then Achish said to his servants, "Behold, you see the man behaving as a madman. Why do you bring him to me?

¹⁵ "Do I lack madmen, that you have brought this one to act the madman in my presence? Shall this one come into my house?"

The Priests Slain at Nob

22 SO DAVID departed from there and escaped to the cave of Adullam; and when his brothers and all his father's household heard *of it,* they went down there to him.

² Everyone who was in distress, and everyone who was in debt, and everyone who was discontented gathered to him; and he became captain over them. Now there were about four hundred men with him.

³ ¶ And David went from there to Mizpah of Moab; and he said to the king of Moab, "Please let my father and my mother come *and stay* with you until I know what God will do for me."

⁴ Then he left them with the king of Moab; and they stayed with him all the time that David was in the stronghold.

⁵ The prophet Gad said to David, "Do not stay in the stronghold; depart, and go into the land of Judah." So David departed and went into the forest of Hereth.

⁶ ¶ Then Saul heard that David and the men who were with him had been discovered. Now Saul was sitting in Gibeah, under the tamarisk tree on the height with his spear in his hand, and all his servants were standing around him.

⁷ Saul said to his servants who stood around him, "Hear now, O Benjamites! Will the son of Jesse also give to all of you fields and vineyards? Will he make you all commanders of thousands and commanders of hundreds?

⁸ "For all of you have conspired against me so that there is no one who discloses to me when my son makes a *covenant* with the son of Jesse, and there is none of you who is sorry for me or discloses to me that my son has stirred up my servant against me to lie in ambush, as *it is* this day."

⁹ Then Doeg the Edomite, who was standing by the servants of Saul, said, "I saw the son of Jesse coming to Nob, to Ahimelech the son of Ahitub.

¹⁰ "He inquired of the LORD for him, gave him provisions, and gave him the sword of Goliath the Philistine."

¹¹ ¶ Then the king sent someone to summon Ahimelech the priest, the son of Ahitub, and all his father's household, the priests who were in Nob; and all of them came to the king.

¹² Saul said, "Listen now, son of Ahitub." And he answered, "Here I am, my lord."

¹³ Saul then said to him, "Why have you and the son of Jesse conspired against me, in that you have given him bread and a sword and have inquired of God for him, so that he would rise up against me by lying in ambush as *it is* this day?"

¹⁴ ¶ Then Ahimelech answered the king and said, "And who among all your servants is as faithful as David, even the king's son-in-law, who is captain over your guard, and is honored in your house?

New International

king of Gath. ¹¹ But the servants of Achish said to him, "Isn't this David, the king of the land? Isn't he the one they sing about in their dances:

" 'Saul has slain his thousands,
　and David his tens of thousands'?"

¹² David took these words to heart and was very much afraid of Achish king of Gath. ¹³ So he pretended to be insane in their presence; and while he was in their hands he acted like a madman, making marks on the doors of the gate and letting saliva run down his beard.

¹⁴ Achish said to his servants, "Look at the man! He is insane! Why bring him to me? ¹⁵ Am I so short of madmen that you have to bring this fellow here to carry on like this in front of me? Must this man come into my house?"

David at Adullam and Mizpah

22 DAVID LEFT Gath and escaped to the cave of Adullam. When his brothers and his father's household heard about it, they went down to him there. ²All those who were in distress or in debt or discontented gathered around him, and he became their leader. About four hundred men were with him.

³From there David went to Mizpah in Moab and said to the king of Moab, "Would you let my father and mother come and stay with you until I learn what God will do for me?" ⁴So he left them with the king of Moab, and they stayed with him as long as David was in the stronghold.

⁵But the prophet Gad said to David, "Do not stay in the stronghold. Go into the land of Judah." So David left and went to the forest of Hereth.

Saul Kills the Priests of Nob

⁶Now Saul heard that David and his men had been discovered. And Saul, spear in hand, was seated under the tamarisk tree on the hill at Gibeah, with all his officials standing around him. ⁷Saul said to them, "Listen, men of Benjamin! Will the son of Jesse give all of you fields and vineyards? Will he make all of you commanders of thousands and commanders of hundreds? ⁸Is that why you have all conspired against me? No one tells me when my son makes a covenant with the son of Jesse. None of you is concerned about me or tells me that my son has incited my servant to lie in wait for me, as he does today."

⁹But Doeg the Edomite, who was standing with Saul's officials, said, "I saw the son of Jesse come to Ahimelech son of Ahitub at Nob. ¹⁰Ahimelech inquired of the LORD for him; he also gave him provisions and the sword of Goliath the Philistine."

¹¹Then the king sent for the priest Ahimelech son of Ahitub and his father's whole family, who were the priests at Nob, and they all came to the king. ¹²Saul said, "Listen now, son of Ahitub."

"Yes, my lord," he answered.

¹³Saul said to him, "Why have you conspired against me, you and the son of Jesse, giving him bread and a sword and inquiring of God for him, so that he has rebelled against me and lies in wait for me, as he does today?"

¹⁴Ahimelech answered the king, "Who of all your servants is as loyal as David, the king's son-in-law, captain of your bodyguard and highly respected in your house-

King James

15Did I then begin to inquire of God for him? be it far from me: let not the king impute *any* thing unto his servant, *nor* to all the house of my father: for thy servant knew nothing of all this, ^rless or more.

16And the king said, Thou shalt surely die, Ahimelech, thou, and all thy father's house.

17 ¶ And the king said unto the ^{s t}footmen that stood about him, Turn, and slay the priests of the LORD; because their hand also *is* with David, and because they knew when he fled, and did not show it to me. But the servants of the king would not put forth their hand to fall upon the priests of the LORD.

18And the king said to Doeg, Turn thou, and fall upon the priests. And Doeg the Edomite turned, and he fell upon the priests, and slew on that day fourscore and five persons that did wear a linen ephod.

19And Nob, the city of the priests, smote he with the edge of the sword, both men and women, children and sucklings, and oxen, and asses, and sheep, with the edge of the sword.

20 ¶ And one of the sons of Ahimelech the son of Ahitub, named Abiathar, escaped, and fled after David.

21And Abiathar showed David that Saul had slain the LORD's priests.

22And David said unto Abiathar, I knew *it* that day, when Doeg the Edomite *was* there, that he would surely tell Saul: I have occasioned *the death* of all the persons of thy father's house.

23Abide thou with me, fear not: for he that seeketh my life seeketh thy life: but with me thou *shalt be* in safeguard.

David at Keilah

23 THEN THEY told David, saying, Behold, the Philistines fight against Keilah, and they rob the threshingfloors.

2Therefore David inquired of the LORD, saying, Shall I go and smite these Philistines? And the LORD said unto David, Go, and smite the Philistines, and save Keilah.

3And David's men said unto him, Behold, we be afraid here in Judah: how much more then if we come to Keilah against the armies of the Philistines?

4Then David inquired of the LORD yet again. And the LORD answered him and said, Arise, go down to Keilah; for I will deliver the Philistines into thine hand.

5So David and his men went to Keilah, and fought with the Philistines, and brought away their cattle, and smote them with a great slaughter. So David saved the inhabitants of Keilah.

6And it came to pass, when Abiathar the son of Ahimelech fled to David to Keilah, *that* he came down *with* an ephod in his hand.

7 ¶ And it was told Saul that David was come to Keilah. And Saul said, God hath delivered him into mine hand; for he is shut in, by entering into a town that hath gates and bars.

8And Saul called all the people together to war, to go down to Keilah, to besiege David and his men.

9 ¶ And David knew that Saul secretly practised mischief against him; and he said to Abiathar the priest, Bring hither the ephod.

10Then said David, O LORD God of Israel, thy servant hath certainly heard that Saul seeketh to come to Keilah, to destroy the city for my sake.

11Will the men of Keilah deliver me up into his hand? will Saul come down, as thy servant hath heard? O LORD God of Israel, I beseech thee, tell thy servant. And the LORD said, He will come down.

12Then said David, Will the men of Keilah ^udeliver me and my men into the hand of Saul? And the LORD said, They will deliver *thee* up.

Amplified

15Have I only today begun inquiring of God for him? No! Let not the king impute any wrong to his servant or to all the house of my father, for your servant has known nothing of all this, little or much.

16[Saul] said, You shall surely die, Ahimelech, you and all your father's house.

17And the king said to the guard that stood about him, Turn and slay the Lord's priests, because their hand also is with David and because they knew that he fled and did not disclose it to me. But the servants of the king would not put forth their hands against the Lord's priests.

18The king said to Doeg, You turn and fall upon the priests. And Doeg the Edomite turned and attacked the priests and slew that day eighty-five persons who wore the priest's linen ephod.

19And Nob, the city of the priests, he smote with the sword; both men and women, children and sucklings, oxen and donkeys and sheep, he put to the sword.

20And one of the sons of Ahimelech son of Ahitub named Abiathar escaped and fled after David.

21And Abiathar told David that Saul had slain the Lord's priests.

22David said to Abiathar, I knew that day, when Doeg the Edomite was there, that he would surely tell Saul. I have occasioned the death of all your father's house.

23Stay with me, fear not; for he who seeks my life seeks your life. But with me you shall be safeguarded.

23 THEN THEY told David, Behold, the Philistines are fighting against Keilah and are robbing the threshing floors.

2So David inquired of the Lord, Shall I go and attack these Philistines? And the Lord said to David, Go, smite the Philistines and save Keilah.

3David's men said to him, Behold, we are afraid here in Judah. How much more, then, if we come to Keilah against the armies of the Philistines?

4Then David inquired of the Lord again. And the Lord answered him, Arise, go down to Keilah, for I will deliver the Philistines into your hand.

5So David and his men went to Keilah and fought the Philistines and brought away their cattle. So David delivered the people of Keilah.

6When Abiathar son of Ahimelech fled to David at Keilah, he came with an ephod in his hand.

7Now it was told Saul that David had come to Keilah. Saul said, God has delivered him into my hand, for he is shut in by going into a town that has gates and bars.

8Saul summoned all the men for war, to go to Keilah to besiege David and his men.

9David knew that Saul was plotting evil against him; and he said to Abiathar the priest, Bring the ephod here.

10Then David said, O Lord, the God of Israel, Your servant has surely heard that Saul intends to come and destroy the city of Keilah on my account.

11Will the men of Keilah deliver me into his hand? Will Saul come down, as Your servant has heard? O Lord, God of Israel, I beseech You, tell Your servant. And the Lord said, He will come down.

12Then David asked, Will the men of Keilah deliver me and my men into Saul's hand? The Lord said, They will deliver you up.

^rHeb. *little or great*   ^sOr, *guard*   ^tHeb. *runners*   ^uHeb. *shut up*

New American Standard

15"Did I *just* begin to inquire of God for him today? Far be it from me! Do not let the king impute anything to his servant *or* to any of the household of my father, for your servant knows nothing at all of this whole affair."

16 But the king said, "You shall surely die, Ahimelech, you and all your father's household!"

17 And the king said to the guards who were attending him, "Turn around and put the priests of the LORD to death, because their hand also is with David and because they knew that he was fleeing and did not reveal it to me." But the servants of the king were not willing to put forth their hands to attack the priests of the LORD.

18 Then the king said to Doeg, "You turn around and attack the priests." And Doeg the Edomite turned around and attacked the priests, and he killed that day eighty-five men who wore the linen ephod.

19 And he struck Nob the city of the priests with the edge of the sword, both men and women, children and infants; also oxen, donkeys, and sheep *he struck* with the edge of the sword.

20 ¶ But one son of Ahimelech the son of Ahitub, named Abiathar, escaped and fled after David.

21 Abiathar told David that Saul had killed the priests of the LORD.

22 Then David said to Abiathar, "I knew on that day, when Doeg the Edomite was there, that he would surely tell Saul. I have brought about *the death* of every person in your father's household.

23"Stay with me; do not be afraid, for he who seeks my life seeks your life, for you are safe with me."

David Delivers Keilah

23 THEN THEY told David, saying, "Behold, the Philistines are fighting against Keilah and are plundering the threshing floors."

2 So David inquired of the LORD, saying, "Shall I go and attack these Philistines?" And the LORD said to David, "Go and attack the Philistines and deliver Keilah."

3 But David's men said to him, "Behold, we are afraid here in Judah. How much more then if we go to Keilah against the ranks of the Philistines?"

4 Then David inquired of the LORD once more. And the LORD answered him and said, "Arise, go down to Keilah, for I will give the Philistines into your hand."

5 So David and his men went to Keilah and fought with the Philistines; and he led away their livestock and struck them with a great slaughter. Thus David delivered the inhabitants of Keilah.

6 ¶ Now it came about, when Abiathar the son of Ahimelech fled to David at Keilah, *that* he came down *with* an ephod in his hand.

7 When it was told Saul that David had come to Keilah, Saul said, "God has delivered him into my hand, for he shut himself in by entering a city with double gates and bars."

8 So Saul summoned all the people for war, to go down to Keilah to besiege David and his men.

9 Now David knew that Saul was plotting evil against him; so he said to Abiathar the priest, "Bring the ephod here."

10 Then David said, "O LORD God of Israel, Your servant has heard for certain that Saul is seeking to come to Keilah to destroy the city on my account.

11"Will the men of Keilah surrender me into his hand? Will Saul come down just as Your servant has heard? O LORD God of Israel, I pray, tell Your servant." And the LORD said, "He will come down."

12 Then David said, "Will the men of Keilah surrender me and my men into the hand of Saul?" And the LORD said, "They will surrender you."

New International

hold? 15Was that day the first time I inquired of God for him? Of course not! Let not the king accuse your servant or any of his father's family, for your servant knows nothing at all about this whole affair."

16But the king said, "You will surely die, Ahimelech, you and your father's whole family."

17Then the king ordered the guards at his side: "Turn and kill the priests of the LORD, because they too have sided with David. They knew he was fleeing, yet they did not tell me."

But the king's officials were not willing to raise a hand to strike the priests of the LORD.

18The king then ordered Doeg, "You turn and strike down the priests." So Doeg the Edomite turned and struck them down. That day he killed eighty-five men who wore the linen ephod. 19He also put to the sword Nob, the town of the priests, with its men and women, its children and infants, and its cattle, donkeys and sheep.

20But Abiathar, a son of Ahimelech son of Ahitub, escaped and fled to join David. 21He told David that Saul had killed the priests of the LORD. 22Then David said to Abiathar: "That day, when Doeg the Edomite was there, I knew he would be sure to tell Saul. I am responsible for the death of your father's whole family. 23Stay with me; don't be afraid; the man who is seeking your life is seeking mine also. You will be safe with me."

David Saves Keilah

23 WHEN DAVID was told, "Look, the Philistines are fighting against Keilah and are looting the threshing floors," 2he inquired of the LORD, saying, "Shall I go and attack these Philistines?"

The LORD answered him, "Go, attack the Philistines and save Keilah."

3But David's men said to him, "Here in Judah we are afraid. How much more, then, if we go to Keilah against the Philistine forces!"

4Once again David inquired of the LORD, and the LORD answered him, "Go down to Keilah, for I am going to give the Philistines into your hand." 5So David and his men went to Keilah, fought the Philistines and carried off their livestock. He inflicted heavy losses on the Philistines and saved the people of Keilah. 6(Now Abiathar son of Ahimelech had brought the ephod down with him when he fled to David at Keilah.)

Saul Pursues David

7Saul was told that David had gone to Keilah, and he said, "God has handed him over to me, for David has imprisoned himself by entering a town with gates and bars." 8And Saul called up all his forces for battle, to go down to Keilah to besiege David and his men.

9When David learned that Saul was plotting against him, he said to Abiathar the priest, "Bring the ephod." 10David said, "O LORD, God of Israel, your servant has heard definitely that Saul plans to come to Keilah and destroy the town on account of me. 11Will the citizens of Keilah surrender me to him? Will Saul come down, as your servant has heard? O LORD, God of Israel, tell your servant."

And the LORD said, "He will."

12Again David asked, "Will the citizens of Keilah surrender me and my men to Saul?"

And the LORD said, "They will."

King James

¹³ ¶ Then David and his men, *which were* about six hundred, arose and departed out of Keilah, and went whithersoever they could go. And it was told Saul that David was escaped from Keilah; and he forbare to go forth.

¹⁴And David abode in the wilderness in strong holds, and remained in a mountain in the wilderness of Ziph. And Saul sought him every day, but God delivered him not into his hand.

Saul pursues David

¹⁵And David saw that Saul was come out to seek his life: and David *was* in the wilderness of Ziph in a wood.

¹⁶ ¶ And Jonathan Saul's son arose, and went to David into the wood, and strengthened his hand in God.

¹⁷And he said unto him, Fear not: for the hand of Saul my father shall not find thee; and thou shalt be king over Israel, and I shall be next unto thee; and that also Saul my father knoweth.

¹⁸And they two made a covenant before the LORD: and David abode in the wood, and Jonathan went to his house.

¹⁹ ¶ Then came up the Ziphites to Saul to Gibeah, saying, Doth not David hide himself with us in strong holds in the wood, in the hill of Hachilah, which *is* ^von the south of ^wJeshimon?

²⁰Now therefore, O king, come down according to all the desire of thy soul to come down; and our part *shall be* to deliver him into the king's hand.

²¹And Saul said, Blessed *be* ye of the LORD; for ye have compassion on me.

²²Go, I pray you, prepare yet, and know and see his place where his ^xhaunt is, *and* who hath seen him there: for it is told me *that* he dealeth very subtly.

²³See therefore, and take knowledge of all the lurking places where he hideth himself, and come ye again to me with the certainty, and I will go with you: and it shall come to pass, if he be in the land, that I will search him out throughout all the thousands of Judah.

²⁴And they arose, and went to Ziph before Saul: but David and his men *were* in the wilderness of Maon, in the plain on the south of Jeshimon.

²⁵Saul also and his men went to seek *him.* And they told David: wherefore he came down ^yinto a rock, and abode in the wilderness of Maon. And when Saul heard *that,* he pursued after David in the wilderness of Maon.

²⁶And Saul went on this side of the mountain, and David and his men on that side of the mountain: and David made haste to get away for fear of Saul; for Saul and his men compassed David and his men round about to take them.

²⁷ ¶ But there came a messenger unto Saul, saying, Haste thee, and come; for the Philistines have ^zinvaded the land.

²⁸Wherefore Saul returned from pursuing after David, and went against the Philistines: therefore they called that place ^aSela-hammahlekoth.

²⁹ ¶ And David went up from thence, and dwelt in strong holds at En-gedi.

David spares Saul

24 AND IT came to pass, when Saul was returned from ^bfollowing the Philistines, that it was told him, saying, Behold, David *is* in the wilderness of En-gedi.

²Then Saul took three thousand chosen men out of all Israel, and went to seek David and his men upon the rocks of the wild goats.

³And he came to the sheepcotes by the way, where *was* a cave; and Saul went in to cover his feet: and David and his men remained in the sides of the cave.

Amplified

¹³Then David and his men, about 600, arose and left Keilah, going wherever they could go. When Saul was told that David had escaped from Keilah, he gave up going there.

¹⁴David remained in the wilderness strongholds in the hill country of the Wilderness of Ziph. Saul sought him every day, but God did not give him into his hands.

¹⁵David saw that Saul had come out to seek his life. David was in the Wilderness of Ziph in the wood [at Horesh].

¹⁶And Jonathan, Saul's son, rose and went into the wood to David [at Horesh] and strengthened his hand in God.

¹⁷He said to him, Fear not; the hand of Saul my father shall not find you. You shall be king over Israel, and I shall be next to you. Saul my father knows that too.

¹⁸And the two of them made a covenant before the Lord. And David remained in the wood [at Horesh], and Jonathan went to his house.

¹⁹Then the Ziphites came to Saul at Gibeah, saying, Does not David hide himself with us in strongholds in the wood [at Horesh], on the hill of Hachilah, which is south of Jeshimon?

²⁰Now come down, O king, according to all your heart's desire to come down, and our part shall be to deliver him into the king's hands.

²¹And Saul said, The Lord bless you, for you have compassion on me.

²²Go, make yet more sure; and know and see where his haunt is and who has seen him there; for I am told he deals very craftily.

²³See and take note of all his hiding places and come back to me with the certain facts, and I will go with you. If he is in the land, I will search him out among all the thousands of Judah.

²⁴So they arose and went to Ziph ahead of Saul. Now David and his men were in the Wilderness of Maon, in the Arabah south of Jeshimon.

²⁵Saul and his men went to seek him. And David was told; so he went down to the rock in the Wilderness of Maon and stayed. When Saul heard that, he pursued David in the Wilderness of Maon.

²⁶And Saul went on one side of the mountain, and David and his men on the other side of the mountain. And David made haste to get away for fear of Saul, for Saul and his men were surrounding [him] and his men to capture them.

²⁷But a messenger came to Saul, saying, Make haste and come, for the Philistines have made a raid on the land.

²⁸So Saul returned from pursuing David and went against the Philistines. So they called that place the Rock of Escape.

²⁹David went up from there and dwelt in the strongholds of En-gedi.

24 WHEN SAUL returned from following the Philistines, he was told, Behold, David is in the Wilderness of En-gedi.

²Then Saul took 3,000 chosen men out of all Israel and went to seek David and his men among the Rocks of the Wild Goats.

³He came to the sheepfolds on the way, where there was a cave, and Saul went in to relieve himself. Now David and his men were sitting in the cave's innermost recesses.

---

^vHeb. *on the right hand*   ^wOr, *The wilderness?*   ^xHeb. *foot shall be*   ^yOr, *from the rock*   ^zHeb. *spread themselves upon*   ^ai.e. *The rock of divisions*   ^bHeb. *after*

New American Standard

13 Then David and his men, about six hundred, arose and departed from Keilah, and they went wherever they could go. When it was told Saul that David had escaped from Keilah, he gave up the pursuit.

14 David stayed in the wilderness in the strongholds, and remained in the hill country in the wilderness of Ziph. And Saul sought him every day, but God did not deliver him into his hand.

Saul Pursues David

15 ¶ Now David became aware that Saul had come out to seek his life while David was in the wilderness of Ziph at Horesh.

16 And Jonathan, Saul's son, arose and went to David at Horesh, and *n*encouraged him in God.

17 Thus he said to him, "Do not be afraid, because the hand of Saul my father will not find you, and you will be king over Israel and I will be next to you; and Saul my father knows that also."

18 So the two of them made a covenant before the LORD; and David stayed at Horesh while Jonathan went to his house.

19 ¶ Then Ziphites came up to Saul at Gibeah, saying, "Is David not hiding with us in the strongholds at Horesh, on the hill of Hachilah, which is on the south of *o*Jeshimon?

20"Now then, O king, come down according to all the desire of your soul to do so; and our part *shall be* to surrender him into the king's hand."

21 Saul said, "May you be blessed of the LORD, for you have had compassion on me.

22"Go now, make more sure, and investigate and see his place where his haunt is, *and* who has seen him there; for I am told that he is very cunning.

23"So look, and learn about all the hiding places where he hides himself and return to me with certainty, and I will go with you; and if he is in the land, I will search him out among all the thousands of Judah."

24 ¶ Then they arose and went to Ziph before Saul. Now David and his men were in the wilderness of Maon, in the Arabah to the south of Jeshimon.

25 When Saul and his men went to seek *him,* they told David, and he came down to the rock and stayed in the wilderness of Maon. And when Saul heard *it,* he pursued David in the wilderness of Maon.

26 Saul went on one side of the mountain, and David and his men on the other side of the mountain; and David was hurrying to get away from Saul, for Saul and his men were surrounding David and his men to seize them.

27 But a messenger came to Saul, saying, "Hurry and come, for the Philistines have made a raid on the land."

28 So Saul returned from pursuing David and went to meet the Philistines; therefore they called that place the Rock of Escape.

29 David went up from there and stayed in the strongholds of Engedi.

David Spares Saul's Life

24 NOW WHEN Saul returned from pursuing the Philistines, he was told, saying, "Behold, David is in the wilderness of Engedi."

2 Then Saul took three thousand chosen men from all Israel and went to seek David and his men in front of the Rocks of the Wild Goats.

3 He came to the sheepfolds on the way, where there *was* a cave; and Saul went in to relieve himself. Now David and his men were sitting in the inner recesses of the cave.

New International

13So David and his men, about six hundred in number, left Keilah and kept moving from place to place. When Saul was told that David had escaped from Keilah, he did not go there.

14David stayed in the desert strongholds and in the hills of the Desert of Ziph. Day after day Saul searched for him, but God did not give David into his hands.

15While David was at Horesh in the Desert of Ziph, he learned that Saul had come out to take his life. 16And Saul's son Jonathan went to David at Horesh and helped him find strength in God. 17"Don't be afraid," he said. "My father Saul will not lay a hand on you. You will be king over Israel, and I will be second to you. Even my father Saul knows this." 18The two of them made a covenant before the LORD. Then Jonathan went home, but David remained at Horesh.

19The Ziphites went up to Saul at Gibeah and said, "Is not David hiding among us in the strongholds at Horesh, on the hill of Hakilah, south of Jeshimon? 20Now, O king, come down whenever it pleases you to do so, and we will be responsible for handing him over to the king."

21Saul replied, "The LORD bless you for your concern for me. 22Go and make further preparation. Find out where David usually goes and who has seen him there. They tell me he is very crafty. 23Find out about all the hiding places he uses and come back to me with definite information.*y* Then I will go with you; if he is in the area, I will track him down among all the clans of Judah."

24So they set out and went to Ziph ahead of Saul. Now David and his men were in the Desert of Maon, in the Arabah south of Jeshimon. 25Saul and his men began the search, and when David was told about it, he went down to the rock and stayed in the Desert of Maon. When Saul heard this, he went into the Desert of Maon in pursuit of David.

26Saul was going along one side of the mountain, and David and his men were on the other side, hurrying to get away from Saul. As Saul and his forces were closing in on David and his men to capture them, 27a messenger came to Saul, saying, "Come quickly! The Philistines are raiding the land." 28Then Saul broke off his pursuit of David and went to meet the Philistines. That is why they call this place Sela Hammahlekoth.*z* 29And David went up from there and lived in the strongholds of En Gedi.

David Spares Saul's Life

24 AFTER SAUL returned from pursuing the Philistines, he was told, "David is in the Desert of En Gedi." 2So Saul took three thousand chosen men from all Israel and set out to look for David and his men near the Crags of the Wild Goats.

3He came to the sheep pens along the way; a cave was there, and Saul went in to relieve himself. David and his

---

n Lit *strengthened his hand*   *o* Or *the desert*

King James

⁴And the men of David said unto him, Behold the day of which the LORD said unto thee, Behold, I will deliver thine enemy into thine hand, that thou mayest do to him as it shall seem good unto thee. Then David arose, and cut off the skirt of ^cSaul's robe privily.

⁵And it came to pass afterward, that David's heart smote him, because he had cut off Saul's skirt.

⁶And he said unto his men, The LORD forbid that I should do this thing unto my master, the LORD'S anointed, to stretch forth mine hand against him, seeing he *is* the anointed of the LORD.

⁷So David ^dstayed his servants with these words, and suffered them not to rise against Saul. But Saul rose up out of the cave, and went on *his* way.

⁸David also arose afterward, and went out of the cave, and cried after Saul, saying, My lord the king. And when Saul looked behind him, David stooped with his face to the earth, and bowed himself.

⁹¶ And David said to Saul, Wherefore hearest thou men's words, saying, Behold, David seeketh thy hurt?

¹⁰Behold, this day thine eyes have seen how that the LORD had delivered thee today into mine hand in the cave: and *some* bade *me* kill thee: but *mine eye* spared thee; and I said, I will not put forth mine hand against my lord; for he *is* the LORD'S anointed.

¹¹Moreover, my father, see, yea, see the skirt of thy robe in my hand: for in that I cut off the skirt of thy robe, and killed thee not, know thou and see that *there is* neither evil nor transgression in mine hand, and I have not sinned against thee; yet thou huntest my soul to take it.

¹²The LORD judge between me and thee, and the LORD avenge me of thee: but mine hand shall not be upon thee.

¹³As saith the proverb of the ancients, Wickedness proceedeth from the wicked: but mine hand shall not be upon thee.

¹⁴After whom is the king of Israel come out? after whom dost thou pursue? after a dead dog, after a flea.

¹⁵The LORD therefore be judge, and judge between me and thee, and see, and plead my cause, and ^edeliver me out of thine hand.

¹⁶¶ And it came to pass, when David had made an end of speaking these words unto Saul, that Saul said, *Is* this thy voice, my son David? And Saul lifted up his voice, and wept.

¹⁷And he said to David, Thou *art* more righteous than I: for thou hast rewarded me good, whereas I have rewarded thee evil.

¹⁸And thou hast shown this day how that thou hast dealt well with me: forasmuch as when the LORD had delivered me into thine hand, thou killedst me not.

¹⁹For if a man find his enemy, will he let him go well away? wherefore the LORD reward thee good for that thou hast done unto me this day.

²⁰And now, behold, I know well that thou shalt surely be king, and that the kingdom of Israel shall be established in thine hand.

²¹Swear now therefore unto me by the LORD, that thou wilt not cut off my seed after me, and that thou wilt not destroy my name out of my father's house.

²²And David sware unto Saul. And Saul went home; but David and his men gat them up unto the hold.

David, Nabal and Abigail

25 AND SAMUEL died; and all the Israelites were gathered together, and lamented him, and buried him in his house at Ramah. And David arose, and went down to the wilderness of Paran.

Amplified

⁴David's men said to him, Behold the day of which the Lord said to you, Behold, I will deliver your enemy into your hands and you shall do to him as it seems good to you. Then David arose [in the darkness] and stealthily cut off the skirt of Saul's robe.

⁵Afterward, David's heart smote him because he had cut off Saul's skirt.

⁶He said to his men, The Lord forbid that I should do this to my master, the Lord's anointed, to put my hand out against him, when he is the anointed of the Lord.

⁷So David checked his men with these words and did not let them rise against Saul. But Saul rose up and left the cave and went on his way.

⁸David also arose afterward and went out of the cave and called after Saul, saying, My lord the king! And when Saul looked behind him, David bowed with his face to the earth and did obeisance.

⁹And David said to Saul, Why do you listen to the words of men who say, David seeks to do you harm?

¹⁰Behold, your eyes have seen how the Lord gave you today into my hands in the cave. Some told me to kill you, but I spared you; I said, I will not put forth my hand against my lord, for he is the Lord's anointed.

¹¹See, my father, see the skirt of your robe in my hand! Since I cut off the skirt of your robe and did not kill you, you know and see that there is no evil or treason in my hands. I have not sinned against you, yet you hunt my life to take it.

¹²May the Lord judge between me and you, and may the Lord avenge me upon you, but my hand shall not be upon you.

¹³As the proverb of the ancients says, Out of the wicked comes forth wickedness; but my hand shall not be against you.

¹⁴After whom has the king of Israel come out? After whom do you pursue? After a dead dog? After a flea?

¹⁵May the Lord be judge and judge between me and you, and see and plead my cause, and deliver me out of your hands. [Ps. 142.]

¹⁶When David had said this to Saul, Saul said, Is this your voice, my son David? And Saul lifted up his voice and wept.

¹⁷He said to David, You are more upright in God's eyes than I, for you have repaid me good, but I have rewarded you evil.

¹⁸You have declared today how you have dealt well with me; for when the Lord gave me into your hand, you did not kill me.

¹⁹For if a man finds his enemy, will he let him go away unharmed? Therefore may the Lord reward you with good for what you have done for me this day.

²⁰And now, behold, I well know that you shall surely be king and that the kingdom of Israel shall be established in your hands.

²¹Swear now therefore to me by the Lord that you will not cut off my descendants after me and that you will not destroy my name out of my father's house.

²²David gave Saul his oath; and Saul went home, but David and his men went up to the stronghold.

25 NOW SAMUEL died, and all the Israelites assembled and mourned for him, and buried him at his house in Ramah. David arose and went to the Wilderness of Paran.

^cHeb. *the robe which* was *Saul's*   ^dHeb. *cut off*   ^eHeb. *judge*

New American Standard

4 The men of David said to him, "Behold, *this is* the day of which the LORD said to you, 'Behold; I am about to give your enemy into your hand, and you shall do to him as it seems good to you.' " Then David arose and cut off the edge of Saul's robe secretly.

5 It came about afterward that David's conscience bothered him because he had cut off the edge of Saul's *robe.*

6 So he said to his men, "Far be it from me because of the LORD that I should do this thing to my lord, the LORD's anointed, to stretch out my hand against him, since he is the LORD's anointed."

7 David persuaded his men with *these* words and did not allow them to rise up against Saul. And Saul arose, left the cave, and went on *his* way.

8 ¶ Now afterward David arose and went out of the cave and called after Saul, saying, "My lord the king!" And when Saul looked behind him, David bowed with his face to the ground and prostrated himself.

9 David said to Saul, "Why do you listen to the words of men, saying, 'Behold, David seeks to harm you'?

10 "Behold, this day your eyes have seen that the LORD had given you today into my hand in the cave, and some said to kill you, but *my eye* had pity on you; and I said, 'I will not stretch out my hand against my lord, for he is the LORD's anointed.'

11 "Now, my father, see! Indeed, see the edge of your robe in my hand! For in that I cut off the edge of your robe and did not kill you, know and perceive that there is no evil or rebellion in my hands, and I have not sinned against you, though you are lying in wait for my life to take it.

12 "May the LORD judge between you and me, and may the LORD avenge me on you; but my hand shall not be against you.

13 "As the proverb of the ancients says, 'Out of the wicked comes forth wickedness'; but my hand shall not be against you.

14 "After whom has the king of Israel come out? Whom are you pursuing? A dead dog, a single flea?

15 "The LORD therefore be judge and decide between you and me; and may He see and plead my cause and deliver me from your hand."

16 ¶ When David had finished speaking these words to Saul, Saul said, "Is this your voice, my son David?" Then Saul lifted up his voice and wept.

17 He said to David, "You are more righteous than I; for you have dealt well with me, while I have dealt wickedly with you.

18 "You have declared today that you have done good to me, that the LORD delivered me into your hand and *yet* you did not kill me.

19 "For if a man finds his enemy, will he let him go away safely? May the LORD therefore reward you with good in return for what you have done to me this day.

20 "Now, behold, I know that you will surely be king, and that the kingdom of Israel will be established in your hand.

21 "So now swear to me by the LORD that you will not cut off my descendants after me and that you will not destroy my name from my father's household."

22 David swore to Saul. And Saul went to his home, but David and his men went up to the stronghold.

Samuel's Death

25 THEN SAMUEL died; and all Israel gathered together and mourned for him, and buried him at his house in Ramah. And David arose and went down to the wilderness of Paran.

New International

men were far back in the cave. 4The men said, "This is the day the LORD spoke of when he said[a] to you, 'I will give your enemy into your hands for you to deal with as you wish.' " Then David crept up unnoticed and cut off a corner of Saul's robe.

5Afterward, David was conscience-stricken for having cut off a corner of his robe. 6He said to his men, "The LORD forbid that I should do such a thing to my master, the LORD's anointed, or lift my hand against him; for he is the anointed of the LORD." 7With these words David rebuked his men and did not allow them to attack Saul. And Saul left the cave and went his way.

8Then David went out of the cave and called out to Saul, "My lord the king!" When Saul looked behind him, David bowed down and prostrated himself with his face to the ground. 9He said to Saul, "Why do you listen when men say, 'David is bent on harming you'? 10This day you have seen with your own eyes how the LORD delivered you into my hands in the cave. Some urged me to kill you, but I spared you; I said, 'I will not lift my hand against my master, because he is the LORD's anointed.' 11See, my father, look at this piece of your robe in my hand! I cut off the corner of your robe but did not kill you. Now understand and recognize that I am not guilty of wrongdoing or rebellion. I have not wronged you, but you are hunting me down to take my life. 12May the LORD judge between you and me. And may the LORD avenge the wrongs you have done to me, but my hand will not touch you. 13As the old saying goes, 'From evildoers come evil deeds,' so my hand will not touch you.

14"Against whom has the king of Israel come out? Whom are you pursuing? A dead dog? A flea? 15May the LORD be our judge and decide between us. May he consider my cause and uphold it; may he vindicate me by delivering me from your hand."

16When David finished saying this, Saul asked, "Is that your voice, David my son?" And he wept aloud. 17"You are more righteous than I," he said. "You have treated me well, but I have treated you badly. 18You have just now told me of the good you did to me; the LORD delivered me into your hands, but you did not kill me. 19When a man finds his enemy, does he let him get away unharmed? May the LORD reward you well for the way you treated me today. 20I know that you will surely be king and that the kingdom of Israel will be established in your hands. 21Now swear to me by the LORD that you will not cut off my descendants or wipe out my name from my father's family."

22So David gave his oath to Saul. Then Saul returned home, but David and his men went up to the stronghold.

David, Nabal and Abigail

25 NOW SAMUEL died, and all Israel assembled and mourned for him; and they buried him at his home in Ramah.

Then David moved down into the Desert of Maon.[b]

King James

2And *there was* a man in Maon, whose *f*possessions *were* in Carmel; and the man *was* very great, and he had three thousand sheep, and a thousand goats: and he was shearing his sheep in Carmel.

3Now the name of the man *was* Nabal; and the name of his wife Abigail: and *she was* a woman of good understanding, and of a beautiful countenance: but the man *was* churlish and evil in his doings; and he *was* of the house of Caleb.

4 ¶ And David heard in the wilderness that Nabal did shear his sheep.

5And David sent out ten young men, and David said unto the young men, Get you up to Carmel, and go to Nabal, and greet him in my name:

6And thus shall ye say to him that liveth *in prosperity,* Peace *be* both to thee, and peace *be* to thine house, and peace *be* unto all that thou hast.

7And now I have heard that thou hast shearers: now thy shepherds which were with us, we *g*hurt them not, neither was there aught missing unto them, all the while they were in Carmel.

8Ask thy young men, and they will show thee. Wherefore let the young men find favour in thine eyes: for we come in a good day: give, I pray thee, whatsoever cometh to thine hand unto thy servants, and to thy son David.

9And when David's young men came, they spake to Nabal according to all those words in the name of David, and *h*ceased.

10 ¶ And Nabal answered David's servants, and said, Who *is* David? and who *is* the son of Jesse? there be many servants now a days that break away every man from his master.

11Shall I then take my bread, and my water, and my *i*flesh that I have killed for my shearers, and give *it* unto men, whom I know not whence they *be?*

12So David's young men turned their way, and went again, and came and told him all those sayings.

13And David said unto his men, Gird ye on every man his sword. And they girded on every man his sword; and David also girded on his sword: and there went up after David about four hundred men; and two hundred abode by the stuff.

14 ¶ But one of the young men told Abigail, Nabal's wife, saying, Behold, David sent messengers out of the wilderness to salute our master; and he *j*railed on them.

15But the men *were* very good unto us, and we were not *g*hurt, neither missed we any thing, as long as we were conversant with them, when we were in the fields:

16They were a wall unto us both by night and day, all the while we were with them keeping the sheep.

17Now therefore know and consider what thou wilt do; for evil is determined against our master, and against all his household: for he *is such* a son of Belial, that *a man* cannot speak to him.

18 ¶ Then Abigail made haste, and took two hundred loaves, and two bottles of wine, and five sheep ready dressed, and five measures of parched *corn,* and an hundred *k*clusters of raisins, and two hundred cakes of figs, and laid *them* on asses.

19And she said unto her servants, Go on before me; behold, I come after you. But she told not her husband Nabal.

20And it was *so, as* she rode on the ass, that she came down by the covert of the hill, and, behold, David and his men came down against her; and she met them.

21Now David had said, Surely in vain have I kept all that this *fellow* hath in the wilderness, so that nothing was missed of all that *pertained* unto him: and he hath requited me evil for good.

Amplified

2A very rich man was in Maon, whose possessions *and* business were in Carmel. He had 3,000 sheep and 1,000 goats, and he was shearing his sheep in Carmel.

3The man's name was Nabal and his wife's name was Abigail; she was a woman of good understanding, and beautiful. But the man was rough and evil in his doings; he was a Calebite.

4David heard in the wilderness that Nabal was shearing his sheep.

5And David sent out ten young men and said to [them], Go up to Carmel to Nabal and greet him in my name;

6And salute him thus: Peace be to you and to your house and to all that you have.

7I have heard that you have shearers. Now your shepherds have been with us and we did them no harm, and they missed nothing all the time they were in Carmel.

8Ask your young men and they will tell you. Therefore let my young men find favor in your sight, for we come at an opportune time. I pray you, give whatever you have at hand to your servants and to your son David.

9And when David's young men came, they said all this to Nabal in the name of David, and then paused.

10And Nabal answered David's servants and said, Who is David? Who is the son of Jesse? There are many servants nowadays who are each breaking away from his master.

11Shall I then take my bread and my water, and my meat that I have killed for my shearers, and give it to men when I do not know where they belong?

12So David's young men turned away, and came and told him all that was said.

13And David said to his men, Every man gird on his sword. And they did so, and David also girded on his sword; and there went up after David about 400 men, and 200 remained with the baggage.

14But one of Nabal's young men told Abigail, Nabal's wife, Behold, David sent messengers out of the wilderness to salute our master, and he railed at them.

15But David's men were very good to us, and we were not harmed, nor did we miss anything as long as we went with them, when we were in the fields.

16They were a wall to us night and day, all the time we were with them keeping the sheep.

17So know this and consider what you will do, for evil is determined against our master and all his house. For he is such a wicked man that one cannot speak to him.

18Then Abigail made haste and took 200 loaves, two skins of wine, five sheep already dressed, five measures of parched grain, 100 clusters of raisins, and 200 cakes of figs, and laid them on donkeys.

19And she said to her servants, Go on before me; behold, I come after you. But she did not tell her husband Nabal.

20As she rode on her donkey, she came down hidden by the mountain, and behold, David and his men came down opposite her, and she met them.

21Now David had said, Surely in vain have I protected all that this fellow has in the wilderness, so that nothing was missed of all that belonged to him; and he has repaid me evil for good.

*f*Or, *business*   *g*Heb. *shamed*   *h*Heb. *rested*   *i*Heb.
slaughter   *j*Heb. *flew upon them*   *k*Or, *lumps*

New American Standard

Nabal and Abigail

2 ¶ Now *there was* a man in Maon whose business was in Carmel; and the man was very rich, and he had three thousand sheep and a thousand goats. And it came about while he was shearing his sheep in Carmel

3 (now the man's name was Nabal, and his wife's name was Abigail. And the woman was intelligent and beautiful in appearance, but the man was harsh and evil in *his* dealings, and he was a Calebite),

4 that David heard in the wilderness that Nabal was shearing his sheep.

5 So David sent ten young men; and David said to the young men, "Go up to Carmel, visit Nabal and greet him in my name;

6 and thus you shall say, 'Have a long life, peace be to you, and peace be to your house, and peace be to all that you have.

7 'Now I have heard that you have shearers; now your shepherds have been with us and we have not insulted them, nor have they missed anything all the days they were in Carmel.

8 'Ask your young men and they will tell you. Therefore let *my* young men find favor in your eyes, for we have come on a festive day. Please give whatever you find at hand to your servants and to your son David.' "

9 ¶ When David's young men came, they spoke to Nabal according to all these words in David's name; then they waited.

10 But Nabal answered David's servants and said, "Who is David? And who is the son of Jesse? There are many servants today who are each breaking away from his master.

11 "Shall I then take my bread and my water and my meat that I have slaughtered for my shearers, and give it to men whose origin I do not know?"

12 So David's young men retraced their way and went back; and they came and told him according to all these words.

13 David said to his men, "Each *of you* gird on his sword." So each man girded on his sword. And David also girded on his sword, and about four hundred men went up behind David while two hundred stayed with the baggage.

14 ¶ But one of the young men told Abigail, Nabal's wife, saying, "Behold, David sent messengers from the wilderness to greet our master, and he scorned them.

15 "Yet the men were very good to us, and we were not insulted, nor did we miss anything as long as we went about with them, while we were in the fields.

16 "They were a wall to us both by night and by day, all the time we were with them tending the sheep.

17 "Now therefore, know and consider what you should do, for evil is plotted against our master and against all his household; and he is such a worthless man that no one can speak to him."

Abigail Intercedes

18 ¶ Then Abigail hurried and took two hundred *loaves* of bread and two jugs of wine and five sheep already prepared and five measures of roasted grain and a hundred clusters of raisins and two hundred cakes of figs, and loaded *them* on donkeys.

19 She said to her young men, "Go on before me; behold, I am coming after you." But she did not tell her husband Nabal.

20 It came about as she was riding on her donkey and coming down by the hidden part of the mountain, that behold, David and his men were coming down toward her; so she met them.

21 Now David had said, "Surely in vain I have guarded all that this *man* has in the wilderness, so that nothing was missed of all that belonged to him; and he has returned me evil for good.

New International

2 A certain man in Maon, who had property there at Carmel, was very wealthy. He had a thousand goats and three thousand sheep, which he was shearing in Carmel. 3 His name was Nabal and his wife's name was Abigail. She was an intelligent and beautiful woman, but her husband, a Calebite, was surly and mean in his dealings.

4 While David was in the desert, he heard that Nabal was shearing sheep. 5 So he sent ten young men and said to them, "Go up to Nabal at Carmel and greet him in my name. 6 Say to him: 'Long life to you! Good health to you and your household! And good health to all that is yours!

7 " 'Now I hear that it is sheep-shearing time. When your shepherds were with us, we did not mistreat them, and the whole time they were at Carmel nothing of theirs was missing. 8 Ask your own servants and they will tell you. Therefore be favorable toward my young men, since we come at a festive time. Please give your servants and your son David whatever you can find for them.' "

9 When David's men arrived, they gave Nabal this message in David's name. Then they waited.

10 Nabal answered David's servants, "Who is this David? Who is this son of Jesse? Many servants are breaking away from their masters these days. 11 Why should I take my bread and water, and the meat I have slaughtered for my shearers, and give it to men coming from who knows where?"

12 David's men turned around and went back. When they arrived, they reported every word. 13 David said to his men, "Put on your swords!" So they put on their swords, and David put on his. About four hundred men went up with David, while two hundred stayed with the supplies.

14 One of the servants told Nabal's wife Abigail: "David sent messengers from the desert to give our master his greetings, but he hurled insults at them. 15 Yet these men were very good to us. They did not mistreat us, and the whole time we were out in the fields near them nothing was missing. 16 Night and day they were a wall around us all the time we were herding our sheep near them. 17 Now think it over and see what you can do, because disaster is hanging over our master and his whole household. He is such a wicked man that no one can talk to him."

18 Abigail lost no time. She took two hundred loaves of bread, two skins of wine, five dressed sheep, five seahs[c] of roasted grain, a hundred cakes of raisins and two hundred cakes of pressed figs, and loaded them on donkeys. 19 Then she told her servants, "Go on ahead; I'll follow you." But she did not tell her husband Nabal.

20 As she came riding her donkey into a mountain ravine, there were David and his men descending toward her, and she met them. 21 David had just said, "It's been useless—all my watching over this fellow's property in the desert so that nothing of his was missing. He has paid me back evil

c 18 That is, probably about a bushel (about 37 liters)

King James	Amplified

King James

[22]So and more also do God unto the enemies of David, if I leave of all that *pertain* to him by the morning light any that pisseth against the wall.

[23]And when Abigail saw David, she hasted, and lighted off the ass, and fell before David on her face, and bowed herself to the ground,

[24]And fell at his feet, and said, Upon me, my lord, *upon me let this* iniquity *be:* and let thine handmaid, I pray thee, speak in thine *l* audience, and hear the words of thine handmaid.

[25]Let not my lord, I pray thee, *m*regard this man of Belial, *even* Nabal: for as his name *is,* so *is* he; *n*Nabal *is* his name, and folly *is* with him: but I thine handmaid saw not the young men of my lord, whom thou didst send.

[26]Now therefore, my lord, *as* the LORD liveth, and *as* thy soul liveth, seeing the LORD hath withholden thee from coming to *shed* blood, and from *o*avenging thyself with thine own hand, now let thine enemies, and they that seek evil to my lord, be as Nabal.

[27]And now this *p*blessing which thine handmaid hath brought unto my lord, let it even be given unto the young men that follow my lord.

[28]I pray thee, forgive the trespass of thine handmaid: for the LORD will certainly make my lord a sure house; because my lord fighteth the battles of the LORD, and evil hath not been found in thee *all* thy days.

[29]Yet a man is risen to pursue thee, and to seek thy soul: but the soul of my lord shall be bound in the bundle of life with the LORD thy God; and the souls of thine enemies, them shall he sling out, *q*as *out* of the middle of a sling.

[30]And it shall come to pass, when the LORD shall have done to my lord according to all the good that he hath spoken concerning thee, and shall have appointed thee ruler over Israel;

[31]That this shall be *r*no grief unto thee, nor offence of heart unto my lord, either that thou hast shed blood causeless, or that my lord hath avenged himself: but when the LORD shall have dealt well with my lord, then remember thine handmaid.

[32] ¶ And David said to Abigail, Blessed *be* the LORD God of Israel, which sent thee this day to meet me:

[33]And blessed *be* thy advice, and blessed *be* thou, which hast kept me this day from coming to *shed* blood, and from avenging myself with mine own hand.

[34]For in very deed, *as* the LORD God of Israel liveth, which hath kept me back from hurting thee, except thou hadst hasted and come to meet me, surely there had not been left unto Nabal by the morning light any that pisseth against the wall.

[35]So David received of her hand *that* which she had brought him, and said unto her, Go up in peace to thine house; see, I have hearkened to thy voice, and have accepted thy person.

[36] ¶ And Abigail came to Nabal; and, behold, he held a feast in his house, like the feast of a king; and Nabal's heart *was* merry within him, for he *was* very drunken: wherefore she told him nothing, less or more, until the morning light.

[37]But it came to pass in the morning, when the wine was gone out of Nabal, and his wife had told him these things, that his heart died within him, and he became *as* a stone.

Amplified

[22]May God do so, and more also, to David *h*if I leave of all who belong to him one male alive by morning.

[23]When Abigail saw David, she hastened and lighted off the donkey, and fell before David on her face and did obeisance.

[24]Kneeling at his feet she said, Upon me alone let this guilt be, my lord. And let your handmaid, I pray you, speak in your presence, and hear the words of your handmaid.

[25]Let not my lord, I pray you, regard this foolish *and* wicked fellow Nabal, for as his name is, so is he—Nabal [foolish, wicked] is his name, and folly is with him. But I, your handmaid, did not see my lord's young men whom you sent.

[26]So now, my lord, as the Lord lives and as your soul lives, seeing that the Lord has prevented you from bloodguiltiness and from avenging yourself with your own hand, now let your enemies and those who seek to do evil to my lord be as Nabal.

[27]And now this gift, which your handmaid has brought my lord, let it be given to the young men who follow my lord.

[28]Forgive, I pray you, the trespass of your handmaid, for the Lord will certainly make my lord a sure house, because my lord is fighting the Lord's battles, and evil has not been found in you all your days.

[29]Though man is risen up to pursue you and to seek your life, yet the life of my lord shall be bound in the living bundle with the Lord your God. And the lives of your enemies—them shall He sling out as out of the center of a sling.

[30]And when the Lord has done to my lord according to all the good that He has promised concerning you and has made you ruler over Israel,

[31]This shall be no staggering grief to you or cause for pangs of conscience to my lord, either that you have shed blood without cause or that my lord has avenged himself. And when the Lord has dealt well with my lord, then [i earnestly] remember your handmaid.

[32]And David said to Abigail, Blessed be the Lord, the God of Israel, Who sent you this day to meet me!

[33]And blessed be your discretion *and* advice, and blessed be you who have kept me today from bloodguiltiness and from avenging myself with my own hand.

[34]For as the Lord, the God of Israel, lives, Who has prevented me from hurting you, if you had not hurried and come to meet me, surely by morning there would not have been left so much as one male to Nabal.

[35]So David accepted what she had brought him and said to her, Go up in peace to your house. See, I have hearkened to your voice and have granted your petition.

[36]And Abigail came to Nabal, and behold, he was holding a feast in his house like the feast of a king. And [his] heart was merry, for he was very drunk; so she told him nothing at all until the morning light.

[37]But in the morning, when the wine was gone out of Nabal, and his wife told him these things, his heart died within him and he became [paralyzed, helpless as] a stone.

h The Septuagint (Greek translation of the Old Testament) so reads. The Hebrew reads "David's enemies."   *i* Whenever God's inspired Word says "[earnestly] remember," one is certain to miss something if he does not stop, look, and really listen to what the Holy Spirit is wanting to tell him—or her. "[Earnestly] remember" Abigail, the woman whom God has specifically held up as a pattern of right behavior in an unfortunate marriage. Here a dozen vital questions are answered through Abigail's example. She could not have known that thousands of years later people in similar circumstances would become "more than conquerors" because of her, but God knew. Study her until you know her God-given secrets of success; then pass them on to the people who are letting an unfortunate marriage wreck them rather than sanctify them for service. F.B. Meyer (*Through the Bible Day by Day*) said, "Never let the evil disposition of one mate hinder the devotion and grace of the other. Never let the difficulties of your home lead you to abdicate your throne. Do not step down to the level of your circumstances, but lift them to your own high calling in Christ. 'Be not conformed . . . but be ye transformed' (Rom. 12:1, 2 KJV)."

*l*Heb. *ears*   *m*Heb. *lay* it *to his heart*   *n* i.e. *Fool*   *o*Heb. *saving thyself*   *p* Or, *present*   *q* Heb. *in the midst of the bought of a sling*   *r* Heb. *no staggering,* or, *stumbling*

New American Standard

²²"May God do so to the enemies of David, and more also, if by morning I leave *as much as* one male of any who belong to him."

²³ ¶ When Abigail saw David, she hurried and dismounted from her donkey, and fell on her face before David and bowed herself to the ground.

²⁴ She fell at his feet and said, "On me alone, my lord, be the blame. And please let your maidservant speak to you, and listen to the words of your maidservant.

²⁵"Please do not let my lord pay attention to this worthless man, Nabal, for as his name is, so is he. Nabal is his name and folly is with him; but I your maidservant did not see the young men of my lord whom you sent.

²⁶ ¶ "Now therefore, my lord, as the LORD lives, and as your soul lives, since the LORD has restrained you from shedding blood, and from avenging yourself by your own hand, now then let your enemies and those who seek evil against my lord, be as Nabal.

²⁷"Now let this gift which your maidservant has brought to my lord be given to the young men who accompany my lord.

²⁸"Please forgive the transgression of your maidservant; for the LORD will certainly make for my lord an enduring house, because my lord is fighting the battles of the LORD, and evil will not be found in you all your days.

²⁹"Should anyone rise up to pursue you and to seek your life, then the life of my lord shall be bound in the bundle of the living with the LORD your God; but the lives of your enemies He will sling out as from the hollow of a sling.

³⁰"And when the LORD does for my lord according to all the good that He has spoken concerning you, and appoints you ruler over Israel,

³¹ this will not cause grief or a troubled heart to my lord, both by having shed blood without cause and by my lord having avenged himself. When the LORD deals well with my lord, then remember your maidservant."

³² ¶ Then David said to Abigail, "Blessed be the LORD God of Israel, who sent you this day to meet me,

³³ and blessed be your discernment, and blessed be you, who have kept me this day from bloodshed and from avenging myself by my own hand.

³⁴"Nevertheless, as the LORD God of Israel lives, who has restrained me from harming you, unless you had come quickly to meet me, surely there would not have been left to Nabal until the morning light *as much as* one male."

³⁵ So David received from her hand what she had brought him and said to her, "Go up to your house in peace. See, I have listened to you and granted your request."

³⁶ ¶ Then Abigail came to Nabal, and behold, he was holding a feast in his house, like the feast of a king. And Nabal's heart was merry within him, for he was very drunk; so she did not tell him anything at all until the morning light.

³⁷ But in the morning, when the wine had gone out of Nabal, his wife told him these things, and his heart died within him so that he became *as* a stone.

New International

for good. ²²May God deal with David,[d] be it ever so severely, if by morning I leave alive one male of all who belong to him!"

²³When Abigail saw David, she quickly got off her donkey and bowed down before David with her face to the ground. ²⁴She fell at his feet and said: "My lord, let the blame be on me alone. Please let your servant speak to you; hear what your servant has to say. ²⁵May my lord pay no attention to that wicked man Nabal. He is just like his name—his name is Fool, and folly goes with him. But as for me, your servant, I did not see the men my master sent.

²⁶"Now since the LORD has kept you, my master, from bloodshed and from avenging yourself with your own hands, as surely as the LORD lives and as you live, may your enemies and all who intend to harm my master be like Nabal. ²⁷And let this gift, which your servant has brought to my master, be given to the men who follow you. ²⁸Please forgive your servant's offense, for the LORD will certainly make a lasting dynasty for my master, because he fights the LORD's battles. Let no wrongdoing be found in you as long as you live. ²⁹Even though someone is pursuing you to take your life, the life of my master will be bound securely in the bundle of the living by the LORD your God. But the lives of your enemies he will hurl away as from the pocket of a sling. ³⁰When the LORD has done for my master every good thing he promised concerning him and has appointed him leader over Israel, ³¹my master will not have on his conscience the staggering burden of needless bloodshed or of having avenged himself. And when the LORD has brought my master success, remember your servant."

³²David said to Abigail, "Praise be to the LORD, the God of Israel, who has sent you today to meet me. ³³May you be blessed for your good judgment and for keeping me from bloodshed this day and from avenging myself with my own hands. ³⁴Otherwise, as surely as the LORD, the God of Israel, lives, who has kept me from harming you, if you had not come quickly to meet me, not one male belonging to Nabal would have been left alive by daybreak."

³⁵Then David accepted from her hand what she had brought him and said, "Go home in peace. I have heard your words and granted your request."

³⁶When Abigail went to Nabal, he was in the house holding a banquet like that of a king. He was in high spirits and very drunk. So she told him nothing until daybreak. ³⁷Then in the morning, when Nabal was sober, his wife told him all these things, and his heart failed him and he

---

d 22 Some Septuagint manuscripts; Hebrew *with David's enemies*

King James

38And it came to pass about ten days *after*, that the LORD smote Nabal, that he died.

39 ¶ And when David heard that Nabal was dead, he said, Blessed *be* the LORD, that hath pleaded the cause of my reproach from the hand of Nabal, and hath kept his servant from evil: for the LORD hath returned the wickedness of Nabal upon his own head. And David sent and communed with Abigail, to take her to him to wife.

40And when the servants of David were come to Abigail to Carmel, they spake unto her, saying, David sent us unto thee, to take thee to him to wife.

41And she arose, and bowed herself on *her* face to the earth, and said, Behold, *let* thine handmaid *be* a servant to wash the feet of the servants of my lord.

42And Abigail hasted, and arose, and rode upon an ass, with five damsels of hers that went after her; and she went after the messengers of David, and became his wife.

43David also took Ahinoam of Jezreel; and they were also both of them his wives.

44 ¶ But Saul had given Michal his daughter, David's wife, to ⁵Phalti the son of Laish, which *was* of Gallim.

David spares Saul again

26 AND THE Ziphites came unto Saul to Gibeah, saying, Doth not David hide himself in the hill of Hachilah, *which is* before Jeshimon?

2Then Saul arose, and went down to the wilderness of Ziph, having three thousand chosen men of Israel with him, to seek David in the wilderness of Ziph.

3And Saul pitched in the hill of Hachilah, which *is* before Jeshimon, by the way. But David abode in the wilderness, and he saw that Saul came after him into the wilderness.

4David therefore sent out spies, and understood that Saul was come in very deed.

5 ¶ And David arose, and came to the place where Saul had pitched: and David beheld the place where Saul lay, and Abner the son of Ner, the captain of his host: and Saul lay in the ᵗtrench, and the people pitched round about him.

6Then answered David and said to Ahimelech the Hittite, and to Abishai the son of Zeruiah, brother to Joab, saying, Who will go down with me to Saul to the camp? And Abishai said, I will go down with thee.

7So David and Abishai came to the people by night: and, behold, Saul lay sleeping within the trench, and his spear stuck in the ground at his bolster: but Abner and the people lay round about him.

8Then said Abishai to David, God hath delivered thine enemy into thine hand this day: now therefore let me smite him, I pray thee, with the spear even to the earth at once, and I will not *smite* him the second time.

9And David said to Abishai, Destroy him not: for who can stretch forth his hand against the LORD's anointed, and be guiltless?

10David said furthermore, *As* the LORD liveth, the LORD shall smite him; or his day shall come to die; or he shall descend into battle, and perish.

11The LORD forbid that I should stretch forth mine hand against the LORD's anointed: but, I pray thee, take thou now the spear that *is* at his bolster, and the cruse of water, and let us go.

12So David took the spear and the cruse of water from Saul's bolster; and they gat them away, and no man saw *it*, nor knew *it*, neither awaked: for they *were* all asleep; because a deep sleep from the LORD was fallen upon them.

13 ¶ Then David went over to the other side, and stood on the top of an hill afar off; a great space *being* between them:

Amplified

38And about ten days after that, the Lord smote Nabal and he died.

39When David heard that Nabal was dead, he said, Blessed be the Lord, Who has pleaded the cause of my reproach at the hand of Nabal, and kept His servant from evil. For the Lord has returned the wickedness of Nabal upon his own head. And David sent and communed with Abigail, to take her to him as his wife.

40And when the servants of David had come to Abigail at Carmel, they said to her, David sent us to you to take you to him to be his wife.

41And she arose and bowed herself to the earth and said, Behold, let your handmaid be a servant to wash the feet of the servants of my lord.

42And Abigail hastened and arose and rode on a donkey, with five of her maids who followed her, and she went after the messengers of David and became his wife.

43David also took Ahinoam of Jezreel, and they both became his wives.

44Saul had given Michal his daughter, David's wife, to Phalti son of Laish, who was of Gallim.

26 THE ZIPHITES came to Saul at Gibeah, saying, Does not David hide himself on the hill of Hachilah, east of Jeshimon?

2So Saul arose and went down to the Wilderness of Ziph, with 3,000 chosen men of Israel, to seek David [there].

3Saul encamped on the hill of Hachilah, which is beside the road east of Jeshimon. But David remained in the wilderness. And when he saw that Saul came after him into the wilderness,

4David sent out spies and learned that Saul had actually come.

5David arose and came to the place where Saul had encamped, and saw where Saul lay with Abner son of Ner, commander of his army; and Saul was lying in the encampment, with the army encamped around him.

6Then David said to Ahimelech the Hittite and to Abishai son of Zeruiah, brother of Joab, Who will go down with me into the camp of Saul? And Abishai said, I will go down with you.

7So David and Abishai went to the army by night, and there Saul lay sleeping within the encampment with his spear stuck in the ground at his head; and Abner and the army lay round about him.

8Then said Abishai to David, God has given your enemy into your hands this day. Now therefore let me smite him to the earth at once with one stroke of the spear, and I will not strike him twice.

9David said to Abishai, Do not destroy him; for who can raise his hand against the Lord's anointed and be guiltless?

10David said, As the Lord lives, [He] will smite him; or his day will come to die or he will go down in battle and perish.

11The Lord forbid that I should raise my hand against the Lord's anointed; but take now the spear that is at his head and the bottle of water, and let us go.

12So David took the spear and the bottle of water from Saul's head, and they got away. And no man saw or knew or wakened, for they were all asleep, because a deep sleep from the Lord had fallen upon them.

13Then David went over to the other side and stood on the top of the mountain afar off, a great space being between them.

---

⁵*Phaltiel* in 2 Sam. 3:15   ᵗOr, *midst of his carriages*

New American Standard

New International

³⁸ About ten days later, the LORD struck Nabal and he died.

David Marries Abigail

³⁹ ¶ When David heard that Nabal was dead, he said, "Blessed be the LORD, who has pleaded the cause of my reproach from the hand of Nabal and has kept back His servant from evil. The LORD has also returned the evildoing of Nabal on his own head." Then David sent a proposal to Abigail, to take her as his wife.

⁴⁰ When the servants of David came to Abigail at Carmel, they spoke to her, saying, "David has sent us to you to take you as his wife."

⁴¹ She arose and bowed with her face to the ground and said, "Behold, your maidservant is a maid to wash the feet of my lord's servants."

⁴² Then Abigail quickly arose, and rode on a donkey, with her five maidens who attended her; and she followed the messengers of David and became his wife.

⁴³ ¶ David had also taken Ahinoam of Jezreel, and they both became his wives.

⁴⁴ ¶ Now Saul had given Michal his daughter, David's wife, to Palti the son of Laish, who was from Gallim.

David Again Spares Saul

26 THEN THE Ziphites came to Saul at Gibeah, saying, "Is not David hiding on the hill of Hachilah, *which is* before ^pJeshimon?"

² So Saul arose and went down to the wilderness of Ziph, having with him three thousand chosen men of Israel, to search for David in the wilderness of Ziph.

³ Saul camped in the hill of Hachilah, which is before ^pJeshimon, beside the road, and David was staying in the wilderness. When he saw that Saul came after him into the wilderness,

⁴ David sent out spies, and he knew that Saul was definitely coming.

⁵ David then arose and came to the place where Saul had camped. And David saw the place where Saul lay, and Abner the son of Ner, the commander of his army; and Saul was lying in the circle of the camp, and the people were camped around him.

⁶ ¶ Then David said to Ahimelech the Hittite and to Abishai the son of Zeruiah, Joab's brother, saying, "Who will go down with me to Saul in the camp?" And Abishai said, "I will go down with you."

⁷ So David and Abishai came to the people by night, and behold, Saul lay sleeping inside the circle of the camp with his spear stuck in the ground at his head; and Abner and the people were lying around him.

⁸ Then Abishai said to David, "Today God has delivered your enemy into your hand; now therefore, please let me strike him with the spear to the ground with one stroke, and I will not strike him the second time."

⁹ But David said to Abishai, "Do not destroy him, for who can stretch out his hand against the LORD'S anointed and be without guilt?"

¹⁰ David also said, "As the LORD lives, surely the LORD will strike him, or his day will come that he dies, or he will go down into battle and perish.

¹¹"The LORD forbid that I should stretch out my hand against the LORD'S anointed; but now please take the spear that is at his head, and the jug of water, and let us go."

¹² So David took the spear and the jug of water from *beside* Saul's head, and they went away, but no one saw or knew *it,* nor did any awake, for they were all asleep, because a sound sleep from the LORD had fallen on them.

¹³ ¶ Then David crossed over to the other side and stood on top of the mountain at a distance *with* a large area between them.

became like a stone. ³⁸About ten days later, the LORD struck Nabal and he died.

³⁹When David heard that Nabal was dead, he said, "Praise be to the LORD, who has upheld my cause against Nabal for treating me with contempt. He has kept his servant from doing wrong and has brought Nabal's wrongdoing down on his own head."

Then David sent word to Abigail, asking her to become his wife. ⁴⁰His servants went to Carmel and said to Abigail, "David has sent us to you to take you to become his wife."

⁴¹She bowed down with her face to the ground and said, "Here is your maidservant, ready to serve you and wash the feet of my master's servants." ⁴²Abigail quickly got on a donkey, and attended by her five maids, went with David's messengers and became his wife. ⁴³David had also married Ahinoam of Jezreel, and they both were his wives. ⁴⁴But Saul had given his daughter Michal, David's wife, to Paltiel^e son of Laish, who was from Gallim.

David Again Spares Saul's Life

26 THE ZIPHITES went to Saul at Gibeah and said, "Is not David hiding on the hill of Hakilah, which faces Jeshimon?"

²So Saul went down to the Desert of Ziph, with his three thousand chosen men of Israel, to search there for David. ³Saul made his camp beside the road on the hill of Hakilah facing Jeshimon, but David stayed in the desert. When he saw that Saul had followed him there, ⁴he sent out scouts and learned that Saul had definitely arrived.^f

⁵Then David set out and went to the place where Saul had camped. He saw where Saul and Abner son of Ner, the commander of the army, had lain down. Saul was lying inside the camp, with the army encamped around him.

⁶David then asked Ahimelech the Hittite and Abishai son of Zeruiah, Joab's brother, "Who will go down into the camp with me to Saul?"

"I'll go with you," said Abishai.

⁷So David and Abishai went to the army by night, and there was Saul, lying asleep inside the camp with his spear stuck in the ground near his head. Abner and the soldiers were lying around him.

⁸Abishai said to David, "Today God has delivered your enemy into your hands. Now let me pin him to the ground with one thrust of my spear; I won't strike him twice."

⁹But David said to Abishai, "Don't destroy him! Who can lay a hand on the LORD's anointed and be guiltless? ¹⁰As surely as the LORD lives," he said, "the LORD himself will strike him; either his time will come and he will die, or he will go into battle and perish. ¹¹But the LORD forbid that I should lay a hand on the LORD's anointed. Now get the spear and water jug that are near his head, and let's go."

¹²So David took the spear and water jug near Saul's head, and they left. No one saw or knew about it, nor did anyone wake up. They were all sleeping, because the LORD had put them into a deep sleep.

¹³Then David crossed over to the other side and stood on top of the hill some distance away; there was a wide space

^e44 Hebrew *Palti*, a variant of *Paltiel*   ^f4 Or *had come to Nacon*

King James

¹⁴And David cried to the people, and to Abner the son of Ner, saying, Answerest thou not, Abner? Then Abner answered and said, Who *art* thou *that* criest to the king?

¹⁵And David said to Abner, *Art* not thou a *valiant* man? and who *is* like to thee in Israel? wherefore then hast thou not kept thy lord the king? for there came one of the people in to destroy the king thy lord.

¹⁶This thing *is* not good that thou hast done. *As* the LORD liveth, ye *are* worthy to die, because ye have not kept your master, the LORD'S anointed. And now see where the king's spear *is,* and the cruse of water that *was* at his bolster.

¹⁷And Saul knew David's voice, and said, *Is* this thy voice, my son David? And David said, *It is* my voice, my lord, O king.

¹⁸And he said, Wherefore doth my lord thus pursue after his servant? for what have I done? or what evil *is* in mine hand?

¹⁹Now therefore, I pray thee, let my lord the king hear the words of his servant. If the LORD have stirred thee up against me, let him ^uaccept an offering: but if *they be* the children of men, cursed *be* they before the LORD; for they have driven me out this day from ^vabiding in the inheritance of the LORD, saying, Go, serve other gods.

²⁰Now therefore, let not my blood fall to the earth before the face of the LORD: for the king of Israel is come out to seek a flea, as when one doth hunt a partridge in the mountains.

²¹ ¶ Then said Saul, I have sinned: return, my son David: for I will no more do thee harm, because my soul was precious in thine eyes this day: behold, I have played the fool, and have erred exceedingly.

²²And David answered and said, Behold the king's spear! and let one of the young men come over and fetch it.

²³The LORD render to every man his righteousness and his faithfulness: for the LORD delivered thee into *my* hand today, but I would not stretch forth mine hand against the LORD'S anointed.

²⁴And, behold, as thy life was much set by this day in mine eyes, so let my life be much set by in the eyes of the LORD, and let him deliver me out of all tribulation.

²⁵Then Saul said to David, Blessed *be* thou, my son David: thou shalt both do great *things,* and also shalt still prevail. So David went on his way, and Saul returned to his place.

David lives with the Philistines

27 AND DAVID said in his heart, I shall now ^wperish one day by the hand of Saul: *there is* nothing better for me than that I should speedily escape into the land of the Philistines; and Saul shall despair of me, to seek me any more in any coast of Israel: so shall I escape out of his hand.

²And David arose, and he passed over with the six hundred men that *were* with him unto Achish, the son of Maoch, king of Gath.

Amplified

¹⁴David called to the army and Abner son of Ner, Will you answer, Abner? Abner replied, Who are you, calling [and disturbing] the king?

¹⁵David said to Abner, Are you not a valiant man? Who is like you in Israel? Why then have you not guarded your lord the king? For one of the people came in [to your camp] to destroy the king your lord.

¹⁶This thing is not good that you have done. As the Lord lives, you deserve to die, because you have not guarded your master, the Lord's anointed. And now see where the king's spear is and the bottle of water that was at his head.

¹⁷And Saul knew David's voice and said, Is this your voice, my son David? And David said, My voice, my lord O king!

¹⁸And David said, Why does my lord thus pursue his servant? What have I done? Or what evil is in my hand [tonight]?

¹⁹Now therefore, I pray you, let my lord the king hear the words of his servant. If the Lord has stirred you up against me, let Him accept an offering; but if it is men, may they be cursed before the Lord, for they have driven me out this day that I should have no share in the inheritance of the Lord, saying, Go, serve other gods.

²⁰Now therefore, let not my blood fall to the earth away from the presence of the Lord; for the king of Israel is come out to seek one flea, as when one hunts a partridge in the mountains.

²¹Then said Saul, I have sinned. Return, my son David, for I will no more do you harm, because my life was precious in your eyes this day. Behold, I have *j*played the fool and have erred exceedingly.

²²David answered, See the king's spear! Let one of the young men come and get it.

²³The Lord rewards every man for his righteousness and his faithfulness; for the Lord delivered you into my hands today, but I would not stretch forth my hand against the Lord's anointed.

²⁴And behold, as your life was precious today in my sight, so let my life be precious in the sight of the Lord, and let Him deliver me out of all tribulation.

²⁵Then Saul said to David, May you be blessed, my son David; you will both do mightily and surely prevail. So David went on his way, and Saul returned to his place.

27 BUT DAVID said in his heart, I shall now perish one day by the hand of Saul. There is nothing better for me than that I should escape into the land of the Philistines. Then Saul will despair of seeking me any more within the borders of Israel, and I shall escape out of his hand.

²So David arose and went over with the 600 men who were with him to Achish son of Maoch, king of Gath.

j "When for a moment a man is off guard, in all probability you will know more truth about him than in all his attempts either to reveal himself or to hide himself. The ever-present consciousness, habitually hidden, flashes forth. Later he may apologize and say he did not mean what he said. The fact is that he was surprised into saying what he was constantly thinking. In all probability Saul had never said that before and would never say it again, but he had been thinking it for a long time—'I played the fool.' There is no escape for any man, as long as reason continues, from the naked truth about himself. He may practice deceit so skillfully as not only to hide himself from his fellowmen, but in his unutterable folly to imagine he has hidden himself from God; but he can never hide himself from **himself**. In some moment of stress and strain he says what he has been thinking all the time . . . . Ere Saul knew it, he had said, 'Behold, I have played the fool.' That is the whole story of the man" (G. Campbell Morgan, cited by J. Sidlow Baxter, *Explore the Book*).

^uHeb. *smell;* see Gen. 8:21; Lev. 26:31   ^vHeb. *cleaving*
^wHeb. *be consumed*

New American Standard

14 David called to the people and to Abner the son of Ner, saying, "Will you not answer, Abner?" Then Abner replied, "Who are you who calls to the king?"

15 So David said to Abner, "Are you not a man? And who is like you in Israel? Why then have you not guarded your lord the king? For one of the people came to destroy the king your lord.

16 "This thing that you have done is not good. As the LORD lives, *all* of you must surely die, because you did not guard your lord, the LORD's anointed. And now, see where the king's spear is and the jug of water that was at his head."

17 ¶ Then Saul recognized David's voice and said, "Is this your voice, my son David?" And David said, "It is my voice, my lord the king."

18 He also said, "Why then is my lord pursuing his servant? For what have I done? Or what evil is in my hand?

19 "Now therefore, please let my lord the king listen to the words of his servant. If the LORD has stirred you up against me, let Him accept an offering; but if it is men, cursed are they before the LORD, for they have driven me out today so that I would have no attachment with the inheritance of the LORD, saying, 'Go, serve other gods.'

20 "Now then, do not let my blood fall to the ground away from the presence of the LORD; for the king of Israel has come out to search for a single flea, just as one hunts a partridge in the mountains."

21 ¶ Then Saul said, "I have sinned. Return, my son David, for I will not harm you again because my life was precious in your sight this day. Behold, I have played the fool and have committed a serious error."

22 David replied, "Behold the spear of the king! Now let one of the young men come over and take it.

23 "The LORD will repay each man *for* his righteousness and his faithfulness; for the LORD delivered you into *my* hand today, but I refused to stretch out my hand against the LORD's anointed.

24 "Now behold, as your life was highly valued in my sight this day, so may my life be highly valued in the sight of the LORD, and may He deliver me from all distress."

25 Then Saul said to David, "Blessed are you, my son David; you will both accomplish much and surely prevail." So David went on his way, and Saul returned to his place.

David Flees to the Philistines

27 THEN DAVID said to himself, "Now I will perish one day by the hand of Saul. There is nothing better for me than to escape into the land of the Philistines. Saul then will despair of searching for me anymore in all the territory of Israel, and I will escape from his hand."

2 So David arose and crossed over, he and the six hundred men who were with him, to Achish the son of Maoch, king of Gath.

New International

between them. 14 He called out to the army and to Abner son of Ner, "Aren't you going to answer me, Abner?"

Abner replied, "Who are you who calls to the king?"

15 David said, "You're a man, aren't you? And who is like you in Israel? Why didn't you guard your lord the king? Someone came to destroy your lord the king. 16 What you have done is not good. As surely as the LORD lives, you and your men deserve to die, because you did not guard your master, the LORD's anointed. Look around you. Where are the king's spear and water jug that were near his head?"

17 Saul recognized David's voice and said, "Is that your voice, David my son?"

David replied, "Yes it is, my lord the king." 18 And he added, "Why is my lord pursuing his servant? What have I done, and what wrong am I guilty of? 19 Now let my lord the king listen to his servant's words. If the LORD has incited you against me, then may he accept an offering. If, however, men have done it, may they be cursed before the LORD! They have now driven me from my share in the LORD's inheritance and have said, 'Go, serve other gods.' 20 Now do not let my blood fall to the ground far from the presence of the LORD. The king of Israel has come out to look for a flea—as one hunts a partridge in the mountains."

21 Then Saul said, "I have sinned. Come back, David my son. Because you considered my life precious today, I will not try to harm you again. Surely I have acted like a fool and have erred greatly."

22 "Here is the king's spear," David answered. "Let one of your young men come over and get it. 23 The LORD rewards every man for his righteousness and faithfulness. The LORD delivered you into my hands today, but I would not lay a hand on the LORD's anointed. 24 As surely as I valued your life today, so may the LORD value my life and deliver me from all trouble."

25 Then Saul said to David, "May you be blessed, my son David; you will do great things and surely triumph."

So David went on his way, and Saul returned home.

David Among the Philistines

27 BUT DAVID thought to himself, "One of these days I will be destroyed by the hand of Saul. The best thing I can do is to escape to the land of the Philistines. Then Saul will give up searching for me anywhere in Israel, and I will slip out of his hand."

2 So David and the six hundred men with him left and went over to Achish son of Maoch king of Gath. 3 David

King James

³And David dwelt with Achish at Gath, he and his men, every man with his household, *even* David with his two wives, Ahinoam the Jezreelitess, and Abigail the Carmelitess, Nabal's wife.

⁴And it was told Saul that David was fled to Gath: and he sought no more again for him.

⁵ ¶ And David said unto Achish, If I have now found grace in thine eyes, let them give me a place in some town in the country, that I may dwell there: for why should thy servant dwell in the royal city with thee?

⁶Then Achish gave him Ziklag that day: wherefore Ziklag pertaineth unto the kings of Judah unto this day.

⁷And ^xthe time that David dwelt in the country of the Philistines was a full year and four months.

⁸ ¶ And David and his men went up, and invaded the Geshurites, and the ^yGezrites, and the Amalekites: for those *nations were* of old the inhabitants of the land, as thou goest to Shur, even unto the land of Egypt.

⁹And David smote the land, and left neither man nor woman alive, and took away the sheep, and the oxen, and the asses, and the camels, and the apparel, and returned, and came to Achish.

¹⁰And Achish said, ^zWhither have ye made a road today? And David said, Against the south of Judah, and against the south of the Jerahmeelites, and against the south of the Kenites.

¹¹And David saved neither man nor woman alive, to bring *tidings* to Gath, saying, Lest they should tell on us, saying, So did David, and so *will be* his manner all the while he dwelleth in the country of the Philistines.

¹²And Achish believed David, saying, He hath made his people Israel ^autterly to abhor him; therefore he shall be my servant for ever.

28 AND IT came to pass in those days, that the Philistines gathered their armies together for warfare, to fight with Israel. And Achish said unto David, Know thou assuredly, that thou shalt go out with me to battle, thou and thy men.

²And David said to Achish, Surely thou shalt know what thy servant can do. And Achish said to David, Therefore will I make thee keeper of mine head for ever.

Saul and the woman at Endor

³ ¶ Now Samuel was dead, and all Israel had lamented him, and buried him in Ramah, even in his own city. And Saul had put away those that had familiar spirits, and the wizards, out of the land.

⁴And the Philistines gathered themselves together, and came and pitched in Shunem: and Saul gathered all Israel together, and they pitched in Gilboa.

⁵And when Saul saw the host of the Philistines, he was afraid, and his heart greatly trembled.

⁶And when Saul inquired of the LORD, the LORD answered him not, neither by dreams, nor by Urim, nor by prophets.

⁷ ¶ Then said Saul unto his servants, Seek me a woman that hath a familiar spirit, that I may go to her, and inquire of her. And his servants said to him, Behold, *there is* a woman that hath a familiar spirit at En-dor.

Amplified

³And David dwelt with Achish at Gath, he and his men, every man with his household, and David with his two wives, Ahinoam the Jezreelitess and Abigail the Carmelitess, Nabal's widow.

⁴When it was told Saul that David had fled to Gath, he sought for him no more.

⁵And David said to Achish, If I have now found favor in your eyes, let me be given a place to dwell in some country town; for why should your servant live in the royal city with you?

⁶Then Achish gave David the town of Ziklag that day. Therefore Ziklag belongs to the kings of Judah to this day.

⁷The time David dwelt in the Philistines' country was a year and four months.

⁸Now David and his men went up and made attacks on the Geshurites, Girzites, and Amalekites [enemies of Israel Joshua had failed to exterminate]. For from of old those nations inhabited the land, as one goes to Shur even to the land of Egypt. [Deut. 25:19; Josh. 13:1, 2, 13.]

⁹And David smote the land and left neither man nor woman alive, and took away the sheep, oxen, donkeys, camels, and the apparel, and returned to Achish.

¹⁰Achish would ask, Against whom have you made a raid today? And David would reply, ^kAgainst the South (Negeb) of Judah, or of the Jerahmeelites, or of the Kenites.

¹¹And David saved neither man nor woman alive to bring tidings to Gath, thinking, Lest they should say about us, So did David, and so will he do as long as he dwells in the Philistines' country.

¹²And Achish believed David, saying, He has made his people Israel utterly abhor him; so he shall be my servant always.

28 IN THOSE days the Philistines gathered their forces for war against Israel. Achish said to David, Understand that you and your men shall go with me to battle.

²David said to Achish, All right, you shall know what your servant can do. Achish said to David, Therefore I will make you my bodyguard always.

³Now Samuel was dead, and all Israel had mourned for him and buried him in Ramah, his own city. And Saul had put the mediums and the wizards out of the land.

⁴And the Philistines assembled and came and encamped at Shunem; and Saul gathered all Israel and they encamped at Gilboa.

⁵When Saul saw the Philistine host, he was afraid; his heart trembled greatly.

⁶When Saul inquired of the Lord, He refused to answer him, either by dreams or by Urim [a symbol worn by the priest when seeking the will of God for Israel] or by the prophets. [Prov. 1:24–30.]

⁷Then Saul said to his servants, Find me a woman who is a medium [between the living and the dead], that I may go and inquire of her. His servants said, Behold, there is a woman who is a medium at Endor.

---

^kHow could David be "a man after His [God's] own heart" (I Sam. 13:14) and lie and deceive like that? God hates lying (Prov. 12:22), and those who deal in falsehood and deception are to be excluded from heaven (Rev. 22:15). The truth is that David had gone through such a long period of persecution and threatening circumstances that he had fallen into a bit of mistrust of God Himself. God had sworn to make him king, to rid him of his enemies, to give him a sure house; yet here he was in a panic, concluding that God had forsaken him and that if he was to remain alive he must manage it himself. It was very dishonoring to God. But God was standing by His stricken child, waiting for the moment when he would realize his own utter helplessness and turn in blessed surrender to the almighty arms of Him who had been watching over him all along. That time came at Ziklag, when, in the bitterest hour of his life, we are told, "But David encouraged *and* strengthened himself in the Lord his God" (I Sam. 30:6), truly "a man after God's own heart."

---

^xHeb. *the number of days*   ^yOr, *Gerzites*   ^zOr, *Did you not make a road*   ^aHeb. *to stink*

New American Standard

³ And David lived with Achish at Gath, he and his men, each with his household, *even* David with his two wives, Ahinoam the Jezreelitess, and Abigail the Carmelitess, Nabal's widow.

⁴ Now it was told Saul that David had fled to Gath, so he no longer searched for him.

⁵ ¶ Then David said to Achish, "If now I have found favor in your sight, let them give me a place in one of the cities in the country, that I may live there; for why should your servant live in the royal city with you?"

⁶ So Achish gave him Ziklag that day; therefore Ziklag has belonged to the kings of Judah to this day.

⁷ The number of days that David lived in the country of the Philistines was a year and four months.

⁸ ¶ Now David and his men went up and raided the Geshurites and the Girzites and the Amalekites; for they were the inhabitants of the land from ancient times, as you come to Shur even as far as the land of Egypt.

⁹ David attacked the land and did not leave a man or a woman alive, and he took away the sheep, the cattle, the donkeys, the camels, and the clothing. Then he returned and came to Achish.

¹⁰ Now Achish said, "Where have you made a raid today?" And David said, "Against the *q*Negev of Judah and against the Negev of the Jerahmeelites and against the Negev of the Kenites."

¹¹ David did not leave a man or a woman alive to bring to Gath, saying, "Otherwise they will tell about us, saying, 'So has David done and so *has been* his practice all the time he has lived in the country of the Philistines.' "

¹² So Achish believed David, saying, "He has surely made himself odious among his people Israel; therefore he will become my servant forever."

Saul and the Spirit Medium

28 NOW IT came about in those days that the Philistines gathered their armed camps for war, to fight against Israel. And Achish said to David, "Know assuredly that you will go out with me in the camp, you and your men."

² David said to Achish, "Very well, you shall know what your servant can do." So Achish said to David, "Very well, I will make you my bodyguard for life."

³ ¶ Now Samuel was dead, and all Israel had lamented him and buried him in Ramah, his own city. And Saul had removed from the land those who were mediums and spiritists.

⁴ So the Philistines gathered together and came and camped in Shunem; and Saul gathered all Israel together and they camped in Gilboa.

⁵ When Saul saw the camp of the Philistines, he was afraid and his heart trembled greatly.

⁶ When Saul inquired of the LORD, the LORD did not answer him, either by dreams or by Urim or by prophets.

⁷ Then Saul said to his servants, "Seek for me a woman who is a medium, that I may go to her and inquire of her." And his servants said to him, "Behold, there is a woman who is a medium at En-dor."

New International

and his men settled in Gath with Achish. Each man had his family with him, and David had his two wives: Ahinoam of Jezreel and Abigail of Carmel, the widow of Nabal. ⁴When Saul was told that David had fled to Gath, he no longer searched for him.

⁵Then David said to Achish, "If I have found favor in your eyes, let a place be assigned to me in one of the country towns, that I may live there. Why should your servant live in the royal city with you?"

⁶So on that day Achish gave him Ziklag, and it has belonged to the kings of Judah ever since. ⁷David lived in Philistine territory a year and four months.

⁸Now David and his men went up and raided the Geshurites, the Girzites and the Amalekites. (From ancient times these peoples had lived in the land extending to Shur and Egypt.) ⁹Whenever David attacked an area, he did not leave a man or woman alive, but took sheep and cattle, donkeys and camels, and clothes. Then he returned to Achish.

¹⁰When Achish asked, "Where did you go raiding today?" David would say, "Against the Negev of Judah" or "Against the Negev of Jerahmeel" or "Against the Negev of the Kenites." ¹¹He did not leave a man or woman alive to be brought to Gath, for he thought, "They might inform on us and say, 'This is what David did.' " And such was his practice as long as he lived in Philistine territory. ¹²Achish trusted David and said to himself, "He has become so odious to his people, the Israelites, that he will be my servant forever."

Saul and the Witch of Endor

28 IN THOSE days the Philistines gathered their forces to fight against Israel. Achish said to David, "You must understand that you and your men will accompany me in the army."

²David said, "Then you will see for yourself what your servant can do."

Achish replied, "Very well, I will make you my bodyguard for life."

³Now Samuel was dead, and all Israel had mourned for him and buried him in his own town of Ramah. Saul had expelled the mediums and spiritists from the land.

⁴The Philistines assembled and came and set up camp at Shunem, while Saul gathered all the Israelites and set up camp at Gilboa. ⁵When Saul saw the Philistine army, he was afraid; terror filled his heart. ⁶He inquired of the LORD, but the LORD did not answer him by dreams or Urim or prophets. ⁷Saul then said to his attendants, "Find me a woman who is a medium, so I may go and inquire of her."

"There is one in Endor," they said.

---

q I.e. South country

King James

Amplified

8And Saul disguised himself, and put on other raiment, and he went, and two men with him, and they came to the woman by night: and he said, I pray thee, divine unto me by the familiar spirit, and bring me *him* up, whom I shall name unto thee.

9And the woman said unto him, Behold, thou knowest what Saul hath done, how he hath cut off those that have familiar spirits, and the wizards, out of the land: wherefore then layest thou a snare for my life, to cause me to die?

10And Saul sware to her by the LORD, saying, *As* the LORD liveth, there shall no punishment happen to thee for this thing.

11Then said the woman, Whom shall I bring up unto thee? And he said, Bring me up Samuel.

12And when the woman saw Samuel, she cried with a loud voice: and the woman spake to Saul, saying, Why hast thou deceived me? for thou *art* Saul.

13And the king said unto her, Be not afraid: for what sawest thou? And the woman said unto Saul, I saw gods ascending out of the earth.

14And he said unto her, *b*What form *is* he of? And she said, An old man cometh up; and he *is* covered with a mantle. And Saul perceived that it *was* Samuel, and he stooped with *his* face to the ground, and bowed himself.

15 ¶ And Samuel said to Saul, Why hast thou disquieted me, to bring me up? And Saul answered, I am sore distressed; for the Philistines make war against me, and God is departed from me, and answereth me no more, neither *c*by prophets, nor by dreams: therefore I have called thee, that thou mayest make known unto me what I shall do.

16Then said Samuel, Wherefore then dost thou ask of me, seeing the LORD is departed from thee, and is become thine enemy?

17And the LORD hath done *d*to him, as he spake by *e*me: for the LORD hath rent the kingdom out of thine hand, and given it to thy neighbour, *even* to David:

18Because thou obeyedst not the voice of the LORD, nor executedst his fierce wrath upon Amalek, therefore hath the LORD done this thing unto thee this day.

19Moreover the LORD will also deliver Israel with thee into the hand of the Philistines: and tomorrow *shalt* thou and thy sons *be* with me: the LORD also shall deliver the host of Israel into the hand of the Philistines.

20Then Saul *f*fell straightway all along on the earth, and was sore afraid, because of the words of Samuel: and there was no strength in him; for he had eaten no bread all the day, nor all the night.

21 ¶ And the woman came unto Saul, and saw that he was sore troubled, and said unto him, Behold, thine handmaid hath obeyed thy voice, and I have put my life in my hand, and have hearkened unto thy words which thou spakest unto me.

22Now therefore, I pray thee, hearken thou also unto the voice of thine handmaid, and let me set a morsel of bread before thee; and eat, that thou mayest have strength, when thou goest on thy way.

23But he refused, and said, I will not eat. But his servants, together with the woman, compelled him; and he hearkened unto their voice. So he arose from the earth, and sat upon the bed.

24And the woman had a fat calf in the house; and she hasted, and killed it, and took flour, and kneaded *it,* and did bake unleavened bread thereof:

25And she brought *it* before Saul, and before his servants; and they did eat. Then they rose up, and went away that night.

8So Saul disguised himself, put on other raiment, and he and two men with him went and came to the woman at night. He said to her, Perceive for me by the familiar spirit and bring up for me the dead person whom I shall name to you.

9The woman said, See here, you know what Saul has done, how he has cut off those who are mediums and wizards out of the land. Why then do you lay a trap for my life to cause my death?

10And Saul swore to her by the Lord, saying, As the Lord lives, there shall no punishment come to you for this.

11The woman said, Whom shall I bring up for you? He said, Bring up Samuel for me.

12And when the woman saw Samuel, she screamed and she said to Saul, Why have you deceived me? For you are Saul!

13The king said to her, Be not afraid; what do you see? The woman said to Saul, I see a god [terrifying superhuman being] coming up out of the earth!

14He said to her, In what form is he? And she said, An old man comes up, covered with a mantle. And Saul perceived that it was Samuel, and he stooped with his face to the ground and made obeisance.

15And Samuel said to Saul, Why have you disturbed me to bring me up? Saul answered, I am bitterly distressed; for the Philistines make war against me, and God has departed from me and answers me no more, either by prophets or by dreams. Therefore I have called you, that you may make known to me what I should do.

16Samuel said, Why then do you ask me, seeing that the Lord has turned from you and has become your enemy?

17The Lord has done to you as He said through me He would do; for [He] has torn the kingdom out of your hands and given it to your neighbor David. [I Sam. 15:22–28.]

18Because you did not obey the voice of the Lord or execute His fierce wrath upon Amalek, therefore the Lord has done this thing to you this day.

19Moreover, the Lord will also give Israel with you into the hands of the Philistines, and tomorrow you and your sons shall be with me [among the dead]. The Lord also will give the army of Israel into the hands of the Philistines.

20Then immediately Saul fell full length upon the earth floor [of the medium's house], and was exceedingly afraid because of Samuel's words. There was no strength in him, for he had eaten nothing all day and all night.

21The woman came to Saul, and seeing that he was greatly troubled, she said to him, Behold, your handmaid has obeyed you, and I have put my life in my hands and have listened to what you said to me.

22So now, I pray you, listen also to the voice of your handmaid and let me set a morsel of food before you, and eat, so you may have strength when you go on your way.

23But he said, I will not eat. But his servants, together with the woman, urged him, and he heeded their words. So he arose from the ground and sat upon the bed.

24The woman had a fat calf in the house; she hurried and killed it, and took flour, kneaded it, and baked unleavened bread.

25Then she brought it before Saul and his servants, and they ate. Then they rose up and went away that night.

---

*b*Heb. *What is his form?*   *c*Heb. *by the hand of prophets*
*d*Or, *for himself*   *e*Heb. *mine hand*   *f*Heb. *made haste, and fell with the fulness of his stature*

New American Standard

8 ¶ Then Saul disguised himself by putting on other clothes, and went, he and two men with him, and they came to the woman by night; and he said, "Conjure up for me, please, and bring up for me whom I shall name to you."

9 But the woman said to him, "Behold, you know what Saul has done, how he has cut off those who are mediums and spiritists from the land. Why are you then laying a snare for my life to bring about my death?"

10 Saul vowed to her by the LORD, saying, "As the LORD lives, no punishment shall come upon you for this thing."

11 Then the woman said, "Whom shall I bring up for you?" And he said, "Bring up Samuel for me."

12 When the woman saw Samuel, she cried out with a loud voice; and the woman spoke to Saul, saying, "Why have you deceived me? For you are Saul."

13 The king said to her, "Do not be afraid; but what do you see?" And the woman said to Saul, "I see a divine being coming up out of the earth."

14 He said to her, "What is his form?" And she said, "An old man is coming up, and he is wrapped with a robe." And Saul knew that it was Samuel, and he bowed with his face to the ground and did homage.

15 ¶ Then Samuel said to Saul, "Why have you disturbed me by bringing me up?" And Saul answered, "I am greatly distressed; for the Philistines are waging war against me, and God has departed from me and no longer answers me, either through prophets or by dreams; therefore I have called you, that you may make known to me what I should do."

16 Samuel said, "Why then do you ask me, since the LORD has departed from you and has become your adversary?

17 "The LORD has done accordingly as He spoke through me; for the LORD has torn the kingdom out of your hand and given it to your neighbor, to David.

18 "As you did not obey the LORD and did not execute His fierce wrath on Amalek, so the LORD has done this thing to you this day.

19 "Moreover the LORD will also give over Israel along with you into the hands of the Philistines, therefore tomorrow you and your sons will be with me. Indeed the LORD will give over the army of Israel into the hands of the Philistines!"

20 ¶ Then Saul immediately fell full length upon the ground and was very afraid because of the words of Samuel; also there was no strength in him, for he had eaten no food all day and all night.

21 The woman came to Saul and saw that he was terrified, and said to him, "Behold, your maidservant has obeyed you, and I have taken my life in my hand and have listened to your words which you spoke to me.

22 "So now also, please listen to the voice of your maidservant, and let me set a piece of bread before you that *you may* eat and have strength when you go on *your* way."

23 But he refused and said, "I will not eat." However, his servants together with the woman urged him, and he listened to them. So he arose from the ground and sat on the bed.

24 The woman had a fattened calf in the house, and she quickly slaughtered it; and she took flour, kneaded it and baked unleavened bread from it.

25 She brought *it* before Saul and his servants, and they ate. Then they arose and went away that night.

New International

8 So Saul disguised himself, putting on other clothes, and at night he and two men went to the woman. "Consult a spirit for me," he said, "and bring up for me the one I name."

9 But the woman said to him, "Surely you know what Saul has done. He has cut off the mediums and spiritists from the land. Why have you set a trap for my life to bring about my death?"

10 Saul swore to her by the LORD, "As surely as the LORD lives, you will not be punished for this."

11 Then the woman asked, "Whom shall I bring up for you?"

"Bring up Samuel," he said.

12 When the woman saw Samuel, she cried out at the top of her voice and said to Saul, "Why have you deceived me? You are Saul!"

13 The king said to her, "Don't be afraid. What do you see?"

The woman said, "I see a spirit*g* coming up out of the ground."

14 "What does he look like?" he asked.

"An old man wearing a robe is coming up," she said.

Then Saul knew it was Samuel, and he bowed down and prostrated himself with his face to the ground.

15 Samuel said to Saul, "Why have you disturbed me by bringing me up?"

"I am in great distress," Saul said. "The Philistines are fighting against me, and God has turned away from me. He no longer answers me, either by prophets or by dreams. So I have called on you to tell me what to do."

16 Samuel said, "Why do you consult me, now that the LORD has turned away from you and become your enemy?

17 The LORD has done what he predicted through me. The LORD has torn the kingdom out of your hands and given it to one of your neighbors—to David.

18 Because you did not obey the LORD or carry out his fierce wrath against the Amalekites, the LORD has done this to you today.

19 The LORD will hand over both Israel and you to the Philistines, and tomorrow you and your sons will be with me. The LORD will also hand over the army of Israel to the Philistines."

20 Immediately Saul fell full length on the ground, filled with fear because of Samuel's words. His strength was gone, for he had eaten nothing all that day and night.

21 When the woman came to Saul and saw that he was greatly shaken, she said, "Look, your maidservant has obeyed you. I took my life in my hands and did what you told me to do.

22 Now please listen to your servant and let me give you some food so you may eat and have the strength to go on your way."

23 He refused and said, "I will not eat."

But his men joined the woman in urging him, and he listened to them. He got up from the ground and sat on the couch.

24 The woman had a fattened calf at the house, which she butchered at once. She took some flour, kneaded it and baked bread without yeast.

25 Then she set it before Saul and his men, and they ate. That same night they got up and left.

g 13 Or see spirits; or see gods

King James

The Philistines dismiss David

29 NOW THE Philistines gathered together all their armies to Aphek: and the Israelites pitched by a fountain which *is* in Jezreel.

2 And the lords of the Philistines passed on by hundreds, and by thousands: but David and his men passed on in the rearward with Achish.

3 Then said the princes of the Philistines, What *do* these Hebrews *here?* And Achish said unto the princes of the Philistines, *Is* not this David, the servant of Saul the king of Israel, which hath been with me these days, or these years, and I have found no fault in him since he fell *unto me* unto this day?

4 And the princes of the Philistines were wroth with him; and the princes of the Philistines said unto him, Make this fellow return, that he may go again to his place which thou hast appointed him, and let him not go down with us to battle, lest in the battle he be an adversary to us: for wherewith should he reconcile himself unto his master? *should it* not *be* with the heads of these men?

5 *Is* not this David, of whom they sang one to another in dances, saying, Saul slew his thousands, and David his ten thousands?

6 ¶ Then Achish called David, and said unto him, Surely, *as* the Lord liveth, thou hast been upright, and thy going out and thy coming in with me in the host *is* good in my sight: for I have not found evil in thee since the day of thy coming unto me unto this day: nevertheless ᵍthe lords favour thee not.

7 Wherefore now return, and go in peace, that thou ʰdisplease not the lords of the Philistines.

8 ¶ And David said unto Achish, But what have I done? and what hast thou found in thy servant so long as I have been ⁱwith thee unto this day, that I may not go fight against the enemies of my lord the king?

9 And Achish answered and said to David, I know that thou *art* good in my sight, as an angel of God: notwithstanding the princes of the Philistines have said, He shall not go up with us to the battle.

10 Wherefore now rise up early in the morning with thy master's servants that are come with thee: and as soon as ye be up early in the morning, and have light, depart.

11 So David and his men rose up early to depart in the morning, to return into the land of the Philistines. And the Philistines went up to Jezreel.

David smites the Amalekites

30 AND IT came to pass, when David and his men were come to Ziklag on the third day, that the Amalekites had invaded the south, and Ziklag, and smitten Ziklag, and burned it with fire;

2 And had taken the women captives, that *were* therein: they slew not any, either great or small, but carried *them* away, and went on their way.

3 ¶ So David and his men came to the city, and, behold, *it was* burned with fire; and their wives, and their sons, and their daughters, were taken captives.

4 Then David and the people that *were* with him lifted up their voice and wept, until they had no more power to weep.

5 And David's two wives were taken captives, Ahinoam the Jezreelitess, and Abigail the wife of Nabal the Carmelite.

6 And David was greatly distressed; for the people spake of stoning him, because the soul of all the people was ʲgrieved, every man for his sons and for his daughters: but David encouraged himself in the Lord his God.

Amplified

29 NOW THE Philistines gathered all their forces at Aphek, and the Israelites encamped by the fountain in Jezreel.

2 As the Philistine lords were passing on by hundreds and by thousands, and David and his men were in the rear with Achish,

3 The Philistine princes said, What are these Hebrews doing here? Achish said to the Philistine princes, Is not this David, the servant of Saul king of Israel, who has been with me these days and years, and I have found no fault in him since he deserted to me to this day?

4 And the Philistine princes were angry with Achish and they said to him, Make this fellow return, that he may go again to his place where you have assigned him, and let him not go down with us to battle, lest in the battle he become an adversary to us. For how could David reconcile himself to his master? Would it not be with the heads of the men here?

5 Is not this David, of whom they sang to one another in dances, Saul slew his thousands, and David his ten thousands?

6 Then Achish called David and said to him, As surely as the Lord lives, you have been honest *and* upright, and for you to go out and come in with me in the army is good in my sight; for I have found no evil in you from the day of your coming to me to this day. Yet the lords do not approve of you.

7 So return now and go peaceably, so as not to displease the Philistine lords.

8 David said to Achish, But what have I done? And what have you found in your servant as long as I have been with you to this day, that I may not go and fight against the enemies of my lord the king?

9 And Achish said to David, I know that you are as blameless in my sight as an angel of God; nevertheless the princes of the Philistines have said, He shall not go up with us to the battle.

10 So now rise up early in the morning, with your master's servants who have come with you, and as soon as you are up and have light, depart.

11 So David and his men rose up early in the morning to return to the land of the Philistines. But the Philistines went up to Jezreel [to fight against Israel].

30 NOW WHEN David and his men came home to Ziklag on the third day, they found that the Amalekites had made a raid on the South (the Negeb) and on Ziklag, and had struck Ziklag and burned it with fire,

2 And had taken the women and all who were there, both great and small, captive. They killed no one, but carried them off and went on their way.

3 So David and his men came to the town, and behold, it was burned, and their wives and sons and daughters were taken captive.

4 Then David and the men with him lifted up their voices and wept until they had no more strength to weep.

5 David's two wives also had been taken captive, Ahinoam the Jezreelitess and Abigail, the widow of Nabal the Carmelite.

6 David was greatly distressed, for the men spoke of stoning him because the souls of them all were bitterly grieved, each man for his sons and daughters. But David encouraged *and* strengthened himself in the Lord his God.

ᵍ Heb. *thou art not good in the eyes of the lords evil in the eyes of the lords*   ⁱ Heb. *before thee*   ʰ Heb. *do not*   ʲ Heb. *bitter*

New American Standard

The Philistines Mistrust David

29 NOW THE Philistines gathered together all their armies to Aphek, while the Israelites were camping by the spring which is in Jezreel.
2 And the lords of the Philistines were proceeding on by hundreds and by thousands, and David and his men were proceeding on in the rear with Achish.
3 Then the commanders of the Philistines said, "What *are* these Hebrews *doing here?*" And Achish said to the commanders of the Philistines, "Is this not David, the servant of Saul the king of Israel, who has been with me these days, or *rather* these years, and I have found no fault in him from the day he deserted *to me* to this day?"
4 But the commanders of the Philistines were angry with him, and the commanders of the Philistines said to him, "Make the man go back, that he may return to his place where you have assigned him, and do not let him go down to battle with us, or in the battle he may become an adversary to us. For with what could this *man* make himself acceptable to his lord? *Would it* not *be* with the heads of these men?
5 "Is this not David, of whom they sing in the dances, saying,

'Saul has slain his thousands,
And David his ten thousands'?"

6 ¶ Then Achish called David and said to him, "*As* the LORD lives, you *have been* upright, and your going out and your coming in with me in the army are pleasing in my sight; for I have not found evil in you from the day of your coming to me to this day. Nevertheless, you are not pleasing in the sight of the lords.
7 "Now therefore return and go in peace, that you may not displease the lords of the Philistines."
8 David said to Achish, "But what have I done? And what have you found in your servant from the day when I came before you to this day, that I may not go and fight against the enemies of my lord the king?"
9 But Achish replied to David, "I know that you are pleasing in my sight, like an angel of God; nevertheless the commanders of the Philistines have said, 'He must not go up with us to the battle.'
10 "Now then arise early in the morning with the servants of your lord who have come with you, and as soon as you have arisen early in the morning and have light, depart."
11 So David arose early, he and his men, to depart in the morning to return to the land of the Philistines. And the Philistines went up to Jezreel.

David's Victory over the Amalekites

30 THEN IT happened when David and his men came to Ziklag on the third day, that the Amalekites had made a raid on the Negev and on Ziklag, and had overthrown Ziklag and burned it with fire;
2 and they took captive the women *and all* who were in it, both small and great, without killing anyone, and carried *them* off and went their way.
3 When David and his men came to the city, behold, it was burned with fire, and their wives and their sons and their daughters had been taken captive.
4 Then David and the people who were with him lifted their voices and wept until there was no strength in them to weep.
5 Now David's two wives had been taken captive, Ahinoam the Jezreelitess and Abigail the widow of Nabal the Carmelite.
6 Moreover David was greatly distressed because the people spoke of stoning him, for all the people were embittered, each one because of his sons and his daughters. But David strengthened himself in the LORD his God.

New International

Achish Sends David Back to Ziklag

29 THE PHILISTINES gathered all their forces at Aphek, and Israel camped by the spring in Jezreel.
2 As the Philistine rulers marched with their units of hundreds and thousands, David and his men were marching at the rear with Achish. 3 The commanders of the Philistines asked, "What about these Hebrews?"

Achish replied, "Is this not David, who was an officer of Saul king of Israel? He has already been with me for over a year, and from the day he left Saul until now, I have found no fault in him."

4 But the Philistine commanders were angry with him and said, "Send the man back, that he may return to the place you assigned him. He must not go with us into battle, or he will turn against us during the fighting. How better could he regain his master's favor than by taking the heads of our own men? 5 Isn't this the David they sang about in their dances:

" 'Saul has slain his thousands,
and David his tens of thousands'?"

6 So Achish called David and said to him, "As surely as the LORD lives, you have been reliable, and I would be pleased to have you serve with me in the army. From the day you came to me until now, I have found no fault in you, but the rulers don't approve of you. 7 Turn back and go in peace; do nothing to displease the Philistine rulers."

8 "But what have I done?" asked David. "What have you found against your servant from the day I came to you until now? Why can't I go and fight against the enemies of my lord the king?"

9 Achish answered, "I know that you have been as pleasing in my eyes as an angel of God; nevertheless, the Philistine commanders have said, 'He must not go up with us into battle.' 10 Now get up early, along with your master's servants who have come with you, and leave in the morning as soon as it is light."

11 So David and his men got up early in the morning to go back to the land of the Philistines, and the Philistines went up to Jezreel.

David Destroys the Amalekites

30 DAVID AND his men reached Ziklag on the third day. Now the Amalekites had raided the Negev and Ziklag. They had attacked Ziklag and burned it, 2 and had taken captive the women and all who were in it, both young and old. They killed none of them, but carried them off as they went on their way.

3 When David and his men came to Ziklag, they found it destroyed by fire and their wives and sons and daughters taken captive. 4 So David and his men wept aloud until they had no strength left to weep. 5 David's two wives had been captured—Ahinoam of Jezreel and Abigail, the widow of Nabal of Carmel. 6 David was greatly distressed because the men were talking of stoning him; each one was bitter in spirit because of his sons and daughters. But David found strength in the LORD his God.

King James

Amplified

7And David said to Abiathar the priest, Ahimelech's son, I pray thee, bring me hither the ephod. And Abiathar brought thither the ephod to David.

8And David inquired at the LORD, saying, Shall I pursue after this troop? shall I overtake them? And he answered him, Pursue: for thou shalt surely overtake *them*, and without fail recover *all.*

9So David went, he and the six hundred men that *were* with him, and came to the brook Besor, where those that were left behind stayed.

10But David pursued, he and four hundred men: for two hundred abode behind, which were so faint that they could not go over the brook Besor.

11 ¶ And they found an Egyptian in the field, and brought him to David, and gave him bread, and he did eat; and they made him drink water;

12And they gave him a piece of a cake of figs, and two clusters of raisins: and when he had eaten, his spirit came again to him: for he had eaten no bread, nor drunk *any* water, three days and three nights.

13And David said unto him, To whom *belongest* thou? and whence *art* thou? And he said, I *am* a young man of Egypt, servant to an Amalekite; and my master left me, because three days agone I fell sick.

14We made an invasion *upon* the south of the Cherethites, and upon *the coast* which *belongeth* to Judah, and upon the south of Caleb; and we burned Ziklag with fire.

15And David said to him, Canst thou bring me down to this company? And he said, Swear unto me by God, that thou wilt neither kill me, nor deliver me into the hands of my master, and I will bring thee down to this company.

16 ¶ And when he had brought him down, behold, *they were* spread abroad upon all the earth, eating and drinking, and dancing, because of all the great spoil that they had taken out of the land of the Philistines, and out of the land of Judah.

17And David smote them from the twilight even unto the evening of *k*the next day: and there escaped not a man of them, save four hundred young men, which rode upon camels, and fled.

18And David recovered all that the Amalekites had carried away: and David rescued his two wives.

19And there was nothing lacking to them, neither small nor great, neither sons nor daughters, neither spoil, nor any *thing* that they had taken to them: David recovered all.

20And David took all the flocks and the herds, *which* they drave before those *other* cattle, and said, This *is* David's spoil.

21 ¶ And David came to the two hundred men, which were so faint that they could not follow David, whom they had made also to abide at the brook Besor: and they went forth to meet David, and to meet the people that *were* with him: and when David came near to the people, he *l*saluted them.

22Then answered all the wicked men and *men* of Belial, of *m*those that went with David, and said, Because they went not with us, we will not give them *aught* of the spoil that we have recovered, save to every man his wife and his children, that they may lead *them* away, and depart.

23Then said David, Ye shall not do so, my brethren, with that which the LORD hath given us, who hath preserved us, and delivered the company that came against us into our hand.

24For who will hearken unto you in this matter? but as his *part is* that goeth down to the battle, so *shall* his part *be* that tarrieth by the stuff: they shall part alike.

25And it was *so* from that day *n*forward, that he made it a statute and an ordinance for Israel unto this day.

26 ¶ And when David came to Ziklag, he sent of the spoil unto the elders of Judah, *even* to his friends, saying, Behold a *o*present for you of the spoil of the enemies of the LORD;

7David said to Abiathar the priest, Ahimelech's son, I pray you, bring me the ephod. And Abiathar brought him the ephod.

8And David inquired of the Lord, saying, Shall I pursue this troop? Shall I overtake them? The Lord answered him, Pursue, for you shall surely overtake them and without fail recover all.

9So David went, he and the 600 men with him, and came to the brook Besor; there those remained who were left behind.

10But David pursued, he and 400 men, for 200 stayed behind who were too exhausted *and* faint to cross the brook Besor.

11They found an Egyptian in the field and brought him to David, and gave him bread and he ate, and water to drink,

12And a piece of a cake of figs and two clusters of raisins; and when he had eaten, his spirit returned to him, for he had eaten no food or drunk any water for three days and three nights.

13And David said to him, To whom do you belong? And from where have you come? He said, I am a young man of Egypt, servant to an Amalekite; and my master left me because three days ago I fell sick.

14We had made a raid on the South (Negeb) of the Cherethites and upon that which belongs to Judah and upon the South (Negeb) of Caleb. And we burned Ziklag with fire.

15And David said to him, Can you take me down to this band? And he said, Swear to me by God that you will neither kill me nor deliver me into the hands of my master, and I will bring you down to this band.

16And when he had brought David down, behold, the raiders were spread abroad over all the land, eating and drinking and dancing because of all the great spoil they had taken from the land of the Philistines and from the land of Judah.

17And David smote them from twilight even to the evening of the next day, and not a man of them escaped, except 400 youths who rode camels and fled.

18David recovered all that the Amalekites had taken and rescued his two wives.

19Nothing was missing, small or great, sons or daughters, spoil or anything that had been taken; David recovered all.

20Also David captured all the flocks and herds [which the enemy had], and the people drove those animals before him and said, This is David's spoil.

21And David came to the 200 men who were so exhausted *and* faint that they could not follow [him] and had been left at the brook Besor [with the baggage]. They came to meet David and those with him, and when he came near to the men, he saluted them.

22Then all the wicked and base men who went with David said, Because they did not go with us, we will give them nothing of the spoil we have recovered, except that every man may lead away his wife and children and depart.

23David said, You shall not do so, my brethren, with what the Lord has given us. He has preserved us and has delivered into our hands the troop that came against us.

24Who would listen to you in this matter? For as is the share of him who goes into the battle, so shall his share be who stays by the baggage. They shall share alike.

25And from that day to this he made it a statute and ordinance for Israel.

26When David came to Ziklag, he sent part of the spoil to the elders of Judah, his friends, saying, Here is a gift for you of the spoil of the enemies of the Lord:

---

*k*Heb. *their morrow*   *l*Or, *asked them how they did*   *m*Heb.
men   *n*Heb. *and forward*   *o*Heb. *blessing*

New American Standard

7 ¶ Then David said to Abiathar the priest, the son of Ahimelech, "Please bring me the ephod." So Abiathar brought the ephod to David.

8 David inquired of the LORD, saying, "Shall I pursue this band? Shall I overtake them?" And He said to him, "Pursue, for you will surely overtake them, and you will surely rescue *all*."

9 So David went, he and the six hundred men who were with him, and came to the brook Besor, *where* those left behind remained.

10 But David pursued, he and four hundred men, for two hundred who were too exhausted to cross the brook Besor remained *behind*.

11 ¶ Now they found an Egyptian in the field and brought him to David, and gave him bread and he ate, and they provided him water to drink.

12 They gave him a piece of fig cake and two clusters of raisins, and he ate; then his spirit revived. For he had not eaten bread or drunk water for three days and three nights.

13 David said to him, "To whom do you belong? And where are you from?" And he said, "I am a young man of Egypt, a servant of an Amalekite; and my master left me behind when I fell sick three days ago.

14 "We made a raid on the Negev of the Cherethites, and on that which belongs to Judah, and on the Negev of Caleb, and we burned Ziklag with fire."

15 Then David said to him, "Will you bring me down to this band?" And he said, "Swear to me by God that you will not kill me or deliver me into the hands of my master, and I will bring you down to this band."

16 ¶ When he had brought him down, behold, they were spread over all the land, eating and drinking and dancing because of all the great spoil that they had taken from the land of the Philistines and from the land of Judah.

17 David slaughtered them from the twilight until the evening of the next day; and not a man of them escaped, except four hundred young men who rode on camels and fled.

18 So David recovered all that the Amalekites had taken, and rescued his two wives.

19 But nothing of theirs was missing, whether small or great, sons or daughters, spoil or anything that they had taken for themselves; David brought *it* all back.

20 So David had captured all the sheep and the cattle *which the people* drove ahead of the *other* livestock, and they said, "This is David's spoil."

The Spoils Are Divided

21 ¶ When David came to the two hundred men who were too exhausted to follow David, who had also been left at the brook Besor, and they went out to meet David and to meet the people who were with him, then David approached the people and greeted them.

22 Then all the wicked and worthless men among those who went with David said, "Because they did not go with us, we will not give them any of the spoil that we have recovered, except to every man his wife and his children, that they may lead *them* away and depart."

23 Then David said, "You must not do so, my brothers, with what the LORD has given us, who has kept us and delivered into our hand the band that came against us.

24 "And who will listen to you in this matter? For as his share is who goes down to the battle, so shall his share be who stays by the baggage; they shall share alike."

25 So it has been from that day forward, that he made it a statute and an ordinance for Israel to this day.

26 ¶ Now when David came to Ziklag, he sent *some* of the spoil to the elders of Judah, to his friends, saying, "Behold, a gift for you from the spoil of the enemies of the LORD:

New International

7 Then David said to Abiathar the priest, the son of Ahimelech, "Bring me the ephod." Abiathar brought it to him, 8 and David inquired of the LORD, "Shall I pursue this raiding party? Will I overtake them?"

"Pursue them," he answered. "You will certainly overtake them and succeed in the rescue."

9 David and the six hundred men with him came to the Besor Ravine, where some stayed behind, 10 for two hundred men were too exhausted to cross the ravine. But David and four hundred men continued the pursuit.

11 They found an Egyptian in a field and brought him to David. They gave him water to drink and food to eat—12 part of a cake of pressed figs and two cakes of raisins. He ate and was revived, for he had not eaten any food or drunk any water for three days and three nights.

13 David asked him, "To whom do you belong, and where do you come from?"

He said, "I am an Egyptian, the slave of an Amalekite. My master abandoned me when I became ill three days ago. 14 We raided the Negev of the Kerethites and the territory belonging to Judah and the Negev of Caleb. And we burned Ziklag."

15 David asked him, "Can you lead me down to this raiding party?"

He answered, "Swear to me before God that you will not kill me or hand me over to my master, and I will take you down to them."

16 He led David down, and there they were, scattered over the countryside, eating, drinking and reveling because of the great amount of plunder they had taken from the land of the Philistines and from Judah. 17 David fought them from dusk until the evening of the next day, and none of them got away, except four hundred young men who rode off on camels and fled. 18 David recovered everything the Amalekites had taken, including his two wives. 19 Nothing was missing: young or old, boy or girl, plunder or anything else they had taken. David brought everything back. 20 He took all the flocks and herds, and his men drove them ahead of the other livestock, saying, "This is David's plunder."

21 Then David came to the two hundred men who had been too exhausted to follow him and who were left behind at the Besor Ravine. They came out to meet David and the people with him. As David and his men approached, he greeted them. 22 But all the evil men and troublemakers among David's followers said, "Because they did not go out with us, we will not share with them the plunder we recovered. However, each man may take his wife and children and go."

23 David replied, "No, my brothers, you must not do that with what the LORD has given us. He has protected us and handed over to us the forces that came against us. 24 Who will listen to what you say? The share of the man who stayed with the supplies is to be the same as that of him who went down to the battle. All will share alike." 25 David made this a statute and ordinance for Israel from that day to this.

26 When David arrived in Ziklag, he sent some of the plunder to the elders of Judah, who were his friends, saying, "Here is a present for you from the plunder of the LORD's enemies."

<table>
<tr><td>

King James

²⁷To *them* which *were* in Beth-el, and to *them* which *were* in south Ramoth, and to *them* which *were* in Jattir,

²⁸And to *them* which *were* in Aroer, and to *them* which *were* in Siphmoth, and to *them* which *were* in Eshtemoa,

²⁹And to *them* which *were* in Rachal, and to *them* which *were* in the cities of the Jerahmeelites, and to *them* which *were* in the cities of the Kenites,

³⁰And to *them* which *were* in Hormah, and to *them* which *were* in Chor-ashan, and to *them* which *were* in Athach,

³¹And to *them* which *were* in Hebron, and to all the places where David himself and his men were wont to haunt.

The death of Saul

31 NOW THE Philistines fought against Israel: and the men of Israel fled from before the Philistines, and fell down *p*slain in mount Gilboa.

²And the Philistines followed hard upon Saul and upon his sons; and the Philistines slew Jonathan, and Abinadab, and Melchi-shua, Saul's sons.

³And the battle went sore against Saul, and the *q*archers *r*hit him; and he was sore wounded of the archers.

⁴Then said Saul unto his armourbearer, Draw thy sword, and thrust me through therewith; lest these uncircumcised come and thrust me through, and *s*abuse me. But his armourbearer would not; for he was sore afraid. Therefore Saul took a sword, and fell upon it.

⁵And when his armourbearer saw that Saul was dead, he fell likewise upon his sword, and died with him.

⁶So Saul died, and his three sons, and his armourbearer, and all his men, that same day together.

⁷ ¶ And when the men of Israel that *were* on the other side of the valley, and *they* that *were* on the other side Jordan, saw that the men of Israel fled, and that Saul and his sons were dead, they forsook the cities, and fled; and the Philistines came and dwelt in them.

⁸And it came to pass on the morrow, when the Philistines came to strip the slain, that they found Saul and his three sons fallen in mount Gilboa.

⁹And they cut off his head, and stripped off his armour, and sent into the land of the Philistines round about, to publish *it in* the house of their idols, and among the people.

¹⁰And they put his armour in the house of Ashtaroth: and they fastened his body to the wall of Beth-shan.

¹¹ ¶ And when the inhabitants of Jabesh-gilead heard *t*of that which the Philistines had done to Saul;

¹²All the valiant men arose, and went all night, and took the body of Saul and the bodies of his sons from the wall of Beth-shan, and came to Jabesh, and burnt them there.

¹³And they took their bones, and buried *them* under a tree at Jabesh, and fasted seven days.

</td><td>

Amplified

²⁷For those in Bethel, Ramoth of the Negeb, Jattir,

²⁸Aroer, Siphmoth, Eshtemoa,

²⁹Racal, the cities of the Jerahmeelites, the cities of the Kenites,

³⁰Hormah, Bor-ashan, Athach,

³¹Hebron, and for those in all the places David and his men had habitually haunted.

31 NOW THE Philistines fought against Israel; and the men of Israel fled before [them] and fell slain on Mount Gilboa.

²And the Philistines pursued Saul and his sons, and slew Jonathan and Abinadab and Malchi-shua, Saul's sons.

³The battle went heavily against Saul, and the archers severely wounded him.

⁴Saul said to his armor-bearer, Draw your sword and thrust me through, lest these uncircumcised come and thrust me through and abuse *and* mock me. But his armor-bearer would not, for he was terrified. So *l*Saul took a sword and fell upon it.

⁵When his armor-bearer saw that Saul was dead, he likewise fell upon his sword and died with him.

⁶So Saul, his three sons, his armor-bearer, and all his men died that day together.

⁷And when the men of Israel on the other side of the valley and beyond the Jordan saw that the Israelites had fled and that Saul and his sons were dead, they forsook the cities and fled; and the Philistines came and dwelt in them.

⁸The next day, when the Philistines came to strip the slain, they found Saul and his three sons fallen on Mount Gilboa.

⁹They cut off Saul's head and stripped off his armor and sent them round about the land of the Philistines to publish it in the house of their idols and among the people.

¹⁰And they put Saul's armor in the house of the Ashtaroth [the idols representing the female deities Ashtoreth and Asherah], and they fastened his body to the wall of Beth-shan.

¹¹When the people of Jabesh-gilead heard what the Philistines had done to Saul,

¹²All the valiant men arose and went all night, and they took the bodies of Saul and his sons from the wall of Beth-shan and came to Jabesh and cremated them there.

¹³And they took their bones and buried them under a tree at Jabesh, and fasted seven days.

</td></tr>
</table>

*l*This account of Saul's death obviously contradicts that given by the Amalekite who came to David with Saul's spear and crown, claiming to have killed him (II Sam. 1:9ff). His story was probably a fabrication. He found the king's body on the battlefield, stripped it, and brought the spoil to David hoping for a reward, as *The Cambridge Bible* comments. However, it is possible that Saul was not entirely dead when the Amalekite found him, though his armor-bearer had thought him dead and had killed himself, in which case the Amalekite's story may have been true.

p Or, *wounded*   *q* Heb. *shooters, men with bows*   *r* Heb. *found him*   *s* Or, *mock me*   *t* Or, *concerning him*

New American Standard

²⁷ to those who were in Bethel, and to those who were in Ramoth of the Negev, and to those who were in Jattir, ²⁸ and to those who were in Aroer, and to those who were in Siphmoth, and to those who were in Eshtemoa, ²⁹ and to those who were in Racal, and to those who were in the cities of the Jerahmeelites, and to those who were in the cities of the Kenites; ³⁰ and to those who were in Hormah, and to those who were in Bor-ashan, and to those who were in Athach, ³¹ and to those who were in Hebron, and to all the places where David himself and his men were accustomed to go."

Saul and His Sons Slain

31 NOW THE Philistines were fighting against Israel, and the men of Israel fled from before the Philistines and fell slain on Mount Gilboa. ² The Philistines overtook Saul and his sons; and the Philistines killed Jonathan and Abinadab and Malchi-shua the sons of Saul. ³ The battle went heavily against Saul, and the archers hit him; and he was badly wounded by the archers. ⁴ Then Saul said to his armor bearer, "Draw your sword and pierce me through with it, otherwise these uncircumcised will come and pierce me through and make sport of me." But his armor bearer would not, for he was greatly afraid. So Saul took his sword and fell on it. ⁵ When his armor bearer saw that Saul was dead, he also fell on his sword and died with him. ⁶ Thus Saul died with his three sons, his armor bearer, and all his men on that day together. ⁷ ¶ When the men of Israel who were on the other side of the valley, with those who were beyond the Jordan, saw that the men of Israel had fled and that Saul and his sons were dead, they abandoned the cities and fled; then the Philistines came and lived in them. ⁸ ¶ It came about on the next day when the Philistines came to strip the slain, that they found Saul and his three sons fallen on Mount Gilboa. ⁹ They cut off his head and stripped off his weapons, and sent *them* throughout the land of the Philistines, to carry the good news to the house of their idols and to the people. ¹⁰ They put his weapons in the temple of Ashtaroth, and they fastened his body to the wall of Beth-shan. ¹¹ Now when the inhabitants of Jabesh-gilead heard what the Philistines had done to Saul, ¹² all the valiant men rose and walked all night, and took the body of Saul and the bodies of his sons from the wall of Beth-shan, and they came to Jabesh and burned them there. ¹³ They took their bones and buried them under the tamarisk tree at Jabesh, and fasted seven days.

New International

²⁷He sent it to those who were in Bethel, Ramoth Negev and Jattir; ²⁸to those in Aroer, Siphmoth, Eshtemoa ²⁹and Racal; to those in the towns of the Jerahmeelites and the Kenites; ³⁰to those in Hormah, Bor Ashan, Athach ³¹and Hebron; and to those in all the other places where David and his men had roamed.

Saul Takes His Life

31 NOW THE Philistines fought against Israel; the Israelites fled before them, and many fell slain on Mount Gilboa. ²The Philistines pressed hard after Saul and his sons, and they killed his sons Jonathan, Abinadab and Malki-Shua. ³The fighting grew fierce around Saul, and when the archers overtook him, they wounded him critically.

⁴Saul said to his armor-bearer, "Draw your sword and run me through, or these uncircumcised fellows will come and run me through and abuse me."

But his armor-bearer was terrified and would not do it; so Saul took his own sword and fell on it. ⁵When the armor-bearer saw that Saul was dead, he too fell on his sword and died with him. ⁶So Saul and his three sons and his armor-bearer and all his men died together that same day.

⁷When the Israelites along the valley and those across the Jordan saw that the Israelite army had fled and that Saul and his sons had died, they abandoned their towns and fled. And the Philistines came and occupied them.

⁸The next day, when the Philistines came to strip the dead, they found Saul and his three sons fallen on Mount Gilboa. ⁹They cut off his head and stripped off his armor, and they sent messengers throughout the land of the Philistines to proclaim the news in the temple of their idols and among their people. ¹⁰They put his armor in the temple of the Ashtoreths and fastened his body to the wall of Beth Shan.

¹¹When the people of Jabesh Gilead heard of what the Philistines had done to Saul, ¹²all their valiant men journeyed through the night to Beth Shan. They took down the bodies of Saul and his sons from the wall of Beth Shan and went to Jabesh, where they burned them. ¹³Then they took their bones and buried them under a tamarisk tree at Jabesh, and they fasted seven days.

King James

THE SECOND BOOK OF

Samuel

OTHERWISE CALLED THE SECOND BOOK OF THE KINGS

The news of Saul's death

1 NOW IT came to pass after the death of Saul, when David was returned from the slaughter of the Amalekites, and David had abode two days in Ziklag;

2It came even to pass on the third day, that, behold, a man came out of the camp from Saul with his clothes rent, and earth upon his head: and *so* it was, when he came to David, that he fell to the earth, and did obeisance.

3And David said unto him, From whence comest thou? And he said unto him, Out of the camp of Israel am I escaped.

4And David said unto him, How went the matter? I pray thee, tell me. And he answered, That the people are fled from the battle, and many of the people also are fallen and dead; and Saul and Jonathan his son are dead also.

5And David said unto the young man that told him, How knowest thou that Saul and Jonathan his son be dead?

6And the young man that told him said, As I happened by chance upon mount Gilboa, behold, Saul leaned upon his spear; and, lo, the chariots and horsemen followed hard after him.

7And when he looked behind him, he saw me, and called unto me. And I answered, *a*Here *am* I.

8And he said unto me, Who *art* thou? And I answered him, I *am* an Amalekite.

9He said unto me again, Stand, I pray thee, upon me, and slay me: for *b*anguish is come upon me, because my life *is* yet whole in me.

10So I stood upon him, and slew him, because I was sure that he could not live after that he was fallen: and I took the crown that *was* upon his head, and the bracelet that *was* on his arm, and have brought them hither unto my lord.

11Then David took hold on his clothes, and rent them; and likewise all the men that *were* with him:

12And they mourned, and wept, and fasted until even, for Saul, and for Jonathan his son, and for the people of the LORD, and for the house of Israel; because they were fallen by the sword.

13 ¶ And David said unto the young man that told him, Whence *art* thou? And he answered, I *am* the son of a stranger, an Amalekite.

14And David said unto him, How wast thou not afraid to stretch forth thine hand to destroy the LORD'S anointed?

15And David called one of the young men, and said, Go near, *and* fall upon him. And he smote him that he died.

16And David said unto him, Thy blood *be* upon thy head; for thy mouth hath testified against thee, saying, I have slain the LORD'S anointed.

David's lament

17 ¶ And David lamented with this lamentation over Saul and over Jonathan his son:

18(Also he bade them teach the children of Judah *the use of* the bow: behold, *it is* written in the book *c*of Jasher.)

19The beauty of Israel is slain upon thy high places: how are the mighty fallen!

20Tell *it* not in Gath, publish *it* not in the streets of Askelon; lest the daughters of the Philistines rejoice, lest the daughters of the uncircumcised triumph.

Amplified

THE SECOND BOOK OF

Samuel

1 NOW AFTER the death of Saul, when David returned from the slaughter of the Amalekites, he had stayed two days in Ziklag,

2When on the third day a man came from Saul's camp with his clothes torn and dust on his head. When he came to David, he fell to the ground and did obeisance.

3David said to him, Where have you come from? He said, I have escaped from the camp of Israel.

4David said to him, How did it go? Tell me. He answered, The men have fled from the battle. Many have fallen and are dead; Saul and Jonathan his son are dead also.

5David said to the young man, How do you know Saul and Jonathan his son are dead?

6The young man said, By chance I happened to be on Mount Gilboa and I saw Saul leaning on his spear, and behold, the chariots and horsemen were close behind him.

7When he looked behind him, he saw me and called to me. I answered, Here I am.

8He asked me, Who are you? I answered, An Amalekite.

9He said to me, Rise up against me and slay me; for terrible dizziness has come upon me, yet my life is still in me [and I will be taken alive].

10So I stood up against him and slew him, because I was sure he could not live after he had fallen. So I took the crown on his head and the bracelet on his arm and have brought them here to my lord. [I Sam. 31:4.]

11Then David grasped his own clothes and tore them; so did all the men with him.

12They mourned and wept for Saul and Jonathan his son, and fasted until evening for the Lord's people and the house of Israel, because of their defeat in battle.

13David said to the young man who told him, Where are you from? He answered, I am the son of a foreigner, an Amalekite.

14David said to him, Why were you not afraid to stretch forth your hand to destroy the Lord's anointed?

15David called one of the young men and said, Go near and fall upon him. And he smote him so that he died.

16David said to [the fallen man], Your blood be upon your own head; for you have testified against yourself, saying, I have slain the Lord's anointed.

17David lamented with this lamentation over Saul and Jonathan his son,

18And he commanded to teach it, [the lament of] the bow, to the Israelites. Behold, it is written in the Book of Jashar:

19Your glory, O Israel, is slain upon your high places. How have the mighty fallen!

20Tell it not in Gath, announce it not in the streets of Ashkelon, lest the daughters of the Philistines rejoice, lest the daughters of the uncircumcised exult.

New American Standard

THE SECOND BOOK OF

Samuel

David Learns of Saul's Death

1 NOW IT came about after the death of Saul, when David had returned from the slaughter of the Amalekites, that David remained two days in Ziklag.

2 On the third day, behold, a man came out of the camp from Saul, with his clothes torn and dust on his head. And it came about when he came to David that he fell to the ground and prostrated himself.

3 Then David said to him, "From where do you come?" And he said to him, "I have escaped from the camp of Israel."

4 David said to him, "How did things go? Please tell me." And he said, "The people have fled from the battle, and also many of the people have fallen and are dead; and Saul and Jonathan his son are dead also."

5 So David said to the young man who told him, "How do you know that Saul and his son Jonathan are dead?"

6 The young man who told him said, "By chance I happened to be on Mount Gilboa, and behold, Saul was leaning on his spear. And behold, the chariots and the horsemen pursued him closely.

7 "When he looked behind him, he saw me and called to me. And I said, 'Here I am.'

8 "He said to me, 'Who are you?' And I answered him, 'I am an Amalekite.'

9 "Then he said to me, 'Please stand beside me and kill me, for agony has seized me because my life still lingers in me.'

10 "So I stood beside him and killed him, because I knew that he could not live after he had fallen. And I took the crown which *was* on his head and the bracelet which *was* on his arm, and I have brought them here to my lord."

11 ¶ Then David took hold of his clothes and tore them, and *so also did* all the men who *were* with him.

12 They mourned and wept and fasted until evening for Saul and his son Jonathan and for the people of the LORD and the house of Israel, because they had fallen by the sword.

13 David said to the young man who told him, "Where are you from?" And he answered, "I am the son of an alien, an Amalekite."

14 Then David said to him, "How is it you were not afraid to stretch out your hand to destroy the LORD'S anointed?"

15 And David called one of the young men and said, "Go, cut him down." So he struck him and he died.

16 David said to him, "Your blood is on your head, for your mouth has testified against you, saying, 'I have killed the LORD's anointed.' "

David's Dirge for Saul and Jonathan

17 ¶ Then David chanted with this lament over Saul and Jonathan his son,

18 and he told *them* to teach the sons of Judah *the song of* the bow; behold, it is written in the book of Jashar.

19 "Your beauty, O Israel, is slain on your high places!
How have the mighty fallen!

20 "Tell *it* not in Gath,
Proclaim it not in the streets of Ashkelon,
Or the daughters of the Philistines will rejoice,
The daughters of the uncircumcised will exult.

New International

2 Samuel

David Hears of Saul's Death

1 AFTER THE death of Saul, David returned from defeating the Amalekites and stayed in Ziklag two days. 2 On the third day a man arrived from Saul's camp, with his clothes torn and with dust on his head. When he came to David, he fell to the ground to pay him honor.

3 "Where have you come from?" David asked him.
He answered, "I have escaped from the Israelite camp."

4 "What happened?" David asked. "Tell me."
He said, "The men fled from the battle. Many of them fell and died. And Saul and his son Jonathan are dead."

5 Then David said to the young man who brought him the report, "How do you know that Saul and his son Jonathan are dead?"

6 "I happened to be on Mount Gilboa," the young man said, "and there was Saul, leaning on his spear, with the chariots and riders almost upon him. 7 When he turned around and saw me, he called out to me, and I said, 'What can I do?'

8 "He asked me, 'Who are you?'
" 'An Amalekite,' I answered.

9 "Then he said to me, 'Stand over me and kill me! I am in the throes of death, but I'm still alive.'

10 "So I stood over him and killed him, because I knew that after he had fallen he could not survive. And I took the crown that was on his head and the band on his arm and have brought them here to my lord."

11 Then David and all the men with him took hold of their clothes and tore them. 12 They mourned and wept and fasted till evening for Saul and his son Jonathan, and for the army of the LORD and the house of Israel, because they had fallen by the sword.

13 David said to the young man who brought him the report, "Where are you from?"
"I am the son of an alien, an Amalekite," he answered.

14 David asked him, "Why were you not afraid to lift your hand to destroy the LORD's anointed?"

15 Then David called one of his men and said, "Go, strike him down!" So he struck him down, and he died. 16 For David had said to him, "Your blood be on your own head. Your own mouth testified against you when you said, 'I killed the LORD's anointed.' "

David's Lament for Saul and Jonathan

17 David took up this lament concerning Saul and his son Jonathan, 18 and ordered that the men of Judah be taught this lament of the bow (it is written in the Book of Jashar):

19 "Your glory, O Israel, lies slain on your
heights.
How the mighty have fallen!

20 "Tell it not in Gath,
proclaim it not in the streets of Ashkelon,
lest the daughters of the Philistines be glad,
lest the daughters of the uncircumcised
rejoice.

King James

²¹Ye mountains of Gilboa, *let there be* no dew, neither *let there be* rain, upon you, nor fields of offerings: for there the shield of the mighty is vilely cast away, the shield of Saul, *as though he had* not *been* anointed with oil.

²²From the blood of the slain, from the fat of the mighty, the bow of Jonathan turned not back, and the sword of Saul returned not empty.

²³Saul and Jonathan *were* lovely and ^dpleasant in their lives, and in their death they were not divided: they were swifter than eagles, they were stronger than lions.

²⁴Ye daughters of Israel, weep over Saul, who clothed you in scarlet, with *other* delights, who put on ornaments of gold upon your apparel.

²⁵How are the mighty fallen in the midst of the battle! O Jonathan, *thou wast* slain in thine high places.

²⁶I am distressed for thee, my brother Jonathan: very pleasant hast thou been unto me: thy love to me was wonderful, passing the love of women.

²⁷How are the mighty fallen, and the weapons of war perished!

David anointed king of Judah

2 AND IT came to pass after this, that David inquired of the LORD, saying, Shall I go up into any of the cities of Judah? And the LORD said unto him, Go up. And David said, Whither shall I go up? And he said, Unto Hebron.

²So David went up thither, and his two wives also, Ahinoam the Jezreelitess, and Abigail Nabal's wife the Carmelite.

³And his men that *were* with him did David bring up, every man with his household: and they dwelt in the cities of Hebron.

⁴And the men of Judah came, and there they anointed David king over the house of Judah. And they told David, saying, *That* the men of Jabesh-gilead *were they* that buried Saul.

⁵ ¶ And David sent messengers unto the men of Jabesh-gilead, and said unto them, Blessed *be* ye of the LORD, that ye have shown this kindness unto your lord, *even* unto Saul, and have buried him.

⁶And now the LORD show kindness and truth unto you: and I also will requite you this kindness, because ye have done this thing.

⁷Therefore now let your hands be strengthened, and ^ebe ye valiant: for your master Saul is dead, and also the house of Judah have anointed me king over them.

War between Israel and Judah

⁸ ¶ But Abner the son of Ner, captain of ^fSaul's host, took ^gIsh-bosheth the son of Saul, and brought him over to Mahanaim;

⁹And made him king over Gilead, and over the Ashurites, and over Jezreel, and over Ephraim, and over Benjamin, and over all Israel.

¹⁰Ish-bosheth Saul's son *was* forty years old when he began to reign over Israel, and reigned two years. But the house of Judah followed David.

¹¹And the ^htime that David was king in Hebron over the house of Judah was seven years and six months.

Amplified

²¹O mountains of Gilboa, let there be no dew or rain upon you, or fields with offerings. For there the shield of the mighty was defiled, the shield of Saul, as though he were not anointed with oil.

²²From the blood of the slain, from the fat of the mighty, the bow of Jonathan turned not back, and the sword of Saul returned not empty.

²³Saul and Jonathan, beloved and lovely! In their lives and in their deaths they were not divided. They were swifter than eagles, they were stronger than lions.

²⁴You daughters of Israel, weep over Saul, who clothed you in scarlet with [other] delights, who put ornaments of gold upon your apparel.

²⁵How have the mighty fallen in the midst of the battle! Jonathan lies slain upon your high places.

²⁶I am distressed for you, my brother Jonathan; very pleasant have you been to me. Your love to me was wonderful, passing the love of women.

²⁷How have the mighty fallen, and the weapons of war perished!

2 AFTER THIS, David inquired of the Lord, saying, Shall I go up into any of the cities of Judah? And the Lord said to him, Go up. David said, To which shall I go up? And He said, To Hebron.

²So David went up there with his two wives, Ahinoam the Jezreelitess and Abigail, the widow of Nabal of Carmel.

³And David brought up his men who were with him, each one with his household, and they dwelt in the towns of Hebron.

⁴And the men of Judah came and there they anointed David king over the house of Judah. They told David, The men of Jabesh-gilead buried Saul. [I Sam. 31:11–13.]

⁵And David sent messengers to the men of Jabesh-gilead, saying, May the Lord bless you because you showed kindness *and* loyalty to Saul your king and buried him.

⁶And now may the Lord show loving-kindness and faithfulness to you. I also will do well by you because you have done this.

⁷So now, let your hands be strengthened and be valiant, for your master Saul is dead, and the house of Judah has anointed me king over them.

⁸Now Abner son of Ner, commander of Saul's army, took Ish-bosheth son of Saul and brought him over to Mahanaim.

⁹And he made him king over Gilead, the Ashurites, Jezreel, Ephraim, Benjamin, and all Israel.

¹⁰Ish-bosheth, Saul's son, was forty years old when he began his two-year reign over Israel. But the house of Judah followed David.

¹¹And David was king in Hebron over the house of Judah for seven years and six months.

---

^dOr, *sweet*   ^eHeb. *be ye the sons of valour*   ^fHeb. *the host which* was *Saul's*   ^gOr, *Esh-baal;* see 1 Chr. 8:33 & 9:39   ^hHeb. *number of days*

New American Standard

21"O mountains of Gilboa,
  Let not dew or rain be on you, nor fields of
    offerings;
  For there the shield of the mighty was defiled,
  The shield of Saul, not anointed with oil.
22"From the blood of the slain, from the fat of the
    mighty,
  The bow of Jonathan did not turn back,
  And the sword of Saul did not return empty.
23"Saul and Jonathan, beloved and pleasant in their
    life,
  And in their death they were not parted;
  They were swifter than eagles,
  They were stronger than lions.
24"O daughters of Israel, weep over Saul,
  Who clothed you luxuriously in scarlet,
  Who put ornaments of gold on your apparel.
25"How have the mighty fallen in the midst of the
    battle!
  Jonathan is slain on your high places.
26"I am distressed for you, my brother Jonathan;
  You have been very pleasant to me.
  Your love to me was more wonderful
  Than the love of women.
27"How have the mighty fallen,
  And the weapons of war perished!"

David Made King over Judah

2 THEN IT came about afterwards that David inquired
  of the LORD, saying, "Shall I go up to one of the cities
of Judah?" And the LORD said to him, "Go up." So David
said, "Where shall I go up?" And He said, "To Hebron."
  2 So David went up there, and his two wives also,
Ahinoam the Jezreelitess and Abigail the widow of Nabal
the Carmelite.
  3 And David brought up his men who *were* with him,
each with his household; and they lived in the cities of
Hebron.
  4 Then the men of Judah came and there anointed David king over the house of Judah.
  ¶ And they told David, saying, "It was the men of
Jabesh-gilead who buried Saul."
  5 David sent messengers to the men of Jabesh-gilead,
and said to them, "May you be blessed of the LORD because you have shown this kindness to Saul your lord, and
have buried him.
  6"Now may the LORD show lovingkindness and truth to
you; and I also will show this goodness to you, because
you have done this thing.
  7"Now therefore, let your hands be strong and be valiant; for Saul your lord is dead, and also the house of Judah
has anointed me king over them."

Ish-bosheth Made King over Israel

  8 ¶ But Abner the son of Ner, commander of Saul's
army, had taken *a*Ish-bosheth the son of Saul and brought
him over to Mahanaim.
  9 He made him king over Gilead, over the Ashurites,
over Jezreel, over Ephraim, and over Benjamin, even over
all Israel.
  10 Ish-bosheth, Saul's son, was forty years old when he
became king over Israel, and he was king for two years.
The house of Judah, however, followed David.
  11 The time that David was king in Hebron over the
house of Judah was seven years and six months.

New International

21"O mountains of Gilboa,
  may you have neither dew nor rain,
    nor fields that yield offerings ⌊of grain⌋.
  For there the shield of the mighty was defiled,
  the shield of Saul—no longer rubbed with
    oil.
22From the blood of the slain,
  from the flesh of the mighty,
  the bow of Jonathan did not turn back,
  the sword of Saul did not return unsatisfied.

23"Saul and Jonathan—
  in life they were loved and gracious,
  and in death they were not parted.
  They were swifter than eagles,
  they were stronger than lions.

24"O daughters of Israel,
  weep for Saul,
  who clothed you in scarlet and finery,
  who adorned your garments with ornaments
    of gold.

25"How the mighty have fallen in battle!
  Jonathan lies slain on your heights.
26I grieve for you, Jonathan my brother;
  you were very dear to me.
  Your love for me was wonderful,
  more wonderful than that of women.

27"How the mighty have fallen!
  The weapons of war have perished!"

David Anointed King Over Judah

2 IN THE course of time, David inquired of the LORD.
  "Shall I go up to one of the towns of Judah?" he
asked.
  The LORD said, "Go up."
  David asked, "Where shall I go?"
  "To Hebron," the LORD answered.
  2So David went up there with his two wives, Ahinoam
of Jezreel and Abigail, the widow of Nabal of Carmel.
3David also took the men who were with him, each with
his family, and they settled in Hebron and its towns. 4Then
the men of Judah came to Hebron and there they anointed
David king over the house of Judah.
  When David was told that it was the men of Jabesh
Gilead who had buried Saul, 5he sent messengers to the
men of Jabesh Gilead to say to them, "The LORD bless you
for showing this kindness to Saul your master by burying
him. 6May the LORD now show you kindness and faithfulness, and I too will show you the same favor because you
have done this. 7Now then, be strong and brave, for Saul
your master is dead, and the house of Judah has anointed
me king over them."

War Between the Houses of David and Saul

  8Meanwhile, Abner son of Ner, the commander of
Saul's army, had taken Ish-Bosheth son of Saul and
brought him over to Mahanaim. 9He made him king over
Gilead, Ashuri*a* and Jezreel, and also over Ephraim, Benjamin and all Israel.
  10Ish-Bosheth son of Saul was forty years old when he
became king over Israel, and he reigned two years. The
house of Judah, however, followed David. 11The length of
time David was king in Hebron over the house of Judah
was seven years and six months.

---

*a*I.e. man of shame; cf 1 Chr 8:33, *Eshbaal*   *a*9 Or *Asher*

King James

12 ¶ And Abner the son of Ner, and the servants of Ish-bosheth the son of Saul, went out from Mahanaim to Gibeon.

13 And Joab the son of Zeruiah, and the servants of David, went out, and met *together* by the pool of Gibeon: and they sat down, the one on the one side of the pool, and the other on the other side of the pool.

14 And Abner said to Joab, Let the young men now arise, and play before us. And Joab said, Let them arise.

15 Then there arose and went over by number twelve of Benjamin, which *pertained* to Ish-bosheth the son of Saul, and twelve of the servants of David.

16 And they caught every one his fellow by the head, and *thrust* his sword in his fellow's side; so they fell down together: wherefore that place was called *j* Helkath-hazzurim, which *is* in Gibeon.

17 And there was a very sore battle that day; and Abner was beaten, and the men of Israel, before the servants of David.

18 ¶ And there were three sons of Zeruiah there, Joab, and Abishai, and Asahel: and Asahel *was as* light *k* of foot *l* as a wild roe.

19 And Asahel pursued after Abner; and in going he turned not to the right hand nor to the left *m* from following Abner.

20 Then Abner looked behind him, and said, *Art* thou Asahel? And he answered, I *am*.

21 And Abner said to him, Turn thee aside to thy right hand or to thy left, and lay thee hold on one of the young men, and take thee his *n* armour. But Asahel would not turn aside from following of him.

22 And Abner said again to Asahel, Turn thee aside from following me: wherefore should I smite thee to the ground? how should I hold up my face to Joab thy brother?

23 Howbeit he refused to turn aside: wherefore Abner with the hinder end of the spear smote him under the fifth *rib*, that the spear came out behind him; and he fell down there, and died in the same place: and it came to pass, *that* as many as came to the place where Asahel fell down and died stood still.

24 Joab also and Abishai pursued after Abner: and the sun went down when they were come to the hill of Ammah, that *lieth* before Giah by the way of the wilderness of Gibeon.

25 ¶ And the children of Benjamin gathered themselves together after Abner, and became one troop, and stood on the top of an hill.

26 Then Abner called to Joab, and said, Shall the sword devour for ever? knowest thou not that it will be bitterness in the latter end? how long shall it be then, ere thou bid the people return from following their brethren?

27 And Joab said, *As* God liveth, unless thou hadst spoken, surely then *o* in the morning the people had *p* gone up every one from following his brother.

28 So Joab blew a trumpet, and all the people stood still, and pursued after Israel no more, neither fought they any more.

29 And Abner and his men walked all that night through the plain, and passed over Jordan, and went through all Bithron, and they came to Mahanaim.

30 And Joab returned from following Abner: and when he had gathered all the people together, there lacked of David's servants nineteen men and Asahel.

31 But the servants of David had smitten of Benjamin, and of Abner's men, *so that* three hundred and threescore men died.

Amplified

12 And Abner son of Ner and the servants of Ish-bosheth son of Saul went out from Mahanaim to Gibeon.

13 Joab son of Zeruiah and the servants of David went out also; and the two groups met by the pool of Gibeon, seating themselves with one group on either side of the pool.

14 And Abner said to Joab, Let the young men now arise and have a contest before us. And Joab said, Let them arise.

15 Then there arose and went over by number—twelve of Benjamin who were with Ish-bosheth son of Saul, and twelve of the servants of David.

16 And each caught his opponent by the head and thrust his sword into his side; so they all fell together. Therefore that place was called the Field of Sharp Knives, which is at Gibeon.

17 A very fierce battle followed, and Abner and the men of Israel were beaten before the servants of David.

18 Three sons of Zeruiah [the half sister of David] were there: Joab, Abishai, and Asahel. Now Asahel was as light of foot as a wild roe *or* antelope.

19 Asahel pursued Abner, and as he ran he turned not to the right hand or to the left from following Abner.

20 Then Abner looked behind him and said, Are you Asahel? He answered, I am.

21 Abner said to him, Turn aside to your right or left, and seize one of the young men and take his armor. But Asahel would not turn aside from following him.

22 And Abner said again to Asahel, Turn aside from following me. Why should I strike you to the ground? How then should I be able to face Joab your brother?

23 Asahel refused to turn aside; so Abner with the rear end of his spear smote him through the abdomen, and he fell and died where he fell. And all who came to the place where Asahel fell and died stood still.

24 But Joab and Abishai [his brothers] pursued Abner; the sun was going down as they came to the hill of Ammah, before Giah on the way to the wilderness of Gibeon.

25 And the Benjamites gathered together behind Abner and became one troop and took their stand on the top of a hill.

26 Then Abner called to Joab, Shall the sword devour forever? Do you not know that bitterness will be the result? How long will it be then before you bid the people to stop pursuing their brethren?

27 Joab said, As God lives, if you had not spoken, surely the men would have stopped pursuing their brethren in the morning.

28 So Joab blew a trumpet, and all the people stood still and pursued Israel no more, nor did they fight any more.

29 Abner and his men went all night through the Arabah [plain], crossed the Jordan, and went through the whole Bithron [district of ravines] and came to Mahanaim.

30 Joab returned from pursuing Abner, and when he had gathered all the people together, there were missing of David's servants nineteen men besides Asahel.

31 But the servants of David had slain of Benjamin 360 of Abner's men.

---

i Heb. *them together*   *j* i.e. *The field of strong men*   *k* Heb. *of his feet*   *l* Heb. *as one of the roes that is in the field*   *m* Heb. *from after Abner*   *n* Or, *spoil*   *o* Heb. *from the morning*   *p* Or, *gone away*

New American Standard

Civil War

12 ¶ Now Abner the son of Ner, went out from Mahanaim to Gibeon with the servants of Ish-bosheth the son of Saul.

13 And Joab the son of Zeruiah and the servants of David went out and met them by the pool of Gibeon; and they sat down, one on the one side of the pool and the other on the other side of the pool.

14 Then Abner said to Joab, "Now let the young men arise and *b*hold a contest before us." And Joab said, "Let them arise."

15 So they arose and went over by count, twelve for Benjamin and Ish-bosheth the son of Saul, and twelve of the servants of David.

16 Each one of them seized his opponent by the head and *thrust* his sword in his opponent's side; so they fell down together. Therefore that place was called *c*Helkath-hazzurim, which is in Gibeon.

17 That day the battle was very severe, and Abner and the men of Israel were beaten before the servants of David.

18 ¶ Now the three sons of Zeruiah were there, Joab and Abishai and Asahel; and Asahel *was as* swift-footed as one of the gazelles which is in the field.

19 Asahel pursued Abner and did not turn to the right or to the left from following Abner.

20 Then Abner looked behind him and said, "Is that you, Asahel?" And he answered, "It is I."

21 So Abner said to him, "Turn to your right or to your left, and take hold of one of the young men for yourself, and take for yourself his spoil." But Asahel was not willing to turn aside from following him.

22 Abner repeated again to Asahel, "Turn aside from following me. Why should I strike you to the ground? How then could I lift up my face to your brother Joab?"

23 However, he refused to turn aside; therefore Abner struck him in the belly with the butt end of the spear, so that the spear came out at his back. And he fell there and died on the spot. And it came about that all who came to the place where Asahel had fallen and died, stood still.

24 ¶ But Joab and Abishai pursued Abner, and when the sun was going down, they came to the hill of Ammah, which is in front of Giah by the way of the wilderness of Gibeon.

25 The sons of Benjamin gathered together behind Abner and became one band, and they stood on the top of a certain hill.

26 Then Abner called to Joab and said, "Shall the sword devour forever? Do you not know that it will be bitter in the end? How long will you refrain from telling the people to turn back from following their brothers?"

27 Joab said, "As God lives, if you had not spoken, surely then the people would have gone away in the morning, each from following his brother."

28 So Joab blew the trumpet; and all the people halted and pursued Israel no longer, nor did they continue to fight anymore.

29 Abner and his men then went through the Arabah all that night; so they crossed the Jordan, walked all morning, and came to Mahanaim.

30 ¶ Then Joab returned from following Abner; when he had gathered all the people together, nineteen of David's servants besides Asahel were missing.

31 But the servants of David had struck down many of Benjamin and Abner's men, *so that* three hundred and sixty men died.

New International

12 Abner son of Ner, together with the men of Ish-Bosheth son of Saul, left Mahanaim and went to Gibeon. 13 Joab son of Zeruiah and David's men went out and met them at the pool of Gibeon. One group sat down on one side of the pool and one group on the other side.

14 Then Abner said to Joab, "Let's have some of the young men get up and fight hand to hand in front of us."

"All right, let them do it," Joab said.

15 So they stood up and were counted off—twelve men for Benjamin and Ish-Bosheth son of Saul, and twelve for David. 16 Then each man grabbed his opponent by the head and thrust his dagger into his opponent's side, and they fell down together. So that place in Gibeon was called Helkath Hazzurim.*b*

17 The battle that day was very fierce, and Abner and the men of Israel were defeated by David's men.

18 The three sons of Zeruiah were there: Joab, Abishai and Asahel. Now Asahel was as fleet-footed as a wild gazelle. 19 He chased Abner, turning neither to the right nor to the left as he pursued him. 20 Abner looked behind him and asked, "Is that you, Asahel?"

"It is," he answered.

21 Then Abner said to him, "Turn aside to the right or to the left; take on one of the young men and strip him of his weapons." But Asahel would not stop chasing him.

22 Again Abner warned Asahel, "Stop chasing me! Why should I strike you down? How could I look your brother Joab in the face?"

23 But Asahel refused to give up the pursuit; so Abner thrust the butt of his spear into Asahel's stomach, and the spear came out through his back. He fell there and died on the spot. And every man stopped when he came to the place where Asahel had fallen and died.

24 But Joab and Abishai pursued Abner, and as the sun was setting, they came to the hill of Ammah, near Giah on the way to the wasteland of Gibeon. 25 Then the men of Benjamin rallied behind Abner. They formed themselves into a group and took their stand on top of a hill.

26 Abner called out to Joab, "Must the sword devour forever? Don't you realize that this will end in bitterness? How long before you order your men to stop pursuing their brothers?"

27 Joab answered, "As surely as God lives, if you had not spoken, the men would have continued the pursuit of their brothers until morning.*c*"

28 So Joab blew the trumpet, and all the men came to a halt; they no longer pursued Israel, nor did they fight anymore.

29 All that night Abner and his men marched through the Arabah. They crossed the Jordan, continued through the whole Bithron*d* and came to Mahanaim.

30 Then Joab returned from pursuing Abner and assembled all his men. Besides Asahel, nineteen of David's men were found missing. 31 But David's men had killed three hundred and sixty Benjamites who were with Abner.

---

b 16 *Helkath Hazzurim means field of daggers or field of hostilities.*
c 27 *Or spoken this morning, the men would not have taken up the pursuit of their brothers; or spoken, the men would have given up the pursuit of their brothers by morning*   *d 29* *Or morning; or ravine; the meaning of the Hebrew for this word is uncertain.*

b Lit *make sport*   *c* I.e. the field of sword-edges

King James

³² ¶ And they took up Asahel, and buried him in the sepulchre of his father, which *was in* Bethlehem. And Joab and his men went all night, and they came to Hebron at break of day.

3 NOW THERE was long war between the house of Saul and the house of David: but David waxed stronger and stronger, and the house of Saul waxed weaker and weaker.

² ¶ And unto David were sons born in Hebron: and his firstborn was Amnon, of Ahinoam the Jezreelitess;

³ And his second, ^qChileab, of Abigail the wife of Nabal the Carmelite; and the third, Absalom the son of Maacah the daughter of Talmai king of Geshur;

⁴ And the fourth, Adonijah the son of Haggith; and the fifth, Shephatiah the son of Abital;

⁵ And the sixth, Ithream, by Eglah David's wife. These were born to David in Hebron.

⁶ ¶ And it came to pass, while there was war between the house of Saul and the house of David, that Abner made himself strong for the house of Saul.

⁷ And Saul had a concubine, whose name *was* Rizpah, the daughter of Aiah: and *Ish-bosheth* said to Abner, Wherefore hast thou gone in unto my father's concubine?

⁸ Then was Abner very wroth for the words of Ish-bosheth, and said, *Am* I a dog's head, which against Judah do show kindness this day unto the house of Saul thy father, to his brethren, and to his friends, and have not delivered thee into the hand of David, that thou chargest me today with a fault concerning this woman?

⁹ So do God to Abner, and more also, except, as the LORD hath sworn to David, even so I do to him;

¹⁰ To translate the kingdom from the house of Saul, and to set up the throne of David over Israel and over Judah, from Dan even to Beer-sheba.

¹¹ And he could not answer Abner a word again, because he feared him.

¹² ¶ And Abner sent messengers to David on his behalf, saying, Whose *is* the land? saying *also,* Make thy league with me, and, behold, my hand *shall be* with thee, to bring about all Israel unto thee.

¹³ And he said, Well; I will make a league with thee: but one thing I require of thee, ^rthat is, Thou shalt not see my face, except thou first bring Michal Saul's daughter, when thou comest to see my face.

¹⁴ And David sent messengers to Ish-bosheth Saul's son, saying, Deliver *me* my wife Michal, which I espoused to me for an hundred foreskins of the Philistines.

¹⁵ And Ish-bosheth sent, and took her from *her* husband, *even* from Phaltiel the son of Laish.

¹⁶ And her husband went with her ^salong weeping behind her to Bahurim. Then said Abner unto him, Go, return. And he returned.

Abner visits David

¹⁷ ¶ And Abner had communication with the elders of Israel, saying, Ye sought for David ^tin times past *to be* king over you:

¹⁸ Now then do *it:* for the LORD hath spoken of David, saying, By the hand of my servant David I will save my people Israel out of the hand of the Philistines, and out of the hand of all their enemies.

¹⁹ And Abner also spake in the ears of Benjamin: and Abner went also to speak in the ears of David in Hebron all that seemed good to Israel, and that seemed good to the whole house of Benjamin.

²⁰ So Abner came to David to Hebron, and twenty men with him. And David made Abner and the men that *were* with him a feast.

Amplified

³² And they took up Asahel and buried him in the tomb of his father at Bethlehem. And Joab and his men walked all night and came to Hebron at daybreak.

3 THERE WAS a long war between the house of Saul and the house of David. But David grew stronger and stronger, and the house of Saul grew weaker and weaker.

² Sons were born to David in Hebron: his firstborn was Amnon, by Ahinoam the Jezreelitess;

³ His second, Chileab, by Abigail widow of Nabal of Carmel; the third, Absalom the son of Maacah daughter of Talmai king of Geshur;

⁴ The fourth, Adonijah the son of Haggith; the fifth, Shephatiah the son of Abital;

⁵ And the sixth, Ithream, by Eglah, David's wife. These were born to David in Hebron.

⁶ While there was war between the houses of Saul and David, Abner was making himself strong in the house of Saul.

⁷ Now Saul had a concubine whose name was Rizpah daughter of Aiah. And Ish-bosheth said to Abner, Why have you gone in to my father's concubine?

⁸ Then Abner was very angry at the words of Ish-bosheth and said, Am I a dog's head [despicable and hostile] against Judah? This day I keep showing kindness *and* loyalty to the house of Saul your father, to his brothers, and his friends, and have not delivered you into the hands of David; and yet you charge me today with a fault concerning this woman!

⁹ May God do so to Abner, and more also, if I do not do for David what the Lord has sworn to him,

¹⁰ To transfer the kingdom from the house of Saul and set the throne of David over Israel and Judah from Dan to Beersheba.

¹¹ And Ish-bosheth could not answer Abner a word, because he feared him.

¹² And Abner sent messengers to David where he was [at Hebron], saying, Whose is the land? Make your league with me, and my hand shall be with you to bring all Israel over to you.

¹³ And David said, Good. I will make a league with you. But I require one thing of you: that is, you shall not see my face unless you first bring Michal, Saul's daughter, when you come to see me.

¹⁴ And David sent messengers to Ish-bosheth, Saul's son, saying, Give me my wife Michal, whom I betrothed for a hundred foreskins of the Philistines.

¹⁵ And Ish-bosheth sent and took her from her [second] husband, from Paltiel son of Laish [to whom Saul had given her].

¹⁶ But her husband went with her, weeping behind her all the way to Bahurim. Then Abner said to him, Go back. And he did so.

¹⁷ Abner talked with the seniors of Israel, saying, In times past you sought to make David king over you.

¹⁸ Now then, do it! For the Lord has spoken of David, saying, By the hand of My servant David I will save My people Israel from the hands of the Philistines and of all their enemies. [I Sam. 9:16.]

¹⁹ Abner also spoke to [the men of] Benjamin. Then [he] went to Hebron to tell David all that seemed good to Israel and the whole house of Benjamin to do.

²⁰ So Abner came to David at Hebron, and twenty men along with him. And David made Abner and the men with him a feast.

^qOr, *Daniel* in 1 Chr. 3:1   ^rHeb. *saying*   ^sHeb. *going and weeping*   ^tHeb. *both yesterday and the third day*

New American Standard

32 And they took up Asahel and buried him in his father's tomb which was in Bethlehem. Then Joab and his men went all night until the day dawned at Hebron.

The House of David Strengthened

3 NOW THERE was a long war between the house of Saul and the house of David; and David grew steadily stronger, but the house of Saul grew weaker continually.

2 ¶ Sons were born to David at Hebron: his firstborn was Amnon, by Ahinoam the Jezreelitess;

3 and his second, Chileab, by Abigail the widow of Nabal the Carmelite; and the third, Absalom the son of Maacah, the daughter of Talmai, king of Geshur;

4 and the fourth, Adonijah the son of Haggith; and the fifth, Shephatiah the son of Abital;

5 and the sixth, Ithream, by David's wife Eglah. These were born to David at Hebron.

Abner Joins David

6 ¶ It came about while there was war between the house of Saul and the house of David that Abner was making himself strong in the house of Saul.

7 Now Saul had a concubine whose name was Rizpah, the daughter of Aiah; and Ish-bosheth said to Abner, "Why have you gone in to my father's concubine?"

8 Then Abner was very angry over the words of Ish-bosheth and said, "Am I a dog's head that belongs to Judah? Today I show kindness to the house of Saul your father, to his brothers and to his friends, and have not delivered you into the hands of David; and yet today you charge me with a guilt concerning the woman.

9 "May God do so to Abner, and more also, if as the LORD has sworn to David, I do not accomplish this for him,

10 to transfer the kingdom from the house of Saul and to establish the throne of David over Israel and over Judah, from Dan even to Beersheba."

11 And he could no longer answer Abner a word, because he was afraid of him.

12 ¶ Then Abner sent messengers to David in his place, saying, "Whose is the land? Make your covenant with me, and behold, my hand shall be with you to bring all Israel over to you."

13 He said, "Good! I will make a covenant with you, but I demand one thing of you, namely, you shall not see my face unless you first bring Michal, Saul's daughter, when you come to see me."

14 So David sent messengers to Ish-bosheth, Saul's son, saying, "Give me my wife Michal, to whom I was betrothed for a hundred foreskins of the Philistines."

15 Ish-bosheth sent and took her from *her* husband, from Paltiel the son of Laish.

16 But her husband went with her, weeping as he went, and followed her as far as Bahurim. Then Abner said to him, "Go, return." So he returned.

17 ¶ Now Abner had consultation with the elders of Israel, saying, "In times past you were seeking for David to be king over you.

18 "Now then, do *it!* For the LORD has spoken of David, saying, 'By the hand of My servant David I will save My people Israel from the hand of the Philistines and from the hand of all their enemies.' "

19 Abner also spoke in the hearing of Benjamin; and in addition Abner went to speak in the hearing of David in Hebron all that seemed good to Israel and to the whole house of Benjamin.

20 ¶ Then Abner and twenty men with him came to David at Hebron. And David made a feast for Abner and the men who were with him.

New International

32 They took Asahel and buried him in his father's tomb at Bethlehem. Then Joab and his men marched all night and arrived at Hebron by daybreak.

3 THE WAR between the house of Saul and the house of David lasted a long time. David grew stronger and stronger, while the house of Saul grew weaker and weaker.

2 Sons were born to David in Hebron:

His firstborn was Amnon the son of Ahinoam of Jezreel;

3 his second, Kileab the son of Abigail the widow of Nabal of Carmel;

the third, Absalom the son of Maacah daughter of Talmai king of Geshur;

4 the fourth, Adonijah the son of Haggith;

the fifth, Shephatiah the son of Abital;

5 and the sixth, Ithream the son of David's wife Eglah.

These were born to David in Hebron.

Abner Goes Over to David

6 During the war between the house of Saul and the house of David, Abner had been strengthening his own position in the house of Saul. 7 Now Saul had had a concubine named Rizpah daughter of Aiah. And Ish-Bosheth said to Abner, "Why did you sleep with my father's concubine?"

8 Abner was very angry because of what Ish-Bosheth said and he answered, "Am I a dog's head—on Judah's side? This very day I am loyal to the house of your father Saul and to his family and friends. I haven't handed you over to David. Yet now you accuse me of an offense involving this woman! 9 May God deal with Abner, be it ever so severely, if I do not do for David what the LORD promised him on oath 10 and transfer the kingdom from the house of Saul and establish David's throne over Israel and Judah from Dan to Beersheba." 11 Ish-Bosheth did not dare to say another word to Abner, because he was afraid of him.

12 Then Abner sent messengers on his behalf to say to David, "Whose land is it? Make an agreement with me, and I will help you bring all Israel over to you."

13 "Good," said David. "I will make an agreement with you. But I demand one thing of you: Do not come into my presence unless you bring Michal daughter of Saul when you come to see me." 14 Then David sent messengers to Ish-Bosheth son of Saul, demanding, "Give me my wife Michal, whom I betrothed to myself for the price of a hundred Philistine foreskins."

15 So Ish-Bosheth gave orders and had her taken away from her husband Paltiel son of Laish. 16 Her husband, however, went with her, weeping behind her all the way to Bahurim. Then Abner said to him, "Go back home!" So he went back.

17 Abner conferred with the elders of Israel and said, "For some time you have wanted to make David your king. 18 Now do it! For the LORD promised David, 'By my servant David I will rescue my people Israel from the hand of the Philistines and from the hand of all their enemies.' "

19 Abner also spoke to the Benjamites in person. Then he went to Hebron to tell David everything that Israel and the whole house of Benjamin wanted to do. 20 When Abner, who had twenty men with him, came to David at Hebron,

King James

21 And Abner said unto David, I will arise and go, and will gather all Israel unto my lord the king, that they may make a league with thee, and that thou mayest reign over all that thine heart desireth. And David sent Abner away; and he went in peace.

22 ¶ And, behold, the servants of David and Joab came from *pursuing* a troop, and brought in a great spoil with them: but Abner *was* not with David in Hebron; for he had sent him away, and he was gone in peace.

23 When Joab and all the host that *was* with him were come, they told Joab, saying, Abner the son of Ner came to the king, and he hath sent him away, and he is gone in peace.

24 Then Joab came to the king, and said, What hast thou done? behold, Abner came unto thee; why *is* it *that* thou hast sent him away, and he is quite gone?

25 Thou knowest Abner the son of Ner, that he came to deceive thee, and to know thy going out and thy coming in, and to know all that thou doest.

Joab kills Abner

26 And when Joab was come out from David, he sent messengers after Abner, which brought him again from the well of Sirah: but David knew *it* not.

27 And when Abner was returned to Hebron, Joab took him aside in the gate to speak with him [u]quietly, and smote him there under the fifth *rib*, that he died, for the blood of Asahel his brother.

28 ¶ And afterward when David heard *it*, he said, I and my kingdom *are* guiltless before the LORD for ever from the [v]blood of Abner the son of Ner:

29 Let it rest on the head of Joab, and on all his father's house; and let there not [w]fail from the house of Joab one that hath an issue, or that is a leper, or that leaneth on a staff, or that falleth on the sword, or that lacketh bread.

30 So Joab and Abishai his brother slew Abner, because he had slain their brother Asahel at Gibeon in the battle.

31 ¶ And David said to Joab, and to all the people that *were* with him, Rend your clothes, and gird you with sackcloth, and mourn before Abner. And king David *himself* followed the [x]bier.

32 And they buried Abner in Hebron: and the king lifted up his voice, and wept at the grave of Abner; and all the people wept.

33 And the king lamented over Abner, and said, Died Abner as a fool dieth?

34 Thy hands *were* not bound, nor thy feet put into fetters: as a man falleth before [y]wicked men, *so* fellest thou. And all the people wept again over him.

35 And when all the people came to cause David to eat meat while it was yet day, David sware, saying, So do God to me, and more also, if I taste bread, or aught else, till the sun be down.

36 And all the people took notice *of it*, and it [z]pleased them: as whatsoever the king did pleased all the people.

37 For all the people and all Israel understood that day that it was not of the king to slay Abner the son of Ner.

38 And the king said unto his servants, Know ye not that there is a prince and a great man fallen this day in Israel?

39 And I *am* this day [a]weak, though anointed king; and these men the sons of Zeruiah *be* too hard for me: the LORD shall reward the doer of evil according to his wickedness.

[u]Or, *peaceably* [v]Heb. *bloods* [w]Heb. *be cut off* [x]Heb. *bed* [y]Heb. *children of iniquity* [z]Heb. *was good in their eyes* [a]Heb. *tender*

Amplified

21 Abner said to David, I will go and gather all Israel to my lord the king, that they may make a league with you, and that you may reign over all that your heart desires. So David sent Abner away in peace.

22 Then the servants of David came with Joab from pursuing a troop and brought much spoil with them. But Abner was not with David in Hebron, for he had sent him away, and he had gone in peace.

23 When Joab and all the army with him had come, it was told to Joab, Abner son of Ner came to the king, and he has sent him away, and he is gone in peace.

24 Then Joab came to the king and said, What have you done? Behold, Abner came to you. Why is it you have sent him away and he is quite gone?

25 You know that Abner son of Ner came to deceive you and to know your going out and coming in and all you are doing.

26 When Joab came from seeing David, he sent messengers after Abner, and they brought him back from the well of Sirah; but David did not know it.

27 And when Abner returned to Hebron, Joab took him aside to the center of the gate to speak to him privately, and there he smote Abner in the abdomen, so that he died to avenge the blood of Asahel, Joab's brother.

28 When David heard of it, he said, I and my kingdom are guiltless before the Lord forever of the blood of Abner son of Ner.

29 Let it fall on the head of Joab and on all his father's house; and let the house of Joab never be without one who has a discharge or is a leper or walks with a crutch *or* is a distaff holder [unfit for war] or who falls by the sword or lacks food!

30 So Joab and Abishai his brother slew Abner because he had slain their brother Asahel at Gibeon in the battle.

31 And David said to Joab and to all the people with him, Rend your clothes, gird yourselves with sackcloth, and mourn before Abner. And King David followed the bier.

32 They buried Abner in Hebron. And the king lifted up his voice and wept at the grave of Abner, and all the people wept.

33 And the king lamented over Abner and said, Should Abner die as a fool dies?

34 Your hands were not bound or your feet put into fetters; as a man falls before wicked men, so you fell. And all the people wept again over him.

35 All the people came to urge David to eat food while it was yet day; but David took an oath, saying, May God do so to me, and more also, if I taste bread or anything else, till the sun is down.

36 And all the people took notice of it, and it pleased them, as whatever the king did pleased all the people.

37 For all the people and all Israel understood that day that it was not the king's will to slay Abner son of Ner.

38 King David said to his servants, Do you not know that a prince and a great man has fallen this day in Israel?

39 And I am this day weak, though anointed [but not crowned] king; these sons of Zeruiah are too hard for me. May the Lord repay the evildoer according to his wickedness!

New American Standard

21 Abner said to David, "Let me arise and go and gather all Israel to my lord the king, that they may make a covenant with you, and that you may be king over all that your soul desires." So David sent Abner away, and he went in peace.

22 ¶ And behold, the servants of David and Joab came from a raid and brought much spoil with them; but Abner was not with David in Hebron, for he had sent him away, and he had gone in peace.

23 When Joab and all the army that was with him arrived, they told Joab, saying, "Abner the son of Ner came to the king, and he has sent him away, and he has gone in peace."

24 Then Joab came to the king and said, "What have you done? Behold, Abner came to you; why then have you sent him away and he is already gone?

25 "You know Abner the son of Ner, that he came to deceive you and to learn of your going out and coming in and to find out all that you are doing."

Joab Murders Abner

26 ¶ When Joab came out from David, he sent messengers after Abner, and they brought him back from the well of Sirah; but David did not know it.

27 So when Abner returned to Hebron, Joab took him aside into the middle of the gate to speak with him privately, and there he struck him in the belly so that he died on account of the blood of Asahel his brother.

28 Afterward when David heard it, he said, "I and my kingdom are innocent before the LORD forever of the blood of Abner the son of Ner.

29 "May it fall on the head of Joab and on all his father's house; and may there not fail from the house of Joab one who has a discharge, or who is a leper, or who takes hold of a distaff, or who falls by the sword, or who lacks bread."

30 So Joab and Abishai his brother killed Abner because he had put their brother Asahel to death in the battle at Gibeon.

David Mourns Abner

31 ¶ Then David said to Joab and to all the people who were with him, "Tear your clothes and gird on sackcloth and lament before Abner." And King David walked behind the bier.

32 Thus they buried Abner in Hebron; and the king lifted up his voice and wept at the grave of Abner, and all the people wept.

33 The king chanted a *lament* for Abner and said,
"Should Abner die as a fool dies?

34 "Your hands were not bound, nor your feet put in fetters;
As one falls before the wicked, you have fallen."
And all the people wept again over him.

35 Then all the people came to persuade David to eat bread while it was still day; but David vowed, saying, "May God do so to me, and more also, if I taste bread or anything else before the sun goes down."

36 Now all the people took note *of it,* and it pleased them, just as everything the king did pleased all the people.

37 So all the people and all Israel understood that day that it had not been *the will* of the king to put Abner the son of Ner to death.

38 Then the king said to his servants, "Do you not know that a prince and a great man has fallen this day in Israel?

39 "I am weak today, though anointed king; and these men the sons of Zeruiah are too difficult for me. May the LORD repay the evildoer according to his evil."

New International

David prepared a feast for him and his men. 21 Then Abner said to David, "Let me go at once and assemble all Israel for my lord the king, so that they may make a compact with you, and that you may rule over all that your heart desires." So David sent Abner away, and he went in peace.

Joab Murders Abner

22 Just then David's men and Joab returned from a raid and brought with them a great deal of plunder. But Abner was no longer with David in Hebron, because David had sent him away, and he had gone in peace. 23 When Joab and all the soldiers with him arrived, he was told that Abner son of Ner had come to the king and that the king had sent him away and that he had gone in peace.

24 So Joab went to the king and said, "What have you done? Look, Abner came to you. Why did you let him go? Now he is gone! 25 You know Abner son of Ner; he came to deceive you and observe your movements and find out everything you are doing."

26 Joab then left David and sent messengers after Abner, and they brought him back from the well of Sirah. But David did not know it. 27 Now when Abner returned to Hebron, Joab took him aside into the gateway, as though to speak with him privately. And there, to avenge the blood of his brother Asahel, Joab stabbed him in the stomach, and he died.

28 Later, when David heard about this, he said, "I and my kingdom are forever innocent before the LORD concerning the blood of Abner son of Ner. 29 May his blood fall upon the head of Joab and upon all his father's house! May Joab's house never be without someone who has a running sore or leprosy[e] or who leans on a crutch or who falls by the sword or who lacks food."

30 (Joab and his brother Abishai murdered Abner because he had killed their brother Asahel in the battle at Gibeon.)

31 Then David said to Joab and all the people with him, "Tear your clothes and put on sackcloth and walk in mourning in front of Abner." King David himself walked behind the bier. 32 They buried Abner in Hebron, and the king wept aloud at Abner's tomb. All the people wept also.

33 The king sang this lament for Abner:

"Should Abner have died as the lawless die?
34   Your hands were not bound,
       your feet were not fettered.
   You fell as one falls before wicked men."

And all the people wept over him again.

35 Then they all came and urged David to eat something while it was still day; but David took an oath, saying, "May God deal with me, be it ever so severely, if I taste bread or anything else before the sun sets!"

36 All the people took note and were pleased; indeed, everything the king did pleased them. 37 So on that day all the people and all Israel knew that the king had no part in the murder of Abner son of Ner.

38 Then the king said to his men, "Do you not realize that a prince and a great man has fallen in Israel this day? 39 And today, though I am the anointed king, I am weak, and these sons of Zeruiah are too strong for me. May the LORD repay the evildoer according to his evil deeds!"

---

[e] 29 The Hebrew word was used for various diseases affecting the skin—not necessarily leprosy.

King James

The murder of Ish-bosheth

4 AND WHEN Saul's son heard that Abner was dead in Hebron, his hands were feeble, and all the Israelites were troubled.

²And Saul's son had two men *that were* captains of bands: the name of the one *was* Baanah, and the name of the *b*other Rechab, the sons of Rimmon a Beerothite, of the children of Benjamin: (for Beeroth also was reckoned to Benjamin:

³And the Beerothites fled to Gittaim, and were sojourners there until this day.)

⁴And Jonathan, Saul's son, had a son *that was* lame of *his* feet. He was five years old when the tidings came of Saul and Jonathan out of Jezreel, and his nurse took him up, and fled: and it came to pass, as she made haste to flee, that he fell, and became lame. And his name *was* *c*Mephibosheth.

⁵And the sons of Rimmon the Beerothite, Rechab and Baanah, went, and came about the heat of the day to the house of Ish-bosheth, who lay on a bed at noon.

⁶And they came thither into the midst of the house, *as though* they would have fetched wheat; and they smote him under the fifth *rib:* and Rechab and Baanah his brother escaped.

⁷For when they came into the house, he lay on his bed in his bedchamber, and they smote him, and slew him, and beheaded him, and took his head, and gat them away through the plain all night.

⁸And they brought the head of Ish-bosheth unto David to Hebron, and said to the king, Behold the head of Ish-bosheth the son of Saul thine enemy, which sought thy life; and the LORD hath avenged my lord the king this day of Saul, and of his seed.

⁹ ¶ And David answered Rechab and Baanah his brother, the sons of Rimmon the Beerothite, and said unto them, As the LORD liveth, who hath redeemed my soul out of all adversity,

¹⁰When one told me, saying, Behold, Saul is dead, *d*thinking to have brought good tidings, I took hold of him, and slew him in Ziklag, *e*who *thought* that I would have given him a reward for his tidings:

¹¹How much more, when wicked men have slain a righteous person in his own house upon his bed? shall I not therefore now require his blood of your hand, and take you away from the earth?

¹²And David commanded his young men, and they slew them, and cut off their hands and their feet, and hanged *them* up over the pool in Hebron. But they took the head of Ish-bosheth, and buried *it* in the sepulchre of Abner in Hebron.

David made king of Israel

5 THEN CAME all the tribes of Israel to David unto Hebron, and spake, saying, Behold, we *are* thy bone and thy flesh.

²Also in time past, when Saul was king over us, thou wast he that leddest out and broughtest in Israel: and the LORD said to thee, Thou shalt feed my people Israel, and thou shalt be a captain over Israel.

³So all the elders of Israel came to the king to Hebron; and king David made a league with them in Hebron before the LORD: and they anointed David king over Israel.

⁴ ¶ David *was* thirty years old when he began to reign, *and* he reigned forty years.

⁵In Hebron he reigned over Judah seven years and six months: and in Jerusalem he reigned thirty and three years over all Israel and Judah.

Amplified

4 WHEN ISH-BOSHETH, Saul's son [king over Israel], heard that Abner was dead in Hebron, his courage failed, and all the Israelites were troubled *and* dismayed.

²Saul's son had two men who were captains of raiding bands. One was named Baanah and the other Rechab, sons of Rimmon the Beerothite of Benjamin—for Beeroth also was reckoned to Benjamin,

³And the Beerothites fled to Gittaim and have been sojourners there to this day.

⁴Jonathan, Saul's son, had a son who was a cripple in his feet. He was five years old when the news came out of Jezreel [of the deaths] of Saul and Jonathan. And the boy's nurse took him up and fled; and in her haste, he fell and became lame. His name was Mephibosheth.

⁵Now the sons of Rimmon the Beerothite, Rechab and Baanah, went about in the heat of the day to the house of Ish-bosheth, who lay resting on his bed at noon.

⁶And they came into the interior of the house as though they were delivering wheat, and they smote him in the body; and Rechab and Baanah his brother escaped.

⁷Now when they had come into the house and he lay on his bed in his bedroom, they [not only] smote and slew him, [but] beheaded him and took his head and went by the way of the plain all night.

⁸And they brought the head of Ish-bosheth to David at Hebron and said to the king, Behold, the head of Ish-bosheth son of Saul, your enemy, who sought your life; and the Lord has avenged my lord the king this day on Saul and on his offspring.

⁹And David answered Rechab and Baanah his brother, sons of Rimmon the Beerothite, As the Lord lives, Who redeemed my life out of all adversity,

¹⁰When one told me, Behold, Saul is dead, thinking he was bringing good news, I seized and slew him in Ziklag who expected me to give him a reward for his news.

¹¹How much more—when wicked men have slain a just man in his own house on his bed—shall I not now require his blood of your hand and remove you from the earth!

¹²David commanded his young men, and they slew them and cut off their hands and feet and hanged them over the pool in Hebron. But they took Ish-bosheth's head and buried it in Hebron in the tomb of Abner [his relative and once chief supporter].

5 THEN ALL the tribes of Israel came to David at Hebron and said, Behold, we are your bone and your flesh.

²In times past, when Saul was king over us, it was you who led out and brought in Israel. And the Lord told you, You shall feed My people Israel and be prince over [them]. [I Sam. 15:27–29; 16:1.]

³So all the elders of Israel came to the king at Hebron, and King David made a covenant with them [there] before the Lord, and they anointed [him] king over Israel.

⁴David was thirty years old when he began his forty-year reign.

⁵In Hebron he reigned over Judah seven years and six months, and in Jerusalem he reigned thirty-three years over all Israel and Judah.

*b*Heb. *second*   *c*Or, *Merib-baal;* see 1 Chr. 8:34 & 9:40
*d*Heb. *he was in his own eyes as a bringer*   *e*Or, *which* was *the reward I gave him for his tidings*

New American Standard

Ish-bosheth Murdered

4 NOW WHEN Ish-bosheth, Saul's son, heard that Abner had died in Hebron, he lost courage, and all Israel was disturbed.

2 Saul's son *had* two men who were commanders of bands: the name of the one was Baanah and the name of the other Rechab, sons of Rimmon the Beerothite, of the sons of Benjamin (for Beeroth is also considered *part* of Benjamin,

3 and the Beerothites fled to Gittaim and have been aliens there until this day).

4 ¶ Now Jonathan, Saul's son, had a son crippled in his feet. He was five years old when the report of Saul and Jonathan came from Jezreel, and his nurse took him up and fled. And it happened that in her hurry to flee, he fell and became lame. And his name was Mephibosheth.

5 ¶ So the sons of Rimmon the Beerothite, Rechab and Baanah, departed and came to the house of Ish-bosheth in the heat of the day while he was taking his midday rest.

6 They came to the middle of the house as if to get wheat, and they struck him in the belly; and Rechab and Baanah his brother escaped.

7 Now when they came into the house, as he was lying on his bed in his bedroom, they struck him and killed him and beheaded him. And they took his head and traveled by way of the Arabah all night.

8 Then they brought the head of Ish-bosheth to David at Hebron and said to the king, "Behold, the head of Ish-bosheth the son of Saul, your enemy, who sought your life; thus the LORD has given my lord the king vengeance this day on Saul and his descendants."

9 ¶ David answered Rechab and Baanah his brother, sons of Rimmon the Beerothite, and said to them, "As the LORD lives, who has redeemed my life from all distress,

10 when one told me, saying, 'Behold, Saul is dead,' and thought he was bringing good news, I seized him and killed him in Ziklag, which was the reward I gave him for *his* news.

11 "How much more, when wicked men have killed a righteous man in his own house on his bed, shall I not now require his blood from your hand and destroy you from the earth?"

12 Then David commanded the young men, and they killed them and cut off their hands and feet and hung them up beside the pool in Hebron. But they took the head of Ish-bosheth and buried it in the grave of Abner in Hebron.

David King over All Israel

5 THEN ALL the tribes of Israel came to David at Hebron and said, "Behold, we are your bone and your flesh.

2 "Previously, when Saul was king over us, you were the one who led Israel out and in. And the LORD said to you, 'You will shepherd My people Israel, and you will be a ruler over Israel.' "

3 So all the elders of Israel came to the king at Hebron, and King David made a covenant with them before the LORD at Hebron; then they anointed David king over Israel.

4 David was thirty years old when he became king, *and* he reigned forty years.

5 At Hebron he reigned over Judah seven years and six months, and in Jerusalem he reigned thirty-three years over all Israel and Judah.

New International

Ish-Bosheth Murdered

4 WHEN ISH-BOSHETH son of Saul heard that Abner had died in Hebron, he lost courage, and all Israel became alarmed. 2Now Saul's son had two men who were leaders of raiding bands. One was named Baanah and the other Recab; they were sons of Rimmon the Beerothite from the tribe of Benjamin—Beeroth is considered part of Benjamin, 3because the people of Beeroth fled to Gittaim and have lived there as aliens to this day.

4(Jonathan son of Saul had a son who was lame in both feet. He was five years old when the news about Saul and Jonathan came from Jezreel. His nurse picked him up and fled, but as she hurried to leave, he fell and became crippled. His name was Mephibosheth.)

5Now Recab and Baanah, the sons of Rimmon the Beerothite, set out for the house of Ish-Bosheth, and they arrived there in the heat of the day while he was taking his noonday rest. 6They went into the inner part of the house as if to get some wheat, and they stabbed him in the stomach. Then Recab and his brother Baanah slipped away.

7They had gone into the house while he was lying on the bed in his bedroom. After they stabbed and killed him, they cut off his head. Taking it with them, they traveled all night by way of the Arabah. 8They brought the head of Ish-Bosheth to David at Hebron and said to the king, "Here is the head of Ish-Bosheth son of Saul, your enemy, who tried to take your life. This day the LORD has avenged my lord the king against Saul and his offspring."

9David answered Recab and his brother Baanah, the sons of Rimmon the Beerothite, "As surely as the LORD lives, who has delivered me out of all trouble, 10when a man told me, 'Saul is dead,' and thought he was bringing good news, I seized him and put him to death in Ziklag. That was the reward I gave him for his news! 11How much more—when wicked men have killed an innocent man in his own house and on his own bed—should I not now demand his blood from your hand and rid the earth of you!"

12So David gave an order to his men, and they killed them. They cut off their hands and feet and hung the bodies by the pool in Hebron. But they took the head of Ish-Bosheth and buried it in Abner's tomb at Hebron.

David Becomes King Over Israel

5 ALL THE tribes of Israel came to David at Hebron and said, "We are your own flesh and blood. 2In the past, while Saul was king over us, you were the one who led Israel on their military campaigns. And the LORD said to you, 'You will shepherd my people Israel, and you will become their ruler.' "

3When all the elders of Israel had come to King David at Hebron, the king made a compact with them at Hebron before the LORD, and they anointed David king over Israel.

4David was thirty years old when he became king, and he reigned forty years. 5In Hebron he reigned over Judah seven years and six months, and in Jerusalem he reigned over all Israel and Judah thirty-three years.

King James

The capture of Jerusalem

6 ¶ And the king and his men went to Jerusalem unto the Jebusites, the inhabitants of the land: which spake unto David, saying, Except thou take away the blind and the lame, thou shalt not come in hither: [f]thinking, David cannot come in hither.

7 Nevertheless David took the strong hold of Zion: the same *is* the city of David.

8 And David said on that day, Whosoever getteth up to the gutter, and smiteth the Jebusites, and the lame and the blind, *that are* hated of David's soul, *he shall be chief and captain.* [g]Wherefore they said, The blind and the lame shall not come into the house.

9 So David dwelt in the fort, and called it the city of David. And David built round about from Millo and inward.

10 And David [h]went on, and grew great, and the Lord God of hosts *was* with him.

11 ¶ And Hiram king of Tyre sent messengers to David, and cedar trees, and carpenters, and [i]masons: and they built David an house.

12 And David perceived that the Lord had established him king over Israel, and that he had exalted his kingdom for his people Israel's sake.

13 ¶ And David took *him* more concubines and wives out of Jerusalem, after he was come from Hebron: and there were yet sons and daughters born to David.

14 And these *be* the names of those that were born unto him in Jerusalem; [j]Shammuah, and Shobab, and Nathan, and Solomon,

15 Ibhar also, and [k]Elishua, and Nepheg, and Japhia,

16 And Elishama, and [l]Eliada, and Eliphalet.

The Philistines defeated

17 ¶ But when the Philistines heard that they had anointed David king over Israel, all the Philistines came up to seek David; and David heard *of it,* and went down to the hold.

18 The Philistines also came and spread themselves in the valley of Rephaim.

19 And David inquired of the Lord, saying, Shall I go up to the Philistines? wilt thou deliver them into mine hand? And the Lord said unto David, Go up: for I will doubtless deliver the Philistines into thine hand.

20 And David came to Baal-perazim, and David smote them there, and said, The Lord hath broken forth upon mine enemies before me, as the breach of waters. Therefore he called the name of that place [m]Baal-perazim.

21 And there they left their images, and David and his men [n]burned them.

22 ¶ And the Philistines came up yet again, and spread themselves in the valley of Rephaim.

23 And when David inquired of the Lord, he said, Thou shalt not go up; *but* fetch a compass behind them, and come upon them over against the mulberry trees.

24 And let it be, when thou hearest the sound of a going in the tops of the mulberry trees, that then thou shalt bestir thyself: for then shall the Lord go out before thee, to smite the host of the Philistines.

25 And David did so, as the Lord had commanded him; and smote the Philistines from Geba until thou come to Gazer.

Bringing the ark to Jerusalem

6 AGAIN, DAVID gathered together all *the* chosen *men* of Israel, thirty thousand.

2 And David arose, and went with all the people that

Amplified

6 And the king and his men went to Jerusalem against the Jebusites, the inhabitants of the land, who said to David, You shall not enter here, for the blind and the lame will prevent you; they thought, David cannot come in here.

7 Nevertheless, David took the stronghold of Zion, that is, the City of David.

8 David said on that day, Whoever smites the Jebusites, let him get up through the water shaft and smite the lame and the blind who are detested by David's soul. So they say, The blind and the lame shall not come into the house.

9 So David dwelt in the stronghold and called it the City of David. And he built round about from the Millo and inward.

10 David became greater and greater, for the Lord God of hosts was with him.

11 Hiram king of Tyre sent messengers to David, and cedar trees, carpenters, and masons; and they built David a house.

12 And David perceived that the Lord had established him king over Israel and that He had exalted his kingdom for His people Israel's sake.

13 And David took more concubines and wives out of Jerusalem, after he came from Hebron, and other sons and daughters were born to [him].

14 And these are the names of those who were born to him in Jerusalem: Shammua, Shobab, Nathan, Solomon,

15 Ibhar, Elishua, Nepheg, Japhia,

16 Elishama, Eliada, and Eliphelet.

17 When the Philistines heard that David had been anointed king over Israel, they all went up to find [him], but [he] heard of it and went down to the stronghold.

18 The Philistines also came and spread themselves in the Valley of Rephaim.

19 David inquired of the Lord, saying, Shall I go up against the Philistines? Will You deliver them into my hand? And the Lord said to David, Go up, for I will surely deliver [them] into your hand.

20 And David came to Baal-perazim, and he smote them there, and said, The Lord has broken through my enemies before me, like the bursting out of great waters. So he called the name of that place Baal-perazim [Lord of breaking through].

21 There the Philistines left their [a]images, and David and his men took them away.

22 The Philistines came up again and spread themselves out in the Valley of Rephaim.

23 When David inquired of the Lord, He said, You shall not go up, but go around behind them and come upon them over opposite the mulberry (or balsam) trees.

24 And when you hear the sound of marching in the tops of the mulberry trees, then bestir yourselves, for then has the Lord gone out before you to smite the army of the Philistines.

25 And David did as the Lord had commanded him, and smote the Philistines from Geba to Gezer.

6 AGAIN DAVID gathered together all the chosen men of Israel, 30,000.

2 And [he] arose and went with all the people who were

---

[f]Or, *saying, David shall not the blind and the lame, He shall not come into the house*   [g]Or, *Because they had said, even went going and growing*   [h]Heb. [i]Heb. *hewers of the stone of the wall* [j]Or, *Shimea;* see 1 Chr. 3:5   [k]Or, *Elishama;* see 1 Chr. 3:6 [l]Or, *Beeliada;* see 1 Chr. 14:7   [m]i.e. *The plain of breaches* [n]Or, *took them away*

[a]The Israelites took as spoil the images of the Philistines, perhaps to display in triumphal procession, though they were afterward burned (I Chron. 14:12) in compliance with the law of Deut. 7:5, 25. Thus the old disgrace of the capture of the ark by the Philistines was avenged (I Sam. 4:4, 10, 11) (*The Cambridge Bible*).

New American Standard

6 ¶ Now the king and his men went to Jerusalem against the Jebusites, the inhabitants of the land, and they said to David, "You shall not come in here, but the blind and lame will turn you away"; thinking, "David cannot enter here."

7 Nevertheless, David captured the stronghold of Zion, that is the city of David.

8 David said on that day, "Whoever would strike the Jebusites, let him reach the lame and the blind, who are hated by David's soul, through the water tunnel." Therefore they say, "The blind or the lame shall not come into the house."

9 So David lived in the stronghold and called it the city of David. And David built all around from the [d]Millo and inward.

10 David became greater and greater, for the LORD God of hosts was with him.

11 ¶ Then Hiram king of Tyre sent messengers to David with cedar trees and carpenters and stonemasons; and they built a house for David.

12 And David realized that the LORD had established him as king over Israel, and that He had exalted his kingdom for the sake of His people Israel.

13 ¶ Meanwhile David took more concubines and wives from Jerusalem, after he came from Hebron; and more sons and daughters were born to David.

14 Now these are the names of those who were born to him in Jerusalem: Shammua, Shobab, Nathan, Solomon,

15 Ibhar, Elishua, Nepheg, Japhia,

16 Elishama, Eliada and Eliphelet.

War with the Philistines

17 ¶ When the Philistines heard that they had anointed David king over Israel, all the Philistines went up to seek out David; and when David heard *of it*, he went down to the stronghold.

18 Now the Philistines came and spread themselves out in the valley of Rephaim.

19 Then David inquired of the LORD, saying, "Shall I go up against the Philistines? Will You give them into my hand?" And the LORD said to David, "Go up, for I will certainly give the Philistines into your hand."

20 So David came to Baal-perazim and defeated them there; and he said, "The LORD has broken through my enemies before me like the breakthrough of waters." Therefore he named that place [e]Baal-perazim.

21 They abandoned their idols there, so David and his men carried them away.

22 ¶ Now the Philistines came up once again and spread themselves out in the valley of Rephaim.

23 When David inquired of the LORD, He said, "You shall not go *directly* up; circle around behind them and come at them in front of the [f]balsam trees.

24 "It shall be, when you hear the sound of marching in the tops of the [f]balsam trees, then you shall act promptly, for then the LORD will have gone out before you to strike the army of the Philistines."

25 Then David did so, just as the LORD had commanded him, and struck down the Philistines from Geba as far as Gezer.

Peril in Moving the Ark

6 NOW DAVID again gathered all the chosen men of Israel, thirty thousand.

2 And David arose and went with all the people who

New International

David Conquers Jerusalem

6 The king and his men marched to Jerusalem to attack the Jebusites, who lived there. The Jebusites said to David, "You will not get in here; even the blind and the lame can ward you off." They thought, "David cannot get in here." 7 Nevertheless, David captured the fortress of Zion, the City of David.

8 On that day, David said, "Anyone who conquers the Jebusites will have to use the water shaft[f] to reach those 'lame and blind' who are David's enemies.[g]" That is why they say, "The 'blind and lame' will not enter the palace."

9 David then took up residence in the fortress and called it the City of David. He built up the area around it, from the supporting terraces[h] inward. 10 And he became more and more powerful, because the LORD God Almighty was with him.

11 Now Hiram king of Tyre sent messengers to David, along with cedar logs and carpenters and stonemasons, and they built a palace for David. 12 And David knew that the LORD had established him as king over Israel and had exalted his kingdom for the sake of his people Israel.

13 After he left Hebron, David took more concubines and wives in Jerusalem, and more sons and daughters were born to him. 14 These are the names of the children born to him there: Shammua, Shobab, Nathan, Solomon, 15 Ibhar, Elishua, Nepheg, Japhia, 16 Elishama, Eliada and Eliphelet.

David Defeats the Philistines

17 When the Philistines heard that David had been anointed king over Israel, they went up in full force to search for him, but David heard about it and went down to the stronghold. 18 Now the Philistines had come and spread out in the Valley of Rephaim; 19 so David inquired of the LORD, "Shall I go and attack the Philistines? Will you hand them over to me?"

The LORD answered him, "Go, for I will surely hand the Philistines over to you."

20 So David went to Baal Perazim, and there he defeated them. He said, "As waters break out, the LORD has broken out against my enemies before me." So that place was called Baal Perazim.[i] 21 The Philistines abandoned their idols there, and David and his men carried them off.

22 Once more the Philistines came up and spread out in the Valley of Rephaim; 23 so David inquired of the LORD, and he answered, "Do not go straight up, but circle around behind them and attack them in front of the balsam trees. 24 As soon as you hear the sound of marching in the tops of the balsam trees, move quickly, because that will mean the LORD has gone out in front of you to strike the Philistine army." 25 So David did as the LORD commanded him, and he struck down the Philistines all the way from Gibeon[j] to Gezer.

The Ark Brought to Jerusalem

6 DAVID AGAIN brought together out of Israel chosen men, thirty thousand in all. 2 He and all his men set out from Baalah of Judah[k] to bring up from there the ark of

---

[d] I.e. citadel   [e] I.e. the master of breakthrough   [f] Or baka-shrubs

[f] 8 Or *use scaling hooks*   [g] 8 Or *are hated by David*   [h] 9 Or *the Millo*   [i] 20 *Baal Perazim* means *the lord who breaks out.*   [j] 25 Septuagint (see also 1 Chron. 14:16); Hebrew *Geba*   [k] 2 That is, Kiriath Jearim; Hebrew *Baale Judah*, a variant of *Baalah of Judah*

King James

were with him from [o]Baale of Judah, to bring up from thence the ark of God, [p]whose name is called by the name of the LORD of hosts that dwelleth *between* the cherubims.

3 And they [q]set the ark of God upon a new cart, and brought it out of the house of Abinadab that *was* in [r]Gibeah: and Uzzah and Ahio, the sons of Abinadab, drave the new cart.

4 And they brought it out of the house of Abinadab which *was* at Gibeah, [s]accompanying the ark of God: and Ahio went before the ark.

5 And David and all the house of Israel played before the LORD on all manner of *instruments made of* fir wood, even on harps, and on psalteries, and on timbrels, and on cornets, and on cymbals.

6 ¶ And when they came to Nachon's threshingfloor, Uzzah put forth *his hand* to the ark of God, and took hold of it; for the oxen [t]shook *it.*

7 And the anger of the LORD was kindled against Uzzah; and God smote him there for *his* [u]error; and there he died by the ark of God.

8 And David was displeased, because the LORD had [v]made a breach upon Uzzah: and he called the name of the place [w]Perez-uzzah to this day.

9 And David was afraid of the LORD that day, and said, How shall the ark of the LORD come to me?

10 So David would not remove the ark of the LORD unto him into the city of David: but David carried it aside into the house of Obed-edom the Gittite.

11 And the ark of the LORD continued in the house of Obed-edom the Gittite three months: and the LORD blessed Obed-edom, and all his household.

12 ¶ And it was told king David, saying, The LORD hath blessed the house of Obed-edom, and all that *pertaineth* unto him, because of the ark of God. So David went and brought up the ark of God from the house of Obed-edom into the city of David with gladness.

13 And it was *so,* that when they that bare the ark of the LORD had gone six paces, he sacrificed oxen and fatlings.

14 And David danced before the LORD with all *his* might; and David *was* girded with a linen ephod.

15 So David and all the house of Israel brought up the ark of the LORD with shouting, and with the sound of the trumpet.

16 And as the ark of the LORD came into the city of David, Michal Saul's daughter looked through a window, and saw king David leaping and dancing before the LORD; and she despised him in her heart.

17 ¶ And they brought in the ark of the LORD, and set it in his place, in the midst of the tabernacle that David had [x]pitched for it: and David offered burnt offerings and peace offerings before the LORD.

18 And as soon as David had made an end of offering burnt offerings and peace offerings, he blessed the people in the name of the LORD of hosts.

19 And he dealt among all the people, *even* among the whole multitude of Israel, as well to the women as men, to every one a cake of bread, and a good piece *of flesh,* and a flagon *of wine.* So all the people departed every one to his house.

20 ¶ Then David returned to bless his household. And Michal the daughter of Saul came out to meet David, and said, How glorious was the king of Israel today, who uncovered himself today in the eyes of the handmaids of his servants, as one of the vain fellows [y]shamelessly uncovereth himself!

[o] Or, *Baalah* i.e. *Kirjath-jearim;* see Josh. 15:9 [p] Or, *at which the name,* even *the name of the LORD of hosts, was called upon* [q] Heb. *made to ride* [r] Or, *The hill* [s] Heb. *with* [t] Or, *stumbled* [u] Or, *rashness* [v] Heb. *broken* [w] i.e. *The breach of Uzzah* [x] Heb. *stretched* [y] Or, *openly*

Amplified

with him to Baale-judah [Kiriath-jearim] to bring up from there the ark of God, which is called by the name of the Lord of hosts, Who sits enthroned above the cherubim.

3 And they set the ark of God upon a new cart and brought it [b]out of the house of Abinadab, which was on the hill; and Uzzah and Ahio, sons of Abinadab, drove the new cart.

4 And they brought it out of the house of Abinadab, which was on the hill, with the ark of God; and Ahio went before the ark.

5 And David and all the house of Israel played before the Lord with all their might, with songs, lyres, harps, tambourines, castanets, and cymbals.

6 And when they came to Nacon's threshing floor, Uzzah put out his hand to the ark of God and took hold of it, for the oxen stumbled *and* shook it.

7 And the anger of the Lord was kindled against Uzzah; and God smote him there for touching the ark, and he died there by the ark of God.

8 David was grieved *and* offended because the Lord had broken forth upon Uzzah, and that place is called Perez-uzzah [the breaking forth upon Uzzah] to this day.

9 David was afraid of the Lord that day and said, How can the ark of the Lord come to me?

10 So David was not willing to take the ark of the Lord to him into the City of David; but he took it aside into the house of Obed-edom the Gittite.

11 And the ark of the Lord remained in the house of Obed-edom the Gittite for three months, and the Lord blessed Obed-edom and all his household.

12 And it was told King David, The Lord has blessed the house of Obed-edom and all that belongs to him, because of the ark of God. So David went and brought up the ark of God from the house of Obed-edom into the City of David with rejoicing;

13 And when those who bore the ark of the Lord had gone six paces, he sacrificed an ox and a fatling.

14 And David danced before the Lord with all his might, clad in a linen ephod [a priest's upper garment].

15 So David and all the house of Israel brought up the ark of the Lord with shouting and with the sound of the trumpet.

16 As the ark of the Lord came into the City of David, Michal, Saul's daughter [David's wife], looked out of the window and saw King David leaping and dancing before the Lord, and she despised him in her heart.

17 They brought in the ark of the Lord and set it in its place inside the tent which David had pitched for it, and David offered burnt offerings and peace offerings before the Lord.

18 When David had finished offering the burnt offerings and peace offerings, he blessed the people in the name [and presence] of the Lord of hosts,

19 And distributed among all the people, the whole multitude of Israel, both to men and women, to each a cake of bread, a portion of meat, and a cake of raisins. So all the people departed, each to his house.

20 Then David returned to bless his household. And [his wife] Michal daughter of Saul came out to meet David and said, How glorious was the king of Israel today, who stripped himself of his kingly robes *and* uncovered himself in the eyes of his servants' maids as one of the worthless fellows shamelessly uncovers himself!

[b] How long had the ark been in the house of Abinadab (see I Sam. 7:2)?

New American Standard

were with him to Baale-judah, to bring up from there the ark of God which is called by the Name, the very name of the LORD of hosts who is enthroned *above* the cherubim.

3 They placed the ark of God on a new cart that they might bring it from the house of Abinadab which was on the hill; and Uzzah and Ahio, the sons of Abinadab, were leading the new cart.

4 So they brought it with the ark of God from the house of Abinadab, which was on the hill; and Ahio was walking ahead of the ark.

5 Meanwhile, David and all the house of Israel were celebrating before the LORD with all kinds of *instruments made of* fir wood, and with lyres, harps, tambourines, castanets and cymbals.

6 ¶ But when they came to the threshing floor of Nacon, Uzzah reached out and took hold of it, for the oxen nearly upset *it*.

7 And the anger of the LORD burned against Uzzah, and God struck him down there for his irreverence; and he died there by the ark of God.

8 David became angry because of the LORD'S outburst against Uzzah, and that place is called *g*Perez-uzzah to this day.

9 So David was afraid of the LORD that day; and he said, "How can the ark of the LORD come to me?"

10 And David was unwilling to move the ark of the LORD into the city of David with him; but David took it aside to the house of Obed-edom the Gittite.

11 Thus the ark of the LORD remained in the house of Obed-edom the Gittite three months, and the LORD blessed Obed-edom and all his household.

The Ark Is Brought to Jerusalem

12 ¶ Now it was told King David, saying, "The LORD has blessed the house of Obed-edom and all that belongs to him, on account of the ark of God." David went and brought up the ark of God from the house of Obed-edom into the city of David with gladness.

13 And so it was, that when the bearers of the ark of the LORD had gone six paces, he sacrificed an ox and a fatling.

14 And David was dancing before the LORD with all *his* might, and David was wearing a linen ephod.

15 So David and all the house of Israel were bringing up the ark of the LORD with shouting and the sound of the trumpet.

16 ¶ Then it happened *as* the ark of the LORD came into the city of David that Michal the daughter of Saul looked out of the window and saw King David leaping and dancing before the LORD; and she despised him in her heart.

17 ¶ So they brought in the ark of the LORD and set it in its place inside the tent which David had pitched for it; and David offered burnt offerings and peace offerings before the LORD.

18 When David had finished offering the burnt offering and the peace offering, he blessed the people in the name of the LORD of hosts.

19 Further, he distributed to all the people, to all the multitude of Israel, both to men and women, a cake of bread and one of dates and one of raisins to each one. Then all the people departed each to his house.

20 ¶ But when David returned to bless his household, Michal the daughter of Saul came out to meet David and said, "How the king of Israel distinguished himself today! He uncovered himself today in the eyes of his servants' maids as one of the foolish ones shamelessly uncovers himself!"

New International

God, which is called by the Name,*l* the name of the LORD Almighty, who is enthroned between the cherubim that are on the ark. 3They set the ark of God on a new cart and brought it from the house of Abinadab, which was on the hill. Uzzah and Ahio, sons of Abinadab, were guiding the new cart 4with the ark of God on it,*m* and Ahio was walking in front of it. 5David and the whole house of Israel were celebrating with all their might before the LORD, with songs*n* and with harps, lyres, tambourines, sistrums and cymbals.

6When they came to the threshing floor of Nacon, Uzzah reached out and took hold of the ark of God, because the oxen stumbled. 7The LORD's anger burned against Uzzah because of his irreverent act; therefore God struck him down and he died there beside the ark of God.

8Then David was angry because the LORD's wrath had broken out against Uzzah, and to this day that place is called Perez Uzzah.*o*

9David was afraid of the LORD that day and said, "How can the ark of the LORD ever come to me?" 10He was not willing to take the ark of the LORD to be with him in the City of David. Instead, he took it aside to the house of Obed-Edom the Gittite. 11The ark of the LORD remained in the house of Obed-Edom the Gittite for three months, and the LORD blessed him and his entire household.

12Now King David was told, "The LORD has blessed the household of Obed-Edom and everything he has, because of the ark of God." So David went down and brought up the ark of God from the house of Obed-Edom to the City of David with rejoicing. 13When those who were carrying the ark of the LORD had taken six steps, he sacrificed a bull and a fattened calf. 14David, wearing a linen ephod, danced before the LORD with all his might, 15while he and the entire house of Israel brought up the ark of the LORD with shouts and the sound of trumpets.

16As the ark of the LORD was entering the City of David, Michal daughter of Saul watched from a window. And when she saw King David leaping and dancing before the LORD, she despised him in her heart.

17They brought the ark of the LORD and set it in its place inside the tent that David had pitched for it, and David sacrificed burnt offerings and fellowship offerings*p* before the LORD. 18After he had finished sacrificing the burnt offerings and fellowship offerings, he blessed the people in the name of the LORD Almighty. 19Then he gave a loaf of bread, a cake of dates and a cake of raisins to each person in the whole crowd of Israelites, both men and women. And all the people went to their homes.

20When David returned home to bless his household, Michal daughter of Saul came out to meet him and said, "How the king of Israel has distinguished himself today, disrobing in the sight of the slave girls of his servants as any vulgar fellow would!"

---

l 2 Hebrew; Septuagint and Vulgate do not have *the Name.*
m 3,4 Dead Sea Scrolls and some Septuagint manuscripts; Masoretic Text *cart* *4and they brought it with the ark of God from the house of Abinadab, which was on the hill*   *n 5* See Dead Sea Scrolls, Septuagint and 1 Chronicles 13:8; Masoretic Text *celebrating before the LORD with all kinds of instruments made of pine.*   *o 8* Perez Uzzah means *outbreak against Uzzah.*   *p 17* Traditionally *peace offerings;* also in verse 18

g I.e. the breakthrough of Uzzah

King James

21And David said unto Michal, *It was* before the LORD, which chose me before thy father, and before all his house, to appoint me ruler over the people of the LORD, over Israel: therefore will I play before the LORD.

22And I will yet be more vile than thus, and will be base in mine own sight: and *z*of the maidservants which thou hast spoken of, of them shall I be had in honour.

23Therefore Michal the daughter of Saul had no child unto the day of her death.

Nathan's prophecy

7 AND IT came to pass, when the king sat in his house, and the LORD had given him rest round about from all his enemies;

2That the king said unto Nathan the prophet, See now, I dwell in an house of cedar, but the ark of God dwelleth within curtains.

3And Nathan said to the king, Go, do all that *is* in thine heart; for the LORD *is* with thee.

4 ¶ And it came to pass that night, that the word of the LORD came unto Nathan, saying,

5Go and tell *a*my servant David, Thus saith the LORD, Shalt thou build me an house for me to dwell in?

6Whereas I have not dwelt in *any* house since the time that I brought up the children of Israel out of Egypt, even to this day, but have walked in a tent and in a tabernacle.

7In all *the places* wherein I have walked with all the children of Israel spake I a word with *b*any of the tribes of Israel, whom I commanded to feed my people Israel, saying, Why build ye not me an house of cedar?

8Now therefore so shalt thou say unto my servant David, Thus saith the LORD of hosts, I took thee from the sheepcote, *c*from following the sheep, to be ruler over my people, over Israel:

9And I was with thee whithersoever thou wentest, and have cut off all thine enemies *d*out of thy sight, and have made thee a great name, like unto the name of the great *men* that *are* in the earth.

10Moreover I will appoint a place for my people Israel, and will plant them, that they may dwell in a place of their own, and move no more; neither shall the children of wickedness afflict them any more, as beforetime,

11And as since the time that I commanded judges *to be* over my people Israel, and have caused thee to rest from all thine enemies. Also the LORD telleth thee that he will make thee an house.

12 ¶ And when thy days be fulfilled, and thou shalt sleep with thy fathers, I will set up thy seed after thee, which shall proceed out of thy bowels, and I will establish his kingdom.

13He shall build an house for my name, and I will stablish the throne of his kingdom for ever.

14I will be his father, and he shall be my son. If he commit iniquity, I will chasten him with the rod of men, and with the stripes of the children of men:

15But my mercy shall not depart away from him, as I took *it* from Saul, whom I put away before thee.

16And thine house and thy kingdom shall be established for ever before thee: thy throne shall be established for ever.

17According to all these words, and according to all this vision, so did Nathan speak unto David.

David's prayer

18 ¶ Then went king David in, and sat before the LORD, and he said, Who *am* I, O Lord GOD? and what *is* my house, that thou hast brought me hitherto?

Amplified

21David said to Michal, It was before the Lord, Who chose me above your father and all his house to appoint me as prince over Israel, the people of the Lord. Therefore will I make merry [in pure enjoyment] before the Lord.

22I will be still more lightly esteemed than this, and will humble *and* lower myself in my own sight [and yours]. But by the maids you mentioned, I will be held in honor.

23And Michal the daughter of Saul had no child to the day of her death.

7 WHEN KING David dwelt in his house and the Lord had given him rest from all his surrounding enemies,

2The king said to Nathan the prophet, See now, I dwell in a house of cedar, but the ark of God dwells within curtains.

3And Nathan said to the king, Go, do all that is in your heart, for the Lord is with you.

4That night the word of the Lord came to Nathan, saying,

5Go and tell My servant David, Thus says the Lord: Shall you build Me a house in which to dwell?

6For I have not dwelt in a house since I brought the Israelites out of Egypt to this day, but have moved about with a tent for My dwelling.

7In all the places where I have moved with all the Israelites, did I speak a word to any from the tribes of Israel whom I commanded to be shepherd of My people Israel, asking, Why do you not build Me a house of cedar?

8So now say this to My servant David, Thus says the Lord of hosts: I took you from the pasture, from following the sheep, to be prince over My people Israel.

9And I was with you wherever you went, and have cut off all your enemies from before you; and I will make you a great name, like [that] of the great men of the earth.

10And I will appoint a place for My people Israel and will plant them, that they may dwell in a place of their own and be moved no more. And wicked men shall afflict them no more, as formerly

11And as from the time that I appointed judges over My people Israel; and I will cause you to rest from all your enemies. Also the Lord declares to you that He will make for you a house:

12And when your days are fulfilled and you sleep with your fathers, I will set up after you your offspring who shall be born to you, and I will establish his kingdom.

13He shall build a house for My *c*Name [and My Presence], and I will establish the throne of his kingdom forever.

14I will be his Father, and he shall be My son. When he commits iniquity, I will chasten him with the rod of men and with the stripes of the sons of men.

15But My mercy *and* loving-kindness shall not depart from him, as I took [them] from Saul, whom I took away from before you.

16And your house and your kingdom shall be made sure forever before you; your throne shall be established forever.

17In accordance with all these words and all this vision Nathan spoke to David.

18Then King David went in and sat before the Lord, and said, Who am I, O Lord God, and what is my house, that You have brought me this far?

---

*z*Or, *of the handmaids* of my servants   *a*Heb. *to my servant, to David*   *b*Or, *any of the judges;* see 1 Chr. 17:6   *c*Heb. *from after*   *d*Heb. *from thy face*

c"Name" is equivalent to "Me" in II Sam. 7:5. See also footnote on Deut. 12:5.

New American Standard

21 So David said to Michal, "*It was* before the LORD, who chose me above your father and above all his house, to appoint me ruler over the people of the LORD, over Israel; therefore I will celebrate before the LORD.

22"I will be more lightly esteemed than this and will be humble in my own eyes, but with the maids of whom you have spoken, with them I will be distinguished."

23 Michal the daughter of Saul had no child to the day of her death.

David Plans to Build a Temple

7 NOW IT came about when the king lived in his house, and the LORD had given him rest on every side from all his enemies,

2 that the king said to Nathan the prophet, "See now, I dwell in a house of cedar, but the ark of God dwells within tent curtains."

3 Nathan said to the king, "Go, do all that is in your mind, for the LORD is with you."

4 ¶ But in the same night the word of the LORD came to Nathan, saying,

5"Go and say to My servant David, 'Thus says the LORD, "Are you the one who should build Me a house to dwell in?

6"For I have not dwelt in a house since the day I brought up the sons of Israel from Egypt, even to this day; but I have been moving about in a tent, even in a tabernacle.

7"Wherever I have gone with all the sons of Israel, did I speak a word with one of the tribes of Israel, which I commanded to shepherd My people Israel, saying, 'Why have you not built Me a house of cedar?' " '

God's Covenant with David

8"Now therefore, thus you shall say to My servant David, 'Thus says the LORD of hosts, "I took you from the pasture, from following the sheep, to be ruler over My people Israel.

9"I have been with you wherever you have gone and have cut off all your enemies from before you; and I will make you a great name, like the names of the great men who are on the earth.

10"I will also appoint a place for My people Israel and will plant them, that they may live in their own place and not be disturbed again, nor will the wicked afflict them any more as formerly,

11 even from the day that I commanded judges to be over My people Israel; and I will give you rest from all your enemies. The LORD also declares to you that the LORD will make a house for you.

12"When your days are complete and you lie down with your fathers, I will raise up your descendant after you, who will come forth from you, and I will establish his kingdom.

13"He shall build a house for My name, and I will establish the throne of his kingdom forever.

14"I will be a father to him and he will be a son to Me; when he commits iniquity, I will correct him with the rod of men and the strokes of the sons of men,

15 but My lovingkindness shall not depart from him, as I took *it* away from Saul, whom I removed from before you.

16"Your house and your kingdom shall endure before Me forever; your throne shall be established forever." ' "

17 In accordance with all these words and all this vision, so Nathan spoke to David.

David's Prayer

18 ¶ Then David the king went in and sat before the LORD, and he said, "Who am I, O Lord GOD, and what is my house, that You have brought me this far?

New International

21David said to Michal, "It was before the LORD, who chose me rather than your father or anyone from his house when he appointed me ruler over the LORD's people Israel—I will celebrate before the LORD. 22I will become even more undignified than this, and I will be humiliated in my own eyes. But by these slave girls you spoke of, I will be held in honor."

23And Michal daughter of Saul had no children to the day of her death.

God's Promise to David

7 AFTER THE king was settled in his palace and the LORD had given him rest from all his enemies around him, 2he said to Nathan the prophet, "Here I am, living in a palace of cedar, while the ark of God remains in a tent."

3Nathan replied to the king, "Whatever you have in mind, go ahead and do it, for the LORD is with you."

4That night the word of the LORD came to Nathan, saying:

5"Go and tell my servant David, 'This is what the LORD says: Are you the one to build me a house to dwell in? 6I have not dwelt in a house from the day I brought the Israelites up out of Egypt to this day. I have been moving from place to place with a tent as my dwelling. 7Wherever I have moved with all the Israelites, did I ever say to any of their rulers whom I commanded to shepherd my people Israel, "Why have you not built me a house of cedar?" '

8"Now then, tell my servant David, 'This is what the LORD Almighty says: I took you from the pasture and from following the flock to be ruler over my people Israel. 9I have been with you wherever you have gone, and I have cut off all your enemies from before you. Now I will make your name great, like the names of the greatest men of the earth. 10And I will provide a place for my people Israel and will plant them so that they can have a home of their own and no longer be disturbed. Wicked people will not oppress them anymore, as they did at the beginning 11and have done ever since the time I appointed leaders*q* over my people Israel. I will also give you rest from all your enemies.

" 'The LORD declares to you that the LORD himself will establish a house for you: 12When your days are over and you rest with your fathers, I will raise up your offspring to succeed you, who will come from your own body, and I will establish his kingdom. 13He is the one who will build a house for my Name, and I will establish the throne of his kingdom forever. 14I will be his father, and he will be my son. When he does wrong, I will punish him with the rod of men, with floggings inflicted by men. 15But my love will never be taken away from him, as I took it away from Saul, whom I removed from before you. 16Your house and your kingdom will endure forever before me*r*; your throne will be established forever.' "

17Nathan reported to David all the words of this entire revelation.

David's Prayer

18Then King David went in and sat before the LORD, and he said:

"Who am I, O Sovereign LORD, and what is my

---

q 11 Traditionally *judges*   *r 16* Some Hebrew manuscripts and Septuagint; most Hebrew manuscripts *you*

King James

¹⁹And this was yet a small thing in thy sight, O Lord God; but thou hast spoken also of thy servant's house for a great while to come. And *is* this the *e*manner of man, O Lord God?

²⁰And what can David say more unto thee? for thou, Lord God, knowest thy servant.

²¹For thy word's sake, and according to thine own heart, hast thou done all these great things, to make thy servant know *them*.

²²Wherefore thou art great, O Lord God: for *there is* none like thee, neither *is there any* God beside thee, according to all that we have heard with our ears.

²³And what one nation in the earth *is* like thy people, *even* like Israel, whom God went to redeem for a people to himself, and to make him a name, and to do for you great things and terrible, for thy land, before thy people, which thou redeemedst to thee from Egypt, *from* the nations and their gods?

²⁴For thou hast confirmed to thyself thy people Israel *to be* a people unto thee for ever: and thou, Lord, art become their God.

²⁵And now, O Lord God, the word that thou hast spoken concerning thy servant, and concerning his house, establish *it* for ever, and do as thou hast said.

²⁶And let thy name be magnified for ever, saying, The Lord of hosts *is* the God over Israel: and let the house of thy servant David be established before thee.

²⁷For thou, O Lord of hosts, God of Israel, hast revealed to thy servant, saying, I will build thee an house: therefore hath thy servant found in his heart to pray this prayer unto thee.

²⁸And now, O Lord God, thou *art* that God, and thy words be true, and thou hast promised this goodness unto thy servant:

²⁹Therefore now *f*let it please thee to bless the house of thy servant, that it may continue for ever before thee: for thou, O Lord God, hast spoken *it*: and with thy blessing let the house of thy servant be blessed for ever.

David's military victories

8 AND AFTER this it came to pass, that David smote the Philistines, and subdued them: and David took *g*Metheg-ammah out of the hand of the Philistines.

²And he smote Moab, and measured them with a line, casting them down to the ground; even with two lines measured he to put to death, and with one full line to keep alive. And *so* the Moabites became David's servants, *and* brought gifts.

³ ¶ David smote also *h*Hadadezer, the son of Rehob, king of Zobah, as he went to recover his border at the river Euphrates.

⁴And David took *i*from him a thousand *j*chariots, and seven hundred horsemen, and twenty thousand footmen: and David houghed all the chariot *horses,* but reserved of them *for* an hundred chariots.

⁵And when the Syrians of Damascus came to succour Hadadezer king of Zobah, David slew of the Syrians two and twenty thousand men.

⁶Then David put garrisons in Syria of Damascus: and the Syrians became servants to David, *and* brought gifts. And the Lord preserved David whithersoever he went.

⁷And David took the shields of gold that were on the servants of Hadadezer, and brought them to Jerusalem.

⁸And from *k*Betah, and from *l*Berothai, cities of Hadadezer, king David took exceeding much brass.

⁹ ¶ When *m*Toi king of Hamath heard that David had smitten all the host of Hadadezer,

Amplified

¹⁹Then as if this were a little thing in Your eyes, O Lord God, You have spoken also of Your servant's house in the far distant future. And this is the law for man, O Lord God!

²⁰What more can David say to You? For You know Your servant, O Lord God.

²¹Because of Your promise and as Your own heart dictates, You have done all these astounding things to make Your servant know *and* understand.

²²Therefore You are great, O Lord God; for none is like You, nor is there any God besides You, according to all [You have made] our ears to hear.

²³What [other] one nation on earth is like Your people Israel, whom God went to redeem to be a people for Himself and to make for Himself a name? You have done great and terrible things for Yourself *and* for Your land, before Your people, whom You redeemed *and* delivered for Yourself from Egypt, from the nations and their gods.

²⁴And You have established for Yourself Your people Israel to be Your people forever, and You, Lord, became their God.

²⁵Now, O Lord God, confirm forever the word You have given as to Your servant and his house; and do as You have said,

²⁶And Your name [and presence] shall be magnified forever, saying, The Lord of hosts is God over Israel; and the house of Your servant David will be made firm before You.

²⁷For You, O Lord of hosts, God of Israel, have revealed this to Your servant: I will build you a house. So Your servant has found courage to pray this prayer to You.

²⁸And now, O Lord God, You are God, and Your words are truth, and You have promised this good thing to Your servant.

²⁹Therefore now let it please You to bless the house of Your servant, that it may continue forever before You; for You, O Lord God, have spoken it, and with Your blessing let [his] house be blessed forever.

8 AFTER THIS David smote the Philistines and subdued them, and he took Metheg-ammah out of the hands of the Philistines.

²He defeated Moab, and measured them with a line, making them lie down on the ground; two lines he measured to be put to death, and one full line to keep alive. And the Moabites became servants to David, bringing tribute.

³David also defeated Hadadezer son of Rehob, king of Zobah, as he went to restore his power at the river [Euphrates].

⁴David took from him 1,700 horsemen and 20,000 foot soldiers; and David hamstrung all the chariot horses, except he reserved enough of them for 100 chariots.

⁵And when the Syrians of Damascus came to help Hadadezer king of Zobah, David slew 22,000 of them.

⁶David put garrisons in Syrian Damascus, and the Syrians became [his] servants and brought tribute. The Lord preserved *and* gave victory to David wherever he went.

⁷And David took the shields of gold that were on the servants of Hadadezer and brought them to Jerusalem.

⁸And from Betah and Berothai, cities of Hadadezer, King David exacted an immense amount of bronze.

⁹When Toi king of Hamath heard about David's defeat of all the forces of Hadadezer,

---

e Heb. *law*
f Heb. *be thou pleased and bless*
g Or, *The bridle of Ammah*
h Or, *Hadarezer;* see 1 Chr. 18:3
i Or, *of his*
j As 1 Chr. 18:4
k Or, *Tibhath*
l Or, *Chun;* see 1 Chr. 18:8
m Tou; see 1 Chr. 18:9

New American Standard

19"And yet this was insignificant in Your eyes, O Lord GOD, for You have spoken also of the house of Your servant concerning the distant future. And this is the custom of man, O Lord GOD.

20"Again what more can David say to You? For You know Your servant, O Lord GOD!

21"For the sake of Your word, and according to Your own heart, You have done all this greatness to let Your servant know.

22"For this reason You are great, O Lord GOD; for there is none like You, and there is no God besides You, according to all that we have heard with our ears.

23"And what one nation on the earth is like Your people Israel, whom God went to redeem for Himself as a people and to make a name for Himself, and to do a great thing for You and awesome things for Your land, before Your people whom You have redeemed for Yourself from Egypt, *from* nations and their gods?

24"For You have established for Yourself Your people Israel as Your own people forever, and You, O LORD, have become their God.

25"Now therefore, O LORD God, the word that You have spoken concerning Your servant and his house, confirm *it* forever, and do as You have spoken,

26 that Your name may be magnified forever, by saying, 'The LORD of hosts is God over Israel'; and may the house of Your servant David be established before You.

27"For You, O LORD of hosts, the God of Israel, have made a revelation to Your servant, saying, 'I will build you a house'; therefore Your servant has found courage to pray this prayer to You.

28"Now, O Lord GOD, You are God, and Your words are truth, and You have promised this good thing to Your servant.

29"Now therefore, may it please You to bless the house of Your servant, that it may continue forever before You. For You, O Lord GOD, have spoken; and with Your blessing may the house of Your servant be blessed forever."

David's Triumphs

8 NOW AFTER this it came about that David defeated the Philistines and subdued them; and David took control of the chief city from the hand of the Philistines.

2 ¶ He defeated Moab, and measured them with the line, making them lie down on the ground; and he measured two lines to put to death and one full line to keep alive. And the Moabites became servants to David, bringing tribute.

3 ¶ Then David defeated Hadadezer, the son of Rehob king of Zobah, as he went to restore his rule at the ʰRiver.

4 David captured from him 1,700 horsemen and 20,000 foot soldiers; and David hamstrung the chariot horses, but reserved *enough* of them for 100 chariots.

5 When the Arameans of Damascus came to help Hadadezer, king of Zobah, David killed 22,000 Arameans.

6 Then David put garrisons among the Arameans of Damascus, and the Arameans became servants to David, bringing tribute. And the LORD helped David wherever he went.

7 David took the shields of gold which were carried by the servants of Hadadezer and brought them to Jerusalem.

8 From Betah and from Berothai, cities of Hadadezer, King David took a very large amount of bronze.

9 ¶ Now when Toi king of Hamath heard that David had defeated all the army of Hadadezer,

New International

family, that you have brought me this far? 19And as if this were not enough in your sight, O Sovereign LORD, you have also spoken about the future of the house of your servant. Is this your usual way of dealing with man, O Sovereign LORD?

20"What more can David say to you? For you know your servant, O Sovereign LORD. 21For the sake of your word and according to your will, you have done this great thing and made it known to your servant.

22"How great you are, O Sovereign LORD! There is no one like you, and there is no God but you, as we have heard with our own ears. 23And who is like your people Israel—the one nation on earth that God went out to redeem as a people for himself, and to make a name for himself, and to perform great and awesome wonders by driving out nations and their gods from before your people, whom you redeemed from Egypt?ˢ 24You have established your people Israel as your very own forever, and you, O LORD, have become their God.

25"And now, LORD God, keep forever the promise you have made concerning your servant and his house. Do as you promised, 26so that your name will be great forever. Then men will say, 'The LORD Almighty is God over Israel!' And the house of your servant David will be established before you.

27"O LORD Almighty, God of Israel, you have revealed this to your servant, saying, 'I will build a house for you.' So your servant has found courage to offer you this prayer. 28O Sovereign LORD, you are God! Your words are trustworthy, and you have promised these good things to your servant. 29Now be pleased to bless the house of your servant, that it may continue forever in your sight; for you, O Sovereign LORD, have spoken, and with your blessing the house of your servant will be blessed forever."

David's Victories

8 IN THE course of time, David defeated the Philistines and subdued them, and he took Metheg Ammah from the control of the Philistines.

2David also defeated the Moabites. He made them lie down on the ground and measured them off with a length of cord. Every two lengths of them were put to death, and the third length was allowed to live. So the Moabites became subject to David and brought tribute.

3Moreover, David fought Hadadezer son of Rehob, king of Zobah, when he went to restore his control along the Euphrates River. 4David captured a thousand of his chariots, seven thousand charioteersᵗ and twenty thousand foot soldiers. He hamstrung all but a hundred of the chariot horses.

5When the Arameans of Damascus came to help Hadadezer king of Zobah, David struck down twenty-two thousand of them. 6He put garrisons in the Aramean kingdom of Damascus, and the Arameans became subject to him and brought tribute. The LORD gave David victory wherever he went.

7David took the gold shields that belonged to the officers of Hadadezer and brought them to Jerusalem. 8From Tebahᵘ and Berothai, towns that belonged to Hadadezer, King David took a great quantity of bronze.

9When Touᵛ king of Hamath heard that David had

ˢ 23 See Septuagint and 1 Chron. 17:21; Hebrew *wonders for your land and before your people, whom you redeemed from Egypt, from the nations and their gods.*   ᵗ 4 Septuagint (see also Dead Sea Scrolls and 1 Chron. 18:4); Masoretic Text *captured seventeen hundred of his charioteers*   ᵘ 8 See some Septuagint manuscripts (see also 1 Chron. 18:8); Hebrew *Betah.*   ᵛ 9 Hebrew *Toi,* a variant of *Tou;* also in verse 10

ʰ I.e. Euphrates

King James

¹⁰Then Toi sent Joram his son unto king David, to ⁿsalute him, and to bless him, because he had fought against Hadadezer, and smitten him: for Hadadezer ^ohad wars with Toi. And *Joram* ^pbrought with him vessels of silver, and vessels of gold, and vessels of brass:

¹¹Which also king David did dedicate unto the LORD, with the silver and gold that he had dedicated of all nations which he subdued;

¹²Of Syria, and of Moab, and of the children of Ammon, and of the Philistines, and of Amalek, and of the spoil of Hadadezer, son of Rehob, king of Zobah.

¹³And David gat *him* a name when he returned from ^qsmiting of the Syrians in the valley of salt, ^rbeing eighteen thousand *men*.

¹⁴ ¶ And he put garrisons in Edom; throughout all Edom put he garrisons, and all they of Edom became David's servants. And the LORD preserved David whithersoever he went.

¹⁵And David reigned over all Israel; and David executed judgment and justice unto all his people.

¹⁶And Joab the son of Zeruiah *was* over the host; and Jehoshaphat the son of Ahilud *was* ^srecorder;

¹⁷And Zadok the son of Ahitub, and Ahimelech the son of Abiathar, *were* the priests; and Seraiah *was* the ^tscribe;

¹⁸And Benaiah the son of Jehoiada *was over* both the Cherethites and the Pelethites; and David's sons were ^uchief rulers.

David and Mephibosheth

9 AND DAVID said, Is there yet any that is left of the house of Saul, that I may show him kindness for Jonathan's sake?

²And *there was* of the house of Saul a servant whose name *was* Ziba. And when they had called him unto David, the king said unto him, *Art* thou Ziba? And he said, Thy servant *is* he.

³And the king said, *Is* there not yet any of the house of Saul, that I may show the kindness of God unto him? And Ziba said unto the king, Jonathan hath yet a son, *which is* lame on *his* feet.

⁴And the king said unto him, Where *is* he? And Ziba said unto the king, Behold, he *is* in the house of Machir, the son of Ammiel, in Lo-debar.

⁵ ¶ Then king David sent, and fetched him out of the house of Machir, the son of Ammiel, from Lo-debar.

⁶Now when ^vMephibosheth, the son of Jonathan, the son of Saul, was come unto David, he fell on his face, and did reverence. And David said, Mephibosheth. And he answered, Behold thy servant!

⁷ ¶ And David said unto him, Fear not: for I will surely show thee kindness for Jonathan thy father's sake, and will restore thee all the land of Saul thy father; and thou shalt eat bread at my table continually.

⁸And he bowed himself, and said, What *is* thy servant, that thou shouldest look upon such a dead dog as I *am?*

⁹ ¶ Then the king called to Ziba, Saul's servant, and said unto him, I have given unto thy master's son all that pertained to Saul and to all his house.

¹⁰Thou therefore, and thy sons, and thy servants, shall till the land for him, and thou shalt bring in *the fruits,* that thy master's son may have food to eat: but Mephibosheth thy master's son shall eat bread always at my table. Now Ziba had fifteen sons and twenty servants.

Amplified

¹⁰[He] sent Joram his son to King David to salute *and* congratulate him about his battle and defeat of Hadadezer. For Hadadezer had had wars with Toi. Joram brought vessels of silver, gold, and bronze.

¹¹These King David dedicated to the Lord, with the silver and gold that he had dedicated from all the nations he subdued:

¹²From Syria, Moab, the Ammonites, the Philistines, Amalek, and from the spoil of Hadadezer son of Rehob, king of Zobah.

¹³David won renown. When he returned he slew 18,000 Edomites in the Valley of Salt.

¹⁴He put garrisons throughout all Edom, and all the Edomites became his servants. And the Lord preserved *and* gave victory to [him] wherever he went.

¹⁵So David reigned over all Israel, and executed justice and righteousness for all his people.

¹⁶Joab son of Zeruiah was over the army; Jehoshaphat son of Ahilud was recorder;

¹⁷Zadok son of Ahitub and Ahimelech son of Abiathar were the [chief] priests, and Seraiah was the scribe;

¹⁸Benaiah son of Jehoiada was over both the Cherethites and Pelethites [the king's bodyguards]; and David's sons were chief [confidential] assistants to the king.

9 AND DAVID said, Is there still anyone left of the house of Saul to whom I may show kindness for Jonathan's sake?

²And of the house of Saul there was a servant whose name was Ziba. When they had called him to David, he said to him, Are you Ziba? He said, I, your servant, am he.

³The king said, Is there not still someone of the house of Saul to whom I may show the [unfailing, unsought, unlimited] mercy *and* kindness of God? Ziba replied, Jonathan has yet a son who is lame in his feet. [I Sam. 20:14–17.]

⁴And the king said, Where is he? Ziba replied, He is in the house of Machir son of Ammiel in Lo-debar.

⁵Then King David sent and brought him from the house of Machir son of Ammiel at Lo-debar.

⁶And Mephibosheth son of Jonathan, the son of Saul, came to David and fell on his face and did obeisance. David said, Mephibosheth! And he answered, Behold your servant!

⁷David said to him, Fear not, for I will surely show you kindness for Jonathan your father's sake, and will restore to you all the land of Saul your father [grandfather], and you shall eat at my table always.

⁸And [the cripple] bowed himself and said, What is your servant, that you should look upon such a dead dog as I am?

⁹Then the king called to Ziba, Saul's servant, and said to him, I have given your master's son [grandson] all that belonged to Saul and to all his house.

¹⁰And you shall till the land for him, you, your sons, and your servants, and you shall bring in the produce, that your master's heir may have food to eat; but Mephibosheth, your master's son [grandson], shall eat always at my table. Now Ziba had fifteen sons and twenty servants.

ⁿHeb. *ask him of peace*   ^oHeb. *was a man of wars with*
^pHeb. *in his hand were*   ^qHeb. *his smiting*   ^rOr, *slaying*
^sOr, *remembrancer,* or, *writer of chronicles*   ^tOr, *secretary*
^uOr, *princes*   ^vCalled *Merib-baal* in 1 Chr. 8:34

New American Standard

¹⁰ Toi sent Joram his son to King David to greet him and bless him, because he had fought against Hadadezer and defeated him; for Hadadezer had been at war with Toi. And *Joram* brought with him articles of silver, of gold and of bronze.

¹¹ King David also dedicated these to the LORD, with the silver and gold that he had dedicated from all the nations which he had subdued:

¹² from *i* Aram and Moab and the sons of Ammon and the Philistines and Amalek, and from the spoil of Hadadezer, son of Rehob, king of Zobah.

¹³ ¶ So David made a name *for himself* when he returned from killing 18,000 *i* Arameans in the Valley of Salt.

¹⁴ He put garrisons in Edom. In all Edom he put garrisons, and all the Edomites became servants to David. And the LORD helped David wherever he went.

¹⁵ ¶ So David reigned over all Israel; and David administered justice and righteousness for all his people.

¹⁶ Joab the son of Zeruiah *was* over the army, and Jehoshaphat the son of Ahilud *was* recorder.

¹⁷ Zadok the son of Ahitub and Ahimelech the son of Abiathar *were* priests, and Seraiah *was* secretary.

¹⁸ Benaiah the son of Jehoiada was over the Cherethites and the Pelethites; and David's sons were chief ministers.

David's Kindness to Mephibosheth

9 THEN DAVID said, "Is there yet anyone left of the house of Saul, that I may show him kindness for Jonathan's sake?"

² Now there was a servant of the house of Saul whose name was Ziba, and they called him to David; and the king said to him, "Are you Ziba?" And he said, "*I am* your servant."

³ The king said, "Is there not yet anyone of the house of Saul to whom I may show the kindness of God?" And Ziba said to the king, "There is still a son of Jonathan who is crippled in both feet."

⁴ So the king said to him, "Where is he?" And Ziba said to the king, "Behold, he is in the house of Machir the son of Ammiel in Lo-debar."

⁵ Then King David sent and brought him from the house of Machir the son of Ammiel, from Lo-debar.

⁶ Mephibosheth, the son of Jonathan the son of Saul, came to David and fell on his face and prostrated himself. And David said, "Mephibosheth." And he said, "Here is your servant!"

⁷ David said to him, "Do not fear, for I will surely show kindness to you for the sake of your father Jonathan, and will restore to you all the land of your grandfather Saul; and you shall eat at my table regularly."

⁸ Again he prostrated himself and said, "What is your servant, that you should regard a dead dog like me?"

⁹ ¶ Then the king called Saul's servant Ziba and said to him, "All that belonged to Saul and to all his house I have given to your master's grandson.

¹⁰ "You and your sons and your servants shall cultivate the land for him, and you shall bring in *the produce* so that your master's grandson may have food; nevertheless Mephibosheth your master's grandson shall eat at my table regularly." Now Ziba had fifteen sons and twenty servants.

New International

defeated the entire army of Hadadezer, ¹⁰he sent his son Joram^w to King David to greet him and congratulate him on his victory in battle over Hadadezer, who had been at war with Tou. Joram brought with him articles of silver and gold and bronze.

¹¹King David dedicated these articles to the LORD, as he had done with the silver and gold from all the nations he had subdued: ¹²Edom^x and Moab, the Ammonites and the Philistines, and Amalek. He also dedicated the plunder taken from Hadadezer son of Rehob, king of Zobah.

¹³And David became famous after he returned from striking down eighteen thousand Edomites^y in the Valley of Salt.

¹⁴He put garrisons throughout Edom, and all the Edomites became subject to David. The LORD gave David victory wherever he went.

David's Officials

¹⁵David reigned over all Israel, doing what was just and right for all his people. ¹⁶Joab son of Zeruiah was over the army; Jehoshaphat son of Ahilud was recorder; ¹⁷Zadok son of Ahitub and Ahimelech son of Abiathar were priests; Seraiah was secretary; ¹⁸Benaiah son of Jehoiada was over the Kerethites and Pelethites; and David's sons were royal advisers.^z

David and Mephibosheth

9 DAVID ASKED, "Is there anyone still left of the house of Saul to whom I can show kindness for Jonathan's sake?"

²Now there was a servant of Saul's household named Ziba. They called him to appear before David, and the king said to him, "Are you Ziba?"

"Your servant," he replied.

³The king asked, "Is there no one still left of the house of Saul to whom I can show God's kindness?"

Ziba answered the king, "There is still a son of Jonathan; he is crippled in both feet."

⁴"Where is he?" the king asked.

Ziba answered, "He is at the house of Makir son of Ammiel in Lo Debar."

⁵So King David had him brought from Lo Debar, from the house of Makir son of Ammiel.

⁶When Mephibosheth son of Jonathan, the son of Saul, came to David, he bowed down to pay him honor.

David said, "Mephibosheth!"

"Your servant," he replied.

⁷"Don't be afraid," David said to him, "for I will surely show you kindness for the sake of your father Jonathan. I will restore to you all the land that belonged to your grandfather Saul, and you will always eat at my table."

⁸Mephibosheth bowed down and said, "What is your servant, that you should notice a dead dog like me?"

⁹Then the king summoned Ziba, Saul's servant, and said to him, "I have given your master's grandson everything that belonged to Saul and his family. ¹⁰You and your sons and your servants are to farm the land for him and bring in the crops, so that your master's grandson may be provided for. And Mephibosheth, grandson of your master, will always eat at my table." (Now Ziba had fifteen sons and twenty servants.)

w 10 A variant of *Hadoram*   *x 12* Some Hebrew manuscripts, Septuagint and Syriac (see also 1 Chron. 18:11); most Hebrew manuscripts *Aram*   *y 13* A few Hebrew manuscripts, Septuagint and Syriac (see also 1 Chron. 18:12); most Hebrew manuscripts *Aram* (that is, Arameans)   *z 18* Or *were priests*

King James

11Then said Ziba unto the king, According to all that my lord the king hath commanded his servant, so shall thy servant do. As for Mephibosheth, *said the king,* he shall eat at my table, as one of the king's sons.

12And Mephibosheth had a young son, whose name *was* Micha. And all that dwelt in the house of Ziba *were* servants unto Mephibosheth.

13So Mephibosheth dwelt in Jerusalem: for he did eat continually at the king's table; and was lame on both his feet.

Victory over the Ammonites

10 AND IT came to pass after this, that the king of the children of Ammon died, and Hanun his son reigned in his stead.

2Then said David, I will show kindness unto Hanun the son of Nahash, as his father showed kindness unto me. And David sent to comfort him by the hand of his servants for his father. And David's servants came into the land of the children of Ammon.

3And the princes of the children of Ammon said unto Hanun their lord, [w]Thinkest thou that David doth honour thy father, that he hath sent comforters unto thee? hath not David *rather* sent his servants unto thee, to search the city, and to spy it out, and to overthrow it?

4Wherefore Hanun took David's servants, and shaved off the one half of their beards, and cut off their garments in the middle, *even* to their buttocks, and sent them away.

5When they told *it* unto David, he sent to meet them, because the men were greatly ashamed: and the king said, Tarry at Jericho until your beards be grown, and *then* return.

6 ¶ And when the children of Ammon saw that they stank before David, the children of Ammon sent and hired the Syrians of Beth-rehob, and the Syrians of Zoba, twenty thousand footmen, and of king Maacah a thousand men, and of [x]Ish-tob twelve thousand men.

7And when David heard of *it,* he sent Joab, and all the host of the mighty men.

8And the children of Ammon came out, and put the battle in array at the entering in of the gate: and the Syrians of Zoba, and of Rehob, and Ish-tob, and Maacah, *were* by themselves in the field.

9When Joab saw that the front of the battle was against him before and behind, he chose of all the choice *men* of Israel, and put *them* in array against the Syrians:

10And the rest of the people he delivered into the hand of Abishai his brother, that he might put *them* in array against the children of Ammon.

11And he said, If the Syrians be too strong for me, then thou shalt help me: but if the children of Ammon be too strong for thee, then I will come and help thee.

12Be of good courage, and let us play the men for our people, and for the cities of our God: and the LORD do that which seemeth him good.

13And Joab drew nigh, and the people that *were* with him, unto the battle against the Syrians: and they fled before him.

14And when the children of Ammon saw that the Syrians were fled, then fled they also before Abishai, and entered into the city. So Joab returned from the children of Ammon, and came to Jerusalem.

15 ¶ And when the Syrians saw that they were smitten before Israel, they gathered themselves together.

16And Hadarezer sent, and brought out the Syrians that *were* beyond [y]the river: and they came to Helam; and [z]Shobach the captain of the host of Hadarezer *went* before them.

[w]Heb. *In thine eyes doth David* [x]Or, *The men of Tob* [y]i.e. Euphrates [z]Or, *Shophach;* see 1 Chr. 19:16

Amplified

11Then Ziba said to the king, Your servant will do according to all my lord the king commands. So Mephibosheth ate at David's table as one of the king's sons.

12Mephibosheth had a young son whose name was Micha. And all who dwelt in Ziba's house were servants to Mephibosheth.

13So Mephibosheth dwelt in Jerusalem, for he ate continually at the king's table, [even though] he was lame in both feet.

10 LATER, THE king of the Ammonites died, and Hanun his son reigned in his stead.

2David said, I will show kindness to Hanun son of Nahash, as his father did to me. So David sent his servants to console him for his father's death; and they came into the land of the Ammonites,

3But the princes of the Ammonites said to Hanun their lord, Do you think that it is because David honors your father that he has sent comforters to you? Has he not rather sent his servants to you to search the city, spy it out, and overthrow it?

4So Hanun took David's servants and shaved off half their beards and cut off their garments in the middle at their hips and sent them away.

5When it was told David, he sent to meet them, for the men were greatly ashamed. And the king said, Tarry at Jericho until your beards are grown, and then return.

6And when the Ammonites saw that they had made themselves obnoxious *and* disgusting to David, they sent and hired the Syrians of Beth-rehob and of Zobah, 20,000 foot soldiers, and of the king of Maacah 1,000 men, and of Tob 12,000 men.

7When David heard of it, he sent Joab and all the army of the mighty men.

8And the Ammonites came out and put the battle in array at the entrance of the gate, but the Syrians of Zobah and of Rehob and the men of Tob and Maacah were stationed by themselves in the open country.

9When Joab saw that the battlefront was against him before and behind, he picked some of all the choice men of Israel and put them in array against the Syrians.

10The rest of the men Joab gave over to Abishai his brother, that he might put them in array against the Ammonites.

11Joab said, If the Syrians are too strong for me, then you shall help me; but if the Ammonites are too strong for you, I will come and help you.

12Be of good courage; let us play the man for our people and the cities of our God. And may the Lord do what seems good to Him.

13And Joab and the people who were with him drew near to battle against the Syrians, and they fled before him.

14And when the Ammonites saw that the Syrians had fled, they also fled before Abishai and entered the city. So Joab returned from battling against the Ammonites and came to Jerusalem.

15When the Syrians saw that they were defeated by Israel, they gathered together.

16Hadadezer sent and brought the Syrians who were beyond the river [Euphrates]; and they came to Helam, with Shobach commander of the army of Hadadezer leading them.

New American Standard

¹¹ Then Ziba said to the king, "According to all that my lord the king commands his servant so your servant will do." So Mephibosheth ate at David's table as one of the king's sons.

¹² Mephibosheth had a young son whose name was Mica. And all who lived in the house of Ziba were servants to Mephibosheth.

¹³ So Mephibosheth lived in Jerusalem, for he ate at the king's table regularly. Now he was lame in both feet.

Ammon and Aram Defeated

10 NOW IT happened afterwards that the king of the Ammonites died, and Hanun his son became king in his place.

² Then David said, "I will show kindness to Hanun the son of Nahash, just as his father showed kindness to me." So David sent some of his servants to console him concerning his father. But when David's servants came to the land of the Ammonites,

³ the princes of the Ammonites said to Hanun their lord, "Do you think that David is honoring your father because he has sent consolers to you? Has David not sent his servants to you in order to search the city, to spy it out and overthrow it?"

⁴ So Hanun took David's servants and shaved off half of their beards, and cut off their garments in the middle as far as their hips, and sent them away.

⁵ When they told *it* to David, he sent to meet them, for the men were greatly humiliated. And the king said, "Stay at Jericho until your beards grow, and *then* return."

⁶ ¶ Now when the sons of Ammon saw that they had become odious to David, the sons of Ammon sent and hired the Arameans of Beth-rehob and the Arameans of Zobah, 20,000 foot soldiers, and the king of Maacah with 1,000 men, and the men of Tob with 12,000 men.

⁷ When David heard *of it,* he sent Joab and all the army, the mighty men.

⁸ The sons of Ammon came out and drew up in battle array at the entrance of the city, while the Arameans of Zobah and of Rehob and the men of Tob and Maacah *were* by themselves in the field.

⁹ ¶ Now when Joab saw that the battle was set against him in front and in the rear, he selected from all the choice men of Israel, and arrayed *them* against the Arameans.

¹⁰ But the remainder of the people he placed in the hand of Abishai his brother, and he arrayed *them* against the sons of Ammon.

¹¹ He said, "If the Arameans are too strong for me, then you shall help me, but if the sons of Ammon are too strong for you, then I will come to help you.

¹²"Be strong, and let us show ourselves courageous for the sake of our people and for the cities of our God; and may the LORD do what is good in His sight."

¹³ So Joab and the people who were with him drew near to the battle against the Arameans, and they fled before him.

¹⁴ When the sons of Ammon saw that the Arameans fled, they *also* fled before Abishai and entered the city. Then Joab returned from *fighting* against the sons of Ammon and came to Jerusalem.

¹⁵ ¶ When the Arameans saw that they had been defeated by Israel, they gathered themselves together.

¹⁶ And Hadadezer sent and brought out the Arameans who were beyond the *j*River, and they came to Helam; and Shobach the commander of the army of Hadadezer led them.

New International

¹¹Then Ziba said to the king, "Your servant will do whatever my lord the king commands his servant to do." So Mephibosheth ate at David's*a* table like one of the king's sons.

¹²Mephibosheth had a young son named Mica, and all the members of Ziba's household were servants of Mephibosheth. ¹³And Mephibosheth lived in Jerusalem, because he always ate at the king's table, and he was crippled in both feet.

David Defeats the Ammonites

10 IN THE course of time, the king of the Ammonites died, and his son Hanun succeeded him as king. ²David thought, "I will show kindness to Hanun son of Nahash, just as his father showed kindness to me." So David sent a delegation to express his sympathy to Hanun concerning his father.

When David's men came to the land of the Ammonites, ³the Ammonite nobles said to Hanun their lord, "Do you think David is honoring your father by sending men to you to express sympathy? Hasn't David sent them to you to explore the city and spy it out and overthrow it?" ⁴So Hanun seized David's men, shaved off half of each man's beard, cut off their garments in the middle at the buttocks, and sent them away.

⁵When David was told about this, he sent messengers to meet the men, for they were greatly humiliated. The king said, "Stay at Jericho till your beards have grown, and then come back."

⁶When the Ammonites realized that they had become a stench in David's nostrils, they hired twenty thousand Aramean foot soldiers from Beth Rehob and Zobah, as well as the king of Maacah with a thousand men, and also twelve thousand men from Tob.

⁷On hearing this, David sent Joab out with the entire army of fighting men. ⁸The Ammonites came out and drew up in battle formation at the entrance to their city gate, while the Arameans of Zobah and Rehob and the men of Tob and Maacah were by themselves in the open country.

⁹Joab saw that there were battle lines in front of him and behind him; so he selected some of the best troops in Israel and deployed them against the Arameans. ¹⁰He put the rest of the men under the command of Abishai his brother and deployed them against the Ammonites. ¹¹Joab said, "If the Arameans are too strong for me, then you are to come to my rescue; but if the Ammonites are too strong for you, then I will come to rescue you. ¹²Be strong and let us fight bravely for our people and the cities of our God. The LORD will do what is good in his sight."

¹³Then Joab and the troops with him advanced to fight the Arameans, and they fled before him. ¹⁴When the Ammonites saw that the Arameans were fleeing, they fled before Abishai and went inside the city. So Joab returned from fighting the Ammonites and came to Jerusalem.

¹⁵After the Arameans saw that they had been routed by Israel, they regrouped. ¹⁶Hadadezer had Arameans brought from beyond the River*b*; they went to Helam, with Shobach the commander of Hadadezer's army leading them.

---

j I.e. Euphrates   *a 11* Septuagint; Hebrew *my*   *b 16* That is, the Euphrates

King James

17And when it was told David, he gathered all Israel together, and passed over Jordan, and came to Helam. And the Syrians set themselves in array against David, and fought with him.

18And the Syrians fled before Israel; and David slew *the men of* seven hundred chariots of the Syrians, and forty thousand horsemen, and smote Shobach the captain of their host, who died there.

19And when all the kings *that were* servants to Hadarezer saw that they were smitten before Israel, they made peace with Israel, and served them. So the Syrians feared to help the children of Ammon any more.

David's sin against Uriah

11 AND IT came to pass, *a*after the year *was* expired, at the time when kings go forth *to battle,* that David sent Joab, and his servants with him, and all Israel; and they destroyed the children of Ammon, and besieged Rabbah. But David tarried still at Jerusalem.

2 ¶ And it came to pass in an eveningtide, that David arose from off his bed, and walked upon the roof of the king's house: and from the roof he saw a woman washing herself; and the woman *was* very beautiful to look upon.

3And David sent and inquired after the woman. And *one* said, *Is* not this *b*Bath-sheba, the daughter of *c*Eliam, the wife of Uriah the Hittite?

4And David sent messengers, and took her; and she came in unto him, and he lay with her; *d*for she was purified from her uncleanness: and she returned unto her house.

5And the woman conceived, and sent and told David, and said, I *am* with child.

6 ¶ And David sent to Joab, *saying,* Send me Uriah the Hittite. And Joab sent Uriah to David.

7And when Uriah was come unto him, David demanded *of him e*how Joab did, and how the people did, and how the war prospered.

8And David said to Uriah, Go down to thy house, and wash thy feet. And Uriah departed out of the king's house, and there *f*followed him a mess *of meat* from the king.

9But Uriah slept at the door of the king's house with all the servants of his lord, and went not down to his house.

10And when they had told David, saying, Uriah went not down unto his house, David said unto Uriah, Camest thou not from *thy* journey? why *then* didst thou not go down unto thine house?

11And Uriah said unto David, The ark, and Israel, and Judah, abide in tents; and my lord Joab, and the servants of my lord, are encamped in the open fields; shall I then go into mine house, to eat and to drink, and to lie with my wife? *as* thou livest, and *as* thy soul liveth, I will not do this thing.

12And David said to Uriah, Tarry here today also, and tomorrow I will let thee depart. So Uriah abode in Jerusalem that day, and the morrow.

13And when David had called him, he did eat and drink before him; and he made him drunk: and at even he went out to lie on his bed with the servants of his lord, but went not down to his house.

14 ¶ And it came to pass in the morning, that David wrote a letter to Joab, and sent *it* by the hand of Uriah.

15And he wrote in the letter, saying, Set ye Uriah in the forefront of the *g*hottest battle, and retire ye *h*from him, that he may be smitten, and die.

16And it came to pass, when Joab observed the city, that he assigned Uriah unto a place where he knew that valiant men *were*.

Amplified

17When David was told, he gathered all Israel, crossed the Jordan, and came to Helam. Then the Syrians set themselves in array against David and fought with him.

18The Syrians fled before Israel, and David slew of [them] the men of 700 chariots and 40,000 horsemen and smote Shobach captain of their army, who died there.

19And when all the kings serving Hadadezer saw that they were defeated by Israel, they made peace with Israel and served them. So the Syrians were afraid to help the Ammonites any more.

11 IN THE spring, when kings go forth to battle, David sent Joab with his servants and all Israel, and they ravaged the Ammonites [country] and besieged Rabbah. But David remained in Jerusalem.

2One evening David arose from his couch and was walking on the roof of the king's house, when from there he saw a woman bathing; and she was very lovely to behold.

3David sent and inquired about the woman. One said, Is not this Bathsheba, the daughter of Eliam and the wife of Uriah the Hittite?

4And David sent messengers and took her. And she came in to him, and he lay with her—for she was purified from her uncleanness. Then she returned to her house.

5And the woman became pregnant and sent and told David, I am with child.

6David sent to Joab, saying, Send me Uriah the Hittite. So Joab sent [him] Uriah.

7When Uriah had come to him, David asked him how Joab was, how the people fared, and how the war progressed.

8David said to Uriah, Go down to your house and wash your feet. Uriah went out of the king's house, and there followed him a mess of food [a gift] from the king.

9But Uriah slept at the door of the king's house with all the servants of his lord and did not go down to his house.

10When they told David, Uriah did not go down to his house, David said to Uriah, Have you not come from a journey? Why did you not go down to your house?

11Uriah said to David, The ark and Israel and Judah live in tents, and my lord Joab and the servants of my lord are camping in the open field. Shall I then go to my house to eat and drink and lie with my wife? As you live and as my soul lives, I will not do this thing.

12And David said to Uriah, Remain here today also, and tomorrow I will let you depart. So Uriah remained in Jerusalem that day and the next.

13David invited him, and he ate with him and drank, so that he made him drunk; but that night he went out to lie on his bed with the servants of his lord and did not go down to his house.

14In the morning David wrote a letter to Joab and sent it with Uriah.

15And he wrote in the letter, Put Uriah in the front line of the heaviest fighting and withdraw from him, that he may be struck down and die.

16So when Joab was besieging the city, he assigned Uriah opposite where he knew the enemy's most valiant men were.

---

a Heb. *at the return of the year*   *b* Or, *Bath-shuah;* see 1 Chr. 3:5
c Or, *Ammiel*   *d* Or, *and when she had purified herself, &c., she returned*   *e* Heb. *of the peace of*   *f* Heb. *went out after him*
g Heb. *strong*   *h* Heb. *from after him*

New American Standard

17. Now when it was told David, he gathered all Israel together and crossed the Jordan, and came to Helam. And the Arameans arrayed themselves to meet David and fought against him.

18. But the Arameans fled before Israel, and David killed 700 charioteers of the Arameans and 40,000 horsemen and struck down Shobach the commander of their army, and he died there.

19. When all the kings, servants of Hadadezer, saw that they were defeated by Israel, they made peace with Israel and served them. So the Arameans feared to help the sons of Ammon anymore.

Bathsheba, David's Great Sin

11 THEN IT happened in the spring, at the time when kings go out *to battle,* that David sent Joab and his servants with him and all Israel, and they destroyed the sons of Ammon and besieged Rabbah. But David stayed at Jerusalem.

2. ¶ Now when evening came David arose from his bed and walked around on the roof of the king's house, and from the roof he saw a woman bathing; and the woman was very beautiful in appearance.

3. So David sent and inquired about the woman. And one said, "Is this not Bathsheba, the daughter of Eliam, the wife of Uriah the Hittite?"

4. David sent messengers and took her, and when she came to him, he lay with her; and when she had purified herself from her uncleanness, she returned to her house.

5. The woman conceived; and she sent and told David, and said, "I am pregnant."

6. ¶ Then David sent to Joab, *saying,* "Send me Uriah the Hittite." So Joab sent Uriah to David.

7. When Uriah came to him, David asked concerning the welfare of Joab and the people and the state of the war.

8. Then David said to Uriah, "Go down to your house, and wash your feet." And Uriah went out of the king's house, and a present from the king was sent out after him.

9. But Uriah slept at the door of the king's house with all the servants of his lord, and did not go down to his house.

10. Now when they told David, saying, "Uriah did not go down to his house," David said to him, "Have you not come from a journey? Why did you not go down to your house?"

11. Uriah said to David, "The ark and Israel and Judah are staying in temporary shelters, and my lord Joab and the servants of my lord are camping in the open field. Shall I then go to my house to eat and to drink and to lie with my wife? By your life and the life of your soul, I will not do this thing."

12. Then David said to Uriah, "Stay here today also, and tomorrow I will let you go." So Uriah remained in Jerusalem that day and the next.

13. Now David called him, and he ate and drank before him, and he made him drunk; and in the evening he went out to lie on his bed with his lord's servants, but he did not go down to his house.

14. ¶ Now in the morning David wrote a letter to Joab and sent *it* by the hand of Uriah.

15. He had written in the letter, saying, "Place Uriah in the front line of the fiercest battle and withdraw from him, so that he may be struck down and die."

16. So it was as Joab kept watch on the city, that he put Uriah at the place where he knew there *were* valiant men.

New International

17. When David was told of this, he gathered all Israel, crossed the Jordan and went to Helam. The Arameans formed their battle lines to meet David and fought against him. 18. But they fled before Israel, and David killed seven hundred of their charioteers and forty thousand of their foot soldiers.[c] He also struck down Shobach the commander of their army, and he died there. 19. When all the kings who were vassals of Hadadezer saw that they had been defeated by Israel, they made peace with the Israelites and became subject to them.

So the Arameans were afraid to help the Ammonites anymore.

David and Bathsheba

11 IN THE spring, at the time when kings go off to war, David sent Joab out with the king's men and the whole Israelite army. They destroyed the Ammonites and besieged Rabbah. But David remained in Jerusalem.

2. One evening David got up from his bed and walked around on the roof of the palace. From the roof he saw a woman bathing. The woman was very beautiful, 3. and David sent someone to find out about her. The man said, "Isn't this Bathsheba, the daughter of Eliam and the wife of Uriah the Hittite?" 4. Then David sent messengers to get her. She came to him, and he slept with her. (She had purified herself from her uncleanness.) Then[d] she went back home. 5. The woman conceived and sent word to David, saying, "I am pregnant."

6. So David sent this word to Joab: "Send me Uriah the Hittite." And Joab sent him to David. 7. When Uriah came to him, David asked him how Joab was, how the soldiers were and how the war was going. 8. Then David said to Uriah, "Go down to your house and wash your feet." So Uriah left the palace, and a gift from the king was sent after him. 9. But Uriah slept at the entrance to the palace with all his master's servants and did not go down to his house.

10. When David was told, "Uriah did not go home," he asked him, "Haven't you just come from a distance? Why didn't you go home?"

11. Uriah said to David, "The ark and Israel and Judah are staying in tents, and my master Joab and my lord's men are camped in the open fields. How could I go to my house to eat and drink and lie with my wife? As surely as you live, I will not do such a thing!"

12. Then David said to him, "Stay here one more day, and tomorrow I will send you back." So Uriah remained in Jerusalem that day and the next. 13. At David's invitation, he ate and drank with him, and David made him drunk. But in the evening Uriah went out to sleep on his mat among his master's servants; he did not go home.

14. In the morning David wrote a letter to Joab and sent it with Uriah. 15. In it he wrote, "Put Uriah in the front line where the fighting is fiercest. Then withdraw from him so he will be struck down and die."

16. So while Joab had the city under siege, he put Uriah at a place where he knew the strongest defenders were.

---

c 18 Some Septuagint manuscripts (see also 1 Chron. 19:18); Hebrew *horsemen*   d 4 Or *with her. When she purified herself from her uncleanness,*

King James

¹⁷And the men of the city went out, and fought with Joab: and there fell *some* of the people of the servants of David; and Uriah the Hittite died also.

¹⁸ ¶ Then Joab sent and told David all the things concerning the war;

¹⁹And charged the messenger, saying, When thou hast made an end of telling the matters of the war unto the king,

²⁰And if so be that the king's wrath arise, and he say unto thee, Wherefore approached ye so nigh unto the city when ye did fight? knew ye not that they would shoot from the wall?

²¹Who smote Abimelech the son of Jerubbesheth? did not a woman cast a piece of a millstone upon him from the wall, that he died in Thebez? why went ye nigh the wall? then say thou, Thy servant Uriah the Hittite is dead also.

²² ¶ So the messenger went, and came and showed David all that Joab had sent him for.

²³And the messenger said unto David, Surely the men prevailed against us, and came out unto us into the field, and we were upon them even unto the entering of the gate.

²⁴And the shooters shot from off the wall upon thy servants; and *some* of the king's servants be dead, and thy servant Uriah the Hittite is dead also.

²⁵Then David said unto the messenger, Thus shalt thou say unto Joab, Let not this thing *i* displease thee, for the sword devoureth *j* one as well as another: make thy battle more strong against the city, and overthrow it: and encourage thou him.

²⁶ ¶ And when the wife of Uriah heard that Uriah her husband was dead, she mourned for her husband.

²⁷And when the mourning was past, David sent and fetched her to his house, and she became his wife, and bare him a son. But the thing that David had done *k* displeased the LORD.

David repents

12 AND THE LORD sent Nathan unto David. And he came unto him, and said unto him, There were two men in one city; the one rich, and the other poor.

²The rich *man* had exceeding many flocks and herds:

³But the poor *man* had nothing, save one little ewe lamb, which he had bought and nourished up: and it grew up together with him, and with his children; it did eat of his own *l* meat, and drank of his own cup, and lay in his bosom, and was unto him as a daughter.

⁴And there came a traveller unto the rich man, and he spared to take of his own flock and of his own herd, to dress for the wayfaring man that was come unto him; but took the poor man's lamb, and dressed it for the man that was come to him.

⁵And David's anger was greatly kindled against the man; and he said to Nathan, *As* the LORD liveth, the man that hath done this *thing* ^m shall surely die:

⁶And he shall restore the lamb fourfold, because he did this thing, and because he had no pity.

⁷ ¶ And Nathan said to David, Thou *art* the man. Thus saith the LORD God of Israel, I anointed thee king over Israel, and I delivered thee out of the hand of Saul;

⁸And I gave thee thy master's house, and thy master's wives into thy bosom, and gave thee the house of Israel and of Judah; and if *that had been* too little, I would moreover have given unto thee such and such things.

⁹Wherefore hast thou despised the commandment of the LORD, to do evil in his sight? thou hast killed Uriah the Hittite with the sword, and hast taken his wife *to be* thy wife, and hast slain him with the sword of the children of Ammon.

Amplified

¹⁷And the men of the city came out and fought with Joab, and some of the servants of David fell. Uriah the Hittite died also.

¹⁸Then Joab sent and told David all the things concerning the war.

¹⁹And he charged the messenger, When you have finished reporting matters of the war to the king,

²⁰Then if the king's anger rises and he says to you, Why did you go so near to the city to fight? Did you not know they would shoot from the wall?

²¹Who killed Abimelech son of Jerubbesheth (Gideon)? Did not a woman cast an upper millstone upon him from the wall, so that he died in Thebez? Why did you go near the wall? Then say, Your servant Uriah the Hittite is dead also. [Judg. 9:35, 53.]

²²So the messenger went and told David all for which Joab had sent him.

²³The messenger said to David, Surely the men prevailed against us and came out to us in the field, but we were upon them even to the entrance of the gate.

²⁴Then the archers shot at your servants from the wall. Some of the king's servants are dead, and your servant Uriah the Hittite is dead also.

²⁵Then David said to the messenger, Say to Joab, Let not this thing disturb you, for the sword devours one as well as another. Strengthen your attack upon the city and overthrow it. And encourage Joab.

²⁶When Uriah's wife heard that her husband was dead, she mourned for Uriah.

²⁷And when the mourning was past, David sent and brought her to his house, and she became his wife and bore him a son. But the thing that David had done was evil in the sight of the Lord.

12 AND THE Lord sent Nathan to David. He came and said to him, There were two men in a city, one rich and the other poor.

²The rich man had very many flocks and herds,

³But the poor man had nothing but one little ewe lamb which he had bought and brought up, and it grew up with him and his children. It ate of his own morsel, drank from his own cup, lay in his bosom, and was like a daughter to him.

⁴Now a traveler came to the rich man, and to avoid taking one of his own flock or herd to prepare for the wayfaring man who had come to him, he took the poor man's lamb and prepared it for his guest.

⁵Then David's anger was greatly kindled against the man, and he said to Nathan, As the Lord lives, the man who has done this is a son [worthy] of death.

⁶He shall restore the lamb fourfold, because he did this thing and had no pity.

⁷Then Nathan said to David, You are the man! Thus says the Lord, the God of Israel: I anointed you king of Israel, and I delivered you out of the hand of Saul.

⁸And I gave you your master's house, and your master's wives into your bosom, and gave you the house of Israel and of Judah; and if that had been too little, I would have added that much again.

⁹Why have you despised the commandment of the Lord, doing evil in His sight? You have slain Uriah the Hittite with the sword and have taken his wife to be your wife. You have murdered him with the sword of the Ammonites. [Lev. 20:10; 24:17.]

ⁱHeb. *be evil in thine eyes*   ^jHeb. *so and such*   ^kHeb. *was evil in the eyes of*   ^lHeb. *morsel*   ^mOr, *is worthy to die,* or, *is a son of death*

New American Standard

17 The men of the city went out and fought against Joab, and some of the people among David's servants fell; and Uriah the Hittite also died.

18 Then Joab sent and reported to David all the events of the war.

19 He charged the messenger, saying, "When you have finished telling all the events of the war to the king,

20 and if it happens that the king's wrath rises and he says to you, 'Why did you go so near to the city to fight? Did you not know that they would shoot from the wall?

21 'Who struck down Abimelech the son of Jerub-besheth? Did not a woman throw an upper millstone on him from the wall so that he died at Thebez? Why did you go so near the wall?'—then you shall say, 'Your servant Uriah the Hittite is dead also.' "

22 ¶ So the messenger departed and came and reported to David all that Joab had sent him *to tell*.

23 The messenger said to David, "The men prevailed against us and came out against us in the field, but we pressed them as far as the entrance of the gate.

24 "Moreover, the archers shot at your servants from the wall; so some of the king's servants are dead, and your servant Uriah the Hittite is also dead."

25 Then David said to the messenger, "Thus you shall say to Joab, 'Do not let this thing displease you, for the sword devours one as well as another; make your battle against the city stronger and overthrow it'; and *so* encourage him."

26 ¶ Now when the wife of Uriah heard that Uriah her husband was dead, she mourned for her husband.

27 When the *time of* mourning was over, David sent and brought her to his house and she became his wife; then she bore him a son. But the thing that David had done was evil in the sight of the LORD.

Nathan Rebukes David

12 THEN THE LORD sent Nathan to David. And he came to him and said,
"There were two men in one city, the one rich and the other poor.

2 "The rich man had a great many flocks and herds.

3 "But the poor man had nothing except one little ewe lamb
Which he bought and nourished;
And it grew up together with him and his children.
It would eat of his bread and drink of his cup and lie in his bosom,
And was like a daughter to him.

4 "Now a traveler came to the rich man,
And he was unwilling to take from his own flock or his own herd,
To prepare for the wayfarer who had come to him;
Rather he took the poor man's ewe lamb and prepared it for the man who had come to him."

5 Then David's anger burned greatly against the man, and he said to Nathan, "As the LORD lives, surely the man who has done this deserves to die.

6 "He must make restitution for the lamb fourfold, because he did this thing and had no compassion."

7 ¶ Nathan then said to David, "You are the man! Thus says the LORD God of Israel, 'It is I who anointed you king over Israel and it is I who delivered you from the hand of Saul.

8 'I also gave you your master's house and your master's wives into your care, and I gave you the house of Israel and Judah; and if *that had been* too little, I would have added to you many more things like these!

9 'Why have you despised the word of the LORD by doing evil in His sight? You have struck down Uriah the Hittite with the sword, have taken his wife to be your wife, and have killed him with the sword of the sons of Ammon.

New International

17 When the men of the city came out and fought against Joab, some of the men in David's army fell; moreover, Uriah the Hittite died.

18 Joab sent David a full account of the battle. 19 He instructed the messenger: "When you have finished giving the king this account of the battle, 20 the king's anger may flare up, and he may ask you, 'Why did you get so close to the city to fight? Didn't you know they would shoot arrows from the wall? 21 Who killed Abimelech son of Jerub-Besheth[e]? Didn't a woman throw an upper millstone on him from the wall, so that he died in Thebez? Why did you get so close to the wall?' If he asks you this, then say to him, 'Also, your servant Uriah the Hittite is dead.' "

22 The messenger set out, and when he arrived he told David everything Joab had sent him to say. 23 The messenger said to David, "The men overpowered us and came out against us in the open, but we drove them back to the entrance to the city gate. 24 Then the archers shot arrows at your servants from the wall, and some of the king's men died. Moreover, your servant Uriah the Hittite is dead."

25 David told the messenger, "Say this to Joab: 'Don't let this upset you; the sword devours one as well as another. Press the attack against the city and destroy it.' Say this to encourage Joab."

26 When Uriah's wife heard that her husband was dead, she mourned for him. 27 After the time of mourning was over, David had her brought to his house, and she became his wife and bore him a son. But the thing David had done displeased the LORD.

Nathan Rebukes David

12 THE LORD sent Nathan to David. When he came to him, he said, "There were two men in a certain town, one rich and the other poor. 2 The rich man had a very large number of sheep and cattle, 3 but the poor man had nothing except one little ewe lamb he had bought. He raised it, and it grew up with him and his children. It shared his food, drank from his cup and even slept in his arms. It was like a daughter to him.

4 "Now a traveler came to the rich man, but the rich man refrained from taking one of his own sheep or cattle to prepare a meal for the traveler who had come to him. Instead, he took the ewe lamb that belonged to the poor man and prepared it for the one who had come to him."

5 David burned with anger against the man and said to Nathan, "As surely as the LORD lives, the man who did this deserves to die! 6 He must pay for that lamb four times over, because he did such a thing and had no pity."

7 Then Nathan said to David, "You are the man! This is what the LORD, the God of Israel, says: 'I anointed you king over Israel, and I delivered you from the hand of Saul. 8 I gave your master's house to you, and your master's wives into your arms. I gave you the house of Israel and Judah. And if all this had been too little, I would have given you even more. 9 Why did you despise the word of the LORD by doing what is evil in his eyes? You struck down Uriah the Hittite with the sword and took his wife to be your own. You killed him with the sword of the Am-

---

e 21 Also known as *Jerub-Baal* (that is, Gideon)

King James

Amplified

[10]Now therefore the sword shall never depart from thine house; because thou hast despised me, and hast taken the wife of Uriah the Hittite to be thy wife.

[11]Thus saith the LORD, Behold, I will raise up evil against thee out of thine own house, and I will take thy wives before thine eyes, and give *them* unto thy neighbour, and he shall lie with thy wives in the sight of this sun.

[12]For thou didst *it* secretly: but I will do this thing before all Israel, and before the sun.

[13]And David said unto Nathan, I have sinned against the LORD. And Nathan said unto David, The LORD also hath put away thy sin; thou shalt not die.

[14]Howbeit, because by this deed thou hast given great occasion to the enemies of the LORD to blaspheme, the child also *that is* born unto thee shall surely die.

[15] ¶ And Nathan departed unto his house. And the LORD struck the child that Uriah's wife bare unto David, and it was very sick.

[16]David therefore besought God for the child; and David *n*fasted, and went in, and lay all night upon the earth.

[17]And the elders of his house arose, *and went* to him, to raise him up from the earth: but he would not, neither did he eat bread with them.

[18]And it came to pass on the seventh day, that the child died. And the servants of David feared to tell him that the child was dead: for they said, Behold, while the child was yet alive, we spake unto him, and he would not hearken unto our voice: how will he then *o*vex himself, if we tell him that the child is dead?

[19]But when David saw that his servants whispered, David perceived that the child was dead: therefore David said unto his servants, Is the child dead? And they said, He is dead.

[20]Then David arose from the earth, and washed, and anointed *himself,* and changed his apparel, and came into the house of the LORD, and worshipped: then he came to his own house; and when he required, they set bread before him, and he did eat.

[21]Then said his servants unto him, What thing *is* this that thou hast done? thou didst fast and weep for the child, *while it was* alive; but when the child was dead, thou didst rise and eat bread.

[22]And he said, While the child was yet alive, I fasted and wept: for I said, Who can tell *whether* GOD will be gracious to me, that the child may live?

[23]But now he is dead, wherefore should I fast? can I bring him back again? I shall go to him, but he shall not return to me.

[24] ¶ And David comforted Bath-sheba his wife, and went in unto her, and lay with her: and she bare a son, and he called his name Solomon: and the LORD loved him.

[25]And he sent by the hand of Nathan the prophet; and he called his name *p*Jedidiah, because of the LORD.

Victory over the Ammonites

[26] ¶ And Joab fought against Rabbah of the children of Ammon, and took the royal city.

[27]And Joab sent messengers to David, and said, I have fought against Rabbah, and have taken the city of waters.

[28]Now therefore gather the rest of the people together, and encamp against the city, and take it: lest I take the city, and *q*it be called after my name.

[10]Now, therefore, the sword shall never depart from your house, because [you have not only despised My command, but] you have despised Me and have taken the wife of Uriah the Hittite to be your wife.

[11]Thus says the Lord, Behold, I will raise up evil against you out of your *d*own house; and I will take your wives before your eyes and give them to your neighbor, and he shall lie with your wives in the sight of this sun.

[12]For you did it secretly, but I will do this thing before all Israel and before the sun. [Fulfilled in II Sam. 16:21, 22.]

[13]And David said to Nathan, I have sinned against the Lord. And Nathan said to David, The Lord also has put away your sin; you shall not die. [Ps. 51.]

[14]Nevertheless, because by this deed you have utterly scorned the Lord *and* given great occasion to the enemies of the Lord to blaspheme, the child that is born to you shall surely die.

[15]Then Nathan departed to his house. And the Lord struck the child that Uriah's widow bore to David, and he was very sick.

[16]David therefore besought God for the child; and David fasted and went in and lay all night [repeatedly] on the floor.

[17]His older house servants arose [in the night] and went to him to raise him up from the floor, but he would not, nor did he eat food with them.

[18]And on the seventh day the child died. David's servants feared to tell him that the child was dead, for they said, While the child was yet alive, we spoke to him and he would not listen to our voices; will he then harm himself if we tell him the child is dead?

[19]But when David saw that his servants whispered, he perceived that the child was dead. So he said to them, Is the child dead? And they said, He is.

[20]Then David arose from the floor, washed, anointed himself, changed his apparel, and went into the house of the Lord and worshiped. Then he came to his own house, and when he asked, they set food before him, and he ate.

[21]Then his servants said to him, What is this that you have done? You fasted and wept while the child was alive, but when the child was dead, you arose and ate food.

[22]David said, While the child was still alive, I fasted and wept; for I said, Who knows whether the Lord will be gracious to me and let the child live?

[23]But now he is dead; why should I fast? Can I bring him back again? I shall go to him, but he will not return to me.

[24]David comforted Bathsheba his wife, and went to her and lay with her; and she bore a son, and she called his name Solomon. And the Lord loved [the child];

[25]He sent [a message] by the hand of Nathan the prophet, and [Nathan] called the boy's [special] name Jedidiah [beloved of the Lord], because the Lord [loved the child].

[26]Now Joab fought against Rabbah of the Ammonites and took the royal city.

[27]And Joab sent messengers to David and said, I have fought against Rabbah, and have taken the city of waters.

[28]Now therefore assemble the rest of the men, encamp against the city, and take it, lest I take the city, and it be called after my name.

---

*d*This sentence was fulfilled in the agony brought on David by his lawless children: Amnon's scandalous behavior with his half sister Tamar (13:14) and his consequent murder by his brother Absalom (13:28, 29); Absalom's escape to a foreign land (13:38) and his return after three years; Absalom without recognition by David for two more years (14:28); Absalom's deliberate, rebellious attempt to win the hearts of the people and supplant his father (15:6); David's flight from Jerusalem, with the mass of the people against him (15:14), the terrible battle in the forest of Ephraim, won by David's forces, with Absalom killed in flight (18:6ff.). David's agony of heart is echoed repeatedly in the history of these tragedies [II Sam. 13:1–19:8] and in some of his psalms. Even when the great king was dying, his son Adonijah was attempting to usurp the throne, and was later executed as a traitor (II Kings 1:5; 2:25).

n Heb. *fasted a fast*   *o* Heb. *do hurt*   *p* i.e. *Beloved of the LORD*
q Heb. *my name be called upon it*

New American Standard

New International

¹⁰ 'Now therefore, the sword shall never depart from your house, because you have despised Me and have taken the wife of Uriah the Hittite to be your wife.'

¹¹"Thus says the LORD, 'Behold, I will raise up evil against you from your own household; I will even take your wives before your eyes and give *them* to your companion, and he will lie with your wives in broad daylight.

¹² 'Indeed you did it secretly, but I will do this thing before all Israel, and under the sun.' "

¹³ Then David said to Nathan, "I have sinned against the LORD." And Nathan said to David, "The LORD also has taken away your sin; you shall not die.

¹⁴"However, because by this deed you have given occasion to the enemies of the LORD to blaspheme, the child also that is born to you shall surely die."

¹⁵ So Nathan went to his house.

Loss of a Child

¶ Then the LORD struck the child that Uriah's widow bore to David, so that he was *very* sick.

¹⁶ David therefore inquired of God for the child; and David fasted and went and lay all night on the ground.

¹⁷ The elders of his household stood beside him in order to raise him up from the ground, but he was unwilling and would not eat food with them.

¹⁸ Then it happened on the seventh day that the child died. And the servants of David were afraid to tell him that the child was dead, for they said, "Behold, while the child was *still* alive, we spoke to him and he did not listen to our voice. How then can we tell him that the child is dead, since he might do *himself* harm!"

¹⁹ But when David saw that his servants were whispering together, David perceived that the child was dead; so David said to his servants, "Is the child dead?" And they said, "He is dead."

²⁰ So David arose from the ground, washed, anointed *himself*, and changed his clothes; and he came into the house of the LORD and worshiped. Then he came to his own house, and when he requested, they set food before him and he ate.

²¹ ¶ Then his servants said to him, "What is this thing that you have done? While the child was alive, you fasted and wept; but when the child died, you arose and ate food."

²² He said, "While the child was *still* alive, I fasted and wept; for I said, 'Who knows, the LORD may be gracious to me, that the child may live.'

²³"But now he has died; why should I fast? Can I bring him back again? I will go to him, but he will not return to me."

Solomon Born

²⁴ ¶ Then David comforted his wife Bathsheba, and went in to her and lay with her; and she gave birth to a son, and he named him Solomon. Now the LORD loved him

²⁵ and sent *word* through Nathan the prophet, and he named him ^kJedidiah for the LORD's sake.

War Again

²⁶ ¶ Now Joab fought against Rabbah of the sons of Ammon and captured the royal city.

²⁷ Joab sent messengers to David and said, "I have fought against Rabbah, I have even captured the city of waters.

²⁸"Now therefore, gather the rest of the people together and camp against the city and capture it, or I will capture the city myself and it will be named after me."

---

monites. ¹⁰Now, therefore, the sword will never depart from your house, because you despised me and took the wife of Uriah the Hittite to be your own.'

¹¹"This is what the LORD says: 'Out of your own household I am going to bring calamity upon you. Before your very eyes I will take your wives and give them to one who is close to you, and he will lie with your wives in broad daylight. ¹²You did it in secret, but I will do this thing in broad daylight before all Israel.' "

¹³Then David said to Nathan, "I have sinned against the LORD."

Nathan replied, "The LORD has taken away your sin. You are not going to die. ¹⁴But because by doing this you have made the enemies of the LORD show utter contempt,^f the son born to you will die."

¹⁵After Nathan had gone home, the LORD struck the child that Uriah's wife had borne to David, and he became ill. ¹⁶David pleaded with God for the child. He fasted and went into his house and spent the nights lying on the ground. ¹⁷The elders of his household stood beside him to get him up from the ground, but he refused, and he would not eat any food with them.

¹⁸On the seventh day the child died. David's servants were afraid to tell him that the child was dead, for they thought, "While the child was still living, we spoke to David but he would not listen to us. How can we tell him the child is dead? He may do something desperate."

¹⁹David noticed that his servants were whispering among themselves and he realized the child was dead. "Is the child dead?" he asked.

"Yes," they replied, "he is dead."

²⁰Then David got up from the ground. After he had washed, put on lotions and changed his clothes, he went into the house of the LORD and worshiped. Then he went to his own house, and at his request they served him food, and he ate.

²¹His servants asked him, "Why are you acting this way? While the child was alive, you fasted and wept, but now that the child is dead, you get up and eat!"

²²He answered, "While the child was still alive, I fasted and wept. I thought, 'Who knows? The LORD may be gracious to me and let the child live.' ²³But now that he is dead, why should I fast? Can I bring him back again? I will go to him, but he will not return to me."

²⁴Then David comforted his wife Bathsheba, and he went to her and lay with her. She gave birth to a son, and they named him Solomon. The LORD loved him; ²⁵and because the LORD loved him, he sent word through Nathan the prophet to name him Jedidiah.^g

²⁶Meanwhile Joab fought against Rabbah of the Ammonites and captured the royal citadel. ²⁷Joab then sent messengers to David, saying, "I have fought against Rabbah and taken its water supply. ²⁸Now muster the rest of the troops and besiege the city and capture it. Otherwise I will take the city, and it will be named after me."

---

^kI.e. beloved of the LORD

f 14 Masoretic Text; an ancient Hebrew scribal tradition *this you have shown utter contempt for the LORD*   *g 25 Jedidiah* means *loved by the LORD.*

King James

²⁹And David gathered all the people together, and went to Rabbah, and fought against it, and took it.

³⁰And he took their king's crown from off his head, the weight whereof *was* a talent of gold with the precious stones: and it was *set* on David's head. And he brought forth the spoil of the city ^rin great abundance.

³¹And he brought forth the people that *were* therein, and put *them* under saws, and under harrows of iron, and under axes of iron, and made them pass through the brickkiln: and thus did he unto all the cities of the children of Ammon. So David and all the people returned unto Jerusalem.

Amnon defiles Tamar

13 AND IT came to pass after this, that Absalom the son of David had a fair sister, whose name *was* Tamar; and Amnon the son of David loved her.

²And Amnon was so vexed, that he fell sick for his sister Tamar; for she *was* a virgin; and ^sAmnon thought it hard for him to do any thing to her.

³But Amnon had a friend, whose name *was* Jonadab, the son of Shimeah David's brother: and Jonadab *was* a very subtle man.

⁴And he said unto him, Why *art* thou, *being* the king's son, ^tlean ^ufrom day to day? wilt thou not tell me? And Amnon said unto him, I love Tamar, my brother Absalom's sister.

⁵And Jonadab said unto him, Lay thee down on thy bed, and make thyself sick: and when thy father cometh to see thee, say unto him, I pray thee, let my sister Tamar come, and give me meat, and dress the meat in my sight, that I may see *it,* and eat *it* at her hand.

⁶ ¶ So Amnon lay down, and made himself sick: and when the king was come to see him, Amnon said unto the king, I pray thee, let Tamar my sister come, and make me a couple of cakes in my sight, that I may eat at her hand.

⁷Then David sent home to Tamar, saying, Go now to thy brother Amnon's house, and dress him meat.

⁸So Tamar went to her brother Amnon's house; and he was laid down. And she took ^vflour, and kneaded *it,* and made cakes in his sight, and did bake the cakes.

⁹And she took a pan, and poured *them* out before him; but he refused to eat. And Amnon said, Have out all men from me. And they went out every man from him.

¹⁰And Amnon said unto Tamar, Bring the meat into the chamber, that I may eat of thine hand. And Tamar took the cakes which she had made, and brought *them* into the chamber to Amnon her brother.

¹¹And when she had brought *them* unto him to eat, he took hold of her, and said unto her, Come lie with me, my sister.

¹²And she answered him, Nay, my brother, do not ^wforce me; for ^xno such thing ought to be done in Israel: do not thou this folly.

¹³And I, whither shall I cause my shame to go? and as for thee, thou shalt be as one of the fools in Israel. Now therefore, I pray thee, speak unto the king; for he will not withhold me from thee.

¹⁴Howbeit he would not hearken unto her voice: but, being stronger than she, forced her, and lay with her.

¹⁵ ¶ Then Amnon hated her ^yexceedingly; so that the hatred wherewith he hated her *was* greater than the love wherewith he had loved her. And Amnon said unto her, Arise, be gone.

¹⁶And she said unto him, *There is* no cause: this evil in sending me away *is* greater than the other that thou didst unto me. But he would not hearken unto her.

Amplified

²⁹So David gathered all the men, went to Rabbah, fought against it, and took it.

³⁰And he took the crown of their king [of Malcham] from his head; the weight of it was a talent of gold, and in it were precious stones; and it was set on David's head. And he brought forth exceedingly much spoil from the city.

³¹And he brought forth the people who were there, and put them to [work with] saws and iron threshing sledges and axes, and made them labor at the brickkiln. And he did this to all the Ammonite cities. Then [he] and all the men returned to Jerusalem.

13 ABSALOM SON of David had a fair sister whose name was Tamar, and Amnon [her half brother] son of David loved her.

²And Amnon was so troubled that he fell sick for his [half] sister Tamar, for she was a virgin, and Amnon thought it impossible for him to do anything to her.

³But Amnon had a friend whose name was Jonadab son of Shimeah, David's brother; and Jonadab was a very crafty man.

⁴He said to Amnon, Why are you, the king's son, so lean and weak-looking from day to day? Will you not tell me? And Amnon said to him, I love Tamar, my [half] brother Absalom's sister.

⁵Jonadab said to him, Go to bed and pretend you are sick; and when your father David comes to see you, say to him, Let my sister Tamar come and give me food and prepare it in my sight, that I may see it and eat it from her hand.

⁶So Amnon lay down and pretended to be sick; and when the king came to see him, Amnon said to the king, I pray you, let my sister Tamar come and make me a couple of cakes in my sight, that I may eat from her hand.

⁷Then David sent home and told Tamar, Go now to your brother Amnon's house and prepare food for him.

⁸So Tamar went to her brother Amnon's house, and he was in bed. And she took dough and kneaded it and made cakes in his sight and baked them.

⁹She took the pan and emptied it out before him, but he refused to eat. And Amnon said, Send everyone out from me. So everyone went out from him.

¹⁰Then Amnon said to Tamar, Bring the food here into the bedroom, so I may eat from your hand. So Tamar took the cakes she had made and brought them into the room to Amnon her brother.

¹¹And when she brought them to him, he took hold of her and said, Come lie with me, my sister.

¹²She replied, No, my brother! Do not force *and* humble me, for no such thing should be done in Israel! Do not do this foolhardy, scandalous thing! [Gen. 34:7.]

¹³And I, how could I rid myself of my shame? And you, you will be [considered] one of the stupid fools in Israel. Now therefore, I pray you, speak to the king, for he will not withhold me from you.

¹⁴But he would not listen to her, and being stronger than she, he forced her and lay with her.

¹⁵Then Amnon hated her exceedingly, so that his hatred for her was greater than the love with which he had loved her. And Amnon said to her, Get up and get out!

¹⁶But she said, No! This great evil of sending me away is worse than what you did to me. But he would not listen to her.

---

^rHeb. *very great*   ^sHeb. *it was marvellous,* or, *hidden in the eyes of Amnon*   ^tHeb. *thin*   ^uHeb. *morning by morning*   ^vOr, *paste*   ^wHeb. *humble me*   ^xHeb. *it ought not so to be done*   ^yHeb. *with great hatred greatly*

New American Standard

²⁹ So David gathered all the people and went to Rabbah, fought against it and captured it.

³⁰ Then he took the crown of their king from his head; and its weight *was* a talent of gold, and *in it was* a precious stone; and it was *placed* on David's head. And he brought out the spoil of the city in great amounts.

³¹ He also brought out the people who were in it, and set *them* under saws, sharp iron instruments, and iron axes, and made them pass through the brickkiln. And thus he did to all the cities of the sons of Ammon. Then David and all the people returned *to* Jerusalem.

Amnon and Tamar

13 NOW IT was after this that Absalom the son of David had a beautiful sister whose name was Tamar, and Amnon the son of David loved her.

² Amnon was so frustrated because of his sister Tamar that he made himself ill, for she was a virgin, and it seemed hard to Amnon to do anything to her.

³ But Amnon had a friend whose name was Jonadab, the son of Shimeah, David's brother; and Jonadab was a very shrewd man.

⁴ He said to him, "O son of the king, why are you so depressed morning after morning? Will you not tell me?" Then Amnon said to him, "I am in love with Tamar, the sister of my brother Absalom."

⁵ Jonadab then said to him, "Lie down on your bed and pretend to be ill; when your father comes to see you, say to him, 'Please let my sister Tamar come and give me *some* food to eat, and let her prepare the food in my sight, that I may see *it* and eat from her hand.' "

⁶ So Amnon lay down and pretended to be ill; when the king came to see him, Amnon said to the king, "Please let my sister Tamar come and make me a couple of cakes in my sight, that I may eat from her hand."

⁷ ¶ Then David sent to the house for Tamar, saying, "Go now to your brother Amnon's house, and prepare food for him."

⁸ So Tamar went to her brother Amnon's house, and he was lying down. And she took dough, kneaded *it,* made cakes in his sight, and baked the cakes.

⁹ She took the pan and dished *them* out before him, but he refused to eat. And Amnon said, "Have everyone go out from me." So everyone went out from him.

¹⁰ Then Amnon said to Tamar, "Bring the food into the bedroom, that I may eat from your hand." So Tamar took the cakes which she had made and brought them into the bedroom to her brother Amnon.

¹¹ When she brought *them* to him to eat, he took hold of her and said to her, "Come, lie with me, my sister."

¹² But she answered him, "No, my brother, do not violate me, for such a thing is not done in Israel; do not do this disgraceful thing!

¹³ "As for me, where could I get rid of my reproach? And as for you, you will be like one of the fools in Israel. Now therefore, please speak to the king, for he will not withhold me from you."

¹⁴ However, he would not listen to her; since he was stronger than she, he violated her and lay with her.

¹⁵ ¶ Then Amnon hated her with a very great hatred; for the hatred with which he hated her was greater than the love with which he had loved her. And Amnon said to her, "Get up, go away!"

¹⁶ But she said to him, "No, because this wrong in sending me away is greater than the other that you have done to me!" Yet he would not listen to her.

New International

²⁹So David mustered the entire army and went to Rabbah, and attacked and captured it. ³⁰He took the crown from the head of their king^h—its weight was a talentⁱ of gold, and it was set with precious stones—and it was placed on David's head. He took a great quantity of plunder from the city ³¹and brought out the people who were there, consigning them to labor with saws and with iron picks and axes, and he made them work at brickmaking.^j He did this to all the Ammonite towns. Then David and his entire army returned to Jerusalem.

Amnon and Tamar

13 IN THE course of time, Amnon son of David fell in love with Tamar, the beautiful sister of Absalom son of David.

²Amnon became frustrated to the point of illness on account of his sister Tamar, for she was a virgin, and it seemed impossible for him to do anything to her.

³Now Amnon had a friend named Jonadab son of Shimeah, David's brother. Jonadab was a very shrewd man. ⁴He asked Amnon, "Why do you, the king's son, look so haggard morning after morning? Won't you tell me?"

Amnon said to him, "I'm in love with Tamar, my brother Absalom's sister."

⁵"Go to bed and pretend to be ill," Jonadab said. "When your father comes to see you, say to him, 'I would like my sister Tamar to come and give me something to eat. Let her prepare the food in my sight so I may watch her and then eat it from her hand.' "

⁶So Amnon lay down and pretended to be ill. When the king came to see him, Amnon said to him, "I would like my sister Tamar to come and make some special bread in my sight, so I may eat from her hand."

⁷David sent word to Tamar at the palace: "Go to the house of your brother Amnon and prepare some food for him." ⁸So Tamar went to the house of her brother Amnon, who was lying down. She took some dough, kneaded it, made the bread in his sight and baked it. ⁹Then she took the pan and served him the bread, but he refused to eat.

"Send everyone out of here," Amnon said. So everyone left him. ¹⁰Then Amnon said to Tamar, "Bring the food here into my bedroom so I may eat from your hand." And Tamar took the bread she had prepared and brought it to her brother Amnon in his bedroom. ¹¹But when she took it to him to eat, he grabbed her and said, "Come to bed with me, my sister."

¹²"Don't, my brother!" she said to him. "Don't force me. Such a thing should not be done in Israel! Don't do this wicked thing. ¹³What about me? Where could I get rid of my disgrace? And what about you? You would be like one of the wicked fools in Israel. Please speak to the king; he will not keep me from being married to you." ¹⁴But he refused to listen to her, and since he was stronger than she, he raped her.

¹⁵Then Amnon hated her with intense hatred. In fact, he hated her more than he had loved her. Amnon said to her, "Get up and get out!"

¹⁶"No!" she said to him. "Sending me away would be a greater wrong than what you have already done to me."

---

^h30 Or *of Milcom* (that is, Molech)   ⁱ30 That is, about 75 pounds (about 34 kilograms)   ^j31 The meaning of the Hebrew for this clause is uncertain.

King James

17Then he called his servant that ministered unto him, and said, Put now this *woman* out from me, and bolt the door after her.

18And *she had* a garment of divers colours upon her: for with such robes were the king's daughters *that were* virgins apparelled. Then his servant brought her out, and bolted the door after her.

19 ¶ And Tamar put ashes on her head, and rent her garment of divers colours that *was* on her, and laid her hand on her head, and went on crying.

20And Absalom her brother said unto her, Hath zAmnon thy brother been with thee? but hold now thy peace, my sister: he *is* thy brother; aregard not this thing. So Tamar remained bdesolate in her brother Absalom's house.

21 ¶ But when king David heard of all these things, he was very wroth.

22And Absalom spake unto his brother Amnon neither good nor bad: for Absalom hated Amnon, because he had forced his sister Tamar.

Absalom kills Amnon

23 ¶ And it came to pass after two full years, that Absalom had sheepshearers in Baal-hazor, which *is* beside Ephraim: and Absalom invited all the king's sons.

24And Absalom came to the king, and said, Behold now, thy servant hath sheepshearers; let the king, I beseech thee, and his servants go with thy servant.

25And the king said to Absalom, Nay, my son, let us not all now go, lest we be chargeable unto thee. And he pressed him: howbeit he would not go, but blessed him.

26Then said Absalom, If not, I pray thee, let my brother Amnon go with us. And the king said unto him, Why should he go with thee?

27But Absalom pressed him, that he let Amnon and all the king's sons go with him.

28 ¶ Now Absalom had commanded his servants, saying, Mark ye now when Amnon's heart is merry with wine, and when I say unto you, Smite Amnon; then kill him, fear not: chave not I commanded you? be courageous, and be dvaliant.

29And the servants of Absalom did unto Amnon as Absalom had commanded. Then all the king's sons arose, and every man egat him up upon his mule, and fled.

30 ¶ And it came to pass, while they were in the way, that tidings came to David, saying, Absalom hath slain all the king's sons, and there is not one of them left.

31Then the king arose, and tare his garments, and lay on the earth; and all his servants stood by with their clothes rent.

32And Jonadab, the son of Shimeah David's brother, answered and said, Let not my lord suppose *that* they have slain all the young men the king's sons; for Amnon only is dead: for by the fappointment of Absalom this hath been gdetermined from the day that he forced his sister Tamar.

33Now therefore let not my lord the king take the thing to his heart, to think that all the king's sons are dead: for Amnon only is dead.

Absalom flees to Geshur

34But Absalom fled. And the young man that kept the watch lifted up his eyes, and looked, and, behold, there came much people by the way of the hill side behind him.

35And Jonadab said unto the king, Behold, the king's sons come: has thy servant said, so it is.

Amplified

17He called the servant who served him and said, Put this woman out of my presence now, and bolt the door after her!

18Now [Tamar] was wearing a long robe with sleeves *and* of various colors, for in such robes were the king's virgin daughters clad of old. Then Amnon's servant brought her out and bolted the door after her.

19And [she] put ashes on her head and tore the long, sleeved robe which she wore, and she laid her hand on her head and went away shrieking *and* wailing.

20And Absalom her brother said to her, Has your brother Amnon been with you? Be quiet now, my sister. He is your brother; take not this matter to heart. So Tamar dwelt in her brother Absalom's house, a desolate woman.

21But when King David heard of all these things, he was very angry.

22And Absalom spoke to Amnon neither good nor bad; for Absalom hated Amnon because he had humbled his sister Tamar.

23After two full years Absalom had sheepshearers at Baal-hazor near Ephraim, and Absalom invited all the king's sons.

24Absalom came to the king and said, Behold, your servant has sheepshearers; I pray you, let the king and his servants go with your servant.

25And the king said to Absalom, No, my son, let us not all go, lest we be burdensome to you. Absalom urged David; still he would not go, but he blessed him.

26Then said Absalom, If not, I pray you, let my brother Amnon go with us. And the king said to him, Why should he go with you?

27But Absalom urged him, and he let Amnon and all the king's sons go with him.

28Now Absalom commanded his servants, Notice now, when Amnon's heart is merry with wine and when I say to you, Strike Amnon, then kill him. Fear not; have I not commanded you? Be courageous and brave.

29And the servants of Absalom did to Amnon as Absalom had commanded. Then all the king's sons arose and every man mounted his mule and fled.

30While they were on the way, the word came to David, Absalom has killed all the king's sons, and not one of them is left.

31Then the king arose and tore his garments and lay on the floor; and all his servants standing by tore their clothes.

32But Jonadab son of Shimeah, David's brother, said, Let not my lord suppose they have killed all the king's sons; for Amnon only is dead. This purpose has shown itself on Absalom's determined mouth ever since the day Amnon humiliated his sister Tamar.

33So let not my lord the king take the thing to heart and think all the king's sons are dead; for Amnon only is dead.

34But Absalom fled. And the young man who kept the watch looked up, and behold, many people were coming by the way of the hillside behind him.

35And Jonadab said to the king, See, the king's sons are coming. It is as your servant said.

---

zHeb. *Aminon*   aHeb. *set not thine heart*   bHeb. *and desolate*   cOr, *will you not, since I have commanded you?*   dHeb. *sons of valour*   eHeb. *rode*   fHeb. *mouth*   gOr, *settled*   hHeb. *according to the word of thy servant*

New American Standard

17 Then he called his young man who attended him and said, "Now throw this woman out of my *presence,* and lock the door behind her."

18 Now she had on a long-sleeved garment; for in this manner the virgin daughters of the king dressed themselves in robes. Then his attendant took her out and locked the door behind her.

19 Tamar put ashes on her head and tore her long-sleeved garment which *was* on her; and she put her hand on her head and went away, crying aloud as she went.

20 ¶ Then Absalom her brother said to her, "Has Amnon your brother been with you? But now keep silent, my sister, he is your brother; do not take this matter to heart." So Tamar remained and was desolate in her brother Absalom's house.

21 Now when King David heard of all these matters, he was very angry.

22 But Absalom did not speak to Amnon either good or bad; for Absalom hated Amnon because he had violated his sister Tamar.

23 ¶ Now it came about after two full years that Absalom had sheepshearers in Baal-hazor, which is near Ephraim, and Absalom invited all the king's sons.

Absalom Avenges Tamar

24 Absalom came to the king and said, "Behold now, your servant has sheepshearers; please let the king and his servants go with your servant."

25 But the king said to Absalom, "No, my son, we should not all go, for we will be burdensome to you." Although he urged him, he would not go, but blessed him.

26 Then Absalom said, "If not, please let my brother Amnon go with us." And the king said to him, "Why should he go with you?"

27 But when Absalom urged him, he let Amnon and all the king's sons go with him.

28 ¶ Absalom commanded his servants, saying, "See now, when Amnon's heart is merry with wine, and when I say to you, 'Strike Amnon,' then put him to death. Do not fear; have not I myself commanded you? Be courageous and be valiant."

29 The servants of Absalom did to Amnon just as Absalom had commanded. Then all the king's sons arose and each mounted his mule and fled.

30 ¶ Now it was while they were on the way that the report came to David, saying, "Absalom has struck down all the king's sons, and not one of them is left."

31 Then the king arose, tore his clothes and lay on the ground; and all his servants were standing by with clothes torn.

32 Jonadab, the son of Shimeah, David's brother, responded, "Do not let my lord suppose they have put to death all the young men, the king's sons, for Amnon alone is dead; because by the intent of Absalom this has been determined since the day that he violated his sister Tamar.

33 "Now therefore, do not let my lord the king take the report to heart, namely, 'all the king's sons are dead,' for only Amnon is dead."

34 ¶ Now Absalom had fled. And the young man who was the watchman raised his eyes and looked, and behold, many people were coming from the road behind him by the side of the mountain.

35 Jonadab said to the king, "Behold, the king's sons have come; according to your servant's word, so it happened."

New International

But he refused to listen to her. 17He called his personal servant and said, "Get this woman out of here and bolt the door after her." 18So his servant put her out and bolted the door after her. She was wearing a richly ornamented[k] robe, for this was the kind of garment the virgin daughters of the king wore. 19Tamar put ashes on her head and tore the ornamented[l] robe she was wearing. She put her hand on her head and went away, weeping aloud as she went.

20Her brother Absalom said to her, "Has that Amnon, your brother, been with you? Be quiet now, my sister; he is your brother. Don't take this thing to heart." And Tamar lived in her brother Absalom's house, a desolate woman.

21When King David heard all this, he was furious. 22Absalom never said a word to Amnon, either good or bad; he hated Amnon because he had disgraced his sister Tamar.

Absalom Kills Amnon

23Two years later, when Absalom's sheepshearers were at Baal Hazor near the border of Ephraim, he invited all the king's sons to come there. 24Absalom went to the king and said, "Your servant has had shearers come. Will the king and his officials please join me?"

25"No, my son," the king replied. "All of us should not go; we would only be a burden to you." Although Absalom urged him, he still refused to go, but gave him his blessing.

26Then Absalom said, "If not, please let my brother Amnon come with us."

The king asked him, "Why should he go with you?" 27But Absalom urged him, so he sent with him Amnon and the rest of the king's sons.

28Absalom ordered his men, "Listen! When Amnon is in high spirits from drinking wine and I say to you, 'Strike Amnon down,' then kill him. Don't be afraid. Have not I given you this order? Be strong and brave." 29So Absalom's men did to Amnon what Absalom had ordered. Then all the king's sons got up, mounted their mules and fled.

30While they were on their way, the report came to David: "Absalom has struck down all the king's sons; not one of them is left." 31The king stood up, tore his clothes and lay down on the ground; and all his servants stood by with their clothes torn.

32But Jonadab son of Shimeah, David's brother, said, "My lord should not think that they killed all the princes; only Amnon is dead. This has been Absalom's expressed intention ever since the day Amnon raped his sister Tamar. 33My lord the king should not be concerned about the report that all the king's sons are dead. Only Amnon is dead."

34Meanwhile, Absalom had fled.

Now the man standing watch looked up and saw many people on the road west of him, coming down the side of the hill. The watchman went and told the king, "I see men in the direction of Horonaim, on the side of the hill."[m]

35Jonadab said to the king, "See, the king's sons are here; it has happened just as your servant said."

---

k 18 The meaning of the Hebrew for this phrase is uncertain.
l 19 The meaning of the Hebrew for this word is uncertain.
m 34 Septuagint; Hebrew does not have this sentence.

King James

³⁶And it came to pass, as soon as he had made an end of speaking, that, behold, the king's sons came, and lifted up their voice and wept: and the king also and all his servants wept ⁱvery sore.

³⁷ ¶ But Absalom fled, and went to Talmai, the son of ^jAmmihud, king of Geshur. And *David* mourned for his son every day.

³⁸So Absalom fled, and went to Geshur, and was there three years.

³⁹And *the soul of* king David ^klonged to go forth unto Absalom: for he was comforted concerning Amnon, seeing he was dead.

Absalom's return

14 NOW JOAB the son of Zeruiah perceived that the king's heart *was* toward Absalom.

²And Joab sent to Tekoah, and fetched thence a wise woman, and said unto her, I pray thee, feign thyself to be a mourner, and put on now mourning apparel, and anoint not thyself with oil, but be as a woman that had a long time mourned for the dead:

³And come to the king, and speak on this manner unto him. So Joab put the words in her mouth.

⁴ ¶ And when the woman of Tekoah spake to the king, she fell on her face to the ground, and did obeisance, and said, ^lHelp, O king.

⁵And the king said unto her, What aileth thee? And she answered, I *am* indeed a widow woman, and mine husband is dead.

⁶And thy handmaid had two sons, and they two strove together in the field, and *there was* ^mnone to part them, but the one smote the other, and slew him.

⁷And, behold, the whole family is risen against thine handmaid, and they said, Deliver him that smote his brother, that we may kill him, for the life of his brother whom he slew; and we will destroy the heir also: and so they shall quench my coal which is left, and shall not leave to my husband *neither* name nor remainder ⁿupon the earth.

⁸And the king said unto the woman, Go to thine house, and I will give charge concerning thee.

⁹And the woman of Tekoah said unto the king, My lord, O king, the iniquity *be* on me, and on my father's house: and the king and his throne *be* guiltless.

¹⁰And the king said, Whosoever saith *aught* unto thee, bring him to me, and he shall not touch thee any more.

¹¹Then said she, I pray thee, let the king remember the LORD thy God, ^othat thou wouldest not suffer the revengers of blood to destroy any more, lest they destroy my son. And he said, *As* the LORD liveth, there shall not one hair of thy son fall to the earth.

¹²Then the woman said, Let thine handmaid, I pray thee, speak *one* word unto my lord the king. And he said, Say on.

¹³And the woman said, Wherefore then hast thou thought such a thing against the people of God? for the king doth speak this thing as one which is faulty, in that the king doth not fetch home again his banished.

¹⁴For we must needs die, and *are* as water spilt on the ground, which cannot be gathered up again; ^pneither doth God respect *any* person: yet doth he devise means, that his banished be not expelled from him.

¹⁵Now therefore that I am come to speak of this thing unto my lord the king, *it is* because the people have made me afraid: and thy handmaid said, I will now speak unto the king; it may be that the king will perform the request of his handmaid.

Amplified

³⁶And as he finished speaking, the king's sons came and lifted up their voices and wept; and the king also and all his servants wept very bitterly.

³⁷But Absalom fled and went to [his mother's father] Talmai son of Ammihud, king of Geshur. And David mourned for his son [Amnon] every day.

³⁸So Absalom fled to Geshur and was there three years.

³⁹And the spirit of King David longed to go forth to Absalom, for he was comforted about Amnon, seeing that he was dead.

14 NOW JOAB son of Zeruiah knew that the king's heart was toward Absalom.

²And Joab sent to Tekoah and brought from there a wise woman and said to her, Pretend to be a mourner; put on mourning apparel, do not anoint yourself with oil, but act like a woman who has long been mourning for the dead.

³And go to the king and speak thus to him. And Joab told her what to say.

⁴When the woman of Tekoah spoke to the king, she fell on her face to the ground and did obeisance, and said, Help, O king!

⁵The king asked her, What troubles you? She said, I am a widow; my husband is dead.

⁶And your handmaid had two sons, and they quarreled with one another in the field. There was no one to separate them, and one struck the other and killed him.

⁷And behold, our whole family has risen against your handmaid, and they say, Deliver him who slew his brother, that we may kill him for the life of his brother whom he slew; and so they would destroy the heir also. And so quenching my coal which is left, they would leave to my husband neither name nor remnant upon the earth.

⁸David said to the woman, Go home, and I will give orders concerning you.

⁹And the woman of Tekoah said to the king, My lord, O king, let the guilt be on me and on my father's house; let the king and his throne be guiltless.

¹⁰The king said, If anyone says anything to you, bring him to me, and he shall not touch you again.

¹¹Then she said, I pray you, let the king remember the Lord your God, that the avenger of blood destroy not any more, lest they destroy my son. And David said, As the Lord lives, there shall not one hair of your son fall to the earth.

¹²Then the woman said, Let your handmaid, I pray you, speak one word to my lord the king. He said, Say on.

¹³[She] said, Why then have you planned such a thing against God's people? For in speaking this word the king is like one who is guilty, in that [he] does not bring home his banished one.

¹⁴We must all die; we are like water spilled on the ground, which cannot be gathered up again. And God does not take away life, but devises means that he who is banished may not be an utter outcast from Him.

¹⁵And now I have come to speak of this thing to my lord the king because the people have made me afraid. And I thought, I will speak to the king; it may be that he will perform the request of his servant.

ⁱHeb. *with a great weeping greatly*   ^jOr, *Ammihur*   ^kOr, *was consumed*   ^lHeb. *Save*   ^mHeb. *no deliverer between them*   ⁿHeb. *upon the face of the earth*   ^oHeb. *that the revenger of blood do not multiply to destroy*   ^pOr, *because God hath not taken away* his *life, he hath also devised means*

New American Standard

36 As soon as he had finished speaking, behold, the king's sons came and lifted their voices and wept; and also the king and all his servants wept very bitterly.

37 ¶ Now Absalom fled and went to Talmai the son of Ammihud, the king of Geshur. And *David* mourned for his son every day.

38 So Absalom had fled and gone to Geshur, and was there three years.

39 *The heart of* King David longed to go out to Absalom; for he was comforted concerning Amnon, since he was dead.

The Woman of Tekoa

14 NOW JOAB the son of Zeruiah perceived that the king's heart *was inclined* toward Absalom.

2 So Joab sent to Tekoa and brought a wise woman from there and said to her, "Please pretend to be a mourner, and put on mourning garments now, and do not anoint yourself with oil, but be like a woman who has been mourning for the dead many days;

3 then go to the king and speak to him in this manner." So Joab put the words in her mouth.

4 ¶ Now when the woman of Tekoa [1]spoke to the king, she fell on her face to the ground and prostrated herself and said, "Help, O king."

5 The king said to her, "What is your trouble?" And she answered, "Truly I am a widow, for my husband is dead.

6 "Your maidservant had two sons, but the two of them struggled together in the field, and there was no [m]one to separate them, so one struck the other and killed him.

7 "Now behold, the whole family has risen against your maidservant, and they say, 'Hand over the one who struck his brother, that we may put him to death for the life of his brother whom he killed, and destroy the heir also.' Thus they will extinguish my coal which is left, so as to leave my husband neither name nor remnant on the face of the earth."

8 ¶ Then the king said to the woman, "Go to your house, and I will give orders concerning you."

9 The woman of Tekoa said to the king, "O my lord, the king, the iniquity is on me and my father's house, but the king and his throne are guiltless."

10 So the king said, "Whoever speaks to you, bring him to me, and he will not touch you anymore."

11 Then she said, "Please let the king remember the LORD your God, *so that* the avenger of blood will not continue to destroy, otherwise they will destroy my son." And he said, "As the LORD lives, not one hair of your son shall fall to the ground."

12 ¶ Then the woman said, "Please let your maidservant speak a word to my lord the king." And he said, "Speak."

13 The woman said, "Why then have you planned such a thing against the people of God? For in speaking this word the king is as one who is guilty, *in that* the king does not bring back his banished one.

14 "For we will surely die and are like water spilled on the ground which cannot be gathered up again. Yet God does not take away life, but plans ways so that the banished one will not be cast out from him.

15 "Now the reason I have come to speak this word to my lord the king is that the people have made me afraid; so your maidservant said, 'Let me now speak to the king, perhaps the king will perform the request of his maidservant.

New International

36 As he finished speaking, the king's sons came in, wailing loudly. The king, too, and all his servants wept very bitterly.

37 Absalom fled and went to Talmai son of Ammihud, the king of Geshur. But King David mourned for his son every day.

38 After Absalom fled and went to Geshur, he stayed there three years. 39 And the spirit of the king[n] longed to go to Absalom, for he was consoled concerning Amnon's death.

Absalom Returns to Jerusalem

14 JOAB SON of Zeruiah knew that the king's heart longed for Absalom. 2 So Joab sent someone to Tekoa and had a wise woman brought from there. He said to her, "Pretend you are in mourning. Dress in mourning clothes, and don't use any cosmetic lotions. Act like a woman who has spent many days grieving for the dead. 3 Then go to the king and speak these words to him." And Joab put the words in her mouth.

4 When the woman from Tekoa went[o] to the king, she fell with her face to the ground to pay him honor, and she said, "Help me, O king!"

5 The king asked her, "What is troubling you?"

She said, "I am indeed a widow; my husband is dead. 6 I your servant had two sons. They got into a fight with each other in the field, and no one was there to separate them. One struck the other and killed him. 7 Now the whole clan has risen up against your servant; they say, 'Hand over the one who struck his brother down, so that we may put him to death for the life of his brother whom he killed; then we will get rid of the heir as well.' They would put out the only burning coal I have left, leaving my husband neither name nor descendant on the face of the earth."

8 The king said to the woman, "Go home, and I will issue an order in your behalf."

9 But the woman from Tekoa said to him, "My lord the king, let the blame rest on me and on my father's family, and let the king and his throne be without guilt."

10 The king replied, "If anyone says anything to you, bring him to me, and he will not bother you again."

11 She said, "Then let the king invoke the LORD his God to prevent the avenger of blood from adding to the destruction, so that my son will not be destroyed."

"As surely as the LORD lives," he said, "not one hair of your son's head will fall to the ground."

12 Then the woman said, "Let your servant speak a word to my lord the king."

"Speak," he replied.

13 The woman said, "Why then have you devised a thing like this against the people of God? When the king says this, does he not convict himself, for the king has not brought back his banished son? 14 Like water spilled on the ground, which cannot be recovered, so we must die. But God does not take away life; instead, he devises ways so that a banished person may not remain estranged from him.

15 "And now I have come to say this to my lord the king because the people have made me afraid. Your servant thought, 'I will speak to the king; perhaps he will do what

---

[1]Many mss and ancient versions read *came between*   [m]Lit *deliverer*

[n]39 Dead Sea Scrolls and some Septuagint manuscripts; Masoretic Text *But the spirit of David the king*   [o]4 Many Hebrew manuscripts, Septuagint, Vulgate and Syriac; most Hebrew manuscripts *spoke*

King James

16For the king will hear, to deliver his handmaid out of the hand of the man *that would* destroy me and my son together out of the inheritance of God.

17Then thine handmaid said, The word of my lord the king shall now be qcomfortable: for as an angel of God, so *is* my lord the king rto discern good and bad: therefore the LORD thy God will be with thee.

18Then the king answered and said unto the woman, Hide not from me, I pray thee, the thing that I shall ask thee. And the woman said, Let my lord the king now speak.

19And the king said, *Is not* the hand of Joab with thee in all this? And the woman answered and said, *As* thy soul liveth, my lord the king, none can turn to the right hand or to the left from aught that my lord the king hath spoken: for thy servant Joab, he bade me, and he put all these words in the mouth of thine handmaid:

20To fetch about this form of speech hath thy servant Joab done this thing: and my lord *is* wise, according to the wisdom of an angel of God, to know all *things* that *are* in the earth.

21 ¶ And the king said unto Joab, Behold now, I have done this thing: go therefore, bring the young man Absalom again.

22And Joab fell to the ground on his face, and bowed himself, and sthanked the king: and Joab said, Today thy servant knoweth that I have found grace in thy sight, my lord, O king, in that the king hath fulfilled the request of this servant.

23So Joab arose and went to Geshur, and brought Absalom to Jerusalem.

24And the king said, Let him turn to his own house, and let him not see my face. So Absalom returned to his own house, and saw not the king's face.

25 ¶ uBut in all Israel there was none to be so much praised as Absalom for his beauty: from the sole of his foot even to the crown of his head there was no blemish in him.

26And when he polled his head, (for it was at every year's end that he polled *it:* because *the hair* was heavy on him, therefore he polled it:) he weighed the hair of his head at two hundred shekels after the king's weight.

27And unto Absalom there were born three sons, and one daughter, whose name *was* Tamar: she was a woman of a fair countenance.

28 ¶ So Absalom dwelt two full years in Jerusalem, and saw not the king's face.

29Therefore Absalom sent for Joab, to have sent him to the king; but he would not come to him: and when he sent again the second time, he would not come.

30Therefore he said unto his servants, See, Joab's field is vnear mine, and he hath barley there; go and set it on fire. And Absalom's servants set the field on fire.

31Then Joab arose, and came to Absalom unto *his* house, and said unto him, Wherefore have thy servants set my field on fire?

32And Absalom answered Joab, Behold, I sent unto thee, saying, Come hither, that I may send thee to the king, to say, Wherefore am I come from Geshur? *it had been* good for me *to have been* there still: now therefore let me see the king's face; and if there be *any* iniquity in me, let him kill me.

33So Joab came to the king, and told him: and when he had called for Absalom, he came to the king, and bowed himself on his face to the ground before the king: and the king kissed Absalom.

Amplified

16For the king will hear to deliver his handmaid from the hand of the man who would destroy me and my son together from [Israel] the inheritance of God.

17And the woman said, The word of my lord the king will now give me rest *and* security, for as an angel of God is my lord the king to hear *and* discern good and evil. May the Lord your God be with you!

18Then the king said to the woman, Hide not from me anything I ask you. And the woman said, Let my lord the king speak.

19The king said, Is the hand of Joab with you in all this? And the woman answered, As your soul lives, my lord the king, none can turn to the right hand or to the left from anything my lord the king has said. It was your servant Joab who directed me; he put all these words in my mouth.

20In order to change the course of matters [between Absalom and his father] your servant Joab did this. But my lord has wisdom like the wisdom of the angel of God—to know all things that are on the earth.

21Then the king said to Joab, Behold now, I grant this; go, bring back the young man Absalom.

22And Joab fell to the ground on his face and did obeisance and thanked the king. And Joab said, Today your servant knows that I have found favor in your sight, my lord, O king, in that the king has performed the request of his servant.

23So Joab arose, went to Geshur, and brought Absalom to Jerusalem.

24And the king said, Let him go to his own house, and let him not see my face. So Absalom went to his own house and did not see the king's face.

25But in all Israel there was none so much to be praised for his beauty as Absalom; from the sole of his foot to the crown of his head there was no blemish in him.

26And when he cut the hair of his head, he weighed it—for at each year's end he cut it, because its weight was a burden to him—and it weighed 200 shekels by the king's weight.

27There were born to Absalom three sons and one daughter whose name was Tamar; she was a beautiful woman.

28Absalom dwelt two full years in Jerusalem and did not see the king's face.

29So Absalom sent for Joab to send him to the king, but he would not come to him; even when he sent again the second time, he would not come.

30Therefore Absalom said to his servants, See, Joab's field is near mine, and he has barley there; go and set it on fire. So Absalom's servants set the field afire.

31Then Joab arose and went to Absalom at his house and said to him, Why have your servants set my field on fire?

32Absalom answered Joab, I sent to you, saying, Come here, that I may send you to the king to ask, Why have I come from Geshur? It would be better for me to be there still. Now therefore [Joab], let me see the king, and if there is iniquity *and* guilt in me, let him kill me.

33So Joab came to the king and told him. And when David had called for Absalom, he came to him and bowed himself on his face to the ground before the king; and [David] kissed Absalom.

---

qHeb. *for rest*   rHeb. *to hear*   sHeb. *blessed*   tOr, *thy*
uHeb. *And as Absalom there was not a beautiful man in all Israel to praise greatly*   vHeb. *near my place*

New American Standard

16 'For the king will hear and deliver his maidservant from the hand of the man who would destroy both me and my son from the inheritance of God.'

17"Then your maidservant said, 'Please let the word of my lord the king be comforting, for as the angel of God, so is my lord the king to discern good and evil. And may the LORD your God be with you.' "

18 ¶ Then the king answered and said to the woman, "Please do not hide anything from me that I am about to ask you." And the woman said, "Let my lord the king please speak."

19 So the king said, "Is the hand of Joab with you in all this?" And the woman replied, "As your soul lives, my lord the king, no one can turn to the right or to the left from anything that my lord the king has spoken. Indeed, it was your servant Joab who commanded me, and it was he who put all these words in the mouth of your maidservant;

20 in order to change the appearance of things your servant Joab has done this thing. But my lord is wise, like the wisdom of the angel of God, to know all that is in the earth."

Absalom Is Recalled

21 ¶ Then the king said to Joab, "Behold now, I will surely do this thing; go therefore, bring back the young man Absalom."

22 Joab fell on his face to the ground, prostrated himself and blessed the king; then Joab said, "Today your servant knows that I have found favor in your sight, O my lord, the king, in that the king has performed the request of his servant."

23 So Joab arose and went to Geshur and brought Absalom to Jerusalem.

24 However the king said, "Let him turn to his own house, and let him not see my face." So Absalom turned to his own house and did not see the king's face.

25 ¶ Now in all Israel was no one as handsome as Absalom, so highly praised; from the sole of his foot to the crown of his head there was no defect in him.

26 When he cut the hair of his head (and it was at the end of every year that he cut it, for it was heavy on him so he cut it), he weighed the hair of his head at 200 shekels by the king's weight.

27 To Absalom there were born three sons, and one daughter whose name was Tamar; she was a woman of beautiful appearance.

28 ¶ Now Absalom lived two full years in Jerusalem, and did not see the king's face.

29 Then Absalom sent for Joab, to send him to the king, but he would not come to him. So he sent again a second time, but he would not come.

30 Therefore he said to his servants, "See, Joab's [n]field is next to mine, and he has barley there; go and set it on fire." So Absalom's servants set the field on fire.

31 Then Joab arose, came to Absalom at his house and said to him, "Why have your servants set my [n]field on fire?"

32 Absalom answered Joab, "Behold, I sent for you, saying, 'Come here, that I may send you to the king, to say, "Why have I come from Geshur? It would be better for me still to be there." ' Now therefore, let me see the king's face, and if there is iniquity in me, let him put me to death."

33 So when Joab came to the king and told him, he called for Absalom. Thus he came to the king and prostrated himself on his face to the ground before the king, and the king kissed Absalom.

New International

his servant asks. 16Perhaps the king will agree to deliver his servant from the hand of the man who is trying to cut off both me and my son from the inheritance God gave us.'

17"And now your servant says, 'May the word of my lord the king bring me rest, for my lord the king is like an angel of God in discerning good and evil. May the LORD your God be with you.' "

18Then the king said to the woman, "Do not keep from me the answer to what I am going to ask you."

"Let my lord the king speak," the woman said.

19The king asked, "Isn't the hand of Joab with you in all this?"

The woman answered, "As surely as you live, my lord the king, no one can turn to the right or to the left from anything my lord the king says. Yes, it was your servant Joab who instructed me to do this and who put all these words into the mouth of your servant. 20Your servant Joab did this to change the present situation. My lord has wisdom like that of an angel of God—he knows everything that happens in the land."

21The king said to Joab, "Very well, I will do it. Go, bring back the young man Absalom."

22Joab fell with his face to the ground to pay him honor, and he blessed the king. Joab said, "Today your servant knows that he has found favor in your eyes, my lord the king, because the king has granted his servant's request."

23Then Joab went to Geshur and brought Absalom back to Jerusalem. 24But the king said, "He must go to his own house; he must not see my face." So Absalom went to his own house and did not see the face of the king.

25In all Israel there was not a man so highly praised for his handsome appearance as Absalom. From the top of his head to the sole of his foot there was no blemish in him. 26Whenever he cut the hair of his head—he used to cut his hair from time to time when it became too heavy for him—he would weigh it, and its weight was two hundred shekels[p] by the royal standard.

27Three sons and a daughter were born to Absalom. The daughter's name was Tamar, and she became a beautiful woman.

28Absalom lived two years in Jerusalem without seeing the king's face. 29Then Absalom sent for Joab in order to send him to the king, but Joab refused to come to him. So he sent a second time, but he refused to come. 30Then he said to his servants, "Look, Joab's field is next to mine, and he has barley there. Go and set it on fire." So Absalom's servants set the field on fire.

31Then Joab did go to Absalom's house and he said to him, "Why have your servants set my field on fire?"

32Absalom said to Joab, "Look, I sent word to you and said, 'Come here so I can send you to the king to ask, "Why have I come from Geshur? It would be better for me if I were still there!" ' Now then, I want to see the king's face, and if I am guilty of anything, let him put me to death."

33So Joab went to the king and told him this. Then the king summoned Absalom, and he came in and bowed down with his face to the ground before the king. And the king kissed Absalom.

---

[n] Lit portion

[p] 26 That is, about 5 pounds (about 2.3 kilograms)

King James

Absalom's revolt against David

15 AND IT came to pass after this, that Absalom prepared him chariots and horses, and fifty men to run before him.

2 And Absalom rose up early, and stood beside the way of the gate: and it was *so,* that when any man that had a controversy *w*came to the king for judgment, then Absalom called unto him, and said, Of what city *art* thou? And he said, Thy servant *is* of one of the tribes of Israel.

3 And Absalom said unto him, See, thy matters *are* good and right; but *x*there is no man *deputed* of the king to hear thee.

4 Absalom said moreover, Oh that I were made judge in the land, that every man which hath any suit or cause might come unto me, and I would do him justice!

5 And it was *so,* that when any man came nigh *to him* to do him obeisance, he put forth his hand, and took him, and kissed him.

6 And on this manner did Absalom to all Israel that came to the king for judgment: so Absalom stole the hearts of the men of Israel.

7 ¶ And it came to pass after forty years, that Absalom said unto the king, I pray thee, let me go and pay my vow, which I have vowed unto the LORD, in Hebron.

8 For thy servant vowed a vow while I abode at Geshur in Syria, saying, If the LORD shall bring me again indeed to Jerusalem, then I will serve the LORD.

9 And the king said unto him, Go in peace. So he arose, and went to Hebron.

10 ¶ But Absalom sent spies throughout all the tribes of Israel, saying, As soon as ye hear the sound of the trumpet, then ye shall say, Absalom reigneth in Hebron.

11 And with Absalom went two hundred men out of Jerusalem, *that were* called; and they went in their simplicity, and they knew not any thing.

12 And Absalom sent for Ahithophel the Gilonite, David's counsellor, from his city, *even* from Giloh, while he offered sacrifices. And the conspiracy was strong; for the people increased continually with Absalom.

David and his household flee

13 ¶ And there came a messenger to David, saying, The hearts of the men of Israel are after Absalom.

14 And David said unto all his servants that *were* with him at Jerusalem, Arise, and let us flee; for we shall not *else* escape from Absalom: make speed to depart, lest he overtake us suddenly, and *y*bring evil upon us, and smite the city with the edge of the sword.

15 And the king's servants said unto the king, Behold, thy servants *are ready to do* whatsoever my lord the king shall *z*appoint.

16 And the king went forth, and all his household *a*after him. And the king left ten women, *which were* concubines, to keep the house.

17 And the king went forth, and all the people after him, and tarried in a place that was far off.

18 And all his servants passed on beside him; and all the Cherethites, and all the Pelethites, and all the Gittites, six hundred men which came after him from Gath, passed on before the king.

19 ¶ Then said the king to Ittai the Gittite, Wherefore goest thou also with us? return to thy place, and abide with the king: for thou *art* a stranger, and also an exile.

20 Whereas thou camest *but* yesterday, should I this day *b*make thee go up and down with us? seeing I go whither I may, return thou, and take back thy brethren: mercy and truth *be* with thee.

21 And Ittai answered the king, and said, As the LORD liveth, and *as* my lord the king liveth, surely in what place my lord the king shall be, whether in death or life, even there also will thy servant be.

Amplified

15 AFTER THIS, Absalom got a chariot and horses, and fifty men to run before him.

2 And [he] rose up early and stood beside the gateway; and when any man who had a controversy came to the king for judgment, Absalom called to him, Of what city are you? And he would say, Your servant is of such and such a tribe of Israel.

3 Absalom would say to him, Your claims are good and right, but there is no man appointed as the king's agent to hear you.

4 Absalom added, Oh, that I were judge in the land! Then every man with any suit or cause might come to me and I would do him justice!

5 And whenever a man came near to do obeisance to him, he would put out his hand, take hold of him, and kiss him.

6 Thus Absalom did to all Israel who came to the king for judgment. So Absalom stole the hearts of the men of Israel.

7 And after [four] years, Absalom said to the king, I pray you, let me go to Hebron [his birthplace] and pay my vow to the Lord.

8 For your servant vowed while I dwelt at Geshur in Syria, If the Lord will bring me again to Jerusalem, then I will serve the Lord [by offering a sacrifice].

9 And the king said to him, Go in peace. So he arose and went to Hebron.

10 But Absalom sent secret messengers throughout all the tribes of Israel, saying, As soon as you hear the sound of the trumpet, then say, Absalom is king at Hebron.

11 With Absalom went 200 men from Jerusalem, who were invited [as guests to his sacrificial feast]; and they went in their simplicity, and they knew not a thing.

12 And while Absalom was offering the sacrifices, he sent for Ahithophel the Gilonite, David's counselor, from his city Giloh. And the conspiracy was strong; the people with Absalom increased continually.

13 And there came a messenger to David, saying, The hearts of the men of Israel have gone after Absalom.

14 David said to all his servants who were with him at Jerusalem, Arise, and let us flee, or else none of us will escape from Absalom. Make haste to depart, lest he overtake us suddenly and bring evil upon us and smite the city with the sword.

15 And the king's servants said to the king, Behold, your servants are ready to do whatever my lord the king says.

16 So the king and all his household after him went forth. But he left ten women who were concubines to keep the house. [II Sam. 12:11; 20:3.]

17 The king went forth with all the people after him, and halted at the last house.

18 All David's servants passed on beside him, along with [his bodyguards] all the Cherethites, Pelethites; also all the Gittites, 600 men who came after him from Gath, passed on before the king.

19 The king said to Ittai the Gittite, Why do you go with us also? Return to your place and remain with the king [Absalom], for you are a foreigner and an exile.

20 Since you came only yesterday, should I make you go up and down with us? Since I must go where I may, you return, and take back your brethren with you. May lovingkindness and faithfulness be with you.

21 But Ittai answered the king, As the Lord lives, and as my lord the king lives, wherever my lord the king shall be, whether for death or life, even there also will your servant be.

---

w Heb. *to come*   *x* Or, *none will hear thee from the king*
downward   *y* Heb. *thrust*   *z* Heb. *choose*   *a* Heb. *at his*
feet   *b* Heb. *make thee wander in going*

New American Standard

Absalom's Conspiracy

15 NOW IT came about after this that Absalom provided for himself a chariot and horses and fifty men as runners before him. 2 Absalom used to rise early and stand beside the way to the gate; and when any man had a suit to come to the king for judgment, Absalom would call to him and say, "From what city are you?" And he would say, "Your servant is from one of the tribes of Israel." 3 Then Absalom would say to him, "See, your claims are good and right, but no man listens to you on the part of the king." 4 Moreover, Absalom would say, "Oh that one would appoint me judge in the land, then every man who has any suit or cause could come to me and I would give him justice." 5 And when a man came near to prostrate himself before him, he would put out his hand and take hold of him and kiss him. 6 In this manner Absalom dealt with all Israel who came to the king for judgment; so Absalom stole away the hearts of the men of Israel.

7 ¶ Now it came about at the end of *o*forty years that Absalom said to the king, "Please let me go and pay my vow which I have vowed to the LORD, in Hebron. 8"For your servant vowed a vow while I was living at Geshur in Aram, saying, 'If the LORD shall indeed bring me back to Jerusalem, then I will serve the LORD.' " 9 The king said to him, "Go in peace." So he arose and went to Hebron. 10 But Absalom sent spies throughout all the tribes of Israel, saying, "As soon as you hear the sound of the trumpet, then you shall say, 'Absalom is king in Hebron.' " 11 Then two hundred men went with Absalom from Jerusalem, who were invited and went innocently, and they did not know anything. 12 And Absalom sent for Ahithophel the Gilonite, David's counselor, from his city Giloh, while he was offering the sacrifices. And the conspiracy was strong, for the people increased continually with Absalom.

David Flees Jerusalem

13 ¶ Then a messenger came to David, saying, "The hearts of the men of Israel are with Absalom." 14 David said to all his servants who were with him at Jerusalem, "Arise and let us flee, for *otherwise* none of us will escape from Absalom. Go in haste, or he will overtake us quickly and bring down calamity on us and strike the city with the edge of the sword." 15 Then the king's servants said to the king, "Behold, your servants *are ready to do* whatever my lord the king chooses." 16 So the king went out and all his household with him. But the king left ten concubines to keep the house. 17 The king went out and all the people with him, and they stopped at the last house. 18 Now all his servants passed on beside him, all the Cherethites, all the Pelethites and all the Gittites, six hundred men who had come with him from Gath, passed on before the king.

19 ¶ Then the king said to Ittai the Gittite, "Why will you also go with us? Return and remain with the king, for you are a foreigner and also an exile; *return* to your own place. 20"You came *only* yesterday, and shall I today make you wander with us, while I go where I will? Return and take back your brothers; mercy and truth be with you." 21 But Ittai answered the king and said, "As the LORD lives, and as my lord the king lives, surely wherever my lord the king may be, whether for death or for life, there also your servant will be."

New International

Absalom's Conspiracy

15 IN THE course of time, Absalom provided himself with a chariot and horses and with fifty men to run ahead of him. 2 He would get up early and stand by the side of the road leading to the city gate. Whenever anyone came with a complaint to be placed before the king for a decision, Absalom would call out to him, "What town are you from?" He would answer, "Your servant is from one of the tribes of Israel." 3 Then Absalom would say to him, "Look, your claims are valid and proper, but there is no representative of the king to hear you." 4 And Absalom would add, "If only I were appointed judge in the land! Then everyone who has a complaint or case could come to me and I would see that he gets justice."

5 Also, whenever anyone approached him to bow down before him, Absalom would reach out his hand, take hold of him and kiss him. 6 Absalom behaved in this way toward all the Israelites who came to the king asking for justice, and so he stole the hearts of the men of Israel.

7 At the end of four*q* years, Absalom said to the king, "Let me go to Hebron and fulfill a vow I made to the LORD. 8 While your servant was living at Geshur in Aram, I made this vow: 'If the LORD takes me back to Jerusalem, I will worship the LORD in Hebron.*r* ' " 9 The king said to him, "Go in peace." So he went to Hebron.

10 Then Absalom sent secret messengers throughout the tribes of Israel to say, "As soon as you hear the sound of the trumpets, then say, 'Absalom is king in Hebron.' " 11 Two hundred men from Jerusalem had accompanied Absalom. They had been invited as guests and went quite innocently, knowing nothing about the matter. 12 While Absalom was offering sacrifices, he also sent for Ahithophel the Gilonite, David's counselor, to come from Giloh, his hometown. And so the conspiracy gained strength, and Absalom's following kept on increasing.

David Flees

13 A messenger came and told David, "The hearts of the men of Israel are with Absalom."

14 Then David said to all his officials who were with him in Jerusalem, "Come! We must flee, or none of us will escape from Absalom. We must leave immediately, or he will move quickly to overtake us and bring ruin upon us and put the city to the sword."

15 The king's officials answered him, "Your servants are ready to do whatever our lord the king chooses."

16 The king set out, with his entire household following him; but he left ten concubines to take care of the palace. 17 So the king set out, with all the people following him, and they halted at a place some distance away. 18 All his men marched past him, along with all the Kerethites and Pelethites; and all the six hundred Gittites who had accompanied him from Gath marched before the king.

19 The king said to Ittai the Gittite, "Why should you come along with us? Go back and stay with King Absalom. You are a foreigner, an exile from your homeland. 20 You came only yesterday. And today shall I make you wander about with us, when I do not know where I am going? Go back, and take your countrymen. May kindness and faithfulness be with you."

21 But Ittai replied to the king, "As surely as the LORD lives, and as my lord the king lives, wherever my lord the king may be, whether it means life or death, there will your servant be."

---

*o*Some ancient versions render *four*

q 7 Some Septuagint manuscripts, Syriac and Josephus; Hebrew *forty*   *r* 8 Some Septuagint manuscripts; Hebrew does not have *in Hebron.*

King James

Amplified

²²And David said to Ittai, Go and pass over. And Ittai the Gittite passed over, and all his men, and all the little ones that *were* with him.

²³And all the country wept with a loud voice, and all the people passed over: the king also himself passed over the brook ^cKidron, and all the people passed over, toward the way of the wilderness.

²⁴ ¶ And lo Zadok also, and all the Levites *were* with him, bearing the ark of the covenant of God: and they set down the ark of God; and Abiathar went up, until all the people had done passing out of the city.

²⁵And the king said unto Zadok, Carry back the ark of God into the city: if I shall find favour in the eyes of the LORD, he will bring me again, and show me *both* it, and his habitation:

²⁶But if he thus say, I have no delight in thee; behold, *here am* I, let him do to me as seemeth good unto him.

²⁷The king said also unto Zadok the priest, *Art not* thou a seer? return into the city in peace, and your two sons with you, Ahimaaz thy son, and Jonathan the son of Abiathar.

²⁸See, I will tarry in the plain of the wilderness, until there come word from you to certify me.

²⁹Zadok therefore and Abiathar carried the ark of God again to Jerusalem: and they tarried there.

³⁰ ¶ And David went up by the ascent of *mount* Olivet, ^dand wept as he went up, and had his head covered, and he went barefoot: and all the people that *was* with him covered every man his head, and they went up, weeping as they went up.

³¹ ¶ And *one* told David, saying, Ahithophel *is* among the conspirators with Absalom. And David said, O LORD, I pray thee, turn the counsel of Ahithophel into foolishness.

³² ¶ And it came to pass, that *when* David was come to the top *of the mount*, where he worshipped God, behold, Hushai the Archite came to meet him with his coat rent, and earth upon his head:

³³Unto whom David said, If thou passest on with me, then thou shalt be a burden unto me:

³⁴But if thou return to the city, and say unto Absalom, I will be thy servant, O king; *as* I *have been* thy father's servant hitherto, so *will* I now also *be* thy servant: then mayest thou for me defeat the counsel of Ahithophel.

³⁵And *hast thou* not there with thee Zadok and Abiathar the priests? therefore it shall be, *that* what thing soever thou shalt hear out of the king's house, thou shalt tell *it* to Zadok and Abiathar the priests.

³⁶Behold, *they have* there with them their two sons, Ahimaaz Zadok's *son*, and Jonathan Abiathar's *son;* and by them ye shall send unto me every thing that ye can hear.

³⁷So Hushai David's friend came into the city, and Absalom came into Jerusalem.

Ziba's lie

16 AND WHEN David was a little past the top *of the hill*, behold, Ziba the servant of Mephibosheth met him, with a couple of asses saddled, and upon them two hundred *loaves* of bread, and an hundred bunches of raisins, and an hundred of summer fruits, and a bottle of wine.

²And the king said unto Ziba, What meanest thou by these? And Ziba said, The asses *be* for the king's household to ride on; and the bread and summer fruit for the young men to eat; and the wine, that such as be faint in the wilderness may drink.

³And the king said, And where *is* thy master's son? And Ziba said unto the king, Behold, he abideth at Jerusalem: for he said, Today shall the house of Israel restore me the kingdom of my father.

²²So David said to Ittai, Go on and pass over [the Kidron]. And Ittai the Gittite passed over and all his men and all the little ones who were with him.

²³All the country wept with a loud voice as all the people passed over. The king crossed the brook Kidron, and all the people went on toward the wilderness.

²⁴Abiathar [the priest] and behold, Zadok came also, and all the Levites with him, bearing the ark of the covenant of God. And they set down the ark of God until all the people had gone from the city.

²⁵Then the king told Zadok, Take back the ark of God to the city. If I find favor in the Lord's eyes, He will bring me back and let me see both it and His house.

²⁶But if He says, I have no delight in you, then here I am; let Him do to me what seems good to Him.

²⁷The king also said to Zadok the priest, Are you not a seer? [You and Abiathar] return to the city in peace, and your two sons with you, Ahimaaz your son and Jonathan son of Abiathar.

²⁸See, I will wait at the fords [at the Jordan] of the wilderness until word comes from you to inform me.

²⁹Zadok, therefore, and Abiathar carried the ark of God back to Jerusalem and they stayed there.

³⁰And David went up over the Mount of Olives and wept as he went, barefoot and his head covered. And all the people who were with him covered their heads, weeping as they went.

³¹David was told, Ahithophel [your counselor] is among the conspirators with Absalom. David said, O Lord, I pray You, turn Ahithophel's counsel into foolishness.

³²When David came to the summit [of Olivet], where he worshiped God, behold, Hushai the Archite came to meet him with his coat rent and earth upon his head.

³³David said to him, If you go with me, you will be a burden to me.

³⁴But if you return to the city and say to Absalom, I will be your servant, O king; as I have been your father's servant in the past, so will I be your servant now, then you may defeat for me the counsel of Ahithophel.

³⁵Will not Zadok and Abiathar the priests be with you? So whatever you hear from the king's house, just tell it to [them].

³⁶Behold, their two sons are there with them, Ahimaaz, Zadok's son and Jonathan, Abiathar's son; and by them send to me everything you hear.

³⁷So Hushai, David's friend, returned, and Absalom also came into Jerusalem.

16 WHEN DAVID was a little past the top [of Olivet], behold, Ziba, the servant of Mephibosheth, met him with a couple of donkeys saddled, and upon them 200 loaves of bread, 100 bunches of raisins, 100 summer fruits, and a skin of wine.

²The king said to Ziba, What do you mean by these? Ziba said, The donkeys are for the king's household to ride on, the bread and summer fruit for the young men to eat, and the wine is for those to drink who become faint in the wilderness.

³The king said, And where is your master's son [grandson Mephibosheth]? Ziba said to the king, Behold, he remains in Jerusalem, for he said, Today the house of Israel will give me back the kingdom of my father [grandfather Saul].

---

^cCalled *Cedron* in John 18:1   ^dHeb. *going up, and weeping*

New American Standard

22 Therefore David said to Ittai, "Go and pass over." So Ittai the Gittite passed over with all his men and all the little ones who *were* with him.

23 While all the country was weeping with a loud voice, all the people passed over. The king also passed over the brook Kidron, and all the people passed over toward the way of the wilderness.

24 ¶ Now behold, Zadok also *came*, and all the Levites with him carrying the ark of the covenant of God. And they set down the ark of God, and Abiathar came up until all the people had finished passing from the city.

25 The king said to Zadok, "Return the ark of God to the city. If I find favor in the sight of the LORD, then He will bring me back again and show me both it and His habitation.

26 "But if He should say thus, 'I have no delight in you,' behold, here I am, let Him do to me as seems good to Him."

27 The king said also to Zadok the priest, "Are you *not* a seer? Return to the city in peace and your two sons with you, your son Ahimaaz and Jonathan the son of Abiathar.

28 "See, I am going to wait at the fords of the wilderness until word comes from you to inform me."

29 Therefore Zadok and Abiathar returned the ark of God to Jerusalem and remained there.

30 ¶ And David went up the ascent of the *Mount of Olives*, and wept as he went, and his head was covered and he walked barefoot. Then all the people who were with him each covered his head and went up weeping as they went.

31 Now someone told David, saying, "Ahithophel is among the conspirators with Absalom." And David said, "O LORD, I pray, make the counsel of Ahithophel foolishness."

32 ¶ It happened as David was coming to the summit, where God was worshiped, that behold, Hushai the Archite met him with his coat torn and dust on his head.

33 David said to him, "If you pass over with me, then you will be a burden to me.

34 "But if you return to the city, and say to Absalom, 'I will be your servant, O king; as I have been your father's servant in time past, so I will now be your servant,' then you can thwart the counsel of Ahithophel for me.

35 "Are not Zadok and Abiathar the priests with you there? So it shall be that whatever you hear from the king's house, you shall report to Zadok and Abiathar the priests.

36 "Behold their two sons are with them there, Ahimaaz, Zadok's son and Jonathan, Abiathar's son; and by them you shall send me everything that you hear."

37 So Hushai, David's friend, came into the city, and Absalom came into Jerusalem.

Ziba, a False Servant

16 NOW WHEN David had passed a little beyond the summit, behold, Ziba the servant of Mephibosheth met him with a couple of saddled donkeys, and on them *were* two hundred loaves of bread, a hundred clusters of raisins, a hundred summer fruits, and a jug of wine.

2 The king said to Ziba, "Why do you have these?" And Ziba said, "The donkeys are for the king's household to ride, and the bread and summer fruit for the young men to eat, and the wine, for whoever is faint in the wilderness to drink."

3 Then the king said, "And where is your master's son?" And Ziba said to the king, "Behold, he is staying in Jerusalem, for he said, 'Today the house of Israel will restore the kingdom of my father to me.' "

New International

22 David said to Ittai, "Go ahead, march on." So Ittai the Gittite marched on with all his men and the families that were with him.

23 The whole countryside wept aloud as all the people passed by. The king also crossed the Kidron Valley, and all the people moved on toward the desert.

24 Zadok was there, too, and all the Levites who were with him were carrying the ark of the covenant of God. They set down the ark of God, and Abiathar offered sacrifices[s] until all the people had finished leaving the city.

25 Then the king said to Zadok, "Take the ark of God back into the city. If I find favor in the LORD's eyes, he will bring me back and let me see it and his dwelling place again. 26 But if he says, 'I am not pleased with you,' then I am ready; let him do to me whatever seems good to him."

27 The king also said to Zadok the priest, "Aren't you a seer? Go back to the city in peace, with your son Ahimaaz and Jonathan son of Abiathar. You and Abiathar take your two sons with you. 28 I will wait at the fords in the desert until word comes from you to inform me." 29 So Zadok and Abiathar took the ark of God back to Jerusalem and stayed there.

30 But David continued up the Mount of Olives, weeping as he went; his head was covered and he was barefoot. All the people with him covered their heads too and were weeping as they went up. 31 Now David had been told, "Ahithophel is among the conspirators with Absalom." So David prayed, "O LORD, turn Ahithophel's counsel into foolishness."

32 When David arrived at the summit, where people used to worship God, Hushai the Arkite was there to meet him, his robe torn and dust on his head. 33 David said to him, "If you go with me, you will be a burden to me. 34 But if you return to the city and say to Absalom, 'I will be your servant, O king; I was your father's servant in the past, but now I will be your servant,' then you can help me by frustrating Ahithophel's advice. 35 Won't the priests Zadok and Abiathar be there with you? Tell them anything you hear in the king's palace. 36 Their two sons, Ahimaaz son of Zadok and Jonathan son of Abiathar, are there with them. Send them to me with anything you hear."

37 So David's friend Hushai arrived at Jerusalem as Absalom was entering the city.

David and Ziba

16 WHEN DAVID had gone a short distance beyond the summit, there was Ziba, the steward of Mephibosheth, waiting to meet him. He had a string of donkeys saddled and loaded with two hundred loaves of bread, a hundred cakes of raisins, a hundred cakes of figs and a skin of wine.

2 The king asked Ziba, "Why have you brought these?"

Ziba answered, "The donkeys are for the king's household to ride on, the bread and fruit are for the men to eat, and the wine is to refresh those who become exhausted in the desert."

3 The king then asked, "Where is your master's grandson?"

Ziba said to him, "He is staying in Jerusalem, because he thinks, 'Today the house of Israel will give me back my grandfather's kingdom.' "

King James

Amplified

⁴Then said the king to Ziba, Behold, thine *are* all that pertained unto Mephibosheth. And Ziba said, *e*I humbly beseech thee *that* I may find grace in thy sight, my lord, O king.

Shimei curses David

⁵ ¶ And when king David came to Bahurim, behold, thence came out a man of the family of the house of Saul, whose name *was* Shimei, the son of Gera: *f*he came forth, and cursed still as he came.

⁶And he cast stones at David, and at all the servants of king David: and all the people and all the mighty men *were* on his right hand and on his left.

⁷And thus said Shimei when he cursed, Come out, come out, thou *g*bloody man, and thou man of Belial:

⁸The LORD hath returned upon thee all the blood of the house of Saul, in whose stead thou hast reigned; and the LORD hath delivered the kingdom into the hand of Absalom thy son: and, *h*behold, thou *art taken* in thy mischief, because thou *art* a bloody man.

⁹ ¶ Then said Abishai the son of Zeruiah unto the king, Why should this dead dog curse my lord the king? let me go over, I pray thee, and take off his head.

¹⁰And the king said, What have I to do with you, ye sons of Zeruiah? so let him curse, because the LORD hath said unto him, Curse David. Who shall then say, Wherefore hast thou done so?

¹¹And David said to Abishai, and to all his servants, Behold, my son, which came forth of my bowels, seeketh my life: how much more now *may this* Benjamite *do it?* let him alone, and let him curse; for the LORD hath bidden him.

¹²It may be that the LORD will look on mine *i*affliction, and that the LORD will requite me good for his cursing this day.

¹³And as David and his men went by the way, Shimei went along on the hill's side over against him, and cursed as he went, and threw stones at him, and *j*cast dust.

¹⁴And the king, and all the people that *were* with him, came weary, and refreshed themselves there.

The advice of Ahithophel

¹⁵ ¶ And Absalom, and all the people the men of Israel, came to Jerusalem, and Ahithophel with him.

¹⁶And it came to pass, when Hushai the Archite, David's friend, was come unto Absalom, that Hushai said unto Absalom, *k*God save the king, God save the king.

¹⁷And Absalom said to Hushai, *Is* this thy kindness to thy friend? why wentest thou not with thy friend?

¹⁸And Hushai said unto Absalom, Nay; but whom the LORD, and this people, and all the men of Israel, choose, his will I be, and with him will I abide.

¹⁹And again, whom should I serve? *should I* not *serve* in the presence of his son? as I have served in thy father's presence, so will I be in thy presence.

²⁰ ¶ Then said Absalom to Ahithophel, Give counsel among you what we shall do.

²¹And Ahithophel said unto Absalom, Go in unto thy father's concubines, which he hath left to keep the house; and all Israel shall hear that thou art abhorred of thy father: then shall the hands of all that *are* with thee be strong.

²²So they spread Absalom a tent upon the top of the house; and Absalom went in unto his father's concubines in the sight of all Israel.

²³And the counsel of Ahithophel, which he counselled in those days, *was* as if a man had inquired at the *l*oracle of God: so *was* all the counsel of Ahithophel both with David and with Absalom.

⁴Then the king said to Ziba, Behold, all that belonged to Mephibosheth is now yours. Ziba said, I do obeisance; let me ever find favor in your sight, my lord O king.

⁵When King David came to Bahurim, a man of the family of the house of Saul, Shimei son of Gera, came out and cursed continually as he came.

⁶And he cast stones at David and at all the servants of King David; and all the people and all the mighty men were on his right hand and on his left.

⁷Shimei said as he cursed, Get out, get out, you man of blood, you base fellow!

⁸The Lord has avenged upon you all the blood of the house of Saul, in whose stead you have reigned; and the Lord has delivered the kingdom into the hands of Absalom your son. Behold, the calamity is upon you because you are a bloody man!

⁹Then said [David's nephew] Abishai son of Zeruiah to the king, Why should this dead dog curse my lord the king? Let me go over and take off his head.

¹⁰The king said, What have I to do with you, you sons of Zeruiah? If he is cursing because the Lord said to him, Curse David, who then shall ask, Why have you done so?

¹¹And David said to Abishai and to all his servants, Behold, my son, who was born to me, seeks my life. With how much more reason now may this Benjamite do it? Let him alone; and let him curse, for the Lord has bidden him to do it.

¹²It may be that the Lord will look on the iniquity done me and will recompense me with good for his cursing this day.

¹³So David and his men went by the road, and Shimei went along on the hillside opposite David and cursed as he went and threw stones and dust at him.

¹⁴And the king and all the people who were with him came [to the Jordan] weary, and he refreshed himself there.

¹⁵And Absalom and all the people, the men of Israel, came to Jerusalem, and Ahithophel with him.

¹⁶And when Hushai the Archite, David's friend, came to Absalom, Hushai said to [him], Long live the king! Long live the king!

¹⁷Absalom said to Hushai, Is this your kindness *and* loyalty to your friend? Why did you not go with your friend?

¹⁸Hushai said to Absalom, No, for whom the Lord and this people and all the men of Israel choose, his will I be, and with him I will remain.

¹⁹And again, whom should I serve? Should it not be his son? As I have served your father, so will I serve you.

²⁰Then Absalom said to Ahithophel, Give your counsel. What shall we do?

²¹And Ahithophel said to Absalom, Go in to your father's concubines whom he has left to keep the house; and all Israel will hear that you are abhorred by your father. Then the hands of all who are with you will be made strong.

²²So they spread for Absalom a tent on the top of the [king's] house, and Absalom went in to his father's harem in the sight of all Israel.

²³And the counsel of Ahithophel in those days was as if a man had consulted the word of God; so was all Ahithophel's counsel considered both by David and by Absalom.

---

*e*Heb. *I do obeisance*   *f*Or, *he still came forth and cursed*
*g*Heb. *man of blood*   *h*Heb. *behold thee in thy evil*   *i*Or,
tears   *j*Heb. *dusted* him *with dust*   *k*Heb. *Let the king live*
*l*Heb. *word*

New American Standard

4 So the king said to Ziba, "Behold, all that belongs to Mephibosheth is yours." And Ziba said, "I prostrate myself; let me find favor in your sight, O my lord, the king!"

David Is Cursed

5 ¶ When King David came to Bahurim, behold, there came out from there a man of the family of the house of Saul whose name was Shimei, the son of Gera; he came out cursing continually as he came.
6 He threw stones at David and at all the servants of King David; and all the people and all the mighty men were at his right hand and at his left.
7 Thus Shimei said when he cursed, "Get out, get out, you man of bloodshed, and worthless fellow!
8 "The LORD has returned upon you all the bloodshed of the house of Saul, in whose place you have reigned; and the LORD has given the kingdom into the hand of your son Absalom. And behold, you are *taken* in your own evil, for you are a man of bloodshed!"
9 ¶ Then Abishai the son of Zeruiah said to the king, "Why should this dead dog curse my lord the king? Let me go over now and cut off his head."
10 But the king said, "What have I to do with you, O sons of Zeruiah? If he curses, and if the LORD has told him, 'Curse David,' then who shall say, 'Why have you done so?' "
11 Then David said to Abishai and to all his servants, "Behold, my son who came out from me seeks my life; how much more now this Benjamite? Let him alone and let him curse, for the LORD has told him.
12 "Perhaps the LORD will look on my affliction and return good to me instead of his cursing this day."
13 So David and his men went on the way; and Shimei went along on the hillside parallel with him and as he went he cursed and cast stones and threw dust at him.
14 The king and all the people who were with him arrived weary and he refreshed himself there.

Absalom Enters Jerusalem

15 ¶ Then Absalom and all the people, the men of Israel, entered Jerusalem, and Ahithophel with him.
16 Now it came about when Hushai the Archite, David's friend, came to Absalom, that Hushai said to Absalom, "*Long* live the king! *Long* live the king!"
17 Absalom said to Hushai, "Is this your loyalty to your friend? Why did you not go with your friend?"
18 Then Hushai said to Absalom, "No! For whom the LORD, this people, and all the men of Israel have chosen, his I will be, and with him I will remain.
19 "Besides, whom should I serve? *Should I* not *serve* in the presence of his son? As I have served in your father's presence, so I will be in your presence."
20 ¶ Then Absalom said to Ahithophel, "Give your advice. What shall we do?"
21 Ahithophel said to Absalom, "Go in to your father's concubines, whom he has left to keep the house; then all Israel will hear that you have made yourself odious to your father. The hands of all who are with you will also be strengthened."
22 So they pitched a tent for Absalom on the roof, and Absalom went in to his father's concubines in the sight of all Israel.
23 The advice of Ahithophel, which he gave in those days, *was* as if one inquired of the word of God; so was all the advice of Ahithophel *regarded* by both David and Absalom.

New International

4 Then the king said to Ziba, "All that belonged to Mephibosheth is now yours."
"I humbly bow," Ziba said. "May I find favor in your eyes, my lord the king."

Shimei Curses David

5 As King David approached Bahurim, a man from the same clan as Saul's family came out from there. His name was Shimei son of Gera, and he cursed as he came out. 6 He pelted David and all the king's officials with stones, though all the troops and the special guard were on David's right and left. 7 As he cursed, Shimei said, "Get out, get out, you man of blood, you scoundrel! 8 The LORD has repaid you for all the blood you shed in the household of Saul, in whose place you have reigned. The LORD has handed the kingdom over to your son Absalom. You have come to ruin because you are a man of blood!"
9 Then Abishai son of Zeruiah said to the king, "Why should this dead dog curse my lord the king? Let me go over and cut off his head."
10 But the king said, "What do you and I have in common, you sons of Zeruiah? If he is cursing because the LORD said to him, 'Curse David,' who can ask, 'Why do you do this?' "
11 David then said to Abishai and all his officials, "My son, who is of my own flesh, is trying to take my life. How much more, then, this Benjamite! Leave him alone; let him curse, for the LORD has told him to. 12 It may be that the LORD will see my distress and repay me with good for the cursing I am receiving today."
13 So David and his men continued along the road while Shimei was going along the hillside opposite him, cursing as he went and throwing stones at him and showering him with dirt. 14 The king and all the people with him arrived at their destination exhausted. And there he refreshed himself.

The Advice of Ahithophel and Hushai

15 Meanwhile, Absalom and all the men of Israel came to Jerusalem, and Ahithophel was with him. 16 Then Hushai the Arkite, David's friend, went to Absalom and said to him, "Long live the king! Long live the king!"
17 Absalom asked Hushai, "Is this the love you show your friend? Why didn't you go with your friend?"
18 Hushai said to Absalom, "No, the one chosen by the LORD, by these people, and by all the men of Israel—his I will be, and I will remain with him. 19 Furthermore, whom should I serve? Should I not serve the son? Just as I served your father, so I will serve you."
20 Absalom said to Ahithophel, "Give us your advice. What should we do?"
21 Ahithophel answered, "Lie with your father's concubines whom he left to take care of the palace. Then all Israel will hear that you have made yourself a stench in your father's nostrils, and the hands of everyone with you will be strengthened." 22 So they pitched a tent for Absalom on the roof, and he lay with his father's concubines in the sight of all Israel.
23 Now in those days the advice Ahithophel gave was like that of one who inquires of God. That was how both David and Absalom regarded all of Ahithophel's advice.

King James

Amplified

17 MOREOVER AHITHOPHEL said unto Absalom, Let me now choose out twelve thousand men, and I will arise and pursue after David this night:

[2]And I will come upon him while he *is* weary and weak handed, and will make him afraid: and all the people that *are* with him shall flee; and I will smite the king only:

[3]And I will bring back all the people unto thee: the man whom thou seekest *is* as if all returned: *so* all the people shall be in peace.

[4]And the saying [m]pleased Absalom well, and all the elders of Israel.

The advice of Hushai

[5]Then said Absalom, Call now Hushai the Archite also, and let us hear likewise [n]what he saith.

[6]And when Hushai was come to Absalom, Absalom spake unto him, saying, Ahithophel hath spoken after this manner: shall we do *after* his [o]saying? if not; speak thou.

[7]And Hushai said unto Absalom, The counsel that Ahithophel hath [p]given *is* not good at this time.

[8]For, said Hushai, thou knowest thy father and his men, that they *be* mighty men, and they *be* [q]chafed in their minds, as a bear robbed of her whelps in the field: and thy father *is* a man of war, and will not lodge with the people.

[9]Behold, he is hid now in some pit, or in some *other* place: and it will come to pass, when some of them be [r]overthrown at the first, that whosoever heareth it will say, There is a slaughter among the people that follow Absalom.

[10]And he also *that is* valiant, whose heart *is* as the heart of a lion, shall utterly melt: for all Israel knoweth that thy father *is* a mighty man, and *they* which *be* with him *are* valiant men.

[11]Therefore I counsel that all Israel be generally gathered unto thee, from Dan even to Beer-sheba, as the sand that *is* by the sea for multitude; and [s]that thou go to battle in thine own person.

[12]So shall we come upon him in some place where he shall be found, and we will light upon him as the dew falleth on the ground: and of him and of all the men that *are* with him there shall not be left so much as one.

[13]Moreover, if he be gotten into a city, then shall all Israel bring ropes to that city, and we will draw it into the river, until there be not one small stone found there.

[14]And Absalom and all the men of Israel said, The counsel of Hushai the Archite *is* better than the counsel of Ahithophel. For the LORD had [t]appointed to defeat the good counsel of Ahithophel, to the intent that the LORD might bring evil upon Absalom.

[15] ¶ Then said Hushai unto Zadok and to Abiathar the priests, Thus and thus did Ahithophel counsel Absalom and the elders of Israel; and thus and thus have I counselled.

[16]Now therefore send quickly, and tell David, saying, Lodge not this night in the plains of the wilderness, but speedily pass over; lest the king be swallowed up, and all the people that *are* with him.

[17]Now Jonathan and Ahimaaz stayed by En-rogel; for they might not be seen to come into the city: and a wench went and told them; and they went and told king David.

[18]Nevertheless a lad saw them, and told Absalom: but they went both of them away quickly, and came to a man's house in Bahurim, which had a well in his court; whither they went down.

[19]And the woman took and spread a covering over the well's mouth, and spread ground corn thereon; and the thing was not known.

17 MOREOVER, AHITHOPHEL said to Absalom, Let me choose 12,000 men and I will set out and pursue David this night.

[2]I will come upon him while he is exhausted and weak, and cause him to panic; all the people with him will flee. Then I will strike down the king alone.

[3]I will bring back all the people to you. [The removal of] the man whom you seek is the assurance that all will return; and all the people will be at peace.

[4]And what he said pleased Absalom well and all the elders of Israel.

[5]Absalom said, Now call Hushai the Archite also, and let us hear what he says.

[6]When Hushai came, Absalom said to him, Ahithophel has counseled thus. Shall we do what he says? If not, speak up.

[7]And Hushai said to Absalom, The counsel that Ahithophel has given is not good at this time.

[8]For, said Hushai, you know your father and his men, that they are mighty men, and they are embittered *and* enraged like a bear robbed of her whelps in the field. And your father is a man of war, and will not lodge with the people.

[9]Behold, he is hidden even now in some pit or other place; and when some of them are overthrown at the first, whoever hears it will say, There is a slaughter among the followers of Absalom.

[10]And even he who is brave, whose heart is as the heart of a lion, will utterly melt, for all Israel knows that your father is a mighty man and that those who are with him are brave men.

[11]Therefore I counsel that all [the men of] Israel be gathered to you, from Dan even to Beersheba, as the sand that is by the sea for multitude, and that you go to battle in your own person.

[12]So shall we come upon [David] some place where he shall be found, and we will light upon him as the dew settles [unseen and unheard] on the ground; and of him and of all the men with him there shall not be left so much as one.

[13]If he withdraws into a city, then shall all Israel bring ropes to that city, and we will drag it into the ravine until not one pebble is left there.

[14]Absalom and all the men of Israel said, The counsel of Hushai the Archite is better than that of Ahithophel. For the Lord had ordained to defeat the good counsel of Ahithophel, so that the Lord might bring evil upon Absalom.

[15]Then said Hushai to Zadok and Abiathar the priests, Thus and thus did Ahithophel counsel Absalom and the elders of Israel, and thus and thus have I counseled.

[16]Now send quickly and tell David, Lodge not this night at the fords [at the Jordan] of the wilderness, but by all means pass over, lest the king be swallowed up and all the people with him.

[17]Now [the youths] Jonathan and Ahimaaz stayed at En-rogel, for they must not be seen coming into the city. But a maidservant went and told them, and they went and told King David.

[18]But a lad saw them and told Absalom; but they left quickly and came to the house of a man in Bahurim, who had a well in his court, and they went down into it.

[19]And the woman spread a covering over the well's mouth and spread ground corn on it; and the thing was not discovered.

---

[m]Heb. *was right in the eyes of*   [n]Heb. *what is in his mouth*
[o]Heb. *word?*   [p]Heb. *counselled*   [q]Heb. *bitter of soul*
[r]Heb. *fallen*   [s]Heb. *that thy face,* or, *presence go*   [t]Heb.
commanded

New American Standard

Hushai's Counsel

17 FURTHERMORE, AHITHOPHEL said to Absalom, "Please let me choose 12,000 men that I may arise and pursue David tonight.

2"I will come upon him while he is weary and exhausted and terrify him, so that all the people who are with him will flee. Then I will strike down the king alone,

3 and I will bring back all the people to you. The return of everyone depends on the man you seek; *then* all the people will be at peace."

4 So the plan pleased Absalom and all the elders of Israel.

5 ¶ Then Absalom said, "Now call Hushai the Archite also, and let us hear what he has to say."

6 When Hushai had come to Absalom, Absalom said to him, "Ahithophel has spoken thus. Shall we carry out his plan? If not, you speak."

7 So Hushai said to Absalom, "This time the advice that Ahithophel has given is not good."

8 Moreover, Hushai said, "You know your father and his men, that they are mighty men and they are fierce, like a bear robbed of her cubs in the field. And your father is an expert in warfare, and will not spend the night with the people.

9"Behold, he has now hidden himself in one of the caves or in another place; and it will be when he falls on them at the first attack, that whoever hears *it* will say, 'There has been a slaughter among the people who follow Absalom.'

10"And even the one who is valiant, whose heart is like the heart of a lion, will completely lose heart; for all Israel knows that your father is a mighty man and those who are with him are valiant men.

11"But I counsel that all Israel be surely gathered to you, from Dan even to Beersheba, as the sand that is by the sea in abundance, and that you personally go into battle.

12"So we shall come to him in one of the places where he can be found, and we will fall on him as the dew falls on the ground; and of him and of all the men who are with him, not even one will be left.

13"If he withdraws into a city, then all Israel shall bring ropes to that city, and we will drag it into the valley until not even a small stone is found there."

14 Then Absalom and all the men of Israel said, "The counsel of Hushai the Archite is better than the counsel of Ahithophel." For the LORD had ordained to thwart the good counsel of Ahithophel, so that the LORD might bring calamity on Absalom.

Hushai's Warning Saves David

15 ¶ Then Hushai said to Zadok and to Abiathar the priests, "This is what Ahithophel counseled Absalom and the elders of Israel, and this is what I have counseled.

16"Now therefore, send quickly and tell David, saying, 'Do not spend the night at the fords of the wilderness, but by all means cross over, or else the king and all the people who are with him will be destroyed.' "

17 Now Jonathan and Ahimaaz were staying at En-rogel, and a maidservant would go and tell them, and they would go and tell King David, for they could not be seen entering the city.

18 But a lad did see them and told Absalom; so the two of them departed quickly and came to the house of a man in Bahurim, who had a well in his courtyard, and they went down into it.

19 And the woman took a covering and spread it over the well's mouth and scattered grain on it, so that nothing was known.

New International

17 AHITHOPHEL SAID to Absalom, "I would[t] choose twelve thousand men and set out tonight in pursuit of David. 2I would[u] attack him while he is weary and weak. I would[u] strike him with terror, and then all the people with him will flee. I would[u] strike down only the king 3and bring all the people back to you. The death of the man you seek will mean the return of all; all the people will be unharmed." 4This plan seemed good to Absalom and to all the elders of Israel.

5But Absalom said, "Summon also Hushai the Arkite, so we can hear what he has to say." 6When Hushai came to him, Absalom said, "Ahithophel has given this advice. Should we do what he says? If not, give us your opinion."

7Hushai replied to Absalom, "The advice Ahithophel has given is not good this time. 8You know your father and his men; they are fighters, and as fierce as a wild bear robbed of her cubs. Besides, your father is an experienced fighter; he will not spend the night with the troops. 9Even now, he is hidden in a cave or some other place. If he should attack your troops first,[v] whoever hears about it will say, 'There has been a slaughter among the troops who follow Absalom.' 10Then even the bravest soldier, whose heart is like the heart of a lion, will melt with fear, for all Israel knows that your father is a fighter and that those with him are brave.

11"So I advise you: Let all Israel, from Dan to Beersheba—as numerous as the sand on the seashore—be gathered to you, with you yourself leading them into battle. 12Then we will attack him wherever he may be found, and we will fall on him as dew settles on the ground. Neither he nor any of his men will be left alive. 13If he withdraws into a city, then all Israel will bring ropes to that city, and we will drag it down to the valley until not even a piece of it can be found."

14Absalom and all the men of Israel said, "The advice of Hushai the Arkite is better than that of Ahithophel." For the LORD had determined to frustrate the good advice of Ahithophel in order to bring disaster on Absalom.

15Hushai told Zadok and Abiathar, the priests, "Ahithophel has advised Absalom and the elders of Israel to do such and such, but I have advised them to do so and so. 16Now send a message immediately and tell David, 'Do not spend the night at the fords in the desert; cross over without fail, or the king and all the people with him will be swallowed up.' "

17Jonathan and Ahimaaz were staying at En Rogel. A servant girl was to go and inform them, and they were to go and tell King David, for they could not risk being seen entering the city. 18But a young man saw them and told Absalom. So the two of them left quickly and went to the house of a man in Bahurim. He had a well in his courtyard, and they climbed down into it. 19His wife took a covering and spread it out over the opening of the well and scattered grain over it. No one knew anything about it.

King James

20And when Absalom's servants came to the woman to the house, they said, Where *is* Ahimaaz and Jonathan? And the woman said unto them, They be gone over the brook of water. And when they had sought and could not find *them,* they returned to Jerusalem.

21And it came to pass, after they were departed, that they came up out of the well, and went and told king David, and said unto David, Arise, and pass quickly over the water: for thus hath Ahithophel counselled against you.

22Then David arose, and all the people that *were* with him, and they passed over Jordan: by the morning light there lacked not one of them that was not gone over Jordan.

23 ¶ And when Ahithophel saw that his counsel was not ᵘfollowed, he saddled *his* ass, and arose, and gat him home to his house, to his city, and ᵛput his household in order, and hanged himself, and died, and was buried in the sepulchre of his father.

24Then David came to Mahanaim. And Absalom passed over Jordan, he and all the men of Israel with him.

25 ¶ And Absalom made Amasa captain of the host instead of Joab: which Amasa *was* a man's son, whose name *was* ʷIthra an Israelite, that went in to ˣAbigail the daughter of ʸNahash, sister to Zeruiah Joab's mother.

26So Israel and Absalom pitched in the land of Gilead.

27 ¶ And it came to pass, when David was come to Mahanaim, that Shobi the son of Nahash of Rabbah of the children of Ammon, and Machir the son of Ammiel of Lo-debar, and Barzillai the Gileadite of Rogelim,

28Brought beds, and ᶻbasins, and earthen vessels, and wheat, and barley, and flour, and parched *corn,* and beans, and lentiles, and parched *pulse,*

29And honey, and butter, and sheep, and cheese of kine, for David, and for the people that *were* with him, to eat: for they said, The people *is* hungry, and weary, and thirsty, in the wilderness.

Absalom killed by Joab

18 AND DAVID numbered the people that *were* with him, and set captains of thousands and captains of hundreds over them.

2And David sent forth a third part of the people under the hand of Joab, and a third part under the hand of Abishai the son of Zeruiah, Joab's brother, and a third part under the hand of Ittai the Gittite. And the king said unto the people, I will surely go forth with you myself also.

3But the people answered, Thou shalt not go forth: for if we flee away, they will not ᵃcare for us; neither if half of us die, will they care for us: but now *thou art* ᵇworth ten thousand of us: therefore now *it is* better that thou ᶜsuccour us out of the city.

4And the king said unto them, What seemeth you best I will do. And the king stood by the gate side, and all the people came out by hundreds and by thousands.

5And the king commanded Joab and Abishai and Ittai, saying, *Deal* gently for my sake with the young man, *even* with Absalom. And all the people heard when the king gave all the captains charge concerning Absalom.

6 ¶ So the people went out into the field against Israel: and the battle was in the wood of Ephraim;

7Where the people of Israel were slain before the servants of David, and there was there a great slaughter that day of twenty thousand *men.*

8For the battle was there scattered over the face of all the country: and the wood ᵈdevoured more people that day than the sword devoured.

Amplified

20For when Absalom's servants came to the woman at the house, they said, Where are Ahimaaz and Jonathan? And the woman said to them, They went over the brook of water. When they had sought and could not find them, they returned to Jerusalem.

21After they had departed, the boys came up out of the well and went and told King David, and said, Arise and pass quickly over the river Jordan; for thus and so has Ahithophel counseled against you.

22David arose and all the people with him and passed over the Jordan. By daybreak, not one was left who had not crossed.

23But when Ahithophel saw that his counsel was not followed, he saddled his donkey, went home to his city, put his household in order, and hanged himself and died, and was buried in the tomb of his father.

24Then David came to Mahanaim. And Absalom passed over the Jordan, he and all the men of Israel with him.

25Absalom made Amasa captain of the army instead of Joab. Amasa was the son of an [Ishmaelite] named Ithra, who married Abigail daughter of Nahash, [half sister of David and] sister of Zeruiah, Joab's mother.

26So Israel and Absalom encamped in the land of Gilead.

27When David came to Mahanaim, Shobi son of Nahash of Rabbah of the Ammonites, and Machir son of Ammiel of Lo-debar, and Barzillai the Gileadite of Rogelim

28Brought beds, basins, earthen vessels, wheat, barley, meal, parched grain, beans, lentils, parched [pulse—seeds of peas and beans],

29Honey, curds, sheep, and cheese of cows for David and the people with him to eat; for they said, The people are hungry, weary, and thirsty in the wilderness.

18 DAVID NUMBERED the men who were with him and set over them commanders of thousands and of hundreds.

2David sent forth the army, a third under command of Joab, a third under Abishai son of Zeruiah, Joab's brother, and a third under Ittai the Gittite. [He] told the men, I myself will go out with you also.

3But the men said, You shall not go out. For if we flee, they will not care about us; if half of us die, they will not care about us. But you are worth 10,000 such as we are. So now it is better that you be able to help us from the city.

4The king said to them, Whatever seems best to you I will do. So he stood beside the gate, and all the army came out by hundreds and by thousands.

5The king commanded Joab, Abishai, and Ittai, saying, Deal gently for my sake with the young man Absalom. And all the people heard when the king gave orders to all the commanders about Absalom.

6So the army went out into the field against Israel, and the battle was fought in the forest of Ephraim.

7[Absalom's] men of Israel were defeated by the servants of David, and there was a great slaughter that day of 20,000 men.

8For the battle spread over the face of all the country, and the forest devoured more men that day than did the sword.

New American Standard

20 Then Absalom's servants came to the woman at the house and said, "Where are Ahimaaz and Jonathan?" And the woman said to them, "They have crossed the brook of water." And when they searched and could not find *them,* they returned to Jerusalem.

21 ¶ It came about after they had departed that they came up out of the well and went and told King David; and they said to David, "Arise and cross over the water quickly for thus Ahithophel has counseled against you."

22 Then David and all the people who *were* with him arose and crossed the Jordan; and by dawn not even one remained who had not crossed the Jordan.

23 ¶ Now when Ahithophel saw that his counsel was not followed, he saddled *his* donkey and arose and went to his home, to his city, and set his house in order, and strangled himself; thus he died and was buried in the grave of his father.

24 ¶ Then David came to Mahanaim. And Absalom crossed the Jordan, he and all the men of Israel with him.

25 Absalom set Amasa over the army in place of Joab. Now Amasa was the son of a man whose name was Ithra the Israelite, who went in to Abigail the daughter of Nahash, sister of Zeruiah, Joab's mother.

26 And Israel and Absalom camped in the land of Gilead.

27 ¶ Now when David had come to Mahanaim, Shobi the son of Nahash from Rabbah of the sons of Ammon, Machir the son of Ammiel from Lo-debar, and Barzillai the Gileadite from Rogelim,

28 brought beds, basins, pottery, wheat, barley, flour, parched *grain,* beans, lentils, parched *seeds,*

29 honey, curds, sheep, and cheese of the herd, for David and for the people who *were* with him, to eat; for they said, "The people are hungry and weary and thirsty in the wilderness."

Absalom Slain

18 THEN DAVID numbered the people who were with him and set over them commanders of thousands and commanders of hundreds.

2 David sent the people out, one third under the command of Joab, one third under the command of Abishai the son of Zeruiah, Joab's brother, and one third under the command of Ittai the Gittite. And the king said to the people, "I myself will surely go out with you also."

3 But the people said, "You should not go out; for if we indeed flee, they will not care about us; even if half of us die, they will not care about us. But you are worth ten thousand of us; therefore now it is better that you *be ready* to help us from the city."

4 Then the king said to them, "Whatever seems best to you I will do." So the king stood beside the gate, and all the people went out by hundreds and thousands.

5 The king charged Joab and Abishai and Ittai, saying, "*Deal* gently for my sake with the young man Absalom." And all the people heard when the king charged all the commanders concerning Absalom.

6 ¶ Then the people went out into the field against Israel, and the battle took place in the forest of Ephraim.

7 The people of Israel were defeated there before the servants of David, and the slaughter there that day was great, 20,000 men.

8 For the battle there was spread over the whole countryside, and the forest devoured more people that day than the sword devoured.

New International

20 When Absalom's men came to the woman at the house, they asked, "Where are Ahimaaz and Jonathan?"

The woman answered them, "They crossed over the brook."[w] The men searched but found no one, so they returned to Jerusalem.

21 After the men had gone, the two climbed out of the well and went to inform King David. They said to him, "Set out and cross the river at once; Ahithophel has advised such and such against you." 22 So David and all the people with him set out and crossed the Jordan. By daybreak, no one was left who had not crossed the Jordan.

23 When Ahithophel saw that his advice had not been followed, he saddled his donkey and set out for his house in his hometown. He put his house in order and then hanged himself. So he died and was buried in his father's tomb.

24 David went to Mahanaim, and Absalom crossed the Jordan with all the men of Israel. 25 Absalom had appointed Amasa over the army in place of Joab. Amasa was the son of a man named Jether,[x] an Israelite[y] who had married Abigail,[z] the daughter of Nahash and sister of Zeruiah the mother of Joab. 26 The Israelites and Absalom camped in the land of Gilead.

27 When David came to Mahanaim, Shobi son of Nahash from Rabbah of the Ammonites, and Makir son of Ammiel from Lo Debar, and Barzillai the Gileadite from Rogelim 28 brought bedding and bowls and articles of pottery. They also brought wheat and barley, flour and roasted grain, beans and lentils,[a] 29 honey and curds, sheep, and cheese from cows' milk for David and his people to eat. For they said, "The people have become hungry and tired and thirsty in the desert."

Absalom's Death

18 DAVID MUSTERED the men who were with him and appointed over them commanders of thousands and commanders of hundreds. 2 David sent the troops out—a third under the command of Joab, a third under Joab's brother Abishai son of Zeruiah, and a third under Ittai the Gittite. The king told the troops, "I myself will surely march out with you."

3 But the men said, "You must not go out; if we are forced to flee, they won't care about us. Even if half of us die, they won't care; but you are worth ten thousand of us.[b] It would be better now for you to give us support from the city."

4 The king answered, "I will do whatever seems best to you."

So the king stood beside the gate while all the men marched out in units of hundreds and of thousands. 5 The king commanded Joab, Abishai and Ittai, "Be gentle with the young man Absalom for my sake." And all the troops heard the king giving orders concerning Absalom to each of the commanders.

6 The army marched into the field to fight Israel, and the battle took place in the forest of Ephraim. 7 There the army of Israel was defeated by David's men, and the casualties that day were great—twenty thousand men. 8 The battle spread out over the whole countryside, and the forest claimed more lives that day than the sword.

w 20 Or "*They passed by the sheep pen toward the water.*"
x 25 Hebrew *Ithra,* a variant of *Jether*   *y 25* Hebrew and some Septuagint manuscripts; other Septuagint manuscripts (see also 1 Chron. 2:17) *Ishmaelite* or *Jezreelite*   *z 25* Hebrew *Abigal,* a variant of *Abigail*   *a 28* Most Septuagint manuscripts and Syriac; Hebrew *lentils, and roasted grain*   *b 3* Two Hebrew manuscripts, some Septuagint manuscripts and Vulgate; most Hebrew manuscripts *care; for now there are ten thousand like us*

King James

Amplified

9 ¶ And Absalom met the servants of David. And Absalom rode upon a mule, and the mule went under the thick boughs of a great oak, and his head caught hold of the oak, and he was taken up between the heaven and the earth; and the mule that *was* under him went away.

10And a certain man saw *it,* and told Joab, and said, Behold, I saw Absalom hanged in an oak.

11And Joab said unto the man that told him, And, behold, thou sawest *him,* and why didst thou not smite him there to the ground? and I would have given thee ten *shekels* of silver, and a girdle.

12And the man said unto Joab, Though I should ᵉreceive a thousand *shekels* of silver in mine hand, *yet* would I not put forth mine hand against the king's son: for in our hearing the king charged thee and Abishai and Ittai, saying, ʲBeware that none *touch* the young man Absalom.

13Otherwise I should have wrought falsehood against mine own life: for there is no matter hid from the king, and thou thyself wouldest have set thyself against *me.*

14Then said Joab, I may not tarry thus ᵍwith thee. And he took three darts in his hand, and thrust them through the heart of Absalom, while he *was* yet alive in the ʰmidst of the oak.

15And ten young men that bare Joab's armour compassed about and smote Absalom, and slew him.

16And Joab blew the trumpet, and the people returned from pursuing after Israel: for Joab held back the people.

17And they took Absalom, and cast him into a great pit in the wood, and laid a very great heap of stones upon him: and all Israel fled every one to his tent.

18 ¶ Now Absalom in his lifetime had taken and reared up for himself a pillar, which *is* in the king's dale: for he said, I have no son to keep my name in remembrance: and he called the pillar after his own name: and it is called unto this day, Absalom's place.

David told of Absalom's death

19 ¶ Then said Ahimaaz the son of Zadok, Let me now run, and bear the king tidings, how that the LORD hath ⁱavenged him of his enemies.

20And Joab said unto him, Thou shalt not ʲbear tidings this day, but thou shalt bear tidings another day: but this day thou shalt bear no tidings, because the king's son is dead.

21Then said Joab to Cushi, Go tell the king what thou hast seen. And Cushi bowed himself unto Joab, and ran.

22Then said Ahimaaz the son of Zadok yet again to Joab, But ᵏhowsoever, let me, I pray thee, also run after Cushi. And Joab said, Wherefore wilt thou run, my son, seeing that thou hast no tidings ˡready?

23But howsoever, *said he,* let me run. And he said unto him, Run. Then Ahimaaz ran by the way of the plain, and overran Cushi.

24And David sat between the two gates: and the watchman went up to the roof over the gate unto the wall, and lifted up his eyes, and looked, and behold a man running alone.

25And the watchman cried, and told the king. And the king said, If he *be* alone, *there is* tidings in his mouth. And he came apace, and drew near.

26And the watchman saw another man running: and the watchman called unto the porter, and said, Behold *another* man running alone. And the king said, He also bringeth tidings.

27And the watchman said, ᵐMe thinketh the running of the foremost is like the running of Ahimaaz the son of Zadok. And the king said, He *is* a good man, and cometh with good tidings.

9Then Absalom [unavoidably] met the servants of David. Absalom rode on a mule, and the mule went under the thick boughs of a great oak, and Absalom's head caught fast [in a fork] of the oak; and the mule under him ran away, leaving him hanging between the heavens and the earth.

10A certain man saw it and told Joab, Behold, I saw Absalom hanging in an oak.

11Joab said to the man, You saw him! Why did you not strike him down to the ground? I would have given you ten shekels of silver and a girdle.

12The man told Joab, Though I should receive 1,000 pieces of silver, yet I would not put forth my hand against the king's son. For in our hearing the king charged you, Abishai, and Ittai, Have a care, whoever you be, for the young man Absalom.

13Otherwise, if I had dealt falsely against his life—for nothing is hidden from the king—you yourself would have taken sides against me.

14Joab said, I will not tarry thus with you. He took three darts in his hand and thrust them into the body of Absalom while he was yet alive in the midst of the oak.

15And ten young men, Joab's armor-bearers, surrounded and struck Absalom and killed him.

16Then Joab blew the trumpet, and the troops returned from pursuing Israel, for Joab restrained *and* spared them.

17They took Absalom and cast him into a great pit in the forest and raised a very great heap of stones upon him. And all Israel fled, everyone to his own home.

18Now Absalom in his lifetime had reared up for himself a pillar which is in the King's Valley, for he said, I have no son to keep my name in remembrance. He called the pillar after his own name, and to this day it is called Absalom's Monument.

19Then said Ahimaaz son of Zadok, Let me now run and bear the king tidings of how the Lord has avenged David of his enemies.

20Joab told him, You shall not carry news today, but another time. Today you shall bear no news, for the king's son is dead.

21Then said Joab to the Cushite [an Ethiopian], Go tell the king what you have seen. And the Cushite bowed to Joab and ran.

22Then said Ahimaaz son of Zadok again to Joab, But anyhow, let me, I pray you, also run after the Cushite. Joab said, Why should you run, my son, seeing you will have no reward, for you have not sufficient tidings?

23But he said, Let me run anyhow. So Joab said to him, Run. Then Ahimaaz ran by the way of the plain and outran the Cushite.

24Now David was sitting between the two gates; and the watchman went up to the roof over the gate by the wall, and when he looked, he saw a man running alone.

25The watchman called out and told the king. The king said, If he is alone, he has news to tell. And he came on and drew near.

26Then the watchman saw another man running, and the watchman called to the gatekeeper, Behold, another man running alone. The king said, He also brings news.

27The watchman said, I think the man in front runs like Ahimaaz son of Zadok. The king said, He is a good man and comes with good tidings.

ᵉ Heb. *weigh upon mine hand*   ʲHeb. *Beware whosoever ye be of*
ᵍ Heb. *before thee*   ʰHeb. *heart*   ⁱHeb. *judged him from the*
hand   ʲHeb. *be a man of tidings*   ᵏHeb. *be what may*
ˡOr, *convenient*   ᵐHeb. *I see the running*

New American Standard

9 ¶ Now Absalom happened to meet the servants of David. For Absalom was riding on *his* mule, and the mule went under the thick branches of a great oak. And his head caught fast in the oak, so he was left hanging between heaven and earth, while the mule that was under him kept going.

10 When a certain man saw *it*, he told Joab and said, "Behold, I saw Absalom hanging in an oak."

11 Then Joab said to the man who had told him, "Now behold, you saw *him!* Why then did you not strike him there to the ground? And I would have given you ten *pieces* of silver and a belt."

12 The man said to Joab, "Even if I should receive a thousand *pieces of* silver in my hand, I would not put out my hand against the king's son; for in our hearing the king charged you and Abishai and Ittai, saying, 'Protect for me the young man Absalom!'

13 "Otherwise, if I had dealt treacherously against his life (and there is nothing hidden from the king), then you yourself would have stood aloof."

14 Then Joab said, "I will not waste time here with you." So he took three spears in his hand and thrust them through the heart of Absalom while he was yet alive in the midst of the oak.

15 And ten young men who carried Joab's armor gathered around and struck Absalom and killed him.

16 ¶ Then Joab blew the trumpet, and the people returned from pursuing Israel, for Joab restrained the people.

17 They took Absalom and cast him into a deep pit in the forest and erected over him a very great heap of stones. And all Israel fled, each to his tent.

18 Now Absalom in his lifetime had taken and set up for himself a pillar which is in the King's Valley, for he said, "I have no son to preserve my name." So he named the pillar after his own name, and it is called Absalom's Monument to this day.

David Is Grief-stricken

19 ¶ Then Ahimaaz the son of Zadok said, "Please let me run and bring the king news that the LORD has freed him from the hand of his enemies."

20 But Joab said to him, "You are not the man to carry news this day, but you shall carry news another day; however, you shall carry no news today because the king's son is dead."

21 Then Joab said to the Cushite, "Go, tell the king what you have seen." So the Cushite bowed to Joab and ran.

22 Now Ahimaaz the son of Zadok said once more to Joab, "But whatever happens, please let me also run after the Cushite." And Joab said, "Why would you run, my son, since you will have no reward for going?"

23 "But whatever happens," *he said,* "I will run." So he said to him, "Run." Then Ahimaaz ran by way of the plain and passed up the Cushite.

24 ¶ Now David was sitting between the two gates; and the watchman went up to the roof of the gate by the wall, and raised his eyes and looked, and behold, a man running by himself.

25 The watchman called and told the king. And the king said, "If he is by himself there is good news in his mouth." And he came nearer and nearer.

26 Then the watchman saw another man running; and the watchman called to the gatekeeper and said, "Behold, *another* man running by himself." And the king said, "This one also is bringing good news."

27 The watchman said, "I think the running of the first one is like the running of Ahimaaz the son of Zadok." And the king said, "This is a good man and comes with good news."

New International

9 Now Absalom happened to meet David's men. He was riding his mule, and as the mule went under the thick branches of a large oak, Absalom's head got caught in the tree. He was left hanging in midair, while the mule he was riding kept on going.

10 When one of the men saw this, he told Joab, "I just saw Absalom hanging in an oak tree."

11 Joab said to the man who had told him this, "What! You saw him? Why didn't you strike him to the ground right there? Then I would have had to give you ten shekels[c] of silver and a warrior's belt."

12 But the man replied, "Even if a thousand shekels[d] were weighed out into my hands, I would not lift my hand against the king's son. In our hearing the king commanded you and Abishai and Ittai, 'Protect the young man Absalom for my sake.[e]' 13 And if I had put my life in jeopardy[f]—and nothing is hidden from the king—you would have kept your distance from me."

14 Joab said, "I'm not going to wait like this for you." So he took three javelins in his hand and plunged them into Absalom's heart while Absalom was still alive in the oak tree. 15 And ten of Joab's armor-bearers surrounded Absalom, struck him and killed him.

16 Then Joab sounded the trumpet, and the troops stopped pursuing Israel, for Joab halted them. 17 They took Absalom, threw him into a big pit in the forest and piled up a large heap of rocks over him. Meanwhile, all the Israelites fled to their homes.

18 During his lifetime Absalom had taken a pillar and erected it in the King's Valley as a monument to himself, for he thought, "I have no son to carry on the memory of my name." He named the pillar after himself, and it is called Absalom's Monument to this day.

David Mourns

19 Now Ahimaaz son of Zadok said, "Let me run and take the news to the king that the LORD has delivered him from the hand of his enemies."

20 "You are not the one to take the news today," Joab told him, "You may take the news another time, but you must not do so today, because the king's son is dead."

21 Then Joab said to a Cushite, "Go, tell the king what you have seen." The Cushite bowed down before Joab and ran off.

22 Ahimaaz son of Zadok again said to Joab, "Come what may, please let me run behind the Cushite."

But Joab replied, "My son, why do you want to go? You don't have any news that will bring you a reward."

23 He said, "Come what may, I want to run."

So Joab said, "Run!" Then Ahimaaz ran by way of the plain[g] and outran the Cushite.

24 While David was sitting between the inner and outer gates, the watchman went up to the roof of the gateway by the wall. As he looked out, he saw a man running alone. 25 The watchman called out to the king and reported it.

The king said, "If he is alone, he must have good news." And the man came closer and closer.

26 Then the watchman saw another man running, and he called down to the gatekeeper, "Look, another man running alone!"

The king said, "He must be bringing good news, too."

27 The watchman said, "It seems to me that the first one runs like Ahimaaz son of Zadok."

"He's a good man," the king said. "He comes with good news."

---

c 11 That is, about 4 ounces (about 115 grams)   *d 12* That is, about 25 pounds (about 11 kilograms)   *e 12* A few Hebrew manuscripts, Septuagint, Vulgate and Syriac; most Hebrew manuscripts may be translated *Absalom, whoever you may be.*   *f 13* Or *Otherwise, if I had acted treacherously toward him*   *g 23* That is, the plain of the Jordan

King James

28And Ahimaaz called, and said unto the king, *n*oAll is well. And he fell down to the earth upon his face before the king, and said, Blessed *be* the LORD thy God, which hath *p*delivered up the men that lifted up their hand against my lord the king.

29And the king said, *q*Is the young man Absalom safe? And Ahimaaz answered, When Joab sent the king's servant, and *me* thy servant, I saw a great tumult, but I knew not what *it was.*

30And the king said *unto him,* Turn aside, *and* stand here. And he turned aside, and stood still.

31And, behold, Cushi came; and Cushi said, *r*Tidings, my lord the king: for the LORD hath avenged thee this day of all them that rose up against thee.

32And the king said unto Cushi, *Is* the young man Absalom safe? And Cushi answered, The enemies of my lord the king, and all that rise against thee to do *thee* hurt, be as *that* young man *is.*

33 ¶ And the king was much moved, and went up to the chamber over the gate, and wept: and as he went, thus he said, O my son Absalom, my son, my son Absalom! would God I had died for thee, O Absalom, my son, my son!

19 AND IT was told Joab, Behold, the king weepeth and mourneth for Absalom.

2And the *s*victory that day was *turned* into mourning unto all the people: for the people heard say that day how the king was grieved for his son.

3And the people gat them by stealth that day into the city, as people being ashamed steal away when they flee in battle.

4But the king covered his face, and the king cried with a loud voice, O my son Absalom, O Absalom, my son, my son!

5And Joab came into the house to the king, and said, Thou hast shamed this day the faces of all thy servants, which this day have saved thy life, and the lives of thy sons and of thy daughters, and the lives of thy wives, and the lives of thy concubines;

6*t*In that thou lovest thine enemies, and hatest thy friends. For thou hast declared this day, *u*that thou regardest neither princes nor servants: for this day I perceive, that if Absalom had lived, and all we had died this day, then it had pleased thee well.

7Now therefore arise, go forth, and speak *v*comfortably unto thy servants: for I swear by the LORD, if thou go not forth, there will not tarry one with thee this night: and that will be worse unto thee than all the evil that befell thee from thy youth until now.

8Then the king arose, and sat in the gate. And they told unto all the people, saying, Behold, the king doth sit in the gate. And all the people came before the king: for Israel had fled every man to his tent.

David's return to Jerusalem

9 ¶ And all the people were at strife throughout all the tribes of Israel, saying, The king saved us out of the hand of our enemies, and he delivered us out of the hand of the Philistines; and now he is fled out of the land for Absalom.

10And Absalom, whom we anointed over us, is dead in battle. Now therefore why *w*speak ye not a word of bringing the king back?

Amplified

28And Ahimaaz called and said to the king, All is well! And he fell down to the ground on his face before the king and said, Blessed be the Lord your God, Who has shut up the men who lifted up their hands against my lord the king.

29The king said, Is the young man Absalom safe? Ahimaaz answered, When Joab sent the king's servant and me, your servant, I saw a great tumult, but I do not know what it was.

30The king told him, Turn aside; stand here. And he turned aside and stood still.

31And behold, the Cushite (Ethiopian) came, and he said, News, my lord the king! For the Lord has delivered you this day from all who rose up against you.

32The king said to the Cushite, Is the young man Absalom safe? The Cushite replied, May the enemies of my lord the king and all who rise against you to do evil be like that young man is.

33And the king was deeply moved and went up to the chamber over the gate and wept. And as he went, he said, O my son Absalom, my son, my son Absalom! Would to God I had died for you, O Absalom, my son, my son!

19 IT WAS told Joab, Behold, the king is weeping and mourning for Absalom.

2So the victory that day was turned into mourning for all the people, for they heard it said, The king grieves for his son.

3The people slipped into the city stealthily that day as humiliated people steal away when they flee in battle.

4But the king covered his face and cried with a loud voice, O my son Absalom, O Absalom, my son, my son!

5And Joab came into the house to the king and said, You have today covered the faces of all your servants with shame, who this day have saved your life and the lives of your sons and your daughters and the lives of your wives and concubines.

6For you love those who hate you and hate those who love you. You have declared today that princes and servants are nothing to you; for today I see that if Absalom had lived and all the rest of us had died, you would be well pleased.

7So now arise, go out and speak kindly and encouragingly to your servants; for I swear by the Lord that if you do not go, not a man will remain with you this night. And this will be worse for you than all the evil that has befallen you from your youth until now.

8Then the king arose and sat in the gate. And all [his followers] were told, The king is sitting in the gate, and they all came before the king. Now Israel [Absalom's troops] had fled, every man to his home.

9And all the people were at strife throughout all the tribes of Israel, saying, The king delivered us from the hands of our enemies, and he saved us from the hands of the Philistines. And now he has fled out of the land from Absalom.

10And Absalom, whom we anointed over us, is dead in battle. So now, why do you say nothing about bringing back the king?

---

n Or, *Peace be to thee*   *o* Heb. *Peace*
p Heb. *shut up*
q Heb. *Is there peace?*   *r* Heb. *Tidings is brought*   *s* Heb.
salvation, or, *deliverance*   *t* Heb. *By loving*   *u* Heb. *that*
princes or, *servants* are *not to thee*   *v* Heb. *to the heart of thy*
servants   *w* Heb. *are ye silent?*

New American Standard

28 ¶ Ahimaaz called and said to the king, "*p*All is well." And he prostrated himself before the king with his face to the ground. And he said, "Blessed is the LORD your God, who has delivered up the men who lifted their hands against my lord the king."

29 The king said, "Is it well with the young man Absalom?" And Ahimaaz answered, "When Joab sent the king's servant, and your servant, I saw a great tumult, but I did not know what *it was.*"

30 Then the king said, "Turn aside and stand here." So he turned aside and stood still.

31 ¶ Behold, the Cushite arrived, and the Cushite said, "Let my lord the king receive good news, for the LORD has freed you this day from the hand of all those who rose up against you."

32 Then the king said to the Cushite, "Is it well with the young man Absalom?" And the Cushite answered, "Let the enemies of my lord the king, and all who rise up against you for evil, be as that young man!"

33 ¶ The king was deeply moved and went up to the chamber over the gate and wept. And thus he said as he walked, "O my son Absalom, my son, my son Absalom! Would I had died instead of you, O Absalom, my son, my son!"

Joab Reproves David's Lament

19 THEN IT was told Joab, "Behold, the king is weeping and mourns for Absalom."

2 The victory that day was turned to mourning for all the people, for the people heard *it* said that day, "The king is grieved for his son."

3 So the people went by stealth into the city that day, as people who are humiliated steal away when they flee in battle.

4 The king covered his face and cried out with a loud voice, "O my son Absalom, O Absalom, my son, my son!"

5 Then Joab came into the house to the king and said, "Today you have covered with shame the faces of all your servants, who today have saved your life and the lives of your sons and daughters, the lives of your wives, and the lives of your concubines,

6 by loving those who hate you, and by hating those who love you. For you have shown today that princes and servants are nothing to you; for I know this day that if Absalom were alive and all of us were dead today, then you would be pleased.

7 "Now therefore arise, go out and speak kindly to your servants, for I swear by the LORD, if you do not go out, surely not a man will pass the night with you, and this will be worse for you than all the evil that has come upon you from your youth until now."

David Restored as King

8 So the king arose and sat in the gate. When they told all the people, saying, "Behold, the king is sitting in the gate," then all the people came before the king.

¶ Now Israel had fled, each to his tent.

9 All the people were quarreling throughout all the tribes of Israel, saying, "The king delivered us from the hand of our enemies and saved us from the hand of the Philistines, but now he has fled out of the land from Absalom.

10 "However, Absalom, whom we anointed over us, has died in battle. Now then, why are you silent about bringing the king back?"

New International

28 Then Ahimaaz called out to the king, "All is well!" He bowed down before the king with his face to the ground and said, "Praise be to the LORD your God! He has delivered up the men who lifted their hands against my lord the king."

29 The king asked, "Is the young man Absalom safe?"

Ahimaaz answered, "I saw great confusion just as Joab was about to send the king's servant and me, your servant, but I don't know what it was."

30 The king said, "Stand aside and wait here." So he stepped aside and stood there.

31 Then the Cushite arrived and said, "My lord the king, hear the good news! The LORD has delivered you today from all who rose up against you."

32 The king asked the Cushite, "Is the young man Absalom safe?"

The Cushite replied, "May the enemies of my lord the king and all who rise up to harm you be like that young man."

33 The king was shaken. He went up to the room over the gateway and wept. As he went, he said: "O my son Absalom! My son, my son Absalom! If only I had died instead of you—O Absalom, my son, my son!"

19 JOAB WAS told, "The king is weeping and mourning for Absalom." 2 And for the whole army the victory that day was turned into mourning, because on that day the troops heard it said, "The king is grieving for his son." 3 The men stole into the city that day as men steal in who are ashamed when they flee from battle. 4 The king covered his face and cried aloud, "O my son Absalom! O Absalom, my son, my son!"

5 Then Joab went into the house to the king and said, "Today you have humiliated all your men, who have just saved your life and the lives of your sons and daughters and the lives of your wives and concubines. 6 You love those who hate you and hate those who love you. You have made it clear today that the commanders and their men mean nothing to you. I see that you would be pleased if Absalom were alive today and all of us were dead. 7 Now go out and encourage your men. I swear by the LORD that if you don't go out, not a man will be left with you by nightfall. This will be worse for you than all the calamities that have come upon you from your youth till now."

8 So the king got up and took his seat in the gateway. When the men were told, "The king is sitting in the gateway," they all came before him.

David Returns to Jerusalem

Meanwhile, the Israelites had fled to their homes. 9 Throughout the tribes of Israel, the people were all arguing with each other, saying, "The king delivered us from the hand of our enemies; he is the one who rescued us from the hand of the Philistines. But now he has fled the country because of Absalom; 10 and Absalom, whom we anointed to rule over us, has died in battle. So why do you say nothing about bringing the king back?"

---

p Lit *Peace*

King James

11 ¶ And king David sent to Zadok and to Abiathar the priests, saying, Speak unto the elders of Judah, saying, Why are ye the last to bring the king back to his house? seeing the speech of all Israel is come to the king, *even* to his house.

12 Ye *are* my brethren, ye *are* my bones and my flesh: wherefore then are ye the last to bring back the king?

13 And say ye to Amasa, *Art* thou not of my bone, and of my flesh? God do so to me, and more also, if thou be not captain of the host before me continually in the room of Joab.

14 And he bowed the heart of all the men of Judah, even as *the heart of* one man; so that they sent *this word* unto the king, Return thou, and all thy servants.

15 So the king returned, and came to Jordan. And Judah came to Gilgal, to go to meet the king, to conduct the king over Jordan.

16 ¶ And Shimei the son of Gera, a Benjamite, which *was* of Bahurim, hasted and came down with the men of Judah to meet king David.

17 And *there were* a thousand men of Benjamin with him, and Ziba the servant of the house of Saul, and his fifteen sons and his twenty servants with him; and they went over Jordan before the king.

18 And there went over a ferry boat to carry over the king's household, and to do ˣwhat he thought good. And Shimei the son of Gera fell down before the king, as he was come over Jordan;

19 And said unto the king, Let not my lord impute iniquity unto me, neither do thou remember that which thy servant did perversely the day that my lord the king went out of Jerusalem, that the king should take it to his heart.

20 For thy servant doth know that I have sinned: therefore, behold, I am come the first this day of all the house of Joseph to go down to meet my lord the king.

21 But Abishai the son of Zeruiah answered and said, Shall not Shimei be put to death for this, because he cursed the LORD's anointed?

22 And David said, What have I to do with you, ye sons of Zeruiah, that ye should this day be adversaries unto me? shall there any man be put to death this day in Israel? for do not I know that I *am* this day king over Israel?

23 Therefore the king said unto Shimei, Thou shalt not die. And the king sware unto him.

24 ¶ And Mephibosheth the son of Saul came down to meet the king, and had neither dressed his feet, nor trimmed his beard, nor washed his clothes, from the day the king departed until the day he came *again* in peace.

25 And it came to pass, when he was come to Jerusalem to meet the king, that the king said unto him, Wherefore wentest not thou with me, Mephibosheth?

26 And he answered, My lord, O king, my servant deceived me: for thy servant said, I will saddle me an ass, that I may ride thereon, and go to the king; because thy servant *is* lame.

27 And he hath slandered thy servant unto my lord the king; but my lord the king *is* as an angel of God: do therefore *what is* good in thine eyes.

28 For all *of* my father's house were but ʸdead men before my lord the king: yet didst thou set thy servant among them that did eat at thine own table. What right therefore have I yet to cry any more unto the king?

29 And the king said unto him, Why speakest thou any more of thy matters? I have said, Thou and Ziba divide the land.

30 And Mephibosheth said unto the king, Yea, let him take all, forasmuch as my lord the king is come again in peace unto his own house.

31 ¶ And Barzillai the Gileadite came down from Rogelim, and went over Jordan with the king, to conduct him over Jordan.

Amplified

11 And King David sent to Zadok and to Abiathar the priests, saying, Say to the elders of Judah, Why are you the last to bring the king back to his house, when the word of all Israel has come to the king, to bring him to his house?

12 You are my kinsmen; you are my bone and my flesh. Why then are you the last to bring back the king?

13 And say to Amasa, Are you not of my bone and of my flesh? May God do so to me, and more also, if you are not commander of my army hereafter in place of Joab.

14 He inclined the hearts of all the men of Judah as one man, so they sent word to [him], Return, you and all your servants.

15 So [David] returned and came to the Jordan. And Judah came to Gilgal to meet the king, to conduct him over the Jordan.

16 And Shimei son of Gera, a Benjamite of Bahurim, hastily came down with the men of Judah to meet King David,

17 And 1,000 men of Benjamin with him. And Ziba, the servant of the house of Saul, and his fifteen sons and twenty servants with him, rushed to the Jordan *and* pressed quickly into the king's presence.

18 And there went over a ferryboat to bring over the king's household and to do what he thought good. And Shimei son of Gera fell down before the king as David came to the Jordan,

19 And said to the king, Let not my lord impute iniquity to me *and* hold me guilty, nor remember what your servant did the day my lord went out of Jerusalem [when Shimei grossly insulted David]; may the king not take it to heart.

20 For your servant knows that I have sinned; therefore, behold, I am today the first of all the house of Joseph to come down to meet my lord the king.

21 But Abishai son of Zeruiah said, Shall not Shimei be put to death for this, because he cursed the Lord's anointed?

22 David said, What have I to do with you, you sons of Zeruiah, that you should be an adversary to me today? Shall anyone be put to death today in Israel? For do not I know that I am this day king over Israel?

23 Therefore the king said to Shimei, You shall not die [at my hand]. And the king gave him his oath. [I Kings 2:44–46.]

24 Mephibosheth the son [grandson] of Saul came down to meet the king, and had not dressed his feet, trimmed his beard, or washed his clothes from the day the king left until he returned in peace *and* safety.

25 And when he came to Jerusalem to meet the king, David said to him, Why did you not go with me, Mephibosheth?

26 He said, My lord O king, my servant [Ziba] deceived me; for I said, Saddle me the donkey that I may ride on it and go to the king, for your servant is lame [but he took the donkey and left without me].

27 He has slandered your servant to my lord the king. But the king is as an angel of God; so do what is good in your eyes.

28 For all of my father's house were but doomed to death before my lord the king; yet you set your servant among those who ate at your own table. What right therefore have I to cry any more to the king?

29 The king said to him, Why speak any more of your affairs? I say, You and Ziba divide the land.

30 Mephibosheth said to the king, Oh, let him take it all, since my lord the king has returned home in safety *and* peace.

31 Now Barzillai the Gileadite came down from Rogelim and went on to the Jordan with the king to conduct him over the Jordan.

ˣHeb. *the good in his eyes*   ʸHeb. *men of death*

New American Standard

11 ¶ Then King David sent to Zadok and Abiathar the priests, saying, "Speak to the elders of Judah, saying, 'Why are you the last to bring the king back to his house, since the word of all Israel has come to the king, *even* to his house?

12 'You are my brothers; you are my bone and my flesh. Why then should you be the last to bring back the king?'

13 "Say to Amasa, 'Are you not my bone and my flesh? May God do so to me, and more also, if you will not be commander of the army before me continually in place of Joab.' "

14 Thus he turned the hearts of all the men of Judah as one man, so that they sent *word* to the king, *saying,* "Return, you and all your servants."

15 The king then returned and came as far as the Jordan. And Judah came to Gilgal in order to go to meet the king, to bring the king across the Jordan.

16 ¶ Then Shimei the son of Gera, the Benjamite who was from Bahurim, hurried and came down with the men of Judah to meet King David.

17 There were a thousand men of Benjamin with him, with Ziba the servant of the house of Saul, and his fifteen sons and his twenty servants with him; and they rushed to the Jordan before the king.

18 Then they kept crossing the ford to bring over the king's household, and to do what was good in his sight. And Shimei the son of Gera fell down before the king as he was about to cross the Jordan.

19 So he said to the king, "Let not my lord consider me guilty, nor remember what your servant did wrong on the day when my lord the king came out from Jerusalem, so that the king would take *it* to heart.

20 "For your servant knows that I have sinned; therefore behold, I have come today, the first of all the house of Joseph to go down to meet my lord the king."

21 But Abishai the son of Zeruiah said, "Should not Shimei be put to death for this, because he cursed the LORD's anointed?"

22 David then said, "What have I to do with you, O sons of Zeruiah, that you should this day be an adversary to me? Should any man be put to death in Israel today? For do I not know that I am king over Israel today?"

23 The king said to Shimei, "You shall not die." Thus the king swore to him.

24 ¶ Then Mephibosheth the *q*son of Saul came down to meet the king; and he had neither cared for his feet, nor trimmed his mustache, nor washed his clothes, from the day the king departed until the day he came *home* in peace.

25 It was when he came from Jerusalem to meet the king, that the king said to him, "Why did you not go with me, Mephibosheth?"

26 So he answered, "O my lord, the king, my servant deceived me; for your servant said, 'I will saddle a donkey for myself that I may ride on it and go with the king,' because your servant is lame.

27 "Moreover, he has slandered your servant to my lord the king; but my lord the king is like the angel of God, therefore do what is good in your sight.

28 "For all my father's household was nothing but dead men before my lord the king; yet you set your servant among those who ate at your own table. What right do I have yet that I should complain anymore to the king?"

29 So the king said to him, "Why do you still speak of your affairs? I have decided, 'You and Ziba shall divide the land.' "

30 Mephibosheth said to the king, "Let him even take it all, since my lord the king has come safely to his own house."

31 ¶ Now Barzillai the Gileadite had come down from Rogelim; and he went on to the Jordan with the king to escort him over the Jordan.

q I.e. grandson

New International

11 King David sent this message to Zadok and Abiathar, the priests: "Ask the elders of Judah, 'Why should you be the last to bring the king back to his palace, since what is being said throughout Israel has reached the king at his quarters? 12 You are my brothers, my own flesh and blood. So why should you be the last to bring back the king?' 13 And say to Amasa, 'Are you not my own flesh and blood? May God deal with me, be it ever so severely, if from now on you are not the commander of my army in place of Joab.' "

14 He won over the hearts of all the men of Judah as though they were one man. They sent word to the king, "Return, you and all your men." 15 Then the king returned and went as far as the Jordan.

Now the men of Judah had come to Gilgal to go out and meet the king and bring him across the Jordan. 16 Shimei son of Gera, the Benjamite from Bahurim, hurried down with the men of Judah to meet King David. 17 With him were a thousand Benjamites, along with Ziba, the steward of Saul's household, and his fifteen sons and twenty servants. They rushed to the Jordan, where the king was. 18 They crossed at the ford to take the king's household over and to do whatever he wished.

When Shimei son of Gera crossed the Jordan, he fell prostrate before the king 19 and said to him, "May my lord not hold me guilty. Do not remember how your servant did wrong on the day my lord the king left Jerusalem. May the king put it out of his mind. 20 For I your servant know that I have sinned, but today I have come here as the first of the whole house of Joseph to come down and meet my lord the king."

21 Then Abishai son of Zeruiah said, "Shouldn't Shimei be put to death for this? He cursed the LORD's anointed."

22 David replied, "What do you and I have in common, you sons of Zeruiah? This day you have become my adversaries! Should anyone be put to death in Israel today? Do I not know that today I am king over Israel?" 23 So the king said to Shimei, "You shall not die." And the king promised him on oath.

24 Mephibosheth, Saul's grandson, also went down to meet the king. He had not taken care of his feet or trimmed his mustache or washed his clothes from the day the king left until the day he returned safely. 25 When he came from Jerusalem to meet the king, the king asked him, "Why didn't you go with me, Mephibosheth?"

26 He said, "My lord the king, since I your servant am lame, I said, 'I will have my donkey saddled and will ride on it, so I can go with the king.' But Ziba my servant betrayed me. 27 And he has slandered your servant to my lord the king. My lord the king is like an angel of God; so do whatever pleases you. 28 All my grandfather's descendants deserved nothing but death from my lord the king, but you gave your servant a place among those who eat at your table. So what right do I have to make any more appeals to the king?"

29 The king said to him, "Why say more? I order you and Ziba to divide the fields."

30 Mephibosheth said to the king, "Let him take everything, now that my lord the king has arrived home safely."

31 Barzillai the Gileadite also came down from Rogelim to cross the Jordan with the king and to send him on his

King James

³²Now Barzillai was a very aged man, *even* fourscore years old: and he had provided the king of sustenance while he lay at Mahanaim; for he *was* a very great man.

³³And the king said unto Barzillai, Come thou over with me, and I will feed thee with me in Jerusalem.

³⁴And Barzillai said unto the king, ^zHow long have I to live, that I should go up with the king unto Jerusalem?

³⁵I *am* this day fourscore years old: *and* can I discern between good and evil? can thy servant taste what I eat or what I drink? can I hear any more the voice of singing men and singing women? wherefore then should thy servant be yet a burden unto my lord the king?

³⁶Thy servant will go a little way over Jordan with the king: and why should the king recompense it me with such a reward?

³⁷Let thy servant, I pray thee, turn back again, that I may die in mine own city, *and be buried* by the grave of my father and of my mother. But behold thy servant Chimham; let him go over with my lord the king; and do to him what shall seem good unto thee.

³⁸And the king answered, Chimham shall go over with me, and I will do to him that which shall seem good unto thee: and whatsoever thou shalt ^arequire of me, *that* will I do for thee.

³⁹And all the people went over Jordan. And when the king was come over, the king kissed Barzillai, and blessed him; and he returned unto his own place.

⁴⁰Then the king went on to Gilgal, and ^bChimham went on with him: and all the people of Judah conducted the king, and also half the people of Israel.

⁴¹¶ And, behold, all the men of Israel came to the king, and said unto the king, Why have our brethren the men of Judah stolen thee away, and have brought the king, and his household, and all David's men with him, over Jordan?

⁴²And all the men of Judah answered the men of Israel, Because the king *is* near of kin to us: wherefore then be ye angry for this matter? have we eaten at all of the king's *cost?* or hath he given us any gift?

⁴³And the men of Israel answered the men of Judah, and said, We have ten parts in the king, and we have also more *right* in David than ye: why then did ye ^cdespise us, that our advice should not be first had in bringing back our king? And the words of the men of Judah were fiercer than the words of the men of Israel.

Sheba leads Israel to revolt

20 AND THERE happened to be there a man of Belial, whose name *was* Sheba, the son of Bichri, a Benjamite: and he blew a trumpet, and said, We have no part in David, neither have we inheritance in the son of Jesse: every man to his tents, O Israel.

²So every man of Israel went up from after David, *and* followed Sheba the son of Bichri: but the men of Judah clave unto their king, from Jordan even to Jerusalem.

³¶ And David came to his house at Jerusalem; and the king took the ten women *his* concubines, whom he had left to keep the house, and put them in ^dward, and fed them, but went not in unto them. So they were ^eshut up unto the day of their death, ^fliving in widowhood.

⁴¶ Then said the king to Amasa, ^gAssemble me the men of Judah within three days, and be thou here present.

⁵So Amasa went to assemble *the men of* Judah: but he tarried longer than the set time which he had appointed him.

⁶And David said to Abishai, Now shall Sheba the son of Bichri do us more harm than *did* Absalom: take thou thy lord's servants, and pursue after him, lest he get him fenced cities, and ^hescape us.

Amplified

³²Now Barzillai was a very aged man, even eighty years old; and he had provided the king with food while he remained at Mahanaim, for he was a very great man.

³³And the king said to Barzillai, Come over with me, and I will provide for you with me in Jerusalem.

³⁴And Barzillai said to the king, How much longer have I to live, that it would be worthwhile for me to go up with the king to Jerusalem?

³⁵I am this day eighty years old. Could I now [be useful as a counselor to] discern between good and evil? Can your servant appreciate what I eat or drink? Can I any longer enjoy the voices of singing men and women? Why then should your servant be still a burden to my lord the king?

³⁶Your servant will only go over the Jordan with the king. Why should the king repay me with such a reward?

³⁷Let your servant turn back again, that I may die in my own city and be buried by the grave of my father and mother. But here is your servant Chimham; let him go over with my lord the king. And do to him what shall seem good to you.

³⁸The king answered, Chimham shall go over with me, and I will do to him what seems good to you; and whatever you ask of me I will do for you.

³⁹So all the people went over the Jordan. When the king had crossed over, he kissed Barzillai and blessed him, and [the great man] returned to his own place.

⁴⁰Then the king went on to Gilgal, and Chimham went with him; and all the people of Judah and also half the people of Israel escorted the king.

⁴¹And all the men of Israel came to the king and said to him, Why have our kinsmen, the men of Judah, stolen you away and have brought the king and his household over the Jordan, and all David's men with him?

⁴²But all the men of Judah answered the men of Israel, Because the king is near of kin to us. Why then be angry about it? Have we eaten at all at the king's expense? Or has he given us any gift?

⁴³Then the men of Israel answered the men of Judah, We have ten [tribes'] shares in the king; and we have more right to David than you have. Why then did you despise *and* ignore us? Were we not the first to speak of our bringing back our king? But the words of the men of Judah were more violent than the charges of the men of Israel.

20 THERE HAPPENED to be there a base *and* contemptible fellow named Sheba son of Bichri, a Benjamite. He blew a trumpet and said, We have no portion in David and no inheritance in the son of Jesse! Every man to his tents, O Israel!

²So all the men of Israel withdrew from David and followed Sheba son of Bichri; but the men of Judah stayed faithfully with their king, from the Jordan to Jerusalem.

³So David came to his house at Jerusalem. And the king took the ten women, his concubines, whom he had left to keep the house, and put them away under guard and provided for them, but did not go in to them. So they were shut up to the day of their death, living in widowhood.

⁴Then said the king to Amasa, Assemble the men of Judah to me within three days, and you be present here.

⁵So Amasa went to assemble the men of Judah, but he tarried longer than the set time which had been appointed him.

⁶And David said to Abishai, Now will Sheba son of Bichri do us more harm than Absalom did. Take your lord's servants and pursue him, lest he get for himself fenced cities and snatch away our very eyes.

^zHeb. *How many days* are *the years of my life?* 　^aHeb. *choose*
^bHeb. *Chimhan* 　^cHeb. *set us at light* 　^dHeb. *an house of ward* 　^eHeb. *bound* 　^fHeb. *in widowhood of life* 　^gHeb. *Call* 　^hHeb. *deliver himself from our eyes*

New American Standard

³² Now Barzillai was very old, being eighty years old; and he had sustained the king while he stayed at Mahanaim, for he was a very great man. ³³ The king said to Barzillai, "You cross over with me and I will sustain you in Jerusalem with me."
³⁴ But Barzillai said to the king, "How long have I yet to live, that I should go up with the king to Jerusalem? ³⁵"I am now eighty years old. Can I distinguish between good and bad? Or can your servant taste what I eat or what I drink? Or can I hear anymore the voice of singing men and women? Why then should your servant be an added burden to my lord the king? ³⁶"Your servant would merely cross over the Jordan with the king. Why should the king compensate me *with* this reward? ³⁷"Please let your servant return, that I may die in my own city near the grave of my father and my mother. However, here is your servant Chimham, let him cross over with my lord the king, and do for him what is good in your sight."
³⁸ The king answered, "Chimham shall cross over with me, and I will do for him what is good in your sight; and whatever you require of me, I will do for you."
³⁹ All the people crossed over the Jordan and the king crossed too. The king then kissed Barzillai and blessed him, and he returned to his place.
⁴⁰ ¶ Now the king went on to Gilgal, and Chimham went on with him; and all the people of Judah and also half the people of Israel accompanied the king.
⁴¹ And behold, all the men of Israel came to the king and said to the king, "Why had our brothers the men of Judah stolen you away, and brought the king and his household and all David's men with him over the Jordan?"
⁴² Then all the men of Judah answered the men of Israel, "Because the king is a close relative to us. Why then are you angry about this matter? Have we eaten at all at the king's *expense,* or has anything been taken for us?"
⁴³ But the men of Israel answered the men of Judah and said, "We have ten parts in the king, therefore we also have more *claim* on David than you. Why then did you treat us with contempt? Was it not our advice first to bring back our king?" Yet the words of the men of Judah were harsher than the words of the men of Israel.

Sheba's Revolt

20 NOW A worthless fellow happened to be there whose name was Sheba, the son of Bichri, a Benjamite; and he blew the trumpet and said,
"We have no portion in David,
Nor do we have inheritance in the son of Jesse;
Every man to his tents, O Israel!"
² So all the men of Israel withdrew from following David *and* followed Sheba the son of Bichri; but the men of Judah remained steadfast to their king, from the Jordan even to Jerusalem.
³ ¶ Then David came to his house at Jerusalem, and the king took the ten women, the concubines whom he had left to keep the house, and placed them under guard and provided them with sustenance, but did not go in to them. So they were shut up until the day of their death, living as widows.
⁴ ¶ Then the king said to Amasa, "Call out the men of Judah for me within three days, and be present here yourself."
⁵ So Amasa went to call out *the men of* Judah, but he delayed longer than the set time which he had appointed him.
⁶ And David said to Abishai, "Now Sheba the son of Bichri will do us more harm than Absalom; take your lord's servants and pursue him, so that he does not find for himself fortified cities and escape from our sight."

New International

way from there. ³²Now Barzillai was a very old man, eighty years of age. He had provided for the king during his stay in Mahanaim, for he was a very wealthy man. ³³The king said to Barzillai, "Cross over with me and stay with me in Jerusalem, and I will provide for you."
³⁴But Barzillai answered the king, "How many more years will I live, that I should go up to Jerusalem with the king? ³⁵I am now eighty years old. Can I tell the difference between what is good and what is not? Can your servant taste what he eats and drinks? Can I still hear the voices of men and women singers? Why should your servant be an added burden to my lord the king? ³⁶Your servant will cross over the Jordan with the king for a short distance, but why should the king reward me in this way? ³⁷Let your servant return, that I may die in my own town near the tomb of my father and mother. But here is your servant Kimham. Let him cross over with my lord the king. Do for him whatever pleases you."
³⁸The king said, "Kimham shall cross over with me, and I will do for him whatever pleases you. And anything you desire from me I will do for you."
³⁹So all the people crossed the Jordan, and then the king crossed over. The king kissed Barzillai and gave him his blessing, and Barzillai returned to his home.
⁴⁰When the king crossed over to Gilgal, Kimham crossed with him. All the troops of Judah and half the troops of Israel had taken the king over.
⁴¹Soon all the men of Israel were coming to the king and saying to him, "Why did our brothers, the men of Judah, steal the king away and bring him and his household across the Jordan, together with all his men?"
⁴²All the men of Judah answered the men of Israel, "We did this because the king is closely related to us. Why are you angry about it? Have we eaten any of the king's provisions? Have we taken anything for ourselves?"
⁴³Then the men of Israel answered the men of Judah, "We have ten shares in the king; and besides, we have a greater claim on David than you have. So why do you treat us with contempt? Were we not the first to speak of bringing back our king?"
But the men of Judah responded even more harshly than the men of Israel.

Sheba Rebels Against David

20 NOW A troublemaker named Sheba son of Bicri, a Benjamite, happened to be there. He sounded the trumpet and shouted,
"We have no share in David,
no part in Jesse's son!
Every man to his tent, O Israel!"

²So all the men of Israel deserted David to follow Sheba son of Bicri. But the men of Judah stayed by their king all the way from the Jordan to Jerusalem.
³When David returned to his palace in Jerusalem, he took the ten concubines he had left to take care of the palace and put them in a house under guard. He provided for them, but did not lie with them. They were kept in confinement till the day of their death, living as widows.
⁴Then the king said to Amasa, "Summon the men of Judah to come to me within three days, and be here yourself." ⁵But when Amasa went to summon Judah, he took longer than the time the king had set for him.
⁶David said to Abishai, "Now Sheba son of Bicri will do us more harm than Absalom did. Take your master's men and pursue him, or he will find fortified cities and escape

King James

⁷And there went out after him Joab's men, and the Cherethites, and the Pelethites, and all the mighty men: and they went out of Jerusalem, to pursue after Sheba the son of Bichri.

⁸When they *were* at the great stone which *is* in Gibeon, Amasa went before them. And Joab's garment that he had put on was girded unto him, and upon it a girdle *with* a sword fastened upon his loins in the sheath thereof; and as he went forth it fell out.

⁹And Joab said to Amasa, *Art* thou in health, my brother? And Joab took Amasa by the beard with the right hand to kiss him.

¹⁰But Amasa took no heed to the sword that *was* in Joab's hand: so he smote him therewith in the fifth *rib,* and shed out his bowels to the ground, and *i*struck him not again; and he died. So Joab and Abishai his brother pursued after Sheba the son of Bichri.

¹¹And one of Joab's men stood by him, and said, He that favoureth Joab, and he that *is* for David, *let him go* after Joab.

¹²And Amasa wallowed in blood in the midst of the highway. And when the man saw that all the people stood still, he removed Amasa out of the highway into the field, and cast a cloth upon him, when he saw that every one that came by him stood still.

¹³When he was removed out of the highway, all the people went on after Joab, to pursue after Sheba the son of Bichri.

¹⁴ ¶ And he went through all the tribes of Israel unto Abel, and to Beth-maachah, and all the Berites: and they were gathered together, and went also after him.

¹⁵And they came and besieged him in Abel of Beth-maachah, and they cast up a bank against the city, and *j*it stood in the trench: and all the people that *were* with Joab *k*battered the wall, to throw it down.

¹⁶ ¶ Then cried a wise woman out of the city, Hear, hear; say, I pray you, unto Joab, Come near hither, that I may speak with thee.

¹⁷And when he was come near unto her, the woman said, *Art* thou Joab? And he answered, I *am he.* Then she said unto him, Hear the words of thine handmaid. And he answered, I do hear.

¹⁸Then she spake, saying, *l*They were wont to speak in old time, saying, They shall surely ask *counsel* at Abel: and so they ended *the matter.*

¹⁹I *am one of them that are* peaceable *and* faithful in Israel: thou seekest to destroy a city and a mother in Israel: why wilt thou swallow up the inheritance of the Lᴏʀᴅ?

²⁰And Joab answered and said, Far be it, far be it from me, that I should swallow up or destroy.

²¹The matter *is* not so: but a man of mount Ephraim, Sheba the son of Bichri *m*by name, hath lifted up his hand against the king, *even* against David: deliver him only, and I will depart from the city. And the woman said unto Joab, Behold, his head shall be thrown to thee over the wall.

²²Then the woman went unto all the people in her wisdom. And they cut off the head of Sheba the son of Bichri, and cast *it* out to Joab. And he blew a trumpet, and they *n*retired from the city, every man to his tent. And Joab returned to Jerusalem unto the king.

²³ ¶ Now Joab *was* over all the host of Israel: and Benaiah the son of Jehoiada *was* over the Cherethites and over the Pelethites:

²⁴And Adoram *was* over the tribute: and Jehoshaphat the son of Ahilud *was* orecorder;

²⁵And Sheva *was* scribe: and Zadok and Abiathar *were* the priests:

²⁶And Ira also the Jairite was *p*a chief ruler about David.

Amplified

⁷And there went after him Joab's men and [David's bodyguards] the Cherethites and Pelethites and all the mighty men; they went out from Jerusalem to pursue Sheba son of Bichri.

⁸When they were at the great stone in Gibeon, Amasa came to meet them. Joab was wearing a soldier's garment, and over it was a sheathed sword fastened around his hips; and as he went forward, it fell out.

⁹Joab said to Amasa, Are you well, my brother? And Joab took Amasa by the beard with the right hand [as if] to kiss him.

¹⁰But Amasa did not notice the sword in Joab's hand. So [Joab] struck him [who was to have been his successor] with it in the body, shedding his bowels to the ground without another blow; and [soon] he died. So Joab and Abishai his brother pursued Sheba son of Bichri.

¹¹And one of Joab's men stood by him and said, Whoever favors Joab and is for David, follow Joab!

¹²And Amasa wallowed in his blood in the highway. And when the man saw that all the people who came by stood still, he removed Amasa out of the highway into the field and spread a cloth over him.

¹³When Amasa was removed from the highway, all the people went on after Joab to pursue Sheba son of Bichri.

¹⁴Joab went through all the tribes of Israel to Abel of Beth-maacah, and all the Berites assembled and also went after [Sheba] ardently.

¹⁵And they came and besieged Sheba in Abel of Beth-maacah, and they cast up a siege mound against the city, and it stood against the rampart; and all the men with Joab battered *and* undermined the wall to make it fall.

¹⁶Then a wise woman of the city cried, Hear, hear! Say to Joab, Come here so I can speak to you.

¹⁷And when he came near her, the woman said, Are you Joab? He answered, I am. Then she said to him, Hear the words of your handmaid. He answered, I am listening.

¹⁸Then she said, People used to say, Let them but ask counsel at Abel, and so they settled the matter.

¹⁹I am one of the peaceable and faithful in Israel. You seek to destroy a city which is a mother in Israel. Why will you swallow up the inheritance of the Lord?

²⁰Joab answered, Far be it, far be it from me that I should swallow up or destroy!

²¹That is not true. But a man of the hill country of Ephraim, Sheba son of Bichri, has lifted up his hand against King David. Deliver him only, and I will depart from the city. And the woman said, Behold, his head shall be thrown to you over the wall.

²²Then the woman in her wisdom went to all the people. And they cut off the head of Sheba son of Bichri and cast it down to Joab. So he blew the trumpet, and they retired from the city, every man to his own home. And Joab returned to Jerusalem to the king. [Eccl. 9:13–16.]

²³Joab was over the host of Israel; Benaiah son of Jehoiada was over [the king's bodyguards] the Cherethites and Pelethites;

²⁴Adoram was over the tribute; Jehoshaphat son of Ahilud was recorder;

²⁵Sheva was scribe; and Zadok and Abiathar were the priests;

²⁶Also Ira the Jairite was chief minister to David.

ⁱHeb. *doubled not his stroke*   ^jOr, *it stood against the outmost wall*   ^kHeb. *marred to throw down*   ^lOr, *They plainly spake in the beginning, saying, Surely they will ask of Abel, and so make an end*   ^mHeb. *by his name*   ⁿHeb. *were scattered*   ^oOr, *remembrancer*   ^pOr, *a prince*

New American Standard

7 So Joab's men went out after him, along with the Cherethites and the Pelethites and all the mighty men; and they went out from Jerusalem to pursue Sheba the son of Bichri.

8 When they were at the large stone which is in Gibeon, Amasa came to meet them. Now Joab was dressed in his military attire, and over it was a belt with a sword in its sheath fastened at his waist; and as he went forward, it fell out.

9 Joab said to Amasa, "Is it well with you, my brother?" And Joab took Amasa by the beard with his right hand to kiss him.

Amasa Murdered

10 But Amasa was not on guard against the sword which was in Joab's hand so he struck him in the belly with it and poured out his inward parts on the ground, and did not *strike* him again, and he died. Then Joab and Abishai his brother pursued Sheba the son of Bichri.

11 Now there stood by him one of Joab's young men, and said, "Whoever favors Joab and whoever is for David, *let him* follow Joab."

12 But Amasa lay wallowing in *his* blood in the middle of the highway. And when the man saw that all the people stood still, he removed Amasa from the highway into the field and threw a garment over him when he saw that everyone who came by him stood still.

Revolt Put Down

13 As soon as he was removed from the highway, all the men passed on after Joab to pursue Sheba the son of Bichri.

14 ¶ Now he went through all the tribes of Israel to Abel, even Beth-maacah, and all the Berites; and they were gathered together and also went after him.

15 They came and besieged him in Abel Beth-maacah, and they cast up a siege ramp against the city, and it stood by the rampart; and all the people who were with Joab were wreaking destruction in order to topple the wall.

16 Then a wise woman called from the city, "Hear, hear! Please tell Joab, 'Come here that I may speak with you.' "

17 So he approached her, and the woman said, "Are you Joab?" And he answered, "I am." Then she said to him, "Listen to the words of your maidservant." And he answered, "I am listening."

18 Then she spoke, saying, "Formerly they used to say, 'They will surely ask *advice* at Abel,' and thus they ended *the dispute.*

19 "I am of those who are peaceable *and* faithful in Israel. You are seeking to destroy a city, even a mother in Israel. Why would you swallow up the inheritance of the LORD?"

20 Joab replied, "Far be it, far be it from me that I should swallow up or destroy!

21 "Such is not the case. But a man from the hill country of Ephraim, Sheba the son of Bichri by name, has lifted up his hand against King David. Only hand him over, and I will depart from the city." And the woman said to Joab, "Behold, his head will be thrown to you over the wall."

22 Then the woman wisely came to all the people. And they cut off the head of Sheba the son of Bichri and threw it to Joab. So he blew the trumpet, and they were dispersed from the city, each to his tent. Joab also returned to the king at Jerusalem.

23 ¶ Now Joab was over the whole army of Israel, and Benaiah the son of Jehoiada was over the Cherethites and the Pelethites;

24 and Adoram was over the forced labor, and Jehoshaphat the son of Ahilud was the recorder;

25 and Sheva was scribe, and Zadok and Abiathar were priests;

26 and Ira the Jairite was also a priest to David.

New International

from us." 7So Joab's men and the Kerethites and Pelethites and all the mighty warriors went out under the command of Abishai. They marched out from Jerusalem to pursue Sheba son of Bicri.

8While they were at the great rock in Gibeon, Amasa came to meet them. Joab was wearing his military tunic, and strapped over it at his waist was a belt with a dagger in its sheath. As he stepped forward, it dropped out of its sheath.

9Joab said to Amasa, "How are you, my brother?" Then Joab took Amasa by the beard with his right hand to kiss him. 10Amasa was not on his guard against the dagger in Joab's hand, and Joab plunged it into his belly, and his intestines spilled out on the ground. Without being stabbed again, Amasa died. Then Joab and his brother Abishai pursued Sheba son of Bicri.

11One of Joab's men stood beside Amasa and said, "Whoever favors Joab, and whoever is for David, let him follow Joab!" 12Amasa lay wallowing in his blood in the middle of the road, and the man saw that all the troops came to a halt there. When he realized that everyone who came up to Amasa stopped, he dragged him from the road into a field and threw a garment over him. 13After Amasa had been removed from the road, all the men went on with Joab to pursue Sheba son of Bicri.

14Sheba passed through all the tribes of Israel to Abel Beth Maacah[h] and through the entire region of the Berites, who gathered together and followed him. 15All the troops with Joab came and besieged Sheba in Abel Beth Maacah. They built a siege ramp up to the city, and it stood against the outer fortifications. While they were battering the wall to bring it down, 16a wise woman called from the city, "Listen! Listen! Tell Joab to come here so I can speak to him." 17He went toward her, and she asked, "Are you Joab?"

"I am," he answered.

She said, "Listen to what your servant has to say."

"I'm listening," he said.

18She continued, "Long ago they used to say, 'Get your answer at Abel,' and that settled it. 19We are the peaceful and faithful in Israel. You are trying to destroy a city that is a mother in Israel. Why do you want to swallow up the LORD's inheritance?"

20"Far be it from me!" Joab replied, "Far be it from me to swallow up or destroy! 21That is not the case. A man named Sheba son of Bicri, from the hill country of Ephraim, has lifted up his hand against the king, against David. Hand over this one man, and I'll withdraw from the city."

The woman said to Joab, "His head will be thrown to you from the wall."

22Then the woman went to all the people with her wise advice, and they cut off the head of Sheba son of Bicri and threw it to Joab. So he sounded the trumpet, and his men dispersed from the city, each returning to his home. And Joab went back to the king in Jerusalem.

23Joab was over Israel's entire army; Benaiah son of Jehoiada was over the Kerethites and Pelethites; 24Adoniram[i] was in charge of forced labor; Jehoshaphat son of Ahilud was recorder; 25Sheva was secretary; Zadok and Abiathar were priests; 26and Ira the Jairite was David's priest.

---

h 14 Or Abel, even Beth Maacah; also in verse 15   i 24 Some Septuagint manuscripts (see also 1 Kings 4:6 and 5:14); Hebrew Adoram

King James

David repays the Gibeonites

21 THEN THERE was a famine in the days of David three years, year after year; and David *q*inquired of the LORD. And the LORD answered, *It is* for Saul, and for *his* bloody house, because he slew the Gibeonites.

2And the king called the Gibeonites, and said unto them; (now the Gibeonites *were* not of the children of Israel, but of the remnant of the Amorites; and the children of Israel had sworn unto them: and Saul sought to slay them in his zeal to the children of Israel and Judah.)

3Wherefore David said unto the Gibeonites, What shall I do for you? and wherewith shall I make the atonement, that ye may bless the inheritance of the LORD?

4And the Gibeonites said unto him, *r*We will have no silver nor gold of Saul, nor of his house; neither for us shalt thou kill any man in Israel. And he said, What ye shall say, *that* will I do for you.

5And they answered the king, The man that consumed us, and that *s*devised against us *that* we should be destroyed from remaining in any of the coasts of Israel,

6Let seven men of his sons be delivered unto us, and we will hang them up unto the LORD in Gibeah of Saul, *t*whom the LORD did choose. And the king said, I will give *them*.

7But the king spared Mephibosheth, the son of Jonathan the son of Saul, because of the LORD'S oath that *was* between them, between David and Jonathan the son of Saul.

8But the king took the two sons of Rizpah the daughter of Aiah, whom she bare unto Saul, Armoni and Mephibosheth; and the five sons of *u*Michal the daughter of Saul, whom she *v*brought up for Adriel the son of Barzillai the Meholathite:

9And he delivered them into the hands of the Gibeonites, and they hanged them in the hill before the LORD: and they fell *all* seven together, and were put to death in the days of harvest, in the first *days,* in the beginning of barley harvest.

10 ¶ And Rizpah the daughter of Aiah took sackcloth, and spread it for her upon the rock, from the beginning of harvest until water dropped upon them out of heaven, and suffered neither the birds of the air to rest on them by day, nor the beasts of the field by night.

11And it was told David what Rizpah the daughter of Aiah, the concubine of Saul, had done.

12 ¶ And David went and took the bones of Saul and the bones of Jonathan his son from the men of Jabesh-gilead, which had stolen them from the street of Beth-shan, where the Philistines had hanged them, when the Philistines had slain Saul in Gilboa:

13And he brought up from thence the bones of Saul and the bones of Jonathan his son; and they gathered the bones of them that were hanged.

14And the bones of Saul and Jonathan his son buried they in the country of Benjamin in Zelah, in the sepulchre of Kish his father: and they performed all that the king commanded. And after that God was entreated for the land.

Victories over the Philistines

15 ¶ Moreover the Philistines had yet war again with Israel; and David went down, and his servants with him, and fought against the Philistines: and David waxed faint.

16And Ishbi-benob, which *was* of the sons of *w*the giant, the weight of whose *x*spear *weighed* three hundred *shekels* of brass in weight, he being girded with a new *sword,* thought to have slain David.

Amplified

21 THERE WAS a three-year famine in the days of David, year after year; and David inquired of the Lord. The Lord replied, It is on account of Saul and his bloody house, for he put to death the Gibeonites.

2So the king called the Gibeonites—now the Gibeonites were not Israelites but of the remnant of the Amorites. The Israelites had sworn to spare them, but Saul in his zeal for the people of Israel and Judah had sought to slay the Gibeonites—

3So David said to the Gibeonites, What shall I do for you? How can I make atonement that you may bless the Lord's inheritance?

4The Gibeonites said to him, We will accept no silver or gold of Saul or of his house; neither for us shall you kill any man in Israel. David said, I will do for you what you say.

5They said to the king, The man who consumed us and planned to prevent us from remaining in any territory of Israel,

6Let seven men of his sons be delivered to us and we will hang them up before the Lord at Gibeah of Saul, [on the mountain] of the Lord. And the king said, I will give them.

7But the king spared Mephibosheth son of Jonathan, the son of Saul, because of the Lord's oath that was between David and Jonathan son of Saul.

8But the king took the two sons of Rizpah daughter of Aiah, whom she bore to Saul, Armoni and Mephibosheth, and the five sons of [Merab] daughter of Saul, whom she bore to Adriel son of Barzillai the Meholathite.

9He delivered them into the hands of the Gibeonites, and they hung them up on the hill before the Lord, and all seven perished together. They were put to death in the first days of barley harvest.

10Rizpah daughter of Aiah took sackcloth and spread it for herself on the rock, from the beginning of harvest until rain fell on them, and she did not allow either the birds of the air to come upon them by day or the beasts of the field by night.

11It was told David what Rizpah daughter of Aiah, the concubine of Saul, had done.

12And David went and took the bones of Saul and Jonathan his son from the men of Jabesh-gilead, who had stolen them from the street of Beth-shan, where the Philistines had hung them up when the Philistines had slain Saul in Gilboa.

13He brought from there the bones of Saul and of Jonathan his son, and they gathered the bones of those who were hung up.

14And the bones of Saul and Jonathan his son they buried in the country of Benjamin in Zelah in the tomb of Kish, [Saul's] father, and they did all that the king commanded. And after that, God heard *and* answered when His people prayed for the land.

15The Philistines had war again with Israel. And David went down and his servants with him and fought against the Philistines, and David became faint.

16Ishbi-benob, who was of the sons of the giants, the weight of whose spear was 300 shekels of bronze, was girded with a new sword, and thought to kill David.

---

*q*Heb. *sought the face*   *r*Or, It is *not silver nor gold that we have to do with Saul or his house, neither* pertains it *to us to kill* *s*Or, *cut us off*   *t*Or, *chosen of the LORD*   *u*Or, *Michal's sister*   *v*Heb. *bare to Adriel;* see 1 Sam. 18:19   *w*Or, *Rapha* *x*Heb. *the staff,* or, *the head*

New American Standard

Gibeonite Revenge

21 NOW THERE was a famine in the days of David for three years, year after year; and David sought the presence of the LORD. And the LORD said, "It is for Saul and his bloody house, because he put the Gibeonites to death."

2 So the king called the Gibeonites and spoke to them (now the Gibeonites were not of the sons of Israel but of the remnant of the Amorites, and the sons of Israel made a covenant with them, but Saul had sought to kill them in his zeal for the sons of Israel and Judah).

3 Thus David said to the Gibeonites, "What should I do for you? And how can I make atonement that you may bless the inheritance of the LORD?"

4 Then the Gibeonites said to him, "We have no *concern* of silver or gold with Saul or his house, nor is it for us to put any man to death in Israel." And he said, "I will do for you whatever you say."

5 So they said to the king, "The man who consumed us and who planned to exterminate us from remaining within any border of Israel,

6 let seven men from his sons be given to us, and we will hang them before the LORD in Gibeah of Saul, the chosen of the LORD." And the king said, "I will give *them.*"

7 ¶ But the king spared Mephibosheth, the son of Jonathan the son of Saul, because of the oath of the LORD which was between them, between David and Saul's son Jonathan.

8 So the king took the two sons of Rizpah the daughter of Aiah, Armoni and Mephibosheth whom she had borne to Saul, and the five sons of Merab the daughter of Saul, whom she had borne to Adriel the son of Barzillai the Meholathite.

9 Then he gave them into the hands of the Gibeonites, and they hanged them in the mountain before the LORD, so that the seven of them fell together; and they were put to death in the first days of harvest at the beginning of barley harvest.

10 ¶ And Rizpah the daughter of Aiah took sackcloth and spread it for herself on the rock, from the beginning of harvest until it rained on them from the sky; and she allowed neither the birds of the sky to rest on them by day nor the beasts of the field by night.

11 When it was told David what Rizpah the daughter of Aiah, the concubine of Saul, had done,

12 then David went and took the bones of Saul and the bones of Jonathan his son from the men of Jabesh-gilead, who had stolen them from the open square of Beth-shan, where the Philistines had hanged them on the day the Philistines struck down Saul in Gilboa.

13 He brought up the bones of Saul and the bones of Jonathan his son from there, and they gathered the bones of those who had been hanged.

14 They buried the bones of Saul and Jonathan his son in the country of Benjamin in Zela, in the grave of Kish his father; thus they did all that the king commanded, and after that God was moved by prayer for the land.

15 ¶ Now when the Philistines were at war again with Israel, David went down and his servants with him; and as they fought against the Philistines, David became weary.

16 Then Ishbi-benob, who was among the descendants of the giant, the weight of whose spear was three hundred *shekels* of bronze in weight, was girded with a new *sword,* and he intended to kill David.

New International

The Gibeonites Avenged

21 DURING THE reign of David, there was a famine for three successive years; so David sought the face of the LORD. The LORD said, "It is on account of Saul and his blood-stained house; it is because he put the Gibeonites to death."

2 The king summoned the Gibeonites and spoke to them. (Now the Gibeonites were not a part of Israel but were survivors of the Amorites; the Israelites had sworn to ⌊spare⌋ them, but Saul in his zeal for Israel and Judah had tried to annihilate them.) 3 David asked the Gibeonites, "What shall I do for you? How shall I make amends so that you will bless the LORD's inheritance?"

4 The Gibeonites answered him, "We have no right to demand silver or gold from Saul or his family, nor do we have the right to put anyone in Israel to death."

"What do you want me to do for you?" David asked.

5 They answered the king, "As for the man who destroyed us and plotted against us so that we have been decimated and have no place anywhere in Israel, 6 let seven of his male descendants be given to us to be killed and exposed before the LORD at Gibeah of Saul—the LORD's chosen one."

So the king said, "I will give them to you."

7 The king spared Mephibosheth son of Jonathan, the son of Saul, because of the oath before the LORD between David and Jonathan son of Saul. 8 But the king took Armoni and Mephibosheth, the two sons of Aiah's daughter Rizpah, whom she had borne to Saul, together with the five sons of Saul's daughter Merab,*j* whom she had borne to Adriel son of Barzillai the Meholathite. 9 He handed them over to the Gibeonites, who killed and exposed them on a hill before the LORD. All seven of them fell together; they were put to death during the first days of the harvest, just as the barley harvest was beginning.

10 Rizpah daughter of Aiah took sackcloth and spread it out for herself on a rock. From the beginning of the harvest till the rain poured down from the heavens on the bodies, she did not let the birds of the air touch them by day or the wild animals by night. 11 When David was told what Aiah's daughter Rizpah, Saul's concubine, had done, 12 he went and took the bones of Saul and his son Jonathan from the citizens of Jabesh Gilead. (They had taken them secretly from the public square at Beth Shan, where the Philistines had hung them after they struck Saul down on Gilboa.) 13 David brought the bones of Saul and his son Jonathan from there, and the bones of those who had been killed and exposed were gathered up.

14 They buried the bones of Saul and his son Jonathan in the tomb of Saul's father Kish, at Zela in Benjamin, and did everything the king commanded. After that, God answered prayer in behalf of the land.

Wars Against the Philistines

15 Once again there was a battle between the Philistines and Israel. David went down with his men to fight against the Philistines, and he became exhausted. 16 And Ishbi-Benob, one of the descendants of Rapha, whose bronze spearhead weighed three hundred shekels*k* and who was

---

j 8 Two Hebrew manuscripts, some Septuagint manuscripts and Syriac (see also 1 Samuel 18:19); most Hebrew and Septuagint manuscripts *Michal*   *k 16* That is, about 7 1/2 pounds (about 3.5 kilograms)

King James

Amplified

¹⁷But Abishai the son of Zeruiah succoured him, and smote the Philistine, and killed him. Then the men of David sware unto him, saying, Thou shalt go no more out with us to battle, that thou quench not the ^ylight of Israel.

¹⁸And it came to pass after this, that there was again a battle with the Philistines at Gob: then Sibbechai the Hushathite slew ^zSaph, which *was* of the sons of ^athe giant.

¹⁹And there was again a battle in Gob with the Philistines, where Elhanan the son of ^bJaare-oregim, a Bethlehemite, slew *the brother of* Goliath the Gittite, the staff of whose spear *was* like a weaver's beam.

²⁰And there was yet a battle in Gath, where was a man of *great* stature, that had on every hand six fingers, and on every foot six toes, four and twenty in number; and he also was born to ^athe giant.

²¹And when he ^cdefied Israel, Jonathan the son of Shimeah the brother of David slew him.

²²These four were born to the giant in Gath, and fell by the hand of David, and by the hand of his servants.

David's psalm of praise

22 AND DAVID spake unto the LORD the words of this song in the day *that* the LORD had delivered him out of the hand of all his enemies, and out of the hand of Saul:

²And he said, The LORD *is* my rock, and my fortress, and my deliverer;

³The God of my rock; in him will I trust: *he is* my shield, and the horn of my salvation, my high tower, and my refuge, my saviour; thou savest me from violence.

⁴I will call on the LORD, *who is* worthy to be praised: so shall I be saved from mine enemies.

⁵When the ^dwaves of death compassed me, the floods of ^eungodly men made me afraid;

⁶The ^fsorrows of hell compassed me about; the snares of death prevented me;

⁷In my distress I called upon the LORD, and cried to my God: and he did hear my voice out of his temple, and my cry *did enter* into his ears.

⁸Then the earth shook and trembled; the foundations of heaven moved and shook, because he was wroth.

⁹There went up a smoke ^gout of his nostrils, and fire out of his mouth devoured: coals were kindled by it.

¹⁰He bowed the heavens also, and came down; and darkness *was* under his feet.

¹¹And he rode upon a cherub, and did fly: and he was seen upon the wings of the wind.

¹²And he made darkness pavilions round about him, ^hdark waters, *and* thick clouds of the skies.

¹³Through the brightness before him were coals of fire kindled.

¹⁴The LORD thundered from heaven, and the most High uttered his voice.

¹⁵And he sent out arrows, and scattered them; lightning, and discomfited them.

¹⁶And the channels of the sea appeared, the foundations of the world were discovered, at the rebuking of the LORD, at the blast of the breath of his nostrils.

¹⁷But Abishai son of Zeruiah came to David's aid, and smote and killed the Philistine. Then David's men charged him, You shall no more go out with us to battle, lest you quench the lamp of Israel.

¹⁸After this, there was again war with the Philistines at Gob (Gezer). Then Sibbecai the Hushathite slew Saph (Sippai), who was a descendant of the giant.

¹⁹There was again war at Gob with the Philistines, and Elhanan son of Jaare-oregim, a Bethlehemite, slew Goliath the Gittite, whose spear shaft was like a weaver's beam.

²⁰And there was again war at Gath, where there was a man of great stature who had six fingers on each hand and six toes on each foot, twenty-four in number; he also was a descendant of the giants.

²¹And when he defied Israel, Jonathan son of Shimei, brother of David, slew him.

²²These four were descended from the giant in Gath, and they fell by the hands of David and his servants.

22 DAVID SPOKE to the Lord the words of this song on the day when the Lord delivered him from the hands of all his enemies and from the hand of Saul.

²He said: The Lord is my Rock [of escape from Saul] and my Fortress [in the wilderness] and my Deliverer; [I Sam. 23:14, 25, 28.]

³My God, my Rock, in Him will I take refuge; my Shield and the Horn of my salvation; my Stronghold and my Refuge, my Savior—You save me from violence. [Gen. 15:1.]

⁴I call on the Lord, Who is worthy to be praised, and I am saved from my enemies.

⁵For the waves of death enveloped me; the torrents of destruction made me afraid.

⁶The cords of Sheol were entangling me; I encountered the snares of death.

⁷In my distress I called upon the Lord; I cried to my God, and He heard my voice from His temple; my cry came into His ears.

⁸Then the earth reeled and quaked, the foundations of the heavens trembled and shook because He was angry.

⁹Smoke went up from His nostrils, and devouring fire from His mouth; coals were kindled by it.

¹⁰He bowed the heavens and came down; thick darkness was under His feet.

¹¹He rode on a cherub and flew; He was seen upon the wings of the wind.

¹²He made darkness His canopy around Him, gathering of waters, thick clouds of the skies.

¹³Out of the brightness before Him coals of fire flamed forth.

¹⁴The Lord thundered from heaven, and the Most High uttered His voice.

¹⁵He sent out arrows and scattered them; lightning confused *and* troubled them.

¹⁶The channels of the sea were visible, the foundations of the world were uncovered at the rebuke of the Lord, at the blast of the breath of His nostrils.

---

^yHeb. *candle,* or, *lamp*   ^zOr, *Sippai*   ^aOr, *Rapha*   ^bOr, *Jair*   ^cOr, *reproached*   ^dOr, *pangs*   ^eHeb. *Belial*   ^fOr, *cords*   ^gHeb. *by*   ^hHeb. *binding of waters*

New American Standard

17 But Abishai the son of Zeruiah helped him, and
struck the Philistine and killed him. Then the men of David swore to him, saying, "You shall not go out again with
us to battle, so that you do not extinguish the lamp of
Israel."

18 ¶ Now it came about after this that there was war
again with the Philistines at Gob; then Sibbecai the Hushathite struck down Saph, who was among the descendants of the giant.

19 There was war with the Philistines again at Gob, and
Elhanan the son of Jaare-oregim the Bethlehemite killed
Goliath the Gittite, the shaft of whose spear was like a
weaver's beam.

20 There was war at Gath again, where there was a man
of *great* stature who had six fingers on each hand and six
toes on each foot, twenty-four in number; and he also had
been born to the giant.

21 When he defied Israel, Jonathan the son of Shimei,
David's brother, struck him down.

22 These four were born to the giant in Gath, and they
fell by the hand of David and by the hand of his servants.

David's Psalm of Deliverance

22 AND DAVID spoke the words of this song to the
LORD in the day that the LORD delivered him from
the hand of all his enemies and from the hand of Saul.

2 He said,
"The LORD is my rock and my fortress and my
deliverer;
3 My God, my rock, in whom I take refuge,
My shield and the horn of my salvation, my
stronghold and my refuge;
My savior, You save me from violence.
4 "I call upon the LORD, who is worthy to be
praised,
And I am saved from my enemies.
5 "For the waves of death encompassed me;
The torrents of destruction overwhelmed me;
6 The cords of Sheol surrounded me;
The snares of death confronted me.
7 "In my distress I called upon the LORD,
Yes, I cried to my God;
And from His temple He heard my voice,
And my cry for help *came* into His ears.
8 "Then the earth shook and quaked,
The foundations of heaven were trembling
And were shaken, because He was angry.
9 "Smoke went up out of His nostrils,
Fire from His mouth devoured;
Coals were kindled by it.
10 "He bowed the heavens also, and came down
With thick darkness under His feet.
11 "And He rode on a cherub and flew;
And He appeared on the wings of the wind.
12 "And He made darkness canopies around Him,
A mass of waters, thick clouds of the sky.
13 "From the brightness before Him
Coals of fire were kindled.
14 "The LORD thundered from heaven,
And the Most High uttered His voice.
15 "And He sent out arrows, and scattered them,
Lightning, and routed them.
16 "Then the channels of the sea appeared,
The foundations of the world were laid bare
By the rebuke of the LORD,
At the blast of the breath of His nostrils.

New International

armed with a new ⌊sword⌋, said he would kill David. 17But
Abishai son of Zeruiah came to David's rescue; he struck
the Philistine down and killed him. Then David's men
swore to him, saying, "Never again will you go out with
us to battle, so that the lamp of Israel will not be extin-
guished."

18In the course of time, there was another battle with the
Philistines, at Gob. At that time Sibbecai the Hushathite
killed Saph, one of the descendants of Rapha.

19In another battle with the Philistines at Gob, Elhanan
son of Jaare-Oregim[l] the Bethlehemite killed Goliath[m]
the Gittite, who had a spear with a shaft like a weaver's
rod.

20In still another battle, which took place at Gath, there
was a huge man with six fingers on each hand and six toes
on each foot—twenty-four in all. He also was descended
from Rapha. 21When he taunted Israel, Jonathan son of
Shimeah, David's brother, killed him.

22These four were descendants of Rapha in Gath, and
they fell at the hands of David and his men.

David's Song of Praise

22 DAVID SANG to the LORD the words of this song
when the LORD delivered him from the hand of all
his enemies and from the hand of Saul. 2He said:

"The LORD is my rock, my fortress and my
deliverer;
3 my God is my rock, in whom I take refuge,
my shield and the horn[n] of my salvation.
He is my stronghold, my refuge and my
savior—
from violent men you save me.
4I call to the LORD, who is worthy of praise,
and I am saved from my enemies.

5"The waves of death swirled about me;
the torrents of destruction overwhelmed me.
6The cords of the grave[o] coiled around me;
the snares of death confronted me.
7In my distress I called to the LORD;
I called out to my God.
From his temple he heard my voice;
my cry came to his ears.

8"The earth trembled and quaked,
the foundations of the heavens[p] shook;
they trembled because he was angry.
9Smoke rose from his nostrils;
consuming fire came from his mouth,
burning coals blazed out of it.
10He parted the heavens and came down;
dark clouds were under his feet.
11He mounted the cherubim and flew;
he soared[q] on the wings of the wind.
12He made darkness his canopy around him—
the dark[r] rain clouds of the sky.
13Out of the brightness of his presence
bolts of lightning blazed forth.
14The LORD thundered from heaven;
the voice of the Most High resounded.
15He shot arrows and scattered ⌊the enemies⌋,
bolts of lightning and routed them.
16The valleys of the sea were exposed
and the foundations of the earth laid bare
at the rebuke of the LORD,
at the blast of breath from his nostrils.

[l] *19* Or *son of Jair the weaver* [m] *19* Hebrew and Septuagint; 1 Chron. 20:5 *son of Jair killed Lahmi the brother of Goliath* [n] *3* *Horn* here symbolizes strength. [o] *6* Hebrew *Sheol* [p] *8* Hebrew; Vulgate and Syriac (see also Psalm 18:7) *mountains* [q] *11* Many Hebrew manuscripts (see also Psalm 18:10); most Hebrew manuscripts *appeared* [r] *12* Septuagint and Vulgate (see also Psalm 18:11); Hebrew *massed*

King James

¹⁷He sent from above, he took me; he drew me out of *i*many waters;

¹⁸He delivered me from my strong enemy, *and* from them that hated me: for they were too strong for me.

¹⁹They prevented me in the day of my calamity: but the LORD was my stay.

²⁰He brought me forth also into a large place: he delivered me, because he delighted in me.

²¹The LORD rewarded me according to my righteousness: according to the cleanness of my hands hath he recompensed me.

²²For I have kept the ways of the LORD, and have not wickedly departed from my God.

²³For all his judgments *were* before me: and *as for* his statutes, I did not depart from them.

²⁴I was also upright *j*before him, and have kept myself from mine iniquity.

²⁵Therefore the LORD hath recompensed me according to my righteousness; according to my cleanness *k*in his eyesight.

²⁶With the merciful thou wilt show thyself merciful, *and* with the upright man thou wilt show thyself upright.

²⁷With the pure thou wilt show thyself pure; and with the froward thou wilt *l*show thyself unsavoury.

²⁸And the afflicted people thou wilt save: but thine eyes *are* upon the haughty, *that* thou mayest bring *them* down.

²⁹For thou *art* my *m*lamp, O LORD: and the LORD will lighten my darkness.

³⁰For by thee I have *n*run through a troop: by my God have I leaped over a wall.

³¹*As for* God, his way *is* perfect; the word of the LORD *is* *o*tried: he *is* a buckler to all them that trust in him.

³²For who *is* God, save the LORD? and who *is* a rock, save our God?

³³God *is* my strength *and* power: and he *p*maketh my way perfect.

³⁴He *q*maketh my feet like hinds' *feet:* and setteth me upon my high places.

³⁵He teacheth my hands *r*to war; so that a bow of steel is broken by mine arms.

³⁶Thou hast also given me the shield of thy salvation: and thy gentleness hath *s*made me great.

³⁷Thou hast enlarged my steps under me; so that my *t*feet did not slip.

³⁸I have pursued mine enemies, and destroyed them; and turned not again until I had consumed them.

³⁹And I have consumed them, and wounded them, that they could not arise: yea, they are fallen under my feet.

⁴⁰For thou hast girded me with strength to battle: them that rose up against me hast thou *u*subdued under me.

⁴¹Thou hast also given me the necks of mine enemies, that I might destroy them that hate me.

⁴²They looked, but *there was* none to save; *even* unto the LORD, but he answered them not.

Amplified

¹⁷He sent from above, He took me; He drew me out of great waters.

¹⁸He delivered me from my strong enemy, from those who hated me, for they were too mighty for me.

¹⁹They came upon me in the day of my calamity, but the Lord was my stay.

²⁰He brought me forth into a large place; He delivered me because He delighted in me.

²¹The Lord rewarded me according to my uprightness with Him; He compensated *and* benefited me according to the cleanness of my hands.

²²For I have kept the ways of the Lord, and have not wickedly departed from my God.

²³For all His ordinances were before me; and from His statutes I did not turn aside.

²⁴I was also blameless before Him and kept myself from guilt *and* iniquity.

²⁵Therefore the Lord has recompensed me according to my righteousness, according to my cleanness in His [holy] sight.

²⁶Toward the loving *and* loyal You will show Yourself loving *and* loyal, and with the upright *and* blameless You will show Yourself upright *and* blameless.

²⁷To the pure You will show Yourself pure, and to the willful You will show Yourself willful.

²⁸And the afflicted people You will deliver, but Your eyes are upon the haughty, whom You will bring down.

²⁹For You, O Lord, are my Lamp; the Lord lightens my darkness.

³⁰For by You I run through a troop; by my God I leap over a wall.

³¹As for God, His way is perfect; the word of the Lord is tried. He is a Shield to all those who trust *and* take refuge in Him.

³²For who is God but the Lord? And who is a Rock except our God?

³³God is my strong Fortress; He guides the blameless in His way *and* sets him free.

³⁴He makes my feet like the hinds' [firm and able]; He sets me secure *and* confident upon the heights.

³⁵He trains my hands for war, so that my arms can bend a bow of bronze.

³⁶You have also given me the shield of Your salvation; and Your condescension *and* gentleness have made me great.

³⁷You have enlarged my steps under me, so that my feet have not slipped.

³⁸I have pursued my enemies and destroyed them; and I did not turn back until they were consumed.

³⁹I consumed them and thrust them through, so that they did not arise; they fell at my feet.

⁴⁰For You girded me with strength for the battle; those who rose up against me You subdued under me.

⁴¹You have made my enemies turn their backs to me, that I might cut off those who hate me.

⁴²They looked, but there was none to save—even to the Lord, but He did not answer them.

---

i Or, *great*   *j* Heb. *to him*   *k* Heb. *before his eyes*   *l* Or, *wrestle*   *m* Or, *candle*   *n* Or, *broken a troop*   *o* Or, *refined*
p Heb. *riddeth, or, looseth*   *q* Heb. *equalleth*   *r* Heb. *for the war*   *s* Heb. *multiplied me*   *t* Heb. *ankles*   *u* Heb. *caused to bow*

New American Standard

17"He sent from on high, He took me;
  He drew me out of many waters.
18"He delivered me from my strong enemy,
  From those who hated me, for they were too
    strong for me.
19"They confronted me in the day of my calamity,
  But the LORD was my support.
20"He also brought me forth into a broad place;
  He rescued me, because He delighted in me.
21"The LORD has rewarded me according to my
    righteousness;
  According to the cleanness of my hands He has
    recompensed me.
22"For I have kept the ways of the LORD,
  And have not acted wickedly against my God.
23"For all His ordinances *were* before me,
  And *as for* His statutes, I did not depart from
    them.
24"I was also blameless toward Him,
  And I kept myself from my iniquity.
25"Therefore the LORD has recompensed me
    according to my righteousness,
  According to my cleanness before His eyes.
26"With the kind You show Yourself kind,
  With the blameless You show Yourself blameless;
27 With the pure You show Yourself pure,
  And with the perverted You show Yourself astute.
28"And You save an afflicted people;
  But Your eyes are on the haughty *whom* You
    abase.
29"For You are my lamp, O LORD;
  And the LORD illumines my darkness.
30"For by You I can ʳrun upon a troop;
  By my God I can leap over a wall.
31"As for God, His way is blameless;
  The word of the LORD is tested;
  He is a shield to all who take refuge in Him.
32"For who is God, besides the LORD?
  And who is a rock, besides our God?
33"God is my strong fortress;
  And He sets the blameless in His way.
34"He makes my feet like hinds' *feet,*
  And sets me on my high places.
35"He trains my hands for battle,
  So that my arms can bend a bow of bronze.
36"You have also given me the shield of Your
    salvation,
  And Your help makes me great.
37"You enlarge my steps under me,
  And my feet have not slipped.
38"I pursued my enemies and destroyed them,
  And I did not turn back until they were
    consumed.
39"And I have devoured them and shattered them, so
    that they did not rise;
  And they fell under my feet.
40"For You have girded me with strength for battle;
  You have subdued under me those who rose up
    against me.
41"You have also made my enemies turn *their* backs
    to me,
  And I destroyed those who hated me.
42"They looked, but there was none to save;
  Even to the LORD, but He did not answer them.

New International

17"He reached down from on high and took
    hold of me;
  he drew me out of deep waters.
18He rescued me from my powerful enemy,
  from my foes, who were too strong for me.
19They confronted me in the day of my disaster,
  but the LORD was my support.
20He brought me out into a spacious place;
  he rescued me because he delighted in me.
21"The LORD has dealt with me according to my
    righteousness;
  according to the cleanness of my hands he
    has rewarded me.
22For I have kept the ways of the LORD;
  I have not done evil by turning from my
    God.
23All his laws are before me;
  I have not turned away from his decrees.
24I have been blameless before him
  and have kept myself from sin.
25The LORD has rewarded me according to my
    righteousness,
  according to my cleannessˢ in his sight.
26"To the faithful you show yourself faithful,
  to the blameless you show yourself
    blameless,
27to the pure you show yourself pure,
  but to the crooked you show yourself
    shrewd.
28You save the humble,
  but your eyes are on the haughty to bring
    them low.
29You are my lamp, O LORD;
  the LORD turns my darkness into light.
30With your help I can advance against a
    troopᵗ;
  with my God I can scale a wall.
31"As for God, his way is perfect;
  the word of the LORD is flawless.
  He is a shield
  for all who take refuge in him.
32For who is God besides the LORD?
  And who is the Rock except our God?
33It is God who arms me with strengthᵘ
  and makes my way perfect.
34He makes my feet like the feet of a deer;
  he enables me to stand on the heights.
35He trains my hands for battle;
  my arms can bend a bow of bronze.
36You give me your shield of victory;
  you stoop down to make me great.
37You broaden the path beneath me,
  so that my ankles do not turn.
38"I pursued my enemies and crushed them;
  I did not turn back till they were destroyed.
39I crushed them completely, and they could not
    rise;
  they fell beneath my feet.
40You armed me with strength for battle;
  you made my adversaries bow at my feet.
41You made my enemies turn their backs in
    flight,
  and I destroyed my foes.
42They cried for help, but there was no one to
    save them—
  to the LORD, but he did not answer.

ˢ 25 Hebrew; Septuagint and Vulgate (see also Psalm 18:24) *to the
cleanness of my hands*   ᵗ 30 Or *can run through a barricade*
ᵘ 33 Dead Sea Scrolls, some Septuagint manuscripts, Vulgate and
Syriac (see also Psalm 18:32); Masoretic Text *who is my strong
refuge*

ʳ Or *crush a troop*

King James

Amplified

43Then did I beat them as small as the dust of the earth, I did stamp them as the mire of the street, *and* did spread them abroad.

44Thou also hast delivered me from the strivings of my people, thou hast kept me *to be* head of the heathen: a people *which* I knew not shall serve me.

45ᵛStrangers shall ʷsubmit themselves unto me: as soon as they hear, they shall be obedient unto me.

46Strangers shall fade away, and they shall be afraid out of their close places.

47The LORD liveth; and blessed *be* my rock; and exalted be the God of the rock of my salvation.

48It *is* God that ˣavengeth me, and that bringeth down the people under me,

49And that bringeth me forth from mine enemies: thou also hast lifted me up on high above them that rose up against me: thou hast delivered me from the violent man.

50Therefore I will give thanks unto thee, O LORD, among the heathen, and I will sing praises unto thy name.

51ᴴe is the tower of salvation for his king: and showeth mercy to his anointed, unto David, and to his seed for evermore.

43Then I beat them small as the dust of the earth; I crushed them as the mire of the street and scattered them abroad.

44You also have delivered me from strife with my people; You kept me as the head of the nations. People whom I had not known served me.

45Foreigners yielded feigned obedience to me; as soon as they heard of me, they became obedient to me.

46Foreigners faded away; they came limping *and* trembling from their strongholds.

47The Lord lives; blessed be my Rock, and exalted be God, the Rock of my salvation.

48It is God Who executes vengeance for me and Who brought down [and disciplined] the peoples under me,

49Who brought me out from my enemies. You also lifted me up above those who rose up against me; You delivered me from the violent man.

50For this I will give thanks *and* extol You, O Lord, among the nations; I will sing praises to Your name.

51He is a Tower of salvation *and* great deliverance to His king, and shows loving-kindness to His anointed, to David and his offspring forever.

David's last words

23 NOW THESE *be* the last words of David. David the son of Jesse said, and the man *who was* raised up on high, the anointed of the God of Jacob, and the sweet psalmist of Israel, said,

2The spirit of the LORD spake by me, and his word *was* in my tongue.

3The God of Israel said, the Rock of Israel spake to me, ʸHe that ruleth over men *must be* just, ruling in the fear of God.

4And *he shall be* as the light of the morning, *when* the sun riseth, *even* a morning without clouds; *as* the tender grass *springing* out of the earth by clear shining after rain.

5Although my house *be* not so with God; yet he hath made with me an everlasting covenant, ordered in all *things,* and sure: for *this is* all my salvation, and all *my* desire, although he make *it* not to grow.

6 ¶ But *the* sons of Belial *shall be* all of them as thorns thrust away, because they cannot be taken with hands:

7But the man *that* shall touch them must be ᶻfenced with iron and the staff of a spear; and they shall be utterly burned with fire in the *same* place.

David's mighty men

8 ¶ These *be* the names of the mighty men whom David had: ᵃThe Tachmonite that sat in the seat, chief among the captains; the same *was* Adino the Eznite: ᵇhe lift up *his spear* against eight hundred, ᶜwhom he slew at one time.

23 NOW THESE are the last words of David: David son of Jesse says, and the man who was raised on high, the anointed of the God of Jacob, and the sweet psalmist of Israel, says,

2The Spirit of the Lord spoke in *and* by me, and His word was upon my tongue.

3The God of Israel spoke, the Rock of Israel said to me, When one rules over men righteously, ruling in the fear of God,

4He dawns on them like the morning light when the sun rises on a cloudless morning, when the tender grass springs out of the earth through clear shining after rain.

5Truly does not my house stand so with God? For He has made with me an everlasting covenant, ordered in all things, and sure. For will He not cause to prosper all my help and my desire?

6But wicked, godless, *and* worthless lives are all like thorns to be thrust away, because they cannot be taken with the hand.

7But the man who touches them arms himself with iron and the shaft of a spear, and they are utterly consumed with fire on the spot.

8These are the names of the mighty men whom David had: Josheb-basshebeth, a Tahchemonite, chief of the Three [heroes], known also as Adino the Eznite; he wielded his spear and went against 800 men, who were slain at one time. [I Chron. 11:11.]

ᵛHeb. *Sons of the stranger*   ʷOr, *yield feigned obedience*
ˣHeb. *giveth avengement for me*   ʸOr, *Be thou ruler*   ᶻHeb.
filled   ᵃOr, *Josheb-bassebet the Tachmonite, head of the three*
ᵇSee 1 Chr. 11:11   ᶜHeb. *slain*

New American Standard

43"Then I pulverized them as the dust of the earth;
I crushed *and* stamped them as the mire of the
streets.
44"You have also delivered me from the contentions
of my people;
You have kept me as head of the nations;
A people whom I have not known serve me.
45"Foreigners pretend obedience to me;
As soon as they hear, they obey me.
46"Foreigners lose heart,
And come trembling out of their fortresses.
47"The LORD lives, and blessed be my rock;
And exalted be God, the rock of my salvation,
48 The God who executes vengeance for me,
And brings down peoples under me,
49 Who also brings me out from my enemies;
You even lift me above those who rise up
against me;
You rescue me from the violent man.
50"Therefore I will give thanks to You, O LORD,
among the nations,
And I will sing praises to Your name.
51"*He* is a tower of ⁵deliverance to His king,
And shows lovingkindness to His anointed,
To David and his descendants forever."

David's Last Song

23 NOW THESE are the last words of David.
David the son of Jesse declares,
The man who was raised on high declares,
The anointed of the God of Jacob,
And the sweet psalmist of Israel,
2"The Spirit of the LORD spoke by me,
And His word was on my tongue.
3"The God of Israel said,
The Rock of Israel spoke to me,
'He who rules over men righteously,
Who rules in the fear of God,
4 Is as the light of the morning *when* the sun rises,
A morning without clouds,
When the tender grass *springs* out of the earth,
Through sunshine after rain.'
5"Truly is not my house so with God?
For He has made an everlasting covenant
with me,
Ordered in all things, and secured;
For all my salvation and all *my* desire,
Will He not indeed make *it* grow?
6"But the worthless, every one of them will be
thrust away like thorns,
Because they cannot be taken in hand;
7 But the man who touches them
Must be armed with iron and the shaft of a spear,
And they will be completely burned with fire in
their place."

His Mighty Men

8 ¶ These are the names of the mighty men whom David had: Josheb-basshebeth a Tahchemonite, chief of the
captains, he was *called* Adino the Eznite, because of eight
hundred slain *by him* at one time;

New International

43I beat them as fine as the dust of the earth;
I pounded and trampled them like mud in
the streets.
44"You have delivered me from the attacks of
my people;
you have preserved me as the head of
nations.
People I did not know are subject to me,
45 and foreigners come cringing to me;
as soon as they hear me, they obey me.
46They all lose heart;
they come trembling^v from their
strongholds.
47"The LORD lives! Praise be to my Rock!
Exalted be God, the Rock, my Savior!
48He is the God who avenges me,
who puts the nations under me,
49 who sets me free from my enemies.
You exalted me above my foes;
from violent men you rescued me.
50Therefore I will praise you, O LORD, among
the nations;
I will sing praises to your name.
51He gives his king great victories;
he shows unfailing kindness to his anointed,
to David and his descendants forever.

The Last Words of David

23 THESE ARE the last words of David:

"The oracle of David son of Jesse,
the oracle of the man exalted by the Most
High,
the man anointed by the God of Jacob,
Israel's singer of songs^w:

2"The Spirit of the LORD spoke through me;
his word was on my tongue.
3The God of Israel spoke,
the Rock of Israel said to me:
'When one rules over men in righteousness,
when he rules in the fear of God,
4he is like the light of morning at sunrise
on a cloudless morning,
like the brightness after rain
that brings the grass from the earth.'

5"Is not my house right with God?
Has he not made with me an everlasting
covenant,
arranged and secured in every part?
Will he not bring to fruition my salvation
and grant me my every desire?
6But evil men are all to be cast aside like
thorns,
which are not gathered with the hand.
7Whoever touches thorns
uses a tool of iron or the shaft of a spear;
they are burned up where they lie."

David's Mighty Men

8These are the names of David's mighty men:
Josheb-Basshebeth,^x a Tahkemonite,^y was chief of
the Three; he raised his spear against eight hundred men,
whom he killed^z in one encounter.

---

^v46 Some Septuagint manuscripts and Vulgate (see also Psalm
18:45); Masoretic Text *they arm themselves.*   ^w1 Or *Israel's
beloved singer*   ^x8 Hebrew; some Septuagint manuscripts
suggest *Ish-Bosheth,* that is, *Esh-Baal* (see also 1 Chron. 11:11
Jashobeam).   ^y8 Probably a variant of *Hacmonite* (see 1 Chron.
11:11)   ^z8 Some Septuagint manuscripts (see also 1 Chron.
11:11); Hebrew and other Septuagint manuscripts *Three; it was
Adino the Eznite who killed eight hundred men*

---

⁵I.e. victories; lit *salvation*

King James

Amplified

9And after him *was* Eleazar the son of Dodo the Ahohite, *one* of the three mighty men with David, when they defied the Philistines *that* were there gathered together to battle, and the men of Israel were gone away:

10He arose, and smote the Philistines until his hand was weary, and his hand clave unto the sword: and the LORD wrought a great victory that day; and the people returned after him only to spoil.

11And after him *was* Shammah the son of Agee the Hararite. And the Philistines were gathered together d into a troop, where was a piece of ground full of lentiles: and the people fled from the Philistines.

12But he stood in the midst of the ground, and defended it, and slew the Philistines: and the LORD wrought a great victory.

13And e three of the thirty chief went down, and came to David in the harvest time unto the cave of Adullam: and the troop of the Philistines pitched in the valley of Rephaim.

14And David *was* then in an hold, and the garrison of the Philistines *was* then *in* Bethlehem.

15And David longed, and said, Oh that one would give me drink of the water of the well of Bethlehem, which *is* by the gate!

16And the three mighty men brake through the host of the Philistines, and drew water out of the well of Bethlehem, that *was* by the gate, and took *it*, and brought *it* to David: nevertheless he would not drink thereof, but poured it out unto the LORD.

17And he said, Be it far from me, O LORD, that I should do this: *is not this* the blood of the men that went in jeopardy of their lives? therefore he would not drink it. These things did these three mighty men.

18And Abishai, the brother of Joab, the son of Zeruiah, was chief among three. And he lifted up his spear against three hundred, f and slew *them*, and had the name among three.

19Was he not most honourable of three? therefore he was their captain: howbeit he attained not unto the *first* three.

20And Benaiah the son of Jehoiada, the son of a valiant man, of Kabzeel, g who had done many acts, he slew h lionlike men of Moab: he went down also and slew a lion in the midst of a pit in time of snow:

21And he slew an Egyptian, i a goodly man: and the Egyptian had a spear in his hand; but he went down to him with a staff, and plucked the spear out of the Egyptian's hand, and slew him with his own spear.

22These *things* did Benaiah the son of Jehoiada, and had the name among three mighty men.

23He was j more honourable than the thirty, but he attained not to the *first* three. And David set him over his k guard.

24Asahel the brother of Joab *was* one of the thirty; Elhanan the son of Dodo of Bethlehem,

25Shammah the Harodite, Elika the Harodite,

26Helez the Paltite, Ira the son of Ikkesh the Tekoite,

27Abiezer the Anethothite, Mebunnai the Hushathite,

28Zalmon the Ahohite, Maharai the Netophathite,

29Heleb the son of Baanah, a Netophathite, Ittai the son of Ribai out of Gibeah of the children of Benjamin,

30Benaiah the Pirathonite, Hiddai of the l brooks of Gaash,

31Abi-albon the Arbathite, Azmaveth the Barhumite,

32Eliahba the Shaalbonite, of the sons of Jashen, Jonathan,

9Next to him among the three mighty men was Eleazar son of Dodo, son of Ahohi. He was with David when they defied the Philistines assembled there for battle, and the men of Israel had departed.

10[Eleazar] arose and struck down the Philistines until his hand was weary and clung to the sword. The Lord wrought a great deliverance *and* victory that day; the men returned after him only to take the spoil.

11Next to [Eleazar] was Shammah son of Agee the Hararite. The Philistines were gathered at Lehi on a piece of ground full of lentils; and the [Israelites] fled from the Philistines.

12But he stood in the midst of the ground and defended it and slew the Philistines; and the Lord wrought a great victory.

13And three of the thirty chief men went down at harvest time to David in the cave of Adullam, and a troop of Philistines was encamped in the Valley of Rephaim.

14And David was then in the stronghold, and the garrison of the Philistines was then in Bethlehem.

15And David said longingly, Oh, that someone would give me a drink of water from the well of Bethlehem by the gate!

16And the three mighty men broke through the army of the Philistines and drew water out of the well of Bethlehem by the gate and brought it to David. But he would not drink it, but poured it out to the Lord.

17And he said, Be it far from me, O Lord, to drink this. Is it not [the same as] the blood of the men who went at the risk of their lives? So he would not drink it. These things did the three mighty men.

18Now Abishai the brother of Joab son of Zeruiah was chief of the Three. He wielded his spear against 300 men and slew them, and won a name beside the Three.

19Was he not most renowned of the Three? So he was their captain; however, he did not attain to the Three.

20And Benaiah son of Jehoiada, a valiant man of Kabzeel, who had done many notable acts, slew two lionlike men of Moab. He went down also and slew a lion in a pit on a snowy day.

21And he slew an Egyptian, a handsome man. The Egyptian had a spear in his hand, but Benaiah went down to him with a staff, snatched the spear out of the Egyptian's hand, and slew the man with his own spear.

22These things Benaiah son of Jehoiada did, and won a name beside the three mighty men.

23He was more renowned than the Thirty, but he attained not to the [first] Three. David set him over his guard *or* council.

24Asahel brother of Joab was one of the Thirty; then Elhanan son of Dodo of Bethlehem,

25Shammah of Harod, Elika of Harod,

26Helez the Paltite, Ira son of Ikkesh of Tekoa,

27Abiezer of Anathoth, Mebunnai the Hushathite,

28Zalmon the Ahohite, Maharai of Netophah,

29Heleb son of Baanah of Netophah, Ittai son of Ribai of Gibeah of the Benjamites.

30Benaiah of Pirathon, Hiddai of the brooks of Gaash,

31Abi-albon the Arbathite, Azmaveth the Barhumite,

32Eliahba of Shaalbon, the sons of Jashen, Jonathan,

---

d Or, *for foraging*   e Or, *the three captains over the thirty*
f Heb. *slain*   g Heb. *great of acts*   h Heb. *lions of God*
i Heb. *a man of countenance,* or, *sight:* called   j Or, *honourable*
among the thirty   k Or, *council*   l Or, *valleys*

New American Standard

⁹ and after him was Eleazar the son of Dodo the Ahohite, one of the three mighty men with David when they defied the Philistines who were gathered there to battle and the men of Israel had withdrawn.

¹⁰ He arose and struck the Philistines until his hand was weary and clung to the sword, and the LORD brought about a great victory that day; and the people returned after him only to strip *the slain.*

¹¹ ¶ Now after him was Shammah the son of Agee a Hararite. And the Philistines were gathered into a troop where there was a plot of ground full of lentils, and the people fled from the Philistines.

¹² But he took his stand in the midst of the plot, defended it and struck the Philistines; and the LORD brought about a great victory.

¹³ ¶ Then three of the thirty chief men went down and came to David in the harvest time to the cave of Adullam, while the troop of the Philistines was camping in the valley of Rephaim.

¹⁴ David was then in the stronghold, while the garrison of the Philistines was then in Bethlehem.

¹⁵ David had a craving and said, "Oh that someone would give me water to drink from the well of Bethlehem which is by the gate!"

¹⁶ So the three mighty men broke through the camp of the Philistines, and drew water from the well of Bethlehem which was by the gate, and took *it* and brought *it* to David. Nevertheless he would not drink it, but poured it out to the LORD;

¹⁷ and he said, "Be it far from me, O LORD, that I should do this. *Shall I drink* the blood of the men who went in *jeopardy* of their lives?" Therefore he would not drink it. These things the three mighty men did.

¹⁸ ¶ Abishai, the brother of Joab, the son of Zeruiah, was chief of the thirty. And he swung his spear against three hundred and killed *them,* and had a name as well as the three.

¹⁹ He was most honored of the thirty, therefore he became their commander; however, he did not attain to the three.

²⁰ ¶ Then Benaiah the son of Jehoiada, the son of a valiant man of Kabzeel, who had done mighty deeds, killed the two *sons of* Ariel of Moab. He also went down and killed a lion in the middle of a pit on a snowy day.

²¹ He killed an Egyptian, an impressive man. Now the Egyptian *had* a spear in his hand, but he went down to him with a club and snatched the spear from the Egyptian's hand and killed him with his own spear.

²² These *things* Benaiah the son of Jehoiada did, and had a name as well as the three mighty men.

²³ He was honored among the thirty, but he did not attain to the three. And David appointed him over his guard.

²⁴ ¶ Asahel the brother of Joab was among the thirty; Elhanan the son of Dodo of Bethlehem,

²⁵ Shammah the Harodite, Elika the Harodite,

²⁶ Helez the Paltite, Ira the son of Ikkesh the Tekoite,

²⁷ Abiezer the Anathothite, Mebunnai the Hushathite,

²⁸ Zalmon the Ahohite, Maharai the Netophathite,

²⁹ Heleb the son of Baanah the Netophathite, Ittai the son of Ribai of Gibeah of the sons of Benjamin,

³⁰ Benaiah a Pirathonite, Hiddai of the brooks of Gaash,

³¹ Abi-albon the Arbathite, Azmaveth the Barhumite,

³² Eliahba the Shaalbonite, the sons of Jashen, Jonathan,

New International

⁹Next to him was Eleazar son of Dodai the Ahohite. As one of the three mighty men, he was with David when they taunted the Philistines gathered ⌊at Pas Dammim⌋*ᵃ* for battle. Then the men of Israel retreated, ¹⁰but he stood his ground and struck down the Philistines till his hand grew tired and froze to the sword. The LORD brought about a great victory that day. The troops returned to Eleazar, but only to strip the dead.

¹¹Next to him was Shammah son of Agee the Hararite. When the Philistines banded together at a place where there was a field full of lentils, Israel's troops fled from them. ¹²But Shammah took his stand in the middle of the field. He defended it and struck the Philistines down, and the LORD brought about a great victory.

¹³During harvest time, three of the thirty chief men came down to David at the cave of Adullam, while a band of Philistines was encamped in the Valley of Rephaim. ¹⁴At that time David was in the stronghold, and the Philistine garrison was at Bethlehem. ¹⁵David longed for water and said, "Oh, that someone would get me a drink of water from the well near the gate of Bethlehem!" ¹⁶So the three mighty men broke through the Philistine lines, drew water from the well near the gate of Bethlehem and carried it back to David. But he refused to drink it; instead, he poured it out before the LORD. ¹⁷"Far be it from me, O LORD, to do this!" he said. "Is it not the blood of men who went at the risk of their lives?" And David would not drink it.

Such were the exploits of the three mighty men.

¹⁸Abishai the brother of Joab son of Zeruiah was chief of the Three.*ᵇ* He raised his spear against three hundred men, whom he killed, and so he became as famous as the Three. ¹⁹Was he not held in greater honor than the Three? He became their commander, even though he was not included among them.

²⁰Benaiah son of Jehoiada was a valiant fighter from Kabzeel, who performed great exploits. He struck down two of Moab's best men. He also went down into a pit on a snowy day and killed a lion. ²¹And he struck down a huge Egyptian. Although the Egyptian had a spear in his hand, Benaiah went against him with a club. He snatched the spear from the Egyptian's hand and killed him with his own spear. ²²Such were the exploits of Benaiah son of Jehoiada; he too was as famous as the three mighty men. ²³He was held in greater honor than any of the Thirty, but he was not included among the Three. And David put him in charge of his bodyguard.

²⁴Among the Thirty were:
Asahel the brother of Joab,
Elhanan son of Dodo from Bethlehem,
²⁵Shammah the Harodite,
Elika the Harodite,
²⁶Helez the Paltite,
Ira son of Ikkesh from Tekoa,
²⁷Abiezer from Anathoth,
Mebunnai*ᶜ* the Hushathite,
²⁸Zalmon the Ahohite,
Maharai the Netophathite,
²⁹Heled*ᵈ* son of Baanah the Netophathite,
Ithai son of Ribai from Gibeah in Benjamin,
³⁰Benaiah the Pirathonite,
Hiddai*ᵉ* from the ravines of Gaash,
³¹Abi-albon the Arbathite,
Azmaveth the Barhumite,
³²Eliahba the Shaalbonite,
the sons of Jashen,

ᵃ9 See 1 Chron. 11:13; Hebrew *gathered there.*   *ᵇ18* Most Hebrew manuscripts (see also 1 Chron. 11:20); two Hebrew manuscripts and Syriac *Thirty*   *ᶜ27* Hebrew; some Septuagint manuscripts (see also 1 Chron. 11:29) *Sibbecai*   *ᵈ29* Some Hebrew manuscripts and Vulgate (see also 1 Chron. 11:30); most Hebrew manuscripts *Heleb*   *ᵉ30* Hebrew; some Septuagint manuscripts (see also 1 Chron. 11:32) *Hurai*

King James

33Shammah the Hararite, Ahiam the son of Sharar the Hararite,

34Eliphelet the son of Ahasbai, the son of the Maachathite, Eliam the son of Ahithophel the Gilonite,

35Hezrai the Carmelite, Paarai the Arbite,

36Igal the son of Nathan of Zobah, Bani the Gadite,

37Zelek the Ammonite, Nahari the Beerothite, armourbearer to Joab the son of Zeruiah,

38Ira an Ithrite, Gareb an Ithrite,

39Uriah the Hittite: thirty and seven in all.

The census of Israel and Judah

24 AND AGAIN the anger of the LORD was kindled against Israel, and he moved David against them to say, Go, number Israel and Judah.

2For the king said to Joab the captain of the host, which *was* with him, *m*Go now through all the tribes of Israel, from Dan even to Beer-sheba, and number ye the people, that I may know the number of the people.

3And Joab said unto the king, Now the LORD thy God add unto the people, how many soever they be, an hundredfold, and that the eyes of my lord the king may see *it:* but why doth my lord the king delight in this thing?

4Notwithstanding the king's word prevailed against Joab, and against the captains of the host. And Joab and the captains of the host went out from the presence of the king, to number the people of Israel.

5 ¶ And they passed over Jordan, and pitched in Aroer, on the right side of the city that *lieth* in the midst of the *n*river of Gad, and toward Jazer:

6Then they came to Gilead, and to the *o*land of Tahtimhodshi; and they came to Dan-jaan, and about to Zidon,

7And came to the strong hold of Tyre, and to all the cities of the Hivites, and of the Canaanites: and they went out to the south of Judah, *even* to Beer-sheba.

8So when they had gone through all the land, they came to Jerusalem at the end of nine months and twenty days.

9And Joab gave up the sum of the number of the people unto the king: and there were in Israel eight hundred thousand valiant men that drew the sword; and the men of Judah *were* five hundred thousand men.

10 ¶ And David's heart smote him after that he had numbered the people. And David said unto the LORD, I have sinned greatly in that I have done: and now, I beseech thee, O LORD, take away the iniquity of thy servant; for I have done very foolishly.

11For when David was up in the morning, the word of the LORD came unto the prophet Gad, David's seer, saying,

12Go and say unto David, Thus saith the LORD, I offer thee three *things;* choose thee one of them, that I may *do it* unto thee.

13So Gad came to David, and told him, and said unto him, Shall seven years of famine come unto thee in thy land? or wilt thou flee three months before thine enemies, while they pursue thee? or that there be three days' pestilence in thy land? now advise, and see what answer I shall return to him that sent me.

14And David said unto Gad, I am in a great strait: let us fall now into the hand of the LORD; for his mercies *are* *p*great: and let me not fall into the hand of man.

33Shammah the Hararite, Ahiam son of Sharar the Hararite,

34Eliphelet son of Ahasbai, son of Maacah, Eliam son of Ahithophel of Giloh,

35Hezro (Hezrai) of Carmel, Paarai the Arbite,

36Igal son of Nathan of Zobah, Bani the Gadite,

37Zelek the Ammonite, Naharai of Beeroth, armorbearer of Joab son of Zeruiah,

38Ira the Ithrite, Gareb the Ithrite,

39Uriah the Hittite—thirty-seven in all.

24 AGAIN THE anger of the Lord was kindled against Israel, and He moved David against them, saying, Go, number Israel and Judah.

2For the king said to Joab the captain of the host who was with him, Go now through all the tribes of Israel, from Dan even to Beersheba, and count the people, that I may know their number.

3And Joab said to the king, May the Lord your God add a hundred times as many people as there are, and let the eyes of my lord the king see it; but why does my lord the king delight in this thing?

4But the king's word prevailed against Joab and the commanders of the army. So they went from the king's presence to number the Israelites.

5They passed over the Jordan and encamped in Aroer, on the south side of the city lying in the midst of the ravine [of the Arnon] toward Gad, and on to Jazer.

6Then they came to Gilead, and to the land of Tahtimhodshi, and they came to Dan-jaan [Dan in the forest] and around to Sidon,

7And came to the stronghold of Tyre and to all the cities of the Hivites and Canaanites; and they went out to the South (the Negeb) of Judah at Beersheba.

8So when they had gone through all the land [taking the census], they came to Jerusalem at the end of nine months and twenty days.

9And Joab gave the sum of the numbering of the people to the king. There were in Israel 800,000 valiant men who drew the sword, and the men of Judah were 500,000.

10But David's heart smote him after he had numbered the people. David said to the Lord, I have sinned greatly in what I have done. I beseech You, O Lord, take away the iniquity of Your servant, for I have done very foolishly.

11When David arose in the morning, the word of the Lord came to the prophet Gad, David's seer, saying,

12Go and say to David, Thus says the Lord, I hold over you three choices; select one of them, so I may bring it upon you.

13So Gad came to David and told him and said, Shall seven years of famine come to your land? Or will you flee three months before your pursuing enemies? Or do you prefer three days of pestilence in your land? Consider and see what answer I shall return to Him Who sent me.

14And David said to Gad, I am in great distress. Let us fall into the hands of the Lord, for His mercies are many *and* great; but let me not fall into the hands of man.

m Or, *Compass*   *n* Or, *valley*   *o* Or, *nether land newly inhabited*   *p* Or, *many*

New American Standard

33 Shammah the Hararite, Ahiam the son of Sharar the Ararite,

34 Eliphelet the son of Ahasbai, the son of the Maacathite, Eliam the son of Ahithophel the Gilonite,

35 Hezro the Carmelite, Paarai the Arbite,

36 Igal the son of Nathan of Zobah, Bani the Gadite,

37 Zelek the Ammonite, Naharai the Beerothite, armor bearers of Joab the son of Zeruiah,

38 Ira the Ithrite, Gareb the Ithrite,

39 Uriah the Hittite; thirty-seven in all.

The Census Taken

24 NOW AGAIN the anger of the LORD burned against Israel, and it incited David against them to say, "Go, number Israel and Judah."

2 The king said to Joab the commander of the army who was with him, "Go about now through all the tribes of Israel, from Dan to Beersheba, and register the people, that I may know the number of the people."

3 But Joab said to the king, "Now may the LORD your God add to the people a hundred times as many as they are, while the eyes of my lord the king *still* see; but why does my lord the king delight in this thing?"

4 Nevertheless, the king's word prevailed against Joab and against the commanders of the army. So Joab and the commanders of the army went out from the presence of the king to register the people of Israel.

5 They crossed the Jordan and camped in Aroer, on the right side of the city that is in the middle of the valley of Gad and toward Jazer.

6 Then they came to Gilead and to 'the land of Tahtim-hodshi, and they came to Dan-jaan and around to Sidon,

7 and came to the fortress of Tyre and to all the cities of the Hivites and of the Canaanites, and they went out to the south of Judah, *to* Beersheba.

8 So when they had gone about through the whole land, they came to Jerusalem at the end of nine months and twenty days.

9 And Joab gave the number of the registration of the people to the king; and there were in Israel eight hundred thousand valiant men who drew the sword, and the men of Judah were five hundred thousand men.

10 ¶ Now David's heart troubled him after he had numbered the people. So David said to the LORD, "I have sinned greatly in what I have done. But now, O LORD, please take away the iniquity of Your servant, for I have acted very foolishly."

11 When David arose in the morning, the word of the LORD came to the prophet Gad, David's seer, saying,

12 "Go and speak to David, 'Thus the LORD says, "I am offering you three things; choose for yourself one of them, which I will do to you." ' "

13 So Gad came to David and told him, and said to him, "Shall seven years of famine come to you in your land? Or will you flee three months before your foes while they pursue you? Or shall there be three days' pestilence in your land? Now consider and see what answer I shall return to Him who sent me."

14 Then David said to Gad, "I am in great distress. Let us now fall into the hand of the LORD for His mercies are great, but do not let me fall into the hand of man."

New International

Jonathan 33son of*f* Shammah the Hararite,
Ahiam son of Sharar*g* the Hararite,
34Eliphelet son of Ahasbai the Maacathite,
Eliam son of Ahithophel the Gilonite,
35Hezro the Carmelite,
Paarai the Arbite,
36Igal son of Nathan from Zobah,
the son of Hagri,*h*
37Zelek the Ammonite,
Naharai the Beerothite, the armor-bearer of Joab
son of Zeruiah,
38Ira the Ithrite,
Gareb the Ithrite
39and Uriah the Hittite.
There were thirty-seven in all.

David Counts the Fighting Men

24 AGAIN the anger of the LORD burned against Israel, and he incited David against them, saying, "Go and take a census of Israel and Judah."

2So the king said to Joab and the army commanders*i* with him, "Go throughout the tribes of Israel from Dan to Beersheba and enroll the fighting men, so that I may know how many there are."

3But Joab replied to the king, "May the LORD your God multiply the troops a hundred times over, and may the eyes of my lord the king see it. But why does my lord the king want to do such a thing?"

4The king's word, however, overruled Joab and the army commanders; so they left the presence of the king to enroll the fighting men of Israel.

5After crossing the Jordan, they camped near Aroer, south of the town in the gorge, and then went through Gad and on to Jazer. 6They went to Gilead and the region of Tahtim Hodshi, and on to Dan Jaan and around toward Sidon. 7Then they went toward the fortress of Tyre and all the towns of the Hivites and Canaanites. Finally, they went on to Beersheba in the Negev of Judah.

8After they had gone through the entire land, they came back to Jerusalem at the end of nine months and twenty days.

9Joab reported the number of the fighting men to the king: In Israel there were eight hundred thousand ablebodied men who could handle a sword, and in Judah five hundred thousand.

10David was conscience-stricken after he had counted the fighting men, and he said to the LORD, "I have sinned greatly in what I have done. Now, O LORD, I beg you, take away the guilt of your servant. I have done a very foolish thing."

11Before David got up the next morning, the word of the LORD had come to Gad the prophet, David's seer: 12"Go and tell David, 'This is what the LORD says: I am giving you three options. Choose one of them for me to carry out against you.' "

13So Gad went to David and said to him, "Shall there come upon you three*j* years of famine in your land? Or three months of fleeing from your enemies while they pursue you? Or three days of plague in your land? Now then, think it over and decide how I should answer the one who sent me."

14David said to Gad, "I am in deep distress. Let us fall into the hands of the LORD, for his mercy is great; but do not let me fall into the hands of men."

---

f33 Some Septuagint manuscripts (see also 1 Chron. 11:34); Hebrew does not have *son of.*   *g33* Hebrew; some Septuagint manuscripts (see also 1 Chron. 11:35) *Sacar*   *h36* Some Septuagint manuscripts (see also 1 Chron. 11:38); Hebrew *Haggadi*   *i2* Septuagint (see also verse 4 and 1 Chron. 21:2); Hebrew *Joab the army commander*   *j13* Septuagint (see also 1 Chron. 21:12); Hebrew *seven*

---

*Or Kadesh in the land of the Hittite

King James

15 ¶ So the LORD sent a pestilence upon Israel from the morning even to the time appointed: and there died of the people from Dan even to Beer-sheba seventy thousand men.

16And when the angel stretched out his hand upon Jerusalem to destroy it, the LORD repented him of the evil, and said to the angel that destroyed the people, It is enough: stay now thine hand. And the angel of the LORD was by the threshingplace of Araunah the Jebusite.

17And David spake unto the LORD when he saw the angel that smote the people, and said, Lo, I have sinned, and I have done wickedly: but these sheep, what have they done? let thine hand, I pray thee, be against me, and against my father's house.

David builds an altar

18 ¶ And Gad came that day to David, and said unto him, Go up, rear an altar unto the LORD in the threshingfloor of qAraunah the Jebusite.

19And David, according to the saying of Gad, went up as the LORD commanded.

20And Araunah looked, and saw the king and his servants coming on toward him: and Araunah went out, and bowed himself before the king on his face upon the ground.

21And Araunah said, Wherefore is my lord the king come to his servant? And David said, To buy the threshingfloor of thee, to build an altar unto the LORD, that the plague may be stayed from the people.

22And Araunah said unto David, Let my lord the king take and offer up what *seemeth* good unto him: behold, *here be* oxen for burnt sacrifice, and threshing instruments and *other* instruments of the oxen for wood.

23All these *things* did Araunah, *as* a king, give unto the king. And Araunah said unto the king, The LORD thy God accept thee.

24And the king said unto Araunah, Nay; but I will surely buy *it* of thee at a price: neither will I offer burnt offerings unto the LORD my God of that which doth cost me nothing. So David bought the threshingfloor and the oxen for fifty shekels of silver.

25And David built there an altar unto the LORD, and offered burnt offerings and peace offerings. So the LORD was entreated for the land, and the plague was stayed from Israel.

Amplified

15So the Lord sent a pestilence upon Israel from the morning even to the time appointed; and there died of the people from Dan even to Beersheba 70,000 men.

16And when the angel stretched out his hand upon Jerusalem to destroy it, the Lord relented of the evil *and* reversed His judgment and said to the destroying angel, It is enough; now stay your hand. And the angel of the Lord was by the threshing floor of Araunah the Jebusite.

17When David saw the angel who was smiting the people, he spoke to the Lord and said, Behold, I have sinned and I have done wickedly; but these sheep, what have they done? Let Your hand, I pray You, be [only] against me and against my father's house.

18Then Gad came to David and said, Go up, rear an altar to the Lord on the threshing floor of Araunah the Jebusite.

19So David went up according to Gad's word, as the Lord commanded.

20Araunah looked and saw the king and his servants coming toward him; and [he] went out and bowed himself before the king with his face to the ground.

21Araunah said, Why has my lord the king come to his servant? And David said, To buy the threshing floor from you, to build there an altar to the Lord, that the plague may be stayed from the people.

22And Araunah said to David, Let my lord the king take and offer up what seems good to him. Behold, here are oxen for burnt sacrifice, and threshing instruments and the yokes of the oxen for wood.

23All this, O king, Araunah gives to the king. And Araunah said to the king, The Lord your God accept you.

24But King David said to Araunah, No, but I will buy it of you for a price. I will not offer burnt offerings to the Lord my God of that which costs me nothing. So David bought the threshing floor and the oxen for fifty shekels of silver.

25David built there an altar to the Lord and offered burnt offerings and peace offerings. So the Lord heeded the prayers for the land, and Israel's plague was stayed.

q Heb. *Araniah*

New American Standard

Pestilence Sent

15 ¶ So the LORD sent a pestilence upon Israel from the morning until the appointed time, and seventy thousand men of the people from Dan to Beersheba died.

16 When the angel stretched out his hand toward Jerusalem to destroy it, the LORD relented from the calamity and said to the angel who destroyed the people, "It is enough! Now relax your hand!" And the angel of the LORD was by the threshing floor of Araunah the Jebusite.

17 Then David spoke to the LORD when he saw the angel who was striking down the people, and said, "Behold, it is I who have sinned, and it is I who have done wrong; but these sheep, what have they done? Please let Your hand be against me and against my father's house."

David Builds an Altar

18 ¶ So Gad came to David that day and said to him, "Go up, erect an altar to the LORD on the threshing floor of Araunah the Jebusite."

19 David went up according to the word of Gad, just as the LORD had commanded.

20 Araunah looked down and saw the king and his servants crossing over toward him; and Araunah went out and bowed his face to the ground before the king.

21 Then Araunah said, "Why has my lord the king come to his servant?" And David said, "To buy the threshing floor from you, in order to build an altar to the LORD, that the plague may be held back from the people."

22 Araunah said to David, "Let my lord the king take and offer up what is good in his sight. Look, the oxen for the burnt offering, the threshing sledges and the yokes of the oxen for the wood.

23 "Everything, O king, Araunah gives to the king." And Araunah said to the king, "May the LORD your God accept you."

24 However, the king said to Araunah, "No, but I will surely buy it from you for a price, for I will not offer burnt offerings to the LORD my God which cost me nothing." So David bought the threshing floor and the oxen for fifty shekels of silver.

25 David built there an altar to the LORD and offered burnt offerings and peace offerings. Thus the LORD was moved by prayer for the land, and the plague was held back from Israel.

New International

15 So the LORD sent a plague on Israel from that morning until the end of the time designated, and seventy thousand of the people from Dan to Beersheba died. 16 When the angel stretched out his hand to destroy Jerusalem, the LORD was grieved because of the calamity and said to the angel who was afflicting the people, "Enough! Withdraw your hand." The angel of the LORD was then at the threshing floor of Araunah the Jebusite.

17 When David saw the angel who was striking down the people, he said to the LORD, "I am the one who has sinned and done wrong. These are but sheep. What have they done? Let your hand fall upon me and my family."

David Builds an Altar

18 On that day Gad went to David and said to him, "Go up and build an altar to the LORD on the threshing floor of Araunah the Jebusite." 19 So David went up, as the LORD had commanded through Gad. 20 When Araunah looked and saw the king and his men coming toward him, he went out and bowed down before the king with his face to the ground.

21 Araunah said, "Why has my lord the king come to his servant?"

"To buy your threshing floor," David answered, "so I can build an altar to the LORD, that the plague on the people may be stopped."

22 Araunah said to David, "Let my lord the king take whatever pleases him and offer it up. Here are oxen for the burnt offering, and here are threshing sledges and ox yokes for the wood. 23 O king, Araunah gives all this to the king." Araunah also said to him, "May the LORD your God accept you."

24 But the king replied to Araunah, "No, I insist on paying you for it. I will not sacrifice to the LORD my God burnt offerings that cost me nothing."

So David bought the threshing floor and the oxen and paid fifty shekels[k] of silver for them. 25 David built an altar to the LORD there and sacrificed burnt offerings and fellowship offerings.[l] Then the LORD answered prayer in behalf of the land, and the plague on Israel was stopped.

---

k 24 That is, about 1 1/4 pounds (about 0.6 kilogram)
l 25 Traditionally peace offerings

THE FIRST BOOK OF THE

Kings

COMMONLY CALLED THE THIRD BOOK OF THE KINGS

Adonijah seeks to be king

1 NOW KING David was old *and* [a]stricken in years; and they covered him with clothes, but he gat no heat. ²Wherefore his servants said unto him, [b]Let there be sought for my lord the king [c]a young virgin: and let her stand before the king, and let her [d]cherish him, and let her lie in thy bosom, that my lord the king may get heat.

³So they sought for a fair damsel throughout all the coasts of Israel, and found Abishag a Shunammite, and brought her to the king.

⁴And the damsel *was* very fair, and cherished the king, and ministered to him: but the king knew her not.

⁵ ¶ Then Adonijah the son of Haggith exalted himself, saying, I will [e]be king: and he prepared him chariots and horsemen, and fifty men to run before him.

⁶And his father had not displeased him [f]at any time in saying, Why hast thou done so? and he also *was a* very goodly *man;* and *his* mother bare him after Absalom.

⁷And [g]he conferred with Joab the son of Zeruiah, and with Abiathar the priest: and they [h]following Adonijah helped *him.*

⁸But Zadok the priest, and Benaiah the son of Jehoiada, and Nathan the prophet, and Shimei, and Rei, and the mighty men which *belonged* to David, were not with Adonijah.

⁹And Adonijah slew sheep and oxen and fat cattle by the stone of Zoheleth, which *is* by [i]En-rogel, and called all his brethren the king's sons, and all the men of Judah the king's servants:

¹⁰But Nathan the prophet, and Benaiah, and the mighty men, and Solomon his brother, he called not.

¹¹ ¶ Wherefore Nathan spake unto Bath-sheba the mother of Solomon, saying, Hast thou not heard that Adonijah the son of Haggith doth reign, and David our lord knoweth *it* not?

¹²Now therefore come, let me, I pray thee, give thee counsel, that thou mayest save thine own life, and the life of thy son Solomon.

¹³Go and get thee in unto king David, and say unto him, Didst not thou, my lord, O king, swear unto thine handmaid, saying, Assuredly Solomon thy son shall reign after me, and he shall sit upon my throne? why then doth Adonijah reign?

¹⁴Behold, while thou yet talkest there with the king, I also will come in after thee, and [j]confirm thy words.

¹⁵ ¶ And Bath-sheba went in unto the king into the chamber: and the king was very old; and Abishag the Shunammite ministered unto the king.

¹⁶And Bath-sheba bowed, and did obeisance unto the king. And the king said, [k]What wouldest thou?

¹⁷And she said unto him, My lord, thou swarest by the LORD thy God unto thine handmaid, *saying,* Assuredly Solomon thy son shall reign after me, and he shall sit upon my throne.

¹⁸And now, behold, Adonijah reigneth; and now, my lord the king, thou knowest *it* not:

THE FIRST BOOK OF THE

Kings

1 AND KING David was old and advanced in years; they covered him with [bed]clothes, but he could not get warm.

²So his servants [the [a]physicians] said to him, Let there be sought for my lord the king a young virgin, and let her wait on and be useful to the king; let her lie in your bosom, that my lord the king may get warm.

³So they sought a fair maiden through all the territory of Israel and found Abishag the Shunammite, and brought her to the king.

⁴The maiden was beautiful; and she waited on and nursed him. But the king had no intercourse with her.

⁵Then Adonijah son of [David's wife] Haggith exalted himself, saying, I [the eldest living son] will be king. And he prepared for himself chariots and horsemen, with fifty men to run before him.

⁶David his father had never in his life displeased him by asking, Why have you done so? He was also a very attractive man and was born after Absalom.

⁷He conferred with [b]Joab son of Zeruiah [David's half sister] and with Abiathar the priest, and they followed Adonijah and helped him.

⁸But Zadok the priest, Benaiah son of Jehoiada, Nathan the prophet, Shimei, Rei, and David's mighty men did not side with Adonijah.

⁹Adonijah sacrificed sheep, oxen, and fatlings by the Stone of Zoheleth, which is beside [the well] En-rogel; and he invited all his brothers, the king's sons, and all the royal officials of Judah.

¹⁰But Nathan the prophet, Benaiah, the mighty men, and Solomon his brother he did not invite.

¹¹Then Nathan said to Bathsheba the mother of Solomon, Have you not heard that Adonijah, the son of Haggith, reigns and David our lord does not know it?

¹²Come now, let me advise you how to save your own life and your son Solomon's.

¹³Go to King David and say, Did you not, my lord, O king, swear to your handmaid, saying, Assuredly Solomon your son shall reign after me, and he shall sit upon my throne? Why then does Adonijah reign?

¹⁴Behold, while you are still talking there with the king, I also will come in after you and confirm your words.

¹⁵So Bathsheba went in to the king in his chamber. Now the king was very old *and* feeble, and Abishag the Shunammite was ministering to [him].

¹⁶Bathsheba bowed and did obeisance to the king. The king said, What do you wish?

¹⁷And she said to him, My lord, you swore by the Lord your God to your handmaid, saying, Assuredly Solomon your son shall reign after me and sit upon my throne.

¹⁸And now, behold, Adonijah is reigning, and, my lord the king, you do not know it.

---

[a]Heb. *entered into days*   [b]Heb. *Let them seek*   [c]Heb. *a damsel, a virgin*   [d]Heb. *be a cherisher unto him*   [e]Heb. *reign*   [f]Heb. *from his days*   [g]Heb. *his words were with Joab*   [h]Heb. *helped after Adonijah*   [i]Or, *The well Rogel*   [j]Heb. *fill up*   [k]Heb. *What to thee?*

[a]Josephus, *Antiquities of the Jews* 14, 3.   [b]The commander of Israel's army.

THE FIRST BOOK OF THE

Kings

David in Old Age

1 NOW KING David was old, advanced in age; and they covered him with clothes, but he could not keep warm.

2 So his servants said to him, "Let them seek a young virgin for my lord the king, and let her attend the king and become his nurse; and let her lie in your bosom, that my lord the king may keep warm."

3 So they searched for a beautiful girl throughout all the territory of Israel, and found Abishag the Shunammite, and brought her to the king.

4 The girl was very beautiful; and she became the king's nurse and served him, but the king did not cohabit with her.

5 ¶ Now Adonijah the son of Haggith exalted himself, saying, "I will be king." So he prepared for himself chariots and horsemen with fifty men to run before him.

6 His father had never crossed him at any time by asking, "Why have you done so?" And he was also a very handsome man, and he was born after Absalom.

7 He had conferred with Joab the son of Zeruiah and with Abiathar the priest; and following Adonijah they helped him.

8 But Zadok the priest, Benaiah the son of Jehoiada, Nathan the prophet, Shimei, Rei, and the mighty men who belonged to David, were not with Adonijah.

9 ¶ Adonijah sacrificed sheep and oxen and fatlings by the ^astone of Zoheleth, which is beside En-rogel; and he invited all his brothers, the king's sons, and all the men of Judah, the king's servants.

10 But he did not invite Nathan the prophet, Benaiah, the mighty men, and Solomon his brother.

Nathan and Bathsheba

11 ¶ Then Nathan spoke to Bathsheba the mother of Solomon, saying, "Have you not heard that Adonijah the son of Haggith has become king, and David our lord does not know *it?*

12 "So now come, please let me give you counsel and save your life and the life of your son Solomon.

13 "Go at once to King David and say to him, 'Have you not, my lord, O king, sworn to your maidservant, saying, "Surely Solomon your son shall be king after me, and he shall sit on my throne"? Why then has Adonijah become king?'

14 "Behold, while you are still there speaking with the king, I will come in after you and confirm your words."

15 ¶ So Bathsheba went in to the king in the bedroom. Now the king was very old, and Abishag the Shunammite was ministering to the king.

16 Then Bathsheba bowed and prostrated herself before the king. And the king said, "What do you wish?"

17 She said to him, "My lord, you swore to your maidservant by the LORD your God, *saying,* 'Surely your son Solomon shall be king after me and he shall sit on my throne.'

18 "Now, behold, Adonijah is king; and now, my lord the king, you do not know *it.*

1 Kings

Adonijah Sets Himself Up as King

1 WHEN KING David was old and well advanced in years, he could not keep warm even when they put covers over him. 2So his servants said to him, "Let us look for a young virgin to attend the king and take care of him. She can lie beside him so that our lord the king may keep warm."

3Then they searched throughout Israel for a beautiful girl and found Abishag, a Shunammite, and brought her to the king. 4The girl was very beautiful; she took care of the king and waited on him, but the king had no intimate relations with her.

5Now Adonijah, whose mother was Haggith, put himself forward and said, "I will be king." So he got chariots and horses^a ready, with fifty men to run ahead of him. 6(His father had never interfered with him by asking, "Why do you behave as you do?" He was also very handsome and was born next after Absalom.)

7Adonijah conferred with Joab son of Zeruiah and with Abiathar the priest, and they gave him their support. 8But Zadok the priest, Benaiah son of Jehoiada, Nathan the prophet, Shimei and Rei^b and David's special guard did not join Adonijah.

9Adonijah then sacrificed sheep, cattle and fattened calves at the Stone of Zoheleth near En Rogel. He invited all his brothers, the king's sons, and all the men of Judah who were royal officials, 10but he did not invite Nathan the prophet or Benaiah or the special guard or his brother Solomon.

11Then Nathan asked Bathsheba, Solomon's mother, "Have you not heard that Adonijah, the son of Haggith, has become king without our lord David's knowing it? 12Now then, let me advise you how you can save your own life and the life of your son Solomon. 13Go in to King David and say to him, 'My lord the king, did you not swear to me your servant: "Surely Solomon your son shall be king after me, and he will sit on my throne"? Why then has Adonijah become king?' 14While you are still there talking to the king, I will come in and confirm what you have said."

15So Bathsheba went to see the aged king in his room, where Abishag the Shunammite was attending him. 16Bathsheba bowed low and knelt before the king.

"What is it you want?" the king asked.

17She said to him, "My lord, you yourself swore to me your servant by the LORD your God: 'Solomon your son shall be king after me, and he will sit on my throne.' 18But now Adonijah has become king, and you, my lord the

---

^aOr *Gliding* or *Serpent Stone*

^a5 Or *charioteers* ^b8 Or *and his friends*

King James

¹⁹And he hath slain oxen and fat cattle and sheep in abundance, and hath called all the sons of the king, and Abiathar the priest, and Joab the captain of the host: but Solomon thy servant hath he not called.

²⁰And thou, my lord, O king, the eyes of all Israel *are* upon thee, that thou shouldest tell them who shall sit on the throne of my lord the king after him.

²¹Otherwise it shall come to pass, when my lord the king shall sleep with his fathers, that I and my son Solomon shall be counted *l*offenders.

²² ¶ And, lo, while she yet talked with the king, Nathan the prophet also came in.

²³And they told the king, saying, Behold Nathan the prophet. And when he was come in before the king, he bowed himself before the king with his face to the ground.

²⁴And Nathan said, My lord, O king, hast thou said, Adonijah shall reign after me, and he shall sit upon my throne?

²⁵For he is gone down this day, and hath slain oxen and fat cattle and sheep in abundance, and hath called all the king's sons, and the captains of the host, and Abiathar the priest; and, behold, they eat and drink before him, and say, *m*God save king Adonijah.

²⁶But me, *even* me thy servant, and Zadok the priest, and Benaiah the son of Jehoiada, and thy servant Solomon, hath he not called?

²⁷Is this thing done by my lord the king, and thou hast not showed *it* unto thy servant, who should sit on the throne of my lord the king after him?

Solomon anointed king

²⁸ ¶ Then king David answered and said, Call me Bath-sheba. And she came *n*into the king's presence, and stood before the king.

²⁹And the king sware, and said, *As* the LORD liveth, that hath redeemed my soul out of all distress,

³⁰Even as I sware unto thee by the LORD God of Israel, saying, Assuredly Solomon thy son shall reign after me, and he shall sit upon my throne in my stead; even so will I certainly do this day.

³¹Then Bath-sheba bowed with *her* face to the earth, and did reverence to the king, and said, Let my lord king David live for ever.

³² ¶ And king David said, Call me Zadok the priest, and Nathan the prophet, and Benaiah the son of Jehoiada. And they came before the king.

³³The king also said unto them, Take with you the servants of your lord, and cause Solomon my son to ride upon *o*mine own mule, and bring him down to Gihon:

³⁴And let Zadok the priest and Nathan the prophet anoint him there king over Israel: and blow ye with the trumpet, and say, God save king Solomon.

³⁵Then ye shall come up after him, that he may come and sit upon my throne; for he shall be king in my stead: and I have appointed him to be ruler over Israel and over Judah.

³⁶And Benaiah the son of Jehoiada answered the king, and said, Amen: the LORD God of my lord the king say so *too.*

³⁷As the LORD hath been with my lord the king, even so be he with Solomon, and make his throne greater than the throne of my lord king David.

³⁸So Zadok the priest, and Nathan the prophet, and Benaiah the son of Jehoiada, and the Cherethites, and the Pelethites, went down, and caused Solomon to ride upon king David's mule, and brought him to Gihon.

³⁹And Zadok the priest took an horn of oil out of the tabernacle, and anointed Solomon. And they blew the trumpet; and all the people said, God save king Solomon.

⁴⁰And all the people came up after him, and the people piped with *p*pipes, and rejoiced with great joy, so that the earth rent with the sound of them.

Amplified

¹⁹He has sacrificed oxen and fatlings and sheep in abundance, and has invited all the king's sons and Abiathar the priest and Joab the commander of the army. But he did not invite Solomon your servant.

²⁰Now, my lord O king, the eyes of all Israel are on you, to tell who shall sit on the throne of my lord the king after you.

²¹Otherwise, when my lord the king shall sleep with his fathers, I and my son Solomon shall be counted as offenders.

²²While she was still talking with the king, Nathan the prophet also came in.

²³The king was told, Here is Nathan the prophet. And when he came before the king, he bowed himself before him with his face to the ground.

²⁴And Nathan said, My lord the king, have you said, Adonijah shall reign after me, and he shall sit on my throne?

²⁵He has gone this day and sacrificed oxen, fatlings, and sheep in abundance, and has invited all the king's sons, the captains of the host, and Abiathar the priest; and they eat and drink before him and say, Long live King Adonijah!

²⁶But me your servant, and Zadok the priest, and Benaiah son of Jehoiada, and your servant Solomon he has not invited.

²⁷Is this done by my lord the king and you have not shown your servants who shall succeed my lord the king?

²⁸Then King David answered, Call Bathsheba. And she came into the king's presence and stood before him.

²⁹And the king took an oath and said, As the Lord lives, Who has redeemed my soul out of all distress,

³⁰Even as I swore to you by the Lord, the God of Israel, saying, Assuredly Solomon your son shall reign after me, and he shall sit upon my throne in my stead—even so will I certainly do this day.

³¹Bathsheba bowed with her face to the ground and did obeisance to the king and said, Let my lord King David live forever!

³²King David said, Call Zadok the priest, Nathan the prophet, and Benaiah son of Jehoiada. And they came before the king.

³³The king told them, Take the servants of your lord and cause Solomon my son to ride on my own mule and bring him down to Gihon [in the Kidron Valley].

³⁴And let Zadok the priest and Nathan the prophet anoint him there king over Israel. Then blow the trumpet and say, Long live King Solomon!

³⁵Then you shall come up after him, and he shall come and sit on my throne, for he shall be king in my stead; I have appointed him ruler over Israel and Judah.

³⁶And Benaiah son of Jehoiada answered the king and said, Amen! May the Lord, the God of my lord the king, say so too.

³⁷As the Lord has been with my lord the king, even so may He be with Solomon and make his throne greater than the throne of my lord King David.

³⁸So Zadok the priest, Nathan the prophet, Benaiah son of Jehoiada, the Cherethites, and the Pelethites [the king's bodyguards] went down and caused Solomon to ride upon King David's mule and brought him to Gihon.

³⁹Zadok the priest took a horn of oil out of the tent and anointed Solomon. They blew the trumpet and all the people said, Long live King Solomon!

⁴⁰All the people followed him; they played on pipes and rejoiced greatly, so that the earth [resounded] with the joyful sound.

---

*l*Heb. *sinners*   *m*Heb. *Let king Adonijah live*   *n*Heb. *before the king*   *o*Heb. *which* belongeth *to me*   *p*Or, *flutes*

New American Standard

¹⁹"He has sacrificed oxen and fatlings and sheep in abundance, and has invited all the sons of the king and Abiathar the priest and Joab the commander of the army, but he has not invited Solomon your servant.

²⁰"As for you now, my lord the king, the eyes of all Israel are on you, to tell them who shall sit on the throne of my lord the king after him.

²¹"Otherwise it will come about, as soon as my lord the king sleeps with his fathers, that I and my son Solomon will be considered offenders."

²² ¶ Behold, while she was still speaking with the king, Nathan the prophet came in.

²³ They told the king, saying, "Here is Nathan the prophet." And when he came in before the king, he prostrated himself before the king with his face to the ground.

²⁴ Then Nathan said, "My lord the king, have you said, 'Adonijah shall be king after me, and he shall sit on my throne'?

²⁵"For he has gone down today and has sacrificed oxen and fatlings and sheep in abundance, and has invited all the king's sons and the commanders of the army and Abiathar the priest, and behold, they are eating and drinking before him; and they say, '*Long* live King Adonijah!'

²⁶"But me, *even* me your servant, and Zadok the priest and Benaiah the son of Jehoiada and your servant Solomon, he has not invited.

²⁷"Has this thing been done by my lord the king, and you have not shown to your servants who should sit on the throne of my lord the king after him?"

²⁸ ¶ Then King David said, "Call Bathsheba to me." And she came into the king's presence and stood before the king.

²⁹ The king vowed and said, "As the LORD lives, who has redeemed my life from all distress,

³⁰ surely as I vowed to you by the LORD the God of Israel, saying, 'Your son Solomon shall be king after me, and he shall sit on my throne in my place'; I will indeed do so this day.'

³¹ Then Bathsheba bowed with her face to the ground, and prostrated herself before the king and said, "May my lord King David live forever."

³² ¶ Then King David said, "Call to me Zadok the priest, Nathan the prophet, and Benaiah the son of Jehoiada." And they came into the king's presence.

³³ The king said to them, "Take with you the servants of your lord, and have my son Solomon ride on my own mule, and bring him down to Gihon.

³⁴"Let Zadok the priest and Nathan the prophet anoint him there as king over Israel, and blow the trumpet and say, '*Long* live King Solomon!'

³⁵"Then you shall come up after him, and he shall come and sit on my throne and be king in my place; for I have appointed him to be ruler over Israel and Judah."

³⁶ Benaiah the son of Jehoiada answered the king and said, "Amen! Thus may the LORD, the God of my lord the king, say.

³⁷"As the LORD has been with my lord the king, so may He be with Solomon, and make his throne greater than the throne of my lord King David!"

Solomon Anointed King

³⁸ ¶ So Zadok the priest, Nathan the prophet, Benaiah the son of Jehoiada, the Cherethites, and the Pelethites went down and had Solomon ride on King David's mule, and brought him to Gihon.

³⁹ Zadok the priest then took the horn of oil from the tent and anointed Solomon. Then they blew the trumpet, and all the people said, "*Long* live King Solomon!"

⁴⁰ All the people went up after him, and the people were playing on flutes and rejoicing with great joy, so that the earth shook at their noise.

New International

king, do not know about it. ¹⁹He has sacrificed great numbers of cattle, fattened calves, and sheep, and has invited all the king's sons, Abiathar the priest and Joab the commander of the army, but he has not invited Solomon your servant. ²⁰My lord the king, the eyes of all Israel are on you, to learn from you who will sit on the throne of my lord the king after him. ²¹Otherwise, as soon as my lord the king is laid to rest with his fathers, I and my son Solomon will be treated as criminals."

²²While she was still speaking with the king, Nathan the prophet arrived. ²³And they told the king, "Nathan the prophet is here." So he went before the king and bowed with his face to the ground.

²⁴Nathan said, "Have you, my lord the king, declared that Adonijah shall be king after you, and that he will sit on your throne? ²⁵Today he has gone down and sacrificed great numbers of cattle, fattened calves, and sheep. He has invited all the king's sons, the commanders of the army and Abiathar the priest. Right now they are eating and drinking with him and saying, 'Long live King Adonijah!' ²⁶But me your servant, and Zadok the priest, and Benaiah son of Jehoiada, and your servant Solomon he did not invite. ²⁷Is this something my lord the king has done without letting his servants know who should sit on the throne of my lord the king after him?"

David Makes Solomon King

²⁸Then King David said, "Call in Bathsheba." So she came into the king's presence and stood before him.

²⁹The king then took an oath: "As surely as the LORD lives, who has delivered me out of every trouble, ³⁰I will surely carry out today what I swore to you by the LORD, the God of Israel: Solomon your son shall be king after me, and he will sit on my throne in my place."

³¹Then Bathsheba bowed low with her face to the ground and, kneeling before the king, said, "May my lord King David live forever!"

³²King David said, "Call in Zadok the priest, Nathan the prophet and Benaiah son of Jehoiada." When they came before the king, ³³he said to them: "Take your lord's servants with you and set Solomon my son on my own mule and take him down to Gihon. ³⁴There have Zadok the priest and Nathan the prophet anoint him king over Israel. Blow the trumpet and shout, 'Long live King Solomon!' ³⁵Then you are to go up with him, and he is to come and sit on my throne and reign in my place. I have appointed him ruler over Israel and Judah."

³⁶Benaiah son of Jehoiada answered the king, "Amen! May the LORD, the God of my lord the king, so declare it. ³⁷As the LORD was with my lord the king, so may he be with Solomon to make his throne even greater than the throne of my lord King David!"

³⁸So Zadok the priest, Nathan the prophet, Benaiah son of Jehoiada, the Kerethites and the Pelethites went down and put Solomon on King David's mule and escorted him to Gihon. ³⁹Zadok the priest took the horn of oil from the sacred tent and anointed Solomon. Then they sounded the trumpet and all the people shouted, "Long live King Solomon!" ⁴⁰And all the people went up after him, playing flutes and rejoicing greatly, so that the ground shook with the sound.

King James

41 ¶ And Adonijah and all the guests that *were* with him heard *it* as they had made an end of eating. And when Joab heard the sound of the trumpet, he said, Wherefore *is this* noise of the city being in an uproar?

42 And while he yet spake, behold, Jonathan the son of Abiathar the priest came: and Adonijah said unto him, Come in; for thou *art* a valiant man, and bringest good tidings.

43 And Jonathan answered and said to Adonijah, Verily our lord king David hath made Solomon king.

44 And the king hath sent with him Zadok the priest, and Nathan the prophet, and Benaiah the son of Jehoiada, and the Cherethites, and the Pelethites, and they have caused him to ride upon the king's mule:

45 And Zadok the priest and Nathan the prophet have anointed him king in Gihon: and they are come up from thence rejoicing, so that the city rang again. This *is* the noise that ye have heard.

46 And also Solomon sitteth on the throne of the kingdom.

47 And moreover the king's servants came to bless our lord king David, saying, God make the name of Solomon better than thy name, and make his throne greater than thy throne. And the king bowed himself upon the bed.

48 And also thus said the king, Blessed *be* the LORD God of Israel, which hath given *one* to sit on my throne this day, mine eyes even seeing *it.*

49 And all the guests that *were* with Adonijah were afraid, and rose up, and went every man his way.

50 ¶ And Adonijah feared because of Solomon, and arose, and went, and caught hold on the horns of the altar.

51 And it was told Solomon, saying, Behold, Adonijah feareth king Solomon: for, lo, he hath caught hold on the horns of the altar, saying, Let king Solomon swear unto me today that he will not slay his servant with the sword.

52 And Solomon said, If he will show himself a worthy man, there shall not an hair of him fall to the earth: but if wickedness shall be found in him, he shall die.

53 So king Solomon sent, and they brought him down from the altar. And he came and bowed himself to king Solomon: and Solomon said unto him, Go to thine house.

David's last words and death

2 NOW THE days of David drew nigh that he should die; and he charged Solomon his son, saying,

2 I go the way of all the earth: be thou strong therefore, and show thyself a man;

3 And keep the charge of the LORD thy God, to walk in his ways, to keep his statutes, and his commandments, and his judgments, and his testimonies, as it is written in the law of Moses, that thou mayest *q*prosper in all that thou doest, and whithersoever thou turnest thyself:

4 That the LORD may continue his word which he spake concerning me, saying, If thy children take heed to their way, to walk before me in truth with all their heart and with all their soul, there shall not *r*fail thee (said he) a man on the throne of Israel.

5 Moreover thou knowest also what Joab the son of Zeruiah did to me, *and* what he did to the two captains of the hosts of Israel, unto Abner the son of Ner, and unto Amasa the son of Jether, whom he slew, and *s*shed the blood of war in peace, and put the blood of war upon his girdle *that was* about his loins, and in his shoes that *were* on his feet.

6 Do therefore according to thy wisdom, and let not his hoar head go down to the grave in peace.

7 But show kindness unto the sons of Barzillai the Gileadite, and let them be of those that eat at thy table: for so they came to me when I fled because of Absalom thy brother.

Amplified

41 And Adonijah and all the guests with him heard it as they finished feasting. When Joab heard the trumpet sound, he said, What does this uproar in the city mean?

42 While he was still speaking, behold, Jonathan son of Abiathar the priest came. And Adonijah said, Come in, for you are a trustworthy man and bring good news.

43 Jonathan replied, Adonijah, truly our lord King David has made Solomon king!

44 The king has sent him with Zadok the priest, Nathan the prophet, Benaiah son of Jehoiada, the Cherethites and the Pelethites, and they have caused him to ride upon the king's mule.

45 Zadok the priest and Nathan the prophet have anointed him king in Gihon; they have come up from there rejoicing, so the city resounds. This is the noise you heard.

46 Solomon sits on the royal throne.

47 Moreover, the king's servants came to congratulate our lord King David, saying, May God make the name of Solomon better than your name and make his throne greater than your throne. And the king bowed himself upon the bed

48 And said, Blessed be the Lord, the God of Israel, Who has granted me to see one of my offspring sitting on my throne this day.

49 And all the guests that were with Adonijah were afraid and rose up and went every man his way.

50 And Adonijah feared because of Solomon, and arose and went [to the tabernacle tent on Mt. Zion] and caught hold of the horns of the altar [as a fugitive's refuge].

51 And it was told Solomon, Behold, Adonijah fears King Solomon, for behold, he has caught hold of the horns of the altar, saying, Let King Solomon swear to me first that he will not slay his servant with the sword.

52 Solomon said, If he will show himself to be a worthy man, not a hair of him shall fall to the ground; but if wickedness is found in him, he shall die.

53 So King Solomon sent, and they brought Adonijah down from the altar [in front of the tabernacle]. He came and bowed himself to King Solomon, and Solomon said to him, Go to your house.

2 WHEN DAVID'S time to die was near, he charged Solomon his son, saying,

2 I go the way of all the earth. Be strong and show yourself a man;

3 Keep the charge of the Lord your God, walk in His ways, keep His statutes, His commandments, His precepts, and His testimonies, as it is written in the Law of Moses, that you may do wisely *and* prosper in all that you do and wherever you turn,

4 That the Lord may fulfill His promise to me, saying, If your sons take heed to their way, to walk before Me in truth with all their heart *and* mind and with all their soul, there shall not fail you [to have] a man on the throne of Israel.

5 You know also what Joab son of Zeruiah did to me, and what he did to the two captains of the hosts of Israel, Abner son of Ner and Amasa son of Jether, whom he murdered, avenging in time of peace blood shed in war, and putting innocent blood of war on the girdle on his loins and on the sandals of his feet.

6 Do therefore according to your wisdom, but let not his hoary head go down to Sheol (the place of the dead) in peace.

7 But show kindness to the sons of Barzillai the Gileadite and let them be among those who eat at your table; for with such kindness they met me when I fled because of Absalom your brother. [II Sam. 17:27–29.]

---

q Or, *do wisely*   *r* Heb. *be cut off from thee from the throne*
s Heb. *put*

New American Standard

⁴¹ ¶ Now Adonijah and all the guests who *were* with him heard *it* as they finished eating. When Joab heard the sound of the trumpet, he said, "Why is the city making such an uproar?"

⁴² While he was still speaking, behold, Jonathan the son of Abiathar the priest came. Then Adonijah said, "Come in, for you are a valiant man and bring good news."

⁴³ But Jonathan replied to Adonijah, "No! Our lord King David has made Solomon king.

⁴⁴"The king has also sent with him Zadok the priest, Nathan the prophet, Benaiah the son of Jehoiada, the Cherethites, and the Pelethites; and they have made him ride on the king's mule.

⁴⁵"Zadok the priest and Nathan the prophet have anointed him king in Gihon, and they have come up from there rejoicing, so that the city is in an uproar. This is the noise which you have heard.

⁴⁶"Besides, Solomon has even taken his seat on the throne of the kingdom.

⁴⁷"Moreover, the king's servants came to bless our lord King David, saying, 'May your God make the name of Solomon better than your name and his throne greater than your throne!' And the king bowed himself on the bed.

⁴⁸"The king has also said thus, 'Blessed be the LORD, the God of Israel, who has granted one to sit on my throne today while my own eyes see *it.*' "

⁴⁹ ¶ Then all the guests of Adonijah were terrified; and they arose and each went on his way.

⁵⁰ And Adonijah was afraid of Solomon, and he arose, went and took hold of the horns of the altar.

⁵¹ Now it was told Solomon, saying, "Behold, Adonijah is afraid of King Solomon, for behold, he has taken hold of the horns of the altar, saying, 'Let King Solomon swear to me today that he will not put his servant to death with the sword.' "

⁵² Solomon said, "If he is a worthy man, not one of his hairs will fall to the ground; but if wickedness is found in him, he will die."

⁵³ So King Solomon sent, and they brought him down from the altar. And he came and prostrated himself before King Solomon, and Solomon said to him, "Go to your house."

David's Charge to Solomon

2 AS DAVID'S time to die drew near, he charged Solomon his son, saying,

²"I am going the way of all the earth. Be strong, therefore, and show yourself a man.

³"Keep the charge of the LORD your God, to walk in His ways, to keep His statutes, His commandments, His ordinances, and His testimonies, according to what is written in the Law of Moses, that you may succeed in all that you do and wherever you turn,

⁴ so that the LORD may carry out His promise which He spoke concerning me, saying, 'If your sons are careful of their way, to walk before Me in ^btruth with all their heart and with all their soul, you shall not lack a man on the throne of Israel.'

⁵ ¶ "Now you also know what Joab the son of Zeruiah did to me, what he did to the two commanders of the armies of Israel, to Abner the son of Ner, and to Amasa the son of Jether, whom he killed; he also shed the blood of war in peace. And he put the blood of war on his belt about his waist, and on his sandals on his feet.

⁶"So act according to your wisdom, and do not let his gray hair go down to Sheol in peace.

⁷"But show kindness to the sons of Barzillai the Gileadite, and let them be among those who eat at your table; for they assisted me when I fled from Absalom your brother.

New International

⁴¹Adonijah and all the guests who were with him heard it as they were finishing their feast. On hearing the sound of the trumpet, Joab asked, "What's the meaning of all the noise in the city?"

⁴²Even as he was speaking, Jonathan son of Abiathar the priest arrived. Adonijah said, "Come in. A worthy man like you must be bringing good news."

⁴³"Not at all!" Jonathan answered. "Our lord King David has made Solomon king. ⁴⁴The king has sent with him Zadok the priest, Nathan the prophet, Benaiah son of Jehoiada, the Kerethites and the Pelethites, and they have put him on the king's mule, ⁴⁵and Zadok the priest and Nathan the prophet have anointed him king at Gihon. From there they have gone up cheering, and the city resounds with it. That's the noise you hear. ⁴⁶Moreover, Solomon has taken his seat on the royal throne. ⁴⁷Also, the royal officials have come to congratulate our lord King David, saying, 'May your God make Solomon's name more famous than yours and his throne greater than yours!' And the king bowed in worship on his bed ⁴⁸and said, 'Praise be to the LORD, the God of Israel, who has allowed my eyes to see a successor on my throne today.' "

⁴⁹At this, all Adonijah's guests rose in alarm and dispersed. ⁵⁰But Adonijah, in fear of Solomon, went and took hold of the horns of the altar. ⁵¹Then Solomon was told, "Adonijah is afraid of King Solomon and is clinging to the horns of the altar. He says, 'Let King Solomon swear to me today that he will not put his servant to death with the sword.' "

⁵²Solomon replied, "If he shows himself to be a worthy man, not a hair of his head will fall to the ground; but if evil is found in him, he will die." ⁵³Then King Solomon sent men, and they brought him down from the altar. And Adonijah came and bowed down to King Solomon, and Solomon said, "Go to your home."

David's Charge to Solomon

2 WHEN THE time drew near for David to die, he gave a charge to Solomon his son.

²"I am about to go the way of all the earth," he said. "So be strong, show yourself a man, ³and observe what the LORD your God requires: Walk in his ways, and keep his decrees and commands, his laws and requirements, as written in the Law of Moses, so that you may prosper in all you do and wherever you go, ⁴and that the LORD may keep his promise to me: 'If your descendants watch how they live, and if they walk faithfully before me with all their heart and soul, you will never fail to have a man on the throne of Israel.'

⁵"Now you yourself know what Joab son of Zeruiah did to me—what he did to the two commanders of Israel's armies, Abner son of Ner and Amasa son of Jether. He killed them, shedding their blood in peacetime as if in battle, and with that blood stained the belt around his waist and the sandals on his feet. ⁶Deal with him according to your wisdom, but do not let his gray head go down to the grave^c in peace.

⁷"But show kindness to the sons of Barzillai of Gilead and let them be among those who eat at your table. They stood by me when I fled from your brother Absalom.

---

^bOr *faithfulness*   ^c6 Hebrew *Sheol*; also in verse 9

King James

8And, behold, *thou hast* with thee Shimei the son of Gera, a Benjamite of Bahurim, which cursed me with a *t*grievous curse in the day when I went to Mahanaim: but he came down to meet me at Jordan, and I sware to him by the LORD, saying, I will not put thee to death with the sword.

9Now therefore hold him not guiltless: for thou *art* a wise man, and knowest what thou oughtest to do unto him; but his hoar head bring thou down to the grave with blood.

10So David slept with his fathers, and was buried in the city of David.

11And the days that David reigned over Israel *were* forty years: seven years reigned he in Hebron, and thirty and three years reigned he in Jerusalem.

12 ¶ Then sat Solomon upon the throne of David his father; and his kingdom was established greatly.

13 ¶ And Adonijah the son of Haggith came to Bath-sheba the mother of Solomon. And she said, Comest thou peaceably? And he said, Peaceably.

14He said moreover, I have somewhat to say unto thee. And she said, Say on.

15And he said, Thou knowest that the kingdom was mine, and *that* all Israel set their faces on me, that I should reign: howbeit the kingdom is turned about, and is become my brother's: for it was his from the LORD.

16And now I ask one petition of thee, *u*deny me not. And she said unto him, Say on.

17And he said, Speak, I pray thee, unto Solomon the king, (for he will not say thee nay,) that he give me Abishag the Shunammite to wife.

18And Bath-sheba said, Well; I will speak for thee unto the king.

19 ¶ Bath-sheba therefore went unto king Solomon, to speak unto him for Adonijah. And the king rose up to meet her, and bowed himself unto her, and sat down on his throne, and caused a seat to be set for the king's mother; and she sat on his right hand.

20Then she said, I desire one small petition of thee; *I pray thee,* say me not nay. And the king said unto her, Ask on, my mother: for I will not say thee nay.

21And she said, Let Abishag the Shunammite be given to Adonijah thy brother to wife.

22And king Solomon answered and said unto his mother, And why dost thou ask Abishag the Shunammite for Adonijah? ask for him the kingdom also; for he *is* mine elder brother; even for him, and for Abiathar the priest, and for Joab the son of Zeruiah.

23Then king Solomon sware by the LORD, saying, God do so to me, and more also, if Adonijah have not spoken this word against his own life.

24Now therefore, *as* the LORD liveth, which hath established me, and set me on the throne of David my father, and who hath made me an house, as he promised, Adonijah shall be put to death this day.

25And king Solomon sent by the hand of Benaiah the son of Jehoiada; and he fell upon him that he died.

26 ¶ And unto Abiathar the priest said the king, Get thee to Anathoth, unto thine own fields; for thou *art* *v*worthy of death: but I will not at this time put thee to death, because thou barest the ark of the Lord GOD before David my father, and because thou hast been afflicted in all wherein my father was afflicted.

27So Solomon thrust out Abiathar from being priest unto the LORD; that he might fulfil the word of the LORD, which he spake concerning the house of Eli in Shiloh.

Amplified

8And you have with you Shimei son of Gera, the Benjamite of Bahurim, who cursed me with a grievous curse in the day when I went to Mahanaim. But he came down to meet me at the Jordan [on my return], and I swore to him by the Lord, saying, I will not put you to death with the sword.

9So do not hold him guiltless; for you are a wise man and know what you should do to him. His hoary head bring down to the grave with blood.

10So David slept with his fathers and was buried in the City of David.

11David reigned over Israel forty years—seven years in Hebron and thirty-three years in Jerusalem.

12Then Solomon sat on the throne of David his father, and his kingdom was firmly established.

13Adonijah, the son of [David and] Haggith, came to Bathsheba, the mother of Solomon. She said, Do you come peaceably? And he said, Peaceably.

14He said, I have something to say to you. And she said, Say on.

15He said, You know that the kingdom belonged to me [as the eldest living son], and all Israel looked to me to reign. However, the kingdom has passed from me to my brother; for it was his from the Lord.

16Now I make one request of you; do not deny me. And she said, Say on.

17He said, I pray you, ask King Solomon, for he will not refuse you, to give me Abishag the Shunammite to be my wife. [I Kings 1:1–4.]

18And Bathsheba said, Very well; I will speak for you to the king.

19So Bathsheba went to King Solomon to speak to him for Adonijah. The king rose to meet her, bowed to her, sat down on his throne, and caused a seat to be set at his right hand for her, the king's mother.

20Then she said, I have one small request to make of you; do not refuse me. The king said to her, Ask on, my mother, for I will not refuse you.

21She said, Give Abishag the Shunammite to Adonijah your brother to be his wife.

22King Solomon answered his mother, And why do you ask Abishag the Shunammite for Adonijah? Ask for him the kingdom also—for he is my elder brother—[ask it] even for him and for [his supporters] Abiathar the priest and Joab son of Zeruiah.

23Then King Solomon swore by the Lord, saying, May God do so to me, and more also, if Adonijah has not requested this against his own life.

24Therefore, as the Lord lives, Who has established me and set me on the throne of David my father and Who has made me a house as He promised, Adonijah shall be put to death this day.

25So King Solomon sent Benaiah son of Jehoiada, who attacked [Adonijah] and he died.

26And to Abiathar the priest the king said, Get to Anathoth to your own estate; for you deserve death, but I will not put you to death now, because you bore the ark of the Lord God before my father David and were afflicted in all my father endured.

27So Solomon expelled Abiathar [descendant of Eli] from being priest to the Lord, fulfilling the word of the Lord which He spoke concerning the house of Eli in Shiloh. [I Sam. 2:27–36.]

*t*Heb. *strong*   *u*Heb. *turn not away my face*   *v*Heb. *a man of death*

New American Standard

8"Behold, there is with you Shimei the son of Gera the Benjamite, of Bahurim; now it was he who cursed me with a violent curse on the day I went to Mahanaim. But when he came down to me at the Jordan, I swore to him by the LORD, saying, 'I will not put you to death with the sword.' 9"Now therefore, do not let him go unpunished, for you are a wise man; and you will know what you ought to do to him, and you will bring his gray hair down to Sheol with blood."

Death of David

10 ¶ Then David slept with his fathers and was buried in the city of David.

11 The days that David reigned over Israel *were* forty years: seven years he reigned in Hebron and thirty-three years he reigned in Jerusalem.

12 And Solomon sat on the throne of David his father, and his kingdom was firmly established.

13 ¶ Now Adonijah the son of Haggith came to Bathsheba the mother of Solomon. And she said, "Do you come peacefully?" And he said, "Peacefully."

14 Then he said, "I have something *to say* to you." And she said, "Speak."

15 So he said, "You know that the kingdom was mine and that all Israel expected me to be king; however, the kingdom has turned about and become my brother's, for it was his from the LORD.

16"Now I am making one request of you; do not ᶜrefuse me." And she said to him, "Speak."

17 Then he said, "Please speak to Solomon the king, for he will not refuse you, that he may give me Abishag the Shunammite as a wife."

18 Bathsheba said, "Very well; I will speak to the king for you."

Adonijah Executed

19 ¶ So Bathsheba went to King Solomon to speak to him for Adonijah. And the king arose to meet her, bowed before her, and sat on his throne; then he had a throne set for the king's mother, and she sat on his right.

20 Then she said, "I am making one small request of you; do not refuse me." And the king said to her, "Ask, my mother, for I will not refuse you."

21 So she said, "Let Abishag the Shunammite be given to Adonijah your brother as a wife."

22 King Solomon answered and said to his mother, "And why are you asking Abishag the Shunammite for Adonijah? Ask for him also the kingdom—for he is my older brother—even for him, for Abiathar the priest, and for Joab the son of Zeruiah!"

23 Then King Solomon swore by the LORD, saying, "May God do so to me and more also, if Adonijah has not spoken this word against his own life.

24"Now therefore, as the LORD lives, who has established me and set me on the throne of David my father and who has made me a house as He promised, surely Adonijah shall be put to death today."

25 So King Solomon sent Benaiah the son of Jehoiada; and he fell upon him so that he died.

26 ¶ Then to Abiathar the priest the king said, "Go to Anathoth to your own field, for you deserve to die; but I will not put you to death at this time, because you carried the ark of the Lord GOD before my father David, and because you were afflicted in everything with which my father was afflicted."

27 So Solomon dismissed Abiathar from being priest to the LORD, in order to fulfill the word of the LORD, which He had spoken concerning the house of Eli in Shiloh.

New International

8"And remember, you have with you Shimei son of Gera, the Benjamite from Bahurim, who called down bitter curses on me the day I went to Mahanaim. When he came down to meet me at the Jordan, I swore to him by the LORD: 'I will not put you to death by the sword.' 9But now, do not consider him innocent. You are a man of wisdom; you will know what to do to him. Bring his gray head down to the grave in blood."

10Then David rested with his fathers and was buried in the City of David. 11He had reigned forty years over Israel—seven years in Hebron and thirty-three in Jerusalem. 12So Solomon sat on the throne of his father David, and his rule was firmly established.

Solomon's Throne Established

13Now Adonijah, the son of Haggith, went to Bathsheba, Solomon's mother. Bathsheba asked him, "Do you come peacefully?"

He answered, "Yes, peacefully." 14Then he added, "I have something to say to you."

"You may say it," she replied.

15"As you know," he said, "the kingdom was mine. All Israel looked to me as their king. But things changed, and the kingdom has gone to my brother; for it has come to him from the LORD. 16Now I have one request to make of you. Do not refuse me."

"You may make it," she said.

17So he continued, "Please ask King Solomon—he will not refuse you—to give me Abishag the Shunammite as my wife."

18"Very well," Bathsheba replied, "I will speak to the king for you."

19When Bathsheba went to King Solomon to speak to him for Adonijah, the king stood up to meet her, bowed down to her and sat down on his throne. He had a throne brought for the king's mother, and she sat down at his right hand.

20"I have one small request to make of you," she said. "Do not refuse me."

The king replied, "Make it, my mother; I will not refuse you."

21So she said, "Let Abishag the Shunammite be given in marriage to your brother Adonijah."

22King Solomon answered his mother, "Why do you request Abishag the Shunammite for Adonijah? You might as well request the kingdom for him—after all, he is my older brother—yes, for him and for Abiathar the priest and Joab son of Zeruiah!"

23Then King Solomon swore by the LORD: "May God deal with me, be it ever so severely, if Adonijah does not pay with his life for this request! 24And now, as surely as the LORD lives—he who has established me securely on the throne of my father David and has founded a dynasty for me as he promised—Adonijah shall be put to death today!" 25So King Solomon gave orders to Benaiah son of Jehoiada, and he struck down Adonijah and he died.

26To Abiathar the priest the king said, "Go back to your fields in Anathoth. You deserve to die, but I will not put you to death now, because you carried the ark of the Sovereign LORD before my father David and shared all my father's hardships." 27So Solomon removed Abiathar from the priesthood of the LORD, fulfilling the word the LORD had spoken at Shiloh about the house of Eli.

ᶜLit *turn away my face*

King James

²⁸ ¶ Then tidings came to Joab: for Joab had turned after Adonijah, though he turned not after Absalom. And Joab fled unto the tabernacle of the LORD, and caught hold on the horns of the altar.

²⁹And it was told king Solomon that Joab was fled unto the tabernacle of the LORD; and, behold, *he is* by the altar. Then Solomon sent Benaiah the son of Jehoiada, saying, Go, fall upon him.

³⁰And Benaiah came to the tabernacle of the LORD, and said unto him, Thus saith the king, Come forth. And he said, Nay; but I will die here. And Benaiah brought the king word again, saying, Thus said Joab, and thus he answered me.

³¹And the king said unto him, Do as he hath said, and fall upon him, and bury him; that thou mayest take away the innocent blood, which Joab shed, from me, and from the house of my father.

³²And the LORD shall return his blood upon his own head, who fell upon two men more righteous and better than he, and slew them with the sword, my father David not knowing *thereof, to wit,* Abner the son of Ner, captain of the host of Israel, and Amasa the son of Jether, captain of the host of Judah.

³³Their blood shall therefore return upon the head of Joab, and upon the head of his seed for ever: but upon David, and upon his seed, and upon his house, and upon his throne, shall there be peace for ever from the LORD.

³⁴So Benaiah the son of Jehoiada went up, and fell upon him, and slew him: and he was buried in his own house in the wilderness.

³⁵ ¶ And the king put Benaiah the son of Jehoiada in his room over the host: and Zadok the priest did the king put in the room of Abiathar.

³⁶ ¶ And the king sent and called for Shimei, and said unto him, Build thee an house in Jerusalem, and dwell there, and go not forth thence any whither.

³⁷For it shall be, *that* on the day thou goest out, and passest over the brook Kidron, thou shalt know for certain that thou shalt surely die: thy blood shall be upon thine own head.

³⁸And Shimei said unto the king, The saying *is* good: as my lord the king hath said, so will thy servant do. And Shimei dwelt in Jerusalem many days.

³⁹And it came to pass at the end of three years, that two of the servants of Shimei ran away unto Achish son of Maachah king of Gath. And they told Shimei, saying, Behold, thy servants *be* in Gath.

⁴⁰And Shimei arose, and saddled his ass, and went to Gath to Achish to seek his servants: and Shimei went, and brought his servants from Gath.

⁴¹And it was told Solomon that Shimei had gone from Jerusalem to Gath, and was come again.

⁴²And the king sent and called for Shimei, and said unto him, Did I not make thee to swear by the LORD, and protested unto thee, saying, Know for a certain, on the day thou goest out, and walkest abroad any whither, that thou shalt surely die? and thou saidst unto me, The word *that* I have heard *is* good.

⁴³Why then hast thou not kept the oath of the LORD, and the commandment that I have charged thee with?

⁴⁴The king said moreover to Shimei, Thou knowest all the wickedness which thine heart is privy to, that thou didst to David my father: therefore the LORD shall return thy wickedness upon thine own head;

⁴⁵And king Solomon *shall be* blessed, and the throne of David shall be established before the LORD for ever.

⁴⁶So the king commanded Benaiah the son of Jehoiada; which went out, and fell upon him, that he died. And the kingdom was established in the hand of Solomon.

Amplified

²⁸When the news came to Joab, for Joab had followed Adonijah though he had not followed Absalom, [he] fled to the tent (tabernacle) of the Lord and caught hold of the horns of the altar [before it].

²⁹King Solomon was told that Joab had fled to the tent of the Lord and was at the altar. Then Solomon sent Benaiah son of Jehoiada, saying, Go, strike him down.

³⁰So Benaiah came to the tent of the Lord and told Joab, The king commands, Come forth. But Joab said, No, I will die here. Then Benaiah brought the king word again, Thus said Joab, and thus he answered me.

³¹The king said to him, Do as he has said. Strike him down and bury him, that you may take away from [me and from] my father's house the innocent blood which Joab shed.

³²The Lord shall return his bloody deeds upon his own head, for he fell upon two men more [uncompromisingly] righteous and honorable than he and slew them with the sword, without my father David knowing of it: Abner son of Ner, captain of the host of Israel, and Amasa son of Jether, captain of the host of Judah.

³³So shall their blood return upon the head of Joab and of his descendants forever. But upon David, his descendants, his house, and his throne, there shall be peace from the Lord forever.

³⁴So Benaiah son of Jehoiada went up and struck and killed Joab, and he was buried at his own house in the wilderness.

³⁵The king put Benaiah son of Jehoiada in Joab's place over the army and put Zadok the priest in place of Abiathar.

³⁶The king sent for Shimei and said to him, Build yourself a house in Jerusalem and dwell there, and do not leave there.

³⁷For on the day you go out and pass over the brook Kidron, know with certainty that you shall die; your blood shall be upon your own head.

³⁸And Shimei said to the king, The saying is good. As my lord the king has said, so your servant will do. And Shimei dwelt in Jerusalem many days.

³⁹But after three years, two of Shimei's servants ran away to Achish son of Maacah, king of Gath. And Shimei was told, Behold, your [runaway] servants are in Gath.

⁴⁰So Shimei arose, saddled his donkey, and went to Gath to King Achish to seek his servants, and brought them from Gath.

⁴¹It was told Solomon that Shimei went from Jerusalem to Gath and had returned.

⁴²And the king sent for Shimei and said to him, Did I not make you swear by the Lord and warn you, saying, Know with certainty, on the day you go out and walk abroad anywhere, you shall surely die? And you said to me, I have heard your word. It is accepted.

⁴³Why then have you not kept the oath of the Lord and the command with which I have charged you?

⁴⁴The king also said to Shimei, You are aware in your own heart of all the evil you did to my father David; so the Lord will return your evil upon your own head.

⁴⁵But King Solomon shall be blessed, and the throne of David shall be established before the Lord forever.

⁴⁶So the king commanded Benaiah son of Jehoiada, who went out and struck down Shimei, and he died. And the kingdom was established in the hands of Solomon.

New American Standard

Joab Executed

28 ¶ Now the news came to Joab, for Joab had followed Adonijah, although he had not followed Absalom. And Joab fled to the tent of the LORD and took hold of the horns of the altar.

29 It was told King Solomon that Joab had fled to the tent of the LORD, and behold, he is beside the altar. Then Solomon sent Benaiah the son of Jehoiada, saying, "Go, fall upon him."

30 So Benaiah came to the tent of the LORD and said to him, "Thus the king has said, 'Come out.'" But he said, "No, for I will die here." And Benaiah brought the king word again, saying, "Thus spoke Joab, and thus he answered me."

31 The king said to him, "Do as he has spoken and fall upon him and bury him, that you may remove from me and from my father's house the blood which Joab shed without cause.

32 "The LORD will return his blood on his own head, because he fell upon two men more righteous and better than he and killed them with the sword, while my father David did not know *it:* Abner the son of Ner, commander of the army of Israel, and Amasa the son of Jether, commander of the army of Judah.

33 "So shall their blood return on the head of Joab and on the head of his descendants forever; but to David and his descendants and his house and his throne, may there be peace from the LORD forever."

34 Then Benaiah the son of Jehoiada went up and fell upon him and put him to death, and he was buried at his own house in the wilderness.

35 The king appointed Benaiah the son of Jehoiada over the army in his place, and the king appointed Zadok the priest in the place of Abiathar.

Shimei Executed

36 Now the king sent and called for Shimei and said to him, "Build for yourself a house in Jerusalem and live there, and do not go out from there to any place.

37 "For on the day you go out and cross over the brook Kidron, you will know for certain that you shall surely die; your blood shall be on your own head."

38 Shimei then said to the king, "The word is good. As my lord the king has said, so your servant will do." So Shimei lived in Jerusalem many days.

39 ¶ But it came about at the end of three years, that two of the servants of Shimei ran away to Achish son of Maacah, king of Gath. And they told Shimei, saying, "Behold, your servants are in Gath."

40 Then Shimei arose and saddled his donkey, and went to Gath to Achish to look for his servants. And Shimei went and brought his servants from Gath.

41 It was told Solomon that Shimei had gone from Jerusalem to Gath, and had returned.

42 So the king sent and called for Shimei and said to him, "Did I not make you swear by the LORD and solemnly warn you, saying, 'You will know for certain that on the day you depart and go anywhere, you shall surely die'? And you said to me, 'The word which I have heard is good.'

43 "Why then have you not kept the oath of the LORD, and the command which I have laid on you?"

44 The king also said to Shimei, "You know all the evil which you acknowledge in your heart, which you did to my father David; therefore the LORD shall return your evil on your own head.

45 "But King Solomon shall be blessed, and the throne of David shall be established before the LORD forever."

46 So the king commanded Benaiah the son of Jehoiada, and he went out and fell upon him so that he died.

¶ Thus the kingdom was established in the hands of Solomon.

New International

28 When the news reached Joab, who had conspired with Adonijah though not with Absalom, he fled to the tent of the LORD and took hold of the horns of the altar. 29 King Solomon was told that Joab had fled to the tent of the LORD and was beside the altar. Then Solomon ordered Benaiah son of Jehoiada, "Go, strike him down!"

30 So Benaiah entered the tent of the LORD and said to Joab, "The king says, 'Come out!'"

But he answered, "No, I will die here."

Benaiah reported to the king, "This is how Joab answered me."

31 Then the king commanded Benaiah, "Do as he says. Strike him down and bury him, and so clear me and my father's house of the guilt of the innocent blood that Joab shed. 32 The LORD will repay him for the blood he shed, because without the knowledge of my father David he attacked two men and killed them with the sword. Both of them—Abner son of Ner, commander of Israel's army, and Amasa son of Jether, commander of Judah's army—were better men and more upright than he. 33 May the guilt of their blood rest on the head of Joab and his descendants forever. But on David and his descendants, his house and his throne, may there be the LORD's peace forever."

34 So Benaiah son of Jehoiada went up and struck down Joab and killed him, and he was buried on his own land[d] in the desert. 35 The king put Benaiah son of Jehoiada over the army in Joab's position and replaced Abiathar with Zadok the priest.

36 Then the king sent for Shimei and said to him, "Build yourself a house in Jerusalem and live there, but do not go anywhere else. 37 The day you leave and cross the Kidron Valley, you can be sure you will die; your blood will be on your own head."

38 Shimei answered the king, "What you say is good. Your servant will do as my lord the king has said." And Shimei stayed in Jerusalem for a long time.

39 But three years later, two of Shimei's slaves ran off to Achish son of Maacah, king of Gath, and Shimei was told, "Your slaves are in Gath." 40 At this, he saddled his donkey and went to Achish at Gath in search of his slaves. So Shimei went away and brought the slaves back from Gath.

41 When Solomon was told that Shimei had gone from Jerusalem to Gath and had returned, 42 the king summoned Shimei and said to him, "Did I not make you swear by the LORD and warn you, 'On the day you leave to go anywhere else, you can be sure you will die'? At that time you said to me, 'What you say is good. I will obey.' 43 Why then did you not keep your oath to the LORD and obey the command I gave you?"

44 The king also said to Shimei, "You know in your heart all the wrong you did to my father David. Now the LORD will repay you for your wrongdoing. 45 But King Solomon will be blessed, and David's throne will remain secure before the LORD forever."

46 Then the king gave the order to Benaiah son of Jehoiada, and he went out and struck Shimei down and killed him.

The kingdom was now firmly established in Solomon's hands.

---

d 34 Or *buried in his tomb*

King James

Amplified

Prayer for wisdom granted

3 AND SOLOMON made affinity with Pharaoh king of Egypt, and took Pharaoh's daughter, and brought her into the city of David, until he had made an end of building his own house, and the house of the LORD, and the wall of Jerusalem round about.

²Only the people sacrificed in high places, because there was no house built unto the name of the LORD, until those days.

³And Solomon loved the LORD, walking in the statutes of David his father: only he sacrificed and burnt incense in high places.

⁴And the king went to Gibeon to sacrifice there; for that *was* the great high place: a thousand burnt offerings did Solomon offer upon that altar.

⁵ ¶ In Gibeon the LORD appeared to Solomon in a dream by night: and God said, Ask what I shall give thee.

⁶And Solomon said, Thou hast shown unto thy servant David my father great ʷmercy, according as he walked before thee in truth, and in righteousness, and in uprightness of heart with thee; and thou hast kept for him this great kindness, that thou hast given him a son to sit on his throne, as *it is* this day.

⁷And now, O LORD my God, thou hast made thy servant king instead of David my father: and I *am but* a little child: I know not *how* to go out or come in.

⁸And thy servant *is* in the midst of thy people which thou hast chosen, a great people, that cannot be numbered nor counted for multitude.

⁹Give therefore thy servant an ˣunderstanding heart to judge thy people, that I may discern between good and bad: for who is able to judge this thy so great a people?

¹⁰And the speech pleased the Lord, that Solomon had asked this thing.

¹¹And God said unto him, Because thou hast asked this thing, and hast not asked for thyself ʸlong life; neither hast asked riches for thyself, nor hast asked the life of thine enemies; but hast asked for thyself understanding ᶻto discern judgment;

¹²Behold, I have done according to thy words: lo, I have given thee a wise and an understanding heart; so that there was none like thee before thee, neither after thee shall any arise like unto thee.

¹³And I have also given thee that which thou hast not asked, both riches, and honour: so that there ᵃshall not be any among the kings like unto thee all thy days.

¹⁴And if thou wilt walk in my ways, to keep my statutes and my commandments, as thy father David did walk, then I will lengthen thy days.

¹⁵And Solomon awoke; and, behold, *it was* a dream. And he came to Jerusalem, and stood before the ark of the covenant of the LORD, and offered up burnt offerings, and offered peace offerings, and made a feast to all his servants.

Solomon's wise decision

¹⁶ ¶ Then came there two women, *that were* harlots, unto the king, and stood before him.

¹⁷And the one woman said, O my lord, I and this woman dwell in one house; and I was delivered of a child with her in the house.

¹⁸And it came to pass the third day after that I was delivered, that this woman was delivered also: and we *were* together; *there was* no stranger with us in the house, save we two in the house.

¹⁹And this woman's child died in the night; because she overlaid it.

3 AND SOLOMON made an alliance with Pharaoh king of Egypt and took Pharaoh's daughter and brought her into the City of David until he had finished building his own house and the house of the Lord, and the wall around Jerusalem.

²But the people sacrificed [to God] in the high places [as the heathen did to their idols], for there was no house yet built to the ᶜName of the Lord.

³Solomon loved the Lord, walking [at first] in the statutes *and* practices of David his father, only he sacrificed and burned incense in the high places.

⁴The king went to Gibeon [near Jerusalem, where stood the tabernacle and the bronze altar] to sacrifice there, for that was the great high place. One thousand burnt offerings Solomon offered on that altar.

⁵In Gibeon the Lord appeared to Solomon in a dream by night. And God said, ᵈAsk what I shall give you.

⁶Solomon said, You have shown to Your servant David my father great mercy *and* loving-kindness, according as he walked before You in faithfulness, righteousness, and uprightness of heart with You; and You have kept for him this great kindness *and* steadfast love, that You have given him a son to sit on his throne this day.

⁷Now, O Lord my God, You have made Your servant king instead of David my father, and I am ᵉbut a lad [in wisdom and experience]; I know not how to go out (begin) or come in (finish).

⁸Your servant is in the midst of Your people whom You have chosen, a great people who cannot be counted for multitude.

⁹So give Your servant an understanding mind *and* a hearing heart to judge Your people, that I may discern between good and bad. For who is able to judge *and* rule this Your great people? [James 1:5.]

¹⁰It pleased the Lord that Solomon had asked this.

¹¹God said to him, Because you have asked this and have not asked for long life or for riches, nor for the lives of your enemies, but have asked for yourself understanding to recognize what is just and right,

¹²Behold, I have done as you asked. I have given you a wise, discerning mind, so that no one before you was your equal, nor shall any arise after you equal to you.

¹³I have also given you what you have not asked, both riches and honor, so that there shall not be any among the kings equal to you all your days.

¹⁴And if you will go My way, keep My statutes and My commandments as your father David did, then I will lengthen your days.

¹⁵Solomon awoke, and behold, it was a dream. He came to Jerusalem, stood before the ark of the covenant of the Lord, and offered burnt offerings and peace offerings, and made a feast for all his servants.

¹⁶Then two women who had become mothers out of wedlock came and stood before the king.

¹⁷And one woman said, O my lord, I and this woman dwell in one house; and I was delivered of a child with her in the house.

¹⁸And the third day after I was delivered, this woman also was delivered. And we were together; no stranger was with us, just we two in the house.

¹⁹And this woman's child died in the night because she lay on him.

ᶜ See footnote on Deut. 12:5.   ᵈ This is the high privilege of the child of God. Each one's life tells what he has asked for—"in heaven above or in the earth beneath." Which shall it be, God's will and glory, or our own?   ᵉ Solomon was already a father (see I Kings 11:42; 14:21).

ʷOr, *bounty*   ˣHeb. *hearing*   ʸHeb. *many days*   ᶻHeb. *to hear*   ᵃOr, *hath not been*

New American Standard

Solomon's Rule Consolidated

3 THEN SOLOMON formed a marriage alliance with Pharaoh king of Egypt, and took Pharaoh's daughter and brought her to the city of David until he had finished building his own house and the house of the LORD and the wall around Jerusalem. 2 The people were still sacrificing on the high places, because there was no house built for the name of the LORD until those days. 3 ¶ Now Solomon loved the LORD, walking in the statutes of his father David, except he sacrificed and burned incense on the high places.

4 The king went to Gibeon to sacrifice there, for that was the great high place; Solomon offered a thousand burnt offerings on that altar. 5 In Gibeon the LORD appeared to Solomon in a dream at night; and God said, "Ask what *you wish* me to give you."

Solomon's Prayer

6 Then Solomon said, "You have shown great lovingkindness to Your servant David my father, according as he walked before You in ᵈtruth and righteousness and uprightness of heart toward You; and You have reserved for him this great lovingkindness, that You have given him a son to sit on his throne, as *it is* this day. 7"Now, O LORD my God, You have made Your servant king in place of my father David, yet I am but a little child; I do not know how to go out or come in. 8"Your servant is in the midst of Your people which You have chosen, a great people who are too many to be numbered or counted. 9"So give Your servant an understanding heart to judge Your people to discern between good and evil. For who is able to judge this great people of Yours?"

God's Answer

10 ¶ It was pleasing in the sight of the Lord that Solomon had asked this thing. 11 God said to him, "Because you have asked this thing and have not asked for yourself long life, nor have asked riches for yourself, nor have you asked for the life of your enemies, but have asked for yourself discernment to understand justice, 12 behold, I have done according to your words. Behold, I have given you a wise and discerning heart, so that there has been no one like you before you, nor shall one like you arise after you. 13"I have also given you what you have not asked, both riches and honor, so that there will not be any among the kings like you all your days. 14"If you walk in My ways, keeping My statutes and commandments, as your father David walked, then I will prolong your days." 15 ¶ Then Solomon awoke, and behold, it was a dream. And he came to Jerusalem and stood before the ark of the covenant of the Lord, and offered burnt offerings and made peace offerings, and made a feast for all his servants.

Solomon Wisely Judges

16 ¶ Then two women who were harlots came to the king and stood before him. 17 The one woman said, "Oh, my lord, this woman and I live in the same house; and I gave birth to a child while she *was* in the house. 18"It happened on the third day after I gave birth, that this woman also gave birth to a child, and we were together. There was no stranger with us in the house, only the two of us in the house. 19"This woman's son died in the night, because she lay on it.

New International

Solomon Asks for Wisdom

3 SOLOMON MADE an alliance with Pharaoh king of Egypt and married his daughter. He brought her to the City of David until he finished building his palace and the temple of the LORD, and the wall around Jerusalem. 2The people, however, were still sacrificing at the high places, because a temple had not yet been built for the Name of the LORD. 3Solomon showed his love for the LORD by walking according to the statutes of his father David, except that he offered sacrifices and burned incense on the high places.

4The king went to Gibeon to offer sacrifices, for that was the most important high place, and Solomon offered a thousand burnt offerings on that altar. 5At Gibeon the LORD appeared to Solomon during the night in a dream, and God said, "Ask for whatever you want me to give you."

6Solomon answered, "You have shown great kindness to your servant, my father David, because he was faithful to you and righteous and upright in heart. You have continued this great kindness to him and have given him a son to sit on his throne this very day.

7"Now, O LORD my God, you have made your servant king in place of my father David. But I am only a little child and do not know how to carry out my duties. 8Your servant is here among the people you have chosen, a great people, too numerous to count or number. 9So give your servant a discerning heart to govern your people and to distinguish between right and wrong. For who is able to govern this great people of yours?"

10The Lord was pleased that Solomon had asked for this. 11So God said to him, "Since you have asked for this and not for long life or wealth for yourself, nor have asked for the death of your enemies but for discernment in administering justice, 12I will do what you have asked. I will give you a wise and discerning heart, so that there will never have been anyone like you, nor will there ever be. 13Moreover, I will give you what you have not asked for—both riches and honor—so that in your lifetime you will have no equal among kings. 14And if you walk in my ways and obey my statutes and commands as David your father did, I will give you a long life." 15Then Solomon awoke—and he realized it had been a dream.

He returned to Jerusalem, stood before the ark of the Lord's covenant and sacrificed burnt offerings and fellowship offerings.ᵉ Then he gave a feast for all his court.

A Wise Ruling

16Now two prostitutes came to the king and stood before him. 17One of them said, "My lord, this woman and I live in the same house. I had a baby while she was there with me. 18The third day after my child was born, this woman also had a baby. We were alone; there was no one in the house but the two of us.

19"During the night this woman's son died because she

ᵈ Or *faithfulness*   ᵉ 15 Traditionally *peace offerings*

King James

Amplified

²⁰And she arose at midnight, and took my son from beside me, while thine handmaid slept, and laid it in her bosom, and laid her dead child in my bosom.

²¹And when I rose in the morning to give my child suck, behold, it was dead: but when I had considered it in the morning, behold, it was not my son, which I did bear.

²²And the other woman said, Nay; but the living *is* my son, and the dead *is* thy son. And this said, No; but the dead *is* thy son, and the living *is* my son. Thus they spake before the king.

²³Then said the king, The one saith, This *is* my son that liveth, and thy son *is* the dead: and the other saith, Nay; but thy son *is* the dead, and my son *is* the living.

²⁴And the king said, Bring me a sword. And they brought a sword before the king.

²⁵And the king said, Divide the living child in two, and give half to the one, and half to the other.

²⁶Then spake the woman whose the living child *was* unto the king, for her bowels ^byearned upon her son, and she said, O my lord, give her the living child, and in no wise slay it. But the other said, Let it be neither mine nor thine, *but* divide *it*.

²⁷Then the king answered and said, Give her the living child, and in no wise slay it: she *is* the mother thereof.

²⁸And all Israel heard of the judgment which the king had judged; and they feared the king: for they saw that the wisdom of God *was* ^cin him, to do judgment.

Appointment of court officials

4 SO KING Solomon was king over all Israel.
²And these *were* the princes which he had; Azariah the son of Zadok ^dthe priest,

³Elihoreph and Ahiah, the sons of Shisha, ^escribes; Jehoshaphat the son of Ahilud, the ^frecorder.

⁴And Benaiah the son of Jehoiada *was* over the host: and Zadok and Abiathar *were* the priests:

⁵And Azariah the son of Nathan *was* over the officers: and Zabud the son of Nathan *was* principal officer, *and* the king's friend:

⁶And Ahishar *was* over the household: and Adoniram the son of Abda *was* over the ^gtribute.

⁷ ¶ And Solomon had twelve officers over all Israel, which provided victuals for the king and his household: each man his month in a year made provision.

⁸And these *are* their names: ^hThe son of Hur, in mount Ephraim:

⁹ⁱThe son of Dekar, in Makaz, and in Shaalbim, and Beth-shemesh, and Elon-beth-hanan:

^{10j}The son of Hesed, in Aruboth; to him *pertained* Sochoh, and all the land of Hepher:

^{11k}The son of Abinadab, in all the region of Dor; which had Taphath the daughter of Solomon to wife:

¹²Baana the son of Ahilud; *to him pertained* Taanach and Megiddo, and all Beth-shean, which *is* by Zartanah beneath Jezreel, from Beth-shean to Abel-meholah, *even* unto *the place that is* beyond Jokneam:

^{13l}The son of Geber, in Ramoth-gilead; to him *pertained* the towns of Jair the son of Manasseh, which *are* in Gilead; to him *also pertained* the region of Argob, which *is* in Bashan, threescore great cities with walls and brasen bars:

¹⁴Ahinadab the son of Iddo *had* ^mMahanaim:

¹⁵Ahimaaz *was* in Naphtali; he also took Basmath the daughter of Solomon to wife:

¹⁶Baanah the son of Hushai *was* in Asher and in Aloth:

¹⁷Jehoshaphat the son of Paruah, in Issachar:

¹⁸Shimei the son of Elah, in Benjamin:

²⁰And she arose at midnight and took my son from beside me while your handmaid slept and laid him in her bosom and laid her dead child in my bosom.

²¹And when I rose to nurse my child, behold, he was dead. But when I had considered him in the morning, behold, it was not the son I had borne.

²²But the other woman said, No! But the living one is my son, and the dead one is your son! And this one said, No! But the dead son is your son, and the living is my son. Thus they spoke before the king.

²³The king said, One says, This is my son that is alive and yours is the dead one. The other woman says, No! But your son is the dead one and mine is the living one.

²⁴And the king said, Bring me a sword. And they brought a sword to the king.

²⁵And the king said, Divide the living child in two and give half to the one and half to the other.

²⁶Then the mother of the living child said to the king, for she yearned over her son, O my lord, give her the living baby, and by no means slay him. But the other said, Let him not be mine or yours, but divide him.

²⁷Then the king said, Give her [who pleads for his life] the living baby, and by no means slay him. She is the child's mother.

²⁸And all Israel heard of the judgment which the king had made, and they stood in awe of him, for they saw that the wisdom of God was in him to do justice.

4 KING SOLOMON was king over all Israel.
²These were his chief officials: Azariah son of Zadok was the [high] priest;

³Elihoreph and Ahijah, sons of Shisha, were secretaries; Jehoshaphat son of Ahilud was recorder;

⁴Benaiah son of Jehoiada commanded the army; Zadok and Abiathar were priests;

⁵Azariah son of Nathan was over the officers; Zabud son of Nathan was priest and the king's friend *and* private advisor;

⁶Ahishar was in charge of the palace; and Adoniram son of Abda was in charge of the forced labor.

⁷Solomon had twelve officers over all Israel, who secured provisions for the king and his household; each man had to provide for a month in a year.

⁸These were their names: Ben-hur, in the hill country of Ephraim;

⁹Ben-deker, in Makaz, Shaalbim, Beth-shemesh, and Elon-beth-hanan;

¹⁰Ben-hesed, in Arubboth (to him belonged Socoh and all the land of Hepher);

¹¹Ben-abinadab, in Naphoth-dor (he had Taphath, Solomon's daughter, as wife);

¹²Baana son of Ahilud, in Taanach, Megiddo, and all Beth-shean which is beside Zarethan below Jezreel, from Beth-shean to Abel-meholah as far as beyond Jokmeam;

¹³Ben-geber, in Ramoth-gilead (to him belonged the villages of Jair son of Manasseh which are in Gilead, also the region of Argob which is in Bashan, sixty great cities with walls and bronze bars);

¹⁴Ahinadab son of Iddo, in Mahanaim;

¹⁵Ahimaaz, in Naphtali (he had taken Basemath, Solomon's daughter, as his wife);

¹⁶Baana son of Hushai, in Asher and Bealoth;

¹⁷Jehoshaphat son of Paruah, in Issachar;

¹⁸Shimei son of Ela, in Benjamin;

^bHeb. *were hot*   ^cHeb. *in the midst of him*   ^dOr, *the chief officer*   ^eOr, *secretaries*   ^fOr, *remembrancer*   ^gOr, *levy*   ^hOr, *Ben-hur*   ⁱOr, *Ben-dekar*   ^jOr, *Ben-hesed*   ^kOr, *Ben-abin-adab*   ^lOr, *Ben-geber*   ^mOr, *to Mahanaim*

New American Standard

20"So she arose in the middle of the night and took my son from beside me while your maidservant slept, and laid him in her bosom, and laid her dead son in my bosom. 21"When I rose in the morning to nurse my son, behold, he was dead; but when I looked at him carefully in the morning, behold, he was not my son, whom I had borne." 22 Then the other woman said, "No! For the living one is my son, and the dead one is your son." But the first woman said, "No! For the dead one is your son, and the living one is my son." Thus they spoke before the king. 23 ¶ Then the king said, "The one says, 'This is my son who is living, and your son is the dead one'; and the other says, 'No! For your son is the dead one, and my son is the living one.' "
24 The king said, "Get me a sword." So they brought a sword before the king. 25 The king said, "Divide the living child in two, and give half to the one and half to the other." 26 Then the woman whose child *was* the living one spoke to the king, for she was deeply stirred over her son and said, "Oh, my lord, give her the living child, and by no means kill him." But the other said, "He shall be neither mine nor yours; divide *him!*" 27 Then the king said, "Give the first woman the living child, and by no means kill him. She is his mother." 28 When all Israel heard of the judgment which the king had handed down, they feared the king, for they saw that the wisdom of God was in him to administer justice.

Solomon's Officials

4 NOW KING Solomon was king over all Israel. 2 These were his officials: Azariah the son of Zadok *was* the priest; 3 Elihoreph and Ahijah, the sons of Shisha *were* secretaries; Jehoshaphat the son of Ahilud *was* the recorder; 4 and Benaiah the son of Jehoiada *was* over the army; and Zadok and Abiathar *were* priests; 5 and Azariah the son of Nathan *was* over the deputies; and Zabud the son of Nathan, a priest, *was* the king's friend; 6 and Ahishar was over the household; and Adoniram the son of Abda *was* over the men subject to forced labor.
7 ¶ Solomon had twelve deputies over all Israel, who provided for the king and his household; each man had to provide for a month in the year. 8 These are their names: Ben-hur, in the hill country of Ephraim; 9 Ben-deker in Makaz and Shaalbim and Beth-shemesh and Elonbeth-hanan; 10 Ben-hesed, in Arubboth (Socoh *was* his and all the land of Hepher); 11 Ben-abinadab, *in* all the height of Dor (Taphath the daughter of Solomon was his wife); 12 Baana the son of Ahilud, *in* Taanach and Megiddo, and all Beth-shean which is beside Zarethan below Jezreel, from Beth-shean to Abel-meholah as far as the other side of Jokmeam; 13 Ben-geber, in Ramoth-gilead (the towns of Jair, the son of Manasseh, which are in Gilead were his: the region of Argob, which is in Bashan, sixty great cities with walls and bronze bars *were* his); 14 Ahinadab the son of Iddo, *in* Mahanaim; 15 Ahimaaz, in Naphtali (he also married Basemath the daughter of Solomon); 16 Baana the son of Hushai, in Asher and Bealoth; 17 Jehoshaphat the son of Paruah, in Issachar; 18 Shimei the son of Ela, in Benjamin;

New International

lay on him. 20So she got up in the middle of the night and took my son from my side while I your servant was asleep. She put him by her breast and put her dead son by my breast. 21The next morning, I got up to nurse my son—and he was dead! But when I looked at him closely in the morning light, I saw that it wasn't the son I had borne." 22The other woman said, "No! The living one is my son; the dead one is yours."

But the first one insisted, "No! The dead one is yours; the living one is mine." And so they argued before the king.

23The king said, "This one says, 'My son is alive and your son is dead,' while that one says, 'No! Your son is dead and mine is alive.' "

24Then the king said, "Bring me a sword." So they brought a sword for the king. 25He then gave an order: "Cut the living child in two and give half to one and half to the other."

26The woman whose son was alive was filled with compassion for her son and said to the king, "Please, my lord, give her the living baby! Don't kill him!"

But the other said, "Neither I nor you shall have him. Cut him in two!"

27Then the king gave his ruling: "Give the living baby to the first woman. Do not kill him; she is his mother."

28When all Israel heard the verdict the king had given, they held the king in awe, because they saw that he had wisdom from God to administer justice.

Solomon's Officials and Governors

4 SO KING Solomon ruled over all Israel. 2And these were his chief officials:

Azariah son of Zadok—the priest;
3Elihoreph and Ahijah, sons of Shisha—secretaries;
Jehoshaphat son of Ahilud—recorder;
4Benaiah son of Jehoiada—commander in chief;
Zadok and Abiathar—priests;
5Azariah son of Nathan—in charge of the district officers;
Zabud son of Nathan—a priest and personal adviser to the king;
6Ahishar—in charge of the palace;
Adoniram son of Abda—in charge of forced labor.

7Solomon also had twelve district governors over all Israel, who supplied provisions for the king and the royal household. Each one had to provide supplies for one month in the year. 8These are their names:

Ben-Hur—in the hill country of Ephraim;
9Ben-Deker—in Makaz, Shaalbim, Beth Shemesh and Elon Bethhanan;
10Ben-Hesed—in Arubboth (Socoh and all the land of Hepher were his);
11Ben-Abinadab—in Naphoth Dor*f* (he was married to Taphath daughter of Solomon);
12Baana son of Ahilud—in Taanach and Megiddo, and in all of Beth Shan next to Zarethan below Jezreel, from Beth Shan to Abel Meholah across to Jokmeam;
13Ben-Geber—in Ramoth Gilead (the settlements of Jair son of Manasseh in Gilead were his, as well as the district of Argob in Bashan and its sixty large walled cities with bronze gate bars);
14Ahinadab son of Iddo—in Mahanaim;
15Ahimaaz—in Naphtali (he had married Basemath daughter of Solomon);
16Baana son of Hushai—in Asher and in Aloth;
17Jehoshaphat son of Paruah—in Issachar;
18Shimei son of Ela—in Benjamin;

f 11 Or in the heights of Dor

King James

¹⁹Geber the son of Uri *was* in the country of Gilead, *in* the country of Sihon king of the Amorites, and of Og king of Bashan; and *he was* the only officer which *was* in the land.

²⁰ ¶ Judah and Israel *were* many, as the sand which *is* by the sea in multitude, eating and drinking, and making merry.

²¹And Solomon reigned over all kingdoms from the river unto the land of the Philistines, and unto the border of Egypt: they brought presents, and served Solomon all the days of his life.

The household provisions

²² ¶ And Solomon's ⁿprovision for one day was thirty ^omeasures of fine flour, and threescore measures of meal;

²³Ten fat oxen, and twenty oxen out of the pastures, and an hundred sheep, beside harts, and roebucks, and fallow-deer, and fatted fowl.

²⁴For he had dominion over all *the region* on this side the river, from Tiphsah even to Azzah, over all the kings on this side the river: and he had peace on all sides round about him.

²⁵And Judah and Israel dwelt ^psafely, every man under his vine and under his fig tree, from Dan even to Beer-sheba, all the days of Solomon.

²⁶ ¶ And Solomon had forty thousand stalls of horses for his chariots, and twelve thousand horsemen.

²⁷And those officers provided victual for king Solomon, and for all that came unto king Solomon's table, every man in his month: they lacked nothing.

²⁸Barley also and straw for the horses and ^qdromedaries brought they unto the place where *the officers* were, every man according to his charge.

Solomon's great wisdom

²⁹ ¶ And God gave Solomon wisdom and understanding exceeding much, and largeness of heart, even as the sand that *is* on the sea shore.

³⁰And Solomon's wisdom excelled the wisdom of all the children of the east country, and all the wisdom of Egypt.

³¹For he was wiser than all men; than Ethan the Ezrahite, and Heman, and Chalcol, and Darda, the sons of Mahol: and his fame was in all nations round about.

³²And he spake three thousand proverbs: and his songs were a thousand and five.

³³And he spake of trees, from the cedar tree that *is* in Lebanon even unto the hyssop that springeth out of the wall: he spake also of beasts, and of fowl, and of creeping things, and of fishes.

³⁴And there came of all people to hear the wisdom of Solomon, from all kings of the earth, which had heard of his wisdom.

Preparing to build the temple

5 AND HIRAM king of Tyre sent his servants unto Solomon; for he had heard that they had anointed him king in the room of his father: for Hiram was ever a lover of David.

²And Solomon sent to Hiram, saying,

³Thou knowest how that David my father could not build an house unto the name of the LORD his God for the wars which were about him on every side, until the LORD put them under the soles of his feet.

Amplified

¹⁹Geber son of Uri, in Gilead, the country of Sihon king of the Amorites and of Og king of Bashan; only one officer was over all the country [at one time, each serving for one month].

²⁰Judah and Israel were many, like the sand which is by the sea in multitude; they ate, drank, and rejoiced.

²¹Solomon reigned ^fover all the kingdoms from the [Euphrates] River to the land of the Philistines and to the border of Egypt; they brought tribute and served Solomon all the days of his life.

²²Solomon's provision for one day was thirty measures of fine flour, sixty measures of meal,

²³Ten fat oxen, twenty pasture-fed cattle, a hundred sheep, besides harts, gazelles, roebucks, and fatted fowl of choice kinds.

²⁴For he had dominion over all the region west of the [Euphrates] River, from Tiphsah to Gaza, over all the kings west of the River, and he had peace on all sides around him.

²⁵Judah and Israel dwelt safely, every man under his vine and fig tree, from Dan to Beersheba, all of Solomon's days.

²⁶Solomon also had 40,000 stalls of horses for his chariots, and 12,000 horsemen.

²⁷And those officers provided food for King Solomon and for all who came to his table, every man in his month; they let nothing be lacking.

²⁸Barley also and straw for the horses and swift steeds they brought to the place where it was needed, each according to his assignment.

²⁹And God gave Solomon exceptionally much wisdom and understanding, and breadth of mind like the sand of the seashore.

³⁰Solomon's wisdom excelled the wisdom of all the people of the East and all the wisdom of Egypt.

³¹For he was wiser ^gthan all other men—than Ethan the Ezrahite, and Heman, Calcol, and Darda, the sons of Mahol. His fame was in all the nations round about.

³²He also originated 3,000 proverbs, and his songs were 1,005.

³³He spoke of trees, from the cedar that is in Lebanon to the hyssop that grows out of the wall; he spoke also of beasts, of birds, of creeping things, and of fish.

³⁴Men came from all peoples to hear the wisdom of Solomon, and from all kings of the earth who had heard of his wisdom.

5 HIRAM KING of Tyre sent his servants to Solomon, when he heard that he was anointed king in place of his father, for Hiram always loved David.

²And Solomon sent to Hiram, saying,

³You know how David my father could not build a house to the Name of the Lord his God because wars were about him on every side, until the Lord put his foes under his feet. [II Sam. 7:4ff.; I Chron. 22:8.]

---

^fThat King Solomon's empire was as great as is definitely indicated here and in II Chron. 9:26 has frequently been questioned because of the great empires of Assyria on the Euphrates and Egypt on the Nile. But archaeological discoveries prove that "precisely during the period 1100-900 B.C., when the kingdom of Israel was being built up, 'the weak and inglorious twenty-first dynasty' was ruling in Egypt and at the same time Assyria went into a period of decline" (J. P. Free, *Archaeology and Bible History*, citing A. T. Olmstead, *History of Assyria*).   ^g"Wiser than all other men," until Christ came. Jesus said, "Someone more *and* greater than Solomon is here" (Matt. 12:42).

ⁿHeb. *bread*   ^oHeb. *cors*   ^pHeb. *confidently*   ^qOr, *mules,*
or, *swift beasts*

New American Standard

19 Geber the son of Uri, in the land of Gilead, the country of Sihon king of the Amorites and of Og king of Bashan; and *he was* the only deputy who *was* in the land.

Solomon's Power, Wealth and Wisdom

20 ¶ Judah and Israel *were* as numerous as the sand that is on the seashore in abundance; *they* were eating and drinking and rejoicing.
21 ¶ Now Solomon ruled over all the kingdoms from the *e*River *to* the land of the Philistines and to the border of Egypt; *they* brought tribute and served Solomon all the days of his life.
22 ¶ Solomon's provision for one day was thirty *f*kors of fine flour and sixty kors of meal,
23 ten fat oxen, twenty pasture-fed oxen, a hundred sheep besides deer, gazelles, roebucks, and fattened fowl.
24 For he had dominion over everything west of the River, from Tiphsah even to Gaza, over all the kings west of the River; and he had peace on all sides around about him.
25 So Judah and Israel lived in safety, every man under his vine and his fig tree, from Dan even to Beersheba, all the days of Solomon.
26 Solomon had *g*40,000 stalls of horses for his chariots, and 12,000 horsemen.
27 Those deputies provided for King Solomon and all who came to King Solomon's table, each in his month; they left nothing lacking.
28 They also brought barley and straw for the horses and swift steeds to the place where it should be, each according to his charge.
29 ¶ Now God gave Solomon wisdom and very great discernment and breadth of mind, like the sand that is on the seashore.
30 Solomon's wisdom surpassed the wisdom of all the sons of the east and all the wisdom of Egypt.
31 For he was wiser than all men, than Ethan the Ezrahite, Heman, Calcol and Darda, the sons of Mahol; and his fame was *known* in all the surrounding nations.
32 He also spoke 3,000 proverbs, and his songs were 1,005.
33 He spoke of trees, from the cedar that is in Lebanon even to the hyssop that grows on the wall; he spoke also of animals and birds and creeping things and fish.
34 Men came from all peoples to hear the wisdom of Solomon, from all the kings of the earth who had heard of his wisdom.

Alliance with King Hiram

5 NOW HIRAM king of Tyre sent his servants to Solomon, when he heard that they had anointed him king in place of his father, for Hiram had always been a friend of David.
2 Then Solomon sent *word* to Hiram, saying,
3 "You know that David my father was unable to build a house for the name of the LORD his God because of the wars which surrounded him, until the LORD put them under the soles of his feet.

New International

19Geber son of Uri—in Gilead (the country of Sihon king of the Amorites and the country of Og king of Bashan). He was the only governor over the district.

Solomon's Daily Provisions

20The people of Judah and Israel were as numerous as the sand on the seashore; they ate, they drank and they were happy. 21And Solomon ruled over all the kingdoms from the River*g* to the land of the Philistines, as far as the border of Egypt. These countries brought tribute and were Solomon's subjects all his life.
22Solomon's daily provisions were thirty cors*h* of fine flour and sixty cors*i* of meal, 23ten head of stall-fed cattle, twenty of pasture-fed cattle and a hundred sheep and goats, as well as deer, gazelles, roebucks and choice fowl. 24For he ruled over all the kingdoms west of the River, from Tiphsah to Gaza, and had peace on all sides. 25During Solomon's lifetime Judah and Israel, from Dan to Beersheba, lived in safety, each man under his own vine and fig tree.
26Solomon had four*j* thousand stalls for chariot horses, and twelve thousand horses.*k*
27The district officers, each in his month, supplied provisions for King Solomon and all who came to the king's table. They saw to it that nothing was lacking. 28They also brought to the proper place their quotas of barley and straw for the chariot horses and the other horses.

Solomon's Wisdom

29God gave Solomon wisdom and very great insight, and a breadth of understanding as measureless as the sand on the seashore. 30Solomon's wisdom was greater than the wisdom of all the men of the East, and greater than all the wisdom of Egypt. 31He was wiser than any other man, including Ethan the Ezrahite—wiser than Heman, Calcol and Darda, the sons of Mahol. And his fame spread to all the surrounding nations. 32He spoke three thousand proverbs and his songs numbered a thousand and five. 33He described plant life, from the cedar of Lebanon to the hyssop that grows out of walls. He also taught about animals and birds, reptiles and fish. 34Men of all nations came to listen to Solomon's wisdom, sent by all the kings of the world, who had heard of his wisdom.

Preparations for Building the Temple

5 WHEN HIRAM king of Tyre heard that Solomon had been anointed king to succeed his father David, he sent his envoys to Solomon, because he had always been on friendly terms with David. 2Solomon sent back this message to Hiram:

3"You know that because of the wars waged against my father David from all sides, he could not build a temple for the Name of the LORD his God until the

---

*g*21 That is, the Euphrates; also in verse 24   *h*22 That is, probably about 185 bushels (about 6.6 kiloliters)   *i*22 That is, probably about 375 bushels (about 13.2 kiloliters)   *j*26 Some Septuagint manuscripts (see also 2 Chron. 9:25); Hebrew *forty*   *k*26 Or *charioteers*

---

*e*I.e. Euphrates   *f*I.e. One kor equals approx 10 bu   *g*One ms reads *4000,* cf 2 Chr 9:25

King James

⁴But now the LORD my God hath given me rest on every side, *so that there is* neither adversary nor evil occurrent.

⁵And, behold, I ^rpurpose to build an house unto the name of the LORD my God, as the LORD spake unto David my father, saying, Thy son, whom I will set upon my throne in thy room, he shall build an house unto my name.

⁶Now therefore command thou that they hew me cedar trees out of Lebanon; and my servants shall be with thy servants: and unto thee will I give hire for thy servants according to all that thou shalt ^rappoint: for thou knowest that *there is* not among us any that can skill to hew timber like unto the Sidonians.

⁷ ¶ And it came to pass, when Hiram heard the words of Solomon, that he rejoiced greatly, and said, Blessed *be* the LORD this day, which hath given unto David a wise son over this great people.

⁸And Hiram sent to Solomon, saying, I have ^sconsidered the things which thou sentest to me for: *and* I will do all thy desire concerning timber of cedar, and concerning timber of fir.

⁹My servants shall bring *them* down from Lebanon unto the sea: and I will convey them by sea in floats unto the place that thou shalt ^tappoint me, and will cause them to be discharged there, and thou shalt receive *them:* and thou shalt accomplish my desire, in giving food for my household.

¹⁰So Hiram gave Solomon cedar trees and fir trees *according to* all his desire.

¹¹And Solomon gave Hiram twenty thousand ^umeasures of wheat *for* food to his household, and twenty measures of pure oil: thus gave Solomon to Hiram year by year.

¹²And the LORD gave Solomon wisdom, as he promised him: and there was peace between Hiram and Solomon; and they two made a league together.

¹³ ¶ And king Solomon raised a ^vlevy out of all Israel; and the levy was thirty thousand men.

¹⁴And he sent them to Lebanon, ten thousand a month by courses: a month they were in Lebanon, *and* two months at home: and Adoniram *was* over the levy.

¹⁵And Solomon had threescore and ten thousand that bare burdens, and fourscore thousand hewers in the mountains;

¹⁶Beside the chief of Solomon's officers which *were* over the work, three thousand and three hundred, which ruled over the people that wrought in the work.

¹⁷And the king commanded, and they brought great stones, costly stones, *and* hewed stones, to lay the foundation of the house.

¹⁸And Solomon's builders and Hiram's builders did hew *them,* and the ^wstonesquarers: so they prepared timber and stones to build the house.

The description of the temple

6 AND IT came to pass in the four hundred and eightieth year after the children of Israel were come out of the land of Egypt, in the fourth year of Solomon's reign over Israel, in the month Zif, which *is* the second month, that he ^xbegan to build the house of the LORD.

²And the house which king Solomon built for the LORD, the length thereof *was* threescore cubits, and the breadth thereof twenty *cubits,* and the height thereof thirty cubits.

³And the porch before the temple of the house, twenty cubits *was* the length thereof, according to the breadth of the house; *and* ten cubits *was* the breadth thereof before the house.

⁴And for the house he made ^ywindows of narrow lights.

Amplified

⁴But now the Lord my God has given me rest on every side, so that there is neither adversary nor evil confronting me.

⁵And I purpose to build a house to the Name of the Lord my God, as the Lord said to David my father, Your son whom I will set on your throne in your place shall build the house to My Name *and* Presence.

⁶So, Hiram, command them to hew me cedar trees out of Lebanon; my servants shall join yours, and I will give you whatever wages you set for your servants. For you know that no one among us can equal the skill of the Sidon men in cutting timber.

⁷When Hiram heard the words of Solomon, he rejoiced greatly and said, Blessed be the Lord this day, Who has given David a wise son to be over this great people.

⁸And Hiram sent to Solomon, saying, I have considered the things for which you sent to me; I will do all you wish concerning the cedar and cypress timber.

⁹My servants shall bring the logs down from Lebanon to the sea, make them into rafts, and float them by sea to the place that you direct. I will have them released there, and you shall take them away. And you shall fulfill my desire by providing food for my household.

¹⁰So Hiram gave Solomon all the cedar and cypress trees he desired,

¹¹And Solomon gave Hiram 20,000 measures of wheat for food for his household, and 20 measures of pure, beaten oil. He gave these to Hiram yearly.

¹²The Lord gave Solomon wisdom, as He promised him; and there was peace between Hiram and Solomon, and they made a treaty.

¹³King Solomon raised a levy [of forced labor] out of all Israel; and the levy was 30,000 men.

¹⁴He sent them to Lebanon, 10,000 a month by divisions; one month they were in Lebanon and two months at home. Adoniram was over the levy.

¹⁵And Solomon had 70,000 burden bearers and 80,000 hewers [of stone] in the hill country of Judah,

¹⁶Besides Solomon's 3,300 overseers in charge of the people doing the work.

¹⁷The king commanded, and they hewed *and* brought out ^hgreat, costly stones in order to lay the foundation of the house with dressed stone.

¹⁸Solomon's builders and Hiram's builders and the men of Gebal did the hewing and prepared the timber and stones to build the house.

6 AND 480 years after the Israelites came out of the land of Egypt, in the fourth year of Solomon's reign over Israel, in the second month, Ziv, he began to build the Lord's house.

²The length of the house Solomon built for the Lord was sixty cubits, its breadth twenty, and its height thirty cubits.

³The length of the vestibule in front of the temple was twenty cubits, equal to the width of the house, and its depth in front of the house was ten cubits.

⁴For the house he made narrow [latticed] windows.

---

^rHeb. *say*   ^sHeb. *heard*   ^tHeb. *send*   ^uHeb. *cors*
^vHeb. *tribute* of men   ^wOr, *Giblites* as Ezek. 27:9   ^xHeb. *built*   ^yOr, *windows broad* within, and *narrow* without: or, *skewed* and *closed*

^hThese great foundation stones remain to this day. One of them is almost thirty-nine feet long, one of the most interesting stones of the world. It is the chief cornerstone of the Mosque of Omar's massive wall, placed in its present position 3,000 years ago. Markings on the stones represent the culture of Phoenicia, the region around Tyre from which Solomon received building materials for the temple.

New American Standard

4 "But now the LORD my God has given me rest on every side; there is neither adversary nor misfortune.

5 "Behold, I intend to build a house for the name of the LORD my God, as the LORD spoke to David my father, saying, 'Your son, whom I will set on your throne in your place, he will build the house for My name.'

6 "Now therefore, command that they cut for me cedars from Lebanon, and my servants will be with your servants; and I will give you wages for your servants according to all that you say, for you know that there is no one among us who knows how to cut timber like the Sidonians."

7 ¶ When Hiram heard the words of Solomon, he rejoiced greatly and said, "Blessed be the LORD today, who has given to David a wise son over this great people."

8 So Hiram sent *word* to Solomon, saying, "I have heard *the message* which you have sent me; I will do what you desire concerning the cedar and cypress timber.

9 "My servants will bring *them* down from Lebanon to the sea; and I will make them into rafts *to go* by sea to the place where you direct me, and I will have them broken up there, and you shall carry *them* away. Then you shall accomplish my desire by giving food to my household."

10 So Hiram gave Solomon as much as he desired of the cedar and cypress timber.

11 Solomon then gave Hiram 20,000 kors of wheat as food for his household, and twenty kors of beaten oil; thus Solomon would give Hiram year by year.

12 The LORD gave wisdom to Solomon, just as He promised him; and there was peace between Hiram and Solomon, and the two of them made a covenant.

Conscription of Laborers

13 ¶ Now King Solomon levied forced laborers from all Israel; and the forced laborers numbered 30,000 men.

14 He sent them to Lebanon, 10,000 a month in relays; they were in Lebanon a month *and* two months at home. And Adoniram *was* over the forced laborers.

15 Now Solomon had 70,000 transporters, and 80,000 hewers *of stone* in the mountains,

16 besides Solomon's 3,300 chief deputies who *were* over the project *and* who ruled over the people who were doing the work.

17 Then the king commanded, and they quarried great stones, costly stones, to lay the foundation of the house with cut stones.

18 So Solomon's builders and Hiram's builders and the Gebalites cut them, and prepared the timbers and the stones to build the house.

The Building of the Temple

6 NOW IT came about in the four hundred and eightieth year after the sons of Israel came out of the land of Egypt, in the fourth year of Solomon's reign over Israel, in the month of Ziv which is the second month, that he began to build the house of the LORD.

2 As for the house which King Solomon built for the LORD, its length *was* sixty [h]cubits and its width twenty *cubits* and its height thirty cubits.

3 The porch in front of the nave of the house *was* twenty cubits in length, corresponding to the width of the house, *and* its depth along the front of the house *was* ten cubits.

4 Also for the house he made windows with *artistic* frames.

[h] I.e. One cubit equals approx 18 in.

New International

LORD put his enemies under his feet. 4 But now the LORD my God has given me rest on every side, and there is no adversary or disaster. 5 I intend, therefore, to build a temple for the Name of the LORD my God, as the LORD told my father David, when he said, 'Your son whom I will put on the throne in your place will build the temple for my Name.'

6 "So give orders that cedars of Lebanon be cut for me. My men will work with yours, and I will pay you for your men whatever wages you set. You know that we have no one so skilled in felling timber as the Sidonians."

7 When Hiram heard Solomon's message, he was greatly pleased and said, "Praise be to the LORD today, for he has given David a wise son to rule over this great nation."

8 So Hiram sent word to Solomon:

"I have received the message you sent me and will do all you want in providing the cedar and pine logs. 9 My men will haul them down from Lebanon to the sea, and I will float them in rafts by sea to the place you specify. There I will separate them and you can take them away. And you are to grant my wish by providing food for my royal household."

10 In this way Hiram kept Solomon supplied with all the cedar and pine logs he wanted, 11 and Solomon gave Hiram twenty thousand cors[l] of wheat as food for his household, in addition to twenty thousand baths[m,n] of pressed olive oil. Solomon continued to do this for Hiram year after year. 12 The LORD gave Solomon wisdom, just as he had promised him. There were peaceful relations between Hiram and Solomon, and the two of them made a treaty.

13 King Solomon conscripted laborers from all Israel—thirty thousand men. 14 He sent them off to Lebanon in shifts of ten thousand a month, so that they spent one month in Lebanon and two months at home. Adoniram was in charge of the forced labor. 15 Solomon had seventy thousand carriers and eighty thousand stonecutters in the hills, 16 as well as thirty-three hundred[o] foremen who supervised the project and directed the workmen. 17 At the king's command they removed from the quarry large blocks of quality stone to provide a foundation of dressed stone for the temple. 18 The craftsmen of Solomon and Hiram and the men of Gebal[p] cut and prepared the timber and stone for the building of the temple.

Solomon Builds the Temple

6 IN THE four hundred and eightieth[q] year after the Israelites had come out of Egypt, in the fourth year of Solomon's reign over Israel, in the month of Ziv, the second month, he began to build the temple of the LORD.

2 The temple that King Solomon built for the LORD was sixty cubits long, twenty wide and thirty high.[r] 3 The portico at the front of the main hall of the temple extended the width of the temple, that is twenty cubits,[s] and projected ten cubits[t] from the front of the temple. 4 He made

[l] *11* That is, probably about 125,000 bushels (about 4,400 kiloliters)
[m] *11* Septuagint (see also 2 Chron. 2:10); Hebrew *twenty cors*
[n] *11* That is, about 115,000 gallons (about 440 kiloliters)
[o] *16* Hebrew; some Septuagint manuscripts (see also 2 Chron. 2:2, 18) *thirty-six hundred*
[p] *18* That is, Byblos
[q] *1* Hebrew; Septuagint *four hundred and fortieth*
[r] *2* That is, about 90 feet (about 27 meters) long and 30 feet (about 9 meters) wide and 45 feet (about 13.5 meters) high
[s] *3* That is, about 30 feet (about 9 meters)
[t] *3* That is, about 15 feet (about 4.5 meters)

King James

5 ¶ And *z*against the wall of the house he built *a*chambers round about, *against* the walls of the house round about, *both* of the temple and of the oracle: and he made *b*chambers round about:

6The nethermost chamber *was* five cubits broad, and the middle *was* six cubits broad, and the third *was* seven cubits broad: for without *in the wall* of the house he made *c*narrowed rests round about, that *the beams* should not be fastened in the walls of the house.

7And the house, when it was in building, was built of stone made ready before it was brought thither: so that there was neither hammer nor axe *nor* any tool of iron heard in the house, while it was in building.

8The door for the middle chamber *was* in the right *d*side of the house: and they went up with winding stairs into the middle *chamber,* and out of the middle into the third.

9So he built the house, and finished it; and covered the house *e*with beams and boards of cedar.

10And *then* he built chambers against all the house, five cubits high: and they rested on the house with timber of cedar.

11 ¶ And the word of the LORD came to Solomon, saying,

12*Concerning* this house which thou art in building, if thou wilt walk in my statutes, and execute my judgments, and keep all my commandments to walk in them; then will I perform my word with thee, which I spake unto David thy father:

13And I will dwell among the children of Israel, and will not forsake my people Israel.

14So Solomon built the house, and finished it.

15And he built the walls of the house within with boards of cedar, *f*both the floor of the house, and the walls of the ceiling: *and* he covered *them* on the inside with wood, and covered the floor of the house with planks of fir.

16And he built twenty cubits on the sides of the house, both the floor and the walls with boards of cedar: he even built *them* for it within, *even* for the oracle, *even* for the most holy *place.*

17And the house, that *is,* the temple before it, was forty cubits *long.*

18And the cedar of the house within *was* carved with *g*knobs and *h*open flowers: all *was* cedar; there was no stone seen.

19And the oracle he prepared in the house within, to set there the ark of the covenant of the LORD.

20And the oracle in the forepart *was* twenty cubits in length, and twenty cubits in breadth, and twenty cubits in the height thereof: and he overlaid it with *i*pure gold; and *so* covered the altar *which was of* cedar.

21So Solomon overlaid the house within with pure gold: and he made a partition by the chains of gold before the oracle; and he overlaid it with gold.

22And the whole house he overlaid with gold, until he had finished all the house: also the whole altar that *was* by the oracle he overlaid with gold.

23 ¶ And within the oracle he made two cherubims *of jk*olive tree, *each* ten cubits high.

24And five cubits *was* the one wing of the cherub, and five cubits the other wing of the cherub: from the uttermost part of the one wing unto the uttermost part of the other *were* ten cubits.

25And the other cherub *was* ten cubits: both the cherubims *were* of one measure and one size.

26The height of the one cherub *was* ten cubits, and so *was it* of the other cherub.

Amplified

5Against the wall of the house he built chambers running round the walls of the house both of the Holy Place and of the Holy of Holies; and he made side chambers all around.

6The first story's side chambers were five cubits wide, those of the middle story six cubits wide, and of the third story seven cubits wide; for around the outside of the wall of the house he made offsets in order that the supporting beams should not be thrust into the walls of the house.

7When the house was being built, its stone was made ready at the quarry, and no hammer, ax, or tool of iron was heard in the house while it was in building.

8The entrance to the lowest side chamber was on the right [or south] side of the house; and one went up winding stairs into the middle chamber and from the middle into the third.

9So Solomon built the temple building and finished it, and roofed the house with beams and boards of cedar.

10Then he built the stories of chambers [the lean-to] against all the house, each [story] five cubits high; and it was joined to the house with timbers of cedar.

11Now the word of the Lord came to Solomon, saying,

12Concerning this house which you are building, if you will walk in My statutes, execute My precepts, and keep all My commandments to walk in them, then I will fulfill to you My promises which I made to David your father.

13And I will dwell among the Israelites and will not forsake My people Israel.

14So Solomon built the house and finished it.

15He built the walls of the house (the Holy Place and the Holy of Holies) within with boards of cedar, from the floor of the house to the rafters of the ceiling. He covered the inside with wood, and the floor of the house with boards of cypress.

16He built twenty cubits of the rear of the house with boards of cedar from the floor to the rafters; he built it within for the sanctuary, the Holy of Holies.

17The [rest of the] house, that is, the temple in front of the Holy of Holies, was forty cubits long.

18The cedar on the house within was carved with gourds and open flowers. All was cedar; no stone was visible.

19And he prepared the Holy of Holies in the inner room in which to set the ark of the covenant of the Lord.

20The Holy of Holies was twenty cubits in length, in breadth, and in height. He overlaid it with pure gold. He also overlaid the cedar altar.

21Solomon overlaid the house within with pure gold, and he drew chains of gold across in front of the Holy of Holies and overlaid it with gold.

22And the whole house he overlaid with gold, until all the house was finished. Also the whole [incense] altar that [stood outside the door but] belonged to the Holy of Holies he overlaid with gold.

23Within the Holy of Holies he made two cherubim of olive wood, each ten cubits high.

24Five cubits was the length of one wing of the cherub and five cubits its other wing; from the tip of one wing to the tip of the other was ten cubits.

25The wings of the other cherub were also ten cubits. Both cherubim were the same,

26The height of one cherub ten cubits, as was the other.

---

*z*Or, *upon,* or, *joining to*   *a*Heb. *floors*   *b*Heb. *ribs*
*c*Heb. *narrowings,* or, *rebatements*   *d*Heb. *shoulder*   *e*Or, *the vault-beams and the ceilings with cedar*   *f*Or, *from the floor of the house unto the walls*   *g*Or, *goards*   *h*Heb. *openings of flowers*   *i*Heb. *shut up*   *j*Or, *oily*   *k*Heb. *trees of oil*

New American Standard

5 Against the wall of the house he built stories encompassing the walls of the house around both the nave and the inner sanctuary; thus he made side chambers all around.

6 The lowest story *was* five cubits wide, and the middle *was* six cubits wide, and the third *was* seven cubits wide; for on the outside he made offsets *in the wall* of the house all around in order that *the beams* would not be inserted in the walls of the house.

7 ¶ The house, while it was being built, was built of stone prepared at the quarry, and there was neither hammer nor axe nor any iron tool heard in the house while it was being built.

8 ¶ The doorway for the *i* lowest side chamber *was* on the right side of the house; and they would go up by winding stairs to the middle *story,* and from the middle to the third.

9 So he built the house and finished it; and he covered the house with beams and planks of cedar.

10 He also built the stories against the whole house, each five cubits high; and they were fastened to the house with timbers of cedar.

11 ¶ Now the word of the LORD came to Solomon saying,

12 "*Concerning* this house which you are building, if you will walk in My statutes and execute My ordinances and keep all My commandments by walking in them, then I will carry out My word with you which I spoke to David your father.

13 "I will dwell among the sons of Israel, and will not forsake My people Israel."

14 ¶ So Solomon built the house and finished it.

15 Then he built the walls of the house on the inside with boards of cedar; from the floor of the house to the ceiling he overlaid *the walls* on the inside with wood, and he overlaid the floor of the house with boards of cypress.

16 He built twenty cubits on the rear part of the house with boards of cedar from the floor to the ceiling; he built *them* for it on the inside as an inner sanctuary, *even* as the most holy place.

17 The house, that is, the nave in front of *the inner sanctuary,* was forty cubits *long.*

18 There was cedar on the house within, carved *in the shape* of gourds and open flowers; all was cedar, there was no stone seen.

19 Then he prepared an inner sanctuary within the house in order to place there the ark of the covenant of the LORD.

20 The inner sanctuary *was* twenty cubits in length, twenty cubits in width, and twenty cubits in height, and he overlaid it with pure gold. He also overlaid the altar with cedar.

21 So Solomon overlaid the inside of the house with pure gold. And he drew chains of gold across the front of the inner sanctuary, and he overlaid it with gold.

22 He overlaid the whole house with gold, until all the house was finished. Also the whole altar which was by the inner sanctuary he overlaid with gold.

23 ¶ Also in the inner sanctuary he made two cherubim of olive wood, each ten cubits high.

24 Five cubits *was* the one wing of the cherub and five cubits the other wing of the cherub; from the end of one wing to the end of the other wing *were* ten cubits.

25 The other cherub *was* ten cubits; both the cherubim were of the same measure and the same form.

26 The height of the one cherub *was* ten cubits, and so *was* the other cherub.

New International

narrow clerestory windows in the temple. 5Against the walls of the main hall and inner sanctuary he built a structure around the building, in which there were side rooms. 6The lowest floor was five cubits*u* wide, the middle floor six cubits*v* and the third floor seven.*w* He made offset ledges around the outside of the temple so that nothing would be inserted into the temple walls.

7In building the temple, only blocks dressed at the quarry were used, and no hammer, chisel or any other iron tool was heard at the temple site while it was being built.

8The entrance to the lowest*x* floor was on the south side of the temple; a stairway led up to the middle level and from there to the third. 9So he built the temple and completed it, roofing it with beams and cedar planks. 10And he built the side rooms all along the temple. The height of each was five cubits, and they were attached to the temple by beams of cedar.

11The word of the LORD came to Solomon: 12"As for this temple you are building, if you follow my decrees, carry out my regulations and keep all my commands and obey them, I will fulfill through you the promise I gave to David your father. 13And I will live among the Israelites and will not abandon my people Israel."

14So Solomon built the temple and completed it. 15He lined its interior walls with cedar boards, paneling them from the floor of the temple to the ceiling, and covered the floor of the temple with planks of pine. 16He partitioned off twenty cubits*y* at the rear of the temple with cedar boards from floor to ceiling to form within the temple an inner sanctuary, the Most Holy Place. 17The main hall in front of this room was forty cubits*z* long. 18The inside of the temple was cedar, carved with gourds and open flowers. Everything was cedar; no stone was to be seen.

19He prepared the inner sanctuary within the temple to set the ark of the covenant of the LORD there. 20The inner sanctuary was twenty cubits long, twenty wide and twenty high.*a* He overlaid the inside with pure gold, and he also overlaid the altar of cedar. 21Solomon covered the inside of the temple with pure gold, and he extended gold chains across the front of the inner sanctuary, which was overlaid with gold. 22So he overlaid the whole interior with gold. He also overlaid with gold the altar that belonged to the inner sanctuary.

23In the inner sanctuary he made a pair of cherubim of olive wood, each ten cubits*b* high. 24One wing of the first cherub was five cubits long, and the other wing five cubits—ten cubits from wing tip to wing tip. 25The second cherub also measured ten cubits, for the two cherubim were identical in size and shape. 26The height of each

u6 That is, about 7 1/2 feet (about 2.3 meters); also in verses 10 and 24   *v6* That is, about 9 feet (about 2.7 meters)   *w6* That is, about 10 1/2 feet (about 3.1 meters)   *x8* Septuagint; Hebrew *middle*   *y16* That is, about 30 feet (about 9 meters)   *z17* That is, about 60 feet (about 18 meters)   *a20* That is, about 30 feet (about 9 meters) long, wide and high   *b23* That is, about 15 feet (about 4.5 meters)

i So with Gr and versions; M.T. *middle*

King James | Amplified

<table>
<tr><td>

27And he set the cherubims within the inner house: and *they stretched forth the wings of the cherubims, so that the wing of the one touched the *one* wall, and the wing of the other cherub touched the other wall; and their wings touched one another in the midst of the house.

28And he overlaid the cherubims with gold.

29And he carved all the walls of the house round about with carved figures of cherubims and palm trees and *open flowers, within and without.

30And the floor of the house he overlaid with gold, within and without.

31 ¶ And for the entering of the oracle he made doors *of* olive tree: the lintel *and* side posts *were* na fifth part *of the wall.*

32The °two doors also *were of* olive tree; and he carved upon them carvings of cherubims and palm trees and *open flowers, and overlaid *them* with gold, and spread gold upon the cherubims, and upon the palm trees.

33So also made he for the door of the temple posts *of* olive tree, Pa fourth part *of the wall.*

34And the two doors *were of* fir tree: the two leaves of the one door *were* folding, and the two leaves of the other door *were* folding.

35And he carved *thereon* cherubims and palm trees and open flowers: and covered *them* with gold fitted upon the carved work.

36 ¶ And he built the inner court with three rows of hewed stone, and a row of cedar beams.

37 ¶ In the fourth year was the foundation of the house of the LORD laid, in the month Zif:

38And in the eleventh year, in the month Bul, which *is* the eighth month, was the house finished *throughout all the parts thereof, and according to all the fashion of it. So was he seven years in building it.

The palace buildings

7 BUT SOLOMON was building his own house thirteen years, and he finished all his house.

2 ¶ He built also the house of the forest of Lebanon; the length thereof *was* an hundred cubits, and the breadth thereof fifty cubits, and the height thereof thirty cubits, upon four rows of cedar pillars, with cedar beams upon the pillars.

3And *it was* covered with cedar above upon the rbeams, that *lay* on forty-five pillars, fifteen *in* a row.

4And *there were* windows *in* three rows, and slight *was* against light *in* three ranks.

5And all the rdoors and posts *were* square, with the windows: and light *was* against light *in* three ranks.

6 ¶ And he made a porch of pillars; the length thereof *was* fifty cubits, and the breadth thereof thirty cubits: and the porch *was* ubefore them: and the *other* pillars and the thick beam *were* ubefore them.

7 ¶ Then he made a porch for the throne where he might judge, *even* the porch of judgment: and *it was* covered with cedar vfrom one side of the floor to the other.

8 ¶ And his house where he dwelt *had* another court within the porch, *which* was of the like work. Solomon made also an house for Pharaoh's daughter, whom he had taken *to* wife, like unto this porch.

9All these *were of* costly stones, according to the measures of hewed stones, sawed with saws, within and without, even from the foundation unto the coping, and *so* on the outside toward the great court.

10And the foundation *was of* costly stones, even great stones, stones of ten cubits, and stones of eight cubits.

</td><td>

27He put the cherubim within the inner sanctuary. Their wings were stretched out, so that the wing of one touched one wall, and the wing of the other cherub touched the other wall, and their inner wings touched in the midst of the room.

28Solomon overlaid the cherubim with gold.

29He carved all the walls of the house (these two holy rooms) round about with figures of cherubim, palm trees, and open flowers, within and without.

30The floor of the house he overlaid with gold, inside and out.

31For the Holy of Holies he made [folding] doors of olive wood; their entire width was one-fifth that of the wall.

32On the two doors of olive wood he carved cherubim, palm trees, and open flowers; he overlaid them with gold, and spread gold on the cherubim and palm trees.

33Also he made for the door of the Holy Place four-sided posts of olive wood.

34The two doors were of cypress wood; the two leaves of each door were folding.

35He carved on them cherubim, palm trees, and open flowers, covered with gold evenly applied on the carved work.

36He built the inner court with three rows of hewn stone and a row of cedar beams.

37In the fourth year the foundation of the Lord's house was laid, in the [second] month, Ziv.

38In the eleventh year, in Bul, the eighth month, the house was finished throughout according to all its specifications. So he was seven years in building it.

7 SOLOMON WAS building his own house ithirteen years, and he finished all of it.

2He built also the Forest of Lebanon House; its length was a hundred cubits, its breadth fifty, and its height thirty cubits, upon four rows of cedar pillars, with cedar beams upon the pillars.

3And it was covered with cedar above the side chambers that were upon the forty-five pillars, fifteen in a row.

4There were window frames in three rows, and window opposite window in three tiers.

5All the doorways and windows were square cut, and window was opposite window in three tiers.

6He also made the Hall of Pillars; its length was fifty cubits and its breadth thirty cubits. There was a porch in front, and pillars and a cornice before them.

7He made the porch for the throne where he was to judge, the Porch of Judgment; it was covered with cedar from floor to ceiling.

8His house where he was to dwell had another court behind the Porch of Judgment of similar work. Solomon also made a house like this porch for Pharaoh's daughter, whom he had married.

9All were of costly stones hewn according to measure, sawed with saws back and front, even from foundation to coping, and from the outside to the great court.

10The foundation was of costly stones, even great stones of eight and ten cubits.

</td></tr>
</table>

---

lOr, *the cherubims stretched forth their wings*   mHeb. *openings of flowers*   nOr, *fivesquare*   oOr, *leaves of the doors*   POr, *foursquare*   qOr, *with all the appurtenances thereof, and with all the ordinances thereof*   rHeb. *ribs*   sHeb. *sight against sight*   tOr, *spaces and pillars were square in prospect*   uOr, *according to them*   vHeb. *from floor to floor*

iSolomon built God's house first, then his own. That his took much longer is no reflection on Solomon, for David had made every possible preparation for building the temple, greatly reducing the time needed to finish it (I Chron. 22:2-5). David even left for Solomon plans and patterns for the temple and loyal friends eager to help (I Kings 5:1; I Chron. 28:14-19).

New American Standard

27 He placed the cherubim in the midst of the inner house, and the wings of the cherubim were spread out, so that the wing of the one was touching the *one* wall, and the wing of the other cherub was touching the other wall. So their wings were touching each other in the center of the house.

28 He also overlaid the cherubim with gold.

29 ¶ Then he carved all the walls of the house round about with carved engravings of cherubim, palm trees, and open flowers, inner and outer *sanctuaries*.

30 He overlaid the floor of the house with gold, inner and outer *sanctuaries*.

31 ¶ For the entrance of the inner sanctuary he made doors of olive wood, the lintel *and* five-sided doorposts.

32 So *he made* two doors of olive wood, and he carved on them carvings of cherubim, palm trees, and open flowers, and overlaid them with gold; and he spread the gold on the cherubim and on the palm trees.

33 ¶ So also he made for the entrance of the nave four-sided doorposts of olive wood

34 and two doors of cypress wood; the two leaves of the one door turned on pivots, and the two leaves of the other door turned on pivots.

35 He carved *on it* cherubim, palm trees, and open flowers; and he overlaid *them* with gold evenly applied on the engraved work.

36 He built the inner court with three rows of cut stone and a row of cedar beams.

37 ¶ In the fourth year the foundation of the house of the LORD was laid, in the month of Ziv.

38 In the eleventh year, in the month of Bul, which is the eighth month, the house was finished throughout all its parts and according to all its plans. So he was seven years in building it.

Solomon's Palace

7 NOW SOLOMON was building his own house thirteen years, and he finished all his house.

2 He built the house of the forest of Lebanon; its length was 100 *j* cubits and its width 50 cubits and its height 30 cubits, on four rows of cedar pillars with cedar beams on the pillars.

3 It was paneled with cedar above the side chambers which were on the 45 pillars, 15 in each row.

4 *There were artistic window* frames in three rows, and window was opposite window in three ranks.

5 All the doorways and doorposts *had* squared *artistic* frames, and window was opposite window in three ranks.

6 ¶ Then he made the hall of pillars; its length was 50 cubits and its width 30 cubits, and a porch *was* in front of them and pillars and a threshold in front of them.

7 ¶ He made the hall of the throne where he was to judge, the hall of judgment, and it was paneled with cedar from floor to floor.

8 ¶ His house where he was to live, the other court inward from the hall, was of the same workmanship. He also made a house like this hall for Pharaoh's daughter, whom Solomon had married.

9 ¶ All these were of costly stones, of stone cut according to measure, sawed with saws, inside and outside; even from the foundation to the coping, and so on the outside to the great court.

10 ¶ The foundation was of costly stones, *even* large stones, stones of ten cubits and stones of eight cubits.

New International

cherub was ten cubits. 27 He placed the cherubim inside the innermost room of the temple, with their wings spread out. The wing of one cherub touched one wall, while the wing of the other touched the other wall, and their wings touched each other in the middle of the room. 28 He overlaid the cherubim with gold.

29 On the walls all around the temple, in both the inner and outer rooms, he carved cherubim, palm trees and open flowers. 30 He also covered the floors of both the inner and outer rooms of the temple with gold.

31 For the entrance of the inner sanctuary he made doors of olive wood with five-sided jambs. 32 And on the two olive wood doors he carved cherubim, palm trees and open flowers, and overlaid the cherubim and palm trees with beaten gold. 33 In the same way he made four-sided jambs of olive wood for the entrance to the main hall. 34 He also made two pine doors, each having two leaves that turned in sockets. 35 He carved cherubim, palm trees and open flowers on them and overlaid them with gold hammered evenly over the carvings.

36 And he built the inner courtyard of three courses of dressed stone and one course of trimmed cedar beams.

37 The foundation of the temple of the LORD was laid in the fourth year, in the month of Ziv. 38 In the eleventh year in the month of Bul, the eighth month, the temple was finished in all its details according to its specifications. He had spent seven years building it.

Solomon Builds His Palace

7 IT TOOK Solomon thirteen years, however, to complete the construction of his palace. 2 He built the Palace of the Forest of Lebanon a hundred cubits long, fifty wide and thirty high,*c* with four rows of cedar columns supporting trimmed cedar beams. 3 It was roofed with cedar above the beams that rested on the columns—forty-five beams, fifteen to a row. 4 Its windows were placed high in sets of three, facing each other. 5 All the doorways had rectangular frames; they were in the front part in sets of three, facing each other.*d*

6 He made a colonnade fifty cubits long and thirty wide.*e* In front of it was a portico, and in front of that were pillars and an overhanging roof.

7 He built the throne hall, the Hall of Justice, where he was to judge, and he covered it with cedar from floor to ceiling.*f* 8 And the palace in which he was to live, set farther back, was similar in design. Solomon also made a palace like this hall for Pharaoh's daughter, whom he had married.

9 All these structures, from the outside to the great courtyard and from foundation to eaves, were made of blocks of high-grade stone cut to size and trimmed with a saw on their inner and outer faces. 10 The foundations were laid with large stones of good quality, some measuring ten

---

j I.e. One cubit equals approx 18 in.

c 2 That is, about 150 feet (about 46 meters) long, 75 feet (about 23 meters) wide and 45 feet (about 13.5 meters) high
d 5 The meaning of the Hebrew for this verse is uncertain.
e 6 That is, about 75 feet (about 23 meters) long and 45 feet (about 13.5 meters) wide   *f* 7 Vulgate and Syriac; Hebrew *floor*

King James

¹¹And above *were* costly stones, after the measures of hewed stones, and cedars.

¹²And the great court round about *was* with three rows of hewed stones, and a row of cedar beams, both for the inner court of the house of the LORD, and for the porch of the house.

The temple furnishings

¹³ ¶ And king Solomon sent and fetched Hiram out of Tyre.

¹⁴He *was* ^wa widow's son of the tribe of Naphtali, and his father *was* a man of Tyre, a worker in brass: and he was filled with wisdom, and understanding, and cunning to work all works in brass. And he came to king Solomon, and wrought all his work.

¹⁵For he ^xcast two pillars of brass, of eighteen cubits high apiece: and a line of twelve cubits did compass either of them about.

¹⁶And he made two chapiters *of* molten brass, to set upon the tops of the pillars: the height of the one chapiter *was* five cubits, and the height of the other chapiter *was* five cubits:

¹⁷*And* nets of checker work, and wreaths of chain work, for the chapiters which *were* upon the top of the pillars; seven for the one chapiter, and seven for the other chapiter.

¹⁸And he made the pillars, and two rows round about upon the one network, to cover the chapiters that *were* upon the top, with pomegranates: and so did he for the other chapiter.

¹⁹And the chapiters that *were* upon the top of the pillars *were* of lily work in the porch, four cubits.

²⁰And the chapiters upon the two pillars *had pomegranates* also above, over against the belly which *was* by the network: and the pomegranates *were* two hundred in rows round about upon the other chapiter.

²¹And he set up the pillars in the porch of the temple: and he set up the right pillar, and called the name thereof ^yJachin: and he set up the left pillar, and called the name thereof ^zBoaz.

²²And upon the top of the pillars *was* lily work: so was the work of the pillars finished.

²³ ¶ And he made a molten sea, ten cubits ^afrom the one brim to the other: *it was* round all about, and his height *was* five cubits: and a line of thirty cubits did compass it round about.

²⁴And under the brim of it round about *there were* knobs compassing it, ten in a cubit, compassing the sea round about: the knobs *were* cast in two rows, when it was cast.

²⁵It stood upon twelve oxen, three looking toward the north, and three looking toward the west, and three looking toward the south, and three looking toward the east: and the sea *was set* above upon them, and all their hinder parts *were* inward.

²⁶And it *was* an handbreadth thick, and the brim thereof was wrought like the brim of a cup, with flowers of lilies: it contained two thousand baths.

²⁷ ¶ And he made ten bases of brass; four cubits *was* the length of one base, and four cubits the breadth thereof, and three cubits the height of it.

²⁸And the work of the bases *was* on this *manner:* they had borders, and the borders *were* between the ledges:

²⁹And on the borders that *were* between the ledges *were* lions, oxen, and cherubims: and upon the ledges *there was* a base above: and beneath the lions and oxen *were* certain additions made of thin work.

³⁰And every base had four brasen wheels, and plates of brass: and the four corners thereof had undersetters: under the laver *were* undersetters molten, at the side of every addition.

Amplified

¹¹And above were costly stones hewn according to measure, and cedar timbers.

¹²Also the great encircling court had three courses of hewn stone and a course of cedar beams, like was around the inner court of the house of the Lord and the porch of the house.

¹³King Solomon brought Hiram from Tyre.

¹⁴He was the son of a widow of the tribe of Naphtali, and his father was a man of Tyre, a worker in bronze. He was full of wisdom, understanding, and skill to do any kind of work in bronze. So he came to King Solomon and did all his [bronze] work.

¹⁵He fashioned the two pillars of bronze, each eighteen cubits high, and a line of twelve cubits measured its circumference.

¹⁶He made two capitals of molten bronze to set upon the tops of the pillars; the height of each capital was five cubits.

¹⁷Nets of checkerwork and wreaths of chainwork for the capitals were on the tops of the pillars, seven for each capital.

¹⁸So Hiram made the pillars. There were two rows of pomegranates encircling each network to cover the capitals that were upon the top.

¹⁹The capitals that were upon the top of the pillars in the porch were of lily work [design], four cubits.

²⁰The capitals were upon the two pillars and also above the rounded projection beside the network. There were 200 pomegranates in two rows round about, and so with the other capital.

²¹Hiram set up the pillars of the porch of the temple; he set up the right pillar and called its name Jachin [he will establish], and he set up the left pillar and called its name Boaz [in strength].

²²On the tops of the pillars was lily work [design]. So the work of the pillars was finished.

²³He made a round molten Sea, ten cubits from brim to brim, five cubits high and thirty cubits in circumference. [Exod. 30:17–21; II Chron. 4:6.]

²⁴Under its brim were gourds encircling the Sea, ten to a cubit; the gourds were in two rows, cast in one piece with it.

²⁵It stood upon twelve oxen, three facing north, three west, three south, and three east; the Sea was set upon them, and all their rears pointed inward.

²⁶It was a handbreadth thick, and its brim was made like the brim of a cup, like a lily blossom. It held 2,000 baths [Hebrew liquid measurement].

²⁷Hiram made ten bronze bases [for the lavers]; their length and breadth were four cubits, and the height three cubits.

²⁸This is the way the bases were made: they had panels between the ledges.

²⁹On the panels between the ledges were lions, oxen, and cherubim; and upon the ledges there was a pedestal above. Beneath the lions and oxen were wreaths of hanging work.

³⁰And every base had four bronze wheels and axles of bronze, and at the four corners were supports for a laver. Beneath the laver the supports were cast, with wreaths at the side of each.

---

^wHeb. *the son of a widow woman* ^xHeb. *fashioned* ^yi.e. *He shall establish* ^zi.e. *In it is strength* ^aHeb. *from his brim to his brim*

New American Standard

11 And above were costly stones, stone cut according to measure, and cedar.

12 So the great court all around *had* three rows of cut stone and a row of cedar beams even as the inner court of the house of the LORD, and the porch of the house.

Hiram's Work in the Temple

13 ¶ Now King Solomon sent and brought Hiram from Tyre.

14 He was a widow's son from the tribe of Naphtali, and his father was a man of Tyre, a worker in bronze; and he was filled with wisdom and understanding and skill for doing any work in bronze. So he came to King Solomon and performed all his work.

15 ¶ He fashioned the two pillars of bronze; eighteen cubits was the height of one pillar, and a line of twelve cubits measured the circumference of both.

16 He also made two capitals of molten bronze to set on the tops of the pillars; the height of the one capital was five cubits and the height of the other capital was five cubits.

17 *There were* nets of network and twisted threads of chainwork for the capitals which were on the top of the pillars; seven for the one capital and seven for the other capital.

18 So he made the pillars, and two rows around on the one network to cover the capitals which were on the top of the pomegranates; and so he did for the other capital.

19 The capitals which *were* on the top of the pillars in the porch were of lily design, four cubits.

20 *There were* capitals on the two pillars, even above *and* close to the rounded projection which was beside the network; and the pomegranates *numbered* two hundred in rows around both capitals.

21 Thus he set up the pillars at the porch of the nave; and he set up the right pillar and named it *k*Jachin, and he set up the left pillar and named it *l*Boaz.

22 On the top of the pillars was lily design. So the work of the pillars was finished.

23 ¶ Now he made the sea of cast *metal* ten cubits from brim to brim, circular in form, and its height was five cubits, and thirty cubits in circumference.

24 Under its brim gourds went around encircling it ten to a cubit, completely surrounding the sea; the gourds were in two rows, cast with the rest.

25 It stood on twelve oxen, three facing north, three facing west, three facing south, and three facing east; and the sea *was set* on top of them, and all their rear parts *turned* inward.

26 It was a handbreadth thick, and its brim was made like the brim of a cup, *as* a lily blossom; it could hold two thousand baths.

27 ¶ Then he made the ten stands of bronze; the length of each stand was four cubits and its width four cubits and its height three cubits.

28 This was the design of the stands: they had borders, even borders between the *m*frames,

29 and on the borders which were between the *m*frames *were* lions, oxen and cherubim; and on the *m*frames there *was* a pedestal above, and beneath the lions and oxen *were* wreaths of hanging work.

30 Now each stand had four bronze wheels with bronze axles, and its four feet had supports; beneath the basin *were* cast supports with wreaths at each side.

New International

cubits*g* and some eight.*h* 11Above were high-grade stones, cut to size, and cedar beams. 12The great courtyard was surrounded by a wall of three courses of dressed stone and one course of trimmed cedar beams, as was the inner courtyard of the temple of the LORD with its portico.

The Temple's Furnishings

13King Solomon sent to Tyre and brought Huram,*i* 14whose mother was a widow from the tribe of Naphtali and whose father was a man of Tyre and a craftsman in bronze. Huram was highly skilled and experienced in all kinds of bronze work. He came to King Solomon and did all the work assigned to him.

15He cast two bronze pillars, each eighteen cubits high and twelve cubits around,*j* by line. 16He also made two capitals of cast bronze to set on the tops of the pillars; each capital was five cubits*k* high. 17A network of interwoven chains festooned the capitals on top of the pillars, seven for each capital. 18He made pomegranates in two rows*l* encircling each network to decorate the capitals on top of the pillars.*m* He did the same for each capital. 19The capitals on top of the pillars in the portico were in the shape of lilies, four cubits*n* high. 20On the capitals of both pillars, above the bowl-shaped part next to the network, were the two hundred pomegranates in rows all around. 21He erected the pillars at the portico of the temple. The pillar to the south he named Jakin*o* and the one to the north Boaz.*p* 22The capitals on top were in the shape of lilies. And so the work on the pillars was completed.

23He made the Sea of cast metal, circular in shape, measuring ten cubits*g* from rim to rim and five cubits high. It took a line of thirty cubits*q* to measure around it. 24Below the rim, gourds encircled it—ten to a cubit. The gourds were cast in two rows in one piece with the Sea.

25The Sea stood on twelve bulls, three facing north, three facing west, three facing south and three facing east. The Sea rested on top of them, and their hindquarters were toward the center. 26It was a handbreadth*r* in thickness, and its rim was like the rim of a cup, like a lily blossom. It held two thousand baths.*s*

27He also made ten movable stands of bronze; each was four cubits long, four wide and three high.*t* 28This is how the stands were made: They had side panels attached to uprights. 29On the panels between the uprights were lions, bulls and cherubim—and on the uprights as well. Above and below the lions and bulls were wreaths of hammered work. 30Each stand had four bronze wheels with bronze axles, and each had a basin resting on four supports, cast

---

g 10,23 That is, about 15 feet (about 4.5 meters)   *h 10* That is, about 12 feet (about 3.6 meters)   *i 13* Hebrew *Hiram*, a variant of *Huram*; also in verses 40 and 45   *j 15* That is, about 27 feet (about 8.1 meters) high and 18 feet (about 5.4 meters) around   *k 16* That is, about 7 1/2 feet (about 2.3 meters); also in verse 23   *l 18* Two Hebrew manuscripts and Septuagint; most Hebrew manuscripts *made the pillars, and there were two rows*   *m 18* Many Hebrew manuscripts and Syriac; most Hebrew manuscripts *pomegranates*   *n 19* That is, about 6 feet (about 1.8 meters); also in verse 38   *o 21* *Jakin* probably means *he establishes.*   *p 21* *Boaz* probably means *in him is strength.*   *q 23* That is, about 45 feet (about 13.5 meters)   *r 26* That is, about 3 inches (about 8 centimeters)   *s 26* That is, probably about 11,500 gallons (about 44 kiloliters); the Septuagint does not have this sentence.   *t 27* That is, about 6 feet (about 1.8 meters) long and wide and about 4 1/2 feet (about 1.3 meters) high

---

k I.e. he shall establish   *l* I.e. in it is strength   *m* Or *crossbars*

King James

³¹And the mouth of it within the chapiter and above *was* a cubit: but the mouth thereof *was* round *after* the work of the base, a cubit and an half: and also upon the mouth of it *were* gravings with their borders, foursquare, not round.

³²And under the borders *were* four wheels; and the axletrees of the wheels *were* *b*joined to the base: and the height of a wheel *was* a cubit and half a cubit.

³³And the work of the wheels *was* like the work of a chariot wheel: their axletrees, and their naves, and their felloes, and their spokes, *were* all molten.

³⁴And *there were* four undersetters to the four corners of one base: *and* the undersetters *were* of the very base itself.

³⁵And in the top of the base *was there* a round compass of half a cubit high: and on the top of the base the ledges thereof and the borders thereof *were* of the same.

³⁶For on the plates of the ledges thereof, and on the borders thereof, he graved cherubims, lions, and palm trees, according to the *c*proportion of every one, and additions round about.

³⁷After this *manner* he made the ten bases: all of them had one casting, one measure, *and* one size.

³⁸ ¶ Then made he ten lavers of brass: one laver contained forty baths: *and* every laver was four cubits: *and* upon every one of the ten bases one laver.

³⁹And he put five bases on the right *d*side of the house, and five on the left side of the house: and he set the sea on the right side of the house eastward over against the south.

⁴⁰ ¶ And *e*Hiram made the lavers, and the shovels, and the basins. So Hiram made an end of doing all the work that he made king Solomon for the house of the LORD:

⁴¹The two pillars, and the *two* bowls of the chapiters that *were* on the top of the two pillars; and the two networks, to cover the two bowls of the chapiters which *were* upon the top of the pillars;

⁴²And four hundred pomegranates for the two networks, *even* two rows of pomegranates for one network, to cover the two bowls of the chapiters that *were* *f*upon the pillars;

⁴³And the ten bases, and ten lavers on the bases;

⁴⁴And one sea, and twelve oxen under the sea;

⁴⁵And the pots, and the shovels, and the basins: and all these vessels, which Hiram made to king Solomon for the house of the LORD, *were of* *g*bright brass.

⁴⁶In the plain of Jordan did the king cast them, *h*in the clay ground between Succoth and Zarthan.

⁴⁷And Solomon left all the vessels *unweighed,* *i*because they were exceeding many: neither was the weight of the brass *j*found out.

⁴⁸And Solomon made all the vessels that *pertained* unto the house of the LORD: the altar of gold, and the table of gold, whereupon the showbread *was,*

⁴⁹And the candlesticks of pure gold, five on the right *side,* and five on the left, before the oracle, with the flowers, and the lamps, and the tongs *of* gold,

⁵⁰And the bowls, and the snuffers, and the basins, and the spoons, and the *k*censers *of* pure gold; and the hinges *of* gold, *both* for the doors of the inner house, the most holy *place, and* for the doors of the house, *to wit,* of the temple.

⁵¹So was ended all the work that king Solomon made for the house of the LORD. And Solomon brought in the *l*things which David his father had dedicated; *even* the silver, and the gold, and the vessels, did he put among the treasures of the house of the LORD.

Amplified

³¹Its mouth within the capital projected upward a cubit, and its mouth was round like the work of a pedestal, a cubit and a half. Also upon its mouth were carvings, and their borders were square, not round.

³²Under the borders were four wheels, and the axles of the wheels were one piece with the base. And the height of a wheel was a cubit and a half.

³³The wheels were made like a chariot wheel: their axles, their rims, their spokes, and their hubs were all cast.

³⁴There were four supports to the four corners of each base; the supports were part of the base itself.

³⁵On the top of the base there was a circular elevation half a cubit high, and on the top of the base its stays and panels were of one piece with it.

³⁶And on the surface of its stays and its panels Hiram carved cherubim, lions, and palm trees, according to the space of each, with wreaths round about.

³⁷Thus he made the ten bases. They all had one casting, one measure, and one form.

³⁸Then he made ten lavers of bronze; each laver held forty baths and measured four cubits, and there was one laver on each of the ten bases.

³⁹He put the bases five on the south side of the house and five on the north side; and he set the Sea at the southeast corner of the house.

⁴⁰Hiram made the lavers, the shovels, and the basins. So Hiram finished all the work that he did for King Solomon on the house of the Lord:

⁴¹The two pillars; and the two bowls of the capitals that were on the tops of the two pillars; and the two networks to cover the two bowls;

⁴²And the 400 pomegranates for the two networks, two rows of pomegranates for each network, to cover the two bowls of the capitals that were upon the pillars;

⁴³The ten bases and the ten lavers on the bases;

⁴⁴One Sea, and the twelve oxen under it;

⁴⁵The pots, the shovels, and the basins. All these vessels which Hiram made for King Solomon in the house of the Lord were of burnished bronze.

⁴⁶In the Jordan plain the king cast them, in clay ground between Succoth and Zarethan.

⁴⁷Solomon left all the vessels unweighed, because they were so many; the weight of the bronze was not found out.

⁴⁸Solomon made all the other vessels of the Lord's house: the [incense] altar of gold; the table of gold for the showbread;

⁴⁹The lampstands of pure gold, five on the right side and five on the left, in front of the Holy of Holies; with the flowers, the lamps, and the tongs of gold;

⁵⁰The cups, snuffers, basins, spoons, firepans—of pure gold; and the hinges of gold for the doors of the innermost room, the Holy of Holies, and for the doors of the Holy Place.

⁵¹So all the work that King Solomon did on the house of the Lord was completed. Solomon brought in the things which David his father had dedicated—the silver, the gold, and the vessels—and put them in the treasuries of the Lord's house.

b Heb. *in the base*   *c* Heb. *nakedness*   *d* Heb. *shoulder*
e Heb. *Hirom;* see ver. 13   *f* Heb. *upon the face of the pillars*
g Heb. *made bright,* or, *scoured*   *h* Heb. *in the thickness of the ground*   *i* Heb. *for the exceeding multitude*   *j* Heb. *searched*
k Heb. *ash pans*   *l* Heb. *holy things of David*

New American Standard

31 Its opening inside the crown at the top *was* a cubit, and its opening *was* round like the design of a pedestal, a cubit and a half; and also on its opening *there were* engravings, and their borders were square, not round. 32 The four wheels *were* underneath the borders, and the axles of the wheels *were* on the stand. And the height of a wheel *was* a cubit and a half. 33 The workmanship of the wheels *was* like the workmanship of a chariot wheel. Their axles, their rims, their spokes, and their hubs *were* all cast. 34 Now *there were* four supports at the four corners of each stand; its supports *were* part of the stand itself. 35 On the top of the stand *there was* a circular form half a cubit high, and on the top of the stand its stays and its borders *were* part of it. 36 He engraved on the plates of its stays and on its borders, cherubim, lions and palm trees, according to the clear space on each, with wreaths *all* around. 37 He made the ten stands like this: all of them had one casting, one measure and one form.

38 ¶ He made ten basins of bronze, one basin held forty baths; each basin *was* four cubits, *and* on each of the ten stands *was* one basin. 39 Then he set the stands, five on the right side of the house and five on the left side of the house; and he set the sea *of cast metal* on the right side of the house eastward toward the south.

40 ¶ Now Hiram made the basins and the shovels and the bowls. So Hiram finished doing all the work which he performed for King Solomon *in* the house of the LORD: 41 the two pillars and the *two* bowls of the capitals which *were* on the top of the two pillars, and the two networks to cover the two bowls of the capitals which *were* on the top of the pillars; 42 and the four hundred pomegranates for the two networks, two rows of pomegranates for each network to cover the two bowls of the capitals which *were* on the tops of the pillars; 43 and the ten stands with the ten basins on the stands; 44 and the one sea and the twelve oxen under the sea; 45 and the pails and the shovels and the bowls; even all these utensils which Hiram made for King Solomon *in* the house of the LORD *were* of polished bronze. 46 In the plain of the Jordan the king cast them, in the clay ground between Succoth and Zarethan. 47 Solomon left all the utensils *unweighed,* because *they were* too many; the weight of the bronze could not be ascertained.

48 ¶ Solomon made all the furniture which *was in* the house of the LORD: the golden altar and the golden table on which *was* the bread of the Presence; 49 and the lampstands, five on the right side and five on the left, in front of the inner sanctuary, of pure gold; and the flowers and the lamps and the tongs, of gold; 50 and the cups and the snuffers and the bowls and the spoons and the firepans, of pure gold; and the hinges both for the doors of the inner house, the most holy place, *and* for the doors of the house, *that is,* of the nave, of gold. 51 ¶ Thus all the work that King Solomon performed *in* the house of the LORD was finished. And Solomon brought in the things dedicated by his father David, the silver and the gold and the utensils, *and* he put them in the treasuries of the house of the LORD.

New International

with wreaths on each side. 31 On the inside of the stand there was an opening that had a circular frame one cubit[u] deep. This opening was round, and with its basework it measured a cubit and a half.[v] Around its opening there was engraving. The panels of the stands were square, not round. 32 The four wheels were under the panels, and the axles of the wheels were attached to the stand. The diameter of each wheel was a cubit and a half. 33 The wheels were made like chariot wheels; the axles, rims, spokes and hubs were all of cast metal.

34 Each stand had four handles, one on each corner, projecting from the stand. 35 At the top of the stand there was a circular band half a cubit[w] deep. The supports and panels were attached to the top of the stand. 36 He engraved cherubim, lions and palm trees on the surfaces of the supports and on the panels, in every available space, with wreaths all around. 37 This is the way he made the ten stands. They were all cast in the same molds and were identical in size and shape.

38 He then made ten bronze basins, each holding forty baths[x] and measuring four cubits across, one basin to go on each of the ten stands. 39 He placed five of the stands on the south side of the temple and five on the north. He placed the Sea on the south side, at the southeast corner of the temple. 40 He also made the basins and shovels and sprinkling bowls.

So Huram finished all the work he had undertaken for King Solomon in the temple of the LORD:

41 the two pillars;
   the two bowl-shaped capitals on top of the pillars;
   the two sets of network decorating the two bowl-shaped capitals on top of the pillars;
42 the four hundred pomegranates for the two sets of network (two rows of pomegranates for each network, decorating the bowl-shaped capitals on top of the pillars);
43 the ten stands with their ten basins;
44 the Sea and the twelve bulls under it;
45 the pots, shovels and sprinkling bowls.

All these objects that Huram made for King Solomon for the temple of the LORD were of burnished bronze. 46 The king had them cast in clay molds in the plain of the Jordan between Succoth and Zarethan. 47 Solomon left all these things unweighed, because there were so many; the weight of the bronze was not determined.

48 Solomon also made all the furnishings that were in the LORD's temple:

the golden altar;
   the golden table on which was the bread of the Presence;
49 the lampstands of pure gold (five on the right and five on the left, in front of the inner sanctuary);
   the gold floral work and lamps and tongs;
50 the pure gold basins, wick trimmers, sprinkling bowls, dishes and censers;
   and the gold sockets for the doors of the innermost room, the Most Holy Place, and also for the doors of the main hall of the temple.

51 When all the work King Solomon had done for the temple of the LORD was finished, he brought in the things his father David had dedicated—the silver and gold and the furnishings—and he placed them in the treasuries of the LORD's temple.

---

u 31 That is, about 1 1/2 feet (about 0.5 meter)   *v 31* That is, about 2 1/4 feet (about 0.7 meter); also in verse 32   *w 35* That is, about 3/4 foot (about 0.2 meter)   *x 38* That is, about 230 gallons (about 880 liters)

King James

The ark brought to the temple

8 THEN SOLOMON assembled the elders of Israel, and all the heads of the tribes, the *m*chief of the fathers of the children of Israel, unto king Solomon in Jerusalem, that they might bring up the ark of the covenant of the LORD out of the city of David, which *is* Zion.

2 And all the men of Israel assembled themselves unto king Solomon at the feast in the month Ethanim, which *is* the seventh month.

3 And all the elders of Israel came, and the priests took up the ark.

4 And they brought up the ark of the LORD, and the tabernacle of the congregation, and all the holy vessels that *were* in the tabernacle, even those did the priests and the Levites bring up.

5 And king Solomon, and all the congregation of Israel, that were assembled unto him, *were* with him before the ark, sacrificing sheep and oxen, that could not be told nor numbered for multitude.

6 And the priests brought in the ark of the covenant of the LORD unto his place, into the oracle of the house, to the most holy *place, even* under the wings of the cherubims.

7 For the cherubims spread forth *their* two wings over the place of the ark, and the cherubims covered the ark and the staves thereof above.

8 And they drew out the staves, that the *n*ends of the staves were seen out in the *o*holy *place* before the oracle, and they were not seen without: and there they are unto this day.

9 *There was* nothing in the ark save the two tables of stone, which Moses put there at Horeb, *p*when the LORD made *a covenant* with the children of Israel, when they came out of the land of Egypt.

10 And it came to pass, when the priests were come out of the holy *place,* that the cloud filled the house of the LORD,

11 So that the priests could not stand to minister because of the cloud: for the glory of the LORD had filled the house of the LORD.

12 ¶ Then spake Solomon, The LORD said that he would dwell in the thick darkness.

13 I have surely built thee an house to dwell in, a settled place for thee to abide in for ever.

14 And the king turned his face about, and blessed all the congregation of Israel: (and all the congregation of Israel stood;)

15 And he said, Blessed *be* the LORD God of Israel, which spake with his mouth unto David my father, and hath with his hand fulfilled *it,* saying,

16 Since the day that I brought forth my people Israel out of Egypt, I chose no city out of all the tribes of Israel to build an house, that my name might be therein; but I chose David to be over my people Israel.

17 And it was in the heart of David my father to build an house for the name of the LORD God of Israel.

18 And the LORD said unto David my father, Whereas it was in thine heart to build an house unto my name, thou didst well that it was in thine heart.

19 Nevertheless thou shalt not build the house; but thy son that shall come forth out of thy loins, he shall build the house unto my name.

20 And the LORD hath performed his word that he spake, and I am risen up in the room of David my father, and sit on the throne of Israel, as the LORD promised, and have built an house for the name of the LORD God of Israel.

21 And I have set there a place for the ark, wherein *is* the covenant of the LORD, which he made with our fathers, when he brought them out of the land of Egypt.

Amplified

8 THEN SOLOMON assembled the elders of Israel and all the heads of the tribes, the chiefs of the fathers' houses of the Israelites, before the king in Jerusalem, to bring up the ark of the covenant of the Lord out of Zion, the City of David.

2 All the men of Israel assembled themselves before King Solomon at the feast in the seventh month, Ethanim.

3 All the elders of Israel came, and the priests took up the ark.

4 And they brought up the ark of the Lord, the Tent of Meeting, and all the holy vessels that were in the tent; the priests and the Levites brought them up.

5 King Solomon and all the congregation of Israel who had assembled before him were with him before the ark, sacrificing sheep and oxen, so many that they could not be reported or counted.

6 And the priests brought the ark of the covenant of the Lord to its place in the Holy of Holies of the house, under the wings of the cherubim.

7 For the cherubim spread forth their two wings over the place of the ark, and the cherubim covered the ark and its poles.

8 The poles were so long that the ends of them were seen from the Holy Place before the Holy of Holies, but they were not seen outside; they are there to this day.

9 There was nothing in the ark except the two tables of stone which Moses put there at Horeb, where the Lord made a covenant with the Israelites when they came out of the land of Egypt. [Deut. 10:2–5.]

10 When the priests had come out of the Holy Place, the cloud filled the Lord's house,

11 So the priests could not stand to minister because of the cloud, for the glory of the Lord had filled the Lord's house.

12 Then Solomon said, The Lord said that He would dwell in the thick darkness.

13 I have surely built You a house of habitation, a settled place for You to dwell in forever.

14 And the king turned his face about and blessed all the assembly of Israel, and all the assembly of Israel stood.

15 He said, Blessed be the Lord, the God of Israel, Who spoke with His mouth to David my father and has with His hand fulfilled it, saying,

16 Since the day that I brought forth My people Israel out of Egypt, I chose no city out of all the tribes of Israel in which to build a house that My Name [and My Presence] might be in it, but I chose David to be over My people Israel.

17 Now it was in the heart of David my father to build a house for the Name [the Presence] of the Lord, the God of Israel.

18 And the Lord said to David my father, Whereas it was in your heart to build a house for My Name, you did well that it was in your heart.

19 Yet you shall not build the house, but your son, who shall be born to you, shall build it to My Name [and My actively present Person].

20 And the Lord has fulfilled His promise which He made: I have risen up in the place of David my father, and sit on the throne of Israel, as the Lord promised, and have built a house for the Name (renown) of the Lord, the God of Israel.

21 And I have made there a place for the ark [the token of *j*His presence], in which is the covenant [the Ten Commandments] of the Lord which He made with our fathers when He brought them out of the land of Egypt. [Exod. 34:28.]

---

j God acknowledged the ark as a token of His presence (Matthew Henry, *Commentary on the Holy Bible*). The ark of the covenant is the pledge of the divine gracious presence, and the cloud that filled the house (I Kings 8:10) is the sign that Yahweh will dwell here (J.P. Lange, *A Commentary*).

m Heb. *princes*　　*n* Heb. *heads*　　*o* Or, *ark* as 2 Chr. 5:9
p Or, *where*

New American Standard

The Ark Brought into the Temple

8 THEN SOLOMON assembled the elders of Israel and all the heads of the tribes, the leaders of the fathers' *households* of the sons of Israel, to King Solomon in Jerusalem, to bring up the ark of the covenant of the LORD from the city of David, which is Zion.

2 All the men of Israel assembled themselves to King Solomon at the feast, in the month Ethanim, which is the seventh month.

3 Then all the elders of Israel came, and the priests took up the ark.

4 They brought up the ark of the LORD and the tent of meeting and all the holy utensils, which were in the tent, and the priests and the Levites brought them up.

5 And King Solomon and all the congregation of Israel, who were assembled to him, were with him before the ark, sacrificing so many sheep and oxen they could not be counted or numbered.

6 Then the priests brought the ark of the covenant of the LORD to its place, into the inner sanctuary of the house, to the most holy place, under the wings of the cherubim.

7 For the cherubim spread *their* wings over the place of the ark, and the cherubim made a covering over the ark and its poles from above.

8 But the poles were so long that the ends of the poles could be seen from the holy place before the inner sanctuary, but they could not be seen outside; they are there to this day.

9 There was nothing in the ark except the two tablets of stone which Moses put there at Horeb, where the LORD made a covenant with the sons of Israel, when they came out of the land of Egypt.

10 It happened that when the priests came from the holy place, the cloud filled the house of the LORD,

11 so that the priests could not stand to minister because of the cloud, for the glory of the LORD filled the house of the LORD.

Solomon Addresses the People

12 ¶ Then Solomon said,
"The LORD has said that He would dwell in the
    thick cloud.

13 "I have surely built You a lofty house,
A place for Your dwelling forever."

14 ¶ Then the king faced about and blessed all the assembly of Israel, while all the assembly of Israel was standing.

15 He said, "Blessed be the LORD, the God of Israel, who spoke with His mouth to my father David and has fulfilled *it* with His hand, saying,

16 'Since the day that I brought My people Israel from Egypt, I did not choose a city out of all the tribes of Israel *in which* to build a house that My name might be there, but I chose David to be over My people Israel.'

17 "Now it was in the heart of my father David to build a house for the name of the LORD, the God of Israel.

18 "But the LORD said to my father David, 'Because it was in your heart to build a house for My name, you did well that it was in your heart.

19 'Nevertheless you shall not build the house, but your son who will be born to you, he will build the house for My name.'

20 "Now the LORD has fulfilled His word which He spoke; for I have risen in place of my father David and sit on the throne of Israel, as the LORD promised, and have built the house for the name of the LORD, the God of Israel.

21 "There I have set a place for the ark, in which is the covenant of the LORD, which He made with our fathers when He brought them from the land of Egypt."

New International

The Ark Brought to the Temple

8 THEN KING Solomon summoned into his presence at Jerusalem the elders of Israel, all the heads of the tribes and the chiefs of the Israelite families, to bring up the ark of the LORD's covenant from Zion, the City of David. 2All the men of Israel came together to King Solomon at the time of the festival in the month of Ethanim, the seventh month.

3When all the elders of Israel had arrived, the priests took up the ark, 4and they brought up the ark of the LORD and the Tent of Meeting and all the sacred furnishings in it. The priests and Levites carried them up, 5and King Solomon and the entire assembly of Israel that had gathered about him were before the ark, sacrificing so many sheep and cattle that they could not be recorded or counted.

6The priests then brought the ark of the LORD's covenant to its place in the inner sanctuary of the temple, the Most Holy Place, and put it beneath the wings of the cherubim. 7The cherubim spread their wings over the place of the ark and overshadowed the ark and its carrying poles. 8These poles were so long that their ends could be seen from the Holy Place in front of the inner sanctuary, but not from outside the Holy Place; and they are still there today. 9There was nothing in the ark except the two stone tablets that Moses had placed in it at Horeb, where the LORD made a covenant with the Israelites after they came out of Egypt.

10When the priests withdrew from the Holy Place, the cloud filled the temple of the LORD. 11And the priests could not perform their service because of the cloud, for the glory of the LORD filled his temple.

12Then Solomon said, "The LORD has said that he would dwell in a dark cloud; 13I have indeed built a magnificent temple for you, a place for you to dwell forever."

14While the whole assembly of Israel was standing there, the king turned around and blessed them. 15Then he said:

"Praise be to the LORD, the God of Israel, who with his own hand has fulfilled what he promised with his own mouth to my father David. For he said, 16'Since the day I brought my people Israel out of Egypt, I have not chosen a city in any tribe of Israel to have a temple built for my Name to be there, but I have chosen David to rule my people Israel.'

17"My father David had it in his heart to build a temple for the Name of the LORD, the God of Israel. 18But the LORD said to my father David, 'Because it was in your heart to build a temple for my Name, you did well to have this in your heart. 19Nevertheless, you are not the one to build the temple, but your son, who is your own flesh and blood—he is the one who will build the temple for my Name.'

20"The LORD has kept the promise he made: I have succeeded David my father and now I sit on the throne of Israel, just as the LORD promised, and I have built the temple for the Name of the LORD, the God of Israel. 21I have provided a place there for the ark, in which is the covenant of the LORD that he made with our fathers when he brought them out of Egypt."

King James

Solomon's prayer of dedication

22 ¶ And Solomon stood before the altar of the LORD in the presence of all the congregation of Israel, and spread forth his hands toward heaven:

23 And he said, LORD God of Israel, *there is* no God like thee, in heaven above, or on earth beneath, who keepest covenant and mercy with thy servants that walk before thee with all their heart:

24 Who hast kept with thy servant David my father that thou promisedst him: thou spakest also with thy mouth, and hast fulfilled *it* with thine hand, as *it is* this day.

25 Therefore now, LORD God of Israel, keep with thy servant David my father that thou promisedst him, saying, *q*There shall not fail thee a man in my sight to sit on the throne of Israel; *r*so that thy children take heed to their way, that they walk before me as thou hast walked before me.

26 And now, O God of Israel, let thy word, I pray thee, be verified, which thou spakest unto thy servant David my father.

27 But will God indeed dwell on the earth? behold, the heaven and heaven of heavens cannot contain thee; how much less this house that I have builded?

28 Yet have thou respect unto the prayer of thy servant, and to his supplication, O LORD my God, to hearken unto the cry and to the prayer, which thy servant prayeth before thee today:

29 That thine eyes may be open toward this house night and day, *even* toward the place of which thou hast said, My name shall be there: that thou mayest hearken unto the prayer which thy servant shall make *s*toward this place.

30 And hearken thou to the supplication of thy servant, and of thy people Israel, when they shall pray *t*toward this place: and hear thou in heaven thy dwellingplace: and when thou hearest, forgive.

31 ¶ If any man trespass against his neighbour, *t*and an oath be laid upon him to cause him to swear, and the oath come before thine altar in this house:

32 Then hear thou in heaven, and do, and judge thy servants, condemning the wicked, to bring his way upon his head; and justifying the righteous, to give him according to his righteousness.

33 ¶ When thy people Israel be smitten down before the enemy, because they have sinned against thee, and shall turn again to thee, and confess thy name, and pray, and make supplication unto thee *u*in this house:

34 Then hear thou in heaven, and forgive the sin of thy people Israel, and bring them again unto the land which thou gavest unto their fathers.

35 ¶ When heaven is shut up, and there is no rain, because they have sinned against thee; if they pray toward this place, and confess thy name, and turn from their sin, when thou afflictest them:

36 Then hear thou in heaven, and forgive the sin of thy servants, and of thy people Israel, that thou teach them the good way wherein they should walk, and give rain upon thy land, which thou hast given to thy people for an inheritance.

37 ¶ If there be in the land famine, if there be pestilence, blasting, mildew, locust, *or* if there be caterpillar; if their enemy besiege them in the land of their *v*cities; whatsoever plague, whatsoever sickness *there be;*

38 What prayer and supplication soever be *made* by any man, *or* by all thy people Israel, which shall know every man the plague of his own heart, and spread forth his hands toward this house:

39 Then hear thou in heaven thy dwellingplace, and forgive, and do, and give to every man according to his ways, whose heart thou knowest; (for thou, *even* thou only, knowest the hearts of all the children of men;)

Amplified

22 Then Solomon stood [in the court] before the Lord's burnt offering altar in the presence of all the assembly of Israel, and spread forth his hands toward heaven

23 And he said, O Lord, the God of Israel, there is no God like You in heaven above or on earth beneath, keeping covenant and showing mercy *and* loving-kindness to Your servants who walk before You with all their heart.

24 You have kept what You promised Your servant David my father. You also spoke with Your mouth and have fulfilled it with Your hand, as it is this day.

25 Therefore now, O Lord, the God of Israel, keep with Your servant David my father what You promised him when You said, There shall not fail you a man before Me to sit on the throne of Israel, if only your children take heed to their way, that they walk before Me as you have done.

26 Now, O God of Israel, let Your word which You spoke to Your servant David my father be confirmed [by experience].

27 But will God indeed dwell with men on the earth? Behold, the heavens and heaven of heavens [in its most extended compass] cannot contain You; how much less this house that I have built?

28 Yet graciously consider the prayer and supplication of Your servant, O Lord my God, to hearken to the [loud] cry and prayer which he prays before You today;

29 That Your eyes may be open toward this house night and day, toward the place of which You have said, My Name [and the token of My presence] shall be there, that You may hearken to the prayer which Your servant shall make in [or facing toward] this place.

30 Hearken to the prayer of Your servant and of Your people Israel when they pray in *or* toward this place. Hear in heaven, Your dwelling place, and when You hear, forgive.

31 Whenever a man sins against his neighbor and is made to take an oath and comes and swears the oath before Your altar in this house,

32 Then hear in heaven and do and judge Your servants, condemning the wicked by bringing his guilt upon his own head and justifying the [uncompromisingly] righteous by rewarding him according to his righteousness (his uprightness, right standing with God).

33 When Your people Israel are struck down before the enemy because they have sinned against You, and they turn again to You, confess Your *k*name (Your revelation of Yourself), and pray, beseeching You in this house,

34 Then hear in heaven and forgive the sin of Your people Israel and return them to the land You gave to their fathers.

35 When heaven is shut up and no rain falls because they have sinned against You, if they pray in [or toward] this place and confess Your name (Your revelation of Yourself) and turn from their sin when You afflict them,

36 Then hear in heaven and forgive the sin of Your servants, Your people Israel, when You teach them the good way in which they should walk. And give rain upon Your land which You have given to Your people as an inheritance.

37 If there is famine in the land or pestilence, blight, mildew, locust, or caterpillar, if their enemy besieges them in the land of their cities, whatever plague, whatever sickness there is,

38 Whatever prayer or supplication is made by any or all of Your people Israel—each man knowing the affliction of his own heart, and spreading forth his hands toward this house [and its pledge of Your presence]—

39 Then hear in heaven, Your dwelling place, and forgive and act and give to every man according to his ways, whose heart You know, for You and You only know the hearts of all the children of men,

---

*q*Heb. *There shall not be cut off unto thee a man from my sight*
*r*Heb. *only if*   *s*Or, *in this place*   *t*Heb. *and he require an oath of him*   *u*Or, *toward*   *v*Or, *jurisdiction*

*k*See footnote on Exod. 3:15.

New American Standard

The Prayer of Dedication

22 ¶ Then Solomon stood before the altar of the LORD in the presence of all the assembly of Israel and spread out his hands toward heaven.

23 He said, "O LORD, the God of Israel, there is no God like You in heaven above or on earth beneath, keeping covenant and *showing* lovingkindness to Your servants who walk before You with all their heart,

24 who have kept with Your servant, my father David, that which You have promised him; indeed, You have spoken with Your mouth and have fulfilled it with Your hand as it is this day.

25 "Now therefore, O LORD, the God of Israel, keep with Your servant David my father that which You have promised him, saying, 'You shall not lack a man to sit on the throne of Israel, if only your sons take heed to their way to walk before Me as you have walked.'

26 "Now therefore, O God of Israel, let Your word, I pray, be confirmed which You have spoken to Your servant, my father David.

27 ¶ "But will God indeed dwell on the earth? Behold, heaven and the highest heaven cannot contain You, how much less this house which I have built!

28 "Yet have regard to the prayer of Your servant and to his supplication, O LORD my God, to listen to the cry and to the prayer which Your servant prays before You today;

29 that Your eyes may be open toward this house night and day, toward the place of which You have said, 'My name shall be there,' to listen to the prayer which Your servant shall pray toward this place.

30 "Listen to the supplication of Your servant and of Your people Israel, when they pray toward this place; hear in heaven Your dwelling place; hear and forgive.

31 ¶ "If a man sins against his neighbor and is made to take an oath, and he comes *and* takes an oath before Your altar in this house,

32 then hear in heaven and act and judge Your servants, condemning the wicked by bringing his way on his own head and justifying the righteous by giving him according to his righteousness.

33 ¶ "When Your people Israel are defeated before an enemy, because they have sinned against You, if they turn to You again and confess Your name and pray and make supplication to You in this house,

34 then hear in heaven, and forgive the sin of Your people Israel, and bring them back to the land which You gave to their fathers.

35 ¶ "When the heavens are shut up and there is no rain, because they have sinned against You, and they pray toward this place and confess Your name and turn from their sin when You afflict them,

36 then hear in heaven and forgive the sin of Your servants and of Your people Israel, indeed, teach them the good way in which they should walk. And send rain on Your land, which You have given Your people for an inheritance.

37 ¶ "If there is famine in the land, if there is pestilence, if there is blight *or* mildew, locust *or* grasshopper, if their enemy besieges them in the land of their cities, whatever plague, whatever sickness *there is,*

38 whatever prayer or supplication is made by any man *or* by all Your people Israel, each knowing the affliction of his own heart, and spreading his hands toward this house;

39 then hear in heaven Your dwelling place, and forgive and act and render to each according to all his ways, whose heart You know, for You alone know the hearts of all the sons of men,

New International

Solomon's Prayer of Dedication

22 Then Solomon stood before the altar of the LORD in front of the whole assembly of Israel, spread out his hands toward heaven 23 and said:

"O LORD, God of Israel, there is no God like you in heaven above or on earth below—you who keep your covenant of love with your servants who continue wholeheartedly in your way. 24 You have kept your promise to your servant David my father; with your mouth you have promised and with your hand you have fulfilled it—as it is today.

25 "Now LORD, God of Israel, keep for your servant David my father the promises you made to him when you said, 'You shall never fail to have a man to sit before me on the throne of Israel, if only your sons are careful in all they do to walk before me as you have done.' 26 And now, O God of Israel, let your word that you promised your servant David my father come true.

27 "But will God really dwell on earth? The heavens, even the highest heaven, cannot contain you. How much less this temple I have built! 28 Yet give attention to your servant's prayer and his plea for mercy, O LORD my God. Hear the cry and the prayer that your servant is praying in your presence this day. 29 May your eyes be open toward this temple night and day, this place of which you said, 'My Name shall be there,' so that you will hear the prayer your servant prays toward this place. 30 Hear the supplication of your servant and of your people Israel when they pray toward this place. Hear from heaven, your dwelling place, and when you hear, forgive.

31 "When a man wrongs his neighbor and is required to take an oath and he comes and swears the oath before your altar in this temple, 32 then hear from heaven and act. Judge between your servants, condemning the guilty and bringing down on his own head what he has done. Declare the innocent not guilty, and so establish his innocence.

33 "When your people Israel have been defeated by an enemy because they have sinned against you, and when they turn back to you and confess your name, praying and making supplication to you in this temple, 34 then hear from heaven and forgive the sin of your people Israel and bring them back to the land you gave to their fathers.

35 "When the heavens are shut up and there is no rain because your people have sinned against you, and when they pray toward this place and confess your name and turn from their sin because you have afflicted them, 36 then hear from heaven and forgive the sin of your servants, your people Israel. Teach them the right way to live, and send rain on the land you gave your people for an inheritance.

37 "When famine or plague comes to the land, or blight or mildew, locusts or grasshoppers, or when an enemy besieges them in any of their cities, whatever disaster or disease may come, 38 and when a prayer or plea is made by any of your people Israel—each one aware of the afflictions of his own heart, and spreading out his hands toward this temple— 39 then hear from heaven, your dwelling place. Forgive and act; deal with each man according to all he does, since you know his heart (for you alone know the hearts of all

King James

⁴⁰That they may fear thee all the days that they live in the land which thou gavest unto our fathers.

⁴¹Moreover concerning a stranger, that *is* not of thy people Israel, but cometh out of a far country for thy name's sake;

⁴²(For they shall hear of thy great name, and of thy strong hand, and of thy stretched out arm;) when he shall come and pray toward this house;

⁴³Hear thou in heaven thy dwellingplace, and do according to all that the stranger calleth to thee for: that all people of the earth may know thy name, to fear thee, as *do* thy people Israel; and that they may know that ʷthis house, which I have builded, is called by thy name.

⁴⁴ ¶ If thy people go out to battle against their enemy, whithersoever thou shalt send them, and shall pray unto the LORD ˣtoward the city which thou hast chosen, and *toward* the house that I have built for thy name:

⁴⁵Then hear thou in heaven their prayer and their supplication, and maintain their ʸcause.

⁴⁶If they sin against thee, (for *there is* no man that sinneth not,) and thou be angry with them, and deliver them to the enemy, so that they carry them away captives unto the land of the enemy, far or near;

⁴⁷Yet if they shall ᶻbethink themselves in the land whither they were carried captives, and repent, and make supplication unto thee in the land of them that carried them captives, saying, We have sinned, and have done perversely, we have committed wickedness;

⁴⁸And *so* return unto thee with all their heart, and with all their soul, in the land of their enemies, which led them away captive, and pray unto thee toward their land, which thou gavest unto their fathers, the city which thou hast chosen, and the house which I have built for thy name:

⁴⁹Then hear thou their prayer and their supplication in heaven thy dwellingplace, and maintain their ʸcause,

⁵⁰And forgive thy people that have sinned against thee, and all their transgressions wherein they have transgressed against thee, and give them compassion before them who carried them captive, that they may have compassion on them:

⁵¹For they *be* thy people, and thine inheritance, which thou broughtest forth out of Egypt, from the midst of the furnace of iron:

⁵²That thine eyes may be open unto the supplication of thy servant, and unto the supplication of thy people Israel, to hearken unto them in all that they call for unto thee.

⁵³For thou didst separate them from among all the people of the earth, *to be* thine inheritance, as thou spakest by the hand of Moses thy servant, when thou broughtest our fathers out of Egypt, O Lord GOD.

⁵⁴And it was *so*, that when Solomon had made an end of praying all this prayer and supplication unto the LORD, he arose from before the altar of the LORD, from kneeling on his knees with his hands spread up to heaven.

⁵⁵And he stood, and blessed all the congregation of Israel with a loud voice, saying,

⁵⁶Blessed *be* the LORD, that hath given rest unto his people Israel, according to all that he promised: there hath not ᵃfailed one word of all his good promise, which he promised by the hand of Moses his servant.

⁵⁷The LORD our God be with us, as he was with our fathers: let him not leave us, nor forsake us:

⁵⁸That he may incline our hearts unto him, to walk in all his ways, and to keep his commandments, and his statutes, and his judgments, which he commanded our fathers.

Amplified

⁴⁰That they may fear *and* revere You all the days that they live in the land which You gave to our fathers.

⁴¹Moreover, concerning a stranger who is not of Your people Israel but comes from a far country for the sake of Your name [and Your active Presence]—

⁴²For they will hear of Your great name (Your revelation of Yourself), Your strong hand, and outstretched arm—when he shall pray in [or toward] this house,

⁴³Hear in heaven, Your dwelling place, and do according to all that the stranger asks of You, so that all peoples of the earth may know Your name [and ˡYour revelation of Your presence] and fear *and* revere You, as do Your people Israel, and may know *and* comprehend that this house which I have built is called by Your Name [and contains the token of Your presence].

⁴⁴If Your people go out to battle against their enemy, wherever You shall send them, and shall pray to the Lord toward the city which You have chosen and the house that I have built for Your Name [and Your revelation of Yourself],

⁴⁵Then hear in heaven their prayer and supplication, and defend their cause *and* maintain their right.

⁴⁶If they sin against You—for there is no man who does not sin—and You are angry with them and deliver them to the enemy, so that they are carried away captive to the enemy's land, far or near;

⁴⁷Yet if they think *and* consider in the land where they were carried captive, and repent and make supplication to You there, saying, We have sinned and have done perversely and wickedly;

⁴⁸If they repent *and* turn to You with all their mind and with all their heart in the land of their enemies who took them captive, and pray to You toward their land which You gave to their fathers, the city which You have chosen, and the house which I have built for Your Name;

⁴⁹Then hear their prayer and their supplication in heaven, Your dwelling place, and defend their cause *and* maintain their right.

⁵⁰And forgive Your people, who have sinned against You, and all their transgressions against You, and grant them compassion before those who took them captive, that they may have pity and be merciful to them;

⁵¹For they are Your people and Your heritage, which You brought out of Egypt, from the midst of the iron furnace.

⁵²Let Your eyes be open to the supplication of Your servant and of Your people Israel, to hearken to them in all for which they call to You.

⁵³For You separated them from among all the peoples of the earth to be Your heritage, as You declared through Moses Your servant when You brought our fathers out of Egypt, O Lord God.

⁵⁴When Solomon finished offering all this prayer and supplication to the Lord, he arose from before the Lord's altar, where he had knelt with hands stretched toward heaven.

⁵⁵And he stood and blessed all the assembly of Israel with a loud voice, saying,

⁵⁶Blessed be the Lord, Who has given rest to His people Israel, according to all that He promised. Not one word has failed of all His good promise which He promised through Moses His servant.

⁵⁷May the Lord our God be with us as He was with our fathers; may He not leave us or forsake us,

⁵⁸That He may incline our hearts to Him, to walk in all His ways and to keep His commandments, His statutes, and His precepts which He commanded our fathers.

ʷHeb. *thy name is called upon this house*   ˣHeb. *the way of the city*   ʸOr, *right*   ᶻHeb. *bring back to their heart*   ᵃHeb. *fallen*

ˡSee footnote on Exod. 3:15.

New American Standard

40 that they may [n]fear You all the days that they live in the land which You have given to our fathers.

41 ¶ "Also concerning the foreigner who is not of Your people Israel, when he comes from a far country for Your name's sake

42 (for they will hear of Your great name and Your mighty hand, and of Your outstretched arm); when he comes and prays toward this house,

43 hear in heaven Your dwelling place, and do according to all for which the foreigner calls to You, in order that all the peoples of the earth may know Your name, to [o]fear You, as *do* Your people Israel, and that they may know that this house which I have built is called by Your name.

44 ¶ "When Your people go out to battle against their enemy, by whatever way You shall send them, and they pray to the LORD toward the city which You have chosen and the house which I have built for Your name,

45 then hear in heaven their prayer and their supplication, and maintain their cause.

46 ¶ "When they sin against You (for there is no man who does not sin) and You are angry with them and deliver them to an enemy, so that they take them away captive to the land of the enemy, far off or near;

47 if they take thought in the land where they have been taken captive, and repent and make supplication to You in the land of those who have taken them captive, saying, 'We have sinned and have committed iniquity, we have acted wickedly';

48 if they return to You with all their heart and with all their soul in the land of their enemies who have taken them captive, and pray to You toward their land which You have given to their fathers, the city which You have chosen, and the house which I have built for Your name;

49 then hear their prayer and their supplication in heaven Your dwelling place, and maintain their cause,

50 and forgive Your people who have sinned against You and all their transgressions which they have transgressed against You, and make them *objects of* compassion before those who have taken them captive, that they may have compassion on them

51 (for they are Your people and Your inheritance which You have brought forth from Egypt, from the midst of the iron furnace),

52 that Your eyes may be open to the supplication of Your servant and to the supplication of Your people Israel, to listen to them whenever they call to You.

53 "For You have separated them from all the peoples of the earth as Your inheritance, as You spoke through Moses Your servant, when You brought our fathers forth from Egypt, O Lord GOD."

Solomon's Benediction

54 ¶ When Solomon had finished praying this entire prayer and supplication to the LORD, he arose from before the altar of the LORD, from kneeling on his knees with his hands spread toward heaven.

55 And he stood and blessed all the assembly of Israel with a loud voice, saying:

56 ¶ "Blessed be the LORD, who has given rest to His people Israel, according to all that He promised; not one word has failed of all His good promise, which He promised through Moses His servant.

57 "May the LORD our God be with us, as He was with our fathers; may He not leave us or forsake us,

58 that He may incline our hearts to Himself, to walk in all His ways and to keep His commandments and His statutes and His ordinances, which He commanded our fathers.

New International

men), 40so that they will fear you all the time they live in the land you gave our fathers.

41"As for the foreigner who does not belong to your people Israel but has come from a distant land because of your name— 42for men will hear of your great name and your mighty hand and your outstretched arm—when he comes and prays toward this temple, 43then hear from heaven, your dwelling place, and do whatever the foreigner asks of you, so that all the peoples of the earth may know your name and fear you, as do your own people Israel, and may know that this house I have built bears your Name.

44"When your people go to war against their enemies, wherever you send them, and when they pray to the LORD toward the city you have chosen and the temple I have built for your Name, 45then hear from heaven their prayer and their plea, and uphold their cause.

46"When they sin against you—for there is no one who does not sin—and you become angry with them and give them over to the enemy, who takes them captive to his own land, far away or near; 47and if they have a change of heart in the land where they are held captive, and repent and plead with you in the land of their conquerors and say, 'We have sinned, we have done wrong, we have acted wickedly'; 48and if they turn back to you with all their heart and soul in the land of their enemies who took them captive, and pray to you toward the land you gave their fathers, toward the city you have chosen and the temple I have built for your Name; 49then from heaven, your dwelling place, hear their prayer and their plea, and uphold their cause. 50And forgive your people, who have sinned against you; forgive all the offenses they have committed against you, and cause their conquerors to show them mercy; 51for they are your people and your inheritance, whom you brought out of Egypt, out of that iron-smelting furnace.

52"May your eyes be open to your servant's plea and to the plea of your people Israel, and may you listen to them whenever they cry out to you. 53For you singled them out from all the nations of the world to be your own inheritance, just as you declared through your servant Moses when you, O Sovereign LORD, brought our fathers out of Egypt."

54When Solomon had finished all these prayers and supplications to the LORD, he rose from before the altar of the LORD, where he had been kneeling with his hands spread out toward heaven. 55He stood and blessed the whole assembly of Israel in a loud voice, saying:

56"Praise be to the LORD, who has given rest to his people Israel just as he promised. Not one word has failed of all the good promises he gave through his servant Moses. 57May the LORD our God be with us as he was with our fathers; may he never leave us nor forsake us. 58May he turn our hearts to him, to walk in all his ways and to keep the commands, decrees and

King James

59And let these my words, wherewith I have made supplication before the LORD, be nigh unto the LORD our God day and night, that he maintain the cause of his servant, and the cause of his people Israel bat all times, as the matter shall require:

60That all the people of the earth may know that the LORD is God, *and that there is* none else.

61Let your heart therefore be perfect with the LORD our God, to walk in his statutes, and to keep his commandments, as at this day.

The offering and feast

62 ¶ And the king, and all Israel with him, offered sacrifice before the LORD.

63And Solomon offered a sacrifice of peace offerings, which he offered unto the LORD, two and twenty thousand oxen, and an hundred and twenty thousand sheep. So the king and all the children of Israel dedicated the house of the LORD.

64The same day did the king hallow the middle of the court that *was* before the house of the LORD: for there he offered burnt offerings, and meat offerings, and the fat of the peace offerings: because the brasen altar that *was* before the LORD *was* too little to receive the burnt offerings, and meat offerings, and the fat of the peace offerings.

65And at that time Solomon held a feast, and all Israel with him, a great congregation, from the entering of Hamath unto the river of Egypt, before the LORD our God, seven days and seven days, *even* fourteen days.

66On the eighth day he sent the people away: and they cblessed the king, and went unto their tents joyful and glad of heart for all the goodness that the LORD had done for David his servant, and for Israel his people.

The covenant with Solomon

9 AND IT came to pass, when Solomon had finished the building of the house of the LORD, and the king's house, and all Solomon's desire which he was pleased to do,

2That the LORD appeared to Solomon the second time, as he had appeared unto him at Gibeon.

3And the LORD said unto him, I have heard thy prayer and thy supplication, that thou hast made before me: I have hallowed this house, which thou hast built, to put my name there for ever; and mine eyes and mine heart shall be there perpetually.

4And if thou wilt walk before me, as David thy father walked, in integrity of heart, and in uprightness, to do according to all that I have commanded thee, *and* wilt keep my statutes and my judgments:

5Then I will establish the throne of thy kingdom upon Israel for ever, as I promised to David thy father, saying, There shall not fail thee a man upon the throne of Israel.

6*But* if ye shall at all turn from following me, ye or your children, and will not keep my commandments *and* my statutes which I have set before you, but go and serve other gods, and worship them:

7Then will I cut off Israel out of the land which I have given them; and this house, which I have hallowed for my name, will I cast out of my sight; and Israel shall be a proverb and a byword among all people:

8And at this house, *which* is high, every one that passeth by it shall be astonished, and shall hiss; and they shall say, Why hath the LORD done thus unto this land, and to this house?

9And they shall answer, Because they forsook the LORD their God, who brought forth their fathers out of the land of Egypt, and have taken hold upon other gods, and have worshipped them, and served them: therefore hath the LORD brought upon them all this evil.

Amplified

59Let these my words, with which I have made supplication before the Lord, be near to the Lord our God day and night, that He may maintain the cause *and* right of His servant and of His people Israel as each day requires,

60That all the earth's people may know that the Lord is God and that there is no other.

61Let your hearts therefore be blameless *and* wholly true to the Lord our God, to walk in His statutes and to keep His commandments, as today.

62And the king and all Israel with him offered sacrifice before the Lord.

63Solomon offered as peace offerings to the Lord: 22,000 oxen and 120,000 sheep. So the king and all the Israelites dedicated the house of the Lord.

64On that same day the king consecrated the middle of the court that was before the Lord's house; there he offered burnt offerings, cereal offerings, and the fat of the peace offerings, because the bronze altar that was before the Lord was too small to receive [all] the offerings.

65So at that time Solomon held the feast, and all Israel with him, a great assembly, from the entrance of Hamath to the Brook of Egypt, before the Lord our God, for seven days [for the dedication] and seven days [for the Feast of Tabernacles], fourteen days in all.

66On the eighth day he sent the people away; they blessed the king and went to their tents with greatest joy and gratitude for all the goodness the Lord had shown to David His servant and Israel His people.

9 WHEN SOLOMON finished the building of the Lord's house and the king's house, and all he desired and was pleased to do,

2The Lord appeared to Solomon the second time, as He had appeared to him at Gibeon.

3The Lord told him, I have heard your prayer and supplication which you have made before Me; I have hallowed this house which you have built, and I have put My Name [and My Presence] there forever. My eyes and My heart shall be there perpetually.

4And if you will walk before Me, as David your father walked, in integrity of heart and uprightness, doing according to all that I have commanded you, keeping My statutes and My precepts,

5Then I will establish your royal throne over Israel forever, as I promised David your father, saying, There shall not fail you [to have] a man upon the throne of Israel.

6But if you turn away from following Me, you or your children, and will not keep My commandments and My statutes which I have set before you but go and serve other gods and worship them,

7Then I will cut off Israel from the land I have given them, and this house I have hallowed for My Name (renown) I will cast from My sight. And Israel shall be a proverb and a byword among all the peoples.

8This house shall become a heap of ruins; every passerby shall be astonished and shall hiss [with surprise] and say, Why has the Lord done thus to this land and to this house?

9Then they will answer, Because they forsook the Lord their God, Who brought their fathers out of the land of Egypt, and have laid hold of other gods and have worshiped and served them; therefore the Lord has brought on them all this evil.

---

bHeb. *the thing of a day in his day*   cOr, *thanked*

New American Standard

59"And may these words of mine, with which I have made supplication before the LORD, be near to the LORD our God day and night, that He may maintain the cause of His servant and the cause of His people Israel, as each day requires,

60 so that all the peoples of the earth may know that the LORD is God; there is no one else.

61"Let your heart therefore be wholly devoted to the LORD our God, to walk in His statutes and to keep His commandments, as at this day."

Dedicatory Sacrifices

62 ¶ Now the king and all Israel with him offered sacrifice before the LORD.

63 Solomon offered for the sacrifice of peace offerings, which he offered to the LORD, 22,000 oxen and 120,000 sheep. So the king and all the sons of Israel dedicated the house of the LORD.

64 On the same day the king consecrated the middle of the court that was before the house of the LORD, because there he offered the burnt offering and the grain offering and the fat of the peace offerings; for the bronze altar that was before the LORD was too small to hold the burnt offering and the grain offering and the fat of the peace offerings.

65 ¶ So Solomon observed the feast at that time, and all Israel with him, a great assembly from the entrance of Hamath to the brook of Egypt, before the LORD our God, for seven days and seven more days, even fourteen days.

66 On the eighth day he sent the people away and they blessed the king. Then they went to their tents joyful and glad of heart for all the goodness that the LORD had shown to David His servant and to Israel His people.

God's Promise and Warning

9 NOW IT came about when Solomon had finished building the house of the LORD, and the king's house, and all that Solomon desired to do,

2 that the LORD appeared to Solomon a second time, as He had appeared to him at Gibeon.

3 The LORD said to him, "I have heard your prayer and your supplication, which you have made before Me; I have consecrated this house which you have built by putting My name there forever, and My eyes and My heart will be there perpetually.

4"As for you, if you will walk before Me as your father David walked, in integrity of heart and uprightness, doing according to all that I have commanded you and will keep My statutes and My ordinances,

5 then I will establish the throne of your kingdom over Israel forever, just as I promised to your father David, saying, 'You shall not lack a man on the throne of Israel.'

6 ¶ "But if you or your sons indeed turn away from following Me, and do not keep My commandments and My statutes which I have set before you, and go and serve other gods and worship them,

7 then I will cut off Israel from the land which I have given them, and the house which I have consecrated for My name, I will cast out of My sight. So Israel will become a proverb and a byword among all peoples.

8"And this house will become a heap of ruins; everyone who passes by will be astonished and hiss and say, 'Why has the LORD done thus to this land and to this house?'

9"And they will say, 'Because they forsook the LORD their God, who brought their fathers out of the land of Egypt, and adopted other gods and worshiped them and served them, therefore the LORD has brought all this adversity on them.' "

New International

regulations he gave our fathers. 59And may these words of mine, which I have prayed before the LORD, be near to the LORD our God day and night, that he may uphold the cause of his servant and the cause of his people Israel according to each day's need, 60so that all the peoples of the earth may know that the LORD is God and that there is no other. 61But your hearts must be fully committed to the LORD our God, to live by his decrees and obey his commands, as at this time."

The Dedication of the Temple

62Then the king and all Israel with him offered sacrifices before the LORD. 63Solomon offered a sacrifice of fellowship offeringsy to the LORD: twenty-two thousand cattle and a hundred and twenty thousand sheep and goats. So the king and all the Israelites dedicated the temple of the LORD.

64On that same day the king consecrated the middle part of the courtyard in front of the temple of the LORD, and there he offered burnt offerings, grain offerings and the fat of the fellowship offerings, because the bronze altar before the LORD was too small to hold the burnt offerings, the grain offerings and the fat of the fellowship offerings.

65So Solomon observed the festival at that time, and all Israel with him—a vast assembly, people from Leboz Hamath to the Wadi of Egypt. They celebrated it before the LORD our God for seven days and seven days more, fourteen days in all. 66On the following day he sent the people away. They blessed the king and then went home, joyful and glad in heart for all the good things the LORD had done for his servant David and his people Israel.

The LORD Appears to Solomon

9 WHEN SOLOMON had finished building the temple of the LORD and the royal palace, and had achieved all he had desired to do, 2the LORD appeared to him a second time, as he had appeared to him at Gibeon. 3The LORD said to him:

"I have heard the prayer and plea you have made before me; I have consecrated this temple, which you have built, by putting my Name there forever. My eyes and my heart will always be there.

4"As for you, if you walk before me in integrity of heart and uprightness, as David your father did, and do all I command and observe my decrees and laws, 5I will establish your royal throne over Israel forever, as I promised David your father when I said, 'You shall never fail to have a man on the throne of Israel.'

6"But if youa or your sons turn away from me and do not observe the commands and decrees I have given youa and go off to serve other gods and worship them, 7then I will cut off Israel from the land I have given them and will reject this temple I have consecrated for my Name. Israel will then become a byword and an object of ridicule among all peoples. 8And though this temple is now imposing, all who pass by will be appalled and will scoff and say, 'Why has the LORD done such a thing to this land and to this temple?' 9People will answer, 'Because they have forsaken the LORD their God, who brought their fathers out of Egypt, and have embraced other gods, worshiping and serving them—that is why the LORD brought all this disaster on them.' "

y63 Traditionally peace offerings; also in verse 64   z65 Or from the entrance to   a6 The Hebrew is plural.

King James

Solomon's accomplishments

10 ¶ And it came to pass at the end of twenty years, when Solomon had built the two houses, the house of the LORD, and the king's house,

11(Now Hiram the king of Tyre had furnished Solomon with cedar trees and fir trees, and with gold, according to all his desire,) that then king Solomon gave Hiram twenty cities in the land of Galilee.

12And Hiram came out from Tyre to see the cities which Solomon had given him; and they *d*pleased him not.

13And he said, What cities *are* these which thou hast given me, my brother? And he called them the land of *e*Cabul unto this day.

14And Hiram sent to the king sixscore talents of gold.

15 ¶ And this *is* the reason of the levy which king Solomon raised; for to build the house of the LORD, and his own house, and Millo, and the wall of Jerusalem, and Hazor, and Megiddo, and Gezer.

16*For* Pharaoh king of Egypt had gone up, and taken Gezer, and burnt it with fire, and slain the Canaanites that dwelt in the city, and given it *for* a present unto his daughter, Solomon's wife.

17And Solomon built Gezer, and Beth-horon the nether,

18And Baalath, and Tadmor in the wilderness, in the land,

19And all the cities of store that Solomon had, and cities for his chariots, and cities for his horsemen, and *f*that which Solomon desired to build in Jerusalem, and in Lebanon, and in all the land of his dominion.

20*And* all the people *that were* left of the Amorites, Hittites, Perizzites, Hivites, and Jebusites, which *were* not of the children of Israel,

21Their children that were left after them in the land, whom the children of Israel also were not able utterly to destroy, upon those did Solomon levy a tribute of bondservice unto this day.

22But of the children of Israel did Solomon make no bondmen: but they *were* men of war, and his servants, and his princes, and his captains, and rulers of his chariots, and his horsemen.

23These *were* the chief of the officers that *were* over Solomon's work, five hundred and fifty, which bare rule over the people that wrought in the work.

24 ¶ But Pharaoh's daughter came up out of the city of David unto her house which *Solomon* had built for her: then did he build Millo.

25 ¶ And three times in a year did Solomon offer burnt offerings and peace offerings upon the altar which he built unto the LORD, and he burnt incense *g*upon the altar that *was* before the LORD. So he finished the house,

26 ¶ And king Solomon made a navy of ships in Ezion-geber, which *is* beside Eloth, on the *h*shore of the Red sea, in the land of Edom.

27And Hiram sent in the navy his servants, shipmen that had knowledge of the sea, with the servants of Solomon.

28And they came to Ophir, and fetched from thence gold, four hundred and twenty talents, and brought *it* to king Solomon.

Amplified

10At the end of twenty years, in which Solomon had built the two houses, the Lord's house and the king's house,

11For which Hiram king of Tyre had furnished Solomon with as much cedar and cypress timber and gold as he desired, King Solomon gave Hiram twenty cities in the land of Galilee.

12And Hiram came from Tyre to see the cities which Solomon had given him, and they did not please him.

13He said, What are these cities worth which you have given me, my brother? So they are called the Cabul [unproductive] Land to this day.

14And Hiram sent to the king 120 talents of gold.

15This is the account of the levy [of forced labor] which King Solomon raised to build the house of the Lord, his own house, the Millo, the wall of Jerusalem, Hazor, Megiddo, and Gezer.

16For Pharaoh king of Egypt had gone up and taken Gezer, burned it with fire, slew the Canaanites who dwelt in the city, and had given it as dowry to his daughter, Solomon's wife.

17So Solomon rebuilt Gezer and Lower Beth-horon,

18Baalath and Tamar (Tadmor) in the wilderness, in the land of Judah,

19And all the store cities which Solomon had and cities for his chariots and cities for his horsemen, and whatever Solomon desired to build *m*for his pleasure in Jerusalem, in Lebanon, and in all the land of his dominion.

20As for all the people who were left of the Amorites, Hittites, Perizzites, Hivites, and Jebusites, who were not Israelites,

21Their children who were left after them in the land, whom the Israelites were not able utterly to destroy, of them Solomon made a forced levy of slaves to this day.

22But Solomon made no slaves of the Israelites; they were the soldiers, his officials, attendants, commanders, captains, chariot officers, and horsemen.

23These were the chief officers over Solomon's work, 550 who had charge of the people who did the work.

24But Pharaoh's daughter came up out of the City of David to her house which Solomon had built for her; then he built the Millo.

25Three times a year Solomon offered burnt offerings and peace offerings on the altar he built to the Lord, and he burned incense with them before the Lord. So he finished the house.

26And King Solomon made a fleet of ships in Ezion-geber, which is beside Eloth, on the shore of the Red Sea, in Edom.

27And Hiram sent with the fleet his servants, shipmen who had knowledge of the sea, with the servants of Solomon.

28They came to Ophir and got 420 talents of gold and brought it to King Solomon.

---

*m*Once on the throne Solomon became a thoroughgoing despot. All political power was taken out of the hands of the tribal sheiks . . . and placed in the hands of officers who were simply puppets of Solomon. The resources of the nation were expended not on works of public utility but on the personal aggrandizement of the monarch. In the means he took to gratify his passions he showed himself to be little better than a savage (James Orr et al., eds., *The International Standard Bible Encyclopedia*). The division of the nation at Solomon's death with all the weakness and misery that it caused [idolatry, ignoring God, captivity, exile, the loss of the ten tribes] through the coming centuries was the direct outgrowth of Solomon's unholy self-indulgence (Amos R. Wells, *Bible Miniatures*). Because of his extensive building program and his extravagant expenditures in the maintenance of his luxurious court, he resorted to forced labor and heavy taxation. Bitter opposition to his rule thus engendered the division of the united kingdom after his death (*The New Jewish Encyclopedia*).

---

*d*Heb. *were not right in his eyes*   *e*i.e. *Displeasing,* or, *Dirty*
*f*Heb. *the desire of Solomon which he desired*   *g*Heb. *upon it*
*h*Heb. *lip*

New American Standard

Cities Given to Hiram

10 ¶ It came about at the end of twenty years in which Solomon had built the two houses, the house of the LORD and the king's house

11 (Hiram king of Tyre had supplied Solomon with cedar and cypress timber and gold according to all his desire), then King Solomon gave Hiram twenty cities in the land of Galilee.

12 So Hiram came out from Tyre to see the cities which Solomon had given him, and they did not please him.

13 He said, "What are these cities which you have given me, my brother?" So they were called the land of ᵖCabul to this day.

14 And Hiram sent to the king 120 talents of gold.

15 ¶ Now this is the account of the forced labor which King Solomon levied to build the house of the LORD, his own house, the ᵠMillo, the wall of Jerusalem, Hazor, Megiddo, and Gezer.

16 For Pharaoh king of Egypt had gone up and captured Gezer and burned it with fire, and killed the Canaanites who lived in the city, and had given it as a dowry to his daughter, Solomon's wife.

17 So Solomon rebuilt Gezer and the lower Beth-horon

18 and Baalath and Tamar in the wilderness, in the land of Judah,

19 and all the storage cities which Solomon had, even the cities for his chariots and the cities for his horsemen, and all that it pleased Solomon to build in Jerusalem, in Lebanon, and in all the land under his rule.

20 As for all the people who were left of the Amorites, the Hittites, the Perizzites, the Hivites and the Jebusites, who were not of the sons of Israel,

21 their descendants who were left after them in the land whom the sons of Israel were unable to destroy utterly, from them Solomon levied forced laborers, even to this day.

22 But Solomon did not make slaves of the sons of Israel; for they were men of war, his servants, his princes, his captains, his chariot commanders, and his horsemen.

23 ¶ These were the chief officers who were over Solomon's work, five hundred and fifty, who ruled over the people doing the work.

24 ¶ As soon as Pharaoh's daughter came up from the city of David to her house which Solomon had built for her, then he built the Millo.

25 ¶ Now three times in a year Solomon offered burnt offerings and peace offerings on the altar which he built to the LORD, burning incense with them on the altar which was before the LORD. So he finished the house.

26 ¶ King Solomon also built a fleet of ships in Ezion-geber, which is near Eloth on the shore of the Red Sea, in the land of Edom.

27 And Hiram sent his servants with the fleet, sailors who knew the sea, along with the servants of Solomon.

28 They went to Ophir and took four hundred and twenty talents of gold from there, and brought it to King Solomon.

New International

Solomon's Other Activities

10 At the end of twenty years, during which Solomon built these two buildings—the temple of the LORD and the royal palace— 11 King Solomon gave twenty towns in Galilee to Hiram king of Tyre, because Hiram had supplied him with all the cedar and pine and gold he wanted. 12 But when Hiram went from Tyre to see the towns that Solomon had given him, he was not pleased with them. 13 "What kind of towns are these you have given me, my brother?" he asked. And he called them the Land of Cabul,ᵇ a name they have to this day. 14 Now Hiram had sent to the king 120 talentsᶜ of gold.

15 Here is the account of the forced labor King Solomon conscripted to build the LORD's temple, his own palace, the supporting terraces,ᵈ the wall of Jerusalem, and Hazor, Megiddo and Gezer. 16 (Pharaoh king of Egypt had attacked and captured Gezer. He had set it on fire. He killed its Canaanite inhabitants and then gave it as a wedding gift to his daughter, Solomon's wife. 17 And Solomon rebuilt Gezer.) He built up Lower Beth Horon, 18 Baalath, and Tadmorᵉ in the desert, within his land, 19 as well as all his store cities and the towns for his chariots and for his horsesᶠ—whatever he desired to build in Jerusalem, in Lebanon and throughout all the territory he ruled.

20 All the people left from the Amorites, Hittites, Perizzites, Hivites and Jebusites (these peoples were not Israelites), 21 that is, their descendants remaining in the land, whom the Israelites could not exterminateᵍ—these Solomon conscripted for his slave labor force, as it is to this day. 22 But Solomon did not make slaves of any of the Israelites; they were his fighting men, his government officials, his officers, his captains, and the commanders of his chariots and charioteers. 23 They were also the chief officials in charge of Solomon's projects—550 officials supervising the men who did the work.

24 After Pharaoh's daughter had come up from the City of David to the palace Solomon had built for her, he constructed the supporting terraces.

25 Three times a year Solomon sacrificed burnt offerings and fellowship offeringsʰ on the altar he had built for the LORD, burning incense before the LORD along with them, and so fulfilled the temple obligations.

26 King Solomon also built ships at Ezion Geber, which is near Elath in Edom, on the shore of the Red Sea.ⁱ 27 And Hiram sent his men—sailors who knew the sea—to serve in the fleet with Solomon's men. 28 They sailed to Ophir and brought back 420 talentsʲ of gold, which they delivered to King Solomon.

ᵇ 13 Cabul sounds like the Hebrew for good-for-nothing.
ᶜ 14 That is, about 4 1/2 tons (about 4 metric tons)   ᵈ 15 Or the Millo; also in verse 24   ᵉ 18 The Hebrew may also be read Tamar.   ᶠ 19 Or charioteers   ᵍ 21 The Hebrew term refers to the irrevocable giving over of things or persons to the LORD, often by totally destroying them.   ʰ 25 Traditionally peace offerings   ⁱ 26 Hebrew Yam Suph; that is, Sea of Reeds   ʲ 28 That is, about 16 tons (about 14.5 metric tons)

ᵖ I.e. as good as nothing   ᵠ I.e. citadel

King James

The visit of the Queen of Sheba

10 AND WHEN the queen of Sheba heard of the fame of Solomon concerning the name of the LORD, she came to prove him with hard questions.

2And she came to Jerusalem with a very great train, with camels that bare spices, and very much gold, and precious stones: and when she was come to Solomon, she communed with him of all that was in her heart.

3And Solomon told her all her *i*questions: there was not *any* thing hid from the king, which he told her not.

4And when the queen of Sheba had seen all Solomon's wisdom, and the house that he had built,

5And the meat of his table, and the sitting of his servants, and the *j*attendance of his ministers, and their apparel, and his *k*cupbearers, and his ascent by which he went up unto the house of the LORD; there was no more spirit in her.

6And she said to the king, It was a true report that I heard in mine own land of thy acts and of thy wisdom.

7Howbeit I believed not the words, until I came, and mine eyes had seen *it:* and, behold, the half was not told me: *l*thy wisdom and prosperity exceedeth the fame which I heard.

8Happy *are* thy men, happy *are* these thy servants, which stand continually before thee, *and* that hear thy wisdom.

9Blessed be the LORD thy God, which delighted in thee, to set thee on the throne of Israel: because the LORD loved Israel for ever, therefore made he thee king, to do judgment and justice.

10And she gave the king an hundred and twenty talents of gold, and of spices very great store, and precious stones: there came no more such abundance of spices as these which the queen of Sheba gave to king Solomon.

11And the navy also of Hiram, that brought gold from Ophir, brought in from Ophir great plenty of *m*almug trees, and precious stones.

12And the king made of the almug trees *n o*pillars for the house of the LORD, and for the king's house, harps also and psalteries for singers: there came no such almug trees, nor were seen unto this day.

13And king Solomon gave unto the queen of Sheba all her desire, whatsoever she asked, beside *that* which Solomon gave her *p*of his royal bounty. So she turned and went to her own country, she and her servants.

The splendor of Solomon

14 ¶ Now the weight of gold that came to Solomon in one year was six hundred threescore and six talents of gold,

15Beside *that he had* of the merchantmen, and of the traffic of the spice merchants, and of all the kings of Arabia, and of the *q*governors of the country.

16 ¶ And king Solomon made two hundred targets *of* beaten gold: six hundred *shekels* of gold went to one target.

17And *he made* three hundred shields *of* beaten gold; three pound of gold went to one shield: and the king put them in the house of the forest of Lebanon.

18 ¶ Moreover the king made a great throne of ivory, and overlaid it with the best gold.

19The throne had six steps, and the top of the throne *was* round *r*behind: and *there were s*stays on either side on the place of the seat, and two lions stood beside the stays.

20And twelve lions stood there on the one side and on the other upon the six steps: there was not *t*the like made in any kingdom.

Amplified

10 WHEN THE queen of Sheba heard of [the constant connection of] the fame of Solomon with the name of the Lord, she came to prove him with hard questions (problems and riddles).

2She came to Jerusalem with a very great train, with camels bearing spices, very much gold, and precious stones. When she had come to Solomon, she communed with him about all that was in her mind.

3Solomon answered all her questions; there was nothing hidden from the king which he failed to explain to her.

4When the queen of Sheba had seen all Solomon's wisdom *and* skill, the house he had built,

5The food of his table, the seating of his officials, the standing at attention of his servants, their apparel, his cupbearers, his ascent by which he went up to the house of the Lord [or the burnt offerings he sacrificed], she was breathless *and* overcome.

6She said to the king, It was a true report I heard in my own land of your acts *and* sayings and wisdom.

7I did not believe it until I came and my eyes had seen. Behold, the half was not told me. You have added wisdom and goodness exceeding the fame I heard.

8Happy are your men! Happy are these your servants who stand continually before you, hearing your wisdom!

9Blessed be the Lord your God, Who delighted in you and set you on the throne of Israel! Because the Lord loved Israel forever, He made you king to execute justice and righteousness.

10And she gave the king 120 talents of gold and of spices a very great store and precious stones. Never again came such abundance of spices as these the queen of Sheba gave King Solomon.

11The navy also of Hiram brought from Ophir gold and a great plenty of almug (algum) wood and precious stones.

12Of the almug wood the king made pillars for the house of the Lord and for the king's house, and lyres also and harps for the singers. No such almug wood came again or has been seen to this day.

13King Solomon gave to the queen of Sheba all she wanted, whatever she asked, besides his gifts to her from his royal bounty. So she returned to her own country, she and her servants.

14Now the weight of gold that came to Solomon in one [particular] year was 666 talents of gold,

15Besides what the traders brought and the traffic of the merchants and from all the [tributary] kings and governors of the land of Arabia.

16King Solomon made 200 large shields of beaten gold; 600 shekels of gold went into each shield.

17And he made 300 shields of beaten gold; three minas of gold went into each shield. The king put them in the House of the Forest of Lebanon.

18Also the king made a great throne of ivory and overlaid it with the finest gold.

19The throne had six steps, and attached at the rear of the top of the throne was a round covering *or* canopy. On either side of the seat were armrests, and two lions stood beside the armrests.

20Twelve lions stood there, one on either end of each of the six steps; there was nothing like it ever made in any kingdom.

---

*i*Heb. *words*   *j*Heb. *standing*   *k*Or, *butlers*   *l*Heb. *thou hast added wisdom and goodness to the fame*   *m*Or, *algum trees*   *n*Or, *rails*   *o*Heb. *a prop*   *p*Heb. *according to the hand of king Solomon*   *q*Or, *captains*   *r*Heb. *on the hinder part thereof*   *s*Heb. *hands*   *t*Heb. *so*

New American Standard

The Queen of Sheba

10 NOW WHEN the queen of Sheba heard about the fame of Solomon concerning the name of the LORD, she came to test him with difficult questions.

2 So she came to Jerusalem with a very large retinue, with camels carrying spices and very much gold and precious stones. When she came to Solomon, she spoke with him about all that was in her heart.

3 Solomon answered all her questions; nothing was hidden from the king which he did not explain to her.

4 When the queen of Sheba perceived all the wisdom of Solomon, the house that he had built,

5 the food of his table, the seating of his servants, the attendance of his waiters and their attire, his cupbearers, and his stairway by which he went up to the house of the LORD, there was no more spirit in her.

6 Then she said to the king, "It was a true report which I heard in my own land about your words and your wisdom.

7 "Nevertheless I did not believe the reports, until I came and my eyes had seen it. And behold, the half was not told me. You exceed *in* wisdom and prosperity the report which I heard.

8 "How blessed are your men, how blessed are these your servants who stand before you continually *and* hear your wisdom.

9 "Blessed be the LORD your God who delighted in you to set you on the throne of Israel; because the LORD loved Israel forever, therefore He made you king, to do justice and righteousness."

10 She gave the king a hundred and twenty talents of gold, and a very great *amount* of spices and precious stones. Never again did such abundance of spices come in as that which the queen of Sheba gave King Solomon.

11 ¶ Also the ships of Hiram, which brought gold from Ophir, brought in from Ophir a very great *number of* almug trees and precious stones.

12 The king made of the almug trees supports for the house of the LORD and for the king's house, also lyres and harps for the singers; such almug trees have not come in *again* nor have they been seen to this day.

13 ¶ King Solomon gave to the queen of Sheba all her desire which she requested, besides what he gave her according to his royal bounty. Then she turned and went to her own land together with her servants.

Wealth, Splendor and Wisdom

14 ¶ Now the weight of gold which came in to Solomon in one year was 666 talents of gold,

15 besides *that* from the traders and the 'wares of the merchants and all the kings of the Arabs and the governors of the country.

16 King Solomon made 200 large shields of beaten gold, using 600 *shekels of* gold on each large shield.

17 *He made* 300 shields of beaten gold, using three minas of gold on each shield, and the king put them in the house of the forest of Lebanon.

18 Moreover, the king made a great throne of ivory and overlaid it with refined gold.

19 *There were* six steps to the throne and a round top to the throne at its rear, and arms on each side of the seat, and two lions standing beside the arms.

20 Twelve lions were standing there on the six steps on the one side and on the other; nothing like *it* was made for any other kingdom.

New International

The Queen of Sheba Visits Solomon

10 WHEN THE queen of Sheba heard about the fame of Solomon and his relation to the name of the LORD, she came to test him with hard questions. 2 Arriving at Jerusalem with a very great caravan—with camels carrying spices, large quantities of gold, and precious stones—she came to Solomon and talked with him about all that she had on her mind. 3 Solomon answered all her questions; nothing was too hard for the king to explain to her. 4 When the queen of Sheba saw all the wisdom of Solomon and the palace he had built, 5 the food on his table, the seating of his officials, the attending servants in their robes, his cupbearers, and the burnt offerings he made at[k] the temple of the LORD, she was overwhelmed.

6 She said to the king, "The report I heard in my own country about your achievements and your wisdom is true. 7 But I did not believe these things until I came and saw with my own eyes. Indeed, not even half was told me; in wisdom and wealth you have far exceeded the report I heard. 8 How happy your men must be! How happy your officials, who continually stand before you and hear your wisdom! 9 Praise be to the LORD your God, who has delighted in you and placed you on the throne of Israel. Because of the LORD's eternal love for Israel, he has made you king, to maintain justice and righteousness."

10 And she gave the king 120 talents[l] of gold, large quantities of spices, and precious stones. Never again were so many spices brought in as those the queen of Sheba gave to King Solomon.

11 (Hiram's ships brought gold from Ophir; and from there they brought great cargoes of almugwood[m] and precious stones. 12 The king used the almugwood to make supports for the temple of the LORD and for the royal palace, and to make harps and lyres for the musicians. So much almugwood has never been imported or seen since that day.)

13 King Solomon gave the queen of Sheba all she desired and asked for, besides what he had given her out of his royal bounty. Then she left and returned with her retinue to her own country.

Solomon's Splendor

14 The weight of the gold that Solomon received yearly was 666 talents,[n] 15 not including the revenues from merchants and traders and from all the Arabian kings and the governors of the land.

16 King Solomon made two hundred large shields of hammered gold; six hundred bekas[o] of gold went into each shield. 17 He also made three hundred small shields of hammered gold, with three minas[p] of gold in each shield. The king put them in the Palace of the Forest of Lebanon.

18 Then the king made a great throne inlaid with ivory and overlaid with fine gold. 19 The throne had six steps, and its back had a rounded top. On both sides of the seat were armrests, with a lion standing beside each of them. 20 Twelve lions stood on the six steps, one at either end of each step. Nothing like it had ever been made for any other

---

r Or *traffic*

k 5 Or *the ascent by which he went up to*   *l* 10 That is, about 4 1/2 tons (about 4 metric tons)   *m* 11 Probably a variant of *algumwood*; also in verse 12   *n* 14 That is, about 25 tons (about 23 metric tons)   *o* 16 That is, about 7 1/2 pounds (about 3.5 kilograms)   *p* 17 That is, about 3 3/4 pounds (about 1.7 kilograms)

King James

²¹ ¶ And all king Solomon's drinking vessels *were of* gold, and all the vessels of the house of the forest of Lebanon *were of* pure gold; ^unone *were of* silver: it was nothing accounted of in the days of Solomon.

²²For the king had at sea a navy of Tharshish with the navy of Hiram: once in three years came the navy of Tharshish, bringing gold, and silver, ^vivory, and apes, and peacocks.

²³So king Solomon exceeded all the kings of the earth for riches and for wisdom.

²⁴ ¶ And all the earth ^wsought to Solomon, to hear his wisdom, which God had put in his heart.

²⁵And they brought every man his present, vessels of silver, and vessels of gold, and garments, and armour, and spices, horses, and mules, a rate year by year.

²⁶ ¶ And Solomon gathered together chariots and horsemen: and he had a thousand and four hundred chariots, and twelve thousand horsemen, whom he bestowed in the cities for chariots, and with the king at Jerusalem.

²⁷And the king ^xmade silver *to be* in Jerusalem as stones, and cedars made he *to be* as the sycamore trees that *are* in the vale, for abundance.

²⁸ ^y ¶ And Solomon had horses brought out of Egypt, and linen yarn: the king's merchants received the linen yarn at a price.

²⁹And a chariot came up and went out of Egypt for six hundred *shekels* of silver, and an horse for an hundred and fifty: and so for all the kings of the Hittites, and for the kings of Syria, did they bring *them* out ^zby their means.

Solomon takes foreign wives

11 BUT KING Solomon loved many strange women, ^atogether with the daughter of Pharaoh, women of the Moabites, Ammonites, Edomites, Zidonians, *and* Hittites;

²Of the nations *concerning* which the LORD said unto the children of Israel, Ye shall not go in to them, neither shall they come in unto you: *for* surely they will turn away your heart after their gods: Solomon clave unto these in love.

³And he had seven hundred wives, princesses, and three hundred concubines: and his wives turned away his heart.

⁴For it came to pass, when Solomon was old, *that* his wives turned away his heart after other gods: and his heart was not perfect with the LORD his God, as *was* the heart of David his father.

⁵For Solomon went after Ashtoreth the goddess of the Zidonians, and after ^bMilcom the abomination of the Ammonites.

⁶And Solomon did evil in the sight of the LORD, and ^cwent not fully after the LORD, as *did* David his father.

⁷Then did Solomon build an high place for Chemosh, the abomination of Moab, in the hill that *is* before Jerusalem, and for Molech, the abomination of the children of Ammon.

⁸And likewise did he for all his strange wives, which burnt incense and sacrificed unto their gods.

Amplified

²¹All King Solomon's drinking vessels were of gold, and all vessels of the House of the Forest of Lebanon were of pure gold. None were of silver; it was accounted as nothing in the days of Solomon.

²²For the king had a fleet of ships of Tarshish at sea with the fleet of Hiram. Once every three years the fleet of ships of Tarshish came bringing gold, silver, ivory, apes, and peacocks.

²³So King Solomon exceeded all the kings of the earth in riches and in wisdom (skill).

²⁴And all the earth sought the presence of Solomon to hear his wisdom which God had put in his mind.

²⁵Every man brought tribute: vessels of silver and gold, garments, equipment, spices, horses, and mules, so much year by year.

²⁶Solomon collected chariots and horsemen; he had 1,400 chariots and 12,000 horsemen, which he stationed in the chariot cities and with the king in Jerusalem.

²⁷The king made silver as common in Jerusalem as stones, and cedars as plentiful as the sycamore trees in the lowlands.

²⁸Solomon's horses were brought out of Egypt, and the king's merchants received them in droves, each at a price. [Deut. 17:15, 16.]

²⁹A chariot could be brought out of Egypt for 600 shekels of silver, and a horse for 150. And so to all the kings of the Hittites and of Syria they were exported by the king's merchants.

11 BUT KING Solomon [defiantly] loved many foreign women—the ⁿdaughter of Pharaoh, women of the Moabites, Ammonites, Edomites, Sidonians, and Hittites.

²They were of the very nations of whom the Lord said to the Israelites, You shall not mingle with them, neither shall they mingle with you, for surely they will turn away your hearts after their gods. Yet Solomon clung to these in love. [Deut. 17:17.]

³He had 700 wives, princesses, and 300 concubines, and his wives turned away his heart from God.

⁴For when Solomon was old, his wives turned away his heart after other gods, and his heart was not perfect (complete and whole) with the Lord his God, as was the heart of David his father.

⁵For Solomon went after Ashtoreth the goddess of the Sidonians, and after Milcom the abominable idol of the Ammonites! [I Kings 9:6–9.]

⁶Solomon did evil in the sight of the Lord, and went not fully after the Lord, as David his father did.

⁷Then Solomon built a high place for Chemosh the abominable idol of Moab, on the hill opposite Jerusalem, and for Molech the abominable idol of the Ammonites.

⁸And he did so ^ofor all of his foreign wives, who burned incense and sacrificed to their gods.

ⁿ "Solomon brought the daughter of Pharaoh out of the City of David into the house he had built for her, for he said, My wife shall not dwell in the house of David king of Israel, because the places are holy to which the ark of the Lord has come" (II Chron. 8:11). God had given Solomon the name "Jedidiah [beloved of the Lord]" (II Sam. 12:25), yet he chose to be the beloved of heathen women instead, in defiance of God's covenant with him. ^o What all this did to Solomon's sweet fellowship with God is to be seen in Ecclesiastes. Take the sun out of the sky, and all earth's beauty and fruitfulness will go also. Take God out of your sky, and life's joys will be turned to dregs, bitterness, and futility. Solomon had deliberately chosen to live "under the sun" instead of under God. In the awareness of his own unquestionable greatness, he had become indifferent to the fact that "here is more than Solomon" (Luke 11:31) and that to scorn or ignore God is fatal. With all his wisdom he failed to recognize that "God will not allow Himself to be sneered at (scorned, disdained, or mocked by mere pretensions or professions or by His precepts being set aside) . . . For whatever a man sows, that *and* that only is what he will reap" (Gal. 6:7).

New American Standard

21 All King Solomon's drinking vessels *were* of gold, and all the vessels of the house of the forest of Lebanon *were* of pure gold. None was of silver; it was not considered *s*valuable in the days of Solomon.

22 For the king had at sea the ships of Tarshish with the ships of Hiram; once every three years the ships of Tarshish came bringing gold and silver, ivory and apes and peacocks.

23 ¶ So King Solomon became greater than all the kings of the earth in riches and in wisdom.

24 All the earth was seeking the presence of Solomon, to hear his wisdom which God had put in his heart.

25 They brought every man his gift, articles of silver and gold, garments, weapons, spices, horses, and mules, so much year by year.

26 ¶ Now Solomon gathered chariots and horsemen; and he had 1,400 chariots and 12,000 horsemen, and he stationed them in the chariot cities and with the king in Jerusalem.

27 The king made silver *as common* as stones in Jerusalem, and he made cedars as plentiful as sycamore trees that are in the *t*lowland.

28 Also Solomon's import of horses was from Egypt and Kue, *and* the king's merchants procured *them* from Kue for a price.

29 A chariot was imported from Egypt for 600 *shekels* of silver, and a horse for 150; and by the same means they exported them to all the kings of the Hittites and to the kings of the Arameans.

Solomon Turns from God

11 NOW KING Solomon loved many foreign women along with the daughter of Pharaoh: Moabite, Ammonite, Edomite, Sidonian, and Hittite women,

2 from the nations concerning which the LORD had said to the sons of Israel, "You shall not associate with them, nor shall you associate with you, *for* they will surely turn your heart away after their gods." Solomon held fast to these in love.

3 He had seven hundred wives, princesses, and three hundred concubines, and his wives turned his heart away.

4 For when Solomon was old, his wives turned his heart away after other gods; and his heart was not *u*wholly devoted to the LORD his God, as the heart of David his father *had been.*

5 For Solomon went after Ashtoreth the goddess of the Sidonians and after Milcom the detestable idol of the Ammonites.

6 Solomon did what was evil in the sight of the LORD, and did not follow the LORD fully, as David his father *had done.*

7 Then Solomon built a high place for Chemosh the detestable idol of Moab, on the mountain which is east of Jerusalem, and for Molech the detestable idol of the sons of Ammon.

8 Thus also he did for all his foreign wives, who burned incense and sacrificed to their gods.

New International

kingdom. 21 All King Solomon's goblets were gold, and all the household articles in the Palace of the Forest of Lebanon were pure gold. Nothing was made of silver, because silver was considered of little value in Solomon's days. 22 The king had a fleet of trading ships*q* at sea along with the ships of Hiram. Once every three years it returned, carrying gold, silver and ivory, and apes and baboons.

23 King Solomon was greater in riches and wisdom than all the other kings of the earth. 24 The whole world sought audience with Solomon to hear the wisdom God had put in his heart. 25 Year after year, everyone who came brought a gift—articles of silver and gold, robes, weapons and spices, and horses and mules.

26 Solomon accumulated chariots and horses; he had fourteen hundred chariots and twelve thousand horses,*r* which he kept in the chariot cities and also with him in Jerusalem. 27 The king made silver as common in Jerusalem as stones, and cedar as plentiful as sycamore-fig trees in the foothills. 28 Solomon's horses were imported from Egypt*s* and from Kue*t*—the royal merchants purchased them from Kue. 29 They imported a chariot from Egypt for six hundred shekels*u* of silver, and a horse for a hundred and fifty.*v* They also exported them to all the kings of the Hittites and of the Arameans.

Solomon's Wives

11 KING SOLOMON, however, loved many foreign women besides Pharaoh's daughter—Moabites, Ammonites, Edomites, Sidonians and Hittites. 2 They were from nations about which the LORD had told the Israelites, "You must not intermarry with them, because they will surely turn your hearts after their gods." Nevertheless, Solomon held fast to them in love. 3 He had seven hundred wives of royal birth and three hundred concubines, and his wives led him astray. 4 As Solomon grew old, his wives turned his heart after other gods, and his heart was not fully devoted to the LORD his God, as the heart of David his father had been. 5 He followed Ashtoreth the goddess of the Sidonians, and Molech*w* the detestable god of the Ammonites. 6 So Solomon did evil in the eyes of the LORD; he did not follow the LORD completely, as David his father had done.

7 On a hill east of Jerusalem, Solomon built a high place for Chemosh the detestable god of Moab, and for Molech the detestable god of the Ammonites. 8 He did the same for all his foreign wives, who burned incense and offered sacrifices to their gods.

---

q 22 Hebrew *of ships of Tarshish*   *r* 26 Or *charioteers*
s 28 Or possibly *Muzur*, a region in Cilicia; also in verse 29
t 28 Probably *Cilicia*   *u* 29 That is, about 15 pounds (about 7 kilograms)   *v* 29 That is, about 3 3/4 pounds (about 1.7 kilograms)   *w* 5 Hebrew *Milcom*; also in verse 33

---

s Lit *anything*   *t* Heb *Shephelah*   *u* Lit *complete with*

King James

9 ¶ And the LORD was angry with Solomon, because his heart was turned from the LORD God of Israel, which had appeared unto him twice,

10And had commanded him concerning this thing, that he should not go after other gods: but he kept not that which the LORD commanded.

11Wherefore the LORD said unto Solomon, Forasmuch as this ᵈis done of thee, and thou hast not kept my covenant and my statutes, which I have commanded thee, I will surely rend the kingdom from thee, and will give it to thy servant.

12Notwithstanding in thy days I will not do it for David thy father's sake: but I will rend it out of the hand of thy son.

13Howbeit I will not rend away all the kingdom; but will give one tribe to thy son for David my servant's sake, and for Jerusalem's sake which I have chosen.

Solomon's adversaries

14 ¶ And the LORD stirred up an adversary unto Solomon, Hadad the Edomite: he was of the king's seed in Edom.

15For it came to pass, when David was in Edom, and Joab the captain of the host was gone up to bury the slain, after he had smitten every male in Edom;

16(For six months did Joab remain there with all Israel, until he had cut off every male in Edom:)

17That Hadad fled, he and certain Edomites of his father's servants with him, to go into Egypt; Hadad being yet a little child.

18And they arose out of Midian, and came to Paran: and they took men with them out of Paran, and they came to Egypt, unto Pharaoh king of Egypt; which gave him an house, and appointed him victuals, and gave him land.

19And Hadad found great favour in the sight of Pharaoh, so that he gave him to wife the sister of his own wife, the sister of Tahpenes the queen.

20And the sister of Tahpenes bare him Genubath his son, whom Tahpenes weaned in Pharaoh's house: and Genubath was in Pharaoh's household among the sons of Pharaoh.

21And when Hadad heard in Egypt that David slept with his fathers, and that Joab the captain of the host was dead, Hadad said to Pharaoh, ᵉLet me depart, that I may go to mine own country.

22Then Pharaoh said unto him, But what hast thou lacked with me, that, behold, thou seekest to go to thine own country? And he answered, ᶠNothing: howbeit let me go in any wise.

23 ¶ And God stirred him up another adversary, Rezon the son of Eliadah, which fled from his lord Hadadezer king of Zobah:

24And he gathered men unto him, and became captain over a band, when David slew them of Zobah: and they went to Damascus, and dwelt therein, and reigned in Damascus.

25And he was an adversary to Israel all the days of Solomon, beside the mischief that Hadad did: and he abhorred Israel, and reigned over Syria.

Jeroboam's rebellion

26 ¶ And Jeroboam the son of Nebat, an Ephrathite of Zereda, Solomon's servant, whose mother's name was Zeruah, a widow woman, even he lifted up his hand against the king.

27And this was the cause that he lifted up his hand against the king: Solomon built Millo, and ᵍrepaired the breaches of the city of David his father.

28And the man Jeroboam was a mighty man of valour: and Solomon seeing the young man that he ʰwas industrious, he made him ruler over all the ⁱcharge of the house of Joseph.

Amplified

9And the Lord was angry with Solomon because his heart was turned from the Lord, the God of Israel, Who had appeared to him twice,

10And had commanded him concerning this thing, that he should not go after other gods, but he did not do what the Lord commanded.

11Therefore the Lord said to Solomon, Because you are doing this and have not kept My covenant and My statutes, which I have commanded you, I will surely rend the kingdom from you and will give it to your servant!

12However, in your days I will not do it, for David your father's sake. But I will rend it out of the hand of your son!

13However, I will not tear away all the kingdom, but will give one tribe to your son for David My servant's sake and for the sake of Jerusalem, which I have chosen.

14The Lord stirred up an adversary against Solomon, Hadad the Edomite; he was of royal descent in Edom.

15For when David was in Edom, and Joab the commander of Israel's army went up to bury the slain, he slew every male in Edom.

16For Joab and all Israel remained there for six months, until he had cut off every male in Edom.

17But Hadad fled, he and certain Edomites of his father's servants, to Egypt, Hadad being yet a little child.

18They set out from Midian and came to Paran, and took men with them out of Paran and came to Egypt, to Pharaoh king of Egypt, who gave [young] Hadad a house and land and ordered provisions for him.

19Hadad found great favor with Pharaoh, so that he gave him in marriage the sister of his own wife Tahpenes the queen.

20The sister of Tahpenes bore Hadad Genubath his son, whom Tahpenes weaned in Pharaoh's house; and Genubath was in Pharaoh's household among the sons of Pharaoh.

21But when Hadad heard in Egypt that David slept with his fathers and that Joab the commander of Israel's army was dead, Hadad said to Pharaoh, Let me depart, that I may go to my own country.

22Then Pharaoh said to him, But what have you lacked with me that now you want to go to your own country? He replied, Nothing. However, let me go anyhow.

23God raised up for [Hadad] another adversary, Rezon son of Eliada, who had fled from his master, Hadadezer king of Zobah.

24Rezon gathered men about him and became leader of a marauding band after the slaughter by David. They went to Damascus and dwelt and made [Rezon] king in Damascus.

25And Rezon was an adversary to Israel all the days of Solomon, besides the mischief that Hadad did. Rezon abhorred Israel and reigned over Syria.

26Jeroboam son of Nebat, an Ephrathite of Zereda, Solomon's servant, whose mother's name was Zeruah, a widow woman, rebelled against the king—

27And for this reason: Solomon built the Millo and repaired the breaches of the city of David his father.

28The man Jeroboam was a mighty man of courage. Solomon, seeing that the young man was industrious, put him in charge over all the [forced] labor of the house of Joseph.

ᵈHeb. is with thee   ᵉHeb. Send me away   ᶠHeb. Not
ᵍHeb. closed   ʰHeb. did work   ⁱHeb. burden

New American Standard

9 ¶ Now the LORD was angry with Solomon because his heart was turned away from the LORD, the God of Israel, who had appeared to him twice,

10 and had commanded him concerning this thing, that he should not go after other gods; but he did not observe what the LORD had commanded.

11 So the LORD said to Solomon, "Because you have done this, and you have not kept My covenant and My statutes, which I have commanded you, I will surely tear the kingdom from you, and will give it to your servant.

12 "Nevertheless I will not do it in your days for the sake of your father David, *but* I will tear it out of the hand of your son.

13 "However, I will not tear away all the kingdom, *but* I will give one tribe to your son for the sake of My servant David and for the sake of Jerusalem which I have chosen."

God Raises Adversaries

14 ¶ Then the LORD raised up an adversary to Solomon, Hadad the Edomite; he was of the royal line in Edom.

15 For it came about, when David was in Edom, and Joab the commander of the army had gone up to bury the slain, and had struck down every male in Edom

16 (for Joab and all Israel stayed there six months, until he had cut off every male in Edom),

17 that Hadad fled to Egypt, he and certain Edomites of his father's servants with him, while Hadad *was* a young boy.

18 They arose from Midian and came to Paran; and they took men with them from Paran and came to Egypt, to Pharaoh king of Egypt, who gave him a house and assigned him food and gave him land.

19 Now Hadad found great favor before Pharaoh, so that he gave him in marriage the sister of his own wife, the sister of Tahpenes the queen.

20 The sister of Tahpenes bore his son Genubath, whom Tahpenes weaned in Pharaoh's house; and Genubath was in Pharaoh's house among the sons of Pharaoh.

21 But when Hadad heard in Egypt that David slept with his fathers and that Joab the commander of the army was dead, Hadad said to Pharaoh, "Send me away, that I may go to my own country."

22 Then Pharaoh said to him, "But what have you lacked with me, that behold, you are seeking to go to your own country?" And he answered, "Nothing; nevertheless you must surely let me go."

23 ¶ God also raised up *another* adversary to him, Rezon the son of Eliada, who had fled from his lord Hadadezer king of Zobah.

24 He gathered men to himself and became leader of a marauding band, after David slew them of *Zobah;* and they went to Damascus and stayed there, and reigned in Damascus.

25 So he was an adversary to Israel all the days of Solomon, along with the evil that Hadad *did;* and he abhorred Israel and reigned over Aram.

26 ¶ Then Jeroboam the son of Nebat, an Ephraimite of Zeredah, Solomon's servant, whose mother's name was Zeruah, a widow, also rebelled against the king.

27 Now this was the reason why he rebelled against the king: Solomon built the Millo, *and* closed up the breach of the city of his father David.

28 Now the man Jeroboam was a valiant warrior, and when Solomon saw that the young man was industrious, he appointed him over all the forced labor of the house of Joseph.

New International

9 The LORD became angry with Solomon because his heart had turned away from the LORD, the God of Israel, who had appeared to him twice. 10 Although he had forbidden Solomon to follow other gods, Solomon did not keep the LORD's command. 11 So the LORD said to Solomon, "Since this is your attitude and you have not kept my covenant and my decrees, which I commanded you, I will most certainly tear the kingdom away from you and give it to one of your subordinates. 12 Nevertheless, for the sake of David your father, I will not do it during your lifetime. I will tear it out of the hand of your son. 13 Yet I will not tear the whole kingdom from him, but will give him one tribe for the sake of David my servant and for the sake of Jerusalem, which I have chosen."

Solomon's Adversaries

14 Then the LORD raised up against Solomon an adversary, Hadad the Edomite, from the royal line of Edom. 15 Earlier when David was fighting with Edom, Joab the commander of the army, who had gone up to bury the dead, had struck down all the men in Edom. 16 Joab and all the Israelites stayed there for six months, until they had destroyed all the men in Edom. 17 But Hadad, still only a boy, fled to Egypt with some Edomite officials who had served his father. 18 They set out from Midian and went to Paran. Then taking men from Paran with them, they went to Egypt, to Pharaoh king of Egypt, who gave Hadad a house and land and provided him with food.

19 Pharaoh was so pleased with Hadad that he gave him a sister of his own wife, Queen Tahpenes, in marriage. 20 The sister of Tahpenes bore him a son named Genubath, whom Tahpenes brought up in the royal palace. There Genubath lived with Pharaoh's own children.

21 While he was in Egypt, Hadad heard that David rested with his fathers and that Joab the commander of the army was also dead. Then Hadad said to Pharaoh, "Let me go, that I may return to my own country."

22 "What have you lacked here that you want to go back to your own country?" Pharaoh asked.

"Nothing," Hadad replied, "but do let me go!"

23 And God raised up against Solomon another adversary, Rezon son of Eliada, who had fled from his master, Hadadezer king of Zobah. 24 He gathered men around him and became the leader of a band of rebels when David destroyed the forces[x] of Zobah; the rebels went to Damascus, where they settled and took control. 25 Rezon was Israel's adversary as long as Solomon lived, adding to the trouble caused by Hadad. So Rezon ruled in Aram and was hostile toward Israel.

Jeroboam Rebels Against Solomon

26 Also, Jeroboam son of Nebat rebelled against the king. He was one of Solomon's officials, an Ephraimite from Zeredah, and his mother was a widow named Zeruah.

27 Here is the account of how he rebelled against the king: Solomon had built the supporting terraces[y] and had filled in the gap in the wall of the city of David his father. 28 Now Jeroboam was a man of standing, and when Solomon saw how well the young man did his work, he put him in charge of the whole labor force of the house of Joseph.

---

x 24 Hebrew *destroyed them*   *y 27* Or *the Millo*

King James

Amplified

King James

29And it came to pass at that time when Jeroboam went out of Jerusalem, that the prophet Ahijah the Shilonite found him in the way; and he had clad himself with a new garment; and they two *were* alone in the field:

30And Ahijah caught the new garment that *was* on him, and rent it *in* twelve pieces:

31And he said to Jeroboam, Take thee ten pieces: for thus saith the LORD, the God of Israel, Behold, I will rend the kingdom out of the hand of Solomon, and will give ten tribes to thee:

32(But he shall have one tribe for my servant David's sake, and for Jerusalem's sake, the city which I have chosen out of all the tribes of Israel:)

33Because that they have forsaken me, and have worshipped Ashtoreth the goddess of the Zidonians, Chemosh the god of the Moabites, and Milcom the god of the children of Ammon, and have not walked in my ways, to do *that which is* right in mine eyes, and *to keep* my statutes and my judgments, as *did* David his father.

34Howbeit I will not take the whole kingdom out of his hand: but I will make him prince all the days of his life for David my servant's sake, whom I chose, because he kept my commandments and my statutes:

35But I will take the kingdom out of his son's hand, and will give it unto thee, *even* ten tribes.

36And unto his son will I give one tribe, that David my servant may have a *j*light always before me in Jerusalem, the city which I have chosen me to put my name there.

37And I will take thee, and thou shalt reign according to all that thy soul desireth, and shalt be king over Israel.

38And it shall be, if thou wilt hearken unto all that I command thee, and wilt walk in my ways, and do *that is* right in my sight, to keep my statutes and my commandments, as David my servant did; that I will be with thee, and build thee a sure house, as I built for David, and give Israel unto thee.

39And I will for this afflict the seed of David, but not for ever.

40Solomon sought therefore to kill Jeroboam. And Jeroboam arose, and fled into Egypt, unto Shishak king of Egypt, and was in Egypt until the death of Solomon.

The death of Solomon

41 ¶ And the rest of the *k*acts of Solomon, and all that he did, and his wisdom, *are* they not written in the book of the acts of Solomon?

42And the *l*time that Solomon reigned in Jerusalem over all Israel *was* forty years.

43And Solomon slept with his fathers, and was buried in the city of David his father: and Rehoboam his son reigned in his stead.

Rehoboam, king of Israel

12 AND REHOBOAM went to Shechem: for all Israel were come to Shechem to make him king.

2And it came to pass, when Jeroboam the son of Nebat, who was yet in Egypt, heard *of it,* (for he was fled from the presence of king Solomon, and Jeroboam dwelt in Egypt;)

3That they sent and called him. And Jeroboam and all the congregation of Israel came, and spake unto Rehoboam, saying,

4Thy father made our yoke grievous: now therefore make thou the grievous service of thy father, and his heavy yoke which he put upon us, lighter, and we will serve thee.

5And he said unto them, Depart yet *for* three days, then come again to me. And the people departed.

6 ¶ And king Rehoboam consulted with the old men, that stood before Solomon his father while he yet lived, and said, How do ye advise that I may answer this people?

Amplified

29At that time, when Jeroboam went out of Jerusalem, the prophet Ahijah the Shilonite met him on the way. Ahijah had clad himself with a new garment; and they were alone in the field.

30Ahijah caught the new garment he wore and tore it into twelve pieces.

31He said to Jeroboam, You take ten pieces, for thus says the Lord, the God of Israel, Behold, I will tear the kingdom from the hand of Solomon and will give you ten tribes.

32But he shall have one tribe, for My servant David's sake and for Jerusalem's sake, the city which I have chosen out of all the tribes of Israel,

33Because they have forsaken Me and have worshiped Ashtoreth the goddess of the Sidonians, Chemosh the god of the Moabites, and Milcom the god of the Ammonites, and have not walked in My ways, to do what is right in My sight, keeping My statutes and My ordinances as did David his father.

34However, I will not take the whole kingdom out of his hand; but I will make him ruler all the days of his life for David My servant's sake, whom I chose because he kept My commandments and My statutes.

35But I will take the kingdom out of his son's hand and give it to you, ten tribes.

36Yet to his son I will give one tribe, that David My servant may always have a light before Me in Jerusalem, the city where I have chosen to put My Name.

37And I will take you, and you shall reign according to all that your soul desires; and you shall be king over Israel.

38And if you will hearken to all I command you and will walk in My ways and do right in My sight, keeping My statutes and My commandments, as David My servant did, I will be with you and build you a sure house, as I built for David, and will give Israel to you.

39And I will for this afflict the descendants of David, but not forever.

40Solomon sought therefore to kill Jeroboam. But Jeroboam arose and fled into Egypt, to Shishak king of Egypt, and was in Egypt until Solomon died.

41The rest of the acts of Solomon—and all that he did, and his wisdom (skill)—are they not written in the book of the acts of Solomon?

42The time Solomon reigned in Jerusalem over all Israel was forty years.

43And Solomon slept with his fathers and was buried in the city of David his father. Rehoboam his son reigned in his stead.

12 REHOBOAM WENT to Shechem, for all Israel had come to Shechem to make him king.

2And when Jeroboam son of Nebat heard of it—for he still dwelt in Egypt, where he had fled from King Solomon—[he] returned from Egypt.

3And they sent and called him, and Jeroboam and all the assembly of Israel came and said to Rehoboam,

4Your father made our yoke heavy; now therefore lighten the hard service and the heavy yoke your father put upon us, and we will serve you.

5He replied, Go away for three days and then return to me. So the people departed.

6And King Rehoboam consulted with the old men who stood before Solomon his father while he yet lived and said, How do you advise me to answer this people?

---

*j*Heb. *lamp,* or, *candle*   *k*Or, *words,* or, *things*   *l*Heb. *days*

New American Standard

New International

29 It came about at that time, when Jeroboam went out of Jerusalem, that the prophet Ahijah the Shilonite found him on the road. Now Ahijah had clothed himself with a new cloak; and both of them were alone in the field.

30 Then Ahijah took hold of the new cloak which was on him and tore it into twelve pieces.

31 He said to Jeroboam, "Take for yourself ten pieces; for thus says the LORD, the God of Israel, 'Behold, I will tear the kingdom out of the hand of Solomon and give you ten tribes

32 (but he will have one tribe, for the sake of My servant David and for the sake of Jerusalem, the city which I have chosen from all the tribes of Israel),

33 because they have forsaken Me, and have worshiped Ashtoreth the goddess of the Sidonians, Chemosh the god of Moab, and Milcom the god of the sons of Ammon; and they have not walked in My ways, doing what is right in My sight and *observing* My statutes and My ordinances, as his father David *did*.

34 'Nevertheless I will not take the whole kingdom out of his hand, but I will make him ruler all the days of his life, for the sake of My servant David whom I chose, who observed My commandments and My statutes;

35 but I will take the kingdom from his son's hand and give it to you, *even* ten tribes.

36 'But to his son I will give one tribe, that My servant David may have a lamp always before Me in Jerusalem, the city where I have chosen for Myself to put My name.

37 'I will take you, and you shall reign over whatever you desire, and you shall be king over Israel.

38 'Then it will be, that if you listen to all that I command you and walk in My ways, and do what is right in My sight by observing My statutes and My commandments, as My servant David did, then I will be with you and build you an enduring house as I built for David, and I will give Israel to you.

39 'Thus I will afflict the descendants of David for this, but not always.' "

40 Solomon sought therefore to put Jeroboam to death; but Jeroboam arose and fled to Egypt to Shishak king of Egypt, and he was in Egypt until the death of Solomon.

The Death of Solomon

41 ¶ Now the rest of the acts of Solomon and whatever he did, and his wisdom, are they not written in the book of the acts of Solomon?

42 Thus the time that Solomon reigned in Jerusalem over all Israel was forty years.

43 And Solomon slept with his fathers and was buried in the city of his father David, and his son Rehoboam reigned in his place.

King Rehoboam Acts Foolishly

12 THEN REHOBOAM went to Shechem, for all Israel had come to Shechem to make him king.

2 Now when Jeroboam the son of Nebat heard *of it,* he was living in Egypt (for he was yet in Egypt, where he had fled from the presence of King Solomon).

3 Then they sent and called him, and Jeroboam and all the assembly of Israel came and spoke to Rehoboam, saying,

4 "Your father made our yoke hard; now therefore lighten the hard service of your father and his heavy yoke which he put on us, and we will serve you."

5 Then he said to them, "Depart for three days, then return to me." So the people departed.

6 ¶ King Rehoboam consulted with the elders who had served his father Solomon while he was still alive, saying, "How do you counsel *me* to answer this people?"

29 About that time Jeroboam was going out of Jerusalem, and Ahijah the prophet of Shiloh met him on the way, wearing a new cloak. The two of them were alone out in the country, 30 and Ahijah took hold of the new cloak he was wearing and tore it into twelve pieces. 31 Then he said to Jeroboam, "Take ten pieces for yourself, for this is what the LORD, the God of Israel, says: 'See, I am going to tear the kingdom out of Solomon's hand and give you ten tribes. 32 But for the sake of my servant David and the city of Jerusalem, which I have chosen out of all the tribes of Israel, he will have one tribe. 33 I will do this because they have[z] forsaken me and worshiped Ashtoreth the goddess of the Sidonians, Chemosh the god of the Moabites, and Molech the god of the Ammonites, and have not walked in my ways, nor done what is right in my eyes, nor kept my statutes and laws as David, Solomon's father, did.

34 " 'But I will not take the whole kingdom out of Solomon's hand; I have made him ruler all the days of his life for the sake of David my servant, whom I chose and who observed my commands and statutes. 35 I will take the kingdom from his son's hands and give you ten tribes. 36 I will give one tribe to his son so that David my servant may always have a lamp before me in Jerusalem, the city where I chose to put my Name. 37 However, as for you, I will take you, and you will rule over all that your heart desires; you will be king over Israel. 38 If you do whatever I command you and walk in my ways and do what is right in my eyes by keeping my statutes and commands, as David my servant did, I will be with you. I will build you a dynasty as enduring as the one I built for David and will give Israel to you. 39 I will humble David's descendants because of this, but not forever.' "

40 Solomon tried to kill Jeroboam, but Jeroboam fled to Egypt, to Shishak the king, and stayed there until Solomon's death.

Solomon's Death

41 As for the other events of Solomon's reign—all he did and the wisdom he displayed—are they not written in the book of the annals of Solomon? 42 Solomon reigned in Jerusalem over all Israel forty years. 43 Then he rested with his fathers and was buried in the city of David his father. And Rehoboam his son succeeded him as king.

Israel Rebels Against Rehoboam

12 REHOBOAM WENT to Shechem, for all the Israelites had gone there to make him king. 2 When Jeroboam son of Nebat heard this (he was still in Egypt, where he had fled from King Solomon), he returned from[a] Egypt. 3 So they sent for Jeroboam, and he and the whole assembly of Israel went to Rehoboam and said to him: 4 "Your father put a heavy yoke on us, but now lighten the harsh labor and the heavy yoke he put on us, and we will serve you."

5 Rehoboam answered, "Go away for three days and then come back to me." So the people went away.

6 Then King Rehoboam consulted the elders who had served his father Solomon during his lifetime. "How would you advise me to answer these people?" he asked.

---

z 33 Hebrew; Septuagint, Vulgate and Syriac *because he has*
a 2 Or *he remained in*

King James

⁷And they spake unto him, saying, If thou wilt be a servant unto this people this day, and wilt serve them, and answer them, and speak good words to them, then they will be thy servants for ever.

⁸But he forsook the counsel of the old men, which they had given him, and consulted with the young men that were grown up with him, *and* which stood before him:

⁹And he said unto them, What counsel give ye that we may answer this people, who have spoken to me, saying, Make the yoke which thy father did put upon us lighter?

¹⁰And the young men that were grown up with him spake unto him, saying, Thus shalt thou speak unto this people that spake unto thee, saying, Thy father made our yoke heavy, but make thou *it* lighter unto us; thus shalt thou say unto them, My little *finger* shall be thicker than my father's loins.

¹¹And now whereas my father did lade you with a heavy yoke, I will add to your yoke: my father hath chastised you with whips, but I will chastise you with scorpions.

¹² ¶ So Jeroboam and all the people came to Rehoboam the third day, as the king had appointed, saying, Come to me again the third day.

¹³And the king answered the people ^mroughly, and forsook the old men's counsel that they gave him;

¹⁴And spake to them after the counsel of the young men, saying, My father made your yoke heavy, and I will add to your yoke: my father *also* chastised you with whips, but I will chastise you with scorpions.

¹⁵Wherefore the king hearkened not unto the people; for the cause was from the LORD, that he might perform his saying, which the LORD spake by Ahijah the Shilonite unto Jeroboam the son of Nebat.

¹⁶ ¶ So when all Israel saw that the king hearkened not unto them, the people answered the king, saying, What portion have we in David? neither *have we* inheritance in the son of Jesse: to your tents, O Israel: now see to thine own house, David. So Israel departed unto their tents.

¹⁷But *as for* the children of Israel which dwelt in the cities of Judah, Rehoboam reigned over them.

¹⁸Then king Rehoboam sent Adoram, who *was* over the tribute; and all Israel stoned him with stones, that he died. Therefore king Rehoboam ⁿmade speed to get him up to his chariot, to flee to Jerusalem.

¹⁹So Israel ^orebelled against the house of David unto this day.

²⁰And it came to pass, when all Israel heard that Jeroboam was come again, that they sent and called him unto the congregation, and made him king over all Israel: there was none that followed the house of David, but the tribe of Judah only.

²¹ ¶ And when Rehoboam was come to Jerusalem, he assembled all the house of Judah, with the tribe of Benjamin, an hundred and fourscore thousand chosen men, which were warriors, to fight against the house of Israel, to bring the kingdom again to Rehoboam the son of Solomon.

²²But the word of God came unto Shemaiah the man of God, saying,

²³Speak unto Rehoboam, the son of Solomon, king of Judah, and unto all the house of Judah and Benjamin, and to the remnant of the people, saying,

²⁴Thus saith the LORD, Ye shall not go up, nor fight against your brethren the children of Israel: return every man to his house; for this thing is from me. They hearkened therefore to the word of the LORD, and returned to depart, according to the word of the LORD.

Two golden calves

²⁵ ¶ Then Jeroboam built Shechem in mount Ephraim, and dwelt therein; and went out from thence, and built Penuel.

²⁶And Jeroboam said in his heart, Now shall the kingdom return to the house of David:

Amplified

⁷And they said to him, If you will be a servant to this people today and serve them and answer them with good words, they will be your servants forever.

⁸But he forsook the counsel the old men gave him and consulted the young men who grew up with him and stood before him.

⁹He said to them, What do you advise that we answer this people who have said, Make the yoke your father put on us lighter?

¹⁰The young men who grew up with him answered, To the people who told you, Your father made our yoke heavy, but you make it lighter for us—say this, My little finger shall be thicker than my father's loins.

¹¹And now whereas my father loaded you with a heavy yoke, I will add to your yoke. My father chastised you with whips, but I will chastise you with scorpions.

¹²So Jeroboam and all the people came to Rehoboam on the third day, as the king had appointed.

¹³And the king answered the people roughly and forsook the counsel the old men had given him,

¹⁴And spoke to them after the counsel of the young men, saying, My father made your yoke heavy, but I will add to your yoke; he chastised you with whips, but I will chastise you with scorpions.

¹⁵So the king did not hearken to the people, for the situation was from the Lord, that He might fulfill His word which He spoke by Ahijah the Shilonite to Jeroboam son of Nebat. [I Kings 11:29–33.]

¹⁶So when all Israel saw that the king did not heed them, they answered the king, What portion have we in David? We have no inheritance in the son of Jesse. To your tents, O Israel! Look now to your own house, David! So Israel went to their tents.

¹⁷But Rehoboam reigned over the Israelites who dwelt in the cities of Judah.

¹⁸Then King Rehoboam sent Adoram, who was over the tribute [taskmaster over the forced labor], and all Israel stoned him to death with stones. So King Rehoboam hastened to get into his chariot to flee to Jerusalem.

¹⁹So Israel has rebelled against the house of David to this day.

²⁰When all Israel heard that Jeroboam had returned, they sent and called him to the assembly and made him king over all Israel. None followed the house of David except the tribe of Judah only.

²¹And when Rehoboam had come to Jerusalem, he assembled all the house of Judah, with the tribe of Benjamin, 180,000 chosen warriors, to fight against the house of Israel to bring the kingdom back to Rehoboam son of Solomon.

²²But the word of God came to Shemaiah the man of God, saying,

²³Tell Rehoboam son of Solomon king of Judah and all the house of Judah and Benjamin and the remnant of the people,

²⁴Thus says the Lord, You shall not go up or fight against your brethren, the Israelites. Return every man to his house, for this thing is from Me. So they hearkened to the Lord's word and returned home, according to the Lord's word.

²⁵Then Jeroboam built Shechem in the hill country of Ephraim and lived there. He went out from there and built Penuel.

²⁶Jeroboam said in his heart, Now the kingdom will return to the house of David.

---

^mHeb. *hardly*   ⁿHeb. *strengthened himself*   ^oOr, *fell away*

New American Standard

7 Then they spoke to him, saying, "If you will be a servant to this people today, and will serve them and grant them their petition, and speak good words to them, then they will be your servants forever."

8 But he forsook the counsel of the elders which they had given him, and consulted with the young men who grew up with him and served him.

9 So he said to them, "What counsel do you give that we may answer this people who have spoken to me, saying, 'Lighten the yoke which your father put on us'?"

10 The young men who grew up with him spoke to him, saying, "Thus you shall say to this people who spoke to you, saying, 'Your father made our yoke heavy, now you make it lighter for us!' But you shall speak to them, 'My little finger is thicker than my father's loins!

11 'Whereas my father loaded you with a heavy yoke, I will add to your yoke; my father disciplined you with whips, but I will discipline you with scorpions.' "

12 ¶ Then Jeroboam and all the people came to Rehoboam on the third day as the king had directed, saying, "Return to me on the third day."

13 The king answered the people harshly, for he forsook the advice of the elders which they had given him,

14 and he spoke to them according to the advice of the young men, saying, "My father made your yoke heavy, but I will add to your yoke; my father disciplined you with whips, but I will discipline you with scorpions."

15 So the king did not listen to the people; for it was a turn *of events* from the LORD, that He might establish His word, which the LORD spoke through Ahijah the Shilonite to Jeroboam the son of Nebat.

The Kingdom Divided; Jeroboam Rules Israel

16 ¶ When all Israel *saw* that the king did not listen to them, the people answered the king, saying,
"What portion do we have in David?
We have no inheritance in the son of Jesse;
To your tents, O Israel!
Now look after your own house, David!"
So Israel departed to their tents.

17 But as for the sons of Israel who lived in the cities of Judah, Rehoboam reigned over them.

18 Then King Rehoboam sent Adoram, who was over the forced labor, and all Israel stoned him to death. And King Rehoboam made haste to mount his chariot to flee to Jerusalem.

19 So Israel has been in rebellion against the house of David to this day.

20 ¶ It came about when all Israel heard that Jeroboam had returned, that they sent and called him to the assembly and made him king over all Israel. None but the tribe of Judah followed the house of David.

21 ¶ Now when Rehoboam had come to Jerusalem, he assembled all the house of Judah and the tribe of Benjamin, 180,000 chosen men who were warriors, to fight against the house of Israel to restore the kingdom to Rehoboam the son of Solomon.

22 But the word of God came to Shemaiah the man of God, saying,

23 "Speak to Rehoboam the son of Solomon, king of Judah, and to all the house of Judah and Benjamin and to the rest of the people, saying,

24 'Thus says the LORD, "You must not go up and fight against your relatives the sons of Israel; return every man to his house, for this thing has come from Me." ' " So they listened to the word of the LORD, and returned and went *their way* according to the word of the LORD.

Jeroboam's Idolatry

25 ¶ Then Jeroboam built Shechem in the hill country of Ephraim, and lived there. And he went out from there and built Penuel.

26 Jeroboam said in his heart, "Now the kingdom will return to the house of David.

New International

7 They replied, "If today you will be a servant to these people and serve them and give them a favorable answer, they will always be your servants."

8 But Rehoboam rejected the advice the elders gave him and consulted the young men who had grown up with him and were serving him. 9 He asked them, "What is your advice? How should we answer these people who say to me, 'Lighten the yoke your father put on us'?"

10 The young men who had grown up with him replied, "Tell these people who have said to you, 'Your father put a heavy yoke on us, but make our yoke lighter'—tell them, 'My little finger is thicker than my father's waist. 11 My father laid on you a heavy yoke; I will make it even heavier. My father scourged you with whips; I will scourge you with scorpions.' "

12 Three days later Jeroboam and all the people returned to Rehoboam, as the king had said, "Come back to me in three days." 13 The king answered the people harshly. Rejecting the advice given him by the elders, 14 he followed the advice of the young men and said, "My father made your yoke heavy; I will make it even heavier. My father scourged you with whips; I will scourge you with scorpions." 15 So the king did not listen to the people, for this turn of events was from the LORD, to fulfill the word the LORD had spoken to Jeroboam son of Nebat through Ahijah the Shilonite.

16 When all Israel saw that the king refused to listen to them, they answered the king:

"What share do we have in David,
    what part in Jesse's son?
To your tents, O Israel!
    Look after your own house, O David!"

So the Israelites went home. 17 But as for the Israelites who were living in the towns of Judah, Rehoboam still ruled over them.

18 King Rehoboam sent out Adoniram,[b] who was in charge of forced labor, but all Israel stoned him to death. King Rehoboam, however, managed to get into his chariot and escape to Jerusalem. 19 So Israel has been in rebellion against the house of David to this day.

20 When all the Israelites heard that Jeroboam had returned, they sent and called him to the assembly and made him king over all Israel. Only the tribe of Judah remained loyal to the house of David.

21 When Rehoboam arrived in Jerusalem, he mustered the whole house of Judah and the tribe of Benjamin—a hundred and eighty thousand fighting men—to make war against the house of Israel and to regain the kingdom for Rehoboam son of Solomon.

22 But this word of God came to Shemaiah the man of God: 23 "Say to Rehoboam son of Solomon king of Judah, to the whole house of Judah and Benjamin, and to the rest of the people, 24 'This is what the LORD says: Do not go up to fight against your brothers, the Israelites. Go home, every one of you, for this is my doing.' " So they obeyed the word of the LORD and went home again, as the LORD had ordered.

Golden Calves at Bethel and Dan

25 Then Jeroboam fortified Shechem in the hill country of Ephraim and lived there. From there he went out and built up Peniel.[c]

26 Jeroboam thought to himself, "The kingdom will now

---

b 18 Some Septuagint manuscripts and Syriac (see also 1 Kings 4:6 and 5:14); Hebrew *Adoram*   c 25 Hebrew *Penuel*, a variant of *Peniel*

King James

27If this people go up to do sacrifice in the house of the LORD at Jerusalem, then shall the heart of this people turn again unto their lord, *even* unto Rehoboam king of Judah, and they shall kill me, and go again to Rehoboam king of Judah.

28Whereupon the king took counsel, and made two calves *of* gold, and said unto them, It is too much for you to go up to Jerusalem: behold thy gods, O Israel, which brought thee up out of the land of Egypt.

29And he set the one in Beth-el, and the other put he in Dan.

30And this thing became a sin: for the people went *to worship* before the one, *even* unto Dan.

31And he made an house of high places, and made priests of the lowest of the people, which were not of the sons of Levi.

32And Jeroboam ordained a feast in the eighth month, on the fifteenth day of the month, like unto the feast that *is* in Judah, *q*sacrificing unto the calves that he had made: and he placed in Beth-el the priests of the high places which he had made.

33So he *p*offered upon the altar which he had made in Beth-el the fifteenth day of the eighth month, *even* in the month which he had devised of his own heart; and ordained a feast unto the children of Israel: and he offered upon the altar, *r*and burnt incense.

The man of God from Judah

13 AND, BEHOLD, there came a man of God out of Judah by the word of the LORD unto Beth-el: and Jeroboam stood by the altar *s*to burn incense.

2And he cried against the altar in the word of the LORD, and said, O altar, altar, thus saith the LORD; Behold, a child shall be born unto the house of David, Josiah by name; and upon thee shall he offer the priests of the high places that burn incense upon thee, and men's bones shall be burnt upon thee.

3And he gave a sign the same day, saying, This *is* the sign which the LORD hath spoken; Behold, the altar shall be rent, and the ashes that *are* upon it shall be poured out.

4And it came to pass, when king Jeroboam heard the saying of the man of God, which had cried against the altar in Beth-el, that he put forth his hand from the altar, saying, Lay hold on him. And his hand, which he put forth against him, dried up, so that he could not pull it in again to him.

5The altar also was rent, and the ashes poured out from the altar, according to the sign which the man of God had given by the word of the LORD.

6And the king answered and said unto the man of God, Entreat now the face of the LORD thy God, and pray for me, that my hand may be restored me again. And the man of God besought *t*the LORD, and the king's hand was restored him again, and became as *it was* before.

7And the king said unto the man of God, Come home with me, and refresh thyself, and I will give thee a reward.

8And the man of God said unto the king, If thou wilt give me half thine house, I will not go in with thee, neither will I eat bread nor drink water in this place:

9For so was it charged me by the word of the LORD, saying, Eat no bread, nor drink water, nor turn again by the same way that thou camest.

10So he went another way, and returned not by the way that he came to Beth-el.

Amplified

27If this people goes up to the house of the Lord at Jerusalem to sacrifice, then the heart of this people will turn again to their lord, to Rehoboam king of Judah; and they will kill me and go back to Rehoboam king of Judah.

28So the king took counsel and made two calves of gold. And he said to the people, It is too much for you to go [all the way] up to Jerusalem. Behold your gods, O Israel, who brought you up out of the land of Egypt.

29And he set the one golden calf in Bethel, and the other he put in Dan.

30And this thing became a sin; for the people went to worship each of them even as far as Dan.

31Jeroboam also made houses on high places and made priests of people who were not Levites.

32And Jeroboam appointed a feast on the fifteenth day of the eighth month, like the feast kept in Judah, and he offered sacrifices upon the altar. So he did in Bethel, sacrificing to the calves he had made. And he placed in Bethel the priests of the high places he had made.

33So he offered upon the altar he had made in Bethel on the fifteenth day of the eighth month, a date which he chose individually; and he appointed a feast for the Israelites and he went up to the altar to burn incense [in defiance of God's law.]

13 AND BEHOLD, there came a man of God out of Judah by the word of the Lord to Bethel. Jeroboam stood by the altar to burn incense.

2The man cried against the altar by the word of the Lord, O altar, altar, thus says the Lord: Behold, a son shall be born to the house of David, Josiah by name; and on you shall he offer the priests of the high places who burn incense on you, and men's bones shall be burned on you.

3And he gave a sign the same day, saying, This is the sign which the Lord has spoken: Behold, the altar shall be split and the ashes upon it shall be poured out. [Fulfilled in II Kings 23:15, 16.]

4When King Jeroboam heard the words the man of God cried against the altar in Bethel, he thrust out his hand, saying, Lay hold on him! And his hand which he put forth against him dried up, so that he could not draw it to him again.

5The altar also was split and the ashes poured out from the altar according to the sign which the man of God had given by the word of the Lord.

6And the king said to the man of God, Entreat now the favor of the Lord your God and pray for me, that my hand may be restored to me. And the man of God entreated the Lord, and the king's hand was restored and became as it was before.

7And the king said to the man of God, Come home with me and refresh yourself, and I will give you a reward.

8And the man of God said to the king, If you give me half your house, I will not go in with you, and I will not eat bread or drink water in this place.

9For I was commanded by the word of the Lord, You shall eat no bread or drink water or return by the way you came.

10So he went another way and did not return by the way that he came to Bethel.

---

*p*Or, *went up to the altar*   *q*Or, *to sacrifice*   *r*Heb. *to burn*
incense   *s*Or, *to offer*   *t*Heb. *the face of the* LORD

New American Standard

27"If this people go up to offer sacrifices in the house of the LORD at Jerusalem, then the heart of this people will return to their lord, *even* to Rehoboam king of Judah; and they will kill me and return to Rehoboam king of Judah."

28 So the king consulted, and made two golden calves, and he said to them, "It is too much for you to go up to Jerusalem; behold your gods, O Israel, that brought you up from the land of Egypt."

29 He set one in Bethel, and the other he put in Dan. 30 Now this thing became a sin, for the people went *to worship* before the one as far as Dan.

31 And he made houses on high places, and made priests from among all the people who were not of the sons of Levi.

32 Jeroboam instituted a feast in the eighth month on the fifteenth day of the month, like the feast which is in Judah, and he went up to the altar; thus he did in Bethel, sacrificing to the calves which he had made. And he stationed in Bethel the priests of the high places which he had made.

33 Then he went up to the altar which he had made in Bethel on the fifteenth day in the eighth month, even in the month which he had devised in his own heart; and he instituted a feast for the sons of Israel and went up to the altar to burn incense.

Jeroboam Warned, Stricken

13 NOW BEHOLD, there came a man of God from Judah to Bethel by the word of the LORD, while Jeroboam was standing by the altar to burn incense.

2 He cried against the altar by the word of the LORD, and said, "O altar, altar, thus says the LORD, 'Behold, a son shall be born to the house of David, Josiah by name; and on you he shall sacrifice the priests of the high places who burn incense on you, and human bones shall be burned on you.' "

3 Then he gave a sign the same day, saying, "This is the sign which the LORD has spoken, 'Behold, the altar shall be split apart and the ashes which are on it shall be poured out.' "

4 Now when the king heard the saying of the man of God, which he cried against the altar in Bethel, Jeroboam stretched out his hand from the altar, saying, "Seize him." But his hand which he stretched out against him dried up, so that he could not draw it back to himself.

5 The altar also was split apart and the ashes were poured out from the altar, according to the sign which the man of God had given by the word of the LORD.

6 The king said to the man of God, "Please ᵛentreat the LORD your God, and pray for me, that my hand may be restored to me." So the man of God ʷentreated the LORD, and the king's hand was restored to him, and it became as it was before.

7 Then the king said to the man of God, "Come home with me and refresh yourself, and I will give you a reward."

8 But the man of God said to the king, "If you were to give me half your house I would not go with you, nor would I eat bread or drink water in this place.

9"For so it was commanded me by the word of the LORD, saying, 'You shall eat no bread, nor drink water, nor return by the way which you came.' "

10 So he went another way and did not return by the way which he came to Bethel.

New International

likely revert to the house of David. 27If these people go up to offer sacrifices at the temple of the LORD in Jerusalem, they will again give their allegiance to their lord, Rehoboam king of Judah. They will kill me and return to King Rehoboam."

28After seeking advice, the king made two golden calves. He said to the people, "It is too much for you to go up to Jerusalem. Here are your gods, O Israel, who brought you up out of Egypt." 29One he set up in Bethel, and the other in Dan. 30And this thing became a sin; the people went even as far as Dan to worship the one there.

31Jeroboam built shrines on high places and appointed priests from all sorts of people, even though they were not Levites. 32He instituted a festival on the fifteenth day of the eighth month, like the festival held in Judah, and offered sacrifices on the altar. This he did in Bethel, sacrificing to the calves he had made. And at Bethel he also installed priests at the high places he had made. 33On the fifteenth day of the eighth month, a month of his own choosing, he offered sacrifices on the altar he had built at Bethel. So he instituted the festival for the Israelites and went up to the altar to make offerings.

The Man of God From Judah

13 BY THE word of the LORD a man of God came from Judah to Bethel, as Jeroboam was standing by the altar to make an offering. 2He cried out against the altar by the word of the LORD: "O altar, altar! This is what the LORD says: 'A son named Josiah will be born to the house of David. On you he will sacrifice the priests of the high places who now make offerings here, and human bones will be burned on you.' " 3That same day the man of God gave a sign: "This is the sign the LORD has declared: The altar will be split apart and the ashes on it will be poured out."

4When King Jeroboam heard what the man of God cried out against the altar at Bethel, he stretched out his hand from the altar and said, "Seize him!" But the hand he stretched out toward the man shriveled up, so that he could not pull it back. 5Also, the altar was split apart and its ashes poured out according to the sign given by the man of God by the word of the LORD.

6Then the king said to the man of God, "Intercede with the LORD your God and pray for me that my hand may be restored." So the man of God interceded with the LORD, and the king's hand was restored and became as it was before.

7The king said to the man of God, "Come home with me and have something to eat, and I will give you a gift."

8But the man of God answered the king, "Even if you were to give me half your possessions, I would not go with you, nor would I eat bread or drink water here. 9For I was commanded by the word of the LORD: 'You must not eat bread or drink water or return by the way you came.' " 10So he took another road and did not return by the way he had come to Bethel.

ᵛLit *soften the face of*   ʷLit *softened the face of*

King James

11 ¶ Now there dwelt an old prophet in Beth-el; and his [u]sons came and told him all the works that the man of God had done that day in Beth-el: the words which he had spoken unto the king, them they told also to their father.

12And their father said unto them, What way went he? For his sons had seen what way the man of God went, which came from Judah.

13And he said unto his sons, Saddle me the ass. So they saddled him the ass; and he rode thereon,

14And went after the man of God, and found him sitting under an oak: and he said unto him, *Art* thou the man of God that camest from Judah? And he said, I *am.*

15Then he said unto him, Come home with me, and eat bread.

16And he said, I may not return with thee, nor go in with thee: neither will I eat bread nor drink water with thee in this place:

17For [v]it was said to me by the word of the LORD, Thou shalt eat no bread nor drink water there, nor turn again to go by the way that thou camest.

18He said unto him, I *am* a prophet also as thou *art;* and an angel spake unto me by the word of the LORD, saying, Bring him back with thee into thine house, that he may eat bread and drink water. *But* he lied unto him.

19So he went back with him, and did eat bread in his house, and drank water.

20 ¶ And it came to pass, as they sat at the table, that the word of the LORD came unto the prophet that brought him back:

21And he cried unto the man of God that came from Judah, saying, Thus saith the LORD, Forasmuch as thou hast disobeyed the mouth of the LORD, and hast not kept the commandment which the LORD thy God commanded thee,

22But camest back, and hast eaten bread and drunk water in the place, of the which *the* LORD did say to thee, Eat no bread, and drink no water; thy carcase shall not come unto the sepulchre of thy fathers.

23 ¶ And it came to pass, after he had eaten bread, and after he had drunk, that he saddled for him the ass, *to wit,* for the prophet whom he had brought back.

24And when he was gone, a lion met him by the way, and slew him: and his carcase was cast in the way, and the ass stood by it, the lion also stood by the carcase.

25And, behold, men passed by, and saw the carcase cast in the way, and the lion standing by the carcase: and they came and told *it* in the city where the old prophet dwelt.

26And when the prophet that brought him back from the way heard *thereof,* he said, It *is* the man of God, who was disobedient unto the word of the LORD: therefore the LORD hath delivered him unto the lion, which hath [w]torn him, and slain him, according to the word of the LORD, which he spake unto him.

27And he spake to his sons, saying, Saddle me the ass. And they saddled *him.*

28And he went and found his carcase cast in the way, and the ass and the lion standing by the carcase: the lion had not eaten the carcase, nor [w]torn the ass.

29And the prophet took up the carcase of the man of God, and laid it upon the ass, and brought it back: and the old prophet came to the city, to mourn and to bury him.

30And he laid his carcase in his own grave; and they mourned over him, *saying,* Alas, my brother!

31And it came to pass, after he had buried him, that he spake to his sons, saying, When I am dead, then bury me in the sepulchre wherein the man of God *is* buried; lay my bones beside his bones:

32For the saying which he cried by the word of the LORD against the altar in Beth-el, and against all the houses of the high places which *are* in the cities of Samaria, shall surely come to pass.

Amplified

11Now there dwelt an old prophet in Bethel; and his sons came and told him all that the man of God had done that day in Bethel; the words which he had spoken to the king they told also to their father.

12Their father asked them, Which way did he go? For his sons had seen which way the man of God who came from Judah had gone.

13He said to his sons, Saddle the donkey for me. So they saddled the donkey and he rode on it

14And went after the man of God. And he found him sitting under an oak, and he said to him, Are you the man of God who came from Judah? And he said, I am.

15Then he said to him, Come home with me and eat bread.

16He said, I may not return with you or go in with you, neither will I eat bread or drink water with you in this place.

17For I was told by the word of the Lord, You shall not eat bread or drink water there or return by the way that you came.

18He answered, I am a prophet also, as you are. And an angel spoke to me by the word of the Lord, saying, Bring him back with you to your house, that he may eat bread and drink water. But he lied to him.

19So the man from Judah went back with him and ate and drank water in his house.

20And as they sat at the table, the word of the Lord came to the prophet who brought him back.

21And he cried to the man of God who came from Judah, Thus says the Lord: Because you have disobeyed the word of the Lord and have not kept the command which the Lord your God commanded you,

22But have come back and have eaten bread and drunk water in the place of which the Lord said to you, Eat no bread and drink no water—your corpse shall not come to the tomb of your fathers.

23And after the prophet of the house had eaten bread and drunk, he saddled the donkey for the man he had brought back.

24And when he had gone, a lion met him by the road and slew him, and his corpse was cast in the way, and the donkey stood by it; the lion also stood by the corpse.

25And behold, men passed by and saw the corpse thrown in the road, and the lion standing by the corpse, and they came and told it in the city where the old prophet dwelt.

26When the prophet who brought him back from the way heard of it, he said, It is the man of God who was disobedient to the word of the Lord; therefore the Lord has given him to the lion, which has torn him and slain him, according to the word of the Lord which He spoke to him.

27And he said to his sons, Saddle the donkey for me. And they saddled it.

28And he went and found the corpse thrown in the road, and the donkey and the lion stood by the body; the lion had not eaten the corpse or torn the donkey.

29The prophet took up the corpse of the man of God and laid it upon the donkey and brought it back, and the old prophet came into the city to mourn and to bury him.

30And he laid the body in his own grave, and they mourned over him, saying, Alas, my brother!

31After he had buried him, he said to his sons, When I am dead, bury me in the grave in which the man of God is buried; lay my bones beside his bones.

32For the saying which he cried by the word of the Lord against the altar in Bethel and against all the houses of the high places which are in the cities of Samaria shall surely come to pass.

[u]Heb. *son*   [v]Heb. *a word* was   [w]Heb. *broken*

New American Standard

The Disobedient Prophet

11 ¶ Now an old prophet was living in Bethel; and his sons came and told him all the deeds which the man of God had done that day in Bethel; the words which he had spoken to the king, these also they related to their father.

12 Their father said to them, "Which way did he go?" Now his sons had seen the way which the man of God who came from Judah had gone.

13 Then he said to his sons, "Saddle the donkey for me." So they saddled the donkey for him and he rode away on it.

14 So he went after the man of God and found him sitting under an oak; and he said to him, "Are you the man of God who came from Judah?" And he said, "I am."

15 Then he said to him, "Come home with me and eat bread."

16 He said, "I cannot return with you, nor go with you, nor will I eat bread or drink water with you in this place.

17 "For a command *came* to me by the word of the LORD, 'You shall eat no bread, nor drink water there; do not return by going the way which you came.' "

18 He said to him, "I also am a prophet like you, and an angel spoke to me by the word of the LORD, saying, 'Bring him back with you to your house, that he may eat bread and drink water.' " *But* he lied to him.

19 So he went back with him, and ate bread in his house and drank water.

20 ¶ Now it came about, as they were sitting down at the table, that the word of the LORD came to the prophet who had brought him back;

21 and he cried to the man of God who came from Judah, saying, "Thus says the LORD, 'Because you have disobeyed the command of the LORD, and have not observed the commandment which the LORD your God commanded you,

22 but have returned and eaten bread and drunk water in the place of which He said to you, "Eat no bread and drink no water"; your body shall not come to the grave of your fathers.' "

23 It came about after he had eaten bread and after he had drunk, that he saddled the donkey for him, for the prophet whom he had brought back.

24 Now when he had gone, a lion met him on the way and killed him, and his body was thrown on the road, with the donkey standing beside it; the lion also was standing beside the body.

25 And behold, men passed by and saw the body thrown on the road, and the lion standing beside the body; so they came and told *it* in the city where the old prophet lived.

26 ¶ Now when the prophet who brought him back from the way heard *it*, he said, "It is the man of God, who disobeyed the command of the LORD; therefore the LORD has given him to the lion, which has torn him and killed him, according to the word of the LORD which He spoke to him."

27 Then he spoke to his sons, saying, "Saddle the donkey for me." And they saddled *it*.

28 He went and found his body thrown on the road with the donkey and the lion standing beside the body; the lion had not eaten the body nor torn the donkey.

29 So the prophet took up the body of the man of God and laid it on the donkey and brought it back, and he came to the city of the old prophet to mourn and to bury him.

30 He laid his body in his own grave, and they mourned over him, *saying,* "Alas, my brother!"

31 After he had buried him, he spoke to his sons, saying, "When I die, bury me in the grave in which the man of God is buried; lay my bones beside his bones.

32 "For the thing shall surely come to pass which he cried by the word of the LORD against the altar in Bethel and against all the houses of the high places which are in the cities of Samaria."

New International

11 Now there was a certain old prophet living in Bethel, whose sons came and told him all that the man of God had done there that day. They also told their father what he had said to the king. 12 Their father asked them, "Which way did he go?" And his sons showed him which road the man of God from Judah had taken. 13 So he said to his sons, "Saddle the donkey for me." And when they had saddled the donkey for him, he mounted it 14 and rode after the man of God. He found him sitting under an oak tree and asked, "Are you the man of God who came from Judah?"

"I am," he replied.

15 So the prophet said to him, "Come home with me and eat."

16 The man of God said, "I cannot turn back and go with you, nor can I eat bread or drink water with you in this place. 17 I have been told by the word of the LORD: 'You must not eat bread or drink water there or return by the way you came.' "

18 The old prophet answered, "I too am a prophet, as you are. And an angel said to me by the word of the LORD: 'Bring him back with you to your house so that he may eat bread and drink water.' " (But he was lying to him.) 19 So the man of God returned with him and ate and drank in his house.

20 While they were sitting at the table, the word of the LORD came to the old prophet who had brought him back. 21 He cried out to the man of God who had come from Judah, "This is what the LORD says: 'You have defied the word of the LORD and have not kept the command the LORD your God gave you. 22 You came back and ate bread and drank water in the place where he told you not to eat or drink. Therefore your body will not be buried in the tomb of your fathers.' "

23 When the man of God had finished eating and drinking, the prophet who had brought him back saddled his donkey for him. 24 As he went on his way, a lion met him on the road and killed him, and his body was thrown down on the road, with both the donkey and the lion standing beside it. 25 Some people who passed by saw the body thrown down there, with the lion standing beside the body, and they went and reported it in the city where the old prophet lived.

26 When the prophet who had brought him back from his journey heard of it, he said, "It is the man of God who defied the word of the LORD. The LORD has given him over to the lion, which has mauled him and killed him, as the word of the LORD had warned him."

27 The prophet said to his sons, "Saddle the donkey for me," and they did so. 28 Then he went out and found the body thrown down on the road, with the donkey and the lion standing beside it. The lion had neither eaten the body nor mauled the donkey. 29 So the prophet picked up the body of the man of God, laid it on the donkey, and brought it back to his own city to mourn for him and bury him. 30 Then he laid the body in his own tomb, and they mourned over him and said, "Oh, my brother!"

31 After burying him, he said to his sons, "When I die, bury me in the grave where the man of God is buried; lay my bones beside his bones. 32 For the message he declared by the word of the LORD against the altar in Bethel and against all the shrines on the high places in the towns of Samaria will certainly come true."

King James

33 ¶ After this thing Jeroboam returned not from his evil way, but ˣmade again of the lowest of the people priests of the high places: whosoever would, he ʸconsecrated him, and he became *one* of the priests of the high places.

34And this thing became sin unto the house of Jeroboam, even to cut *it* off, and to destroy *it* from off the face of the earth.

The prophecy against Jeroboam

14 AT THAT time Abijah the son of Jeroboam fell sick.

2And Jeroboam said to his wife, Arise, I pray thee, and disguise thyself, that thou be not known to be the wife of Jeroboam; and get thee to Shiloh: behold, there *is* Ahijah the prophet, which told me that I *should be* king over this people.

3And take ᶻwith thee ten loaves, and ᵃcracknels, and a ᵇcruse of honey, and go to him: he shall tell thee what shall become of the child.

4And Jeroboam's wife did so, and arose, and went to Shiloh, and came to the house of Ahijah. But Ahijah could not see; for his eyes ᶜwere set by reason of his age.

5 ¶ And the LORD said unto Ahijah, Behold, the wife of Jeroboam cometh to ask a thing of thee for her son; for he *is* sick: thus and thus shalt thou say unto her: for it shall be, when she cometh in, that she shall feign herself *to be* another *woman*.

6And it was *so,* when Ahijah heard the sound of her feet, as she came in at the door, that he said, Come in, thou wife of Jeroboam; why feignest thou thyself *to be* another? for I *am* sent to thee *with* ᵈheavy *tidings*.

7Go, tell Jeroboam, Thus saith the LORD God of Israel, Forasmuch as I exalted thee from among the people, and made thee prince over my people Israel,

8And rent the kingdom away from the house of David, and gave it thee: and *yet* thou hast not been as my servant David, who kept my commandments, and who followed me with all his heart, to do *that* only *which was* right in mine eyes;

9But hast done evil above all that were before thee: for thou hast gone and made thee other gods, and molten images, to provoke me to anger, and hast cast me behind thy back:

10Therefore, behold, I will bring evil upon the house of Jeroboam, and will cut off from Jeroboam him that pisseth against the wall, *and* him that is shut up and left in Israel, and will take away the remnant of the house of Jeroboam, as a man taketh away dung, till it be all gone.

11Him that dieth of Jeroboam in the city shall the dogs eat; and him that dieth in the field shall the fowls of the air eat: for the LORD hath spoken *it*.

12Arise thou therefore, get thee to thine own house: *and* when thy feet enter into the city, the child shall die.

13And all Israel shall mourn for him, and bury him: for he only of Jeroboam shall come to the grave, because in him there is found *some* good thing toward the LORD God of Israel in the house of Jeroboam.

Amplified

33After this thing, Jeroboam turned not from his evil way, but made priests for the high places again from among all the people. Whoever would, he consecrated, that there might be priests for the high places.

34And this thing became the sin of the dynasty of Jeroboam that caused it to be abolished and destroyed from the face of the earth.

14 THEN ABIJAH [the little] son of Jeroboam became sick.

2And Jeroboam said to his wife, Arise, I pray you, and disguise yourself, that you may not be recognized as Jeroboam's wife, and go to Shiloh. Behold, Ahijah the prophet is there, who told me that I should be king over this people.

3Take ten loaves, some cakes, and a bottle of honey, and go to him. He will tell you what shall happen to the child.

4Jeroboam's wife did so. She arose and went [twenty miles] to Shiloh and came to the house of Ahijah. Ahijah could not see, for his eyes were dim because of his age.

5And the Lord said to Ahijah, Behold, the ᵖwife of Jeroboam is coming to ask you concerning her son, for he is sick. Thus and thus shall you say to her. When she came, she pretended to be another woman.

6But when Ahijah heard the sound of her feet as she came in at the door, he said, Come in, wife of Jeroboam. Why do you pretend to be another? For I am charged with heavy news for you.

7Go, tell Jeroboam, Thus says the Lord, the God of Israel: Because I exalted you from among the people and made you leader over My people Israel

8And rent the kingdom away from the house of David and gave it to you—and yet you have not been as My servant David, who kept My commandments and followed Me with all his heart, to do only what was right in My eyes,

9But have done evil above all who were before you; for you have made yourself other gods, molten images, to provoke Me to anger and have cast Me behind your back—

10Therefore behold, I will bring evil upon the house of Jeroboam and will cut off from [him] every male, both bond and free, in Israel, and will utterly sweep away the house of Jeroboam as a man sweeps away dung, till it is all gone.

11Anyone belonging to Jeroboam who dies in the city the dogs shall eat, and any who dies in the field the birds of the heavens shall eat. For the Lord has spoken it.

12Arise therefore [Ano, Jeroboam's wife], get to your own house. When your feet enter the city, the child shall die.

13And all Israel shall mourn for him and bury him; for he only of Jeroboam's family shall come to the grave, because in him there is found something good *and* pleasing to the Lord, the God of Israel, in the house of Jeroboam.

ᵖ The Hebrew text gives no particulars about the background of Jeroboam's wife, but there is an insertion in *The Septuagint* (Greek translation of the Old Testament), found in the Vatican manuscript after I Kings 12:24, in which we find further information about her. When Jeroboam, then taskmaster over the forced labor of the house of Joseph, fled to Egypt to escape death at the hands of King Solomon, he went to King Shishak of Egypt and was with him until the death of Solomon. Jeroboam asked permission of King Shishak to return to his own land, and the king told him, "Ask of me a request, and I will give it to you." And he gave to Jeroboam Ano, the elder sister of his own wife Thekemina (Tahpenes), to be his wife. She was great among the daughters of the king, and bore to Jeroboam Abias (Abijah) his son [who in this chapter lies dying in the palace of Jeroboam while Queen Ano, his mother, is about to hear what the old prophet has been required by God to tell her] (Charles Ellicott, *A Bible Commentary*).

ˣHeb. *returned and made thine hand*   ᵃOr, *cakes*   ᵇOr, *bottle*   ᶜHeb. *stood for his hoariness*   ʸHeb. *filled his hand*   ᶻHeb. *in*   ᵈHeb. *hard*

New American Standard

33 ¶ After this event Jeroboam did not return from his evil way, but again he made priests of the high places from among all the people; any who would, he ordained, to be priests of the high places.

34 This event became sin to the house of Jeroboam, even to blot *it* out and destroy *it* from off the face of the earth.

Ahijah Prophesies against the King

14 AT THAT time Abijah the son of Jeroboam became sick.

2 Jeroboam said to his wife, "Arise now, and disguise yourself so that they will not know that you are the wife of Jeroboam, and go to Shiloh; behold, Ahijah the prophet is there, who spoke concerning me *that I would be* king over this people.

3 "Take ten loaves with you, *some* cakes and a jar of honey, and go to him. He will tell you what will happen to the boy."

4 ¶ Jeroboam's wife did so, and arose and went to Shiloh, and came to the house of Ahijah. Now Ahijah could not see, for his eyes were dim because of his age.

5 Now the LORD had said to Ahijah, "Behold, the wife of Jeroboam is coming to inquire of you concerning her son, for he is sick. You shall say thus and thus to her, for it will be when she arrives that she will pretend to be another woman."

6 ¶ When Ahijah heard the sound of her feet coming in the doorway, he said, "Come in, wife of Jeroboam, why do you pretend to be another woman? For I am sent to you with a harsh *message*.

7 "Go, say to Jeroboam, 'Thus says the LORD God of Israel, "Because I exalted you from among the people and made you leader over My people Israel,

8 and tore the kingdom away from the house of David and gave it to you—yet you have not been like My servant David, who kept My commandments and who followed Me with all his heart, to do only that which was right in My sight;

9 you also have done more evil than all who were before you, and have gone and made for yourself other gods and molten images to provoke Me to anger, and have cast Me behind your back—

10 therefore behold, I am bringing calamity on the house of Jeroboam, and will cut off from Jeroboam every male person, both bond and free in Israel, and I will make a clean sweep of the house of Jeroboam, as one sweeps away dung until it is all gone.

11 "Anyone belonging to Jeroboam who dies in the city the dogs will eat. And he who dies in the field the birds of the heavens will eat; for the LORD has spoken *it*." '

12 "Now you, arise, go to your house. When your feet enter the city the child will die.

13 "All Israel shall mourn for him and bury him, for he alone of Jeroboam's *family* will come to the grave, because in him something good was found toward the LORD God of Israel in the house of Jeroboam.

New International

33 Even after this, Jeroboam did not change his evil ways, but once more appointed priests for the high places from all sorts of people. Anyone who wanted to become a priest he consecrated for the high places. 34 This was the sin of the house of Jeroboam that led to its downfall and to its destruction from the face of the earth.

Ahijah's Prophecy Against Jeroboam

14 AT THAT time Abijah son of Jeroboam became ill, 2 and Jeroboam said to his wife, "Go, disguise yourself, so you won't be recognized as the wife of Jeroboam. Then go to Shiloh. Ahijah the prophet is there—the one who told me I would be king over this people. 3 Take ten loaves of bread with you, some cakes and a jar of honey, and go to him. He will tell you what will happen to the boy." 4 So Jeroboam's wife did what he said and went to Ahijah's house in Shiloh.

Now Ahijah could not see; his sight was gone because of his age. 5 But the LORD had told Ahijah, "Jeroboam's wife is coming to ask you about her son, for he is ill, and you are to give her such and such an answer. When she arrives, she will pretend to be someone else."

6 So when Ahijah heard the sound of her footsteps at the door, he said, "Come in, wife of Jeroboam. Why this pretense? I have been sent to you with bad news. 7 Go, tell Jeroboam that this is what the LORD, the God of Israel, says: 'I raised you up from among the people and made you a leader over my people Israel. 8 I tore the kingdom away from the house of David and gave it to you, but you have not been like my servant David, who kept my commands and followed me with all his heart, doing only what was right in my eyes. 9 You have done more evil than all who lived before you. You have made for yourself other gods, idols made of metal; you have provoked me to anger and thrust me behind your back.

10 " 'Because of this, I am going to bring disaster on the house of Jeroboam. I will cut off from Jeroboam every last male in Israel—slave or free. I will burn up the house of Jeroboam as one burns dung, until it is all gone. 11 Dogs will eat those belonging to Jeroboam who die in the city, and the birds of the air will feed on those who die in the country. The LORD has spoken!'

12 "As for you, go back home. When you set foot in your city, the boy will die. 13 All Israel will mourn for him and bury him. He is the only one belonging to Jeroboam who will be buried, because he is the only one in the house of Jeroboam in whom the LORD, the God of Israel, has found anything good.

King James

14Moreover the LORD shall raise him up a king over Israel, who shall cut off the house of Jeroboam that day: but what? even now.

15For the LORD shall smite Israel, as a reed is shaken in the water, and he shall root up Israel out of this good land, which he gave to their fathers, and shall scatter them beyond the river, because they have made their groves, provoking the LORD to anger.

16And he shall give Israel up because of the sins of Jeroboam, who did sin, and who made Israel to sin.

17 ¶ And Jeroboam's wife arose, and departed, and came to Tirzah: and when she came to the threshold of the door, the child died;

18And they buried him; and all Israel mourned for him, according to the word of the LORD, which he spake by the hand of his servant Ahijah the prophet.

19And the rest of the acts of Jeroboam, how he warred, and how he reigned, behold, they *are* written in the book of the chronicles of the kings of Israel.

20And the days which Jeroboam reigned *were* two and twenty years: and he *e*slept with his fathers, and Nadab his son reigned in his stead.

Rehoboam, king of Judah

21 ¶ And Rehoboam the son of Solomon reigned in Judah. Rehoboam *was* forty and one years old when he began to reign, and he reigned seventeen years in Jerusalem, the city which the LORD did choose out of all the tribes of Israel, to put his name there. And his mother's name *was* Naamah an Ammonitess.

22And Judah did evil in the sight of the LORD, and they provoked him to jealousy with their sins which they had committed, above all that their fathers had done.

23For they also built them high places, and *f*images, and groves, on every high hill, and under every green tree.

24And there were also sodomites in the land: *and* they did according to all the abominations of the nations which the LORD cast out before the children of Israel.

25 ¶ And it came to pass in the fifth year of king Rehoboam, *that* Shishak king of Egypt came up against Jerusalem:

26And he took away the treasures of the house of the LORD, and the treasures of the king's house; he even took away all: and he took away all the shields of gold which Solomon had made.

27And king Rehoboam made in their stead brasen shields, and committed *them* unto the hands of the chief of the *g*guard, which kept the door of the king's house.

28And it was *so*, when the king went into the house of the LORD, that the guard bare them, and brought them back into the guard chamber.

29 ¶ Now the rest of the acts of Rehoboam, and all that he did, *are* they not written in the book of the chronicles of the kings of Judah?

30And there was war between Rehoboam and Jeroboam all *their* days.

31And Rehoboam slept with his fathers, and was buried with his fathers in the city of David. And his mother's name *was* Naamah an Ammonitess. And Abijam his son reigned in his stead.

Amplified

14Moreover, the Lord will raise up for Himself a king over Israel who shall cut off the house of Jeroboam this day. From now on

15The Lord will smite Israel, as a reed is shaken in the water; and He will root up Israel out of this good land which He gave to their fathers, and will scatter them beyond the [Euphrates] River, because they have made their Asherim [idolatrous symbols of the goddess Asherah], provoking the Lord to anger.

16He will give Israel up because of the sins of Jeroboam which he has sinned and made Israel to sin.

17So Jeroboam's wife departed and came to Tirzah. When she came to the threshold of the house, the child died.

18And all Israel buried him and mourned for him, according to the word of the Lord spoken by His servant Ahijah the prophet.

19The rest of the acts of Jeroboam, how he warred and how he reigned, behold, they are written in the Book of the Chronicles of the Kings of Israel.

20Jeroboam reigned for twenty-two years, and he slept with his fathers; and Nadab his son reigned in his stead.

21And Rehoboam son of Solomon reigned in Judah. Rehoboam was forty-one years old when he began to reign, and he reigned seventeen years in Jerusalem, the city the Lord chose out of all the tribes of Israel to put His Name [and the pledge of His presence] there. His mother's name was Naamah the Ammonitess.

22And Judah did evil in the sight of the Lord, Whom they provoked to jealousy with the sins they committed, above all that their fathers had done.

23For they also built themselves [idolatrous] high places, pillars, and Asherim [idolatrous symbols of the goddess Asherah] on every high hill and under every green tree.

24There were also sodomites (male cult prostitutes) in the land. They did all the abominations of the nations whom the Lord cast out before the Israelites.

25In the fifth year of King Rehoboam, Shishak king of Egypt [Jeroboam's brother-in-law] came up against Jerusalem.

26He took away the treasures of the house of the Lord and of the king's house; he took away all, including all the shields of gold which Solomon had made.

27King Rehoboam made in their stead bronze shields and committed them to the hands of the captains of the guard who kept the door of the king's house.

28And as often as the king went into the house of the Lord, the guards bore them and brought them back into the guardroom.

29The rest of the acts of Rehoboam, and all that he did, are they not written in the Book of the Chronicles of the Kings of Judah?

30There was war between Rehoboam and Jeroboam continually.

31Rehoboam slept with his fathers and was buried with them in the City of David. His mother's name was Naamah the Ammonitess. Abijam (Abijah) his son reigned in his stead.

---

e Heb. *lay down*   *f* Or, *standing images,* or, *statues*   *g* Heb. *runners*

New American Standard

14"Moreover, the LORD will raise up for Himself a king over Israel who will cut off the house of Jeroboam this day and from now on.

15 ¶ "For the LORD will strike Israel, as a reed is shaken in the water; and He will uproot Israel from this good land which He gave to their fathers, and will scatter them beyond the *Euphrates* River, because they have made their *x*Asherim, provoking the LORD to anger.

16"He will give up Israel on account of the sins of Jeroboam, which he committed and with which he made Israel to sin."

17 ¶ Then Jeroboam's wife arose and departed and came to Tirzah. As she was entering the threshold of the house, the child died.

18 All Israel buried him and mourned for him, according to the word of the LORD which He spoke through His servant Ahijah the prophet.

19 ¶ Now the rest of the acts of Jeroboam, how he made war and how he reigned, behold, they are written in the Book of the Chronicles of the Kings of Israel.

20 The time that Jeroboam reigned *was* twenty-two years; and he slept with his fathers, and Nadab his son reigned in his place.

Rehoboam Misleads Judah

21 ¶ Now Rehoboam the son of Solomon reigned in Judah. Rehoboam was forty-one years old when he became king, and he reigned seventeen years in Jerusalem, the city which the LORD had chosen from all the tribes of Israel to put His name there. And his mother's name was Naamah the Ammonitess.

22 Judah did evil in the sight of the LORD, and they provoked Him to jealousy more than all that their fathers had done, with the sins which they committed.

23 For they also built for themselves high places and *sacred* pillars and Asherim on every high hill and beneath every luxuriant tree.

24 There were also male cult prostitutes in the land. They did according to all the abominations of the nations which the LORD dispossessed before the sons of Israel.

25 ¶ Now it happened in the fifth year of King Rehoboam, that Shishak the king of Egypt came up against Jerusalem.

26 He took away the treasures of the house of the LORD and the treasures of the king's house, and he took everything, even taking all the shields of gold which Solomon had made.

27 So King Rehoboam made shields of bronze in their place, and committed them to the care of the commanders of the *y*guard who guarded the doorway of the king's house.

28 Then it happened as often as the king entered the house of the LORD, that the *z*guards would carry them and would bring them back into the guards' room.

29 ¶ Now the rest of the acts of Rehoboam and all that he did, are they not written in the Book of the Chronicles of the Kings of Judah?

30 There was war between Rehoboam and Jeroboam continually.

31 And Rehoboam slept with his fathers and was buried with his fathers in the city of David; and his mother's name was Naamah the Ammonitess. And Abijam his son became king in his place.

New International

14"The LORD will raise up for himself a king over Israel who will cut off the family of Jeroboam. This is the day! What? Yes, even now.*d* 15And the LORD will strike Israel, so that it will be like a reed swaying in the water. He will uproot Israel from this good land that he gave to their forefathers and scatter them beyond the River,*e* because they provoked the LORD to anger by making Asherah poles.*f* 16And he will give up Israel because of the sins Jeroboam has committed and has caused Israel to commit."

17Then Jeroboam's wife got up and left and went to Tirzah. As soon as she stepped over the threshold of the house, the boy died. 18They buried him, and all Israel mourned for him, as the LORD had said through his servant the prophet Ahijah.

19The other events of Jeroboam's reign, his wars and how he ruled, are written in the book of the annals of the kings of Israel. 20He reigned for twenty-two years and then rested with his fathers. And Nadab his son succeeded him as king.

Rehoboam King of Judah

21Rehoboam son of Solomon was king in Judah. He was forty-one years old when he became king, and he reigned seventeen years in Jerusalem, the city the LORD had chosen out of all the tribes of Israel in which to put his Name. His mother's name was Naamah; she was an Ammonite.

22Judah did evil in the eyes of the LORD. By the sins they committed they stirred up his jealous anger more than their fathers had done. 23They also set up for themselves high places, sacred stones and Asherah poles on every high hill and under every spreading tree. 24There were even male shrine prostitutes in the land; the people engaged in all the detestable practices of the nations the LORD had driven out before the Israelites.

25In the fifth year of King Rehoboam, Shishak king of Egypt attacked Jerusalem. 26He carried off the treasures of the temple of the LORD and the treasures of the royal palace. He took everything, including all the gold shields Solomon had made. 27So King Rehoboam made bronze shields to replace them and assigned these to the commanders of the guard on duty at the entrance to the royal palace. 28Whenever the king went to the LORD's temple, the guards bore the shields, and afterward they returned them to the guardroom.

29As for the other events of Rehoboam's reign, and all he did, are they not written in the book of the annals of the kings of Judah? 30There was continual warfare between Rehoboam and Jeroboam. 31And Rehoboam rested with his fathers and was buried with them in the City of David. His mother's name was Naamah; she was an Ammonite. And Abijah*g* his son succeeded him as king.

---

d 14 The meaning of the Hebrew for this sentence is uncertain.
e 15 That is, the Euphrates   *f 15* That is, symbols of the goddess Asherah; here and elsewhere in 1 Kings   *g 31* Some Hebrew manuscripts and Septuagint (see also 2 Chron. 12:16); most Hebrew manuscripts *Abijam*

---

*x*I.e. wooden symbols of a female deity   *y*Lit *runner*   *z*Lit *runners*

King James

Abijam, king of Judah

15 NOW IN the eighteenth year of king Jeroboam the son of Nebat reigned Abijam over Judah.

²Three years reigned he in Jerusalem. And his mother's name *was* Maachah, the daughter of Abishalom.

³And he walked in all the sins of his father, which he had done before him: and his heart was not perfect with the LORD his God, as the heart of David his father.

⁴Nevertheless for David's sake did the LORD his God give him a ʰlamp in Jerusalem, to set up his son after him, and to establish Jerusalem:

⁵Because David did *that which was* right in the eyes of the LORD, and turned not aside from any *thing* that he commanded him all the days of his life, save only in the matter of Uriah the Hittite.

⁶And there was war between Rehoboam and Jeroboam all the days of his life.

⁷Now the rest of the acts of Abijam, and all that he did, *are* they not written in the book of the chronicles of the kings of Judah? And there was war between Abijam and Jeroboam.

⁸And Abijam slept with his fathers; and they buried him in the city of David: and Asa his son reigned in his stead.

Asa, king of Judah

⁹ ¶ And in the twentieth year of Jeroboam king of Israel reigned Asa over Judah.

¹⁰And forty and one years reigned he in Jerusalem. And his ⁱmother's name *was* Maachah, the daughter of Abishalom.

¹¹And Asa did *that which was* right in the eyes of the LORD, as *did* David his father.

¹²And he took away the sodomites out of the land, and removed all the idols that his fathers had made.

¹³And also Maachah his mother, even her he removed from *being* queen, because she had made an idol in a grove; and Asa ʲdestroyed her idol, and burnt *it* by the brook Kidron.

¹⁴But the high places were not removed: nevertheless Asa's heart was perfect with the LORD all his days.

¹⁵And he brought in the ᵏthings which his father had dedicated, and the things which himself had dedicated, into the house of the LORD, silver, and gold, and vessels.

¹⁶ ¶ And there was war between Asa and Baasha king of Israel all their days.

¹⁷And Baasha king of Israel went up against Judah, and built Ramah, that he might not suffer any to go out or come in to Asa king of Judah.

¹⁸Then Asa took all the silver and the gold *that were* left in the treasures of the house of the LORD, and the treasures of the king's house, and delivered them into the hand of his servants: and king Asa sent them to Ben-hadad, the son of Tabrimon, the son of Hezion, king of Syria, that dwelt at Damascus, saying,

¹⁹*There is* a league between me and thee, *and* between my father and thy father: behold, I have sent unto thee a present of silver and gold; come and break thy league with Baasha king of Israel, that he may ˡdepart from me.

²⁰So Ben-hadad hearkened unto king Asa, and sent the captains of the hosts which he had against the cities of Israel, and smote Ijon, and Dan, and Abel-beth-maachah, and all Cinneroth, with all the land of Naphtali.

²¹And it came to pass, when Baasha heard *thereof,* that he left off building of Ramah, and dwelt in Tirzah.

²²Then king Asa made a proclamation throughout all Judah; none *was* ᵐexempted: and they took away the stones of Ramah, and the timber thereof, wherewith Baasha had builded; and king Asa built with them Geba of Benjamin, and Mizpah.

Amplified

15 IN THE eighteenth year of King Jeroboam son of Nebat, Abijam began to reign over Judah.

²He reigned three years in Jerusalem. His mother was Maacah (Micaiah) daughter [granddaughter] of Abishalom (Absalom).

³He walked in all the sins of his father [Rehoboam] before him; and his heart was not blameless with the Lord his God, as the heart of David his father [forefather].

⁴Nevertheless, for David's sake the Lord his God gave him a lamp in Jerusalem, setting up his son after him and establishing Jerusalem,

⁵Because David did what was right in the eyes of the Lord and turned not aside from anything that He commanded him all the days of his life, except in the matter of Uriah the Hittite.

⁶There was war between [Abijam's father] Rehoboam and Jeroboam all the days of [Rehoboam's] life.

⁷The rest of the acts of Abijam, and all that he did, are they not written in the Book of the Chronicles of the Kings of Judah? And there was war between Abijam and Jeroboam.

⁸Abijam slept with his fathers and they buried him in the City of David. Asa his son reigned in his stead.

⁹In the twentieth year of Jeroboam king of Israel, Asa began to reign over Judah.

¹⁰Forty-one years he reigned in Jerusalem. His mother was [also named] Maacah (Micaiah) daughter of Abishalom (Absalom). [I Kings 15:2.]

¹¹And Asa did right in the eyes of the Lord, as did David his father [forefather].

¹²He put away the sodomites (male cult prostitutes) out of the land and removed all the idols that his fathers [Solomon, Rehoboam, and Abijam] had made *or* promoted. [I Kings 11:5–11; 14:22.]

¹³Also Maacah his mother he removed from being queen mother, because she had an image made for [the goddess] Asherah. Asa destroyed her image, burning it by the brook Kidron.

¹⁴But the high places were not removed. Yet Asa's heart was blameless with the Lord all his days.

¹⁵He brought the things which his father had dedicated and the things which he himself had dedicated into the house of the Lord—silver, gold, and vessels.

¹⁶There was war between Asa and Baasha king of Israel all their days.

¹⁷Baasha king of Israel went up against Judah and built up Ramah, that he might allow no one to go out or come in to Asa king of Judah.

¹⁸Then Asa took all the silver and gold left in the treasuries of the house of the Lord and of the king's house and delivered them into the hands of his servants. And King Asa sent them to Ben-hadad son of Tabrimmon, the son of Hezion, king of Syria, who dwelt at Damascus, saying,

¹⁹Let there be a league between me and you, as was between my father and your father. Behold, I am sending you a present of silver and gold; go, break your league with Baasha king of Israel, that he may withdraw from me.

²⁰So Ben-hadad hearkened to king Asa and sent the commanders of his armies against the cities of Israel, and smote Ijon, Dan, Abel-beth-maacah, and all Chinneroth, with all the land of Naphtali.

²¹When Baasha heard of it, he quit building up Ramah and dwelt in Tirzah.

²²Then King Asa made a proclamation to all Judah—none was exempted. They carried away the stones of Ramah and its timber with which Baasha had been building. And King Asa built up with them Geba of Benjamin, and also Mizpah.

ʰ Or, candle   ⁱ i.e. grandmother's; see ver. 2   ʲ Heb. cut off
ᵏ Heb. holy   ˡ Heb. go up   ᵐ Heb. free

New American Standard

Abijam Reigns over Judah

15 NOW IN the eighteenth year of King Jeroboam, the son of Nebat, Abijam became king over Judah. ² He reigned three years in Jerusalem; and his mother's name was Maacah the daughter of Abishalom. ³ He walked in all the sins of his father which he had committed before him; and his heart was not wholly devoted to the LORD his God, like the heart of his father David. ⁴ But for David's sake the LORD his God gave him a lamp in Jerusalem, to raise up his son after him and to establish Jerusalem; ⁵ because David did what was right in the sight of the LORD, and had not turned aside from anything that He commanded him all the days of his life, except in the case of Uriah the Hittite. ⁶ There was war between Rehoboam and Jeroboam all the days of his life. ⁷ ¶ Now the rest of the acts of Abijam and all that he did, are they not written in the Book of the Chronicles of the Kings of Judah? And there was war between Abijam and Jeroboam.

Asa Succeeds Abijam

⁸ And Abijam slept with his fathers and they buried him in the city of David; and Asa his son became king in his place. ⁹ ¶ So in the twentieth year of Jeroboam the king of Israel, Asa began to reign as king of Judah. ¹⁰ He reigned forty-one years in Jerusalem; and his mother's name was Maacah the daughter of Abishalom. ¹¹ Asa did what was right in the sight of the LORD, like David his father. ¹² He also put away the male cult prostitutes from the land and removed all the idols which his fathers had made. ¹³ He also removed Maacah his mother from *being* queen mother, because she had made a horrid image as an Asherah; and Asa cut down her horrid image and burned *it* at the brook Kidron. ¹⁴ But the high places were not taken away; nevertheless the heart of Asa was wholly devoted to the LORD all his days. ¹⁵ He brought into the house of the LORD the dedicated things of his father and his own dedicated things: silver and gold and utensils. ¹⁶ ¶ Now there was war between Asa and Baasha king of Israel all their days. ¹⁷ Baasha king of Israel went up against Judah and fortified Ramah in order to prevent *anyone* from going out or coming in to Asa king of Judah. ¹⁸ Then Asa took all the silver and the gold which were left in the treasuries of the house of the LORD and the treasuries of the king's house, and delivered them into the hand of his servants. And King Asa sent them to Ben-hadad the son of Tabrimmon, the son of Hezion, king of Aram, who lived in Damascus, saying, ¹⁹"*Let there be* a treaty between you and me, *as* between my father and your father. Behold, I have sent you a present of silver and gold; go, break your treaty with Baasha king of Israel so that he will withdraw from me." ²⁰ So Ben-hadad listened to King Asa and sent the commanders of his armies against the cities of Israel, and conquered Ijon, Dan, Abel-beth-maacah and all Chinneroth, besides all the land of Naphtali. ²¹ When Baasha heard *of it,* he ceased fortifying Ramah and remained in Tirzah. ²² Then King Asa made a proclamation to all Judah—none was exempt—and they carried away the stones of Ramah and its timber with which Baasha had built. And King Asa built with them Geba of Benjamin and Mizpah.

New International

Abijah King of Judah

15 IN THE eighteenth year of the reign of Jeroboam son of Nebat, Abijah[h] became king of Judah, ²and he reigned in Jerusalem three years. His mother's name was Maacah daughter of Abishalom.[i] ³He committed all the sins his father had done before him; his heart was not fully devoted to the LORD his God, as the heart of David his forefather had been. ⁴Nevertheless, for David's sake the LORD his God gave him a lamp in Jerusalem by raising up a son to succeed him and by making Jerusalem strong. ⁵For David had done what was right in the eyes of the LORD and had not failed to keep any of the LORD's commands all the days of his life—except in the case of Uriah the Hittite.

⁶There was war between Rehoboam[j] and Jeroboam throughout ⌊Abijah's⌋ lifetime. ⁷As for the other events of Abijah's reign, and all he did, are they not written in the book of the annals of the kings of Judah? There was war between Abijah and Jeroboam. ⁸And Abijah rested with his fathers and was buried in the City of David. And Asa his son succeeded him as king.

Asa King of Judah

⁹In the twentieth year of Jeroboam king of Israel, Asa became king of Judah, ¹⁰and he reigned in Jerusalem forty-one years. His grandmother's name was Maacah daughter of Abishalom.

¹¹Asa did what was right in the eyes of the LORD, as his father David had done. ¹²He expelled the male shrine prostitutes from the land and got rid of all the idols his fathers had made. ¹³He even deposed his grandmother Maacah from her position as queen mother, because she had made a repulsive Asherah pole. Asa cut the pole down and burned it in the Kidron Valley. ¹⁴Although he did not remove the high places, Asa's heart was fully committed to the LORD all his life. ¹⁵He brought into the temple of the LORD the silver and gold and the articles that he and his father had dedicated.

¹⁶There was war between Asa and Baasha king of Israel throughout their reigns. ¹⁷Baasha king of Israel went up against Judah and fortified Ramah to prevent anyone from leaving or entering the territory of Asa king of Judah.

¹⁸Asa then took all the silver and gold that was left in the treasuries of the LORD's temple and of his own palace. He entrusted it to his officials and sent them to Ben-Hadad son of Tabrimmon, the son of Hezion, the king of Aram, who was ruling in Damascus. ¹⁹"Let there be a treaty between me and you," he said, "as there was between my father and your father. See, I am sending you a gift of silver and gold. Now break your treaty with Baasha king of Israel so he will withdraw from me."

²⁰Ben-Hadad agreed with King Asa and sent the commanders of his forces against the towns of Israel. He conquered Ijon, Dan, Abel Beth Maacah and all Kinnereth in addition to Naphtali. ²¹When Baasha heard this, he stopped building Ramah and withdrew to Tirzah. ²²Then King Asa issued an order to all Judah—no one was exempt—and they carried away from Ramah the stones and timber Baasha had been using there. With them King Asa built up Geba in Benjamin, and also Mizpah.

---

h 1 Some Hebrew manuscripts and Septuagint (see also 2 Chron. 12:16); most Hebrew manuscripts *Abijam;* also in verses 7 and 8 *i 2* A variant of *Absalom;* also in verse 10   *j 6* Most Hebrew manuscripts; some Hebrew manuscripts and Syriac *Abijam* (that is, Abijah)

King James

23The rest of all the acts of Asa, and all his might, and all that he did, and the cities which he built, *are* they not written in the book of the chronicles of the kings of Judah? Nevertheless in the time of his old age he was diseased in his feet.

24And Asa slept with his fathers, and was buried with his fathers in the city of David his father: and Jehoshaphat his son reigned in his stead.

Nadab, king of Israel

25 ¶ And Nadab the son of Jeroboam ⁿbegan to reign over Israel in the second year of Asa king of Judah, and reigned over Israel two years.

26And he did evil in the sight of the LORD, and walked in the way of his father, and in his sin wherewith he made Israel to sin.

27 ¶ And Baasha the son of Ahijah, of the house of Issachar, conspired against him; and Baasha smote him at Gibbethon, which *belonged* to the Philistines; for Nadab and all Israel laid siege to Gibbethon.

28Even in the third year of Asa king of Judah did Baasha slay him, and reigned in his stead.

29And it came to pass, when he reigned, *that* he smote all the house of Jeroboam; he left not to Jeroboam any that breathed, until he had destroyed him, according unto the saying of the LORD, which he spake by his servant Ahijah the Shilonite:

30Because of the sins of Jeroboam which he sinned, and which he made Israel sin, by his provocation wherewith he provoked the LORD God of Israel to anger.

31 ¶ Now the rest of the acts of Nadab, and all that he did, *are* they not written in the book of the chronicles of the kings of Israel?

32And there was war between Asa and Baasha king of Israel all their days.

Baasha, king of Israel

33In the third year of Asa king of Judah began Baasha the son of Ahijah to reign over all Israel in Tirzah, twenty and four years.

34And he did evil in the sight of the LORD, and walked in the way of Jeroboam, and in his sin wherewith he made Israel to sin.

16 THEN THE word of the LORD came to Jehu the son of Hanani against Baasha, saying,

2Forasmuch as I exalted thee out of the dust, and made thee prince over my people Israel; and thou hast walked in the way of Jeroboam, and hast made my people Israel to sin, to provoke me to anger with their sins;

3Behold, I will take away the posterity of Baasha, and the posterity of his house; and will make thy house like the house of Jeroboam the son of Nebat.

4Him that dieth of Baasha in the city shall the dogs eat; and him that dieth of his in the fields shall the fowls of the air eat.

5Now the rest of the acts of Baasha, and what he did, and his might, *are* they not written in the book of the chronicles of the kings of Israel?

6So Baasha slept with his fathers, and was buried in Tirzah: and Elah his son reigned in his stead.

7And also by the hand of the prophet Jehu the son of Hanani came the word of the LORD against Baasha, and against his house, even for all the evil that he did in the sight of the LORD, in provoking him to anger with the work of his hands, in being like the house of Jeroboam; and because he killed him.

Amplified

23The rest of all the acts of Asa, all his might, all that he did, and the cities which he built, are they not written in the Book of the Chronicles of the Kings of Judah? But in the time of his old age he was diseased in his feet.

24Asa slept with his fathers and was buried with them in the city of David his father. Jehoshaphat his son reigned in his stead.

25Nadab son of Jeroboam began to reign over Israel in the second year of Asa king of Judah, and reigned two years.

26He did evil in the sight of the Lord and walked in the way of his father and in his sin, with which he made Israel sin.

27Baasha son of Ahijah of the house of Issachar conspired against Nadab, and Baasha smote him at Gibbethon, which belonged to the Philistines, for Nadab and all Israel were laying siege to Gibbethon.

28In the third year of Asa king of Judah Baasha slew Nadab and reigned in his stead.

29As soon as he was king, Baasha killed all the household of Jeroboam. He left to [it] not one who breathed, until he had destroyed it, according to the word of the Lord which He spoke by His servant Ahijah the Shilonite— [I Kings 14:9–16.]

30Because of the sins of Jeroboam which he sinned and by which he made Israel to sin, and because of his provocation of the Lord, the God of Israel, to anger.

31The rest of Nadab's acts, and all that he did, are they not written in the Book of the Chronicles of the Kings of Israel?

32There was war between Asa and Baasha king of Israel all their days.

33In the third year of Asa king of Judah, Baasha son of Ahijah began his reign of twenty-four years over all Israel in Tirzah.

34He did evil in the sight of the Lord and walked in the way of Jeroboam and in his sin, with which he made Israel sin.

16 AND THE word of the Lord came to Jehu son of Hanani against Baasha, saying,

2Because I exalted you [Baasha] out of the dust and made you leader over My people Israel, and you have walked in the way of Jeroboam and have made My people Israel sin, to provoke Me to anger with their sins,

3Behold, I will utterly sweep away Baasha and his house, and will make your house like [that] of Jeroboam son of Nebat.

4Any of Baasha's family who dies in the city the dogs shall eat, and any who dies in the field the birds of the heavens shall eat.

5Now the rest of the acts of Baasha, what he did and his might, are they not written in the Book of the Chronicles of the Kings of Israel?

6Baasha slept with his fathers and was buried in Tirzah. Elah his son reigned in his stead.

7Also the word of the Lord against Baasha and his house came through the prophet Jehu son of Hanani for all the evil that Baasha did in the sight of the Lord in provoking Him to anger with the work of his hands [idols], in being like the house of Jeroboam, and also because he destroyed it [the family of Jeroboam, of his own accord].

ⁿHeb. *reigned*

New American Standard

Jehoshaphat Succeeds Asa

23 ¶ Now the rest of all the acts of Asa and all his might and all that he did and the cities which he built, are they not written in the Book of the Chronicles of the Kings of Judah? But in the time of his old age he was diseased in his feet.

24 And Asa slept with his fathers and was buried with his fathers in the city of David his father; and Jehoshaphat his son reigned in his place.

Nadab, then Baasha, Rules over Israel

25 ¶ Now Nadab the son of Jeroboam became king over Israel in the second year of Asa king of Judah, and he reigned over Israel two years.

26 He did evil in the sight of the LORD, and walked in the way of his father and in his sin which he made Israel sin.

27 Then Baasha the son of Ahijah of the house of Issachar conspired against him, and Baasha struck him down at Gibbethon, which belonged to the Philistines, while Nadab and all Israel were laying siege to Gibbethon.

28 ¶ So Baasha killed him in the third year of Asa king of Judah and reigned in his place.

29 It came about as soon as he was king, he struck down all the household of Jeroboam. He did not leave to Jeroboam any persons alive, until he had destroyed them, according to the word of the LORD, which He spoke by His servant Ahijah the Shilonite,

30 *and* because of the sins of Jeroboam which he sinned, and which he made Israel sin, because of his provocation with which he provoked the LORD God of Israel to anger.

31 ¶ Now the rest of the acts of Nadab and all that he did, are they not written in the Book of the Chronicles of the Kings of Israel?

War with Judah

32 There was war between Asa and Baasha king of Israel all their days.

33 ¶ In the third year of Asa king of Judah, Baasha the son of Ahijah became king over all Israel at Tirzah, *and reigned* twenty-four years.

34 He did evil in the sight of the LORD, and walked in the way of Jeroboam and in his sin which he made Israel sin.

Prophecy against Baasha

16 NOW THE word of the LORD came to Jehu the son of Hanani against Baasha, saying,

2 "Inasmuch as I exalted you from the dust and made you leader over My people Israel, and you have walked in the way of Jeroboam and have made My people Israel sin, provoking Me to anger with their sins,

3 behold, I will consume Baasha and his house, and I will make your house like the house of Jeroboam the son of Nebat.

4 "Anyone of Baasha who dies in the city the dogs will eat, and anyone of his who dies in the field the birds of the heavens will eat."

5 ¶ Now the rest of the acts of Baasha and what he did and his might, are they not written in the Book of the Chronicles of the Kings of Israel?

The Israelite Kings

6 And Baasha slept with his fathers and was buried in Tirzah, and Elah his son became king in his place.

7 Moreover, the word of the LORD through the prophet Jehu the son of Hanani also came against Baasha and his household, both because of all the evil which he did in the sight of the LORD, provoking Him to anger with the work of his hands, in being like the house of Jeroboam, and because he struck it.

New International

23 As for all the other events of Asa's reign, all his achievements, all he did and the cities he built, are they not written in the book of the annals of the kings of Judah? In his old age, however, his feet became diseased. 24 Then Asa rested with his fathers and was buried with them in the city of his father David. And Jehoshaphat his son succeeded him as king.

Nadab King of Israel

25 Nadab son of Jeroboam became king of Israel in the second year of Asa king of Judah, and he reigned over Israel two years. 26 He did evil in the eyes of the LORD, walking in the ways of his father and in his sin, which he had caused Israel to commit.

27 Baasha son of Ahijah of the house of Issachar plotted against him, and he struck him down at Gibbethon, a Philistine town, while Nadab and all Israel were besieging it. 28 Baasha killed Nadab in the third year of Asa king of Judah and succeeded him as king.

29 As soon as he began to reign, he killed Jeroboam's whole family. He did not leave Jeroboam anyone that breathed, but destroyed them all, according to the word of the LORD given through his servant Ahijah the Shilonite— 30 because of the sins Jeroboam had committed and had caused Israel to commit, and because he provoked the LORD, the God of Israel, to anger.

31 As for the other events of Nadab's reign, and all he did, are they not written in the book of the annals of the kings of Israel? 32 There was war between Asa and Baasha king of Israel throughout their reigns.

Baasha King of Israel

33 In the third year of Asa king of Judah, Baasha son of Ahijah became king of all Israel in Tirzah, and he reigned twenty-four years. 34 He did evil in the eyes of the LORD, walking in the ways of Jeroboam and in his sin, which he had caused Israel to commit.

16 THEN THE word of the LORD came to Jehu son of Hanani against Baasha: 2 "I lifted you up from the dust and made you leader of my people Israel, but you walked in the ways of Jeroboam and caused my people Israel to sin and to provoke me to anger by their sins. 3 So I am about to consume Baasha and his house, and I will make your house like that of Jeroboam son of Nebat. 4 Dogs will eat those belonging to Baasha who die in the city, and the birds of the air will feed on those who die in the country."

5 As for the other events of Baasha's reign, what he did and his achievements, are they not written in the book of the annals of the kings of Israel? 6 Baasha rested with his fathers and was buried in Tirzah. And Elah his son succeeded him as king.

7 Moreover, the word of the LORD came through the prophet Jehu son of Hanani to Baasha and his house, because of all the evil he had done in the eyes of the LORD, provoking him to anger by the things he did, and becoming like the house of Jeroboam—and also because he destroyed it.

King James

Elah, king of Israel

8 ¶ In the twenty and sixth year of Asa king of Judah began Elah the son of Baasha to reign over Israel in Tirzah, two years.

9 And his servant Zimri, captain of half *his* chariots, conspired against him, as he was in Tirzah, drinking himself drunk in the house of Arza °steward of *his* house in Tirzah.

10 And Zimri went in and smote him, and killed him, in the twenty and seventh year of Asa king of Judah, and reigned in his stead.

11 ¶ And it came to pass, when he began to reign, as soon as he sat on his throne, *that* he slew all the house of Baasha: he left him not one that pisseth against a wall, ᵖneither of his kinsfolks, nor of his friends.

12 Thus did Zimri destroy all the house of Baasha, according to the word of the LORD, which he spake against Baasha ᑫby Jehu the prophet,

13 For all the sins of Baasha, and the sins of Elah his son, by which they sinned, and by which they made Israel to sin, in provoking the LORD God of Israel to anger with their vanities.

14 Now the rest of the acts of Elah, and all that he did, *are* they not written in the book of the chronicles of the kings of Israel?

Zimri, king of Israel

15 ¶ In the twenty and seventh year of Asa king of Judah did Zimri reign seven days in Tirzah. And the people *were* encamped against Gibbethon, which *belonged* to the Philistines.

16 And the people *that were* encamped heard say, Zimri hath conspired, and hath also slain the king: wherefore all Israel made Omri, the captain of the host, king over Israel that day in the camp.

17 And Omri went up from Gibbethon, and all Israel with him, and they besieged Tirzah.

18 And it came to pass, when Zimri saw that the city was taken, that he went into the palace of the king's house, and burnt the king's house over him with fire, and died,

19 For his sins which he sinned in doing evil in the sight of the LORD, in walking in the way of Jeroboam, and in his sin which he did, to make Israel to sin.

20 Now the rest of the acts of Zimri, and his treason that he wrought, *are* they not written in the book of the chronicles of the kings of Israel?

Omri, king of Israel

21 ¶ Then were the people of Israel divided into two parts: half of the people followed Tibni the son of Ginath, to make him king; and half followed Omri.

22 But the people that followed Omri prevailed against the people that followed Tibni the son of Ginath: so Tibni died, and Omri reigned.

23 ¶ In the thirty and first year of Asa king of Judah began Omri to reign over Israel, twelve years: six years reigned he in Tirzah.

24 And he bought the hill Samaria of Shemer for two talents of silver, and built on the hill, and called the name of the city which he built, after the name of Shemer, owner of the hill, ʳSamaria.

25 ¶ But Omri wrought evil in the eyes of the LORD, and did worse than all that *were* before him.

26 For he walked in all the way of Jeroboam the son of Nebat, and in his sin wherewith he made Israel to sin, to provoke the LORD God of Israel to anger with their vanities.

27 Now the rest of the acts of Omri which he did, and his might that he showed, *are* they not written in the book of the chronicles of the kings of Israel?

Amplified

8 In the twenty-sixth year of Asa king of Judah, Elah son of Baasha began his reign of two years over Israel in Tirzah.

9 Elah's servant Zimri, captain of half his chariots, conspired against Elah. He was in Tirzah, drinking himself drunk in the house of Arza, who was over the household in Tirzah.

10 Zimri came in and smote and killed him in the twenty-seventh year of Asa king of Judah, and reigned in his stead.

11 When he began to reign, as soon as he sat on his throne, he killed all the household of Baasha; he left not one male of his kinsmen or his friends.

12 Thus Zimri destroyed all the house of Baasha, according to the word of the Lord which He spoke against Baasha through Jehu the prophet, [I Kings 16:3.]

13 For all the sins of Baasha and of Elah his son by which they sinned and made Israel sin, in provoking the Lord, the God of Israel, to anger with their idols.

14 The rest of the acts of Elah, and all he did, are they not written in the Book of the Chronicles of the Kings of Israel?

15 In the twenty-seventh year of Asa king of Judah, Zimri reigned for seven days in Tirzah. The troops were encamped against Gibbethon, which belonged to the Philistines,

16 And they heard the rumor, Zimri has conspired and slain the king! So all Israel made Omri, the commander of the army, king over Israel that day in the camp.

17 So Omri went up from Gibbethon, and all Israel with him, and they besieged Tirzah.

18 And when Zimri saw that the city was taken, he went into the stronghold of the king's house and burned the king's house over him with fire and died,

19 Because of his sins committed in doing evil in the sight of the Lord, in walking in the way of Jeroboam, and his sin in causing Israel to sin.

20 The rest of the acts of Zimri, and his deeds of treason, are they not written in the Book of the Chronicles of the Kings of Israel?

21 Then the people of Israel were divided into two factions. Half of the people followed Tibni son of Ginath, to make him king, and half followed Omri.

22 But the people who followed Omri prevailed against those who followed Tibni son of Ginath. So Tibni died and Omri reigned.

23 In the thirty-first year of Asa king of Judah, Omri began his reign of twelve years over Israel. He reigned six years in Tirzah.

24 Omri bought the hill Samaria from Shemer for two talents of silver. He built a city on the hill *and* fortified it, and called it Samaria (Shomeron), after the owner of the hill, Shemer.

25 But Omri did evil in the eyes of the Lord, even worse than all who were before him.

26 He walked in all the ways of Jeroboam son of Nebat and in his sin, by which he made Israel sin, to provoke the Lord, the God of Israel, to anger with their idols.

27 The rest of the acts of Omri, and his might that he showed, are they not written in the Book of the Chronicles of the Kings of Israel?

ᵒHeb. *which was over*   ᵖOr, *both his kingsmen and his friends*
ᑫHeb. *by the hand of*   ʳHeb. *Shomeron*

New American Standard

8 ¶ In the twenty-sixth year of Asa king of Judah, Elah the son of Baasha became king over Israel at Tirzah, *and reigned* two years.

9 His servant Zimri, commander of half his chariots, conspired against him. Now he *was* at Tirzah drinking himself drunk in the house of Arza, who *was* over the household at Tirzah.

10 Then Zimri went in and struck him and put him to death in the twenty-seventh year of Asa king of Judah, and became king in his place.

11 It came about when he became king, as soon as he sat on his throne, that he killed all the household of Baasha; he did not leave a single male, neither of his relatives nor of his friends.

12 ¶ Thus Zimri destroyed all the household of Baasha, according to the word of the LORD, which He spoke against Baasha through Jehu the prophet,

13 for all the sins of Baasha and the sins of Elah his son, which they sinned and which they made Israel sin, provoking the LORD God of Israel to anger with their idols.

14 Now the rest of the acts of Elah and all that he did, are they not written in the Book of the Chronicles of the Kings of Israel?

15 ¶ In the twenty-seventh year of Asa king of Judah, Zimri reigned seven days at Tirzah. Now the people were camped against Gibbethon, which belonged to the Philistines.

16 The people who were camped heard it said, "Zimri has conspired and has also struck down the king." Therefore all Israel made Omri, the commander of the army, king over Israel that day in the camp.

17 Then Omri and all Israel with him went up from Gibbethon and besieged Tirzah.

18 When Zimri saw that the city was taken, he went into the citadel of the king's house and burned the king's house over him with fire, and died,

19 because of his sins which he sinned, doing evil in the sight of the LORD, walking in the way of Jeroboam, and in his sin which he did, making Israel sin.

20 Now the rest of the acts of Zimri and his conspiracy which he carried out, are they not written in the Book of the Chronicles of the Kings of Israel?

21 ¶ Then the people of Israel were divided into two parts: half of the people followed Tibni the son of Ginath, to make him king; the *other* half followed Omri.

22 But the people who followed Omri prevailed over the people who followed Tibni the son of Ginath. And Tibni died and Omri became king.

23 In the thirty-first year of Asa king of Judah, Omri became king over Israel *and reigned* twelve years; he reigned six years at Tirzah.

24 He bought the hill Samaria from Shemer for two talents of silver; and he built on the hill, and named the city which he built Samaria, after the name of Shemer, the owner of the hill.

25 ¶ Omri did evil in the sight of the LORD, and acted more wickedly than all who *were* before him.

26 For he walked in all the way of Jeroboam the son of Nebat and in his sins which he made Israel sin, provoking the LORD God of Israel with their idols.

27 Now the rest of the acts of Omri which he did and his might which he showed, are they not written in the Book of the Chronicles of the Kings of Israel?

New International

Elah King of Israel

8 In the twenty-sixth year of Asa king of Judah, Elah son of Baasha became king of Israel, and he reigned in Tirzah two years.

9 Zimri, one of his officials, who had command of half his chariots, plotted against him. Elah was in Tirzah at the time, getting drunk in the home of Arza, the man in charge of the palace at Tirzah. 10 Zimri came in, struck him down and killed him in the twenty-seventh year of Asa king of Judah. Then he succeeded him as king.

11 As soon as he began to reign and was seated on the throne, he killed off Baasha's whole family. He did not spare a single male, whether relative or friend. 12 So Zimri destroyed the whole family of Baasha, in accordance with the word of the LORD spoken against Baasha through the prophet Jehu— 13 because of all the sins Baasha and his son Elah had committed and had caused Israel to commit, so that they provoked the LORD, the God of Israel, to anger by their worthless idols.

14 As for the other events of Elah's reign, and all he did, are they not written in the book of the annals of the kings of Israel?

Zimri King of Israel

15 In the twenty-seventh year of Asa king of Judah, Zimri reigned in Tirzah seven days. The army was encamped near Gibbethon, a Philistine town. 16 When the Israelites in the camp heard that Zimri had plotted against the king and murdered him, they proclaimed Omri, the commander of the army, king over Israel that very day there in the camp. 17 Then Omri and all the Israelites with him withdrew from Gibbethon and laid siege to Tirzah. 18 When Zimri saw that the city was taken, he went into the citadel of the royal palace and set the palace on fire around him. So he died, 19 because of the sins he had committed, doing evil in the eyes of the LORD and walking in the ways of Jeroboam and in the sin he had committed and had caused Israel to commit.

20 As for the other events of Zimri's reign, and the rebellion he carried out, are they not written in the book of the annals of the kings of Israel?

Omri King of Israel

21 Then the people of Israel were split into two factions; half supported Tibni son of Ginath for king, and the other half supported Omri. 22 But Omri's followers proved stronger than those of Tibni son of Ginath. So Tibni died and Omri became king.

23 In the thirty-first year of Asa king of Judah, Omri became king of Israel, and he reigned twelve years, six of them in Tirzah. 24 He bought the hill of Samaria from Shemer for two talents[k] of silver and built a city on the hill, calling it Samaria, after Shemer, the name of the former owner of the hill.

25 But Omri did evil in the eyes of the LORD and sinned more than all those before him. 26 He walked in all the ways of Jeroboam son of Nebat and in his sin, which he had caused Israel to commit, so that they provoked the LORD, the God of Israel, to anger by their worthless idols.

27 As for the other events of Omri's reign, what he did and the things he achieved, are they not written in the book

---

k 24 That is, about 150 pounds (about 70 kilograms)

King James

²⁸So Omri slept with his fathers, and was buried in Samaria: and Ahab his son reigned in his stead.

Ahab, king of Israel

²⁹ ¶ And in the thirty and eighth year of Asa king of Judah began Ahab the son of Omri to reign over Israel: and Ahab the son of Omri reigned over Israel in Samaria twenty and two years.

³⁰And Ahab the son of Omri did evil in the sight of the LORD above all that *were* before him.

³¹And it came to pass, ^sas if it had been a light thing for him to walk in the sins of Jeroboam the son of Nebat, that he took to wife Jezebel the daughter of Ethbaal king of the Zidonians, and went and served Baal, and worshipped him.

³²And he reared up an altar for Baal in the house of Baal, which he had built in Samaria.

³³And Ahab made a grove; and Ahab did more to provoke the LORD God of Israel to anger than all the kings of Israel that were before him.

³⁴ ¶ In his days did Hiel the Beth-elite build Jericho: he laid the foundation thereof in Abiram his firstborn, and set up the gates thereof in his youngest *son* Segub, according to the word of the LORD, which he spake by Joshua the son of Nun.

Elijah fed by ravens

17 AND ^tELIJAH the Tishbite, *who was* of the inhabitants of Gilead, said unto Ahab, *As* the LORD God of Israel liveth, before whom I stand, there shall not be dew nor rain these years, but according to my word.

²And the word of the LORD came unto him, saying,

³Get thee hence, and turn thee eastward, and hide thyself by the brook Cherith, that *is* before Jordan.

⁴And it shall be, *that* thou shalt drink of the brook; and I have commanded the ravens to feed thee there.

⁵So he went and did according unto the word of the LORD: for he went and dwelt by the brook Cherith, that *is* before Jordan.

⁶And the ravens brought him bread and flesh in the morning, and bread and flesh in the evening; and he drank of the brook.

⁷And it came to pass ^uafter a while, that the brook dried up, because there had been no rain in the land.

Elijah raises the widow's son

⁸ ¶ And the word of the LORD came unto him, saying,

⁹Arise, get thee to Zarephath, which *belongeth* to Zidon, and dwell there: behold, I have commanded a widow woman there to sustain thee.

¹⁰So he arose and went to Zarephath. And when he came to the gate of the city, behold, the widow woman *was* there gathering of sticks: and he called to her, and said, Fetch me, I pray thee, a little water in a vessel, that I may drink.

¹¹And as she was going to fetch *it*, he called to her, and said, Bring me, I pray thee, a morsel of bread in thine hand.

¹²And she said, *As* the LORD thy God liveth, I have not a cake, but an handful of meal in a barrel, and a little oil in a cruse: and, behold, I *am* gathering two sticks, that I may go in and dress it for me and my son, that we may eat it, and die.

¹³And Elijah said unto her, Fear not; go *and* do as thou hast said: but make me thereof a little cake first, and bring *it* unto me, and after make for thee and for thy son.

¹⁴For thus saith the LORD God of Israel, The barrel of meal shall not waste, neither shall the cruse of oil fail, until the day *that* the LORD ^vsendeth rain upon the earth.

¹⁵And she went and did according to the saying of Elijah: and she, and he, and her house, did eat ^w*many* days.

²⁸So Omri slept with his fathers and was buried in Samaria. Ahab his son reigned in his stead.

²⁹In the thirty-eighth year of Asa king of Judah, Ahab son of Omri began his reign of twenty-two years over Israel in Samaria.

³⁰And Ahab son of Omri did evil in the sight of the Lord above all before him.

³¹As if it had been a light thing for Ahab to walk in the sins of Jeroboam son of Nebat, he took for a wife Jezebel daughter of Ethbaal king of the Sidonians, and served Baal and worshiped him.

³²He erected an altar for Baal in the house of Baal which he built in Samaria.

³³And Ahab made an Asherah [idolatrous symbol of the goddess Asherah]. Ahab did more to provoke the Lord, the God of Israel, to anger than all the kings of Israel before him.

³⁴In his days, Hiel the Bethelite built Jericho. He laid its foundations at the cost of the life of Abiram his firstborn, and set up its gates with the loss of his youngest son Segub, according to the word of the Lord which He spoke through Joshua son of Nun. [Josh. 6:26.]

17 ELIJAH THE Tishbite, of the temporary residents of Gilead, said to Ahab, As the Lord, the God of Israel, lives, before Whom I stand, there shall not be dew or rain these years but according to My word.

²And the word of the Lord came to him, saying,

³Go from here and turn east and hide yourself by the brook Cherith, east of the Jordan.

⁴You shall drink of the brook, and I have commanded the ravens to feed you there.

⁵So he did according to the word of the Lord; he went and dwelt by the brook Cherith, east of the Jordan.

⁶And the ravens brought him bread and flesh in the morning and bread and flesh in the evening, and he drank of the brook.

⁷After a while the brook dried up because there was no rain in the land.

⁸And the word of the Lord came to him:

⁹Arise, go to Zarephath, which belongs to Sidon, and dwell there. Behold, I have commanded a widow there to provide for you.

¹⁰So he arose and went to Zarephath. When he came to the gate of the city, behold, a widow was there gathering sticks. He called to her, Bring me a little water in a vessel, that I may drink.

¹¹As she was going to get it, he called to her and said, Bring me a morsel of bread in your hand.

¹²And she said, As the Lord your God lives, I have not a loaf baked but only a handful of meal in the jar and a little oil in the bottle. See, I am gathering two sticks, that I may go in and bake it for me and my son, that we may eat it—and die.

¹³Elijah said to her, Fear not; go and do as you have said. But make me a little cake of [it] first and bring it to me, and afterward prepare some for yourself and your son.

¹⁴For thus says the Lord, the God of Israel: The jar of meal shall not waste away or the bottle of oil fail until the day that the Lord sends rain on the earth.

¹⁵She did as Elijah said. And she and he and her household ate for many days.

---

^sHeb. *was it a light thing*   ^tHeb. *Elijahu;* in Luke 1:17 & 4:25, he is called *Elias*   ^uHeb. *at the end of days*   ^vHeb. *giveth*   ^wOr, *a full year*

New American Standard

²⁸ So Omri slept with his fathers and was buried in Samaria; and Ahab his son became king in his place.

²⁹ ¶ Now Ahab the son of Omri became king over Israel in the thirty-eighth year of Asa king of Judah, and Ahab the son of Omri reigned over Israel in Samaria twenty-two years.

³⁰ Ahab the son of Omri did evil in the sight of the LORD more than all who were before him.

³¹ ¶ It came about, as though it had been a trivial thing for him to walk in the sins of Jeroboam the son of Nebat, that he married Jezebel the daughter of Ethbaal king of the Sidonians, and went to serve Baal and worshiped him.

³² So he erected an altar for Baal in the house of Baal which he built in Samaria.

³³ Ahab also made the ^aAsherah. Thus Ahab did more to provoke the LORD God of Israel than all the kings of Israel who were before him.

³⁴ In his days Hiel the Bethelite built Jericho; he laid its foundations with the *loss of* Abiram his firstborn, and set up its gates with the *loss of* his youngest son Segub, according to the word of the LORD, which He spoke by Joshua the son of Nun.

Elijah Predicts Drought

17 NOW ELIJAH the Tishbite, who was of the settlers of Gilead, said to Ahab, "As the LORD, the God of Israel lives, before whom I stand, surely there shall be neither dew nor rain these years, except by my word."

² The word of the LORD came to him, saying,

³"Go away from here and turn eastward, and hide yourself by the brook Cherith, which is east of the Jordan.

⁴"It shall be that you will drink of the brook, and I have commanded the ravens to provide for you there."

⁵ So he went and did according to the word of the LORD, for he went and lived by the brook Cherith, which is east of the Jordan.

⁶ The ravens brought him bread and meat in the morning and bread and meat in the evening, and he would drink from the brook.

⁷ It happened after a while that the brook dried up, because there was no rain in the land.

⁸ ¶ Then the word of the LORD came to him, saying,

⁹"Arise, go to Zarephath, which belongs to Sidon, and stay there; behold, I have commanded a widow there to provide for you."

¹⁰ So he arose and went to Zarephath, and when he came to the gate of the city, behold, a widow was there gathering sticks; and he called to her and said, "Please get me a little water in a jar, that I may drink."

¹¹ As she was going to get *it,* he called to her and said, "Please bring me a piece of bread in your hand."

¹² But she said, "As the LORD your God lives, I have no bread, only a handful of flour in the bowl and a little oil in the jar; and behold, I am gathering a few sticks that I may go in and prepare for me and my son, that we may eat it and die."

¹³ Then Elijah said to her, "Do not fear; go, do as you have said, but make me a little bread cake from it first and bring *it* out to me, and afterward you may make *one* for yourself and for your son.

¹⁴"For thus says the LORD God of Israel, 'The bowl of flour shall not be exhausted, nor shall the jar of oil be empty, until the day that the LORD sends rain on the face of the earth.' "

¹⁵ So she went and did according to the word of Elijah, and she and he and her household ate for *many* days.

New International

of the annals of the kings of Israel? ²⁸Omri rested with his fathers and was buried in Samaria. And Ahab his son succeeded him as king.

Ahab Becomes King of Israel

²⁹In the thirty-eighth year of Asa king of Judah, Ahab son of Omri became king of Israel, and he reigned in Samaria over Israel twenty-two years. ³⁰Ahab son of Omri did more evil in the eyes of the LORD than any of those before him. ³¹He not only considered it trivial to commit the sins of Jeroboam son of Nebat, but he also married Jezebel daughter of Ethbaal king of the Sidonians, and began to serve Baal and worship him. ³²He set up an altar for Baal in the temple of Baal that he built in Samaria. ³³Ahab also made an Asherah pole and did more to provoke the LORD, the God of Israel, to anger than did all the kings of Israel before him.

³⁴In Ahab's time, Hiel of Bethel rebuilt Jericho. He laid its foundations at the cost of his firstborn son Abiram, and he set up its gates at the cost of his youngest son Segub, in accordance with the word of the LORD spoken by Joshua son of Nun.

Elijah Fed by Ravens

17 NOW ELIJAH the Tishbite, from Tishbe*^l* in Gilead, said to Ahab, "As the LORD, the God of Israel, lives, whom I serve, there will be neither dew nor rain in the next few years except at my word."

²Then the word of the LORD came to Elijah: ³"Leave here, turn eastward and hide in the Kerith Ravine, east of the Jordan. ⁴You will drink from the brook, and I have ordered the ravens to feed you there."

⁵So he did what the LORD had told him. He went to the Kerith Ravine, east of the Jordan, and stayed there. ⁶The ravens brought him bread and meat in the morning and bread and meat in the evening, and he drank from the brook.

The Widow at Zarephath

⁷Some time later the brook dried up because there had been no rain in the land. ⁸Then the word of the LORD came to him: ⁹"Go at once to Zarephath of Sidon and stay there. I have commanded a widow in that place to supply you with food." ¹⁰So he went to Zarephath. When he came to the town gate, a widow was there gathering sticks. He called to her and asked, "Would you bring me a little water in a jar so I may have a drink?" ¹¹As she was going to get it, he called, "And bring me, please, a piece of bread."

¹²"As surely as the LORD your God lives," she replied, "I don't have any bread—only a handful of flour in a jar and a little oil in a jug. I am gathering a few sticks to take home and make a meal for myself and my son, that we may eat it—and die."

¹³Elijah said to her, "Don't be afraid. Go home and do as you have said. But first make a small cake of bread for me from what you have and bring it to me, and then make something for yourself and your son. ¹⁴For this is what the LORD, the God of Israel, says: 'The jar of flour will not be used up and the jug of oil will not run dry until the day the LORD gives rain on the land.' "

¹⁵She went away and did as Elijah had told her. So there was food every day for Elijah and for the woman and her

---

^aI.e. wooden symbol of a female deity   *l* 1 Or *Tishbite, of the settlers*

King James

¹⁶*And* the barrel of meal wasted not, neither did the cruse of oil fail, according to the word of the LORD, which he spake *x*by Elijah.

¹⁷ ¶ And it came to pass after these things, *that* the son of the woman, the mistress of the house, fell sick; and his sickness was so sore, that there was no breath left in him.

¹⁸And she said unto Elijah, What have I to do with thee, O thou man of God? art thou come unto me to call my sin to remembrance, and to slay my son?

¹⁹And he said unto her, Give me thy son. And he took him out of her bosom, and carried him up into a loft, where he abode, and laid him upon his own bed.

²⁰And he cried unto the LORD, and said, O LORD my God, hast thou also brought evil upon the widow with whom I sojourn, by slaying her son?

²¹And he *y*stretched himself upon the child three times, and cried unto the LORD, and said, O LORD my God, I pray thee, let this child's soul come *z*into him again.

²²And the LORD heard the voice of Elijah; and the soul of the child came into him again, and he revived.

²³And Elijah took the child, and brought him down out of the chamber into the house, and delivered him unto his mother: and Elijah said, See, thy son liveth.

²⁴ ¶ And the woman said to Elijah, Now by this I know that thou *art* a man of God, *and* that the word of the LORD in thy mouth *is* truth.

Elijah and Obadiah meet

18 AND IT came to pass *after* many days, that the word of the LORD came to Elijah in the third year, saying, Go, show thyself unto Ahab; and I will send rain upon the earth.

²And Elijah went to show himself unto Ahab. And *there was* a sore famine in Samaria.

³And Ahab called *a*Obadiah, which *was* *b*the governor of *his* house. (Now Obadiah feared the LORD greatly:

⁴For it was *so,* when *c*Jezebel cut off the prophets of the LORD, that Obadiah took an hundred prophets, and hid them by fifty in a cave, and fed them with bread and water.)

⁵And Ahab said unto Obadiah, Go into the land, unto all fountains of water, and unto all brooks: peradventure we may find grass to save the horses and mules alive, *d*that we lose not all the beasts.

⁶So they divided the land between them to pass throughout it: Ahab went one way by himself, and Obadiah went another way by himself.

⁷ ¶ And as Obadiah was in the way, behold, Elijah met him: and he knew him, and fell on his face, and said, *Art* thou that my lord Elijah?

⁸And he answered him, I *am:* go, tell thy lord, Behold, Elijah *is here.*

⁹And he said, What have I sinned, that thou wouldest deliver thy servant into the hand of Ahab, to slay me?

¹⁰*As* the LORD thy God liveth, there is no nation or kingdom, whither my lord hath not sent to seek thee: and when they said, *He is* not *there;* he took an oath of the kingdom and nation, that they found thee not.

¹¹And now thou sayest, Go, tell thy lord, Behold, Elijah *is here.*

¹²And it shall come to pass, *as soon as* I am gone from thee, that the spirit of the LORD shall carry thee whither I know not; and *so* when I come and tell Ahab, and he cannot find thee, he shall slay me: but I thy servant fear the LORD from my youth.

Amplified

¹⁶The jar of meal was not spent nor did the bottle of oil fail, according to the word which the Lord spoke through Elijah.

¹⁷After these things, the son of the woman, the mistress of the house, became sick; and his sickness was so severe that there was no breath left in him.

¹⁸And she said to Elijah, What have you against me, O man of God? Have you come to me to call my sin to remembrance and to slay my son?

¹⁹He said to her, Give me your son. And he took him from her bosom and carried him up into the chamber where he stayed and laid him upon his own bed.

²⁰And Elijah cried to the Lord and said, O Lord my God, have You brought further calamity upon the widow with whom I sojourn, by slaying her son?

²¹And he stretched himself upon the child three times and cried to the Lord and said, O Lord my God, I pray You, let this child's soul come back into him.

²²And the Lord heard the voice of Elijah, and the soul of the child came into him again, and he revived.

²³And Elijah took the child, and brought him down out of the chamber into the [lower part of the] house and gave him to his mother; and Elijah said, See, your son is alive!

²⁴And the woman said to Elijah, By this I know that you are a man of God and that the word of the Lord in your mouth is truth.

18 AFTER MANY days, the word of the Lord came to Elijah in the third year, saying, Go, show yourself to Ahab, and I will send rain upon the earth.

²So Elijah went to show himself to Ahab. Now the famine was severe in Samaria.

³And Ahab called Obadiah, who was the governor of his house. (Now Obadiah feared the Lord greatly;

⁴For when Jezebel cut off the prophets of the Lord, Obadiah took a hundred prophets and hid them by fifties in a cave and fed them with bread and water.)

⁵And Ahab said to Obadiah, Go into the land to all the fountains of water and to all the brooks; perhaps we may find grass to keep the horses and mules alive, that we lose none of the beasts.

⁶So they divided the land between them to pass through it. Ahab went one way and Obadiah went another way, each by himself.

⁷As Obadiah was on the way, behold, Elijah met him. He recognized him and fell on his face and said, Are you my lord Elijah?

⁸He answered him, It is I. Go tell your lord, Behold, Elijah is here.

⁹And he said, What sin have I committed, that you would deliver your servant into the hands of Ahab to be slain?

¹⁰As the Lord your God lives, there is no nation or kingdom where my lord has not sent to seek you. And when they said, He is not here, he took an oath from the kingdom or nation that they had not found you.

¹¹And now you say, Go tell your lord, Behold, Elijah is here.

¹²And as soon as I have gone out from you, the Spirit of the Lord will carry you I know not where; so when I come and tell Ahab and he cannot find you, he will kill me. But I your servant have feared *and* revered the Lord from my youth.

---

x Heb. *by the hand of*   *y* Heb. *measured*   *z* Heb. *into his inward parts*   *a* Heb. *Obadiahu*   *b* Heb. *over his house*   *c* Heb. *Izebel*   *d* Heb. *that we cut not off* ourselves *from the beasts*

New American Standard

16 The bowl of flour was not exhausted nor did the jar of oil become empty, according to the word of the LORD which He spoke through Elijah.

Elijah Raises the Widow's Son

17 ¶ Now it came about after these things that the son of the woman, the mistress of the house, became sick; and his sickness was so severe that there was no breath left in him. 18 So she said to Elijah, "What do I have to do with you, O man of God? You have come to me to bring my iniquity to remembrance and to put my son to death!" 19 He said to her, "Give me your son." Then he took him from her bosom and carried him up to the upper room where he was living, and laid him on his own bed. 20 He called to the LORD and said, "O LORD my God, have You also brought calamity to the widow with whom I am staying, by causing her son to die?" 21 Then he stretched himself upon the child three times, and called to the LORD and said, "O LORD my God, I pray You, let this child's life return to him." 22 The LORD heard the voice of Elijah, and the life of the child returned to him and he revived. 23 Elijah took the child and brought him down from the upper room into the house and gave him to his mother; and Elijah said, "See, your son is alive." 24 Then the woman said to Elijah, "Now I know that you are a man of God and that the word of the LORD in your mouth is truth."

Obadiah Meets Elijah

18 NOW IT happened *after* many days that the word of the LORD came to Elijah in the third year, saying, "Go, show yourself to Ahab, and I will send rain on the face of the earth." 2 So Elijah went to show himself to Ahab. Now the famine *was* severe in Samaria. 3 Ahab called Obadiah who *was* over the household. (Now Obadiah *b*feared the LORD greatly; 4 for when Jezebel destroyed the prophets of the LORD, Obadiah took a hundred prophets and hid them by fifties in a cave, and provided them with bread and water.) 5 Then Ahab said to Obadiah, "Go through the land to all the springs of water and to all the valleys; perhaps we will find grass and keep the horses and mules alive, and not have to kill some of the cattle." 6 So they divided the land between them to survey it; Ahab went one way by himself and Obadiah went another way by himself. 7 ¶ Now as Obadiah was on the way, behold, Elijah met him, and he recognized him and fell on his face and said, "Is this you, Elijah my master?" 8 He said to him, "It is I. Go, say to your master, 'Behold, Elijah *is here.*' " 9 He said, "What sin have I committed, that you are giving your servant into the hand of Ahab to put me to death? 10 "As the LORD your God lives, there is no nation or kingdom where my master has not sent to search for you; and when they said, 'He is not *here,*' he made the kingdom or nation swear that they could not find you. 11 "And now you are saying, 'Go, say to your master, "Behold, Elijah *is here."* ' 12 "It will come about when I leave you that the Spirit of the LORD will carry you where I do not know; so when I come and tell Ahab and he cannot find you, he will kill me, although *I* your servant have feared the LORD from my youth.

New International

family. 16 For the jar of flour was not used up and the jug of oil did not run dry, in keeping with the word of the LORD spoken by Elijah.

17 Some time later the son of the woman who owned the house became ill. He grew worse and worse, and finally stopped breathing. 18 She said to Elijah, "What do you have against me, man of God? Did you come to remind me of my sin and kill my son?"

19 "Give me your son," Elijah replied. He took him from her arms, carried him to the upper room where he was staying, and laid him on his bed. 20 Then he cried out to the LORD, "O LORD my God, have you brought tragedy also upon this widow I am staying with, by causing her son to die?" 21 Then he stretched himself out on the boy three times and cried to the LORD, "O LORD my God, let this boy's life return to him!"

22 The LORD heard Elijah's cry, and the boy's life returned to him, and he lived. 23 Elijah picked up the child and carried him down from the room into the house. He gave him to his mother and said, "Look, your son is alive!"

24 Then the woman said to Elijah, "Now I know that you are a man of God and that the word of the LORD from your mouth is the truth."

Elijah and Obadiah

18 AFTER A long time, in the third year, the word of the LORD came to Elijah: "Go and present yourself to Ahab, and I will send rain on the land." 2 So Elijah went to present himself to Ahab.

Now the famine was severe in Samaria, 3 and Ahab had summoned Obadiah, who was in charge of his palace. (Obadiah was a devout believer in the LORD. 4 While Jezebel was killing off the LORD's prophets, Obadiah had taken a hundred prophets and hidden them in two caves, fifty in each, and had supplied them with food and water.) 5 Ahab had said to Obadiah, "Go through the land to all the springs and valleys. Maybe we can find some grass to keep the horses and mules alive so we will not have to kill any of our animals." 6 So they divided the land they were to cover, Ahab going in one direction and Obadiah in another.

7 As Obadiah was walking along, Elijah met him. Obadiah recognized him, bowed down to the ground, and said, "Is it really you, my lord Elijah?"

8 "Yes," he replied. "Go tell your master, 'Elijah is here.' "

9 "What have I done wrong," asked Obadiah, "that you are handing your servant over to Ahab to be put to death? 10 As surely as the LORD your God lives, there is not a nation or kingdom where my master has not sent someone to look for you. And whenever a nation or kingdom claimed you were not there, he made them swear they could not find you. 11 But now you tell me to go to my master and say, 'Elijah is here.' 12 I don't know where the Spirit of the LORD may carry you when I leave you. If I go and tell Ahab and he doesn't find you, he will kill me. Yet I your servant have worshiped the LORD since my youth.

b Or *revered*

| King James | Amplified |

King James

13Was it not told my lord what I did when Jezebel slew the prophets of the LORD, how I hid an hundred men of the LORD'S prophets by fifty in a cave, and fed them with bread and water?

14And now thou sayest, Go, tell thy lord, Behold, Elijah *is here:* and he shall slay me.

15And Elijah said, As the LORD of hosts liveth, before whom I stand, I will surely show myself unto him today.

16So Obadiah went to meet Ahab, and told him: and Ahab went to meet Elijah.

Elijah on mount Carmel

17 ¶ And it came to pass, when Ahab saw Elijah, that Ahab said unto him, *Art* thou he that troubleth Israel?

18And he answered, I have not troubled Israel; but thou, and thy father's house, in that ye have forsaken the commandments of the LORD, and thou hast followed Baalim.

19Now therefore send, *and* gather to me all Israel unto mount Carmel, and the prophets of Baal four hundred and fifty, and the prophets of the groves four hundred, which eat at Jezebel's table.

20So Ahab sent unto all the children of Israel, and gathered the prophets together unto mount Carmel.

21And Elijah came unto all the people, and said, How long halt ye between two ᵉopinions? if the LORD *be* God, follow him: but if Baal, *then* follow him. And the people answered him not a word.

22Then said Elijah unto the people, I, *even* I only, remain a prophet of the LORD; but Baal's prophets *are* four hundred and fifty men.

23Let them therefore give us two bullocks; and let them choose one bullock for themselves, and cut it in pieces, and lay *it* on wood, and put no fire *under:* and I will dress the other bullock, and lay *it* on wood, and put no fire *under:*

24And call ye on the name of your gods, and I will call on the name of the LORD: and the God that answereth by fire, let him be God. And all the people answered and said, ᶠIt is well spoken.

25And Elijah said unto the prophets of Baal, Choose you one bullock for yourselves, and dress *it* first; for ye *are* many; and call on the name of your gods, but put no fire *under.*

26And they took the bullock which was given them, and they dressed *it,* and called on the name of Baal from morning even until noon, saying, O Baal, ᵍhear us. But *there* was no voice, nor any that ʰanswered. And they ⁱleaped upon the altar which was made.

27And it came to pass at noon, that Elijah mocked them, and said, Cry ʲaloud: for he *is* a god; either ᵏhe is talking, or he ˡis pursuing, or he is in a journey, *or* peradventure he sleepeth, and must be awaked.

28And they cried aloud, and cut themselves after their manner with knives and lancets, till ᵐthe blood gushed out upon them.

29And it came to pass, when midday was past, and they prophesied until the *time* of the ⁿoffering of the *evening* sacrifice, that *there was* neither voice, nor any to answer, nor any ᵒthat regarded.

30And Elijah said unto all the people, Come near unto me. And all the people came near unto him. And he repaired the altar of the LORD *that was* broken down.

31And Elijah took twelve stones, according to the number of the tribes of the sons of Jacob, unto whom the word of the LORD came, saying, Israel shall be thy name:

32And with the stones he built an altar in the name of the LORD: and he made a trench about the altar, as great as would contain two measures of seed.

Amplified

13Was it not told my lord what I did when Jezebel slew the prophets of the Lord, how I hid a hundred men of the Lord's prophets by fifties in a cave and fed them with bread and water?

14And now you say, Go tell your lord, Behold, Elijah is here; and he will kill me.

15Elijah said, As the Lord of hosts lives, before Whom I stand, I will surely show myself to Ahab today.

16So Obadiah went to meet Ahab and told him, and Ahab went to meet Elijah.

17When Ahab saw Elijah, Ahab said to him, Are you he who troubles Israel?

18Elijah replied, I have not troubled Israel, but you have, and your father's house, by forsaking the commandments of the Lord and by following the Baals.

19Therefore send and gather to me all Israel at Mount Carmel, and the 450 prophets of Baal and the 400 prophets of [the goddess] Asherah, who eat at [Queen] Jezebel's table.

20So Ahab sent to all the Israelites and assembled the prophets at Mount Carmel.

21Elijah came near to all the people and said, How long will you halt *and* limp between two opinions? If the Lord is God, follow Him! But if Baal, then follow him. And the people did not answer him a word.

22Then Elijah said to the people, I, I only, remain a prophet of the Lord, but Baal's prophets are 450 men.

23Let two bulls be given us; let them choose one bull for themselves and cut it in pieces and lay it on the wood but put no fire to it. I will dress the other bull, lay it on the wood, and put no fire to it.

24Then you call on the name of your god, and I will call on the name of the Lord; and the One Who answers by fire, let Him be God. And all the people answered, It is well spoken.

25Elijah said to the prophets of Baal, Choose one bull for yourselves and dress it first, for you are many; and call on the name of your god, but put no fire under it.

26So they took the bull given them, dressed it, and called on the name of Baal from morning until noon, saying, O Baal, hear *and* answer us! But there was no voice; no one answered. And they leaped upon *or* limped about the altar they had made.

27At noon Elijah mocked them, saying, Cry aloud, for he is a god; either he is musing, or he has gone aside, or he is on a journey, or perhaps he is asleep and must be awakened.

28And they cried aloud and cut themselves after their custom with knives and lances until the blood gushed out upon them.

29Midday passed, and they played the part of prophets until the time for offering the evening sacrifice, but there was no voice, no answer, no one who paid attention.

30Then Elijah said to all the people, Come near to me. And all the people came near him. And he repaired the [old] altar of the Lord that had been broken down [by Jezebel]. [I Kings 18:13; 19:10.]

31Then Elijah took twelve stones, according to the number of the tribes of the sons of Jacob, to whom the word of the Lord came, saying, Israel shall be your name. [Gen. 32:28.]

32And with the stones Elijah built an altar in the name [and self-revelation] of the Lord. He made a trench about the altar as great as would contain two measures of seed.

ᵉOr, *thoughts?*   ᶠHeb. *The word is good*   ᵍOr, *answer*
ʰOr, *heard*   ⁱOr, *leaped up and down at the altar*   ʲHeb.
with a great voice   ᵏOr, *he meditateth*   ˡHeb. *hath a pursuit*
ᵐHeb. *poured out blood upon them*   ⁿHeb. *ascending*
ᵒHeb. *attention*

New American Standard

¹³"Has it not been told to my master what I did when Jezebel killed the prophets of the LORD, that I hid a hundred prophets of the LORD by fifties in a cave, and provided them with bread and water?

¹⁴"And now you are saying, 'Go, say to your master, "Behold, Elijah *is here*" '; he will then kill me."

¹⁵ Elijah said, "As the LORD of hosts lives, before whom I stand, I will surely show myself to him today."

¹⁶ So Obadiah went to meet Ahab and told him; and Ahab went to meet Elijah.

¹⁷ ¶ When Ahab saw Elijah, Ahab said to him, "Is this you, you troubler of Israel?"

¹⁸ He said, "I have not troubled Israel, but you and your father's house *have*, because you have forsaken the commandments of the LORD and you have followed the Baals.

¹⁹"Now then send *and* gather to me all Israel at Mount Carmel, *together* with 450 prophets of Baal and 400 prophets of the Asherah, who eat at Jezebel's table."

God or Baal on Mount Carmel

²⁰ ¶ So Ahab sent *a message* among all the sons of Israel and brought the prophets together at Mount Carmel.

²¹ Elijah came near to all the people and said, "How long *will* you hesitate between two opinions? If the LORD is God, follow Him; but if Baal, follow him." But the people did not answer him a word.

²² Then Elijah said to the people, "I alone am left a prophet of the LORD, but Baal's prophets are 450 men.

²³"Now let them give us two oxen; and let them choose one ox for themselves and cut it up, and place it on the wood, but put no fire *under it;* and I will prepare the other ox and lay it on the wood, and I will not put a fire *under it.*

²⁴"Then you call on the name of your god, and I will call on the name of the LORD, and the God who answers by fire, He is God." And all the people said, "^cThat is a good idea."

²⁵ ¶ So Elijah said to the prophets of Baal, "Choose one ox for yourselves and prepare it first for you are many, and call on the name of your god, but put no fire *under it.*"

²⁶ Then they took the ox which was given them and they prepared it and called on the name of Baal from morning until noon saying, "O Baal, answer us." But there was no voice and no one answered. And they leaped about the altar which they made.

²⁷ It came about at noon, that Elijah mocked them and said, "Call out with a loud voice, for he is a god; either he is occupied or gone aside, or is on a journey, or perhaps he is asleep and needs to be awakened."

²⁸ So they cried with a loud voice and cut themselves according to their custom with swords and lances until the blood gushed out on them.

²⁹ When midday was past, they raved until the time of the offering of the *evening* sacrifice; but there was no voice, no one answered, and no one paid attention.

³⁰ ¶ Then Elijah said to all the people, "Come near to me." So all the people came near to him. And he repaired the altar of the LORD which had been torn down.

³¹ Elijah took twelve stones according to the number of the tribes of the sons of Jacob, to whom the word of the LORD had come, saying, "Israel shall be your name."

³² So with the stones he built an altar in the name of the LORD, and he made a trench around the altar, large enough to hold two measures of seed.

New International

¹³Haven't you heard, my lord, what I did while Jezebel was killing the prophets of the LORD? I hid a hundred of the LORD's prophets in two caves, fifty in each, and supplied them with food and water. ¹⁴And now you tell me to go to my master and say, 'Elijah is here.' He will kill me!"

¹⁵Elijah said, "As the LORD Almighty lives, whom I serve, I will surely present myself to Ahab today."

Elijah on Mount Carmel

¹⁶So Obadiah went to meet Ahab and told him, and Ahab went to meet Elijah. ¹⁷When he saw Elijah, he said to him, "Is that you, you troubler of Israel?"

¹⁸"I have not made trouble for Israel," Elijah replied. "But you and your father's family have. You have abandoned the LORD's commands and have followed the Baals. ¹⁹Now summon the people from all over Israel to meet me on Mount Carmel. And bring the four hundred and fifty prophets of Baal and the four hundred prophets of Asherah, who eat at Jezebel's table."

²⁰So Ahab sent word throughout all Israel and assembled the prophets on Mount Carmel. ²¹Elijah went before the people and said, "How long will you waver between two opinions? If the LORD is God, follow him; but if Baal is God, follow him."

But the people said nothing.

²²Then Elijah said to them, "I am the only one of the LORD's prophets left, but Baal has four hundred and fifty prophets. ²³Get two bulls for us. Let them choose one for themselves, and let them cut it into pieces and put it on the wood but not set fire to it. I will prepare the other bull and put it on the wood but not set fire to it. ²⁴Then you call on the name of your god, and I will call on the name of the LORD. The god who answers by fire—he is God."

Then all the people said, "What you say is good."

²⁵Elijah said to the prophets of Baal, "Choose one of the bulls and prepare it first, since there are so many of you. Call on the name of your god, but do not light the fire." ²⁶So they took the bull given them and prepared it.

Then they called on the name of Baal from morning till noon. "O Baal, answer us!" they shouted. But there was no response; no one answered. And they danced around the altar they had made.

²⁷At noon Elijah began to taunt them. "Shout louder!" he said. "Surely he is a god! Perhaps he is deep in thought, or busy, or traveling. Maybe he is sleeping and must be awakened." ²⁸So they shouted louder and slashed themselves with swords and spears, as was their custom, until their blood flowed. ²⁹Midday passed, and they continued their frantic prophesying until the time for the evening sacrifice. But there was no response, no one answered, no one paid attention.

³⁰Then Elijah said to all the people, "Come here to me." They came to him, and he repaired the altar of the LORD, which was in ruins. ³¹Elijah took twelve stones, one for each of the tribes descended from Jacob, to whom the word of the LORD had come, saying, "Your name shall be Israel." ³²With the stones he built an altar in the name of the LORD, and he dug a trench around it large enough to

^cLit *The matter is good*

King James

³³And he put the wood in order, and cut the bullock in pieces, and laid *him* on the wood, and said, Fill four barrels with water, and pour *it* on the burnt sacrifice, and on the wood.

³⁴And he said, Do *it* the second time. And they did *it* the second time. And he said, Do *it* the third time. And they did *it* the third time.

³⁵And the water ^pran round about the altar; and he filled the trench also with water.

³⁶And it came to pass at *the time of* the offering of the *evening* sacrifice, that Elijah the prophet came near, and said, LORD God of Abraham, Isaac, and of Israel, let it be known this day that thou *art* God in Israel, and *that* I *am* thy servant, and *that* I have done all these things at thy word.

³⁷Hear me, O LORD, hear me, that this people may know that thou *art* the LORD God, and *that* thou hast turned their heart back again.

³⁸Then the fire of the LORD fell, and consumed the burnt sacrifice, and the wood, and the stones, and the dust, and licked up the water that *was* in the trench.

³⁹And when all the people saw *it,* they fell on their faces: and they said, The LORD, he *is* the God; the LORD, he *is* the God.

⁴⁰And Elijah said unto them, ^qTake the prophets of Baal; let not one of them escape. And they took them: and Elijah brought them down to the brook Kishon, and slew them there.

⁴¹ ¶ And Elijah said unto Ahab, Get thee up, eat and drink; for *there is* ^ra sound of abundance of rain.

⁴²So Ahab went up to eat and to drink. And Elijah went up to the top of Carmel; and he cast himself down upon the earth, and put his face between his knees,

⁴³And said to his servant, Go up now, look toward the sea. And he went up, and looked, and said, *There is* nothing. And he said, Go again seven times.

⁴⁴And it came to pass at the seventh time, that he said, Behold, there ariseth a little cloud out of the sea, like a man's hand. And he said, Go up, say unto Ahab, ^sPrepare *thy chariot,* and get thee down, that the rain stop thee not.

⁴⁵And it came to pass in the mean while, that the heaven was black with clouds and wind, and there was a great rain. And Ahab rode, and went to Jezreel.

⁴⁶And the hand of the LORD was on Elijah; and he girded up his loins, and ran before Ahab ^tto the entrance of Jezreel.

Elijah flees from Jezebel

19 AND AHAB told Jezebel all that Elijah had done, and withal how he had slain all the prophets with the sword.

²Then Jezebel sent a messenger unto Elijah, saying, So let the gods do *to me,* and more also, if I make not thy life as the life of one of them by to morrow about this time.

³And when he saw *that,* he arose, and went for his life, and came to Beer-sheba, which *belongeth* to Judah, and left his servant there.

⁴ ¶ But he himself went a day's journey into the wilderness, and came and sat down under a juniper tree: and he requested ^ufor himself that he might die; and said, It is enough; now, O LORD, take away my life; for I *am* not better than my fathers.

⁵And as he lay and slept under a juniper tree, behold, then an angel touched him, and said unto him, Arise *and* eat.

⁶And he looked, and, behold, *there was* a cake baked on the coals, and a cruse of water at his ^vhead. And he did eat and drink, and laid him down again.

Amplified

³³He put the wood in order and cut the bull in pieces and laid it on the wood and said, Fill four jars with water and pour it on the burnt offering and the wood.

³⁴And he said, Do it the second time. And they did it the second time. And he said, Do it the third time. And they did it the third time.

³⁵The water ran round about the altar, and he filled the trench also with water.

³⁶At the time of the offering of the evening sacrifice, Elijah the prophet came near and said, O Lord, the God of Abraham, Isaac, and Israel, let it be known this day that You are God in Israel and that I am Your servant and that I have done all these things at Your word.

³⁷Hear me, O Lord, hear me, that this people may know that You, the Lord, are God, and have turned their hearts back [to You].

³⁸Then the fire of the Lord fell and consumed the burnt sacrifice and the wood and the stones and the dust, and also licked up the water that was in the trench.

³⁹When all the people saw it, they fell on their faces and they said, The Lord, He is God! The Lord, He is God!

⁴⁰And Elijah said, Seize the prophets of Baal; let not one escape. They seized them, and Elijah brought them down to the brook Kishon, and [as God's law required] slew them there. [Deut. 13:5; 18:20.]

⁴¹And Elijah said to Ahab, Go up, eat and drink, for there is the sound of abundance of rain.

⁴²So Ahab went up to eat and to drink. And Elijah went up to the top of Carmel; and he bowed himself down upon the earth and put his face between his knees

⁴³And said to his servant, Go up now, look toward the sea. And he went up and looked and said, There is nothing. Elijah said, Go again seven times.

⁴⁴And at the seventh time the servant said, A cloud as small as a man's hand is arising out of the sea. And Elijah said, Go up, say to Ahab, Hitch your chariot and go down, lest the rain stop you.

⁴⁵In a little while, the heavens were black with windswept clouds, and there was a great rain. And Ahab went to Jezreel.

⁴⁶The hand of the Lord was on Elijah. He girded up his loins and ran before Ahab to the entrance of Jezreel [nearly twenty miles].

19 AHAB TOLD Jezebel all that Elijah had done and how he had slain all the prophets [of Baal] with the sword.

²Then Jezebel sent a messenger to Elijah, saying, So let the gods do to me, and more also, if I make not your life as the life of one of them by this time tomorrow.

³Then he was afraid and arose and went for his life and came to Beersheba of Judah [over eighty miles, and out of Jezebel's realm] and left his servant there.

⁴But he himself went a day's journey into the wilderness and came and sat down under a lone broom *or* juniper tree and asked that he might die. He said, It is enough; now, O Lord, take away my life; for I am no better than my fathers.

⁵As he lay asleep under the broom *or* juniper tree, behold, an angel touched him and said to him, Arise and eat.

⁶He looked, and behold, there was a cake baked on the coals, and a bottle of water at his head. And he ate and drank and lay down again.

---

^pHeb. *went*   ^qOr, *Apprehend*   ^rOr, *a sound of a noise of rain*   ^sHeb. *Tie, or, Bind*   ^tHeb. *till thou come to Jezreel*   ^uHeb. *for his life*   ^vHeb. *bolster*

New American Standard

33 Then he arranged the wood and cut the ox in pieces and laid *it* on the wood.

34 And he said, "Fill four pitchers with water and pour *it* on the burnt offering and on the wood." And he said, "Do it a second time," and they did it a second time. And he said, "Do it a third time," and they did it a third time.

35 The water flowed around the altar and he also filled the trench with water.

Elijah's Prayer

36 At the time of the offering of the *evening* sacrifice, Elijah the prophet came near and said, "O LORD, the God of Abraham, Isaac and Israel, today let it be known that You are God in Israel and that I am Your servant and I have done all these things at Your word.

37 "Answer me, O LORD, answer me, that this people may know that You, O LORD, are God, and *that* You have turned their heart back again."

38 Then the fire of the LORD fell and consumed the burnt offering and the wood and the stones and the dust, and licked up the water that was in the trench.

39 When all the people saw it, they fell on their faces; and they said, "The LORD, He is God; the LORD, He is God."

40 Then Elijah said to them, "Seize the prophets of Baal; do not let one of them escape." So they seized them; and Elijah brought them down to the brook Kishon, and slew them there.

41 ¶ Now Elijah said to Ahab, "Go up, eat and drink; for there is the sound of the roar of a *heavy* shower."

42 So Ahab went up to eat and drink. But Elijah went up to the top of Carmel; and he crouched down on the earth and put his face between his knees.

43 He said to his servant, "Go up now, look toward the sea." So he went up and looked and said, "There is nothing." And he said, "Go back" seven times.

44 It came about at the seventh *time,* that he said, "Behold, a cloud as small as a man's hand is coming up from the sea." And he said, "Go up, say to Ahab, 'Prepare *your chariot* and go down, so that the *heavy* shower does not stop you.'"

45 In a little while the sky grew black with clouds and wind, and there was a heavy shower. And Ahab rode and went to Jezreel.

46 Then the hand of the LORD was on Elijah, and he girded up his loins and outran Ahab to Jezreel.

Elijah Flees from Jezebel

19 NOW AHAB told Jezebel all that Elijah had done, and how he had killed all the prophets with the sword.

2 Then Jezebel sent a messenger to Elijah, saying, "So may the gods do to me and even more, if I do not make your *d*life as the life of one of them by tomorrow about this time."

3 And he was afraid and arose and ran for his *d*life and came to Beersheba, which belongs to Judah, and left his servant there.

4 But he himself went a day's journey into the wilderness, and came and sat down under a juniper tree; and he requested for himself that he might die, and said, "It is enough; now, O LORD, take my *d*life, for I am not better than my fathers."

5 He lay down and slept under a juniper tree; and behold, there was an angel touching him, and he said to him, "Arise, eat."

6 Then he looked and behold, there was at his head a bread cake *baked on* hot stones, and a jar of water. So he ate and drank and lay down again.

New International

hold two seahs*m* of seed. 33 He arranged the wood, cut the bull into pieces and laid it on the wood. Then he said to them, "Fill four large jars with water and pour it on the offering and on the wood."

34 "Do it again," he said, and they did it again.

"Do it a third time," he ordered, and they did it the third time. 35 The water ran down around the altar and even filled the trench.

36 At the time of sacrifice, the prophet Elijah stepped forward and prayed: "O LORD, God of Abraham, Isaac and Israel, let it be known today that you are God in Israel and that I am your servant and have done all these things at your command. 37 Answer me, O LORD, answer me, so these people will know that you, O LORD, are God, and that you are turning their hearts back again."

38 Then the fire of the LORD fell and burned up the sacrifice, the wood, the stones and the soil, and also licked up the water in the trench.

39 When all the people saw this, they fell prostrate and cried, "The LORD—he is God! The LORD—he is God!"

40 Then Elijah commanded them, "Seize the prophets of Baal. Don't let anyone get away!" They seized them, and Elijah had them brought down to the Kishon Valley and slaughtered there.

41 And Elijah said to Ahab, "Go, eat and drink, for there is the sound of a heavy rain." 42 So Ahab went off to eat and drink, but Elijah climbed to the top of Carmel, bent down to the ground and put his face between his knees.

43 "Go and look toward the sea," he told his servant. And he went up and looked.

"There is nothing there," he said.

Seven times Elijah said, "Go back."

44 The seventh time the servant reported, "A cloud as small as a man's hand is rising from the sea."

So Elijah said, "Go and tell Ahab, 'Hitch up your chariot and go down before the rain stops you.'"

45 Meanwhile, the sky grew black with clouds, the wind rose, a heavy rain came on and Ahab rode off to Jezreel. 46 The power of the LORD came upon Elijah and, tucking his cloak into his belt, he ran ahead of Ahab all the way to Jezreel.

Elijah Flees to Horeb

19 NOW AHAB told Jezebel everything Elijah had done and how he had killed all the prophets with the sword. 2 So Jezebel sent a messenger to Elijah to say, "May the gods deal with me, be it ever so severely, if by this time tomorrow I do not make your life like that of one of them."

3 Elijah was afraid*n* and ran for his life. When he came to Beersheba in Judah, he left his servant there, 4 while he himself went a day's journey into the desert. He came to a broom tree, sat down under it and prayed that he might die. "I have had enough, LORD," he said. "Take my life; I am no better than my ancestors." 5 Then he lay down under the tree and fell asleep.

All at once an angel touched him and said, "Get up and eat." 6 He looked around, and there by his head was a cake of bread baked over hot coals, and a jar of water. He ate and drank and then lay down again.

d Lit *soul*

m 32 That is, probably about 13 quarts (about 15 liters)
n 3 Or *Elijah saw*

King James

7And the angel of the LORD came again the second time, and touched him, and said, Arise and eat; because the journey is too great for thee.

8And he arose, and did eat and drink, and went in the strength of that meat forty days and forty nights unto Horeb the mount of God.

Elijah in the mountain cave

9 ¶ And he came thither unto a cave, and lodged there; and, behold, the word of the LORD came to him, and he said unto him, What doest thou here, Elijah?

10And he said, I have been very jealous for the LORD God of hosts: for the children of Israel have forsaken thy covenant, thrown down thine altars, and slain thy prophets with the sword; and I, even I only, am left; and they seek my life, to take it away.

11And he said, Go forth, and stand upon the mount before the LORD. And, behold, the LORD passed by, and a great and strong wind rent the mountains, and brake in pieces the rocks before the LORD; but the LORD was not in the wind: and after the wind an earthquake; but the LORD was not in the earthquake:

12And after the earthquake a fire; but the LORD was not in the fire: and after the fire a still small voice.

13And it was so, when Elijah heard it, that he wrapped his face in his mantle, and went out, and stood in the entering in of the cave. And, behold, there came a voice unto him, and said, What doest thou here, Elijah?

14And he said, I have been very jealous for the LORD God of hosts: because the children of Israel have forsaken thy covenant, thrown down thine altars, and slain thy prophets with the sword; and I, even I only, am left; and they seek my life, to take it away.

15And the LORD said unto him, Go, return on thy way to the wilderness of Damascus: and when thou comest, anoint Hazael to be king over Syria:

16And Jehu the son of Nimshi shalt thou anoint to be king over Israel: and Elisha the son of Shaphat of Abel-meholah shalt thou anoint to be prophet in thy room.

17And it shall come to pass, that him that escapeth the sword of Hazael shall Jehu slay: and him that escapeth from the sword of Jehu shall Elisha slay.

18Yet wI have left me seven thousand in Israel, all the knees which have not bowed unto Baal, and every mouth which hath not kissed him.

Elijah and Elisha

19 ¶ So he departed thence, and found Elisha the son of Shaphat, who was plowing with twelve yoke of oxen before him, and he with the twelfth: and Elijah passed by him, and cast his mantle upon him.

20And he left the oxen, and ran after Elijah, and said, Let me, I pray thee, kiss my father and my mother, and then I will follow thee. And he said unto him, xGo back again: for what have I done to thee?

21And he returned back from him, and took a yoke of oxen, and slew them, and boiled their flesh with the instruments of the oxen, and gave unto the people, and they did eat. Then he arose, and went after Elijah, and ministered unto him.

Amplified

7The angel of the Lord came the second time and touched him and said, Arise and eat, for the journey is too great for you.

8So he arose and ate and drank, and went in the strength of that food forty days and nights to Horeb, the mount of God.

9There he came to a cave and lodged in it; and behold, the word of the Lord came to him, and He said to him, What are you doing here, Elijah?

10He replied, I have been very jealous for the Lord God of hosts; for the Israelites have forsaken Your covenant, thrown down Your altars, and killed Your prophets with the sword. And I, I only, am left; and they seek my life, to take it away.

11And He said, Go out and stand on the mount before the Lord. And behold, the Lord passed by, and a great and strong wind rent the mountains and broke in pieces the rocks before the Lord, but the Lord was not in the wind; and after the wind an earthquake, but the Lord was not in the earthquake;

12And after the earthquake a fire, but the Lord was not in the fire; and after the fire [a sound of gentle stillness and] a still, small voice.

13When Elijah heard the voice, he wrapped his face in his mantle and went out and stood in the entrance of the cave. And behold, there came a voice to him and said, What are you doing here, Elijah?

14He said, I have been very jealous for the Lord God of hosts, because the Israelites have forsaken Your covenant, thrown down Your altars, and slain Your prophets with the sword. And I, I only, am left, and they seek my life, to destroy it.

15And the Lord said to him, Go, return on your way to the Wilderness of Damascus; and when you arrive, anoint Hazael to be king over Syria.

16And anoint Jehu son of Nimshi to be king over Israel, and anoint Elisha son of Shaphat of Abel-meholah to be prophet in your place.

17And him who escapes from the sword of qHazael Jehu shall slay, and him who escapes the sword of Jehu Elisha shall slay.

18Yet I will leave Myself 7,000 in Israel, all the knees that have not bowed to Baal and every mouth that has not kissed him.

19So Elijah left there and found Elisha son of Shaphat, whose plowing was being done with twelve yoke of oxen, and he drove the twelfth. Elijah crossed over to him and cast his mantle upon him.

20He left the oxen and ran after Elijah and said, Let me kiss my father and mother, and then I will follow you. And he [testing Elisha] said, Go on back. What have I done to you? [Settle it for yourself.]

21So Elisha went back from him. Then he took a yoke of oxen, slew them, boiled their flesh with the oxen's yoke [as fuel], and gave to the people, and they ate. Then he arose, followed Elijah, and served him. [II Kings 3:11.]

---

qAhab had again fallen under the sway of Jezebel. Therefore, Baal worship would recover from the blow dealt it by Elijah. Elijah is accordingly instructed to take the necessary steps for the destruction of Baal worship. They were three. First, Ahab was to be attacked from without by the Syrians, and for that purpose warlike Hazael was to take the Syrian throne. Second, when Ahab was thus weakened, Jehu was to seize his throne, since Jehu was a known opponent of Baal worship, and also a ruthless soldier. Third, Elijah was to appoint as his own successor the vigorous and wholehearted Elisha, who might be trusted under Jehu to complete the destruction of the adherents of Baal (The Cambridge Bible).

wOr, I will leave   xHeb. Go return

New American Standard

7 The angel of the LORD came again a second time and touched him and said, "Arise, eat, because the journey is too great for you."

8 So he arose and ate and drank, and went in the strength of that food forty days and forty nights to Horeb, the mountain of God.

Elijah at Horeb

9 ¶ Then he came there to a cave and lodged there; and behold, the word of the LORD *came* to him, and He said to him, "What are you doing here, Elijah?"

10 He said, "I have been very zealous for the LORD, the God of hosts; for the sons of Israel have forsaken Your covenant, torn down Your altars and killed Your prophets with the sword. And I alone am left; and they seek my life, to take it away."

11 ¶ So He said, "Go forth and stand on the mountain before the LORD." And behold, the LORD was passing by! And a great and strong wind was rending the mountains and breaking in pieces the rocks before the LORD; *but* the LORD *was* not in the wind. And after the wind an earthquake, *but* the LORD *was* not in the earthquake.

12 After the earthquake a fire, *but* the LORD *was* not in the fire; and after the fire a sound of a gentle blowing.

13 When Elijah heard *it,* he wrapped his face in his mantle and went out and stood in the entrance of the cave. And behold, a voice *came* to him and said, "What are you doing here, Elijah?"

14 Then he said, "I have been very zealous for the LORD, the God of hosts; for the sons of Israel have forsaken Your covenant, torn down Your altars and killed Your prophets with the sword. And I alone am left; and they seek my life, to take it away."

15 ¶ The LORD said to him, "Go, return on your way to the wilderness of Damascus, and when you have arrived, you shall anoint Hazael king over Aram;

16 and Jehu the son of Nimshi you shall anoint king over Israel; and Elisha the son of Shaphat of Abel-meholah you shall anoint as prophet in your place.

17 "It shall come about, the one who escapes from the sword of Hazael, Jehu shall put to death, and the one who escapes from the sword of Jehu, Elisha shall put to death.

18 "Yet I will leave 7,000 in Israel, all the knees that have not bowed to Baal and every mouth that has not kissed him."

19 ¶ So he departed from there and found Elisha the son of Shaphat, while he was plowing with twelve pairs *of oxen* before him, and he with the twelfth. And Elijah passed over to him and threw his mantle on him.

20 He left the oxen and ran after Elijah and said, "Please let me kiss my father and my mother, then I will follow you." And he said to him, "Go back again, for what have I done to you?"

21 So he returned from following him, and took the pair of oxen and sacrificed them and boiled their flesh with the implements of the oxen, and gave *it* to the people and they ate. Then he arose and followed Elijah and ministered to him.

New International

7 The angel of the LORD came back a second time and touched him and said, "Get up and eat, for the journey is too much for you." 8 So he got up and ate and drank. Strengthened by that food, he traveled forty days and forty nights until he reached Horeb, the mountain of God. 9 There he went into a cave and spent the night.

The LORD Appears to Elijah

And the word of the LORD came to him: "What are you doing here, Elijah?"

10 He replied, "I have been very zealous for the LORD God Almighty. The Israelites have rejected your covenant, broken down your altars, and put your prophets to death with the sword. I am the only one left, and now they are trying to kill me too."

11 The LORD said, "Go out and stand on the mountain in the presence of the LORD, for the LORD is about to pass by."

Then a great and powerful wind tore the mountains apart and shattered the rocks before the LORD, but the LORD was not in the wind. After the wind there was an earthquake, but the LORD was not in the earthquake. 12 After the earthquake came a fire, but the LORD was not in the fire. And after the fire came a gentle whisper. 13 When Elijah heard it, he pulled his cloak over his face and went out and stood at the mouth of the cave.

Then a voice said to him, "What are you doing here, Elijah?"

14 He replied, "I have been very zealous for the LORD God Almighty. The Israelites have rejected your covenant, broken down your altars, and put your prophets to death with the sword. I am the only one left, and now they are trying to kill me too."

15 The LORD said to him, "Go back the way you came, and go to the Desert of Damascus. When you get there, anoint Hazael king over Aram. 16 Also, anoint Jehu son of Nimshi king over Israel, and anoint Elisha son of Shaphat from Abel Meholah to succeed you as prophet. 17 Jehu will put to death any who escape the sword of Hazael, and Elisha will put to death any who escape the sword of Jehu. 18 Yet I reserve seven thousand in Israel—all whose knees have not bowed down to Baal and all whose mouths have not kissed him."

The Call of Elisha

19 So Elijah went from there and found Elisha son of Shaphat. He was plowing with twelve yoke of oxen, and he himself was driving the twelfth pair. Elijah went up to him and threw his cloak around him. 20 Elisha then left his oxen and ran after Elijah. "Let me kiss my father and mother good-by," he said, "and then I will come with you."

"Go back," Elijah replied. "What have I done to you?"

21 So Elisha left him and went back. He took his yoke of oxen and slaughtered them. He burned the plowing equipment to cook the meat and gave it to the people, and they ate. Then he set out to follow Elijah and became his attendant.

King James

Ahab defeats Ben-hadad

20 AND BEN-HADAD the king of Syria gathered all his host together: and *there were* thirty and two kings with him, and horses, and chariots: and he went up and besieged Samaria, and warred against it.

²And he sent messengers to Ahab king of Israel into the city, and said unto him, Thus saith Ben-hadad,

³Thy silver and thy gold *is* mine; thy wives also and thy children, *even* the goodliest, *are* mine.

⁴And the king of Israel answered and said, My lord, O king, according to thy saying, I *am* thine, and all that I have.

⁵And the messengers came again, and said, Thus speaketh Ben-hadad, saying, Although I have sent unto thee, saying, Thou shalt deliver me thy silver, and thy gold, and thy wives, and thy children;

⁶Yet I will send my servants unto thee tomorrow about this time, and they shall search thine house, and the houses of thy servants; and it shall be, *that* whatsoever is ʸpleasant in thine eyes, they shall put *it* in their hand, and take *it* away.

⁷Then the king of Israel called all the elders of the land, and said, Mark, I pray you, and see how this *man* seeketh mischief: for he sent unto me for my wives, and for my children, and for my silver, and for my gold; and ᶻI denied him not.

⁸And all the elders and all the people said unto him, Hearken not *unto him,* nor consent.

⁹Wherefore he said unto the messengers of Ben-hadad, Tell my lord the king, All that thou didst send for to thy servant at the first I will do: but this thing I may not do. And the messengers departed, and brought him word again.

¹⁰And Ben-hadad sent unto him, and said, The gods do so unto me, and more also, if the dust of Samaria shall suffice for handfuls for all the people that ᵃfollow me.

¹¹And the king of Israel answered and said, Tell *him,* Let not him that girdeth on *his harness* boast himself as he that putteth it off.

¹²And it came to pass, when *Ben-hadad* heard this ᵇmessage, as he *was* drinking, he and the kings in the ᶜpavilions, that he said unto his servants, ᵈSet *yourselves in array.* And they set *themselves in array* against the city.

¹³ ¶ And, behold, there ᵉcame a prophet unto Ahab king of Israel, saying, Thus saith the LORD, Hast thou seen all this great multitude? behold, I will deliver it into thine hand this day; and thou shalt know that I *am* the LORD.

¹⁴And Ahab said, By whom? And he said, Thus saith the LORD, *Even* by the ᶠyoung men of the princes of the provinces. Then he said, Who shall ᵍorder the battle? And he answered, Thou.

¹⁵Then he numbered the young men of the princes of the provinces, and they were two hundred and thirty two: and after them he numbered all the people, *even* all the children of Israel, *being* seven thousand.

¹⁶And they went out at noon. But Ben-hadad *was* drinking himself drunk in the pavilions, he and the kings, the thirty and two kings that helped him.

¹⁷And the young men of the princes of the provinces went out first; and Ben-hadad sent out, and they told him, saying, There are men come out of Samaria.

¹⁸And he said, Whether they be come out for peace, take them alive; or whether they be come out for war, take them alive.

¹⁹So these young men of the princes of the provinces came out of the city, and the army which followed them.

²⁰And they slew every one his man: and the Syrians fled; and Israel pursued them: and Ben-hadad the king of Syria escaped on an horse with the horsemen.

Amplified

20 BEN-HADAD KING of Syria gathered all his army together; thirty-two kings were with him, and horses and chariots. And he went up and besieged Samaria, warring against it.

²He sent messengers into Samaria to Ahab king of Israel and said to him, Thus says Ben-hadad:

³Your silver and your gold are mine; your wives and your children, even the fairest, also are mine.

⁴And the king of Israel answered and said, My lord, O king, according to what you say, I am yours, and all that I have.

⁵The messengers came again and said, Thus says Ben-hadad: Although I have sent to you, saying, You shall deliver to me your silver, your gold, your wives, and your children—

⁶Yet I will send my servants to you tomorrow about this time, and they shall search your house and the houses of your servants; and all the desire of your eyes they shall lay hands upon and take away.

⁷Then the king of Israel called all the elders of the land and said, Notice now and see how this man is seeking our destruction. He sent to me for my wives, my children, my silver, and my gold, and I did not refuse him.

⁸And all the elders and all the people said to him, Do not heed him or consent.

⁹So he said to Ben-hadad's messengers, Tell my lord the king, All you first sent for to your servant I will do, but this thing I cannot do. And the messengers left; then they brought him word again.

¹⁰Ben-hadad sent to him and said, May the gods do so to me, and more also, if the rubbish of Samaria shall be enough for each one of all the people who are at my feet *and* follow me to get a handful.

¹¹The king of Israel answered, Tell him: Let not him who girds on his harness boast as he who puts it off.

¹²When Ben-hadad heard this message as he and the kings were drinking in the booths, he said to his servants, Set the army in array. And they set themselves in array against [Samaria].

¹³Then a prophet came to Ahab king of Israel and said, Thus says the Lord: Have you seen all this great multitude? Behold, I will deliver it into your hand today, and you shall know *and* realize that I am the Lord.

¹⁴Ahab said, By whom? And he said, Thus says the Lord: By the young men [the attendants or bodyguards] of the governors of the districts. Then Ahab said, Who shall order the battle? And he answered, You.

¹⁵Ahab numbered the attendants of the governors of the districts, and they were 232. After them he numbered all the people of [the army of] Israel, 7,000. [I Kings 19:18.]

¹⁶And they went out at noon. But Ben-hadad was drinking himself drunk in the booths, he and the thirty-two kings who helped him.

¹⁷The servants of the governors of the districts went out first; and Ben-hadad sent out, and they told him, saying, There are men come out of Samaria.

¹⁸And he said, Whether they have come out for peace or for war, take them alive.

¹⁹So these [strong young guards] of the governors of the districts went out of [Samaria], and the army followed them.

²⁰And each one killed his man; the Syrians fled, and Israel pursued them. Ben-hadad king of Syria escaped on a horse with the horsemen.

ʸHeb. *desirable*   ᶻHeb. *I kept not back from him*   ᵃHeb. are *at my feet*   ᵇHeb. *word*   ᶜOr, *tents*   ᵈOr, *Place* the engines *And they placed* engines   ᵉHeb. *approached*   ᶠOr, *servants*   ᵍHeb. *bind,* or, *tie*

New American Standard

War with Aram

20 NOW BEN-HADAD king of Aram gathered all his army, and there *were* thirty-two kings with him, and horses and chariots. And he went up and besieged Samaria and fought against it. ² Then he sent messengers to the city to Ahab king of Israel and said to him, "Thus says Ben-hadad, ³ 'Your silver and your gold are mine; your most beautiful wives and children are also mine.'" ⁴ The king of Israel replied, "It is according to your word, my lord, O king; I am yours, and all that I have." ⁵ Then the messengers returned and said, "Thus says Ben-hadad, 'Surely, I sent to you saying, "You shall give me your silver and your gold and your wives and your children," ⁶ but about this time tomorrow I will send my servants to you, and they will search your house and the houses of your servants; and whatever is desirable in your eyes, they will take in their hand and carry away.'" ⁷ ¶ Then the king of Israel called all the elders of the land and said, "Please observe and see how this man is looking for trouble; for he sent to me for my wives and my children and my silver and my gold, and I did not refuse him." ⁸ All the elders and all the people said to him, "Do not listen or consent." ⁹ So he said to the messengers of Ben-hadad, "Tell my lord the king, 'All that you sent for to your servant at the first I will do, but this thing I cannot do.'" And the messengers departed and brought him word again. ¹⁰ Ben-hadad sent to him and said, "May the gods do so to me and more also, if the dust of Samaria will suffice for handfuls for all the people who follow me." ¹¹ Then the king of Israel replied, "Tell *him*, 'Let not him who girds on *his armor* boast like him who takes *it* off.'" ¹² When *Ben-hadad* heard this message, as he was drinking with the kings in the temporary shelters, he said to his servants, "Station *yourselves*." So they stationed *themselves* against the city.

Ahab Victorious

¹³ ¶ Now behold, a prophet approached Ahab king of Israel and said, "Thus says the LORD, 'Have you seen all this great multitude? Behold, I will deliver them into your hand today, and you shall know that I am the LORD.'" ¹⁴ Ahab said, "By whom?" So he said, "Thus says the LORD, 'By the young men of the rulers of the provinces.'" Then he said, "Who shall begin the battle?" And he answered, "You." ¹⁵ Then he mustered the young men of the rulers of the provinces, and there were 232; and after them he mustered all the people, *even* all the sons of Israel, 7,000. ¹⁶ ¶ They went out at noon, while Ben-hadad was drinking himself drunk in the temporary shelters with the thirty-two kings who helped him. ¹⁷ The young men of the rulers of the provinces went out first; and Ben-hadad sent out and they told him, saying, "Men have come out from Samaria." ¹⁸ Then he said, "If they have come out for peace, take them alive; or if they have come out for war, take them alive." ¹⁹ ¶ So these went out from the city, the young men of the rulers of the provinces, and the army which followed them. ²⁰ They killed each his man; and the Arameans fled and Israel pursued them, and Ben-hadad king of Aram escaped on a horse with horsemen.

New International

Ben-Hadad Attacks Samaria

20 NOW BEN-HADAD king of Aram mustered his entire army. Accompanied by thirty-two kings with their horses and chariots, he went up and besieged Samaria and attacked it. ²He sent messengers into the city to Ahab king of Israel, saying, "This is what Ben-Hadad says: ³'Your silver and gold are mine, and the best of your wives and children are mine.'" ⁴The king of Israel answered, "Just as you say, my lord the king. I and all I have are yours." ⁵The messengers came again and said, "This is what Ben-Hadad says: 'I sent to demand your silver and gold, your wives and your children. ⁶But about this time tomorrow I am going to send my officials to search your palace and the houses of your officials. They will seize everything you value and carry it away.'" ⁷The king of Israel summoned all the elders of the land and said to them, "See how this man is looking for trouble! When he sent for my wives and my children, my silver and my gold, I did not refuse him." ⁸The elders and the people all answered, "Don't listen to him or agree to his demands." ⁹So he replied to Ben-Hadad's messengers, "Tell my lord the king, 'Your servant will do all you demanded the first time, but this demand I cannot meet.'" They left and took the answer back to Ben-Hadad. ¹⁰Then Ben-Hadad sent another message to Ahab: "May the gods deal with me, be it ever so severely, if enough dust remains in Samaria to give each of my men a handful." ¹¹The king of Israel answered, "Tell him: 'One who puts on his armor should not boast like one who takes it off.'" ¹²Ben-Hadad heard this message while he and the kings were drinking in their tents,ᵒ and he ordered his men: "Prepare to attack." So they prepared to attack the city.

Ahab Defeats Ben-Hadad

¹³Meanwhile a prophet came to Ahab king of Israel and announced, "This is what the LORD says: 'Do you see this vast army? I will give it into your hand today, and then you will know that I am the LORD.'" ¹⁴"But who will do this?" asked Ahab.

The prophet replied, "This is what the LORD says: 'The young officers of the provincial commanders will do it.'"

"And who will start the battle?" he asked.

The prophet answered, "You will." ¹⁵So Ahab summoned the young officers of the provincial commanders, 232 men. Then he assembled the rest of the Israelites, 7,000. ¹⁶They set out at noon while Ben-Hadad and the 32 kings allied with him were in their tents getting drunk. ¹⁷The young officers of the provincial commanders went out first.

Now Ben-Hadad had dispatched scouts, who reported, "Men are advancing from Samaria." ¹⁸He said, "If they have come out for peace, take them alive; if they have come out for war, take them alive." ¹⁹The young officers of the provincial commanders marched out of the city with the army behind them ²⁰and each one struck down his opponent. At that, the Arameans fled, with the Israelites in pursuit. But Ben-Hadad king of Aram escaped on horseback with some of his horsemen.

ᵒ 12 Or in Succoth; also in verse 16

King James

21And the king of Israel went out, and smote the horses and chariots, and slew the Syrians with a great slaughter.

22 ¶ And the prophet came to the king of Israel, and said unto him, Go, strengthen thyself, and mark, and see what thou doest: for at the return of the year the king of Syria will come up against thee.

23And the servants of the king of Syria said unto him, Their gods *are* gods of the hills; therefore they were stronger than we; but let us fight against them in the plain, and surely we shall be stronger than they.

24And do this thing, Take the kings away, every man out of his place, and put captains in their rooms:

25And number thee an army, like the army *h*that thou hast lost, horse for horse, and chariot for chariot: and we will fight against them in the plain, *and* surely we shall be stronger than they. And he hearkened unto their voice, and did so.

26And it came to pass at the return of the year, that Ben-hadad numbered the Syrians, and went up to Aphek, *i*to fight against Israel.

27And the children of Israel were numbered, and *j*were all present, and went against them: and the children of Israel pitched before them like two little flocks of kids; but the Syrians filled the country.

28 ¶ And there came a man of God, and spake unto the king of Israel, and said, Thus saith the LORD, Because the Syrians have said, The LORD *is* God of the hills, but he *is* not God of the valleys, therefore will I deliver all this great multitude into thine hand, and ye shall know that I *am* the LORD.

29And they pitched one over against the other seven days. And *so* it was, that in the seventh day the battle was joined: and the children of Israel slew of the Syrians an hundred thousand footmen in one day.

30But the rest fled to Aphek, into the city; and *there* a wall fell upon twenty and seven thousand of the men *that were* left. And Ben-hadad fled, and came into the city, *k l*into an inner chamber.

31 ¶ And his servants said unto him, Behold now, we have heard that the kings of the house of Israel *are* merciful kings: let us, I pray thee, put sackcloth on our loins, and ropes upon our heads, and go out to the king of Israel: peradventure he will save thy life.

32So they girded sackcloth on their loins, and *put* ropes on their heads, and came to the king of Israel, and said, Thy servant Ben-hadad saith, I pray thee, let me live. And he said, *Is* he yet alive? he *is* my brother.

33Now the men did diligently observe whether *any thing would come* from him, and did hastily catch *it:* and they said, Thy brother Ben-hadad. Then he said, Go ye, bring him. Then Ben-hadad came forth to him; and he caused him to come up into the chariot.

34And *Ben-hadad* said unto him, The cities, which my father took from thy father, I will restore; and thou shalt make streets for thee in Damascus, as my father made in Samaria. Then *said Ahab,* I will send thee away with this covenant. So he made a covenant with him, and sent him away.

Ahab judged

35 ¶ And a certain man of the sons of the prophets said unto his neighbour in the word of the LORD, Smite me, I pray thee. And the man refused to smite him.

36Then said he unto him, Because thou hast not obeyed the voice of the LORD, behold, as soon as thou art departed from me, a lion shall slay thee. And as soon as he was departed from him, a lion found him, and slew him.

37Then he found another man, and said, Smite me, I pray thee. And the man smote him, *m*so that in smiting he wounded *him.*

Amplified

21The king of Israel went out and smote [the riders of] the horses and chariots and slew the Syrians with a great slaughter.

22The prophet came to the king of Israel and said to him, Go, fortify yourself and become strong and give attention to what you must do, for at the first of next year the king of Syria will return against you.

23And the servants of the king of Syria said to him, Israel's gods are gods of the hills; therefore they were stronger than we. But let us fight against them in the plain, and surely we shall be stronger than they.

24And do this thing: Remove the kings, each from his place, and put governors in their stead.

25And muster yourself an army like the army you have lost, horse for horse and chariot for chariot. And we will fight against them in the plain, and surely we shall be stronger than they. And he heeded their speech and did so.

26And at the return of the year, Ben-hadad mustered the Syrians and went up to Aphek to fight against Israel.

27The Israelites were counted and, all present, went against them. The Israelites encamped before the enemy like two little flocks of lost kids [absolutely everything against them but Almighty God], but the Syrians filled the country.

28A man of God came and said to the king of Israel, Thus says the Lord: Because the Syrians have said, The Lord is God of the hills but He is not God of the valleys, therefore I will deliver all this great multitude into your hands, and you shall know *and* recognize by experience that I am the Lord. [Phil. 4:13.]

29They encamped opposite each other seven days. Then the battle was joined; and the Israelites slew of the Syrians 100,000 foot soldiers in one day.

30But the rest fled to the city of Aphek, and the wall fell upon 27,000 men who were left. Ben-hadad fled into the city *and* from chamber to chamber.

31His servants said to him, We have heard that the kings of the house of Israel are merciful kings. Let us put sackcloth on our loins and ropes about our necks, and go out to the king of Israel; perhaps he will spare your life.

32So they girded sackcloth on their loins and put ropes on their necks, and came to the king of Israel and said, Your servant Ben-hadad says, I pray you, let me live. And King [Ahab] said, Is he yet alive? He is my brother.

33Now the men took it as an omen and they hastily took it up and said, Yes, your brother Ben-hadad. Then the king said, Go, bring him. Then Ben-hadad came forth to him, and the victorious king caused him to come up into the chariot.

34Ben-hadad [tempting him] said, The cities which my father took from your father I will restore; and you may maintain bazaars of your own in Damascus, as my father did in Samaria. Then, said Ahab, I will send you away on these terms. So he made a covenant with him and sent him away.

35And a certain man of the sons of the prophets said to his neighbor, At the command of the Lord, strike me, I pray you. And the man refused to strike him.

36Then said he to him, Because you have not obeyed the voice of the Lord, behold, as soon as you have left me a lion will slay you. And as soon as he departed from him, a lion found him and killed him.

37Then [the prophet] found another man and said, Strike me, I pray you. And the man struck him, so that in striking, he wounded him.

---

*h*Heb. *that was fallen*   *i*Heb. *to the war with Israel*   *j*Or,
were victualled   *k*Or, *from chamber to chamber*   *l*Heb. *into
a chamber within a chamber*   *m*Heb. *smiting and wounding*

New American Standard

21 The king of Israel went out and struck the horses and chariots, and killed the Arameans with a great slaughter.

22 ¶ Then the prophet came near to the king of Israel and said to him, "Go, strengthen yourself and observe and see what you have to do; for at the turn of the year the king of Aram will come up against you."

23 ¶ Now the servants of the king of Aram said to him, "Their gods are gods of the mountains, therefore they were stronger than we; but rather let us fight against them in the plain, *and* surely we will be stronger than they.

24"Do this thing: remove the kings, each from his place, and put captains in their place,

25 and muster an army like the army that you have lost, horse for horse, and chariot for chariot. Then we will fight against them in the plain, and surely we will be stronger than they." And he listened to their voice and did so.

Another Aramean War

26 ¶ At the turn of the year, Ben-hadad mustered the Arameans and went up to Aphek to fight against Israel.

27 The sons of Israel were mustered and were provisioned and went to meet them; and the sons of Israel camped before them like two little flocks of goats, but the Arameans filled the country.

28 Then a man of God came near and spoke to the king of Israel and said, "Thus says the LORD, 'Because the Arameans have said, "The LORD is a god of *the* mountains, but He is not a god of *the* valleys," therefore I will give all this great multitude into your hand, and you shall know that I am the LORD.' "

29 So they camped one over against the other seven days. And on the seventh day the battle was joined, and the sons of Israel killed *of* the Arameans 100,000 foot soldiers in one day.

30 But the rest fled to Aphek into the city, and the wall fell on 27,000 men who were left. And Ben-hadad fled and came into the city into an inner chamber.

31 ¶ His servants said to him, "Behold now, we have heard that the kings of the house of Israel are merciful kings, please let us put sackcloth on our loins and ropes on our heads, and go out to the king of Israel; perhaps he will save your life."

32 So they girded sackcloth on their loins and *put* ropes on their heads, and came to the king of Israel and said, "Your servant Ben-hadad says, 'Please let me live.' " And he said, "Is he still alive? He is my brother."

33 Now the men took this as an omen, and quickly catching his word said, "Your brother Ben-hadad." Then he said, "Go, bring him." Then Ben-hadad came out to him, and he took him up into the chariot.

34 *Ben-hadad* said to him, "The cities which my father took from your father I will restore, and you shall make streets for yourself in Damascus, as my father made in Samaria." *Ahab said,* "And I will let you go with this covenant." So he made a covenant with him and let him go.

35 ¶ Now a certain man of the sons of the prophets said to another by the word of the LORD, "Please strike me." But the man refused to strike him.

36 Then he said to him, "Because you have not listened to the voice of the LORD, behold, as soon as you have departed from me, a lion will kill you." And as soon as he had departed from him a lion found him and killed him.

37 Then he found another man and said, "Please strike me." And the man struck him, wounding him.

New International

21The king of Israel advanced and overpowered the horses and chariots and inflicted heavy losses on the Arameans.

22Afterward, the prophet came to the king of Israel and said, "Strengthen your position and see what must be done, because next spring the king of Aram will attack you again."

23Meanwhile, the officials of the king of Aram advised him, "Their gods are gods of the hills. That is why they were too strong for us. But if we fight them on the plains, surely we will be stronger than they. 24Do this: Remove all the kings from their commands and replace them with other officers. 25You must also raise an army like the one you lost—horse for horse and chariot for chariot—so we can fight Israel on the plains. Then surely we will be stronger than they." He agreed with them and acted accordingly.

26The next spring Ben-Hadad mustered the Arameans and went up to Aphek to fight against Israel. 27When the Israelites were also mustered and given provisions, they marched out to meet them. The Israelites camped opposite them like two small flocks of goats, while the Arameans covered the countryside.

28The man of God came up and told the king of Israel, "This is what the LORD says: 'Because the Arameans think the LORD is a god of the hills and not a god of the valleys, I will deliver this vast army into your hands, and you will know that I am the LORD.' "

29For seven days they camped opposite each other, and on the seventh day the battle was joined. The Israelites inflicted a hundred thousand casualties on the Aramean foot soldiers in one day. 30The rest of them escaped to the city of Aphek, where the wall collapsed on twenty-seven thousand of them. And Ben-Hadad fled to the city and hid in an inner room.

31His officials said to him, "Look, we have heard that the kings of the house of Israel are merciful. Let us go to the king of Israel with sackcloth around our waists and ropes around our heads. Perhaps he will spare your life."

32Wearing sackcloth around their waists and ropes around their heads, they went to the king of Israel and said, "Your servant Ben-Hadad says: 'Please let me live.' "

The king answered, "Is he still alive? He is my brother."

33The men took this as a good sign and were quick to pick up his word. "Yes, your brother Ben-Hadad!" they said.

"Go and get him," the king said. When Ben-Hadad came out, Ahab had him come up into his chariot.

34"I will return the cities my father took from your father," Ben-Hadad offered. "You may set up your own market areas in Damascus, as my father did in Samaria."

⌊Ahab said,⌋ "On the basis of a treaty I will set you free." So he made a treaty with him, and let him go.

A Prophet Condemns Ahab

35By the word of the LORD one of the sons of the prophets said to his companion, "Strike me with your weapon," but the man refused.

36So the prophet said, "Because you have not obeyed the LORD, as soon as you leave me a lion will kill you." And after the man went away, a lion found him and killed him.

37The prophet found another man and said, "Strike me,

King James	Amplified

King James

38So the prophet departed, and waited for the king by the way, and disguised himself with ashes upon his face.

39And as the king passed by, he cried unto the king: and he said, Thy servant went out into the midst of the battle; and, behold, a man turned aside, and brought a man unto me, and said, Keep this man: if by any means he be missing, then shall thy life be for his life, or else thou shalt *n*pay a talent of silver.

40And as thy servant was busy here and there, *o*he was gone. And the king of Israel said unto him, So *shall* thy judgment *be; thyself hast decided *it.

41And he hasted, and took the ashes away from his face; and the king of Israel discerned him that he *was* of the prophets.

42And he said unto him, Thus saith the LORD, Because thou hast let go out of *thy* hand a man whom I appointed to utter destruction, therefore thy life shall go for his life, and thy people for his people.

43And the king of Israel went to his house heavy and displeased, and came to Samaria.

Naboth's vineyard

21 AND IT came to pass after these things, *that* Naboth the Jezreelite had a vineyard, which *was* in Jezreel, hard by the palace of Ahab king of Samaria.

2And Ahab spake unto Naboth, saying, Give me thy vineyard, that I may have it for a garden of herbs, because it *is* near unto my house: and I will give thee for it a better vineyard than it; *or,* if it *p*seem good to thee, I will give thee the worth of it in money.

3And Naboth said to Ahab, The LORD forbid it me, that I should give the inheritance of my fathers unto thee.

4And Ahab came into his house heavy and displeased because of the word which Naboth the Jezreelite had spoken to him: for he had said, I will not give thee the inheritance of my fathers. And he laid him down upon his bed, and turned away his face, and would eat no bread.

5 ¶ But Jezebel his wife came to him, and said unto him, Why is thy spirit so sad, that thou eatest no bread?

6And he said unto her, Because I spake unto Naboth the Jezreelite, and said unto him, Give me thy vineyard for money; or else, if it please thee, I will give thee *another* vineyard for it: and he answered, I will not give thee my vineyard.

7And Jezebel his wife said unto him, Dost thou now govern the kingdom of Israel? arise, *and* eat bread, and let thine heart be merry: I will give thee the vineyard of Naboth the Jezreelite.

8So she wrote letters in Ahab's name, and sealed *them* with his seal, and sent the letters unto the elders and to the nobles that *were* in his city, dwelling with Naboth.

9And she wrote in the letters, saying, Proclaim a fast, and set Naboth *q*on high among the people:

10And set two men, sons of Belial, before him, to bear witness against him, saying, Thou didst blaspheme God and the king. And *then* carry him out, and stone him, that he may die.

11And the men of his city, *even* the elders and the nobles who were the inhabitants in his city, did as Jezebel had sent unto them, *and* as it *was* written in the letters which she had sent unto them.

12They proclaimed a fast, and set Naboth on high among the people.

13And there came in two men, children of Belial, and sat before him: and the men of Belial witnessed against him, *even* against Naboth, in the presence of the people, saying, Naboth did blaspheme God and the king. Then they carried him forth out of the city, and stoned him with stones, that he died.

Amplified

38So the prophet departed and waited for King Ahab by the way, and disguised himself with ashes upon his face.

39And as the king passed by, the [prophet] cried out to him, Your servant went out into the midst of the battle, and behold, a man turned aside and brought a man to me and said, Keep this man. If for any reason he is missing, then your life shall be required for his life, or else you shall pay a talent of silver.

40But while your servant was busy here and there, he was gone. And the king of Israel said to him, Such is your own verdict; you yourself have decided it.

41The man hastily removed the ashes from his face, and Ahab king of Israel recognized him as one of the prophets.

42And he said to the king, Thus says the Lord: Because you have let go out of your hand the man I had devoted to destruction, therefore your life shall go for his life, and your people for his people.

43And King [Ahab] of Israel went to his house resentful and sullen, and came to Samaria. [I Kings 22:34–36.]

21 NOW NABOTH the Jezreelite had a vineyard in Jezreel, close beside the palace of Ahab king of Samaria; and after these things,

2Ahab said to Naboth, Give me your vineyard, that I may have it for a garden of herbs, because it is near my house. I will give you a better vineyard for it or, if you prefer, I will give you its worth in money.

3Naboth said to Ahab, The Lord forbid that I should give the inheritance of my fathers to you.

4And Ahab [already depressed by the Lord's message to him] came into his house [more] resentful and sullen because of what Naboth the Jezreelite had said to him; for he had said, I will not give you the inheritance of my fathers. And he lay down on his bed, turned away his face, and would eat no food.

5But Jezebel his wife came and said to him, Why is your spirit so troubled that you eat no food?

6And he said to her, Because I spoke to Naboth the Jezreelite and said to him, Give me your vineyard for money; or if you prefer, I will give you another vineyard for it. And he answered, I will not give you my vineyard.

7Jezebel his wife said to him, Do you not govern Israel? Arise, eat food, and let your heart be happy. I will give you the vineyard of Naboth the Jezreelite.

8So she wrote letters in Ahab's name and sealed them with his seal and sent them to the elders and nobles who dwelt with Naboth in his city.

9And in the letters she said, Proclaim a fast and set Naboth up high among the people.

10And set two men, base fellows, before him, and let them bear witness against him, saying, You cursed *and* renounced God and the king. Then carry him out and stone him to death.

11And the men of his city, the elders and the nobles who dwelt there, did as Jezebel had directed in the letters sent them.

12They proclaimed a fast and set Naboth on high among the people.

13Two base fellows came in and sat opposite him and they charged Naboth before the people, saying, Naboth cursed *and* renounced God and the king. Then he was carried out of the city and stoned to death.

---

*n*Heb. *weigh*   *o*Heb. *he was not*   *p*Heb. *be good in thine eyes*   *q*Heb. *in the top of the people*

New American Standard

38 So the prophet departed and waited for the king by the way, and disguised himself with a bandage over his eyes.

39 As the king passed by, he cried to the king and said, "Your servant went out into the midst of the battle; and behold, a man turned aside and brought a man to me and said, 'Guard this man; if for any reason he is missing, then your life shall be for his life, or else you shall pay a talent of silver.'

40 "While your servant was busy here and there, he was gone." And the king of Israel said to him, "So shall your judgment be; you yourself have decided it."

41 Then he hastily took the bandage away from his eyes, and the king of Israel recognized him that he was of the prophets.

42 He said to him, "Thus says the LORD, 'Because you have let go out of your hand the man whom I had devoted to destruction, therefore your life shall go for his life, and your people for his people.'"

43 So the king of Israel went to his house sullen and vexed, and came to Samaria.

Ahab Covets Naboth's Vineyard

21 NOW IT came about after these things that Naboth the Jezreelite had a vineyard which was in Jezreel beside the palace of Ahab king of Samaria.

2 Ahab spoke to Naboth, saying, "Give me your vineyard, that I may have it for a vegetable garden because it is close beside my house, and I will give you a better vineyard than it in its place; if you like, I will give you the price of it in money."

3 But Naboth said to Ahab, "The LORD forbid me that I should give you the inheritance of my fathers."

4 So Ahab came into his house sullen and vexed because of the word which Naboth the Jezreelite had spoken to him; for he said, "I will not give you the inheritance of my fathers." And he lay down on his bed and turned away his face and ate no food.

5 ¶ But Jezebel his wife came to him and said to him, "How is it that your spirit is so sullen that you are not eating food?"

6 So he said to her, "Because I spoke to Naboth the Jezreelite and said to him, 'Give me your vineyard for money; or else, if it pleases you, I will give you a vineyard in its place.' But he said, 'I will not give you my vineyard.'"

7 Jezebel his wife said to him, "Do you now reign over Israel? Arise, eat bread, and let your heart be joyful; I will give you the vineyard of Naboth the Jezreelite."

8 ¶ So she wrote letters in Ahab's name and sealed them with his seal, and sent letters to the elders and to the nobles who were living with Naboth in his city.

9 Now she wrote in the letters, saying, "Proclaim a fast and seat Naboth at the head of the people;

10 and seat two worthless men before him, and let them testify against him, saying, 'You cursed God and the king.' Then take him out and stone him to death."

Jezebel's Plot

11 ¶ So the men of his city, the elders and the nobles who lived in his city, did as Jezebel had sent word to them, just as it was written in the letters which she had sent them.

12 They proclaimed a fast and seated Naboth at the head of the people.

13 Then the two worthless men came in and sat before him; and the worthless men testified against him, even against Naboth, before the people, saying, "Naboth cursed God and the king." So they took him outside the city and stoned him to death with stones.

New International

please." So the man struck him and wounded him. 38 Then the prophet went and stood by the road waiting for the king. He disguised himself with his headband down over his eyes. 39 As the king passed by, the prophet called out to him, "Your servant went into the thick of the battle, and someone came to me with a captive and said, 'Guard this man. If he is missing, it will be your life for his life, or you must pay a talent*p* of silver.' 40 While your servant was busy here and there, the man disappeared."

"That is your sentence," the king of Israel said. "You have pronounced it yourself."

41 Then the prophet quickly removed the headband from his eyes, and the king of Israel recognized him as one of the prophets. 42 He said to the king, "This is what the LORD says: 'You have set free a man I had determined should die.*q* Therefore it is your life for his life, your people for his people.'" 43 Sullen and angry, the king of Israel went to his palace in Samaria.

Naboth's Vineyard

21 SOME TIME later there was an incident involving a vineyard belonging to Naboth the Jezreelite. The vineyard was in Jezreel, close to the palace of Ahab king of Samaria. 2 Ahab said to Naboth, "Let me have your vineyard to use for a vegetable garden, since it is close to my palace. In exchange I will give you a better vineyard or, if you prefer, I will pay you whatever it is worth."

3 But Naboth replied, "The LORD forbid that I should give you the inheritance of my fathers."

4 So Ahab went home, sullen and angry because Naboth the Jezreelite had said, "I will not give you the inheritance of my fathers." He lay on his bed sulking and refused to eat.

5 His wife Jezebel came in and asked him, "Why are you so sullen? Why won't you eat?"

6 He answered her, "Because I said to Naboth the Jezreelite, 'Sell me your vineyard; or if you prefer, I will give you another vineyard in its place.' But he said, 'I will not give you my vineyard.'"

7 Jezebel his wife said, "Is this how you act as king over Israel? Get up and eat! Cheer up. I'll get you the vineyard of Naboth the Jezreelite."

8 So she wrote letters in Ahab's name, placed his seal on them, and sent them to the elders and nobles who lived in Naboth's city with him. 9 In those letters she wrote:

"Proclaim a day of fasting and seat Naboth in a prominent place among the people. 10 But seat two scoundrels opposite him and have them testify that he has cursed both God and the king. Then take him out and stone him to death."

11 So the elders and nobles who lived in Naboth's city did as Jezebel directed in the letters she had written to them. 12 They proclaimed a fast and seated Naboth in a prominent place among the people. 13 Then two scoundrels came and sat opposite him and brought charges against Naboth before the people, saying, "Naboth has cursed both God and the king." So they took him outside the city and

---

p 39 That is, about 75 pounds (about 34 kilograms)
q 42 The Hebrew term refers to the irrevocable giving over of things or persons to the LORD, often by totally destroying them.

King James

¹⁴Then they sent to Jezebel, saying, Naboth is stoned, and is dead.

¹⁵ ¶ And it came to pass, when Jezebel heard that Naboth was stoned, and was dead, that Jezebel said to Ahab, Arise, take possession of the vineyard of Naboth the Jezreelite, which he refused to give thee for money: for Naboth is not alive, but dead.

¹⁶And it came to pass, when Ahab heard that Naboth was dead, that Ahab rose up to go down to the vineyard of Naboth the Jezreelite, to take possession of it.

¹⁷ ¶ And the word of the LORD came to Elijah the Tishbite, saying,

¹⁸Arise, go down to meet Ahab king of Israel, which *is* in Samaria: behold, *he is* in the vineyard of Naboth, whither he is gone down to possess it.

¹⁹And thou shalt speak unto him, saying, Thus saith the LORD, Hast thou killed, and also taken possession? And thou shalt speak unto him, saying, Thus saith the LORD, In the place where dogs licked the blood of Naboth shall dogs lick thy blood, even thine.

²⁰And Ahab said to Elijah, Hast thou found me, O mine enemy? And he answered, I have found *thee:* because thou hast sold thyself to work evil in the sight of the LORD.

²¹Behold, I will bring evil upon thee, and will take away thy posterity, and will cut off from Ahab him that pisseth against the wall, and him that is shut up and left in Israel,

²²And will make thine house like the house of Jeroboam the son of Nebat, and like the house of Baasha the son of Ahijah, for the provocation wherewith thou hast provoked *me* to anger, and made Israel to sin.

²³And of Jezebel also spake the LORD, saying, The dogs shall eat Jezebel by the ^rwall of Jezreel.

²⁴Him that dieth of Ahab in the city the dogs shall eat; and him that dieth in the field shall the fowls of the air eat.

²⁵ ¶ But there was none like unto Ahab, which did sell himself to work wickedness in the sight of the LORD, whom Jezebel his wife ^sstirred up.

²⁶And he did very abominably in following idols, according to all *things* as did the Amorites, whom the LORD cast out before the children of Israel.

²⁷And it came to pass, when Ahab heard those words, that he rent his clothes, and put sackcloth upon his flesh, and fasted, and lay in sackcloth, and went softly.

²⁸And the word of the LORD came to Elijah the Tishbite, saying,

²⁹Seest thou how Ahab humbleth himself before me? because he humbleth himself before me, I will not bring the evil in his days; *but* in his son's days will I bring the evil upon his house.

Micaiah's prophecy

22 AND THEY continued three years without war between Syria and Israel.

²And it came to pass in the third year, that Jehoshaphat the king of Judah came down to the king of Israel.

³And the king of Israel said unto his servants, Know ye that Ramoth in Gilead *is* ours, and we *be* ^tstill, *and* take it not out of the hand of the king of Syria?

⁴And he said unto Jehoshaphat, Wilt thou go with me to battle to Ramoth-gilead? And Jehoshaphat said to the king of Israel, I *am* as thou *art,* my people as thy people, my horses as thy horses.

⁵And Jehoshaphat said unto the king of Israel, Inquire, I pray thee, at the word of the LORD today.

⁶Then the king of Israel gathered the prophets together, about four hundred men, and said unto them, Shall I go against Ramoth-gilead to battle, or shall I forbear? And they said, Go up; for the Lord shall deliver *it* into the hand of the king.

Amplified

¹⁴Then they sent to Jezebel, saying, Naboth has been stoned and is dead.

¹⁵Then Jezebel said to Ahab, Arise, take possession of the vineyard of Naboth the Jezreelite which he refused to sell you, for Naboth is not alive, but dead.

¹⁶When Ahab heard that, he arose to go down to the vineyard of Naboth the Jezreelite to take possession of it.

¹⁷Then the word of the Lord came to Elijah the Tishbite, saying,

¹⁸Arise, go down to meet Ahab king of Israel in Samaria. He is in the vineyard of Naboth, where he has gone to possess it.

¹⁹Say to him, Thus says the Lord: Have you killed and also taken possession? Thus says the Lord: In the place where dogs licked the blood of Naboth shall dogs lick your blood, even yours.

²⁰And Ahab said to Elijah, Have you found me, O my enemy? And he answered, I have found you, because you have sold yourself to do evil in the sight of the Lord.

²¹See [says the Lord], I will bring evil on you and utterly sweep away and cut off from Ahab every male, bond and free,

²²And will make your household like that of Jeroboam son of Nebat and like the household of Baasha son of Ahijah, for the provocation with which you have provoked Me to anger and made Israel to sin.

²³Also the Lord said of Jezebel: The dogs shall eat Jezebel by the wall of Jezreel.

²⁴Any belonging to Ahab who dies in the city the dogs shall eat, and any who dies in the field the birds of the air shall eat. [I Kings 14:11; 16:4.]

²⁵For there was no one who sold himself to do evil in the sight of the Lord as did Ahab, incited by his wife Jezebel.

²⁶He did very abominably in going after idols, as had the Amorites, whom the Lord cast out before the Israelites.

²⁷When Ahab heard those words of Elijah, he tore his clothes, put sackcloth on his flesh, fasted, lay in sackcloth, and went quietly.

²⁸And the word of the Lord came to Elijah the Tishbite, saying,

²⁹Do you see how Ahab humbles himself before Me? Because he humbles himself before Me, I will not bring the evil in his lifetime, but in his son's day I will bring the evil upon his house.

22 SYRIA AND Israel continued without war for three years.

²In the third year Jehoshaphat king of Judah came down to the king of Israel.

³And [Ahab] king of Israel said to his servants, Do you know that Ramoth in Gilead is ours, and we keep silence and do not take it from the king of Syria?

⁴And [Ahab] said to Jehoshaphat, Will you go with me to Ramoth-gilead to battle? Jehoshaphat said to the king of Israel, I am as you are, my people as your people, my horses as your horses.

⁵But Jehoshaphat said to the king of Israel, Inquire first, I pray you, for the word of the Lord today.

⁶Then [Ahab] king of Israel gathered the prophets together, about 400 men, and said to them, Shall I go against Ramoth-gilead to battle, or shall I hold back? And they said, Go up, for the Lord will deliver it into the hand of the king.

^rOr, ditch　　^sOr, incited　　^tHeb. silent from taking it

New American Standard

14 Then they sent *word* to Jezebel, saying, "Naboth has been stoned and is dead."

15 ¶ When Jezebel heard that Naboth had been stoned and was dead, Jezebel said to Ahab, "Arise, take possession of the vineyard of Naboth, the Jezreelite, which he refused to give you for money; for Naboth is not alive, but dead."

16 When Ahab heard that Naboth was dead, Ahab arose to go down to the vineyard of Naboth the Jezreelite, to take possession of it.

17 ¶ Then the word of the LORD came to Elijah the Tishbite, saying,

18 "Arise, go down to meet Ahab king of Israel, who is in Samaria; behold, he is in the vineyard of Naboth where he has gone down to take possession of it.

19 "You shall speak to him, saying, 'Thus says the LORD, "Have you murdered and also taken possession?" ' And you shall speak to him, saying, 'Thus says the LORD, "In the place where the dogs licked up the blood of Naboth the dogs will lick up your blood, even yours." ' "

20 ¶ Ahab said to Elijah, "Have you found me, O my enemy?" And he answered, "I have found *you,* because you have sold yourself to do evil in the sight of the LORD.

21 "Behold, I will bring evil upon you, and will utterly sweep you away, and will cut off from Ahab every male, both bond and free in Israel;

22 and I will make your house like the house of Jeroboam the son of Nebat, and like the house of Baasha the son of Ahijah, because of the provocation with which you have provoked *Me* to anger, and *because* you have made Israel sin.

23 "Of Jezebel also has the LORD spoken, saying, 'The dogs will eat Jezebel in the district of Jezreel.'

24 "The one belonging to Ahab, who dies in the city, the dogs will eat, and the one who dies in the field the birds of heaven will eat."

25 ¶ Surely there was no one like Ahab who sold himself to do evil in the sight of the LORD, because Jezebel his wife incited him.

26 He acted very abominably in following idols, according to all that the Amorites had done, whom the LORD cast out before the sons of Israel.

27 ¶ It came about when Ahab heard these words, that he tore his clothes and put on sackcloth and fasted, and he lay in sackcloth and went about despondently.

28 Then the word of the LORD came to Elijah the Tishbite, saying,

29 "Do you see how Ahab has humbled himself before Me? Because he has humbled himself before Me, I will not bring the evil in his days, *but* I will bring the evil upon his house in his son's days."

Ahab's Third Campaign against Aram

22 THREE YEARS passed without war between Aram and Israel.

2 In the third year Jehoshaphat the king of Judah came down to the king of Israel.

3 Now the king of Israel said to his servants, "Do you know that Ramoth-gilead belongs to us, and we are still doing nothing to take it out of the hand of the king of Aram?"

4 And he said to Jehoshaphat, "Will you go with me to battle at Ramoth-gilead?" And Jehoshaphat said to the king of Israel, "I am as you are, my people as your people, my horses as your horses."

5 ¶ Moreover, Jehoshaphat said to the king of Israel, "Please inquire first for the word of the LORD."

6 Then the king of Israel gathered the prophets together, about four hundred men, and said to them, "Shall I go against Ramoth-gilead to battle or shall I refrain?" And they said, "Go up, for the Lord will give *it* into the hand of the king."

New International

stoned him to death. 14 Then they sent word to Jezebel: "Naboth has been stoned and is dead."

15 As soon as Jezebel heard that Naboth had been stoned to death, she said to Ahab, "Get up and take possession of the vineyard of Naboth the Jezreelite that he refused to sell you. He is no longer alive, but dead." 16 When Ahab heard that Naboth was dead, he got up and went down to take possession of Naboth's vineyard.

17 Then the word of the LORD came to Elijah the Tishbite: 18 "Go down to meet Ahab king of Israel, who rules in Samaria. He is now in Naboth's vineyard, where he has gone to take possession of it. 19 Say to him, 'This is what the LORD says: Have you not murdered a man and seized his property?' Then say to him, 'This is what the LORD says: In the place where dogs licked up Naboth's blood, dogs will lick up your blood—yes, yours!' "

20 Ahab said to Elijah, "So you have found me, my enemy!"

"I have found you," he answered, "because you have sold yourself to do evil in the eyes of the LORD. 21 'I am going to bring disaster on you. I will consume your descendants and cut off from Ahab every last male in Israel—slave or free. 22 I will make your house like that of Jeroboam son of Nebat and that of Baasha son of Ahijah, because you have provoked me to anger and have caused Israel to sin.'

23 "And also concerning Jezebel the LORD says: 'Dogs will devour Jezebel by the wall of[r] Jezreel.'

24 "Dogs will eat those belonging to Ahab who die in the city, and the birds of the air will feed on those who die in the country."

25 (There was never a man like Ahab, who sold himself to do evil in the eyes of the LORD, urged on by Jezebel his wife. 26 He behaved in the vilest manner by going after idols, like the Amorites the LORD drove out before Israel.)

27 When Ahab heard these words, he tore his clothes, put on sackcloth and fasted. He lay in sackcloth and went around meekly.

28 Then the word of the LORD came to Elijah the Tishbite: 29 "Have you noticed how Ahab has humbled himself before me? Because he has humbled himself, I will not bring this disaster in his day, but I will bring it on his house in the days of his son."

Micaiah Prophesies Against Ahab

22 FOR THREE years there was no war between Aram and Israel. 2 But in the third year Jehoshaphat king of Judah went down to see the king of Israel. 3 The king of Israel had said to his officials, "Don't you know that Ramoth Gilead belongs to us and yet we are doing nothing to retake it from the king of Aram?"

4 So he asked Jehoshaphat, "Will you go with me to fight against Ramoth Gilead?"

Jehoshaphat replied to the king of Israel, "I am as you are, my people as your people, my horses as your horses." 5 But Jehoshaphat also said to the king of Israel, "First seek the counsel of the LORD."

6 So the king of Israel brought together the prophets—about four hundred men—and asked them, "Shall I go to war against Ramoth Gilead, or shall I refrain?"

"Go," they answered, "for the Lord will give it into the king's hand."

r23 Most Hebrew manuscripts; a few Hebrew manuscripts, Vulgate and Syriac (see also 2 Kings 9:26) *the plot of ground at*

King James

⁷And Jehoshaphat said, *Is there* not here a prophet of the LORD besides, that we might inquire of him?

⁸And the king of Israel said unto Jehoshaphat, *There is* yet one man, Micaiah the son of Imlah, by whom we may inquire of the LORD: but I hate him; for he doth not prophesy good concerning me, but evil. And Jehoshaphat said, Let not the king say so.

⁹Then the king of Israel called an ᵘofficer, and said, Hasten *hither* Micaiah the son of Imlah.

¹⁰And the king of Israel and Jehoshaphat the king of Judah sat each on his throne, having put on their robes, in a ᵛvoid place in the entrance of the gate of Samaria; and all the prophets prophesied before them.

¹¹And Zedekiah the son of Chenaanah made him horns of iron: and he said, Thus saith the LORD, With these shalt thou push the Syrians, until thou have consumed them.

¹²And all the prophets prophesied so, saying, Go up to Ramoth-gilead, and prosper: for the LORD shall deliver *it* into the king's hand.

¹³And the messenger that was gone to call Micaiah spake unto him, saying, Behold now, the words of the prophets *declare* good unto the king with one mouth: let thy word, I pray thee, be like the word of one of them, and speak *that which is* good.

¹⁴And Micaiah said, *As* the LORD liveth, what the LORD saith unto me, that will I speak.

¹⁵ ¶ So he came to the king. And the king said unto him, Micaiah, shall we go against Ramoth-gilead to battle, or shall we forbear? And he answered him, Go, and prosper: for the LORD shall deliver *it* into the hand of the king.

¹⁶And the king said unto him, How many times shall I adjure thee that thou tell me nothing but *that which is* true in the name of the LORD?

¹⁷And he said, I saw all Israel scattered upon the hills, as sheep that have not a shepherd: and the LORD said, These have no master: let them return every man to his house in peace.

¹⁸And the king of Israel said unto Jehoshaphat, Did I not tell thee that he would prophesy no good concerning me, but evil?

¹⁹And he said, Hear thou therefore the word of the LORD: I saw the LORD sitting on his throne, and all the host of heaven standing by him on his right hand and on his left.

²⁰And the LORD said, Who shall ʷpersuade Ahab, that he may go up and fall at Ramoth-gilead? And one said on this manner, and another said on that manner.

²¹And there came forth a spirit, and stood before the LORD, and said, I will persuade him.

²²And the LORD said unto him, Wherewith? And he said, I will go forth, and I will be a lying spirit in the mouth of all his prophets. And he said, Thou shalt persuade *him*, and prevail also: go forth, and do so.

²³Now therefore, behold, the LORD hath put a lying spirit in the mouth of all these thy prophets, and the LORD hath spoken evil concerning thee.

²⁴But Zedekiah the son of Chenaanah went near, and smote Micaiah on the cheek, and said, Which way went the spirit of the LORD from me to speak unto thee?

²⁵And Micaiah said, Behold, thou shalt see in that day, when thou shalt go ˣinto ʸan inner chamber to hide thyself.

²⁶And the king of Israel said, Take Micaiah, and carry him back unto Amon the governor of the city, and to Joash the king's son;

²⁷And say, Thus saith the king, Put this *fellow* in the prison, and feed him with bread of affliction and with water of affliction, until I come in peace.

Amplified

⁷Jehoshaphat said, Is there not another prophet of the Lord here whom we may ask?

⁸[Ahab] king of Israel said to Jehoshaphat, There is yet one man, Micaiah son of Imlah, by whom we may inquire of the Lord, but I hate him, for he never prophesies good for me, but evil. Jehoshaphat said, Let not the king say that.

⁹Then [Ahab] king of Israel told an officer, Bring quickly Micaiah son of Imlah.

¹⁰Now the king of Israel and Jehoshaphat king of Judah were sitting in [royal] robes [or armor], each on his throne in an open place [on a threshing floor] at the entrance of the gate of Samaria; and all the prophets prophesied before them.

¹¹And Zedekiah son of Chenaanah made him horns of iron and said, Thus says the Lord: With these you shall push the Syrians until they are destroyed.

¹²And all the prophets agreed, saying, Go up to Ramoth-gilead and prosper, for the Lord will deliver it into the king's hand.

¹³The messenger who went to call Micaiah said to him, Behold now, the prophets unanimously declare good to the king. Let your answer, I pray you, be like theirs, and say what is good.

¹⁴But Micaiah said, As the Lord lives, I will speak what the Lord says to me.

¹⁵So he came to the king. King [Ahab] said, Micaiah, shall we go against Ramoth-gilead to battle, or shall we hold back? And he answered, Go and prosper, for the Lord will deliver it into the king's hand.

¹⁶And the king said to him, How many times must I charge you to tell me nothing but the truth in the name of the Lord?

¹⁷And he said, I saw all Israel scattered upon the hills as sheep that have no shepherd, and the Lord said, These have no master. Let them return every man to his house in peace.

¹⁸Then the king of Israel said to Jehoshaphat, Did I not tell you that he would prophesy no good concerning me, but evil?

¹⁹And Micaiah said, Hear the word of the Lord: I saw the Lord sitting on His throne, and all the host of heaven standing by Him on His right hand and on His left.

²⁰And the Lord said, Who will entice Ahab to go up and fall at Ramoth-gilead? One said this way, another said that way.

²¹Then there came forth a spirit [of whom I am about to tell] and stood before the Lord and said, I will entice him.

²²The Lord said to him, By what means? And he said, I will go forth and be a lying spirit in the mouths of all his prophets. [The Lord] said, You shall entice him and succeed also. Go forth and do it.

²³So the Lord has put a lying spirit in the mouths of all these prophets; and the Lord has spoken evil concerning you.

²⁴But Zedekiah son of Chenaanah went near and struck Micaiah on the cheek and said, Which way went the Spirit of the Lord from me to speak to you?

²⁵Micaiah said, Behold, you shall see on that day when you go into an inner chamber to hide yourself.

²⁶[Ahab] king of Israel said, Take Micaiah, carry him back to Amon the governor of the city and to Joash the king's son,

²⁷And say, The king says, Put this fellow in prison and feed him with bread and water of affliction until I come in peace.

ᵘOr, *eunuch*   ᵛHeb. *floor*   ʷOr, *deceive*   ˣOr, *from chamber to chamber*   ʸHeb. *a chamber in a chamber*

New American Standard

7 But Jehoshaphat said, "Is there not yet a prophet of the LORD here that we may inquire of him?"

8 The king of Israel said to Jehoshaphat, "There is yet one man by whom we may inquire of the LORD, but I hate him, because he does not prophesy good concerning me, but evil. *He is* Micaiah son of Imlah." But Jehoshaphat said, "Let not the king say so."

9 Then the king of Israel called an officer and said, "Bring quickly Micaiah son of Imlah."

10 Now the king of Israel and Jehoshaphat king of Judah were sitting each on his throne, arrayed in *their* robes, at the threshing floor at the entrance of the gate of Samaria; and all the prophets were prophesying before them.

11 Then Zedekiah the son of Chenaanah made horns of iron for himself and said, "Thus says the LORD, 'With these you will gore the Arameans until they are consumed.'"

12 All the prophets were prophesying thus, saying, "Go up to Ramoth-gilead and prosper, for the LORD will give *it* into the hand of the king."

Micaiah Predicts Defeat

13 ¶ Then the messenger who went to summon Micaiah spoke to him saying, "Behold now, the words of the prophets are uniformly favorable to the king. Please let your word be like the word of one of them, and speak favorably."

14 But Micaiah said, "As the LORD lives, what the LORD says to me, that I shall speak."

15 ¶ When he came to the king, the king said to him, "Micaiah, shall we go to Ramoth-gilead to battle, or shall we refrain?" And he answered him, "Go up and succeed, and the LORD will give *it* into the hand of the king."

16 Then the king said to him, "How many times must I adjure you to speak to me nothing but the truth in the name of the LORD?"

17 So he said,

"I saw all Israel
Scattered on the mountains,
Like sheep which have no shepherd.
And the LORD said, 'These have no master.
Let each of them return to his house in peace.'"

18 Then the king of Israel said to Jehoshaphat, "Did I not tell you that he would not prophesy good concerning me, but evil?"

19 ¶ Micaiah said, "Therefore, hear the word of the LORD. I saw the LORD sitting on His throne, and all the host of heaven standing by Him on His right and on His left.

20 "The LORD said, 'Who will entice Ahab to go up and fall at Ramoth-gilead?' And one said this while another said that.

21 "Then a spirit came forward and stood before the LORD and said, 'I will entice him.'

22 "The LORD said to him, 'How?' And he said, 'I will go out and be a deceiving spirit in the mouth of all his prophets.' Then He said, 'You are to entice *him* and also prevail. Go and do so.'

23 "Now therefore, behold, the LORD has put a deceiving spirit in the mouth of all these your prophets; and the LORD has proclaimed disaster against you."

24 ¶ Then Zedekiah the son of Chenaanah came near and struck Micaiah on the cheek and said, "How did the Spirit of the LORD pass from me to speak to you?"

25 Micaiah said, "Behold, you shall see on that day when you enter an inner room to hide yourself."

26 Then the king of Israel said, "Take Micaiah and return him to Amon the governor of the city and to Joash the king's son;

27 and say, 'Thus says the king, "Put this man in prison and feed him sparingly with bread and water until I return safely."'"

New International

7But Jehoshaphat asked, "Is there not a prophet of the LORD here whom we can inquire of?"

8The king of Israel answered Jehoshaphat, "There is still one man through whom we can inquire of the LORD, but I hate him because he never prophesies anything good about me, but always bad. He is Micaiah son of Imlah."

"The king should not say that," Jehoshaphat replied.

9So the king of Israel called one of his officials and said, "Bring Micaiah son of Imlah at once."

10Dressed in their royal robes, the king of Israel and Jehoshaphat king of Judah were sitting on their thrones at the threshing floor by the entrance of the gate of Samaria, with all the prophets prophesying before them. 11Now Zedekiah son of Kenaanah had made iron horns and he declared, "This is what the LORD says: 'With these you will gore the Arameans until they are destroyed.'"

12All the other prophets were prophesying the same thing. "Attack Ramoth Gilead and be victorious," they said, "for the LORD will give it into the king's hand."

13The messenger who had gone to summon Micaiah said to him, "Look, as one man the other prophets are predicting success for the king. Let your word agree with theirs, and speak favorably."

14But Micaiah said, "As surely as the LORD lives, I can tell him only what the LORD tells me."

15When he arrived, the king asked him, "Micaiah, shall we go to war against Ramoth Gilead, or shall I refrain?"

"Attack and be victorious," he answered, "for the LORD will give it into the king's hand."

16The king said to him, "How many times must I make you swear to tell me nothing but the truth in the name of the LORD?"

17Then Micaiah answered, "I saw all Israel scattered on the hills like sheep without a shepherd, and the LORD said, 'These people have no master. Let each one go home in peace.'"

18The king of Israel said to Jehoshaphat, "Didn't I tell you that he never prophesies anything good about me, but only bad?"

19Micaiah continued, "Therefore hear the word of the LORD: I saw the LORD sitting on his throne with all the host of heaven standing around him on his right and on his left. 20And the LORD said, 'Who will entice Ahab into attacking Ramoth Gilead and going to his death there?'

"One suggested this, and another that. 21Finally, a spirit came forward, stood before the LORD and said, 'I will entice him.'

22"'By what means?' the LORD asked.

"'I will go out and be a lying spirit in the mouths of all his prophets,' he said.

"'You will succeed in enticing him,' said the LORD. 'Go and do it.'

23"So now the LORD has put a lying spirit in the mouths of all these prophets of yours. The LORD has decreed disaster for you."

24Then Zedekiah son of Kenaanah went up and slapped Micaiah in the face. "Which way did the spirit from[s] the LORD go when he went from me to speak to you?" he asked.

25Micaiah replied, "You will find out on the day you go to hide in an inner room."

26The king of Israel then ordered, "Take Micaiah and send him back to Amon the ruler of the city and to Joash the king's son 27and say, 'This is what the king says: Put this fellow in prison and give him nothing but bread and water until I return safely.'"

s 24 Or *Spirit of*

King James

Amplified

28And Micaiah said, If thou return at all in peace, the LORD hath not spoken by me. And he said, Hearken, O people, every one of you.

Ahab's defeat and death

29So the king of Israel and Jehoshaphat the king of Judah went up to Ramoth-gilead.

30And the king of Israel said unto Jehoshaphat, zI will disguise myself, and enter into the battle; but put thou on thy robes. And the king of Israel disguised himself, and went into the battle.

31But the king of Syria commanded his thirty and two captains that had rule over his chariots, saying, Fight neither with small nor great, save only with the king of Israel.

32And it came to pass, when the captains of the chariots saw Jehoshaphat, that they said, Surely it is the king of Israel. And they turned aside to fight against him: and Jehoshaphat cried out.

33And it came to pass, when the captains of the chariots perceived that it was not the king of Israel, that they turned back from pursuing him.

34And a certain man drew a bow at a venture, and smote the king of Israel between the ajoints of the harness: wherefore he said unto the driver of his chariot, Turn thine hand, and carry me out of the host; for I am bwounded.

35And the battle cincreased that day: and the king was stayed up in his chariot against the Syrians, and died at even: and the blood ran out of the wound into the dmidst of the chariot.

36And there went a proclamation throughout the host about the going down of the sun, saying, Every man to his city, and every man to his own country.

37 ¶ So the king died, and ewas brought to Samaria; and they buried the king in Samaria.

38And one washed the chariot in the pool of Samaria; and the dogs licked up his blood; and they washed his armour; according unto the word of the LORD which he spake.

39Now the rest of the acts of Ahab, and all that he did, and the ivory house which he made, and all the cities that he built, are they not written in the book of the chronicles of the kings of Israel?

40So Ahab slept with his fathers; and Ahaziah his son reigned in his stead.

Jehoshaphat, king of Judah

41 ¶ And Jehoshaphat the son of Asa began to reign over Judah in the fourth year of Ahab king of Israel.

42Jehoshaphat was thirty and five years old when he began to reign; and he reigned twenty and five years in Jerusalem. And his mother's name was Azubah the daughter of Shilhi.

43And he walked in all the ways of Asa his father; he turned not aside from it, doing that which was right in the eyes of the LORD: nevertheless the high places were not taken away; for the people offered and burnt incense yet in the high places.

44And Jehoshaphat made peace with the king of Israel.

45Now the rest of the acts of Jehoshaphat, and his might that he showed, and how he warred, are they not written in the book of the chronicles of the kings of Judah?

46And the remnant of the sodomites, which remained in the days of his father Asa, he took out of the land.

47There was then no king in Edom: a deputy was king.

48Jehoshaphat fmade ships of Tharshish to go to Ophir for gold: but they went not; for the ships were broken at Ezion-geber.

49Then said Ahaziah the son of Ahab unto Jehoshaphat, Let my servants go with thy servants in the ships. But Jehoshaphat would not.

Amplified

28Micaiah said, If you return at all in peace, the Lord has not spoken by me. He [added], Hear, O people, every one of you!

29So [Ahab] king of Israel and Jehoshaphat the king of Judah went up to Ramoth-gilead.

30And the king of Israel said to Jehoshaphat, I will disguise myself and enter the battle, but you put on your [royal] clothing. And the king of Israel disguised himself and went into the battle.

31But the king of Syria had commanded the thirty-two captains of his chariots, Fight neither with small nor great, but only with [Ahab] king of Israel.

32And when the captains of the chariots saw Jehoshaphat, they said, Surely it is the king of Israel. They turned to fight against him, but Jehoshaphat cried out.

33And when the captains of the chariots saw that it was not the king of Israel, they turned back from pursuing him.

34But a certain man drew a bow at a venture and smote [Ahab] the king of Israel between the joints of the armor. So he said to the driver of his chariot, Turn around and carry me out of the army, for I am wounded.

35The battle increased that day, and [Ahab] the king was propped up in his chariot facing the Syrians, and at nightfall he died. And the blood of his wound flowed onto the floor of the chariot.

36And there went a cry throughout the army about sundown, saying, Every man to his city and his own country,

37For the king is dead! And [Ahab] was brought to Samaria, where they buried him.

38And they washed [his] chariot by the pool of Samaria, where the harlots bathed, and the dogs licked up his blood, as the Lord had predicted. [I Kings 21:19.]

39The rest of Ahab's acts, all he did, the ivory palace and all the cities he built, are they not written in the Book of the Chronicles of the Kings of Israel?

40So Ahab slept with his fathers. Ahaziah his son reigned in his stead.

41Jehoshaphat son of Asa began to reign over Judah in the fourth year of Ahab king of Israel.

42Jehoshaphat was thirty-five years old when he began to reign, and he reigned twenty-five years in Jerusalem. His mother was Azubah daughter of Shilhi.

43He walked in all the ways or customs of Asa his father, never swerving from it, doing right in the sight of the Lord. However, the [idolatrous] high places were not taken away; for the people still sacrificed and burned incense in the high places.

44And Jehoshaphat made peace with Israel's king.

45The rest of the acts of Jehoshaphat, his might that he showed and how he warred, are they not written in the Book of the Chronicles of the Kings of Judah?

46And the remnant of the sodomites (the male cult prostitutes) who remained in the days of his father Asa, [Jehoshaphat] expelled from the country.

47There was no king in Edom; a deputy was acting king.

48Jehoshaphat ordered ships of Tarshish to go to Ophir for gold, but they did not go, for the ships were wrecked at Ezion-geber.

49When Ahaziah son of Ahab said to Jehoshaphat, Let my servants go with your servants in the ships, Jehoshaphat refused.

---

zOr, when he was to disguise himself, and enter into the battle
aHeb. joints and the breastplate   bHeb. made sick   cHeb. ascended   dHeb. bosom   eHeb. came   fOr, had ten ships

New American Standard

28 Micaiah said, "If you indeed return safely the LORD has not spoken by me." And he said, "Listen, all you people."

Defeat and Death of Ahab

29 ¶ So the king of Israel and Jehoshaphat king of Judah went up against Ramoth-gilead.
30 The king of Israel said to Jehoshaphat, "I will disguise myself and go into the battle, but you put on your robes." So the king of Israel disguised himself and went into the battle.
31 Now the king of Aram had commanded the thirty-two captains of his chariots, saying, "Do not fight with small or great, but with the king of Israel alone."
32 So when the captains of the chariots saw Jehoshaphat, they said, "Surely it is the king of Israel," and they turned aside to fight against him, and Jehoshaphat cried out.
33 When the captains of the chariots saw that it was not the king of Israel, they turned back from pursuing him.
34 ¶ Now a certain man drew his bow at random and struck the king of Israel in a joint of the armor. So he said to the driver of his chariot, "Turn around and take me out of the fight; for I am severely wounded."
35 The battle raged that day, and the king was propped up in his chariot in front of the Arameans, and died at evening, and the blood from the wound ran into the bottom of the chariot.
36 Then a cry passed throughout the army close to sunset, saying, "Every man to his city and every man to his country."
37 ¶ So the king died and was brought to Samaria, and they buried the king in Samaria.
38 They washed the chariot by the pool of Samaria, and the dogs licked up his blood (now the harlots bathed themselves *there*), according to the word of the LORD which He spoke.
39 Now the rest of the acts of Ahab and all that he did and the ivory house which he built and all the cities which he built, are they not written in the Book of the Chronicles of the Kings of Israel?
40 So Ahab slept with his fathers, and Ahaziah his son became king in his place.

The New Rulers

41 ¶ Now Jehoshaphat the son of Asa became king over Judah in the fourth year of Ahab king of Israel.
42 Jehoshaphat was thirty-five years old when he became king, and he reigned twenty-five years in Jerusalem. And his mother's name was Azubah the daughter of Shilhi.
43 He walked in all the way of Asa his father; he did not turn aside from it, doing right in the sight of the LORD. However, the high places were not taken away; the people still sacrificed and burnt incense on the high places.
44 Jehoshaphat also made peace with the king of Israel.
45 ¶ Now the rest of the acts of Jehoshaphat, and his might which he showed and how he warred, are they not written in the Book of the Chronicles of the Kings of Judah?
46 The remnant of the sodomites who remained in the days of his father Asa, he expelled from the land.
47 ¶ Now there was no king in Edom; a deputy was king.
48 Jehoshaphat made ships of Tarshish to go to Ophir for gold, but they did not go for the ships were broken at Ezion-geber.
49 Then Ahaziah the son of Ahab said to Jehoshaphat, "Let my servants go with your servants in the ships." But Jehoshaphat was not willing.

New International

28 Micaiah declared, "If you ever return safely, the LORD has not spoken through me." Then he added, "Mark my words, all you people!"

Ahab Killed at Ramoth Gilead

29 So the king of Israel and Jehoshaphat king of Judah went up to Ramoth Gilead. 30 The king of Israel said to Jehoshaphat, "I will enter the battle in disguise, but you wear your royal robes." So the king of Israel disguised himself and went into battle.
31 Now the king of Aram had ordered his thirty-two chariot commanders, "Do not fight with anyone, small or great, except the king of Israel." 32 When the chariot commanders saw Jehoshaphat, they thought, "Surely this is the king of Israel." So they turned to attack him, but when Jehoshaphat cried out, 33 the chariot commanders saw that he was not the king of Israel and stopped pursuing him.
34 But someone drew his bow at random and hit the king of Israel between the sections of his armor. The king told his chariot driver, "Wheel around and get me out of the fighting. I've been wounded." 35 All day long the battle raged, and the king was propped up in his chariot facing the Arameans. The blood from his wound ran onto the floor of the chariot, and that evening he died. 36 As the sun was setting, a cry spread through the army: "Every man to his town; everyone to his land!"
37 So the king died and was brought to Samaria, and they buried him there. 38 They washed the chariot at a pool in Samaria (where the prostitutes bathed),[t] and the dogs licked up his blood, as the word of the LORD had declared.
39 As for the other events of Ahab's reign, including all he did, the palace he built and inlaid with ivory, and the cities he fortified, are they not written in the book of the annals of the kings of Israel? 40 Ahab rested with his fathers. And Ahaziah his son succeeded him as king.

Jehoshaphat King of Judah

41 Jehoshaphat son of Asa became king of Judah in the fourth year of Ahab king of Israel. 42 Jehoshaphat was thirty-five years old when he became king, and he reigned in Jerusalem twenty-five years. His mother's name was Azubah daughter of Shilhi. 43 In everything he walked in the ways of his father Asa and did not stray from them; he did what was right in the eyes of the LORD. The high places, however, were not removed, and the people continued to offer sacrifices and burn incense there. 44 Jehoshaphat was also at peace with the king of Israel.
45 As for the other events of Jehoshaphat's reign, the things he achieved and his military exploits, are they not written in the book of the annals of the kings of Judah? 46 He rid the land of the rest of the male shrine prostitutes who remained there even after the reign of his father Asa. 47 There was then no king in Edom; a deputy ruled.
48 Now Jehoshaphat built a fleet of trading ships[u] to go to Ophir for gold, but they never set sail—they were wrecked at Ezion Geber. 49 At that time Ahaziah son of Ahab said to Jehoshaphat, "Let my men sail with your men," but Jehoshaphat refused.

---

t 38 Or *Samaria and cleaned the weapons of Tarshish*   *u 48* Hebrew *of ships of Tarshish*

King James

⁵⁰ ¶ And Jehoshaphat slept with his fathers, and was buried with his fathers in the city of David his father: and Jehoram his son reigned in his stead.

Ahaziah, king of Israel

⁵¹ ¶ Ahaziah the son of Ahab began to reign over Israel in Samaria the seventeenth year of Jehoshaphat king of Judah, and reigned two years over Israel.

⁵²And he did evil in the sight of the LORD, and walked in the way of his father, and in the way of his mother, and in the way of Jeroboam the son of Nebat, who made Israel to sin:

⁵³For he served Baal, and worshipped him, and provoked to anger the LORD God of Israel, according to all that his father had done.

Amplified

⁵⁰Jehoshaphat slept with his fathers and was buried with them in the city of David his father [forefather]. And Jehoram his son reigned in his stead.

⁵¹Ahaziah son of Ahab began his two-year reign over Israel in Samaria in the seventeenth year of Jehoshaphat king of Judah.

⁵²He did evil in the sight of the Lord and walked in the ways of his father [Ahab] and of his mother [Jezebel] and of Jeroboam son of Nebat, who made Israel sin.

⁵³He served Baal and worshiped him and provoked the Lord, the God of Israel, to anger in all the ways his father had done.

New American Standard

50 And Jehoshaphat slept with his fathers and was buried with his fathers in the city of his father David, and Jehoram his son became king in his place.

51 ¶ Ahaziah the son of Ahab became king over Israel in Samaria in the seventeenth year of Jehoshaphat king of Judah, and he reigned two years over Israel.

52 He did evil in the sight of the LORD and walked in the way of his father and in the way of his mother and in the way of Jeroboam the son of Nebat, who caused Israel to sin.

53 So he served Baal and worshiped him and provoked the LORD God of Israel to anger, according to all that his father had done.

New International

50Then Jehoshaphat rested with his fathers and was buried with them in the city of David his father. And Jehoram his son succeeded him.

Ahaziah King of Israel

51Ahaziah son of Ahab became king of Israel in Samaria in the seventeenth year of Jehoshaphat king of Judah, and he reigned over Israel two years. 52He did evil in the eyes of the LORD, because he walked in the ways of his father and mother and in the ways of Jeroboam son of Nebat, who caused Israel to sin. 53He served and worshiped Baal and provoked the LORD, the God of Israel, to anger, just as his father had done.

THE SECOND BOOK OF THE

Kings

COMMONLY CALLED THE FOURTH BOOK
OF THE KINGS

Elijah's prophecy to Ahaziah

1 THEN MOAB rebelled against Israel after the death of Ahab.

2 And Ahaziah fell down through a lattice in his upper chamber that *was* in Samaria, and was sick: and he sent messengers, and said unto them, Go, inquire of Baal-zebub the god of Ekron whether I shall recover of this disease.

3 But the angel of the LORD said to Elijah the Tishbite, Arise, go up to meet the messengers of the king of Samaria, and say unto them, *Is it* not because *there is* not a God in Israel, *that* ye go to inquire of Baal-zebub the god of Ekron?

4 Now therefore thus saith the LORD, *a*Thou shalt not come down from that bed on which thou art gone up, but shalt surely die. And Elijah departed.

5 ¶ And when the messengers turned back unto him, he said unto them, Why are ye now turned back?

6 And they said unto him, There came a man up to meet us, and said unto us, Go, turn again unto the king that sent you, and say unto him, Thus saith the LORD, *Is it* not because *there is* not a God in Israel, *that* thou sendest to inquire of Baal-zebub the god of Ekron? therefore thou shalt not come down from that bed on which thou art gone up, but shalt surely die.

7 And he said unto them, *b*What manner of man *was he* which came up to meet you, and told you these words?

8 And they answered him, *He was* an hairy man, and girt with a girdle of leather about his loins. And he said, It *is* Elijah the Tishbite.

9 Then the king sent unto him a captain of fifty with his fifty. And he went up to him: and, behold, he sat on the top of an hill. And he spake unto him, Thou man of God, the king hath said, Come down.

10 And Elijah answered and said to the captain of fifty, If I *be* a man of God, then let fire come down from heaven, and consume thee and thy fifty. And there came down fire from heaven, and consumed him and his fifty.

11 Again also he sent unto him another captain of fifty with his fifty. And he answered and said unto him, O man of God, thus hath the king said, Come down quickly.

12 And Elijah answered and said unto them, If I *be* a man of God, let fire come down from heaven, and consume thee and thy fifty. And the fire of God came down from heaven, and consumed him and his fifty.

13 ¶ And he sent again a captain of the third fifty with his fifty. And the third captain of fifty went up, and came and *c*fell on his knees before Elijah, and besought him, and said unto him, O man of God, I pray thee, let my life, and the life of these fifty thy servants, be precious in thy sight.

14 Behold, there came fire down from heaven, and burnt up the two captains of the former fifties with their fifties: therefore let my life now be precious in thy sight.

15 And the angel of the LORD said unto Elijah, Go down with him: be not afraid of him. And he arose, and went down with him unto the king.

THE SECOND BOOK OF THE

Kings

1 MOAB REBELLED against Israel after the death of Ahab.

2 [King] Ahaziah fell down through a lattice in his upper chamber in Samaria and lay sick. He sent messengers, saying, Go, ask Baal-zebub, the god of [Philistine] Ekron, if I shall recover from this illness.

3 But the angel of the Lord said to Elijah the Tishbite, Arise, go up to meet the messengers of the king in Samaria and say to them, Is it because there is no God in Israel that you are going to inquire of Baal-zebub, the god of Ekron?

4 Therefore the Lord says: You [Ahaziah] shall not leave the bed on which you lie, but shall surely die. And Elijah departed.

5 When the messengers returned to Ahaziah, he said, Why have you turned back?

6 They replied, A man came up to meet us who said, Go back to the king who sent you and tell him, Thus says the Lord: Is there no God in Israel that you send to inquire of Baal-zebub, the god of Ekron? Therefore you shall not leave the bed on which you lie, but shall surely die.

7 The king asked, What was the man like who came to meet you saying these things?

8 They answered, He was a hairy man with a girdle of leather about his loins. And he said, It is Elijah the Tishbite.

9 Then the king sent to Elijah a captain of fifty men with his fifty [to seize him]. He found Elijah sitting on a hilltop and said, Man of God, the king says, Come down.

10 Elijah said to the captain of fifty, If I am a man of God, then let fire come down from heaven and consume you and your fifty. And fire fell from heaven and consumed him and his fifty.

11 Again King [Ahaziah] sent to him another captain of fifty with his fifty. And he said to Elijah, Man of God, the king has said, Come down quickly!

12 And Elijah answered, If I am a man of God, let fire come down from heaven and consume you and your fifty. And the fire of God came down from heaven and consumed him and his fifty.

13 Ahaziah sent again a captain of a third fifty with his fifty. And the third captain of fifty went up and fell on his knees before Elijah and besought him and said to him, O man of God, I pray you, let my life and the lives of these fifty, your servants, be precious in your sight.

14 Behold, fire came down from heaven and burned up the two captains of the former fifties with their fifties. Therefore let my life now be precious in your sight.

15 The angel of the Lord said to Elijah, Go down with him; do not be afraid of him. So he arose and went with him to the king.

---

a Heb. *The bed whither thou art gone up, thou shall not come down from it*   *b* Heb. *What* was *the manner of the man?*   *c* Heb. *bowed*

THE SECOND BOOK OF THE

Kings

2 Kings

Ahaziah's Messengers Meet Elijah

1 NOW MOAB rebelled against Israel after the death of Ahab.

2 And Ahaziah fell through the lattice in his upper chamber which *was* in Samaria, and became ill. So he sent messengers and said to them, "Go, inquire of Baal-zebub, the god of Ekron, whether I will recover from this sickness."

3 But the angel of the LORD said to Elijah the Tishbite, "Arise, go up to meet the messengers of the king of Samaria and say to them, 'Is it because there is no God in Israel *that* you are going to inquire of Baal-zebub, the god of Ekron?'

4 "Now therefore thus says the LORD, 'You shall not come down from the bed where you have gone up, but you shall surely die.' " Then Elijah departed.

5 ¶ When the messengers returned to him he said to them, "Why have you returned?"

6 They said to him, "A man came up to meet us and said to us, 'Go, return to the king who sent you and say to him, "Thus says the LORD, 'Is it because there is no God in Israel *that* you are sending to inquire of Baal-zebub, the god of Ekron? Therefore you shall not come down from the bed where you have gone up, but shall surely die.' " ' "

7 He said to them, "What kind of man was he who came up to meet you and spoke these words to you?"

8 They answered him, "*He was* a hairy man with a leather girdle bound about his loins." And he said, "It is Elijah the Tishbite."

9 ¶ Then *the king* sent to him a captain of fifty with his fifty. And he went up to him, and behold, he was sitting on the top of the hill. And he said to him, "O man of God, the king says, 'Come down.' "

10 Elijah replied to the captain of fifty, "If I am a man of God, let fire come down from heaven and consume you and your fifty." Then fire came down from heaven and consumed him and his fifty.

11 ¶ So he again sent to him another captain of fifty with his fifty. And he said to him, "O man of God, thus says the king, 'Come down quickly.' "

12 Elijah replied to them, "If I am a man of God, let fire come down from heaven and consume you and your fifty." Then the fire of God came down from heaven and consumed him and his fifty.

13 ¶ So he again sent the captain of a third fifty with his fifty. When the third captain of fifty went up, he came and bowed down on his knees before Elijah, and begged him and said to him, "O man of God, please let my life and the lives of these fifty servants of yours be precious in your sight.

14 "Behold fire came down from heaven and consumed the first two captains of fifty with their fifties; but now let my life be precious in your sight."

15 The angel of the LORD said to Elijah, "Go down with him; do not be afraid of him." So he arose and went down with him to the king.

The LORD's Judgment on Ahaziah

1 AFTER AHAB'S death, Moab rebelled against Israel. 2 Now Ahaziah had fallen through the lattice of his upper room in Samaria and injured himself. So he sent messengers, saying to them, "Go and consult Baal-Zebub, the god of Ekron, to see if I will recover from this injury."

3 But the angel of the LORD said to Elijah the Tishbite, "Go up and meet the messengers of the king of Samaria and ask them, 'Is it because there is no God in Israel that you are going off to consult Baal-Zebub, the god of Ekron?' 4 Therefore this is what the LORD says: 'You will not leave the bed you are lying on. You will certainly die!' " So Elijah went.

5 When the messengers returned to the king, he asked them, "Why have you come back?"

6 "A man came to meet us," they replied. "And he said to us, 'Go back to the king who sent you and tell him, "This is what the LORD says: Is it because there is no God in Israel that you are sending men to consult Baal-Zebub, the god of Ekron? Therefore you will not leave the bed you are lying on. You will certainly die!" ' "

7 The king asked them, "What kind of man was it who came to meet you and told you this?"

8 They replied, "He was a man with a garment of hair and with a leather belt around his waist."

The king said, "That was Elijah the Tishbite."

9 Then he sent to Elijah a captain with his company of fifty men. The captain went up to Elijah, who was sitting on the top of a hill, and said to him, "Man of God, the king says, 'Come down!' "

10 Elijah answered the captain, "If I am a man of God, may fire come down from heaven and consume you and your fifty men!" Then fire fell from heaven and consumed the captain and his men.

11 At this the king sent to Elijah another captain with his fifty men. The captain said to him, "Man of God, this is what the king says, 'Come down at once!' "

12 "If I am a man of God," Elijah replied, "may fire come down from heaven and consume you and your fifty men!" Then the fire of God fell from heaven and consumed him and his fifty men.

13 So the king sent a third captain with his fifty men. This third captain went up and fell on his knees before Elijah. "Man of God," he begged, "please have respect for my life and the lives of these fifty men, your servants! 14 See, fire has fallen from heaven and consumed the first two captains and all their men. But now have respect for my life!"

15 The angel of the LORD said to Elijah, "Go down with him; do not be afraid of him." So Elijah got up and went down with him to the king.

King James

¹⁶And he said unto him, Thus saith the LORD, Forasmuch as thou hast sent messengers to inquire of Baalzebub the god of Ekron, *is it* not because *there is* no God in Israel to inquire of his word? therefore thou shalt not come down off that bed on which thou art gone up, but shalt surely die.

¹⁷ ¶ So he died according to the word of the LORD which Elijah had spoken. And ^dJehoram reigned in his stead in the second year of Jehoram the son of Jehoshaphat king of Judah; because he had no son.

¹⁸Now the rest of the acts of Ahaziah which he did, *are* they not written in the book of the chronicles of the kings of Israel?

Elijah taken up to heaven

2 AND IT came to pass, when the LORD would take up Elijah into heaven by a whirlwind, that Elijah went with Elisha from Gilgal.

²And Elijah said unto Elisha, Tarry here, I pray thee; for the LORD hath sent me to Beth-el. And Elisha said *unto him, As* the LORD liveth, and *as* thy soul liveth, I will not leave thee. So they went down to Beth-el.

³And the sons of the prophets that *were* at Beth-el came forth to Elisha, and said unto him, Knowest thou that the LORD will take away thy master from thy head today? And he said, Yea, I know *it;* hold ye your peace.

⁴And Elijah said unto him, Elisha, tarry here, I pray thee; for the LORD hath sent me to Jericho. And he said, As the LORD liveth, and *as* thy soul liveth, I will not leave thee. So they came to Jericho.

⁵And the sons of the prophets that *were* at Jericho came to Elisha, and said unto him, Knowest thou that the LORD will take away thy master from thy head today? And he answered, Yea, I know *it;* hold ye your peace.

⁶And Elijah said unto him, Tarry, I pray thee, here; for the LORD hath sent me to Jordan. And he said, *As* the LORD liveth, and *as* thy soul liveth, I will not leave thee. And they two went on.

⁷And fifty men of the sons of the prophets went, and stood ^eto view afar off: and they two stood by Jordan.

⁸And Elijah took his mantle, and wrapped *it* together, and smote the waters, and they were divided hither and thither, so that they two went over on dry ground.

⁹ ¶ And it came to pass, when they were gone over, that Elijah said unto Elisha, Ask what I shall do for thee, before I be taken away from thee. And Elisha said, I pray thee, let a double portion of thy spirit be upon me.

¹⁰And he said, ^fThou hast asked a hard thing: *nevertheless,* if thou see me *when I am* taken from thee, it shall be so unto thee; but if not, it shall not be *so.*

¹¹And it came to pass, as they still went on, and talked, that, behold, *there appeared* a chariot of fire, and horses of fire, and parted them both asunder; and Elijah went up by a whirlwind into heaven.

¹² ¶ And Elisha saw *it,* and he cried, My father, my father, the chariot of Israel, and the horsemen thereof. And he saw him no more: and he took hold of his own clothes, and rent them in two pieces.

Beginning of Elisha's ministry

¹³He took up also the mantle of Elijah that fell from him, and went back, and stood by the ^gbank of Jordan;

¹⁴And he took the mantle of Elijah that fell from him, and smote the waters, and said, Where *is* the LORD God of Elijah? and when he also had smitten the waters, they parted hither and thither: and Elisha went over.

Amplified

¹⁶Elijah said to [King] Ahaziah, Thus says the Lord: Since you have sent messengers to inquire of Baal-zebub, god of Ekron, is it because there is no God in Israel of Whom to inquire His word? Therefore you shall not leave the bed on which you lie, but shall surely die.

¹⁷So Ahaziah died according to the word of the Lord which Elijah had spoken. ^aJoram [also a son of Ahab] reigned in Israel in his stead in the second year of Jehoram son of Jehoshaphat king of Judah, because Ahaziah had no son [but his brother].

¹⁸Now the rest of the acts of Ahaziah, are they not written in the Book of the Chronicles of the Kings of Israel?

2 WHEN THE Lord was about to take Elijah up to heaven by a whirlwind, Elijah and Elisha were going from Gilgal.

²And Elijah said to Elisha, Tarry here, I pray you, for the Lord has sent me to Bethel. But Elisha replied, As the Lord lives and as your soul lives, I will not leave you. So they went down to Bethel.

³The prophets' sons who were at Bethel came to Elisha and said, Do you know that the Lord will take your master away from you today? He said, Yes, I know it; hold your peace.

⁴Elijah said to him, Elisha, tarry here, I pray you, for the Lord has sent me to Jericho. But he said, As the Lord lives and as your soul lives, I will not leave you. So they came to Jericho.

⁵The sons of the prophets who were at Jericho came to Elisha and said, Do you know that the Lord will take your master away from you today? And he answered, Yes, I know it; hold your peace.

⁶Elijah said to him, Tarry here, I pray you, for the Lord has sent me to the Jordan. But he said, As the Lord lives and as your soul lives, I will not leave you. And the two of them went on.

⁷Fifty men of the sons of the prophets also went and stood [to watch] afar off; and the two of them stood by the Jordan.

⁸And Elijah took his mantle and rolled it up and struck the waters, and they divided this way and that, so that the two of them went over on dry ground.

⁹And when they had gone over, Elijah said to Elisha, Ask what I shall do for you before I am taken from you. And Elisha said, I pray you, let a double portion of your spirit be upon me.

¹⁰He said, You have asked a hard thing. However, if you see me when I am taken from you, it shall be so for you—but if not, it shall not be so.

¹¹As they still went on and talked, behold, a chariot of fire and horses of fire parted the two of them, and Elijah went up by a whirlwind into heaven.

¹²And Elisha saw it and he cried, My father, my father! The chariot of Israel and its horsemen! And he saw him no more. And he took hold of his own clothes and tore them in two pieces.

¹³He took up also the mantle of Elijah that fell from him and went back and stood by the bank of the Jordan.

¹⁴And he took the mantle that fell from Elijah and struck the waters and said, Where is the Lord, the God of Elijah? And when he had struck the waters, they parted this way and that, and Elisha went over.

---

^dThe second year that *Jehoram* was *Prorex,* and the eighteenth of *Jehoshaphat;* see ch. 3:1   ^eHeb. *in sight,* or, *over against*   ^fHeb. *Thou hast done hard in asking*   ^gHeb. *lip*

^aHebrew *Jehoram,* a variant of *Joram.*

New American Standard

16 Then he said to him, "Thus says the LORD, 'Because you have sent messengers to inquire of Baal-zebub, the god of Ekron—is it because there is no God in Israel to inquire of His word?—therefore you shall not come down from the bed where you have gone up, but shall surely die.' "

Jehoram Reigns over Israel

17 ¶ So Ahaziah died according to the word of the LORD which Elijah had spoken. And because he had no son, Jehoram became king in his place in the second year of Jehoram the son of Jehoshaphat, king of Judah.

18 Now the rest of the acts of Ahaziah which he did, are they not written in the Book of the Chronicles of the Kings of Israel?

Elijah Taken to Heaven

2 AND IT came about when the LORD was about to take up Elijah by a whirlwind to heaven, that Elijah went with Elisha from Gilgal.

2 Elijah said to Elisha, "Stay here please, for the LORD has sent me as far as Bethel." But Elisha said, "As the LORD lives and as you yourself live, I will not leave you." So they went down to Bethel.

3 Then the sons of the prophets who *were* at Bethel came out to Elisha and said to him, "Do you know that the LORD will take away your master from over you today?" And he said, "Yes, I know; be still."

4 ¶ Elijah said to him, "Elisha, please stay here, for the LORD has sent me to Jericho." But he said, "As the LORD lives, and as you yourself live, I will not leave you." So they came to Jericho.

5 The sons of the prophets who *were* at Jericho approached Elisha and said to him, "Do you know that the LORD will take away your master from over you today?" And he answered, "Yes, I know; be still."

6 Then Elijah said to him, "Please stay here, for the LORD has sent me to the Jordan." And he said, "As the LORD lives, and as you yourself live, I will not leave you." So the two of them went on.

7 ¶ Now fifty men of the sons of the prophets went and stood opposite *them* at a distance, while the two of them stood by the Jordan.

8 Elijah took his mantle and folded it together and struck the waters, and they were divided here and there, so that the two of them crossed over on dry ground.

9 ¶ When they had crossed over, Elijah said to Elisha, "Ask what I shall do for you before I am taken from you." And Elisha said, "Please, let a double portion of your spirit be upon me."

10 He said, "You have asked a hard thing. *Nevertheless,* if you see me when I am taken from you, it shall be so for you; but if not, it shall not be *so.*"

11 As they were going along and talking, behold, *there appeared* a chariot of fire and horses of fire which separated the two of them. And Elijah went up by a whirlwind to heaven.

12 Elisha saw *it* and cried out, "My father, my father, the chariots of Israel and its horsemen!" And he saw Elijah no more. Then he took hold of his own clothes and tore them in two pieces.

13 He also took up the mantle of Elijah that fell from him and returned and stood by the bank of the Jordan.

14 He took the mantle of Elijah that fell from him and struck the waters and said, "Where is the LORD, the God of Elijah?" And when he also had struck the waters, they were divided here and there; and Elisha crossed over.

New International

16 He told the king, "This is what the LORD says: Is it because there is no God in Israel for you to consult that you have sent messengers to consult Baal-Zebub, the god of Ekron? Because you have done this, you will never leave the bed you are lying on. You will certainly die!"

17 So he died, according to the word of the LORD that Elijah had spoken.

Because Ahaziah had no son, Joram[a] succeeded him as king in the second year of Jehoram son of Jehoshaphat king of Judah. 18 As for all the other events of Ahaziah's reign, and what he did, are they not written in the book of the annals of the kings of Israel?

Elijah Taken Up to Heaven

2 WHEN THE LORD was about to take Elijah up to heaven in a whirlwind, Elijah and Elisha were on their way from Gilgal. 2 Elijah said to Elisha, "Stay here; the LORD has sent me to Bethel."

But Elisha said, "As surely as the LORD lives and as you live, I will not leave you." So they went down to Bethel.

3 The company of the prophets at Bethel came out to Elisha and asked, "Do you know that the LORD is going to take your master from you today?"

"Yes, I know," Elisha replied, "but do not speak of it."

4 Then Elijah said to him, "Stay here, Elisha; the LORD has sent me to Jericho."

And he replied, "As surely as the LORD lives and as you live, I will not leave you." So they went to Jericho.

5 The company of the prophets at Jericho went up to Elisha and asked him, "Do you know that the LORD is going to take your master from you today?"

"Yes, I know," he replied, "but do not speak of it."

6 Then Elijah said to him, "Stay here; the LORD has sent me to the Jordan."

And he replied, "As surely as the LORD lives and as you live, I will not leave you." So the two of them walked on.

7 Fifty men of the company of the prophets went and stood at a distance, facing the place where Elijah and Elisha had stopped at the Jordan. 8 Elijah took his cloak, rolled it up and struck the water with it. The water divided to the right and to the left, and the two of them crossed over on dry ground.

9 When they had crossed, Elijah said to Elisha, "Tell me, what can I do for you before I am taken from you?"

"Let me inherit a double portion of your spirit," Elisha replied.

10 "You have asked a difficult thing," Elijah said, "yet if you see me when I am taken from you, it will be yours—otherwise not."

11 As they were walking along and talking together, suddenly a chariot of fire and horses of fire appeared and separated the two of them, and Elijah went up to heaven in a whirlwind. 12 Elisha saw this and cried out, "My father! My father! The chariots and horsemen of Israel!" And Elisha saw him no more. Then he took hold of his own clothes and tore them apart.

13 He picked up the cloak that had fallen from Elijah and went back and stood on the bank of the Jordan. 14 Then he took the cloak that had fallen from him and struck the water with it. "Where now is the LORD, the God of Elijah?" he asked. When he struck the water, it divided to the right and to the left, and he crossed over.

---

a 17 Hebrew *Jehoram,* a variant of *Joram*

King James

¹⁵And when the sons of the prophets which *were* to view at Jericho saw him, they said, The spirit of Elijah doth rest on Elisha. And they came to meet him, and bowed themselves to the ground before him.

¹⁶ ¶ And they said unto him, Behold now, there be with thy servants fifty ^hstrong men; let them go, we pray thee, and seek thy master: lest peradventure the spirit of the LORD hath taken him up, and cast him upon ⁱsome mountain, or into some valley. And he said, Ye shall not send.

¹⁷And when they urged him till he was ashamed, he said, Send. They sent therefore fifty men; and they sought three days, but found him not.

¹⁸And when they came again to him, (for he tarried at Jericho,) he said unto them, Did I not say unto you, Go not?

¹⁹ ¶ And the men of the city said unto Elisha, Behold, I pray thee, the situation of this city *is* pleasant, as my lord seeth: but the water *is* naught, and the ground ^jbarren.

²⁰And he said, Bring me a new cruse, and put salt therein. And they brought *it* to him.

²¹And he went forth unto the spring of the waters, and cast the salt in there, and said, Thus saith the LORD, I have healed these waters; there shall not be from thence any more death or barren *land.*

²²So the waters were healed unto this day, according to the saying of Elisha which he spake.

²³ ¶ And he went up from thence unto Beth-el: and as he was going up by the way, there came forth little children out of the city, and mocked him, and said unto him, Go up, thou bald head; go up, thou bald head.

²⁴And he turned back, and looked on them, and cursed them in the name of the LORD. And there came forth two she bears out of the wood, and tare forty and two children of them.

²⁵And he went from thence to mount Carmel, and from thence he returned to Samaria.

Jehoram's siege against Moab

3 NOW JEHORAM the son of Ahab began to reign over Israel in Samaria the eighteenth year of Jehoshaphat king of Judah, and reigned twelve years.

²And he wrought evil in the sight of the LORD; but not like his father, and like his mother: for he put away the ^kimage of Baal that his father had made.

³Nevertheless he cleaved unto the sins of Jeroboam the son of Nebat, which made Israel to sin; he departed not therefrom.

⁴ ¶ And Mesha king of Moab was a sheepmaster, and rendered unto the king of Israel an hundred thousand lambs, and a hundred thousand rams, with the wool.

⁵But it came to pass, when Ahab was dead, that the king of Moab rebelled against the king of Israel.

⁶ ¶ And king Jehoram went out of Samaria the same time, and numbered all Israel.

⁷And he went and sent to Jehoshaphat the king of Judah, saying, The king of Moab hath rebelled against me: wilt thou go with me against Moab to battle? And he said, I will go up: I *am* as thou *art,* my people as thy people, and my horses as thy horses.

⁸And he said, Which way shall we go up? And he answered, The way through the wilderness of Edom.

Amplified

¹⁵When the sons of the prophets who were [watching] at Jericho saw him, they said, The spirit of Elijah rests on Elisha. And they came to meet him and bowed themselves to the ground before him.

¹⁶And they said to him, Behold now, there are among your servants fifty strong men; let them go, we pray you, and seek your master. It may be that the Spirit of the Lord has taken him up and cast him on some mountain or into some valley. And he said, You shall not send.

¹⁷But when they urged him till he was embarrassed, he said, Send. So they sent fifty men, who sought for three days but did not find him.

¹⁸When they returned to Elisha, who had waited at Jericho, he said to them, Did I not tell you, Do not go?

¹⁹And the men of the city said to Elisha, Behold, inhabiting of this city is pleasant, as my lord sees, but the water is bad and the locality causes miscarriage *and* barrenness [in all animals].

²⁰He said, Bring me a new bowl and put salt [the symbol of God's purifying power] in it. And they brought it to him.

²¹Then Elisha went to the spring of the waters and cast the salt in it and said, Thus says the Lord: I [not the salt] have healed these waters; there shall not be any more death, miscarriage *or* barrenness [and bereavement] because of it.

²²So the waters were healed to this day, as Elisha had said.

²³He went up from Jericho to Bethel. On the way, ^byoung [maturing and accountable] boys came out of the city and mocked him and said to him, Go up [in a whirlwind], you baldhead! Go up, you baldhead!

²⁴And he turned around and looked at them and called a curse down on them in the name of the Lord. And two she-bears came out of the woods and ripped up forty-two of the boys.

²⁵Elisha went from there to Mount Carmel, and from there he returned to Samaria.

3 JORAM SON of Ahab began to reign over Israel in Samaria in the eighteenth year of Jehoshaphat king of Judah, and reigned twelve years.

²He did evil in the sight of the Lord, but not like his father and mother; for he put away the pillar of Baal that his father had made.

³Yet he clung to the sins of Jeroboam son of Nebat, which made Israel to sin; he departed not from them.

^{4c}Mesha king of Moab was a sheepmaster, and paid in tribute to the king of Israel [annually] 100,000 lambs and 100,000 rams, with the wool.

⁵But when Ahab died, the king of Moab rebelled against the king of Israel.

⁶So King Joram went out of Samaria at that time and mustered all Israel.

⁷And he sent to Jehoshaphat king of Judah, saying, The king of Moab has rebelled against me. Will you go with me to war against Moab? And he said, I will go; I am as you are, my people as your people, my horses as your horses.

⁸Joram said, Which way shall we go up? Jehoshaphat answered, The way through the Wilderness of Edom.

^b This incident has long been misunderstood because the Hebrew word "naar" was translated "little boys." That these characteristic juvenile delinquents were old enough to be fully accountable is obvious from the use of the word elsewhere. For example, it was used by David of his son Solomon and translated "young and inexperienced," when Solomon was a father (I Chron. 22:5; cf. I Kings 14:21 and II Chron. 9:30). It was used of Joseph when he was seventeen (Gen. 37:2). In fact, not less than seventy times in the *King James Version* this word "naar" is translated "young man" or "young men."   ^c This name of the king of Moab occurs in the first line of the Moabite Stone. In that inscription the Moabite king mentions his successes against Omri and Omri's successor (I Kings 16:23).

New American Standard

Elisha Succeeds Elijah

15 ¶ Now when the sons of the prophets who *were* at Jericho opposite *him* saw him, they said, "The spirit of Elijah rests on Elisha." And they came to meet him and bowed themselves to the ground before him.

16 They said to him, "Behold now, there are with your servants fifty strong men, please let them go and search for your master; perhaps the Spirit of the LORD has taken him up and cast him on some mountain or into some valley." And he said, "You shall not send."

17 But when they urged him until he was ashamed, he said, "Send." They sent therefore fifty men; and they searched three days but did not find him.

18 They returned to him while he was staying at Jericho; and he said to them, "Did I not say to you, 'Do not go'?"

19 ¶ Then the men of the city said to Elisha, "Behold now, the situation of this city is pleasant, as my lord sees; but the water is bad and the land is unfruitful."

20 He said, "Bring me a new jar, and put salt in it." So they brought *it* to him.

21 He went out to the spring of water and threw salt in it and said, "Thus says the LORD, 'I have purified these waters; there shall not be from there death or unfruitfulness any longer.' "

22 So the waters have been purified to this day, according to the word of Elisha which he spoke.

23 ¶ Then he went up from there to Bethel; and as he was going up by the way, young lads came out from the city and mocked him and said to him, "Go up, you baldhead; go up, you baldhead!"

24 When he looked behind him and saw them, he cursed them in the name of the LORD. Then two female bears came out of the woods and tore up forty-two lads of their number.

25 He went from there to Mount Carmel, and from there he returned to Samaria.

Jehoram Meets Moab Rebellion

3 NOW JEHORAM the son of Ahab became king over Israel at Samaria in the eighteenth year of Jehoshaphat king of Judah, and reigned twelve years.

2 He did evil in the sight of the LORD, though not like his father and his mother; for he put away the *sacred* pillar of Baal which his father had made.

3 Nevertheless, he clung to the sins of Jeroboam the son of Nebat, which he made Israel sin; he did not depart from them.

4 ¶ Now Mesha king of Moab was a sheep breeder, and used to pay the king of Israel 100,000 lambs and the wool of 100,000 rams.

5 But when Ahab died, the king of Moab rebelled against the king of Israel.

6 And King Jehoram went out of Samaria at that time and mustered all Israel.

7 Then he went and sent *word* to Jehoshaphat the king of Judah, saying, "The king of Moab has rebelled against me. Will you go with me to fight against Moab?" And he said, "I will go up; I am as you are, my people as your people, my horses as your horses."

8 He said, "Which way shall we go up?" And he answered, "The way of the wilderness of Edom."

New International

15 The company of the prophets from Jericho, who were watching, said, "The spirit of Elijah is resting on Elisha." And they went to meet him and bowed to the ground before him. 16 "Look," they said, "we your servants have fifty able men. Let them go and look for your master. Perhaps the Spirit of the LORD has picked him up and set him down on some mountain or in some valley."

"No," Elisha replied, "do not send them."

17 But they persisted until he was too ashamed to refuse. So he said, "Send them." And they sent fifty men, who searched for three days but did not find him. 18 When they returned to Elisha, who was staying in Jericho, he said to them, "Didn't I tell you not to go?"

Healing of the Water

19 The men of the city said to Elisha, "Look, our lord, this town is well situated, as you can see, but the water is bad and the land is unproductive."

20 "Bring me a new bowl," he said, "and put salt in it." So they brought it to him.

21 Then he went out to the spring and threw the salt into it, saying, "This is what the LORD says: 'I have healed this water. Never again will it cause death or make the land unproductive.' " 22 And the water has remained wholesome to this day, according to the word Elisha had spoken.

Elisha Is Jeered

23 From there Elisha went up to Bethel. As he was walking along the road, some youths came out of the town and jeered at him. "Go on up, you baldhead!" they said. "Go on up, you baldhead!" 24 He turned around, looked at them and called down a curse on them in the name of the LORD. Then two bears came out of the woods and mauled forty-two of the youths. 25 And he went on to Mount Carmel and from there returned to Samaria.

Moab Revolts

3 JORAM[b] SON of Ahab became king of Israel in Samaria in the eighteenth year of Jehoshaphat king of Judah, and he reigned twelve years. 2 He did evil in the eyes of the LORD, but not as his father and mother had done. He got rid of the sacred stone of Baal that his father had made. 3 Nevertheless he clung to the sins of Jeroboam son of Nebat, which he had caused Israel to commit; he did not turn away from them.

4 Now Mesha king of Moab raised sheep, and he had to supply the king of Israel with a hundred thousand lambs and with the wool of a hundred thousand rams. 5 But after Ahab died, the king of Moab rebelled against the king of Israel. 6 So at that time King Joram set out from Samaria and mobilized all Israel. 7 He also sent this message to Jehoshaphat king of Judah: "The king of Moab has rebelled against me. Will you go with me to fight against Moab?"

"I will go with you," he replied. "I am as you are, my people as your people, my horses as your horses."

8 "By what route shall we attack?" he asked.

"Through the Desert of Edom," he answered.

---

b 1 Hebrew *Jehoram*, a variant of *Joram*; also in verse 6

King James

9So the king of Israel went, and the king of Judah, and the king of Edom: and they fetched a compass of seven days' journey: and there was no water for the host, and for the cattle *l*that followed them.

10And the king of Israel said, Alas! that the LORD hath called these three kings together, to deliver them into the hand of Moab!

11But Jehoshaphat said, *Is there* not here a prophet of the LORD, that we may inquire of the LORD by him? And one of the king of Israel's servants answered and said, Here *is* Elisha the son of Shaphat, which poured water on the hands of Elijah.

12And Jehoshaphat said, The word of the LORD is with him. So the king of Israel and Jehoshaphat and the king of Edom went down to him.

13And Elisha said unto the king of Israel, What have I to do with thee? get thee to the prophets of thy father, and to the prophets of thy mother. And the king of Israel said unto him, Nay: for the LORD hath called these three kings together, to deliver them into the hand of Moab.

14And Elisha said, *As* the LORD of hosts liveth, before whom I stand, surely, were it not that I regard the presence of Jehoshaphat the king of Judah, I would not look toward thee, nor see thee.

15But now bring me a minstrel. And it came to pass, when the minstrel played, that the hand of the LORD came upon him.

16And he said, Thus saith the LORD, Make this valley full of ditches.

17For thus saith the LORD, Ye shall not see wind, neither shall ye see rain; yet that valley shall be filled with water, that ye may drink, both ye, and your cattle, and your beasts.

18And this is *but* a light thing in the sight of the LORD: he will deliver the Moabites also into your hand.

19And ye shall smite every fenced city, and every choice city, and shall fell every good tree, and stop all wells of water, and *m*mar every good piece of land with stones.

20And it came to pass in the morning, when the meat offering was offered, that, behold, there came water by the way of Edom, and the country was filled with water.

21 ¶ And when all the Moabites heard that the kings were come up to fight against them, they *n*gathered all that were able to *o*put on armour, and upward, and stood in the border.

22And they rose up early in the morning, and the sun shone upon the water, and the Moabites saw the water on the other side *as* red as blood:

23And they said, This *is* blood: the kings are surely *p*slain, and they have smitten one another: now therefore, Moab, to the spoil.

24And when they came to the camp of Israel, the Israelites rose up and smote the Moabites, so that they fled before them: but *q*they went forward smiting the Moabites, even in *their* country.

25And they beat down the cities, and on every good piece of land cast every man his stone, and filled it; and they stopped all the wells of water, and felled all the good trees: *r*only in Kir-haraseth left they the stones thereof; howbeit the slingers went about *it,* and smote it.

26 ¶ And when the king of Moab saw that the battle was too sore for him, he took with him seven hundred men that drew swords, to break through *even* unto the king of Edom: but they could not.

27Then he took his eldest son that should have reigned in his stead, and offered him *for* a burnt offering upon the wall. And there was great indignation against Israel: and they departed from him, and returned to *their* own land.

Amplified

9So the king of Israel went with the king of Judah and the king of Edom. They made a circuit of seven days' journey, but there was no water for the army or for the animals following them.

10Then the king of Israel said, Alas! The Lord has called [us] three kings together to be delivered into Moab's hand!

11But Jehoshaphat said, Is there no prophet of the Lord here by whom we may inquire of the Lord? One of the king of Israel's servants answered, Elisha son of Shaphat, who served Elijah, is here.

12Jehoshaphat said, The word of the Lord is with him. So Joram king of Israel and Jehoshaphat and the king of Edom went down to Elisha.

13And Elisha said to the king of Israel, What have I to do with you? Go to the prophets of your [wicked] father Ahab and your [wicked] mother Jezebel. But the king of Israel said to him, No, for the Lord has called [us] three kings together to be delivered into the hand of Moab.

14And Elisha said, As the Lord of hosts lives, before Whom I stand, surely, were it not that I respect the presence of Jehoshaphat king of Judah, I would neither look at you nor see you [King Joram].

15But now bring me a minstrel. And while the minstrel played, the hand *and* power of the Lord came upon [Elisha].

16And he said, Thus says the Lord: Make this [dry] brook bed full of trenches.

17For thus says the Lord: You shall not see wind or rain, yet that ravine shall be filled with water, so you, your cattle, and your beasts [of burden] may drink.

18This is but a light thing in the sight of the Lord. He will deliver the Moabites also into your hands.

19You shall smite every fenced city and every choice city, and shall fell every good tree and stop all wells of water and mar every good piece of land with stones.

20In the morning, when the sacrifice was offered, behold, there came water by the way of Edom, and the country was filled with water.

21When all the Moabites heard that the kings had come up to fight against them, all who were able to put on armor, young and old, gathered and drew up at the border.

22When they rose up early next morning, and the sun shone upon the water, the Moabites saw the water across from them as red as blood.

23And they said, This is blood; the kings have surely been fighting and have slain one another. Now then, Moab, to the spoil!

24But when they came to the camp of Israel, the Israelites rose up and smote the Moabites, so that they fled before them. And they went forward, slaying the Moabites as they went.

25They beat down the cities [walls], and on every good piece of land every man cast a stone, covering it [with stones]. And they stopped all the springs of water and felled all the good trees, until only the stones [of the walls of Moab's capital city] of Kir-hareseth were left standing, and the slingers surrounded and took it.

26And when the king of Moab saw that the battle was against him, he took with him 700 swordsmen to break through to the king of Edom, but they could not.

27Then he [Moab's king] took his eldest son, who was to reign in his stead, and offered him for a burnt offering on the wall [in full view of the horrified enemy kings]. And there was great indignation, wrath, *and* bitterness against Israel; and they [his allies Judah and Edom] withdrew from [Joram] and returned to their own land.

---

l Heb. *at their feet*   *m* Heb. *grieve*   *n* Heb. *were cried together*
o Heb. *gird himself with a girdle*   *p* Heb. *destroyed*   *q* Or, *they smote in it even smiting*   *r* Heb. *until he left the stones thereof in Kir-haraseth*

New American Standard

9 ¶ So the king of Israel went with the king of Judah and the king of Edom; and they made a circuit of seven days' journey, and there was no water for the army or for the cattle that followed them.

10 Then the king of Israel said, "Alas! For the LORD has called these three kings to give them into the hand of Moab."

11 But Jehoshaphat said, "Is there not a prophet of the LORD here, that we may inquire of the LORD by him?" And one of the king of Israel's servants answered and said, "Elisha the son of Shaphat is here, who used to pour water on the hands of Elijah."

12 Jehoshaphat said, "The word of the LORD is with him." So the king of Israel and Jehoshaphat and the king of Edom went down to him.

13 ¶ Now Elisha said to the king of Israel, "What do I have to do with you? Go to the prophets of your father and to the prophets of your mother." And the king of Israel said to him, "No, for the LORD has called these three kings *together* to give them into the hand of Moab."

14 Elisha said, "As the LORD of hosts lives, before whom I stand, were it not that I regard the presence of Jehoshaphat the king of Judah, I would not look at you nor see you.

15 "But now bring me a minstrel." And it came about, when the minstrel played, that the hand of the LORD came upon him.

16 He said, "Thus says the LORD, 'Make this valley full of trenches.'

17 "For thus says the LORD, 'You shall not see wind nor shall you see rain; yet that valley shall be filled with water, so that you shall drink, both you and your cattle and your beasts.

18 'This is but a slight thing in the sight of the LORD; He will also give the Moabites into your hand.

19 'Then you shall strike every fortified city and every choice city, and fell every good tree and stop all springs of water, and mar every good piece of land with stones.' "

20 It happened in the morning about the time of offering the sacrifice, that behold, water came by the way of Edom, and the country was filled with water.

21 ¶ Now all the Moabites heard that the kings had come up to fight against them. And all who were able to put on armor and older were summoned and stood on the border.

22 They rose early in the morning, and the sun shone on the water, and the Moabites saw the water opposite *them* as red as blood.

23 Then they said, "This is blood; the kings have surely fought together, and they have slain one another. Now therefore, Moab, to the spoil!"

24 But when they came to the camp of Israel, the Israelites arose and struck the Moabites, so that they fled before them; and they went forward into the land, slaughtering the Moabites.

25 Thus they destroyed the cities; and each one threw a stone on every piece of good land and filled it. So they stopped all the springs of water and felled all the good trees, until in Kir-haraseth *only* they left its stones; however, the slingers went about *it* and struck it.

26 When the king of Moab saw that the battle was too fierce for him, he took with him 700 men who drew swords, to break through to the king of Edom; but they could not.

27 Then he took his oldest son who was to reign in his place, and offered him as a burnt offering on the wall. And there came great wrath against Israel, and they departed from him and returned to their own land.

New International

9 So the king of Israel set out with the king of Judah and the king of Edom. After a roundabout march of seven days, the army had no more water for themselves or for the animals with them.

10 "What!" exclaimed the king of Israel. "Has the LORD called us three kings together only to hand us over to Moab?"

11 But Jehoshaphat asked, "Is there no prophet of the LORD here, that we may inquire of the LORD through him?"

An officer of the king of Israel answered, "Elisha son of Shaphat is here. He used to pour water on the hands of Elijah.*c*"

12 Jehoshaphat said, "The word of the LORD is with him." So the king of Israel and Jehoshaphat and the king of Edom went down to him.

13 Elisha said to the king of Israel, "What do we have to do with each other? Go to the prophets of your father and the prophets of your mother."

"No," the king of Israel answered, "because it was the LORD who called us three kings together to hand us over to Moab."

14 Elisha said, "As surely as the LORD Almighty lives, whom I serve, if I did not have respect for the presence of Jehoshaphat king of Judah, I would not look at you or even notice you. 15 But now bring me a harpist."

While the harpist was playing, the hand of the LORD came upon Elisha 16 and he said, "This is what the LORD says: Make this valley full of ditches. 17 For this is what the LORD says: You will see neither wind nor rain, yet this valley will be filled with water, and you, your cattle and your other animals will drink. 18 This is an easy thing in the eyes of the LORD; he will also hand Moab over to you. 19 You will overthrow every fortified city and every major town. You will cut down every good tree, stop up all the springs, and ruin every good field with stones."

20 The next morning, about the time for offering the sacrifice, there it was—water flowing from the direction of Edom! And the land was filled with water.

21 Now all the Moabites had heard that the kings had come to fight against them; so every man, young and old, who could bear arms was called up and stationed on the border. 22 When they got up early in the morning, the sun was shining on the water. To the Moabites across the way, the water looked red—like blood. 23 "That's blood!" they said. "Those kings must have fought and slaughtered each other. Now to the plunder, Moab!"

24 But when the Moabites came to the camp of Israel, the Israelites rose up and fought them until they fled. And the Israelites invaded the land and slaughtered the Moabites. 25 They destroyed the towns, and each man threw a stone on every good field until it was covered. They stopped up all the springs and cut down every good tree. Only Kir Hareseth was left with its stones in place, but men armed with slings surrounded it and attacked it as well.

26 When the king of Moab saw that the battle had gone against him, he took with him seven hundred swordsmen to break through to the king of Edom, but they failed. 27 Then he took his firstborn son, who was to succeed him as king, and offered him as a sacrifice on the city wall. The fury against Israel was great; they withdrew and returned to their own land.

---

c 11 That is, he was Elijah's personal servant.

King James

The widow's pot of oil

4 NOW THERE cried a certain woman of the wives of the sons of the prophets unto Elisha, saying, Thy servant my husband is dead; and thou knowest that thy servant did fear the LORD: and the creditor is come to take unto him my two sons to be bondmen.

²And Elisha said unto her, What shall I do for thee? tell me, what hast thou in the house? And she said, Thine handmaid hath not any thing in the house, save a pot of oil.

³Then he said, Go, borrow thee vessels abroad of all thy neighbours, *even* empty vessels; ⁵borrow not a few.

⁴And when thou art come in, thou shalt shut the door upon thee and upon thy sons, and shalt pour out into all those vessels, and thou shalt set aside that which is full.

⁵So she went from him, and shut the door upon her and upon her sons, who brought *the vessels* to her; and she poured out.

⁶And it came to pass, when the vessels were full, that she said unto her son, Bring me yet a vessel. And he said unto her, *There is* not a vessel more. And the oil stayed.

⁷Then she came and told the man of God. And he said, Go, sell the oil, and pay thy ᵗdebt, and live thou and thy children of the rest.

The Shunammite's son

8 ¶ And ᵘit fell on a day, that Elisha passed to Shunem, where *was* a great woman; and she ᵛconstrained him to eat bread. And *so* it was, *that* as oft as he passed by, he turned in thither to eat bread.

⁹And she said unto her husband, Behold now, I perceive that this *is* an holy man of God, which passeth by us continually.

¹⁰Let us make a little chamber, I pray thee, on the wall; and let us set for him there a bed, and a table, and a stool, and a candlestick: and it shall be, when he cometh to us, that he shall turn in thither.

¹¹And it fell on a day, that he came thither, and he turned into the chamber, and lay there.

¹²And he said to Gehazi his servant, Call this Shunammite. And when he had called her, she stood before him.

¹³And he said unto him, Say now unto her, Behold, thou hast been careful for us with all this care; what *is* to be done for thee? wouldest thou be spoken for to the king, or to the captain of the host? And she answered, I dwell among mine own people.

¹⁴And he said, What then *is* to be done for her? And Gehazi answered, Verily she hath no child, and her husband is old.

¹⁵And he said, Call her. And when he had called her, she stood in the door.

¹⁶And he said, About this ʷseason, according to the time of life, thou shalt embrace a son. And she said, Nay, my lord, *thou* man of God, do not lie unto thine handmaid.

¹⁷And the woman conceived, and bare a son at that season that Elisha had said unto her, according to the time of life.

18 ¶ And when the child was grown, it fell on a day, that he went out to his father to the reapers.

¹⁹And he said unto his father, My head, my head. And he said to a lad, Carry him to his mother.

²⁰And when he had taken him, and brought him to his mother, he sat on her knees till noon, and *then* died.

²¹And she went up, and laid him on the bed of the man of God, and shut *the door* upon him, and went out.

²²And she called unto her husband, and said, Send me, I pray thee, one of the young men, and one of the asses, that I may run to the man of God, and come again.

²³And he said, Wherefore wilt thou go to him today? *it is* neither new moon, nor sabbath. And she said, *It shall be* ˣwell.

Amplified

4 NOW THE wife of a son of the prophets cried to Elisha, Your servant my husband is dead, and you know that your servant feared the Lord. But the creditor has come to take my two sons to be his slaves.

²Elisha said to her, What shall I do for you? Tell me, what have you [of sale value] in the house? She said, Your handmaid has nothing in the house except a jar of oil.

³Then he said, Go around and borrow vessels from all your neighbors, empty vessels—and not a few.

⁴And when you come in, shut the door upon you and your sons. Then pour out [the oil you have] into all those vessels, setting aside each one when it is full.

⁵So she went from him and shut the door upon herself and her sons, who brought to her the vessels as she poured the oil.

⁶When the vessels were all full, she said to her son, Bring me another vessel. And he said to her, There is not a one left. Then the oil stopped multiplying.

⁷Then she came and told the man of God. He said, Go, sell the oil and pay your debt, and you and your sons live on the rest.

⁸One day Elisha went on to Shunem, where a rich and influential woman lived, who insisted on his eating a meal. Afterward, whenever he passed by, he stopped there for a meal.

⁹And she said to her husband, Behold now, I perceive that this is a holy man of God who passes by continually.

¹⁰Let us make a small chamber on the [housetop] and put there for him a bed, a table, a chair, and a lamp. Then whenever he comes to us, he can go [up the outside stairs and rest] here.

¹¹One day he came and turned into the chamber and lay there.

¹²And he said to Gehazi his servant, Call this Shunammite. When he had called her, she stood before him.

¹³And he said to Gehazi, Say now to her, You have been most painstakingly *and* reverently concerned for us; what is to be done for you? Would you like to be spoken for to the king or to the commander of the army? She answered, I dwell among my own people [they are sufficient].

¹⁴Later Elisha said, What then is to be done for her? Gehazi answered, She has no child and her husband is old.

¹⁵He said, Call her. [Gehazi] called her, and she stood in the doorway.

¹⁶Elisha said, At this season when the time comes round, you shall embrace a son. She said, No, my lord, you man of God, do not lie to your handmaid.

¹⁷But the woman conceived and bore a son at that season when the time came round, as Elisha had said to her.

¹⁸When the child had grown, he went out one day to his father with the reapers.

¹⁹But he said to his father, My head, my head! The man said to his servant, Carry him to his mother.

²⁰And when he was brought to his mother, he sat on her knees till noon, and then died.

²¹And she went up and laid him on the bed of the man of God, and shut the door upon him and went out.

²²And she called to her husband and said, Send me one of the servants and one of the donkeys, that I may go quickly to the man of God and come back again.

²³And he said, Why go to him today? It is neither the New Moon nor the Sabbath. And she said, It will be all right.

ˢOr, *scant not*   ᵗOr, *creditor*   ᵘHeb. *there was a day*
ᵛHeb. *laid hold on him*   ʷHeb. *set time*   ˣHeb. *peace*

New American Standard

The Widow's Oil

4 NOW A certain woman of the wives of the sons of the prophets cried out to Elisha, "Your servant my husband is dead, and you know that your servant feared the LORD; and the creditor has come to take my two children to be his slaves."

2 Elisha said to her, "What shall I do for you? Tell me, what do you have in the house?" And she said, "Your maidservant has nothing in the house except a jar of oil."

3 Then he said, "Go, borrow vessels at large for yourself from all your neighbors, *even* empty vessels; do not get a few.

4 "And you shall go in and shut the door behind you and your sons, and pour out into all these vessels, and you shall set aside what is full."

5 So she went from him and shut the door behind her and her sons; they were bringing *the vessels* to her and she poured.

6 When the vessels were full, she said to her son, "Bring me another vessel." And he said to her, "There is not one vessel more." And the oil stopped.

7 Then she came and told the man of God. And he said, "Go, sell the oil and pay your debt, and you *and* your sons can live on the rest."

The Shunammite Woman

8 ¶ Now there came a day when Elisha passed over to Shunem, where there was a prominent woman, and she persuaded him to eat food. And so it was, as often as he passed by, he turned in there to eat food.

9 She said to her husband, "Behold now, I perceive that this is a holy man of God passing by us continually.

10 "Please, let us make a little walled upper chamber and let us set a bed for him there, and a table and a chair and a lampstand; and it shall be, when he comes to us, *that* he can turn in there."

11 ¶ One day he came there and turned in to the upper chamber and rested.

12 Then he said to Gehazi his servant, "Call this Shunammite." And when he had called her, she stood before him.

13 He said to him, "Say now to her, 'Behold, you have been careful for us with all this care; what can I do for you? Would you be spoken for to the king or to the captain of the army?' " And she answered, "I live among my own people."

14 So he said, "What then is to be done for her?" And Gehazi answered, "Truly she has no son and her husband is old."

15 He said, "Call her." When he had called her, she stood in the doorway.

16 Then he said, "At this season next year you will embrace a son." And she said, "No, my lord, O man of God, do not lie to your maidservant."

17 ¶ The woman conceived and bore a son at that season the next year, as Elisha had said to her.

The Shunammite's Son

18 ¶ When the child was grown, the day came that he went out to his father to the reapers.

19 He said to his father, "My head, my head." And he said to his servant, "Carry him to his mother."

20 When he had taken him and brought him to his mother, he sat on her lap until noon, and *then* died.

21 She went up and laid him on the bed of the man of God, and shut *the door* behind him and went out.

22 Then she called to her husband and said, "Please send me one of the servants and one of the donkeys, that I may run to the man of God and return."

23 He said, "Why will you go to him today? It is neither new moon nor sabbath." And she said, "*It will be* well."

New International

The Widow's Oil

4 THE WIFE of a man from the company of the prophets cried out to Elisha, "Your servant my husband is dead, and you know that he revered the LORD. But now his creditor is coming to take my two boys as his slaves."

2 Elisha replied to her, "How can I help you? Tell me, what do you have in your house?"

"Your servant has nothing there at all," she said, "except a little oil."

3 Elisha said, "Go around and ask all your neighbors for empty jars. Don't ask for just a few. 4 Then go inside and shut the door behind you and your sons. Pour oil into all the jars, and as each is filled, put it to one side."

5 She left him and afterward shut the door behind her and her sons. They brought the jars to her and she kept pouring. 6 When all the jars were full, she said to her son, "Bring me another one."

But he replied, "There is not a jar left." Then the oil stopped flowing.

7 She went and told the man of God, and he said, "Go, sell the oil and pay your debts. You and your sons can live on what is left."

The Shunammite's Son Restored to Life

8 One day Elisha went to Shunem. And a well-to-do woman was there, who urged him to stay for a meal. So whenever he came by, he stopped there to eat. 9 She said to her husband, "I know that this man who often comes our way is a holy man of God. 10 Let's make a small room on the roof and put in it a bed and a table, a chair and a lamp for him. Then he can stay there whenever he comes to us."

11 One day when Elisha came, he went up to his room and lay down there. 12 He said to his servant Gehazi, "Call the Shunammite." So he called her, and she stood before him. 13 Elisha said to him, "Tell her, 'You have gone to all this trouble for us. Now what can be done for you? Can we speak on your behalf to the king or the commander of the army?' "

She replied, "I have a home among my own people."

14 "What can be done for her?" Elisha asked.

Gehazi said, "Well, she has no son and her husband is old."

15 Then Elisha said, "Call her." So he called her, and she stood in the doorway. 16 "About this time next year," Elisha said, "you will hold a son in your arms."

"No, my lord," she objected. "Don't mislead your servant, O man of God!"

17 But the woman became pregnant, and the next year about that same time she gave birth to a son, just as Elisha had told her.

18 The child grew, and one day he went out to his father, who was with the reapers. 19 "My head! My head!" he said to his father.

His father told a servant, "Carry him to his mother." 20 After the servant had lifted him up and carried him to his mother, the boy sat on her lap until noon, and then he died. 21 She went up and laid him on the bed of the man of God, then shut the door and went out.

22 She called her husband and said, "Please send me one of the servants and a donkey so I can go to the man of God quickly and return."

23 "Why go to him today?" he asked. "It's not the New Moon or the Sabbath."

"It's all right," she said.

King James

²⁴Then she saddled an ass, and said to her servant, Drive, and go forward; ʸslack not *thy* riding for me, except I bid thee.

²⁵So she went and came unto the man of God to mount Carmel. And it came to pass, when the man of God saw her afar off, that he said to Gehazi his servant, Behold, *yonder is* that Shunammite:

²⁶Run now, I pray thee, to meet her, and say unto her, *Is it* well with thee? *is it* well with thy husband? *is it* well with the child? And she answered, *It is* well.

²⁷And when she came to the man of God to the hill, she caught ᶻhim by the feet: but Gehazi came near to thrust her away. And the man of God said, Let her alone; for her soul *is* ᵃvexed within her: and the LORD hath hid *it* from me, and hath not told me.

²⁸Then she said, Did I desire a son of my lord? did I not say, Do not deceive me?

²⁹Then he said to Gehazi, Gird up thy loins, and take my staff in thine hand, and go thy way: if thou meet any man, salute him not; and if any salute thee, answer him not again: and lay my staff upon the face of the child.

³⁰And the mother of the child said, *As* the LORD liveth, and *as* thy soul liveth, I will not leave thee. And he arose, and followed her.

³¹And Gehazi passed on before them, and laid the staff upon the face of the child; but *there was* neither voice, nor ᵇhearing. Wherefore he went again to meet him, and told him, saying, The child is not awaked.

³²And when Elisha was come into the house, behold, the child was dead, *and* laid upon his bed.

³³He went in therefore, and shut the door upon them twain, and prayed unto the LORD.

³⁴And he went up, and lay upon the child, and put his mouth upon his mouth, and his eyes upon his eyes, and his hands upon his hands: and he stretched himself upon the child; and the flesh of the child waxed warm.

³⁵Then he returned, and walked in the house ᶜto and fro; and went up, and stretched himself upon him: and the child sneezed seven times, and the child opened his eyes.

³⁶And he called Gehazi, and said, Call this Shunammite. So he called her. And when she was come in unto him, he said, Take up thy son.

³⁷Then she went in, and fell at his feet, and bowed herself to the ground, and took up her son, and went out.

Poisonous food made harmless

³⁸ ¶ And Elisha came again to Gilgal: and *there was* a dearth in the land; and the sons of the prophets *were* sitting before him: and he said unto his servant, Set on the great pot, and seethe pottage for the sons of the prophets.

³⁹And one went out into the field to gather herbs, and found a wild vine, and gathered thereof wild gourds his lap full, and came and shred *them* into the pot of pottage: for they knew *them* not.

⁴⁰So they poured out for the men to eat. And it came to pass, as they were eating of the pottage, that they cried out, and said, O *thou* man of God, *there is* death in the pot. And they could not eat *thereof*.

⁴¹But he said, Then bring meal. And he cast *it* into the pot; and he said, Pour out for the people, that they may eat. And there was no ᵈharm in the pot.

The feeding of the hundred men

⁴² ¶ And there came a man from Baal-shalisha, and brought the man of God bread of the firstfruits, twenty loaves of barley, and full ears of corn ᵉin the husk thereof. And he said, Give unto the people, that they may eat.

⁴³And his servitor said, What, should I set this before an hundred men? He said again, Give the people, that they may eat: for thus saith the LORD, They shall eat, and shall leave *thereof*.

Amplified

²⁴Then she saddled the donkey and said to her servant, Ride fast; do not slacken your pace for me unless I tell you.

²⁵So she set out and came to the man of God at Mount Carmel. When the man of God saw her afar off, he said to Gehazi his servant, Behold, yonder is that Shunammite.

²⁶Run to meet her and say, Is it well with you? Well with your husband? Well with the child? And she answered, It is well.

²⁷When she came to the mountain to the man of God, she clung to his feet. Gehazi came to thrust her away, but the man of God said, Let her alone, for her soul is bitter *and* vexed within her, and the Lord has hid it from me and has not told me.

²⁸Then she said, Did I desire a son of my lord? Did I not say, Do not deceive me?

²⁹Then he said to Gehazi, Gird up your loins and take my staff in your hand and go lay my staff on the face of the child. If you meet any man, do not salute him. If he salutes you, do not answer him.

³⁰The mother of the child said, As the Lord lives and as my soul lives, I will not leave you. And he arose and followed her.

³¹Gehazi passed on before them and laid the staff on the child's face, but the boy neither spoke nor heard. So he went back to meet Elisha and said to him, The child has not awakened.

³²When Elisha arrived in the house, the child was dead and laid upon his bed.

³³So he went in, shut the door on the two of them, and prayed to the Lord.

³⁴He went up and lay on the child, put his mouth on his mouth, his eyes on his eyes, and his hands on his hands. And as he stretched himself on him *and* embraced him, the child's flesh became warm.

³⁵Then he returned and walked in the house to and fro and went up again and stretched himself upon him. And the child sneezed seven times, and then opened his eyes.

³⁶Then [Elisha] called Gehazi and said, Call this Shunammite. So he called her. And when she came, he said, Take up your son.

³⁷She came and fell at his feet, bowing herself to the ground. Then she took up her son and went out.

³⁸Elisha came back to Gilgal during a famine in the land. The sons of the prophets were sitting before him, and he said to his servant, Set on the big pot and cook pottage for the sons of the prophets.

³⁹Then one went into the field to gather herbs and gathered from a wild vine his lap full of wild gourds, and returned and cut them up into the pot of pottage, for they were unknown to them.

⁴⁰So they poured it out for the men to eat. But as they ate of the pottage, they cried out, O man of God, there is death in the pot! And they could not eat it.

⁴¹But he said, Bring meal [as a symbol of God's healing power]. And he cast it into the pot and said, Pour it out for the people that they may eat. Then there was no harm in the pot.

⁴²[At another time] a man from Baal-shalisha came and brought the man of God bread of the firstfruits, twenty loaves of barley, and fresh ears of grain [in the husk] in his sack. And Elisha said, Give to the men that they may eat.

⁴³His servant said, How am I to set [only] this before a hundred [hungry] men? He said, Give to the men that they may eat. For thus says the Lord: They shall be fed and have some left.

ʸ Heb. *restrain not for me to ride*   ᶻ Heb. *by his feet*   ᵃ Heb. *bitter*   ᵇ Heb. *attention*   ᶜ Heb. *once hither, and once thither*   ᵈ Heb. *evil thing*   ᵉ Or, *in his scrip, or, garment*

New American Standard

24 Then she saddled a donkey and said to her servant, "Drive and go forward; do not slow down the pace for me unless I tell you."

25 So she went and came to the man of God to Mount Carmel.

¶ When the man of God saw her at a distance, he said to Gehazi his servant, "Behold, there is the Shunammite.

26 "Please run now to meet her and say to her, 'Is it well with you? Is it well with your husband? Is it well with the child?'" And she answered, "It is well."

27 When she came to the man of God to the hill, she caught hold of his feet. And Gehazi came near to push her away; but the man of God said, "Let her alone, for her soul is troubled within her; and the LORD has hidden it from me and has not told me."

28 Then she said, "Did I ask for a son from my lord? Did I not say, 'Do not deceive me'?"

29 ¶ Then he said to Gehazi, "Gird up your loins and take my staff in your hand, and go your way; if you meet any man, do not salute him, and if anyone salutes you, do not answer him; and lay my staff on the lad's face."

30 The mother of the lad said, "As the LORD lives and as you yourself live, I will not leave you." And he arose and followed her.

31 Then Gehazi passed on before them and laid the staff on the lad's face, but there was no sound or response. So he returned to meet him and told him, "The lad has not awakened."

32 ¶ When Elisha came into the house, behold the lad was dead and laid on his bed.

33 So he entered and shut the door behind them both and prayed to the LORD.

34 And he went up and lay on the child, and put his mouth on his mouth and his eyes on his eyes and his hands on his hands, and he stretched himself on him; and the flesh of the child became warm.

35 Then he returned and walked in the house once back and forth, and went up and stretched himself on him; and the lad sneezed seven times and the lad opened his eyes.

36 He called Gehazi and said, "Call this Shunammite." So he called her. And when she came in to him, he said, "Take up your son."

37 Then she went in and fell at his feet and bowed herself to the ground, and she took up her son and went out.

The Poisonous Stew

38 ¶ When Elisha returned to Gilgal, *there was* a famine in the land. As the sons of the prophets were sitting before him, he said to his servant, "Put on the large pot and boil stew for the sons of the prophets."

39 Then one went out into the field to gather herbs, and found a wild vine and gathered from it his lap full of wild gourds, and came and sliced them into the pot of stew, for they did not know *what they were*.

40 So they poured *it* out for the men to eat. And as they were eating of the stew, they cried out and said, "O man of God, there is death in the pot." And they were unable to eat.

41 But he said, "Now bring meal." He threw it into the pot and said, "Pour *it* out for the people that they may eat." Then there was no harm in the pot.

42 ¶ Now a man came from Baal-shalishah, and brought the man of God bread of the first fruits, twenty loaves of barley and fresh ears of grain in his sack. And he said, "Give *them* to the people that they may eat."

43 His attendant said, "What, will I set this before a hundred men?" But he said, "Give *them* to the people that they may eat, for thus says the LORD, 'They shall eat and have *some* left over.'"

New International

24 She saddled the donkey and said to her servant, "Lead on; don't slow down for me unless I tell you." 25 So she set out and came to the man of God at Mount Carmel.

When he saw her in the distance, the man of God said to his servant Gehazi, "Look! There's the Shunammite! 26 Run to meet her and ask her, 'Are you all right? Is your husband all right? Is your child all right?'"

"Everything is all right," she said.

27 When she reached the man of God at the mountain, she took hold of his feet. Gehazi came over to push her away, but the man of God said, "Leave her alone! She is in bitter distress, but the LORD has hidden it from me and has not told me why."

28 "Did I ask you for a son, my lord?" she said. "Didn't I tell you, 'Don't raise my hopes'?"

29 Elisha said to Gehazi, "Tuck your cloak into your belt, take my staff in your hand and run. If you meet anyone, do not greet him, and if anyone greets you, do not answer. Lay my staff on the boy's face."

30 But the child's mother said, "As surely as the LORD lives and as you live, I will not leave you." So he got up and followed her.

31 Gehazi went on ahead and laid the staff on the boy's face, but there was no sound or response. So Gehazi went back to meet Elisha and told him, "The boy has not awakened."

32 When Elisha reached the house, there was the boy lying dead on his couch. 33 He went in, shut the door on the two of them and prayed to the LORD. 34 Then he got on the bed and lay upon the boy, mouth to mouth, eyes to eyes, hands to hands. As he stretched himself out upon him, the boy's body grew warm. 35 Elisha turned away and walked back and forth in the room and then got on the bed and stretched out upon him once more. The boy sneezed seven times and opened his eyes.

36 Elisha summoned Gehazi and said, "Call the Shunammite." And he did. When she came, he said, "Take your son." 37 She came in, fell at his feet and bowed to the ground. Then she took her son and went out.

Death in the Pot

38 Elisha returned to Gilgal and there was a famine in that region. While the company of the prophets was meeting with him, he said to his servant, "Put on the large pot and cook some stew for these men."

39 One of them went out into the fields to gather herbs and found a wild vine. He gathered some of its gourds and filled the fold of his cloak. When he returned, he cut them up into the pot of stew, though no one knew what they were. 40 The stew was poured out for the men, but as they began to eat it, they cried out, "O man of God, there is death in the pot!" And they could not eat it.

41 Elisha said, "Get some flour." He put it into the pot and said, "Serve it to the people to eat." And there was nothing harmful in the pot.

Feeding of a Hundred

42 A man came from Baal Shalishah, bringing the man of God twenty loaves of barley bread baked from the first ripe grain, along with some heads of new grain. "Give it to the people to eat," Elisha said.

43 "How can I set this before a hundred men?" his servant asked.

But Elisha answered, "Give it to the people to eat. For this is what the LORD says: 'They will eat and have some

King James

Amplified

44So he set *it* before them, and they did eat, and left *thereof,* according to the word of the LORD.

The cure of Naaman the leper

5 NOW NAAMAN, captain of the host of the king of Syria, was a great man *f*with his master, and *g h*honourable, because by him the LORD had given *i*deliverance unto Syria: he was also a mighty man in valour, *but he was* a leper.

2And the Syrians had gone out by companies, and had brought away captive out of the land of Israel a little maid; and she *j*waited on Naaman's wife.

3And she said unto her mistress, Would God my lord *were f*with the prophet that *is* in Samaria! for he would *k*recover him of his leprosy.

4And *one* went in, and told his lord, saying, Thus and thus said the maid that *is* of the land of Israel.

5And the king of Syria said, Go to, go, and I will send a letter unto the king of Israel. And he departed, and took *l*with him ten talents of silver, and six thousand *pieces* of gold, and ten changes of raiment.

6And he brought the letter to the king of Israel, saying, Now when this letter is come unto thee, behold, I have *therewith* sent Naaman my servant to thee, that thou mayest recover him of his leprosy.

7And it came to pass, when the king of Israel had read the letter, that he rent his clothes, and said, *Am* I God, to kill and to make alive, that this man doth send unto me to recover a man of his leprosy? wherefore consider, I pray you, and see how he seeketh a quarrel against me.

8 ¶ And it was *so,* when Elisha the man of God had heard that the king of Israel had rent his clothes, that he sent to the king, saying, Wherefore hast thou rent thy clothes? let him come now to me, and he shall know that there is a prophet in Israel.

9So Naaman came with his horses and with his chariot, and stood at the door of the house of Elisha.

10And Elisha sent a messenger unto him, saying, Go and wash in Jordan seven times, and thy flesh shall come again to thee, and thou shalt be clean.

11But Naaman was wroth, and went away, and said, Behold, *m n*I thought, He will surely come out to me, and stand, and call on the name of the LORD his God, and *o*strike his hand over the place, and recover the leper.

12*Are* not *p*Abana and Pharpar, rivers of Damascus, better than all the waters of Israel? may I not wash in them, and be clean? So he turned and went away in a rage.

13And his servants came near, and spake unto him, and said, My father, *if* the prophet had bid thee *do some* great thing, wouldest thou not have done *it?* how much rather then, when he saith to thee, Wash, and be clean?

14Then went he down, and dipped himself seven times in Jordan, according to the saying of the man of God: and his flesh came again like unto the flesh of a little child, and he was clean.

15 ¶ And he returned to the man of God, he and all his company, and came, and stood before him: and he said, Behold, now I know that *there is* no God in all the earth, but in Israel: now therefore, I pray thee, take a blessing of thy servant.

16But he said, *As* the LORD liveth, before whom I stand, I will receive none. And he urged him to take *it;* but he refused.

17And Naaman said, Shall there not then, I pray thee, be given to thy servant two mules' burden of earth? for thy servant will henceforth offer neither burnt offering nor sacrifice unto other gods, but unto the LORD.

44So he set it before them, and they ate and left some, as the Lord had said.

5 NAAMAN, COMMANDER of the army of the king of Syria, was a great man with his master, accepted [and acceptable], because by him the Lord had given victory to Syria. He was also a mighty man of valor, but he was a leper.

2The Syrians had gone out in bands and had brought away captive out of the land of Israel a little maid, and she waited on Naaman's wife.

3She said to her mistress, Would that my lord were with the prophet who is in Samaria! For he would heal him of his leprosy.

4[Naaman] went in and told his king, Thus and thus said the maid from Israel.

5And the king of Syria said, Go now, and I will send a letter to the king of Israel. And he departed and took with him ten talents of silver, 6,000 shekels of gold, and ten changes of raiment.

6And he brought the letter to the king of Israel. It said, When this letter comes to you, I will with it have sent to you my servant Naaman, that you may cure him of leprosy.

7When the king of Israel read the letter, he rent his clothes and said, Am I God, to kill and to make alive, that this man sends to me to heal a man of his leprosy? Just consider and see how he is seeking a quarrel with me.

8When Elisha the man of God heard that the king of Israel had rent his clothes, he sent to the king, asking, Why have you rent your clothes? Let Naaman come now to me and he shall know that there is a prophet in Israel.

9So Naaman came with his horses and chariots and stopped at Elisha's door.

10Elisha sent a messenger to him, saying, Go and wash in the Jordan seven times, and your flesh shall be restored and you shall be clean.

11But Naaman was angry and went away and said, Behold, I thought he would surely come out to me and stand and call on the name of the Lord his God, and wave his hand over the place and heal the leper.

12Are not Abana and Pharpar, the rivers of Damascus, better than all the waters of Israel? May I not wash in them and be clean? So he turned and went away in a rage.

13And his servants came near and said to him, My father, if the prophet had bid you to do some great thing, would you not have done it? How much rather, then, when he says to you, Wash and be clean?

14Then he went down and dipped himself seven times in the Jordan, as the man of God had said, and his flesh was restored like that of a little child, and he was clean.

15Then Naaman returned to the man of God, he and all his company, and stood before him. He said, Behold, now I know that there is no God in all the earth but in Israel. So now accept a gift from your servant.

16Elisha said, As the Lord lives, before Whom I stand, I will accept none. He urged him to take it, but Elisha refused.

17Naaman said, Then, I pray you, let there be given to me, your servant, two mules' burden of earth. For your servant will henceforth offer neither burnt offering nor sacrifice to other gods, but only to the Lord.

---

*f*Heb. *before countenance*   *g*Or, *gracious*   *h*Heb. *lifted up,* or, *accepted in gather in*   *i*Or, *victory*   *j*Heb. *was before*   *k*Heb. *with myself, He will surely come out*   *l*Heb. *in his hand*   *m*Heb. *I said*   *n*Or, *I said*   *o*Heb. *move up and down*   *p*Or, *Amana*

New American Standard

44 So he set *it* before them, and they ate and had *some* left over, according to the word of the LORD.

Naaman Is Healed

5 NOW NAAMAN, captain of the army of the king of Aram, was a great man with his master, and highly respected, because by him the LORD had given victory to Aram. The man was also a valiant warrior, *but he was* a leper.
2 Now the Arameans had gone out in bands and had taken captive a little girl from the land of Israel; and she waited on Naaman's wife.
3 She said to her mistress, "I wish that my master were with the prophet who is in Samaria! Then he would cure him of his leprosy."
4 Naaman went in and told his master, saying, "Thus and thus spoke the girl who is from the land of Israel."
5 Then the king of Aram said, "Go now, and I will send a letter to the king of Israel." He departed and took with him ten talents of silver and six thousand *shekels* of gold and ten changes of clothes.
6 ¶ He brought the letter to the king of Israel, saying, "And now as this letter comes to you, behold, I have sent Naaman my servant to you, that you may cure him of his leprosy."
7 When the king of Israel read the letter, he tore his clothes and said, "Am I God, to kill and to make alive, that this man is sending *word* to me to cure a man of his leprosy? But consider now, and see how he is seeking a quarrel against me."
8 ¶ It happened when Elisha the man of God heard that the king of Israel had torn his clothes, that he sent *word* to the king, saying, "Why have you torn your clothes? Now let him come to me, and he shall know that there is a prophet in Israel."
9 So Naaman came with his horses and his chariots and stood at the doorway of the house of Elisha.
10 Elisha sent a messenger to him, saying, "Go and wash in the Jordan seven times, and your flesh will be restored to you and *you will* be clean."
11 But Naaman was furious and went away and said, "Behold, I thought, 'He will surely come out to me and stand and call on the name of the LORD his God, and wave his hand over the place and cure the leper.'
12 "Are not Abanah and Pharpar, the rivers of Damascus, better than all the waters of Israel? Could I not wash in them and be clean?" So he turned and went away in a rage.
13 Then his servants came near and spoke to him and said, "My father, had the prophet told you *to do some* great thing, would you not have done *it?* How much more *then,* when he says to you, 'Wash, and be clean'?"
14 So he went down and dipped *himself* seven times in the Jordan, according to the word of the man of God; and his flesh was restored like the flesh of a little child and he was clean.

Gehazi's Greed

15 ¶ When he returned to the man of God with all his company, and came and stood before him, he said, "Behold now, I know that there is no God in all the earth, but in Israel; so please take a present from your servant now."
16 But he said, "As the LORD lives, before whom I stand, I will take nothing." And he urged him to take *it,* but he refused.
17 Naaman said, "If not, please let your servant at least be given two mules' load of earth; for your servant will no longer offer burnt offering nor will he sacrifice to other gods, but to the LORD.

New International

left over.' " **44** Then he set it before them, and they ate and had some left over, according to the word of the LORD.

Naaman Healed of Leprosy

5 NOW NAAMAN was commander of the army of the king of Aram. He was a great man in the sight of his master and highly regarded, because through him the LORD had given victory to Aram. He was a valiant soldier, but he had leprosy.[d]
2 Now bands from Aram had gone out and had taken captive a young girl from Israel, and she served Naaman's wife.
3 She said to her mistress, "If only my master would see the prophet who is in Samaria! He would cure him of his leprosy."
4 Naaman went to his master and told him what the girl from Israel had said.
5 "By all means, go," the king of Aram replied. "I will send a letter to the king of Israel." So Naaman left, taking with him ten talents[e] of silver, six thousand shekels[f] of gold and ten sets of clothing.
6 The letter that he took to the king of Israel read: "With this letter I am sending my servant Naaman to you so that you may cure him of his leprosy."
7 As soon as the king of Israel read the letter, he tore his robes and said, "Am I God? Can I kill and bring back to life? Why does this fellow send someone to me to be cured of his leprosy? See how he is trying to pick a quarrel with me!"
8 When Elisha the man of God heard that the king of Israel had torn his robes, he sent him this message: "Why have you torn your robes? Have the man come to me and he will know that there is a prophet in Israel."
9 So Naaman went with his horses and chariots and stopped at the door of Elisha's house.
10 Elisha sent a messenger to say to him, "Go, wash yourself seven times in the Jordan, and your flesh will be restored and you will be cleansed."
11 But Naaman went away angry and said, "I thought that he would surely come out to me and stand and call on the name of the LORD his God, wave his hand over the spot and cure me of my leprosy.
12 Are not Abana and Pharpar, the rivers of Damascus, better than any of the waters of Israel? Couldn't I wash in them and be cleansed?" So he turned and went off in a rage.
13 Naaman's servants went to him and said, "My father, if the prophet had told you to do some great thing, would you not have done it? How much more, then, when he tells you, 'Wash and be cleansed'!"
14 So he went down and dipped himself in the Jordan seven times, as the man of God had told him, and his flesh was restored and became clean like that of a young boy.
15 Then Naaman and all his attendants went back to the man of God. He stood before him and said, "Now I know that there is no God in all the world except in Israel. Please accept now a gift from your servant."
16 The prophet answered, "As surely as the LORD lives, whom I serve, I will not accept a thing." And even though Naaman urged him, he refused.
17 "If you will not," said Naaman, "please let me, your servant, be given as much earth as a pair of mules can carry, for your servant will never again make burnt offer-

d 1 The Hebrew word was used for various diseases affecting the skin—not necessarily leprosy; also in verses 3, 6, 7, 11 and 27.
e 5 That is, about 750 pounds (about 340 kilograms)   *f 5* That is, about 150 pounds (about 70 kilograms)

King James

¹⁸In this thing the LORD pardon thy servant, *that* when my master goeth into the house of Rimmon to worship there, and he leaneth on my hand, and I bow myself in the house of Rimmon: when I bow down myself in the house of Rimmon, the LORD pardon thy servant in this thing.

¹⁹And he said unto him, Go in peace. So he departed from him a little way.

²⁰ ¶ But Gehazi, the servant of Elisha the man of God, said, Behold, my master hath spared Naaman this Syrian, in not receiving at his hands that which he brought: but, *as* the LORD liveth, I will run after him, and take somewhat of him.

²¹So Gehazi followed after Naaman. And when Naaman saw *him* running after him, he lighted down from the chariot to meet him, and said, *q*Is all well?

²²And he said, All *is* well. My master hath sent me, saying, Behold, even now there be come to me from mount Ephraim two young men of the sons of the prophets: give them, I pray thee, a talent of silver, and two changes of garments.

²³And Naaman said, Be content, take two talents. And he urged him, and bound two talents of silver in two bags, with two changes of garments, and laid *them* upon two of his servants; and they bare *them* before him.

²⁴And when he came to the *r*tower, he took *them* from their hand, and bestowed *them* in the house: and he let the men go, and they departed.

²⁵But he went in, and stood before his master. And Elisha said unto him, Whence *comest thou*, Gehazi? And he said, Thy servant went *s*no whither.

²⁶And he said unto him, Went not mine heart *with thee*, when the man turned again from his chariot to meet thee? *Is it* a time to receive money, and to receive garments, and oliveyards, and vineyards, and sheep, and oxen, and menservants, and maidservants?

²⁷The leprosy therefore of Naaman shall cleave unto thee, and unto thy seed for ever. And he went out from his presence a leper *as white* as snow.

Recovery of the lost axe head

6 AND THE sons of the prophets said unto Elisha, Behold now, the place where we dwell with thee is too strait for us.

²Let us go, we pray thee, unto Jordan, and take thence every man a beam, and let us make us a place there, where we may dwell. And he answered, Go ye.

³And one said, Be content, I pray thee, and go with thy servants. And he answered, I will go.

⁴So he went with them. And when they came to Jordan, they cut down wood.

⁵But as one was felling a beam, the *t*axe head fell into the water: and he cried, and said, Alas, master! for it was borrowed.

⁶And the man of God said, Where fell it? And he showed him the place. And he cut down a stick, and cast *it* in thither; and the iron did swim.

⁷Therefore said he, Take *it* up to thee. And he put out his hand, and took it.

Elisha strikes the Syrians blind

⁸ ¶ Then the king of Syria warred against Israel, and took counsel with his servants, saying, In such and such a place *shall be* my *u*camp.

⁹And the man of God sent unto the king of Israel, saying, Beware that thou pass not such a place; for thither the Syrians are come down.

¹⁰And the king of Israel sent to the place which the man of God told him and warned him of, and saved himself there, not once nor twice.

Amplified

¹⁸In this thing may the Lord pardon your servant: when my master [the king] goes into the house of [his god] Rimmon to worship there, and he leans on my hand and I bow myself in the house of Rimmon, when I bow down myself in the house of Rimmon, may the Lord pardon your servant in this thing.

¹⁹Elisha said to him, Go in peace. So Naaman departed from him a little way.

²⁰But Gehazi, the servant of Elisha the man of God, said, Behold, my master spared this Naaman the Syrian, in not receiving from his hands what he brought. But as the Lord lives, I will run after him and get something from him.

²¹So Gehazi followed after Naaman. When Naaman saw one running after him, he lighted down from the chariot to meet him and said, Is all well?

²²And he said, All is well. My master has sent me to say, There have just come to me from the hill country of Ephraim two young men of the sons of the prophets. I pray you, give them a talent of silver and two changes of garments.

²³And Naaman said, Be pleased to take two talents. And he urged him, and bound two talents of silver in two bags with two changes of garments and laid them upon two of his servants, and they bore them before Gehazi.

²⁴When he came to the hill, he took them from their hands and put them in the house; and he sent the men away, and they left.

²⁵He went in and stood before his master. Elisha said, Where have you been, Gehazi? He said, Your servant went nowhere.

²⁶Elisha said to him, Did not my spirit go with you when the man turned from his chariot to meet you? Was it a time to accept money, garments, olive orchards, vineyards, sheep, oxen, menservants, and maidservants?

²⁷Therefore the leprosy of Naaman shall cleave to you and to your offspring forever. And Gehazi went from his presence a leper as white as snow.

6 THE SONS of the prophets said to Elisha, Look now, the place where we live before you is too small for us.

²Let us go to the Jordan, and each man get there a [house] beam; and let us make us a place there where we may dwell. And he answered, Go.

³One said, Be pleased to go with your servants. He answered, I will go.

⁴So he went with them. And when they came to the Jordan, they cut down trees.

⁵But as one was felling his beam, the axhead fell into the water; and he cried, Alas, my master, for it was borrowed!

⁶The man of God said, Where did it fall? When shown the place, Elisha cut off a stick and threw it in there, and the iron floated.

⁷He said, Pick it up. And he put out his hand and took it.

⁸When the king of Syria was warring against Israel, after counseling with his servants, he said, In such and such a place shall be my camp.

⁹Then the man of God sent to the king of Israel, saying, Beware that you pass not such a place, for the Syrians are coming down there.

¹⁰Then the king of Israel sent to the place of which [Elisha] told *and* warned him; and thus he protected *and* saved himself there repeatedly.

---

*q*Heb. Is there *peace?* *r*Or, *secret place* *s*Heb. *not hither or thither* *t*Heb. *iron* *u*Or, *encamping*

New American Standard

¹⁸"In this matter may the LORD pardon your servant: when my master goes into the house of Rimmon to worship there, and he leans on my hand and I bow myself in the house of Rimmon, when I bow myself in the house of Rimmon, the LORD pardon your servant in this matter."

¹⁹ He said to him, "Go in peace." So he departed from him some distance.

²⁰ ¶ But Gehazi, the servant of Elisha the man of God, thought, "Behold, my master has spared this Naaman the Aramean, by not receiving from his hands what he brought. As the LORD lives, I will run after him and take something from him."

²¹ So Gehazi pursued Naaman. When Naaman saw one running after him, he came down from the chariot to meet him and said, "Is all well?"

²² He said, "All is well. My master has sent me, saying, 'Behold, just now two young men of the sons of the prophets have come to me from the hill country of Ephraim. Please give them a talent of silver and two changes of clothes.' "

²³ Naaman said, "Be pleased to take two talents." And he urged him, and bound two talents of silver in two bags with two changes of clothes and gave them to two of his servants; and they carried *them* before him.

²⁴ When he came to the hill, he took them from their hand and deposited them in the house, and he sent the men away, and they departed.

²⁵ But he went in and stood before his master. And Elisha said to him, "Where have you been, Gehazi?" And he said, "Your servant went nowhere."

²⁶ ¶ Then he said to him, "Did not my heart go *with you*, when the man turned from his chariot to meet you? Is it a time to receive money and to receive clothes and olive groves and vineyards and sheep and oxen and male and female servants?

²⁷"Therefore, the leprosy of Naaman shall cling to you and to your descendants forever." So he went out from his presence a leper *as white* as snow.

The Axe Head Recovered

6 NOW THE sons of the prophets said to Elisha, "Behold now, the place before you where we are living is too limited for us.

²"Please let us go to the Jordan and each of us take from there a beam, and let us make a place there for ourselves where we may live." So he said, "Go."

³ Then one said, "Please be willing to go with your servants." And he answered, "I shall go."

⁴ So he went with them; and when they came to the Jordan, they cut down trees.

⁵ But as one was felling a beam, the axe head fell into the water; and he cried out and said, "Alas, my master! For it was borrowed."

⁶ Then the man of God said, "Where did it fall?" And when he showed him the place, he cut off a stick and threw *it* in there, and made the iron float.

⁷ He said, "Take it up for yourself." So he put out his hand and took it.

The Arameans Plot to Capture Elisha

⁸ ¶ Now the king of Aram was warring against Israel; and he counseled with his servants saying, "In such and such a place shall be my camp."

⁹ The man of God sent *word* to the king of Israel saying, "Beware that you do not pass this place, for the Arameans are coming down there."

¹⁰ The king of Israel sent to the place about which the man of God had told him; thus he warned him, so that he guarded himself there, more than once or twice.

New International

ings and sacrifices to any other god but the LORD. ¹⁸But may the LORD forgive your servant for this one thing: When my master enters the temple of Rimmon to bow down and he is leaning on my arm and I bow there also—when I bow down in the temple of Rimmon, may the LORD forgive your servant for this."

¹⁹"Go in peace," Elisha said.

After Naaman had traveled some distance, ²⁰Gehazi, the servant of Elisha the man of God, said to himself, "My master was too easy on Naaman, this Aramean, by not accepting from him what he brought. As surely as the LORD lives, I will run after him and get something from him."

²¹So Gehazi hurried after Naaman. When Naaman saw him running toward him, he got down from the chariot to meet him. "Is everything all right?" he asked.

²²"Everything is all right," Gehazi answered. "My master sent me to say, 'Two young men from the company of the prophets have just come to me from the hill country of Ephraim. Please give them a talent^g of silver and two sets of clothing.' "

²³"By all means, take two talents," said Naaman. He urged Gehazi to accept them, and then tied up the two talents of silver in two bags, with two sets of clothing. He gave them to two of his servants, and they carried them ahead of Gehazi. ²⁴When Gehazi came to the hill, he took the things from the servants and put them away in the house. He sent the men away and they left. ²⁵Then he went in and stood before his master Elisha.

"Where have you been, Gehazi?" Elisha asked.

"Your servant didn't go anywhere," Gehazi answered.

²⁶But Elisha said to him, "Was not my spirit with you when the man got down from his chariot to meet you? Is this the time to take money, or to accept clothes, olive groves, vineyards, flocks, herds, or menservants and maidservants? ²⁷Naaman's leprosy will cling to you and to your descendants forever." Then Gehazi went from Elisha's presence and he was leprous, as white as snow.

An Axhead Floats

6 THE COMPANY of the prophets said to Elisha, "Look, the place where we meet with you is too small for us. ²Let us go to the Jordan, where each of us can get a pole; and let us build a place there for us to live."

And he said, "Go."

³Then one of them said, "Won't you please come with your servants?"

"I will," Elisha replied. ⁴And he went with them.

They went to the Jordan and began to cut down trees. ⁵As one of them was cutting down a tree, the iron axhead fell into the water. "Oh, my lord," he cried out, "it was borrowed!"

⁶The man of God asked, "Where did it fall?" When he showed him the place, Elisha cut a stick and threw it there, and made the iron float. ⁷"Lift it out," he said. Then the man reached out his hand and took it.

Elisha Traps Blinded Arameans

⁸Now the king of Aram was at war with Israel. After conferring with his officers, he said, "I will set up my camp in such and such a place."

⁹The man of God sent word to the king of Israel: "Beware of passing that place, because the Arameans are going down there." ¹⁰So the king of Israel checked on the place indicated by the man of God. Time and again Elisha warned the king, so that he was on his guard in such places.

---

^g 22 That is, about 75 pounds (about 34 kilograms)

King James

Amplified

¹¹Therefore the heart of the king of Syria was sore troubled for this thing; and he called his servants, and said unto them, Will ye not show me which of us *is* for the king of Israel?

¹²And one of his servants said, ^vNone, my lord, O king: but Elisha, the prophet that *is* in Israel, telleth the king of Israel the words that thou speakest in thy bedchamber.

¹³ ¶ And he said, Go and spy where he *is*, that I may send and fetch him. And it was told him, saying, Behold, *he is* in Dothan.

¹⁴Therefore sent he thither horses, and chariots, and a ^wgreat host: and they came by night, and compassed the city about.

¹⁵And when the ^xservant of the man of God was risen early, and gone forth, behold, an host compassed the city both with horses and chariots. And his servant said unto him, Alas, my master! how shall we do?

¹⁶And he answered, Fear not: for they that *be* with us *are* more than they that *be* with them.

¹⁷And Elisha prayed, and said, LORD, I pray thee, open his eyes, that he may see. And the LORD opened the eyes of the young man; and he saw: and, behold, the mountain *was* full of horses and chariots of fire round about Elisha.

¹⁸And when they came down to him, Elisha prayed unto the LORD, and said, Smite this people, I pray thee, with blindness. And he smote them with blindness according to the word of Elisha.

¹⁹ ¶ And Elisha said unto them, This *is* not the way, neither *is* this the city: ^yfollow me, and I will bring you to the man whom ye seek. But he led them to Samaria.

²⁰And it came to pass, when they were come into Samaria, that Elisha said, LORD, open the eyes of these *men*, that they may see. And the LORD opened their eyes, and they saw; and, behold, *they were* in the midst of Samaria.

²¹And the king of Israel said unto Elisha, when he saw them, My father, shall I smite *them*? shall I smite *them*?

²²And he answered, Thou shalt not smite *them*: wouldest thou smite those whom thou hast taken captive with thy sword and with thy bow? set bread and water before them, that they may eat and drink, and go to their master.

²³And he prepared great provision for them: and when they had eaten and drunk, he sent them away, and they went to their master. So the bands of Syria came no more into the land of Israel.

Famine in Samaria

²⁴ ¶ And it came to pass after this, that Ben-hadad king of Syria gathered all his host, and went up, and besieged Samaria.

²⁵And there was a great famine in Samaria: and, behold, they besieged it, until an ass's head was *sold* for fourscore *pieces* of silver, and the fourth part of a cab of dove's dung for five *pieces* of silver.

²⁶And as the king of Israel was passing by upon the wall, there cried a woman unto him, saying, Help, my lord, O king.

²⁷And he said, ^zIf the LORD do not help thee, whence shall I help thee? out of the barnfloor, or out of the winepress?

²⁸And the king said unto her, What aileth thee? And she answered, This woman said unto me, Give thy son, that we may eat him today, and we will eat my son tomorrow.

²⁹So we boiled my son, and did eat him: and I said unto her on the ^anext day, Give thy son, that we may eat him: and she hath hid her son.

³⁰ ¶ And it came to pass, when the king heard the words of the woman, that he rent his clothes; and he passed by upon the wall, and the people looked, and, behold, *he had* sackcloth within upon his flesh.

¹¹Therefore the mind of the king of Syria was greatly troubled by this thing. He called his servants and said, Will you show me who of us is for the king of Israel?

¹²One of his servants said, None, my lord O king; but Elisha, the prophet who is in Israel, tells the king of Israel the words that you speak in your bedchamber.

¹³He said, Go and see where he is, that I may send and seize him. And it was told him, He is in Dothan.

¹⁴So [the Syrian king] sent there horses, chariots, and a great army. They came by night and surrounded the city.

¹⁵When the servant of the man of God rose early and went out, behold, an army with horses and chariots was around the city. Elisha's servant said to him, Alas, my master! What shall we do?

¹⁶[Elisha] answered, Fear not; for those with us are more than those with them.

¹⁷Then Elisha prayed, Lord, I pray You, open his eyes that he may see. And the Lord opened the young man's eyes, and he saw, and behold, the mountain was full of horses and chariots of fire round about Elisha.

¹⁸And when the Syrians came down to him, Elisha prayed to the Lord, Smite this people with blindness, I pray You. And God smote them with blindness, as Elisha asked.

¹⁹Elisha said to the Syrians, This is not the way or the city. Follow me, and I will bring you to the man whom you seek. And he led them to Samaria.

²⁰And when they had come into Samaria, Elisha said, Lord, open the eyes of these men that they may see. And the Lord opened their eyes, and they saw. Behold, they were in the midst of Samaria!

²¹When the king of Israel saw them, he said to Elisha, My father, shall I slay them? Shall I slay them?

²²[Elisha] answered, You shall not slay them. Would you slay those you have taken captive with your sword and bow? Set bread and water before them, that they may eat and drink and return to their master.

²³So [the king] prepared great provision for them, and when they had eaten and drunk, he sent them away, and they went to their master. And the bands of Syria came no more into the land of Israel.

²⁴Afterward, Ben-hadad king of Syria gathered his whole army and went up and besieged Samaria,

²⁵And a great famine came to Samaria. They besieged it until a donkey's head was sold for eighty shekels of silver, and a fourth of a kab of dove's dung [a wild vegetable] for five shekels of silver.

²⁶As the king of Israel was passing by upon the wall, a woman cried to him, Help, my lord, O king!

²⁷He said, [For] if he does not help you [No, let the Lord help you!], from where can I get you help? Out of the threshing floor, or out of the winepress?

²⁸And the king said to her, What ails you? She answered, This woman said to me, Give me your son so we may eat him today, and we will eat my son tomorrow.

²⁹So we boiled my son and ate him. The next day I said to her, Give your son so we may eat him, but she had hidden her son.

³⁰When the king heard the woman's words, he rent his clothes. As he went on upon the wall, the people looked, and behold, he wore sackcloth inside on his flesh.

New American Standard

11. ¶ Now the heart of the king of Aram was enraged over this thing; and he called his servants and said to them, "Will you tell me which of us is for the king of Israel?"

12 One of his servants said, "No, my lord, O king; but Elisha, the prophet who is in Israel, tells the king of Israel the words that you speak in your bedroom."

13 So he said, "Go and see where he is, that I may send and take him." And it was told him, saying, "Behold, he is in Dothan."

14 He sent horses and chariots and a great army there, and they came by night and surrounded the city.

15 ¶ Now when the attendant of the man of God had risen early and gone out, behold, an army with horses and chariots was circling the city. And his servant said to him, "Alas, my master! What shall we do?"

16 So he answered, "Do not fear, for those who are with us are more than those who are with them."

17 Then Elisha prayed and said, "O LORD, I pray, open his eyes that he may see." And the LORD opened the servant's eyes and he saw; and behold, the mountain was full of horses and chariots of fire all around Elisha.

18 When they came down to him, Elisha prayed to the LORD and said, "Strike this people with blindness, I pray." So He struck them with blindness according to the word of Elisha.

19 Then Elisha said to them, "This is not the way, nor is this the city; follow me and I will bring you to the man whom you seek." And he brought them to Samaria.

20 ¶ When they had come into Samaria, Elisha said, "O LORD, open the eyes of these *men*, that they may see." So the LORD opened their eyes and they saw; and behold, they were in the midst of Samaria.

21 Then the king of Israel when he saw them, said to Elisha, "My father, shall I kill them? Shall I kill them?"

22 He answered, "You shall not kill *them*. Would you kill those you have taken captive with your sword and with your bow? Set bread and water before them, that they may eat and drink and go to their master."

23 So he prepared a great feast for them; and when they had eaten and drunk he sent them away, and they went to their master. And the marauding bands of Arameans did not come again into the land of Israel.

The Siege of Samaria—Cannibalism

24 ¶ Now it came about after this, that Ben-hadad king of Aram gathered all his army and went up and besieged Samaria.

25 There was a great famine in Samaria; and behold, they besieged it, until a donkey's head was sold for eighty *shekels* of silver, and a fourth of a ᵃkab of dove's dung for five *shekels* of silver.

26 As the king of Israel was passing by on the wall a woman cried out to him, saying, "Help, my lord, O king!"

27 He said, "If the LORD does not help you, from where shall I help you? From the threshing floor, or from the wine press?"

28 And the king said to her, "What is the matter with you?" And she answered, "This woman said to me, 'Give your son that we may eat him today, and we will eat my son tomorrow.'

29 "So we boiled my son and ate him; and I said to her on the next day, 'Give your son, that we may eat him'; but she has hidden her son."

30 When the king heard the words of the woman, he tore his clothes—now he was passing by on the wall—and the people looked, and behold, he had sackcloth beneath on his body.

New International

11 This enraged the king of Aram. He summoned his officers and demanded of them, "Will you not tell me which of us is on the side of the king of Israel?"

12 "None of us, my lord the king," said one of his officers, "but Elisha, the prophet who is in Israel, tells the king of Israel the very words you speak in your bedroom."

13 "Go, find out where he is," the king ordered, "so I can send men and capture him." The report came back: "He is in Dothan." 14 Then he sent horses and chariots and a strong force there. They went by night and surrounded the city.

15 When the servant of the man of God got up and went out early the next morning, an army with horses and chariots had surrounded the city. "Oh, my lord, what shall we do?" the servant asked.

16 "Don't be afraid," the prophet answered. "Those who are with us are more than those who are with them."

17 And Elisha prayed, "O LORD, open his eyes so he may see." Then the LORD opened the servant's eyes, and he looked and saw the hills full of horses and chariots of fire all around Elisha.

18 As the enemy came down toward him, Elisha prayed to the LORD, "Strike these people with blindness." So he struck them with blindness, as Elisha had asked.

19 Elisha told them, "This is not the road and this is not the city. Follow me, and I will lead you to the man you are looking for." And he led them to Samaria.

20 After they entered the city, Elisha said, "LORD, open the eyes of these men so they can see." Then the LORD opened their eyes and they looked, and there they were, inside Samaria.

21 When the king of Israel saw them, he asked Elisha, "Shall I kill them, my father? Shall I kill them?"

22 "Do not kill them," he answered. "Would you kill men you have captured with your own sword or bow? Set food and water before them so that they may eat and drink and then go back to their master." 23 So he prepared a great feast for them, and after they had finished eating and drinking, he sent them away, and they returned to their master. So the bands from Aram stopped raiding Israel's territory.

Famine in Besieged Samaria

24 Some time later, Ben-Hadad king of Aram mobilized his entire army and marched up and laid siege to Samaria. 25 There was a great famine in the city; the siege lasted so long that a donkey's head sold for eighty shekelsʰ of silver, and a quarter of a cabⁱ of seed podsʲ for five shekels.ᵏ

26 As the king of Israel was passing by on the wall, a woman cried to him, "Help me, my lord the king!"

27 The king replied, "If the LORD does not help you, where can I get help for you? From the threshing floor? From the winepress?" 28 Then he asked her, "What's the matter?"

She answered, "This woman said to me, 'Give up your son so we may eat him today, and tomorrow we'll eat my son.' 29 So we cooked my son and ate him. The next day I said to her, 'Give up your son so we may eat him,' but she had hidden him."

30 When the king heard the woman's words, he tore his robes. As he went along the wall, the people looked, and

---

ᵃ I.e. One kab equals approx 2 qts

ʰ 25 That is, about 2 pounds (about 1 kilogram)   ⁱ 25 That is, probably about 1/2 pint (about 0.3 liter)   ʲ 25 Or *of doves' dung*
ᵏ 25 That is, about 2 ounces (about 55 grams)

King James

³¹Then he said, God do so and more also to me, if the head of Elisha the son of Shaphat shall stand on him this day.

The prophecy of Elisha

³²But Elisha sat in his house, and the elders sat with him; and *the king* sent a man from before him: but ere the messenger came to him, he said to the elders, See ye how this son of a murderer hath sent to take away mine head? look, when the messenger cometh, shut the door, and hold him fast at the door: *is* not the sound of his master's feet behind him?

³³And while he yet talked with them, behold, the messenger came down unto him: and he said, Behold, this evil *is* of the LORD; what should I wait for the LORD any longer?

7 THEN ELISHA said, Hear ye the word of the LORD; Thus saith the LORD, Tomorrow about this time *shall* a measure of fine flour *be sold* for a shekel, and two measures of barley for a shekel, in the gate of Samaria.

²Then ᵇa lord on whose hand the king leaned answered the man of God, and said, Behold, *if* the LORD would make windows in heaven, might this thing be? And he said, Behold, thou shalt see *it* with thine eyes, but shalt not eat thereof.

³ ¶ And there were four leprous men at the entering in of the gate: and they said one to another, Why sit we here until we die?

⁴If we say, We will enter into the city, then the famine *is* in the city, and we shall die there: and if we sit still here, we die also. Now therefore come, and let us fall unto the host of the Syrians: if they save us alive, we shall live; and if they kill us, we shall but die.

⁵And they rose up in the twilight, to go unto the camp of the Syrians: and when they were come to the uttermost part of the camp of Syria, behold, *there was* no man there.

⁶For the Lord had made the host of the Syrians to hear a noise of chariots, and a noise of horses, *even* the noise of a great host: and they said one to another, Lo, the king of Israel hath hired against us the kings of the Hittites, and the kings of the Egyptians, to come upon us.

⁷Wherefore they arose and fled in the twilight, and left their tents, and their horses, and their asses, even the camp as it *was,* and fled for their life.

⁸And when these lepers came to the uttermost part of the camp, they went into one tent, and did eat and drink, and carried thence silver, and gold, and raiment, and went and hid *it;* and came again, and entered into another tent, and carried thence *also,* and went and hid *it.*

⁹Then they said one to another, We do not well: this day *is* a day of good tidings, and we hold our peace: if we tarry till the morning light, ᶜsome mischief will come upon us: now therefore come, that we may go and tell the king's household.

¹⁰So they came and called unto the porter of the city: and they told them, saying, We came to the camp of the Syrians, and, behold, *there was* no man there, neither voice of man, but horses tied, and asses tied, and the tents as they *were.*

¹¹And he called the porters; and they told *it* to the king's house within.

¹² ¶ And the king arose in the night, and said unto his servants, I will now shew you what the Syrians have done to us. They know that we *be* hungry; therefore are they gone out of the camp to hide themselves in the field, saying, When they come out of the city, we shall catch them alive, and get into the city.

Amplified

³¹Then he said, May God do so to me, and more also, if the head of Elisha son of Shaphat shall stand on him this day!

³²Now Elisha sat in his house, and the elders sat with him. And the king sent a man from before him [to behead Elisha]. But before the messenger arrived, Elisha said to the elders, See how this son of [Jezebel] a murderer is sending to remove my head? Look, when the messenger comes, shut the door and hold it fast against him. Is not the sound of his master's feet [just] behind him?

³³And while Elisha was talking with them, behold, [the messenger] came to him [and then the king came also]. And [the relenting king] said, This evil is from the Lord! Why should I any longer wait [expecting Him to withdraw His punishment? What, Elisha, can be done now]?

7 THEN ELISHA said, Hear the word of the Lord. Thus says the Lord: Tomorrow about this time a measure of fine flour will sell for a shekel and two measures of barley for a shekel in the gate of Samaria!

²Then the captain on whose hand the king leaned answered the man of God and said, If the Lord should make windows in heaven, could this thing be? But Elisha said, You shall see it with your own eyes, but you shall not eat of it.

³Now four men who were lepers were at the entrance of the city's gate; and they said to one another, Why do we sit here until we die?

⁴If we say, We will enter the city—then the famine is in the city, and we shall die there; and if we sit still here, we die also. So now come, let us go over to the army of the Syrians. If they spare us alive, we shall live; and if they kill us, we shall but die.

⁵So they arose in the twilight and went to the Syrian camp. But when they came to the edge of the camp, no man was there.

⁶For the Lord had made the Syrian army hear a noise of chariots and horses, the noise of a great army. They had said to one another, The king of Israel has hired the Hittite and Egyptian kings to come upon us.

⁷So the Syrians arose and fled in the twilight and left their tents, horses, donkeys, even the camp as it was, and fled for their lives.

⁸And when these lepers came to the edge of the camp, they went into one tent and ate and drank, and carried away silver, gold, and clothing, and went and hid them [in the darkness]. Then they entered another tent and carried from there also and went and hid it.

⁹Then they said one to another, We are not doing right. This is a day of [glad] good news and we are silent *and* do not speak up! If we wait until daylight, some punishment will come upon us [for not reporting at once]. So now come, let us go and tell the king's household.

¹⁰So they came and called to the gatekeepers of the city. They told them, We came to the camp of the Syrians, and behold, there was neither sight nor sound of man there—only the horses and donkeys tied, and the tents as they were.

¹¹Then the gatekeepers called out, and it was told to the king's household within.

¹²And the king rose in the night and said to his servants, I will tell you what the Syrians have done to us. They know that we are hungry; therefore they have gone out of the camp to hide themselves in the open country, thinking, When they come out of the city, we shall take them alive and get into the city.

ᵇ Heb. *a lord which* belonged *to the king leaning upon his hand*
ᶜ Heb. *we shall find punishment*

New American Standard

31 Then he said, "May God do so to me and more also, if the head of Elisha the son of Shaphat remains on him today."

32 ¶ Now Elisha was sitting in his house, and the elders were sitting with him. And *the king* sent a man from his presence; but before the messenger came to him, he said to the elders, "Do you see how this son of a murderer has sent to take away my head? Look, when the messenger comes, shut the door and hold the door shut against him. Is not the sound of his master's feet behind him?"

33 While he was still talking with them, behold, the messenger came down to him and he said, "Behold, this evil is from the LORD; why should I wait for the LORD any longer?"

Elisha Promises Food

7 THEN ELISHA said, "Listen to the word of the LORD; thus says the LORD, 'Tomorrow about this time a measure of fine flour will be *sold* for a shekel, and two measures of barley for a shekel, in the gate of Samaria.'"

2 The royal officer on whose hand the king was leaning answered the man of God and said, "Behold, if the LORD should make windows in heaven, could this be?" Then he said, "Behold, you will see it with your own eyes, but you will not eat of it."

Four Lepers Relate Arameans' Flight

3 ¶ Now there were four leprous men at the entrance of the gate; and they said to one another, "Why do we sit here until we die?

4 "If we say, 'We will enter the city,' then the famine is in the city and we will die there; and if we sit here, we die also. Now therefore come, and let us go over to the camp of the Arameans. If they spare us, we will live; and if they kill us, we will but die."

5 They arose at twilight to go to the camp of the Arameans; when they came to the outskirts of the camp of the Arameans, behold, there was no one there.

6 For the Lord had caused the army of the Arameans to hear a sound of chariots and a sound of horses, *even* the sound of a great army, so that they said to one another, "Behold, the king of Israel has hired against us the kings of the Hittites and the kings of the Egyptians, to come upon us."

7 Therefore they arose and fled in the twilight, and left their tents and their horses and their donkeys, *even* the camp just as it was, and fled for their life.

8 When these lepers came to the outskirts of the camp, they entered one tent and ate and drank, and carried from there silver and gold and clothes, and went and hid *them;* and they returned and entered another tent and carried from there *also,* and went and hid *them.*

9 ¶ Then they said to one another, "We are not doing right. This day is a day of good news, but we are keeping silent; if we wait until morning light, punishment will overtake us. Now therefore come, and let us go and tell the king's household."

10 So they came and called to the gatekeepers of the city, and they told them, saying, "We came to the camp of the Arameans, and behold, there was no one there, nor the voice of man, only the horses tied and the donkeys tied, and the tents just as they were."

11 The gatekeepers called and told *it* within the king's household.

12 Then the king arose in the night and said to his servants, "I will now tell you what the Arameans have done to us. They know that we are hungry; therefore they have gone from the camp to hide themselves in the field, saying, 'When they come out of the city, we will capture them alive and get into the city.'"

New International

there, underneath, he had sackcloth on his body. 31He said, "May God deal with me, be it ever so severely, if the head of Elisha son of Shaphat remains on his shoulders today!"

32Now Elisha was sitting in his house, and the elders were sitting with him. The king sent a messenger ahead, but before he arrived, Elisha said to the elders, "Don't you see how this murderer is sending someone to cut off my head? Look, when the messenger comes, shut the door and hold it against him. Is not the sound of his master's footsteps behind him?"

33While he was still talking to them, the messenger came down to him. And ⌊the king⌋ said, "This disaster is from the LORD. Why should I wait for the LORD any longer?"

7 ELISHA SAID, "Hear the word of the LORD. This is what the LORD says: About this time tomorrow, a seah[l] of flour will sell for a shekel[m] and two seahs[n] of barley for a shekel at the gate of Samaria."

2The officer on whose arm the king was leaning said to the man of God, "Look, even if the LORD should open the floodgates of the heavens, could this happen?"

"You will see it with your own eyes," answered Elisha, "but you will not eat any of it!"

The Siege Lifted

3Now there were four men with leprosy[o] at the entrance of the city gate. They said to each other, "Why stay here until we die? 4If we say, 'We'll go into the city'—the famine is there, and we will die. And if we stay here, we will die. So let's go over to the camp of the Arameans and surrender. If they spare us, we live; if they kill us, then we die."

5At dusk they got up and went to the camp of the Arameans. When they reached the edge of the camp, not a man was there, 6for the Lord had caused the Arameans to hear the sound of chariots and horses and a great army, so that they said to one another, "Look, the king of Israel has hired the Hittite and Egyptian kings to attack us!" 7So they got up and fled in the dusk and abandoned their tents and their horses and donkeys. They left the camp as it was and ran for their lives.

8The men who had leprosy reached the edge of the camp and entered one of the tents. They ate and drank, and carried away silver, gold and clothes, and went off and hid them. They returned and entered another tent and took some things from it and hid them also.

9Then they said to each other, "We're not doing right. This is a day of good news and we are keeping it to ourselves. If we wait until daylight, punishment will overtake us. Let's go at once and report this to the royal palace."

10So they went and called out to the city gatekeepers and told them, "We went into the Aramean camp and not a man was there—not a sound of anyone—only tethered horses and donkeys, and the tents left just as they were." 11The gatekeepers shouted the news, and it was reported within the palace.

12The king got up in the night and said to his officers, "I will tell you what the Arameans have done to us. They know we are starving; so they have left the camp to hide in the countryside, thinking, 'They will surely come out, and then we will take them alive and get into the city.'"

[l] 1 That is, probably about 7 quarts (about 7.3 liters); also in verses 16 and 18   [m] 1 That is, about 2/5 ounce (about 11 grams); also in verses 16 and 18   [n] 1 That is, probably about 13 quarts (about 15 liters); also in verses 16 and 18   [o] 3 The Hebrew word is used for various diseases affecting the skin—not necessarily leprosy; also in verse 8.

King James

13And one of his servants answered and said, Let *some* take, I pray thee, five of the horses that remain, which are left *d*in the city, (behold, they *are* as all the multitude of Israel that are left in it: behold, *I say,* they *are* even as all the multitude of the Israelites that are consumed:) and let us send and see.

14They took therefore two chariot horses; and the king sent after the host of the Syrians, saying, Go and see.

15And they went after them unto Jordan: and, lo, all the way *was* full of garments and vessels, which the Syrians had cast away in their haste. And the messengers returned, and told the king.

16And the people went out, and spoiled the tents of the Syrians. So a measure of fine flour was *sold* for a shekel, and two measures of barley for a shekel, according to the word of the LORD.

17 ¶ And the king appointed the lord on whose hand he leaned to have the charge of the gate: and the people trode upon him in the gate, and he died, as the man of God had said, who spake when the king came down to him.

18And it came to pass as the man of God had spoken to the king, saying, Two measures of barley for a shekel, and a measure of fine flour for a shekel, shall be tomorrow about this time in the gate of Samaria:

19And that lord answered the man of God, and said, Now, behold, *if* the LORD should make windows in heaven, might such a thing be? And he said, Behold, thou shalt see it with thine eyes, but shalt not eat thereof.

20And so it fell out unto him: for the people trode upon him in the gate, and he died.

The Shunammite comes home

8 THEN SPAKE Elisha unto the woman, whose son he had restored to life, saying, Arise, and go thou and thine household, and sojourn wheresoever thou canst sojourn: for the LORD hath called for a famine; and it shall also come upon the land seven years.

2And the woman arose, and did after the saying of the man of God: and she went with her household, and sojourned in the land of the Philistines seven years.

3And it came to pass at the seven years' end, that the woman returned out of the land of the Philistines: and she went forth to cry unto the king for her house and for her land.

4And the king talked with Gehazi the servant of the man of God, saying, Tell me, I pray thee, all the great things that Elisha hath done.

5And it came to pass, as he was telling the king how he had restored a dead body to life, that, behold, the woman, whose son he had restored to life, cried to the king for her house and for her land. And Gehazi said, My lord, O king, this *is* the woman, and this *is* her son, whom Elisha restored to life.

6And when the king asked the woman, she told him. So the king appointed unto her a certain *e*officer, saying, Restore all that *was* hers, and all the fruits of the field since the day that she left the land, even until now.

Hazael anointed king of Syria

7 ¶ And Elisha came to Damascus; and Ben-hadad the king of Syria was sick; and it was told him, saying, The man of God is come hither.

8And the king said unto Hazael, Take a present in thine hand, and go, meet the man of God, and inquire of the LORD by him, saying, Shall I recover of this disease?

Amplified

13One of his servants said, Let some men take five of the remaining horses; [if they are caught and killed] they will be no worse off than all the multitude of Israel left in the city to be consumed. Let us send and see.

14So they took two chariot horses, and the king sent them after the Syrian army, saying, Go and see.

15They went after them to the Jordan. All the way was strewn with clothing and equipment which the Syrians had cast away in their flight. And the messengers returned and told the king.

16Then the people went out and plundered the tents of the Syrians. So a measure of fine flour was sold for a shekel, and two measures of barley for a shekel, as the Lord had spoken [through Elisha]. [II Kings 7:1.]

17The king had appointed the captain on whose hand he leaned to have charge of the gate, and the [starving] people trampled him in the gate [as they struggled to get through for food], and he died, as the man of God had foretold when the king came down to him.

18When the man of God had told the king, Two measures of barley shall sell for a shekel and a measure of fine flour for a shekel tomorrow about this time in the gate of Samaria,

19The captain had told the man of God, If the Lord should make windows in heaven, could such a thing be? And he said, You shall see it with your own eyes, but you shall not eat of it. [II Kings 7:2.]

20And so it was fulfilled to him, for the people trampled on him in the gate, and he died.

8 NOW ELISHA had said to the woman whose son he had restored to life, Arise and go with your household and sojourn wherever you can, for the Lord has called for a famine, and moreover, it will come upon the land for seven years.

2So the woman arose and did as the man of God had said. She went with her household and sojourned in the land of the Philistines seven years.

3At the end of the seven years the woman returned from the land of the Philistines, and she went to appeal to the king for her house and land.

4The king talked with Gehazi, the servant of the man of God, saying, Tell me all the great things Elisha has done.

5And as Gehazi was telling the king how [Elisha] had restored the dead to life, behold, the woman whose son he had restored to life appealed to the king for her house and land. And Gehazi said, My lord O king, this is the woman, and this is her son whom Elisha brought back to life.

6When the king asked the woman, she told him. So the king appointed to her a certain officer, saying, Restore all that was hers, and all the fruits of the field since the day that she left the land even until now.

7Elisha came to Damascus, and Ben-hadad king of Syria was sick; and he was told, The man of God has come here.

8And the king said to Hazael, Take a present in your hand and go meet the man of God, and inquire of the Lord by him, saying, Shall I recover from this disease?

New American Standard

13 One of his servants said, "Please, let some *men* take five of the horses which remain, which are left in the city. Behold, they *will be in any case* like all the multitude of Israel who are left in it; behold, they *will be in any case* like all the multitude of Israel who have already perished, so let us send and see."

14 They took therefore two chariots with horses, and the king sent after the army of the Arameans, saying, "Go and see."

The Promise Fulfilled

15 They went after them to the Jordan, and behold, all the way was full of clothes and equipment which the Arameans had thrown away in their haste. Then the messengers returned and told the king.

16 ¶ So the people went out and plundered the camp of the Arameans. Then a measure of fine flour *was sold* for a shekel and two measures of barley for a shekel, according to the word of the LORD.

17 Now the king appointed the royal officer on whose hand he leaned to have charge of the gate; but the people trampled on him at the gate, and he died just as the man of God had said, who spoke when the king came down to him.

18 It happened just as the man of God had spoken to the king, saying, "Two measures of barley for a shekel and a measure of fine flour for a shekel, will be *sold* tomorrow about this time at the gate of Samaria."

19 Then the royal officer answered the man of God and said, "Now behold, if the LORD should make windows in heaven, could such a thing be?" And he said, "Behold, you will see it with your own eyes, but you will not eat of it."

20 And so it happened to him, for the people trampled on him at the gate and he died.

Jehoram Restores the Shunammite's Land

8 NOW ELISHA spoke to the woman whose son he had restored to life, saying, "Arise and go with your household, and sojourn wherever you can sojourn; for the LORD has called for a famine, and it will even come on the land for seven years."

2 So the woman arose and did according to the word of the man of God, and she went with her household and sojourned in the land of the Philistines seven years.

3 At the end of seven years, the woman returned from the land of the Philistines; and she went out to appeal to the king for her house and for her field.

4 Now the king was talking with Gehazi, the servant of the man of God, saying, "Please relate to me all the great things that Elisha has done."

5 As he was relating to the king how he had restored to life the one who was dead, behold, the woman whose son he had restored to life appealed to the king for her house and for her field. And Gehazi said, "My lord, O king, this is the woman and this is her son, whom Elisha restored to life."

6 When the king asked the woman, she related *it* to him. So the king appointed for her a certain officer, saying, "Restore all that was hers and all the produce of the field from the day that she left the land even until now."

Elisha Predicts Evil from Hazael

7 ¶ Then Elisha came to Damascus. Now Ben-hadad king of Aram was sick, and it was told him, saying, "The man of God has come here."

8 The king said to Hazael, "Take a gift in your hand and go to meet the man of God, and inquire of the LORD by him, saying, 'Will I recover from this sickness?'"

New International

13 One of his officers answered, "Have some men take five of the horses that are left in the city. Their plight will be like that of all the Israelites left here—yes, they will only be like all these Israelites who are doomed. So let us send them to find out what happened."

14 So they selected two chariots with their horses, and the king sent them after the Aramean army. He commanded the drivers, "Go and find out what has happened." 15 They followed them as far as the Jordan, and they found the whole road strewn with the clothing and equipment the Arameans had thrown away in their headlong flight. So the messengers returned and reported to the king. 16 Then the people went out and plundered the camp of the Arameans. So a seah of flour sold for a shekel, and two seahs of barley sold for a shekel, as the LORD had said.

17 Now the king had put the officer on whose arm he leaned in charge of the gate, and the people trampled him in the gateway, and he died, just as the man of God had foretold when the king came down to his house. 18 It happened as the man of God had said to the king: "About this time tomorrow, a seah of flour will sell for a shekel and two seahs of barley for a shekel at the gate of Samaria."

19 The officer had said to the man of God, "Look, even if the LORD should open the floodgates of the heavens, could this happen?" The man of God had replied, "You will see it with your own eyes, but you will not eat any of it!" 20 And that is exactly what happened to him, for the people trampled him in the gateway, and he died.

The Shunammite's Land Restored

8 NOW ELISHA had said to the woman whose son he had restored to life, "Go away with your family and stay for a while wherever you can, because the LORD has decreed a famine in the land that will last seven years." 2 The woman proceeded to do as the man of God said. She and her family went away and stayed in the land of the Philistines seven years.

3 At the end of the seven years she came back from the land of the Philistines and went to the king to beg for her house and land. 4 The king was talking to Gehazi, the servant of the man of God, and had said, "Tell me about all the great things Elisha has done." 5 Just as Gehazi was telling the king how Elisha had restored the dead to life, the woman whose son Elisha had brought back to life came to beg the king for her house and land.

Gehazi said, "This is the woman, my lord the king, and this is her son whom Elisha restored to life." 6 The king asked the woman about it, and she told him.

Then he assigned an official to her case and said to him, "Give back everything that belonged to her, including all the income from her land from the day she left the country until now."

Hazael Murders Ben-Hadad

7 Elisha went to Damascus, and Ben-Hadad king of Aram was ill. When the king was told, "The man of God has come all the way up here," 8 he said to Hazael, "Take a gift with you and go to meet the man of God. Consult the LORD through him; ask him, 'Will I recover from this illness?'"

King James

9So Hazael went to meet him, and took a present *f*with him, even of every good thing of Damascus, forty camels' burden, and came and stood before him, and said, Thy son Ben-hadad king of Syria hath sent me to thee, saying, Shall I recover of this disease?

10And Elisha said unto him, Go, say unto him, Thou mayest certainly recover: howbeit the LORD hath shown me that he shall surely die.

11And he settled his countenance *g*stedfastly, until he was ashamed: and the man of God wept.

12And Hazael said, Why weepeth my lord? And he answered, Because I know the evil that thou wilt do unto the children of Israel: their strong holds wilt thou set on fire, and their young men wilt thou slay with the sword, and wilt dash their children, and rip up their women with child.

13And Hazael said, But what, *is* thy servant a dog, that he should do this great thing? And Elisha answered, The LORD hath shown me that thou *shalt be* king over Syria.

14So he departed from Elisha, and came to his master; who said to him, What said Elisha to thee? And he answered, He told me *that* thou shouldest surely recover.

15And it came to pass on the morrow, that he took a thick cloth, and dipped *it* in water, and spread *it* on his face, so that he died: and Hazael reigned in his stead.

Jehoram, king of Judah

16 ¶ And in the fifth year of Joram the son of Ahab king of Israel, Jehoshaphat *being* then king of Judah, Jehoram the son of Jehoshaphat king of Judah *h*began to reign.

17Thirty and two years old was he when he began to reign; and he reigned eight years in Jerusalem.

18And he walked in the way of the kings of Israel, as did the house of Ahab: for the daughter of Ahab was his wife: and he did evil in the sight of the LORD.

19Yet the LORD would not destroy Judah for David his servant's sake, as he promised him to give him always a *i*light, *and* to his children.

20 ¶ In his days Edom revolted from under the hand of Judah, and made a king over themselves.

21So Joram went over to Zair, and all the chariots with him: and he rose by night, and smote the Edomites which compassed him about, and the captains of the chariots: and the people fled into their tents.

22*j*Yet Edom revolted from under the hand of Judah unto this day. Then Libnah revolted at the same time.

23And the rest of the acts of Joram, and all that he did, *are* they not written in the book of the chronicles of the kings of Judah?

24And Joram slept with his fathers, and was buried with his fathers in the city of David: and *k*Ahaziah his son reigned in his stead.

Ahaziah, king of Judah

25 ¶ In the twelfth year of Joram the son of Ahab king of Israel did Ahaziah the son of Jehoram king of Judah begin to reign.

26Two and twenty years old *was* Ahaziah when he began to reign; and he reigned one year in Jerusalem. And his mother's name *was* Athaliah, the *l*daughter of Omri king of Israel.

27And he walked in the way of the house of Ahab, and did evil in the sight of the LORD, as *did* the house of Ahab: for he *was* the son-in-law of the house of Ahab.

28 ¶ And he went with Joram the son of Ahab to the war against Hazael king of Syria in Ramoth-gilead; and the Syrians wounded Joram.

Amplified

9So Hazael went to meet Elisha and took a present with him of every good thing of Damascus, forty camel loads, and came and stood before him and said, Your son Ben-hadad king of Syria has sent me to you, asking, Shall I recover from this disease?

10And Elisha said, Go, say to him, You shall certainly recover; but the Lord has shown me that he shall certainly die.

11Elisha stared steadily at him until Hazael was embarrassed. And the man of God wept.

12And Hazael said, Why do you weep, my lord? He answered, Because I know the evil that you will do to the Israelites. You will burn their strongholds, slay their young men with the sword, dash their infants in pieces, and rip up their pregnant women.

13And Hazael said, What is your servant, only a dog, that he should do this monstrous thing? And Elisha answered, The Lord has shown me that you will be king over Syria.

14Then [Hazael] departed from Elisha and came to his master, who said to him, What did Elisha say to you? And he answered, He told me you would surely recover.

15But the next day Hazael took the bedspread and dipped it in water and spread it on [the Syrian king's] face, so that he died. And Hazael reigned in his stead.

16In the fifth year of Joram son of Ahab king of Israel, Jehoshaphat being then king of Judah, Jehoram son of Jehoshaphat king of Judah began to reign.

17He was thirty-two years old when he began to reign, and he reigned eight years in Jerusalem.

18He walked in the ways of the kings of Israel, as did the house of Ahab, for [Athaliah] the daughter of Ahab was his wife. He did evil in the sight of the Lord.

19Yet, for David His servant's sake, the Lord would not destroy Judah, for He promised to give him and his sons a lamp forever.

20In his days, Edom revolted from the rule of Judah and set up a king over themselves.

21So Jehoram [of Judah] went over to Zair with all his chariots. He and his chariot commanders rose up by night and slew the Edomites who had surrounded them; and [escaping] his army fled home.

22So Edom revolted from the rule of Judah to this day. Then Libnah revolted at the same time.

23The rest of the acts of Jehoram, and all that he did, are they not written in the Book of the Chronicles of the Kings of Judah?

24Jehoram slept with his fathers and was buried with [them] in the City of David. Ahaziah his son reigned in his stead.

25In the twelfth year of Joram son of Ahab king of Israel, Ahaziah son of Jehoram king of Judah began to reign.

26Ahaziah was twenty-two years old when he began to reign, and he reigned one year in Jerusalem. His mother's name was Athaliah, the granddaughter of Omri king of Israel.

27He walked in the ways of the house of Ahab and did evil in the sight of the Lord, as did the house of Ahab, for his father was son-in-law of Ahab.

28Ahaziah went with Joram son of Ahab to war against Hazael king of Syria in Ramoth-gilead; and the Syrians wounded Joram.

---

*f*Heb. *in his hand*   *g*Heb. *and set it*   *h*Heb. *reigned.* Began to reign in consort with his father   *i*Heb. *candle,* or, *lamp*
*j*And see fulfilled in Gen. 27:40   *k*Called *Azariah* in 2 Chr. 22:6 and *Jehoahaz* in 2 Chr. 21:17 & 25:23   *l*Or, *granddaughter;* see ver. 18

New American Standard

⁹ So Hazael went to meet him and took a gift in his hand, even every kind of good thing of Damascus, forty camels' loads; and he came and stood before him and said, "Your son Ben-hadad king of Aram has sent me to you, saying, 'Will I recover from this sickness?' "

¹⁰ Then Elisha said to him, "Go, say to him, 'You will surely recover,' but the LORD has shown me that he will certainly die."

¹¹ He fixed his gaze steadily *on him* until he was ashamed, and the man of God wept.

¹² Hazael said, "Why does my lord weep?" Then he answered, "Because I know the evil that you will do to the sons of Israel: their strongholds you will set on fire, and their young men you will kill with the sword, and their little ones you will dash in pieces, and their women with child you will rip up."

¹³ Then Hazael said, "But what is your servant, *who is but* a dog, that he should do this great thing?" And Elisha answered, "The LORD has shown me that you will be king over Aram."

¹⁴ So he departed from Elisha and returned to his master, who said to him, "What did Elisha say to you?" And he answered, "He told me that you would surely recover."

¹⁵ On the following day, he took the cover and dipped it in water and spread it on his face, so that he died. And Hazael became king in his place.

Another Jehoram Reigns in Judah

¹⁶ ¶ Now in the fifth year of Joram the son of Ahab king of Israel, Jehoshaphat being then the king of Judah, Jehoram the son of Jehoshaphat king of Judah became king.

¹⁷ He was thirty-two years old when he became king, and he reigned eight years in Jerusalem.

¹⁸ He walked in the way of the kings of Israel, just as the house of Ahab had done, for the daughter of Ahab became his wife; and he did evil in the sight of the LORD.

¹⁹ However, the LORD was not willing to destroy Judah, for the sake of David His servant, since He had promised him to give a lamp to him through his sons always.

²⁰ ¶ In his days Edom revolted from under the hand of Judah, and made a king over themselves.

²¹ Then Joram crossed over to Zair, and all his chariots with him. And he arose by night and struck the Edomites who had surrounded him and the captains of the chariots; but *his* army fled to their tents.

²² So Edom revolted against Judah to this day. Then Libnah revolted at the same time.

²³ The rest of the acts of Joram and all that he did, are they not written in the Book of the Chronicles of the Kings of Judah?

Ahaziah Succeeds Jehoram in Judah

²⁴ So Joram slept with his fathers and was buried with his fathers in the city of David; and Ahaziah his son became king in his place.

²⁵ ¶ In the twelfth year of Joram the son of Ahab king of Israel, Ahaziah the son of Jehoram king of Judah began to reign.

²⁶ Ahaziah *was* twenty-two years old when he became king, and he reigned one year in Jerusalem. And his mother's name *was* Athaliah the granddaughter of Omri king of Israel.

²⁷ He walked in the way of the house of Ahab and did evil in the sight of the LORD, like the house of Ahab *had done*, because he was a son-in-law of the house of Ahab.

²⁸ ¶ Then he went with Joram the son of Ahab to war against Hazael king of Aram at Ramoth-gilead, and the Arameans wounded Joram.

New International

⁹Hazael went to meet Elisha, taking with him as a gift forty camel-loads of all the finest wares of Damascus. He went in and stood before him, and said, "Your son Ben-Hadad king of Aram has sent me to ask, 'Will I recover from this illness?' "

¹⁰Elisha answered, "Go and say to him, 'You will certainly recover'; but*p* the LORD has revealed to me that he will in fact die." ¹¹He stared at him with a fixed gaze until Hazael felt ashamed. Then the man of God began to weep.

¹²"Why is my lord weeping?" asked Hazael.

"Because I know the harm you will do to the Israelites," he answered. "You will set fire to their fortified places, kill their young men with the sword, dash their little children to the ground, and rip open their pregnant women." ¹³Hazael said, "How could your servant, a mere dog, accomplish such a feat?"

"The LORD has shown me that you will become king of Aram," answered Elisha.

¹⁴Then Hazael left Elisha and returned to his master. When Ben-Hadad asked, "What did Elisha say to you?" Hazael replied, "He told me that you would certainly recover." ¹⁵But the next day he took a thick cloth, soaked it in water and spread it over the king's face, so that he died. Then Hazael succeeded him as king.

Jehoram King of Judah

¹⁶In the fifth year of Joram son of Ahab king of Israel, when Jehoshaphat was king of Judah, Jehoram son of Jehoshaphat began his reign as king of Judah. ¹⁷He was thirty-two years old when he became king, and he reigned in Jerusalem eight years. ¹⁸He walked in the ways of the kings of Israel, as the house of Ahab had done, for he married a daughter of Ahab. He did evil in the eyes of the LORD. ¹⁹Nevertheless, for the sake of his servant David, the LORD was not willing to destroy Judah. He had promised to maintain a lamp for David and his descendants forever.

²⁰In the time of Jehoram, Edom rebelled against Judah and set up its own king. ²¹So Jehoram*q* went to Zair with all his chariots. The Edomites surrounded him and his chariot commanders, but he rose up and broke through by night; his army, however, fled back home. ²²To this day Edom has been in rebellion against Judah. Libnah revolted at the same time.

²³As for the other events of Jehoram's reign, and all he did, are they not written in the book of the annals of the kings of Judah? ²⁴Jehoram rested with his fathers and was buried with them in the City of David. And Ahaziah his son succeeded him as king.

Ahaziah King of Judah

²⁵In the twelfth year of Joram son of Ahab king of Israel, Ahaziah son of Jehoram king of Judah began to reign. ²⁶Ahaziah was twenty-two years old when he became king, and he reigned in Jerusalem one year. His mother's name was Athaliah, a granddaughter of Omri king of Israel. ²⁷He walked in the ways of the house of Ahab and did evil in the eyes of the LORD, as the house of Ahab had done, for he was related by marriage to Ahab's family.

²⁸Ahaziah went with Joram son of Ahab to war against Hazael king of Aram at Ramoth Gilead. The Arameans

---

p 10 The Hebrew may also be read *Go and say, 'You will certainly not recover,' for.*   *q 21* Hebrew *Joram,* a variant of *Jehoram*; also in verses 23 and 24

King James

²⁹And king Joram went back to be healed in Jezreel of the wounds ᵐwhich the Syrians had given him at ⁿRamah, when he fought against Hazael king of Syria. And Ahaziah the son of Jehoram king of Judah went down to see Joram the son of Ahab in Jezreel, because he was ᵒsick.

Jehu anointed king of Israel

9 AND ELISHA the prophet called one of the children of the prophets, and said unto him, Gird up thy loins, and take this box of oil in thine hand, and go to Ramoth-gilead:

²And when thou comest thither, look out there Jehu the son of Jehoshaphat the son of Nimshi, and go in, and make him arise up from among his brethren, and carry him to an ᵖinner chamber;

³Then take the box of oil, and pour *it* on his head, and say, Thus saith the LORD, I have anointed thee king over Israel. Then open the door, and flee, and tarry not.

⁴ ¶ So the young man, *even* the young man the prophet, went to Ramoth-gilead.

⁵And when he came, behold, the captains of the host *were* sitting; and he said, I have an errand to thee, O captain. And Jehu said, Unto which of all us? And he said, To thee, O captain.

⁶And he arose, and went into the house; and he poured the oil on his head, and said unto him, Thus saith the LORD God of Israel, I have anointed thee king over the people of the LORD, *even* over Israel.

⁷And thou shalt smite the house of Ahab thy master, that I may avenge the blood of my servants the prophets, and the blood of all the servants of the LORD, at the hand of Jezebel.

⁸For the whole house of Ahab shall perish: and I will cut off from Ahab him that pisseth against the wall, and him that is shut up and left in Israel:

⁹And I will make the house of Ahab like the house of Jeroboam the son of Nebat, and like the house of Baasha the son of Ahijah:

¹⁰And the dogs shall eat Jezebel in the portion of Jezreel, and *there shall be* none to bury *her.* And he opened the door, and fled.

¹¹ ¶ Then Jehu came forth to the servants of his lord: and *one* said unto him, *Is* all well? wherefore came this mad *fellow* to thee? And he said unto them, Ye know the man, and his communication.

¹²And they said, *It is* false; tell us now. And he said, Thus and thus spake he to me, saying, Thus saith the LORD, I have anointed thee king over Israel.

¹³Then they hasted, and took every man his garment, and put *it* under him on the top of the stairs, and blew with trumpets, saying, Jehu ᵠis king.

Jehu kills Joram and Ahaziah

¹⁴So Jehu the son of Jehoshaphat the son of Nimshi conspired against Joram. (Now Joram had kept Ramoth-gilead, he and all Israel, because of Hazael king of Syria.

¹⁵But ʳJoram was returned to be healed in Jezreel of the wounds which the Syrians ˢhad given him, when he fought with Hazael king of Syria.) And Jehu said, If it be your minds, *then* ᵗlet none go forth *nor* escape out of the city to go to tell *it* in Jezreel.

¹⁶So Jehu rode in a chariot, and went to Jezreel; for Joram lay there. And Ahaziah king of Judah was come down to see Joram.

¹⁷And there stood a watchman on the tower in Jezreel, and he spied the company of Jehu as he came, and said, I see a company. And Joram said, Take an horseman, and send to meet them, and let him say, *Is it* peace?

Amplified

²⁹King Joram returned to Jezreel to be healed of the wounds which the Syrians had given him at Ramah when he fought with Hazael king of Syria. And Ahaziah son of Jehoram king of Judah went down to see Joram son of Ahab in Jezreel, because he was sick.

9 AND ELISHA the prophet called one of the sons of the prophets and said to him, Gird up your loins, take this flask of oil in your hand, and go to Ramoth-gilead.

²When you arrive, look there for Jehu son of Jehoshaphat son of Nimshi; and go in and have him arise from among his brethren and lead him to an inner chamber.

³Then take the cruse of oil and pour it on his head and say, Thus says the Lord: I have anointed you king over Israel. Then open the door and flee; do not tarry.

⁴So the young man, the young prophet, went to Ramoth-gilead.

⁵And when he came, the captains of the army were sitting outside; and he said, I have a message for you, O captain. Jehu said, To which of us? And he said, To you, O captain.

⁶And Jehu arose, and they went into the house. And the prophet poured the oil on Jehu's head and said to him, Thus says the Lord, the God of Israel: I have anointed you king over the people of the Lord, even over Israel.

⁷You shall strike down the house of Ahab your master, that I may avenge the blood of My servants the prophets and of all the servants of the Lord [who have died] at the hands of Jezebel.

⁸For the whole house of Ahab shall perish, and I will cut off from Ahab every male, bond or free, in Israel.

⁹I will make the house of Ahab like the house of Jeroboam son of Nebat and like the house of Baasha son of Ahijah. [I Kings 21:22.]

¹⁰And the dogs shall eat Jezebel in the portion of Jezreel, and none shall bury her. And he opened the door and fled. [Fulfilled in II Kings 9:33–37.]

¹¹When Jehu came out to the servants of his master, one said to him, Is all well? Why did this mad fellow come to you? And he said to them, You know that class of man and what he would say.

¹²And they said, That is false; tell us now. And he said, Thus and thus he spoke to me, saying, Thus says the Lord: I have anointed you king over Israel.

¹³Then they hastily took every man his garment and put it [for a cushion] under Jehu on the top of the [outside] stairs, and blew with trumpets, saying, Jehu is king!

¹⁴So Jehu son of Jehoshaphat, the son of Nimshi, conspired against Joram [to dethrone and slay him]. Now Joram was holding Ramoth-gilead, he and all Israel, against Hazael king of Syria.

¹⁵But King Joram had returned to be healed in Jezreel of the wounds which the Syrians had given him when he fought with Hazael king of Syria. And Jehu said, If this is your mind, let no one make his escape from the city [Ramoth-gilead] to go and tell it in Jezreel [the capital].

¹⁶So Jehu rode in a chariot and went to Jezreel, for Joram lay there. And Ahaziah king of Judah had come down to see Joram.

¹⁷A watchman on the tower in Jezreel spied the company of Jehu as he came, and said, I see a company. And Joram said, Send a horseman to meet them and have him ask, Do you come in peace?

ᵐHeb. *wherewith the Syrians had wounded*   ⁿCalled *Ramoth* in ver. 28   ᵒHeb. *wounded*   ᵖHeb. *chamber in a chamber* ᵠHeb. *reigneth*   ʳHeb. *Jehoram*   ˢHeb. *smote*   ᵗHeb. *let no escaper go*

New American Standard

New International

²⁹ So King Joram returned to be healed in Jezreel of the wounds which the Arameans had inflicted on him at Ramah when he fought against Hazael king of Aram. Then Ahaziah the son of Jehoram king of Judah went down to see Joram the son of Ahab in Jezreel because he was sick.

Jehu Reigns over Israel

9 NOW ELISHA the prophet called one of the sons of the prophets and said to him, "Gird up your loins, and take this flask of oil in your hand and go to Ramoth-gilead. ²"When you arrive there, search out Jehu the son of Jehoshaphat the son of Nimshi, and go in and bid him arise from among his brothers, and bring him to an inner room. ³"Then take the flask of oil and pour it on his head and say, 'Thus says the LORD, "I have anointed you king over Israel." ' Then open the door and flee and do not wait."

⁴ ¶ So the young man, the servant of the prophet, went to Ramoth-gilead. ⁵ When he came, behold, the captains of the army were sitting, and he said, "I have a word for you, O captain." And Jehu said, "For which *one* of us?" And he said, "For you, O captain."

⁶ He arose and went into the house, and he poured the oil on his head and said to him, "Thus says the LORD, the God of Israel, 'I have anointed you king over the people of the LORD, *even* over Israel.

⁷ 'You shall strike the house of Ahab your master, that I may avenge the blood of My servants the prophets, and the blood of all the servants of the LORD, at the hand of Jezebel.

⁸ 'For the whole house of Ahab shall perish, and I will cut off from Ahab every male person both bond and free in Israel.

⁹ 'I will make the house of Ahab like the house of Jeroboam the son of Nebat, and like the house of Baasha the son of Ahijah.

¹⁰ 'The dogs shall eat Jezebel in the territory of Jezreel, and none shall bury *her.*' " Then he opened the door and fled.

¹¹ ¶ Now Jehu came out to the servants of his master, and one said to him, "Is all well? Why did this mad fellow come to you?" And he said to them, "You know *very well* the man and his talk."

¹² They said, "It is a lie, tell us now." And he said, "Thus and thus he said to me, 'Thus says the LORD, "I have anointed you king over Israel." ' "

¹³ Then they hurried and each man took his garment and placed it under him on the bare steps, and blew the trumpet, saying, "Jehu is king!"

Jehoram (Joram) Is Assassinated

¹⁴ ¶ So Jehu the son of Jehoshaphat the son of Nimshi conspired against Joram. Now Joram with all Israel was defending Ramoth-gilead against Hazael king of Aram, ¹⁵ but King ^bJoram had returned to Jezreel to be healed of the wounds which the Arameans had inflicted on him when he fought with Hazael king of Aram. So Jehu said, "If this is your mind, *then* let no one escape *or* leave the city to go tell *it* in Jezreel."

¹⁶ Then Jehu rode in a chariot and went to Jezreel, for Joram was lying there. Ahaziah king of Judah had come down to see Joram.

¹⁷ ¶ Now the watchman was standing on the tower in Jezreel and he saw the company of Jehu as he came, and said, "I see a company." And Joram said, "Take a horseman and send him to meet them and let him say, 'Is it peace?' "

wounded Joram; ²⁹so King Joram returned to Jezreel to recover from the wounds the Arameans had inflicted on him at Ramoth^r in his battle with Hazael king of Aram.

Then Ahaziah son of Jehoram king of Judah went down to Jezreel to see Joram son of Ahab, because he had been wounded.

Jehu Anointed King of Israel

9 THE PROPHET Elisha summoned a man from the company of the prophets and said to him, "Tuck your cloak into your belt, take this flask of oil with you and go to Ramoth Gilead. ²When you get there, look for Jehu son of Jehoshaphat, the son of Nimshi. Go to him, get him away from his companions and take him into an inner room. ³Then take the flask and pour the oil on his head and declare, 'This is what the LORD says: I anoint you king over Israel.' Then open the door and run; don't delay!"

⁴So the young man, the prophet, went to Ramoth Gilead. ⁵When he arrived, he found the army officers sitting together. "I have a message for you, commander," he said.

"For which of us?" asked Jehu.

"For you, commander," he replied.

⁶Jehu got up and went into the house. Then the prophet poured the oil on Jehu's head and declared, "This is what the LORD, the God of Israel, says: 'I anoint you king over the LORD's people Israel. ⁷You are to destroy the house of Ahab your master, and I will avenge the blood of my servants the prophets and the blood of all the LORD's servants shed by Jezebel. ⁸The whole house of Ahab will perish. I will cut off from Ahab every last male in Israel—slave or free. ⁹I will make the house of Ahab like the house of Jeroboam son of Nebat and like the house of Baasha son of Ahijah. ¹⁰As for Jezebel, dogs will devour her on the plot of ground at Jezreel, and no one will bury her.' " Then he opened the door and ran.

¹¹When Jehu went out to his fellow officers, one of them asked him, "Is everything all right? Why did this madman come to you?"

"You know the man and the sort of things he says," Jehu replied.

¹²"That's not true!" they said. "Tell us."

Jehu said, "Here is what he told me: 'This is what the LORD says: I anoint you king over Israel.' "

¹³They hurried and took their cloaks and spread them under him on the bare steps. Then they blew the trumpet and shouted, "Jehu is king!"

Jehu Kills Joram and Ahaziah

¹⁴So Jehu son of Jehoshaphat, the son of Nimshi, conspired against Joram. (Now Joram and all Israel had been defending Ramoth Gilead against Hazael king of Aram, ¹⁵but King Joram^s had returned to Jezreel to recover from the wounds the Arameans had inflicted on him in the battle with Hazael king of Aram.) Jehu said, "If this is the way you feel, don't let anyone slip out of the city to go and tell the news in Jezreel." ¹⁶Then he got into his chariot and rode to Jezreel, because Joram was resting there and Ahaziah king of Judah had gone down to see him.

¹⁷When the lookout standing on the tower in Jezreel saw Jehu's troops approaching, he called out, "I see some troops coming."

"Get a horseman," Joram ordered. "Send him to meet them and ask, 'Do you come in peace?' "

---

^bHeb *Jehoram*

^r 29 Hebrew *Ramah*, a variant of *Ramoth*   ^s 15 Hebrew *Jehoram*, a variant of *Joram*; also in verses 17 and 21-24

King James

18So there went one on horseback to meet him, and said, Thus saith the king, *Is it* peace? And Jehu said, What hast thou to do with peace? turn thee behind me. And the watchman told, saying, The messenger came to them, but he cometh not again.

19Then he sent out a second on horseback, which came to them, and said, Thus saith the king, *Is it* peace? And Jehu answered, What hast thou to do with peace? turn thee behind me.

20And the watchman told, saying, He came even unto them, and cometh not again: and the *u*driving *is* like the driving of Jehu the son of Nimshi; for he driveth *v*furiously.

21And Joram said, *w*Make ready. And his chariot was made ready. And Joram king of Israel and Ahaziah king of Judah went out, each in his chariot, and they went out against Jehu, and *x*met him in the portion of Naboth the Jezreelite.

22And it came to pass, when Joram saw Jehu, that he said, *Is it* peace, Jehu? And he answered, What peace, so long as the whoredoms of thy mother Jezebel and her witchcrafts *are so* many?

23And Joram turned his hands, and fled, and said to Ahaziah, *There is* treachery, O Ahaziah.

24And Jehu *y*drew a bow with his full strength, and smote Jehoram between his arms, and the arrow went out at his heart, and he *z*sunk down in his chariot.

25Then said *Jehu* to Bidkar his captain, Take up, *and* cast him in the portion of the field of Naboth the Jezreelite: for remember how that, when I and thou rode together after Ahab his father, the LORD laid this burden upon him;

26Surely I have seen yesterday the *a*blood of Naboth, and the blood of his sons, saith the LORD; and I will requite thee in this *b*plat, saith the LORD. Now therefore take *and* cast him into the plat *of ground,* according to the word of the LORD.

27 ¶ But when Ahaziah the king of Judah saw *this,* he fled by the way of the garden house. And Jehu followed after him, and said, Smite him also in the chariot. *And they did so* at the going up to Gur, which *is* by Ibleam. And he fled to Megiddo, and died there.

28And his servants carried him in a chariot to Jerusalem, and buried him in his sepulchre with his fathers in the city of David.

29And in the eleventh year of Joram the son of Ahab began Ahaziah to reign over Judah.

The death of Jezebel

30 ¶ And when Jehu was come to Jezreel, Jezebel heard *of it;* and she *c*painted her face, and tired her head, and looked out at a window.

31And as Jehu entered in at the gate, she said, *Had* Zimri peace, who slew his master?

32And he lifted up his face to the window, and said, Who *is* on my side? who? And there looked out to him two *or* three *d*eunuchs.

33And he said, Throw her down. So they threw her down: and *some* of her blood was sprinkled on the wall, and on the horses: and he trode her under foot.

34And when he was come in, he did eat and drink, and said, Go, see now this cursed *woman,* and bury her: for she *is* a king's daughter.

35And they went to bury her: but they found no more of her than the skull, and the feet, and the palms of *her* hands.

36Wherefore they came again, and told him. And he said, This *is* the word of the LORD, which he spake *e*by his servant Elijah the Tishbite, saying, In the portion of Jezreel shall dogs eat the flesh of Jezebel:

Amplified

18So one on horseback went to meet him and said, Thus says the king: Is it peace? And Jehu said, What have you to do with peace? Rein in behind me. And the watchman reported, The messenger came to them, but he does not return.

19Then Joram sent out a second man on horseback, who came to them and said, Thus says the king: Is it peace? Jehu replied, What have you to do with peace? Ride behind me.

20And the watchman reported, He came to them, but does not return; also the driving is like the driving of Jehu son of Nimshi, for he drives furiously.

21Joram said, Make ready. When his chariot was made ready, Joram king of Israel and Ahaziah king of Judah went out, each in his chariot. Thus they went out to meet Jehu and met him in the field of Naboth the Jezreelite.

22When Joram saw Jehu, he said, Is it peace, Jehu? And he answered, How can peace exist as long as the fornications of your mother Jezebel and her witchcrafts are so many?

23Then Joram reined about and fled, and he said to Ahaziah, Treachery, Ahaziah!

24But Jehu drew his bow with his full strength and shot Joram between his shoulders; and the arrow went out through his heart, and he sank down in his chariot.

25Then said Jehu to Bidkar his captain, Take [Joram] up and cast him in the plot of Naboth the Jezreelite's field; for remember how, when I and you rode together after Ahab his father, the Lord uttered this prophecy against him:

26As surely as I saw yesterday the blood of Naboth and the blood of his sons, says the Lord, I will repay you on this plot of ground, says the Lord. Now therefore, take and cast Joram into the plot of ground [of Naboth], as the word of the Lord said. [I Kings 21:15–29.]

27When Ahaziah king of Judah saw this, he fled by the way of the garden house. Jehu followed him and said, Smite him also in the chariot. And they did so at the ascent to Gur, which is by Ibleam. And [Ahaziah] fled to Megiddo and died there.

28His servants took him in a chariot to Jerusalem, and buried him in his sepulcher with his fathers in the City of David.

29In the eleventh year of Joram son of Ahab, Ahaziah's reign over Judah began.

30Now when Jehu came to Jezreel, Jezebel heard of it, and she painted her eyes and beautified her head and looked out of [an upper] window.

31And as Jehu entered in at the gate, she said, [Have you come in] peace, you Zimri, who slew his master? [I Kings 16:9, 10.]

32Jehu lifted up his face to the window and said, Who is on my side? Who? And two or three eunuchs looked out at him.

33And he said, Throw her down! So they threw her down, and some of her blood splattered on the wall and on the horses, and he drove over her.

34When he came in, he ate and drank, and said, See now to this cursed woman and bury her, for she is a king's daughter.

35They went to bury her, but they found nothing left of her except the skull, feet, and palms of her hands.

36They came again and told Jehu. He said, This is the word of the Lord which He spoke by His servant Elijah the Tishbite, In the portion of Jezreel shall dogs eat the flesh of Jezebel. [I Kings 21:23.]

---

*u*Or, *marching*   *v*Heb. *in madness*   *w*Heb. *Bind*   *x*Heb. *found*   *y*Heb. *filled his hand with a bow*   *z*Heb. *bowed*
*a*Heb. *bloods*   *b*Or, *portion*   *c*Heb. *put her eyes in painting*
*d*Or, *chamberlains*   *e*Heb. *by the hand of*

New American Standard

18 So a horseman went to meet him and said, "Thus says the king, 'Is it peace?' " And Jehu said, "What have you to do with peace? Turn behind me." And the watchman reported, "The messenger came to them, but he did not return."

19 Then he sent out a second horseman, who came to them and said, "Thus says the king, 'Is it peace?' " And Jehu answered, "What have you to do with peace? Turn behind me."

20 The watchman reported, "He came even to them, and he did not return; and the driving is like the driving of Jehu the son of Nimshi, for he drives furiously."

21 ¶ Then Joram said, "Get ready." And they made his chariot ready. Joram king of Israel and Ahaziah king of Judah went out, each in his chariot, and they went out to meet Jehu and found him in the property of Naboth the Jezreelite.

22 When Joram saw Jehu, he said, "Is it peace, Jehu?" And he answered, "What peace, so long as the harlotries of your mother Jezebel and her witchcrafts are so many?"

23 So Joram reined about and fled and said to Ahaziah, *There is* treachery, O Ahaziah!"

24 And Jehu drew his bow with his full strength and shot Joram between his arms; and the arrow went through his heart and he sank in his chariot.

25 Then *Jehu* said to Bidkar his officer, "Take *him* up and cast him into the ᶜproperty of the field of Naboth the Jezreelite, for I remember when you and I were riding together after Ahab his father, that the LORD laid this oracle against him:

26 'Surely I have seen yesterday the blood of Naboth and the blood of his sons,' says the LORD, 'and I will repay you in this ᶜproperty,' says the LORD. Now then, take and cast him into the property, according to the word of the LORD."

Jehu Assassinates Ahaziah

27 ¶ When Ahaziah the king of Judah saw *this*, he fled by the way of the garden house. And Jehu pursued him and said, "Shoot him too, in the chariot." *So they shot him* at the ascent of Gur, which is at Ibleam. But he fled to Megiddo and died there.

28 Then his servants carried him in a chariot to Jerusalem and buried him in his grave with his fathers in the city of David.

29 ¶ Now in the eleventh year of Joram, the son of Ahab, Ahaziah became king over Judah.

30 ¶ When Jehu came to Jezreel, Jezebel heard *of it,* and she painted her eyes and adorned her head and looked out the window.

31 As Jehu entered the gate, she said, "Is it well, Zimri, your master's murderer?"

32 Then he lifted up his face to the window and said, "Who is on my side? Who?" And two or three officials looked down at him.

Jezebel Is Slain

33 He said, "Throw her down." So they threw her down, and some of her blood was sprinkled on the wall and on the horses, and he trampled her under foot.

34 When he came in, he ate and drank; and he said, "See now to this cursed woman and bury her, for she is a king's daughter."

35 They went to bury her, but they found nothing more of her than the skull and the feet and the palms of her hands.

36 Therefore they returned and told him. And he said, "This is the word of the LORD, which He spoke by His servant Elijah the Tishbite, saying, 'In the property of Jezreel the dogs shall eat the flesh of Jezebel;

New International

18 The horseman rode off to meet Jehu and said, "This is what the king says: 'Do you come in peace?' "

"What do you have to do with peace?" Jehu replied. "Fall in behind me."

The lookout reported, "The messenger has reached them, but he isn't coming back."

19 So the king sent out a second horseman. When he came to them he said, "This is what the king says: 'Do you come in peace?' "

Jehu replied, "What do you have to do with peace? Fall in behind me."

20 The lookout reported, "He has reached them, but he isn't coming back either. The driving is like that of Jehu son of Nimshi—he drives like a madman."

21 "Hitch up my chariot," Joram ordered. And when it was hitched up, Joram king of Israel and Ahaziah king of Judah rode out, each in his own chariot, to meet Jehu. They met him at the plot of ground that had belonged to Naboth the Jezreelite. 22 When Joram saw Jehu he asked, "Have you come in peace, Jehu?"

"How can there be peace," Jehu replied, "as long as all the idolatry and witchcraft of your mother Jezebel abound?"

23 Joram turned about and fled, calling out to Ahaziah, "Treachery, Ahaziah!"

24 Then Jehu drew his bow and shot Joram between the shoulders. The arrow pierced his heart and he slumped down in his chariot. 25 Jehu said to Bidkar, his chariot officer, "Pick him up and throw him on the field that belonged to Naboth the Jezreelite. Remember how you and I were riding together in chariots behind Ahab his father when the LORD made this prophecy about him: 26 'Yesterday I saw the blood of Naboth and the blood of his sons, declares the LORD, and I will surely make you pay for it on this plot of ground, declares the LORD.'ᵗ Now then, pick him up and throw him on that plot, in accordance with the word of the LORD."

27 When Ahaziah king of Judah saw what had happened, he fled up the road to Beth Haggan.ᵘ Jehu chased him, shouting, "Kill him too!" They wounded him in his chariot on the way up to Gur near Ibleam, but he escaped to Megiddo and died there. 28 His servants took him by chariot to Jerusalem and buried him with his fathers in his tomb in the City of David. 29 (In the eleventh year of Joram son of Ahab, Ahaziah had become king of Judah.)

Jezebel Killed

30 Then Jehu went to Jezreel. When Jezebel heard about it, she painted her eyes, arranged her hair and looked out of a window. 31 As Jehu entered the gate, she asked, "Have you come in peace, Zimri, you murderer of your master?"ᵛ

32 He looked up at the window and called out, "Who is on my side? Who?" Two or three eunuchs looked down at him. 33 "Throw her down!" Jehu said. So they threw her down, and some of her blood spattered the wall and the horses as they trampled her underfoot.

34 Jehu went in and ate and drank. "Take care of that cursed woman," he said, "and bury her, for she was a king's daughter." 35 But when they went out to bury her, they found nothing except her skull, her feet and her hands. 36 They went back and told Jehu, who said, "This is the word of the LORD that he spoke through his servant Elijah the Tishbite: On the plot of ground at Jezreel dogs

ᵗ26 See 1 Kings 21:19.   ᵘ27 Or *fled by way of the garden house*
ᵛ31 Or *"Did Zimri have peace, who murdered his master?"*

ᶜLit *portion*

King James

Amplified

³⁷And the carcase of Jezebel shall be as dung upon the face of the field in the portion of Jezreel; *so* that they shall not say, This *is* Jezebel.

Ahab's kin destroyed

10 AND AHAB had seventy sons in Samaria. And Jehu wrote letters, and sent to Samaria, unto the rulers of Jezreel, to the elders, and to *f*them that brought up Ahab's *children,* saying,

²Now as soon as this letter cometh to you, seeing your master's sons *are* with you, and *there are* with you chariots and horses, a fenced city also, and armour;

³Look even out the best and meetest of your master's sons, and set *him* on his father's throne, and fight for your master's house.

⁴But they were 'exceedingly afraid, and said, Behold, two kings stood not before him: how then shall we stand?

⁵And he that *was* over the house, and he that *was* over the city, the elders also, and the bringers up *of the children,* sent to Jehu, saying, *We are* thy servants, and will do all that thou shalt bid us; we will not make any king: do thou *that which* is good in thine eyes.

⁶Then he wrote a letter the second time to them, saying, If ye *be* ᵍmine, and *if* ye will hearken unto my voice, take ye the heads of the men your master's sons, and come to me to Jezreel by tomorrow this time. Now the king's sons, *being* seventy persons, *were* with the great men of the city, which brought them up.

⁷And it came to pass, when the letter came to them, that they took the king's sons, and slew seventy persons, and put their heads in baskets, and sent him *them* to Jezreel.

8 ¶ And there came a messenger, and told him, saying, They have brought the heads of the king's sons. And he said, Lay ye them in two heaps at the entering in of the gate until the morning.

⁹And it came to pass in the morning, that he went out, and stood, and said to all the people, Ye *be* righteous: behold, I conspired against my master, and slew him: but who slew all these?

¹⁰Know now that there shall fall unto the earth nothing of the word of the LORD, which the LORD spake concerning the house of Ahab: for the LORD hath done *that* which he spake ʰby his servant Elijah.

¹¹So Jehu slew all that remained of the house of Ahab in Jezreel, and all his great men, and his ⁱkinsfolks, and his priests, until he left him none remaining.

12 ¶ And he arose and departed, and came to Samaria. *And* as he *was* at the ʲshearing house in the way,

¹³Jehu ᵏmet with the brethren of Ahaziah king of Judah, and said, Who *are* ye? And they answered, We *are* the brethren of Ahaziah; and we go down ˡto salute the children of the king and the children of the queen.

¹⁴And he said, Take them alive. And they took them alive, and slew them at the pit of the shearing house, *even* two and forty men: neither left he any of them.

15 ¶ And when he was departed thence, He ᵏlighted on Jehonadab the son of Rechab *coming* to meet him: and he ᵐsaluted him, and said to him, Is thine heart right, as my heart *is* with thy heart? And Jehonadab answered, It is. If it be, give *me* thine hand. And he gave *him* his hand; and he took him up to him into the chariot.

¹⁶And he said, Come with me, and see my zeal for the LORD. So they made him ride in his chariot.

¹⁷And when he came to Samaria, he slew all that remained unto Ahab in Samaria, till he had destroyed him, according to the saying of the LORD, which he spake to Elijah.

Amplified

³⁷The corpse of Jezebel shall be like dung upon the face of the field in the portion of Jezreel, so that they shall not say, This is Jezebel.

10 AHAB HAD seventy [grandsons] in Samaria. So Jehu wrote letters and sent them from Jezreel to the rulers of Samaria, to the elders, and to those who brought up Ahab's [grandsons], saying,

²Now as soon as this letter comes to you, seeing your master [Joram's] sons are with you and also chariots and horses, a fortified city, and weapons,

³Select the best and most fit of your master's sons and set him on his father's throne; and fight for your master's house.

⁴But they were exceedingly afraid and reasoned, The two kings could not stand before [Jehu]; how then can we stand?

⁵And he who was over the household, he who was over the city, the elders also, and the guardians *and* tutors sent to Jehu, saying, We are your servants and will do all that you bid us; [but] we will not make any man king; do what is good in your eyes.

⁶Then [Jehu] wrote a second letter to them, saying, If you are with me and will obey me, take the heads of your master [Joram's] sons and come to me at Jezreel by tomorrow this time. Now the [dead] king's sons, seventy persons, were with the great men of the city, who were bringing them up.

⁷When the letter came to these men, they took the king's sons and slew them, seventy persons, and put their heads in baskets and sent them to Jehu at Jezreel.

⁸When a messenger came and told him, They have brought the heads of the king's sons, he said, Lay them in two heaps at the entrance of the city gate until morning.

⁹The next morning he went out and stood and said to all the people, You are just *and* innocent. Behold, I conspired against my master and slew him, but who smote all these?

¹⁰Know now that nothing which the Lord spoke concerning the house of Ahab shall be unfulfilled *or* ineffective; for the Lord has done what He said through His servant Elijah.

¹¹So Jehu slew all that remained of the house of Ahab in Jezreel, and all his great men, his familiar friends, and his priests, until he left him none remaining.

¹²And he arose and went to Samaria. And as he was at the shearing house of the shepherds on the way,

¹³Jehu met the kinsmen of Ahaziah king of Judah and said, Who are you? They answered, We are the kinsmen of Ahaziah, and we came down to visit the royal princes and the sons of [Jezebel] the queen mother.

¹⁴He said, Take them alive. And they did so and slew them at the cistern of the shearing house, forty-two men; he left none of them.

¹⁵When Jehu left there, he met Jehonadab son of Rechab coming to meet him. He saluted him and said to him, Is your heart right, as my heart is with yours? Jehonadab answered, It is. [Jehu said] If it is, give me your hand. He gave him his hand, and Jehu took him up into the chariot.

¹⁶And he said, Come with me and see my zeal for the Lord. So they made [the Rechabite] ride in Jehu's chariot.

¹⁷When Jehu came to Samaria, he slew all who remained of Ahab's family in Samaria, till he had destroyed them all, according to what the Lord said to Elijah.

ᶠHeb. *nourishers*   ᵍHeb. *for me*   ʰHeb. *by the hand of*
ⁱOr, *acquaintance*   ʲHeb. *house of shepherds binding* sheep
ᵏHeb. *found*   ˡHeb. *to the peace of*   ᵐHeb. *blessed*

New American Standard

37 and the corpse of Jezebel will be as dung on the face of the field in the property of Jezreel, so they cannot say, "This is Jezebel."' "

Judgment upon Ahab's House

10 NOW AHAB had seventy sons in Samaria. And Jehu wrote letters and sent *them* to Samaria, to the rulers of Jezreel, the elders, and to the guardians of *the children of* Ahab, saying,

2"Now, when this letter comes to you, since your master's sons are with you, as well as the chariots and horses and a fortified city and the weapons,

3 select the best and dfittest of your master's sons, and set *him* on his father's throne, and fight for your master's house."

4 But they feared greatly and said, "Behold, the two kings did not stand before him; how then can we stand?"

5 And the one who *was* over the household, and he who *was* over the city, the elders, and the guardians of *the children,* sent *word* to Jehu, saying, "We are your servants, all that you say to us we will do, we will not make any man king; do what is good in your sight."

6 Then he wrote a letter to them a second time saying, "If you are on my side, and you will listen to my voice, take the heads of the men, your master's sons, and come to me at Jezreel tomorrow about this time." Now the king's sons, seventy persons, *were* with the great men of the city, *who* were rearing them.

7 When the letter came to them, they took the king's sons and slaughtered *them,* seventy persons, and put their heads in baskets, and sent *them* to him at Jezreel.

8 When the messenger came and told him, saying, "They have brought the heads of the king's sons," he said, "Put them in two heaps at the entrance of the gate until morning."

9 Now in the morning he went out and stood and said to all the people, "You are innocent; behold, I conspired against my master and killed him, but who killed all these?

10"Know then that there shall fall to the earth nothing of the word of the LORD, which the LORD spoke concerning the house of Ahab, for the LORD has done what He spoke through His servant Elijah."

11 So Jehu killed all who remained of the house of Ahab in Jezreel, and all his great men and his acquaintances and his priests, until he left him without a survivor.

12 ¶ Then he arose and departed and went to Samaria. On the way while he was at eBeth-eked of the shepherds,

13 Jehu met the relatives of Ahaziah king of Judah and said, "Who are you?" And they answered, "We are the relatives of Ahaziah; and we have come down to greet the sons of the king and the sons of the queen mother."

14 He said, "Take them alive." So they took them alive and killed them at the pit of Beth-eked, forty-two men; and he left none of them.

15 ¶ Now when he had departed from there, he met Jehonadab the son of Rechab *coming* to meet him; and he greeted him and said to him, "Is your heart right, as my heart is with your heart?" And Jehonadab answered, "It is." *Jehu said,* "If it is, give *me* your hand." And he gave him his hand, and he took him up to him into the chariot.

16 He said, "Come with me and see my zeal for the LORD." So he made him ride in his chariot.

17 When he came to Samaria, he killed all who remained to Ahab in Samaria, until he had destroyed him, according to the word of the LORD which He spoke to Elijah.

New International

will devour Jezebel's flesh.w 37Jezebel's body will be like refuse on the ground in the plot at Jezreel, so that no one will be able to say, 'This is Jezebel.' "

Ahab's Family Killed

10 NOW THERE were in Samaria seventy sons of the house of Ahab. So Jehu wrote letters and sent them to Samaria: to the officials of Jezreel,x to the elders and to the guardians of Ahab's children. He said, 2"As soon as this letter reaches you, since your master's sons are with you and you have chariots and horses, a fortified city and weapons, 3choose the best and most worthy of your master's sons and set him on his father's throne. Then fight for your master's house."

4But they were terrified and said, "If two kings could not resist him, how can we?"

5So the palace administrator, the city governor, the elders and the guardians sent this message to Jehu: "We are your servants and we will do anything you say. We will not appoint anyone as king; you do whatever you think best."

6Then Jehu wrote them a second letter, saying, "If you are on my side and will obey me, take the heads of your master's sons and come to me in Jezreel by this time tomorrow."

Now the royal princes, seventy of them, were with the leading men of the city, who were rearing them. 7When the letter arrived, these men took the princes and slaughtered all seventy of them. They put their heads in baskets and sent them to Jehu in Jezreel. 8When the messenger arrived, he told Jehu, "They have brought the heads of the princes."

Then Jehu ordered, "Put them in two piles at the entrance of the city gate until morning."

9The next morning Jehu went out. He stood before all the people and said, "You are innocent. It was I who conspired against my master and killed him, but who killed all these? 10Know then, that not a word the LORD has spoken against the house of Ahab will fail. The LORD has done what he promised through his servant Elijah." 11So Jehu killed everyone in Jezreel who remained of the house of Ahab, as well as all his chief men, his close friends and his priests, leaving him no survivor.

12Jehu then set out and went toward Samaria. At Beth Eked of the Shepherds, 13he met some relatives of Ahaziah king of Judah and asked, "Who are you?"

They said, "We are relatives of Ahaziah, and we have come down to greet the families of the king and of the queen mother."

14"Take them alive!" he ordered. So they took them alive and slaughtered them by the well of Beth Eked—forty-two men. He left no survivor.

15After he left there, he came upon Jehonadab son of Recab, who was on his way to meet him. Jehu greeted him and said, "Are you in accord with me, as I am with you?"

"I am," Jehonadab answered.

"If so," said Jehu, "give me your hand." So he did, and Jehu helped him up into the chariot. 16Jehu said, "Come with me and see my zeal for the LORD." Then he had him ride along in his chariot.

17When Jehu came to Samaria, he killed all who were left there of Ahab's family; he destroyed them, according to the word of the LORD spoken to Elijah.

---

dLit *most upright*   eI.e. house of binding

w36 See 1 Kings 21:23.   x1 Hebrew; some Septuagint manuscripts and Vulgate of the city

King James

Massacre of Baal worshippers

18 ¶ And Jehu gathered all the people together, and said unto them, Ahab served Baal a little; *but* Jehu shall serve him much.

19 Now therefore call unto me all the prophets of Baal, all his servants, and all his priests; let none be wanting: for I have a great sacrifice *to do* to Baal; whosoever shall be wanting, he shall not live. But Jehu did *it* in subtilty, to the intent that he might destroy the worshippers of Baal.

20 And Jehu said, *n*Proclaim a solemn assembly for Baal. And they proclaimed *it*.

21 And Jehu sent through all Israel: and all the worshippers of Baal came, so that there was not a man left that came not. And they came into the house of Baal; and the house of Baal was *o*full from one end to another.

22 And he said unto him that *was* over the vestry, Bring forth vestments for all the worshippers of Baal. And he brought them forth vestments.

23 And Jehu went, and Jehonadab the son of Rechab, into the house of Baal, and said unto the worshippers of Baal, Search, and look that there be here with you none of the servants of the LORD, but the worshippers of Baal only.

24 And when they went in to offer sacrifices and burnt offerings, Jehu appointed fourscore men without, and said, *If* any of the men whom I have brought into your hands escape, *he that letteth him go,* his life *shall be* for the life of him.

25 And it came to pass, as soon as he had made an end of offering the burnt offering, that Jehu said to the guard and to the captains, Go in, *and* slay them; let none come forth. And they smote them with *p*the edge of the sword; and the guard and the captains cast *them* out, and went to the city of the house of Baal.

26 And they brought forth the *q*images out of the house of Baal, and burned them.

27 And they brake down the image of Baal, and brake down the house of Baal, and made it a draught house unto this day.

28 Thus Jehu destroyed Baal out of Israel.

29 ¶ Howbeit *from* the sins of Jeroboam the son of Nebat, who made Israel to sin, Jehu departed not from after them, *to wit,* the golden calves that *were* in Beth-el, and that *were* in Dan.

30 And the LORD said unto Jehu, Because thou hast done well in executing *that which is* right in mine eyes, *and* hast done unto the house of Ahab according to all that *was* in mine heart, thy children of the fourth *generation* shall sit on the throne of Israel.

31 But Jehu *r*took no heed to walk in the law of the LORD God of Israel with all his heart: for he departed not from the sins of Jeroboam, which made Israel to sin.

32 ¶ In those days the LORD began *s*to cut Israel short: and Hazael smote them in all the coasts of Israel;

33 From Jordan *t*eastward, all the land of Gilead, the Gadites, and the Reubenites, and the Manassites, from Aroer, which *is* by the river Arnon, *u*even Gilead and Bashan.

34 Now the rest of the acts of Jehu, and all that he did, and all his might, *are* they not written in the book of the chronicles of the kings of Israel?

35 And Jehu slept with his fathers: and they buried him in Samaria. And Jehoahaz his son reigned in his stead.

36 And *v*the time that Jehu reigned over Israel in Samaria *was* twenty and eight years.

Amplified

18 Jehu assembled all the people and said to them, Ahab served Baal a little; but Jehu will serve him much.

19 So call to me all the prophets of Baal, all his worshipers, and all his priests. Let none be missing, for I have a great sacrifice to make to Baal; whoever is missing shall not live. But Jehu did it with trickery, intending to destroy the Baal worshipers.

20 Jehu said, Sanctify a solemn assembly for Baal. And they proclaimed it.

21 Jehu sent through all Israel, and all the worshipers of Baal came; not a man failed to come. They went to the house *or* temple of Baal, filling it from one end to the other.

22 And he said to the man over the vestry, Bring vestments for all the worshipers of Baal. And he brought them vestments.

23 Then Jehu with Jehonadab son of Rechab went into the house of Baal and said to the worshipers of Baal, Search and see that there are here with you none of the servants of the Lord—but Baal worshipers only.

24 And when they went in to offer sacrifices and burnt offerings, Jehu appointed eighty men outside and said, If any of the men whom I have brought into your hands escape, he who lets him go shall forfeit his own life for his life.

25 As soon as he had finished offering the burnt offering, Jehu said to the guards and to the officers, Go in and slay them; let none escape. And they smote them with the sword; and the guards *or* runners [before the king] and the officers threw their bodies out and went into the inner dwelling of the house of Baal.

26 They brought out the pillars *or* obelisks of the house of Baal and burned them.

27 They broke down the pillars of Baal and the house of Baal, and made it [forever unclean] a privy to this day.

28 Thus Jehu rooted Baal out of Israel.

29 But Jehu did not give up the sins of Jeroboam son of Nebat, by which he made Israel to sin, that is, the golden calves at Bethel and Dan. [I Kings 12:28ff.]

30 And the Lord said to Jehu, Because you have executed well what is right in My eyes and have done to the house of Ahab as I willed, your sons to the fourth generation shall sit on Israel's throne. [Fulfilled in II Kings 15:12.]

31 But Jehu paid no attention to walking in the law of the Lord, the God of Israel, with all his heart. He did not quit the sins with which Jeroboam made Israel to sin.

32 [So] in those days the Lord began to cut off parts of Israel. Hazael [of Syria] defeated them in all the [across the Jordan] territory of Israel

33 From the Jordan east, all the land of Gilead, the Gadites, Reubenites, and Manassites, from Aroer which is by the Valley of the Arnon, even Gilead and Bashan.

34 The rest of the acts of Jehu, and all that he did, and all his might, are they not written in the Book of the Chronicles of the Kings of Israel?

35 Jehu slept with his fathers. They buried him in Samaria. Jehoahaz his son reigned in his stead.

36 The time that Jehu reigned over Israel in Samaria was twenty-eight years.

---

n Heb. *Sanctify*   *o* Or, so *full,* that they stood *mouth to mouth*
p Heb. *the mouth*   *q* Heb. *statues*   *r* Heb. *observed not*
s Heb. *to cut off the ends*   *t* Heb. *toward the rising of the sun*
u Or, *even to Gilead and Bashan*   *v* Heb. *the days* were

New American Standard

Jehu Destroys Baal Worshipers

18 ¶ Then Jehu gathered all the people and said to them, "Ahab served Baal a little; Jehu will serve him much.

19 "Now, summon all the prophets of Baal, all his worshipers and all his priests; let no one be missing, for I have a great sacrifice for Baal; whoever is missing shall not live." But Jehu did it in cunning, so that he might destroy the worshipers of Baal.

20 And Jehu said, "Sanctify a solemn assembly for Baal." And they proclaimed it.

21 Then Jehu sent throughout Israel and all the worshipers of Baal came, so that there was not a man left who did not come. And when they went into the house of Baal, the house of Baal was filled from one end to the other.

22 He said to the one who was in charge of the wardrobe, "Bring out garments for all the worshipers of Baal." So he brought out garments for them.

23 Jehu went into the house of Baal with Jehonadab the son of Rechab; and he said to the worshipers of Baal, "Search and see that there is here with you none of the servants of the LORD, but only the worshipers of Baal."

24 Then they went in to offer sacrifices and burnt offerings.

¶ Now Jehu had stationed for himself eighty men outside, and he had said, "The one who permits any of the men whom I bring into your hands to escape shall give up his life in exchange."

25 ¶ Then it came about, as soon as he had finished offering the burnt offering, that Jehu said to the guard and to the royal officers, "Go in, kill them; let none come out." And they killed them with the edge of the sword; and the guard and the royal officers threw them out, and went to the inner room of the house of Baal.

26 They brought out the sacred pillars of the house of Baal and burned them.

27 They also broke down the sacred pillar of Baal and broke down the house of Baal, and made it a latrine to this day.

28 ¶ Thus Jehu eradicated Baal out of Israel.

29 However, as for the sins of Jeroboam the son of Nebat, which he made Israel sin, from these Jehu did not depart, even the golden calves that were at Bethel and that were at Dan.

30 The LORD said to Jehu, "Because you have done well in executing what is right in My eyes, and have done to the house of Ahab according to all that was in My heart, your sons of the fourth generation shall sit on the throne of Israel."

31 But Jehu was not careful to walk in the law of the LORD, the God of Israel, with all his heart; he did not depart from the sins of Jeroboam, which he made Israel sin.

32 ¶ In those days the LORD began to cut off portions from Israel; and Hazael defeated them throughout the territory of Israel:

33 from the Jordan eastward, all the land of Gilead, the Gadites and the Reubenites and the Manassites, from Aroer, which is by the valley of the Arnon, even Gilead and Bashan.

Jehoahaz Succeeds Jehu

34 Now the rest of the acts of Jehu and all that he did and all his might, are they not written in the Book of the Chronicles of the Kings of Israel?

35 And Jehu slept with his fathers, and they buried him in Samaria. And Jehoahaz his son became king in his place.

36 Now the time which Jehu reigned over Israel in Samaria was twenty-eight years.

New International

Ministers of Baal Killed

18 Then Jehu brought all the people together and said to them, "Ahab served Baal a little; Jehu will serve him much. 19 Now summon all the prophets of Baal, all his ministers and all his priests. See that no one is missing, because I am going to hold a great sacrifice for Baal. Anyone who fails to come will no longer live." But Jehu was acting deceptively in order to destroy the ministers of Baal.

20 Jehu said, "Call an assembly in honor of Baal." So they proclaimed it. 21 Then he sent word throughout Israel, and all the ministers of Baal came; not one stayed away. They crowded into the temple of Baal until it was full from one end to the other. 22 And Jehu said to the keeper of the wardrobe, "Bring robes for all the ministers of Baal." So he brought out robes for them.

23 Then Jehu and Jehonadab son of Recab went into the temple of Baal. Jehu said to the ministers of Baal, "Look around and see that no servants of the LORD are here with you—only ministers of Baal." 24 So they went in to make sacrifices and burnt offerings. Now Jehu had posted eighty men outside with this warning: "If one of you lets any of the men I am placing in your hands escape, it will be your life for his life."

25 As soon as Jehu had finished making the burnt offering, he ordered the guards and officers: "Go in and kill them; let no one escape." So they cut them down with the sword. The guards and officers threw the bodies out and then entered the inner shrine of the temple of Baal. 26 They brought the sacred stone out of the temple of Baal and burned it. 27 They demolished the sacred stone of Baal and tore down the temple of Baal, and people have used it for a latrine to this day.

28 So Jehu destroyed Baal worship in Israel. 29 However, he did not turn away from the sins of Jeroboam son of Nebat, which he had caused Israel to commit—the worship of the golden calves at Bethel and Dan.

30 The LORD said to Jehu, "Because you have done well in accomplishing what is right in my eyes and have done to the house of Ahab all I had in mind to do, your descendants will sit on the throne of Israel to the fourth generation." 31 Yet Jehu was not careful to keep the law of the LORD, the God of Israel, with all his heart. He did not turn away from the sins of Jeroboam, which he had caused Israel to commit.

32 In those days the LORD began to reduce the size of Israel. Hazael overpowered the Israelites throughout their territory 33 east of the Jordan in all the land of Gilead (the region of Gad, Reuben and Manasseh), from Aroer by the Arnon Gorge through Gilead to Bashan.

34 As for the other events of Jehu's reign, all he did, and all his achievements, are they not written in the book of the annals of the kings of Israel?

35 Jehu rested with his fathers and was buried in Samaria. And Jehoahaz his son succeeded him as king. 36 The time that Jehu reigned over Israel in Samaria was twenty-eight years.

King James

Jehoash, king of Judah

11 AND WHEN Athaliah the mother of Ahaziah saw that her son was dead, she arose and destroyed all the ᵂseed royal.

2But ˣJehosheba, the daughter of king Joram, sister of Ahaziah, took ʸJoash the son of Ahaziah, and stole him from among the king's sons *which were* slain; and they hid him, *even* him and his nurse, in the bedchamber from Athaliah, so that he was not slain.

3And he was with her hid in the house of the LORD six years. And Athaliah did reign over the land.

4 ¶ And the seventh year Jehoiada sent and fetched the rulers over hundreds, with the captains and the guard, and brought them to him into the house of the LORD, and made a covenant with them, and took an oath of them in the house of the LORD, and showed them the king's son.

5And he commanded them, saying, This *is* the thing that ye shall do; A third part of you that enter in on the sabbath shall even be keepers of the watch of the king's house;

6And a third part *shall be* at the gate of Sur; and a third part at the gate behind the guard: so shall ye keep the watch of the house, ᶻthat it be not broken down.

7And two ᵃᵇparts of all you that go forth on the sabbath, even they shall keep the watch of the house of the LORD about the king.

8And ye shall compass the king round about, every man with his weapons in his hand: and he that cometh within the ranges, let him be slain: and be ye with the king as he goeth out and as he cometh in.

9And the captains over the hundreds did according to all *things* that Jehoiada the priest commanded: and they took every man his men that were to come in on the sabbath, with them that should go out on the sabbath, and came to Jehoiada the priest.

10And to the captains over hundreds did the priest give king David's spears and shields, that *were* in the temple of the LORD.

11And the guard stood, every man with his weapons in his hand, round about the king, from the right ᶜcorner of the temple to the left corner of the temple, *along* by the altar and the temple.

12And he brought forth the king's son, and put the crown upon him, and *gave him* the testimony; and they made him king, and anointed him; and they clapped their hands, and said, God ᵈsave the king.

13 ¶ And when Athaliah heard the noise of the guard *and* of the people, she came to the people into the temple of the LORD.

14And when she looked, behold, the king stood by a pillar, as the manner *was,* and the princes and the trumpeters by the king, and all the people of the land rejoiced, and blew with trumpets: and Athaliah rent her clothes, and cried, Treason, Treason.

15But Jehoiada the priest commanded the captains of the hundreds, the officers of the host, and said unto them, Have her forth without the ranges: and him that followeth her kill with the sword. For the priest had said, Let her not be slain in the house of the LORD.

16And they laid hands on her; and she went by the way by the which the horses came into the king's house: and there was she slain.

17 ¶ And Jehoiada made a covenant between the LORD and the king and the people, that they should be the LORD'S people; between the king also and the people.

18And all the people of the land went into the house of Baal, and brake it down; his altars and his images brake they in pieces thoroughly, and slew Mattan the priest of Baal before the altars. And the priest appointed ᵉofficers over the house of the LORD.

Amplified

11 WHEN ATHALIAH the mother of [King] Ahaziah [of Judah] saw that her son was dead, she arose and destroyed all the royal descendants.

2But Jehosheba, the daughter of King Jehoram, [half] sister of Ahaziah, stole Joash son of Ahaziah from among the king's sons, who were to be slain, even him and his nurse, and hid them from Athaliah in an inner storeroom for beds; so he was not slain.

3Joash was with his nurse hidden in the house of the Lord for six years. And Athaliah reigned over the land.

4In the seventh year Jehoiada [the priest, Jehosheba's husband] sent for the captains over hundreds of the Carites and of the guards *or* runners and brought them to him in the house of the Lord and made a covenant with them and took an oath from them in the house of the Lord and showed them the king's [hidden] son.

5And he commanded them, saying, This is the thing you shall do: a third of you who come in on the Sabbath shall keep watch of the king's house,

6A third shall be at the gate Sur, and a third at the gate behind the guard. So you shall keep watch of the palace [from three places] and be a barrier.

7And two divisions of all you who should go off duty on the Sabbath shall keep the watch of the house of the Lord to [protect] the king.

8You shall surround the [little] king, every man with his weapons in his hand. And let anyone who breaks through the ranks be put to death. You be with the king when he goes out and when he comes in.

9The captains over the hundreds did all that Jehoiada the priest commanded; and they took every man his men who were to come on duty on the Sabbath with those who should go off duty on the Sabbath, and came to Jehoiada the priest.

10To the captains over hundreds the priest gave the spears and shields that had been King David's, which were in the house of the Lord.

11And the guards stood, every man with his weapons in his hand, from the right corner to the left corner of the temple area, along by the altar [in the court] and the temple proper.

12And Jehoiada brought out the king's son and put the crown on him and gave him the Testimony [the Mosaic Law]; and they proclaimed him king and anointed him, and they clapped their hands and said, Long live the king!

13When Athaliah heard the noise of the guards and the people, she went into the house of the Lord to the people.

14When she looked, there stood the king [on the platform] by the pillar, as was customary [on such occasions], and the captains and the trumpeters beside the king, with all the people of the land rejoicing and blowing trumpets. And Athaliah rent her clothes and cried, Treason! Treason!

15Then Jehoiada the priest commanded the captains of hundreds set over the army and said to them, Take her forth outside the ranks, and him who follows her kill with the sword. For the priest had said, Let her not be slain in the house of the Lord.

16They seized her, and she went through the horses' entrance to the king's house, and there she was slain.

17And Jehoiada made a covenant between the Lord, the king, and the people that they would be the Lord's people—and also between the king and the people.

18Then all the people of the land went to the house of Baal and destroyed it. His altar and his images they broke completely in pieces, and Mattan the priest of Baal they slew before the altars. And [Jehoiada] the priest appointed watchmen to guard the house of the Lord.

ᵂHeb. *seed of the kingdom*   ˣ*Jehoshabeath* in 2 Chr. 22:11
ʸOr, *Jehoash*   ᶻOr, *from breaking up*   ᵃOr, *companies*
ᵇHeb. *hands*   ᶜHeb. *shoulder*   ᵈHeb. *Let the king live*
ᵉHeb. *offices*

New American Standard

Athaliah Queen of Judah

11 WHEN ATHALIAH the mother of Ahaziah saw that her son was dead, she rose and destroyed all the royal offspring.

2 But Jehosheba, the daughter of King Joram, sister of Ahaziah, took Joash the son of Ahaziah and stole him from among the king's sons who were being put to death, and placed him and his nurse in the bedroom. So they hid him from Athaliah, and he was not put to death.

3 So he was hidden with her in the house of the LORD six years, while Athaliah was reigning over the land.

4 ¶ Now in the seventh year Jehoiada sent and brought the captains of hundreds of the Carites and of the *f*guard, and brought them to him in the house of the LORD. Then he made a covenant with them and put them under oath in the house of the LORD, and showed them the king's son.

5 He commanded them, saying, "This is the thing that you shall do: one third of you, who come in on the sabbath and keep watch over the king's house

6 (one third also *shall be* at the gate Sur, and one third at the gate behind the *f*guards), shall keep watch over the house for defense.

7 "Two parts of you, *even* all who go out on the sabbath, shall also keep watch over the house of the LORD for the king.

8 "Then you shall surround the king, each with his weapons in his hand; and whoever comes within the ranks shall be put to death. And be with the king when he goes out and when he comes in."

9 ¶ So the captains of hundreds did according to all that Jehoiada the priest commanded. And each one of them took his men who were to come in on the sabbath, with those who were to go out on the sabbath, and came to Jehoiada the priest.

10 The priest gave to the captains of hundreds the spears and shields that *had been* King David's, which *were* in the house of the LORD.

11 The guards stood each with his weapons in his hand, from the right side of the house to the left side of the house, by the altar and by the house, around the king.

12 Then he brought the king's son out and put the crown on him and *gave him* the testimony; and they made him king and anointed him, and they clapped their hands and said, "*Long* live the king!"

13 ¶ When Athaliah heard the noise of the guard *and of* the people, she came to the people in the house of the LORD.

14 She looked and behold, the king was standing by the pillar, according to the custom, with the captains and the trumpeters beside the king; and all the people of the land rejoiced and blew trumpets. Then Athaliah tore her clothes and cried, "Treason! Treason!"

15 And Jehoiada the priest commanded the captains of hundreds who were appointed over the army and said to them, "Bring her out between the ranks, and whoever follows her put to death with the sword." For the priest said, "Let her not be put to death in the house of the LORD."

16 So they seized her, and when she arrived at the horses' entrance of the king's house, she was put to death there.

17 ¶ Then Jehoiada made a covenant between the LORD and the king and the people, that they would be the LORD's people, also between the king and the people.

18 All the people of the land went to the house of Baal, and tore it down; his altars and his images they broke in pieces thoroughly, and killed Mattan the priest of Baal before the altars. And the priest appointed officers over the house of the LORD.

New International

Athaliah and Joash

11 WHEN ATHALIAH the mother of Ahaziah saw that her son was dead, she proceeded to destroy the whole royal family. 2But Jehosheba, the daughter of King Jehoram[y] and sister of Ahaziah, took Joash son of Ahaziah and stole him away from among the royal princes, who were about to be murdered. She put him and his nurse in a bedroom to hide him from Athaliah; so he was not killed. 3He remained hidden with his nurse at the temple of the LORD for six years while Athaliah ruled the land.

4In the seventh year Jehoiada sent for the commanders of units of a hundred, the Carites and the guards and had them brought to him at the temple of the LORD. He made a covenant with them and put them under oath at the temple of the LORD. Then he showed them the king's son. 5He commanded them, saying, "This is what you are to do: You who are in the three companies that are going on duty on the Sabbath—a third of you guarding the royal palace, 6a third at the Sur Gate, and a third at the gate behind the guard, who take turns guarding the temple— 7and you who are in the other two companies that normally go off Sabbath duty are all to guard the temple for the king. 8Station yourselves around the king, each man with his weapon in his hand. Anyone who approaches your ranks[z] must be put to death. Stay close to the king wherever he goes."

9The commanders of units of a hundred did just as Jehoiada the priest ordered. Each one took his men—those who were going on duty on the Sabbath and those who were going off duty—and came to Jehoiada the priest. 10Then he gave the commanders the spears and shields that had belonged to King David and that were in the temple of the LORD. 11The guards, each with his weapon in his hand, stationed themselves around the king—near the altar and the temple, from the south side to the north side of the temple.

12Jehoiada brought out the king's son and put the crown on him; he presented him with a copy of the covenant and proclaimed him king. They anointed him, and the people clapped their hands and shouted, "Long live the king!"

13When Athaliah heard the noise made by the guards and the people, she went to the people at the temple of the LORD. 14She looked and there was the king, standing by the pillar, as the custom was. The officers and the trumpeters were beside the king, and all the people of the land were rejoicing and blowing trumpets. Then Athaliah tore her robes and called out, "Treason! Treason!"

15Jehoiada the priest ordered the commanders of units of a hundred, who were in charge of the troops: "Bring her out between the ranks[a] and put to the sword anyone who follows her." For the priest had said, "She must not be put to death in the temple of the LORD." 16So they seized her as she reached the place where the horses enter the palace grounds, and there she was put to death.

17Jehoiada then made a covenant between the LORD and the king and people that they would be the LORD's people. He also made a covenant between the king and the people. 18All the people of the land went to the temple of Baal and tore it down. They smashed the altars and idols to pieces and killed Mattan the priest of Baal in front of the altars.

Then Jehoiada the priest posted guards at the temple of

---

*f*Lit *runners*

y2 Hebrew *Joram,* a variant of *Jehoram*   z8 Or *approaches the precincts*   a15 Or *out from the precincts*

King James

19And he took the rulers over hundreds, and the captains, and the guard, and all the people of the land; and they brought down the king from the house of the LORD, and came by the way of the gate of the guard to the king's house. And he sat on the throne of the kings.

20And all the people of the land rejoiced, and the city was in quiet: and they slew Athaliah with the sword *beside* the king's house.

21Seven years old *was* Jehoash when he began to reign.

12 IN THE seventh year of Jehu Jehoash began to reign; and forty years reigned he in Jerusalem. And his mother's name *was* Zibiah of Beer-sheba.

2And Jehoash did *that which was* right in the sight of the LORD all his days wherein Jehoiada the priest instructed him.

3But the high places were not taken away: the people still sacrificed and burnt incense in the high places.

Jehoash repairs the temple

4 ¶ And Jehoash said to the priests, All the money of the *f* *g*dedicated things that is brought into the house of the LORD, *even* the money of every one that passeth *the account,* *h*the money that every man is set at, *and* all the money that *i*cometh into any man's heart to bring into the house of the LORD,

5Let the priests take *it* to them, every man of his acquaintance: and let them repair the breaches of the house, wheresoever any breach shall be found.

6But it was *so, that* *j*in the three and twentieth year of king Jehoash the priests had not repaired the breaches of the house.

7Then king Jehoash called for Jehoiada the priest, and the *other* priests, and said unto them, Why repair ye not the breaches of the house? now therefore receive no *more* money of your acquaintance, but deliver it for the breaches of the house.

8And the priests consented to receive no *more* money of the people, neither to repair the breaches of the house.

9But Jehoiada the priest took a chest, and bored a hole in the lid of it, and set it beside the altar, on the right side as one cometh into the house of the LORD: and the priests that kept the *k*door put therein all the money *that was* brought into the house of the LORD.

10And it was *so,* when they saw that *there was* much money in the chest, that the king's *l*scribe and the high priest came up, and they *m*put up in bags, and told the money that was found in the house of the LORD.

11And they gave the money, being told, into the hands of them that did the work, that had the oversight of the house of the LORD: and they *n*laid it out to the carpenters and builders, that wrought upon the house of the LORD,

12And to masons, and hewers of stone, and to buy timber and hewed stone to repair the breaches of the house of the LORD, and for all that *o*was laid out for the house to repair *it.*

13Howbeit there were not made for the house of the LORD bowls of silver, snuffers, basins, trumpets, any vessels of gold, or vessels of silver, of the money *that was* brought into the house of the LORD:

14But they gave that to the workmen, and repaired therewith the house of the LORD.

15Moreover they reckoned not with the men, into whose hand they delivered the money to be bestowed on workmen: for they dealt faithfully.

Amplified

19Then he took the rulers over hundreds, the captains, the guard, and all the people of the land, and they brought the king down from the house of the Lord and came by way of the guards' gate to the king's house. And [little] Joash was seated on the throne of the kings.

20So all the people of the land rejoiced, and the city was quiet after Athaliah had been slain with the sword beside the king's house.

21Joash was seven years old when he began to reign.

12 IN THE seventh year of Jehu, *d*Joash began to reign, and he reigned forty years in Jerusalem. His mother was Zibiah of Beersheba.

2Joash did right in the sight of the Lord all his days in which Jehoiada the priest instructed him.

3Yet the high places were not taken away; the people still sacrificed and burned incense in the high places.

4And Joash said to the priests, All the current money brought into the house of the Lord to provide the dedicated things, also the money [which the priests by command have] assessed on all those bound by vows, also all the money that it comes into any man's heart voluntarily to bring into the house of the Lord,

5Let the priests solicit *and* receive such contributions, every man from his acquaintance, and let them repair the Lord's house wherever any such need may be found.

6But in the twenty-third year of King Joash's reign the priests had not made the needed repairs on the Lord's house.

7Then King Joash called for Jehoiada the priest and the other priests and said to them, Why are you not repairing the [Lord's] house? Do not take any more money from your acquaintances, but turn it all over for the repair of the house. [You are no longer responsible for this work. I will take it into my own hands.]

8And the priests consented to receive no more money from the people, nor to repair the breaches of the house.

9Then Jehoiada the priest took a chest and bored a hole in the lid of it and set it beside the altar on the right side as one entered the house of the Lord; and the priests who guarded the door put in the chest all the money that was brought into the house of the Lord.

10And whenever they saw that there was much money in the chest, the king's scribe and the high priest came up and counted the money that was found in the house of the Lord and tied it up in bags.

11Then they gave the money, when it was weighed, into the hands of those who were doing the work, who had the oversight of the house of the Lord; and they paid it out to the carpenters and builders who worked on the house of the Lord

12And to the masons and stonecutters, and to buy timber and hewn stone for making the repairs on the house of the Lord, and for all that was outlay for repairing the house.

13However, there were not made for the house of the Lord basins of silver, snuffers, bowls, trumpets, any vessels of gold or of silver, from the money that was brought into the house of the Lord.

14But they gave that to the workmen, and repaired with it the house of the Lord.

15Moreover, they did not require an accounting from the men into whose hands they delivered the money to be paid to the workmen, for they dealt faithfully.

---

*f*Or, *holy things*　　*g*Heb. *holinesses*　　*h*Heb. *the money of the souls of his estimation*　　*i*Heb. *ascendeth upon the heart of a man*　　*j*Heb. *in the twentieth year and third year*　　*k*Heb. *threshold*　　*l*Or, *secretary*　　*m*Heb. *bound up*　　*n*Heb. *brought it forth*　　*o*Heb. *went forth*

*d*Judah and Israel each had a king named Joash or Jehoash, and the Hebrew uses the two forms of the name interchangeably. Since the time of their reigns overlapped, it became difficult not to confuse them. So this version will call the first one Joash, referring to the king of Judah who began his reign at seven years of age, and the other one Jehoash (as the Hebrew does in II Kings 13:10 and 14:17), referring to the king of Israel who began his reign thirty-seven years later.

New American Standard

¹⁹ He took the captains of hundreds and the Carites and the guards and all the people of the land; and they brought the king down from the house of the LORD, and came by the way of the gate of the guards to the king's house. And he sat on the throne of the kings.

²⁰ So all the people of the land rejoiced and the city was quiet. For they had put Athaliah to death with the sword at the king's house.

²¹ ¶ Jehoash was seven years old when he became king.

Joash (Jehoash) Reigns over Judah

12 IN THE seventh year of Jehu, Jehoash became king, and he reigned forty years in Jerusalem; and his mother's name was Zibiah of Beersheba.

² Jehoash did right in the sight of the LORD all his days in which Jehoiada the priest instructed him.

³ Only the high places were not taken away; the people still sacrificed and burned incense on the high places.

The Temple to Be Repaired

⁴ ¶ Then Jehoash said to the priests, "All the money of the sacred things which is brought into the house of the LORD, in current money, *both* the money of each man's assessment *and* all the money which any man's heart prompts him to bring into the house of the LORD,

⁵ let the priests take it for themselves, each from his acquaintance; and they shall repair the ^gdamages of the house wherever any damage may be found."

⁶ ¶ But it came about that in the twenty-third year of King Jehoash the priests had not repaired the damages of the house.

⁷ Then King Jehoash called for Jehoiada the priest, and for the *other* priests and said to them, "Why do you not repair the damages of the house? Now therefore take no *more* money from your acquaintances, but pay it for the damages of the house."

⁸ So the priests agreed that they would take no *more* money from the people, nor repair the damages of the house.

⁹ ¶ But Jehoiada the priest took a chest and bored a hole in its lid and put it beside the altar, on the right side as one comes into the house of the LORD; and the priests who guarded the threshold put in it all the money which was brought into the house of the LORD.

¹⁰ When they saw that there was much money in the chest, the king's scribe and the high priest came up and tied *it* in bags and counted the money which was found in the house of the LORD.

¹¹ They gave the money which was weighed out into the hands of those who did the work, who had the oversight of the house of the LORD; and they paid it out to the carpenters and the builders who worked on the house of the LORD;

¹² and to the masons and the stonecutters, and for buying timber and hewn stone to repair the damages to the house of the LORD, and for all that was laid out for the house to repair it.

¹³ But there were not made for the house of the LORD silver cups, snuffers, bowls, trumpets, any vessels of gold, or vessels of silver from the money which was brought into the house of the LORD;

¹⁴ for they gave that to those who did the work, and with it they repaired the house of the LORD.

¹⁵ Moreover, they did not require an accounting from the men into whose hand they gave the money to pay to those who did the work, for they dealt faithfully.

New International

the LORD. ¹⁹He took with him the commanders of hundreds, the Carites, the guards and all the people of the land, and together they brought the king down from the temple of the LORD and went into the palace, entering by way of the gate of the guards. The king then took his place on the royal throne, ²⁰and all the people of the land rejoiced. And the city was quiet, because Athaliah had been slain with the sword at the palace.

²¹Joash^b was seven years old when he began to reign.

Joash Repairs the Temple

12 IN THE seventh year of Jehu, Joash^c became king, and he reigned in Jerusalem forty years. His mother's name was Zibiah; she was from Beersheba. ²Joash did what was right in the eyes of the LORD all the years Jehoiada the priest instructed him. ³The high places, however, were not removed; the people continued to offer sacrifices and burn incense there.

⁴Joash said to the priests, "Collect all the money that is brought as sacred offerings to the temple of the LORD—the money collected in the census, the money received from personal vows and the money brought voluntarily to the temple. ⁵Let every priest receive the money from one of the treasurers, and let it be used to repair whatever damage is found in the temple."

⁶But by the twenty-third year of King Joash the priests still had not repaired the temple. ⁷Therefore King Joash summoned Jehoiada the priest and the other priests and asked them, "Why aren't you repairing the damage done to the temple? Take no more money from your treasurers, but hand it over for repairing the temple." ⁸The priests agreed that they would not collect any more money from the people and that they would not repair the temple themselves.

⁹Jehoiada the priest took a chest and bored a hole in its lid. He placed it beside the altar, on the right side as one enters the temple of the LORD. The priests who guarded the entrance put into the chest all the money that was brought to the temple of the LORD. ¹⁰Whenever they saw that there was a large amount of money in the chest, the royal secretary and the high priest came, counted the money that had been brought into the temple of the LORD and put it into bags. ¹¹When the amount had been determined, they gave the money to the men appointed to supervise the work on the temple. With it they paid those who worked on the temple of the LORD—the carpenters and builders, ¹²the masons and stonecutters. They purchased timber and dressed stone for the repair of the temple of the LORD, and met all the other expenses of restoring the temple.

¹³The money brought into the temple was not spent for making silver basins, wick trimmers, sprinkling bowls, trumpets or any other articles of gold or silver for the temple of the LORD; ¹⁴it was paid to the workmen, who used it to repair the temple. ¹⁵They did not require an accounting from those to whom they gave the money to pay the workers, because they acted with complete hones-

---

^gLit *breaches*, and so through v 12   ^b21 Hebrew *Jehoash*, a variant of *Joash*   ^c1 Hebrew *Jehoash*, a variant of *Joash*; also in verses 2, 4, 6, 7 and 18

King James

[16]The trespass money and sin money was not brought into the house of the LORD: it was the priests'.

[17] ¶ Then Hazael king of Syria went up, and fought against Gath, and took it: and Hazael set his face to go up to Jerusalem.

[18]And Jehoash king of Judah took all the hallowed things that Jehoshaphat, and Jehoram, and Ahaziah, his fathers, kings of Judah, had dedicated, and his own hallowed things, and all the gold *that was* found in the treasures of the house of the LORD, and in the king's house, and sent *it* to Hazael king of Syria: and he [p]went away from Jerusalem.

[19] ¶ And the rest of the acts of Joash, and all that he did, *are* they not written in the book of the chronicles of the kings of Judah?

[20]And his servants arose, and made a conspiracy, and slew Joash in the [q]house of Millo, which goeth down to Silla.

[21]For Jozabad the son of Shimeath, and Jehozabad the son of [r]Shomer, his servants, smote him, and he died; and they buried him with his fathers in the city of David: and Amaziah his son reigned in his stead.

Jehoahaz, king of Israel

13 IN [s]THE three and twentieth year of Joash the son of Ahaziah king of Judah Jehoahaz the son of Jehu began to reign over Israel in Samaria, *and reigned* seventeen years.

[2]And he did *that which was* evil in the sight of the LORD, and [t]followed the sins of Jeroboam the son of Nebat, which made Israel to sin; he departed not therefrom.

[3] ¶ And the anger of the LORD was kindled against Israel, and he delivered them into the hand of Hazael king of Syria, and into the hand of Ben-hadad the son of Hazael, all *their* days.

[4]And Jehoahaz besought the LORD, and the LORD hearkened unto him: for he saw the oppression of Israel, because the king of Syria oppressed them.

[5](And the LORD gave Israel a saviour, so that they went out from under the hand of the Syrians: and the children of Israel dwelt in their tents, [u]as beforetime.

[6]Nevertheless they departed not from the sins of the house of Jeroboam, who made Israel sin, *but* [v]walked therein: and there [w]remained the grove also in Samaria.)

[7]Neither did he leave of the people to Jehoahaz but fifty horsemen, and ten chariots, and ten thousand footmen; for the king of Syria had destroyed them, and had made them like the dust by threshing.

[8] ¶ Now the rest of the acts of Jehoahaz, and all that he did, and his might, *are* they not written in the book of the chronicles of the kings of Israel?

[9]And Jehoahaz slept with his fathers; and they buried him in Samaria: and [x]Joash his son reigned [y]in his stead.

Jehoash, king of Israel

[10] ¶ In the thirty and seventh year of Joash king of Judah began [z]Jehoash the son of Jehoahaz to reign over Israel in Samaria, *and reigned* sixteen years.

[11]And he did *that which was* evil in the sight of the LORD; he departed not from all the sins of Jeroboam the son of Nebat, who made Israel sin: *but* he walked therein.

[12]And the rest of the acts of Joash, and all that he did, and his might wherewith he fought against Amaziah king of Judah, *are* they not written in the book of the chronicles of the kings of Israel?

Amplified

[16]The money from the guilt offerings and sin offerings was not brought into the house of the Lord; it was the priests'.

[17]Then Hazael king of Syria went up, fought against Gath [in Philistia], and took it. And Hazael set his face to go up to Jerusalem.

[18]And Joash king of Judah took all the hallowed things that Jehoshaphat, Jehoram, and Ahaziah, his [forefathers], kings of Judah, had dedicated and his own hallowed things and all the gold that was found in the treasuries of the house of the Lord and in the king's house, and sent them to Hazael king of Syria; and Hazael went away from Jerusalem.

[19]The rest of the acts of Joash, and all that he did, are they not written in the Book of the Chronicles of the Kings of Judah?

[20]His servants arose and made a conspiracy and slew Joash [in revenge] in the house of Millo, on the way that goes down to Silla. [II Chron. 24:22–25.]

[21]It was Jozachar son of Shimeath and Jehozabad son of Shomer, his servants, who smote him so that he died. They buried [Joash] with his fathers in the City of David. Amaziah his son reigned in his stead.

13 IN THE twenty-third year of Joash son of Ahaziah king of Judah, Jehoahaz son of Jehu began to reign over Israel in Samaria, and reigned seventeen years.

[2]He did evil in the sight of the Lord and followed the sins of Jeroboam son of Nebat, which made Israel to sin, and did not depart from them.

[3]The anger of the Lord was kindled against Israel, and He delivered them into the hand of Hazael king of Syria and of Ben-hadad son of Hazael continually.

[4]But Jehoahaz besought the Lord, and the Lord hearkened to him, for He saw the oppression of Israel, how the king of Syria burdened them.

[5]Then the Lord gave Israel a savior [one to rescue and give them peace], so that they escaped from under the hand of the Syrians; and the Israelites dwelt in their tents *or* homes as before.

[6]Yet they did not depart from the sins of the house of Jeroboam, who made Israel sin; but the nation walked in them. And the Asherah [symbol of the goddess Asherah] remained in Samaria.

[7][Ben-hadad] of Syria did not leave to Jehoahaz of [Israel] an army of more than fifty horsemen, ten chariots, and 10,000 footmen, for the Syrian king had destroyed them and made them like dust to be trampled.

[8]The rest of the acts of Jehoahaz, all that he did and his might, are they not written in the Book of the Chronicles of the Kings of Israel?

[9]Jehoahaz slept with his fathers, and they buried him in Samaria. [e]Jehoash his son reigned in his stead.

[10]In the thirty-seventh year of Joash king of Judah, Jehoash son of Jehoahaz began to reign over Israel in Samaria, and reigned sixteen years.

[11]He did evil in the sight of the Lord; he departed not from all the sins of Jeroboam son of Nebat, who made Israel sin; he walked in them.

[12]The rest of the acts of Jehoash, all that he did, and his might with which he fought against Amaziah king of Judah, are they not written in the Book of the Chronicles of the Kings of Israel?

---

[p]Heb. *went up*   [q]Or, *Beth-millo*   [r]Or, *Shimrith*   [s]Heb. *the twentieth year and third year*   [t]Heb. *walked after*   [u]Heb. *as yesterday,* and *third day*   [v]Heb. *he walked*   [w]Heb. *stood*   [x]*Jehoash* in ver. 10   [y]Alone   [z]In consort with his father; see ch. 14:1

[e]See footnote on II Kings 12:1.

New American Standard

16 The money from the guilt offerings and the money from the sin offerings was not brought into the house of the LORD; it was for the priests.

17 ¶ Then Hazael king of Aram went up and fought against Gath and captured it, and Hazael set his face to go up to Jerusalem.

18 Jehoash king of Judah took all the sacred things that Jehoshaphat and Jehoram and Ahaziah, his fathers, kings of Judah, had dedicated, and his own sacred things and all the gold that was found among the treasuries of the house of the LORD and of the king's house, and sent *them* to Hazael king of Aram. Then he went away from Jerusalem.

Joash (Jehoash) Succeeded by Amaziah in Judah

19 ¶ Now the rest of the acts of Joash and all that he did, are they not written in the Book of the Chronicles of the Kings of Judah?

20 His servants arose and made a conspiracy and struck down Joash at the house of Millo *as he was* going down to Silla.

21 For Jozacar the son of Shimeath and Jehozabad the son of Shomer, his servants, struck *him* and he died; and they buried him with his fathers in the city of David, and Amaziah his son became king in his place.

Kings of Israel: Jehoahaz and Jehoash

13 IN THE twenty-third year of Joash the son of Ahaziah, king of Judah, Jehoahaz the son of Jehu became king over Israel at Samaria, *and he reigned* seventeen years.

2 He did evil in the sight of the LORD, and followed the sins of Jeroboam the son of Nebat, with which he made Israel sin; he did not turn from them.

3 So the anger of the LORD was kindled against Israel, and He gave them continually into the hand of Hazael king of Aram, and into the hand of Ben-hadad the son of Hazael.

4 Then Jehoahaz entreated the favor of the LORD, and the LORD listened to him; for He saw the oppression of Israel, how the king of Aram oppressed them.

5 The LORD gave Israel a ^h deliverer, so that they escaped from under the hand of the Arameans; and the sons of Israel lived in their tents as formerly.

6 Nevertheless they did not turn away from the sins of the house of Jeroboam, with which he made Israel sin, but walked in them; and the Asherah also remained standing in Samaria.

7 For he left to Jehoahaz of the army not more than fifty horsemen and ten chariots and 10,000 footmen, for the king of Aram had destroyed them and made them like the dust at threshing.

8 Now the rest of the acts of Jehoahaz, and all that he did and his might, are they not written in the Book of the Chronicles of the Kings of Israel?

9 And Jehoahaz slept with his fathers, and they buried him in Samaria; and Joash his son became king in his place.

10 ¶ In the thirty-seventh year of Joash king of Judah, Jehoash the son of Jehoahaz became king over Israel in Samaria, *and reigned* sixteen years.

11 He did evil in the sight of the LORD; he did not turn away from all the sins of Jeroboam the son of Nebat, with which he made Israel sin, but he walked in them.

12 Now the rest of the acts of Joash and all that he did and his might with which he fought against Amaziah king of Judah, are they not written in the Book of the Chronicles of the Kings of Israel?

New International

ty. 16 The money from the guilt offerings and sin offerings was not brought into the temple of the LORD; it belonged to the priests.

17 About this time Hazael king of Aram went up and attacked Gath and captured it. Then he turned to attack Jerusalem. 18 But Joash king of Judah took all the sacred objects dedicated by his fathers—Jehoshaphat, Jehoram and Ahaziah, the kings of Judah—and the gifts he himself had dedicated and all the gold found in the treasuries of the temple of the LORD and of the royal palace, and he sent them to Hazael king of Aram, who then withdrew from Jerusalem.

19 As for the other events of the reign of Joash, and all he did, are they not written in the book of the annals of the kings of Judah? 20 His officials conspired against him and assassinated him at Beth Millo, on the road down to Silla. 21 The officials who murdered him were Jozabad son of Shimeath and Jehozabad son of Shomer. He died and was buried with his fathers in the City of David. And Amaziah his son succeeded him as king.

Jehoahaz King of Israel

13 IN THE twenty-third year of Joash son of Ahaziah king of Judah, Jehoahaz son of Jehu became king of Israel in Samaria, and he reigned seventeen years. 2 He did evil in the eyes of the LORD by following the sins of Jeroboam son of Nebat, which he had caused Israel to commit, and he did not turn away from them. 3 So the LORD's anger burned against Israel, and for a long time he kept them under the power of Hazael king of Aram and Ben-Hadad his son.

4 Then Jehoahaz sought the LORD's favor, and the LORD listened to him, for he saw how severely the king of Aram was oppressing Israel. 5 The LORD provided a deliverer for Israel, and they escaped from the power of Aram. So the Israelites lived in their own homes as they had before. 6 But they did not turn away from the sins of the house of Jeroboam, which he had caused Israel to commit; they continued in them. Also, the Asherah pole^d remained standing in Samaria.

7 Nothing had been left of the army of Jehoahaz except fifty horsemen, ten chariots and ten thousand foot soldiers, for the king of Aram had destroyed the rest and made them like the dust at threshing time.

8 As for the other events of the reign of Jehoahaz, all he did and his achievements, are they not written in the book of the annals of the kings of Israel? 9 Jehoahaz rested with his fathers and was buried in Samaria. And Jehoash^e his son succeeded him as king.

Jehoash King of Israel

10 In the thirty-seventh year of Joash king of Judah, Jehoash son of Jehoahaz became king of Israel in Samaria, and he reigned sixteen years. 11 He did evil in the eyes of the LORD and did not turn away from any of the sins of Jeroboam son of Nebat, which he had caused Israel to commit; he continued in them.

12 As for the other events of the reign of Jehoash, all he did and his achievements, including his war against Amaziah king of Judah, are they not written in the book of the

---

^h Or savior

^d 6 That is, a symbol of the goddess Asherah; here and elsewhere in 2 Kings   ^e 9 Hebrew *Joash*, a variant of *Jehoash*; also in verses 12-14 and 25

King James

13And Joash slept with his fathers; and Jeroboam sat upon his throne: and Joash was buried in Samaria with the kings of Israel.

The death of Elisha

14 ¶ Now Elisha was fallen sick of his sickness whereof he died. And Joash the king of Israel came down unto him, and wept over his face, and said, O my father, my father, the chariot of Israel, and the horsemen thereof.

15And Elisha said unto him, Take bow and arrows. And he took unto him bow and arrows.

16And he said to the king of Israel, *a*Put thine hand upon the bow. And he put his hand *upon it:* and Elisha put his hands upon the king's hands.

17And he said, Open the window eastward. And he opened *it.* Then Elisha said, Shoot. And he shot. And he said, The arrow of the LORD'S deliverance, and the arrow of deliverance from Syria: for thou shalt smite the Syrians in Aphek, till thou have consumed *them.*

18And he said, Take the arrows. And he took *them.* And he said unto the king of Israel, Smite upon the ground. And he smote thrice, and stayed.

19And the man of God was wroth with him, and said, Thou shouldest have smitten five or six times; then hadst thou smitten Syria till thou hadst consumed *it:* whereas now thou shalt smite Syria *but* thrice.

20 ¶ And Elisha died, and they buried him. And the bands of the Moabites invaded the land at the coming in of the year.

21And it came to pass, as they were burying a man, that, behold, they spied a band *of men;* and they cast the man into the sepulchre of Elisha: and when the man *b*was let down, and touched the bones of Elisha, he revived, and stood up on his feet.

22 ¶ But Hazael king of Syria oppressed Israel all the days of Jehoahaz.

23And the LORD was gracious unto them, and had compassion on them, and had respect unto them, because of his covenant with Abraham, Isaac, and Jacob, and would not destroy them, neither cast he them from his *c*presence as yet.

24So Hazael king of Syria died; and Ben-hadad his son reigned in his stead.

25And Jehoash the son of Jehoahaz *d*took again out of the hand of Ben-hadad the son of Hazael the cities, which he had taken out of the hand of Jehoahaz his father by war. Three times did Joash beat him, and recovered the cities of Israel.

Amaziah, king of Judah

14 IN THE second year of Joash son of Jehoahaz king of Israel reigned Amaziah the son of Joash king of Judah.

2He was twenty and five years old when he began to reign, and reigned twenty and nine years in Jerusalem. And his mother's name *was* Jehoaddan of Jerusalem.

3And he did *that which was* right in the sight of the LORD, yet not like David his father: he did according to all things as Joash his father did.

4Howbeit the high places were not taken away: as yet the people did sacrifice and burnt incense on the high places.

5 ¶ And it came to pass, as soon as the kingdom was confirmed in his hand, that he slew his servants which had slain the king his father.

6But the children of the murderers he slew not: according unto that which is written in the book of the law of Moses, wherein the LORD commanded, saying, The fathers shall not be put to death for the children, nor the children be put to death for the fathers; but every man shall be put to death for his own sin.

Amplified

13Jehoash slept with his fathers, and Jeroboam [II] sat on his throne. Jehoash was buried in Samaria with the kings of Israel.

14Now Elisha [previously] had become ill of the illness of which he died. And Jehoash king of Israel came down to him and wept over him and said, O my father, my father, the chariot of Israel and the horsemen of it! [II Kings 2:12.]

15And Elisha said to him, Take bow and arrows. And he took bow and arrows.

16And he said to the king of Israel, Put your hand upon the bow. And he put his hand upon it, and Elisha put his hands upon the king's hands.

17And he said, Open the window to the east. And he opened it. Then Elisha said, Shoot. And he shot. And he said, The Lord's arrow of victory, the arrow of victory over Syria. For you shall smite the Syrians in Aphek till you have destroyed them.

18Then he said, Take the arrows. And he took them. And he said to the king of Israel, Strike on the ground. And he struck three times and stopped.

19And the man of God was angry with him and said, You should have struck five or six times; then you would have struck down Syria until you had destroyed it. But now you shall strike Syria down only three times.

20Elisha died, and they buried him. Bands of the Moabites invaded the land in the spring of the next year.

21As a man was being buried [on an open bier], such a band was seen coming; and the man was cast into Elisha's grave. And when the man being let down touched the bones of Elisha, he revived and stood on his feet.

22Hazael king of Syria oppressed Israel all the days of Jehoahaz.

23But the Lord was gracious to them and had compassion on them and turned toward them because of *f*His covenant with Abraham, Isaac, and Jacob, and would not destroy them or cast them from His presence yet. [Mal. 3:6.]

24Hazael king of Syria died; Ben-hadad his son reigned in his stead.

25Jehoash son of Jehoahaz recovered from Ben-hadad son of Hazael the cities which he had taken from Jehoahaz his father by war. Three times Jehoash defeated him, and recovered the cities of Israel. [II Kings 13:19.]

14 IN THE second year of Jehoash son of Jehoahaz king of Israel, Amaziah son of Joash king of Judah reigned.

2He was twenty-five years old when he began his twenty-nine-year reign in Jerusalem. His mother was Jehoaddin of Jerusalem.

3He did right in the sight of the Lord, yet not like David his [forefather]. He did all things as Joash his father did.

4But the high places were not removed; the people still sacrificed and burned incense on the high places.

5As soon as the kingdom was established in Amaziah's hand, he slew his servants who had slain the king his father. [II Kings 12:20.]

6But he did not slay the children of the murderers, in compliance with what is written in the Book of the Law of Moses, in which the Lord commanded, The fathers shall not be put to death for the children, nor the children for the fathers; but every man shall die for his own sin only.

---

a Heb. *Make thine hand to ride*   *b* Heb. *went down*   *c* Heb. *face*   *d* Heb. *returned and took*

f Abraham, Isaac, and Jacob had been dead a thousand years, yet God's covenant with them was undiminishingly effective.

New American Standard

13 So Joash slept with his fathers, and Jeroboam sat on his throne; and Joash was buried in Samaria with the kings of Israel.

Death of Elisha

14 ¶ When Elisha became sick with the illness of which he was to die, Joash the king of Israel came down to him and wept over him and said, "My father, my father, the chariots of Israel and its horsemen!"
15 Elisha said to him, "Take a bow and arrows." So he took a bow and arrows.
16 Then he said to the king of Israel, "Put your hand on the bow." And he put his hand *on it,* then Elisha laid his hands on the king's hands.
17 He said, "Open the window toward the east," and he opened *it.* Then Elisha said, "Shoot!" And he shot. And he said, "The LORD'S arrow of victory, even the arrow of victory over Aram; for you will defeat the Arameans at Aphek until you shall have destroyed *them.*"
18 Then he said, "Take the arrows," and he took them. And he said to the king of Israel, "Strike the ground," and he struck *it* three times and stopped.
19 So the man of God was angry with him and said, "You should have struck five or six times, then you would have struck Aram until you would have destroyed *it.* But now you shall strike Aram *only* three times."
20 ¶ Elisha died, and they buried him. Now the bands of the Moabites would invade the land in the spring of the year.
21 As they were burying a man, behold, they saw a marauding band; and they cast the man into the grave of Elisha. And when the man touched the bones of Elisha he revived and stood up on his feet.
22 ¶ Now Hazael king of Aram had oppressed Israel all the days of Jehoahaz.
23 But the LORD was gracious to them and had compassion on them and turned to them because of His covenant with Abraham, Isaac, and Jacob, and would not destroy them or cast them from His presence until now.
24 ¶ When Hazael king of Aram died, Ben-hadad his son became king in his place.
25 Then Jehoash the son of Jehoahaz took again from the hand of Ben-hadad the son of Hazael the cities which he had taken in war from the hand of Jehoahaz his father. Three times Joash defeated him and recovered the cities of Israel.

Amaziah Reigns over Judah

14 IN THE second year of Joash son of Joahaz king of Israel, Amaziah the son of Joash king of Judah became king.
2 He was twenty-five years old when he became king, and he reigned twenty-nine years in Jerusalem. And his mother's name was Jehoaddin of Jerusalem.
3 He did right in the sight of the LORD, yet not like David his father; he did according to all that Joash his father had done.
4 Only the high places were not taken away; the people still sacrificed and burned incense on the high places.
5 Now it came about, as soon as the kingdom was firmly in his hand, that he killed his servants who had slain the king his father.
6 But the sons of the slayers he did not put to death, according to what is written in the book of the Law of Moses, as the LORD commanded, saying, "The fathers shall not be put to death for the sons, nor the sons be put to death for the fathers; but each shall be put to death for his own sin."

New International

annals of the kings of Israel? 13Jehoash rested with his fathers, and Jeroboam succeeded him on the throne. Jehoash was buried in Samaria with the kings of Israel.
14Now Elisha was suffering from the illness from which he died. Jehoash king of Israel went down to see him and wept over him. "My father! My father!" he cried. "The chariots and horsemen of Israel!"
15Elisha said, "Get a bow and some arrows," and he did so. 16"Take the bow in your hands," he said to the king of Israel. When he had taken it, Elisha put his hands on the king's hands.
17"Open the east window," he said, and he opened it. "Shoot!" Elisha said, and he shot. "The LORD's arrow of victory, the arrow of victory over Aram!" Elisha declared. "You will completely destroy the Arameans at Aphek."
18Then he said, "Take the arrows," and the king took them. Elisha told him, "Strike the ground." He struck it three times and stopped. 19The man of God was angry with him and said, "You should have struck the ground five or six times; then you would have defeated Aram and completely destroyed it. But now you will defeat it only three times."
20Elisha died and was buried.
Now Moabite raiders used to enter the country every spring. 21Once while some Israelites were burying a man, suddenly they saw a band of raiders; so they threw the man's body into Elisha's tomb. When the body touched Elisha's bones, the man came to life and stood up on his feet.
22Hazael king of Aram oppressed Israel throughout the reign of Jehoahaz. 23But the LORD was gracious to them and had compassion and showed concern for them because of his covenant with Abraham, Isaac and Jacob. To this day he has been unwilling to destroy them or banish them from his presence.
24Hazael king of Aram died, and Ben-Hadad his son succeeded him as king. 25Then Jehoash son of Jehoahaz recaptured from Ben-Hadad son of Hazael the towns he had taken in battle from his father Jehoahaz. Three times Jehoash defeated him, and so he recovered the Israelite towns.

Amaziah King of Judah

14 IN THE second year of Jehoash*ᶠ* son of Jehoahaz king of Israel, Amaziah son of Joash king of Judah began to reign. 2He was twenty-five years old when he became king, and he reigned in Jerusalem twenty-nine years. His mother's name was Jehoaddin; she was from Jerusalem. 3He did what was right in the eyes of the LORD, but not as his father David had done. In everything he followed the example of his father Joash. 4The high places, however, were not removed; the people continued to offer sacrifices and burn incense there.
5After the kingdom was firmly in his grasp, he executed the officials who had murdered his father the king. 6Yet he did not put the sons of the assassins to death, in accordance with what is written in the Book of the Law of Moses where the LORD commanded: "Fathers shall not be put to death for their children, nor children put to death for their fathers; each is to die for his own sins."*ᵍ*

ƒ 1 Hebrew *Joash,* a variant of *Jehoash*; also in verses 13, 23 and 27
ᵍ 6 Deut. 24:16

King James

7He slew of Edom in the valley of salt ten thousand, and took *e*Selah by war, and called the name of it Joktheel unto this day.

8 ¶ Then Amaziah sent messengers to Jehoash, the son of Jehoahaz son of Jehu, king of Israel, saying, Come, let us look one another in the face.

9And Jehoash the king of Israel sent to Amaziah king of Judah, saying, The thistle that *was* in Lebanon sent to the cedar that *was* in Lebanon, saying, Give thy daughter to my son to wife: and there passed by a wild beast that *was* in Lebanon, and trode down the thistle.

10Thou hast indeed smitten Edom, and thine heart hath lifted thee up: glory *of this*, and tarry *f*at home: for why shouldest thou meddle to *thy* hurt, that thou shouldest fall, *even* thou, and Judah with thee?

11But Amaziah would not hear. Therefore Jehoash king of Israel went up; and he and Amaziah king of Judah looked one another in the face at Beth-shemesh, which *belongeth* to Judah.

12And Judah *g*was put to the worse before Israel; and they fled every man to their tents.

13And Jehoash king of Israel took Amaziah king of Judah, the son of Jehoash the son of Ahaziah, at Beth-shemesh, and came to Jerusalem, and brake down the wall of Jerusalem from the gate of Ephraim unto the corner gate, four hundred cubits.

14And he took all the gold and silver, and all the vessels that were found in the house of the LORD, and in the treasures of the king's house, and hostages, and returned to Samaria.

15 ¶ Now the rest of the acts of Jehoash which he did, and his might, and how he fought with Amaziah king of Judah, *are* they not written in the book of the chronicles of the kings of Israel?

16And Jehoash slept with his fathers, and was buried in Samaria with the kings of Israel; and Jeroboam his son reigned in his stead.

17 ¶ And Amaziah the son of Joash king of Judah lived after the death of Jehoash son of Jehoahaz king of Israel fifteen years.

18And the rest of the acts of Amaziah, *are* they not written in the book of the chronicles of the kings of Judah?

19Now they made a conspiracy against him in Jerusalem: and he fled to Lachish; but they sent after him to Lachish, and slew him there.

20And they brought him on horses: and he was buried at Jerusalem with his fathers in the city of David.

21 ¶ And all the people of Judah took Azariah, which *was* sixteen years old, and made him king instead of his father Amaziah.

22He built Elath, and restored it to Judah, after that the king slept with his fathers.

Jeroboam II, king of Israel

23 ¶ In the fifteenth year of Amaziah the son of Joash king of Judah Jeroboam the son of Joash king of Israel began to reign in Samaria, *and reigned* forty and one years,

24And he did *that which was* evil in the sight of the LORD: he departed not from all the sins of Jeroboam the son of Nebat, who made Israel to sin.

25He restored the coast of Israel from the entering of Hamath unto the sea of the plain, according to the word of the LORD God of Israel, which he spake by the hand of his servant Jonah, the son of Amittai, the prophet, which *was* of Gath-hepher.

26For the LORD saw the affliction of Israel, *that it was* very bitter: for *there was* not any shut up, nor any left, nor any helper for Israel.

27And the LORD said not that he would blot out the name of Israel from under heaven: but he saved them by the hand of Jeroboam the son of Joash.

Amplified

7Amaziah slew of Edom in the Valley of Salt 10,000, and took Sela (Greek *petra* [rock]) by war, and called it Joktheel, which is the name of it to this day.

8Then Amaziah sent messengers to Jehoash son of Jehoahaz, the son of Jehu, king of Israel, saying, Come, let us look one another in the face *and* test each other.

9Jehoash king of Israel replied to Amaziah king of Judah, The thistle in Lebanon sent to the cedar in Lebanon, saying, Give your daughter to my son as wife. And a wild beast of Lebanon passed by and trampled the thistle [leaving the cedar unharmed].

10You have indeed smitten Edom, and your heart has lifted you up. Glory in that, and stay at home; for why should you meddle to your hurt *and* provoke calamity, causing you to fall, you and Judah with you?

11But Amaziah would not hear. So Jehoash king of Israel went up; and he and Amaziah king of Judah measured swords at Beth-shemesh, which belongs to Judah.

12But Judah was defeated by Israel, and every man fled home.

13And Jehoash king of Israel captured Amaziah king of Judah, son of Joash, the son of Ahaziah, at Beth-shemesh, and came to Jerusalem and broke down the wall of Jerusalem from the Ephraim Gate to the Corner Gate, 400 cubits.

14He seized all the gold and silver and all the vessels found in the Lord's house and in the treasuries of the king's house, also hostages, and returned to Samaria.

15The rest of the acts of Jehoash, his might, and how he fought with Amaziah king of Judah, are they not written in the Book of the Chronicles of Israel's Kings?

16Jehoash slept with his fathers, and was buried in Samaria with Israel's kings. Jeroboam [II] reigned in his stead.

17Amaziah son of Joash king of Judah lived after the death of Jehoash son of Jehoahaz king of Israel fifteen years.

18The rest of the acts of Amaziah, are they not written in the Book of the Chronicles of the Kings of Judah?

19Now a conspiracy was made against him in Jerusalem, and Amaziah fled to Lachish; but they sent after him to Lachish and slew him there.

20They brought him on horses and he was buried at Jerusalem with his fathers in the City of David.

21And all the people of Judah took Azariah, sixteen years old, and made him king instead of his father Amaziah.

22He built Elath and restored it to Judah after the king [his father] died.

23In the fifteenth year of Amaziah son of Joash king of Judah Jeroboam [II] son of Jehoash king of Israel began to reign in Samaria, and reigned forty-one years.

24He did evil in the sight of the Lord; he did not depart from all the sins of Jeroboam [I] son of Nebat, with which he made Israel to sin.

25Jeroboam restored Israel's border from the entrance of Hamath to the [Dead] Sea of the Arabah, according to the word of the Lord, the God of Israel, which He spoke through His servant Jonah son of Amittai, the prophet from Gath-hepher.

26For the Lord saw as very bitter the affliction of Israel; there was no one left, bond or free, nor any helper for Israel.

27But the Lord had not said that He would blot out the name of Israel from under the heavens, so He saved them by the hand of Jeroboam [II] son of Jehoash.

---

e Or, The rock   *f* Heb. *at thy house*   *g* Heb. *was smitten*

New American Standard

7 ¶ He killed *of* Edom in the Valley of Salt 10,000 and took Sela by war, and named it Joktheel to this day.

8 ¶ Then Amaziah sent messengers to Jehoash, the son of Jehoahaz son of Jehu, king of Israel, saying, "Come, let us face each other."

9 Jehoash king of Israel sent to Amaziah king of Judah, saying, "The thorn bush which was in Lebanon sent to the cedar which was in Lebanon, saying, 'Give your daughter to my son in marriage.' But there passed by a wild beast that was in Lebanon, and trampled the thorn bush.

10 "You have indeed defeated Edom, and your heart has become proud. Enjoy your glory and stay at home; for why should you provoke trouble so that you, even you, would fall, and Judah with you?"

11 ¶ But Amaziah would not listen. So Jehoash king of Israel went up; and he and Amaziah king of Judah faced each other at Beth-shemesh, which belongs to Judah.

12 Judah was defeated by Israel, and they fled each to his tent.

13 Then Jehoash king of Israel captured Amaziah king of Judah, the son of Jehoash the son of Ahaziah, at Beth-shemesh, and came to Jerusalem and tore down the wall of Jerusalem from the Gate of Ephraim to the Corner Gate, 400 cubits.

14 He took all the gold and silver and all the utensils which were found in the house of the LORD, and in the treasuries of the king's house, the hostages also, and re-turned to Samaria.

Jeroboam II Succeeds Jehoash in Israel

15 ¶ Now the rest of the acts of Jehoash which he did, and his might and how he fought with Amaziah king of Judah, are they not written in the Book of the Chronicles of the Kings of Israel?

16 So Jehoash slept with his fathers and was buried in Samaria with the kings of Israel; and Jeroboam his son became king in his place.

Azariah (Uzziah) Succeeds Amaziah in Judah

17 ¶ Amaziah the son of Joash king of Judah lived fifteen years after the death of Jehoash son of Jehoahaz king of Israel.

18 Now the rest of the acts of Amaziah, are they not written in the Book of the Chronicles of the Kings of Judah?

19 They conspired against him in Jerusalem, and he fled to Lachish; but they sent after him to Lachish and killed him there.

20 Then they brought him on horses and he was buried at Jerusalem with his fathers in the city of David.

21 All the people of Judah took Azariah, who *was* sixteen years old, and made him king in the place of his father Amaziah.

22 He built Elath and restored it to Judah after the king slept with his fathers.

23 ¶ In the fifteenth year of Amaziah the son of Joash king of Judah, Jeroboam the son of Joash king of Israel became king in Samaria, *and reigned* forty-one years.

24 He did evil in the sight of the LORD; he did not depart from all the sins of Jeroboam the son of Nebat, which he made Israel sin.

25 He restored the border of Israel from the entrance of Hamath as far as the Sea of the Arabah, according to the word of the LORD, the God of Israel, which He spoke through His servant Jonah the son of Amittai, the prophet, who was of Gath-hepher.

26 For the LORD saw the affliction of Israel, *which was* very bitter; for there was neither bond nor free, nor was there any helper for Israel.

27 The LORD did not say that He would blot out the name of Israel from under heaven, but He saved them by the hand of Jeroboam the son of Joash.

New International

7 He was the one who defeated ten thousand Edomites in the Valley of Salt and captured Sela in battle, calling it Joktheel, the name it has to this day.

8 Then Amaziah sent messengers to Jehoash son of Jehoahaz, the son of Jehu, king of Israel, with the challenge: "Come, meet me face to face."

9 But Jehoash king of Israel replied to Amaziah king of Judah: "A thistle in Lebanon sent a message to a cedar in Lebanon, 'Give your daughter to my son in marriage.' Then a wild beast in Lebanon came along and trampled the thistle underfoot. 10 You have indeed defeated Edom and now you are arrogant. Glory in your victory, but stay at home! Why ask for trouble and cause your own downfall and that of Judah also?"

11 Amaziah, however, would not listen, so Jehoash king of Israel attacked. He and Amaziah king of Judah faced each other at Beth Shemesh in Judah. 12 Judah was routed by Israel, and every man fled to his home. 13 Jehoash king of Israel captured Amaziah king of Judah, the son of Joash, the son of Ahaziah, at Beth Shemesh. Then Jehoash went to Jerusalem and broke down the wall of Jerusalem from the Ephraim Gate to the Corner Gate—a section about six hundred feet long.[h] 14 He took all the gold and silver and all the articles found in the temple of the LORD and in the treasuries of the royal palace. He also took hostages and returned to Samaria.

15 As for the other events of the reign of Jehoash, what he did and his achievements, including his war against Amaziah king of Judah, are they not written in the book of the annals of the kings of Israel? 16 Jehoash rested with his fathers and was buried in Samaria with the kings of Israel. And Jeroboam his son succeeded him as king.

17 Amaziah son of Joash king of Judah lived for fifteen years after the death of Jehoash son of Jehoahaz king of Israel. 18 As for the other events of Amaziah's reign, are they not written in the book of the annals of the kings of Judah?

19 They conspired against him in Jerusalem, and he fled to Lachish, but they sent men after him to Lachish and killed him there. 20 He was brought back by horse and was buried in Jerusalem with his fathers, in the City of David.

21 Then all the people of Judah took Azariah,[i] who was sixteen years old, and made him king in place of his father Amaziah. 22 He was the one who rebuilt Elath and restored it to Judah after Amaziah rested with his fathers.

Jeroboam II King of Israel

23 In the fifteenth year of Amaziah son of Joash king of Judah, Jeroboam son of Jehoash king of Israel became king in Samaria, and he reigned forty-one years. 24 He did evil in the eyes of the LORD and did not turn away from any of the sins of Jeroboam son of Nebat, which he had caused Israel to commit. 25 He was the one who restored the boundaries of Israel from Lebo[j] Hamath to the Sea of the Arabah,[k] in accordance with the word of the LORD, the God of Israel, spoken through his servant Jonah son of Amittai, the prophet from Gath Hepher.

26 The LORD had seen how bitterly everyone in Israel, whether slave or free, was suffering; there was no one to help them. 27 And since the LORD had not said he would blot out the name of Israel from under heaven, he saved them by the hand of Jeroboam son of Jehoash.

---

h 13 Hebrew *four hundred cubits* (about 180 meters)   *i* 21 Also called *Uzziah*   *j* 25 Or *from the entrance to*   *k* 25 That is, the Dead Sea

<table>
<tr><td>

King James

</td><td>

Amplified

</td></tr>
</table>

King James

28 ¶ Now the rest of the acts of Jeroboam, and all that he did, and his might, how he warred, and how he recovered Damascus, and Hamath, *which belonged* to Judah, for Israel, *are* they not written in the book of the chronicles of the kings of Israel?

29And Jeroboam slept with his fathers, *even* with the kings of Israel; and Zachariah his son reigned in his stead.

Azariah, king of Judah

15 IN THE twenty and seventh year of Jeroboam king of Israel began Azariah son of Amaziah king of Judah to reign.

2Sixteen years old was he when he began to reign, and he reigned two and fifty years in Jerusalem. And his mother's name *was* Jecholiah of Jerusalem.

3And he did *that which was* right in the sight of the LORD, according to all that his father Amaziah had done;

4Save that the high places were not removed: the people sacrificed and burnt incense still on the high places.

5 ¶ And the LORD smote the king, so that he was a leper unto the day of his death, and dwelt in a several house. And Jotham the king's son *was* over the house, judging the people of the land.

6And the rest of the acts of Azariah, and all that he did, *are* they not written in the book of the chronicles of the kings of Judah?

7So Azariah slept with his fathers; and they buried him with his fathers in the city of David: and Jotham his son reigned in his stead.

Zechariah, king of Israel

8 ¶ In the thirty and eighth year of Azariah king of Judah did Zachariah the son of Jeroboam reign over Israel in Samaria six months.

9And he did *that which was* evil in the sight of the LORD, as his fathers had done: he departed not from the sins of Jeroboam the son of Nebat, who made Israel to sin.

10And Shallum the son of Jabesh conspired against him, and smote him before the people, and slew him, and reigned in his stead.

11And the rest of the acts of Zachariah, behold, they *are* written in the book of the chronicles of the kings of Israel.

12This *was* the word of the LORD which he spake unto Jehu, saying, Thy sons shall sit on the throne of Israel unto the fourth *generation*. And so it came to pass.

Shallum, king of Israel

13 ¶ Shallum the son of Jabesh began to reign in the nine and thirtieth year of Uzziah king of Judah; and he reigned [h]a full month in Samaria.

14For Menahem the son of Gadi went up from Tirzah, and came to Samaria, and smote Shallum the son of Jabesh in Samaria, and slew him, and reigned in his stead.

15And the rest of the acts of Shallum, and his conspiracy which he made, behold, they *are* written in the book of the chronicles of the kings of Israel.

16 ¶ Then Menahem smote Tiphsah, and all that *were* therein, and the coasts thereof from Tirzah: because they opened not *to him,* therefore he smote *it; and* all the women therein that were with child he ripped up.

Menahem, king of Israel

17In the nine and thirtieth year of Azariah king of Judah began Menahem the son of Gadi to reign over Israel, *and reigned* ten years in Samaria.

18And he did *that which was* evil in the sight of the LORD: he departed not all his days from the sins of Jeroboam the son of Nebat, who made Israel to sin.

Amplified

28The rest of the acts of Jeroboam [II], all that he did, his might, how he warred, and how he recovered for Israel Damascus and Hamath, which had belonged to Judah, are they not written in the Book of the Chronicles of the Kings of Israel?

29Jeroboam [II] slept with his fathers, the kings of Israel. Zechariah his son reigned in his stead.

15 IN THE twenty-seventh year of Jeroboam [II] king of Israel, Azariah (Uzziah) son of Amaziah king of Judah began to reign.

2He was sixteen years old when he began his fifty-two-year reign in Jerusalem. His mother was Jecoliah of Jerusalem.

3He did right in the Lord's sight, in keeping with all his father Amaziah had done—

4Except the high places were not removed; the people sacrificed and burned incense still on the high places.

5And the Lord smote the king, so that he was a leper to his dying day, and dwelt in a separate house. Jotham the king's son was over the household, judging the people of the land. [II Chron. 26:16–21.]

6The rest of Azariah's acts, all that he did, are they not written in the Book of the Chronicles of the Kings of Judah?

7Azariah slept with his fathers, and they buried him with them in the City of David. Jotham his son reigned in his stead.

8In the thirty-eighth year of Azariah king of Judah Zechariah son of Jeroboam [II] reigned over Israel in Samaria six months.

9He did evil in the sight of the Lord, as his fathers had done; he departed not from the sins of Jeroboam [I] son of Nebat, with which he made Israel to sin.

10Shallum son of Jabesh conspired against Zechariah and struck and killed him before the people and reigned in his stead.

11The rest of the acts of Zechariah, see, they are written in the Book of the Chronicles of the Kings of Israel.

12This was the fulfillment of the promise to Jehu from the Lord: Your sons shall sit on the throne of Israel to the fourth generation. And so it came to pass. [II Kings 10:30.]

13Shallum son of Jabesh, in the thirty-ninth year of Uzziah king of Judah, began his reign of a full month in Samaria.

14For Menahem son of Gadi went up from Tirzah and came to Samaria, and smote and killed Shallum son of Jabesh in Samaria and reigned in his stead.

15The rest of Shallum's acts, his conspiracy, see, they are written in the Book of the Chronicles of the Kings of Israel.

16Then Menahem smote Tiphsah and all who were in it and its territory from Tirzah on; he attacked it because they did not open to him. And all [g]the women there who were with child he ripped up.

17In the thirty-ninth year of Azariah king of Judah, Menahem son of Gadi began his ten-year reign over Israel in Samaria.

18He did evil in the sight of the Lord; he did not depart all his days from the sins of Jeroboam son of Nebat, which he caused Israel to sin.

[g]This savage conduct was among the enormities that a heathen ruler might perpetrate, but only here do we find such cruelty employed by an Israelite. It shows the great degradation and barbarity of the times (*The Cambridge Bible*).

[h]Heb. *a month of days*

New American Standard

Zechariah Reigns over Israel

28 ¶ Now the rest of the acts of Jeroboam and all that he did and his might, how he fought and how he recovered for Israel, Damascus and Hamath, *which had belonged* to Judah, are they not written in the Book of the Chronicles of the Kings of Israel?

29 And Jeroboam slept with his fathers, even with the kings of Israel, and Zechariah his son became king in his place.

Series of Kings: Azariah (Uzziah) over Judah

15 IN THE twenty-seventh year of Jeroboam king of Israel, Azariah son of Amaziah king of Judah became king.

2 He was sixteen years old when he became king, and he reigned fifty-two years in Jerusalem; and his mother's name was Jecoliah of Jerusalem.

3 He did right in the sight of the LORD, according to all that his father Amaziah had done.

4 Only the high places were not taken away; the people still sacrificed and burned incense on the high places.

5 The LORD struck the king, so that he was a leper to the day of his death. And he lived in a separate house, while Jotham the king's son was over the household, judging the people of the land.

6 Now the rest of the acts of Azariah and all that he did, are they not written in the Book of the Chronicles of the Kings of Judah?

7 And Azariah slept with his fathers, and they buried him with his fathers in the city of David, and Jotham his son became king in his place.

Zechariah over Israel

8 ¶ In the thirty-eighth year of Azariah king of Judah, Zechariah the son of Jeroboam became king over Israel in Samaria *for* six months.

9 He did evil in the sight of the LORD, as his fathers had done; he did not depart from the sins of Jeroboam the son of Nebat, which he made Israel sin.

10 Then Shallum the son of Jabesh conspired against him and struck him before the people and killed him, and reigned in his place.

11 Now the rest of the acts of Zechariah, behold they are written in the Book of the Chronicles of the Kings of Israel.

12 This is the word of the LORD which He spoke to Jehu, saying, "Your sons to the fourth generation shall sit on the throne of Israel." And so it was.

13 ¶ Shallum son of Jabesh became king in the thirty-ninth year of Uzziah king of Judah, and he reigned one month in Samaria.

14 Then Menahem son of Gadi went up from Tirzah and came to Samaria, and struck Shallum son of Jabesh in Samaria, and killed him and became king in his place.

15 Now the rest of the acts of Shallum and his conspiracy which he made, behold they are written in the Book of the Chronicles of the Kings of Israel.

16 Then Menahem struck Tiphsah and all who were in it and its borders from Tirzah, because they did not open *to him;* therefore he struck *it* and ripped up all its women who were with child.

Menahem over Israel

17 ¶ In the thirty-ninth year of Azariah king of Judah, Menahem son of Gadi became king over Israel *and reigned* ten years in Samaria.

18 He did evil in the sight of the LORD; he did not depart all his days from the sins of Jeroboam the son of Nebat, which he made Israel sin.

New International

28 As for the other events of Jeroboam's reign, all he did, and his military achievements, including how he recovered for Israel both Damascus and Hamath, which had belonged to Yaudi,[l] are they not written in the book of the annals of the kings of Israel? 29 Jeroboam rested with his fathers, the kings of Israel. And Zechariah his son succeeded him as king.

Azariah King of Judah

15 IN THE twenty-seventh year of Jeroboam king of Israel, Azariah son of Amaziah king of Judah began to reign. 2 He was sixteen years old when he became king, and he reigned in Jerusalem fifty-two years. His mother's name was Jecoliah; she was from Jerusalem. 3 He did what was right in the eyes of the LORD, just as his father Amaziah had done. 4 The high places, however, were not removed; the people continued to offer sacrifices and burn incense there.

5 The LORD afflicted the king with leprosy[m] until the day he died, and he lived in a separate house.[n] Jotham the king's son had charge of the palace and governed the people of the land.

6 As for the other events of Azariah's reign, and all he did, are they not written in the book of the annals of the kings of Judah? 7 Azariah rested with his fathers and was buried near them in the City of David. And Jotham his son succeeded him as king.

Zechariah King of Israel

8 In the thirty-eighth year of Azariah king of Judah, Zechariah son of Jeroboam became king of Israel in Samaria, and he reigned six months. 9 He did evil in the eyes of the LORD, as his fathers had done. He did not turn away from the sins of Jeroboam son of Nebat, which he had caused Israel to commit.

10 Shallum son of Jabesh conspired against Zechariah. He attacked him in front of the people,[o] assassinated him and succeeded him as king. 11 The other events of Zechariah's reign are written in the book of the annals of the kings of Israel. 12 So the word of the LORD spoken to Jehu was fulfilled: "Your descendants will sit on the throne of Israel to the fourth generation."[p]

Shallum King of Israel

13 Shallum son of Jabesh became king in the thirty-ninth year of Uzziah king of Judah, and he reigned in Samaria one month. 14 Then Menahem son of Gadi went from Tirzah up to Samaria. He attacked Shallum son of Jabesh in Samaria, assassinated him and succeeded him as king.

15 The other events of Shallum's reign, and the conspiracy he led, are written in the book of the annals of the kings of Israel.

16 At that time Menahem, starting out from Tirzah, attacked Tiphsah and everyone in the city and its vicinity, because they refused to open their gates. He sacked Tiphsah and ripped open all the pregnant women.

Menahem King of Israel

17 In the thirty-ninth year of Azariah king of Judah, Menahem son of Gadi became king of Israel, and he reigned in Samaria ten years. 18 He did evil in the eyes of the LORD. During his entire reign he did not turn away from the sins of Jeroboam son of Nebat, which he had caused Israel to commit.

---

[l] 28 Or *Judah*　　[m] 5 The Hebrew word was used for various diseases affecting the skin—not necessarily leprosy.　　[n] 5 Or *in a house where he was relieved of responsibility*　　[o] 10 Hebrew; some Septuagint manuscripts *in Ibleam*　　[p] 12 2 Kings 10:30

King James	Amplified

King James

[19]*And* Pul the king of Assyria came against the land: and Menahem gave Pul a thousand talents of silver, that his hand might be with him to confirm the kingdom in his hand.

[20]And Menahem *exacted the money of Israel, *even* of all the mighty men of wealth, of each man fifty shekels of silver, to give to the king of Assyria. So the king of Assyria turned back, and stayed not there in the land.

[21] ¶ And the rest of the acts of Menahem, and all that he did, *are* they not written in the book of the chronicles of the kings of Israel?

[22]And Menahem slept with his fathers; and Pekahiah his son reigned in his stead.

Pekahiah, king of Israel

[23] ¶ In the fiftieth year of Azariah king of Judah Pekahiah the son of Menahem began to reign over Israel in Samaria, *and reigned* two years.

[24]And he did *that which was* evil in the sight of the LORD: he departed not from the sins of Jeroboam the son of Nebat, who made Israel to sin.

[25]But Pekah the son of Remaliah, a captain of his, conspired against him, and smote him in Samaria, in the palace of the king's house, with Argob and Arieh, and with him fifty men of the Gileadites: and he killed him, and reigned in his room.

[26]And the rest of the acts of Pekahiah, and all that he did, behold, they *are* written in the book of the chronicles of the kings of Israel.

Pekah, king of Israel

[27] ¶ In the two and fiftieth year of Azariah king of Judah Pekah the son of Remaliah began to reign over Israel in Samaria, *and reigned* twenty years.

[28]And he did *that which was* evil in the sight of the LORD: he departed not from the sins of Jeroboam the son of Nebat, who made Israel to sin.

[29]In the days of Pekah king of Israel came Tiglath-pileser king of Assyria, and took Ijon, and Abel-beth-maachah, and Janoah, and Kedesh, and Hazor, and Gilead, and Galilee, all the land of Naphtali, and carried them captive to Assyria.

[30]And Hoshea the son of Elah made a conspiracy against Pekah the son of Remaliah, and smote him, and slew him, and reigned in his stead, in the twentieth year of Jotham the son of Uzziah.

[31]And the rest of the acts of Pekah, and all that he did, behold, they *are* written in the book of the chronicles of the kings of Israel.

Jotham, king of Judah

[32] ¶ In the second year of Pekah the son of Remaliah king of Israel began Jotham the son of Uzziah king of Judah to reign.

[33]Five and twenty years old was he when he began to reign, and he reigned sixteen years in Jerusalem. And his mother's name *was* Jerusha, the daughter of Zadok.

[34]And he did *that which was* right in the sight of the LORD: he did according to all that his father Uzziah had done.

[35] ¶ Howbeit the high places were not removed: the people sacrificed and burned incense still in the high places. He built the higher gate of the house of the LORD.

[36] ¶ Now the rest of the acts of Jotham, and all that he did, *are* they not written in the book of the chronicles of the kings of Judah?

[37]In those days the LORD began to send against Judah Rezin the king of Syria, and Pekah the son of Remaliah.

[38]And Jotham slept with his fathers, and was buried with his fathers in the city of David his father: and Ahaz his son reigned in his stead.

Amplified

[19]There came against the land Pul king of Assyria, and Menahem gave Pul 1,000 talents of silver, that he might help him to confirm his kingship.

[20]Menahem exacted the money from Israel, from all the men of wealth, from each man fifty shekels of silver to give to the king of Assyria. So the king of Assyria turned back and did not stay in the land.

[21]The rest of Menahem's acts, all that he did, are they not written in the Book of the Chronicles of the Kings of Israel?

[22]Menahem slept with his fathers; Pekahiah his son reigned in his stead.

[23]In the fiftieth year of Azariah king of Judah, Pekahiah son of Menahem began his two-year reign over Israel in Samaria.

[24]He did evil in the sight of the Lord; he did not depart from the sins of Jeroboam [I] son of Nebat, which he made Israel sin.

[25]But Pekah son of Remaliah, his captain, conspired against [Pekahiah] and attacked him in Samaria, in the citadel of the king's house, with Argob and Arieh; [for] with [Pekah] were fifty Gileadites. And he killed him and reigned in his stead.

[26]The rest of the acts of Pekahiah, all he did, see, they are written in the Book of the Chronicles of the Kings of Israel.

[27]In the fifty-second year of Azariah king of Judah, Pekah son of Remaliah began his twenty-year reign over Israel in Samaria.

[28]He did evil in the Lord's sight; he did not depart from the sins of Jeroboam [I] son of Nebat, which he made Israel sin.

[29]In the days of Pekah king of Israel, Tiglath-pileser king of Assyria came and took Ijon, Abel-beth-maacah, Janoah, Kedesh, Hazor, Gilead, and Galilee, all the land of Naphtali, and carried the people captive to Assyria.

[30]Hoshea son of Elah conspired against Pekah son of Remaliah [of Israel]; he smote and killed him, and reigned in his stead in the twentieth year of Jotham son of Uzziah king of Judah.

[31]The rest of Pekah's acts, all that he did, behold, they are written in the Book of the Chronicles of Israel's Kings.

[32]In the second year of Pekah son of Remaliah king of Israel, Jotham son of Uzziah king of Judah became king.

[33]When he was twenty-five years old, he began his reign of sixteen years in Jerusalem. His mother was Jerusha daughter of Zadok.

[34]He did right in the Lord's sight, according to all his father Uzziah had done.

[35]Yet the high places were not removed; the people sacrificed and burned incense still on the high places. He built the Upper Gate of the house of the Lord.

[36]The rest of the acts of Jotham, all he did, are they not written in the Book of the Chronicles of Judah's Kings?

[37]In those days the Lord began sending Rezin king of Syria and Pekah son of Remaliah against Judah.

[38]Jotham slept with his fathers and was buried [with them] in the city of David his [forefather]. Ahaz his son succeeded him.

---

i Heb. *caused to come forth*

New American Standard

19 ¶ Pul, king of Assyria, came against the land, and Menahem gave Pul a thousand talents of silver so that his hand might be with him to strengthen the kingdom under his rule.

20 Then Menahem exacted the money from Israel, even from all the mighty men of wealth, from each man fifty shekels of silver to pay the king of Assyria. So the king of Assyria returned and did not remain there in the land.

21 Now the rest of the acts of Menahem and all that he did, are they not written in the Book of the Chronicles of the Kings of Israel?

22 And Menahem slept with his fathers, and Pekahiah his son became king in his place.

Pekahiah over Israel

23 ¶ In the fiftieth year of Azariah king of Judah, Pekahiah son of Menahem became king over Israel in Samaria, *and reigned* two years.

24 He did evil in the sight of the LORD; he did not depart from the sins of Jeroboam son of Nebat, which he made Israel sin.

25 Then Pekah son of Remaliah, his officer, conspired against him and struck him in the castle of the king's house with Argob and Arieh; and with him were fifty men of the Gileadites, and he killed him and became king in his place.

26 Now the rest of the acts of Pekahiah and all that he did, behold they are written in the Book of the Chronicles of the Kings of Israel.

Pekah over Israel

27 ¶ In the fifty-second year of Azariah king of Judah, Pekah son of Remaliah became king over Israel in Samaria, *and reigned* twenty years.

28 He did evil in the sight of the LORD; he did not depart from the sins of Jeroboam son of Nebat, which he made Israel sin.

29 ¶ In the days of Pekah king of Israel, Tiglath-pileser king of Assyria came and captured Ijon and Abel-beth-maacah and Janoah and Kedesh and Hazor and Gilead and Galilee, all the land of Naphtali; and he carried them captive to Assyria.

30 And Hoshea the son of Elah made a conspiracy against Pekah the son of Remaliah, and struck him and put him to death and became king in his place, in the twentieth year of Jotham the son of Uzziah.

31 Now the rest of the acts of Pekah and all that he did, behold, they are written in the Book of the Chronicles of the Kings of Israel.

Jotham over Judah

32 ¶ In the second year of Pekah the son of Remaliah king of Israel, Jotham the son of Uzziah king of Judah became king.

33 He was twenty-five years old when he became king, and he reigned sixteen years in Jerusalem; and his mother's name *was* Jerusha the daughter of Zadok.

34 He did what was right in the sight of the LORD; he did according to all that his father Uzziah had done.

35 Only the high places were not taken away; the people still sacrificed and burned incense on the high places. He built the upper gate of the house of the LORD.

36 Now the rest of the acts of Jotham and all that he did, are they not written in the Book of the Chronicles of the Kings of Judah?

37 In those days the LORD began to send Rezin king of Aram and Pekah the son of Remaliah against Judah.

38 And Jotham slept with his fathers, and he was buried with his fathers in the city of David his father; and Ahaz his son became king in his place.

New International

19Then Pul[q] king of Assyria invaded the land, and Menahem gave him a thousand talents[r] of silver to gain his support and strengthen his own hold on the kingdom. 20Menahem exacted this money from Israel. Every wealthy man had to contribute fifty shekels[s] of silver to be given to the king of Assyria. So the king of Assyria withdrew and stayed in the land no longer.

21As for the other events of Menahem's reign, and all he did, are they not written in the book of the annals of the kings of Israel? 22Menahem rested with his fathers. And Pekahiah his son succeeded him as king.

Pekahiah King of Israel

23In the fiftieth year of Azariah king of Judah, Pekahiah son of Menahem became king of Israel in Samaria, and he reigned two years. 24Pekahiah did evil in the eyes of the LORD. He did not turn away from the sins of Jeroboam son of Nebat, which he had caused Israel to commit. 25One of his chief officers, Pekah son of Remaliah, conspired against him. Taking fifty men of Gilead with him, he assassinated Pekahiah, along with Argob and Arieh, in the citadel of the royal palace at Samaria. So Pekah killed Pekahiah and succeeded him as king.

26The other events of Pekahiah's reign, and all he did, are written in the book of the annals of the kings of Israel.

Pekah King of Israel

27In the fifty-second year of Azariah king of Judah, Pekah son of Remaliah became king of Israel in Samaria, and he reigned twenty years. 28He did evil in the eyes of the LORD. He did not turn away from the sins of Jeroboam son of Nebat, which he had caused Israel to commit.

29In the time of Pekah king of Israel, Tiglath-Pileser king of Assyria came and took Ijon, Abel Beth Maacah, Janoah, Kedesh and Hazor. He took Gilead and Galilee, including all the land of Naphtali, and deported the people to Assyria. 30Then Hoshea son of Elah conspired against Pekah son of Remaliah. He attacked and assassinated him, and then succeeded him as king in the twentieth year of Jotham son of Uzziah.

31As for the other events of Pekah's reign, and all he did, are they not written in the book of the annals of the kings of Israel?

Jotham King of Judah

32In the second year of Pekah son of Remaliah king of Israel, Jotham son of Uzziah king of Judah began to reign. 33He was twenty-five years old when he became king, and he reigned in Jerusalem sixteen years. His mother's name was Jerusha daughter of Zadok. 34He did what was right in the eyes of the LORD, just as his father Uzziah had done. 35The high places, however, were not removed; the people continued to offer sacrifices and burn incense there. Jotham rebuilt the Upper Gate of the temple of the LORD.

36As for the other events of Jotham's reign, and what he did, are they not written in the book of the annals of the kings of Judah? 37(In those days the LORD began to send Rezin king of Aram and Pekah son of Remaliah against Judah.) 38Jotham rested with his fathers and was buried with them in the City of David, the city of his father. And Ahaz his son succeeded him as king.

q 19 Also called *Tiglath-Pileser*   *r 19* That is, about 37 tons
(about 34 metric tons)   *s 20* That is, about 1 1/4 pounds (about
0.6 kilogram)

King James	Amplified

Ahaz, king of Judah

16 IN THE seventeenth year of Pekah the son of Remaliah Ahaz the son of Jotham king of Judah began to reign.

²Twenty years old *was* Ahaz when he began to reign, and reigned sixteen years in Jerusalem, and did not *that which was* right in the sight of the LORD his God, like David his father.

³But he walked in the way of the kings of Israel, yea, and made his son to pass through the fire, according to the abominations of the heathen, whom the LORD cast out from before the children of Israel.

⁴And he sacrificed and burnt incense in the high places, and on the hills, and under every green tree.

⁵ ¶ Then Rezin king of Syria and Pekah son of Remaliah king of Israel came up to Jerusalem to war: and they besieged Ahaz, but could not overcome *him*.

⁶At that time Rezin king of Syria recovered Elath to Syria, and drave the Jews from *j*Elath: and the Syrians came to Elath, and dwelt there unto this day.

⁷So Ahaz sent messengers to *k*Tiglath-pileser king of Assyria, saying, I *am* thy servant and thy son: come up, and save me out of the hand of the king of Syria, and out of the hand of the king of Israel, which rise up against me.

⁸And Ahaz took the silver and gold that was found in the house of the LORD, and in the treasures of the king's house, and sent *it for* a present to the king of Assyria.

⁹And the king of Assyria hearkened unto him: for the king of Assyria went up against *l*Damascus, and took it, and carried *the people of* it captive to Kir, and slew Rezin.

¹⁰ ¶ And king Ahaz went to Damascus to meet Tiglath-pileser king of Assyria, and saw an altar that *was* at Damascus: and king Ahaz sent to Urijah the priest the fashion of the altar, and the pattern of it, according to all the workmanship thereof.

¹¹And Urijah the priest built an altar according to all that king Ahaz had sent from Damascus: so Urijah the priest made *it* against king Ahaz came from Damascus.

¹²And when the king was come from Damascus, the king saw the altar: and the king approached to the altar, and offered thereon.

¹³And he burnt his burnt offering and his meat offering, and poured his drink offering, and sprinkled the blood of *m*his peace offerings, upon the altar.

¹⁴And he brought also the brasen altar, which *was* before the LORD, from the forefront of the house, from between the altar and the house of the LORD, and put it on the north side of the altar.

¹⁵And king Ahaz commanded Urijah the priest, saying, Upon the great altar burn the morning burnt offering, and the evening meat offering, and the king's burnt sacrifice, and his meat offering, with the burnt offering of all the people of the land, and their meat offering, and their drink offerings; and sprinkle upon it all the blood of the burnt offering, and all the blood of the sacrifice: and the brasen altar shall be for me to inquire *by*.

¹⁶Thus did Urijah the priest, according to all that king Ahaz commanded.

¹⁷ ¶ And king Ahaz cut off the borders of the bases, and removed the laver from off them; and took down the sea from off the brasen oxen that *were* under it, and put it upon a pavement of stones.

¹⁸And the covert for the sabbath that they had built in the house, and the king's entry without, turned he from the house of the LORD for the king of Assyria.

16 IN THE seventeenth year of Pekah son of Remaliah, Ahaz son of Jotham king of Judah became king.

²Ahaz was twenty years old when he began his sixteen-year reign in Jerusalem. He did not do right in the sight of the Lord his God, like David his [forefather].

³But he walked in the ways of Israel's kings, yes, and made his son pass through the fire [and offered him as a sacrifice], in accord with the abominable [idolatrous] practices of the [heathen] nations whom the Lord drove out before the Israelites.

⁴He sacrificed and burned incense in the high places, on the hills, and under every green tree.

⁵Then Rezin king of Syria and Pekah son of Remaliah king of Israel came up to Jerusalem to wage war; they besieged Ahaz, but could not conquer him.

⁶At that time, Rezin king of Syria got back Elath [in Edom] for Syria and drove the Jews from [it]. The Syrians came to Elath and dwell there to this day.

⁷So Ahaz sent messengers to Tiglath-pileser king of Assyria, saying, I am your servant and son. Come up and save me out of the hands of the kings of Syria and of Israel, who are attacking me.

⁸And Ahaz took the silver and gold in the house of the Lord and in the treasuries of the king's house and sent a present to the king of Assyria.

⁹Assyria's king hearkened to him; he went up against Damascus, took it, carried its people captive to Kir, and slew Rezin.

¹⁰King Ahaz went to Damascus to meet Tiglath-pileser king of Assyria, and saw there their [heathen] altar. King Ahaz sent to Urijah the priest a model of the altar and an exact pattern for its construction.

¹¹So Urijah the priest built an altar according to all that King Ahaz had sent from Damascus, finishing it before King Ahaz returned.

¹²When the king came from Damascus, he looked at the altar and offered on it.

¹³King Ahaz burned his burnt offering and his cereal offering, poured his drink offering, and dashed the blood of his peace offerings upon that altar.

¹⁴The bronze altar which was before the Lord he removed from the front of the house, from between his [new] altar and the house of the Lord, and put it on the north side of his altar.

¹⁵And King Ahaz commanded Urijah the priest: Upon the principal (the new) altar, burn the morning burnt offering, the evening cereal offering, the king's burnt sacrifice and his cereal offering, with the burnt offering and cereal offering and drink offering of all the people of the land; and dash upon the [new] altar all the blood of the burnt offerings and the sacrifices. But the [old] bronze altar shall be kept for me to use to inquire by [of the Lord].

¹⁶Urijah the priest did all this as King Ahaz commanded.

¹⁷[To keep Assyria's king from getting them] King Ahaz cut off the panels of the bases [of the ten lavers] and removed the laver from each of them; and he took down the Sea from off the bronze oxen that were under it and put it upon stone supports.

¹⁸And the covered way for the Sabbath that they had built in the temple court, and the king's outer entrance, he removed from the house of the Lord, because of the king of Assyria [who if he heard of them might seize them].

---

*j*Heb. *Eloth*   *k*Heb. *Tilgath-pileser;* 1 Chr. 5:26 & 2 Chr. 28:20 have *Tilgath-pilneser*   *l*Heb. *Dammesek*   *m*Heb. *which were his*

New American Standard

Ahaz Reigns over Judah

16 IN THE seventeenth year of Pekah the son of Remaliah, Ahaz the son of Jotham, king of Judah, became king.

2 Ahaz *was* twenty years old when he became king, and he reigned sixteen years in Jerusalem; and he did not do what was right in the sight of the LORD his God, as his father David *had done.*

3 But he walked in the way of the kings of Israel, and even made his son pass through the fire, according to the abominations of the nations whom the LORD had driven out from before the sons of Israel.

4 He sacrificed and burned incense on the high places and on the hills and under every green tree.

5 ¶ Then Rezin king of Aram and Pekah son of Remaliah, king of Israel, came up to Jerusalem to *wage* war; and they besieged Ahaz, but could not overcome him.

6 At that time Rezin king of Aram recovered Elath for Aram, and cleared the Judeans out of Elath entirely; and the Arameans came to Elath and have lived there to this day.

Ahaz Seeks Help of Aram

7 ¶ So Ahaz sent messengers to Tiglath-pileser king of Assyria, saying, "I am your servant and your son; come up and deliver me from the hand of the king of Aram and from the hand of the king of Israel, who are rising up against me."

8 Ahaz took the silver and gold that was found in the house of the LORD and in the treasuries of the king's house, and sent a present to the king of Assyria.

9 So the king of Assyria listened to him; and the king of Assyria went up against Damascus and captured it, and carried *the people of* it away into exile to Kir, and put Rezin to death.

Damascus Falls

10 ¶ Now King Ahaz went to Damascus to meet Tiglath-pileser king of Assyria, and saw the altar which *was* at Damascus; and King Ahaz sent to Urijah the priest the pattern of the altar and its model, according to all its workmanship.

11 So Urijah the priest built an altar; according to all that King Ahaz had sent from Damascus, thus Urijah the priest made *it,* before the coming of King Ahaz from Damascus.

12 When the king came from Damascus, the king saw the altar; then the king approached the altar and went up to it,

13 and burned his burnt offering and his meal offering, and poured his drink offering and sprinkled the blood of his peace offerings on the altar.

14 The bronze altar, which *was* before the LORD, he brought from the front of the house, from between *his* altar and the house of the LORD, and he put it on the north side of *his* altar.

15 Then King Ahaz commanded Urijah the priest, saying, "Upon the great altar burn the morning burnt offering and the evening meal offering and the king's burnt offering and his meal offering, with the burnt offering of all the people of the land and their meal offering and their drink offerings; and sprinkle on it all the blood of the burnt offering and all the blood of the sacrifice. But the bronze altar shall be for me to inquire *by.*"

16 So Urijah the priest did according to all that King Ahaz commanded.

17 ¶ Then King Ahaz cut off the borders of the stands, and removed the laver from them; he also took down the sea from the bronze oxen which were under it and put it on a pavement of stone.

18 The covered way for the sabbath which they had built in the house, and the outer entry of the king, he removed from the house of the LORD because of the king of Assyria.

New International

Ahaz King of Judah

16 IN THE seventeenth year of Pekah son of Remaliah, Ahaz son of Jotham king of Judah began to reign. 2 Ahaz was twenty years old when he became king, and he reigned in Jerusalem sixteen years. Unlike David his father, he did not do what was right in the eyes of the LORD his God. 3 He walked in the ways of the kings of Israel and even sacrificed his son in*[t]* the fire, following the detestable ways of the nations the LORD had driven out before the Israelites. 4 He offered sacrifices and burned incense at the high places, on the hilltops and under every spreading tree.

5 Then Rezin king of Aram and Pekah son of Remaliah king of Israel marched up to fight against Jerusalem and besieged Ahaz, but they could not overpower him. 6 At that time, Rezin king of Aram recovered Elath for Aram by driving out the men of Judah. Edomites then moved into Elath and have lived there to this day.

7 Ahaz sent messengers to say to Tiglath-Pileser king of Assyria, "I am your servant and vassal. Come up and save me out of the hand of the king of Aram and of the king of Israel, who are attacking me." 8 And Ahaz took the silver and gold found in the temple of the LORD and in the treasuries of the royal palace and sent it as a gift to the king of Assyria. 9 The king of Assyria complied by attacking Damascus and capturing it. He deported its inhabitants to Kir and put Rezin to death.

10 Then King Ahaz went to Damascus to meet Tiglath-Pileser king of Assyria. He saw an altar in Damascus and sent to Uriah the priest a sketch of the altar, with detailed plans for its construction. 11 So Uriah the priest built an altar in accordance with all the plans that King Ahaz had sent from Damascus and finished it before King Ahaz returned. 12 When the king came back from Damascus and saw the altar, he approached it and presented offerings*[u]* on it. 13 He offered up his burnt offering and grain offering, poured out his drink offering, and sprinkled the blood of his fellowship offerings*[v]* on the altar. 14 The bronze altar that stood before the LORD he brought from the front of the temple—from between the new altar and the temple of the LORD—and put it on the north side of the new altar.

15 King Ahaz then gave these orders to Uriah the priest: "On the large new altar, offer the morning burnt offering and the evening grain offering, the king's burnt offering and his grain offering, and the burnt offering of all the people of the land, and their grain offering and their drink offering. Sprinkle on the altar all the blood of the burnt offerings and sacrifices. But I will use the bronze altar for seeking guidance." 16 And Uriah the priest did just as King Ahaz had ordered.

17 King Ahaz took away the side panels and removed the basins from the movable stands. He removed the Sea from the bronze bulls that supported it and set it on a stone base. 18 He took away the Sabbath canopy*[w]* that had been built at the temple and removed the royal entryway outside the temple of the LORD, in deference to the king of Assyria.

---

[t]3 Or *even made his son pass through*   *[u]12* Or *and went up*
[v]13 Traditionally *peace offerings*   *[w]18* Or *the dais of his throne*
(see Septuagint)

King James

Amplified

19 ¶ Now the rest of the acts of Ahaz which he did, *are* they not written in the book of the chronicles of the kings of Judah?

20And Ahaz slept with his fathers, and was buried with his fathers in the city of David: and Hezekiah his son reigned in his stead.

Samaria captured by Assyria

17 IN THE twelfth year of Ahaz king of Judah began Hoshea the son of Elah to reign in Samaria over Israel nine years.

2And he did *that which was* evil in the sight of the LORD, but not as the kings of Israel that were before him.

3 ¶ Against him came up Shalmaneser king of Assyria; and Hoshea became his servant, and gave him "presents.

4And the king of Assyria found conspiracy in Hoshea: for he had sent messengers to So king of Egypt, and brought no present to the king of Assyria, as *he had done* year by year: therefore the king of Assyria shut him up, and bound him in prison.

5 ¶ Then the king of Assyria came up throughout all the land, and went up to Samaria, and besieged it three years.

6 ¶ In the ninth year of Hoshea the king of Assyria took Samaria, and carried Israel away into Assyria, and placed them in Halah and in Habor *by* the river of Gozan, and in the cities of the Medes.

The sins of Israel and Judah

7For *so* it was, that the children of Israel had sinned against the LORD their God, which had brought them up out of the land of Egypt, from under the hand of Pharaoh king of Egypt, and had feared other gods,

8And walked in the statutes of the heathen, whom the LORD cast out from before the children of Israel, and of the kings of Israel, which they had made.

9And the children of Israel did secretly *those* things that *were* not right against the LORD their God, and they built them high places in all their cities, from the tower of the watchmen to the fenced city.

10And they set them up °images and groves in every high hill, and under every green tree:

11And there they burnt incense in all the high places, as *did* the heathen whom the LORD carried away before them; and wrought wicked things to provoke the LORD to anger:

12For they served idols, whereof the LORD had said unto them, Ye shall not do this thing.

13Yet the LORD testified against Israel, and against Judah, *Pby* all the prophets, *and by* all the seers, saying, Turn ye from your evil ways, and keep my commandments *and* my statutes, according to all the law which I commanded your fathers, and which I sent to you by my servants the prophets.

14Notwithstanding they would not hear, but hardened their necks, like to the neck of their fathers, that did not believe in the LORD their God.

15And they rejected his statutes, and his covenant that he made with their fathers, and his testimonies which he testified against them; and they followed vanity, and became vain, and went after the heathen that *were* round about them, *concerning* whom the LORD had charged them, that they should not do like them.

16And they left all the commandments of the LORD their God, and made them molten images, *even* two calves, and made a grove, and worshipped all the host of heaven, and served Baal.

19The rest of the acts of Ahaz, are they not written in the Book of the Chronicles of the Kings of Judah?

20Ahaz slept with his fathers and was buried [with them] in the City of David. Hezekiah his son reigned in his stead.

17 IN THE twelfth year of Ahaz king of Judah, Hoshea son of Elah began his nine-year reign in Samaria over Israel.

2He did evil in the sight of the Lord, but not as Israel's kings before him did.

3Against him came up Shalmaneser king of Assyria, and Hoshea became his servant and brought him tribute.

4But the king of Assyria found treachery in Hoshea, for he had sent messengers to So king of Egypt and offered no tribute to the king of Assyria, as he had done year by year; therefore the king of Assyria shut him up and bound him in prison.

5Then the king of Assyria invaded all the land and went up to Samaria and besieged it for three years.

6In the ninth year of Hoshea, the king of Assyria took Samaria and carried the Israelites away into Assyria, and placed them in Halah and in Habor by the river of Gozan and in the cities of the Medes.

7This was so because the Israelites had sinned against the Lord their God, Who had brought them out of the land of Egypt, from under the hand of Pharaoh king of Egypt; and they had feared other gods

8And walked in the customs of the [heathen] nations whom the Lord drove out before the Israelites, customs the kings of Israel had introduced.

9The Israelites did secretly against the Lord their God things not right. They built for themselves high places in all their towns, from [lonely] watchtower to [populous] fortified city.

10They set up for themselves pillars and Asherim [symbols of the goddess Asherah] on every high hill and under every green tree.

11There they burned incense on all the high places, as did the nations whom the Lord carried away before them; and they did wicked things provoking the Lord to anger.

12And they served idols, of which the Lord had said to them, You shall not do this thing.

13Yet the Lord warned Israel and Judah through all the prophets and all the seers, saying, Turn from your evil ways and keep My commandments and My statutes, according to all the Law which I commanded your fathers and which I sent to you by My servants the prophets.

14Yet they would not hear, but hardened their necks as did their fathers who did not believe (trust in, rely on, and remain steadfast to) the Lord their God.

15They despised *and* rejected His statutes and His covenant which He made with their fathers and His warnings to them, and they followed vanity (false gods—falsehood, emptiness, and futility) and [they themselves and their prayers] became false (empty and futile). They went after the heathen round about them, of whom the Lord had charged them that they should not do as they did.

16And they forsook all the commandments of the Lord their God and made for themselves molten images, even two calves, and made an Asherah and worshiped all the [starry] hosts of the heavens and served Baal.

New American Standard

Hezekiah Reigns over Judah

19 Now the rest of the acts of Ahaz which he did, are they not written in the Book of the Chronicles of the Kings of Judah?

20 So Ahaz slept with his fathers, and was buried with his fathers in the city of David; and his son Hezekiah reigned in his place.

Hoshea Reigns over Israel

17 IN THE twelfth year of Ahaz king of Judah, Hoshea the son of Elah became king over Israel in Samaria, *and reigned* nine years.

2 He did evil in the sight of the LORD, only not as the kings of Israel who were before him.

3 Shalmaneser king of Assyria came up against him, and Hoshea became his servant and paid him tribute.

4 But the king of Assyria found conspiracy in Hoshea, who had sent messengers to So king of Egypt and had offered no tribute to the king of Assyria, as *he had done* year by year; so the king of Assyria shut him up and bound him in prison.

5 ¶ Then the king of Assyria invaded the whole land and went up to Samaria and besieged it three years.

Israel Captive

6 In the ninth year of Hoshea, the king of Assyria captured Samaria and carried Israel away into exile to Assyria, and settled them in Halah and Habor, *on* the river of Gozan, and in the cities of the Medes.

Why Israel Fell

7 ¶ Now *this* came about because the sons of Israel had sinned against the LORD their God, who had brought them up from the land of Egypt from under the hand of Pharaoh, king of Egypt, and they had *i* feared other gods

8 and walked in the customs of the nations whom the LORD had driven out before the sons of Israel, and *in the customs* of the kings of Israel which they had introduced.

9 The sons of Israel did things secretly which were not right against the LORD their God. Moreover, they built for themselves high places in all their towns, from watchtower to fortified city.

10 They set for themselves *sacred* pillars and *j* Asherim on every high hill and under every green tree,

11 and there they burned incense on all the high places as the nations *did* which the LORD had carried away to exile before them; and they did evil things provoking the LORD,

12 They served idols, concerning which the LORD had said to them, "You shall not do this thing."

13 Yet the LORD warned Israel and Judah through all His prophets *and* every seer, saying, "Turn from your evil ways and keep My commandments, My statutes according to all the law which I commanded your fathers, and which I sent to you through My servants the prophets."

14 However, they did not listen, but stiffened their neck like their fathers, who did not believe in the LORD their God.

15 They rejected His statutes and His covenant which He made with their fathers and His warnings with which He warned them. And they followed vanity and became vain, and *went* after the nations which surrounded them, concerning which the LORD had commanded them not to do like them.

16 They forsook all the commandments of the LORD their God and made for themselves molten images, *even* two calves, and made an Asherah and worshiped all the host of heaven and served Baal.

New International

19 As for the other events of the reign of Ahaz, and what he did, are they not written in the book of the annals of the kings of Judah? 20 Ahaz rested with his fathers and was buried with them in the City of David. And Hezekiah his son succeeded him as king.

Hoshea Last King of Israel

17 IN THE twelfth year of Ahaz king of Judah, Hoshea son of Elah became king of Israel in Samaria, and he reigned nine years. 2 He did evil in the eyes of the LORD, but not like the kings of Israel who preceded him.

3 Shalmaneser king of Assyria came up to attack Hoshea, who had been Shalmaneser's vassal and had paid him tribute. 4 But the king of Assyria discovered that Hoshea was a traitor, for he had sent envoys to So*x* king of Egypt, and he no longer paid tribute to the king of Assyria, as he had done year by year. Therefore Shalmaneser seized him and put him in prison. 5 The king of Assyria invaded the entire land, marched against Samaria and laid siege to it for three years. 6 In the ninth year of Hoshea, the king of Assyria captured Samaria and deported the Israelites to Assyria. He settled them in Halah, in Gozan on the Habor River and in the towns of the Medes.

Israel Exiled Because of Sin

7 All this took place because the Israelites had sinned against the LORD their God, who had brought them up out of Egypt from under the power of Pharaoh king of Egypt. They worshiped other gods 8 and followed the practices of the nations the LORD had driven out before them, as well as the practices that the kings of Israel had introduced. 9 The Israelites secretly did things against the LORD their God that were not right. From watchtower to fortified city they built themselves high places in all their towns. 10 They set up sacred stones and Asherah poles on every high hill and under every spreading tree. 11 At every high place they burned incense, as the nations whom the LORD had driven out before them had done. They did wicked things that provoked the LORD to anger. 12 They worshiped idols, though the LORD had said, "You shall not do this."*y* 13 The LORD warned Israel and Judah through all his prophets and seers: "Turn from your evil ways. Observe my commands and decrees, in accordance with the entire Law that I commanded your fathers to obey and that I delivered to you through my servants the prophets."

14 But they would not listen and were as stiff-necked as their fathers, who did not trust in the LORD their God. 15 They rejected his decrees and the covenant he had made with their fathers and the warnings he had given them. They followed worthless idols and themselves became worthless. They imitated the nations around them although the LORD had ordered them, "Do not do as they do," and they did the things the LORD had forbidden them to do.

16 They forsook all the commands of the LORD their God and made for themselves two idols cast in the shape of calves, and an Asherah pole. They bowed down to all the

---

i Lit *revered*, and so throughout the ch   *j* I.e. wooden symbols of a female deity

x 4 Or *to Sais, to the*; *So* is possibly an abbreviation for *Osorkon*.
y 12 Exodus 20:4, 5

King James

¹⁷And they caused their sons and their daughters to pass through the fire, and used divination and enchantments, and sold themselves to do evil in the sight of the Lord, to provoke him to anger.

¹⁸Therefore the Lord was very angry with Israel, and removed them out of his sight: there was none left but the tribe of Judah only.

¹⁹Also Judah kept not the commandments of the Lord their God, but walked in the statutes of Israel which they made.

²⁰And the Lord rejected all the seed of Israel, and afflicted them, and delivered them into the hand of spoilers, until he had cast them out of his sight.

²¹For he rent Israel from the house of David; and they made Jeroboam the son of Nebat king: and Jeroboam drave Israel from following the Lord, and made them sin a great sin.

²²For the children of Israel walked in all the sins of Jeroboam which he did; they departed not from them;

²³Until the Lord removed Israel out of his sight, as he had said by all his servants the prophets. So was Israel carried away out of their own land to Assyria unto this day.

Israel resettled with Assyrians

²⁴ ¶ And the king of Assyria brought *men* from Babylon, and from Cuthah, and from Ava, and from Hamath, and from Sepharvaim, and placed *them* in the cities of Samaria instead of the children of Israel: and they possessed Samaria, and dwelt in the cities thereof.

²⁵And *so* it was at the beginning of their dwelling there, *that* they feared not the Lord: therefore the Lord sent lions among them, which slew *some* of them.

²⁶Wherefore they spake to the king of Assyria, saying, The nations which thou hast removed, and placed in the cities of Samaria, know not the manner of the God of the land: therefore he hath sent lions among them, and, behold, they slay them, because they know not the manner of the God of the land.

²⁷Then the king of Assyria commanded, saying, Carry thither one of the priests whom ye brought from thence; and let them go and dwell there, and let him teach them the manner of the God of the land.

²⁸Then one of the priests whom they had carried away from Samaria came and dwelt in Beth-el, and taught them how they should fear the Lord.

²⁹Howbeit every nation made gods of their own, and put *them* in the houses of the high places which the Samaritans had made, every nation in their cities wherein they dwelt.

³⁰And the men of Babylon made Succoth-benoth, and the men of Cuth made Nergal, and the men of Hamath made Ashima,

³¹And the Avites made Nibhaz and Tartak, and the Sepharvites burnt their children in fire to Adrammelech and Anammelech, the gods of Sepharvaim.

³²So they feared the Lord, and made unto themselves of the lowest of them priests of the high places, which sacrificed for them in the houses of the high places.

³³They feared the Lord, and served their own gods, after the manner of the nations ^qwhom they carried away from thence.

³⁴Unto this day they do after the former manners: they fear not the Lord, neither do they after their statutes, or after their ordinances, or after the law and commandment which the Lord commanded the children of Jacob, whom he named Israel;

³⁵With whom the Lord had made a covenant, and charged them, saying, Ye shall not fear other gods, nor bow yourselves to them, nor serve them, nor sacrifice to them:

Amplified

¹⁷They caused their sons and their daughters to pass through the fire and used divination and enchantments and sold themselves to do evil in the sight of the Lord, provoking Him to anger.

¹⁸Therefore the Lord was very angry with Israel and removed them out of His sight. None was left but the tribe of Judah.

¹⁹Judah also did not keep the commandments of the Lord their God, but walked in the customs which Israel introduced.

²⁰The Lord rejected all the descendants of Israel and afflicted them and delivered them into the hands of spoilers, until He had cast them out of His sight.

²¹For He tore Israel from the house of David; and they made Jeroboam son of Nebat king. And Jeroboam drew *and* drove Israel away from following the Lord and made them sin a great sin.

²²For the Israelites walked in all the sins Jeroboam committed; they departed not from them

²³Until the Lord removed Israel from His sight, as He had foretold by all His servants the prophets. So Israel was carried away from their own land to Assyria to this day.

²⁴The king of Assyria brought men from Babylon, Cuthah, Avva, Hamath, and Sepharvaim and placed them in the cities of Samaria instead of the Israelites. They possessed Samaria and dwelt in its cities.

²⁵At the beginning of their dwelling there, they did not fear *and* revere the Lord. Therefore the Lord sent lions among them, which killed some of them.

²⁶So the king of Assyria was told: The nations you removed and placed in the cities of Samaria do not know the manner in which the God of the land requires their worship. Therefore He has sent lions among them, and behold, they are killing them, because they do not know the manner of [worship demanded by] the God of the land.

²⁷Then the king of Assyria commanded, Take to Samaria one of the priests you brought from there, and let him [and his helpers] go and live there and let him teach the people the law of the God of the land.

²⁸So one of the priests whom they had carried away from Samaria came and dwelt in Bethel and taught them how they should fear *and* revere the Lord.

²⁹But every nationality still made gods of their own and put them in the shrines of the high places which the Samaritans had made, every nationality in the city in which they dwelt.

³⁰The men of Babylon made [and worshiped their deity] Succoth-benoth, the men of Cuth made Nergal, the men of Hamath made Ashima,

³¹The Avvites made Nibhaz and Tartak, and the Sepharvites burned their children in the fire to Adrammelech and Anammelech, the gods of Sepharvaim.

³²So they feared the Lord, yet appointed from among themselves, whether high or low, priests of the high places, who sacrificed for them in the shrines of the high places.

³³They feared the Lord, yet served their own gods, as did the nations from among whom they had been carried away.

³⁴Unto this day they do after their former custom: they do not fear the Lord [as God sees it], neither do they obey the statutes or the ordinances or the law and commandment which the Lord commanded the children of Jacob, whom He named Israel,

³⁵With whom the Lord had made a covenant and commanded them, You shall not fear other gods or bow yourselves to them or serve them or sacrifice to them.

New American Standard

17 Then they made their sons and their daughters pass through the fire, and practiced divination and enchantments, and sold themselves to do evil in the sight of the LORD, provoking Him.

18 So the LORD was very angry with Israel and removed them from His sight; none was left except the tribe of Judah.

19 ¶ Also Judah did not keep the commandments of the LORD their God, but walked in the customs which Israel had introduced.

20 The LORD rejected all the descendants of Israel and afflicted them and gave them into the hand of plunderers, until He had cast them out of His sight.

21 ¶ When He had torn Israel from the house of David, they made Jeroboam the son of Nebat king. Then Jeroboam drove Israel away from following the LORD and made them commit a great sin.

22 The sons of Israel walked in all the sins of Jeroboam which he did; they did not depart from them

23 until the LORD removed Israel from His sight, as He spoke through all His servants the prophets. So Israel was carried away into exile from their own land to Assyria until this day.

Cities of Israel Filled with Strangers

24 ¶ The king of Assyria brought *men* from Babylon and from Cuthah and from Avva and from Hamath and Sephar-vaim, and settled *them* in the cities of Samaria in place of the sons of Israel. So they possessed Samaria and lived in its cities.

25 At the beginning of their living there, they did not fear the LORD; therefore the LORD sent lions among them which killed some of them.

26 So they spoke to the king of Assyria, saying, "The nations whom you have carried away into exile in the cities of Samaria do not know the custom of the god of the land; so he has sent lions among them, and behold, they kill them because they do not know the custom of the god of the land."

27 ¶ Then the king of Assyria commanded, saying, "Take there one of the priests whom you carried away into exile and let him go and live there; and let him teach them the custom of the god of the land."

28 So one of the priests whom they had carried away into exile from Samaria came and lived at Bethel, and taught them how they should fear the LORD.

29 ¶ But every nation still made gods of its own and put them in the houses of the high places which the people of Samaria had made, every nation in their cities in which they lived.

30 The men of Babylon made Succoth-benoth, the men of Cuth made Nergal, the men of Hamath made Ashima,

31 and the Avvites made Nibhaz and Tartak; and the Sepharvites burned their children in the fire to Adrammelech and Anammelech the gods of Sepharvaim.

32 They also feared the LORD and appointed from among themselves priests of the high places, who acted for them in the houses of the high places.

33 They feared the LORD and served their own gods according to the custom of the nations from among whom they had been carried away into exile.

34 ¶ To this day they do according to the earlier customs: they do not fear the LORD, nor do they follow their statutes or their ordinances or the law, or the commandments which the LORD commanded the sons of Jacob, whom He named Israel;

35 with whom the LORD made a covenant and commanded them, saying, "You shall not fear other gods, nor bow down yourselves to them nor serve them nor sacrifice to them.

New International

starry hosts, and they worshiped Baal. 17They sacrificed their sons and daughters in= the fire. They practiced divination and sorcery and sold themselves to do evil in the eyes of the LORD, provoking him to anger.

18So the LORD was very angry with Israel and removed them from his presence. Only the tribe of Judah was left, 19and even Judah did not keep the commands of the LORD their God. They followed the practices Israel had introduced. 20Therefore the LORD rejected all the people of Israel; he afflicted them and gave them into the hands of plunderers, until he thrust them from his presence.

21When he tore Israel away from the house of David, they made Jeroboam son of Nebat their king. Jeroboam enticed Israel away from following the LORD and caused them to commit a great sin. 22The Israelites persisted in all the sins of Jeroboam and did not turn away from them 23until the LORD removed them from his presence, as he had warned through all his servants the prophets. So the people of Israel were taken from their homeland into exile in Assyria, and they are still there.

Samaria Resettled

24The king of Assyria brought people from Babylon, Cuthah, Avva, Hamath and Sepharvaim and settled them in the towns of Samaria to replace the Israelites. They took over Samaria and lived in its towns. 25When they first lived there, they did not worship the LORD; so he sent lions among them and they killed some of the people. 26It was reported to the king of Assyria: "The people you deported and resettled in the towns of Samaria do not know what the god of that country requires. He has sent lions among them, which are killing them off, because the people do not know what he requires."

27Then the king of Assyria gave this order: "Have one of the priests you took captive from Samaria go back to live there and teach the people what the god of the land requires." 28So one of the priests who had been exiled from Samaria came to live in Bethel and taught them how to worship the LORD.

29Nevertheless, each national group made its own gods in the several towns where they settled, and set them up in the shrines the people of Samaria had made at the high places. 30The men from Babylon made Succoth Benoth, the men from Cuthah made Nergal, and the men from Hamath made Ashima; 31the Avvites made Nibhaz and Tartak, and the Sepharvites burned their children in the fire as sacrifices to Adrammelech and Anammelech, the gods of Sepharvaim. 32They worshiped the LORD, but they also appointed all sorts of their own people to officiate for them as priests in the shrines at the high places. 33They worshiped the LORD, but they also served their own gods in accordance with the customs of the nations from which they had been brought.

34To this day they persist in their former practices. They neither worship the LORD nor adhere to the decrees and ordinances, the laws and commands that the LORD gave the descendants of Jacob, whom he named Israel. 35When the LORD made a covenant with the Israelites, he commanded them: "Do not worship any other gods or bow

---

z 17 Or They made their sons and daughters pass through

King James

³⁶But the LORD, who brought you up out of the land of Egypt with great power and a stretched out arm, him shall ye fear, and him shall ye worship, and to him shall ye do sacrifice.

³⁷And the statutes, and the ordinances, and the law, and the commandment, which he wrote for you, ye shall observe to do for evermore; and ye shall not fear other gods.

³⁸And the covenant that I have made with you ye shall not forget; neither shall ye fear other gods.

³⁹But the LORD your God ye shall fear; and he shall deliver you out of the hand of all your enemies.

⁴⁰Howbeit they did not hearken, but they did after their former manner.

⁴¹So these nations feared the LORD, and served their graven images, both their children, and their children's children: as did their fathers, so do they unto this day.

Hezekiah, king of Judah

18 NOW IT came to pass in the third year of Hoshea son of Elah king of Israel, *that* Hezekiah the son of Ahaz king of Judah began to reign.

²Twenty and five years old was he when he began to reign; and he reigned twenty and nine years in Jerusalem. His mother's name also *was* Abi, the daughter of Zachariah.

³And he did *that which was* right in the sight of the LORD, according to all that David his father did.

4 ¶ He removed the high places, and brake the ʳimages, and cut down the groves, and brake in pieces the brasen serpent that Moses had made: for unto those days the children of Israel did burn incense to it: and he called it ˢNehushtan.

⁵He trusted in the LORD God of Israel; so that after him was none like him among all the kings of Judah, nor *any* that were before him.

⁶For he clave to the LORD, *and* departed not ᵗfrom following him, but kept his commandments, which the LORD commanded Moses.

⁷And the LORD was with him; *and* he prospered whithersoever he went forth: and he rebelled against the king of Assyria, and served him not.

⁸He smote the Philistines, *even* unto ᵘGaza, and the borders thereof, from the tower of the watchmen to the fenced city.

9 ¶ And it came to pass in the fourth year of king Hezekiah, which *was* the seventh year of Hoshea son of Elah king of Israel, *that* Shalmaneser king of Assyria came up against Samaria, and besieged it.

¹⁰And at the end of three years they took it: *even* in the sixth year of Hezekiah, that *is* the ninth year of Hoshea king of Israel, Samaria was taken.

¹¹And the king of Assyria did carry away Israel unto Assyria, and put them in Halah and in Habor *by* the river of Gozan, and in the cities of the Medes:

¹²Because they obeyed not the voice of the LORD their God, but transgressed his covenant, *and* all that Moses the servant of the LORD commanded, and would not hear *them,* nor do *them.*

13 ¶ Now in the fourteenth year of king Hezekiah did ᵛSennacherib king of Assyria come up against all the fenced cities of Judah, and took them.

¹⁴And Hezekiah king of Judah sent to the king of Assyria to Lachish, saying, I have offended; return from me: that which thou puttest on me will I bear. And the king of Assyria appointed unto Hezekiah king of Judah three hundred talents of silver and thirty talents of gold.

Amplified

³⁶But you shall [reverently] fear, bow yourselves to, and sacrifice to the Lord, Who brought you out of the land of Egypt with great power and an outstretched arm.

³⁷And the statutes, ordinances, law, and commandment which He wrote for you you shall observe and do forevermore; you shall not fear other gods.

³⁸And the covenant that I have made with you you shall not forget; you shall not fear other gods.

³⁹But the Lord your God you shall [reverently] fear; then He will deliver you out of the hands of all your enemies.

⁴⁰However, they did not listen, but they did as they had done formerly.

⁴¹So these nations [vainly] feared the Lord and also served their graven images, as did their children and their children's children. As their fathers did, so do they to this day.

18 IN THE third year of Hoshea son of Elah king of Israel, Hezekiah son of Ahaz king of Judah began to reign.

²He was twenty-five years old when he began his twenty-nine-year reign in Jerusalem. His mother was Abi daughter of Zechariah.

³Hezekiah did right in the sight of the Lord, according to all that David his [forefather] had done.

⁴He removed the high places, broke the images, cut down the Asherim, and broke in pieces the bronze serpent that Moses had made, for until then the Israelites had burned incense to it; but he called it Nehushtan [a bronze trifle].

⁵Hezekiah trusted in, leaned on, *and* was confident in the Lord, the God of Israel; so that neither after him nor before him was any one of all the kings of Judah like him.

⁶For he clung *and* held fast to the Lord and ceased not to follow Him, but kept His commandments, as the Lord commanded Moses.

⁷And the Lord was with Hezekiah; he prospered wherever he went. And he rebelled against the king of Assyria and refused to serve him.

⁸He smote the Philistines, even to Gaza [the most distant city] and its borders, from the [isolated] watchtower to the [populous] fortified city.

⁹In the fourth year of King Hezekiah, which was the seventh of Hoshea son of Elah king of Israel, Shalmaneser king of Assyria came up against Samaria and besieged it.

¹⁰After three years it was taken; in the sixth year of Hezekiah, which was the ninth year of Hoshea king of Israel, Samaria was taken.

¹¹The king of Assyria carried Israel away to Assyria, and put them in Halah, and on the Habor, the river of Gozan, and in the cities of the Medes,

¹²Because they did not obey the voice of the Lord their God, but transgressed His covenant, even all that Moses the servant of the Lord commanded, and would not hear it or do it.

¹³In the fourteenth year of Hezekiah, Sennacherib king of Assyria came up against all the fortified cities of Judah and took them.

¹⁴Then Hezekiah king of Judah sent to the king of Assyria at Lachish, saying, I have done wrong. Depart from me; what you put on me I will bear. And the king of Assyria exacted of Hezekiah king of Judah 300 talents of silver and thirty talents of gold.

ʳHeb. *statues*   ˢi.e. *A piece of brass*   ᵗHeb. *from after him*
ᵘHeb. *Azzah*   ᵛHeb. *Sanherib*

New American Standard

36"But the LORD, who brought you up from the land of Egypt with great power and with an outstretched arm, Him you shall fear, and to Him you shall bow yourselves down, and to Him you shall sacrifice.

37"The statutes and the ordinances and the law and the commandment which He wrote for you, you shall observe to do forever; and you shall not fear other gods.

38"The covenant that I have made with you, you shall not forget, nor shall you fear other gods.

39"But the LORD your God you shall fear; and He will deliver you from the hand of all your enemies."

40 However, they did not listen, but they did according to their earlier custom.

41 So while these nations feared the LORD, they also served their idols; their children likewise and their grandchildren, as their fathers did, so they do to this day.

Hezekiah Reigns over Judah

18 NOW IT came about in the third year of Hoshea, the son of Elah king of Israel, that Hezekiah the son of Ahaz king of Judah became king.

2 He was twenty-five years old when he became king, and he reigned twenty-nine years in Jerusalem; and his mother's name was Abi the daughter of Zechariah.

3 He did right in the sight of the LORD, according to all that his father David had done.

4 He removed the high places and broke down the *sacred* pillars and cut down the *k*Asherah. He also broke in pieces the bronze serpent that Moses had made, for until those days the sons of Israel burned incense to it; and it was called *l*Nehushtan.

5 He trusted in the LORD, the God of Israel; so that after him there was none like him among all the kings of Judah, nor *among those* who were before him.

6 For he clung to the LORD; he did not depart from following Him, but kept His commandments, which the LORD had commanded Moses.

Hezekiah Victorious

7 And the LORD was with him; wherever he went he prospered. And he rebelled against the king of Assyria and did not serve him.

8 He defeated the Philistines as far as Gaza and its territory, from watchtower to fortified city.

9 ¶ Now in the fourth year of King Hezekiah, which was the seventh year of Hoshea son of Elah king of Israel, Shalmaneser king of Assyria came up against Samaria and besieged it.

10 At the end of three years they captured it; in the sixth year of Hezekiah, which was the ninth year of Hoshea king of Israel, Samaria was captured.

11 Then the king of Assyria carried Israel away into exile to Assyria, and put them in Halah and on the Habor, the river of Gozan, and in the cities of the Medes,

12 because they did not obey the voice of the LORD their God, but transgressed His covenant, *even* all that Moses the servant of the LORD commanded; they would neither listen nor do *it.*

Invasion of Judah

13 ¶ Now in the fourteenth year of King Hezekiah, Sennacherib king of Assyria came up against all the fortified cities of Judah and seized them.

14 Then Hezekiah king of Judah sent to the king of Assyria at Lachish, saying, "I have done wrong. Withdraw from me; whatever you impose on me I will bear." So the king of Assyria required of Hezekiah king of Judah three hundred talents of silver and thirty talents of gold.

New International

down to them, serve them or sacrifice to them. 36But the LORD, who brought you up out of Egypt with mighty power and outstretched arm, is the one you must worship. To him you shall bow down and to him offer sacrifices. 37You must always be careful to keep the decrees and ordinances, the laws and commands he wrote for you. Do not worship other gods. 38Do not forget the covenant I have made with you, and do not worship other gods. 39Rather, worship the LORD your God; it is he who will deliver you from the hand of all your enemies."

40They would not listen, however, but persisted in their former practices. 41Even while these people were worshiping the LORD, they were serving their idols. To this day their children and grandchildren continue to do as their fathers did.

Hezekiah King of Judah

18 IN THE third year of Hoshea son of Elah king of Israel, Hezekiah son of Ahaz king of Judah began to reign. 2He was twenty-five years old when he became king, and he reigned in Jerusalem twenty-nine years. His mother's name was Abijah*a* daughter of Zechariah. 3He did what was right in the eyes of the LORD, just as his father David had done. 4He removed the high places, smashed the sacred stones and cut down the Asherah poles. He broke into pieces the bronze snake Moses had made, for up to that time the Israelites had been burning incense to it. (It was called*b* Nehushtan.*c*)

5Hezekiah trusted in the LORD, the God of Israel. There was no one like him among all the kings of Judah, either before him or after him. 6He held fast to the LORD and did not cease to follow him; he kept the commands the LORD had given Moses. 7And the LORD was with him; he was successful in whatever he undertook. He rebelled against the king of Assyria and did not serve him. 8From watchtower to fortified city, he defeated the Philistines, as far as Gaza and its territory.

9In King Hezekiah's fourth year, which was the seventh year of Hoshea son of Elah king of Israel, Shalmaneser king of Assyria marched against Samaria and laid siege to it. 10At the end of three years the Assyrians took it. So Samaria was captured in Hezekiah's sixth year, which was the ninth year of Hoshea king of Israel. 11The king of Assyria deported Israel to Assyria and settled them in Halah, in Gozan on the Habor River and in towns of the Medes. 12This happened because they had not obeyed the LORD their God, but had violated his covenant—all that Moses the servant of the LORD commanded. They neither listened to the commands nor carried them out.

13In the fourteenth year of King Hezekiah's reign, Sennacherib king of Assyria attacked all the fortified cities of Judah and captured them. 14So Hezekiah king of Judah sent this message to the king of Assyria at Lachish: "I have done wrong. Withdraw from me, and I will pay whatever you demand of me." The king of Assyria exacted from Hezekiah king of Judah three hundred talents*d* of silver

---

a 2 Hebrew *Abi,* a variant of *Abijah*   *b 4* Or *He called it*
c 4 *Nehushtan* sounds like the Hebrew for *bronze* and *snake* and *unclean thing.*   *d 14* That is, about 11 tons (about 10 metric tons)

---

k I.e. a wooden symbol of a female deity   *l* I.e. a piece of bronze

King James

¹⁵And Hezekiah gave *him* all the silver that was found in the house of the LORD, and in the treasures of the king's house.

¹⁶At that time did Hezekiah cut off *the gold from* the doors of the temple of the LORD, and *from* the pillars which Hezekiah king of Judah had overlaid, and gave ^wit to the king of Assyria.

The Assyrian threats

¹⁷ ¶ And the king of Assyria sent Tartan and Rabsaris and Rab-shakeh from Lachish to king Hezekiah with a ^xgreat host against Jerusalem. And they went up and came to Jerusalem. And when they were come up, they came and stood by the conduit of the upper pool, which *is* in the highway of the fuller's field.

¹⁸And when they had called to the king, there came out to them Eliakim the son of Hilkiah, which *was* over the household, and Shebna the ^yscribe, and Joah the son of Asaph the recorder.

¹⁹And Rab-shakeh said unto them, Speak ye now to Hezekiah, Thus saith the great king, the king of Assyria, What confidence *is* this wherein thou trustest?

²⁰Thou ^zsayest, (but *they are but* ^avain words,) ^b*I have* counsel and strength for the war. Now on whom dost thou trust, that thou rebellest against me?

²¹Now, behold, thou ^ctrustest upon the staff of this bruised reed, *even* upon Egypt, on which if a man lean, it will go into his hand, and pierce it: so *is* Pharaoh king of Egypt unto all that trust on him.

²²But if ye say unto me, We trust in the LORD our God: *is* not that he, whose high places and whose altars Hezekiah hath taken away, and hath said to Judah and Jerusalem, Ye shall worship before this altar in Jerusalem?

²³Now therefore, I pray thee, give ^dpledges to my lord the king of Assyria, and I will deliver thee two thousand horses, if thou be able on thy part to set riders upon them.

²⁴How then wilt thou turn away the face of one captain of the least of my master's servants, and put thy trust on Egypt for chariots and for horsemen?

²⁵Am I now come up without the LORD against this place to destroy it? The LORD said to me, Go up against this land, and destroy it.

²⁶Then said Eliakim the son of Hilkiah, and Shebna, and Joah, unto Rab-shakeh, Speak, I pray thee, to thy servants in the Syrian language; for we understand *it:* and talk not with us in the Jews' language in the ears of the people that *are* on the wall.

²⁷But Rab-shakeh said unto them, Hath my master sent me to thy master, and to thee, to speak these words? *hath he* not *sent me* to the men which sit on the wall, that they may eat their own dung, and drink ^etheir own piss with you?

²⁸Then Rab-shakeh stood and cried with a loud voice in the Jews' language, and spake, saying, Hear ye the word of the great king, the king of Assyria:

²⁹Thus saith the king, Let not Hezekiah deceive you: for he shall not be able to deliver you out of his hand:

³⁰Neither let Hezekiah make you trust in the LORD, saying, The LORD will surely deliver us, and this city shall not be delivered into the hand of the king of Assyria.

³¹Hearken not to Hezekiah: for thus saith the king of Assyria, ^{f g}Make *an agreement* with me by a present, and come out to me, and *then* eat ye every man of his own vine, and every one of his fig tree, and drink ye every one the waters of his ^hcistern:

Amplified

¹⁵And Hezekiah gave him all the silver that was found in the house of the Lord and in the treasuries of the king's house.

¹⁶Then Hezekiah stripped off the gold from the doors of the temple of the Lord and from the doorposts which he as king of Judah had overlaid, and gave it to the king of Assyria.

¹⁷And the king of Assyria sent the Tartan, the Rabsaris, and the Rabshakeh [the high officials] from Lachish to King Hezekiah at Jerusalem with a great army. They went up to Jerusalem, and when they arrived, they came and stood by the canal of the Upper Pool, which is on the highway to the Fuller's Field. [II Chron. 32:9–19; Isa. 36:1–22.]

¹⁸When they called for the king, there came out to them Eliakim son of Hilkiah, who was over the king's household, and Shebna the scribe, and Joah son of Asaph the recorder.

¹⁹The Rabshakeh told them, Say to Hezekiah, Thus says the great king of Assyria: What justifies this confidence of yours?

²⁰You say—but they are empty words—There is counsel and strength for war. Now on whom do you rely, that you rebel against me?

²¹Behold, you are relying on Egypt, that broken reed of a staff; if a man leans on it, it will pierce his hand. So is Pharaoh king of Egypt to all who trust *and* rely on him.

²²But if you tell me, We trust in *and* rely on the Lord our God, is it not He Whose high places and altars Hezekiah has removed, saying to Judah and Jerusalem, You shall worship before this altar in Jerusalem?

²³So now, make a wager *and* give pledges to my lord the king of Assyria: I will deliver you 2,000 horses—if you can on your part put riders on them.

²⁴How then can you beat back one captain among the least of my master's servants, when your trust is put in Egypt for chariots and horsemen?

²⁵Have I come up without the Lord against this place to destroy it? The Lord said to me, Go up against this land and destroy it.

²⁶Then Eliakim son of Hilkiah and Shebna and Joah said to the Rabshakeh, We pray you, speak to your servants in the Aramaic (Syrian) language, for we understand it; and do not speak to us in the Jews' language in the hearing of the people on the wall.

²⁷But the Rabshakeh said to them, Has my master sent me to your master and you only to say these things? Has he not sent me to the men who sit on the wall [whom Hezekiah has doomed to be forced] to eat their own dung and drink their own urine along with you?

²⁸Then the Rabshakeh stood and cried with a loud voice in the Jews' language, Hear the word of the great king of Assyria!

²⁹Thus says the king: Let not Hezekiah deceive you. For he will not be able to deliver you out of my hand.

³⁰Nor let Hezekiah make you trust in *and* rely on the Lord, saying, The Lord will surely deliver us, and this city will not be given into the hand of Assyria's king.

³¹Hearken not to Hezekiah, for thus says the king of Assyria: Make your peace with me and come out to me, and eat every man from his own vine and fig tree and drink every man the waters of his own cistern,

---

^wHeb. *them*   ^xHeb. *heavy*   ^yOr, *secretary*   ^zOr, *talkest*
^aHeb. *word of the lips*   ^bOr, *But counsel and strength* are *for the war*   ^cHeb. *trustest thee*   ^dOr, *hostages*   ^eHeb. *the water of their feet*   ^fOr, *Seek my favour*   ^gHeb. *Make with me a blessing*   ^hOr, *pit*

New American Standard

¹⁵ Hezekiah gave *him* all the silver which was found in the house of the LORD, and in the treasuries of the king's house.

¹⁶ At that time Hezekiah cut off *the gold from* the doors of the temple of the LORD, and *from* the doorposts which Hezekiah king of Judah had overlaid, and gave it to the king of Assyria.

¹⁷ ¶ Then the king of Assyria sent Tartan and Rab-saris and Rabshakeh from Lachish to King Hezekiah with a large army to Jerusalem. So they went up and came to Jerusalem. And when they went up, they came and stood by the conduit of the upper pool, which is on the highway of the ^mfuller's field.

¹⁸ When they called to the king, Eliakim the son of Hilkiah, who was over the household, and Shebnah the scribe and Joah the son of Asaph the recorder, came out to them.

¹⁹ ¶ Then Rabshakeh said to them, "Say now to Hezekiah, 'Thus says the great king, the king of Assyria, "What is this confidence that you have?

²⁰"You say (but *they are* only empty words), '*I have* counsel and strength for the war.' Now on whom do you rely, that you have rebelled against me?

²¹"Now behold, you rely on the staff of this crushed reed, *even* on Egypt; on which if a man leans, it will go into his hand and pierce it. So is Pharaoh king of Egypt to all who rely on him.

²²"But if you say to me, 'We trust in the LORD our God,' is it not He whose high places and whose altars Hezekiah has taken away, and has said to Judah and to Jerusalem, 'You shall worship before this altar in Jerusalem'?

²³"Now therefore, come, make a bargain with my master the king of Assyria, and I will give you two thousand horses, if you are able on your part to set riders on them.

²⁴"How then can you repulse one official of the least of my master's servants, and rely on Egypt for chariots and for horsemen?

²⁵"Have I now come up without the LORD'S approval against this place to destroy it? The LORD said to me, 'Go up against this land and destroy it.' " ' "

²⁶ ¶ Then Eliakim the son of Hilkiah, and Shebnah and Joah, said to Rabshakeh, "Speak now to your servants in Aramaic, for we understand *it;* and do not speak with us in Judean in the hearing of the people who are on the wall."

²⁷ But Rabshakeh said to them, "Has my master sent me only to your master and to you to speak these words, *and* not to the men who sit on the wall, *doomed* to eat their own dung and drink their own urine with you?"

²⁸ ¶ Then Rabshakeh stood and cried with a loud voice in Judean, saying, "Hear the word of the great king, the king of Assyria.

²⁹"Thus says the king, 'Do not let Hezekiah deceive you, for he will not be able to deliver you from my hand;

³⁰ nor let Hezekiah make you trust in the LORD, saying, "The LORD will surely deliver us, and this city will not be given into the hand of the king of Assyria."

³¹ 'Do not listen to Hezekiah, for thus says the king of Assyria, "Make your peace with me and come out to me, and eat each of his vine and each of his fig tree and drink each of the waters of his own cistern,

New International

and thirty talents*e* of gold. ¹⁵So Hezekiah gave him all the silver that was found in the temple of the LORD and in the treasuries of the royal palace.

¹⁶At this time Hezekiah king of Judah stripped off the gold with which he had covered the doors and doorposts of the temple of the LORD, and gave it to the king of Assyria.

Sennacherib Threatens Jerusalem

¹⁷The king of Assyria sent his supreme commander, his chief officer and his field commander with a large army, from Lachish to King Hezekiah at Jerusalem. They came up to Jerusalem and stopped at the aqueduct of the Upper Pool, on the road to the Washerman's Field. ¹⁸They called for the king; and Eliakim son of Hilkiah the palace administrator, Shebna the secretary, and Joah son of Asaph the recorder went out to them.

¹⁹The field commander said to them, "Tell Hezekiah:

" 'This is what the great king, the king of Assyria, says: On what are you basing this confidence of yours? ²⁰You say you have strategy and military strength—but you speak only empty words. On whom are you depending, that you rebel against me? ²¹Look now, you are depending on Egypt, that splintered reed of a staff, which pierces a man's hand and wounds him if he leans on it! Such is Pharaoh king of Egypt to all who depend on him. ²²And if you say to me, "We are depending on the LORD our God"—isn't he the one whose high places and altars Hezekiah removed, saying to Judah and Jerusalem, "You must worship before this altar in Jerusalem"?

²³" 'Come now, make a bargain with my master, the king of Assyria: I will give you two thousand horses—if you can put riders on them! ²⁴How can you repulse one officer of the least of my master's officials, even though you are depending on Egypt for chariots and horsemen*f*? ²⁵Furthermore, have I come to attack and destroy this place without word from the LORD? The LORD himself told me to march against this country and destroy it.' "

²⁶Then Eliakim son of Hilkiah, and Shebna and Joah said to the field commander, "Please speak to your servants in Aramaic, since we understand it. Don't speak to us in Hebrew in the hearing of the people on the wall."

²⁷But the commander replied, "Was it only to your master and you that my master sent me to say these things, and not to the men sitting on the wall—who, like you, will have to eat their own filth and drink their own urine?"

²⁸Then the commander stood and called out in Hebrew: "Hear the word of the great king, the king of Assyria! ²⁹This is what the king says: Do not let Hezekiah deceive you. He cannot deliver you from my hand. ³⁰Do not let Hezekiah persuade you to trust in the LORD when he says, 'The LORD will surely deliver us; this city will not be given into the hand of the king of Assyria.'

³¹"Do not listen to Hezekiah. This is what the king of Assyria says: Make peace with me and come out to me. Then every one of you will eat from his own vine and fig

---

^mI.e. launderer's

^e*14* That is, about 1 ton (about 1 metric ton)
^f*24* Or *charioteers*

King James

Amplified

32Until I come and take you away to a land like your own land, a land of corn and wine, a land of bread and vineyards, a land of oil olive and of honey, that ye may live, and not die: and hearken not unto Hezekiah, when he *i*persuadeth you, saying, The LORD will deliver us.

33Hath any of the gods of the nations delivered at all his land out of the hand of the king of Assyria?

34Where *are* the gods of Hamath, and of Arpad? where *are* the gods of Sepharvaim, Hena, and Ivah? have they delivered Samaria out of mine hand?

35Who *are* they among all the gods of the countries, that have delivered their country out of mine hand, that the LORD should deliver Jerusalem out of mine hand?

36But the people held their peace, and answered him not a word: for the king's commandment was, saying, Answer him not.

37Then came Eliakim the son of Hilkiah, which *was* over the household, and Shebna the scribe, and Joah the son of Asaph the recorder, to Hezekiah with *their* clothes rent, and told him the words of Rab-shakeh.

Hezekiah sends to Isaiah

19 AND IT came to pass, when king Hezekiah heard *it*, that he rent his clothes, and covered himself with sackcloth, and went into the house of the LORD.

2And he sent Eliakim, which *was* over the household, and Shebna the scribe, and the elders of the priests, covered with sackcloth, to Isaiah the prophet the son of Amoz.

3And they said unto him, Thus saith Hezekiah, This day *is* a day of trouble, and of rebuke, and *j*blasphemy: for the children are come to the birth, and *there is* not strength to bring forth.

4It may be the LORD thy God will hear all the words of Rab-shakeh, whom the king of Assyria his master hath sent to reproach the living God; and will reprove the words which the LORD thy God hath heard: wherefore lift up *thy* prayer for the remnant that are *k*left.

5So the servants of king Hezekiah came to Isaiah.

6 ¶ And Isaiah said unto them, Thus shall ye say to your master, Thus saith the LORD, Be not afraid of the words which thou hast heard, with which the servants of the king of Assyria have blasphemed me.

7Behold, I will send a blast upon him, and he shall hear a rumour, and shall return to his own land; and I will cause him to fall by the sword in his own land.

8 ¶ So Rab-shakeh returned, and found the king of Assyria warring against Libnah: for he had heard that he was departed from Lachish.

9And when he heard say of Tirhakah king of Ethiopia, Behold, he is come out to fight against thee: he sent messengers again unto Hezekiah, saying,

10Thus shall ye speak to Hezekiah king of Judah, saying, Let not thy God in whom thou trustest deceive thee, saying, Jerusalem shall not be delivered into the hand of the king of Assyria.

11Behold, thou hast heard what the kings of Assyria have done to all lands, by destroying them utterly: and shalt thou be delivered?

12Have the gods of the nations delivered them which my fathers have destroyed; *as* Gozan, and Haran, and Rezeph, and the children of Eden which *were* in Thelasar?

13Where *is* the king of Hamath, and the king of Arpad, and the king of the city of Sepharvaim, of Hena, and Ivah?

Hezekiah's prayer

14 ¶ And Hezekiah received the letter of the hand of the messengers, and read it: and Hezekiah went up into the house of the LORD, and spread it before the LORD.

32Until I come and take you away to a land like your own, a land of grain and vintage fruit, of bread and vineyards, of olive trees and honey, that you may live and not die. Do not listen to Hezekiah when he urges you, saying, The Lord will deliver us.

33Has any one of the gods of the nations ever delivered his land out of the hand of the king of Assyria?

34Where are the gods of Hamath and Arpad [in Syria]? Where are the gods of Sepharvaim, Hena, and Ivvah [in the Euphrates Valley]? Have they delivered Samaria [Israel's capital] out of my hand?

35Who of all the gods of the countries has delivered their country out of my hand, that the Lord should deliver Jerusalem out of my hand?

36But the people were silent and answered him not a word, for Hezekiah had commanded, Do not answer him.

37Then Eliakim son of Hilkiah, who was over the royal household, and Shebna the scribe, and Joah son of Asaph the recorder came to Hezekiah with their clothes rent, and told him what the Rabshakeh had said.

19 WHEN KING Hezekiah heard it, he rent his clothes and covered himself with sackcloth and went into the house of the Lord. [Isa. 37:1–13.]

2And he sent Eliakim, who was over his household, Shebna the scribe, and the older priests, covered with sackcloth, to Isaiah the prophet the son of Amoz.

3They said to him, Hezekiah says: This is a day of [extreme danger and] distress, of rebuke *and* chastisement, and blasphemous *and* insolent insult; for children have come to the birth, and there is no strength to bring them forth.

4It may be that the Lord your God will hear all the words of the Rabshakeh, whom the king of Assyria has sent to mock, reproach, insult, *and* defy the living God, and will rebuke the words which the Lord your God has heard. So raise your prayer for the remnant [of His people] that is left.

5So the servants of King Hezekiah came to Isaiah.

6Isaiah said to them, Say to your master, Thus says the Lord: Do not be afraid because of the words you have heard, with which the servants of the king of Assyria have reviled *and* blasphemed Me.

7Behold, I will put a spirit in him so that he will hear a rumor and return to his own land, and I will cause him to fall by the sword in his own country.

8So the Rabshakeh returned and found the king of Assyria fighting against Libnah [a fortified city of Judah]; for he had heard that the king had left Lachish.

9And Sennacherib king of Assyria heard concerning Tirhakah king of Ethiopia, He has come to make war against you. And when he heard it, he sent messengers again to Hezekiah, saying,

10Say this to Hezekiah king of Judah: Let not your God on Whom you rely deceive you by saying, Jerusalem shall not be delivered into the hand of the king of Assyria.

11Behold, you have heard what the Assyrian kings have done to all lands, destroying them utterly. And shall you be delivered?

12Have the gods of the nations delivered those whom my ancestors have destroyed, as Gozan, Haran [of Mesopotamia], Rezeph, and the people of Eden who were in Telassar?

13Where are the kings of Hamath, of Arpad [of northern Syria], of the city of Sepharvaim, of Hena, and Ivvah?

14Hezekiah received the letter from the hand of the messengers and read it. And he went up into the house of the Lord and spread it before the Lord. [Isa. 37:14–20.]

---

*i*Or, *deceiveth*   *j*Or, *provocation*   *k*Heb. *found*

New American Standard

³² until I come and take you away to a land like your own land, a land of grain and new wine, a land of bread and vineyards, a land of olive trees and honey, that you may live and not die." But do not listen to Hezekiah when he misleads you, saying, "The LORD will deliver us."

³³ 'Has any one of the gods of the nations delivered his land from the hand of the king of Assyria?

³⁴ 'Where are the gods of Hamath and Arpad? Where are the gods of Sepharvaim, Hena and Ivvah? Have they delivered Samaria from my hand?

³⁵ 'Who among all the gods of the lands have delivered their land from my hand, that the LORD should deliver Jerusalem from my hand?' "

³⁶ ¶ But the people were silent and answered him not a word, for the king's commandment was, "Do not answer him."

³⁷ Then Eliakim the son of Hilkiah, who was over the household, and Shebna the scribe and Joah the son of Asaph, the recorder, came to Hezekiah with their clothes torn and told him the words of Rabshakeh.

Isaiah Encourages Hezekiah

19 AND WHEN King Hezekiah heard *it*, he tore his clothes, covered himself with sackcloth and entered the house of the LORD.

² Then he sent Eliakim who was over the household with Shebna the scribe and the elders of the priests, covered with sackcloth, to Isaiah the prophet the son of Amoz.

³ They said to him, "Thus says Hezekiah, 'This day is a day of distress, rebuke, and rejection; for children have come to birth and there is no strength to *deliver.*

⁴ 'Perhaps the LORD your God will hear all the words of Rabshakeh, whom his master the king of Assyria has sent to reproach the living God, and will rebuke the words which the LORD your God has heard. Therefore, offer a prayer for the remnant that is left.' "

⁵ So the servants of King Hezekiah came to Isaiah.

⁶ Isaiah said to them, "Thus you shall say to your master, 'Thus says the LORD, "Do not be afraid because of the words that you have heard, with which the servants of the king of Assyria have blasphemed Me.

⁷ "Behold, I will put a spirit in him so that he will hear a rumor and return to his own land. And I will make him fall by the sword in his own land." ' "

Sennacherib Defies God

⁸ ¶ Then Rabshakeh returned and found the king of Assyria fighting against Libnah, for he had heard that the king had left Lachish.

⁹ When he heard *them* say concerning Tirhakah king of Cush, "Behold, he has come out to fight against you," he sent messengers again to Hezekiah saying,

¹⁰ "Thus you shall say to Hezekiah king of Judah, 'Do not let your God in whom you trust deceive you saying, "Jerusalem will not be given into the hand of the king of Assyria."

¹¹ 'Behold, you have heard what the kings of Assyria have done to all the lands, destroying them completely. So will you be spared?

¹² 'Did the gods of those nations which my fathers destroyed deliver them, *even* Gozan and Haran and Rezeph and the sons of Eden who *were* in Telassar?

¹³ 'Where is the king of Hamath, the king of Arpad, the king of the city of Sepharvaim, and *of* Hena and Ivvah?' "

Hezekiah's Prayer

¹⁴ ¶ Then Hezekiah took the letter from the hand of the messengers and read it, and he went up to the house of the LORD and spread it out before the LORD.

New International

tree and drink water from his own cistern, ³²until I come and take you to a land like your own, a land of grain and new wine, a land of bread and vineyards, a land of olive trees and honey. Choose life and not death!

"Do not listen to Hezekiah, for he is misleading you when he says, 'The LORD will deliver us.' ³³Has the god of any nation ever delivered his land from the hand of the king of Assyria? ³⁴Where are the gods of Hamath and Arpad? Where are the gods of Sepharvaim, Hena and Ivvah? Have they rescued Samaria from my hand? ³⁵Who of all the gods of these countries has been able to save his land from me? How then can the LORD deliver Jerusalem from my hand?"

³⁶But the people remained silent and said nothing in reply, because the king had commanded, "Do not answer him."

³⁷Then Eliakim son of Hilkiah the palace administrator, Shebna the secretary and Joah son of Asaph the recorder went to Hezekiah, with their clothes torn, and told him what the field commander had said.

Jerusalem's Deliverance Foretold

19 WHEN KING Hezekiah heard this, he tore his clothes and put on sackcloth and went into the temple of the LORD. ²He sent Eliakim the palace administrator, Shebna the secretary and the leading priests, all wearing sackcloth, to the prophet Isaiah son of Amoz. ³They told him, "This is what Hezekiah says: This day is a day of distress and rebuke and disgrace, as when children come to the point of birth and there is no strength to deliver them. ⁴It may be that the LORD your God will hear all the words of the field commander, whom his master, the king of Assyria, has sent to ridicule the living God, and that he will rebuke him for the words the LORD your God has heard. Therefore pray for the remnant that still survives."

⁵When King Hezekiah's officials came to Isaiah, ⁶Isaiah said to them, "Tell your master, 'This is what the LORD says: Do not be afraid of what you have heard—those words with which the underlings of the king of Assyria have blasphemed me. ⁷Listen! I am going to put such a spirit in him that when he hears a certain report, he will return to his own country, and there I will have him cut down with the sword.' "

⁸When the field commander heard that the king of Assyria had left Lachish, he withdrew and found the king fighting against Libnah.

⁹Now Sennacherib received a report that Tirhakah, the Cushite[g] king of Egypt, was marching out to fight against him. So he again sent messengers to Hezekiah with this word: ¹⁰"Say to Hezekiah king of Judah: Do not let the god you depend on deceive you when he says, 'Jerusalem will not be handed over to the king of Assyria.' ¹¹Surely you have heard what the kings of Assyria have done to all the countries, destroying them completely. And will you be delivered? ¹²Did the gods of the nations that were destroyed by my forefathers deliver them: the gods of Gozan, Haran, Rezeph and the people of Eden who were in Tel Assar? ¹³Where is the king of Hamath, the king of Arpad, the king of the city of Sepharvaim, or of Hena or Ivvah?"

Hezekiah's Prayer

¹⁴Hezekiah received the letter from the messengers and read it. Then he went up to the temple of the LORD and

King James

15And Hezekiah prayed before the LORD, and said, O LORD God of Israel, which dwellest *between* the cherubims, thou art the God, *even* thou alone, of all the kingdoms of the earth; thou hast made heaven and earth.

16LORD, bow down thine ear, and hear: open, LORD, thine eyes, and see: and hear the words of Sennacherib, which hath sent him to reproach the living God.

17Of a truth, LORD, the kings of Assyria have destroyed the nations and their lands,

18And have [l]cast their gods into the fire: for they *were* no gods, but the work of men's hands, wood and stone: therefore they have destroyed them.

19Now therefore, O LORD our God, I beseech thee, save thou us out of his hand, that all the kingdoms of the earth may know that thou *art* the LORD God, *even* thou only.

The divine deliverance

20 ¶ Then Isaiah the son of Amoz sent to Hezekiah, saying, Thus saith the LORD God of Israel, *That* which thou hast prayed to me against Sennacherib king of Assyria I have heard.

21This *is* the word that the LORD hath spoken concerning him; The virgin the daughter of Zion hath despised thee, *and* laughed thee to scorn; the daughter of Jerusalem hath shaken her head at thee.

22Whom hast thou reproached and blasphemed? and against whom hast thou exalted *thy* voice, and lifted up thine eyes on high? *even* against the Holy *One* of Israel.

23[m]By thy messengers thou hast reproached the Lord, and hast said, With the multitude of my chariots I am come up to the height of the mountains, to the sides of Lebanon, and will cut down [n]the tall cedar trees thereof, *and* the choice fir trees thereof: and I will enter into the lodgings of his borders, *and into* [o]the forest of his Carmel.

24I have digged and drunk strange waters, and with the sole of my feet have I dried up all the rivers of [p]besieged places.

25[q]Hast thou not heard long ago *how* I have done it, *and* of ancient times that I have formed it? now have I brought it to pass, that thou shouldest be to lay waste fenced cities *into* ruinous heaps.

26Therefore their inhabitants were [r]of small power, they were dismayed and confounded; they were *as* the grass of the field, and *as* the green herb, *as* the grass on the housetops, and *as corn* blasted before it be grown up.

27But I know thy [s]abode, and thy going out, and thy coming in, and thy rage against me.

28Because thy rage against me and thy tumult is come up into mine ears, therefore I will put my hook in thy nose, and my bridle in thy lips, and I will turn thee back by the way by which thou camest.

29And this *shall be* a sign unto thee, Ye shall eat this year such things as grow of themselves, and in the second year that which springeth of the same; and in the third year sow ye, and reap, and plant vineyards, and eat the fruits thereof.

30And [t]the remnant that is escaped of the house of Judah shall yet again take root downward, and bear fruit upward.

[l]Heb. *given* [m]Heb. *By the hand of* [n]Heb. *the tallness*
[o]Or, *the forest* and *his fruitful field;* see Is. 10:18 [p]Or, *fenced*
[q]Or, *Hast thou not heard* how *I have made it long ago, and formed it of ancient times? should I now bring it to be laid waste,* and *fenced cities* to be *ruinous heaps?* [r]Heb. *short of hand*
[s]Or, *sitting* [t]Heb. *the escaping of the house of Judah that remaineth*

Amplified

15And Hezekiah prayed: O Lord, the God of Israel, Who [in symbol] is enthroned above the cherubim [of the ark in the temple], You are the God, You alone, of all the kingdoms of the earth. You have made the heavens and the earth.

16Lord, bow down Your ear and hear; Lord, open Your eyes and see; hear the words of Sennacherib which he has sent to mock, reproach, insult, *and* defy the living God.

17It is true, Lord, that the Assyrian kings have laid waste the nations and their lands

18And have cast the gods of those peoples into the fire, for they were not gods but the work of men's hands, wood and stone. So they [could destroy and] have destroyed them.

19Now therefore, O Lord our God, I beseech You, save us out of his hand, that all the kingdoms of the earth may know *and* understand that You, O Lord, are God alone.

20Then Isaiah son of Amoz sent to Hezekiah, saying, Thus says the Lord, the God of Israel: Your prayer to Me about Sennacherib king of Assyria I have heard. [Isa. 37:21–38.]

21This is the word that the Lord has spoken concerning him: The Virgin Daughter of Zion has despised you and laughed you to scorn; the Daughter of Jerusalem has wagged her head behind you.

22Whom have you mocked *and* reviled and insulted *and* blasphemed? Against Whom have you raised your voice and haughtily lifted your eyes? Against the Holy One of Israel!

23By your messengers you have mocked, reproached, insulted, *and* defied the Lord, and have said, With my many chariots I have gone up to the heights of the mountains, to the far recesses of Lebanon. I cut down its tall cedar trees and its choicest cypress trees. I entered its most distant retreat, its densest forest.

24I dug wells and drank foreign waters, and with the sole of my feet have I dried up all [the defense and] the streams of Egypt.

25[But, says the God of Israel] Have you not heard how I ordained long ago what now I have brought to pass? I planned it in olden times, that you [king of Assyria] should [be My instrument to] lay waste fortified cities, making them ruinous heaps.

26That is why their inhabitants had little power, they were dismayed and confounded; they were like plants of the field, the green herb, the grass on the housetops, blasted before it is grown up.

27But [O Sennacherib] I [the Lord] know your sitting down, your going out, your coming in, and your raging against Me.

28Because your raging against Me and your arrogance *and* careless ease have come to My ears, therefore I will put My hook in your nose and My bridle in your lips, and I will turn you back by the way you came, O king of Assyria.

29And [Hezekiah, says the Lord] this shall be the sign [of these things] to you: you shall eat this year what grows of itself, also in the second year what springs up voluntarily. But in the third year sow and reap, plant vineyards and eat their fruit.

30And the remnant that has survived of the house of Judah shall again take root downward and bear fruit upward.

New American Standard

15 Hezekiah prayed before the LORD and said, "O LORD, the God of Israel, who are enthroned *above* the cherubim, You are the God, You alone, of all the kingdoms of the earth. You have made heaven and earth.

16"Incline Your ear, O LORD, and hear; open Your eyes, O LORD, and see; and listen to the words of Sennacherib, which he has sent to reproach the living God.

17"Truly, O LORD, the kings of Assyria have devastated the nations and their lands

18 and have cast their gods into the fire, for they were not gods but the work of men's hands, wood and stone. So they have destroyed them.

19"Now, O LORD our God, I pray, deliver us from his hand that all the kingdoms of the earth may know that You alone, O LORD, are God."

God's Answer through Isaiah

20 ¶ Then Isaiah the son of Amoz sent to Hezekiah saying, "Thus says the LORD, the God of Israel, 'Because you have prayed to Me about Sennacherib king of Assyria, I have heard *you.*'

21"This is the word that the LORD has spoken against him:
'She has despised you and mocked you,
The virgin daughter of Zion;
She has shaken *her* head behind you,
The daughter of Jerusalem!
22 'Whom have you reproached and blasphemed?
And against whom have you raised *your* voice,
And haughtily lifted up your eyes?
Against the Holy One of Israel!
23 'Through your messengers you have reproached
    the Lord,
And you have said, "With my many chariots
I came up to the heights of the mountains,
To the remotest parts of Lebanon;
And I cut down its tall cedars *and* its choice
    cypresses.
And I entered its farthest lodging place, its
    thickest forest.
24"I dug *wells* and drank foreign waters,
And with the sole of my feet I dried up
All the rivers of Egypt."

25 ¶ 'Have you not heard?
Long ago I did it;
From ancient times I planned it.
Now I have brought it to pass,
That you should turn fortified cities into ruinous
    heaps.
26 'Therefore their inhabitants were short of strength,
They were dismayed and put to shame;
They were as the vegetation of the field and as
    the green herb,
As grass on the housetops is scorched before it is
    grown up.
27 'But I know your sitting down,
And your going out and your coming in,
And your raging against Me.
28 'Because of your raging against Me,
And because your arrogance has come up to My
    ears,
Therefore I will put My hook in your nose,
And My bridle in your lips,
And I will turn you back by the way which you
    came.

29 ¶ 'Then this shall be the sign for you: you will eat this year what grows of itself, in the second year what springs from the same, and in the third year sow, reap, plant vineyards, and eat their fruit.

30 'The surviving remnant of the house of Judah will again take root downward and bear fruit upward.

New International

spread it out before the LORD. 15And Hezekiah prayed to the LORD: "O LORD, God of Israel, enthroned between the cherubim, you alone are God over all the kingdoms of the earth. You have made heaven and earth. 16Give ear, O LORD, and hear; open your eyes, O LORD, and see; listen to the words Sennacherib has sent to insult the living God.

17"It is true, O LORD, that the Assyrian kings have laid waste these nations and their lands. 18They have thrown their gods into the fire and destroyed them, for they were not gods but only wood and stone, fashioned by men's hands. 19Now, O LORD our God, deliver us from his hand, so that all kingdoms on earth may know that you alone, O LORD, are God."

Isaiah Prophesies Sennacherib's Fall

20Then Isaiah son of Amoz sent a message to Hezekiah: "This is what the LORD, the God of Israel, says: I have heard your prayer concerning Sennacherib king of Assyria. 21This is the word that the LORD has spoken against him:

" 'The Virgin Daughter of Zion
    despises you and mocks you.
The Daughter of Jerusalem
    tosses her head as you flee.
22Who is it you have insulted and blasphemed?
    Against whom have you raised your voice
and lifted your eyes in pride?
    Against the Holy One of Israel!
23By your messengers
    you have heaped insults on the Lord.
And you have said,
    "With my many chariots
I have ascended the heights of the mountains,
    the utmost heights of Lebanon.
I have cut down its tallest cedars,
    the choicest of its pines.
I have reached its remotest parts,
    the finest of its forests.
24I have dug wells in foreign lands
    and drunk the water there.
With the soles of my feet
    I have dried up all the streams of Egypt."

25" 'Have you not heard?
    Long ago I ordained it.
In days of old I planned it;
    now I have brought it to pass,
that you have turned fortified cities
    into piles of stone.
26Their people, drained of power,
    are dismayed and put to shame.
They are like plants in the field,
    like tender green shoots,
like grass sprouting on the roof,
    scorched before it grows up.

27" 'But I know where you stay
    and when you come and go
    and how you rage against me.
28Because you rage against me
    and your insolence has reached my ears,
I will put my hook in your nose
    and my bit in your mouth,
and I will make you return
    by the way you came.'

29"This will be the sign for you, O Hezekiah:

"This year you will eat what grows by itself,
    and the second year what springs from that.
But in the third year sow and reap,
    plant vineyards and eat their fruit.
30Once more a remnant of the house of Judah
    will take root below and bear fruit above.

King James   Amplified

³¹For out of Jerusalem shall go forth a remnant, and ᵘthey that escape out of mount Zion: the zeal of the LORD *of hosts* shall do this.

³²Therefore thus saith the LORD concerning the king of Assyria, He shall not come into this city, nor shoot an arrow there, nor come before it with shield, nor cast a bank against it.

³³By the way that he came, by the same shall he return, and shall not come into this city, saith the LORD.

³⁴For I will defend this city, to save it, for mine own sake, and for my servant David's sake.

³⁵ ¶ And it came to pass that night, that the angel of the LORD went out, and smote in the camp of the Assyrians an hundred fourscore and five thousand: and when they arose early in the morning, behold, they *were* all dead corpses.

³⁶So Sennacherib king of Assyria departed, and went and returned, and dwelt at Nineveh.

³⁷And it came to pass, as he was worshipping in the house of Nisroch his god, that Adrammelech and Sharezer his sons smote him with the sword: and they escaped into the land of ᵛArmenia. And Esar-haddon his son reigned in his stead.

The sickness of Hezekiah

20 IN THOSE days was Hezekiah sick unto death. And the prophet Isaiah the son of Amoz came to him, and said unto him, Thus saith the LORD, ʷSet thine house in order; for thou shalt die, and not live.

²Then he turned his face to the wall, and prayed unto the LORD, saying,

³I beseech thee, O LORD, remember now how I have walked before thee in truth and with a perfect heart, and have done *that which is* good in thy sight. And Hezekiah wept ˣsore.

⁴And it came to pass, afore Isaiah was gone out into the middle ʸcourt, that the word of the LORD came to him, saying,

⁵Turn again, and tell Hezekiah the captain of my people, Thus saith the LORD, the God of David thy father, I have heard thy prayer, I have seen thy tears: behold, I will heal thee: on the third day thou shalt go up unto the house of the LORD.

⁶And I will add unto thy days fifteen years; and I will deliver thee and this city out of the hand of the king of Assyria; and I will defend this city for mine own sake, and for my servant David's sake.

⁷And Isaiah said, Take a lump of figs. And they took and laid *it* on the boil, and he recovered.

³¹For out of Jerusalem shall go forth a remnant, and a band of survivors out of Mount Zion. The zeal of the Lord of hosts shall perform this.

³²Therefore thus says the Lord concerning the king of Assyria: He shall not come into this city or shoot an arrow here or come before it with shield or cast up a siege mound against it.

³³By the way that he came, by that way shall he return, and he shall not come into this city, says the Lord.

³⁴For I will defend this city to save it, for My own sake and for My servant David's sake.

³⁵And it all came to pass, for that night the ʰAngel of the Lord went forth and slew 185,000 in the camp of the Assyrians; and when [the living] arose early in the morning, behold, all these were dead bodies.

³⁶So Sennacherib king of Assyria departed and returned and dwelt at Nineveh.

³⁷And as he was worshiping in the house of Nisroch his god, Adrammelech and Sharezer his sons killed him with the sword, and they escaped to the land of Armenia *or* Ararat. Esarhaddon his son reigned in his stead.

20 IN THOSE days Hezekiah became deadly ill. The prophet Isaiah son of Amoz came and said to him, Thus says the Lord: Set your house in order, for you shall die; you shall not recover. [II Chron. 32:24–26; Isa. 38:1–8.]

²Then Hezekiah turned his face to the wall and prayed to the Lord, saying,

³I beseech You, O Lord, [earnestly] remember now how I have walked before You in faithfulness *and* truth and with a whole heart [entirely devoted to You] and have done what is good in Your sight. And Hezekiah wept bitterly.

⁴Before Isaiah had gone out of the middle court, the word of the Lord came to him:

⁵Turn back and tell Hezekiah, the leader of My people, Thus says the Lord, the God of David your [forefather]: I have heard your prayer, I have seen your tears; behold, I will heal you. On the third day you shall go up to the house of the Lord.

⁶I will ⁱadd to your life fifteen years and deliver you and this city [Jerusalem] out of the hand of the king of Assyria; and I will defend this city for My own sake and for My servant David's sake.

⁷And Isaiah said, Bring a cake of figs. Let them lay it on the burning inflammation, that he may recover.

ʰ See footnote on Gen. 16:7.   ⁱ Good King Hezekiah's prayer life holds a mighty challenge and a clear and terrible warning for every believer. In his nation's darkest hour (18:13-17), he prayed (19:15), and God performed a miracle, one He had foretold (19:20, 32-37). It is a wonderful thing to have such power as that with God! But in this chapter (20) and the next, that power has become a terrible thing; for Hezekiah had put himself on God's "ways and means committee," as chairman in fact. God virtually said, "Your time has come to die" (20:1). But Hezekiah's words and tears implied, "No! I want to live and have sons who will do mighty things, and I myself have my best years ahead of me!" Read this chapter and the next, and note at least ten terrible things (see also footnote on II Kings 20:17) that resulted which only God could foresee and that only Hezekiah's death executed at the time God intended it would have prevented. But Hezekiah interfered. The only safe prayer policy is "God's will; nothing more; nothing less; nothing else; at any cost" (see Luke 22:42, Acts 21:14). It pays triumphantly! Martin Luther is quoted as saying, "Blessed is he who submits to the will of God; he can never be unhappy. Men may deal with him as they will . . . ; he is without care; he knows that 'all things work together for good' for him" (Rom. 8:28) (Martin Luther, cited by J.P. Lange, *A Commentary*).

ᵘHeb. *the escaping concerning thine house*   ᵛHeb. *Ararat*   ʷHeb. *Give charge*   ˣHeb. *with a great weeping*   ʸOr, *city*

New American Standard

31 'For out of Jerusalem will go forth a remnant, and out of Mount Zion survivors. The zeal of *n*the LORD will perform this.

32 ¶ 'Therefore thus says the LORD concerning the king of Assyria, "He will not come to this city or shoot an arrow there; and he will not come before it with a shield or throw up a siege ramp against it.

33"By the way that he came, by the same he will return, and he shall not come to this city," ' declares the LORD.

34 'For I will defend this city to save it for My own sake and for My servant David's sake.' "

35 ¶ Then it happened that night that the angel of the LORD went out and struck 185,000 in the camp of the Assyrians; and when men rose early in the morning, behold, all of them were dead.

36 So Sennacherib king of Assyria departed and returned *home,* and lived at Nineveh.

37 It came about as he was worshiping in the house of Nisroch his god, that Adrammelech and Sharezer killed him with the sword; and they escaped into the land of Ararat. And Esarhaddon his son became king in his place.

Hezekiah's Illness and Recovery

20 IN THOSE days Hezekiah became mortally ill. And Isaiah the prophet the son of Amoz came to him and said to him, "Thus says the LORD, 'Set your house in order, for you shall die and not live.' "

2 Then he turned his face to the wall and prayed to the LORD, saying,

3"Remember now, O LORD, I beseech You, how I have walked before You in truth and with a whole heart and have done what is good in Your sight." And Hezekiah wept bitterly.

4 Before Isaiah had gone out of the middle court, the word of the LORD came to him, saying,

5"Return and say to Hezekiah the leader of My people, 'Thus says the LORD, the God of your father David, "I have heard your prayer, I have seen your tears; behold, I will heal you. On the third day you shall go up to the house of the LORD.

6"I will add fifteen years to your life, and I will deliver you and this city from the hand of the king of Assyria; and I will defend this city for My own sake and for My servant David's sake." ' "

7 Then Isaiah said, "Take a cake of figs." And they took and laid *it* on the boil, and he recovered.

New International

31For out of Jerusalem will come a remnant,
    and out of Mount Zion a band of survivors.

The zeal of the LORD Almighty will accomplish this.

32"Therefore this is what the LORD says concerning the king of Assyria:

   "He will not enter this city
       or shoot an arrow here.
   He will not come before it with shield
       or build a siege ramp against it.
   33By the way that he came he will return;
       he will not enter this city,
                       declares the LORD.
   34I will defend this city and save it,
       for my sake and for the sake of David my
           servant."

35That night the angel of the LORD went out and put to death a hundred and eighty-five thousand men in the Assyrian camp. When the people got up the next morning—there were all the dead bodies! 36So Sennacherib king of Assyria broke camp and withdrew. He returned to Nineveh and stayed there.

37One day, while he was worshiping in the temple of his god Nisroch, his sons Adrammelech and Sharezer cut him down with the sword, and they escaped to the land of Ararat. And Esarhaddon his son succeeded him as king.

Hezekiah's Illness

20 IN THOSE days Hezekiah became ill and was at the point of death. The prophet Isaiah son of Amoz went to him and said, "This is what the LORD says: Put your house in order, because you are going to die; you will not recover."

2Hezekiah turned his face to the wall and prayed to the LORD, 3"Remember, O LORD, how I have walked before you faithfully and with wholehearted devotion and have done what is good in your eyes." And Hezekiah wept bitterly.

4Before Isaiah had left the middle court, the word of the LORD came to him: 5"Go back and tell Hezekiah, the leader of my people, 'This is what the LORD, the God of your father David, says: I have heard your prayer and seen your tears; I will heal you. On the third day from now you will go up to the temple of the LORD. 6I will add fifteen years to your life. And I will deliver you and this city from the hand of the king of Assyria. I will defend this city for my sake and for the sake of my servant David.' "

7Then Isaiah said, "Prepare a poultice of figs." They did so and applied it to the boil, and he recovered.

n Some ancient mss read *the* LORD *of hosts*

King James

8 ¶And Hezekiah said unto Isaiah, What *shall be* the sign that the LORD will heal me, and that I shall go up into the house of the LORD the third day?

9And Isaiah said, This sign shalt thou have of the LORD, that the LORD will do the thing that he hath spoken: shall the shadow go forward ten degrees, or go back ten degrees?

10And Hezekiah answered, It is a light thing for the shadow to go down ten degrees: nay, but let the shadow return backward ten degrees.

11And Isaiah the prophet cried unto the LORD: and he brought the shadow ten degrees backward, by which it had gone down in the ᶻdial of Ahaz.

Hezekiah's foolishness

12 ¶At that time ᵃBerodach-baladan, the son of Baladan, king of Babylon, sent letters and a present unto Hezekiah: for he had heard that Hezekiah had been sick.

13And Hezekiah hearkened unto them, and showed them all the house of his ᵇprecious things, the silver, and the gold, and the spices, and the precious ointment, and *all* the house of his ᶜᵈarmour, and all that was found in his treasures: there was nothing in his house, nor in all his dominion, that Hezekiah showed them not.

14 ¶Then came Isaiah the prophet unto king Hezekiah, and said unto him, What said these men? and from whence came they unto thee? And Hezekiah said, They are come from a far country, *even* from Babylon.

15And he said, What have they seen in thine house? And Hezekiah answered, All *the things* that *are* in mine house have they seen: there is nothing among my treasures that I have not showed them.

16And Isaiah said unto Hezekiah, Hear the word of the LORD.

17Behold, the days come, that all that *is* in thine house, and that which thy fathers have laid up in store unto this day, shall be carried into Babylon: nothing shall be left, saith the LORD.

18And of thy sons that shall issue from thee, which thou shalt beget, shall they take away; and they shall be eunuchs in the palace of the king of Babylon.

19Then said Hezekiah unto Isaiah, Good *is* the word of the LORD which thou hast spoken. And he said, ᵉ*Is it* not *good,* if peace and truth be in my days?

20 ¶And the rest of the acts of Hezekiah, and all his might, and how he made a pool, and a conduit, and brought water into the city, *are* they not written in the book of the chronicles of the kings of Judah?

21And Hezekiah slept with his fathers: and Manasseh his son reigned in his stead.

Manasseh, king of Judah

21 MANASSEH *WAS* twelve years old when he began to reign, and reigned fifty and five years in Jerusalem. And his mother's name *was* Hephzibah.

2And he did *that which was* evil in the sight of the LORD, after the abominations of the heathen, whom the LORD cast out before the children of Israel.

3For he built up again the high places which Hezekiah his father had destroyed; and he reared up altars for Baal, and made a grove, as did Ahab king of Israel; and worshipped all the host of heaven, and served them.

4And he built altars in the house of the LORD, of which the LORD said, In Jerusalem will I put my name.

Amplified

8Hezekiah said to Isaiah, What shall be the sign that the Lord will heal me and that I shall go up into the house of the Lord on the third day?

9And Isaiah said, This is the sign to you from the Lord that He will do the thing He has promised: shall the shadow [denoting the time of day] go forward ten steps, or go back ten steps?

10Hezekiah answered, It is an easy matter for the shadow to go forward ten steps; so let the shadow go back ten steps.

11So Isaiah the prophet cried to the Lord, and He brought the shadow the ten steps backward by which it had gone down on the sundial of Ahaz.

12At that time Merodach-baladan son of Baladan king of Babylon sent letters and a present to Hezekiah, for he had heard of Hezekiah's illness. [Isa. 39:1–8.]

13And Hezekiah rejoiced *and* welcomed the embassy and showed them all his treasure-house—the silver, gold, spices, precious ointment, his armory, and all that was found in his treasuries. There was nothing in his house or in all his realm that Hezekiah did not show them.

14Then Isaiah the prophet came to King Hezekiah and said, What did these men say? From where did they come to you? Hezekiah said, They are from a far country, from Babylon.

15Isaiah said, What have they seen in your house? Hezekiah answered, They have seen all that is in my house. There is no treasure of mine that I have not shown them.

16Then Isaiah said to Hezekiah, Hear the word of the Lord!

17Behold, the time is coming when ʲall that is in your house, and that which your forefathers have stored up till this day, shall be carried to Babylon; nothing shall be left, says the Lord.

18And some of your sons who shall be born to you shall be taken away, and they shall be eunuchs in the palace of Babylon's king.

19Then said Hezekiah to Isaiah, The word of the Lord you have spoken is good. For he thought, Is it not good, if [all this evil is meant for the future and] peace and security shall be in my days?

20The rest of the acts of Hezekiah, and all his might, and how he made the pool and the canal and brought water into the city, are they not written in the Book of the Chronicles of the Kings of Judah?

21Hezekiah slept with his fathers. Manasseh his son reigned in his stead.

21 MANASSEH WAS twelve years old when he began his fifty-five-year [wicked] reign in Jerusalem. His mother's name was Hephzibah.

2He [Hezekiah's son] did evil in the sight of the Lord, after the [idolatrous] practices of the [heathen] nations whom the Lord cast out before the Israelites.

3For he built up again the high places which Hezekiah his father had destroyed; and he reared up altars for Baal and made an Asherah, as did Ahab king of Israel, and worshiped all the [starry] hosts of the heavens and served them!

4And he built [heathen] altars in the house of the Lord, of which the Lord said, In Jerusalem will I put My ᵏName [and the pledge of My presence].

ʲThis is the first of ten tragic results of Hezekiah's self-willed prayer, which God's plan for Hezekiah's death would have prevented (see the footnote on 20:6). For a listing of these results see II Kings 20:18; 21:1, 3, 4, 6, 9, 14, 16, 20.   ᵏSee footnote on Deut. 12:5.

ᶻHeb. *degrees*   ᵃOr, *Merodach-baladan*   ᵇOr, *spicery*
ᶜOr, *jewels*   ᵈHeb. *vessels*   ᵉOr, *Shall there not be peace and truth*

New American Standard

8 ¶ Now Hezekiah said to Isaiah, "What will be the sign that the LORD will heal me, and that I shall go up to the house of the LORD the third day?"

9 Isaiah said, "This shall be the sign to you from the LORD, that the LORD will do the thing that He has spoken: shall the shadow go forward ten steps or go back ten steps?"

10 So Hezekiah answered, "It is easy for the shadow to decline ten steps; no, but let the shadow turn backward ten steps."

11 Isaiah the prophet cried to the LORD, and He brought the shadow on the stairway back ten steps by which it had gone down on the stairway of Ahaz.

Hezekiah Shows Babylon His Treasures

12 ¶ At that time Berodach-baladan a son of Baladan, king of Babylon, sent letters and a present to Hezekiah, for he heard that Hezekiah had been sick.

13 Hezekiah listened to them, and showed them all his treasure house, the silver and the gold and the spices and the precious oil and the house of his armor and all that was found in his treasuries. There was nothing in his house nor in all his dominion that Hezekiah did not show them.

14 Then Isaiah the prophet came to King Hezekiah and said to him, "What did these men say, and from where have they come to you?" And Hezekiah said, "They have come from a far country, from Babylon."

15 He said, "What have they seen in your house?" So Hezekiah answered, "They have seen all that is in my house; there is nothing among my treasuries that I have not shown them."

16 ¶ Then Isaiah said to Hezekiah, "Hear the word of the LORD.

17 'Behold, the days are coming when all that is in your house, and all that your fathers have laid up in store to this day will be carried to Babylon; nothing shall be left,' says the LORD.

18 'Some of your sons who shall issue from you, whom you will beget, will be taken away; and they will become officials in the palace of the king of Babylon.' "

19 Then Hezekiah said to Isaiah, "The word of the LORD which you have spoken is good." For he thought, "Is it not so, if there will be peace and truth in my days?"

20 ¶ Now the rest of the acts of Hezekiah and all his might, and how he made the pool and the conduit and brought water into the city, are they not written in the Book of the Chronicles of the Kings of Judah?

21 So Hezekiah slept with his fathers, and Manasseh his son became king in his place.

Manasseh Succeeds Hezekiah

21 MANASSEH WAS twelve years old when he became king, and he reigned fifty-five years in Jerusalem; and his mother's name was Hephzibah.

2 He did evil in the sight of the LORD, according to the abominations of the nations whom the LORD dispossessed before the sons of Israel.

3 For he rebuilt the high places which Hezekiah his father had destroyed; and he erected altars for Baal and made an Asherah, as Ahab king of Israel had done, and worshiped all the host of heaven and served them.

4 He built altars in the house of the LORD, of which the LORD had said, "In Jerusalem I will put My name."

New International

8Hezekiah had asked Isaiah, "What will be the sign that the LORD will heal me and that I will go up to the temple of the LORD on the third day from now?"

9Isaiah answered, "This is the LORD's sign to you that the LORD will do what he has promised: Shall the shadow go forward ten steps, or shall it go back ten steps?"

10"It is a simple matter for the shadow to go forward ten steps," said Hezekiah. "Rather, have it go back ten steps."

11Then the prophet Isaiah called upon the LORD, and the LORD made the shadow go back the ten steps it had gone down on the stairway of Ahaz.

Envoys From Babylon

12At that time Merodach-Baladan son of Baladan king of Babylon sent Hezekiah letters and a gift, because he had heard of Hezekiah's illness. 13Hezekiah received the messengers and showed them all that was in his storehouses—the silver, the gold, the spices and the fine oil—his armory and everything found among his treasures. There was nothing in his palace or in all his kingdom that Hezekiah did not show them.

14Then Isaiah the prophet went to King Hezekiah and asked, "What did those men say, and where did they come from?"

"From a distant land," Hezekiah replied. "They came from Babylon."

15The prophet asked, "What did they see in your palace?"

"They saw everything in my palace," Hezekiah said. "There is nothing among my treasures that I did not show them."

16Then Isaiah said to Hezekiah, "Hear the word of the LORD: 17The time will surely come when everything in your palace, and all that your fathers have stored up until this day, will be carried off to Babylon. Nothing will be left, says the LORD. 18And some of your descendants, your own flesh and blood, that will be born to you, will be taken away, and they will become eunuchs in the palace of the king of Babylon."

19"The word of the LORD you have spoken is good," Hezekiah replied. For he thought, "Will there not be peace and security in my lifetime?"

20As for the other events of Hezekiah's reign, all his achievements and how he made the pool and the tunnel by which he brought water into the city, are they not written in the book of the annals of the kings of Judah? 21Hezekiah rested with his fathers. And Manasseh his son succeeded him as king.

Manasseh King of Judah

21 MANASSEH WAS twelve years old when he became king, and he reigned in Jerusalem fifty-five years. His mother's name was Hephzibah. 2He did evil in the eyes of the LORD, following the detestable practices of the nations the LORD had driven out before the Israelites. 3He rebuilt the high places his father Hezekiah had destroyed; he also erected altars to Baal and made an Asherah pole, as Ahab king of Israel had done. He bowed down to all the starry hosts and worshiped them. 4He built altars in the temple of the LORD, of which the LORD had said, "In

King James

5And he built altars for all the host of heaven in the two courts of the house of the LORD.

6And he made his son pass through the fire, and observed times, and used enchantments, and dealt with familiar spirits and wizards: he wrought much wickedness in the sight of the LORD, to provoke *him* to anger.

7And he set a graven image of the grove that he had made in the house, of which the LORD said to David, and to Solomon his son, In this house, and in Jerusalem, which I have chosen out of all tribes of Israel, will I put my name for ever:

8Neither will I make the feet of Israel move any more out of the land which I gave their fathers; only if they will observe to do according to all that I have commanded them, and according to all the law that my servant Moses commanded them.

9But they hearkened not: and Manasseh seduced them to do more evil than did the nations whom the LORD destroyed before the children of Israel.

10 ¶ And the LORD spake by his servants the prophets, saying,

11Because Manasseh king of Judah hath done these abominations, *and* hath done wickedly above all that the Amorites did, which *were* before him, and hath made Judah also to sin with his idols:

12Therefore thus saith the LORD God of Israel, Behold, I *am* bringing *such* evil upon Jerusalem and Judah, that whosoever heareth of it, both his ears shall tingle.

13And I will stretch over Jerusalem the line of Samaria, and the plummet of the house of Ahab: and I will wipe Jerusalem as *a man* wipeth a dish, *f*wiping *it,* and turning *it* upside down.

14And I will forsake the remnant of mine inheritance, and deliver them into the hand of their enemies; and they shall become a prey and a spoil to all their enemies;

15Because they have done *that which was* evil in my sight, and have provoked me to anger, since the day their fathers came forth out of Egypt, even unto this day.

16Moreover Manasseh shed innocent blood very much, till he had filled Jerusalem *g*from one end to another; beside his sin wherewith he made Judah to sin, in doing *that which was* evil in the sight of the LORD.

17 ¶ Now the rest of the acts of Manasseh, and all that he did, and his sin that he sinned, *are* they not written in the book of the chronicles of the kings of Judah?

18And Manasseh slept with his fathers, and was buried in the garden of his own house, in the garden of Uzza: and Amon his son reigned in his stead.

Amon, king of Judah

19 ¶ Amon *was* twenty and two years old when he began to reign, and he reigned two years in Jerusalem. And his mother's name *was* Meshullemeth, the daughter of Haruz of Jotbah.

20And he did *that which was* evil in the sight of the LORD, as his father Manasseh did.

21And he walked in all the way that his father walked in, and served the idols that his father served, and worshipped them:

22And he forsook the LORD God of his fathers, and walked not in the way of the LORD.

23 ¶ And the servants of Amon conspired against him, and slew the king in his own house.

24And the people of the land slew all them that had conspired against king Amon; and the people of the land made Josiah his son king in his stead.

25Now the rest of the acts of Amon which he did, *are* they not written in the book of the chronicles of the kings of Judah?

26And he was buried in his sepulchre in the garden of Uzza: and Josiah his son reigned in his stead.

Amplified

5And he [good Hezekiah's son] built altars for all the hosts of the heavens in the two courts of the house of the Lord!

6And he made his son pass through the fire *and* burned him as an offering [to Molech]; he practiced soothsaying and augury, and dealt with mediums and wizards! He did much wickedness in the sight of the Lord, provoking Him to anger.

7He made a graven image of [the goddess] Asherah and set it in the house, of which the Lord said to David and to Solomon his son, In this house and in Jerusalem, which I have chosen out of all the tribes of Israel, will I put My Name [and the pledge of My presence] forever;

8And I will not cause the feet of Israel to wander any more out of the land which I gave their fathers, if only they will observe to do according to all that I have commanded them and according to all the law that My servant Moses commanded them.

9But they would not listen; and Manasseh seduced them to do more evil than the nations did whom the Lord destroyed before the Israelites!

10And the Lord said through His servants the prophets:

11Because Manasseh king of Judah has committed these abominations, and has done wickedly above all that the Amorites did who were before him, and has made Judah also to sin with his idols,

12Therefore thus says the Lord, the God of Israel: Behold, I am bringing such evil upon Jerusalem and Judah, that whoever hears of it, both his ears shall tingle!

13And I will stretch over Jerusalem the measuring line of Samaria and the plummet of the house of Ahab; and I will wipe Jerusalem as one wipes a dish, wiping it and turning it upside down.

14And I will cast off the rest of My inheritance and deliver them into the hands of their enemies; and they shall become a prey and a spoil to all their enemies,

15For they have done evil in My sight and have provoked Me to anger since their fathers came out of Egypt to this day.

16Moreover, Manasseh shed very much innocent blood, filling Jerusalem from one end to another—besides his sin in making Judah sin, by doing evil in the sight of the Lord! [II Chron. 33:1–10.]

17The rest of the acts of Manasseh, all that he did, and his sin that he committed, are they not written in the Book of the Chronicles of the Kings of Judah?

18Manasseh slept with his fathers and was buried in the garden of his own house, in the garden of Uzza. Amon his son reigned in his stead.

19Amon was twenty-two years old when he began his two-year reign in Jerusalem. His mother was Meshullemeth daughter of Haruz of Jotbah.

20[But] he also did evil in the sight of the Lord, as his father Manasseh had done. [II Kings 23:26, 27; 24:3, 4.]

21He walked in all the ways of his father; and he served the idols that his father served, and worshiped them;

22He forsook the Lord, the God of his [forefathers], and did not walk in the way of the Lord.

23The servants of Amon conspired against him and killed the king in his own house.

24But the people of the land killed all those who had conspired against King Amon, and made Josiah his son king in his stead.

25The rest of the acts of Amon, are they not written in the Book of the Chronicles of the Kings of Judah?

26He was buried in his tomb in the garden of Uzza. Josiah his son succeeded him.

---

*f*Heb. *he wipeth and turneth* it *upon the face thereof*   *g*Heb. *from mouth to mouth*

New American Standard

5 For he built altars for all the host of heaven in the two courts of the house of the LORD.

6 He made his son pass through the fire, practiced witchcraft and used divination, and dealt with mediums and spiritists. He did much evil in the sight of the LORD provoking *Him to anger.*

7 Then he set the carved image of Asherah that he had made, in the house of which the LORD said to David and to his son Solomon, "In this house and in Jerusalem, which I have chosen from all the tribes of Israel, I will put My name forever.

8 "And I will not make the feet of Israel wander anymore from the land which I gave their fathers, if only they will observe to do according to all that I have commanded them, and according to all the law that My servant Moses commanded them."

9 But they did not listen, and Manasseh seduced them to do evil more than the nations whom the LORD destroyed before the sons of Israel.

The King's Idolatries Rebuked

10 ¶ Now the LORD spoke through His servants the prophets, saying,

11 "Because Manasseh king of Judah has done these abominations, having done wickedly more than all the Amorites did who *were* before him, and has also made Judah sin with his idols;

12 therefore thus says the LORD, the God of Israel, 'Behold, I am bringing *such* calamity on Jerusalem and Judah, that whoever hears of it, both his ears will tingle.

13 'I will stretch over Jerusalem the line of Samaria and the plummet of the house of Ahab, and I will wipe Jerusalem as one wipes a dish, wiping it and turning it upside down.

14 'I will abandon the remnant of My inheritance and deliver them into the hand of their enemies, and they will become as plunder and spoil to all their enemies;

15 because they have done evil in My sight, and have been provoking Me to anger since the day their fathers came from Egypt, even to this day.' "

16 ¶ Moreover, Manasseh shed very much innocent blood until he had filled Jerusalem from one end to another; besides his sin with which he made Judah sin, in doing evil in the sight of the LORD.

17 Now the rest of the acts of Manasseh and all that he did and his sin which he committed, are they not written in the Book of the Chronicles of the Kings of Judah?

18 And Manasseh slept with his fathers and was buried in the garden of his own house, in the garden of Uzza, and Amon his son became king in his place.

Amon Succeeds Manasseh

19 ¶ Amon was twenty-two years old when he became king, and he reigned two years in Jerusalem; and his mother's name *was* Meshullemeth the daughter of Haruz of Jotbah.

20 He did evil in the sight of the LORD, as Manasseh his father had done.

21 For he walked in all the way that his father had walked, and served the idols that his father had served and worshiped them.

22 So he forsook the LORD, the God of his fathers, and did not walk in the way of the LORD.

23 The servants of Amon conspired against him and killed the king in his own house.

24 Then the people of the land killed all those who had conspired against King Amon, and the people of the land made Josiah his son king in his place.

25 Now the rest of the acts of Amon which he did, are they not written in the Book of the Chronicles of the Kings of Judah?

26 He was buried in his grave in the garden of Uzza, and Josiah his son became king in his place.

New International

Jerusalem I will put my Name." 5 In both courts of the temple of the LORD, he built altars to all the starry hosts. 6 He sacrificed his own son in[h] the fire, practiced sorcery and divination, and consulted mediums and spiritists. He did much evil in the eyes of the LORD, provoking him to anger.

7 He took the carved Asherah pole he had made and put it in the temple, of which the LORD had said to David and to his son Solomon, "In this temple and in Jerusalem, which I have chosen out of all the tribes of Israel, I will put my Name forever. 8 I will not again make the feet of the Israelites wander from the land I gave their forefathers, if only they will be careful to do everything I commanded them and will keep the whole Law that my servant Moses gave them." 9 But the people did not listen. Manasseh led them astray, so that they did more evil than the nations the LORD had destroyed before the Israelites.

10 The LORD said through his servants the prophets: 11 "Manasseh king of Judah has committed these detestable sins. He has done more evil than the Amorites who preceded him and has led Judah into sin with his idols. 12 Therefore this is what the LORD, the God of Israel, says: I am going to bring such disaster on Jerusalem and Judah that the ears of everyone who hears of it will tingle. 13 I will stretch out over Jerusalem the measuring line used against Samaria and the plumb line used against the house of Ahab. I will wipe out Jerusalem as one wipes a dish, wiping it and turning it upside down. 14 I will forsake the remnant of my inheritance and hand them over to their enemies. They will be looted and plundered by all their foes, 15 because they have done evil in my eyes and have provoked me to anger from the day their forefathers came out of Egypt until this day."

16 Moreover, Manasseh also shed so much innocent blood that he filled Jerusalem from end to end—besides the sin that he had caused Judah to commit, so that they did evil in the eyes of the LORD.

17 As for the other events of Manasseh's reign, and all he did, including the sin he committed, are they not written in the book of the annals of the kings of Judah? 18 Manasseh rested with his fathers and was buried in his palace garden, the garden of Uzza. And Amon his son succeeded him as king.

Amon King of Judah

19 Amon was twenty-two years old when he became king, and he reigned in Jerusalem two years. His mother's name was Meshullemeth daughter of Haruz; she was from Jotbah. 20 He did evil in the eyes of the LORD, as his father Manasseh had done. 21 He walked in all the ways of his father; he worshiped the idols his father had worshiped, and bowed down to them. 22 He forsook the LORD, the God of his fathers, and did not walk in the way of the LORD.

23 Amon's officials conspired against him and assassinated the king in his palace. 24 Then the people of the land killed all who had plotted against King Amon, and they made Josiah his son king in his place.

25 As for the other events of Amon's reign, and what he did, are they not written in the book of the annals of the kings of Judah? 26 He was buried in his grave in the garden of Uzza. And Josiah his son succeeded him as king.

h 6 Or He made his own son pass through

King James

Amplified

The book of the law found

22 JOSIAH *WAS* eight years old when he began to reign, and he reigned thirty and one years in Jerusalem. And his mother's name *was* Jedidah, the daughter of Adaiah of Boscath.

2And he did *that which was* right in the sight of the LORD, and walked in all the way of David his father, and turned not aside to the right hand or to the left.

3 ¶ And it came to pass in the eighteenth year of king Josiah, *that* the king sent Shaphan the son of Azaliah, the son of Meshullam, the scribe, to the house of the LORD, saying,

4Go up to Hilkiah the high priest, that he may sum the silver which is brought into the house of the LORD, which the keepers of the *h*door have gathered of the people:

5And let them deliver it into the hand of the doers of the work, that have the oversight of the house of the LORD: and let them give it to the doers of the work which *is* in the house of the LORD, to repair the breaches of the house,

6Unto carpenters, and builders, and masons, and to buy timber and hewn stone to repair the house.

7Howbeit there was no reckoning made with them of the money that was delivered into their hand, because they dealt faithfully.

8 ¶ And Hilkiah the high priest said unto Shaphan the scribe, I have found the book of the law in the house of the LORD. And Hilkiah gave the book to Shaphan, and he read it.

9And Shaphan the scribe came to the king, and brought the king word again, and said, Thy servants have *i*gathered the money that was found in the house, and have delivered it into the hand of them that do the work, that have the oversight of the house of the LORD.

10And Shaphan the scribe showed the king, saying, Hilkiah the priest hath delivered me a book. And Shaphan read it before the king.

11And it came to pass, when the king had heard the words of the book of the law, that he rent his clothes.

12And the king commanded Hilkiah the priest, and Ahikam the son of Shaphan, and Achbor the son of *j*Michaiah, and Shaphan the scribe, and Asahiah a servant of the king's, saying,

13Go ye, inquire of the LORD for me, and for the people, and for all Judah, concerning the words of this book that is found: for great *is* the wrath of the LORD that is kindled against us, because our fathers have not hearkened unto the words of this book, to do according unto all that which is written concerning us.

14So Hilkiah the priest, and Ahikam, and Achbor, and Shaphan, and Asahiah, went unto Huldah the prophetess, the wife of Shallum the son of Tikvah, the son of *k*Harhas, keeper of the *l*wardrobe; (now she dwelt in Jerusalem *m*in the college;) and they communed with her.

15 ¶ And she said unto them, Thus saith the LORD God of Israel, Tell the man that sent you to me,

16Thus saith the LORD, Behold, I will bring evil upon this place, and upon the inhabitants thereof, *even* all the words of the book which the king of Judah hath read:

17Because they have forsaken me, and have burned incense unto other gods, that they might provoke me to anger with all the works of their hands; therefore my wrath shall be kindled against this place, and shall not be quenched.

18But to the king of Judah which sent you to inquire of the LORD, thus shall ye say to him, Thus saith the LORD God of Israel, *As touching* the words which thou hast heard;

22 JOSIAH WAS eight years old when he began his thirty-one-year reign in Jerusalem. His mother was Jedidah daughter of Adaiah of Bozkath.

2He did right in the sight of the Lord and walked in all the ways of David his [forefather], and turned not aside to the right hand or to the left.

3In the eighteenth year of King Josiah, he sent Shaphan son of Azaliah, the son of Meshullam, the scribe, to the Lord's house, saying,

4Go up to Hilkiah the high priest, that he may count the money brought into the house of the Lord, to give to the keepers of the door have gathered from the people. [II Kings 12:4ff.]

5And let them deliver it into the hands of the workmen who have oversight of the Lord's house, to give to the laborers engaged in the repairing of the Lord's house—

6That is, to the carpenters, builders, and masons—and to buy timber and hewn stone to repair the house.

7However, there was no accounting required of them for the money delivered into their hands, because they dealt faithfully.

8Hilkiah the high priest said to Shaphan the scribe, I have found the Book of the Law in the house of the Lord! Hilkiah gave the book to Shaphan, and he read it.

9And Shaphan the scribe came to the king and reported to him: Your servants have gathered the money that was found in the house and have delivered it into the hands of the workmen who have oversight of the house of the Lord.

10Then Shaphan the scribe told the king, Hilkiah the priest has given me a book. And Shaphan read it before the king.

11And when the king heard the words of the Book of the Law, he rent his clothes.

12And the king commanded Hilkiah the priest, Ahikam son of Shaphan, Achbor son of Micaiah, Shaphan the scribe, and Asaiah servant of the king,

13Go, inquire of the Lord for me and for the people and for all Judah concerning the words of this book that has been found. For great is the wrath of the Lord that is kindled against us because our fathers have not listened *and* obeyed the words of this book, to do according to all that is written concerning us.

14So Hilkiah the priest, Ahikam, Achbor, Shaphan, and Asaiah went to Huldah the prophetess, the wife of Shallum son of Tikvah, the son of Harhas, keeper of the wardrobe—now she dwelt in Jerusalem, in the Second Quarter—and they talked with her.

15She said to them, Thus says the Lord, the God of Israel: Tell the man who sent you to me,

16Thus says the Lord: Behold, I will bring evil upon this place and upon its inhabitants, according to all the words of the book which the king of Judah has read.

17Because they have forsaken Me and have burned incense to other gods, provoking Me to anger with all the work of their hands, therefore My wrath will be kindled against this place and will not be quenched.

18But to the king of Judah, who sent you to inquire of the Lord, say this, Thus says the Lord, the God of Israel, regarding the words you have heard:

---

*h*Heb. *threshold*   *i*Heb. *melted*   *j*Or, *Micah*   *k*Or, *Hasrah*
*l*Heb. *garments*   *m*Or, *in the second part*

New American Standard

Josiah Succeeds Amon

22 JOSIAH WAS eight years old when he became king, and he reigned thirty-one years in Jerusalem; and his mother's name *was* Jedidah the daughter of Adaiah of Bozkath.

2 He did right in the sight of the LORD and walked in all the way of his father David, nor did he turn aside to the right or to the left.

3 ¶ Now in the eighteenth year of King Josiah, the king sent Shaphan, the son of Azaliah the son of Meshullam the scribe, to the house of the LORD saying,

4 "Go up to Hilkiah the high priest that he may count the money brought in to the house of the LORD which the doorkeepers have gathered from the people.

5 "Let them deliver it into the hand of the workmen who have the oversight of the house of the LORD, and let them give it to the workmen who are in the house of the LORD to repair the damages of the house,

6 to the carpenters and the builders and the masons and for buying timber and hewn stone to repair the house.

7 "Only no accounting shall be made with them for the money delivered into their hands, for they deal faithfully."

The Lost Book

8 ¶ Then Hilkiah the high priest said to Shaphan the scribe, "I have found the book of the law in the house of the LORD." And Hilkiah gave the book to Shaphan who read it.

9 Shaphan the scribe came to the king and brought back word to the king and said, "Your servants have emptied out the money that was found in the house, and have delivered it into the hand of the workmen who have the oversight of the house of the LORD."

10 Moreover, Shaphan the scribe told the king saying, "Hilkiah the priest has given me a book." And Shaphan read it in the presence of the king.

11 ¶ When the king heard the words of the book of the law, he tore his clothes.

12 Then the king commanded Hilkiah the priest, Ahikam the son of Shaphan, Achbor the son of Micaiah, Shaphan the scribe, and Asaiah the king's servant saying,

13 "Go, inquire of the LORD for me and the people and all Judah concerning the words of this book that has been found, for great is the wrath of the LORD that burns against us, because our fathers have not listened to the words of this book, to do according to all that is written concerning us."

Huldah Predicts

14 ¶ So Hilkiah the priest, Ahikam, Achbor, Shaphan, and Asaiah went to Huldah the prophetess, the wife of Shallum the son of Tikvah, the son of Harhas, keeper of the wardrobe (now she lived in Jerusalem in the Second Quarter); and they spoke to her.

15 She said to them, "Thus says the LORD God of Israel, 'Tell the man who sent you to me,

16 thus says the LORD, 'Behold, I bring evil on this place and on its inhabitants, *even* all the words of the book which the king of Judah has read.

17 "Because they have forsaken Me and have burned incense to other gods that they might provoke Me to anger with all the work of their hands, therefore My wrath burns against this place, and it shall not be quenched." '

18 "But to the king of Judah who sent you to inquire of the LORD thus shall you say to him, 'Thus says the LORD God of Israel, "*Regarding* the words which you have heard,

New International

The Book of the Law Found

22 JOSIAH WAS eight years old when he became king, and he reigned in Jerusalem thirty-one years. His mother's name was Jedidah daughter of Adaiah; she was from Bozkath. 2He did what was right in the eyes of the LORD and walked in all the ways of his father David, not turning aside to the right or to the left.

3In the eighteenth year of his reign, King Josiah sent the secretary, Shaphan son of Azaliah, the son of Meshullam, to the temple of the LORD. He said: 4"Go up to Hilkiah the high priest and have him get ready the money that has been brought into the temple of the LORD, which the doorkeepers have collected from the people. 5Have them entrust it to the men appointed to supervise the work on the temple. And have these men pay the workers who repair the temple of the LORD— 6the carpenters, the builders and the masons. Also have them purchase timber and dressed stone to repair the temple. 7But they need not account for the money entrusted to them, because they are acting faithfully."

8Hilkiah the high priest said to Shaphan the secretary, "I have found the Book of the Law in the temple of the LORD." He gave it to Shaphan, who read it. 9Then Shaphan the secretary went to the king and reported to him: "Your officials have paid out the money that was in the temple of the LORD and have entrusted it to the workers and supervisors at the temple." 10Then Shaphan the secretary informed the king, "Hilkiah the priest has given me a book." And Shaphan read from it in the presence of the king.

11When the king heard the words of the Book of the Law, he tore his robes. 12He gave these orders to Hilkiah the priest, Ahikam son of Shaphan, Acbor son of Micaiah, Shaphan the secretary and Asaiah the king's attendant: 13"Go and inquire of the LORD for me and for the people and for all Judah about what is written in this book that has been found. Great is the LORD's anger that burns against us because our fathers have not obeyed the words of this book; they have not acted in accordance with all that is written there concerning us."

14Hilkiah the priest, Ahikam, Acbor, Shaphan and Asaiah went to speak to the prophetess Huldah, who was the wife of Shallum son of Tikvah, the son of Harhas, keeper of the wardrobe. She lived in Jerusalem, in the Second District.

15She said to them, "This is what the LORD, the God of Israel, says: Tell the man who sent you to me, 16'This is what the LORD says: I am going to bring disaster on this place and its people, according to everything written in the book the king of Judah has read. 17Because they have forsaken me and burned incense to other gods and provoked me to anger by all the idols their hands have made,*i* my anger will burn against this place and will not be quenched.' 18Tell the king of Judah, who sent you to inquire of the LORD, 'This is what the LORD, the God of

---

i 17 Or by everything they have done

King James

19Because thine heart was tender, and thou hast humbled thyself before the LORD, when thou heardest what I spake against this place, and against the inhabitants thereof, that they should become a desolation and a curse, and hast rent thy clothes, and wept before me; I also have heard *thee,* saith the LORD.

20Behold therefore, I will gather thee unto thy fathers, and thou shalt be gathered into thy grave in peace; and thine eyes shall not see all the evil which I will bring upon this place. And they brought the king word again.

The renewal of the covenant

23 AND THE king sent, and they gathered unto him all the elders of Judah and of Jerusalem.

2And the king went up into the house of the LORD, and all the men of Judah and all the inhabitants of Jerusalem with him, and the priests, and the prophets, and all the people, *n*both small and great: and he read in their ears all the words of the book of the covenant which was found in the house of the LORD.

3 ¶ And the king stood by a pillar, and made a covenant before the LORD, to walk after the LORD, and to keep his commandments and his testimonies and his statutes with all *their* heart and all *their* soul, to perform the words of this covenant that were written in this book. And all the people stood to the covenant.

4And the king commanded Hilkiah the high priest, and the priests of the second order, and the keepers of the door, to bring forth out of the temple of the LORD all the vessels that were made for Baal, and for the grove, and for all the host of heaven: and he burned them without Jerusalem in the fields of Kidron, and carried the ashes of them unto Beth-el.

5And he *o*put down the *p*idolatrous priests, whom the kings of Judah had ordained to burn incense in the high places in the cities of Judah, and in the places round about Jerusalem; them also that burned incense unto Baal, to the sun, and to the moon, and to the *q*planets, and to all the hosts of heaven.

6And he brought out the grove from the house of the LORD, without Jerusalem, unto the brook Kidron, and burned it at the brook Kidron, and stamped *it* small to powder, and cast the powder thereof upon the graves of the children of the people.

7And he brake down the houses of the sodomites, that *were* by the house of the LORD, where the women wove *r*hangings for the grove.

8And he brought all the priests out of the cities of Judah, and defiled the high places where the priests had burned incense, from Geba to Beer-sheba, and brake down the high places of the gates that *were* in the entering in of the gate of Joshua the governor of the city, which *were* on a man's left hand at the gate of the city.

9Nevertheless the priests of the high places came not up to the altar of the LORD in Jerusalem, but they did eat of the unleavened bread among their brethren.

10And he defiled Topheth, which *is* in the valley of the children of Hinnom, that no man might make his son or his daughter to pass through the fire to Molech.

11And he took away the horses that the kings of Judah had given to the sun, at the entering in of the house of the LORD, by the chamber of Nathan-melech the *s*chamberlain, which *was* in the suburbs, and burned the chariots of the sun with fire.

12And the altars that *were* on the top of the upper chamber of Ahaz, which the kings of Judah had made, and the altars which Manasseh had made in the two courts of the house of the LORD, did the king beat down, and *t*brake *them* down from thence, and cast the dust of them into the brook Kidron.

Amplified

19Because your heart was [tender and] penitent and you humbled yourself before the Lord when you heard what I said against this place and against its inhabitants, that they should become a desolation, [an astonishment and] a curse, and you have rent your clothes and wept before Me, I also have heard you, says the Lord.

20Behold, therefore [King Josiah], I will gather you to your fathers, taken to your grave in peace, and your eyes shall not see all the evil which I will bring on this place. And they brought the king word.

23 KING JOSIAH sent and gathered to him all the elders of Judah and of Jerusalem.

2The king went up to the house of the Lord, and with him all the men of Judah, all the inhabitants of Jerusalem, the priests, the prophets, and all the people, both small and great. And he read in their ears all the words of the Book of the Covenant, which was found in the Lord's house.

3The king stood [on the platform] by the pillar and made a covenant before the Lord—to walk after the Lord and to keep His commandments, His testimonies, and His statutes with all his heart and soul, to confirm the words of this covenant that were written in this book. And all the people stood to join in the covenant.

4And the king commanded Hilkiah the high priest and the priests of the second rank and the keepers of the threshold to bring out of the temple of the Lord all the vessels made for Baal, for [the goddess] Asherah, and for all the hosts of the heavens; and he burned them outside Jerusalem in the fields of the Kidron, and carried their ashes to Bethel [where Israel's idolatry began]. [I Kings 12:28, 29.]

5He put away the idolatrous priests whom the kings of Judah had ordained to burn incense in the high places in Judah's cities and round about Jerusalem—also those who burned incense to Baal, to the sun, to the moon, to the constellations [or twelve signs of the zodiac], and to all the hosts of the heavens.

6And Josiah brought the Asherah from the house of the Lord to outside Jerusalem to the brook Kidron and burned it there, and beat it to dust and cast its dust upon the graves of the common people [who had sacrificed to it].

7And he broke down the houses of the male cult prostitutes, which were by the house of the Lord, where the women wove [tent] hangings for the Asherah [shrines].

8And [Josiah] brought all the [idolatrous] priests out of the city of Judah and defiled the high places, where the priests had burned incense, from Geba to Beersheba [north to south], and broke down the high places both at the entrance of the Gate of Joshua the governor of the city and that which was on one's left at the city's gate.

9However, the priests of the high places were not allowed to sacrifice upon the Lord's altar in Jerusalem, but they ate unleavened bread among their brethren.

10And Josiah defiled Topheth, which is in the Valley of Ben-hinnom [son of Hinnom], that no man might ever burn there his son or his daughter as an offering to Molech. [Ezek. 16:21.]

11And he removed the horses that the kings of Judah had devoted to the sun from the entrance of the house of the Lord, by the chamber of Nathan-melech the chamberlain, which was in the area, and he burned the chariots of the sun with fire.

12And the altars on the roof of the upper chamber of Ahaz, which the kings of Judah had made, and the altars which Manasseh had made in the two courts of the house of the Lord, [Josiah] pulled down and beat them in pieces, and he [ran and] cast their dust into the brook Kidron.

---

*n*Heb. *from small even unto great*   *o*Heb. *caused to cease*
*p*Heb. *Chemarim*   *q*Or, *twelve signs,* or, *constellations*
*r*Heb. *houses*   *s*Or, *eunuch,* or, *officer*   *t*Or, *ran from thence*

New American Standard

19 because your heart was tender and you humbled yourself before the LORD when you heard what I spoke against this place and against its inhabitants that they should become a desolation and a curse, and you have torn your clothes and wept before Me, I truly have heard you," declares the LORD.

20"Therefore, behold, I will gather you to your fathers, and you will be gathered to your grave in peace, and your eyes will not see all the evil which I will bring on this place." ' " So they brought back word to the king.

Josiah's Covenant

23 THEN THE king sent, and they gathered to him all the elders of Judah and of Jerusalem.

2 The king went up to the house of the LORD and all the men of Judah and all the inhabitants of Jerusalem with him, and the priests and the prophets and all the people, both small and great; and he read in their hearing all the words of the book of the covenant which was found in the house of the LORD.

3 The king stood by the pillar and made a covenant before the LORD, to walk after the LORD, and to keep His commandments and His testimonies and His statutes with all *his* heart and all *his* soul, to carry out the words of this covenant that were written in this book. And all the people entered into the covenant.

Reforms under Josiah

4 ¶ Then the king commanded Hilkiah the high priest and the priests of the second order and the doorkeepers, to bring out of the temple of the LORD all the vessels that were made for Baal, for *o*Asherah, and for all the host of heaven; and he burned them outside Jerusalem in the fields of the Kidron, and carried their ashes to Bethel.

5 He did away with the idolatrous priests whom the kings of Judah had appointed to burn incense in the high places in the cities of Judah and in the surrounding area of Jerusalem, also those who burned incense to Baal, to the sun and to the moon and to the constellations and to all the host of heaven.

6 He brought out the Asherah from the house of the LORD outside Jerusalem to the brook Kidron, and burned it at the brook Kidron, and ground *it* to dust, and threw its dust on the graves of the common people.

7 He also broke down the houses of the *male* cult prostitutes which *were* in the house of the LORD, where the women were weaving hangings for the Asherah.

8 Then he brought all the priests from the cities of Judah, and defiled the high places where the priests had burned incense, from Geba to Beersheba; and he broke down the high places of the gates which *were* at the entrance of the gate of Joshua the governor of the city, which *were* on one's left at the city gate.

9 Nevertheless the priests of the high places did not go up to the altar of the LORD in Jerusalem, but they ate unleavened bread among their brothers.

10 He also defiled *p*Topheth, which is in the valley of the son of Hinnom, that no man might make his son or his daughter pass through the fire for Molech.

11 He did away with the horses which the kings of Judah had given to the sun, at the entrance of the house of the LORD, by the chamber of Nathan-melech the official, which *was* in the precincts; and he burned the chariots of the sun with fire.

12 The altars which *were* on the roof, the upper chamber of Ahaz, which the kings of Judah had made, and the altars which Manasseh had made in the two courts of the house of the LORD, the king broke down; and he *q*smashed them there and threw their dust into the brook Kidron.

New International

Israel, says concerning the words you heard: 19Because your heart was responsive and you humbled yourself before the LORD when you heard what I have spoken against this place and its people, that they would become accursed and laid waste, and because you tore your robes and wept in my presence, I have heard you, declares the LORD. 20Therefore I will gather you to your fathers, and you will be buried in peace. Your eyes will not see all the disaster I am going to bring on this place.' "

So they took her answer back to the king.

Josiah Renews the Covenant

23 THEN THE king called together all the elders of Judah and Jerusalem. 2He went up to the temple of the LORD with the men of Judah, the people of Jerusalem, the priests and the prophets—all the people from the least to the greatest. He read in their hearing all the words of the Book of the Covenant, which had been found in the temple of the LORD. 3The king stood by the pillar and renewed the covenant in the presence of the LORD—to follow the LORD and keep his commands, regulations and decrees with all his heart and all his soul, thus confirming the words of the covenant written in this book. Then all the people pledged themselves to the covenant.

4The king ordered Hilkiah the high priest, the priests next in rank and the doorkeepers to remove from the temple of the LORD all the articles made for Baal and Asherah and all the starry hosts. He burned them outside Jerusalem in the fields of the Kidron Valley and took the ashes to Bethel. 5He did away with the pagan priests appointed by the kings of Judah to burn incense on the high places of the towns of Judah and on those around Jerusalem—those who burned incense to Baal, to the sun and moon, to the constellations and to all the starry hosts. 6He took the Asherah pole from the temple of the LORD to the Kidron Valley outside Jerusalem and burned it there. He ground it to powder and scattered the dust over the graves of the common people. 7He also tore down the quarters of the male shrine prostitutes, which were in the temple of the LORD and where women did weaving for Asherah.

8Josiah brought all the priests from the towns of Judah and desecrated the high places, from Geba to Beersheba, where the priests had burned incense. He broke down the shrines*j* at the gates—at the entrance to the Gate of Joshua, the city governor, which is on the left of the city gate. 9Although the priests of the high places did not serve at the altar of the LORD in Jerusalem, they ate unleavened bread with their fellow priests.

10He desecrated Topheth, which was in the Valley of Ben Hinnom, so no one could use it to sacrifice his son or daughter in*k* the fire to Molech. 11He removed from the entrance to the temple of the LORD the horses that the kings of Judah had dedicated to the sun. They were in the court near the room of an official named Nathan-Melech. Josiah then burned the chariots dedicated to the sun.

12He pulled down the altars the kings of Judah had erected on the roof near the upper room of Ahaz, and the altars Manasseh had built in the two courts of the temple of the LORD. He removed them from there, smashed them to

---

o I.e. a wooden symbol of a female deity, and so throughout the ch   *p* I.e. place of burning   *q* Or *ran from there*

j 8 Or *high places*   *k* 10 Or *to make his son or daughter pass through*

King James

¹³And the high places that *were* before Jerusalem, which *were* on the right hand of ^uthe mount of corruption, which Solomon the king of Israel had builded for Ashtoreth the abomination of the Zidonians, and for Chemosh the abomination of the Moabites, and for Milcom the abomination of the children of Ammon, did the king defile.

¹⁴And he brake in pieces the ^yimages, and cut down the groves, and filled their places with the bones of men.

¹⁵ ¶ Moreover the altar that *was* at Beth-el, *and* the high place which Jeroboam the son of Nebat, who made Israel to sin, had made, both that altar and the high place he brake down, and burned the high place, *and* stamped *it* small to powder, and burned the grove.

¹⁶And as Josiah turned himself, he spied the sepulchres that *were* there in the mount, and sent, and took the bones out of the sepulchres, and burned *them* upon the altar, and polluted it, according to the word of the LORD which the man of God proclaimed, who proclaimed these words.

¹⁷Then he said, What title *is* that that I see? And the men of the city told him, *It is* the sepulchre of the man of God, which came from Judah, and proclaimed these things that thou hast done against the altar of Beth-el.

¹⁸And he said, Let him alone; let no man move his bones. So they let his bones ^walone, with the bones of the prophet that came out of Samaria.

¹⁹And all the houses also of the high places that *were* in the cities of Samaria, which the kings of Israel had made to provoke *the* LORD to anger, Josiah took away, and did to them according to all the acts that he had done in Beth-el.

²⁰And he ^xslew all the priests of the high places that *were* there upon the altars, and burned men's bones upon them, and returned to Jerusalem.

²¹ ¶ And the king commanded all the people, saying, Keep the passover unto the LORD your God, as *it is* written in the book of this covenant.

²²Surely there was not holden such a passover from the days of the judges that judged Israel, nor in all the days of the kings of Israel, nor of the kings of Judah;

²³But in the eighteenth year of king Josiah, *wherein* this passover was holden to the LORD in Jerusalem.

²⁴ ¶ Moreover the *workers with* familiar spirits, and the wizards, and the ^yimages, and the idols, and all the abominations that were spied in the land of Judah and in Jerusalem, did Josiah put away, that he might perform the words of the law which were written in the book that Hilkiah the priest found in the house of the LORD.

²⁵And like unto him was there no king before him, that turned to the LORD with all his heart, and with all his soul, and with all his might, according to all the law of Moses; neither after him arose there *any* like him.

²⁶ ¶ Notwithstanding the LORD turned not from the fierceness of his great wrath, wherewith his anger was kindled against Judah, because of all the ^zprovocations that Manasseh had provoked him withal.

²⁷And the LORD said, I will remove Judah also out of my sight, as I have removed Israel, and will cast off this city Jerusalem which I have chosen, and the house of which I said, My name shall be there.

²⁸Now the rest of the acts of Josiah, and all that he did, *are* they not written in the book of the chronicles of the kings of Judah?

²⁹ ¶ In his days Pharaoh-nechoh king of Egypt went up against the king of Assyria to the river Euphrates: and king Josiah went against him; and he slew him at Megiddo, when he had seen him.

³⁰And his servants carried him in a chariot dead from Megiddo, and brought him to Jerusalem, and buried him in his own sepulchre. And the people of the land took Jehoahaz the son of Josiah, and anointed him, and made him king in his father's stead.

Amplified

¹³And the king defiled the high places east of Jerusalem, south of the Mount of Corruption, which Solomon the king of Israel had built for Ashtoreth the abominable [goddess] of the Sidonians, for Chemosh the abominable god of the Moabites, and for Milcom the abominable [god] of the Ammonites.

¹⁴He broke in pieces the pillars (images) and cut down the Asherim and replaced them with the bones of men [to defile the places forever].

¹⁵Moreover, the altar at Bethel, the high place made by Jeroboam son of Nebat, who made Israel to sin, that altar with the high place Josiah tore down *and* broke in pieces its stones, beating them to dust, and burned the Asherah.

¹⁶And as Josiah turned, he saw the tombs across on the mount, and he sent and brought the bones out of the tombs and burned them upon the altar and defiled it, in fulfillment of the word of the Lord which the man of God prophesied, who predicted these things [about this altar, naming Josiah before he was born]. [I Kings 13:2–5.]

¹⁷Josiah said, What is that monument I see? The men of the city told him, It is the tomb of the man of God who came from Judah and foretold these things that you have just done against the altar of Bethel.

¹⁸He said, Let him alone; let no man move his bones. So they let his bones alone, with the bones of the prophet that came out of Samaria. [I Kings 13:31, 32.]

¹⁹Also Josiah took away all the houses of the high places in the cities of Samaria which the kings of Israel had made, provoking the Lord to anger, and he did to them all that he had done in Bethel.

²⁰He slew all the priests of the high places that were there upon the altars and burned men's bones upon them [to defile the places forever]. Then he returned to Jerusalem.

²¹The king commanded all the people, Keep the Passover to the Lord your God, as it is written in this Book of the Covenant.

²²Surely such a Passover was not held from the days of Israel's judges, even in all the days of the kings of Israel or Judah.

²³But in the eighteenth year of King Josiah, this Passover was kept to the Lord in Jerusalem.

²⁴Moreover, Josiah put away the mediums, the wizards, the teraphim (household gods), the idols, and all the abominations that were seen in Judah and in Jerusalem, that he might establish the words of the law written in the book found by Hilkiah the priest in the house of the Lord.

²⁵There was no king like him before or after [Josiah] who turned to the Lord with all his heart and all his soul and all his might, according to all the Law of Moses.

²⁶Still the Lord did not turn from the fierceness of His great wrath, kindled against Judah because of all the provocations with which Manasseh had provoked Him.

²⁷And the Lord said, I will remove Judah also out of My sight as I have removed Israel, and will cast off this city, Jerusalem, which I have chosen, and the house, of which I said, My Name [and the pledge of My presence] shall be there.

²⁸The rest of the acts of Josiah, all that he did, are they not written in the Book of the Chronicles of Judah's Kings?

²⁹In his days Pharaoh Necho king of Egypt went up against the king of Assyria to the river Euphrates. King Josiah went out against him, but he slew Josiah at Megiddo when he saw him.

³⁰Josiah's servants carried him dead in a chariot from Megiddo, brought him to Jerusalem, and buried him in his own tomb. The people of the land anointed Jehoahaz son of Josiah king in his stead.

---

^ui.e. the mount of Olives   ^yHeb. *statues*   ^wHeb. *to escape*
^xOr, *sacrificed*   ^yOr, *teraphim*   ^zHeb. *angers*

New American Standard

13 The high places which *were* before Jerusalem, which *were* on the right of the mount of destruction which Solomon the king of Israel had built for Ashtoreth the abomination of the Sidonians, and for Chemosh the abomination of Moab, and for Milcom the abomination of the sons of Ammon, the king defiled.

14 He broke in pieces the *sacred* pillars and cut down the Asherim and filled their places with human bones.

15 ¶ Furthermore, the altar that *was* at Bethel *and* the high place which Jeroboam the son of Nebat, who made Israel sin, had made, even that altar and the high place he broke down. Then he demolished its stones, ground them to dust, and burned the Asherah.

16 Now when Josiah turned, he saw the graves that *were* there on the mountain, and he sent and took the bones from the graves and burned *them* on the altar and defiled it according to the word of the LORD which the man of God proclaimed, who proclaimed these things.

17 Then he said, "What is this monument that I see?" And the men of the city told him, "It is the grave of the man of God who came from Judah and proclaimed these things which you have done against the altar of Bethel."

18 He said, "Let him alone; let no one disturb his bones." So they left his bones undisturbed with the bones of the prophet who came from Samaria.

19 Josiah also removed all the houses of the high places which *were* in the cities of Samaria, which the kings of Israel had made provoking the LORD; and he did to them just as he had done in Bethel.

20 All the priests of the high places who *were* there he slaughtered on the altars and burned human bones on them; then he returned to Jerusalem.

Passover Reinstituted

21 ¶ Then the king commanded all the people saying, "Celebrate the Passover to the LORD your God as it is written in this book of the covenant."

22 Surely such a Passover had not been celebrated from the days of the judges who judged Israel, nor in all the days of the kings of Israel and of the kings of Judah.

23 But in the eighteenth year of King Josiah, this Passover was observed to the LORD in Jerusalem.

24 ¶ Moreover, Josiah removed the mediums and the spiritists and the teraphim and the idols and all the abominations that were seen in the land of Judah and in Jerusalem, that he might confirm the words of the law which were written in the book that Hilkiah the priest found in the house of the LORD.

25 Before him there was no king like him who turned to the LORD with all his heart and with all his soul and with all his might, according to all the law of Moses; nor did any like him arise after him.

26 ¶ However, the LORD did not turn from the fierceness of His great wrath with which His anger burned against Judah, because of all the provocations with which Manasseh had provoked Him.

27 The LORD said, "I will remove Judah also from My sight, as I have removed Israel. And I will cast off Jerusalem, this city which I have chosen, and the temple of which I said, 'My name shall be there.' "

Jehoahaz Succeeds Josiah

28 ¶ Now the rest of the acts of Josiah and all that he did, are they not written in the Book of the Chronicles of the Kings of Judah?

29 In his days Pharaoh Neco king of Egypt went up to the king of Assyria to the river Euphrates. And King Josiah went to meet him, and when *Pharaoh Neco* saw him he killed him at Megiddo.

30 His servants drove his body in a chariot from Megiddo, and brought him to Jerusalem and buried him in his own tomb. Then the people of the land took Jehoahaz the son of Josiah and anointed him and made him king in place of his father.

New International

pieces and threw the rubble into the Kidron Valley. 13The king also desecrated the high places that were east of Jerusalem on the south of the Hill of Corruption—the ones Solomon king of Israel had built for Ashtoreth the vile goddess of the Sidonians, for Chemosh the vile god of Moab, and for Molech*l* the detestable god of the people of Ammon. 14Josiah smashed the sacred stones and cut down the Asherah poles and covered the sites with human bones.

15Even the altar at Bethel, the high place made by Jeroboam son of Nebat, who had caused Israel to sin—even that altar and high place he demolished. He burned the high place and ground it to powder, and burned the Asherah pole also. 16Then Josiah looked around, and when he saw the tombs that were there on the hillside, he had the bones removed from them and burned on the altar to defile it, in accordance with the word of the LORD proclaimed by the man of God who foretold these things.

17The king asked, "What is that tombstone I see?"

The men of the city said, "It marks the tomb of the man of God who came from Judah and pronounced against the altar of Bethel the very things you have done to it."

18"Leave it alone," he said. "Don't let anyone disturb his bones." So they spared his bones and those of the prophet who had come from Samaria.

19Just as he had done at Bethel, Josiah removed and defiled all the shrines at the high places that the kings of Israel had built in the towns of Samaria that had provoked the LORD to anger. 20Josiah slaughtered all the priests of those high places on the altars and burned human bones on them. Then he went back to Jerusalem.

21The king gave this order to all the people: "Celebrate the Passover to the LORD your God, as it is written in this Book of the Covenant." 22Not since the days of the judges who led Israel, nor throughout the days of the kings of Israel and the kings of Judah, had any such Passover been observed. 23But in the eighteenth year of King Josiah, this Passover was celebrated to the LORD in Jerusalem.

24Furthermore, Josiah got rid of the mediums and spiritists, the household gods, the idols and all the other detestable things seen in Judah and Jerusalem. This he did to fulfill the requirements of the law written in the book that Hilkiah the priest had discovered in the temple of the LORD. 25Neither before nor after Josiah was there a king like him who turned to the LORD as he did—with all his heart and with all his soul and with all his strength, in accordance with all the Law of Moses.

26Nevertheless, the LORD did not turn away from the heat of his fierce anger, which burned against Judah because of all that Manasseh had done to provoke him to anger. 27So the LORD said, "I will remove Judah also from my presence as I removed Israel, and I will reject Jerusalem, the city I chose, and this temple, about which I said, 'There shall my Name be.'*m* "

28As for the other events of Josiah's reign, and all he did, are they not written in the book of the annals of the kings of Judah?

29While Josiah was king, Pharaoh Neco king of Egypt went up to the Euphrates River to help the king of Assyria. King Josiah marched out to meet him in battle, but Neco faced him and killed him at Megiddo. 30Josiah's servants brought his body in a chariot from Megiddo to Jerusalem and buried him in his own tomb. And the people of the land took Jehoahaz son of Josiah and anointed him and made him king in place of his father.

l 13 Hebrew Milcom   m 27 1 Kings 8:29

King James

Jehoahaz, king of Judah

31 ¶ [a]Jehoahaz *was* twenty and three years old when he began to reign; and he reigned three months in Jerusalem. And his mother's name *was* Hamutal, the daughter of Jeremiah of Libnah.

32And he did *that which was* evil in the sight of the LORD, according to all that his fathers had done.

33And Pharaoh-nechoh put him in bands at Riblah in the land of Hamath, [b]that he might not reign in Jerusalem; and [c]put the land to a tribute of an hundred talents of silver, and a talent of gold.

34And Pharaoh-nechoh made Eliakim the son of Josiah king in the room of Josiah his father, and turned his name to Johoiakim, and took Jehoahaz away: and he came to Egypt, and died there.

35And Jehoiakim gave the silver and the gold to Pharaoh; but he taxed the land to give the money according to the commandment of Pharaoh: he exacted the silver and the gold of the people of the land, of every one according to his taxation, to give *it* unto Pharaoh-nechoh.

Jehoiakim, king of Judah

36 ¶ Jehoiakim *was* twenty and five years old when he began to reign; and he reigned eleven years in Jerusalem. And his mother's name *was* Zebudah, the daughter of Pedaiah of Rumah.

37And he did *that which was* evil in the sight of the LORD, according to all that his fathers had done.

24 IN HIS days Nebuchadnezzar king of Babylon came up, and Jehoiakim became his servant three years: then he turned and rebelled against him.

2And the LORD sent against him bands of the Chaldees, and bands of the Syrians, and bands of the Moabites, and bands of the children of Ammon, and sent them against Judah to destroy it, according to the word of the LORD, which he spake [d]by his servants the prophets.

3Surely at the commandment of the LORD came *this* upon Judah, to remove *them* out of his sight, for the sins of Manasseh, according to all that he did;

4And also for the innocent blood that he shed: for he filled Jerusalem with innocent blood; which the LORD would not pardon.

5 ¶ Now the rest of the acts of Jehoiakim, and all that he did, *are* they not written in the book of the chronicles of the kings of Judah?

6So Jehoiakim slept with his fathers: and Jehoiachin his son reigned in his stead.

7And the king of Egypt came not again any more out of his land: for the king of Babylon had taken from the river of Egypt unto the river Euphrates all that pertained to the king of Egypt.

Jehoiachin, king of Judah

8e ¶ Jehoiachin *was* eighteen years old when he began to reign, and he reigned in Jerusalem three months. And his mother's name *was* Nehushta, the daughter of Elnathan of Jerusalem.

9And he did *that which was* evil in the sight of the LORD, according to all that his father had done.

10 ¶ At that time the servants of Nebuchadnezzar king of Babylon came up against Jerusalem, and the city [f]was besieged.

11And Nebuchadnezzar king of Babylon came against the city, and his servants did besiege it.

Amplified

31Jehoahaz was twenty-three years old when he began his three-month reign in Jerusalem. His mother was Hamutal daughter of Jeremiah of Libnah.

32He did evil in the sight of the Lord, according to all [the evil] his forefathers had done.

33And Pharaoh Necho put him in bonds at Riblah in the land of Hamath, that he might not reign in Jerusalem, and laid a tribute of a hundred talents of silver and a talent of gold upon the land.

34Pharaoh Necho made Eliakim son of Josiah king in place of Josiah and changed his name to Jehoiakim. But he took Jehoahaz away to Egypt, where he died.

35Jehoiakim gave the silver and the gold to Pharaoh, but he taxed the land to give the money as Pharaoh commanded. He exacted the silver and gold of the people of the land, from everyone according to his assessment, to give it to Pharaoh Necho.

36Jehoiakim was twenty-five years old when he began his eleven-year reign in Jerusalem. His mother was Zebidah daughter of Pedaiah of Rumah.

37He did evil in the sight of the Lord, like all his [forefathers] had done.

24 IN HIS days, Nebuchadnezzar king of Babylon came up, and Jehoiakim became his servant for three years; then he turned and rebelled against him.

2The Lord sent against Jehoiakim bands of Chaldeans, of Syrians, of Moabites, and of Ammonites. And He sent them against Judah to destroy it, according to the word of the Lord which He spoke by His servants the prophets.

3Surely this came upon Judah at the command of the Lord, to remove them out of His sight because of the sins of Manasseh according to all he had done,

4And also for the innocent blood that he shed. For he filled Jerusalem with innocent blood, and the Lord would not pardon.

5The rest of the acts of Jehoiakim, all that he did, are they not written in the Book of the Chronicles of Judah's Kings?

6So Jehoiakim slept with his fathers. Jehoiachin his son reigned in his stead.

7The king of Egypt came no more out of his land, for the king of Babylon had taken all that belonged to Egypt's king, from the River of Egypt to the river Euphrates.

8Jehoiachin was eighteen years old when he began his three-month reign in Jerusalem. His mother was Nehushta daughter of Elnathan of Jerusalem.

9And he did evil in the sight of the Lord, in keeping with all his father had done.

10At that time the servants of Nebuchadnezzar king of Babylon came up to Jerusalem, and the city was besieged.

11Nebuchadnezzar king of Babylon came to the city while his servants were besieging it.

---

[a]Called *Shallum* in 1 Chr. 3:15; Jer. 22:11　　[b]Or, *because he reigned*　[c]Heb. *set a mulct upon the land*　[d]Heb. *by the hand of*　[e]Called *Jeconiah* in 1 Chr. 3:16; Jer. 24:1 and *Coniah* in Jer. 22:24　[f]Heb. *came into siege*

New American Standard

31 ¶ Jehoahaz was twenty-three years old when he became king, and he reigned three months in Jerusalem; and his mother's name was Hamutal the daughter of Jeremiah of Libnah.

32 He did evil in the sight of the LORD, according to all that his fathers had done.

33 Pharaoh Neco imprisoned him at Riblah in the land of Hamath, that he might not reign in Jerusalem; and he imposed on the land a fine of one hundred talents of silver and a talent of gold.

Jehoiakim Made King by Pharaoh

34 Pharaoh Neco made Eliakim the son of Josiah king in the place of Josiah his father, and changed his name to Jehoiakim. But he took Jehoahaz away and brought *him* to Egypt, and he died there.

35 So Jehoiakim gave the silver and gold to Pharaoh, but he taxed the land in order to give the money at the command of Pharaoh. He exacted the silver and gold from the people of the land, each according to his valuation, to give it to Pharaoh Neco.

36 ¶ Jehoiakim was twenty-five years old when he became king, and he reigned eleven years in Jerusalem; and his mother's name *was* Zebidah the daughter of Pedaiah of Rumah.

37 He did evil in the sight of the LORD, according to all that his fathers had done.

Babylon Controls Jehoiakim

24 IN HIS days Nebuchadnezzar king of Babylon came up, and Jehoiakim became his servant *for* three years; then he turned and rebelled against him.

2 The LORD sent against him bands of Chaldeans, bands of Arameans, bands of Moabites, and bands of Ammonites. So He sent them against Judah to destroy it, according to the word of the LORD which He had spoken through His servants the prophets.

3 Surely at the command of the LORD it came upon Judah, to remove *them* from His sight because of the sins of Manasseh, according to all that he had done,

4 and also for the innocent blood which he shed, for he filled Jerusalem with innocent blood; and the LORD would not forgive.

5 Now the rest of the acts of Jehoiakim and all that he did, are they not written in the Book of the Chronicles of the Kings of Judah?

Jehoiachin Reigns

6 So Jehoiakim slept with his fathers, and Jehoiachin his son became king in his place.

7 The king of Egypt did not come out of his land again, for the king of Babylon had taken all that belonged to the king of Egypt from the brook of Egypt to the river Euphrates.

8 ¶ Jehoiachin was eighteen years old when he became king, and he reigned three months in Jerusalem; and his mother's name *was* Nehushta the daughter of Elnathan of Jerusalem.

9 He did evil in the sight of the LORD, according to all that his father had done.

Deportation to Babylon

10 ¶ At that time the servants of Nebuchadnezzar king of Babylon went up to Jerusalem, and the city came under siege.

11 And Nebuchadnezzar the king of Babylon came to the city, while his servants were besieging it.

New International

Jehoahaz King of Judah

31 Jehoahaz was twenty-three years old when he became king, and he reigned in Jerusalem three months. His mother's name was Hamutal daughter of Jeremiah; she was from Libnah. **32** He did evil in the eyes of the LORD, just as his fathers had done. **33** Pharaoh Neco put him in chains at Riblah in the land of Hamath[n] so that he might not reign in Jerusalem, and he imposed on Judah a levy of a hundred talents[o] of silver and a talent[p] of gold. **34** Pharaoh Neco made Eliakim son of Josiah king in place of his father Josiah and changed Eliakim's name to Jehoiakim. But he took Jehoahaz and carried him off to Egypt, and there he died. **35** Jehoiakim paid Pharaoh Neco the silver and gold he demanded. In order to do so, he taxed the land and exacted the silver and gold from the people of the land according to their assessments.

Jehoiakim King of Judah

36 Jehoiakim was twenty-five years old when he became king, and he reigned in Jerusalem eleven years. His mother's name was Zebidah daughter of Pedaiah; she was from Rumah. **37** And he did evil in the eyes of the LORD, just as his fathers had done.

24 DURING JEHOIAKIM'S reign, Nebuchadnezzar king of Babylon invaded the land, and Jehoiakim became his vassal for three years. But then he changed his mind and rebelled against Nebuchadnezzar. **2** The LORD sent Babylonian,[q] Aramean, Moabite and Ammonite raiders against him. He sent them to destroy Judah, in accordance with the word of the LORD proclaimed by his servants the prophets. **3** Surely these things happened to Judah according to the LORD's command, in order to remove them from his presence because of the sins of Manasseh and all he had done, **4** including the shedding of innocent blood. For he had filled Jerusalem with innocent blood, and the LORD was not willing to forgive.

5 As for the other events of Jehoiakim's reign, and all he did, are they not written in the book of the annals of the kings of Judah? **6** Jehoiakim rested with his fathers. And Jehoiachin his son succeeded him as king.

7 The king of Egypt did not march out from his own country again, because the king of Babylon had taken all his territory, from the Wadi of Egypt to the Euphrates River.

Jehoiachin King of Judah

8 Jehoiachin was eighteen years old when he became king, and he reigned in Jerusalem three months. His mother's name was Nehushta daughter of Elnathan; she was from Jerusalem. **9** He did evil in the eyes of the LORD, just as his father had done.

10 At that time the officers of Nebuchadnezzar king of Babylon advanced on Jerusalem and laid siege to it, **11** and Nebuchadnezzar himself came up to the city while his

n 33 Hebrew; Septuagint (see also 2 Chron. 36:3) Neco at Riblah in Hamath removed him   o 33 That is, about 3 3/4 tons (about 3.4 metric tons)   p 33 That is, about 75 pounds (about 34 kilograms)   q 2 Or Chaldean

King James

¹²And Jehoiachin the king of Judah went out to the king of Babylon, he, and his mother, and his servants, and his princes, and his ^gofficers: and the king of Babylon took him in the eighth year of his reign.

¹³And he carried out thence all the treasures of the house of the LORD, and the treasures of the king's house, and cut in pieces all the vessels of gold which Solomon king of Israel had made in the temple of the LORD, as the LORD had said.

¹⁴And he carried away all Jerusalem, and all the princes, and all the mighty men of valour, *even* ten thousand captives, and all the craftsmen and smiths: none remained, save the poorest sort of the people of the land.

¹⁵And he carried away Jehoiachin to Babylon, and the king's mother, and the king's wives, and his ^gofficers, and the mighty of the land, *those* carried he into captivity from Jerusalem to Babylon.

¹⁶And all the men of might, *even* seven thousand, and craftsmen and smiths a thousand, all *that were* strong *and* apt for war, even them the king of Babylon brought captive to Babylon.

¹⁷ ¶ And the king of Babylon made Mattaniah his father's brother king in his stead, and changed his name to Zedekiah.

Zedekiah, king of Judah

¹⁸Zedekiah *was* twenty and one years old when he began to reign, and he reigned eleven years in Jerusalem. And his mother's name *was* Hamutal, the daughter of Jeremiah of Libnah.

¹⁹And he did *that which was* evil in the sight of the LORD, according to all that Jehoiakim had done.

²⁰For through the anger of the LORD it came to pass in Jerusalem and Judah, until he had cast them out from his presence, that Zedekiah rebelled against the king of Babylon.

Jerusalem destroyed

25 AND IT came to pass in the ninth year of his reign, in the tenth month, in the tenth *day* of the month, *that* Nebuchadnezzar king of Babylon came, he, and all his host, against Jerusalem, and pitched against it; and they built forts against it round about.

²And the city was besieged unto the eleventh year of king Zedekiah.

³And on the ninth *day* of the *fourth* month the famine prevailed in the city, and there was no bread for the people of the land.

⁴ ¶ And the city was broken up, and all the men of war *fled* by night by the way of the gate between two walls, which *is* by the king's garden: (now the Chaldees *were* against the city round about:) and *the king* went the way toward the plain.

⁵And the army of the Chaldees pursued after the king, and overtook him in the plains of Jericho: and all his army were scattered from him.

⁶So they took the king, and brought him up to the king of Babylon to Riblah; and they ^hgave judgment upon him.

⁷And they slew the sons of Zedekiah before his eyes, and ⁱput out the eyes of Zedekiah, and bound him with fetters of brass, and carried him to Babylon.

⁸ ¶ And in the fifth month, on the seventh *day* of the month, which *is* the nineteenth year of king Nebuchadnezzar king of Babylon, came Nebuzar-adan, ^jcaptain of the guard, a servant of the king of Babylon, unto Jerusalem:

⁹And he burnt the house of the LORD, and the king's house, and all the houses of Jerusalem, and every great *man's* house burnt he with fire.

Amplified

¹²Jehoiachin king of Judah surrendered to the king of Babylon, he, his mother, his servants, princes, and palace officials. The king of Babylon took him prisoner in the eighth year of Nebuchadnezzar's reign.

¹³He carried off all the treasures of the Lord's house and the king's house, and cut in pieces all the vessels of gold in the temple of the Lord, which Solomon king of Israel had made, as the Lord had said.

¹⁴He carried away all Jerusalem, all the princes, all the mighty men of valor, 10,000 captives, and all the craftsmen and smiths. None remained except the poorest of the land.

¹⁵Nebuchadnezzar took captive to Babylon King Jehoiachin; his mother, his wives, his officials, and the chief *and* mighty men of the land [the prophet Ezekiel included] he took from Jerusalem to Babylon into exile. [Ezek. 1:1.]

¹⁶And the king of Babylon brought captive to Babylon all the men of valor, 7,000, and craftsmen and smiths, 1,000, all strong and fit for war.

¹⁷And the king of Babylon made Mattaniah, Jehoiachin's uncle, king in his stead and changed his name to Zedekiah.

¹⁸Zedekiah was twenty-one years old when he began his eleven-year reign in Jerusalem. His mother was Hamutal daughter of Jeremiah of Libnah.

¹⁹He did evil in the sight of the Lord, in keeping with all Jehoiakim had done.

²⁰For because of the anger of the Lord it came to the point in Jerusalem and Judah that He cast them out of His presence. And Zedekiah rebelled against the king of Babylon.

25 IN THE ninth year of Zedekiah's reign, on the tenth day of the tenth month, Nebuchadnezzar king of Babylon came with all his army against Jerusalem and laid siege to it, and they built siege works against it round about.

²The city was besieged [nearly two years] until the eleventh year of King Zedekiah.

³On the ninth day of the fourth month the famine was complete in the city; there was no food for the people of the land.

⁴Then the city was broken through; the king and all the warriors fled by night by way of the gate between the two walls by the king's garden, though the Chaldeans were round about the city. [The king] went by the way toward the Arabah (the plain).

⁵The Chaldean army pursued the king and overtook him in the plains of Jericho. All his army was scattered from him.

⁶So they captured Zedekiah and brought him to the king of Babylon at Riblah, and sentence was passed on him.

⁷And they slew the sons of Zedekiah before his eyes and put out the eyes of Zedekiah and bound him in double fetters [hands and feet] and carried him to Babylon. [Foretold in Jer. 34:3; Ezek. 12:13.]

⁸On the seventh day of the fifth month of the nineteenth year of King Nebuchadnezzar of Babylon, Nebuzaradan, captain of the Babylonian king's guard, came to Jerusalem.

⁹He burned the house of the Lord, the king's house, and all the houses of Jerusalem; every great house he burned down.

---

^gOr, *eunuchs*   ^hHeb. *spake judgment with him*   ⁱHeb. *made blind*   ^jOr, *chief marshal*

New American Standard

12 Jehoiachin the king of Judah went out to the king of Babylon, he and his mother and his servants and his captains and his officials. So the king of Babylon took him captive in the eighth year of his reign.

13 He carried out from there all the treasures of the house of the LORD, and the treasures of the king's house, and cut in pieces all the vessels of gold which Solomon king of Israel had made in the temple of the LORD, just as the LORD had said.

14 Then he led away into exile all Jerusalem and all the captains and all the mighty men of valor, ten thousand captives, and all the craftsmen and the smiths. None remained except the poorest people of the land.

15 ¶ So he led Jehoiachin away into exile to Babylon; also the king's mother and the king's wives and his officials and the leading men of the land, he led away into exile from Jerusalem to Babylon.

16 All the men of valor, seven thousand, and the craftsmen and the smiths, one thousand, all strong and fit for war, and these the king of Babylon brought into exile to Babylon.

Zedekiah Made King

17 Then the king of Babylon made his uncle Mattaniah king in his place, and changed his name to Zedekiah.

18 ¶ Zedekiah was twenty-one years old when he became king, and he reigned eleven years in Jerusalem; and his mother's name was Hamutal the daughter of Jeremiah of Libnah.

19 He did evil in the sight of the LORD, according to all that Jehoiakim had done.

20 For through the anger of the LORD *this* came about in Jerusalem and Judah until He cast them out from His presence. And Zedekiah rebelled against the king of Babylon.

Nebuchadnezzar Besieges Jerusalem

25 NOW IN the ninth year of his reign, on the tenth day of the tenth month, Nebuchadnezzar king of Babylon came, he and all his army, against Jerusalem, camped against it and built a siege wall all around it.

2 So the city was under siege until the eleventh year of King Zedekiah.

3 On the ninth day of the *fourth* month the famine was so severe in the city that there was no food for the people of the land.

4 Then the city was broken into, and all the men of war *fled* by night by way of the gate between the two walls beside the king's garden, though the Chaldeans were all around the city. And they went by way of the Arabah.

5 But the army of the Chaldeans pursued the king and overtook him in the plains of Jericho and all his army was scattered from him.

6 Then they captured the king and brought him to the king of Babylon at Riblah, and he passed sentence on him.

7 They slaughtered the sons of Zedekiah before his eyes, then put out the eyes of Zedekiah and bound him with bronze fetters and brought him to Babylon.

Jerusalem Burned and Plundered

8 ¶ Now on the seventh day of the fifth month, which was the nineteenth year of King Nebuchadnezzar, king of Babylon, Nebuzaradan the captain of the guard, a servant of the king of Babylon, came to Jerusalem.

9 He burned the house of the LORD, the king's house, and all the houses of Jerusalem; even every great house he burned with fire.

New International

officers were besieging it. 12 Jehoiachin king of Judah, his mother, his attendants, his nobles and his officials all surrendered to him.

In the eighth year of the reign of the king of Babylon, he took Jehoiachin prisoner. 13 As the LORD had declared, Nebuchadnezzar removed all the treasures from the temple of the LORD and from the royal palace, and took away all the gold articles that Solomon king of Israel had made for the temple of the LORD. 14 He carried into exile all Jerusalem: all the officers and fighting men, and all the craftsmen and artisans—a total of ten thousand. Only the poorest people of the land were left.

15 Nebuchadnezzar took Jehoiachin captive to Babylon. He also took from Jerusalem to Babylon the king's mother, his wives, his officials and the leading men of the land. 16 The king of Babylon also deported to Babylon the entire force of seven thousand fighting men, strong and fit for war, and a thousand craftsmen and artisans. 17 He made Mattaniah, Jehoiachin's uncle, king in his place and changed his name to Zedekiah.

Zedekiah King of Judah

18 Zedekiah was twenty-one years old when he became king, and he reigned in Jerusalem eleven years. His mother's name was Hamutal daughter of Jeremiah; she was from Libnah. 19 He did evil in the eyes of the LORD, just as Jehoiakim had done. 20 It was because of the LORD's anger that all this happened to Jerusalem and Judah, and in the end he thrust them from his presence.

The Fall of Jerusalem

Now Zedekiah rebelled against the king of Babylon.

25 SO IN the ninth year of Zedekiah's reign, on the tenth day of the tenth month, Nebuchadnezzar king of Babylon marched against Jerusalem with his whole army. He encamped outside the city and built siege works all around it. 2 The city was kept under siege until the eleventh year of King Zedekiah. 3 By the ninth day of the ⌊fourth⌋*r* month the famine in the city had become so severe that there was no food for the people to eat. 4 Then the city wall was broken through, and the whole army fled at night through the gate between the two walls near the king's garden, though the Babylonians*s* were surrounding the city. They fled toward the Arabah,*t* 5 but the Babylonian*u* army pursued the king and overtook him in the plains of Jericho. All his soldiers were separated from him and scattered, 6 and he was captured. He was taken to the king of Babylon at Riblah, where sentence was pronounced on him. 7 They killed the sons of Zedekiah before his eyes. Then they put out his eyes, bound him with bronze shackles and took him to Babylon.

8 On the seventh day of the fifth month, in the nineteenth year of Nebuchadnezzar king of Babylon, Nebuzaradan commander of the imperial guard, an official of the king of Babylon, came to Jerusalem. 9 He set fire to the temple of the LORD, the royal palace and all the houses of Jerusa-

---

r 3 See Jer. 52:6.   *s* 4 Or *Chaldeans*; also in verses 13, 25 and 26
t 4 Or *the Jordan Valley*   *u* 5 Or *Chaldean*; also in verses 10 and 24

King James

[10]And all the army of the Chaldees, that *were with* the captain of the guard, brake down the walls of Jerusalem round about.

[11]Now the rest of the people *that were* left in the city, and the *k*fugitives that fell away to the king of Babylon, with the remnant of the multitude, did Nebuzar-adan the captain of the guard carry away.

[12]But the captain of the guard left of the poor of the land *to be* vinedressers and husbandmen.

[13]And the pillars of brass that *were* in the house of the LORD, and the bases, and the brasen sea that *was* in the house of the LORD, did the Chaldees break in pieces, and carried the brass of them to Babylon.

[14]And the pots, and the shovels, and the snuffers, and the spoons, and all the vessels of brass wherewith they ministered, took they away.

[15]And the firepans, and the bowls, *and* such things as *were* of gold, *in* gold, and of silver, *in* silver, the captain of the guard took away.

[16]The two pillars, *l*one sea, and the bases which Solomon had made for the house of the LORD; the brass of all these vessels was without weight.

[17]The height of the one pillar *was* eighteen cubits, and the chapiter upon it *was* brass: and the height of the chapiter three cubits; and the wreathen work, and pomegranates upon the chapiter round about, all of brass: and like unto these had the second pillar with wreathen work.

[18] ¶ And the captain of the guard took Seraiah the chief priest, and Zephaniah the second priest, and the three keepers of the *m*door:

[19]And out of the city he took an *n*officer that was set over the men of war, and five men of them that *o*were in the king's presence, which were found in the city, and the *p*principal scribe of the host, which mustered the people of the land, and threescore men of the people of the land *that were* found in the city:

[20]And Nebuzar-adan captain of the guard took these, and brought them to the king of Babylon to Riblah:

[21]And the king of Babylon smote them, and slew them at Riblah in the land of Hamath. So Judah was carried away out of their land.

[22] ¶ And *as for* the people that remained in the land of Judah, whom Nebuchadnezzar king of Babylon had left, even over them he made Gedaliah the son of Ahikam, the son of Shaphan, ruler.

[23]And when all the captains of the armies, they and their men, heard that the king of Babylon had made Gedaliah governor, there came to Gedaliah to Mizpah, even Ishmael the son of Nethaniah, and Johanan the son of Careah, and Seraiah the son of Tanhumeth the Netophathite, and Jaazaniah the son of a Maachathite, they and their men.

[24]And Gedaliah sware to them, and to their men, and said unto them, Fear not to be the servants of the Chaldees: dwell in the land, and serve the king of Babylon; and it shall be well with you.

[25]But it came to pass in the seventh month, that Ishmael the son of Nethaniah, the son of Elishama, of the seed *q*royal, came, and ten men with him, and smote Gedaliah, that he died, and the Jews and the Chaldees that were with him at Mizpah.

[26]And all the people, both small and great, and the captains of the armies, arose, and came to Egypt: for they were afraid of the Chaldees.

Jehoiachin in captivity

[27] ¶ And it came to pass in the seven and thirtieth year of the captivity of Jehoiachin king of Judah, in the twelfth month, on the seven and twentieth *day* of the month, *that* Evil-merodach king of Babylon in the year that he began to reign did lift up the head of Jehoiachin king of Judah out of prison;

[10]All the army of the Chaldeans who were with the captain of the [Babylonian] guard broke down the walls around Jerusalem.

[11]Now the rest of the people left in the city, and the deserters who fell away to the king of Babylon, along with the rest of the multitude, Nebuzaradan the captain of the guard carried into exile.

[12]But the captain of the guard left some of the poorest of the land to be vinedressers and soil tillers.

[13]The bronze pillars in the Lord's house and [its] bases and the bronze Sea the Chaldeans smashed and carried the bronze to Babylon.

[14]And they took away the pots, shovels, snuffers, dishes for incense, all the bronze vessels used in the temple service,

[15]The firepans, and bowls. Such things as were of gold the captain of the guard took away as gold, and what was of silver [he took away] as silver.

[16]The two pillars, the one Sea, and the bases, which Solomon had made for the house of the Lord, the bronze of all these articles was incalculable.

[17]The height of the one pillar was eighteen cubits, and upon it was a capital of bronze. The height of the capital was three cubits; a network and pomegranates round about the capital were all of bronze. And the second pillar had the same as these, with a network.

[18]The captain of the guard took Seraiah the chief priest, Zephaniah the second priest, and the three keepers of the threshold.

[19]And out of the city he took an officer who was in command of the men of war and five men of the king's personal advisors, who were found in the city, and the scribe of the captain of the army who mustered the people of the land and sixty men of the people who were found in the city.

[20]Nebuzaradan the captain of the guard took these and brought them to the king of Babylon at Riblah.

[21]The king of Babylon smote and killed them at Riblah in the land of Hamath [north of Damascus]. So Judah was taken into exile.

[22]Over the people whom Nebuchadnezzar king of Babylon had left in the land of Judah he appointed as governor Gedaliah son of Ahikam, the son of Shaphan.

[23]And when all the captains of the forces and their men heard that the king of Babylon had made Gedaliah governor, they came with their men to Gedaliah at Mizpah, namely, Ishmael son of Nethaniah, Johanan son of Kareah, Seraiah son of Tanhumeth the Netophathite, and Jaazaniah son of the Maacathite.

[24]And Gedaliah swore to them and their men, saying, Do not be afraid of the Chaldean officials. Dwell in the land and serve the king of Babylon, and it shall be well with you.

[25]But in the seventh month Ishmael son of Nethaniah, the son of Elishama, of the royal family [so having a claim to be governor], came with ten men and smote and killed Gedaliah and the Jews and the Chaldeans who were with him at Mizpah.

[26]Then all the people, both small and great, and the captains of the forces arose and went to Egypt, for they were afraid of the Chaldeans.

[27]And in the thirty-seventh year of the captivity of Jehoiachin king of Judah, on the twenty-seventh day of the twelfth month, Evil-merodach king of Babylon, in the year that he began to reign, showed favor to Jehoiachin king of Judah *and* released him from prison;

*k*Heb. *fallen away*   *l*Heb. *the one sea*   *m*Heb. *threshold*
*n*Or, *eunuch*   *o*Heb. *saw the king's face*   *p*Or, *scribe of the captain of the host*   *q*Heb. *of the kingdom*

New American Standard

10 So all the army of the Chaldeans who *were with* the captain of the guard broke down the walls around Jerusalem.

11 Then the rest of the people who were left in the city and the deserters who had deserted to the king of Babylon and the rest of the people, Nebuzaradan the captain of the guard carried away into exile.

12 But the captain of the guard left some of the poorest of the land to be vinedressers and plowmen.

13 ¶ Now the bronze pillars which were in the house of the LORD, and the stands and the bronze sea which were in the house of the LORD, the Chaldeans broke in pieces and carried the bronze to Babylon.

14 They took away the pots, the shovels, the snuffers, the spoons, and all the bronze vessels which were used in *temple* service.

15 The captain of the guard also took away the firepans and the basins, what was fine gold and what was fine silver.

16 The two pillars, the one sea, and the stands which Solomon had made for the house of the LORD—the bronze of all these vessels was beyond weight.

17 The height of the one pillar was eighteen cubits, and a bronze capital was on it; the height of the capital was three cubits, with a network and pomegranates on the capital all around, all of bronze. And the second pillar was like these with network.

18 ¶ Then the captain of the guard took Seraiah the chief priest and Zephaniah the second priest, with the three officers of the temple.

19 From the city he took one official who was overseer of the men of war, and five of the king's advisers who were found in the city; and the scribe of the captain of the army who mustered the people of the land; and sixty men of the people of the land who were found in the city.

20 Nebuzaradan the captain of the guard took them and brought them to the king of Babylon at Riblah.

21 Then the king of Babylon struck them down and put them to death at Riblah in the land of Hamath. So Judah was led away into exile from its land.

Gedaliah Made Governor

22 ¶ Now *as for* the people who were left in the land of Judah, whom Nebuchadnezzar king of Babylon had left, he appointed Gedaliah the son of Ahikam, the son of Shaphan over them.

23 When all the captains of the forces, they and *their* men, heard that the king of Babylon had appointed Gedaliah *governor,* they came to Gedaliah to Mizpah, namely, Ishmael the son of Nethaniah, and Johanan the son of Kareah, and Seraiah the son of Tanhumeth the Netophathite, and Jaazaniah the son of the Maacathite, they and their men.

24 Gedaliah swore to them and their men and said to them, "Do not be afraid of the servants of the Chaldeans; live in the land and serve the king of Babylon, and it will be well with you."

25 ¶ But it came about in the seventh month, that Ishmael the son of Nethaniah, the son of Elishama, of the royal family, came with ten men and struck Gedaliah down so that he died along with the Jews and the Chaldeans who were with him at Mizpah.

26 Then all the people, both small and great, and the captains of the forces arose and went to Egypt; for they were afraid of the Chaldeans.

27 ¶ Now it came about in the thirty-seventh year of the exile of Jehoiachin king of Judah, in the twelfth month, on the twenty-seventh *day* of the month, that Evil-merodach king of Babylon, in the year that he became king, released Jehoiachin king of Judah from prison;

New International

lem. Every important building he burned down. 10The whole Babylonian army, under the commander of the imperial guard, broke down the walls around Jerusalem. 11Nebuzaradan the commander of the guard carried into exile the people who remained in the city, along with the rest of the populace and those who had gone over to the king of Babylon. 12But the commander left behind some of the poorest people of the land to work the vineyards and fields.

13The Babylonians broke up the bronze pillars, the movable stands and the bronze Sea that were at the temple of the LORD and they carried the bronze to Babylon. 14They also took away the pots, shovels, wick trimmers, dishes and all the bronze articles used in temple service. 15The commander of the imperial guard took away the censers and sprinkling bowls—all that were made of pure gold or silver.

16The bronze from the two pillars, the Sea and the movable stands, which Solomon had made for the temple of the LORD, was more than could be weighed. 17Each pillar was twenty-seven feet[v] high. The bronze capital on top of one pillar was four and a half feet[w] high and was decorated with a network and pomegranates of bronze all around. The other pillar, with its network, was similar.

18The commander of the guard took as prisoners Seraiah the chief priest, Zephaniah the priest next in rank and the three doorkeepers. 19Of those still in the city, he took the officer in charge of the fighting men and five royal advisers. He also took the secretary who was chief officer in charge of conscripting the people of the land and sixty of his men who were found in the city. 20Nebuzaradan the commander took them all and brought them to the king of Babylon at Riblah. 21There at Riblah, in the land of Hamath, the king had them executed.

So Judah went into captivity, away from her land.

22Nebuchadnezzar king of Babylon appointed Gedaliah son of Ahikam, the son of Shaphan, to be over the people he had left behind in Judah. 23When all the army officers and their men heard that the king of Babylon had appointed Gedaliah as governor, they came to Gedaliah at Mizpah—Ishmael son of Nethaniah, Johanan son of Kareah, Seraiah son of Tanhumeth the Netophathite, Jaazaniah the son of the Maacathite, and their men. 24Gedaliah took an oath to reassure them and their men. "Do not be afraid of the Babylonian officials," he said. "Settle down in the land and serve the king of Babylon, and it will go well with you."

25In the seventh month, however, Ishmael son of Nethaniah, the son of Elishama, who was of royal blood, came with ten men and assassinated Gedaliah and also the men of Judah and the Babylonians who were with him at Mizpah. 26At this, all the people from the least to the greatest, together with the army officers, fled to Egypt for fear of the Babylonians.

Jehoiachin Released

27In the thirty-seventh year of the exile of Jehoiachin king of Judah, in the year Evil-Merodach[x] became king of Babylon, he released Jehoiachin from prison on the

---

King James

28And he spake *r*kindly to him, and set his throne above the throne of the kings that *were* with him in Babylon;

29And changed his prison garments: and he did eat bread continually before him all the days of his life.

30And his allowance *was* a continual allowance given him of the king, a daily rate for every day, all the days of his life.

Amplified

28He spoke kindly to him and ranked him above the kings with him in Babylon.

29Jehoiachin put off his prison garments, and he dined regularly at the king's table the remainder of his life.

30And his allowance, a continual one, was given him by the king, every day a portion, for the rest of his life.

r Heb. *good things with him*

New American Standard

28 and he spoke kindly to him and set his throne above the throne of the kings who *were* with him in Babylon.

29 Jehoiachin changed his prison clothes and had his meals in the king's presence regularly all the days of his life;

30 and for his allowance, a regular allowance was given him by the king, a portion for each day, all the days of his life.

New International

twenty-seventh day of the twelfth month. 28He spoke kindly to him and gave him a seat of honor higher than those of the other kings who were with him in Babylon. 29So Jehoiachin put aside his prison clothes and for the rest of his life ate regularly at the king's table. 30Day by day the king gave Jehoiachin a regular allowance as long as he lived.

THE FIRST BOOK OF THE

Chronicles

THE FIRST BOOK OF THE

Chronicles

Descendants of the patriarchs

1 ADAM, SHETH, Enosh,
  2Kenan, Mahalaleel, Jered,
  3Henoch, Methuselah, Lamech,
  4Noah, Shem, Ham, and Japheth.
  5 ¶ The sons of Japheth; Gomer, and Magog, and Madai, and Javan, and Tubal, and Meshech, and Tiras.
  6And the sons of Gomer; Ashchenaz, and aRiphath, and Togarmah.
  7And the sons of Javan; Elishah, and Tarshish, Kittim, and bDodanim.
  8 ¶ The sons of Ham; Cush, and Mizraim, Put, and Canaan.
  9And the sons of Cush; Seba, and Havilah, and Sabta, and Raamah, and Sabtecha. And the sons of Raamah; Sheba, and Dedan.
  10And Cush begat Nimrod: he began to be mighty upon the earth.
  11And Mizraim begat Ludim, and Anamim, and Lehabim, and Naphtuhim,
  12And Pathrusim, and Casluhim, (of whom came the Philistines,) and Caphthorim.
  13And Canaan begat Zidon his firstborn, and Heth,
  14The Jebusite also, and the Amorite, and the Girgashite,
  15And the Hivite, and the Arkite, and the Sinite,
  16And the Arvadite, and the Zemarite, and the Hamathite.
  17 ¶ The sons of Shem; Elam, and Asshur, and Arphaxad, and Lud, and Aram, and Uz, and Hul, and Gether, and cMeshech.
  18And Arphaxad begat Shelah, and Shelah begat Eber.
  19And unto Eber were born two sons: the name of the one *was* dPeleg; because in his days the earth was divided: and his brother's name *was* Joktan.
  20And Joktan begat Almodad, and Sheleph, and Hazarmaveth, and Jerah,
  21Hadoram also, and Uzal, and Diklah,
  22And Ebal, and Abimael, and Sheba,
  23And Ophir, and Havilah, and Jobab. All these *were* the sons of Joktan.
  24 ¶ Shem, Arphaxad, Shelah,
  25Eber, Peleg, Reu,

1 ADAM [HIS genealogical line], Seth, Enosh,
  2Kenan, Mahalalel, Jared,
  3Enoch, Methuselah, Lamech,
  4Noah, Shem, Ham, and Japheth.
  5The sons of Japheth: Gomer, Magog, Madai, Javan, Tubal, Meshech, and Tiras.
  6The sons of Gomer: Ashkenaz, Diphath, and Togarmah.
  7The sons of Javan: Elishah, Tarshish, Kittim, and Rodanim.
  8The sons of Ham: Cush, Mizraim (Egypt), Put, and Canaan.
  9The sons of Cush: Seba, Havilah, Sabta, Raamah, and Sabteca. The sons of Raamah: Sheba and Dedan.
  10Cush was the father of Nimrod; he began to be a mighty one upon the earth.
  11Mizraim (Egypt) was the father of the Ludim, Anamim, Lehabim, Naphtuhim,
  12Pathrusim, Casluhim, from whom came the Philistines, and the Caphtorim.
  13Canaan was the father of Sidon his firstborn, and Heth,
  14The Jebusites, Amorites, Girgashites,
  15Hivites, Arkites, Sinites,
  16Arvadites, Zemarites, and Hamathites.
  17The sons of Shem: Elam, Asshur, Arpachshad, Lud, Aram, Uz, Hul, Gether, and Meshech.
  18Arpachshad was the father of Shelah, Shelah of Eber.
  19To Eber were born two sons: the name of the one was Peleg, because in his days [the population of] the earth was divided [according to its languages], and his brother's name was Joktan.
  20Joktan was the father of Almodad, Sheleph, Hazarmaveth, Jerah,
  21Hadoram, Uzal, Diklah,
  22Ebal, Abimael, Sheba,
  23Ophir, Havilah, and Jobab. All these were the sons of Joktan.
  24Shem, Arpachshad, Shelah,
  25Eber, Peleg, Reu,

New American Standard

THE FIRST BOOK OF THE

Chronicles

Genealogy from Adam

1 ADAM, SETH, Enosh,
2 Kenan, Mahalalel, Jared,
3 Enoch, Methuselah, Lamech,
4 Noah, Shem, Ham and Japheth.
5 ¶ The sons of Japheth *were* Gomer, Magog, Madai, Javan, Tubal, Meshech and Tiras.
6 The sons of Gomer *were* Ashkenaz, Diphath, and Togarmah.
7 The sons of Javan *were* Elishah, Tarshish, Kittim and Rodanim.
8 ¶ The sons of Ham *were* Cush, Mizraim, Put, and Canaan.
9 The sons of Cush *were* Seba, Havilah, Sabta, Raama and Sabteca; and the sons of Raamah *were* Sheba and Dedan.
10 Cush became the father of Nimrod; he began to be a mighty one in the earth.
11 ¶ Mizraim became the father of the people of Lud, Anam, Lehab, Naphtuh,
12 Pathrus, Casluh, from which the Philistines came, and Caphtor.
13 ¶ Canaan became the father of Sidon, his firstborn, Heth,
14 and the Jebusites, the Amorites, the Girgashites,
15 the Hivites, the Arkites, the Sinites,
16 the Arvadites, the Zemarites and the Hamathites.
17 ¶ The sons of Shem *were* Elam, Asshur, Arpachshad, Lud, Aram, Uz, Hul, Gether and Meshech.
18 Arpachshad became the father of Shelah and Shelah became the father of Eber.
19 Two sons were born to Eber, the name of the one was Peleg, for in his days the earth was divided, and his brother's name was Joktan.
20 Joktan became the father of Almodad, Sheleph, Hazarmaveth, Jerah,
21 Hadoram, Uzal, Diklah,
22 Ebal, Abimael, Sheba,
23 Ophir, Havilah and Jobab; all these *were* the sons of Joktan.
24 ¶ Shem, Arpachshad, Shelah,
25 Eber, Peleg, Reu,

New International

1 Chronicles

Historical Records From Adam to Abraham

To Noah's Sons

1 ADAM, SETH, Enosh, 2Kenan, Mahalalel, Jared, 3Enoch, Methuselah, Lamech, Noah.

4The sons of Noah:a
Shem, Ham and Japheth.

The Japhethites

5The sonsb of Japheth:
Gomer, Magog, Madai, Javan, Tubal, Meshech and Tiras.
6The sons of Gomer:
Ashkenaz, Riphathc and Togarmah.
7The sons of Javan:
Elishah, Tarshish, the Kittim and the Rodanim.

The Hamites

8The sons of Ham:
Cush, Mizraim,d Put and Canaan.
9The sons of Cush:
Seba, Havilah, Sabta, Raamah and Sabteca.
The sons of Raamah:
Sheba and Dedan.
10Cush was the fathere of
Nimrod, who grew to be a mighty warrior on earth.
11Mizraim was the father of
the Ludites, Anamites, Lehabites, Naphtuhites, 12Pathrusites, Casluhites (from whom the Philistines came) and Caphtorites.
13Canaan was the father of
Sidon his firstborn,f and of the Hittites, 14Jebusites, Amorites, Girgashites, 15Hivites, Arkites, Sinites, 16Arvadites, Zemarites and Hamathites.

The Semites

17The sons of Shem:
Elam, Asshur, Arphaxad, Lud and Aram.
The sons of Aramg:
Uz, Hul, Gether and Meshech.
18Arphaxad was the father of Shelah,
and Shelah the father of Eber.
19Two sons were born to Eber:
One was named Peleg,h because in his time the earth was divided; his brother was named Joktan.
20Joktan was the father of
Almodad, Sheleph, Hazarmaveth, Jerah, 21Hadoram, Uzal, Diklah, 22Obal,i Abimael, Sheba, 23Ophir, Havilah and Jobab. All these were sons of Joktan.

24Shem, Arphaxad,j Shelah,
25Eber, Peleg, Reu,

---

a4 Septuagint; Hebrew does not have *The sons of Noah:*
b5 *Sons* may mean *descendants* or *successors* or *nations*; also in verses 6-10, 17 and 20. c6 Many Hebrew manuscripts and Vulgate (see also Septuagint and Gen. 10:3); most Hebrew manuscripts *Diphath* d8 That is, Egypt; also in verse 11
e10 *Father* may mean *ancestor* or *predecessor* or *founder*; also in verses 11, 13, 18 and 20. f13 Or *of the Sidonians, the foremost* g17 One Hebrew manuscript and some Septuagint manuscripts (see also Gen. 10:23); most Hebrew manuscripts do not have this line.
h19 *Peleg* means *division.* i22 Some Hebrew manuscripts and Syriac (see also Gen. 10:28); most Hebrew manuscripts *Ebal* j24 Hebrew; some Septuagint manuscripts *Arphaxad, Cainan* (see also note at Gen. 11:10)

King James

26Serug, Nahor, Terah,
27Abram; the same *is* Abraham.
28The sons of Abraham; Isaac, and Ishmael.
29 ¶ These *are* their generations: The firstborn of Ishmael, Nebaioth; then Kedar, and Adbeel, and Mibsam,
30Mishma, and Dumah, Massa, *e*Hadad, and Tema,
31Jetur, Naphish, and Kedemah. These are the sons of Ishmael.
32 ¶ Now the sons of Keturah, Abraham's concubine: she bare Zimran, and Jokshan, and Medan, and Midian, and Ishbak, and Shuah. And the sons of Jokshan; Sheba, and Dedan.
33And the sons of Midian; Ephah, and Epher, and Henoch, and Abida, and Eldaah. All these *are* the sons of Keturah.
34And Abraham begat Isaac. The sons of Isaac; Esau and Israel.
35 ¶ The sons of Esau; Eliphaz, Reuel, and Jeush, and Jaalam, and Korah.
36The sons of Eliphaz; Teman, and Omar, *f*Zephi, and Gatam, Kenaz, and Timna, and Amalek.
37The sons of Reuel; Nahath, Zerah, Shammah, and Mizzah.
38And the sons of Seir; Lotan, and Shobal, and Zibeon, and Anah, and Dishon, and Ezar, and Dishan.
39And the sons of Lotan; Hori, and *g*Homam: and Timna *was* Lotan's sister.
40The sons of Shobal; *h*Alian, and Manahath, and Ebal, *i*Shephi, and Onam. And the sons of Zibeon; Aiah, and Anah.
41The sons of Anah; Dishon. And the sons of Dishon; *j*Amram, and Eshban, and Ithran, and Cheran.
42The sons of Ezer; Bilhan, and Zavan, *and* *k*Jakan. The sons of Dishan; Uz, and Aran.

The kings of Edom

43 ¶ Now these *are* the kings that reigned in the land of Edom before *any* king reigned over the children of Israel; Bela the son of Beor: and the name of his city *was* Dinhabah.
44And when Bela was dead, Jobab the son of Zerah of Bozrah reigned in his stead.

Amplified

26Serug, Nahor, Terah,
27Abram, the same as Abraham.
28The sons of Abraham: Isaac and Ishmael.
29These are their descendants: The firstborn of Ishmael, Nebaioth; Kedar, Adbeel, Mibsam,
30Mishma, Dumah, Massa, Hadad, Tema,
31Jetur, Naphish, and Kedemah. These are the sons of Ishmael.
32Now the sons of Keturah, Abraham's concubine: she bore Zimran, Jokshan, Medan, Midian, Ishbak, and Shuah. The sons of Jokshan: Sheba and Dedan.
33The sons of Midian: Ephah, Epher, Hanoch, Abida, and Eldaah. All these are the sons [and grandsons] of Keturah.
34Abraham was the father of Isaac. The sons of Isaac: Esau and Israel.
35The sons of Esau: Eliphaz, Reuel, Jeush, Jalam, and Korah.
36The sons of Eliphaz: Teman, Omar, Zephi, Gatam, Kenaz, Timna, and Amalek.
37The sons of Reuel: Nahath, Zerah, Shammah, and Mizzah.
38The sons of Seir: Lotan, Shobal, Zibeon, Anah, Dishon, Ezer, and Dishan.
39The sons of Lotan: Hori and Homam; and Timna was Lotan's sister.
40The sons of Shobal: Alian, Manahath, Ebal, Shephi, and Onam. The sons of Zibeon: Aiah and Anah.
41The son of Anah: Dishon. The sons of Dishon: Hamran, Eshban, Ithran, and Cheran.
42The sons of Ezer: Bilhan, Zaavan, [and] Jaakan. The sons of Dishan: Uz and Aran.
43These are the kings who reigned in the land of Edom before any king reigned over the Israelites: Bela son of Beor; the name of his city was Dinhabah.
44When Bela died, Jobab son of Zerah of Bozrah reigned in his stead.

*e*Or, *Hadar;* see Gen. 25:15   *f*Or, *Zepho;* see Gen. 36:11
*g*Or, *Heman;* see Gen. 36:22   *h*Or, *Alvan;* see Gen. 36:23
*i*Or, *Shepho;* see Gen. 36:23   *j*Or, *Hemdan;* see Gen. 36:26
*k*Or, *Akan;* see Gen. 36:27

New American Standard

26 Serug, Nahor, Terah,
27 Abram, that is Abraham.

Descendants of Abraham

28 ¶ The sons of Abraham *were* Isaac and Ishmael.
29 These are their genealogies: the firstborn of Ishmael *was* Nebaioth, then Kedar, Adbeel, Mibsam,
30 Mishma, Dumah, Massa, Hadad, Tema,
31 Jetur, Naphish and Kedemah; these *were* the sons of Ishmael.
32 The sons of Keturah, Abraham's concubine, *whom* she bore, *were* Zimran, Jokshan, Medan, Midian, Ishbak and Shuah. And the sons of Jokshan *were* Sheba and Dedan.
33 The sons of Midian were Ephah, Epher, Hanoch, Abida and Eldaah. All these were the sons of Keturah.
34 ¶ Abraham became the father of Isaac. The sons of Isaac *were* Esau and Israel.
35 The sons of Esau *were* Eliphaz, Reuel, Jeush, Jalam and Korah.
36 The sons of Eliphaz *were* Teman, Omar, Zephi, Gatam, Kenaz, Timna and Amalek.
37 The sons of Reuel *were* Nahath, Zerah, Shammah and Mizzah.
38 The sons of Seir *were* Lotan, Shobal, Zibeon, Anah, Dishon, Ezer and Dishan.
39 The sons of Lotan *were* Hori and Homam; and Lotan's sister *was* Timna.
40 The sons of Shobal *were* Alian, Manahath, Ebal, Shephi and Onam. And the sons of Zibeon *were* Aiah and Anah.
41 The son of Anah *was* Dishon. And the sons of Dishon *were* Hamran, Eshban, Ithran and Cheran.
42 The sons of Ezer *were* Bilhan, Zaavan and Jaakan. The sons of Dishan *were* Uz and Aran.
43 ¶ Now these are the kings who reigned in the land of Edom before any king of the sons of Israel reigned. Bela was the son of Beor, and the name of his city was Dinhabah.
44 When Bela died, Jobab the son of Zerah of Bozrah became king in his place.

New International

26Serug, Nahor, Terah
27and Abram (that is, Abraham).

The Family of Abraham

28The sons of Abraham:
  Isaac and Ishmael.

Descendants of Hagar

29These were their descendants:
  Nebaioth the firstborn of Ishmael, Kedar, Adbeel, Mibsam, 30Mishma, Dumah, Massa, Hadad, Tema, 31Jetur, Naphish and Kedemah. These were the sons of Ishmael.

Descendants of Keturah

32The sons born to Keturah, Abraham's concubine:
  Zimran, Jokshan, Medan, Midian, Ishbak and Shuah.
  The sons of Jokshan:
  Sheba and Dedan.
33The sons of Midian:
  Ephah, Epher, Hanoch, Abida and Eldaah.
  All these were descendants of Keturah.

Descendants of Sarah

34Abraham was the father of Isaac.
  The sons of Isaac:
  Esau and Israel.

Esau's Sons

35The sons of Esau:
  Eliphaz, Reuel, Jeush, Jalam and Korah.
36The sons of Eliphaz:
  Teman, Omar, Zepho,[k] Gatam and Kenaz;
  by Timna: Amalek.[l]
37The sons of Reuel:
  Nahath, Zerah, Shammah and Mizzah.

The People of Seir in Edom

38The sons of Seir:
  Lotan, Shobal, Zibeon, Anah, Dishon, Ezer and Dishan.
39The sons of Lotan:
  Hori and Homam. Timna was Lotan's sister.
40The sons of Shobal:
  Alvan,[m] Manahath, Ebal, Shepho and Onam.
  The sons of Zibeon:
  Aiah and Anah.
41The son of Anah:
  Dishon.
  The sons of Dishon:
  Hemdan,[n] Eshban, Ithran and Keran.
42The sons of Ezer:
  Bilhan, Zaavan and Akan.[o]
  The sons of Dishan[p]:
  Uz and Aran.

The Rulers of Edom

43These were the kings who reigned in Edom before any Israelite king reigned[q]:
  Bela son of Beor, whose city was named Dinhabah.
44When Bela died, Jobab son of Zerah from Bozrah succeeded him as king.

[k] 36 Many Hebrew manuscripts, some Septuagint manuscripts and Syriac (see also Gen. 36:11); most Hebrew manuscripts *Zephi*
[l] 36 Some Septuagint manuscripts (see also Gen. 36:12); Hebrew *Gatam, Kenaz, Timna and Amalek*   [m] 40 Many Hebrew manuscripts and some Septuagint manuscripts (see also Gen. 36:23); most Hebrew manuscripts *Alian*   [n] 41 Many Hebrew manuscripts and some Septuagint manuscripts (see also Gen. 36:26); most Hebrew manuscripts *Hamran*   [o] 42 Many Hebrew and Septuagint manuscripts (see also Gen. 36:27); most Hebrew manuscripts *Zaavan, Jaakan*   [p] 42 Hebrew *Dishon*, a variant of *Dishan*   [q] 43 Or *before an Israelite king reigned over them*

King James

⁴⁵And when Jobab was dead, Husham of the land of the Temanites reigned in his stead.

⁴⁶And when Husham was dead, Hadad the son of Bedad, which smote Midian in the field of Moab, reigned in his stead: and the name of his city *was* Avith.

⁴⁷And when Hadad was dead, Samlah of Masrekah reigned in his stead.

⁴⁸And when Samlah was dead, Shaul of Rehoboth by the river reigned in his stead.

⁴⁹And when Shaul was dead, Baal-hanan the son of Achbor reigned in his stead.

⁵⁰And when Baal-hanan was dead, *l*Hadad reigned in his stead: and the name of his city *was* *m*Pai; and his wife's name *was* Mehetabel, the daughter of Matred, the daughter of Mezahab.

⁵¹ ¶ Hadad died also. And the dukes of Edom were; duke Timnah, duke *n*Aliah, duke Jetheth,

⁵²Duke Aholibamah, duke Elah, duke Pinon,

⁵³Duke Kenaz, duke Teman, duke Mibzar,

⁵⁴Duke Magdiel, duke Iram. These *are* the dukes of Edom.

From Israel to David

2 THESE *ARE* the sons of *o*Israel; Reuben, Simeon, Levi, and Judah, Issachar, and Zebulun,

²Dan, Joseph, and Benjamin, Naphtali, Gad, and Asher.

³ ¶ The sons of Judah; Er, and Onan, and Shelah: *which* three were born unto him of the daughter of Shua the Canaanitess. And Er, the firstborn of Judah, was evil in the sight of the LORD; and he slew him.

⁴And Tamar his daughter-in-law bare him Pharez and Zerah. All the sons of Judah *were* five.

⁵The sons of Pharez; Hezron, and Hamul.

⁶And the sons of Zerah; *p*Zimri, and Ethan, and Heman, and Calcol, and *q*Dara: five of them in all.

⁷And the sons of Carmi; *r*Achar, the troubler of Israel, who transgressed in the thing accursed.

⁸And the sons of Ethan; Azariah.

⁹The sons also of Hezron, that were born unto him; Jerahmeel, and *s*Ram, and *t*Chelubai.

¹⁰And Ram begat Amminadab; and Amminadab begat Nahshon, prince of the children of Judah;

¹¹And Nahshon begat *u*Salma, and Salma begat Boaz,

¹²And Boaz begat Obed, and Obed begat Jesse.

¹³ ¶ And Jesse begat his firstborn Eliab, and Abinadab the second, and *v*Shimma the third,

¹⁴Nethaneel the fourth, Raddai the fifth.

¹⁵Ozem the sixth, David the seventh:

¹⁶Whose sisters *were* Zeruiah, and Abigail. And the sons of Zeruiah; Abishai, and Joab, and Asahel, three.

Amplified

⁴⁵When Jobab died, Husham of the land of the Temanites reigned in his stead.

⁴⁶When Husham died, Hadad [I of Edom] son of Bedad, who defeated Midian in the field of Moab, reigned in his stead; his city was Avith.

⁴⁷When Hadad [I] died, Samlah of Masrekah reigned in his stead.

⁴⁸When Samlah died, Shaul of Rehoboth, on the River [Euphrates] reigned in his stead.

⁴⁹When Shaul died, Baal-hanan son of Achbor reigned in his stead.

⁵⁰When Baal-hanan died, Hadad [II] reigned in his stead; his city was Pai; his wife was Mehetabel daughter of Matred, the daughter of Mezahab.

⁵¹Hadad died also. The chiefs of Edom were: chiefs Timna, Aliah, Jetheth,

⁵²Oholibamah, Elah, Pinon,

⁵³Kenaz, Teman, Mibzar,

⁵⁴Magdiel, and Iram. These are the chiefs of Edom.

2 THESE ARE the sons of Israel: Reuben, Simeon, Levi, Judah, Issachar, Zebulun,

²Dan, Joseph, Benjamin, Naphtali, Gad, and Asher.

³The sons of Judah: Er, Onan, and Shelah, whom Shua's daughter the Canaanitess bore him. Er, Judah's eldest, was evil in the Lord's sight, and He slew him.

⁴Tamar, Judah's daughter-in-law, bore him Pharez and Zerah. All Judah's sons were five.

⁵The sons of Pharez: Hezron and Hamul.

⁶The sons of Zerah: Zimri, Ethan, Heman, Calcol, and Dara—five in all. [I Kings 4:31.]

⁷The son of Carmi: Achar, the troubler of Israel, who transgressed in the matter of the devoted things. [Josh. 7:1.]

⁸The son of Ethan: Azariah.

⁹The sons of Hezron who were born to him: Jerahmeel, Ram, and Chelubai (that is, Caleb).

¹⁰Ram was the father of Amminadab, and Amminadab of Nahshon, prince of the sons of Judah.

¹¹Nahshon was the father of Salma, Salma of Boaz,

¹²Boaz of Obed, and Obed of Jesse.

¹³Jesse was the father of Eliab his firstborn, Abinadab second, Shimea third,

¹⁴Nethanel fourth, Raddai fifth,

¹⁵Ozem sixth, David seventh.

¹⁶Their sisters were Zeruiah and Abigail. The sons of Zeruiah: Abishai, Joab, and Asahel, three.

New American Standard

45 When Jobab died, Husham of the land of the Temanites became king in his place.

46 When Husham died, Hadad the son of Bedad, who defeated Midian in the field of Moab, became king in his place; and the name of his city *was* Avith.

47 When Hadad died, Samlah of Masrekah became king in his place.

48 When Samlah died, Shaul of Rehoboth by the River became king in his place.

49 When Shaul died, Baal-hanan the son of Achbor became king in his place.

50 When Baal-hanan died, Hadad became king in his place; and the name of his city was Pai, and his wife's name was Mehetabel, the daughter of Matred, the daughter of Mezahab.

51 Then Hadad died.

¶ Now the chiefs of Edom were: chief Timna, chief Aliah, chief Jetheth,

52 chief Oholibamah, chief Elah, chief Pinon,

53 chief Kenaz, chief Teman, chief Mibzar,

54 chief Magdiel, chief Iram. These *were* the chiefs of Edom.

Genealogy: Twelve Sons of Jacob (Israel)

2 THESE ARE the sons of Israel: Reuben, Simeon, Levi, Judah, Issachar, Zebulun,

2 Dan, Joseph, Benjamin, Naphtali, Gad and Asher.

3 ¶ The sons of Judah *were* Er, Onan and Shelah; *these* three were born to him by Bath-shua the Canaanitess. And Er, Judah's firstborn, was wicked in the sight of the LORD, so He put him to death.

4 Tamar his daughter-in-law bore him Perez and Zerah. Judah had five sons in all.

5 ¶ The sons of Perez *were* Hezron and Hamul.

6 The sons of Zerah *were* Zimri, Ethan, Heman, Calcol and Dara; five of them in all.

7 The son of Carmi *was* Achar, the troubler of Israel, who violated the ban.

8 The son of Ethan *was* Azariah.

Genealogy of David

9 ¶ Now the sons of Hezron, who were born to him *were* Jerahmeel, Ram and Chelubai.

10 Ram became the father of Amminadab, and Amminadab became the father of Nahshon, leader of the sons of Judah;

11 Nahshon became the father of Salma, Salma became the father of Boaz,

12 Boaz became the father of Obed, and Obed became the father of Jesse;

13 and Jesse became the father of Eliab his firstborn, then Abinadab the second, Shimea the third,

14 Nethanel the fourth, Raddai the fifth,

15 Ozem the sixth, David the seventh;

16 and their sisters *were* Zeruiah and Abigail. And the three sons of Zeruiah *were* Abshai, Joab and Asahel.

New International

45When Jobab died, Husham from the land of the Temanites succeeded him as king.

46When Husham died, Hadad son of Bedad, who defeated Midian in the country of Moab, succeeded him as king. His city was named Avith.

47When Hadad died, Samlah from Masrekah succeeded him as king.

48When Samlah died, Shaul from Rehoboth on the river[r] succeeded him as king.

49When Shaul died, Baal-Hanan son of Acbor succeeded him as king.

50When Baal-Hanan died, Hadad succeeded him as king. His city was named Pau,[s] and his wife's name was Mehetabel daughter of Matred, the daughter of Me-Zahab. 51Hadad also died.

The chiefs of Edom were:

Timna, Alvah, Jetheth, 52Oholibamah, Elah, Pinon, 53Kenaz, Teman, Mibzar, 54Magdiel and Iram. These were the chiefs of Edom.

Israel's Sons

2 THESE WERE the sons of Israel: Reuben, Simeon, Levi, Judah, Issachar, Zebulun, 2Dan, Joseph, Benjamin, Naphtali, Gad and Asher.

Judah

To Hezron's Sons

3The sons of Judah:

Er, Onan and Shelah. These three were born to him by a Canaanite woman, the daughter of Shua. Er, Judah's firstborn, was wicked in the LORD's sight; so the LORD put him to death. 4Tamar, Judah's daughter-in-law, bore him Perez and Zerah. Judah had five sons in all.

5The sons of Perez:

Hezron and Hamul.

6The sons of Zerah:

Zimri, Ethan, Heman, Calcol and Darda[t]—five in all.

7The son of Carmi:

Achar,[u] who brought trouble on Israel by violating the ban on taking devoted things.[v]

8The son of Ethan:

Azariah.

9The sons born to Hezron were:

Jerahmeel, Ram and Caleb.[w]

From Ram Son of Hezron

10Ram was the father of

Amminadab, and Amminadab the father of Nahshon, the leader of the people of Judah. 11Nahshon was the father of Salmon,[x] Salmon the father of Boaz, 12Boaz the father of Obed and Obed the father of Jesse.

13Jesse was the father of

Eliab his firstborn; the second son was Abinadab, the third Shimea, 14the fourth Nethanel, the fifth Raddai, 15the sixth Ozem and the seventh David. 16Their sisters were Zeruiah and Abigail. Zeruiah's three sons were Abishai, Joab and Asahel.

r48 Possibly the Euphrates   s50 Many Hebrew manuscripts, some Septuagint manuscripts, Vulgate and Syriac (see also Gen. 36:39); most Hebrew manuscripts *Pai*   t6 Many Hebrew manuscripts, some Septuagint manuscripts and Syriac (see also 1 Kings 4:31); most Hebrew manuscripts *Dara*   u7 *Achar* means *trouble*; *Achar* is called *Achan* in Joshua.   v7 The Hebrew term refers to the irrevocable giving over of things or persons to the LORD, often by totally destroying them.   w9 Hebrew *Kelubai*, a variant of *Caleb*   x11 Septuagint (see also Ruth 4:21); Hebrew *Salma*

King James

¹⁷And Abigail bare Amasa: and the father of Amasa *was* ^wJether the Ishmaelite.

¹⁸ ¶ And Caleb the son of Hezron begat *children* of Azubah *his* wife, and of Jerioth: her sons *are* these; Jesher, and Shobab, and Ardon.

¹⁹And when Azubah was dead, Caleb took unto him Ephrath, which bare him Hur.

²⁰And Hur begat Uri, and Uri begat Bezaleel.

²¹ ¶ And afterward Hezron went in to the daughter of Machir the father of Gilead, whom he ^xmarried when he *was* threescore years old; and she bare him Segub.

²²And Segub begat Jair, who had three and twenty cities in the land of Gilead.

²³And he took Geshur, and Aram, with the towns of Jair, from them, with Kenath, and the towns thereof, *even* threescore cities. All these *belonged to* the sons of Machir the father of Gilead.

²⁴And after that Hezron was dead in Caleb-ephratah, then Abiah Hezron's wife bare him Ashur the father of Tekoa.

²⁵ ¶ And the sons of Jerahmeel the firstborn of Hezron were, Ram the firstborn, and Bunah, and Oren, and Ozem, *and* Ahijah.

²⁶Jerahmeel had also another wife, whose name *was* Atarah; she *was* the mother of Onam.

²⁷And the sons of Ram the firstborn of Jerahmeel were, Maaz, and Jamin, and Eker.

²⁸And the sons of Onam were, Shammai, and Jada. And the sons of Shammai; Nadab, and Abishur.

²⁹And the name of the wife of Abishur *was* Abihail, and she bare him Ahban, and Molid.

³⁰And the sons of Nadab; Seled, and Appaim: but Seled died without children.

³¹And the sons of Appaim; Ishi. And the sons of Ishi; Sheshan. And the children of Sheshan; Ahlai.

³²And the sons of Jada the brother of Shammai; Jether, and Jonathan: and Jether died without children.

³³And the sons of Jonathan; Peleth, and Zaza. These were the sons of Jerahmeel.

³⁴ ¶ Now Sheshan had no sons, but daughters. And Sheshan had a servant, an Egyptian, whose name *was* Jarha.

³⁵And Sheshan gave his daughter to Jarha his servant to wife; and she bare him Attai.

³⁶And Attai begat Nathan, and Nathan begat Zabad,

³⁷And Zabad begat Ephlal, and Ephlal begat Obed,

³⁸And Obed begat Jehu, and Jehu begat Azariah,

³⁹And Azariah begat Helez, and Helez begat Eleasah,

⁴⁰And Eleasah begat Sisamai, and Sisamai begat Shallum,

⁴¹And Shallum begat Jekamiah, and Jekamiah begat Elishama.

⁴² ¶ Now the sons of Caleb the brother of Jerahmeel *were*, Mesha his firstborn, which *was* the father of Ziph; and the sons of Mareshah the father of Hebron.

⁴³And the sons of Hebron; Korah, and Tappuah, and Rekem, and Shema.

⁴⁴And Shema begat Raham, the father of Jorkoam: and Rekem begat Shammai.

Amplified

¹⁷Abigail bore Amasa, and the father of Amasa was Jether the Ishmaelite.

¹⁸And Caleb son of Hezron had sons by his wife Azubah and by Jerioth. [Azubah's] sons were: Jesher, Shobab, and Ardon.

¹⁹Azubah died, and Caleb married Ephrath, who bore him Hur.

²⁰Hur was the father of Uri, and Uri of Bezalel [the skillful craftsman who made the furnishings of the tabernacle]. [Exod. 31:2–5.]

²¹Later, when Hezron was sixty years old, he married the daughter of Machir the father of Gilead, and she bore him Segub.

²²Segub was the father of Jair, who had twenty-three cities in the land of Gilead.

²³But Geshur and Aram took from them Havvoth-jair, with Kenath and its villages, sixty towns. All these were the descendants of Machir the father of Gilead.

²⁴After Hezron died in Caleb-ephrathah, Abiah, Hezron's wife, bore to him Ashhur the father of Tekoa.

²⁵The sons of Jerahmeel the firstborn of Hezron: Ram the firstborn, Bunah, Oren, Ozem, and Ahijah.

²⁶Jerahmeel had another wife, named Atarah; she was the mother of Onam.

²⁷The sons of Ram the firstborn of Jerahmeel were: Maaz, Jamin, and Eker.

²⁸The sons of Onam: Shammai and Jada. The sons of Shammai: Nadab and Abishur.

²⁹Abishur's wife was Abihail; she bore him Ahban and Molid.

³⁰The sons of Nadab: Seled and Appaim. Seled died childless.

³¹The son of Appaim: Ishi. The son of Ishi: Sheshan. The son of Sheshan: Ahlai.

³²The sons of Jada the brother of Shammai: Jether and Jonathan. Jether died childless.

³³The sons of Jonathan: Peleth and Zaza. These were the descendants of Jerahmeel.

³⁴Sheshan had no sons—only daughters. But Sheshan had a servant, an Egyptian, whose name was Jarha.

³⁵Sheshan gave his daughter to Jarha his servant as wife; she bore him Attai.

³⁶Attai was the father of Nathan, and Nathan of Zabad.

³⁷Zabad was the father of Ephlal, and Ephlal of Obed.

³⁸Obed was the father of Jehu, and Jehu of Azariah.

³⁹Azariah was the father of Helez, and Helez of Eleasah.

⁴⁰Eleasah was the father of Sismai, and Sismai of Shallum.

⁴¹Shallum was the father of Jekamiah, and Jekamiah of Elishama.

⁴²The sons of Caleb the brother of Jerahmeel: Mesha his firstborn was the father of Ziph; and his son Mareshah [he was] the father of Hebron.

⁴³The sons of Hebron: Korah, Tappuah, Rekem, and Shema.

⁴⁴Shema was the father of Raham, the father of Jorkeam. And Rekem was the father of Shammai.

---

^w Or, *Ithra an Israelite;* see 2 Sam. 17:25   ^x Heb. *took*

New American Standard

17 Abigail bore Amasa, and the father of Amasa was Jether the Ishmaelite.

18 ¶ Now Caleb the son of Hezron had sons by Azubah *his* wife, and by Jerioth; and these were her sons: Jesher, Shobab, and Ardon.

19 When Azubah died, Caleb married Ephrath, who bore him Hur.

20 Hur became the father of Uri, and Uri became the father of Bezalel.

21 ¶ Afterward Hezron went in to the daughter of Machir the father of Gilead, whom he married when he was sixty years old; and she bore him Segub.

22 Segub became the father of Jair, who had twenty-three cities in the land of Gilead.

23 But Geshur and Aram took the towns of Jair from them, with Kenath and its villages, *even* sixty cities. All these were the sons of Machir, the father of Gilead.

24 After the death of Hezron in Caleb-ephrathah, Abijah, Hezron's wife, bore him Ashhur the father of Tekoa.

25 ¶ Now the sons of Jerahmeel the firstborn of Hezron were Ram the firstborn, then Bunah, Oren, Ozem *and* Ahijah.

26 Jerahmeel had another wife, whose name was Atarah; she was the mother of Onam.

27 The sons of Ram, the firstborn of Jerahmeel, were Maaz, Jamin and Eker.

28 The sons of Onam were Shammai and Jada. And the sons of Shammai *were* Nadab and Abishur.

29 The name of Abishur's wife *was* Abihail, and she bore him Ahban and Molid.

30 The sons of Nadab *were* Seled and Appaim, and Seled died without sons.

31 The son of Appaim *was* Ishi. And the son of Ishi *was* Sheshan. And the son of Sheshan *was* Ahlai.

32 The sons of Jada the brother of Shammai *were* Jether and Jonathan, and Jether died without sons.

33 The sons of Jonathan *were* Peleth and Zaza. These were the sons of Jerahmeel.

34 Now Sheshan had no sons, only daughters. And Sheshan had an Egyptian servant whose name was Jarha.

35 Sheshan gave his daughter to Jarha his servant in marriage, and she bore him Attai.

36 Attai became the father of Nathan, and Nathan became the father of Zabad,

37 and Zabad became the father of Ephlal, and Ephlal became the father of Obed,

38 and Obed became the father of Jehu, and Jehu became the father of Azariah,

39 and Azariah became the father of Helez, and Helez became the father of Eleasah,

40 and Eleasah became the father of Sismai, and Sismai became the father of Shallum,

41 and Shallum became the father of Jekamiah, and Jekamiah became the father of Elishama.

42 ¶ Now the sons of Caleb, the brother of Jerahmeel, *were* Mesha his firstborn, who was the father of Ziph; and his son was Mareshah, the father of Hebron.

43 The sons of Hebron *were* Korah and Tappuah and Rekem and Shema.

44 Shema became the father of Raham, the father of Jorkeam; and Rekem became the father of Shammai.

New International

17 Abigail was the mother of Amasa, whose father was Jether the Ishmaelite.

Caleb Son of Hezron

18 Caleb son of Hezron had children by his wife Azubah (and by Jerioth). These were her sons: Jesher, Shobab and Ardon. 19 When Azubah died, Caleb married Ephrath, who bore him Hur. 20 Hur was the father of Uri, and Uri the father of Bezalel.

21 Later, Hezron lay with the daughter of Makir the father of Gilead (he had married her when he was sixty years old), and she bore him Segub. 22 Segub was the father of Jair, who controlled twenty-three towns in Gilead. 23 (But Geshur and Aram captured Havvoth Jair,^{y} as well as Kenath with its surrounding settlements—sixty towns.) All these were descendants of Makir the father of Gilead.

24 After Hezron died in Caleb Ephrathah, Abijah the wife of Hezron bore him Ashhur the father^z of Tekoa.

Jerahmeel Son of Hezron

25 The sons of Jerahmeel the firstborn of Hezron:
Ram his firstborn, Bunah, Oren, Ozem and^a Ahijah. 26 Jerahmeel had another wife, whose name was Atarah; she was the mother of Onam.

27 The sons of Ram the firstborn of Jerahmeel:
Maaz, Jamin and Eker.

28 The sons of Onam:
Shammai and Jada.

The sons of Shammai:
Nadab and Abishur.

29 Abishur's wife was named Abihail, who bore him Ahban and Molid.

30 The sons of Nadab:
Seled and Appaim. Seled died without children.

31 The son of Appaim:
Ishi, who was the father of Sheshan.
Sheshan was the father of Ahlai.

32 The sons of Jada, Shammai's brother:
Jether and Jonathan. Jether died without children.

33 The sons of Jonathan:
Peleth and Zaza.

These were the descendants of Jerahmeel.

34 Sheshan had no sons—only daughters.
He had an Egyptian servant named Jarha. 35 Sheshan gave his daughter in marriage to his servant Jarha, and she bore him Attai.

36 Attai was the father of Nathan,
Nathan the father of Zabad,

37 Zabad the father of Ephlal,
Ephlal the father of Obed,

38 Obed the father of Jehu,
Jehu the father of Azariah,

39 Azariah the father of Helez,
Helez the father of Eleasah,

40 Eleasah the father of Sismai,
Sismai the father of Shallum,

41 Shallum the father of Jekamiah,
and Jekamiah the father of Elishama.

The Clans of Caleb

42 The sons of Caleb the brother of Jerahmeel:
Mesha his firstborn, who was the father of Ziph, and his son Mareshah,^{b} who was the father of Hebron.

43 The sons of Hebron:
Korah, Tappuah, Rekem and Shema. 44 Shema was the father of Raham, and Raham the father of Jor-

y 23 Or *captured the settlements of Jair* z 24 *Father* may mean *civic leader* or *military leader*; also in verses 42, 45, 49-52 and possibly elsewhere. a 25 Or *Oren and Ozem, by* b 42 The meaning of the Hebrew for this phrase is uncertain.

King James

45And the son of Shammai *was* Maon: and Maon *was* the father of Beth-zur.

46And Ephah, Caleb's concubine, bare Haran, and Moza, and Gazez: and Haran begat Gazez.

47And the sons of Jahdai; Regem, and Jotham, and Gesham, and Pelet, and Ephah, and Shaaph.

48Maachah, Caleb's concubine, bare Sheber, and Tirhanah.

49She bare also Shaaph the father of Madmannah, Sheva the father of Machbenah, and the father of Gibea: and the daughter of Caleb *was* Achsah.

50 ¶ These were the sons of Caleb the son of Hur, the firstborn of *y*Ephratah; Shobal the father of Kirjath-jearim,

51Salma the father of Bethlehem, Hareph the father of Beth-gader.

52And Shobal the father of Kirjath-jearim had sons; *z*Haroeh, *and *a*half of the Manahethites.

53And the families of Kirjath-jearim; the Ithrites, and the Puhites, and the Shumathites, and the Mishraites; of them came the Zareathites, and the Eshtaulites.

54The sons of Salma; Bethlehem, and the Netophathites, *b*Ataroth, the house of Joab, and half of the Manahethites, the Zorites.

55And the families of the scribes which dwelt at Jabez; the Tirathites, the Shimeathites, *and* Suchathites. These *are* the Kenites that came of Hemath, the father of the house of Rechab.

The family of David

3 NOW THESE were the sons of David, which were born unto him in Hebron; the firstborn Amnon, of Ahinoam the Jezreelitess; the second *c*Daniel, of Abigail the Carmelitess:

2The third, Absalom the son of Maachah the daughter of Talmai king of Geshur: the fourth, Adonijah the son of Haggith:

3The fifth, Shephatiah of Abital: the sixth, Ithream by Eglah his wife.

4*These* six were born unto him in Hebron; and there he reigned seven years and six months: and in Jerusalem he reigned thirty and three years.

5And these were born unto him in Jerusalem; *d*Shimea, and Shobab, and Nathan, and Solomon, four, of *e*Bathshua the daughter of *f*Ammiel:

6Ibhar also, and *g*Elishama, and Eliphelet,

7And Nogah, and Nepheg, and Japhia,

8And Elishama, and *h*Eliada, and Eliphelet, nine.

9*These were* all the sons of David, beside the sons of the concubines, and Tamar their sister.

The family of Solomon

10 ¶ And Solomon's son *was* Rehoboam, *i*Abia his son, Asa his son, Jehoshaphat his son,

11Joram his son, *j*Ahaziah his son, Joash his son,

12Amaziah his son, *k*Azariah his son, Jotham his son,

Amplified

45The son of Shammai was Maon; Maon's son was Beth-zur.

46Ephah, Caleb's concubine, bore Haran, Moza, and Gazez; Haran was the father of Gazez.

47The sons of Jahdai: Regem, Jotham, Geshan, Pelet, Ephah, and Shaaph.

48Maacah, Caleb's concubine, bore Sheber and Tirhanah, and also

49Shaaph the father of Madmannah and Sheva the father of Machbenah and of Gibea; and the daughter of Caleb was Achsah.

50These were the descendants of Caleb. The sons of Hur the firstborn of Ephrathah: Shobal the father of Kiriath-jearim,

51Salma the father of Bethlehem, and Hareph the father of Beth-gader.

52Shobal the father of Kiriath-jearim had [other] descendants: Haroeh, half [of the inhabitants] of Menuhoth [in Judah],

53And the families of Kiriath-jearim: the Ithrites, Puthites, Shumathites, and Mishraites. From these came the Zorathites and the Eshtaolites.

54The descendants of Salma: Bethlehem, the Netophathites, Atroth-beth-joab, and half of the Manahathites, [and] the Zorites,

55And the families of scribes who dwelt at Jabez: the Tirathites, Shimeathites, and Sucathites. These are the Kenites who came from Hammath, the father of the house of Rechab.

3 THESE SONS of David were born to him in Hebron: the firstborn was Amnon, of Ahinoam the Jezreelitess; second, Daniel (Chileab), of Abigail the Carmelitess;

2Third, Absalom the son of Maacah daughter of Talmai king of Geshur; fourth, Adonijah, of Haggith;

3Fifth, Shephatiah, of Abital; sixth, Ithream, of his wife Eglah.

4These six were born to David in Hebron; there he reigned seven years and six months, and in Jerusalem he reigned thirty-three years.

5These were born to [David] in Jerusalem: Shimea, Shobab, Nathan, Solomon—four of Bathshua (Bathsheba) daughter of Ammiel (Eliam);

6Then Ibhar, Elishama, Eliphelet,

7Nogah, Nepheg, Japhia,

8Elishama, Eliada, and Eliphelet—nine in all.

9These were all the sons of David, besides the sons of the concubines. And Tamar was their sister.

10Solomon's descendants [omitting nonreigning offspring] were: his son Rehoboam. Abijah was his son, Asa his son, Jehoshaphat his son,

11Jehoram (Joram) his son, Ahaziah his son, Joash his son,

12Amaziah his son, Azariah his son, Jotham his son,

New American Standard

45 The son of Shammai was Maon, and Maon *was* the father of Bethzur.

46 Ephah, Caleb's concubine, bore Haran, Moza and Gazez; and Haran became the father of Gazez.

47 The sons of Jahdai *were* Regem, Jotham, Geshan, Pelet, Ephah and Shaaph.

48 Maacah, Caleb's concubine, bore Sheber and Tirhanah.

49 She also bore Shaaph the father of Madmannah, Sheva the father of Machbena and the father of Gibea; and the daughter of Caleb *was* Achsah.

50 These were the sons of Caleb.

¶ The sons of Hur, the firstborn of Ephrathah, *were* Shobal the father of Kiriath-jearim,

51 Salma the father of Bethlehem *and* Hareph the father of Beth-gader.

52 Shobal the father of Kiriath-jearim had sons: Haroeh, half of the Manahathites,

53 and the families of Kiriath-jearim: the Ithrites, the Puthites, the Shumathites and the Mishraites; from these came the Zorathites and the Eshtaolites.

54 The sons of Salma *were* Bethlehem and the Netophathites, Atroth-beth-joab and half of the Manahathites, the Zorites.

55 The families of scribes who lived at Jabez *were* the Tirathites, the Shimeathites *and* the Sucathites. Those are the Kenites who came from Hammath, the father of the house of Rechab.

Family of David

3 NOW THESE were the sons of David who were born to him in Hebron: the firstborn *was* Amnon, by Ahinoam the Jezreelitess; the second *was* Daniel, by Abigail the Carmelitess;

2 the third *was* Absalom the son of Maacah, the daughter of Talmai king of Geshur; the fourth *was* Adonijah the son of Haggith;

3 the fifth *was* Shephatiah, by Abital; the sixth *was* Ithream, by his wife Eglah.

4 Six were born to him in Hebron, and there he reigned seven years and six months. And in Jerusalem he reigned thirty-three years.

5 These were born to him in Jerusalem: Shimea, Shobab, Nathan and Solomon, four, by Bath-shua the daughter of Ammiel;

6 and Ibhar, Elishama, Eliphelet,

7 Nogah, Nepheg and Japhia,

8 Elishama, Eliada and Eliphelet, nine.

9 All *these were* the sons of David, besides the sons of the concubines; and Tamar *was* their sister.

10 ¶ Now Solomon's son *was* Rehoboam, Abijah *was* his son, Asa his son, Jehoshaphat his son,

11 Joram his son, Ahaziah his son, Joash his son,

12 Amaziah his son, Azariah his son, Jotham his son,

New International

keam. Rekem was the father of Shammai. 45The son of Shammai was Maon, and Maon was the father of Beth Zur.

46Caleb's concubine Ephah was the mother of Haran, Moza and Gazez. Haran was the father of Gazez.

47The sons of Jahdai:

Regem, Jotham, Geshan, Pelet, Ephah and Shaaph.

48Caleb's concubine Maacah was the mother of Sheber and Tirhanah. 49She also gave birth to Shaaph the father of Madmannah and to Sheva the father of Macbenah and Gibea. Caleb's daughter was Acsah. 50These were the descendants of Caleb.

The sons of Hur the firstborn of Ephrathah:

Shobal the father of Kiriath Jearim, 51Salma the father of Bethlehem, and Hareph the father of Beth Gader.

52The descendants of Shobal the father of Kiriath Jearim were:

Haroeh, half the Manahathites, 53and the clans of Kiriath Jearim: the Ithrites, Puthites, Shumathites and Mishraites. From these descended the Zorathites and Eshtaolites.

54The descendants of Salma:

Bethlehem, the Netophathites, Atroth Beth Joab, half the Manahathites, the Zorites, 55and the clans of scribes[c] who lived at Jabez: the Tirathites, Shimeathites and Sucathites. These are the Kenites who came from Hammath, the father of the house of Recab.[d]

The Sons of David

3 THESE WERE the sons of David born to him in Hebron:

The firstborn was Amnon the son of Ahinoam of Jezreel;

the second, Daniel the son of Abigail of Carmel;

2the third, Absalom the son of Maacah daughter of Talmai king of Geshur;

the fourth, Adonijah the son of Haggith;

3the fifth, Shephatiah the son of Abital;

and the sixth, Ithream, by his wife Eglah.

4These six were born to David in Hebron, where he reigned seven years and six months.

David reigned in Jerusalem thirty-three years, 5and these were the children born to him there:

Shammua,[e] Shobab, Nathan and Solomon. These four were by Bathsheba[f] daughter of Ammiel. 6There were also Ibhar, Elishua,[g] Eliphelet, 7Nogah, Nepheg, Japhia, 8Elishama, Eliada and Eliphelet—nine in all. 9All these were the sons of David, besides his sons by his concubines. And Tamar was their sister.

The Kings of Judah

10Solomon's son was Rehoboam,
Abijah his son,
Asa his son,
Jehoshaphat his son,
11Jehoram[h] his son,
Ahaziah his son,
Joash his son,
12Amaziah his son,
Azariah his son,
Jotham his son,

---

c 55 Or of the Sopherites   d 55 Or father of Beth Recab
e 5 Hebrew Shimea, a variant of Shammua   f 5 One Hebrew manuscript and Vulgate (see also Septuagint and 2 Samuel 11:3); most Hebrew manuscripts Bathshua   g 6 Two Hebrew manuscripts (see also 2 Samuel 5:15 and 1 Chron. 14:5); most Hebrew manuscripts Elishama   h 11 Hebrew Joram, a variant of Jehoram

King James

¹³Ahaz his son, Hezekiah his son, Manasseh his son,
¹⁴Amon his son, Josiah his son.
¹⁵And the sons of Josiah *were,* the firstborn *l*Johanan, the second *m*Jehoiakim, the third *n*Zedekiah, the fourth Shallum.
¹⁶And the sons of Jehoiakim: *o*Jeconiah his son, Zedekiah his son.
¹⁷ ¶ And the sons of Jeconiah; Assir, *p*Salathiel his son,
¹⁸Malchiram also, and Pedaiah, and Shenazar, Jecamiah, Hoshama, and Nedabiah.
¹⁹And the sons of Pedaiah *were,* Zerubbabel, and Shimei: and the sons of Zerubbabel; Meshullam, and Hananiah, and Shelomith their sister:
²⁰And Hashubah, and Ohel, and Berechiah, and Hasadiah, Jushab-hesed, five.
²¹And the sons of Hananiah; Pelatiah, and Jesaiah: the sons of Rephaiah, the sons of Arnan, the sons of Obadiah, the sons of Shechaniah.
²²And the sons of Shechaniah; Shemaiah: and the sons of Shemaiah; Hattush, and Igeal, and Bariah, and Neariah, and Shaphat, six.
²³And the sons of Neariah; Elioenai, and *q*Hezekiah, and Azrikam, three.
²⁴And the sons of Elioenai *were,* Hodaiah, and Eliashib, and Pelaiah, and Akkub, and Johanan, and Dalaiah, and Anani, seven.

Amplified

¹³Ahaz his son, Hezekiah his son, Manasseh his son,
¹⁴Amon his son, Josiah his son.
¹⁵The descendants of Josiah: firstborn, Johanan; second, Jehoiakim; third, Zedekiah; fourth, Shallum.
¹⁶The descendants of Jehoiakim: Jehoiachin (Jeconiah) his son, Zedekiah his son.
¹⁷The descendants of Jehoiachin the captive: Shealtiel his son,
¹⁸Malchiram, Pedaiah, Shenazzar, Jekamiah, Hoshama, and Nedabiah.
¹⁹The sons of Pedaiah: Zerubbabel and Shimei. The sons of Zerubbabel: Meshullam, Hananiah. And Shelomith was their sister;
²⁰And Hashubah, Ohel, Berechiah, Hasadiah, [and] Jushab-hesed—five [the sons of Meshullam?].
²¹The sons of Hananiah: Pelatiah and Jeshaiah, whose son was Rephaiah, his son Arnan, his son Obadiah, his son Shecaniah.
²²The son of Shecaniah: Shemaiah. The sons of Shemaiah: Hattush, Igal, Bariah, Neariah, and Shaphat—six in all.
²³The sons of Neariah: Elioenai, Hizkiah, and Azrikam—three in all.
²⁴The sons of Elioenai: Hodaviah, Eliashib, Pelaiah, Akkub, Johanan, Delaiah, and Anani—seven in all.

The family of Judah

4 THE SONS of Judah; Pharez, Hezron, and *r*Carmi, and Hur, and Shobal.
²And *s*Reaiah the son of Shobal begat Jahath; and Jahath begat Ahumai, and Lahad. These *are* the families of the Zorathites.
³And these *were of* the father of Etam; Jezreel, and Ishma, and Idbash: and the name of their sister *was* Hazelelponi:
⁴And Penuel the father of Gedor, and Ezer the father of Hushah. These *are* the sons of Hur, the firstborn of Ephratah, the father of Bethlehem.
⁵ ¶ And Ashur the father of Tekoa had two wives, Helah and Naarah.
⁶And Naarah bare him Ahuzam, and Hepher, and Temeni, and Haahashtari. These *were* the sons of Naarah.
⁷And the sons of Helah *were,* Zereth, and Jezoar, and Ethnan.
⁸And Coz begat Anub, and Zobebah, and the families of Aharhel the son of Harum.
⁹ ¶ And Jabez was more honourable than his brethren: and his mother called his name *t*Jabez, saying, Because I bare him with sorrow.
¹⁰And Jabez called on the God of Israel, saying, *u*Oh that thou wouldest bless me indeed, and enlarge my coast, and that thine hand might be with me, and that thou wouldest *v*keep *me* from evil, that it may not grieve me! And God granted him that which he requested.

4 THE SONS of Judah: Perez, Hezron, Carmi, Hur, and Shobal.
²Reaiah son of Shobal was the father of Jahath, and Jahath of Ahumai and Lahad. These were the families of the Zorathites.
³These were the sons of [Hur] the father of Etam: Jezreel, Ishma, and Idbash. And their sister was Hazzelelponi.
⁴And Penuel was the father of Gedor, and Ezer the father of Hushah. These were the sons of Hur, the eldest of Ephrathah (Ephrath), the father of Bethlehem.
⁵Ashur the father of Tekoa had two wives, Helah and Naarah.
⁶Naarah bore him Ahuzzam, Hepher, Temeni, and Haahashtari. These were Naarah's sons.
⁷The sons of Helah: Zereth, Izhar, and Ethnan.
⁸Koz was the father of Anub, Zobebah, and the families of Aharhel son of Harum.
⁹Jabez was honorable above his brothers; but his mother named him Jabez [sorrow maker], saying, Because I bore him in pain.
¹⁰Jabez cried to the God of Israel, saying, Oh, that You would bless me and enlarge my border, and that Your hand might be with me, and You would keep me from evil so it might not hurt me! And God granted his request.

---

^lCalled *Jehoahaz* in 2 Ki. 23:30   ^mCalled *Eliakim* in 2 Ki. 23:34
ⁿCalled *Mattaniah* in 2 Ki. 24:17   ^oCalled *Jehoiachin* in 2 Ki.
24:6; *Coniah* in Jer. 22:24   ^pHeb. *Shealtiel*   ^qHeb. *Hiskijahu*
^rCalled *Chelubai* in ch. 2:9; *Caleb* in ch. 2:18   ^sOr, *Haroeh;*
see ch. 2:52   ^ti.e. *sorrowful*   ^uHeb. *If thou wilt*   ^vHeb.
do me

New American Standard

13 Ahaz his son, Hezekiah his son, Manasseh his son,
14 Amon his son, Josiah his son.
15 The sons of Josiah were Johanan the firstborn, and the second was Jehoiakim, the third Zedekiah, the fourth Shallum.
16 The sons of Jehoiakim were Jeconiah his son, Zedekiah his son.
17 The sons of Jeconiah, the prisoner, were Shealtiel his son,
18 and Malchiram, Pedaiah, Shenazzar, Jekamiah, Hoshama and Nedabiah.
19 The sons of Pedaiah were Zerubbabel and Shimei. And the sons of Zerubbabel were Meshullam and Hananiah, and Shelomith was their sister;
20 and Hashubah, Ohel, Berechiah, Hasadiah and Jushab-hesed, five.
21 The sons of Hananiah were Pelatiah and Jeshaiah, the sons of Rephaiah, the sons of Arnan, the sons of Obadiah, the sons of Shecaniah.
22 The ᵃdescendants of Shecaniah were Shemaiah, and the sons of Shemaiah: Hattush, Igal, Bariah, Neariah and Shaphat, six.
23 The sons of Neariah were Elioenai, Hizkiah and Azrikam, three.
24 The sons of Elioenai were Hodaviah, Eliashib, Pelaiah, Akkub, Johanan, Delaiah and Anani, seven.

Line of Hur, Asher

4 THE SONS of Judah were Perez, Hezron, Carmi, Hur and Shobal.
2 Reaiah the son of Shobal became the father of Jahath, and Jahath became the father of Ahumai and Lahad. These were the families of the Zorathites.
3 These were the sons of Etam: Jezreel, Ishma and Idbash; and the name of their sister was Hazzelelponi.
4 Penuel was the father of Gedor, and Ezer the father of Hushah. These were the sons of Hur, the firstborn of Ephrathah, the father of Bethlehem.
5 Ashhur, the father of Tekoa, had two wives, Helah and Naarah.
6 Naarah bore him Ahuzzam, Hepher, Temeni and Haahashtari. These were the sons of Naarah.
7 The sons of Helah were Zereth, Izhar and Ethnan.
8 Koz became the father of Anub and Zobebah, and the families of Aharhel the son of Harum.
9 Jabez was more honorable than his brothers, and his mother named him Jabez saying, "Because I bore him with pain."
10 Now Jabez called on the God of Israel, saying, "Oh that You would bless me indeed and enlarge my border, and that Your hand might be with me, and that You would keep me from harm that it may not pain me!" And God granted him what he requested.

New International

13Ahaz his son,
　Hezekiah his son,
　Manasseh his son,
14Amon his son,
　Josiah his son.
15The sons of Josiah:
　Johanan the firstborn,
　Jehoiakim the second son,
　Zedekiah the third,
　Shallum the fourth.
16The successors of Jehoiakim:
　Jehoiachinⁱ his son,
　and Zedekiah.

The Royal Line After the Exile

17The descendants of Jehoiachin the captive:
　Shealtiel his son, 18Malkiram, Pedaiah, Shenazzar, Jekamiah, Hoshama and Nedabiah.
19The sons of Pedaiah:
　Zerubbabel and Shimei.
　The sons of Zerubbabel:
　Meshullam and Hananiah.
　Shelomith was their sister.
20There were also five others:
　Hashubah, Ohel, Berekiah, Hasadiah and Jushab-Hesed.
21The descendants of Hananiah:
　Pelatiah and Jeshaiah, and the sons of Rephaiah, of Arnan, of Obadiah and of Shecaniah.
22The descendants of Shecaniah:
　Shemaiah and his sons:
　Hattush, Igal, Bariah, Neariah and Shaphat—six in all.
23The sons of Neariah:
　Elioenai, Hizkiah and Azrikam—three in all.
24The sons of Elioenai:
　Hodaviah, Eliashib, Pelaiah, Akkub, Johanan, Delaiah and Anani—seven in all.

Other Clans of Judah

4 THE DESCENDANTS of Judah:
　Perez, Hezron, Carmi, Hur and Shobal.
2Reaiah son of Shobal was the father of Jahath, and Jahath the father of Ahumai and Lahad. These were the clans of the Zorathites.
3These were the sonsʲ of Etam:
　Jezreel, Ishma and Idbash. Their sister was named Hazzelelponi. 4Penuel was the father of Gedor, and Ezer the father of Hushah.
These were the descendants of Hur, the firstborn of Ephrathah and fatherᵏ of Bethlehem.
5Ashhur the father of Tekoa had two wives, Helah and Naarah.
6Naarah bore him Ahuzzam, Hepher, Temeni and Haahashtari. These were the descendants of Naarah.
7The sons of Helah:
　Zereth, Zohar, Ethnan, 8and Koz, who was the father of Anub and Hazzobebah and of the clans of Aharhel son of Harum.

9Jabez was more honorable than his brothers. His mother had named him Jabez,ˡ saying, "I gave birth to him in pain." 10Jabez cried out to the God of Israel, "Oh, that you would bless me and enlarge my territory! Let your hand be with me, and keep me from harm so that I will be free from pain." And God granted his request.

ⁱ16 Hebrew *Jeconiah*, a variant of *Jehoiachin*; also in verse 17
ʲ3 Some Septuagint manuscripts (see also Vulgate); Hebrew *father*
ᵏ4 *Father* may mean *civic leader* or *military leader*; also in verses 12, 14, 17, 18 and possibly elsewhere.　ˡ9 *Jabez* sounds like the Hebrew for *pain*.

ᵃLit *sons*

King James

Amplified

¹¹ ¶ And Chelub the brother of Shuah begat Mehir, which *was* the father of Eshton.

¹²And Eshton begat Beth-rapha, and Paseah, and Tehinnah the father of ʷIr-nahash. These *are* the men of Rechah.

¹³And the sons of Kenaz; Othniel, and Seraiah: and the sons of Othniel; ˣHathath.

¹⁴And Meonothai begat Ophrah: and Seraiah begat Joab, the father of the ʸvalley of ᶻCharashim; for they were craftsmen.

¹⁵And the sons of Caleb the son of Jephunneh; Iru, Elah, and Naam: and the sons of Elah, ᵃeven Kenaz.

¹⁶And the sons of Jehaleleel; Ziph, and Ziphah, Tiria, and Asareel.

¹⁷And the sons of Ezra *were*, Jether, and Mered, and Epher, and Jalon: and she bare Miriam, and Shammai, and Ishbah the father of Eshtemoa.

¹⁸And his wife ᵇJehudijah bare Jered the father of Gedor, and Heber the father of Socho, and Jekuthiel the father of Zanoah. And these *are* the sons of Bithiah the daughter of Pharaoh, which Mered took.

¹⁹And the sons of *his* wife ᶜHodiah the sister of Naham, the father of Keilah the Garmite, and Eshtemoa the Maachathite.

²⁰And the sons of Shimon *were*, Amnon, and Rinnah, Ben-hanan, and Tilon. And the sons of Ishi *were*, Zoheth, and Ben-zoheth.

²¹ ¶ The sons of Shelah the son of Judah *were*, Er the father of Lecah, and Laadah the father of Mareshah, and the families of the house of them that wrought fine linen, of the house of Ashbea.

²²And Jokim, and the men of Chozeba, and Joash, and Saraph, who had the dominion in Moab, and Jashubilehem. And *these are* ancient things.

²³These *were* the potters, and those that dwelt among plants and hedges: there they dwelt with the king for his work.

The family of Simeon

²⁴ ¶ The sons of Simeon *were*, ᵈNemuel, and Jamin, ᵉJarib, Zerah, *and* Shaul:

²⁵Shallum his son, Mibsam his son, Mishma his son.

²⁶And the sons of Mishma; Hamuel his son, Zacchur his son, Shimei his son.

²⁷And Shimei had sixteen sons and six daughters; but his brethren had not many children, neither did all their family multiply, ᶠlike to the children of Judah.

²⁸And they dwelt at Beer-sheba, and Moladah, and Hazar-shual,

²⁹And at ᵍBilhah, and at Ezem, and at ʰTolad,

³⁰And at Bethuel, and at Hormah, and at Ziklag,

³¹And at Beth-marcaboth, and ⁱHazar-susim, and at Beth-birei, and at Shaaraim. These *were* their cities unto the reign of David.

³²And their villages *were*, ʲEtam, and Ain, Rimmon, and Tochen, and Ashan, five cities:

³³And all their villages that *were* round about the same cities, unto ᵏBaal. These *were* their habitations, and ˡtheir genealogy.

³⁴And Meshobab, and Jamlech, and Joshah the son of Amaziah,

³⁵And Joel, and Jehu the son of Josibiah, the son of Seraiah, the son of Asiel,

³⁶And Elioenai, and Jaakobah, and Jeshohaiah, and Asaiah, and Adiel, and Jesimiel, and Benaiah,

³⁷And Ziza the son of Shiphi, the son of Allon, the son of Jedaiah, the son of Shimri, the son of Shemaiah;

¹¹Chelub the brother of Shuhah was the father of Mehir, the father of Eshton.

¹²Eshton was the father of Beth-rapha, Paseah, and Tehinnah the father of Ir-nahash. These are the men of Recah.

¹³The sons of Kenaz: Othniel and Seraiah. The sons of Othniel: Hathath [and Meonothai].

¹⁴Meonothai was father of Ophrah, and Seraiah of Joab the father of Ge-harashim [the Valley of Craftsmen], so named because they were craftsmen.

¹⁵The sons of Caleb [Joshua's companion] son of Jephunneh: Iru, Elah, and Naam. The son of Elah: Kenaz.

¹⁶The sons of Jehallel: Ziph, Ziphah, Tiria, and Asarel.

¹⁷The sons of Ezrah: Jether, Mered, Epher, and Jalon. ᵃThese are the sons of Bithiah daughter of Pharaoh, whom Mered married: she bore Miriam, Shammai, and Ishbah the father of Eshtemoa.

¹⁸And Mered's Jewish wife bore Jered the father of Gedor, Heber the father of Soco, and Jekuthiel the father of Zanoah.

¹⁹The sons of the wife of Hodiah, the sister of Naham, were: the father of Keilah the Garmite, and Eshtemoa the Maacathite.

²⁰The sons of Shimon: Amnon, Rinnah, Ben-hanan, and Tilon. The sons of Ishi: Zoheth and Ben-zoheth.

²¹The sons of Shelah son of Judah: Er the father of Lecah, and Laadah the father of Mareshah, and the families of the house of the linen workers at Beth-ashbea,

²²And Jokim, the men of Cozeba, Joash, and Saraph, who ruled in Moab, and returned to [Bethlehem]. These are ancient matters.

²³These were the potters and those who dwelt among plantations and hedges at Netaim and Gederah; there they dwelt with the king for his work.

²⁴The sons of Simeon: Nemuel, Jamin, Jarib, Zerah, and Shaul;

²⁵Shallum was his [Shaul's] son, Mibsam his son, Mishma his son.

²⁶The sons of Mishma: Hammuel his son, Zaccur his son, Shimei his son.

²⁷Shimei had sixteen sons and six daughters, but his brothers did not have many children; neither did all their family multiply like the children of Judah.

²⁸They dwelt at Beersheba, Moladah, Hazar-shual,

²⁹Bilhah, Ezem, Tolad,

³⁰Bethuel, Hormah, Ziklag,

³¹Beth-marcaboth, Hazar-susim, Beth-biri, and at Shaaraim. These were their towns [and villages] until the reign of David.

³²There were also Etam, Ain, Rimmon, Tochen, and Ashan—five towns—

³³And all their villages that were round about these towns, as far as Baal[-ath-beer]. These were their settlements, and they had their genealogical record.

³⁴Meshobab, Jamlech, Joshah son of Amaziah,

³⁵Joel, Jehu son of Joshibiah, the son of Seraiah, the son of Asiel,

³⁶Also Elioenai, Jaakobah, Jeshohaiah, Asaiah, Adiel, Jesimiel, Benaiah,

³⁷Ziza son of Shiphi, the son of Allon, the son of Jedaiah, the son of Shimri, the son of Shemaiah.

ʷOr, *the city of Nahash*   ˣOr, *Hathath* and *Meonothai, who begat*   ʸOr, inhabitants *of the valley*   ᶻi.e. *Craftsmen*   ᵃOr, *Uknaz*   ᵇOr, *the Jewess*   ᶜOr, *Jehudijah,* mentioned before   ᵈOr, *Jemuel;* see Gen. 46:10; Ex. 6:15; Num. 26:12   ᵉOr, *Jachin, Zohar,*   ᶠHeb. *unto*   ᵍOr, *Balah;* see Josh. 19:3   ʰOr, *Eltolad;* see Josh. 19:4   ⁱOr, *Hazar-susah;* see Josh. 19:5   ʲOr, *Ether;* see Josh. 19:7   ᵏOr, *Baalath-beer;* see Josh. 19:8   ˡOr, *as they divided themselves by nations among them*

ᵃThis clause, "These are the sons of Bithiah daughter of Pharaoh, whom Mered married," has been transposed from I Chron. 4:18 to I Chron. 4:17.

New American Standard

11 ¶ Chelub the brother of Shuhah became the father of Mehir, who was the father of Eshton.
12 Eshton became the father of Beth-rapha and Paseah, and Tehinnah the father of Ir-nahash. These are the men of Recah.
13 ¶ Now the sons of Kenaz *were* Othniel and Seraiah. And the sons of Othniel *were* Hathath and Meonothai.
14 Meonothai became the father of Ophrah, and Seraiah became the father of Joab the father of Ge-harashim, for they were craftsmen.
15 The sons of Caleb the son of Jephunneh *were* Iru, Elah and Naam; and the son of Elah *was* Kenaz.
16 The sons of Jehallelel *were* Ziph and Ziphah, Tiria and Asarel.
17 The sons of Ezrah *were* Jether, Mered, Epher and Jalon. (And these are the sons of Bithia the daughter of Pharaoh, whom Mered took) and she conceived *and bore* Miriam, Shammai and Ishbah the father of Eshtemoa.
18 His Jewish wife bore Jered the father of Gedor, and Heber the father of Soco, and Jekuthiel the father of Zanoah.
19 The sons of the wife of Hodiah, the sister of Naham, *were* the fathers of Keilah the Garmite and Eshtemoa the Maacathite.
20 The sons of Shimon *were* Amnon and Rinnah, Ben-hanan and Tilon. And the sons of Ishi *were* Zoheth and Ben-zoheth.
21 The sons of Shelah the son of Judah *were* Er the father of Lecah and Laadah the father of Mareshah, and the families of the house of the linen workers at Beth-ashbea;
22 and Jokim, the men of Cozeba, Joash, Saraph, who ruled in Moab, and Jashubi-lehem. And the records are ancient.
23 These were the potters and the inhabitants of Netaim and Gederah; they lived there with the king for his work.

Descendants of Simeon

24 ¶ The sons of Simeon *were* Nemuel and Jamin, Jarib, Zerah, Shaul;
25 Shallum his son, Mibsam his son, Mishma his son.
26 The sons of Mishma *were* Hammuel his son, Zaccur his son, Shimei his son.
27 Now Shimei had sixteen sons and six daughters; but his brothers did not have many sons, nor did all their family multiply like the sons of Judah.
28 They lived at Beersheba, Moladah and Hazar-shual,
29 at Bilhah, Ezem, Tolad,
30 Bethuel, Hormah, Ziklag,
31 Beth-marcaboth, Hazar-susim, Beth-biri and Shaaraim. These *were* their cities until the reign of David.
32 Their villages *were* Etam, Ain, Rimmon, Tochen and Ashan, five cities;
33 and all their villages that *were* around the same cities as far as Baal. These *were* their settlements, and they have their genealogy.
34 ¶ Meshobab and Jamlech and Joshah the son of Amaziah,
35 and Joel and Jehu the son of Joshibiah, the son of Seraiah, the son of Asiel,
36 and Elioenai, Jaakobah, Jeshohaiah, Asaiah, Adiel, Jesimiel, Benaiah,
37 Ziza the son of Shiphi, the son of Allon, the son of Jedaiah, the son of Shimri, the son of Shemaiah;

New International

11 Kelub, Shuhah's brother, was the father of Mehir, who was the father of Eshton. 12 Eshton was the father of Beth Rapha, Paseah and Tehinnah the father of Ir Nahash.^m These were the men of Recah.

13 The sons of Kenaz:
Othniel and Seraiah.
The sons of Othniel:
Hathath and Meonothai.^n 14 Meonothai was the father of Ophrah.
Seraiah was the father of Joab,
the father of Ge Harashim.^o It was called this because its people were craftsmen.
15 The sons of Caleb son of Jephunneh:
Iru, Elah and Naam.
The son of Elah:
Kenaz.
16 The sons of Jehallelel:
Ziph, Ziphah, Tiria and Asarel.
17 The sons of Ezrah:
Jether, Mered, Epher and Jalon. One of Mered's wives gave birth to Miriam, Shammai and Ishbah the father of Eshtemoa. 18 (His Judean wife gave birth to Jered the father of Gedor, Heber the father of Soco, and Jekuthiel the father of Zanoah.) These were the children of Pharaoh's daughter Bithiah, whom Mered had married.
19 The sons of Hodiah's wife, the sister of Naham:
the father of Keilah the Garmite, and Eshtemoa the Maacathite.
20 The sons of Shimon:
Amnon, Rinnah, Ben-Hanan and Tilon.
The descendants of Ishi:
Zoheth and Ben-Zoheth.
21 The sons of Shelah son of Judah:
Er the father of Lecah, Laadah the father of Mareshah and the clans of the linen workers at Beth Ashbea, 22 Jokim, the men of Cozeba, and Joash and Saraph, who ruled in Moab and Jashubi Lehem. (These records are from ancient times.) 23 They were the potters who lived at Netaim and Gederah; they stayed there and worked for the king.

Simeon

24 The descendants of Simeon:
Nemuel, Jamin, Jarib, Zerah and Shaul;
25 Shallum was Shaul's son, Mibsam his son and Mishma his son.
26 The descendants of Mishma:
Hammuel his son, Zaccur his son and Shimei his son.
27 Shimei had sixteen sons and six daughters, but his brothers did not have many children; so their entire clan did not become as numerous as the people of Judah. 28 They lived in Beersheba, Moladah, Hazar Shual, 29 Bilhah, Ezem, Tolad, 30 Bethuel, Hormah, Ziklag, 31 Beth Marcaboth, Hazar Susim, Beth Biri and Shaaraim. These were their towns until the reign of David. 32 Their surrounding villages were Etam, Ain, Rimmon, Token and Ashan—five towns— 33 and all the villages around these towns as far as Baalath.^p These were their settlements. And they kept a genealogical record.

34 Meshobab, Jamlech, Joshah son of Amaziah, 35 Joel, Jehu son of Joshibiah, the son of Seraiah, the son of Asiel, 36 also Elioenai, Jaakobah, Jeshohaiah, Asaiah, Adiel, Jesimiel, Benaiah, 37 and Ziza son of Shiphi, the son of Allon, the son of Jedaiah, the son of Shimri, the son of Shemaiah.

---

^m 12 Or *of the city of Nahash*　　^n 13 Some Septuagint manuscripts and Vulgate; Hebrew does not have *and Meonothai.*
^o 14 *Ge Harashim* means *valley of craftsmen.*　　^p 33 Some Septuagint manuscripts (see also Joshua 19:8); Hebrew *Baal*

King James

[38]These *m*mentioned by *their* names *were* princes in their families: and the house of their fathers increased greatly.

[39] ¶ And they went to the entrance of Gedor, *even* unto the east side of the valley, to seek pasture for their flocks.

[40]And they found fat pasture and good, and the land *was* wide, and quiet, and peaceable; for *they* of Ham had dwelt there of old.

[41]And these written by name came in the days of Hezekiah king of Judah, and smote their tents, and the habitations that were found there, and destroyed them utterly unto this day, and dwelt in their rooms: because *there was* pasture there for their flocks.

[42]And *some* of them, *even* of the sons of Simeon, five hundred men, went to mount Seir, having for their captains Pelatiah, and Neariah, and Rephaiah, and Uzziel, the sons of Ishi.

[43]And they smote the rest of the Amalekites that were escaped, and dwelt there unto this day.

The family of Reuben

5 NOW THE sons of Reuben the firstborn of Israel, (for he *was* the firstborn; but, forasmuch as he defiled his father's bed, his birthright was given unto the sons of Joseph the son of Israel: and the genealogy is not to be reckoned after the birthright.

[2]For Judah prevailed above his brethren, and of him came the chief *n*ruler; but the birthright *was* Joseph's:)

[3]The sons, *I say,* of Reuben the firstborn of Israel *were,* Hanoch, and Pallu, Hezron, and Carmi.

[4]The sons of Joel; Shemaiah his son, Gog his son, Shimei his son,

[5]Micah his son, Reaia his son, Baal his son,

[6]Beerah his son, whom *o*Tilgath-pilneser king of Assyria carried away *captive:* he *was* prince of the Reubenites.

[7]And his brethren by their families, when the genealogy of their generations was reckoned, *were* the chief, Jeiel, and Zechariah,

[8]And Bela the son of Azaz, the son of *p*Shema, the son of Joel, who dwelt in Aroer, even unto Nebo and Baal-meon:

[9]And eastward he inhabited unto the entering in of the wilderness from the river Euphrates: because their cattle were multiplied in the land of Gilead.

[10]And in the days of Saul they made war with the Hagarites, who fell by their hand: and they dwelt in their tents *q*throughout all the east *land* of Gilead.

The family of Gad

[11] ¶ And the children of Gad dwelt over against them, in the land of Bashan unto Salcah:

[12]Joel the chief, and Shapham the next, and Jaanai, and Shaphat in Bashan.

[13]And their brethren of the house of their fathers *were,* Michael, and Meshullam, and Sheba, and Jorai, and Jachan, and Zia, and Heber, seven.

[14]These *are* the children of Abihail the son of Huri, the son of Jaroah, the son of Gilead, the son of Michael, the son of Jeshishai, the son of Jahdo, the son of Buz;

[15]Ahi the son of Abdiel, the son of Guni, chief of the house of their fathers.

[16]And they dwelt in Gilead in Bashan, and in her towns, and in all the suburbs of Sharon, upon *r*their borders.

Amplified

[38]These mentioned by name were princes in their families; and their fathers' houses increased greatly [so they needed more room].

[39]And they journeyed to the entrance of Gedor to the east side of the valley to seek pasture for their flocks.

[40]And they found rich, good pasture, and the [cleared] land was wide, quiet, and peaceful, because people of Ham had dwelt there of old [and had left it a better place for those who came after them].

[41]And these registered by name came in the days of Hezekiah king of Judah and destroyed their tents and the Meunim [foreigners] who were found there and exterminated them to this day, and they settled in their stead, because there was pasture for their flocks.

[42]And some of them from the sons of Simeon, 500 men, went to Mount Seir, having for their leaders Pelatiah, and Neariah, Rephaiah, and Uzziel, the sons of Ishi.

[43]They destroyed the remnant of the Amalekites who had escaped, and they have dwelt there to this day.

5 NOW [WE come to] the sons of Reuben the firstborn of Israel. For [Reuben] was the eldest, but because he polluted his father's couch [with Bilhah his father's concubine] his birthright was given to the sons of Joseph [favorite] son of Israel; so the genealogy is not to be reckoned according to the birthright. [Gen. 35:22; 48:15–22; 49:3, 4.]

[2]Judah prevailed above his brethren, and from him came the prince *and* leader [and eventually the Messiah]; yet the birthright was Joseph's. [Gen. 49:10; Mic. 5:2.]

[3]The sons of Reuben the firstborn of Israel: Hanoch, Pallu, Hezron, and Carmi.

[4]The sons of Joel: Shemaiah his son, Gog his son, Shimei his son,

[5]Micah his son, Reaiah his son, Baal his son,

[6]Beerah his son, whom Tilgath-pilneser king of Assyria carried away captive; he was a prince of the Reubenites.

[7]And his brethren by their families, when the genealogy of their generations was reckoned: the chief Jeiel, and Zechariah,

[8]Bela son of Azaz, the son of Shema, the son of Joel, who dwelt in Aroer as far as Nebo and Baal-meon.

[9]Eastward [Bela] inhabited the land as far as the entrance into the desert this [west] side of the river Euphrates, because their cattle had multiplied in the land of Gilead.

[10]In the days of [King] Saul they made war with the Hagrites *or* Ishmaelites, who fell by their hands; they dwelt in their tents in all the land east of Gilead.

[11]The children of Gad who dwelt opposite them in the land of Bashan, as far as Salecah:

[12]Joel the chief, Shapham the next, Janai, and Shaphat in Bashan.

[13]Their kinsmen of the houses of their fathers: Michael, Meshullam, Sheba, Jorai, Jacan, Zia, and Eber—seven in all.

[14]These were the sons of Abihail son of Huri, the son of Jaroah, the son of Gilead, the son of Michael, the son of Jeshishai, the son of Jahdo, the son of Buz.

[15]Ahi son of Abdiel, the son of Guni, was chief in their fathers' houses.

[16]They dwelt in Gilead, in Bashan and in its towns, and in all the suburbs *and* pasturelands of Sharon to their limits.

---

m Heb. *coming*   *n* Or, *prince*   *o* Or, *Tilgath-pileser;* see 2 Ki.
15:29 & 16:7   *p* Or, *Shemaiah;* see ver. 4   *q* Heb. *upon all*
the face of the east   *r* Heb. *their goings forth*

New American Standard

38 these mentioned by name *were* leaders in their families; and their fathers' houses increased greatly.

39 They went to the entrance of Gedor, even to the east side of the valley, to seek pasture for their flocks.

40 They found rich and good pasture, and the land was broad and quiet and peaceful; for those who lived there formerly *were* Hamites.

41 These, recorded by name, came in the days of Hezekiah king of Judah, and attacked their tents and the Meunites who were found there, and destroyed them utterly to this day, and lived in their place, because there was pasture there for their flocks.

42 From them, from the sons of Simeon, five hundred men went to Mount Seir, with Pelatiah, Neariah, Rephaiah and Uzziel, the sons of Ishi, as their leaders.

43 They destroyed the remnant of the Amalekites who escaped, and have lived there to this day.

Genealogy from Reuben

5 NOW THE sons of Reuben the firstborn of Israel (for he was the firstborn, but because he defiled his father's bed, his birthright was given to the sons of Joseph the son of Israel; so that he is not enrolled in the genealogy according to the birthright).

2 Though Judah prevailed over his brothers, and from him *came* the leader, yet the birthright belonged to Joseph),

3 the sons of Reuben the firstborn of Israel *were* Hanoch and Pallu, Hezron and Carmi.

4 The sons of Joel *were* Shemaiah his son, Gog his son, Shimei his son,

5 Micah his son, Reaiah his son, Baal his son,

6 Beerah his son, whom Tilgath-pilneser king of Assyria carried away into exile; he was leader of the Reubenites.

7 His kinsmen by their families, in the genealogy of their generations, *were* Jeiel the chief, then Zechariah

8 and Bela the son of Azaz, the son of Shema, the son of Joel, who lived in Aroer, even to Nebo and Baal-meon.

9 To the east he settled as far as the entrance of the wilderness from the river Euphrates, because their cattle had increased in the land of Gilead.

10 In the days of Saul they made war with the Hagrites, who fell by their hand, so that they occupied their tents throughout all the land east of Gilead.

11 ¶ Now the sons of Gad lived opposite them in the land of Bashan as far as Salecah.

12 Joel *was* the chief and Shapham the second, then Janai and Shaphat in Bashan.

13 Their kinsmen of their fathers' households *were* Michael, Meshullam, Sheba, Jorai, Jacan, Zia and Eber, seven.

14 These *were* the sons of Abihail, the son of Huri, the son of Jaroah, the son of Gilead, the son of Michael, the son of Jeshishai, the son of Jahdo, the son of Buz;

15 Ahi the son of Abdiel, the son of Guni, *was* head of their fathers' households.

16 They lived in Gilead, in Bashan and in its towns, and in all the pasture lands of Sharon, as far as their borders.

New International

38The men listed above by name were leaders of their clans. Their families increased greatly, 39and they went to the outskirts of Gedor to the east of the valley in search of pasture for their flocks. 40They found rich, good pasture, and the land was spacious, peaceful and quiet. Some Hamites had lived there formerly.

41The men whose names were listed came in the days of Hezekiah king of Judah. They attacked the Hamites in their dwellings and also the Meunites who were there and completely destroyed[q] them, as is evident to this day. Then they settled in their place, because there was pasture for their flocks. 42And five hundred of these Simeonites, led by Pelatiah, Neariah, Rephaiah and Uzziel, the sons of Ishi, invaded the hill country of Seir. 43They killed the remaining Amalekites who had escaped, and they have lived there to this day.

Reuben

5 THE SONS of Reuben the firstborn of Israel (he was the firstborn, but when he defiled his father's marriage bed, his rights as firstborn were given to the sons of Joseph son of Israel; so he could not be listed in the genealogical record in accordance with his birthright, 2and though Judah was the strongest of his brothers and a ruler came from him, the rights of the firstborn belonged to Joseph)— 3the sons of Reuben the firstborn of Israel:

Hanoch, Pallu, Hezron and Carmi.

4The descendants of Joel:
Shemaiah his son, Gog his son,
Shimei his son, 5Micah his son,
Reaiah his son, Baal his son,
6and Beerah his son, whom Tiglath-Pileser[r] king of Assyria took into exile. Beerah was a leader of the Reubenites.

7Their relatives by clans, listed according to their genealogical records:
Jeiel the chief, Zechariah, 8and Bela son of Azaz, the son of Shema, the son of Joel. They settled in the area from Aroer to Nebo and Baal Meon. 9To the east they occupied the land up to the edge of the desert that extends to the Euphrates River, because their livestock had increased in Gilead.

10During Saul's reign they waged war against the Hagrites, who were defeated at their hands; they occupied the dwellings of the Hagrites throughout the entire region east of Gilead.

Gad

11The Gadites lived next to them in Bashan, as far as Salecah:
12Joel was the chief, Shapham the second, then Janai and Shaphat, in Bashan.
13Their relatives, by families, were:
Michael, Meshullam, Sheba, Jorai, Jacan, Zia and Eber—seven in all.
14These were the sons of Abihail son of Huri, the son of Jaroah, the son of Gilead, the son of Michael, the son of Jeshishai, the son of Jahdo, the son of Buz.
15Ahi son of Abdiel, the son of Guni, was head of their family.
16The Gadites lived in Gilead, in Bashan and its outlying villages, and on all the pasturelands of Sharon as far as they extended.

---

q41 The Hebrew term refers to the irrevocable giving over of things or persons to the LORD, often by totally destroying them.
r6 Hebrew *Tilgath-Pilneser*, a variant of *Tiglath-Pileser*; also in verse 26

King James

¹⁷All these were reckoned by genealogies in the days of Jotham king of Judah, and in the days of Jeroboam king of Israel.

¹⁸ ¶ The sons of Reuben, and the Gadites, and half the tribe of Manasseh, ^sof valiant men, men able to bear buckler and sword, and to shoot with bow, and skilful in war, *were* four and forty thousand seven hundred and threescore, that went out to the war.

¹⁹And they made war with the Hagarites, with Jetur, and Nephish, and Nodab.

²⁰And they were helped against them, and the Hagarites were delivered into their hand, and all that *were* with them: for they cried to God in the battle, and he was entreated of them; because they put their trust in him.

²¹And they ^ttook away their cattle; of their camels fifty thousand, and of sheep two hundred and fifty thousand, and of asses two thousand, and of ^umen an hundred thousand.

²²For there fell down many slain, because the war *was* of God. And they dwelt in their steads until the captivity.

The half tribe of Manasseh

²³ ¶ And the children of the half tribe of Manasseh dwelt in the land: they increased from Bashan unto Baal-hermon and Senir, and unto mount Hermon.

²⁴And these *were* the heads of the house of their fathers, even Epher, and Ishi, and Eliel, and Azriel, and Jeremiah, and Hodaviah, and Jahdiel, mighty men of valour, ^vfamous men, *and* heads of the house of their fathers.

²⁵ ¶ And they transgressed against the God of their fathers, and went a-whoring after the gods of the people of the land, whom God destroyed before them.

²⁶And the God of Israel stirred up the spirit of Pul king of Assyria, and the spirit of Tilgath-pilneser king of Assyria, and he carried them away, even the Reubenites, and the Gadites, and the half tribe of Manasseh, and brought them unto Halah, and Habor, and Hara, and to the river Gozan, unto this day.

The family of Levi

6 THE SONS of Levi; ^wGershon, Kohath, and Merari.
²And the sons of Kohath; Amram, Izhar, and Hebron, and Uzziel.

³And the children of Amram; Aaron, and Moses, and Miriam. The sons also of Aaron; Nadab, and Abihu, Eleazar, and Ithamar.

⁴ ¶ Eleazar begat Phinehas, Phinehas begat Abishua,
⁵And Abishua begat Bukki, and Bukki begat Uzzi,
⁶And Uzzi begat Zerahiah, and Zerahiah begat Meraioth,
⁷Meraioth begat Amariah, and Amariah begat Ahitub,
⁸And Ahitub begat Zadok, and Zadok begat Ahimaaz,
⁹And Ahimaaz begat Azariah, and Azariah begat Johanan,
¹⁰And Johanan begat Azariah, (he *it is* that executed the priest's office ^xin the temple that Solomon built in Jerusalem:)
¹¹And Azariah begat Amariah, and Amariah begat Ahitub,
¹²And Ahitub begat Zadok, and Zadok begat ^yShallum,
¹³And Shallum begat Hilkiah, and Hilkiah begat Azariah,
¹⁴And Azariah begat Seraiah, and Seraiah begat Jehozadak,

Amplified

¹⁷All these were enrolled by genealogies in the days of Jotham king of Judah and in the days of Jeroboam [II] king of Israel.

¹⁸The sons of Reuben, the Gadites, and the half-tribe of Manasseh—valiant men able to bear buckler and sword and to shoot with bow and skillful in war—were 44,760 able *and* ready to go forth to war.

¹⁹And [these Israelites, on the east side of the Jordan River] made war with the Hagrites [a tribe of northern Arabia], Jetur, Naphish, and Nodab.

²⁰They were given help against them, and the Hagrites *or* Ishmaelites were delivered into their hands, and all who were allied with them, for they cried to God in the battle; and He granted their entreaty, because they relied on, clung to, *and* trusted in Him.

²¹And [these Israelites] took away their adversaries' herds: of their camels 50,000, and of sheep 250,000, and of donkeys 2,000, and of the lives of men 100,000.

²²For a great number fell mortally wounded, because the battle was God's. And [these Israelites] dwelt in their territory until the captivity [by Assyria more than five centuries later]. [II Kings 15:29.]

²³And the people of the half-tribe of Manasseh dwelt in the land; their settlements spread from Bashan to Baal-hermon, Senir, and Mount Hermon.

²⁴And these were the heads of their fathers' houses: Epher, Ishi, Eliel, Azriel, Jeremiah, Hodaviah, and Jahdiel, mighty men of strength of mind *and* spirit [enabling them to encounter danger with firmness and personal bravery], famous men, and heads of the houses of their fathers.

²⁵They transgressed against the God of their fathers and played the harlot [by unfaithfulness to their own God and running] after the gods of the native peoples, whom God had destroyed before them.

²⁶So the God of Israel stirred up the spirit of Pul king of Assyria, [that is,] the spirit of Tilgath-pilneser king of Assyria, and he carried them away, the Reubenites, Gadites, and half-tribe of Manasseh and brought them to Halah, Habor, Hara, and the river Gozan, to this day.

6 THE SONS of Levi: Gershom, Kohath, and Merari.
²The sons of Kohath: Amram, Izhar, Hebron, and Uzziel.

³The children of Amram: Aaron, Moses, and Miriam. The sons also of Aaron: Nadab, Abihu, Eleazar, and Ithamar.

⁴Eleazar was the father of Phinehas, Phinehas of Abishua,
⁵Abishua was the father of Bukki, and Bukki of Uzzi,
⁶Uzzi of Zerahiah, and Zerahiah of Meraioth,
⁷Meraioth of Amariah, and Amariah of Ahitub,
⁸Ahitub of Zadok, and Zadok of Ahimaaz,
⁹Ahimaaz of Azariah, and Azariah of Johanan,
¹⁰Johanan of Azariah, who was priest in the temple Solomon built in Jerusalem,
¹¹Azariah of Amariah, and Amariah of Ahitub,
¹²Ahitub of Zadok, and Zadok of Shallum,
¹³Shallum of Hilkiah, and Hilkiah of Azariah,
¹⁴Azariah of Seraiah, and Seraiah of Jehozadak;

---

^sHeb. *sons of valour*   ^tHeb. *led captive*   ^uHeb. *souls of men*
^vHeb. *men of names*   ^wOr, *Gershom;* see ver. 16   ^xHeb. *in the house*   ^yOr, *Meshullam;* see ch. 9:11

New American Standard

17 All of these were enrolled in the genealogies in the days of Jotham king of Judah and in the days of Jeroboam king of Israel.

18 ¶ The sons of Reuben and the Gadites and the half-tribe of Manasseh, *consisting* of valiant men, men who bore shield and sword and shot with bow and *were* skillful in battle, *were* 44,760, who went to war.

19 They made war against the Hagrites, Jetur, Naphish and Nodab.

20 They were helped against them, and the Hagrites and all who *were* with them were given into their hand; for they cried out to God in the battle, and He answered their prayers because they trusted in Him.

21 They took away their cattle: their 50,000 camels, 250,000 sheep, 2,000 donkeys; and 100,000 men.

22 For many fell slain, because the war *was* of God. And they settled in their place until the exile.

23 ¶ Now the sons of the half-tribe of Manasseh lived in the land; from Bashan to Baal-hermon and Senir and Mount Hermon they were numerous.

24 These were the heads of their fathers' households, even Epher, Ishi, Eliel, Azriel, Jeremiah, Hodaviah and Jahdiel, mighty men of valor, famous men, heads of their fathers' households.

25 ¶ But they acted treacherously against the God of their fathers and played the harlot after the gods of the peoples of the land, whom God had destroyed before them.

26 So the God of Israel stirred up the spirit of Pul, king of Assyria, even the spirit of Tilgath-pilneser king of Assyria, and he carried them away into exile, namely the Reubenites, the Gadites and the half-tribe of Manasseh, and brought them to Halah, Habor, Hara and to the river of Gozan, to this day.

Genealogy: The Priestly Line

6 THE SONS of Levi *were* Gershon, Kohath and Merari.

2 The sons of Kohath *were* Amram, Izhar, Hebron and Uzziel.

3 The children of Amram *were* Aaron, Moses and Miriam. And the sons of Aaron *were* Nadab, Abihu, Eleazar and Ithamar.

4 Eleazar became the father of Phinehas, *and* Phinehas became the father of Abishua,

5 and Abishua became the father of Bukki, and Bukki became the father of Uzzi,

6 and Uzzi became the father of Zerahiah, and Zerahiah became the father of Meraioth,

7 Meraioth became the father of Amariah, and Amariah became the father of Ahitub,

8 and Ahitub became the father of Zadok, and Zadok became the father of Ahimaaz,

9 and Ahimaaz became the father of Azariah, and Azariah became the father of Johanan,

10 and Johanan became the father of Azariah (it was he who served as the priest in the house which Solomon built in Jerusalem),

11 and Azariah became the father of Amariah, and Amariah became the father of Ahitub,

12 and Ahitub became the father of Zadok, and Zadok became the father of Shallum,

13 and Shallum became the father of Hilkiah, and Hilkiah became the father of Azariah,

14 and Azariah became the father of Seraiah, and Seraiah became the father of Jehozadak;

New International

17 All these were entered in the genealogical records during the reigns of Jotham king of Judah and Jeroboam king of Israel.

18 The Reubenites, the Gadites and the half-tribe of Manasseh had 44,760 men ready for military service—able-bodied men who could handle shield and sword, who could use a bow, and who were trained for battle. 19 They waged war against the Hagrites, Jetur, Naphish and Nodab. 20 They were helped in fighting them, and God handed the Hagrites and all their allies over to them, because they cried out to him during the battle. He answered their prayers, because they trusted in him. 21 They seized the livestock of the Hagrites—fifty thousand camels, two hundred fifty thousand sheep and two thousand donkeys. They also took one hundred thousand people captive, 22 and many others fell slain, because the battle was God's. And they occupied the land until the exile.

The Half-Tribe of Manasseh

23 The people of the half-tribe of Manasseh were numerous; they settled in the land from Bashan to Baal Hermon, that is, to Senir (Mount Hermon).

24 These were the heads of their families: Epher, Ishi, Eliel, Azriel, Jeremiah, Hodaviah and Jahdiel. They were brave warriors, famous men, and heads of their families. 25 But they were unfaithful to the God of their fathers and prostituted themselves to the gods of the peoples of the land, whom God had destroyed before them. 26 So the God of Israel stirred up the spirit of Pul king of Assyria (that is, Tiglath-Pileser king of Assyria), who took the Reubenites, the Gadites and the half-tribe of Manasseh into exile. He took them to Halah, Habor, Hara and the river of Gozan, where they are to this day.

Levi

6 THE SONS of Levi:
Gershon, Kohath and Merari.

2 The sons of Kohath:
Amram, Izhar, Hebron and Uzziel.

3 The children of Amram:
Aaron, Moses and Miriam.
The sons of Aaron:
Nadab, Abihu, Eleazar and Ithamar.

4 Eleazar was the father of Phinehas,
Phinehas the father of Abishua,

5 Abishua the father of Bukki,
Bukki the father of Uzzi,

6 Uzzi the father of Zerahiah,
Zerahiah the father of Meraioth,

7 Meraioth the father of Amariah,
Amariah the father of Ahitub,

8 Ahitub the father of Zadok,
Zadok the father of Ahimaaz,

9 Ahimaaz the father of Azariah,
Azariah the father of Johanan,

10 Johanan the father of Azariah (it was he who served as priest in the temple Solomon built in Jerusalem),

11 Azariah the father of Amariah,
Amariah the father of Ahitub,

12 Ahitub the father of Zadok,
Zadok the father of Shallum,

13 Shallum the father of Hilkiah,
Hilkiah the father of Azariah,

14 Azariah the father of Seraiah,
and Seraiah the father of Jehozadak.

King James

Amplified

15And Jehozadak went *into captivity,* when the LORD carried away Judah and Jerusalem by the hand of Nebuchadnezzar.

16 ¶ The sons of Levi; *z*Gershom, Kohath, and Merari.

17And these *be* the names of the sons of Gershom; Libni, and Shimei.

18And the sons of Kohath *were,* Amram, and Izhar, and Hebron, and Uzziel.

19The sons of Merari; Mahli, and Mushi. And these *are* the families of the Levites according to their fathers.

20Of Gershom; Libni his son, Jahath his son, Zimmah his son,

21*a*Joah his son, *b*Iddo his son, Zerah his son, *c*Jeaterai his son.

22The sons of Kohath; *d*Amminadab his son, Korah his son, Assir his son,

23Elkanah his son, and Ebiasaph his son, and Assir his son,

24Tahath his son, *e*Uriel his son, Uzziah his son, and Shaul his son.

25And the sons of Elkanah; Amasai, and Ahimoth.

26*As for* Elkanah: the sons of Elkanah; *f*Zophai his son, and Nahath his son,

27Eliab his son, Jeroham his son, Elkanah his son.

28And the sons of Samuel; the firstborn *g*Vashni, and Abiah.

29The sons of Merari; Mahli, Libni his son, Shimei his son, Uzza his son,

30Shimea his son, Haggiah his son, Asaiah his son.

31And these *are they* whom David set over the service of song in the house of the LORD, after that the ark had rest.

32And they ministered before the dwellingplace of the tabernacle of the congregation with singing, until Solomon had built the house of the LORD in Jerusalem: and *then* they waited on their office according to their order.

33And these *are* they that *h*waited with their children. Of the sons of the Kohathites: Heman a singer, the son of Joel, the son of Shemuel,

34The son of Elkanah, the son of Jeroham, the son of Eliel, the son of *i*Toah,

35The son of *j*Zuph, the son of Elkanah, the son of Mahath, the son of Amasai,

36The son of Elkanah, the son of Joel, the son of Azariah, the son of Zephaniah,

37The son of Tahath, the son of Assir, the son of Ebiasaph, the son of Korah,

38The son of Izhar, the son of Kohath, the son of Levi, the son of Israel.

39And his brother Asaph, who stood on his right hand, *even* Asaph the son of Berachiah, the son of Shimea,

40The son of Michael, the son of Baaseiah, the son of Malchiah,

41The son of Ethni, the son of Zerah, the son of Adaiah,

15Jehozadak went into captivity when the Lord sent Judah and Jerusalem into exile by the hand of Nebuchadnezzar.

16The sons of Levi: Gershom, Kohath, and Merari.

17These are the names of the sons of Gershom: Libni and Shimei.

18The sons of Kohath: Amram, Izhar, Hebron, and Uzziel.

19The sons of Merari: Mahli and Mushi. These are the families of the Levites according to their fathers:

20Of Gershom: Libni his son, Jahath his son, Zimmah his son,

21Joah his son, Iddo his son, Zerah his son, Jeatherai his son.

22The sons of Kohath: Amminadab his son, Korah his son, Assir his son,

23Elkanah his son, Ebiasaph his son, Assir his son,

24Tahath his son, Uriel his son, Uzziah his son, and Shaul his son.

25And the sons of Elkanah: Amasai, Ahimoth,

26Elkanah his son, Zophai his son, Nahath his son,

27Eliab his son, Jeroham his son, Elkanah [Samuel's father] his son.

28The sons of Samuel: the firstborn [Joel] and Abijah.

29The sons of Merari: Mahli, Libni his son, Shimei his son, Uzza his son,

30Shimea his son, Haggiah his son, Asaiah his son.

31These David put over the service of song in the house of the Lord after the ark of the covenant rested there [after being taken by the Philistines and later placed in the house of Abinadab, where it remained for nearly 100 years during the rest of Samuel's judgeship and Saul's entire reign and into David's reign].

32They ministered before the tabernacle of the Tent of Meeting with singing until Solomon had built the Lord's house in Jerusalem, performing their service in due order.

33These and their sons served of the Kohathites: Heman, the singer, the son of Joel, the son of Samuel [the great prophet and judge],

34The son of Elkanah [III], the son of Jeroham, the son of Eliel, the son of Toah,

35The son of Zuph, the son of Elkanah [II], the son of Mahath, the son of Amasai,

36The son of Elkanah [I], the son of Joel, the son of Azariah, the son of Zephaniah,

37The son of Tahath, the son of Assir, the son of Ebiasaph, the son of Korah,

38The son of Izhar, the son of Kohath, the son of Levi, the son of Israel (Jacob).

39Heman's [tribal] brother Asaph stood at his right hand: Asaph son of Berechiah, the son of Shimea,

40The son of Michael, the son of Baaseiah, the son of Malchijah,

41The son of Ethni, the son of Zerah, the son of Adaiah,

z Or, *Gershon;* see ver. 1   *a* Or, *Ethan;* see ver. 42   *b* Or, *Adaiah;* see ver. 41   *c* Or, *Ethni;* see ver. 41   *d* Or, *Izhar;* see ver. 2,18   *e* Or, *Zephaniah, Azariah, Joel;* see ver. 36   *f* Or, *Zuph;* see ver. 35; 1 Sam. 1:1   *g* Called also *Joel* in ver. 33; 1 Sam. 8:2   *h* Heb. *stood*   *i* Or, *Nahath;* see ver. 26   *j* Or, *Zophai*

New American Standard

15 and Jehozadak went *along* when the LORD carried Judah and Jerusalem away into exile by Nebuchadnezzar.

16 ¶ The sons of Levi *were* Gershom, Kohath and Merari.

17 These are the names of the sons of Gershom: Libni and Shimei.

18 The sons of Kohath *were* Amram, Izhar, Hebron and Uzziel.

19 The sons of Merari *were* Mahli and Mushi. And these are the families of the Levites according to their fathers' *households.*

20 Of Gershom: Libni his son, Jahath his son, Zimmah his son,

21 Joah his son, Iddo his son, Zerah his son, Jeatherai his son.

22 The sons of Kohath *were* Amminadab his son, Korah his son, Assir his son,

23 Elkanah his son, Ebiasaph his son and Assir his son,

24 Tahath his son, Uriel his son, Uzziah his son and Shaul his son.

25 The sons of Elkanah *were* Amasai and Ahimoth.

26 *As for* Elkanah, the sons of Elkanah *were* Zophai his son and Nahath his son,

27 Eliab his son, Jeroham his son, Elkanah his son.

28 The sons of Samuel *were* Joel the firstborn, and Abijah the second.

29 The sons of Merari *were* Mahli, Libni his son, Shimei his son, Uzzah his son,

30 Shimea his son, Haggiah his son, Asaiah his son.

31 ¶ Now these are those whom David appointed over the service of song in the house of the LORD, after the ark rested *there.*

32 They ministered with song before the tabernacle of the tent of meeting, until Solomon had built the house of the LORD in Jerusalem; and they served in their office according to their order.

33 These are those who served with their sons: From the sons of the Kohathites *were* Heman the singer, the son of Joel, the son of Samuel,

34 the son of Elkanah, the son of Jeroham, the son of Eliel, the son of Toah,

35 the son of Zuph, the son of Elkanah, the son of Mahath, the son of Amasai,

36 the son of Elkanah, the son of Joel, the son of Azariah, the son of Zephaniah,

37 the son of Tahath, the son of Assir, the son of Ebiasaph, the son of Korah,

38 the son of Izhar, the son of Kohath, the son of Levi, the son of Israel.

39 *Heman's* brother Asaph stood at his right hand, even Asaph the son of Berechiah, the son of Shimea,

40 the son of Michael, the son of Baaseiah, the son of Malchijah,

41 the son of Ethni, the son of Zerah, the son of Adaiah,

New International

15 Jehozadak was deported when the LORD sent Judah and Jerusalem into exile by the hand of Nebuchadnezzar.

16 The sons of Levi:
Gershom,*s* Kohath and Merari.

17 These are the names of the sons of Gershon:
Libni and Shimei.

18 The sons of Kohath:
Amram, Izhar, Hebron and Uzziel.

19 The sons of Merari:
Mahli and Mushi.

These are the clans of the Levites listed according to their fathers:

20 Of Gershon:
Libni his son, Jehath his son,
Zimmah his son, 21 Joah his son,
Iddo his son, Zerah his son
and Jeatherai his son.

22 The descendants of Kohath:
Amminadab his son, Korah his son,
Assir his son, 23 Elkanah his son,
Ebiasaph his son, Assir his son,

24 Tahath his son, Uriel his son,
Uzziah his son and Shaul his son.

25 The descendants of Elkanah:
Amasai, Ahimoth,

26 Elkanah his son,*t* Zophai his son,
Nahath his son, 27 Eliab his son,
Jeroham his son, Elkanah his son
and Samuel his son.*u*

28 The sons of Samuel:
Joel*v* the firstborn
and Abijah the second son.

29 The descendants of Merari:
Mahli, Libni his son,
Shimei his son, Uzzah his son,

30 Shimea his son, Haggiah his son
and Asaiah his son.

The Temple Musicians

31 These are the men David put in charge of the music in the house of the LORD after the ark came to rest there.

32 They ministered with music before the tabernacle, the Tent of Meeting, until Solomon built the temple of the LORD in Jerusalem. They performed their duties according to the regulations laid down for them.

33 Here are the men who served, together with their sons:

From the Kohathites:
Heman, the musician,
the son of Joel, the son of Samuel,

34 the son of Elkanah, the son of Jeroham,
the son of Eliel, the son of Toah,

35 the son of Zuph, the son of Elkanah,
the son of Mahath, the son of Amasai,

36 the son of Elkanah, the son of Joel,
the son of Azariah, the son of Zephaniah,

37 the son of Tahath, the son of Assir,
the son of Ebiasaph, the son of Korah,

38 the son of Izhar, the son of Kohath,
the son of Levi, the son of Israel;

39 and Heman's associate Asaph, who served at his right hand:
Asaph son of Berekiah, the son of Shimea,

40 the son of Michael, the son of Baaseiah,*w*
the son of Malkijah, 41 the son of Ethni,
the son of Zerah, the son of Adaiah,

s 16 Hebrew *Gershom,* a variant of *Gershon*; also in verses 17, 20, 43, 62 and 71   *t 26* Some Hebrew manuscripts, Septuagint and Syriac; most Hebrew manuscripts *Ahimoth 26and Elkanah. The sons of Elkanah:*   *u 27* Some Septuagint manuscripts (see also 1 Samuel 1:19,20 and 1 Chron. 6:33,34); Hebrew does not have *and Samuel his son.*   *v 28* Some Septuagint manuscripts and Syriac (see also 1 Samuel 8:2 and 1 Chron. 6:33); Hebrew does not have *Joel.*   *w 40* Most Hebrew manuscripts; some Hebrew manuscripts, one Septuagint manuscript and Syriac *Maaseiah*

King James

⁴²The son of Ethan, the son of Zimmah, the son of Shimei,

⁴³The son of Jahath, the son of Gershom, the son of Levi.

⁴⁴And their brethren the sons of Merari *stood* on the left hand: ^kEthan the son of ^lKishi, the son of Abdi, the son of Malluch,

⁴⁵The son of Hashabiah, the son of Amaziah, the son of Hilkiah,

⁴⁶The son of Amzi, the son of Bani, the son of Shamer,

⁴⁷The son of Mahli, the son of Mushi, the son of Merari, the son of Levi.

⁴⁸Their brethren also the Levites *were* appointed unto all manner of service of the tabernacle of the house of God.

The family of Aaron

⁴⁹ ¶ But Aaron and his sons offered upon the altar of the burnt offering, and on the altar of incense, *and were appointed* for all the work of the *place* most holy, and to make an atonement for Israel, according to all that Moses the servant of God had commanded.

⁵⁰And these *are* the sons of Aaron; Eleazar his son, Phinehas his son, Abishua his son,

⁵¹Bukki his son, Uzzi his son, Zerahiah his son,

⁵²Meraioth his son, Amariah his son, Ahitub his son,

⁵³Zadok his son, Ahimaaz his son.

⁵⁴ ¶ Now these *are* their dwelling places throughout their castles in their coasts, of the sons of Aaron, of the families of the Kohathites: for theirs was the lot.

⁵⁵And they gave them Hebron in the land of Judah, and the suburbs thereof round about it.

⁵⁶But the fields of the city, and the villages thereof, they gave to Caleb the son of Jephunneh.

⁵⁷And to the sons of Aaron they gave the cities of Judah, *namely,* Hebron, *the city* of refuge, and Libnah with her suburbs, and Jattir, and Eshtemoa, with their suburbs,

⁵⁸And ^mHilen with her suburbs, Debir with her suburbs,

⁵⁹And ⁿAshan with her suburbs, and Beth-shemesh with her suburbs:

⁶⁰And out of the tribe of Benjamin; Geba with her suburbs, and ^oAlemeth with her suburbs, and Anathoth with her suburbs. All their cities throughout their families *were* thirteen cities.

⁶¹And unto the sons of Kohath, *which were* left of the family of that tribe, *were cities given* out of the half tribe, *namely, out of* the half *tribe* of Manasseh, by lot, ten cities.

⁶²And to the sons of Gershom throughout their families out of the tribe of Issachar, and out of the tribe of Asher, and out of the tribe of Naphtali, and out of the tribe of Manasseh in Bashan, thirteen cities.

⁶³Unto the sons of Merari *were given* by lot, throughout their families, out of the tribe of Reuben, and out of the tribe of Gad, and out of the tribe of Zebulun, twelve cities.

⁶⁴And the children of Israel gave to the Levites *these* cities with their suburbs.

⁶⁵And they gave by lot out of the tribe of the children of Judah, and out of the tribe of the children of Simeon, and out of the tribe of the children of Benjamin, these cities, which are called by *their* names.

⁶⁶And *the residue* of the families of the sons of Kohath had cities of their coasts out of the tribe of Ephraim.

⁶⁷And they gave unto them, *of* the cities of refuge, Shechem in mount Ephraim with her suburbs; *they gave* also Gezer with her suburbs,

⁶⁸And Jokmeam with her suburbs, and Beth-horon with her suburbs,

⁶⁹And Aijalon with her suburbs, and Gath-rimmon with her suburbs:

⁷⁰And out of the half tribe of Manasseh; Aner with her suburbs, and Bileam with her suburbs, for the family of the remnant of the sons of Kohath.

Amplified

⁴²The son of Ethan, the son of Zimmah, the son of Shimei,

⁴³The son of Jahath, the son of Gershom, the son of Levi.

⁴⁴Their kinsmen the sons of Merari stood at the left hand: Ethan son of Kishi, the son of Abdi, the son of Malluch,

⁴⁵The son of Hashabiah, the son of Amaziah, the son of Hilkiah,

⁴⁶The son of Amzi, the son of Bani, the son of Shemer,

⁴⁷The son of Mahli, the son of Mushi, the son of Merari, the son of Levi.

⁴⁸And their brethren the Levites [who were not descended from Aaron] were appointed for all other kinds of service of the tabernacle of the house of God.

⁴⁹But [the line of] Aaron and his sons offered upon the altar of burnt offering and the altar of incense, ministering for all the work of the Holy of Holies, and to make atonement for Israel, according to all that Moses, God's servant, had commanded.

⁵⁰The sons of Aaron: Eleazar his son, Phinehas his son, Abishua his son,

⁵¹Bukki his son, Uzzi his son, Zerahiah his son,

⁵²Meraioth his son, Amariah his son, Ahitub his son,

⁵³Zadok his son, Ahimaaz his son.

⁵⁴Their dwelling places are according to their settlements within their borders: to the sons of Aaron of the families of the Kohathites, for theirs was the [first] lot— [Josh. 21:10.]

⁵⁵To them they gave Hebron in the land of Judah and its surrounding suburbs.

⁵⁶But the fields of the city and its villages they gave to Caleb son of Jephunneh.

⁵⁷To the sons of Aaron they gave the city of refuge, Hebron; also Libnah with its pasturelands, Jattir, Eshtemoa with its pasturelands, [Josh. 21:13.]

⁵⁸Hilen with its pasturelands, Debir with its pasturelands,

⁵⁹Ashan with its pasturelands, and Beth-shemesh with its pasturelands.

⁶⁰And out of the tribe of Benjamin: Geba, Alemeth, and Anathoth, with their pasturelands. All their cities according to their families were thirteen.

⁶¹And to the rest of the Kohathites ten cities were given by lot out of the family of the tribe [of Ephraim and of Dan and], of the half-tribe, the half of Manasseh. [Josh. 21:5.]

⁶²To the Gershomites, according to their families, [were allotted] thirteen cities out of the tribes of Issachar, Asher, Naphtali, and Manasseh in Bashan.

⁶³To the Merarites were given by lot, according to their families, twelve cities out of the tribes of Reuben, Gad, and Zebulun.

⁶⁴And the Israelites gave to the Levites these cities with their pasturelands.

⁶⁵They gave by lot out of the tribes of Judah, Simeon, and Benjamin these cities whose names are mentioned.

⁶⁶Some of the families of the Kohathites had cities in the allotted territory out of the tribe of Ephraim.

⁶⁷And [the Ephraimites] gave to [the Levites] the city of refuge, Shechem in the hill country of Ephraim; also Gezer, [both] with their suburbs *and* pasturelands;

⁶⁸Jokmeam, Beth-horon,

⁶⁹Aijalon, and Gath-rimmon, with their suburbs *and* pasturelands;

⁷⁰And out of the half-tribe of Manasseh [these cities], with their suburbs *and* pasturelands: Aner and Bileam, for the rest of the families of the sons of Kohath.

---

^kCalled *Jeduthun* in ch. 9:16 & 25:1,3,6   ^lOr, *Kushaiah;* see ch. 15:17   ^mOr, *Holon;* see Josh. 21:15   ⁿOr, *Ain;* see Josh. 21:16   ^oOr, *Almon;* see Josh. 21:18

New American Standard

42 the son of Ethan, the son of Zimmah, the son of Shimei, 43 the son of Jahath, the son of Gershom, the son of Levi.

44 On the left hand *were* their kinsmen the sons of Merari: Ethan the son of Kishi, the son of Abdi, the son of Malluch, 45 the son of Hashabiah, the son of Amaziah, the son of Hilkiah, 46 the son of Amzi, the son of Bani, the son of Shemer, 47 the son of Mahli, the son of Mushi, the son of Merari, the son of Levi.

48 Their kinsmen the Levites were appointed for all the service of the tabernacle of the house of God.

49 ¶ But Aaron and his sons offered on the altar of burnt offering and on the altar of incense, for all the work of the most holy place, and to make atonement for Israel, according to all that Moses the servant of God had commanded.

50 These are the sons of Aaron: Eleazar his son, Phinehas his son, Abishua his son, 51 Bukki his son, Uzzi his son, Zerahiah his son, 52 Meraioth his son, Amariah his son, Ahitub his son, 53 Zadok his son, Ahimaaz his son.

54 ¶ Now these are their settlements according to their camps within their borders. To the sons of Aaron of the families of the Kohathites (for theirs was the *first* lot), 55 to them they gave Hebron in the land of Judah and its pasture lands around it; 56 but the fields of the city and its villages, they gave to Caleb the son of Jephunneh.

57 To the sons of Aaron they gave the *following* cities of refuge: Hebron, Libnah also with its pasture lands, Jattir, Eshtemoa with its pasture lands, 58 Hilen with its pasture lands, Debir with its pasture lands, 59 Ashan with its pasture lands and Beth-shemesh with its pasture lands; 60 and from the tribe of Benjamin: Geba with its pasture lands, Allemeth with its pasture lands, and Anathoth with its pasture lands. All their cities throughout their families were thirteen cities.

61 ¶ Then to the rest of the sons of Kohath *were given* by lot, from the family of the tribe, from the half-tribe, the half of Manasseh, ten cities.

62 To the sons of Gershom, according to their families, *were given* from the tribe of Issachar and from the tribe of Asher, the tribe of Naphtali, and the tribe of Manasseh, thirteen cities in Bashan.

63 To the sons of Merari *were given* by lot, according to their families, from the tribe of Reuben, the tribe of Gad and the tribe of Zebulun, twelve cities.

64 So the sons of Israel gave to the Levites the cities with their pasture lands.

65 They gave by lot from the tribe of the sons of Judah, the tribe of the sons of Simeon and the tribe of the sons of Benjamin, these cities which are mentioned by name.

66 ¶ Now some of the families of the sons of Kohath had cities of their territory from the tribe of Ephraim.

67 They gave to them the *following* cities of refuge: Shechem in the hill country of Ephraim with its pasture lands, Gezer also with its pasture lands, 68 Jokmeam with its pasture lands, Beth-horon with its pasture lands, 69 Aijalon with its pasture lands and Gath-rimmon with its pasture lands; 70 and from the half-tribe of Manasseh: Aner with its pasture lands and Bileam with its pasture lands, for the rest of the family of the sons of Kohath.

New International

42 the son of Ethan, the son of Zimmah,
the son of Shimei, 43 the son of Jahath,
the son of Gershon, the son of Levi;
44 and from their associates, the Merarites, at his left hand:
Ethan son of Kishi, the son of Abdi,
the son of Malluch, 45 the son of Hashabiah,
the son of Amaziah, the son of Hilkiah,
46 the son of Amzi, the son of Bani,
the son of Shemer, 47 the son of Mahli,
the son of Mushi, the son of Merari,
the son of Levi.

48 Their fellow Levites were assigned to all the other duties of the tabernacle, the house of God. 49 But Aaron and his descendants were the ones who presented offerings on the altar of burnt offering and on the altar of incense in connection with all that was done in the Most Holy Place, making atonement for Israel, in accordance with all that Moses the servant of God had commanded.

50 These were the descendants of Aaron:
Eleazar his son, Phinehas his son,
Abishua his son, 51 Bukki his son,
Uzzi his son, Zerahiah his son,
52 Meraioth his son, Amariah his son,
Ahitub his son, 53 Zadok his son
and Ahimaaz his son.

54 These were the locations of their settlements allotted as their territory (they were assigned to the descendants of Aaron who were from the Kohathite clan, because the first lot was for them): 55 They were given Hebron in Judah with its surrounding pasturelands. 56 But the fields and villages around the city were given to Caleb son of Jephunneh.

57 So the descendants of Aaron were given Hebron (a city of refuge), and Libnah,[x] Jattir, Eshtemoa, 58 Hilen, Debir, 59 Ashan, Juttah[y] and Beth Shemesh, together with their pasturelands. 60 And from the tribe of Benjamin they were given Gibeon,[z] Geba, Alemeth and Anathoth, together with their pasturelands.

These towns, which were distributed among the Kohathite clans, were thirteen in all.

61 The rest of Kohath's descendants were allotted ten towns from the clans of half the tribe of Manasseh.

62 The descendants of Gershon, clan by clan, were allotted thirteen towns from the tribes of Issachar, Asher and Naphtali, and from the part of the tribe of Manasseh that is in Bashan.

63 The descendants of Merari, clan by clan, were allotted twelve towns from the tribes of Reuben, Gad and Zebulun.

64 So the Israelites gave the Levites these towns and their pasturelands. 65 From the tribes of Judah, Simeon and Benjamin they allotted the previously named towns.

66 Some of the Kohathite clans were given as their territory towns from the tribe of Ephraim.

67 In the hill country of Ephraim they were given Shechem (a city of refuge), and Gezer,[a] 68 Jokmeam, Beth Horon, 69 Aijalon and Gath Rimmon, together with their pasturelands.

70 And from half the tribe of Manasseh the Israelites gave Aner and Bileam, together with their pasturelands, to the rest of the Kohathite clans.

---

[x] 57 See Joshua 21:13; Hebrew *given the cities of refuge: Hebron, Libnah.*   [y] 59 Syriac (see also Septuagint and Joshua 21:16); Hebrew does not have *Juttah.*   [z] 60 See Joshua 21:17; Hebrew does not have *Gibeon.*   [a] 67 See Joshua 21:21; Hebrew *given the cities of refuge: Shechem, Gezer.*

King James

71Unto the sons of Gershom *were given* out of the family of the half tribe of Manasseh, Golan in Bashan with her suburbs, and Ashtaroth with her suburbs:

72And out of the tribe of Issachar; Kedesh with her suburbs, Daberath with her suburbs,

73And Ramoth with her suburbs, and Anem with her suburbs:

74And out of the tribe of Asher; Mashal with her suburbs, and Abdon with her suburbs,

75And Hukok with her suburbs, and Rehob with her suburbs:

76And out of the tribe of Naphtali; Kedesh in Galilee with her suburbs, and Hammon with her suburbs, and Kirjathaim with her suburbs.

77Unto the rest of the children of Merari *were given* out of the tribe of Zebulun, Rimmon with her suburbs, Tabor with her suburbs:

78And on the other side Jordan by Jericho, on the east side of Jordan, *were given them* out of the tribe of Reuben, Bezer in the wilderness with her suburbs, and Jahzah with her suburbs,

79Kedemoth also with her suburbs, and Mephaath with her suburbs:

80And out of the tribe of Gad; Ramoth in Gilead with her suburbs, and Mahanaim with her suburbs,

81And Heshbon with her suburbs, and Jazer with her suburbs.

The family of Issachar

7 NOW THE sons of Issachar *were,* Tola, and *P*Puah, Jashub, and Shimrom, four.

2And the sons of Tola; Uzzi, and Rephaiah, and Jeriel, and Jahmai, and Jibsam, and Shemuel, heads of their father's house, *to wit,* of Tola: *they were* valiant men of might in their generations; whose number *was* in the days of David two and twenty thousand and six hundred.

3And the sons of Uzzi; Izrahiah: and the sons of Izrahiah; Michael and Obadiah, and Joel, Ishiah, five: all of them chief men.

4And with them, by their generations, after the house of their fathers, *were* bands of soldiers for war, six and thirty thousand *men:* for they had many wives and sons.

5And their brethren among all the families of Issachar *were* valiant men of might, reckoned in all by their genealogies fourscore and seven thousand.

The family of Benjamin

6 ¶ *The* sons of Benjamin: Bela, and Becher, and Jediael, three.

7And the sons of Bela; Ezbon, and Uzzi, and Uzziel, and Jerimoth, and Iri, five; heads of the house of *their* fathers, mighty men of valour; and were reckoned by their genealogies twenty and two thousand and thirty and four.

8And the sons of Becher; Zemira, and Joash, and Eliezer, and Elioenai, and Omri, and Jerimoth, and Abiah, and Anathoth, and Alameth. All these *are* the sons of Becher.

9And the number of them, after their genealogy by their generations, heads of the house of their fathers, mighty men of valour, *was* twenty thousand and two hundred.

10The sons also of Jediael; Bilhan: and the sons of Bilhan; Jeush, and Benjamin, and Ehud, and Chenaanah, and Zethan, and Tharshish, and Ahishahar.

11All these the sons of Jediael, by the heads of their fathers, mighty men of valour, *were* seventeen thousand and two hundred *soldiers,* fit to go out for war *and* battle.

12Shuppim also, and Huppim, the children of *q*Ir, *and* Hushim, the sons of *r*Aher.

Amplified

71To the Gershomites were given out of the half-tribe of Manasseh: Golan in Bashan and Ashtaroth, with their suburbs *and* pasturelands;

72Out of the tribe of Issachar, with their suburbs *and* pasturelands: Kedesh, Daberath,

73Ramoth, and Anem;

74Out of the tribe of Asher, with their suburbs *and* pasturelands: Mashal, Abdon,

75Hukok, and Rehob;

76And out of the tribe of Naphtali, with their suburbs *and* pasturelands: Kedesh in Galilee, Hammon, and Kiriathaim.

77To the rest of the Merarites were given from the tribe of Zebulun: Rimmono and Tabor, with their suburbs *and* pasturelands;

78On the other side of the Jordan, on the east side by Jericho, the Levites were given out of the tribe of Reuben [these cities], with their suburbs *and* pasturelands: Bezer in the wilderness, Jahzah,

79Kedemoth, and Mephaath;

80Out of the tribe of Gad [these cities], with their suburbs *and* pasturelands: Ramoth in Gilead, Mahanaim,

81Heshbon, and Jazer.

7 THE SONS of Issachar were: Tola, Puah, Jashub, and Shimron—four in all.

2The sons of Tola: Uzzi, Rephaiah, Jeriel, Jahmai, Ibsam, Shemuel (Samuel)—heads of their fathers' houses, descendants of Tola. They were mighty men of valor in their generations; their number in David's days was 22,600.

3The son of Uzzi: Izrahiah. The sons of Izrahiah: Michael, Obadiah, Joel, Isshiah—five, all of them chief men.

4And with them by their generations according to their fathers' houses were units of the army for war, 36,000, for they had many wives and children [with them].

5Their kinsmen from all the families of Issachar, mighty men of valor, registered by genealogies, were in all 87,000.

6The sons of Benjamin: Bela, Becher, and Jediael—three in all.

7The sons of Bela: Ezbon, Uzzi, Uzziel, Jerimoth, and Iri—five, heads of the houses of their fathers, mighty men of valor. By their genealogies they numbered 22,034.

8The sons of Becher: Zemirah, Joash, Eliezer, Elioenai, Omri, Jeremoth, Abijah, Anathoth, and Alemeth, all sons of Becher.

9The number of them by their genealogies by generations, as heads of their fathers' houses, mighty warriors, was 20,200.

10The son of Jediael: Bilhan. The sons of Bilhan: Jeush, Benjamin, Ehud, Chenaanah, Zethan, Tarshish, and Ahishahar.

11All these were the sons of Jediael, according to the heads of their fathers' houses, mighty men of valor, 17,200, able *and* fit for service in war.

12Shuppim and Huppim were the sons of Ir, and Hushim the son of Aher.

P Phuvah, Job *q Or, Iri;* see ver. 7 *r Or, Ahiram;* see
Num. 26:38

New American Standard

71 ¶ To the sons of Gershom *were given,* from the family of the half-tribe of Manasseh: Golan in Bashan with its pasture lands and Ashtaroth with its pasture lands;

72 and from the tribe of Issachar: Kedesh with its pasture lands, Daberath with its pasture lands,

73 and Ramoth with its pasture lands, Anem with its pasture lands;

74 and from the tribe of Asher: Mashal with its pasture lands, Abdon with its pasture lands,

75 Hukok with its pasture lands and Rehob with its pasture lands;

76 and from the tribe of Naphtali: Kedesh in Galilee with its pasture lands, Hammon with its pasture lands and Kiriathaim with its pasture lands.

77 ¶ To the rest of *the Levites,* the sons of Merari, *were given,* from the tribe of Zebulun: Rimmono with its pasture lands, Tabor with its pasture lands;

78 and beyond the Jordan at Jericho, on the east side of the Jordan, *were given,* from the tribe of Reuben: Bezer in the wilderness with its pasture lands, Jahzah with its pasture lands,

79 Kedemoth with its pasture lands and Mephaath with its pasture lands;

80 and from the tribe of Gad: Ramoth in Gilead with its pasture lands, Mahanaim with its pasture lands,

81 Heshbon with its pasture lands and Jazer with its pasture lands.

Genealogy from Issachar

7 NOW THE sons of Issachar *were* four: Tola, Puah, Jashub and Shimron.

2 The sons of Tola *were* Uzzi, Rephaiah, Jeriel, Jahmai, Ibsam and Samuel, heads of their fathers' households. *The sons of* Tola *were* mighty men of valor in their generations; their number in the days of David was 22,600.

3 The son of Uzzi *was* Izrahiah. And the sons of Izrahiah *were* Michael, Obadiah, Joel, Isshiah; all five of them *were* chief men.

4 With them by their generations according to their fathers' households were 36,000 troops of the army for war, for they had many wives and sons.

5 Their relatives among all the families of Issachar *were* mighty men of valor, enrolled by genealogy, in all 87,000.

Descendants of Benjamin

6 ¶ *The sons of* Benjamin *were* three: Bela and Becher and Jediael.

7 The sons of Bela were five: Ezbon, Uzzi, Uzziel, Jerimoth and Iri. They *were* heads of fathers' households, mighty men of valor, and were 22,034 enrolled by genealogy.

8 The sons of Becher *were* Zemirah, Joash, Eliezer, Elioenai, Omri, Jeremoth, Abijah, Anathoth and Alemeth. All these *were* the sons of Becher.

9 They were enrolled by genealogy, according to their generations, heads of their fathers' households, 20,200 mighty men of valor.

10 The son of Jediael *was* Bilhan. And the sons of Bilhan *were* Jeush, Benjamin, Ehud, Chenaanah, Zethan, Tarshish and Ahishahar.

11 All these *were* sons of Jediael, according to the heads of their fathers' households, 17,200 mighty men of valor, who were ready to go out with the army to war.

12 Shuppim and Huppim *were* the sons of Ir; Hushim *was* the son of Aher.

New International

71 The Gershonites received the following:
  From the clan of the half-tribe of Manasseh
    they received Golan in Bashan and also Ashtaroth, together with their pasturelands;

72 from the tribe of Issachar
    they received Kedesh, Daberath, 73 Ramoth and Anem, together with their pasturelands;

74 from the tribe of Asher
    they received Mashal, Abdon, 75 Hukok and Rehob, together with their pasturelands;

76 and from the tribe of Naphtali
    they received Kedesh in Galilee, Hammon and Kiriathaim, together with their pasturelands.

77 The Merarites (the rest of the Levites) received the following:
  From the tribe of Zebulun
    they received Jokneam, Kartah,[b] Rimmono and Tabor, together with their pasturelands;

78 from the tribe of Reuben across the Jordan east of Jericho
    they received Bezer in the desert, Jahzah, 79 Kedemoth and Mephaath, together with their pasturelands;

80 and from the tribe of Gad
    they received Ramoth in Gilead, Mahanaim, 81 Heshbon and Jazer, together with their pasturelands.

Issachar

7 THE SONS of Issachar:
  Tola, Puah, Jashub and Shimron—four in all.

2 The sons of Tola:
  Uzzi, Rephaiah, Jeriel, Jahmai, Ibsam and Samuel—heads of their families. During the reign of David, the descendants of Tola listed as fighting men in their genealogy numbered 22,600.

3 The son of Uzzi:
  Izrahiah.
  The sons of Izrahiah:
  Michael, Obadiah, Joel and Isshiah. All five of them were chiefs. 4 According to their family genealogy, they had 36,000 men ready for battle, for they had many wives and children.

5 The relatives who were fighting men belonging to all the clans of Issachar, as listed in their genealogy, were 87,000 in all.

Benjamin

6 Three sons of Benjamin:
  Bela, Beker and Jediael.

7 The sons of Bela:
  Ezbon, Uzzi, Uzziel, Jerimoth and Iri, heads of families—five in all. Their genealogical record listed 22,034 fighting men.

8 The sons of Beker:
  Zemirah, Joash, Eliezer, Elioenai, Omri, Jeremoth, Abijah, Anathoth and Alemeth. All these were the sons of Beker. 9 Their genealogical record listed the heads of families and 20,200 fighting men.

10 The son of Jediael:
  Bilhan.
  The sons of Bilhan:
  Jeush, Benjamin, Ehud, Kenaanah, Zethan, Tarshish and Ahishahar. 11 All these sons of Jediael were heads of families. There were 17,200 fighting men ready to go out to war.

12 The Shuppites and Huppites were the descendants of Ir, and the Hushites the descendants of Aher.

---

b 77 See Septuagint and Joshua 21:34; Hebrew does not have Jokneam, Kartah.

King James

The family of Naphtali

13 ¶ The sons of Naphtali; Jahziel, and Guni, and Jezer, and Shallum, the sons of Bilhah.

14 ¶ The sons of Manasseh; Ashriel, whom she bare: (but his concubine the Aramitess bare Machir the father of Gilead:

15 And Machir took to wife the sister of Huppim and Shuppim, whose sister's name was Maachah;) and the name of the second was Zelophehad: and Zelophehad had daughters.

16 And Maachah the wife of Machir bare a son, and she called his name Peresh; and the name of his brother was Sheresh; and his sons were Ulam and Rakem.

17 And the sons of Ulam; Bedan. These were the sons of Gilead, the son of Machir, the son of Manasseh.

18 And his sister Hammoleketh bare Ishod, and Abiezer, and Mahalah.

19 And the sons of Shemidah were, Ahian, and Shechem, and Likhi, and Aniam.

The family of Ephraim

20 ¶ And the sons of Ephraim; Shuthelah, and Bered his son, and Tahath his son, and Eladah his son, and Tahath his son,

21 ¶ And Zabad his son, and Shuthelah his son, and Ezer, and Elead, whom the men of Gath that were born in that land slew, because they came down to take away their cattle.

22 And Ephraim their father mourned many days, and his brethren came to comfort him.

23 ¶ And when he went in to his wife, she conceived, and bare a son, and he called his name Beriah, because it went evil with his house.

24 (And his daughter was Sherah, who built Beth-horon the nether, and the upper, and Uzzen-sherah.)

25 And Rephah was his son, also Resheph, and Telah his son, and Tahan his son,

26 Laadan his son, Ammihud his son, Elishama his son,

27 [s]Non his son, Jehoshuah his son.

28 ¶ And their possessions and habitations were, Bethel and the towns thereof, and eastward Naaran, and westward Gezer, with the [t]towns thereof; Shechem also and the towns thereof, unto Gaza and the towns thereof:

29 And by the borders of the children of Manasseh, Bethshean and her towns, Taanach and her towns, Megiddo and her towns, Dor and her towns. In these dwelt the children of Joseph the son of Israel.

The family of Asher

30 ¶ The sons of Asher; Imnah, and Isuah, and Ishuai, and Beriah, and Serah their sister.

31 And the sons of Beriah; Heber, and Malchiel, who is the father of Birzavith.

32 And Heber begat Japhlet, and Shomer, and Hotham, and Shua their sister.

33 And the sons of Japhlet; Pasach, and Bimhal, and Ashvath. These are the children of Japhlet.

34 And the sons of Shamer; Ahi, and Rohgah, Jehubbah, and Aram.

35 And the sons of his brother Helem; Zophah, and Imna, and Shelesh, and Amal.

36 The sons of Zophah; Suah, and Harnepher, and Shual, and Beri, and Imrah,

Amplified

13 The sons of Naphtali: Jahziel, Guni, Jezer, and Shallum, whose [grandmother] was Bilhah.

14 The sons of Manasseh: Ashriel, whom his concubine the Aramitess bore; she bore Machir the father of Gilead.

15 And Machir took as wife the sister of Huppim and Shuppim; her name was Maacah. The name of a second [and later descendant, the first being Gilead], was Zelophehad; and Zelophehad had daughters [only]. [Num. 27:1–7.]

16 Maacah the wife of Machir bore a son; she called his name Peresh. The name of his brother was Sheresh; his sons were Ulam and Rakem.

17 The son of Ulam: Bedan. These were the sons of Gilead son of Machir, the son of Manasseh.

18 His sister Hammolecheth bore Ishbod, Abiezer, and Mahlah.

19 The sons of Shemida were: Ahian, Shechem, Likhi, and Aniam.

20 The sons of Ephraim: Shuthelah, Bered his son, Tahath [I] his son, Eleadah his son, Tahath [II] his son,

21 Zabad his son, and Shuthelah his son. [During Ephraim's lifetime, his sons] Ezer and Elead were slain by men of Gath born in the land, who had come down to steal the cattle [of the Ephraimites, probably before the Israelites left Egypt].

22 And Ephraim their father mourned many days, and his brethren came to comfort him.

23 Then his wife conceived and bore a son, and he called his name Beriah [in evil], because calamity had befallen his house.

24 [Beriah's] daughter was Sheerah, who built both Lower and Upper Beth-horon, and also Uzzen-sheerah.

25 Rephah was his son, and Resheph [his son]; Resheph's son was Telah, Tahan his son,

26 Ladan his son, Ammihud his son, Elishama his son,

27 Nun his son, Joshua [Moses' successor] his son.

28 And their possessions and settlements were Bethel and its towns, and eastward Naaran, and westward Gezer, and Shechem, and as far as Azzah (Gaza) with all their towns,

29 And along the borders of the Manassites, Beth-shean, Taanach, Megiddo, Dor, with all their towns. In these dwelt the sons of Joseph son of Israel.

30 The sons of Asher: Imnah, Ishvah, Ishvi, Beriah; and Serah their sister.

31 The sons of Beriah: Heber and Malchiel, who was the father of Birzaith.

32 Heber was the father of Japhlet, Shomer, Hotham, and Shua their sister.

33 The sons of Japhlet: Pasach, Bimhal, and Ashvath. These were the sons of Japhlet.

34 The sons of Shemer (Shomer) his brother: Rohgah, Jehubbah, and Aram.

35 The sons of his brother Helem (Hotham): Zophah, Imna, Shelesh, and Amal.

36 The sons of Zophah: Suah, Harnepher, Shual, Beri, Imrah,

---

[s]Or, Nun; see Num. 13:8,16   [t]Heb. daughters

New American Standard

Sons of Naphtali

13 ¶ The sons of Naphtali *were* Jahziel, Guni, Jezer, and Shallum, the sons of Bilhah.

Descendants of Manasseh

14 ¶ The sons of Manasseh *were* Asriel, whom his Aramean concubine bore; she bore Machir the father of Gilead.

15 Machir took a wife for Huppim and Shuppim, whose sister's name was Maacah. And the name of the second was Zelophehad, and Zelophehad had daughters.

16 Maacah the wife of Machir bore a son, and she named him Peresh; and the name of his brother *was* Sheresh, and his sons *were* Ulam and Rakem.

17 The son of Ulam *was* Bedan. These *were* the sons of Gilead the son of Machir, the son of Manasseh.

18 His sister Hammolecheth bore Ishhod and Abiezer and Mahlah.

19 The sons of Shemida were Ahian and Shechem and Likhi and Aniam.

Descendants of Ephraim

20 ¶ The sons of Ephraim *were* Shuthelah and Bered his son, Tahath his son, Eleadah his son, Tahath his son,

21 Zabad his son, Shuthelah his son, and Ezer and Elead whom the men of Gath who were born in the land killed, because they came down to take their livestock.

22 Their father Ephraim mourned many days, and his relatives came to comfort him.

23 Then he went in to his wife, and she conceived and bore a son, and he named him Beriah, because misfortune had come upon his house.

24 His daughter was Sheerah, who built lower and upper Beth-horon, also Uzzen-sheerah.

25 Rephah was his son *along* with Resheph, Telah his son, Tahan his son,

26 Ladan his son, Ammihud his son, Elishama his son,

27 Non his son and Joshua his son.

28 ¶ Their possessions and settlements *were* Bethel with its towns, and to the east Naaran, and to the west Gezer with its towns, and Shechem with its towns as far as Ayyah with its towns,

29 and along the borders of the sons of Manasseh, Bethshean with its towns, Taanach with its towns, Megiddo with its towns, Dor with its towns. In these lived the sons of Joseph the son of Israel.

Descendants of Asher

30 ¶ The sons of Asher *were* Imnah, Ishvah, Ishvi and Beriah, and Serah their sister.

31 The sons of Beriah *were* Heber and Malchiel, who was the father of Birzaith.

32 Heber became the father of Japhlet, Shomer and Hotham, and Shua their sister.

33 The sons of Japhlet *were* Pasach, Bimhal and Ashvath. These were the sons of Japhlet.

34 The sons of Shemer *were* Ahi and Rohgah, Jehubbah and Aram.

35 The sons of his brother Helem *were* Zophah, Imna, Shelesh and Amal.

36 The sons of Zophah *were* Suah, Harnepher, Shual, Beri and Imrah,

New International

Naphtali

13 The sons of Naphtali:
Jahziel, Guni, Jezer and Shillem[c] —the descendants of Bilhah.

Manasseh

14 The descendants of Manasseh:
Asriel was his descendant through his Aramean concubine. She gave birth to Makir the father of Gilead. 15 Makir took a wife from among the Huppites and Shuppites. His sister's name was Maacah.
Another descendant was named Zelophehad, who had only daughters.

16 Makir's wife Maacah gave birth to a son and named him Peresh. His brother was named Sheresh, and his sons were Ulam and Rakem.

17 The son of Ulam:
Bedan.
These were the sons of Gilead son of Makir, the son of Manasseh. 18 His sister Hammoleketh gave birth to Ishhod, Abiezer and Mahlah.

19 The sons of Shemida were:
Ahian, Shechem, Likhi and Aniam.

Ephraim

20 The descendants of Ephraim:
Shuthelah, Bered his son,
Tahath his son, Eleadah his son,
Tahath his son, 21 Zabad his son
and Shuthelah his son.
Ezer and Elead were killed by the native-born men of Gath, when they went down to seize their livestock. 22 Their father Ephraim mourned for them many days, and his relatives came to comfort him. 23 Then he lay with his wife again, and she became pregnant and gave birth to a son. He named him Beriah,[d] because there had been misfortune in his family. 24 His daughter was Sheerah, who built Lower and Upper Beth Horon as well as Uzzen Sheerah.

25 Rephah was his son, Resheph his son,[e] Telah his son, Tahan his son,

26 Ladan his son, Ammihud his son, Elishama his son, 27 Nun his son and Joshua his son.

28 Their lands and settlements included Bethel and its surrounding villages, Naaran to the east, Gezer and its villages to the west, and Shechem and its villages all the way to Ayyah and its villages. 29 Along the borders of Manasseh were Beth Shan, Taanach, Megiddo and Dor, together with their villages. The descendants of Joseph son of Israel lived in these towns.

Asher

30 The sons of Asher:
Imnah, Ishvah, Ishvi and Beriah. Their sister was Serah.

31 The sons of Beriah:
Heber and Malkiel, who was the father of Birzaith.

32 Heber was the father of Japhlet, Shomer and Hotham and of their sister Shua.

33 The sons of Japhlet:
Pasach, Bimhal and Ashvath.
These were Japhlet's sons.

34 The sons of Shomer:
Ahi, Rohgah,[f] Hubbah and Aram.

35 The sons of his brother Helem:
Zophah, Imna, Shelesh and Amal.

36 The sons of Zophah:

---

c 13 Some Hebrew and Septuagint manuscripts (see also Gen. 46:24 and Num. 26:49); most Hebrew manuscripts *Shallum*
d 23 *Beriah* sounds like the Hebrew for *misfortune*.   e 25 Some Septuagint manuscripts; Hebrew does not have *his son*.
f 34 Or *of his brother Shomer: Rohgah*

King James

³⁷Bezer, and Hod, and Shamma, and Shilshah, and Ithran, and Beera.

³⁸And the sons of Jether; Jephunneh, and Pispah, and Ara.

³⁹And the sons of Ulla; Arah, and Haniel, and Rezia.

⁴⁰All these *were* the children of Asher, heads of *their* father's house, choice *and* mighty men of valour, chief of the princes. And the number throughout the genealogy of them that were apt to the war *and* to battle *was* twenty and six thousand men.

The family of Benjamin

8 NOW BENJAMIN begat Bela his firstborn, Ashbel the second, and Aharah the third,

²Nohah the fourth, and Rapha the fifth.

³And the sons of Bela were, ᵘAddar, and Gera, and Abihud,

⁴And Abishua, and Naaman, and Ahoah,

⁵And Gera, and ᵛShephuphan, and Huram.

⁶And these *are* the sons of Ehud: these are the heads of the fathers of the inhabitants of Geba, and they removed them to Manahath:

⁷And Naaman, and Ahiah, and Gera, he removed them, and begat Uzza, and Ahihud.

⁸And Shaharaim begat *children* in the country of Moab, after he had sent them away; Hushim and Baara *were* his wives.

⁹And he begat of Hodesh his wife, Jobab, and Zibia, and Mesha, and Malcham,

¹⁰And Jeuz, and Shachia, and Mirma. These *were* his sons, heads of the fathers.

¹¹And of Hushim he begat Abitub, and Elpaal.

¹²The sons of Elpaal; Eber, and Misham, and Shamed, who built Ono, and Lod, with the towns thereof:

¹³Beriah also, and Shema, who *were* heads of the fathers of the inhabitants of Aijalon, who drove away the inhabitants of Gath:

¹⁴And Ahio, Shashak, and Jeremoth,

¹⁵And Zebadiah, and Arad, and Ader,

¹⁶And Michael, and Ispah, and Joha, the sons of Beriah;

¹⁷And Zebadiah, and Meshullam, and Hezeki, and Heber,

¹⁸Ishmerai also, and Jezliah, and Jobab, the sons of Elpaal;

¹⁹And Jakim, and Zichri, and Zabdi,

²⁰And Elienai, and Zilthai, and Eliel,

²¹And Adaiah, and Beraiah, and Shimrath, the sons of ʷShimhi;

²²And Ishpan, and Heber, and Eliel,

²³And Abdon, and Zichri, and Hanan,

²⁴And Hananiah, and Elam, and Antothijah,

²⁵And Iphedeiah, and Penuel, the sons of Shashak;

²⁶And Shamsherai, and Shehariah, and Athaliah,

²⁷And Jaresiah, and Eliah, and Zichri, the sons of Jeroham.

²⁸These *were* heads of the fathers, by their generations, chief *men*. These dwelt in Jerusalem.

²⁹And at Gibeon dwelt the ˣfather of Gibeon; whose wife's name *was* Maachah:

³⁰And his firstborn son Abdon, and Zur, and Kish, and Baal, and Nadab,

³¹And Gedor, and Ahio, and ʸZacher.

³²And Mikloth begat ᶻShimeah. And these also dwelt with their brethren in Jerusalem, over against them.

³³ ¶ And Ner begat Kish, and Kish begat Saul, and Saul begat Jonathan, and Malchi-shua, and Abinadab, and ᵃEsh-baal.

Amplified

³⁷Bezer, Hod, Shamma, Shilshah, Ithran, and Beera.

³⁸The sons of Jether: Jephunneh, Pispa, and Ara.

³⁹The sons of Ulla: Arah, Hanniel, and Rizia.

⁴⁰All these were offspring of Asher, heads of their fathers' houses, approved men, mighty warriors, chief of the princes. Their number enrolled by genealogies for service in war, was 26,000 men.

8 BENJAMIN WAS the father of Bela his firstborn, Ashbel the second, Aharah the third,

²Nohah the fourth, and Rapha the fifth.

³Bela's sons were: Addar, Gera, Abihud,

⁴Abishua, Naaman, Ahoah,

⁵Gera, Shephuphan, and Huram.

⁶The sons of Ehud: These are the heads of the fathers' houses of the inhabitants of Geba; they were exiled to Manahath:

⁷Naaman, Ahijah, and Gera, that is, Heglam, who was the father of Uzza and Ahihud.

⁸Shaharaim had sons in the country of Moab after he had [divorced and] sent away Hushim and Baara his wives.

⁹And by Hodesh his [Moabitish] wife he was the father of Jobab, Zibia, Mesha, Malcam,

¹⁰Jeuz, Sachia, and Mirmah. These were his sons, heads of fathers' houses.

¹¹By Hushim [divorced] he had had sons: Abitub and Elpaal.

¹²The sons of Elpaal: Eber, Misham, and Shemed, who built Ono and Lod with its towns,

¹³And Beriah and Shema, who were heads of fathers' houses of the inhabitants of Aijalon, who put to flight the inhabitants of Gath,

¹⁴And Ahio, Shashak, and Jeremoth,

¹⁵The sons of Beriah: Zebadiah, Arad, Eder,

¹⁶Michael, Ishpah, and Joha.

¹⁷Zebadiah, Meshullam, Hizki, Heber,

¹⁸Ishmerai, Izliah, and Jobab were the sons of Elpaal.

¹⁹Jakim, Zichri, Zabdi,

²⁰Elienai, Zillethai, Eliel,

²¹Adaiah, Beraiah, and Shimrath were the sons of Shimei.

²²Ishpan, Eber, Eliel,

²³Abdon, Zichri, Hanan,

²⁴Hananiah, Elam, Anthothijah,

²⁵Iphdeiah, and Penuel were the sons of Shashak.

²⁶Shamsherai, Shehariah, Athaliah,

²⁷Jaareshiah, Elijah, and Zichri were the sons of Jeroham.

²⁸These were heads of the fathers' houses, according to their generations, chief men. These dwelt in Jerusalem.

²⁹At Gibeon dwelt [Jeiel] the father of Gibeon, whose wife's name was Maacah.

³⁰His firstborn son was Abdon, then Zur, Kish, Baal, Nadab,

³¹Gedor, Ahio, Zecher,

³²And Mikloth the father of Shimeah. These dwelt together opposite their kinsmen in Jerusalem.

³³Ner was the father of Kish, and Kish of [King] Saul the father of Jonathan, Malchi-shua, Abinadab, and Eshbaal (Ish-bosheth).

ᵘOr, *Ard;* see Gen. 46:21   ᵛOr, *Shupham;* see Num. 26:39; see ch. 7:12   ʷOr, *Shema;* see ver. 13   ˣCalled *Jehiel* in ch. 9:35   ʸOr, *Zechariah;* see ch. 9:37   ᶻOr, *Shimeam;* see ch. 9:38   ᵃOr, *Ishbosheth;* see 2 Sam. 2:8

New American Standard

[37] Bezer, Hod, Shamma, Shilshah, Ithran and Beera.
[38] The sons of Jether *were* Jephunneh, Pispa and Ara.
[39] The sons of Ulla *were* Arah, Hanniel and Rizia.
[40] All these *were* the sons of Asher, heads of the fathers' houses, choice and mighty men of valor, heads of the princes. And the number of them enrolled by genealogy for service in war was 26,000 men.

Genealogy from Benjamin

8 AND BENJAMIN became the father of Bela his firstborn, Ashbel the second, Aharah the third,
[2] Nohah the fourth and Rapha the fifth.
[3] Bela had sons: Addar, Gera, Abihud,
[4] Abishua, Naaman, Ahoah,
[5] Gera, Shephuphan and Huram.
[6] These are the sons of Ehud: these are the heads of fathers' *households* of the inhabitants of Geba, and they carried them into exile to Manahath,
[7] namely, Naaman, Ahijah and Gera—he carried them into exile; and he became the father of Uzza and Ahihud.
[8] Shaharaim became the father of children in the country of Moab after he had sent away Hushim and Baara his wives.
[9] By Hodesh his wife he became the father of Jobab, Zibia, Mesha, Malcam,
[10] Jeuz, Sachia, Mirmah. These were his sons, heads of fathers' *households.*
[11] By Hushim he became the father of Abitub and Elpaal.
[12] The sons of Elpaal *were* Eber, Misham, and Shemed, who built Ono and Lod, with its towns;
[13] and Beriah and Shema, who were heads of fathers' *households* of the inhabitants of Aijalon, who put to flight the inhabitants of Gath;
[14] and Ahio, Shashak and Jeremoth.
[15] Zebadiah, Arad, Eder,
[16] Michael, Ishpah and Joha *were* the sons of Beriah.
[17] Zebadiah, Meshullam, Hizki, Heber,
[18] Ishmerai, Izliah and Jobab *were* the sons of Elpaal.
[19] Jakim, Zichri, Zabdi,
[20] Elienai, Zillethai, Eliel,
[21] Adaiah, Beraiah and Shimrath *were* the sons of Shimei.
[22] Ishpan, Eber, Eliel,
[23] Abdon, Zichri, Hanan,
[24] Hananiah, Elam, Anthothijah,
[25] Iphdeiah and Penuel *were* the sons of Shashak.
[26] Shamsherai, Shehariah, Athaliah,
[27] Jaareshiah, Elijah and Zichri *were* the sons of Jeroham.
[28] These were heads of the fathers' *households* according to their generations, chief men who lived in Jerusalem.
[29] ¶ Now in Gibeon, *Jeiel,* the father of Gibeon lived, and his wife's name was Maacah;
[30] and his firstborn son *was* Abdon, then Zur, Kish, Baal, Nadab,
[31] Gedor, Ahio and Zecher.
[32] Mikloth became the father of Shimeah. And they also lived with their relatives in Jerusalem opposite their *other* relatives.

Genealogy from King Saul

[33] Ner became the father of Kish, and Kish became the father of Saul, and Saul became the father of Jonathan, Malchi-shua, Abinadab and Eshbaal.

New International

Suah, Harnepher, Shual, Beri, Imrah, [37]Bezer, Hod, Shamma, Shilshah, Ithran[g] and Beera.
[38]The sons of Jether:
    Jephunneh, Pispah and Ara.
[39]The sons of Ulla:
    Arah, Hanniel and Rizia.
[40]All these were descendants of Asher—heads of families, choice men, brave warriors and outstanding leaders. The number of men ready for battle, as listed in their genealogy, was 26,000.

The Genealogy of Saul the Benjamite

8 BENJAMIN WAS the father of Bela his firstborn, Ashbel the second son, Aharah the third,
[2]Nohah the fourth and Rapha the fifth.
[3]The sons of Bela were:
    Addar, Gera, Abihud,[h] [4]Abishua, Naaman, Ahoah, [5]Gera, Shephuphan and Huram.
[6]These were the descendants of Ehud, who were heads of families of those living in Geba and were deported to Manahath:
[7]Naaman, Ahijah, and Gera, who deported them and who was the father of Uzza and Ahihud.
[8]Sons were born to Shaharaim in Moab after he had divorced his wives Hushim and Baara. [9]By his wife Hodesh he had Jobab, Zibia, Mesha, Malcam, [10]Jeuz, Sakia and Mirmah. These were his sons, heads of families. [11]By Hushim he had Abitub and Elpaal.
[12]The sons of Elpaal:
    Eber, Misham, Shemed (who built Ono and Lod with its surrounding villages), [13]and Beriah and Shema, who were heads of families of those living in Aijalon and who drove out the inhabitants of Gath.
[14]Ahio, Shashak, Jeremoth, [15]Zebadiah, Arad, Eder, [16]Michael, Ishpah and Joha were the sons of Beriah.
[17]Zebadiah, Meshullam, Hizki, Heber, [18]Ishmerai, Izliah and Jobab were the sons of Elpaal.
[19]Jakim, Zicri, Zabdi, [20]Elienai, Zillethai, Eliel, [21]Adaiah, Beraiah and Shimrath were the sons of Shimei.
[22]Ishpan, Eber, Eliel, [23]Abdon, Zicri, Hanan, [24]Hananiah, Elam, Anthothijah, [25]Iphdeiah and Penuel were the sons of Shashak.
[26]Shamsherai, Shehariah, Athaliah, [27]Jaareshiah, Elijah and Zicri were the sons of Jeroham.
[28]All these were heads of families, chiefs as listed in their genealogy, and they lived in Jerusalem.
[29]Jeiel[i] the father[j] of Gibeon lived in Gibeon.
    His wife's name was Maacah, [30]and his firstborn son was Abdon, followed by Zur, Kish, Baal, Ner,[k] Nadab, [31]Gedor, Ahio, Zeker [32]and Mikloth, who was the father of Shimeah. They too lived near their relatives in Jerusalem.
[33]Ner was the father of Kish, Kish the father of Saul, and Saul the father of Jonathan, Malki-Shua, Abinadab and Esh-Baal.[l]

King James

34And the son of Jonathan *was* bMerib-baal; and Merib-baal begat Micah.

35And the sons of Micah *were,* Pithon, and Melech, and cTarea, and Ahaz.

36And Ahaz begat Jehoadah; and Jehoadah begat Alemeth, and Azmaveth, and Zimri; and Zimri begat Moza,

37And Moza begat Binea: Rapha *was* his son, Eleasah his son, Azel his son:

38And Azel had six sons, whose names *are* these, Azrikam, Bocheru, and Ishmael, and Sheariah, and Obadiah, and Hanan. All these *were* the sons of Azel.

39And the sons of Eshek his brother *were,* Ulam his firstborn, Jehush the second, and Eliphelet the third.

40And the sons of Ulam were mighty men of valour, archers, and had many sons, and sons' sons, an hundred and fifty. All these *are* of the sons of Benjamin.

Inhabitants in Jerusalem

9 SO ALL Israel were reckoned by genealogies; and, behold, they *were* written in the book of the kings of Israel and Judah, *who* were carried away to Babylon for their transgression.

2 ¶ Now the first inhabitants that *dwelt* in their possessions in their cities *were,* the Israelites, the priests, Levites, and the Nethinims.

3And in Jerusalem dwelt of the children of Judah, and of the children of Benjamin, and of the children of Ephraim, and Manasseh;

4Uthai the son of Ammihud, the son of Omri, the son of Imri, the son of Bani, of the children of Pharez the son of Judah.

5And of the Shilonites; Asaiah the firstborn, and his sons.

6And of the sons of Zerah; Jeuel, and their brethren, six hundred and ninety.

7And of the sons of Benjamin; Sallu the son of Meshullam, the son of Hodaviah, the son of Hasenuah,

8And Ibneiah the son of Jeroham, and Elah the son of Uzzi, the son of Michri, and Meshullam the son of Shephathiah, the son of Reuel, the son of Ibnijah;

9And their brethren, according to their generations, nine hundred and fifty and six. All these men *were* chief of the fathers in the house of their fathers.

10 ¶ And of the priests; Jedaiah, and Jehoiarib, and Jachin,

11And dAzariah the son of Hilkiah, the son of Meshullam, the son of Zadok, the son of Meraioth, the son of Ahitub, the ruler of the house of God;

12And Adaiah the son of Jeroham, the son of Pashur, the son of Malchijah, and Maasiai the son of Adiel, the son of Jahzerah, the son of Meshullam, the son of Meshillemith, the son of Immer;

13And their brethren, heads of the house of their fathers, a thousand and seven hundred and threescore; every able men for the work of the service of the house of God.

14And of the Levites; Shemaiah the son of Hasshub, the son of Azrikam, the son of Hashabiah, of the sons of Merari;

15And Bakbakkar, Heresh, and Galal, and Mattaniah the son of Micah, the son of Zichri, the son of Asaph;

16And Obadiah the son of Shemaiah, the son of Galal, the son of Jeduthun, and Berechiah the son of Asa, the son of Elkanah, that dwelt in the villages of the Netophathites.

17And the porters *were,* Shallum, and Akkub, and Talmon, and Ahiman, and their brethren: Shallum *was* the chief;

Amplified

34The son of Jonathan was Merib-baal (Mephibosheth) the father of Micah.

35The sons of Micah: Pithon, Melech, Tarea, and Ahaz.

36Ahaz was the father of Jehoaddah, and Jehoaddah of Alemeth, Azmaveth, and Zimri; Zimri was the father of Moza.

37Moza was the father of Binea; Raphah his son, Eleasah his son, Azel his son.

38Azel had six sons: Azrikam, Bocheru, Ishmael, Sheariah, Obadiah, and Hanan. All these were the sons of Azel.

39The sons of Eshek his brother: Ulam his firstborn, Jehush the second, Eliphelet the third.

40The sons of Ulam were mighty warriors, archers, with many sons and grandsons—150 in all. All these were Benjamites.

9 SO ALL Israel was enrolled by genealogies; and they are written in the Book of the Kings of Israel. And Judah was carried away captive to Babylon for their unfaithfulness to God.

2Now the first [of the returned exiles] to dwell again in their possessions in the cities of Israel were the priests, Levites, and the Nethinim [the temple servants].

3In Jerusalem dwelt some of the people of Judah, Benjamin, Ephraim, and Manasseh:

4Uthai son of Ammihud, the son of Omri, the son of Imri, the son of Bani, of the sons of Pharez son of Judah.

5Of the Shilonites: Asaiah the firstborn and his sons.

6Of the sons of Zerah: Jeuel and their kinsmen, 690.

7Of the Benjamites: Sallu son of Meshullam, the son of Hodaviah, the son of Hassenuah;

8Ibneiah son of Jeroham; Elah son of Uzzi, the son of Michri; and Meshullam son of Shephatiah, the son of Reuel, the son of Ibnijah;

9And their kinsmen, according to their generations, 956. All these were heads of fathers' houses according to their fathers' houses.

10Of the priests: Jedaiah; Jehoiarib; Jachin;

11Azariah son of Hilkiah, the son of Meshullam, the son of Zadok, the son of Meraioth, the son of Ahitub, the chief officer of God's house;

12And Adaiah son of Jeroham, the son of Pashhur, the son of Malchijah; Massai son of Adiel, the son of Jahzerah, the son of Meshullam, the son of Meshillemith, the son of Immer;

13And their kinsmen, heads of their fathers' houses, 1,760—very able men for the work of the service of the house of God.

14Of the Levites: Shemaiah son of Hasshub, the son of Azrikam, the son of Hashabiah, of the sons of Merari;

15And Bakbakkar, Heresh, Galal, and Mattaniah son of Mica, the son of Zichri, the son of Asaph;

16Obadiah son of Shemaiah, the son of Galal, the son of Jeduthun; and Berechiah son of Asa, the son of Elkanah, who dwelt in the villages of the Netophathites [near Jerusalem].

17The gatekeepers were: Shallum, Akkub, Talmon, Ahiman, and their kinsmen, Shallum being the chief

bOr, *Mephibosheth;* see 2 Sam. 4:4 & 9:6,10   cOr, *Tahrea;* see ch. 9:41   dOr, *Seraiah;* see Neh. 11:11   eHeb. *mighty men of valour*

New American Standard

34 The son of Jonathan *was* Merib-baal, and Merib-baal became the father of Micah.

35 The sons of Micah *were* Pithon, Melech, Tarea and Ahaz.

36 Ahaz became the father of Jehoaddah, and Jehoaddah became the father of Alemeth, Azmaveth and Zimri; and Zimri became the father of Moza.

37 Moza became the father of Binea; Raphah *was* his son, Eleasah his son, Azel his son.

38 Azel had six sons, and these *were* their names: Azrikam, Bocheru, Ishmael, Sheariah, Obadiah and Hanan. All these *were* the sons of Azel.

39 The sons of Eshek his brother *were* Ulam his firstborn, Jeush the second and Eliphelet the third.

40 The sons of Ulam were mighty men of valor, archers, and had many sons and grandsons, 150 *of them.* All these *were* of the sons of Benjamin.

People of Jerusalem

9 SO ALL Israel was enrolled by genealogies; and behold, they are written in the Book of the Kings of Israel. And Judah was carried away into exile to Babylon for their unfaithfulness.

2 ¶ Now the first who lived in their possessions in their cities *were* Israel, the priests, the Levites and the temple servants.

3 Some of the sons of Judah, of the sons of Benjamin and of the sons of Ephraim and Manasseh lived in Jerusalem:

4 Uthai the son of Ammihud, the son of Omri, the son of Imri, the son of Bani, from the sons of Perez the son of Judah.

5 From the Shilonites *were* Asaiah the firstborn and his sons.

6 From the sons of Zerah *were* Jeuel and their relatives, 690 *of them.*

7 From the sons of Benjamin *were* Sallu the son of Meshullam, the son of Hodaviah, the son of Hassenuah,

8 and Ibneiah the son of Jeroham, and Elah the son of Uzzi, the son of Michri, and Meshullam the son of Shephatiah, the son of Reuel, the son of Ibnijah;

9 and their relatives according to their generations, 956. All these *were* heads of fathers' *households* according to their fathers' houses.

10 ¶ From the priests *were* Jedaiah, Jehoiarib, Jachin,

11 and Azariah the son of Hilkiah, the son of Meshullam, the son of Zadok, the son of Meraioth, the son of Ahitub, the chief officer of the house of God;

12 and Adaiah the son of Jeroham, the son of Pashhur, the son of Malchijah, and Maasai the son of Adiel, the son of Jahzerah, the son of Meshullam, the son of Meshillemith, the son of Immer;

13 and their relatives, heads of their fathers' households, 1,760 very able men for the work of the service of the house of God.

14 ¶ Of the Levites *were* Shemaiah the son of Hasshub, the son of Azrikam, the son of Hashabiah, of the sons of Merari;

15 and Bakbakkar, Heresh and Galal and Mattaniah the son of Mica, the son of Zichri, the son of Asaph,

16 and Obadiah the son of Shemaiah, the son of Galal, the son of Jeduthun, and Berechiah the son of Asa, the son of Elkanah, who lived in the villages of the Netophathites.

17 ¶ Now the gatekeepers *were* Shallum and Akkub and Talmon and Ahiman and their relatives (Shallum the chief

New International

34The son of Jonathan:
Merib-Baal,*m* who was the father of Micah.

35The sons of Micah:
Pithon, Melech, Tarea and Ahaz.

36Ahaz was the father of Jehoaddah, Jehoaddah was the father of Alemeth, Azmaveth and Zimri, and Zimri was the father of Moza. 37Moza was the father of Binea; Raphah was his son, Eleasah his son and Azel his son.

38Azel had six sons, and these were their names:
Azrikam, Bokeru, Ishmael, Sheariah, Obadiah and Hanan. All these were the sons of Azel.

39The sons of his brother Eshek:
Ulam his firstborn, Jeush the second son and Eliphelet the third. 40The sons of Ulam were brave warriors who could handle the bow. They had many sons and grandsons—150 in all.

All these were the descendants of Benjamin.

The People in Jerusalem

9 ALL ISRAEL was listed in the genealogies recorded in the book of the kings of Israel.

The People in Jerusalem

The people of Judah were taken captive to Babylon because of their unfaithfulness. 2Now the first to resettle on their own property in their own towns were some Israelites, priests, Levites and temple servants.

3Those from Judah, from Benjamin, and from Ephraim and Manasseh who lived in Jerusalem were:

4Uthai son of Ammihud, the son of Omri, the son of Imri, the son of Bani, a descendant of Perez son of Judah.

5Of the Shilonites:
Asaiah the firstborn and his sons.

6Of the Zerahites:
Jeuel.
The people from Judah numbered 690.

7Of the Benjamites:
Sallu son of Meshullam, the son of Hodaviah, the son of Hassenuah;

8Ibneiah son of Jeroham; Elah son of Uzzi, the son of Micri; and Meshullam son of Shephatiah, the son of Reuel, the son of Ibnijah.

9The people from Benjamin, as listed in their genealogy, numbered 956. All these men were heads of their families.

10Of the priests:
Jedaiah; Jehoiarib; Jakin;

11Azariah son of Hilkiah, the son of Meshullam, the son of Zadok, the son of Meraioth, the son of Ahitub, the official in charge of the house of God;

12Adaiah son of Jeroham, the son of Pashhur, the son of Malkijah; and Maasai son of Adiel, the son of Jahzerah, the son of Meshullam, the son of Meshillemith, the son of Immer.

13The priests, who were heads of families, numbered 1,760. They were able men, responsible for ministering in the house of God.

14Of the Levites:
Shemaiah son of Hasshub, the son of Azrikam, the son of Hashabiah, a Merarite; 15Bakbakkar, Heresh, Galal and Mattaniah son of Mica, the son of Zicri, the son of Asaph; 16Obadiah son of Shemaiah, the son of Galal, the son of Jeduthun; and Berekiah son of Asa, the son of Elkanah, who lived in the villages of the Netophathites.

17The gatekeepers:
Shallum, Akkub, Talmon, Ahiman and their broth-

King James

18Who hitherto *waited* in the king's gate eastward: they *were* porters in the companies of the children of Levi.

19And Shallum the son of Kore, the son of Ebiasaph, the son of Korah, and his brethren, of the house of his father, the Korahites, *were* over the work of the service, keepers of the *f*gates of the tabernacle: and their fathers, *being* over the host of the LORD, *were* keepers of the entry.

20And Phinehas the son of Eleazar was the ruler over them in time past, *and* the LORD *was* with him.

21*And* Zechariah the son of Meshelemiah *was* porter of the door of the tabernacle of the congregation.

22All these *which were* chosen to be porters in the gates *were* two hundred and twelve. These were reckoned by their genealogy in their villages, whom David and Samuel the seer *g*did ordain in their *h*set office.

23So they and their children *had* the oversight of the gates of the house of the LORD, *namely,* the house of the tabernacle, by wards.

24In four quarters were the porters, toward the east, west, north, and south.

25And their brethren, *which were* in their villages, *were* to come after seven days from time to time with them.

26For these Levites, the four chief porters, were in *their h*set office, and were over the *i*chambers and treasuries of the house of God.

27 ¶ And they lodged round about the house of God, because the charge *was* upon them, and the opening thereof every morning *pertained* to them.

28And *certain* of them had the charge of the ministering vessels, that they should *j*bring them in and out by tale.

29*Some* of them also *were* appointed to oversee the vessels, and all the *k*instruments of the sanctuary, and the fine flour, and the wine, and the oil, and the frankincense, and the spices.

30And *some* of the sons of the priests made the ointment of the spices.

31And Mattithiah, *one* of the Levites, who *was* the firstborn of Shallum the Korahite, had the *h*set office over the things that were made *l*in the pans.

32And *other* of their brethren, of the sons of the Kohathites, *were* over the *m*showbread, to prepare *it* every sabbath.

33And these *are* the singers, chief of the fathers of the Levites, *who remaining* in the chambers *were* free: for *n*they were employed in *that* work day and night.

34These chief fathers of the Levites *were* chief throughout their generations; these dwelt at Jerusalem.

The family of Saul

35 ¶ And in Gibeon dwelt the father of Gibeon, Jehiel, whose wife's name *was* Maachah:

36And his firstborn son Abdon, then Zur, and Kish, and Baal, and Ner, and Nadab,

37And Gedor, and Ahio, and Zechariah, and Mikloth.

38And Mikloth begat Shimeam. And they also dwelt with their brethren at Jerusalem, over against their brethren.

39And Ner begat Kish; and Kish begat Saul; and Saul begat Jonathan, and Malchi-shua, and Abinadab, and Esh-baal.

40And the son of Jonathan *was* Merib-baal: and Merib-baal begat Micah.

41And the sons of Micah *were,* Pithon, and Melech, and Tahrea, *and* Ahaz.

42And Ahaz begat Jarah; and Jarah begat Alemeth, and Azmaveth, and Zimri; and Zimri begat Moza;

43And Moza begat Binea; and Rephaiah his son, Eleasah his son, Azel his son.

Amplified

18Who hitherto was assigned to the king's east side gate. They were the gatekeepers of the camp of the Levites.

19Shallum son of Kore, the son of Ebiasaph, the son of Korah, and his kinsmen of his father's house, the Korahites, were in charge of the work of the service, keepers of the thresholds of the Tent, as their fathers had been in charge of the camp of the Lord, keepers of the entrance.

20Phinehas son of Eleazar was ruler over them in times past, and the Lord was with him.

21Zechariah son of Meshelemiah was gatekeeper at the entrance of the Tent of Meeting.

22All these chosen to be keepers at the thresholds were 212. These were enrolled by their genealogies in their villages [around Jerusalem], these men [whose grandfathers] David and Samuel the seer had established to their office of trust.

23So they and their sons had oversight of the gates of the Lord's house, that is, the house of the tabernacle, by wards.

24The gatekeepers were stationed on the four sides [of the house of the Lord]—on the east, west, north, and south.

25Their brethren in their villages were to come in every seven days to be with them.

26But these Levites, the four chief gatekeepers, were in charge of the chambers and treasuries of the house of God.

27They lodged round about God's house, for the duty [of watching] was theirs, as well as the opening of the house every morning.

28Some of them had charge of the serving utensils, being required to count them when they brought them in or took them out.

29Some of them also were appointed over the furniture and over all the sacred utensils, as well as over the fine flour, wine, oil, frankincense, and spices.

30Other sons of the priests prepared the ointment of spices.

31Mattithiah, one of the Levites, the firstborn of Shallum the Korahite, was responsible for the things baked in pans.

32Of their Kohathite kinsmen, some were to prepare the showbread every Sabbath.

33These are the singers, heads of the fathers' houses of the Levites, dwelling in the temple chambers, free from other service because they were on duty day and night.

34These were heads of fathers' houses of the Levites, according to their generations, chief men, who lived in Jerusalem.

35In Gibeon dwelt the father of Gibeon, Jeiel, whose wife's name was Maacah,

36His firstborn son Abdon, then Zur, Kish, Baal, Ner, Nadab,

37Gedor, Ahio, Zechariah, and Mikloth.

38Mikloth was the father of Shimeam. They also dwelt beside their brethren, opposite their kinsmen in Jerusalem.

39Ner was the father of Kish, Kish of [King] Saul, Saul of Jonathan, Malchi-shua, Abinadab, and Esh-baal.

40The son of Jonathan was Merib-baal (Mephibosheth); Merib-baal was the father of Micah.

41The sons of Micah: Pithon, Melech, Tahrea, and Ahaz.

42Ahaz was the father of Jarah, and Jarah of Alemeth, Azmaveth, and Zimri; Zimri was the father of Moza,

43Moza of Binea; Rephaiah was his son, Eleasah his son, Azel his son.

---

*f*Heb. *thresholds*   *g*Heb. *founded*   *h*Or, *trust*   *i*Or, *storehouses*   *j*Heb. *bring them in by tale, and carry them out by tale*   *k*Or, *vessels*   *l*Or, *on flat plates,* or, *slices*   *m*Heb. *bread of ordering*   *n*Heb. *upon them*

New American Standard

18 *being stationed* until now at the king's gate to the east). These *were* the gatekeepers for the camp of the sons of Levi.

19 Shallum the son of Kore, the son of Ebiasaph, the son of Korah, and his relatives of his father's house, the Korahites, *were* over the work of the service, keepers of the thresholds of the tent; and their fathers had been over the camp of the LORD, keepers of the entrance.

20 Phinehas the son of Eleazar was ruler over them previously, *and* the LORD was with him.

21 Zechariah the son of Meshelemiah was gatekeeper of the entrance of the tent of meeting.

22 All these who were chosen to be gatekeepers at the thresholds were 212. These were enrolled by genealogy in their villages, whom David and Samuel the seer appointed in their office of trust.

23 So they and their sons had charge of the gates of the house of the LORD, *even* the house of the tent, as guards.

24 The gatekeepers were on the four sides, to the east, west, north and south.

25 Their relatives in their villages *were* to come in every seven days from time to time *to be* with them;

26 for the four chief gatekeepers who *were* Levites, were in an office of trust, and were over the chambers and over the treasuries in the house of God.

27 They spent the night around the house of God, because the watch was committed to them; and they *were* in charge of opening *it* morning by morning.

28 ¶ Now some of them had charge of the utensils of service, for they counted them when they brought them in and when they took them out.

29 Some of them also were appointed over the furniture and over all the utensils of the sanctuary and over the fine flour and the wine and the oil and the frankincense and the spices.

30 Some of the sons of the priests prepared the mixing of the spices.

31 Mattithiah, one of the Levites, who was the firstborn of Shallum the Korahite, had the responsibility over the things which were baked in pans.

32 Some of their relatives of the sons of the Kohathites *were* over the showbread to prepare it every sabbath.

33 ¶ Now these are the singers, heads of fathers' *households* of the Levites, *who lived* in the chambers *of the temple* free *from other service;* for they were engaged in their work day and night.

34 These were heads of fathers' *households* of the Levites according to their generations, chief men, who lived in Jerusalem.

Ancestry and Descendants of Saul

35 ¶ In Gibeon Jeiel the father of Gibeon lived, and his wife's name was Maacah,

36 and his firstborn son *was* Abdon, then Zur, Kish, Baal, Ner, Nadab,

37 Gedor, Ahio, Zechariah and Mikloth.

38 Mikloth became the father of Shimeam. And they also lived with their relatives in Jerusalem opposite their *other* relatives.

39 Ner became the father of Kish, and Kish became the father of Saul, and Saul became the father of Jonathan, Malchi-shua, Abinadab and Eshbaal.

40 The son of Jonathan *was* Merib-baal; and Merib-baal became the father of Micah.

41 The sons of Micah *were* Pithon, Melech, Tahrea *and* Ahaz.

42 Ahaz became the father of Jarah, and Jarah became the father of Alemeth, Azmaveth and Zimri; and Zimri became the father of Moza,

43 and Moza became the father of Binea and Rephaiah his son, Eleasah his son, Azel his son.

New International

ers, Shallum their chief [18]being stationed at the King's Gate on the east, up to the present time. These were the gatekeepers belonging to the camp of the Levites. [19]Shallum son of Kore, the son of Ebiasaph, the son of Korah, and his fellow gatekeepers from his family (the Korahites) were responsible for guarding the thresholds of the Tent[n] just as their fathers had been responsible for guarding the entrance to the dwelling of the LORD. [20]In earlier times Phinehas son of Eleazar was in charge of the gatekeepers, and the LORD was with him. [21]Zechariah son of Meshelemiah was the gatekeeper at the entrance to the Tent of Meeting.

[22]Altogether, those chosen to be gatekeepers at the thresholds numbered 212. They were registered by genealogy in their villages. The gatekeepers had been assigned to their positions of trust by David and Samuel the seer. [23]They and their descendants were in charge of guarding the gates of the house of the LORD—the house called the Tent. [24]The gatekeepers were on the four sides: east, west, north and south. [25]Their brothers in their villages had to come from time to time and share their duties for seven-day periods. [26]But the four principal gatekeepers, who were Levites, were entrusted with the responsibility for the rooms and treasuries in the house of God. [27]They would spend the night stationed around the house of God, because they had to guard it; and they had charge of the key for opening it each morning.

[28]Some of them were in charge of the articles used in the temple service; they counted them when they were brought in and when they were taken out. [29]Others were assigned to take care of the furnishings and all the other articles of the sanctuary, as well as the flour and wine, and the oil, incense and spices. [30]But some of the priests took care of mixing the spices. [31]A Levite named Mattithiah, the firstborn son of Shallum the Korahite, was entrusted with the responsibility for baking the offering bread. [32]Some of their Kohathite brothers were in charge of preparing for every Sabbath the bread set out on the table.

[33]Those who were musicians, heads of Levite families, stayed in the rooms of the temple and were exempt from other duties because they were responsible for the work day and night.

[34]All these were heads of Levite families, chiefs as listed in their genealogy, and they lived in Jerusalem.

The Genealogy of Saul

[35]Jeiel the father[o] of Gibeon lived in Gibeon.

His wife's name was Maacah, [36]and his firstborn son was Abdon, followed by Zur, Kish, Baal, Ner, Nadab, [37]Gedor, Ahio, Zechariah and Mikloth. [38]Mikloth was the father of Shimeam. They too lived near their relatives in Jerusalem.

[39]Ner was the father of Kish, Kish the father of Saul, and Saul the father of Jonathan, Malki-Shua, Abinadab and Esh-Baal.[p]

[40]The son of Jonathan:

Merib-Baal,[q] who was the father of Micah.

[41]The sons of Micah:

Pithon, Melech, Tahrea and Ahaz.[r]

[42]Ahaz was the father of Jadah, Jadah[s] was the father of Alemeth, Azmaveth and Zimri, and Zimri was the father of Moza. [43]Moza was the father of Binea; Rephaiah was his son, Eleasah his son and Azel his son.

---

[n]19 That is, the temple; also in verses 21 and 23　　[o]35 *Father* may mean *civic leader* or *military leader.*　　[p]39 Also known as *Ish-Bosheth*　　[q]40 Also known as *Mephibosheth*　　[r]41 Vulgate and Syriac (see also Septuagint and 1 Chron. 8:35); Hebrew does not have *and Ahaz.*　　[s]42 Some Hebrew manuscripts and Septuagint (see also 1 Chron. 8:36); most Hebrew manuscripts *Jarah, Jarah*

King James

44And Azel had six sons, whose names *are* these, Azrikam, Bocheru, and Ishmael, and Sheariah, and Obadiah, and Hanan: these *were* the sons of Azel.

Saul killed on mount Gilboa

10 NOW THE Philistines fought against Israel; and the men of Israel fled from before the Philistines, and fell down *o*slain in mount Gilboa.

2And the Philistines followed hard after Saul, and after his sons; and the Philistines slew Jonathan, and *p*Abinadab, and Malchi-shua, the sons of Saul.

3And the battle went sore against Saul, and the *q*archers *r*hit him, and he was wounded of the archers.

4Then said Saul to his armourbearer, Draw thy sword, and thrust me through therewith; lest these uncircumcised come and *s*abuse me. But his armourbearer would not; for he was sore afraid. So Saul took a sword, and fell upon it.

5And when his armourbearer saw that Saul was dead, he fell likewise on the sword, and died.

6So Saul died, and his three sons, and all his house died together.

7And when all the men of Israel that *were* in the valley saw that they fled, and that Saul and his sons were dead, then they forsook their cities, and fled: and the Philistines came and dwelt in them.

8 ¶ And it came to pass on the morrow, when the Philistines came to strip the slain, that they found Saul and his sons fallen in mount Gilboa.

9And when they had stripped him, they took his head, and his armour, and sent into the land of the Philistines round about, to carry tidings unto their idols, and to the people.

10And they put his armour in the house of their gods, and fastened his head in the temple of Dagon.

11 ¶ And when all Jabesh-gilead heard all that the Philistines had done to Saul,

12They arose, all the valiant men, and took away the body of Saul, and the bodies of his sons, and brought them to Jabesh, and buried their bones under the oak in Jabesh, and fasted seven days.

13 ¶ So Saul died for his transgression which he *t*committed against the LORD, *even* against the word of the LORD, which he kept not, and also for asking *counsel* of one that had a familiar spirit, to inquire *of it;*

14And inquired not of the LORD: therefore he slew him, and turned the kingdom unto David the son of *u*Jesse.

David, king of all Israel

11 THEN ALL Israel gathered themselves to David unto Hebron, saying, Behold, we *are* thy bone and thy flesh.

2And moreover *v*in time past, even when Saul was king, thou *wast* he that leddest out and broughtest in Israel: and the LORD thy God said unto thee, Thou shalt *w*feed my people Israel, and thou shalt be ruler over my people Israel.

3Therefore came all the elders of Israel to the king to Hebron; and David made a covenant with them in Hebron before the LORD; and they anointed David king over Israel, according to the word of the LORD *x*by Samuel.

4 ¶ And David and all Israel went to Jerusalem, which *is* Jebus; where the Jebusites *were,* the inhabitants of the land.

5And the inhabitants of Jebus said to David, Thou shalt not come hither. Nevertheless David took the castle of Zion, which *is* the city of David.

Amplified

44Azel had six sons: Azrikam, Bocheru, Ishmael, Sheariah, Obadiah, and Hanan. These were the sons of Azel.

10 NOW THE Philistines fought against Israel; and the men of Israel fled from before them and fell slain on Mount Gilboa.

2And the Philistines followed close after Saul and his sons *and* overtook them, and the Philistines slew Jonathan, Abinadab, and Malchi-shua, the sons of Saul.

3And the battle raged about Saul, and the archers found and wounded him.

4Then Saul said to his armor-bearer, Draw your sword and thrust me through with it, lest these uncircumcised come and abuse *and* make sport of me. But his armor-bearer would not, for he was terrified. So Saul took his own sword and fell on it.

5When his armor-bearer saw that Saul was dead, he also fell on his sword and died.

6So Saul died; he and his three sons and all his house died together.

7And when all the men of Israel who were in the valley saw that the army had fled and that Saul and his sons were dead, they forsook their cities and fled; and the Philistines came and dwelt in them.

8The next day, when the Philistines came to strip the slain, they found Saul and his sons fallen on Mount Gilboa.

9They stripped [Saul] and took his head and his armor, and sent [them] round about in Philistia to carry the news to their idols and to the people.

10And they put [Saul's] armor in the house of their gods and fastened his head in the temple of Dagon.

11When all Jabesh-gilead heard all that the Philistines had done to Saul,

12All the brave men arose, took away the bodies of Saul and his sons, brought them to Jabesh, and buried their bones under the oak in Jabesh; then they fasted seven days. [I Sam. 31:12.]

13So Saul died for his trespass against the Lord [in sparing Amalek], for his unfaithfulness in not keeping God's word, and also for consulting [a medium with] a spirit of the dead to inquire pleadingly of it,

14And inquired not so of the Lord [in earnest penitence]. Therefore the Lord slew him and turned the kingdom over to David son of Jesse. [I Sam. 28:6.]

11 THEN [AFTER the death of Ish-bosheth, Saul's son, who ruled over eleven tribes of Israel for two troubled years after Saul's death] all Israel gathered at Hebron and said to David, Behold, we are your bone and your flesh. [II Sam. 2:8–10.]

2In times past, even when Saul was king, it was you who led out and brought in Israel; and the Lord your God said to you, You shall be shepherd of My people Israel, and you shall be prince *and* leader over [them].

3So all the elders of Israel came to the king at Hebron, and David made a covenant with them there before the Lord, and they anointed [him] king over Israel, according to the word of the Lord through Samuel. [I Sam. 16:1, 12, 13.]

4And David and all Israel went to Jerusalem, that is Jebus, where the Jebusites, the inhabitants of the land, were.

5Then the Jebusites said to David, You shall not come in here! But David took the stronghold of Zion, that is, the City of David.

---

*o*Or, *wounded*   *p*Or, *Ishui;* see 1 Sam. 14:49   *q*Heb. *shooters with bows*   *r*Heb. *found him*   *s*Or, *mock me*   *t*Heb. *transgressed*   *u*Heb. *Isai*   *v*Heb. *both yesterday and the third day*   *w*Or, *rule*   *x*Heb. *by the hand of*

New American Standard

44 Azel had six sons whose names are these: Azrikam, Bocheru and Ishmael and Sheariah and Obadiah and Hanan. These were the sons of Azel.

Defeat and Death of Saul and His Sons

10 NOW THE Philistines fought against Israel; and the men of Israel fled before the Philistines and fell slain on Mount Gilboa.

2 The Philistines closely pursued Saul and his sons, and the Philistines struck down Jonathan, Abinadab and Malchi-shua, the sons of Saul.

3 The battle became heavy against Saul, and the archers overtook him; and he was wounded by the archers.

4 Then Saul said to his armor bearer, "Draw your sword and thrust me through with it, otherwise these uncircumcised will come and abuse me." But his armor bearer would not, for he was greatly afraid. Therefore Saul took his sword and fell on it.

5 When his armor bearer saw that Saul was dead, he likewise fell on his sword and died.

6 Thus Saul died with his three sons, and all *those* of his house died together.

7 ¶ When all the men of Israel who were in the valley saw that they had fled, and that Saul and his sons were dead, they forsook their cities and fled; and the Philistines came and lived in them.

8 ¶ It came about the next day, when the Philistines came to strip the slain, that they found Saul and his sons fallen on Mount Gilboa.

9 So they stripped him and took his head and his armor and sent *messengers* around the land of the Philistines to carry the good news to their idols and to the people.

10 They put his armor in the *house* of their gods and fastened his head in the house of Dagon.

Jabesh-gilead's Tribute to Saul

11 When all Jabesh-gilead heard all that the Philistines had done to Saul,

12 all the valiant men arose and took away the body of Saul and the bodies of his sons and brought them to Jabesh, and they buried their bones under the oak in Jabesh, and fasted seven days.

13 ¶ So Saul died for his trespass which he committed against the LORD, because of the word of the LORD which he did not keep; and also because he asked counsel of a medium, making inquiry *of it*,

14 and did not inquire of the LORD. Therefore He killed him and turned the kingdom to David the son of Jesse.

David Made King over All Israel

11 THEN ALL Israel gathered to David at Hebron and said, "Behold, we are your bone and your flesh.

2 "In times past, even when Saul was king, you *were* the one who led out and brought in Israel; and the LORD your God said to you, 'You shall shepherd My people Israel, and you shall be prince over My people Israel.' "

3 So all the elders of Israel came to the king at Hebron, and David made a covenant with them in Hebron before the LORD; and they anointed David king over Israel, according to the word of the LORD through Samuel.

Jerusalem, Capital City

4 ¶ Then David and all Israel went to Jerusalem (that is, Jebus); and the Jebusites, the inhabitants of the land, *were* there.

5 The inhabitants of Jebus said to David, "You shall not enter here." Nevertheless David captured the stronghold of Zion (that is, the city of David).

New International

44 Azel had six sons, and these were their names: Azrikam, Bokeru, Ishmael, Sheariah, Obadiah and Hanan. These were the sons of Azel.

Saul Takes His Life

10 NOW THE Philistines fought against Israel; the Israelites fled before them, and many fell slain on Mount Gilboa. 2 The Philistines pressed hard after Saul and his sons, and they killed his sons Jonathan, Abinadab and Malki-Shua. 3 The fighting grew fierce around Saul, and when the archers overtook him, they wounded him.

4 Saul said to his armor-bearer, "Draw your sword and run me through, or these uncircumcised fellows will come and abuse me."

But his armor-bearer was terrified and would not do it; so Saul took his own sword and fell on it. 5 When the armor-bearer saw that Saul was dead, he too fell on his sword and died. 6 So Saul and his three sons died, and all his house died together.

7 When all the Israelites in the valley saw that the army had fled and that Saul and his sons had died, they abandoned their towns and fled. And the Philistines came and occupied them.

8 The next day, when the Philistines came to strip the dead, they found Saul and his sons fallen on Mount Gilboa. 9 They stripped him and took his head and his armor, and sent messengers throughout the land of the Philistines to proclaim the news among their idols and their people. 10 They put his armor in the temple of their gods and hung up his head in the temple of Dagon.

11 When all the inhabitants of Jabesh Gilead heard of everything the Philistines had done to Saul, 12 all their valiant men went and took the bodies of Saul and his sons and brought them to Jabesh. Then they buried their bones under the great tree in Jabesh, and they fasted seven days.

13 Saul died because he was unfaithful to the LORD; he did not keep the word of the LORD and even consulted a medium for guidance, 14 and did not inquire of the LORD. So the LORD put him to death and turned the kingdom over to David son of Jesse.

David Becomes King Over Israel

11 ALL ISRAEL came together to David at Hebron and said, "We are your own flesh and blood. 2 In the past, even while Saul was king, you were the one who led Israel on their military campaigns. And the LORD your God said to you, 'You will shepherd my people Israel, and you will become their ruler.' "

3 When all the elders of Israel had come to King David at Hebron, he made a compact with them at Hebron before the LORD, and they anointed David king over Israel, as the LORD had promised through Samuel.

David Conquers Jerusalem

4 David and all the Israelites marched to Jerusalem (that is, Jebus). The Jebusites who lived there 5 said to David, "You will not get in here." Nevertheless, David captured the fortress of Zion, the City of David.

King James

⁶And David said, Whosoever smiteth the Jebusites first shall be ^ychief and captain. So Joab the son of Zeruiah went first up, and was chief.

⁷And David dwelt in the castle; therefore they called ^zit the city of David.

⁸And he built the city round about, even from Millo round about: and Joab ^arepaired the rest of the city.

⁹So David ^bwaxed greater and greater: for the LORD of hosts *was* with him.

David's mighty men

¹⁰ ¶ These also *are* the chief of the mighty men whom David had, who ^cstrengthened themselves with him in his kingdom, *and* with all Israel, to make him king, according to the word of the LORD concerning Israel.

¹¹And this *is* the number of the mighty men whom David had; Jashobeam, ^dan Hachmonite, the chief of the captains: he lifted up his spear against three hundred slain *by him* at one time.

¹²And after him *was* Eleazar the son of Dodo, the Ahohite, who *was one* of the three mighties.

¹³He was with David at ^ePas-dammim, and there the Philistines were gathered together to battle, where was a parcel of ground full of barley; and the people fled from before the Philistines.

¹⁴And they ^fset themselves in the midst of *that* parcel, and delivered it, and slew the Philistines; and the LORD saved *them* by a great deliverance.

¹⁵ ¶ Now ^gthree of the thirty captains went down to the rock to David, into the cave of Adullam; and the host of the Philistines encamped in the valley of Rephaim.

¹⁶And David *was* then in the hold, and the Philistines' garrison *was* then at Bethlehem.

¹⁷And David longed, and said, Oh that one would give me drink of the water of the well of Bethlehem, that *is* at the gate!

¹⁸And the three brake through the host of the Philistines, and drew water out of the well of Bethlehem, that *was* by the gate, and took *it,* and brought *it* to David: but David would not drink *of* it, but poured it out to the LORD,

¹⁹And said, My God forbid it me, that I should do this thing: shall I drink the blood of these men ^hthat have put their lives in jeopardy? for with *the jeopardy of* their lives they brought it. Therefore he would not drink it. These things did these three mightiest.

²⁰ ¶ And Abishai the brother of Joab, he was chief of the three: for lifting up his spear against three hundred, he slew *them,* and had a name among the three.

²¹Of the three, he was more honourable than the two; for he was their captain: howbeit he attained not to the *first* three.

²²Benaiah the son of Jehoiada, the son of a valiant man of Kabzeel, ⁱwho had done many acts; he slew two lion-like men of Moab: also he went down and slew a lion in a pit in a snowy day.

²³And he slew an Egyptian, ^ja man of *great* stature, five cubits high; and in the Egyptian's hand *was* a spear like a weaver's beam; and he went down to him with a staff, and plucked the spear out of the Egyptian's hand, and slew him with his own spear.

²⁴These *things* did Benaiah the son of Jehoiada, and had the name among the three mighties.

²⁵Behold, he was honourable among the thirty, but attained not to the *first* three: and David set him over his guard.

²⁶ ¶ Also the valiant men of the armies *were,* Asahel the brother of Joab, Elhanan the son of Dodo of Bethlehem,

²⁷^kShammoth the ^lHarorite, Helez the ^mPelonite,

Amplified

⁶And David said, Whoever smites the Jebusites first shall be chief and commander. Joab son of Zeruiah [David's half sister] went up first, and so he was made chief.

⁷David dwelt in the stronghold; so it was called the City of David.

⁸He built the city from the Millo [a fortification] on around; and Joab repaired *and* revived the rest of the [old Jebusite] city.

⁹And David became greater and greater, for the Lord of hosts was with him.

¹⁰Now these are the chiefs of David's mighty men, who strongly supported him in his kingdom, together with all Israel, to make him king, according to the word of the Lord concerning Israel.

¹¹And this is the number [thirty, and list] of David's mighty men: Jashobeam, a Hachmonite, the chief of the Thirty [captains]. He lifted up his spear against 300, whom he slew at one time.

¹²Next to him in rank was Eleazar son of Dodo the Ahohite, one of the three mighty men.

¹³He was with David at Pas-dammim [where David had long before slain Goliath], and there the Philistines were gathered for battle, where there was a plot of ground full of barley *or* lentils; and the men [of Israel] fled before the Philistines.

¹⁴And Eleazar [one of the Three] stood in the midst of that plot and defended it and slew the Philistines [until his hand was weary, and his hand cleaved to the sword], and the Lord saved by a great victory *and* deliverance. [II Sam. 23:9, 10.]

¹⁵Three of the thirty chief men went down to the rock to David, into the cave of Adullam, and the army of the Philistines was encamped in the Valley of Rephaim.

¹⁶David was then in the stronghold, and the Philistines' garrison was in Bethlehem.

¹⁷And David longingly said, Oh, that someone would give me water to drink from the well of Bethlehem which is by the gate!

¹⁸Then the Three [mighty men] broke through the camp of the Philistines and drew water out of the well of Bethlehem which was by the gate and brought it to David. But David would not drink it; he poured it out to the Lord,

¹⁹And said, My God forbid that I should do this thing. Shall I drink the blood of these men who have put their lives in jeopardy? For at the risk of their lives they brought it. So he would not drink it. These things did these three mighty men.

²⁰Abishai the brother of Joab was chief of the Three. For he lifted up his spear against 300 and slew them, and was named among the Three.

²¹Of the Three [in the second rank] he was more renowned than the two, and became their captain; however, he attained not to the first three.

²²Benaiah son of Jehoiada, whose father was a valiant man of Kabzeel, had done mighty deeds. He slew the two sons of Ariel of Moab. Also he went down and slew a lion in a pit in time of snow.

²³He slew an Egyptian also, a man of great stature, five cubits tall. The Egyptian held a spear like a weaver's beam, and [Benaiah] went to him with a staff and plucked the spear out of the Egyptian's hand and slew him with the man's own spear.

²⁴These things did Benaiah son of Jehoiada, and won a name beside the three mighty men.

²⁵He was renowned among the Thirty, but he did not attain to the rank of the first three. David put him over his guard *and* council.

²⁶Also the mighty men of the armies were: Asahel the brother of Joab, Elhanan son of Dodo of Bethlehem,

²⁷Shammoth of Harod, Helez the Pelonite,

^yHeb. *head*   ^zi.e. *Zion;* see 2 Sam. 5:7   ^aHeb. *revived*
^bHeb. *went in going and increasing*   ^cOr, *held strongly with him*   ^dOr, *son of Hachmoni*   ^eOr, *Ephes-dammim;* see
1 Sam. 17:1   ^fOr, *stood*   ^gOr, *three captains over the thirty*
^hHeb. *with their lives?*   ⁱHeb. *great of deeds*   ^jHeb. *a man of measure*   ^kOr, *Shammah*   ^lOr, *Harodite;* see 2 Sam. 23:25
^mOr, *Paltite;* see 2 Sam. 23:26

New American Standard

6 Now David had said, "Whoever strikes down a Jebusite first shall be chief and commander." Joab the son of Zeruiah went up first, so he became chief.

7 Then David dwelt in the stronghold; therefore it was called the city of David.

8 He built the city all around, from the *b*Millo even to the surrounding area; and Joab repaired the rest of the city.

9 David became greater and greater, for the LORD of hosts *was* with him.

David's Mighty Men

10 ¶ Now these are the heads of the mighty men whom David had, who gave him strong support in his kingdom, together with all Israel, to make him king, according to the word of the LORD concerning Israel.

11 These *constitute* the list of the mighty men whom David had: Jashobeam, the son of a Hachmonite, the chief of the thirty; he lifted up his spear against three hundred whom he killed at one time.

12 ¶ After him was Eleazar the son of Dodo, the Ahohite, who *was* one of the three mighty men.

13 He was with David at Pasdammim when the Philistines were gathered together there to battle, and there was a plot of ground full of barley; and the people fled before the Philistines.

14 They took their stand in the midst of the plot and defended it, and struck down the Philistines; and the LORD saved them by a great victory.

15 ¶ Now three of the thirty chief men went down to the rock to David, into the cave of Adullam, while the army of the Philistines was camping in the valley of Rephaim.

16 David was then in the stronghold, while the garrison of the Philistines *was* then in Bethlehem.

17 David had a craving and said, "Oh that someone would give me water to drink from the well of Bethlehem, which is by the gate!"

18 So the three broke through the camp of the Philistines and drew water from the well of Bethlehem which *was* by the gate, and took *it* and brought *it* to David; nevertheless David would not drink it, but poured it out to the LORD;

19 and he said, "Be it far from me before my God that I should do this. Shall I drink the blood of these men *who went* at the risk of their lives? For at the risk of their lives they brought it." Therefore he would not drink it. These things the three mighty men did.

20 ¶ As for Abshai the brother of Joab, he was chief of the thirty, and he swung his spear against three hundred and killed them; and he had a name as well as the thirty.

21 Of the three in the second *rank* he was the most honored and became their commander; however, he did not attain to the *first* three.

22 ¶ Benaiah the son of Jehoiada, the son of a valiant man of Kabzeel, mighty in deeds, struck down the two *sons* of Ariel of Moab. He also went down and killed a lion inside a pit on a snowy day.

23 He killed an Egyptian, a man of *great* stature five cubits tall. Now in the Egyptian's hand *was* a spear like a weaver's beam, but he went down to him with a club and snatched the spear from the Egyptian's hand and killed him with his own spear.

24 These *things* Benaiah the son of Jehoiada did, and had a name as well as the three mighty men.

25 Behold, he was honored among the thirty, but he did not attain to the three; and David appointed him over his guard.

26 ¶ Now the mighty men of the armies *were* Asahel the brother of Joab, Elhanan the son of Dodo of Bethlehem,

27 Shammoth the Harorite, Helez the Pelonite,

New International

6David had said, "Whoever leads the attack on the Jebusites will become commander-in-chief." Joab son of Zeruiah went up first, and so he received the command.

7David then took up residence in the fortress, and so it was called the City of David. 8He built up the city around it, from the supporting terraces*t* to the surrounding wall, while Joab restored the rest of the city. 9And David became more and more powerful, because the LORD Almighty was with him.

David's Mighty Men

10These were the chiefs of David's mighty men—they, together with all Israel, gave his kingship strong support to extend it over the whole land, as the LORD had promised— 11this is the list of David's mighty men:

Jashobeam,*u* a Hacmonite, was chief of the officers*v*; he raised his spear against three hundred men, whom he killed in one encounter.

12Next to him was Eleazar son of Dodai the Ahohite, one of the three mighty men. 13He was with David at Pas Dammim when the Philistines gathered there for battle. At a place where there was a field full of barley, the troops fled from the Philistines. 14But they took their stand in the middle of the field. They defended it and struck the Philistines down, and the LORD brought about a great victory.

15Three of the thirty chiefs came down to David to the rock at the cave of Adullam, while a band of Philistines was encamped in the Valley of Rephaim. 16At that time David was in the stronghold, and the Philistine garrison was at Bethlehem. 17David longed for water and said, "Oh, that someone would get me a drink of water from the well near the gate of Bethlehem!" 18So the Three broke through the Philistine lines, drew water from the well near the gate of Bethlehem and carried it back to David. But he refused to drink it; instead, he poured it out before the LORD. 19"God forbid that I should do this!" he said. "Should I drink the blood of these men who went at the risk of their lives?" Because they risked their lives to bring it back, David would not drink it.

Such were the exploits of the three mighty men.

20Abishai the brother of Joab was chief of the Three. He raised his spear against three hundred men, whom he killed, and so he became as famous as the Three. 21He was doubly honored above the Three and became their commander, even though he was not included among them.

22Benaiah son of Jehoiada was a valiant fighter from Kabzeel, who performed great exploits. He struck down two of Moab's best men. He also went down into a pit on a snowy day and killed a lion. 23And he struck down an Egyptian who was seven and a half feet*w* tall. Although the Egyptian had a spear like a weaver's rod in his hand, Benaiah went against him with a club. He snatched the spear from the Egyptian's hand and killed him with his own spear. 24Such were the exploits of Benaiah son of Jehoiada; he too was as famous as the three mighty men. 25He was held in greater honor than any of the Thirty, but he was not included among the Three. And David put him in charge of his bodyguard.

26The mighty men were:
Asahel the brother of Joab,
Elhanan son of Dodo from Bethlehem,
27Shammoth the Harorite,
Helez the Pelonite,

---

b I.e. citadel

t 8 Or *the Millo*   *u* 11 Possibly a variant of *Jashob-Baal*
v 11 Or *Thirty*; some Septuagint manuscripts *Three* (see also
2 Samuel 23:8)   *w* 23 Hebrew *five cubits* (about 2.3 meters)

<table>
<tr><td>

King James

</td><td>

Amplified

</td></tr>
</table>

King James	Amplified

<table>
<tr><td>

28Ira the son of Ikkesh the Tekoite, Abiezer the Antoth-ite,

29nSibbecai the Hushathite, oIlai the Ahohite,

30Maharai the Netophathite, pHeled the son of Baanah the Netophathite,

31Ithai the son of Ribai of Gibeah, *that pertained* to the children of Benjamin, Benaiah the Pirathonite,

32qHurai of the brooks of Gaash, rAbiel the Arbathite,

33Azmaveth the Baharumite, Eliahba the Shaalbonite,

34The sons of sHashem the Gizonite, Jonathan the son of Shage the Hararite,

35Ahiam the son of tSacar the Hararite, uEliphal the son of vUr,

36Hepher the Mecherathite, Ahijah the Pelonite,

37wHezro the Carmelite, xNaarai the son of Ezbai,

38Joel the brother of Nathan, Mibhar ythe son of Haggeri,

39Zelek the Ammonite, Naharai the Berothite, the armourbearer of Joab the son of Zeruiah,

40Ira the Ithrite, Gareb the Ithrite,

41Uriah the Hittite, Zabad the son of Ahlai,

42Adina the son of Shiza the Reubenite, a captain of the Reubenites, and thirty with him,

43Hanan the son of Maachah, and Joshaphat the Mithnite,

44Uzzia the Ashterathite, Shama and Jehiel the sons of Hothan the Aroerite,

45Jediael the zson of Shimri, and Joha his brother, the Tizite,

46Eliel the Mahavite, and Jeribai, and Joshaviah, the sons of Elnaam, and Ithmah the Moabite,

47Eliel, and Obed, and Jasiel the Mesobaite.

</td><td>

28Ira son of Ikkesh of Tekoa, Abiezer of Anathoth,

29Sibbecai the Hushathite, Ilai the Ahohite,

30Maharai of Netophah, Heled son of Baanah of Netophah,

31Ithai son of Ribai of Gibeah of the Benjamites, Benaiah of Pirathon,

32Hurai of the brooks of Gaash, Abiel the Arbathite,

33Azmaveth of Baharum, Eliahba of Shaalbon,

34The sons of Hashem the Gizonite, Jonathan son of Shagee the Hararite,

35Ahiam son of Sacar the Hararite, Eliphal son of Ur,

36Hepher the Mecherathite, Ahijah the Pelonite,

37Hezro of Carmel, Naarai son of Ezbai,

38Joel the brother of Nathan, Mibhar son of Hagri,

39Zelek the Ammonite, Naharai the Berothite, the armor-bearer of Joab son of Zeruiah [David's half sister],

40Ira the Ithrite, Gareb the Ithrite,

41Uriah the Hittite [Bathsheba's husband], Zabad son of Ahlai,

42Adina son of Shiza, a leader of the Reubenites, and thirty heroes with him,

43Hanan son of Maacah, and Joshaphat the Mithnite,

44Uzzia the Ashterathite, Shama and Jeiel the sons of Hotham the Aroerite,

45Jediael son of Shimri, and Joha his brother, the Tizite,

46Eliel the Mahavite, Jeribai and Joshaviah sons of Elnaam, Ithmah the Moabite,

47Eliel, Obed, and Jaasiel the Mezobaite.

</td></tr>
</table>

David's supporters

<table>
<tr><td>

12 NOW THESE *are* they that came to David to Ziklag, awhile he yet kept himself close because of Saul the son of Kish: and they *were* among the mighty men, helpers of the war.

2*They were* armed with bows, and could use both the right hand and the left in *hurling* stones and *shooting* arrows out of a bow, *even* of Saul's brethren of Benjamin.

3The chief *was* Ahiezer, then Joash, the sons of bShemaah the Gibeathite; and Jeziel, and Pelet, the sons of Azmaveth; and Berachah, and Jehu the Antothite,

4And Ismaiah the Gibeonite, a mighty man among the thirty, and over the thirty; and Jeremiah, and Jahaziel, and Johanan, and Josabad the Gederathite,

5Eluzai, and Jerimoth, and Bealiah, and Shemariah, and Shephatiah the Haruphite,

6Elkanah, and Jesiah, and Azareel, and Joezer, and Jashobeam, the Korhites,

7And Joelah, and Zebadiah, the sons of Jeroham of Gedor.

8And of the Gadites there separated themselves unto David into the hold to the wilderness men of might, *and* men cof war *fit* for the battle, that could handle shield and buckler, whose faces *were like* the faces of lions, and *were* das swift as the roes upon the mountains;

</td><td>

12 THESE ARE the ones who came to David at Ziklag, while he yet concealed himself because of Saul son of Kish; they were among the mighty men, his helpers in war.

2They were bowmen and could use the right hand or the left to sling stones or shoot arrows from the bow; they were of Saul's kinsmen of Benjamin.

3The chief was Ahiezer and then Joash the sons of Shemaah of Gibeah; Jeziel and Pelet the sons of Azmaveth; Beracah, and Jehu of Anathoth,

4Ishmaiah of Gibeon, a mighty man among the Thirty and a [leader] over them; Jeremiah, Jahaziel, Johanan, Jozabad of Gederah,

5Eluzai, Jerimoth, Bealiah, Shemariah, Shephatiah the Haruphite;

6Elkanah, Isshiah, Azarel, Joezer, and Jashobeam, the Korahites;

7Joelah and Zebadiah the sons of Jeroham of Gedor.

8Of the Gadites there went over to David to the stronghold in the wilderness men of might, men trained for war who could handle shield and spear, whose faces were like the faces of lions, and who were swift as gazelles on the mountains:

</td></tr>
</table>

nOr, *Mebunnai*   oOr, *Zalmon*   pOr, *Heleb*   qOr, *Hiddai*
rOr, *Abi-albon*   sOr, *Jashen; see* 2 Sam. 23:32,33   tOr,
Sharar   uOr, *Eliphelet*   vOr, *Ahasbai*   wOr, *Hezrai*
xOr, *Paarai the Arbite*   yOr, *the Haggerite*   zOr, *Shimrite*
aHeb. *being yet shut up*   bOr, *Hasmaah*   cHeb. *of the host*
dHeb. *as the roes upon the mountains to make haste*

New American Standard

28 Ira the son of Ikkesh the Tekoite, Abiezer the Anathothite,
29 Sibbecai the Hushathite, Ilai the Ahohite,
30 Maharai the Netophathite, Heled the son of Baanah
the Netophathite,
31 Ithai the son of Ribai of Gibeah of the sons of Benjamin, Benaiah the Pirathonite,
32 Hurai of the brooks of Gaash, Abiel the Arbathite,
33 Azmaveth the Baharumite, Eliahba the Shaalbonite,
34 the sons of Hashem the Gizonite, Jonathan the son of
Shagee the Hararite,
35 Ahiam the son of Sacar the Hararite, Eliphal the son
of Ur,
36 Hepher the Mecherathite, Ahijah the Pelonite,
37 Hezro the Carmelite, Naarai the son of Ezbai,
38 Joel the brother of Nathan, Mibhar the son of Hagri,
39 Zelek the Ammonite, Naharai the Berothite, the armor bearer of Joab the son of Zeruiah,
40 Ira the Ithrite, Gareb the Ithrite,
41 Uriah the Hittite, Zabad the son of Ahlai,
42 Adina the son of Shiza the Reubenite, a chief of the
Reubenites, and thirty with him,
43 Hanan the son of Maacah and Joshaphat the Mithnite,
44 Uzzia the Ashterathite, Shama and Jeiel the sons of
Hotham the Aroerite,
45 Jediael the son of Shimri and Joha his brother, the
Tizite,
46 Eliel the Mahavite and Jeribai and Joshaviah, the
sons of Elnaam, and Ithmah the Moabite,
47 Eliel and Obed and Jaasiel the Mezobaite.

David's Supporters in Ziklag

12 NOW THESE are the ones who came to David at
Ziklag, while he was still restricted because of
Saul the son of Kish; and they were among the mighty
men who helped *him* in war.
2 They were equipped with bows, using both the right
hand and the left *to sling* stones and *to shoot* arrows from
the bow; *they were* Saul's kinsmen from Benjamin.
3 The chief was Ahiezer, then Joash, the sons of Shemaah the Gibeathite; and Jeziel and Pelet, the sons of
Azmaveth, and Beracah and Jehu the Anathothite,
4 and Ishmaiah the Gibeonite, a mighty man among the
thirty, and over the thirty. Then Jeremiah, Jahaziel, Johanan, Jozabad the Gederathite,
5 Eluzai, Jerimoth, Bealiah, Shemariah, Shephatiah the
Haruphite,
6 Elkanah, Isshiah, Azarel, Joezer, Jashobeam, the Korahites,
7 and Joelah and Zebadiah, the sons of Jeroham of
Gedor.
8 ¶ From the Gadites there came over to David in the
stronghold in the wilderness, mighty men of valor, men
trained for war, who could handle shield and spear, and
whose faces were like the faces of lions, and *they were* as
swift as the gazelles on the mountains.

New International

28 Ira son of Ikkesh from Tekoa,
Abiezer from Anathoth,
29 Sibbecai the Hushathite,
Ilai the Ahohite,
30 Maharai the Netophathite,
Heled son of Baanah the Netophathite,
31 Ithai son of Ribai from Gibeah in Benjamin,
Benaiah the Pirathonite,
32 Hurai from the ravines of Gaash,
Abiel the Arbathite,
33 Azmaveth the Baharumite,
Eliahba the Shaalbonite,
34 the sons of Hashem the Gizonite,
Jonathan son of Shagee the Hararite,
35 Ahiam son of Sacar the Hararite,
Eliphal son of Ur,
36 Hepher the Mekerathite,
Ahijah the Pelonite,
37 Hezro the Carmelite,
Naarai son of Ezbai,
38 Joel the brother of Nathan,
Mibhar son of Hagri,
39 Zelek the Ammonite,
Naharai the Berothite, the armor-bearer of Joab
son of Zeruiah,
40 Ira the Ithrite,
Gareb the Ithrite,
41 Uriah the Hittite,
Zabad son of Ahlai,
42 Adina son of Shiza the Reubenite, who was chief
of the Reubenites, and the thirty with him,
43 Hanan son of Maacah,
Joshaphat the Mithnite,
44 Uzzia the Ashterathite,
Shama and Jeiel the sons of Hotham the Aroerite,
45 Jediael son of Shimri,
his brother Joha the Tizite,
46 Eliel the Mahavite,
Jeribai and Joshaviah the sons of Elnaam,
Ithmah the Moabite,
47 Eliel, Obed and Jaasiel the Mezobaite.

Warriors Join David

12 THESE WERE the men who came to David at
Ziklag, while he was banished from the presence of
Saul son of Kish (they were among the warriors who
helped him in battle; 2 they were armed with bows and
were able to shoot arrows or to sling stones right-handed
or left-handed; they were kinsmen of Saul from the tribe
of Benjamin):

3 Ahiezer their chief and Joash the sons of Shemaah
the Gibeathite; Jeziel and Pelet the sons of Azmaveth;
Beracah, Jehu the Anathothite, 4 and Ishmaiah the Gibeonite, a mighty man among the Thirty, who was a
leader of the Thirty; Jeremiah, Jahaziel, Johanan, Jozabad the Gederathite, 5 Eluzai, Jerimoth, Bealiah,
Shemariah and Shephatiah the Haruphite; 6 Elkanah,
Isshiah, Azarel, Joezer and Jashobeam the Korahites;
7 and Joelah and Zebadiah the sons of Jeroham from
Gedor.

8 Some Gadites defected to David at his stronghold in the
desert. They were brave warriors, ready for battle and able
to handle the shield and spear. Their faces were the faces
of lions, and they were as swift as gazelles in the mountains.

King James

⁹Ezer the first, Obadiah the second, Eliab the third,

¹⁰Mishmannah the fourth, Jeremiah the fifth,

¹¹Attai the sixth, Eliel the seventh,

¹²Johanan the eighth, Elzabad the ninth,

¹³Jeremiah the tenth, Machbanai the eleventh.

¹⁴These *were* of the sons of Gad, captains of the host: *e*one of the least *was* over an hundred, and the greatest over a thousand.

¹⁵These *are* they that went over Jordan in the first month, when it had *f*overflown all his banks; and they put to flight all *them* of the valleys, *both* toward the east, and toward the west.

¹⁶And there came of the children of Benjamin and Judah to the hold unto David.

¹⁷And David went out *g*to meet them, and answered and said unto them, If ye be come peaceably unto me to help me, mine heart shall *h*be knit unto you: but if *ye be come* to betray me to mine enemies, seeing *there is* no *i*wrong in mine hands, the God of our fathers look *thereon,* and rebuke *it.*

¹⁸Then *j*the spirit came upon Amasai, *who was* chief of the captains, *and he said,* Thine *are* we, David, and on thy side, thou son of Jesse: peace, peace *be* unto thee, and peace *be* to thine helpers; for thy God helpeth thee. Then David received them, and made them captains of the band.

¹⁹And there fell *some* of Manasseh to David, when he came with the Philistines against Saul to battle: but they helped them not: for the lords of the Philistines upon advisement sent him away, saying, He will fall to his master Saul *k*to *the jeopardy of* our heads.

²⁰As he went to Ziklag, there fell to him of Manasseh, Adnah, and Jozabad, and Jediael, and Michael, and Jozabad, and Elihu, and Zilthai, captains of the thousands that *were* of Manasseh.

²¹And they helped David *l*against the band *of the rovers:* for they *were* all mighty men of valour, and were captains in the host.

²²For at *that* time day by day there came to David to help him, until *it was* a great host, like the host of God.

The number of David's men

²³ ¶ And these *are* the numbers of the *m n*bands *that were* ready armed to the war, *and* came to David to Hebron, to turn the kingdom of Saul to him, according to the word of the LORD.

²⁴The children of Judah that bare shield and spear *were* six thousand and eight hundred, ready *o*armed to the war.

²⁵Of the children of Simeon, mighty men of valour for the war, seven thousand and one hundred.

²⁶Of the children of Levi four thousand and six hundred.

²⁷And Jehoiada *was* the leader of the Aaronites, and with him *were* three thousand and seven hundred;

²⁸And Zadok, a young man mighty of valour, and of his father's house twenty and two captains.

²⁹And of the children of Benjamin, the *p*kindred of Saul, three thousand: for hitherto *q*the greatest part of them had kept the ward of the house of Saul.

³⁰And of the children of Ephraim twenty thousand and eight hundred, mighty men of valour, *r*famous throughout the house of their fathers.

³¹And of the half tribe of Manasseh eighteen thousand, which were expressed by name, to come and make David king.

³²And of the children of Issachar, *which were men* that had understanding of the times, to know what Israel ought to do; the heads of them *were* two hundred; and all their brethren *were* at their commandment.

Amplified

⁹Ezer the chief, Obadiah the second, Eliab the third,

¹⁰Mishmannah the fourth, Jeremiah the fifth,

¹¹Attai the sixth, Eliel the seventh,

¹²Johanan the eighth, Elzabad the ninth,

¹³Jeremiah the tenth, Machbannai the eleventh.

¹⁴These Gadites were officers of the army. The lesser was equal to *and* over a hundred, and the greater equal to *and* over a thousand.

¹⁵These are the men who went over the Jordan in the first month when it had overflowed all its banks, and put to flight all those in the valleys, east and west.

¹⁶There came some of the men of Benjamin and Judah to the stronghold to David.

¹⁷David went out to meet them and said to them, If you have come peaceably to me to help me, my heart shall be knit to you; but if you have come to betray me to my adversaries, although there is no violence *or* wrong in my hands, may the God of our fathers look upon and rebuke you.

¹⁸Then the Spirit came upon Amasai, who was chief of the captains, and he said, Yours we are, David, and on your side, you son of Jesse! Peace, peace be to you, and peace be to your helpers, for your God helps you. Then David received them and made them officers of his troops.

¹⁹Some of the men of Manasseh deserted to David when he came with the Philistines for the battle against Saul. But [David's] men did not actually fight with them, for the lords of the Philistines, upon advisement, sent him away, saying, He will desert to his master Saul at the risk of our heads. [I Sam. 29:2-9.]

²⁰As David went to Ziklag, there deserted to him of Manasseh: Adnah, Jozabad, Jediael, Michael, Jozabad, Elihu, and Zillethai, chiefs of thousands in Manasseh.

²¹They helped David against the band of raiders, for they were all mighty men of courage, and [all seven] became commanders in [his] army.

²²For at that time day by day men kept coming to David to help him, until there was a great army, like the army of God.

²³These are the numbers of the armed divisions who came to David at Hebron to turn the kingdom of Saul to him, according to the word of the Lord:

²⁴Those of Judah, who bore shield and spear, were 6,800 armed for war;

²⁵Those of Simeon, mighty and brave warriors, 7,100;

²⁶Those of Levi, 4,600—

²⁷Jehoiada was the leader of the Aaronite [priests], and with him were 3,700,

²⁸And Zadok, a young man mighty in valor, and twenty-two captains from his own father's house;

²⁹Of the Benjamites, the kindred of [King] Saul, 3,000—hitherto the majority of them had kept their allegiance [to Saul] *and* the charge of the house of Saul;

³⁰Of the Ephraimites, 20,800, mighty in valor, famous in their fathers' houses;

³¹Of the half-tribe of Manasseh, 18,000, who were mentioned by name to come and make David king;

³²And of Issachar, men who had understanding of the times to know what Israel ought to do, 200 chiefs; and all their kinsmen were under their command;

---

*e*Or, *one that was least* could resist *an hundred, and the greatest a thousand*   *f*Heb. *filled over*   *g*Heb. *before them*   *h*Heb. *be one*   *i*Or, *violence*   *j*Heb. *the spirit clothed Amasai*   *k*Heb. *on our heads*   *l*Or, *with a band*   *m*Or, *captains, or, men*   *n*Heb. *heads*   *o*Or, *prepared*   *p*Heb. *brethren*   *q*Heb. *a multitude of them*   *r*Heb. *men of names*

New American Standard

⁹ Ezer *was* the first, Obadiah the second, Eliab the third,

¹⁰ Mishmannah the fourth, Jeremiah the fifth,

¹¹ Attai the sixth, Eliel the seventh,

¹² Johanan the eighth, Elzabad the ninth,

¹³ Jeremiah the tenth, Machbannai the eleventh.

¹⁴ These of the sons of Gad were captains of the army; he who was least was equal to a hundred and the greatest to a thousand.

¹⁵ These are the ones who crossed the Jordan in the first month when it was overflowing all its banks and they put to flight all those in the valleys, both to the east and to the west.

¹⁶ ¶ Then some of the sons of Benjamin and Judah came to the stronghold to David.

¹⁷ David went out to meet them, and said to them, "If you come peacefully to me to help me, my heart shall be united with you; but if to betray me to my adversaries, since there is no wrong in my hands, may the God of our fathers look on *it* and decide."

¹⁸ Then the Spirit came upon Amasai, who was the chief of the thirty, *and he said,*
"*We* are yours, O David,
And with you, O son of Jesse!
Peace, peace to you,
And peace to him who helps you;
Indeed, your God helps you!"
Then David received them and made them captains of the band.

¹⁹ ¶ From Manasseh also some defected to David when he was about to go to battle with the Philistines against Saul. But they did not help him, for the lords of the Philistines after consultation sent him away, saying, "At *the cost of* our heads he may defect to his master Saul."

²⁰ As he went to Ziklag there defected to him from Manasseh: Adnah, Jozabad, Jediael, Michael, Jozabad, Elihu and Zillethai, captains of thousands who belonged to Manasseh.

²¹ They helped David against the band of raiders, for they were all mighty men of valor, and were captains in the army.

²² For day by day *men* came to David to help him, until there was a great army like the army of God.

Supporters Gathered at Hebron

²³ ¶ Now these are the numbers of the divisions equipped for war, who came to David at Hebron, to turn the kingdom of Saul to him, according to the word of the LORD.

²⁴ The sons of Judah who bore shield and spear *were* 6,800, equipped for war.

²⁵ Of the sons of Simeon, mighty men of valor for war, 7,100.

²⁶ Of the sons of Levi 4,600.

²⁷ Now Jehoiada was the leader of *the house of* Aaron, and with him were 3,700,

²⁸ also Zadok, a young man mighty of valor, and of his father's house twenty-two captains.

²⁹ Of the sons of Benjamin, Saul's kinsmen, 3,000; for until now the greatest part of them had kept their allegiance to the house of Saul.

³⁰ Of the sons of Ephraim 20,800, mighty men of valor, famous men in their fathers' households.

³¹ Of the half-tribe of Manasseh 18,000, who were designated by name to come and make David king.

³² Of the sons of Issachar, men who understood the times, with knowledge of what Israel should do, their chiefs *were* two hundred; and all their kinsmen *were* at their command.

New International

⁹Ezer was the chief,
Obadiah the second in command, Eliab the third,

¹⁰Mishmannah the fourth, Jeremiah the fifth,

¹¹Attai the sixth, Eliel the seventh,

¹²Johanan the eighth, Elzabad the ninth,

¹³Jeremiah the tenth and Macbannai the eleventh.

¹⁴These Gadites were army commanders; the least was a match for a hundred, and the greatest for a thousand. ¹⁵It was they who crossed the Jordan in the first month when it was overflowing all its banks, and they put to flight everyone living in the valleys, to the east and to the west.

¹⁶Other Benjamites and some men from Judah also came to David in his stronghold. ¹⁷David went out to meet them and said to them, "If you have come to me in peace, to help me, I am ready to have you unite with me. But if you have come to betray me to my enemies when my hands are free from violence, may the God of our fathers see it and judge you."

¹⁸Then the Spirit came upon Amasai, chief of the Thirty, and he said:

"We are yours, O David!
We are with you, O son of Jesse!
Success, success to you,
and success to those who help you,
for your God will help you."

So David received them and made them leaders of his raiding bands.

¹⁹Some of the men of Manasseh defected to David when he went with the Philistines to fight against Saul. (He and his men did not help the Philistines because, after consultation, their rulers sent him away. They said, "It will cost us our heads if he deserts to his master Saul.") ²⁰When David went to Ziklag, these were the men of Manasseh who defected to him: Adnah, Jozabad, Jediael, Michael, Jozabad, Elihu and Zillethai, leaders of units of a thousand in Manasseh. ²¹They helped David against raiding bands, for all of them were brave warriors, and they were commanders in his army. ²²Day after day men came to help David, until he had a great army, like the army of God.ˣ

Others Join David at Hebron

²³These are the numbers of the men armed for battle who came to David at Hebron to turn Saul's kingdom over to him, as the LORD had said:

²⁴men of Judah, carrying shield and spear—6,800 armed for battle;

²⁵men of Simeon, warriors ready for battle—7,100;

²⁶men of Levi—4,600, ²⁷including Jehoiada, leader of the family of Aaron, with 3,700 men, ²⁸and Zadok, a brave young warrior, with 22 officers from his family;

²⁹men of Benjamin, Saul's kinsmen—3,000, most of whom had remained loyal to Saul's house until then;

³⁰men of Ephraim, brave warriors, famous in their own clans—20,800;

³¹men of half the tribe of Manasseh, designated by name to come and make David king—18,000;

³²men of Issachar, who understood the times and knew what Israel should do—200 chiefs, with all their relatives under their command;

ˣ22 Or *a great and mighty army*

King James

33Of Zebulun, such as went forth to battle, sexpert in war, with all instruments of war, fifty thousand, which could tkeep rank: they were unot of double heart.

34And of Naphtali a thousand captains, and with them with shield and spear thirty and seven thousand.

35And of the Danites expert in war twenty and eight thousand and six hundred.

36And of Asher, such as went forth to battle, vexpert in war, forty thousand.

37And on the other side of Jordan, of the Reubenites, and the Gadites, and of the half tribe of Manasseh, with all manner of instruments of war for the battle, an hundred and twenty thousand.

38All these men of war, that could keep rank, came with a perfect heart to Hebron, to make David king over all Israel: and all the rest also of Israel were of one heart to make David king.

39And there they were with David three days, eating and drinking: for their brethren had prepared for them.

40Moreover they that were nigh them, even unto Issachar and Zebulun and Naphtali, brought bread on asses, and on camels, and on mules, and on oxen, and wmeat, meal, cakes of figs, and bunches of raisins, and wine, and oil, and oxen, and sheep abundantly: for there was joy in Israel.

The ark taken to Obed-edom

13 AND DAVID consulted with the captains of thousands and hundreds, and with every leader.

2And David said unto all the congregation of Israel, If it seem good unto you, and that it be of the LORD our God, xlet us send abroad unto our brethren every where, that are left in all the land of Israel, and with them also to the priests and Levites which are yin their cities and suburbs, that they may gather themselves unto us:

3And let us zbring again the ark of our God to us: for we inquired not at it in the days of Saul.

4And all the congregation said that they would do so: for the thing was right in the eyes of all the people.

5So David gathered all Israel together, from Shihor of Egypt even unto the entering of Hemath, to bring the ark of God from Kirjath-jearim.

6And David went up, and all Israel, to Baalah, that is, to Kirjath-jearim, which belonged to Judah, to bring up thence the ark of God the LORD, that dwelleth between the cherubims, whose name is called on it.

7And they acarried the ark of God in a new cart out of the house of Abinadab: and Uzza and Ahio drave the cart.

8And David and all Israel played before God with all their might, and with bsinging, and with harps, and with psalteries, and with timbrels, and with cymbals, and with trumpets.

9 ¶ And when they came unto the threshingfloor of cChidon, Uzza put forth his hand to hold the ark; for the oxen dstumbled.

10And the anger of the LORD was kindled against Uzza, and he smote him, because he put his hand to the ark: and there he died before God.

11And David was displeased, because the LORD had made a breach upon Uzza: wherefore that place is called ePerez-uzza to this day.

12And David was afraid of God that day, saying, How shall I bring the ark of God home to me?

13So David fbrought not the ark home to himself to the city of David, but carried it aside into the house of Obed-edom the Gittite.

Amplified

33Of Zebulun, 50,000 experienced troops, fitted out with all kinds of weapons and instruments of war that could order and set the battle in array, men not of double purpose but stable and trustworthy.

34Of Naphtali, 1,000 captains, and with them 37,000 [of the rank and file armed] with shield and spear;

35Of Dan, 28,600, men who could set the battle in array;

36Of Asher, men able to go forth to battle, fit for active service, 40,000;

37On the other [the east] side of the Jordan River, of Reuben and Gad and the half-tribe of Manasseh, 120,000 men, armed with all the weapons and instruments of war.

38All these, being men of war arrayed in battle order, came with a perfect and sincere heart to Hebron to make David king over all Israel; and all the rest also of Israel were of one mind to make David king.

39And they were there with David for three days, eating and drinking, for their brethren had prepared for them.

40Also those who were near them from as far as Issachar, Zebulun, and Naphtali brought food on donkeys, camels, mules, and oxen, abundant supplies of meal, cakes of figs, bunches of raisins, wine, oil, oxen, and sheep, for there was joy in Israel.

13 DAVID CONSULTED the captains of thousands and hundreds, even with every leader.

2And David said to all the assembly of Israel, If it seems good to you and if it is of the Lord our God, let us send abroad everywhere to our brethren who are left in all the land of Israel, and with them to the priests and Levites in their cities that have suburbs and pasturelands, that they may gather together with us.

3And let us bring again the ark of our God to us, for we did not seek it during the days of Saul.

4And all the assembly agreed to do so, for the thing seemed right in the eyes of all the people.

5So David gathered all Israel together, from the Shihor, the brook of Egypt [that marked the southeast border of Palestine], to the entrance of Hemath, to bring the ark of God from Kiriath-jearim.

6And David and all Israel went up to Baalah, that is, to Kiriath-jearim which belonged to Judah, to bring up from there the ark of God the Lord, which is called by the name of Him Who sits [enthroned] above the cherubim.

7And they carried the ark of God on a new cart and brought it out of the house of Abinadab, and Uzza and Ahio [his brother] drove the cart.

8And David and all Israel merrily celebrated before God with all their might, with songs and lyres and harps and tambourines and cymbals and trumpets.

9And when they came to the threshing floor of Chidon, Uzza put out his hand to steady the ark, for the oxen [that were drawing the cart] stumbled and were restive.

10And the anger of the Lord was kindled against Uzza, and He smote him because he touched the ark; and there he died before God. [Num. 4:15.]

11And David was offended because the Lord had broken forth upon Uzza; that place to this day is called Perez-uzza [the breaking forth upon Uzza].

12And David was afraid of God that day, and he said, How can I bring the ark of God home to me?

13So David did not bring the ark home to the City of David, but carried it aside into the house of Obed-edom the Gittite [a Levitical porter born in Gath-rimmon]. [Josh. 21:20, 24; I Chron. 15:24.]

New American Standard

33 Of Zebulun, there were 50,000 who went out in the army, who could draw up in battle formation with all kinds of weapons of war and helped *David* with an undivided heart.

34 Of Naphtali *there were* 1,000 captains, and with them 37,000 with shield and spear.

35 Of the Danites who could draw up in battle formation, *there were* 28,600.

36 Of Asher *there were* 40,000 who went out in the army to draw up in battle formation.

37 From the other side of the Jordan, of the Reubenites and the Gadites and of the half-tribe of Manasseh, *there were* 120,000 with all *kinds* of weapons of war for the battle.

38 ¶ All these, being men of war who could draw up in battle formation, came to Hebron with a perfect heart to make David king over all Israel; and all the rest also of Israel were of one mind to make David king.

39 They were there with David three days, eating and drinking, for their kinsmen had prepared for them.

40 Moreover those who were near to them, *even* as far as Issachar and Zebulun and Naphtali, brought food on donkeys, camels, mules and on oxen, great quantities of flour cakes, fig cakes and bunches of raisins, wine, oil, oxen and sheep. There was joy indeed in Israel.

Peril in Transporting the Ark

13 THEN DAVID consulted with the captains of the thousands and the hundreds, even with every leader.

2 David said to all the assembly of Israel, "If it seems good to you, and if it is from the LORD our God, let us send everywhere to our kinsmen who remain in all the land of Israel, also to the priests and Levites who are with them in their cities with pasture lands, that they may meet with us;

3 and let us bring back the ark of our God to us, for we did not seek it in the days of Saul."

4 Then all the assembly said that they would do so, for the thing was right in the eyes of all the people.

5 ¶ So David assembled all Israel together, from the Shihor of Egypt even to the entrance of Hamath, to bring the ark of God from Kiriath-jearim.

6 David and all Israel went up to Baalah, *that is,* to Kiriath-jearim, which belongs to Judah, to bring up from there the ark of God, the LORD who is enthroned *above* the cherubim, where His name is called.

7 They carried the ark of God on a new cart from the house of Abinadab, and Uzza and Ahio drove the cart.

8 David and all Israel were celebrating before God with all *their* might, even with songs and with lyres, harps, tambourines, cymbals and with trumpets.

9 ¶ When they came to the threshing floor of Chidon, Uzza put out his hand to hold the ark, because the oxen nearly upset *it.*

10 The anger of the LORD burned against Uzza, so He struck him down because he put out his hand to the ark; and he died there before God.

11 Then David became angry because of the LORD's outburst against Uzza; and he called that place *c*Perez-uzza this day.

12 David was afraid of God that day, saying, "How can I bring the ark of God *home* to me?"

13 So David did not take the ark with him to the city of David, but took it aside to the house of Obed-edom the Gittite.

New International

33 men of Zebulun, experienced soldiers prepared for battle with every type of weapon, to help David with undivided loyalty—50,000;

34 men of Naphtali—1,000 officers, together with 37,000 men carrying shields and spears;

35 men of Dan, ready for battle—28,600;

36 men of Asher, experienced soldiers prepared for battle—40,000;

37 and from east of the Jordan, men of Reuben, Gad and the half-tribe of Manasseh, armed with every type of weapon—120,000.

38 All these were fighting men who volunteered to serve in the ranks. They came to Hebron fully determined to make David king over all Israel. All the rest of the Israelites were also of one mind to make David king. 39 The men spent three days there with David, eating and drinking, for their families had supplied provisions for them. 40 Also, their neighbors from as far away as Issachar, Zebulun and Naphtali came bringing food on donkeys, camels, mules and oxen. There were plentiful supplies of flour, fig cakes, raisin cakes, wine, oil, cattle and sheep, for there was joy in Israel.

Bringing Back the Ark

13 DAVID CONFERRED with each of his officers, the commanders of thousands and commanders of hundreds. 2 He then said to the whole assembly of Israel, "If it seems good to you and if it is the will of the LORD our God, let us send word far and wide to the rest of our brothers throughout the territories of Israel, and also to the priests and Levites who are with them in their towns and pasturelands, to come and join us. 3 Let us bring the ark of our God back to us, for we did not inquire of*y* it*z* during the reign of Saul." 4 The whole assembly agreed to do this, because it seemed right to all the people.

5 So David assembled all the Israelites, from the Shihor River in Egypt to Lebo*a* Hamath, to bring the ark of God from Kiriath Jearim. 6 David and all the Israelites with him went to Baalah of Judah (Kiriath Jearim) to bring up from there the ark of God the LORD, who is enthroned between the cherubim—the ark that is called by the Name.

7 They moved the ark of God from Abinadab's house on a new cart, with Uzzah and Ahio guiding it. 8 David and all the Israelites were celebrating with all their might before God, with songs and with harps, lyres, tambourines, cymbals and trumpets.

9 When they came to the threshing floor of Kidon, Uzzah reached out his hand to steady the ark, because the oxen stumbled. 10 The LORD's anger burned against Uzzah, and he struck him down because he had put his hand on the ark. So he died there before God.

11 Then David was angry because the LORD's wrath had broken out against Uzzah, and to this day that place is called Perez Uzzah.*b*

12 David was afraid of God that day and asked, "How can I ever bring the ark of God to me?" 13 He did not take the ark to be with him in the City of David. Instead, he took

---

c I.e. the breakthrough of Uzza

y 3 Or *we neglected*　　*z 3* Or *him*　　*a 5* Or *to the entrance to*
b 11 *Perez Uzzah* means *outbreak against Uzzah.*

King James

14And the ark of God remained with the family of Obed-edom in his house three months. And the LORD blessed the house of Obed-edom, and all that he had.

David defeats the Philistines

14 NOW HIRAM king of Tyre sent messengers to David, and timber of cedars, with masons and carpenters, to build him an house.

2And David perceived that the LORD had confirmed him king over Israel, for his kingdom was lifted up on high, because of his people Israel.

3 ¶ And David took *g*more wives at Jerusalem: and David begat more sons and daughters.

4Now these *are* the names of *his* children which he had in Jerusalem; Shammua, and Shobab, Nathan, and Solomon,

5And Ibhar, and Elishua, and Elpalet,

6And Nogah, and Nepheg, and Japhia,

7And Elishama, and *h*Beeliada, and Eliphalet.

8 ¶ And when the Philistines heard that David was anointed king over all Israel, all the Philistines went up to seek David. And David heard *of it,* and went out against them.

9And the Philistines came and spread themselves in the valley of Rephaim.

10And David inquired of God, saying, Shall I go up against the Philistines? and wilt thou deliver them into mine hand? And the LORD said unto him, Go up; for I will deliver them into thine hand.

11So they came up to Baal-perazim; and David smote them there. Then David said, God hath broken in upon mine enemies by mine hand like the breaking forth of waters: therefore they called the name of that place *i*Baal-perazim.

12And when they had left their gods there, David gave a commandment, and they were burned with fire.

13And the Philistines yet again spread themselves abroad in the valley.

14Therefore David inquired again of God; and God said unto him, Go not up after them; turn away from them, and come upon them over against the mulberry trees.

15And it shall be, when thou shalt hear a sound of going in the tops of the mulberry trees, *that* then thou shalt go out to battle: for God is gone forth before thee to smite the host of the Philistines.

16David therefore did as God commanded him: and they smote the host of the Philistines from Gibeon even to Gazer.

17And the fame of David went out into all lands; and the LORD brought the fear of him upon all nations.

The ark brought to Jerusalem

15 AND *DAVID* made him houses in the city of David, and prepared a place for the ark of God, and pitched for it a tent.

2Then David said, *j*None ought to carry the ark of God but the Levites: for them hath the LORD chosen to carry the ark of God, and to minister unto him for ever.

3And David gathered all Israel together to Jerusalem, to bring up the ark of the LORD unto his place, which he had prepared for it.

4And David assembled the children of Aaron, and the Levites:

5Of the sons of Kohath; Uriel the chief, and his *k*brethren an hundred and twenty:

6Of the sons of Merari; Asaiah the chief, and his brethren two hundred and twenty:

Amplified

14And the ark of God remained with the family of Obed-edom in his house three months. And the Lord blessed the house of Obed-edom and all that he had.

14 AND HIRAM king of Tyre sent messengers to David, and cedar timbers, with masons and carpenters, to build him a house.

2And David perceived that the Lord had established *and* confirmed him as king over Israel, for his kingdom was exalted highly for His people Israel's sake.

3And David took more wives to Jerusalem, and [he] became the father of more sons and daughters.

4Now these are the names of the children whom he had in Jerusalem: Shammua, Shobab, Nathan, Solomon,

5Ibhar, Elishua, Elpelet,

6Nogah, Nepheg, Japhia,

7Elishama, Beeliada, and Eliphelet.

8And when the Philistines heard that David was anointed king over all Israel, [they] all went up to seek David. And [he] heard of it and went out before them.

9Now the Philistines had come and made a raid in the Valley of Rephaim.

10David asked God, Shall I go up against the Philistines? And will You deliver them into my hand? And the Lord said, Go up, and I will deliver them into your hand.

11So [Israel] came up to Baal-perazim, and David smote [the Philistines] there. Then David said, God has broken my enemies by my hand, like the bursting forth of waters. Therefore they called the name of that place Baal-perazim [Lord of breaking through].

12[The Philistines] left their gods there; David commanded and they were burned.

13And the Philistines again made a raid in the valley.

14And David inquired again of God, and God said to him, Do not go up after them; turn away from them and come [around] upon them over opposite the mulberry trees.

15And when you hear a sound of marching in the tops of the mulberry *or* balsam trees, then go out to battle, for God has gone out before you to smite the Philistine host.

16So David did as God commanded him, and they smote the army of the Philistines from Gibeon even to Gezer.

17And the fame of David went out into all lands, and the Lord brought the fear of him upon all nations.

15 DAVID MADE for himself houses in the City of David, and he prepared a place for the ark of God and pitched a tent for it.

2Then David said, None should carry the ark of God but the Levites, for the Lord chose them to carry the ark of God and to minister to Him forever.

3And David assembled all Israel at Jerusalem to bring up the ark of the Lord to its place, which he had prepared for it.

4And David gathered together the sons of Aaron and the Levites:

5Of the sons of Kohath, Uriel the chief, with 120 kinsmen;

6Of the sons of Merari, Asaiah the chief, with 220 kinsmen;

---

g Heb. *yet breaches*　　*h* Or, *Eliada;* see 2 Sam. 5:16　　*i* i.e. *A place of Levites*　　*j* Heb. It is *not to carry the ark of God, but for the Levites*　　*k* Or, *kinsmen*

New American Standard

14 Thus the ark of God remained with the family of Obed-edom in his house three months; and the LORD blessed the family of Obed-edom with all that he had.

David's Family Enlarged

14 NOW HIRAM king of Tyre sent messengers to David with cedar trees, masons and carpenters, to build a house for him. 2 And David realized that the LORD had established him as king over Israel, *and* that his kingdom was highly exalted, for the sake of His people Israel.

3 ¶ Then David took more wives at Jerusalem, and David became the father of more sons and daughters. 4 These are the names of the children born *to him* in Jerusalem: Shammua, Shobab, Nathan, Solomon, 5 Ibhar, Elishua, Elpelet, 6 Nogah, Nepheg, Japhia, 7 Elishama, Beeliada and Eliphelet.

Philistines Defeated

8 ¶ When the Philistines heard that David had been anointed king over all Israel, all the Philistines went up in search of David; and David heard of it and went out against them. 9 Now the Philistines had come and made a raid in the valley of Rephaim. 10 David inquired of God, saying, "Shall I go up against the Philistines? And will You give them into my hand?" Then the LORD said to him, "Go up, for I will give them into your hand." 11 So they came up to Baal-perazim, and David defeated them there; and David said, "God has broken through my enemies by my hand, like the breakthrough of waters." Therefore they named that place *d*Baal-perazim. 12 They abandoned their gods there; so David gave the order and they were burned with fire. 13 ¶ The Philistines made yet another raid in the valley. 14 David inquired again of God, and God said to him, "You shall not go up after them; circle around behind them and come at them in front of the balsam trees. 15 "It shall be when you hear the sound of marching in the tops of the balsam trees, then you shall go out to battle, for God will have gone out before you to strike the army of the Philistines." 16 David did just as God had commanded him, and they struck down the army of the Philistines from Gibeon even as far as Gezer. 17 Then the fame of David went out into all the lands; and the LORD brought the fear of him on all the nations.

Plans to Move the Ark to Jerusalem

15 NOW *DAVID* built houses for himself in the city of David; and he prepared a place for the ark of God and pitched a tent for it. 2 Then David said, "No one is to carry the ark of God but the Levites; for the LORD chose them to carry the ark of God and to minister to Him forever." 3 And David assembled all Israel at Jerusalem to bring up the ark of the LORD to its place which he had prepared for it. 4 David gathered together the sons of Aaron and the Levites: 5 of the sons of Kohath, Uriel the chief, and 120 of his relatives; 6 of the sons of Merari, Asaiah the chief, and 220 of his relatives;

New International

it aside to the house of Obed-Edom the Gittite. 14 The ark of God remained with the family of Obed-Edom in his house for three months, and the LORD blessed his household and everything he had.

David's House and Family

14 NOW HIRAM king of Tyre sent messengers to David, along with cedar logs, stonemasons and carpenters to build a palace for him. 2 And David knew that the LORD had established him as king over Israel and that his kingdom had been highly exalted for the sake of his people Israel.

3 In Jerusalem David took more wives and became the father of more sons and daughters. 4 These are the names of the children born to him there: Shammua, Shobab, Nathan, Solomon, 5 Ibhar, Elishua, Elpelet, 6 Nogah, Nepheg, Japhia, 7 Elishama, Beeliada*c* and Eliphelet.

David Defeats the Philistines

8 When the Philistines heard that David had been anointed king over all Israel, they went up in full force to search for him, but David heard about it and went out to meet them. 9 Now the Philistines had come and raided the Valley of Rephaim; 10 so David inquired of God: "Shall I go and attack the Philistines? Will you hand them over to me?"

The LORD answered him, "Go, I will hand them over to you."

11 So David and his men went up to Baal Perazim, and there he defeated them. He said, "As waters break out, God has broken out against my enemies by my hand." So that place was called Baal Perazim.*d* 12 The Philistines had abandoned their gods there, and David gave orders to burn them in the fire.

13 Once more the Philistines raided the valley; 14 so David inquired of God again, and God answered him, "Do not go straight up, but circle around them and attack them in front of the balsam trees. 15 As soon as you hear the sound of marching in the tops of the balsam trees, move out to battle, because that will mean God has gone out in front of you to strike the Philistine army." 16 So David did as God commanded him, and they struck down the Philistine army, all the way from Gibeon to Gezer.

17 So David's fame spread throughout every land, and the LORD made all the nations fear him.

The Ark Brought to Jerusalem

15 AFTER DAVID had constructed buildings for himself in the City of David, he prepared a place for the ark of God and pitched a tent for it. 2 Then David said, "No one but the Levites may carry the ark of God, because the LORD chose them to carry the ark of the LORD and to minister before him forever."

3 David assembled all Israel in Jerusalem to bring up the ark of the LORD to the place he had prepared for it. 4 He called together the descendants of Aaron and the Levites: 5 From the descendants of Kohath,
    Uriel the leader and 120 relatives;
6 from the descendants of Merari,
    Asaiah the leader and 220 relatives;

---

*d*I.e. the master of breakthrough

c 7 A variant of *Eliada*   *d 11 Baal Perazim* means *the lord who breaks out.*

King James

Amplified

7Of the sons of Gershom; Joel the chief, and his brethren an hundred and thirty:

8Of the sons of Elizaphan; Shemaiah the chief, and his brethren two hundred:

9Of the sons of Hebron; Eliel the chief, and his brethren fourscore:

10Of the sons of Uzziel; Amminadab the chief, and his brethren an hundred and twelve.

11And David called for Zadok and Abiathar the priests, and for the Levites, for Uriel, Asaiah, and Joel, Shemaiah, and Eliel, and Amminadab,

12And said unto them, Ye *are* the chief of the fathers of the Levites: Sanctify yourselves, *both* ye and your brethren, that ye may bring up the ark of the LORD God of Israel unto *the place that* I have prepared for it.

13For because ye *did it* not at the first, the LORD our God made a breach upon us, for that we sought him not after the due order.

14So the priests and the Levites sanctified themselves to bring up the ark of the LORD God of Israel.

15And the children of the Levites bare the ark of God upon their shoulders with the staves thereon, as Moses commanded according to the word of the LORD.

16And David spake to the chief of the Levites to appoint their brethren *to be* the singers with instruments of music, psalteries and harps and cymbals, sounding, by lifting up the voice with joy.

17So the Levites appointed Heman the son of Joel; and of his brethren, Asaph the son of Berechiah; and of the sons of Merari their brethren, Ethan the son of Kushaiah;

18And with them their brethren of the second *degree*, Zechariah, Ben, and Jaaziel, and Shemiramoth, and Jehiel, and Unni, Eliab, and Benaiah, and Maaseiah, and Mattithiah, and Elipheleh, and Mikneiah, and Obed-edom, and Jeiel, the porters.

19So the singers, Heman, Asaph, and Ethan, *were appointed* to sound with cymbals of brass;

20And Zechariah, and *I*Aziel, and Shemiramoth, and Jehiel, and Unni, and Eliab, and Maaseiah, and Benaiah, with psalteries on Alamoth;

21And Mattithiah, and Elipheleh, and Mikneiah, and Obed-edom, and Jeiel, and Azaziah, with harps on the Sheminith to excel.

22And Chenaniah, chief of the Levites, *m*was for *n*song: he instructed about the song, because he *was* skilful.

23And Berechiah and Elkanah *were* doorkeepers for the ark.

24And Shebaniah, and Jehoshaphat, and Nethaneel, and Amasai, and Zechariah, and Benaiah, and Eliezer, the priests, did blow with the trumpets before the ark of God: and Obed-edom and Jehiah *were* doorkeepers for the ark.

25 ¶ So David, and the elders of Israel, and the captains over thousands, went to bring up the ark of the covenant of the LORD out of the house of Obed-edom with joy.

26And it came to pass, when God helped the Levites that bare the ark of the covenant of the LORD, that they offered seven bullocks and seven rams.

27And David *was* clothed with a robe of fine linen, and all the Levites that bare the ark, and the singers, and Chenaniah the master of the *o*song with the singers: David also *had* upon him an ephod of linen.

28Thus all Israel brought up the ark of the covenant of the LORD with shouting, and with sound of the cornet, and with trumpets, and with cymbals, making a noise with psalteries and harps.

29 ¶ And it came to pass, *as* the ark of the covenant of the LORD came to the city of David, that Michal the daughter of Saul looking out at a window saw king David dancing and playing: and she despised him in her heart.

7Of the sons of Gershom, Joel the chief, with 130 kinsmen;

8Of the sons of Elizaphan, Shemaiah the chief, with 200 kinsmen;

9Of the sons of Hebron, Eliel the chief, with 80 kinsmen;

10Of the sons of Uzziel, Amminadab the chief, with 112 kinsmen.

11And David called for Zadok and Abiathar the priests, and for the Levites—Uriel, Asaiah, Joel, Shemaiah, Eliel, and Amminadab,

12And said to them, You are the heads of the fathers' houses of the Levites; sanctify yourselves, both you and your brethren, that you may bring up the ark of the Lord, the God of Israel, to the place that I have prepared for it.

13For because you bore it not [as God directed] at the first, the Lord our God broke forth upon us—because we did not seek Him in the way He ordained. [Num. 1:50; I Chron. 13:7–10.]

14So the priests and the Levites sanctified themselves to bring up the ark of the Lord, the God of Israel.

15The Levites carried the ark of God on their shoulders with the poles, as Moses commanded by the word of the Lord.

16David told the chief Levites to appoint their brethren the singers with instruments of music—harps, lyres, and cymbals—to play loudly and lift up their voices with joy.

17So the Levites appointed Heman son of Joel; and of his brethren, Asaph son of Berechiah; and of the sons of Merari their brethren, Ethan son of Kushaiah;

18And with them their brethren of the second class: Zechariah, Ben, Jaaziel, Shemiramoth, Jehiel, Unni, Benaiah, Maaseiah, Mattithiah, Eliphelehu, and Mikneiah, and also the gatekeepers, Obed-edom and Jeiel.

19So the singers Heman, Asaph, and Ethan, were appointed to sound bronze cymbals;

20Zechariah, Aziel, Shemiramoth, Jehiel, Unni, Eliab, Maaseiah, and Benaiah were to play harps [resembling guitars] set to Alamoth [probably the treble voice];

21Mattithiah, Eliphelehu, Mikneiah, Obed-edom, Jeiel, and Azaziah were to lead with lyres set to Sheminith [the bass voice].

22Chenaniah, leader of the Levites in singing, was put in charge of carrying the ark *and* lifting up song. He instructed about these matters because he was skilled *and* able.

23Berechiah and Elkanah were gatekeepers for the ark.

24Shebaniah, Joshaphat, Nethanel, Amasai, Zechariah, Benaiah, and Eliezer the priests were to blow the trumpets before the ark of God. And Obed-edom and Jehiah (Jeiel) were also gatekeepers for the ark.

25So David, the elders of Israel, and the captains over thousands went to bring up the ark of the covenant of the Lord out of the house of Obed-edom with joy.

26And when God helped the Levites who carried the ark of the covenant of the Lord [with a safe start], they offered seven bulls and seven rams.

27David was clothed with a robe of fine linen, as were the Levites who bore the ark, and the singers, and Chenaniah, director of the music of the singers. David also wore an ephod [a priestly upper garment] of linen;

28Thus all Israel brought up the ark of the covenant of the Lord with shouting, sound of the cornet, trumpets, and cymbals, sounding aloud with harps and lyres.

29As the ark of the covenant of the Lord came to the City of David, Michal [David's wife] daughter of Saul, looking from a window, saw King David leaping as in sport, and she despised him in her heart.

---

*I*Or, *Jaaziel;* see ver. 18   *m*Or, was *for the carriage: he instructed about the carriage*   *n*Heb. *lifting up*   *o*Or,
carriage

New American Standard

7 of the sons of Gershom, Joel the chief, and 130 of his relatives;

8 of the sons of Elizaphan, Shemaiah the chief, and 200 of his relatives;

9 of the sons of Hebron, Eliel the chief, and 80 of his relatives;

10 of the sons of Uzziel, Amminadab the chief, and 112 of his relatives.

11 ¶ Then David called for Zadok and Abiathar the priests, and for the Levites, for Uriel, Asaiah, Joel, Shemaiah, Eliel and Amminadab,

12 and said to them, "You are the heads of the fathers' *households* of the Levites; consecrate yourselves both you and your relatives, that you may bring up the ark of the LORD God of Israel to *the place* that I have prepared for it.

13 "Because you did not *carry it* at the first, the LORD our God made an outburst on us, for we did not seek Him according to the ordinance."

14 So the priests and the Levites consecrated themselves to bring up the ark of the LORD God of Israel.

15 The sons of the Levites carried the ark of God on their shoulders with the poles thereon, as Moses had commanded according to the word of the LORD.

16 ¶ Then David spoke to the chiefs of the Levites to appoint their relatives the singers, with instruments of music, harps, lyres, loud-sounding cymbals, to raise sounds of joy.

17 So the Levites appointed Heman the son of Joel, and from his relatives, Asaph the son of Berechiah; and from the sons of Merari their relatives, Ethan the son of Kushaiah,

18 and with them their relatives of the second rank, Zechariah, Ben, Jaaziel, Shemiramoth, Jehiel, Unni, Eliab, Benaiah, Maaseiah, Mattithiah, Eliphelehu, Mikneiah, Obed-edom and Jeiel, the gatekeepers.

19 So the singers, Heman, Asaph and Ethan *were appointed* to sound aloud cymbals of bronze;

20 and Zechariah, Aziel, Shemiramoth, Jehiel, Unni, Eliab, Maaseiah and Benaiah, with harps *tuned* to alamoth;

21 and Mattithiah, Eliphelehu, Mikneiah, Obed-edom, Jeiel and Azaziah, to lead with lyres tuned to the sheminith.

22 Chenaniah, chief of the Levites, was *in charge of* the singing; he gave instruction in singing because he was skillful.

23 Berechiah and Elkanah were gatekeepers for the ark.

24 Shebaniah, Joshaphat, Nethanel, Amasai, Zechariah, Benaiah and Eliezer, the priests, blew the trumpets before the ark of God. Obed-edom and Jehiah also *were* gatekeepers for the ark.

25 ¶ So *it was* David, with the elders of Israel and the captains over thousands, who went to bring up the ark of the covenant of the LORD from the house of Obed-edom with joy.

26 Because God was helping the Levites who were carrying the ark of the covenant of the LORD, they sacrificed seven bulls and seven rams.

27 Now David was clothed with a robe of fine linen with all the Levites who were carrying the ark, and the singers and Chenaniah the leader of the singing *with* the singers. David also wore an ephod of linen.

28 Thus all Israel brought up the ark of the covenant of the LORD with shouting, and with sound of the horn, with trumpets, with loud-sounding cymbals, with harps and lyres.

29 ¶ It happened when the ark of the covenant of the LORD came to the city of David, that Michal the daughter of Saul looked out of the window and saw King David leaping and celebrating; and she despised him in her heart.

New International

7 from the descendants of Gershon,*e*
    Joel the leader and 130 relatives;

8 from the descendants of Elizaphan,
    Shemaiah the leader and 200 relatives;

9 from the descendants of Hebron,
    Eliel the leader and 80 relatives;

10 from the descendants of Uzziel,
    Amminadab the leader and 112 relatives.

11 Then David summoned Zadok and Abiathar the priests, and Uriel, Asaiah, Joel, Shemaiah, Eliel and Amminadab the Levites. 12 He said to them, "You are the heads of the Levitical families; you and your fellow Levites are to consecrate yourselves and bring up the ark of the LORD, the God of Israel, to the place I have prepared for it. 13 It was because you, the Levites, did not bring it up the first time that the LORD our God broke out in anger against us. We did not inquire of him about how to do it in the prescribed way." 14 So the priests and Levites consecrated themselves in order to bring up the ark of the LORD, the God of Israel. 15 And the Levites carried the ark of God with the poles on their shoulders, as Moses had commanded in accordance with the word of the LORD.

16 David told the leaders of the Levites to appoint their brothers as singers to sing joyful songs, accompanied by musical instruments: lyres, harps and cymbals.

17 So the Levites appointed Heman son of Joel; from his brothers, Asaph son of Berekiah; and from their brothers the Merarites, Ethan son of Kushaiah; 18 and with them their brothers next in rank: Zechariah,*f* Jaaziel, Shemiramoth, Jehiel, Unni, Eliab, Benaiah, Maaseiah, Mattithiah, Eliphelehu, Mikneiah, Obed-Edom and Jeiel,*g* the gatekeepers.

19 The musicians Heman, Asaph and Ethan were to sound the bronze cymbals; 20 Zechariah, Aziel, Shemiramoth, Jehiel, Unni, Eliab, Maaseiah and Benaiah were to play the lyres according to *alamoth,*h 21 and Mattithiah, Eliphelehu, Mikneiah, Obed-Edom, Jeiel and Azaziah were to play the harps, directing according to *sheminith.*h 22 Kenaniah the head Levite was in charge of the singing; that was his responsibility because he was skillful at it.

23 Berekiah and Elkanah were to be doorkeepers for the ark. 24 Shebaniah, Joshaphat, Nethanel, Amasai, Zechariah, Benaiah and Eliezer the priests were to blow trumpets before the ark of God. Obed-Edom and Jehiah were also to be doorkeepers for the ark.

25 So David and the elders of Israel and the commanders of units of a thousand went to bring up the ark of the covenant of the LORD from the house of Obed-Edom, with rejoicing. 26 Because God had helped the Levites who were carrying the ark of the covenant of the LORD, seven bulls and seven rams were sacrificed. 27 Now David was clothed in a robe of fine linen, as were all the Levites who were carrying the ark, and as were the singers, and Kenaniah, who was in charge of the singing of the choirs. David also wore a linen ephod. 28 So all Israel brought up the ark of the covenant of the LORD with shouts, with the sounding of rams' horns and trumpets, and of cymbals, and the playing of lyres and harps.

29 As the ark of the covenant of the LORD was entering the City of David, Michal daughter of Saul watched from a window. And when she saw King David dancing and celebrating, she despised him in her heart.

King James

16 SO THEY brought the ark of God, and set it in the midst of the tent that David had pitched for it: and they offered burnt sacrifices and peace offerings before God.

2 And when David had made an end of offering the burnt offerings and the peace offerings, he blessed the people in the name of the LORD.

3 And he dealt to every one of Israel, both man and woman, to every one a loaf of bread, and a good piece of flesh, and a flagon *of wine.*

4 ¶ And he appointed *certain* of the Levites to minister before the ark of the LORD, and to record, and to thank and praise the LORD God of Israel:

5 Asaph the chief, and next to him Zechariah, Jeiel, and Shemiramoth, and Jehiel, and Mattithiah, and Eliab, and Benaiah, and Obed-edom: and Jeiel [p]with psalteries and with harps; but Asaph made a sound with cymbals;

6 Benaiah also and Jahaziel the priests with trumpets continually before the ark of the covenant of God.

David's psalm of gratitude

7 ¶ Then on that day David delivered first *this psalm* to thank the LORD into the hand of Asaph and his brethren.

8 Give thanks unto the LORD, call upon his name, make known his deeds among the people.

9 Sing unto him, sing psalms unto him, talk ye of all his wondrous works.

10 Glory ye in his holy name: let the heart of them rejoice that seek the LORD.

11 Seek the LORD and his strength, seek his face continually.

12 Remember his marvellous works that he hath done, his wonders, and the judgments of his mouth;

13 O ye seed of Israel his servant, ye children of Jacob, his chosen ones.

14 He *is* the LORD our God; his judgments *are* in all the earth.

15 Be ye mindful always of his covenant; the word *which* he commanded to a thousand generations;

16 *Even of the covenant* which he made with Abraham, and of his oath unto Isaac;

17 And hath confirmed the same to Jacob for a law, *and* to Israel *for* an everlasting covenant,

18 Saying, Unto thee will I give the land of Canaan, [q]the lot of your inheritance;

19 When ye were but [r]few, even a few, and strangers in it.

20 And *when* they went from nation to nation, and from *one* kingdom to another people;

21 He suffered no man to do them wrong: yea, he reproved kings for their sakes,

22 *Saying,* Touch not mine anointed, and do my prophets no harm.

23 Sing unto the LORD, all the earth; show forth from day to day his salvation.

24 Declare his glory among the heathen; his marvellous works among all nations.

25 For great *is* the LORD, and greatly to be praised: he also *is* to be feared above all gods.

26 For all the gods of the people *are* idols: but the LORD made the heavens.

27 Glory and honour *are* in his presence; strength and gladness *are* in his place.

[p] Heb. *with instruments of psalteries and harps* [q] Heb. *the cord*
[r] Heb. *men of number*

Amplified

16 SO THEY brought the ark of God and set it in the midst of the tent which David had pitched for it, and they offered burnt offerings and peace offerings before God.

2 And when David had finished offering the burnt offerings and the peace offerings, he blessed the people in the name of the Lord.

3 And he distributed to everyone of Israel, both man and woman, to everyone a loaf of bread, a portion of meat, and a cake of raisins.

4 He appointed Levites to minister before the ark of the Lord and to celebrate [by calling to mind], thanking and praising the Lord, the God of Israel:

5 Asaph was the chief, next to him Zechariah, Jeiel (Jaaziel), Shemiramoth, Jehiel, Mattithiah, Eliab, and Benaiah, Obed-edom and Jeiel, who were to play harps and lyres; Asaph was to sound the cymbals;

6 Benaiah and Jahaziel the priests were to blow trumpets continually before the ark of the covenant of God.

7 Then on that day David first entrusted to Asaph and his brethren the singing of thanks to the Lord [as their chief task]:

8 O give thanks to the Lord, call on His name; make known His doings among the peoples!

9 Sing to Him, sing praises to Him; meditate on *and* talk of all His wondrous works *and* devoutly praise them!

10 Glory in His holy name; let the hearts of those rejoice who seek the Lord!

11 Seek the Lord and His strength; yearn for *and* seek His face *and* to be in His presence continually!

12 [Earnestly] remember the marvelous deeds which He has done, His miracles, and the judgments He uttered [as in Egypt],

13 O you offspring of [Abraham and] of Israel His servants, you children of Jacob, His chosen ones!

14 He is the Lord our God; His judgments are in all the earth.

15 Be mindful of His covenant forever, the promise which He commanded *and* established to a thousand generations,

16 The covenant which He made with Abraham, and His sworn promise to Isaac.

17 He confirmed it as a statute to Jacob, and to Israel for an everlasting covenant, [Gen. 35:11, 12.]

18 Saying, To you I will give the land of Canaan, the measured portion of your possession *and* inheritance.

19 When they were but few, even a very few, and only temporary residents *and* strangers in it,

20 When they went from nation to nation, and from one kingdom to another people,

21 He allowed no man to do them wrong; yes, He reproved kings for their sakes, [Gen. 12:17; 20:3; Exod. 7:15–18.]

22 Saying, Touch not My anointed, and do My prophets no harm. [Gen. 20:7.]

23 Sing to the Lord, all the earth; show forth from day to day His salvation.

24 Declare His glory among the nations, His marvelous works among all peoples.

25 For great is the Lord and greatly to be praised; He also is to be [reverently] feared above all so-called gods.

26 For all the gods of the people are [lifeless] idols, but the Lord made the heavens.

27 Honor and majesty are [found] in His presence; strength and joy are [found] in His sanctuary.

New American Standard

A Tent for the Ark

16 AND THEY brought in the ark of God and placed it inside the tent which David had pitched for it, and they offered burnt offerings and peace offerings before God.
2 When David had finished offering the burnt offering and the peace offerings, he blessed the people in the name of the LORD.
3 He distributed to everyone of Israel, both man and woman, to everyone a loaf of bread and a portion *of meat* and a raisin cake.
4 ¶ He appointed some of the Levites *as* ministers before the ark of the LORD, even to celebrate and to thank and praise the LORD God of Israel:
5 Asaph the chief, and second to him Zechariah, *then* Jeiel, Shemiramoth, Jehiel, Mattithiah, Eliab, Benaiah, Obed-edom and Jeiel, with musical instruments, harps, lyres; also Asaph *played* loud-sounding cymbals,
6 and Benaiah and Jahaziel the priests *blew* trumpets continually before the ark of the covenant of God.
7 ¶ Then on that day David first assigned Asaph and his relatives to give thanks to the LORD.

Psalm of Thanksgiving

8 Oh give thanks to the LORD, call upon His name;
Make known His deeds among the peoples.
9 Sing to Him, sing praises to Him;
*e*Speak of all His wonders.
10 Glory in His holy name;
Let the heart of those who seek the LORD be glad.
11 Seek the LORD and His strength;
Seek His face continually.
12 Remember His wonderful deeds which He has done,
His marvels and the judgments from His mouth,
13 O seed of Israel His servant,
Sons of Jacob, His chosen ones!
14 He is the LORD our God;
His judgments are in all the earth.
15 Remember His covenant forever,
The word which He commanded to a thousand generations,
16 *The covenant* which He made with Abraham,
And His oath to Isaac.
17 He also confirmed it to Jacob for a statute,
To Israel as an everlasting covenant,
18 Saying, "To you I will give the land of Canaan,
As the portion of your inheritance."
19 When they were only a few in number,
Very few, and strangers in it,
20 And they wandered about from nation to nation,
And from *one* kingdom to another people,
21 He permitted no man to oppress them,
And He reproved kings for their sakes, *saying,*
22 "Do not touch My anointed ones,
And do My prophets no harm."
23 Sing to the LORD, all the earth;
Proclaim good tidings of His salvation from day to day.
24 Tell of His glory among the nations,
His wonderful deeds among all the peoples.
25 For great is the LORD, and greatly to be praised;
He also is to be feared above all gods.
26 For all the gods of the peoples are idols,
But the LORD made the heavens.
27 Splendor and majesty are before Him,
Strength and joy are in His place.

New International

16 THEY BROUGHT the ark of God and set it inside the tent that David had pitched for it, and they presented burnt offerings and fellowship offerings[i] before God. 2After David had finished sacrificing the burnt offerings and fellowship offerings, he blessed the people in the name of the LORD. 3Then he gave a loaf of bread, a cake of dates and a cake of raisins to each Israelite man and woman.
4He appointed some of the Levites to minister before the ark of the LORD, to make petition, to give thanks, and to praise the LORD, the God of Israel: 5Asaph was the chief, Zechariah second, then Jeiel, Shemiramoth, Jehiel, Mattithiah, Eliab, Benaiah, Obed-Edom and Jeiel. They were to play the lyres and harps, Asaph was to sound the cymbals, 6and Benaiah and Jahaziel the priests were to blow the trumpets regularly before the ark of the covenant of God.

David's Psalm of Thanks

7That day David first committed to Asaph and his associates this psalm of thanks to the LORD:

8Give thanks to the LORD, call on his name;
make known among the nations what he has done.
9Sing to him, sing praise to him;
tell of all his wonderful acts.
10Glory in his holy name;
let the hearts of those who seek the LORD rejoice.
11Look to the LORD and his strength;
seek his face always.
12Remember the wonders he has done,
his miracles, and the judgments he pronounced,
13O descendants of Israel his servant,
O sons of Jacob, his chosen ones.
14He is the LORD our God;
his judgments are in all the earth.
15He remembers[j] his covenant forever,
the word he commanded, for a thousand generations,
16the covenant he made with Abraham,
the oath he swore to Isaac.
17He confirmed it to Jacob as a decree,
to Israel as an everlasting covenant:
18"To you I will give the land of Canaan
as the portion you will inherit."
19When they were but few in number,
few indeed, and strangers in it,
20they[k] wandered from nation to nation,
from one kingdom to another.
21He allowed no man to oppress them;
for their sake he rebuked kings:
22"Do not touch my anointed ones;
do my prophets no harm."
23Sing to the LORD, all the earth;
proclaim his salvation day after day.
24Declare his glory among the nations,
his marvelous deeds among all peoples.
25For great is the LORD and most worthy of praise;
he is to be feared above all gods.
26For all the gods of the nations are idols,
but the LORD made the heavens.
27Splendor and majesty are before him;
strength and joy in his dwelling place.

---

*i 1 Traditionally peace offerings; also in verse 2   j 15 Some
Septuagint manuscripts (see also Psalm 105:8); Hebrew Remember
k 18-20 One Hebrew manuscript, Septuagint and Vulgate (see also
Psalm 105:12); most Hebrew manuscripts inherit, / 19though you are
but few in number, / few indeed, and strangers in it." / 20They*

e Or Meditate on

King James

²⁸Give unto the LORD, ye kindreds of the people, give unto the LORD glory and strength.

²⁹Give unto the LORD the glory *due* unto his name: bring an offering, and come before him: worship the LORD in the beauty of holiness.

³⁰Fear before him, all the earth: the world also shall be stable, that it be not moved.

³¹Let the heavens be glad, and let the earth rejoice: and let *men* say among the nations, The LORD reigneth.

³²Let the sea roar, and the fulness thereof: let the fields rejoice, and all that *is* therein.

³³Then shall the trees of the wood sing out at the presence of the LORD, because he cometh to judge the earth.

³⁴O give thanks unto the LORD; for *he is* good; for his mercy *endureth* for ever.

³⁵And say ye, Save us, O God of our salvation, and gather us together, and deliver us from the heathen, that we may give thanks to thy holy name, *and* glory in thy praise.

³⁶Blessed *be* the LORD God of Israel for ever and ever. And all the people said, Amen, and praised the LORD.

³⁷ ¶ So he left there before the ark of the covenant of the LORD Asaph and his brethren, to minister before the ark continually, as every day's work required:

³⁸And Obed-edom with their brethren, threescore and eight; Obed-edom also the son of Jeduthun and Hosah *to be* porters.

³⁹And Zadok the priest, and his brethren the priests, before the tabernacle of the LORD in the high place that *was* at Gibeon,

⁴⁰To offer burnt offerings unto the LORD upon the altar of the burnt offering continually ˢmorning and evening, and *to do* according to all that is written in the law of the LORD, which he commanded Israel;

⁴¹And with them Heman and Jeduthun, and the rest that were chosen, who were expressed by name, to give thanks to the LORD, because his mercy *endureth* for ever;

⁴²And with them Heman and Jeduthun with trumpets and cymbals for those that should make a sound, and with musical instruments of God. And the sons of Jeduthun *were* ᵗporters.

⁴³And all the people departed every man to his house: and David returned to bless his house.

Nathan's warning to David

17 NOW IT came to pass, as David sat in his house, that David said to Nathan the prophet, Lo, I dwell in an house of cedars, but the ark of the covenant of the LORD *remaineth* under curtains.

²Then Nathan said unto David, Do all that *is* in thine heart; for God *is* with thee.

³ ¶ And it came to pass the same night, that the word of God came to Nathan, saying,

⁴Go and tell David my servant, Thus saith the LORD, Thou shalt not build me an house to dwell in:

⁵For I have not dwelt in an house since the day that I brought up Israel unto this day; but ᵘhave gone from tent to tent, and from *one* tabernacle *to another*.

⁶Wheresoever I have walked with all Israel, spake I a word to any of the judges of Israel, whom I commanded to feed my people, saying, Why have ye not built me an house of cedars?

Amplified

²⁸Ascribe to the Lord, you families of the peoples, ascribe to the Lord glory and strength,

²⁹Ascribe to the Lord the glory due His name. Bring an offering and come before Him; worship the Lord in the beauty of holiness *and* in holy array.

³⁰Tremble *and* reverently fear before Him, all the earth's peoples; the world also shall be established, so it cannot be moved.

³¹Let the heavens be glad and let the earth rejoice; and let men say among the nations, The Lord reigns!

³²Let the sea roar, and all the things that fill it; let the fields rejoice, and all that is in them.

³³Then shall the trees of the wood sing out for joy before the Lord, for He comes to judge *and* govern the earth.

³⁴O give thanks to the Lord, for He is good; for His mercy *and* loving-kindness endure forever!

³⁵And say, Save us, O God of our salvation; gather us together and deliver us from the nations, that we may give thanks to Your holy name and glory in Your praise.

³⁶Blessed be the Lord, the God of Israel, forever and ever! And all the people said Amen! and praised the Lord.

³⁷So David left Asaph and his brethren before the ark of the covenant of the Lord to minister before the ark continually, as each day's work required,

³⁸And Obed-edom with [his] sixty-eight kinsmen. Also Obed-edom son of Jeduthun, and Hosah, were to be gate-keepers.

³⁹And David left Zadok the priest and his brethren the priests before the tabernacle of the Lord in the high place that was at Gibeon

⁴⁰To offer burnt offerings to the Lord upon the altar of burnt offering continually, morning and evening, and to do all that is written in the Law of the Lord which He commanded Israel.

⁴¹With them were Heman and Jeduthun and the rest who were chosen and expressly named to give thanks to the Lord, for His mercy *and* loving-kindness endure forever.

⁴²With them were Heman and Jeduthun with trumpets and cymbals for those who should sound aloud, and instruments for accompanying the songs of God. And the sons of Jeduthun were to be at the gate.

⁴³Then all the people departed, each man to his house, and David returned home to bless his household.

17 AS DAVID sat in his house, he said to Nathan the prophet, Behold, I dwell in a house of cedars, but the ark of the covenant of the Lord remains under tent curtains.

²Then Nathan said to David, Do all that is in your heart, for God is with you.

³And that same night the word of God came to Nathan, saying,

⁴Go and tell David My servant, Thus says the Lord: You shall not build Me a house to dwell in,

⁵For I have not dwelt in a house since the day that I brought up Israel from Egypt until this day; but I have gone from tent to tent, and from one tabernacle to another.

⁶Wherever I have walked with all Israel, did I say a word to any of the judges of Israel whom I commanded to feed My people, saying, Why have you not built Me a house of cedar?

ˢHeb. *in the morning, and in the evening*   ᵗHeb. *for the gate*
ᵘHeb. *have been*

New American Standard

28 Ascribe to the LORD, O families of the peoples,
Ascribe to the LORD glory and strength.
29 Ascribe to the LORD the glory due His name;
Bring an offering, and come before Him;
Worship the LORD in holy array.
30 Tremble before Him, all the earth;
Indeed, the world is firmly established, it will not
be moved.
31 Let the heavens be glad, and let the earth rejoice;
And let them say among the nations, "The LORD
reigns."
32 Let the sea roar, and all it contains;
Let the field exult, and all that is in it.
33 Then the trees of the forest will sing for joy
before the LORD;
For He is coming to judge the earth.
34 O give thanks to the LORD, for He is good;
For His lovingkindness is everlasting.
35 Then say, "Save us, O God of our salvation,
And gather us and deliver us from the nations,
To give thanks to Your holy name,
And glory in Your praise."
36 Blessed be the LORD, the God of Israel,
From everlasting even to everlasting.
Then all the people said, "Amen," and praised the LORD.

Worship before the Ark

37 ¶ So he left Asaph and his relatives there before the
ark of the covenant of the LORD to minister before the ark
continually, as every day's work required;
38 and Obed-edom with his 68 relatives; Obed-edom,
also the son of Jeduthun, and Hosah as gatekeepers.
39 He left Zadok the priest and his relatives the priests
before the tabernacle of the LORD in the high place which
was at Gibeon,
40 to offer burnt offerings to the LORD on the altar of
burnt offering continually morning and evening, even according to all that is written in the law of the LORD, which
He commanded Israel.
41 With them were Heman and Jeduthun, and the rest
who were chosen, who were designated by name, to give
thanks to the LORD, because His lovingkindness is everlasting.
42 And with them were Heman and Jeduthun with trumpets and cymbals for those who should sound aloud, and
with instruments for the songs of God, and the sons of
Jeduthun for the gate.
43 ¶ Then all the people departed each to his house, and
David returned to bless his household.

God's Covenant with David

17 AND IT came about, when David dwelt in his
house, that David said to Nathan the prophet, "Behold, I am dwelling in a house of cedar, but the ark of the
covenant of the LORD is under curtains."
2 Then Nathan said to David, "Do all that is in your
heart, for God is with you."
3 ¶ It came about the same night that the word of God
came to Nathan, saying,
4 "Go and tell David My servant, 'Thus says the LORD,
"You shall not build a house for Me to dwell in;
5 for I have not dwelt in a house since the day that I
brought up Israel to this day, but I have gone from tent to
tent and from one dwelling place to another.
6 "In all places where I have walked with all Israel, have
I spoken a word with any of the judges of Israel, whom I
commanded to shepherd My people, saying, 'Why have
you not built for Me a house of cedar?' " '

New International

28 Ascribe to the LORD, O families of nations,
ascribe to the LORD glory and strength,
29 ascribe to the LORD the glory due his name.
Bring an offering and come before him;
worship the LORD in the splendor of his[l]
holiness.
30 Tremble before him, all the earth!
The world is firmly established; it cannot be
moved.
31 Let the heavens rejoice, let the earth be glad;
let them say among the nations, "The LORD
reigns!"
32 Let the sea resound, and all that is in it;
let the fields be jubilant, and everything in
them!
33 Then the trees of the forest will sing,
they will sing for joy before the LORD,
for he comes to judge the earth.
34 Give thanks to the LORD, for he is good;
his love endures forever.
35 Cry out, "Save us, O God our Savior;
gather us and deliver us from the nations,
that we may give thanks to your holy name,
that we may glory in your praise."
36 Praise be to the LORD, the God of Israel,
from everlasting to everlasting.

Then all the people said "Amen" and "Praise the LORD."

37 David left Asaph and his associates before the ark of
the covenant of the LORD to minister there regularly, according to each day's requirements. 38 He also left Obed-
Edom and his sixty-eight associates to minister with them.
Obed-Edom son of Jeduthun, and also Hosah, were gatekeepers.
39 David left Zadok the priest and his fellow priests before the tabernacle of the LORD at the high place in Gibeon
40 to present burnt offerings to the LORD on the altar of
burnt offering regularly, morning and evening, in accordance with everything written in the Law of the LORD,
which he had given Israel. 41 With them were Heman and
Jeduthun and the rest of those chosen and designated by
name to give thanks to the LORD, "for his love endures
forever." 42 Heman and Jeduthun were responsible for the
sounding of the trumpets and cymbals and for the playing
of the other instruments for sacred song. The sons of Jeduthun were stationed at the gate.
43 Then all the people left, each for his own home, and
David returned home to bless his family.

God's Promise to David

17 AFTER DAVID was settled in his palace, he said
to Nathan the prophet, "Here I am, living in a
palace of cedar, while the ark of the covenant of the LORD
is under a tent."
2 Nathan replied to David, "Whatever you have in mind,
do it, for God is with you."
3 That night the word of God came to Nathan, saying:
4 "Go and tell my servant David, 'This is what the
LORD says: You are not the one to build me a house
to dwell in. 5 I have not dwelt in a house from the day
I brought Israel up out of Egypt to this day. I have
moved from one tent site to another, from one dwelling place to another. 6 Wherever I have moved with all
the Israelites, did I ever say to any of their leaders[m]
whom I commanded to shepherd my people, "Why
have you not built me a house of cedar?" '

---

l 29 Or LORD with the splendor of   m 6 Traditionally judges; also
in verse 10

King James

7Now therefore thus shalt thou say unto my servant David, Thus saith the LORD of hosts, I took thee from the sheepcote, even vfrom following the sheep, that thou shouldest be ruler over my people Israel:

8And I have been with thee whithersoever thou hast walked, and have cut off all thine enemies from before thee, and have made thee a name like the name of the great men that *are* in the earth.

9Also I will ordain a place for my people Israel, and will plant them, and they shall dwell in their place, and shall be moved no more; neither shall the children of wickedness waste them any more, as at the beginning,

10And since the time that I commanded judges *to be* over my people Israel. Moreover I will subdue all thine enemies. Furthermore I tell thee that the LORD will build thee an house.

11 ¶ And it shall come to pass, when thy days be expired that thou must go *to be* with thy fathers, that I will raise up thy seed after thee, which shall be of thy sons; and I will establish his kingdom.

12He shall build me an house, and I will establish his throne for ever.

13I will be his father, and he shall be my son: and I will not take my mercy away from him, as I took *it* from *him* that was before thee:

14But I will settle him in mine house and in my kingdom for ever: and his throne shall be established for evermore.

15According to all these words, and according to all this vision, so did Nathan speak unto David.

David's prayer

16 ¶ And David the king came and sat before the LORD, and said, Who *am* I, O LORD God, and what *is* mine house, that thou hast brought me hitherto?

17And *yet* this was a small thing in thine eyes, O God; for thou hast *also* spoken of thy servant's house for a great while to come, and hast regarded me according to the estate of a man of high degree, O LORD God.

18What can David *speak* more to thee for the honour of thy servant? for thou knowest thy servant.

19O LORD, for thy servant's sake, and according to thine own heart, hast thou done all this greatness, in making known all *these* wgreat things.

20O LORD, *there is* none like thee, neither *is there any* God beside thee, according to all that we have heard with our ears.

21And what one nation in the earth *is* like thy people Israel, whom God went to redeem *to be* his own people, to make thee a name of greatness and terribleness, by driving out nations from before thy people, whom thou hast redeemed out of Egypt?

22For thy people Israel didst thou make thine own people for ever; and thou, LORD, becamest their God.

23Therefore now, LORD, let the thing that thou hast spoken concerning thy servant and concerning his house be established for ever, and do as thou hast said.

24Let it even be established, that thy name may be magnified for ever, saying, The LORD of hosts *is* the God of Israel, *even* a God to Israel: and *let* the house of David thy servant *be* established before thee.

Amplified

7Now therefore, thus shall you say to My servant David, Thus says the Lord of hosts: I took you from the sheepfold, from following the sheep, that you should be prince over My people Israel.

8And I have been with you wherever you have gone, and I have cut off all your enemies from before you, and I will make your name like the name of the great ones of the earth.

9Also I will appoint a place for My people Israel and will plant them, that they may dwell in their own place and be moved no more; neither shall the children of wickedness waste them any more, as at the first,

10Since the time that I commanded judges to be over My people Israel. Moreover, I will subdue all your enemies. Furthermore, I foretell to you that the Lord will build you a house (a blessed posterity).

11And it shall come to pass that when your days are fulfilled to go to be with your fathers, I will raise up your offspring after you, one of your own sons, and I will establish his kingdom.

12He shall build Me a house, and I will establish his throne forever. [I Chron. 28:7.]

13I will be his father, and he shall be My son; and I will not take My mercy *and* steadfast love away from him, as I took it from him [King Saul] who was before you. [Heb. 1:5, 6.]

14But I will settle bhim (Him) in My house and in My kingdom forever; and his (His) throne shall be established forevermore. [Isa. 9:7.]

15According to all these words and according to all this vision, so Nathan spoke to David.

16And David the king went in and sat before the Lord and said, Who am I, O Lord God, and what is my house *and* family, that You have brought me up to this?

17And yet this was a small thing in Your eyes, O God; for You have spoken of Your servant's house for a great while to come, and have regarded me according to the estate of a man of high degree, O Lord God!

18What more can David say to You for thus honoring Your servant? For You know Your servant.

19O Lord, for Your servant's sake and in accord with Your own heart, You have wrought all this greatness, to make known all these great things.

20O Lord, there is none like You, nor is there any God beside You, according to all that our ears have heard.

21And what nation on the earth is like Your people Israel, whom God went to redeem to Himself as a people, making Yourself a name by great and terrible things, by driving out nations from before Your people, whom You redeemed out of Egypt?

22You made Your people Israel Your own forever, and You, Lord, became their God.

23Therefore now, Lord, let the word which You have spoken concerning Your servant and his house be established forever, and do as You have said.

24Let it be established and let Your name [and the character that name denotes] be magnified forever, saying, The Lord of hosts, the God of Israel, is Israel's God; and the house of David Your servant will be established before You.

---

bThe "house" or "kingdom of God," in which this preservation or confirming of the seed of David is to take place, has two points of reference: first, the Old Testament theocracy [government of a state by the immediate direction of God], and second, the Messianic kingdom of the new covenant. The text of II Sam. 7:16 (KJV) differs: "And thine house and thy kingdom shall be established forever before thee, and thy throne shall be established forever." The sense of both is Messianic [though the writer in earlier verses definitely referred not to Christ but to Solomon (I Chron. 17:11-13 and II Sam. 7:13, 14)] (J.P. Lange, *A Commentary*). "The reference in this prophecy looks beyond Solomon to Him of Whom the greatest princes of the house of David were but imperfect types" (Charles Ellicott, *A Bible Commentary*).

vHeb. *from after*   wHeb. *greatnesses*

New American Standard

7"Now, therefore, thus shall you say to My servant David, 'Thus says the LORD of hosts, "I took you from the pasture, from following the sheep, to be leader over My people Israel.

8"I have been with you wherever you have gone, and have cut off all your enemies from before you; and I will make you a name like the name of the great ones who are in the earth.

9"I will appoint a place for My people Israel, and will plant them, so that they may dwell in their own place and not be moved again; and the wicked will not waste them anymore as formerly,

10 even from the day that I commanded judges *to be* over My people Israel. And I will subdue all your enemies.

¶ Moreover, I tell you that the LORD will build a house for you.

11"When your days are fulfilled that you must go *to be* with your fathers, that I will set up *one of* your descendants after you, who will be of your sons; and I will establish his kingdom.

12"He shall build for Me a house, and I will establish his throne forever.

13"I will be his father and he shall be My son; and I will not take My lovingkindness away from him, as I took it from him who was before you.

14"But I will settle him in My house and in My kingdom forever, and his throne shall be established forever." ' "

15 According to all these words and according to all this vision, so Nathan spoke to David.

David's Prayer in Response

16 ¶ Then David the king went in and sat before the LORD and said, "Who am I, O LORD God, and what is my house that You have brought me this far?

17"This was a small thing in Your eyes, O God; but You have spoken of Your servant's house for a great while to come, and have regarded me according to the standard of a man of high degree, O LORD God.

18"What more can David still *say* to You concerning the honor *bestowed* on Your servant? For You know Your servant.

19"O LORD, for Your servant's sake, and according to Your own heart, You have wrought all this greatness, to make known all these great things.

20"O LORD, there is none like You, nor is there any God besides You, according to all that we have heard with our ears.

21"And what one nation in the earth is like Your people Israel, whom God went to redeem for Himself *as* a people, to make You a name by great and terrible things, in driving out nations from before Your people, whom You redeemed out of Egypt?

22"For Your people Israel You made Your own people forever, and You, O LORD, became their God.

23 ¶ "Now, O LORD, let the word that You have spoken concerning Your servant and concerning his house be established forever, and do as You have spoken.

24"Let Your name be established and magnified forever, saying, 'The LORD of hosts is the God of Israel, *even* a God to Israel; and the house of David Your servant is established before You.'

New International

7"Now then, tell my servant David, 'This is what the LORD Almighty says: I took you from the pasture and from following the flock, to be ruler over my people Israel. 8I have been with you wherever you have gone, and I have cut off all your enemies from before you. Now I will make your name like the names of the greatest men of the earth. 9And I will provide a place for my people Israel and will plant them so that they can have a home of their own and no longer be disturbed. Wicked people will not oppress them anymore, as they did at the beginning 10and have done ever since the time I appointed leaders over my people Israel. I will also subdue all your enemies.

" 'I declare to you that the LORD will build a house for you: 11When your days are over and you go to be with your fathers, I will raise up your offspring to succeed you, one of your own sons, and I will establish his kingdom. 12He is the one who will build a house for me, and I will establish his throne forever. 13I will be his father, and he will be my son. I will never take my love away from him, as I took it away from your predecessor. 14I will set him over my house and my kingdom forever; his throne will be established forever.' "

15Nathan reported to David all the words of this entire revelation.

David's Prayer

16Then King David went in and sat before the LORD, and he said:

"Who am I, O LORD God, and what is my family, that you have brought me this far? 17And as if this were not enough in your sight, O God, you have spoken about the future of the house of your servant. You have looked on me as though I were the most exalted of men, O LORD God.

18"What more can David say to you for honoring your servant? For you know your servant, 19O LORD. For the sake of your servant and according to your will, you have done this great thing and made known all these great promises.

20"There is no one like you, O LORD, and there is no God but you, as we have heard with our own ears. 21And who is like your people Israel—the one nation on earth whose God went out to redeem a people for himself, and to make a name for yourself, and to perform great and awesome wonders by driving out nations from before your people, whom you redeemed from Egypt? 22You made your people Israel your very own forever, and you, O LORD, have become their God.

23"And now, LORD, let the promise you have made concerning your servant and his house be established forever. Do as you promised, 24so that it will be established and that your name will be great forever. Then men will say, 'The LORD Almighty, the God over Israel, is Israel's God!' And the house of your servant David will be established before you.

King James

25For thou, O my God, xhast told thy servant that thou wilt build him an house: therefore thy servant hath found *in his heart* to pray before thee.

26And now, LORD, thou art God, and hast promised this goodness unto thy servant:

27Now therefore ylet it please thee to bless the house of thy servant, that it may be before thee for ever: for thou blessest, O LORD, and *it shall be* blessed for ever.

David's victories

18 NOW AFTER this it came to pass, that David smote the Philistines, and subdued them, and took Gath and her towns out of the hand of the Philistines.

2And he smote Moab; and the Moabites became David's servants, *and* brought gifts.

3 ¶ And David smote zHadarezer king of Zobah unto Hamath, as he went to stablish his dominion by the river Euphrates.

4And David took from him a thousand chariots, and seven thousand horsemen, and twenty thousand footmen: David also houghed all the chariot *horses,* but reserved of them an hundred chariots.

5And when the Syrians of aDamascus came to help Hadarezer king of Zobah, David slew of the Syrians two and twenty thousand men.

6Then David put *garrisons* in Syria-damascus; and the Syrians became David's servants, *and* brought gifts. Thus the LORD preserved David whithersoever he went.

7And David took the shields of gold that were on the servants of Hadarezer, and brought them to Jerusalem.

8Likewise from bTibhath, and from Chun, cities of Hadarezer, brought David very much brass, wherewith Solomon made the brasen sea, and the pillars, and the vessels of brass.

9 ¶ Now when cTou king of Hamath heard how David had smitten all the host of Hadarezer king of Zobah;

10He sent dHadoram his son to king David, eto inquire of his welfare, and fto congratulate him, because he had fought against Hadarezer, and smitten him; (for Hadarezer ghad war with Tou;) and *with him* all manner of vessels of gold and silver and brass.

11 ¶ Them also king David dedicated unto the LORD, with the silver and the gold that he brought from all *these* nations; from Edom, and from Moab, and from the children of Ammon, and from the Philistines, and from Amalek.

12Moreover hAbishai the son of Zeruiah slew of the Edomites in the valley of salt eighteen thousand.

13 ¶ And he put garrisons in Edom; and all the Edomites became David's servants. Thus the LORD preserved David whithersoever he went.

14 ¶ So David reigned over all Israel, and executed judgment and justice among all his people.

15And Joab the son of Zeruiah *was* over the host; and Jehoshaphat the son of Ahilud, irecorder.

16And Zadok the son of Ahitub, and jAbimelech the son of Abiathar, *were* the priests; and kShavsha was scribe;

17And Benaiah the son of Jehoiada *was* over the Cherethites and the Pelethites; and the sons of David *were* chief labout the king.

Amplified

25For You, O my God, have told Your servant that You will build for him a house (a blessed posterity); therefore Your servant has found courage *and* confidence to pray before You.

26And now, Lord, You are God, and have promised this good thing to Your servant.

27Therefore may it please You to bless the house (posterity) of Your servant, that it may continue before You forever; for what You bless, O Lord, is blessed forever.

18 AFTER THIS, David smote and subdued the Philistines, and took Gath and its villages out of the hand of the Philistines.

2He smote Moab, and the Moabites became David's servants and brought tribute.

3Also David defeated Hadadezer king of Zobah toward Hamath, as he went to establish his dominion by the river Euphrates.

4David took from him 1,000 chariots, 7,000 horsemen, and 20,000 foot soldiers. David also hamstrung all the chariot horses, but reserved enough for 100 chariots.

5When the Syrians of Damascus came to help Hadadezer king of Zobah, David slew of the Syrians 22,000 men.

6Then David put garrisons in Syria, [whose capital was] Damascus; the Syrians became David's servants and brought tribute. Thus the Lord preserved *and* gave victory to David wherever he went.

7David took the shields of gold that were carried by the servants of Hadadezer and brought them to Jerusalem.

8Likewise from Tibhath and from Cun, cities of Hadadezer, David brought very much bronze, with which Solomon later made the bronze laver, the pillars, and the vessels of bronze.

9When Tou king of Hamath heard how David had defeated all the hosts of Hadadezer king of Zobah,

10He sent Hadoram his son to King David to salute him and to congratulate him because he had fought and defeated Hadadezer, for Hadadezer had had wars with Tou. And Hadoram brought with him all manner of vessels of gold, silver, and bronze.

11King David dedicated them also to the Lord, with the silver and the gold he brought from all these nations: Edom, Moab, the Ammonites, the Philistines, and the Amalekites.

12Also Abishai son of Zeruiah slew 18,000 of the Edomites in the Valley of Salt.

13He put garrisons in Edom, and all the Edomites became David's servants. Thus the Lord preserved *and* gave victory to David wherever he went.

14So David reigned over all Israel and executed judgment and justice among all his people.

15Joab son of Zeruiah [David's half sister] was over the army; and Jehoshaphat son of Ahilud was the recorder;

16Zadok son of Ahitub and Abimelech son of Abiathar were the priests; and Shavsha was secretary [of state];

17Benaiah son of Jehoiada was over [David's bodyguards] the Cherethites and the Pelethites; and David's sons were chiefs next to the king.

---

xHeb. *hast revealed the ear of thy servant*   yOr, *it hath pleased thee*   zOr, *Hadadezer;* see 2 Sam. 8:3   aHeb. *Darmesek*
bCalled *Betah* and *Berothai* in 2 Sam. 8:8   cOr, *Toi;* see 2 Sam. 8:9   dOr, *Joram;* see 2 Sam. 8:10   eOr, *to salute*   fHeb. *to bless*   gHeb. *was the man of wars*   hHeb. *Abshai*
iOr, *remembrancer*   jCalled *Ahimelech* in 2 Sam. 8:17
kCalled *Seraiah* in 2 Sam. 8:17 and *Shisha* in 1 Ki. 4:3   lHeb. *at the hand of the king*

New American Standard

25"For You, O my God, have revealed to Your servant that You will build for him a house; therefore Your servant has found *courage* to pray before You.
26"Now, O LORD, You are God, and have promised this good thing to Your servant.
27"And now it has pleased You to bless the house of Your servant, that it may continue forever before You; for You, O LORD, have blessed, and it is blessed forever."

David's Kingdom Strengthened

18 NOW AFTER this it came about that David defeated the Philistines and subdued them and took Gath and its towns from the hand of the Philistines.
2 He defeated Moab, and the Moabites became servants to David, bringing tribute.
3 ¶ David also defeated Hadadezer king of Zobah *as far as* Hamath, as he went to establish his rule to the Euphrates River.
4 David took from him 1,000 chariots and 7,000 horsemen and 20,000 foot soldiers, and David hamstrung all the chariot horses, but reserved *enough* of them for 100 chariots.
5 ¶ When the Arameans of Damascus came to help Hadadezer king of Zobah, David killed 22,000 men of the Arameans.
6 Then David put *garrisons* among the Arameans of Damascus; and the Arameans became servants to David, bringing tribute. And the LORD helped David wherever he went.
7 David took the shields of gold which were carried by the servants of Hadadezer and brought them to Jerusalem.
8 Also from Tibhath and from Cun, cities of Hadadezer, David took a very large amount of bronze, with which Solomon made the bronze sea and the pillars and bronze utensils.
9 ¶ Now when Tou king of Hamath heard that David had defeated all the army of Hadadezer king of Zobah,
10 he sent Hadoram his son to King David to greet him and to bless him, because he had fought against Hadadezer and had defeated him; for Hadadezer had been at war with Tou. And *Hadoram brought* all kinds of articles of gold and silver and bronze.
11 King David also dedicated these to the LORD with the silver and the gold which he had carried away from all the nations: from Edom, Moab, the sons of Ammon, the Philistines, and from Amalek.
12 ¶ Moreover Abishai the son of Zeruiah defeated 18,000 Edomites in the Valley of Salt.
13 Then he put garrisons in Edom, and all the Edomites became servants to David. And the LORD helped David wherever he went.
14 ¶ So David reigned over all Israel; and he administered justice and righteousness for all his people.
15 Joab the son of Zeruiah *was* over the army, and Jehoshaphat the son of Ahilud *was* recorder;
16 and Zadok the son of Ahitub and Abimelech the son of Abiathar *were* priests, and Shavsha *was* secretary;
17 and Benaiah the son of Jehoiada *was* over the Cherethites and the Pelethites, and the sons of David were chiefs at the king's side.

New International

25"You, my God, have revealed to your servant that you will build a house for him. So your servant has found courage to pray to you. 26O LORD, you are God! You have promised these good things to your servant. 27Now you have been pleased to bless the house of your servant, that it may continue forever in your sight; for you, O LORD, have blessed it, and it will be blessed forever."

David's Victories

18 IN THE course of time, David defeated the Philistines and subdued them, and he took Gath and its surrounding villages from the control of the Philistines.
2David also defeated the Moabites, and they became subject to him and brought tribute.
3Moreover, David fought Hadadezer king of Zobah, as far as Hamath, when he went to establish his control along the Euphrates River. 4David captured a thousand of his chariots, seven thousand charioteers and twenty thousand foot soldiers. He hamstrung all but a hundred of the chariot horses.
5When the Arameans of Damascus came to help Hadadezer king of Zobah, David struck down twenty-two thousand of them. 6He put garrisons in the Aramean kingdom of Damascus, and the Arameans became subject to him and brought tribute. The LORD gave David victory everywhere he went.
7David took the gold shields carried by the officers of Hadadezer and brought them to Jerusalem. 8From Tebah[n] and Cun, towns that belonged to Hadadezer, David took a great quantity of bronze, which Solomon used to make the bronze Sea, the pillars and various bronze articles.
9When Tou king of Hamath heard that David had defeated the entire army of Hadadezer king of Zobah, 10he sent his son Hadoram to King David to greet him and congratulate him on his victory in battle over Hadadezer, who had been at war with Tou. Hadoram brought all kinds of articles of gold and silver and bronze.
11King David dedicated these articles to the LORD, as he had done with the silver and gold he had taken from all these nations: Edom and Moab, the Ammonites and the Philistines, and Amalek.
12Abishai son of Zeruiah struck down eighteen thousand Edomites in the Valley of Salt. 13He put garrisons in Edom, and all the Edomites became subject to David. The LORD gave David victory everywhere he went.

David's Officials

14David reigned over all Israel, doing what was just and right for all his people. 15Joab son of Zeruiah was over the army; Jehoshaphat son of Ahilud was recorder; 16Zadok son of Ahitub and Ahimelech[o] son of Abiathar were priests; Shavsha was secretary; 17Benaiah son of Jehoiada was over the Kerethites and Pelethites; and David's sons were chief officials at the king's side.

---

n 8 Hebrew *Tibhath*, a variant of *Tebah*   o 16 Some Hebrew manuscripts, Vulgate and Syriac (see also 2 Samuel 8:17); most Hebrew manuscripts *Abimelech*

King James

David and the Ammonites

19 NOW IT came to pass after this, that Nahash the king of the children of Ammon died, and his son reigned in his stead.

2And David said, I will show kindness unto Hanun the son of Nahash, because his father showed kindness to me. And David sent messengers to comfort him concerning his father. So the servants of David came into the land of the children of Ammon to Hanun, to comfort him.

3But the princes of the children of Ammon said to Hanun, *m*Thinkest thou that David doth honour thy father, that he hath sent comforters unto thee? are not his servants come unto thee for to search, and to overthrow, and to spy out the land?

4Wherefore Hanun took David's servants, and shaved them, and cut off their garments in the midst hard by their buttocks, and sent them away.

5Then there went *certain,* and told David how the men were served. And he sent to meet them: for the men were greatly ashamed. And the king said, Tarry at Jericho until your beards be grown, and *then* return.

6 ¶ And when the children of Ammon saw that they had made themselves *n*odious to David, Hanun and the children of Ammon sent a thousand talents of silver to hire them chariots and horsemen out of Mesopotamia, and out of Syria-maachah, and out of Zobah.

7So they hired thirty and two thousand chariots, and the king of Maachah and his people; who came and pitched before Medeba. And the children of Ammon gathered themselves together from their cities, and came to battle.

8And when David heard *of it,* he sent Joab, and all the host of the mighty men.

9And the children of Ammon came out, and put the battle in array before the gate of the city: and the kings that were come *were* by themselves in the field.

10Now when Joab saw that *o*the battle was set against him before and behind, he chose out of all the *p*choice of Israel, and put *them* in array against the Syrians.

11And the rest of the people he delivered unto the hand of *q*Abishai his brother, and they set *themselves* in array against the children of Ammon.

12And he said, If the Syrians be too strong for me, then thou shalt help me: but if the children of Ammon be too strong for thee, then I will help thee.

13Be of good courage, and let us behave ourselves valiantly for our people, and for the cities of our God: and let the LORD do *that which is* good in his sight.

14So Joab and the people that *were* with him drew nigh before the Syrians unto the battle; and they fled before him.

15And when the children of Ammon saw that the Syrians were fled, they likewise fled before Abishai his brother, and entered into the city. Then Joab came to Jerusalem.

16 ¶ And when the Syrians saw that they were put to the worse before Israel, they sent messengers, and drew forth the Syrians that *were* beyond the *r*river: and *s*Shophach the captain of the host of Hadarezer *went* before them.

17And it was told David; and he gathered all Israel, and passed over Jordan, and came upon them, and set *the battle* in array against them. So when David had put the battle in array against the Syrians, they fought with him.

18But the Syrians fled before Israel; and David slew of the Syrians seven thousand *men which fought in* chariots, and forty thousand footmen, and killed Shophach the captain of the host.

19And when the servants of Hadarezer saw that they were put to the worse before Israel, they made peace with David, and became his servants: neither would the Syrians help the children of Ammon any more.

Amplified

19 AFTER THIS, Nahash king of the Ammonites died, and his son reigned in his stead.

2David said, I will show kindness to Hanun son of Nahash, because his father showed kindness to me. And David sent messengers to comfort him concerning his father's death. So the servants of David came into the land of the Ammonites to comfort Hanun.

3But the princes of the Ammonites said to Hanun, Do you think that David has sent comforters to you because he honors your father? Have his servants not come to you to search, to overthrow, and to spy out the land?

4Therefore Hanun took David's servants, shaved them, cut off their garments in the middle near their buttocks, and sent them away.

5When David was told how the men were served, he sent to meet them, for [they] were greatly shamed *and* embarrassed. The king said, Stay in Jericho until your beards are grown, and then return.

6When the Ammonites saw that they had made themselves hateful to David, Hanun and [his people] sent 1,000 talents of silver to hire chariots and horsemen from Mesopotamia and Aram-maacah and Zobah.

7So they hired 32,000 chariots, and the king of Maacah and his troops, who came and pitched before Medeba. And the Ammonites gathered from their cities and came to battle.

8When David heard of it, he sent Joab and all the army of mighty men.

9And the Ammonites came out and lined up in battle array before the entrance of the city [Medeba], and the kings who had come were by themselves in the open country.

10When Joab saw that the battle was set against him before and behind, he chose from all the choice men of Israel and put them in array against the Syrians.

11The rest of the soldiers he delivered to Abishai his brother, and they were arrayed against the Ammonites.

12And he said, If the Syrians are too strong for me, then you help me; but if the Ammonites are too strong for you, I will help you.

13Be of good courage and let us behave ourselves courageously for our people and for the cities of our God; and may the Lord do what is good in His sight.

14So Joab and the people who were with him drew near before the Syrians for battle, and they fled before him.

15And when the Ammonites saw that the Syrians fled, they likewise fled before Abishai, Joab's brother, and entered into the city [Medeba]. Then Joab came to Jerusalem.

16When the Syrians saw that they were defeated by Israel, they sent messengers and drew forth the Syrians who were beyond the Euphrates River, with Shophach the commander of the army of Hadadezer at their head.

17It was told to David, and he gathered all Israel and crossed the Jordan and drew up his army against them. So when David set the battle in array against the Syrians, they fought with him.

18But the Syrians fled before Israel, and David slew of the Syrians 7,000 men in chariots and 40,000 foot soldiers, and killed Shophach the commander of the army.

19When the servants of Hadadezer saw that they were defeated before Israel, they made peace with David and became subject to him; nor would the Syrians any longer help the Ammonites.

---

*m*Heb. *In thine eyes doth David*   *n*Heb. *to stink*   *o*Heb. *the face of the battle was*   *p*Or, *young men*   *q*Heb. *Abshai*   *r*i.e. *Euphrates*   *s*Or, *Shobach;* see 2 Sam. 10:16

New American Standard

David's Messengers Abused

19 NOW IT came about after this, that Nahash the king of the sons of Ammon died, and his son became king in his place.

2 Then David said, "I will show kindness to Hanun the son of Nahash, because his father showed kindness to me." So David sent messengers to console him concerning his father. And David's servants came into the land of the sons of Ammon to Hanun to console him.

3 But the princes of the sons of Ammon said to Hanun, "Do you think that David is honoring your father, in that he has sent comforters to you? Have not his servants come to you to search and to overthrow and to spy out the land?"

4 So Hanun took David's servants and shaved them and cut off their garments in the middle as far as their hips, and sent them away.

5 Then *certain persons* went and told David about the men. And he sent to meet them, for the men were greatly humiliated. And the king said, "Stay at Jericho until your beards grow, and *then* return."

6 ¶ When the sons of Ammon saw that they had made themselves odious to David, Hanun and the sons of Ammon sent 1,000 talents of silver to hire for themselves chariots and horsemen from Mesopotamia, from Aram-maacah and from Zobah.

7 So they hired for themselves 32,000 chariots, and the king of Maacah and his people, who came and camped before Medeba. And the sons of Ammon gathered together from their cities and came to battle.

8 When David heard *of it,* he sent Joab and all the army, the mighty men.

9 The sons of Ammon came out and drew up in battle array at the entrance of the city, and the kings who had come were by themselves in the field.

Ammon and Aram Defeated

10 ¶ Now when Joab saw that the battle was set against him in front and in the rear, he selected from all the choice men of Israel and they arrayed themselves against the Arameans.

11 But the remainder of the people he placed in the hand of Abshai his brother; and they arrayed themselves against the sons of Ammon.

12 He said, "If the Arameans are too strong for me, then you shall help me; but if the sons of Ammon are too strong for you, then I will help you.

13 "Be strong, and let us show ourselves courageous for the sake of our people and for the cities of our God; and may the LORD do what is good in His sight."

14 So Joab and the people who were with him drew near to the battle against the Arameans, and they fled before him.

15 When the sons of Ammon saw that the Arameans fled, they also fled before Abshai his brother and entered the city. Then Joab came to Jerusalem.

16 ¶ When the Arameans saw that they had been defeated by Israel, they sent messengers and brought out the Arameans who were beyond the *f* River, with Shophach the commander of the army of Hadadezer leading them.

17 When it was told David, he gathered all Israel together and crossed the Jordan, and came upon them and drew up in formation against them. And when David drew up in battle array against the Arameans, they fought against him.

18 The Arameans fled before Israel, and David killed of the Arameans 7,000 charioteers and 40,000 foot soldiers, and put to death Shophach the commander of the army.

19 So when the servants of Hadadezer saw that they were defeated by Israel, they made peace with David and served him. Thus the Arameans were not willing to help the sons of Ammon anymore.

New International

The Battle Against the Ammonites

19 IN THE course of time, Nahash king of the Ammonites died, and his son succeeded him as king. 2David thought, "I will show kindness to Hanun son of Nahash, because his father showed kindness to me." So David sent a delegation to express his sympathy to Hanun concerning his father.

When David's men came to Hanun in the land of the Ammonites to express sympathy to him, 3the Ammonite nobles said to Hanun, "Do you think David is honoring your father by sending men to you to express sympathy? Haven't his men come to you to explore and spy out the country and overthrow it?" 4So Hanun seized David's men, shaved them, cut off their garments in the middle at the buttocks, and sent them away.

5When someone came and told David about the men, he sent messengers to meet them, for they were greatly humiliated. The king said, "Stay at Jericho till your beards have grown, and then come back."

6When the Ammonites realized that they had become a stench in David's nostrils, Hanun and the Ammonites sent a thousand talents*p* of silver to hire chariots and charioteers from Aram Naharaim,*q* Aram Maacah and Zobah. 7They hired thirty-two thousand chariots and charioteers, as well as the king of Maacah with his troops, who came and camped near Medeba, while the Ammonites were mustered from their towns and moved out for battle.

8On hearing this, David sent Joab out with the entire army of fighting men. 9The Ammonites came out and drew up in battle formation at the entrance to their city, while the kings who had come were by themselves in the open country.

10Joab saw that there were battle lines in front of him and behind him; so he selected some of the best troops in Israel and deployed them against the Arameans. 11He put the rest of the men under the command of Abishai his brother, and they were deployed against the Ammonites. 12Joab said, "If the Arameans are too strong for me, then you are to rescue me; but if the Ammonites are too strong for you, then I will rescue you. 13Be strong and let us fight bravely for our people and the cities of our God. The LORD will do what is good in his sight."

14Then Joab and the troops with him advanced to fight the Arameans, and they fled before him. 15When the Ammonites saw that the Arameans were fleeing, they too fled before his brother Abishai and went inside the city. So Joab went back to Jerusalem.

16After the Arameans saw that they had been routed by Israel, they sent messengers and had Arameans brought from beyond the River,*r* with Shophach the commander of Hadadezer's army leading them.

17When David was told of this, he gathered all Israel and crossed the Jordan; he advanced against them and formed his battle lines opposite them. David formed his lines to meet the Arameans in battle, and they fought against him. 18But they fled before Israel, and David killed seven thousand of their charioteers and forty thousand of their foot soldiers. He also killed Shophach the commander of their army.

19When the vassals of Hadadezer saw that they had been defeated by Israel, they made peace with David and became subject to him.

So the Arameans were not willing to help the Ammonites anymore.

---

f I.e. Euphrates

*p*6 That is, about 37 tons (about 34 metric tons)   *q*6 That is, Northwest Mesopotamia   *r*16 That is, the Euphrates

King James

Amplified

War with the Philistines

20 AND IT came to pass, that *after the year was expired, at the time that kings go out *to battle,* Joab led forth the power of the army, and wasted the country of the children of Ammon, and came and besieged Rabbah. But David tarried at Jerusalem. And Joab smote Rabbah, and destroyed it.

2And David took the crown of their king from off his head, and found it *uto weigh a talent of gold, and *there were* precious stones in it; and it was set upon David's head: and he brought also exceeding much spoil out of the city.

3And he brought out the people that *were* in it, and cut *them* with saws, and with harrows of iron, and with axes. Even so dealt David with all the cities of the children of Ammon. And David and all the people returned to Jerusalem.

4 ¶ And it came to pass after this, that there *vw*arose war at *x*Gezer with the Philistines; at which time Sibbechai the Hushathite slew *y*Sippai, *that was* of the children of *z*the giant: and they were subdued.

5And there was war again with the Philistines; and Elhanan the son of *a*Jair slew Lahmi the brother of Goliath the Gittite, whose spear staff *was* like a weaver's beam.

6And yet again there was war at Gath, where was *b*a man of *great* stature, whose fingers and toes *were* four and twenty, six *on each hand,* and six *on each foot:* and he also was *c*the son of the giant.

7But when he *d*defied Israel, Jonathan the son of *e*Shimea David's brother slew him.

8These were born unto the giant in Gath; and they fell by the hand of David, and by the hand of his servants.

20 AFTER THE end of the year, when kings go out to battle, Joab led forth the army and devastated the land of the Ammonites, and came and besieged Rabbah. But David tarried at Jerusalem. Joab smote Rabbah and overthrew it.

2David took their king's crown from off his head and found that it weighed a talent of gold and that precious stones were in it. It was set upon David's head. He brought also very much spoil out of the city of Rabbah.

3He brought out the people who were in it and set them at cutting with saws, iron wedges, and axes. So David dealt with all the Ammonite cities. And David and all the army returned to Jerusalem.

4After this, there arose war at Gezer with the Philistines; then Sibbecai the Hushathite slew Sippai, of the sons of the giant, and they were subdued.

5There was war again with the Philistines, and Elhanan son of Jair slew Lahmi the brother of Goliath the Gittite, the staff of whose spear was like a weaver's beam.

6And again there was war at Gath, where was a man of great stature who had twenty-four fingers and toes, six on each hand and each foot. He also was born to the giant.

7And when he reproached *and* defied Israel, Jonathan son of Shimea, David's brother, slew him.

8These were born to the giant [clan] in Gath, and they fell by the hands of David and his servants.

David's census

21 AND SATAN stood up against Israel, and provoked David to number Israel.

2And David said to Joab and to the rulers of the people, Go, number Israel from Beer-sheba even to Dan; and bring the number of them to me, that I may know *it.*

3And Joab answered, The LORD make his people an hundred times so many more as they *be:* but, my lord the king, *are* they not all my lord's servants? why then doth my lord require this thing? why will he be a cause of trespass to Israel?

4Nevertheless the king's word prevailed against Joab. Wherefore Joab departed, and went throughout all Israel, and came to Jerusalem.

5 ¶ And Joab gave the sum of the number of the people unto David. And all *they of* Israel were a thousand thousand and an hundred thousand men that drew sword: and Judah *was* four hundred threescore and ten thousand men that drew sword.

6But Levi and Benjamin counted he not among them: for the king's word was abominable to Joab.

7*f*And God was displeased with this thing; therefore he smote Israel.

8And David said unto God, I have sinned greatly, because I have done this thing: but now, I beseech thee, do away the iniquity of thy servant; for I have done very foolishly.

9 ¶ And the LORD spake unto Gad, David's seer, saying,

10Go and tell David, saying, Thus saith the LORD, I *g*offer thee three *things:* choose thee one of them, that I may do *it* unto thee.

11So Gad came to David, and said unto him, Thus saith the LORD, *h*Choose thee

21 SATAN [an adversary] stood up against Israel and stirred up David to number Israel.

2David said to Joab and the rulers of the people, Go, number Israel from Beersheba to Dan, and bring me the total, that I may know it.

3And Joab answered, May the Lord multiply His people a hundred times! But, my lord the king, are they not all my lord's servants? Why then does my lord require this? Why will he bring guilt upon Israel?

4But the king's word prevailed against Joab. So Joab departed and went throughout all Israel and came to Jerusalem.

5Joab gave the total number of the people to David. And all of Israel were 1,100,000 who drew the sword, and of Judah 470,000 who drew the sword.

6But Levi and Benjamin he did not include among them, for the king's order was detestable to Joab.

7And God was displeased with this [reliance on human resources], and He smote Israel.

8And David said to God, I have sinned greatly because I have done this thing. But now, I beseech You, take away the hateful wickedness of Your servant; for I have done very foolishly.

9And the Lord said to Gad, David's seer,

10Go and tell David, Thus says the Lord: I offer you three things; choose one of them, that I may do it to you.

11So Gad came to David and said to him, Thus says the Lord: Take which one you will:

---

*t*Heb. *at the return of the year*   *u*Heb. *the weight of*   *v*Or,
continued   *w*Heb. *stood*   *x*Or, *Gob*   *y*Or, *Saph;* see
2 Sam. 21:18   *z*Or, *Rapha*   *a*Called *Jaareoregim* in 2 Sam.
21:19   *b*Heb. *a man of measure*   *c*Heb. *born to the giant,* or,
Rapha   *d*Or, *reproached*   *e*Called *Shammah* in 1 Sam. 16:9
*f*Heb. *And it was evil in the eyes of the LORD concerning this thing*
*g*Heb. *stretch out*   *h*Heb. *Take to thee*

New American Standard

War with Philistine Giants

20 THEN IT happened in the spring, at the time when kings go out *to battle,* that Joab led out the army and ravaged the land of the sons of Ammon, and came and besieged Rabbah. But David stayed at Jerusalem. And Joab struck Rabbah and overthrew it.

2 David took the crown of their king from his head, and he found it to weigh a talent of gold, and there was a precious stone in it; and it was placed on David's head. And he brought out the spoil of the city, a very great amount.

3 He brought out the people who *were* in it, and cut *them* with saws and with sharp instruments and with axes. And thus David did to all the cities of the sons of Ammon. Then David and all the people returned *to* Jerusalem.

4 ¶ Now it came about after this, that war broke out at Gezer with the Philistines; then Sibbecai the Hushathite killed Sippai, one of the descendants of the giants, and they were subdued.

5 And there was war with the Philistines again, and Elhanan the son of Jair killed Lahmi the brother of Goliath the Gittite, the shaft of whose spear *was* like a weaver's beam.

6 Again there was war at Gath, where there was a man of *great* stature who had twenty-four fingers and toes, six *fingers on each hand* and six *toes on each foot;* and he also was descended from the giants.

7 When he taunted Israel, Jonathan the son of Shimea, David's brother, killed him.

8 These were descended from the giants in Gath, and they fell by the hand of David and by the hand of his servants.

Census Brings Pestilence

21 THEN SATAN stood up against Israel and moved David to number Israel.

2 So David said to Joab and to the princes of the people, "Go, number Israel from Beersheba even to Dan, and bring me *word* that I may know their number."

3 Joab said, "May the LORD add to His people a hundred times as many as they are! But, my lord the king, are they not all my lord's servants? Why does my lord seek this thing? Why should he be a cause of guilt to Israel?"

4 Nevertheless, the king's word prevailed against Joab. Therefore, Joab departed and went throughout all Israel, and came to Jerusalem.

5 Joab gave the number of the census of *all* the people to David. And all Israel were 1,100,000 men who drew the sword; and Judah *was* 470,000 men who drew the sword.

6 But he did not number Levi and Benjamin among them, for the king's command was abhorrent to Joab.

7 ¶ God was displeased with this thing, so He struck Israel.

8 David said to God, "I have sinned greatly, in that I have done this thing. But now, please take away the iniquity of Your servant, for I have done very foolishly."

9 ¶ The LORD spoke to Gad, David's seer, saying,

10 "Go and speak to David, saying, 'Thus says the LORD, "I offer you three things; choose for yourself one of them, which I will do to you." ' "

11 So Gad came to David and said to him, "Thus says the LORD, 'Take for yourself

New International

The Capture of Rabbah

20 IN THE spring, at the time when kings go off to war, Joab led out the armed forces. He laid waste the land of the Ammonites and went to Rabbah and besieged it, but David remained in Jerusalem. Joab attacked Rabbah and left it in ruins. 2David took the crown from the head of their king[s]—its weight was found to be a talent[t] of gold, and it was set with precious stones—and it was placed on David's head. He took a great quantity of plunder from the city 3and brought out the people who were there, consigning them to labor with saws and with iron picks and axes. David did this to all the Ammonite towns. Then David and his entire army returned to Jerusalem.

War With the Philistines

4In the course of time, war broke out with the Philistines, at Gezer. At that time Sibbecai the Hushathite killed Sippai, one of the descendants of the Rephaites, and the Philistines were subjugated.

5In another battle with the Philistines, Elhanan son of Jair killed Lahmi the brother of Goliath the Gittite, who had a spear with a shaft like a weaver's rod.

6In still another battle, which took place at Gath, there was a huge man with six fingers on each hand and six toes on each foot—twenty-four in all. He also was descended from Rapha. 7When he taunted Israel, Jonathan son of Shimea, David's brother, killed him.

8These were descendants of Rapha in Gath, and they fell at the hands of David and his men.

David Numbers the Fighting Men

21 SATAN ROSE up against Israel and incited David to take a census of Israel. 2So David said to Joab and the commanders of the troops, "Go and count the Israelites from Beersheba to Dan. Then report back to me so that I may know how many there are."

3But Joab replied, "May the LORD multiply his troops a hundred times over. My lord the king, are they not all my lord's subjects? Why does my lord want to do this? Why should he bring guilt on Israel?"

4The king's word, however, overruled Joab; so Joab left and went throughout Israel and then came back to Jerusalem. 5Joab reported the number of the fighting men to David: In all Israel there were one million one hundred thousand men who could handle a sword, including four hundred and seventy thousand in Judah.

6But Joab did not include Levi and Benjamin in the numbering, because the king's command was repulsive to him. 7This command was also evil in the sight of God; so he punished Israel.

8Then David said to God, "I have sinned greatly by doing this. Now, I beg you, take away the guilt of your servant. I have done a very foolish thing."

9The LORD said to Gad, David's seer, 10"Go and tell David, 'This is what the LORD says: I am giving you three options. Choose one of them for me to carry out against you.' "

11So Gad went to David and said to him, "This is what

---

[s]2 Or *of Milcom,* that is, Molech   [t]2 That is, about 75 pounds (about 34 kilograms)

King James

¹²Either three years' famine; or three months to be destroyed before thy foes, while that the sword of thine enemies overtaketh *thee;* or else three days the sword of the LORD, even the pestilence, in the land, and the angel of the LORD destroying throughout all the coasts of Israel. Now therefore advise thyself what word I shall bring again to him that sent me.

¹³And David said unto Gad, I am in a great strait: let me fall now into the hand of the LORD; for very *i* great *are* his mercies: but let me not fall into the hand of man.

¹⁴ ¶ So the LORD sent pestilence upon Israel: and there fell of Israel seventy thousand men.

¹⁵And God sent an angel unto Jerusalem to destroy it: and as he was destroying, the LORD beheld, and he repented him of the evil, and said to the angel that destroyed, It is enough, stay now thine hand. And the angel of the LORD stood by the threshingfloor of *j*Ornan the Jebusite.

¹⁶And David lifted up his eyes, and saw the angel of the LORD stand between the earth and the heaven, having a drawn sword in his hand stretched out over Jerusalem. Then David and the elders *of Israel, who were* clothed in sackcloth, fell upon their faces.

¹⁷And David said unto God, *Is it* not I *that* commanded the people to be numbered? even I it is that have sinned and done evil indeed; but *as for* these sheep, what have they done? let thine hand, I pray thee, O LORD my God, be on me, and on my father's house; but not on thy people, that they should be plagued.

¹⁸ ¶ Then the angel of the LORD commanded Gad to say to David, that David should go up, and set up an altar unto the LORD in the threshingfloor of Ornan the Jebusite.

¹⁹And David went up at the saying of Gad, which he spake in the name of the LORD.

²⁰*k*And Ornan turned back, and saw the angel; and his four sons with him hid themselves. Now Ornan was threshing wheat.

²¹And as David came to Ornan, Ornan looked and saw David, and went out of the threshingfloor, and bowed himself to David with *his* face to the ground.

²²Then David said to Ornan, *l*Grant me the place of *this* threshingfloor, that I may build an altar therein unto the LORD: thou shalt grant it me for the full price: that the plague may be stayed from the people.

²³And Ornan said unto David, Take *it* to thee, and let my lord the king do *that which is* good in his eyes: lo, I give *thee* the oxen *also* for burnt offerings, and the threshing instruments for wood, and the wheat for the meat offering; I give it all.

²⁴And king David said to Ornan, Nay; but I will verily buy it for the full price: for I will not take *that* which *is* thine for the LORD, nor offer burnt offerings without cost.

²⁵So David gave to Ornan for the place six hundred shekels of gold by weight.

²⁶And David built there an altar unto the LORD, and offered burnt offerings and peace offerings, and called upon the LORD; and he answered him from heaven by fire upon the altar of burnt offering.

²⁷And the LORD commanded the angel; and he put up his sword again into the sheath thereof.

²⁸ ¶ At that time when David saw that the LORD had answered him in the threshingfloor of Ornan the Jebusite, then he sacrificed there.

²⁹For the tabernacle of the LORD, which Moses made in the wilderness, and the altar of the burnt offering, *were* at that season in the high place at Gibeon.

³⁰But David could not go before it to inquire of God: for he was afraid because of the sword of the angel of the LORD.

Amplified

¹²Either three years of famine, or three months of devastation before your foes, while the sword of your enemies overtakes you, or else three days of the sword of the Lord and pestilence in the land, and the angel of the Lord destroying throughout all the borders of Israel. Now therefore, consider what answer I shall return to Him Who sent me.

¹³And David said to Gad, I am in great *and* distressing perplexity; let me fall, I pray you, into the hands of the Lord, for very great *and* many are His mercies; but let me not fall into the hands of man.

¹⁴So the Lord sent a pestilence upon Israel, and there fell of Israel 70,000 men.

¹⁵God sent an angel to Jerusalem to destroy it, and as he was destroying, the Lord beheld, and He regretted *and* relented of the evil and said to the destroying angel, It is enough; now stay your hand. And the angel of the Lord stood by the threshing floor of Ornan the Jebusite.

¹⁶David lifted up his eyes and saw the angel of the Lord standing between earth and the heavens, having a drawn sword in his hand stretched out over Jerusalem. Then David and the elders, clothed in sackcloth, fell upon their faces.

¹⁷And David said to God, Is it not I who commanded the people to be numbered? It is I who has sinned and done evil indeed; but as for these sheep, what have they done? Let Your hand, I pray You, O Lord my God, be on me and on my father's house; but not on Your people, that they should be plagued.

¹⁸Then the angel of the Lord commanded Gad to say to David that David should go up and set up an altar to the Lord in the threshing floor of Ornan the Jebusite.

¹⁹So David went up at Gad's word, which he spoke in the name of the Lord.

²⁰Now Ornan was threshing wheat, and he turned back and saw the angel; and his four sons hid themselves.

²¹And as David came to Ornan, Ornan looked and saw him, and went out from the threshing floor and bowed himself to David with his face to the ground.

²²Then David said to Ornan, Grant me the site of this threshing floor, that I may build an altar on it to the Lord. You shall charge me the full price for it, that the plague may be averted from the people.

²³Ornan said to David, Take it; and let my lord the king do what is good in his eyes. I give you the oxen also for burnt offerings and the threshing sledges for wood and the wheat for the meal offering. I give it all.

²⁴And King David said to Ornan, No, but I will pay the full price. I will not take what is yours for the Lord, nor offer burnt offerings which cost me nothing.

²⁵So David gave to Ornan for the site 600 shekels of gold by weight.

²⁶And David built there an altar to the Lord and offered burnt offerings and peace offerings and called upon the Lord; and He answered him by fire from heaven upon the altar of burnt offering.

²⁷Then the Lord commanded the [avenging] angel, and he put his sword back into its sheath.

²⁸When David saw that the Lord had answered him at the threshing floor of Ornan the Jebusite, he sacrificed there.

²⁹For the tabernacle of the Lord, which Moses made in the wilderness, and the altar of burnt offering were at that time in the high place at Gibeon.

³⁰But David could not go before it to inquire of God, for he was afraid of the sword of the angel of the Lord.

---

i Or, *many*   *j* Or, *Araunah;* see 2 Sam. 24:18   *k* Or, *When Ornan turned back and saw the angel,* then he *and his four sons with him hid themselves.*   *l* Heb. *Give*

New American Standard

¹² either three years of famine, or three months to be swept away before your foes, while the sword of your enemies overtakes *you*, or else three days of the sword of the LORD, even pestilence in the land, and the angel of the LORD destroying throughout all the territory of Israel.' Now, therefore, consider what answer I shall return to Him who sent me."

¹³ David said to Gad, "I am in great distress; please let me fall into the hand of the LORD, for His mercies are very great. But do not let me fall into the hand of man."

¹⁴ ¶ So the LORD sent a pestilence on Israel; 70,000 men of Israel fell.

¹⁵ And God sent an angel to Jerusalem to destroy it; but as he was about to destroy *it,* the LORD saw and was sorry over the calamity, and said to the destroying angel, "It is enough; now relax your hand." And the angel of the LORD was standing by the threshing floor of Ornan the Jebusite.

¹⁶ Then David lifted up his eyes and saw the angel of the LORD standing between earth and heaven, with his drawn sword in his hand stretched out over Jerusalem. Then David and the elders, covered with sackcloth, fell on their faces.

¹⁷ David said to God, "Is it not I who commanded to count the people? Indeed, I am the one who has sinned and done very wickedly, but these sheep, what have they done? O LORD my God, please let Your hand be against me and my father's household, but not against Your people that they should be plagued."

David's Altar

¹⁸ ¶ Then the angel of the LORD commanded Gad to say to David, that David should go up and build an altar to the LORD on the threshing floor of Ornan the Jebusite.

¹⁹ So David went up at the word of Gad, which he spoke in the name of the LORD.

²⁰ Now Ornan turned back and saw the angel, and his four sons *who were* with him hid themselves. And Ornan was threshing wheat.

²¹ As David came to Ornan, Ornan looked and saw David, and went out from the threshing floor and prostrated himself before David with his face to the ground.

²² Then David said to Ornan, "Give me the site of *this* threshing floor, that I may build on it an altar to the LORD; for the full price you shall give it to me, that the plague may be restrained from the people."

²³ Ornan said to David, "Take *it* for yourself; and let my lord the king do what is good in his sight. See, I will give the oxen for burnt offerings and the threshing sledges for wood and the wheat for the grain offering; I will give *it* all."

²⁴ But King David said to Ornan, "No, but I will surely buy *it* for the full price; for I will not take what is yours for the LORD, or offer a burnt offering which costs me nothing."

²⁵ So David gave Ornan 600 shekels of gold by weight for the site.

²⁶ Then David built an altar to the LORD there and offered burnt offerings and peace offerings. And he called to the LORD and He answered him with fire from heaven on the altar of burnt offering.

²⁷ The LORD commanded the angel, and he put his sword back in its sheath.

²⁸ ¶ At that time, when David saw that the LORD had answered him on the threshing floor of Ornan the Jebusite, he offered sacrifice there.

²⁹ For the tabernacle of the LORD, which Moses had made in the wilderness, and the altar of burnt offering *were* in the high place at Gibeon at that time.

³⁰ But David could not go before it to inquire of God, for he was terrified by the sword of the angel of the LORD.

New International

the LORD says: 'Take your choice: ¹²three years of famine, three months of being swept away[u] before your enemies, with their swords overtaking you, or three days of the sword of the LORD—days of plague in the land, with the angel of the LORD ravaging every part of Israel.' Now then, decide how I should answer the one who sent me."

¹³David said to Gad, "I am in deep distress. Let me fall into the hands of the LORD, for his mercy is very great; but do not let me fall into the hands of men."

¹⁴So the LORD sent a plague on Israel, and seventy thousand men of Israel fell dead. ¹⁵And God sent an angel to destroy Jerusalem. But as the angel was doing so, the LORD saw it and was grieved because of the calamity and said to the angel who was destroying the people, "Enough! Withdraw your hand." The angel of the LORD was then standing at the threshing floor of Araunah[v] the Jebusite.

¹⁶David looked up and saw the angel of the LORD standing between heaven and earth, with a drawn sword in his hand extended over Jerusalem. Then David and the elders, clothed in sackcloth, fell facedown.

¹⁷David said to God, "Was it not I who ordered the fighting men to be counted? I am the one who has sinned and done wrong. These are but sheep. What have they done? O LORD my God, let your hand fall upon me and my family, but do not let this plague remain on your people."

¹⁸Then the angel of the LORD ordered Gad to tell David to go up and build an altar to the LORD on the threshing floor of Araunah the Jebusite. ¹⁹So David went up in obedience to the word that Gad had spoken in the name of the LORD.

²⁰While Araunah was threshing wheat, he turned and saw the angel; his four sons who were with him hid themselves. ²¹Then David approached, and when Araunah looked and saw him, he left the threshing floor and bowed down before David with his face to the ground.

²²David said to him, "Let me have the site of your threshing floor so I can build an altar to the LORD, that the plague on the people may be stopped. Sell it to me at the full price."

²³Araunah said to David, "Take it! Let my lord the king do whatever pleases him. Look, I will give the oxen for the burnt offerings, the threshing sledges for the wood, and the wheat for the grain offering. I will give all this."

²⁴But King David replied to Araunah, "No, I insist on paying the full price. I will not take for the LORD what is yours, or sacrifice a burnt offering that costs me nothing."

²⁵So David paid Araunah six hundred shekels[w] of gold for the site. ²⁶David built an altar to the LORD there and sacrificed burnt offerings and fellowship offerings.[x] He called on the LORD, and the LORD answered him with fire from heaven on the altar of burnt offering.

²⁷Then the LORD spoke to the angel, and he put his sword back into its sheath. ²⁸At that time, when David saw that the LORD had answered him on the threshing floor of Araunah the Jebusite, he offered sacrifices there. ²⁹The tabernacle of the LORD, which Moses had made in the desert, and the altar of burnt offering were at that time on the high place at Gibeon. ³⁰But David could not go before it to inquire of God, because he was afraid of the sword of the angel of the LORD.

u 12 Hebrew; Septuagint and Vulgate (see also 2 Samuel 24:13) *of fleeing*   *v 15* Hebrew *Ornan,* a variant of *Araunah;* also in verses 18-28   *w 25* That is, about 15 pounds (about 7 kilograms)   *x 26* Traditionally *peace offerings*

King James

Amplified

22 THEN DAVID said, This *is* the house of the LORD God, and this *is* the altar of the burnt offering for Israel.

Preparing to build the temple

2 And David commanded to gather together the strangers that *were* in the land of Israel; and he set masons to hew wrought stones to build the house of God.

3 And David prepared iron in abundance for the nails for the doors of the gates, and for the joinings; and brass in abundance without weight;

4 Also cedar trees in abundance: for the Zidonians and they of Tyre brought much cedar wood to David.

5 And David said, Solomon my son *is* young and tender, and the house *that is* to be builded for the LORD *must be* exceeding magnifical, of fame and of glory throughout all countries: I will *therefore* now make preparation for it. So David prepared abundantly before his death.

6 ¶ Then he called for Solomon his son, and charged him to build an house for the LORD God of Israel.

7 And David said to Solomon, My son, as for me, it was in my mind to build an house unto the name of the LORD my God:

8 But the word of the LORD came to me, saying, Thou hast shed blood abundantly, and hast made great wars: thou shalt not build an house unto my name, because thou hast shed much blood upon the earth in my sight.

9 Behold, a son shall be born to thee, who shall be a man of rest; and I will give him rest from all his enemies round about: for his name shall be *m*Solomon, and I will give peace and quietness unto Israel in his days.

10 He shall build an house for my name; and he shall be my son, and I *will be* his father; and I will establish the throne of his kingdom over Israel for ever.

11 Now, my son, the LORD be with thee; and prosper thou, and build the house of the LORD thy God, as he hath said of thee.

12 Only the LORD give thee wisdom and understanding, and give thee charge concerning Israel, that thou mayest keep the law of the LORD thy God.

13 Then shalt thou prosper, if thou takest heed to fulfil the statutes and judgments which the LORD charged Moses with concerning Israel: be strong, and of good courage; dread not, nor be dismayed.

14 Now, behold, *n*in my trouble I have prepared for the house of the LORD an hundred thousand talents of gold, and a thousand thousand talents of silver; and of brass and iron without weight; for it is in abundance: timber also and stone have I prepared; and thou mayest add thereto.

15 Moreover *there are* workmen with thee in abundance, hewers and *o*workers of stone and timber, and all manner of cunning men for every manner of work.

16 Of the gold, the silver, and the brass, and the iron, *there is* no number. Arise *therefore*, and be doing, and the LORD be with thee.

17 ¶ David also commanded all the princes of Israel to help Solomon his son, *saying*,

18 *Is* not the LORD your God with you? and hath he *not* given you rest on every side? for he hath given the inhabitants of the land into mine hand; and the land is subdued before the LORD, and before his people.

19 Now set your heart and your soul to seek the LORD your God; arise therefore, and build ye the sanctuary of the LORD God, to bring the ark of the covenant of the LORD, and the holy vessels of God, into the house that is to be built to the name of the LORD.

22 THEN DAVID said, Here shall be the house of the Lord God, and here the altar of the burnt offering for Israel.

2 David commanded to gather together the strangers who were in the land of Israel, and he set stonecutters to hew out stones to build the house of God.

3 David prepared iron in abundance for nails for the doors of the gates and for the couplings, and bronze in abundance without weighing,

4 Also cedar trees without number, for the Sidonians and they of Tyre brought much cedar timber to David.

5 David said, Solomon my son is young and inexperienced, and the house that is to be built for the Lord must be exceedingly magnificent, of fame and glory throughout all lands. I will therefore make preparation for it. So David prepared abundantly before his death.

6 Then he called for Solomon his son and charged him to build a house for the Lord, the God of Israel.

7 David said to Solomon, My son, it was in my heart to build a house to the *c*Name *and* [for the symbol of] the Presence of the Lord my God.

8 But the word of the Lord came to me, saying, You have shed much blood and have waged great wars; you shall not build a house to My Name, because you have shed much blood on the earth in My sight.

9 Behold, a son shall be born to you who shall be a man of peace. I will give him rest from all his enemies round about; for his name shall be Solomon [peaceable], and I will give peace and quiet to Israel in his days. [II Sam. 12:24, 25.]

10 He shall build a house for My Name *and* [the symbol of My] Presence. He shall be My son, and I will be his father; and I will establish his royal throne over Israel forever.

11 Now, my son, the Lord be with and prosper you in building the house of the Lord your God, as He has spoken concerning you.

12 Only may the Lord give you wisdom and understanding as you are put in charge of Israel, that you may keep the law of the Lord your God.

13 Then you will prosper if you are careful to keep *and* fulfill the statutes and ordinances with which the Lord charged Moses concerning Israel. Be strong and of good courage. Dread not *and* fear not; be not dismayed.

14 In my affliction *and* trouble I have provided for the house of the Lord 100,000 talents of gold, 1,000,000 talents of silver, and bronze and iron without weighing. I have also provided timber and stone; you must add to them.

15 You have workmen in abundance: hewers, workers of stone and timber, and all kinds of craftsmen without number, skillful in doing every kind of work

16 With gold, silver, bronze, and iron. So arise and be doing, and the Lord be with you!

17 David also commanded all the princes of Israel to help Solomon his son, saying,

18 Is not the Lord your God with you? And has He not given you peace on every side? For He has given the inhabitants of the land into my hand, and the land is subdued before the Lord and His people.

19 Now set your mind and heart to seek (inquire of and require as your vital necessity) the Lord your God. Arise and build the sanctuary of the Lord God, so that the ark of the covenant of the Lord and the holy vessels of God may be brought into the house built to the Name *and* renown of the Lord.

---

*m*i.e. *Peaceable*   *n*Or, *in my poverty*   *o*i.e. *masons and carpenters*

*c*See footnote on Deut. 12:5.

New American Standard

David Prepares for Temple Building

22 THEN DAVID said, "This is the house of the LORD God, and this is the altar of burnt offering for Israel."

2 ¶ So David gave orders to gather the foreigners who were in the land of Israel, and he set stonecutters to hew out stones to build the house of God.

3 David prepared large quantities of iron to make the nails for the doors of the gates and for the clamps, and more bronze than could be weighed;

4 and timbers of cedar logs beyond number, for the Sidonians and Tyrians brought large quantities of cedar timber to David.

5 David said, "My son Solomon is young and inexperienced, and the house that is to be built for the LORD shall be exceedingly magnificent, famous and glorious throughout all lands. *Therefore* now I will make preparation for it." So David made ample preparations before his death.

Solomon Charged with the Task

6 ¶ Then he called for his son Solomon, and charged him to build a house for the LORD God of Israel.

7 David said to Solomon, "My son, I had intended to build a house to the name of the LORD my God.

8 "But the word of the LORD came to me, saying, 'You have shed much blood and have waged great wars; you shall not build a house to My name, because you have shed *so* much blood on the earth before Me.

9 'Behold, a son will be born to you, who shall be a man of rest; and I will give him rest from all his enemies on every side; for his name shall be gSolomon, and I will give peace and quiet to Israel in his days.

10 'He shall build a house for My name, and he shall be My son and I will be his father; and I will establish the throne of his kingdom over Israel forever.'

11 "Now, my son, the LORD be with you that you may be successful, and build the house of the LORD your God just as He has spoken concerning you.

12 "Only the LORD give you discretion and understanding, and give you charge over Israel, so that you may keep the law of the LORD your God.

13 "Then you will prosper, if you are careful to observe the statutes and the ordinances which the LORD commanded Moses concerning Israel. Be strong and courageous, do not fear nor be dismayed.

14 "Now behold, with great pains I have prepared for the house of the LORD 100,000 talents of gold and 1,000,000 talents of silver, and bronze and iron beyond weight, for they are in great quantity; also timber and stone I have prepared, and you may add to them.

15 "Moreover, there are many workmen with you, stonecutters and masons of stone and carpenters, and all men who are skillful in every kind of work.

16 "Of the gold, the silver and the bronze and the iron there is no limit. Arise and work, and may the LORD be with you."

17 ¶ David also commanded all the leaders of Israel to help his son Solomon, *saying,*

18 "Is not the LORD your God with you? And has He not given you rest on every side? For He has given the inhabitants of the land into my hand, and the land is subdued before the LORD and before His people.

19 "Now set your heart and your soul to seek the LORD your God; arise, therefore, and build the sanctuary of the LORD God, so that you may bring the ark of the covenant of the LORD and the holy vessels of God into the house that is to be built for the name of the LORD."

New International

22 THEN DAVID said, "The house of the LORD God is to be here, and also the altar of burnt offering for Israel."

Preparations for the Temple

2 So David gave orders to assemble the aliens living in Israel, and from among them he appointed stonecutters to prepare dressed stone for building the house of God. 3 He provided a large amount of iron to make nails for the doors of the gateways and for the fittings, and more bronze than could be weighed. 4 He also provided more cedar logs than could be counted, for the Sidonians and Tyrians had brought large numbers of them to David.

5 David said, "My son Solomon is young and inexperienced, and the house to be built for the LORD should be of great magnificence and fame and splendor in the sight of all the nations. Therefore I will make preparations for it." So David made extensive preparations before his death.

6 Then he called for his son Solomon and charged him to build a house for the LORD, the God of Israel. 7 David said to Solomon: "My son, I had it in my heart to build a house for the Name of the LORD my God. 8 But this word of the LORD came to me: 'You have shed much blood and have fought many wars. You are not to build a house for my Name, because you have shed much blood on the earth in my sight. 9 But you will have a son who will be a man of peace and rest, and I will give him rest from all his enemies on every side. His name will be Solomon,y and I will grant Israel peace and quiet during his reign. 10 He is the one who will build a house for my Name. He will be my son, and I will be his father. And I will establish the throne of his kingdom over Israel forever.'

11 "Now, my son, the LORD be with you, and may you have success and build the house of the LORD your God, as he said you would. 12 May the LORD give you discretion and understanding when he puts you in command over Israel, so that you may keep the law of the LORD your God. 13 Then you will have success if you are careful to observe the decrees and laws that the LORD gave Moses for Israel. Be strong and courageous. Do not be afraid or discouraged.

14 "I have taken great pains to provide for the temple of the LORD a hundred thousand talentsz of gold, a million talentsa of silver, quantities of bronze and iron too great to be weighed, and wood and stone. And you may add to them. 15 You have many workmen: stonecutters, masons and carpenters, as well as men skilled in every kind of work 16 in gold and silver, bronze and iron—craftsmen beyond number. Now begin the work, and the LORD be with you."

17 Then David ordered all the leaders of Israel to help his son Solomon. 18 He said to them, "Is not the LORD your God with you? And has he not granted you rest on every side? For he has handed the inhabitants of the land over to me, and the land is subject to the LORD and to his people. 19 Now devote your heart and soul to seeking the LORD your God. Begin to build the sanctuary of the LORD God, so that you may bring the ark of the covenant of the LORD and the sacred articles belonging to God into the temple that will be built for the Name of the LORD."

---

g I.e. peaceful

y 9 *Solomon* sounds like and may be derived from the Hebrew for *peace.*   z 14 That is, about 3,750 tons (about 3,450 metric tons)
a 14 That is, about 37,500 tons (about 34,500 metric tons)

King James

Priests and Levites assembled

23 SO WHEN David was old and full of days, he made Solomon his son king over Israel.

2 ¶ And he gathered together all the princes of Israel, with the priests and the Levites.

3 Now the Levites were numbered from the age of thirty years and upward: and their number by their polls, man by man, was thirty and eight thousand.

4 Of which, twenty and four thousand *were* Pto set forward the work of the house of the LORD; and six thousand *were* officers and judges:

5 Moreover four thousand *were* porters; and four thousand praised the LORD with the instruments which I made, *said David,* to praise *therewith.*

6 And David divided them into qcourses among the sons of Levi, *namely,* Gershon, Kohath, and Merari.

7 ¶ Of the Gershonites *were,* rLaadan, and Shimei.

8 The sons of Laadan; the chief *was* Jehiel, and Zetham, and Joel, three.

9 The sons of Shimei; Shelomith, and Haziel, and Haran, three. These *were* the chief of the fathers of Laadan.

10 And the sons of Shimei *were,* Jahath, sZina, and Jeush, and Beriah. These four *were* the sons of Shimei.

11 And Jahath was the chief, and Zizah the second: but Jeush and Beriah thad not many sons; therefore they were in one reckoning, according to *their* father's house.

12 ¶ The sons of Kohath; Amram, Izhar, Hebron, and Uzziel, four.

13 The sons of Amram; Aaron and Moses: and Aaron was separated, that he should sanctify the most holy things, he and his sons for ever, to burn incense before the LORD, to minister unto him, and to bless in his name for ever.

14 Now *concerning* Moses the man of God, his sons were named of the tribe of Levi.

15 The sons of Moses *were,* Gershom, and Eliezer.

16 Of the sons of Gershom, uShebuel *was* the chief.

17 And the sons of Eliezer *were,* Rehabiah vthe chief. And Eliezer had none other sons; but the sons of Rehabiah wwere very many.

18 Of the sons of Izhar; xShelomith the chief.

19 Of the sons of Hebron; Jeriah the first, Amariah the second, Jahaziel the third, and Jekameam the fourth.

20 Of the sons of Uzziel; Michah the first, and Jesiah the second.

21 ¶ The sons of Merari; Mahli, and Mushi. The sons of Mahli; Eleazar, and Kish.

22 And Eleazar died, and had no sons, but daughters: and their ybrethren the sons of Kish took them.

23 The sons of Mushi; Mahli, and Eder, and Jeremoth, three.

The duties of the Levites

24 ¶ These *were* the sons of Levi after the house of their fathers; *even* the chief of the fathers, as they were counted by number of names by their polls, that did the work for the service of the house of the LORD, from the age of twenty years and upward.

Amplified

23 WHEN DAVID was old and full of days, he made Solomon his son king over Israel.

2 David assembled all the leaders of Israel, with the priests and Levites.

3 The Levites thirty years old and upward numbered, man by man, 38,000.

4 Of whom d24,000 were to oversee the work of the house of the Lord and 6,000 were to be officers and judges.

5 And, said David, 4,000 shall be gatekeepers and 4,000 are to praise the Lord with the instruments which I made for praise.

6 And David organized them in sections according to the sons of Levi: Gershon, Kohath, and Merari.

7 Of the Gershonites: Ladan (Libni) and Shimei.

8 The sons of Ladan: Jehiel the chief, Zetham, and Joel—three in all.

9 The sons of Shimei: Shelomith, Haziel, and Haran—three in all. These were the heads of the fathers' houses of Ladan.

10 And the sons of Shimei: Jahath, Zina (Zizah), Jeush, and Beriah. Of these four sons of Shimei,

11 Jahath was chief and Zizah the second, but Jeush and Beriah had not many sons [not enough for a father's house or clan]; so they were counted together as one father's house.

12 The sons of Kohath: Amram, Izhar, Hebron, and Uzziel—four in all.

13 The sons of Amram: Aaron and Moses. Aaron was set apart to sanctify him as most holy *and* to consecrate the most holy things, that he and his sons forever might burn incense before the Lord, minister to Him, and bless in His name [and the character which that name denotes] forever.

14 But the sons of Moses the man of God were named among the tribe of Levi.

15 The sons of Moses: Gershom and Eliezer.

16 The son of Gershom: Shebuel the chief.

17 The son of Eliezer: Rehabiah the chief. Eliezer had no other sons, but Rehabiah's sons were very many.

18 The sons of Izhar: Shelomith was the chief.

19 The sons of Hebron: Jeriah the first, Amariah the second, Jahaziel the third, and Jekameam the fourth.

20 The sons of Uzziel: Micah the first and Isshiah the second.

21 The sons of Merari: Mahli and Mushi. The sons of Mahli: Eleazar and Kish.

22 Eleazar died and had no sons, but daughters only, and their kinsmen, sons of Kish, took them as wives.

23 The sons of Mushi: Mahli, Eder, and Jeremoth—three in all.

24 These were the Levites by their fathers' houses, the heads of the fathers' houses of those registered, according to the number of names of the individuals who were the servants of the house of the Lord, from twenty years old and upward.

---

dThe reader may be tempted to consider these figures absurdly high if he does not get the whole picture. Note these features of it: 1. The Levites were divided into twenty-four rotating divisions (I Chron. 24:6-19). 2. One thousand Levites on duty at one time for Solomon's temple, considering the many purposes and cost of the building, its ornate ritual, and the scale of the work, is not unreasonable according to authorities. 3. In the primitive simplicity of the wilderness, the worshiper killed the animal he brought for an offering, skinned it, cut it in pieces, and washed the entrails and legs. But now all these services were the duty of the Levites or Nethinim (servants of the temple); in addition, the number of worshipers had greatly increased (hence the need for a large number of Levites).

---

pOr, *to oversee*   qHeb. *divisions*   rOr, *Libni;* see ch. 6:17
sOr, *Zizah*   tHeb. *did not multiply sons*   uOr, *Shubael;* see
ch. 24:20   vOr, *the first*   wHeb. *were highly multiplied*
xOr, *Shelomoth;* see ch. 24:22   yOr, *kinsmen*

New American Standard

Solomon Reigns

23 NOW WHEN David reached old age, he made his son Solomon king over Israel.
2 And he gathered together all the leaders of Israel with the priests and the Levites.

Offices of the Levites

3 The Levites were numbered from thirty years old and upward, and their number by census of men was 38,000.
4 Of these, 24,000 were to oversee the work of the house of the LORD; and 6,000 *were* officers and judges,
5 and 4,000 *were* gatekeepers, and 4,000 *were* praising the LORD with the instruments which David made for giving praise.
6 David divided them into divisions according to the sons of Levi: Gershon, Kohath, and Merari.

Gershonites

7 ¶ Of the Gershonites *were* Ladan and Shimei.
8 The sons of Ladan *were* Jehiel the first and Zetham and Joel, three.
9 The sons of Shimei *were* Shelomoth and Haziel and Haran, three. These were the heads of the fathers' *households* of Ladan.
10 The sons of Shimei *were* Jahath, Zina, Jeush and Beriah. These four *were* the sons of Shimei.
11 Jahath was the first and Zizah the second; but Jeush and Beriah did not have many sons, so they became a father's household, one class.

Kohathites

12 ¶ The sons of Kohath were four: Amram, Izhar, Hebron and Uzziel.
13 The sons of Amram were Aaron and Moses. And Aaron was set apart to sanctify him as most holy, he and his sons forever, to burn incense before the LORD, to minister to Him and to bless in His name forever.
14 But *as for* Moses the man of God, his sons were named among the tribe of Levi.
15 The sons of Moses *were* Gershom and Eliezer.
16 The son of Gershom *was* Shebuel the chief.
17 The son of Eliezer was Rehabiah the chief; and Eliezer had no other sons, but the sons of Rehabiah were very many.
18 The son of Izhar was Shelomith the chief.
19 The sons of Hebron *were* Jeriah the first, Amariah the second, Jahaziel the third and Jekameam the fourth.
20 The sons of Uzziel *were* Micah the first and Isshiah the second.

Merarites

21 ¶ The sons of Merari were Mahli and Mushi. The sons of Mahli *were* Eleazar and Kish.
22 Eleazar died and had no sons, but daughters only, so their brothers, the sons of Kish, took them *as wives.*
23 The sons of Mushi *were* three: Mahli, Eder and Jeremoth.

Duties Revised

24 ¶ These were the sons of Levi according to their fathers' households, *even* the heads of the fathers' *households* of those of them who were counted, in the number of names by their census, doing the work for the service of the house of the LORD, from twenty years old and upward.

New International

The Levites

23 WHEN DAVID was old and full of years, he made his son Solomon king over Israel.
2He also gathered together all the leaders of Israel, as well as the priests and Levites. 3The Levites thirty years old or more were counted, and the total number of men was thirty-eight thousand. 4David said, "Of these, twenty-four thousand are to supervise the work of the temple of the LORD and six thousand are to be officials and judges. 5Four thousand are to be gatekeepers and four thousand are to praise the LORD with the musical instruments I have provided for that purpose."
6David divided the Levites into groups corresponding to the sons of Levi: Gershon, Kohath and Merari.

Gershonites

7Belonging to the Gershonites:
Ladan and Shimei.
8The sons of Ladan:
Jehiel the first, Zetham and Joel—three in all.
9The sons of Shimei:
Shelomoth, Haziel and Haran—three in all.
These were the heads of the families of Ladan.
10And the sons of Shimei:
Jahath, Ziza,*b* Jeush and Beriah.
These were the sons of Shimei—four in all.
11Jahath was the first and Ziza the second, but Jeush and Beriah did not have many sons; so they were counted as one family with one assignment.

Kohathites

12The sons of Kohath:
Amram, Izhar, Hebron and Uzziel—four in all.
13The sons of Amram:
Aaron and Moses.
Aaron was set apart, he and his descendants forever, to consecrate the most holy things, to offer sacrifices before the LORD, to minister before him and to pronounce blessings in his name forever.
14The sons of Moses the man of God were counted as part of the tribe of Levi.
15The sons of Moses:
Gershom and Eliezer.
16The descendants of Gershom:
Shubael was the first.
17The descendants of Eliezer:
Rehabiah was the first.
Eliezer had no other sons, but the sons of Rehabiah were very numerous.
18The sons of Izhar:
Shelomith was the first.
19The sons of Hebron:
Jeriah the first, Amariah the second, Jahaziel the third and Jekameam the fourth.
20The sons of Uzziel:
Micah the first and Isshiah the second.

Merarites

21The sons of Merari:
Mahli and Mushi.
The sons of Mahli:
Eleazar and Kish.
22Eleazar died without having sons: he had only daughters. Their cousins, the sons of Kish, married them.
23The sons of Mushi:
Mahli, Eder and Jerimoth—three in all.

24These were the descendants of Levi by their families—the heads of families as they were registered under their names and counted individually, that is, the workers twenty years old or more who served in the temple of the

King James

²⁵For David said, The LORD God of Israel hath given rest unto his people, ^zthat they may dwell in Jerusalem for ever:

²⁶And also unto the Levites; they shall no *more* carry the tabernacle, nor any vessels of it for the service thereof.

²⁷For by the last words of David the Levites *were* ^anumbered from twenty years old and above:

²⁸Because ^btheir office *was* to wait on the sons of Aaron for the service of the house of the LORD, in the courts, and in the chambers, and in the purifying of all holy things, and the work of the service of the house of God;

²⁹Both for the showbread, and for the fine flour for meat offering, and for the unleavened cakes, and for *that which is baked in* the ^cpan, and for that which is fried, and for all manner of measure and size;

³⁰And to stand every morning to thank and praise the LORD, and likewise at even;

³¹And to offer all burnt sacrifices unto the LORD in the sabbaths, in the new moons, and on the set feasts, by number, according to the order commanded unto them, continually before the LORD:

³²And that they should keep the charge of the tabernacle of the congregation, and the charge of the holy *place,* and the charge of the sons of Aaron their brethren, in the service of the house of the LORD.

The division of the priests

24 NOW *THESE* are the divisions of the sons of Aaron. The sons of Aaron; Nadab, and Abihu, Eleazar, and Ithamar.

²But Nadab and Abihu died before their father, and had no children: therefore Eleazar and Ithamar executed the priest's office.

³And David distributed them, both Zadok of the sons of Eleazar, and Ahimelech of the sons of Ithamar, according to their offices in their service.

⁴And there were more chief men found of the sons of Eleazar than of the sons of Ithamar; and *thus* were they divided. Among the sons of Eleazar *there were* sixteen chief men of the house of *their* fathers, and eight among the sons of Ithamar according to the house of their fathers.

⁵Thus were they divided by lot, one sort with another; for the governors of the sanctuary, and governors *of the house* of God, were of the sons of Eleazar, and of the sons of Ithamar.

⁶And Shemaiah the son of Nethaneel the scribe, *one* of the Levites, wrote them before the king, and the princes, and Zadok the priest, and Ahimelech the son of Abiathar, and *before* the chief of the fathers of the priests and Levites: one ^dprincipal household being taken for Eleazar, and *one* taken for Ithamar.

⁷Now the first lot came forth to Jehoiarib, the second to Jedaiah,

⁸The third to Harim, the fourth to Seorim,

⁹The fifth to Malchijah, the sixth to Mijamin,

¹⁰The seventh to Hakkoz, the eighth to Abijah,

¹¹The ninth to Jeshuah, the tenth to Shecaniah,

¹²The eleventh to Eliashib, the twelfth to Jakim,

¹³The thirteenth to Huppah, the fourteenth to Jeshebeab,

¹⁴The fifteenth to Bilgah, the sixteenth to Immer,

¹⁵The seventeenth to Hezir, the eighteenth to Aphses,

¹⁶The nineteenth to Pethahiah, the twentieth to Jehezekel,

¹⁷The one and twentieth to Jachin, the two and twentieth to Gamul,

¹⁸The three and twentieth to Delaiah, the four and twentieth to Maaziah.

Amplified

²⁵For David said, The Lord, the God of Israel has given peace *and* rest to His people, and He dwells in Jerusalem forever.

²⁶So the Levites no more have need to carry the tabernacle and all its vessels for its service.

²⁷For by the last words *and* acts of David, these were the number of the Levites from twenty years old and above.

²⁸But their duty should be to wait on [the priests] the sons of Aaron in the service of the house of the Lord, caring for the courts, the chambers, the cleansing of all holy things, and any work of the service of God's house,

²⁹For the showbread also, and for the fine flour for a cereal offering, whether of unleavened wafers or of what is baked on the griddle or soaked [in oil], and for all measuring of amount and size [as the Law of Moses required].

³⁰They are also to stand every morning to thank and praise the Lord, and likewise at evening,

³¹And to assist in offering all burnt sacrifices to the Lord on Sabbaths, New Moon festivals, and set feast days by number according to the ordinance concerning them, continually before the Lord.

³²So they shall keep charge of the Tent of Meeting and the Holy Place and shall attend to the sons of Aaron their kinsmen, for the service of the house of the Lord.

24 THE COURSES *or* divisions of the priests, the sons of Aaron, were these: The sons of Aaron: Nadab, and Abihu, Eleazar, and Ithamar.

²But Nadab and Abihu died before their father and had no children; therefore Eleazar and Ithamar executed the priest's office.

³And David, with Zadok of the sons of Eleazar and Ahimelech of the sons of Ithamar, divided *and* distributed them according to their assigned duties.

⁴Since there were more chief men found among the sons of Eleazar [because of the misfortunes of Eli, and Saul's slaughter of the priests at Nob] than among the sons of Ithamar, they were divided thus: sixteen heads of fathers' houses of the sons of Eleazar and eight of the sons of Ithamar according to their fathers' houses.

⁵Thus were they divided by lot, one group with the other, for there were chiefs of the sanctuary and chiefs of God [high priests] drawn both from the sons of Eleazar and from the sons of Ithamar.

⁶Shemaiah the scribe, son of Nethanel, a Levite, recorded them in the presence of the king, the princes, Zadok the priest, Ahimelech son of Abiathar [the priest who escaped being killed at Nob by Saul and fled to David], and the heads of the fathers' houses of the priests and Levites— one father's house being taken alternately for Eleazar and one for Ithamar.

⁷The lots fell, the first one to Jehoiarib, the second to Jedaiah,

⁸The third to Harim, the fourth to Se-orim,

⁹The fifth to Malchijah, the sixth to Mijamin,

¹⁰The seventh to Hakkoz, the eighth to Abijah,

¹¹The ninth to Jeshua, the tenth to Shecaniah,

¹²The eleventh to Eliashib, the twelfth to Jakim,

¹³The thirteenth to Huppah, the fourteenth to Jeshebeab,

¹⁴The fifteenth to Bilgah, the sixteenth to Immer,

¹⁵The seventeenth to Hezir, the eighteenth to Happizzez,

¹⁶The nineteenth to Pethahiah, the twentieth to Jehezkel,

¹⁷The twenty-first to Jachin, the twenty-second to Gamul,

¹⁸The twenty-third to Delaiah, the twenty-fourth to Maaziah.

---

^zOr, *and he dwelleth in Jerusalem*   ^aHeb. *number*   ^bHeb. *their station* was *at the hand of the sons of Aaron*   ^cOr, *flat plate*   ^dHeb. *house of the father*

New American Standard

25 For David said, "The LORD God of Israel has given rest to His people, and He dwells in Jerusalem forever. 26 "Also, the Levites will no longer need to carry the tabernacle and all its utensils for its service." 27 For by the last words of David the sons of Levi *were* numbered from twenty years old and upward. 28 For their office is to assist the sons of Aaron with the service of the house of the LORD, in the courts and in the chambers and in the purifying of all holy things, even the work of the service of the house of God, 29 and with the showbread, and the fine flour for a grain offering, and unleavened wafers, or *what is baked in the* pan or what is well-mixed, and all measures of volume and size. 30 They are to stand every morning to thank and to praise the LORD, and likewise at evening, 31 and to offer all burnt offerings to the LORD, on the sabbaths, the new moons and the fixed festivals in the number *set* by the ordinance concerning them, continually before the LORD.

32 Thus they are to keep charge of the tent of meeting, and charge of the holy place, and charge of the sons of Aaron their relatives, for the service of the house of the LORD.

Divisions of Levites

24 NOW THE divisions of the descendants of Aaron *were these:* the sons of Aaron *were* Nadab, Abihu, Eleazar and Ithamar.

2 But Nadab and Abihu died before their father and had no sons. So Eleazar and Ithamar served as priests.

3 David, with Zadok of the sons of Eleazar and Ahimelech of the sons of Ithamar, divided them according to their offices for their ministry.

4 Since more chief men were found from the descendants of Eleazar than the descendants of Ithamar, they divided them thus: *there were* sixteen heads of fathers' households of the descendants of Eleazar and eight of the descendants of Ithamar, according to their fathers' households.

5 Thus they were divided by lot, the one as the other; for they were officers of the sanctuary and officers of God, both from the descendants of Eleazar and the descendants of Ithamar.

6 Shemaiah, the son of Nethanel the scribe, from the Levites, recorded them in the presence of the king, the princes, Zadok the priest, Ahimelech the son of Abiathar, and the heads of the fathers' *households* of the priests and of the Levites; one father's household taken for Eleazar and one taken for Ithamar.

7 ¶ Now the first lot came out for Jehoiarib, the second for Jedaiah,

8 the third for Harim, the fourth for Seorim,

9 the fifth for Malchijah, the sixth for Mijamin,

10 the seventh for Hakkoz, the eighth for Abijah,

11 the ninth for Jeshua, the tenth for Shecaniah,

12 the eleventh for Eliashib, the twelfth for Jakim,

13 the thirteenth for Huppah, the fourteenth for Jeshebeab,

14 the fifteenth for Bilgah, the sixteenth for Immer,

15 the seventeenth for Hezir, the eighteenth for Happizzez,

16 the nineteenth for Pethahiah, the twentieth for Jehezkel,

17 the twenty-first for Jachin, the twenty-second for Gamul,

18 the twenty-third for Delaiah, the twenty-fourth for Maaziah.

New International

LORD. 25 For David had said, "Since the LORD, the God of Israel, has granted rest to his people and has come to dwell in Jerusalem forever, 26 the Levites no longer need to carry the tabernacle or any of the articles used in its service." 27 According to the last instructions of David, the Levites were counted from those twenty years old or more. 28 The duty of the Levites was to help Aaron's descendants in the service of the temple of the LORD: to be in charge of the courtyards, the side rooms, the purification of all sacred things and the performance of other duties at the house of God. 29 They were in charge of the bread set out on the table, the flour for the grain offerings, the unleavened wafers, the baking and the mixing, and all measurements of quantity and size. 30 They were also to stand every morning to thank and praise the LORD. They were to do the same in the evening 31 and whenever burnt offerings were presented to the LORD on Sabbaths and at New Moon festivals and at appointed feasts. They were to serve before the LORD regularly in the proper number and in the way prescribed for them.

32 And so the Levites carried out their responsibilities for the Tent of Meeting, for the Holy Place and, under their brothers the descendants of Aaron, for the service of the temple of the LORD.

The Divisions of Priests

24 THESE WERE the divisions of the sons of Aaron: The sons of Aaron were Nadab, Abihu, Eleazar and Ithamar. 2 But Nadab and Abihu died before their father did, and they had no sons; so Eleazar and Ithamar served as the priests. 3 With the help of Zadok a descendant of Eleazar and Ahimelech a descendant of Ithamar, David separated them into divisions for their appointed order of ministering. 4 A larger number of leaders were found among Eleazar's descendants than among Ithamar's, and they were divided accordingly: sixteen heads of families from Eleazar's descendants and eight heads of families from Ithamar's descendants. 5 They divided them impartially by drawing lots, for there were officials of the sanctuary and officials of God among the descendants of both Eleazar and Ithamar.

6 The scribe Shemaiah son of Nethanel, a Levite, recorded their names in the presence of the king and of the officials: Zadok the priest, Ahimelech son of Abiathar and the heads of families of the priests and of the Levites—one family being taken from Eleazar and then one from Ithamar.

7 The first lot fell to Jehoiarib,
    the second to Jedaiah,
8 the third to Harim,
    the fourth to Seorim,
9 the fifth to Malkijah,
    the sixth to Mijamin,
10 the seventh to Hakkoz,
    the eighth to Abijah,
11 the ninth to Jeshua,
    the tenth to Shecaniah,
12 the eleventh to Eliashib,
    the twelfth to Jakim,
13 the thirteenth to Huppah,
    the fourteenth to Jeshebeab,
14 the fifteenth to Bilgah,
    the sixteenth to Immer,
15 the seventeenth to Hezir,
    the eighteenth to Happizzez,
16 the nineteenth to Pethahiah,
    the twentieth to Jehezkel,
17 the twenty-first to Jakin,
    the twenty-second to Gamul,
18 the twenty-third to Delaiah
    and the twenty-fourth to Maaziah.

King James

9Now the first lot came forth for Asaph to Joseph: the second to Gedaliah, who with his brethren and sons *were* twelve:

10The third to Zaccur, *he,* his sons, and his brethren, *were* twelve:

11The fourth to Izri, *he,* his sons, and his brethren, *were* twelve:

12The fifth to Nethaniah, *he,* his sons, and his brethren, *were* twelve:

13The sixth to Bukkiah, *he,* his sons, and his brethren, *were* twelve:

14The seventh to Jesharelah, *he,* his sons, and his brethren, *were* twelve:

15The eighth to Jeshaiah, *he,* his sons, and his brethren, *were* twelve:

16The ninth to Mattaniah, *he,* his sons, and his brethren, *were* twelve:

17The tenth to Shimei, *he,* his sons, and his brethren, *were* twelve:

18The eleventh to Azareel, *he,* his sons, and his brethren, *were* twelve:

19The twelfth to Hashabiah, *he,* his sons, and his brethren, *were* twelve:

20The thirteenth to Shubael, *he,* his sons, and his brethren, *were* twelve:

21The fourteenth to Mattithiah, *he,* his sons, and his brethren, *were* twelve:

22The fifteenth to Jeremoth, *he,* his sons, and his brethren, *were* twelve:

23The sixteenth to Hananiah, *he,* his sons, and his brethren, *were* twelve:

24The seventeenth to Joshbekashah, *he,* his sons, and his brethren, *were* twelve:

25The eighteenth to Hanani, *he,* his sons, and his brethren, *were* twelve:

26The nineteenth to Mallothi, *he,* his sons, and his brethren, *were* twelve:

27The twentieth to Eliathah, *he,* his sons, and his brethren, *were* twelve:

28The one and twentieth to Hothir, *he,* his sons, and his brethren, *were* twelve:

29The two and twentieth to Giddalti, *he,* his sons, and his brethren, *were* twelve:

30The three and twentieth to Mahazioth, *he,* his sons, and his brethren, *were* twelve:

31The four and twentieth to Romamti-ezer, *he,* his sons, and his brethren, *were* twelve.

The arrangements for porters

26 CONCERNING THE divisions of the porters: Of the Korhites *was* ¹Meshelemiah the son of Kore, of the sons of ᵐAsaph.

2And the sons of Meshelemiah *were,* Zechariah the firstborn, Jediael the second, Zebadiah the third, Jathniel the fourth,

3Elam the fifth, Jehohanan the sixth, Elioenai the seventh.

4Moreover the sons of Obed-edom *were,* Shemaiah the firstborn, Jehozabad the second, Joah the third, and Sacar the fourth, and Nethaneel the fifth,

Amplified

9The first lot fell for Asaph to Joseph; the second to Gedaliah, to him, his brethren and his sons, twelve;

10The third to Zaccur, his sons and his brethren, twelve;

11The fourth to Izri, his sons and his brethren, twelve;

12The fifth to Nethaniah, his sons and his brethren, twelve;

13The sixth to Bukkiah, his sons and his brethren, twelve;

14The seventh to Jesharelah, his sons and his brethren, twelve;

15The eighth to Jeshaiah, his sons and his brethren, twelve;

16The ninth to Mattaniah, his sons and his brethren, twelve;

17The tenth to Shimei, his sons and his brethren, twelve;

18The eleventh to Azarel, his sons and his brethren, twelve;

19The twelfth to Hashabiah, his sons and his brethren, twelve;

20The thirteenth to Shubael, who had no sons, twelve;

21The fourteenth to Mattithiah, his sons and his brethren, twelve;

22The fifteenth to Jeremoth, his sons and his brethren, twelve;

23The sixteenth to Hananiah, his sons and his brethren, twelve;

24The seventeenth of Joshbekashah, his sons and his brethren, twelve;

25The eighteenth to Hanani, his sons and his brethren, twelve;

26The nineteenth to Mallothi, his sons and his brethren, twelve;

27The twentieth to Eliathah, his sons and his brethren, twelve;

28The twenty-first to Hothir, his sons and his brethren, twelve;

29The twenty-second to Giddalti, his sons and his brethren, twelve;

30The twenty-third to Mahazioth, his sons and his brethren, twelve;

31The twenty-fourth to Romamti-ezer, his sons and his brethren, twelve.

26 FOR THE divisions of the gatekeepers: Of the Korahites was: Meshelemiah son of Kore, of the sons of Asaph.

2And Meshelemiah had sons: Zechariah the firstborn, Jediael the second, Zebadiah the third, Jathniel the fourth,

3Elam the fifth, Jehohanan the sixth, Eliehoenai the seventh.

4Obed-edom had sons: Shemaiah the firstborn, Jehozabad the second, Joah the third, Sacar the fourth, Nethanel the fifth,

New American Standard

9 ¶ Now the first lot came out for Asaph to Joseph, the second for Gedaliah, he with his relatives and sons *were* twelve;
10 the third to Zaccur, his sons and his relatives, twelve;
11 the fourth to Izri, his sons and his relatives, twelve;
12 the fifth to Nethaniah, his sons and his relatives, twelve;
13 the sixth to Bukkiah, his sons and his relatives, twelve;
14 the seventh to Jesharelah, his sons and his relatives, twelve;
15 the eighth to Jeshaiah, his sons and his relatives, twelve;
16 the ninth to Mattaniah, his sons and his relatives, twelve;
17 the tenth to Shimei, his sons and his relatives, twelve;
18 the eleventh to Azarel, his sons and his relatives, twelve;
19 the twelfth to Hashabiah, his sons and his relatives, twelve;
20 for the thirteenth, Shubael, his sons and his relatives, twelve;
21 for the fourteenth, Mattithiah, his sons and his relatives, twelve;
22 for the fifteenth to Jeremoth, his sons and his relatives, twelve;
23 for the sixteenth to Hananiah, his sons and his relatives, twelve;
24 for the seventeenth to Joshbekashah, his sons and his relatives, twelve;
25 for the eighteenth to Hanani, his sons and his relatives, twelve;
26 for the nineteenth to Mallothi, his sons and his relatives, twelve;
27 for the twentieth to Eliathah, his sons and his relatives, twelve;
28 for the twenty-first to Hothir, his sons and his relatives, twelve;
29 for the twenty-second to Giddalti, his sons and his relatives, twelve;
30 for the twenty-third to Mahazioth, his sons and his relatives, twelve;
31 for the twenty-fourth to Romamti-ezer, his sons and his relatives, twelve.

Divisions of the Gatekeepers

26 FOR THE divisions of the gatekeepers *there were* of the Korahites, Meshelemiah the son of Kore, of the sons of Asaph.
2 Meshelemiah had sons: Zechariah the firstborn, Jediael the second, Zebadiah the third, Jathniel the fourth,
3 Elam the fifth, Johanan the sixth, Eliehoenai the seventh.
4 Obed-edom had sons: Shemaiah the firstborn, Jehozabad the second, Joah the third, Sacar the fourth, Nethanel the fifth,

New International

9 The first lot, which was for Asaph, fell to Joseph,
   his sons and relatives, [f]   12 [g]
the second to Gedaliah,
   he and his relatives and sons,   12
10 the third to Zaccur,
   his sons and relatives,   12
11 the fourth to Izri, [h]
   his sons and relatives,   12
12 the fifth to Nethaniah,
   his sons and relatives,   12
13 the sixth to Bukkiah,
   his sons and relatives,   12
14 the seventh to Jesarelah, [i]
   his sons and relatives,   12
15 the eighth to Jeshaiah,
   his sons and relatives,   12
16 the ninth to Mattaniah,
   his sons and relatives,   12
17 the tenth to Shimei,
   his sons and relatives,   12
18 the eleventh to Azarel, [j]
   his sons and relatives,   12
19 the twelfth to Hashabiah,
   his sons and relatives,   12
20 the thirteenth to Shubael,
   his sons and relatives,   12
21 the fourteenth to Mattithiah,
   his sons and relatives,   12
22 the fifteenth to Jerimoth,
   his sons and relatives,   12
23 the sixteenth to Hananiah,
   his sons and relatives,   12
24 the seventeenth to Joshbekashah,
   his sons and relatives,   12
25 the eighteenth to Hanani,
   his sons and relatives,   12
26 the nineteenth to Mallothi,
   his sons and relatives,   12
27 the twentieth to Eliathah,
   his sons and relatives,   12
28 the twenty-first to Hothir,
   his sons and relatives,   12
29 the twenty-second to Giddalti,
   his sons and relatives,   12
30 the twenty-third to Mahazioth,
   his sons and relatives,   12
31 the twenty-fourth to Romamti-Ezer,
   his sons and relatives,   12

The Gatekeepers

26 THE DIVISIONS of the gatekeepers:

From the Korahites: Meshelemiah son of Kore, one of the sons of Asaph.
2 Meshelemiah had sons:
   Zechariah the firstborn,
   Jediael the second,
   Zebadiah the third,
   Jathniel the fourth,
   3 Elam the fifth,
   Jehohanan the sixth
   and Eliehoenai the seventh.
4 Obed-Edom also had sons:
   Shemaiah the firstborn,
   Jehozabad the second,
   Joah the third,
   Sacar the fourth,
   Nethanel the fifth,

---

f 9   See Septuagint; Hebrew does not have *his sons and relatives*.
g 9   See the total in verse 7; Hebrew does not have *twelve*.
h 11   A variant of *Zeri*   i 14   A variant of *Asarelah*
j 18   A variant of *Uzziel*

King James

5Ammiel the sixth, Issachar the seventh, Peulthai the eighth: for God blessed *n*him.

6Also unto Shemaiah his son were sons born, that ruled throughout the house of their father: for they *were* mighty men of valour.

7The sons of Shemaiah; Othni, and Rephael, and Obed, Elzabad, whose brethren *were* strong men, Elihu, and Semachiah.

8All these of the sons of Obed-edom: they and their sons and their brethren, able men for strength for the service, *were* threescore and two of Obed-edom.

9And Meshelemiah had sons and brethren, strong men, eighteen.

10Also Hosah, of the children of Merari, had sons; Simri the chief, (for *though* he was not the firstborn, yet his father made him the chief;)

11Hilkiah the second, Tebaliah the third, Zechariah the fourth: all the sons and brethren of Hosah *were* thirteen.

12Among these *were* the divisions of the porters, *even* among the chief men, *having* wards one against another, to minister in the house of the LORD.

13 ¶ And they cast lots, *o*as well the small as the great, according to the house of their fathers, for every gate.

14And the lot eastward fell to *p*Shelemiah. Then for Zechariah his son, a wise counsellor, they cast lots; and his lot came out northward.

15To Obed-edom southward; and to his sons the house of *q*Asuppim.

16To Shuppim and Hosah *the lot came forth* westward, with the gate Shallecheth, by the causeway of the going up, ward against ward.

17Eastward *were* six Levites, northward four a day, southward four a day, and toward Asuppim two *and* two.

18At Parbar westward, four at the causeway, *and* two at Parbar.

19These *are* the divisions of the porters among the sons of Kore, and among the sons of Merari.

The arrangements for treasures

20 ¶ And of the Levites, Ahijah *was* over the treasures of the house of God, and over the treasures of the *r*dedicated things.

21*As concerning* the sons of *s*Laadan; the sons of the Gershonite Laadan, chief fathers, *even* of Laadan the Gershonite, *were* *t*Jehieli.

22The sons of Jehieli; Zetham, and Joel his brother, *which were* over the treasures of the house of the LORD.

23Of the Amramites, *and* the Izharites, the Hebronites, *and* the Uzzielites:

24And Shebuel the son of Gershom, the son of Moses, *was* ruler of the treasures.

25And his brethren by Eliezer; Rehabiah his son, and Jeshaiah his son, and Joram his son, and Zichri his son, and Shelomith his son.

26Which Shelomith and his brethren *were* over all the treasures of the dedicated things, which David the king, and the chief fathers, the captains over thousands and hundreds, and the captains of the host, had dedicated.

27*u*Out of the spoils won in battles did they dedicate to maintain the house of the LORD.

28And all that Samuel the seer, and Saul the son of Kish, and Abner the son of Ner, and Joab the son of Zeruiah, had dedicated; *and* whosoever had dedicated *any thing, it was* under the hand of Shelomith, and of his brethren.

The officers and judges

29 ¶ Of the Izharites, Chenaniah and his sons *were* for the outward business over Israel, for officers and judges.

Amplified

5Ammiel the sixth, Issachar the seventh, Peullethai the eighth; for God blessed him.

6Also to Shemaiah his son were sons born, who were rulers in their fathers' houses, for they were mighty men of ability *and* courage.

7The sons of Shemaiah: Othni, Rephael, Obed, and Elzabad, whose brethren were strong *and* able men, Elihu and Semachiah.

8All these were sons of Obed-edom [in whose house the ark was kept], with their sons and brethren, strong *and* able men for the service—sixty-two in all. [I Chron. 13:13, 14.]

9Meshelemiah had sons and brethren, strong *and* able men—eighteen in all.

10Also Hosah, of the sons of Merari, had sons: Shimri the chief (he was not the firstborn, yet his father made him chief),

11Hilkiah the second, Tebaliah the third, Zechariah the fourth; all the sons and brethren of Hosah were thirteen in all.

12Of these were the divisions of the gatekeepers, even of the chief men, having duties, as did their brethren, to minister in the house of the Lord.

13And they cast lots by fathers' houses, small and great alike, for every gate.

14The lot for the east fell to Shelemiah. They cast lots also for Zechariah his son, a wise counselor, and his lot came out for the north.

15To Obed-edom it came out for the south, and to his sons the storehouse was allotted.

16To Shuppim and Hosah the lot fell for the west, by the refuse gate that goes into the ascending highway, post opposite post.

17On the east were six Levites, on the north four a day, on the south four a day, and two by two at the storehouse.

18At the *e*colonnade on the west side [of the outer court of the temple], there were four at the road and two at the colonnade.

19These were the divisions of the gatekeepers among the Korahites and the sons of Merari.

20Of the Levites, Ahijah was over the treasuries of the house of God and the treasuries of the dedicated gifts.

21The sons of Ladan, the descendants of Gershon through Ladan, the heads of families of Ladan the Gershonite: Jehieli;

22The sons of Jehieli, Zetham and Joel his brother, who were over the treasuries of the house of the Lord.

23Of the Amramites, Izharites, Hebronites, and Uzzielites:

24Shebuel son of Gershom, the son of Moses, was ruler over the treasuries.

25His brethren from Eliezer were his son Rehabiah, his son Jeshaiah, his son Joram, his son Zichri, and his son Shelomoth.

26This Shelomoth and his brethren were over all the treasuries of the dedicated gifts, which King David, the heads of the fathers' houses, the officers over thousands and hundreds, and the commanders of the army had dedicated.

27From spoil won in battles they dedicated gifts to maintain the house of the Lord.

28Also all that Samuel the seer, Saul son of Kish, Abner son of Ner, and Joab son of Zeruiah had dedicated, and whatever anyone had dedicated, it was in the charge of Shelomoth and his brethren.

29Of the Izharites: Chenaniah and his sons were appointed to outside duties for Israel, as officers and judges.

---

n i.e. Obed-edom as ch. 13:14   *o* Or, *as well for the small as for the great*   *p* Called *Meshelemiah* in ver. 1   *q* Heb. *Gatherings*   *r* Heb. *holy things*   *s* Or, *Libni;* see ch. 6:17   *t* Or, *Jehiel;* see ch. 23:8 & 29:8   *u* Heb. *Out of the battles and spoils*

e Hebrew *Parbar,* possibly court or colonnade.

New American Standard

⁵ Ammiel the sixth, Issachar the seventh *and* Peullethai the eighth; God had indeed blessed him.

⁶ Also to his son Shemaiah sons were born who ruled over the house of their father, for they were mighty men of valor.

⁷ The sons of Shemaiah *were* Othni, Rephael, Obed and Elzabad, whose brothers, Elihu and Semachiah, were valiant men.

⁸ All these *were* of the sons of Obed-edom; they and their sons and their relatives *were* able men with strength for the service, 62 from Obed-edom.

⁹ Meshelemiah had sons and relatives, 18 valiant men.

¹⁰ Also Hosah, *one* of the sons of Merari had sons: Shimri the first (although he was not the firstborn, his father made him first),

¹¹ Hilkiah the second, Tebaliah the third, Zechariah the fourth; all the sons and relatives of Hosah *were* 13.

¹² ¶ To these divisions of the gatekeepers, the chief men, *were given* duties like their relatives to minister in the house of the LORD.

¹³ They cast lots, the small and the great alike, according to their fathers' households, for every gate.

¹⁴ The lot to the east fell to Shelemiah. Then they cast lots *for* his son Zechariah, a counselor with insight, and his lot came out to the north.

¹⁵ For Obed-edom *it fell* to the south, and to his sons went the storehouse.

¹⁶ For Shuppim and Hosah *it was* to the west, by the gate of Shallecheth, on the ascending highway. Guard corresponded to guard.

¹⁷ On the east there were six Levites, on the north four daily, on the south four daily, and at the storehouse two by two.

¹⁸ At the *ⁱ*Parbar on the west *there were* four at the highway and two at the Parbar.

¹⁹ These were the divisions of the gatekeepers of the sons of Korah and of the sons of Merari.

Keepers of the Treasure

²⁰ ¶ *ʲ*The Levites, their relatives, had charge of the treasures of the house of God and of the treasures of the dedicated gifts.

²¹ The sons of Ladan, the sons of the Gershonites belonging to Ladan, *namely,* the Jehielites, *were* the heads of the fathers' *households,* belonging to Ladan the Gershonite.

²² ¶ The sons of Jehieli, Zetham and Joel his brother, had charge of the treasures of the house of the LORD.

²³ As for the Amramites, the Izharites, the Hebronites and the Uzzielites,

²⁴ Shebuel the son of Gershom, the son of Moses, was officer over the treasures.

²⁵ His relatives by Eliezer *were* Rehabiah his son, Jeshaiah his son, Joram his son, Zichri his son and Shelomoth his son.

²⁶ This Shelomoth and his relatives had charge of all the treasures of the dedicated gifts which King David and the heads of the fathers' *households,* the commanders of thousands and hundreds, and the commanders of the army, had dedicated.

²⁷ They dedicated part of the spoil won in battles to repair the house of the LORD.

²⁸ And all that Samuel the seer had dedicated and Saul the son of Kish, Abner the son of Ner and Joab the son of Zeruiah, everyone who had dedicated *anything, all of this* was in the care of Shelomoth and his relatives.

Outside Duties

²⁹ ¶ As for the Izharites, Chenaniah and his sons were *assigned* to outside duties for Israel, as officers and judges.

New International

⁵Ammiel the sixth,
 Issachar the seventh
 and Peullethai the eighth.
 (For God had blessed Obed-Edom.)

⁶His son Shemaiah also had sons, who were leaders in their father's family because they were very capable men. ⁷The sons of Shemaiah: Othni, Rephael, Obed and Elzabad; his relatives Elihu and Semakiah were also able men. ⁸All these were descendants of Obed-Edom; they and their sons and their relatives were capable men with the strength to do the work—descendants of Obed-Edom, 62 in all.

⁹Meshelemiah had sons and relatives, who were able men—18 in all.

¹⁰Hosah the Merarite had sons: Shimri the first (although he was not the firstborn, his father had appointed him the first), ¹¹Hilkiah the second, Tabaliah the third and Zechariah the fourth. The sons and relatives of Hosah were 13 in all.

¹²These divisions of the gatekeepers, through their chief men, had duties for ministering in the temple of the LORD, just as their relatives had. ¹³Lots were cast for each gate, according to their families, young and old alike.

¹⁴The lot for the East Gate fell to Shelemiah.*ᵏ* Then lots were cast for his son Zechariah, a wise counselor, and the lot for the North Gate fell to him. ¹⁵The lot for the South Gate fell to Obed-Edom, and the lot for the storehouse fell to his sons. ¹⁶The lots for the West Gate and the Shalleketh Gate on the upper road fell to Shuppim and Hosah.

Guard was alongside of guard: ¹⁷There were six Levites a day on the east, four a day on the north, four a day on the south and two at a time at the storehouse. ¹⁸As for the court to the west, there were four at the road and two at the court itself.

¹⁹These were the divisions of the gatekeepers who were descendants of Korah and Merari.

The Treasurers and Other Officials

²⁰Their fellow Levites were*ˡ* in charge of the treasuries of the house of God and the treasuries for the dedicated things.

²¹The descendants of Ladan, who were Gershonites through Ladan and who were heads of families belonging to Ladan the Gershonite, were Jehieli, ²²the sons of Jehieli, Zetham and his brother Joel. They were in charge of the treasuries of the temple of the LORD.

²³From the Amramites, the Izharites, the Hebronites and the Uzzielites:

²⁴Shubael, a descendant of Gershom son of Moses, was the officer in charge of the treasuries. ²⁵His relatives through Eliezer: Rehabiah his son, Jeshaiah his son, Joram his son, Zicri his son and Shelomith his son. ²⁶Shelomith and his relatives were in charge of all the treasuries for the things dedicated by King David, by the heads of families who were the commanders of thousands and commanders of hundreds, and by the other army commanders. ²⁷Some of the plunder taken in battle they dedicated for the repair of the temple of the LORD. ²⁸And everything dedicated by Samuel the seer and by Saul son of Kish, Abner son of Ner and Joab son of Zeruiah, and all the other dedicated things were in the care of Shelomith and his relatives.

²⁹From the Izharites: Kenaniah and his sons were assigned duties away from the temple, as officials and judges over Israel.

ⁱ Possibly *court* or *colonnade*   *ʲ* So Gr; Heb *As for the Levites, Ahijah had*   *ᵏ* 14 A variant of *Meshelemiah*   *ˡ* 20 Septuagint; Hebrew *As for the Levites, Ahijah was*

King James

³⁰*And* of the Hebronites, Hashabiah and his brethren, men of valour, a thousand and seven hundred, *were* ^vofficers among them of Israel on this side Jordan westward in all the business of the LORD, and in the service of the king.

³¹Among the Hebronites *was* Jerijah the chief, *even* among the Hebronites, according to the generations of his fathers. In the fortieth year of the reign of David they were sought for, and there were found among them mighty men of valour at Jazer of Gilead.

³²And his brethren, men of valour, *were* two thousand and seven hundred chief fathers, whom king David made rulers over the Reubenites, the Gadites, and the half tribe of Manasseh, for every matter pertaining to God, and ^waffairs of the king.

Military and civil officials

27 NOW THE children of Israel after their number, *to wit*, the chief fathers and captains of thousands and hundreds, and their officers that served the king in any matter of the courses, which came in and went out month by month throughout all the months of the year, of every course *were* twenty and four thousand.

²Over the first course for the first month *was* Jashobeam the son of Zabdiel: and in his course *were* twenty and four thousand.

³Of the children of Perez *was* the chief of all the captains of the host for the first month.

⁴And over the course of the second month *was* ^xDodai an Ahohite, and of his course *was* Mikloth also the ruler: in his course likewise *were* twenty and four thousand.

⁵The third captain of the host for the third month *was* Benaiah the son of Jehoiada, a ^ychief priest: and in his course *were* twenty and four thousand.

⁶This *is that* Benaiah, *who was* mighty *among* the thirty, and above the thirty: and in his course *was* Ammizabad his son.

⁷The fourth *captain* for the fourth month *was* Asahel the brother of Joab, and Zebadiah his son after him: and in his course *were* twenty and four thousand.

⁸The fifth captain for the fifth month *was* Shamhuth the Izrahite: and in his course *were* twenty and four thousand.

⁹The sixth *captain* for the sixth month *was* Ira the son of Ikkesh the Tekoite: and in his course *were* twenty and four thousand.

¹⁰The seventh *captain* for the seventh month *was* Helez the Pelonite, of the children of Ephraim: and in his course *were* twenty and four thousand.

¹¹The eighth *captain* for the eighth month *was* Sibbecai the Hushathite, of the Zarhites: and in his course *were* twenty and four thousand.

¹²The ninth *captain* for the ninth month *was* Abiezer the Anetothite, of the Benjamites: and in his course *were* twenty and four thousand.

¹³The tenth *captain* for the tenth month *was* Maharai the Netophathite, of the Zarhites: and in his course *were* twenty and four thousand.

¹⁴The eleventh *captain* for the eleventh month *was* Benaiah the Pirathonite, of the children of Ephraim: and in his course *were* twenty and four thousand.

¹⁵The twelfth *captain* for the twelfth month *was* ^zHeldai the Netophathite, of Othniel: and in his course *were* twenty and four thousand.

¹⁶ ¶ Furthermore over the tribes of Israel: the ruler of the Reubenites *was* Eliezer the son of Zichri: of the Simeonites, Shephatiah the son of Maachah:

¹⁷Of the Levites, Hashabiah the son of Kemuel: of the Aaronites, Zadok:

¹⁸Of Judah, Elihu, *one* of the brethren of David: of Issachar, Omri the son of Michael:

Amplified

³⁰Of the Hebronites: Hashabiah and his brethren, men of courage *and* ability, 1,700 in all, were officers over Israel on the west side of the Jordan in all the Lord's business and the king's service.

³¹Of the Hebronites: Jerijah was the chief, according to their generations by fathers' houses. In the fortieth year of David's reign a search was made, and men of great courage *and* ability were found among them at Jazer in Gilead.

³²Jerijah's kinsmen, men of courage *and* ability, were 2,700 heads of fathers' houses; King David made them overseers of the Reubenites, the Gadites, and the half-tribe of Manasseh, for everything pertaining to God and for the affairs of the king.

27 THIS IS the list of the Israelites, the heads of fathers' houses, the commanders of thousands and hundreds, and their officers who served the king in all matters of the divisions that came and went, month by month throughout the year, each division numbering 24,000.

²Over the first division for the first month was Jashobeam son of Zabdiel. In his division were 24,000.

³He was descended from Perez and was chief of all the commanders of the army for the first month.

⁴Over the division for the second month was Dodai the Ahohite; and of his division Mikloth was the chief officer. In his division were 24,000.

⁵The third commander of the army for the third month was Benaiah son of Jehoiada the priest, as chief. In his division were 24,000.

⁶This is the Benaiah who was a mighty man of the Thirty and over the Thirty; and in his division was Ammizabad his son.

⁷The fourth, for the fourth month, Asahel brother of Joab, and Zebadiah his son after him. In his division were 24,000.

⁸The fifth, for the fifth month, Shamhuth the Izrahite. In his division were 24,000.

⁹The sixth, for the sixth month, Ira son of Ikkesh the Tekoite. In his division were 24,000.

¹⁰The seventh, for the seventh month, Helez the Pelonite, of the Ephraimites. In his division were 24,000.

¹¹The eighth, for the eighth month, Sibbecai the Hushathite, of the Zarahites. In his division were 24,000.

¹²The ninth, for the ninth month, Abiezer of Anathoth, a Benjamite. In his division were 24,000.

¹³The tenth, for the tenth month, Maharai from Netophah, of the Zerahites. In his division were 24,000.

¹⁴The eleventh, for the eleventh month, Benaiah the Pirathonite, of the sons of Ephraim. In his division were 24,000.

¹⁵The twelfth, for the twelfth month, Heldai the Netophathite, of Othniel. In his division were 24,000.

¹⁶Also over the tribes of Israel: of the Reubenites: Eliezer son of Zichri was chief officer; of the Simeonites: Shephatiah son of Maachah;

¹⁷Of Levi: Hashabiah son of Kemuel; of Aaron: Zadok;

¹⁸Of Judah: Elihu, one of David's brothers; of Issachar: Omri son of Michael;

---

^vHeb. *over the charge*   ^wHeb. *thing*   ^xOr, *Dodo;* see 2 Sam. 23:9   ^yOr, *principal officer;* see 1 Ki. 4:5   ^zOr, *Heled;* see ch. 11:30

New American Standard

30 As for the Hebronites, Hashabiah and his relatives, 1,700 capable men, had charge of the affairs of Israel west of the Jordan, for all the work of the LORD and the service of the king.
31 As for the Hebronites, Jerijah the chief (these Hebronites were investigated according to their genealogies and fathers' *households,* in the fortieth year of David's reign, and men of outstanding capability were found among them at Jazer of Gilead)
32 and his relatives, capable men, *were* 2,700 in number, heads of fathers' *households.* And King David made them overseers of the Reubenites, the Gadites and the half-tribe of the Manassites concerning all the affairs of God and of the king.

Commanders of the Army

27 NOW *THIS is* the enumeration of the sons of Israel, the heads of fathers' *households,* the commanders of thousands and of hundreds, and their officers who served the king in all the affairs of the divisions which came in and went out month by month throughout all the months of the year, each division *numbering* 24,000:
2 ¶ Jashobeam the son of Zabdiel *k*had charge of the first division for the first month; and in his division *were* 24,000.
3 *He was* from the sons of Perez, *and was* chief of all the commanders of the army for the first month.
4 Dodai the Ahohite and his division had charge of the division for the second month, Mikloth *being* the chief officer; and in his division *were* 24,000.
5 The third commander of the army for the third month *was* Benaiah, the son of Jehoiada the priest, *as* chief; and in his division *were* 24,000.
6 This Benaiah *was* the mighty man of the thirty, and had charge of thirty; and over his division was Ammizabad his son.
7 The fourth for the fourth month *was* Asahel the brother of Joab, and Zebadiah his son after him; and in his division *were* 24,000.
8 The fifth for the fifth month *was* the commander Shamhuth the Izrahite; and in his division *were* 24,000.
9 The sixth for the sixth month *was* Ira the son of Ikkesh the Tekoite; and in his division *were* 24,000.
10 The seventh for the seventh month *was* Helez the Pelonite of the sons of Ephraim; and in his division *were* 24,000.
11 The eighth for the eighth month *was* Sibbecai the Hushathite of the Zerahites; and in his division *were* 24,000.
12 The ninth for the ninth month *was* Abiezer the Anathothite of the Benjamites; and in his division *were* 24,000.
13 The tenth for the tenth month *was* Maharai the Netophathite of the Zerahites; and in his division *were* 24,000.
14 The eleventh for the eleventh month *was* Benaiah the Pirathonite of the sons of Ephraim; and in his division *were* 24,000.
15 The twelfth for the twelfth month *was* Heldai the Netophathite of Othniel; and in his division *were* 24,000.

Chief Officers of the Tribes

16 ¶ Now in charge of the tribes of Israel: chief officer for the Reubenites was Eliezer the son of Zichri; for the Simeonites, Shephatiah the son of Maacah;
17 for Levi, Hashabiah the son of Kemuel; for Aaron, Zadok;
18 for Judah, Elihu, *one* of David's brothers; for Issachar, Omri the son of Michael;

New International

30 From the Hebronites: Hashabiah and his relatives— seventeen hundred able men—were responsible in Israel west of the Jordan for all the work of the LORD and for the king's service. 31 As for the Hebronites, Jeriah was their chief according to the genealogical records of their families. In the fortieth year of David's reign a search was made in the records, and capable men among the Hebronites were found at Jazer in Gilead. 32 Jeriah had twenty-seven hundred relatives, who were able men and heads of families, and King David put them in charge of the Reubenites, the Gadites and the half-tribe of Manasseh for every matter pertaining to God and for the affairs of the king.

Army Divisions

27 THIS IS the list of the Israelites—heads of families, commanders of thousands and commanders of hundreds, and their officers, who served the king in all that concerned the army divisions that were on duty month by month throughout the year. Each division consisted of 24,000 men.

2 In charge of the first division, for the first month, was Jashobeam son of Zabdiel. There were 24,000 men in his division. 3 He was a descendant of Perez and chief of all the army officers for the first month.
4 In charge of the division for the second month was Dodai the Ahohite; Mikloth was the leader of his division. There were 24,000 men in his division.
5 The third army commander, for the third month, was Benaiah son of Jehoiada the priest. He was chief and there were 24,000 men in his division. 6 This was the Benaiah who was a mighty man among the Thirty and was over the Thirty. His son Ammizabad was in charge of his division.
7 The fourth, for the fourth month, was Asahel the brother of Joab; his son Zebadiah was his successor. There were 24,000 men in his division.
8 The fifth, for the fifth month, was the commander Shamhuth the Izrahite. There were 24,000 men in his division.
9 The sixth, for the sixth month, was Ira the son of Ikkesh the Tekoite. There were 24,000 men in his division.
10 The seventh, for the seventh month, was Helez the Pelonite, an Ephraimite. There were 24,000 men in his division.
11 The eighth, for the eighth month, was Sibbecai the Hushathite, a Zerahite. There were 24,000 men in his division.
12 The ninth, for the ninth month, was Abiezer the Anathothite, a Benjamite. There were 24,000 men in his division.
13 The tenth, for the tenth month, was Maharai the Netophathite, a Zerahite. There were 24,000 men in his division.
14 The eleventh, for the eleventh month, was Benaiah the Pirathonite, an Ephraimite. There were 24,000 men in his division.
15 The twelfth, for the twelfth month, was Heldai the Netophathite, from the family of Othniel. There were 24,000 men in his division.

Officers of the Tribes

16 The officers over the tribes of Israel:

over the Reubenites: Eliezer son of Zicri;
over the Simeonites: Shephatiah son of Maacah;
17 over Levi: Hashabiah son of Kemuel;
over Aaron: Zadok;
18 over Judah: Elihu, a brother of David;
over Issachar: Omri son of Michael;

---

k Lit *was over,* and so throughout the ch

King James

[19]Of Zebulun, Ishmaiah the son of Obadiah: of Naphtali, Jerimoth the son of Azriel:

[20]Of the children of Ephraim, Hoshea the son of Azaziah: of the half tribe of Manasseh, Joel the son of Pedaiah:

[21]Of the half *tribe* of Manasseh in Gilead, Iddo the son of Zechariah: of Benjamin, Jaasiel the son of Abner:

[22]Of Dan, Azareel the son of Jeroham. These *were* the princes of the tribes of Israel.

[23] ¶ But David took not the number of them from twenty years old and under: because the LORD had said he would increase Israel like to the stars of the heavens.

[24]Joab the son of Zeruiah began to number, but he finished not, because there fell wrath for it against Israel; neither *a*was the number put in the account of the chronicles of king David.

[25] ¶ And over the king's treasures *was* Azmaveth the son of Adiel: and over the storehouses in the fields, in the cities, and in the villages, and in the castles, *was* Jehonathan the son of Uzziah:

[26]And over them that did the work of the field for tillage of the ground *was* Ezri the son of Chelub:

[27]And over the vineyards *was* Shimei the Ramathite: *b*over the increase of the vineyards for the wine cellars *was* Zabdi the Shiphmite:

[28]And over the olive trees and the sycamore trees that *were* in the low plains *was* Baal-hanan the Gederite: and over the cellars of oil *was* Joash:

[29]And over the herds that fed in Sharon *was* Shitrai the Sharonite: and over the herds *that were* in the valleys *was* Shaphat the son of Adlai:

[30]Over the camels also *was* Obil the Ishmaelite: and over the asses *was* Jehdeiah the Meronothite:

[31]And over the flocks *was* Jaziz the Hagerite. All these *were* the rulers of the substance which *was* king David's.

[32]Also Jonathan David's uncle was a counsellor, a wise man, and a *c*scribe: and Jehiel the *d*son of Hachmoni *was* with the king's sons:

[33]And Ahithophel *was* the king's counsellor: and Hushai the Archite *was* the king's companion:

[34]And after Ahithophel *was* Jehoiada the son of Benaiah, and Abiathar: and the general of the king's army *was* Joab.

David's instructions to Solomon

28 AND DAVID assembled all the princes of Israel, the princes of the tribes, and the captains of the companies that ministered to the king by course, and the captains over the thousands, and captains over the hundreds, and the stewards over all the substance and *e*possession of the king, *f*and of his sons, with the *g*officers, and with the mighty men, and with all the valiant men, unto Jerusalem.

[2]Then David the king stood up upon his feet, and said, Hear me, my brethren, and my people: *As for me,* I *had* in mine heart to build an house of rest for the ark of the covenant of the LORD, and for the footstool of our God, and had made ready for the building:

[3]But God said unto me, Thou shalt not build an house for my name, because thou *hast been* a man of war, and hast shed *h*blood.

Amplified

[19]Of Zebulun: Ishmaiah son of Obadiah; of Naphtali: Jerimoth son of Azriel;

[20]Of the Ephraimites: Hoshea son of Azaziah; of the half-tribe of Manasseh: Joel son of Pedaiah;

[21]Of the half-tribe of Manasseh in Gilead: Iddo son of Zechariah; of Benjamin: Jaasiel son of Abner;

[22]Of Dan: Azarel son of Jeroham. These were the leaders of the tribes of Israel.

[23]But David did not number those under twenty years of age, for the Lord had promised to make Israel as the stars of the heavens.

[24]Joab son of Zeruiah began a census but did not finish, because the census brought wrath upon Israel, and the number was not recorded in the chronicles of King David.

[25]Over the king's treasuries was Azmaveth son of Adiel; and over the treasuries in the country, cities, villages, and towers *or* forts was Jonathan son of Uzziah;

[26]Over those who did the work of the field of tilling the soil was Ezri son of Chelub;

[27]Over the vineyards was Shimei the Ramathite; over the produce of the vineyards for the wine cellars, Zabdi the Shiphmite;

[28]Over the olive and sycamore trees in the low plains, Baal-hanan the Gederite; over the stores of oil, Joash;

[29]Over the herds pasturing in Sharon, Shitrai the Sharonite; over the herds in the valleys, Shaphat son of Adlai;

[30]Over the camels, Obil the Ishmaelite; over the she-donkeys, Jehdeiah the Meronothite;

[31]And over the flocks, Jaziz the Hagrite. All these were stewards of King David's property.

[32]Also Jonathan, David's uncle, was a counselor, a wise man and a scribe; he and Jehiel son of Hachmoni attended the king's sons [as tutors]. [II Kings 10:6.]

[33]Ahithophel was the king's counselor; Hushai the Archite was the king's companion *and* friend.

[34]Ahithophel was succeeded by Jehoiada son of Benaiah and by Abiathar. Joab was the commander of the king's army.

28 DAVID ASSEMBLED at Jerusalem all the leaders of Israel and of the tribes, the officers of the divisions that served the king in courses, and those over thousands and hundreds, and the stewards over all the property and livestock of the king and his sons, with the palace officers, the mighty men, and all the mighty warriors.

[2]Then David the king rose to his feet and said, Hear me, my brethren and my people. I myself intended to build a house of rest for the ark of the covenant of the Lord, as a footstool for our God, and I prepared materials for the building.

[3]But God said to me, You shall not build a house for My Name [and Presence], because you have been a man of war and have shed blood.

---

a Heb. *ascended*   *b* Heb. *over that which was of the vineyards*
c Or, *secretary*   *d* Or, *Hachmonite*   *e* Or, *cattle*   *f* Or, *and his sons*   *g* Or, *eunuchs*   *h* Heb. *bloods*

New American Standard

19 for Zebulun, Ishmaiah the son of Obadiah; for Naphtali, Jeromoth the son of Azriel;
20 for the sons of Ephraim, Hoshea the son of Azaziah; for the half-tribe of Manasseh, Joel the son of Pedaiah;
21 for the half-tribe of Manasseh in Gilead, Iddo the son of Zechariah; for Benjamin, Jaasiel the son of Abner;
22 for Dan, Azarel the son of Jeroham. These *were* the princes of the tribes of Israel.
23 But David did not count those twenty years of age and under, because the LORD had said He would multiply Israel as the stars of heaven.
24 Joab the son of Zeruiah had begun to count *them*, but did not finish; and because of this, wrath came upon Israel, and the number was not included in the account of the chronicles of King David.

Various Overseers

25 ¶ Now Azmaveth the son of Adiel had charge of the king's storehouses. And Jonathan the son of Uzziah had charge of the storehouses in the country, in the cities, in the villages and in the towers.
26 Ezri the son of Chelub had charge of the agricultural workers who tilled the soil.
27 Shimei the Ramathite had charge of the vineyards; and Zabdi the Shiphmite had charge of the produce of the vineyards *stored* in the wine cellars.
28 Baal-hanan the Gederite had charge of the olive and sycamore trees in the *l*Shephelah; and Joash had charge of the stores of oil.
29 Shitrai the Sharonite had charge of the cattle which were grazing in Sharon; and Shaphat the son of Adlai had charge of the cattle in the valleys.
30 Obil the Ishmaelite had charge of the camels; and Jehdeiah the Meronothite had charge of the donkeys.
31 Jaziz the Hagrite had charge of the flocks. All these were overseers of the property which belonged to King David.

Counselors

32 ¶ Also Jonathan, David's uncle, *was* a counselor, a man of understanding, and a scribe; and Jehiel the son of Hachmoni tutored the king's sons.
33 Ahithophel *was* counselor to the king; and Hushai the Archite *was* the king's friend.
34 Jehoiada the son of Benaiah, and Abiathar succeeded Ahithophel; and Joab was the commander of the king's army.

David's Address about the Temple

28 NOW DAVID assembled at Jerusalem all the officials of Israel, the princes of the tribes, and the commanders of the divisions that served the king, and the commanders of thousands, and the commanders of hundreds, and the overseers of all the property and livestock belonging to the king and his sons, with the officials and the mighty men, even all the valiant men.
2 Then King David rose to his feet and said, "Listen to me, my brethren and my people; I had *m*intended to build a *n*permanent home for the ark of the covenant of the LORD and for the footstool of our God. So I had made preparations to build *it*.
3 "But God said to me, 'You shall not build a house for My name because you are a man of war and have shed blood.'

New International

19 over Zebulun: Ishmaiah son of Obadiah;
    over Naphtali: Jerimoth son of Azriel;
20 over the Ephraimites: Hoshea son of Azaziah;
    over half the tribe of Manasseh: Joel son of Pedaiah;
21 over the half-tribe of Manasseh in Gilead: Iddo son of Zechariah;
    over Benjamin: Jaasiel son of Abner;
22 over Dan: Azarel son of Jeroham.
    These were the officers over the tribes of Israel.

23 David did not take the number of the men twenty years old or less, because the LORD had promised to make Israel as numerous as the stars in the sky. 24 Joab son of Zeruiah began to count the men but did not finish. Wrath came on Israel on account of this numbering, and the number was not entered in the book*m* of the annals of King David.

The King's Overseers

25 Azmaveth son of Adiel was in charge of the royal storehouses.
Jonathan son of Uzziah was in charge of the storehouses in the outlying districts, in the towns, the villages and the watchtowers.
26 Ezri son of Kelub was in charge of the field workers who farmed the land.
27 Shimei the Ramathite was in charge of the vineyards.
Zabdi the Shiphmite was in charge of the produce of the vineyards for the wine vats.
28 Baal-Hanan the Gederite was in charge of the olive and sycamore-fig trees in the western foothills.
Joash was in charge of the supplies of olive oil.
29 Shitrai the Sharonite was in charge of the herds grazing in Sharon.
Shaphat son of Adlai was in charge of the herds in the valleys.
30 Obil the Ishmaelite was in charge of the camels.
Jehdeiah the Meronothite was in charge of the donkeys.
31 Jaziz the Hagrite was in charge of the flocks.
All these were the officials in charge of King David's property.

32 Jonathan, David's uncle, was a counselor, a man of insight and a scribe. Jehiel son of Hacmoni took care of the king's sons.
33 Ahithophel was the king's counselor.
Hushai the Arkite was the king's friend. 34 Ahithophel was succeeded by Jehoiada son of Benaiah and by Abiathar.
Joab was the commander of the royal army.

David's Plans for the Temple

28 DAVID SUMMONED all the officials of Israel to assemble at Jerusalem: the officers over the tribes, the commanders of the divisions in the service of the king, the commanders of thousands and commanders of hundreds, and the officials in charge of all the property and livestock belonging to the king and his sons, together with the palace officials, the mighty men and all the brave warriors.
2 King David rose to his feet and said: "Listen to me, my brothers and my people. I had it in my heart to build a house as a place of rest for the ark of the covenant of the LORD, for the footstool of our God, and I made plans to build it. 3 But God said to me, 'You are not to build a house for my Name, because you are a warrior and have shed blood.'

---

l Or *lowlands*   *m* Lit *in my heart*   *n* Lit *house of rest*   *m* 24 Septuagint; Hebrew *number*

King James

4Howbeit the LORD God of Israel chose me before all the house of my father to be king over Israel for ever: for he hath chosen Judah *to be* the ruler; and of the house of Judah, the house of my father; and among the sons of my father he liked me to make *me* king over all Israel:

5And of all my sons, (for the LORD hath given me many sons,) he hath chosen Solomon my son to sit upon the throne of the kingdom of the LORD over Israel.

6And he said unto me, Solomon thy son, he shall build my house and my courts: for I have chosen him *to be* my son, and I will be his father.

7Moreover I will establish his kingdom for ever, if he be *i*constant to do my commandments and my judgments, as at this day.

8Now therefore in the sight of all Israel the congregation of the LORD, and in the audience of our God, keep and seek for all the commandments of the LORD your God: that ye may possess this good land, and leave *it* for an inheritance for your children after you for ever.

9 ¶ And thou, Solomon my son, know thou the God of thy father, and serve him with a perfect heart and with a willing mind: for the LORD searcheth all hearts, and understandeth all the imaginations of the thoughts: if thou seek him, he will be found of thee; but if thou forsake him, he will cast thee off for ever.

10Take heed now; for the LORD hath chosen thee to build an house for the sanctuary: be strong, and do *it*.

11 ¶ Then David gave to Solomon his son the pattern of the porch, and of the houses thereof, and of the treasuries thereof, and of the upper chambers thereof, and of the inner parlours thereof, and of the place of the mercy seat,

12And the pattern *j*of all that he had by the spirit, of the courts of the house of the LORD, and of all the chambers round about, of the treasuries of the house of God, and of the treasuries of the dedicated things:

13Also for the courses of the priests and the Levites, and for all the work of the service of the house of the LORD, and for all the vessels of service in the house of the LORD.

14*He gave* of gold by weight for *things* of gold, for all instruments of all manner of service; *silver also* for all instruments of silver by weight, for all instruments of every kind of service:

15Even the weight for the candlesticks of gold, and for their lamps of gold, by weight for every candlestick, and for the lamps thereof: and for the candlesticks of silver by weight, *both* for the candlestick, and *also* for the lamps thereof, according to the use of every candlestick.

16And by weight *he gave* gold for the tables of showbread, for every table; and *likewise* silver for the tables of silver:

17Also pure gold for the fleshhooks, and the bowls, and the cups: and for the golden basins *he gave gold* by weight for every basin; and *likewise silver* by weight for every basin of silver:

Amplified

4However, the Lord, the God of Israel, chose me before all my father's house to be king over Israel forever. For He chose Judah to be the ruler; and of the house of Judah he chose the house of my father; and among the sons of my father He was pleased to make me king over all Israel;

5And of all my sons, for the Lord has given me many sons, He has chosen Solomon my son to sit upon the throne of the kingdom of the Lord over Israel.

6And He said to me, Solomon your son shall build My house and My courts, for I have chosen him to be My son, and I will be his father.

7I will establish his kingdom forever if he loyally *and* continuously obeys My commandments and My ordinances, as he does today.

8Now therefore, in the sight of all Israel, the assembly of the Lord, and in the hearing of our God, keep and seek [to be familiar with] all the commandments of the Lord your God, that you may possess this good land and leave it as an inheritance for your children after you forever.

9And you, Solomon my son, know the God of your father [have personal knowledge of Him, be acquainted with, and understand Him; appreciate, heed, and cherish Him] and serve Him with a blameless heart and a willing mind. For the Lord searches all hearts *and* minds and understands all the wanderings of the thoughts. If you seek Him [inquiring for and of Him and requiring Him as your first and vital necessity] you will find Him; but *f*if you forsake Him, He will cast you off forever!

10Take heed now, for the Lord has chosen you to build a house for the sanctuary. Be strong and do it!

11Then David gave Solomon his son the plan of the vestibule of the temple, its houses, its treasuries, its upper chambers, its inner rooms, and of the place for the [ark and its] mercy seat;

12And the plan of all that he had in mind [by the Spirit] for the courts of the house of the Lord, all the surrounding chambers, the treasuries of the house of God, and the treasuries for the dedicated gifts;

13The plan for the divisions of the priests and the Levites, for all the work of the service in the house of the Lord; for all the vessels for service in the house of the Lord:

14The weight of gold and silver for all the gold and silver articles of every kind of service—

15The weight of the golden lampstands and their lamps, the weight of gold or silver for each lampstand and its lamps, according to the use of each lampstand;

16The gold by weight for each table of showbread, and the silver for the tables of silver;

17Also pure gold for the forks, basins, and cups; for the golden bowls by weight of each; for the silver bowls by weight of each;

---

*f*God's promises to men and women invariably are dependent upon the other party to the covenant meeting His conditions, whether He says so at the time or not. In I Chron. 28:7 we find God promising to establish Solomon's kingdom forever. Yet in I Kings 11:9-11 we find that God became angry with Solomon for all his degenerate and abominable conduct and his treachery of heart toward Him; and without mercy, except for David's sake, God declared that the kingdom would be torn from him. Was God breaking His covenant with Solomon? No, Solomon had broken and nullified that covenant long before; it no longer existed. There was now no promise for God to keep. Christians are prone to think that God will keep His part of a bargain whether they do or not, but the wisest man who ever lived died knowing that God is not mocked; "[He inevitably deludes himself who attempts to delude God.] For whatever a man sows, that *and* that only is what he will reap" (Gal. 6:7). "If you seek Him [inquiring for and of Him and requiring Him as your first and vital necessity], you will find Him; but if you forsake Him, He will cast you off forever!" David was telling Solomon all this, but as the new king grew in power, popularity, and personal aggrandizement, step by step he set himself up as privileged to ignore God. In all his wisdom he failed to comprehend that "Something greater *and* more exalted *and* more majestic than the temple is here! . . . Someone more *and* greater than Solomon is here" (Matt. 12:6, 42).

*i*Heb. *strong*   *j*Heb. *of all that was with him*

New American Standard

4"Yet, the LORD, the God of Israel, chose me from all the house of my father to be king over Israel forever. For He has chosen Judah to be a leader; and in the house of Judah, my father's house, and among the sons of my father He took pleasure in me to make *me* king over all Israel. 5"Of all my sons (for the LORD has given me many sons), He has chosen my son Solomon to sit on the throne of the kingdom of the LORD over Israel. 6"He said to me, 'Your son Solomon is the one who shall build My house and My courts; for I have chosen him to be a son to Me, and I will be a father to him. 7'I will establish his kingdom forever if he resolutely performs My commandments and My ordinances, as is done now.'

8"So now, in the sight of all Israel, the assembly of the LORD, and in the hearing of our God, observe and seek after all the commandments of the LORD your God so that you may possess the good land and bequeath *it* to your sons after you forever.

9 ¶ "As for you, my son Solomon, know the God of your father, and serve Him with a whole heart and a willing mind; for the LORD searches all hearts, and understands every intent of the thoughts. If you seek Him, He will let you find Him; but if you forsake Him, He will reject you forever.

10"Consider now, for the LORD has chosen you to build a house for the sanctuary; be courageous and act."

11 ¶ Then David gave to his son Solomon the plan of the porch *of the temple,* its buildings, its storehouses, its upper rooms, its inner rooms and the room for the mercy seat; 12 and the plan of all that he had in mind, for the courts of the house of the LORD, and for all the surrounding rooms, for the storehouses of the house of God and for the storehouses of the dedicated things; 13 also for the divisions of the priests and the Levites and for all the work of the service of the house of the LORD and for all the utensils of service in the house of the LORD; 14 for the golden *utensils,* the weight of gold for all utensils for every kind of service; for the silver utensils, the weight *of silver* for all utensils for every kind of service; 15 and the weight *of gold* for the golden lampstands and their golden lamps, with the weight of each lampstand and its lamps; and *the weight of silver* for the silver lampstands, with the weight of each lampstand and its lamps according to the use of each lampstand; 16 and the gold by weight for the tables of showbread, for each table; and silver for the silver tables; 17 and the forks, the basins, and the pitchers of pure gold; and for the golden bowls with the weight for each bowl; and for the silver bowls with the weight for each bowl;

New International

4"Yet the LORD, the God of Israel, chose me from my whole family to be king over Israel forever. He chose Judah as leader, and from the house of Judah he chose my family, and from my father's sons he was pleased to make me king over all Israel. 5Of all my sons—and the LORD has given me many—he has chosen my son Solomon to sit on the throne of the kingdom of the LORD over Israel. 6He said to me: 'Solomon your son is the one who will build my house and my courts, for I have chosen him to be my son, and I will be his father. 7I will establish his kingdom forever if he is unswerving in carrying out my commands and laws, as is being done at this time.'

8"So now I charge you in the sight of all Israel and of the assembly of the LORD, and in the hearing of our God: Be careful to follow all the commands of the LORD your God, that you may possess this good land and pass it on as an inheritance to your descendants forever.

9"And you, my son Solomon, acknowledge the God of your father, and serve him with wholehearted devotion and with a willing mind, for the LORD searches every heart and understands every motive behind the thoughts. If you seek him, he will be found by you; but if you forsake him, he will reject you forever. 10Consider now, for the LORD has chosen you to build a temple as a sanctuary. Be strong and do the work."

11Then David gave his son Solomon the plans for the portico of the temple, its buildings, its storerooms, its upper parts, its inner rooms and the place of atonement. 12He gave him the plans of all that the Spirit had put in his mind for the courts of the temple of the LORD and all the surrounding rooms, for the treasuries of the temple of God and for the treasuries for the dedicated things. 13He gave him instructions for the divisions of the priests and Levites, and for all the work of serving in the temple of the LORD, as well as for all the articles to be used in its service. 14He designated the weight of gold for all the gold articles to be used in various kinds of service, and the weight of silver for all the silver articles to be used in various kinds of service: 15the weight of gold for the gold lampstands and their lamps, with the weight for each lampstand and its lamps; and the weight of silver for each silver lampstand and its lamps, according to the use of each lampstand; 16the weight of gold for each table for consecrated bread; the weight of silver for the silver tables; 17the weight of pure gold for the forks, sprinkling bowls and pitchers; the weight of gold for each gold dish; the weight of silver for

King James

¹⁸And for the altar of incense refined gold by weight; and gold for the pattern of the chariot of the cherubims, that spread out *their wings,* and covered the ark of the covenant of the LORD.

¹⁹All *this, said David,* the LORD made me understand in writing by *his* hand upon me, *even* all the works of this pattern.

²⁰And David said to Solomon his son, Be strong and of good courage, and do *it:* fear not, nor be dismayed: for the LORD God, *even* my God, *will be* with thee; he will not fail thee, nor forsake thee, until thou hast finished all the work for the service of the house of the LORD.

²¹And, behold, the courses of the priests and the Levites, *even they shall be with thee* for all the service of the house of God: and *there shall be* with thee for all manner of workmanship every willing skilful man, for any manner of service: also the princes and all the people *will be* wholly at thy commandment.

David invites the people to give

29 FURTHERMORE DAVID the king said unto all the congregation, Solomon my son, whom alone God hath chosen, *is yet* young and tender, and the work *is* great: for the palace *is* not for man, but for the LORD God.

²Now I have prepared with all my might for the house of my God the gold for *things to be made* of gold, and the silver for *things* of silver, and the brass for *things* of brass, the iron for *things* of iron, and wood for *things* of wood; onyx stones, and *stones* to be set, glistering stones, and of divers colours, and all manner of precious stones, and marble stones in abundance.

³Moreover, because I have set my affection to the house of my God, I have of mine own proper good, of gold and silver, *which* I have given to the house of my God, over and above all that I have prepared for the holy house,

⁴*Even* three thousand talents of gold, of the gold of Ophir, and seven thousand talents of refined silver, to overlay the walls of the houses *withal:*

⁵The gold for *things* of gold, and the silver for *things* of silver, and for all manner of work *to be made* by the hands of artificers. And who *then* is willing *k*to consecrate his service this day unto the LORD?

⁶ ¶ Then the chief of the fathers and princes of the tribes of Israel, and the captains of thousands and of hundreds, with the rulers of the king's work, offered willingly,

⁷And gave for the service of the house of God of gold five thousand talents and ten thousand drams, and of silver ten thousand talents, and of brass eighteen thousand talents, and one hundred thousand talents of iron.

⁸And they with whom *precious* stones were found gave *them* to the treasure of the house of the LORD, by the hand of Jehiel the Gershonite.

⁹Then the people rejoiced, for that they offered willingly, because with perfect heart they offered willingly to the LORD: and David the king also rejoiced with great joy.

David's prayer

¹⁰ ¶ Wherefore David blessed the LORD before all the congregation: and David said, Blessed *be* thou, LORD God of Israel our father, for ever and ever.

¹¹Thine, O LORD, *is* the greatness, and the power, and the glory, and the victory, and the majesty: for all *that is* in the heaven and in the earth *is thine;* thine *is* the kingdom, O LORD, and thou art exalted as head above all.

Amplified

¹⁸For the incense altar refined gold by weight, and gold for the plan of the chariot of the cherubim that spread their wings and covered the ark of the Lord's covenant.

¹⁹All this the Lord made me understand by the writing by His hand upon me, all the work to be done according to the plan.

²⁰Also David told Solomon his son, Be strong and courageous, and do it. Fear not, be not dismayed, for the Lord God, my God, is with you. He will not fail or forsake you until you have finished all the work for the service of the house of the Lord.

²¹And see, [you have] the divisions of the priests and Levites for all the service of God's house, and with you in all the kinds of work will be every willing, skillful man for any kind of service. Also the officers and all the people will be wholly at your command.

29 AND KING David said to all the assembly, Solomon my son, whom alone God has chosen, is yet young, tender, *and* inexperienced; and the work is great, for the palace is not to be for man but for the Lord God.

²So I have provided with all my might for the house of my God the gold for things to be of gold, silver for things of silver, bronze for things of bronze, iron for things of iron, and wood for things of wood, as well as onyx *or* beryl stones, stones to be set, stones of antimony, stones of various colors, and all sorts of precious stones, and marble stones in abundance.

³Moreover, because I have set my affection on the house of my God, in addition to all I have prepared for the holy house, I have a private treasure of gold and silver which I give for the house of my God:

⁴It is 3,000 talents of gold, gold of Ophir, 7,000 talents of refined silver for overlaying the walls of the house,

⁵Gold for the uses of gold, silver for the uses of silver, and for every work to be done by craftsmen. Now who will offer willingly to fill his hand [and consecrate it] today to the Lord [like one consecrating himself to the priesthood]?

⁶Then the chiefs of the fathers and princes of the tribes of Israel and the captains of thousands and of hundreds, with the rulers of the king's work, offered willingly

⁷And gave for the service of the house of God—of gold 5,000 talents and 10,000 darics, of silver 10,000 talents, of bronze 18,000 talents, and 100,000 talents of iron.

⁸And whoever had precious stones gave them to the treasury of the house of the Lord in the care of Jehiel the Gershonite.

⁹Then the people rejoiced because these had given willingly, for with a whole *and* blameless heart they had offered freely to the Lord. King David also rejoiced greatly.

¹⁰Therefore David blessed the Lord before all the assembly and said, Be praised, adored, *and* thanked, O Lord, the God of Israel our [forefather], forever and ever.

¹¹Yours, O Lord, is the greatness and the power and the glory and the victory and the majesty, for all that is in the heavens and the earth is Yours; Yours is the kingdom, O Lord, and Yours it is to be exalted as Head over all.

---

*k*Heb. *to fill his hand*

New American Standard

18 and for the altar of incense refined gold by weight; and gold for the model of the chariot, *even* the cherubim that spread out *their wings* and covered the ark of the covenant of the LORD.

19 ¶ "All *this*," said David, "the LORD made me understand in writing by His hand upon me, all the details of this pattern."

20 ¶ Then David said to his son Solomon, "Be strong and courageous, and act; do not fear nor be dismayed, for the LORD God, my God, is with you. He will not fail you nor forsake you until all the work for the service of the house of the LORD is finished.

21 "Now behold, *there are* the divisions of the priests and the Levites for all the service of the house of God, and every willing man of any skill will be with you in all the work for all kinds of service. The officials also and all the people will be entirely at your command."

Offerings for the Temple

29 THEN KING David said to the entire assembly, "My son Solomon, whom alone God has chosen, is still young and inexperienced and the work is great; for the temple is not for man, but for the LORD God.

2 "Now with all my ability I have provided for the house of my God the gold for the *things of* gold, and the silver for the *things of* silver, and the bronze for the *things of* bronze, the iron for the *things of* iron, and wood for the *things of* wood, onyx stones and inlaid *stones,* stones of antimony and stones of various colors, and all kinds of precious stones and alabaster in abundance.

3 "Moreover, in my delight in the house of my God, the treasure I have of gold and silver, I give to the house of my God, over and above all that I have already provided for the holy *o*temple,

4 *namely,* 3,000 talents of gold, of the gold of Ophir, and 7,000 talents of refined silver, to overlay the walls of the buildings;

5 of gold for the *things of* gold and of silver for the *things of* silver, that is, for all the work done by the craftsmen. Who then is willing to consecrate himself this day to the LORD?"

6 ¶ Then the rulers of the fathers' *households,* and the princes of the tribes of Israel, and the commanders of thousands and of hundreds, with the overseers over the king's work, offered willingly;

7 and for the service for the house of God they gave 5,000 talents and 10,000 darics of gold, and 10,000 talents of silver, and 18,000 talents of brass, and 100,000 talents of iron.

8 Whoever possessed *precious* stones gave them to the treasury of the house of the LORD, in care of Jehiel the Gershonite.

9 Then the people rejoiced because they had offered so willingly, for they made their offering to the LORD with a whole heart, and King David also rejoiced greatly.

David's Prayer

10 ¶ So David blessed the LORD in the sight of all the assembly; and David said, "Blessed are You, O LORD God of Israel our father, forever and ever.

11 "Yours, O LORD, is the greatness and the power and the glory and the victory and the majesty, indeed everything that is in the heavens and the earth; Yours is the dominion, O LORD, and You exalt Yourself as head over all.

New International

each silver dish; 18and the weight of the refined gold for the altar of incense. He also gave him the plan for the chariot, that is, the cherubim of gold that spread their wings and shelter the ark of the covenant of the LORD.

19"All this," David said, "I have in writing from the hand of the LORD upon me, and he gave me understanding in all the details of the plan."

20David also said to Solomon his son, "Be strong and courageous, and do the work. Do not be afraid or discouraged, for the LORD God, my God, is with you. He will not fail you or forsake you until all the work for the service of the temple of the LORD is finished. 21The divisions of the priests and Levites are ready for all the work on the temple of God, and every willing man skilled in any craft will help you in all the work. The officials and all the people will obey your every command."

Gifts for Building the Temple

29 THEN KING David said to the whole assembly: "My son Solomon, the one whom God has chosen, is young and inexperienced. The task is great, because this palatial structure is not for man but for the LORD God. 2With all my resources I have provided for the temple of my God—gold for the gold work, silver for the silver, bronze for the bronze, iron for the iron and wood for the wood, as well as onyx for the settings, turquoise,*n* stones of various colors, and all kinds of fine stone and marble— all of these in large quantities. 3Besides, in my devotion to the temple of my God I now give my personal treasures of gold and silver for the temple of my God, over and above everything I have provided for this holy temple: 4three thousand talents*o* of gold (gold of Ophir) and seven thousand talents*p* of refined silver, for the overlaying of the walls of the buildings, 5for the gold work and the silver work, and for all the work to be done by the craftsmen. Now, who is willing to consecrate himself today to the LORD?"

6Then the leaders of families, the officers of the tribes of Israel, the commanders of thousands and commanders of hundreds, and the officials in charge of the king's work gave willingly. 7They gave toward the work on the temple of God five thousand talents*q* and ten thousand darics*r* of gold, ten thousand talents*s* of silver, eighteen thousand talents*t* of bronze and a hundred thousand talents*u* of iron. 8Any who had precious stones gave them to the treasury of the temple of the LORD in the custody of Jehiel the Gershonite. 9The people rejoiced at the willing response of their leaders, for they had given freely and wholeheartedly to the LORD. David the king also rejoiced greatly.

David's Prayer

10David praised the LORD in the presence of the whole assembly, saying,

"Praise be to you, O LORD,
    God of our father Israel,
    from everlasting to everlasting.
11Yours, O LORD, is the greatness and the
      power
    and the glory and the majesty and the
      splendor,
    for everything in heaven and earth is yours.
Yours, O LORD, is the kingdom;
    you are exalted as head over all.

---

n 2 The meaning of the Hebrew for this word is uncertain.
o 4 That is, about 110 tons (about 100 metric tons)   *p 4* That is, about 260 tons (about 240 metric tons)   *q 7* That is, about 190 tons (about 170 metric tons)   *r 7* That is, about 185 pounds (about 84 kilograms)   *s 7* That is, about 375 tons (about 345 metric tons)   *t 7* That is, about 675 tons (about 610 metric tons)   *u 7* That is, about 3,750 tons (about 3,450 metric tons)

o Lit *house*

THE SECOND BOOK OF THE
Chronicles

THE SECOND BOOK OF THE
Chronicles

King James

Solomon asks for wisdom

1 AND SOLOMON the son of David was strengthened in his kingdom, and the LORD his God *was* with him, and magnified him exceedingly.

2 Then Solomon spake unto all Israel, to the captains of thousands and of hundreds, and to the judges, and to every governor in all Israel, the chief of the fathers.

3 So Solomon, and all the congregation with him, went to the high place that *was* at Gibeon; for there was the tabernacle of the congregation of God, which Moses the servant of the LORD had made in the wilderness.

4 But the ark of God had David brought up from Kirjath-jearim to *the place which* David had prepared for it: for he had pitched a tent for it at Jerusalem.

5 Moreover the brasen altar, that Bezaleel the son of Uri, the son of Hur, had made, *a*he put before the tabernacle of the LORD: and Solomon and the congregation sought unto it.

6 And Solomon went up thither to the brasen altar before the LORD, which *was* at the tabernacle of the congregation, and offered a thousand burnt offerings upon it.

7 ¶ In that night did God appear unto Solomon, and said unto him, Ask what I shall give thee.

8 And Solomon said unto God, Thou hast shown great mercy unto David my father, and hast made me to reign in his stead.

9 Now, O LORD God, let thy promise unto David my father be established: for thou hast made me king over a people *b*like the dust of the earth in multitude.

10 Give me now wisdom and knowledge, that I may go out and come in before this people: for who can judge this thy people, *that is so* great?

11 And God said to Solomon, Because this was in thine heart, and thou hast not asked riches, wealth, or honour, nor the life of thine enemies, neither yet hast asked long life; but hast asked wisdom and knowledge for thyself, that thou mayest judge my people, over whom I have made thee king:

12 Wisdom and knowledge *is* granted unto thee; and I will give thee riches, and wealth, and honour, such as none of the kings have had that *have been* before thee, neither shall there any after thee have the like.

13 ¶ Then Solomon came *from his journey* to the high place that *was* at Gibeon to Jerusalem, from before the tabernacle of the congregation, and reigned over Israel.

14 And Solomon gathered chariots and horsemen: and he had a thousand and four hundred chariots, and twelve thousand horsemen, which he placed in the chariot cities, and with the king at Jerusalem.

15 And the king *c*made silver and gold at Jerusalem *as* plenteous as stones, and cedar trees made he as the sycamore trees that *are* in the vale for abundance.

16 And *d*Solomon had horses brought out of Egypt, and linen yarn: the king's merchants received the linen yarn at a price.

17 And they fetched up, and brought forth out of Egypt a chariot for six hundred *shekels* of silver, and an horse for an hundred and fifty: and so brought they out *horses* for all the kings of the Hittites, and for the kings of Syria, *e*by their means.

Amplified

1 SOLOMON SON of David was strengthened in his kingdom, and the Lord his God was with him and made him exceedingly great.

2 Solomon spoke to all Israel, to the captains of thousands and of hundreds, and to the judges, and to every prince in all Israel, the heads of the fathers' houses.

3 And Solomon and all the assembly [a united nation] with him went to the high place that was at Gibeon, for the Tent of Meeting of God, which Moses the servant of the Lord had made in the wilderness, was there [where the Canaanites had habitually worshiped].

4 But David had brought up the ark of God from Kiriath-jearim to the place which David had prepared for it, for he had pitched a tent for it at Jerusalem.

5 Moreover, the bronze altar that Bezalel son of Uri, son of Hur, had made was there before the tabernacle of the Lord, and Solomon and the assembly sought [the Lord].

6 Solomon went up there to the bronze altar before the Lord at the Tent of Meeting and offered 1,000 burnt offerings on it.

7 That night God appeared to Solomon and said to him, Ask what I shall give you.

8 And Solomon said to God, You have shown great mercy and loving-kindness to David my father and have made me king in his place.

9 Now, O Lord God, let Your promise to David my father be fulfilled, for you have made me king over a people like the dust of the earth in multitude.

10 Give me now wisdom and knowledge to go out and come in before this people, for who can rule this Your people who are so great?

11 God replied to Solomon, Because this was in your heart and you have not asked for riches, possessions, honor, *and* glory, or the life of your foes, or even for long life, but have asked wisdom and knowledge for yourself, that you may rule *and* judge My people over whom I have made you king,

12 Wisdom and knowledge are granted you. And I will give you riches, possessions, honor, *and* glory, such as none of the kings had before you, and none after you shall have their equal.

13 Then Solomon came from the high place at Gibeon, from before the Tent of Meeting, to Jerusalem. And he reigned over Israel.

14 Solomon gathered chariots and horsemen; he had 1,400 chariots and 12,000 horsemen, which he placed in the cities [suited for the use] of chariots and with the king at Jerusalem.

15 And the king made silver and gold in Jerusalem as common as stones, and he made cedar as plentiful as the sycamores of the lowland.

16 Solomon's horses were brought out of Egypt; the king's merchants received them in droves, *a*each drove at a price.

17 They imported from Egypt a chariot for 600 shekels of silver, and a horse for 150; so they brought out horses for all the Hittite and Syrian kings as export agents.

---

*a*Or, was *there*   *b*Heb. *much as the dust of the earth*   *c*Heb. gave   *d*Heb. *the going forth of the horses which* was *Solomon's*   *e*Heb. *by their hand*

*a*Solomon's actions were in violation of the commands given through Moses in Deut. 17:16, 17 (see also I Kings 4:26; I Kings 10:26-11:1-4).

THE SECOND BOOK OF THE

Chronicles

2 Chronicles

Solomon Worships at Gibeon

1 NOW SOLOMON the son of David established him- self securely over his kingdom, and the LORD his God *was* with him and exalted him greatly.

2 ¶ Solomon spoke to all Israel, to the commanders of thousands and of hundreds and to the judges and to every leader in all Israel, the heads of the fathers' *households.*

3 Then Solomon and all the assembly with him went to the high place which was at Gibeon, for God's tent of meeting was there, which Moses the servant of the LORD had made in the wilderness.

4 However, David had brought up the ark of God from Kiriath-jearim to the place he had prepared for it, for he had pitched a tent for it in Jerusalem.

5 Now the bronze altar, which Bezalel the son of Uri, the son of Hur, had made, was there before the tabernacle of the LORD, and Solomon and the assembly sought it out.

6 Solomon went up there before the LORD to the bronze altar which *was* at the tent of meeting, and offered a thou- sand burnt offerings on it.

7 ¶ In that night God appeared to Solomon and said to him, "Ask what I shall give you."

Solomon's Prayer for Wisdom

8 Solomon said to God, "You have dealt with my fa- ther David with great lovingkindness, and have made me king in his place.

9"Now, O LORD God, Your promise to my father Da- vid is fulfilled, for You have made me king over a people as numerous as the dust of the earth.

10"Give me now wisdom and knowledge, that I may go out and come in before this people, for who can rule this great people of Yours?"

11 God said to Solomon, "Because you had this in mind, and did not ask for riches, wealth or honor, or the life of those who hate you, nor have you even asked for long life, but you have asked for yourself wisdom and knowledge that you may rule My people over whom I have made you king,

12 wisdom and knowledge have been granted to you. And I will give you riches and wealth and honor, such as none of the kings who were before you has possessed nor those who will come after you."

13 So Solomon went from the high place which was at Gibeon, from the tent of meeting, to Jerusalem, and he reigned over Israel.

Solomon's Wealth

14 ¶ Solomon amassed chariots and horsemen. He had 1,400 chariots and 12,000 horsemen, and he stationed them in the chariot cities and with the king at Jerusalem.

15 The king made silver and gold as plentiful in Jerusa- lem as stones, and he made cedars as plentiful as syca- mores in the lowland.

16 Solomon's horses were imported from Egypt and from Kue; the king's traders procured them from Kue for a price.

17 They imported chariots from Egypt for 600 *shekels* of silver apiece and horses for 150 apiece, and by the same means they exported them to all the kings of the Hittites and the kings of Aram.

Solomon Asks for Wisdom

1 SOLOMON SON of David established himself firmly over his kingdom, for the LORD his God was with him and made him exceedingly great.

2Then Solomon spoke to all Israel—to the commanders of thousands and commanders of hundreds, to the judges and to all the leaders in Israel, the heads of families— 3and Solomon and the whole assembly went to the high place at Gibeon, for God's Tent of Meeting was there, which Mo- ses the LORD's servant had made in the desert. 4Now Da- vid had brought up the ark of God from Kiriath Jearim to the place he had prepared for it, because he had pitched a tent for it in Jerusalem. 5But the bronze altar that Bezalel son of Uri, the son of Hur, had made was in Gibeon in front of the tabernacle of the LORD; so Solomon and the assembly inquired of him there. 6Solomon went up to the bronze altar before the LORD in the Tent of Meeting and offered a thousand burnt offerings on it.

7That night God appeared to Solomon and said to him, "Ask for whatever you want me to give you."

8Solomon answered God, "You have shown great kind- ness to David my father and have made me king in his place. 9Now, LORD God, let your promise to my father David be confirmed, for you have made me king over a people who are as numerous as the dust of the earth. 10Give me wisdom and knowledge, that I may lead this people, for who is able to govern this great people of yours?"

11God said to Solomon, "Since this is your heart's desire and you have not asked for wealth, riches or honor, nor for the death of your enemies, and since you have not asked for a long life but for wisdom and knowledge to govern my people over whom I have made you king, 12therefore wisdom and knowledge will be given you. And I will also give you wealth, riches and honor, such as no king who was before you ever had and none after you will have."

13Then Solomon went to Jerusalem from the high place at Gibeon, from before the Tent of Meeting. And he reigned over Israel.

14Solomon accumulated chariots and horses; he had fourteen hundred chariots and twelve thousand horses,[a] which he kept in the chariot cities and also with him in Jerusalem. 15The king made silver and gold as common in Jerusalem as stones, and cedar as plentiful as sycamore-fig trees in the foothills. 16Solomon's horses were imported from Egypt[b] and from Kue[c]—the royal merchants pur- chased them from Kue. 17They imported a chariot from Egypt for six hundred shekels[d] of silver, and a horse for a hundred and fifty.[e] They also exported them to all the kings of the Hittites and of the Arameans.

---

[a]14 Or charioteers   [b]16 Or possibly Muzur, a region in Cilicia; also in verse 17   [c]16 Probably Cilicia   [d]17 That is, about 15 pounds (about 7 kilograms)   [e]17 That is, about 3 3/4 pounds (about 1.7 kilograms)

King James

Preparing to build the temple

2 AND SOLOMON determined to build an house for the name of the LORD, and an house for his kingdom. [2]And Solomon told out threescore and ten thousand men to bear burdens, and fourscore thousand to hew in the mountain, and three thousand and six hundred to oversee them.

[3] ¶ And Solomon sent to fHuram the king of Tyre, saying, As thou didst deal with David my father, and didst send him cedars to build him an house to dwell therein, even so deal with me.

[4]Behold, I build an house to the name of the LORD my God, to dedicate it to him, and to burn before him gsweet incense, and for the continual showbread, and for the burnt offerings morning and evening, on the sabbaths, and on the new moons, and on the solemn feasts of the LORD our God. This is an ordinance for ever to Israel.

[5]And the house which I build is great: for great is our God above all gods.

[6]But who his able to build him an house, seeing the heaven and heaven of heavens cannot contain him? who am I then, that I should build him an house, save only to burn sacrifice before him?

[7]Send me now therefore a man cunning to work in gold, and in silver, and in brass, and in iron, and in purple, and crimson, and blue, and that can skill ito grave with the cunning men that are with me in Judah and in Jerusalem, whom David my father did provide.

[8]Send me also cedar trees, fir trees, and jalgum trees, out of Lebanon: for I know that thy servants can skill to cut timber in Lebanon; and, behold, my servants shall be with thy servants,

[9]Even to prepare me timber in abundance: for the house which I am about to build shall be kwonderful great.

[10]And, behold, I will give to thy servants, the hewers that cut timber, twenty thousand measures of beaten wheat, and twenty thousand measures of barley, and twenty thousand baths of wine, and twenty thousand baths of oil.

[11] ¶ Then Huram the king of Tyre answered in writing, which he sent to Solomon, Because the LORD hath loved his people, he hath made thee king over them.

[12]Huram said moreover, Blessed be the LORD God of Israel, that made heaven and earth, who hath given to David the king a wise son, lendued with prudence and understanding, that might build an house for the LORD, and an house for his kingdom.

[13]And now I have sent a cunning man, endued with understanding, of Huram my father's,

[14]The son of a woman of the daughters of Dan, and his father was a man of Tyre, skilful to work in gold, and in silver, in brass, in iron, in stone, and in timber, in purple, in blue, and in fine linen, and in crimson; also to grave any manner of graving, and to find out every device which shall be put to him, with thy cunning men, and with the cunning men of my lord David thy father.

[15]Now therefore the wheat, and the barley, the oil, and the wine, which my lord hath spoken of, let him send unto his servants:

[16]And we will cut wood out of Lebanon, mas much as thou shalt need: and we will bring it to thee in floats by sea to nJoppa; and thou shalt carry it up to Jerusalem.

[17] ¶ And Solomon numbered all othe strangers that were in the land of Israel, after the numbering wherewith David his father had numbered them; and they were found an hundred and fifty thousand and three thousand and six hundred.

Amplified

2 SOLOMON DETERMINED to build a temple for the bName of the Lord and a royal capitol. [2]And Solomon counted out 70,000 men to bear burdens, 80,000 to be stonecutters in the hill country, and 3,600 overseers.

[3]And Solomon sent to Hiram king of Tyre, saying, As you dealt with David my father and sent him cedars to build himself a house in which to dwell, even so deal with me.

[4]Behold, I am about to build a house for the Name of the Lord my God, dedicated to Him for the burning of incense of sweet spices before Him, for the continual showbread, and for the burnt offerings morning and evening, on the Sabbaths, New Moons, and on the solemn feasts of the Lord our God, as ordained forever for Israel.

[5]The house which I am to build is great, for our God is greater than all gods.

[6]But who is able to build Him a house, since heaven, even highest heaven, cannot contain Him? Who am I to build Him a house, except as a place to burn incense in worship before Him?

[7]Now therefore, send a man skilled to work in gold, silver, bronze, and iron, and in purple, crimson, and blue colors, who is a trained engraver, to work with the skilled men who are with me in Judah and Jerusalem, whom David my father provided.

[8]Send me also from Lebanon cedar, cypress, and algum timber, for I know your servants can skillfully cut timber in Lebanon; and my servants will be with your servants,

[9]To prepare for me timber in abundance, for the house I am about to build shall be great and wonderful.

[10]And I will give to your servants who cut timber 20,000 measures of crushed wheat and also of barley, and 20,000 baths of wine and also of oil.

[11]Then Hiram king of Tyre replied in writing sent to Solomon, Because the Lord loves His people, He has made you king over them.

[12]Hiram said also, Blessed be the Lord, the God of Israel, Who made heaven and earth, Who has given to David the king a wise son, endued with prudence and understanding, who should build a house for the Lord and a royal palace as his capitol.

[13]Now I have sent a skilled man, endued with understanding, even Huram-abi, my trusted counselor,

[14]The son of a woman of the daughters of cDan; his father was a man of Tyre. He is a trained worker in gold, silver, bronze, iron, stone, and wood; in purple, blue, and crimson colors, and in fine linen; and also to engrave any type of engraving and to carry out any design given him, with your skilled men and those of my lord, David your father.

[15]Now therefore, the wheat, barley, oil, and wine of which my lord has spoken, let him send them to his servants,

[16]And we will cut whatever timber you need from Lebanon and bring it to you in rafts by sea to Joppa, so you may take it up to Jerusalem.

[17]Then Solomon took a census of all the aliens in the land of Israel, like the census of them which his father David had taken. They were found to be 153,600.

---

fOr, Hiram   gHeb. incense of spices   hHeb. hath retained, or, obtained strength   iHeb. to grave gravings   jOr, almuggim; see 1 Ki. 10:11   kHeb. great and wonderful   lHeb. knowing prudence and understanding   mHeb. according to all thy need   nHeb. Japho; see Josh. 19:46; Acts 9:36   oHeb. the men the strangers

bSee footnote on Deut. 12:5.   cI Kings 7:14 says that this woman was of the tribe of Naphtali. Doubtless her mother's marriage identified her with a tribe of which she was not a native.

New American Standard

Solomon Will Build a Temple and Palace

2 NOW SOLOMON decided to build a house for the
name of the LORD and a royal palace for himself.
² So Solomon assigned 70,000 men to carry loads and
80,000 men to quarry *stone* in the mountains and 3,600 to
supervise them.
³ ¶ Then Solomon sent *word* to Huram the king of
Tyre, saying, "As you dealt with David my father and sent
him cedars to build him a house to dwell in, so do for me.
⁴"Behold, I am about to build a house for the name of
the LORD my God, dedicating it to Him, to burn fragrant
incense before Him and *to set out* the showbread continually, and to offer burnt offerings morning and evening, on
sabbaths and on new moons and on the appointed feasts of
the LORD our God, this *being required* forever in Israel.
⁵"The house which I am about to build *will be* great, for
greater is our God than all the gods.
⁶"But who is able to build a house for Him, for the
heavens and the highest heavens cannot contain Him? So
who am I, that I should build a house for Him, except to
ᵃburn *incense* before Him?
⁷"Now send me a skilled man to work in gold, silver,
brass and iron, and in purple, crimson and violet *fabrics,*
and who knows how to make engravings, to *work* with the
skilled men whom I have in Judah and Jerusalem, whom
David my father provided.
⁸"Send me also cedar, cypress and algum timber from
Lebanon, for I know that your servants know how to cut
timber of Lebanon; and indeed my servants *will work* with
your servants,
⁹ to prepare timber in abundance for me, for the house
which I am about to build *will be* great and wonderful.
¹⁰"Now behold, I will give to your servants, the woodsmen who cut the timber, 20,000 ᵇkors of crushed wheat
and 20,000 kors of barley, and 20,000 baths of wine and
20,000 baths of oil."

Huram to Assist

¹¹ ¶ Then Huram, king of Tyre, answered in a letter sent
to Solomon: "Because the LORD loves His people, He has
made you king over them."
¹² Then Huram continued, "Blessed be the LORD, the
God of Israel, who has made heaven and earth, who has
given King David a wise son, endowed with discretion and
understanding, who will build a house for the LORD and a
royal palace for himself.
¹³ ¶ "Now I am sending Huram-abi, a skilled man, endowed with understanding,
¹⁴ the son of a Danite woman and a Tyrian father, who
knows how to work in gold, silver, bronze, iron, stone and
wood, *and* in purple, violet, linen and crimson fabrics, and
who knows how to make all kinds of engravings, *to work*
with your skilled men and with those of my lord David
your father.
¹⁵"Now then, let my lord send to his servants wheat and
barley, oil and wine, of which he has spoken.
¹⁶"We will cut whatever timber you need from Lebanon
and bring it to you on rafts by sea to Joppa, so that you
may carry it up to Jerusalem."
¹⁷ ¶ Solomon numbered all the aliens who *were* in the
land of Israel, following the census which his father David
had taken; and 153,600 were found.

New International

Preparations for Building the Temple

2 SOLOMON GAVE orders to build a temple for the
Name of the LORD and a royal palace for himself. ²He
conscripted seventy thousand men as carriers and eighty
thousand as stonecutters in the hills and thirty-six hundred
as foremen over them.
³Solomon sent this message to Hiramᶠ king of Tyre:

"Send me cedar logs as you did for my father David
when you sent him cedar to build a palace to live in.
⁴Now I am about to build a temple for the Name of the
LORD my God and to dedicate it to him for burning
fragrant incense before him, for setting out the consecrated bread regularly, and for making burnt offerings
every morning and evening and on Sabbaths and New
Moons and at the appointed feasts of the LORD our
God. This is a lasting ordinance for Israel.
⁵"The temple I am going to build will be great,
because our God is greater than all other gods. ⁶But
who is able to build a temple for him, since the heavens, even the highest heavens, cannot contain him?
Who then am I to build a temple for him, except as a
place to burn sacrifices before him?
⁷"Send me, therefore, a man skilled to work in gold
and silver, bronze and iron, and in purple, crimson and
blue yarn, and experienced in the art of engraving, to
work in Judah and Jerusalem with my skilled craftsmen, whom my father David provided.
⁸"Send me also cedar, pine and algumᵍ logs from
Lebanon, for I know that your men are skilled in
cutting timber there. My men will work with yours ⁹to
provide me with plenty of lumber, because the temple
I build must be large and magnificent. ¹⁰I will give
your servants, the woodsmen who cut the timber,
twenty thousand corsʰ of ground wheat, twenty thousand cors of barley, twenty thousand bathsⁱ of wine
and twenty thousand baths of olive oil."

¹¹Hiram king of Tyre replied by letter to Solomon:

"Because the LORD loves his people, he has made
you their king."

¹²And Hiram added:

"Praise be to the LORD, the God of Israel, who made
heaven and earth! He has given King David a wise
son, endowed with intelligence and discernment, who
will build a temple for the LORD and a palace for
himself.
¹³"I am sending you Huram-Abi, a man of great
skill, ¹⁴whose mother was from Dan and whose father
was from Tyre. He is trained to work in gold and
silver, bronze and iron, stone and wood, and with
purple and blue and crimson yarn and fine linen. He
is experienced in all kinds of engraving and can execute any design given to him. He will work with your
craftsmen and with those of my lord, David your father.
¹⁵"Now let my lord send his servants the wheat and
barley and the olive oil and wine he promised, ¹⁶and
we will cut all the logs from Lebanon that you need
and will float them in rafts by sea down to Joppa. You
can then take them up to Jerusalem."

¹⁷Solomon took a census of all the aliens who were in
Israel, after the census his father David had taken; and they

---

f 3 Hebrew *Huram,* a variant of *Hiram*; also in verses 11 and 12
g 8 Probably a variant of *almug*; possibly juniper　　*h 10* That is,
probably about 125,000 bushels (about 4,400 kiloliters)
i 10 That is, probably about 115,000 gallons (about 440 kiloliters)

ᵃLit *offer up in smoke*　　ᵇI.e. One kor equals approx 10 bu

King James

Amplified

¹⁸And he set threescore and ten thousand of them *to be* bearers of burdens, and fourscore thousand *to be* hewers in the mountain, and three thousand and six hundred overseers to set the people awork.

Building the temple

3 THEN SOLOMON began to build the house of the LORD at Jerusalem in mount Moriah, *p*where *the* LORD appeared unto David his father, in the place that David had prepared in the threshingfloor of *q*Ornan the Jebusite.

²And he began to build in the second *day* of the second month, in the fourth year of his reign.

³ ¶ Now these *are the things wherein* Solomon was *r*instructed for the building of the house of God. The length by cubits after the first measure *was* threescore cubits, and the breadth twenty cubits.

⁴And the porch that *was* in the front *of the house,* the length *of it was* according to the breadth of the house, twenty cubits, and the height *was* an hundred and twenty: and he overlaid it within with pure gold.

⁵And the greater house he ceiled with fir tree, which he overlaid with fine gold, and set thereon palm trees and chains.

⁶And he *s*garnished the house with precious stones for beauty: and the gold *was* gold of Parvaim.

⁷He overlaid also the house, the beams, the posts, and the walls thereof, and the doors thereof, with gold; and graved cherubims on the walls.

⁸And he made the most holy house, the length whereof *was* according to the breadth of the house, twenty cubits, and the breadth thereof twenty cubits: and he overlaid it with fine gold, *amounting* to six hundred talents.

⁹And the weight of the nails *was* fifty shekels of gold. And he overlaid the upper chambers with gold.

¹⁰And in the most holy house he made two cherubims *t*of image work, and overlaid them with gold.

¹¹ ¶ And the wings of the cherubims *were* twenty cubits long: one wing *of the one cherub was* five cubits, reaching to the wall of the house: and the other wing *was likewise* five cubits, reaching to the wing of the other cherub.

¹²And *one* wing of the other cherub *was* five cubits, reaching to the wall of the house: and the other wing *was* five cubits *also,* joining to the wing of the other cherub.

¹³The wings of these cherubims spread themselves forth twenty cubits: and they stood on their feet, and their faces *were u*inward.

¹⁴ ¶ And he made the veil *of* blue, and purple, and crimson, and fine linen, and *v*wrought cherubims thereon.

¹⁵Also he made before the house two pillars of thirty and five cubits *w*high, and the chapiter that *was* on the top of each of them *was* five cubits.

¹⁶And he made chains, *as* in the oracle, and put *them* on the heads of the pillars; and made an hundred pomegranates, and put *them* on the chains.

¹⁷And he reared up the pillars before the temple, one on the right hand, and the other on the left; and called the name of that on the right hand *x*Jachin, and the name of that on the left *y*Boaz.

¹⁸And he assigned 70,000 of them to be burden bearers, 80,000 to work in the mountain quarries, and 3,600 as overseers to direct the people's work.

3 THEN SOLOMON began to build the house of the Lord at Jerusalem on Mount Moriah, where the Lord appeared to David his father, in the place that David had appointed, on the threshing floor of Ornan the Jebusite. [I Chron. 21:20–22.]

²And Solomon began to build on the second day of the second month in the fourth year of his reign.

³Now these are the measurements for the foundations which Solomon laid for the house of God. The length in cubits by the former measure was sixty cubits, and the breadth twenty cubits.

⁴The porch *or* vestibule across the front of the house was the same length as the house's breadth, twenty cubits, and the *d*height 120 cubits. He overlaid it inside with pure gold.

⁵And the greater house (the Holy Place) he lined with cypress and overlaid it with fine gold and made palm trees and chains on it.

⁶And he adorned the house with precious stones for beauty; and the gold was gold of Parvaim.

⁷He lined the house (the Holy Place), its beams, thresholds, walls, and doors with gold, and engraved cherubim on the walls.

⁸He made the Most Holy Place, its length equaling the breadth of the house, twenty cubits, and its breadth twenty cubits; he overlaid it with 600 talents of fine gold.

⁹The weight of the nails was fifty shekels of gold. And he lined the upper chambers with gold.

¹⁰And in the Most Holy Place he made two cherubim of image work, and they were overlaid with gold.

¹¹And the wings of the cherubim [combined] extended twenty cubits: one wing of one cherub was five cubits, reaching to the wall of the house, and its other wing of five cubits touched the other cherub's wing.

¹²And of the other cherub one wing of five cubits touched the wall of the house, and the other wing, also five cubits, joined the wing of the first cherub.

¹³The wings of these cherubim extended twenty cubits; the cherubim stood on their feet, their faces toward the Holy Place.

¹⁴And he made the veil [between the Holy Place and the Most Holy Place] of blue, purple, and crimson colors, and fine linen, and embroidered cherubim on it.

¹⁵Before the house he made two pillars, 35 cubits high, with a capital on the top of each which was five cubits.

¹⁶He made chains like a necklace and put them on the heads of the pillars, and he made 100 pomegranates and put them on the chains.

¹⁷He erected the pillars before the temple, one on the right, the other on the left, and called the one on the right Jachin [he shall establish] and the one on the left Boaz [in it is strength].

---

*p*Or, *which was seen of David his father*　　*q*Or, *Araunah;* see 2 Sam. 24:18　　*r*Heb. *founded*　　*s*Heb. *covered*　　*t*Or, (as some think) *of moveable work*　　*u*Or, *toward the house* *v*Heb. *caused to ascend*　　*w*Heb. *long*　　*x*i.e. *He shall establish* *y*i.e. *In it is strength*

*d*This extreme height is believed by most scholars to be a copyist's error, but II Chron. 7:21 seems to confirm it. It reads, "... this house, which was so high ..."

New American Standard

18 He appointed 70,000 of them to carry loads and 80,000 to quarry *stones* in the mountains and 3,600 supervisors to make the people work.

The Temple Construction in Jerusalem

3 THEN SOLOMON began to build the house of the LORD in Jerusalem on Mount Moriah, where *the* LORD had appeared to his father David, at the place that David had prepared on the threshing floor of Ornan the Jebusite.

2 He began to build on the second *day* in the second month of the fourth year of his reign.

Dimensions and Materials of the Temple

3 Now these are the foundations which Solomon laid for building the house of God. The length in [c]cubits, according to the old standard *was* sixty cubits, and the width twenty cubits.

4 The porch which was in front of the house was as long as the width of the house, twenty cubits, and the height 120; and inside he overlaid it with pure gold.

5 He overlaid the main room with cypress wood and overlaid it with fine gold, and ornamented it with palm trees and chains.

6 Further, he adorned the house with precious stones; and the gold was gold from Parvaim.

7 He also overlaid the house with gold—the beams, the thresholds and its walls and its doors; and he carved cherubim on the walls.

8 ¶ Now he made the room of the holy of holies: its length across the width of the house *was* twenty cubits, and its width *was* twenty cubits; and he overlaid it with fine gold, *amounting* to 600 talents.

9 The weight of the nails was fifty shekels of gold. He also overlaid the upper rooms with gold.

10 ¶ Then he made two sculptured cherubim in the room of the holy of holies and overlaid them with gold.

11 The wingspan of the cherubim *was* twenty cubits; the wing of one, of five cubits, touched the wall of the house, and *its* other wing, of five cubits, touched the wing of the other cherub.

12 The wing of the other cherub, of five cubits, touched the wall of the house; and *its* other wing of five cubits was attached to the wing of the first cherub.

13 The wings of these cherubim extended twenty cubits, and they stood on their feet facing the *main* room.

14 He made the veil of violet, purple, crimson and fine linen, and he worked cherubim on it.

15 ¶ He also made two pillars for the front of the house, thirty-five cubits high, and the capital on the top of each *was* five cubits.

16 He made chains in the inner sanctuary and placed *them* on the tops of the pillars; and he made one hundred pomegranates and placed *them* on the chains.

17 He erected the pillars in front of the temple, one on the right and the other on the left, and named the one on the right Jachin and the one on the left Boaz.

[c]I.e. One cubit equals approx 18 in.

New International

were found to be 153,600. 18 He assigned 70,000 of them to be carriers and 80,000 to be stonecutters in the hills, with 3,600 foremen over them to keep the people working.

Solomon Builds the Temple

3 THEN SOLOMON began to build the temple of the LORD in Jerusalem on Mount Moriah, where the LORD had appeared to his father David. It was on the threshing floor of Araunah[j] the Jebusite, the place provided by David. 2 He began building on the second day of the second month in the fourth year of his reign.

3 The foundation Solomon laid for building the temple of God was sixty cubits long and twenty cubits wide[k] (using the cubit of the old standard). 4 The portico at the front of the temple was twenty cubits[l] long across the width of the building and twenty cubits[m] high.

He overlaid the inside with pure gold. 5 He paneled the main hall with pine and covered it with fine gold and decorated it with palm tree and chain designs. 6 He adorned the temple with precious stones. And the gold he used was gold of Parvaim. 7 He overlaid the ceiling beams, doorframes, walls and doors of the temple with gold, and he carved cherubim on the walls.

8 He built the Most Holy Place, its length corresponding to the width of the temple—twenty cubits long and twenty cubits wide. He overlaid the inside with six hundred talents[n] of fine gold. 9 The gold nails weighed fifty shekels.[o] He also overlaid the upper parts with gold.

10 In the Most Holy Place he made a pair of sculptured cherubim and overlaid them with gold. 11 The total wingspan of the cherubim was twenty cubits. One wing of the first cherub was five cubits[p] long and touched the temple wall, while its other wing, also five cubits long, touched the wing of the other cherub. 12 Similarly one wing of the second cherub was five cubits long and touched the other temple wall, and its other wing, also five cubits long, touched the wing of the first cherub. 13 The wings of these cherubim extended twenty cubits. They stood on their feet, facing the main hall.[q]

14 He made the curtain of blue, purple and crimson yarn and fine linen, with cherubim worked into it.

15 In the front of the temple he made two pillars, which ⌊together⌋ were thirty-five cubits[r] long, each with a capital on top measuring five cubits. 16 He made interwoven chains[s] and put them on top of the pillars. He also made a hundred pomegranates and attached them to the chains. 17 He erected the pillars in the front of the temple, one to the south and one to the north. The one to the south he named Jakin[t] and the one to the north Boaz.[u]

[j] *1* Hebrew *Ornan,* a variant of *Araunah* [k] *3* That is, about 90 feet (about 27 meters) long and 30 feet (about 9 meters) wide [l] *4* That is, about 30 feet (about 9 meters); also in verses 8, 11 and 13 [m] *4* Some Septuagint and Syriac manuscripts; Hebrew *and a hundred and twenty* [n] *8* That is, about 23 tons (about 21 metric tons) [o] *9* That is, about 1 1/4 pounds (about 0.6 kilogram) [p] *11* That is, about 7 1/2 feet (about 2.3 meters); also in verse 15 [q] *13* Or *facing inward* [r] *15* That is, about 52 feet (about 16 meters) [s] *16* Or possibly *made chains in the inner sanctuary*; the meaning of the Hebrew for this phrase is uncertain. [t] *17* *Jakin* probably means *he establishes.* [u] *17* *Boaz* probably means *in him is strength.*

| King James | Amplified |

The furnishings of the temple

4 MOREOVER HE made an altar of brass, twenty cubits the length thereof, and twenty cubits the breadth thereof, and ten cubits the height thereof.

2 ¶ Also he made a molten sea of ten cubits ᶻfrom brim to brim, round in compass, and five cubits the height thereof; and a line of thirty cubits did compass it round about.

3 And under it *was* the similitude of oxen, which did compass it round about: ten in a cubit, compassing the sea round about. Two rows of oxen *were* cast, when it was cast.

4 It stood upon twelve oxen, three looking toward the north, and three looking toward the west, and three looking toward the south, and three looking toward the east: and the sea *was* set above upon them, and all their hinder parts *were* inward.

5 And the thickness of it *was* an handbreadth, and the brim of it like the work of the brim of a cup, ᵃwith flowers of lilies; *and* it received and held three thousand baths.

6 ¶ He made also ten lavers, and put five on the right hand, and five on the left, to wash in them: ᵇsuch things as they offered for the burnt offering they washed in them; but the sea *was* for the priests to wash in.

7 And he made ten candlesticks of gold according to their form, and set *them* in the temple, five on the right hand, and five on the left.

8 He made also ten tables, and placed *them* in the temple, five on the right side, and five on the left. And he made an hundred ᶜbasins of gold.

9 ¶ Furthermore he made the court of the priests, and the great court, and doors for the court, and overlaid the doors of them with brass.

10 And he set the sea on the right side of the east end, over against the south.

11 And Huram made the pots, and the shovels, and the ᶜbasins. And Huram ᵈfinished the work that he was to make for king Solomon for the house of God;

12 ᵀo wit, the two pillars, and the pommels, and the chapiters *which were* on the top of the two pillars, and the two wreaths to cover the two pommels of the chapiters which *were* on the top of the pillars;

13 And four hundred pomegranates on the two wreaths; two rows of pomegranates on each wreath, to cover the two pommels of the chapiters which *were* ᵉupon the pillars.

14 He made also bases, and ᶠlavers made he upon the bases;

15 One sea, and twelve oxen under it.

16 The pots also, and the shovels, and the fleshhooks, and all their instruments, did Huram his father make to king Solomon for the house of the LORD of ᵍbright brass.

17 In the plain of Jordan did the king cast them, in the ʰclay ground between Succoth and Zeredathah.

18 Thus Solomon made all these vessels in great abundance: for the weight of the brass could not be found out.

19 ¶ And Solomon made all the vessels that *were for* the house of God, the golden altar also, and the tables whereon the showbread *was set;*

20 Moreover the candlesticks with their lamps, that they should burn after the manner before the oracle, of pure gold;

21 And the flowers, and the lamps, and the tongs, *made he of* gold, *and* that ⁱperfect gold;

22 And the snuffers, and the ᶜbasins, and the spoons, and the censers, *of* pure gold: and the entry of the house, the inner doors thereof for the most holy *place*, and the doors of the house of the temple, *were of* gold.

4 ALSO SOLOMON made an altar of bronze, its top twenty by twenty cubits and its height ten cubits.

2 Also he made a round Sea of molten metal, ten cubits from brim to brim and five cubits high, and a line of thirty cubits measured around it.

3 Under it were figures of oxen encircling it, ten to a cubit. The oxen were in two rows, cast in one piece with it.

4 It stood upon twelve oxen, three looking north, three west, three south, three east; and the Sea rested upon them, and all their hind parts were inward.

5 Its thickness was a handbreadth; its brim was like the brim of a cup, like the flower of a lily; it held 3,000 baths (measures).

6 He made also ten lavers in which to wash and put five on the right (south) side and five on the left (north). Such things as they offered for the burnt offering they washed in them, but the Sea was for the priests to wash in.

7 And he made ten golden lampstands as directed and set them in the temple, five on the right side and five on the left.

8 He made also ten tables and placed them in the temple, five each on the right and left sides, and 100 basins of gold.

9 Moreover, he made the priests' court, and the great court and doors for the court, and overlaid their doors with bronze.

10 And he set the Sea at the southeast corner of the house.

11 And Huram made the pots, shovels, and basins. So Huram finished the work that he did for King Solomon:

12 The two pillars; the bowls; the capitals on top of the two pillars; and the two networks to cover the two bowls of the capitals on top of the pillars;

13 And 400 pomegranates for the two networks, two rows of pomegranates for each network, to cover the two bowls of the capitals upon the pillars.

14 He made also bases *or* stands and lavers upon the bases;

15 One Sea and the twelve oxen under it;

16 The pots, shovels, and fleshhooks, and all their equipment Huram his trusted counselor made of burnished bronze for King Solomon for the house of the Lord.

17 In the plain of the Jordan the king cast them, in the clay ground between Succoth and Zeredah.

18 Solomon made all these things in such great numbers that the weight of the bronze was not computed.

19 And Solomon made all the vessels for the house of God: the golden altar also; and the tables for the showbread (the bread of the Presence);

20 And the lampstands with their lamps of pure gold, to burn before the inner sanctuary (the Holy of Holies) as directed;

21 The flowers, lamps, and tongs, of purest gold;

22 The snuffers, basins, dishes for incense, and firepans, of pure gold; and for the temple entry, the inner doors for the Most Holy Place and the doors of the Holy Place were of gold.

ᶻHeb. *from his brim to his brim*   ᵃOr, *like a lilyflower*
ᵇHeb. *the work of burnt offering*   ᶜOr, *bowls*   ᵈHeb. *finished*
to make   ᵉHeb. *upon the face*   ᶠOr, *caldrons*   ᵍHeb.
made bright, or, scoured   ʰHeb. *thicknesses of the ground*
ⁱHeb. *perfections of gold*

New American Standard

Furnishings of the Temple

4 THEN HE made a bronze altar, twenty cubits in length and twenty cubits in width and ten cubits in height.

2 Also he made the cast *metal* sea, ten cubits from brim to brim, circular in form, and its height *was* five cubits and its circumference thirty cubits.

3 Now figures like oxen *were* under it *and* all around it, ten cubits, entirely encircling the sea. The oxen *were* in two rows, cast in one piece.

4 It stood on twelve oxen, three facing the north, three facing west, three facing south and three facing east; and the sea *was set* on top of them and all their hindquarters turned inwards.

5 It was a handbreadth thick, and its brim was made like the brim of a cup, *like* a lily blossom; it could hold 3,000 baths.

6 He also made ten basins in which to wash, and he set five on the right side and five on the left to rinse things for the burnt offering; but the sea *was* for the priests to wash in.

7 ¶ Then he made the ten golden lampstands in the way prescribed for them and he set them in the temple, five on the right side and five on the left.

8 He also made ten tables and placed them in the temple, five on the right side and five on the left. And he made one hundred golden bowls.

9 Then he made the court of the priests and the great court and doors for the court, and overlaid their doors with bronze.

10 He set the sea on the right side *of the house* toward the southeast.

11 ¶ Huram also made the pails, the shovels and the bowls. So Huram finished doing the work which he performed for King Solomon in the house of God:

12 the two pillars, the bowls and the two capitals on top of the pillars, and the two networks to cover the two bowls of the capitals which were on top of the pillars,

13 and the four hundred pomegranates for the two networks, two rows of pomegranates for each network to cover the two bowls of the capitals which were on the pillars.

14 He also made the stands and he made the basins on the stands,

15 *and* the one sea with the twelve oxen under it.

16 The pails, the shovels, the forks and all its utensils, Huram-abi made of polished bronze for King Solomon for the house of the LORD.

17 On the plain of the Jordan the king cast them in the clay ground between Succoth and Zeredah.

18 Thus Solomon made all these utensils in great quantities, for the weight of the bronze could not be found out.

19 ¶ Solomon also made all the things that *were* in the house of God: even the golden altar, the tables with the bread of the Presence on them,

20 the lampstands with their lamps of pure gold, to burn in front of the inner sanctuary in the way prescribed;

21 the flowers, the lamps, and the tongs of gold, of purest gold;

22 and the snuffers, the bowls, the spoons and the firepans of pure gold; and the entrance of the house, its inner doors for the holy of holies and the doors of the house, *that is,* of the nave, of gold.

New International

The Temple's Furnishings

4 HE MADE a bronze altar twenty cubits long, twenty cubits wide and ten cubits high.[v] 2He made the Sea of cast metal, circular in shape, measuring ten cubits from rim to rim and five cubits[w] high. It took a line of thirty cubits[x] to measure around it. 3Below the rim, figures of bulls encircled it—ten to a cubit.[y] The bulls were cast in two rows in one piece with the Sea.

4The Sea stood on twelve bulls, three facing north, three facing west, three facing south and three facing east. The Sea rested on top of them, and their hindquarters were toward the center. 5It was a handbreadth[z] in thickness, and its rim was like the rim of a cup, like a lily blossom. It held three thousand baths.[a]

6He then made ten basins for washing and placed five on the south side and five on the north. In them the things to be used for the burnt offerings were rinsed, but the Sea was to be used by the priests for washing.

7He made ten gold lampstands according to the specifications for them and placed them in the temple, five on the south side and five on the north.

8He made ten tables and placed them in the temple, five on the south side and five on the north. He also made a hundred gold sprinkling bowls.

9He made the courtyard of the priests, and the large court and the doors for the court, and overlaid the doors with bronze. 10He placed the Sea on the south side, at the southeast corner.

11He also made the pots and shovels and sprinkling bowls.

So Huram finished the work he had undertaken for King Solomon in the temple of God:

12the two pillars;
the two bowl-shaped capitals on top of the pillars;
the two sets of network decorating the two bowl-shaped capitals on top of the pillars;

13the four hundred pomegranates for the two sets of network (two rows of pomegranates for each network, decorating the bowl-shaped capitals on top of the pillars);

14the stands with their basins;

15the Sea and the twelve bulls under it;

16the pots, shovels, meat forks and all related articles.

All the objects that Huram-Abi made for King Solomon for the temple of the LORD were of polished bronze. 17The king had them cast in clay molds in the plain of the Jordan between Succoth and Zarethan.[b] 18All these things that Solomon made amounted to so much that the weight of the bronze was not determined.

19Solomon also made all the furnishings that were in God's temple:

the golden altar;
the tables on which was the bread of the Presence;

20the lampstands of pure gold with their lamps, to burn in front of the inner sanctuary as prescribed;

21the gold floral work and lamps and tongs (they were solid gold);

22the pure gold wick trimmers, sprinkling bowls, dishes and censers; and the gold doors of the temple: the inner doors to the Most Holy Place and the doors of the main hall.

v 1 That is, about 30 feet (about 9 meters) long and wide, and about 15 feet (about 4.5 meters) high   w 2 That is, about 7 1/2 feet (about 2.3 meters)   x 2 That is, about 45 feet (about 13.5 meters)   y 3 That is, about 1 1/2 feet (about 0.5 meter)   z 5 That is, about 3 inches (about 8 centimeters)   a 5 That is, about 17,500 gallons (about 66 kiloliters)   b 17 Hebrew *Zeredatha*, a variant of *Zarethan*

King James

5 THUS ALL the work that Solomon made for the house of the LORD was finished: and Solomon brought in *all* the things that David his father had dedicated; and the silver, and the gold, and all the instruments, put he among the treasures of the house of God.

Bringing the ark to the temple

2 ¶ Then Solomon assembled the elders of Israel, and all the heads of the tribes, the chief of the fathers of the children of Israel, unto Jerusalem, to bring up the ark of the covenant of the LORD out of the city of David, which *is* Zion.

3Wherefore all the men of Israel assembled themselves unto the king in the feast which *was* in the seventh month.

4And all the elders of Israel came; and the Levites took up the ark.

5And they brought up the ark, and the tabernacle of the congregation, and all the holy vessels that *were* in the tabernacle, these did the priests *and* the Levites bring up.

6Also king Solomon, and all the congregation of Israel that were assembled unto him before the ark, sacrificed sheep and oxen, which could not be told nor numbered for multitude.

7And the priests brought in the ark of the covenant of the LORD unto his place, to the oracle of the house, into the most holy *place, even* under the wings of the cherubims:

8For the cherubims spread forth *their* wings over the place of the ark, and the cherubims covered the ark and the staves thereof above.

9And they drew out the staves *of the ark,* that the ends of the staves were seen from the ark before the oracle; but they were not seen without. And there it is unto this day.

10*There was* nothing in the ark save the two tables which Moses put *therein* at Horeb, *j*when the LORD made *a covenant* with the children of Israel, when they came out of Egypt.

11 ¶ And it came to pass, when the priests were come out of the holy *place:* (for all the priests *that were* *k*present were sanctified, *and* did not *then* wait by course:

12Also the Levites *which were* the singers, all of them of Asaph, of Heman, of Jeduthun, with their sons and their brethren, *being* arrayed in white linen, having cymbals and psalteries and harps, stood at the east end of the altar, and with them an hundred and twenty priests sounding with trumpets:)

13It came even to pass, as the trumpeters and singers *were* as one, to make one sound to be heard in praising and thanking the LORD; and when they lifted up *their* voice with the trumpets and cymbals and instruments of music, and praised the LORD, *saying,* For *he is* good; for his mercy *endureth* for ever: that *then* the house was filled with a cloud, *even* the house of the LORD;

14So that the priests could not stand to minister by reason of the cloud: for the glory of the LORD had filled the house of God.

6 THEN SAID Solomon, The LORD hath said that he would dwell in the thick darkness.

2But I have built an house of habitation for thee, and a place for thy dwelling for ever.

3And the king turned his face, and blessed the whole congregation of Israel: and all the congregation of Israel stood.

4And he said, Blessed *be* the LORD God of Israel, who hath with his hands fulfilled *that* which he spake with his mouth to my father David, saying,

Amplified

5 THUS ALL the work that Solomon did for the house of the Lord was finished. He brought in all the things that David his father had dedicated, and the silver, the gold, and all the vessels he put in the treasuries of the house of God.

2Then Solomon assembled the elders of Israel and all the heads of the tribes, the chiefs of the fathers' houses of the Israelites, to Jerusalem to bring up the ark of the covenant of the Lord out of the City of David, which is Zion.

3All the men of Israel gathered to the king at the feast in the seventh month.

4And all the elders of Israel came, and the Levites took up the ark.

5And the priests and Levites brought up the ark, the Tent of Meeting, and all the holy vessels that were in the Tent.

6Also King Solomon and all the assembly of Israel who were gathered to him before the ark sacrificed sheep and oxen so numerous that they could not be counted or reported.

7And the priests brought the ark of the covenant of the Lord to its place, to the sanctuary of the house, into the Holy of Holies, under the wings of the cherubim;

8For the cherubim spread out their wings over the place of the ark, making a covering above the ark and its poles.

9And they drew out the poles of the ark, so that the ends of the poles protruding from the ark were visible from the front of the Holy of Holies, but were not visible from without. It is there to this day.

10There was nothing in the ark except the two tables [the Ten Commandments] which Moses put in it at Mount Horeb, when the Lord made a covenant with the Israelites when they came out of Egypt.

11And when the priests had come out of the Holy Place—for all the priests present had sanctified themselves, separating themselves from everything that defiles, without regard to their divisions;

12And all the Levites who were singers—all of those of Asaph, Heman, and Jeduthun, with their sons and kinsmen, arrayed in fine linen, having cymbals, harps, and lyres—stood at the east end of the altar, and with them 120 priests blowing trumpets;

13And when the trumpeters and singers were joined in unison, making one sound to be heard in praising and thanking the Lord, and when they lifted up their voice with the trumpets and cymbals and other instruments for song and praised the Lord, saying, For He is good, for His mercy *and* loving-kindness endure forever, then the house of the Lord was filled with a cloud,

14So that the priests could not stand to minister because of the cloud, for the glory of the Lord filled the house of God.

6 THEN SOLOMON said, The Lord has said that He would dwell in the thick darkness;

2I have built You a house, [in which the dark Holy of Holies seems] a [fitting] abode for You, a place for You to dwell in forever.

3And the king turned his face and blessed all the assembly of Israel, and they all stood.

4And he said, Blessed be the Lord, the God of Israel, Who has fulfilled with His hands what He promised with His mouth to David my father, saying,

---

j Or, *where*   *k* Heb. *found*

New American Standard

The Ark Is Brought into the Temple

5 THUS ALL the work that Solomon performed for the house of the LORD was finished. And Solomon brought in the things that David his father had dedicated, even the silver and the gold and all the utensils, *and* put *them* in the treasuries of the house of God.

2 ¶ Then Solomon assembled to Jerusalem the elders of Israel and all the heads of the tribes, the leaders of the fathers' *households* of the sons of Israel, to bring up the ark of the covenant of the LORD out of the city of David, which is Zion.

3 All the men of Israel assembled themselves to the king at the feast, that is *in* the seventh month.

4 Then all the elders of Israel came, and the Levites took up the ark.

5 They brought up the ark and the tent of meeting and all the holy utensils which *were* in the tent; the Levitical priests brought them up.

6 And King Solomon and all the congregation of Israel who were assembled with him before the ark, were sacrificing so many sheep and oxen that they could not be counted or numbered.

7 Then the priests brought the ark of the covenant of the LORD to its place, into the inner sanctuary of the house, to the holy of holies, under the wings of the cherubim.

8 For the cherubim spread their wings over the place of the ark, so that the cherubim made a covering over the ark and its poles.

9 The poles were so long that the ends of the poles of the ark could be seen in front of the inner sanctuary, but they could not be seen outside; and they are there to this day.

10 There was nothing in the ark except the two tablets which Moses put *there* at Horeb, where the LORD made a covenant with the sons of Israel, when they came out of Egypt.

The Glory of God Fills the Temple

11 ¶ When the priests came forth from the holy place (for all the priests who were present had sanctified themselves, without regard to divisions),

12 and all the Levitical singers, Asaph, Heman, Jeduthun, and their sons and kinsmen, clothed in fine linen, with cymbals, harps and lyres, standing east of the altar, and with them one hundred and twenty priests blowing trumpets

13 in unison when the trumpeters and the singers were to make themselves heard with one voice to praise and to glorify the LORD, and when they lifted up their voice accompanied by trumpets and cymbals and instruments of music, and when they praised the LORD *saying,* "*He* indeed is good for His lovingkindness is everlasting," then the house, the house of the LORD, was filled with a cloud,

14 so that the priests could not stand to minister because of the cloud, for the glory of the LORD filled the house of God.

Solomon's Dedication

6 THEN SOLOMON said,
"The LORD has said that He would dwell in the thick cloud.

2 "I have built You a lofty house,
And a place for Your dwelling forever."

3 ¶ Then the king faced about and blessed all the assembly of Israel, while all the assembly of Israel was standing.

4 He said, "Blessed be the LORD, the God of Israel, who spoke with His mouth to my father David and has fulfilled *it* with His hands, saying,

New International

5 WHEN ALL the work Solomon had done for the temple of the LORD was finished, he brought in the things his father David had dedicated—the silver and gold and all the furnishings—and he placed them in the treasuries of God's temple.

The Ark Brought to the Temple

2 Then Solomon summoned to Jerusalem the elders of Israel, all the heads of the tribes and the chiefs of the Israelite families, to bring up the ark of the LORD's covenant from Zion, the City of David. 3 And all the men of Israel came together to the king at the time of the festival in the seventh month.

4 When all the elders of Israel had arrived, the Levites took up the ark, 5 and they brought up the ark and the Tent of Meeting and all the sacred furnishings in it. The priests, who were Levites, carried them up; 6 and King Solomon and the entire assembly of Israel that had gathered about him were before the ark, sacrificing so many sheep and cattle that they could not be recorded or counted.

7 The priests then brought the ark of the LORD's covenant to its place in the inner sanctuary of the temple, the Most Holy Place, and put it beneath the wings of the cherubim. 8 The cherubim spread their wings over the place of the ark and covered the ark and its carrying poles. 9 These poles were so long that their ends, extending from the ark, could be seen from in front of the inner sanctuary, but not from outside the Holy Place; and they are still there today. 10 There was nothing in the ark except the two tablets that Moses had placed in it at Horeb, where the LORD made a covenant with the Israelites after they came out of Egypt.

11 The priests then withdrew from the Holy Place. All the priests who were there had consecrated themselves, regardless of their divisions. 12 All the Levites who were musicians—Asaph, Heman, Jeduthun and their sons and relatives—stood on the east side of the altar, dressed in fine linen and playing cymbals, harps and lyres. They were accompanied by 120 priests sounding trumpets. 13 The trumpeters and singers joined in unison, as with one voice, to give praise and thanks to the LORD. Accompanied by trumpets, cymbals and other instruments, they raised their voices in praise to the LORD and sang:

"He is good;
his love endures forever."

Then the temple of the LORD was filled with a cloud, 14 and the priests could not perform their service because of the cloud, for the glory of the LORD filled the temple of God.

6 THEN SOLOMON said, "The LORD has said that he would dwell in a dark cloud; 2 I have built a magnificent temple for you, a place for you to dwell forever."

3 While the whole assembly of Israel was standing there, the king turned around and blessed them. 4 Then he said:

"Praise be to the LORD, the God of Israel, who with his hands has fulfilled what he promised with his

King James

5Since the day that I brought forth my people out of the land of Egypt I chose no city among all the tribes of Israel to build an house in, that my name might be there; neither chose I any man to be a ruler over my people Israel:

6But I have chosen Jerusalem, that my name might be there; and have chosen David to be over my people Israel.

7Now it was in the heart of David my father to build an house for the name of the LORD God of Israel.

8But the LORD said to David my father, Forasmuch as it was in thine heart to build an house for my name, thou didst well in that it was in thine heart:

9Notwithstanding thou shalt not build the house; but thy son which shall come forth out of thy loins, he shall build the house for my name.

10The LORD therefore hath performed his word that he hath spoken: for I am risen up in the room of David my father, and am set on the throne of Israel, as the LORD promised, and have built the house for the name of the LORD God of Israel.

11And in it have I put the ark, wherein *is* the covenant of the LORD, that he made with the children of Israel.

Solomon's prayer of dedication

12 ¶ And he stood before the altar of the LORD in the presence of all the congregation of Israel, and spread forth his hands:

13For Solomon had made a brasen scaffold, of five cubits *l*long, and five cubits broad, and three cubits high, and had set it in the midst of the court: and upon it he stood, and kneeled down upon his knees before all the congregation of Israel, and spread forth his hands toward heaven,

14And said, O LORD God of Israel, *there is* no God like thee in the heaven, nor in the earth; which keepest covenant, and *showest* mercy unto thy servants, that walk before thee with all their hearts:

15Thou which hast kept with thy servant David my father that which thou hast promised him; and spakest with thy mouth, and hast fulfilled *it* with thine hand, as *it is* this day.

16Now therefore, O LORD God of Israel, keep with thy servant David my father that which thou hast promised him, saying, *m*There shall not fail thee a man in my sight to sit upon the throne of Israel; yet so that thy children take heed to their way to walk in my law, as thou hast walked before me.

17Now then, O LORD God of Israel, let thy word be verified, which thou hast spoken unto thy servant David.

18But will God in very deed dwell with men on the earth? behold, heaven and the heaven of heavens cannot contain thee; how much less this house which I have built!

19Have respect therefore to the prayer of thy servant, and to his supplication, O LORD my God, to hearken unto the cry and the prayer which thy servant prayeth before thee:

20That thine eyes may be open upon this house day and night, upon the place whereof thou hast said that thou wouldest put thy name there; to hearken unto the prayer which thy servant prayeth *n*toward this place.

21Hearken therefore unto the supplications of thy servant, and of thy people Israel, which they shall *o*make toward this place: hear thou from thy dwelling place, *even* from heaven; and when thou hearest, forgive.

22 ¶ If a man sin against his neighbour, *p*and an oath be laid upon him to make him swear, and the oath come before thine altar in this house;

Amplified

5Since the day that I brought My people out of the land of Egypt, I chose no city among all the tribes of Israel to build a house in, that My Name might be there, *e*neither chose I any man to be a ruler over My people Israel;

6But I have chosen Jerusalem, that My Name [and the symbol of My presence] might be there, and I have chosen David to be over My people Israel.

7Now it was in the heart of David my father to build a house for the Name *and* renown of the Lord, the God of Israel.

8But the Lord said to David my father, Since it was in your heart to build a house for My Name *and* renown, you did well that it was in your heart.

9Yet you shall not build the house, but your son, who shall be born to you—he shall build the house for My Name.

10The Lord therefore has performed His word that He has spoken, for I have risen up in the place of David my father and sit on the throne of Israel, as the Lord promised, and have built the house for the Name of the Lord, the God of Israel.

11In it have I put the ark [the symbol of His presence], in which is the covenant of the Lord [the Ten Commandments] which He made with the people of Israel.

12And Solomon stood before the altar of the Lord in the presence of all the assembly of Israel and spread forth his hands.

13For he had made a bronze scaffold, five cubits square and three cubits high, and had set it in the midst of the court; upon it he stood, and he knelt upon his knees before all the assembly of Israel and spread forth his hands toward heaven,

14And said, O Lord, God of Israel, there is no God like You in the heavens or in the earth, keeping covenant and showing mercy *and* loving-kindness to Your servants who walk before You with all their hearts,

15You Who have kept Your promises to my father David and fulfilled with Your hand what You spoke with Your mouth, as it is today.

16Now therefore, O Lord, God of Israel, keep with Your servant David my father that which You promised him, saying, There shall not fail a man in My sight to sit on the throne of Israel, provided your children are careful to walk in My law as you, David, have walked before Me.

17Now then, O Lord, God of Israel, let Your word to Your servant David be verified.

18But will God actually dwell with men on the earth? Behold, heaven and the heaven of heavens cannot contain You; how much less this house which I have built!

19Yet have respect for the prayer of Your servant and for his supplication, O Lord my God, to listen to the cry and the prayer which Your servant prays before You,

20That Your eyes may be open upon this house day and night, toward the place in which You have said You would put Your Name [and the symbol of your presence], to listen to *and* heed the prayer which Your servant prays facing this place.

21So listen to *and* heed the requests of Your servant and Your people Israel which they shall make facing this place. Hear from Your dwelling place, heaven; and when You hear, forgive.

22If a man sins against his neighbor, and he is required to take an oath, and the oath comes before Your altar in this house,

---

*e*God is plainly saying here that it was not His desire for Israel to have a king. To be sure, when to Samuel's attempt to dissuade them they replied, "No! We will have a king over us, that we also may be like all the nations" (I Sam. 8:19-20), God said to Samuel, "They have rejected Me, that I should not be King over them . . . appoint them a king" (I Sam. 8:7, 22). But Saul was originally the people's choice, not God's choice. The Bible nowhere teaches that "the voice of the people is the voice of God." But it does teach that when people make demands of God that are not in harmony with His will, He may grant them to their sorrow, and send "leanness into their souls" (Ps. 106:15).

---

*l*Heb. *the length thereof off* *m*Heb. *There shall not a man be cut off* *n*Or, *in this place require an oath of him* *o*Heb. *pray* *p*Heb. *and he*

New American Standard

5 'Since the day that I brought My people from the land of Egypt, I did not choose a city out of all the tribes of Israel *in which* to build a house that My name might be there, nor did I choose any man for a leader over My people Israel;

6 but I have chosen Jerusalem that My name might be there, and I have chosen David to be over My people Israel.'

7"Now it was in the heart of my father David to build a house for the name of the LORD, the God of Israel.

8"But the LORD said to my father David, 'Because it was in your heart to build a house for My name, you did well that it was in your heart.

9 'Nevertheless you shall not build the house, but your son who will be born to you, he shall build the house for My name.'

10"Now the LORD has fulfilled His word which He spoke; for I have risen in the place of my father David and sit on the throne of Israel, as the LORD promised, and have built the house for the name of the LORD, the God of Israel.

11"There I have set the ark in which is the covenant of the LORD, which He made with the sons of Israel."

Solomon's Prayer of Dedication

12 ¶ Then he stood before the altar of the LORD in the presence of all the assembly of Israel and spread out his hands.

13 Now Solomon had made a bronze platform, five cubits long, five cubits wide and three cubits high, and had set it in the midst of the court; and he stood on it, knelt on his knees in the presence of all the assembly of Israel and spread out his hands toward heaven.

14 He said, "O LORD, the God of Israel, there is no god like You in heaven or on earth, keeping covenant and *showing* lovingkindness to Your servants who walk before You with all their heart;

15 who has kept with Your servant David, my father, that which You have promised him; indeed You have spoken with Your mouth and have fulfilled it with Your hand, as it is this day.

16"Now therefore, O LORD, the God of Israel, keep with Your servant David, my father, that which You have promised him, saying, 'You shall not lack a man to sit on the throne of Israel, if only your sons take heed to their way, to walk in My law as you have walked before Me.'

17"Now therefore, O LORD, the God of Israel, let Your word be confirmed which You have spoken to Your servant David.

18 ¶ "But will God indeed dwell with mankind on the earth? Behold, heaven and the highest heaven cannot contain You; how much less this house which I have built.

19"Yet have regard to the prayer of Your servant and to his supplication, O LORD my God, to listen to the cry and to the prayer which Your servant prays before You;

20 that Your eye may be open toward this house day and night, toward the place of which You have said that *You would* put Your name there, to listen to the prayer which Your servant shall pray toward this place.

21"Listen to the supplications of Your servant and of Your people Israel when they pray toward this place; hear from Your dwelling place, from heaven; hear and forgive.

22 ¶ "If a man sins against his neighbor and is made to take an oath, and he comes *and* takes an oath before Your altar in this house,

New International

mouth to my father David. For he said, 5 'Since the day I brought my people out of Egypt, I have not chosen a city in any tribe of Israel to have a temple built for my Name to be there, nor have I chosen anyone to be the leader over my people Israel. 6But now I have chosen Jerusalem for my Name to be there, and I have chosen David to rule my people Israel.'

7"My father David had it in his heart to build a temple for the Name of the LORD, the God of Israel. 8But the LORD said to my father David, 'Because it was in your heart to build a temple for my Name, you did well to have this in your heart. 9Nevertheless, you are not the one to build the temple, but your son, who is your own flesh and blood—he is the one who will build the temple for my Name.'

10"The LORD has kept the promise he made. I have succeeded David my father and now I sit on the throne of Israel, just as the LORD promised, and I have built the temple for the Name of the LORD, the God of Israel. 11There I have placed the ark, in which is the covenant of the LORD that he made with the people of Israel."

Solomon's Prayer of Dedication

12Then Solomon stood before the altar of the LORD in front of the whole assembly of Israel and spread out his hands. 13Now he had made a bronze platform, five cubits*c* long, five cubits wide and three cubits*d* high, and had placed it in the center of the outer court. He stood on the platform and then knelt down before the whole assembly of Israel and spread out his hands toward heaven. 14He said:

"O LORD, God of Israel, there is no God like you in heaven or on earth—you who keep your covenant of love with your servants who continue wholeheartedly in your way. 15You have kept your promise to your servant David my father; with your mouth you have promised and with your hand you have fulfilled it—as it is today.

16"Now LORD, God of Israel, keep for your servant David my father the promises you made to him when you said, 'You shall never fail to have a man to sit before me on the throne of Israel, if only your sons are careful in all they do to walk before me according to my law, as you have done.' 17And now, O LORD, God of Israel, let your word that you promised your servant David come true.

18"But will God really dwell on earth with men? The heavens, even the highest heavens, cannot contain you. How much less this temple I have built! 19Yet give attention to your servant's prayer and his plea for mercy, O LORD my God. Hear the cry and the prayer that your servant is praying in your presence. 20May your eyes be open toward this temple day and night, this place of which you said you would put your Name there. May you hear the prayer your servant prays toward this place. 21Hear the supplications of your servant and of your people Israel when they pray toward this place. Hear from heaven, your dwelling place; and when you hear, forgive.

22"When a man wrongs his neighbor and is required to take an oath and he comes and swears the oath

---

c 13 That is, about 7 1/2 feet (about 2.3 meters)　　*d 13* That is, about 4 1/2 feet (about 1.3 meters)

King James

23Then hear thou from heaven, and do, and judge thy servants, by requiting the wicked, by recompensing his way upon his own head; and by justifying the righteous, by giving him according to his righteousness.

24 ¶ And if thy people Israel qbe put to the worse before the enemy, because they have sinned against thee; and shall return and confess thy name, and pray and make supplication before thee rin this house;

25Then hear thou from the heavens, and forgive the sin of thy people Israel, and bring them again unto the land which thou gavest to them and to their fathers.

26 ¶ When the heaven is shut up, and there is no rain, because they have sinned against thee; yet if they pray toward this place, and confess thy name, and turn from their sin, when thou dost afflict them;

27Then hear thou from heaven, and forgive the sin of thy servants, and of thy people Israel, when thou hast taught them the good way, wherein they should walk; and send rain upon thy land, which thou hast given unto thy people for an inheritance.

28 ¶ If there be dearth in the land, if there be pestilence, if there be blasting, or mildew, locusts, or caterpillars; if their enemies besiege them sin the cities of their land; whatsoever sore or whatsoever sickness there be:

29Then what prayer or what supplication soever shall be made of any man, or of all thy people Israel, when every one shall know his own sore and his own grief, and shall spread forth his hands tin this house:

30Then hear thou from heaven thy dwellingplace, and forgive, and render unto every man according unto all his ways, whose heart thou knowest; (for thou only knowest the hearts of the children of men:)

31That they may fear thee, to walk in thy ways, uso long as they live vin the land which thou gavest unto our fathers.

32 ¶ Moreover concerning the stranger, which is not of thy people Israel, but is come from a far country for thy great name's sake, and thy mighty hand, and thy stretched out arm; if they come and pray in this house;

33Then hear thou from the heavens, even from thy dwellingplace, and do according to all that the stranger calleth to thee for; that all people of the earth may know thy name, and fear thee, as doth thy people Israel, and may know that wthis house which I have built is called by thy name.

34If thy people go out to war against their enemies by the way that thou shalt send them, and they pray unto thee toward this city which thou hast chosen, and the house which I have built for thy name;

35Then hear thou from the heavens their prayer and their supplication, and maintain their xcause.

36If they sin against thee, (for there is no man which sinneth not,) and thou be angry with them, and deliver them over before their enemies, and ythey carry them away captives unto a land far off or near;

37Yet if they zbethink themselves in the land whither they are carried captive, and turn and pray unto thee in the land of their captivity, saying, We have sinned, we have done amiss, and have dealt wickedly;

38If they return to thee with all their heart and with all their soul in the land of their captivity, whither they have carried them captives, and pray toward their land, which thou gavest unto their fathers, and toward the city which thou hast chosen, and toward the house which I have built for thy name:

39Then hear thou from the heavens, even from thy dwellingplace, their prayer and their supplications, and maintain their xcause, and forgive thy people which have sinned against thee.

Amplified

23Then hear from heaven and do; and judge Your servants, requiting the wicked by bringing his conduct upon his own head, and justifying the [uncompromisingly] righteous by giving him according to his righteousness (his uprightness and right standing with God).

24If Your people Israel have been defeated before the enemy because they have sinned against You, and shall return, confess Your name [and You Yourself], and pray and make supplication before You in this house,

25Then hear from heaven and forgive the sin of Your people Israel and bring them again to the land which You gave to them and their fathers.

26When the heavens are shut up and there is no rain because Your people have sinned against You, yet if they pray toward this place, confess your name [and You Yourself], and turn from their sin when You afflict them,

27Then hear from heaven and forgive the sin of Your servants, [all of] Your people Israel, when You have taught them the good way in which they should walk. And send rain upon Your land which You have given to Your people for an inheritance.

28If there is famine in the land, if there is pestilence, blight, mildew, locusts, or caterpillars, if their enemies besiege them in any of their cities, whatever plague or sickness there may be,

29Then whatever prayer or supplication any man or all of Your people Israel shall make—each knowing his own affliction and his own sorrow and stretching out his hands toward this house—

30Then hear from heaven, Your dwelling place, and forgive, and render to every man according to all his ways, whose heart You know; for You, You only, know men's hearts,

31That they may fear You and walk in Your ways as long as they live in the land which You gave to our fathers.

32Also concerning the stranger who is not of Your people Israel but has come from a far country for Your great name's sake and Your mighty power and Your outstretched arm—if he comes and prays toward this house,

33Hear from heaven, from Your dwelling place, and do all for which the stranger calls to You, that all peoples of the earth may know Your name and fear You [reverently and worshipfully], as do Your people Israel, and may know that this house which I have built is called by Your Name.

34If Your people go out to war against their enemies by the way that You send them, and they pray to You facing this city [Jerusalem] which You have chosen and the house which I have built for Your Name,

35Then hear from heaven their prayer and supplication, and maintain their cause.

36If they sin against You—for there is no man who does not sin—and You are angry with them and give them to enemies who take them captive to a land far or near;

37Yet if they repent in the land to which they have been carried captive, and turn and pray there, saying, We have sinned, we have done wrong, and have dealt wickedly;

38If they return to You with all their heart and soul in the land of their captivity, and pray facing their land which You gave to their fathers and toward the city which You have chosen and the house which I have built for Your Name;

39Then hear from heaven, Your dwelling place, their prayer and supplications, and maintain their cause; and forgive Your people, who have sinned against You.

---

q Or, be smitten   r Or, toward
gates   t Or, toward this house   s Heb. in the land of their
v Heb. upon the face of the land   u Heb. all the days which
this house   x Or, right   w Heb. thy name is called upon
carry them away   z Heb. bring back to their heart   y Heb. they that take them captives

New American Standard

23 then hear from heaven and act and judge Your servants, punishing the wicked by bringing his way on his own head and justifying the righteous by giving him according to his righteousness.

24 ¶ "If Your people Israel are defeated before an enemy because they have sinned against You, and they return *to You* and confess Your name, and pray and make supplication before You in this house,

25 then hear from heaven and forgive the sin of Your people Israel, and bring them back to the land which You have given to them and to their fathers.

26 ¶ "When the heavens are shut up and there is no rain because they have sinned against You, and they pray toward this place and confess Your name, and turn from their sin when You afflict them;

27 then hear in heaven and forgive the sin of Your servants and Your people Israel, indeed, teach them the good way in which they should walk. And send rain on Your land which You have given to Your people for an inheritance.

28 ¶ "If there is famine in the land, if there is pestilence, if there is blight or mildew, if there is locust or grasshopper, if their enemies besiege them in the land of their cities, whatever plague or whatever sickness *there is,*

29 whatever prayer or supplication is made by any man or by all Your people Israel, each knowing his own affliction and his own pain, and spreading his hands toward this house,

30 then hear from heaven Your dwelling place, and forgive, and render to each according to all his ways, whose heart You know for You alone know the hearts of the sons of men,

31 that they may ᵈfear You, to walk in Your ways as long as they live in the land which You have given to our fathers.

32 ¶ "Also concerning the foreigner who is not from Your people Israel, when he comes from a far country for Your great name's sake and Your mighty hand and Your outstretched arm, when they come and pray toward this house,

33 then hear from heaven, from Your dwelling place, and do according to all for which the foreigner calls to You, in order that all the peoples of the earth may know Your name, and ᵈfear You as *do* Your people Israel, and that they may know that this house which I have built is called by Your name.

34 ¶ "When Your people go out to battle against their enemies, by whatever way You shall send them, and they pray to You toward this city which You have chosen and the house which I have built for Your name,

35 then hear from heaven their prayer and their supplication, and maintain their cause.

36 ¶ "When they sin against You (for there is no man who does not sin) and You are angry with them and deliver them to an enemy, so that they take them away captive to a land far off or near,

37 if they take thought in the land where they are taken captive, and repent and make supplication to You in the land of their captivity, saying, 'We have sinned, we have committed iniquity and have acted wickedly';

38 if they return to You with all their heart and with all their soul in the land of their captivity, where they have been taken captive, and pray toward their land which You have given to their fathers and the city which You have chosen, and toward the house which I have built for Your name,

39 then hear from heaven, from Your dwelling place, their prayer and supplications, and maintain their cause and forgive Your people who have sinned against You.

New International

before your altar in this temple, 23then hear from heaven and act. Judge between your servants, repaying the guilty by bringing down on his own head what he has done. Declare the innocent not guilty and so establish his innocence.

24"When your people Israel have been defeated by an enemy because they have sinned against you and when they turn back and confess your name, praying and making supplication before you in this temple, 25then hear from heaven and forgive the sin of your people Israel and bring them back to the land you gave to them and their fathers.

26"When the heavens are shut up and there is no rain because your people have sinned against you, and when they pray toward this place and confess your name and turn from their sin because you have afflicted them, 27then hear from heaven and forgive the sin of your servants, your people Israel. Teach them the right way to live, and send rain on the land you gave your people for an inheritance.

28"When famine or plague comes to the land, or blight or mildew, locusts or grasshoppers, or when enemies besiege them in any of their cities, whatever disaster or disease may come, 29and when a prayer or plea is made by any of your people Israel—each one aware of his afflictions and pains, and spreading out his hands toward this temple— 30then hear from heaven, your dwelling place. Forgive, and deal with each man according to all he does, since you know his heart (for you alone know the hearts of men), 31so that they will fear you and walk in your ways all the time they live in the land you gave our fathers.

32"As for the foreigner who does not belong to your people Israel but has come from a distant land because of your great name and your mighty hand and your outstretched arm—when he comes and prays toward this temple, 33then hear from heaven, your dwelling place, and do whatever the foreigner asks of you, so that all the peoples of the earth may know your name and fear you, as do your own people Israel, and may know that this house I have built bears your Name.

34"When your people go to war against their enemies, wherever you send them, and when they pray to you toward this city you have chosen and the temple I have built for your Name, 35then hear from heaven their prayer and their plea, and uphold their cause.

36"When they sin against you—for there is no one who does not sin—and you become angry with them and give them over to the enemy, who takes them captive to a land far away or near; 37and if they have a change of heart in the land where they are held captive, and repent and plead with you in the land of their captivity and say, 'We have sinned, we have done wrong and acted wickedly'; 38and if they turn back to you with all their heart and soul in the land of their captivity where they were taken, and pray toward the land you gave their fathers, toward the city you have chosen and toward the temple I have built for your Name; 39then from heaven, your dwelling place, hear their prayer and their pleas, and uphold their cause. And forgive your people, who have sinned against you.

ᵈOr *reverence*

King James

40Now, my God, let, I beseech thee, thine eyes be open, and *let* thine ears *be* attent a unto the prayer *that is made* in this place.

41Now therefore arise, O LORD God, into thy resting place, thou, and the ark of thy strength: let thy priests, O LORD God, be clothed with salvation, and let thy saints rejoice in goodness.

42O LORD God, turn not away the face of thine anointed: remember the mercies of David thy servant.

Dedicating the house of God

7 NOW WHEN Solomon had made an end of praying, the fire came down from heaven, and consumed the burnt offering and the sacrifices; and the glory of the LORD filled the house.

2And the priests could not enter into the house of the LORD, because the glory of the LORD had filled the LORD'S house.

3And when all the children of Israel saw how the fire came down, and the glory of the LORD upon the house, they bowed themselves with their faces to the ground upon the pavement, and worshipped, and praised the LORD, *saying,* For he is good; for his mercy *endureth* for ever.

4 ¶ Then the king and all the people offered sacrifices before the LORD.

5And king Solomon offered a sacrifice of twenty and two thousand oxen, and an hundred and twenty thousand sheep: so the king and all the people dedicated the house of God.

6And the priests waited on their offices: the Levites also with instruments of music of the LORD, which David the king had made to praise the LORD, because his mercy *endureth* for ever, when David praised b by their ministry; and the priests sounded trumpets before them, and all Israel stood.

7Moreover Solomon hallowed the middle of the court that *was* before the house of the LORD: for there he offered burnt offerings, and the fat of the peace offerings, because the brasen altar which Solomon had made was not able to receive the burnt offerings, and the meat offerings, and the fat.

8 ¶ Also at the same time Solomon kept the feast seven days, and all Israel with him, a very great congregation, from the entering in of Hamath unto the river of Egypt.

9And in the eighth day they made c a solemn assembly: for they kept the dedication of the altar seven days, and the feast seven days.

Amplified

40Now, O my God, I beseech You, let Your eyes be open and Your ears attentive to the prayer offered in this temple.

41So now arise, O Lord God, and come into Your resting place, You and the ark of Your strength *and* power. Let Your priests, O Lord God, be clothed with salvation, and let Your saints (Your zealous ones) rejoice in good *and in* Your goodness.

42O Lord God, f turn not away the face of [me] Your anointed one; [earnestly] remember Your good deeds, mercy, *and* steadfast love for David Your servant.

7 WHEN SOLOMON had finished praying, the fire came down from heaven and consumed the burnt offering and the sacrifices, and the glory of the Lord filled the house.

2The priests could not enter the house of the Lord, because the glory of the Lord had filled the Lord's house.

3And when all the people of Israel saw how the fire came down and the glory of the Lord upon the house, they bowed with their faces upon the pavement and worshiped and praised the Lord, saying, For He is good, for His mercy *and* loving-kindness endure forever.

4Then the king and all the people offered sacrifices before the Lord.

5King Solomon offered a sacrifice of 22,000 oxen and 120,000 sheep. So the king and all the people dedicated God's house.

6The priests stood at their posts, and the Levites also, with instruments of music to the Lord, which King David had made to praise *and* give thanks to the Lord—for His mercy *and* loving-kindness endure forever—whenever David praised through their ministry; the priests blew trumpets before them, and all Israel stood.

7Moreover, Solomon consecrated the middle of the court that was before the house of the Lord, for there he offered burnt offerings and the fat of the peace offerings, because the bronze altar which [he] had made was not sufficient to receive the burnt offerings, the cereal offerings, and the fat.

8At that time Solomon held the feast for seven days, and all Israel with him, a very great assembly, from the entrance of Hamath to the Brook of Egypt.

9The eighth day they made a solemn assembly, for they had kept the dedication of the altar and the feast, each for seven days.

f Young Solomon seems, and doubtless is, utterly sincere as he offers this prayer of which God shows His approval by the miraculous demonstration of His presence in the next verse. It raises the ever-present question, How could Solomon have begun his career like this, and have written his unquestionably divinely inspired books, and yet have fallen eventually into utter defiance of God's will? Not as the result of one false step, as with David, but as the habit of his life for the remainder of his days! Not broken with unspeakable sorrow for his awful sin, as was his penitent father (Ps. 51), but without ever apparently repenting or confessing his awful defiance of God and His explicit commands and warnings, given specifically to Solomon himself (II Chron. 7:17-22). Possibly in this closing sentence of Solomon's prayer we detect the fallacy in the young king's thinking. He seems to be saying in substance, "O Lord God, I am **Your responsibility** now; it will be for **You** to see that my face does not turn away from You; and not for my sake, but [since my name is identified with this temple as well as Yours, You must keep my face turned toward You] for Your own sake!" God lost no unnecessary time in attempting to set the young man straight as to whose is the responsibility for sin—in his case specifically (II Chron. 7:12, 17-22). But there is no evidence that Solomon applied it to himself; though he preached a bit to others, he seems to have considered himself exempt from obeying God's commands—an attitude which has brought disaster upon every person who has ever taken it, however great, or wise, or rich, or otherwise sufficient.

a Heb. *to the prayer of this place*   b Heb. *by their hand*
c Heb. *a restraint*

New American Standard

40 ¶ "Now, O my God, I pray, let Your eyes be open and Your ears attentive to the prayer *offered* in this place.
41 ¶ "Now therefore arise, O LORD God, to Your resting place, You and the ark of Your might; let Your priests, O LORD God, be clothed with salvation and let Your godly ones rejoice in what is good.
42 ¶ "O LORD God, do not turn away the face of Your anointed; remember *Your* lovingkindness to Your servant David."

The Shekinah Glory

7 NOW WHEN Solomon had finished praying, fire came down from heaven and consumed the burnt offering and the sacrifices, and the glory of the LORD filled the house.
2 The priests could not enter into the house of the LORD because the glory of the LORD filled the LORD'S house.
3 All the sons of Israel, seeing the fire come down and the glory of the LORD upon the house, bowed down on the pavement with their faces to the ground, and they worshiped and gave praise to the LORD, *saying*, "Truly He is good, truly His lovingkindness is everlasting."

Sacrifices Offered

4 ¶ Then the king and all the people offered sacrifice before the LORD.
5 King Solomon offered a sacrifice of 22,000 oxen and 120,000 sheep. Thus the king and all the people dedicated the house of God.
6 The priests stood at their posts, and the Levites also, with the instruments of music to the LORD, which King David had made for giving praise to the LORD—"for His lovingkindness is everlasting"—whenever he gave praise by their means, while the priests on the other side blew trumpets; and all Israel was standing.
7 ¶ Then Solomon consecrated the middle of the court that *was* before the house of the LORD, for there he offered the burnt offerings and the fat of the peace offerings because the bronze altar which Solomon had made was not able to contain the burnt offering, the grain offering and the fat.

The Feast of Dedication

8 ¶ So Solomon observed the feast at that time for seven days, and all Israel with him, a very great assembly *who came* from the entrance of Hamath to the brook of Egypt.
9 On the eighth day they held a solemn assembly, for the dedication of the altar they observed seven days and the feast seven days.

New International

40"Now, my God, may your eyes be open and your ears attentive to the prayers offered in this place.
41"Now arise, O LORD God, and come to
   your resting place,
   you and the ark of your might.
May your priests, O LORD God, be
   clothed with salvation,
   may your saints rejoice in your
     goodness.
42O LORD God, do not reject your anointed
   one.
Remember the great love promised to
   David your servant."

The Dedication of the Temple

7 WHEN SOLOMON finished praying, fire came down from heaven and consumed the burnt offering and the sacrifices, and the glory of the LORD filled the temple.
2The priests could not enter the temple of the LORD because the glory of the LORD filled it. 3When all the Israelites saw the fire coming down and the glory of the LORD above the temple, they knelt on the pavement with their faces to the ground, and they worshiped and gave thanks to the LORD, saying,

"He is good;
   his love endures forever."

4Then the king and all the people offered sacrifices before the LORD. 5And King Solomon offered a sacrifice of twenty-two thousand head of cattle and a hundred and twenty thousand sheep and goats. So the king and all the people dedicated the temple of God. 6The priests took their positions, as did the Levites with the LORD's musical instruments, which King David had made for praising the LORD and which were used when he gave thanks, saying, "His love endures forever." Opposite the Levites, the priests blew their trumpets, and all the Israelites were standing.

7Solomon consecrated the middle part of the courtyard in front of the temple of the LORD, and there he offered burnt offerings and the fat of the fellowship offerings,*e* because the bronze altar he had made could not hold the burnt offerings, the grain offerings and the fat portions.

8So Solomon observed the festival at that time for seven days, and all Israel with him—a vast assembly, people from Lebo*f* Hamath to the Wadi of Egypt. 9On the eighth day they held an assembly, for they had celebrated the dedication of the altar for seven days and the festival for

---

e 7 Traditionally peace offerings   f 8 Or from the entrance to

King James

¹⁰And on the three and twentieth day of the seventh month he sent the people away into their tents, glad and merry in heart for the goodness that the LORD had shown unto David, and to Solomon, and to Israel his people.

The LORD's promise to Solomon

¹¹Thus Solomon finished the house of the LORD, and the king's house: and all that came into Solomon's heart to make in the house of the LORD, and in his own house, he prosperously effected.

¹² ¶ And the LORD appeared to Solomon by night, and said unto him, I have heard thy prayer, and have chosen this place to myself for an house of sacrifice.

¹³If I shut up heaven that there be no rain, or if I command the locusts to devour the land, or if I send pestilence among my people;

¹⁴If my people, ^dwhich are called by my name, shall humble themselves, and pray, and seek my face, and turn from their wicked ways; then will I hear from heaven, and will forgive their sin, and will heal their land.

¹⁵Now mine eyes shall be open, and mine ears attent ^eunto the prayer *that is made* in this place.

¹⁶For now have I chosen and sanctified this house, that my name may be there for ever: and mine eyes and mine heart shall be there perpetually.

¹⁷And as for thee, if thou wilt walk before me, as David thy father walked, and do according to all that I have commanded thee, and shalt observe my statutes and my judgments;

¹⁸Then will I stablish the throne of thy kingdom, according as I have covenanted with David thy father, saying, ^fThere shall not fail thee a man *to be* ruler in Israel.

¹⁹But if ye turn away, and forsake my statutes and my commandments, which I have set before you, and shall go and serve other gods, and worship them;

²⁰Then will I pluck them up by the roots out of my land which I have given them; and this house, which I have sanctified for my name, will I cast out of my sight, and will make it *to be* a proverb and a byword among all nations.

²¹And this house, which is high, shall be an astonishment to every one that passeth by it; so that he shall say, Why hath the LORD done thus unto this land, and unto this house?

²²And it shall be answered, Because they forsook the LORD God of their fathers, which brought them forth out of the land of Egypt, and laid hold on other gods, and worshipped them, and served them: therefore hath he brought all this evil upon them.

Solomon's other achievements

8 AND IT came to pass at the end of twenty years, wherein Solomon had built the house of the LORD, and his own house,

²That the cities which Huram had restored to Solomon, Solomon built them, and caused the children of Israel to dwell there.

³And Solomon went to Hamath-zobah, and prevailed against it.

⁴And he built Tadmor in the wilderness, and all the store cities, which he built in Hamath.

⁵Also he built Beth-horon the upper, and Beth-horon the nether, fenced cities, with walls, gates, and bars;

⁶And Baalath, and all the store cities that Solomon had, and all the chariot cities, and the cities of the horsemen, and ^gall that Solomon desired to build in Jerusalem, and in Lebanon, and throughout all the land of his dominion.

⁷ ¶As for all the people *that were* left of the Hittites, and the Amorites, and the Perizzites, and the Hivites, and the Jebusites, which *were* not of Israel,

Amplified

¹⁰And on the twenty-third day of the seventh month he sent the people away to their homes, glad and merry in heart for the goodness that the Lord had shown to David, to Solomon, and to Israel His people.

¹¹Thus Solomon finished the Lord's house and the king's house; all that [he] had planned to do in the Lord's house and his own house he accomplished successfully.

¹²And the Lord appeared to Solomon by night and said to him: I have heard your prayer and have chosen this place for Myself as a house of sacrifice.

¹³If I shut up heaven so no rain falls, or if I command locusts to devour the land, or if I send pestilence among My people,

¹⁴If My people, who are called by My name, shall humble themselves, pray, seek, crave, *and* require of necessity My face and turn from their wicked ways, then will I hear from heaven, forgive their sin, and heal their land.

¹⁵Now My eyes will be open and My ears attentive to prayer offered in this place.

¹⁶For I have chosen and sanctified (set apart for holy use) this house, that My Name may be here forever, and My eyes and My heart will be here perpetually.

¹⁷As for you [Solomon], if you will walk before me as David your father walked, and do all I have commanded you, and observe My statutes and My ordinances, [I Kings 11:1–11.]

¹⁸Then I will establish the throne of your kingdom, as I covenanted with David your father, saying, There shall not fail you a man to be ruler in Israel.

¹⁹But if you [people] turn away and forsake My statutes and My commandments which I have set before you and go and serve other gods and worship them,

²⁰Then will I pluck [Israel] up by the roots out of My land which I have given [them]; and this house which I have hallowed for My Name will I cast out of My sight, and will make it to be a proverb and a byword among all nations. [Jer. 24:9, 10.]

²¹And this house, which was so high, shall be an astonishment to everyone passing it, and they will say, Why has the Lord done thus to this land and to this house?

²²Then men will say, Because they forsook the Lord, the God of their fathers, Who brought them out of Egypt, and they laid hold of other gods and worshiped and served them; therefore has He brought all this evil upon them.

8 AT THE end of twenty years, in which Solomon had built the house of the Lord and his own house,

²The cities which Huram had given to [him] Solomon rebuilt *and* fortified, and caused the Israelites to dwell there.

³And Solomon took Hamath-zobah.

⁴He built Tadmor in the wilderness and all his store cities in Hamath.

⁵Also he built Upper Beth-horon and Lower Beth-horon, fortified cities with walls, gates, and bars,

⁶And Baalath and all the store cities [he] had, and all the cities for his chariots and the cities for his horsemen, and all that Solomon desired to build in Jerusalem, in Lebanon, and in all his dominion.

⁷All the people who were left of the Hittites, Amorites, Perizzites, Hivites, and Jebusites, who were not of Israel,

---

^dHeb. *upon whom my name is called*   ^eHeb. *to the prayer of this place*   ^fHeb. *There shall not be cut off to thee*   ^gHeb. *all the desire of Solomon which he desired to build*

New American Standard

10 Then on the twenty-third day of the seventh month he sent the people to their tents, rejoicing and happy of heart because of the goodness that the LORD had shown to David and to Solomon and to His people Israel.

God's Promise and Warning

11 ¶ Thus Solomon finished the house of the LORD and the king's palace, and successfully completed all that he had planned on doing in the house of the LORD and in his palace.

12 ¶ Then the LORD appeared to Solomon at night and said to him, "I have heard your prayer and have chosen this place for Myself as a house of sacrifice.

13 "If I shut up the heavens so that there is no rain, or if I command the locust to devour the land, or if I send pestilence among My people,

14 and My people who are called by My name humble themselves and pray and seek My face and turn from their wicked ways, then I will hear from heaven, will forgive their sin and will heal their land.

15 "Now My eyes will be open and My ears attentive to the prayer *offered* in this place.

16 "For now I have chosen and consecrated this house that My name may be there forever, and My eyes and My heart will be there perpetually.

17 "As for you, if you walk before Me as your father David walked, even to do according to all that I have commanded you, and will keep My statutes and My ordinances,

18 then I will establish your royal throne as I covenanted with your father David, saying, 'You shall not lack a man *to be* ruler in Israel.'

19 ¶ "But if you turn away and forsake My statutes and My commandments which I have set before you, and go and serve other gods and worship them,

20 then I will uproot you from My land which I have given you, and this house which I have consecrated for My name I will cast out of My sight and I will make it a proverb and a byword among all peoples.

21 "As for this house, which was exalted, everyone who passes by it will be astonished and say, 'Why has the LORD done thus to this land and to this house?'

22 "And they will say, 'Because they forsook the LORD, the God of their fathers who brought them from the land of Egypt, and they adopted other gods and worshiped them and served them; therefore He has brought all this adversity on them.' "

Solomon's Activities and Accomplishments

8 NOW IT came about at the end of the twenty years in which Solomon had built the house of the LORD and his own house

2 that he built the cities which Huram had given to him, and settled the sons of Israel there.

3 ¶ Then Solomon went to Hamath-zobah and captured it.

4 He built Tadmor in the wilderness and all the storage cities which he had built in Hamath.

5 He also built upper Beth-horon and lower Beth-horon, fortified cities *with* walls, gates and bars;

6 and Baalath and all the storage cities that Solomon had, and all the cities for his chariots and cities for his horsemen, and all that it pleased Solomon to build in Jerusalem, in Lebanon, and in all the land under his rule.

7 ¶ All of the people who were left of the Hittites, the Amorites, the Perizzites, the Hivites and the Jebusites, who were not of Israel,

New International

seven days more. 10 On the twenty-third day of the seventh month he sent the people to their homes, joyful and glad in heart for the good things the LORD had done for David and Solomon and for his people Israel.

The LORD Appears to Solomon

11 When Solomon had finished the temple of the LORD and the royal palace, and had succeeded in carrying out all he had in mind to do in the temple of the LORD and in his own palace, 12 the LORD appeared to him at night and said:

"I have heard your prayer and have chosen this place for myself as a temple for sacrifices.

13 "When I shut up the heavens so that there is no rain, or command locusts to devour the land or send a plague among my people, 14 if my people, who are called by my name, will humble themselves and pray and seek my face and turn from their wicked ways, then will I hear from heaven and will forgive their sin and will heal their land. 15 Now my eyes will be open and my ears attentive to the prayers offered in this place. 16 I have chosen and consecrated this temple so that my Name may be there forever. My eyes and my heart will always be there.

17 "As for you, if you walk before me as David your father did, and do all I command, and observe my decrees and laws, 18 I will establish your royal throne, as I covenanted with David your father when I said, 'You shall never fail to have a man to rule over Israel.'

19 "But if you[g] turn away and forsake the decrees and commands I have given you[g] and go off to serve other gods and worship them, 20 then I will uproot Israel from my land, which I have given them, and will reject this temple I have consecrated for my Name. I will make it a byword and an object of ridicule among all peoples. 21 And though this temple is now so imposing, all who pass by will be appalled and say, 'Why has the LORD done such a thing to this land and to this temple?' 22 People will answer, 'Because they have forsaken the LORD, the God of their fathers, who brought them out of Egypt, and have embraced other gods, worshiping and serving them—that is why he brought all this disaster on them.' "

Solomon's Other Activities

8 AT THE end of twenty years, during which Solomon built the temple of the LORD and his own palace, 2 Solomon rebuilt the villages that Hiram[h] had given him, and settled Israelites in them. 3 Solomon then went to Hamath Zobah and captured it. 4 He also built up Tadmor in the desert and all the store cities he had built in Hamath. 5 He rebuilt Upper Beth Horon and Lower Beth Horon as fortified cities, with walls and with gates and bars, 6 as well as Baalath and all his store cities, and all the cities for his chariots and for his horses[i]—whatever he desired to build in Jerusalem, in Lebanon and throughout all the territory he ruled.

7 All the people left from the Hittites, Amorites, Perizzites, Hivites and Jebusites (these peoples were not Israel-

g 19 The Hebrew is plural. Hiram; also in verse 18   h 2 Hebrew *Huram*, a variant of   i 6 Or *charioteers*

⁸*But* of their children, who were left after them in the land, whom the children of Israel consumed not, them did Solomon make to pay tribute until this day.

⁹But of the children of Israel did Solomon make no servants for his work; but they *were* men of war, and chief of his captains, and captains of his chariots and horsemen.

¹⁰And these *were* the chief of king Solomon's officers, *even* two hundred and fifty, that bare rule over the people.

¹¹ ¶ And Solomon brought up the daughter of Pharaoh out of the city of David unto the house that he had built for her: for he said, My wife shall not dwell in the house of David king of Israel, because *the places are* ʰholy, whereunto the ark of the LORD hath come.

¹² ¶ Then Solomon offered burnt offerings unto the LORD on the altar of the LORD, which he had built before the porch,

¹³Even after a certain rate every day, offering according to the commandment of Moses, on the sabbaths, and on the new moons, and on the solemn feasts, three times in the year, *even* in the feast of unleavened bread, and in the feast of weeks, and in the feast of tabernacles.

¹⁴ ¶ And he appointed, according to the order of David his father, the courses of the priests to their service, and the Levites to their charges, to praise and minister before the priests, as the duty of every day required: the porters also by their courses at every gate: for ⁱso had David the man of God commanded.

¹⁵And they departed not from the commandment of the king unto the priests and Levites concerning any matter, or concerning the treasures.

¹⁶Now all the work of Solomon was prepared unto the day of the foundation of the house of the LORD, and until it was finished. *So* the house of the LORD was perfected.

¹⁷ ¶ Then went Solomon to Ezion-geber, and to ʲEloth, at the sea side in the land of Edom.

¹⁸And Huram sent him by the hands of his servants ships, and servants that had knowledge of the sea; and they went with the servants of Solomon to Ophir, and took thence four hundred and fifty talents of gold, and brought *them* to king Solomon.

The visit of the queen of Sheba

9 AND WHEN the queen of Sheba heard of the fame of Solomon, she came to prove Solomon with hard questions at Jerusalem, with a very great company, and camels that bare spices, and gold in abundance, and precious stones: and when she was come to Solomon, she communed with him of all that was in her heart.

²And Solomon told her all her questions: and there was nothing hid from Solomon which he told her not.

³And when the queen of Sheba had seen the wisdom of Solomon, and the house that he had built,

⁴And the meat of his table, and the sitting of his servants, and the attendance of his ministers, and their apparel; his ᵏcupbearers also, and their apparel; and his ascent by which he went up into the house of the LORD; there was no more spirit in her.

⁵And she said to the king, *It was* a true ˡreport which I heard in mine own land of thine ᵐacts, and of thy wisdom:

⁶Howbeit I believed not their words, until I came, and mine eyes had seen *it:* and, behold, the one half of the greatness of thy wisdom was not told me: *for* thou exceedest the fame that I heard.

⁷Happy *are* thy men, and happy *are* these thy servants, which stand continually before thee, and hear thy wisdom.

⁸But descendants of those who were left in the land, whom the Israelites had not destroyed—of them Solomon made a levy for forced labor to this day.

⁹But of the Israelites Solomon made no slaves for his work; but they were men of war, chiefs of his captains, and captains of his chariots and horsemen.

¹⁰These were the chiefs of King Solomon's officers, 250 in authority over the people.

¹¹Solomon brought the daughter of Pharaoh out of the City of David into the house he had built for her, for he said, My wife shall not dwell in the house of David king of Israel, because the places are holy to which the ark of the Lord has come.

¹²Then Solomon offered burnt offerings to the Lord on the Lord's altar which he had built before the [temple] porch *or* vestibule,

¹³A certain number every day, offering as Moses commanded for the Sabbaths, the New Moons, and the solemn feast days three times in the year—the Feasts of Unleavened Bread, of Weeks, and of Tabernacles.

¹⁴And he appointed, as ordered by David his father, the divisions of the priests for their service, and the Levites to their offices to praise and to serve before the priests as the duty of every day required, and the gatekeepers also by their divisions at every gate; for so had David the man of God commanded.

¹⁵And they did not turn from the command of the king to the priests and Levites in any respect or concerning the treasuries.

¹⁶Thus all the work of Solomon was prepared from the day the foundation of the Lord's house was laid until it was finished. So the house of the Lord was completed.

¹⁷Then Solomon went to Ezion-geber and to Eloth on the shore of the [Red] Sea in the land of Edom.

¹⁸And Huram sent him by his servants ships and servants familiar with the sea; and they went with the servants of Solomon to Ophir and took from there 450 talents of gold and brought them to King Solomon.

9 WHEN THE queen of Sheba heard of the fame of Solomon, she came to Jerusalem to test him with hard questions, accompanied by very many attendants and camels bearing spices, much gold, and precious stones. And when she came to Solomon, she talked with him of all that was on her mind.

²And Solomon answered all her questions; there was nothing hidden from [him] which he was unable to make clear to her.

³And when the queen of Sheba had seen Solomon's wisdom, the house he had built,

⁴The food of his table, the seating of his officials, the [standing at] attention of his servants, their apparel, his cupbearers also and their apparel, and his burnt offerings which he offered at the house of the Lord, there was no more spirit in her.

⁵She said to the king, The report which I heard in my own land of your acts *and* sayings and of your wisdom was true,

⁶But I did not believe their words until I came and my eyes had seen it. Behold, the half of the greatness of your wisdom was not told me; you surpass the fame that I heard of you.

⁷Happy are your wives *and* men, and happy are these your servants who stand continually before you and hear your wisdom!

ʰHeb. *holiness*   ⁱHeb. *so was the commandment of David the man of God*   ʲOr, *Elath;* see Deut. 2:8; 2 Ki. 14:22   ᵏOr, *butlers*   ˡHeb. *word*   ᵐOr, *sayings*

New American Standard

8 *namely,* from their descendants who were left after them in the land whom the sons of Israel had not destroyed, them Solomon raised as forced laborers to this day.

9 But Solomon did not make slaves for his work from the sons of Israel; they were men of war, his chief captains and commanders of his chariots and his horsemen.

10 These were the chief officers of King Solomon, two hundred and fifty who ruled over the people.

11 ¶ Then Solomon brought Pharaoh's daughter up from the city of David to the house which he had built for her, for he said, "My wife shall not dwell in the house of David king of Israel, because the places are holy where the ark of the LORD has entered."

12 ¶ Then Solomon offered burnt offerings to the LORD on the altar of the LORD which he had built before the porch;

13 and *did so* according to the daily rule, offering *them* up according to the commandment of Moses, for the sabbaths, the new moons and the three annual feasts—the Feast of Unleavened Bread, the Feast of Weeks and the Feast of Booths.

14 Now according to the ordinance of his father David, he appointed the divisions of the priests for their service, and the Levites for their duties of praise and ministering before the priests according to the daily rule, and the gatekeepers by their divisions at every gate; for David the man of God had so commanded.

15 And they did not depart from the commandment of the king to the priests and Levites in any manner or concerning the storehouses.

16 ¶ Thus all the work of Solomon was carried out from the day of the foundation of the house of the LORD, and until it was finished. So the house of the LORD was completed.

17 ¶ Then Solomon went to Ezion-geber and to Eloth on the seashore in the land of Edom.

18 And Huram by his servants sent him ships and servants who knew the sea; and they went with Solomon's servants to Ophir, and took from there four hundred and fifty talents of gold and brought them to King Solomon.

Visit of the Queen of Sheba

9 NOW WHEN the queen of Sheba heard of the fame of Solomon, she came to Jerusalem to test Solomon with difficult questions. She had a very large retinue, with camels carrying spices and a large amount of gold and precious stones; and when she came to Solomon, she spoke with him about all that was on her heart.

2 Solomon answered all her questions; nothing was hidden from Solomon which he did not explain to her.

3 When the queen of Sheba had seen the wisdom of Solomon, the house which he had built,

4 the food at his table, the seating of his servants, the attendance of his ministers and their attire, his cupbearers and their attire, and his stairway by which he went up to the house of the LORD, she was breathless.

5 Then she said to the king, "It was a true report which I heard in my own land about your words and your wisdom.

6"Nevertheless I did not believe their reports until I came and my eyes had seen it. And behold, the half of the greatness of your wisdom was not told me. You surpass the report that I heard.

7"How blessed are your men, how blessed are these your servants who stand before you continually and hear your wisdom.

New International

ites), 8that is, their descendants remaining in the land, whom the Israelites had not destroyed—these Solomon conscripted for his slave labor force, as it is to this day. 9But Solomon did not make slaves of the Israelites for his work; they were his fighting men, commanders of his captains, and commanders of his chariots and charioteers. 10They were also King Solomon's chief officials—two hundred and fifty officials supervising the men.

11Solomon brought Pharaoh's daughter up from the City of David to the palace he had built for her, for he said, "My wife must not live in the palace of David king of Israel, because the places the ark of the LORD has entered are holy."

12On the altar of the LORD that he had built in front of the portico, Solomon sacrificed burnt offerings to the LORD, 13according to the daily requirement for offerings commanded by Moses for Sabbaths, New Moons and the three annual feasts—the Feast of Unleavened Bread, the Feast of Weeks and the Feast of Tabernacles. 14In keeping with the ordinance of his father David, he appointed the divisions of the priests for their duties, and the Levites to lead the praise and to assist the priests according to each day's requirement. He also appointed the gatekeepers by divisions for the various gates, because this was what David the man of God had ordered. 15They did not deviate from the king's commands to the priests or to the Levites in any matter, including that of the treasuries.

16All Solomon's work was carried out, from the day the foundation of the temple of the LORD was laid until its completion. So the temple of the LORD was finished.

17Then Solomon went to Ezion Geber and Elath on the coast of Edom. 18And Hiram sent him ships commanded by his own officers, men who knew the sea. These, with Solomon's men, sailed to Ophir and brought back four hundred and fifty talents*j* of gold, which they delivered to King Solomon.

The Queen of Sheba Visits Solomon

9 WHEN THE queen of Sheba heard of Solomon's fame, she came to test him with hard questions. Arriving with a very great caravan—with camels carrying spices, large quantities of gold, and precious stones—she came to Solomon and talked with him about all she had on her mind. 2Solomon answered all her questions; nothing was too hard for him to explain to her. 3When the queen of Sheba saw the wisdom of Solomon, as well as the palace he had built, 4the food on his table, the seating of his officials, the attending servants in their robes, the cupbearers in their robes and the burnt offerings he made at*k* the temple of the LORD, she was overwhelmed.

5She said to the king, "The report I heard in my own country about your achievements and your wisdom is true. 6But I did not believe what they said until I came and saw with my own eyes. Indeed, not even half the greatness of your wisdom was told me; you have far exceeded the report I heard. 7How happy your men must be! How happy your officials, who continually stand before you and hear

j18 That is, about 17 tons (about 16 metric tons)   k4 Or the ascent by which he went up to

King James

8Blessed be the LORD thy God, which delighted in thee to set thee on his throne, *to be* king for the LORD thy God: because thy God loved Israel, to establish them for ever, therefore made he thee king over them, to do judgment and justice.

9And she gave the king an hundred and twenty talents of gold, and of spices great abundance, and precious stones: neither was there any such spice as the queen of Sheba gave king Solomon.

10And the servants also of Huram, and the servants of Solomon, which brought gold from Ophir, brought algum trees and precious stones.

11And the king made *of* the algum trees *n*oterraces to the house of the LORD, and to the king's palace, and harps and psalteries for singers: and there were none such seen before in the land of Judah.

12And king Solomon gave to the queen of Sheba all her desire, whatsoever she asked, beside *that* which she had brought unto the king. So she turned, and went away to her own land, she and her servants.

Solomon's wealth and wisdom

13 ¶ Now the weight of gold that came to Solomon in one year was six hundred and threescore and six talents of gold;

14Beside *that which* chapmen and merchants brought. And all the kings of Arabia and *p*governors of the country brought gold and silver to Solomon.

15 ¶ And king Solomon made two hundred targets *of* beaten gold: six hundred *shekels* of beaten gold went to one target.

16And three hundred shields *made he of* beaten gold: three hundred *shekels* of gold went to one shield. And the king put them in the house of the forest of Lebanon.

17Moreover the king made a great throne of ivory, and overlaid it with pure gold.

18And *there were* six steps to the throne, with a footstool of gold, *which were* fastened to the throne, and *q*stays on each side of the sitting place, and two lions standing by the stays:

19And twelve lions stood there on the one side and on the other upon the six steps. There was not the like made in any kingdom.

20 ¶ And all the drinking vessels of king Solomon *were of* gold, and all the vessels of the house of the forest of Lebanon *were of* *r*pure gold: *s*none *were of* silver; it was *not* any thing accounted of in the days of Solomon.

21For the king's ships went to Tarshish with the servants of Huram: every three years once came the ships of Tarshish bringing gold, and silver, *t*ivory, and apes, and peacocks.

22And king Solomon passed all the kings of the earth in riches and wisdom.

23 ¶ And all the kings of the earth sought the presence of Solomon, to hear his wisdom, that God had put in his heart.

24And they brought every man his present, vessels of silver, and vessels of gold, and raiment, harness, and spices, horses, and mules, a rate year by year.

25 ¶ And Solomon had four thousand stalls for horses and chariots, and twelve thousand horsemen; whom he bestowed in the chariot cities, and with the king at Jerusalem.

26 ¶ And he reigned over all the kings from the *u*river even unto the land of the Philistines, and to the border of Egypt.

27And the king *v*made silver in Jerusalem as stones, and cedar trees made he as the sycamore trees that *are* in the low plains in abundance.

28And they brought unto Solomon horses out of Egypt, and out of all lands.

Amplified

8Blessed be the Lord your God, Who delighted in you and set you on His throne to be king for the Lord your God! Because your God loved Israel and would establish them forever, He made you king over them, to do justice and righteousness.

9She gave the king 120 talents of gold, a very large quantity of spices, and precious stones; such spice was not anywhere as that which the queen of Sheba gave King Solomon.

10The servants of Huram and [those] of Solomon, who brought gold from Ophir, also brought algum trees and precious stones.

11The king made of the algum trees terraces *or* walks to the house of the Lord and to the king's palace, and lyres and harps for the singers; none such had ever been seen before in the land of Judah.

12And King Solomon gave to the queen of Sheba all her desire, whatever she asked, besides what she had brought to the king. So she with her servants returned to her own land.

13Now the weight of gold that came to Solomon in one year was 666 talents,

14Besides what traders and merchants brought; and all the kings of Arabia and governors of the country brought gold and silver to Solomon.

15And King Solomon made 200 large shields *or* bucklers of beaten gold; 600 shekels of beaten gold went into each shield.

16And he made 300 shields of beaten gold, with 300 shekels of gold spread on each shield. And the king put them in the House of the Forest of Lebanon.

17Moreover, [he] made a great throne of ivory and overlaid it with pure gold.

18There were six steps to the throne and a gold footstool attached to the throne, and arms on each side of the seat, with two lions standing beside the arms.

19And twelve lions stood there one on either end of each of the six steps. The like of it was never made in any kingdom before.

20King Solomon's drinking vessels were all of gold, and all the vessels of the House of the Forest of Lebanon were of pure gold; silver was not counted as anything in the days of Solomon.

21For the king's ships went to Tarshish with Huram's servants; once every three years the ships of Tarshish came bringing gold, silver, ivory, apes, and peacocks.

22King Solomon surpassed all the kings of the earth in riches and wisdom.

23And all the kings of the earth sought the presence of Solomon to hear his wisdom which God had put into his mind.

24And every man brought his tribute: silver and gold articles, robes, armor, spices, horses, and mules, so much year by year.

25Solomon had 4,000 stalls for horses and chariots, and 12,000 horsemen, stationed in chariot cities or at Jerusalem with the king. [Deut. 17:16, 17.]

26And he ruled over *g*all the kings from the [Euphrates] River to the land of Philistia and to the frontier of Egypt.

27The king made silver in Jerusalem as common as stones, and cedar wood as plentiful as sycamore trees in the lowlands.

28And they imported horses for Solomon from Egypt and from all lands.

---

*n*Or, *stairs*   *o*Heb. *highways*   *p*Or, *captains*   *q*Heb. *hands*   *r*Heb. *shut up*   *s*Or, there was *no silver* in them   *t*Or, *elephants' teeth*   *u*i.e. Euphrates   *v*Heb. *gave*

*g*See footnote on I Kings 4:21 for proof for this statement.

New American Standard

8 "Blessed be the LORD your God who delighted in you, setting you on His throne as king for the LORD your God; because your God loved Israel establishing them forever, therefore He made you king over them, to do justice and righteousness."

9 Then she gave the king one hundred and twenty talents of gold and a very great *amount of* spices and precious stones; there had never been spice like that which the queen of Sheba gave to King Solomon.

10 ¶ The servants of Huram and the servants of Solomon who brought gold from Ophir, also brought algum trees and precious stones.

11 From the algum trees the king made steps for the house of the LORD and for the king's palace, and lyres and harps for the singers; and none like that was seen before in the land of Judah.

12 ¶ King Solomon gave to the queen of Sheba all her desire which she requested besides *a return for* what she had brought to the king. Then she turned and went to her own land with her servants.

Solomon's Wealth and Power

13 ¶ Now the weight of gold which came to Solomon in one year was 666 talents of gold,

14 besides that which the traders and merchants brought; and all the kings of Arabia and the governors of the country brought gold and silver to Solomon.

15 King Solomon made 200 large shields of beaten gold, using 600 *shekels of* beaten gold on each large shield.

16 *He made* 300 shields of beaten gold, using three hundred shekels of gold on each shield, and the king put them in the house of the forest of Lebanon.

17 ¶ Moreover, the king made a great throne of ivory and overlaid it with pure gold.

18 *There were* six steps to the throne and a footstool in gold attached to the throne, and arms on each side of the seat, and two lions standing beside the arms.

19 Twelve lions were standing there on the six steps on the one side and on the other; nothing like *it* was made for any *other* kingdom.

20 All King Solomon's drinking vessels *were* of gold, and all the vessels of the house of the forest of Lebanon *were* of pure gold; silver was not considered valuable in the days of Solomon.

21 For the king had ships which went to Tarshish with the servants of Huram; once every three years the ships of Tarshish came bringing gold and silver, ivory and apes and peacocks.

22 ¶ So King Solomon became greater than all the kings of the earth in riches and wisdom.

23 And all the kings of the earth were seeking the presence of Solomon, to hear his wisdom which God had put in his heart.

24 They brought every man his gift, articles of silver and gold, garments, weapons, spices, horses and mules, so much year by year.

25 ¶ Now Solomon had 4,000 stalls for horses and chariots and 12,000 horsemen, and he stationed them in the chariot cities and with the king in Jerusalem.

26 He was the ruler over all the kings from the Euphrates River even to the land of the Philistines, and as far as the border of Egypt.

27 The king made silver *as common* as stones in Jerusalem, and he made cedars as plentiful as sycamore trees that are in the lowland.

28 And they were bringing horses for Solomon from Egypt and from all countries.

New International

your wisdom! 8 Praise be to the LORD your God, who has delighted in you and placed you on his throne as king to rule for the LORD your God. Because of the love of your God for Israel and his desire to uphold them forever, he has made you king over them, to maintain justice and righteousness."

9 Then she gave the king 120 talents[l] of gold, large quantities of spices, and precious stones. There had never been such spices as those the queen of Sheba gave to King Solomon.

10 (The men of Hiram and the men of Solomon brought gold from Ophir; they also brought algumwood[m] and precious stones. 11 The king used the algumwood to make steps for the temple of the LORD and for the royal palace, and to make harps and lyres for the musicians. Nothing like them had ever been seen in Judah.)

12 King Solomon gave the queen of Sheba all she desired and asked for; he gave her more than she had brought to him. Then she left and returned with her retinue to her own country.

Solomon's Splendor

13 The weight of the gold that Solomon received yearly was 666 talents,[n] 14 not including the revenues brought in by merchants and traders. Also all the kings of Arabia and the governors of the land brought gold and silver to Solomon.

15 King Solomon made two hundred large shields of hammered gold; six hundred bekas[o] of hammered gold went into each shield. 16 He also made three hundred small shields of hammered gold, with three hundred bekas[p] of gold in each shield. The king put them in the Palace of the Forest of Lebanon.

17 Then the king made a great throne inlaid with ivory and overlaid with pure gold. 18 The throne had six steps, and a footstool of gold was attached to it. On both sides of the seat were armrests, with a lion standing beside each of them. 19 Twelve lions stood on the six steps, one at either end of each step. Nothing like it had ever been made for any other kingdom. 20 All King Solomon's goblets were gold, and all the household articles in the Palace of the Forest of Lebanon were pure gold. Nothing was made of silver, because silver was considered of little value in Solomon's day. 21 The king had a fleet of trading ships[q] manned by Hiram's[r] men. Once every three years it returned, carrying gold, silver and ivory, and apes and baboons.

22 King Solomon was greater in riches and wisdom than all the other kings of the earth. 23 All the kings of the earth sought audience with Solomon to hear the wisdom God had put in his heart. 24 Year after year, everyone who came brought a gift—articles of silver and gold, and robes, weapons and spices, and horses and mules.

25 Solomon had four thousand stalls for horses and chariots, and twelve thousand horses,[s] which he kept in the chariot cities and also with him in Jerusalem. 26 He ruled over all the kings from the River[t] to the land of the Philistines, as far as the border of Egypt. 27 The king made silver as common in Jerusalem as stones, and cedar as plentiful as sycamore-fig trees in the foothills. 28 Solomon's horses were imported from Egypt[u] and from all other countries.

King James

Solomon's death and successor

29 ¶ Now the rest of the acts of Solomon, first and last, *are* they not written in the [w]book of Nathan the prophet, and in the prophecy of Ahijah the Shilonite, and in the visions of Iddo the seer against Jeroboam the son of Nebat?

30 And Solomon reigned in Jerusalem over all Israel forty years.

31 And Solomon slept with his fathers, and he was buried in the city of David his father: and Rehoboam his son reigned in his stead.

Rehoboam's harsh rule

10 AND REHOBOAM went to Shechem: for to Shechem were all Israel come to make him king.

2 And it came to pass, when Jeroboam the son of Nebat, who *was* in Egypt, whither he had fled from the presence of Solomon the king, heard *it,* that Jeroboam returned out of Egypt.

3 And they sent and called him. So Jeroboam and all Israel came and spake to Rehoboam, saying,

4 Thy father made our yoke grievous: now therefore ease thou somewhat the grievous servitude of thy father, and his heavy yoke that he put upon us, and we will serve thee.

5 And he said unto them, Come again unto me after three days. And the people departed.

6 ¶ And king Rehoboam took counsel with the old men that had stood before Solomon his father while he yet lived, saying, What counsel give ye *me* to return answer to this people?

7 And they spake unto him, saying, If thou be kind to this people, and please them, and speak good words to them, they will be thy servants for ever.

8 But he forsook the counsel which the old men gave him, and took counsel with the young men that were brought up with him, that stood before him.

9 And he said unto them, What advice give ye that we may return answer to this people, which have spoken to me, saying, Ease somewhat the yoke that thy father did put upon us?

10 And the young men that were brought up with him spake unto him, saying, Thus shalt thou answer the people that spake unto thee, saying, Thy father made our yoke heavy, but make thou *it* somewhat lighter for us; thus shalt thou say unto them, My little *finger* shall be thicker than my father's loins.

11 For whereas my father [x]put a heavy yoke upon you, I will put more to your yoke: my father chastised you with whips, but I *will chastise you* with scorpions.

12 So Jeroboam and all the people came to Rehoboam on the third day, as the king bade, saying, Come again to me on the third day.

13 And the king answered them roughly; and king Rehoboam forsook the counsel of the old men,

14 And answered them after the advice of the young men, saying, My father made your yoke heavy, but I will add thereto: my father chastised you with whips, but I *will chastise you* with scorpions.

15 So the king hearkened not unto the people: for the cause was of God, that the LORD might perform his word, which he spake by the hand of Ahijah the Shilonite to Jeroboam the son of Nebat.

16 ¶ And when all Israel *saw* that the king would not hearken unto them, the people answered the king, saying, What portion have we in David? and *we have* none inheritance in the son of Jesse: every man to your tents, O Israel: *and* now, David, see to thine own house. So all Israel went to their tents.

17 But *as for* the children of Israel that dwelt in the cities of Judah, Rehoboam reigned over them.

Amplified

29 Now the rest of the acts of Solomon, from first to last, are they not written in the history of Nathan the prophet and in the prophecy of Ahijah the Shilonite and in the visions of Iddo the seer concerning Jeroboam the son of Nebat?

30 Solomon reigned in Jerusalem over all Israel forty years.

31 Then Solomon slept with his fathers; he was buried in the city of David his father. Rehoboam his son reigned in his stead.

10 REHOBOAM WENT to Shechem, for all Israel had gone to Shechem to make him king.

2 Jeroboam the son of Nebat was in Egypt, where he had fled from the presence of King Solomon, when he heard about the new king; so Jeroboam returned from Egypt.

3 And the people sent for him. So Jeroboam and all Israel came to Rehoboam, saying,

4 Your father [King Solomon] made our yoke grievous. So now make lighter the grievous service of your father and his heavy yoke that he put upon us, and we will serve you.

5 Rehoboam replied, Come again to me after three days. And the people departed.

6 King Rehoboam took counsel with the old men who stood before Solomon his father while he was alive, saying, What counsel do you give me in reply to the people?

7 And they answered him, If you are kind to [these] people and please them and speak good words to them, they will be your servants forever.

8 But the king forsook the counsel which the old men gave him and took counsel with the young men who were brought up with him and stood before him.

9 And he said to them, What answer do you advise that we give to the demand of [these] people, Make the yoke your father put upon us lighter?

10 The young men who were brought up with him said to him, Tell the people who said to you, Your father made our yoke heavy, but you make it lighter: My little finger is thicker than my father's loins.

11 For whereas my father put a heavy yoke upon you, I will add to your yoke. My father chastised you with whips, but I will chastise you with scorpions.

12 The third day Jeroboam and all the people returned to Rehoboam as he had said.

13 And the king answered them harshly, forsaking the counsel of the old men,

14 And answered them after the advice of the young men, saying, My father made your yoke heavy, but I will add to it; my father chastised you with whips, but I will chastise you with scorpions.

15 So the king did not heed the people, for it was [h]brought about of God, that the Lord might perform His word which He spoke by Ahijah the Shilonite to Jeroboam son of Nebat. [I Kings 11:29–39.]

16 And when all Israel saw that the king would not listen to *and* heed them, they answered [him], What portion have we in David? We have no inheritance in the son of Jesse. Every man to your tents, O Israel! Now, David [tribe of Judah], see to your own house [under your tyrant King Rehoboam]! So all Israel went to their homes.

17 But as for the Israelites who dwelt in Judah's cities, Rehoboam ruled over them.

---

[h] God permitted the revolt of the northern tribes, intending it as a punishment of the house of David for Solomon's apostasy (Robert Jamieson, A.R. Fausset and David Brown, *A Commentary*).

[w] Heb. *words*   [x] Heb. *laded*

New American Standard

29 ¶ Now the rest of the acts of Solomon, from first to last, are they not written in the records of Nathan the prophet, and in the prophecy of Ahijah the Shilonite, and in the visions of Iddo the seer concerning Jeroboam the son of Nebat?

30 Solomon reigned forty years in Jerusalem over all Israel.

Death of Solomon

31 And Solomon slept with his fathers and was buried in the city of his father David; and his son Rehoboam reigned in his place.

Rehoboam's Reign of Folly

10 THEN REHOBOAM went to Shechem, for all Israel had come to Shechem to make him king.

2 When Jeroboam the son of Nebat heard *of it* (for he was in Egypt where he had fled from the presence of King Solomon), Jeroboam returned from Egypt.

3 So they sent and summoned him. When Jeroboam and all Israel came, they spoke to Rehoboam, saying,

4 "Your father made our yoke hard; now therefore lighten the hard service of your father and his heavy yoke which he put on us, and we will serve you."

5 He said to them, "Return to me again in three days." So the people departed.

6 ¶ Then King Rehoboam consulted with the elders who had served his father Solomon while he was still alive, saying, "How do you counsel *me* to answer this people?"

7 They spoke to him, saying, "If you will be kind to this people and please them and speak good words to them, then they will be your servants forever."

8 But he forsook the counsel of the elders which they had given him, and consulted with the young men who grew up with him and served him.

9 So he said to them, "What counsel do you give that we may answer this people, who have spoken to me, saying, 'Lighten the yoke which your father put on us'?"

10 The young men who grew up with him spoke to him, saying, "Thus you shall say to the people who spoke to you, saying, 'Your father made our yoke heavy, but you make it lighter for us.' Thus you shall say to them, 'My little finger is thicker than my father's loins!

11 'Whereas my father loaded you with a heavy yoke, I will add to your yoke; my father disciplined you with whips, but I *will discipline you* with scorpions.' "

12 ¶ So Jeroboam and all the people came to Rehoboam on the third day as the king had directed, saying, "Return to me on the third day."

13 The king answered them harshly, and King Rehoboam forsook the counsel of the elders.

14 He spoke to them according to the advice of the young men, saying, "My father made your yoke heavy, but I will add to it; my father disciplined you with whips, but I *will discipline you* with scorpions."

15 So the king did not listen to the people, for it was a turn *of events* from God that the LORD might establish His word, which He spoke through Ahijah the Shilonite to Jeroboam the son of Nebat.

16 ¶ When all Israel *saw* that the king did not listen to them the people answered the king, saying,

"What portion do we have in David?
   We have no inheritance in the son of Jesse.
Every man to your tents, O Israel;
   Now look after your own house, David."
So all Israel departed to their tents.

17 But as for the sons of Israel who lived in the cities of Judah, Rehoboam reigned over them.

New International

Solomon's Death

29 As for the other events of Solomon's reign, from beginning to end, are they not written in the records of Nathan the prophet, in the prophecy of Ahijah the Shilonite and in the visions of Iddo the seer concerning Jeroboam son of Nebat? 30 Solomon reigned in Jerusalem over all Israel forty years. 31 Then he rested with his fathers and was buried in the city of David his father. And Rehoboam his son succeeded him as king.

Israel Rebels Against Rehoboam

10 REHOBOAM WENT to Shechem, for all the Israelites had gone there to make him king. 2 When Jeroboam son of Nebat heard this (he was in Egypt, where he had fled from King Solomon), he returned from Egypt. 3 So they sent for Jeroboam, and he and all Israel went to Rehoboam and said to him: 4 "Your father put a heavy yoke on us, but now lighten the harsh labor and the heavy yoke he put on us, and we will serve you."

5 Rehoboam answered, "Come back to me in three days." So the people went away.

6 Then King Rehoboam consulted the elders who had served his father Solomon during his lifetime. "How would you advise me to answer these people?" he asked.

7 They replied, "If you will be kind to these people and please them and give them a favorable answer, they will always be your servants."

8 But Rehoboam rejected the advice the elders gave him and consulted the young men who had grown up with him and were serving him. 9 He asked them, "What is your advice? How should we answer these people who say to me, 'Lighten the yoke your father put on us'?"

10 The young men who had grown up with him replied, "Tell the people who have said to you, 'Your father put a heavy yoke on us, but make our yoke lighter'—tell them, 'My little finger is thicker than my father's waist. 11 My father laid on you a heavy yoke; I will make it even heavier. My father scourged you with whips; I will scourge you with scorpions.' "

12 Three days later Jeroboam and all the people returned to Rehoboam, as the king had said, "Come back to me in three days." 13 The king answered them harshly. Rejecting the advice of the elders, 14 he followed the advice of the young men and said, "My father made your yoke heavy; I will make it even heavier. My father scourged you with whips; I will scourge you with scorpions." 15 So the king did not listen to the people, for this turn of events was from God, to fulfill the word the LORD had spoken to Jeroboam son of Nebat through Ahijah the Shilonite.

16 When all Israel saw that the king refused to listen to them, they answered the king:

"What share do we have in David,
   what part in Jesse's son?
To your tents, O Israel!
   Look after your own house, O David!"

So all the Israelites went home. 17 But as for the Israelites who were living in the towns of Judah, Rehoboam still ruled over them.

King James

¹⁸Then king Rehoboam sent Hadoram that *was* over the tribute; and the children of Israel stoned him with stones, that he died. But king Rehoboam *y*made speed to get him up to *his* chariot, to flee to Jerusalem.

¹⁹And Israel rebelled against the house of David unto this day.

Rehoboam builds strongholds

11 AND WHEN Rehoboam was come to Jerusalem, he gathered of the house of Judah and Benjamin an hundred and fourscore thousand chosen *men*, which were warriors, to fight against Israel, that he might bring the kingdom again to Rehoboam.

²But the word of the LORD came to Shemaiah the man of God, saying,

³Speak unto Rehoboam the son of Solomon, king of Judah, and to all Israel in Judah and Benjamin, saying,

⁴Thus saith the LORD, Ye shall not go up, nor fight against your brethren: return every man to his house: for this thing is done of me. And they obeyed the words of the LORD, and returned from going against Jeroboam.

⁵ ¶ And Rehoboam dwelt in Jerusalem, and built cities for defence in Judah.

⁶He built even Bethlehem, and Etam, and Tekoa,

⁷And Beth-zur, and Shoco, and Adullam,

⁸And Gath, and Mareshah, and Ziph,

⁹And Adoraim, and Lachish, and Azekah,

¹⁰And Zorah, and Aijalon, and Hebron, which *are* in Judah and in Benjamin fenced cities.

¹¹And he fortified the strong holds, and put captains in them, and store of victual, and of oil and wine.

¹²And in every several city *he put* shields and spears, and made them exceeding strong, having Judah and Benjamin on his side.

¹³ ¶ And the priests and the Levites that *were* in all Israel *z*resorted to him out of all their coasts.

¹⁴For the Levites left their suburbs and their possession, and came to Judah and Jerusalem: for Jeroboam and his sons had cast them off from executing the priest's office unto the LORD:

¹⁵And he ordained him priests for the high places, and for the devils, and for the calves which he had made.

¹⁶And after them out of all the tribes of Israel such as set their hearts to seek the LORD God of Israel came to Jerusalem, to sacrifice unto the LORD God of their fathers.

¹⁷So they strengthened the kingdom of Judah, and made Rehoboam the son of Solomon strong, three years: for three years they walked in the way of David and Solomon.

Rehoboam's many wives

¹⁸ ¶ And Rehoboam took him Mahalath the daughter of Jerimoth the son of David to wife, *and* Abihail the daughter of Eliab the son of Jesse;

¹⁹Which bare him children; Jeush, and Shamariah, and Zaham.

²⁰And after her he took Maachah the daughter of Absalom; which bare him Abijah, and Attai, and Ziza, and Shelomith.

²¹And Rehoboam loved Maachah the daughter of Absalom above all his wives and his concubines: (for he took eighteen wives, and threescore concubines; and begat twenty and eight sons, and threescore daughters.)

²²And Rehoboam made Abijah the son of Maachah the chief, *to be* ruler among his brethren: for *he thought* to make him king.

²³And he dealt wisely, and dispersed of all his children throughout all the countries of Judah and Benjamin, unto every fenced city: and he gave them victual in abundance. And he desired *a*many wives.

Amplified

¹⁸Then King Rehoboam sent Hadoram, who was over the forced labor, and the Israelites stoned him and he died. But King Rehoboam hastened to get up to his royal chariot to flee to Jerusalem.

¹⁹And Israel has rebelled against the house of David to this day.

11 AND WHEN Rehoboam came to Jerusalem, he assembled of the house of Judah and Benjamin 180,000 chosen warriors to fight against [the ten rebellious tribes of] Israel to bring the kingdom again to Rehoboam.

²But the word of the Lord came to Shemaiah the man of God, saying,

³Say to Rehoboam son of Solomon king of Judah and to all Israel in Judah and Benjamin,

⁴Thus says the Lord: You shall not go up or fight against your brethren. Return every man to his house, for this thing is from Me. And they obeyed the Lord and returned from going against Jeroboam.

⁵Rehoboam dwelt in Jerusalem and built cities for defense in Judah.

⁶He built Bethlehem, Etam, Tekoa,

⁷Beth-zur, Soco, Adullam,

⁸Gath, Mareshah, Ziph,

⁹Adoraim, Lachish, Azekah,

¹⁰Zorah, Aijalon, and Hebron, which are fortified cities in Judah and Benjamin.

¹¹He fortified the strongholds and put captains in them, with stores of food, oil, and vintage fruits.

¹²And in each city he put shields and spears, and made them very strong. So he held Judah and Benjamin.

¹³And the priests and the Levites who were in all Israel came over to Rehoboam from wherever they lived.

¹⁴For the Levites left their suburbs and their possessions and came to Judah and Jerusalem, for Jeroboam and his sons had cast them out from executing the priest's office to the Lord.

¹⁵And he appointed his own priests for the high places and for the [idols of demon] he-goats, and calves he had made. [I Kings 12:28.]

¹⁶And after them out of all the tribes of Israel there came to Jerusalem those who set their hearts to seek *and* inquire of the Lord, the God of Israel, to sacrifice to the Lord, the God of their fathers.

¹⁷So they strengthened the kingdom of Judah and upheld Rehoboam son of Solomon for three years; for they walked in the ways of David and Solomon for three years.

¹⁸Rehoboam took as wife Mahalath, whose father was Jerimoth son of David; her mother was Abihail daughter of Eliab son of Jesse.

¹⁹She bore him sons: Jeush, Shamariah, and Zaham.

²⁰And after her he took Maacah daughter [granddaughter] of Absalom, who bore him Abijah, Attai, Ziza, and Shelomith.

²¹And Rehoboam loved Maacah daughter [granddaughter] of Absalom more than all his wives and concubines—for he took eighteen wives and sixty concubines, and he had twenty-eight sons and sixty daughters.

²²And Rehoboam made Abijah son of Maacah the chief prince among his brethren, for he intended to make him king.

²³And he dealt understandingly and dispersed his children throughout all Judah and Benjamin to every fortified city. He gave them abundant supplies, and he sought many wives for them.

---

*y*Heb. *strengthened himself*   *z*Heb. *presented themselves to him*
*a*Heb. *a multitude of wives*

New American Standard

18 Then King Rehoboam sent Hadoram, who was over the forced labor, and the sons of Israel stoned him to death. And King Rehoboam made haste to mount his chariot to flee to Jerusalem.

19 So Israel has been in rebellion against the house of David to this day.

Rehoboam Reigns over Judah and Builds Cities

11 NOW WHEN Rehoboam had come to Jerusalem, he assembled the house of Judah and Benjamin, 180,000 chosen men who were warriors, to fight against Israel to restore the kingdom to Rehoboam.

2 But the word of the LORD came to Shemaiah the man of God, saying,

3 "Speak to Rehoboam the son of Solomon, king of Judah, and to all Israel in Judah and Benjamin, saying,

4 'Thus says the LORD, "You shall not go up or fight against your relatives; return every man to his house, for this thing is from Me." ' " So they listened to the words of the LORD and returned from going against Jeroboam.

5 ¶ Rehoboam lived in Jerusalem and built cities for defense in Judah.

6 Thus he built Bethlehem, Etam, Tekoa,

7 Beth-zur, Soco, Adullam,

8 Gath, Mareshah, Ziph,

9 Adoraim, Lachish, Azekah,

10 Zorah, Aijalon and Hebron, which are fortified cities in Judah and in Benjamin.

11 He also strengthened the fortresses and put officers in them and stores of food, oil and wine.

12 *He put* shields and spears in every city and strengthened them greatly. So he held Judah and Benjamin.

13 ¶ Moreover, the priests and the Levites who were in all Israel stood with him from all their districts.

Jeroboam Appoints False Priests

14 For the Levites left their pasture lands and their property and came to Judah and Jerusalem, for Jeroboam and his sons had excluded them from serving as priests to the LORD.

15 He set up priests of his own for the high places, for the satyrs and for the calves which he had made.

16 Those from all the tribes of Israel who set their hearts on seeking the LORD God of Israel followed them to Jerusalem, to sacrifice to the LORD God of their fathers.

17 They strengthened the kingdom of Judah and supported Rehoboam the son of Solomon for three years, for they walked in the way of David and Solomon for three years.

Rehoboam's Family

18 ¶ Then Rehoboam took as a wife Mahalath the daughter of Jerimoth the son of David *and of* Abihail the daughter of Eliab the son of Jesse,

19 and she bore him sons: Jeush, Shemariah and Zaham.

20 After her he took Maacah the daughter of Absalom, and she bore him Abijah, Attai, Ziza and Shelomith.

21 Rehoboam loved Maacah the daughter of Absalom more than all his *other* wives and concubines. For he had taken eighteen wives and sixty concubines and fathered twenty-eight sons and sixty daughters.

22 Rehoboam appointed Abijah the son of Maacah as head and leader among his brothers, for he *intended* to make him king.

23 He acted wisely and distributed some of his sons through all the territories of Judah and Benjamin to all the fortified cities, and he gave them food in abundance. And he sought many wives *for them.*

New International

18 King Rehoboam sent out Adoniram,[v] who was in charge of forced labor, but the Israelites stoned him to death. King Rehoboam, however, managed to get into his chariot and escape to Jerusalem. 19 So Israel has been in rebellion against the house of David to this day.

11 WHEN REHOBOAM arrived in Jerusalem, he mustered the house of Judah and Benjamin—a hundred and eighty thousand fighting men—to make war against Israel and to regain the kingdom for Rehoboam.

2 But this word of the LORD came to Shemaiah the man of God: 3 "Say to Rehoboam son of Solomon king of Judah and to all the Israelites in Judah and Benjamin, 4 'This is what the LORD says: Do not go up to fight against your brothers. Go home, every one of you, for this is my doing.' " So they obeyed the words of the LORD and turned back from marching against Jeroboam.

Rehoboam Fortifies Judah

5 Rehoboam lived in Jerusalem and built up towns for defense in Judah: 6 Bethlehem, Etam, Tekoa, 7 Beth Zur, Soco, Adullam, 8 Gath, Mareshah, Ziph, 9 Adoraim, Lachish, Azekah, 10 Zorah, Aijalon and Hebron. These were fortified cities in Judah and Benjamin. 11 He strengthened their defenses and put commanders in them, with supplies of food, olive oil and wine. 12 He put shields and spears in all the cities, and made them very strong. So Judah and Benjamin were his.

13 The priests and Levites from all their districts throughout Israel sided with him. 14 The Levites even abandoned their pasturelands and property, and came to Judah and Jerusalem because Jeroboam and his sons had rejected them as priests of the LORD. 15 And he appointed his own priests for the high places and for the goat and calf idols he had made. 16 Those from every tribe of Israel who set their hearts on seeking the LORD, the God of Israel, followed the Levites to Jerusalem to offer sacrifices to the LORD, the God of their fathers. 17 They strengthened the kingdom of Judah and supported Rehoboam son of Solomon three years, walking in the ways of David and Solomon during this time.

Rehoboam's Family

18 Rehoboam married Mahalath, who was the daughter of David's son Jerimoth and of Abihail, the daughter of Jesse's son Eliab. 19 She bore him sons: Jeush, Shemariah and Zaham. 20 Then he married Maacah daughter of Absalom, who bore him Abijah, Attai, Ziza and Shelomith. 21 Rehoboam loved Maacah daughter of Absalom more than any of his other wives and concubines. In all, he had eighteen wives and sixty concubines, twenty-eight sons and sixty daughters.

22 Rehoboam appointed Abijah son of Maacah to be the chief prince among his brothers, in order to make him king. 23 He acted wisely, dispersing some of his sons throughout the districts of Judah and Benjamin, and to all the fortified cities. He gave them abundant provisions and took many wives for them.

---

v 18 Hebrew *Hadoram,* a variant of *Adoniram*

| King James | Amplified |

Egyptians raid Jerusalem

12 AND IT came to pass, when Rehoboam had established the kingdom, and had strengthened himself, he forsook the law of the LORD, and all Israel with him.

2And it came to pass, *that* in the fifth year of king Rehoboam Shishak king of Egypt came up against Jerusalem, because they had transgressed against the LORD,

3With twelve hundred chariots, and threescore thousand horsemen: and the people *were* without number that came with him out of Egypt; the Lubims, the Sukkiims, and the Ethiopians.

4And he took the fenced cities which *pertained* to Judah, and came to Jerusalem.

5¶ Then came Shemaiah the prophet to Rehoboam, and *to* the princes of Judah, that were gathered together to Jerusalem because of Shishak, and said unto them, Thus saith the LORD, Ye have forsaken me, and therefore have I also left you in the hand of Shishak.

6Whereupon the princes of Israel and the king humbled themselves; and they said, The LORD *is* righteous.

7And when the LORD saw that they humbled themselves, the word of the LORD came to Shemaiah, saying, They have humbled themselves; *therefore* I will not destroy them, but I will grant them [b]some deliverance; and my wrath shall not be poured out upon Jerusalem by the hand of Shishak.

8Nevertheless they shall be his servants; that they may know my service, and the service of the kingdoms of the countries.

9So Shishak king of Egypt came up against Jerusalem, and took away the treasures of the house of the LORD, and the treasures of the king's house; he took all: he carried away also the shields of gold which Solomon had made.

10Instead of which king Rehoboam made shields of brass, and committed *them* to the hands of the chief of the guard, that kept the entrance of the king's house.

11And when the king entered into the house of the LORD, the guard came and fetched them, and brought them again into the guard chamber.

12And when he humbled himself, the wrath of the LORD turned from him, that he would not destroy *him* altogether: [c]and also in Judah things went well.

13¶ So king Rehoboam strengthened himself in Jerusalem, and reigned: for Rehoboam *was* one and forty years old when he began to reign, and he reigned seventeen years in Jerusalem, the city which the LORD had chosen out of all the tribes of Israel, to put his name there. And his mother's name *was* Naamah an Ammonitess.

14And he did evil, because he [d]prepared not his heart to seek the LORD.

15Now the acts of Rehoboam, first and last, *are* they not written in the [e]book of Shemaiah the prophet, and of Iddo the seer concerning genealogies? And *there were* wars between Rehoboam and Jeroboam continually.

16And Rehoboam slept with his fathers, and was buried in the city of David: and Abijah his son reigned in his stead.

Abijah, king of Judah

13 NOW IN the eighteenth year of king Jeroboam began Abijah to reign over Judah.

2He reigned three years in Jerusalem. His mother's name also *was* Michaiah the daughter of Uriel of Gibeah. And there was war between Abijah and Jeroboam.

12 WHEN REHOBOAM had established the kingdom and had strengthened himself, he forsook the law of the Lord, and all Israel with him.

2And in the fifth year of King Rehoboam, because they had transgressed *and* been unfaithful to the Lord, Shishak king of Egypt came up against Jerusalem

3With 1,200 chariots and 60,000 horsemen, and the people were without number who came with him from Egypt—the Libyans, Sukkiim, and Ethiopians.

4And he took the fortified cities of Judah and came on to Jerusalem.

5Then Shemaiah the prophet came to Rehoboam and the princes of Judah who had gathered at Jerusalem because of Shishak, and said to them, Thus says the Lord: You have forsaken Me, so I have abandoned you into the hands of Shishak.

6Then the princes of Israel and the king humbled themselves and said, The Lord is righteous.

7And when the Lord saw that they humbled themselves, the word of the Lord came to Shemaiah, saying, They have humbled themselves, so I will not destroy them, but I will grant them some deliverance; and My wrath shall not be poured out upon Jerusalem by the hand of Shishak.

8Nevertheless, they shall be his servants, that they may know [the difference between] My service and the service of the kingdoms of the countries.

9So Shishak king of Egypt came up against Jerusalem; he took away the treasures of the house of the Lord and of the king's house. He took everything. He took away also the shields of gold Solomon had made.

10Instead of them King Rehoboam made shields of bronze and committed them to the hands of the officers of the guard who kept the door of the king's house.

11And whenever the king entered the Lord's house, the guards came and got the shields of bronze and brought them again into the guard chamber.

12When Rehoboam humbled himself, the wrath of the Lord turned from him, so as not to destroy him entirely; also in Judah conditions were good.

13So King Rehoboam established *and* strengthened himself in Jerusalem and reigned. Rehoboam was forty-one years old when he began to reign, and he reigned seventeen years in Jerusalem, the city in which the Lord had chosen out of all the tribes of Israel to put His Name [and the symbol of His presence]. His mother was Naamah an Ammonitess.

14And he did evil because he did not set his heart to seek (inquire of, yearn for) the Lord with all his desire.

15Now the acts of Rehoboam, from first to last, are they not written in the histories of Shemaiah the prophet and of Iddo the seer regarding genealogies? There were wars between Rehoboam and Jeroboam of Israel continually.

16And Rehoboam slept with his fathers and was buried in the City of David; and Abijah his son reigned in his stead.

13 IN THE eighteenth year of King Jeroboam, Abijah began to reign over Judah.

2He reigned three years in Jerusalem. His mother was Micaiah daughter of Uriel of Gibeah. And there was war between Abijah and Jeroboam of Israel.

[b]Or, *a little while* [c]Or, *and yet in Judah there were good things* [d]Or, *fixed* [e]Heb. *words*

New American Standard

Shishak of Egypt Invades Judah

12 WHEN THE kingdom of Rehoboam was established and strong, he and all Israel with him forsook the law of the LORD. 2 And it came about in King Rehoboam's fifth year, because they had been unfaithful to the LORD, that Shishak king of Egypt came up against Jerusalem 3 with 1,200 chariots and 60,000 horsemen. And the people who came with him from Egypt were without number: the Lubim, the Sukkiim and the Ethiopians. 4 He captured the fortified cities of Judah and came as far as Jerusalem. 5 Then Shemaiah the prophet came to Rehoboam and the princes of Judah who had gathered at Jerusalem because of Shishak, and he said to them, "Thus says the LORD, 'You have forsaken Me, so I also have forsaken you to Shishak.' " 6 So the princes of Israel and the king humbled themselves and said, "The LORD is righteous." 7 ¶ When the LORD saw that they humbled themselves, the word of the LORD came to Shemaiah, saying, "They have humbled themselves *so* I will not destroy them, but I will grant them some *measure* of deliverance, and My wrath shall not be poured out on Jerusalem by means of Shishak. 8 "But they will become his slaves so that they may learn *the difference between* My service and the service of the kingdoms of the countries."

Plunder Impoverishes Judah

9 ¶ So Shishak king of Egypt came up against Jerusalem, and took the treasures of the house of the LORD and the treasures of the king's palace. He took everything; he even took the golden shields which Solomon had made. 10 Then King Rehoboam made shields of bronze in their place and committed them to the care of the commanders of the guard who guarded the door of the king's house. 11 As often as the king entered the house of the LORD, the guards came and carried them and *then* brought them back into the guards' room. 12 And when he humbled himself, the anger of the LORD turned away from him, so as not to destroy *him* completely; and also conditions were good in Judah. 13 ¶ So King Rehoboam strengthened himself in Jerusalem and reigned. Now Rehoboam was forty-one years old when he began to reign, and he reigned seventeen years in Jerusalem, the city which the LORD had chosen from all the tribes of Israel, to put His name there. And his mother's name was Naamah the Ammonitess. 14 He did evil because he did not set his heart to seek the LORD. 15 ¶ Now the acts of Rehoboam, from first to last, are they not written in the records of Shemaiah the prophet and of Iddo the seer, according to genealogical enrollment? And *there were* wars between Rehoboam and Jeroboam continually. 16 And Rehoboam slept with his fathers and was buried in the city of David; and his son Abijah became king in his place.

Abijah Succeeds Rehoboam

13 IN THE eighteenth year of King Jeroboam, Abijah became king over Judah. 2 He reigned three years in Jerusalem; and his mother's name was Micaiah the daughter of Uriel of Gibeah. ¶ Now there was war between Abijah and Jeroboam.

New International

Shishak Attacks Jerusalem

12 AFTER REHOBOAM'S position as king was established and he had become strong, he and all Israel[w] with him abandoned the law of the LORD. 2 Because they had been unfaithful to the LORD, Shishak king of Egypt attacked Jerusalem in the fifth year of King Rehoboam. 3 With twelve hundred chariots and sixty thousand horsemen and the innumerable troops of Libyans, Sukkites and Cushites[x] that came with him from Egypt, 4 he captured the fortified cities of Judah and came as far as Jerusalem.

5 Then the prophet Shemaiah came to Rehoboam and to the leaders of Judah who had assembled in Jerusalem for fear of Shishak, and he said to them, "This is what the LORD says, 'You have abandoned me; therefore, I now abandon you to Shishak.' "

6 The leaders of Israel and the king humbled themselves and said, "The LORD is just."

7 When the LORD saw that they humbled themselves, this word of the LORD came to Shemaiah: "Since they have humbled themselves, I will not destroy them but will soon give them deliverance. My wrath will not be poured out on Jerusalem through Shishak. 8 They will, however, become subject to him, so that they may learn the difference between serving me and serving the kings of other lands."

9 When Shishak king of Egypt attacked Jerusalem, he carried off the treasures of the temple of the LORD and the treasures of the royal palace. He took everything, including the gold shields Solomon had made. 10 So King Rehoboam made bronze shields to replace them and assigned these to the commanders of the guard on duty at the entrance to the royal palace. 11 Whenever the king went to the LORD's temple, the guards went with him, bearing the shields, and afterward they returned them to the guardroom.

12 Because Rehoboam humbled himself, the LORD's anger turned from him, and he was not totally destroyed. Indeed, there was some good in Judah.

13 King Rehoboam established himself firmly in Jerusalem and continued as king. He was forty-one years old when he became king, and he reigned seventeen years in Jerusalem, the city the LORD had chosen out of all the tribes of Israel in which to put his Name. His mother's name was Naamah; she was an Ammonite. 14 He did evil because he had not set his heart on seeking the LORD.

15 As for the events of Rehoboam's reign, from beginning to end, are they not written in the records of Shemaiah the prophet and of Iddo the seer that deal with genealogies? There was continual warfare between Rehoboam and Jeroboam. 16 Rehoboam rested with his fathers and was buried in the City of David. And Abijah his son succeeded him as king.

Abijah King of Judah

13 IN THE eighteenth year of the reign of Jeroboam, Abijah became king of Judah, 2 and he reigned in Jerusalem three years. His mother's name was Maacah,[y] a daughter[z] of Uriel of Gibeah.

There was war between Abijah and Jeroboam. 3 Abijah

---

w 1 That is, Judah, as frequently in 2 Chronicles   x 3 That is, people from the upper Nile region   y 2 Most Septuagint manuscripts and Syriac (see also 2 Chron. 11:20 and 1 Kings 15:2); Hebrew *Micaiah*   z 2 Or *granddaughter*

King James

³And Abijah ^fset the battle in array with an army of valiant men of war, *even* four hundred thousand chosen men: Jeroboam also set the battle in array against him with eight hundred thousand chosen men, *being* mighty men of valour.

⁴ ¶ And Abijah stood up upon mount Zemaraim, which *is* in mount Ephraim, and said, Hear me, thou Jeroboam, and all Israel;

⁵Ought ye not to know that the LORD God of Israel gave the kingdom over Israel to David for ever, *even* to him and to his sons by a covenant of salt?

⁶Yet Jeroboam the son of Nebat, the servant of Solomon the son of David, is risen up, and hath rebelled against his lord.

⁷And there are gathered unto him vain men, the children of Belial, and have strengthened themselves against Rehoboam the son of Solomon, when Rehoboam was young and tender-hearted, and could not withstand them.

⁸And now ye think to withstand the kingdom of the LORD in the hand of the sons of David; and ye *be* a great multitude, and *there are* with you golden calves, which Jeroboam made you for gods.

⁹Have ye not cast out the priests of the LORD, the sons of Aaron, and the Levites, and have made you priests after the manner of *other* lands? so that whosoever cometh ^gto consecrate himself with a young bullock and seven rams, *the same* may be a priest of *them that are* no gods.

¹⁰But as for us, the LORD *is* our God, and we have not forsaken him; and the priests, which minister unto the LORD, *are* the sons of Aaron, and the Levites *wait* upon *their* business:

¹¹And they burn unto the LORD every morning and every evening burnt sacrifices and sweet incense: the showbread also *set they in order* upon the pure table; and the candlestick of gold with the lamps thereof, to burn every evening: for we keep the charge of the LORD our God; but ye have forsaken him.

¹²And, behold, God himself *is* with us for *our* captain, and his priests with sounding trumpets to cry alarm against you. O children of Israel, fight ye not against the LORD God of your fathers; for ye shall not prosper.

¹³ ¶ But Jeroboam caused an ambushment to come about behind them: so they were before Judah, and the ambushment *was* behind them.

¹⁴And when Judah looked back, behold, the battle *was* before and behind: and they cried unto the LORD, and the priests sounded with the trumpets.

¹⁵Then the men of Judah gave a shout: and as the men of Judah shouted, it came to pass, that God smote Jeroboam and all Israel before Abijah and Judah.

¹⁶And the children of Israel fled before Judah: and God delivered them into their hand.

¹⁷And Abijah and his people slew them with a great slaughter: so there fell down slain of Israel five hundred thousand chosen men.

¹⁸Thus the children of Israel were brought under at that time, and the children of Judah prevailed, because they relied upon the LORD God of their fathers.

¹⁹And Abijah pursued after Jeroboam, and took cities from him, Beth-el with the towns thereof, and Jeshanah with the towns thereof, and Ephrain with the towns thereof.

²⁰Neither did Jeroboam recover strength again in the days of Abijah: and the LORD struck him, and he died.

²¹ ¶ But Abijah waxed mighty, and married fourteen wives, and begat twenty and two sons, and sixteen daughters.

²²And the rest of the acts of Abijah, and his ways, and his sayings, *are* written in the ^hstory of the prophet Iddo.

Amplified

³And Abijah prepared for battle with an army of valiant men of war, 400,000 chosen men. Jeroboam set the battle in array against him with 800,000 chosen men, mighty men of valor.

⁴And Abijah stood on Mount Zemaraim, in the hill country of Ephraim, and said, Hear me, O Jeroboam and all Israel!

⁵Ought you not to know that the Lord, the God of Israel, gave the kingship over Israel to David forever, even to him and to his sons by a covenant of salt?

⁶Yet Jeroboam son of Nebat, a servant of Solomon of David, rose up and rebelled against his lord [the king].

⁷And there gathered to him worthless men, base fellows, who strengthened themselves against Rehoboam son of Solomon when Rehoboam was young [as king], irresolute, *and* inexperienced and did not withstand them with firmness and strength.

⁸And now you think to withstand the kingdom of the Lord which is in the hands of the sons of David, because you are a great multitude and you have with you the golden calves which Jeroboam made for you for gods.

⁹Have you not driven out the priests of the Lord, the sons of Aaron, and the Levites, and made priests for yourselves like the peoples of other lands? So whoever comes to consecrate himself with a young bull and seven rams may be a priest of idols that are not gods.

¹⁰But as for us, the Lord is our God, and we have not forsaken Him. We have priests ministering to the Lord who are sons of Aaron, and Levites for their service.

¹¹They offer to the Lord every morning and every evening burnt sacrifices and incense of sweet spices; they set in order the showbread on the table of pure gold and attend to the golden lampstand, that its lamps may be lighted every evening. For we keep the charge of the Lord our God, but you have forsaken Him.

¹²Behold, God Himself is with us at our head, and His priests with their battle trumpets to sound an alarm against you. O Israelites, fight not against the Lord, the God of your fathers, for you cannot prosper.

¹³But Jeroboam caused an ambushment to come around them from behind, so his troops were before Judah and the ambush behind.

¹⁴When Judah looked, behold, the battle was before and behind; and they cried to the Lord, and the priests blew the trumpets.

¹⁵Then the men of Judah gave a shout; and as they shouted, God smote Jeroboam and all Israel before Abijah and Judah.

¹⁶And the Israelites fled before Judah, and God delivered them into their hands.

¹⁷And Abijah and his people slew them with a great slaughter, so there fell of Israel 500,000 chosen men.

¹⁸Thus the Israelites were brought low at that time, and the people of Judah prevailed because they relied upon the Lord, the God of their fathers.

¹⁹And Abijah pursued Jeroboam and took some cities from him, Bethel, Jeshanah, and Ephraim (Ephron), with their towns.

²⁰Jeroboam did not recover strength again in the days of Abijah. And the Lord smote him and he died.

²¹But Abijah became mighty. He married fourteen wives and had twenty-two sons and sixteen daughters.

²²And the rest of the acts of Abijah, his ways and his sayings, are written in the story of the prophet Iddo.

New American Standard

3 Abijah began the battle with an army of valiant warriors, 400,000 chosen men, while Jeroboam drew up in battle formation against him with 800,000 chosen men *who were* valiant warriors.

Civil War

4 ¶ Then Abijah stood on Mount Zemaraim, which is in the hill country of Ephraim, and said, "Listen to me, Jeroboam and all Israel:

5"Do you not know that the LORD God of Israel gave the rule over Israel forever to David and his sons by a covenant of salt?

6"Yet Jeroboam the son of Nebat, the servant of Solomon the son of David, rose up and rebelled against his master,

7 and worthless men gathered about him, scoundrels, who proved too strong for Rehoboam, the son of Solomon, when he was young and timid and could not hold his own against them.

8 ¶ "So now you intend to resist the kingdom of the LORD through the sons of David, being a great multitude and *having* with you the golden calves which Jeroboam made for gods for you.

9"Have you not driven out the priests of the LORD, the sons of Aaron and the Levites, and made for yourselves priests like the peoples of *other* lands? Whoever comes to consecrate himself with a young bull and seven rams, even he may become a priest of *what are* no gods.

10"But as for us, the LORD is our God, and we have not forsaken Him; and the sons of Aaron are ministering to the LORD as priests, and the Levites attend to their work.

11"Every morning and evening they burn to the LORD burnt offerings and fragrant incense, and the showbread is *set* on the clean table, and the golden lampstand with its lamps is *ready* to light every evening; for we keep the charge of the LORD our God, but you have forsaken Him.

12"Now behold, God is with us at *our* head and His priests with the signal trumpets to sound the alarm against you. O sons of Israel, do not fight against the LORD God of your fathers, for you will not succeed."

13 ¶ But Jeroboam had set an ambush to come from the rear, so that *Israel* was in front of Judah and the ambush was behind them.

14 When Judah turned around, behold, they were attacked both front and rear; so they cried to the LORD, and the priests blew the trumpets.

15 Then the men of Judah raised a war cry, and when the men of Judah raised the war cry, then it was that God routed Jeroboam and all Israel before Abijah and Judah.

16 When the sons of Israel fled before Judah, God gave them into their hand.

17 Abijah and his people defeated them with a great slaughter, so that 500,000 chosen men of Israel fell slain.

18 Thus the sons of Israel were subdued at that time, and the sons of Judah conquered because they trusted in the LORD, the God of their fathers.

19 Abijah pursued Jeroboam and captured from him *several* cities, Bethel with its villages, Jeshanah with its villages and Ephron with its villages.

Death of Jeroboam

20 Jeroboam did not again recover strength in the days of Abijah; and the LORD struck him and he died.

21 ¶ But Abijah became powerful; and took fourteen wives to himself, and became the father of twenty-two sons and sixteen daughters.

22 Now the rest of the acts of Abijah, and his ways and his words are written in the treatise of the prophet Iddo.

New International

went into battle with a force of four hundred thousand able fighting men, and Jeroboam drew up a battle line against him with eight hundred thousand able troops.

4Abijah stood on Mount Zemaraim, in the hill country of Ephraim, and said, "Jeroboam and all Israel, listen to me! 5Don't you know that the LORD, the God of Israel, has given the kingship of Israel to David and his descendants forever by a covenant of salt? 6Yet Jeroboam son of Nebat, an official of Solomon son of David, rebelled against his master. 7Some worthless scoundrels gathered around him and opposed Rehoboam son of Solomon when he was young and indecisive and not strong enough to resist them.

8"And now you plan to resist the kingdom of the LORD, which is in the hands of David's descendants. You are indeed a vast army and have with you the golden calves that Jeroboam made to be your gods. 9But didn't you drive out the priests of the LORD, the sons of Aaron, and the Levites, and make priests of your own as the peoples of other lands do? Whoever comes to consecrate himself with a young bull and seven rams may become a priest of what are not gods.

10"As for us, the LORD is our God, and we have not forsaken him. The priests who serve the LORD are sons of Aaron, and the Levites assist them. 11Every morning and evening they present burnt offerings and fragrant incense to the LORD. They set out the bread on the ceremonially clean table and light the lamps on the gold lampstand every evening. We are observing the requirements of the LORD our God. But you have forsaken him. 12God is with us; he is our leader. His priests with their trumpets will sound the battle cry against you. Men of Israel, do not fight against the LORD, the God of your fathers, for you will not succeed."

13Now Jeroboam had sent troops around to the rear, so that while he was in front of Judah the ambush was behind them. 14Judah turned and saw that they were being attacked at both front and rear. Then they cried out to the LORD. The priests blew their trumpets 15and the men of Judah raised the battle cry. At the sound of their battle cry, God routed Jeroboam and all Israel before Abijah and Judah. 16The Israelites fled before Judah, and God delivered them into their hands. 17Abijah and his men inflicted heavy losses on them, so that there were five hundred thousand casualties among Israel's able men. 18The men of Israel were subdued on that occasion, and the men of Judah were victorious because they relied on the LORD, the God of their fathers.

19Abijah pursued Jeroboam and took from him the towns of Bethel, Jeshanah and Ephron, with their surrounding villages. 20Jeroboam did not regain power during the time of Abijah. And the LORD struck him down and he died.

21But Abijah grew in strength. He married fourteen wives and had twenty-two sons and sixteen daughters.

22The other events of Abijah's reign, what he did and what he said, are written in the annotations of the prophet Iddo.

King James

Amplified

Asa, king of Judah

14 SO ABIJAH slept with his fathers, and they buried him in the city of David: and Asa his son reigned in his stead. In his days the land was quiet ten years.

²And Asa did *that which was* good and right in the eyes of the LORD his God:

³For he took away the altars of the strange *gods,* and the high places, and brake down the *ⁱ*images, and cut down the groves:

⁴And commanded Judah to seek the LORD God of their fathers, and to do the law and the commandment.

⁵Also he took away out of all the cities of Judah the high places and the *ʲ*images: and the kingdom was quiet before him.

⁶ ¶ And he built fenced cities in Judah: for the land had rest, and he had no war in those years; because the LORD had given him rest.

⁷Therefore he said unto Judah, Let us build these cities, and make about *them* walls, and towers, gates, and bars, *while* the land *is* yet before us; because we have sought the LORD our God, we have sought *him,* and he hath given us rest on every side. So they built and prospered.

⁸And Asa had an army *of men* that bare targets and spears, out of Judah three hundred thousand; and out of Benjamin, that bare shields and drew bows, two hundred and fourscore thousand: all these *were* mighty men of valour.

⁹ ¶ And there came out against them Zerah the Ethiopian with an host of a thousand thousand, and three hundred chariots; and came unto Mareshah.

¹⁰Then Asa went out against him, and they set the battle in array in the valley of Zephathah at Mareshah.

¹¹And Asa cried unto the LORD his God, and said, LORD, *it is* nothing with thee to help, whether with many, or with them that have no power: help us, O LORD our God; for we rest on thee, and in thy name we go against this multitude. O LORD, thou *art* our God; let not *ᵏ*man prevail against thee.

¹²So the LORD smote the Ethiopians before Asa, and before Judah; and the Ethiopians fled.

¹³And Asa and the people that *were* with him pursued them unto Gerar: and the Ethiopians were overthrown, that they could not recover themselves; for they were *ˡ*destroyed before the LORD, and before his host; and they carried away very much spoil.

¹⁴And they smote all the cities round about Gerar; for the fear of the LORD came upon them: and they spoiled all the cities; for there was exceeding much spoil in them.

¹⁵They smote also the tents of cattle, and carried away sheep and camels in abundance, and returned to Jerusalem.

Asa's reform movement

15 AND THE spirit of God came upon Azariah the son of Oded:

²And he went out *ᵐ*to meet Asa, and said unto him, Hear ye me, Asa, and all Judah and Benjamin; The LORD *is* with you, while ye be with him; and if ye seek him, he will be found of you; but if ye forsake him, he will forsake you.

³Now for a long season Israel *hath been* without the true God, and without a teaching priest, and without law.

⁴But when they in their trouble did turn unto the LORD God of Israel, and sought him, he was found of them.

⁵And in those times *there was* no peace to him that went out, nor to him that came in, but great vexations *were* upon all the inhabitants of the countries.

14 SO ABIJAH slept with his fathers, and they buried him in the City of David; and Asa his son reigned in his stead. In his days the land was at rest for ten years.

²And Asa did what was good and right in the eyes of the Lord his God.

³He took away the foreign altars and high places and broke down the idol pillars *or* obelisks and cut down the Asherim [symbols of the goddess Asherah]

⁴And commanded Judah to seek the Lord, the God of their fathers [to inquire of and for Him and crave Him as a vital necessity], and to obey the law and the commandment.

⁵Also Asa took out of all the cities of Judah the idolatrous high places and the incense altars. And the kingdom had rest under his reign.

⁶And he built fortified cities in Judah, for the land had rest. He had no war in those years, for the Lord gave him peace.

⁷Therefore he said to Judah, Let us build these cities and surround them with walls, towers, gates, and bars. The land is still ours, because we sought the Lord our God; we have sought Him [yearning for Him with all our desire] and He has given us rest *and* peace on every side. So they built and prospered.

⁸Asa had an army of 300,000 men out of Judah, who bore bucklers and spears, and 280,000 out of Benjamin, who bore shields and drew bows, all mighty men of courage.

⁹There came out against Judah Zerah the Ethiopian with a host of a million [that is, too many to be numbered] and 300 chariots, and came as far as Mareshah.

¹⁰Then Asa went out against him, and they set up their lines of battle in the Valley of Zephathah at Mareshah.

¹¹Asa cried to the Lord his God, O Lord, there is none besides You to help, and it makes no difference to You whether the one You help is mighty or powerless. Help us, O Lord our God! For we rely on You, and we go against this multitude in Your name. O Lord, You are our God; let no man prevail against You!

¹²So the Lord smote the Ethiopians before Asa and Judah, and the Ethiopians fled.

¹³Asa and the people with him pursued them to Gerar; and the Ethiopians were overthrown, so that none remained alive; for they were destroyed before the Lord and His host, who carried away very much booty.

¹⁴And they smote all the cities round about Gerar, for the fear of the Lord came upon them. They plundered all the cities, for there was much plunder in them.

¹⁵They smote also the cattle encampments and carried away sheep in abundance and camels; and they returned to Jerusalem.

15 THE SPIRIT of God came upon Azariah son of Oded.

²And he went out to meet Asa and said to him, Hear me, Asa, and all Judah and Benjamin: the Lord is with you while you are with Him. If you seek Him [inquiring for and of Him, craving Him as your soul's first necessity], He will be found by you; but if you [become indifferent and] forsake Him, He will forsake you.

³Now for a long time Israel was without the true God, without a teaching priest, and without law.

⁴But when they in their trouble turned to the Lord, the God of Israel, and [in desperation earnestly] sought Him, He was found by them.

⁵And in those times there was no peace to him who went out nor to him who came in, but great *and* vexing afflictions *and* disturbances were upon all the inhabitants of the countries.

---

*ⁱ*Heb. *statues*   *ʲ*Heb. *sun images*   *ᵏ*Or, *mortal man*
*ˡ*Heb. *broken*   *ᵐ*Heb. *before Asa*

New American Standard

Asa Succeeds Abijah in Judah

14 SO ABIJAH slept with his fathers, and they buried him in the city of David, and his son Asa became king in his place. The land was undisturbed for ten years during his days.

2 ¶ Asa did good and right in the sight of the LORD his God,

3 for he removed the foreign altars and high places, tore down the *sacred* pillars, cut down the ᵉAsherim,

4 and commanded Judah to seek the LORD God of their fathers and to observe the law and the commandment.

5 He also removed the high places and the incense altars from all the cities of Judah. And the kingdom was undisturbed under him.

6 He built fortified cities in Judah, since the land was undisturbed, and there was no one at war with him during those years, because the LORD had given him rest.

7 For he said to Judah, "Let us build these cities and surround *them* with walls and towers, gates and bars. The land is still ours because we have sought the LORD our God; we have sought Him, and He has given us rest on every side." So they built and prospered.

8 Now Asa had an army of 300,000 from Judah, bearing large shields and spears, and 280,000 from Benjamin, bearing shields and wielding bows; all of them were valiant warriors.

9 ¶ Now Zerah the Ethiopian came out against them with an army of a million men and 300 chariots, and he came to Mareshah.

10 So Asa went out to meet him, and they drew up in battle formation in the valley of Zephathah at Mareshah.

11 Then Asa called to the LORD his God and said, "LORD, there is no one besides You to help *in the battle* between the powerful and those who have no strength; so help us, O LORD our God, for we trust in You, and in Your name have come against this multitude. O LORD, You are our God; let not man prevail against You."

12 So the LORD routed the Ethiopians before Asa and before Judah, and the Ethiopians fled.

13 Asa and the people who *were* with him pursued them as far as Gerar; and so many Ethiopians fell that they could not recover, for they were shattered before the LORD and before His army. And they carried away very much plunder.

14 They destroyed all the cities around Gerar, for the dread of the LORD had fallen on them; and they despoiled all the cities, for there was much plunder in them.

15 They also struck down those who owned livestock, and they carried away large numbers of sheep and camels. Then they returned to Jerusalem.

The Prophet Azariah Warns Asa

15 NOW THE Spirit of God came on Azariah the son of Oded,

2 and he went out to meet Asa and said to him, "Listen to me, Asa, and all Judah and Benjamin: the LORD is with you when you are with Him. And if you seek Him, He will let you find Him; but if you forsake Him, He will forsake you.

3 "For many days Israel was without the true God and without a teaching priest and without law.

4 "But in their distress they turned to the LORD God of Israel, and they sought Him, and He let them find Him.

5 "In those times there was no peace to him who went out or to him who came in, for many disturbances afflicted all the inhabitants of the lands.

New International

14 AND ABIJAH rested with his fathers and was buried in the City of David. Asa his son succeeded him as king, and in his days the country was at peace for ten years.

Asa King of Judah

2Asa did what was good and right in the eyes of the LORD his God. 3He removed the foreign altars and the high places, smashed the sacred stones and cut down the Asherah poles.ᵃ 4He commanded Judah to seek the LORD, the God of their fathers, and to obey his laws and commands. 5He removed the high places and incense altars in every town in Judah, and the kingdom was at peace under him. 6He built up the fortified cities of Judah, since the land was at peace. No one was at war with him during those years, for the LORD gave him rest.

7"Let us build up these towns," he said to Judah, "and put walls around them, with towers, gates and bars. The land is still ours, because we have sought the LORD our God; we sought him and he has given us rest on every side." So they built and prospered.

8Asa had an army of three hundred thousand men from Judah, equipped with large shields and with spears, and two hundred and eighty thousand from Benjamin, armed with small shields and with bows. All these were brave fighting men.

9Zerah the Cushite marched out against them with a vast armyᵇ and three hundred chariots, and came as far as Mareshah. 10Asa went out to meet him, and they took up battle positions in the Valley of Zephathah near Mareshah.

11Then Asa called to the LORD his God and said, "LORD, there is no one like you to help the powerless against the mighty. Help us, O LORD our God, for we rely on you, and in your name we have come against this vast army. O LORD, you are our God; do not let man prevail against you."

12The LORD struck down the Cushites before Asa and Judah. The Cushites fled, 13and Asa and his army pursued them as far as Gerar. Such a great number of Cushites fell that they could not recover; they were crushed before the LORD and his forces. The men of Judah carried off a large amount of plunder. 14They destroyed all the villages around Gerar, for the terror of the LORD had fallen upon them. They plundered all these villages, since there was much booty there. 15They also attacked the camps of the herdsmen and carried off droves of sheep and goats and camels. Then they returned to Jerusalem.

Asa's Reform

15 THE SPIRIT of God came upon Azariah son of Oded. 2He went out to meet Asa and said to him, "Listen to me, Asa and all Judah and Benjamin. The LORD is with you when you are with him. If you seek him, he will be found by you, but if you forsake him, he will forsake you. 3For a long time Israel was without the true God, without a priest to teach and without the law. 4But in their distress they turned to the LORD, the God of Israel, and sought him, and he was found by them. 5In those days it was not safe to travel about, for all the inhabitants of

---

ᵉ I.e. wooden symbols of a female deity

King James

Amplified

<table>
<tr><td>

⁶And nation was ⁿdestroyed of nation, and city of city: for God did vex them with all adversity.

⁷Be ye strong therefore, and let not your hands be weak: for your work shall be rewarded.

⁸And when Asa heard these words, and the prophecy of Oded the prophet, he took courage, and put away the ^oabominable idols out of all the land of Judah and Benjamin, and out of the cities which he had taken from mount Ephraim, and renewed the altar of the LORD, that *was* before the porch of the LORD.

⁹And he gathered all Judah and Benjamin, and the strangers with them out of Ephraim and Manasseh, and out of Simeon: for they fell to him out of Israel in abundance, when they saw that the LORD his God *was* with him.

¹⁰So they gathered themselves together at Jerusalem in the third month, in the fifteenth year of the reign of Asa.

¹¹And they offered unto the LORD ^pthe same time, of the spoil *which* they had brought, seven hundred oxen and seven thousand sheep.

¹²And they entered into a covenant to seek the LORD God of their fathers with all their heart and with all their soul;

¹³That whosoever would not seek the LORD God of Israel should be put to death, whether small or great, whether man or woman.

¹⁴And they sware unto the LORD with a loud voice, and with shouting, and with trumpets, and with cornets.

¹⁵And all Judah rejoiced at the oath: for they had sworn with all their heart, and sought him with their whole desire; and he was found of them: and the LORD gave them rest round about.

¹⁶ ¶ And also *concerning* Maachah the ^qmother of Asa the king, he removed her from *being* queen, because she had made an ^ridol in a grove: and Asa cut down her idol, and stamped *it,* and burnt *it* at the brook Kidron.

¹⁷But the high places were not taken away out of Israel: nevertheless the heart of Asa was perfect all his days.

¹⁸ ¶ And he brought into the house of God the things that his father had dedicated, and that he himself had dedicated, silver, and gold, and vessels.

¹⁹And there was no *more* war unto the five and thirtieth year of the reign of Asa.

The end of Asa's reign

16 IN THE six and thirtieth year of the reign of Asa Baasha king of Israel came up against Judah, and built Ramah, to the intent that he might let none go out or come in to Asa king of Judah.

²Then Asa brought out silver and gold out of the treasures of the house of the LORD and of the king's house, and sent to Ben-hadad king of Syria, that dwelt at ^sDamascus, saying,

³*There is* a league between me and thee, as *there was* between my father and thy father: behold, I have sent thee silver and gold; go, break thy league with Baasha king of Israel, that he may depart from me.

⁴And Ben-hadad hearkened unto king Asa, and sent the captains of ^this armies against the cities of Israel; and they smote Ijon, and Dan, and Abel-maim, and all the store cities of Naphtali.

⁵And it came to pass, when Baasha heard *it,* that he left off building of Ramah, and let his work cease.

⁶Then Asa the king took all Judah; and they carried away the stones of Ramah, and the timber thereof, wherewith Baasha was building; and he built therewith Geba and Mizpah.

</td><td>

⁶Nation was broke in pieces against nation, and city against city, for God vexed *and* troubled them with all sorts of adversity.

⁷Be strong, therefore, and let not your hands be weak *and* slack, for your work shall be rewarded.

⁸And when Asa heard these words, the prophecy of Oded the prophet, he took courage and put away the abominable idols from all the land of Judah and Benjamin and from the cities which he had taken in the hill country of Ephraim; and he repaired the altar [of burnt offering] of the Lord which was in front of the porch *or* vestibule [of the house] of the Lord.

⁹And he gathered all Judah and Benjamin and the strangers with them out of Ephraim, Manasseh, and Simeon, for they came over to Asa out of Israel in large numbers when they saw that the Lord his God was with him.

¹⁰So they gathered at Jerusalem in the third month of the fifteenth year of the reign of Asa.

¹¹And they sacrificed to the Lord on that day from the spoil which they had brought—700 oxen and 7,000 sheep.

¹²And they entered into a covenant to seek the Lord, the God of their fathers, *and* to yearn for Him with all their heart's desire and with all their soul;

¹³And that whoever would not seek the Lord, the God of Israel, should be put to death, whether young or old, man or woman.

¹⁴They took an oath to the Lord with a loud voice, with shouting, with trumpets, and with cornets.

¹⁵And all Judah rejoiced at the oath, for they had sworn with all their heart and sought Him [yearning for Him] with their whole desire, and He was found by them. And the Lord gave them rest *and* peace round about.

¹⁶Also Maacah, King Asa's mother, he removed from being queen mother, because she had made an abominable image for [the goddess] Asherah. Asa cut down her idol, crushed it, and burned it at the brook Kidron.

¹⁷But the high places were not taken out of Israel. Nevertheless, the heart of Asa was blameless all his days.

¹⁸And he brought into the house of God the things that his father [Abijah] had dedicated and those he himself had dedicated—silver and gold and vessels.

¹⁹And there was no more war until the thirty-fifth year of the reign of Asa.

16 IN THE thirty-sixth year of Asa's reign, Baasha king of Israel came up against Judah, and built (fortified) Ramah intending to intercept anyone going out or coming in to Asa king of Judah.

²Then Asa brought silver and gold out of the treasuries of the house of the Lord and of the king's house and sent them to Ben-hadad king of Syria, who dwelt at Damascus, saying,

³Let there be a league between me and you, as was between my father and your father. Behold, I am sending you silver and gold; go, break your league with Baasha king of Israel, that he may withdraw from me.

⁴And Ben-hadad hearkened to King Asa and sent the captains of his armies against the cities of Israel; and they smote Ijon, Dan, Abel-maim, and all the store cities of Naphtali.

⁵And when Baasha heard it, he stopped building Ramah and let his work cease.

⁶Then King Asa took all Judah, and they carried away the stones of Ramah and its timber with which Baasha had been building, and with them he built Geba and Mizpah.

</td></tr>
</table>

ⁿ Heb. *beaten in pieces*   ^o Heb. *abominations*   ^p Heb. *in that day*   ^q i.e. *grandmother;* see 1 Ki. 15:2,10   ^r Heb. *horror*   ^s Heb. *Darmesek*   ^t Heb. *which were his*

New American Standard

⁶"Nation was crushed by nation, and city by city, for God troubled them with every kind of distress.

⁷"But you, be strong and do not lose courage, for there is reward for your work."

Asa's Reforms

⁸ ¶ Now when Asa heard these words and the prophecy which Azariah the son of Oded the prophet spoke, he took courage and removed the abominable idols from all the land of Judah and Benjamin and from the cities which he had captured in the hill country of Ephraim. He then restored the altar of the LORD which was in front of the porch of the LORD.

⁹ He gathered all Judah and Benjamin and those from Ephraim, Manasseh and Simeon who resided with them, for many defected to him from Israel when they saw that the LORD his God was with him.

¹⁰ So they assembled at Jerusalem in the third month of the fifteenth year of Asa's reign.

¹¹ They sacrificed to the LORD that day 700 oxen and 7,000 sheep from the spoil they had brought.

¹² They entered into the covenant to seek the LORD God of their fathers with all their heart and soul;

¹³ and whoever would not seek the LORD God of Israel should be put to death, whether small or great, man or woman.

¹⁴ Moreover, they made an oath to the LORD with a loud voice, with shouting, with trumpets and horns.

¹⁵ All Judah rejoiced concerning the oath, for they had sworn with their whole heart and had sought Him earnestly, and He let them find Him. So the LORD gave them rest on every side.

¹⁶ ¶ He also removed Maacah, the mother of King Asa, from the *position of* queen mother, because she had made a horrid image as an Asherah, and Asa cut down her horrid image, crushed *it* and burned *it* at the brook Kidron.

¹⁷ But the high places were not removed from Israel; nevertheless Asa's heart was blameless all his days.

¹⁸ He brought into the house of God the dedicated things of his father and his own dedicated things: silver and gold and utensils.

¹⁹ And there was no more war until the thirty-fifth year of Asa's reign.

Asa Wars against Baasha

16 IN THE thirty-sixth year of Asa's reign Baasha king of Israel came up against Judah and fortified Ramah in order to prevent *anyone* from going out or coming in to Asa king of Judah.

² Then Asa brought out silver and gold from the treasuries of the house of the LORD and the king's house, and sent them to Ben-hadad king of Aram, who lived in Damascus, saying,

³"*Let there be* a treaty between you and me, *as* between my father and your father. Behold, I have sent you silver and gold; go, break your treaty with Baasha king of Israel so that he will withdraw from me."

⁴ So Ben-hadad listened to King Asa and sent the commanders of his armies against the cities of Israel, and they conquered Ijon, Dan, Abel-maim and all the store cities of Naphtali.

⁵ When Baasha heard *of it,* he ceased fortifying Ramah and stopped his work.

⁶ Then King Asa brought all Judah, and they carried away the stones of Ramah and its timber with which Baasha had been building, and with them he fortified Geba and Mizpah.

New International

the lands were in great turmoil. ⁶One nation was being crushed by another and one city by another, because God was troubling them with every kind of distress. ⁷But as for you, be strong and do not give up, for your work will be rewarded."

⁸When Asa heard these words and the prophecy of Azariah son of[c] Oded the prophet, he took courage. He removed the detestable idols from the whole land of Judah and Benjamin and from the towns he had captured in the hills of Ephraim. He repaired the altar of the LORD that was in front of the portico of the LORD's temple.

⁹Then he assembled all Judah and Benjamin and the people from Ephraim, Manasseh and Simeon who had settled among them, for large numbers had come over to him from Israel when they saw that the LORD his God was with him.

¹⁰They assembled at Jerusalem in the third month of the fifteenth year of Asa's reign. ¹¹At that time they sacrificed to the LORD seven hundred head of cattle and seven thousand sheep and goats from the plunder they had brought back. ¹²They entered into a covenant to seek the LORD, the God of their fathers, with all their heart and soul. ¹³All who would not seek the LORD, the God of Israel, were to be put to death, whether small or great, man or woman. ¹⁴They took an oath to the LORD with loud acclamation, with shouting and with trumpets and horns. ¹⁵All Judah rejoiced about the oath because they had sworn it wholeheartedly. They sought God eagerly, and he was found by them. So the LORD gave them rest on every side.

¹⁶King Asa also deposed his grandmother Maacah from her position as queen mother, because she had made a repulsive Asherah pole. Asa cut the pole down, broke it up and burned it in the Kidron Valley. ¹⁷Although he did not remove the high places from Israel, Asa's heart was fully committed to the LORD all his life. ¹⁸He brought into the temple of God the silver and gold and the articles that he and his father had dedicated.

¹⁹There was no more war until the thirty-fifth year of Asa's reign.

Asa's Last Years

16 IN THE thirty-sixth year of Asa's reign Baasha king of Israel went up against Judah and fortified Ramah to prevent anyone from leaving or entering the territory of Asa king of Judah.

²Asa then took the silver and gold out of the treasuries of the LORD's temple and of his own palace and sent it to Ben-Hadad king of Aram, who was ruling in Damascus. ³"Let there be a treaty between me and you," he said, "as there was between my father and your father. See, I am sending you silver and gold. Now break your treaty with Baasha king of Israel so he will withdraw from me."

⁴Ben-Hadad agreed with King Asa and sent the commanders of his forces against the towns of Israel. They conquered Ijon, Dan, Abel Maim[d] and all the store cities of Naphtali. ⁵When Baasha heard this, he stopped building Ramah and abandoned his work. ⁶Then King Asa brought all the men of Judah, and they carried away from Ramah the stones and timber Baasha had been using. With them he built up Geba and Mizpah.

---

[c] 8 Vulgate and Syriac (see also Septuagint and verse 1); Hebrew does not have *Azariah son of.*   [d] 4 Also known as *Abel Beth Maacah*

King James

7 ¶ And at that time Hanani the seer came to Asa king of Judah, and said unto him, Because thou hast relied on the king of Syria, and not relied on the LORD thy God, therefore is the host of the king of Syria escaped out of thine hand.

8Were not the Ethiopians and the Lubims *a huge host, with very many chariots and horsemen? yet, because thou didst rely on the LORD, he delivered them into thine hand.

9For the eyes of the LORD run to and fro throughout the whole earth, *to show himself strong in the behalf of *them whose heart *is perfect toward him. Herein thou hast done foolishly: therefore from henceforth thou shalt have wars.

10Then Asa was wroth with the seer, and put him in a prison house; for *he was in a rage with him because of this thing. And Asa *oppressed *some of the people the same time.

11 ¶ And, behold, the acts of Asa, first and last, lo, they *are written in the book of the kings of Judah and Israel.

12And Asa in the thirty and ninth year of his reign was diseased in his feet, until his disease *was exceeding *great: yet in his disease he sought not to the LORD, but to the physicians.

13 ¶ And Asa slept with his fathers, and died in the one and fortieth year of his reign.

14And they buried him in his own sepulchres, which he had *made for himself in the city of David, and laid him in the bed which was filled with sweet odours and divers kinds of spices prepared by the apothecaries' art: and they made a very great burning for him.

Jehoshaphat, king of Judah

17 AND JEHOSHAPHAT his son reigned in his stead, and strengthened himself against Israel.

2And he placed forces in all the fenced cities of Judah, and set garrisons in the land of Judah, and in the cities of Ephraim, which Asa his father had taken.

3And the LORD was with Jehoshaphat, because he walked in the first ways *of his father David, and sought not unto Baalim;

4But sought to the LORD God of his father, and walked in his commandments, and not after the doings of Israel.

5Therefore the LORD stablished the kingdom in his hand; and all Judah *brought to Jehoshaphat presents; and he had riches and honour in abundance.

6And his heart *was lifted up in the ways of the LORD: moreover he took away the high places and groves out of Judah.

7 ¶ Also in the third year of his reign he sent to his princes, even to Ben-hail, and to Obadiah, and to Zechariah, and to Nethaneel, and to Michaiah, to teach in the cities of Judah.

8And with them he sent Levites, even Shemaiah, and Nethaniah, and Zebadiah, and Asahel, and Shemiramoth, and Jehonathan, and Adonijah, and Tobijah, and Tobadonijah, Levites; and with them Elishama and Jehoram, priests.

9And they taught in Judah, and had the book of the law of the LORD with them, and went about throughout all the cities of Judah, and taught the people.

10 ¶ And the fear of the LORD *fell upon all the kingdoms of the lands that were round about Judah, so that they made no war against Jehoshaphat.

11Also some of the Philistines brought Jehoshaphat presents, and tribute silver; and the Arabians brought him flocks, seven thousand and seven hundred rams, and seven thousand and seven hundred he goats.

12 ¶ And Jehoshaphat waxed great exceedingly; and he built in Judah *castles, and cities of store.

Amplified

7At that time Hanani the seer came to Asa king of Judah and said to him, Because you relied on the king of Syria and not on the Lord your God, the army of the king of Syria has escaped you.

8Were not the Ethiopians and Libyans a huge host with very many chariots and horsemen? Yet because you relied then on the Lord, He gave them into your hand.

9For the eyes of the Lord run to and fro throughout the whole earth to show Himself strong in behalf of those whose hearts are blameless toward Him. You have done foolishly in this; therefore, from now on you shall have wars.

10Then Asa was angry with the seer and put him in prison [in the stocks], for he was enraged with him because of this. Asa oppressed some of the people at the same time.

11The acts of Asa, from first to last, are written in the Book of the Kings of Judah and Israel.

12In the thirty-ninth year of his reign Asa was diseased in his feet—until his disease became very severe; yet in his disease he did not seek the Lord, but relied on the physicians.

13And Asa slept with his fathers, dying in the forty-first year of his reign.

14And they buried him in his own tomb which he had hewn out for himself in the City of David, and they laid him on a bier which was filled with sweet odors and various kinds [of spices] prepared by the perfumers' art; and they made a very great burning [of spices] in his honor.

17 JEHOSHAPHAT HIS son reigned in Asa's stead and strengthened himself against Israel.

2And he placed forces in all the fortified cities of Judah and set garrisons in the land of Judah and in the cities of Ephraim which Asa his father had taken.

3The Lord was with Jehoshaphat because he walked in the first ways of his father [David]. He did not seek the Baals

4But sought and yearned with all his desire for the Lord, the God of his father, and walked in His commandments and not after the ways of Israel.

5Therefore the Lord established the kingdom in his hand; and all Judah brought tribute to Jehoshaphat, and he had great riches and honor.

6His heart was cheered and his courage was high in the ways of the Lord; moreover, he took away the high places and the Asherim out of Judah.

7Also in the third year of his reign he sent his princes Ben-hail, Obadiah, Zechariah, Nethanel, and Micaiah to teach in the cities of Judah;

8And with them were the Levites—Shemaiah, Nethaniah, Zebadiah, Asahel, Shemiramoth, Jehonathan, Adonijah, Tobijah, and Tob-adonijah; and with these Levites were the priests Elishama and Jehoram.

9And they taught in Judah, and had the Book of the Law of the Lord with them; they went about throughout all the cities of Judah and taught among the people.

10And a terror from the Lord fell upon all the kingdoms of the lands that were round about Judah, so that they made no war against Jehoshaphat.

11And some of the Philistines brought Jehoshaphat gifts and tribute silver, and the Arabs brought him flocks: 7,700 each of rams and of he-goats.

12And Jehoshaphat became very great. He built in Judah fortresses and store cities,

---

*Heb. in abundance   *Or, strongly to hold with them   *Heb. crushed   *Heb. digged   *Or, of his father, and of David   *Heb. gave   *i.e. was encouraged   *Heb. was   *Or, palaces

New American Standard

Asa Imprisons the Prophet

7 ¶ At that time Hanani the seer came to Asa king of Judah and said to him, "Because you have relied on the king of Aram and have not relied on the LORD your God, therefore the army of the king of Aram has escaped out of your hand.

8 "Were not the Ethiopians and the Lubim an immense army with very many chariots and horsemen? Yet because you relied on the LORD, He delivered them into your hand.

9 "For the eyes of the LORD move to and fro throughout the earth that He may strongly support those whose heart is completely His. You have acted foolishly in this. Indeed, from now on you will surely have wars."

10 Then Asa was angry with the seer and put him in prison, for he was enraged at him for this. And Asa oppressed some of the people at the same time.

11 ¶ Now, the acts of Asa from first to last, behold, they are written in the Book of the Kings of Judah and Israel.

12 In the thirty-ninth year of his reign Asa became diseased in his feet. His disease was severe, yet even in his disease he did not seek the LORD, but the physicians.

13 So Asa slept with his fathers, having died in the forty-first year of his reign.

14 They buried him in his own tomb which he had cut out for himself in the city of David, and they laid him in the resting place which he had filled with spices of various kinds blended by the perfumers' art; and they made a very great fire for him.

Jehoshaphat Succeeds Asa

17 JEHOSHAPHAT HIS son then became king in his place, and made his position over Israel firm.

2 He placed troops in all the fortified cities of Judah, and set garrisons in the land of Judah and in the cities of Ephraim which Asa his father had captured.

His Good Reign

3 The LORD was with Jehoshaphat because he followed the example of his father David's earlier days and did not seek the Baals,

4 but sought the God of his father, followed His commandments, and did not act as Israel did.

5 So the LORD established the kingdom in his control, and all Judah brought tribute to Jehoshaphat, and he had great riches and honor.

6 He took great pride in the ways of the LORD and again removed the high places and the Asherim from Judah.

7 ¶ Then in the third year of his reign he sent his officials, Ben-hail, Obadiah, Zechariah, Nethanel and Micaiah, to teach in the cities of Judah;

8 and with them the Levites, Shemaiah, Nethaniah, Zebadiah, Asahel, Shemiramoth, Jehonathan, Adonijah, Tobijah and Tobadonijah, the Levites; and with them Elishama and Jehoram, the priests.

9 They taught in Judah, *having* the book of the law of the LORD with them; and they went throughout all the cities of Judah and taught among the people.

10 ¶ Now the dread of the LORD was on all the kingdoms of the lands which *were* around Judah, so that they did not make war against Jehoshaphat.

11 Some of the Philistines brought gifts and silver as tribute to Jehoshaphat; the Arabians also brought him flocks, 7,700 rams and 7,700 male goats.

12 So Jehoshaphat grew greater and greater, and he built fortresses and store cities in Judah.

New International

7 At that time Hanani the seer came to Asa king of Judah and said to him: "Because you relied on the king of Aram and not on the LORD your God, the army of the king of Aram has escaped from your hand. 8 Were not the Cushites*e* and Libyans a mighty army with great numbers of chariots and horsemen*f*? Yet when you relied on the LORD, he delivered them into your hand. 9 For the eyes of the LORD range throughout the earth to strengthen those whose hearts are fully committed to him. You have done a foolish thing, and from now on you will be at war."

10 Asa was angry with the seer because of this; he was so enraged that he put him in prison. At the same time Asa brutally oppressed some of the people.

11 The events of Asa's reign, from beginning to end, are written in the book of the kings of Judah and Israel. 12 In the thirty-ninth year of his reign Asa was afflicted with a disease in his feet. Though his disease was severe, even in his illness he did not seek help from the LORD, but only from the physicians. 13 Then in the forty-first year of his reign Asa died and rested with his fathers. 14 They buried him in the tomb that he had cut out for himself in the City of David. They laid him on a bier covered with spices and various blended perfumes, and they made a huge fire in his honor.

Jehoshaphat King of Judah

17 JEHOSHAPHAT HIS son succeeded him as king and strengthened himself against Israel. 2 He stationed troops in all the fortified cities of Judah and put garrisons in Judah and in the towns of Ephraim that his father Asa had captured.

3 The LORD was with Jehoshaphat because in his early years he walked in the ways his father David had followed. He did not consult the Baals 4 but sought the God of his father and followed his commands rather than the practices of Israel. 5 The LORD established the kingdom under his control; and all Judah brought gifts to Jehoshaphat, so that he had great wealth and honor. 6 His heart was devoted to the ways of the LORD; furthermore, he removed the high places and the Asherah poles from Judah.

7 In the third year of his reign he sent his officials Ben-Hail, Obadiah, Zechariah, Nethanel and Micaiah to teach in the towns of Judah. 8 With them were certain Levites—Shemaiah, Nethaniah, Zebadiah, Asahel, Shemiramoth, Jehonathan, Adonijah, Tobijah and Tob-Adonijah—and the priests Elishama and Jehoram. 9 They taught throughout Judah, taking with them the Book of the Law of the LORD; they went around to all the towns of Judah and taught the people.

10 The fear of the LORD fell on all the kingdoms of the lands surrounding Judah, so that they did not make war with Jehoshaphat. 11 Some Philistines brought Jehoshaphat gifts and silver as tribute, and the Arabs brought him flocks: seven thousand seven hundred rams and seven thousand seven hundred goats.

12 Jehoshaphat became more and more powerful; he built

---

e 8 That is, people from the upper Nile region
f 8 Or *charioteers*

King James

Amplified

Reforms by Jehoshaphat

19 AND JEHOSHAPHAT the king of Judah returned to his house in peace to Jerusalem.

²And Jehu the son of Hanani the seer went out to meet him, and said to king Jehoshaphat, Shouldest thou help the ungodly, and love them that hate the LORD? therefore *is* wrath upon thee from before the LORD.

³Nevertheless there are good things found in thee, in that thou hast taken away the groves out of the land, and hast prepared thine heart to seek God.

⁴And Jehoshaphat dwelt at Jerusalem: and *s*he went out again through the people from Beer-sheba to mount Ephraim, and brought them back unto the LORD God of their fathers.

⁵ ¶ And he set judges in the land throughout all the fenced cities of Judah, city by city,

⁶And said to the judges, Take heed what ye do: for ye judge not for man, but for the LORD, who *is* with you *t*in the judgment.

⁷Wherefore now let the fear of the LORD be upon you; take heed and do *it:* for *there is* no iniquity with the LORD our God, nor respect of persons, nor taking of gifts.

⁸ ¶ Moreover in Jerusalem did Jehoshaphat set of the Levites, and *of* the priests, and of the chief of the fathers of Israel, for the judgment of the LORD, and for controversies, when they returned to Jerusalem.

⁹And he charged them, saying, Thus shall ye do in the fear of the LORD, faithfully, and with a perfect heart.

¹⁰And what cause soever shall come to you of your brethren that dwell in their cities, between blood and blood, between law and commandment, statutes and judgments, ye shall even warn them that they trespass not against the LORD, and *so* wrath come upon you, and upon your brethren: this do, and ye shall not trespass.

¹¹And, behold, Amariah the chief priest *is* over you in all matters of the LORD; and Zebadiah the son of Ishmael, the ruler of the house of Judah, for all the king's matters: also the Levites *shall be* officers before you. *u*Deal courageously, and the LORD shall be with the good.

Moab and Ammon defeated

20 IT CAME to pass after this also, *that* the children of Moab, and the children of Ammon, and with them *other* beside the Ammonites, came against Jehoshaphat to battle.

²Then there came some that told Jehoshaphat, saying, There cometh a great multitude against thee from beyond the sea on this side Syria; and, behold, they *be* in Hazazon-tamar, which *is* En-gedi.

³And Jehoshaphat feared, and set *v*himself to seek the LORD, and proclaimed a fast throughout all Judah.

⁴And Judah gathered themselves together, to ask *help* of the LORD: even out of all the cities of Judah they came to seek the LORD.

⁵ ¶ And Jehoshaphat stood in the congregation of Judah and Jerusalem, in the house of the LORD, before the new court,

⁶And said, O LORD God of our fathers, *art* not thou God in heaven? and rulest *not* thou over all the kingdoms of the heathen? and in thine hand *is there not* power and might, so that none is able to withstand thee?

⁷*Art* not thou our God, *w*who didst drive out the inhabitants of this land before thy people Israel, and gavest it to the seed of Abraham thy friend for ever?

⁸And they dwelt therein, and have built thee a sanctuary therein for thy name, saying,

19 JEHOSHAPHAT THE king of Judah returned safely to his house in Jerusalem.

²Jehu son of Hanani, the seer, went out to meet him and said to Jehoshaphat, Should you help the ungodly and love those who hate the Lord? Because of this, wrath has gone out against you from the Lord.

³But there are good things found in you, for you have destroyed the Asherim out of the land and have set your heart to seek God [with all your soul's desire].

⁴Jehoshaphat dwelt at Jerusalem, and he went out again among the people from Beersheba to the hill country of Ephraim and brought them back to the Lord, the God of their fathers.

⁵He appointed judges throughout all the fortified cities of Judah, city by city,

⁶And said to the judges, Be careful what you do, for you judge not for man but for the Lord, and He is with you in the matter of judgment.

⁷So now let the reverence *and* fear of the Lord be upon you; take heed what you do, for there is no injustice with the Lord our God, or partiality or taking of bribes.

⁸Also in Jerusalem, Jehoshaphat set certain Levites, priests, and heads of families of Israel to give judgment for the Lord and decide controversies. When they [of the commission] returned to Jerusalem,

⁹The king charged them, Do this in the fear of the Lord, faithfully, with integrity *and* a blameless heart.

¹⁰Whenever any controversy shall come to you from your brethren who dwell in their cities, between blood and blood, between law and commandment, statutes and judgments, you shall warn *and* instruct them that they may not be guilty before the Lord; otherwise wrath will come upon you and your brethren. Do this and you will not be guilty.

¹¹And behold, Amariah the chief priest is over you in all matters of the Lord, and Zebadiah son of Ishmael, the governor of the house of Judah, in all the king's matters; also the Levites will serve you as officers. Deal courageously [be strong and do], and may the Lord be with the good!

20 AFTER THIS, the Moabites, the Ammonites, and with them the Meunites came against Jehoshaphat to battle.

²It was told Jehoshaphat, A great multitude has come against you from beyond the [Dead] Sea, from Edom; and behold they are in Hazazon-tamar, which is En-gedi.

³Then Jehoshaphat feared, and set himself [determinedly, as his vital need] to seek the Lord; he proclaimed a fast in all Judah.

⁴And Judah gathered together to ask help from the Lord; even out of all the cities of Judah they came to seek the Lord [yearning for Him with all their desire].

⁵And Jehoshaphat stood in the assembly of Judah and Jerusalem in the house of the Lord before the new court,

⁶And said, O Lord, God of our fathers, are You not God in heaven? And do You not rule over all the kingdoms of the nations? In Your hand are power and might, so that none is able to withstand You.

⁷Did not You, O our God, drive out the inhabitants of this land before Your people Israel and give it forever to the descendants of Abraham Your friend?

⁸They dwelt in it and have built You a sanctuary in it for Your Name, saying,

---

s Heb. *he returned and went out*   *t* Heb. *in the matter of*
judgment   *u* Heb. *Take courage and do*   *v* Heb. *his face*
w Heb. *thou*

New American Standard

Jehu Rebukes Jehoshaphat

19 THEN JEHOSHAPHAT the king of Judah returned in safety to his house in Jerusalem.
2 Jehu the son of Hanani the seer went out to meet him and said to King Jehoshaphat, "Should you help the wicked and love those who hate the LORD and so *bring* wrath on yourself from the LORD?
3 "But there is *some* good in you, for you have removed the Asheroth from the land and you have set your heart to seek God."
4 ¶ So Jehoshaphat lived in Jerusalem and went out again among the people from Beersheba to the hill country of Ephraim and brought them back to the LORD, the God of their fathers.

Reforms Instituted

5 He appointed judges in the land in all the fortified cities of Judah, city by city.
6 He said to the judges, "Consider what you are doing, for you do not judge for man but for the LORD who is with you when you render judgment.
7 "Now then let the fear of the LORD be upon you; be very careful what you do, for the LORD our God will have no part in unrighteousness or partiality or the taking of a bribe."
8 ¶ In Jerusalem also Jehoshaphat appointed some of the Levites and priests, and some of the heads of the fathers' *households* of Israel, for the judgment of the LORD and to judge disputes among the inhabitants of Jerusalem.
9 Then he charged them saying, "Thus you shall do in the fear of the LORD, faithfully and wholeheartedly.
10 "Whenever any dispute comes to you from your brethren who live in their cities, between blood and blood, between law and commandment, statutes and ordinances, you shall warn them so that they may not be guilty before the LORD, and wrath may *not* come on you and your brethren. Thus you shall do and you will not be guilty.
11 "Behold, Amariah the chief priest will be over you in all that pertains to the LORD, and Zebadiah the son of Ishmael, the ruler of the house of Judah, in all that pertains to the king. Also the Levites shall be officers before you. Act resolutely, and the LORD be with the upright."

Judah Invaded

20 NOW IT came about after this that the sons of Moab and the sons of Ammon, together with some of the Meunites, came to make war against Jehoshaphat.
2 Then some came and reported to Jehoshaphat, saying, "A great multitude is coming against you from beyond the sea, out of Aram and behold, they are in Hazazon-tamar (that is Engedi)."
3 Jehoshaphat was afraid and turned his attention to seek the LORD, and proclaimed a fast throughout all Judah.
4 So Judah gathered together to seek help from the LORD; they even came from all the cities of Judah to seek the LORD.

Jehoshaphat's Prayer

5 ¶ Then Jehoshaphat stood in the assembly of Judah and Jerusalem, in the house of the LORD before the new court,
6 and he said, "O LORD, the God of our fathers, are You not God in the heavens? And are You not ruler over all the kingdoms of the nations? Power and might are in Your hand so that no one can stand against You.
7 "Did You not, O our God, drive out the inhabitants of this land before Your people Israel and give it to the descendants of Abraham Your friend forever?
8 "They have lived in it, and have built You a sanctuary there for Your name, saying,

New International

19 WHEN JEHOSHAPHAT king of Judah returned safely to his palace in Jerusalem, 2Jehu the seer, the son of Hanani, went out to meet him and said to the king, "Should you help the wicked and love*ʰ* those who hate the LORD? Because of this, the wrath of the LORD is upon you. 3There is, however, some good in you, for you have rid the land of the Asherah poles and have set your heart on seeking God."

Jehoshaphat Appoints Judges

4Jehoshaphat lived in Jerusalem, and he went out again among the people from Beersheba to the hill country of Ephraim and turned them back to the LORD, the God of their fathers. 5He appointed judges in the land, in each of the fortified cities of Judah. 6He told them, "Consider carefully what you do, because you are not judging for man but for the LORD, who is with you whenever you give a verdict. 7Now let the fear of the LORD be upon you. Judge carefully, for with the LORD our God there is no injustice or partiality or bribery."
8In Jerusalem also, Jehoshaphat appointed some of the Levites, priests and heads of Israelite families to administer the law of the LORD and to settle disputes. And they lived in Jerusalem. 9He gave them these orders: "You must serve faithfully and wholeheartedly in the fear of the LORD. 10In every case that comes before you from your fellow countrymen who live in the cities—whether bloodshed or other concerns of the law, commands, decrees or ordinances—you are to warn them not to sin against the LORD; otherwise his wrath will come on you and your brothers. Do this, and you will not sin.
11 "Amariah the chief priest will be over you in any matter concerning the LORD, and Zebadiah son of Ishmael, the leader of the tribe of Judah, will be over you in any matter concerning the king, and the Levites will serve as officials before you. Act with courage, and may the LORD be with those who do well."

Jehoshaphat Defeats Moab and Ammon

20 AFTER THIS, the Moabites and Ammonites with some of the Meunites*ⁱ* came to make war on Jehoshaphat.
2Some men came and told Jehoshaphat, "A vast army is coming against you from Edom,*ʲ* from the other side of the Sea.*ᵏ* It is already in Hazazon Tamar" (that is, En Gedi). 3Alarmed, Jehoshaphat resolved to inquire of the LORD, and he proclaimed a fast for all Judah. 4The people of Judah came together to seek help from the LORD; indeed, they came from every town in Judah to seek him.
5Then Jehoshaphat stood up in the assembly of Judah and Jerusalem at the temple of the LORD in the front of the new courtyard 6and said:

"O LORD, God of our fathers, are you not the God who is in heaven? You rule over all the kingdoms of the nations. Power and might are in your hand, and no one can withstand you. 7O our God, did you not drive out the inhabitants of this land before your people Israel and give it forever to the descendants of Abraham your friend? 8They have lived in it and have built

*ʰ*2 Or *and make alliances with*　　*ⁱ*1 Some Septuagint manuscripts; Hebrew *Ammonites*　　*ʲ*2 One Hebrew manuscript; most Hebrew manuscripts, Septuagint and Vulgate *Aram*　　*ᵏ*2 That is, the Dead Sea

King James

⁹If, *when* evil cometh upon us, *as* the sword, judgment, or pestilence, or famine, we stand before this house, and in thy presence, (for thy name *is* in this house,) and cry unto thee in our affliction, then thou wilt hear and help.

¹⁰And now, behold, the children of Ammon and Moab and mount Seir, whom thou wouldest not let Israel invade, when they came out of the land of Egypt, but they turned from them, and destroyed them not;

¹¹Behold, *I say, how* they reward us, to come to cast us out of thy possession, which thou hast given us to inherit.

¹²O our God, wilt thou not judge them? for we have no might against this great company that cometh against us; neither know we what to do: but our eyes *are* upon thee.

¹³And all Judah stood before the LORD, with their little ones, their wives, and their children.

¹⁴ ¶ Then upon Jahaziel the son of Zechariah, the son of Benaiah, the son of Jeiel, the son of Mattaniah, a Levite of the sons of Asaph, came the spirit of the LORD in the midst of the congregation;

¹⁵And he said, Hearken ye, all Judah, and ye inhabitants of Jerusalem, and thou king Jehoshaphat, Thus saith the LORD unto you, Be not afraid nor dismayed by reason of this great multitude; for the battle *is* not yours, but God's.

¹⁶Tomorrow go ye down against them: behold, they come up by the ˣcliff of Ziz; and ye shall find them at the end of the ʸbrook, before the wilderness of Jeruel.

¹⁷Ye shall not *need* to fight in this *battle:* set yourselves, stand ye *still,* and see the salvation of the LORD with you, O Judah and Jerusalem: fear not, nor be dismayed; tomorrow go out against them: for the LORD *will be* with you.

¹⁸And Jehoshaphat bowed his head with *his* face to the ground: and all Judah and the inhabitants of Jerusalem fell before the LORD, worshipping the LORD.

¹⁹And the Levites, of the children of the Kohathites, and of the children of the Korhites, stood up to praise the LORD God of Israel with a loud voice on high.

²⁰ ¶ And they rose early in the morning, and went forth into the wilderness of Tekoa: and as they went forth, Jehoshaphat stood and said, Hear me, O Judah, and ye inhabitants of Jerusalem; Believe in the LORD your God, so shall ye be established; believe his prophets, so shall ye prosper.

²¹And when he had consulted with the people, he appointed singers unto the LORD, and ᶻthat should praise the beauty of holiness, as they went out before the army, and to say, Praise the LORD; for his mercy *endureth* for ever.

²² ¶ ᵃAnd when they began ᵇto sing and to praise, the LORD set ambushments against the children of Ammon, Moab, and mount Seir, which were come against Judah; and ᶜthey were smitten.

²³For the children of Ammon and Moab stood up against the inhabitants of mount Seir, utterly to slay and destroy *them:* and when they had made an end of the inhabitants of Seir, every one helped ᵈto destroy another.

²⁴And when Judah came toward the watchtower in the wilderness, they looked unto the multitude, and, behold, they *were* dead bodies fallen to the earth, and ᵉnone escaped.

²⁵And when Jehoshaphat and his people came to take away the spoil of them, they found among them in abundance both riches with the dead bodies, and precious jewels, which they stripped off for themselves, more than they could carry away: and they were three days in gathering of the spoil, it was so much.

Amplified

⁹If evil comes upon us, the sword of judgment, or pestilence, or famine, we will stand before this house and before You—for Your Name [and the symbol of Your presence] is in this house—and cry to You in our affliction, and You will hear and save.

¹⁰And now behold, the men of Ammon, Moab, and Mount Seir, whom You would not let Israel invade when they came from the land of Egypt, and whom they turned from and did not destroy—[Deut. 2:9.]

¹¹Behold, they reward us by coming to drive us out of Your possession which You have given us to inherit.

¹²O our God, will You not exercise judgment upon them? For we have no might to stand against this great company that is coming against us. We do not know what to do, but our eyes are upon You.

¹³And all Judah stood before the Lord, with their children and their wives.

¹⁴Then the Spirit of the Lord came upon Jahaziel son of Zechariah, the son of Benaiah, the son of Jeiel, the son of Mattaniah, a Levite of the sons of Asaph, in the midst of the assembly.

¹⁵He said, Hearken, all Judah, you inhabitants of Jerusalem, and you King Jehoshaphat. The Lord says this to you: Be not afraid or dismayed at this great multitude; for the battle is not yours, but God's.

¹⁶Tomorrow go down to them. Behold, they will come up by the Ascent of Ziz, and you will find them at the end of the ravine before the Wilderness of Jeruel.

¹⁷You shall not need to fight in this battle; take your positions, stand still, and see the deliverance of the Lord [Who is] with you, O Judah and Jerusalem. Fear not nor be dismayed. Tomorrow go out against them, for the Lord is with you.

¹⁸And Jehoshaphat bowed his head with his face to the ground, and all Judah and the inhabitants of Jerusalem fell down before the Lord, worshiping Him.

¹⁹And some Levites of the Kohathites and Korahites stood up to praise the Lord, the God of Israel, with a very loud voice.

²⁰And they rose early in the morning and went out into the Wilderness of Tekoa; and as they went out, Jehoshaphat stood and said, Hear me, O Judah, and you inhabitants of Jerusalem! Believe in the Lord your God and you shall be established; believe *and* remain steadfast to His prophets and you shall prosper.

²¹When he had consulted with the people, he appointed singers to sing to the Lord and praise Him in their holy [priestly] garments as they went out before the army, saying, Give thanks to the Lord, for His mercy *and* lovingkindness endure forever!

²²And when they began to sing and to praise, the Lord set ambushments against the men of Ammon, Moab, and Mount Seir who had come against Judah, and they were [self-] slaughtered;

²³For [suspecting betrayal] the men of Ammon and Moab rose against those of Mount Seir, utterly destroying them. And when they had made an end of the men of Seir, they all helped to destroy one another.

²⁴And when Judah came to the watchtower of the wilderness, they looked at the multitude, and behold, they were dead bodies fallen to the earth, and none had escaped!

²⁵When Jehoshaphat and his people came to take the spoil, they found among them much cattle, goods, garments, and precious things which they took for themselves, more than they could carry away, so much they were three days in gathering the spoil.

ˣHeb. *ascent*   ʸOr, *valley*   ᶻHeb. *praisers*   ᵃHeb. *And in the time that they*   ᵇHeb. *in singing and praise*   ᶜOr, *they smote one another*   ᵈHeb. *for the destruction*   ᵉHeb. *there was not an escaping*

New American Standard

9 'Should evil come upon us, the sword, *or* judgment, or pestilence, or famine, we will stand before this house and before You (for Your name is in this house) and cry to You in our distress, and You will hear and deliver *us.*'

10"Now behold, the sons of Ammon and Moab and Mount Seir, whom You did not let Israel invade when they came out of the land of Egypt (they turned aside from them and did not destroy them),

11 see *how* they are rewarding us by coming to drive us out from Your possession which You have given us as an inheritance.

12"O our God, will You not judge them? For we are powerless before this great multitude who are coming against us; nor do we know what to do, but our eyes are on You."

13 ¶ All Judah was standing before the LORD, with their infants, their wives and their children.

Jahaziel Answers the Prayer

14 Then in the midst of the assembly the Spirit of the LORD came upon Jahaziel the son of Zechariah, the son of Benaiah, the son of Jeiel, the son of Mattaniah, the Levite of the sons of Asaph;

15 and he said, "Listen, all Judah and the inhabitants of Jerusalem and King Jehoshaphat: thus says the LORD to you, 'Do not fear or be dismayed because of this great multitude, for the battle is not yours but God's.

16"Tomorrow go down against them. Behold, they will come up by the ascent of Ziz, and you will find them at the end of the valley in front of the wilderness of Jeruel.

17'You *need* not fight in this *battle;* station yourselves, stand and see the salvation of the LORD on your behalf, O Judah and Jerusalem.' Do not fear or be dismayed; tomorrow go out to face them, for the LORD is with you."

18 ¶ Jehoshaphat bowed his head with *his* face to the ground, and all Judah and the inhabitants of Jerusalem fell down before the LORD, worshiping the LORD.

19 The Levites, from the sons of the Kohathites and of the sons of the Korahites, stood up to praise the LORD God of Israel, with a very loud voice.

Enemies Destroy Themselves

20 ¶ They rose early in the morning and went out to the wilderness of Tekoa; and when they went out, Jehoshaphat stood and said, "Listen to me, O Judah and inhabitants of Jerusalem, put your trust in the LORD your God and you will be established. Put your trust in His prophets and succeed."

21 When he had consulted with the people, he appointed those who sang to the LORD and those who praised *Him* in holy attire, as they went out before the army and said, "Give thanks to the LORD, for His lovingkindness is everlasting."

22 When they began singing and praising, the LORD set ambushes against the sons of Ammon, Moab and Mount Seir, who had come against Judah; so they were routed.

23 For the sons of Ammon and Moab rose up against the inhabitants of Mount Seir destroying *them* completely; and when they had finished with the inhabitants of Seir, they helped to destroy one another.

24 ¶ When Judah came to the lookout of the wilderness, they looked toward the multitude, and behold, they *were* corpses lying on the ground, and no one had escaped.

25 When Jehoshaphat and his people came to take their spoil, they found much among them, *including* goods, garments and valuable things which they took for themselves, more than they could carry. And they were three days taking the spoil because there was so much.

New International

in it a sanctuary for your Name, saying, 9'If calamity comes upon us, whether the sword of judgment, or plague or famine, we will stand in your presence before this temple that bears your Name and will cry out to you in our distress, and you will hear us and save us.'

10"But now here are men from Ammon, Moab and Mount Seir, whose territory you would not allow Israel to invade when they came from Egypt; so they turned away from them and did not destroy them.

11See how they are repaying us by coming to drive us out of the possession you gave us as an inheritance.

12O our God, will you not judge them? For we have no power to face this vast army that is attacking us. We do not know what to do, but our eyes are upon you."

13All the men of Judah, with their wives and children and little ones, stood there before the LORD.

14Then the Spirit of the LORD came upon Jahaziel son of Zechariah, the son of Benaiah, the son of Jeiel, the son of Mattaniah, a Levite and descendant of Asaph, as he stood in the assembly.

15He said: "Listen, King Jehoshaphat and all who live in Judah and Jerusalem! This is what the LORD says to you: 'Do not be afraid or discouraged because of this vast army. For the battle is not yours, but God's. 16Tomorrow march down against them. They will be climbing up by the Pass of Ziz, and you will find them at the end of the gorge in the Desert of Jeruel. 17You will not have to fight this battle. Take up your positions; stand firm and see the deliverance the LORD will give you, O Judah and Jerusalem. Do not be afraid; do not be discouraged. Go out to face them tomorrow, and the LORD will be with you.' "

18Jehoshaphat bowed with his face to the ground, and all the people of Judah and Jerusalem fell down in worship before the LORD. 19Then some Levites from the Kohathites and Korahites stood up and praised the LORD, the God of Israel, with a very loud voice.

20Early in the morning they left for the Desert of Tekoa. As they set out, Jehoshaphat stood and said, "Listen to me, Judah and people of Jerusalem! Have faith in the LORD your God and you will be upheld; have faith in his prophets and you will be successful." 21After consulting the people, Jehoshaphat appointed men to sing to the LORD and to praise him for the splendor of his[l] holiness as they went out at the head of the army, saying:

"Give thanks to the LORD,
    for his love endures forever."

22As they began to sing and praise, the LORD set ambushes against the men of Ammon and Moab and Mount Seir who were invading Judah, and they were defeated. 23The men of Ammon and Moab rose up against the men from Mount Seir to destroy and annihilate them. After they finished slaughtering the men from Seir, they helped to destroy one another.

24When the men of Judah came to the place that overlooks the desert and looked toward the vast army, they saw only dead bodies lying on the ground; no one had escaped. 25So Jehoshaphat and his men went to carry off their plunder, and they found among them a great amount of equipment and clothing[m] and also articles of value—more than they could take away. There was so much plunder that it

---

l 21 Or *him with the splendor of*   *m 25* Some Hebrew manuscripts and Vulgate; most Hebrew manuscripts *corpses*

King James

²⁶ ¶ And on the fourth day they assembled themselves in the valley of *f*Berachah; for there they blessed the LORD: therefore the name of the same place was called, The valley of Berachah, unto this day.

²⁷Then they returned, every man of Judah and Jerusalem, and Jehoshaphat in the *g*forefront of them, to go again to Jerusalem with joy; for the LORD had made them to rejoice over their enemies.

²⁸And they came to Jerusalem with psalteries and harps and trumpets unto the house of the LORD.

²⁹And the fear of God was on all the kingdoms of *those* countries, when they had heard that the LORD fought against the enemies of Israel.

³⁰So the realm of Jehoshaphat was quiet: for his God gave him rest round about.

The death of Jehoshaphat

³¹ ¶ And Jehoshaphat reigned over Judah: *he was* thirty and five years old when he began to reign, and he reigned twenty and five years in Jerusalem. And his mother's name *was* Azubah the daughter of Shilhi.

³²And he walked in the way of Asa his father, and departed not from it, doing *that which was* right in the sight of the LORD.

³³Howbeit the high places were not taken away: for as yet the people had not prepared their hearts unto the God of their fathers.

³⁴Now the rest of the acts of Jehoshaphat, first and last, behold, they *are* written in the *h*book of Jehu the son of Hanani, who *i*is mentioned in the book of the kings of Israel.

³⁵ ¶ And after this did Jehoshaphat king of Judah join himself with Ahaziah king of Israel, who did very wickedly:

³⁶*j*And he joined himself with him to make ships to go to Tarshish: and they made the ships in Ezion-geber.

³⁷Then Eliezer the son of Dodavah of Mareshah prophesied against Jehoshaphat, saying, Because thou hast joined thyself with Ahaziah, the LORD hath broken thy works. And the ships were broken, that they were not able to go to Tarshish.

Jehoram, king of Judah

21 NOW JEHOSHAPHAT slept with his fathers, and was buried with his fathers in the city of David. And Jehoram his son *k*reigned in his stead.

²And he had brethren the sons of Jehoshaphat, Azariah, and Jehiel, and Zechariah, and Azariah, and Michael, and Shephatiah: all these *were* the sons of Jehoshaphat king of Israel.

³And their father gave them great gifts of silver, and of gold, and of precious things, with fenced cities in Judah: but the kingdom gave he to *l*Jehoram; because he *was* the firstborn.

⁴Now when Jehoram was risen up to the kingdom of his father, he strengthened himself, and slew all his brethren with the sword, and *divers* also of the princes of Israel.

⁵ ¶ Jehoram *was* thirty and two years old when he began to reign, and he reigned eight years in Jerusalem.

⁶And he walked in the way of the kings of Israel, like as did the house of Ahab: for he had the daughter of Ahab to wife: and he wrought *that which was* evil in the eyes of the LORD.

⁷Howbeit the LORD would not destroy the house of David, because of the covenant that he had made with David, and as he promised to give a *m*light to him and to his sons for ever.

Amplified

²⁶On the fourth day they assembled in the Valley of Beracah. There they blessed the Lord. So the name of the place is still called the Valley of Beracah [blessing].

²⁷Then they returned, every man of Judah and Jerusalem, Jehoshaphat leading them, to Jerusalem with joy, for the Lord had made them to rejoice over their enemies.

²⁸They came to Jerusalem with harps, lyres, and trumpets to the house of the Lord.

²⁹And the fear of God came upon all the kingdoms of those countries when they heard that the Lord had fought against the enemies of Israel.

³⁰So the realm of Jehoshaphat was quiet, for his God gave him rest round about.

³¹Thus Jehoshaphat reigned over Judah. He was thirty-five years old when he began his twenty-five-year reign in Jerusalem. His mother was Azubah daughter of Shilhi.

³²And he walked in the ways of Asa his father and departed not from it, doing what was right in the sight of the Lord.

³³But the high places [of idolatry] were not taken away, for the people had not yet set their hearts on their fathers' God.

³⁴Now the rest of the acts of Jehoshaphat, from first to last, they are written in the records of Jehu son of Hanani, which are in the Book of the Kings of Israel.

³⁵After this, Jehoshaphat king of Judah joined with Ahaziah king of Israel, who did very wickedly.

³⁶He joined him in building ships to go to Tarshish, building them in Ezion-geber.

³⁷Then Eliezer son of Dodavahu of Mareshah prophesied against Jehoshaphat, saying, Because you have joined Ahaziah, the Lord will destroy your works. So the ships were wrecked and unable to go to Tarshish.

21 JEHOSHAPHAT SLEPT with his fathers and was buried with [them] in the City of David. Jehoram his son reigned in his stead.

²He had brothers: Azariah, Jehiel, Zechariah, Azariah, Michael, and Shephatiah, all the sons of Jehoshaphat king of Israel.

³Their father gave them great gifts of silver, gold, and precious things, together with fortified cities in Judah, but the kingdom he gave to Jehoram, the firstborn.

⁴When Jehoram had ascended to the kingship of his father, he strengthened himself and slew all his brethren with the sword and also some of Israel's princes.

⁵Jehoram at thirty-two years of age began his eight-year reign in Jerusalem.

⁶He walked in the ways of the kings of Israel, as did the house of Ahab, for he married the daughter of Ahab and did what was evil in the eyes of the Lord.

⁷But the Lord would not destroy the house of David, because He had made a covenant with David and promised to give a light to him and to his sons forever.

*f*i.e. *Blessing*   *g*Heb. *head*   *h*Heb. *words*   *i*Heb. *was made to ascend*   *j*At first Jehoshaphat was unwilling; see 1 Ki. 22:49   *k*Alone   *l*Jehoram made partner of the kingdom with his father; see 2 Ki. 8:16   *m*Heb. *lamp,* or, *candle*

New American Standard

Triumphant Return to Jerusalem

26 Then on the fourth day they assembled in the valley of Beracah, for there they blessed the LORD. Therefore they have named that place "The Valley of [f]Beracah" until today.

27 Every man of Judah and Jerusalem returned with Jehoshaphat at their head, returning to Jerusalem with joy, for the LORD had made them to rejoice over their enemies.

28 They came to Jerusalem with harps, lyres and trumpets to the house of the LORD.

29 And the dread of God was on all the kingdoms of the lands when they heard that the LORD had fought against the enemies of Israel.

30 So the kingdom of Jehoshaphat was at peace, for his God gave him rest on all sides.

31 ¶ Now Jehoshaphat reigned over Judah. He *was* thirty-five years old when he became king, and he reigned in Jerusalem twenty-five years. And his mother's name *was* Azubah the daughter of Shilhi.

32 He walked in the way of his father Asa and did not depart from it, doing right in the sight of the LORD.

33 The high places, however, were not removed; the people had not yet directed their hearts to the God of their fathers.

34 ¶ Now the rest of the acts of Jehoshaphat, first to last, behold, they are written in the annals of Jehu the son of Hanani, which is recorded in the Book of the Kings of Israel.

Alliance Displeases God

35 ¶ After this Jehoshaphat king of Judah allied himself with Ahaziah king of Israel. He acted wickedly in so doing.

36 So he allied himself with him to make ships to go to Tarshish, and they made the ships in Ezion-geber.

37 Then Eliezer the son of Dodavahu of Mareshah prophesied against Jehoshaphat saying, "Because you have allied yourself with Ahaziah, the LORD has destroyed your works." So the ships were broken and could not go to Tarshish.

Jehoram Succeeds Jehoshaphat in Judah

21 THEN JEHOSHAPHAT slept with his fathers and was buried with his fathers in the city of David, and Jehoram his son became king in his place.

2 He had brothers, the sons of Jehoshaphat: Azariah, Jehiel, Zechariah, Azaryahu, Michael and Shephatiah. All these *were* the sons of Jehoshaphat king of Israel.

3 Their father gave them many gifts of silver, gold and precious things, with fortified cities in Judah, but he gave the kingdom to Jehoram because he was the firstborn.

4 ¶ Now when Jehoram had taken over the kingdom of his father and made himself secure, he killed all his brothers with the sword, and some of the rulers of Israel also.

5 Jehoram *was* thirty-two years old when he became king, and he reigned eight years in Jerusalem.

6 He walked in the way of the kings of Israel, just as the house of Ahab did (for Ahab's daughter was his wife), and he did evil in the sight of the LORD.

7 Yet the LORD was not willing to destroy the house of David because of the covenant which He had made with David, and since He had promised to give a lamp to him and his sons forever.

[f]I.e. blessing

New International

took three days to collect it. 26On the fourth day they
assembled in the Valley of Beracah, where they praised
the LORD. This is why it is called the Valley of Beracah[n]
to this day.
27Then, led by Jehoshaphat, all the men of Judah and
Jerusalem returned joyfully to Jerusalem, for the LORD had
given them cause to rejoice over their enemies. 28They
entered Jerusalem and went to the temple of the LORD with
harps and lutes and trumpets.
29The fear of God came upon all the kingdoms of the
countries when they heard how the LORD had fought
against the enemies of Israel. 30And the kingdom of Jehoshaphat was at peace, for his God had given him rest on
every side.

The End of Jehoshaphat's Reign

31So Jehoshaphat reigned over Judah. He was thirty-five
years old when he became king of Judah, and he reigned
in Jerusalem twenty-five years. His mother's name was
Azubah daughter of Shilhi. 32He walked in the ways of his
father Asa and did not stray from them; he did what was
right in the eyes of the LORD. 33The high places, however,
were not removed, and the people still had not set their
hearts on the God of their fathers.
34The other events of Jehoshaphat's reign, from beginning to end, are written in the annals of Jehu son of Hanani, which are recorded in the book of the kings of Israel.
35Later, Jehoshaphat king of Judah made an alliance
with Ahaziah king of Israel, who was guilty of wickedness. 36He agreed with him to construct a fleet of trading
ships.[o] After these were built at Ezion Geber, 37Eliezer
son of Dodavahu of Mareshah prophesied against Jehoshaphat, saying, "Because you have made an alliance with
Ahaziah, the LORD will destroy what you have made." The
ships were wrecked and were not able to set sail to trade.[p]

21 THEN JEHOSHAPHAT rested with his fathers
and was buried with them in the City of David.
And Jehoram his son succeeded him as king. 2Jehoram's
brothers, the sons of Jehoshaphat, were Azariah, Jehiel,
Zechariah, Azariahu, Michael and Shephatiah. All these
were sons of Jehoshaphat king of Israel.[q] 3Their father
had given them many gifts of silver and gold and articles
of value, as well as fortified cities in Judah, but he had
given the kingdom to Jehoram because he was his firstborn son.

Jehoram King of Judah

4When Jehoram established himself firmly over his father's kingdom, he put all his brothers to the sword along
with some of the princes of Israel. 5Jehoram was thirty-
two years old when he became king, and he reigned in
Jerusalem eight years. 6He walked in the ways of the kings
of Israel, as the house of Ahab had done, for he married a
daughter of Ahab. He did evil in the eyes of the LORD.
7Nevertheless, because of the covenant the LORD had
made with David, the LORD was not willing to destroy the
house of David. He had promised to maintain a lamp for
him and his descendants forever.

[n]26 *Beracah* means *praise.* [o]36 Hebrew *of ships that could go to Tarshish* [p]37 Hebrew *sail for Tarshish* [q]2 That is, Judah, as frequently in 2 Chronicles

King James

8 ¶ In his days the Edomites revolted from under the [n]dominion of Judah, and made themselves a king.

9 Then Jehoram went forth with his princes, and all his chariots with him: and he rose up by night, and smote the Edomites which compassed him in, and the captains of the chariots.

10 So the Edomites revolted from under the hand of Judah unto this day. The same time also did Libnah revolt from under his hand; because he had forsaken the LORD God of his fathers.

11 Moreover he made high places in the mountains of Judah, and caused the inhabitants of Jerusalem to commit fornication, and compelled Judah thereto.

12 ¶ And there came a writing to him from Elijah the prophet, saying, Thus saith the LORD God of David thy father, Because thou hast not walked in the ways of Jehoshaphat thy father, nor in the ways of Asa king of Judah,

13 But hast walked in the way of the kings of Israel, and hast made Judah and the inhabitants of Jerusalem to go a-whoring, like to the whoredoms of the house of Ahab, and also hast slain thy brethren of thy father's house, which were better than thyself:

14 Behold, with [o]a great plague will the LORD smite thy people, and thy children, and thy wives, and all thy goods:

15 And thou shalt have great sickness by disease of thy bowels, until thy bowels fall out by reason of the sickness day by day.

16 ¶ Moreover the LORD stirred up against Jehoram the spirit of the Philistines, and of the Arabians, that were near the Ethiopians:

17 And they came up into Judah, and brake into it, and [p]carried away all the substance that was found in the king's house, and his sons also, and his wives; so that there was never a son left him, save [q]Jehoahaz, the youngest of his sons.

18 ¶ And after all this the LORD smote him in his bowels with an incurable disease.

19 And it came to pass, that in process of time, after the end of two years, his bowels fell out by reason of his sickness: so he died of sore diseases. And his people made no burning for him, like the burning of his fathers.

20 Thirty and two years old was he when he began to reign, and he reigned in Jerusalem eight years, and departed without being desired. Howbeit they buried him in the city of David, but not in the sepulchres of the kings.

Ahaziah, king of Judah

22 AND THE inhabitants of Jerusalem made Ahaziah his youngest son king in his stead: for the band of men that came with the Arabians to the camp had slain all the eldest. So Ahaziah the son of Jehoram king of Judah reigned.

2 Forty and two years old was Ahaziah when he began to reign, and he reigned one year in Jerusalem. His mother's name was also Athaliah the daughter of Omri.

3 He also walked in the ways of the house of Ahab: for his mother was his counsellor to do wickedly.

4 Wherefore he did evil in the sight of the LORD like the house of Ahab: for they were his counsellors after the death of his father to his destruction.

5 ¶ He walked also after their counsel, and went with Jehoram the son of Ahab king of Israel to war against Hazael king of Syria at Ramoth-gilead: and the Syrians smote Joram.

Amplified

8 In Jehoram's days, the Edomites revolted from the rule of Judah and set up for themselves a king.

9 Then Jehoram passed over [the Jordan] with his captains and all his chariots, and rose up by night and smote the Edomites who had surrounded him and his chariot captains.

10 So Edom revolted from the rule of Judah to this day. Then Libnah also revolted from Jehoram's rule, because he had forsaken the Lord, the God of his fathers.

11 Moreover, he made idolatrous high places in the hill country of Judah and debauched spiritually the inhabitants of Jerusalem and led Judah astray [compelling the people's cooperation].

12 And there came a letter to Jehoram from Elijah the prophet, saying, Thus says the Lord, the God of David your father [forefather]: Because you have not walked in the ways of Jehoshaphat your father nor in the ways of Asa king of Judah,

13 But have walked in the ways of Israel's kings, and made Judah and the inhabitants of Jerusalem play the harlot like the [spiritual] harlotry of Ahab's house, and also have slain your brothers of your father's house, who were better than you,

14 Behold, the Lord will smite your people, and your children, your wives, and all your possessions with a great plague.

15 And you yourself shall have a severe illness because of an intestinal disease, until your bowels fall out because of the sickness, day after day.

16 And the Lord stirred up against Jehoram the anger of the Philistines and of the Arabs who were near the Ethiopians.

17 They came against Judah, invaded it, and carried away all the possessions found in and around the king's house, together with his sons and his wives; so there was not a son left to him except Jehoahaz, the youngest.

18 And after all this, the Lord smote [Jehoram] with an incurable intestinal disease.

19 In process of time, after two years, his bowels fell out because of his disease. So he died in severe distress. And his people made no funeral fire to honor him, like the fires for his fathers.

20 Thirty-two years old was Jehoram when he began to reign, and he reigned in Jerusalem eight years, and departed without being wanted. Yet they buried him in the City of David, but not in the tombs of the kings.

22 THE PEOPLE of Jerusalem made Ahaziah, his youngest son, king in his stead, for the troop that came with the Arabs to the camp had slain all the older sons. So Ahaziah son of Jehoram king of Judah reigned.

2 Forty-two years old was Ahaziah when he began his one-year reign in Jerusalem. His mother was Athaliah, a granddaughter of Omri. [II Kings 8:26.]

3 He also walked in the ways of the house of Ahab, for his mother was his counselor to do wickedly.

4 So he did evil in the sight of the Lord like the house of Ahab, for they were his counselors after his father's death, to his destruction.

5 He followed their counsel and even went with [i]Joram son of Ahab king of Israel to war against Hazael king of Syria at Ramoth-gilead. And the Syrians wounded Joram; [II Kings 8:28ff.]

---

[n] Heb. hand; see ch. 22:1　　[o] Heb. a great stroke　　[p] Heb. carried captive; [q] Or, Ahaziah in ch. 22:1, or, Azariah in ch. 22:6

[i] See footnote on II Kings 1:17.